MW01096580

THE TROUSER PRESS

The All-New Fifth Edition of
The Trouser Press Record Guide

GUIDE TO '90s ROCK

Ira A. Robbins
Editor

David Sprague
Deputy Editor

A Fireside Book
Published by Simon & Schuster

FIRESIDE
Rockefeller Center
1230 Avenue of the Americas
New York, NY 10020

Designed by Elina D. Nudelman

Manufactured in the United States of America
1 3 5 7 9 10 8 6 4 2

Library of Congress Cataloging-in-Publication Data

The Trouser Press guide to '90s rock : the all-new
fifth edition of The Trouser Press record guide / Ira A.
Robbins, editor ; David Sprague, deputy editor.
p. cm.
Used in conjunction with the 4th ed. The editors
assume most readers will own or have access to the
4th ed. which is available on the World Wide Web.
Rev. ed. of: The Trouser Press record guide. 4th ed. 1991.
1. Rock music—1991–2000—Discography. 2. Rock
music—1991–2000—History and criticism. 3. Sound
recordings—Reviews. I. Robbins, Ira A. II. Sprague,
David, music critic. III. Trouser Press record guide.
ML156.4.R6T75 1997
016.78166'0266—dc20 96-41087
CIP
MN

ISBN 0-684-81437-4

The Trouser Press Record Guide fourth edition (published in 1991) is available on the World Wide Web (www.trouserpress.com). The site is also a forum for communicating with the editors of the book and other readers and rock fans.

C·O·N·T·E·N·T·S

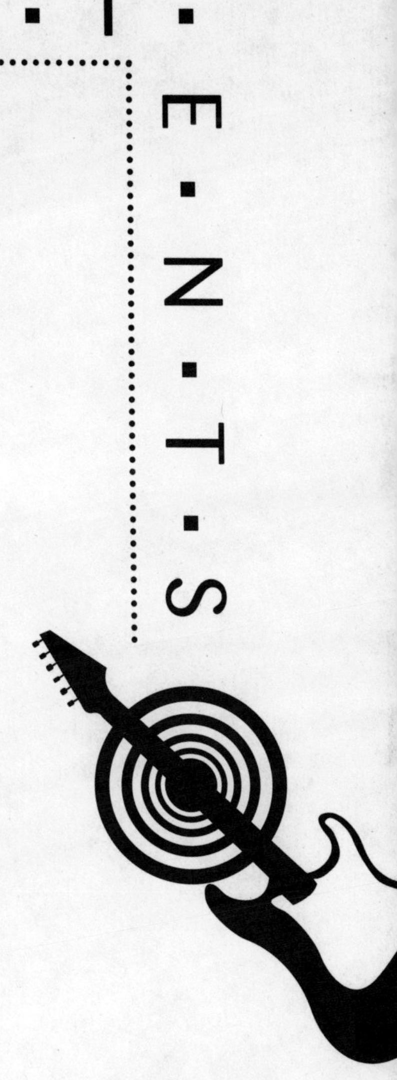

PREFACE

In 1983, *Trouser Press,* a New York–based international music monthly then in its ninth year of publication, assembled and put its name to a slim volume of capsule reviews that covered most of the albums in a field that, at the time, was known as new wave. The genre, like the magazine, soon shuffled into the annals of past cultural history, but the book was off and running. Under a title that has undergone various permutations, updated and substantially expanded revisions of the *Record Guide* were published in 1985, 1989 and 1991. Over time, those four paperbacks have come to define the Trouser Press name (borrowed, with love, from a Bonzo Dog Band song) and aesthetic principles (music over money), even for those who never encountered the magazine.

The publication of the book's fourth edition at the end of 1991 was precipitously if not propitiously timed. The exploding success of Nirvana's **Nevermind** (which came out in September and was therefore a hair too late for coverage in the book) made "alternative music" a household term and attracted an enormous audience for music once thought to be permanently outside the putative mainstream. More important, it led to an enormous upsurge in the vitality of independent record companies and the openness of major labels to signing bands that would previously have been deemed too ratty, bratty or ridiculous for corporate support and national exposure.

It was ironic that a project whose values were elementary to this upheaval was, in a marketing sense, left behind when the barricades were finally stormed. By a thoughtless fluke of timing, the book covered everything up to the moment of impact, and little was done to make the commercial connection for readers not already familiar with the era or the effort. Nonetheless, there were those who recognized the continuum, and they soon began pressing me for the sequel, which—given the deluge of new bands and releases that have since emerged—seemed an absurdity. It took a while, but ultimately enough friends, serious music fans and professionals in possession of my e-mail address hounded me into thinking about the next edition. Once I started warming up to the idea that the rock world truly *needed* another record guide, I had to contend with the fact that adding five years' worth of new bands and records to a book that already filled 750 pages and contained nearly as much coverage of the '70s as the '80s was patently unfeasible.

Furthermore, the connection of this decade's developments to the music that first kicked down some of the corporate barricades and opened the DIY doors for business led to the inevitable conclusion that the '90s were shaping up as a clear and distinct era, with **Nevermind** conveniently serving as the inaugural message of Lollapaloozalot. I concluded that the only way to do it again was to start with a clean slate. (It was also high time to jettison old reviews—some of them originally written in 1982—made out of date by long-obsolete reference points and shifts in the musical landscape. Yesterday's innovations are most assuredly tomorrow's clichés.)

So that's what I did. Other than a few thousand words carried over from the fourth edition to prevent whiplash by abrupt full-velocity entry into the middle of an artist's recording career, this edition is completely new. In other words, hold on to your fourth edition—this in no way replaces or supplants it. Adding a simple guideline to the seat-of-the-pants concept that has always guided *The Trouser Press Record Guide*'s editorial decision-making, this book covers only artists who have released full-length albums in the '90s. Rather than maintaining the cumulative designs of the first four editions, this one starts from scratch, using 1990–91 as ground zero.

The idea, simple and practical in principle, proved fairly intricate in editorial execution. Acts that were not around at the time of the last edition were easy to weigh, but veterans who have continued to release records also had to be considered for inclusion, with a present-tense judgment made of their significance and relevance here. This was a tricky problem, and I hasten to acknowledge that reasonable cases could be mounted to counter some of those decisions. Also, the rectification of some past omissions—most notably Last Exit, Last Poets, Yoko Ono, Richard Thompson, Frank Zappa and John Zorn, all of whom have long since displayed a valid ticket for the direction of today's music—is not covered by either aspect of that evaluation process. At the same time, defunct outfits with recent reissues didn't generally qualify, while some active artists covered in depth in the last edition hadn't added enough of consequence to their canon to warrant inclusion.

In order to get the contents of this book to actually fit between two covers, one basic and essential assumption had to be made: that the majority of those who would buy *The Trouser Press Guide to '90s Rock* already own (or have access to) and will retain *The Trouser Press Record Guide* from 1991. For artists covered in both books, that premise allowed the excision of holdovers' old reviews (not discographies, which have been preserved complete). In their place, brief (sometimes not-so-brief) critical summaries of the artist's pre-'90s oeuvre precede a detailed appraisal of recent work. (The abbreviation TPRG in the cross-reference line at the bottom of an entry means that an entry for this artist, containing substantial additional material, can be found in the previous edition of the book.)

Contributing to the challenge here is the troubling glut of releases. Whatever the initial modest impulses of the DIY movement, the '90s has witnessed a harrowing replay of old-school superstar indulgence, with many indie bands and labels stuck in recording sprawl, producing side projects on top of remix albums in addition to solo ventures, cassette quickies, spoken word ventures, B-side collections and the occasional live LP. With record contracts now openly structured to allow all sorts of corporate creeping around, today's active artists can't seem to keep their mouths shut or their hands in their pockets when tape is rolling; the acceptance of lo-fi sound and the availability of respectable home-studio gear have considerably abetted the velocity and the volume. Nobody, it seems, is satisfied being in just one band at a time; the complications of interlocking memberships have made covering the field a fluid organizational nightmare. I have attempted to put it all in clear and logical order, following as many branches of family trees as brush up against the retail window. As always, no distinctions are made between tiny pressings, self-released cassettes and major-label roll-outs. If a piece of music was ever available for sale, even only by mail order, it very well may be reviewed here. As a result, no implication is made that any title is currently in print or commercially available. This is a critique, not a catalogue.

One of indie-rock's dubious virtues is its early admissions program. In the old world, bands used to spend years finding their stylistic selves, settling on formats and lineups, creating and culling material, working on presentation and purpose—in short, growing up to be what their musical genes ordained—before risking/getting the chance to make a record. Anxious labels' club-level A&R (often supplanted by full-on DIY) no longer lets that developmental process take place without documentation; ready or not, young bands hit the studio as soon as they've got a set and a buzz, making albums as snapshots along the way to . . . whatever. Murky and embarrassing pictures of "whatever" can get formed as a result. Adolescence is a gawky and thoughtless time, and the act of committing various stages of it to posterity makes the moments appear more profound than they might ultimately turn out to be. Wearing a wide-lapel purple-checked Qiana shirt when you're thirteen is no big deal; having people remember you in it and ask where it is a decade later may not feel as comfortable. (Then again . . .)

That said, some artists are truly worth picking apart; everything they've committed to posterity bears some critical scrutiny. Unlike other record guide editors, I don't presume to boil artists down to their widely known works, or forgive them their early missteps. This is an egalitarian exercise: within the stylistic and philosophical framework in effect here, those who declare themselves musicians and produce work for public consumption are treated seriously regardless of success or obscurity. That's why a prolific and intriguing artist who has never sold in the five figures might well be covered in an entry far longer than an obvious platinum act with two albums. It's about the music, not the numbers.

My goal here was to say something about the era as much as its records; some entries, it will be noted, are as much topical essays as record-by-record critiques. This was far too much work to have been fun, but communing with contemporary music as a hundred-hour-a-week job for seven months has been an enlightening and rewarding experience. Welcome to the '90s.

—Ira Robbins

ACKNOWLEDGMENTS

More than fifty writers from all over the United States (and one from England) contributed to this book; a handful went way beyond the call of duty in devotion to the team effort. Gold stars go to Lydia Anderson, Jem Aswad, Greg Fasolino, David Fricke, Marlene Goldman, Gary Graff, Greg Kot, Fred Mills, Tom Moon, Kurt B. Reighley, Douglas Wolk and Katherine Yeske.

Deputy Editor David Sprague has been a crucial collaborator from the very beginning of this project in the spring of 1995. Beyond the voluminous evidence of his critical perceptions contained in these pages, his expertise, taste and friendship are reflected in many of the editorial decisions that shaped the book.

Many of our pals in the music industry went out of their way to provide needed records, advice or information in a most supportive manner. Thanks are due especially to Bruce Adams, Tim Adams, Cary Baker, Shira Berk, Nils Bernstein, Amy Bloebaum, Jennie Boddy, John C. Brand, Julie Butterfield, Debra Chapman, Dan Cohen, Stacey Conde, Gordon Conrad, Steve Daly, Glenn Dicker, David Dorn, Drag City, Bruce Duff, Toni Eng, Jeff Feuerzeig, Jennifer Fisher, Bobbie Gale, Liz Garo, Yvonne Garrett, Spencer Gates, Mary Melia Giambalvo, Debbie Gibbs, Robert Griffin, Michelle Gutenstein, Ed Haber, Carl Hanni, Bruce Hartley, Andrew Jacobs, Steven Joerg, Neil Lawi, Keith Lyle, Maria Malta, Sue Marcus, Matthew McAllester, Jim Merlis, Judy Miller, Barbara Mitchell, the Nasty Little Man gang, Molly Neuman, Deborah Orr, Steve Pilon, Michael Reed, Jim Reynolds, Michael Ribas, Jill Richmond, Mark Robinson, Michelle Roche, Rey Roldan, Denise Royal, Donna Russo, Stacey Sanner, Andy Schwartz, Ada Shore, Tim Sommer, Brian Spevak, Cece Stelljas, Carrie Svingen, Jeff Tartakov, Lydia Tomkiw, Jill Tomlinson, Jenny Toomey, Chris Vanderloo, Naomi Walker, Ken Weinstein, Amy Welch, Meryl Wheeler, Howard Wuelfing, Steve Yegelwel and Tracy Zamot.

I am indebted to others for encouragement, information, translation, patience and advice: John Dunbar, Gayle Eisner, Richard Gehr, Sylviane Gold, Jim Green, Janas Hoyt, Scott Isler, Kris Juzaitis, Linda Lutzak, Freddie Patterson, Linda Robbins, Fred Wasser. And, beyond that, I'd like to acknowledge my friends Wayne King, Regina Joskow Dunton, Alan Fielding and Ron Decker for helping out in myriad ways. My literary agent, Sarah Lazin, has been enormously helpful by keeping me in the loop and out of the line of fire. David Dunton, the former Fireside editor who convinced me to do this book, and Michael Pietsch, the editor who got this project going in the first place, have both my respect and my gratitude. So do, as ever, my parents, Louis and Estelle Robbins.

Most of all, I'd like to thank Leslie Morgan, who helped me get through this ordeal as no one else could with her patience, support and love (plus download technology and home-cooked meals). No thanks to Bobo.

This book was entirely written and edited on a Toshiba Satellite T1910 laptop running Xywrite. Very nearly all of the copy flow was managed electronically via e-mail on America Online and other services. AOL was also very helpful for various types of research; numerous sites on the World Wide Web also yielded essential discographical and biographical information.

—Ira Robbins
New York City
1 May 1996

HEADINGS

The format is straightforward: entries are arranged in pure alphabetical order by the last names of individuals and the first word of group names, with no precedence given to acronyms, numerals, abbreviations (except for "St.," which is understood to be short for Saint) or the like. Groups named for a member (even one who uses a pseudonym, like Elvis Hitler, in the H's) are alphabetized as if an individual; fabricated group names for which there is no corresponding member (Ed Hall, in the E's) go by first letter of the first word. MC and DJ titles are considered part of the name; one-letter surnames (Warren G, Paul K) are now the basis for alphabetization. All articles in band names have been omitted from the headings and ignored in alphabetization unless they are an integral part of the name (The For Carnation, A Band Called Bud), intentionally misspelled (Thee Hypnotics, Th Faith Healers), unlikely to be correctly presumed in context (the The) or in a foreign language (Los Lobos, Die Toten Hosen). In order to avoid chronological confusion, multiple-name artists like Foetus and Jazz Butcher have been given an overall heading this time; additionally, several headings employ parentheses to combine an artist's work under variant names. Records devoted to the songs of an artist are filed with their subjects.

The years noted are the original date of release; a second date follows a "+" when the same label issued the same record with some significant change in content. Foreign reissues are noted only when there is some content variation in the record or there is no other version available. A few minor style changes have been instituted for this edition. Two labels divided by a slash now denote joint or licensed releases, not international distinctions (but not in the typographically exceptional cases of the Tim/Kerr, Bar/None and Twin\Tone labels). All releases are US unless otherwise indicated, and all UK releases are specifically noted as such. In cases where a long-running artist's '80s (or '70s) records have been reissued more than once, some of the intermediate editions that were listed in previous editions have been omitted. Also, for the sake of streamlining and maintaining the book's contemporary focus, some '80s EPs and subordinate-heading albums that were listed in previous editions have been deleted from the discographies here.

Most significantly, this edition reflects the format shift that has rendered CDs the standard and vinyl the exception (leaving cassettes in the same third-rate limbo as before). No attempt has been made to distinguish between vinyl and CD availability this time. Furthermore, the progression from one format to another (tape to CD, for instance) was not deemed significant enough to detail. The text will mention if an album was initially issued only on cassette; if it has since been issued in other formats, the heading will not detail that. Discographies make no effort to differentiate between records that are in print and impossibly rare: this is a critical guide, not a catalogue.

EPs: Basically, the guideline for the format between single and album is four to six songs, but there are exceptions: a 7-inch with more than six songs will also be designated an EP, a full-length album (roughly forty minutes, but nobody's counting) with six or fewer songs will not. Neither will a record of more than six songs in which multiple mixes of a song account for the excess of tracks. Although there's no excuse for it, some significant releases of only three songs (especially when the record has an actual title) have been listed as EPs; such deviations are noted in the text.

Titles that appear within quotation marks designate singles, which are listed and mentioned only in cases of special significance. This stylistic convention necessitated the omission of quotation marks from titles that appear with them on record covers, but in this instance consistency was valued over slavish accuracy. Likewise, idiosyncratic type case conventions (and needless punctuation marks) in band names, titles and labels have been respected only when there seems to be both consistency and general acceptance for such use.

The most recent releases covered in this edition are from the middle of 1996; because of inconsistent availability of advance tapes and suchlike, there is no reason to assume an overall cutoff date. In other words, there are undoubtedly records that aren't reviewed here that were released before some that were. When reliably available close to the editorial deadline, titles are listed without any further mention.

Bylines appear as lowercase initials in brackets at the end of entries. (Regular readers should not assume absolute consistency in initial coding from past editions.) Pieces written by more than one critic are noted in the approximate order their contributions appear. In a few cases, cross-references at the bottom of entries provide direction to related artists, with incidental appearances (such as production work) not generally noted.

As ever, some bands that were going to be covered in this edition for one or more reasons aren't. The list of notable yes-I-know omissions: Barkmarket, Blackwatch, Tracy Bonham, Bouncing Souls, Boyracer, Cake, Dandelion, Dazzling Killmen, Die Warzau, Dog Faced Hermans, Doughboys, Down by Law, Drunken Boat, Dusted Bloods, Edsel Auctioneer, Flophouse, Front Line Assembly, Greg Ginn, Mick Harvey, Kinky Machine, Legendary Pink Dots, Les Thugs, Arto Lindsay, Helen Love, Morning Glories, Nectarine No. 9, Nitzer Ebb, No Doubt, Odds, Ozric Tentacles, Psychic TV, Zoogz Rift, Scarce, Sexpod, Shootyz Groove, Shoulders, Single Gun Theory, Skin Yard, Sleeper, Azalia Snail, Sparklehorse, Spirea X, Supreme Dicks, Sweet Lizard Illtet, Swell, 311, Universal Congress Of, Voice of the Beehive, Volebeats, Vanilla Trainwreck, Wallflowers, Steve Westfield, X-Tal, Xymox . . .

Comments, complaints, corrections, quibbles and kudos all gladly accepted. I can't promise to reply, but all correspondence will certainly be read and considered.

Address snailmail and musical offerings to:

Trouser Press Record Guide
c/o Fireside Books
1230 Avenue of the Americas
New York, NY 10020

Address e-mail to: TrouserHQ@aol.com

ABBREVIATIONS AND CONVENTIONS USED IN THE HEADINGS

[tape]: cassette-only release

[CD]: CD-only release

[8-track]: 8-track cartridge

EP: a record with more than three and fewer than seven songs

EP3: an EP released on 3-inch CD only

EP7: an EP released on 7-inch vinyl only

EP10: an EP released on 10-inch vinyl only

" ": titles that appear within quotation marks designate singles

(no label): there is no record company name indicated on the release

(self-released): informal cassettes issued without label identification

Nationality of Release:

Aus.	Australia
Aut.	Austria
Bel.	Belgium
Braz.	Brazil
Can.	Canada
Fin.	Finland
Fr.	France
Ger.	Germany
Gr.	Greece
Hol.	Netherlands
Ice.	Iceland
It.	Italy
Japan.	Japan
Mex.	Mexico
Nor.	Norway
NZ	New Zealand
Sp.	Spain
Sw.	Switzerland
Swed.	Sweden
UK	Great Britain
US	United States

The abbreviation TPRG in the cross-reference line means that an entry for this artist, containing substantial additional material, appears in the fourth edition of *The Trouser Press Record Guide* (1991).

CONTRIBUTORS

bw	Bill Wyman
db	Doug Brod
dbg	David Greenberger
ddw	Douglas Wolk
df	David Fricke
dps	Denise Sheppard
ds	Dave Schulps
dss	David Sprague
fm	Fred Mills
ga	Grant Alden
gef	Greg Fasolino
gg	Gary Graff
gk	Greg Kot
i	Ira Robbins
ic	Ian Christe
icm	Ian McCaleb
ja	Jem Aswad
jc	Jason Cohen
jdr	Jim DeRogatis
jf	Jason Ferguson
jg	Jim Green
jmb	John M. Borack
jo	Jordan Oakes
jp	j. poet
jr	Jack Rabid
jt	Jim Testa
jy	Jon Young
jzc	Jeff Chang
kbr	Kurt B. Reighley
ky	Katherine Yeske
la	Lydia Anderson
ma	Michael Azerrad
mf	Megan Frampton
mg	Marlene Goldman
mgk	Michael Krugman
mk	Matthew Kaplan
mrk	Mark Kemp
mww	Mark Woodlief
nds	Natasha Stovall
ns	Neil Strauss
ph	Peter Howell
pl	Paul Lukas
pm	Peter Margasak
pnm	Peter Momtchiloff
re	Robin Eisgrau
rl	Robert Levine
roc	Rob O'Connor
rxe	Robin Edgerton
sf	Scott Frampton
sm	Steven Mirkin
ss	Scott Schinder
tja	Troy J. Augusto
tm	Tom Moon
tr	Terry Rompers
ts	Tom Sinclair
vg	Vickie Gilmer

Ira Robbins didn't set out to be a music journalist. He was a full-time electrical engineering student when, armed with little more than a handful of encouraging rejection letters from Lester Bangs, his father's mimeograph machine and the proselytic need to rave in print about bands he liked, he co-founded *Trouser Press* in 1974. Since the magazine's demise a decade later, he has alternated between staff jobs at such publications as *Video* magazine and *New York Newsday* and lengthy bouts of freelance work. Born and raised in New York City, he resides there with his cat Bobo (a prince) and many walls of records. When not writing about music, he sings and plays guitar in Utensil.

David Sprague decided to pursue a career in rock criticism after seeing how much hate mail he could generate with a single record review in his high-school paper. A native of Cleveland, Sprague began freelance writing while pursuing a journalism degree at New York University. His work has appeared in such publications as *Rolling Stone, Billboard, Newsday, Request* and *Creem* (where he also served as editor in chief). He lives in Queens, New York, with his cat Fang and far, far too many of the records written about in these pages.

Grant Alden is a freelance writer, editor, art gallery co-owner and generally unemployable sort temporarily based in Los Angeles. He was the managing editor of *The Rocket* and is now managing editor at *huH.*

Lydia Anderson is the managing editor of *CMJ New Music Report,* an associate editor and writer for *CMJ New Music Monthly* and an avid music fan who resides in New York City.

One rainy afternoon in 1968, **Jem Aswad**'s mother brought home **Sgt. Pepper;** the following year, she brought home Lillian Roxon's *Rock Encyclopedia.* At the age of six, his fate was sealed.

Troy J. Augusto, a radio producer and writer living in Los Angeles, still admits to listening to Rush.

The music editor of the SonicNet Web site (http://www.sonicnet.com), **Michael Azerrad** is the author of *Come As You Are: The Story of Nirvana* (Doubleday/Main Street, 1993) and a frequent contributor to many of your favorite rock magazines. He also drums in New York's Utensil.

John M. Borack is a California-based freelance journalist who writes for *Goldmine, Audities, Yellow Pills* and *The Garden Grove Journal.*

Doug Brod is a senior editor at *Entertainment Weekly* and works on the Manhattan Cable TV show *Beyond Vaudeville.*

California-based writer and DJ **Jeff Chang** uses the alias "Zen" when he's feeling mischievous.

Ian Christe is a contributing editor to *HotWired,* a columnist for *Warp* and *CMJ New Music Monthly* and a writer for much else. He lives in Williamsburg, Brooklyn.

Jason Cohen lives in Austin, Texas, where he writes about music and popular culture for *Rolling Stone, Texas Monthly* and various other publications. He is the co-author of *Generation Ecch!* and is "at work" on a book about American indie-rock labels.

Jim DeRogatis, a former senior editor at *Rolling Stone,* is the author of *Kaleidoscope Eyes: Psychedelic Rock From the '60s to the '90s* (Citadel Underground).

Robin Edgerton knows how to read, write and talk, and is music directress at WFMU radio in New Jersey.

Robin Eisgrau has been writing about alternative music since 1989. She is a featured columnist for *Paper,* the founding editor of *Net* and a former associate editor of *Seventeen.* She freelances for publications that will pay her and/or treat her well.

Greg Fasolino, a former editor of *Reflex* and current freelance writer and professional genealogist, lives in Huntington, New York, with his Antilles pinktoe tarantula and many, many records.

Jason Ferguson is a South Carolina–based freelance writer who is a regular contributor to *Alternative Press, Raygun, Urb* and other publications.

Megan Frampton is editor-in-chief of the *CMJ New Music Report,* lives in Brooklyn and likes Jane Austen and fashion as much as she likes music.

Scott Frampton is editor-in-chief of *CMJ New Music Monthly.* He lives in Brooklyn and is a Knicks fan.

David Fricke has been a writer and editor at *Rolling Stone* since 1985 and is the American correspondent for the British music weekly *Melody Maker.*

Vickie Gilmer is a freelance editor and writer based in Minneapolis; her work has appeared in *Request, Saint Paul Pioneer Press, City Pages, Rolling Stone Online, Minneapolis Star Tribune* and *Sassy.*

Marlene Goldman is a San Francisco–based writer and broadcaster.

Gary Graff is a Detroit–based music journalist whose work appears in a variety of newspapers as well as *Guitar World,* Mr. Showbiz, Compuserve Wow! and other online services.

Jim Green is trying to learn how to write and how to act in Los Angeles, where tons of people already do these things (most of them badly).

David Greenberger has been creating *The Duplex Planet* in its various forms (magazines, books, comics, CDs and performances) since 1979.

Peter Howell is the pop and rock critic for the *Toronto Star.*

Matthew Kaplan is an attorney and radio DJ in New Jersey.

Mark Kemp is a senior editor at *Rolling Stone.* He was the editor of *Option* from 1991 to 1996 and has written for a variety of publications including *Creem, L.A. Weekly, San Francisco Bay Guardian, Spin* and the *Village Voice.*

Greg Kot is the rock critic for the *Chicago Tribune.*

Michael Krugman is a writer and nationally syndicated radio personality who divides his time between London, Brooklyn and Austin.

Robert Levine is an editor at *HotWired* and also contributes to *Option* and the *San Francisco Chronicle.*

Paul Lukas lives in Brooklyn, where he publishes *Beer Frame: The Journal of Inconspicuous Consumption.*

Peter Margasak is a staff writer at the *Chicago Reader* and publishes *Butt Rag* with astonishing inconsistency.

Ian McCaleb is a Washington, DC–based wire service reporter and freelance writer.

Fred Mills is a freelance music writer for *Option, Magnet, The Bob, Goldmine* and many other publications; in his spare time he pens liner notes for reissues and grows cactus on his Tucson, Arizona, beachfront property.

Steven Mirkin is a freelance writer based in New York.

Peter Momtchiloff plays guitar in Heavenly.

Tom Moon is a music critic for the *Philadelphia Inquirer.*

Jordan Oakes publishes *Yellow Pills* magazine and has compiled a CD series of the same name. He writes about pop and rock music for the *Riverfront Times* in St. Louis.

Rob O'Connor is the editor of *Throat Culture,* a fanzine that may never have a fourth issue, and a contributor to *Rolling Stone, BAM* and *Launch.*

j. poet (poebeat@aol.com) has written about world music and pop culture for several decades and contributes regularly to *RhythmMusic, Utne Reader, Wired, Pulse!* and other local and national publications.

Jack Rabid became a music writer in 1979 and has published his (now) 200-page magazine *The Big Takeover* from his home in the Big Apple for over sixteen years.

Kurt B. Reighley has written for more publications than he cares to recall, including *Details, Interview* and *Out.*

Terry Rompers is a shadowy figure who writes about popular music from various places in the United States.

Scott Schinder, who shares a birthday with Boy George, lives in Queens, New York, with a lot of records and a bunch of cats.

Dave Schulps, the co-founder of *Trouser Press* magazine, lives in Los Angeles where he works on daily music news services for MJI Broadcasting while preparing for the senior tour.

Denise Sheppard is a Vancouver freelancer who loves sunset walks, candlelit dinners and writing for *Raygun, huH, Pulse* and *The Rocket.*

Tom Sinclair, author of the children's fantasy novel *Tales of a Wandering Warthog* (Albert Whitman, 1985), is a staff writer in the music department of *Entertainment Weekly.*

Natasha Stovall is a writer living in Brooklyn. Her work has appeared in *The Village Voice, Newsday, Spin* and *The New York Times.*

Neil Strauss is a pop music critic and reporter at *The New York Times* and the editor of *Radiotext(e),* a collection of radio-related writings.

Jim Testa, a freelance writer whose work frequently appears in *Request, Guitar World* and *The Jersey Journal,* is the editor of *Jersey Beat* fanzine, which he has published continuously since 1982.

Douglas Wolk is the managing editor of *CMJ New Music Monthly,* lives in Queens, and sometimes does other stuff too.

Mark Woodlief was the first editorial intern at the *Village Voice Rock and Roll Quarterly,* has contributed to the *Orange County Register, Option, Raygun, L.A. View, The Rocket, The Bob* and other publications, and is currently managing editor at *Warp* magazine.

Bill Wyman is the arts editor of the *San Francisco Weekly.* He was formerly a staff writer at the *Chicago Reader.*

Katherine Yeske, a freelance writer and perpetual wanderer, contributes regularly to *B-Side, Hits* and various regional publications.

Jon Young is an aging rock'n'roll fan whose favorite singers are (in alphabetical order) Billy Fury, Wynonie Harris, Barbara Lynn, Doug Sahm and Del Shannon.

A BAND CALLED BUD

See *Grifters.*

ABLE TASMANS

The Tired Sun EP (NZ Flying Nun) 1985
A Cuppa Tea and a Lie Down (NZ Flying Nun) 1987
Hey Spinner! (NZ Flying Nun) 1991
Somebody Ate My Planet (NZ Flying Nun) 1992
The Shape of Dolls EP (NZ Flying Nun) 1993
Store in a Cool Place (NZ Flying Nun) 1996

In New Zealand, where bands routinely break up, trade members and then form anew in order to requalify for state-sponsored funding grants, the Able Tasmans managed to stay the course for over a decade. The group—whose moniker is a pun based on the name of seventeenth-century Dutch explorer Abel Tasman, who discovered New Zealand—was able to maintain most of its original lineup from the mid-'80s through the mid-'90s, all the while peddling a unique brand of guitar/keyboard pop of consistently high quality.

The Tasmans' early output, most of it quite good, is available on the CD version of **A Cuppa Tea and a Lie Down,** which also includes the band's debut EP, **The Tired Sun,** and a few items from assorted compilations. The group really came into its own, however, with **Hey Spinner!,** one of the finest records ever to emerge from New Zealand. The band's signature sound defined by the interplay between Peter Keen's soaring, angelic voice and Leslie Jonkers' keyboards is used to its fullest effect. Despite some adornments that would sink less talented outfits (like the occasional use of a cello or clarinet and the periodic Victorian flourishes in Jonkers' playing), the intelligent scope of the lyrics and the expertly sculpted songcraft make this a major pleasure from start to finish.

The following year's **Somebody Ate My Planet** is, depending on one's perspective, either a slight advance or a small step backward. The production adds a bit more hard-edged rock to the guitars on several tracks; it's welcome at some junctures but overall tends to give a more "normal" dimension to a group better served by its eclecticism. Still, the lyrics continue to plumb the intellectual and emotional depths of modern life; this, combined with a sensational over-the-top vocal performance by guitarist Graeme Humphreys on "Weight of Love," makes **Somebody Ate My Planet** a solidly recommended listen, if not quite as stellar as its predecessor.

The five-song **The Shape of Dolls** is a reassuring return to form, and a fine example of rock'n'roll maturity. The slow, stately title track, with its ambling gait and gorgeous harmonies, stands as an apt summation of the band's work to this point: unhurried, calmly effective and quietly beautiful.

The Tasmans decided to call it quits shortly after recording 1996's **Store in a Cool Place,** which serves as a curious exit point. Saddled with a number of instrumentals, most of them aimless and unnecessary, the record is bloated to well over an hour in length; it could easily have been trimmed by a quarter. If you can get past the excess baggage, though, the remaining tunes are among the quintet's best, with Keen characteristically burying a few of his sharpest emotional daggers amidst some of the more outwardly placid tracks. Though the Tasmans were never one of Flying Nun's most celebrated acts, either in America or in New Zealand, their recorded legacy stands with the label's best. [pl]

A-BONES

Tempo Tantrum EP10 (Ger. Exile) 1986
Free Beer for Life! EP (Norton) 1988
The Life of Riley (Norton) 1991 (Japan. 1+2) 1991
I Was a Teenage Mummy (Norton) 1992
Music Minus Five (Norton) 1993

As proprietors of the reliably terrific Norton label and the estimable if infrequent *Kicks* fanzine, Brooklyn's Billy Miller and Miriam Linna (onetime Cramps skin-beater) have built their deep-rooted affinity for trashy, primitive rock'n'roll and R&B into a mini-empire. As frontman and drummer, respectively, of New York's A-Bones, the couple put their love of stone-age sounds into practice, delivering unpretentiously greasy lo-fi fun that's consistently engaging in its try-anything spirit. Taking the more formal rockabilly of Miller and Linna's previous combo, the Zantees, to new levels of sloppy enthusiasm, the A-Bones' joyously cruddy sound is built on Linna's simple but effective pounding, Miller's manly grunt, Bruce Bennett's unexpectedly inventive guitar work and (from **The Life of Riley** onward) saxist Lars Espensen's spirited honking.

The four-song 10-inch **Tempo Tantrum** and the six-song 12-inch **Free Beer for Life!** are both fun, but the band really comes into its own on the full-length **Life of Riley,** which benefits from the leaders' record-collecting acumen with swell covers of obscurities by the likes of the Royal Teens, Benny Joy, Doug Sahm and the Surfaris. The album's Japanese edition has different cover art and adds the contents of **Free Beer for Life!,** plus two extra tracks. The nine-song **I Was a Teenage Mummy** (soundtrack to an ultra-low-budget horror flick in which the band appears) demonstrates an unlikely exotic bent manifested in a howling version of the Coasters' "Little Egypt" and the four-and-a-half-minute (epic by A-Bones standards) instrumental "Kashmiriam."

The A-Bones closed their career on a high note with **Music Minus Five,** the cover art of which cleverly refers to the Yardbirds. Produced at Seattle's Egg Studios by PopLlama owner Conrad Uno, the album boasts a higher concentration of originals and (somewhat) improved sonic fidelity on catchy originals like "The Claw" and "Bonomo Twine Time," a fine Gene Vincent cover and a syntactically mischievous version of "Hully Gully" featuring backing vocals by Japan's 5.6.7.8's.

The A-Bones released a passel of non-album singles for a variety of indie labels, including Norton. The band called it quits in 1994, but Norton has promised a posthumous album of Benny Joy covers. [ss]

ABOVE THE LAW

Livin' Like Hustlers (Ruthless/Epic) 1990
Vocally Pimpin' EP (Ruthless/Epic) 1991
Black Mafia Life (Ruthless) 1992
Uncle Sam's Curse (Ruthless) 1994

Capable if unimaginative rappers, Los Angeles' Above the Law were primordial gangstas, taking the violence and misogyny pioneered by N.W.A and others another step further down the road to ugly nihilism. Entertaining only in the most dismal sense, **Livin' Like Hustlers** (which features Ruthless label boss Eazy-E and lead producer Dr. Dre on "The Last Song") is less intimidating than it is unpleasant. Over handsome beats constructed from '70s soul classics (Cameo, Isaac Hayes, James Brown) as well as live guitar, bass and keyboards, self-styled hustlers Cold 187um (Gregory Hutchison), KM.G the Illustrator (Kevin Dulley), Go Mack (Arthur Goodman) and Total K-oss (Anthony Stewart) rhyme about cold-blooded violence (the Mega Side) and cold-hearted sex (the Ranching Side).

Vocally Pimpin' is a lengthy EP of new tracks (the most captivating of which, "Wicked," reveals an incidental political sensibility), studio chat, remixes—including three dissimilar versions of the non-LP "4 the Funk of It"—and promotional announcements for the then-upcoming second album.

Black Mafia Life, ably produced to an alternately fuzzy and frisky funk bump by Cold 187um, partly defuses the quartet's anger and vulgarity, integrating Above the Law into the growing gangsta mainstream with highly styled and obvious playacting (these guys should definitely call their agents about film work) and familiar MC boasts in the "black mafia mindset." "G-rupies Best Friend" (complete with ecstatic female moans) is as obnoxious as it has to be, but a good-natured lack of conviction—even on tracks like "Pimp Clinic" and "Pimpology 101"—and cozy grooves soften **Black Mafia Life** into a relatively appealing party. The guest shot by Eazy-E adds just the right touch of whiny bravado; ragga rapper Kokane freestyles on "Game Wreck-Oniz-Iz Game."

Exchanging sophisticated finery for casual threads, Above the Law get serious—about racism and oppression—on **Uncle Sam's Curse,** blaming the titular malediction for a variety of urban ills. The trio's political depth doesn't go much beyond "the system is always trying to keeping us down" (as "Set Free" inarticulates), however, and most of the album is a pernicious return to the gangsta banality of **Livin' Like Hustlers.** Cold 187um kicks more good grooves as producer, but he can't smooth over the lyrical nonsense. "Uncle Sam's Curse" can hardly be held responsible for the crude booty calls of "Everything Will Be Alright," the banging of "The 'G' in Me" or the multipurpose sex-and-drugs-and-guns "Who Ryde," in which Tone-Lōc makes an effective guest appearance. Ending with "Gangsta Madness," ATL borrows Ice Cube's vocal inflection for a solemn dedication to dead homies, acknowledging one law even these roughnecks can't pretend to be above. [i]

ABSOLUTE GREY

See *Pat Thomas.*

ACETONE

Acetone EP (Vernon Yard) 1993
Cindy (Vernon Yard) 1993
I Guess I Would (Vernon Yard) 1994
If You Only Knew (Vernon Yard) 1996

Once the rhythm section in Los Angeles garage-rockers Spinout, guitarist Mark Lightcap, drummer Steve Hadley and bassist Richie Lee became Acetone in the early '90s to make nearly rhythmless music more suited for the bedroom than the garage. The debut EP immediately establishes the trio's sound, a downbeat drone in the style of Luna or Low. But Acetone has yet to completely settle its identity, which allows for stretched-out explorations of everything from punk to country. Burning off its aggression in the first fifteen seconds of "I'm Gone" with a burst of three-chord rock, Acetone slowly strips the sound of melody and energy; by the fourth and last song, the eight-minute "Cindy," the band is making more mood than music.

The full-length **Cindy** doesn't include that song; the ten tracks vary in style and substance, including the feedback-drenched pop of "Come On," the '80s schlock rock of "Endless Summer" and a three-and-a-half-minute instrumental entitled "Intermission."

Acetone finds its focus on **I Guess I Would,** but the subject is surprising: country music. The trio performs sleepy-eyed versions of the Flying Burrito Brothers' "Juanita," John Prine's "The Late John Garfield Blues" and five other favorites, taking all that is languid and atmospheric from the originals (except for the relatively raucous eleven-minute version of Kris Kristofferson's "Border Lord") and leaving the rest behind.

The results of **I Guess I Would**'s roots searching linger on **If You Only Knew,** adding a weepy undercurrent of emotion to the band's low-key songs of relationship trouble. "I've Enjoyed as Much of This as I Can Stand" and "99" trudge with all the restrained power of a Neil Young slow-roller. Only on "The Final Say," for which Acetone turns the distortion pedal and metronome up a few notches, does the music's medicated veneer wear away, revealing a great '60s-style garage-rock band. Appropriately, it's in the lyrics to "The Final Say" that Acetone offers its best perspective on the motivation (or lack thereof) behind its music: "I'm so tired, but I'm on fire." [ns]

ACEYALONE

See *Freestyle Fellowship.*

ACID TEST

Trip on This (Can. Eggplant) 1992
Drop (Sire/Reprise) 1993

Lots of bands have members whose fame endures after their death, but guitarist Steve Fall of Toronto dance-pop quintet Acid Test was famous as a dead man before his life attracted public notice: he played the bothersome corpse in *Highway 61,* a devilish 1992 black comedy by award-winning Canadian filmmaker Bruce McDonald. Fall's work on the movie led to the creation of Acid Test with bassist Lucy Di Santo and their contribution of two strong songs ("Mr. Skin," "Dance") to its soundtrack. That the media-savvy group seemed destined for success was reinforced when Acid Test was signed by an American major. The hitch was that Fall and Di Santo lacked songwriting skills; rather than woodshed to work out the problem, they just kept releasing different mixes of "Mr. Skin" and "Dance." **Trip on This** contains three redundant mixes of the former and two of the latter; **Drop** adds yet another version of "Mr. Skin" to a passel of weaker songs that do nothing to advance the band's cause. Faced with withering criticism and a paucity of sales and radio play, Acid Test quietly retreated, and hasn't been heard from since. [ph]

A CONFEDERACY OF DUNCES

Tsk, Tsk, Tsk (Old School) 1989
Dunces With Wolves (Old School) 1991

JOHN DUNBAR

The Man Who Never Learns (Heartpunch) 1996

Informed enthusiasm for the British Invasion sound (mainly the jaunty folk-rock end of the Kinks and Hollies) doesn't prevent New York City power pop auteur John Dunbar from writing and singing about the here and now. The talented multi-instrumentalist with a light, sincere tenor is ambitious enough to create music for an off-Broadway show (*The Last Hand Laundry in Chinatown*) and homebrew fully realized concept albums (an as-yet-unreleased Rutles-like tribute entitled **Konks**), but—following the model of hero Ray Davies—inclined to do so by telescoping his vision down to modest and sympathetic appraisals of nobodies.

Dunbar recorded his first two albums with a quartet he named after the John Kennedy Toole novel. The delightful **Tsk, Tsk, Tsk** is a simply effective debut, shunning explicit retro styling in the catchy tunes and well-drawn portraits of people who could be neighbors ("Live for Lotto," "She Hates Good Looking Guys," "Don't Mess With Marge," "The Bride Has Braces"). Made with a different band lineup (lead guitarist Joe Pampel is a valuable addition), **Dunces With Wolves** replaces the debut's rudimentary production with well-defined studio sound that reveals the band's resemblance to Squeeze. Other than a few clumsy constructions, Dunbar's songwriting is more assured and meaningful. The memorable "Everybody's Nice ('Til You Know Them)" and "How She Used to Feel" reveal a streak of disillusionment, while "Hating Me Again" (a monthly emotional barometer) and "Betsey Johnson Dress" apply gentle humor to good effect. His multi-tracked singing on the most alluring melodies ("I Still Have Him," "The Land of Opposites," "The Fine Art of Settling") is positively uplifting.

The Dunces fell apart, and Dunbar became a solo artist. **The Man Who Never Learns,** his first album in five years, is an extended character study, a demoralized chronicle of frustration and loneliness ultimately redeemed by love. The intricately overdubbed vocal arrangement of the a cappella "Insecurity Guard" and the group-sing finale, "Don't We All," are technically impressive; the phony British accent and kazoo of "Frankly, the Idea Bores Me" add a comic touch. Ultimately, though, it's the haunting piano ballad "When She Says Goodbye" that stands out. [i]

ACTION SWINGERS

Action Swingers (Primo Scree/Caroline) 1991
More Fast Numbers EP (UK Wiiija) 1992
Decimation Blvd. (Caroline) 1993
Quit While You're Ahead (Caroline) 1994

Punk rock doesn't usually need or encourage auteurs, but there's no other word to describe New Yorker Ned Hayden, whose skeletal songs, raw Iggy-derived vocals and scrabbly guitar were the only constant element in the Action Swingers' burnin' garage.

Joined by guitarist/singer Julia Cafritz (on her way out of Pussy Galore), bassist Pete Shore (of Unsane) and drummer Bob Bert (ex–Sonic Youth/Bewitched/Pussy Galore), Hayden brings the surly attitude and a deliciously raw caveman stomp—but too few real songs—to the distorted studio compression of **Action Swingers.** The conceptual cleverness of "Song" and "Instrumental" (which it is) can't be overlooked, but swiping bits from Donovan and the Doors for "Funky Manc" is about as memorable as the debut gets. **Quit While You're Ahead** is an arduous compilation of pre-album slash 'n' screamers. Half of the ten tracks are from early singles—including the calamitous 1990 gutter-classic debut "Kicked in the Head" b/w "Bum My Trip," and "Fear of a Fucked Up Planet" b/w "Blow Job"—while the rest are noisy scrapheap findings, including two ("In the Hole" and "Losing My Cool") with drumming by J Mascis.

The Swingers then ceased to exist for more than a year, but re-formed (minus Cafritz and Shore, plus guitarist Bruce Bennett of the A-Bones and bassist Howie Pyro of D Generation) for a '92 UK tour and the **More Fast Numbers** EP, a five-songer that includes the legendary "Courtney Love." Bert and Bennett then split, leaving Hayden to make the Action Swingers' *chef d'oeuvre* with three no-name sidemen. The pressure-cooking **Decimation Blvd.** (a Sweet joke), tidily co-produced by Hayden and Nitebob Czaykowski, bumrushes hardcore with a postdated Dolls/Stooges rock sensibility, sounding for all the world like the hellhound spawn of the Ramones, MC5 and Shadows of Knight. Hayden declares his disgust and self-loathing in such jovial dizbusters as "I Don't Wanna Be This Way," "Glad to Be Gone," "Fooled Again" and "You Better Keep Your Big Mouth Shut," filling out the spectacular fourteen-song blur (a near-perfect twenty-one minutes in all!) with compulsory declarations of ennui ("Searching for Kicks," "I Can't Get No Action," "How Do You Work This Thing") that contribute mightily to the moving-violation fun. [i/jf]

See also *Unsane.*

OLETA ADAMS

See *Tears for Fears.*

BARRY ADAMSON

The Man With the Golden Arm EP (UK Mute) 1988
Moss Side Story (Mute/Restless) 1989

The Taming of the Shrewd EP (UK Mute) 1989
Delusion (Mute) 1991
Soul Murder (UK Mute) 1992
Cinema Is King EP (UK Mute) 1992
The Negro Inside Me (Mute) 1993

VARIOUS ARTISTS

Gas Food Lodging (Mute) 1992

On his first three solo releases, ex-Magazine/Bad Seeds bassist Barry Adamson created what were essentially voluptuous, ambitious soundtracks to non-existent films noir and, in the process, became an acknowledged influence on such higher-profile trip-hoppers as Portishead. The producers of 1991's witty American neo-noir *Delusion* were wise to secure the Mancunian to compose its actual soundtrack. Revealing a playful side mostly lacking from his forthright solo records, Adamson drenches the grooves with menacing organ, flamenco guitar and spaghetti western sass that perfectly evokes the film's double dealings. Also included: the recording debut of Miranda Sex Garden (whom Adamson discovered) on "Il Solitario" and a twisted, chugging rendition of "These Boots Are Made for Walking," featuring petulant vocals by Nick Cave cohort Anita Lane.

Returning to his movies of the mind, **Soul Murder** is a sketchbook of often brilliant ideas—crime jazz, sinewy dance, smoky bossa nova—all peppered with strange samples (including one from TV prison documentary *Scared Straight*) and spoken-word bits (the Fall's Marcia Schofield narrates "A Gentle Man of Colour," the gruesome tale of a young black man falsely accused of raping a white woman). For all the inventiveness on display, it's surprising that the highlight is a reinterpretation of the 007 theme that alternates between rock-steady ska and big-band attack. (**Cinema Is King** collects one track each from all the preceding releases save for the first and offers a concise sampler of Adamson's movie music.)

The six-track, album-length **The Negro Inside Me** is Adamson's most accessible recording yet. The Hammond-heavy jazz-funk of "The Snowball Effect" reiterates his gift for innovative sampling—in this case, an answering machine message left by his publicist. On the porno-dance "Je T'Aime . . . Moi Non Plus," he tackles the work of Serge Gainsbourg two years before fellow Bad Seed Mick Harvey recorded a tribute album to the steamy French crooner.

Adamson shared scoring duties for Alison Anders' debut film *Gas Food Lodging* with Dinosaur Jr's J Mascis. Amid a diverse set of vocal and instrumental tracks from other Mute artists, Adamson subtly sets moods with simple keyboard orchestrations in a half-dozen short pieces that aren't as discernibly Latin as several Spanish titles might imply. [db/i]

See also *Nick Cave and the Bad Seeds, Miranda Sex Garden.*

ADORABLE

Against Perfection (Creation/SBK) 1993
Fake (UK Creation) 1994

Although hailed by the British press for a pair of gloriously heavy first singles—"Sunshine Smile" and "I'll Be Your Saint"—this talented foursome from Coventry regrettably shot themselves in the media foot. In subsequent interviews, singer/guitarist Piotr Fijalkowski and bassist Wil (just Wil) snidely, stridently insisted that every other band of the time was crap and that young Adorable was a dead cert for immortality. That sealed their fate with an appalled music establishment and obscured the actual qualities of two extremely worthy albums of resplendent whomp-rock with jagged edges that are best described as post–Echo and the Bunnymen/early House of Love. In America, Adorable was foiled by a more traditional nemesis: being licensed to an indifferent US company.

Against Perfection is very nearly a greatest-hits collection—in fact, it yielded no fewer than three UK singles in addition to "Sunshine Smile" and "I'll Be Your Saint"—with sharp, varied songs that are by turns pretty, soaring and brooding. Fijalkowski's intentionally dramatic, full voice mixes Ian McCulloch with harsher tones, at times spitting out distaste and rancor, elsewhere all but shouting or coolly basking in the drenched melodies. The album's highlights include two of its singles: the dance-beat "Sistine Chapel Ceiling" and the neo-punk crashing of "Favorite Fallen Idol." Very strong.

Although unissued in America, **Fake** meets the sophomore challenge with surprising grace and ease. A more coherent, ambitious album that flows far better than its predecessor, it possesses twice the bite, more interesting guitar passages and an underlying obstinacy that fuels the immaculately built tunes. "Vendetta" is especially searing, mixing a furious New Order–style dance groove with heavy, ringing, darting guitars and a surprisingly vulnerable vocal. In the same lyrical vein, Fijalkowski takes clever aim at the antagonistic British press in "Kangaroo Court" ("I know I'm losing my appeal/Because I was hung, drawn and quartered before my trial/Without the privilege of denial") as if he knows the end is near. Sadly, it in fact was. The bitter band capitulated, stunning a Brussels audience in November 1994 by announcing it as their farewell performance. When last heard of, the disillusioned singer was working in his home studio, dabbling with, of all things, Pet Shop Boys–style facile pop. [jr]

AENONE

See *Nyack.*

AFGHAN WHIGS

Big Top Halloween (Ultrasuede) 1988
Retarded EP (Ger. Sub Pop) 1990
Up in It (Sub Pop) 1990
Congregation (Sub Pop) 1992
Uptown Avondale EP (Sub Pop) 1993
Gentlemen (Sub Pop/Elektra) 1994
Debonair EP (UK Blast First) 1994
What Jail Is Like (Sub Pop/Elektra) 1994
Honky's Ladder EP (UK Mute) 1996
Black Love (Sub Pop/Elektra) 1996

Every decade needs its ambassador of bad juju, the kind of sneering, self-involved superstud who bewitches, bothers and bewilders ordinarily intelligent women (and a smattering of men, no doubt) with his sheer pheremonal aura. Greg Dulli has done a neat job of claiming that role for himself: the frontman of Cincinnati's Afghan Whigs is possessed of an impressive swagger and one of the more (melo)dramatic voices this side of Jim Morrison. Dulli comports himself like a throwback to a pre-(sexual)-revolutionary era when women were unsuspecting prey just waiting to fall victim to a rod-packin' Romeo.

There's a surprising amount of subtlety—sophistication, even—rustling beneath the boozy, gutter-rat surface of the quartet's self-released debut. While Dulli's desperate, breathless rasp recalls **Hootenanny**-era Paul Westerberg (as does his uncommon wordsmithery: check out the bittersweet "Here Comes Jesus"), the rest of the band stirs '70s rock—from punk to pomp—into an aural hurricane with one hypnotic eye. An altogether terrific debut.

Typically gauzy Jack Endino production instantly brands **Up in It** as a Sub Pop issue. While the increased volume follows suit, the Whigs still wax more lyrical than their thrash'n'burn label contemporaries. There's more implied in the affecting "I Know Your Little Secret" and the disjointed country swing of "Son of the South" than mere sonic overkill, an effect somewhat reflected in the sleeve art's understated creepiness. (Three tracks from **Big Top Halloween** are included on the **Up in It** CD.)

The strangely flamboyant **Congregation** marks the beginning of Dulli's metamorphosis from everypunk wallflower to rakish scoundrel with a heart of glass. At various points on the spaciously constructed set, the singer portrays himself as obscure object of desire ("Conjure Me"), subjugate lover (the coy smack anecdote "I'm Her Slave") and, most convincingly, sexual predator ("Tonight"). The remaining Whigs do an impressive job of contriving panoramic images through judicious use of wah-wah guitar (Rick McCollum's contribution to the breathless "Turn on the Water") and the tribal drumbeats with which Steven Earle invokes an air of ritualistic surrender. The all-covers **Uptown Avondale** reveals a heretofore hidden facet of the band's art: its ability to delve into classic soul music without sounding patronizing or ironic. Dulli doesn't miss a vocal trick on bodice-rippers like Freda Payne's "Band of Gold" and—more surprisingly—gives a sensitive, nuanced reading of Dallas Frazier's "True Love Travels on a Gravel Road."

There's no such subtlety on **Gentlemen,** an album that threatens to give pomposity a good name. The ironically titled (and provocatively art-directed) disc is dauntingly exhaustive in its first-person survey of infidelity and perfidy, making it the first concept album where the protagonist's survival is kind of a drag. Dulli's over-the-top emoting—he goes from a whisper to a scream on track after track, most engagingly on "Debonair" and the lasciviously cocky "Be Sweet"—is matched by appropriately imperious arrangements that allow McCollum plenty of room to roam. Just when the ambience gets overly oppressive, the Whigs introduce some fresh air in the form of "My Curse," a sparse, piano-bar ballad sung by Scrawl's Marcy Mays. The lengthy **What Jail Is Like** mini-album offers two versions (one live) of its title track (from **Gentlemen**), along with several non-LP items, including Dan Penn's soul standard "The Dark End of the Street" and a live medley of the Supremes' "I Hear a Symphony" and "My World Is Empty Without You."

That blacker-than-thou attitude led the Whigs (who replaced Earle with Paul Buchignani in 1994) to cover Barry White's "Can't Get Enough of Your Love, Babe" on the soundtrack of Ted Demme's *Beautiful Girls,* a film in which they essentially serve the same role the Feelies did in Jonathan Demme's *Something Wild.* On **Black Love,** however, Dulli borders on minstrel-show shtick, chewing scenery non-stop through arena-soul ditties like the pimpspeak "Honky's Ladder" (which also features Prince vocal doppelgänger/Pigeonhed frontman Shawn Smith). Thankfully, the ghetto-ese abates on the album's more somber songs (like the gripping "Blame, Etc."), which allows the artful subtext of Dulli's ruminations on betrayal to shine through. [dss]

AFX

See *Aphex Twin.*

A HANDFUL OF DUST

See *Dead C.*

A HOUSE

On Our Big Fat Merry-Go-Round (Sire/Reprise) 1988
I Want Too Much (Sire/Reprise) 1990
I Am the Greatest (Setanta/Radioactive) 1992
Wide Eyed and Ignorant (Setanta/Radioactive) 1995

A House singer Dave Couse crafts literate (not to mention wordy) treatises on romance and frustration that should send most rock lyricists scrambling for a thesaurus. Unpredictable and relentlessly smart, the Dublin quartet's first two albums toy with a buoyant folkiness the group wholly embraced on the next two. **On Our Big Fat Merry-Go-Round** soars with the joyous, charging "Call Me Blue"; **I Want Too Much** is typified by the witty pop of "The Patron Saint of Mediocrity" and "I Think I'm Going Mad."

The group recorded **I Am the Greatest** pared down to three core members, with help from, among others, Mekons violinist Susie Honeyman. Sympathetically produced by Edwyn Collins, the album is simply stunning, opening with a grating yet powerful shit list ("I Don't Care") but quickly easing into lilting fiddle-accented pop that recalls the best of Dexy's Midnight Runners, the Violent Femmes and the Pogues. "Take It Easy on Me" and "You're Too Young" are just two standouts; the US edition inexplicably deletes three tracks from the import.

Mostly produced by Collins, **Wide Eyed and Ignorant** is not much of a departure, though the domestic version again deletes three tracks while adding two. "Curious" and "Here Come the Good Times" showcase the trio at the peak of its hook-crafting powers. Couse bemoans his broken heart with such average-guy likability on the delightful "Why Me?" that you can't help but feel for him. [db]

AINTS

See *Ed Kuepper.*

AIRLINES

Airlines (Quixotic) 1994

GIANT MUMS

The Giant Mums (Quixotic) 1993

Something like a better-adjusted Feelies with loosened wigs or Yo La Tengo on a coffee rush, New York's Airlines perforates its brisk, understated rhythm guitar pop with pure, sustained distortion leads. In "10,000 Days," the effect recalls Robert Fripp's evanescent sound paintings. Singer/guitarist John Tanzer (ex–Ex–Lion Tamers, the Wire cover band that toured with its idols in 1987), guitarist/singer Joe Arcidiacono and bassist John Neilson all write, which provides a degree of stylistic diversity within the quintet's relatively narrow framework and makes **Airlines** an uneven debut. Neilson's "Steady Goes" is gorgeous and intense, with a folky undercurrent; Arcidiacono's "Interval" bends the Feelies influence back to one of its sources—Television—and Tanzer's "No. 2" owes some of its herkyjerk tempo to early Talking Heads. But "Weekend," recorded live, is an annoying gripe about waiting for the phone to ring.

Several years after Airlines got off the ground in 1988, Tanzer launched another band, the Giant Mums, which actually beat the parent group to market. Compared to Airlines, the trio has stranger concepts ("Minutes Later, Nothing Gets Out Every Stain" and "Sheep in the Blacklight Room" are only two of the odd titles on **The Giant Mums;** the chorus of "We Made It Sing" begins "meow meow meow") as well as a singular sensibility and, for the most part, an aggressive, jagged guitar attack. Wharton Tiers' production makes the most of intriguing compositions, shaping the band's fill-the-void playing and Tanzer's singing into moderate wind-shear excursions that keep moving forward. [i]

AIR MIAMI

See *Unrest.*

ALANIS

See *Alanis Morissette.*

ALASKA

See *Chris Stamey.*

WILLIE ALEXANDER AND THE BOOM BOOM BAND

Willie Alexander and the Boom Boom Band (MCA) 1978
Meanwhile . . . Back in the States (MCA) 1979

WILLIE ("LOCO") ALEXANDER

Solo Loco (Fr. New Rose) 1981 (Bomp!) 1981
Autre Chose (Fr. New Rose) 1982
A Girl Like You (Fr. New Rose) 1982
Taxi-Stand Diane EP (Fr. New Rose) 1984
Greatest Hits (Fr. New Rose) 1985
Tap Dancing on My Piano (Fr. New Rose) 1986
The Dragons Are Still Out (Fr. New Rose) 1988
Fifteen Years of Rock'n'Roll (Fr. Fan Club) 1991
Willie Loco Boom Boom Ga Ga 1975–1991 (Northeastern) 1992
Private WA (Tourmaline) 1992

WILLIE ALEXANDER'S PERSISTENCE OF MEMORY ORCHESTRA

Willie Alexander's Persistence of Memory Orchestra (Accurate/Distortion) 1993

Boston scene patriarch and would-be Beat Generation holdout Alexander (whose best-known song remains the tributary "Kerouac," first unveiled on a 1975 single) is an intriguing and unique historical figure, the eternal ghost of the Rat who has raved and played through more musical eras than most musicians have even survived. The irrepressible singer/pianist's redoubtable résumé goes back to the '60s and includes such groups as the Lost, Bagatelle, Bluesberry Jam, Grass Menagerie—even a stint in the post–Lou Reed Velvet Underground. If he was never really a punk (despite such conceptually righteous songs as 1976's "Hit Her wid de Axe"), Alexander's intelligence and commitment to rock'n'roll purity (minus the eternal adolescence) made him a part of the punks' underworld; maturity and boundless enthusiasm for writing and performing music has sustained him into the '90s.

In the late '70s, Alexander and the Boom Boom Band snuck onto a major label (MCA) and made two albums of routine bar-band rock. In the early '80s, his more artistic, keyboard-based Tom Waitsy jazz-cabaret-Stones-rock'n'roll mélange—**Autre Chose** and **A Girl Like You** backed by his band, the Confessions, and solo work alike—was only issued in France. It's only been in recent years that his music has become domestically available again.

In light of Alexander's discographical complexity, **Willie Loco Boom Boom Ga Ga 1975–1991** is better than one-stop shopping, it's the only opportunity for a newcomer to glean a sensible career summary without spending years searching out now-rare import vinyl. The sloppy, spirited festival of bands, unpretentious sounds and songs (twenty-two in all) is neatly annotated by the star. (Sample: "I wrote this ['Kerouac'] in my bathtub in two minutes after thinking about Jack for 20 years.") There's nothing fancy here, but Alexander's plainspoken writing and skilled from-the-heart delivery of original songs that chronicle people ("Taxi-Stand Diane," "Abel and Elvis," "Dirty Eddie") and places ("Mass. Ave.," "At the Rat") make this an invaluable diary of a rocker (not, it needs to be noted, a rapper).

Alexander is also one hell of a spoken-word artist, and that's an area he's been exploring to good effect of late. **Private WA,** a collection of studio recitations and diary entries with ambient keyboard accompaniment recorded between 1984 and 1990, makes the personal compelling and sharp-focuses the universal. A bit heavy on the Burroughsian delivery at times (once a would-be Beat, always a would-be Beat), but consistently revealing and engaging.

The most contemporary track on **1975–1991** is the previously unreleased debut of the Persistence of Memory Orchestra. A full album by that quartet—Willie singing and playing piano with two horn players and a drummer—became his first new American all-music release in a dozen years. "I'm like Rip Van Winkle waking up from his nap," sings Alexander in the autobiographical "Fishtown Horrible," and it's true: this hairyassed but somehow cogent rock/fusion jazz/rock (all loosely laced, with hip-hop and Suicide-al techno accessories) has the recharged imagination of a young turk rubbing his eyes in anticipation, not an aging dozer settling in for the late innings. With wholly reimagined versions of such oldies as "Mystery Train" and Alexander's own "Shopping Cart Louie," the record is—smartly produced, bizarre and thoroughly unpredictable—an improbably welcome creative rebirth. [i]

See also *TPRG.*

ALGEBRA SUICIDE

Algebra Suicide EP7 (Buzzerama) 1982
An Explanation for That Flock of Crows EP7 (Buzzerama) 1984

Big Skin (Cause & Effect) 1986 (Buzzerama) 1988
The Secret Like Crazy (RRR/DOM) 1988 (RRR/Cargo America) 1992
Real Numbers (Ger. Pursuit of Market Share) 1989
Alpha Cue (Bel. Body) 1990
Swoon (Widely Distributed) 1991
Tongue Wrestling (Widely Distributed) 1994

LYDIA TOMKIW

Incorporated (Widely Distributed) 1995

Of the many vocalist/instrumentalist duos to emerge in and around the new wave, this Chicago couple was unique, a fascinating marriage of guitarist/synthesist Don Hedeker's music and poet/vocalist Lydia Tomkiw's romantic-with-an-absurd-streak texts. Over the course of its career, Algebra Suicide flirted with pop forms and occasionally shared stylistic ground with both Laurie Anderson and the Velvet Underground but never wavered from its own individual identity. Algebra Suicide isn't rock'n'roll, but even those with an aversion to modern poetry should test the pair's waters.

The eponymous debut, a four-song 7-inch, offers a sketchy but atmospheric mix of guitar and rhythm box behind Tomkiw's coolly intoned short texts, which include the haunting and memorable "True Romance at the World's Fair," among the group's most enduring pieces. **An Explanation for That Flock of Crows** adds bass, better sound and new vocal inflections (Tomkiw nearly sings "Tonight") to the recitation of four more numbers made accessible—even catchy—by tangible, occasionally narrative ideas and strong internal tempos.

Originally issued on cassette with a lyric booklet and later revamped on vinyl, **Big Skin** introduces piano and simple synthesizers to Hedeker's increasingly complex and dynamic music. The duo occasionally stumbles in its efforts to synchronize the verbal/instrumental rhythms, but both the song-form music and the lyrical content (such as a fascinating, wry discussion of death entitled "Little Dead Body Poem") are engrossing.

The Secret Like Crazy is a generous compilation: three tracks from each EP, half of **Big Skin,** four oldies from various sources and three new cuts. **Real Numbers** is a convivial 1988 live album, recorded with tapes supplementing Hedeker's onstage guitar work. Introducing new material and revisiting more than a dozen oldies, it's an ear-opener for a band that might otherwise seem studio-bound.

Alpha Cue ups the couple's production ambitions, employing a guest to play bass and piano on two numbers and delivering carefully formed tracks with a credible band sound and enough chordal structure to easily support melodies. Tomkiw's multi-tracked vocals occasionally resemble tune-shy singing more than recitation. Sample: "What's inside me is rampant/Wanting ice bath or alcohol sponge/Something to extract it into a test tube/Glowing in the dark like Madame Curie's lover."

Her carefully measured flow and his one-man arrangements both continue to gain style and confidence on **Swoon,** a CD that includes all of **Alpha Cue.** The poetess' structural experiments go so far as "Tender Red Net," a series of palindromes, but the bulk of her provocative prose is personal contemplations riddled with anxious emotions and aroused with sexual imagery. A nouveau rock star turns out to be a big-headed jerk in "He's Famous Now," but even the changing of the seasons ("After Busy Summer") is described as "big lipped, hyper, with bawdy tone"; the fog in "Charming Twilight Haze" is "sexy . . . thick enough to choke on."

Tomkiw doesn't mince words—or maybe that's exactly what she does—in "What I Like Doing Best," the unrestrained paean to kissing that opens **Tongue Wrestling,** Algebra Suicide's final album and easily their best. Hedeker outdoes himself with grand backing tracks that sift through early '80s new wave idioms (think of the sweeping guitar/synth vistas of A Flock of Seagulls, Big Country and Human League) and update them; Tomkiw's ticklish vocals have enough up-and-down motion to be free-style singing. Though the words and music don't exactly seem related or connected, the two elements still play off the moods and catch the angled light of each other, turning tracks like "Thank You" ("I have no sleeves, no pockets or secret hiding places/Except my head, my heart and other such tiny empty holes"), "One Night I Fell in Love" (a harrowing hallucination about obsession: "So very much in love, so I got up and drank a fifth of gin/And smoked a million cigarettes, and thought about/All the dead people I knew to make me drowsy . . .") and "Loose Change," a powerful meditation on the meaning of money: "I am living to find a new method/Of measuring success."

Relocating to New York, Tomkiw made her solo debut, using various musicians—including the Chicago trio Reality Scare, the Cleveland quartet Sosumi, Britain's Martin Bowes (ex-Attrition) and Edward Ka-Spel with some of his Legendary Pink Dots—to provide strong, surging tracks of atmospheric rock and adventurous ambient techno. In a voice that lacks some of the singsong delight of her previous work, Tomkiw recites pieces like "Iris," which makes effectively sensual use of vocal distortion, "Thief" (personality transfer set to what could be a film score) and "Saturn Makes a Move," a relationship-ending slap delivered with steely bitterness over coldly electronic industrial noises. The backing of "Pretty Something" has an otherworldly quality; the edgy, wistful relationship lyrics, however, are clear and real: "Because it was hopeless/I turned my face toward you and let you color my skin." [i]

See also *TPRG.*

ALICE DONUT

Donut Comes Alive (Alternative Tentacles) 1988
Bucketfulls of Sickness and Horror in an Otherwise Meaningless Life (Alternative Tentacles) 1989
Mule (Alternative Tentacles) 1990
Revenge Fantasies of the Impotent (Alternative Tentacles) 1991
The Untidy Suicides of Your Degenerate Children (Alternative Tentacles) 1992
Dry Humping the Cash Cow (Alternative Tentacles) 1994
Pure Acid Park (Alternative Tentacles) 1995

To paraphrase Donny and Marie, this durable New York combo is a little bit Zappa, a little bit cacophonous punk. That combination makes its quirkcore expeditions either grin-inducing or grating, depending on one's ability to stomach the *unique* vocal-style of frontman Tomas Antona, whose high-pitched screech falls somewhere between Perry Farrell and Sparks frontman Russell Mael on the weed-o-meter. While it took the band a while to find its footing—the first two albums are little more than extended, grad–school fortified fart jokes—Alice Donut did develop a knack for sniggeringly malevolent tweaking of mainstream and underground mores alike.

Donut Comes Alive proves man cannot live by snot alone. The band's gleeful vivisection of public figures as far-flung as Mason Reese and Joan of Arc is mean-spirited, but that's a less fundamental problem than Antona's insistently telegraphed punchlines. In case you didn't grow tired of hippie lampoons a decade before, the band even takes the time to eviscerate Donovan's "Sunshine Superman." The targets selected over the course of the jauntily titled **Bucketfulls of Sickness and Horror in an Otherwise Meaningless Life** aren't any more ambulatory, but at least most of them are contemporary (see "Sinéad O'Connor on MTV"). The artily slurred guitar tones—which on occasion draw attention away from Antona's yowl—are, however, a more effective conduit than the debut's direct punk-pop.

Mule sheds the band's juvenile skin to reveal tight intricacy and more incisive social commentary. Tomas' discovery of more listenable ways to express himself is happily coupled with vast improvements in the band's playing; city life, however, seems to be getting to them. "J Train Downtown: A Nest of Murder," "Bottom of the Chain" and "Roaches in the Sink" betray enough misery for a week's worth of *New York Post*s.

Although a temporary three-guitar front line occasionally lends an alterna–Molly Hatchet feel to **Revenge Fantasies of the Impotent,** the album benefits from Antona's growing familiarity with composure. By lowering both the pitch of his voice and the tone of his rhetoric, Antona increases his slugging percentage considerably, connecting with full force on the sinuous "Telebloodprintmediadeathwhore." The band even seems to have learned to work its irony meter, judging by the wacked-out instrumental version of Black Sabbath's "War Pigs" (which supplants the sludgy guitar riff at the center of the original with Steve Moses' slurry trombone). The quintet regresses slightly on **The Untidy Suicides of Your Degenerate Children,** contenting themselves with making silly noises and drawing broad caricatures of suburban losers. Moses, who's also the drummer, shines on complex rhythmic structures like those underpinning "Untidy Suicides" and the Dixieland-screech "She Loves You She Wants You It's Amazing How Much Head Wounds Bleed," but most of the album recalls Frank Zappa at his worst.

Tongues are planted in cheeks even before the first note of the live **Dry Humping the Cash Cow** is struck—with stadium-volume crowd noise spliced in as a replacement for the CBGB audience that actually witnessed the show firsthand. The precision and pop-savvy of the band's playing—particularly on the part of bassist Sissi Schulmeister—on songs like "Green Meat Stew" (a rewrite of the first album's "Green Pea Soup") and the previously unreleased "Hose" come as something of a surprise, as does the power mustered without the benefit of studio gewgaws. The electricity even pervades Antona's surreal spoken-word shtick, in full effect on "The Son of a Disgruntled X–Postal Worker Reflects on His Life While Getting Stoned in the Parking Lot of a Winn Dixie While Listening to Metallica." A good introduction.

There's nothing remotely subdued about **Pure Acid Park,** a daffily psychedelic set that incorporates everything from banjo and washboard to remarkably ugly spuzz-guitar into dour millennialist rants like "Dreaming in Cuban" (which allows Antona to revisit his heritage) and "Shining Path." The band's most focused and affecting release, **Pure Acid Park** crystallizes its maverick raving and boundary-pushing instrumentation with a thoroughness that poseurs like Perry Farrell could never imagine. Alice Donut broke up after playing its one thousandth show in January 1996. [dss]

ALICE IN CHAINS

Facelift (Columbia) 1990
Sap EP (Columbia) 1991
Dirt (Columbia) 1992
Jar of Flies (Columbia) 1993
Alice in Chains (Columbia) 1995
MTV Unplugged (Columbia) 1996

MAD SEASON

Above (Columbia) 1995

It was all so simple before Led Zeppelin. Despite some overlap (Deep Purple), it was pretty easy to tell which hard-rock bands were seeking to beat audiences into submission and which were expecting credit for melody, dynamics and at least a pretense of innovation. Then came Page, Plant, Bonham and Jones to trample the line away with abusive drumming, super riffology and screaming id-iocy crossed with rustic acoustics, intricately ambitious arrangements and lyrics sprung from sources other than horror movies and superhero comics.

Flash forward to the American Northwest, circa 1989. The region's burgeoning hard-rock scene comes in three varieties: ex-punks who worship Led Zeppelin, non-punks who worship Led Zeppelin and permanent punks who just don't give a fuck. While the third category produced the erratic tradition-busting of Mudhoney and Nirvana, the first two yielded Tad, Soundgarden, Alice in Chains and Pearl Jam, retroids whose essential differences from vintage metal have less to do with the sound of music than their distinctive senses of self and purpose. Soundgarden wants to be the serious modern equal to its idol, gods of '90s thunder, while Pearl Jam strives to nullify the issue with compelling faith in its own individuality. That leaves Alice in Chains, predestined by its torpid unoriginality to contentedly embody dumb-rock as if the '70s were still in full swing. Mediocre to the core and with at least one member regrettably quick to make the same heroin mistake as misguided Charlie Parker acolytes seeking unattainable inspiration via substance abuse, the quartet owes its dramatic tug to the personal messes chronicled on its records. If it wasn't for bad shit, Alice in Chains wouldn't have no shit (to sing about) at all.

Trotting out one of the hoariest clichés in the punkmetal phrase book and setting the agenda for much of what follows, guitarist/songwriter Jerry Cantrell has singer Layne Staley open the thuggish bore that is **Facelift** by declaring "We Die Young." Attempting poetry-as-a-second-language, the songs rock hard in the service of such lunkheaded lines (some attributable to the vocalist) as "Walls of thought, strong and high/As my castle crumbles with time" and "Here I sit writing on the paper/Trying to make the words you can't ignore." Such inanity would be excusable if the music supplied the missing imagination or wit, but **Facelift** is dismayingly consistent in that regard.

The five new songs on **Sap** amplify the band's Led Zep exertions with ruminative rusticity ("Brother," the all-acoustic "Right Turn"), moody bluesiness ("Got Me Wrong") and not-the-real-thing-but-big-fans guest appearance by Chris Cornell of Soundgarden and the dreadful Ann Wilson of Heart. (Mudhoney's Mark Arm, who doesn't emit Plant-like noises in public, also sings along.) Inarticulating his programmatic bleak vision in "Am I Inside," Staley sticks the only memorable hook here into "Black is all I feel/So this is how it feels to be free." The unlisted fifth track is a pastiche of dance-hall piano, silly samples, industrial pounding and sound effects that teases a surprising lighter side from a generally dismal band.

Taking structural cues from Metallica and Pearl Jam (and getting an assist from Slayer's Tom Araya), Alice in Chains and producer Dave Jerden fry up a sizzling metal platter with a thunderous bottom (credit bassist Mike Starr and drummer Sean Kinney) on **Dirt;** lockstep riffs move songs along like machinery performing intricate and repetitive assembly line maneuvers. The songs aren't musically involving as such, but the intensity and density of their performances gives them an effectively menacing aura. What's more memorable about **Dirt,** however, is its unguarded (if obliquely cast) Staley diaries of drug addiction. (As explicit as it gets: "What's my drug of choice?/Well, what have you got?/I don't go broke and I do it a lot.") Appalling in their death obsessions and relentless wretchedness, songs like "God Smack," "Hate to Feel" and "Junkhead" wallow miserably without any promise of long-term redemption. "Ah, what's the difference I'll die/In this sick world of mine," Staley sings in "Sickman," and echoes that thought in nearly every song. All of which leads to unanswerable questions of intent: gutsy self-examination, wolf-crying sensationalism or queasy self-exploitation? Tragedy is ideal source material for art, but it's highly unsettling to hear a band in the middle of a crisis fill an album with reports on how bad it feels. And no matter how grim the strung-out life is pictured to be, living through it in public without evidence of doing anything to escape an avowedly suicidal existence sends a dangerously seductive message of acquiescence.

Written and recorded in a week with new bassist Mike Inez, the self-produced, mostly unplugged **Jar of Flies** repeats the loud LP/quiet EP pattern established by the juxtaposition of **Facelift** and **Sap,** adding seven new songs, strings and an intriguing semi-electric stylistic plateau (erected on mood rings borrowed from R.E.M., America, the Allman Brothers Band and Mountain's "Nantucket Sleighride") to the repertoire. Redressing **Dirt**'s moral failing in a quizzical blend of bluntness and obfuscation, Cantrell clarifies the band's view of drug addiction with "Don't Follow." Although it vividly enumerates the cost ("Forgot my woman, lost my friends . . . sleep in sweat . . . my face it's growin' old . . . scared to death . . ."), the best advice the song can offer is "Say goodbye, don't follow/Misery is so hollow." That's not much to go on. The affecting "Rotten Apple," "Nutshell" and two others co-written by Inez reach previously unexplored melodic terrain and indicate a more tuneful future for the band's music. That, and the fact that Staley's steely voice actually suits the restrained ambience of these songs, makes the group's arena metal seem even more misguided.

The group evidently realized that, at least enough to fiddle the formula and gimmickify its next album. Inez calmly leads the music out of the metal woods to a poppier clearing on nearly half the tracks (three others he didn't write head that way as well, but his influence is manifestly substantial). **Alice in Chains** starts with a typical roar ("Grind") but immediately downshifts into the charged atmospherics and controlled feedback symphony of "Brush Away" and continues switching between bellowing force and various restrained alternatives. The blaring songs send Staley's voice through distortion processors to corny effect, but the singer rises (lowers?) to the challenge of such engagingly low-key tracks as "Frogs," "Shame in You" and "Heaven Beside You." His ability to come down off his rock chariot and show reserve and subtlety (not to mention attractive harmonies) is impressive, but not as encouraging as the newfound will to survive and romantic dedication of the lyrics. However dubious the impulse, Staley seems genuinely concerned (in "Sludge Factory") that "the body of one soul I adore wants to die . . . I say stay long enough to repay all those who caused strife." The craggy prayer of "God Am" includes an encouraging request: "All of this death you're sending/Best throw some free heart mending." Cantrell reflects the same recovery mindset: "You'd be well advised not to plan my funeral before the body dies," he warns in "Grind," adding (in the CSN-ish "Over Now") "Guess it's over now/I seem alive somehow." The band's last word on addiction, one hopes, **Alice in Chains** (which bears remarkable similarity in thinking to the Red Hot Chili Peppers' **One Hot Minute,** released a month or two earlier in the fall of '95) clears away old business but leaves open the question of what topic Alice might find up its sleeve for an encore.

Side projects have become as common among Northwest bands as cigarette lighters at Melissa Etheridge concerts, and Alice in Chains is not about to be an exception to that rule. Recorded during a band breakup between **Jar of Flies** and **Alice in Chains,** Mad Season's **Above** unites Staley, Pearl Jam guitarist Mike McCready, drummer Barrett Martin of Screaming Trees and bassist John Baker Saunders in a boring tribute to arena rock and blues-rock of the late '70s. (Anyone looking for a sandwich of P-Jam and Chains is better recommended to a shuffle-play CD changer.) The record's actual significance is in Staley's confessional lyrics, which serve as something of a bridge between the desolation of **Dirt** and the cleanliness of **Alice in Chains.** "Long Gone Day" finds him drowning in tears, clutching a silver spoon and an open flame but acknowledging that he's lost his way; "I Don't Know Anything" goes even further in accepting the wrongness of his situation. Finally, the admission (in "River of Deceit") that "My pain is self-chosen" effectively negates the pathos of everything else he has to say in song, which makes it the closest he's ever come to real art. [i]

See also *Guns n' Roses, My Sister's Machine, Pearl Jam, Screaming Trees.*

ALKAHOLIKS

21 & Over (Loud/RCA) 1993
Coast II Coast (Loud/RCA) 1995

Part of the '90s West Coast revival of old-school rap sensibilities, San Fernando Valley's Alkaholiks take the "party-and-bullshit" theme to its inevitable falling-down-drunk-and-hurling end. Fortunately they've managed to avoid becoming a one-joke act with a slick combination of E-Swift's razor-sharp beats and Tash and (especially) J-Ro's hilarious rhymes. Clocking in at all of thirty-six minutes, **21 & Over** captures the adrenaline of a rocking house party with Mom and Dad gone for the weekend. When J-Ro burps his way (on-beat) groggily through a verse of "Only When I'm Drunk" that refers to "Iko Iko," it even sounds like art.

Coast II Coast finds E-Swift's music as incisive as ever, while Tash and J-Ro try to move past their obvious shtick to consider music's past and future. "WLIX" (an ode to on-air freestyles and breakbeat records), "Flashback" (a tribute to old-school routines) and "2014" (in which J-Ro projects the survival of hip-hop two decades into the future) make their point without coming off preachy. But only the two tracks produced by Diamond D ("Let It Out" and "The Next Level") recall the first album's lighthearted spirit. Confronting kids at the corner liquor store, "21 and Under" even reveals some ambivalence about the group's personae. This party isn't over yet. [jzc]

ALL

Allroy Sez. . . . (Cruz) 1988
Allroy for Prez . . . (Cruz) 1988
Allroy's Revenge (Cruz) 1989
Trailblazer (Cruz) 1990
Allroy Saves (Cruz) 1990
Percolater (Cruz) 1992
Breaking Things (Cruz) 1993
Pummel (Interscope/Atlantic) 1995

TONYALL

New Girl, Old Story (Cruz) 1991

In 1987, the Descendents parted ways with vocalist Milo Aukerman, bringing ex–Dag Nasty singer Dave Smalley in to take over, and—using the title of the group's final album for a name—transmuted into All, drummer (and ex–Black Flagger) Bill Stevenson's long-brewing caffeine concept quartet with bassist Karl Alvarez and guitarist Stephen Egerton. The Lomita, California, band began by putting a melodic spin and a goofy, good-natured lyrical twist on punky, clear guitar rock, but through enormous productivity and a procession of lead singers (the weakest link in All's chain) has developed into a more substantial and serious proposition.

At the first LP's silliest point, All sings a Dickies-ish ode to a fast-food joint ("Alfredo's") in the hopes of getting free food. But it's not All jokes: "Just Perfect," "#10 (Wet)" and "Hooidge" have killer hooks and a beach-blanket sound energized by hardcore leftovers. **Allroy for Prez . . .** dispenses with the humor for eight (six on vinyl) rocking love songs. The playing and production are great, but the material (written individually by all hands) doesn't consistently connect. Between Smalley's bitter "Wrong Again," Alvarez's cynical "I Hate to Love" and Stevenson's idyllic "Just Perfect" (added to the CD from a prior 12-inch), the disc gains melodic momentum, peaking on "Postage," an overdriven Shoes-like power pop hummer.

Scott Reynolds replaced Smalley in time for **Allroy's Revenge,** a speedy, punkier-sounding album of broadening artistic ambition that lacks the production clarity, melodic strength and carefree demeanor of All's early work. Existential anxieties and problems with women set a serious tone unleavened by the hard-edged music. (Released as a single, the delightful "She's My Ex" is the exception that best demonstrates the problem.) Still, a snappy bonus rendition of "Hot Rod Lincoln" proves that All hasn't entirely lost its taste for fun.

In a clever bit of continuity, the live **Trailblazer,** recorded at New York's CBGB in July 1989, begins with the song that ends **Revenge** and goes on to draw more than half of its material from that album. Flat, mushy sound and unspectacular performances make it an easy show to skip.

The pursuit of the mythic All then brought the group to **Allroy Saves,** a complex and sophisticated album that trades in difficult rhythms and intricate guitar figures, pop melodies and thoughtful lyrics. With Reynolds taking the lead writing role, conversational narratives about losers, fools, cops and frogs make **Saves** fascinating and provocative; the rough music alternates All-some catchiness (as on old pal Milo Aukerman's Gen X–y "Just Like Them") with a challenging attack that approaches an unpretentious punk Police. (The high end of Reynolds' voice does have a Sting-like quality to it.)

Temporarily reuniting with erstwhile Descendents bassist Tony Lombardo, All became Tonyall to cut an album of his songs. Lombardo, Reynolds and Alvarez take turns singing lead on **New Girl, Old Story,** a flimsy power pop outing in which goony sentimental lyrics are the only serious fly in its inoffensive ointment. "I've got your picture in my guitar case/I guess that I am just a hopeless case . . ."

The excellent **Percolater** reheats All's inventive pop-punk variation without missing a conceptual beat. Having relocated to Brookfield, Missouri, the foursome continues to break barriers and bridge styles with growing skill, humor and strength in varied directions. When the tightly arranged music isn't incorporating sophisticated Police-y rhythmic shifts or showboating fusion guitar figures (in the instrumental "Birds"), All could pass for Squeeze's punk-schooled cousins (see the prosaic family report of "Wonder," the craggy cow manure of "Missouri 63"), the Ramones' big brothers ("Minute" calmly speeds through its three-chord melody) or Midwest rockers ("Empty" mixes elements of Cheap Trick, Soul Asylum and the Magnolias). Ultimately, this natural progression of wit and wood is all All, All good.

Following another change in HQ (this time pitching tent in Fort Collins, Colorado) and lead singers (trading Reynolds for Chad Price), All loosened up, dropped its grown-up demeanor and made an entertaining, uncomplicated punk-rock record. Loud, hard, fast and totally lacking in the subtlety, details and dynamics that made **Percolater** so special, **Breaking Things** tears along densely at full tilt, navigating firm melodies, super hooks and troubled lyrics with the easy confidence of Bad Religion. Although the material is uneven ("Politics" is unmitigated thrash, the likes of which All hasn't played in years), the pop-cool quality of the best songs is uncompromised, just served up without sonic trimmings. Stevenson's "Shreen" is a disconsolate romantic dynamo with a superb anthem chorus worthy of the Replacements; his miserable

"Guilty" and "Birthday I.O.U." are nearly as good. Alvarez's terse "Right" gets through a complete and memorable crash course in under two minutes and leaves the tune lingering in the air. Price's voice suits hardcore better than Reynolds' ever did, and the band seems to have settled toward that sound without any embarrassment at the implications of such an uncomplicated approach.

All of which cleared the decks and prepared All for its major-label debut, **Pummel.** With valuable writing contributions by Price and no specific stylistic axes to swing or bury (except the one obviously being sharpened for an unnamed but evidently real rock journalist in the venomous "Uncle Critic"), the quartet rares back and fires off a rock mulligan that has big, meaty chunks of everything in All's arsenal. Unrecognizable as the All of old, the group lashes Egerton's intricate guitar power and Price's throaty voice to typically well-crafted songs that become harsh punk ("Stalker," "This World") and racing popcore ("Button It") as convincingly as charged rock ("Self-Righteous," "Black Sky") or lovable loud pop ("Miranda," "Long Distance," "Breakin' Up"). The lyrics rake over the coals of failed relationships and antagonistic acquaintances (and, in Egerton's "On Foot," mechanical transportation), generally sticking to the band's thoughtful standards until abandoning them completely for the whiny stupidity of Stevenson's "Hetero" ("I never get any chicks/But it's better than a gun/Or a dick in the mouth"). Other than that lapse, **Pummel** is a winning combination of mighty tunes, power and intelligence. [i]

DAEVID ALLEN & KRAMER

See *Kramer.*

MARC ALMOND

Vermin in Ermine (UK Some Bizzare/Phonogram) 1984
Stories of Johnny (UK Some Bizzare/Virgin) 1985
A Woman's Story (UK Some Bizzare/Virgin) 1986
Violent Silence EP (Bel. Virgin) 1986
Melancholy Rose EP (UK Some Bizzare/Virgin) 1987
Mother Fist . . . and Her Five Daughters (UK Some Bizzare/Virgin) 1987
Singles 1984–1987 (UK Some Bizzare/Virgin) 1987
The Stars We Are (Some Bizzare/Capitol) 1988
Jacques (Some Bizzare/Rough Trade) 1989
Enchanted (Some Bizzare/Capitol) 1990
Tenement Symphony (Some Bizzare/Sire/Reprise) 1991
A Virgin's Tale Vol. I (UK Some Bizzare/Virgin) 1992
A Virgin's Tale Vol. II (UK Some Bizzare/Virgin) 1992
12 Years of Tears (Some Bizzare/Sire/Reprise) 1993
Absinthe: The French Album (UK Some Bizzare) 1994
Treasure Box (Some Bizzare/EMI) 1995
Fantastic Star (UK Mercury) 1996

MARC AND THE MAMBAS

Untitled (UK Some Bizzare) 1983
Torment and Toreros (UK Some Bizzare) 1983

SOFT CELL/MARC ALMOND

Memorabilia: The Singles (Polydor) 1991

Listeners who acknowledge Marc Almond only as the voice behind Soft Cell's "Tainted Love" do the English singer a great disservice. Since that electropop landmark in 1981, Almond has steadfastly devoted his career to exploring the art of the song. As an interpreter, he has successfully taken on Jacques Brel (on **Jacques**), '60s obscurities (on the mini-album **A Woman's Story**), Brecht and Weill ("Surabaya Johnny" and "Pirate Jenny" on the EP of "Melancholy Rose")—even Madonna ("Like a Prayer"). His original compositions draw inspiration from subjects as diverse (or not) as French sensualist Georges Bataille (**Violent Silence**) and Judy Garland ("Saint Judy" on **Mother Fist**). In addition, Almond has collaborated with Coil, Bronski Beat, Jim "Foetus" Thirlwell, Nico, Psychic TV, Sally Timms of the Mekons and Andi Sex Gang. One of the most uncommercial commercial artists in pop, Almond has bounced from label to label, but his devoted fans—and his ability to occasionally launch a record into the European charts (**The Stars We Are**'s "Something's Gotten Hold of My Heart," redone as a duet with Gene Pitney, who first had a British hit with the Cook/Greenaway oldie in 1967, topped the British singles chart in 1989)—ensure that he always finds a home. That wayfarer status, coupled with Almond's prodigious output, guarantees a plethora of compilations. Issued after the self-explanatory **Singles 1984–1987, A Virgin's Tale**—two individual CDs composed of almost all Almond's EPs and B-sides from 1985 through 1987—is especially rich in strong material. Heavily loaded with remixes and demos, the two-CD (but could have been one) **Treasure Box** covers rarities from 1988 to 1990.

The singer got his umpteenth fresh start in 1991 with two releases, one providing a sense of closure on what had gone before, the other looking to the future. **Memorabilia** collects thirteen cuts (plus two remixes) from both Soft Cell and Almond's solo career. With regard to the latter, the album omits anything from **Vermin in Ermine, Stories of Johnny** and **Mother Fist** (not to mention his two prior Marc and the Mambas albums), focusing instead on more accessible material. In what has to be seen as a belated admission of their original inadequacy, Almond offered to lay down new vocals for three Soft Cell songs he felt ready to improve upon: "Memorabilia," "Say Hello, Wave Goodbye" and (of course) "Tainted Love," which promptly shot back into the British Top 10.

The concurrent **Tenement Symphony** is a muddled affair. The record suffers from a surplus of polish; Trevor Horn, who produced the titular second-half suite, threatens to bury Almond in the mix. When the singer rises to the occasion, the chemistry proves explosive, as on flamboyant readings of Brel's "Jacky" and David MacWilliams' "The Days of Pearly Spencer." The beautiful original "My Hand Over My Heart," which reunites Almond with Soft Cell keyboard partner Dave Ball (now working with Richard Norris as the Grid), does not fare as well; two other such collaborations ("Meet Me in My Dream" and the defiantly homoerotic "I've Never Seen Your Face") produced by the Grid bear up far better.

Recorded at London's Royal Albert Hall in September 1992, **12 Years of Tears** boils down a two-and-a-half-hour show—featuring dancers, a full band and orchestra—to a single fourteen-song CD. Although Almond takes a while to get up to speed (his notoriously dodgy pitch is especially flat on "Champagne" and the musicians on "Tears Run Rings" sound canned), the momentum never sags once he's up and running, revisiting tunes from his entire repertoire. The album's high point (and one of Almond's finest moments ever) is his poignant reading of Charles Aznavour's "What Makes a Man," a ballad sung from the point of view of a transvestite.

Almond abruptly changed tack once more for his next release. **Absinthe,** an attempt (aided by translator Paul Buck) to affect the French *chanson* tradition in English, began life as early as 1986 (five of the tracks feature Almond's previous ensemble, La Magia). The finished project is ambitious in scope and difficult for the untrained ear to digest, but ultimately rewarding both as pure entertainment and from a musicological standpoint. A raucous, bawdy "Undress Me (Déshabillez-Moi)," a staple for Juliette Gréco (the album's primary muse), and the wistful "Lost Paradise (Le Paradis Perdu)" are especially noteworthy.

Almond released three diverse singles in 1995: "Adored and Explored" introduces elements of techno, coupled with harmonica by David Johansen; "The Idol" is a Gary Glitter–style stomp about the nature of fame; and "Child Star" is a sweeping ballad worthy of Shirley Bassey. Those songs, along with a new single ("Out There"), the trip-hoppy "Sweet Assassin" and eleven other cuts, make up 1996's **Fantastic Star.** [kbr]

See also *TPRG.*

ALT

See *Crowded House.*

ALTERED BEATS

See *Bill Laswell.*

DAVE ALVIN

Every Night About This Time (UK Demon) 1987
Romeo's Escape (Epic) 1988 (Razor & Tie) 1995
Blue Blvd (Hightone) 1991
Museum of Heart (Hightone) 1993
King of California (Hightone) 1994
Interstate City (Hightone) 1996

SONNY BURGESS WITH DAVE ALVIN

Tennessee Border (Hightone) 1992

Much the way Robbie Robertson served as the creative mainspring for the Band, guitarist/writer Dave Alvin was the guiding force behind the Blasters, providing his brother, singer Phil Alvin, with stellar, Americana-soaked tunes. After leaving that band (high and dry) and signing on with X for a short stint, Alvin embarked on what could have been an ill-fated solo career: "blessed" with the kind of raspy, technically suspect voice that would only be tolerated in rock'n'roll, Alvin has continued to pen emotionally powerful tunes of everyday life, while putting his limited abilities as a singer to surprisingly good use.

Romeo's Escape (released in the UK under the less catchy title **Every Night About This Time**) is a promising if ragged beginning that sets the tempo for subsequent works. The boy boogies ("New Tattoo"), celebrates the common man ("Brother on the Line") and recycles his best compositions, including the Blasters' "Long White Cadillac" and X's "Fourth of July."

Leaving the major-label ranks, Alvin resettled on the rootsy indie Hightone, a more appropriate home for his rough-hewn art. Alvin began to hit his stride with **Blue Blvd.** The grooves are familiar, touching on everything from spirituals ("Gospel Night") to mutant Chicago blues ("Brand New Heart") and moody acoustic laments ("Dry River"). Though Alvin's in good company—the cast includes Los Lobos' David Hidalgo, ex-Blaster sax great Lee Allen and California cowpoke Dwight Yoakam—his no-frills singing sometimes fails to hold the spotlight, especially when the backing players crank up.

Museum of Heart is a more relaxed and assured work—Alvin will never give Pavarotti pause, but he's comfortable within his narrow range, letting his pithy songwriting carry the load. Among the highlights are "A Woman's Got a Right" (a nasty putdown of a rejected lover), the greasy "Burning in Water Drowning in Flame," the sorrowful "As She Slowly Turns to Leave" and the stark, scary "Stranger in Town" (not the Del Shannon song, but undoubtedly inspired by it). Guests include Syd Straw and X's John Doe. Why don't more people cover this guy's stuff? Kindred spirit Bruce Springsteen, for one, would benefit enormously by sampling Alvin's more diverse material.

Alvin's latest opus is also his best. A stripped-down acoustic record (if he were a bigger star, it'd be marketed as his long-awaited unplugged album), **King of California** mixes moldy blues ("Mother Earth"), new tunes (the almost funky "Barn Burning") and yet one more review of his "greatest hits," including "Fourth of July," "Every Night About This Time," "Little Honey" and "Border Radio." These renditions can safely stand as the definitive versions. Amidst the steel guitars, mandolins and acoustic guitars, Alvin finally seems comfortable at the mic, confidently emphasizing the content of the songs instead of trying to put on a big show. And don't miss the poignant duet with Syd Straw on the George Jones heartbreaker "What Am I Worth."

The live **Interstate City,** recorded in Austin with the Guilty Men, includes both new songs and Blasters oldies amid past solo album selections.

Alvin produced, arranged and contributed guitar to **Tennessee Border,** starring rockabilly cult figure Sonny Burgess, one of the great overlooked talents of ye olden days. While Burgess, having grown noticeably hoarser over the years, is no longer quite the wildman who belted out "Red Headed Woman" for Sun Records back in the '50s, this is still a solid set of honky-tonk rock'n'country, highlighted by a rollicking cover of Lefty Frizzell's "Old, Old Man." Burgess deserves the same respect accorded more celebrated peers like Carl Perkins and Jerry Lee Lewis, though he'll probably never get it. Nice going, Dave. [jy]

See also *Mojo Nixon, X.*

PHIL ALVIN

Un"Sung" Stories (Slash) 1986
County Fair 2000 (Hightone) 1994

BLASTERS

The Blasters Collection (Slash/Warner Bros.) 1991

Singer Phil Alvin co-founded the Blasters in Los Angeles with his guitar-slinging kid brother Dave in 1979; the blues-roots-rocking band ended its recording career in the mid-'80s and, shortly thereafter, except for the occasional reunion gig, folded its tent for a while. (The twenty-cut compilation issued in 1991 offers a fine summary of the group's four studio albums and live-in-London EP.) Before dedicating himself to academics (getting graduate degrees in esoteric math disciplines), Phil cut a delightful solo album of blues, gospel and jazz goodies (including Cab Calloway's "Minnie the Moocher"), featuring Sun Ra and the Arkestra on three tracks.

Nearly a decade later, with the Blasters back on the road again, Alvin finally followed his debut with **County Fair 2000,** another impressive and winning visit to the record library in the college of Phil's musical knowledge. Relying a shade more on fantasy antique store originals than genuine oldies ("Old Rugged Cross" and Sammy Fain's "Low Down Rhythm" being among them), the album embraces a staggering assortment of idioms—Dixieland, blues, swing, folk, modern jazz, country and spirituals—performed with a parade of hep pals (such as Top Jimmy, Jerome Bowman, Cesar Rosas) and sympathetic musical organizations, all of which (save the Dirty Dozen Brass Band) he holds membership in: the Faultline Syncopators, the Guada La Habrians, the Blasters. Billy Boy Arnold joins him for an amusing automotive grudge match ("Wreck Your V-8 Ford"), Mary Franklin insults him in "What's the Reason I'm Not Pleasin' You" and trumpeter Ike Williams and drummer Jerry Angel back his piano rendition of Sun Ra's "Ankh." There's lots more, and it's all good. It's a marvel to hear such musty chapters from music's history books brought to robust modern life in the hands of such a well-versed scholar. [i]

See also *TPRG.*

AMAZING DELORES

Stop Messin' With My Mind (Upstart) 1994

This Appalachian wildwoman may look like your aunt Sophie all dolled up for the bus to Atlantic City, but she sounds like Bessie Smith reincarnated as a roadhouse rockabilly diva. The Amazing Delores (Boyd)—born and bred in Mudlick, West Virginia (!)—is gifted with a raspy, raunchy voice that can recall Captain Beefheart (on "Love Magic") or a cat in heat (on the loopy "Rats in My Trailer"). She's also clearly gotten her soul caught in the same God-versus-Satan tug-o-war that's addled fellow southerners from Jerry Lee Lewis to Daniel Johnston. The ecstatic intensity with which she rebukes underworld spirits ("Stop Testifyin' to the Devil") seemingly gives the edge to the Man Upstairs, but the hormone-drenched "Do the In and Out" evens the playing field somewhat. A variety of local musicians—including producer/multi-instrumentalist Michael Lipton, whose answering machine messages from Delores provide suitably spooky between-song punctuation—keep a low blue flame burning beneath the splendidly spicy stew. [dss]

ERIC AMBEL

Roscoe's Gang (Enigma) 1988

ERIC AMBEL & ROSCOE'S GANG

Loud & Lonesome (East Side Digital) 1993

Since leaving the Del-Lords in 1990, New York singer/guitarist Eric "Roscoe" Ambel has made a name for himself as a producer specializing in unpretentious rock with a distinct country edge. Working out of Coyote Studios hard by Brooklyn's Gowanus Canal, Ambel has manned the board (and sometimes played guitar) for records by such rootsy acts as the Bottle Rockets, Blue Mountain, Blood Oranges, Simon and the Bar Sinisters, Go to Blazes, Mojo Nixon and Nils Lofgren.

Recorded while Ambel was still a Del-Lord, **Roscoe's Gang** is a casual good-time rock'n'roll session with the Skeletons, Peter Holsapple and other likeminded pals. In the joyful party atmosphere, cover versions of Swamp Dogg, Bob Dylan and Neil Young songs meld easily with originals by Ambel, co-producer Lou Whitney, Holsapple and then-bandmate Scott Kempner. Ambel takes center stage more confidently on **Loud & Lonesome,** writing with members of a gang that includes Terry Anderson, Kevin Salem, Dan Baird and former Del Fuego Dan Zanes. (Ambel, Anderson and Baird have since coalesced into a loose part-time combo dubbed the Yayhoos.) With his overdriven, wailing guitar and reedy vocals, Roscoe favors the more rock side of the (don't-call-it) cowpunk equation, sounding like a less-ravaged Neil Young. "Way Outside" and "I'm Not Alone" would not sound out of place on **Ragged Glory.** [sm]

See also *Kevin Salem; TPRG.*

AMERICAN MUSIC CLUB

The Restless Stranger (Grifter) 1986
Engine (Grifter/Frontier) 1987
California (Grifter/Frontier) 1988
United Kingdom (UK Demon) 1990
Everclear (Alias) 1991
Rise EP (Alias) 1991
Mercury (Reprise) 1993
San Francisco (Reprise) 1994
Hello Amsterdam EP (Reprise) 1995

MARK EITZEL

Songs of Love Live (UK Demon) 1991
60 Watt Silver Lining (Warner Bros.) 1996

Rock'n'roll, especially the fringier areas thereof, has always been awash with beautiful losers. Maybe that's why American Music Club mastermind Mark Eitzel is so refreshing. His desperate confessional songs reveal a man with little doubt that he's a loser but can't for the life of him see any beauty in said condition. With a no-frills Bay Area aggregation providing bare-bones backing, Eitzel's pointedly non-metaphorical writing sails past self-revelation on its way to self-evisceration.

The singer's unipolar, Ian Curtis–like vocal drone dominates **The Restless Stranger**'s tales of solitude and delirium tremens to perhaps too great a degree. That affectation, and occasionally ponderous arrangements (Eitzel has cited, without irony, early Yes as an influence), blunt some of the songs' impact, though "Room Above the Bar" and "$1,000,000 Song" bull through. A lineup juggle that preceded **Engine** (producer Tom Mallon stepped in to handle guitar—and, more important, arranging—chores) nudges the band toward stark but gently applied folk-rock structure. On "Outside This Bar," a Bukowski-like attempt to maintain the hermetic seal around the singer's world, Eitzel wails almost unaccompanied; in this context, when the backing grows more strident (as on the harrowing "Art of Love"), the edge becomes even sharper.

Like a particularly cruel maze, **California** is exceedingly difficult to enter and all but impossible to escape. Though it incongruously contains the spitting brawler "Bad Liquor," **California** is even more austere than the band's prior ventures. The cumulative emotional overload (particularly on "Laughingstock") is positively anesthetizing. Dispensing with its predecessors' vague adherence to folk-rock structure, **United**

Kingdom lacks obvious songs and melodies as such and, in its starkness, recalls nothing so much as Big Star's **Sister Lovers.** Perhaps the most interesting thing (besides the fact that the three live tracks lack any standard concert-recording evidence of an audience) is "The Hula Maiden," the first document of Eitzel's occasional stage retreat into the safe harbor of broad Vegas schmaltz. With its wild mood swings—from morose to mocking—**United Kingdom** is a fine document of an erratic, invigorating and frightening band. (The CD contains all of **California** as well.)

Everclear recasts American Music Club as a bona fide rock band, with mixed results. The anthemic "Rise" turns an uncommonly hopeful eye on the topic of AIDS, hailing its protagonist as a (potentially) conquering hero. But more often than not, slickened production works against the band, encouraging Eitzel's tendency toward bombast and inflating longtime guitarist Vudi's sound to illogically arena-esque proportions. The **Rise** EP combines the title track with some restrained material, most notably the rhapsodic "Chanel #5."

Every one of **Mercury**'s fourteen songs sounds like an apology for Eitzel's very existence. He may couch some of his rending sentiments in feigned indifference ("I've been praying a lot lately/Because I no longer have a TV") or tried-and-true slapstick (there's a song entitled "What Godzilla Said to God When His Name Wasn't Found in the Book of Life"), but those tricks are reminiscent of sad-sack pathos masters like Harold Lloyd. Part exorcism and part party trick, songs like the narcotically slow "Gratitude Walks" (one of several here that implicitly address the AIDS-related deaths of several friends) cast Eitzel in the role of street-corner preacher. Typically, when he meets one of the deities in his pantheistic universe (in "Johnny Mathis' Feet"), said idol dismisses him as a hopeless mess. A postcard from the edge.

While a good bit of the exceedingly muted **San Francisco** (particularly "The Thorn in My Side Is Gone") reveals Eitzel to be descending to yet another level on his tour of the psychic abyss, he seems more willing to stumble toward what few rays of light exist down there. The spy-flick throb of "It's Your Birthday" sees him encouraging a pal to accept the love of a partner, "Even though she hasn't been a girl for very long"; the dynamic "Wish the World Away" seeks its solace in mood-alterers as varied as TV and good ol' bad liquor. There's even a moment of black comedy: in "Hello Amsterdam," Eitzel addresses the band's continued commercial failure, noting "They didn't even like us when we played 'Dancing Queen.'" No ABBA covers materialize on **Hello Amsterdam,** an EP that incorporates that song and a handful of otherwise unavailable tracks, including an alternate version of "The Thorn in My Side Is Gone") and the wry, rock-star–baiting "The President's Test for Physical Fitness." (Simplifying matters for collectors, the EP contains "I Just Took My Two Sleeping Pills and Now I'm Like a Bridegroom Standing at the Altar," which was added to **San Francisco**'s abridged vinyl edition.) With that, Eitzel broke up the band at the end of 1995.

Songs of Love Live, documenting a then-rare solo show, was recorded in London in January of 1991 and captures Eitzel in varying stages of drunkenness and equally varying degrees of control. The between-song shtick seems to have been partially excised, which is unfortunate, since even a mediocre Eitzel performance (which this one is) can be redeemed by the guy's rants. The studiofied **60 Watt Silver Lining** provides a different, virtually adult-contemporary setting for Eitzel's lyrical gems. His voice, which has grown mellower and less prone to sudden cracks over the years, sounds almost soothing on typically downtempo songs like the acoustic, flute-filigreed "Wild Sea" and the loungy, Tom Waits–like "Some Bartenders Have the Gift of Pardon" (which invests a mythical mixmaster with godlike qualities). Those with an affinity for Eitzel's more messed-up excesses needn't fret: "Cleopatra Jones" leaps into blaxploitation melodrama with the skewed kinship only a self-professed loser could muster. [dss]

See also *Toiling Midgets.*

AMINIATURE

Plexiwatt (Scheming Intelligentsia) 1992 (Restless) 1994
Depth Five Rate Six (Restless) 1994
Murk Time Cruiser (Restless) 1995

In the early '90s, with no warning, San Diego began spewing out an endless supply of high-octane punk bands, most of them following in the footsteps of either Rocket From the Crypt (sloppy, slightly retro garage-rock) or Drive Like Jehu (rhythmically complex prog-punk). From the start, aMINIATURE set its own agenda, with a rhythm section that provided the thump and wallop of traditional hardcore but a guitar sound built on weird tunings, harmonics and melodic dissonance. That's not to say that **Depth Five Rate Six** is all noise, it's just that the quartet continually pushes the envelope on how many different sounds, textures and rhythms can be assimilated into the formerly narrow confines of punk rock. Like vintage Dylan, guitarist/vocalist John Lee's stream-of-consciousness lyrics rarely make sense on the printed page yet connect emotionally, often punctuated by Christian Hoffman's scattershot drumbeats that pepper the repetitive, sing-song riffs. Songs like "Towner on the B-Side" and "Showdowned" follow few of the traditional rules of pop music; their anthemic choruses stick in your head anyway. Other bands (such as Wire and Superchunk, in different ways) have explored similar territory, but few have succeeded in fusing the excitement and immediacy of hardcore with such adventurous sonic bedlam.

After a lineup shuffle, **Murk Time Cruiser** finds the band expanding on the '94 album's blueprint. New drummer Mark Trombino dominates nearly every track, providing pounding ferocity for emphasis and intricate fills for effect; his doubletracked off-kilter rhythms on "The Prizefighters" are nothing short of amazing, making it seem as if the tape is running backward! Lee continues to explore unusual guitar textures that eschew simple effects like feedback and distortion pedals for unusual fingerings and unexpected chord changes. But no matter how ambitious the music, aMINIATURE remains a punk-rock band at heart. If the ambition is to incite gleeful head-bobbing enthusiasm, the jaunty, exhilarating "He, the Bad Feeler," "Long Live Soul Miner" and especially "Flux Is Flux" succeed admirably. [jt]

AMORPHOUS ANDROGYNOUS

See *Future Sound of London.*

TORI AMOS

Little Earthquakes (Atlantic) 1991
Crucify EP (Atlantic) 1992 (UK EastWest) 1992
Winter EP (Atlantic) 1992 (UK EastWest) 1992
China EP (UK EastWest) 1992
Under the Pink (Atlantic) 1994
God EP (Atlantic) 1994
Cornflake Girl EP (Atlantic) 1994 (UK EastWest) 1994
Caught a Lite Sneeze EP (Atlantic) 1996
Boys for Pele (Atlantic) 1996

Y KANT TORI READ

Y Kant Tori Read (Atlantic) 1988

As befits the daughter of a preacherman, Tori Amos is blessed with a heady voice of intense, wine-like richness. Drunk with feeling and aurally intimate, it is nearly operatic in its ornate agility and inextricable link to her resonant, purposefully asymmetrical piano playing. The entire **Little Earthquakes** album—led by "Silent All These Years," the song that introduced Amos to her public—follows this simple voice-and-keys blueprint and is strongly reminiscent of the first two Kate Bush albums. A variety of producers layer on oblique orchestration, stringed instruments and percussion; the spare piano sound is so distinct, however, that such embellishments are barely noticeable. The string-laden ballad "Winter" is elegantly tender and evocative of snowdrifts and childhood fantasies; "China" is nearly as lovely. "Tear in Your Hand" drops references to Neil Gaiman's masterful *Sandman* comic-book series (the two are mutual admirers). "Happy Phantom" strikes an uncharacteristically jaunty chord, as Amos delights in her own imagination, while "Crucify" accurately skewers the psychological architecture of guilt. Amos struck a feminist chord with the emotionally raw, even confrontational sexual tone of some lyrics ("Precious Things" issues the devastating put-down "So you can make me cum/That doesn't make you Jesus"; "Leather" begins "Look I'm standing naked before you/Don't you want more than my sex"), paving the way for Alanis Morissette. But she quashed any unsympathetic prurient interest in the stunning a cappella "Me and a Gun," which starkly, unflinchingly details her own rape experience. With hardly a weak moment to detract from its introspective womanliness, **Little Earthquakes** is a legitimate '90s analogue to Carole King's **Tapestry.**

While not as consistently striking as its predecessor, **Under the Pink** doesn't slavishly repeat the **Earthquakes** formula, and Amos' stylistic experimentation makes for excellent, challenging listening. The opening "Pretty Good Year" begins innocently enough with familiar gentle piano melodies but the calm is eventually broken by a savage crescendo; at the album's close, "Yes, Anastasia" endlessly rises and falls with orchestrated orgasmic aplomb. In between, the brief, brittle "Icicle" wittily remembers childhood masturbation in the shadow of religion ("When they say 'take of his body,' I think I'll take from mine instead"), and Nine Inch Nails auteur Trent Reznor (another mutual fan: check the lyrics of "Precious Things") guests to good effect on the elegiac "Past the Mission." But a cranky tirade against "The Waitress" (murderous mantra: "I believe in peace, bitch") quickly grows irritating. The album's most intriguing tracks—"God" (with its sultry groove and squawking guitar) and the sauntering cascade of "Cornflake Girl"—use a full band sound as the organic foundation instead of mere layering. With the quasi-danceable "Space Dog" (a rare lyrical flop; who could relate to gibberish like "Colonel Dirtyfishydishcloth"?), Amos again follows Kate Bush, in the embrace of electronics and dance rhythms.

Self-produced in Ireland and New Orleans, **Boys for Pele** is more Amos than most people can handle: eighteen diverse tracks adding blues ("Professional Widow," "In the Springtime of His Voodoo") and gospel ("Way Down") to the more familiar pure piano gems ("Horses," "Twinkle") and **Under the Pink**'s fuller percussive pop ("Caught a Lite Sneeze"). Thematically, **Boys for Pele** appears to be a statement of independence from a former boyfriend and other male mentors. (The cover photo of her lounging on a ramshackle porch with a rifle nestled in her lap, a snake tangled in her rocker and a pair of dead birds hanging past her shoulder certainly sends a clear enough message.) Pop-culture references (Mr. Sulu, Angie Dickinson and so forth) abound, but the lyrics' essential meanings are utterly personal. If Amos has become more obsessive—even obtuse—fine, because her songwriting here is superb. The mystic muse whose inattention left **Under the Pink** inconsistent has returned in force. Most exciting of all is her use of harpsichord for many cuts, letting its authoritative baroque tone infuse "Blood Roses" and "Talula" with richness and resonance. In sum, her best to date.

Amos commendably follows the British model in jam-packing her CD singles with at least three discrete extra tracks per disc (at this point, nearly two albums' worth!) rather than redundant remixes. Three particularly great originals—as fine as anything on the first two albums—are the melancholy gem "Upside Down" (found on the domestic **Winter** EP, a good five-song value), the delicate "Honey" (from the American **Cornflake Girl**) and the soaring live favorite "Flying Dutchman" **(China).** The US **Crucify** and the UK **Winter** EPs both feature three fascinatingly rearranged (for voice and piano) covers: the Stones' "Angie," Led Zeppelin's "Thank You" and a muted "Smells Like Teen Spirit" (which Nirvana had released only months earlier). The import **Crucify** is actually a live EP, offering warm versions of four **Little Earthquakes** songs recorded in Cambridge in April '92. **God** shows off Amos' piano prowess with an abstract rendition of the old "Home on the Range" and two instrumentals ("All the Girls Hate Her" and "Over It"), while the inclusion of three more hauntingly performed covers—Joni Mitchell's "A Case of You," Jimi Hendrix's "If 6 Was 9" (the start of piano grunge?) and Billie Holiday's "Strange Fruit"—makes the UK **Cornflake Girl** EP a delectable purchase. **Caught a Lite Sneeze** comes with an additional five-track suite entitled "Silly Songs," which includes two short, sharp ditties ("Graveyard" and "Toodles Mr. Jim") and the oddball "This Old Man" and "That's What I Like Mick."

Several years before her makeover as a sensitive alternative goddess, Amos recorded an excruciatingly bad album issued under the even worse moniker **Y Kant Tori Read.** Though marketed as a Vixenish rouge-and-hairspray metal babe, YKTR's music is an artless plunder of mid-'80s commercial pop, from

True Blue–period Madonna ("Cool on Your Island," "Floating City") to Paula Abdul ("Fayth") and even sour hints of Heart and Bon Jovi. (One of the album's two drummers is future Guns n' Roses replacement Matt Sorum.) Aside from the relatively unscathed neo-Celtic balladry of "Etienne," any hints of Amos' piano-based approach (in the wailing chorus of "On the Boundary" and the intro to "Heart Attack at 23") are ruthlessly swamped by nauseatingly slick synth riffs and studio-muso hackwork. Her voice and trite wordplay sound forced throughout; "Pirates" and "You Go to My Head" ("I'm such a lush for your love") are particularly dumb. Although Tori's own liner notes conspicuously thank an exec for "letting me make the record I wanted to make," she later disowned the hapless album, blaming its utter commercial and artistic failure on "corporate pressures." [gef]

AMPS

See *Breeders.*

BRUCE ANDERSON

Brutality I . . . America/Iran [tape] (Quadruped) 1987
Brutality II . . . Israel/Palestine [tape] (Quadruped) 1988
Brutality (Quadruped/Atavistic) 1995

MX-80

Existential Lover [tape] (Quadruped) 1987
Das Love Boat (A&R) 1990 (Atavistic) 1995
Out of Control (Quadruped/T.E.C. Tones) 1992 (Atavistic) 1995
Big Hits/Hard Attack (Atavistic) 1995

Guitarist Bruce Anderson, a founder of MX-80 Sound and more recently a member of that band's O-Type and Gizzards offshoots with **Brutality** producer Dale Sophiea, truly brings the noise on his full-length 1995 album, a compilation of the two solo cassettes plus ten minutes' worth of nation-named tracks ("Lebanon" and "Greece," which diverge from the remainder by having Sophiea's bass and sample contributions) from a 1986 O-Type release. Half the places visited on **Brutality** are wordless layered 4-track guitar cacophonies—impressive in their density but not good for much beyond emergency lease-breaking campaigns. The remaining spots on this obscure self-indulgence are spare one-or-two-guitar improvisations that sometimes incorporate Frippertronic sustain melodies but rarely surpass the imaginative structure level of random warmup exercises.

Having dropped the "Sound" from its name (thereby encouraging confusion with Virginia garage-blues quartet the M-80's), MX-80—which began in Indiana in the mid-'70s and eventually relocated to San Francisco following a hookup with the Residents' Ralph Records label—has remained active in the '90s. In addition to singles and a 1990 instrumental album, the band recently saw to the reissue of its original catalogue: 1980's **Out of the Tunnel** and 1981's **Crowd Control** were combined on CD as **Out of Control,** while 1976's seven-song **Big Hits** 7-inch and 1977's **Hard Attack** were packaged together with a bonus outtake from the latter. [i]

See also *TPRG.*

CARLEEN ANDERSON

See *Young Disciples.*

LAURIE ANDERSON

Big Science (Warner Bros.) 1982
Mister Heartbreak (Warner Bros.) 1984
United States Live (Warner Bros.) 1984
Home of the Brave (Warner Bros.) 1986
Strange Angels (Warner Bros.) 1989
Bright Red/Tightrope (Warner Bros.) 1994
In Our Sleep EP (Warner Bros.) 1995
The Ugly One With the Jewels and Other Stories (Warner Bros.) 1995

After kicking around the New York art scene for a decade, Chicago native Laurie Anderson reached the masses in the early 1980s when the improbable UK single success of "O Superman" suddenly made her the world's most famous performance artist. Singing in a droll deadpan and playing violin and keyboards, she followed up on her surprise stardom with two albums of haunting, thought-provoking and high-tech explorations of language and technology buoyed by deadpan irony, all of which made Anderson very much a creature of the '80s. She continued her recording career with the five-vinyl-disc (later four-CD) summation **United States Live** (**Big Science** was first subtitled *Songs From United States I–IV*) and the soundtrack album to her film, *Home of the Brave.* **Strange Angels** is an extremely well-crafted but disappointing stab at highbrow mainstream pop access, with featured performances by Bobby McFerrin.

Anderson waited a long time before making a record in the '90s, co-producing **Bright Red/Tightrope** with Brian Eno. The results of this post-modern dream team don't even remotely live up to expectations; oddly enough, Eno's contribution is virtually undetectable. Even appearances by Lou Reed, Adrian Belew and downtown Manhattan luminaries like Arto Lindsay and Joey Baron can't redeem the flat music, which recalls Yoko Ono's blander latter-day moments. Still, as Anderson softly declaims over the polished, skeletal synth and rhythm tracks, some fine poetry does emerge, especially on "World Without End" (from the first half, dubbed **Bright Red**) and "Love Among the Sailors" and "Night in Baghdad," from the **Tightrope** portion.

The Ugly One With the Jewels, recorded live in London, is Anderson's idea of an unplugged record, basically a spoken-word performance with sound effects that takes its text from Anderson's book, *Stories From the Nerve Bible.* Full of the dry, ironic wit and cultural insights that made her famous, the best tracks—"The End of the World," the Andy Kaufman reminiscence "The Rotowhirl" and "The Night Flight from Houston"—celebrate the surreality of the mundane (and, often, of Anderson's career). The sounds complement the text beautifully and the effect is riveting, evocative and cinematic—the best way to listen to this album is to wait for a quiet evening, dim the lights and kick back. Then again, at over seventy minutes, two quiet evenings might be required. [ma/i]

See also *TPRG.*

AN EMOTIONAL FISH

An Emotional Fish (Atlantic) 1990
Junk Puppets (Atlantic) 1993
Sloper (Ger. ZYX) 1995 (Pure) 1996

Polite and well-meaning, passionate and witlessly thoughtful ("One thing about colours is that colours always speak their minds"—hunh?), Dublin's An Emotional Fish was too deeply in the thrall of U2 and Simple Minds to make a debut album of any consequence. The Dylan-meets-the-Waterboys blend of the taut "Celebrate" suggests an incipient personality, but a lot of **An Emotional Fish** is the sketchbook of untalented amateurs attempting to jot down the work of a master: the echoing guitar pings (David Frew), thrusting basslines (Enda Wyatt) and surging vocal power (Gerard Whelan) are all there on the palette, but the labors betray no hint of the motivation or invention underlying the real thing. If originality wasn't an option for the young band, careful mimicry might have sufficed, but these lads didn't have the heart to do that, either.

"I'll forget everything I ever said," sings Whelan on "Rain," the song that inaugurates **Junk Puppets,** and he's not kidding. The stuttering, guitar-charged dance track renounces every stylistic feature of **An Emotional Fish** for a whole new landscape. Produced into a split personality by Alan Moulder, David A. Stewart and Clive Langer, the album maps out a dramatic, kinetic surge of pointed, textured rhythmic noise-pop that is, at times, not entirely unlike the clamorous sound of U2's **Achtung Baby.** Going out on a conceptual limb with numbers like the speculative "If God Was a Girl" (which quietly appropriates a bit of "Jesus Christ Superstar") and "Hole in My Heaven," overstretching material that has inadequate structural stamina, An Emotional Fish doesn't knock this one out of the park (for one thing, too many lyrics encourage chortles), but it's still a great leap forward.

Having made that hard left turn, AEF threw the map away for the calmer, more intimate **Sloper.** Nothing like either of its predecessors, the self-produced album is a riot of borrowed idioms: Lou Reed, Bowie (by way of Suede), rootsy pop, soul, Waterboys folk, disco—even a sappy country duet. The whole thing is daft but engaging, a musical kaleidoscope bound together by Whelan's gentle singing. Other than consistency, lyrics that don't suck remain the band's most elusive challenge. Recipe for a fine Fish dish: keep lines like "It seems obvious to me that you'll still be there tomorrow/With the happiness that you borrowed from the clowns" out of the mix, settle on a few favored genres and get back to work. [i]

ANGELFISH

See *Garbage.*

ANGRY SAMOANS

See *Metal Mike.*

ADAM ANT

Friend or Foe (Epic) 1982
Strip (Epic) 1983
Vive le Rock (Epic) 1985
Hits (UK CBS) 1986
Manners & Physique (MCA) 1990
Antics in the Forbidden Zone (Epic) 1990
Antmusic: The Very Best of Adam Ant (UK Arcade/Sony) 1993
B-Side Babies (Epic Legacy) 1994
Wonderful (Capitol) 1995

Making good on his lyrical ant-threat—"You cut off his head, legs come looking for you"—Adam Ant found a third professional life in the 1990s with **Wonderful.** Outlasting the absurd glam punk theatrics of Adam and the Ants, the former Stuart Goddard completed the '80s with a solo career that wobbled between delightful (**Friend or Foe** and **Vive le Rock**) and dire (**Strip**) and then wound up in a surprising disco variation (**Manners & Physique**). After that, the London-born singer/actor took a studio powder, leaving his former label to bring out a trio of compilations all billed solely to the star: the sketchy but adequate **Antics in the Forbidden Zone** (twenty-one tracks, taken from all of the Ants' albums and his first three solo records), the English-only **Antmusic** (some copies of which included a bonus live disc) and **B-Side Babies,** a sixteen-song collection of flipsides and bonus tracks from the same period.

Whatever convinced Adam to exchange the walloping funk grooves of **Manners & Physique** for the quiet balladry of **Wonderful,** it didn't change his obsessions any: songs about sex ("Beautiful Dream," "Gotta Be a Sin"), prickly personal irritation ("Won't Take That Talk"), cultural observation ("Vampires") and narcissism ("Image of Yourself") are topically familiar, even if they're wrapped in soft, fuzzy bundles. While the lyrics are loaded with provocative bits—the waterlogged "Wonderful" alludes to domestic violence, the pop-rocking "Alien" touches on English nationalism and the solitude of "Very Long Ride" requires pistol possession—much of the music is intrinsically dull and soporifically produced. Patently contrived errors like the gentle calypso bounce of "Beautiful Dream" and the rap verses of "Very Long Ride" point to a hack's lack of stylistic conviction and leave a sour taste. Permanent sidekick Marco Pirroni plays a lot of acoustic guitar on the album; outside of the merry old-style "Gotta Be a Sin" and a couple of T. Rex impressions, Adam sings in a quiet voice extracted from the yipping joy of his early hits. **Wonderful** won't wake the children, but neither could it arouse the ants. [tr]

See also *TPRG.*

ANTENNA

Sway (Mammoth) 1991
Sleep EP (Mammoth) 1992
Hideout (Mammoth) 1993
(For Now) EP (Mammoth) 1993

VELO-DELUXE

Superelastic (Mammoth) 1994

MYSTERIES OF LIFE

Keep a Secret (Citizen X/RCA) 1996

The silver-lined divorce that terminated the Blake Babies and freed Juliana Hatfield to begin a solo career sent the other two—guitarist John Strohm and drummer Freda Love—back to Indiana, from whence they had come and where they erected their next musical endeavor, Antenna. With bassist Jake Smith and guitarist Vess Ruhtenberg (ex–Datura Seeds) completing the lineup, Antenna made **Sway,** an album that released all the pent-up rock energy implicit in the Babies' restrained pop. Strohm's tuneful verse-chorus songs betray a country influence, begin with bits of film dialogue and have the nerve to quote Donna Summer and Jimmy Webb (in the intricate "All I Need" and the stormy "Blood Red," respectively). Many of them receive brash, invigorated guitar crunch treatment but have the fortitude to keep their twinky sparkle. **Sway**'s biggest problem is its facelessness: Strohm's artless voice, although effective for the unpretentious arrangements (local violinist Lisa Germano plays a small guest role), isn't distinctive or memorable. A good first step, but not a conclusive tune-in.

Sleep combines two of **Sway**'s best tracks with a pair of subsequent demos (of Smith's "Wall Paper" and Wire's "Outdoor Miner"), recorded with Ruhtenberg out and drummer Patrick Spurgeon replacing Love. The same trio, aided by guitarist Ed Ackerson (then of Minneapolis' 27 Various, later of Polara; in between, he toured as Antenna's fourth member), cut **Hideout.** If **Sway** was spiked pop, the seething distortion of **Hideout** forms a loud, confident bridge to shoegazing sensuality, the span of which can be measured between the simple, diffident "Wall Paper" demo and the album's roaring noise monster version. With producer Paul Mahern helping shape the Strohm/Smith songs into burly but alluring volume assaults, Antenna radiates its tuneful shock waves, painting pretty pictures and peeling the canvas back at the same time. The band's essential paradox is nicely mirrored in the enigma of "Easy Listening," the chorus of which observes, "It's easy listening to someone else, but it's hard to make up your mind." After all the careful consideration, sometimes blind rage is all we have.

Antenna then ended, leaving the poignantly titled four-song **(For Now)** EP, which extracts "Wallpaper" from **Hideout** and surrounds it with three tunes recorded by Strohm, Love and Smith. "Swoon" and "Given Way" are fine, but the roaring, funhouse-mirror pop of "For Now" is one of those devastating parting glances that makes you instantly sorry for what you're losing.

Strohm formed Velo-Deluxe with bassist Kenny Childers and drummer Mitch Harris, continuing his ascent into the joyous buzz of evanescent noise-pop on the powerful **Superelastic.** Getting outside help on various instruments (saxophone, trumpet, organ and, on the country exception "Saturday," pedal steel) and borrowing some of the vibrant sonic designs (like sickly bent chords) from My Bloody Valentine's **Loveless,** Strohm propels **Superelastic** with strong melodies that are perfect for chewing through the thick pile of the band's briskly moving carpet. The chorus of "Dirtass"—"I feel sick and I feel dirty/Might be dead before I'm thirty"—sets the dark tone for these adventures in discordance, which channel various forms of articulate anguish into majestic storms of craggy distortion and top them with seductively sweet melodies, occasionally dissolving into fun-with-sounds indulgence (see "Miracle") or taking a Jesus and Mary Chain–styled acoustic time-out ("Eleven"). As a starting point for a band with loads of potential, **Superelastic** is kickass cool.

After Antenna, Smith took over the bass job in the Indianapolis wing of the Vulgar Boatmen; the elemental intensity of that group's frugal folk-pop strongly informs the Mysteries of Life, the delightful Bloomington group he and cymbal-shy wife Freda Love unveiled in 1995. But, to a lesser degree, so does the unbound electrification of **Hideout**-era Antenna, and those two poles furnish **Keep a Secret** with stylistic tension and dynamic variety. "Hesitate" keeps extraneous sounds out, letting Geraldine Haas' cello, the bass (played by Smith) and Love's snare balance Smith's sweet voice (with backing vocals by Boatmen leader Dale Lawrence) and plucky guitar figures; "Alibi," a deliciously pretty song of guilt and honesty he loaned Velo-Deluxe for **Superelastic,** begins with a similar skeletal arrangement and then erupts in feedback squeals and surging guitar strums. "Feel My Way" accents the swinging Stealers Wheel honeysnap with angry fuzz chords; "I Guess I'm in Luck" adopts a jaunty calypso bounce and rides it with the merriment of a Jonathan Richman confection. Whether the Mysteries of Life is tamping down the ferocity or amping up the gentleness, **Keep a Secret** is neither obvious nor dull—and frequently wonderful. (In a bit of post-LP circle completion, ex-Antenna guitarist Vess Ruhtenberg became the Mysteries of Life bassist.) [i]

See also *Juliana Hatfield, 27 Various.*

ANTHRAX

Fistful of Metal (Megaforce) 1984
Armed and Dangerous EP (Megaforce) 1985
Spreading the Disease (Megaforce/Island) 1985
Among the Living (Megaforce/Island) 1987
I'm the Man EP (Megaforce/Island) 1987
State of Euphoria (Megaforce/Island) 1988
Persistence of Time (Megaforce/Island) 1990
Attack of the Killer B's (Megaforce/Island) 1991
Sound of White Noise (Elektra) 1993
Live: The Island Years (Megaforce/Island) 1994
Stomp 442 (Elektra) 1995

BELLADONNA

Belladonna (Mausoleum/BMG) 1995

One of the most fertile products of the cross between metal and punk, New York's Anthrax helped establish speed metal in the mid-'80s, fused its hard-guitar attack with rap rhythms in 1987 and attained widespread popularity with 1990's **Persistence of Time,** a survey of urban decay and psychological tumult that jumbled together all sorts of information horror classics and hate crimes, apocalyptic visions and meditations on gridlock. Down-to-earth and streetwise, neatly straddling the worlds of cool and killer, Anthrax carved itself a unique role as full-blown rockers not entirely lost to the mentality of the moshpit.

Since changing labels in the '90s, however, the group has had far less impact on a scene dominated by bands inspired by "the old Anthrax"—everyone from Helmet to Green Day owes a debt. It lost lead singer Joey Belladonna in '92; he went on to form an eponymous quartet and was replaced by ex–Armored Saint belter John Bush. Before work began on 1995's **Stomp 442,** original guitarist Danny Spitz also departed, leaving a quartet in which guitarist Scott Ian and drummer Charlie Benante are the only remnants of the band that made **Fistful of Metal.**

The band's '90s output does have important moments, however: **Attack of the Killer B's,** a contract-fulfilling odds'n'sods collection, contains reasonably crunchy alternate tracks and signature covers, including a version of "Bring the Noise" that features Public Enemy's Chuck D and Flavor Flav. **Live: The Island Years,** recorded mainly in 1991 (four tracks are from a '92 radio broadcast), offers a more vital look at a band in peak form. Whether shouting down prejudice ("Keep It in the Family") or remaking Kiss' "Parasite" to their more exacting specifications, Anthrax is able to bring an awe-inspiring measure of precision to blindingly fast music played at a consistently athletic level of intensity.

Bush made his debut on the bland **Sound of White Noise.** The instrumental tracks are no less electric, but Bush hadn't yet settled in, and his vocals sound strained, as if he's trying to copy Belladonna's phrasing exactly.

Co-produced by the Butcher Brothers (Urge Overkill) and named after a particularly powerful automobile engine, **Stomp 442** restores some of the band's former glory. Bush makes himself much more at home, the rhythm section (Benante and bassist Frank Bello) seems hungry again and the songwriting—at least on the funky "American Pompeii," the throttling "Tester" and the anthemic "Fueled"—revisits the flammable mixture of social responsibility and physical agitation that hallmarked Anthrax in the '80s. A variety of guest stars—including Dimebag Darrell of Pantera—fill the lead guitar slot but, as was true in its heyday, Anthrax's no-frills rhythm section remains the real catalyst. [tm]

See also *TPRG*.

ANTIETAM

Antietam (Homestead) 1985
Music From Elba (Homestead) 1986
Burgoo (Triple X) 1990
Everywhere Outside (Triple X) 1991
Antietam Comes Alive! (Triple X) 1992
Rope-a-Dope (Homestead) 1994

TARA KEY

Bourbon County (Homestead) 1994
Ear and Echo (Homestead) 1995

BABYLON DANCE BAND

Four on One (Matador) 1994

While you'd never know it from listening to the undeniably pleasant but comparatively lightweight indie-pop that comprises this up-from-Louisville New York trio's early records, Antietam possesses one of the most stealthy weapons in the post-punk sphere—the utterly transcendent guitar discourse of frontwoman Tara Key. Whether it was a trip down to the crossroads or merely a move to an apartment that allowed for more volume-intensive jam sessions, Antietam (named after the site of a pivotal Civil War battle) underwent a sea change sometime in the early '90s, one that transformed it into a juggernaut capable of tearing the roof off any venue on any given night.

The two mid-'80s releases are marred by an overabundance of restraint: Just when Key and her bass-playing significant other Tim Harris start to approach liftoff, they seem to think better of it and remain content to chug along on terra firma. There's nothing really wrong with either disc—save some sub-standard harmonizing that makes X sound like the New Christy Minstrels—but the songs are a bit too inconspicuous, too gentle to really grab the listener by the lapels. **Burgoo** tweaks the formula somewhat, focusing more attention on Key's angular playing—no doubt a function of producers Georgia Hubley and Ira Kaplan's sympathetic ears—and planing away the sound's softer edges. It's a big step in the right direction, but the band clearly needs to hook up with a more effective drummer than Charles Schultz (not the cartoonist, who could probably keep time as effectively) if it's to be anything more than pleasant.

Key and Harris found a more sympathetic third member in drummer Josh Madell, whose playing imbues **Everywhere Outside** with a combination of freeform restlessness and Cream-styled bottom-end vigor, both of which contrast nicely with Key's increasingly complex songs. Although it's a quantum leap forward in terms of both storm and stress, the self-produced album still doesn't replicate the urgency of the trio's live shows. The subsequent release, however, captures a particularly fine one: recorded at Antietam's de facto home base, CBGB, **Antietam Comes Alive!** hits with the room-spinning displacement of a furious tequila buzz. The ropy guitar soloing that permeates the Dream Syndicate–styled instrumental "Track 13" lets Key set an ecstatic (in the spiritual sense) tone straightaway as she trance-ports the band through a fifty-minute firewalk that reaches peak intensity on a cover of Patti Smith's "Ask the Angels." Truly revelatory.

Rope-a-Dope transfers a good bit of that assurance to the studio environment: the trio positively swaggers through the garage-rock prototype "Hands Down" (which gets an added dose of spunk from Kaplan's crisp organ playing) and a cover of Dead Moon's gnashing "Graveyard." As borne out by songs like the gently psychedelic "Pine," Key has settled into a wafting lower register that accentuates the spooky qualities of her voice; she's also found a way to channel some of her manic onstage attack (as on the heady "What She Will"). An encouraging sign of things to come.

Although Harris and Madell play on both, there's not a whit of Antietam's explosiveness in evidence on Key's solo albums—which is by no means a criticism. The bucolic ambience of **Bourbon County** (which also features cameos by Hubley and Kaplan of Yo La Tengo, Rick Rizzo, Janet Beveridge Bean and Wink O'Bannon of Eleventh Dream Day and Sue Garner and Rick Brown of Run On) is steeped in old-school hippie-country values. The looseness of songs like "Jack of Hearts" and "Northern Star" replicates the innocence of a stoned campfire singalong to such a wonderful extent that it's possible to overlook the indulgence of several formless instrumental numbers.

Ear and Echo is a more "serious" and fully realized set. Even when it seems as if you're listening to a few drinking buddies killin' some time (as on the gentle instrumental "All Lit Up"), the album belies a definite focus. It's evident that the crew paid as much attention to sonic details—like Key's accordion fillips on the airy "Breakin' In" and Harris' lovely cello shadings on "In Absinthe"—as to the beer list so lovingly detailed in the CD booklet. **Ear and Echo** is not the kind of album that seizes your attention, but it doesn't take too long to seep into your consciousness.

Before their New York relocation, Key and Harris led Louisville's Babylon Dance Band, an engagingly wound-up foursome that split the difference between brittle Dixie-funk and angular guitar whittlings that would have sounded at home in the Mission of Burma catalogue. The Matador disc, recorded after a decade-long hiatus, reveals the formula to have aged well. Lead vocalist Chip Nold has one of those urgent bellows that works best when he's delivering monosyllabic spurts (as on "Bold Beginnings") and drummer

Sean Mulhall maintains a skittery pulse that emphasizes the pressurization of songs like "The Reckoning" and a cover of "Shake!" (a Kasenetz-Katz factory product originally recorded by the Shadows of Knight). [dss]

APACHE INDIAN

No Reservations (Mango) 1993
Make Way for the Indian (Mango) 1995

Bhangra is a product of Britain's growing Asian community, a mixture of Punjabi folk music and techno, jungle, house, rock and dancehall reggae. Traditionally, bhangra was played at harvest festivals where one of the chief products was hemp (bhang), which helps explain the trance-inducing beat. Although considered too Western by Indian parents fearful of assimilation, the music currently rules Britain's Asian music charts.

Apache Indian, who hails from Hansworth (home of Steel Pulse and UB40), is primarily a ragamuffin DJ, although many of his tunes have elements of the bhangra beat. **No Reservations** was recorded in Jamaica; along with "Feel It Fe Real," a duet with reggae crooner Maxi Priest, it features three UK hits: "Chok There," chanted in Jamaican/English patois and riding a bubbly *dhol* (double-headed drum) riddim, and the typical dancehall boasts of "Don Raja" and "Move Over India." The most Indian track on the disc is "Arranged Marriage," which samples bits of Indian *filmi* music, uses tabla and expounds culturally conscious lyrics that deal with one of the traditions that cause tribulation for more assimilated Asian youth in the UK.

On **Make Way,** Apache uses a more folkloric bhangra sound with his dancehall and adds elements of roots reggae, jungle, hip-hop, R&B, rock steady and rock. "Boomshackalak," Apache's first UK pop crossover hit, is a mélange of various Motown samples married to a chunky reggae guitar, "Armagideon Time" (an oldie popularly covered by the Clash) has a biblical roots reggae tone and a catchy chorus, "Born for a Purpose" is a traditional R&B/reggae ballad, "Boba" mixes acoustic bhangra with a modified funk beat to poke fun at assimilated Indians in Hindi/patois and "Who Say?" would be at home at any rave with its heavy, techno jungle feel. Tim Dog, Yami Bolo and Frankie Paul all have featured vocal spots. [jp]

APHEX TWIN

Aphex Twin EP (UK Mighty Force) 1991
Didgeridoo EP (Bel. R&S) 1992
Xylem Tube EP (Bel. R&S) 1992
Selected Ambient Works '85–'92 (Bel. R&S) 1992
On EP (Sire/Warner Bros.) 1993
Madreporic Plate Remixes EP (UK Warp) 1993
Selected Ambient Works Volume II (Warp/Sire/Warner Bros.) 1994
Classics (Bel. R&S) 1995
Ventolin EP (Warp/Sire) 1995
. . . I Care Because You Do (Warp/Sire) 1995
Donkey Rhubarb (Warp/Sire) 1995

AFX

Analogue Bubblebath EP (UK Mighty Force) 1991 (Mighty Force/TVT) 1994
Analogue Bubblebath Vol. 2 (UK Rabbit City) 1992 (UK Rephlex) 1992
Analogue Bubblebath 3 (UK Rephlex) 1993

POLYGON WINDOW

Artificial Intelligence (UK Warp) 1992
Surfing on Sine Waves (Warp/Wax Trax!/TVT) 1993
Quoth EP (Warp/Wax Trax!/TVT) 1993

MIKE & RICH

Expert Knob Twiddlers (UK Rephlex) 1996

Richard James may not be any monkey with a sampler, but the unstructured aspect of the twiddly wallpaper records and forceful rhythm commands the ambient techno auteur has created and issued under a multitude of names makes him (if no more so than other avatars of the genres) seem like something less than a serious artist to those stuck with obsolete expectations of the music they consume. Still, it's fascinating how such a functionally minded idiom as dance music could be the catalyst by which such anti-participation sounds were able to leap from scorned proximity to Muzak and gain cutting-edge credibility (if not intimidating trendiness) as drug/trance zone-out art and skittering beat hallucinations. Times, and perceptions, do change.

Since emerging from his Cornwall bedroom to partake of the rave culture as a DJ (moving to London to launch himself as a musician), James has been the very model of the modern young egghead with his finger on the electronic pulse. While the gentler end of his vocal-less sonic ablutions has earned him ambient comparisons to Brian Eno, there's a stronger visceral component to James' work: still in his early twenties, he has not yet lost his connection to the dancefloor. When he means to rock the party, he does so with prodigious power, but even when on a more cerebral plane, he sets the pulse of his productions racing with a shade more energy, playful imagination and organized rhythmic force than other techno-grads-cum-soundscapers. In other words, he's a far more striking breed of bore.

Like many of his peers, James is far too prolific for casual consideration. Not counting outside production and remix work, his discography is an international morass of releases as the Aphex Twin, AFX, Polygon Window, Metapharstic, Caustic Window, Joyrex, Blue Calx, the Dice Man and so on. His American releases, however, have not been many.

The **Analogue Bubblebath** EP (1991) contains formative efforts that are more routine techno than escapist ambient: aggressively sequenced dance rhythms underpin the synthesized squonks, plonks and samples. "Isopropophlex" is especially collar-grabbing in a most non-atmospheric manner. The **On** EP leans into a balance of insistent beat-itude, pop formalism and ancillary sonic action: the title track (also offered in a soft, billowy remix) sets a busily tinkling piano figure working against meteorological events and other samples in what almost sounds like a concession to chart-pop catchiness. The other two tracks on the disc jump into jungle skitter with predictably unsettling don't-sit-down-don't-move spasmodic results.

Selected Ambient Works Volume II is, good to its title, concertedly and consistently mood-setting. The slices of subtle delicacy meander gracefully in clearly conceptualized pathways where very little happens. The Aphex Twin's work here travels without arriving, yet he invariably makes it a pleasant journey with pretty audio scenery. Two discs of this stuff ask a lot of the listener, but none of it is so distracting that it would interfere with other activities—like, say, listening to music. **Classics** compiles much of the early R&S material, including the complete **Didgeridoo** and **Xylem Tube** EPs (eight tracks in all), plus five more studio numbers and a live version of "Didgeridoo."

. . . I Care Because You Do starts out with a slow drum pattern, squiggly synth fillips and friendly organ chords in "Acrid Avid Jam Shred," but soon revs up into the harsh thicket of frenzied jungle beats. James thoughtfully introduces other elements into the mix—languorous keyboard strains, ricocheting sequencer tones, an ear-splitting whistle, dramatic strings, spoken bits—but by "Start as You Mean to Go On" (the first song on the non-literal Side 3), the Aphex Twin is in full calamitous gear, leaving room for nothing but mute heart-pounding submission. (Or instantaneous push-button escape.) The album calms down after that—"Alberto Balsalm" is seductively light in tone and tempo—and concludes in most enigmatic fashion with a very natural-sounding and percussion-free orchestral fugue, "Next Heap With." Oh that Aphex boy!

Expert Knob Twiddlers is James' collaboration with Michael Paradinas, the techie also known as μ-Ziq. [i]

APPLES

The Apples EP7 (Elephant 6) 1993

APPLES IN STEREO

Fun Trick Noisemaker (spinART) 1995

In a rock era that seems to have lost sight of the distinction between playfully childlike and willfully childish, the Denver-based Apples are a refreshing change of pace. The guitar-pop group's self-titled debut EP—six songs pressed on apple-green vinyl—comes stuffed to the gills with amusing stickers and other assorted fun inserts. (The sleeve itself is actually a twelve-page booklet, complete with a great color cover.) Most groups attempting to go the bouncy-jumpy-happy route end up failing miserably, but the Apples get away with it, mainly because they never sound like they're trying too hard—their giddy enthusiasm seems natural, not feigned. The group's basic sound, perky but resilient (imagine the Sex Clark Five with a fuzzbox), works to perfection on tracks like "Tidal Wave" and "Haley." This is what an indie 7-inch is supposed to be—fun, exciting, personal and completely unexpected.

Worried about potential lawsuits from other bands with the same name, the group became the Apples in Stereo for their first album, **Fun Trick Noisemaker,** a nifty little record that shows they didn't use up all the best tunes on the EP. The bevy of sparkling pop tunes, highlighted by "Lucky Charm" and "Dots 1-2-3," is an object lesson in how a band can reference bubblegum culture without being kitschy or sounding like a case of arrested emotional development. Serious fun for (and by) adults who were never afraid to grow up in the first place. [pl]

AQUANETTAS

Love With the Proper Stranger (Nettwerk/IRS) 1990
Roadhaüs EP (Rockville) 1993

It takes a determined mindset to write and perform convincing time-capsule songs like "Beach Party," but that's what New York's girlsapoppin' Aquanettas do on **Love With the Proper Stranger.** Without pushing it as a gimmicky signature, singer/guitarist Deborah Schwartz's mighty voice is redolent of West Coast '60s folk-rockers like the Mamas and the Papas (and, therefore, the early Bangles as well); drummer Stephanie Seymour's high harmonies enhance and elevate the effect, as do the acoustic strummings and Jill Richmond's tradition-packed lead guitar interjections. Pushing Schwartz's wry lyrics about problems with the opposite sex ("Diplomat," "Faults," "15 Men") and lifestyles of the poor and obscure ("Pictures of Italy," "Up!"), the quartet turns casual simplicity to its advantage, allowing the vintage spirit to inhabit them as if to the '60s born.

There's an equally timeless air to **Roadhaüs,** but erratic production styles and other problems disconnect the five songs, leaving the EP hobbled and lacking a focal point. The sexy "Run," a toast to drinking, is a good'un ("I feel like Persephone freed from hell/Now I'd like to be freed from my mind as well"), but the band's best-ever song, "Mind Full of Worry," slumps from absolute knockout to thorough disappointment in a bout of dismally sour singing. The group broke up in '94. Schwartz has been pursuing a solo art-folk career; Richmond formed the Mean Reds. [tr]

AQUA VELVETS

The Aqua Velvets (Riptide) 1992 (Heyday) 1993
Surfmania (Mesa) 1995
Nomad (Milan) 1996

Nobody knows how or why, but the early '90s saw dozens of San Francisco bands pulling out their best retro-'60s chops and pickin' away on twangy, reverb-heavy guitars. In a city known more for foggy B-movie atmospherics than suntanned beach bunnies, a cult began to grow, led by new wave and world beat dropouts like the Aqua Velvets (lead guitarist Miles Corbin, bassist/keyboardist/accordionist Michael Lindner, rhythm guitarist Hank Maninger and drummer Donn Spindt). Although this revival is certainly steeped in intellectual cool and a sometimes smug world-weary irony, there's no denying the musical smarts and killer backbeats that drive every track the Velvets have committed to disc.

The eponymous debut officially kicked off the Great San Francisco Surf Revival. The self-released album was quickly picked up by Heyday and brought the movement a national profile. (Tracks popped up on MTV's *House of Style Swimsuit Special,* ESPN's *Max Out* and the soundtrack to *Blazing Longboards.*) Corbin has clearly studied the Big Book of '60s Instrumentals, and tips his hat to Dick Dale, the Ventures, Ennio Morricone, Link Wray and other iconic dynamos, but the Aqua Velvets transcend influences to create their own cozy bit of dreamy ocean-front property.

Surfmania continues the magic with more neo-classical sounds that transport you to a place where the sun never sets, the waves are perfect, the guitars are always in tune, the lounge is always open, the drinks are never watered and the boys and girls never age. Corbin's compositions here are even stronger than those on the band's debut. The faux Latin of "Mexican Rooftop Afternoon," the faux Polynesia of "Martin Denny, Esq." and the faux noir of "Raymond Chandler Evening" continue the winning combination of hot licks and cool irony. [jp]

TASMIN ARCHER

Great Expectations (SBK) 1993
Shipbuilding (SBK) 1994
Bloom (UK EMI) 1996

Like countryman Seal, English singer Tasmin Archer sets a course through the thorny woods of sophisticated modern pop by giving tuneful, well-crafted and lyrically substantial songs snappy arrangements that cherrypick elements from dance music, soul, rock and Top 40. A chart contender who owes more to Joni Mitchell than Janet Jackson, the Bradford native fills her first album with catchy, stylistically untethered tunes about unemployment ("Steeltown"), ecology ("Sleeping Satellite"), power brokers ("Lords of the New Church," but not the Stiv Bator song) and anxiety ("When It Comes Down to It"). Alluring, smart, well-produced (primarily by Pet Shop Boys collaborator Julian Mendelsohn) and handsomely sung, **Great Expectations** is an effortlessly great record, full-strength music for grownups.

For her next trick, Archer tackled four from the Elvis Costello songbook, pairing them with live renditions of three **Great Expectations** songs and a jazzy acoustic piano version of a fourth. Archer's well-intentioned poke at "Shipbuilding" misses the mark, turning this harrowing political poem into lugubrious grand theater. Elvis' country confessional, "Deep Dark Truthful Mirror" (from **Spike**), fares much better as Archer succumbs to its rueful hangover. Likewise, she picks her way safely through "New Amsterdam" by not getting too cute or sarcastic. Her Elton John–styled interpretation of "All Grown Up" sounds ready for Broadway and is just as memorable here as it was on **Mighty Like a Rose.** [i]

ARCHERS OF LOAF

Icky Mettle (Alias) 1993
Archers of Loaf vs the Greatest of All Time EP (Alias) 1994
Vee Vee (Alias) 1995
The Speed of Cattle (Alias) 1996

BARRY BLACK

Barry Black (Alias) 1995

Like many towns (Athens, Seattle, Austin) before it, Chapel Hill, North Carolina, became an indie mecca in the early 1990s. Like the other bands—scene leaders Superchunk, the wondrous Polvo, Small—to emerge from the area at the time, Archers of Loaf creates provocative guitar rock with distinctive, if collegiate, melodic dissonance.

Icky Mettle showcases the particularly crafty dual-guitar efforts of Eric Johnson and singer Eric Bachmann, who allows (in "Web in Front"), "There's a chance that things'll get weird." While they certainly do, there are enough hooks—especially on "Wrong," the swirly "Hate Paste," "Learo, You're a Hole" and "Slow Worm"—to lure in even a casual listener. Affecting the personality of an intelligent, reflective loner, Bachmann battles between nasal plaints and frustrated hollering. Drummer Mark Price is intriguingly unconventional but solid, and bassist Matt Gentling lopes effectively in the mix.

Engineered by Shellac's Bob Weston, the five-song **. . . vs the Greatest of All Time** captures a different sound for the Archers, one that somewhat bridges the gap between full-length releases. While "Audiowhore" is more experimental than most of **Icky Mettle,** the ringing guitars and low, rumbling bass of "Lowest Part Is Free!" are more familiar. After a free-form guitar solo introduction, "Revenge" melds spaghetti western, reverby surf and quirky pop.

Evidently satisfied with Weston, the Archers returned to Chicago to make the excellent **Vee Vee.** Both as musicians and as songwriters, the band is better-developed and more dynamic, progress which pays off in the moving opener, "Step Into the Light," poignant "Greatest of All Time," Polvoid "Underdogs of Nipomo," raw "Nostalgia" and even the odd "Underachievers March and Fight Song." Bachmann's stunning "Harnessed in Slums" is one of the best protest songs in indie-rock. Noisy as ever, the Archers really get weird here, and steep in the gritty buoyancy of Bachmann and Johnson's tangled guitars.

The Speed of Cattle, an eighteen-track collection of Peel sessions, B-sides and other rarities, is more than just a fans-only necessity. It includes the group's first single ("Wrong" b/w "South Carolina"), the "Web in Front" demo, a version of Treepeople's "Funnelhead" and other hard-to-find roughhewn gems.

Like prolific neighbor Mac McCaughan (Superchunk/Portastatic), Bachmann has a solo project, one that points to the various musical subcultures revolving around the Chapel Hill scene. The breezy, ambitious and mostly instrumental Barry Black incorporates jazz, folk, rock and other genres; the adventurous arrangements include rainsticks, cello, fiddle, trumpet, trombone and sax. The band's loose lineup includes former Red Clay Rambler Bill Hicks (fiddle), former Ugly American Chris Eubanks (cello) and pianist Ben Folds as himself; guest scenester Frank Heath (owner of Chapel Hill club Cat's Cradle) adds vocals. **Barry Black** includes the surfy "Cockroaches," the Coltrane homage "Train of Pain," the lovely, minimalist "I Can't Breathe" and "Animals Are for Eating," sort of underground Raymond Scott. Only "Golden Throat" truly resembles the Archers, as Bachmann takes the lead vocal on a snaky guitar-rock (with banjo) offering. [mww]

See also *Small.*

ARCWELDER

Jacket Made in Canada (Big Money) 1991
Pull (Touch and Go) 1993
Xerxes (Touch and Go) 1994
Entropy (Touch and Go) 1996

TILT-A-WHIRL

This (Big Money) 1990

Like the sizzle of hot sparks hitting cold metal, Minneapolis' Arcwelder splatters impassioned vocals over a chilling backdrop. There's a frayed fury that lingers behind even the strongest hooks, the same tension-building mix that in the past has proven explosive for bands like Naked Raygun and Hüsker Dü, to which Arcwelder has most often been compared. With vibrant melodies that jump out of penetrating grooves, Arcwelder's albums also tend toward more subdued soundscapes. If the Hüsker match doesn't always apply, Arcwelder's singing does owe something to Bob Mould's disaffected tone. Drummer Scott Macdonald and guitarist Bill Graber share vocal duties—sometimes harmonizing, but often taking on differing melodies.

Completed by brother Rob Graber (bass/guitar), the trio debuted in 1988 as Tilt-a-Whirl and released its first album, **This,** under that moniker two years later. But the manufacturers of the carnival ride threatened to sue, and Tilt-a-Whirl became Arcwelder.

"Harmonic Instrumental" starts **Jacket Made in Canada** off with a characteristic mix of buoyant melodies and bottled aggression. Vocals on several cuts (the outstanding "Staback and Favor") fall into the Mould pocket, but other tracks display the band's experimental side, venturing into country parody on "I Hates to Lose" and essaying a surprising instrumental, "Bob Sez."

Armed with such terse pop constructions as "Raleigh" and "Remember to Forget," **Pull** again hits with harsh Big Blackened aggression and rhythms that churn and grind. A few tracks slow the pace, yet still seethe with anguish: see "What Did You Call It That For." Though the repetition of lyrics and riffs gets monotonous, the vocal interplay adds a caustic beauty to the basic melodies of "Finish My Song," "Lahabim" and "And Then Again."

The appeal of **Xerxes** again rests on the band's vocals; the second half of "Pound" pits two competing vocals over a hyper beat. The song constructions are more stylized, though the deliberate rhythms of "All My Want for Need" and "Change" have far less impact than the livelier tracks. "All Mixed Together" and the instrumental "Freebird" (not *that* one) provide punchy energy spurts. "The Carpal Tunnel Song" sounds like a punk interpretation of Brian Eno's **Here Come the Warm Jets,** but nothing can top the snappy "Down to the Wire," a fireball that keeps gathering heat as it goes.

Entropy continues Arcwelder's successful quest to sharpen provocative lyrics and shapely song structures with a medium-grit abrasive edge, roughening the attack but staying inside the accessible safety zone of Midwest clangor. Pulling free of past stylistic associations, the trio ventures a more distinctive melodic noise, using dissonance, nagging guitar repetition, rhythmic invention and typically impressive singing to make its way. Graber's "Doubt," "Unknown" and "Blowin' Smoke," Macdonald's "I Promise Not to Be an Asshole" and the collaborative "Snake Oil" are a varied and exciting set of multi-faceted winners; the rest of the album doesn't lag far behind. (Crediting members of Boston for performing "Turn To" is an inexplicable joke, though.) [mg/i]

A.R.KANE

Lolita EP (UK 4AD) 1987
Up Home! EP (UK Rough Trade) 1988
Sixty Nine (Rough Trade) 1988
i (UK Rough Trade) 1989
rem"i"xes EP (UK Rough Trade) 1990
Americana (Luaka Bop/Sire) 1992
New Clear Child (3rd Stone/Luaka Bop/Warner Bros.) 1994

SUFI

Life's Rising (Caroline) 1995

A.R.Kane, the London duo of Alex (Ayuli) and Rudy (Tambala), helped usher in two significant musical movements in England. The 12-inch dance single "Pump Up the Volume," a 1987 collaboration with members of Colourbox in the ad hoc group M/A/R/R/S, introduced the scratching and sampling aesthetic of American hip-hop and house music to the British mainstream, where it remains an integral part of rave culture and its outgrowths. Then, with the lulling noisescapes of the **Up Home!** EP and **Sixty Nine,** the duo (who dubbed their music "dreampop") exerted a profound sonic influence on the legion of trippy shoegazer guitar bands that would emerge a few years later in the UK.

Up Home! and **Sixty Nine** make a virtue of vagueness, with voices like murmuring ghosts, vapor-trail guitars and echo-laden rhythms that suggest a dub reggae remix more than any kind of rock production. The EP's "Up," a shimmering, six-minute plunge into weightlessness, is a virtual sonic blueprint for Lush and Slowdive.

A.R.Kane branched into pop on the double-album-length **i,** employing a variety of dance rhythms, female vocalists and more overt melodic hooks, but the music retains its otherworldliness. "Snow Joke" quotes Philly soul, "In a Circle" has the austere beauty of chamber music, "Crack Up" rides a giddy ska beat and "Love From Outer Space" is a brooding slice of dance soul. As the disc progresses, the mood hardens, climaxing with the biting guitar opus "Super Vixens," which updates the murderous sentiments of "Hey Joe" and "Down by the River": ". . . killing her was the best thing I ever did." The **rem"i"xes** EP pulls five tracks from **i** ("Crack Up" is redone twice by Cocteau Twin Robin Guthrie), including "Miles Apart" and "Catch My Drift."

Americana is a solid fifteen-song compilation that draws from the two albums and early 12-inch releases. With its piano-and-saxophone sentimentality and "holding on for love" lyric, the one new track, "Water," serves as a bridge to the more conventional pop of **New Clear Child.** Although the duo's 1994 album retains some of the off-kilter allure of the early work, the vocals are now clearly up front in the mix, and the noisy intrusions have been muted, thus depriving A.R.Kane of whatever originality it had left.

Sufi is Tambala's trip-hop venture with his sister, Margaret Alice Tambala. Her light, jazzy coo of a voice is the most appealing aspect of **Life's Rising,** a collection of weakly written pop songs ("Lostaday," "Lover," "Into the Blue") turned into sonically uninspired ambient soul doodles. [gk/i]

ARMAGEDDON DILDOS

That's Armageddon (Ger. Zoth Ommog) 1991
Homicidal Dolls (Sire/Warner Bros.) 1993
Lost (Sire/Warner Bros.) 1995

The domestic release of two records by Armageddon Dildos is the only fruit, and bitter at that, of Sire's licensing agreement with German techno label Zoth Ommog. Under the guidance of Bigod 20's Talla 2XLC, Zoth Ommog's exported releases had a big influence on the American post-house underground club scene of the late '80s, taking sterility to new dancefloor highs. **Homicidal Dolls,** however, verges on both the cold precision of German techno and the well-trodden path of Belgian industrial exemplified by Front 242. The Kassel duo's main asset is singer Uwe Kanka, whose strong voice croons through Dirk Krause's frantic beats, providing the songs with their only semblance of melody.

Lost is a stronger, but still not terribly original, mix of guitars, processed rhythms and pop melodies. The chilly club sound that characterized the group's earlier work is subsumed by guitars that run along the Ministry/Nine Inch Nails corridor. Not as endearingly harsh as either of those two bands, but more adept at the transition than later Depeche Mode, **Lost** is a reasonably enjoyable mixed bag. (But mope-rock fans would do well to skip the seething version of Morrissey's "Everyday Is Like Sunday.") [sf]

JOAN ARMATRADING

Whatever's for Us (UK Cube) 1972 (A&M) 1973
Back to the Night (A&M) 1975
Joan Armatrading (A&M) 1976
Show Some Emotion (A&M) 1977
To the Limit (A&M) 1978
Steppin' Out (A&M) 1979
Me Myself I (A&M) 1980
Walk Under Ladders (A&M) 1981
The Key (A&M) 1983
Track Record (A&M) 1983
Secret Secrets (A&M) 1985
Sleight of Hand (A&M) 1986
Classics Vol. 21 (A&M) 1986
The Shouting Stage (A&M) 1988
Hearts and Flowers (A&M) 1990
The Very Best of Joan Armatrading (UK A&M) 1991
Square the Circle (A&M) 1992
What's Inside (RCA Victor) 1995

For twenty-five years, English singer/guitarist/songwriter Joan Armatrading—born in the West Indies, raised in Birmingham—has been making records of warm, emotional music matching a sturdy, subtly controlled voice with eloquent, personal songwriting. Having never managed to move beyond a dedicated mid-sized following in the US, Armatrading had to watch as the singer/songwriter resurgence of the late '80s sent likeminded artists (including nominal soundalike Tracy Chapman) catapulting past her hard-earned level of success with music that was not substantially different from hers. The subsequent slowing of her album output can certainly be presumed to have something to do with the more densely populated field into which it is now being released.

Although the intimate essence of her romantic candor has never wavered, the duration of her career has led Armatrading to tinker with her approach in various ways, attempting to embolden or glamorize her sound over the years. After working with an array of stellar instrumentalists and producers as diverse as Glyn Johns (**Joan Armatrading, Show Some Emotion,** the live **Steppin' Out**), Richard Gottehrer (**Me Myself I**), Steve Lillywhite (**Walk Under Ladders, The Key**), Armatrading began producing herself. On **Sleight of Hand,** using just a drummer, bassist and keyboardist (plus a few guests in minor roles), she acquits herself well behind the board. Even more encouraging, the lyrics leave behind the anguish of **Secret Secrets** to bring in a new era of personal happiness and stability. **The Shouting Stage** tests a smooth and jazzy adult contemporary vein that doesn't suit her, although the album does contain some strong songs ("Did I Make You Up," "Watch Your Step"). Japan bassist Mick Karn makes a noticeable contribution to **Hearts and Flowers,** a handsomely slick and modern realization of Armatrading's traditional artistic values.

Square the Circle has no overriding flavor, just ten clearly expressed and resonant songs of devotion ("True Love"), uncertainty ("Wrapped Around Her"), remorse ("Can't Get Over (How I Broke Your Heart)") and idyllic feminism ("If Women Ruled the World"). The arrangements are tasteful but pointed—more Laura Nyro than Carole King, although "Weak Woman" and "Can I Get Next to You" put a little Aretha gusto into the mix—and Armatrading even flashes a rare bit of humor by quoting herself in "Crazy."

Ending a two-decade stint on A&M, Armatrading redoubled her creative ambitions for **What's Inside,** an elegant, rich and intricate album with strings (by a London orchestra and the Kronos Quartet), horns, male backup singers and a superb band featuring drummer Manu Katche, Benmont Tench and Tony Levin. Based as much on piano as guitar (although she plays a surprising amount of lead, and one track employs pedal steel for a novel country effect), the album relies on simply effective material performed with imaginative skill—stylistically, instrumentally and vocally. "Shapes and Sizes" makes striking use of the Kronos Quartet and little else; "Lost the Love" slides from a jazzy standards swing into a sizzling blues, while "Can't Stop Loving You" (punched up by the Memphis Horns) is one of the most uplifting and engaging pop songs in Armatrading's repertoire. If all it takes for Joan to make an album this great is a new recording contract, she should jump ship annually from now on. [i]

See also *TPRG*.

ARRESTED DEVELOPMENT

3 Years, 5 Months and 2 Days in the Life of . . . (Chrysalis) 1991
Unplugged (Chrysalis) 1993
Zingalamaduni (Chrysalis) 1994

SPEECH

Speech (Chrysalis) 1996

GUMBO!

Dropping Soulful H20 on the Fiber (Chrysalis) 1993

May all your wishes be granted, goes the ominous blessing. And how can Speech complain? The leader of Atlanta's Arrested Development saw every would-be rock-star dream come true. He made the record he wanted, sold millions and had his shot at reforming the face of pop music. It hardly seems fair that the now-defunct band's name is almost synonymous with failed promise.

Speech is Todd Thomas, whose parents published a small Milwaukee newspaper. **3 Years, 5 Months and 2 Days in the Life of . . .** (the title memorializes how long after forming at the Art Institute of Atlanta it took the band to sign a recording contract) is quite a debut, a logorrheic spill of irresistible rhythms, by turns uncompromising and lovey-dovey rhetoric and, oh yes, a pair of amazing hit singles in "People Everyday" and "Tennessee." The album epitomizes the goal of alternative hip-hop: to harness the energy and immediacy of the music but drop the less savory elements that had come to define it in the eyes of many, thereby creating a worthy successor to the music of both Sly Stone and the Last Poets. Looked at one way, the record pulls it off. "Tennessee," a truly wonderful and unconventional song, is a sobering and deeply religious tale of racial self-reflection and uneasy history. Overfamiliarity may have blinded listeners to the originality of its funky, off-beat beginning, dead-on lyrics ("Walk the roads my forefathers walked/Climb the trees my forefathers hung from") and the passionate, beautiful wails from Dionne Farris at song's end. In "Fishin' 4 Religion," Speech aims a bazooka blast at black churches ("They're praising a god that watches you weep/And doesn't want you to do a damn thing about it") and, in a rewrite of Stone's "Everyday People," goes after gangsta rap, explicitly and violently. Speech's hippiesque, new agey vision—which has obscured the tougher side of his persona—is uncovered here: one of his objections to gangsta rap is that its brand of violence is nihilistic and self-defeating, not that it's violent per se. "Brothers wit their AK's and the 9mms/Need to learn how to correctly shoot them/Save those rounds for a revolution." Speech can be a drag: his efforts to write about positive role models and such can be smarmy, his feel-good rhetoric can be annoying and, despite his attempts in that direction, he's definitely not a love man. But when he pulls it together—as on the lulling electronic construction and moving recitation that make up the closing "Washed Away"—it's possible to believe that much better things might be coming.

On top of the world, Arrested Development was asked to contribute a song to Spike Lee's *Malcolm X* and delivered "Revolution," a minor-strength raveup based on an African chant. **Unplugged** was a disappointment, too. The record has eleven songs from the MTV special, and then, inexplicably, seven of the same tracks with the vocals mixed out.

In 1993, Arrested Development did Lollapalooza; that same year, Speech spread his enterprising wings and provided music, production, scratches and the words to one song for **Dropping Soulful H20 on the Fiber,** the debut by Milwaukee's Gumbo! Telescoping AD's sweeping reach and analytical outlook down to a more intimate setting, the soulful Afro-centric trio's engaging album disproves the presumptions of clonedom: although some are voiced by Deanna Dawn, precocious seventeen-year-old mainman Fulani Faluke's lyrical ideas are his own.

The true followup album to **3 Years, 5 Months and 2 Days, Zingalamaduni** (the title is purportedly Swahili for "beehive of culture") was a major commercial flop. But the worst that can be said of the record is that it's more of the same, and there's nothing wrong with that. "Ease My Mind" and "Shell" have simple and unaffected grooves, and Speech still seems to be able to construct radio-worthy songs, even if none of these actually made it there. But a couple of things about the album are worrisome. One is that Speech's lyrics are less subtle; he can't seem to move out of political base-touching and on to tougher and more personal topics. The second is that when he tries, he sounds like a kook. "Mister Landlord" is unattractively strident; worse is "Warm Sentiments," in which the singer chides his girlfriend for having an abortion without consulting him and comes off incredibly insufferable and paternalistic.

In January '96, Speech returned with a self-titled solo album and the announcement that Arrested Development had disbanded. **Speech** shows that he can still construct a lulling, even groovy song cycle, but at this point he just doesn't have the lyrical chops to give it substance. The album is far too dependent on pat sloganeering ("If you think the system's workin'/Ask somebody who ain't") and filler, like a yawn-inducing recitation of hip-hop honors ("Impregnated Tid Bits of Dope Hits"). The kookiness hasn't left, either. This time, the submission is "Ghetto Sex." Speech thinks there's too much of it, and guess which sex he points the finger at? Hint: It's the one that wears tight dresses. [bw]

See also *Dionne Farris.*

DANIEL ASH

See *Love and Rockets.*

ASHTRAY BOY

See *Cannanes.*

ASS PONYS

Mr. Superlove (OKra) 1990
Grim (OKra) 1992 (Safe House) 1993
Electric Rock Music (A&M) 1994
The Known Universe (A&M) 1996

Seeking to remedy rock's sickly lack of humor, Cincinnati's Ass Ponys prescribe some wildly oddball tales of underappreciated aspects of America. The foursome coalesced in 1989, when singer/guitarist Chuck Cleaver (a veteran of the Lunchbuddies and Gomez) and ex-Libertines bassist Randy Cheek threw in their lot together. **Mr. Superlove** (produced by Afghan Whigs bassist and Cincy homeboy John Curley) touches on such uniquely American topics as roadkill ("Hey Swifty"), twisting them in a way that will make liberal types cringe. (Instead of offering sympathy, Cleaver's protagonist repeatedly runs over the animal.) The frontman's slightly nasal, oddly high-pitched vocal tricks most definitely aren't for everyone, but his hell-bent strains give the Ass Ponys an instantly likable quality.

Distribution problems left **Mr. Superlove** by the wayside, but **Grim** proved the band unwilling to abandon its twisted route: if anything, the Ponys are more determined in their folk-rock vision. Where the previous release used John Erhardt's slide and pedal steel to infuse a rootsy sound, **Grim** sees him sprinkling lighter flourishes into the mix. Maybe it's the occasionally muffled production that takes the fun down a peg, but **Grim** takes the "more serious" mission too seriously.

Curley takes the production reins again for **Electric Rock Music;** his return is good for the Ass Ponys. On the best of its albums, the band handles pop melodies, acoustic meanderings and country influences with equal aplomb: call the resultant hybrid Pavement-meets-Hank-Williams (with less heartbreak). The band's humor is back in full effect, tackling such sacred topics as familial knickknacks ("Earth to Grandma"), the socially challenged ("Peanut '93") and unfulfilling relationships ("Otter Slide"). The Ass Ponys aren't afraid to let you look into the mind of a kook; hell, they'll even split the skull wide open for your convenience.

By **The Known Universe,** however, it's not just the cosmology that's starting to seem familiar, it's the group's hackneyed idea of wit. Sounding like slapdash country kin of the Barenaked Ladies, the Ass Ponys retread familiar soil, relying on exhausted film jokes ("God Tells Me To") and mild outrage ("Cancer

Show"), all the while belaboring clichés like "I could rule the world if . . ." (a self-mocking line Tin Huey used to better effect fifteen years earlier) and real-life oddities like the oft-derided "Satin lives in hell" graffiti. While the semi-acoustic music is good-naturedly upbeat (breaking the mold, "And She Drowned" is impressive in its chunky pop-punk spunk), Cleaver's wavery voice remains a possible deal-breaker. [vg/i]

MICHAEL ASTON

See *Edith Grove, Gene Loves Jezebel.*

NATACHA ATLAS

See *Transglobal Underground, Jah Wobble's Invaders of the Heart.*

A TRIBE CALLED QUEST

People's Instinctive Travels and the Paths of Rhythm (Jive) 1990
The Low End Theory (Jive) 1991
Revised Quest for the Seasoned Traveller (UK Jive) 1992
Midnight Marauders (Jive) 1993
Beats, Rhymes and Life (Jive) 1996

Once the young'uns of the New York–area Native Tongues posse (De La Soul, Jungle Brothers), A Tribe Called Quest have proven to be its greatest and most consistent exponent. While the trio's stunning debut quickly aligned them with the others' formalist revisionism (an expansive range of samples, from Lou Reed to Stevie Wonder) and attitudinal adjustments (humanist consideration and good humor in place of violence and misogyny), the effortless flow of raps by Q-Tip, Phife Dog and Jarobi (DJ Ali Shaheed Muhammad completed the original quartet) suggested an inherent rhythmic sophistication that would later manifest itself in the group's innovative appropriations of jazz. Quest's slightly fantastic and sometimes absurdist narrative acumen masterfully guides the rhymes. Whether pleading to wild but conjured dream girls ("Bonita Applebum"), fearing cholesterol ("Ham 'n' Eggs") or offering bravado-free self-portraits ("Youthful Expression"), the first album maintains a perfect balance of style and substance.

Down to a trio with the departure of Jarobi, the band made its real breakthrough on **The Low End Theory**—fatback acoustic basslines lifted from old bebop records (and a real-time performance by Ron Carter on "Verses From the Abstract") and propelled by jeep beats. Perhaps the first hip-hop album to incorporate an unfettered jazz influence, it's among the most artistically successful of such fusions. Pairing roomy rhythmic patterns and lots of tensile basslines with more of their simpatico easy-flowing raps, Quest delivers a thoroughly enmeshed blend that understands the rhythmic looseness of jazz without imagining that hip-hop's beat rigidity can flex enough to swallow it whole. The record finds them broadening their lyrical scope as well: "Excursions" offers a vision of unified black cultural achievement, "Show Business" spews fumes of disgust with the music industry, "The Infamous Date Rape" thoughtfully ponders the complexity of refused sexual advances and "What?" spouts an endless stream of twisted wordplay-soaked riddles. An unqualified masterpiece. **Revised Quest for the Seasoned Traveller** is a collection of interesting, varied remixes of tracks from the first two albums.

Although **Midnight Marauders** builds upon the huge advances of **The Low End Theory,** it can't help but smother some of them. The jazzy fluidity remains, but instead of the previous album's brilliant and economical sense of space, this one brings the occasional gloppy sonic overload. Ultimately, however, such complaints are minor; the album catches Quest confidently tightening up previous accomplishments, not just breaking the same impressive ground. Amid the ceaseless fury of stale gangsta rap gestures, A Tribe Called Quest remains the brightest and steadiest light of realism-tempered positivity. [pm]

BACHIR ATTAR AND ELLIOTT SHARP

See *Elliott Sharp.*

MURRAY ATTAWAY

In Thrall (DGC) 1993

Through four Guadalcanal Diaries albums in the 1980s, Georgia singer/guitarist Murray Attaway was an intelligent, slightly bent auteur of New South roots pop, steering an imaginative course in a regional sea of post-punks, R.E.M. clones and recidivist rockers. The group never really caught on, and ended as the decade did; when Attaway resurfaced, it was with **In Thrall,** a mature solo debut with more mainstream craft and less lyrical eccentricity. Looking at his existence from the other side of some great divide, Attaway ponders "Living in Another Time" and tenses the past in "My Book" ("I have walked between the lines for years . . ."). Contemplating an old photograph in "Fall So Far," he asks, "Great godamighty, is this really me?" Using top-drawer sessioneers (Steve Nieve, Jim Keltner, the since-deceased Nicky Hopkins, Robbie Blunt, Benmont Tench) and background vocals on one song each by Jackson Browne and Aimee Mann, Attaway and producer/guitarist Tony Berg (Michael Penn, Ted Hawkins) turn his compositions into various stripes of modern pop. Still, the carefully wrought **In Thrall** comes across a bit more tepid than its title, leaving the conviction of Attaway's observations easier to believe in than his music. [i]

ATTILA & OTWAY

See *John Otway & Wild Willy Barrett.*

AUTEURS

New Wave (Caroline) 1993
Now I'm a Cowboy (Hut USA/Vernon Yard) 1994
Light Aircraft on Fire EP (UK Hut) 1996
After Murder Park (Hut USA/Vernon Yard) 1996

μ-ZIQ VS THE AUTEURS

μ-Ziq Vs the Auteurs (Hut USA/Astralwerks) 1995

With a purposefully self-conscious name, the Auteurs write perfectly self-conscious British guitar pop with strong Bowie overtones but a tamed interpretation of his grit. Songwriter Luke Haines heads the London trio with his taut guitar, refined piano and strained vocals, which give life to his crisply wrought story-like songs.

The Auteurs made a propitious debut with **New Wave,** a calculated but nonetheless graceful collection. In a dozen spare songs, Haines effectively captures the dullness of everyday life and the desire for a glittery escape with poignant songs like the strident single

"Showgirl," the sing-songy, piano-based "Junk Shop Clothes" and the delicate "Starstruck." His voice retains a Bowiesque lilt throughout, though his vocal range and the scope of his songs are narrower. The music is well-thought-out as well, using guest cellist James Banbury's lithe dips and swoops to adorn the songs like tasteful costume jewelry. The sympathetic rhythm section (bassist Alice Readman and drummer Glenn Collins) never over-asserts itself.

The promise of **New Wave** was not outdone by **Now I'm a Cowboy,** but neither was it negated. There are still rousing rockers like the single "Lenny Valentino," while wistful songs about a "New French Girlfriend," "The Upper Classes" and "Modern History" reveal Haines' and co-producer Phil Vinall's ear for a careful arrangement. (Banbury is credited as a full-time member.) While the overall sound is crisper and cleaner than that of its predecessor, the album lacks the energy of a group mining newly discovered ground, and suffers from a little too much self-awareness.

If the Auteurs weren't up to taking any stylistic leaps on their own, they were ready to let others do so for them. Electronic musician Michael Paradinas (who records under a variety of pseudonyms, including µ-Ziq, Jake Slazenger and Kid Spatula) was initially enlisted to remix a few **New Wave** cuts; what he did was create a brilliant, sample-driven album. Paradinas is deft at rearranging sounds into highly textural, yet strangely melodic soundscapes. The songs on **µ-Ziq Vs the Auteurs** aren't listed by name (nor is the origin of each cut's components), making it look and sound more like a record by µ-Ziq than the Auteurs.

Without exactly changing their tune, the Auteurs go for a heavier sound on **After Murder Park,** recorded by Steve Albini, whose love for sharp edges and crisp, noisy guitars doesn't suffocate some of the more delicately arranged songs. Haines' lyrics focus less on the glitzy and more on the gritty; you can practically feel the sting of the venom he spews in "Everything You Say Will Destroy You." For its sing-songy tone, "Unsolved Child Murder" grapples with dark subject matter. Complementing the lyrical bite is harsher, more metallic guitar and ominous organ from Banbury (whose cello playing remains a highlight of the band's sound).

Although the original single version of "Light Aircraft on Fire" is pretty brisk on its own, the Albini version on the album stresses the angularity of Haines' guitar line and toughens up the song's jerky rhythm (but lacks the rousing cello finish of the initial recording). The EP is fleshed out by a four-track demo of "Buddha" (it appears in finished form on the album), which reveals that Haines was heading in a noisier guitar direction even without Albini's input, and two non-LP cuts. Points to the band for having the courage to put a new face on its sound. [la]

AUTOCLAVE

See *Helium, Slant 6.*

AUTOMATON

See *Bill Laswell.*

ASTER AWEKE

Aster (UK Triple Earth) 1989 (Columbia) 1990
Kabu (Columbia) 1991

Aster Aweke grew up in Addis Ababa, surrounded by traditional Ethiopian sounds, Euro-pop, disco and American soul music. She got her start singing with various traditional and "popular" groups, although Ethiopian pop music is heavily based on traditional styles. Her first cassettes, recorded by Ali Tango (one of the country's best producers), were hits, but the repressive post-Selassie dictatorship sent Aweke into self-imposed exile by 1979. She settled in the African diplomatic community of Washington, DC, intending to pursue a university degree, but music took precedence. After a sold-out run at Ronnie Scott's famous jazz club in London, Aweke was contacted by Iain Scott and Bunt Stafford Clark, producers of Anglo-Indian singer Najma, and recorded her Western debut for London's Triple Earth label. Columbia picked Aweke's album up for domestic release in '90, touting her as an Ethiopian "soul singer," probably overestimating her commercial appeal and misunderstanding her artistry and music.

The horn charts on **Aster** may lean westward, but the slightly off-center rhythms and Aweke's soulful Amharic wail and ululating Arabic vocal style don't sound like any kind of music Americans are familiar with. Aweke's singing is impressive, but the linear construction of the tunes makes repeated listenings a must for most Westerners. "Tizita (Memories)," a traditional lament to lost love that's backed by a solo *oud,* is a low-key sizzler, while "Teyim (Sepia)," with its "Whiter Shade of Pale" organ and bluesy guitar, is as close to American R&B as Aweke gets. The rest of the album is solidly Ethiopian, despite the Western instruments.

Kabu is slightly less African than Aweke's debut, and heavy on midtempo grooves and ballads. "Yedi Gosh (My Guy)" opens the disc with a bit of Motown in its bouncy rhythm, but the album otherwise explores the band's richly atmospheric playing. The synthesizer on "Kabu (Sacred Rock)" mimics a bass kalimba while Aweke's vocals swoop and soar like a hummingbird; "Eyoha" is solidly funky; "Bitchengna (Loneliness)" is as bluesy and moody as anything Anita Baker has cut; "Tchewata ("Romance")," the token traditional track, is one of its standouts. [jp]

AXIOM AMBIENT/AXIOM FUNK

See *Bill Laswell.*

AZTEC CAMERA

High Land, Hard Rain (Sire) 1983
Knife (Sire) 1984
Backwards and Forwards EP10 (Sire) 1985
Love (Sire) 1987
Stray (Sire/Reprise) 1990
Dreamland (Sire/Reprise) 1993
Frestonia (Reprise) 1995

Scottish pop auteur Roddy Frame—founder, longtime leader and now solitary embodiment of Aztec Camera—traffics in the corniest romantic clichés, yet somehow makes them seem original. His wistful crooning, lush melodies and endless obsession with love's ups and downs make his flavorful light pop the attitudinal descendant of Nat "King" Cole or the young Frank Sinatra rather than fodder for the hip set, except for one thing: there's barely a hint of the cheesy sentimentality commonly associated with old-fashioned easy-listening slush. Frame cuts through the bull and makes the affairs of the heart seem like late-breaking news.

The striking **High Land, Hard Rain** is a smashing debut, with airy, haunting original tunes like "Oblivious," "We Could Send Letters" and "Walk Out to Winter." Dire Straits honcho Mark Knopfler produced **Knife,** adding an earthier feel to Frame's music—which inevitably dissipates some of the dreamy magic. The **Backwards and Forwards** EP offers five odds and ends, among them a lazy, unlikely cover of Van Halen's "Jump" that's thoroughly delightful.

Recorded with a variety of American producers and abandoning the illusion of Aztec Camera being a band, **Love** is somewhat unfocused, but boasts two of Frame's finest songs: the heart-rending "How Men Are" and "Somewhere in My Heart," a soaring, complex love song with a chorus that won't quit.

Frame retreated to the UK for the self-produced (with engineer Eric Calvi) **Stray,** turning out a more focused album with highlights such as "The Crying Scene" (not to be confused with "The Crying Game") and "Notting Hill Blues." His boisterous duet with Big Audio Dynamiter Mick Jones on "Good Morning Britain" proves conclusively that social commentary ain't his bag, however.

Co-producing with ambient meister Ryuichi Sakamoto on the aptly named **Dreamland,** Frame approaches a nirvana of cerebral passion on "Valium Summer," "Let Your Love Decide" and other ethereal treats. The haze occasionally becomes a bit cloying—which only goes to show how true Frame's aim is the rest of the time.

Frestonia (a place? a chemical element?) underscores the apparently endless resilience of Frame's art, depicting the usual romantic travails with eloquent vigor. "Rainy Season" is a dramatic kiss-off to a lover, while "Debutante" and "Beautiful Girl" probe for truths beneath the obvious. "I got laid just to see/My reflection burning bright," Frame sings in "Imperfectly," just in case anyone thinks he's lost his edge. [jy]

See also *TPRG*.

B

BABBLE
The Stone (Reprise) 1994
Ether (Reprise) 1996

THOMPSON TWINS
A Product of . . . (UK T) 1981
Set (UK T) 1982
In the Name of Love (Arista) 1982
Quick Step & Side Kick (UK Arista) 1983
Side Kicks (Arista) 1983
Into the Gap (Arista) 1984
Here's to Future Days (Arista) 1985
Close to the Bone (Arista) 1987
Greatest Mixes: The Best of Thompson Twins (Arista) 1988
Big Trash (Red Eye/Warner Bros.) 1989
Queer (Warner Bros.) 1991

Reaching the late '80s reduced to the two-person lineup always suggested by the band's name, the Thompson Twins—Englishman Tom Bailey and New Zealander Alannah Currie, both singing/songwriting multi-instrumentalists—made three albums before retiring the name and reorganizing the partnership as Babble. With **Greatest Mixes** providing a club-powered primer in the Twins' unconventionally crafty commercial dance-pop (before the hit-free **Close to the Bone**)—such career essentials as "Lies," "Hold Me Now," "Love on Your Side," "Doctor! Doctor!" and a previously unreleased remix of "In the Name of Love"—the group wrote its penultimate chapter in **Big Trash,** an uninspired mess of grade-school rhymes and bland music that is, at best, self-imitative. Ill-conceived and feebly written ("Kiss your wife goodbye/'Cos you know it's time to die/There are bombers in the sky" isn't even the creative nadir here), the album lacks nothing but effort, conviction and value.

The tense, erratic penmanship with which **Queer**'s lyrics are scrawled in the CD booklet suggests a change of creative heart (or an emotional upset of some severity), but the album is a largely successful return to the Twins' bouncy appeal. There is a dark, edgy undercurrent to Bailey's singing—like eau de Foetus, diluted to a safe concentration—and in the arrangements of songs like "Come Inside" (proffered in two mixes), "Groove On" and "The Saint," but the album's general tone is upbeat, atmospheric and clubby. (A description that doesn't quite cover "The Invisible Man," a sinuous crypto-Moroccan trance novelty of greater import down the line.) While "Strange Jane" and "Wind It Up" revisit the Bolanesque simplicity of **Big Trash**'s lyric writing, the album's overall intelligence level (and hook quotient) is pitched somewhat higher. The Thompson Twins had lost their momentum for good, but at least they hadn't lost their dignity.

As if acknowledging that no one was breathlessly awaiting another Thompson Twins album, Bailey and Currie became Babble, releasing **The Stone,** an album that chills out the tone of their late-'80s work to navigate less-rhythmatized, more restrained musical currents. The tranquilizing influence of ambient techno, occasionally colored in with world music elements (the title track is a veritable Middle Eastern sonic bazaar), gives the record its appealing character, a nearly there experiment to balance pop's explicit desires with ambient house's coy grooves. (If only Currie did more of the singing . . .) **Ether** continues the pair's progress into pop trippery, letting cushiony drones of atmospheric sequencers underpin quietly sly songs like Bailey's "The Circle" and Currie's "Love Has No Name." While the duo's knack for keeping things catchy makes **Ether** go down easy, they lack the stylistic conviction to abandon accessible tunefulness completely and wind up sounding like dilettantes rather than adventurers. [i]

See also *TPRG*.

BABES IN TOYLAND
Spanking Machine (Twin\Tone) 1990
To Mother (Twin\Tone) 1991
The Peel Sessions (Strange Fruit/Dutch East India Trading) 1992
Fontanelle (Reprise) 1992
Painkillers (Reprise) 1993
Nemesisters (Reprise) 1995

CRUNT
Crunt (Trance Syndicate) 1993

Babes in Toyland's origins lie in Sugar Baby Doll, a mid-'80s San Francisco supergrrroup of sorts involving Oregon-born high-school friends Kat(hy) Bjelland (pronounced, suitably enough, "be-yellin'") and Courtney Love, augmented by future L7 guitarist Jennifer Finch and a drummer whose name no one seems to remember. The group apparently never performed or recorded, although a very funny photograph survives; Kat also played with the charmingly named Italian Whore Nuns. Kat and Courtney soon moved to Minneapolis, but whether the latter was ever actually a member of Babes in Toyland depends upon whose memory is being prodded.

Around a nucleus of guitarist Bjelland and novice drummer Lori Barbero, the Babes plodded along as a four-piece through 1987–88 before Kat took over the vocal slot and bassist Michelle Leon joined. The trio made its debut with the scrawny and brawling declaration of intent, **Spanking Machine.** Produced in Seattle by Jack Endino, the album makes up in spunk what it lacks in instrumental fluency: the group thuds cathartic tribal punk (not worlds away from the Slits crossed with Bauhaus) while Bjelland screeches like an otherworldly pairing of Bon Scott and Linda Blair. **Spanking Machine** wears thin pretty quickly, but is awesome in small doses, especially "He's My Thing" and "Swamp Pussy."

Recorded in London with John Loder, **To Mother** is doomier and only slightly more instrumentally accomplished, but the songwriting quality is considerably improved, especially in the scathing "Spit to See the Shine" and "Mad Pilot" (although "The Quiet Room" instrumental is a shameless cop of Bauhaus' "King Volcano"). The eight-song **Peel Sessions** combines two sessions from '90 and '91 and serves as a demi–"greatest hits." Leon quit literally days before the band recorded its next album and was replaced by Maureen Herman.

Fontanelle, co-produced by Bjelland and Sonic Youth's Lee Ranaldo, blasts off with one of the group's best songs, "Bruise Violet," allegedly a swipe at Courtney, who had already taken media heat for appropriating Bjelland's kinderpunk fashions. (The song's airing on *Beavis and Butt-head,* combined with Lollapalooza tour exposure, actually coalesced a bit of a suburban following for the group.) All told, the Babes roar through fifteen songs with a minimum of repetition; while the drastic upgrade in sonic clarity counts for a lot, **Fontanelle**'s strength is that the trio has mastered its game without compromise.

The six-cut **Painkillers** contains a re-recording of "He's My Thing" along with some B-sides and "Fontanellette," a thirty-four-minute live rendition of the album taken from a raunchy April '92 CBGB set that finds Bjelland's psychobabble in rare form. (For the fan who must have everything, there's the promo-only **Live at the Academy,** documenting eleven songs recorded two months after the CBGB gig.)

Released after a three-year studio gap, the plodding **Nemesisters** might as well have been called **Lamesisters.** The album begins promisingly with the slow and snarling "Hello," but quickly devolves into weak songs and self-indulgence, including a horrendous butchering of Eric Carmen's "All by Myself" and an incongruously perky take on Sister Sledge's "We Are Family." Even the great cover artwork doesn't make up for what's inside.

Crunt is a cantankerous side-project by Bjelland (playing bass), her husband, Lubricated Goat frontal lobe Stuart Gray (aka Stu Spasm), and Jon Spencer Blues Explosion drummer Russell Simins, making a typically muscular contribution. Apart from one Kat vocal, this enthusiastic if offhand outing—recorded in Seattle—is pretty much Stuart's show. [ja]

See also *Hole.*

BABE THE BLUE OX

(BOX) (Homestead) 1993
Je m'Appelle Babe EP (Homestead) 1993
Color Me Babe (Homestead) 1994
People (RCA) 1996

By the sounds of it, this Brooklyn threesome, who met at Brown University, make their open-ended backyard music as if they'd read the instruction manual backward and then set out to translate it into a foreign language. Drummer Hanna Fox, guitarist Tim Thomas and bassist Rosalee Thomson (all sing) don't do anything as obvious as don different genre attire on their records, all of which are pretty well rooted in the advanced precision of jazz-pop eccentricity. No, where Babe the Blue OX opens the floodgates is in the second-to-second diversity of its invention. As one small illustrative example, the debut's "Booty" careens along on Thomas' urgently whispered vocals ("a baptism of jism/through the prisms of ism") over a spastic skeleton of firmly held fusion-factory art-funk complexity—until it turns a corner with a knock-knock joke and launches into shouts and a wriggly electric drive-by, a two-line refrain at a completely different syncopated rhythm and then a spare instrumental bridge. No hyperkinetic video game could run through as many different landscapes in three minutes, and certainly not with such provocatively clever lyrics as "National Geographic": "I didn't recognize the mom of the world/Til I saw her global fridgerator covered with boys and girls/From thousands of years, spanned all countries and races."

(BOX) can be remarkably entertaining. "Chicken Head Bone Sucker" finds a stunning common ground between the Butthole Surfers and King Crimson; "Spatula" digs a groove between Basehead and Soul Coughing; "Born Again," Thomson's ironic self-help screed, is roaring punkish fun. But the album is also exhausting, with challenging tempos, overcaffeinated tension and music that does everything imaginable to avoid stepping into a simple melodic structure. Although a fascinating animal that merits further investigation, Babe the Blue OX is not the easiest creature to wrap your arms around.

For most of the encouraging six-song **Je m'Appelle Babe,** the trio focuses the skittish mania of its presentation while maintaining the feverish level of think-tank activity. "S'Good" actually has a regular-type chorus; "Tattoos" and "Agent 6950" are almost normal enough to play safely with the other children, while "Everybody Want$ You" sets Thomas' own wordplay against a relatively straight rendition of the 1982 Billy Squier hit. But any presumption that the trio's artistic resolve might be softening evaporates in "Spin the Bottle," a disturbing Adrian-Belew-meets-Devo space exploration.

Establishing a band habit of borrowing titles from Barbra Streisand LPs, **Color Me Babe** pushes through to a new, more accessible plane of Babeness. Without giving any artistic ground, the thicker rock textures, bolder melodies (and singing) and a notch less restlessness conspire to hammer typically oddball ideas like "Ego Pimps," "Axl" (Fox's womanly dig at the rude rock star), "9/10" and "Health" into inviting shapes that sublimate instrumental arm-waving for less stimulation and greater satisfaction. The distraction level rises from moderate to intense as the album proceeds toward "There's a Hole in the Crotch of My Work Pants," but the folky "King of the Rain"—despite some adroit noise-guitar incursions—is unabashedly lovely, vivid proof of the tender human heart driving this vigorously cerebral corps.

The move to a major label did not go unnoted by the trio; while retaining enough confusion-is-sex extremism here and there, **People** is Babe at its most straightforward and ingratiatingly rock-like. (Another view would call it calculatingly commercial, but that doesn't seem to be what's going on here.) Sounding unnervingly like the Presidents of the United States of America at times (most pointedly on the tense, bass-heavy "Can't Stand Up," "Rube Goldberg" and the explosive "Family Picnic"), the album peels away the band's difficult exterior for such best-behavior charmers as "Breathe," "Stand by Your Man" (no, not that one), the sweet-sounding/sour-tongued "Memphis" and Thomson's gorgeous "Wake Up," which could pass for a lost Lisa Loeb single. If **People** attracts new fans who won't care much for the band's trickier back catalogue, it's clear that the same wry intelligence and highly individual musical ambition is at work both here and there. [i]

BABYLON DANCE BAND

See *Antietam.*

BAD BRAINS

Bad Brains (ROIR) 1982 (Dutch East India Trading) 1991 (ROIR) 1996
Bad Brains EP (UK Alternative Tentacles) 1982
I and I Survive EP (Important) 1982
Rock for Light (PVC) 1983 (Caroline) 1991
I Against I (SST) 1986
Live (SST) 1988
Attitude: The ROIR Sessions (In-Effect/Relativity) 1989
Quickness (Caroline) 1989
The Youth Are Getting Restless (Caroline) 1990
Spirit Electricity (SST) 1991
Rise (Epic) 1993
God of Love (Maverick/Warner Bros.) 1995

At their best, Bad Brains are a band to make the hairs on the back of your neck ripple in awe. Rastafarians from Washington, DC, by way of New York City, Bad Brains play a groundbreaking, incendiary mixture of raging hardcore punk, deftly thudding metal and heartfelt, liquid reggae, bristling with spiritual fervor. Visionary frontman H.R. (Paul Hudson) has the lungs of a lion, able to morph from sweetly soulful crooner to fiery banshee wailer; guitar wizard Dr. Know erupts with serpentine squealing leads and charging, crunching chords; the churning heartbeat rhythms are forged by limber bassist Darryl Jenifer and stoic drummer (and H.R.'s brother) Earl Hudson.

The quartet's problem is its internal volatility: the Bad Brains have broken up and re-formed more times than Liz Taylor has walked down the aisle. While such tumult hasn't diminished the band's tremendous influence (not only on obvious progeny like Living Colour and 24-7 Spyz, but on the likes of Rollins, Red Hot Chili Peppers, Beastie Boys and Jane's Addiction as well), it has precluded large-scale success. Nonetheless, Bad Brains continue to reunite, tilting gloriously at the windmills of Babylon.

Much of the band's early motherlode—lethal thrash classics like "Banned in D.C.," "Big Takeover," "Sailin' On," "Attitude" and "Pay to Cum"—can be found in rawer versions on **Bad Brains** and in slicker, Ric Ocasek–produced takes on **Rock for Light.** (The latter's CD reissue—completely remixed and resequenced by Ocasek and Jenifer—contains three bonus tracks.) The group's first implosion lasted several years, but led to one of their best reunion records, 1986's **I Against I,** which skillfully introduces spicy funk and soul elements. Another split followed, during which time the Hudson brothers released records under the H.R. name, and Know and Jenifer briefly led an alternate Bad Brains with another singer and Cro-Mags drummer Mackie, who plays on the bulldozer comeback, **Quickness,** with H.R back behind the mic. (Earl rejoined before the record's release and is pictured on it.) Again, Bad Brains collapsed.

The quartet entered the '90s in limbo, issuing a spate of live discs, all recorded during the **I Against I** period. (For the record, **Live** sounds best. The harder-rocking **The Youth Are Getting Restless** has a lot more tracks, while **Spirit Electricity** can boast of its otherwise unreleased title cut.) That stasis ended in 1993 when a new lineup—Dr. Know, Darryl Jenifer, Mackie and singer Israel Joseph-I (a dead ringer, vocally, for H.R.)—signed the band's first major-label deal and cut the surprisingly solid **Rise.** Galloping thrashers like "Unidentified" and "Coming in Numbers" really get the adrenaline flowing, while delicious reggae numbers like "Love Is the Answer" and "Yes Jah" allow Israel Joseph-I to take a credible stab at Bob Marley stylings. A snazzy version of Graham Central Station's "Hair" is apropos lyrically ("I just don't believe it's fair/To judge a man by the length of his hair"). Predictably, this outfit didn't stay together long.

Reuniting once again with H. R. and Earl Hudson (not to mention producer Ocasek), and signed to Madonna's Maverick label, the original rasta-blastas sound as powerful as ever on **God of Love**'s crisp, chord-driven openers, "Cool Mountaineer" and "Justice Keepers." The title track and "Tongue Tee Tie" are familiar metallic riffsters driven by big, funky Bonhamian beats in the tradition of such past bruisers as "Re-Ignition," "With the Quickness" and "Rise." Interesting dub/dancehall textures and synths enliven "Long Time" and the reggae-rocking "How I Love Thee." But despite H.R.'s leonine presence, **God of Love** is uneven and oddly uninspiring. Vocals and arrangements seem awkwardly off on several cuts ("Darling I Need You," "Thank Jah" and the curdled ballad "Overs the Water"); the poorly sequenced record is simply not one of the band's best. Following the album's release, Bad Brains split up yet again. [gef]

See also *TPRG.*

BAD EXAMPLES

Bad Is Beautiful (Waterdog) 1991
Cheap Beer Night (Waterdog) 1992

One of the salutary side effects of rock's indie-fueled progression leftward has been a general elevation of bar-band standards. The number of balding journeymen bashing out today's chart hits for tonight's barflies probably hasn't shrunk, but today's population of knockabout groups with tried and true virtues, a thorough lack of trendy pretensions *and* the burning ambition to write and record their own material have appreciably more on the ball than those Johnny-B.-Goode-enough rockers largely displaced when underground modernists took over most urban sinkholes possessing a stage and a sink.

The Bad Examples is a good example of this upward trend. In its poppy Beatlisms, the Chicago quartet bears more than a passing resemblance to another onetime bar band, Squeeze. Singer/guitarist Ralph Covert writes solidly tuneful songs in a variety of Midwest rock veins (one of which favors the Spin Doctors); the group plays 'em all with engaging skill—if an unfortunate weakness for shmaltz. Although there's absolutely no need for another desolate number about waiting for the phone to ring ("Statue by the Phone"), and the phrase "sick and tired of being sick and tired" (used in "Ashes of My Heart") is hereby banished to the songwriters' book of untouchable clichés, most of the numbers on **Bad Is Beautiful** say something original in an easily familiar way. "Faces in Picasso's Notebook" is a touching post-breakup get-together; "One Perfect Moment" removes a skeptical curtain from romance; "Stranger Than Fiction" and "Promises in the Dark" both acknowledge encroaching adulthood: "Someone as old as you should never look for the truth/In promises made in the dark."

Recorded in a Chicago club after two years of touring (with latecomer lead guitarist John Duich joining Covert, drummer Terry Wathen and bassist Pickles Piekarski), **Cheap Beer Night** is aptly described in the liner notes as "real people playing & singing real music on real instruments." The band is tight enough that the rockers sound like a studio record until the applause roars up, but the spirited delivery that comes from kicking it live explains the strategic wisdom of doing it this way. There's a surprising amount of restrained pop mush for a concert that contains a rip-snorting rendition of the first album's defiant "Not Dead Yet," but the Bad Examples also crank it good on "Hey St. Peter," "The Secret of Television" and the Tom Petty–like "Bad Girl." The novelty of "Sammy the Dog," the autogeographical "Long Drive Back From Madison" and a reliable yes-we're-a-bar-band cover of Bo Diddley's "Mona" add to the entertainment. [i]

BAD LIVERS

Dust on the Bible (no label) 1991 (Quarterstick) 1993
Delusions of Banjer (Quarterstick) 1992
The Golden Years EP (UK Southern Studios) 1992
Horses in the Mines (Quarterstick) 1994

Representing perhaps the most true-blue wing of the mid-'90s alternative country movement, Austin's Bad Livers—Danny Barnes (vocals, banjo, guitar), Mark Rubin (upright bass, tuba) and Ralph White III (fiddle, accordion)—first made a name as the folks who could whip out bluegrass covers of punk classics and toured with the Butthole Surfers. It might seem like gimmickry, but what they're really doing is bringing bluegrass to today's kids—and besides, the music's forebears had speed-demon chops and bad-ass attitude, too. Fans of SST-era Meat Puppets might well dig this stuff, although just about any rocker could appreciate the Bad Livers—the music is full of the bluegrass equivalent of heavy riffs, the lyrics are generally about outlaws, drunks and alienated types, and the tempos occasionally attain hardcore velocity.

Delusions of Banjer was straightforwardly produced by Butthole Surfer Paul Leary, who also contributed a number called "The Adventures of Pee Pee the Sailor." It's a tribute to the Livers' authenticity that, though the songs sound like bluegrass and old-timey country chestnuts, most are originals. Topped by Barnes' twangy vocals, songs like "Shit Creek," "Uncle Lucius" and "If It Runs" are a fine match for the band's formidable chops. Although generally traditional-sounding, the album does allow one concession to modernity: an amazing free-bluegrass break on the old standard "Crow Black Chicken."

A home recording initially self-released on cassette as a Christmas present for the band's family and friends in 1991, **Dust on the Bible** contains covers of a dozen gospel and spiritual standards.

Recorded on an 8-track board with vintage tube microphones—reportedly in a woodshed—**Horses in the Mines** uncovers blues and New Orleans second-line rhythms sneaking into the pathos of "Turpentine Willie," a gentle country swing in the rueful "Time and Time Again" and an aching desolation in the slow, spare title track. While the emphasis is on heartfelt songs framed by well-wrought arrangements (like the ambitious—and successful—art-bluegrass instrumental "Puke Grub"), there's fabulous high-velocity picking on a version of Ed Shelton's banjo colossus, "Blue Ridge Express." For the most part, though, **Horses in the Mines** is more reflective, less rollicking than its predecessor. The album's depth and sincerity prove that the Bad Livers are indeed no gimmick. [ma]

BAD RELIGION

Bad Religion EP7 (Epitaph) 1981
How Could Hell Be Any Worse? (Epitaph) 1982
Into the Unknown (Epitaph) 1983
Back to the Known EP (Epitaph) 1984
Suffer (Epitaph) 1988
No Control (Epitaph) 1989
Against the Grain (Epitaph) 1990
80–85 (Epitaph) 1991
Generator (Epitaph) 1992
Recipe for Hate (Epitaph) 1993 (Epitaph/Atlantic) 1993
Stranger Than Fiction (Atlantic) 1994
All Ages (Epitaph) 1995
The Gray Race (Atlantic) 1996

Armed with four chords and a higher education, Southern California's Bad Religion offers compelling proof that blistering punk-rock energy and provocative, artistic intelligence can do better than merely coexist—they can meld into something of much broader cultural consequence. After an early career that looks fairly hapless in retrospect, Bad Religion was able to find itself, set an agenda and stick to it without compromise, reaching adulthood and achieving major-league stardom—playing music once considered too rugged for mass appeal—without bending an inch to any outside will.

Inspirational in its work and achievement, able to accept major-label involvement without allowing interference, Bad Religion defies the genre's typical preaching-to-the-converted limits by offering two reasons to believe: the invigorating music's raw, atavistic power sets fire to one audience while the lyrics' thoughtful sophistication can speak to and hold the attention of another. (Whatever mingling there is comes as a social bonus.) Bolstered by the concurrent growth of founding guitarist Brett Gurewitz's Epitaph label (home of the Offspring, Rancid, NOFX, Pennywise, and others)—which has had a greater impact on the sound and style of '90s rock than most corporate ogres—Bad Religion has come to stand for more than it actually amounts to. That the group's creative growth has been incremental (the stylistic differences between, say, **Suffer** and **Generator** are barely worth noting) is disappointing; consistency is not the only attribute a band this important needs to uphold.

The San Fernando Valley rockers spent their early

years changing lineups and playing a brand of hardcore that stood out from the headbanging crowd. The first album adds singer Greg Graffin's piano and university-grade lyrics to a full dose of ramalama crunch. Making a rule of the debut's exceptions, **Into the Unknown** shifts gears completely, adopting a nifty '70s keyboard-pop sound that owes something to Todd Rundgren, Deep Purple, Mott the Hoople and David Bowie and nothing to Black Flag or the Damned. But Bad Religion had serious second thoughts about that direction, broke up and, upon regrouping, reversed its allegiance, taking pains to renounce eclecticism on the all-punk **Back to the Known.**

It wasn't until **Suffer,** four years after getting **Back to the Known,** that the latter-day Bad Religion got itself squared away as a quintet: Graffin (who had acquired a master's degree in geology from UCLA in the interim; he later earned a doctorate in biology from Cornell—take that, you lowlifes!), Gurewitz ("Mr. Brett"), guitarist Greg Hetson (ex–Circle Jerks) and the founding rhythm section of drummer Pete Finestone and bassist Jay Bentley, who had quit early in the **Unknown** sessions. Considering how much time had elapsed between records, **Suffer**'s youthful fury is a revelation. While most turn-of-the-decade LA punks had fallen off or succumbed to hackneyed metal-faced cliché, Bad Religion simply surged forward: the album is faster, meaner and leaner than any in the band's past. The attack is ablaze with unusual hooks (sea chanteys seem to be a primary source for song shapes, which give the band an abiding folk-roots undercurrent), pointed riffs and pretentious pseudo-erudition. Unfortunately—and typically—the playing's relentless velocity makes it hard to distinguish among the songs.

Suffer was just a warmup, however, for **No Control,** an awesome achievement in an otherwise moribund genre. Perhaps one of the best hardcore albums ever, **No Control** recaptures all of the form's exhilarating attributes, with inspired songwriting, vocal harmonies, transfixing visionary lyrics ("Change of Ideas," "I Want to Conquer the World," "Progress," "I Want Something More"), explosive playing and Graffin's pleading, tearing voice. The lack of rhythmic and stylistic variety can't sabotage this firecracker, as the sheer power of might meeting melody is too satisfying.

Maintaining **No Control**'s pace, **Against the Grain** is another unbelted rollercoaster ride. The band's smoking self-production makes Graffin's voice seem especially sinister on such tracks as "Get Off," "Anesthesia" and "Operation Rescue," a scathing indictment of the anti-abortion movement. A few slow songs (like "Faith Alone") test his range, but he delivers consistently dramatic performances. Although this first rendition of it is turgid and sloppy compared to the **Stranger Than Fiction** remake, "21st Century (Digital Boy)"—in which Mr. Brett rewrites the Kinks and King Crimson in one blistering swoop—is one of the band's strongest, catchiest songs.

Other than the new face behind the drums (Bobby Schayer) and individual songwriting credits (which the faster/louder Graffin and poppier/rockier Mr. Brett had been sharing since **Suffer**), the riveting **Generator** doesn't provide much to remark on beyond the intellectual meat on the songs' familiar bones. Taking a firm stand against conformity in "No Direction," Graffin turns the tables on those who look up to their cultural idols: "No Bad Religion song can make your life complete . . . you'll get no direction from me." The diabolical title track—as usual, the album's best—seethes with philosophical passion ("Like a rock/Like a planet/Like a fucking atom bomb/I'll remain unperturbed by the joy and the madness that I encounter everywhere I turn") forced into precision stop-start rhythms that heighten the tension. Rich harmony vocals give "Too Much to Ask" and "Heaven Is Falling" extra juice, recalling nothing so much as prime X.

Recipe for Hate struggles vainly against the band's stylistic straitjacket, but the slide guitar (which had to be played by a sessioneer) that gives "Man With a Mission" its wry country flavor sticks out like a minuet in the middle of a wrestling match. Graffin's impressive multi-tracked vocals (aided by such choirboys as Eddie Vedder) and a few songs that consciously try to move beyond standard structures ("Portrait of Authority," "All Good Soldiers," "Struck a Nerve") aren't enough to keep the record away from been-there-heard-that fatigue. Racing 4/4 beats can be a sturdy platform or a barbed-wire fence; here they rope-a-dope Bad Religion with a simple slip knot.

Bringing in Andy Wallace as co-producer of **Stranger Than Fiction** got the band a more varied and musical drum sound and opened the door to some unprecedented approaches. The central Bad Religion thesis remains fast, taut, rhythm-guitar rock with Graffin's articulate pontification, but other ideas are given room to develop; small details throughout the writing and arrangements spread the songs into a wider panorama. "The Handshake" has an especially conscious lyric; "Infected" and the folky verses of "Slumber" vary the pace to land on new emotional planes. "Television" simply revs into overdrive, but with an above-average pop melody that makes it refreshing anyway. The much-improved encore of "21st Century (Digital Boy)" supplies this crucial album—the band's first for Atlantic—with a reliable catalogue item, but Gurewitz equals it with "Stranger Than Fiction," a mobile descending riff, catchy pop chorus and lyrics that compare reality to literature: "Life is the crummiest book I ever read/There isn't a hook, just a lot of cheap shots/Pictures to shock and characters an amateur would never dream up." (We know what you meant, Brett.)

Stranger Than Fiction was Gurewitz's final album. In late '94, when the band hit the road to tour behind their first major-label record, he stayed behind to devote himself to Epitaph. Punk veteran Brian Baker (Minor Threat/Dag Nasty/Junkyard) took over his rhythm guitar slot and stayed in the lineup to put an extra charge into **The Gray Race.** Neither Baker nor Ric Ocasek's co-production nor the fact that the songs are all Graffin's drastically affects the sound of the record, other than to make it a bit less catchy and take further advantage of the group's less strictured approach and vary the textures within familiar walls. Graffin's lyrics are especially invigorating: following the sarcasm of "Punk Rock Song," "Come Join Us" repeats an old sentiment with fresh enthusiasm.

The **80–85** CD—a consolidation of **Bad Religion, How Could Hell Be Any Worse?** and **Back to the Known** in full, plus a handful of compilation cuts—simply bypasses **Into the Unknown** as if it were a dog puddle. **All Ages** does the same thing in less conspicuous fashion: only two of the songs predate 1985, and one of them ("Fuck Armageddon . . . This Is Hell") appears in a '94 live-in-Sweden version (as does **Suffer**'s "Do What You Want"). Otherwise, the retrospective cherrypicks the four albums released between 1988 and 1992 (unwisely including the inferior first version of "21st Century (Digital Boy)"), thereby making the band's prime pre-stardom years easily available to late arrivals.

In mid-'96, Gurewitz unveiled his new musical project, a studio quartet named the Daredevils, with a CD single of "Hate You" and "Rules, Hearts." For all the spite motivating his efforts (the band's bio refers to Bad Religion as the "bloody corpse of Thesaurus Rock"), the A-side's doubletracked vocals, big, chunky chord progression and gutsy, proud lyrics sound mighty familiar. [i/jr]

See also *Circle Jerks; TPRG.*

CHRIS BAILEY

Casablanca (Fr. New Rose) 1983
What We Did on Our Holidays (Fr. New Rose) 1984
Demons (Fr. New Rose) 1991
Savage Entertainment (Fr. New Rose) 1992
54 Days at Sea (Fr. New Rose) 1994

SAINTS

(I'm) Stranded (Sire) 1977
Eternally Yours (Sire) 1978
Prehistoric Sounds (UK Harvest) 1978
Prehistoric Songs (Fr. Harvest) 1981
The Monkey Puzzle (Fr. New Rose) 1981
Out in the Jungle . . . (UK Flicknife) 1982
A Little Madness to Be Free (Fr. New Rose) 1984
Live in a Mud Hut (Fr. New Rose) 1985
Best of the Saints (UK Razor) 1986
All Fools Day (TVT) 1987
Prodigal Son (TVT) 1988
Scarce Saints (Aus. Raven) 1989
Box Set (Aus. Mushroom) 1989
The New Rose Years (Fr. Fan Club) 1989
Songs of Salvation 1976–1988 (Aus. Raven) 1991
The Most Primitive Band in the World (Live From the Twilight Zone–Brisbane 1974) (Hot/Restless) 1995

When Chris Bailey stopped using the Saints moniker in 1989, he was just coming clean; all of the Saints' 1980s albums were truly solo records, using a constant but revolving cast of backing characters. The actual Saints had not existed since the late '70s, when guitarist/songwriter Ed Kuepper split from the Australian group that had blazed its country's punk trail.

Bailey's first two solo albums date from those '80s Saints days. In fact, **Casablanca** consists of Bailey's voice-and-guitar demos for 1982's **Out in the Jungle,** and was released against his wishes. Good thing, though: three excellent originals were not re-recorded for that LP, and the stark presentation enlivens a batch of folk/blues troubadour covers.

The authorized **What We Did on Our Holidays** is also no big deal. As indicated by its title, Bailey was just having some fun—with one exception, it's all covers. Half of it is acoustic folk and blues, the other full-band soul raveups, a good workout for Bailey's rich voice. The CD adds eight of **Casablanca**'s twelve songs.

Seventeen years into his career, **Demons** is the first proper Bailey solo album released as such. And it's largely an improvement on **Prodigal Son,** the good but overproduced album that ended the Saints' nominal career in 1988. The title track, "Marquis of Queensbury," "Running Away From Home" and others may not recall the heights of the Saints' **A Little Madness to Be Free** and **All Fools Day,** but they do showcase lush, smartly conceived and arranged music, from boisterous rock to blues.

Savage Entertainment returns Bailey more completely to his past glory. Finally eschewing the bloated production, he keeps it simple—just voice and guitar, with other instruments as color, not competition. With the exception of the heavy, bluesed-out "Queen of the Hour," Bailey doesn't bellow much here, but is no less effective a vocalist. The standout is the single, "Do They Come From You": a circling piano underpinned by strings and Bailey's plaintive wail. Other tracks delve into bitter ironies, self-deprecation and inner torment.

Continuing the thread, **54 Days at Sea** again plays to his strengths: superior song construction, a booming, bluesy voice and fluid, flowery, spot-on arrangements, including unobtrusive touches of flute, clarinet and piano. "Vampyres" and "Lazarus" point the album's theme to the horror of coming to grips with severe disappointment—sparked by his own failed marriage—but offset the introspection with breezy tunes. Bailey pulls the listener into this emotional warfare brilliantly, without the whiskey-soaked lamentations of the latter-day Saints. [jr]

See also *TPRG.*

DEREK BAILEY/GEORGE LEWIS/ JOHN ZORN

See *John Zorn.*

BAILTER SPACE

Nelsh Bailter Space EP (NZ Flying Nun) 1987
Tanker (NZ Flying Nun) 1988
Grader Spader EP (NZ Flying Nun) 1988
Thermos (NZ Flying Nun) 1990
The Aim EP (Matador) 1992
Robot World (Matador) 1993
B•E•I•P (Matador) 1993
Vortura (Matador) 1994
Wammo (Matador) 1995

Formed as an outgrowth of New Zealand noise-exploration trio the Gordons, Bailter Space was, in the late '80s, doing something similar to what Sonic Youth sold in the '90s—hard, droning, unforgiving guitar music with occasional lapses into verse/chorus regularity. Only Bailter Space wasn't quite as interested in accessibility. Right from the band's debut EP, **Nelsh,** guitarist John Halvorsen specialized in an abrasive, almost pitchless assault that could feel as polished and smooth as sheet metal, and his foils—ex-Gordons guitarist Alister Parker, Clean drummer Hamish Kilgour (later replaced by Gordons drummer Brent McLachlan when Kilgour settled in the New York area and formed the Mad Scene)—worked to feed that sound, contributing feedback gales and arty, disjointed backbeats that never felt fully settled.

Tanker takes baby steps toward convention. The songs have recognizable forms, and there are times when the disaffected vocals actually penetrate, revealing Bailter Space as unexpectedly subversive students of pop. This aspect of the band's personality is evident on some subsequent projects, and curiously missing from others: it's there on the hooky 1988 EP **Grader Spader** and in spots on the morose and dissonant **Thermos,** but absent from the curiously cold **Robot World.** (**B•E•I•P** pairs two songs from **Robot World** with "X" and "Projects" from the same sessions.)

The Aim marks the first time these divergent strains unite. The result is music that has distinct melodic character atop a supple and more listener-friendly sheen of noise. This balance defines Bailter Space's later works. Never lapsing into imitation, the group's muddy and apologetic vocals and multi-layered guitar textures manage to wink at everything from the Velvet Underground to the Beatles without subordinating mood-setting skills all its own.

Vortura leans toward the Velvets, with slow dirges and moping medium tempos that conjure languid, late-afternoon reveries. There are more extroverted single-note guitar statements, and the vocals are no longer buried in the mix; still, the shape-shifting instrumental play is much more interesting than the compositions. The pseudo-concept-album **Wammo** lurches back toward accessibility: despite the art-school conceit of the sleeve note that seven of the ten songs "were originally entitled Wammo," Bailter Space flirts with power chords and pop hooks. On the uncharacteristically catchy "Retro" as well as "Splat" and "At Five We Drive," it's possible to hear Halvorsen searching for a way to personalize the post-Nirvana punk-pop crunch. Just as often, though, the band is happy brooding, finding new ways to link the conventional with open-ended exploration. [tm]

See also *Clean; TPRG.*

ED BALL

Welcome to the Wonderful World of Ed Ball (UK Creation) 1995
If a Man Ever Loved a Woman (UK Creation) 1995

O-LEVEL

1977–1980 A Day in the Life of Gilbert and George (UK Rev-Ola) 1992

Going back to 1982, the complete album discography of London's Ed Ball as the leader (at times, sole member) of the modpop-turned-rave-then-techno Times numbers well over dozen; add in two albums of early work as the Teenage Filmstars; three more by his pseudonymous solo dance machine, Love Corporation; one by the Conspiracy of Noise (a violent rock collaboration with the singer of Extreme Noise Terror) and miscellaneous "side" projects like L'Orange Mechanik, and you've got a shelf full from this eclectically talented co-founder of the Television Personalities, a man who actually makes his living playing in the Boo Radleys and working as a Creation Records staffer. Amazingly, none of Ball's work has ever been released on this side of the Atlantic.

Thanks to the lack of album attribution, as well as inscrutable selection logic and mad sequencing by compiler (and Creation boss and one-album Times member) Alan McGee, novices won't be able to glean much more than a random sense of career highlights from the two CDs of **Welcome to the Wonderful World of Ed Ball.** As an introduction, it's a delightful journey that leads those not already familiar down a blind alley. The primeval "We Love Malcolm" (a 1978 rewrite of a Television Personalities song by the pre-Times O-Level) follows a 1993 dub track that mixes raggamuffin toaster Tippa Irie into a Scritti Politti song. Whoa! The Times' ingenious mod kernels (1983's "I Helped Patrick McGoohan Escape" and "This Is London") are set next to more modern bits of whimsy (like 1989's scene-ribbing "Manchester" from the acid-synched **E Is for Edward**) and theatrical ambition ("Up Against It," the title track of an album based on Joe Orton's rejected script for a Beatles movie); among the stranger juxtapositions are a delightful (if badly pronounced) French version of New Order's "Blue Monday" next to eleven endless minutes of Love Corporation's club-pumping "Give Me Some Love." This hodgepodge won't encourage many converts from the vast audience segment that has never encountered Ball's amazing adventures in style, but those who have some idea of his unchartable course will find plenty of times to enjoy. (For fans of early London twee-pop, however, the O-Level reissue—half of which is actually by the Teenage Filmstars, a subsequent Ball band with head TV Personality Dan Treacy—provides a much smarter and focused treat.)

If a Man Ever Loved a Woman is, then, Ball's first official solo album. A subdued acoustic epitaph to a relationship, the poignant folk-pop record is painfully heartfelt; after all the years of erecting facile constructions in whatever idiom strikes his momentary fancy, Ball is so accustomed to artifice that revealing himself risks emotional overexposure. Joined by such musical associates as Andy Bell of Ride, Nick Heyward, Idha, McGee and the Boo Radleys, Ball—sounding like Ray Davies at his absolute worst—pours it all out in desolate postmortems like "She's Just High Maintenance, Baby," "Firehorse," "A Ton of Blues" and "It's Kinda Lonely Where I Am" (twice). Shoehorning unmediated lyrics like "When we were together there was never victory, only varying degrees of defeat" (from "You're an Idiot Babe") into uninspired melodies makes for songs that could be lifted straight from answering-machine messages. Despite flashes of art in the writing and unfailing aptness in the presentation, Ball is so clearly overwhelmed by misery that he can't find much music in his pain. [i]

See also *Boo Radleys, Television Personalities.*

VICTOR BANANA

See *April March.*

BAND OF BLACKY RANCHETTE

See *Giant Sand.*

BAND OF SUSANS

Blessing and Curse EP (Trace Elements) 1987
Hope Against Hope (Furthur/Blast First) 1988
Love Agenda (Blast First/Restless) 1989
The Word and the Flesh (Restless) 1991
The Peel Sessions EP (Strange Fruit) 1992
Now EP (Restless) 1992
Veil (Restless) 1993
Wired for Sound–Band of Susans 1986–1993 (UK Blast First) 1995
Here Comes Success (Restless) 1995

ROBERT POSS

Sometimes [tape] (Trace Elements) 1986

ROBERT POSS/NICOLAS COLLINS

Inverse Guitar [tape] (Trace Elements) 1988

Of the three original Susans who named this noise-loving New York group in the mid-'80s, only bassist/singer Susan Stenger emerged as a mainstay alongside guitarist/singer Robert Poss. Together, they've navigated the band through high-powered sonic experiments in the realm of rock songdom. With-connections to noted downtown composer (and earplug posterboy) Rhys Chatham's ensembles as well as more conventional bands, the early BoS efforts set simple, repetitive chord/bass patterns in motion and then slather on layers of vocals and noisy guitar to produce a brisk, visceral flow of magmatic melodicism. An improvement on the debut EP (the only document of a six-piece lineup with vocalist Alva Rogers), **Hope Against Hope** is loud but never strident, the sensually potent sound of a band that can't seem to get enough guitar tracks on tape to satisfy itself.

A different, smaller company (the quintet here includes future Helmet founder Page Hamilton) made **Love Agenda** with no diminution in power; the band's ability to harness distortion, wall-shaking volume and feedback into well-structured song forms remains a marvelous achievement; the pretentiously poetic art-school lyrics are another matter. The same incarnation appears on the 1988 segment of **The Peel Sessions:** a motor-city cover of Gang of Four's "I Found That Essence Rare," one bruising song each from the two previous albums and a lumbering version of the Rolling Stones' "Child of the Moon" (a studio version of which was added as a bonus track to the CD of **Love Agenda**). Adding to the genealogical complexity, the **Peel** EP's other two tracks, from 1989, capture an otherwise lost inter-album permutation of players doing **Love Agenda**'s "Which Dream Came True" and Wire's "Too Late." Unlike many such essentially live-in-the-studio efforts, this one is well worth owning, and not just as a historical curiosity.

Despite the presence of two new axe-grinders, **The Word and the Flesh** maintains, even fine-tunes, the Susans' dedication to both content and presentation. Neither Poss nor Stenger is much of a vocalist, but the band's failings in that department are swallowed by the resolute maelstrom of guitar pressure, which—as distinct from the Jesus and Mary Chain's fuzz—is kept on a strict low-reverb diet and carefully assembled into a roar of distinct instruments rather than one hazy propwash. For an out-and-out lease-breaker, this is a richly rewarding and surprisingly accessible piece of music. In tribute to its former employer, the group ends the album with a cover of Chatham's "Guitar Trio."

Now's remix of "Now Is Now" (from **The Word and the Flesh**) is fine but unessential, as is the quintet's seductively subdued interpretation of the Stones' "Paint It, Black." Since two of the EP's three new songs also crop up on **Veil,** it's strictly a footnote. But it's also a dividing line, separating the band's original self-made deluge from a reorientation, first intimated in the wavering density and stylistic peregrinations of **Veil.** Letting their generally strong songwriting slide a notch, Poss and Stenger (with stalwart drummer Ron Spitzer and a pair of guitarists) back up the noise truck and unload crank-it-to-eleven radioactive landfill in shapeless piles. Lacking the spiny concentration that made it all go forward in cogent doses in the past, **Veil** is a long, tedious drone, more like a dry run for material yet to be written than an album. Shifting close to British shoegaze sloth at times, **Veil** lacks the melodies and structural designs that would validate the medium-over-message approach.

Wired for Sound is a two-CD (three-LP) British retrospective; **Here Comes Success,** however, is an all-new album that explains where Band of Susans was headed but didn't reach on **Veil.** The central thesis remains thick, vibrant guitar textures that inscribe slow kaleidoscopic circles around propulsive beats and occasionally stand back for vocals, but the group embraces dynamics like never before: "Elizabeth Stride (1843–1888)" makes calm progress from quiet to monumental, getting the album off on a rewardingly different foot. Other tracks explore similarly sloped terrain. "Stone Like a Heart" puts angular guitar slashes and feedback behind an uncommon percussion pattern, while "Pardon My French" jumps back to pithy songdom and "Two Jacks," taking a page from Sonic Youth, narrows the attack to a manageable ribbon of skipping aggression. The monolithic slab of "In the Eye of the Beholder (For Rhys)" casts out the demons and pays further homage to Chatham at the same time. Although it's the least colorful undertaking on this invigorated, invigorating record, the track is clearly therapeutic. Success lies ahead. [i]

See also *Helmet.*

BARDO POND

Bufo Alvarius, Amen 29:15 (Drunken Fish) 1995
Big Laughing Jym (Compulsiv) 1995
Amanita (Drunken Fish/Matador) 1996

Perhaps as an equal-and-opposite reaction to the ubiquity of mosh-happy riff-merchants, a sort of head music revival got underway in the '90s, focusing on sounds designed to exercise the brainpan more than the biceps. Like most of its ilk, this Philadelphia quintet defies the video era's short-attention-span format with drawn-out, undulating jams that require the listener to exert a fair amount of effort in order to stay afloat amidst the waves of crashing sound. Not that Bardo Pond is entirely unfair about it; the band does throw out a tow line in the form of the ravishingly pretty flute melodies conjured up by primary vocalist Isobel Sollenberger.

In a clever (but not altogether surprising) titling move, the quintet borrowed the Latin name of the hallucinogen-secreting Colorado River toad for **Bufo Alvarius,** an album that's every bit as synapse-destroying as its namesake. More consistently aggressive than like-minded drone-dreamers Magic Hour and Spiritualized, Bardo Pond recalls Hawkwind's headier days in psychedelic sludgestorms like the half-hour-long "Amen 29:15." The bottom-end heft is countered by Sollenberger's ethereal vocals—which bear a passing resemblance to those of Renaissance art-rock songbird Annie Haslam—and her playing, which is so striking that it just about absolves the flute for the sins of Ian Anderson.

Big Laughing Jym, a seven-song collection of album outtakes and home-studio stuff, accentuates the scrungier elements of the band's sound, namely the hepatic guitar rumblings winnowed out by the brotherly tandem of John and Michael Gibbons on "Dispersion" and "Clearhead." The premeditated lack of infrastructure makes it a chore to maintain equilibrium (see the lunging "Champ"), but the outer-ear pleasures more than make up for the inner-ear discomfort.

Amanita finds the band reconsidering the dosage on the prescriptions it writes—average song length is way shorter—without sacrificing intensity or effect. The free-form guitar scrawls of "Limerick" and "Tantric Porno" refract chaos in much the same way prog-rock forefathers like Ash Ra Tempel did—but by compacting the commotion into four- and five-minute bursts and all but eliminating passages of blissed-out trance, Bardo Pond makes sure not to lose control of the universe it has created. [dss]

BARENAKED LADIES

Bare Naked Lunch EP [tape] (Can. self-released) 1990
Bare Naked Ladies EP [tape] (Can. self-released) 1991
Gordon (Sire/Reprise) 1992
Maybe You Should Drive (Sire/Reprise) 1994
Shoe Box E.P. EP (Reprise) 1996
Born on a Pirate Ship (Reprise) 1996

DON'T TALK, DANCE!

Don't Talk, Dance! (Can. WEA) 1995

BROTHERS CREEGGAN

The Brothers Creeggan (Can. Fat Chicken/WEA) 1995

As cute as a baby and as appealing as a loaded diaper, Toronto's Barenaked Ladies—in truth, a bunch of guys whose only discernible fashion statement is their heinous haircuts—rope together the hyperactive lyrical imagination of They Might Be Giants, the overbearing sentimentality of Harry Chapin, the folk-rocky musical conviction of Jimmy Buffett (the group most often sounds like it's hitting the Squeeze sample button on its stylistic synthesizer) and the hip rock sensibilities of a high-school principal to produce a gut course for impressionable liberal arts majors. (You haven't fully loathed a concert crowd until you've seen boxloads of dry Kraft macaroni and cheese gaily thrown onstage in ritual response to a line from **Gordon**'s "If I Had a $1000000.")

The group made a huge initial splash in Canada, where the self-released **Bare Naked Ladies**—a demo-quality five-song cassette informally known as **The Yellow Tape**—sold seventy-five thousand copies. All four originals were re-recorded for **Gordon;** the parody cover of Public Enemy's "Fight the Power" was thankfully left behind. (Slightly less accomplished and far more obscure, the prior **Bare Naked Lunch** tape was sold only at shows. It has some overlap but contains the otherwise unreleased "The Trouble With Tracy" and "Night Photographs.")

Gordon is spoonfed smartypants pop. The role-playing rock references are strictly grade-school culture history: "Brian Wilson" ("Lying in bed just like Brian Wilson did . . . just listening and relistening to **Smiley Smile** . . . and if you want to find me I'll be out in the sandbox"), "Be My Yoko Ono" ("You can follow me wherever I go"), "New Kid (On the Block)" ("So we may not write the songs we sing but look at Elvis . . ."), "Box Set" ("So now my fans are crying sellout . . ."). The music—mild ska, white-bread pop, watery new wave and lightly swinging folk-rock—is equally well-crafted and unchallenging. Getting lots of harmony support from his bandmates, Steven Page sings in a characterless—but exceedingly chipper—Vegas voice, whose intensely sincere side comes in handy for incongruously serious songs about physical abuse in a relationship ("The Flag") and societal pressures on childhood ("What a Good Boy" and the flip but substantial "Grade 9").

Produced by k.d. lang collaborator Ben Mink, **Maybe You Should Drive** is a more mature and reserved—even somber—album that evinces a narrower stylistic focus in the gentle music (imagine a Squeeze tribute album produced by Natalie Merchant) and avoids topical subjects (except for "Alternative Girlfriend" and "Jane," a crush song—co-written by Stephen Duffy—that uses Juliana [Hatfield] and Evan [Dando] for comparison) in favor of romantic breakup lyrics ("You Will Be Waiting," "Intermittently," "A," "Am I the Only One?"). Cutting back on the humor reduces the quintet's ability to irritate, but the seriousness of **Maybe You Should Drive** doesn't suit the group any better.

Too bad, since **Born on a Pirate Ship** is all about romantic doubt, personal collapse and thoughts of self-destruction. "Mental health is overrated," avers Page at one point, and he doesn't appear to be kidding. Other than a few fantasy episodes, the songs describe a thoroughly miserable personality, offering lots of shame and not much humor. Recorded as a quartet (keyboardist Andy Creeggan having opted for school in '95), the music is as glibly upbeat as ever, but the Ladies can't smooth over all this emotional dyspepsia by dancing a merry jig. Neither entertaining nor redemptive (unless there's something in the CD-ROM track that redeems the whole sorry venture), **Born on a Pirate Ship** is too much like eavesdropping on happy hour at the suicide prevention line to be any fun. (Never mind that the title was evidently chosen for its Butt-headed utility in a hold-your-tongue pronunciation joke.)

Released before the third album, **Shoe Box** contains the titular song from it (already unveiled on the *Friends* TV soundtrack LP) in two versions, as well as the previously unreleased "Trust Me," the folky acoustic **Yellow Tape** version of "If I Had a $1000000" and CD-ROM videos, a bio, performance footage, song samples and a load of other great stuff.

Don't Talk, Dance!, a side project led by Ladies drummer Tyler Stewart, was a cheesy disco-funk trio with Chris Brown of Bourbon Tabernacle Choir and guitarist/singer Gordie Johnson of Big Sugar (words that evidently mean "Canned Heat" in Canadian). The Brothers Creeggan (originally known as Van Creeggan, ha-ha) is, as billed, a duo of Andy and bassist Jim; their album of jazz-tinged rock includes backup singing on one track ("Places") by Alanis Morissette. [i]

BARK PSYCHOSIS

Hex (Caroline) 1994
Independency (UK 3rd Stone) 1994

Having released their first single ("All Different Things") when the band members' average age was around seventeen, East London's Bark Psychosis hardly seemed likely candidates to cause critic Simon Reynolds to identify an entirely new musical sub-genus ("post-rock" found its first mention—at least since writer Ellen Willis used it in 1968—in his review of **Hex**), much less reshape the context of pre-millennial rock'n'roll. However, the quartet managed to do both. Over the course of five singles (four of which are collected on **Independency**), the group's music slowly metamorphosed from spacious rockscapes (the percussive "By-Blow" recalls some of Talk Talk's better moments) into truly epic visions of ambience (the ultra-sinister twenty-three minutes of the vaguely improvisational "Scum"). With the release of **Hex,** the band's music—as well as its reputation—solidified.

Ironically, though Bark Psychosis had earned a bit of notoriety for lengthy songs, the tracks on **Hex** are hardly the double-digit exercises in mind expansion the earlier singles were. Rather, excepting the nine minutes of hazy ambience called "Pendulum Man," the songs seem decidedly more structured than their predecessors. Although still working outside the typical expectations of "rock" music—no choruses, no solos . . . hell, not too many verses or repeated refrains—**Hex** shows a band that has learned to employ the dynamics of dilation without resorting to noodly, space-rock jams. The music is delicate and accomplished, relying on atmospherics that are reminiscent of early A.R.Kane (minus all the post-Romantic angst drama) or the enveloping pizzicato of Durutti Column. Beautifully tense, strangely relaxed and unexpectedly visionary. [jf]

LOU BARLOW (AND FRIENDS)

See *Sebadoh.*

BARNABYS

Delightful Browns EP (spinART) 1992
Augustus Loop (spinART) 1993

The Barnabys typify the second generation of America's indie-pop scene. The trio, formed in Philadelphia in 1990, grew up listening to all the right records; when they synthesize those sounds, the results can be either pop perfection or musical mediocrity. On **Delightful Browns,** singer/guitarist Joey Sweeney shows that he knows how to craft a good indie-rock song: one part off-kilter vocals (à la Scott McCaughey of the Young Fresh Fellows), a chorus the kids can sing along with and a sense of naïvete to make it all endearing. The production is clean, crisp and radio-friendly when it counts—which, of the eight tracks, is only on "Global Teen." More often than not, though, the group comes off as a second-rate Violent Femmes clone, all acoustic guitars and fractured vocals.

The ambitious **Augustus Loop** is much better. While it reprises three tracks from **Delightful Browns,** those previously forgettable songs come off stronger and well worth the second look. With a certain resemblance to the folk-pop sound of Small Factory, the Barnabys get by on Sweeney's pleading adenoidal vocals, which contain more than a hint of Robert Smith's weary charm. He sings about everything from feeling out of place in an upscale eatery ("Yuppie Restaurant"), to feeling out of place in the suburbs ("Wilmington"). Of guest note are the Garth Hudson–like organ Matt Keating adds to "Room 17" and the lovely violin Rosie Macnamara plays throughout. [mk]

RICHARD BARONE

Cool Blue Halo (Passport) 1987
Primal Dream (Paradox/MCA) 1990
Primal Cuts EP (Ger. Line) 1990
Clouds Over Eden (Mesa) 1993
Between Heaven and Cello (Ger. Line) 1994

RICHARD BARONE/JAMES MASTRO

Nuts and Bolts (Passport) 1983

Following the breakup of Hoboken's Bongos in 1986, singer/songwriter Richard Barone moved across the river to New York and set about retooling his trademark amalgam of British Invasion, glam and American jangle-pop into more mature, less frenetic music. Recorded live at New York's Bottom Line in 1987, **Cool Blue Halo** finds Barone fronting an acoustic/electric "chamber-rock" quartet of two guitars, cello and percussion. A hushed combination of Bongos favorites, a few new songs and nods to his influences (in the form of Marc Bolan's "The Visit," the Beatles' "Cry Baby Cry" and David Bowie's "The Man Who Sold the World," in a treatment similar to the one Nirvana would give the song six years later on **MTV Unplugged in New York**), the results are intimate but confused. Cellist Jane Scarpantoni and percussionist Valerie Naranjo (who would go on to work with David Byrne) provide restrained backing, but Barone's sometimes coy vocals can break the mood.

Primal Dream, his first studio album, sounds like a step backward. Produced by Barone, Don Dixon and Richard Gottehrer, the forced tempos, chattering keyboards and big, treated drums give the busy album a retro new wave feel, overwhelming a fine set of yearning love songs and (on the CD) a sensitive cover of the Velvet Underground's "I'll Be Your Mirror." Just how badly the songs were served can be heard on the German-only **Primal Cuts.** Along with two mixes of the album's "Mr. Used-to-Be," the EP includes live acoustic versions of **Primal Dream**'s two best songs, "Where the Truth Lies" and "River to River."

Moved by the death of a friend, author Nicholas Schaffner, Barone came up with **Clouds Over Eden,** the great album fans always imagined him making. While the components of his work remain the same, they take on a darker edge in the gloomy "Within These Walls," the eerie rush of keyboards on "Forbidden," the loneliness of "Nobody Knows Me" and the "Eleanor Rigby"–ish arrangement of the title track. It's not a completely somber affair. "Waiting for the Train," a duet with Jill Sobule, provides a welcome respite. The production, by Hugh Jones, is a fuller, more muscular take on the rock with strings sound of **Cool Blue Halo.** Barone's singing is also improved, losing the precious self-consciousness that mars previous outings. A wrenching and thoroughly worthwhile album.

Rather than follow **Clouds** with another studio album, Barone recorded the live **Between Heaven and Cello,** a return to the familiar guitar/strings setting. While the record doesn't break any new ground for Barone, two cellists (Scarpantoni and Lisa Haney) make it a diverting listen. [sm]

See also *TPRG.*

BARRY BLACK

See *Archers of Loaf.*

BARTLEBEES

The Bartlebees (Ger. Little Teddy) 1993
Finally We Did It (Ger. Little Teddy) 1993
What Is It All About? (Ger. Little Teddy) 1994
Bartland EP (Ger. Little Teddy) 1995
From Path of Pain to Jewels of Glory (18 Wheeler) 1995
Miracles for Sale (Ger. Little Teddy) 1995

With evident aspirations to be Germany's most convincing naïfs, this lo-fi trio plies its adorable pop trade largely in stylistic emulation of the Television Personalities. Tunefully singing sweet-and-sour love lyrics in quietly accented (and slightly flat) English against brash guitar strums and a puppy-like rhythm section, the ultra-sensitive Bartlebees carefully press the tender leaves of supposed adolescence between the pages of a tear-stained diary. Unlike the flashy culture references and anguished passions of the TVPs (whose leader, Dan Treacy, plays organ on two of the first album's tracks), the Bartlebees are a blandly genial lot, posting their concise and alluring missives to unnamed romantic correspondents.

The group's skills have improved over the course of four longplayers (**From Path of Pain to Jewels of Glory,** the Bartlebees' only US album, is a twenty-six-song CD combining the first two German releases and three bonus tracks), but never far exceed the minimum standards required to convey a shapely melody. Guitarist Patrick's singing and the playing (especially Armen's slapdash drumming) on **The Bartlebees** (also referred to as **Diary of a Youngblood**) are on the cavalier side of simple; still, originals like "No Stories," "Someday I'll Send You a Rainbow," "Love the Moment" and "I Laugh Again" demonstrate the band's genuine facility for upholding tradition without coming off like mere copycats. (The members' actual names are notoriously hard to pin down: the American release identifies them as both Toby, Less and Keith and Smokey, Randy and Bonzo.)

The better-balanced sound on **Finally We Did It** is matched by a squinch more self-assurance in the unfussy, uncomplicated performances. But the songwriting is not quite as reliable, and a guitar tuner would have been useful. Consequently, while "First Love," the Ramonesy "I Want to Know You're Happy" and the instrumental "Rock and Roll President" are fine showings, a full-bodied cover of the Vaselines' "Jesus Wants Me for a Sunbeam" (covered more famously by Nirvana) stands out more than it probably should.

What Is It All About? puts all the pieces together in a prime platter of modest pop craft. The spot introduction of acoustic rhythm guitar adds a welcome dose of cream to the sonic tea, while strong melodies, longer songs, bolder arrangements, better playing (compare the piano remake of "Rock and Roll President" to the original version) and cannier lyrics ("My Invisible Friend" praises the subject for not signing with David Geffen; "I Would Have Left You Anyway" betrays an advanced state of emotional candor) all contribute to the maturation of a cool combo that doesn't need to hide behind its imaginings of youth. Topped off with a very pretty cover of "Angela Jones" (a 1960 British hit for Joe Meek protégé Michael Cox), **What Is It All About?** contains the real scoop on the Bartlebees.

Although it breaks tradition with a surprisingly boisterous rocker ("You Will Make It") and the ludicrously languid French-language "La Chanson de Prevert," the ten-song 10-inch **Miracles for Sale** genially maintains the trio's idyllic pop breeze in such girl-loving/girl-hurting lullabies as "Hello Stranger," "You're Not the Only One," "This Is What I Was Made For" and "Don't Make Me Fall in Love With You," the pronunciation of which reveals a Teutonic hazard in this kind of *lied.* [i]

BASEHEAD

Play With Toys (Emigre) 1991 (Imago) 1992
2000 BC EP (Imago) 1992
Not in Kansas Anymore (Imago) 1993
Split Personality EP (Imago) 1993
Faith (Imago) 1996

B.Y.O.B

B.Y.O.B (13/Rykodisc) 1994

A brilliant Prince of low-key hip-hop, Michael Ivey (vocals, guitar, bass, keyboards, programming) made the first Basehead album while studying film at Howard University in the nation's capital. Other than another Pittsburgh native, Brian Hendrix, on drums and DJ Paul Howard kicking in delicate scratches, **Play With Toys** is a one-man endeavor—and a masterful, unique accomplishment. (The critic who characterized it as "Galaxie 500 meets De La Soul" wasn't far off the mark; the subsequent emergence of Spearhead offers another point of reference for the blunted geniality of Basehead's lazy funk.)

Ivey brings amazing imagination to bear on the task of filling a record with engrossing music: the surreal sonic experience integrates songs with settings that repeatedly upend the musician's usual role in making a record. There's fake stagework (the intro has "Jethro and the Graham Crackers" giving James Brown a cornpone country poke), dialogues (the soulful "Ode to My Favorite Beer" is offered in response to a pal's request to hear what Ivey is working on; the sloblo funk of "Evening News" stops for a bit of channel surfing and gets creative direction from other viewers, who end up arguing as Ivey jams away in the background) and fourth-wall-busting breaks in the lyrical action. "Hair," a softly sung complaint of infidelity set to a spare, juicy groove and the sampled sound of a woman moaning, is interrupted by a scabrous remark from the woman being sung to; Ivey's answer restarts the song. The most alluring track—the gorgeous, atmospheric romance of "Not Over You"—has to end so the friend with whom the dispirited singer is hanging can search the radio for a song to brighten his mood. After drifting through the quiet storm and a Bill Withers oldie, the dial alights on . . . "Not Over You." Ingenious. Evidently incapable of repeating himself, thoughtful in his social and political observations, winningly charismatic and musically generous, Michael Ivey is an incredible talent, and **Play With Toys** is one of hip-hop's finest (forty-minute) hours. (The "BC" in the album track pulled off for a single refers to brain cells.)

The similarly constructed **Not in Kansas Anymore** is a shade less ambitious but nearly as good. The advent of harsher lyrics tests the skillful music's unfailing good mood without doing any serious damage. Ivey's obsessions here are honest sex (both "Do You Wanna Fuck (Or What)?" and "Nite Out on the Town" express doubts about the sincerity of the mating ritual), the smokable solution ("I Need a Joint," "Pass the Thought"), racism (the two-part "Brown Kisses," "Shouldna Dunnit," "Split Personality") and violence ("Greener Pastures"), but the album also includes thoughts about pets ("Fluffy and Richard") and growing up ("Not the Same"). Hendrix is still on hand; a full live band performed three of the tracks.

Ivey next continued along his singular path with B.Y.O.B, a sort-of group in which he relinquishes exclusive songwriting rights and has lots more instrumental and vocal assistance than in Basehead. **B.Y.O.B** (don't ask me where that last period went; the record makes a running joke of what the acronym stands for), as a result, has more straight-up hip-hop beats—as well as some go-go (Clarence Greenwood's "The Rackett"), mushy soul ("Where Ya Going To?" and "Too Good to Let Go," sung by Justine Hall), even fusion ("Go Jazz Go," a track that Ivey produced but does not appear on) and trippy instrumental atmospherics ("Outerspacegethithang"). While that makes for a rambly, disjointed album that is more energetic and less engaging than prior Basehead releases, Ivey does make sure to get some pointed ideas across. Using a telephoned invitation to a B.Y.O.B. "party in your mind" as a schematic catalyst, the sprawling tracks articulately excoriate role-playing—in the pretense of gangsta rap ("Change It"), political correctness, the acceptance of crack and guns, fake celebrations of freedom and the predictable patterns of sexual and racial behavior. Typical of Ivey's individuality, the party dialogue of "Rambilfications of Getting & Saying Hi gh" pokes fun at African-American objections to interracial dating.

In mid-'96, Ivey revived the Basehead handle and released the all-new **Faith** album. [i]

BASH & POP

Friday Night Is Killing Me (Sire/Reprise) 1993

Following the Replacements, bassist (and junior member) Tommy Stinson switched to guitar, formed a quartet and cut a sharp but uncompelling tribute to one facet of the Mats' multiple personality—the bluesy, boozy, shambling rock they learned from old Faces albums. Stinson's constricted voice is the best thing here; while the songs bear evidence (especially the frantic chorus of "Fast & Hard") of a decade spent in the company of Paul Westerberg, Stinson can only lift chord patterns and manage weak echoes of his former bandmate's lacerating wit. Lacking the rock-sucks-let's-do-something-better ambition that kept repeated choruses and time-wasting vamps to a minimum on Replacements vinyl, he wallows in abnormal ordinariness. That Stinson can do a credible imitation of Rod Stewart's lurch and rasp might be enough for a journeyman career, but **Friday Night** is hardly the adult achievement his alma mater primed him for.

Bash & Pop didn't last long enough to record again. In '96, Stinson returned to work at the helm of a new band called Perfect. [i]

JIM BASNIGHT

See *Moberlys.*

BATS

By Night EP (NZ Flying Nun) 1984
And Here Is 'Music for the Fireside'! (NZ Flying Nun) 1985
Made Up in Blue EP (UK Flying Nun) 1986
Compiletely Bats (NZ Flying Nun) 1987 (Communion) 1991
Daddy's Highway (NZ Flying Nun) 1988 (Communion) 1988 (Flying Nun/Mammoth) 1994
Four Songs EP (NZ Flying Nun) 1988
The Law of Things (NZ Flying Nun) 1990 (Communion) 1990 (Flying Nun/Mammoth) 1994
Fear of God (NZ Flying Nun) 1991 (Flying Nun/Mammoth) 1992
Silverbeet (Flying Nun/Mammoth) 1993
Courage EP (Flying Nun/Mammoth) 1993
Live at WFMU EP7 (Merge) 1994
Spill the Beans EP (Flying Nun/Mammoth) 1994
Couchmaster (Flying Nun/Mammoth) 1995

ELECTRIC BLOOD

Electric Easter (Aus. EST) 1984 (Beehive Rebellion) 1994

MAGICK HEADS

Before We Go Under (NZ Flying Nun) 1995

The Bats' taut jangle has become nearly synonymous with both New Zealand's pop underground and Flying Nun's rich roster. The quartet of singer/guitarists Robert Scott (also of the Clean) and Kaye Woodward, bassist Paul Kean and drummer Malcolm Grant has been writing and recording delicious pop gems since 1983, but didn't get around to recording a proper full-length album until 1988's **Daddy's Highway.** (**Compiletely Bats** unites the three tracks of **Made Up in Blue,** all seven from **Music for the Fireside** and five of **By Night's** six.)

The same year **Compiletely Bats** received a belated American release (joining **Daddy's Highway** and **The Law of Things** in the group's US catalogue), the Bats released **Fear of God.** Recorded with producer Nicholas Sansano (Sonic Youth, Public Enemy), the album dissipates the cloudiness hovering over the Bats' earlier work (which was never an entirely bad thing) while respecting the group's crisp arrangements and sugary melodic centers. Scott's sweet, nasal vocals carry the buoyant, sing-song tunes, perfectly matched by Woodward's pretty, plain-jane harmonizing; touches of viola add a rootsy strain. "The Black and the Blue," "Boogey Man" and "Fear of God" epitomize all that is wonderful and perfect about the three-minute Bats song.

Moving on to a different American producer, Lou Giordano (Sugar, Lemonheads, Goo Goo Dolls), didn't improve—or damage—the Bats on their next album. While **Silverbeet** adds another enjoyable chapter in the Bats tale, it doesn't refine or redirect their sound; if anything, the quartet seems to have settled in too comfortably. (Woodward's vocal contributions are notably less prominent.) "Courage," also released as a single, is listless, but "Sighting the Sound" and "No Time for Your Kind" offer the requisite jaunty pop and rippling guitar lines; the driving "Green" and "Half Way to Nowhere" find the Bats pushing gently on the perimeter of their stylistic confines.

The **Courage** EP adds three **Silverbeet** outtakes; the loose, one-take sound and fluid piano of "The Wind Is Sad" offers a nice break to the samey flow of the EP. Recorded in New Jersey in July '93, **Live at WFMU** contains three of the Bats' finest ("Sighting the Sound," "Block of Wood" and "North by North"), plus a cover of Harlan Howard's (by way of Gram Parsons) "Streets of Baltimore," which adds a twang to the Bats' beautiful billowing sound.

The thicker guitar sound of **Spill the Beans**' "Under the Law" points to the Bats' growing affinity for American indie-rock. The EP's four other cuts, recorded in Raleigh, North Carolina, feature Superchunk leader Mac McCaughan's expressive guitar playing rippling through the Bats' strum'n'hum effervescence. He's integrated particularly well on the title song and "Give Into the Sands," both of which make effective use of acoustic/electric guitar dialogue.

While in many ways a retreat—it was recorded in New Zealand without a producer and has a more introspective timbre—**Couchmaster** is actually a boundary-stretching breakthrough. The guitars have a warm electric glow (not unlike Yo La Tengo's electric reflections); the songs are less formulaic and a little more adventurous, broader in length and scope on "Afternoon in Bed" and the hypnotic "Crow Song." While the quartet still offers a handful of familiarly winged pop songs ("Land 'o' Lakes," "Out of Bounds"), the slide guitar on "Work It Out" and the instrumental "Supernova" introduce new elements. The dark, slow "Shoeshine" features Woodward's first lead vocal.

Scott formed Electric Blood after the Clean's first breakup in the early '80s; it existed concurrently with the Bats for several years. A dozen songs recorded at a practice space in 1984, **Electric Easter** (initially cassette-only) has a loose, pleasant feel led by Scott's strained vocals, nifty psychedelic-tinged guitar and lots of warm, fuzzy strumming. "Earwig" eventually became a Bats song, and is included on **Compiletely Bats.**

A decade later, Electric Blood drummer Jimmy Strang resurfaced with Scott on the Magick Heads' **Before We Go Under.** Vocalist Jane Sinnott takes the lead on most of the thirteen lovely songs, although Scott's voice and fluttery arrangements are integral to the group's sound. (Scott actually wrote the title song for Barbara Manning, who recorded it as "B4 We Go Under" with Bay Area band Flophouse and released it as a single on TeenBeat.) Fiery guitar playing by David Mitchell (also of the 3Ds) meshes surprisingly well, adding an extra dimension to the songs without overwhelming them with electricity. With all that and the Celtic accent coming from Alan Starrett's graceful violin, accordion and hammer dulcimer, the album positively soars. [la]

See also *Clean, Chris Knox; TPRG.*

BEACON HILL BILLIES

See *Blood Oranges.*

BEASTIE BOYS

Polly Wog Stew EP (Rat Cage) 1982 (UK Southern Studios) 1988
"Rock Hard" (Def Jam) 1984
Licensed to Ill (Def Jam/Columbia) 1986
Paul's Boutique (Capitol) 1989
Check Your Head (Grand Royal/Capitol) 1992
Some Old Bullshit (Grand Royal) 1994
Ill Communication (Grand Royal/Capitol) 1994
Root Down (Grand Royal/Capitol) 1995
Aglio & Olio (Grand Royal/Capitol) 1995
The In Sound From Way Out (Grand Royal/Capitol) 1995

HURRICANE

The Hurra (Grand Royal/Capitol) 1995

MONEY MARK

Mark's Keyboard Repair (UK Pinto/Mo Wax) 1995 (Pinto/Mo Wax/ffrr) 1996

Somewhere along the line, this New York trio "progressed" from relentless beer-spewing assailants on good taste to self-appointed arbiters of a one-world youth culture wherein B-boys, skatepunks and art-nerds meet to share in stoopid fresh communion. Sometimes, as in the Beasties' fluid miscegenation of vintage Afro-funk and the hardcore punk that is their more proximate roots, it's a brilliant concept. Of course, that self-elevation has also led to the pomposity that oozes from the band's intensifying notion that every note it records merits commercial release—not to mention coverage in the pages of its back-slapping fanzine, *Grand Royal.*

Initially, the Beastie Boys—then composed of singer Michael Diamond and bassist Adam Yauch, as well as guitarist John Berry and drummer Kate Schellenbach (now of Luscious Jackson)—were New York University's contribution to the city's nascent hardcore scene, playing the young, fast and nose-thumbing role carved out by the Dictators some years before. **Polly Wog Stew**'s eight light-speed blasts lambaste standard targets like police ("Transit Cop"), but also veer into off-kilter slapstick like the ranting "Egg Raid on Mojo." Schellenbach and Berry left, Adam Horowitz (who had played in the Young and the Useless) joined and the band traded in its hardcore for rap, a new obsession that surfaced on 1983's "Cooky Puss," a single that was dismissed as parody but actually reveals abundant empathy for hip-hop culture (and a straight-outta-junior-high sensayuma).

In 1984, the Beasties made the stylistic move official with the release of "Rock Hard," a 12-inch co-produced by NYU chum Rick Rubin and released on Def Jam, the label he and Russell Simmons had just launched. Unmistakably white and more than middle class, the group wisely acknowledged its '70s rock heritage in hunks of guitar: AC/DC riffs pop up in "Rock Hard" and "Party's Gettin' Rough," Led Zep shards fill "Beastie Groove." The band then appeared in the film *Krush Groove,* for which they cut "She's on It," a fun, dumb stomper with a great guitar hook and obnoxious couplets like "She'd get down on her knees/If we'd only say *please.*" The Beasties—now going by the names King Ad-Rock (Horowitz), Mike D (Diamond) and MCA (Yauch)—had reached a new plateau of offensiveness and were squinting upward.

Licensed to Ill turned what had seemed like a self-indulgent novelty into a platinum cultural phenomenon. Self-consciously moronic celebrations of stupidity like "Fight for Your Right (To Party)," "No Sleep Till Brooklyn," "Time to Get Ill" and "Girls" may have been parodies of the baser levels of both rock and hip-hop, but the good-natured record's net effect was to erase the distinctions between the genres in the irresistible bluster of fratboys with a beat. Combined with the whining nasal roar of the three stooges' unabashed invention, Rubin's brilliant stew—boiled up from old tracks by the Stones, Led Zep, Clash and many others—created a perfectly timed sound of adolescent freedom no other group from either side of the divide has ever quite matched.

After a long, ugly legal war, the band split with Rubin and issued **Paul's Boutique,** a thickly textured, deceptively subtle album that distanced the Boys from both the controversy-for-controversy's-sake mindset and the getting-tired rock'n'rap fusion formula. The album makes extensive use of a remarkable array of samples—thanks in part to the Dust Brothers' stoner-friendly production—and shows an impressive affinity for funk at its deepest. Tracks like "High Plains Drifter" and the whining anthem "Johnny Ryall" merge West Coast cool with East Coast tension, propelled by a swagger unlike anything the group had previously mastered. Even the moments of utter goofiness—like "Egg Man" and the Mr. Wizard-gone-bad "The Sounds of Science"—are handled more nimble-mindedly. An indispensable item in any hip-hop library.

In the wake of **Paul's Boutique, Check Your Head** is a bit of a letdown. Oh sure, the grooves roll out in impressive enough fashion, most intriguingly on the insinuating "Funky Boss" and "So What'cha Want" (which are fairly close to being two mixes of the same track, anyway), but, too often, the Boys are simply passengers on a Jeep blasting the beats. The live instrumentation—a funk-rock fusion alternately reminiscent of Mandrill and '70s TV themes—doesn't do much for "Jimmy James" or "Gratitude," although those tracks are far superior to tired sample pastiches like "Lighten Up." (The band's flair for odd sample juxtapositions is still there, though, as evidenced by "The Biz-vs-The Nuge," which pits Biz Markie against Mr. Ted Bowhunter himself.) Perhaps the most pleasant surprise is the roots-revisiting hardcore splatter of "Time For Livin'." (Incidentally, that first voice you hear belongs to Robin Zander, sampled from **Cheap Trick at Budokan.**)

There's even more hammer-down HC on **Ill Communication,** a maddeningly inconsistent but whip-smart journey to the heart of urban youth culture. Alternating testosterone-fueled rockers like "Heart Attack Man" and "Tough Guy" with acid-jazz-imbued pieces like "Sure Shot" and "Flute Loop" (both of which employ chilled-out flute samples, from records by, respectively, Jeremy Steig and the Blues Project), the trio whips up a mighty vertiginous storm. Sampling from (or referencing) pop culture deities from Russell Simmons to Moms Mabley, the Beasties remain defiantly—and studiedly—post-modern. But with a few glaring exceptions (like "Bodhisattva Vow," one of Yauch's overly pious paeans to his newly accepted Buddhist faith), the band wears its cultural hodgepodge well.

Some Old Bullshit is a compilation of the band's embryonic material, comprising both the **Polly Wog Stew** EP and the long out-of-print "Cooky Puss" single (an ice cream put-on that did not go down smoothly at the house of Carvel). The packaging, which includes reprints of flyers, set lists and vintage photos—as well as an amusing band history penned by Diamond—is in itself enough of a purchase incentive for fans, even those who own the rare original vinyl.

Root Down is another, far less interesting, product of the Boys' vault-vacuuming. Built around three versions of the title track, the ten-song disc appends live renditions of material both old ("Time to Get Ill," "Flute Loop") or in-progress (the Baretta-meets-Barbieri jam "Sabrosa," which would turn up in its studio version on **The In Sound From Way Out**). It's strictly a vanity pressing. In an effort to relive their hardcore adolescence, the Beasties whipped out **Aglio & Olio,** a breathless compendium of no-speed-limit thrashers (eight songs, twelve minutes) marked by equal parts puerile lyrical juvenilia and brainpan-bashing guitar sledgehammering. A brief blast from the stylistic past.

The all-instrumental **The In Sound From Way Out** is an intermittently successful attempt to bridge Afro-funk fusion and kitschy '60s "electronic pop music of the future." While there's no disputing the instrumental dexterity at play—especially on Yauch's part—in the grooves of "Bobo on the Corner" and "Son of Neckbone," the Beasties slip too often from tribute to duplication—right down to the title and cover, both of which were "borrowed" from an album by '60s Moog masters Perrey-Kingsley. More than anything else, this collection is reminiscent—in spirit—of Frank Zappa's early post-Mothers work. It's too early to say where the efforts to cast off past goofiness and replace it with a more serious composerly attitude will lead.

The band's longtime mixmaster, DJ Hurricane (who often takes a featured turn in the Beasties' increasingly protracted concerts) cuts a surprisingly powerful figure as frontman on his solo bow, **The Hurra.** His rhymes aren't particularly original, focusing as they do on the gat-centric worldview long ago parodied by the Beasties (particularly "Pass Me the Gun"), but Hurricane's sinewy delivery and low-rider funk backing tracks make songs like "Elbow Room" and "Four Fly Guys" perfect for late-night beer-swilling.

Money Mark (Mark Ramos Nishita), the band's keyboardist for the past several years, waxes more experimental on **Mark's Keyboard Repair,** a thirty-track collection that, at its best, recalls some chance collaboration between Sebadoh and Parliament. The scratchy funk grooves of songs like the lead-off "Pretty Pain" are mottled with bedsit vocals and diffident melodies, while aural in-jokes like "Have Clav Will Travel" are well-steeped in a post-modern bath. Still, when Mark hits a stone groove—as on the too-brief "Spooky" and "Sunday Gardena Blvd."—it's strictly old-school, and strictly phat. [dss/i]

See also *Luscious Jackson; TPRG.*

BEASTS OF PARADISE

Nobody Knew the Time EP (City of Tribes) 1994
Gathered on the Edge (City of Tribes) 1995

Picture five musicians shadow dancing on a butterfly's wings, and you'll begin to understand the fragile grace of San Francisco's Beasts of Paradise. Eda Maxym's vocal incantations oscillate far above the earth, even as the multitude of instruments used to make the music flutter and spin spans its far reaches. At the center are Nancy Kaspar's double bass, Geoffrey Gordon's exotic array of percussion and Stephen Kent's didgeridoo—though it's not as prominent as with his other outfit, Trance Mission. Combined, they create enough gravitational pull to balance Maxym's drifting vocals and Barbara Imhoff's feathery harp.

The title track of the five-song debut is a mix of atypical rhythms, with both Middle Eastern and Indian lilts. Aside from the harp and didgeridoo, the record's instrumentation includes *dumbek,* Zambian drums and world music master Jai Uttal's *dotar.* Kenneth Newby, a percussionist in Trance Mission, shows off his exotic throat singing. Despite the loose arrangement, "Nobody Knew the Time" is the most grounded of the tracks, and the best vehicle for Maxym's wafting vocals. Both "Falling" and "Limehouse Chambers," which employs a toy piano and one-string *rebab,* are as ephemeral as a tide pool in the Sahara. But Maxym's introspective presence keeps the songs from evaporating completely. Buzzcocks fans may balk at harps taking the place of electric guitar on a cover of "Why Can't I Touch It," but Maxym makes the question her own.

Gathered on the Edge was produced by Simon Tassano, a former bandmate of Kent's in Lights in a Fat City. The instrumental augmentation again runs the gamut: *ngoma, kanjira,* tabla, marimba. "Flickering Blue" is the group's most cohesive track to date. The dreamy music offsets darkly veiled lyrics: "Work all day sleep all night/Live in the cracks in between." Kent's haunting didgeridoo on "Red Rock" is an ideal setting for Maxym's enchanting cry about our disintegrating environment. And the Beasts' soothing tones on "River" are an elegant canvas for Maxym's heavy thoughts about the loss of innocence. Several tracks start out soft and serene and gradually turn more earthly and upbeat—an approach that keeps the mood from becoming too pensive—and the jazzy groove of "The Smile" (based on a William Blake poem) keeps the album from getting lost in its own sentiment. [mg]

See also *Trance Mission.*

BEAT FARMERS

Tales of the New West (Rhino) 1985
Glad'n'Greasy EP (UK Demon) 1986 (Rhino) 1991
Van Go (Curb/MCA) 1986
The Pursuit of Happiness (Curb/MCA) 1987
Poor & Famous (Curb/MCA) 1989
Loud and Plowed and . . . Live!! (Curb) 1990
Viking Lullabys (Sector 2) 1994
Manifold (Sector 2) 1995
Best of the Beat Farmers (Curb) 1995

COUNTRY DICK MONTANA

The Devil Lied to Me (Bar/None) 1996

These San Diego bar-band delinquents rightly earned their reputation as an ace live act, thanks in large part to the beer-soaked antics of drummer and part-time vocalist Country Dick Montana, whose booming basso and larger-than-life persona were the band's most identifiable features. On record, though, the band had a tougher time striking a balance between his clowning and the melodic roots-rock of its non-Montana numbers. Although all of the Beat Farmers' albums have something to recommend them, the band never quite managed to resolve their better qualities into a fully satisfying whole.

Tales of the New West is an immensely likable debut, with some good originals by singer/guitarists Buddy Blue and Jerry Raney, snappy covers of Springsteen, John Stewart and the Velvet Underground, and Montana's signature tunes: "Happy Boy" and "California Kid." The six-song **Glad'n'Greasy** is, track for track, even stronger, boasting a good cover of Neil Young's "Powderfinger." The Beat Farmers re-recorded the song on the amiable but rather thin **Van Go,** which attempts to tone down the band's eccentricities (less Country Dick) but fails to compensate with much in the way of songwriting, save for Blue's witty "Gun Sale at the Church" and band pal Paul Kamanski's jangly "Road of Ruin."

Joey Harris (formerly of the Speedsters, who recorded one album for MCA in 1983) replaced Blue for the more substantial **The Pursuit of Happiness,** which benefits from better material, notably Kamanski's epic "Hollywood Hills" and Harris' "God Is Here Tonight," as well as a hearty Montana reading of Johnny Cash's "Big River." Despite terrific cover art and a couple of catchy tunes, **Poor & Famous** is a confusing mess that tries to cover too many stylistic bases. The drunk-and-in-person **Loud and Plowed and . . . Live!!**—with on-target covers of the Kinks, George Jones and Kenny Rogers—does a better job of capturing the Beat Farmers' scruffy charm than any of its studio predecessors.

After a five-year studio layoff, the Farmers bounced back with the solid, tuneful **Viking Lullabys,** which finally lands a balance between sincerity and silliness. Harris' "Southern Cross" and Raney's "Atomic Age Mutants" are among the group's strongest and catchiest songs, while Montana's "Are You Drinkin' With Me Jesus?" (co-written by Mojo Nixon, with whom Montana had done a Pleasure Barons album) and "Baby's Liquor'd Up" showcase him without sticking out like sore thumbs.

On the other hand, the self-produced **Manifold** has its moments, but suffers from ill-advised stabs at a heavier—and rather anonymous—blues-rock sound, which tends to smother the personality of songs like Harris' "Mystery," Raney's "Got It Bad" and Montana's amusing yet heartfelt protest tune "Whale•Oil•Beef•Hooked." The album also adds Dylan's "Positively 4th Street" to the Beat Farmers' dossier of well-executed covers.

In early November 1995, Country Dick Montana collapsed on stage in Canada and died of a heart attack. (Despite the possible presumption that it was a hasty cash-in, the Curb compilation—ten songs, seemingly chosen at random from the band's four albums for the label—was already in stores at the time of the tragedy.) In mid-'96, Bar/None posthumously released Montana's solo album, a robust, semi-serious version of country balladry. [ss]

See also *Mojo Nixon; TPRG.*

BEAT HAPPENING

Beat Happening EP [tape] (K) 1984
Three Tea Breakfast EP [tape] (K) 1984
Beat Happening (K) 1985 + 1996
Crashing Through EP (UK 53rd & 3rd) 1988
Jamboree (K/Rough Trade) 1988 (K/Sub Pop) 1992
Black Candy (K) 1989 (K/Sub Pop) 1992
1983–85 (K/Feel Good All Over) 1990
Dreamy (Sub Pop) 1991
You Turn Me On (K/Sub Pop) 1992

BEAT HAPPENING/SCREAMING TREES

Beat Happening/Screaming Trees EP (K/Homestead) 1988

VARIOUS ARTISTS

Fortune Cookie Prize (Simple Machines/Cargo) 1992

Maybe it was one of life's Newtonian formulations about equal and opposite reactions, or some Einstein thing concerning the duality of the university and matter/anti-matter. Maybe it was a case of identical concepts being explored on two very different volume settings. Maybe it was nothing more than anti-hipster nonconformity run wild. In any case, as one musical upheaval—grunge/punk (grunk?)—was gestating in and emanating loudly from Seattle, its antithesis, a spare, minimalist adorable pop concoction dubbed love-rock or cuddlecore and casually marketed as the International Pop Underground, was bubbling up quietly in the nearby state capital, Olympia. At the center of this latter phenomenon stood Calvin Johnson, his band Beat Happening and the K Records label he founded.

As profoundly archetypal in its way as the Velvet

Underground, the influential and delightful Beat Happening demonstrated that punk's rebel spirit could be expressed just as well by defying rock's conventions as by defying society's. Hence the contrived (or sincere, you get to guess) anti-star innocence and cuteness: first names only, scanty, handwritten credits, blurry photos and crude drawings, sardonically trivial lyrics, singing that treats melody and key with cavalier apathy, disorganized and seemingly impromptu concert appearances. Structurally, the trio—Johnson, Heather (Lewis) and Bret (Lunsford)—pulled off one of orthodoxy's wings by repeating a feat first tested by the Cramps (another obvious stylistic source; add Jonathan Richman's self-willed flimsy to that short list) and doing without bass. (Perhaps they assumed Johnson's astonishingly deep voice could provide all the notes needed in that register.) Finally, the group certified the insignificance of instrumental skill by democratically rotating guitar and drum responsibilities among its members.

After releasing two five-song tapes, Beat Happening made its monumental album debut in 1985, produced (well . . .) by Greg Sage of the Wipers. A fresh breeze of one-take pop ingenuity, songs like "I Spy," "Down at the Sea" and the Crampsy "Bad Seeds" are remorselessly amateurish but loaded with charm and invention. (The twenty-six-song **1983–85** brings the story up to date with the trio's first single, the first album, **Three Tea Breakfast,** several compilation contributions and some otherwise unreleased tracks. The '96 K CD of **Beat Happening** has twenty-three of the same selections but better artwork.)

While repeating **Beat Happening**'s gambit of ending an album with a live cut, **Jamboree**—co-produced by Mark Lanegan and Gary Lee Conner of Screaming Trees and Steve Fisk—is a bit more intricate and electric, but not enough to hurt. What makes the trio so special is its innate ability to turn raw, crude ingredients into friendly, nice music without getting all mushy about it. So, while "Hangman" gets a ferocious Cramps roar going, the vocals are thoroughly mild. Similarly, the alluring (and oft-covered) "Indian Summer" paints an idyllic lyrical picture over an innocuous drone. Indicative of a deft internal compass, the pathos-laden "Cat Walk" has enough of a spine not to whimper.

The four songs on the joint Beat Happening/Screaming Trees 12-inch (the record melds the two groups without specific credits) suggest that a boxload of Cream's **Disraeli Gears** had recently arrived in town. (The wah-wah and mock–Ginger Baker drumming is a dead giveaway.) "Polly Pereguin" and the pointedly titled "Tales of Brave Aphrodite," a loopy confessional, are rough-cut electric pop with definite '60s ambience. If nothing else, the EP demonstrates how open-ended the group's musical ambitions could be.

Beat Happening lost its poise on **Black Candy,** a disappointing album that's more careless than casual, with vocals (almost all by Calvin) that wander nervously around melodies over guitars and drums that are too often intrusively aggressive (and, in "Knick Knack," gravely out of tune). The album contains a couple of great songs ("Black Candy" and "Cast a Shadow"), but that's about it.

The darkly painted **Dreamy,** inconspicuously produced by Fisk, continues in the scrabbly stylistic direction of **Black Candy** but is a much better, more consistent LP with none of its predecessor's sloppiest shortcomings. Calvin's resonant voice is the concise album's dominant feature (Heather sings three: the lightly tuneful "Left Behind," the wistful "Fortune Cookie Prize" and the racing, feedback-drenched "Collide"); the raw and undeveloped electric music supports him with easy grace, making the most of inspired—and only occasionally Crampsy (see the surly and sexy "Nancy Sin")—minimalism. The album is loaded with cool tunes: the ominous "Me Untamed," the Shonen Knife– like "Hot Chocolate Boy," the '60s-ish "Cry for a Shadow" and the bodacious "Red Head Walking."

If it proves to be Beat Happening's final long-player, **You Turn Me On** leaves the group in a different place than it began. Carefully performed and produced with startling clarity by (separately) Fisk and Stuart Moxham (an avatar of '70s new wave minimalism in the Young Marble Giants, another crucial ingredient in the foundation of Calvinism), it takes forty-five minutes to present nine numbers in what actually sound like planned arrangements. Stretching out songs that are as structurally ambitious as usual—which is to say not in the slightest—merely makes them longer. (Unlike many minimalists, Beat Happening has never made a fetish of brevity.) So while there's nothing in the four-plus minutes of Calvin's gritty "You Turn Me On" or the nine-plus of Heather's pretty "Godsend" that couldn't have been achieved in half (or a quarter) of the time, neither is seriously damaged by its interminability. That said, the material's exceptionally high quality would have been more obvious if each song didn't hang around so long. (Besides the title track, "Pinebox Derby," "Bury the Hammer," "Tiger Trap" and "Sleepyhead" are all keepers, and not just to the bands who named themselves after the last two.) Beat Happening has not released a record since—Johnson has busied himself in two other bands—but there is talk of a new album on the way.

Considering how many like-minded artists have covered Beat Happening songs over the years, the tribute album, despite good intentions (artistic, educational and fund-raising), is surprising stinky. Indie bands like Velocity Girl, Seaweed, Scrawl and half of Sonic Youth put their fat-fingered handprints on a bass-ackwards selection of tunes (and an awful Unrest original called "I Love Calvin") that lose most of their personality in the process. Superchunk's seething "Nancy Sin" and the Tsunami-related Geek's raging rendition of "Night Moves on the Catwalk" (the deep male voice of which sounds suspiciously like one of the album's honorees) are the prizes of **Fortune Cookie Prize.** [i]

See also *Dub Narcotic Sound System, Halo Benders, Screaming Trees; TPRG.*

BEATNIK BEATCH

See *Jellyfish.*

BEATNIK FILMSTARS

Maharishi (UK Big Sky) 1991
Themes From Foreverdrone EP (UK Vinyl Japan) 1992
Laid Back and English (La-di-da America) 1994
Astronaut House (La-di-da America) 1995

This English quintet spits back shards of US influences like Pavement, Sebadoh and Sonic Youth, but the group's rough-hewn, druggy, post-Velvets flavor leaves it a tad behind more commercial countrymen in the bid to conquer America. And while Beatnik Filmstars come from Bristol, the group's lo-fi three-guitar assault has nothing in common with such trendy trip-hop hometowners as Massive Attack, Tricky and Portishead.

The production on **Laid Back and English** is cloudy, but its sixteen songs are edgy, jagged and occasionally buoyant in spite of the murky sound. Singer/songwriter/guitarist Andrew Jarrett's pop sensibilities are bent but honed. His prim, almost melancholy vocals are poignant enough for the group's melodic material ("Clean," "Kick It in the Head," "Skill") but don't offer a lot of range. While unremarkable, **Laid Back and English** has a groovy kind of innocence; also, the guitar interplay among Jarrett, Tim Rippington and John Austin is quite good (especially on "Missed"). Aside from a throwaway attempt at shocking noise ("Swillyagro") and a few arty indulgences, it's a solid, psychedelic debut.

From the first fractious chords of "La Fruitmousse," **Astronaut House** is a major improvement, with more surprises and fewer affectations. The three guitarists careen and cut boldly, and Jarrett adopts a new, angrier tone to match: "Don't listen to the radio," he commands. "Wreck My Style" betters the first record's style with snaky melodies and exotic guitar sounds; that segues into the belligerent, Fall-ish title track. If Jarrett was shy on the debut, he's well out of his shell here, and the band responds with rhythmic frenzy and spastic abandon. Even the pretty ballad ("Protein +") is interrupted with an ear-scorching noise-guitar eruption. "What Goes Around Comes Around" again confirms Pavement debts, but it's followed by the ironic (?) "New Improved Formula" and "Best Idea Probably," which features guitars that sound like—no shit—helicopters. Apocalypse now. [mww]

BEATNUTS

Intoxicated Demons EP (Violator/Relativity) 1993
The Beatnuts (Violator/Relativity) 1994

New York Latino hip-hoppers Psycho Les (Lester Fernandez) and JuJu (Jerry Tineo), joined in mid-career by Fashion (Berntony Smalls)—the Beatnuts—initially made their reputation as versatile producers, working the samplers and boards for a slew of artists, including Chi Ali, Monie Love, Jungle Brothers, Pete Nice and Kurious. Then they began making their own records. Under the trio's deft hands, Afro-Cuban percussion breaks, fuzzy guitar runs, acoustic basslines, horn choruses and organ solos are re-cut and transformed into memorable, hook-dense tunes ("No Equal" from the eleven-track, six-song **Intoxicated Demons;** "Are You Ready," "Hellraiser" and "Yeah You Get Props" from the full-length album).

Beatnuts records take their ambience from early-'70s Prestige or Westbound wax and their technique from late-'80s innovators A Tribe Called Quest and De La Soul, but the lyrics are something else entirely. When they're not in battle mode, the Beatnuts just act ill. The chorus to **Intoxicated Demons**' "Psycho Dwarf" goes, "I wanna fuck, drink beer and smoke some shit!" For those who can't get enough, **The Beatnuts** offers an extended version of the song. [jzc]

BEAUTICIANS

See *Smugglers.*

BEAUTIFUL PEOPLE LTD.

See *Swans.*

BEAUTIFUL SOUTH

Welcome to the Beautiful South (Go! Discs/Elektra) 1989
Choke (Go! Discs/Elektra) 1990
0898 Beautiful South (Go! Discs/Elektra) 1992
Miaow (UK Go! Discs) 1994
The Best of the Beautiful South: Carry on Up the Charts (UK Go! Discs) 1994 (Go! Discs/Mercury) 1995

After disbanding England's ironically poppy—and, at home, wildly popular—Housemartins in 1988, frontman Paul Heaton wasted little time in maintaining the Hull band's chart momentum with the less jangly but similarly double-edged Beautiful South. (Another ex-member launched Beats International.) Though the new combo replaces the plangent guitars with a more mature, keyboard-driven MOR-pop sound, it maintains the pointed juxtaposition of attractively crafted tunes and Heaton's barbed lyrical sentiments.

With ex-Housemartins drummer Dave Hemingway sharing vocal duties (but not playing drums), **Welcome to the Beautiful South** sets the tone with "Song for Whoever," an irresistible melody supporting a biting lyric nailing the cynicism just below the surface of commercial love songs. Elsewhere, the material—co-written by Heaton and guitarist David Rotheray—is most effective when Heaton lets his guard down and shows some vulnerability (as he does in "You Keep It All In" and "I'll Sail This Ship Alone") and less so when taking gratuitous potshots at obvious targets. **Choke** ventures closer to outright misanthropy, but it does so with undeniable wit and style, balancing the biliousness with consistently gorgeous music. "Tonight I Fancy Myself" and "I Hate You (But You're Interesting)" encapsulate Heaton's withering view of romance. An added female vocalist, Briana Corrigan, isn't given much to do, but she brings a welcome edge to "Should've Kept My Eyes Shut," which sets harrowing lyrics of domestic abuse against bouncy pop dynamics.

0898 Beautiful South features even more uplifting melodies and more balanced lyrics: "Old Red Eyes Is Back," "We Are Each Other" and the Corrigan-sung "Bell-Bottomed Tear" benefit immeasurably by demonstrating a bit more compassion for their subjects. **Miaow** is similarly satisfying, with such tunes as "Good as Gold (Stupid as Mud)" and "Prettiest Eyes" focusing more on intimate details rather than the sweeping generalizations all too common on the band's early discs. New singer Jacqueline Abbott (who replaces Corrigan and is similarly underused) steps out front for a competent but pointless reading of Fred Neil's "Everybody's Talkin'." Those **Miaow** tunes made it to the States via the fifteen-song compilation, a decent sampler that includes two new numbers, the anthemic "One Last Love Song" and a snappy Abbott-sung cover of the pop chestnut "Dream a Little Dream of Me." [ss]

See also *TPRG.*

BECK

Golden Feelings [tape] (Sonic Enemy) 1993
"Loser" (Bong Load) 1993 (DGC) 1994
Mellow Gold (Bong Load/DGC) 1994
Stereopathetic Soulmanure (Flipside) 1994

One Foot in the Grave (K) 1994
A Western Harvest Field by Moonlight (Fingerpaint) 1994
Beercan EP (DGC) 1995
Odelay (Bong Load/DGC) 1996

Once upon a time, every passing season brought another guitar-slinger with aspirations of being knighted the New Dylan, but it's hard to recall a single one able to fill the role as well as this smart-alecky bicoastal expectation-tweaker. Like Dylan, Beck (Hansen) has reinvented his personal history countless times—frequently claiming to be a lower-middle-class yutz from Kansas City, since his third-generation bohemian background (mom ran LA's legendary Masque club in the '70s, grandpa was a pioneer in the Fluxus art movement a generation before) didn't have the right cachet. An initial fling at folk—or anti-folk, if you want to nitpick—in the Big Apple didn't pan out, although he did manage to sneak onto a few bills topped by acoustic-punk potentates like Kirk Kelly and Roger Manning. Having lost the battle on the eastern front, Beck took the struggle to the thriving boho community of Los Angeles' Silverlake district, discarded his surname and commenced to radicalizing his approach.

When next heard from, Beck was spouting a stripe of stream-of-consciousness slacker poetry not all that different from his all-acoustic days, but he'd augmented the folk instrumentation with beatbox, tape loops and all manner of gadgetry. An embryonic single, "MTV Makes Me Wanna Smoke Crack," drew some appreciative smirks from fellow enemies of, er, The Man, but received little attention east of LA's city limits; ditto the homebrew cassette. Beck remedied that with his next release. The Delta-rap "Loser" looked set to follow its predecessor into obscurity—the single's thousand-copy pressing didn't immediately leap from record store shelves—until a few sympathetic radio types began teasing locals with the annoying/insistent/infectious anti-anthem often enough to put the phrase "I'm a loser, baby, so why don't you kill me" on the lips of every beaten-generation devotee within earshot. Although the lo-fi smirk-hop ditty was actually recorded nearly two years before its release, "Loser" became a national phenomenon, climbing the charts and helping expose the rest of Beck's markedly less-populist savantry to the masses.

Although a few catchy ditties are strewn across the surface of **Mellow Gold,** the bulk of the album is given over to aggressively ironic bricolage that allows the artiste to empty his sonic bag of tricks (and assert his affinity for a particular four-letter word that crops up in more than half the disc's songs and two of its titles). But even weighed down with all the self-consciously post-modern baggage, **Mellow Gold** makes a case for Beck as auteur-despite-himself. Delve beneath the stoner patter of "Nitemare Hippy Girl" and "Pay No Mind (Snoozer)," and you'll find a writer with an intuitive ability to lance the boils on the face of pop culture, even when that means turning the dagger inward: the latter song's anti-materialist stance plants the suggestion that listeners "give the finger to the rock'n'roll singer as he's dancing upon your paycheck." Not all of Beck's detours lead to the promised land—"Whiskeyclone, Hotel City 1997" is a flat faux-Bukowski rummy tale and "Soul Suckin Jerk" merely reprises the shtick introduced on "Loser"—but by the time **Mellow Gold** winds down, Highway 61 seems to be on the horizon.

Simultaneously safeguarding his hipster cachet and offering newfound fans a real reason to shout the title of his hit (a song he routinely "forgot" to play when touring behind **Mellow Gold**), Beck concurrently released a handful of albums that betray his inability to differentiate between the ridiculous and the sublime. **Stereopathetic Soulmanure** falls almost exclusively into the former category. Composed of two dozen studio experiments dating from 1988 to 1993, the album is, for all its jabbing at frat-boy culture, little more than a soundtrack to nickel-beer night at an art-school Animal House—as should be evident from tracks like "Satan Gave Me a Taco" and "Rollins Power Sauce" (okay, the latter *is* worth a chuckle or two). Dominated by distorted, tenaciously tuneless trifles like "Pink Noise (Rock Me Amadeus)" and "Thunder Peel"—both of which sound like the product of too much Zappa combined with too much helium inhalation—**Stereopathetic Soulmanure** mistakes idiocy for idiosyncrasy.

Both of his other indie releases, however, belie the sincerity beneath the ever-present smirk—at least when it comes to his facility with the building blocks of bona fide folk music. The 10-inch **A Western Harvest Field by Moonlight** is less than riveting, thanks in no small part to its lower-than-low fidelity and a surfeit of sardonic sidestepping on the part of Beck himself, but **One Foot in the Grave** is most assuredly a revelation. Recorded before his commercial breakthrough, the largely acoustic album replicates the feel of a vintage Folkways release, to the point that you can hear the vibration of virtually every guitar string on a song like the Appalachian-styled call to arms "He's a Mighty Good Leader." On several songs (notably "I Get Lonesome"), Beck is joined by Calvin Johnson (K Records/Beat Happening), whose bass vocals provide a campfire-suitable counterpoint. The refreshingly simple approach allows plenty of room for Beck's determinedly rudimentary guitar picking to resonate—and forces his writing into newly emotional territory. Even the songs that threaten to collapse under insistent heaps of non sequitur (like "Sleeping Bag") end up leaving more than a punch line as a legacy.

The **Beercan** EP surrounds one of **Mellow Gold**'s lesser tracks with a handful of ineffectual studio improvisations. In retrospect, though, such digressions can be seen as the necessary burning of crops to produce a more bountiful future harvest, which **Odelay** surely is. Co-produced by the Dust Brothers, this monumental compost heap of lazy beats, witty po-mo lyrical/instrumental detritus and Donovanesque '60s trippiness is rendered as a relaxed but kinetic audio channel surf that spews blues, country, folk, rap and rock with unfailing offhand charm. Bizarre and captivating, with messages amid the muzzy relaxation, **Odelay** is Beck's shockingly mature statement on his endless childhood. [dss]

See also *Lync.*

BEDHEAD

WhatFunLifeWas (Trance Syndicate) 1994
4songCDEP19:10 EP (Trance Syndicate) 1994
The Dark Ages EP (Trance Syndicate) 1996
Beheaded (Trance Syndicate) 1996

Spawned in early 1992 in the unlikely locale of Dallas, Bedhead was an early harbinger of the mid-'90s slowcore semi-movement. The key word here is "languid," even when the quartet (guitar-playing brothers Bubba and Matt Kadane, bassist Kris Wheat and drummer Trini Martinez) is playing hard: Matt's lazy vocals, the unhurried tempos and intricately interwoven guitar/bass patterns that bear footprints of Spacemen 3 and New Order, as well as the occasional tread of Galaxie 500 and Codeine. (Bedhead covers Joy Division's "Disorder" on **4songCDEP19:10,** which was recorded live to stereo in one take.) Yet unlike those groups, Bedhead evidently uses no gearboxes, its clean sonic sheets conveying enough tension and intensity to render effects unnecessary. [ja]

ADRIAN BELEW

Lone Rhino (Island) 1982
Twang Bar King (Island) 1983
Desire Caught by the Tail (Island) 1986
Mr. Music Head (Atlantic) 1989
Young Lions (Atlantic) 1990
Desire of the Rhino King (Island) 1991
Inner Revolution (Atlantic) 1992
Here (Caroline) 1994

BEARS

The Bears (Primitive Man) 1987
Rise and Shine (Primitive Man) 1988

The guitarist aging art-rockers turn to for a sublime and stirring mixture of solid chops and wild-eyed invention, Adrian Belew (born in Kentucky, raised in Ohio) has played a crucial long-term role in the careers of David Bowie and King Crimson, while also making important contributions to Frank Zappa, Talking Heads, the Tom Tom Club and others. In between commitments like Bowie's endless Sound+Vision tour, Belew has found the time to pursue a pop career of his own, recording seven solo albums (letting a few guests help out here and there but essentially DIYing it all the way) and a pair with the Bears, a quartet of old pals he led in the late '80s. Nearly every LP contains at least one or two songs in which Belew's Beatlesque songwriting, unpretentious humanism, MIDI-processed guitar adventures and yelping vocals ring the delightful popcraft bell. At times, he seems very much like a latter-day Todd Rundgren with smaller computers.

Mixing straightforward songs and sonic explorations (**Desire** is all-instrumental), the first three albums are usefully boiled down on the twenty-one-track **Desire of the Rhino King.** His subsequent Atlantic triptych increasingly gets down to chart-potential cases with musical enticements accessible enough to make you forget the fringey artistic abilities of their creator. **Mr. Music Head** contains the absolutely delightful "Oh Daddy" (with guest vocals by daughter Audie); **Young Lions** adds the catchy "Pretty Pink Rose" and a new version of King Crimson's "Heartbeat" to the collection.

Inner Revolution shifts into high vintage-pop gear for a full-blown collection of fab inventions that resemble—perhaps a shade too closely—the Beatles, Traveling Wilburys and, most of all, the bridge between those two bands, ELO. A charming and diverse set that makes equally good use of Belew's dexterous guitar reach, copycat arranging facility and engaging voice, the album is down-to-earth and upbeat (except for the rousingly sung breakup autobiography, "The War in the Gulf Between Us").

Here refines that approach to subtler, less lapel-tugging effect, cutting the retro bounce for lighter, sonically ambitious designs. "Burned by the Fire We Made" and others are fairly consistent with the previous album, but several tracks are scarcely identifiable as Belew. (Or, to his credit, anyone else.) The lyrics' new agey philosophizing is a drag, but Belew manages to sing his golly-gee contemplations, quandaries, homilies and realizations without getting too precious or clumsy. The record doesn't suffer unduly from all the sensitive sharing, and a couple of howling guitar solos (especially in "Never Enough" and "Brave New World") go a long way in dispersing the therapy aroma. [i]

See also *David Bowie, King Crimson; TPRG.*

CHRIS BELL

See *Big Star.*

BELLTOWER

Exploration Day EP (UK Ultimate) 1991
In Hollow EP (UK Ultimate) 1991
Popdropper (EastWest) 1992

Formed in New York by three Americans but resident in England, the Belltower washes its pretty pop songs in lush, moderately distorted instrumental textures. If not nearly as overwhelming as, say, My Bloody Valentine, the quartet heads in that general direction with far more instrumental aptitude than many fuzzbox collectors. But while their collective guitar playing is impressive, Britta Phillips and Jody Porter don't really have the right kind of voices for this kind of music—hers has a harsh edge, his is actually too wispy. Fortunately, the gently stirring rock atmospheres are seductive enough to reduce the vocals to a minor distraction.

Popdropper is a compilation of tracks from various British singles and EPs; "Outshine the Sun" and "Solstice," both from **Exploration Day,** were produced by Levitation's Terry Bickers and are the clearest, strongest and most effectively integrated expositions of the Belltower's pleasurable skills. [i]

BELLY

Slow Dust EP (UK 4AD) 1992
Star (Sire/Reprise) 1993
King (Sire/Reprise) 1995

As if to make it easier for those post-graduates who never understood what all the hoohah was about Throwing Muses, Belly—the band formed by Rhode Island singer/guitarist Tanya Donelly after tasting freedom in the Breeders—gets down to pop tacks with a minimum of airy artiness. The band sets its table with the snappy beats, forthright presentation and tangible melodies that were never indispensable to the Throwing Muses lifestyle.

Joined by brothers Tom (guitar) and Chris (drums) Gorman, with former Musemate Fred Abong playing bass in the studio, Donelly didn't cut the stylistic cord completely at first. **Slow Dust,** a four-song EP produced in Liverpool by old studio friend Gil Norton, raises the music's rock quotient without fully extracting the wispy preciousness from its vocal component. Still, it contains the potent "Dusted," the memorable "Slow Dog" and "Low Red Moon" to demonstrate the catchy accessibility and tuneful fortitude that would separate the sound of Belly from its predecessor.

Star folds those three tracks and a session leftover—"Feed the Tree," a jangly hookfest that made Belly's career when released as the album's first single—together with the eleven produced in Nashville by the trio and engineer Tracy Chisholm. Donelly, who was the junior writing partner to stepsister Kristin Hersh in Throwing Muses, makes a few missteps on the way to finding her feet as a strong creative leader. But the album gains stylish intrigue from her elliptical, disquieting lyrics ("Baby's playing dead in the cellar/Gave her water, just got paler/Grass stains, back burns, she's a screamer/She's just dusted, leave her") and adequate sonic allure from arrangements that embellish her airy melodies with overdubbed harmony vocals and subtle instrumental accessories. Still, the sense of a new band searching out its stylistic voice on the fly compromises the most poised creations ("Full Moon, Empty Heart," "White Belly," "Stay") by revealing all the test-runs, and prevents **Star** from reaching the potential to which it clearly alludes.

Donelly's evident goal of normalizing relations with the rock-pop mainstream take real root on **King**, a much-improved followup smartly produced by English rock master Glyn Johns (Who, Eagles, Faces, Eric Clapton). As a Grammy-nominated four-piece (bassist Gail Greenwood joined after the first album) with a lot to live up to, Belly hits the spot. The group asserts itself in a steady, thrilling electric pop attack that offsets the residual aridness and challenges Donelly to hold her own—which she ably does in a deeper, stronger voice. Co-writing the better half of the album's songs with Greenwood or Tom Gorman, Donelly sifts out the enigmatism for easier lyrical access, and lashes the results to immediately appealing structures in the majestic "Silverfish," the giddy "Red," the Cranberries-like "King" and the star-harshing "Super-Connected." This is where Belly belongs. [i]

See also *Breeders, Throwing Muses.*

BEME SEED

Beme Seed (Blast First) 1989
Lights Unfold (No. 6) 1990
Purify (No. 6) 1992

Beme Seed singer Kathleen Lynch was "the Stripper," whose stage antics helped propel Butthole Surfers to infamy. In most ways, her band is on its own plane—the quartet opened an entire tour for the Surfers simply by showing up at gigs unannounced, setting up and playing. Lacking the minimal organization of even the Sun City Girls, Beme Seed captures unique psychic qualities on its three opaque and unsettling records.

For starters, **Beme Seed** is one long, orgiastic tuneup, with lots of chanting and squealing over guitar feedback and erratic pulsing rumble. Lynch's band has the same paranormal quality as her dance act. The few snippets of sustained songs are simplistic and ceremonial—complete with speaking in tongues. Sounding more like a hazy memory than an actual recording of music, the album's unrelenting tension can be panic-inducing. Whether the band is coming or going, it leaves a bewildering impression.

Lights Unfold further explores the outsides of abstraction. Beme Seed grabs the equivalent of break-beats from psychedelic and noise music in an attempt to build something new and inspiring. Pagan paeans like "Old New Song" begin in climax and reach for enlightenment from there. Hand-lettered lyrics show Lynch is a sha(wo)man with a mission: "Move your body like you move your mind/Celebrate life, it's on time."

Recorded in New York with Wharton Tiers, **Purify** takes a stab at regular-sounding songs, where you can feel the beat and guess the changes. Accordingly, Lynch's tranced-out moans and Michael Albin's endless fried guitar wailing have a calming effect on incantations like "Inner Life Is Calling." Encroaching '60s sensibilities aside, the rainbow dance "I'm So Glad That Love Is Travelling All Around the World" is a provocative spaced-out mix of Jefferson Airplane and the Banshees.

The band broke up soon after. With even the Buttholes having lost their love of insanity by 1992, underground rock became nice and safe, and the riddle of Beme Seed was paved over without ever really being solved. [ic]

BENT-BACKED TULIPS

See *Dramarama.*

STEVE BERESFORD/DAVID TOOP/ JOHN ZORN/TONIE MARSHALL

See *John Zorn.*

STEVEN JESSE BERNSTEIN

Prison (Sub Pop) 1992

Seattle performance poet Steven Jesse Bernstein brought his own despairing misery and emotional violence to the grimy disgust of William Burroughs' familiar vistas; the landscape of his personal experience and vision produced a hellish text of sex, drugs, shit, disease, decadence, shame, incarceration, noise and crushing alienation. When the forty-year-old committed suicide in 1991, he was in the early stages of a project to pair his recorded readings with musical accompaniment by local composer/producer Steve Fisk.

Prison is the posthumously completed result of that collaboration, a masterful match of prose and the music it inspired. As Bernstein recites his gruesome fantasies (?) and sardonic treatises, Fisk responds to both mood and content, latching on to and enfolding the words in diverse music and concrete sounds—screeching saw noises and techno beats for "The Sport (Part One)," a '60s super-agent soundtrack that gives way to a merry jingle and then an unsettling roil in "No No Man (Part One)"; a soulful groove for "Party Balloon"; boho bongo jazz for "This Clouded Heart." At times, the album manages the illusion of Bernstein—who spoke these pieces alone—fighting to be heard above the din, yet Fisk has the artistic insight and control to add nothing more than distant thunder to sanctify the traumatic "Face," an epic and appalling "fictional" reminiscence. "At two, my face already looked like the face of a convict . . ." Bernstein was a compelling, tormented poet, but Fisk is every bit the master of this **Prison.** [i]

See also *Pell Mell.*

HEIDI BERRY

Firefly EP (UK Creation) 1987
Below the Waves (UK Creation) 1989 (Rockville) 1990

Love (UK 4AD) 1991
Heidi Berry (4AD) 1993
Miracle (4AD) 1996

Without fitting into any particular scene, Heidi Berry (born in Boston but raised in the UK) has developed her own aesthetic, one clearly based on early folk/rock singer/songwriter models and approached from a Celtic angle. Nonetheless, her wavering, emotive soprano refracts other styles, and **Firefly** fits in comfortably with Creation's late-'80s stable. Backing her on these six songs are members of the Weather Prophets and Felt keyboardist Martin Duffy, whose colorful piano playing spices up the pleasant amalgam of Sandy Denny–esque folk and crisp guitar pop. Fittingly, this coherent EP features moody, folky-sounding ruminations ("Houses Made of Wood") and sprightly pop ("Firefly"), along with an occasional shower from the Weather Prophets ("Nobody Tells on You").

While **Firefly**'s cover art depicts Berry hanging out in jeans and a western shirt, **Below the Waves** sees her in all black, lounging on a red sofa with a cigarette dangling from her fingers; the image shift underscores the album's more contemplative, less jangly tone. "It's quiet here/It's warm here/It's peaceful/It's dark," she sings over the title cut's sparse arrangement, setting the album's introspective mood. The accompaniment is also different, as the Weather Prophets' jaunty, sparkling chords are replaced by the subtle acoustic guitar picking of Berry's brother Christopher. The opening "Ribbons" intertwines Berry's better-controlled voice with a curving violin line and simple autoguitar strums. The melancholy, fuller-sounding "Northshore Train," reinforced by a larger string section, and the sunnier, piano-based "All for You" hint at broader stylistic possibilities. While **Below the Waves** is a pleasant dip into new waters for Berry, the album is not as fully realized as her subsequent explorations would be. The domestic CD of **Below the Waves** includes **Firefly.**

Love retains the personal tone but beefs it up slightly with fuller, more mood-sculpting arrangements, adding synthesizer, impressionistic electric guitar by Terry Bickers (House of Love, Levitation) and warm fretless bass from Levitation's Laurence O'Keefe (who also co-wrote a song here). Weather Prophets Peter Astor and Dave Morgan also return to help out. In addition to the usual beautifully presented originals—including the languorous "Gloria" and the uplifting "Wake"—Berry attempts her first cover version, bringing a graceful interpretation of Bob Mould's "Up in the Air" to life with her distinctive, studied voice.

"Mercury," the opening cut of **Heidi Berry,** sets the stage for an album of even fuller arrangements, stronger atmospheres and more lively and varied structures, making it her most sure-footed, confident LP to date. Most of **Love**'s cast returns, augmented by Kitchens of Distinction guitarist Julian Swales (credited with "guitar shimmers"). Many of the songs—including "The Moon and the Sun," "Darling Companion" and "Distant Thunder"—even rub elbows with a rock sound and structure, making them approachable without sacrificing any of Berry's personality. In addition to two O'Keefe collaborations, Berry presents a telling take on Anna McGarrigle's "Heart Like a Wheel," linking her further to a period and a sound. [la]

CINDY LEE BERRYHILL

Who's Gonna Save the World? (Rhino) 1987
Naked Movie Star (Rhino) 1989
Garage Orchestra (Earth Music) 1994
Straight Outta Marysville (Earth Music) 1996
Pony EP (Earth Music) 1996

First emerging as a witty, self-aware West Coast delegate to the mid-'80s fast folk movement, Cindy Lee Berryhill always bore a broader agenda than what could be achieved with a single guitar. Not that she wasn't perfectly able to put over clever original songs like "Damn, I Wish I Was a Man" and "Who's Gonna Save the World?" (on the lighthearted, mostly acoustic first album; the second is serious and electric) with simple apparatus, but Berryhill didn't reach her creative stride until her rebirth as a more ambitious pop auteur on 1994's delightfully baroque **Garage Orchestra.** With an army of instrumentalists—playing everything from clarinet and cello to banjo, vibraphone and tympani—at her disposal, Berryhill comes across with inventive, thoughtful, entertaining songs that fully deserve the diverse junior Phil Spector productions. And her singing—never much more than serviceable in the past—is luminously entrancing, as in the astonishing harmony exercise "Gary Handeman," an academic ode that sounds in spots like the Association, and the swooping waves of the intrinsically absurd "Etude for Ph. Machine." Berryhill pumps out ideas—great, wack and in between—like a fountain, delivering the dream fantasy of "Song for Brian" (Wilson), the genial idealism of "I Want Stuff" and a boppy sci-fi epic ("UFO Suite") as if such ingenuity grew in garages.

Recorded with three core alumni of the Garage Orchestra, **Straight Outta Marysville** brings Berryhill back to modest folk-pop with vibes and tympani adding cool touches; a couple of the autobiographical songs are performed solo on acoustic guitar. (She also turns the clock back in a rambling, jazzy raconteur rendition of Donovan's "Season of the Witch" that's almost as long as the one on the 1968 Al Kooper/Mike Bloomfield **Super Session** LP.) But while the arrangements are neat and clean, Berryhill's singing employs irritating stylistic maneuvers that leave her sounding like Edie Brickell gone native. About half of the songs cross from being revealing to being self-indulgent, reminiscences that don't resonate beyond the singer's world. [i]

BEST KISSERS IN THE WORLD

Best Kissers in the World EP (Sub Pop) 1991
Puddin' EP (MCA) 1993
Been There (MCA) 1993

These snappily monickered Oregonians started off as a beautifully scrawny fusion of Cheap Trick/Replacements pop brawn, but quickly lost inspiration, degenerating into tepid riffs and tired melodies. The quartet's 7-inch debut ("Take Me Home," which brilliantly lifts the riff from the untitled live fragment at the end of Cheap Trick's **Heaven Tonight** LP) and the five-track Sub Pop EP show the Kissers at their best. Produced by the Posies' Jonathan Auer, snotty attitude and power-poparama are driven to the fore, peaking on the awesome "Workin' on Donita" and ending with the jokey country lament "Hungover Together" (a duet with Hammerbox/Goodness singer Carrie Akre).

The five-song **Puddin'** retains the spirit but loses

the irresistible hooks; **Been There**'s title tells all. The band recorded a slightly better album called **Yellow Brick Roadkill** that disappeared from MCA's release schedule early in '96. [ja]

BETTER THAN EZRA

Surprise [tape] (Swell) 1990
Deluxe (Swell) 1993 (Swell/Elektra) 1995
friction, baby (Swell/Elektra) 1996

After more than half a decade, the Louisiana-bred Better Than Ezra—an unwitting beneficiary of the sine wave of musical style that can come along and lift flotsam right out of the water as if self-propelled—suddenly found a beachhead in 1995 for its clean-cut pop. Although marketed as alternative (hah!), the earnest trio has a generic sound blander than Gin Blossoms or Toad the Wet Sprocket—if singer/guitarist Kevin Griffin had a stronger voice, a substantial resemblance to Hootie and the Blowfish would be worth noting. On **Deluxe** (self-released and then given a major-label reissue), Better Than Ezra plies its inoffensive craft with the dedication of well-behaved students, doing their own work but peeking around the room to crib a little folk-anthem passion from Live, a melody from Cat Stevens (compare the chorus of "Teenager" to "The First Cut Is the Deepest"), a song title ("The Killer Inside") from Jim Thompson and a heavy grunge joke (the untitled bonus track, following the equally unconvincing country fakery of "Coyote") from some band they must have seen on MTV. [i]

BETTIE SERVEERT

Palomine (UK Guernica) 1992 (Matador) 1993 (Atlantic) 1993
Tom Boy EP (Matador) 1992
Kid's Allright EP (Matador) 1993
Crutches EP (Matador) 1995
Lamprey (Matador/Atlantic) 1995
Ray Ray Rain EP (UK Beggars Banquet) 1995
Something So Wild EP (Matador) 1995

DE ARTSEN

Conny Waves With a Shell (Hol. Why Are There People Like Frank?) 1989 (Ger. Glitterhouse) 1990 (Hol. Brinkman) 1993
Out of Sack (Ger. Glitterhouse) 1990

JOOST VISSER

Partners in Hair (Brinkman/Ajax) 1994

It's not as if Dutch rock completely sucked before Bettie Serveert—if nothing else, the recorded evidence of the band's immediate predecessor, De Artsen, puts paid to that—but when a country's greatest international contributions are Golden Earring, Focus and the Nits, low expectations can be understood. The very idea that a quartet from Amsterdam should make a year's best indie-rock album ('92, when the debut arrived in the UK) upends basic premises on which international culture rests. Good.

Between the carefully arranged seduction of Canadian-born Carol van Dijk's lyrical, faintly accented English vocals and the smeary aggression of Peter Visser's piercing guitar leads, **Palomine** achieves an uncanny standoff of passions rare in pop music. Without stepping outside its powerfully melodic setting or sounding anything but casual in the practice of its pop craft, Bettie Serveert (the name comes from the title of a tennis instruction book authored by onetime Wimbledon contender Betty Stöve) manages whisper-to-a-scream (and right back again) transitions better than anyone. The group subtly rides the intensity faders from folky guitar strums and drummer Berend Dubbe's light-fingered rhythms to raging storms of Crazy-Horse-channeling-Tom-Verlaine noise, making each song a thrilling series of unexpected emotional events. In the album-opening "Leg," Visser's searing rock intensity creeps up on van Dijk's gentle strums and airy singing like a pickpocket. It's an ominous shadow in the background through the second verse, rising up in curls of lead smoke and then exploding over vibrant organ chord swells as she slings her defiance like a cudgel: "You won't have me worried/I can still take care of myself somehow." In the sturdy and distinctive songs, musical complications amplify the quirky uncertainties of van Dijk's plainspoken lyrics, recollections—with misgivings about decisions long since made—about childhood ("Tom Boy," "Kid's Alright"), love ("Brain-Tag," "Leg") and the blurry lines between friendship and romance ("Balentine," "Palomine").

The excellent four-song **Tom Boy** EP (with the disturbing unwashed and somewhat slightly dazed cover photo of bassist Herman Bunskoeke's girlfriend) includes a wistful semi-acoustic version of "Balentine," a careening demo of the non-LP "Maggot" and the top-notch but otherwise unreleased "Smile."

Poorly modulated production screws up the band's dynamic tension on **Lamprey,** maintaining an action-packed energy level that just can't settle itself down to the hushed sparseness of **Palomine**'s most enticing moments. Even during quiet passages, there's too much going on; instrumental restlessness keeps getting the better of the band. That's no impediment to the hectic "Totally Freaked Out," but it diminishes the sonic ironies of "Crutches" and "Keepsake," turning songs that could have been magnificent plain. The songwriting on **Lamprey** shows no slackoff—if less imagination is evident in the chord structures, there's no shortage of affecting melodies or engaging lyrics. (The most notable is "Something So Wild," a volatile spew of disdain for another woman's overbearing boyfriend.) Still, the second album labors where the first danced; the band simply rocks out when it used to think twice and then hold back. Track for track, the songs hold up to **Palomine**'s extraordinary standard, but as a totality, add up to less. And while the two albums present the same number of songs in the same amount of time, **Lamprey** seems to take a lot longer. (The 10-inch of "Crutches," a song for which Come is profusely thanked for its guitar riff, contains two non-LP B-sides, the piano ballad "Shades" and the sedately electric "Entire Races," both of which are quite lovely. The import-only **Ray Ray Rain** and the American **Something So Wild** three-song EPs both contain "What Friend" and a cover of the Television Personalities' "Look Back in Anger" as their B-sides.)

De Artsen, which existed throughout the second half of the '80s and contained Visser and Bunskoeke (Dubbe was the quartet's roadie), was primarily a vehicle for Peter's brother, singer/random lyricist Joost Visser. (While in de Artsen, Peter and Herman also played in an early incarnation of Bettie Serveert as a side project with de Artsen's sound mixer, Carol van

Dijk.) Intriguing and promising but not exactly good, **Conny Waves With a Shell** betrays familiar traces of guitar and bass (and, inexplicably, rhythmic) technique and otherwise bears scant resemblance to its members' future endeavors. Despite Joost's squawky, unaccented voice and a dry tone influenced by somber auteurs like Lloyd Cole, Nick Cave, Dan Stuart and Tom Verlaine, the album finds poetic grace in such Americanized creations as "10 Grains," "Miss Understood" and the echoey '60s drone of "She's in Love." A nifty cover of Daniel Johnston's "Hey Joe" indicates a mindset impossible to glean from anything else on the record. (**Out of Sack** is a limited-edition vinyl release of rehearsal recordings and demos from 1986–88.)

So it makes a perfect kind of sense that Joost's post–de Artsen solo album should display some of the self-contained alienated inexplicability of Johnston's work. With ambient noise cropping up everywhere, the arduous **Partners in Hair** consists of nineteen simply recorded tracks, some using a band (reproducing the driving monotony of de Artsen, but with both hands off the steering wheel), the rest solo on acoustic guitar. In the latter category, the appealing folk sound of "Fingers in the Wind," "Press Your Lips" and "Some Use the Mekons" contrasts strongly with the strange and oblique lyrical assertions. [i]

BEVIS FROND

Miasma (Reckless) 1987
Inner Marshland (Reckless) 1987
Triptych (Reckless) 1988
Bevis Through the Looking Glass (Reckless) 1988
Acid Jam (UK Woronzow) 1988
The Auntie Winnie Album (Reckless) 1989
Any Gas Faster (Reckless) 1990
Ear Song EP (Reckless) 1990
New River Head (Reckless) 1991
A Gathering of Fronds (Reckless) 1992
London Stone (UK Woronzow) 1992
It Just Is (UK Woronzow) 1993
Sprawl (UK Woronzow) 1994
Superseeder (UK Woronzow) 1995

The Bevis Frond is Londoner Nick Saloman, whose staunch devotion to the spirit of vintage psychedelia has yielded a series of unmistakably '60s-derived albums. But there's more to the Bevis Frond's extensive catalogue than mere hippie revival. The singer/multi-instrumentalist's twisted pop tunes, reflective acoustic excursions and extended guitar freakouts carry a quirkily personal edge and a distinctive melodic sensibility that raises them well above mere stylistic fetishism. Increasingly, his songs are finding their way into the repertoires of American indie-rockers, and that has increased his profile even among those daunted by the prospect of a substantial oeuvre.

The home-recorded, relatively lo-fi **Miasma, Inner Marshland, Triptych** and **The Auntie Winnie Album** are pretty much of a piece, exploring Saloman's various obsessions with abundant spirit and flashes of absurdist humor. (Reckless' CD editions of these titles offer excellent value for money, appending jam-intensive bonus tracks drawn from the vinyl-only **Bevis Through the Looking Glass** and **Acid Jam;** indeed, virtually every Bevis Frond CD is filled to the gills, time-wise.)

With **Any Gas Faster,** Saloman upgraded the Frond's sonic fidelity without sacrificing the music's character, and that approach has continued, with minor variations, through his '90s releases. **New River Head** features some of his most mature and disciplined material—specifically the bittersweet title track and the heartbreaking "Thankless Task." Since an eighty-minute CD wasn't enough to contain all of the music on the album's double-disc vinyl configuration, **A Gathering of Fronds** CD was subsequently assembled from the six tracks left off the **New River Head** CD, plus ten more singles, compilation and vinyl-only tracks—including unlikely but well-executed covers of Muddy Waters and Iron Butterfly. **London Stone,** despite its fiddle-instrumental intro, sticks largely to heavier rock numbers; it's not bad, but the lack of variety makes it less compelling than it ought to be. **It Just Is** follows largely in the same vein, but boasts a pair of ace pop tunes in "I Can't Catch Up With You" and "Everyday Sunshine." True to its title, **Sprawl** concentrates on the Frond's spacey jamming side, and even includes a twenty-minute-plus meditation entitled "Right On (Hippie Dream)." Despite the presence of tracks clocking in at eleven and seventeen minutes, **Superseeder** restores the eclectic balance of Saloman's best albums, stressing tunefulness and melodic wit on tracks like "Stoned Train Driver" and the humorously autobiographical "Animal Tracks." [ss]

BEWITCHED

Bewitched EP (Shove) 1986
Brain Eraser (No. 6) 1990
Harshing My Mellow (No. 6) 1991

Bewitched started as a joke. While on tour, Sonic Youth's Thurston Moore told the English music press that the group's former drummer, Bob Bert, had put together an exciting new band when, in fact, Bert had done nothing of the sort. Still, Paul Smith of London's Blast First read the story and offered to release the group's first record. Bert, who had recently ended his stint as drummer for Pussy Galore and needed a new gig, slapped together a post-psychedelic noise collage that proved so unlistenable that Smith rescinded the offer. Bert wound up releasing the disc himself, and the momentum from that project eventually led to the existence of an actual band.

For **Brain Eraser,** the first Bewitched full-lengther, Bert transferred his accumulated rhythmic skills to a drum machine, although he does get behind the drum kit for two instrumentals. Guitarist Jim Fu and bassist Chris Ward generate a dense, throbbing buzz, enhanced by turntable wiz Dave P's scratching and samples. In many ways, **Brain Eraser** is the best album Sonic Youth never made; Fu eschews standard guitar rock, preferring to wring twisted shards of sound from his instrument, while Bert's deadpan, monotone-chanted vocals mirror the delivery of former bandmate Kim Gordon.

On **Harshing My Mellow,** produced by Steve Albini, the swap of Jim Fu for Art Reinitz provides a more rockish guitar sound. But the band's grinding proto-industrial riffs are only a backdrop to Bewitched's real strengths: Bert's acidic sense of humor, encyclopedic knowledge of the current indie-rock scene and goofy, off-the-wall lyrics, like the bad acid trip described in "Orange Owsley," or "No. 1," a parody of big-time rock'n'roll in which Bert imagines himself sharing the stage with Axl Rose and "Mikey" Stipe. [jt]

See also *Action Swingers, Chrome Cranks, Sonic Youth.*

B-52'S

The B-52's (Warner Bros.) 1979
Wild Planet (Warner Bros.) 1980
Party Mix! EP (Warner Bros.) 1981
Mesopotamia EP (Warner Bros.) 1982
Whammy! (Warner Bros.) 1983
Bouncing off the Satellites (Warner Bros.) 1986
Cosmic Thing (Reprise) 1989
Dance This Mess Around: The Best of the B-52's (UK Island) 1990
Party Mix!/Mesopotamia (Reprise) 1991
Good Stuff (Reprise) 1992

FRED SCHNEIDER

Fred Schneider & the Shake Society (Warner Bros.) 1984 (Reprise) 1991
Just . . . Fred (Reprise) 1996

The charmed rise of the Athens, Georgia, sillies who first brought kitschy luncheonette camp and kinetic pogo power to the American underground during (and after) the new wave era came to a tragic end in October 1985, when guitarist Ricky Wilson died of AIDS shortly after the recording of **Bouncing off the Satellites.** (Upon its delayed release, the bittersweet, uneven album was dedicated to him.) Already on the brink of creative exhaustion and heartbroken by Wilson's death, the B-52's seemed over, but the four survivors slowly pulled themselves together and continued. Inevitably, though, the playful innocence that defined the group was gone, replaced by a self-conscious determination to have fun while supporting socially conscious activism. Drummer Keith Strickland switched to guitar and, with half-and-half production by Don Was and Nile Rodgers (kudos to both), the quartet cut **Cosmic Thing,** a forced-sounding record with a few great songs ("Roam," "Love Shack," "Deadbeat Club") and a lot of halfhearted ones. While not fully divining the lost soul of planet B, the album at least takes great advantage of the bit it did recapture. But rather than making sport of their beloved sources, the B-52's seem to be making campy fun of themselves.

Ironically (or understandably, depending on one's cynicism meter setting), **Cosmic Thing** became the B-52's' platinum-selling breakthrough. One long-shot winner couldn't pave over all of the band's internal bumps, however, and it took three years to get another album out of the gate. (In the interim, a remix of the David Byrne–produced **Mesopotamia** was issued on a joint CD with **Party Mix!,** offering easy access to the band's least-known records. For neophytes, the prime purchases are **The B-52's,** with "Rock Lobster" and "52 Girls," and **Wild Planet,** which boasts "Private Idaho" and "Party Out of Bounds." **Whammy!** is nearly essential for "Legal Tender" and "Song for a Future Generation.")

The mysterious departure of singer Cindy Wilson left the trio of Strickland, singer Fred Schneider and singer/keyboardist Kate Pierson to make **Good Stuff,** again produced by the Was/Rodgers tag team. It's another uneven collection. "Good Stuff," with its powerhouse harmony bridge, and the rich UFO fantasy of "Is That You Mo-Dean?" are primo nonsense, and "Revolution Earth" boasts a gorgeous Pierson vocal, but skimpy songwriting and creeping seriousness undercut the record's superficially appealing spirit. "Vision of a Kiss" is straight romantic stuff; fashion nostalgia can't separate Fred Schneider's "Hot Pants" from the obviousness of its desire; and the idealism of "Breezin'" dissolves into drivel ("We got to get it together" ???). All the sonic giddiness Was and Rodgers can cobble together just can't make the B-52's' cheerfulness seem sincere.

Schneider's first album was very much in keeping with the band's joyful charms; his second is quite the opposite. With producer Steve Albini riding noisy herd on three groovy backing bands—Shadowy Men on a Shadowy Planet, Six Finger Satellite and the Deadly Cupcake (a pickup trio drafted from the ranks of Tar, the Supersuckers and the Jon Spencer Blues Explosion), **Just . . . Fred** mistakenly attempts to reposition the beloved entertainer as an indie shouter. Straining like the neighborhood nerd making a fool of himself auditioning for the local punk combo, Fred's hapless efforts to keep up with the unfamiliar rock aggression on songs like "Whip," "Sugar in My Hog" and "Bad Dream" strand him in vocal hell. A bad idea on paper, the record is worse in the hearing, an embarrassing square peg/round hole disaster. [i]

See also *TPRG.*

JELLO BIAFRA

No More Cocoons (Alternative Tentacles) 1987
High Priest of Harmful Matter–Tales From the Trial (Alternative Tentacles) 1989
I Blow Minds for a Living (Alternative Tentacles) 1991
Beyond the Valley of the Gift Police (Alternative Tentacles) 1994

LARD

The Power of Lard EP (Alternative Tentacles) 1988
The Last Temptation of Reid (Alternative Tentacles) 1990

JELLO BIAFRA WITH D.O.A.

Last Scream of the Missing Neighbors EP (Alternative Tentacles) 1990

JELLO BIAFRA WITH NOMEANSNO

The Sky Is Falling and I Want My Mommy (Alternative Tentacles) 1991

TUMOR CIRCUS

Tumor Circus (Alternative Tentacles) 1991

JELLO BIAFRA WITH PLAINFIELD

Jello Biafra With Plainfield EP (Alternative Tentacles) 1993

JELLO BIAFRA WITH MOJO NIXON

Will the Fetus Be Aborted? EP (Alternative Tentacles) 1993
Prairie Home Invasion (Alternative Tentacles) 1994

VARIOUS ARTISTS

Terminal City Ricochet (Alternative Tentacles) 1989

Since the shuttering of San Franciscan political punk provocateurs Dead Kennedys in the late '80s, Jello Biafra (born Eric Boucher in Boulder, Colorado) has continued to ply his prankster-cum-missionary trade with spoken-word records and enough intriguing musical collaborations to qualify him as the Julio Iglesias of the underground set. Until he was set upon by skinheads and seriously injured in the fabled East Bay 924 Gilman club in May '94, Biafra was busily and enthusiastically proving that even old punks can change their musical stripes without endangering their synergistic sense of humor *and* outrage.

The political satire of **No More Cocoons** was recorded at college appearances, radio interviews and readings. Biafra has found his ideal medium here, and this is as sharp, funny and informative as any Dead Kennedys record. Biafra applies his acerbic wit, endless outrage, abundant intelligence and theatricality to a variety of concerns, making the record highly worthwhile and grimly amusing. Those old enough to remember Lenny Bruce or even Mort Sahl in his prime may consider this topical comedy in the grand tradition; younger listeners may find it a fruitful inkling of what Biafra was singing about in the DKs.

As someone whose outspoken opinions and freethinking actions are enough to bring down the legal wrath of the land's moral guardians, it's convenient that Biafra has an independent record label on which to rebut his accusers. Following his 1987 acquittal for "distribution of harmful matter to minors" (a case resulting from artwork included in the DKs' **Frankenchrist**), Biafra spewed out **High Priest of Harmful Matter,** an absurdist post-mortem on his frightening brush with the justice system. On **I Blow Minds for a Living,** recorded on tour in late '90 and early '91, he rants merrily about then-president George Bush, censorship, petroleum politics and the Gulf War, censorship, his actual mayoral campaign, censorship, pot, censorship and another one of his favorite topics, censorship. Good, angry fun, dripping sarcasm through a sharpened point. **Beyond the Valley of the Gift Police,** arising from several 1994 appearances, fills an attention-daring three CDs with further lectures on (no points for this one) censorship, retailers' suppression, anti-gay amendments and the like. In addition, Biafra offers a serio-comic wish list for the future and a resonantly entertaining news-driven reminiscence of his curious childhood. Other than its daunting length, the set's major flaw is the cloddish editing, which inserts brief, jarringly different-sounding bits.

In between making two records by Lard (a promising partnership with Ministry that didn't quite mesh), Biafra starred in and performed on the soundtrack of *Terminal City Ricochet.* The 1989 Canadian film's soundtrack contains tracks by assorted Alternative Tentacles bands as well as Biafra's musical collaborations with D.O.A., NoMeansNo and Keith LeBlanc. As a side effect, he took a step toward resuming his musical career with **Last Scream of the Missing Neighbors,** a roaring rock record that puts his trademark whiny vocals and songs to D.O.A.'s meat-and-cojones guitar power. Through a half-dozen numbers like "Wish I Was in El Salvador," "Attack of the Peacekeepers" and the epic "Full Metal Jackoff," **Last Scream** proudly re-hoists the DK flag in all but name.

With that test successfully fluttering in the Canadian rock breeze, Biafra was off and running. He teamed with high-pressure British Columbia prog/thrash jokers NoMeansNo for **The Sky Is Falling and I Want My Mommy,** a dense explosion of political punk vehemence. Returning to the quivering vocal frequencies of the Dead Kennedys, Biafra paces the racing music slam for slam. Except for the evenly paced and horn-charged "Bruce's Diary," the eight songs whiz by in a hypertense blur of topical aggression. Typically, Biafra overloads his shopping cart with brightly packaged issues—bio-engineering ("Sharks in the Gene Pool"), urban decay ("Chew"), hypocrisy ("The Myth Is Real—Let's Eat"), space junk (the title track)—but he also displays a more humane side here. Despite a spot of structural anxiety, "Ride the Flume" actually enthuses about an amusement park attraction (and quotes the "George of the Jungle" theme).

The groaning, moaning grub-soaking crud of **Tumor Circus** finds Biafra slinging demi-melodic gutter poetry like a revved-up Nick Cave in a group made up of San Francisco's Steel Pole Bath Tub and guitarist Charlie Tolnay of Australia's King Snake Roost. Over a godawful racket that provides a horrific rock analogue to the delirium tremens, a suitably loose-sounding Biafra roars lengthy texts of news headlines ("Take Me Back or I'll Drown Our Dog"), secret societies ("Hazing for Success"), metaphoric illness ("Swine Flu") and metaphoric pinball ("Fireball"). "Meathook Up My Rectum" pulls out a gamut of things that get him mad. A load of filthy rubbish—and one of the best things Biafra has ever done. At the other end of the spectrum, the pointlessly stupid **Jello Biafra With Plainfield** is his own take on Beavis and Butt-head make a record. Guitarist Smelly Mustafa, bassist Cooties and drummer Edward Gein (ha-ha) thrash away sloppily as Biafra and Smelly engage in crude, offensive and boring low-rent sketch comedy for nineteen unendurable minutes.

Not content with sinking that low, Biafra married himself into Mojo Nixon's loopy clan, the Toadliquors, for a lusciously lurid roots-rock romp. The duo previewed their joint album with a topical single of "Will the Fetus Be Aborted?" (a parody of "Will the Circle Be Unbroken?" written by Darryl Cherney and Judi Bari); the CD EP also contains a second album track, the non-LP "Lost World" and an unrelated country spoof by Eugene Chadbourne and Evan Johns.

Biafra hardly has the voice or style for the rustic music on **Prairie Home Invasion,** but it don't make no nevermind. Whether updating Phil Ochs' "Love Me, I'm a Liberal," ripping meet-the-new-boss sellout bands in "Buy My Snake Oil," deflating cultural illusions in "Nostalgia for an Age That Never Existed" or trotting out that irreverent standby, "Plastic Jesus," JB makes Mojo's bud-guzzling country honk work for him with cavalier aplomb. For his part, king dick Nixon is moved to serious current events concern in "Hamlet Chicken Plant Disaster," although his other spotlight numbers are the more typical "Let's Go Burn Ole Nashville Down" and "Are You Drinkin' With Me Jesus," an inebriated howler he co-wrote for the Beat Farmers, which dares the deity: "I know you can walk on water/But can you walk on this much beer?" [i]

See also *Mojo Nixon, Pigface, Steel Pole Bath Tub; TPRG.*

BIFF BANG POW!

Pass the Paintbrush, Honey . . . (UK Creation) 1985
Love's Going Out of Fashion EP (UK Creation) 1986
The Girl Who Runs the Beat Hotel (UK Creation) 1987
Oblivion (Creation/Relativity) 1987
Love Is Forever (Creation/Relativity) 1988

The Acid House Album (UK Creation) 1989
Songs for the Sad Eyed Girl (UK Creation) 1990
L'amour, Demure, Steinhousemuir. A Compilation 1984–1991 (UK Creation) 1991
Me (UK Creation) 1991
Debasement Tapes (UK Creation) 1992
Bertula Pop (Creation/TriStar Music) 1994

For the better part of a decade, Biff Bang Pow!—the music-making endeavor of Creation Records founder/leader Alan McGee—has been a touchstone to the influential label's definition and development, albeit one that never assumed the limelight or achieved any major hits. (Having named his label for the great '60s aggro-art-mod group, it was probably inevitable that the Glaswegian's band, which has never used the Creation for specific musical cues, would take its moniker from a Creation song.) From the initial recordings, rife with brisk, neo-psychedelic garage pop, to the spare, acoustic laments at the end, Biff Bang Pow! ambled along, releasing a string of well-conceived and -executed singles and albums that still sound fresh. (The smoothly accomplished **Oblivion** is the most immediately appealing of the bunch; the psychedelicized **Pass the Paintbrush, Honey** and the well-written but poorly produced **The Girl Who Runs the Beat Hotel** are worthy of investigation as well.)

The group's final record, **Me,** is subtitled *More Songs for the Sad Eyed Girl,* which makes sense, since it builds on the legacy of that 1990 album with a solitary sound unlike the fleshier arrangements of prior albums. The ten songs are, for the most part, acoustic ballads alternately celebrating and crying over love. "There's only one thing worth living for and it's love," McGee sorrowfully notes on "Miss You," as mournful slide guitar and an uncommonly thick atmosphere well up around his vocals and gentle strumming. McGee's lovelorn lyrics do become a bit self-obsessed, but as a study in the delicate affairs of the heart, **Me** works.

"Miss You" is one of two cuts from **Me** on the American **Bertula Pop** compilation, which culls Biff Pang Pow!'s entire oeuvre, including **The Acid House Album,** a misleadingly titled collection of outtakes, alternate versions and demos. The five fervently strummed acoustic cuts from **Love Is Forever** (including the wonderful "She Paints" and "She Haunts") stand proudly here, as does the jangly "She's Got Diamonds in Her Hair," the lone cut from **Oblivion.** The organ-drenched "Someone Stole My Wheels" (one of two from **The Girl Who Runs the Beat Hotel**) is a reminder that McGee was once pissed off as well as sad as hell, while **Songs for the Sad Eyed Girl**'s lonesome version of the Television Personalities' "Someone to Share My Life With" is equally effective. [la]

See also *TPRG.*

BIG AUDIO DYNAMITE

This Is Big Audio Dynamite (Columbia) 1985
No. 10, Upping St. (Columbia) 1986
Tighten Up Vol. 88 (Columbia) 1988
Megatop Phoenix (Columbia) 1989
F-Punk (Radioactive) 1995
Planet BAD: Greatest Hits (Columbia) 1995

BIG AUDIO DYNAMITE II

Kool-Aid (UK CBS) 1990
The Globe (Columbia) 1991
On the Road '92 EP (Columbia) 1992
Lost Treasures of Big Audio Dynamite I & II (Japan. Sony) 1993

BIG AUDIO

Higher Power (Columbia) 1994
Looking for a Song (Columbia) 1994

Big Audio Dynamite's first two albums, **This Is Big Audio Dynamite** and **No. 10, Upping Street,** were not just excellent but also hugely influential, spawning a dubious slew of early-'90s guitar'n'sample bands: EMF, Urban Dance Squad, Jesus Jones and others. With former Clash guitarist Mick Jones' homely everyman vocals and dance beats anchoring some fairly ambitious sonic collagery by filmmaker/DJ Don Letts, the music reflected the trendiest club and hip-hop sounds of the day. Through various lineups and name permutations, none of Jones' ensuing albums have matched the catchy sing-song melodies, cinematic sampling and sheer innovation of the first two, which contain such staples as "E=MC2" and "The Bottom Line" (**Big Audio Dynamite**) and "C'mon Every Beatbox" and the Strummer/Jones-written "V. Thirteen" (**No. 10**). The problem lies in the fact that, for all the resourceful soundbiting and up-to-the-minute dance beats, Big Audio Dynamite is ultimately a pop band—and as such lives or dies by the strength of its songwriting.

Jones dissolved the original lineup after **Megatop Phoenix** and reconvened the group as Big Audio Dynamite II, with bassist Gary Stonadge, guitarist Nick Hawkins and drummer Chris Kavanagh, late of Sigue Sigue Sputnik. The new lineup was unveiled on the limited-edition scattered **Kool-Aid** (an eight-song stopgap containing a version of "Free," the band's contribution to the *Flashback* soundtrack), and given its full debut on **The Globe.** The album's first four tracks bode well for the new outfit. The minor MTV hit "Rush" (with its witty "Baba O'Riley" sample) is an inspired blend of art and commerce. A not-so-distant cousin of the Replacements' "Can't Hardly Wait," "Can't Wait" is a bit of hi-tech uptempo soul punctuated by the group's trademark sampling of upper-class Englishmen reciting pompous doggerel; "I Don't Know" introduces a refreshing note of foreboding. Finishing up the quartet, the title track is a bone-simple party stomper. After that, **The Globe** falls off axis precipitously, bottoming out with the maudlin ballad "Innocent Child" and an ill-advised medley, "The Tea Party." (The following year's tour yielded **On the Road,** an EP containing live versions of the album's "Kool-Aid," "Can't Wait," "Innocent Child" and "Rush," plus **Megatop**'s "Contact.")

While Jones dropped the Dynamite for **Higher Power,** the band itself swelled to a sextet, adding turntablist Mickey "Lord Zonka" Custance and B.A.D. producer Andre Shapps on keyboards. Nonetheless, **Higher Power** finds Jones and company operating at a decidedly lower level. The hip dance-music sounds are there, but the tunes most certainly aren't. "It ain't as easy as it looks/Coming up with all those hooks," Jones sings on the unintentionally ironic "Looking for a Song." A couple of fair tracks—"Some People" and "Over the Rise"—are not nearly enough to save the show. Props are due, however, for sampling Leadbelly on the Kinksy closer, "Hope."

The limited-edition **Looking for a Song** valiantly

attempts to prop up a weak number (presented in three mixes) with dispensable '94 live takes on "Medicine Show" and "Rush" and a fifteen-track bonus disc, **Greatest Hits—The Radio Edits,** which includes such past triumphs as "E=MC2," "C'mon Every Beatbox," "Contact," "Just Play Music" and "The Globe."

By the time of 1995's **F-Punk** (a witty play on "P-Funk"), Jones must surely have taken notice of the Clash comparisons being accorded California's new generation of platinum upstarts. "I Turned Out a Punk," the lead-off track, is a smug, blatant attempt to exploit his own legendary résumé (as is the album cover's shameless reference to **London Calling**). The rest of the album is apparently Jones' attempt to cash in on his formidable legacy by largely abandoning dance sounds for unexceptional, straight-ahead rock—it's emblematic of the band's stylistic change that "Push Those Blues Away" drops a promising jungle beat for plain-jane rock. Still, modern techno steps excitingly to the fore on "It's a Jungle Out There," while "Psycho Wing" is the album's only credible rocker.

As the producer of the **Planet BAD** retrospective, Jones turns a blind eye to some of his own strengths (giving **No. 10 Upping Street** and the underrated **Megatop Phoenix** short shrift) and weaknesses (too much '90s-era material). Yet **Planet BAD** hits some high points and accurately documents the band's story in that its quality diminishes as the disc wears on. Having made the huge stylistic leap from the Clash to Big Audio Dynamite, Mick Jones has already reinvented himself once. Perhaps it's time to do it again. [ma]

See also *TPRG*.

BIG BLACK

See *Shellac*.

BIG CHIEF

Drive It Off (Get Hip) 1991
Face (UK Repulsion) 1991 (Sup Pop) 1992
Mack Avenue Skullgame (Sub Pop) 1993
Big Chief Brand Product EP (Ger. Sub Pop) 1993
Platinum Jive (Greatest Hits 1966–99) (Revolution/Capitol) 1994

THORNETTA DAVIS WITH THE BIG CHIEF BAND

Shout Out EP (Ger. Sub Pop) 1994

With a grungey guitar attack and sludgy sonics, Big Chief's early records sound like prototypical '90s Seattle—except the band is from Ann Arbor, Michigan. Formed by members of a number of popular local groups (Laughing Hyenas, Necros, McDonalds, Posse From Hell), Big Chief embraced a wide swath of hard-rock influences, ranging from righteous homeboys the MC5 and the Stooges to Black Sabbath, Blue Cheer and Black Flag. The twist is in the funk, however; Big Chief hails from George Clinton country, too, and their debt to Dr. Funkenstein—an obligation none of their forebears knew from—would become obvious later on.

It was all balls to the wall in the beginning. Forming in 1989, Big Chief eschewed the Detroit/Ann Arbor club scene and took its act worldwide, drumming up attention in Britain with the series of singles that are collected on **Drive It Off.** Heavy and savage, the album had more to offer than much of the hardcore scene at the time, though it lacked cohesiveness. That problem was resolved with **Face,** a titanium monster that ranks among the best albums produced in Michigan's rich rock heritage. "Fresh Vines" kicks things off with a murky, Sabbath-style intro lumbering into a molten groove of grinding guitars (Mark Dancey and Phil Durr) and a thundering rhythm section (bassist Matt O'Brien and drummer Mike Danner); Detroit R&B diva Thornetta Davis provides a striking counterpoint to Barry Henssler's guttural roar. The rest of **Face** is filled with steel-booted stomps ("The Ballad of Dylan Cohl," "Drive It Off," "500 Reasons") as well as murky mood pieces like "Desert Jam." A primal delight.

Mack Avenue Skullgame is a different animal entirely, a film soundtrack that's an oddity in the Big Chief oeuvre. It's more the work of a collective than a band, as Big Chief expands its ranks and its sound; there's much more spare, almost ambient funk and incidental musical passages. The album contains its share of good songs—"Soul on a Roll," "Let's Do It Again," "Cut to the Chase"—but it's not nearly as satisfying as **Face.**

The quintet more than makes amends, though, on its major-label debut, **Platinum Jive.** The rock/funk synthesis is even more seamless, resulting in heavy music that drives hard and with great invention—including ample spicy sonic details provided by flutes, horns and deftly arranged backup vocals. There's a rap number ("Bona Fide," with Schoolly D) and a soul croon called "Simply Barry," but mostly **Platinum Jive** rocks and roils, from the slamming opener "Lion's Mouth" through the trippy "Your Days Are Numbered" and the relentlessly rhythmic "The Liquor Talkin'." Kudos also to the packaging, a hilarious sendup of greatest-hits albums that even lists fictional solo records by the individual Big Chiefs (Henssler's is called **The Sexual Intellectual**). The group's outside activities—including the irreverent *Motorbooty* magazine, which Dancey edits—tend to put a bit of time between Big Chief's releases, but the next one can't come too soon.

The six-cut **Big Chief Brand Product** has items from **Face** and **Mack Avenue** as well as non-LP matter; the five-songer with Thornetta Davis (now recording as a solo artist on Sub Pop) includes a **Mack Avenue** tune and a couple of funk covers. [gg]

BIG COUNTRY

The Crossing (Mercury) 1983
Steeltown (Mercury) 1984
The Seer (Mercury) 1986
Peace in Our Time (Reprise) 1988
Through a Big Country: Greatest Hits (UK Mercury) 1990
No Place Like Home (UK Phonogram) 1991
The Buffalo Skinners (Fox) 1993
The Best of Big Country (Mercury) 1994
Radio 1 Sessions (Dutch East India Trading) 1994
BBC Live in Concert (UK Windsong International) 1995
Why the Long Face (Pure) 1995

Although continued British chart success gives lie to the perception, Big Country sure has made a lot of records for a band that hit its creative peak on its first two singles ("Fields of Fire" and "In a Big Country," both included on **The Crossing**) in 1983. Graduates of the punk era, Big Country harnessed ex-Skids Stuart Adamson's distinctive Scottish accent, grand romantic sensibilities and bagpipe-aping guitar lines (bolstered by second stringman Bruce Watson) to muscular rock power and participated in the '80s effort to shunt the new wave's creative ambition off into credible commercial rock. Smart (or lucky) enough to establish an enduringly potent signature sound right off the bat, Big Country never had a second great idea but has still been able to coast for more than a decade on uneven, largely redundant songwriting.

As the first step in a path that led straight down to the antiseptic, technologically overrun **Peace in Our Time, The Crossing**—brilliantly produced by Steve Lillywhite—is nearly all the Big Country anyone needs. As a useful companion that ties up the loose ends, **The Best of Big Country**—and its UK equivalent, **Through a Big Country**—includes "Wonderland," "East of Eden" and a few other subsequent worthies with all the crap (running up through 1991's **No Place Like Home**).

Following a five-year absence from the American record racks (and an even longer US touring gap)—during which time drummer Mark Brzezicki left and returned—Big Country dropped back into sight with **The Buffalo Skinners,** a zealous, self-produced wheel-spinner with loads of urgent, anthemic guitar. It's not that far in sound from Bon Jovi or Bryan Adams, but no amount of instrumental flash can hide knuckleheaded verses like this, from "Long Way Home": "Out upon the China Sea/Boats will run eternally . . . Half-million Nixon babies/Some with toys and some with rabies." Elsewhere, Adamson continues a trait inaugurated on **No Place Like Home,** relocating the geographical loci of his lyrics in "The Selling of America" and "We're Not in Kansas."

Why the Long Face ably integrates Big Country's familiar strengths into a much tastier brew, one that steers clear of egregious lyrical minefields and soaks deep in the band's original Scot-o-sonic rock formula. Not surprisingly, there isn't a single untested idea here—unless the terrible cover of Lou Reed's "Vicious" or an unplugged bumpkin version of "In a Big Country" (both tracks added as bonuses to the album's American issue) count—but unabashed vitality redeems the band's traditionalism. In Adamson's words, "I'm not ashamed of the things I've done/I took the blame when I could have run." If there's a musical ethos in there somewhere, good on him.

The simply played, weakly mixed studio broadcast performances on **Radio 1 Sessions** date from '82 and '83; six of the eight songs come off **The Crossing,** although no singles are among them. The genuine 1989 London show documented on the full-length **BBC Live in Concert,** on the other hand, has all the early songs anyone would want to hear given full-on renditions before an audibly enthusiastic audience. Adamson's haiverin' song introductions are an amusing bonus. [i]

See also *TPRG*.

BIG DRILL CAR

Small Block EP (Varient) 1988 (Cruz) 1990
Album Type Thing (Cruz) 1989
Tape Type Thing [tape] (Cruz) 1989
CD Type Thing [CD] (Cruz) 1989
Batch (Cruz) 1991
Toured (A Live Album) (Headhunter/Cargo) 1992
No Worse for the Wear (Headhunter/Cargo) 1994

Orange County, California's Big Drill Car specializes in bouncy punk-pop, full of hooks, harmonies and exuberant playing. Frank Daly's earnest and clear vocals and Mark Arnold's sharp, efficient guitar work brighten the six-song **Small Block,** a near-perfect introduction to a very likable quartet. The inexplicably French-titled "Les Cochons Sans Poils," which suggests the group has listened to as much Cheap Trick as Black Flag, stands out on a record whose only disappointment is its brevity. The band's first full-length opus (the title of which is format-specific) mines similar terrain, though only a couple of the tracks are as immediately catchy. Still, as the jaunty "16 Lines," "No Need" and "About Us" prove, you'd be hard-pressed to find a band straddling the hardcore, power pop and hard rock fences with more finesse and enthusiasm.

Batch upholds the group's stylistic consistency: riffs, tunes and punchy rhythms collide in an enjoyable blend of big rock, vampy thrashfunk and nicely detailed pop that hardly belongs on a punk-rooted indie label. The originals (with typically loopy titles like "Freep," "Ick" and "Restless Habs") are engaging without quite reaching irresistibility ("Faster" comes close); the metal-edged cover of Devo's "Freedom of Choice" is pointless.

The live **Toured** was recorded for $215 at CBGB in the fall of '91; capping off a brisk half-hour of the band's zippiest rock originals is a distressingly sober rock cover of Billy Joel's gruesome "Big Shot."

No Worse for the Wear might describe Daly and Arnold on the Big Drillers' third studio full-length, but the band's original rhythm section didn't make it and was replaced. Otherwise, the album continues into a loud power-pop domain not far from Material Issue, Smoking Popes or the Lemonheads—all informed by abiding Cheap Trick instincts. Tight, focused and nearly free of **Batch**'s incipient arena proclivities, **No Worse** is Big Drill Car's best, a bracing blast of nifty chord maneuvers, songcraft and harmony-brushed singing. Oh, and the song titles are fashioned to standard specifications ("Nagaina," "Hye"). [db/i]

BIG ELECTRIC CAT

Dreams of a Mad King (Cleopatra) 1994
Burning Embers (Cleopatra) 1995

Maybe Big Electric Cat's thoroughly original interpretation of the gothic sound results from being based in Sydney, Australia, maybe not. In any case, the band's surprisingly enthusiastic method is on spirited display in **Dreams of a Mad King.** Guitarist Paul Sadler's emotional vocals alternate from a sensual purr to a menacing snarl, all the while sounding a lot like INXS's Michael Hutchence. His instrumental efforts produce a shimmery, slinky mix of acoustic and electric melodies. Bassist David Block and keyboardist/programmer Deborah Denton wrap the material in haunting, dramatic flourishes and undercurrents, crafting a sound that's moody and atmospheric, with a twist of decidedly non-goth warmth and color. In fact, the only emotionless element here is the drum machine.

Burning Embers is an unfortunate attempt to milk more mileage from the debut. Remixes of songs from **Dreams of a Mad King** recklessly turn the once-powerful, provocative compositions into generic club-oriented bits of nightmarish offal. [ky]

BIG F

The Big F (fff/Elektra) 1989
Patience Peregrine EP (fff/Chrysalis) 1993
The Big F Is (fff/Chrysalis) 1993

TERRI NUNN

Moment of Truth (DGC) 1991

As if '80s sexed-up synth-pop fluke Berlin wasn't enough cultural frottage for one batch of Californians to inflict, the group's two main figures continued to record (separately) into the early '90s. Bassist/singer John Crawford and drummer Rob Brill formed the Big F, a loud power trio that came out swinging (although cloaked in anonymity) with an album of overheated pre-grunge brutery. Other than Crawford's guttural singing and pretentiously malevolent lyrics, **The Big F** is passably awful, a middle-of-the-gutter compromise between thuggish metal and sluggish thrash.

That smug effort fell before the onslaught of bands with more conviction and style, and it was four years until the trio put something else in the racks. The four-song EP and album (which also contains "Patience Peregrine") generally peruse the same raging hard-rock vein, although co-producers Ed Stasium and Simon Hanhart help sculpt an intriguingly surly sound; **The Big F Is** goes afield enough to include a trumpet solo (on the instrumentally restrained "Lube") and the nearly acoustic "Mother Mary." Without adding anything original, the lengthy slabs of tumescent guitar raunch have muscle, skill and scraps of melody, making this uninspired utilitarian post–Zep/sub–Pearl Jam melodrama ideal for those who can't get enough of the Cult, Stone Temple Pilots or Porno for Pyros. But the phony growl and nonsensical apocalypse imagery ("True faith, conquer the globe/Soul chain, sinners and saviors") draw a big zero, as does the album's ludicrous liner-note admonishment, "Get fucked to: each and every fascist." That'll fix their wagons.

For *her* futile second act, Berlin singer Terri Nunn (actually, a Los Angeles native whose early career was as a TV actress) hooked up with onetime Prince associate David Z, who produced and drummed, and Underworld guitarist Karl Hyde, who played and co-wrote four numbers. This dull-as-dirt generic rock pancake fails to establish Nunn as anything but . . . the former singer of Berlin. On "89 Lines," she makes her borrowed political statement: "When I flag down a cab it doesn't stop/Not because I look dangerous or nothing like that/It's not 'cause he's off duty/It's 'cause I'm black." (Shades of Steve Martin . . .) In the more relevant "Desire Me," Nunn runs down her trusty list—"Birth/Love/Pain/Sex/Desire"—as if it were the pinnacle of wit and insight. In the little world of **Moment of Truth**—which more than anything sounds like late-'80s Pat Benatar outtakes—it is. [i]

BIG FISH ENSEMBLE

Extra Spicy [tape] (Sardine) 1990
Way Out West [tape] (Sardine) 1991
Field Trip (Long Play) 1992
I Hate Parties (Long Play) 1993
Lucky (Long Play) 1995

Atlanta's Big Fish Ensemble is one of the best relatively unknown pop bands in America. The Georgia group's laid-back music combines snatches of folk, rock, country and blues, adding a lyrical slant that mixes satire and an exaggerated kind of peculiar populism that goes back to the tall tales of the rural South. Now and again, hints of Talking Heads, Velvet Underground, Camper Van Beethoven and other intellectual popsters surface in their sound, but Big Fish is its own ensemble, and both the group's musical prowess and the cleverness of its tunes have grown by leaps and bounds over its first five years.

The Big Fish Ensemble began as a strictly improvisational gang of artists with no set musical goals. They banged on pots and pans and made up the words to songs as they went along. This early incarnation, dubbed Big Wall of Shit, was locally legendary for its anarchic shows. By the late '80s, they had settled down and become a "regular" band, and soon began issuing original cassettes. Five multi-instrumentalists allowed the group to range far and wide in the indulgence of their unique eclecticism. Paul Schwartz sings and plays guitar and trombone; Sheila Doyle handles violin and bass; Leigh Finlayson plays bass, bass clarinet, trumpet and sings; main songwriter Michael Lorant (who, like Doyle, has contributed instrumentally to several Indigo Girls albums) is the drummer as well as a vocalist and acoustic guitarist; David Clair plays guitar, sax and vocals.

Originally recorded as a demo, **Field Trip** is crammed with absurdist humor, high intellectual concepts, real melodies and impressive chops—imagine Talking Heads fronted by Dan Hicks. Despite its humble beginnings, the album has no shortage of memorable moments: a hallucinogenic cowboy ballad ("Way Out West"), a tune about alienation and pretensions that sports a Bacharach-ish horn chart ("Young Artists") and a cynical rocker ("Message From Ferdinand") that could keep company with the best work of XTC.

I Hate Parties includes material that predates **Field Trip,** songs considered too happy or too goofy. The wit and musicianship is sharper than on the debut—no mean feat. (The Indigo Girls sing harmonies on "Animal.") The title track sounds like a falling-down-drunk frat anthem—until you listen to the words. "I wish I'd stayed at home and watched TV/I hate parties more than anything." Other potential hits: "Greenland" (a string-drenched bit of cynical Anglo pop), "Amy No" (a fatalistic lament accented by Doyle's mournful mountain fiddle), "Bad Driver" (a chooglin' ode to the dark side of the road) and the cheery "Where the Fuckheads Roam."

David Clair left the band just after recording **Lucky;** while the new live quartet is reported to be louder and more aggressive, the album's scattershot pop is still quietly quirky. **Lucky** follows the Big Fish blueprint, although the subject matter is more downbeat and the music bluesier. Most of the songs explore the wreckage of failed relationships, and dead-end lives fueled by booze and bad luck. But there's more: "Robert" is a doleful tune that limns Dole's spinelessness, "Devil" gets into the mind of a paranoid right-winger and "Sunday Morning" delivers a typical secular humanist's nightmares about religion with plenty of metallic crunch. The Indigos lend their pipes to the harmonies on "City of Sin," another sad tale of futile love, while Kelly Hogan (ex–Jody Grind) sings on "Blue Streak" and "Some Heroic Punk." [jp]

BIGGEST SQUARE THING

See *Shams.*

BIG HEAD TODD AND THE MONSTERS

Another Mayberry (Big) 1989 (Giant) 1994
Midnight Radio (Big) 1990 (Giant) 1994
Sister Sweetly (Giant/Reprise) 1992
Live EP (Giant/Reprise) 1993
Strategem (Giant) 1994

Seldom is releasing a live album the best career advice to offer a fledgling band, but Big Head Todd and the Monsters is an exception. A Colorado member of the improvisation-loving H.O.R.D.E. community, this three-piece fully realizes itself only in concert, where its indulgences are actually strengths. Todd Park Mohr is a tasteful guitarist who seldom repeats himself and who *doesn't* want to be Jimi Hendrix—an important distinction in the trio format. The Monsters—bassist Rob Squires and drummer Brian Nevin—are a supple and sympathetic rhythm section, versatile enough to follow whatever rock, roots, blues or jazz path Mohr chooses.

The band's chief problem has always been songwriting; as a composer, Mohr is a terrific player. On the self-released **Another Mayberry** and **Midnight Radio,** the songs often sound like thin frameworks for jams, though the latter has an early version of "Bittersweet" and "The Moose Song," while **Another Mayberry**'s title track is likable enough. **Sister Sweetly,** produced by David Z, is a revelation, however. By taking on mostly shorter songs, Mohr forces his writing to be tighter and more economical. The irony is that the delicately constructed "Bittersweet," at six minutes the album's longest cut, actually snared the group some radio play. But the rest of the album rewards those who come on board, offering a stylistic sweep from blues ("Circle," "Ellis Island") to the rhythmic "Groove Thing," the soulful "It's Alright," the chiming, spooky love song "Tomorrow Never Comes" and the strutting, funky title track.

The three-song **Live** EP, recorded during the 1993 H.O.R.D.E. tour, offers solid, expansive renderings of "Bittersweet" and "Circle" (plus a needless cover of Sly and the Family Stone's "Everyday People"), but doesn't fill the need for a full-fledged Monsters live album. Meanwhile, **Strategem** takes a step backward, lacking the songwriting focus Mohr appeared to be finding on **Sister Sweetly.** [gg]

BIG MIKE

See *Geto Boys.*

BIG STAR

#1 Record (Ardent) 1972
Radio City (Ardent) 1974
3rd (PVC) 1978
Sister Lovers (PVC) 1985
Big Star's Biggest (Ger. Line) 1987
Third/Sister Lovers (Rykodisc) 1992
Live (Rykodisc) 1992
#1 Record/Radio City (Stax/Fantasy) 1992
Columbia: Live at Missouri University 4/25/93 (Zoo) 1993

CHRIS BELL

I Am the Cosmos (Rykodisc) 1992

The '70s American power-pop group to which all good indie melodicists pray, Memphis' Big Star (named, prosaically enough, after a supermarket chain) released exactly two studio albums, **#1 Record** and **Radio City,** during its little-noticed lifespan; a third record meant as an Alex Chilton solo project and completed by the remnants of the shrinking group in 1974 wasn't even issued until the singer/guitarist/fuckup genius had thrown in the towel, knocked around various haunts and finally alighted in New York, where he formed a Bowery band with local pop undergrounders and started a new wave solo career. Loaded with timeless adult creations that have burrowed their way deep into the fertile topsoil out in left field, Big Star's albums have been reissued more times than anyone need know about. The last, variously titled **3rd, Sister Lovers** and a combination of the two, has been repeatedly resequenced, all the while picking up tracks like passengers on a commuter train. The 1992 edition—the original fourteen songs plus five outtakes, including covers of "Whole Lotta Shakin' Goin' On" and the Kinks' "Till the End of the Day"—seems definitive enough to last for a while.

Concurrent with that re-release, Rykodisc arranged for the posthumous issue of **I Am the Cosmos,** a beautiful and disturbing Syd-Barrett-by-way-of-Badfinger album of erratic, haunted pop music by Big Star cofounder Chris Bell. (The dope-and-depression-troubled guitarist, singer and songwriter quit after **#1 Record** and was killed in a 1978 car crash.) The label also fished out a 1974 Long Island radio broadcast—a pretty but uninspired and thin-sounding set by Chilton (performing solo acoustic for a third of the program), stalwart drummer/singer Jody Stephens and stand-in bassist John Lightman—complete with an interview segment and issued it as **Live.**

The appearance of a vintage Big Star concert album proved surprisingly portentous when an invitation extended to Stephens and Chilton to re-form their old group—twenty years after—for a spring festival date at Missouri University was unexpectedly accepted. Drafting Jon Auer (guitar/vocals) and Ken Stringfellow (bass/vocals) from Seattle's Posies—whose employment application was their PopLlama single of Big Star's "Feel" b/w Bell's "I Am the Cosmos"—to complete the intergenerational lineup, Stephens and Chilton did the gig in April '93, preserving the remarkable one-off for posterity on **Columbia.** (Confounding expectations further, the quartet has since actually toured.) Using all four vocalists to do loose-limbed justice to Big Star's best memories, this enthusiastic live greatest-hits is as good as it could possibly be. The under-rehearsed playing, if hardly air-tight, is free of preciousness and nostalgia and vibrantly on the emotional money; the sloppy singing is hearty and tuneful. Most incredibly, the bubbling energy level totally belies the age of these artifacts. (The songs, that is.) With the thoughtful inclusion of "I Am the Cosmos" as a tribute to their late bandmate, Big Star achieves a seamless time warp that reflects brilliantly on the past, the present and all concerned. [i]

See also *Alex Chilton, Posies; TPRG.*

BIG WHEEL

East End (Giant) 1989
Holiday Manor (Mammoth) 1992
Slowtown (Mammoth) 1993

STARBILLY

Master Vibrator (Buzz) 1994

Peter Searcy's gritty vocals helped make Louisville, Kentucky's Squirrel Bait the rage of indie-rock in the mid-'80s, when most of the band was still in high school. Big Wheel teamed him with the all-too-collegiate trio of guitarist Glenn Taylor, drummer Scott Langford and bassist Mike Bradon. (The band photo on the CD sleeve shows them shooting hoops.) Although "Bang, Bang, Bang," the first track on **East End,** comes close to capturing the feisty, Hüsker Dü–ish roar of Squirrel Bait, most of **East End** takes a much mellower tack—melodic, heartfelt campfire songs played on electric guitars.

Despite that promising debut, things did not go well for Big Wheel; **Holiday Manor,** released after a lengthy legal wrangle with Giant Records, finds the band on a new label with a new drummer, Tom Tompkins. Recording at Ardent Studios in Memphis, the quartet trades in whatever rough edges existed in its sound for facile, commercial pop; the slick production strips Searcy's vocals of any bite and makes him sound like Elton John crooning his treacliest ballads.

Happily, the band rebounded on its final album, **Slowtown.** Producer Paul Mahern (of the legendary midwestern punk band Zero Boys) relocates the sardonic edge in Searcy's vocals, and the songs of twentysomething angst and yearning make the perfect vehicle. Lyrically, the album's a complete downer, filled with songs of loss and mourning, missed opportunities and wrong choices. The poignant "Pete Rose" eulogizes the downfall of an American hero, while "Lazy Days" tenderly expresses the belief that tomorrow won't be any better than today ("Maybe we'll smile, maybe not/Maybe is all I've got in these lazy days"). In many ways, Big Wheel's generational angst mirrored the sentiments of the era's biggest hitmakers, but Taylor's clean, '70s-styled guitar leads distanced Big Wheel from the grunge bandwagon, and the group dissolved without ever finding an audience.

After Big Wheel's demise, Searcy and drummer Tom Tompkins put together Starbilly, recruiting two new guitar players and a bassist but changing very little else. Searcy still plays the tortured romantic on **Master Vibrator,** his throaty vocals wracked with regret and sadness. The singer effectively milks the songs for all the pathos they're worth, and never more so than on the aching, ballad-tempo cover of Hüsker Dü's speed-metal anthem, "Diane." Starbilly's two guitars give it a fuller sound than Big Wheel, but the group still draws its influences from '70s pop and metal, resisting the obvious commercial temptations to go grunge or punk. Instead, Searcy remains true to his original vision of middle-of-the-road, midwestern pop for fans who might feel threatened by bands trendier than themselves. [jt]

BIKINI KILL

Revolution Girl Style Now [tape] (no label) 1991
Bikini Kill EP (Kill Rock Stars) 1992
New Radio EP7 (Kill Rock Stars) 1993
Peel Sessions EP7 (no label) 1993
Pussy Whipped (Kill Rock Stars) 1993
The C.D. Version of the First Two Records (Kill Rock Stars) 1994
The Anti-Pleasure Dissertation EP7 (Kill Rock Stars) 1995
Reject All American (Kill Rock Stars) 1996

BIKINI KILL/HUGGY BEAR

Yeah Yeah Yeah Yeah/Our Troubled Youth (Kill Rock Stars/Catcall) 1993

VIVA KNIEVAL

Viva Knieval EP7 (Ultra-Sound) 1994

FAKES

Real Fiction (Chainsaw) 1995

On the strength of its legendary live shows, Bikini Kill—the archetypal riot grrrl band—was packing clubs before it even had a record out. Singer Kathleen Hanna, an American incarnation of X-Ray Spex's Poly Styrene, worked the crowd like a master preacher, singing, speechifying and switching between a little-girl voice and a full-throated howl, bringing girls to the front and attacking obnoxious guys, sometimes verbally, sometimes physically. Meanwhile, the band—guitarist Billy Karren (aka Billy Boredom), bassist Kathi Wilcox and drummer Tobi Vail (formerly half of the Go Team's core membership, with Beat Happening's Calvin Johnson)—bashed out passionate three-chord punk behind her; every so often, Vail would take over the mic for an even more confrontational number.

The eight-song tape **Revolution Girl Style Now,** sold at shows, is blandly recorded but gets down on tape the band's earliest anthems and their basic message: girls should be empowered, molesting children is bad and so forth. Subtle they're not, but sometimes a two-by-four is the only prescription. The six-song vinyl-only **Bikini Kill** EP includes "Carnival" from the cassette, plus new versions of four more of those songs, re-recorded with Ian MacKaye and Don Zientara. It also includes "Thurston Hearts the Who," a live recording of the band churning away, Vail ranting and Molly Neuman of Bratmobile furiously reading a magazine article that had the gall to be critical of Hanna and company. The record's politics are a little suspect ("Eat meat/Hate Blacks/Beat your fuckin wife/Its all the same thing"), but the ardor is unmistakable, especially on the anthemic "Feels Blind" and "Suck My Left One."

Unfortunately, that ardor is much harder to hear on **Yeah Yeah Yeah Yeah,** Bikini Kill's side of a split LP with British pals Huggy Bear. The wretched recording quality nearly ruins good songs like "This Is Not a Test," "Rebel Girl" and "White Boy"; the generally listless, sloppy performances don't help much either. (**Yeah Yeah Yeah Yeah** and **Bikini Kill** were later collected on a CD helpfully called **The C.D. Version of the First Two Records.**) "Rebel Girl" makes a much more successful second appearance on the three-song **New Radio** EP, produced by Bikini Kill role model Joan Jett, who joins in with a little guitar and singing. The title track is pretty hot too ("Come here baby let me kiss you like a boy does," Hanna yells). Both "New Radio" and "Demirep" also appear in not-so-great versions on the four-song **Peel Sessions** authorized bootleg.

For the definitive Bikini Kill record, look to the explosive **Pussy Whipped:** twelve songs (including a *third* "Rebel Girl"), twenty-four minutes, no prisoners. The high point is a white-hot diptych on sexual frustration, "Sugar" and "Star Bellied Boy"—by the end, Hanna is screaming her throat out, and the band matches her blow for blow. Vail gets in her best song yet ("Hamster Baby," a hilarious megaphone-assisted rant about British rock crit and riot grrrl bandwagoneer Everett True) and Wilcox, singing for the first time on record, nearly gets drowned out by her own song ("Speed Heart"). The closing love song, "For Tammy Rae," is instrumentally crude and a little out-of-tune, but really touching.

After a long absence, the band's reappearance with the four-song **Anti-Pleasure Dissertation** EP shows, more than anything else, that they've been listening to a lot of Huggy Bear. It's a dense little record: two hookless anthems and two short rants.

After another disappointing non-album single, "I Like Fucking," Bikini Kill mostly returned to form with **Reject All American.** For the first five minutes or so, it's raw electricity—the band charges out of the gate on "Statement of Vindication," and Hanna lets loose with an awesome bellow on the chorus of "Jet Ski." After that, though, the record gradually loses steam. Wilcox's "False Start" is surprisingly pretty, and Vail's two vocals serve basically the same purpose as John Entwistle's on Who records, but they both break the flow of the album, as does Hanna's dreadful ballad "R.I.P." And, maybe since they couldn't justify recording "Rebel Girl" again, its cousin—the title track—appears this time.

Members of Bikini Kill have recorded in a handful of side projects. Vail has made a half-dozen or so EPs with the Frumpies. Hanna's "Rock Star," a spoken-word piece on a single with Kill Rock Stars owner Slim Moon, is shattering, almost unbearably powerful; the EP by her pre–Bikini Kill band Viva Knieval, though, is dull, tough listening. The sole album by the Fakes, Hanna's project with Nation of Ulysses' Tim Green (and a guest cast of thousands) is a concept record in search of a concept, though it includes a sweet, sad piece she sings along with a music box playing the theme from **Love Story.** [ddw]

See also *Joan Jett.*

BIOHAZARD

Biohazard (Maze) 1990
Urban Discipline (Roadrunner) 1992
State of the World Address (Warner Bros.) 1994
Mata Leáo (Warner Bros.) 1996

While bands have traded in gang imagery since rock's beginnings, few have done so with the thuggish authenticity of this big, ugly cabal of blue-collar Brooklynites. Every bit as steely and rugged as the hardcore rappers who developed in the same borough—albeit a few neighborhoods over—the quartet manifests both anticipated macho posturing and bare-knuckled social commentary. Recently, it has augmented those characteristics with music that stimulates something besides the mosh reflex.

In the late '80s, when its members did everything but drive the shuttle bus between downtown Manhattan's hardcore punk hangouts and Brooklyn's metal clubs, Biohazard was known for a violent following and morally ambiguous songs that seemed to pick up where Charles Bronson's *Death Wish* character left off. The foursome's unrelentingly heavy debut is riddled with lurid imagery of the simpleminded boot-boy variety—as evidenced by "Survival of the Fittest" and "Retribution." Bassist and primary vocalist Evan Seinfeld (no relation) has a drill-sergeant bark that powers some of the more iffy ideas home on the strength of jut-jawed authority alone, but there's absolutely no way to defend the odious "Howard Beach," which reproaches the media for its harsh indictment of the white neighborhood that fomented a racially based murder that made national headlines.

Urban Discipline isn't exactly an about-face, but there is a sense that Biohazard has learned to think before making pronouncements like "Black and White and Red All Over," a cryptic missive that seems to call for racial brotherhood. (The band walked that walk when it teamed with the equally obstreperous Onyx on "Slam" and the theme to *Judgment Night,* neither of which is included here.) Guitarists Billy Graziadei and Bobby Hambel pull away ever so slightly from textbook thrash progressions, adding some impressively distended riffs into the icy "Chamber Spins Three" and "Business." While they spend altogether too much time ranting about uniting against the outside world (so much so, you'd swear David Koresh was one of the songwriters), there's the seed of—believe it or not—a sense of humor. At least one would hope there's some comic intent behind "We're Only Gonna Die (From Our Own Arrogance)."

The Onyx collaboration clearly had a big effect on Biohazard, since **State of the World Address** is shot through with hip-hop tinges, both obvious ("How It Is" has a cameo by Cypress Hill's Sen Dog) and subtle (Seinfeld's newfound hip-swang). Likewise, rather than simply switch off one song at a time, the vocalists pass the microphone line by line on tracks like "Tales From the Hard Side," evincing the dizzying on-point alacrity of a polished posse like Wu-Tang. And while there are still moments (the absurd "Human Animal") when you wish they'd shelve that dog-eared Nietzsche Cliff's Notes once and for all, they're even beginning to manifest traces of incontestably adult thought—see the downtrodden-working-man's anthem, "Five Blocks to the Subway." [dss]

BIZARR SEX TRIO

See *Pigface.*

BIZ MARKIE

Goin' Off (Cold Chillin'/Warner Bros.) 1988
The Biz Never Sleeps (Cold Chillin'/Warner Bros.) 1989
I Need a Haircut (Cold Chillin'/Warner Bros.) 1991
All Samples Cleared! (Cold Chillin'/Warner Bros.) 1993
Biz's Baddest Beats (Cold Chillin') 1994

Highly respected and well connected as both performer and producer among old-schoolers, New York rapper Biz Markie's juvenile sense of humor and shameless desire to entertain made his records the comic relief of late-'80s hip-hop. Between his relaxed backporch flow, good cheer and uninhibited silliness, the Biz (Marcel Hall) took the seriousness out of beatbox music. As crudely embarrassing as stuff on early albums like **Goin' Off** could be, occasional songs like "Just a Friend" and "Spring Again" (both on **The Biz Never Sleeps**) match Jonathan Winters' ability to pluck joy and laughs from the simplest things.

Biz Markie's playful career sank in the '90s when a song on **I Need a Haircut** left him the loser in a sample clearance court case that forced the album's recall and inspired the title of its followup. On a fairly diverting record that could have been suppressed on the basis of good taste—"T.S.R. (Toilet Stool Rap)" describes a sitdown creative process no one needs to hear about—what caused the ruckus was "Alone Again," a winsome rejection tale in which the Biz sang the chorus and bit the piano track of Gilbert O'Sullivan's "Alone Again (Naturally)."

"I don't give a damn if my record gets banned," declares the Biz within the first minute of **All Samples Cleared!**, a harder-edged album on which the cover depicts him in prison stripes pleading his case before a wigged-out judge. With so much detailed information in the booklet that there are probably cleared samples that aren't even on the record, (nobody beats the) Biz doesn't dwell on his recent legal troubles; instead, his songs touch on old-school nostalgia and complain about people calling him ugly and the women he's hot for. Still, the episode seems to have shaken his innocence. Other than "I'm Singin'," a lumbering stroll through pop standards like "Over the Rainbow" and "Singin' in the Rain," and the bluesy "Bad by Myself," the clown prince doesn't sound like he's having much fun. Now that's a crime.

Biz's Baddest Beats is a straightforward career anthology. [i]

See also *TPRG*.

BJÖRK

Björk (Ice. Falkinn) 1977
Debut (Elektra) 1993
Venus as a Boy EP (Elektra) 1993
Post (Elektra) 1995

BJÖRK GUDMUNDSDÓTTIR & TRIO GUDMUNDAR INGÓLFSSONAR

Gling-Gló (UK Smekkleysa/Mother/One Little Indian) 1990

Iceland's Björk Gudmundsdóttir sings with the nonlinear abandon of a jazz vocalist, squeals like a gradeschooler on Christmas morning and purrs with the feral lustiness of a big cat in pursuit of a meal. The spaced-out kewpie-doll vocal mannerisms can be wearying, but Björk's devotion to quirkiness has led to some of the most forward-looking dance-pop of the '90s.

Debut (the title is a misnomer: she actually recorded an album of children's songs at age twelve) is as much a triumph of Nellee Hooper's skills as a producer as it is of Björk's vocal abilities. With the Sugarcubes, the singer's vocabulary of warbles, trills and grrrs was just another layer in her bandmates' cacophony. Hooper, who redefined dance rhythm in his sensual Soul II Soul projects, clears away the sonic rubble and frames Björk's voice in a variety of flattering settings: the clubland churn of "Violently Happy," the winsome strings-and-things of the technicolor romance "Venus as a Boy," the space-bliss ambience of "Come to Me" and the sweet-and-sour horns of "The Anchor Song." But on the lesser tracks, Björk's vocal shortcomings are left painfully exposed. Her voice frayed and off-key, she mangles the standard "Like Someone in Love"; on "One Day," she goos and coos like a child—a pixiefied persona she has been mining with diminishing results since the days of the Sugarcubes' breakthrough "Birthday" single in 1987.

Hooper and Björk are reunited on a portion of **Post**, but this time the singer spreads the work among various producers of the moment, including Tricky, 808 State's Graham Massey and Mo Wax's Howie Bernstein. The result is a stunningly assured and diverse album, a tour of club-savvy beats, techno atmospherics and avant-garde filigrees, with Björk turning in her most assured batch of vocal performances ever. As usual, she lets her eccentricities gush, this time with a knowing wink on "Hyper-ballad": "Every morning I walk towards the edge/And throw little things off/Like car-parts, bottles and cutlery/Or whatever I find lying around." The album runs a stylistic gamut from the ominous bass-heavy throb of "Army of Me" to the brassy cover of "It's Oh So Quiet," a big-band oldie recorded by actress/singer Betty Hutton. Björk nails every nuance with previously unheard subtlety: pensive compassion on "You've Been Flirting Again," coy sensuality on "Possibly Maybe," hushed wonderment on "Cover Me." She's still the Girl Who Fell to Earth, but this time she brought along plenty of cool songs.

On **Gling-Gló**, recorded as a jovial digression while she was still a 'Cube, Björk—backed by a jazz trio making nice and snappy on piano, string bass and drums—gives her all to a collection of Icelandic pop classics. (Actually, the album contains two American ringers, Leiber/Stoller's "Ruby Baby" and Oscar Hammerstein II/Jerome Kern's "I Can't Help Loving That Man," which are its only English lyrics.) The novelty of another nation's unknown musical heritage aside, the album's charm is in Björk's robust singing—a typical panoply of tricks, delicacies and unpredictable explosions. It comes as no surprise that Björk is a truly amazing vocal stylist, but this ices the cake with wonderfully pure sweetness. [gk/i]

BJÖRN AGAIN

Flashback!/Live Album (UK M&G) 1994

Two things tribute bands don't usually do: make records and become international stars. Australia's Björn Again—a full-costume replica of ABBA, down to the mock-Swedish accents—has done both. (As a measure of the magnitude of the group's achievement and notoriety, Björn Again engaged Erasure in a playful—and well-publicized—vinyl joust. After the English duo cut a '92 EP of covers entitled **Abba-esque**, Björn Again defended their adopted franchise by replying with **Erasure-ish**, charting in the UK with an EP of that band's tunes.)

Riding the global wave of enthusiasm for all things '70s, the theatrical surrogates (a front line of ersatz Björn, Benny, Agnetha and Frida, plus a rhythm section led by bassist Rod Woolley, the brains behind the clone) take full advantage of the growing kitsch popularity of a band that closed up shop in 1982. But they know better than to compete directly with their mega-platinum idols. Although **Flashback!** is carefully calculated to sound like a mid-'70s ABBA album, the thumping, uptempo Euro-disco renditions are all of other people's hits: "Flashdance," "Denis," "Concrete and Clay," "Will You Love Me Tomorrow," "Band of Gold," "So You Win Again." Total garbage doesn't get much weirder or more entertaining than this.

The bonus live album, recorded in '94 in London, is—except for an intentionally incongruous instrumental slice of "Smells Like Teen Spirit"—nothing but reverently rendered ABBA classics. The stage patter is awful, but the singing is great, and it's hard to imagine that the real deal could have performed "Waterloo," "Fernando," "Mamma Mia," "Dancing Queen" or "S.O.S." with any greater verve or skill. [i]

FRANK BLACK

Frank Black (4AD/Elektra) 1993
Teenager of the Year (4AD/Elektra) 1994
The Cult of Ray (American) 1996

Portraying himself as an average suburban nobody—his singing voice is artless, his guitar playing average and he's certainly not pretty—Frank Black, aka Black Francis, aka Charles Thompson IV, is an extroverted mystery, an irony-coated creature of unexplained obsessions. His oblique, often opaque songs singe the hairs of self-amusement for reasons that are impossible to discern. Although he'd probably like folks to wonder if he's the son of dada or just an esoteric goofball, he's really just a semi-talent in postmodern leisure wear.

In the Pixies, Black Francis' grinding, explosive taste for rock drama gave the band its raw power and magisterial sense of occasion; on the other hand, indulgences like alphabetical set lists, merciless shrieking and such pointless exercises as covering the Jesus and Mary Chain made the group less titanic than it might have been. When the group ended, he changed his name as well as his life, becoming Frank Black and hooking up with keyboardist/producer Eric Drew Feldman (a veteran of both Pere Ubu and Captain Beefheart's Magic Band) for a more modestly scaled solo career. **Frank Black** downplays but doesn't discard the Pixies' roaring aggression—the first sound you hear is acoustic guitar, but "Los Angeles" drops an all-electric shoe loudly twenty seconds later—and shapes up with generally simpler, poppier, more accessible tunes, produced with arch imagination and fine musicianship. (The firm rock cover of Brian Wilson's "Hang on to Your Ego"—which the Beach Boys rejected until he turned it into "I Know There's an Answer"—is incisive, effective and illustrative.) But Black's dry wit pours Pernod all over the album's ice cream: lines like "I had so many problems/And then I got me a Walkman" lead nowhere, turning enjoyment into a challenge of meanings hidden and otherwise. He's capable of creative clarity—"Two Spaces" mounts a rational argument against gravity—but the surreal landscapes of the mostly geographical songs (try "Old Black Dawning": "I hung around/On the planet Mabel/She tried to stand/But she was not able") turn potential sonic pleasure into a frustrating chore.

The science-and-technology-themed **Teenager of the Year,** however, makes the careful travels of its predecessor seem like see-Frank-run. "(I Want to Live on an) Abstract Plain" details the depth of Black's Beefheartian self-consciousness. Again co-produced by Feldman, the album spews out half-baked ideas with abandon—twenty-two complete songs in all—rushing through guitar-loaded gusts of Pixiesque fury, pretty slices of mocking pop and crypto-country, all of it impenetrably odd and none of it especially well developed. Either trivial ("Whatever Happened to Pong?"), whimsical ("Space Is Gonna Do Me Good") or impossibly weird ("Fiddle Riddle"), if these were the high-grade demos they sound to be, at least half of the free-association incidents of words and chords wouldn't have been worth completing. Keepers: "Calistan," "Speedy Marie," "Headache," "I Could Stay Here Forever," "White Noise Maker," "Pie in the Sky."

The Cult of Ray, self-produced with a new band that doesn't include Feldman, is generic Black-ness, a slack repetition of formula that makes the vacuum-packed flatness of Frank's songwriting all too plain. Other than a couple of catchy tunes ("Dance War" is the late standout), there's nothing here he hasn't done better before. And twice was plenty. [i]

See also *Pixies.*

BLACKBIRD

BlackBird (Iloki) 1988
BlackBird (Iloki) 1989
BlackBird (Ger. Fundamental) 1991
BlackBird (Scotti Bros.) 1992

After leading the leftist agit-punk Dils and cowpunk-pioneering Rank and File, brothers Chip and Tony Kinman reinvented themselves as BlackBird, a brooding duo whose clattery low-tech electro-garage sound and dystopic lyrical attitude presaged some of what would come to be known as industrial music. But, while most such combos generally attach a mechanical sound to equally machinelike compositions, BlackBird uses its technology as a counterpoint to its consistently well-crafted songs.

The band's discography is a mite confusing since all four self-titled albums are separate entities with overlapping material. The two Iloki LPs (the one with the red sleeve is the first, the one with the pink lizard on the cover is the second) maintain a compelling balance between the brothers' grumpy, forbidding sonic approach and the strong melodies that consistently lurk below the surface. The Fundamental import is a compilation of the Iloki albums.

By the time BlackBird released yet another eponymous album on Scotti Bros., the Kinmans had lightened up enough to allow themselves to place relatively straightforward love songs like "Take Me" and "Be My Friend" alongside the darker material. The album also recycles tunes ("Howl," "Quicksand") from the first two discs in clearer, less abrasive remixes that bring out their lyrical and melodic strengths without losing their original tension. It also features a timely reworking of the Dils' classic "Class War."

BlackBird subsequently returned to Iloki for a single, "Big Train." (Mike Watt later covered the song on his 1995 album.) With that as a finale, the Kinmans put BlackBird to rest but have continued working together, now using the handle Chipandtony. [ss]

See also *TPRG.*

BLACK CROWES

Shake Your Money Maker (Def American) 1990
The Southern Harmony and Musical Companion (Def American) 1992
Amorica (American) 1994
Three Snakes and One Charm (American) 1996

Led by the brothers Robinson, Atlanta's pot-loving Black Crowes (previously a jangly R.E.M. clone band) lit up the dawn of the '90s with a then-surprising nod to the hard-driving arena sounds of the '70s. Arriving in a brief pre-grunge window of time when rock was still dominated by the dying gasps of hair metal and the bloated excess of the once-promising Guns n' Roses, these neo-hippie vagabonds' pure bluesy rock sounded positively divine. Though at first savaged by critics bemoaning their indebtedness to the Faces, Humble Pie and Rolling Stones (much as Aerosmith had been fifteen years earlier), the quintet nonetheless made a lot of people realize that "classic rock" didn't have to remain moribund (or hamstrung by cheesy Van Halen–derived technique). Given a hot young band with real songwriting ability and energy and passion to burn—plus a sympathetic producer, George Drakoulias—history could sound damn fine again.

Those retro influences may have been obvious on **Shake Your Money Maker**—Faces, Free, Allmans, Otis Redding, early Aerosmith and especially Mick-Taylor-era Stones—but the overall effect is actually refreshing. Swaggering rockers dominated by Rich Robinson's chunky rhythm guitar ("Jealous Again," the saucy slide showcase "Twice as Hard," a rollicking hit version of Redding's "Hard to Handle") alternate with organ-tinged, "Wild Horses"–style ballads like "Seeing Things," "Sister Luck" and the sublime "She Talks to Angels." There are a few weak spots near the end (the generic "Struttin' Blues," to name one), but **Shake Your Money Maker** started the Crowes ball rolling.

The Southern Harmony and Musical Companion, again produced with rootsy vigor by Drakoulias, features a much fuller Southern-fried sound and a bit of internal shuffling that replaced flighty lead guitarist Jeff Cease with the more accomplished Marc Ford and a full-time keyboardist, Ed Hawrysch. The Crowes had clearly grown up, moving beyond simple blues raveups into more soulful material; Chris Robinson's singing is more expansive and detailed, his lyrics tend toward the spiritual. The sophisticated arrangements and textures suggest Traffic; gospelly female backing vocals are key (resplendent on the juicy rocker "Remedy"). "Sometimes Salvation" and "My Morning Song" are bruisingly emotional, as Chris rips his throat to lovely shreds the way Rod Stewart no longer has the fire in his belly to do. "No Speak No Slave" grinds out an ascending riff reminiscent of early Zep or Beck (Jeff, that is); "Black Moon Creeping" walls its thick grooves with harmonica and talk-box. In "Thorn in My Pride," Ford's lovely solos imbue the pensive blend of acoustic guitar and muted organ with a haunting inner light. Closing the masterfully sequenced record, the Crowes show off their range and arranging ability with an excellent recasting of Bob Marley's "Time Will Tell." All in all, a great rock 'n' roll album that does not suffer in comparison to **Sticky Fingers** or **Eat a Peach.**

Co-produced by Jellyfish producer Jack Joseph Puig (that band's Andy Sturmer guests), **Amorica** is a leaner, grittier, more uptempo beast, as evidenced by the tough opener "Gone" and "She Gave Good Sunflower." Bruce (American Music Club) Kaphan's pedal steel adds a country flavor to the subtle "Wiser Time," while "Downtown Money Waster" invokes the simmering slide aura of Robert Johnson. The Latin percussion augmenting several tracks is a great addition; as a result, "High Head Blues" cooks up a zesty congafied War flavor. While not as consistently rewarding a creation as the lush **Southern Harmony, Amorica** gets down and dirty with an invigorating sense of heightened sonic libido. [gef]

BLACK 47

Black 47 (BLK) 1992
Black 47 EP (SBK) 1992
Fire of Freedom (SBK) 1993
Home of the Brave (SBK/EMI) 1994
Green Suede Shoes (Tim/Kerr/Mercury) 1996

New York singer/guitarist—and self-published playwright—Larry Kirwan is, first and foremost, for better and much worse, a dramatist. If that makes his rock credibility suspect, it's not for want of onstage exertion or long-term effort to find the most effective vehicle for his narrative compulsions. In the late '70s, he and fellow Irish expatriate Pierce Turner recorded as Turner and Kirwan of Wexford, a shaggy bearded duo crafting folky art-rock that namechecked Frodo and cursed medieval dawns pregnant with minions' cries. The following decade, the two resurfaced as East Village new wavers, alternately chanting "Avenue B" over tribal drum machines and emoting Human League–like in the Major Thinkers. By the '90s, however, Kirwan had become an uptown guy (the Fordham section of the Bronx, where many recent arrivals from Ireland have settled) and was beating his ethno-political breast and pumping his fist in the roots-rocking Black 47, whose sizable following, primarily among Irish-Americans, was amassed over an extended residency at a Manhattan bar.

Named to invoke memories of Ireland's nineteenth-century potato famine (the one Sinéad O'Connor claims didn't actually occur), Black 47 is a bizarre and clumsy stew of horns, hip-hopping electronic percussion, Gaelic traditionalism, electric guitar and gurgly overwrought vocals. (Imagine a band built with the wrong parts taken from the Pogues, Clash and Bruce Springsteen.) The sextet graced its fans with an eponymous self-released album and then signed to a major label. The five archetypal songs co-produced by Kirwan and Ric Ocasek for **Black 47** make it the only record anyone need own by the band, whose theatrical overzealousness, topical grandstanding and forced stylistic blend frequently conspire to make it unbearable. The cinematic, autobiographical "Funky Céili (Bridie's Song)" rewrites Squeeze's "Up the Junction" (minus the morose restraint); Kirwan sings out about the woman he left behind as if his heart were about to burst from the passion of it all. The rest of the disc mixes historical righteousness (the anti-British "James Connolly" and "Black 47") and personal rambunctiousness ("Maria's Wedding," "Our Lady of the Bronx") in a welter that is overwrought and exhausting.

The full-length **Fire of Freedom** repeats four of those songs, adding the abominable "Rockin' the Bronx," a rapped story-of-the-band (with tin whistle and uilleann pipes), and a bunch of numbers that reprise the EP's essential formula without any further development or imagination. Autobiography is Kirwan's weakness: "New York, NY 10009" explains why he formed the Major Thinkers and proceeds to detail that band's career, but the specific romantic reminiscence of "Banks of the Hudson" is no more involving or tolerable. Ocasek's co-production shapes the music into presentable pointlessness, but it's hard to hear anything beyond Kirwan's singing and lyrics.

Switching from one old new wave star to another, Black 47 got ex–Talking Head Jerry Harrison to produce **Home of the Brave** in wan imitation of the R&B phase of Dexy's Midnight Runners, the horn-driven band in which Black 47 saxman Geoff Blythe is said to have once played. "Different Drummer" dances a merry jig, but otherwise the album cuts way back on the music's Irish component in favor of such absurd culture escapades as the reggaefied "Voodoo City," the rap-dancehall-ska mess of "Black Rose" and "Time to Go," written and rapped (well . . .) by Seanchaí, aka Chris Byrne, Black 47's pipe-and-whistle-playing ex-cop. (Byrne also rhymes in a Gaelic hip-hop side band, Paddy a Go Go.) "Blood Wedding," sung as a duet with guest Claudette Sierra, sounds like Meat Loaf. Beyond the usual real-life characters of "Oh Maureen" and "Danny Boy" (about an Irish AIDS victim), Kirwan has to strain for functional song subjects. With the gears obviously whirring for the scripts he could be writing, Kirwan sings in the first person about "Paul Robeson" (arranged for maximum incongruity as a glib soul-funk extravaganza, complete with readings of Robeson's words) and wonders "Who Killed Bobby Fuller?" as the existential response to his own mistreatment by muggers and lovers. [i]

BLACKGIRLS

See *Dish.*

BLACK GRAPE

See *Happy Mondays.*

BLACK TRAIN JACK

No Reward (Roadrunner) 1993
You're Not Alone (Roadrunner) 1994

Green Day might have grabbed the headlines and the multi-platinum sales figures, but New York's Black Train Jack proves there's more than one approach to latter-day pop-punk. The adamantly anti-drug foursome, formed when guitarist Ernie Parada's hardcore combo Token Entry (in which he played drums) disbanded in 1992, specializes in lightning-quick tempos and effusive choruses—and unlike many of their peers, advocate such un-slacker ideas as self-discipline and personal responsibility.

No Reward is all haywire energy and fight-or-flight adrenaline, a blitz of surprisingly melodic vocal declarations supported by buzzing guitar. More than one track champions clean living with a straight-edge zeal that borders on righteousness: "The Newest One" turns on the chorus "Put to the test and I still come out on top/Put down by the rest, looking back they're the ones who flopped."

You're Not Alone is no less severe, although it is slightly more compassionate. "Not Alone" proclaims, "I don't hurt myself internally, I'm poison-free intentionally," and other selections celebrate the virtues of being clear-headed—at breakneck speed. Exhibiting a taste for more daring (almost virtuosic) musical settings here, the band wisely avoids passing judgment or sounding sanctimonious, but comes close on "The Lottery": "You can't compare an effortless gamble with a consistent valiant try." Other bands might get crucified for such messages, but because the music is delivered with such all-or-nothing intensity, the end result is mesmerizing. In a world of poseurs and dime-a-dozen slogans, Black Train Jack mean what they say. [tm]

BLACK VELVET FLAG

Come Recline With Black Velvet Flag (Go-Kart) 1994

Trends may come and trends may go, but shtick springs eternal. This mock-rock trio's gimmick may be a simple one—vintage West Coast hardcore classics reinvented as lounge-music ditties—but the execution (to say nothing of the timing) is pretty darn impeccable. New York's Black Velvet Flag doesn't miss a beat, going so far as to reproduce the cover of **The Decline of Western Civilization,** picturing singer Fred Stesney doing his best Darby Crash impression (albeit wearing eyeglasses and a tuxedo). **Come Recline** is actually quite witty the first few times through, teeming as it is with absurdities like a finger-poppin' take on Fear's "I Don't Care About You" (which conjures up images of Stesney shooting his cuffs and pointing out audience members one by one as he croons the title phrase) and a version of Suicidal Tendencies' "Institutionalized" that Vic Damone would be proud to call his own. Ultimately, the album falls somewhere between Dread Zeppelin feebdom and a '90's approximation of Frank Sinatra's late-'60's hipster era, during which Ol' Blue Eyes tried his best to bask in the glow of the summer of love—not that either assessment will keep Black Velvet Flag from the next century's thrift store bargain bins. [dss]

BLAKE BABIES

See *Antenna, Juliana Hatfield.*

BLASTERS

See *Phil Alvin.*

BLEACH

Killing Time (Dali/Chameleon) 1992

This quartet from Ipswich recorded three EPs inside a year's time and received an inordinate amount of British press accolades for them. Scoring an American deal with the soon-to-be-bankrupt Chameleon label, Bleach released a compilation of those EPs and then apparently disappeared off the face of the earth. An unenviable fate to be sure, but Bleach's music didn't deserve much more. With tribal rhythms and sheets of razor-wire guitar backing Salli Carson's dry, monotonic vocals, the only thing providing much of a melodic impulse on **Killing Time** is Nick Singleton's bass playing. A near soundalike to the far superior Th Faith Healers, Bleach's wholly uninteresting take on British guitar rock is almost redeemed by the swirly psychedelia of "Shotgun." Almost. [jf]

PETER BLEGVAD

The Naked Shakespeare (UK Virgin) 1983
Knights Like This (UK Virgin) 1985
Downtime (UK ReR) 1988
King Strut and Other Stories (UK Silvertone) 1990
Just Woke Up (East Side Digital) 1995

PETER BLEGVAD & JOHN GREAVES

Kew. Rhone (UK Virgin) 1977 (Europa) 1977
Unearthed (Bel. Sub Rosa) 1995

SLAPP HAPPY

Sort Of (Ger. Polydor) 1972
Slapp Happy (UK Virgin) 1973
Acnalbasac Noom (UK Recommended) 1982 (Cuneiform) 1988
Casablanca Moon/Desperate Straights (UK Virgin) 1993

HENRY COW/SLAPP HAPPY

Desperate Straights (UK Virgin) 1975 (UK ReR) 1982

HENRY COW

In Praise of Learning (UK Virgin) 1975 (Red) 1979 (East Side Digital) 1991

LODGE

Smell of a Friend (Island) 1988

Peter Blegvad's work contains some of the most oblique and poetic wordplay to ever make its way to song. It's a testament to his hard work and clear vision that, though his references can sometimes be too arcane, literary or personal to be widely recognized, the completed form of his work is generally downright friendly and inviting. This is in no small part due to dry wit and a voice that can bring forth everything from anger to vulnerability with a folkish naturalism. Which is not to say that Blegvad's a folksinger, just that folk music's dictum of celebrating the natural, honest resonance of everyman's voice is the path he follows. Further testimony comes by way of his songs' having been covered by, among others, Fairport Convention, Leo Sayer and Bongwater.

Born in Connecticut but living in England, Blegvad started Slapp Happy around 1971 with Anthony Moore, whom he'd met at boarding school, and singer Dagmar Krause, Moore's wife. The trio released three albums before being fully absorbed into Henry Cow, a confederation from which Blegvad was ejected for not fitting in. (Slapp Happy had a reunion of sorts in 1991 when British television commissioned an hour-long opera, *Camera,* which had music by Moore, a libretto by Blegvad and was performed by Krause. It aired in 1993, but, to date, has not been issued on either album or video.)

Resident in New York in the '80s, Blegvad hooked up with various musicians working the downtown scene that eventually coalesced around the Knitting Factory. As a member of Anton Fier's floating Golden Palominos, Blegvad's songs helped shape the identity of 1986's **Blast of Silence** album. Blegvad also contributed to Syd Straw's 1989 solo album, long after they'd both flown the Palominos stable.

Back in the UK, Blegvad pursued a solo career. **The Naked Shakespeare,** produced by Andy Partridge, offers some fine moments, just not enough of them. The album's noticeable problems were exacerbated on **Knights Like This,** wherein producer David Lord, in a misguided attempt to make Blegvad a pop sensation, buried the songs under a mound of overarrangement and filigree.

Downtime finally found him in more suitably simple surroundings. Working sporadically over the course of three years with Chris Cutler (who had been Henry Cow's drummer), they fashioned an album that suited Blegvad's songs and singing, released on Cutler's label, an outpost for uncompromising and idiosyncratic music.

With a bigger recording budget, Blegvad chose to be produced by Chris Stamey (with whom he'd worked in the Golden Palominos). Stamey brought the appropriate settings of **Downtime** into sharp, perfect focus on **King Strut,** Blegvad's peak effort to date. (As part of its promotional effort, Silvertone issued **Peter Who?,** a disc of live and demo versions as well an infuriatingly catchy jingle, sung and played by Andy Partridge, that teaches the correct pronunciation of the singer's name: "Peter Blegvad, rhymes with egg-bad.")

Performed as a trio with ex–Henry Cow bassist John Greaves and Cutler (with notable help from Peter's guitarist brother Kristoffer and pedal steel player B. J. Cole), **Just Woke Up** is the first proper American release of Blegvad's solo career. A masterpiece of confident simplicity, produced with rhythmic intricacy but exquisite clarity and nuance, the album is a perfect introduction to Blegvad's work, rescuing three **Knights Like This** songs from under the layers of production that originally buried them and including a remake of the Golden Palominos' "(Something Else Is) Working Harder." Blegvad's easygoing delivery—now in line with thoughtful semi-acoustic artists like Simon Bonney, Leonard Cohen, Daniel Lanois and Peter Case, but with a bit of recent XTC around the edges—smoothly paves his reflective, philosophical musings. "It's a full-time occupation leaving well-enough alone" begins "You & Me," and what follows suggests Blegvad's incapacity for that intellectual job. In "Bee Dream," which ends in a shattering feedback freakout, he observes, "Each of us has in our soul/A portion of eagle, a portion of mole," while "Driver's Seat" asks "There are two kinds of people/Ask anyone you meet/Would you prefer to be a passenger/Or in the driver's seat?"

Blegvad has also worked in Greaves' band, the Lodge, with whom he recorded **Smell of a Friend;** the two also collaborated on **Kew. Rhone,** a dense song cycle, and **Unearthed,** a set of Blegvad's stories (many of them already published in a 1994 book, *Headcheese)* told over a variety of musical backdrops. In London, where he currently lives, Blegvad is less widely known for his music than for *Leviathan,* a weekly cartoon he draws for *The Independent.*

Belated discographical clarifications department: nearly a decade after the release of Slapp Happy's eponymous second album—which contains the song "Casablanca Moon" but does not bear that title—the band issued its original demos as **Acnalbasac Noom.** Although there are some songs in common, this is an entirely different album from **Slapp Happy.** In 1993, British Virgin confusingly reissued **Slapp Happy** and **Desperate Straights** on a single CD as **Casablanca Moon/Desperate Straights,** omitting Henry Cow's name—which had appeared on the latter's original cover. [dbg/i]

See also *Golden Palominos, John Zorn; TPRG.*

BLIND MELON

Blind Melon (Capitol) 1992

Change EP (Capitol) 1994

Soup (Capitol) 1995

For a lot of young bands, the classified ad that assembled the troops is easy to conjecture. ("Influences: Dinosaur Jr, Sonic Youth, Pavement," that sort of thing.) But what pitch could possibly have brought the five members of Southern California's Blind Melon together? "We have: a raspy singer who can't carry a tune and an obnoxiously condescending name. We need: two bland guitarists (one rock, one folk) and a rhythm section that can mess up Jane's Addiction thrash and white-boy funk and is willing to sit out the acoustic numbers."

Its inexplicable success (much of which can be attributed to the popular bee-girl "No Rain" video) aside, **Blind Melon** is a complete mess. The band switches derivative idioms at will, bringing an equal absence of originality, intelligence and skill to riffy Led Zeppelin thump ("Soak the Sin"), jam-band partydown syncopation ("Tones of Home," "Time"), hippie-dude fake folk ("Change"), Allmanesque boogie ("Holyman"), Dead-like aimlessness ("No Rain") and vintage folk-rock ("Deserted," "Sleepyhouse"). Where other groups might inject their own sound into such an assortment of genres, Blind Melon roots around in search of an identity and comes up empty. The band's songwriting is lazy, amelodic and shapeless; the trippy lyrics do their signifying without the inconvenience of substance. Rick Parashar's co-production is hopeless. Worst of all, Shannon Hoon is an atrocious singer, and he's the only distinctive element in a band that seems to have been concocted from a hand-me-down sense of the '60s.

During the three years it took Blind Melon to record a followup, the **Change** EP appeared as a placeholder: two versions of the titular album track, a couple of dozy acoustic remakes and an idiotic rural version of the Velvet Underground's "Candy Says."

Co-producer Andy Wallace whipped Blind Melon into some sonic shape on **Soup,** lashing the band's diversity to a cohesive center so the riff flareups and acoustic porch-swings—if not the jug-band arrangement of "Skinned"—can be understood as oases in the generic melodic rock zone. But while the quintet is able to escape its reliance on obvious influences, it still couldn't come up with much worthwhile material. (This really seems like a case of attempting to milk a bull.) Regardless of the album's carefully fashioned window dressing, the tunes run strictly on energy, as Hoon repeatedly squanders fragments of melody. At best, the lyrics are calculated to disturb. "Car Seat" fantasizes about being buried by one's father; the narrator of "Walk" wakes up "in a pile of puke" and literalizes the expression "bang my head against this wall." "Skinned" threatens to "make a lampshade of durable skin." Suicide fantasies and self-loathing permeate the album, but only one idea carries the weight of real reflective intelligence: in "New Life," Hoon wonders if looking into the eyes of his new baby will "bring new life into me." Evidently not. On October 21, 1995, several months after the record's release, Hoon was found dead from a cocaine overdose on the band's tour bus in New Orleans. [i]

BLISTERS

Off My Back (Albertine) 1991
Pissed to Meet Me (Ger. Incognito) 1992
Meow: The Claude Coleman Sessions EP [tape] (no label) 1995

These chronic underachievers form one of the longest-lived and least-appreciated pop-punk outfits to ever come out of New Jersey. Beginning in 1987 with a string of singles and compilation cuts, the group established itself as a favorite in the Garden State's punk-rock underground by seamlessly blending Ramones-influenced three-chord rock'n'roll with Replacements-ish garage-punk. Chief among the Blisters' charms is bassist Steve "Nitti" Bahr's boyish vocals, as sincere and ingratiating as Paul Westerberg's more famous midwestern drawl and the perfect vehicle for the group's sweet, boy-next-door persona.

Off My Back is a near-perfect collection of infectiously catchy and upbeat tunes capturing the bitter-sweet freedom of early adulthood. "Off My Back," "My Room" and "Gimme Some Time" chug along like vintage Ramones, powered by guitarist Dennis Marmon's energetic power-chord strums and Bil Kleemeyer's concise, emphatic drums. But like the Ramones, the Blisters can be unexpectedly poignant, too: "Turn 21" laments the changes that adulthood and responsibility can bring to a relationship, while "Change My World" exposes the band's romantic side in a surprisingly touching love song set to a slow-dance tempo.

Pissed to Meet Me presents a markedly changed and matured Blisters. Kleemeyer had been replaced by headbanger Tony DiLeo; Jersey scenester (and *Maximumrocknroll* columnist) Sam Schiffman joined the group briefly on rhythm guitar. The harder drums and the twin guitars yield a much fuller and heavier sound, freeing Marmon to inject feisty metallish guitar solos on top of the familiar churn. The songs are darker and less happy sounding, although Bahr's ebullient vocals continue to buoy even broken-hearted love songs like "Don't Rewind" with optimistic hooks ("Don't give up on tomorrow, don't rewind"). Schiffman's contributions include a frenetic noise-collage called "Shmuel" ("Sam" in Yiddish).

After struggling through years of near-constant personnel shifts and a changing club scene, the Blisters re-emerged in 1995 with **Meow: The Claude Coleman Sessions,** a five-song tape produced by the titular Ween drummer. Only Bahr and Marmon remain from the original lineup; while the former's vocals still sound about the same, Marmon's guitar has gone totally metal, especially on the Guns n' Roses–styled lead that introduces the power ballad "Eleventh Hour." The new lineup rekindles some of the poppy, punky energy of the band's early years on "John Wilkes Booth" and "Ride the Sky," albeit with heavier guitars, more complex arrangements and longer solos, while "Banshee" provides another showcase for Bahr's huge stylistic debt to Westerberg. An over-the-top cover of Deep Purple's "Highway Star" ends the tape on a playfully cheesy note. [jt]

BLOHOLE

Leave It to Blohole (Triple X) 1992

Mike Scaccia, who played guitar on Ministry's **Psalm 69,** is one-third of Blohole, a hoarse combo that reduces the relentless beat and harsh volume of industrial rage to its simple hardcore basis—and winds up sounding mighty lightweight for its troubles. When **Leave It to Blohole** isn't being an entirely ordinary generic punk record with no distinguishing features (unless covering ZZ Top's "Beer Drinkers and Hell Raisers" in straight boogie-rock fashion counts as defiance), Blohole unleashes guitar solos over medium tempos and does the metal thing with equal futility. Bassist Casey Orr has an unpleasant gargly voice; the writing, production and playing are adequate and nothing more. [tr]

See also *Ministry.*

BLONDE REDHEAD

Blonde Redhead (Smells Like) 1994
La Mia Vita Violenta (Smells Like) 1995

As the name (which actually comes from a DNA song) suggests, New York's Blonde Redhead incorporates a rich variety of sometimes contrasting ideas. Formed by twin Italian brothers (on guitar and drums) and two unrelated Japanese women (on guitar and bass), the group fuses a hodgepodge of post-punk sounds into a tasty melting pot.

The quartet's first album led to its reputation as a Sonic Youth protégé too deeply in thrall to that band's influence—and not without cause. SY drummer Steve Shelley produced and released the album on his own label, and his group's guitar sound and song structures clearly inform **Blonde Redhead**'s eight songs, which include both warped pop nuggets ("Sciuri Sciura") and trippy guitar forays ("I Don't Want U"). As guitarists Kazu Makino and Amedeo Pace trade off vocals on these alternately catchy and groovy songs, what makes the record substantial is the group's application of these familiar ideas in new, creative ways. There's much more at work here than mere flattery.

Having lost its bassist, Blonde Redhead recorded **La Mia Vita Violenta** as a trio, displaying a far more distinctive sound—not abandoning the warm, fuzzy Sonic-isms but allowing its own personalities to take the lead. The vocals are much stronger and clearer in the mix—Pace's fuller, Makino's transformed into a passionate, high-pitched (at times cloying) squeal. Their guitar playing is likewise improved, producing a glistening tangle of melodic sounds. The punky "(I Am Taking Out My Eurotrash) I Still Get Rocks Off" is strengthened by a malleable structure within the confines of a pretty catchy tune, while the sitar-laced "Harmony" reveals an open ear for altogether different aural landscapes. [la]

BLOOD CIRCUS

Primal Rock Therapy EP (Sub Pop) 1989
Primal Rock Therapy (Sub Pop) 1992

Before grunge became a marketing concept it was a pretty good way of describing the fusion of suburban metal and urban punk. And in Seattle's summer of '88, Blood Circus (Doug Day, Michael Anderson, T-Man and Geoff Robinson) vied with Mudhoney, Soundgarden and Mother Love Bone to see who might fill arenas first. (Sub Pop also got in the habit of booking a scared trio from Aberdeen as their opening act.) For a time Blood Circus even seemed likely to win, as theirs was the simplest, least ironic and most ferocious sound in town.

The MC5-like band was never quite able to live up to the promise of its debut single, "Six Foot Under," though it was once a landmark of equal weight to Mudhoney's "Touch Me I'm Sick." The **Primal Rock Therapy** EP was released to horrendous reviews and general apathy in the winter of '89 (nearly a year after it was recorded), and the quartet broke up. In 1992, Sub Pop recklessly re-released the entire Blood Circus oeuvre (one single, one EP), plus five previously unissued tracks from an aborted album recorded in the spring of 1989, as the full-length **Primal Rock Therapy.** [ga]

BLOOD FROM THE SOUL

See *Napalm Death.*

BLOODLOSS

See *Mudhoney.*

BLOOD OF ABRAHAM

Future Profits (Ruthless) 1993

One minute hip-hop is bubbling up, pure and unrefined, in South Bronx playgrounds; fifteen years later, it's flowing over cultural barriers like water through a chain-link fence. For better or worse (depending on the resolution of debates over community property and artistic appropriation), musical rhyming has become a ready tool to anyone with beats in the bag and something to say. Blood of Abraham—Los Angeles MCs Benyad (an Israeli native raised in Nigeria) and Mazik (a Las Vegan)—are hip, serious-minded, moderately funky Afrocentric Jewish rappers with the blessing of Eazy-E. Although Blood of Abraham dabbles in typical topics—passing the pot in "3-2-1 Contact"—on the album, what sets **Future Profits** apart is the provocative lyrical uses the unorthodox duo finds for religion, Ethiopian heritage and ethnic identity. "Stick to Your Own Kind" preaches solidarity between Jews and blacks; over a Ramsey Lewis sample, "Stabbed by the Steeple" takes rash and unexplained potshots at Christianity; the daring we-can-say-it epithet-laden "Niggaz and Jews (Some Say Kikes)," featuring Eazy-E, castigates racists and anti-Semites. A simple, low-key album whose subject matter can be overlooked as easily (or not) as the thoughtless bigotry that pollutes some rap records, **Future Profits** is most notable for containing shoutouts to Ruth, Jeff, Max and Aunt Lillie. [i]

BLOOD ORANGES

Corn River (East Side Digital) 1990
Lone Green Valley EP (East Side Digital) 1992
The Crying Tree (East Side Digital) 1994

BEACON HILL BILLIES

Duffield Station (East Side Digital) 1993
More Songs of Love and Murder (East Side Digital) 1994
A Better Place (East Side Digital) 1996

SUNDAY'S WELL

We Don't Care Where Your Grandparents Are From (East Side Digital) 1994

WOODEN LEG

Wooden Leg (East Side Digital) 1996

CHERI KNIGHT

The Knitter (East Side Digital) 1996

The Boston-bred Blood Oranges are one of America's finest and least formulaic roots-rock combos, balancing stylistic know-how and instrumental skill with a timeless emotional thrust, all the while consistently avoiding the genre's clichés. **Corn River** is an accomplished debut, showcasing singer/mandolinist Jimmy Ryan's bluegrass expertise and guitarist Mark Spencer's inventive picking on catchy tunes like "Pounding Pipes" and "Heart of Mud." (Bassist Cheri Knight threatens to steal the show on her vocal showcase, "Thief.") The band's arrangement of the country standard "High on a Mountaintop" is so authoritative that Nashville's own Marty Stuart lifted it whole for his hit version. The four new songs on **Lone Green Valley** (which also includes **Corn River**'s recording of the traditional "Shady Grove") benefit from Eric Ambel's lucid production and the sensitive bashing of new drummer Keith Levreault, with tunes like Ryan's power-poppish "Fire Escape" and Knight's dark "All the Way Down" demonstrating increased musical and lyrical sophistication.

The Oranges really blossom on **The Crying Tree,** a holistic Ambel-produced balance of the eclectic foursome's disparate elements. Ryan contributes fine, rollicking workouts like "Halfway 'Round the World" and "Titanic," but the real revelation here is the dusky-voiced Knight, whose four songs include the epic "Crying Tree" and the heart-rending ballad "Shadow of You."

Blood Oranges has spawned a variety of side projects, most of them Ryan's. The Beacon Hill Billies (aka Beacon Hillbillies) is an ace bluegrass-based trio in which he shares the spotlight with singer/guitarist John McGann, while Sunday's Well (in which Ryan, billed as Séamus O' Ríain, and McGann play supporting roles; McGann also produced **We Don't Care Where Your Grandparents Are From**), led by Sean Cunningham, is an acoustic octet specializing in modified Irish traditionals. The more rockish Wooden Leg, which also features Mark Spencer (who also produced) and Levreault, places Ryan's songs, voice and mandolin in an eclectic array of acoustic and electric settings, with some tracks reminiscent of the Blood Oranges' country-rock stylings and others a bit more ethno-spacey.

Knight's solo album displays some subtle but significant variations on her contributions to the Blood Oranges. With Ambel producing and playing guitar, the music has a rougher edge that's well-suited to Knight's luminously mournful vocals. The images of loss, resignation and resurrection contained in richly emotional tunes like "Light in the Road," "That I Might See" and the title number reach an organic depth to which other roots-rockers might aspire. [ss]

See also *Crush, Sr., Madder Rose.*

LUKA BLOOM

Riverside (Reprise) 1990
The Acoustic Motorbike (Reprise) 1992
Turf (Reprise) 1994

Luka Bloom is a traveler, a nomad. It's no accident the Irish singer/songwriter's three albums have names inspired by geography or vehicles; they reflect the songs, which are linked by their sense of place and motion. Of course, Bloom has been a traveling kind of guy. Born Barry Moore—the younger brother of Irish folk legend Christy Moore—he recorded three albums in his homeland before moving in 1986 to New York, where he forged a performing name from Suzanne Vega's hit and the protagonist of James Joyce's *Ulysses.*

Although it contains a reflection on the suicide of Pablo Picasso's second wife ("Gone to Pablo"), **Riverside** is mostly about an Irishman living in New York, gazing at the Statue of Liberty ("Hudson Lady"), looking for love or something approximating it ("An Irishman in Chinatown") or simply surveying the landscape ("Dreams in America"). Despite numerous musicians—including Hothouse Flowers' Liam Ó Maonlai and Iranian finger drummer Ali Fatemi—Bloom and producer Jeffrey Wood keep **Riverside**'s arrangements in check, going for a spare, open sound driven by his full-bodied, ringing acoustic guitar. This is one debut that has aged well.

Bloom returned to Ireland and made **The Acoustic Motorbike,** a far more frenetic and eclectic work, in Dublin. He carried New York back with him, though, in a cover of LL Cool J's "I Need Love," on which brother Christy plays the traditional *bodhran* drum in synch with a drum machine. "Bridge of Sorrow" also incorporates raps, while "Listen to the Hoofbeat" offers Bloom's sympathetic views on the plight of Native Americans. He also covers Elvis Presley's "Can't Help Falling in Love." **The Acoustic Motorbike** leans towards fuller, band-oriented instrumentation—Ed Tomney (ex-Necessaries/Rage to Live) plays a lot more electric guitar this time—but it's unfocused, not entirely abandoning **Riverside**'s simple melodicism but not forwarding that album's strengths, either.

Turf, then, seems like a retrenchment. Bloom's coffeehouse album is just him, an acoustic guitar and Mairéad Ni Mhaonaigh of the Irish band Altan harmonizing on "Sunny Sailor Boy," a Mike Scott song Bloom has long performed in concert. Bloom and his co-producers, Paul Ashe-Browne and Brian Masterson, achieve a big, rich sound for such a simple presentation, putting some muscle behind his warm tenor and propulsive guitar work. The best songs—"Cold Comfort," "Holding Back the River," "The Fertile Rock," "Background Noise"—are career highs, while Bloom's assured performance very nearly rescues flimsier moments like "Freedom Song" and the doe-eyed "Black Is the Colour." [gg]

BLOW POPS

Charmed I'm Sure (Get Hip) 1992
American Beauties (Get Hip) 1994

Singer/guitarist Mike Jarvis—a former road member of the group Green—and one Tim Buckley front this nifty Milwaukee power-pop quartet. Re-creating a British Invasion aura with echoed Hollies-like harmonies over chiming guitar strums, the Blow Pops bring a fresh breeze of innocence to solidly tuneful girl-titled (and girl-related) songs on **Charmed I'm Sure.** The simply produced album's census includes "Wake Up Mary," "I Know Nancy," "Stiff Priscilla" and "Martha's Mourning Morning." It also contains a sterling cover of the Who's challenging "I Can't Reach You" and an ambitious ten-minute song cycle ("Under the Big Top") about a circus, which gets off to a fine start but makes an abrupt exit. Unpretentious, enthusiastic, skilled and unfailingly pleasant, the Blow Pops make their first impression a good one.

American Beauties' title reflects a salutary stylistic relocation from the debut's prevailing Anglophilia; with producer Jeff Murphy of Shoes burnishing the sound to a glistening brightness, the band plays taut guitar-pop with increased force and confidence and less of an audible debt to swingin' England. That AM radio of the '60s remains the Blow Pops' touchstone makes a certain British accent unavoidable ("Without Reason" sounds like an outtake from **The Rutles),** but this change—more of a course correction than a turnaround—moves the group forward, sacrificing nothing in the process. The best tune on this long album (the CD of which adds two bonus tracks from a single) is "Halloween," while the sharpest tribute is the pointedly Green-like "All Night Long." [i]

See also *Green.*

BLUE AEROPLANES

Bop Art (UK Abstract) 1984 (UK Regeneration) 1994
Action Painting and Other Original Works EP (UK Fire) 1985
Lover and Confidante and Other Stories of Travel, Religion and Heartbreak (UK Fire) 1986

Tolerance (UK Fire) 1986
Bury Your Love Like Treasure EP (UK Fire) 1987
Spitting Out Miracles (Fire/Restless) 1987
Veils of Colour EP (UK Fire) 1988
Friendloverplane (UK Fire) 1988 (Fire/Restless) 1989
Swagger (Ensign/Chrysalis) 1990
Loved EP (UK Ensign) 1990
World View Blue (Ensign/Chrysalis) 1990
Beatsongs (Ensign/Chrysalis) 1991
Yr Own World EP (UK Ensign) 1991
Friendloverplane 2: Up in a Down World (UK Ensign) 1993
Broken & Mended E.P. EP (UK Beggars Banquet) 1994
Life Model (Beggars Banquet) 1994
Up in a Down World EP (UK Fantastic Plastic) 1994
Detective Song EP (UK Beggars Banquet) 1994
Rough Music (Beggars Banquet) 1995
Sugared Almond EP (UK Beggars Banquet) 1995
Fruit (Live 1983–1995) (UK Fire) 1996

The Blue Aeroplanes are so arty that their lineup includes a full-time dancer, but this ever-mutating Bristol combo has the talent and vision to justify its pretensions. Leader (and sole original member) Gerard Langley's lyrics, unlike those of most literate rock writers, are genuinely absorbing and poetic, while his band—which has maintained a consistently sterling standard of musicianship through numerous personnel shakeups—spins intricate yet accessible folk-rock epics that range from mildly gorgeous to full-on breathtaking.

Worthy as the Aeroplanes' '80s indie releases were, the band really came into its own on the Gil Norton–produced **Swagger,** wherein Langley's ambitious verbiage and sly sung/spoken vocals meet their match in a strong and sensitive band lineup featuring guitarists Angelo Bruschini, Alex Lee and Rodney Allen, whose inventive textures shine on "Jacket Hangs," ". . . And Stones" and "What It Is" (which features a discreet guest appearance by Michael Stipe). Elsewhere, Langley mines a Sylvia Plath poem for the lyrics of "The Applicant," and Allen steps up to the mic to sing his own fresh-faced pop tune, "Careful Boy." The eight-track **World View Blue** is a footnote to **Swagger**'s US release, with the non-album single "You (Are Loved)," the hard-edged "Razor Walk," another catchy Allen tune, covers of Lou Reed, Bob Dylan and Richard Thompson, live tracks and an acoustic rendition of the title number, the original version of which appeared on **Swagger.**

Beatsongs is even more impressive than **Swagger,** mixing jangly pop ("Yr Own World," "Fun"), folky introspection ("Cardboard Box," "Colour Me") and majestic art-rock extravaganzas ("Sixth Continent," "My Hurricane"). The excess of talent contained in the Aeroplanes' **Swagger/Beatsongs** configuration is demonstrated handily on **Friendloverplane 2,** a generous assortment of B-sides and outtakes (including a brilliant cover of the Kinks' "Big Sky") compiled into an album as cohesive as its two immediate predecessors.

After an extended layoff brought on by record company politics, Langley and company came back with **Life Model,** a transitional effort recorded with a couple of different lineups. Though it has its moments ("Broken & Mended" and "Ghost-Nets" among them), it largely misses the multi-leveled magnificence of the band's best work. Altogether more impressive is **Rough Music,** for which Langley augments the latest Aeroplanes lineup with return appearances by various alumni. The sprawling cast—featuring no fewer than twenty instrumentalists, including the Jazz Butcher, who co-wrote the haunting "Whatever Happened to Our Golden Birds?"—is well-suited to the task, as evidenced by the rockers ("Detective Song," "Contact High!") given tense, full-bodied treatments as well as subtler numbers ("A Map Below," "James"). The four-song pre-LP EP of **Detective Song** contains, quizzically enough, a cover of the Smithereens' "Top of the Pops." [ss]

See also *TPRG.*

BLUE MOUNTAIN

Blue Mountain (4 Barrel) 1993
Dog Days (Roadrunner) 1995

HILLTOPS

Big Black River (Fishtone) 1993

Produced in Missouri by New Yorker Eric Ambel, this Oxford, Mississippi, trio (recently returned from a year-long sojourn in Los Angeles) essentially relives **After the Gold Rush** with a similar disparity of impulses on its first nationally distributed album. (The group had previously released **Blue Mountain** and, under its original name, the Hilltops, **Big Black River.**) "Wink" and the original Elvis tribute of "Epitaph" provide tender acoustic folk balladry; "ZZQ," about a local radio station, and "Let's Ride" are rootsy southern rock; and, best of all, "Slow Suicide" and "Soul Sister" surge with Crazy Horse slow guitar storming. Drawing other related styles from its quiver, Blue Mountain hits the target with stomping heartland rock (the knockabout mythology of "A Band Called Bud," inspired by the Grifters) and sends a few shots awry with the electric bluegrass of the biographical "Jimmy Carter," a loud dose of twelve-bar ("Special Rider Blues") and mealy country pop ("Mountain Girl," "Blue Canoe"). Although singer/guitarist Cary Hudson, bassist Laurie Stirratt and drummer Frank Coutch do good, unpretentious work throughout the album, there are too many different Blue Mountains here. A single **Dog Day** would have made a longer-lasting impression. [i]

BLUE NILE

A Walk Across the Rooftops (Linn/Virgin/A&M) 1984
Hats (Linn/Virgin/A&M) 1989
Peace at Last (Warner Bros.) 1996

A vast seven-year gap yawned between the Blue Nile's second and third albums. During that time (which included a time-consuming process of securing a new record deal), the perfectionist Glaswegian trio's only visible activities were one tour and three collaborations. They recorded a cover of Joni Mitchell's "Big Yellow Taxi" on Clannad vocalist Máire Brennan's **Misty Eyed Adventures,** a live British B-side with Rickie Lee Jones and "The Gift," a song the threesome co-wrote with Annie Lennox for her **Diva** album; Lennox certified her satisfaction by including the Blue Nile's "Downtown Lights" on her **Medusa** collection.

Recorded (somewhat tellingly) in Los Angeles, **Peace at Last** is by far the atmospheric group's most diverse, accessible and fully realized work. Generally more upbeat and conventional than the first two, the album uses vastly different instrumentation—acoustic guitars, strings, even a gospel choir on "Happiness"—yet retains the group's distinctive melancholy, panoramic feel. The pop ideas explored rather clumsily on **Hats** are infinitely more assured here; while the horn-speckled "Sentimental Man" summons frightening visions of Phil Collins, "Body and Soul" slithers brilliantly on- and off-beat, showing how thoroughly the group has managed to integrate groove into its sound. Although the unmistakable whiff of VH1-friendliness imbues the proceedings—there's even a lump-in-the-throat Christmas ballad called "Family Life"—**Peace at Last** is a natural and dramatic progression for a group that one hopes will again bear fruit before the end of this millennium. [ja]

See also *TPRG.*

BLUES TRAVELER

Blues Traveler (A&M) 1990
Travelers & Thieves (A&M) 1991
Save His Soul (A&M) 1993
Four (A&M) 1994
Live From the Fall (A&M) 1996

JONO MANSON BAND

Almost Home (A&M) 1995

One of the unforeseen pop music movements of the late '80s was a passel of bands that decided to do something about the absence of improvisatory jamming, a feature that had faded out of rock's mainstream along with summer festivals after the mid-'70s. This generation of groups found a spiritual forebear in the Grateful Dead, not only musically but also in an audience-friendly marketing approach of fan clubs, hot lines, Internet sites and near-constant touring. Not surprisingly, such grass-roots efforts attracted followings of high-school and college kids, career-oriented but hungry for rootsy, nomadic summer breaks of granola, Hacky Sack, pot and tunes that, like roads, go on forever.

Blues Traveler was at the forefront of this; leader John Popper even conceived the annual H.O.R.D.E. tour to give the movement a mantle. Formed during 1983 in Princeton, New Jersey, by school friends Popper and drummer Brendan Hill, the group became a serious proposition after a knee injury scotched the ample singer's fledgling football career. Guitarist Chan Kinchla and bassist Bobby Sheehan hopped on board, and the quartet—then known simply as Blues Band—relocated to Brooklyn and became Manhattan club favorites. Their music was, and is, more about chops than songs; fortunately, they're all exciting players, and the weapon-packing Popper's harmonica virtuosity—he brings a guitarist's sensibility to the instrument, which makes him more utilitarian than simply a soloist—is a source of endless delights. And he's no slouch as a blues belter, either.

The knock that Blues Traveler *can't* write songs isn't quite accurate. There are lots of compelling hooks and melodies on **Blues Traveler,** but the group too often hurries through them to get to the jams. Thus the longer tracks ("Crystal Flame," "Alone") tend to be the most fully realized, allowing the group to take its time developing the composition and still have plenty left for the solos. But some of the shorter numbers do work. The gentle, swaying "100 Years," bolstered by Arnie Lawrence's soprano sax solo, has remained a favorite of the band's live set, while "Gotta Get Mean" is a punchy blues grind driven by one of Kinchla's tastiest licks.

Travelers & Thieves boasts a similar mix of virtues and problems, though some of the latter are more pronounced. The song constructions still aren't complete; Popper tries to fill more space with words and frequently slips into verbosity. "Onslaught" and "Ivory Tusk" are heavy—both in their tone and in their socially conscious lyrics—and sound forced within the context of Blues Traveler's normally good-natured, wiggly grooves. Popper displays a new Creole flavor in his playing on "Optimistic Thought" and "Support Your Local Emperor." The best cut by far (and the longest) is a winding nine-minute workout, "Mountain Cry," that alternates slow blues and funk grooves and features Gregg Allman on organ.

Save His Soul is a significant step forward. The quartet's songwriting is tighter, and Popper—who was seriously injured in a motorcycle accident while the album was being made—is starting to find his voice as a social commentator. (He still tends to get preachy and hasn't dropped the cartoonish bad-dude persona that crops up in the bar-room braggadocio of "Defense & Desire.") "Trina Magna" brings Latin flavors into the mix, while the group employs strings to flesh out the arrangement of "Fledgling." "Go Outside & Drive" lays a chugging rhythm under Popper's stream-of-consciousness vocal, "Believe Me" kicks into a convincing southern rock shuffle and "Manhattan Bridge" is, shockingly, the first instrumental Blues Traveler has ever put on record. Once again, the longest track ("Whoops") shines, and the folkish "Letter From a Friend," with a tough, poignant lyric about death ("We can't change that he left us/But it's up to you to stay"), is a standout.

Blues Traveler tightened its songs further for **Four,** yielding a pop hit in the Latiny swirl of "Run-Around." "Hook," "Price to Pay" and the Dead-like "Stand" are also fully realized compositions, in which the solos serve the song rather than the other way around. "The Mountains Win Again" is another victorious step into southern rock, while "Fallible" and "Freedom" attack heavier grooves without sacrificing the band's natural swing. The playing also benefits from the improved songwriting: Popper's harp blasts sound particularly focused and Kinchla delivers a career-topping solo in "Just Wait." Guest shots by keyboardist Chuck Leavell and guitarist Warren Haynes strengthen an already outstanding effort.

Answering the clamor for a concert document, Blues Traveler delivered **Live From the Fall,** a double-length souvenir from the **Four** tour. Showcasing the quartet's live virtues—particularly Popper's harmonica gymnastics and nimble scat singing—the album doubles as a solid overview of the group's best material. The one-two punch of "Gina" and "But Anyway" is electrifying, as is the smooth segue from "Mulling It Over" into "Closing Down the Park" (one of two new songs: the other is "Regarding Steven"). Fifteen minutes of "Alone" is pushing it a little, but the late-show jam on "Go Outside & Drive"—which uses "Tequila," "Low Rider" and Beck's "Loser" to wind toward the big hit "Run-Around"—is a treat.

Kinchla and Sheehan compose half of the Jono Manson Band on **Almost Home,** turning in fine performances backing up their old scene pal on an appealing, earthy album that sounds a lot like John Hiatt's rock/R&B side. Popper, who played behind the rootsy singer/guitarist in the '80s, blows his face out on three tracks. [gg/i]

BLUE UP?

Cake and Eat It (Catacombs) 1992
Spool Forka Dish (Columbia) 1995

I'll take Anything but Muzak for two hundred, Alex. Three brash and colorful young rock women from Minneapolis? Who are . . . Babes in Toyland? *Darn.* I thought I had that one.

If the Babes were leather-coated tenth-graders who magic-markered Iggy Pop's name on their backpacks and read *Maximumrocknroll,* Rachael Olson—who sings, plays guitar and writes the songs for the Blue Up?—must have been more of the feline Kate Bush/Salvador Dalí type. The trio's second album, **Spool Forka Dish,** attempts a rapprochement between a flip indie attitude, a rarefied sense of psychedelia and the potentially precious artiness of Tori Amos; the result, as produced by former Prince drummer Bobby Z, is a bizarre kitchen sink that shifts blithely from small-scale acoustic folkiness ("Feel Me Dying," "Beautiful Hysterical") to punk screaming ("Come Alive," "Exhibitionist") to panoramic ambient house dreams ("Capture This") to Heart-like rock grandiosity ("Shine," "Breathe You Out") to out-and-out nonsense ("H. Sidakr of Loops," which—as might be guessed from the reverse title—is the album played backward). Materially, Rachael is not above the silly title-naming of "Blasting XTC," but she's also capable of the feminist freedom declaration of "Exhibitionist" and the whimsical reveries of "Spoons for Seven." All of which makes for an inconsistent, not always pleasant but invariably attention-getting frolic in a fascinating artist's uncommon world. And how often does a twenty-nine-year-old urge listeners to "go buy **S. F. Sorrow** and **Parachute** by the Pretty Things" anymore? [i]

BLUMFELD

Ich Maschine (Ger. What's So Funny About/ZickZack) 1992
L'Etat et Moi (Ger. ZickZack) 1994 (ZickZack/Big Cat) 1995
Verstärker EP (ZickZack/Big Cat) 1995

Though some may dispute the point, German is not the language most conducive to singing rock. Teutonic death metal, Deutsche industrial extrusions and Wagnerian opera may be one thing, but otherwise it's a tongue that music trips off with difficulty. True, David Bowie, Peter Gabriel, Nena, Kraftwerk, Trio, D.A.F. and Nina Hagen have all issued appealing material in German, but the country has been stymied in its ability to feed untranslated indigenous pop to the Anglo-American pipeline. That barrier may be falling a bit, thanks to the international lingua franca of indie-pop. The Bartlebees do all their tweeing in the king's English, but Pavement pals Blumfeld's **L'Etat et Moi** (French LP title, Elvis Presley parody cover and English song titles notwithstanding) is 98 percent German, and it makes not the slightest whit of difference. In fact, when singer/guitarist/pianist Jochen Distelmeyer does spoken-word, German actually works to his audible benefit.

On its second album, the Hamburg group—which includes bassist/guitarist/harmonicat Eike Bohlken and drummer Andre Rattay; guitarist Tobias Levin joined afterward—explores various approaches to bright electric and acoustic pop merriment by borrowing conceptual and textural ideas from Sonic Youth, the Fall, the Smiths and Aztec Camera, devoting more than five minutes to the unaccompanied recitation of the title track and generally making music that is easy to enjoy if not understand. Distelmeyer has a pleasantly serious and expressive pop voice, and his habit of occasionally dropping an English phrase without missing a beat adds a provocative footnote to "Sing Sing," "Ich—Wie Es Wirklich War" ("I—As It Really Was"), "Evergreen" and "L'Etat et Moi (Mein Vorgehen in 4, 5 Sätzen)," which ends by fudging Dylan: "And if my thought dreams could be seen/They'd probably put my head in an ich-machine."

Taking its magnificent New Ordery title track (which translates as "Amplifier") from the middle of **L'Etat et Moi,** the **Verstärker** EP adds three 1992 tracks that—appropriately—betray a strong Joy Division influence in the trio's droney down-strummed guitar presence. [i]

BLUR

Leisure (Food/SBK) 1991
Modern Life Is Rubbish (UK Food) 1992 (Food/SBK) 1993
Parklife (Food/SBK) 1994
The Great Escape (Food/Parlophone/Virgin) 1995

The career of this arch cadre of middle-class art-school grads from Colchester (though the band took shape in London in the late '80s and was originally known as Seymour) has unfolded with such intense speed that you'd swear you were experiencing Blur's evolution via some sort of time-lapse technology. In the process of its giddy genre-jumping, however, the quartet has matured into a potent (if occasionally backward-looking) force on the Britpop scene, with singer Damon Albarn emerging as the '90s heir to the social-commentator-cum-curmudgeon throne variously held by Ray Davies, Pete Townshend and Paul Weller.

The semi-diverting **Leisure** positioned Blur on the milder (read: less self-destructive) end of the dance-pop revival scene dominated by such pharmaceutically enhanced spirits as Happy Mondays. The "baggy" crowd never fully embraced the band, however, and bubbly confections like "There's No Other Way" and "She's So High" (both of which bobble along to the omnipresent Manchester groove) proved to have very limited shelf lives.

When the band reappeared, it was as old-school mods with all the accouterments: scooters, parkas, even carefully practiced Cockney accents. It would be easy to dismiss **Modern Life Is Rubbish** as dilettantish, except that it stands up astonishingly well on its own merits. Sure, you've heard slices of working-class life like "Pressure on Julian" and "Chemical World" before, but Graham Coxon's jagged, post-punk guitar lines and Albarn's clever sociological commentary elevate them above revival-band mediocrity. Blur gets bonus points for assembling a comprehensive package, complete with **Who Sell Out**–styled fake adverts and a lyric booklet that also incorporates the chord changes for aspiring musos.

Parklife, which elevated Blur to superstar status

across Europe, is quite a bit more multi-dimensional in terms of sound, encompassing everything from jaunty Eurodisco (on the coolly insinuating "Girls and Boys," a single that satirizes the ambisexual debauchery on the UK spring break circuit) to the Cockney-speak title track (which boasts narration by *Quadrophenia* star Phil Daniels). The really important development, however, is the maturation of Albarn's steadfastly Anglocentric deadpan observations, which cut cleanly through the jostle of punky guitars, lush strings and faux-soul arrangements. Despite the dour outlook—"Bank Holiday" practically revels in Britain's state of diminished socio-economic expectations—**Parklife** brims with the sort of pub-ready melodies that evoke images of sturdy dole-queue denizens packing their evenings with hard-won fun. A strikingly adult record—one that stands head and shoulders above the perpetually adolescent angst so common in '90s pop—**Parklife** merits inclusion on the short list of truly compelling concept albums.

Parklife's success obviously gave Blur an emphatic confidence boost, inspiring the group to redouble its efforts to switch its American label and gain itself free rein to record the wryly named **The Great Escape** to its own creative specifications. Again, Albarn sets his sights on British society, but this time, he takes on characters with whom he's more intimately familiar—the more well-heeled suburbanites of his youth. In "Stereotypes," the strident "Mr. Robinson's Quango" and the mockingly peppy "Charmless Man," these ostensible model citizens sneak off for interludes of extramarital sex and drug abuse; lovingly detailed character sketches like "Ernold Same" and "Dan Abnormal" are so vivid a courtroom artist would have little trouble drawing perfect images of their subjects. The music's growth continues apace, most evidently on "The Universal," a grandiose (but not over-inflated) ballad that sweeps up even jaded types as it soars toward the millennium with wistful pessimism. [dss]

BMX BANDITS

The Day Before Tomorrow EP (UK 53rd & 3rd) 1986
C86 (UK Click!) 1990 (UK Vinyl Japan) 1992
Totally Groovy Live Experience! (UK Avalanche) 1990
Come Clean EP (UK Vinyl Japan) 1991
Star Wars (UK Vinyl Japan) 1991
Gordon Keen and His BMX Bandits (UK Sunflower) 1992
Serious Drugs EP (UK Creation) 1992
Kylie's Got a Crush on Us EP (UK Creation) 1993
Life Goes On (Creation/TriStar Music) 1993
Little Hands EP (UK Creation) 1993
Gettin' Dirty (UK Creation) 1995
That Summer Feeling EP (UK Creation) 1995

The British blues scene had John Mayall for a prep-school headmaster; similarly, to become somebody in the downtown New York noise-art world, you first had to play with Glenn Branca. For the past decade or so, Scottish youth preparing to move out into the real music world have pledged their temporary troth to the unsteady musical vision of Duglas T. Stewart, the fair-haired singer/songwriter at the center of the fringes of Glasgow indie-pop. Members of Teenage Fanclub, the Soup Dragons, Superstar and Eugenius have all played a co-dependent role in the loosely configured wry on the rocks known as the BMX Bandits. More than just a crucial genealogical Scot-pop locus and overseas counterpart to such outfits as Luna, Velvet Crush, Beat Happening and the Gigolo Aunts, the band has introduced an inconsistently likable body of music to the international pop underground.

Initially conceived as a one-off by Stewart (ex–Pretty Flowers) and Sean Dickson (pre–Soup Dragons), the group soon settled into the formless state of permanence that has sustained it ever since. The BMX Bandits began releasing charming lighter-than-air pop singles in 1986, finally reaching full-length form on **C86** four years later. Written and recorded by Stewart, future Fanclubbers Francis Macdonald (drums) and Norman Blake (guitar), future Eugenius guitarist Gordon Keen and future Superstar leader Joe McAlinden on bass, the album is whimsical, simple, romantic and catchy—very much the sum of its parts. ("Whirlpool" is an unmistakable blueprint for early Teenage Fanclub.) Plucky enough to make fun of an entire musical movement and un-self-conscious enough to include the love song "Disco Girl" in two dinky versions, **C86** is less a revolutionary scene-setter than an engaging love-rock ground-clearer.

Recorded and played presentably well (but no more) at a Scottish hotel in January 1989, **Totally Groovy Live Experience!** draws songs from the first album ("Disco Girl," "Your Class," "Whirlpool") and early singles ("E102," "The Day Before Tomorrow"), adding noisy covers of Neil Young ("Like a Hurricane"), the Dead Kennedys ("Nazi Punks Fuck Off") and head Television Personality Daniel Treacy ("Girl at the Bus Stop") as well as winning stage patter to the effort.

"Come Clean" not only appears twice on the EP named for it, the mildly diverting number does the same again on the succeeding album. (The EP is rounded out by the acoustic "Retitled," also on **Star Wars,** and **C86**'s "Let Mother Nature Be Your Guide.") With Macdonald free of his Fanclub commitments and Blake doing double duty here, **Star Wars** adds Eugene Kelly (ex-Vaselines, in the process of getting Captain America, later renamed Eugenius, off the ground) to the creative porridge. In addition, the album takes a decidedly more refined, semi-mature tone. Between the finespun production, careful (but sometimes inept) harmony vocals, restrained energy (no "Nazi Punks" raves here), piano, strings and things, **Star Wars** is a handsome enough affair, but the songwriting and playing are short on sparkle. Luna-like electricity makes "Think Tank" notable, and an enthusiastic cover of Daniel Johnston's "Do You Really Love Me?" leaps right out; otherwise, **Star Wars** is a fairly forgettable skirmish.

Gordon Keen and His BMX Bandits is a nifty/silly seven-track studio detour, with two versions of "Girl at the Bus Stop," a reincarnation of **C86**'s wonderful "Your Class," a raw cover of Badfinger's "Come and Get It," the giddy "Kylie's Got a Crush on Us" (written by Gerry Love of the Fanclub, who also plays on the novelty track), an a cappella gospel throwdown ("King of the Fools") and "Hot Bandito No. 1" (which owes only the inspiration of its title to Gram Parsons).

Following the Fanclub to Creation, the BMX Bandits made "Serious Drugs," the best single of the band's career. In this perfectly shaped romantic ode phrased for deadpan eyebrow elevation, pharmaceutical imperatives are evenly invoked without significance; the deadpan provocation is just part of a desperate romantic campaign. "I'd cut off my hair if you want me to/I'd cut off a finger if it'd get me you/Serious love." Other than a demo of the song, the rest of the EP built around it doesn't give "Drugs" any competition.

The cleaned-up remake of "Kylie's Got a Crush on Us" is a solid also-ran in the group's upper echelons; the four-song EP also contains a very pretty rendition of Brian Wilson's "Thinkin' 'Bout You Baby," a dissenting parodic original entitled "My Generation" and a hoarse demo of "Hole in My Heart." That last song also appears in finished form on **Life Goes On,** the first BMX Bandits album recorded as a full-time band—Stewart, Francis Macdonald, bassist Finlay Macdonald and guitarist John Hogarty—free of moonlighters. (It's also the band's sole US release to date.) **Life Goes On** gets a rise from "Serious Drugs," "Kylie's Got a Crush on Us" and a sweet cover of Beat Happening's "Cast a Shadow," but too many of the new originals are smoothed down and gussied up to a pristine pop breeze blowing sweetly between Haircut One Hundred and Aztec Camera. The familiar melody and trumpet make "Space Girl" call to mind Herb Alpert's 1968 hit, "This Guy's in Love With You"; like the whole quiet album, the song could be taken for camp if it weren't so studiously serious. When's the fun begin? [i]

See also *Eugenius, Soup Dragons, Superstar, Teenage Fanclub.*

BODEANS

Love & Hope & Sex & Dreams (Slash) 1986
Outside Looking In (Slash) 1987
Home (Slash) 1989
Black and White (Slash/Reprise) 1991
Go Slow Down (Slash/Reprise) 1993
Joe Dirt Car (Slash/Reprise) 1995

John Mellencamp's excursion into mandolin, fiddles and hammer dulcimer aside, there was no notable roots rock movement afoot in 1986 when BoDeans emerged from Waukesha, Wisconsin. The quartet's earnest sound was fresh not trendy, with captivating harmonies by guitarists Kurt Neumann and Sammy Llanas. Picking a line from the Rolling Stones' "Shattered" for the first album's title was a clever little stroke, too. It was only after repeated listenings that BoDeans' inherent flaws began to show. The songs were tuneful enough, but the writing was a little on the thin side and often repetitive. By the time of **Home,** BoDeans—which also includes bassist Bob Griffin but has trouble holding on to drummers—seemed willing to try anything, from U2-ish power rock to Motown-y R&B and '50s-style raveups. The topics had broadened, but the band's social commentary wasn't nearly as good as its more personal songs. Things were getting messy.

They don't get better on **Black and White.** With Prince cohort David Z producing, the album is awash in twinkly synthesizers and Linn drums—sounds baldly at odds with the kind of straightforward melodies Neumann and Llanas write. That renders rockers like "Black, White and Blood Red," "Naked" and "Long Hard Day" anonymous, and turns "Any Given Day" into a candidate for some '80s pop compilation—even though it came out in '91. What's frustrating is that **Black and White** also has some of BoDeans' best material, including the infectious, Latin-tinged "Paradise," the fiery "True Devotion" and a pair of mature love songs, "Good Things" and "Forever on My Mind."

Go Slow Down is a welcome return to form and BoDeans' best, most consistent album. Neumann shares the drum stool with the always superb Kenny Aronoff; T-Bone Burnett, who helmed **Love & Hope & Sex & Dreams,** is back as executive producer. The group strides across its familiar terrain of American music, stopping for a little funk in "Freedom" and a little twang on "In Trow/Texas Ride Song," but mostly perusing rock'n'roll. "Closer to Free" and the lusty "Feed the Fire" work up convincing heads of steam, while "Save a Little" and "Idaho" are smoother and sparser, taking full advantage of the Neumann/Llanas harmonies. "The Other Side" deals with suicide, but the album's emotional standout is "Cold Winter's Day," a simple but nicely drawn account of a Christmas Day reunion with an old friend.

If erratic in the studio, BoDeans has always been a solid concert band. The overdue live double-album **Joe Dirt Car** is an essential addition to the story. Mining all five albums—plus a soundcheck recording of the B-side "Ooh (She's My Baby)"—from shows between 1989 and 1994, the set provides a good sense of BoDeans' ebullient performances, abundantly spirited and harder rocking than any of the other releases. The song selection provides a thorough overview (even though just one features Aronoff), and Llanas' solo rendition of "True Devotion" is a treat. Coming in the wake of **Go Slow Down,** this may be a sign that BoDeans are hitting the stride that was expected after **Love & Hope & Sex & Dreams.** [gg]

See also *Violent Femmes.*

BODECO

Bone, Hair and Hide (Homestead) 1992
Callin' All Dogs (Safe House) 1995

MATTHEW O'BANNON

Wink (Safe House) 1993

One of the most underappreciated combos in the early-to-mid-'90s indie roots-rock movement (Gibson Bros, '68 Comeback, Reverend Horton Heat, Southern Culture on the Skids), Bodeco—take the Bo from Diddley and the 'deco from zydeco—shake, rattle and roll out celebratory party rawk. Sing the praises of the Jon Spencer Blues Explosion's arch blues deconstructions all day; Bodeco wallops with an allegiant muscle that unabashedly lacks irony.

Guitarist Ricky "Shaggy" Feather leads the band through the kind of rumbles that might have inspired his nickname; **Bone, Hair and Hide**'s full of 'em, fueled by Link Wray/Duane Eddy–inspired guitar riffs (shared with Matthew "Wink" O'Bannon) as Feather's gruff throat blasts out Mardi Gras–tinged tales of fast living ("Crazy Wild," "Dead Broke and Dirty"), hot rods ("Suicide Ride," "Holy Rollers Rockin' in a Killin' Machine") and psychobilly mischief ("Whole Lotta Trouble," "Spank Your Fanny," "Hoe Dad"). Sharp, jumpin' instrumentals like "Happy Guitar Boogie" and "Casillero del Diablo" are a specialty, and Bodeco delivers them with aw-shucks economy.

The delayed followup reinforces Bodeco's simple genius by turning up the slop right from the get-go. Percussionist Gary Stillwell makes an immediate impression on "Crazy Sexy Baby," his bells and shakers accenting the steady, in-the-pocket rhythms of drummer/co-founder Brian Burkett and bassist Jimmy Brown. The guitars are hotter here and, beyond the expected fire ("Wicked Mean & Evil" is a superior sequel to "Dead Broke and Dirty"), the band's instrumental work is varied and improved. Guest saxophone brings fat, smoky resonance to "High Window," "Chicken Shifter" and a sassy cover of "La Cucaracha." "Bright Lights at the End of the Road" is raw and raunchy; "Lucky 13" is a percolating ode to biker slang for pot. The album includes studio versions of "Rock and Roll Till the Cows Come Home" and "Hill and Gully Rider," both of which appear as live raves on **Bone, Hair and Hide.**

In the liner notes to **Wink,** O'Bannon (who spent much of '93 and '94 as a member of Eleventh Dream Day) writes "This big turd was recorded at various times between 1984 and 1993—a sordid, unpleasant decade." In fact, it's a pretty charming—if mangy—little turd. Singing simple rock, country and blues songs in a lazy, unsteady voice over minimal accompaniment—guitar, bass, drums, an occasional spot of sax, with very little involvement of his Bodeco brothers—O'Bannon registers chronic dissipation. He's there but he's not happy, regardless of what the wry lyrics say. (A fragmentary one-word ode entitled "Penis," which elicits howls of protest from a woman in the studio, is about as merry as this gets.) Where O'Bannon really comes alive is in the instrumentals, which touch on surf twang, Wray-man rumbles, Memphis boogie, Chuck Berry rock'n'roll and crisp country picking without ever leaving Louisville, Kentucky. [mww/i]

See also *Eleventh Dream Day.*

BODY COUNT

See *Ice-T.*

BOGEYMEN

See *Masters of Reality.*

BOLLWEEVILS

Stick Your Neck Out! (Dr. Strange) 1994
The History of the Bollweevils, Part One (Dr. Strange) 1994
Heavyweight (Dr. Strange) 1995

Chicago's Bollweevils betray their roots with a grinding, buzzsaw guitar sound, very much in the Chicago hardcore tradition of Naked Raygun and the Effigies. Add cascading bass riffs, rapid-fire drums, a snotty lead vocalist and plenty of speed, and you've got an energetic and entertaining punk band that can hold its own in any mosh pit in America. On **Stick Your Neck Out!,** the band relies on the power of lead singer Daryl's (no last names) vocals, which are strong enough to carry the band's soundalike thrash anthems and supply whatever melody the songs possess. Although the lyrics generally root around familiar punk themes—friendship, loyalty, broken hearts and scene politics—they tend to be more literate than the usual pop-punk fare, especially the stark, eerie "John Doe," which examines the plight of a homeless man turned medical cadaver, wondering what kind of life ended in such squalid anonymity. A hidden bonus track—a cover of Tommy Tutone's "867-5309/Jenny"—ends the album with a bit of puckish wit.

The Bollweevils are nothing if not prolific; the group's second album collects previously released tracks from four EPs, several compilations and even a Christmas song. The recording quality varies, but not the basic formula: power-chord guitar sound and rallying vocals.

The band shows a bit of growth on **Heavyweight,** with more complex arrangements and the addition of rousing background vocals to augment Daryl's fiery leads. Everything still rushes along at breakneck tempos, but the lyrics tackle the more complicated, tangled emotions of post-adolescence. "There's a place I've heard of where perfection is standard," Daryl sings in "Utopia." "Where I come from, we don't know it/if you live there, overthrow it." "Major Problems" takes a poke at the legions of punk bands fleeing the indie underground for major labels: "Your music is the rage, 15 minutes it's your fame," Daryl warns angrily. The album concludes with a raveup cover of the Bad Brains' thrash classic, "Pay to Cum," followed by a twelve-minute audio tour diary—a waste of time, but good for a few chuckles the first time you hear it. [jt]

BONE MACHINE

See *His Name Is Alive.*

BONE THUGS-N-HARMONY

Creepin on ah Come Up (Ruthless) 1994
E. 1999 Eternal (Ruthless) 1995

It may have taken Cleveland a while to make its mark on the national hip-hop scene (an ironic development, given its R&B heritage stretching back through the Dazz Band to the O'Jays and Screamin' Jay Hawkins), but this quintet broke the city's drought with one of the 1990s' most distinctive takes on hardcore rap. It's easy to see why Eazy-E took Bone under his wing: the unapologetic (but braggadocio-free) gangsta parables are authentic enough that you can practically smell the sulfurous aftermath of the gun battles they chronicle. But what's really fascinating is the group's close-harmony melodic flow. Jazzily scatting, fluid and mercurial, Bone Thugs—Bizzy Bone, Wish Bone, Krayzie Bone, Flesh-n-Bone and Layzie Bone—are capable of braking from breakneck vocal sprints to lissome stalking without so much as a backward glance. On the tracks where they croon handsomely about murderous brutality, Bone Thugs set up a daring dichotomy that actually works.

The eight-track **Creepin on ah Come Up** is an extremely impressive debut, although it's difficult to assess how much of its three-million-selling stature springs from the songs—which are certainly colorful enough—and how much from the guest turns taken by folks like Eazy himself (who drops in for "For tha Love of $"). The selection of producers is likewise wide, although DJ Uneek's contributions (particularly to the tongue-twisting "Thuggish Ruggish Bone") are the freshest.

The full-length album (which knocked Michael Jackson's **HIStory** from the top spot on the pop album chart upon its release) is considerably stronger. Loosely tied with a linear narrative thread, the rambling set kicks off on a spooky note with the muezzin-like wailing of "Da Introduction," which dovetails into the sepulchral "East 1999." Uneek, who handles the controls on all seventeen tracks, outdoes himself on "Budsmokers Only" (which spirals off a breezy Earth

Wind & Fire sample) and the jarring "Mo' Murda." The body count (not to mention the bud count) may be high enough to induce dizziness, but the terpsichorean grace with which Bone rolls out such morsels as "1st of tha Month" (an advisory on dubious uses for welfare checks) keeps indignation from setting in. A native's note: the band's map of its Cleve-town 'hood is most assuredly not AAA-authorized. [dss]

SIMON BONNEY

Forever (Mute) 1992
Everyman (Mute) 1995

The well-traveled Simon Bonney has changed his tune. The former lead vocalist of Crime and the City Solution (a band joined in the mid-'80s by two ex-members of Australia's grating and innovative Birthday Party) has reinvented himself so effectively that listeners unfamiliar with his extensive back catalogue are bound to think him a product of America's heartland—a firsthand witness to the demise of the midwestern industrial town, and the pain and chaos caused by common social disaster.

Now based in Los Angeles, Bonney is a product of places both removed and relevant. The farm-raised Australian spent a significant amount of his Crime career in Berlin, where the band trademarked and exported its own gloomy brand of experimental art-infused dirge. In the two years between Crime's swan song and Bonney's first solo album, the singer tired of Europe and took a growing interest in American country-western of the late '60s and early '70s, with a heavy emphasis placed on the "western" portion of the phrase. (Crime had shown some very slight leanings in that direction after the departure of Rowland S. Howard from the band in 1987; evidence of Bonney's evolution can be traced from the group's **Shine** album as well as **Paradise Discotheque.**)

Free of the complications of a full band, Bonney—joined by former Dwight Yoakam guitarist J. D. Foster, erstwhile True Believer Jon Dee Graham (lap steel, Dobro) and ex-Crime violinist Bronwyn Adams, among others—unloads a full range of American-bred introspection on **Forever,** the sort that can only be characterized as the result of numerous heartbreaks and a succession of minor letdowns. Much of the stupendous record is purposefully languid and calculated to the last note and final sentiment; it could serve equally well in a Wim Wenders film or a seedy Texas bar. "A Part of You" and "Someone Loves You" marry roadhouse sensibilities to the kind of warmth and wisdom displayed by Green on Red in the early '80s, while the title track fosters an urge for a shot or two of Wild Turkey and a good cry. **Forever** is a yeoman effort, well worth a good listen or ten.

Everyman, a heartland concept album, is even more credible than **Forever.** Although Bonney tries too hard to apply his powers of observation and analysis to **Everyman**'s big picture, the material within is still admirable. Drawn in broad strokes, **Everyman** tells a story of an itinerant on the hunt for odd jobs throughout the Southwest in a nearly vain attempt to keep his family alive. The small towns he hits once seemed to have bright futures, but now seem useful only to truckers who stop for a meal. He meets old girlfriends along the way, battles temptations of nearly every sort and wishes to more peaceably accept what little he has. "Blue Eyes Crying in the Rain" and the finale, "This Is What You Made Me," are gently touching and revealing, while the most accessible number, "Don't Walk Away From Love," sounds like Chris Isaak on a bad day—and that's a compliment. [icm]

See also *TPRG.*

BOODLERS

See *Elliott Sharp.*

BOOGIE DOWN PRODUCTIONS

Criminal Minded (B-Boy) 1987
Man and His Music (B-Boy) 1987
By All Means Necessary (Jive/RCA) 1988
Ghetto Music: The Blueprint of Hip Hop (Jive/RCA) 1989
Edutainment (Jive/RCA) 1990
Live Hardcore Worldwide (Jive/RCA) 1991
Sex and Violence (Jive) 1992

KRS-ONE

Return of the Boom Bap (Jive) 1993
KRS-One (Jive) 1995

In the matter of KRS-One, it's difficult to separate the man from the myth. Raised in poverty by a single mother, Lawrence Krsna Parker left home at a young age. The library-loving autodidact wound up living at a Bronx homeless shelter where he met social worker Scott Sterling, aka DJ Scott LaRock. They soon formed Boogie Down Productions and hooked up with producer Ced Gee to cut "South Bronx" and "The Bridge Is Over," monumental records that toppled the Queens-based Juice Crew and cemented the boogie-down Bronx's place in the active history of hip-hop. These tracks, along with the sublime "Poetry" and the shocking "9mm Goes Bang," formed the basis of **Criminal Minded.**

Hip-hop has always been about competition and leveling—thus its fascination with violent metaphor and its insistence that heroes be "real." But because rap arose during a period of racial polarization and political reaction, it has also been looked to as an authentic source of social commentary. Dropped at a crucial moment, the lasting brilliance of **Criminal Minded** lies in the way it encapsulates these essentially divergent functions. Some loved the extravagant desecration of the music coming out of the Queensbridge projects. Others appreciated that the KRS-One name stood for "Knowledge Reigns Supreme Over Nearly Everybody"—and that Parker meant it.

Shortly after the record took off, Scott LaRock was shot to death while coming to the aid of rapper D-Nice. (**Man and His Music** is an unessential posthumous collection of remixes and early demos, including a track by D-Nice.) All of twenty-two but worldly wise, KRS-One bounced back with **By All Means Necessary,** appearing on the cover toting an Uzi in a self-defense stance carefully echoing a famous photograph of Malcolm X. In his newly articulated roles as metaphysician and teacher, Parker condemns self-destruction in "Stop the Violence" and shows impatience for hypocritical outsiders on "Necessary." BDP's most coherent record musically and lyrically, each track resonates powerfully, from the far-ranging manifesto "My Philosophy" to the drug conspiracies of "Illegal Business" and the battle-ready rhymes of "I'm Still #1."

Ghetto Music presents BDP as a full-fledged crew—including D-Nice, Willie D., Ms. Melodie and

Harmony—while experimenting with a crossover dancehall/hip-hop sound. KRS-One's tendency toward self-righteous humorlessness makes his knowledge go down like medicine, not music, and the album's generally uninspiring and murky beats make his lessons even less inviting. Only the singles "Why Is That?," "You Must Learn" and "Jack of Spades" pack real punch. **Edutainment** is better, incorporating sinuous jazz, funk, rock steady and ska grooves behind Parker's loose rhymes on cultural pride.

The **Live Hardcore Worldwide** collection of concert performances is an excellent document, both in terms of the group's onstage power and as a retrospective, but seemed like a holding action against the inevitable. Likewise, **Sex and Violence** did nothing to quell fears that the mighty was falling. Most of the album sounds as it if had been better done before; "13 and Good" is a one-note joke that isn't very funny.

Finally, KRS-One jettisoned the crew, went solo to cut the amazing single "Black Cop" and the self-analytical "Outta Here," and then turned in his most memorable record since **By All Means Necessary.** The title track of **Return of the Boom Bap** strips the sound ("It's the return of the real hard beats and real rap") and his attitude ("I'm an around the way guy with a baseball cap") back to basic elements. DJ Premier's propulsive production is a revelation, a perfect fit with KRS-One's aggressive rhyming. Catching a second creative wind, KRS has since produced records for members of the new BDP posse, including Channel Live and Mad Lion, and released an excellent B-side, "Hip Hop Vs. Rap." The eponymous followup maintains **Boom Bap**'s high standards, particularly on the irrepressibly funky "Rappaz R.N. Dainja," in which Premier styles a hip-hop march for KRS-One to tear the roof off like a bayou hurricane. [jzc]

See also *TPRG*.

BOOGIEMONSTERS

Riders of the Storm: The Underwater Album (Pendulum) 1994

Formed at Virginia State University, this eminently likable New York foursome follows in the footsteps of the Native Tongues (De La Soul, Jungle Brothers and A Tribe Called Quest). Lowdown, muted grooves provide the backdrop as Yodared (Al Myers), Myntric (Sean Myers), Mondo McCann and Vex (Sean Pollard) seek to transcend troublesome reality, offering lamentations for Mother Earth ("Mark of the Beast") and reflecting on everyday insanity ("Recognized Thresholds of Negative Stress"). The quartet's spacey, artfully offhand approach produces deceptively powerful mood music that may lack the brassy urgency of more commercial MCs, but repays repeated listenings with provocative mind excursions. [jy]

BOOK OF LOVE

Book of Love (I Square/Sire) 1984
Lullaby (I Square/Sire) 1988
Candy Carol (I Square/Sire/Warner Bros.) 1991
Lovebubble (I Square/Sire/Warner Bros.) 1993

A New York art-school quartet led by two unrelated Connecticut natives with the same surname, Book of Love introduced themselves with a then-innovative debut that cleverly synthesized catchy electro-pop minimalism and dance-driven rhythmatics. On **Book of Love**'s most atmospheric standouts, Susan Ottaviano's breathy, almost spoken vocals neatly offset the simple, spacious arrangements. (Special note to aficionados of esoteric cover versions: Book of Love tackles Liliput's "Diematrosen.")

From such fringey beginnings, Book of Love made the mistake of abandoning stylish economy and reaching for mainstream success on **Lullaby.** The imaginative group's knowing junk-culture side surfaces on a driving club interpretation of "Tubular Bells," but Susan O's sex-kitten singing, Ted Ottaviano's dumb lyrics and the routine sound of hyperactive sequencers get to be a drag.

The all-keyboards-and-vocals quartet (with a few guest guitarists) found its place again on **Candy Carol,** a toned-down and frequently enticing appliqué of flower-power style and lush pop harmonies. The synth arrangements run from trite ("Butterfly") to clever (the title track makes cute use of a melody that came pre-programmed on every thirty-dollar Casio). So do the lyrics: "Quiver" is simple and dumb, while "Flower Parade" presents an a cappella list of floral species, and "Orange Flip" is a kicky little ode to lipstick colors.

For much of **Lovebubble,** Ted Ottaviano's production keeps Book of Love current by relegating dance beats to a semi-ambient role; the band focuses on breezy harmonies and seductive audio collages as rhythms percolate gently underneath songs like "Sunday A.M." (shades of early OMD) and the Madonna-like (in sound, not attitude) good-riddance number, "Happily Ever After." In their strong melodic spines, firm rock beats and layers of harmony vocal frosting, "Hunny Hunny," "Flower in My Hand" and the delightfully flip "Tambourine" suggest an electronic ABBA for a post-ABBA world. Its stylistic diversity ensured by the consciously retro "Boy Pop," two ambient-house "Chatterbox" raps and a cover of Osibisa's "Woyaya," sung by Ted Ottaviano to the sole accompaniment of crowd noises, **Lovebubble** is an airy, relaxing charmer. The cover of David Bowie's "Sound and Vision," however, can't decide if it's reverent or mocking, and jags out like a bad note here. [i]

SONIC BOOM

See *Spacemen 3*.

BOO RADLEYS

Ichabod and I (UK Action) 1990
Kaleidoscope EP (UK Rough Trade) 1990
Every Heaven EP (UK Rough Trade) 1991
Boo Up EP (UK Rough Trade) 1991
Adrenaline EP (UK Creation) 1992
Everything's Alright Forever (Columbia) 1992
Boo Forever! EP (UK Creation) 1992
Giant Steps (Columbia) 1993
Learning to Walk (UK Rough Trade) 1994
Wake Up! (Columbia) 1995

EGGMAN

First Fruits (UK Creation) 1996

Though the central cast of characters has been the same all along, it seems as if there's been three Boo Radleys. From nutty noise merchants to schizophrenic dreampoppers to classic pop thoroughbreds gone Top 40 in the UK, it's been a long and strange path to European stardom for this Liverpool group that has never managed to crack the US.

Few people seem aware of **Ichabod and I.** Almost every writeup calls **Everything's Alright Forever** "the first album," and the band apparently wishes it were, having more or less disowned this primitive effort. A shambolic, untogether, unrealized work of a band that has just formed and is thrashing around in the dark, **Ichabod** isn't a complete bust: a decent melody threatens to peek its way out of "Kaleidoscope," and there are other such moments that portend the better things to come. But little here justifies the effort and expense required to procure a copy on the collector's market.

In contrast, **Everything's Alright Forever** finds the quartet diving headlong into the burgeoning shoegazer movement. Between the discordant tendencies, sheets of harsh sound and buried vocals as a (tuneful) afterthought, "Losing It (Song for Abigail)," "Skyscraper" and "Memory Babe" could be mistaken for My Bloody Valentine. Though the album is woefully inconsistent, its magnificent half throws the spectral, refracted guitar of songwriter Martin Carr into a melodic framework, thus approaching the spatial luster of the Pale Saints. It takes a while to get used to the album's excursion into the sea of sound, but at its best it's an aural paradise.

Giant Steps' advancement is Carr's maturing fascination with '60s sensibilities, not only with the decade's structure and sounds but also with its variety. Named for a John Coltrane LP, the album aspires to the multi-influenced repertoire that distinguished the mid-'60s Beatles, Kinks, Zombies, Hollies and especially the Beach Boys, whose specter looms large here. The Boo Radleys somehow pull it off, weaving seventeen incongruous songs into a fascinating tapestry rather than sounding like seventeen different tribute bands. Singer Sice croons impressively on such enigmatic, tense tunes as "Upon 9th and Fairchild" and the colossal "Lazarus" (dig those trumpets) and such baroque ditties as "Best Lose the Fear." A far-reaching album as challenging as it is enjoyable, loud and pretty.

Learning to Walk, a compilation of the first three EPs released between **Ichabod and I** and **Everything's Alright Forever,** might as well be the band's true second album, since "Kaleidoscope" is the only one of the dozen songs that appeared on either adjacent longplayer. Had it been released as such, it would have been the Boos' best ever. Although beset by Ride comparisons for similar shoegaze antics (the overdriven float-guitars), Carr goes on a hot streak on the last eight selections (from **Every Heaven** and **Boo Up**), with his best tunes and lyrics meeting jumpy basslines and stabbing guitars. With its dripping, lonely melody and haunting lyrics, "Everybird" is the pinnacle of the band's career. "Sometime Soon She Said" is equally exciting at double the tempo, and "The Finest Kiss" and the hypnotic "Naomi" are almost as spectacular. Any best-of-dream-pop compilation would need to include these. **Learning to Walk** also includes two otherwise unreleased John Peel session covers of songs by Love and New Order.

If **Learning to Walk** is track-for-track the band's best collection, **Wake Up!** is its most consistent start-to-finish proper LP. Alternately masterful and wonderfully strange, the album fits disparate parts together into an even flow, in much the same way the band's Liverpool ancestors could let George Harrison's Indian raga be followed by Paul McCartney pretending he was a dance-hall smoothie. In fact, the Boos save their finest work for midway through the album, where the near-perfect trio of "Reaching out From Here," "Martin, Doom! It's Seven O'Clock" and "Stuck on Amber" appear. The horn sections and busy strings on these tracks are especially deft; most bands attempting this would likely produce a pitiable nostalgia pastiche. **Wake Up!** takes a long time to develop and to convey its impact, but it truly does reward patience.

In '96, Sice released a solo album as the Eggman. [jr]

See also *Ed Ball.*

BOOTSTRAPPERS

See *Elliott Sharp.*

B.O.R.B.

See *Magic Hour.*

BORBETOMAGUS

Borbetomagus (Agaric) 1980
Work on What Has Been Spoiled (Agaric) 1981
Borbetomagus (Agaric) 1982
Barbed Wire Maggots (Agaric) 1983
Zurich (Agaric) 1984
New York Performances (Agaric) 1986
Snuff Jazz (Agaric) 1988
Seven Reasons for Tears (Purge Sound League) 1989
Borbeto Jam (Cadence Jazz) 1990
Experience the Magic (Agaric) 1991
Buncha Hair That Long (Agaric) 1992
Live at In-Roads (Japan. PSF) 1993

BORBETOMAGUS & FRIENDS

Industrial Strength (Leo) 1983

BORBETOMAGUS AND VOICE CRACK

Fish That Sparkling Bubble (UP06/Agaric) 1987
Asbestos Shake (Agaric) 1992

BORBETOMAGUS & THE SHAKING COELCANTH

Borbetomagus and the Shaking Coelcanth (Agaric) 1991

SAUTER/DIETRICH

Bells Together (Agaric) 1985

JIM SAUTER/DON DIETRICH/THURSTON MOORE

Barefoot in the Head (Forced Exposure) 1990 (Shock) 1991

DONALD MILLER

A Little Treatise on Morals (Audiofile) 1987 (Audible Hiss) 1995

If you don't think of jazz as a full-contact sport, you've obviously never spent any time in a room with the music of this durable upstate New York trio. "Punishing" doesn't even begin to describe the loud, assaultive—and often earthily beautiful—sound the members coax from guitar and two saxophones, instruments that here seldom uphold their conventional identities, thanks to innovative use of tone splitting, harmonic distortion and out-and-out brute force.

Initially formed at the tail end of the '70s—concurrent with, but not actually part of, New York's no wave scene—Borbetomagus imbued its free-squealing with a vividly blue-collar style, evident in both the members' biker-ish appearance and the sheer brawn with which Don Dietrich, Donald Miller and Jim Sauter handle their various "axes." The first self-titled disc—on which the core trio is abetted by sine-wave master Brian Doherty (his work is reminiscent of Allen Ravenstine's more jagged essays in Pere Ubu)—holds the seeds of what would become the Borbeto style, most notably Miller's jet-engine guitar roar, which occasionally wanes long enough to reveal him plucking strings like a mad harpist.

It wasn't until the 1982 release that the sheer otherness of the group manifested itself fully. Early performances may have manipulated a fairly wide range of horrible noise, but this one set up stakes around a tiny patch of what would come to be sacrosanct ground for Borbetomagus. Improvising vertically rather than horizontally, there's no release, only tension heaped upon tension. The three members scrape at each other's sore spots and howl with raw fury when the scraping gets too close to the bone. There's nothing remotely cyclical in these untitled improvisations—highlighted by a spatially disconcerting piece recorded before a clearly befuddled audience in Nyack, New York, in early '79—which sets Borbetomagus' new thing apart from even the radical blasts volleyed by Ornette Coleman et al. back in the day.

The forty-minute improvised piece that makes up **Barbed Wire Maggots,** while mottled with passages that are identifiable as jazz—notably a stretch of about five minutes in when Dietrich and Sauter trade fleet, squawking runs in the manner of Albert Ayler and Charles Tyler circa "Bells"—is as otherworldly in its power as anything the trio has ever produced. There are moments when Miller's guitar re-creates the sound of a dentist's drill in the mouth of a screaming patient—if the mic were attached to said patient's tonsils. Draining in every conceivable way.

The double-album **Zurich** and **New York Performances** record a portion of the Borbetomagus live experience, but fail to capture the sheer density, the non-aural undertow that comes from immersion in the uncommon frequencies the trio tends to inhabit. The latter, recorded in three parts during the summer of 1986, is especially effective in establishing the band's ability to build something other than a tsunami of sound. **Seven Reasons for Tears,** on which tape-manipulation expert Adam Nodelman guests, is one of Borbetomagus' most insidious releases, underlaid as it is with a constant dream-state drone that lulls even while the players manifest the will to provoke. A real soul-tearer.

The trio shifts gears to a degree on **Buncha Hair That Long,** which maintains the apocalyptic petitioning tone in a format that's considerably more discrete. Not only do the pieces have titles this time, the reedmen even make use of discernible phrasing: "Friendly Fire" practically ignites in a moment where the saxes, in unison, play what could pass for a baritone squonk variation on the coda from "Marquee Moon." To top it all off, the live-at-CBGB version of "Blue Jay Way" could easily reunite the Beatles for good if it were played in the presence of the surviving trio. **Live at In-Roads** is a sonically pristine reissue of an early cassette-only release documenting one of the band's confrontational New York shows.

Borbetomagus takes on an entirely different edge when locked in a room with Norbert Moslang and Andy Guhl (aka the Swiss electro-shock duo Voice Crack). Creating rhythms without percussion and sophisticated harmonics without chords per se, they wrest both philosophical manifestos and tribal primitivism from the randomly generated sizzle that permeates **Fish That Sparkling Bubble.** On the followup, the bent is more clearly cerebral, with Moslang and Guhl imparting a more scientific approach to the voltage-sapping entreaties contained herein.

The **Shaking Coelcanth** 10-inch incorporates the strangely Luddite electronics (mostly homemade patch synthesizers and radically deconstructed percussive devices) manipulated by Tennessee-based wiz Dennis Ray Levis, whose junkyard noise can also be sampled on albums released under the Shaking Ray Levis imprimatur. It's an exquisite mix of over (amplified) and out (of their mind) elements. The earlier **Industrial Strength** is quite a bit less powerful, not because the onslaught is any less fierce, but because the three Borbeto men tend to allow the multitude of fellow travelers too much autonomy. The excessively diffuse nature of the hit-and-miss improv clusters attest to the necessity of keeping free combos as compact as possible.

Sonic Youth guitarist Thurston Moore steps into—and almost fills—Miller's shoes on **Barefoot in the Head.** Playing with percussive force, Moore sticks to underpinning "All Doors Look Alike" (which features some remarkable high-end blowing by one of the reedmen) and leans into a leering grind on "Concerning the Sun as a Cool Solid" with such glee one can actually infer some truth behind the liner-note assertion that he was begging to be "freed from the shackles of the Peggy Lee–descended dogshit" of his day job. **Bells Together** is a deceptively simple description of the Dietrich/Sauter album, long stretches of which consist of the two saxists placing the bells of their instruments together and blowing—a maneuver that seems to allow them to play each other's very lungs as much as the instruments themselves.

Sauter has also played and recorded with the Blue Humans, an incendiary no-wave-cum-free-skronk outfit led by Ed Wood biographer Rudolph Grey, who can also count drummer Rashied Ali among his collaborators. Miller has provided jolts on several albums by drummer William Hooker (as well as the industro-trance group Lhasa Cement Plant). The guitarist's solo album, **A Little Treatise on Morals,** is given over to more subtle uses of space than most of his work with the band. There are certainly outbursts where power electronics have their way (especially on the grinding "Deploration") but, by and large, the textured string-play shows a kinder (if not necessarily gentler) side to the noise titan. [dss]

See also *William Hooker, Sonic Youth.*

BOREDOMS

Anal by Anal (Japan. Trans) 1986
Osorezan to Stooges Kyo (Japan. Selfish) 1988
Onanie Bomb Meets the Sex Pistols (Japan. WEA) 1989 (Warner Bros.) 1994
Soul Discharge (Shimmy-Disc) 1991 + 1992
Pop Tatari (Japan. WEA) 1992 (Reprise) 1993
Wow-2 (Japan. Avant) 1993
Super Roots EP (Japan. WEA) 1993 (Reprise) 1994
Chocolate Synthesizer (Japan. WEA) 1994 (Reprise) 1995
Super Roots 2 EP (Japan. WEA) 1994

Super Roots 3 (Japan. WEA) 1994
Super Roots 5 (Japan. WEA) 1995
Super Roots 6 (Reprise) 1996

UFO OR DIE

Bee Haibu [tape] (Japan. SSS) 1990
UOD [tape] (Japan. Bron) 1991
Cassettetape Superstar (Time Bomb/Public Bath) 1993

OMOIDE HATOBA

Daiongaku (Japan. Alchemy) 1990
Suichi Joe (Japan. Alchemy) 1991
Black Hawaii (Japan. Alchemy) 1992
Mantako (Public Bath) 1994
Livers & Giggers (Japan. Overseas) 1994
Kinsei (Japan. Meldac) 1995

AUDIO SPORTS

3-6-9 EP (Japan. Bron) 1991
Eat Buy Eat EP (Japan. All Access) 1992
Era of Glittering Gas (Japan. All Access) 1992

HANADENSHA

The Golden Age of Heavy Blood (Japan. Alchemy) 1992
Hanaden Bless All (Japan. Alchemy) 1993

DEKOBOKO HAJIME/YAMANTAKA EYE

Nani Nani (Tzadik) 1995

MYSTIC FUGU ORCHESTRA

Zohar (Tzadik) 1995

HANATARASH

Hanatarashi (Japan. Alchemy) 1985
2 (Japan. Alchemy) 1987
3 (RRR) 1990
The Hanatarash and His Eye EP (Public Bath) 1992
Live! 84 Dec 16 Zabo Kyoto (Japan. Mom n Dad) 1992
Live! 88 Feb 21 Antiknock Tokyo (Japan. Mom n Dad) 1992
4 (AIDS-a-Delic) (Public Bath) 1994

SONIC YOUTH/EYE YAMATSUKA

Shit TV EP (Ecstatic Peace!) 1994

This ever-evolving Osaka-based band's confoundingly intricate sound resembles a head-on collision between the less showbizzy, free-form efforts of Sun Ra's Arkestra and the scatological nihilism of early Butthole Surfers—fronted by the hollers and gibbers of a couple of guys who can't decide whether they'd rather be Beastie Boys or Residents. But even that doesn't really describe the sheer sense of otherness that pervades the Boredoms aesthetic, which appears to stem from a desire to short-circuit the game of telephone that passes for cultural exchange in these post-post-modern times. Or maybe they simply *are* from Mars.

On **Anal by Anal,** Boredoms engage in a veritable scatalog of potty-probing, including such enduring classics as "Anal Eater" and "Born to Anal." Things really start to get weird on **Osorezan to Stooges Kyo,** which would sound like an outer-space interception of eclectic FM transmissions circa 1966 a million or so light-years away if combating frontmen Eye Yamatsuka and Toyohito Yoshikawa (who rant almost exclusively in an invented language not at all unlike that used by Magma in the '70s) weren't so near-at-hand. Structure-free sonic whirlwinds like "Call Me God" and "Feedbackfuck" are simultaneously far funnier than any quirk-rock smirk-fest you'd care to name and far scarier than any death-metal posing in recent memory. The first two releases were combined into **Onanie Bomb Meets the Sex Pistols,** subsequently issued in the US in different packaging.

Soul Discharge has marginally more terrestrial reference points—like the snuff-film B-52's cop "52 Boredom" and the Funkadelic-on-strychnine "funk" of "JB Dick + Tin Turner Pussy Badsmell"—but it's still a daunting challenge to figure out how the sextet has gotten from point A to point 396. Guitarist Yamamoto, whose thrust-and-parry figures rarely last more than a bar or two, nevertheless demonstrates a prescient improv style, especially when he and drummer P-We YY (aka Yoshimi P-Wee) dive headlong into their Three Stooges slap-shtick. Subsequent CD pressings added fourteen bonus tracks, some new (like the mondo obstreperous "Jah Called AC/DC") and some alternate versions of previously released tracks. Shadowy ancillary member God Mama "became invisible" (to use official Bore-speak) after this release.

Pop Tatari may well be the apex of Borecore, with its endless procession of sideshow audio spectacle, self-aggrandizing (and self-lampooning) conceit and remarkably intricate free-jazz-as-demolition-derby sonic wackiness. Two drummers (including the irrepressible P-Wee, who also pitches in with wordless dog whistle screeches from time to time) alternate between pushing the band forward and setting up roadblocks in its path, making songs like "Bod" and "Okinawa Rasta Beef (Mockin' Fuzz2)" into virtual-rock Rosetta Stones. Yamatsuka's glottal acrobatics (he frequently deep-throats the mic) highlight "Heeba" and "Telehorse Uma," while "Cheeba," a clever cross-cultural cop, turns the Peggy Lee classic "Fever" into a nine-minute pro-pot paean. And if you haven't had enough excess by album's end, the band purees thirty-five years of rock'n'roll into ten minutes of psychobabble on "Cory & the Mandara Suicide Pyramid Action or Gas Satori."

Although its intent is no less twisted, **Chocolate Synthesizer** (which apparently revolves around the concept of electronic music's invention in the caves of prehistoric Japan) seems to have been recorded after the discovery of the Ritalin patch. While traveling carnival spine-jolters like "Shock City" and "Anarchy in the UKK" maintain the everything-all-at-once-forever methodology of Borecore of yore, the album is mottled with ambient pieces that often veer too far toward the Zappa realm. Seemingly cut from the same swath of sound, "Tomato Synthesizer," "Synthesizer Guide Book on Fire" and "Action Synthesizer Hero" do little to instill the sense of wonder the band seldom miscarried in the past.

The **Super Roots** series is dominated by unedited freakouts, with later volumes consisting of one long piece of what Yamatsuka has characterized as "ambient hardcore." It's possible to accept the ambient portion of that description only if your everyday living situation puts you in close proximity to either a jet-testing facility or a slaughterhouse (ideally both). The first edition is the most overtly playful, with skittery schoolyard giggles like "Ear? Wig? Web?" and "Budokan Tape Try (500 Tapes High)" setting a giddy mood. That carries over to **Super Roots 2,** which will keep you on the edge of your seat, if only for the numerous long silences that cleave songs like "Magic Milk" and "White Plastic See-Through Finger." Later editions (there is no **Super Roots 4** as yet) are more byzantine in structure, ranging from the third set's thirty-minute "Karaoke of Cosmos" to the utterly incomprehensible hour-long "Go!" on **5.**

There are numerous ephemeral Boredoms releases, most of which stem from Yamatsuka's situationist perspective on record-making. He's been known to cut single-copy editions of items (like "Born to Be Wild") to be pressed and sold in the same day. The cassettes he's issued under the Boretronix moniker (think Frippertronics with attitude) are slightly more obtainable.

For fans of space-a-delic rap, the band offers that in its Audio Sports side project, which resembles nothing so much as the Beastie Boys being choreographed by a tag team of Neil Tennant and John Zorn. With its surreal cutting (provided by DJ Kool Jazz Takemura) and stun-gun BPM levels, **Eat Buy Eat** uses basic hip-hop elements as a base for wiggy gibbers and rasps that effectively skewer consumer culture icons. Yamatsuka is less of a presence on **Era of Glittering Gas,** but his hijinks add an edgy goofiness to the maliciously playful "Outlaw in Wonderland."

UFO or Die (anchored by Yamatsuka and Yoshimi) takes its inspiration directly from neo-aboriginal '60s combos like the Godz and the Fugs: the very name (an acronym for Unlimited Freak Out) is taken from a song by the latter band, and a cover of the former's "Radar Eyes" is one of the multiple highlights on the endlessly entertaining **Cassettetape Superstar.** Perhaps the most Boredoms-like of the myriad spin-off bands, UFO or Die undertakes some of the more extreme regressions "rock" music has seen in the '90s, what with Eye grunting neanderthal monosyllables over a backing of seemingly random percussion (on "Dog Wave"). There's no real intent to pass any of this off as legitimate outsider stuff: it never takes long before the band lapses into purposeful funk deconstruction ("Kendo Machine Smokin' ") or meta-rock insight (as on "MC5 or 6"). The most unlikely—but enjoyable—party album of the '90s.

Omoide Hatoba provides a vehicle for guitarist Yamamoto to mobilize his own set of noise-guitar forces. While he never quite reaches the astral heights of peers like Zeni Geva's KK Null or Fusitsusha's Keiji Haino, he does put the six-string through some truly dizzying paces. His scrabbling on **Black Hawaii** fuses muscle and whimsy in a way one might expect from a (Groucho) Marxist version of Sonny Sharrock, especially on "Zen Beat Manifesto" and what's allegedly a version of Country Joe's "Feel Like I'm Fixin' to Die Rag." The trio takes a similar tack on **Mantako,** though the freak-outs that burble through the surface of "Come On! Me!" are a bit rote. Yamamoto expands the band's lineup for **Kinsei,** and the elusive bleats of baritone sax and tuba give the whole suite (titular translations are not provided) an inscrutable, provocative air.

Don't let the altered surname spelling put you off the scent of **Nani Nani,** one of many projects in which Yamatsuka (aka Yamantaka) engages in non-stop headbutting with John Zorn (aka Dekoboko Hajime). Zorn's sax playing is unmistakable, but he actually spends more time weaving off-kilter spazzadelia on harmonium and sitar, which adds an element of brown acid trippiness to tracks like "Yoga Dollar" and the appropriately titled "Bad Hawkwind." Eye squeaks happily on an array of toy instruments and tinker-toy percussion; that staging makes his inhuman vocal histrionics sound agreeably cartoonish. Using another set of aliases, the duo also convened as Mystic Fugu Orchestra (the *fugu* being the Japanese delicacy that can cause either gustatory orgasm or serious illness, depending on the skill of the chef). **Zohar** is a far more solemn, Teutonic-sounding collection, dominated by Zorn's harmonium washes, but it never achieves any real level of intensity.

Longtime Boredoms bassist Hira also serves as "singer" for the deconstructionist-blues outfit Hanadensha, which more or less transports Blue Cheer–styled thud to the top of a musical Tower of Babel. **The Golden Age of Heavy Blood** is an improbably thick wall of sludge, peppered with Hira's razor-cut stage whispering and injured yowls—which are most effective on the head-spinning "Mary Mary Mary." The double-CD **Hanaden Bless All** is even more excessive: Although it trims the two-bass lineup to a more manageable power trio, the lava-like progression of songs like "God Only Needs Hanadensha" could easily be field recordings of a particularly primitive cargo cult.

Before the Boredoms, Yamatsuka was the prime mover in (and eventually the sole member of) the Hanatarash, a post–Einstürzende Neubauten exercise in power-tool abuse and tape manipulation. The doggedly phallocentric first album, which includes such tracks as "Power Cock" and "Cock Victory," is dominated by Christian Marclay–styled turntable deconstruction, but the loopiness subverts any real effect. Guitarist Jojo Hiroshige brings more menace to the mix of **2** with the howling feedback and rancorous sheet-metal shriek he adds to songs like "Vortex Shit" and "Boat People Hate Fuck." The live albums are probably the most accurate (not to say the most listenable) documents of the Hanatarash experience, replete as they are with shattering glass, exploding metal and the omnipresent sound of a machine shop full of grinding gears. Yamatsuka eventually backed off the injurious confrontation—partly as a result of nearly severing a leg when one of the stage constructions (literally) backfired. [dss]

See also *Naked City, Painkiller, Sonic Youth, John Zorn.*

BO$$

Born Gangstaz (DJ West/Chaos/Columbia) 1993

The line between female empowerment, cynical image-mongering and a B-girl variant of exploitative self-abuse evaporates in the mic work of Lichelle Laws, the chronic-smoking, fuck-not-giving voice and mind of Bo$$. Joined by partner Irene Moore and an all-star cast of producers headed by Erick Sermon, MC Serch, Jam Master Jay and Def Jef, Laws fronts a full-on gangsta pose—spewing animosity, talking sex, recalling bank jobs and promising violence on convincingly hardass tracks like "Drive By," "2 to da Head," "Born Gangsta," "Recipe of a Hoe" and "Diary of a Mad Bitch." Punctuated by death-happy vignettes, **Born Gangstaz** is made fascinating by Laws' tacit acknowledgment that she's play-acting: phone messages from her mother and father detail a middle-class Catholic-school/tap-dancing/piano-playing upbringing that doesn't exactly mesh with the album's relentless crudity and senseless violence. Some gangstas, it seems, are made, not born. [i]

BOSS HOG

Drinkin, Lechin' & Lyin' EP (Amphetamine Reptile) 1989
Cold Hands (Amphetamine Reptile) 1990
Action Box EP (Amphetamine Reptile) 1991
Girl+ EP (Amphetamine Reptile) 1992
Boss Hog (DGC) 1995

This loosely configured hipster conglomerate began as a conceptual exercise in art-rock carnality (talk about an oxymoron!) and surreptitiously developed into a legit, earthy dirt-blues *band.* It'd be hard to anticipate that sort of validity from the smirky debut, which does come swathed in one of the most eye-catching covers—a full-frontal nude photo of the band's frontwoman, Cristina Martinez—to cross the threshold in modern times. The disc's innards, heavily skewed toward the kind of deconstructionist garage-rock proffered by Pussy Galore (a band led by Martinez's husband and Boss Hog bandmate Jon Spencer), don't match up.

Cold Hands, (un)dressed in another impressive Cristina-as-art statement on the front, is a bit more lucid, but its reliance on in-jokes—songs are named in tribute to such band pals as "Gerard" (Cosloy, a writer turned record executive) and "Pete Shore" (the Unsane bassist who guests here)—and calculatedly rakish rhythmic stratagems make it the aural equivalent of a vanity press book. In terms of pure hedonism, it'd be hard to top **Action Box** (the non-cheesecake cover aside). Over the course of four songs, Martinez casts the sex act as both demolition derby ("Bunny Fly") and down-at-the-crossroads soul-swap ("Big Fish," wherein she and Spencer engage in a sexy crawlin'-blues duet). **Girl+** spends the bulk of its time in similarly dusky territory, from the muted-trumpet strut of "Ruby" to the ominously whispered terrorfest "Some Sara." The consolidation of a tenable lineup helps matters dramatically: of particular note is the bracingly erotic bass playing by Jens Jurgensen, also the post-scum scene's most noted filmmaker.

After a long absence from recording, Boss Hog (a quartet with the pseudonymous Hollis Queens on drums) returned to action none the worse for wear on its major-label bow. In the interim, both Spencer and Martinez discovered that it don't mean a thing if it ain't got that swing—and songs like "What the Fuck" and "Green Shirt" (definitely not an Elvis Costello cover) have got it in spades. A full pelvic workout. [dss]

See also *Action Swingers, Gibson Bros, Jon Spencer Blues Explosion.*

ANNE RICHMOND BOSTON

See *Ottoman Empire.*

BOTTLE ROCKETS

Bottle Rockets (East Side Digital) 1993
The Brooklyn Side (ESD) 1994 (ESD/Tag/Atlantic) 1995

If you're gonna play highway-driving, bar-haunting, trailer-parking, lovesick scruffy T-shirt roots-rock, there are probably worse places to come from than Festus, Missouri. After all, it's a small town right by a big city, both midwestern *and* southern. Fueled by the purified essence of roadhouse rock'n'roll but sweet on country swing and steering the bus with intelligence and a temperate sense of humor, the Bottle Rockets can play it safe when they want—and then floor the noise pedal in a Crazy Horse explosion of controlled fury. Judging by their first two albums, these experienced club veterans can do it with their eyes closed, but know that it's more fun when you get to watch.

Having evolved from a group called Chicken Truck, the car-obsessed quartet cut its first album in Athens, Georgia. Produced by John Keane and featuring guest appearances by Jeff Tweedy and Jay Farrar of Uncle Tupelo (on whose **March 16–20, 1992** Bottle Rockets frontman Brian Henneman played), **Bottle Rockets** is eager and excitable, fun but sometimes clumsy. Ingenuous enough to obsess about a filling station "Gas Girl" and pitch woo with a car bumper in "Every Kinda Everything," the Bottle Rockets are also ready to condemn rebel hostility in "Wave That Flag" and funny enough to chronicle the culture incongruities of "Manhattan Countryside." Singer/guitarist Henneman has a burly voice better suited to the randy slobber of "Trailer Mama" than the sensitive restraint of "Got What I Wanted," but when he tells the story of a burned-out trailer in "Kerosene," cutting Keane's pretty pedal steel with angry indignation, it's obvious he's listening to the words he's singing.

Made in New York with Eric Ambel at the board, **The Brooklyn Side** is a sharper, harder, more cosmopolitan collection that brings the band's strengths into cohesive focus with infinitely better songs. (So much for the sophomore jinx.) The thick, roaring "1000 Dollar Car" is a wry, hard-won lesson in previously owned automotive economics; "Radar Gun" offers more motoring fun (and a way to make a quick buck). Over a stormy Neil Young sound in "Sunday Sports," Henneman describes a couch potato making his weekly escape from life. The twangy "Idiot's Revenge" takes a cue from Merle Haggard in pissing all over someone who "likes Dinosaur Jr but she can't tell you why/Says you like country music, man you deserve to die." On the serious romantic tip, the surging, memorably melodic "I'll Be Comin' Around" holds out an insistent back-door-hand to someone already in a relationship—"If he ever breaks your heart/Decides he wants to make a new start/Or if you just want to be vile/And he steps out for a while." An album unguarded enough to brush up against Jimi Hendrix in one song ("Stuck in a Rut") and mention Hank Williams in another ("Queen of the World"), **The Brooklyn Side** is the rollercoaster to ride. [i]

DAVID BOWIE

Man of Words/Man of Music (Mercury) 1969
The Man Who Sold the World (Mercury) 1970 (RCA) 1972 (Rykodisc) 1990
Hunky Dory (RCA) 1971 (Rykodisc) 1990
The Rise and Fall of Ziggy Stardust and the Spiders From Mars (RCA) 1972 (Rykodisc) 1990
Space Oddity (RCA) 1972 (Rykodisc) 1990
Images 1966–1967 (London) 1973
Aladdin Sane (RCA) 1973 (Rykodisc) 1990
Pin Ups (RCA) 1973 (Rykodisc) 1990
Diamond Dogs (RCA) 1974 (Rykodisc) 1990
David Live (RCA) 1974 (Rykodisc) 1990
Young Americans (RCA) 1975 (Rykodisc) 1991
Station to Station (RCA) 1976 (Rykodisc) 1991
Changesonebowie (RCA) 1976
Low (RCA) 1977 (Rykodisc) 1991

Starting Point (London) 1977
Heroes (RCA) 1977 (Rykodisc) 1991
Stage (RCA) 1978 (Rykodisc) 1991
Lodger (RCA) 1979 (Rykodisc) 1991
Scary Monsters (RCA) 1980 (Rykodisc) 1992
Changestwobowie (RCA) 1981
Let's Dance (EMI America) 1983 (Virgin) 1995
Ziggy Stardust: The Motion Picture (RCA) 1983 (Rykodisc) 1992
Golden Years (RCA) 1983
Tonight (EMI America) 1984 (Virgin) 1995
Fame and Fashion (RCA) 1984
Never Let Me Down (EMI America) 1987 (Virgin) 1995
Sound+Vision (Rykodisc) 1989 + 1995
Changesbowie (Rykodisc) 1990
Early On (1964–1966) (Rhino) 1991
Black Tie White Noise (Savage) 1993 (Virgin) 1995
The Buddha of Suburbia (UK Arista/BMG) 1993 (Virgin) 1995
The Singles 1969 to 1993 (Rykodisc) 1993
Outside: The Nathan Adler Diaries (Virgin) 1995

TIN MACHINE

Tin Machine (EMI) 1989 (Virgin) 1995
Tin Machine II (Victory) 1991
Tin Machine Live: Oy Vey, Baby (Victory) 1992

David Bowie may no longer have a lucid plan for how to keep up with the stylistic grandchildren—his 1995 tour with Nine Inch Nails proved to be a generation-gap disaster as young Reznorfarians turned their backs on the funny old guy doing a bunch of songs that weren't half as fuckinamazin as "Closer"—but he certainly hasn't lost his will to try. If Bowie's attempts to be as inventive as he was a quarter-century ago have been marked by ideas less likely to redirect the course of rock (or, occasionally, produce listenable albums) than the costume-illusion distancing of **Ziggy Stardust,** the '70s soul rapprochement of **Young Americans** or the avant-garde sound of **Station to Station,** his unflagging enthusiasm and curiosity have at least kept him a credible and provocative figure. Leading an unchartable multi-media course of stylistic discontinuity and precipitous reinvention—doing whatever total change of pace comes naturally—London boy David Jones is still productively making it up as he goes along.

After enjoying the just commercial desserts of his deftly club-*and*-pop-geared **Let's Dance** (followed, less enjoyably all around, by the musical and monetary hangovers of **Tonight** and **Never Let Me Down**) in the mid-'80s, Bowie hit upon one of the diminishing number of personal options he had not previously entertained: forming a low-profile group that would not bear his name. Thus was born Tin Machine, a semi-collaborative quartet with native New York guitarist Reeves Gabrels and the fraternal rhythm section of Hunt and Tony Sales, whose lengthy résumé includes a substantial '70s stint with Iggy Pop.

The group's debut, **Tin Machine,** presents an uneven (thanks mostly to bouts of Gabrels' idiotic guitar-god riffwank) but entertaining rough'n'ready vision of contemporary rock as blunt, vulgar, violent, ephemeral and derivative—in short, the direct antithesis of Bowie's prevailing artistic ethos. The title track is an amusing rewrite of the Yardbirds' "Over Under Sideways Down" (a **Pin Ups** flashback, perhaps?); "Under the God" addresses neo-fascism with a sly Ramones citation ("Beating on blacks with a baseball bat"), while "Crack City" ("Louie, Louie" recast as a **Diamond Dogs** outtake) ludicrously sets out to slay a dragon—or at the very least indignantly call drug dealers bad names. The cover of John Lennon's "Working Class Hero" is fair but irrelevant, and the album's catchiest melody ("Baby Can Dance") is oddly saved for the very end. All in all, Bowie's exercise in self-denial doesn't actually trim much out of the diet—it's not a great leap forward, but a fun ride all the same. (The Virgin reissue adds a live version of "Bus Stop.")

The ancient nude statuary on the front of **Tin Machine II** outraged retail moralists, who declined to stock the album and forced a redesign. Such disfavor would have been easier to accept if they'd simply listened to the thing. Making it obvious that Bowie's agenda for the band involves self-conscious slumming and a desire to revisit his past under cover of an autonomous timeline (thereby escaping accusations of regression), the album displays a singing style (on "Baby Universal") that hasn't been heard in years; a cover of Roxy Music's glam-era "If There Is Something" and nonsense originals like "You Belong in Rock & Roll" all suggest a futile effort to reclaim lost innocence. Whatever Bowie's motivations, Tin Machine was clearly designed for instant obsolescence. It only takes drummer Hunt Sales stepping up to sing the generic blues "Stateside" for Bowie's experiment in democracy to collapse in a miserable heap.

Nevertheless, the group (augmented on tour by an extra guitarist) pressed on long enough to leave an egregious live album, **Oy Vey, Baby,** as its final squalling-guitar statement. Between crummy sound, Gabrels' numbing fill-every-space onslaught and rearrangements that exacerbate an irrational set list (not to mention Bowie's always dangerous saxophone exercises), it's a woeful epitaph in any language. (The U2 joke of the title is cute, though.)

After that escapade, Bowie wisely returned to his own monotheistic world; unfortunately, the record he chose to make was **Black Tie White Noise,** an ill-conceived if reasonably well-executed (by Nile Rodgers) adventure into acid-jazz—or whatever other description might characterize a pretentious album of mildly ambient dance grooves with trumpeter Lester Bowie (no relation, ha-ha) blowing his horn in half-hearted opposition to a third of the tracks. (Other guests, including onetime Spiders From Mars Mick Ronson and Mike Garson, complicate the remainder.) Covers of Cream's "I Feel Free" and Morrissey's "I Know It's Going to Happen Someday" (from **Your Arsenal,** an album Ronson produced) are capricious red herrings. So is the hapless Bowie/Bowie horn jam, "Looking for Lester." The title number is a glossy R&B duet (with Al B. Sure!) that cites both Marvin Gaye and "We Are the World" in an oblique consideration of the LA riots. Although the album's main theme is a sense of racial and personal harmony resulting from Bowie's marriage to model Iman ("The Wedding" even opens the procession with church bells), its most compelling track digs at the other end of life's yard. "Jump" is a vague take on society's deadly power.

Ironically, the little-noticed **Buddha of Suburbia,** an album expanded from the soundtrack work Bowie did for a BBC-TV mini-series of the Hanif Kureishi novel, takes a far more effective and enthralling spin on the modern dancefloor. Recorded quickly as a two-man endeavor with multi-instrumentalist Erdal Kizilcay, the album benefits from a paradoxically random simplicity (of sound, not designs: like his confrère Eno, Bowie sets and meets arbitrary conceptual challenges here). Although fully realized, the scattered pop songs—"Strangers When We Meet," the Pet Shoppy "Dead Against It," the "Fame"-like "Bleed Like Crazy, Dad," "Buddha of Suburbia," one version of which has a hideous Lenny Kravitz guitar solo—have an ebullience and directness, an ingratiating why-not-try-this? aspect that counteracts Bowie's implicit high-art seriousness. The rest of the album meanders through fascinating rhythms and varied atmospheres like a wealthy shopper in a fine department store, picking up the latest styles, trying them on and then scampering on to the next rack. Bowie's liner notes make the whole thing seem obnoxiously self-conscious, but you've got to love a brilliant piss-artist who can admit to repeating bits "at varying intervals so giving the impression of forethought." Downplaying the source and eliminating Bowie's exegesis, the belated American issue has a completely different cover and booklet than the import.

Bowie reunited with Eno as co-writer, co-producer and instrumental collaborator for **Outside,** which is subtitled *The Art-Ritual Murder of Baby Grace Blue* and described as "A non-linear Gothic Drama Hypercycle." So much for humor and humility. ("A convoluted load of bollocks," would be a more apt underline.) Flying in the face of all we know to be true about concept albums, Bowie cobbles together a lurid meta-plot and peoples it with processed-voice characters. As is often the case with such preposterous projects, the construction process involves some quality songs, and it hardly matters that the bubbling techno calm of "We Prick You" is indicated as being sung by members of the Court of Justice, that Leon Blank renders "The Motel" or that Detective Nathan Adler delivers "The Hearts Filthy Lesson," a dance track loaded up with random instrumental action. If there's nothing else self-evident about the artist, it's that Bowie—in whatever guise he affects—is always Bowie. **Outside**'s raucous highlights include "Hallo Spaceboy," a pulverizing industrial flip of the nine-inch tail, and "Voyeur of Utter Destruction (As Beauty)," a powerful, King Crimson–like charge lanced by lines of feedback and colliding rhythms. The album also contains passages of orchestral grace and quiet solace, like the febrile piano/drum jazz inventions at the heart of "A Small Plot of Land" and the nearly subliminal buildup of "The Motel." The story of **Outside** is not one worth telling, but the master of musical language still festoons it with brilliant sonic poetry.

Rykodisc's wholesale reissue of Bowie's catalogue, which began with the 1989 boxed set **Sound+Vision,** refurbished the sound, artwork and contents of his '70s and '80s albums, adding bonus tracks—B-sides, outtakes, alternate versions, non-LP singles, live bits—to all but two of them (**Aladdin Sane** and the thanks-I've-had-enough Ziggy Stardust concert film soundtrack). The studio **Ziggy Stardust** received extra-posh treatment in a special edition with its own booklet and slipcase, as well as five extra items, including the original demos for "Ziggy Stardust" and "Lady Stardust." (In 1995, having already replaced **Sound+Vision Plus,** the audio/video bonus disc that originally came in the box, with a more current CD-ROM, Ryko redesigned the set to eliminate the twelve-by-twelve design and the multi-media item altogether, leaving three music discs in a regular-sized case.)

Virgin subsequently acquired the rights to what was left and brought out augmented CDs of Bowie's three '80s records on EMI America and the lost-on-arrival **Black Tie White Noise.** "Under Pressure," Bowie's memorable 1982 45 collaboration with Queen, is the bonus track on **Let's Dance. Tonight** goes to the movies for Bowie's soundtrack contributions to *The Falcon and the Snowman* ("This Is Not America"), *Labyrinth* ("As the World Falls Down") and *Absolute Beginners* ("Absolute Beginners"). The new version of **Never Let Me Down** effects a swap, deleting "Too Dizzy" but adding two B-sides from the album's singles and another movie theme ("When the Wind Blows").

Meanwhile, Rhino packaged up a nifty set of Bowie's earliest singles (and some outtakes) as **Early On,** thereby putting the amusing music from some previously highly prized 7-inch obscurities within easy reach. Rykodisc then trumped its own **Changesbowie** (and, in the process, the two similarly named RCA compilations it had replaced, as well as the slapdash **Golden Years** and **Fame and Fashion**) with a prodigious thirty-nine-track greatest-hits, **The Singles 1969 to 1993,** two discs that follow Bowie's musical saga all the way from "Space Oddity"—the leadoff track of 1969's **Man of Words/Man of Music** (later retitled **Space Oddity**)—right up to the doorstep of **Outside.** (Early copies of the compilation included a bonus third CD of Bowie's warmhearted Christmas duet with Bing Crosby.) Whether or not it was planned this way, **The Singles** neatly complements **Sound+Vision**—a beautifully appointed three-CD collection of classics, obscurities, outtakes, concert recordings, etc. that is everything but a greatest-hits—with a minimum of overlap. [i]

See also *TPRG*.

BOY GEORGE

Sold (Virgin) 1987
Tense Nervous Headache (UK Virgin) 1988
Boyfriend (Ger. Virgin) 1989
High Hat (Virgin) 1989
The Martyr Mantras (Virgin) 1991
Cheapness and Beauty (Virgin) 1995

BOY GEORGE AND CULTURE CLUB

At Worst . . . The Best of Boy George and Culture Club (SBK) 1993

Boy George's solo career, launched in the wake of Culture Club, didn't get off to a good start: **Sold** is overblown and forgettable, possessing none of the flair his former band once had. The album's dubious high point is an absurd reggaefied version of Bread's "Everything I Own," modeled after Ken Boothe's mid-'70s interpretation. The former George O'Dowd's next American album, stitched together from two overseas releases (one of which didn't even come out in England), appeared as **High Hat:** slick, assembly-line R&B without a shred of personality. For a performer who built a huge career on stylized outrage, such musical anonymity is amazing.

The Martyr Mantras, a dance-oriented remix compilation of non-LP singles and newer tracks recorded with a variety of producers (including one collaboration with ex–Culture Clubber Jon Moss), is a significant improvement. Though most of the material is more functional than inspired, the uncluttered extended settings allow George to deliver some genuinely soulful vocal performances, particularly on the social-activist disco number "Generations of Love" (included in two versions) and the ballad "One on One." Showing a little political awareness, "No Clause 28" is an effectively good-humored anti-oppression rant.

Released to take advantage of the singer's 1992 commercial rebirth via a Pet Shop Boys–produced version of "The Crying Game," **At Worst** retraces his steps, from 1982's "Do You Really Want to Hurt Me" through **The Martyr Mantras** and beyond: 1993's "Love Hurts" (not the Everly Brothers classic) and PM Dawn's George-sung "More Than Likely" (from the duo's **Bliss Album**). Whether or not there's much evidence of creative progress here, that cushy voice remains easy on the ears, and the degree of craft and cozy warmth stays high even when the choice or design of the material falters. Summarizing an era subject to extreme degrees of personal trouble and strife (chronicled in a 1995 autobiography, *Take It Like a Man*), **At Worst** is an impressively even-tempered report.

No such description suits **Cheapness and Beauty,** Boy George's shameless, conflicted and semi-cool rock album. Backed on about half the songs by a speeding guitar/synths-charged quartet produced to a fine Billy Idol–like roar by Jessica Corcoran, George's strong voice is almost indistinguishable as the soulful crooner of yore. Elsewhere, a more temperate tone prevails, and there are acoustic numbers, straight pop and even an orchestral extravaganza. Separated by phone messages and spoken-word scraps, and making frequent reference to drugs and addiction, the songs run the gamut of George's obsessions. He proffers rough self-analysis ("God Don't Hold a Grudge," "I'll Adore," the string-y "If I Could Fly"), expresses different devotion ("Your Love Is What I Am," the restrained "Cheapness & Beauty") and gay pride (the folky "Same Thing in Reverse"), and indulges mean-spirited vendettas. The sadistically gloating "Sad" and the touchingly acoustic but bitter "Unfinished Business" are clearly meant to injure guilty parties, but it's difficult to be sure diatribes like "Satan's Child" ("You're sick and you're twisted/Irreverent, so beautiful") aren't about his nibs. [i/ss]

See also *TPRG.*

BRACKET

924 Forestville St. (Caroline) 1994
4-Wheel Vibe (Caroline) 1995

It's almost impossible not to think of Bracket as a minor-league Green Day. The two bands have an undeniable similarity in style and sound—the same catchy melodies, power-chord guitars and bratty vocals—and Bracket's signing came hard on the heels of Green Day's multi-platinum **Dookie.** The quartet from the northern California town of Forestville even borrows the Green Day device of stopping the instruments for a few beats so the vocals can hammer home a hook.

But that's not to say that **924 Forestville St.** doesn't have charms of its own. Unlike the snarl and slacker angst of **Dookie,** Bracket offers a sunnier, more lighthearted variety of pop-punk, with lots of sweet harmonizing and a few tasty (but regulation short) guitar solos. Bouncy, slaphappy cuts like "Huge Balloon" and "Why Should Eye?" chug along with head-bobbing energy to spare, and the band even adds a dollop of reggae to the verses of "J. Weed."

Bracket trips over its own ambition on **4-Wheel Vibe,** stuck in an uneasy compromise between its pop-punk roots and a heavier, ostensibly more commercial, sound. Don Fleming's production beefs up the band's bottom end and adds a metallish tinge to the guitars (there's even a track called "Metal"), but the incessant tempo changes and busier arrangements just bog things down. Louder, faster and more emphatic equals less fun here. By the time Bracket takes its stab at a power ballad ("Pessimist"), it's clear the band's new direction has been a monumental wrong turn. [jt]

BRAD

Shame (Epic Associated) 1993

SATCHEL

EDC (Epic) 1994
The Family (Epic) 1996

PIGEONHED

Pigeonhed (UK Sub Pop) 1993 (Sub Pop) 1994

Seattle singer/keyboardist Shawn Smith is the common denominator of Brad, Satchel and Pigeonhed—and probably a bunch of other bands that haven't released albums. A soulful, papery voice and the apparent ability to work cooperatively in different setups (not to mention whatever it takes to persuade people to issue albums of his various undertakings) has made Smith one of the city's most prolific rockers; he has, however, yet to match local activity with widespread stardom.

Shame, written and self-produced over a fortnight in October '92, is the collective soul of Smith, Pearl Jam guitarist Stone Gossard, drummer Regan Hagar (ex-Malfunkshun) and bassist Jeremy Toback. The moody and restrained rock record benefits from Smith's expressive voice and some soulfully atmospheric songs ("Buttercup," "My Fingers," "Nadine," "Good News"), but the rushed pace of the process and limited idea resources didn't yield an entire album of equal quality. Where the good tunes strike an effective equilibrium between on-the-spot inspiration and a cohesive band effort, too much of the material sounds undeveloped in composition and improvised in arrangement, turning the corner from casual/sharp to casual/slack, finally resorting to jam-a-loo time-sucking. After establishing an excellent funky riff and organ pocket for "20th Century," Brad seems at a loss to do anything with it; the song doesn't fade out so much as slink away.

The more collaborative and stylistically expansive Satchel pairs Smith and Hagar with guitarist John Hoag and one of two bassists. All of the music on **EDC** is credited to the group as a whole, but Smith is the sole (and dreary) lyricist in an erratic, indulgent proposition that sounds like Pearl Jam one song and Yes the next, with sound bites from *Reservoir Dogs* scattered for no obvious reason. Smith affects a Prince-ly falsetto for much of the time; long passages are given over to vaguely floating instrumental assemblages and ad libs. Perhaps the liner-note defense of marijuana helps explain the dreamy quality and aimless shapes (and perhaps the cover clouds) of this numbing exercise.

If Satchel is unpredictably offbeat, Pigeonhed—a

continuation of Smith's partnership with producer/keyboardist Steve Fisk that began when they teamed up to remix an Afghan Whigs song—is downright certifiable. Joined on **Pigeonhed** by guest guitarist Kim Thayil of Soundgarden, the duo postulates what Sylvester Stewart might have come up with if locked in a studio too long with Prince and Thrill Kill Kult. Stitched together from combinations of funky beats and techno drive-throughs, baying dogs, meteorological phenomena and other sound effects, extraneous keyboard bits and Smith's treated voice and meandering falsetto croon, each long track is less a song (although the soul-stirring romantic "Her" certainly qualifies in that category) than an exotic aural collage that could run behind the credits of a different underground film. Engrossing. [i]

See also *Mother Love Bone, Pearl Jam, Pell Mell, Soundgarden.*

BILLY BRAGG

Life's a Riot With Spy vs. Spy (UK Utility) 1983 (UK Utility/Go! Discs) 1983
Brewing Up With Billy Bragg (UK Go! Discs) 1984 (CD Presents) 1984
Between the Wars EP7 (UK Go! Discs) 1985
Life's a Riot Etc (Utility/CD Presents) 1985
Talking With the Taxman About Poetry (Go! Discs/Elektra) 1986
Back to Basics (Go! Discs/Elektra) 1987
The Peel Sessions EP (UK Strange Fruit) 1987 (Strange Fruit/Dutch East India Trading) 1991
Help Save the Youth of America EP (Go! Discs/Elektra) 1988
Workers Playtime (Go! Discs/Elektra) 1988
The Internationale (Utility/Elektra) 1990
Don't Try This at Home (Go! Discs/Elektra) 1991
The Peel Session Album (Strange Fruit/Dutch East India Trading) 1991
Accident Waiting to Happen EP (UK Go! Discs) 1992
William Bloke (Elektra) 1996

For all the indefatigable stumping he's done as a left-wing activist, Billy Bragg has always understood the comical absurdity of running a chart race in the name of political righteousness. On **Workers Playtime,** a major-label album whose proletarian Chinese cover art bears the self-abnegating slogan "Capitalism is killing music," the Englishman makes a thin and telling joke of his singular predicament. In addition to invoking Camelot and Castro, the cynical "Waiting for the Great Leap Forwards" offers this sardonic couplet: "Mixing pop and politics he asks me what the use is/I offer him embarrassment and my usual excuses." Too smart to imagine himself some kind of plugged-in savior, far too gifted to be an ordinary topical troubadour and too conscientious to let it go with a check written to Greenpeace, this brilliant auteur remains a tragic figure whose most commendable impulses explain his commercial futility.

When high-minded righteousness gets the better of him, Bragg can be a tunefully wry pedantic imposition, something amply proven on **The Internationale** (a well-meaning but misbegotten seven-song collection of left-wing paraders and his own dubious contributions to the genre) and, to a lesser degree, on the largely live **Help Save the Youth of America,** a witty but precious six-track tract. But when he's left the world to sort itself out and allowed himself off the hook, Bragg is an exceptionally sharp songwriter and adenoidally accented singer of enormous rough-hewn charm. "A New England" **(Life's a Riot With Spy vs. Spy),** "Levi Stubbs' Tears" and "Greetings to the New Brunette" **(Talking With the Taxman About Poetry),** "The Short Answer" and "Must I Paint You a Picture" **(Workers Playtime)** are heartrendingly beautiful creations peppered with pungent observations and enough tenderness to bring a tear to the eye. When Bragg's public vision turns personal—as in "Between the Wars" and **Taxman**'s Dylan-quoting "Ideology"—his work can pack the same folk-rooted resonance and prove that no excuses are needed for the concept of mixing pop and politics. It's just the tricky business of getting the balance right.

Whether presented as a-boy-and-his-electric-guitar demos (like the seven socially observant songs of the brilliant debut, **Life's a Riot With Spy vs. Spy),** dressed up in tasteful band arrangements (a tactic which works wonders on **Workers Playtime** but proves an inadequate antidote to Bragg's disheartened condition on **Don't Try This at Home**) or calmly falling in between (the modestly ambitious **Brewing Up** and the sublimely stupendous **Talking With the Taxman About Poetry),** Billy Bragg is Elvis Costello reinvented as the guy sitting next to you on the bus.

Bragg was nearly invisible in the first half of the '90s, bowing out of the spotlight after reaching a dead end with **Don't Try This at Home.** The most musically sophisticated of Bragg's albums, it contains developments both good and bad. The fleshy but familiar-sounding pub rock ("Accident Waiting to Happen," "Sexuality"), countryfied folkery ("You Woke Up My Neighbourhood," with half of R.E.M. guesting) and flat-out rock'n'roll ("North Sea Bubble") are swell, but solemn acoustic chamber pop ("Moving the Goalposts," "God's Footballer," "Rumours of War") and junior-league Spector-osity ("Cindy of a Thousand Lives," with guests Johnny Marr and Kirsty MacColl) point up the difficulty Bragg has putting on airs. He's just not that kind of guy. At the nadir of this deeply disappointing album, Bragg croons the soul ballad "Wish You Were Her" in an unrecognizable falsetto. A live EP of "Accident Waiting to Happen," "North Sea Bubble" and two older songs followed the album, but it was four years before Bragg would again tour the US, and he made it to '96 before delivering a new record.

Life's a Riot Etc is a handy American release that combines the first mini-album with **Between the Wars. Back to Basics** goes that effort one better by assembling **Life's a Riot, Between the Wars** and **Brewing Up.** The **Peel Sessions** EP, recorded in 1983 for radio broadcast, contains renditions of "A New England," "Love Gets Dangerous," John Cale's "Fear" and a hilarious Britain-specific exploration of "Route 66." **The Peel Session Album** incorporates all of those tracks as bonuses to a baker's dozen collected from five subsequent visits (1984–88) to the BBC 1 radio studios. [i]

See also *TPRG.*

BRAINIAC

Super Duper Seven EP EP7 (Limited Potential) 1992
Smack Bunny Baby (Grass) 1993

Bonsai Superstar (Grass) 1994
Internationale EP (Touch and Go) 1995
Hissing Prigs in Static Couture (Touch and Go) 1996

O-MATIC

Dog Years (Grass) 1996

Right around the time neighbors Guided by Voices were emerging from obscurity into critical darlingdom, this crack(ed) Dayton quartet reached into Ohio's rich musical history (can you say Devo? Pere Ubu? Rocket From the Tombs?) for a handful of back-to-the-futuristic cool wave influences. And it was good.

Really good. Armed with a Realistic Moog synthesizer and aggressive, unforgettable stage presence, frontman Tim Taylor led the outfit on a series of early tours supporting better-known colleagues like the Jesus Lizard and Girls Against Boys, whose Eli Janney twisted the knobs on Brainiac's first three albums. On **Smack Bunny Baby,** titles like "Martian Dance Invasion" and "I, Fuzzbot" are sure clues to the group's arty approach to new wave. Taylor's Moog is another key, furiously punctuating the menacing playfulness. The best tracks—"Cultural Zero," "Ride," "Draag," "Get Away"—cleverly deconstruct early new wave, using what the band likes, discarding the rest and adding its own innovative ideas to the process. A solid effort from a young band still in its formative stages.

Slathered in schizoid punk, synth belches, abstract noise compositions and rhythmic heat, **Bonsai Superstar** is a tour de force. From the herky-jerky spazz of "Hot Metal Dobermans" and "Hands of the Genius" to the sexy "Flypaper" and "Fucking With the Altimeter" to the Moog/samples-damaged "Transmissions After Zero," the album is engaging, frenetic and fucked up in all the right ways. Blasting garbled, catchy pop, Taylor sounds soulful, affected and completely lost in his art, especially on "Sexual Frustration," "To the Baby-Counter," "Radio Apeshot" and "Status: Choke." The arrival of guitarist John Schmersal (replacing Michelle O'Dean, aka Michelle Bodine, now of O-matic) brings a more formidable attacker who takes the band to a truly otherworldly level of discordant tunings and staccato structures. Bassist Juan Monasterio and drummer Tyler Trent form a relentless foundation for his skronk and Taylor's manic disorder. Here's one band that's intelligently reconfigured new wave with an eye toward the future as well as the past. **Internationale** is a three-song EP of new material (none of it repeated on the subsequent LP) "decoded" by Kim Deal of the Breeders/Amps.

Delivering on the promise of **Bonsai Superstar,** Brainiac turns in another spastic gem with **Hissing Prigs in Static Couture,** a white-hot slab of new wave dada-punk. In electrifying performances with more Moog and more freaky vocals, Brainiac squawks out new sonic oddities ("I Am a Cracked Machine," "Pussyfootin'," "Hot Seat Can't Sit Down," "Kiss Me, U Jacked Up Jerk") and, in "Indian Poker [Part 2]," manages to sound like the children's electronic toy, Simon.

Guitarist Michelle Bodine formed O-matic in 1994 with bassist Rob Tarbell, guitarist/brother Scott Bodine and drummer Will Gates. With studio advice from Dayton pals like Kim Deal and Mitch Mitchell (Guided by Voices), a car-culture fetish and a bunch of overdriven, guitar-fueled songs, **Dog Years** is more straight-ahead than Brainiac, but no less wild. [mww]

BRAIN SURGEONS

Eponymous (Cellsum) 1994
Trepanation (Cellsum) 1996

Only a rock critic (or serious readers of rock magazines, like R.E.M.) would name her first album **Eponymous.** And, indeed, the head Brain Surgeons are none other than veteran New York journalist Deborah Frost and her husband, ex–Blue Öyster Cult drummer Albert Bouchard. On **Eponymous,** the singing-songwriting-rocking couple gets assistance from a bassist, three hornmen and such co-composers as Richard Meltzer and David Roter, resulting in an entertaining if self-conscious album that covers the Del-Lords and Coasters, conjures up the sonic influence of Danielle Dax, Public Image, Nina Hagen, Blondie and Foetus and even pokes absurdist fun at metal's dark obsession in "(666) Devil Got Your Mother."

The more ambitious and serious **Trepanation** reconfigures the Brain Surgeons as a quintet in which Frost does most of the singing—in various voices, some (like the ligature-popping rasp she trots out for a rocking rendition of Robert Johnson's "Stones in My Passway") less appealing than others. (It's not clear if her imitation of Robert Plant on "Ramblin' Rose" is meant in tribute, parody or error.) Still, Frost demonstrates effective restraint in "Everything Is Blue" and lets it all roar in the AC/DC-like "Bad Habit." Patti Smith and Helen Wheels (like Meltzer and Roter, alumni of the BÖC brain trust) each co-wrote a number here; the collaborations yield everything from the dada picnic ruminations of "Hansel and Gretel" to the dreamy folk-rock poetry of "If U Come Close" and the accusatory bramble of "Sally." [i]

GLENN BRANCA

Lesson #1 EP (99) 1980
The Ascension (99) 1981
Music for the Dance *Bad Smells* (GPS) 1982
Symphony No. 1 (Tonal Plexus) (ROIR) 1983 (Fr. Danceteria) 1992
Symphony No. 3 (Gloria) (Neutral) 1983 (Atavistic) 1993
Soundtrack for *The Belly of an Architect* (UK Factory) 1987
Symphony No. 6 (Devil Choirs at the Gates of Heaven) (Blast First) 1989 (Atavistic) 1993
The World Upside Down (Bel. Les Disques du Crépuscule) 1992 (Atavistic) 1994
Symphony No. 2 (The Peak of the Sacred) (Atavistic) 1992
Symphony Nos. 8 & 10 (The Mysteries) (Atavistic) 1994
Symphony No. 9 (L'eve Future) (Point Music) 1995
Songs '77–'79 (The Static & Theoretical Girls) (Atavistic) 1996
Symphony No. 5 (Describing Planes of an Expanding Hypersphere) (Atavistic) 1996

Rock's impact on the music of New York composer Glenn Branca is clear, but the reverse is equally obvious as well. It's easy to hear the influence of Branca's cacophonous but transcendent electric guitar chorales on bands like Sonic Youth and Helmet (both of whom include alumni of Branca's ensemble) and, by extension, their myriad progeny.

Branca's power-classical makes an art of the phenomenon of overtones, wherein combined frequencies produce phantom tones. Although the effect is much more dramatic live and at concert volume, Branca has also managed to make some thrilling records with the overpowering, monolithic grandeur of a Richard Serra sculpture, as if the crescendo of "A Day in the Life" were extended into full-length symphonies. For the best of the early days, check out **The Ascension, Symphony No. 3 (Gloria)** or **Symphony No. 6 (Devil Choirs at the Gates of Heaven)**—although just about anything Branca has released is quite capable of blowing your mind.

Symphony No. 8 (The Mystery) is as brilliant as Branca gets. With the composer conducting a ten-piece guitar orchestra, the first movement ("The Passion") runs through teeming, vertiginous scales, producing a downright Hitchcockian sense of high anxiety. The second movement ("Spiritual Anarchy") unleashes the full arsenal—illusions of heavenly choirs, French horns, tuned gongs, strings and other sonic mirages all emerge from Branca's colossal tone clusters, combining with Virgil Moorefield's pounding drums to reach one unimaginably intense plateau after another. You've already got your money's worth but then there's **Symphony No. 10 (The Mystery Pt. 2)**. Densely packed with massive black storm clouds of electric discord, like heavy metal Penderecki, the first movement ("The Final Problem") is exultantly malevolent, while the second ("The Horror") seethes with relentless, frenetic clangor.

Perhaps to save his hearing, perhaps to woo the classical establishment, perhaps to investigate different timbral realms, Branca abandoned the electric guitar and began writing music for traditional classical instruments and even voice. And yet the master's harmonic fingerprint is all over the rapturous **World Upside Down,** a seven-movement work for symphony orchestra. The stunning piece marks a crucial stylistic leap, especially in the slowly swirling, oceanic first, fifth and final movements. Here Branca unveils a new harmonic palette, new rhythms and a clear affinity for unalloyed beauty.

A symphony for orchestra and wordless choir in one forty-seven-minute movement, **Symphony No. 9 (L'eve Future)** continues Branca's exploration of nonlinear composition, a collage of sensations rather than a narrative. The tones are softer (although no less intense), the solemn, almost ambient mood inviting critical comparisons to Górecki. A cryptic liner note reference to a post-apocalyptic theme seems almost redundant, given the piece's overwhelmingly vivid sense of hope and fear. In what amounts to a bonus track, the vibrant eleven-minute "Freeform" could almost be a missing allegro movement from the symphony, its relatively hectic pace only underscoring the great strides Branca has made with the stately **Symphony No. 9.** [ma]

See also *TPRG*.

BRANCH MANAGER

Top Scale Speed EP7 (Sweet Portable You) 1993
Branch Manager (Dischord) 1995

Top Scale Speed, the first missile from Washington, DC's Branch Manager, is too cheeky for a 7-inch record; the trio tries to bite off more than it can give back. Singer/guitarist Ron Winters squashes the unpredictability of Bad Brain H. R. and the brash, ersatz insecurity of **Armed Forces**–era Elvis Costello together for an untidy but compelling little package in both "Floored and to the Left" and "Sharp," which culminates in a rollercoaster of unexpected dips and rolls. The other two songs could have been left off.

Branch Manager succeeds in accomplishing what the EP tried to do: blend a variety of musical styles into a fairly complete package, though not song by song. The group trots out a bit of jazz, some tongue-in-cheek suburban funk, a burst of hardcore and a jolt of power-chord-heavy prog-rock. Stretching out on a full-length CD, Winters is better able to open the occasional door into what he would have listeners believe are the recesses of his soul, as in "Smoke and Mirrors" "Hate, Resentment and Jealousy" and "The Best Sleep Is Behind Me," a dizzy lounge ditty. Meanwhile, drummer Derek Decker (ex-Iceboxers) and bassist Dave Allen demonstrate rhythms that are inhumanly precise ("Gameface") or just sloppy enough to trust ("Spirit Boy 2000"). The disc does have weak links, however, none more damaging than the choice of an ineffectual instrumental, "Bent Flagpole," as its opening track. [icm]

BRAND NEW HEAVIES

The Brand New Heavies (UK Acid Jazz) 1990 (Delicious Vinyl) 1991 (Delicious Vinyl/Capitol) 1996
Heavy Rhyme Experience: Vol. 1 (Delicious Vinyl) 1992 (Delicious Vinyl/Capitol) 1996
Brother Sister (Delicious Vinyl) 1994 (Delicious Vinyl/Capitol) 1996
Original Flava (Acid Jazz/Hollywood) 1995
Excursions: Remixes & Rare Grooves (Delicious Vinyl/Capitol) 1996

The Brand New Heavies is one of the few recent hybrids able to break down once-daunting genre boundaries and still outlive the glare of media fascination. Boasting a genuine cultural mixture (Britons and Americans, whites and blacks, men and women) in its ranks, the London-based group plays a groovy meld of '70s funk, rare groove and jazz flavor. While this combination isn't always practical—the band is a jack-of-all-genres more than a master of one, not hip enough for the hipsters and not soulful enough for the R&B audience—when it does take, the band's crossbred funk is splendid.

A stylish mix of smoky jazz club ambience and Average White Band/Wild Cherry funk, the best tracks on **The Brand New Heavies** feature N'Dea Davenport, an Atlanta expatriate whose sultry soul vocals make up in emotion and depth what they lack in range. (She wasn't on the original UK issue, which featured Jaye Ella Ruth. Tracks were recut and added for the Stateside release.) In addition to the band's five-man core, a horn section ups the '70s feel. On "Never Stop" and "Dream Come True," these copycats are cooking with gas, and the band members seem to be having a great time playing music they clearly love.

Pared to a trio on **Heavy Rhyme Experience: Vol. 1,** guitarist Simon Bartholomew, bassist Andrew Levy and drummer Jan Kincaid get a procession of rap notables (including the Pharcyde, Main Source, Kool G. Rap, Ed O.G., Jamalski and Masta Ace) in to help them explore the soul/jazz/hip-hop connection. Gang Starr's Guru adds his husky, confident rhymes to the live, jamming band laying down a solid groove in "It's Gettin Hectic." Grand Puba, who raps smoothly on "Who Makes the Loot?," describes the music being created as "some real live funky funky get down on the getdown . . . the bass player's real and the drummer's real." Throughout the album, that combination of band and rappers makes it an innovative standout in the continuing mixture of hip-hop with other styles of rhythm music.

Davenport sat out the second album, working instead with Guru on his first **Jazzmatazz** project; the songs on which she appears are some of the best moments on that stellar record. She returned to the Heavies for **Brother Sister,** however, an album that finds the band back making soul music, easing up on the funk to go with a glossier, moderately discofied sound. "Dream on Dreamer" is a frothy, catchy pop tune that shows little of the band's characteristic innovation. "Fake," on the other hand, is a total funk throwdown, a strong woman's putdown of a disrespectful lover. Back to fusing funk, jazz and soul, "Back to Love," "Spend Some Time" and the stomping workout, "Snake Hips," are almost as cool.

Original Flava collects rarities and previously unreleased tracks from the band's past efforts. Although it contains some outtakes and rare cuts, **Excursions** is mainly an album of remixes, assembled to coincide with the prior albums' reissues. [mf]

See also *Gang Starr.*

BRAND NUBIAN

One for All (Elektra) 1990
In God We Trust (Elektra) 1992
Everything Is Everything (Elektra) 1994

GRAND PUBA

Reel to Reel (Elektra) 1992
2000 (Elektra) 1995

MASTERS OF CEREMONY

Dynamite (4th & Broadway) 1988

New York's Masters of Ceremony first drew attention with the single "Cracked Out," an anti-drug blast set to an "Atomic Dog"–style track. Led by the high-pitched Grand Puba (Maxwell Dixon), the trio explored the intersection of raggamuffin styles with more traditional breakbeat-based hip-hop, landing solid punches with "Sexy," "Master Move" and "One to the Knot." But it was Grand Puba's next group that would significantly influence the early '90s New York sound.

The masterfully loose rhyme styles of Lord Jamar and especially the party-ready Puba and Derek X, plus the loop-and-go freedom of sampling technology, define the Brand Nubian sound, attaching it to Derek X's anti-racist activism (in the wake of the Bensonhurst killing of Yusuf Hawkins) and the crew's controversial adherence to 5% Nation (a sectarian branch of the Nation of Islam) orthodoxy. The endlessly sampled **One for All** is a high point of East Coast hip-hop; see the exciting "All for One," "Concerto in X Minor," "Step to the Rear," "Wake Up" and "Who Can Get Busy Like This Man." But it's also controversial for its religious radicalism, most evident on "Drop the Bomb." Brand Nubian boldly transforms Edie Brickell's hippychick music into a groove masterpiece on "Slow Down," a hypocritical dose of sexual politics ("A 40 and a blunt/That's all she really wants"). The album's most innocuous-seeming cut—Grand Puba's unlistenable stab at new jack swing, "Try to Do Me"—is perhaps its most prescient. Brand Nubian's marriage of party groove and polemical grit could not last.

After Puba's departure for a solo career, New Rochelle natives Sadat X (the former Derek X) and Lord Jamar, joined by DJ Sincere, stepped decidedly to the right on the heavier **In God We Trust.** Musically more textured and moody, it elaborates on their spiritual beliefs (in the Minister Farrakhan speech of "Meaning of the 5%" as well as "Ain't No Mystery" and "Allah and Justice") and flirts with images of street violence ("Pass the Gat," the homophobic "Punks Jump Up to Get Beat Down"). Edgy and unyielding.

Everything Is Everything caught the group behind the curve, however, tritely slowing down the tempos to a drive-by crawl and employing Dr. Dre–like dramatics. The only tracks that stand out are the freestyle session, "Straight off da Head," the old-school Average White Band bounce of "Word Is Bond" and the solemn reworking of Simply Red's "Hold On."

On his own, Grand Puba tries to keep the party live. With the exception of the title track, "Ya Know How It Goes" and "Soul Controller," **Reel to Reel** is generally light, resting on Puba's ample reputation more than any great expense of new effort. But **2000** may disclose his ultimate intentions, as it contains his half-serious flirtation with R&B crooning. Sadat X released his first solo album, **Wild Cowboys** (Loud/RCA), in the summer of '96. [jzc]

BRATMOBILE

Pottymouth (Kill Rock Stars) 1993
The Real Janelle EP (Kill Rock Stars) 1994
The Peel Session EP (Strange Fruit/Dutch East India Trading) 1994

The flaw in most '70s punk bands was their lack of true commitment to chaos. It took '90s riot grrrl bands like the belligerent tease that was Bratmobile to show oldtimers how to fall together and fall apart with equal conviction. Singer Allison Wolfe, drummer Molly Neuman and guitarist Erin Smith made their daredevil punk debut in the summer of '91 at K Records' International Pop Underground convention in Olympia, Washington, and spent the next three years sporadically ruffling indie-rock feathers (mostly via 45s) with calamitous minimalism and the id-ful caterwauling of Wolfe's blunt, often antagonistic, lyrics.

Although it sounds like the efforts of one rowdy afternoon, **Pottymouth** was recorded in '91 and '92 (the bandmembers' geographical dispersion—California, Olympia and Maryland—was always a problem). Mustering seventeen songs, including a relatively protracted bash at the Runaways' seminal "Cherry Bomb," in under a half-hour, the album is like a slap in the face: it's over before you realize what you're feeling but its sting lasts a good long while. Spewed out in the simplest, rawest manner possible, the songs' conflicting emotions have the unfocused frenzy of adolescence: lust one minute, spite the next, anger at enemies and self, jealousy, disdain, fitting in, standing out. Between the demanding sexuality of "Juswanna (FUK U.)" and "P.R.D.C.T." (Punk Rock Dream Come True) and the confrontational rancor of "Bitch Theme," "Love Thing" and "Fuck Yr. Fans," however, Bratmobile has a charming way with silly love songs, revealing a softer side in "Queenie," "Kiss and Ride" (aka "Fuck and Ride") and the troubled "Throway." Best scene trope (from "Cool Schmool"): "I don't want to sit around and talk about the Wipers/Weren't those the good ole days . . . "

Raising its musical skills to the next level (more of a mezzanine than a genuine second stage), Bratmobile cut six songs, including a cover of the Misfits' crudely defensive "Where Eagles Dare" (with vocals by Kill Rock Stars head/Olympia poet-in-residence Slim Moon), for the twelve-minute **The Real Janelle.** The title track is an upbeat cheer ("Janelle, Janelle—she's so swell!"); other songs are either hard ("Brat Girl," a murderous revenge fantasy about the infamous Spur Posse), unhinged ("Die," in which death is both the alternative to friendship and the test of love), Oedipal ("And I Live in a Town Where the Boys Amputate Their Hearts," which announces "I can't go home again/But I'm still a good tax break") or winsomely mild (Neuman's "Yeah, Huh?").

For the clearest blast of Brat, try the BBC broadcast, which dates from July '93. Playing exceptionally well (perhaps because of the presence of an actual producer), the unexpectedly tight trio rips through five songs, including "Bitch Theme" and "Make Me Miss America," in under nine minutes. Neuman now drums and sings in the Peechees, who released a '96 LP **Do the Math** on KRS. Wolfe and Smith are in Cold Cold Hearts. [i]

BREEDERS

Pod (4AD) 1990 (Elektra) 1992
Safari EP (4AD/Elektra) 1992
Last Splash (4AD/Elektra) 1993
Cannonball EP (4AD/Elektra) 1993
Live in Stockholm (Breeders Digest) 1994

AMPS

Pacer (4AD/Elektra) 1995

KELLEY DEAL 6000

Go to the Sugar Altar (Nice) 1996

It's a truism of romantic relationships that dysfunctional ones don't usually end for good until something better comes along to replace them. For Kim Deal, the Breeders—formed as a side project with Tanya Donelly (moonlighting from Throwing Muses on her way to forming Belly) as a parallel to the Pixies, which had increasingly come to be dominated by her bandmate, Black Francis—became not just an escape route from a dead-end and deteriorating situation but an entirely new and better way of life.

The Breeders' initial dynamic on **Pod** was a mess of conflicting impulses and untested strengths mediated by Steve Albini in one of his most restrained "engineering" efforts. Deal, singing and playing guitar (rather than the bass she shouldered in the Pixies), and Donelly (guitar/vocals) at least pretend to search for an equilibrium between the former's need for unchallenged turbulent discharge and the latter's predilection for firmly structured pop. But the band is clearly Deal's deal. Donelly scores but one co-writing credit, and **Pod**'s sound consistently favors the Pixies far more than the Muses; even the melodicism of "Doe" and "Fortunately Gone" can't simmer down to credible gentleness. A cover of John Lennon's "Happiness Is a Warm Gun" lacks context, but adds a useful frisson of creepiness to the unpolished enthusiasms. With Josephine Wiggs (soon to be ex–Perfect Disaster) on bass and Slint drummer Britt Walford (using the name Shannon Doughton), the quartet is loose and casually aggressive; whatever internal tension there might have been only feeds the album's edgy hunger. Hindered by lax, unfinished songwriting and arrangements, **Pod** is distinctly an extracurricular effort, but an encouraging and frequently exciting one.

Deal was an ex-Pixie by the time the Breeders resurfaced on record, so the four-song **Safari** became a banner of her full-time future. Meanwhile, the addition of her twin sister Kelley (untrained guitar/vocals) to the lineup signaled the transition that would ultimately reshape the group. The Breeders' elements are better organized into a distinctive sound—undersung vocals with ferocious loud/soft guitar dynamics over a deliberate beat—but material weakness remains a problem. A bottom-heavy harmony cover of the Who's "So Sad About Us" without an ending is the dubious highlight here, and that's no breakthrough for '90s alternakids.

That was enough second-bananadom for Donelly, and she left. Drummer Jim MacPherson arrived to join Wiggs in the rhythm pen and—with a confident, spectacular album as their calling card—the Deals became rock's best-known sister act since Heart. **Last Splash** pulls all the pieces together in a stirring display of teeth, claws, fuzzy distortion and cagey melodies, sung with ethereal sweetness—an instantly recognizable sonic signature layered on like fluffy blankets strewn with sand. This enigmatic explosion of id teases and kicks, tightening and relaxing its grip around a soft, firm center, whether wiggling like a funky worm on a hook ("Cannonball"), thundering through drippy '70s pop ("Divine Hammer," "Invisible Man"), ripping apart Pixiesque punk (two versions of "Roi," "Hag"), deconstructing Beatlisms ("Saints"), accessing country-rock ("Drivin' on 9") or taking a surf-rock break (the instrumental "Flipside"). Indicative of how much more accomplished the group has become, a new version of the EP's longing "Do You Love Me Now?" is altogether better. Flirty, sexy and stocked with enigmas that could only be in-jokes, **Last Splash** turns un-self-consciousness into a multi-faceted blast of female personality. The **Cannonball** EP contains an Aerosmith cover.

Live in Stockholm is a fan club CD that loudly documents twenty minutes in May ('94). The set includes a half-dozen **Last Splash** songs, **Pod**'s "Hellbound," the non-LP "Shocker in Gloomtown" and Kim's recipe for a mudslide (equal parts vodka, Kahlua and Bailey's).

Quite unlike the creative desires that led to the Breeders, legal problems—namely her sister's 1995 drug bust—led Kim Deal to put the band on hold and convoke a side project, the Amps, with MacPherson and two non-Breeders, bassist Luis Lerma and guitarist/singer Nathan Farley. Addressing the impairment issue in "Hoverin," Deal announces "Yeah, we're straight—we get high on music," offering this advice, which could be to Kelley and could concern either band participation or life expectancy: "Don't do it if you plan to stick around." Sounding like **Last Splash** with a good deal of the life, joy and imagination sucked out, **Pacer** delivers perfectly good Breeder-like songs ("I Am Decided," "She's a Girl," "Mom's Drunk" and "Bragging Party," which isn't far off a rewrite of "Divine Hammer") in disappointing small-scale arrangements. Other than the fine title track and a few others, the performances are forced and lackluster; the production varies between flat and colorless. Deal's desire to keep busy is understandable, but **Pacer** slumps halfheartedly in the wrong direction.

For her part, Kelley Deal returned to action in '96 with a new quartet and a self-released album. [i]

See also *Belly, Pixies, Slint, Throwing Muses.*

BRICK LAYER CAKE

Eye for an Eye, Tooth for a Tooth EP (Ruthless) 1990
Call It a Day EP (Touch and Go) 1991
Tragedy-Tragedy (Touch and Go) 1994

From Ringo on down, rock protocol has decreed that drummers' solo projects, regardless of merit, are not to be taken seriously. Little else can explain the cold shoulder given to Brick Layer Cake, the brilliant vehicle for Todd Trainer. He is best known as the manic drummer for such midwestern powerhouses as Breaking Circus, Rifle Sport and, most recently, Shellac—fine groups all, but even their best work is easily matched and usually surpassed by Trainer's criminally neglected Brick Layer Cake output.

The Cake, which consists of Trainer on guitar and vocals and a shifting cast of co-conspirators that typically includes Gerald Boissy or Brian Paulson (or both) on guitar and, in live settings, Steve Albini on drums, debuted in 1990 with **Eye for an Eye, Tooth for a Tooth,** a six-song EP that establishes Trainer's signature sound: skeletal song structures delivered at a dirge-like pace, huge, ringing major chords with plenty of distortion, slow, rasping vocals tinged with a convincing sense of righteousness and clever lyrics that breathe new life into such long-clichéd subject areas as death, drinking and decay. The overall effect, while probably not for everyone, is extremely powerful and surprisingly tuneful, with whopper hooks lurking beneath the guitar onslaught. (See "Clockwork" and "Happy Hour.")

The following year's **Call It a Day** EP (the CD of which includes all of **Eye for an Eye**) takes things a step further, with fuller production that turns Trainer's bare-bones compositions into monstrous pop tunes. The lyrics, which had previously contented themselves with cynical witticisms, are stronger too, with a stinging indictment of the fashion and image industries ("Sitting Pretty"), a genuinely frightening tale of a childhood friend's murder ("Killer") and one of rock's best songs about AIDS ("Kiss of Death"). This is Brick Layer Cake at its finest.

Tragedy-Tragedy, Trainer's first full-length effort, mines essentially the same territory with similarly devastating results. He may be treading on thin creative ice by repeatedly hammering away at such tired topics as death ("Cold Day in Hell"), alcohol ("Thirteenth Drink") and the apocalypse ("Doomsday"), but the dark obsessions somehow continue to sound fresh. If Trainer ever gets around to writing a love song, it'll be a beaut. [pl]

See also *Flour, Shellac.*

BRICKS

See *Superchunk.*

BRISE-GLACE

See *Jim O'Rourke.*

JUSTIN K. BROADRICK/ANDY HAWKINS

See *Godflesh.*

MICHAEL BROOK

Hybrid (Editions EG) 1985
Cobalt Blue (4AD) 1992
Live at the Aquarium (4AD) 1993
Shona (UK Sine) 1995

EDGE WITH MICHAEL BROOK

Captive (Virgin) 1987

PIETER NOOTEN/MICHAEL BROOK

Sleeps With the Fishes (UK 4AD) 1987

U. SRINIVAS & MICHAEL BROOK

Dream (Real World) 1995

NUSRAT FATEH ALI KHAN & MICHAEL BROOK

Night Song (Real World) 1996

Martha and the Muffins alumnus, collaborator with Eno, Daniel Lanois, Robert Fripp, the Edge and other hipsters, all-round clever sonic guy—Canada's Michael Brook ventures into the solo spotlight for his **Cobalt Blue** album. Showcasing his aptly named "infinite guitar," which—thanks to various electronic treatments—seems to come from another dimension, the dozen "songs" on this ambient work are actually different facets of one constantly shifting, undulating piece. A grown-up alternative to Mike Oldfield's **Tubular Bells** or an intelligent reappraisal of new age music (if such a thing is possible), this evocative dreamscape evaporates if observed closely, yet makes fine background music. Recorded at the London press party for **Cobalt Blue, Live at the Aquarium** follows the same strategy, though it features Brook alone, rather than with backing musicians. Repeating many of the same tracks, it ought to be an exercise in redundancy, but there's a sharper edge to his playing that makes this the more exciting album.

In 1987, Brook and U2 guitarist the Edge scored the film *Captive.* Their understated acoustic guitar/piano excursions and gripping synthesizer/electric guitar adventures are passingly evocative, but overshadowed by the appearance of Sinéad O'Connor, who makes her first album appearance anywhere singing the theme song.

Brook also produced and played guitar, bass and keyboards on **Sleeps With the Fishes,** a dreamy set of synth-driven instrumentals, with occasional delicate vocals, by the wistful Pieter Nooten, lately of Xymox, on whose **Phoenix** album Brook later guested. The perfect soundtrack for pond-gazing on a sleepy summer afternoon. Fans will also want to check out **Night Song,** Brook's collaboration with Pakistan's charismatic Sufi trance singer Nusrat Fateh Ali Khan. The tasteful ambient shadings testify to Brook's restraint, as well as to Nusrat's overpowering presence.

"Originally the plan was to record a traditional album of Srinivas' music . . ." writes Brook in the liner notes to **Dream,** an album on which he is co-billed with the famed Indian mandolin player. As W. C. Fields once said, "Things happened . . ." What resulted from the collaboration (which eventually employed English showboat violinist Nigel Kennedy, Canadian singer Jane Siberry, Brazilian percussionist/vocalist Nana Vasconcelos, American Stick player Trey Gunn and others) couldn't be further from a world music album if it were recorded on Pluto. The set of four quietly meandering ambient pieces was sampled and shaped in the studio with Enoesque initiative; Srinivas's mandolin is one of the least prominent elements. So much for the Real World. [jy/i]

See also *David Sylvian.*

BROTHERHOOD OF LIZARDS

See *Martin Newell.*

BROTHER JT

See *Original Sins.*

CASPAR BRÖTZMANN MASSAKER

The Tribe (Ger. Zensor) 1987
Black Axis (Ger. Marat/Zensor) 1989
Der Abend der Schwarzen Folklore (Ger. Our Choice/Rough Trade) 1992
Koksofen (Ger. Our Choice/Rough Trade) 1992 (Homestead) 1993
Home (Thirsty Ear) 1995

CASPAR BRÖTZMANN/PETER BRÖTZMANN

Last Home (UK Pathological) 1990

F. M. EINHEIT/CASPAR BRÖTZMANN

Merry Christmas (Thirsty Ear) 1995

As a second-generation avant-noise provocateur, this crunch-rock-dallying free-jazz guitarist has yet to develop the visceral improvisational extravagance shown by dad Peter (the hard-blowing saxophonist who's recorded with Sonny Sharrock and Bill Laswell in Last Exit). He has, however, demonstrated a heartening willingness to perpetuate the more-is-more attitude synthesized by the raucous proponents of post-Ornette ear-blister (that despite an unhealthy proximity to Berlin's goth-rock contingent).

The first Massaker album, recorded when Caspar was a mere snip of a lad, is easily identified as a debut. The guitarist is feeling his way around in search of a voice—one which he *almost* manages to cobble together from bits of Sharrock-styled muscle-flex and icily jagged single-note projectiles inspired by Blixa Bargeld's Einstürzende Neubauten work. More a curio than anything else. By the time of **Black Axis,** Brötzmann had matured considerably. With little apparent effort, he, bassist Eduardo Delgado Lopez and drummer Frank Neumeier manage to sustain some comparatively epic-length songs (most impressively the fourteen-minute title track) by asserting enough cyclical themes to buoy the largely improvised music just this side of shapelessness' breakwall.

Der Abend der Schwarzen Folklore only sporadically emphasizes the monochromatic industrial hues on which the trio had previously lit. Brötzmann (who spends too much time flaunting his Nick Cave–like groan—he'd be better off if, in the words of Frank Zappa, he'd shut up and play his guitar) and Lopez are joined this time by the more Neubauten-esque percussionist Danny Lommen (ex–Gore) who brings a mechanical precision to forbidding pieces like "Bass Totem." Fortunately, Brötzmann spends much of **Koksofen** following Zappa's admonition, guiding Massaker through five live-in-the-studio improvisations that establish a much more finely tuned dynamic grasp: "Hymne" buries the guitarist's isolated note flurries in stoic, discreet percussive underbrush; "Kerkersong" storms from thrash-metal into Last Exit–styled swagger halfway through its eleven-minute run. **Home** consists of the trio's radically changed re-recordings of early tracks (mostly from the first two Massaker albums); the contrasts are marked, both in Brötzmann's confidence level and in his willingness to act as poised bandleader rather than sonic dictator.

Neubauten "percussionist" F. M. Einheit (who produced **Home**) brings his usual array of metal constructions and *objets trouvés* out to play on **Merry Christmas,** a mistitled, misanthropic collection of sound collages and aggressive ambient pieces. Brötzmann is up to the challenge, splaying elephant screams across the breadth of "Nizzary" and entrapping "Federn Fuckhouse" in a note-bending primordial ooze. On **Last Home,** the guitarist's collaboration with his father ranges from strangely poignant to outright hostile—the overall tone is not unlike one of those coming-of-age films wherein Dad blusters about his accomplishments loud and long enough to prompt a raging retort from the young whippersnapper being challenged. In 1990, at least, the iron-lunged saxophonist got the better of his offspring: time will tell if Caspar can turn the tables. [dss]

See also *Einstürzende Neubauten, Last Exit.*

JUNIOR BROWN

12 Shades of Brown (UK Demon) 1990 (Curb) 1993
Guit With It (Curb) 1993
Junior High EP (MCG/Curb) 1995
Semi Crazy (MCG/Curb) 1996

The strangest star in today's country-circling galaxy, Junior (Jamieson) Brown combines unreconstructed traditionalism modeled on Ernest Tubb and Bob Wills and unprecedented guitar playing. Using his patented guit-steel, a cumbersome-looking two-necked contraption, he jumps from lap slide to twangy fingering—and back—without missing a blistering, lyrical lick. That he's a student of Jimi Hendrix who habitually incorporates the southpaw's riffs, as well as muffled cottonpicking and angry distortion, into his roadhouse rock sets Brown, an Indiana native based in Austin, Texas, apart from a world of facile players. Meanwhile, the witty, offbeat sensibility that permeates his superficial normalcy further distances this talented oddity with a rich, commanding baritone from anything coming out of Nashville nowadays.

Brown needs to be seen live (peering out from under a ten-gallon white hat, accompanied by his power-strumming missus, Tanya Rae, a string bassist and a minimalist snare drummer) to be fully appreciated. On record, although all four are careful to exhibit his unique instrument on their covers, it's Brown's songwriting smarts, clever jokes and voice that give his tactile virtuosity the balance needed to make him an all-around entertainer, not a hayseed shredder.

Originally a cassette sold at shows and then a vinyl release in Britain, the self-produced **12 Shades of Brown** covers all of Brown's bases: novelty swing ("My Baby Don't Dance to Nothing but Ernest Tubb,"

"Hillbilly Hula Gal," "What's Left Just Won't Go Right," "Coconut Island"), wry moral rig-rock ("Too Many Nights in a Roadhouse," "Broke Down South of Dallas"), Hank-y roots country blues ("Moan All Night Along") and serious social sermonizing ("They Don't Choose to Live That Way," "Don't Sell the Farm"). Throughout, Brown's easy confidence and excellent playing make for a delightful diversion.

Brown tones down his colorful personality a bit on **Guit With It,** devoting more effort to sentimental ballads ("So Close Yet So Far Away," sung as a duet with Tanya Rae), instrumental showboating (Hank Garland's "Sugarfoot Rag," which ends with a "Wind Cries Mary" citation; the eleven-minute "Guit-Steel Blues") and straight-faced country ("Doin' What Comes Easy to a Fool," "You Didn't Have to Go All the Way"). The music is fine, it's the songs that are disappointing. The record does include a pair of peppy wisecracks (the old "Highway Patrol" and the calamitous "My Wife Thinks You're Dead"; "Holding Pattern" is just a corny pun), but the net reduction of wit takes too much of the fun out.

Despite the steady elevation of his national profile—Brown's popularity is greater outside country circles than within them—his studio output has been meager. Ending a two-year wait in late '95, Brown released an EP that contains crisp re-recordings of three **Guit With It** numbers (needless except for the over-the-top frenzy of this rendition of "Sugarfoot Rag"), a mock-Polynesian cover ("Lovely Hula Hands") and one new original, the heartfelt "That's Easy for You to Say." [i]

BRUJERIA

Machetazos! EP (Alternative Tentacles) 1993
Matando Güeros (Roadrunner) 1993
Raza Odiada (Roadrunner) 1995

With so many gory alienation fantasies in death metal, it's difficult to find the truly fine-grade chops. Brujeria are incendiary Spanish-language death-grind raiders who deal with the everyday gore of life in Latin America. (The mysterious group seems to make its albums only during periods when members of Fear Factory, Faith No More and Napalm Death all have free time.)

Machetazos! is a landmark in aural atrocity, employing a violent hell on earth as the backdrop for a blistering, aggressive onslaught of religious and greed-induced horror. On **Matando Güeros,** Brujeria further glorifies the dark arts of blood worship and heroin trafficking with bellowed lyrics like, "Trafficando drogas, coca y mota/La bendición Satánica, quien nos para." "Molestando Niños Muertos" describes even more gruesome pursuits. The sleeve's positively appalling color photographs of a head and a decapitated, dismembered body underscore that the criminal lyrics are based wholly in reality. Compared to these machete-wielding hate bandits, Skinny Puppy is holding a toothpick and Unsane is waving a potato peeler.

Anything beyond **Matando Güeros** seems redundant, but **Raza Odiada** is up to snuff, with equal doses of sluggish pounding and claustrophobic speed. On the opening cut, the band pumps a stream of bullets into California governor "Pito" Wilson (portrayed by Jello Biafra) as he delivers an anti-immigration speech. On track after punishing track, Brujeria is anthemic, brutal and dynamic, toasting perverse idols like the rebels of the Chiapas uprising, Colombian drug boss Pablo Escobar and that favorite scourge of Catholicism, Lucifer. [ic]

See also *Faith No More, Napalm Death.*

FRANKLIN BRUNO

See *Nothing Painted Blue.*

BRUTAL JUICE

How Tasty Was My Little Timmy? [tape] (Homus Boyus) 1991
I Love the Way They Scream When They Die (Sound Virus) 1994 (Alternative Tentacles) 1994
Mutilation Makes Identification Difficult (Interscope/Atlantic) 1995

This may be the last entertaining bit of OJ trivia left: an old Hertz commercial shows Simpson and Arnold Palmer yakking about car rental rates. When OJ confesses to overpaying, Arnie commiserates, "Brutal, Juice, brutal." That was enough for this fascinating rock band from Denton, Texas, whose best work is like a steamroller massage but includes irregular time signatures and unusual chord progressions. Harmonies contrast the screamed vocal leads discoursing on intolerance, women, murder, space opera, women, murder, women, snobbiness, women . . . and Nietzsche. The pummeling drums, anchored by rugged bass, hurtle along energetically, carrying great sheets of rhythm guitar and spacy/noisy quasi-psychedelic solos. With one foot in a sophisticated variation on death metal, a taste for the frenzied energy of industrial, the destructive urges of the old Butthole Surfers and an abiding pop sense that's more shocking than any of those impulses, the carefully controlled Brutal Juice is a smart bomb timed to blow up right in your face.

Founded by singer, guitarist and chief songwriter Gordon Gibson (who holds an M.A. in political philosophy) and powerhouse drummer Ben Burt, the band eventually added guitarist Ted Wood, soundman Sam McCall on bass and co–lead singer Craig Welch, the unholy spawn of Iggy Pop and Huntz Hall (neither of whom has ever been known to put cigarettes out on his head as Welch does). **How Tasty Was My Little Timmy?** was cut before McCall joined the quintet, but six of its songs turn up again on the live **I Love the Way They Scream When They Die.** (**Mutilation Makes Identification Difficult** contains three numbers that are on both plus five more from the second.)

Mutilation Makes Identification Difficult, which was originally going to be titled **Everything's Coming Up Toilets** (likely inspired by the bloody porcelain photo in the booklet), has only five previously unreleased songs, but it's still the place to start. Opening with the harrowing menace of "Kentucky Fuck Daddy" rattling along at a swift 5/4 pace, the band dives into the hitman memoir of "Burpgun" (from whence comes the line "I love the way they scream when they die") and then "The Vaginals," an almost poppy ditty about girls who are "ugly on the inside." After those newcomers, Brutal Juice proceeds to improve on all but one of the older songs recut for the album. Only "Whorehouse of Screams" receives a dubious rethink: the grim tale is well told and the first three minutes of frenzied jamming are compelling, but the last half of the twenty-minute (!) track is just dicking around.

I Love the Way They Scream When They Die is largely made redundant by **Mutilation,** but it does include versions of the band's first two A-sides ("Black Moment of Panic" and "Punk Fuck") and an otherwise unreleased piece of nasty noise, "Pull the Plug." **Timmy** is more worthwhile as it includes "Rock Town," the catchy B-side of "Black Moment of Panic," and "Dominick," which contrasts dual-guitar riffola and primal scream mayhem. [jg]

BRUTAL TRUTH

Extreme Conditions Demand Extreme Responses (Earache/Relativity) 1992
Perpetual Conversion EP (Earache/Relativity) 1992
Need to Control (Earache) 1994

MALFORMED EARTHBORN

Defiance of the Ugly by the Merely Repulsive (Relapse) 1995

This hyper-aggressive New York foursome ambitiously pushes the death-metal genre to new limits by amplifying the speed and terror while incorporating outside influences like hardcore techno and power tools. Such growth in grindcore comes courtesy singer/journalist Kevin Sharp and bassist Dan Lilker, notable for co-founding and then quitting Anthrax, Nuclear Assault and the infamous Stormtroopers of Death.

Extreme Conditions presents a hip alternative to the adolescent satanic gore-mongering of rivals like Deicide and Obituary. "Walking Corpse" and "Birth of Ignorance" take the tough stance of metal to the advanced political mindset of British earachers. Unlike the special grooviness of Carcass, however, this debut has little to offer non-believers except a vision of sheer hardcore metal intensity and a debt to Napalm Death.

The five-track **Perpetual Conversion** companion piece expands on tangential interests, featuring an electronic remix of the title track, an interesting ten-minute noise collage by Lilker ("Bed Sheet"), the previous album's convincing Death tribute ("Walking Corpses") and a Black Sabbath cover ("Lord of This World"). As is typical for heavy bands, the Sabbath worship is two-dimensional and wooden—inhuman vocals and noise power is not sufficient to re-create the emotion of a classic.

Need to Control pushes metal until it ruptures into experimental noise. Unpredictable songs like "Black Door Mine" are masked in a frantic blur of saturated sound. New drummer Rich Hoak's frenetic circular playing is one of several innovations; "Godplayer" opens with the low rattle of a didgeridoo, the ultimate bass rumble. The new chaos and complexity are a paralyzing combination, forming the most paranormal metal since Voivod. The group has subsequently collaborated with John Zorn, the Boredoms and God Is My Co-Pilot.

Joined by Shane Embury of Napalm Death, Lilker and former Brutal Truth drummer Scott Lewis are Malformed Earthborn, a studio project that takes the band's dense, jagged ethos to the sample bank, injecting waves of exotic snippets into dance-y rhythms with psychedelic results. Despite their metalhead front, the musicians prove themselves articulate, creative overachievers—if a little too enamored of Skinny Puppy. [ic]

BRUTE

See *Vic Chesnutt.*

BUCCINATOR

See *Ethyl Meatplow.*

JEFF BUCKLEY

Live at Sin-é EP (Columbia) 1993
Grace (Columbia) 1994

Operatic and Romantic with a capital R, Jeff Buckley's extraordinary singing draws on sources as diverse as Robert Plant, Edith Piaf, Nusrat Fateh Ali Khan, Freddie Mercury and Billie Holiday—and, much as he protests the comparison, even a blind taste test would reveal a noticeable vocal resemblance to his late father, folk-jazz legend Tim Buckley. He is a rare artist for his generation: totally unashamed to draw on his formidable technique and putting no post-modern irony or cool posturing between himself and the deep, vivid emotions he portrays. Some might consider that unhip, others find it refreshingly honest.

Live at Sin-é is a four-song EP recorded at the East Village Irish café where Buckley served a celebrated solo residency through the summer of '93. After a lot of hype and even with Buckley's prodigious vocal chops, the disc is a bit of a letdown. There's a pretentious take on Piaf's "Je N'en Connais Pas la Fin" and an interminable ten minutes of Van Morrison's "The Way Young Lovers Do." Buckley's own "Eternal Life" is hopelessly self-indulgent, while "Mojo Pin," written with erstwhile collaborator Gary Lucas, simply begs to be fleshed out with full-on rock instrumentation.

Buckley did just that on **Grace.** With an excellent band and appropriately wide-screen production by Andy Wallace, this stunning debut album delivers on the hints and promises of the EP. With his remarkable pipes sounding the charge, Buckley's old-fashioned troubadourism and spotlessly grunge-free music combines the pastoral stomp of Led Zeppelin with jazzy chord voicings laced with exotic Third Worldisms and English folk cadences. On the quiet side, he covers both Benjamin Britten (an incandescent "Corpus Christi Carol") and Leonard Cohen (a spine-chilling "Hallelujah"). Unafraid to pull such a rockist move as an archetypal epic title track, Buckley sometimes slips into bombast, but even that is so gloriously over the top that it just becomes part of the act. Things do fall off slightly after the jaw-dropping remake of "Mojo Pin," "Last Goodbye" and "So Real," but no matter—this guy is amazing. [ma]

BUFFALO TOM

Buffalo Tom (SST) 1989 (Beggars Banquet/Megadisc/EastWest) 1994
Birdbrain (Beggars Banquet/RCA) 1990
Let Me Come Over (Beggars Banquet/RCA) 1992
[Sodajerk] EP (UK Beggars Banquet/Megadisc) 1993
[Big Red Letter Day] (Beggars Banquet/Megadisc/EastWest) 1993
Sleepy Eyed (Beggars Banquet/Megadisc/EastWest) 1995

Although Buffalo Tom began with the stated intention of capturing the din of a "guitar army," the Amherst, Massachusetts, trio later did an about-face to invoke the unplugged sound and fury of a small platoon of folkies. The band's penchant for melody-laced amps-on-stun racket (and its chummy relationship to Dinosaur Jr's J Mascis) earned a nickname of "Dinosaur Jr Jr." from smartass rock critics, but that sobriquet does capture the essence of Buffalo Tom's early records as well as anything. The debut kicks up a satisfying squall as guitarist Bill Janovitz's earnestly overwrought vocals vie to be heard over the six-string turbulence of songs like "Sunflower Suit" and "500,000 Warnings." Mascis, who co-produced the album, contributes lead guitar to "Impossible."

Mascis took the same studio role (sharing credit with Sean Slade and the band) on **Birdbrain,** which boasts most of Buffalo Tom's best songs. The exquisite "Enemy" features a dramatic chorus nailed down by a killer riff; "Baby" is an unpretentiously lovely throwaway. The giddy propulsion of "Guy Who Is Me" and "Directive" make the tracks as invigorating as a cold shower. Providing a taste of things to come, the CD closes with two acoustic bonus tracks, "Reason Why" (a song off the first LP) and a cover of the Psychedelic Furs' "Heaven."

Let Me Come Over marks a jarring shift in direction as the boys unplug in a big way (a puzzling move, considering that grunge was at its height at the time of its release). Although the electric "Velvet Roof" is a revved-up delight and the pristine "Mineral" a minor classic, the album's folk-hearted plangency and heart-on-sleeve lyrics add up to a deeply drippy listening experience. **[Big Red Letter Day]** continues in the same vein, a shotgun marriage between folk and rock sensibilities that amounts to a brave failure. The plainspoken sincerity of songs like "I'm Allowed" and "Would Not Be Denied" is admirable, but it's hard to imagine Buffalo Tom getting much wimpier without alienating its core audience.

Produced by John Agnello (Cell, Kerosene, Chainsaw Kittens), **Sleepy Eyed** restores much of the guitar firepower to the trio's sound—and not a moment too soon. Simultaneously grungy and clean, anthemic singalongs like "Tangerine" and "It's You" do a lot to restore Buffalo Tom's erstwhile status as everyone's favorite raucously sincere college rockers. A rewarding synthesis of the two approaches. [ts]

BUILT TO SPILL

Ultimate Alternative Wavers (C/Z) 1993
There's Nothing Wrong With Love (Up) 1994
The Normal Years (K) 1996

BUILT TO SPILL/CAUSTIC RESIN

Built to Spill Caustic Resin EP (Up) 1995

CAUSTIC RESIN

Body Love Body Hate (C/Z) 1993
Fly Me to the Moon (Up) 1995

BUTTERFLY TRAIN

Building Distrust From Trust (Up) 1994
Distorted, Retarded, Peculiar (Up) 1996

In 1993, Doug Martsch of Seattle's Treepeople returned to Boise, Idaho, to escape the city, stop touring and record with an open-ended cast of backup musicians as Built to Spill. Over the next few albums and singles, Martsch proved himself to be one of indie-rock's most striking songwriters and guitarists. His songs are divided into sections that go beyond verse-chorus-verse form, with pop ditties that stop halfway and turn into glorious landscapes of mangled guitar strings. His lyrics reflect on life and love with intellectual angst.

The magic of **Ultimate Alternative Wavers** is that, although the unwound post-punk songs reach and even exceed the nine-minute mark, Martsch (here spelling his given name Dug) manages to endow each jagged, twisted guitar line with the emotion of the song, whether it be anger, introspection or love. "Revolution" and the band's theme song, "Built to Spill," are both excellent, but the standout is the infectious "Nowhere Nothin' Fuckup," which begins as a critical anthem for losers and slackers and ends as a requiem for the entire country, with Martsch chanting, "In America/Every puddle/Gasoline rainbow."

There's Nothing Wrong With Love telescopes Martsch's experimental urges into a focused album of three-to-four-minute deconstructed pop songs about growing up. "Cleo," named after Martsch's son, Benjamin Cleo, may be the least corny rock song ever written from the point of view of a baby being born. Singing "Living in the womb, running out of room, got to greet the sun and moon and—" Martsch breaks off mid-sentence for some serious string-twisting. "Twin Falls" begins with Martsch at age two as he traces the evolution of his first crush on a girl, from a family Christmas to physical contact in an elementary-school game of seven-up. And "Distopian Dream Girl" boils down all the anger and frustration of adolescence into a disagreement over musical taste: "My stepfather looks just like David Bowie, but he hates David Bowie/I think Bowie's cool, I think **Lodger** rules—step-dad's a fool." One of the album's cleverest moments comes at the end, when a voice announces a "preview of the next Built to Spill record." The band then proceeds to deliver a series of fifteen-second song clips that, one by one, parody punk, new wave, power pop and metal ballad.

The Normal Years is a ten-song rarities compilation of tracks by every lineup of the band between 1993 and '95. It includes a cover of "Some Things Last a Long Time," co-written by Jad Fair and Daniel Johnston.

Teaming up with Caustic Resin, a Boise band led by Brett Netson (who played on the first Built to Spill album), Martsch returned to more stretched-out songs on **Built to Spill Caustic Resin.** The EP mixes two of Martsch's songs, the advice-laden opuses "When Not Being Stupid Is Not Enough" and "One Thing," a Caustic Resin number (the instrumental "Shit Brown Eyes") and a Kicking Giant cover, the punky love song "She's Real."

If Built to Spill makes rock on the verge of collapse, Caustic Resin's music epitomizes the collapse. The band's songs are acid-rock nightmares, a mess of fuzzy guitar, distorted vocals and meandering drumbeats. The trio's first album, **Body Love Body Hate,** is filled with cocky loathing. Agonized screams and lyrics (the few intelligible lines are about suicide, murder and pain) combine with songs that explore density and recording-studio knobs at the expense of melody and linearity.

Fly Me to the Moon is an improvement. Caustic Resin comes off like a cross between the Jimi Hendrix Experience and Jesus Lizard. Thick, coagulated guitar-and-bass jams threaten to smother Netson's lyrics, which are better and clearer than the last album's, even if the topics are the same: "Kill You If You Want Me To," "A Fistful of Violence."

This is where the lineage gets confusing. Brett Nelson (not Netson), who was one-third of Built to Spill on the second album, leads Butterfly Train, anchoring lyrics of lost love to gently driving pop-punk on **Building Distrust From Trust.** Singing in the dulcet but cracking voice of a jilted lover, Nelson vacillates between affection for the past and hate for the present, switching between haltingly strummed verses and furious choruses. He comes off so sweet and so hurt that, by the end of the album, one wonders what kind of monster could have broken up with him. [ns]

See also *Halo Benders, Treepeople.*

BUNNYGRUNT

Standing Hampton EP7 (No Life) 1994
Action Pants! (No Life) 1995

Exporting glorious tweerock from St. Louis, bUNNYgRUNT is the gifted trio of Karen Reid (drums), Matt Hamish (guitar) and Jen Wolfe (bass). Sandwiching the eight catchy songs on **Action Pants!** between two coolly casual singers—the wispy Reid and the boyish Hamish—the group underpins its brisk jangle-pop with occasional blasts of afterburner racket power. Those lulled into a false sense of cuddlecore giddiness by the folky rush of "Superstar 666," "Transportation Pants" and the organ-flecked "Just Like Suppertime," and not sufficiently alerted by the sterner presence of the autobiographical "I Am Curious Partridge," may be knocked for a loop by the clattering intensity of "G. I. 2K" and "Tadpole." Musically adorable and not at all coy, bUNNYgRUNT cuts a colorful swath of free-wheeling style through what is often a refuge for the plain and unassertive, giving **Action Pants!** the sharp creases that stand out from the crowd. [i]

MARK BURGESS AND THE SONS OF GOD

Zima Junction (Pivot) 1994
Manchester 1993 (Pivot) 1994
Spring Blooms Tra-la (Ger. Strangeways/Indigo) 1994

MARK BURGESS AND YVES ALTANA

Paradyning (UK Dead Dead Good) 1995

CHAMELEONS

Here Today . . . Gone Tomorrow (UK Imaginary) 1992
The Radio 1 Evening Show Sessions (Nighttracks/Dutch East India Trading) 1993
Live in Toronto (UK Imaginary) 1993
Live at the Gallery Club Manchester 18 December 1982 (UK Visionary/Cherry Red) 1996

After the breakups of the revered Chameleons and the Sun and the Moon, bassist/singer Mark Burgess embarked on a sort-of solo excursion that found him creating intriguing new music while heading what turned out to be one of alternative rock's most glorious live nostalgia acts. **Zima Junction,** consisting of demos "for an album that was never to be" largely performed by Burgess himself, stands on its own as an interesting collection, merging the Chameleons' epic song structures with vulnerable folk-rock. Acoustic guitars dominate, with cheesy synths occasionally approximating string and horn sections. "Refugees" carries forward the Chameleons' tradition of virtual songs within songs, while "Happy New Life" builds to a shiver-inducing melancholic chorus, something the old band did as well. A stunning cover of Philip Glass' "Facades" (with lyrics by a Shetland poet) foreshadows a direction Burgess would later take.

To the delight of Burgess diehards, the touring Sons of God (a different lineup from the album) was virtually the Chameleons Mark II, though its leader had switched to guitar. The limited-edition live **Manchester 1993** (sold at shows during the Sons of God's '94 North American Tour) features eight Chameleons classics and two **Zima Junction** songs. Solidly played and well-recorded, it's a passionate, thrilling document of a seminal band, even if it is, by definition, secondhand.

Recorded and released in Germany, **Spring Blooms Tra-la** contains different live versions of a half-dozen Chameleons songs that also appear on **Manchester 1993,** six additional Chameleons numbers plus one **Zima Junction** track. To make things even more confusing, **Spring Blooms** contains a bonus CD of three tracks from **Manchester 1993.** A boon for completists.

By mid-decade, Burgess dissolved the Sons of God and, with its guitarist, Yves Altana, released **Paradyning,** his first proper studio album since the Sun and the Moon's 1988 debut. Amidst new agey guitar washes and simpler arrangements, the duo (with the help of some sidemen) craft dreamy soundscapes with rocky underpinnings—far from Burgess' most memorable material but an intriguing development nonetheless. The charmingly titled "You Opened My Mind (Then the Acid Kicked In)" is the highlight, while "Stop Talking," a vindictive personal complaint (to a former Chameleon, perhaps?), displays a self-righteousness not heard since Burgess' first group's heyday.

The Chameleons' posthumous **Radio 1** album gathers nine tracks recorded by different lineups of the quintet in '83 and '85 and adds a previously unheard leftover from the vaults. **Here Today . . . Gone Tomorrow** likewise documents the group from British radio sessions in '82 and '85. **Live in Toronto** and **Live at the Gallery Club** are both vintage concert recordings. There are others. [db]

See also *Reegs; TPRG.*

SONNY BURGESS WITH DAVE ALVIN

See *Dave Alvin.*

BUSH

Sixteen Stone (Trauma) 1994 (Trauma/Interscope) 1994

Platitudes about flattery don't go very far in justifying Bush's unnatural attachment to the fabulous sounds of the Pacific Northwest. On **Sixteen Stone,** the thunderous English quartet displays the manipulative skill of bionic engineers, playing stylistic charades in a gene pool stocked with the sounds of Pearl Jam, Nirvana, Soundgarden, Alice in Chains and Mudhoney. The sizzlingly raw, carefully inexact production by Clive Langer and Alan Winstanley is as commercially calculated as a gambling casino, alternately wrapping singer/guitarist Gavin Rossdale's thick, quivering passion in distorted blankets of barbed-wire guitar overdrive and claustrophobic emptiness. Haphazardly abstruse-going-on-dumb lyrics and songs clumsily hooked together from discontinuous bits (the worst offender in both regards being "Everything Zen," the hodgepodge hit that switches from a climactic chant of "I don't believe that Elvis is dead" to end with the unrelated and equally nonsensical anthem, "There's no sex in your violence") are actually a bigger problem than the shameless sonic appropriation. Bush goes about its dirty business with such intense conviction and pride that it's nearly impossible to begrudge the band its pretensions. [i]

KATE BUSH

The Kick Inside (Harvest) 1978
Lionheart (EMI America) 1978
Never For Ever (EMI America) 1980
The Dreaming (EMI America) 1982
Kate Bush EP (EMI America) 1983
Hounds of Love (EMI America) 1985
The Whole Story (EMI America) 1986
The Sensual World (Columbia) 1989
The Red Shoes (Columbia) 1993

Though she took years between projects, rarely performed live and generally wasn't around very much, Kate Bush cast a spell over the '80s. On **The Dreaming** and **Hounds of Love,** England's high priestess of production created moody soundscapes—sending Peter Gabriel and others back to the drawing board—in pursuit of a brainy, thickly layered brand of pop that only comes from endless hours spent in the studio. **The Sensual World,** her 1989 concept album, provides a passport to a dark, mysterious place, with strange voices (the Bulgarian Women's Choir) and surreal textures cushioning treatises on physical and metaphysical love.

Bush has been far less influential in the '90s. Though professing a love for alternative rock, she hasn't altered her own sound much—**The Red Shoes** is another pristine, carefully orchestrated collection notable for its chiming vocal harmonies and crafty use of guest stars. Bush still generates fantastical, image-rich songs—"Lily" celebrates the wisdom of a mystic, "Top of the City" uses the New York skyline to ponder the meaning of life—but the most interesting aspects of **The Red Shoes** come from other people. Eric Clapton contributes wrenching guitar counterpoint to "And So Is Love," and Prince animates the otherwise canned funk attempt "Why Should I Love You?" [tm]

See also *TPRG*.

BUSHWICK BILL

See *Geto Boys*.

BUTTERFLY TRAIN

See *Built to Spill*.

BUTTERGLORY

Alexander Bends EP7 (Merge) 1992
Our Heads EP7 (Merge) 1993
Cursive EP7 (Little Brother) 1994
Crumble (Merge) 1994
Wait for Me EP7 (Merge) 1995
Downed: A Singles Collection (Merge) 1995
are you building a temple in heaven? (Merge) 1996
She's Got the Akshun! EP (Merge) 1996

Like Pavement and the Archers of Loaf, this lo-fi indie-rock duo (relocated to Lawrence, Kansas, from Visalia, California) proves that pop songs can be instantly infectious even if it's hard to tell where they'll go next. Butterglory's songs are unpredictable, unpolished, off-kilter gems; they buzz with guitar feedback then drop back into catchy melodies with little warning. Despite the band's arty edge, though, there's not a single turkey of a tune amid all the fuzz and feedback of **Crumble.** Instead, Matt Suggs and Debby Vander Wall (the pair fills out the live sound with other musicians) craft loose, two-minute songs full of both razor-edge tension and, sometimes, disarming innocence. Songs like "Waiting on the Guns" and "The Skills of the Star Pilot" would be almost anthemic if not for their sloppy production values—which make them even more affecting.

Downed: A Singles Collection consists of eighteen songs originally released on the first four 7-inch EPs. The songs that post-date **Crumble** sound a bit more mature, perhaps a little better thought-out, than the earlier efforts, but nearly everything here is pretty similar to the first album. That's a good thing, though, and Butterglory's songs seem tailor-made for the collected singles format. Despite its method of assembly, **Downed** is an amazingly solid collection, far more consistent than many intentional albums.

Joined for its second album and subsequent tour by bassist Stephen Naron, Butterglory finds a more distinctive musical voice on **are you building a temple in heaven?** with more complex, slightly less chaotic-sounding songs. Unfortunately, some of them don't live up to the band's previous material. Textural tracks like "Boy Burning Down" and "The Lion Weeps Tonight" are effective in their own right, but they lack the raw energy of Butterglory's earlier work—not to mention this album's tense, feedback-filled gems, "Sit in the Car" and "Rivers." The three-song **She's Got the Akshun!** EP combines its title track—one of the album's stronger songs—with two previously unavailable tunes, one of which ("Places in Mind") is an exceptionally catchy song with the manic tension Butterglory brought to **Crumble.** [rl]

BUTTHOLE SURFERS

Butthole Surfers (Alternative Tentacles) 1983
Live PCPPEP (Alternative Tentacles) 1984
Psychic . . . Powerless . . . Another Man's Sac (Touch and Go) 1985
Cream Corn from the Socket of Davis EP (Touch and Go) 1985
Rembrandt Pussyhorse (Touch and Go) 1986
Locust Abortion Technician (Touch and Go) 1987
Hairway to Steven (Touch and Go) 1988
Double Live (Latino Buggerveil) 1989
Widowermaker! EP (Touch and Go) 1989
piouhgd (Rough Trade) 1991 (Capitol) 1992
Independent Worm Saloon (Capitol) 1994
The Hole Truth . . . and Nothing Butt! (Trance Syndicate) 1995
Electriclarryland (Capitol) 1996

JACKOFFICERS

Digital Dump (Rough Trade) 1990

DADDY LONGHEAD

Cheatos (Touch and Go) 1991

PAUL LEARY

The History of Dogs (Rough Trade) 1991

DRAIN

Pick Up Heaven (Trance Syndicate) 1992

P

P (Capitol) 1995

Granted, the world didn't come screeching to an explosive climax followed by a stunned silence, but every other useful standard of measure registered the Butthole Surfers' 1992 signing to a major label—and not just any old major label, but Capitol, the conservative corporate preserve of the Beatles, the Beach Boys and Steve Miller—as a major cataclysm in the cultural order of things. For big business to give money and allocate resources to a band as perversely devoted to grotesque noise, wanton offensiveness and conceptual sedition ("The Shah Sleeps in Lee Harvey's Grave"? "The Revenge of Anus Presley"?? "Bar-B-Q Pope"???) as the influential Texans only proves how deeply the "alternative" developments of 1991 altered the rational foundation of pop music. The rich irony of the matter, of course, is that the Buttholes had already lost their taste for truly shocking aural degradation.

The veteran quartet's bigtime bow came via the re-release of a record whose original issue went blooey when Rough Trade closed up shop in America. The uneven **piouhgd** (pronounced "p-o'd") is a well-produced disappointment that scrounges around in half-baked ideas like Donovan's "Hurdy Gurdy Man" (without perceptible irony) and "Revolution" (one part of which consists of an unobtrusive stew of synthetic strings, noise-guitar, a ringing phone and police sirens over which singer Gibby Haynes keeps calling out Garry Shandling's name). Besides such nonsense—and "Lonesome Bulldog," a comedic cowboy ballad in four segments—**piouhgd** stoops to a spot-on parody of the Jesus and Mary Chain that is a pointless waste of effort for a band so geared to give offense. The reassuring appearance of several slabs of typical Buttholian psycho-acoustics proves the band isn't completely soft; still, **piouhgd** lacks a certain psumbthaenng. (The CD bonus, "Barking Dogs," is an extended sound collage with brief canine contributions.)

In between his years of Led Zeppelin fame and such fringier '90s undertakings as a duo with Diamanda Galás, bassist John Paul Jones produced **Independent Worm Saloon,** the Buttholes' unbalanced attempt at reconciliation with both the real world and the underground cesspool from which it emerged. The riff-rock of "Who Was in My Room Last Night?" is nostalgic in a seemingly serious vein. "You Don't Know Me" and "Leave Me Alone" could be Cheap Trick; the antagonistic posturing of songs like "Goofy's Concern" ("I don't give a fuck about the FBI/I don't give a fuck about the CIA/I don't give a fuck about the kids on the street/I don't give a fuck about anything") sounds forced and, worse, half-hearted. Although Gibby holds his genially deranged own and guitarist Paul Leary sends out endless plumes of flamethrower guitar distortion and feedback, their efforts don't go nearly far, deep or wide enough to rattle any windows at this late date. The puke prelude to "Clean It Up" is visceral but pitifully old hat—only "The Annoying Song" is deserving of its honorable title. As inconceivable as the thought of the Butthole Surfers' ever being tame and boring is, this album is the proof that such tragedies can occur.

Electriclarryland (available on vinyl, with one of four sides devoted to band etchings) gets off to a snorting good start with the manic storm of "Birds," but the rest of the album mainly serves to reconfirm the band's loss of sonic nerve. As the songs make a point of mounting goofball platforms in concept ("Jingle of a Dog's Collar," "The Lord Is a Monkey," "Ulcer Break-out"), the music is spineless and dull, taking half-hearted jokey toe-dips into polluted waters the Buttholes once walked on with sweaty pride.

The Hole Truth, a compilation of sloppy live tracks (1985–93) plus two '83 demos and an uproarious vintage radio interview (complete with an in-studio musical tribute to Gordon Lightfoot), is much more like it. Captured in its natural state—driving blind drunk down a dirt road with the headlights flashing madly—the band raises a toxic cloud of sonic dirt in mindboggling guitar windstorms ("USSA"), deliciously skeevy vocal showcases ("Moving to Florida," "Cherub," "Bon Song") and barely coordinated band meltdowns ("Psychedelic," a hearteningly ear-busting '93 version of "The Shah Sleeps in Lee Harvey's Grave"). Among the illuminating items in this marauding mess: a primeval studio version of "Butthole Surfer" and a twisted take on "Hurdy Gurdy Man" five years older than the studio track.

Before his departure (and temporary replacement, for some of **Electriclarryland,** by ex–Rollins Band bassist Andrew Weiss), Jeff Pinkus made a couple of extracurricular records. Paired with Gibby as the Jack-officers, he fiddled around with synthesizers to make **Digital Dump,** a sample-heavy simulation of silly dance songs. As Daddy Longhead—with drummer Rey Washam (who graduated from Scratch Acid to Steve Albini's Rapeman), guitarist/fiddler Jim Yongue (Waste King Universal) and help from Leary and Butthole drummer King Coffey—Pinkus (vocals, bass, guitar) made **Cheatos,** an out-of-control hard-rock record with all the crazed invention of the Buttholes and none of the Gibbyness. The layers of furious shredmetal riff-ology that overwhelm several songs reduce them to showoff filler—whatever wit there is in the lyrics of "Back in '69" or "20 Lb. Jockey," for instance, is swamped out by Yongue's flashy fingerwork—but Pinkus' irredeemable shrieking in "Scar Spangled Boner" makes it clear that extraordinary forces are at work. Agony Column's Richie Turner puts growling death-metal vocals to "Pine Box," adding a cacophony that doesn't so much signify the evil that lurks in the hearts of men as amplify it to the point of random violence. In "The Post" (a "traditional" better known to jam-band concertgoers as "Whipping Post"), Daddy Longhead comes across as the southern boogie band from another planet, eviscerating the genre while glibly respecting most of its standard features.

So far, Leary (who has produced albums for the Meat Puppets, Daniel Johnston and Supersuckers, among others) is the only Surfer to release an official solo album. **The History of Dogs,** undertaken with no help whatsoever, offers his topical commentary on the Gulf War, Native American rights and space travel, sung (frequently double-tracked in high and low voices) over restrained arrangements in a variety of non-Buttholian modes: mock-symphonics, acoustic pop, heavy rock, dance-hall piano. Although **The History of Dogs** is surprising in its relative propriety, Leary still manages to make his seriousness sound mocking.

In his spare time, King Coffey runs the concertedly left-field Trance Syndicate label and records as Drain, a trio with guitarist David McCreath and bassist Owen McMann of the Cherubs. With vocals kept at bay behind distortion and disregard, **Pick Up Heaven** slackly piles together rugged guitar, driving rhythms, keyboards and (on the incongruous techno-styled "Instant Hippie") samples for a weenie-roast as noisy as it is pointless.

Besides the Surfers, the Jackofficers, guest shots with Ministry, album production for the Rev. Horton Heat and a radio show in Austin, Gibby sings in a quartet called P with Austin guitarist/songwriter Bill Carter, actor/guitarist Johnny Depp and actor/drummer Sal Jenco. Although shaped into a Texas roots-rock boogie sound, **P** is everything a Butthole Surfers album should be: sick and twisted, dayglo, vulgar, ugly and funny, mean-spirited and self-abusive, out of control and shameless. Gibby is in top form, describing a funhouse ride of vocal hysterics; he even whips out an impressive scrawling noise-guitar solo. Beyond the nearly sincere cover of ABBA's "Dancing Queen" and a full-frontal clambake (complete with electric sitar) of Daniel Johnston's queasy "I Save Cigarette Butts," the group's own inventions are richly absurd, whether taking friendly pop aim at "Michael Stipe," exploring the depths of dub in "Jon Glenn (Mega Mix)" or wailing out a rugged twelve-bar, "White Man Sings the Blues." In light of the overexertion of his real band's underwhelming efforts of late, maybe P is Gibby's heavenly option. [i]

See also *Beme Seed, Ministry; TPRG.*

BUTT TRUMPET

Primitive Enema (Hell Yeah) 1994 (Chrysalis/EMI) 1994

The vulgarity goes in before the proud name goes on. The double-bassist Los Angeles quintet (not to be confused with Buttsteak, Blohole or the Ass Ponys) is strictly out to offend on **Primitive Enema,** wielding a two-pronged fork of blaring punk aggression and tastelessly crude lyrics that make outrageous jokes of the three S's: scatology, sex and stoopidity. (That this harmless but appalling nonsense wound up being reissued on a titanic record label must have cost *someone* their key to the executive bidet.) The album is funny in spots: "Shutup" has the rest of the band shouting down frontman Thom Bone's attempts to sing the thing; "I'm Ugly and I Don't Know Why," a vocal cameo by bassist Sharon Needles, makes good sport of school-age cruelty, and "I've Been So Mad Lately" consists of little more than bassist Bianca Butthole using her hillbilly-from-hell screech to scream cathartically pure invective. But it's also cumulatively overpowering in its headache-inducing awfulness. Merry odes to anal sex (an unlisted bonus), defecation (the title track), promiscuity ("Clusterfuck"), yeast infections ("Ten Seconds of Heaven") and romantic aroma therapy ("Yesterday") fill the septic tank of Butt Trumpet's bad-joke novelties to the brim and then some. Yeuch. [i]

BUZZCOCKS

Another Music in a Different Kitchen (UK UA) 1978
Love Bites (UK UA) 1978
A Different Kind of Tension (UK UA) 1979 (IRS) 1989
Singles Going Steady (IRS) 1979
Parts One, Two, Three EP (IRS) 1984
The Peel Sessions EP (UK Strange Fruit) 1988
Lest We Forget (ROIR) 1988
Live at the Roxy Club April '77 (UK Absolutely Free) 1989 (UK Receiver) 1990
Product (Restless Retro) 1989
The Peel Sessions Album (UK Strange Fruit) 1989 (Strange Fruit/Dutch East India Trading) 1991
Operators Manual: Buzzcocks Best (IRS) 1991
Alive Tonight EP (UK Planet Pacific) 1991
Entertaining Friends: Live at the Hammersmith Odeon March 1979 (IRS) 1992
Trade Test Transmissions (UK Essential/Castle Communications) 1993 (Caroline) 1993
French (IRS) 1996
All Set (IRS) 1996

STEVE DIGGLE

Heated and Rising EP (UK Three Thirty) 1993

VARIOUS ARTISTS

Something's Gone Wrong Again: The Buzzcocks' Covers Compilation (C/Z) 1992

Having broken up in 1980, the Buzzcocks—Manchester's pop pride in the class of '77, and perhaps the best singles band to come out of the initial new wave explosion—saw fit to end the decade by answering the question once posed in song ("Whatever Happened To?") and fulfilling the dream of "Nostalgia": "I look up at the sky and I wonder what it'll be like in days gone by/I'm surfing on a wave of nostalgia for an age yet to come." Sparked in part by the attention attending the classy **Product** boxed set (which contains the post–Howard Devoto band's entire studio issue—three albums and a dozen 45s—plus an outtake and eight songs from a '78 gig), singer/guitarist Pete Shelley, guitarist/singer Steve Diggle, bassist Steve Garvey and (briefly) original hyper-drummer John Maher mounted a reunion tour in 1989, and kept going from there.

Inspired in turn by *that* unexpected turn of events, the group's past label put out **Operators Manual,** a concise twenty-five-track career condensation, and **Entertaining Friends,** a great 1979 concert document. For their part, Shelley and Diggle weathered the departure of Garvey and Maher (eventually drafting a new rhythm section of bassist Tony Barber and drummer Phil Barker) and set about, separately, writing songs. The first result of their renewed labors was **Alive Tonight,** an encouraging but diffident four-song 12-inch that doesn't resemble the old band much beyond Shelley's inimitable giddy vocals and flashback melody on "Last to Know," a catchy case of romantic nerves.

"Last to Know" and Diggle's "Alive Tonight" wound up being redone for the full-length **Trade Test Transmissions,** the first new Buzzcocks studio album in fourteen years. With a bigger, more distorted guitar backdrop and forceful production as the only notable evidence of time's arrow, whatever went into the Buzzcocks' mixmaster way back when seems to have been relocated and recharged: Shelley shelves the stylistic alter ego of his intervening solo career to bang out rushing pop joys like "Innocent," "Never Gonna Give It Up," "Who'll Help Me to Forget?" and "Palm of Your Hand" (a song about masturbation that nicely bookends 1977's "Orgasm Addict"), stamping them all with the unmistakable sound that launched a thousand pogos. A more equitable division of labor—Diggle wrote and sings nearly a third of the augmented American edition—may have been necessary to maintain peace, but Diggle, whose singing is much improved from the old days and who has developed into a fine pop craftsman, sounds (as he did then) like he's fronting a different band. For all his sexual enthusiasm, Shelley still comes from another plane as his bandmate, decrying fascism ("Crystal Night") and irony ("369") while Diggle doesn't raise his sights much higher than basic survival ("Alive Tonight") and ideas ("Energy," "Isolation"). Rather than attempt to establish some working dynamic that integrates their concerns, the once and future 'Cocks simply present themselves as a two-headed monster and leave it at that. A different kind of tension . . .

French is a live album recorded in Paris in April 1995; the twenty-three-song set runs the discographical gamut from "Orgasm Addict," "Noise Annoys" and "Why She's a Girl From the Chainstore" through "Energy," "Isolation" and "Innocent."

Diggle and Shelley prove the reliability of their resurgence on **All Set,** another new studio record of memorable originals with familiar virtues. Highlights: "Totally From the Heart," "Hold Me Close," "Point of No Return" and "Back With You."

Among the punks having a go at fourteen Buzzcocks classics on **Something's Gone Wrong Again** are the Fluid, Didjits, Alice Donut and Naked Raygun. Coffin Break barely follows the melody of "What Do I Get?," Lunachicks make a joke of "Noise Annoys" before jumping into "Promises" and Porn Orchard insert an inane rap and prank phone call into "Why Can't I Touch It?" Doing fair frontier justice to, respectively, "I Don't Mind" and "Everybody's Happy Nowadays," Big Drill Car and Dose are the only bands here that seem genuinely interested in paying tribute to the group. [i]

See also *TPRG*.

BUZZ HUNGRY

See *Sugar*.

B.Y.O.B

See *Basehead*.

DAVID BYRNE AND BRIAN ENO

My Life in the Bush of Ghosts (Sire) 1981

DAVID BYRNE

Songs From the Broadway Production of "The Catherine Wheel" (Sire) 1981
Music for *The Knee Plays* (ECM) 1985
Rei Momo (Luaka Bop/Sire) 1989
The Forest (Luaka Bop/Sire/Warner Bros.) 1991
Forestry EP (Luaka Bop/Sire/Warner Bros.) 1991
Uh-Oh (Luaka Bop/Sire/Warner Bros.) 1992
David Byrne (Luaka Bop/Sire/Warner Bros.) 1994

DAVID BYRNE ET AL.

Sounds From True Stories (Sire) 1986

RYUICHI SAKAMOTO, DAVID BYRNE AND CONG SU

The Last Emperor (Virgin Movie Music) 1988

TALKING HEADS

Sand in the Vaseline: Popular Favorites (Sire/Warner Bros.) 1992

David Byrne conducted a broad variety of solo experiments before finally cutting the string that connected the Talking Heads. The successful tape and found-sound test of **My Life in the Bush of Ghosts** wouldn't have done for a proper band album at the time. **Songs From . . . "The Catherine Wheel"** (a score that is complete only on cassette), a series of pieces to which choreographer Twyla Tharp set an ambitious dance program, isn't a big musical departure from his work within the band, and particularly echoes **Remain in Light** remixes. **Music for *The Knee Plays,*** inspired by the Dirty Dozen Brass Band and composed for Robert Wilson's play/opera/dance, presages the role horns would take on the Heads' 1988 album, **Naked.** The songs generally work best as incidental music, much like Byrne's subsequent soundtrack work.

Still, for all its Latin musics (and supporting cast), **Rei Momo** is a surprisingly tentative solo debut. Although Byrne announces his sovereignty in the opening track, "Independence Day" ("Waiting such a long time/Till Independence Day"), **Rei Momo** is the first record in which he attempts to subordinate his own strong voice. It consequently lacks Byrne's usual rhythmic sharpness, wants for one or two of his commanding left hooks and plays like incidental music for a film or a tropical restaurant.

The followup is vastly more ambitious. **The Forest** takes an orchestral whack at the ancient Sumerian epic of Gilgamesh; some of the music was also used in a theatrical collaboration with Robert Wilson. As with John Cale's **Fragments of a Rainy Season, The Forest** betrays a remarkably conservative approach to orchestral music. Byrne had spent better than a decade aggressively exploring a broad variety of sounds, but his frame of reference here has little to do with twentieth-century composers (not even Copland or Bernstein); rather, he willfully invokes the traditions of eighteenth-century European court composers—if you can imagine David Byrne's voice singing along at the odd moment. Byrne handed two of the pieces off to Meat Beat Manifesto's Jack Dangers and A.R.Kane's Rudy Tambala, who (separately) remixed them for the five-track **Forestry** EP. It is not an altogether happy marriage of sensibilities.

Uh-Oh, by contrast, is exactly that: an exultant union of Byrne's widely varied impulses. Having studied many ethnic musics, both as musician and as the taste-setting entrepreneur behind Luaka Bop's international roster, Byrne is finally able to stop thinking about music and resume playing it. The songs swing with a goofy, infectious joy, buoyed by evidence that Byrne can let down his artistic hair and have fun for a change. The supporting cast, drawn from his ever-expanding galaxy of musical associates, provides a broad range of sounds—all of which tumble together in the infectious "Something Ain't Right."

David Byrne sets an altogether different mood, alternating between contemplative and somber. Even bouncy tracks like "Lilies of the Valley" and "You & Eye" are understated and spare in their presentation. Instead of the dense congregations of musicians who added complicated layers of texture to previous releases, the small groupings here provide simpler, largely acoustic settings for songs notable for their craft and their seriousness. Lyrically, he's working under a heavy cloud. "A Long Time Ago" combines allusions to blood-borne infection with the closing of a disco; "Angels" mentions Tiananmen Square; "Crash" begins "I met my love at a funeral/I'm tired of goodbyes and burials." For all its haunted images and global anxieties, though, the album has a grace and strength that speaks to its author's abundant ability to make the music he hears, unhindered by the memories of what he has already produced.

As a fascinating, enlightening and amusingly annotated souvenir of Talking Heads, the posthumous two-CD **Sand in the Vaseline** is a fine place to meet the band. [ga/i]

See also *Brian Eno; TPRG*

CHRIS CACAVAS AND JUNK YARD LOVE

Chris Cacavas and Junk Yard Love (Heyday) 1989
Good Times (Heyday) 1992
Pale Blonde Hell (Ger. Normal) 1994
Dwarf Star (Ger. Return to Sender/Normal) 1995
New Improved Pain (Ger. Normal) 1996

CHRIS CACAVAS

Six String Soapbox (Ger. Return to Sender/Normal) 1994

On his own records, former Green on Red keyboardist Chris Cacavas treads spiky southwestern guitar-rock turf that should be vaguely familiar to admirers of such combos as Green on Red, the Dream Syndicate and Giant Sand (all of which Cacavas has recorded with). But Cacavas' own records—on which he sings, writes and plays guitar as well as keys—reveal both an individual musical sensibility and a plainspoken songwriting talent that establishes his significance beyond those past associations.

The Steve Wynn–produced **Chris Cacavas and Junk Yard Love** is a worthy if tentative debut, as the Arizona native sings his songs in a dry, unadorned voice that underlines their straightforward observations. The ironically titled **Good Times** (which Cacavas co-produced with Bad Religion's Brett Gurewitz) is generally less reflective and more aggressive, in the activist streak of numbers like "Did You Hear What She Said?" and "Many Splintered Thing," in the harder-hitting arrangements and in the artist's assertive vocal performances. He also sounds noticeably more confident on the acoustic numbers ("Chain of Roses," "Rocking Chair"). The self-produced, relationship-oriented **Pale Blonde Hell** has an especially organic feel, as Cacavas and band rock with force and subtlety on such tunes as "Rejection as Usual" and "Let You Down." **New Improved Pain** is Cacavas' best yet, with rockers ("Heart of Sand") and moodier numbers ("Freak") boasting full-bodied performances and lyrics that take on personal and political matters with equal lucidity.

Dwarf Star and **Six String Soapbox** are both part of the German Return to Sender series of limited-edition releases by American artists. The former features unadorned band performances of eight otherwise unavailable originals, plus an oddly effective reworking of Matthew Sweet's "Someone to Pull the Trigger" and an unlisted jazz-piano bonus track. The latter consists of mostly solo renditions of eight songs, some of which (including the title track) appear in fuller versions on other albums. [ss]

CAFE TACUBA

Cafe Tacuba (Mex. WEA Latina) 1992
Re (Mex. WEA Latina) 1994

In America and England, where new wave is just another flavor of nostalgia, bands that make music with those values can't escape the taint of parody or contrived style-mongering. In Mexico, however, the energetic sound of early-'80s jumparound music hasn't yet lost its currency, and offbeat rockers like Caifanes and Cafe Tacuba can still rev up cheesy organ and skittery ska rhythms without making an issue of it. Fronted by flamboyant brat singer Cosme (aka Juan; his given name is Rubén Albarrán), who shapes his fire-red hair into devil horns, the un-self-conscious and eclectic quartet from Mexico City makes a pan-cultural game of *rock en español,* throwing hip-hop, acoustic pop, romantic balladry, *ranchera, mariachi,* funk, new wave and whatever happens across the radar screen into the mix on the infectious **Cafe Tacuba.** The instrumentation switches as often as the tempos—piano, melodica, string bass, acoustic and electric guitars, synthesizers and percussion (as well as accordion by Flaco Jiménez and trumpet) all shape the whimsical songs—but Cosme's melodramatic delivery is what holds the energetic party together. Pick hit (for its dead-catchy chorus): "Noche Oscura" ("Dark Night").

Re is a far more ambitious undertaking, as a dozen guests help the newly politicized Cafe Tacuba through a musical funhouse that yanks open doors to reveal an endless array of idioms and traditions. The band shifts gears repeatedly, often within songs: "El Ciclinto" is a wild Sly Stone/Beatles/Plastic Bertrand/Manfred Mann/Sugarcubes mix-and-match. "El Borrego" goes for a distorted Ministry-like techno kill, while "Ixtepec" can only be called flamenco house, "El Metro" is pop-funk, "El Fin de la Infancia" is speedy *mariachi,* "Pez" is spare pop and "Las Flores" bounces to a ska beat. "El Baile y el Salón" quotes Labelle; "La Pinta" rips a mighty electric guitar hole. Making eclectic unpredictability its strong stylistic statement, **Re** amazingly holds together. [i]

CAIFANES

Caifanes (Mex. RCA) 1988
El Diablito (Mex. RCA) 1990
El Silencio (Mex. RCA/BMG International) 1992
El Nervio del Volcan (Mex. RCA/BMG) 1994

More fun from Mexico City: loosely bound by two very different musical traditions—indigenous folk and the fading influence of imported new wave (mostly of the Police, but also Duran Duran, U2 and the Cure)—Caifanes produces high-gloss pop, mixing stylistic metaphors and eras into a modern blend that can lead toward sodden sentimentality ("Amarrate a una Escoba y Vuela Lejos," on **El Diablito**) at one end and rousing guitar-rock ("La Vida No Es Eterna," a CD bonus track on the same album) at the other, with an early predilection for dramatic synth-pop (**Caifanes**' "Cuentame Tu Vida") and even glitzed-up *cumbia* (the debut's "La Negra Tomasa," Caifanes' first big hit) on either side. If the group's albums don't push any international envelopes, the songs (written by singer/guitarist Saúl Hernandez) speak powerfully to Mexican youth via dramatically impressionist lyrics about souls, love, alienation and metaphysical transformations.

The first album is the most new wavey ("Perdi Mi Ojo de Venado" lodges your basic bored-teenagers complaint); the phantoms of Gary Numan and Nick Rhodes alternately operate the keyboards as Hernandez explores the pompous reaches of his sturdy baritone. The substantially improved **El Diablito** refines Caifanes' sound with more sophisticated instrumental textures and less stylistic meandering. "Detras de Ti" slides through its minor key and rhythmic permutations with smooth confidence (the Cars reborn as a Latin ska group?), while "Antes de Que Nos Olviden" gathers a potent atmosphere around Alejandro Marcovich's tensely pinging guitar nibbles before releasing a dreamy chorus and then finding room for a wiggly fretless bass solo by Sabo Romo.

Adrian Belew, who produced **El Silencio** (is there a theme here? Phil Manzanera, another adventurous guitar wanger from way back, produced Brazil's Paralamas do Sucesso) in Wisconsin, coaxed edgier rock and a smart stylistic upgrade out of Caifanes. "Nubes" integrates Latin percussion and horns for a salsa inflection; "Piedra" floats off on a raft of MIDI tubas and trumpets; "No Dejes Que . . ." modernizes the Tin Pan pop of bands like Haircut 100 with glorious results; and "Debajo de Tu Piel" strikes a balance between the Beatles and David Bowie. Not surprisingly, **El Silencio** is a night of a thousand guitar sounds, but the songwriting and arrangements are just as fascinating.

Warren Zevon/Toto regular Greg Ladanyi co-produced **El Nervio del Volcan,** which nonetheless leaves the blocks accompanied by a very Belew-like guitar figure in "Afuera," a song drawn from Argentinian and Bolivian musics. Reduced to a trio (listing the album's bassist and keyboard player as guests), Caifanes retrenches from the previous record's advances a bit. Without settling for a single rock idiom, the album evinces a more practical measure of ambition. Other than the clattery distortions of "Hasta Que Dejes de Respirar" and the string-laden acoustic dalliance of "Ayer Me Dijo un Ave," Caifanes rocks with focused power at a fairly consistent and effective dynamic level. At the band's most surreal, "Quisiera Ser Alcohol" ("I Wish I Was Alcohol") asserts the desire to "evaporate inside you/And learn what passion means." Take that, Prince Charles. [i]

CAKEKITCHEN

Cake Kitchen EP (NZ Flying Nun) 1989
Time Flowing Backwards (Homestead) 1991
World of Sand (Homestead) 1992
Far From the Sun (Homestead) 1993
Stompin' Thru the Boneyard (Merge) 1995
Bald Old Bear EP (Merge/Raffmond) 1996
The Devil and the Deep Blue Sea (Ger. Raffmond) 1996 (Merge) 1996

GRAEME JEFFERIES

Messages for the Cakekitchen (NZ Flying Nun) 1988 (Ajax) 1993

THIS KIND OF PUNISHMENT

A Beard of Bees (NZ TKP) 1984 [tape] (NZ Xpressway) 1990 (Xpressway/Ajax) 1993
5 by Four EP (NZ Flying Nun) 1985
In the Same Room (NZ Flying Nun) 1987
Live '85 [tape] (NZ Xpressway) 1989
In the Same Room. 5 by Four. (Ajax) 1993
This Kind of Punishment (Ajax) 1996

NOCTURNAL PROJECTIONS

Another Year EP (NZ Hit Singles) 1982
Understanding Another Year in Darkness EP (NZ Hit Singles) 1983
Nerve Ends in Power Lines (Ger. Raffmond) 1995

Graeme Jefferies has made an indelible mark on New Zealand's fertile underground scene, most notably with Cakekitchen and his prior band, This Kind of Punishment, a collaboration with his equally influential brother Peter. Both men possess thick, deep voices which, along with their use of 4- and 8-track recording equipment, elemental sounds and non-traditional rock instrumentation (violin, recorder), distinguishes their music from that of their contemporaries.

Although billed as a solo record, **Messages for the Cakekitchen** is effectively the first Cakekitchen album. Sparser and darker than the official band work to follow, it's more in keeping with the homemade recordings of his Xpressway label brethren. At times, his vocals sound vaguely gothic ("Reason to Keep Swimming"), while the music alternates between tension-filled electric guitar arrangements ("All the Colours Run Dry"), deliberate acoustic ones ("Nothing That's New") and combinations of the two ("Prisoner of a Single Passion"). Although not as fully realized as its immediate successor, **Messages** details Jefferies' signature elements and his keen, individual songwriting style.

Previewed on an eponymous 1989 four-song EP, **Time Flowing Backwards** begins with the enormous guitar sound of "Dave the Pimp," which sets the album's intense mood, washing over the droning melody and burly rhythm like a tidal wave. Though certainly intense, the rest of the album tucks Jefferies' delicious melodies into subtler settings (like "Silence of the Sirens"). The drone remains crucial to "One + One = One," while the noisy "Walked Over Texas" boasts a 3Ds-like lurch (3Ds guitarist David Mitchell guests on the track). Surely one of Jefferies' most accomplished albums, **Time Flowing Backwards** also introduces the Cakekitchen's first solid lineup—a trio with bassist Rachael King and drummer Robert Key.

World of Sand ranges from sweet melodies drawn by Jefferies' subtle acoustic guitar playing and given depth by his guttural voice ("World of Sand," "Dogs and Cats") to vibrant displays of his electric six-string fury ("Walking on Glass," "This Perfect Day"), with additional "noises" spicing up the mix. Noted NZ violinist Alastair Galbraith makes an appearance on the title track; the album is brought to a promising conclusion by a rousing duet with another 3Ds member, Denise Roughan, on "Crimson to Gunmetal."

Having relocated to London, Jefferies assembled a new rhythm section (bassist Keith McLean and drummer Huw Dainow) and recorded **Far From the Sun.** As usual, the album displays both Jefferies' denser, electric side ("Stranger Than Paradise," "Man in the Mirror") and his contemplative singer/songwriter side ("Greater Windmill Street Blues," the title track), both of which are given a bittersweet melancholy by the low lonesome sound of his voice. Jefferies reveals a penchant for experimentation, incorporating odd sounds into several arrangements: his gentle acoustic playing in "Overexcited" is violently disrupted by what sounds like a jackhammer, while "Far From the Sun" begins with the sound of water dripping.

Another year, another Cakekitchen lineup: **Stompin' Thru the Boneyard** was primarily recorded by Jefferies and Jean-Yves Douet, a Frenchman whose aggressive drumming underscores the albums's rough-around-the-edges but poppy sound. Despite somewhat muddy, hollow production, Jefferies sprawls out stylistically. "Tell Me Why You Lie" is concise pop; the multi-part "Hole in My Shoe" ends with a longish instrumental segment; "The Mad Clarinet" is a highly textured acoustic piece complicated by Galbraith's fervent violin playing.

The material on **The Devil and the Deep Blue Sea** appears to have been recorded contemporaneously with that on **Stompin',** although its overall tone is more serious and less immediately catchy, the production a little fuller. The core lineup remains Jefferies and Douet, with contributions from Hamish Kilgour of the Clean/Mad Scene (percussion on "Ballad of Oxford Circus") and Galbraith (violin on "Escape to Fire Island"). On the sober, lilting melody of "I Know You Know," Jefferies is accompanied solely by his own acoustic strumming and violin playing; the spare "You Make a God of Money" promises goose pimples as Jefferies sings, "And I'm so scared that I am going to die/It makes me feel so very fragile," before the song's "rock" segment kicks in. As if to balance out the album's personal, reflective aura, "Baby I Luv You" is a revved-up, Lou Reed–like rocker, and "Everything Turned Orange" hearkens back to the more driving, droning guitar sounds that bored their way through earlier Cakekitchen material. Picking up on the previous album's more experimental leanings, the eleven-and-a-half-minute opener, "Old Grey Ghost," labors through five minutes of amelodic noise before reaching the song; "Take It Easy With Me" incorporates tape loops and some wild non-verbal vocals, and the instrumental "Escape to Fire Island" begins as a harsh noise collage before erupting into sweet guitar/violin/piano interplay. The **Bald Old Bear** EP includes the title track and four otherwise unavailable songs recorded with members of the Hausmusik collective; one is a cover of Michael Hurley's "Wild Geeses."

Before focusing full-time on the Cakekitchen, Graeme recorded as This Kind of Punishment with his brother Peter and a revolving cast of locals. Captured on Xpressway's favorite machine, a Teac 4-track, the nine songs on 1984's **A Beard of Bees** ripple with an edginess enhanced by the intimate recording quality and rich arrangements, also featuring a variety of instrumentation. Peter's poetic piano playing colors the proceedings in dark hues, deepened by both Jefferies' eerie baritones. Most, but not all, of Graeme's contributions are on the guitar.

While similar in mood, the stronger **In the Same Room** album (recorded 1986–87) is driven by more traditional rock instrumentation (Peter plays drums more often than piano here), making the whole thing more approachable, the songs easier to grasp. "Holding," written and sung by Michael Morley of the Dead C, also features Shayne Carter (Straitjacket Fits) on "subliminal" guitar, while Galbraith makes another appearance on "Left Turns Right." The tension really explodes on "Words Fail Me," a taut encapsulation of the Jefferies' complementary talents: Peter's rumbling beats put the force behind Graeme's turbulent guitar playing, against the waves of which Peter's vocals battle, seeming to gasp for each breath. **5 by Four**—five songs recorded by the Jefferies, Chris Matthews and Johnny Pierce—dates from 1985 (between the first two albums) and dips back into darker, more experimental waters. The songs are edgy: "Mr. Tic Toc" is essentially a spoken-word piece, while the instrumental "North Head" features industrial-sounding percussion.

In the early '80s, the Jefferies brothers played together in Nocturnal Projections, Graeme on guitar and Peter on vocals. The group released one 7-inch and two EPs, all in very limited editions, and had a track ("Walk in a Straight Line") on the influential Xpressway **Pile=Up** compilation. The belated **Nerve Ends in Power Lines** offers an overview, including both "In Purgatory" (on which Peter's vocals sound particularly goth-y, via Joy Division) and "Nerve Ends in Power Lines" from the 7-inch, three tracks from the two EPs, four live cuts and two previously unreleased studio tracks. The raw, angsty sound of these early recordings sounds only slightly dated today, as the group's snarling, punk/isolationist edge shines through tension-filled songs that hold up surprisingly well. Graeme's informative, personal liner notes on each track are also welcome. [la]

See also *Peter Jefferies, 3Ds.*

CAKE LIKE

Delicious (Japan. Avant) 1994
Mr. Fireman EP7 (Genius) 1995

This New York trio of singer/bassist Kerri Kenney (an actress on MTV's *The State*), guitarist/singer Nina Hellman and drummer Jody Seifert revels in the sort of indie-rock simplicity that made the Breeders' **Pod** such a shocking debut. Between Eli Janney's sparkling, vocals-up-front production and the driving, fractured, short-song structures and lyrical absurdities ("your dad works for my dad/my dad") of the music, **Delicious** is immediately accessible to those ready for aggressive, independent-minded pop by women who know how to write a song without painting anything on their bellies. Cake Like's pared-down intellectualism makes it clear that when you hear something like the "la-la-la-la-la-la-la-la" on "Fruitcake" break down into the percussive loose-hewn squall of "Suck," there's something far greater going on than simple cutesy chick-rock. **Mr. Fireman** ("Bring your goddamned truck and some water!") is a three-song single produced by Ric Ocasek. [jf]

JOHN CALE

Vintage Violence (Columbia) 1970
Church of Anthrax (Columbia) 1971
The Academy in Peril (Reprise) 1972 (Warner Archives) 1994
Paris 1919 (Reprise) 1973 (Warner Archives) 1994
Fear (Island) 1974
Slow Dazzle (Island) 1975
Helen of Troy (UK Island) 1975
Guts (Island) 1977
Animal Justice EP (UK Illegal) 1977
Sabotage/Live (Spy) 1979
Honi Soit . . . (A&M) 1981
Music for a New Society (ZE/Passport) 1982 (Rhino) 1994

Caribbean Sunset (ZE/Island) 1984
John Cale Comes Alive (ZE/Island) 1984
Artificial Intelligence (Beggars Banquet/PVC) 1985
Words for the Dying (Opal/Warner Bros.) 1989
Even Cowgirls Get the Blues (ROIR) 1991
Fragments of a Rainy Season (Hannibal) 1992
Paris S'Eveille (Bel. Les Disques du Crépuscule) 1994
Seducing Down the Door: A Collection 1970–1990 (Rhino) 1994
Antártida (Bel. Les Disques du Crépuscule) 1995
N'Oublie Pas Que Tu Vas Mourir (Bel. Les Disques du Crépuscule) 1995
The Island Years (Island) 1996

LOU REED/JOHN CALE

Songs for Drella (Sire/Warner Bros.) 1990

ENO/CALE

Wrong Way Up (Opal/Warner Bros.) 1990

JOHN CALE/BOB NEUWIRTH

Last Day on Earth (MCA) 1994

For all his creative perseverance in the 1990s, John Cale found time to go back over old ground, adding a much-deserved and highly useful career compilation, two live solo albums and a document of the highly vaunted but short-lived Velvet Underground reunion to his exceptionally diverse catalogue. The two decades covered for better and worse by **Seducing Down the Door** follow the Welsh-born singer, composer and multi-instrumentalist (primarily viola, guitar and keyboards) through his literate forays into numerous realms of classically influenced new music, song pop, movie music and fringe-oriented rock, all of it finely reflective of the people with whom he chooses to work and the changing environment—though not necessarily the most obvious or dominant one—in which he finds himself. As someone who began with far more musical training than his peers, Cale has spent a lifetime getting over those theoretical limitations, inserting himself into alien worlds and reaching his own understanding of their stylistic possibilities. If that makes him a dilettante, Cale's never gone for easy marks: his original intelligence has always brought something unique and beneficial to his fields of vision.

With lovely historical symmetry, **Seducing Down the Door** (the title is a lyric from "A Child's Christmas in Wales") is an extremely judicious two-CD sampler of every record (including two live albums and the punk-era **Animal Justice** EP) Cale released between his departure from the Velvet Underground in 1968 and his 1990 collaborations with Lou Reed and Brian Eno. Primped up with three outtakes (the previously unknown 1971 pop shmaltz of "Dixieland and Dixie" proves someone's sense of humor), the excellently annotated collection reduces the saga of Cale's musical development to concise but detailed manageability. It's possible that few have followed him all the way from the panoramic production pop of "Big White Cloud" (from **Vintage Violence**) to the solo piano of "Temper" (from **The Academy in Peril**) to the coldhearted rock of "Fear Is a Man's Best Friend" (from the essential **Fear,** the **Guts** compilation and **The Island Years**) to the brutal meltdown demolition of "Heartbreak Hotel" (**Slow Dazzle**) to the grim art-balladry of "Hedda Gabbler" (**Animal Justice**) to the twisted deconstruction of "Walkin' the Dog" (**Sabotage/Live**)—and then through the '80s as well—but fitting the pieces together like this makes the winding course of Cale's progress most compelling.

Adding to the retrospective atmosphere, **Even Cowgirls Get the Blues** and **Fragments of a Rainy Season** are both live John Cale albums, although they could scarcely be more different. The former was recorded with members of the Patti Smith Group at CBGB in 1978 and '79 (the years of Cale's noisy punk involvement) and includes some hair-raising feedback excusions. **Fragments of a Rainy Season** finds him alone onstage with an acoustic piano or guitar, providing a handsome auto-retrospective that stretches from "Paris 1919" to "Cordoba" (from **Wrong Way Up**) and fills in some of the gaps ("Ship of Fools," "Darling I Need You," "Buffalo Ballet") left by the compilation. The consistently styled performances of twenty songs originally recorded in nearly as many divergent styles proves that Cale is not pop's most resourceful songwriter, but he brings characteristically ornery invention to what, in other hands, could well be a dry, bland ordeal. The freakout endings of "Guts" and "Fear Is a Man's Best Friend," the dramatic vocalizing of "Leaving It Up to You" and the sharpened piano notes of "Do Not Go Gentle Into That Good Night" (one of the Dylan Thomas poems Cale put music to on **Words for the Dying**) all evince a sensitive artist who can play rough when he wants.

Paris S'Eveille, Antártida and **N'Oublie Pas Que Tu Vas Mourir** are scores Cale composed for French films; he also contributed to the soundtrack of 1996's *I Shot Andy Warhol.*

Cale's equal-partner collaborations have been hit-and-miss; what he brings to the table doesn't vary much, but his interactions with Lou Reed and Brian Eno (if not Terry Riley, with whom he made **Church of Anthrax**) veer into unpredictable zones. That's certainly true of **Last Day on Earth,** an unfortunate concept album (forgive me, "song cycle/performance piece" and "blueprint for theatre") written and recorded with Bob Neuwirth, the New York folk-scene footnote who hung around Dylan in the early '60s and co-wrote "Mercedes Benz" for Janis Joplin. This sprawling and discouraging slab of folk, rock, brass, strings, soundtrack mush and recitation makes the distance between the gullible hick sincerity in Neuwirth's voice and the dramatic self-importance of Cale's an unbreachable gulf. What's more, **Last Day on Earth** has a stagey sound that diminishes the songs and a stylistic randomness that distracts from the end-time theme. Although not overly unpleasant in little bits, the hour-plus of quixotic pretensions virtually dares you to make it all the way through. [i]

See also *Brian Eno, Lou Reed, Velvet Underground; TPRG.*

ALI CAMPBELL

See *UB40.*

CANDLEBOX

Candlebox (Maverick/Sire) 1993
Lucy (Maverick) 1995

Much as Bon Jovi put a net on hair metal, Candlebox's primary function was to put a final stamp of megaselling irrelevance on the rotten corpse of Big Northwest Noise. Swept along in the Pearl Jam backdraft (another negative factor to improve PJ's standing in the creative food chain), the Seattle quartet arrived—on Madonna's label, no less—in mid-'93 with a debut that exhausted the region's clichés in one thundering, colorless roar. Free of irony, independence or imagination—which more or less makes Candlebox this decade's Grand Funk Railroad—the good-natured group hybridizes grunge and raunch (graunch?) with such generic witlessness that it would be overstating things to call them derivative. Unimproved by occasional lyrical dips into the social-concern pool (the anti-drug putdown of "You," the homeless pathos of "He Calls Home"), Peter Klett's hackneyed guitar flash, the lumbering rhythm section of Bardi Martin (bass) and Scott Mercado (drums) and Kevin (no relation) Martin's macho, overheated vocals add up to a big, noisy nothing.

Other than stylistic inklings of U2, Bad Company and Robin Trower (go figure) on **Lucy,** the pressures of a triple-platinum debut had no audible effect on Candlebox. Beyond its self-possession, the band's second album exhibits added variety and texture in the sound of its robust rock, but nothing short of a power outage could improve the imbecilic songs or third-rate guitar heroics of this dismal throwback. [i]

CANDY SKINS

Space I'm In (DGC) 1991
Fun? (DGC) 1993

Named for a Fire Engines song, Oxford, England's Candy Skins provide consistently pleasant if far from earthshaking pop'n'roll on **Space I'm In.** The eleven originals—and a needless cover of Stephen Stills' "For What It's Worth"—are all crammed with jangly guitars, hummable melodies and Nick Cope's slightly edgy lead vocals. The quartet aims to evoke a blissful, happy vibe on such poppy tunes as "Get Together" and "Freedom Bus," but **Space I'm In** lacks warmth and conviction.

With Pat Collier back as producer and the group upped to a fivesome thanks to the addition of ex-Colourfield bassist Karl Shale, things improve on **Fun?** The disc opens with a blast of fiery, Buzzcockian tuneage (the nostalgic "Wembley") and includes nods to the Beatles ("Tired of Being Happy," which sort of nicks the "Paperback Writer" riff) and Stone Roses (the nearly funky, pulsating "Fun"). Overall, the band sounds a lot more comfortable in the studio: the guitars have more bite and the songs grab and hold, especially the pretty "Everybody Loves You," the mournful ballad "All Over Now" and the powerful "Dig It Deep." [jmb]

CANNANES

Bored, Angry & Jealous EP (Aus. Distant Violins) 1986
The African Man's Tomato (Aus. no label) 1988
A Love Affair With Nature (Aus. no label) 1989 (Feel Good All Over) 1990 (Ajax) 1995
Broken Bottles EP (UK Bi-Joopiter) 1992
Stumpvision EP (Ajax) 1992
Caveat Emptor (Feel Good All Over) 1993
Witchetty Pole (Feel Good All Over) 1993
Short Poppy Syndrome (Ajax) 1994
Prototype EP (Ger. Little Teddy) 1994
Simple Question EP (Ajax) 1996
The Cannanes (Ajax) 1996
Arty Barbeque (Ajax) 1996

NICE

Nice (Feel Good All Over) 1992
Apple Pie (Feel Good All Over) 1993

ASHTRAY BOY

The Honeymoon Suite (Feel Good All Over) 1993
Macho Champions (Ajax) 1994
Candypants Beach (Ajax) 1995
The Everyman's 4th Dimension (Ajax) 1996

Folks who revel in the notion that love-rock means never having to tune your guitar will no doubt grow weak in the knees upon first exposure to the Cannanes. The fluid Australian combo is willfully amateurish and occasionally a bit too cute for its own good, but the utterly unpretentious purity of the band's output is hard to deny. Their closest American corollary would probably be Beat Happening, but the Cannanes are slightly folkier, less prone to outbursts of rock primitivism. The band's debut EP is charmingly unsteady on virtually every level, from the cracks in Annabel Bleach's sweet warble to the audible string squeak that accompanies each acoustic guitar chord change. The informality only adds to the charm of songs like "You're So Groovy" and the quietly caustic "I Don't Want to Talk About Your Problems."

By the time **The African Man's Tomato** was recorded, the Cannanes had already experienced the first of what would be many lineup changes—and consequent shifts in direction—with the vocal onus largely placed on Randall Lee. Slightly more fleshed-out (some of the songs recall early Go-Betweens) and darker in tone, the album still focuses on life's simpler pleasures and pains in whimsical inventions like "Corn Chips," "We Drink Bitter" and the tender "Love Takes Only a Minute." **The African Man's Tomato** and **Bored, Angry & Jealous** were later combined on **Witchetty Pole,** an anthology that also includes the utterly daft "Felicia," a theme song of sorts that essentially concedes the Cannanes have no reason to exist. The early incarnation's finest moment.

Perhaps as a result of Lee's departure, **A Love Affair With Nature** brings a return to the more shambolic charm of the band's first recordings. The vocals are shared by bassist Frances Gibson and guitarist Stephen O'Neil, both of whom are given over to fits of pique and melancholy—or, in the case of O'Neil's "Take Me to the Hotel Johanna (and Let's Trash the Joint)," both. For better *and* worse, the album is imbued with an omnipresent sense of nostalgia. The trio is certainly adept at conveying the frame of mind, but the reference points are specific enough that non-Antipodeans will probably be left scratching their heads. The 1995 reissue adds a dozen previously unreleased tracks, some performed by the Lee-fronted lineup, others (including the long, loopy "Marco Polo Suite") featuring Susan Grigg's superb violin playing.

Both **Stumpvision,** which contains the (comparatively) lush "Singing to Satellites," and **Caveat Emptor** follow the same pattern: Gibson's sweet, regretful wisps of song contrast with the edgier contributions from O'Neil and drummer David Nichols—with the bonus of more trumpet playing from O'Neil. On **Short Poppy Syndrome** (like all the band's records, annotated with self-deprecating caprice), the core trio is joined by bassist Gavin Butler. More intricate arrangements and electric instruments don't detract from the bedsit intimacy of songs like "Perfect Light" and "Chosen One." As usual, there are moments when the studied unsophistication gets overweening: Butler's vocal on "Cocaine" is all but unlistenable, and twinky toy instrumentation doesn't exactly advance "Red Smoke Across the Square."

In comparison, the self-titled disc is positively professional. From the appropriately woozy strains of "Drug-Induced Delirum" (a sort of pharmacological children's round) to the jittery, Feelies-styled rocker "Asleep," there's surprisingly little shamble. Fortunately, the band's newfound interest in conventional quality control can't outweigh the charm that emanates from eminently joyful songs like "Swing, You Little Red Devil." The Cannanes' steadfast refusal to acquiesce to commercial mandates (they've toured but once and have pledged to never do so again) may make them an anachronism, but at least they'll never be accused of being dilettantes.

After leaving the Cannanes, Randall Lee formed Nice, a professional-sounding trio rounded out by bassist Susannah Stuart-Lindsay and drummer Jo Packer. The gist of the band's debut is very much the same as the Go-Betweens or Verlaines: baroque, romantic pop songs punctuated by odd lyric flights. ("Dear John" finds Lee musing about stealing away to a distant mansion to make babies with a fantasy man.) Stuart-Lindsay also writes and sings; her dark-hued songs steer the band into choppier waters that recall the Velvet Underground's third album. **Apple Pie** sees a more even division of the spotlight, with Stuart-Lindsay moving to guitar (new bassist Mark King gets into the act, singing his own "Fucked Around"). While there are certainly standout tracks—Lee's "On My Back in the Madhouse," for one—the album has neither the piquancy nor the distinctiveness of Nice's debut.

After Nice, Lee began splitting his time between Sydney and Chicago and, to entangle the family tree even further, formed and maintained a separate-but-equal incarnation of his new band, Ashtray Boy, in each city. **The Honeymoon Suite,** which features the American lineup, is colored by David Trumfio's stately double-bass playing as well as guest backing vocals by Liz Phair, who helps out on the wry "Shirley MacLaine" and "Infidel." The album is remarkably diverse, ranging from the Fairport Convention–styled allegory "How Charles Destroyed the Inland Sea" to the funk-tinged gore-cartoon "Hit." Mighty odd stuff. The somewhat schizy **Macho Champions** is split between the two combos, with the Aussie version (rounded out by Thomas Tallis and Neil Johnston) sticking more closely to typical local jangle-folk—with the exception of the enjoyable surreal lounge-pop "Amy Grant Super Number."

Homesickness apparently got the better of Lee, and he recorded the bulk of the meaty **Candypants Beach** down under. As times goes on, he's more prone to explore his voice's powerful lower register—witness the Beat Happening–like "Dead Body in the Surf" and the Gallic-tinged "She's Taken Up Snoring" (which bursts with ancillary noisemakers like accordion and xylophone). Lee has always been a like a fascinating character actor; the continued evolution of Ashtray Boy is pushing him closer and closer to leading man status. [dss]

CAPTAIN AMERICA

See *Eugenius.*

CAPTAIN HOWDY

See *Kramer.*

CAPTAINS OF INDUSTRY

See *Wreckless Eric.*

CARDIGANS

Emmerdale (Swed. Trampolene) 1994
Life (Swed. Stockholm) 1995 (UK Stockholm/Polydor) 1995 (Minty Fresh) 1996
The First Band on the Moon (Mercury) 1996

Five winsome young Swedish beatniks sharing a house in Malmö and a penchant for wistful melodies with light, sophisticated lounge arrangements: the Cardigans. The cherubic Nina Persson's cool vocals (in English) are matched by the deft instrumental touch of her male colleagues; what they offer is a distance from rock'n'roll, something they cheerfully profess to hate. Nonetheless, the group shares with many of their fellow Scandinavians a fondness for death metal, perhaps understandable in the light of the fact that Malmö is the religious center of Sweden. For the Cardigans, this enthusiasm finds expression through delicate close-harmony versions of Ozzy Osbourne songs, revealing an elegance often overlooked in the work of the Midlands gloom guvner.

Emmerdale (the title is from a dull English rural soap opera) shows the Cardigans already fully formed stylistically, but still somewhat introverted. A high point is "Sabbath Bloody Sabbath," which is somehow lured into a Rive Gauche nightclub, emerging with a jade cigarette holder and lipstick on its collar. For **Life,** the Cardigans leave the more languid stuff behind, resulting in an assured and happy cocktail of melodic invention and '60s motifs. The obligatory vibraphone is joined by woodwinds, brass, strings and finger snaps; the immaculately cheesy jazz guitars are occasionally turned up past the "mellow" marker; the rhythm section even shows it can pump out a soul groove. Persson sings as softly and precisely as Peggy Lee; at one point she gets carried away and essays a "la la la doobie doobie doo." Look out. **Life** appears in three different versions: the UK and US releases both delete tracks from the Swedish original in order to reprise some of the catchier tunes (like "Sabbath Bloody Sabbath") from **Emmerdale.** [pnm]

CARDINAL

Cardinal (Flydaddy) 1994

MOLES

Untune the Sky EP (Aus. Seaside) 1990
Tendrils and Paracetamol EP (Aus. Seaside) 1991
Untune the Sky (Aus. Seaside) 1992
The Moles: Double Single EP7 (Ringers Lactate) 1992 (Aus. Seaside) 1992
Instinct (Flydaddy) 1994

ERIC MATTHEWS

It's Heavy in Here (Sub Pop) 1995

RICHARD DAVIES

There's Never Been a Crowd Like This (Flydaddy) 1996

While everybody else was singing "I Got Dem Ol' Kozmik Twentysomething Angst Blues Again," Cardinal set about making pristine, Anglocentric chamber pop about the heartbreak of heartbreak. Australian

Richard Davies wrote and sings most of the tunes on Cardinal's self-titled album, while Oregonian Eric Matthews concentrates on arrangements, employing pastoral horns, piano, strings, marimba, harpsichord and, most important, a keen sense of space. With subdued yet ornate drumming, the quiet music unerringly recalls Love, the Left Banke and late-era Zombies. Matthews' meticulously elegant arrangements perfectly mirror Davies' eloquent dissections of romantic melancholy. Although some tracks scud by almost unnoticed, ravishing numbers like "You've Lost Me There" and "Silver Machines" make **Cardinal** a keeper.

On their own, Davies' and Matthews' individual projects would seem to show that Cardinal, although reportedly riven by internal strife, is (was?) more than the sum of its parts. Davies arrived an international pop underground legend via Sydney's Moles, whose first American release was a pair of 7-inch singles that, in four songs recorded in New York, display some of the Australian quartet's very divergent instincts. In "What's the New Mary Jane," Davies borrows the title from a legendary Beatles outtake and piles on brass and cacophonous guitar distortion that suddenly parts to reveal a lovely bit of vintage psychedeli-pop; "Saint Jack" sounds like a long-lost '60s beat-group hit; except for blasts of guitar distortion and David Newgarden's guest trumpet intrusions, the cover of Don Nix's "Going Down" follows the song's southern-rock blueprints with lo-fi care.

The Moles' major US issue is the nine-song, twenty-four-minute **Instinct,** a dryly rendered record of sparse, disjointed music, several steps abstracted from its pop sources, full of odd spaces, anxious changes and lyrics like "Drink until you're blind/And you'll feel like Ray Charles." Somewhere between early Van Dyke Parks and Guided by Voices at their strangest (especially on the title track), tunes like "Eros Lunch (1963)" and "Did You See the Red Queen?" are not without their stately charms, although the musicianly approach doesn't always jibe with a sensibility that's weird going on creepy.

Following the Cardinal album, Matthews made an interesting but ultimately failed self-produced solo record. Not exactly little symphonies for the kids, the tunes are more like little string quartest for slackers. Cloaked in arrangements even more baroque than those on **Cardinal, It's Heavy in Here** wears the vestments of pop—favoring melodic flourishes over sheer beat-noise—but somehow manages to avoid pop's most distinguishing characteristic: catchiness. Matthews attempts intriguing experiments with song structure but, combined with his opaque lyrics, the songs offer no way into whatever it is that's on his mind (arty titles such as "Forging Plastic Pain" and "Distant Mother Reality" are a tip-off). However pleasurable the music is from moment to moment—and that's often the case—it rarely adds up to anything.

There's Never Been a Crowd Like This, Davies' first post-Cardinal missive, is more enticing and substantial than that. Taking it upon himself to create the first album to bear close comparison to the ineffable '70s wry rustic folk-pop of England's Stackridge, Davies avoids the baroque constructs of **Cardinal** in favor of uncomplicated light pop to carry his finespun melodies and lyrical fantasies. "My father was Stewart Granger . . ." begins the album-opening "Transcontinental," and that's not the half of it. "Sipping American beer/Thinking how it would be/To live in the green trees/Like Chip Rafferty." "Why Not Bomb the Movies?" Smartly self-produced with a bass-drums-guitar-piano quartet, an occasional trumpeter and a pair of backing singers (Davies is credited only with vocals and harmonica), this lost-in-time album is inscrutably eccentric and equally engaging. [ma/i]

BELINDA CARLISLE

See *Go-Go's.*

CARNEY-HILD-KRAMER

See *Kramer.*

CARNIVAL STRIPPERS

Reveal (Fox) 1994

LOEY NELSON

Venus Kissed the Moon (Warner Bros.) 1990

The diverse and shadowy sonic intrigue organized by producers David Kershenbaum and Paul McKenna can't disguise Loey Nelson's clunky songwriting and starchy, uncertain singing on **Venus Kissed the Moon,** the Milwaukeean's not-quite-promising 1990 debut. Faced with a finely set table, she delivers an unimpressive menu of warmed-over made-it-myself disappointments, served with too much audible concern for how they're going over with the guests. Stylishly presented as small-scale jazz-pop, the title tune is a minor treat; nothing else comes close, and the fussed-over artiness slathered on "To Sir With Love" all but hides the song completely.

Four years later, Nelson resurfaced as the centerpiece of Carnival Strippers, a Milwaukee quartet with guitarist Mike Hoffman (ex-E*I*E*I*O), bassist Keith Brammer (ex–Die Kreuezen/Wreck) and drummer Kirk McFarlin (ex-Ecoteur). With such in-house experience, Steve Jordan's supposed production expertise and a mix involving the usually tasteful Niko Bolas, the awfulness of **Reveal** is surprising. A distracting tin-can snare clank, endless, shapeless songs that oscillate between acoustic folkiness and loud rock spuzz in several familiar flavors, singing that only intermittently matches the instruments' chromatic exertions, kitchen-sink effects (like group whistling, sleigh bells and dulcimer) where they are truly unneeded—need to hear any more? [i]

See also *Waco Brothers.*

CAROLINER

Rear End Hernia Puppet Show (Subterranean) 1986
I'm Armed With Quarts of Blood (Nuf Sed) 1989
Rise of the Common Woodpile (Nuf Sed) 1990
The Cooking Stove Beast (Nuf Sed) 1991
Strike Them Hard, Drag Them to Church (Nuf Sed) 1992
The Sabre Waving Saracen Wall (Nuf Sed) 1993
Banknotes, Dreams & Signatures (Nuf Sed) 1994
Rings on the Awkward Shadow (Nuf Sed) 1995
Sell Heal Holler (Nuf Sed) 1995

Claiming the solitary influence of "Caroliner—the Famous Singing Bull of the 1800's," San Francisco's Caroliner is one of America's most original and difficult musical entities. Vaguely indicated by the tag "industrial bluegrass," the vehemently indescribable band consists of futuristic Luddites in the moral center of an avant-garde for erratic minds, covering turf wider than all alternative rock combined. The wealth of material ranges from shrill musique concrète to believable theater tunes, all pointing back to cowboy songs heard on dusty Victrolas.

Behind an ever-shifting facade of pseudonyms stands the dictatorial "singer from Caroliner"; the band's only predictable element is that each hand-packaged record will be credited to "Caroliner Rainbow something of the something something," and will include a double-sided photocopied lyric sheet meant to be read along with the music.

Rear End Hernia Puppet Show introduces the basic Caroliner concept. Simple, repetitive rhyme-songs are formed around the bass, with embellishing bells, whistles and unpredictable vocals upsetting the proceedings in various ways. Images of madness, bad health, broken wagons, gamblers and raging earth spirits weave together the genesis of the heightened-awareness Caroliner world. Primary influences—the Residents, Throbbing Gristle and Tom Waits—are evident, but even those touchstones become faint points of departure for the bewildering mass of references that follow.

The band's mindset is better elucidated on **I'm Armed With Quarts of Blood;** the album has a Grand Guignol pop-up and bits of hair, dirt and cockroaches glued to the cover. It begins with four hysterical locked grooves, which the liner notes recommend be listened to for a solid week each before pressing forth. Catchy ditties like "Corn Red Moon" and "Barrel Horses & Window Crackers" describe extreme remedies for problems of mind and farm as errant fiddles squeal and lopsided voices caterwaul. A violent and twisted euphoria of the imagination.

Rise of the Common Woodpile is Caroliner at its most accessible, radiating a ghostly prettiness in the midst of haunted squeaking doors and other dangers. The delicate synthesis of disparate and competing incongruities is a real achievement. "Burdensome Blood" and "Child Heart of Dirt Pump" are sweet but morbid bluegrass banjo songs rearranged as surrealist film scores, interrupted by immense slamming noises and assorted racketry. The band is at a creative high, and the next album benefits from the gold rush as well.

Some of the pieces on the clamorous **Cooking Stove Beast** were probably recorded at the same time as the previous two albums; indeterminacy, inconsistency and obscurity are among Caroliner's habitual modes. Fuller of bellowing distortion and monolithic dirges, the record contains "Hanna's Medicinal Tick Collection" among an unforgettable array of other disturbances.

Caroliner moves into a more mannered, less rocking phase with **Strike Them Hard, Drag Them to Church.** The lengthy title track is a suite of simple choral music, promoting the major thematic element of eerie organ alongside deep gurgling vocals, squeaky disembodied squeals and assorted groaning of a whole community of child-like phantoms. Eastern influences appear, the off-pitch *erhu* warble and buzzing sitar edging Asian-tinged aspects into Caroliner's testaments of hard times in the Old West.

An undertaker's organ and an idiot's banjo team up with sitars, trumpets and shattering glass to forward the oral tradition of an insane agrarian society on **The Sabre Waving Saracen Wall.** Ragtime piano, mouth harps and a bossa nova beat enliven the confident ruckus. Exemplifying the Caroliner trick of letting a sound define a song's content, a warbled trumpet toot inspires "Misery Pipe in the Fray," a number about an inept military bugler who stumbles into victory from the brink of death. Steady beats, discernible melodies and intelligible vocals come and go amid the chaos.

The double-album **Rings on the Awkward Shadow** was purportedly mastered on antique wire-spool equipment, rendering a trebly monophonic din that suits Caroliner perfectly. The record's extra length matches a return to simpler arrangements, jaggedly introducing the Oriental whistle burlesque of "Land Mace" and the somber meditations of "Sprillowed Sprawling Prediction on Our Future." Abrupt electronic anachronisms summon the image of an alien presence on the prairie.

Without waiting for the world to recover from that double-whammy, Caroliner shipped **Sell Heal Holler,** sort of a history of twentieth-century music as performed by students from an insect elementary school. Minimalism, soul, noise, rock drums and digital blips form a subtle set of enjoyable nocturnes. "Air-Blasted Earth" seems to push along to the pulse of a distorted barking dog toy. With so much deliberate and unintentional button-pushing to digest over its first nine albums, Caroliner seems near its goal of covering over the outside world with its own enlightened universe. [ic]

See also *Zip Code Rapists*.

CARS

See *Ric Ocasek*.

LORI CARSON

See *Golden Palominos*.

CARTER THE UNSTOPPABLE SEX MACHINE

101 Damnations (UK Big Cat) 1990 (Big Cat/Chrysalis) 1991
30 Something (Chrysalis) 1991
Bloodsport for All EP (Rough Trade) 1992
1992 The Love Album (Chrysalis) 1992
Post Historic Monsters (UK Chrysalis) 1993 (IRS) 1994
Starry Eyed and Bollock Naked (UK Chrysalis) 1994
Worry Bomb (UK Chrysalis) 1995
Straw Donkey . . . The Singles (UK Chrysalis) 1995

Carter the Unstoppable Smartalecks is more like it. Two of the brightest bulbs ever to hook themselves to a drum machine and let rip, South London's Fruitbat (Leslie Carter, guitar) and Jim Bob (Morrison, vocals)—veterans of a dozen years together in various obscure bands—seem like the kind of overstimulated chums who would have given teachers fits in school. Their energetic albums employ the clattering drive and sampling inserts of industrial music, the hyperverbosity of rap, the bratty topical posturing of punk's intellectual wing and the melodies of chart pop. Packed to the gills with product and people names, inverted puns, non-didactic political outrage and persistent rock gripping in its breathless enthusiasm, the runaway sequencer-driven doses of scattershot literate whimsy (shades of Dylan on acid) can be far too chaotic and complicated. But for those raised on *Mad* magazine and methedrine, Carter is a dream come true, a contact high of instant culture overload. If only the ultra-British records came with footnotes.

"Sheriff Fatman," a wild hallucinatory biography of a person or persons unknown ("At six foot six and a hundred tons/The undisputed king of the slums/With more aliases than Klaus Barbie/The master butcher of Leigh-on-Sea"), is the key spot on **101 Damnations,** a fully realized debut that also contains such resonant ironies as "The Taking of Peckham 123," "A Perfect Day to Drop the Bomb" (which incorporates the hook from Grandmaster Flash's "The Message") and "Midnight on the Murder Mile," which crosses Wilson Pickett and the KLF, quoting the Unit 4+2 and paraphrasing Chuck Berry in what appears to be a narrative about a street beating ("I was marinaded, regurgitated and served up as cold meat . . . my kingdom for a phone box"). Dedicated to "everyone we've ever harangued into a corner," **101 Damnations** is mind-blowing in the most stimulating sense.

Adding the soccer chant "You Fat Bastard!" to the global vernacular, **30 Something** opens with the frantic dance instrumental "Surfin' USM" (thanks to David Bowie) and then moves into "My Second to Last Will and Testament" ("only a rough draft, a handwritten estimate"). The record addresses such eclectic issues as retail ("Shoppers' Paradise," with a sampled bit of Clash), drinking ("A Prince in a Pauper's Grave"), the army ("Bloodsport for All"), drinking ("Anytime Anyplace Anywhere," title borrowed from the Monkees), the dead-end pathology of hunger ("Billy's Smart Circus") and drinking ("The Final Comedown"). Between a mild effort to broaden the band's stylistic vocabulary—lots of synth horns, a grandiose waltz and a rhythm borrowed from the Fall are among the small innovations—and the disappointing narrowing of its lyrical frame, the not-at-all-bad **30 Something** is the most easily overlooked of Carter's LPs. **Bloodsport for All** adds five strong studio tracks—including two loopy covers (Soft Cell's "Bedsitter," given an Eddie-Cochran-by-way-of-Sigue-Sigue-Sputnik treatment, and the Monkees' "Alternate Title"), the nifty "Re-Educating Rita" and an instrumental ("Randy Sarf Git," another Monkees reference)—to the titular album cut.

With personally reflective lyrics that are more depressed than amused, Carter unevenly advances its stylistic reach on **1992 The Love Album.** Jim Bob and Fruitbat perpetrate a jaunty boulevardier fraud ("England"), camp away at piano pop ("Is Wrestling Fixed?," a contemplation on happiness) and rustle up both rustic restraint and jazzy sprawl for the urban defunding of "While You Were Out." The grandiose pop of "Skywest and Crooked" and a dryly serious cover of "The Impossible Dream" are wretched, but "Do Re Me, So Far So Good" kicks with the first album's vigor, mentioning Elvis while quoting Public Enemy and borrowing its singalong melody from Slade. The easy highlight, which rips a page from the Paul Simon title book, is "The Only Living Boy in New Cross," which shakes a brightly colored and catchy tailfeather while casting a cynical eye at the current state of London pop society ("The gypsies, the travelers and the thieves/The good, bad, the average and unique/The grebos, the crusties and the goths . . .").

Post Historic Monsters sends the Carters back to basics, railing in highly amusing dudgeon at fascists, political strife, war, ethnic cleansing, moral collapse, royal celebrations, racists, unnamed people you would have to be English to recognize, pop stars, pop songs and a whole lot more. Other than a few usefully contrasting digressions—acoustic guitar folk ("Suicide Isn't Painless"), mainstream shmaltz ("Under the Thumb and Over the Moon"), cocktail jazz ("Being Here")—the Unstoppables keep their music to a safe straight and narrow, slashing at guitars and setting sequencers chattering madly in thick barrages of electronic rock power. When not asking the imponderable in "The Music That Nobody Likes" ("If love is the answer/What was the question/And can it cure my indigestion?"), the duo confronts the truth. In "Commercial Fucking Suicide Part 1," after calling Michael Jackson a liar and noting that Bono is not "the new messiah," Jim Bob blurts out, "If you buy this record today/It's not true what the advertisements say/Your life won't be greatly improved/But Christ you've got nothing to lose/And we've got so much to gain." Honesty—what a sick concept. (Perhaps significantly, the song was added to the US edition and omitted from the UK.)

Straw Donkey . . . The Singles is a British singles compilation; **Starry Eyed and Bollock Naked** recapitulates their flipsides. In between all that looking backward, Carter—expanded to a trio with the addition of drummer Wez—walloped out the all-new **Worry Bomb** (initial CD copies of which came with a full-length bonus live album, the crashingly great and articulate **Doma Sportova . . . Live in Zagreb, 20/5/94**). Having duly elected themselves the sardonic social commentators of the 1990s, Fruitbat and Jim Bob have at a staggering variety of topics, usually a couple per feverish non-linear song. "Airplane Food/Airplane Fast Food," for instance, chronicles two friends who go different emblematic ways before settling into an airborne tray of "Buttered scones that can't be trusted/Warm blancmange and lumpy custard." After swearing off drink in the lulling piano introduction to "Cheap-'n'Cheesy," the song bursts into a moan about "I've got no family for my family car"; a few tracks later, "Let's Get Tattoos" has the protagonist getting wrecked and doing dumb stuff, while "Senile Delinquent" raises the possibility of being awarded an Order of the British Empire for "services to serious drinking." Similarly, contrast the anti-suicide message in "Gas (Man)" with the dispirited whining of "My Defeatist Attitude," which throws in the towel with a clever flick of the wrist ("I'd fight the system/But what's the use/It's fire resistant/And waterproof"). Multiplying the engrossing confusion of this ace album, the music is broader, more dynamic and imaginative than in the past, suggesting that for all their misery, the boys are getting stronger in their resolve to enjoy it. For their deliciously corrosive and grimly amused outlook, Carter the Unstoppable Senile Delinquent earn the right to print the Martin Amis quote that explains the album's title. [i]

PETER CASE

Peter Case (Geffen) 1986
The Man With the Blue Postmodern Fragmented Neo-Traditionalist Guitar (Geffen) 1989
Six-Pack of Love (Geffen) 1992
Sings Like Hell (Vanguard) 1994
Torn Again (Vanguard) 1995

Setting aside the new wavey rock approach of his former bands (the Nerves and the Plimsouls), Buffalo-born singer/songwriter Peter Case stepped into the role of literate troubadour in the mid-'80s. He sorted himself out nicely over the course of his first two solo albums, sharpening his material and investigating lean, diverse arrangements with help from such folks as T-Bone Burnett, Mitchell Froom, David Lindley, Jim Keltner and David Hidalgo. Indicative of his progress, **The Man With the Blue Postmodern Fragmented Neo-Traditionalist Guitar** is the more distinctive, a collection of startlingly precise character studies, stark emotional dramas and carefully observed sense-of-place vignettes.

Case got back to rocking on **Six-Pack of Love,** a gritty pop record on which he plays a lot of piano, displays a John Lennon–ish voice and circles around the threat of romance as warily as an alley cat coming across a dead body. Co-producing with Froom and co-writing with such offbeat elders as John Prine, Billy Swan and Tonio K, Case extricates himself and his beat-up feelings from the frustration of "Vanishing Act" and the threat of "Never Comin' Home" to find the dubious optimism of "Why Don't We Give It a Go?" ("Let's light it up and see if it blows") and the defiant willfulness of "It Don't Matter What People Say." Nicely balanced between articulate expression and evocative emotionalism, the energetic album paints Case into a corner (he doesn't seem to have given much thought to what would happen if it does blow), letting him writhe happily while pondering the romantic apocalypse.

Dropping out of the major-label world, Case picked up his acoustic guitar and harmonica and slung out **Sings Like Hell,** a stark and stirring album of blues oldies he wears like a cracked pair of old shoes. Getting only minor assists from producer Marvin Etzioni on mandolin and several other musicians (but playing his own barrelhouse piano on "Down in the Alley" and "Well Run Dry"), Case sheds his modern rock'n'roll baggage, drops his defenses and lets it howl, finding himself in the strength of strings. Digging deep and passionate one-take burrows into the fertile mud of folksongs like "Rovin' Gambler," "Matchbox Blues," "Rose Conolly" and "Lakes of Ponchartrain," Case repeats the feat of Dylan's **World Gone Wrong** and **Good As I Been to You,** using old patterns to shape an intensely moving original work. A gem.

Returning to his own composiitons with a band and full studio production on the rich and rewarding **Torn Again,** Case emerges as an itinerant folkie cousin of John Hiatt and Nick Lowe, strumming an old hollow-body and singing working-class stories that drift around the fringes of America. Case's characters hang out in bars, drink in cars, steal airplanes, run afoul of the law and catch love when they can. "Workin' for the Enemy," "Turnin' Blue" and "Wilderness" sketch out unhappy tales with telling detail; the singer's own lyrical role, when he has one, is strictly as victim. "Anything that you love will bring you to your knees," he swears; "I thought I had you but you had me." More painful than love's wounds, however, "Baltimore" finds him beaten in the street with a shovel. Although he promises "A Little Wind (Could Blow Me Away)" in a number co-written with Tom Russell, Case sounds a lot sturdier and steader than that. [i]

CAST

See *La's.*

CATHEDRAL

Echoes of Dirges Into the Naves EP (Mex. MM/PPR) 1990
Forest of Equilibrium (Earache/Relativity) 1992
Soul Sacrifice EP (Earache/Columbia) 1992
The Ethereal Mirror (Earache/Columbia) 1993
Statik Majik EP (UK Earache) 1994
Cosmic Requiem EP (Earache/Columbia) 1994
In Memorium EP (UK Rough Trade) 1994
Carnival Bizarre (Earache) 1995

Grindcore pioneers Napalm Death were one of the fastest bands ever. Perverse logic would therefore dictate that when vocalist Lee Dorrian left in 1989, he would form the slowest, most detuned and dirge-like doom-metal outfit ever to plod this increasingly mortal coil. Thus the monstrously heavy Cathedral arose from the deepest bowels of the British Midlands, the regional spawning ground of Black Sabbath and Judas Priest. Reverent enough to include the names of favorite bands in its albums' thank-you lists, Cathedral worships at the altars of Sabbath, Celtic Frost. St. Vitus, Trouble and countless early-'80s metal bands, throwing in stretches of laughably pretentious prog-rock for good measure.

Operating around the slogan "A dark celebration of jaded misery," **Forest of Equilibrium**—with suitably mind-altering artwork by Dave Patchett—features an average song-time of eight minutes, an average BPM of about forty-five . . . how much more do you need to know? **In Memorium,** a belatedly issued 1990 demo, contains a couple of non-LP tracks (including the awesome "Mourning of a New Day") but is generally of interest only to the converted. Likewise, **Echoes of Dirges Into the Naves** is a hopelessly rare five-song live official bootleg released on a Mexican indie label.

Its doomy deeds done (dirt cheap, even), Cathedral set out on a new course: to fuse Judas Priest and Thin Lizzy into the ultimate velvet bell-bottomed early-'70s heavy metal sound. **Soul Sacrifice** unveils this approach, with "Autumn Twilight" and three lesser efforts. The songs are generally shorter, faster and a lot more melodic, although no number can end until Garry Jennings and Adam Lehan have pealed off at least two squealing twin lead guitar solos. **The Ethereal Mirror** continues in the same vein, but gets lost in overly complex instrumental sections that distract from the heavy grooves that are Cathedral's greatest strength (see "Ride"). What's more entertaining is the band's ability to be reverent and irreverent at the same time: Dorrian has a habit of interjecting shouts like "Dyn-o-mite!" and "Disco, man!" at moments of peak heaviness.

Cosmic Requiem (titled **Statik Majik** overseas) presents five new songs that—with the exception of the twenty-three-minute "Voyage of the Homeless Sapien"—bring a little conciseness to the style of **The Ethereal Mirror.**

Cathedral's lineup has always been fairly fluid; and **Carnival Bizarre** finds Dorrian and co-founder Jennings united with another new rhythm section. With its Sabbath-worship at an all-time high, the band achieves its crowning moment of glory (or redundancy) by featuring that group's Tony Iommi on a song that sounds astonishingly like "Planet Caravan" (there's even one called "Electric Grave," which sounds nothing like Sabbath's "Electric Funeral," lifting the riff from Zep's "Moby Dick" instead!). Pagan idolatry aside, **Carnival Bizarre** is Cathedral's best and tightest album yet, rectifying many of the indulgences of the past and concentrating on throbbing grooves and viscous riffage—and a shout-out to Huggy Bear. [ja]

See also *Napalm Death.*

CATHERINE

Sleepy EP (March) 1993 (TVT) 1994
Sorry (TVT) 1994
Hot Saki & Bedtime Stories (TVT) 1996

It's not altogether surprising that this Chicago-based guitar army would find a nesting spot under the wing of Smashing Pumpkins—the bands are related not only by marriage (Catherine drummer Kerry Brown to Pumpkins bassist D'Arcy Wretzky) but by a deep-seated disposition towards the big bold sounds of '70s prog-rock. (The quintet's slogan is "Better Living Through Noise.") Co-produced by Billy Corgan, **Sleepy**'s oversized sonic webs succeed in drawing listeners into the band's more abstract pieces, but not in making a lasting impact. **Sorry** is imbued with a similarly transitory nature. With its wispy, soaring harmonies and flaky layers of amp noise, "Songs About Girls" is worthy of inclusion in a psych-pop 101 primer, and singer/guitarist Neil Jendon proves proficient at sugar-coating some tantalizingly acrid riffs. Half an hour after listening, however, you're not likely to retain more than a hint of vaguely pleasant aftertaste. [dss]

CATHERINE WHEEL

She's My Friend EP (UK Wilde Club) 1990
Painful Thing EP (UK Wilde Club) 1991
Ferment (UK Fontana) 1991 (Fontana/Mercury) 1992
30 Century Man EP (UK Fontana) 1992
Chrome (Fontana/Mercury) 1993
Happy Days (Fontana/Mercury) 1995

Right from their first album, this Yarmouth quartet blew the doors off the maze of post–My Bloody Valentine shoegaze guitar bands by going back to older UK outfits such as the House of Love (whom they covered) and especially the gigantic crushing beauty of the early Comsat Angels.

Containing remakes of two songs from each of the band's early EPs, **Ferment** gained the Catherine Wheel a solid foothold in the US with "I Want to Touch You," which has a repeating, echoed guitar line that digs in like nails in your back, and "Black Metallic," which builds, quiets and percolates like Echo and the Bunnymen, complete with a devastating tremolo-pan guitar solo. With soaring choruses and producer Tim Friese-Greene's shimmering textures, the entire album—both delicate and demonstrative—sparkles and smolders.

Pixies producer Gil Norton toughened the sound on **Chrome,** an album that combines songwriting prowess with more raging playing, pop tunes gone kablooey and a huge bonfire sound with a faint metal edge. Rob Dickinson (whose cousin Bruce was the vocalist of Iron Maiden) sings as if to choke on his words but never loses the gritty determination of his and Brian Futter's guitars. Amidst the delicious fallout, Catherine Wheel mixes in more quiet, moody tracks (the resplendent "The Nude," "Fripp"); the single "Crank" is as spindly as it is catchy. No sophomore slump here.

Happy Days, also produced by Norton, is an even more monstrous bomb drop. The metallisms are more pronounced, but don't mar the album's mindboggling assault. Huge shards of guitar and furious, pounding bass drums dominate, implying the intelligent onslaught of bands like Nirvana and Sugar. Highlighted by the blistering single "Waydown" and the crushing, string-bending "Empty Head," the album is a restless, passionate emotional overload. The first half favors hyper rev-ups; the second is more playful and includes "Judy Staring at the Sun," a sweet duet by Dickinson and Belly's Tanya Donelly. Best song title: "Eat My Dust You Insensitive Fuck." [jr]

CAULFIELDS

Whirligig (A&M) 1995

This Delaware power-pop quartet packs exactly the sort of angst one would expect from a band named after the confused teen of J. D. Salinger's *The Catcher in the Rye.* Singer/guitarist John Faye chronicles slacker life in a sleepy college town, addressing alienation and the perceived hypocrisy of the adult world in short, catchy modern pop songs that occasionally betray his grave concerns about important matters. "Ask a little girl if she wants a piece of candy / And you'll find yourself in front of a lynch mob for a jury / And they'll read the riot act along with your Miranda warning." The lyrics are clever if uninspired, his anger concealed inside sugar-coated melodies. There's not much here that hasn't been done before; still, the Caulfields do it well, and the band's catchy songs have easy appeal. [rl]

CAUSTIC RESIN

See *Built to Spill.*

NICK CAVE AND THE BAD SEEDS

From Her to Eternity (UK Mute) 1984 (Mute/Restless) 1990 (Mute) 1994
The Firstborn Is Dead (Mute/Homestead) 1985 (Mute) 1994
Tupelo EP (Homestead) 1985
Kicking Against the Pricks (Homestead) 1986 (Mute) 1994
Your Funeral . . . My Trial (Homestead) 1986 (Mute) 1994
Tender Prey (Mute/Enigma) 1988 (Mute/Elektra) 1992
The Good Son (Mute/Enigma) 1990 (Mute/Elektra) 1990
Henry's Dream (Mute/Elektra) 1992
Live Seeds (Mute/Elektra) 1993
Let Love In (Mute/Elektra) 1994
Murder Ballads (Mute/Reprise) 1996

NICK CAVE/MICK HARVEY/BLIXA BARGELD

Ghosts . . . of the Civil Dead (Mute) 1989

NICK CAVE & SHANE MACGOWAN

What a Wonderful World EP (Mute/Elektra) 1992

ANITA LANE

Dirty Sings EP (Mute/Restless) 1989
Dirty Pearl (Mute) 1995

After Australia's chaos-wreaking Birthday Party immolated in the early '80s, singer Nick Cave set out to explore and refine the bleak, twisted ideas he had developed and begun to test out about American country music, spiritual music and Delta blues. Bringing together top caliber players—bassist Barry Adamson (ex-Magazine), guitarist Blixa Bargeld (moonlighting from Einstürzende Neubauten) and drummer Mick

Harvey (the Birthday Party's former guitarist and keyboardist)—as the Bad Seeds, Cave slowed the old band's dynamic evil to a crawl and began to assay more prose-like lyrical conceits. **The Firstborn Is Dead,** in particular, captures Cave's hoodoo-voodoo (with a grim Elvis Presley fixation to boot) at its most ripe and primal. The CD incorporates the three non-LP tracks of **Tupelo,** including Cave's disarming cover of the Elvis hit "In the Ghetto." Going deeper into that realm, **Kicking Against the Pricks** is a collection of covers ("All Tomorrow's Parties," "By the Time I Get to Phoenix," John Lee Hooker's "I'm Gonna Kill That Woman," Johnny Cash's "The Folksinger") that simultaneously helps explain where Cave had come from and where he was hoping to go. By the time of **Tender Prey,** the Bad Seeds had reorganized, with Adamson gone, Harvey shifting back to guitar, bass and keyboards and two newcomers, drummer Thomas Wydler and guitarist Kid Congo Powers (ex-Cramps), on hand.

The dawn of the '90s saw the emergence of a more subdued Cave. After publishing his novel, *And the Ass Saw the Angel,* he released his most "mature"—for better and worse—work. Recorded in Brazil, **The Good Son** finds Cave caught up in stately material that attempts to showcase him as a singer—a crooner, even. The result is more lyrically compressed and musically restrained, but poignant ("The Ship Song," "Sorrow's Child"), dramatic ("The Good Son," "The Hammer Song") and over-reaching ("Foi Na Cruz," sung in Portuguese, no less). On initial British copies, acoustic versions of **Tender Prey**'s "The Mercy Seat," "City of Refuge" and "Deanna" were included as a bonus.

Henry's Dream is Cave's attempt to reintegrate the rhythmic thrust of his previous work into his newfound, well-groomed charm. Produced by David Briggs, the album has a disciplined air about it, a direction that seems counterproductive to Cave's true gifts. Though sonically impressive, the playing lacks the kinetic interplay that marks Cave's best work. Not that the songwriting is entirely up to snuff, either: "Papa Won't Leave You, Henry," "Straight to You" and "Brother, My Cup Is Empty" are all decent compositions, but a sameness pervades much of the material. **Live Seeds** was recorded in Europe and Australia during the band's 1992–93 world tour and includes a photo-diary by Peter Milne. The thirteen tracks fairly represent the Bad Seeds at this juncture, with the older material clearly showing up the previous album's work.

Let Love In, however, is thoroughly re-energized. Though not as focused as Cave's first few albums, the disc unleashes a galvanized Bad Seeds, poking through with the Isaac Hayes–style strut of "Loverman," the aching balladry of "Nobody's Baby Now" and an onslaught of other fine songs ("Do You Love Me?," "I Let Love In," "Jangling Jack"). Cave is forever obsessed with his usual themes of sex, death, the devil and rhythm, but here he relocates the elusive energy that had gone out from much of his '90s material.

Upholding his creative pattern, Cave next released **Murder Ballads,** a collection of songs focusing on—you guessed it—death, and the blues inspired by it. Though the sound is familiarly Cave-like, he thoughtfully imports several different guests for duets. Australian pop star Kylie Minogue adds a layer of sublime gentleness to the ravaged dialogue between murderer and victim in "Where the Wild Roses Grow," while Bob Dylan's "Death Is Not the End" gets the royal treatment from Cave and an all-star chorus including Minogue, Shane MacGowan (with whom Cave had previously essayed "What a Wonderful World" on a '92 single), Anita Lane and PJ Harvey, who also duets with Cave on the traditional folk tale, "Henry Lee." If nothing else, **Murder Ballads** suggests that Cave has truly come to grips with his fringe existence.

In addition to his own albums, Cave has contributed tracks to the soundtracks of Wim Wenders' *Wings of Desire, Until the End of the World* and *Faraway, So Close;* he has also tried his hand at acting, appearing in *Wings of Desire, Johnny Suede* and the Australian *Ghosts of the Civil Dead,* for which he and two bandmates wrote and performed the eerie, slow-moving score.

Anita Lane was for a time Cave's girlfriend and wrote a few lyrics for his projects. On **Dirty Sings,** accompanied by the uncredited Bad Seeds, she warbles through four songs, including Chic's "Lost in Music." In 1995, Mute Records appended the EP to a full album of material, **Dirty Pearl.** Lane's vocal skills haven't gotten any better over time, but the record does boast "The Fullness of His Coming," a track recorded with members of the Birthday Party for a compilation on a Berlin label that went belly-up before its release. [roc]

See also *Barry Adamson, Congo Norvell, Cramps, Einstürzende Neubauten, Gun Club, Pogues; TPRG.*

CELL

Slo*Blo (Ger. City Slang) 1992 (Ecstatic Peace!/DGC) 1993
Living Room (DGC) 1994

Operating under the rationale that songs and singing don't matter much if you've got a bombass guitar sound that screams indie cred and supportive pals like Sonic Youth (who've certainly coasted down that same carpool lane on more than one occasion) in your corner, New York's Cell made an exceedingly underwhelming bow on **Slo*Blo,** shaking the walls in a rich, tuneless blare. Singing guitarists Ian James and Jerry DiRienzo mash together roaring, boring textures while drummer Keith Nealy (a onetime Sonic Youth guitar tech) and bassist David Motamed (ex–Das Damen) kick the tracks along in vari-speed drive; if commercial post-punk noise were to get more formulaic than this, it'd have to be stacked in the generic-brand aisle. "Two" mounts a usable Led Zeppelin beat and something approaching a melody (to carry along the timeless "Your world's in trouble and I'm seeing double"); the acoustic digression of "Bad Day" suggests **Love It to Death**–era Alice Cooper (though the opera singer that filters in from somewhere at the quietest moments doesn't figure in that equation). Although "Hills" reaches for some pop purpose, Cell doesn't get a firm grip, and jamming lets it slip away.

Firmly wacked into a presentable state by producer John Agnello, **Living Room** makes a concerted effort to tone down and shape up something better (setting the thresher controls closer to Crazy Horse)—and to a degree succeeds. It's amazing what a difference a little loud/not-loud dynamic variety can make. Beyond the refurbished sound, DiRienzo's songwriting is functional ("Goodbye" roughs up an attractive descending figure and serviceable pop melody), but even the better ones (including "Milky," "Fly," "Soft Ground" and the

Johnny Thunders–styling "Sad & Beautiful") are limited by the lack of an able singer and the are-we-done-yet? slouch that underlies all of Cell's work.

Following Cell's demise, DiRienzo launched a new quartet, Ugly Beauty, in 1996. [i]

See also *Versus.*

EXENE CERVENKA

See *Lydia Lunch, X.*

EUGENE CHADBOURNE WITH EVAN JOHNS AND THE H-BOMBS

Vermin of the Blues (Fundamental) 1987

EUGENE CHADBOURNE & EVAN JOHNS

Terror Has Some Strange Kinfolk (Alternative Tentacles) 1993

EVAN JOHNS AND THE H-BOMBS

Giddy Up Girl EP10 (Deco) 1980
Rollin' Through the Night (Alternative Tentacles) 1986 + 1992
Evan Johns and the H-Bombs (Jungle) 1986
Bombs Away (Speedo/Rykodisc) 1989
Please Mr. Santa Claus (Rykodisc) 1990
Rockit Fuel Only! (Rykodisc) 1991

Re-pairing loopy North Carolina country-pop terrorist Eugene Chadbourne (he of the electric rake and the vast Shockabilly/solo catalogue) with Virginia-born roots-rocker Evan Johns (minus his long-running Austin band, the H-Bombs, who contributed immeasurably to the duo's uproarious **Vermin of the Blues**), **Terror Has Some Strange Kinfolk** tempers the furies for a good-natured but noisy stomp through the backwoods tangle where Nashville meets the refugees from a politically conscious Martian boobyhatch. On "Redneck Jazz," the guitar-totin' Johns and a snappy rhythm section confidently run through their paces while Chadbourne tries to fuck shit up with all the random noise he can muster on guitar, banjo and rake. Turning the tables, "I Cut the Wrong Man" and "Killbillies" find Evan, bassist Buggs Coombs and drummer Mike Buck attempting to follow Eugene's ectoplasmic lyrical inventions as best they can. In between, there are drunken nonsense scraps ("I Gotta Pee," "Missing Engineer"), acoustic guitar and banjo topicals ("George Bush's Bones Jig," "Desert Storm Chewing Gum"), conscious parodies ("Achey Rakey Heart"), tape manipulations, even a few moments of poignant semi-seriousness ("Checkers of Blood," a wordless "Got the Blues & Can't Be Satisfied"). The collaborators make apt foils: Chadbourne's clever, provocative words colorize Johns' solid musical chops, which, in turn, haul chunks of the record closer to Planet Reality than Chadbourne usually orbits. (For those concerned with his erratic rotations, the good doctor surfaced in '95, playing a little banjo on the Feral Chickens' **Only a Mother** LP.)

Johns, who was prolific in the '80s, hasn't released much of late. Nonetheless, his two albums on Rykodisc remain positively ballistic (not true of the primarily instrumental Xmas record); the '92 CD reissue of **Rollin' Through the Night** (in which Alternative Tentacles owner Jello Biafra credits a "record reviewer from *Trouser Press* magazine" for introducing him to Johns' work—it wasn't me) adds three previously unreleased cuts. [i]

See also *Jello Biafra, John Zorn; TPRG.*

CHAIN GANG

Deuce Package EP7 (Kapitalist) 1979
Mondo Manhattan (Lost) 1987
Kill for You EP7 (Matador) 1990
Perfumed (Matador) 1993

Like the Loch Ness monster, this venerable New York quartet creates both heated excitement and intense apprehension among those who've followed its murky existence through more than two decades of irregular surfacings. Chain Gang began with the onset of New York's first punk scene, having played its initial gigs (under a prior name) in the early part of 1975; the band's aggressive, occasionally outright violent, approach would have fit right in if the deportment of its devotees hadn't gotten the group banned from most of the city's venues.

After releasing a handful of singles, Chain Gang went underground in the early '80s, only to return with the blindingly intense **Mondo Manhattan,** the soundtrack to a mythical video project the group purportedly spent years working on before abandoning. Picking up where *Taxi Driver* left off, squalid songs like "Are You Wearing Gold Tonight" and "Gross Out on 40 Deuce" chronicle the Big Apple's slow slide into the void—an inevitability that doesn't seem to bother singer Ricky Luanda all that much. Although parts of the album are likely to be all but impenetrable to those living west of the Hudson, the guitar splatter that surges from the heart of songs like "Kill the Bouncers at the Ritz" and "I Read" (captured live, in a 1982 version enhanced by the sax honking of scene stalwart Bud Struggle) is absolutely universal.

Another stretch of self-imposed exile came to an end when the band recorded the **Kill for You** double 7-inch and then compiled **Perfumed,** matching those studio tracks with live material from various eras—evidence that the quartet has carefully preserved every ounce of the nihilistic vitriol it's emitted over the years. Luanda proves as sharp as ever when it comes to anti-authority harangues like "Cut off the Drug Czar's Head." (In a show of solidarity for Body Count, Chain Gang challenged every band in America to follow its lead and integrate a version of "Cop Killer" into their sets.) Larry Gee's pinned-pupil guitar scratching adds more than enough menace to anti-everything missives like "Murder for the Millions." But don't let those titles give you the idea that Chain Gang plays only punk rock. As evidenced by the mid-'70s recording of O. V. Wright's soul classic "That's How Strong My Love Is" and the contorted funk of "Beijing" (which spotlights the freakishly synchronous bond between bassist Ted Twist and drummer Phil Von Rome), it's far more out there than that. This is the *real* sound of the decline of Western civilization. [dss]

CHAINSAW KITTENS

Violent Religion (Mammoth) 1990
Flipped Out in Singapore (Mammoth) 1992
High in High School EP (Mammoth) 1992
Angel on the Range (Mammoth) 1993
Pop Heiress (Mammoth/Atlantic) 1994
Chainsaw Kittens (Scratchie/Mercury) 1996

FOR LOVE NOT LISA

For Love Not Lisa EP (Indivision) 1992
Merge (EastWest) 1993
Information Superdriveway (EastWest) 1995

Cross-dressing singer Tyson Todd Meade crawled from the wreckage of Norman, Oklahoma's Defenestration to form Chainsaw Kittens as a low-rent Bowie-cum-New-York-Dolls glam unit. Displaying the rudiments of the quartet's sound (romping, guitar-goosed melodies, theatrically fey vocals), **Violent Religion** is a promising first album with some memorable tunes ("Here at the End," the Syd Barrett–like "Feel Like a Drugstore") and spirited playing throughout. The Anglophiliac sheen of Meade's vocals, as well as his sharply developed pop sense, serves to reinforce the aesthetic differences between the Kittens and most of their mid-American indie-rock peers.

Recorded as a quintet with a new rhythm section and a second guitarist joining co-founder Mark Metzger, **Flipped Out in Singapore** (produced by Butch Vig) ups the brute force quotient. Amid the overdriven guitars, Meade continues to assert his I'm-a-freak-and-I-dig-it persona on songs like "High in High School" and "Shannon's Fellini Movie." The gloriously transcendent "Never to Be Found" demonstrates Meade's genuine gift for writing an affecting power ballad.

High in High School reprises two songs from the album and includes a cover of Harry Nilsson's schlock classic "One." The seven-song **Angel on the Range,** recorded with a third rhythm section and Metzger gone, showcases the band in prime, hard-rocking form, with brief forays into churning psychedelia ("Lazy Little Dove") and willful silliness ("Little Fishies," sung by remaining guitarist Trent Bell).

Pop Heiress is the Kittens' finest album, thanks to a combination of strong hooks, masterful production (by John Agnello) and the confidence that goes with such assets. Beginning with the raging blast of "Sore on the Floor," the Kittens careen through twelve memorable tunes, ranging from the romantically wistful "Loneliest China Place" to the sleekly propulsive "Silver Millionaire." **Pop Heiress** should have lifted the Kittens out of the indie-rock ghetto once and for all; instead, the band was dropped shortly after its release. Go figure.

The rhythm section on **Singapore** and **High School**—drummer Aaron Preston and bassist Clint McBay—went on, singly, to join For Love Not Lisa, a band formed by singer/guitarist Mike Lewis and guitarist Miles (just Miles) in Oklahoma City but nurtured in Southern California. Defying its title, **Merge** is an accomplished but eclectic record that catapults easily from mersh grunge ("Softhand") to swoony dream-pop ("Travis Hoffman"), psychedelic recitation ("Just a Phase") to arena-scaled rock ("Mother's Faith"). The quartet can't seem to land on any lily pad for more than three minutes, but nifty items like the fiery power pop of "Traces" makes the constant head-spinning worthwhile.

Information Superdriveway takes a narrower path through terse, taut tuneful rock with clangy guitars and hustling rhythms. A glaring Replacements influence coming off the Goo Goo Dolls makes "Coming Into Focus" a surging treat, while a striking Fugazi design sharpens the band's knives to fine effect on "Seasick." If a bit short on clear-cut personality (ironically, the diversity of **Merge** reveals more of the band's own), it's still an exciting blast gounded in strong songwriting and controlled fury. [ts/tr]

See also *TPRG*.

SHEILA CHANDRA

Out on My Own (UK Indipop) 1984 (Indipop/Caroline) 1996
Quiet (UK Indipop) 1984 (Indipop/Caroline) 1996
The Struggle (UK Indipop) 1985 (Indipop/Caroline) 1995
Nada Brahma (UK Indipop) 1985 (Indipop/Caroline) 1995
Roots and Wings (UK Indipop) 1990
Silk (Shanachie) 1991
Weaving My Ancestors' Voices (Real World/Caroline) 1992
The Zen Kiss (Real World/Caroline) 1994
ABoneCroneDrone (Real World/Caroline) 1996

MONSOON

Third Eye (UK Mobile Suit Corp.) 1983 (UK Great Expectations) 1989

First heard in 1983 as the exotic teenaged star of the offbeat British contrivance Monsoon—a chartworthy hybrid that fed Indian raga sounds into organically homegrown danceable techno-pop—London-born actress/singer Sheila Chandra outlasted the gimmicky group to become an important fusion figure in world music. In creative and corporate partnership (in the Indipop label) with Monsoon songwriter/producer Steve Coe, with contributions from Coe's collaborator, Martin Smith, Chandra became a solo artist in 1984, releasing four albums inside of two years. **Out on My Own,** the most ingratiatingly mainstream of them, tones down the ethnic component in favor of an accented Eurovision sound; sitars eddy and race, tablas batter along, but the songs—statements of love, strength and independence—are strictly from the ABBA school of peppy jingles. **Quiet** eschews obvious song structure for wordless contemplative sound paintings; Coe's piano and various Indian instruments support Chandra's multi-tracked vocal exercises, which range from rhythmic scat inventions to Laurie Anderson nabobbing to breathy sustains—not quite a new age, but getting there.

The Struggle picks up from **Out on My Own** with a tougher, harder dance presence and more determined lyrics in English and Hindi. After the exotic appointments and vocal tactics Chandra tested on **Quiet,** the backbeat stubbornly redirects **The Struggle** westward. **Nada Brahma,** the fourth album of this prolific phase of Chandra's career, tilts the balance back towards Indian music; the twenty-seven-minute "Nada Brahma (Sound Is God)" is a drummerless raga, an evocative if overextended piece (especially the a cappella segment) featuring Chandra, Coe and their regular sitar player, Dharambir Singh. Throughout the album, the organic blend of sitar, piano, tabla and voice is particularly handsome.

Chandra then took an extended powder, finally returning to action in 1990 with **Roots and Wings.** Moving well outside the realm of tarted-up pop music (relinquishing electronic keyboards once and for all), Chandra and Coe create weightless atmospheres; they delve into Indian music and extract elements of it for their own purposes, adding nothing but lyrics, a subtle and not altogether incongruous Celtic strain (in "Lament of McCrimmon/Song of the Banshee") and the chromatic scale to the ancient drones and rhythms. If the seductive fruit of their labor winds up as foreign sonic wallpaper in somebody's Soho waiting room, so be it.

Silk is a handy sampler of ten tracks from all of Chandra's preceding albums except **Nada Brahma**—plenty for all but the most determined enthusiasts.

Chandra's prodigious vocal facility and diversity makes **Weaving My Ancestors' Voices** a most impressive showing. She does a credible scat imitation of a blazing tabla in "Speaking in Tongues I" and then trots out the gorgeous "Dhyana and Donalogue," an Irish folk ballad she renders unaccompanied. The sophisticated album, released on the Real World label (highbrow home for many of the world's leading folk musicians), contains rarefied remakes of two Monsoon songs ("Ever So Lonely" and "Eyes"), an English traditional song ("The Enchantment") and North African chanting. A serious, irreverent work of intercultural musicology, and beautiful to boot.

Deepening the most surprising ventures of **Weaving My Ancestors' Voices, The Zen Kiss** moves Chandra into a fantastic new realm, one in which the elemental, nonsectarian purity of singing is all that matters. "La Sagesse (Women, I'm Calling You)" is a solo invocation that owes as much to American blues and gospel as to any Asian prayer tradition; "Love It Is a Killing Thing" is an equally unadorned Anglo-Saxon ballad; "En Mireal del Penal" extends the explicit universality of her music to Latin America. When Chandra brings sitar quietly into the picture (as in "A Sailor's Life," the larklike "Waiting" and the maternal/erotic recitation "Woman and Child"), the droning undercurrent could just as easily be bagpipe. There's a valuable lesson in this disorienting and engrossing album. [i]

See also *TPRG*.

CHANNEL LIGHT VESSEL

See *Roger Eno.*

CHAOS FACE

See *Bill Laswell.*

TRACY CHAPMAN

Tracy Chapman (Elektra) 1988
Crossroads (Elektra) 1989
Matters of the Heart (Elektra) 1992
New Beginning (Elektra) 1995

Chapman's powerful lyrics and deep, emotion-packed voice (shockingly similar, on first brush, to Joan Armatrading's) gave the Cleveland-born singer/songwriter's exceptional debut the impact of a smooth stone wrapped in unprocessed cotton. The unadorned electric and acoustic arrangements of David Kershenbaum's tasteful production focus attention on Chapman's knockout performances of resonantly passionate songs: "Fast Car," "Behind the Wall," "Talkin' Bout a Revolution." The odes to romance ("Baby Can I Hold You," "For My Lover," "For You") leaven her anger with undiminished intensity and conviction.

Acknowledging the intrusive challenge presented by her sudden and massive success, Chapman channeled the threats to her privacy and independence (most bluntly addressed in the title song) into broadly relevant songs of personal freedom—romantic, social and political—on the satisfying second album. Beyond that, **Crossroads**—which safely incorporates more varied and expansive instrumentation and production—upholds the debut's commitment to social protest, supporting Nelson Mandela ("Freedom Now") and idealism ("All That You Have Is Your Soul"), while drawing a critical bead on governmental neglect ("Subcity") and upward mobility ("Material World"). Chapman saves the most affecting lyrics on **Crossroads** for relationships, where she mines wounds and anxieties for aching odes to love and loneliness.

Having neatly sidestepped the sophomore jinx, Chapman then fell into a gaping career hole. For her third album, she took some extra time, brought in coproducer Jimmy Iovine and a new breed of sessionmen (Mike Campbell, Roy Bittan, Tony Levin and Manu Katche in place of Denny Fongheiser, Larry Klein and Russ Kunkel) and made **Matters of the Heart,** a dull record that is no major stylistic departure other than sounding incrementally more like a Joni Mitchell record. Emotionally, Chapman sounds despondent, self-critical and unsettled; although she paints a grim portrait of the gun culture's devastating impact (in the lead-off "Bang Bang Bang") and offers a fragment of generalized feminism in "Woman's Work," she can't concentrate on social commentary. Her lyrics all turn inward and, with the exception of the incongruously idealistic "Dreaming on a World," down. "All we know will cease to be," she promises in the vaguely ecological "Short Supply"; "I sit and rot behind these padded walls," she announces in "I Used to Be a Sailor." Singing "I only have nightmares" and "Why don't I dream anymore" in one song and "I'll keep on dreaming" in another, Chapman belies the strength and confidence of her voice with the wavering uncertainty of her vision. Only on "Open Arms," the first of two love songs that close the record, does she regain her composure, offering solace and support with compelling grace.

Handsomely if plainly produced by Chapman and Don Gehman, the belated **New Beginning** doesn't even begin to live up to its title in any sense other than commercial. (The beaming photographs are likewise misleading.) Rather than relocate the burning heart of her passionate artistry, set off down some surprising stylistic path or even address her need for a personal renaissance, Chapman somberly offers prosaic philosophy, familiar romantic pledges and abject self-doubt in songs alternately too preachy and personal to be entertaining. "The whole world's broke and it ain't worth fixing/It's time to start all over, make a new beginning," she sings in the title track, and that's about as deep as it gets. In "Heaven's Here on Earth," she calls for "peace and love and understanding"—commendable sentiments, to be sure, but hardly stimulating notions, and shallow expression for such a gifted poet. Likewise, "The Rape of the World" adds nothing to the musical literature on ecological destruction. The quiet, intimate intensity of Chapman's singing is undiminished, but none of the sentiments is nearly as potent as the tenderness of her voice. She dons a hair shirt in "At This Point in My Life"—"I've done so many things wrong, I don't know if I can do right"—but it's a mystery why, and there goes an otherwise affecting creation. In closing **New Beginning** at the point where it should have begun, Chapman offers "I'm Ready." Too late. (Following that finale, there's an unlisted love song as unadorned and attractive as anything on the album.) [i]

See also *TPRG*.

CHAPTERHOUSE

Whirlpool (Dedicated/RCA) 1991
Blood Music (Dedicated/Arista) 1993
Blood Music; Pentamerous Metamorphosis (UK Dedicated) 1993

Chapterhouse had plenty of time to refine its trancey pop atmospherics: the young Reading quintet was together more than three years before piling together British singles (including "Pearl") and new tracks into the descriptively titled **Whirlpool.** Gauzy dream-pop with a solid structural center, Chapterhouse's songs are not the usual vague, floating clouds but exceptionally agreeable bolts of catchiness dressed for a long winter in comfortable layers of echoey guitar fuzz and wispy voices. A surprisingly cohesive (if not exactly consistent) album despite an abundance of distinctive producers (Robin Guthrie and Stephen Hague, among others) and two equally tuneful writers in singer/guitarists Andrew Sherriff and Stephen Patman, **Whirpool** gets added points for sticking to a brisk timetable, energetically moved along by Ashley Bates' firmly economical drumming. A better breed of shoegazing.

Although **Whirpool**'s "Falling Down" does hit a forceful acid dance groove, the band's beat-crazy second album is still a shock. All that careful preparation evidently didn't ensure stability regarding the bigger picture, but few bands could survive such a major redirection without doing substantial damage to themselves. Chapterhouse get away scot-free, sounding as good as new. Discharging their drummer to immerse themselves in rhythm on **Blood Music,** the remaining quartet keeps an airy vocal presence while bringing guitars down from the clouds, turning to keyboards, samples, heavy electronic percussion and producer Pascal Gabriel (Inspiral Carpets, EMF, Peter Murphy). Another tuneful delight in a different kitchen, **Blood Music** hustles and bustles, putting emphatic rhythms into songs that could have been cut from the first album's sparkling pop cloth. "Summer's Gone," "On the Way to Fly," the jangly "Greater Power" and the sharp-toothed guitar rockers "We Are the Beautiful" and "She's a Vision" are good examples. Even longwinded adventures like "Deli" and the trippy "Love Forever" have songs lurking in there someplace. Initial copies of **Blood Music** contain a bonus disc with two double-length Hague club mixes of "We Are the Beautiful," the beguiling non-LP "Frost" and a hypnotic fifteen-minute sonic happening entitled "Picnic." **Blood Music: Pentamerous Metamorphosis** is an hour of "retranslation" by Global Communication (Mark Pritchard and Tom Middleton). [i]

CHARLATANS (UK)

The Only One I Know EP (Dead Dead Good/Beggars Banquet/RCA) 1990
Some Friendly (Dead Dead Good/Beggars Banquet/RCA) 1990
Between 10th and 11th (Beggars Banquet/RCA) 1992
Up to Our Hips (Beggars Banquet/Atlantic) 1994
The Charlatans UK (Beggars Banquet/Atlantic) 1995
The Charlatans UK v. the Chemical Brothers EP (Beggars Banquet/Atlantic) 1995

Initially pegged as Stone Roses wannabes with an attendant likely short shelf life, this quintet from outside Manchester (Northwich, actually) managed to parlay its derivative yet endearingly poppy neo-psychedelic dance-rock into a real career. They certainly got off on the right foot, as the first EP and **Some Friendly** both contain "The Only One I Know," still their best (and best-known) song. **Between 10th and 11th** likewise successfully blends up-to-the-minute dance technology (courtesy of ace producer Flood) with song-oriented shoegazing, highlighted by "Weirdo," a fiery Hammond organ (Rob Collins) workout. That "Can't Even Be Bothered" nicks the bassline from "Under My Thumb" is just a sign of things to come.

Working with producer (and '70s prog-rock guitar god) Steve Hillage on **Up to Our Hips** yielded lackluster results, dulling the group's dance drive in guitar-oriented doodling, underplaying singer Tim Burgess' calmly seductive voice amid sluggish tempos and a general lack of dynamic juice. In "Feel Flows," "Autograph," "Another Rider Up in Flames" and the organ-churning title track, the band sounds as if it misread the speed limit and is going as slow as humanly possible. It's only on the still-measured "Patrol" and the slide-powered "Jesus Hairdo" that the Charlatans manage to rev up any appreciable measure of energy.

For reasons unknown, **Up to Our Hips** was released in America without the "UK" name appendage, although it was reattached for the eponymous fourth album. **The Charlatans UK,** partly produced by Hillage, finds the group falling off the Madchester bandwagon for good—if not exactly for better. Though the supremely funky opening near-instrumental "Nine Acre Court" and the pleasant single "Just Lookin'" capitalize on the band's strengths, the rest of the disc is a mixed bag of trippy, stream-of-consciousness lyrics and retro-boogie—especially on the Stonesy "Just When You're Thinkin' Things Over."

Rob Collins died in a car crash in Wales in July 1996. [db/i]

See also *TPRG.*

PAUL CHASTAIN

See *Velvet Crush.*

CHAVEZ

Gone Glimmering (Matador) 1995
Pentagram Ring EP (Matador) 1995

SKUNK

Last American Virgin (Twin\Tone) 1989
Laid (Twin\Tone) 1991

Singer/guitarist Matt Sweeney first came to light with the New Jersey punk band Skunk, whose two records feature sophomoric album titles with juvenile lyrics and aimless vocals to match, although both are stylistically diverse and **Laid** shows real progress toward a fully realized sound. When Skunk dissolved, Sweeney served a stint in the New York group Wider, whose ranks included ex–Live Skull drummer James Lo. When Wider likewise splintered, Sweeney and Lo hooked up with bassist Scott Masciarelli and former Bullet LaVolta guitarist Clay Tarver to form Chavez. (Meanwhile, ex-Skunk bassist Matt Quigley formed a Move-sounding dress-up glam duo, Vaganza. **Last American Virgin** guitarist Stephan Apicella spent some time in H.P. Zinker, as had Sweeney; drummer Claude "Matt" Coleman has worked with Chris Harford and Ween.)

A pair of tracks originally recorded for a demo tape became Chavez' magnificent debut 7-inch, "Repeat the Ending" b/w "Hack the Sides Away," both sides of which feature huge, lurching rhythmic shifts that give way to anthemic choruses rooted in classic hard rock and show that Sweeney had developed into an extremely powerful songwriter and front presence. This single, combined with a series of incendiary live shows, made Chavez the hottest band on the New York club scene in the latter part of 1994. The quartet's first album, **Gone Glimmering,** issued the following year, is somewhat more rhythmically straightforward than the 45 (and also finds Sweeney's vocals sounding curiously like Kurt Cobain's at several points) but only barely less effective. Whether playing on a high-energy adrenaline rush ("Nailed to the Blank Spot," "Pentagram Ring") or doing a slow burn ("Break Up Your Band," "The Ghost by the Sea"), Chavez sounds utterly assured and delivers a stun-gun guitar charge all the way through. Lone gripe: the album clocks in at only thirty minutes.

The **Pentagram Ring** EP is an excellent introduction to Chavez, featuring the best cut from **Gone Glimmering,** both sides of the great debut single and two new tracks—one of which, "You Faded," is as strong as anything in the Chavez songbook. [pl]

See also *Blisters, H.P. Zinker, Ween; TPRG.*

CHEEPSKATES

Run Better Run (Midnight) 1984
Second and Last (Midnight) 1986
Remember (Ger. Music Maniac) 1987
It Wings Above (Ger. Music Maniac) 1988
Waiting for Unta (Ger. Music Maniac) 1989
Songs Volume One–Perry Como EP (Ger. Music Maniac) 1989
Confessional (Ger. Music Maniac) 1990
Songs Volume Two–The Residents EP (Ger. Music Maniac) 1992

SHANE FAUBERT

Kalkara (Ger. Music Maniac) 1990
San Blass (Ger. Music Maniac) 1993

The Cheepskates began as an appealingly retro garage group, eventually transforming into an original pop combo featuring the warm, expressive lead vocals of Shane Faubert. The New York quartet's two Midnight albums are filled with wonderful Farfisa organ, a few great songs and authentic lo-fi production.

After losing Keith and guitarist David John Herrera (who went on to release the underwhelming **A Handout From a Cheepskate** in 1989), the 'Skates continued as a trio of Faubert, bassist Tony Low and new drummer Jeremy Lee. **Remember** took the boys out of the garage and into the realm of charming power pop, upping the production values and placing more emphasis on smooth vocal arrangements.

It Wings Above continues the Cheepskates' creative ascent: it's a small-scale pop revelation with sturdy tracks like the breezy "Someday," the haunting, beautifully constructed "Baybee" and the vividly descriptive, boppy "Cathode Prison." **Songs Volume One—Perry Como** is a five-song curio that finds Faubert wrapping his pipes around such standards as "Catch a Falling Star" and "Dream on Little Dreamer." Strange, yet somehow fitting—and not nearly as strange as **Songs Volume Two,** which contains Cheepskates interpretations of six Residents tunes.

Recorded in Berlin in 1988, the live **Waiting for Unta** is a loose, generous eighteen-song set that includes a bundle of Faubert-written songs from the band's ample back catalogue as well as covers of the Equals' "Baby Come Back," the Everly Brothers' "Bye Bye Love," the Beach Boys' "Little Honda" and, oddly, Peggy Lee's "Fever." Slightly ragged, but definitely energetic.

Guitarist Rich Punzi joined for 1990's consistently successful **Confessional.** Among the fourteen tracks are chewy pop morsels that run the gamut from the cheery primer "How to Pick Up Girls in Germany" to the downcast "How Long Can It Rain" and the joyously romantic "Come Close to Me." Unnecessary, dopey cover: "Sixteen Tons." (One hopes there isn't a **Songs Volume Three—Tennessee Ernie Ford** in the cards.)

Faubert's two solo albums follow an introspective singer/songwriter path (not unlike Richard Barone's chamber-pop excursions). **Kalkara**'s high points include the sadly beautiful "I Wanna Hide" and "Just a Girl," while the more focused **San Blass** finds Faubert aided by Rich Punzi and Lane Hollend (aka Lane Steinberg of Noel Coward's Ghost; he also produced and plays on **It Wings Above**), as well as other New York scene vets. Stirring and compelling, **San Blass** includes Faubert's take on Dave Davies' "Death of a Clown."

Opting out of the Cheepskates in 1992, bassist Tony Low and drummer Jeremy Lee formed their own group, which became, by mid-decade, a tuneful hard-rock quartet named Static 13. [jmb]

See also *Noel Coward's Ghost; TPRG.*

CHEMICAL BROTHERS

Exit Planet Dust (Junior Boy's Own/Freestyle Dust/Astralwerks) 1995
Loops of Fury EP (Junior Boy's Own/Freestyle Dust/Astralwerks) 1996

DUST BROTHERS

"Song to the Siren" (UK no label) 1992 (UK Junior Boy's Own) 1993
Fourteenth Century Sky EP (UK Junior Boy's Own) 1994
My Mercury Mouth EP (UK Junior Boy's Own) 1994

Facing legal action from the American team with the same moniker, Manchester's Dust Brothers—players/producers Tom Rowlands and Ed Simons—became the Chemical Brothers in time for the release of **Exit Planet Dust,** one of the strongest debut techno albums of the mid-'90s. Before crystallizing their own vision, the DJs/musicians spent much of the early part of the decade making singles under their original handle and doing remixes for such British bands as Bomb the Bass, the Charlatans, Manic Street Preachers, Primal Scream and Saint Etienne.

Exit Planet Dust begins with the fiery "Leave Home," a euphoric musical concoction that rides a driving fuzz-bassline and drum track and incorporates edgy, distorted guitar and a vocal loop from Blake Baxter's "Brothers Gonna Work It Out." The song combines the power of punk and metal with the cut-up creativity of techno and hip-hop. Though nothing else on **Exit Planet Dust** reaches that dizzying peak, the remainder is nearly as hard-hitting. Fittingly, "In Dust

We Trust" shows off the duo's turntable scratching prowess, while a live-in-clubland version of the Brothers' original nightlife hit, "Song to the Siren," layers screeching voices into a minimal collage of sirens and other urban sounds. The album's only weakness is its sequencing, which kicks an odd change of pace near the end, importing actual singing voices and more traditional pop structure to "Life Is Sweet" (which features Tim Burgess of the Charlatans) and the folk-flavored, ambient dub of "Alive Alone" (Beth Orton).

The subsequent EP combines a remix of the album's "Chemical Beats" with "Loops of Fury" and two other new tracks. [mrk]

See also *Charlatans (UK).*

CHEMICAL PEOPLE

So Sexist! (Cruz) 1988
Ten-Fold Hate (Cruz) 1989
The Right Thing (Cruz) 1990
Overdosed On . . . (UK Vinyl Solution) 1990
Angels'n'Devils EP (Two Inch Pecker) 1990 (Cruz) 1991
Soundtracks (Cruz) 1991
Chemical People (Cruz) 1992

This aggressively melodic Southern California punk-pop trio got a reputation for its juvenile porn-movie fetishism (the first two albums feature skinflick stars as cover models). But the simple, uptempo music is smarter and catchier than the band's imagery would suggest, even if the lyrics are stupid as often as they're clever.

So Sexist! (produced, like **Ten-Fold Hate** and **The Right Thing,** by Descendents/All drummer Bill Stevenson) is an understandably uneven debut, divided into a side each of songs written and sung by guitarist Blair Jobe (who left the band after his tunes were recorded) and drummer Dave Nazworthy (late of the Last). Side Blair is fairly unremarkable, but the rawer Side Dave shows some spirit, and kindred spirit Tesco Vee (of Meatmen infamy) shows up to deliver some of his trademark rants. The more spirited **Ten-Fold Hate** presents Chemical People as a more focused trio (with bassist Ed Urlik and guitarist Jaime Pina), with Nazworthy taking over most of the writing and singing; the songs are concerned with such pet topics as porn (naturally), junk food, VD, Aquaman and Metallica, but there's also an energetic cover of the Go-Go's' "Vacation." **The Right Thing** isn't radically different, but it finds Chemical People drifting dangerously close to the doctrinaire humorlessness of hardcore. Fortunately, the six-song **Angels'n'Devils** (originally a self-released 7-inch, then a Cruz CD) is a big improvement, with some snappy originals (including a rap tune), a good acoustic number and a surprisingly effective version of Patti Smith's "Ask the Angels."

Soundtracks consists of instrumental jams the bands originally recorded for porn-film soundtracks; the compact pieces range from catchy metal riffs to moodier pieces, but only diehards (of either the band or cheesy cinema) are likely to care. Pina's departure left Nazworthy and Urlik to record **Chemical People** as a duo, overdubbing the guitars themselves with help from Robert Hecker (ex–Redd Kross) while experimenting with a horn section on three tracks (Nazworthy plays tenor sax on two more). The resulting melodic guitar rock is almost completely lacking in the energy of the band's prior work but it has its moments. [ss]

See also *Jeff Dahl Group; TPRG.*

NENEH CHERRY

Raw Like Sushi (Virgin) 1989
Homebrew (Virgin) 1992

Neneh Cherry created her own post–hip-hop world—as imagined by a strong, sexy woman unafraid to combine the contrasting methodologies of stripped-down new wave disco and rap. Although Cherry is not particularly skilled as a vocalist, her sass and confidence are so omnipresent they're practically another musician. Her background—both musical (she began her career with the British art-punk noise band Rip Rig + Panic) and personal (born of a Swedish-African union, she's the step-daughter of the late trumpeter Don Cherry)—helps explain her readiness to challenge longstanding traditions. In partnership with her producer/husband Cameron McVey (from the Bristol ether of Massive Attack, Portishead and Soul II Soul), Cherry works around her shortcomings, and the innovative result is a refreshing change of pace.

Raw Like Sushi is highlighted by the ultra-catchy dance hit, "Buffalo Stance," the Madonna-like percolating pop of "Kisses on the Wind" and such forthright sexual delights as "So Here I Come" and "Outré Risqué Locomotive." On **Homebrew,** Cherry and McVey struggle to make the formula work as well the second time. Rather than reinvent the wheel, they broaden the focus to include more of a rock/alternative flavor. Cherry's thin vocal style is propped up by two prominent (and very different) guest stars who also co-wrote their featured tracks. Gang Starr rapper Guru's back-and-forth flirty repartee with Cherry on "Sassy" yields one of the album's best numbers; for "Trout," she chooses a persona that compliments Michael Stipe's earnest vocals. "Buddy X," a scathing attack on a cheating husband, plays Cherry's international homegirl image to the hilt; its call and response chorus is both smart and smart-alecky. [mf]

See also *TPRG.*

CHER U.K.

She's a Weird Little Snack (Red Decibel) 1993
Go-Go Fish (Red Decibel) 1994

While the scenery that surrounds its hometown (Kansas City, Missouri) may give the illusion of serenity, the wryly named Cher U.K. does its best to disturb the peace with metallically inclined garage-rock that dissects the local environment with a smirk. On the trio's first album—a dozen brash ditties in thirty-three minutes—the jerky, skittering rhythms of "24 Hour Breakfast Menu Macabre" would make the Meat Puppets proud, while "College Song" smears gobs of punk snot all over.

Frontman Mike McCoy's plaintive squawk and bassist Heather Grehan's steady stepping weave together in the threads of Lisa McKenzie's drumming on **Go-Go Fish.** Ripping through "Court" and lifting the Velvet Underground's "Femme Fatale" for "Baldie" (slowing the tempo and replacing the VU verse with "everybody knows you cut your hair"), the group maintains the debut's manic energy while varying the stylistic approaches. [vg]

VIC CHESNUTT

Little (Texas Hotel) 1990
West of Rome (Texas Hotel) 1992
Drunk (Texas Hotel) 1994
Is the Actor Happy? (Texas Hotel) 1995
About to Choke (Capitol) 1996

BRUTE

Nine High a Pallet (Capricorn) 1995

VARIOUS ARTISTS

Sweet Relief II: Gravity of the Situation (The Songs of Vic Chesnutt) (Columbia) 1996

Countless artists can produce convincing creative facsimiles of heartbreak and its many guises—alienation, guilt, regret, self-flagellating misery—in song, but none meets the task with more bitter pleasure, honesty or crooked-smile charm than the inimitable Vic Chesnutt. Phrasing his lyrics idiosyncratically in a cracked, unsteady voice, strumming simple acoustic guitar patterns from his wheelchair, the real auteur of Athens, Georgia, produces aggressively vulnerable records that turn predictable emotions inside out, using the wrenching pathos of his sublime (but intentionally rough-hewn), self-effacing poetry. For an illuminating introduction to a unique figure, Peter Sillen's half-hour 1993 documentary film *Speed Racer: Welcome to the World of Vic Chesnutt* is available on videocassette.

This colorful and witty storyteller doesn't need to be reminded of his failings—he's more than ready to sing about them, in a synergy of life and art that closes around his slight figure like a noose. In the bleak corrosion of Chesnutt's tender idealism, a highly literate mind in a ruined body becomes a willful primitive with a ferocious and highly developed sense of irony. His skilled songwriting burns with reality's pain while glowing with imagination.

Little was recorded in one 1988 day through the good offices of hometown pal Michael Stipe, who produced and hooked up the slow-cooking record deal. ("Production" in this case seems to have involved getting Vic in front of a microphone, although there is a trace of synthesizer on "Speed Racer." "Stevie Smith," which begins with a sound bite of the English poet, was cut separately with a small acoustic band.) In a reminiscence about the "Rabbit Box" he built as a child, Chesnutt catches a possum and a kitten, sets them free and breathes a sigh of relief, noting—with typical winsomeness—"We all three escaped safely." In "Mr. Riely," he passes along the bad news about "Joan, our ex-newspaper girl," who has hung herself. "They found her by the frozen lake but it wasn't frozen enough to skate but by the look on her face it must have been awful tempting."

Stipe's ambitious production—incorporating a handful of musicians to casually play cello, bass, drums and keyboards—elevates the sound of **West of Rome** all the way up to rudimentary. Chesnutt's singing on "my second squirt" is concomitantly more assured and accomplished, which is about all that keeps the naked emotions surfacing in his songs from overwhelming him. He's able to focus the jealousy and hurt in "Where Were You" enough to land a square, somber blow for romantic reliability, and the stark "Stupid Preoccupations" climbs down the abyss of self-loathing on sharp-tongued pitons tipped in poison, but the raw pain in "Withering" is beyond his control; the quiet dirge might as well be an anguished scream. Chesnutt settles for cryptic wordplay on "Lucinda Williams," "Sponge" and "Latent/Blatant." Elsewhere, Vic sends his arrows flying with pinpoint accuracy. He levels "Florida" as the "perfect place to retire from life," slags off malicious gossips in "Soggy Tongues" and makes a delightful game out of his guarded optimism in "Steve Willoughby": "Someday I'll be a paragon/Like Louis Farrakhan/But today I simply am a mess." No other mess ever recorded anything as lovely as the untitled two-guitar madrigal that ends this most challenging album.

Drunk is a great leap forward—in sound (some of it smartly electric), songwriting and vocal skill. The absence of Stipe is noted without prejudice. When not singing a tragic Stevie Smith poem or goofing around (as in "Super Tuesday"), Vic reviews his medical experiences ("Gluefoot," "Supernatural") and his trail of troubles ("When I Ran Off and Left Her," "Kick My Ass," "Dodge") with a mischievous streak of amusement about the pickles he gets himself into. The consistency of tone and the quiet quality of the music bring Chesnutt to a newly accessible stage.

"I wrote you an eloquent postcard once/About this most exquisite onion soup/But of course I never mailed it though/Cause it was your turn in the loop." **Is the Actor Happy?** brings Vic into the realm of utterly presentable commercial recording, as producer John Keane and a low-key trio deliver the eccentricity of his creations and voice with loving empathy. Casting his songwriting eye as far as "Thailand" and as near as "Thumbtack," he balances humor and determination in the "Gravity of the Situation," taking serious things in stride, mocking himself without assigning blame. His grasp of language and construction is better than ever, to the point where the songs here manage to juggle streamlined musical power and crackpot invention without falling over. "Free of Hope," a rocked-up haunted blues as brilliant and chilling as anything he's ever written, paints a scorching portrait of despair ("Thank you God of Nothing—I'm free at last") by deftly sidestepping self-pity, a luxury he has long since abandoned. Chesnutt alone knows the price he's paid for his art, and he's no martyr.

Brute is a bad but innocuous idea, a one-off studio project that finds Chesnutt backed by five-sixths of local rockers Widespread Panic. The tastefully efficient country-soul-rock accompaniment neither improves nor damages a genial (except for "Miserable" and the spiteful "PC," and maybe the breakup epilogue of "Let's Get Down to Business" and, oh yeah, the turned-down disappointment of "Blight") collection of excellent new Chesnutt originals. The band may be gaining some much-needed hip cred here, but Chesnutt takes the ride with his usual unflappable calm. Given that his vocal personality is strong enough to obscure whatever else is going on, and too quirky for the sonic finish to make any commercial difference, **Nine High a Pallet** is, ultimately, another Vic Chesnutt record, one that proves what his music can withstand more than where it should be headed. When he sings "Good Morning Mr. Hard-on," a crisp funk beat and pumping piano don't stand a chance of being taken seriously. And it hardly matters what goes on behind a vivid image like "Daddy is asleep, just home from work/In his comfy chair in his yellowed undershirt/Sister is sad she just got the curse/I am fairly happy 'cause my go-kart kind of works." The surging rock power in "Protein

Drink" and "Sewing Machine" come as a surprise, but the band plays it like Crazy Horse, leaving Chesnutt to be a southern Neil Young at the center of the storm. As Chesnutt sings, "I will float again/When they're done dredging." [i]

See also *Widespread Panic.*

CHARLIE CHESTERMAN

From the Book of Flames (Slow River) 1994
Studebakersfield (Slow River) 1996

As leader of Boston's rocking Scruffy the Cat, guitarist Charlie Chesterman kept moving his band toward a rootsy sensibility (Scruffy's 1988 **Moons of Jupiter** was produced by Memphis mud king Jim Dickinson). With that credible background, his solo rebirth into the '90s vogue for refreshing singer/songwriter rock with unprecedented amounts of country honk sounds right on time. **From the Book of Flames** is one of those unadorned one-take rustic winners that gets down to cases, making the you-and-me lyrics ring powerfully true no matter where one stands on the universal roundabout. Singing evocative lyrics that don't mince words in suffering the reverses of romance, Chesterman dresses up his serious emotions in occasional horn charts ("Got You Bad," "Hello Judy!") and silly song titles. "Sexy Rickenbacker" slides a hairline of difference between Byrds country and power pop to ask "could you be the one for me?" and mean it; "Sleeping With Nero and Dreaming of Smokey the Bear" is a soulful (and direct) tearjerker with pedal steel; "Pink Lemonade" needs only one acoustic guitar to say "I'm not joking now I'm blue/When I think about the day I fell for you." Likewise, the album's most moving song, "If You Were Mine," is an uncertain but unmistakably real cry from the heart that Chesterman does alone on clinky electric guitar. Too unassuming to sound premeditated, **From the Book of Flames** comes straight from a creative place heated to a pungent simmer.

Although there's still some western swing–styled rock, horns and cello on **Studebakersfield,** Chesterman's second album is pretty much a country record, albeit an eclectic, irreverent one. While basting himself in the genre's usual emotionalism ("Heart of a Fool," "Lonesome Cowboy's Lament," "Mister Blue"), he still cleverly manages to stay out of clichés' clutches. If Chesterman can't quite make a fertile spread of this strip-mined wasteland, he has no trouble cultivating a nice little patch of it for his own sweet garden. [i]

BILLY CHILDISH

I've Got Everything Indeed (UK Hangman) 1987
The 1982 Cassetes (UK Hangman) 1987
i remember . . . (UK Hangman) 1987
Poems of Laughter and Violence (UK Hangman) 1988
50 Albums Great (UK Hangman) 1990
I Am the Billy Childish (Sub Pop) 1991
The Sudden Fart of Laughter (Aus. Dog Meat) 1992
Native American Sampler–A History 1983–1993 (Sub Pop) 1993
Hunger at the Moon (Sympathy for the Record Industry) 1993

BILLY CHILDISH AND THE BLACK HANDS

Captain Calypso's Hoodoo Party (UK Hangman) 1988
The Original Chatham Jack (Sub Pop) 1992
Live in the Netherlands (UK Hangman) 1993

BILLY CHILDISH & THE SINGING LOINS

At the Bridge (UK Hangman) 1993

THEE HEADCOATS

Headcoats Down! (UK Hangman) 1989
The Earls of Suavedom (Crypt) 1990
The Kids Are All Square–This Is Hip! (UK Hangman) 1990
Beach Bums Must Die (Crypt) 1990
Heavens to Murgatroyd, Even! It's Thee Headcoats (Already) (Sub Pop) 1990
Troubled Times EP (Aus. Dog Meat) 1990
Sect EP (UK Hangman) 1991
Headcoatitude (UK Shakin' Street) 1991 (Get Hip) 1993
Bo in Thee Garage (UK Hangman) 1991 (Get Hip) 1993
Cavern by the Sea EP (K) 1991
The Würst Is Yet to Come (Live in Schaffhausen 18 Sept. 1990) (Sw. Tom Product) 1992
Beached Earls (Crypt) 1993
The Good Times Are Killing Me (UK Vinyl Japan) 1993
Conundrum (UK Hangman's Daughter) 1994

THEE HEADCOATEES

Girlsville (UK Hangman) 1991 (Get Hip) 1994
Have Love Will Travel (UK Vinyl Japan) 1992
Ballad of an Insolent Pup (UK Vinyl Japan) 1994

THEE HEADCOATS/THEE HEADCOATEES

The Kids Are All Square/Girlsville (UK Damaged Goods) 1993
Wild Billy Childish and His Famous Headcoats Live! At the Wild Western Room London, featuring Thee Headcoatees! (UK Damaged Goods) 1994
The Sound of the Baskervilles (UK Overground) 1995

The albums listed above represent some portion of the oeuvre produced by Bill Hamper, the iconoclastic bandleader/producer/poet/painter/publisher known, among other pseudonyms, as The/Thee/Wild Billy Childish. Behind the tangled discography lies the singular, if proudly derivative, vision of an Englishman whose insanely prolific output stresses unpolished immediacy over quality control, taking the DIY ethos to ridiculous extremes. Thus has Mr. Childish—working under various band names and in an endless variety of personnel permutations—amassed a huge catalogue of musical products that vary greatly in quality but share a consistent lo-fi passion underlining their creator's obsessive sense of mission.

Childish first came on the scene in 1979 with the Pop Rivets, a sloppy mod-punk combo whose three self-released studio albums were a lot more enthusiastic than inspired. By 1982, the Pop Rivets had mutated into the (sometimes Thee, initially Mickey and the) Milkshakes, whose energetic garage rock—possessed by the spirit of Bo Diddley, the early Kinks and a legion of obscure no-hit wonders—was considerably catchier and more competently played. Though the Milkshakes' best work matched the fervor of their influences, the band was equally impressive for the prodigious volume of its output (in 1984, its most productive year, the band released no fewer than seven albums—four of them on the same day). Singer/guitarist Childish and Milkshakes partner Mickey Hampshire also served as behind-the-scenes Svengalis for sister group the Delmonas, who originally convened to sing backup with the Milkshakes and ended up releasing several discs of their own. In the mid-'80s, Childish traded the Milkshakes for the not-dissimilar Thee Mighty Caesars, whose original lineup included the Milkshakes' rhythm section and maintained a typically prolific output—much of it on Billy's own Hangman imprint, whose book-publishing arm has issued dozens of volumes of his left-wing poems and rants—through the second half of the decade.

During the Caesars' lifespan, Childish began churning out solo and side projects, working in a variety of collaborations and under an assortment of assumed names. **I've Got Everything Indeed** and **i remember** offer his idiosyncratic take on the blues; **The 1982 Cassetes** consists of even-more-ragged-than-usual early recordings. **Poems of Laughter and Violence** is a venomous spoken-word effort whose you-are-there ambience is a large part of its appeal. The dodgy **50 Albums Great** is a retrospective of sorts, with raw solo remakes of several items from previous releases.

Since 1989, the main vehicle for Billy's more accessible rock'n'roll impulses has been Thee Headcoats, a trio that includes Pop Rivets/Milkshakes/Mighty Caesars drummer Bruce Brand. The **Beached Earls** CD combines the vinyl releases **Beach Bums Must Die** and **The Earls of Suavedom** for a heaping thirty-song helping emphasizing Thee Headcoats' '60s garage-trash leanings. With a neat cover by Dan Clowes, **Heavens to Murgatroyd** (proudly proclaimed to be "mastered directly from vinyl") and **Headcoatitude** each feature plenty of catchy R&B/pop numbers. **Bo in Thee Garage** is a careless but frequently compelling Bo Diddley tribute.

The enjoyable live albums **Live! At the Wild Western Room** and **The Sound of the Baskervilles** are split between Thee Headcoats and the all-girl Headcoatees (actually, a reshuffled Delmonas), whose own releases are produced and largely written by Childish and employ Thee Headcoats (for fair play, if no other reason) as their backup group. Other Childish diversions include the Black Hands, a lineup with accordion, banjo and trumpet that plays deceptively bouncy, cheery-sounding music contrasted by Childish's harsh megaphone-filtered vocals and leftist finger-pointing.

Childish's continued insistence on making all of his musical whims available to the buying public leaves catalogue-surfing him a very tricky proposition, but careful sifting will reward the effort. Curious neophytes without unlimited free time, cash or patience are immediately recommended to **I Am the Billy Childish** (subtitled *Fifty Songs From Fifty Records*), a handy two-CD sampler of numerous outfits throughout the '80s complete with an extensive (no, make that daunting) discography, a printed interview and samples of Billy's painting and poetry. The eighteen-track **Native American Sampler**—which collects previously released Native American–themed cuts by various Childish-led/affiliated bands as a benefit for the tribal-rights organization Survival International—is a decent companion piece. [ss]

See also *TPRG*.

CHILDMAN

See *Consolidated.*

TONI CHILDS

Union (A&M) 1988
House of Hope (A&M) 1991
The Woman's Boat (DGC) 1994

Lumping Toni Childs in with other confessional singer/songwriters is too simple—and an unjustice. Childs brings an international tableau of sounds and experiences to her three albums. The Southern California native has lived all over the western United States and in England; her early musical experiences including playing with future members of the Red Hot Chili Peppers, the Bangles, World Party, Shriekback and Peter Gabriel's band, as well as fronting the first incarnation of Berlin. By the time she got around to recording on her own, the husky-voiced singer was homing in on a distinctive musical vision.

Union is stirring and captivating, a collection of mostly joyful emotions dressed up in world music tones, including backing vocals from African troupes in Zambia and Swaziland. Collaborating with David Ricketts (of David + David) and producer David Tickle, Childs alternates wide-angle messages—such as a plea for world peace, "Zimbabwae"—with more personal ruminations on self-realization ("Tin Drum") and the value of relationships ("Where's the Ocean"). There's a hypnotic, ambient quality to the music that nicely complements Childs' passionate emotive vocals.

House of Hope is a darker record; as it begins, Childs is struggling with a decision to leave her mate in "I've Got to Go Now" ("Must be addicted to all this pain/'Cause I keep coming back for the shame"). "Daddy's Song" hints at dark, buried secrets of the past, and many of the other tracks ("Where's the Light," "Put This Fire Out," the title song) trace an unrequited yearning for inner peace. The album raises more provocative questions than **Union,** but it misses that album's celebratory quality.

On **The Woman's Boat,** Childs goes for the whole kaboodle—life itself. Recorded mostly at Gabriel's Real World Studio in England, her third album starts with "Womb" and ends with "Death," mulling over virtually every other life experience during the nine songs in between. Inspired partially by a trip to Nepal, **The Woman's Boat** is filled with winding, rhythmic and moody songs that show both Indian and African influences. Members of the vocal group Zap Mama provide the uplifting background chorales, while a ringer's list of musicians includes Pakistani great Nusrat Fateh Ali Khan, Robert Fripp and Trey Gunn. Childs employs an exotic restraint for much of the album, though she cuts loose on the clanging "Predator," the bouncy title track and the driving "Lay Down Your Pain." This time, as the song cycle nears its end with "Long Time Coming" and "Death," Childs announces a sense of peace—a fulfilling resolution that one hopes won't preclude her making more music in the future. [gg]

CHILLS

The Lost EP (NZ Flying Nun) 1985 (Homestead) 1988
Kaleidoscope World (UK Creation) 1986 (Homestead) 1990
Brave Words (NZ Flying Nun) 1987 (Homestead) 1988
Submarine Bells (Slash/Warner Bros.) 1990
Soft Bomb (Slash/Reprise) 1992
Heavenly Pop Hits: The Best of the Chills (Aus. Flying Nun) 1994

MARTIN PHILLIPPS & THE CHILLS

Sunburnt (NZ Flying Nun) 1996

POP ART TOASTERS

Pop Art Toasters EP (Aus. Flying Nun) 1994

Perhaps the most widely known and beloved combo of New Zealand's '80s indie-pop boom, Dunedin's Chills—led by singer/writer/guitarist and sole charter member Martin Phillipps—made clean, understated, catchy music whose consistent taste and subtlety conspired to keep the band from having real commercial success in this country. At its best, the Chills' work boasted an undercurrent of dark uneasiness that clearly marked it as a vehicle for personal expression rather than mere genre exercise. **Kaleidoscope World,** which collects most of the band's early singles and compilation tracks, is a cornerstone of NZ pop; Homestead's CD version adds **The Lost** EP plus four more tracks. **Brave Words,** the band's first proper album, is disappointingly flawed, but still contains such gems as "House With 100 Rooms" and "Wet Blanket."

By the time the group (at this point a quartet with bassist Justin Harwood, keyboardist Andrew Todd and drummer James Stephenson) clinched a deal with a mainstream US label for **Submarine Bells,** the Chills had evolved a mature, restrained and affectingly personal approach that belied its original reputation as a singles band. Produced by Gary Smith, the album is a quietly authoritative winner, with songs like "Part Past Part Fiction," "Don't Be—Memory" and even the ostensibly cheery "Heavenly Pop Hit" carrying a muted air of all-encompassing heartbreak. The hushed title track concludes the album on a haunting note of faith.

Recorded in Los Angeles with a largely American cast (including Peter Holsapple, Lisa Mednick and Clay Idols leader Steve Schayer), the conceptually ambitious **Soft Bomb** finds Phillipps addressing personal themes while producing some of his most engaging music to date. The romantic "Double Summer" and the rueful "The Male Monster From the Id" take on tricky inter-sex issues, while "Song for Randy Newman Etc." movingly ponders the role of the artist in a philistine culture without condescension or self-congratulation, namechecking such kindred spirits as Brian Wilson, Syd Barrett, Scott Walker and Nick Drake. Van Dyke Parks' haunting orchestral arrangement for "Water Wolves" accentuates the song's chilling fatalism.

After touring behind **Soft Bomb,** Phillipps announced that he was putting the band name to rest and would henceforth release records under his own name. But the first thing to appear was the **Pop Art Toasters** EP, in which Phillipps and fellow New Zealand scene veterans David Kilgour and Noel Ward proffer five fluffy covers of obscure and semi-obscure vintage pop gems.

Heavenly Pop Hits is a good sixteen-track sampler drawn from the Chills' entire catalogue; initial pressings included a six-track rarities disc. [ss]

See also *Luna[2]; TPRG.*

ALEX CHILTON

Singer Not the Song EP7 (Ork) 1977
Like Flies on Sherbert (Peabody) 1979 (UK Aura) 1980 (Cooking Vinyl) 1996
Bach's Bottom (Ger. Line) 1981 (Razor & Tie) 1993
Live in London (UK Aura) 1982
Feudalist Tarts EP (Big Time) 1985 (Razor & Tie) 1994
Alex Chilton's Lost Decade (Fr. Fan Club) 1985
Document (UK Aura) 1985
Stuff (Fr. New Rose) 1987
High Priest (Big Time) 1987 (Razor & Tie) 1994
Black List EP (Fr. New Rose) 1990
19 Years: A Collection of Alex Chilton (Rhino) 1991
Clichés (Ardent) 1994
A Man Called Destruction (Ardent) 1995
1970 (Ardent) 1996

The unmistakable footprints of a legend do traipse indolently through **19 Years;** what you get in the workaday worlds of Alex Chilton's individual albums, however, is a lot more mortal. So much faith has been invested in this man who has never claimed to be anything more than what he is—an unhappy, standoffish Memphis singer and songwriter with the face of an altar boy and a knack for memorable, occasionally transcendent, pop tunes—that each time he releases one of his homey, smaller-than-life records, every time he sings "Volaré" rather than "Holocaust," it's as if he was willfully denying the legacy Big Star fans expect him to so proudly tote.

At his haunted best, Chilton sings like someone with a gun being held to his head; reluctance and release flow together in a prurient lifeforce sap being forced from the orchard's sorriest tree. (At his worst, he sounds like someone's holding a checkbook on him; few reputable performers can sound as distracted or uninterested in a studio performance.) Wisely, at least for Chilton, he got over the self-immolating allure of his endeavors early on, dropping out of the music grind for much of the '80s—after barely contributing to it in the half of the '70s left when Big Star collapsed. By 1985, at which time he unrusted his gears to produce the six charmingly mild-mannered (and New Orleans–inflected) R&B/pop songs of **Feudalist Tarts,** Chilton's decade-long solo career consisted of a live disc and two haphazardly created studio albums (**Bach's Bottom,** an intriguing stop/start hodgepodge expanded, minorly overdubbed and remixed for its 1993 CD edition, and **Like Flies on Sherbert**); the next nine years yielded a three-song single (1986's "No Sex" 12-inch), the six-song **Black List,** one new album (the casually winning, mostly covers **High Priest,** the 1994 CD of which adds four bonus tunes and the entire **Black List**) plus a bunch of compilations. The useful if sketchy **19 Years** mixes Big Star and Chilton recordings, overlooking **Bach's Bottom** but otherwise outlining the reeling stylistic progress of Chilton's sporadic music-making.

Perhaps spurred on by Big Star's intervening reunion, Chilton hit the mid-'90s in an unprecedented surge of recording (if not songwriting) productivity: two new studio albums in as many years. The first, **Clichés,** sails past his beloved "Volaré" into a full-blown concept and contains nothing but pre-rock pop standards sung and played alone on acoustic guitar (plus, briefly, an unsettling background rumble that sounds suspiciously like bleed from a heavy time-keeping foot). If that sounds ordinary or dull, think again—Chilton's spent his adulthood becoming an offhandedly brilliant vocalist, and his sensitive, naturalistic renderings of such oldies as "My Baby Just Cares for Me," "Let's Get Lost," "There Will Never Be Another You," "All of You" and Mel Tormé's "The Christmas Song" (plus a Bach gavotte and a Slide Hampton blues that underscore his matching instrumental sophistication) are unique and extraordinary, scruffily heartfelt.

Altogether different but nearly as wonderful, **A Man Called Destruction** sets a half-dozen Chilton originals and a typically offbeat array of covers (among them "Il Ribelle," "What's Your Sign Girl," Chris Kenner's "Sick and Tired" and Jan and Dean's "New Girl in School," complete with soaring falsetto) into a brassy electric soul/blues setting with swinging Memphis drumming, a stirring Leslied organ presence and Chilton's stabbing guitar leads for punctuation. The company's idiosyncratic version of spirited '60s southern soul makes the grooves glow with a comfortable warmth that Chilton rides and rolls with easy confidence and what might even be the sound of him enjoying the work. In this state of sonic bliss, Chilton's unexcited delivery helps sell even the silliest bits in the modest new songs, most of which find him at home in or around the blues: "Boplexity" is a blaring jam, "Devil Girl" puts his drink on R&B Coasters and "You're Lookin' Good" does its leering to a sturdy twelve-bar workout. Chilton may not be reaching for eternity here, but the music raises him right off the ground. [i]

See also *Big Star; TPRG.*

CHOCOLATE USA

All Jets Are Gonna Fall Today (Bar/None) 1993
Smoke Machine (Bar/None) 1994

Basking in the same warm lo-fi aesthetic as Sebadoh, Chocolate USA specializes in romantic reveries and catchy pop songs, sung in the voice of an innocent but precocious adolescent and backed by an orchestral array of cheap acoustic and toy instruments. Chocolate USA is primarily the vehicle of singer/guitarist/bassist Julian Koster, who formed the group as a high-school student in Tampa, Florida, naming it Miss America but changing the name when the pageant threatened to sue.

Besides starting a radio show, tape club and annual indie-rock festival, Koster and some friends recorded **All Jets Are Gonna Fall Today,** which they initially self-released on cassette. Sincerity drives his songwriting and the results are sweetly endearing. Listening to acoustic numbers like "The Shower Song," "Two Dogs" or "Luniks Furniture" is like eavesdropping on a moody teenager strumming his guitar alone in his bedroom. But Chocolate USA is nothing if not eclectic; although most of the album is acoustic slacker pop, "Skyphilis/Air Raid" kicks off as a pastiche of Tommy Dorsey's big band sound and glides into an extended free-jazz fantasy. Besides violin, guitar, bass, accordion and drums, the record employs toy piano, cardboard box, french horn, clarinet and turntable scratching; the tracks are interspersed with funny samples from TV, radio and snippets of a tape correspondence between two elderly women.

Following school and the reissue of the first album by Bar/None, Koster moved to Athens, Georgia, and then Queens, New York. Recorded in, among other places, an Athens attic, a Long Island basement and a Hoboken studio, **Smoke Machine** retains the determinedly unpretentious vibe of the first album, but the songwriting and arrangements are surer and more fully realized. His plaintive vocals—surrounded by a new group of gifted eccentrics (only violinist Liza Wakeman remains from the first LP) playing guitar, bass, concertina, viola, drums and piano—continue to find beauty in sadness and sadness in the most comical situations. It doesn't matter what the songs are about—bookbags, milk, cherry bombs, cows, "The Boy Who Stuck His Head in the Dryer (And Whirl'd Round n' Round)"—they come out sounding like the musings of a lonely little boy with a broken heart. [jt]

See also *Swales.*

CHOO CHOO TRAIN

See *Velvet Crush.*

CHOPPER

4play EP (Animal 5) 1989
Chopper (Aus. Zero Hour) 1991
Slogans and Jingles (Big Deal) 1993
Supersmile EP (Big Deal) 1994
Madhouse on Castle Street (Big Deal) 1995

Connecticut singer/songwriters Steven Deal and Robert Dietrich are Chopper. With a revolving assortment of bassists and drummers, the guitar-playing duo has released three full-length albums of hook-filled pop visions. Each disc is as rewarding as it is different.

Recorded as a trio, the 12-inch **4play** contains four songs, including "Caitlin Cries" and "Nice Girls (Don't Explode)." **Chopper,** however, does explode with a healthy ration of mod-influenced power chords and nifty melodies. Surrounding a rough yet reverent cover of the Creation's classic "How Does It Feel to Feel" are a slew of originals in the same spirit. The disc's highlight is the terse rocker "You're Tearing Me Up," reprised from **4play.**

The two packed away the mod influences on **Slogans and Jingles,** instead traveling the classic, chiming three-minute pop song route. The results are stunning: fourteen tracks of consistently enjoyable, boyishly sung numbers like the cutesy "Swirling Girl," the bubblegummy "Is It Love Inside?!?!" (which borrows its lead guitar riff from the Jaggerz' 1970 hit, "The Rapper") and a totally appropriate cover of the Records' "The Same Mistakes." The **Supersmile** EP contains two tunes from **Slogans and Jingles,** as well as covers of Stealers Wheel's "Stuck in the Middle With You," the Plimsouls' "Hush, Hush" (from an Australian tribute album) and the Buzzcocks' "Ever Fallen in Love?," given a delicate acoustic reading.

Another stylistic shift of sorts occurred with the release of **Madhouse on Castle Street,** which takes Chopper partway into country-rock. There's still some pure pop (most notably the opening "Run Away"), but the addition of mandolin and pedal steel guitar is a radical departure. The jaunty "Walter Byrd" scores points in the country vein, but the often melancholy song stylings of **Madhouse** are, on the whole, something of a disappointment after the fresh-faced pop of **Slogans and Jingles.** [jmb]

CHRISTIAN DEATH

Only Theatre of Pain (Frontier) 1982
Death Wish EP (Fr. L'Invitation au Suicide) 1984
Catastrophe Ballet (Fr. L'Invitation au Suicide) 1984 (It. Contempo) 1987 (Nostradamus) 1990
Ashes (Nostradamus) 1985 (Ger. Normal) 1988
The Wind Kissed Pictures EP (It. Supporti Fonografici) 1985 (Nostradamus/Chameleon) 1986
The Decomposition of Violets [tape] (ROIR) 1985 (It. Contempo) 1990

An Official Anthology of "Live" Bootlegs (UK Nostradamus) 1986
Atrocities (Ger. Normal) 1986
Jesus Christ Proudly Presents Christian Death (Ger. Normal) 1987
The Scriptures (UK Jungle) 1987
The Wind Kissed Pictures (past & present) (It. Supporti Fonografici) 1988
Sex and Drugs and Jesus Christ (UK Jungle) 1988 (Nostradamus/Dutch East India Trading) 1989
The Heretics Alive (UK Jungle) 1989 (Nostradamus/Dutch East India Trading) 1990
All the Love All the Hate Part One: All the Love (UK Jungle) 1989
All the Love All the Hate Part Two: All the Hate (UK Jungle) 1989
The Wind Kissed Pictures (past present & future) (It. Supporti Fonografici) 1990
Insanus, Ultio, Proditio, Misericordia Que (It. Supporti Fonografici) 1990
Jesus Points the Bone at You (Century Media) 1991
The Iron Mask (Cleopatra) 1992
Skeleton Kiss EP (Cleopatra) 1992
The Path of Sorrows (Cleopatra) 1993
Iconologia: Apparitions Dreams and Nightmares (Triple X) 1993
Sleepless Nights: Live 1990 (Cleopatra) 1993
Invocations: 1981–1989 (Cleopatra) 1993
The Doll's Theatre (Cleopatra) 1994
Sexy Death God (Nostradamus) 1994
The Rage of Angels (Cleopatra) 1994
Tales of Innocence: A Continued Anthology (Cleopatra) 1994
Death in Detroit (Cleopatra) 1995

ROZZ WILLIAMS

Every King a Bastard Son (Cleopatra) 1992
Whorse's Mouth (Triple X) 1996

SHADOW PROJECT

Shadow Project (Triple X) 1991
Dreams for the Dying (Triple X) 1992
In Tuned Out–Live '93 (Triple X) 1994

PREMATURE EJACULATION

Necessary Discomforts (Cleopatra) 1993
Estimating the Time of Death (Triple X) 1994

DAUCUS KAROTA

Shrine EP (Triple X) 1994

ROZZ WILLIAMS/HELTIR

Neue Sachlichkeit (Triple X) 1994

GITANE DEMONE

A Heavenly Melancholy EP (Hol. Cult Music) 1992
Lullabies for a Troubled World EP (Hol. Cult Music) 1993
Facets of Blue (Cleopatra) 1993
With Love & Dementia (Cleopatra) 1995

ROZZ WILLIAMS AND GITANE DEMONE

Dream Home Heartache (Triple X) 1995

EVA O

Past Time (Cleopatra) 1993

EVA O. HALO EXPERIENCE

A Demon's Fall for an Angel's Kiss (Cleopatra) 1994

SUPER HEROINES

Love and Pain (Cleopatra) 1993

In the early '80s, an androgynous teenaged street performer named Rozz Williams founded Christian Death in Los Angeles, creating what would become one of the most prolific, enduring and beloved gothic acts of all time. (Bauhaus fans have had plenty to chew over with this crowd.) But few groups have histories as tangled as Christian Death's: the band has gone through countless lineup changes and thrown off a multitude of side projects and solo careers. There have also been vicious altercations between Williams and guitarist Valor over rights to the name. Williams was there first, but Valor claims *he* deserves sole use of it since he's been the lineup's only constant for the past decade. For a time, the two men led separate versions of Christian Death; Williams' higher profile and sheer volume of releases make him the undeclared victor of this battle.

Valor's side attempts to prove its superiority with **Jesus Points the Bone at You,** a best-of sampling of singles from 1986 through 1991. The rambling, pretentious and often nonsensical liner notes provide much more entertainment than the bombastic music: ". . . Christian Death music always resounds the conflict between mankind and the natural order, albeit chaos." Whatever. Valor's gruff voice would be more appropriate in a metal or hard-rock setting; he lacks the elegant sensuality that marks great goth vocalists. Also included is **All the Hate**'s self-indulgent (but amusing) "I Hate You," which features Valor's snotty five-year-old son gleefully screeching out profanity-laden lyrics over crunchy punk/metal guitar riffs.

The Iron Mask finds Williams taking a brief break from his other projects to hoist the Christian Death banner once again. Along with ex–Super Heroines guitarist/vocalist Eva O., Williams reworks songs originally released on Christian Death's first three albums (the ones with which he established the group a decade earlier). Despite the changes, longtime fans will quickly recognize old favorites like "Figurative Theatre" **(Only Theatre of Pain)** and "Death Wish." Williams sounds strangely subdued throughout most of the gritty, trying-hard-to-be-ghastly material, and things truly drag without his theatrical delivery. The songs were much better the first time around.

As if the **Iron Mask** round of do-overs wasn't enough, Williams and the band rework those same old songs once again for the **Skeleton Kiss** EP, which contains two versions of "Skeleton Kiss" and one of "Spiritual Cramp." The EP also includes a live recording of the first album's "Resurrection." Again, there's nothing terribly exciting or different about the versions.

Williams rediscovers his charismatic, energetic self on **The Path of Sorrows.** There are some remarkably good songs here, as well as such misguided curiosities as a strange cover of the Velvet Underground's "Venus in Furs." But the tension-packed, wailing "Book of Lies" is first-rate, as is the eerie, bleakly atmospheric "Mother" (which *strongly* resembles Bauhaus' classic "Hollow Hills"). And "Psalm (Maggot's Lair)," a scathing spoken-word piece that attacks Jesus Christ and glorifies murder (paradoxically backed by a soothing choir), is among Williams' best pieces.

In 1993, Williams reunited the original Christian Death lineup (veteran punk guitarist Rikk Agnew and drummer George Belanger, but not bassist James Gearty) for a show in Los Angeles; the event is preserved on **Iconologia.** The rough-edged live set includes songs from **Only Theatre of Pain** (the only full-length studio album this particular incarnation recorded), Lou Reed's "Kill Your Sons" and two new songs. Aside from a disturbing-but-fascinating intro featuring a jarring array of samples, this historical document is less intriguing and exciting than it might appear to be.

Sleepless Nights documents another of Williams' Christian Death career-overview performances, this one from 1990 and featuring both Agnew and Eva O. on guitars. The sound is horrible, the performances competent but perfunctory. But **Sleepless Nights** seems like a rollicking good time next to the indescribably bad **Invocations: 1981–1989.** a collection of bootleg recordings from various Christian Death shows so unlistenable that it actually includes the band's apology for the sound quality. **Invocations** also tacks on an early studio version of "Sleepwalk" (which appeared in a different form on 1984's **Catastrophe Ballet**), as well as three previously unreleased demos from the band's first years. None of these additions justify making fans pay for this dreadful release, though.

Yet another so-so live recording, this one from Halloween '81, **The Doll's Theatre** is a limited-edition CD that's essentially another excuse to make loyal followers waste money as they try to keep their collections complete. How many live versions of "Cavity" or "Figurative Theatre" does a person really need to hear?

Breaking the live-album thread, the band returned to the studio for **The Rage of Angels,** which Williams again opens with a sacrilegious spoken-word piece, "Trust (The Sacred and Unclean)." Except for a jaunty, likable cover of David Bowie's "Panic in Detroit," the album is virtually indistinguishable from **The Path of Sorrows:** the same melodramatic vocal delivery dwelling on the same lyrical subjects, all set to the same jagged guitar and spooky effects.

Death in Detroit consists of remixes of various Christian Death classics ("Spiritual Cramp," "Figurative Theatre," "Skeleton Kiss") by members of Spahn Ranch, Rosetta Stone, Die Krupps and others. The album also contains covers of "Panic in Detroit" and "Venus in Furs" that would leave David Bowie and Lou Reed in shock. With varying degrees of success, the songs veer from grating industrial bombast to eerie sensuality. A sinewy version of "Figurative Theatre" by Jürgen Engler of Die Krupps and the multi-layered take on "Panic in Detroit" by Zero Gravity's Len Del Rio are truly original interpretations of the material.

Williams and Valor put out a vast amount of material as a unified Christian Death before becoming competitors; some of their best work together is compiled on **Tales of Innocence: A Continued Anthology.** Other than several studio outtakes, the tracks are mainly concert recordings. As with most Christian Death live albums, the fidelity is dicey and the performances strangely unenthusiastic. Still, the album has the distinction of recording Williams and Valor working compatibly together. And some of Valor's songs do turn out extremely well, after all. The Cult-ish "Jezebel's Tribulation" is spirited fun, while "Strange Fortune" finds him crooning with surprising delicacy, accompanied by spare acoustic guitar and slightly ominous percussion.

Williams' spoken-word **Every King a Bastard Son** is the most hair-raising poetry likely to be encountered outside a satanic cult read-in. Sickening knives-scraping-bones sound effects embellish "Mind Fuck (Soundtrack to a Murder)" as he gleefully spits out lines like, "He has, among other things, been decapitated . . . Solid metal stripping off his skin . . ." Unless you're an actual sadist, you *really* don't want to know about the rest of this deliberately horrific creation. Williams continues the nightmarish journey on **Whorse's Mouth.** If anything, his recitations are even more graphically disgusting. On "Raped," for example, a Williams cohort languidly describes (in excruciating detail) how he's going to rape a woman he's apparently been stalking, how he'll glory in her pain and humiliation. It's a stretch to imagine who would actually *enjoy* this, but that's undoubtedly the point. If Williams' aim is to make listeners exceedingly queasy, he surely succeeds.

Challenging himself to lead a successful band without relying on the drawing power of the Christian Death name, Williams formed Shadow Project with Eva O. on vocals and guitars, keyboardist Paris and a terminally unstable rhythm section. Fans remained loyal, but that probably has a lot to do with the fact that **Shadow Project** doesn't sound any different. In his trademark feline croon, Williams tackles pet topics: organized religion, violence and death. "Death Plays His Role," "Holy Hell" and "Red Handed" make his beliefs unsettlingly vivid. Eva's guitar work is appropriately heavy-handed, and she frequently joins Williams for wailing, chilling choruses in her strong, throaty alto. Paris contributes subtly ominous synth effects to sharpen the edgy undercurrents.

Paris opens **Dreams for the Dying** with a dramatic organ instrumental passage before the bruising guitar and howling harmonies start in earnest. Williams' lyrics are, of course, obsessed with the obvious: death ("Funeral Rites"), religion ("Static Jesus," "Thy Kingdom Come") and violence ("Night Stalker"). The music is notably more spacious and melodic, but still aims to provide the usual unease.

Most of the songs on Shadow Project's first two albums appear on **In Tuned Out—Live '93,** taped before an appreciative Los Angeles audience. The renditions aren't substantially different from the studio versions, however. There's no between-song chatter—the band determinedly plows through one song after another with scant pause. The studio albums are a safer bet; the production values are much better and they reveal just as much personality.

Premature Ejaculation is Williams' uninspired collaboration with Chuck Collision. **Necesary Discomforts** contains six long, dreary, monotonous instrumentals: hell's version of Muzak? With typical calculated-to-offend taste, the cover photo shows an angel-faced young boy in a suggestive, full-frontal nude pose. Likewise, **Estimating the Time of Death** overflows with ho-hum instrumental "soundscapes"—boring collages of haphazard samples—that are even more slow-moving and unimaginative than the debut. Nine and a half minutes of dragging-chains sound effects make up one "song." The only imaginable use for this is as a Halloween novelty joke, to scare the water out of the costumed tykes at your door.

Williams fares *much* better in Daucus Karota, the band he formed with bassist Mark Barone, drummer Christian Omar Madrigal Izzo and guitarist Roxy. The enjoyable **Shrine** offers up flashy, slightly glammy rock, while Williams abandons his gore-drenched goth ways and instead imitates Bryan Ferry (especially on the sauntering "Angel"). Daucus Karota also pays homage to another idol, Iggy Pop, with a deft cover of

"Raw Power." (The EP was co-produced by former Iggy/Bowie sideman Hunt Sales.) Unfortunately, at only five tracks, **Shrine**'s good time doesn't last nearly long enough. It figures. Just when Williams finally hits on a winning formula, he suddenly decides to get miserly with it.

Not content with the many projects already on his résumé, Williams formed Heltir and released **Neue Sachlichkeit** ("new objectivity"), a needless collage of weird samples and distorted loops that shows slightly more life and imagination than Premature Ejaculation.

Proving she can do more than sing in wailing goth style, Christian Death keyboardist/sometime-vocalist Gitane Demone turned to club-ready dance music in her solo work. On **A Heavenly Melancholy,** her vocals veer from impressively broad-ranged to Liza-like overstatement. The title track is a bouncy, fluffy bit that would fit in nicely at some Euro-trash soirée; über-sleek and pseudo-sophisticated, but good fun. Except for the ever-present dominatrix gear, Demone tones it way down on **Lullabies for a Troubled World,** possibly the most enjoyable music released by anyone in the Christian Death camp. Simple, pretty piano provides the main accompaniment for Demone's classy, expressive vocals. She's finally learned how to sing with emotion—and not go over the top. It's hard to believe this is the same woman whose shrieks and screams made some of Christian Death's albums such perilous listening. The somber, haunting "Sounds of War" and the evocative, quietly elegant "Lullaby for a Troubled Man" display her considerable talent with commendable panache.

The contents of both **A Heavenly Melancholy** and **Lullabies for a Troubled World** appear on **Facets of Blue**—along with some amazing live tracks recorded in Holland: "Golden Age," "Little Birds" and Cole Porter's "Love for Sale." The gorgeous "Golden Age" (slightly marred by her zeal) is actually a Christian Death song written by Valor. **With Love & Dementia** documents a 1994 Demone performance in France; Rozz Williams assists with vocals on two tracks. Like her previous releases, the album features Demone's solo work alongside piano-based versions of older Christian Death material ("Tales of Innocence," "Lament") and a pop standard ("I Only Have Eyes for You"). Unfortunately, the mood is destroyed on "Sleepwalk," wherein Demone and Williams proffer the same kind of screeching, cats-in-heat performance that characterized much of their work together in Christian Death.

Demone and Williams only occasionally slip into that headache-inducing style on **Dream Home Heartache,** their first official duo album. Williams indulges his adulation for Bryan Ferry in a slo-motion cover of Roxy Music's "In Every Dream Home a Heartache." Unlike the original, however, this one never kicks in at the end, and instead spirals away on Demone's frantic wailing. The rest of the songs mesh her lounge act style with his hyper-dramatic tendencies, making for a surreal experience that could be the score to some warped, shadowy Broadway musical.

After playing in the Speed Queens, Eva O. led LA's Super Heroines in the '80s; this tough metal band, which briefly included future Hole bassist Jill Emery, disbanded in '87 when Eva left to form Shadow Project with Williams. (Emery followed her, and is the bassist on **Shadow Project,** for which she did a spot of writing as well.) **Love and Pain** contains tracks from an unreleased album as well as two early songs and some live tracks. The sound is poor, especially on the concert recordings, but even that can't mask Super Heroines' immense power.

When Shadow Project disbanded and her involvement with Williams' new Christian Death gained speed, Eva released **Past Time** as a sampler of her career. Three new solo songs join tracks by the Speed Queens, Super Heroines and Christian Death. The early material is frustratingly muddy; better production would've done wonders.

Eva's next move was shocking but probably predictable for someone in the Christian Death circle: she became a born-again Christian and released **A Demon's Fall for an Angel's Kiss.** As with every Christian Death–affiliated project, the album's lyrics dwell on the war between good and evil . . . but this time, evil *doesn't* conquer. A relatively delicate acoustic ballad, "Take a Jesus," demonstrates a previously unrealized knack for subtlety. Still, much of **Demon's Fall** incorporates her usual heavy-handed guitar technique—which, combined with the religious lyrics, brings her uncomfortably close to Stryper. [ky]

See also *Faith & the Muse, Hole, Mephisto Walz; TPRG.*

CHRISTMAS

See *Combustible Edison.*

CHROME CRANKS

Chrome Cranks (PCP) 1994
Dead Cool (Crypt) 1995
Love in Exile (PCP) 1996

CHROME CRANKS/FOETUS

Vice Squad Dick EP (PCP) 1994

Put a couple of sanitation engineers together in a room and, before long, you'll be inundated with yarns about the unearthing of everything from diamond rings to human heads (and, more than likely, an argument or two about which of those makes a better find). The same is true of junk hoarders like Chrome Cranks' Peter Aaron and Jerry Teel (the former conductor of New York sleaze supremos the Honeymoon Killers), whose collective obsession with primitive garage-rock, backwoods rockabilly—indeed, no-budget recreation of all stripes—provides plenty of common ground for the erection of this trash-culture landfill.

The quartet's self-titled debut could easily pass for a reincarnation of Teel's old band, with sonic debris piled just as high as the lyrics' softcore debauchery—not that there's anything wrong with that. "Doll in a Dress" and "Lo-End Buzz" don't offer much in the way of, uh, subtext, but the claret-splattered guitar of William Weber (late of GG Allin's Murder Junkies) provides plenty of sinister B-movie edge. The collaboration with Foetus never really gets on track, since the co-conspirators seem to have very different ideas about what constitutes a pulp-fiction vibe, with the Cranks favoring a hard-drinking Raymond Chandler portrayal, while Thirlwell shifts into deep James Ellroy–fueled psychodrama.

The ominous bass/maracas duel that opens the stuttering sludge-a-billy title track sets the tone for **Dead Cool,** a gristly swamp-trawl that threatens to tunnel out of the Lower East Side and not stop until it reaches the

Big Easy. With ex–Sonic Youth/Pussy Galore/Bewitched drummer Bob Bert aboard, the Cranks are free to slip one level further into the primordial ooze, which clearly sparks Aaron. His interjections—he's content to groan, yelp and whisper curt phrases into the squall—charge the air with a Pentecostal fervor. One man's trash is another man's treasure. [dss]

CIBO MATTO

Cibo Matto EP (El Diablo) 1995
Viva! La Woman (Warner Bros.) 1996

New York voice-and-keyboards duo Cibo Matto (the name is Italian for "food madness") began as a side project of the legendary short-lived Laito Lychee. The two Japanese expatriates in that group, Miho Hatori and Yuka Honda, started writing songs inspired by the tremendous variety of comestibles available in NYC. They quickly evolved into an unconventional but delightful live act: tiny Hatori whispering, shouting, singing and rapping into her microphone, Honda behind her keyboard, impassively drawing out one wildly funky, unrecognizable sample after another. ("Apple" briefly uses a riff from Gilberto Gil's "Ponto de Lanca Africana"; that's as close as they ever get to obviousness, which is to say, not very.)

Viva! La Woman, the pair's first full-length album, contains most of Cibo Matto's early live staples—"Sugar Water," "Beef Jerky," "Birthday Cake" (with its unforgettable "shut up and eeeeeat!" chorus)—together with a couple of ringers, like the languid "White Pepper Ice Cream" and a very peculiar cover of Anthony Newley's "The Candy Man." Hatori plays up the cute-Japanese-chick thing, aided by her *very* strong accent, but consistently tricky, witty lyrics save her: "We love LSD/We die easily/Can we just say *c'est la vie*?" And Honda is amazing, gracing the fast songs with snatches of soulful organ (she *was* briefly in Brooklyn Funk Essentials) and the slow ones with great weird stuff, like the keening tone at the end of "Artichoke."

The **Cibo Matto** EP collects two early singles—initial versions of "Birthday Cake" and "Beef Jerky," a ferocious take on "Know Your Chicken" with Russell Simins (of the Jon Spencer Blues Explosion, also a member of Butter 08, the Cibo Matto women's side band) drumming and a creamy cover of Soundgarden's "Black Hole Sun"—and tosses in an improvised instrumental, "Crumbs." [ddw]

CICCONE YOUTH

See *Sonic Youth.*

CIRCLE JERKS

Group Sex (Frontier) 1980
Wild in the Streets (Faulty Products) 1982
Golden Shower of Hits (LAX) 1983 (Avenue) 1992
Wönderful (Combat Core) 1985
VI (Relativity) 1987
Group Sex/Wild in the Streets (Frontier) 1988
Gig (Relativity) 1992
Oddities Abnormalities and Curiosities (Mercury) 1995

VARIOUS ARTISTS

The Decline of Western Civilization (Slash) 1980

Singer Keith Morris, who left Black Flag after appearing on its debut single, formed the Circle Jerks with ex–Redd Kross guitarist Greg Hetson in Los Angeles in 1980. Fast, loud and loose, the Jerks became one of the region's most popular and durable slam bands. Except for the bored-sounding **Wönderful,** the '80s albums give a fair studio shake to the band's crude live shambles, complete with typically loopy cover choices like Jackie DeShannon's "Put a Little Love in Your Heart" (on **Wild in the Streets**) and the stack of classics that became the riotous "Jerks on 45" medley on **Golden Shower of Hits.**

The quartet—which, by **Wönderful,** had come to include Zander Schloss on bass and Keith Clark on drums—ran out of gas in the late '80s, however, and its members moved on to other enterprises. Morris passed along what he knew to the Hangmen (whom he managed) and worked behind the scenes with other bands as well. Hetson joined Bad Religion. Schloss collaborated with Joe Strummer on a number of projects, joined Thelonious Monster briefly and formed the Low and Sweet Orchestra, which has come to include actor Dermot Mulroney and a member of the Pogues. But the Circle Jerks never officially disbanded—a fact loudly confirmed in 1992 on a raging and rude live album. Recorded at shows in California and Mexico, **Gig** rips up the floorboards with twenty-two doses of essential Jerkdom, including "When the Shit Hits the Fan," "Wild in the Streets," "Beat Me Senseless" and "Coup d'Etat." Sure it's fifteen years too late, but the quartet plays 'em like it means 'em, and the hot sound (courtesy producer Paul du Gré) does justice to the spirited performances.

That blast across the world's bow was followed by the group's first studio album in eight years. **Oddities Abnormalities and Curiosities** finds Morris, Hetson, Schloss and Clark slashing away enthusiastically at songs that have teenage energy and adult lyrics. Striking a Peter Pan pose, at least they don't pretend to be anything they're not—namely, young kids. (Ironically, Robyn Hitchcock's "I Wanna Destroy You," with guest vocals by notorious raver Debbie Gibson and L7's Suzi Gardner, is the only song with real punk conviction.) Producer Niko Bolas keeps the sound loose and raunchy, and the band lands somewhere between post-Rotten Pistols and mid-'70s Stones, making the better-than-fair album more of a mature second start than a continuation of the Circle Jerks' original slouching bratcore. [i]

See also *Bad Religion, Redd Kross, Thelonious Monster; TPRG.*

CIV

Set Your Goals (Revelation/Lava/Atlantic) 1995

GORILLA BISCUITS

Start Today (Revelation) 1989

Much as Green Day magically rendered an old musical genre fresh and understandable to the adults who run MTV (and thereby millions of know-nothings too young to be bothered by historical precedence), New York's CIV put business suits on hardcore punk and dived into the mainstream moshpit as if they had just discovered the cure for boredom. Able to claim real roots in the scene—singer Civ (Anthony Civocelli), bassist Arthur (Smilios) and drummer Sammy (Siegler) all spent their favorite years in late-'80s Queens punks Gorilla Biscuits; **Set Your Goals** co-producer Walter Schreifels of Quicksand was one of that band's two guitarists—the quartet keeps the hardcore hard while including other, more accessible, styles on **Set Your Goals.** Armed with a clearheaded pop sense, CIV makes punk rock intensity palatable without sugarcoating it.

Looting the record store alongside Rancid and others, CIV plunders the past with impunity. On **Set Your Goals,** the quartet does a credible imitation of the mid-'70s Dictators, ties together elements of British new wave (subtly quoting the Clash in "Choices Made," blatantly imitating the Sex Pistols in "Boring Summer," re-creating a cheeralong atmosphere somewhere between Generation X and Sham 69 for "So Far, So Good . . . So What"), honors pioneer thrash (covering Kraut's "All Twisted") and even acknowledges a Stray Cats strut ("Set Your Goals") in service of well-crafted songs that deliver their tough, uplifting messages and standard gripes with impressive pop smarts. Making the most of clear sound, tight, unfussy playing and a full complement of rhythmic shifts (these guys remember when moshing was a dance tempo, not a slamming catch-all), CIV recycles with detailed dignity.

As a prelude, **Start Today** has all the speed, intensity and raw-throated aggression—but a less pronounced pop streak—of CIV and expresses sensible opinions about the same sorts of things. This exceptionally intelligent, articulate, well-played and clearly recorded hardcore rip would be totally killer if Civ's voice weren't so harsh. Still, highlights include an attack on prejudgment ("Two Sides"), an objection to racist punks ("Degradation") and a motivational message about "Competition," complete with a whistled bit. [i]

See also *Quicksand.*

CLARISSA

See *Snatches of Pink.*

SONNY CLARK MEMORIAL QUARTET

See *John Zorn.*

GILBY CLARKE

See *Guns n' Roses.*

CLAWHAMMER

Poor Robert EP (Aus. Grown Up Wrong) 1989
Get Yer Heh Heh's Out [tape] (Trigon) 1989
Clawhammer (Sympathy for the Record Industry) 1990
Double Pack Whack Attack EP (Sympathy for the Record Industry) 1990
Q: Are We Not Men? A: We Are Not Devo (Sympathy for the Record Industry) 1991
Ramwhale (Sympathy for the Record Industry) 1992
Pablum (Epitaph) 1993
Thank the Holder Uppers (Interscope/Atlantic) 1995

With a moniker cribbed from Captain Beefheart, you wouldn't suspect ex–Pontiac Brothers guitarist Jon Wahl's baby to mewl forth much in the way of pub-rock revivalism. And you'd be mostly right. Locked into a stupefyingly precise dada-blues/hard-rock fusion on **Poor Robert,** the quartet zooms along like a dragster doing 110 mph with cruise control (particularly on a hard-as-nails version of the Fab Four's less-than-robust "Everybody's Got Something to Hide . . .").

Unfettered by standard song structure on much of the eponymous longplayer, Wahl's mercurial yelp skitters across measures like Richard Hell at his most dislocated. At times ("Papa's Got Us All Tied in Knots"), Clawhammer sounds like Half Japanese gone classic rock. Then again, at the end of the finale, the group indulges in a spate of angular jamming that sounds like vintage Allman Brothers. That they never actually parrot the good Captain is to Clawhammer's credit; that they can evoke his spirit as convincingly as they do on "Warm Spring Night" is nothing short of eerie. On **Double Pack Whack Attack,** Wahl and his cohorts inflict varied degrees of damage to faves by Patti Smith, Pere Ubu and Devo, a band that seems to be a sort of talisman for Clawhammer. Taking a whack at covering (with the blessing of Mark Mothersbaugh) the spudboys' seminal debut album in its entirety yields an end product that falls somewhere between tribute and rumination.

Ramwhale's vicious production can't mask the fact that this mostly unsatisfying, overly boogie-drenched collection indicates Wahl is holding back (or is perhaps impeded by his double duty as drummer/token male in his wife's band, the Red Aunts—not to mention guitarist Chris Bagarozzi's moonlighting in thrash-funk outfit Down by Law). **Pablum** loosens the wingnuts palpably: Wahl barrels from gravel-gargle (on the visceral "Vigil Smile") to muezzin wail (on the Bill Burroughs biograph, "William Tell") without so much as popping a lozenge. Clawhammer also forges a welcome return to its radar-gun-defying speedball antics on the tequila-and-ephedrine paroxysm "Montezuma's Hands."

On its overdue major-label bow, **Thank the Holder Uppers,** the foursome caper rowdily like (dead end) kids set loose in a candy store. The sonic debris launched—particularly on the protracted "Five Fifths Dead"—ushers in a whole new era of reasons to duck and cover. [dss]

See also *Wayne Kramer & Mick Farren; TPRG.*

CLEAN

Boodle Boodle Boodle EP (NZ Flying Nun) 1981
Great Sounds (NZ Flying Nun) 1982
Oddities (NZ Flying Nun) 1983 (UK Flying Nun) 1994
Live Dead Clean EP (NZ Flying Nun) 1986
Compilation (NZ Flying Nun) 1986 (Homestead) 1988
In-a-Live EP (NZ Flying Nun) 1989
Vehicle (Rough Trade) 1990
Modern Rock (NZ Flying Nun) 1994 (Summershine) 1995

GREAT UNWASHED

Clean Out of Our Minds (NZ Flying Nun) 1983
Singles (NZ Flying Nun) 1984
Collection (NZ Flying Nun) 1992

CLEAN/GREAT UNWASHED

Oddities 2 [tape] (NZ Flying Nun) 1988

VARIOUS ARTISTS

Cleaned Out EP7 (Dark Beloved Cloud) 1992

The first band to appear on New Zealand's vaunted Flying Nun label (with the "Tally-Ho!" 7-inch in 1981), the Clean technically existed for a mere eighteen months before sending its members (David Kilgour, Hamish Kilgour, Robert Scott and, at times, Peter Gutteridge) off to a multitude of other projects. But over the years, the trio, which always wrote collectively, with all three members switching off on lead vocals, has reunited with inconsistent consistency, resulting in a bunch of new records and live performances from a group most fans thought they'd never hear or see again.

Just as amazing as its short life is the fact that the band's essential output consisted of two EPs: the five-track **Boodle Boodle Boodle** and the seven-track **Great Sounds** (which theoretically has a much longer title, and is referred to on the jacket spine as **Yet Another Clean EP**). Both records were "produced" by Tall Dwarf Chris Knox (that is, he provided the Teac 4-track) and offer up short sharp shots of super-shambolic, super-perky garage-pop that's deceptive in its simplicity. From the groovy organ swing of "Beatnik" to the loping "Anything Could Happen" and the lengthier drone of "Point That Thing Somewhere Else," Clean songs were exercises in unbridled minimalism and maximum impact. David Kilgour didn't play a lot of notes, but his guitar provided a haunting, half-psychedelic, half-spy-movie tone, with sleek, fuzzy lines that could lay down a trance *and* inspire sing-song silliness. The Clean was folksy, lo-fi, precious, aggressive, baroque and naïve all at once, and always knew just how many times to repeat a hook.

Compilation collects some, but not all, of the early stuff, including highlights from the two EPs and "Tally Ho!"; the import CD tacks on six live tracks. **Odditties** is just that, the veritable odds-and-sods collection; originally released on cassette, the CD also has extra material. And as the title would suggest, **Live Dead Clean** (recorded in '81 and '82, with several songs not found on the previous vinyl releases) was thought to be posthumous. But before that record even came out, there was already the Great Unwashed, which saw the Kilgour brothers taking up with original bassist (and one-time Chill, though practically every Kiwi musician can say that) Peter Gutteridge in the place of Robert Scott, who'd gone and started the Bats. Just to further confuse the discography, the **Odditties 2** cassette mingles outtakes and live tracks (from '79 to '84) by the Clean and the Great Unwashed.

Now then. In 1988, Kilgour, Kilgour and Scott played a reunion gig in London, resulting in the sublime and frenzied **In-a-Live** EP, which features five of the band's best old songs, recorded, amazingly enough, on a 16-track board. At the same time, thanks to the Homestead reissue of **Compilation** (as well as the efforts of the Chills, the Tall Dwarfs and the Verlaines), there was more international interest than ever in the band. Next thing you know, the Clean made what was technically its very first album. **Vehicle** finds the band in immaculate form, churning out little diamond cuts of nervous guitar, earnest vocal harmonies and pesky little hooks that sting, tickle and shock. The sound quality is better and the rhythms more elastic, but otherwise it's as if they never left. "Draw(in)g to a (W)hole," "Dunes," "Big Cat" and "Diamond Shine" would all be candidates for the best little singles in the world if they came in 7-inch form; songs like "Home" and "I Can See" are gorgeously shimmering ballads.

The Clean toured some in support of **Vehicle** and then scattered again. David began a solo career, Robert continued with the Bats and Hamish moved to New York, where he and his wife formed the Mad Scene (before that, he briefly played with Bailter Space). In 1994, with little fanfare—basically, the three of them found out they were going to be in Dunedin at the same time—**Modern Rock** was recorded and released. Suggesting influences like the Velvet Underground, Nick Drake and maybe even Stereolab (though the Clean has always wielded the same sort of rolling keyboard trickery), it's a more grown-up affair that floats off-kilter melodies and tiny tensile guitar in a slower, softer swirl of cloudy organ lines and spacey electric piano textures, with liberal use of strings and folk instruments. The old teenage energy is missed, but the sweet deadpan vocals and reliably airy textures still deliver, resulting in a record that's pretty, experimental and highly atmospheric.

Cleaned Out is an American tribute 7-inch (plus a one-song flexi), with contributions by Sleepyhead, Uncle Wiggly, Kickstand, Airlines and Giant Mums. The sleeve drawing is by Hamish Kilgour, who also thought up the title. And in an unprecedented bout of activity (by Clean standards), the band began working on another record not long after **Modern Rock** [jc]

See also *Bailter Space, Bats, David Kilgour, Mad Scene; TPRG.*

CLEANERS FROM VENUS

See *Martin Newell.*

CLICK

See *E-40.*

GEORGE CLINTON

Computer Games (Capitol) 1982
You Shouldn't-Nuf Bit Fish (Capitol) 1983
Some of My Best Jokes Are Friends (Capitol) 1985
R&B Skeletons in the Closet (Capitol) 1986
The Mothership Connection (Live From Houston) (Capitol) 1986
The Best of George Clinton (Capitol) 1986
Atomic Clinton! [tape] (Capitol) 1988
The Cinderella Theory (Paisley Park/Warner Bros.) 1989
Sample Some of Disc–Sample Some of DAT (AEM) 1993
Hey Man . . . Smell My Finger (Paisley Park/Warner Bros.) 1993

GEORGE CLINTON AND THE P-FUNK ALLSTARS

T.A.P.O.A.F.O.M. (550 Music/Epic) 1996

George Clinton will never lose the respect of the children of the P, not as long as hip-hoppers continue sampling such Rosetta Stones of funk as "Atomic Dog," "Flashlight" and "One Nation Under a Groove." Actually, that isn't the point at all: his unassailable stature as the primary architect of booty-moving funk is as solid and reliable as the monumental grooves of his music. That's a given. The tricky bit for an active musical legend like Clinton is staying in the game as a contemporary contender, not just the beloved igniter of an eternal flame. In a culture so dependent on change, there are precious few veterans who can—if they even opt to try—keep doing the hip moves without looking like grandpa in bellbottoms.

Clinton in the '90s has been aided immeasurably by his crazy cool, his easy rapport with rap stars raised on the crypto-spiritual essence of his P-Funk records, the corporate support of an influential fan, the growing knowledge of vintage funk among a wide audience exposed to it via roundabout channels and the election of a funk-free president with the same surname. As a result, Clinton hasn't fallen off much from where he stood in his commercial heyday two decades earlier. An endless road of muscle-relaxing, mind-boggling four-hour partyjam throwdowns (trimmed back to a mere blip in time for the short-attention-span Lollapalooza crowd in '94) keeps Clinton's reputation for doing it until everyone's satisfied intact, while an intermittent flow of reissues (like **Tear the Roof Off 1974–1980,** an annotated two-CD compilation of classics released in '93) is slowly making his voluminous back catalogue available to those who need it.

The only area where the 1941-born (in North Carolina) titan has slowed way down is in the record-making department. Signing to Prince's ill-fated Paisley Park label added only two new albums to his discography (which had stalled out with the end of his Capitol deal in the mid-'80s; **Atomic** is a cassette of remixes). **The Cinderella Theory** and **Hey Man . . . Smell My Finger** are similar in that they both find room for enormous rosters of celebrity vocalists (given more to do than simply tributary shootouts) and manage to preserve Clinton's brightly hued personality and rhythmic primacy in comfortably modern settings. That said, the first is appreciably more self-conscious in its attempt to reassert relevance to the R&B mainstream, while the followup shows Clinton's growing ease in and around hip-hop. (He even does the most conventional thing imaginable: sample old P-Funk jams!)

The Cinderella Theory's "Why Should I Dog U Out?" inverts Clinton's influence on Prince with falsetto vocals and crisp one-chord guitar action, but the whimsical lyrics (and interpolation of "How Much Is That Doggie in the Window?") are strictly George's. Otherwise, the album is a bit plain, making a few good ideas go a long way, and relying heavily on Public Enemy's Flavor Flav and Chuck D for the music-analyzing "Tweakin'," bits of which found their way to **Smell My Finger**'s "Paint the White House Black."

The second of Clinton's Paisley Park albums is stronger fun, boasting the epic "White House," the chanted anthem "Rhythm and Rhyme" and the Rodney King–defending "Martial Law." (It also has "If True Love," a soggy soul ballad co-written and sung by Clinton's son Trey Lewd, and "The Big Pump," a dopey club collaboration with Prince.) Among the cameos popping out of the speakers are Ice Cube, Bootsy Collins, Kam, Dr. Dre, Humpty Hump (Digital Underground), Anthony Kiedis (Red Hot Chili Peppers) and Yo Yo. If Clinton sometimes seems to have left the building while his fans do the work (he produced—but didn't have a hand in writing—all the tracks, and his audible contributions are intermittent), **Smell My Finger** is nonetheless his record through and through. But then so are plenty of others that were recorded with only his spirit in the house. [i]

See also *TPRG*.

COAL PORTERS

Rebels Without Applause (Aus. Rubber) 1992 (UK Utility) 1992
Land of Hope and Crosby (UK Prima) 1993 (Temple Bar) 1994
Los London (UK Prima) 1995

LONG RYDERS

10-5-60 EP (PVC) 1983 (Frontier) 1992
Native Sons (Frontier) 1984 + 1992
State of Our Union (Island) 1985 (UK Prima) 1992
Two Fisted Tales (Island) 1987
Metallic B.O. (Long Ryders Fan Club) 1989 (UK Overground) 1990

After the breakup of Los Angeles' retro-country-rocking Long Ryders, Kentucky-born singer/guitarist Sid Griffin (also the author of a Gram Parsons biography) and the band's drummer, Greg Sowders, formed the Coal Porters with English bassist Ian Thomson. A few years later, Thomson returned to London with Griffin, who married ex–Dream Academy reed player Kate St. John and continued his all-American recording career from a foreign perch.

Rebels Without Applause was first released in Australia as an EP, gaining tracks (including "Sittin' in an Isle of Palms," recorded at a '90 BBC session) for its nine-song English issue. While sticking to the Byrds-inflected hybrid that originally sparked the Long Ryders (and, as those groups generally did, eschewing the obvious sound of pedal steel), the Coal Porters make a poor showing on their debut. Griffin's not an overpowering singer or tunesmith (lyrics are a special problem), and this project serves straight to his weaknesses. The encouraging exceptions are the long, rocking "Roll Columbia Roll" and "Rhythm and Blue Angel," a surging singalong inexplicably preceded by a bitter phone call from an unidentified musician with a grudge.

Assembling tracks by various lineups (variously including St. John, Sowders, Thomson, ex–Green on Red organist Chris Cacavas and ex-Rockpiler Billy Bremner), the full-length **Land of Hope and Crosby** provides further evidence that Griffin is more adept at rocking than twanging. A horn section led by St. John kicks "Imperial Beach" into a soulful cool-jerk; the excellent "What Am I Doin' (In This Thing Called Love)" doses up on the Anglo-American roots sound, prompting Bremner to add a corking guitar solo. An organ sound straight outta the Augie Meyers school of Texas border fun spices up the peppy romantic enthusiasm of "What About Tomorrow." But the Byrdsy tendencies of the flat-footed "Death Like a Valentine" amount to little more than twelve-string flourishes, an incongruous pop bounce spoils the tear-in-my-beer country stylings of "Everybody's Fault but Mine" and neither pedal steel nor oboe can make peace with the old-timey acoustic heart of "You Can See Them There." Of the country-rockers, only "Windy City" gets the balance right, giving the Nashville-styled ode to Chicago an English '60s art-rock twist with an oboe part that actually works.

Other than a couple of sodden ballads (including Gram Parsons' "Apple Tree") that wash it in sickly soapsuds, **Los London** displays Griffin's prudent dedication to the Coal Porters' most winnable causes: bouncy country ("Crackin' at the Seams"), horn-powered roots rock (the Long Ryders–recalling "It Happened to Me"), heartland passion ("A Woman to Love"), Byrdsy nostalgia ("Chasing Rainbows"). His lyrics and vocals are most often good-natured and effective; the arrangements are more considered and complex than in the past. A minor pleasure to be sure, but it's reassuring to know country-rock still has credible friends in faraway places.

A good chunk of the Long Ryders' catalogue has been reissued in the '90s. Frontier slapped its two titles together on a single CD as **10-5-60/Native Sons,** while Griffin's own London-based Prima label got the rights to **State of Our Union** (the group's one shining commercial moment, thanks to the wretched semi-hit "Looking for Lewis and Clark") and put it out on CD with four added rarities, including an acoustic number sung as a duet by guitarist Stephen McCarthy and Christine Collister, plus a lighthearted geographical seasonal, "Christmas in New Zealand." [i]

See also *TPRG.*

COBRA VERDE

Viva la Muerte (Scat) 1994
Vintage Crime EP (Scat) 1995

GEM

Hexed (Restless) 1995

Freeing themselves of the diabolical fashions of flamboyant drummer Steve-o, the three serious members of Cleveland's gritty Death of Samantha—singer/guitarist/journalist John Petkovic, guitarist/singer Doug Gillard and bassist Dave Swanson (shifting to drums)—regrouped in the '90s as Cobra Verde, adding bassist Don Depew to complete the lineup. Operating under the slogan "Death in small doses," the quartet made its longplaying debut with **Viva la Muerte,** a solid center of tough, literate songs reflecting various eras of rock influence (from the rerun Television melodicism of "Was It Good" to the taut boogiemonster riffology of "Gimmie Your Heart") wrapped in a thick curtain of stirring clubland ferocity and decorated with venomous razor nicks of barbed guitar. Although "Montenegro," the lovely in parts "Already Dead" and the verses of the epic "I Thought You Knew (What Pleasure Was)" gently dip into an expansive, romantic undercurrent, the album's typical tactic—in songs like the Bunnymen-informed "Until the Killing Time" and "Cease to Exist" (*not* the Charles Manson song)—is to jag along, energized to the point of nervous exhaustion.

The six-song **Vintage Crime** is more accomplished, controlled and diverse: effective settings for Petkovic's expressions of cynical disgust at public trendoids ("Media Whore"), performers ("Every God for Himself"), the future ("World Doesn't End") and public alienation ("Wish I Was Here"). The lively mix well serves the vivid arrangements and gives increased prominence to Petkovic's wavery baritone. Jody Reynolds' late-'50s chestnut "Fire of Love" receives a full dose of vintage atmosphere and a fine vocal performance in clear tribute to the Gun Club's baleful rendition.

Guitarist Doug Gillard, Prisonshake drummer Scott Pickering and Four Coyotes guitarist Tim Tobias lead Gem, a group whose primary qualification for membership seems to be past involvement in My Dad Is Dead. **Hexed** is a tuneful rush of smart, catchy and simple rhythm guitar pop-rock—sort of grown-up Weezer without the anxious pretensions. Although contributions from the others aren't as crafty, main songwriter Gillard comes across with the woolly and weird chant of "Sheep," the bracing T. Rex borrowings of "Your Heroes Hate You" and the countryfied pun of "Only a Loan." [i]

See also *My Dad Is Dead, Prisonshake.*

COCTAILS

Hip Hip Hooray (Hi-Ball) 1990
Here Now Today (Hi-Ball) 1991
Songs for Children EP (Hi-Ball) 1991
Early Hi-Ball Years (Carrot Top) 1992
Long Sound (Hi-Ball) 1993 (Carrot Top) 1993
3/4 Time EP (Hi-Ball) 1993
Winter Wonderland EP (Hi-Ball) 1993
Peel (Hi-Ball) 1994 (Carrot Top) 1994
The Coctails EP (Hello Recording Club) 1995
The Coctails (Carrot Top) 1995

The Coctails made their debut in Kansas City, wearing matching yellow tuxes with burgundy bowties, quietly butchering a Miles Davis song at an art-gallery opening for the bass player's girlfriend. The quartet's initial albums exploited this sense of nerdy, nervy cool, blending the hygienic graphics and sparse black-and-white cover art of '50s jazz releases with the bewildering musical eclecticism of the '90s lo-fi underground. The effect was charming if gimmicky, and it brought the band some undue notoriety as avatars of the lounge-rock movement, later popularized by Love Jones and Combustible Edison. By the time that unfortunate revival had become fodder for media trend pieces, the Coctails had set themselves apart with the variety and depth of their songwriting.

The best work from the first two albums and EP is collected on the **Early Hi-Ball Years,** released after a move to Chicago, where the band established a self-contained music industry with two record labels (Carrot Top and the vinyl-only Hi-Ball), a pressing plant and a line of handmade merchandise. The music ranges from polkas, doo-wop and klezmer tunes to twisted jazz instrumentals and garage-rock, with songs often exploiting one or more of the menagerie of instruments in the quartet's collection, including tenor saw, vibraphone, saxophone, clarinet, lap steel and trumpet—in addition to keyboards, guitars, drums and bass.

Multi-instrumentalists John Upturch, Mark Greenberg, Archer Prewitt and Barry Phipps developed a sound and a set list for every occasion, playing everything from weddings to club gigs with Shellac, mutant Christmas carols to deceptively simplistic children's music (the latter two genres documented on the **Winter Wonderland** and **Songs for Children** EPs).

Other aspects of that vast repertoire are the focus of the **3/4 Time** EP of waltzes and **Long Sound,** devoted entirely to the group's jazz-leaning instrumentals. While hardly virtuosos, the Coctails play with low-key humor and create a series of soundscapes—by turns muted and buoyant, lush and fractured—that evoke heroes from Billy Strayhorn to Sun Ra. Lending instrumental sizzle are ringers Ken Vandermark, Poi Dog Pondering's Dave Crawford and NRG Ensemble founder Hal Russell, in one of the last recording sessions before his death.

Peel is the Coctails' crowning achievement, a sprawling pop album full of sneaky hooks ("Miss Maple," "2000," "Even Time") and spidery guitar lines, spiked with noisy intrusions and the odd musical saw solo ("Cottonbelt"). In its range and ambition, **Peel** recalls the best work of another underappreciated Chicago group, Shrimp Boat. Although none of the band members is much of a singer, the tunes are so strong it almost doesn't matter. (As with **Long Sound,** the vinyl edition is on Hi-Ball, the CD on Carrot Top.)

The Coctails EP, issued on the subscription-only Hello label, is all-instrumental, but considerably different in tone from **Long Sound.** With wan whistling, a snippet of dialogue, ambling banjo and eerie musical saw, it's a richly atmospheric soundtrack to an unmade movie and hints at the darker-tinged music to follow.

The Coctails LP was issued to coincide with the group's farewell concert, on December 31, 1995. The songs are more understated and atmospheric, the album more cohesive—if less buoyant—than **Peel.** With the exception of the garage-punk clatter of "Cast Stones," the disc is dominated by brooding instrumentals, sparse ballads and muted vocals. But the melancholy majesty of "So Low" and the rural plaintiveness of "Low Road" and "Hey" reach an emotional depth to which the Coctails only previously hinted. [gk]

See also *Rachel's, Shrimp Boat.*

COCTEAU TWINS

Garlands (UK 4AD) 1982 (4AD/Capitol) 1991
Head Over Heels (UK 4AD) 1983 (4AD/Capitol) 1991
Sunburst and Snowblind EP (UK 4AD) 1983
Pearly Dewdrops' Drop EP (UK 4AD) 1984
Treasure (UK 4AD) 1984 (4AD/Capitol) 1991
Aikea-Guinea EP (UK 4AD) 1985
Tiny Dynamine EP (UK 4AD) 1985
Echoes in a Shallow Bay EP (UK 4AD) 1985
Tiny Dynamine/Echoes in a Shallow Bay (UK 4AD) 1986
The Pink Opaque (4AD/Relativity) 1986
Victorialand (UK 4AD) 1986 (4AD/Capitol) 1991
Love's Easy Tears EP (4AD/Relativity) 1986
Blue Bell Knoll (4AD/Capitol) 1988
Iceblink Luck EP (4AD/Capitol) 1990
Heaven or Las Vegas (4AD/Capitol) 1990
Cocteau Twins (4AD/Capitol) 1991
Four-Calender Café (Capitol) 1993
Twinlights EP (Capitol) 1995
Otherness EP (Capitol) 1995
Milk & Kisses (Capitol) 1996

HAROLD BUDD/ELIZABETH FRASER/ ROBIN GUTHRIE/SIMON RAYMONDE

The Moon and the Melodies (4AD/Relativity) 1986

In their prolific '80s output, Scotland's influential Cocteau Twins mined a non-linear, richly ethereal style built around Elizabeth Fraser's otherworldly vocals and the adventurous instrumental textures of Robin Guthrie and Simon Raymonde. The band's early efforts—before Raymonde's arrival in late 1983—are agreeably meandering, more style than substance, but **Treasure,** recorded as a trio, displays enough musical and emotional concentration to make the work more than just a seductive stylistic oddity. Fraser's voice effortlessly conveys a range of emotions (though her impressionistic lyrics remain largely undecipherable); the music sounds similarly purposeful. Subsequent '80s efforts—culminating in the soporific **Blue Bell Knoll**—are disappointingly uninspired. The group seems content to produce exotic mood music rather than challenge themselves or their audience.

As the '90s dawned, though, the Cocteau Twins dramatically regained their bearings with **Heaven or Las Vegas.** Such numbers as "Cherry-Coloured Funk" and "Iceblink Luck" are focused and emotionally involving, yet don't skimp on the trademark atmospherics; Fraser even sings some of her lyrics in recognizable English. The album plays not like an attempt at commercialism so much as a genuine effort to communicate more clearly.

Four-Calendar Café continues the trend toward clarity, adding a slightly earthy edge that nicely balances the ethereality. Standout tracks like "Know Who You Are at Every Age," "Bluebeard" and "Squeeze-Wax" rank with the group's most memorable and melodically accessible work.

The two 1995 EPs find the Cocteaus exploring alternative approaches with mixed success. **Twinlights** features acoustic versions of three new songs and 1985's "Pink Orange Red"; it's the Cocteaus at their most restrained and unadorned, and unfussy clarity makes it a low-key winner. The ambient-flavored **Otherness** combines two new songs with "Cherry-Coloured Funk" and "Feet Like Fins" (from **Victorialand**), all remixed by Mark Clifford of Seefeel; the result is vaguely interesting as a convergence of disparate genres, but not a particularly fulfilling listen.

Milk & Kisses reprises "Rilkean Heart" from **Twinlights** and "Violaine" and "Seekers Who Are Lovers" from **Otherness,** all in more characteristically Cocteauesque versions. Elsewhere, the album maintains the organic, approachable mood of **Heaven or Las Vegas** and **Four-Calendar Café,** making it one of the Twins' smoothest—and most satisfying—concoctions.

Cocteau Twins (1991) is a deluxe boxed set of CDs that repackages the group's 4AD EPs (**Sunburst and Snowblind, Pearly Dewdrops' Drop, Aikea-Guinea, Tiny Dynamine, Echoes in a Shallow Bay, Love's Easy Tears** and **Iceblink Luck**), adding a four-track bonus disc. [ss]

See also *TPRG.*

CODEINE

Frigid Stars (Ger. Glitterhouse) 1990 (Sub Pop) 1991
Barely Real EP (Ger. Sub Pop) 1992 (Sub Pop) 1993
The White Birch (Sub Pop) 1994

REX

Rex (Southern) 1995

These slowcore progenitors were just about the first band to risk terminal transmission damage by operating in perpetual low gear, dragging their chassis through all manner of psychosexual detritus in the process. Codeine's glacial pace—languid enough to fit a beer run between the notes of some songs—allows you the chance to connect the music's dots for yourself, no doubt sketching some provocatively sinister images along the way.

Frigid Stars is a draggy, druggy and somewhat placid (in relation to the trio's often apocalyptically loud live shows) crawl through a world where the clocks always read 4:00 A.M. Codeine's sheer cranial woolliness is amazingly refreshing when viewed in the gleam of the chrome 'n' crystal polish slathered over so many of its peers' releases. The fact that "beat" is an all but meaningless concept to rigidly disciplined drummer Chris Brokaw (who concurrently served as guitarist in Come, the band to which he eventually defected) is just the first chapter in Codeine's story: bassist Stephen Immerwahr's clenched-jaw delivery of defeatist anti-anthems like "Pickup Song" may make **Frigid Stars** seem like an all-or-nothing proposition. But when John Engle's sustained guitar waves break just so—as on "New Year's" and "D"—Codeine dispenses the most succubus-like music you'll have the pleasure of losing your soul to.

The trio steps into the first notes of **Barely Real** without so much as (no pun intended) missing a beat: the gossamer-thin wave of feedback that Engle stretches through "Realize" provides just enough equilibrium to keep Immerwahr's fragile vocal line from crumbling entirely. They do tinker with the formula a bit—"JR" features a noise-guitar cameo from Bitch Magnet's Jon Fine, while Bastro's David Grubbs provides a sumptuous piano interlude on "W."—but Codeine isn't about to start obeying rock's speed edicts. Brokaw left before the release of **The White Birch,** but his replacement, Douglas Scharin, plays with similar rigor, punctuating the sepulchral "Sea" with military-funeral snare snaps and maintaining an ascetic stillness during hushed pieces like "Loss Leader." Immerwahr's intensifying reticence allows more space for the band's slowly unfolding improvisations to bloom.

Scharin also serves as a foundation-builder for Rex, a Brooklyn-based foursome that's as terse as—but somewhat more scholarly than—Codeine. That schooling is evident in both the band's eloquent use of strings and the careful chamber-styled arrangements of songs like "A Good Time to Die." As Him, he also released 1996's **Egg** (Southern): seven slices of dub instrumental work. [dss]

See also *Come, Rodan.*

COFFIN BREAK

Psychosis (C/Z) 1989
Rupture (C/Z) 1990
Crawl (Epitaph) 1991
No Sleep 'til the Stardust Motel (C/Z) 1991
Thirteen (Epitaph) 1992

To those who didn't bother to keep track of every bit of minutiae flowing from the Seattle rock scene in the early '90s, Coffin Break was likely just another face in the long line of indistinguishable faces. Why the band never reached any measure of national prominence is a no-brainer—the trio clung to its hardcore and heavy metal roots too tenaciously to gain widespread acceptance. That the band never even achieved the cult status of the Young Fresh Fellows (a major influence) is also easy to figger: none of Coffin Break's material displays the underhanded cheekiness the Fellows consistently offered.

Psychosis, a shortplayer of sloppy hardcore, adds just a dash of metal to sour the flavor a bit, but standouts like "Stupid Love Song" also nod directly toward the Fellows, down to bassist/singer Rob Skinner's pursed-lips imitation of Scott McCaughey's campy, smart but insecure vocalizations. "Hopeless" tightens Coffin Break's grip on straightforward punk rock, while the discordant metallic intro to "Promise" sheds a bit of light on things to come.

What was to come was 1990's **Rupture,** a record made distinct from its predecessor by a few run-of-the-speed-metal guitar solos and the attempt by singer/guitarist Peter Litwin to expand his vocal range to metallic flourishes better left to Soundgarden's Chris Cornell. (Actually, he comes off sounding more like Ronnie James Dio easing himself back to consciousness after a long nap.) "Vision of Never" and "Rosy Picture" pack some decent punk-rock wallop, but Skinner's clever "Kill the President" could be the YFFs themselves. The record also features a competent cover of Hüsker Dü's frightening "Diane." (One C/Z CD combines **Rupture** and **Psychosis.)**

A label switch did Coffin Break some good. The combo benefits from improved studio work, but sharp stylistic divisions are beginning to show. Skinner's writing and singing are markedly improved on **Crawl,** and his talent for catchy, hooky pop-punk is beginning to peak. Litwin, on the other hand, continues to seek refuge in the hoariest metal clichés, turning what could be a terrific album (if Skinner held the reins) into a disjointed handful of diamonds and a whole lotta rough. "Wiser" is an unforgettable bit of punky bubblegum pop that shows Skinner has finally been able to catapult past the obvious references and become his own fellow. "For Beth" and "Cry" are also winners, but "Stop" is a shameful piece of anti-censorship tripe.

Having released a number of Coffin Break singles, C/Z put them together on **No Sleep 'til the Stardust Motel.** As many of the singles were also album tracks, the main novelties here are a sendup of Lynyrd Skynyrd's "Free Bird" (yawn) and a not-bad cover of the Beatles' "We Can Work It Out." Litwin's material dominates the compilation, but his stuff doesn't seem so horrible here. In fact, "The Drive," from Coffin Break's first demo tape, is fairly captivating, but it's the rough recording that helps it along.

It was only a matter of time before Coffin Break would get around to a Black Sabbath cover, and that's what the band does on its final album, **Thirteen,** for which guitarist Jeff Lorien was added to bolster the combo's metal punch. The album has the requisite Skinner punky raveups ("Wasted Time," "Old n' Jaded"); even Litwin proves willing to take some silly pills and lighten up a bit. "Our World Now" merges his hard-edged metal with a nifty pop sensibility. But the whole thing goes straight to hell at the halfway point, as Litwin heads right back to his trite metal shenanigans. Memo to C/Z and Epitaph: re-release each guy's compositions on separate discs. [icm]

COGS

See *Ween.*

LEONARD COHEN

Songs of Leonard Cohen (Columbia) 1968
Songs from a Room (Columbia) 1969
Songs of Love and Hate (Columbia) 1971
Live Songs (Columbia) 1972
New Skin for the Old Ceremony (Columbia) 1974
Best of Leonard Cohen (Columbia) 1975
Death of a Ladies' Man (Warner Bros.) 1977 (Columbia) 1988
Recent Songs (Columbia) 1979
Various Positions (Passport) 1985 (Columbia) 1995
I'm Your Man (Columbia) 1988
The Future (Columbia) 1992
Cohen Live (Columbia) 1994

VARIOUS ARTISTS

I'm Your Fan (Atlantic) 1991
Tower of Song: The Songs of Leonard Cohen (A&M) 1995

JENNIFER WARNES

Famous Blue Raincoat (Cypress) 1986

Because he is better known from usually inferior cover versions of his songs (Judy Collins' "Suzanne" being the blandest), Montreal's Leonard Cohen has frequently been taken for a singer/songwriter in a sullen variation on the James Taylor sensitive mold. But this world-weary, ironic commentator on romantic despair has more in common with Serge Gainsbourg, Bryan Ferry and Bertolt Brecht than Jackson Browne. It's not for nothing his 1966 novel is entitled *Beautiful Losers.*

Which is not to say there are not congruences between Cohen and the singer/songwriter world. His early albums betray their roots as poems set to rudimentary chords. Cohen's vocals are half-sung/half-talked, like a rock'n'roll Rex Harrison but, like Dylan, he is a talented non-singer, able to extract a wide range of emotion from a limited range. (Over the years it has lowered from an ardent, almost earnest tenor to a gruff, insinuating growl.) But "Chelsea Hotel" (from **New Skin for the Old Ceremony**) and "Famous Blue Raincoat" (from **Songs of Love and Hate**) exhibit an exquisite sense of place; the cantorial "Who by Fire?" (**New Skin**) and "Hey, That's No Way to Say Goodbye" (from **Songs of Leonard Cohen**) have their moments. The **Best of** album is a worthy sampler of this era.

His next move was a label change and a puzzling collaboration with Phil Spector. Almost twenty years later, **Death of a Ladies' Man** doesn't sound like the unmitigated disaster critics (and the artist) considered it to be at the time. There's no denying the album was flawed from conception: Spector's wall of sound was created to contain black-and-white, adolescent emotions; it would be hard to name a songwriter who inhabits a larger gray area than Cohen. The production overwhelms Cohen (it also overwhelms Dylan, who is credited but impossible to detect as a background vocalist), although some worthy songs are there to be heard beneath the rubble: "True Love Leaves No Traces" and "I Can't Forget." Cohen took something away from those sessions; his subsequent albums have been steadily more produced. The mariachi-accented **Recent Songs** is intriguing but the songs don't really measure up.

Cohen moved to Greece in the late '70s and appears to have lived the life of the gentleman artist. While his latter-day bohemianism has slowed his production (he averages an album every four years), the quality of his work had never been higher. On **Various Positions,** Cohen shares the vocals with Jennifer Warnes (whose subsequent **Famous Blue Raincoat** consists entirely of his songs). The material is darker, the arrangements sparser, setting off Cohen's apocalyptic imagination ("Dance Me to the End of Love," the surreal "The Law") and his continued fascination with religious imagery (the extraordinary "Hallelujah," "If It Be Your Will").

Cohen's best album, **I'm Your Man,** is also his most sophisticated, with the artist exhibiting a sure sense of, and control over, his music. A panoply of keyboards and driving basslines hints at the hedonism of dance music, but the arrangements echo the high, spacey, unresolved harmonies of Weimar Berlin. All told, they form an ironic counterpoint to the songs' pessimism about the music industry and the modern world. "First We Take Manhattan" is Cohen's fantasy of commercial success, conflated with fascism, a vision of victory undercut by the spoils of a battle not really worth winning. In "Everybody Knows," a worried lover meditates on faithlessness and AIDS; in "The Tower of Song," he ruefully contemplates his career. "I was born like this, I had no choice," Cohen deadpans, "I was born with the gift of a golden voice."

The Future suffers only by comparison. While song for song the equal to **I'm Your Man,** it lacks the prior album's impact. In the title track, while a gospel-tinged soul groove churns behind him, Cohen longs for a return to the days of "the Berlin Wall/and anal sex" because he's "seen the future/and it's murder." A minor-key country two-step plays during the desperate erotic scramble of last call in "Closing Time." And there's an eight-minute version of Irving Berlin's "Always" that turns the lyric into a not-so-veiled threat. **Cohen Live** is a fine souvenir of one of Cohen's infrequent tours.

As if to underscore Cohen's appeal and influence, he's been the subject of two major-label tribute albums. **I'm Your Fan,** the better option, posits Cohen as an alternative-rock godfather. R.E.M., the Pixies, Lloyd Cole and Nick Cave (who covered Cohen's "Cabin Fever" on **From Her to Eternity**) state the case best, easily making Cohen's songs their own. Cave's version of "Tower of Song" has to be heard to be believed—it takes the title literally, doing each line in a different style. The singer rethinks the material so radically that it's almost unrecognizable; a more conservative version by Robert Forster (of the Go-Betweens) is also included.

Tower of Song, which has no overriding agenda, is worth hearing for Bono's techno rendition of "Hallelujah," Aaron Neville's country soul take on "Ain't No Cure for Love" and Suzanne Vega's respectful "Story of Isaac." But Don Henley and Billy Joel miss Cohen's irony, turning their selections ("Everybody Knows" and "Light as the Breeze," respectively) into empty, heavy-handed lite-rock ballads. [sm]

HOLLY COLE

See *Tom Waits.*

LLOYD COLE AND THE COMMOTIONS

Ratttlesnakes (Geffen) 1984 (Capitol) 1988
Easy Pieces (Geffen) 1985 (Capitol) 1988
Mainstream (UK Polydor) 1987 (Capitol) 1988
1984–1989 (Capitol) 1989

LLOYD COLE

Lloyd Cole (Capitol) 1990
Don't Get Weird on Me, Babe (Capitol) 1991
Bad Vibes (UK Phonogram) 1993 (Rykodisc) 1994
Love Story (Rykodisc) 1995

Lloyd Cole is a pretentious twit—in the nicest possible sense. Which is to say the Scottish singer/songwriter is highly literate and ultra-sensitive. Always has been, ever since he first turned up in 1984 with **Rattlesnakes.** Coming on like a typical new Dylan/Reed in the nascent R.E.M./Smiths era, Cole speaks French ("2cv"), drops names (Arthur Lee, Norman Mailer), rewrites novelists (Renata Adler, Joan Didion), deliberately mispronounces "Eva Marie Saint" (to rhyme with "On the Waterfront") and lets his voice break with wounded affect in all the right places. That he manages to do so with some levity, while the Commotions veer between forceful thrumming (a little hometown Postcard Records influence there) and moody heartbreakers, makes the record a treat, albeit an instantly nostalgic one. Its naïfish, momentarily novel pleasures were not to be equaled.

Easy Pieces is hit-and-miss, the only new developments being ill-advised soul touches and producer-imposed horns. **Mainstream** isn't quite that, but it is streamlined and more rhythmically bubbly, ushering out the Commotions in brooding and tuneful fashion. The retrospective boils down the three albums and adds two early British B-sides for collectible good measure.

The end of the Commotions didn't much matter—it was always Cole's show. Besides, the band's keyboardist (and Cole's co-writer) Blair Cowan and, eventually, guitarist Neil Clark, remained among the star's key collaborators, even after he moved to New York and took up with drummer/producer Fred Maher and guitarist Robert Quine (who brought in a bassist named Matthew Sweet). Quine's reliably understated seething is in large part what makes **Lloyd Cole** decent. Slow-starting numbers like "Don't Look Back" and "No Blue Skies" benefit greatly from Quine's nervous tension; Cole's glibness and glumness carry the day on the ballads "Undressed" and "To the Church."

Cole then went to extremes—the strength of **Don't Get Weird on Me, Babe** and the weakness of **Bad Vibes.** The former is definitively divided between rousing pop songs and yearning, Paul Buckmaster–orchestrated epics. Cole has since said he wishes he'd gone whole-hog on the symphonic tip, but that's selling his zippy little guitar-rockers short, especially the Quine-addled "Tell Your Sister," the muscular "Weeping Wine" and the ultra-hooky, seemingly fatuous "She's a Girl and I'm a Man," which is actually a touching exercise in self-deprecation. Yet the ominous urgency of the flipside (metaphorically speaking) is in fact superior, with Cole's uncomplicated romantic angst made fleshy and devastating by the surrounding lushness of woodwinds, strings, percussion, piano and female backing vocals. A great record.

Not so its successor. Quine is gone, replaced by ex-Banshee John Carruthers; the producer is Adam Peters, late of the Flowerpot Men (he also co-auteured the Triffids' fussiest record). While Cole can't help but pen a few memorable songs, including his usual dose of clever-or-stupid wordsmithery (for example, "Everybody knows that she's worse than religion"), **Bad Vibes** is a cluttered work that sinks under the weight of busy electronics, strained psychedelic atmosphere and—ugh!—misbegotten funk. (Fun fact: due to either bizarre coincidence or simple cheek, Cole's old Glasgow mates del Amitri rephrased the opening lines of Cole's "So You'd Like to Save the World" in "Start With Me" on their **Twisted** album.)

"The more I learn, the less I know," Cole sings on **Love Story**'s second song. Never mind that "will you make mine straight Absolut?" completes the couplet; maybe it's supposed to be a pun. And so he's back where he started—for this minimal record, Neil Clark joins Quine on guitars, and Peters reins himself in considerably—but filtered through the sensibility of a wistful thirtysomething rather than a wordy newcomer. Writing a whole album of songs like "Baby," "Sentimental Fool" and the devoted-doormat lament "Happy for You," however, is very nearly an adolescent exercise—you'd get just as much insight into the heart's complexities from the Shirelles. But simplicity is the point, and the music animates the lyrics. There's certainly nothing lacking in the spare, well-crafted songwriting or Cole's frequently beauteous (and ever-breaking) shaggy-dog voice. Lovely, precious and sappy—in the nicest possible sense. [jc]

See also *del Amitri; TPRG.*

EDWYN COLLINS

Hope and Despair (UK Demon) 1989
Hellbent on Compromise (UK Demon) 1990
Gorgeous George (UK Setanta) 1994 (Bar/None) 1995
Hope and Despair/Hellbent on Compromise (UK Demon) 1995

After the Orange Juice ended its influential pop reign in the mid-'80s, sonorous Scottish singer/guitarist Edwyn Collins made a couple of false starts at a solo career before finally seeing **Hope and Despair**—produced and played on by old ally Dennis Bovell (with instrumental assistance from Aztec Camera–man Roddy Frame and others)—through to release in 1989. Between Collins' handsome conversational voice and skilled, offbeat songcraft (done up tastefully as everything from frisky country rock to downcast pop soul and Bowie bluejean bop), the album is wonderfully engaging, a strong statement from a precursor of many suave/hip crooners to come. As idiosyncratic and unself-conscious as Morrissey but equipped with his own set of emotional bristles, Collins climbs the album's titular poles in such songs as "You're Better Than You Know" and "The Beginning of the End."

Bovell's absence from **Hellbent on Compromise** is entirely too noticeable; while the record isn't strenuously different from the debut, too many keyboards, synthetic drums and the mildly unctuous tone of the bland arrangements unbalance Collins' precarious stylistic perch and leave the flat outing sounding like something Leonard Cohen was made to do against his better judgment. The songs go on too long; other than "It Might as Well Be You" and "Now That It's Love," there are few highlights: even Smokey Robinson's "My Girl Has Gone" is squandered by filling the track with incongruous Dobro slide guitar.

Collins spent the next few years producing other artists (A House, Vic Godard) and getting together a pair of Orange Juice reissues: **Ostrich Churchyard,** a collection of demos, and **The Heather's on Fire,** a singles retrospective.

Highlighted by "A Girl Like You," a catchy whiff of retro atmosphere used to primp up two different '95 films (*Empire Records* and *Never Talk to Strangers*), **Gorgeous George** introduces Collins to America as a smooth operator with a soulful side and a vicious cranky streak. Backed by Sex Pistols drummer Paul Cook and bassist Claire Kenny, Collins uses his composed baritone and diverse guitar sounds to vent bitterly at various buffoons and phonies: musicians in "The Campaign for Real Rock" ("the overrated hit the stage/Overpaid and over here/And their idea of counter-culture's/Momma's charge account at Sears') and "North of Heaven" ("Some mother's talking 'bout Guns n' Roses/As if I give a fuck/At best I think they suck/I'm too preoccupied with my memories/Not nonentities") and whoever the title track is about ("the last of the go-getters . . . a dandy to the letter/you really should know better"). All this snide condescension would be insufferably pompous or, at the very least, meaningless if the music weren't styled so ingeniously.

"A Girl Like You" employs an Iggy-like croon, wiggly fuzz guitar, a cool vibraphone lick and echoey backing vocals to summon up an incongruous and distinctive lounge-pop groove. "Low Expectations" is a stately folksong, while "If You Could Love Me" beds down in comfy Philly soul. Collins' skill at conveying specific moods with simple implements is impressive—at times more so than his content—but it's ultimately **Gorgeous George**'s cocky indifference that makes its translucent designs shimmer. [i]

CHRISTINE COLLISTER

See *Clive Gregson & Christine Collister.*

COLORBLIND JAMES EXPERIENCE

The Colorblind James Experience (Fundamental) 1987
Why Should I Stand Up? (Cooking Vinyl/Death Valley/ Gold Castle) 1989
The Peel Sessions EP (UK Strange Fruit) 1989 (Strange Fruit/Dutch East India Trading) 1991
Solid! Behind the Times (Red House) 1992
I Saved Your Life (Ger. Scout) 1996

COLORBLIND JAMES AND THE DEATH VALLEY BOYS

Strange Sounds From the Basement (Cooking Vinyl/Death Valley) 1990

The seven-piece from Rochester, New York, is led by Colorblind James (guitar, vibraphone, vocals), who's seen nearly two dozen players pass through the band's friendly gates. The alumni association includes eight bassists, five guitarists, three trombonists and a host of others. Throughout it all, however, the Experience's sound has remained incredibly stable, which is, of course, a testament to the clearly defined character and easy command of its namesake's songs and musical vision. Elements of string-band music, honkytonk, country blues, polkas and more invite hybrid descriptive handles like Nino Rota Jug Band or Memphis Slim Cabaret Orchestra.

The eponymous debut sets the tone for all subsequent releases: James' world-weary but hopeful musings on one's lot in life, delivered in a neighborly midrange that explores the line between singing and speaking. The band manages to make an easy pace sound exuberant, and nearly every number features a unison melodic line, repeated with infectious delight. Not to be missed: the comically deadpan song of loss and betrayal, "A Different Bob."

British airplay for the debut led to a number of tours there and on the continent, where they quickly amassed a following far in excess of any response back home. The band's next two records were released first in England and then licensed to an American outlet. Taking a mild spin in country, **Why Should I Stand Up?** also adds two horn players; **Strange Sounds From the Basement** strips everyone down to acoustic instruments (hence the modified ensemble name). **The Peel Sessions** EP contains four songs from a live '88 radio broadcast (during the group's first trip to the UK).

Solid! Behind the Times makes a fine entry point into the CBJE oeuvre, with more songs that mix humor, gentility and compassion. The funny stuff always leads you in, rather than slapping you on the head or squirting you in the eye.

A German label picked up the ball for **I Saved Your Life,** and the album features a strong and stable (three years and counting) lineup; Rita Coulter's vocals add a perfect foil to the mixture. In particular, she brings warmth and confidence to "I'll Never Get Tired," a simple celebration of undying love that wouldn't have been possible without her. As usual, the songs win with characters that spring to life; the range of indignities, discomforts and doubts suffered may bewilder, but never overwhelm, them. They're never looking for redemption or intervention, rather, just some company for commiseration. As Colorblind James sings in "I Can Be Your Guide," "If you want to find your way home, I'll just step aside/But if you're lost and want to stay lost, I could be your guide." [dbg]

See also *TPRG.*

COMBUSTIBLE EDISON

I, Swinger (Sub Pop) 1994
Four Rooms: Original Motion Picture Soundtrack (Elektra) 1995
Schizophonic! (Sub Pop) 1996

CHRISTMAS

In Excelsior Dayglo (Big Time) 1986
Ultraprophets of Thee Psykick Revolution (IRS) 1989
Vortex (Matador) 1993

As the band that poured the first shot in the Cocktail Revolution, this Boston-area combo brought lounge music into the '90s—or, more accurately, transported tastemakers back to the suburbia of the '50s—with strikingly authentic interpretations of some of the most unauthentic sounds known to mankind. Gleefully embracing the ersatz ethnicity and sybaritic sophistication of spiritual forefathers like Martin Denny and Esquivel, the quintet slinks into its easy listening groove with martinis in hand and tongues in cheek, proving once and for all that trend-chasers will swallow absolutely any next big thing served to them.

I, Swinger is a faithful replication of bargain-bin exotica, right down to a sleeve festooned with cocktail recipes and calculatedly dated hep-cat liner notes. Majordomo Michael Cudahy (aka "The Millionaire") puts the band through paces as varied as bossa nova ("Breakfast at Denny's") and retro-futuristic space-pop ("Carnival of Souls") with deadpan precision, exploiting the "possibilities" of stereophonic sound via the panning, phasing and soundplay excess of the composer/performers who ushered in the hi-fi era. Armed with all manner of ancillary percussion, drummer Liz "Miss Lily Banquette" Cox and vibraphonist Aaron Oppenheimer craft supremely tacky travelogues that transport listeners from Gay Parée to the Amazon River basin—while Peter Dixon's dairy-state organ trills make it clear they've never actually left the shopping mall. To give credit where credit is due, Combustible Edison does a credible job when tackling covers like "Cry Me a River" (sung, like all the band's non-instrumentals, by the agreeably brandy-voiced Cox) and Nino Rota's "Cadillac."

Considering the degree to which the band has conceptualized its own songs as soundtracks for non-existent films (**I, Swinger** ends with a track called "Theme from 'The Tiki Wonder Hour'"), it's hardly surprising that they'd link with fellow vulture of trash culture Quentin Tarantino to create a real soundtrack—particularly one for a film set in their spiritual homeland of Las Vegas. Since the music on **Four Rooms** is primarily incidental in nature, most of it doesn't hold up to careful scrutiny without the visual accompaniment, but there are revelatory moments: Cox's giddy scat-singing on the "Vertigogo" theme is positively intoxicating; "Four Rooms Swing" melts into a sensual love-puddle right before your ears. Elsewhere, the charm wears thin: a decontextualized (if faithful) remake of the theme from *Bewitched* triggers involuntary eye-rolling. Exotica aficionados will no doubt be pleased to note that genre pioneer Esquivel looms not only in spirit, but in the flesh: his smashing renditions of "Harlem Nocturne" and "Sentimental Journey" are among the soundtrack's high points.

Since progress is obviously not an option for Combustible Edison, the stasis of **Schizophonic!** can't really be called a disappointment. The album can't be called remotely interesting, either. Yes, the combo delivers the obligatory exotica ("One Eyed Monkey") and Cox her required torch songs ("Bluebeard"), but having painted itself into a stylistic corner, Combustible Edison seems content to simply stand around and watch that paint dry.

Before their rebirth as lounge lizards, Cox and Cudahy were two-thirds of the Christmas, an absurdist folk-pop combo with a flair for trippy concepts often hamstrung by an affinity for too-straightforward songwriting. The fragile-sounding debut doesn't hold up particularly well, although a paean to Pee-wee Herman should elicit a chuckle or two. The band relocated to Las Vegas in the late '80s (a harbinger of things to come) and released **Ultraprophets of Thee Psykick Revolution,** which rocks quite a bit harder and takes fuller advantage of the creamy harmonies Cox and Cudahy can conjure up.

Vortex was recorded in 1990, but rejected by IRS; by the time Matador licensed and released it, Christmas was over. Too bad, since the band (by this point containing bassist James McNew, soon to join Yo La Tengo) had begun to match its considerable verbal skills with equal melodic invention, particularly on the tribal "Painted Savages," the X-styled "Jupiter, Florida" and the goofball country-raga "Medicine." [dss]

See also *Yo La Tengo; TPRG.*

COME

Eleven: Eleven (Matador) 1992
Don't Ask Don't Tell (Matador) 1994
Near Life Experience (Matador) 1996

UZI

Sleep Asylum EP (Homestead) 1986 (Matador) 1993

Surprisingly orthodox for a band generated by such "out" bloodlines, Come spends much of its time poking about in the more opiated, murkier corners of post-Stones blues-noise. Led by the charismatic Thalia Zedek—whose mightily lascivious vocals take their just place in the spotlight for the first time in a decade-long career—the quartet heaps tension atop tension, rarely providing even a semblance of release. (An ironic state of affairs, given the moniker.)

Eleven: Eleven is very much a guitar tour de force, drenched as it is in the sweaty fluids that come forth when the six-strings of Zedek (a veteran of Boston's Dangerous Birds and New York's Live Skull) and Chris Brokaw (who served concurrently as Codeine's drummer until 1993) rub against each other. The guitarists seldom settle into standard lead/rhythm roles; rather, they hydroplane in roughly parallel arcs over the steadfast rhythms laid down by drummer Arthur Johnson (formerly a member of spazz-punk ensemble the Bar-B-Q Killers) and bassist Sean O'Brien (who played with the Kilkenny Cats). On tracks like "Brand New Vein" and "Submerge," the atmosphere verges on the oppressive, the air heavy and blue-black with a pharmacological ennui that only abates on the double-barreled windup of "Fast Piss Blues" and a cover of the Stones' "I Got the Blues."

The hues don't get much brighter on **Don't Ask Don't Tell,** but the odd sliver of light does peek through the between-notes fissures. The mere fact that those cracks exist not only leavens the claustrophobia of more dynamic tracks (the dervish-like "Yr Reign") but also accentuates the power fomented when the foursome re-thickens the mood, as on the Iberian-tinged dirge "Finish Line." Again, both Brokaw and Zedek coax all manner of licentious notes into the darker corners of tracks like "Poison" and the slow-dance enchantment "Let's Get Lost," but this time the mood that lingers is one of liberation rather than pressure buildup.

Johnson and O'Brien departed before the recording of **Near Life Experience,** which was completed using two different rhythm sections—the team of Bundy Brown (Tortoise) and Mac McNeilly (Jesus Lizard) and ex-Rodan bandmates Tara Jane O'Neil and Kevin Coultas. Zedek's affinity for narcoleptic waltz-time constructions—like the one that wraps around "Hurricane"—has never been more apropos, given the dazed tone of most of the album's eight songs, particularly the pair that ramble forward led by Brokaw's parched lead vocals.

Between the Dangerous Birds and her relocation to New York, Zedek fronted Uzi, a gloomy, overly elliptical band that concealed her raspy singing behind a veil of murky guitar effects and tape manipulation, the latter provided by Boston scene vet Phil Milstein (more recently of Pep Lester & His Pals and a solo career). The Matador reissue of **Sleep Asylum** adds the previously unreleased, but scarcely indispensable, "Underneath." [dss]

See also *Codeine, Rodan, Steve Wynn.*

COMET GAIN

Casino Classics (Wiiija/X-mas) 1995

The soul bus let off the pop children in Oxford, England, and what sprouted was Comet Gain, a simply appointed and thoroughly enticing bedsit quintet that afflicts the alluring tunefulness of Heavenly with equally mild doses of guitar punk, garage-rock and the impulse that once directed Paul Weller toward the world of Curtis Mayfield. Sarah Bleach and guitarist David Christian take turns giving amateurish airy voice to catchy songs that aren't, in fact, as lyrically intriguing as their titles ("Ghost of the Roman Empire," "Chevron Action Flash," "Original Arrogance") promise. Still, the blend of Jax's organ and Hoffner Burns' snappy drumming give the best tracks a solid dose of beamed-in '60s, feeding a pointedly English effort and resulting in such winners as "A Million and Nine," "Stay With Me Til Morning" and the horn-charged revue blast, "A Kind of Loving." Daniel Treacy of the Television Personalities wrote the liner notes for **Casino Classics,** which says more about who the band's friends are than how their adorable sound leans. The American edition adds a couple of tracks from a 1993 Wiiija compilation single to the original UK issue. [tr]

COMMON SENSE

Can I Borrow a Dollar? (Relativity) 1992
Resurrection (Relativity) 1994

Although Common Sense's first album arrived around the same time as Arrested Development's and introduces a similarly laid-back and melodic rapper with more on his mind than blunts and gats, the conscious avoidance of gunplay and death in his rhymes doesn't exactly make the Chicago MC a wholesome positivist. Sounding like a belated Midwest echo of the East Coast's Native Tongues pumped with testosterone, **Can I Borrow a Dollar?** is a laid-back crib in which Common Sense slings endless pop/consumer culture references and enough crude desire (see "Charms Alarm" and "Tricks Up My Sleeve" for instant proof) to fully earn his parental advisory sticker. The gentle soul bounce of "Take It EZ" alludes to a modest, placid center for his individualism, and indeed Common Sense runs with a minimum of free-standing belligerence: even when he rips apart a woman in "Heidi Hoe" (the one track here produced by the Beatnuts), the rapper doesn't generalize the put-down. Promising in sensibility but short of thought, the debut introduces a smart young guy who still needs to find himself.

Fortunately, he did. **Resurrection** is all good, a considered and evocative reflection on growing up African-American in Chi-town. The outlook expressed in "Thisisme" is emblematic of a hardcore album free of violence and gratuitous vulgarity: the only kind of gangsta Common Sense wants to be in the song is the "gangsta of love." (Does that make Steve Miller a hip-hop pioneer?) Maturity hasn't cost Common Sense anything: the record is chockablock with mesmerizingly hyperactive rhymes, an uncommon vocabulary (how often do rappers "rebuke" people or compare MC styles to computer languages?) and ear-tickling citations of records, bands, TV shows, products and other pop ephemera. ("My style is too developed to be arrested," and "I didn't learn the facts of life by watching Tootie" are typical.) Wrapped in burnished soul beats by producer No I.D., Common Sense demonstrates his ingenuity by personalizing a chronicle of the hip-hop nation's chameleon style shifts ("I Used to Love H.E.R."), sketching an outline of racial economics in "Chapter 13 (Rich Man vs. Poor Man)" and summarizing his position in the modestly titled "Sum Shit I Wrote." He even gets his dad to offer some pacific wisdom of his own ("Pop's Rap"). But while the inclusion of a track called "Communism" suggests a resurgent left-wing orthodoxy in rap politics, the track is just a play on the rapper's name—a litany of words that begin with "com." [i]

COMPTONS MOST WANTED

It's a Compton Thang! (Orpheus) 1990
Straight Checkn 'Em (Orpheus/Epic) 1991
Music to Driveby (Orpheus/Epic) 1992

MC EIHT FEATURING CMW

We Come Strapped (Epic Street) 1994
Death Threatz (Epic Street) 1996

Making their initial mark in 1989 with the singles "Rhymes Too Funky" and "This Is Compton," Comptons Most Wanted was one of the first crews to take advantage of N.W.A's gangsta breakthrough. Originally made up of Unknown DJ, DJ Mike T, DJ Slip, the Chill MC and MC Eiht, the group boiled down to a trio and made its debut with **It's a Compton Thang!,** issued in two versions: full-on (featuring "Rhymes Too Funky" and "Give It Up") and censored (replacing those cuts with "We Made It"). Although not an especially gripping hardcore record, the inclusion of "One Time Gaffled Em Up," a CMW variation on "(Fuck) tha Police," brought the group some street credibility. On CMW's subsequent single, "Growin' Up in the Hood," a moody *Cleopatra Jones* loop and a stark drum break serve as the backdrop for Eiht and Chill as they capture the hopeless desperation of the downbeat *Boyz n the Hood,* the film for which it was commissioned.

Straight Checkn 'Em is an overlooked classic of the gangsta genre, important primarily for the music selected by DJ Slip and Unknown. Chill MC was incarcerated halfway through the recording, and lyricist/rapper Eiht began to find his cool-and-deadly voice on "Def Wish" (the first entry in the DJ Quik/MC Eiht diss war) and "Compton's Lynchin."

The provocatively titled **Music to Driveby** is actually less involving than that. Eiht goes after females in "Hoodrat" and does an unconvincing blues on "Niggaz Strugglin." But "Hood Took Me Under" picks up where "Growin' Up in the Hood" left off, proving Eiht to be a storyteller with a keen eye. Besides making a star-turn appearance in the movie *Menace II Society,* Eiht provided the stunning single "Streiht Up Menace" for the soundtrack, which substantially raised his profile.

With the group reduced to a duo, the sound is dramatically different on **We Come Strapped,** an album on which MC Eiht gets top billing. DJ Slip experiments with a more spacious, largely sample-free sound dominated by synth hooks and enormous bass, while Eiht slows his delivery and ups his dramatics. The best tracks—"Take 2 With Me," "Compton Cyco" and "All for the Money"—achieve a nearly cinematic scope, an apex of reality in music.

Likewise, **Death Threatz** keeps Eiht on his distinctive sonic path, working grooves unrelated to any contemporary hip-hop clichés. Although nothing more than a couple of keyboardists are credited, Slip's slow-rolling '70s-styling beats have a live feel that sets off Eiht's tough, incisive staccato-accented rhymes. The criminal-minded (and Cypress Hill–quoting) "Run 4 Your Life" and the hostile "Fuc Em All" are especially potent; although the subject matter is similar, the lush "Late Nite Hype Part 2" tones down the delivery for a nearly seductive expression of violence. [jzc/i]

COMPULSION

Compulsion EP (UK Fabulon) 1992
Casserole EP (UK Fabulon) 1993
Safety EP (UK One Little Indian) 1993
Boogie Woogie EP (Elektra) 1994
Comforter (Interscope/Atlantic) 1994
The Future Is Medium (UK One Little Indian) 1996

THEE AMAZING COLOSSAL MEN

Totale (UK Siren/Virgin) 1990

In a constellation of retro-looking and -sounding bands, London's Compulsion—three Irishmen and a Dutch drummer—is the great spiky hope for punk-like rock. Combining the best of Nirvana's quiet-loud dynamics and the Pixies' axemanship with incredibly forceful presentation (both live and on record), the band has forged a pummeling, absolutely individual sound.

Aging angry young man singer Josephmary and fellow Dubliner bassist Sid Rainey first hooked up in the '60s-inspired Thee Amazing Colossal Men. With the addition of guitarist Garret Lee and drummer Jan-Willem Alkema, they formed Compulsion and released two powerful vinyl-only EPs on their own label; **Compulsion** and **Casserole** were later collected on a bonus CD available in initial UK copies of **Comforter;** a few of the EPs' best tracks compose the band's American debut, **Boogie Woogie.**

After bailing on a deal with Elektra, Compulsion issued its brilliant debut album, **Comforter,** on Interscope. Over vividly chunky riffs and ringing epic guitar (most notably on the gruesome "Accident Ahead" and Nirvana-echoing "Lovers"), Josephmary proffers muscular gravelly vocals, the likes of which should have neighbors complaining in a jif. After delivering aggro shoutathons ("Find Time") and speedy pop-punk ("Easterman"), the band shows off its technical prowess on the instrumentals "Late Again" and "Dick, Dale, Rick, and Rickey," which surf a decidedly Pixie-ish guitar wave. A remarkable new band.

Despite its Devo-esque cover photo, the second album offers more of the same—tuneful if not exactly subtle punky growlers with cumbersome song titles like "Question Time for the Proles" and "Juvenile Scene Detective." [db]

CONCRETE BLONDE

Concrete Blonde (IRS) 1987
Free (IRS) 1989
Bloodletting (IRS) 1990
Walking in London (IRS) 1992
Mexican Moon (IRS/Capitol) 1993
Still in Hollywood (IRS) 1994
Recollection (IRS) 1996

VOWEL MOVEMENT

Vowel Movement (Mammoth) 1995

PRETTY & TWISTED

Pretty & Twisted (Warner Bros.) 1995

Concrete Blonde, the Los Angeles partnership of singer/bassist (and guitarist) Johnette Napolitano and ex-Sparks guitarist Jim Mankey, evolved from a group called Dream 6 and made its debut in 1987 with a terrible album that could be half-finished demos. Napolitano's untrained voice is remarkably unappealing (especially when she tries too hard to ape Chrissie Hynde); the pair's guitar work is patently derivative and the songs thrust along with neither focus nor flair.

The better-sounding **Free,** recorded as a quartet, is a loud, textured rock record with Harry Rushakoff's clunky drumming and singing that is only occasionally overzealous. The two songs that stand out (for opposite reasons) are the sweet, catchy "Happy Birthday" and "Roses Grow," a bizarre and inept stab at rap.

In Concrete Blonde's third incarnation, Napolitano (taking sole songwriting credit and putting down her guitar) and Mankey were joined by ex–Roxy Music drummer Paul Thompson. Erstwhile metal producer Chris Tsangarides makes a tentative attempt to move the trio toward the mainstream on **Bloodletting,** roughing/punching up the sound a bit, adding instrumental and theatrical vocal layers without appreciably raising the band's volume. But the songs—other than those inspired by Anne Rice's fiction, almost all about a failed relationship—haven't got the melodic content to hold the charge. "Joey," a Heart-like ballad to an addict ("And if you're somewhere out there/Passed out on the floor/Oh Joey, I'm not angry anymore"), rewrites "Love Hurts" to sappy effect.

Rushakoff returned for **Walking in London,** a record that consolidates witchy-woman Napolitano's metaphysical obsessions and dubious feminism. With Tsangarides helping organize a restrained environment of stylish atmosphe-rock (and Cheap Trick's Tom Petersson playing "additional bass," whatever that means), Napolitano's blustery singing and why-wouldn't-they like-it? songwriting are the only intemperate elements left (as if anything else mattered). "Ghost of a Texas Ladies' Man," the multilingual "Les Coeurs Jumeaux" and "City Screaming" are ridiculous inventions; another bout of the hip-hops ("I Wanna Be Your Friend Again") is dismal. And "Woman to Woman" is about competition, not solidarity. A female-sung cover of James Brown's "It's a Man's Man's Man's World" is unfortunately typical of the dim-bulb invention and imagination on which this band appears to function.

Musical (drum) chairs left Thompson and Rushakoff sharing the honors on **Mexican Moon,** an eclectic, inflamed major-label debut that veers from the roaring melodrama of "Jenny I Read" and "Heal It Up" to the swirling acoustic guitars and hoarsely whispered (if patronizingly accented) singing of the title track; "Jonestown" employs a sample of Jim Jones and distortion on Napolitano's voice for effect. Including songs by Steve Wynn ("When You Smile," given feedback-edged menace) and Bryan Ferry (an attempt to shoehorn "End of the Line," from Roxy Music's **Siren,** into jovial ordinariness), collaborating with cow-punk volcano Texacala Jones (of Tex and the Horseheads) and generally brewing up a frenetic Day of the Dead religious apocalypse in a teapot, Napolitano—who is still a mighty bad singer and doesn't seem to know it—gives her headstrong, knicker-twisting all to the effort, and very nearly gets by on sheer gumption.

With the star off to try other things under different names, Concrete Blonde ended, its passing marked by the **Still in Hollywood** compilation of non-album matter: B-sides, soundtrack contributions, live cuts (including an acoustic "Joey") and outtakes. For better and worse, the retrospective is heavy with other people's songs: Leonard Cohen, Rick Nielsen, Nick Cave, Jimi Hendrix and Bob Dylan are among the notables whose work gets the Concrete Blonde cement-overshoes treatment. With such low points as a live "Roses Grow," this stays close to wretched from start to finish.

On the way to her next pit stop, Napolitano made **Vowel Movement,** a largely improvised and sporadically entertaining goddesses-of-thunder bash with drummer/guitarist/singer Holly Vincent. She then cemented a longstanding palship with Wall of Voodoo by forming Pretty & Twisted with that group's ex-guitarist,

Marc Moreland (who lasted for one P&T album and tour before bowing out, to be replaced by English veteran Knox Chandler); drummer Danny Montgomery completes the trio. While **Pretty & Twisted** simplifies things and cuts away the artsier pretensions of latter-day Concrete Blonde, it replaces them with dopier ego indulgences: a humiliating fan-letter/song to Marlon Brando ("I'd like to come and visit if you'd give me a call . . . You are the coolest of the cool/I hope you call"), a song that sets Charles Bukowski poetry to music (wow! what a *cool* idea) and a sappy homage to a drag queen. Back to her old cover tricks, Napolitano turns Roxy Music's elegant "Mother of Pearl" into an imbecilic choogle. The bassist essays songwriting collaborations with persons living (Moreland, Paul Westerberg, Chris Bailey) and dead (Janis Joplin is credited with the words to "Come Away With Me"). The high incidence of sensitive ballads and pop stylings (both oddly inflected with bits of feedback and guitar noise low in the mix—is that the "alternative" sound we've been hearing so much about?) might have been beneficial if Napolitano's voice were more intrinsically appealing or her respect for melody more reliable. Still, "Train Song (Edge of Desperation)" is moodily effective, and the harmony-laden "¡Ride!" comes as close as anything in her recorded repertoire to packing genuine vocal allure. [i]

See also *Holly Vincent; TPRG.*

CONGO NORVELL

Lullabies EP10 (Fiasco) 1993
Music to Remember Him By (Basura!/Priority) 1994
The Dope, the Lies, the Vaseline (Basura!/Priority) 1996

KRISTIAN HOFFMAN

I Don't Love My Guru Anymore (Eggbert) 1993

Los Angeles' Congo Norvell, the namesake partnership of guitarist Kid Congo Powers (Cramps, Gun Club, Bad Seeds) and singer Sally Norvell (Prohibition), is said to have begun at the deathbed of a mutual friend. After that dramatic beginning, the two set about assembling a band of eccentrics that, by its very nature, would produce eccentric music. So far, so good.

The **Lullabies** EP is so quiet it nearly lives up to its title, but the four torch songs and druggy apostrophes would not inspire very sweet dreams. Space is a primary instrument, and the songs are filled with emptiness, setting the melodies against vast silences that give them even more of a desperate feel than Norvell's melodramatic way with a melody. "Lullaby" and a cover of Crime and the City Solution's "Angel" are the most successful tracks.

By contrast, **Music to Remember Him By** is a cabaret show. Norvell's throaty voice and anthemic phrasings are enough to make Helen Merrill fans weak at the knees as Powers' spaghetti western guitar lines play off the theatrical keyboard stylings by Kristian Hoffman (formerly of the Swinging Madisons and New York's Lance Loud–led Mumps, more recently a solo folkie) and spare percussion (bongos are a favorite) by drummer Joseph Berardi (James White, Stan Ridgway). Considering all the elements at work, the music is spectacularly understated, allowing Norvell to take a star turn. Alone in the spotlight, she radiates heartache in "My Midnight" and "Drift Away," hitting every note like a spurned housewife drunk on cooking sherry and Jackie Collins. The postmodern coffeehouse feel is, at times, an uncomfortably kitschy mix, but it's creepy and compelling just the same. [sf]

See also *Nick Cave and the Bad Seeds, Cramps, Gun Club.*

CONNELLS

Darker Days (Black Park) 1985 (TVT) 1987
Boylan Heights (TVT) 1987
Fun & Games (TVT) 1989
One Simple Word (TVT) 1990
Ring (TVT) 1993
New Boy EP (TVT) 1994
Weird Food & Devastation (TVT) 1996

GEORGE HUNTLEY

brain junk (TVT) 1996

Fronted by guitarist Mike Connell (his brother David is the bassist), this Raleigh, North Carolina, quintet mixes singer/songwriter introspection and college radio guitar-pop with generally effective results. Formed in the early part of the '80s and working hard through that decade, the earnest band greeted the '90s with its strongest album, the smart, punchy **One Simple Word.**

The Connells' debut, **Darker Days,** is awkward, but its pleasant, jangly pop shows quite a bit of promise. **Boylan Heights** is subtler and more sophisticated, but also darker—and not nearly so much fun. Though its name might seem to imply otherwise, the edgier **Fun & Games** (to which guitarist George Huntley contributed four songs; Mike Connell is the band's primary writer) is almost as brooding, but the Connells more ably balance melancholy with melody—especially on the title track and "Inside My Head."

One Simple Word is the band's tightest and least mopey album. Doug MacMillan's singing carries more authority; the songs are both catchy and clever. "Stone Cold Yesterday" and "Get a Gun" are guitar-pop gems—two of the band's best—and the Huntley-penned "The Joke" is witty and melodic, making it his best contribution to the band's songbook.

The next album lacks much of **One Simple Word**'s punch, yet the appropriately titled **Ring** does just that—at least the guitars do, on songs like "Slack-jawed" and "New Boy." The record contains some brilliant pieces of pop songcraft ("Carry My Picture," "Eyes on the Ground") and some bittersweet lyrical ruminations, but slower numbers like "'74–'75" are so sweet they border on cloying. For all its solid virtues, the **Ring** still sounds tentative compared to its predecessor.

Fun but basically disposable, the **New Boy** EP combines live and studio versions of its title track (from **Ring**) with two previously unreleased songs, a second live number and a cover. The new studio tunes are unexceptionally decent, but the pop-inflected rendition of Jethro Tull's "Living in the Past" is a goof that quickly wears thin; while introspective and powerful, the live "Fun & Games" is not nearly enough to carry the record.

Huntley's solo album—which he didn't quit the Connells to record—is an attempt to get back to his southern roots. Unfortunately, only a few of the songs on **brain junk** effectively combine country and pop. The rest aren't as catchy or clever as most of the tunes Huntley has written for the Connells, and his debut is disappointing compared with the group's recent albums. [rl]

See also *TPRG.*

CHRIS CONNELLY

Whiplash Boychild (Wax Trax!) 1991
Phenobarb Bambalam (Wax Trax!) 1992
Shipwreck (Wax Trax!) 1994

Wiping off the industrial grit, burning flames and sleazy sampler ooze of his night jobs in Revolting Cocks, Ministry and Pigface, Edinburgh-born/Chicago-resident singer, guitarist and pianist Chris Connelly (*not* the MTV film-show host/*Premiere* magazine editor but the former Fini Tribe member) has made three restrained solo albums that increase the peace and are, at heart, more pop than anything else. Paying proud homage to moody Anglo-American pop legend Scott Walker in both the style and title of **Whiplash Boychild** (credit also goes to the Velvet Underground's "Venus in Furs" for the phrase), Connelly starts things off plain and obvious with the restrained Bowiesque balladry of "Daredevil" and "Ghost of a Saint" (both of which sound precisely like **Scary Monsters** demos) and the dolorous piano and paper-thin singing of "This Edge of Midnight," but soon winds his way onto craggier terrain: "Stowaway" (especially the "daydream mix") takes a mild ride down the techno road, "The Game Is All Yours" does the clubland house boogie and "Confessions of the Highest Bidder" is a distracted tape collage. An ambitious lyricist who doesn't quite have poetry within his reach, Connelly is an able, mannered singer with some intriguing ideas. Covering Walker's bizarrely mundane exposition, "The Amorous Humphrey Plugg," isn't one of them, however.

Phenobarb Bambalam, which Connelly recorded in the aftermath of his girlfriend's suicide and dedicated to her memory, cuts back on the Walker/Bowie devotions for a bit of the sterner rock aggression and dance rhythms of Connelly's other endeavors. (Although the downcast '60s inflections of "Too Good to Be True" and the guilty feedback miseries of "Heartburn" do follow **Whiplash Boychild**'s lead; a dramatic cover of Tom Verlaine's "Souvenir From a Dream" introduces a new design entirely.) Keeping the sound pressure beneath drastic levels, Connelly sounds like all the wind has been sucked out of his sails; the bleak record winds along aimlessly on auto-pilot, avoiding sharp turns and great ambitions, often letting the grooves shape the songwriting rather than the other way around. Although hauntingly effective in conveying gloom, **Phenobarb Bambalam** shunts much of the suffering in the lyrics away; Connelly's resigned singing leaves the album's emotional door wide open, and all the claustrophobia in the music rushes right out.

Shipwreck brings Connelly triumphantly back to shore in a swimmingly (sorry) integrated blend of unabashed pop songcraft, artfully inspired singing and diverse stylistic imagination. A wordy personal recollection of religion and family, "Spoonfed Celeste" bounces along in a vintage dance-hall idiom; the lonely, alienated portraiture of "Anyones' Mistake" becomes a gorgeous, finely detailed waltz. Drummer William Rieflin (of Ministry, Pigface and other bands), who played on **Whiplash Boychild** as well, fires up a breathtaking attack on "Drench" and settles into a snappy stride for "The Early Nighters," a sublimely tuneful jazz-pop eulogy for River Phoenix. Using the consistency of his voice to seam together smooth restraint and demi-bludgeonry, Connelly lets guitarists Chris Bruce and William Tucker and bassist Bruce McNulty load up the tanks for the oppressive density of "Meridian Afterburn," then floats calm emotional crooning over it all like a lord and master observing the battle from the safety of a castle tower. Connelly's pronounced vocal resemblance to Bowie remains disarming throughout **Shipwreck**'s eleven fascinating chapters, but as long as the real thing shows no inclination of creating music this affecting and accessible, Connelly might as well make the most of it. [i]

See also *Killing Joke, Ministry, Pigface, Revolting Cocks; TPRG.*

TONY CONRAD

See *Faust.*

CONSCIOUS DAUGHTERS

See *Paris.*

CONSOLIDATED

¡Consolidated! EP (Can. Nettwerk) 1989
The Myth of Rock (Nettwerk/IRS) 1990
Friendly Fa$cism (Nettwerk/IRS) 1991
Play More Music (Nettwerk/IRS) 1992
Business of Punishment (London) 1994

CHILDMAN

Childman (Can. Nettwerk) 1993

Consolidated (lyricist/singer Adam Sherburne, drum programmer Philip Steir and keyboard "operator" Mark Pistel) say their mission is to take revolution to the dancefloor. Using house, hip-hop, rock, funk, rap, industrial noise and an endless flurry of samples, the band's devout message includes anti-sexist, anti-racist and anti-capitalist rants as well as a militant stance in favor of reproductive choice, animal rights and vegetarianism.

Sherburne was born a military brat and raised in Monterey; he trained to be a professional athlete but threw it away to play music. His musical career eventually led him to Until December, a San Francisco new wave group. Pistel was born in Minnesota where his father worked rehabilitating handicapped people; he started his first rock'n'roll band at age nine. Steir grew up in Piedmont, an ultra-rich and conservative neighborhood of Oakland. They met when Pistel and Steir replaced departed members of Until December.

As Consolidated, the trio vowed to make music that mattered, an industrial-strength assault on what they call "the racist, sexist, capitalist system known as the music business." The harsh, stripped-down six-song **¡Consolidated!** EP (which contains the proclamation of purpose "Consolidated" in two mixes) was followed by **Myth of Rock.** The set has a dark industrial edge, but the music is undermined by the humorless, patronizing tone of the vocals. On tracks like "Dysfunctional Relationship" and "Message to the People," the band is preaching, not entertaining; the message may be politically correct but the stance is as sanctimonious as that of any right-wing fundamentalist.

Early on, the band made a point of engaging its fans in dialectic conversations during and after gigs; on **Friendly Fa$cism,** Consolidated experiments with "inter-active democracy" by dropping sampled snippets of these dialogues into their tunes. Ironically, "Unity of Oppression," a track that slams America's corporate mentality, made MTV's Top 10 video list for '91. Still, the insufferably self-righteous tone again makes the disc hard to listen to.

Play More Music has guest appearances by Paris, who adds some much-needed street cred, and feisty Berkeley feminist rap trio the Yeastie Girlz (on "You Suck"), who bring some much-needed humor to the proceedings, but neither can stop the beats from sinking under the weight of Consolidated's self-important rhetoric. Making a politically daring move to a major label for **Business of Punishment,** the trio sounds like any other industro-metal-rap band. The lyrical density that undermines the dance beats remains in full effect, although there are flashes of bitter (if unintentional) humor in "Dog + Pony Show," a detailed screed against the band's record company ("This will be the last time a label tries to jerk us 'cause we can get worked on Nettwerk . . . and no you can't have the fucking back catalog . . ."), while "Woman Shoots John," a "Superfly" parody in which a prostitute kills a customer, proves the band capable of compassionate and compelling music when they put their minds to it.

Sherburne waxes funky, lets down his romantic hair and even sings (after a Peter Wolf-y oomagooma fashion) in his side project, but makes a point of clinging to his impossible moral high ground and obsessive guilt on **Childman.** Dispensing with hard techno beats, the bizarre ride includes Hendrixy guitar rock ("3 Reasons"), a grim pregnancy story ("False Positive") recited over a wailing siren, the audio documentary of a birth ("Lily J.A.C."), newsreel samples and some grooves as musically inviting as Spearhead's. Although it's obvious Sherburne is working to humanize and soften his approach here, the ridiculous "Refuse to Be a Man" is as absurd as anything in Consolidated's repertoire. [jp/i]

CONTAINE

See *Versus.*

CONTINENTAL DRIFTERS

Continental Drifters (Monkey Hill) 1994

For most of 1992, Tuesday nights in Hollywood meant that the Continental Drifters could be found on the stage of Raji's. Instigated the previous year by drummer/singer Carlo Nuccio (who had been in an early-'80s New Orleans precursor to the Subdudes by the same name) and guitarist/singer Ray Ganucheau—Louisiana émigrés getting some buddies together to write and play for fun—the residency turned into an indie-scene happening that attracted the cream of a likeminded crop. The weekly roots-rock hootenanny eventually solidified into an absurdly talented family containing multi-instrumentalist/singer Peter Holsapple (ex-dB's), bassist Mark Walton (ex–Dream Syndicate) and singer/guitarists Vicki Peterson (ex-Bangles) and Susan Cowsill (ex-Cowsills).

By the time of the group's debut album, Ganucheau was gone and the lineup had settled down to a six-piece with five gifted songwriters and four lead singers. A powerful, superbly played record of indescribable diversity—put pins in the Band, the Bangles and the soulful side of John Hiatt and connect the dots, that at least describes the perimeter—**Continental Drifters** is a passionate, populist winner in which everyone has a say worth hearing. If the singing lacks precision, the depth of emotions put into—and drawn from—the songs more than makes up for it.

Cowsill sings Walton's angry "Get Over It" with the surety of a woman who's been through it all and renders Goffin/King's "I Can't Make It Alone" with aching sadness and love; the rough edges of her own "Desperate Love" can't obscure its fiery core. Peterson's frustration at the "Mixed Messages" she's getting is palpable, as is her determination in Mike Nesmith's "Some of Shelly's Blues." Holsapple gives a handsome burnish to "Soul Deep" (a Wayne Thompson song done by the Box Tops) and tells an enigmatic romantic tale in the swaying "Invisible Boyfriend." Nuccio bounces through life's ups and downs in "New York" and "Mezzanine." Rather than a sampler of co-dependent solo artists, **Continental Drifters** is a sympathetic collective of individual hearts, minds and voices strengthening each other. [i]

See also *Chris Stamey.*

CONTROL PANEL

See *His Name Is Alive.*

CONVICTS

See *Geto Boys.*

COO COO ROCKIN TIME

See *Half Japanese.*

COOLIES

See *Ottoman Empire.*

COOLIO

It Takes a Thief (Tommy Boy) 1994
Gangsta's Paradise (Tommy Boy) 1995

WC AND THE MAAD CIRCLE

Ain't a Damn Thang Changed (Priority) 1991
Curb Servin' (Payday/London) 1995

Coolio has achieved a rare thing in the music world: maintaining his underground credibility while playing the pop game for all the exposure it can give him. His braids-to-the-sky hairdo has become a trademark as familiar as Michael Jackson's mono-glove, and every one of his hits to date has relied on a single formula, a wise rap riding on the back of a '70s sample. His past, however, lies in Compton's mean streets: ten months in juvenile detention for his connection with a murder a friend committed during a mugging and several years of crack addiction. Though Coolio (born Artis Ivey) had been rapping since he was fifteen, it wasn't until he cleaned himself up (quitting drugs to become a firefighter) that his career began. He was thirty—well over the hill in hip-hop time—when he had his first hit.

Coolio made his recorded debut (braids down) on WC and the MAAD Circle's first album, **Ain't a Damn Thang Changed.** With the patronage of Ice Cube, the band (whose leader, WC, was once in the rap duo Low Profile with DJ Aladdin) raps tag-team style over mid-tempo drum-machine beats, funky basslines and the occasional live instrument and sample. (Tears for Fears' "Shout" mysteriously pops up in "Caught n a Fad.") The album's subject is real-life tales of the ghetto, from the abusive, alcoholic, cheating father ("Fuck My Daddy") to the monetary advantages of robbing and dealing over straight jobs ("You Don't Work, U Don't Eat"). The best song, "Dress Code," talks about prejudice toward not just skin color but also formality of attire.

Coolio's chosen topic on the MAAD Circle album is his time in prison and how he's not going back; on his solo debut, **It Takes a Thief,** he amplifies on that desire in songs that are mostly reflections on the past. In "Fantastic Voyage," its chorus taken from the 1980 Lakeside song of the same name, Coolio name-checks two WC and the MAAD Circle songs and imagines a dream neighborhood where "Everybody got a stack, and it ain't no crack/And it really don't matter if you're white or black." For the better part of the album, Coolio portrays himself as a ghetto cartoon, offering songs that are half-joke, half–real life: "Mama, I'm in Love wit a Gangsta" and "Smokin' Stix." "I Remember," with a hook from Al Green's "Tomorrow's Dream," most skillfully fuses fact and whimsy, as Coolio and friends reminisce on pre-pubescent days of poverty and innocence like a comedy team trying to deliver a moral without breaking the light-hearted mood.

Coolio continues his ghetto morality play on **Gangsta's Paradise,** rhyming with the laid-back voice of experience. The excellent title track, taken from the film *Dangerous Minds,* became the biggest single of 1995. In the verses, Coolio sings from the point of view of a headstrong, trigger-happy twenty-three-year-old; the choruses, half Stevie Wonder's "Pastime Paradise" and half the soulful vocals of a singer known as L.V. (which stands for "large variety"), pull back to weep over the fate of a good rat caught in an inhumane maze. Much of the album, which is slower and more R&B-oriented than **It Takes a Thief,** seems to have been thrown together to capitalize on the success of "Gangsta's Paradise." In "Too Hot," Coolio delivers a safe-sex message over smooth, lackluster R&B. And in "For My Sistas," he reverses the position of last album's "Ugly Bitches" to pay respect to the female record-buying demographic.

After several years spent getting out of its contract with Priority Records, WC and the MAAD Circle returned with **Curb Servin'.** Taking a tip from Coolio (who performs on one song, "In a Twist"), the band finds fuel for its songs in R&B classics. At the same time, it sticks to its tough, streetwise rhymes. The combination is unwieldy and the results are uninventive. [ns]

JULIAN COPE

World Shut Your Mouth (UK Mercury) 1984
Fried (UK Mercury) 1984
Saint Julian (Island) 1987
My Nation Underground (Island) 1988
Skellington (UK CopeCo/Zippo) 1990 (UK K.A.K. Ltd.) 1994
Droolian (UK MoFoCo/Zippo) 1990
Peggy Suicide (Island) 1991
Jehovahkill (Island) 1992
Floored Genius: The Best of Julian Cope and The Teardrop Explodes 1979–91 (Island) 1992
Floored Genius 2: Julian Cope—Best of the BBC Sessions 1983–91 (Nighttracks/Dutch East India Trading) 1993
Autogeddon (American) 1994
Rite (UK K.A.K. Ltd.) 1994
Queen Elizabeth (UK Echo Special Products) 1994
Julian Cope Presents 20 Mothers (American) 1995

There are essentially three phases to the long and twisted career of Julian Cope, the man who merged Iggy Pop and Syd Barrett with his own warped psychedelic punk/pop sensibility. Born in Wales but raised in the small mining town of Tamworth, he undertook the first part of his tale in the druggy saga of Liverpool's premier new wave "bubblegum trance" band, The Teardrop Explodes. (The full story can be read in the first volume of Cope's autobiography, *Head-On: Memories of the Liverpool Punk Scene and the Story of The Teardrop Explodes, 1976–82,* published by his own Ma-Gog Books.) The second phase encompasses Cope's efforts to fine-tune different elements of his sound as a solo artist—the big, bouncy pop tunes and the stark acid campfire songs—starting with **World Shut Your Mouth** in 1984 and stretching through a pair of do-it-yourself releases in '90, **Skellington** and **Droolian.** The two **Floored Genius** collections offer a condensed but very rewarding overview of both of these periods, and they're highly recommended for anyone who wants a quick introduction before exploring Cope's '90s work, which in many ways is his strongest and most original.

Leaving behind his late-'80s image as a cynical, burned-out Barrett-like character ("Namdam am I, I'm a madman," he had announced in the liner notes to **Fried**), Cope reinvented himself as an elder statesman of weirdness, a stay-at-home family man who nevertheless has a burning desire to make rock that explores such esoteric interests as environmentalism, stone circles, religious conspiracies and incest. **Peggy Suicide** is a surprising introduction to this new Cope; it's also a masterpiece of pop-rock weirdness and the single best album of his career. The sprawling record is a concept effort about the sorry plight of the title character, essentially a stand-in for Mother Earth. But unlike bloated concept efforts from the '70s, every one of the eighteen songs is strong enough to stand on its own. Raw, immediate tunes such as "Beautiful Love," "East Easy Rider" and "Safesurfer" draw you in with seductive grooves, bubbling synthesizers, echoed guitars and singalong choruses that work even if you don't quite buy the lyrical messages about the destructive power of automobiles or the horrors of love in the age of AIDS.

Cope tried to repeat the formula of **Peggy Suicide** on his next two concept efforts, which veer a bit closer to trippy wankery. **Jehovahkill** tackles the themes of ancient stone formations such as Stonehenge and what Cope considers a Christian conspiracy to suppress pagan symbols. (The album's subtitle, *That'll Be the Deicide*—like **Peggy Suicide,** a pun on a Buddy Holly song—was mangled in the US so the cover reads *That'll Be the Decide.*) After a bitter split with Island, Cope moved to American Records for **Autogeddon,** an album prompted by the spontaneous explosion of his car in the driveway one Christmas Eve. Lyrically, it continues the anti-auto tirades and environmental concerns of **Peggy Suicide,** but Cope neglects hooks in favor of a jam-happy sound derived from such early '70s German psychedelic bands as Amon Düül II, Neu! and Can, favorites from Cope's teenage years. He continued to pay tribute to these groups in another book, *Krautrocksampler,* and two DIY instrumental albums, **Rite** and **Queen Elizabeth,** which are only for true krautrock aficionados. A little bit of gurgling analog synthesizer and echoplexed guitar goes an awfully long way.

The man who once declared himself Saint Julian quit the noodling and returned to crafting short, sharp pop songs in 1995. Ostensibly a concept disc about incest (though that storyline is pretty hard to detect), the twenty tunes on **20 Mothers** again feature those trademark bouncy hooks, in addition to the weird synth sounds and production tricks and Cope's strong Iggy-inflected baritone. Cope did a handful of gigs to support the album—he has generally shied away from the stage throughout the '90s—but hopes for a full-blown tour were short-lived. Meanwhile, the prolific artist shows no signs of slowing down, and he promises another volume of his autobiography, a book about the ancient stones, more full-blown solo albums and offbeat DIY releases in the years to come. [jdr]

See also *TPRG.*

COP SHOOT COP

Headkick Facsimile EP (Japan. Supernatural Organization) 1989
Piece Man EP (Vertical) 1989
Consumer Revolt (Circuit) 1990 (Big Cat) 1992
White Noise (Big Cat) 1991
Suck City EP (Interscope/Atlantic) 1992
Ask Questions Later (Interscope/Atlantic) 1993
Release (Interscope/Atlantic) 1995

MOTHERHEAD BUG

Zambodia (Pow Wow) 1993

Anyone unfamiliar with this Lower East Side mob of miscreants might well ascertain all they need to know by taking a look (and a sniff) at the cover of an early single that came spattered in (very real) pig's blood. All of those left in the room after first exposure will no doubt revel in the sternum-crushing rhythms and bewildering sample overload emanating from the speakers—and give extra points for the luridly anti-authority (heck, anti-*everything*) slogans that lead snarler Tod Ashley lobs into the mix.

Cop Shoot Cop formed out of the ashes of noise-masters Dig Dat Hole and exceedingly confrontational junk-blues potentates Black Snakes (a band that counted among its members transgressive filmmaker Richard Kern). The quartet wasted no time establishing a reputation for sonic fuckery through use of sheet-metal percussion and guitar disavowal (Ashley and Jack Natz both play bass, with the former taking credit for "high end" version of the instrument). The early self-released EPs move with a decidedly mechanical grind, but sidestep industrial pigeonholding thanks to the inventive found-sound sampling of "Cripple" Jim Filer. **Consumer Revolt** (which disappeared almost instantly after its initial release on a flimsy Long Island indie) finds Ashley formulating a barbed, whipsmart perspective on American society, accented by fractured backing tracks that always manage to fall away when the frontman is about to deliver his punchline. Black humor beats black metal any day.

Passing judgments like "Injustice is never an accident/Repression is only a state of mind" ("Traitor/Martyr") on the shapely, song-strong **White Noise** suggest that there is a moral gyroscope to all this. Still, Ashley saves his best lines for the usual topics: "Corporate Protopop" (foreshadowing an obsession that would get further consideration on the next release) promises "Your needs are our main concern" and urges consumers to "nurture your desires . . . cultivate your desires . . . let them grow and flower into the blossom that is greed."

In characteristic fashion, **Suck City** steamrolls anyone who'd cry "major-label sellout" by shamelessly presenting the four-song EP as just that: A sleeve line even suggests that buyers should "file under '90s nostalgia." Although most of the material is subdued, almost funereal, the title track swings with an exaggerated swagger as Ashley unravels a self-mocking, post-"Truckin'" bio ("We'll be history by 34/there's always the reunion tour . . . suck city, here we come") that should put the tired genre to rest once and for all. The ensuing **Ask Questions Later** maintains that acrimony, wrapping Ashley's ever-virulent neo-anarchist rhetoric (which proves particularly potent on "$10 Bill" and "Got No Soul") in elaborate arrangements that employ a three-man horn section keyed by trombonist David Ouimet.

For **Release,** the band broke with (or caved in to) tradition by adding a guitarist, Steve McMillen, even though the still-bass-heavy sound of songs like "Interference" and the Mancini-on-methadone "Last Legs" indicates they don't seem to have found a lot for him to do. Nevertheless, the crisper overall sound and scrupulous inclusion of previously superfluous frills like easy hooks and singalong choruses ("It Only Hurts When I Breathe" strives oh-so-hard for anthemic status) paint a picture of a band sneaking surreptitiously toward the mainstream.

After playing in a nascent version of Cop Shoot Cop, David Ouimet formed Motherhead Bug, a purposefully disconcerting industrial orchestra. On **Zambodia,** the free-flowing aggregation appears as a nine-piece, with three drummers, two string players and a horn trio carving out rough-hewn noisebursts. The instrumentation and Ouimet's theatrical vocals lend a decadent grandeur to Weill-esque numbers like "Demon Erection" and "My Sweet Milstar." It may be burlesque, but it's still pretty scary stuff. [dss]

CORNERSHOP

In the Days of Ford Cortina EP7 (UK Wiiija) 1993
Lock, Stock and Double-Barrel EP (UK Wiiija) 1993
Elvis Sex-Change EP (UK Wiiija) 1993
Hold on It Hurts (UK Wiiija) 1994 (Wiiija/Merge) 1995
Readers' Wives EP (UK Wiiija) 1994
Born Disco; Died Heavy Metal EP7 (UK Wiiija) 1994 (Merge) 1994
Woman's Gotta Have It (Wiiija/Luaka Bop/Warner Bros.) 1995

Leicester, England's prolific Cornershop launched its career with the buzzy **In the Days of Ford Cortina,** a four-song EP, at the beginning of 1993 and hasn't bothered to look back. (Or, judging by the deluge of singles and EPs the group released that same year, for the studio exit door, either.) Led by brothers Tjinder (vocals/bass) and Avtar (guitar) Singh with three others, including self-described "token honky" Dave Chambers on drums and sitar/keyboard player Anthony Saffrey, this remarkable band has grown immensely through the recording process and has survived the suffocating, fickle and often dim-witted adoration heaped upon it by the notoriously shallow British pop music press.

In the Days of Ford Cortina isn't a pretty effort, but it demonstrates the outfit's knowledge of traditional Indian stylings (illustrated on the flute-and-sitar-rich "Waterlogged") as well as its ability to play distortion-laden punk rock ("Moonshine"). Of the other shortplayers released by the quartet in 1993, the strongest by far is the four-song **Lock, Stock and Double-Barrel,** a screaming, pounding little masterpiece of youthful, anger-soaked sloppiness. A reprise of the previously released "England's Dreaming," written in tribute to author Jon Savage's new wave history of the same title, opens the disc with aplomb in a disjointed, discordant three-and-a-half-minute punk puzzle (with a Hindi count-off, no less) whose pieces joyously don't exactly fit together. "Trip Easy" drapes sitar over an uneasy psychedelic foundation, while "Breaking Every Rule Language English" pokes wry fun at Asian assimilation and acceptance in Great Britain. **Lock, Stock and Double-Barrel** was appended to the US edition of the first album.

Hold on It Hurts is a politically charged popfest, ten tracks (fifteen in the US) of noisy delights that meld incisive social commentary ("You Always Said My Language Would Get Me Into Trouble") with a firm hold on British post-punk. From the opening drive of "Jason Donovan/Tessa Sanderson" to the earnest "Where D'U Get Your Information," **Hold on It Hurts** upholds its aggression and intelligence. The album's forward motion is interrupted occasionally, but to very strong effect. "Counteraction" is a straight-up Indian pop tune free of any outright Western influence, and the narrative "Tera Mera Pyar" tells the story of a self-obsessed Indian film star. The combination of incongruous styles may appear unappealing on paper, but the songs blend as well as the ingredients of a smooth highball, one that's a lot more potent than it tastes. **Hold on It Hurts** is brilliant. (Which can't exactly be said of the unlisted track in which an American trucker croons a country recipe for ground beef hash.)

Following two EPs built around album tracks, Cornershop signed a major-label deal and had to consider the challenge of America. The group's response was the relatively slick and very different **Woman's Gotta Have It.** Many of the tracks are longer than any in the band's past; the record leans more toward Indian pop than Western rock. When the album fixes on rock stylings, the results abandon straightforward aggression-laden concision for ponderous expositions ("Roof Rack") or choppy looseness (the Fall-like "Hong Kong Book of Kung Fu"). "Jansimram King" sticks closest to Cornershop's previous pounding form, but still demonstrates a new level of sophistication. Like **Hold on It Hurts, Woman's Gotta Have It** is recommended, but for very different reasons. The Eastern-oriented "6 A.M. Jullander Shere," "My Dancing Days Are Done" and "7:20 A.M. Jullander Shere" are easily its most enchanting and captivating tracks. [icm]

KLAUS CORNFIELD & LOTSI LAPISLAZULI

See *Throw That Beat in the Garbagecan!*

ANGEL CORPUS CHRISTI

I Love New York (UK Criminal Damage) 1984
Wake Up & Cry (UK Criminal Damage) 1985
Dim the Lights [tape] (a&r/ENT) 1987
Accordion Pop Vol. I [tape] (Stim) 1989
The 80's (a&r/ENT) 1989
White Courtesy Phone (Almo Sounds) 1995

Where so many have dug nothing but worthless nostalgia out of passé styles—claiming credit for their discerning taste rather than any creative imagination—San Francisco singer/accordionist Angel Corpus Christi (Andrea Ross) is one of a select breed that makes productive modern use of vintage templates. She began her eccentric career with a series of independent singles and albums written, recorded and released with her husband, guitarist/singer Rich Stim (whose distinguished career in DIY fringe-rock dates back to 1976, when the pioneering MX-80 Sound began blasting away in Bloomington, Indiana), and his musical cohorts. The early works (available domestically on a&r/ENT cassette only) include a themed set of Gotham-related covers, with songs by the Ramones, Suicide and Lou Reed (**I Love New York**), the nearly all-original **Wake Up & Cry** and **Dim the Lights** and an unaccompanied collection of squeeze-box covers (**Accordion Pop Vol. I**). Her first CD, **The 80's,** is half-retrospective and half-new, containing one of Angel's celebrity songs ("John Cassavetes") and a nifty remake of Alice Cooper's "I'm 18."

Ascending to a mainstream label in 1995, Corpus Christi rared back and popped out the year's best new wave album. Surrounding her carbon-dated canned vocal presence with diverse synth-draped arrangements that manage to sound simultaneously complex and rinkydink, Angel croons the elementary melodies of supremely ingenious hook-filled songs that bounce and bop in an echo of early-'80s dance-club pogo fare by Toni Basil, Lene Lovich, Martha and the Muffins, Algebra Suicide, Hilary and so forth. Adopting a stance of mildly bemused enthusiasm, she sings offhand lyrics about the crumbling state of the world ("Big Black Cloud," "Nature Girl"), her own shortcomings ("Lazy," "Threw It Away"), sex ("Dim the Lights," "Candy") and a presumptuous lover ("Been There Done That"). The anachronistic derivation would be just a gimmick if the tuneful songs weren't so great. But with an album as confidently, instantly lovable as **White Courtesy Phone,** it doesn't matter where she's calling from. Fine-tuning what Angel had already outlined on **The 80's,** Craig Leon produced and played all the keyboards; label co-owner Herb Alpert blows an undercurrent of sax on a remake of "John Cassavetes." [i]

See also *Bruce Anderson.*

CORPUS DELICTI

Twilight (Fr. Glasnost) 1993
Sylphes (Fr. Glasnost) 1994
Obsessions (Fr. WMD Music) 1995 (Etherhaus) 1996
Sarabands (Cleopatra) 1996

The touristy city of Nice on the sunny Riviera might seem an unlikely hometown for Corpus Delicti, France's only goth band of international repute. Any doubts about Gallic suitability for that gloomy genre are quickly laid to rest by **Twilight:** Sebastian (vocals), Roma (drums/synths), Chrys (bass) and Frank (guitars) serve up by-the-book heaviness on all eleven tracks, laying it on particularly thick for "Poisoned Dead Flowers" (!!!) and "Haunted Picture." Early Bauhaus records obviously played a pivotal role in forming Corpus Delicti's sound, especially when it comes to Sebastian's suspiciously Peter Murphy–like vocal delivery. The English-language lyrics are unfortunate—the romance of the French language would perfectly convey goth's seductive side.

Sylphes continues in the same vampiric vein as **Twilight.** These folks aren't breathing any new life into the idiom, but the album is still good solid goth rock. Two notable exceptions—"Saraband," with a sprightly verse and pulsating, sinewy chorus, and a haunting version of "Noxious (The Demon's Game)"—display bolstered confidence.

Obsessions finds Corpus Delicti finally well on its way to perfecting a distinctive goth sound. Sebastian's lyrics show a new sensitivity and subtlety, and his French-accented singing (which still sounds like Peter Murphy) gives the material that crucial swoon factor. The fragile, melancholia-soaked "Motherland" is one of the band's finest compositions; with a winding melody and rousing chorus, "Treasures" is another standout.

For its first American release, Corpus reworked the best material from the first two albums, adding more layers and atmospheric touches. As a result, **Sarabands** is by far the most satisfying Corpus Delicti album yet. There are also a few new additions, which stand up well against the earlier work. The only failure is an over-the-top cover of David Bowie's "Suffragette City." [ky]

ELVIS COSTELLO

My Aim Is True (Columbia) 1977 (Rykodisc) 1994
This Years Model (Columbia) 1978 (Rykodisc) 1994
Taking Liberties (Columbia) 1980
King of America (Columbia) 1986 (Rykodisc) 1995
Spike (Warner Bros.) 1989
Mighty Like a Rose (Warner Bros.) 1991
Brutal Youth (Warner Bros.) 1994
Elvis Costello's Kojak Variety (Warner Bros.) 1995

ELVIS COSTELLO AND THE ATTRACTIONS

Armed Forces (Columbia) 1979 (Rykodisc) 1994
Get Happy!! (Columbia) 1980 (Rykodisc) 1994
Ten Bloody Marys & Ten How's Your Fathers (UK F-Beat) 1980 (UK Demon) 1984
Trust (Columbia) 1981 (Rykodisc) 1994
Almost Blue (Columbia) 1982 (Rykodisc) 1994
Imperial Bedroom (Columbia) 1982 (Rykodisc) 1994
Punch the Clock (Columbia) 1983 (Rykodisc) 1995
Goodbye Cruel World (Columbia) 1984 (Rykodisc) 1995
The Best of Elvis Costello and the Attractions (Columbia) 1985
The Man: The Best of Elvis Costello (UK Telstar) 1985 (UK Demon) 1987
Blood & Chocolate (Columbia) 1986 (Rykodisc) 1995
Girls + £ ÷ Girls = $ & Girls (UK Demon) 1989 (Columbia) 1990
2 1/2 Years (Rykodisc) 1993
The Very Best of Elvis Costello and the Attractions (Rykodisc) 1994
All This Useless Beauty (Warner Bros.) 1996

ELVIS COSTELLO AND THE BRODSKY QUARTET

The Juliet Letters (Warner Bros.) 1993

ELVIS COSTELLO & RICHARD HARVEY

G.B.H. (UK Demon Soundtrack) 1991 (Rykodisc) 1994
Jake's Progress (UK Demon Soundtrack) 1995

ELVIS COSTELLO AND BILL FRISELL

Deep Dead Blue Live 25 June 1995 (UK Warner Bros.) 1995

VARIOUS ARTISTS

Out of Our Idiot (UK Demon) 1987
The Courier (Virgin Movie Music) 1988

If Elvis Costello had a motto for the first half of the '90s, it would be Advance in All Directions at Once. While taking experimental flyers with the Brodsky String Quartet and modern jazz guitarist Bill Frisell, composing TV film scores and exploring other paths of progress, he also released an album of vintage covers and cleaned out the attic, overseeing a vast reissue program of his back catalogue. Most surprisingly for this man in constant motion, he wrote off an old personal feud and reunited with the Attractions.

The net effect of all this activity was to force even the most devoted fans to give new consideration to what arguably amounts to—and grows with hindsight as—modern pop's greatest single-artist oeuvre, second only to Bob Dylan's. Although the onetime punk pioneer has hung in long enough to mellow into adulthood and become part of the pop furniture (just what the world needs: another Randy Newman), for those who were young enough to embrace **This Years Model** as one of 1978's most compelling pieces of plastic, Costello has never lost his youthful enthusiasm for making albums of extraordinary ambition, complexity and expression.

Despite unwavering audience ambivalence—in America at least—Costello keeps churning it out, a brilliant musical novelist who has more intriguing and original ideas per album than most artists muster in a lifetime. Regardless of what people make of his idiosyncratic singing (crooning now a speciality) or stylistic peregrinations, the fact is that no other rock-rooted songwriter can match Costello in terms of consistency, volume, imagination and variety. In a time when the genius appellation is slapped on everyone with three salable ideas, Declan Patrick Aloysius McManus should be able to fill a couple of mantels with the statues he deserves.

Accompanied by the first American label change of his career, Costello ended his longest album layoff (more than two years) with 1989's **Spike.** Working apart from the great Attractions (their last album together being **Blood & Chocolate**), he and an all-star cast presented a challenging and eclectic production job that brings masterful artistry to the great issues of the late '80s: God, infidelity, aging, honesty, capital punishment, Margaret Thatcher, the personal cost of war.

After that bravura blowout, however, **Mighty Like a Rose** was a disappointing retrenchment; despite their verbose complexities, the unwieldy songs—most given lush, glib arrangements—suggest creative fatigue. Imitating the Band ("Playboy to a Man") is only the most irritating of the album's pyrrhic exercises in cleverness. Significantly (especially in retrospect), two of the most immediately engaging tracks ("The Other Side of Summer" and "How to Be Dumb," a devastating slam at Attractions bassist Bruce Thomas for his tacky play-and-tell "novel," *The Big Wheel*) return Costello to his sound of the late '70s. "Hurry Down Doomsday (The Bugs Are Taking Over)" doesn't go quite that far, alighting on a revisit to **Trust**'s "Lover's Walk."

The Juliet Letters, on the other hand, is without precedent in Costello's career. Writing and recording (live in the studio, without overdubs) a theatrical concept album of fantasy correspondence with an open-minded classical string quartet, Costello threw himself completely off the tracks, leaving his guitar home to venture into previously untested compositional and vocal realms. Did he succeed? The mere fact of his newly developed arranging skill is impressive; that he can unhitch himself from rock and make credible chamber pop suggests a grand mastery of music's possibilities—as if a photographer had suddenly unveiled skill as a sculptor. Is it easy on the ears? Generally. Does it make for an engrossing, stimulating hour's worth of entertainment? No. For all the exquisite pop bowing and Costello's careful vocal exertions, the melodies sound like afterthoughts, rambling ups and downs of operatic convenience that spark memories of an eighth-grade music-appreciation teacher attempting to make *Don Giovanni* meaningful to a class full of adolescents. (Besides "This Sad Burlesque" and the tender "The First to Leave," which actually sounds like an ordinary Costello item given an uncommon rendering, the album's most striking song, "I Almost Had a Weakness," reworks a familiar cartoon theme, which obliterates its power.) The lyrics are curioser and curioser, too oddly canted to create any forward narrative motion. Good for you, Elvis, now can we have something else we might actually like to hear?

Good as done. **Brutal Youth** proves that even aging sophisticates can visit old haunts without being sucked in by nostalgia. In a byzantine sequence of coincidences—that included Costello's desire to try something quick and dirty straightaway after **The Juliet Letters,** his running into ex-Attractions keyboard ace Steve Nieve at a Sam Moore session, Wendy James asking drummer Pete Thomas if he could persuade his sometime employer to write her a song and Nick Lowe's disinclination to play tricky bass parts, thereby necessitating a differences-settling phone call to Bruce Thomas—the Attractions were reassembled.

Like an old lover who breezes back in the door after a protracted absence with no more than an indolent shrug and a sly smile, **Brutal Youth** pulls the angry twentysomething bile-spewer out of mothballs to meet his thoughtful, accomplished adult self. Wielding all the creative energy of **Armed Forces** with a far more skilled hand, Elvis, the Attractions *and* Nick Lowe (who might as well have been an official member for his pivotal production role on those early records) light a fire under his mature sensibilities; few albums that sound so simple are the result of such commanding artistry. Armed with a set of top-shelf tunes designed for uncomplicated small band assessments, Costello works across his entire dynamic range, waxing gorgeously romantic on "Still Soon to Know" and "All the Rage" but ripping up the floorboards on "Sulky Girl" and "20% Amnesia" (which, recalling the worst public-relations disaster of Costello's brutal youth, renders the phrase "strip jack naked" as if it were something far less innocuous). Besides taking brisk strolls down **My Aim Is True** lane for "Clown Strike" and "Just About Glad," he stirs up a breathtaking chorus for "Pony St.," crosses a soulful generation gap in "You Tripped at Every Step," uses genial folk-rock to express amazement at the diminishing Englishness of his hometown in "London's Brilliant Parade" and kicks tremoloed aggression to decry a military rape and its coverup in the cinematic "Kinder Murder." Throughout, deft instrumental touches, superb singing and the easy confidence of a still-competitive athlete returning to the scene of his greatest triumph make this another effortless win.

Recorded before **Mighty Like a Rose, Kojak Variety** brings Costello's typical taste and craft to the task of making a covers album. Ignoring those artists who reach for the Top 40 book in the hopes of getting mileage out of recognizable songs, he dredges up an amazing array of choice items from the R&B, country, soul and pop-standard cabinets of his evidently vast record collection. Backed by a small combo of skilled professionals, Costello whips up generally reverent interpretations that (to their abundant credit) sound like live band blows after a few quick run-throughs. The well-known (Bob Dylan's "I Threw It All Away," Little Willie John's Beatles-covered "Leave My Kitten Alone," Little Richard's "Bama Lama Bama Loo," the Kinks' "Days") and the obscure (Walter Hawkins' "Strange," Mose Allison's "Everybody's Crying Mercy," Holland/Dozier/Holland's "Remove This Doubt" and Bill Anderson's "Must You Throw Dirt in My Face," which segues into the James Carr–popularized "Pouring Water on a Drowning Man") alike benefit from Costello's enthusiastic ministrations. More than a curio, **Kojak Variety** puts the unmistakable Costello imprimatur on songs that he might well have written, while undoubtedly encouraging curiosity about their actual sources.

Although it's predominately originals, the brief **Deep Dead Blue** seems like a covers record (or at least somebody else's record), as it finds Costello—backed on a London stage by American guitarist Bill Frisell—indulging his vibrato-laden crooneristic desires to their slushy hilt on Charles Mingus' "Weird Nightmare" and Lerner/Loewe's "Gigi" (never imagined *that* one in his repertoire), as well as **Spike**'s "Baby Plays Around" (the only number that really soars in this setting), **Goodbye Cruel World**'s "Love Field," "Poor Napoleon" and co-compositions with Frisell and Rubén Blades. Tenderly rendered but hard to swallow, Costello's suave aspirations have a pinched, square-peg feeling, and Frisell's cocktail lounge arpeggios (and volume-knob wiggles) don't humidify the arid environment enough to make it cozy.

All This Useless Beauty, a full-fledged reunion with the Attractions, was originally mooted as a collection of songs written for or with other artists. It would have done well to have stayed that way. The prismatic enlightenment of "You Bowed Down" (originally recorded by Roger McGuinn and riffled here in unmistakable twelve-string flourishes), the cagey rock'n'roll summit of "Shallow Grave" (co-written with Paul McCartney), "All This Useless Beauty" (an over-reserved, under-melodic stab at pop standard-hood), "Why Can't a Man Stand Alone" (a torchy soul tune penned for Stax legend Sam Moore), the ill-conceived "Complicated Shadows" (at least for its intended singer, Johnny Cash) and "Other End of the Telescope," an oil-and-water Aimee Mann collaboration cut by 'Til Tuesday, would have stood as a footnote sort of album, a minor but respectable elaboration on one aspect of Costello's work. But the inclusion of some fine ("It's Time," "Little Atoms") and foul ("Distorted Angel" and "I Want to Vanish," a wan ballad accompanied by the Brodsky Quartet) new numbers that don't fall under that category queers the deal. Forced to be considered as the successor to **Brutal Youth, All This Useless Beauty** is too dainty to hold that honor.

On the soundtrack front, Costello has forged a '90s partnership with composer/conductor Richard Harvey, adding two full orchestral scores for British Channel 4 TV films to his cinematic résumé (which already included contributions to *The Courier* and Alex Cox's *Straight to Hell*). The exact nature of his role in penning the swelling dramatic atmospheres of **G.B.H.** is hard to reckon, but, really, it's the achievement and exercise that count here, not the music.

Other artists sit back and let labels reissue their back titles for an ego stroke and a quick buck. Not Costello. He took the opportunity to reassess and refurbish a decade's worth of work, annotating each album with illuminating explanations and amplifications, resolving willful US/UK repertoire disparities and adding copious amounts of contemporaneous (or otherwise related) material as bonuses. As potent as a written autobiography—and ironic, considering how journalistically tight-lipped he was for so long—the overhauled albums are obligatory for anyone with more than a casual interest in Costello's universe.

In its reincarnation, **My Aim Is True**—the here-comes-the-nerd pub-rock debut produced by Lowe on the computer-operator's days off with members of California's Clover and others—gains nine tracks, including pre-album demos, a circa-'75 track by the band Flip City and early country leftovers, "Radio Sweetheart" and "Stranger in the House." **This Years Model,** his groundshaking introduction to the Attractions (who didn't receive cover billing), is presented in its original English configuration and augmented by solo acoustic demos for the next album's "Green Shirt" and "Big Boys" (as well as the otherwise undocumented "Running Out of Angels"), the soundtrack contribution "Crawling to the U.S.A.," the B-side "Big Tears" (with Mick Jones of the Clash providing nearly inaudible lead guitar) and "Radio Radio," a single that was added to the US edition and became the group's bitter calling card to the unfriendly American media outlets that shunned the surly foreign snots.

Armed Forces, the even-better successor to **This Years Model,** incorporates three trenchant live tracks (a suave pre-LP "Accidents Will Happen," "Alison" and "Watching the Detectives," from a '78 Hollywood High show originally issued as a bonus single), "Wednesday Week" and "Talking in the Dark" (from a giveaway 45) and three non-disposable B-sides: "Tiny Steps," "Clean Money" and "My Funny Valentine," the first intriguing evidence of his Sinatraesque aspirations. The breathless, soul-gauged and amazingly gem-packed **Get Happy!!**—which already contained twenty fragmentary tracks in fifty minutes and really needed the mastering tuneup that relieves the original's weird, thin tone—is expanded by another eleven tunes, including the three that filled out 1980's **New Amsterdam** EP, such B-sides as "Girls Talk" (an EC original done to better commercial effect by Dave Edmunds), "Getting Mighty Crowded" and "Hoover Factory," as well as outtake versions of the album's "Riot Act" and "Clowntime Is Over" and an unlisted demo of "Love for Tender."

The uneven **Trust** has a firm, multi-leveled production grasp on such excellent songs as "Clubland," "Strict Time," "New Lace Sleeves" and "Watch Your Step" (as well as "From a Whisper to a Scream," a duet with Squeeze's Glenn Tilbrook) but contains too many weak numbers, making it Costello's first notable creative stumble. The nine bonus tracks, most of them never previously released, are as inconsistent as the album itself, although the creative process illustrated by the swell piano demo of "Boy With a Problem" (recut for **Imperial Bedroom**) and the progress of the so-what "Twenty-Five to Twelve" into the sweeping "Seconds of Pleasure" (a song Rockpile didn't bother recording for the album they gave its title) is as ear-opening as the songs.

Almost Blue, an album of reliable country ballads (from the catalogues, if not the pens, of Hank Williams, Patsy Cline, George Jones and Merle Haggard, as well as Gram Parsons), was produced in Nashville by local legend Billy Sherrill. Time has found the record a more organic place in Costello's creative stream; the eleven stylistically connected bonus tracks come from a 1979 Los Angeles club date, a 1981 Scottish show, a 1982 London concert with the Royal Philharmonic Orchestra and the Sherrill sessions.

After that vocally centered record, Costello pursued the Tin Pan Alley side of his personality with mainstream pop producer Geoff Emerick on **Imperial Bedroom,** a complex, classy and heavily worked-over collection that fortunately has the songs ("Man Out of Time," "Almost Blue," "Human Hands," "Kid About It," "Beyond Belief," "The Loved Ones," "You Little Fool") to carry the extra instrumental load, finessing ballads between bouts of grandiose, atmospheric rock. Among the nine added numbers are non-LP singles (all covers: "From Head to Toe," "The World of Broken Hearts," "Night Time"), demos for "Shabby Doll," the unused "Imperial Bedroom" and the final rendition of "Seconds of Pleasure"—before it was cannibalized for **Punch the Clock**'s "The Invisible Man."

Punch the Clock, produced by the commercially minded but more stylistically agile Clive Langer and Alan Winstanley, coincided with Costello's return to the immediate reality of his surroundings, and politically potent poetry like "Shipbuilding," "Pills and Soap" and "TKO (Boxing Day)" balance such neutral pop achievements as "Everyday I Write the Book" and the brassy "Let Them All Talk." While the arrangements invariably benefit the songs, a certain distance and dryness in the writing prevents okay-to-great numbers from coalescing into a truly estimable album. Brisk pre-album live versions of "The World and His Wife" and "Everyday I Write the Book" join an edgy cover of Yoko Ono's "Walking on Thin Ice" and four more significant studio items as bonus tracks.

Costello's other Langer/Winstanley album, **Goodbye Cruel World,** is similarly troubled; the artist's liner notes blame the dissolution of his marriage and a general lack of spirit for what he calls "our worst album." In fact, the quiet protest song, "Peace in Our Time," is absolutely brilliant; with the vocal presence of Daryl Hall, "The Only Flame in Town" is presentably slick soul-pop. In between those bookends, however, there's a little good ("Home Truth," "Inch by Inch") and a lot of just-OKs, shouldn't-have-beens and nice tries, many of them inexplicably afflicted by electronic percussion and keyboards. In other words, the uneven album is not altogether different in effect from the two that precede it. The ten (one of which is unlisted) bonus tracks—including the acrid and angry pairing of "Get Yourself Another Fool" and an unreleased early version of "I Hope You're Happy Now," a quiet studio duet with Lowe on the Shirelles' "Baby It's You" and a handful from Costello's extraordinary 1984 solo tour—are embarrassingly better than the album they augment.

Taking a one-album trial separation from the Attractions (who back him on "Suit of Lights" anyway), Costello—billed as The Costello Show—made **King of America,** a staggering return to folk-shaped rock form rich with moving, articulate and memorable songs and inspired, passionate performances using a couple of crackerjack American pickup bands. His first undeniable classic since **Get Happy!!,** the album contains almost as many highlights as tracks. Try these on for instant recognition: "Brilliant Mistake," "American Without Tears," "Indoor Fireworks," "The Big Light" and a searing slow cover of "Don't Let Be Misunderstood" that nearly challenges the Animals for rights to the song. Overflowing with extras, the package adds five studio tracks (including a pair by the Coward Brothers, a duo with **King of America** co-producer T-Bone Burnett) and a short second disc from Costello's 1986 Broadway concert stand with the Confederates, most of them **King of America** veterans, performing "The Big Light" and a half-dozen obscure covers.

Blood & Chocolate, Costello's second album of '86, ended his relationships with Columbia Records permanently and the Attractions for the better part of a decade. A tumultuous, tough-hearted rock record with lots of great songs given ripping, live-in-the-studio renditions, it tends to get overlooked, probably because of the casual, forbidding tone of the performances. But the album has a spiny integrity and a tense feel of bad feelings being fed into lively playing. "Uncomplicated" and a lethal version of "I Hope You're Happy Now" open it, with further testimony taking such form as "Home Is Anywhere You Hang Your Head," "Honey Are You Straight or Are You Blind?" and "Blue Chair." Turning anger into obsession, Costello unleashes seven minutes of "I Want You," a hypnotic mash note that has undoubtedly replaced the unrelated Bob Dylan song on countless flirty mix tapes. Bonuses include alternate versions of "Blue Chair" and "American Without Tears" (a fascinating lyrical sequel to the **King of America** song), film soundtrack work for *Straight to Hell* and *Club Paradise* ("Seven Day Weekend," with Jimmy Cliff) and two more studio tracks, one unreleased and the other a B-side. Initial quantities included a bonus interview disc.

Costello's discography is heavy with compilations and other repackages. **2 1/2 Years** puts a box around the first three albums (**My Aim Is True, This Years Model, Armed Forces**—an essential collection if ever there was one) with a bonus disc of **Live at the El Mocambo,** the frequently bootlegged fourteen-song radio broadcast from 1978. **The Very Best of Elvis Costello and the Attractions** one-ups **The Best of Elvis Costello and the Attractions** by subtracting five and adding eight with significantly better packaging and sound. Neither, of course, is any sort of a match for **Girls + £ ÷ Girls = $ & Girls,** a double-length retrospective that sports a maddeningly different (and not in the simple food-chain way one would expect) set list on CD, cassette and vinyl. All of the B-sides and other non-LP leftovers that compose the respective US and UK rarities sets, **Taking Liberties** and **Ten Bloody Marys & Ten How's Your Fathers,** have since become bonus tracks on the '90s reissues of the first four albums. Likewise, all but a couple of the twenty-one outtakes, soundtrack ventures and outside collaborations (under a stultifying variety of names, hence the various-artists designation) that fill **Out of Our Idiot** have subsequently been redistributed, with chronological and creative logic, among the reissues. [i]

See also *Tasmin Archer, Wendy James; TPRG.*

COUNTING CROWS

August and Everything After (DGC) 1993

SORDID HUMOR

Light Music for Dying People (Capricorn) 1994

ENGINE 88

Clean Your Room (Caroline) 1995

Drawing a bead on the narrow singer/songwriter tunnel between Bruce Springsteen, Bob Dylan and Van Morrison (with an excessive debt to all three), San Francisco's Counting Crows are a middle-aged rock critic's wet dream: a commercially certified young band with poetic intelligence, rustic resonance, credible passion and excellent musicianship. Y'know, the kind of band that *used* to walk the earth back when music was *really* good. Early fans were seen clutching their copies of **Tupelo Honey, Blood on the Tracks, The Heart of Saturday Night** and **Nebraska** as they sang the praises of **August and Everything After.** (Alternate title: **1984 and Everything Before.**) As produced by T-Bone Burnett, the pristinely rendered folk-rock grooves are smooth and the singing assured. Yes, singer Adam Duritz sounds like Van Morrison, complete with the "sha-la-la" refrain of the catchy hit single, "Mr. Jones." So go tell a Pavement fan.

After a strong beginning ("Round Here," "Mr. Jones," the restrained "Perfect Blue Buildings"), the album bogs down into sluggish tempos and indistinguishable melodies. The languid pace forces the focus onto the lyrics, which are frequently too full of themselves to be taken seriously. "I took the cannonball down to the ocean/Across the desert from sea to shining sea/I rode a ladder that climbs across the nation/Fifty million feet of earth between the buried and me." Yeah, whatever. The quintet's ensemble playing is impressive, but over the course of eleven songs, Duritz is unable to maintain the melodic invention on which to safely hang his beautiful loser clichés.

Sordid Humor, a Bay Area band led between 1987 and 1992 by singer/guitarist Tom Barnes (now at the helm of the rocking Engine 88), is connected genealogically to Counting Crows via bassist David Immerglück (also of the Monks of Doom), a Duritz pal who played guitar, mandolin and pedal steel on **August and Everything After**. **Light Music for Dying People** was assembled and released posthumously in the wake of the Crows' success (especially as the group made a habit of including Sordid Humor's "Jumping Jesus," from a 1989 EP, in its set). With seven tracks co-produced by Crows rhythm guitarist Dave Bryson, the album—which amazingly doesn't contain "Jumping Jesus"—is pleasant but undistinguished electric folk-rock; Duritz sings backup and co-wrote the song "Barbarossa." [i/roc]

See also *Monks of Doom.*

COWBOY JUNKIES

Whites off Earth Now!! (Can. Latent) 1986 (RCA) 1991
The Trinity Session (RCA) 1988
The Caution Horses (RCA) 1990
Black Eyed Man (RCA) 1992
Pale Sun, Crescent Moon (RCA) 1993
200 More Miles: Live Performances 1985–1994 (RCA) 1995
Lay It Down (Geffen) 1995

Toronto's Cowboy Junkies consists of three siblings—Margo, Michael and Peter Timmins—and a friend, Alan Anton, attracted to rural blues and honky-tonk. They began by blending a rudimentary production aesthetic, gauzy vocals, exquisite taste in covers and subtle group dynamics into a soft-focus sound that, depending on one's viewpoint, is either catatonic or mesmerizing. But before slumber or charges of gimmickry set in, the low-key quartet discovered how to make equally affecting music at higher volume.

Whites off Earth Now!! is steeped in blusey introspection, with covers of Robert Johnson and John Lee Hooker classics. It also evokes Bruce Springsteen's stark **Nebraska,** from which it draws "State Trooper." While veering dangerously close to elevator music, the disc has an intriguing subtext: in a lullaby voice, Margo Timmins pulls a sex reversal on the harsher blues vignettes, vowing on the Johnson tune, "I'm gonna beat my man/Until I get satisfied."

Covers also dominate **The Trinity Session,** and the Junkies take the tentative, stripped-down sound of the debut to its glorious extreme. Setting up in a church with a single microphone, the group circled 'round Timmins and created a masterpiece of noir atmosphere. Anchored by dirge-like versions of Hank Williams' "I'm So Lonesome I Could Cry" and Lou Reed's "Sweet Jane," the core group embellishes its country/blues hybrid with fiddle, mandolin, pedal steel and harmonica players.

The deceptively tough female persona that glimmered on **Whites off Earth Now!!** emerges more forcefully on **The Caution Horses,** as Margo Timmins interprets the songs of her brother Michael, the band's guitarist and primary writer. In general, the material and performances are more strident, with mixed results. "Your body for my soul . . . fair swap," she sings with chilling finality on " 'Cause Cheap Is How I Feel," while "Sun Comes Up, It's Tuesday Morning" is a bitter declaration of independence. But a tepid version of Neil Young's "Powderfinger" breaks the band's string of dazzling covers.

Black Eyed Man shakes off the last vestiges of drowsiness, with punchier arrangements and singing. Bassist Anton's rubbery grooves are reminiscent of the Grateful Dead's Phil Lesh; like the Dead in **American Beauty** mode, the Junkies veer toward rustic rock. Michael Timmins indulges his literary pretensions with songs that read more like exercises in southern gothic imagery, but he's outdone by Texas blues mystic Townes Van Zandt, who contributes "Cowboy Junkies Lament" and "To Live Is to Fly." Even with Van Zandt's help, the disc feels mannered and distant.

On **Pale Sun, Crescent Moon,** the Junkies drop most of the string-band sidemen to incorporate, of all things, guitar feedback. With the songs once again more personal in tone—this time focusing on domestic scenes of redemption and violence—the band sounds newly energized. A cover of Dinosaur Jr's "The Post," while hardly definitive, is a gateway to the new sound, with Michael's guitar twisting around his sister's ardent yet nuanced delivery on the glowing "Anniversary Song" and the terror-stricken "Hunted."

The next stop for this deceptively reserved bunch was a grand live retrospective, a bold and gripping demonstration of how the group has been able to sustain its hypnotic spell equally at subliminal and extroverted energy levels on a near-decade's worth of stages. The two-CD **200 More Miles** pulls together small club dates and Royal Albert Hall triumphs, revisiting familiar covers ("Sweet Jane," "I'm So Lonesome I Could Cry," "Walking After Midnight," "Blue Moon") and prime originals (" 'Cause Cheap Is How I Feel," "If You Were the Woman and I Was the Man"), all receiving subtle, sturdy, stirring, painterly renditions.

With the quartet moving to a new label, **Lay It Down** returns the group to its sparest musical setting since the debut, with the four core members only occasionally augmented by organ, strings and pedal steel. "Small blessings laid upon us/Small mysteries unfold," sings Timmins, and she might as well be describing the album's modest intentions. Despite the occasional strident fuzz chord, the group mostly hunkers down in unrushed, bluesy intimacy—without actually playing the blues. By now the Junkies are as easy to take for granted as a well-worn sofa, but few groups imbue absence (of a lover, or feeling itself) with such beauty ("Lonely Sinking Feeling," "Now I Know") or explore the commonplace with such moving insight ("Bea's Song," "Musical Key"). [gk]

See also *TPRG.*

COWBOY MOUTH

Word of Mouth (Domino) 1992
Mouthing Off (Live + More) (Viceroy) 1993
It Means Escape (Monkey Hill) 1994
Are You With Me? (MCA) 1996

Ex–Dash Rip Rock drummer/singer Fred LeBlanc's New Orleans–based combo with guitarist John Thomas Griffith (ex–Red Rockers), bassist Steve Walters (ex-Normals) and guitarist Paul Sanchez (ex-Backbeats), has two studio albums and a live set to its credit. **Word of Mouth,** produced by Gene Holder, is weak-willed roots rock that owes nothing to its cultural milieu. With varying measures of country and rock flavor, the foursquare adult songwriting (by all hands but Walters) is skillfully presented at mid-power in various plain ways. The four voices of experience use familiar approaches, some more melodically nourishing than others, to describe women past and present: "Running Into You," "The Stars Remind Me of You," "Rose on Fire," "Maggie Don't Two-Step." LeBlanc's "Jenny Says," one of the album's strongest and most exciting numbers, was done first by Dash Rip Rock (on **Ace of Clubs**).

Holder also produced the mostly live **Mouthing Off,** which wisely repeats only three **Word of Mouth** tunes. Leading the set off with two studio tracks—the lame "Listen to What I Say" and a snappy rendition of Loretta Lynn's fearsome. "Don't Come Home a Drinkin' (With Lovin' on Your Mind)"—Cowboy Mouth moves it on over to a stage in Rennes, France, where the quartet cranks up four spunky new originals and a snappy range of covers, including "Tears Towards Heaven" (a Mercyland song written by Dave Barbe before his tenure in Sugar), Bo Diddley's "I Can Tell" and the old gospel "Down by the Riverside."

It Means Escape packs a stronger rock bite ("Everyone Is Waiting" really roars) and more diverse topics ("Looked Like a Woman" is a confusing confused-identity tale; "Here I Sit in Prison (Yipee-I-Yay)" is a rotting-on-remand plaint) than **Word of Mouth.** Thoughtfully written, sharply arranged and delivered with mature energy, the album maintains Cowboy Mouth's geographical ambiguity without fixing a stylistic purpose. Holder and Peter Holsapple guest.

"Jenny Says" makes yet another appearance as the leadoff track of the band's engaging major-label bow, **Are You With Me?** The album veers between adroit sentimentality ("Peacemaker," "Louisiana Lowdown," "Laughable," "Man on the Run") and maudlin preditability ("God Makes the Rain," "So Sad About Me"), relaunching Cowboy Mouth as easygoing roots rock for the AAA set.

Sanchez has also released a pair of solo albums: 1992's **Jet Black and Jealous** and 1994's **Wasted Lives and Bluegrass.** [i]

See also *Dash Rip Rock.*

COWS

Taint Pluribus Taint Unum (Treehouse) 1987
Daddy Has a Tail! (Amphetamine Reptile) 1989
Effete and Impudent Snobs (Amphetamine Reptile) 1990
Peacetika (Amphetamine Reptile) 1991
Cunning Stunts (Amphetamine Reptile) 1992
Sexy Pee Story (Amphetamine Reptile) 1993
Orphan's Tragedy (Amphetamine Reptile) 1995
Whorn (Amphetamine Reptile) 1996
Old Gold 1989–1991 (Amphetamine Reptile) 1996

Though located squarely within the Amphetamine Reptile aesthetic—loud, loud guitars, lyrics full of hate (including self-hate)—Cows inject their little corner of the stable with more humor than such labelmates as Surgery and Vertigo. Taking a poke-in-the-eye approach to poking fun, the Minneapolis quartet aims to provoke its audience to express dissatisfaction with, well, everything. Onstage, singer Shannon Selberg has sported business suits with a stuffed animal on the crotch, football uniforms rendered in fake fur, shaving cream and not much else, a love doll remade as a second skin and other bizarre costumes. He presents himself as a character; literally drawing on new characteristics with a magic marker (not just tattoos, but facial hair and facial expressions), he transforms himself and pulls the immediate world down to his uncomfortable cartoon level.

After **Daddy Has a Tail!** and **Effete and Impudent Snobs,** Cows abandoned its original sound—industrial-grade sandpaper guitar ripping over a jug-band playing with scalpels—in favor of a chunky, stop-start style that makes most hardcore punk easy listening in comparison. Starting with **Peacetika,** the group also traded its twisted sense of humor for more screaming and pained chunks of noise in songs that hit, gut-level, over and over. The spectacular "Hitting the Wall" begins the album with pounding and whistling organized mayhem, which the weaker following tracks can't equal.

Selberg's tuneless, beaten and dented bugle had always appeared sparingly on Cows records; on **Cunning Stunts** (now *there's* an old joke), the songs are peppered with its unusual, warbly depressed punctuation marks. Cows' lyrics create an environment of distance: the thoughts, actions and lives are described so brutally you can only hope they're meant to be ironic. **Sexy Pee Story** continues in this mode, adding themes of being cheated—by yourself, your pals, the boss, the government—to the usual torrent of hopelessness and disgust. The band's previous musical punch gives way to a toppling cascade of instruments.

The mediocre and disappointing **Orphan's Tragedy** opens up an empty warehouse of sound, but—with meandering, plodding guitars and more instrumentals than usual—Cows don't begin to fill it up. Bookending songs with opaque, unusual noises doesn't make up for the empty middles.

The not dissimilar **Whorn** makes even greater use of horn. Two songs favor that lowly bugle over guitar: "Organized Meat" and "A Oven." The rest are one big morass, lightened (very occasionally) by some cute/eerie whistling and faint piano (!). In places, the guitars dip so low they're merely a deep vibrating sludge. "A Gift Called Life" maintains Cows' usual stance—a rant at everybody—yet reinjects that theme with some freshness and spontaneity.

Old Gold is a collection of tracks from Cows' early albums. [rxe]

See also *TPRG.*

CRACKER

Cracker (Virgin) 1992
Tucson EP (Virgin) 1992
Kerosene Heat (Virgin) 1993
Low EP (Virgin) 1994
The Golden Age (Virgin) 1996

After Camper Van Beethoven broke up—the band's members apparently divided over whether to focus on their experimental leanings or pure pop songcraft—singer/guitarist David Lowery formed Cracker with two high-school pals, guitarist Johnny Hickman and bassist Davey Faragher (the group has never had a permanent drummer), to do the latter. On **Cracker,** Lowery strips rock down to its muscular essence, avoiding any of the fancy flourishes Camper Van Beethoven used that might have hurt—or strengthened—this album of catchy, clever and disarmingly ironic songs. The most sarcastic tune, "Teen Angst (What the World Needs Now)," became somewhat of a hit on the very alternative radio airwaves it seemed to mock, and "This Is Cracker Soul" has a funk-driven edginess that's irresistible—even if the song lives up to its name a little too well.

The four songs, recorded live in the studio, that form **Tucson** were originally meant to be the core of Cracker's second album. From the punchy pop of "I Ride My Bike" to the sing-song cynicism of "Bad Vibes Everybody," there's little on this EP that the band hadn't done already, but it's good, solid, between-album fun.

Cracker broadens its horizons slightly on **Kerosene Hat** by incorporating more of a country-fried feel. This approach works some of the time—a cover of the Grateful Dead's "Loser" is surprisingly convincing, even if the lyrics to "Sweet Potato" are a bit much. Luckily, Lowery takes his irony with him, and affectionately parodies teen angst and pop conventions on pleasantly punchy songs like "Sick of Goodbyes" and "Let's Go for a Ride." The ballads ("Take Me Down to the Infirmary," the title track) come off a bit flat, but it's hard to deny their good-natured appeal.

Low contains the first album's "I See the Light," the second's "Low" and two outtakes from it, plus "Steve's Hornpipe," which predates both.

Cracker added former Silo Bob Rupe on bass before cutting its third album (Faragher had left after the second was recorded), which offers an all too familiar—if somewhat more polished—mix of appealing uptempo rockers and less effective ballads. Such songs as "I Hate My Generation" are as catchy and cynically funny as earlier Lowery efforts, but the singer's curmudgeon pose wears a bit thin, and **The Golden Age** suffers as a result. Far more appealing are the songs on which Cracker stretches out musically, including the surprisingly spacey "I Can't Forget You." [rl]

See also *John Hiatt, Monks of Doom, Silos.*

CRACKERBASH

Crackerbash (eMpTy) 1992
Tin Toy (eMpTy) 1993

Like a big boy with a little head (or Neil Young on a grunge-pop adventure), Portland, Oregon's Crackerbash started off putting squingey pop singing atop a fat-bottomed indie-rock buzz. **Crackerbash** diverges from standard Northwest noise by giving the hapless (but winsomely tuneful) vocals prominence over the peppy punk playing. An adorable little monster, the album screams a little, rocks a lot and generally displays as much songwriting creativity as sloppy performing enthusiasm. The catchy chorus of "Jasper" hides an unsettling and stormy half-step coda; "Human Alarm Clock" triples a spongy bassline with gaping guitar and distorted vocals but manages to avoid lockstep obviousness. Good ideas occasionally make the band's execution disappointing: "Bad Karma," a soaring harmony (well . . .) charmer, especially cries out for a more careful rendering. (The vinyl and CD each contain a different bonus track.)

Except for the uproariously earnest attempt at vocal-group swooniness (the organ-driven "Lovelights"), Crackerbash doesn't derive much audible benefit from Kurt Bloch's production on the seven-song **Tin Toy.** Jagging along with harsher, harder punk mettle and more decisive drumming than on the debut, the band slouches toward generic pop aggression, although there's more behind "Orion" (which sounds like a Spinanes song given a blustery supercharge), "Hollow" (a bomb-dropping skeleton) and "La La La" (an edgy, atmospheric drive through Los Angeles) than that. [i]

CRADLE OF THORNS

Feed-Us (Triple X) 1994
Download This! (Triple X) 1994

Bakersfield, California's Cradle of Thorns melds metal/hard rock with funk, goth, industrial, a little jazz and even a touch of opera to create a sound that, while not always pleasant, is at the very least intriguing. **Feed-Us** presents a young band that's as musically ambitious and ambiguous as Jane's Addiction once was. Countered by Tamera Slayton's lovely operatic soprano, Ty Elam's painfully ragged vocal style sounds like Alice in Chains vocalist Layne Staley's trademark growl—but even Staley doesn't revel in throat-scorching howls this much. Although the lyrics address the usual overdone controversy-stirring topics, the music itself is impressive: guitarist David File, drummer Kris Kohls, keyboardist/sampler Rohan and bassist Scat Elis handle a dizzying array of styles with admirable ease. The alternately crunching, lilting "Transparent Jesus" is especially noteworthy—it would sound right at home on any Metallica album.

Cradle of Thorns doesn't integrate its personality any better on **Download This!;** if anything, there are even more genres in the mix. Unfortunately, musical prowess is once again overshadowed by the inanely grotesque obnoxiousness of the lyrics. Want a laugh? Try "Bulimia Blow-Job," "Thirsty 4 Sex," "Cocaine 4 Breakfast," "Roaches 4 Roaches" and "The Golden Butt Plug Puppet Show." [ky]

CRAMPS

Gravest Hits EP (Illegal) 1979
Songs the Lord Taught Us (Illegal/IRS) 1980
Psychedelic Jungle (IRS) 1981
. . . Off the Bone (UK Illegal) 1983
Smell of Female (Enigma) 1983 (Restless) 1994
Bad Music for Bad People (IRS) 1984
A Date With Elvis (UK Big Beat) 1986 (Enigma) 1990 (Restless) 1994
Rockinnreelininaucklandnewzealandxxx (UK Vengeance) 1987 (Vengeance/Restless) 1994
Gravest Hits/Psychedelic Jungle (IRS) 1989
Stay Sick! (Enigma) 1990
All Women Are Bad EP (UK Enigma) 1990
Look Mom No Head! (Restless) 1991
FlameJob (Medicine) 1994 (Epitaph) 1994

Punk's greatest living rockabilly zombies had a fittingly up and down time in the '80s. After inventing and perfecting leering psychotronic rock on such wild-eyed ravefests as **Gravest Hits** and **Songs the Lord Taught Us,** New York's Cramps—Ohio-born vocalist Lux Interior (Erick Purkhiser, clearly a student of Cleveland television's Ghoulardi), native California guitarist Poison Ivy Rorschach (Kirsty Wallace) and assorted cohorts (drummer Miriam Linna, guitarist Bryan Gregory, drummer Nick Knox and guitarist Kid Congo Powers)—began rotting away. Although the group's ability to rip it up live has never faltered (the in-concert **Smell of Female,** issued in both six-song and nine-song configurations, is evidence of that), **Psychedelic Jungle**—which nonetheless contains the classic "Goo Goo Muck"—cut down on the Cramps' manic intensity; after that, they gave up entirely, leaving only the compilations **Bad Music for Bad People** and **Off the Bone** to mark the band's remains.

With the dedication of genuine zombies, though, the Cramps roused themselves again in late '85 for **A Date With Elvis,** a new sex-crazed studio album dedicated to Ricky Nelson. The lyrics make a nostalgically suggestive party joke of horniness: "Can Your Pussy Do the Dog" is typical. A bit more professional (breaking the band's bottomless tradition, Ivy plays bass as well as guitar) and less stylized, perhaps, but as happily crazed as ever.

Concurrent with the beginning of a four-year studio layoff, the Cramps toured some of the world's nether regions; the cruddy-sounding (you expected maybe Mobile Fidelity?) **Rockinnreelininaucklandnewzealandxxx** documents an August '86 show down under. Lux is in fine fettle; the set includes more than half the songs on **A Date With Elvis** plus typically choice covers ("Sunglasses After Dark," "Heartbreak Hotel," "Do the Clam"). As good as any bootleg!

With full-time bassist Candy Del Mar joining and Ivy taking the producer's chair, **Stay Sick!** got the Cramps back to the racks, their high low-culture standards upheld with the usual colorful enthusiasm. While "Bikini Girls With Machine Guns," "All Women Are Bad" and "Journey to the Center of a Girl" all reflect Lux's bewildered bedevilment by the opposite sex, "Mama Oo Pow Pow" takes a good swig from the same trashcan that originally fueled the Cramps' wild-eyed vision. (The artistic motives for covering "Shortnin' Bread" and "Muleskinner Blues," however, are completely open to debate.) The CD adds a nifty version of Carl Perkins' "Her Love Rubbed Off"; meanwhile, the **All Women Are Bad** 12-inch comes with three new B-music tracks: "King of the Drapes," "Teenage Rage" and "High School Hellcats."

Ivy and Lux have two new playmates (veteran drummer Jim Sclavunos and bassist Slim Chance) on **Look Mom No Head!**, a half-baked genre exercise that, true to its title, is short on original ideas. Singing with only a taste of his usual shuddering passion, Lux follows his lust into lurid originals—"Dames, Booze, Chains and Boots" (which inexplicably paraphrases Elvis Costello's "Pump It Up"), "Two Headed Sex Change" ("If your clam's in a jam/Baby I know what to do"), "I Wanna Get in Your Pants" and "Bend Over, I'll Drive"—with a notable lack of enthusiasm and a surprising degree of vulgarity. Iggy Pop makes a cameo on "Miniskirt Blues," and the rote album has a couple of relevant obscure closet classics ("Hipsville 29 B.C."), but there's no substitute for a full shake of the Cramps' own special sauce.

FlameJob is more like it. Co-produced by Lux and Ivy, with new drummer Harry Drumdini replacing Sclavunos, the album (also available as a limited-edition CD doublepack with a thirteen-song career retrospective) doesn't work so hard to fester the band's garbage aesthetic, doesn't hide its crudity under a bushel—"Let's Get Fucked Up" is by far the coarsest item in the Cramps catalogue, with "Inside Out and Upside Down (With You)" a close second—and doesn't even waste much effort on stylistic fidgeting. The songs are simple, stupid, direct and as raw as a scraped knee. Poison Ivy plays her ass off, and Lux sings like he means it. His gurgling rendition of "How Come You Do Me?" is spectacular proof of his rockabilly chops; the rest of the album finds him no less engaged or exciting. If a booklet quotation about aesthetics from Man Ray strikes a bum note, these precious "Sinners" otherwise run right into the dirt-filled mainstream of '90s traffic, dodging oncoming cars with a wicked grin and a manic laugh. Even "Route 66" sounds like a creepy place in the Cramps' capable clutches. [i]

See also *Nick Cave and the Bad Seeds, Congo Norvell, Gun Club; TPRG.*

CRANBERRIES

Everybody Else Is Doing It, So Why Can't We? (Island) 1993
No Need to Argue (Island) 1994
Doors and Windows EP (Island) 1995
To the Faithful Departed (Island) 1996

Hooking up with a Limerick trio (guitarist Noel Hogan, his bass-playing brother Mike Hogan and drummer Feargal Lawler) that had been backing a different singer under the name the Cranberry Saw Us, Dolores O'Riordan became the frontwoman and lyricist for the rechristened Cranberries. Drawing on the folky traditions of her nation's music, the Irish singer/guitarist informs the band's music with old-school melodies, a breathy Gaelic lilt and gasping yodel-like yelps. If O'Riordan has nowhere near the artistic reach or vision of Sinéad O'Connor, don't tell her that.

As the band's success has grown, so have O'Riordan's creative ambitions and vocal confidence. The dreamy love ballads (all but three co-written with Noel) that fill **Everybody Else Is Doing It, So Why Can't We?** (produced by Smiths collaborator Stephen Street) are rendered with gentle semi-acoustic allure, casting the group as a weak Irish response to England's Sundays. O'Riordan sings with shy grace but little assertive energy, as the plush arrangements of the driven "Dreams" and "Linger" (complete with dancing strings and cooing backing vocals) glow with a comforting blend of warm folk and pop. Two lesser songs, "Pretty" and "Waltzing Back," reveal the edge and latent strength of her voice, while Hogan's location of his fuzz pedal in "Not Sorry" suggests another side to the Cranberries. But most of the album glides on easy-listening gear with scant variety in the arrangements, writing or delivery.

The twenty-two-year-old O'Riordan's presence is far bolder and more compelling on **No Need to Argue;** she sings out, employing a more pronounced brogue and mannered aggression that makes it clear which countrywoman's records *she's* been listening to. (The hushed title track, sung over nothing but a bit of organ, adds credence to that supposition.) She also asserts her creative domination of the band. Besides adding keyboards and electric guitar to her instrumental responsibilities and taking care of all the string charts, she wrote half the songs herself, leaving Hogan only shares of the remaining musical credits. Broadening her sights to offer a condescending and diffident "Ode to My Family" ("My father, he liked me, does anyone care?"), passionately decry man's inhumanity to child in Northern Ireland ("Zombie"), celebrate a literary treasure ("Yeats' Grave") and ask, in "Empty," if "my identity has been taken," O'Riordan goes out on a lyrical limb and ends up self-conscious, self-obsessed and more than a little clumsy at times. The fuzz-rocking "Zombie," which became a hit single, does follow a powerfully atmospheric descending minor-key course, but her endless repetition of the title is maddening; "Ridiculous Thoughts" has a pretty bed of strummed guitars, but a multi-tracked O'Riordan alternately wails wordlessly like Enya and sings lyrics through clenched teeth. The liner notes thank "all those who enjoyed and understood our debut. Here's hoping you will understand this one." Too bad the record doesn't come with a money-back guarantee for those disinclined to the indulgence of such arrogance.

The CD-ROM **Doors and Windows** includes three alternate versions of "Zombie," a live version of "Dreams" and three previously unreleased tracks.

Regressing at a frightening pace, aided by Aerosmith producer Bruce Fairbairn, the Cranberries follow the stylistic lead of "Zombie" like a treasure map and make like a fired-up rock band for most of **To the Faithful Departed,** an ineffectually loud and risibly simpleminded joined-in-progress chronicle of the world's tragedies. Armed with heaps more commercial clout than creative sense (never mind anything like insight), O'Riordan comes off like an ignorant young idealist staring in indignant disbelief at a video entitled *History Since 1960.* Considering the dream factory of "Hollywood," she announces, "The greatest irony of all/It's not so glamorous at all," as if she had stumbled onto a blinding discovery. Her lyrics about the deaths of public figures are no less insipid, and bizarrely backdated to boot: "I Just Shot John Lennon" sounds as if the event was recent news to her, while Kurt Cobain and JFK are namechecked side by side in "I'm Still Remembering." "Free to Decide" contains the revelation, "There's a war in Russia/And Sarajevo, too," and leaves it at that. (The song "Bosnia" does little to elucidate the Cranberries' view of this complex conflict.) The racing "Forever Yellow Skies" builds to a repeated refrain of "I'll be forever holding you respon-si-ble" without providing the faintest hint of who or what's got her so agitated. Even romance ("When You're Gone") is reduced to childish black-and-white terms. O'Riordan's woeful lyrics might not be such an impediment if the music provided some distraction, but the amped-up redundancy—which drives the hook of "Salvation" into the ground—is no use at all. The only notable innovations (notwithstanding the ponderous strings that underscore the lachrymose sentimentality of "War Child" and the nostalgia of "The Rebels") are the band's absence of effort, imagination and subtlety. [vg/i]

CRANES

Wings of Joy (Dedicated/RCA) 1991
Forever (Dedicated/RCA) 1993
Loved (Dedicated/RCA) 1994
The Tragedy of Orestes & Electre (UK Dedicated) 1995

Monolithic and minimal, **Wings of Joy** conjures up the idea that Cocteau Twins and Swans once exchanged their musical DNA. A twilight marble edifice of lonely, ominous piano and stark beats marked by the occasional shocking bursts of industrial-strength guitar fuzz (as on the tremendous "Starblood"), it's a difficult but ultimately rewarding record. The neo-classical sonic watercolors are intriguing (the pretty "Tomorrow's Tears" is as haunting as anything from the **17 Seconds/Faith**-era Cure; "Watersong" was appropriately ethereal enough for perfumier Guerlain to use it as the theme for a European ad campaign), but it's obvious that Cranes, a quartet from Portsmouth, England, transcends the constraints of this bleak backdrop by dint of chanteuse Alison Shaw. Her faraway, childlike tone instantly recalls Claire Grogan of Altered Images (though Shaw is dead serious—not bubbly) and, to a lesser extent, Cocteau warbler Liz Fraser (but never as obscure). The contrast built up between Shaw's obsessive sing-song reveries and the forbidding music (composed entirely by her brother Jim) gives the whole thing a special frisson. "Beautiful Sadness" aptly described the entire disc.

Even with improved designs, Cranes still sound relatively minimal on **Forever,** but the arrangements are allowed to breathe, adding color and humanity to the aloof core of darkness. "Far Away" and "And Ever" are dominated by warm piano. The keening opener "Everywhere" and "Jewel" have lush acoustic strumming. (A remix of the latter by avid fan Robert Smith—he'd earlier chosen Cranes as the Cure's opening band—resulted in a European hit.) The corrugated guitar ferocity of the debut's "Starblood" is reawakened on "Sun and Sky" and "Clear," which also incorporates sirens and congas. Creepy yet joyous, the single "Adrift" best showcases Cranes' essential stylistic contrasts.

Cranes began plotting a double-set encompassing regular Cranes songs as well as pieces influenced by French-literature-fan Shaw's interest in *The Flies,* an expressionistic play by Sartre. Ultimately, the two projects were divided, and the former portion was released as **Loved,** Cranes' most accomplished and diverse disc to date. "Shining Road" has an enchanting pop melody and rushing guitar pulse, "Lilies" flirts with fragile funkiness and "Paris and Rome" feels like a European music-box waltz. Using odd squeaking noises and distant whammy-bar twangs, "Beautiful Friend" cunningly fashions an unusual ambient/western hybrid; the title track actually rocks. The CD appends top-notch remixes of three songs by Flood and Michael Brauer.

The Sartre material was issued a year later as the **Tragedy of Orestes & Electre** mini-album. Shaw emotes solely (and fetchingly) in French throughout. The semi-industrial soundscapes, built mainly of samples and simple, circus-like piano/string motifs, resemble some of Philip Glass' and Tom Waits' soundtracks—if interpreted by Coil or Foetus. Interesting, but for existentialists and Cranatics only.

Before signing with Dedicated, the Shaw siblings recorded two primitive efforts as a duo—the self-released cassette-only **Fuse,** and a vinyl mini-LP, **Self Non Self,** later reissued on CD in the UK by Dedicated. [gef]

CRASH TEST DUMMIES

The Ghosts That Haunt Me (Arista) 1991
God Shuffled His Feet (Arista) 1993

Canada's Crash Test Dummies was a hit even before releasing an album or firming up its five-member lineup. Before the release of **The Ghosts That Haunt Me,** the band had a fan in Cowboy Junkies singer Margo Timmins, who told *Rolling Stone* in March 1990 that its demo tape was one of her favorite albums of the previous year. At the time, Crash Test Dummies had a revolving cast of musicians—some still employed as coat-check people and other support staff at Winnipeg's Blue Note club—undecided about making the band their full-time profession. The tape that grabbed Timmins' attention, and also that of Los Lobos' Steve Berlin (who quickly signed on to produce the debut album), included "Superman's Song," which became the band's first hit.

Recorded as a quartet of Brad Roberts (vocals, guitar), Ellen Reid (vocals, keyboards), Benjamin Darvill (harmonica, mandolin) and brother Dan Roberts (bass)—drummer Michel Dorge joined afterward—**The Ghosts That Haunt Me** includes that number and others in a Celtic-rock vein—"Winter Song," "Here on Earth (I'll Have My Cake)"—as well as a cover of the Replacements' "Androgynous." The album (and band) gets its distinctive personality from Roberts' unusually deep baritone singing and deadpan off-kilter lyrics: the hostel trip of "The Voyage," the rural cure of "The Country Life," the angry criticisms of "Thick-necked Man." Crash Test Dummies was quickly embraced in certain circles as an intelligent, sophisticated and accessible blast of fresh air.

Roberts overhauled the group's sound on the second album. He purged the Celtic citations and hired ex–Talking Head Jerry Harrison as co-producer to develop a more layered style. He got what he wanted on **God Shuffled His Feet,** a record just left-of-center enough to qualify as "alternative" on American radio yet friendly enough to mass taste. Released as a single, "Mmm Mmm Mmm Mmm" established the Dummies as quirky originals in the US, but the song (as well as "Swimming in Your Ocean" and "How Does a Duck Know?") failed to get much airplay in Canada, causing a rift between the band and its Canadian critics, who wondered if the Dummies had sanded off the rougher edges for America's benefit. [ph]

HELIOS CREED

X-Rated Fairy Tales (Subterranean) 1985 (Cleopatra) 1994
Superior Catholic Finger (Subterranean) 1989 (Cleopatra) 1994
The Last Laugh (Amphetamine Reptile) 1989
Boxing the Clown (Amphetamine Reptile) 1990
Lactating Purple (Amphetamine Reptile) 1991
Kiss to the Brain (Amphetamine Reptile) 1992
Busting Through the Van Allen Belt (Cleopatra) 1994
Cosmic Assault (Cleopatra) 1995

After Chrome disbanded in 1983, the subsequent solo careers of its two members left little doubt about where most of the creative energies in the pioneering San Francisco proto-industrial synth-rock group resided. Helios Creed's eight solo LPs are scary stuff, dark psychedelia filled with blasts of chaotic guitar and disorienting tape manipulations. Damon Edge's solo work, on the other hand, is kind of like Count Floyd shouting "scary noises!" where something frightening should actually happen. (Edge died in late 1995.)

After **X-Rated Fairy Tales** and the much better **Superior Catholic Finger** (later issued on a single CD by Cleopatra), Creed signed to Amphetamine Reptile, which not only brought the veteran a cachet of indie cool, but paired him with rhythm sections capable of rooting Creed to time signatures found in the real world.

The primary pitfall of Creed's space-rock is that its intensity goes way down when there's more space than rock, and hence the quality of the cut-up sound collages can fluctuate wildly from one project to the next. **Lactating Purple**'s vast stretches of disconnectedness can be too trippy, even for Creed. And while you never expect to hear someone say "You know, I was humming side one of **Half Machine Lip Moves** the other day . . . ," Rey Washam's drumming on **Boxing the Clown** is too recent a reminder of how powerful that familiar flattened wah-wah guitar sound can be when there's a song chugging away under the thick strata of dissonance.

Thanks to bassist Pauk Kirk and drummer Paul Della Pelle, **Kiss to the Brain** is more successful. This time, the guitar pops up as more than just a guidepost, and the contrast makes the moments of otherworldly radio static, menacing vocorder distortions and sci-fi freakouts all the more effective. Having blasted through the comparatively formulaic "Malavia Meltdown" and "Throw Away the Rind," the respite Creed offers in the Pink Floyd **Animals**-like acoustic intro of the mini-epic title track seems all the more inspired.

Signing to the gothic/industrial label Cleopatra seems to have encouraged Creed to unwisely emphasize that side of his music. For someone who likely has more acid in his system than a Sears Die-Hard, a little creative structure goes a long way, and the drum machines that click time on **Busting Through the Van Allen Belt** and **Cosmic Assault** are no match for the bands he had in his AmRep years. That's not to say these aren't fine records—and it's true there is a certain degree of hair-splitting when comparing fairly similar works of menacingly psychedelic proto-industrial noise—just that they are more likely to fall prey to the "heard one Helios Creed record, heard 'em all" sentiment. Still, the long moments of atmospheric disassociation here are among the prettiest things he's ever done. Could Helios Creed be mellowing in his old age? [sf]

See also *TPRG.*

CREEDLE

See *Rust.*

MARSHALL CRENSHAW

Marshall Crenshaw (Warner Bros.) 1982
Field Day (Warner Bros.) 1983
Downtown (Warner Bros.) 1985
Mary Jean & 9 Others (Warner Bros.) 1987
Good Evening (Warner Bros.) 1989
Life's Too Short (Paradox/MCA) 1991
. . . My Truck Is My Home (Razor & Tie) 1994
Miracle of Science (Razor & Tie) 1996

Detroit-born singer/guitarist Crenshaw spent some time in a road company of *Beatlemania* before moving to New York, where his own songs became local new wave faves in the early '80s. Although he was seen as a latter-day Buddy Holly at the outset (a comparison renewed when he actually portrayed Buddy onscreen in 1987's *La Bamba*), Crenshaw soon proved too talented and original to be anyone but himself. Over the course of five albums in the '80s, he emerged as, first, a songwriter of extraordinary skill and, second, a winning performer. Except for **Good Evening,** on which the best material isn't his, each of the Warner Bros. records contains an ample supply of sparkling, tuneful gems that are both instantly appealing and enduringly memorable. Among the solid winners in his song catalogue: "Someday, Someway" and "Cynical Girl" (**Marshall Crenshaw**), "Whenever You're on My Mind" (**Field Day**), "The Distance Between," "Like a Vague Memory" and "Yvonne" (**Downtown**), "Calling Out for Love (At Crying Time)" (**Mary Jean**).

Produced by Ed Stasium to a bright, rocky consistency, with firm instrumental underpinning by bassist Fernando Saunders and drummer Kenny Aronoff, **Life's Too Short** is another good 'un. Shedding the commercial anxiety that ruined **Good Evening,** Crenshaw comes across with such enchanting originals as "Better Back Off," "Don't Disappear Now" (both co-written with Tom Teeley), the jazzy and lighthearted

"Fantastic Planet of Love" and the gorgeous "Somewhere Down the Line."

He didn't soon return to the studio, but Crenshaw—whose c.v. already included outside record production, journalism and the compilation of a hillbilly music anthology album—did edit *Hollywood Rock* (1994), a useful reference book about rock movies. **. . . My Truck Is My Home** is a compendium of not-overly-clean-sounding concert recordings made around the country and Belgium between 1982 and 1994. That nearly half the tunes are covers—including ABBA's "Knowing Me, Knowing You" and the MC5's "Tonight," both of which receive insightful renditions, and the instrumental "Twine Time," which ties organist Glen Burtnick up in a stinging Crenshaw guitar solo—limits the reflection of the artist's own repertoire, but that doesn't present a problem. Rather than grandstanding, the point of this eye-opening, ear-pleasing collection seems to be good songs sung with thought, care and enthusiasm.

Crenshaw got into the charts in 1995 via the Gin Blossoms' "Til I Hear It From You," which he co-wrote. The following summer, **Miracle of Science** became his first new studio album in five years. [i]

See also *TPRG.*

CRITICS

Braintree (Black Vinyl) 1995

Following the pop-rocky road paved by Cheap Trick, Shoes, Off Broadway and the like, the Critics are another in the long line of great Illinois power-pop combos. The talented trio (vocalist/guitarist Kevin Mantegna, drummer Marty Winer and bassist Todd Rusin) worked as the house band for Danny Bonaduce's Chicago-area radio show before recording **Braintree** with a little help from pals like the Elvis Brothers' Rob Elvis and the Idea's Phil Angotti. (Before the Critics, Mantegna released a fine solo album entitled **Communicate.**)

Issued on Shoes' label, **Braintree** falls somewhere between that group's wistful pop and the muscular rock of **In Color**–era Cheap Trick. The songs (written by Mantegna and Winer, separately and in collaboration) are across-the-board fine; the band's sharp playing, crisp harmonies and uncanny melodic know-how mesh perfectly. Listen to the early-Who-influenced "You Can't Lie," the pslightly psychedelic "Love Discreet" and the forceful-but-not-overbearing "Got No Heart" and "Lucky Thing." [jmb]

DALE CROVER

See *Melvins.*

ROB CROW

See *Heavy Vegetable.*

SHERYL CROW

Tuesday Night Music Club (A&M) 1993
Sheryl Crow (A&M) 1996

Sheryl Crow is not all that. She's a vague, dull live performer, the recipient of far more adult-rock acclaim and success than her music deserves and, worst of all, not much of a singer. The actual content of her debut is among the least of the Missouri native's cultural offenses. The result of a weekly Los Angeles songwriting get-together with David Baerwald, David Ricketts (aka David + David), Kevin Gilbert and producer Bill Bottrell, **Tuesday Night Music Club** (released in lieu of a previously completed debut Crow scrapped) is appealing if wishy-washy, a fussy studio undertaking that dresses strong emotions in the rustic hues of folky rock-pop. It's a record Bonnie Raitt might have made had she never encountered the blues, or a John Hiatt outing filtered through a half-dozen different sensibilities. As the music meanders through digressions into atmospheric artiness ("Leaving Las Vegas"), John Lennonish declamation ("The Na-Na Song"), genteel funk ("Solidify"), Eagles country ("No One Said It Would Be Easy") and Stealers Wheel party swing ("All I Wanna Do"), the collaborative songwriting likewise reflects various outlooks. "Strong Enough" is a quietly stirring search for one good man; "Run, Baby, Run" portrays a damaged daughter of politicos; "We Do What We Can" sketches out a life portrait of a horn-playing neighbor; "All I Wanna Do" adopts the role of a barfly to offer mindless encouragement of goodtime indulgence. Since each number was written by a different assortment of up to seven people, the lack of a singular artistic vision is no surprise, but it does counter the effectiveness of individual songs. Although the focus remains clearly on her singing, Crow doesn't always seem like the star of the album. (Incidentally, the novel on which the 1995 film *Leaving Las Vegas* was based predates Crow's album by several years.) [i]

CROWDED HOUSE

Crowded House (Capitol) 1986
Temple of Low Men (Capitol) 1988
Woodface (Capitol) 1991
Together Alone (Capitol) 1993
Recurring Dream: The Very Best of Crowded House (Capitol) 1996

TIM FINN

Escapade (Oz/A&M) 1983
Big Canoe (UK Virgin) 1986 (Virgin) 1988
Tim Finn (Capitol) 1989
Before & After (Capitol) 1993

ALT

Altitude (Cooking Vinyl America) 1995

FINN

Finn (UK Parlophone) 1995

FINN BROTHERS

Finn Brothers (Discovery) 1996

In Crowded House, New Zealand's Finn brothers—Tim (older, vocals, songs, spot of keyboards, etc.) and Neil (younger, vocals, songs, lead guitar, etc.)—played out an inversion of what happened in their previous band, Split Enz. This time, Tim joined Neil's band after a couple of albums. The eponymous debut was short on production (by keyboardist Mitchell Froom) but long on songs. The second (again produced by Froom) had far better and more varied sound, but was not as accomplished compositionally; it's humorless and dour to boot.

Woodface seems to integrate Tim into the band as though he were meant to be a part of it; in fact, it started out to be a Finn Brothers record. Co-writing most of the best songs with Neil, Tim seems to have helped focus the pain into poignancy ("Tall Trees") and even occasionally lift the mood to snidely beguiling black humor ("Chocolate Cake," "There Goes God") or even (gulp) enchantment ("Everywhere you go you always take the weather with you"). Froom co-produced with Neil Finn, blithely blending in such outsider contributors as Los Lobos' David Hidalgo on accordion and ex–Beach Boy Ricky Fataar sitting in for drummer Paul Hester on three tracks. (Nice cover painting by bassist Nick Seymour, too.)

Tim came to feel redundant as an onstage band-member and took an amicable powder. With a change of producer (Youth, the Killing Joke veteran who has branched into many other genres as a producer), the remaining trio came up with the ingratiating **Together Alone.** It's fairly Beatles-influenced, both obviously (like the "Taxman"-style verses of "In My Command," the "Norwegian Wood" tone of "Pineapple Head," the out-and-out Lennonesque rocker "Locked Out") and less overtly, in the whimsical and ambitiously "produced" feel. There's also a decidedly New Zealand–ish spin from the get-go: "Kare Kare," named for the beach locale of the recording studio, opens the album declaring "I stood on top of the wave/And then I made the drop." The title track incorporates a Maori choir; "Private Universe" features Micronesian log drummers. **Together Alone** isn't outright happy, but it's definitely Crowded House's brightest album.

Tim, meanwhile, cut his most consistent solo album to date—despite the number of producers (David Leonard, Ricky Fataar, Langer/Winstanley) and songwriting collaborators involved. Neil Finn co-wrote two songs (leftovers from **Woodface**), Richard Thompson contributed to the modest but resonant "Protected" and Hothouse Flowers' Liam Ó Maonlai took part as well. To be sure, **Escapade, Big Canoe** and **Tim Finn** all have their moments, but just one or two per disc (usually a juicy ballad). **Before & After,** however, is balanced and mature in a positive way. Finn took a ten-day silent retreat before making the album, and embodies his spiritual aspect in the closing "I Found It," which keeps tongue firmly in cheek and never identifies what "it" actually is. The album opens with the mid-tempo "Hit the Ground Running," which sets the tone with a disarming, seemingly effortless soul-lite style to convey the story of a friend-of-a-friend's fight against AIDS and succeeds by understatement rather than the arrangement overkill resorted to on previous solo outings. Other highlights: the Dave Edmunds–like "Funny Way" and the wistful soul-pop of "Always Never Now." "In Love With It All" and "Strangeness and Charm," the pair of songs Neil co-wrote, were cut in Dublin with backing by Hothouse Flowers; during those sessions, a pub-crawling incident induced Tim, Ó Maonlai and his singer/songwriter buddy Andy White to whip up "Many's the Time," a catchy observation on celebrity.

That one-off proved such a satisfying collaboration that it developed into a trio, ALT (Andy, Liam, Tim). Ó Maonlai and White camped out at Tim's New Zealand home studio long enough to write and record **Altitude,** playing everything but drums. An invitation to massive self-gratification? Sure, but that's not to say the album is without appeal. The first few tracks are charming, with a coherent if playful ambience, but the enthusiasm peters out as the album runs its course.

Meanwhile, in Auckland sessions in late '94 and early '95, Tim and Neil reunited as Finn (aka the Finn Brothers) writing together, playing all but one bass part and producing **Finn** (released in the US as **Finn Brothers**) with Tchad Blake. Sounding like it was as much fun to make as **Altitude,** this album is miles more entertaining for the listener. Beatlisms abound, in Neil's vocals, in the McCartneyesque feel of his "Last Day of June" and the "I Dig a Pony" vibe of the pseudo-live "Kiss the Road to Raratonga" and in such specific allusions as the simulated musique concrète coda of "Eyes of the World" and the "Helter Skelter"-like descending riff late in "Suffer Never." It's all done with an irresistibly frolicsome spirit, and none of the songs actually depend on purloined Merseysounds. The album is leavened by the poignant "Only Talking Sense" and "Where Is My Soul," the endearingly sweet "Angels Heap," the groove-rocking "Niwhai" and the goofy noir of "Bullets in My Hairdo." If this isn't quite a masterwork, it's still the most consistently enjoyable thing either brother has done in ages. And the booklet has a great photo of the two playing guitar that dates back to before Neil could shave. [jg]

See also *TPRG.*

CRUNT

See *Babes in Toyland.*

CRUSH

Crush (EastWest) 1993

A useful reminder that you can't judge a band by its genealogy, this witless melodic modern-rock quartet boasts original Killing Joke drummer Paul Ferguson and mid-'80s Siouxsie and the Banshees guitarist John Valentine Carruthers (also ex-Clock DVA, Lloyd Cole). That singer Fred Schreck is a New Jersey goth veteran is more salient. None too smart, utterly ordinary (woven together from bits of Big Country, Bad Company, Simple Minds and Rage Against the Machine—the band should have been called Big, Bad & Simple Machine) and produced to a glossy pallor by Pat Moran, **Crush** is a generic waste of plastic. [i]

See also *Lloyd Cole and the Commotions, Siouxsie and the Banshees.*

CRUSH, SR.

The Clown Sessions (Rockville) 1993

Bigtime rock gods may go three to four years between albums, but you can't keep indie-rockers out of the studio with a padlock. Recorded in Boston in the late '80s and partly leaked out piecemeal on three 45s, **The Clown Sessions** documents a collaboration between guitarist/keyboardist Gary Waleik (ex–Big Dipper), bassist Bob Weston (between Volcano Suns and Shellac), drummer Bob Fay (a contributor to Sebadoh's **Smash Your Head on the Punk Rock,** lately the leader of Deluxx) and vocalist Ron Ward, who was the drummer in the Blood Oranges and more recently the singer of Speedball Baby. Improvising scraggly rock matter with a lively sense of humor—"Corndog" leads Ward to paraphrase a cigarette slogan in the service of fowl; "Sweet Cheetah" ("she's my little chiquita") emerges from an unseeing, unknowing cover of "Public Image"; Weston's introductory trumpeting on "Livin' Like a Pimp" only adds to the track's overall twisted fist of funk—Crush, Sr. wrestles **The Clown Sessions** to a draw between inspired slash'n'holler and noisy shit. Now ain't that punk rock, baby? [i]

See also *Blood Oranges, Madder Rose, Shellac.*

CRUST

Sacred Heart of Crust EP (Trance Syndicate) 1990
Crust (Trance Syndicate) 1991
Crusty Love (Trance Syndicate) 1994

Gleefully depicting the life of deviants and incompetents, Austin's Crust explores dementia with sound in the great tradition of Black Sabbath (depression), Black Flag (psychosis) and the Butthole Surfers (schizophrenia). **Sacred Heart of Crust** offers convoluted industrial Mexican dirges like "Tiny Shoes" and the screaming short-wave radio funk of "Black Tuesday."

The trio's buzz seems as varied as whatever pills they choke down, and the self-titled album gnaws away at claustrophobic dialogues on such topics as roadside crime, public institutions and sexually transmitted disease. Eschewing the sacrilegious bent of the EP (also bundled onto the album's CD), the band portrays life on the skids with insight in first-person accounts like "Head Lice" and "Diet Tray." In sonic synch with friends/patrons the Butthole Surfers, Crust's music is a grandiose sonata of harnessed chaos, using distorted voices, droning bass and various noisemakers (electric door springs, toolbox, car springs) that perennially seem on the verge of breaking down.

Crust really gets going on **Crusty Love,** where the trio (Jerry Page, Richard Smith and John Hawkins) reveals an ability to cultivate anxiety more artfully. Uncomfortable anthems like "Chlamydia Is Not a Flower" are ridiculous and frightening, continually surpassing expectations of their own awfulness. Without losing its delusional down-and-out scariness, the music has real force, comparable to Alice Donut and Cop Shoot Cop but infinitely more disturbing. [ic]

CRYSTALIZED MOVEMENTS

See *Magic Hour.*

CUB

Pep EP7 (Can. Mint) 1992
Hot Dog EP7 (Can. Mint) 1993
Betti-Cola (Can. Mint) 1993
Come Out Come Out (Can. Mint) 1994
Box of Hair (Mint/Lookout!) 1996

Vancouver's Cub formed in '92 just across the border from the gravitational pull of Olympia, Washington's K Records/Beat Happening scene and first appeared on a pair of pleasingly amateurish six-song 7-inchers. Genial, sweet, simple and sturdy enough to rock away the coyness that could ruin guitar-pop tunes like "A Party" and "My Chinchilla," the self-declared cuddlecore trio proves that cute *can* be differentiated from cutesy.

The **Betti-Cola** album, with an original cover illustration of the band by Archies Comics artist Dan DeCarlo, recapitulates most of those EPs and then moves on with fifteen subsequent tracks, originals and otherwise, that evince increasing musical strength and confidence (especially on the part of guitarist Robynn Iwata and singer/bassist Lisa Marr; a procession of drummers make rhythmic progress impossible to chart). Besides nifty numbers like the idyllic "Pretty Pictures," the hopeful "Someday" and the buzzingly superstitious "Lucky 7," there's a lovely rendition of Beat Happening's "Cast a Shadow," a peppy bop through Brian Wilson's "Surfer Girl" and an indifferent version of Daniel Johnston's poignant "Tell Me Now." Typical of Cub's casual goodness, the twenty-four-song album ends with a cover of the band's own "What the Water Gave Me" by NFA, a male Canadian trio from New Brunswick. (**Betti-Cola** was also released as a double 7-inch with two bonus tracks added to selections from the LP.)

It's tempting to make too much of the stripped-down cover of the Go-Go's' "Vacation" that ends the much-improved **Come Out Come Out** (released on CD and *triple* 7-inch), but it's impossible to gauge whether the song is being milked for camp or enjoyed for its own merits rather than meant as a tribute to the pioneer rock women. In fact, it doesn't matter, as Cub is well on the way to defining itself. Marr's singing has plenty of vulnerable but self-possessed personality; Iwata's fuzz-guitar power fleshes out the band's sonic presence; drummer Lisa G punches the beat with brisk authority and no frills. Ultimately, though, it's the lyrics—about crushes on girls ("Ticket to Spain"), sexual roles ("You be Doris, I'll be Rock" is a crushing throwaway in "Your Bed"), romantic disillusion ("Life of Crime") and unfailing devotion ("So Far Apart")—that give the album the weight intentionally absent from the breathless music. Incidentally, a very surprising unlabeled bonus track starts five minutes after the end of "Vacation." [i]

CUD

When in Rome, Kill Me (UK Imaginary) 1989
Elvis Belt (UK Imaginary) 1990
Leggy Mambo (UK Imaginary) 1990
The Cud Band E.P. EP (A&M) 1991
Asquarius (A&M) 1992
Showbiz (UK A&M) 1994

By the time Leeds' irredeemably quirky Cud made its Stateside debut, the quartet had shaken off much of the parodic obscureness of its early releases (**Elvis Belt** is a singles compilation that dates back to 1987) and embraced a groove-heavy mix of power-pop bounce and hard-rock guitars. **The Cud Band E.P.** takes four of **Leggy Mambo**'s catchier tracks, adds a dance remix (of "Magic") and sets a course for the band's unfortunate beeline to cut-out bins everywhere. It's a shame, too, since the subsequent domestic album, **Asquarius** (almost entirely produced by Mekon Jon Langford), delivers on the rockist promise only hinted at in the band's embryonic efforts. With Carl Puttnam's cocksure faux-Vegas delivery and generally upbeat lyrics, the Stonesy guitar ranch of "Sometimes Rightly, Sometimes Wrongly" and joyous boogie of "Rich and Strange" and "Pink Flamingo" sound downright fresh.

Showbiz steers this versatile band in a funkier direction, though "Waving and Drowning" and "Slip Away" suggest the guys had been listening to far too much Spin Doctors. No matter that "One Giant Love" is a virtual rewrite of "Pink Flamingo," its touching idealism and the infectious ebullience of "You Lead Me" make Cud a band that deserves to be heard. [db]

See also *TPRG.*

CUL DE SAC

Ecim (UK Capella) 1992 (Northeastern/Lunar Rotation) 1993
I Don't Want to Go to Bed (Nuf Sed) 1995
China Gate (Thirsty Ear) 1996

This instrumental quartet from Boston flies in the face of the dictionary definition of its name; Cul de Sac possesses a much more expansive and hard-to-pinpoint structural arrangement. The group delights in the link between sources as seemingly diverse as John Fahey and Can. Guitarist Glenn Jones uses everything from Middle Eastern tonalities and scales to pure noise soundscapes (for which he's apt to use the Contraption, a homemade stringed apparatus loaded to the gills with electronic hardware). Robin Amos' synthesizer (first heard in the legendary Girls, from which he went on to form Shut Up, which also included Jones) stresses the instrument's unique potential; rather than melodic input, he creates the weather—every condition under the sun—the rest of the band marches through.

On **Ecim,** drummer Chris Guttmacher (from Bullet LaVolta) and bassist Chris Fujiwara create a regularly metered foundation that continuously slices and frames the elements provided by Jones and Amos, like a musical sequence of Muybridge photographs. After Guttmacher left in late '93 (replaced by John Proudman, ex–Men & Volts), the group assembled **I Don't Want to Go to Bed** from hours of improvisation. **China Gate** evinces a broadened palette, in terms of both the ensemble's interplay and Jones' compositions. Proudman is an extremely musical drummer, who can hold down the fort while taking off on flights of fancy with the liquidly propulsive Fujiwara. [tr]

CULT

Dreamtime (UK Beggars Banquet) 1984
Love (Sire) 1985
Electric (Beggars Banquet/Sire) 1987
Sonic Temple (Beggars Banquet/Sire/Reprise) 1989
Ceremony (Beggars Banquet/Sire/Reprise) 1991
The Cult (Beggars Banquet/Sire/Reprise) 1994

HOLY BARBARIANS

Cream (Beggars Banquet/Reprise) 1996

Electric made the Cult a mighty force in the musclebound world of post-Zeppelin poseur rock—the macho realm that prefigured the aesthetic core of Pearl Jam and their imitators several years alter. Although the standard-issue **Sonic Temple** kept it on a platinum plateau, the English quartet subsequently went into a creative and commercial tailspin, the logical result of inadequate imagination in the face of unearned success. A year after **The Cult**'s release, singer Ian Astbury and guitarist Billy Duffy—having rebuilt their band from the sessionmen festival that was **Ceremony**—threw in the towel.

The Cult always had a revolving drum chair, but Astbury and Duffy had to rely completely on hired hands to make the tedious **Ceremony.** With mainstream metal hack Richie Zito producing, such strangers to the genre as bassist Charlie Drayton and keyboardist Benmont Tench assist the two in recalling the lumbering roar of Mountain and indulging an intense interest in Native Americans. While Duffy lays on a hellish roar of cranked-up guitar slabbage, Astbury bellows his best Jim Morrison melodrama and Robert Plant "oooobabybabybaby" pleading in nonsense like the mock-'70s title track ("Funky style music got you good now children"), the flamboyant power ballad "Sweet Salvation," "Earth Mofo," the cello-driven "Indian" ("Standing at the forest awaiting your penance") and the even more ludicrous "Heart of Soul," which announces, "You got to bleed a little while you sing/Less the words don't mean a thing." His dopey words ain't gonna mean a thing, no matter how much he cuts himself.

The returning Bob Rock (producer of **Sonic Temple**) keeps the Cult from sounding quite so stupid on its harsh-edged finale. Duffy outdoes himself in filling every iota of **The Cult** with messy razor-burn noise; new drummer Scott Garrett clatters away on a horribly tuned kit. Over it all, Astbury sings wildly, as if he were being chased down a narrow alley. The chaotic results sound excited more than exciting, but there's a compelling quality to the manic intensity of the sizzling mix. A few digressions—like the Plastic Ono Band guitar citation of the Doorsy "Joy" and the restrained ramble of "Universal You"—provide beneficial contrast to the mindless thunder. Despite the obligatory '60s-fixation indulgences (the somber "Sacred Life" mentions Abbie Hoffman as well as River Phoenix, Kurt Cobain and Andrew Wood), Astbury's reflexive lyrics are weirder and more intriguing than usual. It's hard to suss what's he's on about, but a few songs ("Naturally High," which also refers to friends dying young) suggest things that might actually be going on in his life. Live and let bleed, I say.

Not content with having finally driven the Cult into the ground, Astbury started again, forming the Holy Barbarians with Garrett, his bassist brother Matt and American guitarist Patrick Sugg, using keyboard-type studio gear to make up for the new band's diminished (not quite banished) heaviosity. Produced with a clumsy feel for '80s prog-rock by Matt Hyde, **Cream** moves to affect mild airs of modern techno currency, trying to entice where the Cult could only bludgeon and bellow. No sale: even when he succeeds in reining in his vocal excesses, Astbury is mired by clumsy lyrics ("Space Junkie," "Opium" and "Cream" all imply a drug obsession the fully conscious music doesn't begin to match; "Bodhisattva" turns his attention to sex), flat, go-nowhere songs and his general melodic incapacity. It would be unfair to say that Billy Duffy was the Cult's only crucial member, but **Cream** sure doesn't taste the same without him. [i]

See also *Eat, Wonder Stuff; TPRG.*

CURE

Three Imaginary Boys (UK Fiction) 1979
Boys Don't Cry (Fiction/PVC) 1980 (Elektra) 1988
Seventeen Seconds (UK Fiction) 1980 (Elektra) 1988
Faith (UK Fiction) 1981 (Elektra) 1988
Carnage Visors [tape] (UK Fiction) 1981
. . . Happily Ever After (Fiction/A&M) 1981
Pornography (Fiction/A&M) 1982 (Elektra) 1988
Japanese Whispers (Fiction/Sire) 1983
The Top (Fiction/Sire) 1984
Concert: The Cure Live (UK Fiction) 1984
Concert and Curiosity (UK Fiction) 1984
The Head on the Door (Elektra) 1985
Standing on a Beach: The Singles (Elektra) 1986
Staring at the Sea: The Singles (Elektra) 1986
Kiss Me Kiss Me Kiss Me (Elektra) 1987
The Peel Sessions EP (UK Strange Fruit) 1988 (Strange Fruit/Dutch East India Trading) 1991
Disintegration (Elektra) 1989
Integration (Elektra) 1990
Mixed Up (Fiction/Elektra) 1990

Entreat (UK Fiction) 1991
Wish (Elektra) 1992
Show (Fiction/Elektra) 1993
Sideshow EP (Fiction/Elektra) 1993
Paris (Fiction/Elektra) 1993
Wild Mood Swings (Fiction/Elektra) 1996

With the Cure's first decade clearly sketched out on **Standing on a Beach** and **Staring at the Sea**—respectively, overlapping vinyl/cassette and CD singles compilations containing such standards as "Killing an Arab," "Boys Don't Cry," "Jumping Someone Else's Train," "Let's Go to Bed," "The Love Cats" and "In-Between Days"—singer/guitarist Robert Smith and his unstable collection of bandmates faced the late-'80s as post-punk titans, beloved survivors of an era that no longer held much currency for their young black-clad goth-pop atmosphere vampires. The what-next question was quickly dispatched with the most ambitious album of the Cure's career—the dense and dynamic arena-ready magnum mope-romance opus **Kiss Me Kiss Me Kiss Me**—and its enervated successor, **Disintegration,** but those records were followed by a series of placeholder releases.

Disintegration yielded four CD EPs, later collected in a boxed set entitled **Integration;** a live show from the tour that followed the album produced the eight-song concert document **Entreat.** In the midst of all this nothing, Smith took the unprecedented step of inviting a variety of studio hounds to have a go at remixing the band's 12-inch catalogue, issuing his selection of the best results as **Mixed Up.** The strange and extremely uneven package contains one new song (the hard-rocking "Never Enough"), re-recordings of "The Walk" and "A Forest," a few previously issued versions of familiar singles and disfiguring reworkings of several Cure classics. "Close to Me" gets a shuffling house beat and horns; "Pictures of You" undergoes a complete dub/house remodeling; the dancefloor "Inbetween Days" is nearly unrecognizable. (The bonus track, "Why Can't I Be You?," is available *only* on vinyl.)

Wish scales back the music to a vibrant, busy intimacy; the group seems content to have it all sound alike, not bothering much about differentiating individual songs. Only the simple '60s lollipop jangle of "Friday I'm in Love" and the elegiac "Trust" stand out clearly from the crowd. The lyrics reveal why highly developed arrangements probably weren't a major concern to the band during the album's production: Smith's harrowing squirm in the spotlight is so loaded down with angst and unhappiness that it's amazing he could actually rouse himself to the enthusiasms he manages here. After acknowledging various forms of extreme discomfort (meaningless social contact in "Open," meaningless sexual contact in "Wendy Time," a meaningfully broken heart in "A Letter to Elise" and "To Wish Impossible Things"), he delivers a crushing pronouncement in the chillingly titled and evocatively despairing "End": "I think I've reached that point/Where giving up and going on/Are both the same dead end to me." In what can only be taken as an unprecedented plea for wholesale fan desertion, Smith repeatedly bawls "Please stop loving me . . . I am none of these things." Heavy shit.

Short of cavalier deception, such a confession doesn't leave much room for a bright and shining future, yet Smith and the Cure hit the road in late '92 to support **Wish** on a tour that produced two live albums (plus an EP) with complementary set lists. **Show,** recorded in Michigan, is heavy on the **Wish** songs; **Sideshow,** an EP of leftovers from the same gig, inexplicably repeats "Just Like Heaven" but appends "Fascination Street," "The Walk," "Let's Go to Bed" and the instrumental intro played on tape before the band's onstage arrival. **Paris** buries a couple of **Wish** bones amid an eccentric and esoteric root through the back catalogue: "Charlotte Sometimes," "Close to Me" and "Lovesong" are the best-known songs here. Although not always a compelling act in concert, the Cure is in fine form—upbeat, detailed, engaged. Wherever Smith left his disconsolate anomie, it's nowhere in evidence. Lol Tolhurst, the Cure's founding drummer—whose role in the group had become increasingly undefined—departed before **Wish,** leaving the Cure a trim quintet of Smith, Simon Gallup (bass), Boris Williams (drums), Porl Thompson (guitar/keyboards, but soon to depart for a year's tour with Robert Plant and Jimmy Page) and newcomer Perry Bamonte (guitar/keyboards). Without further instrumental assistance, both concert discs are heavy on thick atmosphere—you can almost smell the church incense seething out from amid the dense drones—and distinguished, as ever, by Smith's unmistakable voice.

In mid-'96, the Cure (reconfigured as a quintet with new members) broke a four-year studio silence by releasing **Wild Mood Swings.** In this potent and sweeping dissertation on melancholy and tentative dreams denied, Smith presents his emotional diffidence and despair with more than the usual musical confidence and enthusiasm. The bittersweet "Strange Attraction"—about a disappointing romance with a letter-writing fan—stands out from this consistently compelling collection for sharing subtle and credible emotions in a most attractive setting. "Numb"? I think not. [i]

See also *Siouxsie and the Banshees; TPRG.*

CURVE

Blindfold EP (UK Anxious) 1991
Frozen EP (UK Anxious/Charisma) 1991
Cherry EP (UK Anxious) 1991
Doppelgänger (Anxious/Charisma) 1992
Pubic Fruit (Anxious/Charisma) 1992
Radio Sessions (UK Anxious) 1993
Cuckoo (Anxious/Charisma) 1993

STATE OF PLAY

Balancing the Scales (UK Virgin) 1986

TONI HALLIDAY

Hearts and Handshakes (WTG) 1989

Chastised as *musique plastique* by critics skeptical of both the band's history and lack thereof, Curve's entirely auspicious bow (a series of three surprisingly accomplished EPs released in under seven months and collected on **Pubic Fruit**) helped deflect accusations of perfectionist hipness. However, the group's core—bassist/guitarist Dean Garcia and vocalist Toni Halliday—was not without its closeted skeletons, having worked together previously in the unsuccessful (yet noxiously commercial) State of Play. Both **Balancing the Scales** and Halliday's solo bow (recorded in 1989 with help from both Garcia and future Curve producer/ancillary guitarist Alan Moulder) are amazing for their complete dearth of original ideas, wallowing in the mushy, pre-rave electro-pop that dominated UK charts in the mid-'80s.

However, they are also remarkable for the astonishing (if illogical) stylistic metamorphosis that Garcia and Halliday underwent in the intervening years. The percussive, guitar-drenched music on **Blindfold** is certainly a far cry from the commercialism of their earlier works, relying on a numb sort of sonic bludgeon to get its point across. Although the formula varies little between the three EPs (as a result, **Pubic Fruit** makes a much better album than many such collections), Halliday's icy sensuality—combined with Garcia's layers of guitars and keyboards—produces an impenetrable top layer carried along by an effective rhythm mixture of live and sequenced drum patterns. Far from either the metallic clichés of industrial music or the fuzzy flailings of My Bloody Valentine hopefuls, Curve's blend of pure sonics and infectious throb works in a way that is truly original.

Having found a functional formula, Halliday and Garcia proceeded to essentially re-record the same song in eleven new ways for **Doppelgänger.** Enjoyable but ultimately monochromatic, Curve's proper debut came as a disappointment in light of the group's initially accelerated innovation. Except for the baroque theatricality of "Faît Accompli" and the dramatic ambience of "Sandpit," Garcia appears to have gotten his drum pattern stuck on "stun" during the sessions; the result is an album that, though certainly well-made, sounds as if it's caught in a loop.

As if to drive the disturbing point home, Curve actually began re-releasing its old music around this time. In addition to **Pubic Fruit,** the **Radio Sessions** CD appeared, arising from a Radio One session that took place as **Blindfold** was released and a session that immediately preceded the release of **Doppelgänger.** Although vaguely informative ("Coast Is Clear" was a day old at the time of the first session and sounds it), it's basically another redundancy in what was shaping up as an incredibly redundant career.

When nobody was paying much attention anymore, Curve released an extraordinary record: **Cuckoo.** Darker, deeper and ultimately more rewarding than any of the band's other work, **Cuckoo**'s gnashing guitar batterie and barely controlled percussion reveal a group that seems to actually be functioning as a live unit rather than as a pair of stars and backup musicians. The album forsakes a good deal of **Doppelgänger**'s sterile finish for an uneasy blend of swirling studio sheen and feedback-driven rock. The band's best moment, **Cuckoo** was also Curve's last. Guitarist Debbie Smith joined Echobelly on a full-time basis. Garcia has devoted his time to—in Halliday's words, making "flying saucer music." Halliday, working with Moulder under the name Scylla, has a very Curve-like track on the *Showgirls* soundtrack. [jf]

See also *Depeche Mode, Echobelly.*

CUSTOMERS

See *Leonards.*

CYCLOPS

See *Peter Jefferies.*

CYCO MIKO

See *Suicidal Tendencies.*

CYCOMOTOGOAT

Cycomotogoat EP (De-es-el) 1992
Alkaline (Sector 2) 1994

Originally known, with a different drummer, as Bah Gah Brothers (the name under which the trio issued **Is There a Doctor in the Fish?**), Cycomotogoat surfaced during the heyday of self-conscious '70s revivalism yet comes off like the real thing on its lengthy self-released EP. The Hoboken trio's dirty boogie suggests a well-preserved Blue Cheer, with lyrical nods to Mercedes cars and Uzi machine guns keeping reality in check. "Serenading Her Soul" and "Tongue and Groove" explore promising terrain, pairing straight-ahead chug with non-flaky psychedelic tendencies. Musically, they surpass more fashionable retro-sludge wankers Monster Magnet and less-dynamic punk-rockers Seaweed.

The full-length **Alkaline** may have suited Cycomotogoat's affiliation with Blues Traveler, but as throwbacks go it's a lackluster likeness. Sporting a cleaner sound than on the EP, the group seems as tired as a bar band and just as low on ideas. Ham-fisted hard-rock numbers gloss over crude spots with Crugie Riccio's Hendrixy guitar solos, while his voice is reduced to a hoarse howl. Cellist Tom Cora sits in on two unrewarding quiet numbers, but the band has slumped enough to merit unflattering comparisons to Steppenwolf. [ic]

CYPRESS HILL

Cypress Hill (Ruffhouse/Columbia) 1991
Black Sunday (Ruffhouse/Columbia) 1993
Cypress Hill III: Temples of Boom (Ruffhouse/Columbia) 1995

To the increasingly outlandish pathology of West Coast gangsta rap, Cypress Hill brings an element of sarcasm and casual, pot-stoked serendipity, embodied by the cartoonish high-sinus drawl of B-Real. At once comical and fierce, Cypress Hill talks about two primary 'hood ornaments—Glocks and blunts—and suggests that the second is a necessity to escape, if only briefly, from the first.

That the interracial trio, from the Latin quarter of Los Angeles near the South Central war zone, had a different take on street violence than its hip-hop peers was immediately apparent on **Cypress Hill.** The opening track, "Pigs," starts off as just another street-thug vignette, but as soon as B-Real starts bustin' rhymes in a nasal whine, it's clear that the Hill gang has a fresh approach. The homophobia in "Pigs" is a pathetic cliché, but it's about the only place on the debut where the group falters. Even at their most explicit, B-Real (Louis Freese) and his wheezing sidekick Sen Dog (Senen Reyes) retain a sense of humor that distinguishes the group from the blinding rage of Ice Cube or the laid-back menace of Snoop Doggy Dog. Just as "Pigs" is a comical inversion of "(Fuck) tha Police," the threat in "Hand on the Pump" is undercut by an absurdly catchy sample from Gene Chandler's "Duke of Earl." The debut is packed with low-rider funk grooves associated with the Dr. Dre–led Cali school, but the group's third principal member and producer DJ Muggs (Lawrence Muggerud) also brings in denser, East Coast flavors: the churning "How I Could Just Kill a Man" bombards the listener with high-pitched squeals in a bring-the-noise mix reminiscent of Public

Enemy. The group also introduces its other key theme in "Light Another" and "Something for the Blunted," which serve primarily as homages to the lethargic bong-hugging "comedy" of Cheech and Chong.

In contrast to the relatively uptempo vibe of its predecessor, **Black Sunday** rolls in like a bad dream, a grim landscape of sawed-off shotguns and deadly encounters that portrays the unglamorous consequences of the gang lifestyle. The mood is set by the migraine-inducing hum that swirls through "I Ain't Goin' Out Like That," punctuated by a few nasty bleats from a saxophone and anchored by the deep tones of a string bass. The narrator in "Lick a Shot" gasps from a lung wound and watches his world go black, while "When the Shit Goes Down" expresses something like remorse for a misdeed chronicled on the first album: "I didn't want to kill a man." Once again, the only relief is inhaled ("Hits From the Bong"); for the second album in a row, there isn't a single female character or even a hint of a romantic, let alone sexual, interest.

This loner attitude dominates **Temples of Boom,** one of the bleakest commentaries on the gangbanger lifestyle ever made. Whereas previous Cypress records offered at least some celebratory moments, **III** is introspective and insular, with creeping rhythms underscored by imploding psychedelic effects, sitars, marimbas, string bass and even the looped voice of an opera singer in full cry (on "Killafornia"). The triumph of "Throw Your Set in the Air" becomes hollow in "Illusions," and the bravado of the barrio stick-up men in "Locotes" is shattered by their deaths. The impact of these narratives is diminished by the tacked-on closer, "Everybody Must Get Stoned," while the swipes at Ice Cube (in "No Rest for the Wicked") and House of Pain (in "Strictly Hip Hop") resort to petty tit-for-tat posturing. Still, for a group that began almost as a caricature of gangsta rap, **III** is a coup, a hardcore album that serves as a critique of the gangsta myth. [gk]

See also *House of Pain.*

D  D

DADDY LONGHEAD

See *Butthole Surfers.*

DADDY-O

You Can Be a Daddy, but Never Daddy-O (Brooktown/Island) 1993

With Stetsasonic out of the picture after topping out creatively with its third album (the brilliant 1991 **Blood, Sweat & No Tears**), Brooklyn rapper/producer Daddy-O made this upbeat, uneventful solo album. Over bumping jeep beats, he tells stories ("Come for Mine") and hurls out good-natured party rhymes (some intriguingly structured in verse-chorus form) in an enthusiastic, articulate sing-song voice. The shoutouts sprinkled throughout the album (an entire track is devoted to Kid Capri) aren't the only ingredient to stir in the old-school flavor; in "Brooklyn Bounce," Daddy-O even acknowledges the direction of his flow. "And if it sounds like something you heard before/It's all the more reason to get on the dancefloor/And rock with the play by play I announce." [i]

JEFF DAHL GROUP

Vomit Wet Kiss (Sympathy for the Record Industry) 1987
Scratch Up Some Action (Aus. Dog Meat) 1989 (Triple X) 1993

JEFF DAHL

I Kill Me (Triple X) 1990
Ultra Under (Triple X) 1991
Wicked (Triple X) 1992
Have Faith EP (Triple X) 1992
Wasted Remains of a Disturbing Childhood (Triple X) 1993
Moonchild (Triple X) 1993
Leather Frankenstein (Triple X) 1994
Bliss (Triple X) 1995
French Cough Syrup (Triple X) 1996

JEFF DAHL AND POISON IDEA

Jeff Dahl . . . Poison Idea (Triple X) 1993

Diehards are a marvelous breed, following a singular vision long after its original benefits—trendiness, reflected glory, creative satisfaction—have expired. Sticking to ancient values makes such intransigents living relics of a bygone age, and the best of the ilk take that responsibility seriously. Hawaiian-born singer/guitarist Jeff Dahl, a devoted, skilled and clear-headed adherent of old-school StoogeDolls spunk, made his recording debut in Washington, DC, in the late '70s but established his career in Los Angeles in the '80s. He spent time in various scene bands (Vox Pop, Angry Samoans, Mentors and Powertrip) before declaring his solo status on the competent but undistinguished **Vomit Wet Kiss.** Continuing an occasional allegiance with ex–Dead Boy guitarist Cheetah Chrome and ex-Adolescent Rikk Agnew (whose 1990 album is entitled **Emotional Vomit**—does the same stomach problem afflict both fellas?), Dahl followed it with **Scratch Up Some Action,** a **Raw Power**–styled roar that makes rocket fuel out of obvious covers ("White Light/White Heat," "1970," "Two-Headed Dog") but runs into trouble on Dahl's originals. (The reissue appends a live fan-club EP, **Pussyfart K.O.)**

Dahl parades his Iggy aspirations on **I Kill Me** (which was actually recorded before, and contains some of the same tracks as, **Vomit Wet Kiss),** most obviously in a spot-on cover of "Search and Destroy." Made in Los Angeles following a move to Arizona, **Ultra Under** energetically maintains Dahl's spirited formula with suitably rocked covers (the Runaways' "Cherry Bomb"), topicals ("Mick & Keith Killed Brian," "Elks Lodge Riot") and other credible originals ("Chemical Eyeballs." "God Don't Care," "Junkies Deserve to Die"). The inclusion of an unabashed piano ballad ("Just Amazin'") shows Dahl is neither afraid to be seen as a softie nor hamstrung by convention. The studio cast includes drummer Dave Nazworthy (of Chemical People) and guitarist Paul Cutler (45 Grave/Dream Syndicate). As low-rent and past-tense as Dahl's records are, they're generally dignified, spry and nearly as entertaining as the era they uphold.

Dahl cut **Wicked** with a lot of the same people and no hint of change in approach from **Ultra Under**—and it's just as good. Amid such generic originals as "Lisa's World," "Real High School Romance" and "Radio Babylon," Dahl shifts his choice of covers a little by doing "The Moon Upstairs" from Mott the Hoople's 1972 **Brain Capers.** Piano continues to be a useful element: John Manikoff's addition to the full-power "Just Like They Should" does the deed here.

Dahl then did the unpunkable and released a limited-edition six-song solo acoustic EP, **Have Faith,** caveating the punk emptors with a cover banner warning of the ampless contents. (As an indication of how unprecedented the idea is, Dahl has to include a liner note thanking Dave Naz for the loan of an acoustic guitar.) Unlikely to be mistaken for a folkie, Dahl is a skilled enough singer and guitarist that the gamble works—and doesn't even sound like a tribute to Johnny Thunders. The more ambitious (bass and drums, guitar overdubs) **Moonchild** repeats the offer with five acoustic demos previewing songs on **Leather Frankenstein** and five otherwise unissued tunes. If **Have Faith** is charmingly casual, this is downright sloppy: the instrumental tracks are rarely in synch with each other. Best moment: Dahl, alone in the studio, exclaiming "Come on!" at the start of "Only Lovers Left Alive."

With Ratboy (of LA's Motorcycle Boy, later to form Pillbox in NYC), longtime bassist John Duffy and Nazworthy on drums, Dahl made the adequate but edgeless **Wasted Remains of a Disturbing Childhood** (requisite borrowing: "1969," from **The Stooges**). A Dollsy album with good derivative tunes ("She's So Cool," "Hey Cinderella," "Positive"), it could have used a producer to move Dahl off the stylistic dime. Other than the hot dueling solos of "A Dash of Prayer," Dahl's blue plate special is getting mighty cold . . .

Two years after the 1990 death of Dead Boys singer Stiv Bator(s), Dahl read an article in which Oregon punks Poison Idea echoed his reverent sentiments toward the singer and lit upon the idea of joining forces to record a tribute. The resulting mini-album contains their fine collaboration on Lords of the New Church's "Open Your Eyes" and a less effective try at the Dead Boys' "Flame Thrower Love," as well as three numbers from each half of the project. Dahl doles out a Ramones cover, the Lords' "Method to My Madness" and his own "Falling Apart," while Poison Idea musters typical original charmers like "Desecration" and "Crippled Angel." Intentions are fine all around, but a single would have sufficed.

The cover bills it to Jeff Dahl and the Spiders From Uranus (yawn), but **Leather Frankenstein** begins Dahl's era of solitary recording. Guitarist Zepp Oberpichler (?) and pianist/violinist Robert Brock contribute to half the tracks, otherwise, it's all Dahl—including the songwriting credits (a technical distinction, of course, although "Only Lovers Left Alive" and "I Think I Lost My Mind" are handsome, punk-free ballads). Except for the fried guitar tone, the experiment in self-reliance is successful, but the patient is still ready for a rest.

A cover of "Gimme Danger" (does he get a washing machine when he completes the eight-song **Raw Power** cycle?) isn't the only overly familiar attribute of **Bliss.** Dahl's not exactly a font of novel ideas, and his endless variations on the same themes—especially as he's become a studio hermit (pianist Brock is the only outsider here)—make his soundalike albums less interchangeable than indistinguishable. If he's gonna keep writing the same tunes over and over, at least he should try varying the timbre or style of his guitar or voice. On **French Cough Syrup,** the electronic drums sound especially crappy, and that's not helpful. The self-aware autobiography of "Circa '70" kicks two lines in a promising power-pop vein, but quickly reverts to form. Some things never change. [i]

See also *Chemical People, Pillbox, Poison Idea; TPRG.*

BLAG DAHLIA

See *Dwarves.*

DAISY CHAINSAW

Love Sick Pleasure EP (Deva/One Little Indian/A&M) 1991
Eleventeen (Deva/One Little Indian/A&M) 1992

Kicking off **Love Sick Pleasure** with a big, brazen bang, wacky waif Katie Jane Garside declaims the tart anti-record-label diatribe "Love Your Money" in a slightly distorted little-girl-gone-vicious vocal pout atop the chunky bed of Richard Adams' fuzz bass and songwriter Crispin Gray's gnashing punk guitar. As acidly enjoyable as a lemon-sour candy, the London quartet happily recalls the loud, noisy hijinx of X-Ray Spex and the Slits while prefiguring poppier bands like Elastica. "Pink Flower" throbs like a runaway train, breathless and unsettled, before devolving into a sweet, strange dirge, harried by chirping effects; the EP is rounded out by the brief, blistering "Sick of Sex," "All the Kids Agree" and seven chaotic minutes in "Room Eleven."

The full-length **Eleventeen** reprises "Love Your Money" and "Pink Flower," adding more of the same wailing fuzz-punk ("Dog with Sharper Teeth," "I Feel Insane"). Variations include the acoustic guitar plunkings and running-water sounds making up "Natural Man" and the eerily ambient "Use Me Use You." "Everything Is Weird," indeed. Garside's departure before a second album could be recorded ended the group. [gef]

DAISYCUTTER

See *Monster Magnet.*

DA LENCH MOB

See *Ice Cube.*

DAMBUILDERS

A Young Person's Guide (Ger. Cuacha!) 1989
Geek Lust (Ger. Cuacha!) 1991
Tough Guy Problem EP (spinART) 1992
Islington Porn Tapes (Ger. Cuacha!) 1993
Dambuilders EP7 (Rockville) 1993
Encendedor (EastWest) 1994
Ruby Red (EastWest) 1995

The Dambuilders' records chronicle the progress of a band that, for better or worse, finally seems to have found an identifiable sonic niche in the mid-'90s. Singer/bassist Dave Derby and guitarist Eric Masunaga evolved the group from the Exactones, the name under which they released several homemade cassettes in their native Hawaii. **A Young Person's Guide**—recorded in the fiftieth state and released by a German label—unveils the Dambuilders searching high and low for a style. Ironically, its very derivativeness is what makes it such an utter delight, as the group jumps from punk to folk to garage to funk to rock to indie-pop, succeeding charmingly at most of it. The Replacements, Violent Femmes, Talking Heads, Ramones, Cheap Trick, R.E.M., Lemonheads, B-52's and Marshall Crenshaw are all likely influences; "Radio Is King" even anticipates the arrival of the Gin Blossoms. It's the only Dambuilders album to feature two guitarists—Masunaga, who also skillfully produced all of the band's records up to **Ruby Red,** and Tryan George, whose acoustic work gives the album much of its flavor. Violinist Debbie Fox guested on a couple of tracks and subsequently joined the group.

The Dambuilders relocated to Boston and also toured Europe between **A Young Person's Guide** and **Geek Lust,** resulting in a change of drummers and the departures of George and Fox. Joan Wasser (ex-Heretix/Lotus Eaters) replaced Fox during the recording of **Geek Lust,** an album that moves the band in a darker, heavier direction, thanks in part to Masunaga's increasing use of guitar distortion. While some of the songs veer closer to grunge than anything on the debut, the album is nearly as melodic and infectious overall.

With the addition of Kevin March, a superb drummer, the band's current lineup finally came together on the five-song **Tough Guy Problem,** which contributes two songs ("Louisiana" and "Idaho") to the group's continuing "50 songs for 50 states" project. (The goal is to write one about, or at least titled after, every state of the Union. For those in need of direction, "New Jersey," "Wyoming" and "Oregon" fill the '93 7-inch.) On **Islington Porn Tapes,** the band's sound continues to grow bigger, darker, more intense and more progressive. The first album seems miles away.

Encendedor, the Dambuilders' full-length US debut, consists of five tracks (including the excellent single "Shrine") from **Islington Porn Tapes,** one from **Geek Lust** (that album's intense peak, the Stooges-like "Fur"), **Tough Guy**'s "Idaho" and three new ones, of which "Delaware" is the most catchy and "Collective" provides the best glimpse into where the band was headed. As usual, Masunaga's production is superb.

Don Gehman produced **Ruby Red,** making everything bigger, pulling Wasser's violin and backing vocals and March's drums to the fore. The result is arena-ready hugeness that subverts the band's sonic variety, especially Masunaga's guitar work. There are some good songs, and Derby does some nice things vocally—his falsetto on "Down" would give Radiohead's Thom Yorke a run for his money—but it's a letdown from a band that has rarely disappointed in the past. [ds]

See also *Shudder to Think.*

DAMON AND NAOMI

More Sad Hits (Shimmy-Disc) 1992
The Wondrous World of Damon and Naomi (Sub Pop) 1995

"Sweetness and light" doesn't accurately describe the gloomily ethereal moods that emanate from the seemingly hermetic universe inhabited by Damon Krukowski and Naomi Yang—"sweetness and dark" is more like it. After leaving Galaxie 500 at the dawn of the '90s, the duo set out to build an entirely different superstructure atop the slowcore foundation they perfected as that band's rhythm section—one based in expansive sonic washes rather than angular riffs, a backdrop that helps accentuate the impersonal yet affecting nature of their songs.

On the meaningfully titled **More Sad Hits,** bassist Yang and drummer/guitarist Krukowski—who share an affinity for watery, unfocused vocals—pass the mic back and forth with such ease that it's tempting to simply float along on the wisps of melody. That would be a mistake, and not just because of the attention to detail that manifests itself in little ways (like the brass shadings coloring the hollow "Information Age," which bemoans a lost love in decidedly cyber-era terms). Concentrating really pays off once you begin to break down the album's unconventional blend of agit-prop gauntlet-throwing (like the Mao-quoting "Little Red Record Co.") and vividly imagistic landscapes ("Boston's Daily Temperature") and reach its core of all-consuming melancholy. Kramer, who produced, is given equal credit with the headliners for instruments and vocals; his contributions include guitar, keyboards and drums. Cool cover: Soft Machine's "Memories."

Despite occasionally busy production (Kramer again), **The Wondrous World** casts off some of the debut's studiocentric layering in favor of an engagingly organic, acoustic-guitar-dominated woodsiness. Originals like the forlorn campfire—make that dying-ember—singalong "In the Morning" are nicely bracketed by a well-chosen array of covers, including the Band's "Whispering Pines" and "Who Am I," a dirge originally recorded by Country Joe and the Fish. Admittedly, it takes some doing to penetrate Krukowski's more oblique dissertations—"The New Historicism" is every bit as bombastic as it sounds—but the prevailing tone is rustic enough to offset such post-mod affectations. [dss]

See also *Magic Hour.*

DANCE HALL CRASHERS

Dance Hall Crashers (Moon) 1990
1989–1992 (Moon) 1993
Lockjaw (510) 1995

Although the group was originally instigated by guitarist Tim Armstrong and bassist Matt Freeman (both of Operation Ivy and, more recently, Rancid) as a ska-core side project, neither East Bay scene activist was involved when the Dance Hall Crashers—solidified into an energetic sextet behind delightful vocalists Elyse Rogers and Karina Deniké—made their debut with an eponymous 1990 album. That done, the band dissolved, but started up again two years later (an event their erstwhile label celebrated by repackaging **Dance Hall Crashers** with some added tracks as **1989–1992**), and was thus well-positioned to benefit from the sudden attention focused on their backyard as ground zero of the Green Day dookie-bomb. Green Day's former managers signed the group to their new label, and Dance Hall Crashers responded with **Lockjaw,** a marvelous surge of mature and catchy power-pop accented with punk juice and set—almost incidentally—to a breathless bluebeat. Although "Sticky" (a devastatingly sardonic observation of putting up with a treacherous boyfriend: "Pull the knife out of my back/Clean the blade and put it back") rips off the control, the band mostly keeps itself in check to favor great songs like "Shelley," "Buried Alive" (another long-suffering romantic lament), "Queen for a Day" (a suspicious view of the record industry), the ambivalent "Go" and the landlord kiss-off "So Sue Us." As joyous and witty as any new wave pop classic, **Lockjaw** is the much-needed skanking soundtrack of 1995, a consciously un-nostalgic treat that will still send you digging for those old Blondie and Madness records. [i]

See also *Rancid.*

DANCING FRENCH LIBERALS OF '48

See *Gits.*

DANDY WARHOLS

The Dandy Warhols (Tim/Kerr) 1995

The umpty-millionth band of tragically self-conscious style-mongers to come sashaying down the noise-pop runway as if they had just bought the place hails from Portland, Oregon. The Dandy Warhols have a regrettable name and a modern time-capsule sound that neatly summarizes a good chunk of what's stopped by *Alternative Nation* sporting an English accent since a week ago Thursday. Both seriously pretentious (glib put-on lyrics about LSD, suicide and TV, aren't-we-clever rock references, the accurately clocked interplanetary monotony of "It's a Fast-Driving Rave-Up With the Dandy Warhols Sixteen Minutes") and pretentiously unserious (a funny parody entitled "(Tony, This Song Is Called) Lou Weed," a pointless nothing called "Grunge Betty"), the quartet is commendably good at teasing a variety of cool sounds from Courtney Taylor's vocal harmonies with keyboard bassist Zia McCabe and his fuzzbox clashes with the band's other guitarist, Peter Holmstrom. But cleverness is no substitute for real songwriting, and that's where the fizz goes out here. Having located the point where the self-amused genre fakery of bands like Denim and the Pooh Sticks becomes hard to distinguish from the sham posturing of phonies like Suede or Menswe@r, the Dandy Warhols—lacking the stylistic commitment to be a full-time anything—use it as a safety zone in which everything is possible but nothing really matters. [i]

DANZIG

Danzig (Def American/Geffen) 1988
Danzig II–Lucifuge (Def American/Geffen) 1990
Danzig III: How the Gods Kill (Def American) 1992
Thrall–Demonsweatlive (Def American) 1993
4 (American) 1994
Blackacidevil (Hollywood) 1996

At the very crest of Misfits cult mania, producer Rick Rubin decided to help ex-'Fits vocalist Glenn Danzig realize a dream of making his current group, Samhain, more professional and focused. It worked. In Danzig, the diminutive New Jersey hunk moved his dark hard rock into the commercial mainstream while remaining true to fans' sanguinary tastes. Although Danzig's satanic pretensions are too much for some to bear, they are easy to set aside or ignore; the group's undeniable might, its songwriting skill and the phlegmy singer's melodramatic bellow cast a far more potent spell than any comic-book malevolence.

With the benefit of a real band—tasteful metallic guitarist John Christ, Samhain holdover Eerie Von (bass) and dexterous drummer Chuck Biscuits (ex-D.O.A., Black Flag and Circle Jerks)—**Danzig** is a crunchy and lusty demonic cross between the Doors, Misfits and Black Sabbath. Roughly half of the album is ominous and mighty ("Twist of Cain," "She Rides," "Soul on Fire" and "Mother"); the rest displays the weak underbelly of Rubin's thinly homogeneous production.

Lucifuge corrects the debut's flaws: Rubin's production is much fleshier, and Glenn exercises the theatrical satanic-pagan muscle-stud angle to entertaining effect. The songs (especially the cool, dank beauty of "Her Black Wings" and the '50s-style melodic tear-jerker, "Blood and Tears") are consistently stronger; a heavy dose of voodoo blues (the stripped-down "I'm the One") adds pungent flavor to the thematic and musical brew.

Producing himself (under Rubin's executive eye), Glenn proves the quartet's intrinsic mettle on **How the Gods Kill,** a roaring slab of leathery rock that isn't overly troubled by his lyrical obsessions. Actually, for an avowed underworld-lover, the thoroughly unintimidating singer sounds a lot like a recovering Catholic ("I couldn't take it anymore/And so you leave me godless"); his lyrics in "Do You Wear the Mark" and "Heart of the Devil" are littered with references to "evil," "devil," "Heaven," "soul" and "blood." As its namesake shows the confidence (or hubris, same difference here) to sing "Sistinas" as a ridiculous croony gothic ballad, the band spends most of this exciting record roaring down the power alley in tight, martial formation, lashing songs to tense riffs that give way to explosions of energy. (The title track's verses are held back for a Blue Öyster Cult–style buildup.) Economical and efficient, an organic blend of vocals and instrumental intensity, **How the Gods Kill** is great bleak fun.

As if to acknowledge his wry insincerity, Danzig recorded a straight-faced version of "Trouble," Leiber and Stoller's innocuous rewrite of "Hoochie Coochie Man" ("Because I'm evil/My middle name is misery/Said I'm evil child/Don't you mess around with me") for Elvis Presley, as one of three new studio tracks on the otherwise live-in-Irvine **Thrall—Demonsweatlive.** ("It's Coming Down" is a worthier, and original, addition to the band's repertoire.) With something from each prior album, the four concert cuts are loud, buzzy and ringed in crowd noise, but—other than Christ's phenomenal displays of fret frenzy—not nearly as exciting as witnessing the real thing in the flesh.

The remainder of **4**'s title is one of those unprintable runic phrases ("Bowling Night"?). The album itself, however, is in English—dark, sinister, violent, theatrically overstated English. Reaching new levels of lurid posturing, Danzig sounds a personal note amid the usual fictional depictions ("Bringer of Death," "Stalker Song"). "I Don't Mind the Pain," "Son of the Morning Star," "Let It Be Captured" and "Cantspeak" disguise what appear to be mundane feelings of loneliness in grandiose imagery, although that doesn't explain the sexual violence of "Little Whip." Elsewhere, he indulges in a little garden-variety self-deification ("Brand New God," "Until You Call on the Dark"). The dynamic variety of the long, ambitious record (complete with a bonus sepulchral chant) is better than ever, but it's an audibly strenuous effort. Too self-conscious by half (the sound effects are a bad sign) and sonically thick-skinned where pervious albums ripped away flesh, **4** is pure but not prime Danzig.

After playing on **4,** Chuck Biscuits left the band and was rebuffed when he asked to rejoin later in '94. Joey Castillo became Danzig's new drummer; Glenn then replaced the rest of the band. [gef/i]

TERENCE TRENT D'ARBY

Introducing the Hardline According to Terence Trent D'Arby (Columbia) 1987
Terence Trent D'Arby's Neither Fish nor Flesh (Columbia) 1989
Terence Trent D'Arby's Symphony or Damn (Columbia) 1993
Terence Trent D'Arby's Vibrator (Work) 1995

TOUCH WITH TERENCE TRENT D'ARBY

Early Works (Ger. IMP/Polydor) 1989

Derivative, arrogant and at times unbearably pretentious, Terence Trent D'Arby is nevertheless so inventive and entertaining (when he's in the mood) that it's hard not to be seduced by his rock'n'soul pastiche. Though he'll never rise to the stirring grace of his number-one role model, Sam Cooke—he's got the inflections and the texture, but little of the warmth—the obvious pleasure D'Arby takes in plying his craft makes even the embarrassing misfires fascinating in a twisted way.

Recorded with British veterans of the pub-rock/new wave wars, the New York native's accomplished debut,

Introducing the Hardline, includes the sultry hit "Wishing Well," which created unrealistic commercial expectations, but it's a fine album in any case. Eager to prove his versatility from the git-go, he wails ("Dance Little Sister"), croons ("Sign Your Name") and rocks out ("If You Let Me Stay"). Good fun all around. (**Early Works** is a 1983 skeleton—a German band D'Arby joined after finishing an Army hitch there—trotted out to capitalize on D'Arby's success.)

Emboldened by his quick success, D'Arby wasted no time embracing the sophomore slump with a vengeance, promptly alienating the mainstream following that needs reassurance to keep coming back for more. Pompously announcing "I will not be defined" at the start of **Neither Fish nor Flesh** (subtitled *A Soundtrack of Love, Faith, Hope & Destruction*), he offers up a murky, lukewarm stew of psychedelic funk, spacey Marvin Gaye soul, a few commercial gestures and plenty of self-indulgent mood pieces. Weirdly intriguing but not at all good.

Despite self-conscious conceptual trappings, D'Arby's two subsequent albums have attempted to reingratiate him with normal buyers. Both are excellent, eclectic pop records that emphasize his strengths and feature a slew of catchy numbers along with a few inevitable stinkers. **Symphony or Damn** *(Exploring the Tension Inside the Sweetness)* sparkles on the upbeat tunes, including the furious "Baby Let Me Share My Love," the glittering "Penelope Please" and the sizzling "She Kissed Me," while the ominous "Succumb to Me" makes lust seem dangerous. To hear the corniest tune ever written, check out the icky "Let Her Down Easy."

Vibrator *(Batteries Included)* is just as diverse, but with a case of the jitters. Featured in Robert Altman's *Pret-a-Porter (Ready to Wear),* "Supermodel Sandwich" is psychedelia lite, a vibe pushed to edgier extremes in "Read My Lips (I Dig Your Scene)." With silly lyrics about the "slow striptease of time" and the like, "TTD's Recurring Dream" is so shamelessly melodramatic that it's great fun. Apparently concerned with balancing the belligerent desire of "C.Y.F.M.L.A.Y?" ("can you feel my love around you") and gentler sentiments, D'Arby includes plenty of drippy stuff, so be prepared to hit the skip button a few times. [jy]

See also *TPRG*.

DARKSIDE

All That Noise (UK Situation Two) 1990 (Beggars Banquet/RCA) 1991
Melomania (Beggars Banquet/RCA) 1992

Rosco and Pete Bassman (né Baines), the original rhythm section of England's extraordinary Spacemen 3, formed the Darkside as a side band in 1986, devoting themselves to it several years later. On **All That Noise,** the Rugby trio has the Doors' old rainy-night bass/drums sound down cold, but that dubious achievement is the album's best feature. The other notable elements on this atmospheric but underwhelming record—Bassman's lazy artless-pop vocals, Rosco's wheedly organ, and guitar work that ranges from a translucent pop drizzle to floods of pseudo-psychedelic distortion—don't amount to much. Other than "Good for Me," the songwriting is too weak to carry the load. Lacking the obsessive intensity of the Spacemen or a strong personality of its own, the Darkside's candle flickers without shedding any light.

Recorded as a quartet, the self-produced **Melomania** (for those without access to an OED, the title means "a mania for music") documents Bassman's second futile try at singing consistently in tune, accompanied by a narrowed dynamic range of stylish quiet and ragged loud, all slathered ineffectually in '60s ambience. With no sign of the first album's Doors fixation, "This Mystic Morning" does ape some of that group's Los Angeles folk-rock contemporaries reasonably well. Ultimately, the Darkside's incoherence, lack of conviction and threadbare compositional ideas go to show that a mania for music is nothing like a talent for it. [i]

See also *Spacemen 3*.

DARLING BUDS

Pop Said . . . (Columbia) 1988
Tiny Machine EP (UK Epic) 1990
Crawdaddy (Columbia) 1990
Erotica Plays EP (UK Epic) 1991
Erotica (Chaos/Columbia) 1992

While **Pop Said . . .** placed this Welsh quartet (whose name comes from a Shakespeare sonnet) squarely in the company of other chirpy British female-fronted pop groups, the Darling Buds' bubblegum gradually morphed into something decidedly less sweet. On **Crawdaddy,** the sound is lusher, with most of the pop and dance morsels coated in feedback.

Singer/co-writer Andrea Lewis comes into her own on the aptly named **Erotica** (like **Crawdaddy,** made with Smiths/Blur producer Stephen Street), an album that sees a fine band maturing in sound, yet still capitalizing on its original strength—brilliant hookcraft. (Incidentally, Madonna's **Erotica** also appeared in '92.) With vaguely menacing distortion added to the seductive sugar-pop attack, practically every track (especially "One Thing Leads to Another," "Gently Fall" and "Angels Fallen") is a single that could have been a hit. And the absolutely lovely "Please Yourself" beats "I Touch Myself" and "She Bop" as modern rock's most joyous ode to carnal solitaire. [db]

See also *TPRG*.

DARYLL-ANN

Daryll-Ann EP (Hut U.S.A./Vernon Yard) 1994
Seaborne West (Hut U.S.A./Vernon Yard) 1995

The near-absence of accent in the pop produced by the four young Dutchmen of Daryll-Ann is both literal and descriptive: while guitarist Jelle Paulusma betrays only the scantest difficulty pronouncing English words in his high, attractive voice, the band's sweet'n'low guitar rock too often drifts off into bland tweeness, early Aztec Camera diluted with too much water. More the windblown product of diverse influences than a stylistically resolved proposition, Daryll-Ann spends its six-song debut (a condensation of two UK EPs) puttering around. The group imagines how David Bowie '70s country rock might sound ("I Could Never Love You"), pastes banjo into the Kinksy bounce of "Come Around" and tries out Hollies harmonies on "Doll," a pre-*Toy Story* song that imagines being on a shelf "next to Superman." The quartet displays ample enthusiasm and a bit of élan, but even lyrics that describe cruel words as "snakes from our mouth" just aren't striking enough to compensate for the music's shocking normalcy.

The full-length **Seaborne West** increases the peace, offering oily commercial chirpiness (except for a fat wah-wah guitar solo, "Stay" sounds like the second coming of Pilot), adding more country and quiet to the mix, and generally paying unironic tribute to wishywashiness in many pale colors. The malt-rock cover of Carly Simon's "You're So Vain" sounds altogether sincere—although guitarist Anne Soldaat does fire off a piercing solo for credibility's sake. Other numbers ("Sheila") owe something to Crosby, Stills and Nash (the Neil Young tributes are separate). As hard as it is to dislike a band that can start the album's hardest-rocking song ("Birthmark") with a murmured "Uh-oh!," sing convincingly about turning in ("Low Light") and make no issue of the line "Little boy you were, you're growing older and I'm scared to lose you," Daryll-Ann repeatedly sidles up to promising ideas and then lets them get away in a whoosh of the wimpy cutes. As bright and jingly as it is, this charm bracelet is just too flimsy to cherish. [i]

DAS EFX

Dead Serious (EastWest) 1992
Straight Up Sewaside (EastWest) 1993
Hold It Down (EastWest) 1995

Armed with a rich, febrile, foul sense of humor and an unmistakably idiosyncratic delivery—a syncopated stutter with dancehall syllable scattering and stop-hold-rush gear-shifting—Das EFX came to market under the production wing of EPMD. The Virginia State University–formed, Brooklyn-based duo of Dre (aka Krazy Drayz, aka Andre Weston) and Skoob (aka Books, aka Willie Hines) don't push the topical envelope any—geography, rhyming and sexing are pretty much the alpha-omega of their menu on the sarcastically titled **Dead Serious.** Fortunately, the pair's rereading of old news yields fresh and funny angles, and they pack the rhymes with ridiculous TV and music references ("like Chico, I'm the man . . . I gave a crew cut to Sinéad O'Connor") certain to tease a smile out of the hardest roughneck. Vocalized in their original and entertaining (not to mention influential: former EPMDer Parrish Smith virtually stole their act on his 1994 solo album) style, songs like "Mic Checka," "Jussummen" (one of two cuts with guitar by future solo blues-rapper Bobby Sichran), the way-rude "Looseys" and "Straight Out the Sewer" make **Dead Serious** a monstrously entertaining debut.

Lines like "I rolled two spliffs, so I guess I'm double-jointed" show that Skoob and Dray [sic] have their brain-teasing wits about them on **Straight Up Sewaside,** but the sophomore album is a let-down, with dull production, streamlined vocals and too many go-nowhere stragglers like the repetitive "Check It Out," "Baknaffek" and "Kaught in da Ak." "It'z Lik Dat" and "Rappaz" are bright moments, but Das EFX's decision to downplay their strengths—combined with such filler as an interview and the majorly annoying gimmick of spinning a radio dial—makes the album a sorry also-ran to the first.

Which still leaves it miles better than the pitiful **Hold It Down.** An audio representation of two minds on drugs—"40 & a Blunt" is all she hadda write—the album finds Hines and Weston dull-wittedly stuck in a mental end groove, repetitively rhyming about skunk and blunts, about getting and staying high, as if they were rehearsing for parts in *The Cheech and Chong Story.* Boring, casually offensive ("faggot" is essential, if non-sexual, vocabulary here; a passing reference to Long Island Railroad mass-murderer Colin Ferguson is in extremely poor taste) and slack to the max; the occasional "diggedy" scat syllables are dropped in as a sad reminder of the duo's once-phenomenal skills. [i]

See also *Ice Cube.*

DASHBOARD SAVIORS

Kitty (Medium Cool/Twin\Tone) 1992
Spinnin on Down (Medium Cool/Twin\Tone) 1993
Love Sorrow Hatred Madness (Medium Cool/Twin\Tone) 1995

The '90s roots-rock revival has allowed some fine bands to gain a deserved foothold. Others have merely had the good fortune to be swept up in their wake: Georgia's Dashboard Saviors are of the second variety. While the band was enough of an Athens favorite to be able to enlist Pete Buck, Mike Mills and Vic Chesnutt to play on **Kitty,** the songs don't amount to much. Keeping good company is fine, but the Dashboard Saviors are at best a tuneful frat band, with forgettable lyrics and an uneventful style. "Dilettante's Ball," for example, shares a pot-smoking high-school memory amid Skynyrd-proud bar-rousing riffs.

With little reliance on the artistic tradition from which they supposedly draw, the quartet sprays out streams of beer-swill rock punctuated by frontman Todd McBride's raspy vocals—which deliver neither the finality of John Prine, nor the desperation of Townes Van Zandt nor even the humor of Todd Snider. Chesnutt swings a lick on **Spinnin on Down,** as does Marlee MacLeod (a labelmate who used Saviors bassist Rob Veal and drummer John Crist as the rhythm section on her 1995 album, **Favorite Ball & Chain**); Jack Logan co-wrote "Pawnbroker" with McBride. But for all their southern culture, the Saviors seem to have picked up little of the gothic storytelling tradition that marks their pals' best work. "Not the Engineer" and "Rand McNally Blues" are the strongest tracks—the band should have stopped there and had itself a dandy single.

The Saviors attempt a sort of transfiguration on **Love Sorrow Hatred Madness,** including more effective acoustic numbers, but the band's slow development is frustrating. (See "Watching You," a painful attempt at mimicking Dylan.) Logan again offers assistance, contributing to "Out in the Back" and the bluesy "Training Wheels." [vg]

DASH RIP ROCK

Dash Rip Rock (688) 1986 (Mammoth) 1989
Ace of Clubs (Mammoth) 1989
Not of This World (Mammoth) 1990
Boiled Alive! (Mammoth) 1991
Tiger Town (Doctor Dream) 1993
Get You Some of Me (Sector 2) 1995

Regardless of the stylistic ingredients poured into the Dash Rip Rock stew pot (and that would include everything between Hank Williams and Bo Diddley), what the Louisiana trio (named after Elly May's movie-star beau on *The Beverly Hillbillies*) ladles out is white lightning rock'n'roll, distilled to its basic essence with the tradition-minded reliability of backwoods bootleggers. "Nothin' fancy" covers it, but these guys can really play, so sloppiness is only the seasoning, not Dash's stock in trade. Singer/guitarist (and onetime Louisiana State U grad student in journalism) Bill Davis, bassist Ned "Hoaky" Hickel and a procession of durable drummers have been tearing up the clubs since the mid-'80s; every year or two, they drop by a recording studio and commit some more purified musical hootch to tape. If none of their work advances the stylistic state of popular culture one inch, Dash Rip Rock never fails to boil up a hearty, spicy concoction that sticks to the ribs and fills a sinful soul.

Dash Rip Rock and **Ace of Clubs** benefit from the presence of original drummer/singer/wildman Fred LeBlanc, who then departed to open his own quartet, Cowboy Mouth, for business. Introducing producer Jim Dickinson and drummer Chris Luckette, Dash got loud and raunchy on **Not of This World,** an album hot enough to light a small studio conflagration. Recorded onstage in Texas and Louisiana, **Boiled Alive!** draws heavily from all three LPs, adding fresh new originals, covers like "Jambalaya" and some typically uproarious Davis platter patter.

Tiger Town keeps the gas on through ravers like "Little Rita," "True Drunk Love," Mojo Nixon's "All Liquored Up," Larry Williams' "Dizzy Miss Lizzy" and the choogling "Swamp Thing." Dash reveals its poppier, more ambitious side in "Loosen Up Your Wig," "Livin' Breathin'," "Walk on the Water" and "Shine a Light," all of which keep the electricity on but apply it more judiciously to songs with real tunes and dynamic control. Growing up without lying down, Davis makes **Tiger Town** a positive stop on the Dash Rip ride.

The self-produced **Get You Some of Me** (Luckette's last blast) spreads the band's reach even further. Guest piano and pedal steel don't seriously alter the sound of elemental Dash: Davis' twangy singing and stinging guitar are the only notes that count. But he can certainly shift his own gears, so the taut razor-rock basics of "Life Flash" and "Shootin' Up Signs" and the retro geo-romp of "Ridin' Into Memphis" (co-written by Davis and LeBlanc) give way to acoustic balladry ("Houseboat") and pop ("The Heart I Break," "Scheme of Things"), lonesome country ("Half Kansas Moon") and high-steppin' rock-funk ("Get You Some of Me"). But the ratio of borrowed tunes (John Doe's "All Day Night," Ben Vaughn's "Houseboat," Danny and the Juniors' "At the Hop," reworked as "Let's Go Smoke Some Pot") suggests that supplies might be running short, and the originals don't all stack up with the band's best. Maybe it's time for a breather. [i]

See also *Cowboy Mouth; TPRG.*

DAS ICH

Die Propheten (Ger. Danse Macabre) 1991 (Etherhaus) 1996
Stigma EP (Ger. Danse Macabre) 1994
Staub (Ger. Danse Macabre) 1994 (Etherhaus) 1996
Feuer (Ger. Danse Macabre) 1995 (Etherhaus) 1996

Das Ich plays hard, *hard*-hitting industrial music, with strictly German lyrics adding to the harsh, foreign atmosphere. The band's bombastic, strident music is not some industrial-by-the-numbers exercise in Nine Inch Nails faux-miserabilism: Das Ich means every howl of anger and estrangement. Stefan Ackermann's alien vocal stylings are the centerpiece of the unsettling **Die Propheten,** with programmer/keyboardist Bruno Kramm's intense, mind-numbing non-melodies crashing in the background. The din lets up only on the final track, "Freuel," which features Ackermann's almost gentle—but spooky—singing over simple carnival-like piano.

Stigma offers more of the same raging, futuristic industrial noise. The EP is composed of the sinewy, hypnotic "Der Schrei" and three versions of "Von der Armut" ("from poverty"): one robotically cold, one that starts off in a dirge-like sequence before latching on to the melody halfway through and a "reverse edit" that makes the band sound like it's playing in a wind tunnel.

Incorporating more orchestral touches and spacious intros, the barrage continues on **Staub.** The band's evolution is especially apparent on the furtive "Gier" and the bleak title track, but not to worry: the clanging "Im Ich" and the reappearance of "Von der Armut" end any fears that Das Ich might be mellowing. Ackermann's vocals are as freaky-creepy as ever.

Feuer, a live album recorded around Germany in early '95, has amazing sound quality and overwhelmingly intense performances of numbers from every Das Ich release, including "Kain und Abel" (from **Die Propheten**) and "Von der Armut." "Jericho," a new ballad, is strongly reminiscent of the first album's fragile "Freuel." Incredibly powerful stuff. [ky]

DAUCUS KAROTA

See *Christian Death.*

DAVID J

See *Love and Rockets.*

THORNETTA DAVIS WITH THE BIG CHIEF BAND

See *Big Chief.*

DA WILLYS

See *Vacant Lot.*

DB'S

See *Chris Stamey.*

DEAD C

Live Dead C [tape] (NZ Xpressway) 1987 (Feel Good All Over) 1992
DR503 (NZ Flying Nun) 1987 (Feel Good all Over) 1992
The Sun Stabbed EP7 (NZ Xpressway) 1989
Trapdoor Fucking Exit [tape] (NZ Precious Metal) 1989 [CD] (Siltbreeze) 1992
DR503B [tape] (NZ Xpressway) 1989
Eusa Kills (NZ Flying Nun) 1989
Helen Said This (Siltbreeze) 1990
Harsh '70s Reality (Siltbreeze) 1992
Clyma Est Mort (Proletariat Idiots Production) 1993 (Siltbreeze) 1994
The Dead C vs. Sebadoh EP7 (Siltbreeze) 1993
The Operation of the Sun (Siltbreeze) 1993
World Peace Hope et al. (UK Shock) 1994
The White House (Siltbreeze) 1995

A HANDFUL OF DUST

Concord (Twisted Village) 1993
The Philosophick Mercury (NZ Corpus Hermeticum) 1994

GATE

Guitar (Majora) 1992
Metric (Majora) 1993
Lounge (Twisted Village) 1994
The Dew Line (Table of the Elements) 1994
Golden (NZ IMD) 1995
Live in Boston, NYC 1994 (Poon Village) 1995

WRECK SMALL SPEAKERS ON EXPENSIVE STEREOS

River Falling Love EP (NZ Flying Nun) 1987
A Child's Guide to . . . [tape] (NZ Xpressway) 1988
River Falling Love (Ajax) 1993

You could be forgiven for thinking of New Zealand as one of those pastoral spots where the sun always shines and the natives are given to the creation of cordial jangle-pop. Every stretch of terra firma has its less-illuminated stretches, however, and few Kiwis have probed their motherland's darker side more effectively than this prolific (yet shadowy) combo. Formed in 1987 by Bruce Russell (founder of the influential Xpressway label), avant-noise veteran Michael Morley and former Verlaines drummer Robbie Yeats, the Dead C has created an uncompromising (some might say undifferentiated) corpus of work that exists in the shadowlands between hell-spawned noise and fallen-angel beauty.

The trio's earliest work was issued in micro-mini editions on cassette only—an appropriate state, given the grit-encrusted lo-fi recordings. By the time **DR503** saw the light of day, there had been a moderate upgrade, but not so much as to frighten off unreconstructed Luddites: "Sun Stabbed" (which turns up in a longer version on the subsequent EP) is carried by a skittering, highly caffeinated rhythm, overlaid by harsh guitar scrapings, while "Angel" buries whatever structure might be present under brittle sheets of electronic discord. A brutal prologue. **Trapdoor Fucking Exit** launches in similarly severe fashion with the practice-space-quality "Heaven," a song that chisels Brit-folk vocals into a bottom-heavy vein of Ubu-esque skronk, while its evil adjunct "Hell Is Now Love" pushes Morley's "singing" to the fore, as Yeats summons a rhythmic paroxysm from what sounds like a single snare drum. The album's true killer, however, is the fisheyed "Bone," which laces a gymnastic fret run around a slo-mo incantation that makes sex dirty all over again.

Helen Said This allows the band to explore plenty of blind alleys, given that its two side-long songs can be timed with a sundial. Still, the dark, oscillating tumult that emanates from both the title track and "Bury (Refutatio Omnium Haeresium)" brings to mind the earliest, most experimental days of the Velvet Underground—back when a forty-five-minute "Sister Ray" was likely to be the most, er, "accessible" thing in earshot. (Siltbreeze later issued **Helen Said This** and **Trapdoor Fucking Exit,** originally a tape-only release on Morley's label, on a single CD under the latter's title.) **Eusa Kills,** which was recorded in 1988, is ever so slightly more digestible, at times redolent of the unfettered sonic discharge of the early Fall: an almost-unrecognizable cover of T. Rex's "Children of the Revolution" is the disc's most malevolent moment.

The double-LP **Harsh '70s Reality** is incontrovertibly the Dead C's masterwork, spanning eighty-odd minutes of purposefully mulched guitar harmonics and furtive tape manipulations. The apex, in terms of pure excess, is the abrasive, side-long "Driver U.F.O.," but there are moments of concord that verge on radiance: "Sea Is Violet" glides somberly across opalescent layers of manipulated sound, while the largely acoustic "Hope" could well be a newly discovered outtake from Neil Young's **Tonight's the Night.** A thorough document of the splendor of squalor. Wittily packaged in a faux-Fall graphic style, the no-fi live **Clyma Est Mort** (a bootleg given an official rerelease) provides an interesting though hardly indispensable companion piece, proving that the trio can be every bit as reckless and indistinct onstage as in the studio.

The trio dives headlong into improv on **The Operation of the Sun,** concentrating on gentle swells rather than overt rock surges and de-emphasizing the role of feedback. Songs like "Mordant Heaven" roll out a carpet of analog synth that Can's various members would be exceedingly comfortable walking across. The concurrently released **World Peace Hope et al.** compiles fourteen odds and ends, spanning five years' worth of particularly noisy moments: not surprisingly, the title isn't a desire for mankind, merely three of the record's song titles. (Completists should note the presence of four short, electrifying tracks originally released in conjunction with *Bananafish* magazine.) **The White House** reestablishes a link to terra firma with a handful of unusually organic mid-tempo songs (and that word is appropriate for a change) that sound like they could have been recorded at a Velvets jam session—on a day when Lou Reed called in sick. Utterly bewitching.

Russell uses the moniker A Handful of Dust to transmit his more academic treatises on sound in all its permutations, cleaving his ever-present array of jerry-rigged frequency-generating appliances with "real" instruments played by associates like Alastair Galbraith (who provides the sumptuous violin lines that vein "God's Love to His People Israel," the thirty-minute centerpiece of **The Philosophick Mercury**). Anyone with a fondness for modern classical music might want to mull these over.

Gate is Morley's solo project, its output often issued on singles that he presses in editions as small as twenty-five copies. On those, as well as a wide array of more fleshed-out albums, he sculpts feedback and oscillating tape noise into remarkable three-dimensional forms. **Live in Boston, NYC 1994** documents two recent East Coast improvised performances, one by Morley and Lee Ranaldo (a frequent Gate participant) and the other with Zeena Parkins joining them. A decade earlier (1980–85), Morley made a slightly more rock-embracing attempt to do the same with Wreck Small Speakers on Expensive Stereos, a duo well represented by Ajax's posthumous **River Falling Love** compilation. [dss]

See also *Mecca Normal, Verlaines.*

DEAD CAN DANCE

Dead Can Dance (UK 4AD) 1984 (4AD) 1994
Garden of the Arcane Delights EP (UK 4AD) 1984
Spleen and Ideal (UK 4AD) 1985 (4AD) 1994
Within the Realm of a Dying Sun (UK 4AD) 1987 (4AD) 1994
The Serpent's Egg (UK 4AD) 1988 (4AD) 1994
Aion (UK 4AD) 1990 (4AD) 1994
A Passage in Time (4AD/Rykodisc) 1991
Into the Labyrinth (4AD) 1993
Toward the Within (4AD) 1994
Spiritchaser (4AD) 1996

LISA GERRARD

The Mirror Pool (4AD) 1995

By 1991's release of **A Passage in Time,** a solemn, scintillating retrospective, the Anglo-Irish (but founded in Australia) duo Dead Can Dance's increasing awareness of European classicism and ancient musics (predominantly Celtic and Middle Eastern) had blossomed into archaic mastery, married to an intriguing lyrical bent for myth and symbolism. Aiming for a coherent mood rather than comprehensiveness, **A Passage in Time** ignores the Cocteau-inflected goth-rock drones of the band's first two records to concentrate on the medieval masterpiece **Aion** and **The Serpent's Egg,** with one selection from **Spleen and Ideal** ("Enigma of the Absolute") and two from **Within the Realm of a Dying Sun.** Additionally, the album includes the newly recorded "Bird" and "Spirit." Many of these masterfully arranged songs whirl headlong into the Renaissance, to a sonic realm where somber Gregorian chants ("The Song of the Sibyl," "Song of Sophia") and jaunty maypole dances ("Saltarello") have never left the hit parade. Subtle semi-orchestral keyboards, spiced with authentic folk instruments (hurdy-gurdy, flute, bagpipes) form the evocative backdrop for Lisa Gerrard's soaring vocals (the seminal, glossolalic "Cantara") and Brendan Perry's darker, silky intonations ("Severance").

Into the Labyrinth finds Dead Can Dance moving away from overwhelming medievalism, incorporating both more organic, non-Western sounds ("Yulunga," the ululating "Saldek") and relatively contemporary influences like historical Irish ballads ("The Wind that Shakes the Barley") and theatrical idioms ("The Carnival Is Over" and a sharp adaption of Bertolt Brecht's "How Fortunate the Man With None").

Toward the Within, recorded live (and filmed for a long-form video) with five added musicians in Santa Monica, California, at the end of the 1993 tour following **Into the Labyrinth,** does an excellent job of displaying not only the mystic richness and pan-ethnic musicianship of the duo's diverse concert presentation, but also a substantial amount of new material. Only four of the fifteen songs are from previous releases; **Toward the Within** is studded with such otherwise unheard treasures as "Tristan," "Desert Song" and "Rakim." The last of those begins with Gerrard's skeletal cascade of *yang ch'in* (Chinese dulcimer) scales, before Perry's heady Arabic exhortations ignite the lush, rhythmic piece. Gerrard's vocal cords are also tested, and achieve gorgeous heights on "Cantara," "Yulunga (Spirit Dance)" and the traditional "Persian Love Song." The backing quintet contributes chanting vocals, keyboards, *uillean* pipes, whistles, bouzouki and various exotic percussion. In particular, Perry's brother Robert shines on the show-stopping "Piece for Solo Flute." Three mainly acoustic Brendan Perry originals—"I Can See Now," "American Dreaming" and "Don't Fade Away"—flirt with pastoral folk, while his increasing Celtic enthusiasm is displayed in a moving rendition of Sinéad O'Connor's obsessive "I Am Stretched on Your Grave."

Residing at opposite ends of the earth (Perry on a river island in Ireland, Gerrard by Australia's Snowy River) and meeting only to unite their sonic visions, it's natural the pair would eventually put Dead Can Dance on a brief hiatus to pursue individual projects. Gerrard was first out of the gate with **The Mirror Pool,** which unsurprisingly devotes the lion's share of attention to her vocal theatrics, buttressed by the Victorian Philharmonic Orchestra and various guest players. "Violina (The Last Embrace)" and "La Bas (Song of the Drowned)" are ominously operatic—static and gorgeous—as are studio recordings of **Toward the Within**'s "Persian Love Song (The Silver Gun)" and "Sanvean (I Am Your Shadow)." The droning "Ajhon" and "The Rite" recall Native American chant, while many of the album's minor-key melodies are reminiscent of the haunting ballads of the thirteenth and fourteenth centuries. The wailing Middle Eastern sway prevalent on latter-day Dead Can Dance material rarely comes to the fore ("Swans" is an exception); without her more visceral partner's input, Gerrard's debut is almost too ethereal. Still, it's an enjoyable audio treatise on the pure beauty of the human voice, exemplified by a stunning rendition of Handel's "Largo." [gef]

See also *TPRG.*

DEAD HOT WORKSHOP

Dead Hot Workshop [tape] (Bong) 1991
White House (Bong) 1994
River Otis EP (Seed) 1994
1001 (Tag/Atlantic) 1995

Hailing from the same town as the Gin Blossoms—Tempe, Arizona—Dead Hot Workshop debuted with a self-released cassette LP, followed several years later by a low-budget album, this one on CD. The relatively subdued **White House** (its recording budget partly offset by a loan from Doug Hopkins of the Gin Blossoms) is full of decent, twangy tunes. Dedicated to Hopkins, the **River Otis** EP continues the quartet's rough-hewn but ballad-heavy (or light, depending on perspective) approach to country rock. Only on the final track, "257," does Dead Hot Workshop cut loose in true blue-collar style—half-ranch, half-raunch—setting the tone for the band's major-label debut.

A true rock'n'roll album at heart, **1001** uses country to give the music its edge rather than the other way around. Where many practitioners hold the genre sacred, Dead Hot Workshop kick country around like a new idea. Iowa native Brent Babb's vocals have a typically cracked drawl, but they go as far as the songs take them, and often it's out of the fields and into the city. Steve Larson's guitar playing is dynamic—equal parts twang and bang—and the rhythm section of G. Brian Scott and Curtis Grippe rolls along sturdily. Melodic gems like "Burger Christ" and "Jesus Revisited" may display a cynical side, but function on more than one level. No matter how introspective the song, the guitars burst hungrily outward, devouring any trace of ennui. [jo]

DEAD MILKMEN

Big Lizard in My Back Yard (Fever/Enigma) 1985
Eat Your Paisley! (Fever/Restless) 1986
Bucky Fellini (Fever/Enigma) 1987
Instant Club Hit (You'll Dance to Anything) EP (Fever/Enigma) 1987
Beelzebubba (Fever/Enigma) 1988
Smokin' Banana Peels EP (Fever/Restless) 1989
Metaphysical Graffiti (Enigma) 1990
Soul Rotation (Hollywood) 1992
Not Richard, but Dick (Hollywood) 1993
Chaos Rules: Live at the Trocadero (Restless) 1994
Stoney's Extra Stout (Pig) (Restless) 1995

There are few things staler than an old joke, and Philadelphia's Dead Milkmen were barely funny when they began a decade-long adventure into the realm of willful punk-rock stupidity. Fortunately, their intelligence grew with age; rather than sink deeper into the cesspool of sophomoric silliness, the quartet eventually developed a mature, thoughtful approach to their mission. So they called it a day.

Starting off with the reckless insults and put-downs on **Big Lizard in My Back Yard** (which contains the career-making "Bitchin' Camaro," a catchy cocktail-jazz/hardcore hybrid that tastelessly makes light of AIDS while poking fun at teenagers, the Doors and sports car owners), the group proceeded through the mildly satirical B-movie fantasies of **Eat Your Paisley!** and the relatively expansive **Bucky Fellini,** which coughed up the clever "Instant Club Hit (You'll Dance to Anything)," subsequently expanded into an EP.

The Milkmen's skimpy charms run very thin on **Beelzebubba,** an album with precisely three assets: a great title, amusing artwork and the catchy but dumb "Punk Rock Girl." **Metaphysical Graffiti** likewise manages some cute song titles ("If You Love Somebody, Set Them on Fire," "In Praise of Sha Na Na" and "I Tripped Over the Ottoman," an ode to Dick Van Dyke), but the tunes themselves are thoroughly lame. Nonetheless, the disco-versed "Smokin' Banana Peels" was remixed by Don and David Was (four separate ways!) as the centerpiece of an EP that contains five flimsy-to-awful (none more so than "The Puking Song") non-LP items.

Moving to a bigger label for a two-album sojourn, the Milkmen—artless singer Rodney Anonymous, drummer Dean Clean, bassist Dave Blood and guitarist Joe Jack Talcum, all of whom have used various pseudonyms (er . . .) over the years—found a suitable studio collaborator in producer Ted Nicely and made the first genuinely good album of their career, **Soul Rotation.** The gentleness of the band's adult humor is well-served by equally unprepossessing eclectic pop-rock that makes varied use of the Uptown Horns and Rodney's keyboard sideline. Between the furious punk goof of "The Conspiracy Song," the funky "How It's Gonna Be," the new wavey rock decimation of "Wonderfully Colored Plastic War Toys" and the ska beat of "Shaft in Greenland," the Milkmen finally locate a comfortable balance of provocative ideas and winning presentation.

The simplified **Not Richard, but Dick** favors down-the-hatch indie-rock, which suits the Milkmen fine but doesn't make for as entertaining an experience. The spoken "I Dream of Jesus" mounts a drastic cinematic fable in evident tribute to King Missile, but religion is dwarfed by psychiatry as the album's lyrical obsession. "Leggo My Ego," "Not Crazy" and "Nobody Falls Like" all shoot from the mind, while "The Woman Who Was Also a Mongoose" at least pays titular homage to Dr. Oliver Sacks. A little bit They Might Be Giants ("The Infant of Prague Customized My Van," the other theological essay here), a little bit Ween ("Let's Get the Baby High"), the album is inoffensive but underwhelming.

Evidently as a result of contractual obligations, songs from the two preceding albums were cut out of **Chaos Rules,** a slapdash greatest-hits concert record inconsistently documenting a pair of shows—two years apart—at Philadelphia's Trocadero club. Other than scattered topical references ("Laundromat Song" mentions John S. Hall, "Right Wing Pigeons" slags off Bill Clinton and the introduction to "Bitchin' Camaro" throws down the gauntlet to a local anti-abortion crusader), most of the renditions are surprisingly worse than the originals.

Their creative stamina waning, the Milkmen ended it all with **Stoney's Extra Stout (Pig),** a **Dick**-like but slack sleepwalk proudly (relievedly?) stickered as "Their Final Studio LP!" Recalling such cutting audience attacks as "You'll Dance to Anything," Rodney comes to life on "The Blues Song," a sharp cultural critique masquerading as a cloddish twelve-bar shuffle: "The blues isn't an art form, a type of music, it's a product . . . a way for white kids to feel that they understand the feelings of black people without ever actually having to meet any." He also revisits amelodic prose to amusing effect in the eavesdropping "Peter Bazooka" and the multiple-personality "Don't Deny Your Inner Child," but the other dozen songs are flat, lazy and instantly forgotten. Typical of the uninspired banality, the final track, "Big Deal," opens with "Life sucks then you die/And your soul gets sucked into the sky." Meanwhile, your records go to the cut-out bins. [i]

See also *TPRG.*

DEAD MOON

In the Graveyard (Tombstone) 1988
Unknown Passage (Tombstone) 1989
Defiance (Tombstone) 1990
Thirteen off My Hook (Ger. Music Maniac) 1990
Dead Moon Night (Tombstone) 1990
Live Evil (Ger. Music Maniac) 1991
Stranded in the Mystery Zone (Tombstone) 1991
Strange Pray Tell (Tombstone) 1992
Crack in the System (Tombstone) 1994
Nervous Sooner Changes (Tombstone) 1995

Fred Cole ended up in Portland, Oregon, in the late '60s with a band of Las Vegas teenagers who called themselves the Weeds and were running from either the draft, the law or both. In any event, they ran out of money, stumbled onto a manager, transformed into the Lollipop Shoppe and released an album on UA Records. Fred didn't like being on a major label, didn't enjoy being (literally) locked up in a rehearsal room and especially didn't like making his girlfriend, Toody, climb in through the window to see him.

Cole resurfaced in the punk-booming late '70s in the Rats (a trio with Toody and a series of drummers), releasing a series of LPs on his own Whizeagle label. He simultaneously operated Tombstone Music, an equipment store that later housed a label of the same name. When the Rats finally disbanded (one too many drummers left), Fred took up country music with the Western Front but decided the pull of rock'n'roll was too strong and formed Dead Moon. The band's lineup has been constant since its 1988 debut: Fred, Toody and Andrew Loomis on drums. (Several records include tracks with other drummers; those are leftover Rats songs.)

Dead Moon usually records in Cole's 8-track studio; though deaf in one ear, he also masters each disc (few titles are available on CD, most are mono only) on the same 1954 Presto-88 disc cutter that inscribed the Kingsmen's definitive "Louie, Louie." His songwriting spans punk and garage traditions, though the band's choice of covers, like "Hey Joe" and "The Times They

Are A-Changin'," underscores his '60s roots. Consistent throughout the oeuvre is a blunt, working-class pragmatism. The band has stubbornly declined to play in the US outside the Pacific Northwest, and consequently is better known in Europe, where Dead Moon tours regularly.

The considerable recorded output isn't exactly interchangeable, but it all sounds very much like Dead Moon; Fred's high, quavering vocals are remarkably expressive but an acquired taste. The fidelity is modest and the group's grasp of tuning nuances sporadic, but the songs bash and pop with the enthusiasm of a first-year driver on the figure-eight circuit (and so what if the car crashes). It sounds like vintage punk rock, or, when there are too many jugs of wine in the room, the Yardbirds stealing new songs.

The simplest starting point is **Live Evil,** on which Toody yells at her husband to tune up (impatient to get on with the task at hand, he doesn't), the band is in splendid shambles and most of its best songs are represented. **Strange Pray Tell** is Dead Moon's strongest, most frenzied release, and includes the stunning "Fire in the Western World." The recent **Nervous Sooner Changes** is a comparatively restrained song cycle (well, kind of) on the theme of infidelity. Fred and Toody have been married twenty-seven years and have three grandchildren. [ga]

DEAD PRESIDENTS

See *Dub Narcotic Sound System.*

DEAD VOICES ON AIR

Hafted Maul (Invisible) 1995
New Words Machine (Hypnotic/Chameleon) 1995
Shap (Invisible) 1996

SPASM

Spasm (Invisible) 1995

After relocating to Vancouver in 1993, England's Mark Spybey adopted the name Dead Voices on Air to continue the experimental audio sculpting he took part in as a member of Newcastle's prolific Zoviet France. That avant-garde group was famed for the extraordinary packaging of its releases. **Hafted Maul** is, alas, an entirely ordinary-looking CD, containing a series of edgy, dramatic urban soundscapes in which loops of found sound (voices, ambient noise, traffic, running water, static and so forth) are accompanied by bits of conscious music (percussion, harmonica, trumpet, string instruments). Pointless but not much more unpleasant than, say, rush hour in a big city, the short tracks—as well as two that break ranks to exceed ten minutes—slice and dice, rub a few processed elements together, let simmer for a while and then turn off the gas and move on to another recipe. The responsibility for discovering actual nourishment in all this abstract impressionism, however, is left to the listener. Thickly textured but equally pointless and frustrating, **Shap** is more of the same, using different sound sources in parallel constructions. **New Words Machine** credits cEVIN Key of Skinny Puppy as a collaborator.

Spasm is a one-off collaboration between Spybey, Martin Atkins (Pigface/Invisible Records), Eric Pounder of Lab Report and Curse Mackey of Evil Mothers. [i]

DE ARTSEN

See *Bettie Serveert.*

DEATH FOLK

See *Pat RuthenSmear.*

DECONSTRUCTION

Deconstruction (American) 1994

Few bands have been more obviously the sum of their parts than Jane's Addiction. After headlining the first Lollapalooza festival in 1991, the LA quartet split in half: the vocalist and drummer went one way (Porno for Pyros), the guitarist and bassist went another (Deconstruction); each suffered painfully from the absence of the other. While **Deconstruction** can claim a few decent songs and Dave Navarro's dazzling guitar work, the album is ruined by utterly toneless vocals—both Navarro and bassist Eric Avery are credited, but whoever is doing the singing makes former bandmate Perry Farrell sound like Pavarotti. The seventy-minute album doesn't work as a whole even instrumentally, although several tracks—especially "L.A. Song," "Fire in the Hole" and the instrumental "Iris"—do feature fine specimens of Navarro's jagged funk riffs and soaring celestial textures: close your eyes and you can imagine what Jane's Addiction's fourth album could have sounded like, or even what *this* album could have sounded like with even an average singer. All of which became moot when, shortly before **Deconstruction**'s release, Navarro announced his long-rumored jump to the Red Hot Chili Peppers. [ja]

See also *Porno for Pyros, Red Hot Chili Peppers.*

WILLIE DEE

See *Geto Boys.*

DEEE-LITE

World Clique (Elektra) 1990
Infinity Within (Elektra) 1992
Dewdrops in the Garden (Elektra) 1994

TOWA TEI

Future Listening! (Elektra) 1995

Downtown New York denizens Deee-Lite burst onto the club scene with, ironically, the B-side of their first single. "Groove Is in the Heart," a deliciously frilly, funky dance song, enchanted modern-day clubbers in every major American city. Thus propelled, the colorful trio—Russian émigré Super DJ Dmitry Brill, Japanese-born Towa Tei and the striking American Lady Miss Kier Kirby (who sports the nuttiest wardrobe this side of *Lost in Space*'s Mrs. Robinson)—tore both dancefloors and trendinistas' living rooms apart with **World Clique.** Getting assistance from rapper Q-Tip (A Tribe Called Quest) and bassist/guitarist Bootsy Collins, Deee-Lite produced a self-consciously kitschy mix of disco and soulful early techno. Though far less skilled or naturally gifted, Lady Miss Kier's vocals recall Diana Ross' post-Supremes range and style and disco singers like Vicki Sue Robinson. The band's inherent superficiality came cloaked in a layer of granola world consciousness, and most of the lyrics have something to do with universality and connection.

Deee-Lite's flakiness starts to show on **Infinity Within;** the band's self-conscious political correctness and the themes of universal grooviness are beginning to grate. Nothing on the second record lives up to the joyousness of the debut, but that doesn't stop the three from taking themselves more seriously: check the humorless public-service number, "I Had a Dream I Was Falling Through a Hole in the Ozone Layer," for corroboration. Although the record boasts as many guests as the debut, none contributes as essentially to the effort; it's obvious that no one, and that includes the band, is having as much fun.

Towa Tei then took a sabbatical, leaving Kier and Dmitry to produce **Dewdrops in the Garden,** a totally flimsy record that takes disco-techno to an embarrassingly skimpy low. None of the band's initial excitement is audible; that sound you hear is the pair clutching at the latest straw. The silver lining to this cloud is Towa Tei's solo record. Exploring those areas overshadowed by the glitz and glitter of Deee-Lite's other two members, **Future Listening!** reveals just who's got the musical talent in the family. Displaying a plethora of influences, **Future Listening!** sample-checks Brazilian bossa nova ("Technova" and "Batucada," in particular), jazz, electronic dance and all sorts of odd sounds. Although Towa Tei's style of creation relies too heavily on repetition, he doesn't lack for imaginative samples and ideas, and is willing to load many styles into the same song. His guests include Ryuichi Sakamoto, Haruomi Hosono and Natasha Diggs. [mf]

DEEP BLUE SOMETHING

Home (Rainmaker) 1994 (Rainmaker/Interscope) 1995

Houston-bred brothers Toby (guitar/vocals) and Todd (bass/vocals) Pipes lead this Texas quartet, which made a commercial splash in late '95 with the catchy romantic power-pap of "Breakfast at Tiffany's." Bringing the brain-dead grandiosity of late-'70s harmony-rockers like Styx and Supertramp to the modern world, Deep Blue Something (formed in '91 at the University of North Texas as Leper Messiah) combines big acoustic/electric strumming and airy, melodramatic singing into a resoundingly hollow album unimproved by its good intentions. (The faintly feminist "Over" sarcastically castigates a drunk's sexual desire, but includes the sure-to-be-misappropriated refrain, "Flip her over, man she is done.") "Souls suffer the landscape / In shrouds of dew, as ghosts." All right, Denton! [i]

CARMAIG DE FOREST

I Shall Be Released (Good Foot) 1987

CARMAIG DE FOREST + BAND

6 Live Cuts EP (Fr. New Rose) 1988

CARMAIG DE FOREST'S DEATH GROOVE LOVE PARTY

Carmaig de Forest's Death Groove Love Party (Factory Outlet) 1993

Fans of Carmaig de Forest's wild ukulele rock (well documented on the 1987 album, produced with creative ferocity by Alex Chilton, and the subsequent in-concert mini-album) may be frustrated that the San Francisco singer/songwriter leaves his little four-stringer home for all but one of the songs on **Death Groove Love Party,** a rollicking collection recorded under various circumstances with an assortment of pals (including such visiting dignitaries as Gordon Gano, Will Rigby and Jim Sclavunos joining a local corps) between 1988 and 1993. No matter. De Forest's guitar playing is passable, and his electric folk/rock songs—funny, sardonic, rude, ribald—are unimpeded by the small instrumental disappointment. Singing in a wavery Lou Reed–like voice, he covers Bob Dylan's "Million Dollar Bash" and makes a federal case out of fashion crimes in "The Ponytail Song" (while wallowing in his own sartorial hypocrisy). He wonders "Why can't your husband be a flaming asshole . . . then I could steal you away from him" (in the covetous "So Happy Together") and faces a series of daily disasters with a shrug in "I Can't Get Used to It." Life as it should be. [i]

See also *TPRG.*

DEL AMITRI

Del Amitri (Chrysalis) 1985
Waking Hours (UK A&M) 1989 (A&M) 1990
Change Everything (A&M) 1992
Twisted (A&M) 1995

Maybe it's just because they come from Glasgow, released their 1983 45 debut on an indie label and have an uncommon name that del Amitri has always been expected to be something more commendable than inconsistent mainstream popsters. The first album, nicely produced by Hugh Jones, introduces a harmlessly enthusiastic folk-country-rock group, politely bubbling with appealing tunes and not a lot on their minds. Bassist Justin Currie's accent is the only sign of unpolished reality in this smooth effort to please.

With a different second guitarist (Michael Slaven) in the lineup and a new producer (Mark Freegard) behind the board, **Waking Hours** has a stronger rock presence but not much more personality than the debut. A few of the songs (notably "When I Want You" and "Kiss This Thing Goodbye") have solid content and catchy choruses, but a disconcerting resemblance to the stolid ordinariness of Dire Straits (minus the stellar fretwork) leaves the album a faint pleasure.

The first del Amitri record to stake a personality claim, **Change Everything** is an unhappy collection of infidelity and breakup songs set to a rocking pop-soul blend sparkling with bits of '70s raunch and country. Featuring an overhauled five-piece lineup (only Currie and founding guitarist Iain Harvie remain from the previous record's quartet) and produced by Gil Norton, the songs point fingers all over the place, including inward ("Be My Downfall," "Just Like a Man"); the burned band backs up all the shame and anger with surging musical conviction. When Currie reaches for a shimmery falsetto to punctuate the line "I wanna die" in "Just Like a Man," he truly sounds like a man on an emotional ledge. Just to spread the misery around, the acoustic "The First Rule of Love" and the Stonesy "the Ones That You Love Lead You Nowhere" bemoan romance in general.

Snorting out of **Twisted**'s gate like a hopping mad the The, del Amitri adds honking guest harmonica and charging slide-guitar power to Currie's quixotically angry distorted-vocal refusal to become "Food for Songs" and follows it with the similarly arranged "Start With Me," upping the self-interest by praising a desire to save the world and then asking, "Is it such a hateful crime to start with me?" The album's abrupt third-song shift into wimpy semi-acoustic balladry

("Here & Now") dilutes its mighty opening, and the remainder—with few exceptions ("Being Somebody Else") a bland plate of restrained pop mush that could be Steve Miller or Air Supply for all it matters—washes the memory away. [i]

See also *Lloyd Cole and the Commotions.*

DE LA SOUL

3 Feet High and Rising (Tommy Boy) 1989
De La Soul Is Dead (Tommy Boy) 1991
Buhloone Mind State (Tommy Boy) 1993
Stakes Is High (Tommy Boy) 1996

Against a background of the ascendant school of aggressive, violent West Coast rap, the loopy, hippiesque debut by Long Island natives (and members, along with A Tribe Called Quest and the Jungle Brothers, of the Native Tongues alternative hip-hop family) De La Soul sounded like it came from another planet. Moving across musical boundaries with breathtaking ease, **3 Feet High and Rising**—a stunningly fresh and original debut in 1989—really did feel like the dawning of a new age. The D.A.I.S.Y. Age, to be exact.

DA Inner Sound, Y'all was announced by the album's dayglo graphics, spacy, laid-back attitudes and pychedelic grooves. In contrast with other rap records in which samples of old R&B and funk jams were merely used to accentuate beats, Posdnous (Kelvyn Mercer), Trugoy the Dove (David Jolicoeur), P.A. Pasemaster Mase (Vincent Mason) and producer Prince Paul (of Stetsasonic and, later, Gravediggaz) used a wider palette, creating musical canvases where a French language instruction record, Otis Redding, Steely Dan, P-Funk and the Turtles (who, in a case that would have been a legal landmark had it not settled out of court, sued over the use of "You Showed Me" on "Transmitting Live From Mars") could intermingle and blend into highly textured soundscapes. Their groove (anyone who doubts the group's ability to lay down a compelling groove via such oblique strategies need only hear the hit "Me Myself and I") was leavened by an un-self-consciously goofy, surreal sense of humor, not unlike George Clinton's.

On **De La Soul Is Dead,** as on the Beastie Boys' **Paul's Boutique,** the band's ambition outstrips its ideas. The feeble, forced skits that dot the album fall flat, and many of the songs can be heard as a reaction to criticism that De La Soul was soft. Unlike "Do As De La Does" (from **3 Feet High and Rising**), where the group puts itself in a leadership position, songs like "Afro Connections at a Hi 5 (In the Eyes of the Hoodlum)" and "Millie Pulled a Pistol on Santa" hew closer to rap convention, with harder-edged lyrics and sound. The album's not bad, but it lacks some of the qualities that made the debut unique.

Superficially, **Buhloone Mind State** is a return to form. While it does resemble the first album, there's a pro forma air to the proceedings that even guests like Fred Wesley and Maceo Parker can't allay; the sound is in the house, but the trio's once-profound inspiration has fled. [sm]

See also *Gravediggaz; TPRG.*

DELILAHS

Delilahs (October) 1994
Dying to Build a Bridge (October) 1995

The Delilahs' two albums offer earnest folk-pop with occasional snapshots of R.E.M.'s infancy. At times reminiscent of a much milder Bob Mould, vocalist Aaron Seymour guides the Minneapolis quintet through cathartic music that flips from happy to sad with less notice than a car wreck. On the band's self-titled debut, "Beats the Hell Out of Me" lets the harmonies do the hooking; "Who's Gonna Stop Me" has a rich sadness evocative of vintage Beau Brummels.

Better production (again by John Munson and John Strawberry Fields) gives **Dying to Build a Bridge** a listener-friendly sheen while presenting a more solemn, message-based set of songs, including "Man on a Mission," "Feels Like a Job" and "Wasting My Time." Even when the band threatens to get too serious, there are harmony vocals to cool things off. [jo]

IRIS DEMENT

Infamous Angel (Philo) 1992 (Warner Bros.) 1993
My Life (Warner Bros.) 1994
The Way I Should (Warner Bros.) 1996

You could scan the contemporary music horizon for a week and still not hear anything quite like Iris DeMent's voice, a full-bodied soprano that bursts with yearning and knowing, while suggesting Loretta Lynn's no-nonsense conviction and Mother Maybelle Carter's purity. DeMent's albums have a pre-rock feel, built on drummer-less string-band arrangements, but her songs avoid the drinkin' and romancin' clichés of hackneyed country to ruminate on God, death and the transforming power of music itself.

Riding a plaintive, gospel-tinged melody in "Let the Mystery Be," the first song on **Infamous Angel,** DeMent brings an agnostic's skepticism to her Pentecostal upbringing in rural Arkansas. In "Our Town," she assumes the perspective of a much older woman forced to move on because of economic hard times. Even the potentially maudlin sentiments of "After You're Gone," about her late father, are transformed by the understated, yet heartfelt, delivery.

If **Infamous Angel** seemed a bit callow as it ached for lost innocence, **My Life** is a mature statement tinged with fatalism. Virtually identical to the debut in its folk-country melodicism, the album boasts a more consistent set of songs in which DeMent's soaring voice turns plain-spoken verse into poetic revelation. "No Time to Cry" returns to the subject of her father's death and examines how her grief has been put on hold by life's relentless passage. Singing lines like "My life, it's only a season/A passing September that no one will recall" (from the title track), she exudes a resigned self-knowledge (as opposed to self-pity) that is almost comforting. In celebrating faith, love, rural simplicity and singing along to the country radio, DeMent seems almost too innocent and simple for an ironic and edgy era, but the astonishing sincerity of her delivery and the pristine beauty of her voice bear a timeless and universal truth. [gk]

GITANE DEMONE

See *Christian Death.*

DENIM

Back in Denim (UK Boys Own) 1992
Denim on Ice (UK Echo) 1996

Ending a low-key decade of Felt that produced a large catalogue of atmospheric pop in stylistic tribute to Tom Verlaine, Lou Reed and Bob Dylan, Lawrence—the prolific but retiring Birmingham singer/guitarist whose unused surname is Hayward—chose a different fabric for his next endeavor. Gathering up a bunch of studio players, he took a splashy dip into ironic glam-rock revisionism with the wry and enormously entertaining Denim. More involved and philosophically purposeful than the similarly motivated Pooh Sticks, Denim fields an uncomplicated rhythm-guitar crunch, dippy synthesizer sounds and the giddy, kidney-punch production style that typified 1973–75 British chart pop (the memory banks of Gary Glitter, Hot Chocolate, Mott the Hoople, Mud, Sparks and Paper Lace heat up here) to present Lawrence's idiosyncratic cultural perspective, which identifies music—but not just any old music—as the essence of young life.

Back in Denim's dreamy eight-minute centerpiece, "The Osmonds," vividly evokes the British '70s with a stream of cringeable references including Chicory Tip, the I.R.A., crushed velvet flares, Lieutenant Pigeon, left-over hippies, "Gilbert O" (Sullivan) and Bell Records, topping off the tour de farce with a passing quotation from David Essex's "Rock On." Having identified an era he at least claims to like, Lawrence then sets about carefully rejecting everything else. The CD-ending "I'm Against the Eighties" announces, "I'm sick of winklepicker kids Mary Chain debris . . . singers with nothing to say . . . Duran Duran fake make-up boys." In "Middle of the Road," a rewrite of Jonathan Richman's "Roadrunner," he goes further, offering a centrist's opposition to everything indulgent, historical or gritty in pop's past. He rails at Chuck Berry, the Stones, Phil Spector, early Dylan, guitar licks, soul and spliffs with snobby vitriol. If the music weren't so delicious—Lawrence has his finger right on the twitching pulse of this cadaver—such arrogance might be irritating, but Denim is so well-made and sublimely thought through that even indefensible perversity suits it fine.

Lawrence then spent some time in New York City, thawing out the band in 1996 with **Denim on Ice.** None the worse for wear, Denim fixes sharply on a new set of targets—"The Great Pub Rock Revival," punk history ("Jane Suck Died in 77"), city planners ("Council Houses")—offering surprisingly rough and blunt views of sex and abortion ("Brumburger," "Grandad's False Teeth") and debauchery ("Glue and Smack"). The musical span is likewise broader: Denim affects a jaunty Gilbert O'Sullivan bop in "Mrs. Mills," goes all drippy for the maudlin "Synthesizers in the Rain" and apes Devo in "Shut Up Sidney," a comical spew against techno-pop and other chart abominations. "Best Song in the World" draws uncomfortably near Poohville, but Lawrence's distinctively inquisitive voice and the project's exquisite musicianship keeps Denim firmly sewn to its own odd domain. [i]

DENISON/KIMBALL TRIO

See *Jesus Lizard.*

DENTISTS

Some People Are on the Pitch: They Think It's Over but It's Not (UK Spruck) 1985
You and Your Bloody Oranges EP (UK Spruck) 1985
Down and Out in Paris and Chatham EP (UK Spruck) 1986
Writhing on the Shagpile EP (UK Tambourine) 1987
Beer Bottle and Banister Symphonies (Bel. Antler) 1987
The Fun Has Arrived EP (UK Spruck) 1988
Heads and How to Read Them (Bel. Integrity) 1991
Naked EP10 (Independent Project) 1991
Dressed (Homestead) 1992
Powdered Lobster Fiasco (Homestead) 1993
Behind the Door I Keep the Universe (EastWest) 1994
Deep 6 (EastWest) 1995

This smart and friendly English foursome (from Medway, in Kent) embodies the best aspects of the Anglo-jangle-pop genre, while maintaining a jittery—sometimes downright loud—rock edge that keeps their playful tunes from straying too far into the land of the twee. After a series of low-key UK and European releases in the second half of the '80s, the Dentists belatedly entered the US market with the six-song **Naked** and the twenty-two-song CD **Dressed.** The latter collects most of **Some People Are on the Pitch** and **Beer Bottle and Banister Symphonies,** albums that themselves were assembled from early singles and EPs. As such, it's a treasure trove of impish wordplay and wall-to-wall hooks, with tunes like "Strawberries Are Growing in My Garden (and It's Wintertime)," "She Dazzled Me With Basil," "I Had an Excellent Dream" and "Just like Oliver Reed" sounding every bit as sharp as their titles. The ten-track **Powdered Lobster Fiasco** is just as tuneful and energetic, with increased lyrical depth that enhances the resonance of tunes like "Charms and the Girl," "Outside Your Inside" and "I Can See Your House From Up Here" (all of which, along with three others on the LP, had previously been issued on a set of three coordinated 7-inch singles by different Amerindie labels).

Behind the Door I Keep the Universe (also released in the US as a limited-edition set of three 7-inch EPs) is the Dentists' most infectious album, as well as its most mature. The band's melodic strengths meld nicely with its increasingly grown-up lyrical perspective. As such, it's a delight from start to finish, with hyperactive pop tunes ("Space Man," "Faces on Stone") and more introspective fare ("Sorry Is Not Enough," "A Smile Like Oil on Water").

The production credit of New York noise-rock specialist Wharton Tiers is a tipoff of the misguided sonic makeover the band attempts on **Deep 6.** The attempt to toughen up the approach only succeeds in making the Dentists sound more like everybody else, but the album still has its moments, including "Shining Like a Star," "Kick Start My Body" and "My Heart Is Like a Town You Moved Away From." Not surprisingly, the souped-up production didn't help the band expand its audience. Soon after, they were dropped by EastWest, guitarist Bob Collins left and the remaining members (singer/guitarist Mick Murphy, drummer Rob Grigg and bassist Mark Matthews) regrouped as the Shot Marilyns, which quickly became Coax. [ss]

DENZIL

Pub (Play/Giant) 1994

Those wrinkles in the brow of Bournemouth singer/songwriter Denzil Thomas seem to have been well earned. A welcome entrant in the English furrow between early Elvis Costello and late Richard Thompson, he's "Too Scared to Be True" on his debut album, wonders "Who Made You So Cynical About Me?," feels the presence of a girl's dad with them in the back of a car and envisions his baby daughter making out with "some great baboon" named Duane and ultimately "Running This Family." Actually, the slippery sands of domestic bliss provide Denzil's worst fears: most of the songs on this winning semi-electric exposition, which describes mundanity with the wry, intimate detail of a Nick Hornby or Roddy Doyle novel, concern family life, especially as it ushers along confessional reflections regarding dad's own befuddled youth. Other topics emerge in the margins: "Cutie" sardonically castigates tabloid readers for their blind prejudices, while "Shame" wags an easy finger at thoughtless evil-doers. Singing memorable tunes in a clear, slightly weedy tenor, tastefully backed by an electric trio, Denzil strikes a level balance between the ups and downs of life, making this public house an inviting semi-private home. [i]

DEPECHE MODE

Speak & Spell (UK Mute) 1981 (Mute/Sire) 1982
A Broken Frame (Mute/Sire) 1982
Construction Time Again (Mute/Sire) 1983
People Are People (Mute/Sire) 1984
Some Great Reward (Mute/Sire) 1984
The Singles '81–'85 (UK Mute) 1985
Catching Up With Depeche Mode (Mute/Sire) 1985
Black Celebration (Mute/Sire) 1986
Music for the Masses (Mute/Sire) 1987
101 (Mute/Sire) 1989
Violator (Mute/Sire/Reprise) 1990
Songs of Faith and Devotion (Mute/Sire/Reprise) 1993
Songs of Faith and Devotion Live (Mute/Sire/Reprise) 1993

RECOIL

Hydrology and 1 + 2 (Mute/Enigma) 1989
Bloodline (Mute/Sire/Reprise) 1992

VARIOUS ARTISTS

Trans-Mode Express (Cleopatra) 1996

Perhaps it was the mirror held up to Depeche Mode by **101,** a concert album and theatrical documentary by D. A. Pennebaker, that caused the gloomy synthesists to unravel. The stability and unanimity of purpose gained early on when Alan Wilder joined (replacing Vince Clarke, who wrote most of the songs on the first album and then left at the end of '81) undoubtedly helped the English quartet from Basildon become wall-poster stars of countless depressed teenagers. They provided solace, if not guidance, in the dense, ominous atmospheres of singles like "Blasphemous Rumours," "Master and Servant," "Never Let Me Down Again" and "Shake the Disease." In the '90s, however, fame and fortune did not provide enough of a panacea for the psychic ache that has manifested itself in the group's personal troubles.

Effectively combining pop catchiness and a cheerless industrial tone to make distinctive music (and disguise singer David Gahan's mannered incompetence), Depeche Mode mastered their sound quickly, but needed some time for Martin Gore's songwriting—bizarre adventures in the skin trade or bleak philosophical conceits—to reach its stride. Finally, on **Some Great Reward,** Depeche Mode got the balance right, feeding quintessential material ("Blasphemous Rumours," "Master and Servant," "People Are People") into a finely tuned assembly line. Seamlessly blending unsettling concrète sounds—factory din, clanking chains and so forth—into the music, the group achieved a masterful music/life mix few of the same mind had approached.

But Gore was evidently not equipped to keep it up indefinitely, and Depeche Mode subsequently allowed moodiness to get the better of his music. A casebook of doubt, disgust and depression, **Black Celebration** has a certain grim power, but not a lot of appeal. The unambitious **Music for the Masses,** though marginally brighter in temperament, finds the band running out of ideas, displaying little beyond Gore's emotional anxieties and Gahan's vocal limitations. Then came **101,** a lengthy live album recorded at a June 1988 stadium show in Pasadena, which served to certify Depeche Mode's mass popularity and provide permanent evidence of the band's—a pitch-impaired singer crucified on racks of keyboards—concert inadequacy. (It might have at least included a church incense scratch-and-sniff.)

The dismal **Violator** (which nonetheless produced more US hit singles—three—than any other DM LP) matches **Music for the Masses** for shallow blandness. A lack of external input locks the insular group in a closed creative circle that shows no signs of opening or expanding. Gore's dearth of meaningful ideas and the introduction of guitars (most notably on the rock-'n'rolly "Personal Jesus") dominates this handsomely performed, tuneless waste. Only the lyrics of the album-ending "Clean" indicate any break in the clouds: "Now that I'm clean . . . I've broken my fall . . . changed my routine."

Routines may be altered, but **Songs of Faith and Devotion** (followed, nine months later—just in time for Christmas shopping—by a track-for-track live version, recorded on tour in Europe and New Orleans with two female backup singers adding much-needed texture and melodic accuracy) is marginally stronger if lyrically grimmer than **Violator.** The album, which needs a warning sticker for underage moralists in the audience, could better be titled **Songs of Sex and Arrogance.** By the second number, "Walking in My Shoes," Gore (via Gahan) is back to moaning about his misbegotten past, wallowing in self-righteous (or at least self-induced) misery: "I would tell you about the things they put me through / The pain I've been subjected to / But the Lord himself would blush." Oh, come on—try him. Gore's dream of remorseless redemption (the '90s zipless fuck?) runs through the record: In "Condemnation" he avers, "I'm not looking for absolution . . . I'll show no repentance / I'll suffer with pride." In "Get Right With Me," he instructs, "Don't waste your energy making apologies." Only "One Caress" actually admits a request for anonymous exculpation: "And I pray to the only one / Who has the strength / To bear the pain / To forgive all the things that I've done." As usual, the central DM industro-pop sound on this understated album is set off by a few stray stylistic elements—ballads (after a fashion) and soul/gospel (after a fashion).

Evidently, the gloom in Depeche Mode's music had some basis in the quartet's reality, although Gore seems able to safely sublimate his demons into hits. Citing "increasing dissatisfaction with the internal relations and working practices of the group," Alan Wilder quit in May '95. A few months later, Dave Gahan was hospitalized in LA after slitting his wrist, reportedly amidst drug and marital problems.

Long before he bailed out of the band, Wilder began exploring extracurricular opportunities under the name Recoil. He unveiled the side project in 1986 with **1 + 2,** a British 12-inch that he later expanded and reissued as the longwinded **Hydrology and 1 + 2.** Accented with ephemeral electronic and vocal noises, the monotonous instrumentals drone aimlessly in several idioms: loud synthesizers, soft synthesizers, pinging synthesizers, chanted vocals and piano. The first track recalls **Tubular Bells,** and that's the record's most provocative feature.

Returning to the enterprise in '92, Wilder made the seven-track **Bloodline,** using such guest vocalists as would-be rapper Moby, Diamanda Galás, Toni Halliday of Curve and a sample of the late bluesman Bukka White. Only sporadically song-like (the title track, sung by Halliday, is an ominous storm cloud of distortion that resolves into a sunny day), the collection favors engrossing ambient exercises with dialogue loops, clattering, atmospheric electronic music and firm clock beats that don't lead anywhere. **Bloodline** hardly sounds like the future for an international pop star, but it does fill the background with enough intriguing sounds to be a keeper.

Trans-Mode Express is a tribute album in which a subdirectory of techno bands covers DM songs. [i]

See also *Erasure; TPRG.*

DES'REE

Mind Adventures (Epic) 1992
I Ain't Movin' (550 Music/Epic) 1994

If every era deserves its very own Melanie—a good-hearted, pure-voiced idealist bringing messages of positive inspiration to a world in deep denial—ours belongs to Des'ree (Weekes). This London-born daughter of Barbados addresses such challenges to modern individualism as competition, despair, weakness, mundanity, cynicism and intimidation. But rather than offer Aquarian Age populism, Des'ree sells I'm-OK-you're-OK solipsism. Essentially, she's a spiritual motivational speaker, delivering her messages in a smoky, handsomely modulated alto amid shimmering adult funk-pop that owes equal debts to Carole King, Sting, Lionel Richie, Joni Mitchell and Kenny G.

Overseen by multi-instrumentalists/producers Phil Legg and Ashley Ingram, **Mind Adventures** is a good start but not quite a good album. Too intent on demonstrating her vocal prowess and dancing around her essential themes, Des'ree strains and stretches—waxing jazzy, bluesy, folky and more—with the overexertion of a nervous novice. She touches on her true ethos with "Stand My Own Ground" and "Competitive World," but spends most of the album pledging her devotion to mother, lover and Lord. The music flits around from tasteful dance grooves to swoony piano ballads; very little of it suits her ethereal presence.

I Ain't Movin' gets the balance right and goes far enough out on a lyrical limb to allow the young optimist to stake out a distinctive place for herself. The self-assuring mantra of "You Gotta Be" became her breakthrough hit, but "Strong Enough," "Crazy Maze" and the title track strike similar philosophical notes; the album is singleminded in its commitment to making a better world via personal bestness. A fine singer who provides herself with alluring, uplifting melodies (given added appeal by sensitive arrangements), Des'ree is, unfortunately, no deep thinker, and her self-help exhortations to "Go ahead release your fears" and "Learn to love yourself/It's a great, great feeling" are naïve and numbing, aphorisms that don't make sweet music. In "Herald the Day," when she offers "Something's gonna happen/It's written in the air/Something's gonna happen/Revolution is everywhere," it becomes evident how trivial these talented musician's opinions really are. [i]

EDDY DETROIT

See *Sun City Girls.*

DEVIANTS

See *Mick Farren.*

DEVIL DOGS

Devil Dogs (Crypt) 1989
Big Beef Bonanza! (Crypt) 1990
The Devil Dogs Live in Tokyo EP7 (Japan. 1+2) 1991
We Three Kings (Crypt) 1992
30 Sizzling Slabs (Crypt) 1992
Saturday Night Fever (Crypt) 1993 (Sympathy for the Record Industry) 1993
Stereodrive! (Japan. 1+2) 1994
Laid Back Motherfuckers EP7 (Headache) 1994

DEVIL DOGS & RAUNCH HANDS

Sink or Swim (Fin. GaGa Goodies) 1990

VIKINGS

Go Berserk! (Japan. 1+2) 1995

New York punk-rock has always been about playing bars on the Bowery where the beer and urinals have a lot in common. The path the Devil Dogs chose followed the hefty footprints of the Dictators and the Ramones. Like those forefathers, the group looked to '50s rock'n'roll to bring back the spark that once made it great.

The basic tracks for the first Devil Dogs album were produced by Billy Childish for release under the name Rat Bastards, but that band split up before the album's completion, sending singer/guitarist Pete Ciccone off to form the Vacant Lot. Renamed the Devil Dogs, bassist/singer Steve Baise, guitarist/singer Andy Gortler and drummer Paul Corio finished up the sixteen songs with production help from Mike Mariconda of the Raunch Hands. Split evenly (if undiscernibly) between originals and covers, the album boasts songs by several generations of greats: DMZ, Dictators, Beach Boys, Ramones and Bob B. Soxx and the Bluejeans. Drawing from the Billy Childish songbook, the band announced its disinclination toward political correctness with "Pussywhipped," "Hosebag" and "Suck the Dog."

After the album's release, Corio left to rejoin Ciccone in the Vacant Lot; he was replaced by Dave Ari (ex–Headless Horsemen). Although **Big Beef Bonanza!** runs only four songs a vinyl side, the group is still able to offend with complaints about Long Island women ("North Shore Bitch") and odes to the joys of drink and drugs ("Stay Out All Night"). Like its predecessor, the record contains some pointed covers: the Shadows of Knight's "I'm Gonna Make You Mine" and Freddy Cannon's "Palisades Park."

By 1990, the Devil Dogs had international stature in the punk underground and toured Europe. In Finland, eight tracks were culled from their first two albums to fill one side of **Sink or Swim,** the other half being given over to the Raunch Hands. That group's Mariconda subsequently joined his pals for a Japanese tour, from which they brought home a 7-inch memento, **The Devil Dogs Live in Tokyo.**

The trio's revolving drum stool took another turn with the arrival of Joe Vincent for the recording of **We Three Kings,** a raw, punchy album composed (with one exception) of hot-blooded garage-punk originals like "Strip Search," "Rock City, U.S.A." and "Whip It Out." With only three songs AWOL, **30 Sizzling Slabs** collates the first three albums.

Along with tighter songwriting, **Saturday Night Fever** is noteworthy as the Devil Dogs' first studio work outside New York. The trio traveled to Seattle, where producer Kurt Bloch (of the Fastbacks) organized the sonic crunch previously missing. The band's renewed energy throws each song into overdrive, with scorching guitar solos on "Back in the City" and a lost punk gem, "Dance With You Baby," originally done by the Victims. Don't miss the tasteful rendition of Gene Pitney's "Backstage" or the near-perfect original "Sweet Like Wine." (Crypt issued the album on vinyl and CD overseas; Sympathy's domestic CD includes four bonus tracks retrieved from singles.)

Japan's 1+2 Records added four tracks to the quartet of songs that appear on the **Laid Back Motherfuckers** EP for **Stereodrive!,** but the thrill was almost gone from the Devil Dogs, who broke up at the end of '94. Baise, who had married a member of Norway's Blind Bats, joined forces with members of three Scandinavian groups and recorded an album as the Vikings. The power-popping **Go Berserk!** puts the enthusiasm back in his singing and playing, replacing a Devil Dogs snarl with harmonies that would make the Who proud. As usual, the covers say it all: among the twenty selections are the Boys' "First Time," Bobby Fuller's "Let Her Dance," the Bay City Rollers' "Let's Go" and Cheap Trick's "Surrender." [mk]

See also *Vacant Lot.*

DEVILHEAD

Your Ice Cream's Dirty (Loosegroove) 1994
Pest Control (Loosegroove) 1996

Since the music on **Your Ice Cream's Dirty**—a witless meander through the backyards of various Seattlooza sounds ('70s Britrock, puerile comedy, a slack version of Rollins Band kick-out-the-thrashjams, stoner country, stoner jazz)—doesn't offer an adequate explanation for this underachiever's major-label-affiliated existence, a little background is in order. In the mid-'80s, Devilhead guitarist Kevin Wood was in the lame Malfunkshun with his younger brother Andrew, who went on to front Mother Love Bone and then OD in 1990, leaving two bandmates—one of whom co-owns Loosegroove with another Malfunkshun alumnus—to form Pearl Jam. Devilhead, which has no fixed lineup but calls Bainbridge Island in Puget Sound home, includes a third Wood, singer/guitarist Brian. Collectors of Seattle ephemera may be compelled, but nothing about **Your Ice Cream's Dirty** otherwise merits a second glance. [i]

See also *Mother Love Bone.*

WILLY DEVILLE

Miracle (A&M) 1987
Victory Mixture (Orleans) 1990
Backstreets of Desire (Forward) 1994
Big Easy Fantasy (Fr. New Rose) 1995

MINK DEVILLE

Mink DeVille (Capitol) 1977 (Era) 1993
Return to Magenta (Capitol) 1978 (Era) 1993
Le Chat Bleu (Capitol) 1980 (Era) 1993
Coup de Grâce (Atlantic) 1981
Savoir Faire (Capitol) 1981
Where Angels Fear to Tread (Atlantic) 1983
Sportin' Life (Atlantic) 1985

At a time when most of his scene mates were stripping rock'n'roll back down to its rawest basics, Willy DeVille was an anomaly on the original New York punk scene. As the suave, streetwise leader of Mink DeVille, he crafted a smoothly passionate, openly romantic style rooted in vintage R&B and soul. DeVille's vision sprang to vibrant life on his band's eponymous debut album, but subsequent efforts like **Return to Magenta, Le Chat Bleu** and **Coup de Grâce** are thin and uninspired. By the time DeVille hit his stride again, with **Where Angels Fear to Tread** and **Sportin' Life,** few—at least in his own country—seemed to notice. (**Savoir Faire** compiles tracks from the three Capitol albums.)

Mink DeVille had ceased to be an actual group long before Willy stopped using the "Mink" moniker on 1987's bland and gimmicky Mark Knopfler-produced **Miracle,** which includes the unaccountably Oscar-nominated "Storybook Love" (from the film *The Princess Bride*). The rootsy covers collection **Victory Mixture** provides a welcome antidote to **Miracle**'s misguided modernity, making the most of the singer's relocation to New Orleans with backup from such local legends as Allen Toussaint, Eddie Bo and Dr. John. By contrast, the mostly self-penned **Backstreets of Desire** skillfully draws on DeVille's prior genre explorations to create music that's wholly contemporary while remaining true to the artist's original vision. The anthemic "All in the Name of Love" is a surefire hit-in-waiting.

Big Easy Fantasy, a mixture of studio tracks and New York concert recordings, is another successful exploration of New Orleans' musical heritage; the re-energized DeVille holds his own while sharing the stage and the spotlight with an even more impressive array of Crescent City luminaries. Initial pressings contain a bonus disc of DeVille performing "All in the Name of Love" and "Hey Joe" with Los Camperos de Nacional Cano Mariachi Orchestra. [ss]

See also *TPRG.*

DEVINE & STATTON

See *Alison Statton & Spike.*

D GENERATION

D Generation (Chrysalis) 1994
No Lunch (Columbia) 1996

Not many people understand that it's possible to draw a (relatively) straight line and connect the truly vital exponents of bad-boy rock'n'roll, regardless of spatial-temporal considerations—Presley, Richards and Thunders were all saying the same thing with each curled lip and thrust hip. That belief anchors D Generation's every—admittedly calculated—move. If the New York quintet sounds like it could have sprung from Max's Kansas City in 1976 or CBGB in 1982, that's because its members were there: bassist Howie Pyro can trace his lineage back to the Blessed, a gaggle of high-schoolers that played some of the Big Apple's earliest punk gigs, while singer Jesse Malin fronted Heart Attack, a seminal band on the nascent hardcore scene.

D Generation's debut, however, owes more to the traditional values laid down in the golden age of glam-punk than anything else. "Feel Like Suicide" and "Sins of America" could easily pass for long-lost Mott the Hoople recordings, with guitarists Richard Bacchus and Danny Sage tossing off indelibly anthemic riffs with unnerving ease. In a classic meta-rock gambit, the band ties its most memorable melody to "Guitar Mafia," a sort of auto-tribute that begins with a recorded message of support from longtime champion/Yardbirds producer Giorgio Gomelsky and pivots on the languishing rockers' lament: "tattoos fade like lovers do." Rock about rock hasn't sounded this fresh in years.

The Ric Ocasek–produced **No Lunch** contains remakes of four songs from **D Generation,** which make the improvements in sound, playing and enthusiasm all the more apparent. Timed for optimum impact in the '96 post-post-punk slipstream, the crisp, tight blast of cosmopolitan tuneage balances the then and the now into an easy font of familiarity that doesn't sound second-hand. The irritating bonus-track phone call from a relative ends the album on a sour note, but everything up to that point timewarps D Gen into the sweet spot of a promising future. [dss]

See also *Action Swingers.*

DICKIES

The Incredible Shrinking Dickies (A&M) 1979
Dawn of the Dickies (A&M) 1979
Stukas Over Disneyland (PVC) 1983 (Restless) 1988
We Aren't the World (ROIR) 1986
Killer Klowns From Outer Space EP (Enigma) 1988
Great Dictations (A&M) 1989
Second Coming (Enigma) 1989
Live in London–Locked 'n' Loaded 1990 (Taang!) 1991
Idjit Savant (Triple X) 1995

VARIOUS ARTISTS

Live from the Masque Vol. 3: Dicks Fight Banks Hate (Year 1) 1996

Leave it to the Dickies. Right after Green Day sells millions by cannibalizing a sound they had failed at commercially for well over a decade, Southern California's kings of Saturday-morning punk release what could be the finest album of their motley career.

As of 1990, the junk culturists' intermittent existence had yielded only four hysterically uneven studio records. Some of the best tracks from the first two, plus a handful of bonus babies from UK singles, make up **Great Dictations,** which contains such classics as "Manny, Moe & Jack" and "Rondo (The Midget's Revenge)." **Stukas Over Disneyland** and the post-reunion **Second Coming** both have their moments as well. **We Aren't the World** is a live compilation spiked with four 1977 demos; the five-song **Killer Klowns** boasts one of the group's actual Z-movie theme songs and a cover of *The Jetsons'* timeless "Eep Opp Ork (Uh, Uh)."

The Dickies welcomed the '90s with another live album, and then finally came across with **Idjit Savant,** proof that the unstable band (basically helium-sucking singer Leonard Graves Phillips and guitarist Stan Lee, plus interchangeable others; original keyboardist Chuck Wagon killed himself in 1981) can still outmaneuver and outplay their snot-nosed offspring/competition. Fully recovered from the production excesses that marred **Second Coming,** the Dickies continue to break loud-fast-rules with a class clown's sense of humor. Originals like "I'm Stuck in a Condo (With Marlon Brando)"—a successor of sorts to the second album's "(I'm Stuck in a Pagoda) With Tricia Toyota"—and "I'm on Crack" give a pretty good indication of the band's lyrical stance, but it's the brilliant cover of Pat Smear's 1987 Cheap Trick tribute, "Golden Boys," that reiterates what a great straight *pop* band these guys are. For the first time since **Stukas Over Disneyland,** the parodic antics that define the Dickies don't overwhelm the tunes, making **Idjit Savant** well worth the six-year wait.

The **Masque** album contains a half-dozen live Dickies tracks recorded in 1978; also featured on the album are the Eyes, Randoms and Black Randy and the Metro Squad. [db]

See also *TPRG.*

DIDJITS

See *Supersuckers.*

DIED PRETTY

Died Pretty EP (UK What Goes On) 1984
Next to Nothing EP (Citadel/What Goes On) 1985
Free Dirt (Citadel/What Goes On) 1986
Pre-Deity (Aus. Citadel) 1987
Lost (Beggars Banquet/RCA) 1988
Every Brilliant Eye (Beggars Banquet/RCA) 1990
Doughboy Hollow (Beggars Banquet/RCA) 1992
Trace (Columbia) 1993
Days EP (Aus. Columbia) 1994

Produced by Radio Birdman Rob Younger, Died Pretty's early efforts lived up to the Australian quintet's evocative name, combining delicate, somber folk and intense guitar scree, with the added attraction of melancholy church organ. Over time, the Sydney group has built up a body of work that's classic rock in the best sense.

Going LA (sort of), the band replaced its longtime bassist and keyboardist and hooked up with producer Jeff Eyrich for **Every Brilliant Eye.** Fortunately, a change of scenery didn't dilute Died Pretty's power. Two years later, back in Sydney with English producer Hugh Jones, Died Pretty harnessed every brilliant virtue of its songwriting (by singer Ronald S. Peno and guitarist Brett Myers) and made its masterstroke, **Doughboy Hollow.** Passionate, dramatic, soothing and catchy as hell, the album features a would-be hit in the gorgeous "Sweetheart." Peno's alternately subtle and cranky croon has matured into a distinctive instrument, even if he actually sounds like Gordon Lightfoot (in the best possible way, of course) on the gradually building epic "Satisfied." The bouncy "Stop Myself" adds power-pop to the unique repertoire of this tightly wound band.

Knowing a good thing when they record one, Died Pretty wisely stuck with Jones for **Trace,** which reveals their true talent—for Outback Heartland rock (check the absolutely devastating "The Rivers"). The fine album's one wrong move is "110 B.P.M.," which might as well be a metal-rap-funk reworking of "Another Brick in the Wall Part 2." [db]

See also *TPRG*.

DIE KRUPPS

See *Metallica.*

DIE TOTEN HOSEN

Opel-Gang (Ger. Virgin) 1983
Unter Falscher Flagge (Ger. Virgin) 1985
Damenwahl (Ger. Virgin) 1986
Never Mind the Hosen, Here's die Rotten Rosen (Ger. Virgin) 1987
Bis Zum Bitteren Ende (Ger. Virgin) 1987
Ein Kleines Bisschen Horroschau (Ger. Virgin) 1988
125 Jahre auf dem Kreuzzug ins Glück (Ger. Virgin) 1990
Learning English, Lesson One (Charisma) 1992 (Atlantic) 1994
Kauf MICH! (Ger. Virgin) 1993
Love, Peace & Money (Atlantic) 1995

Born in the early '80s from the remnants of two Düsseldorf bands, Die Toten Hosen (literally, "the dead trousers"; idiomatically, "dead boring" or "bad in bed") combined reckless spirit, roaring musicianship, think-big buffoonery and soccer-stadium rabble-rousing to become Germany's biggest homegrown rock band by the end of the decade. Never settling for cliché or getting stuck in nostalgic ruts, the good-natured group has pushed forward with concept albums, can-you-top-this concert stunts and a calamitous food-fight image that has steered clear of dire disasters by clinging tenaciously to the safe side of the border where spirited abandon turns to chaos. Reliably entertaining and unpredictably outrageous, Die Toten Hosen will never do anything totally original, but its records—trademarked by anthem-like choruses that owe as much to Slade and Gary Glitter as the rebellious British bands that supplanted them later in the '70s—are can't-go-wrong propositions that wrong all rights and rock like crazy.

That said, **Opel-Gang** isn't an impressive debut, rather a timid take on the Clash Pistols with too much pop and too little aggression. By **Damenwahl,** however, the quintet's silly streak, confidence and sound (a mid-tempo rhythm-guitar précis of the slow-learners section of the class of '77, it sometimes resembles the post-Rotten Pistols afterbirth) are in full effect. The cover pictures them dressed like Duran Duran and the Ants; "Disco in Moskau," "Agent X" (a Glitter beat horribly rendered in English), "Helmstedt Blues" and a moronic drinking song, "Das Altbierlied," capture the giddy mood. Even the streamlined rockers—"Verschwende Deine Zeit" ("Waste Your Time"), for instance—can't help but mess about, paraphrasing "Telstar" and suchlike.

Ein Kleines Bisschen Horroschau (subtitled *Die Lieder aus Clockwork Orange und Andere Schmutzige Melodien*) is, as billed, a ridiculous concept album of original songs about Alex and his droogs; in keeping with the character's obsession, Beethoven is the cover star, and a touch of his music crops up amid the accomplished and appealing rock. The ambitious and powerful **125 Jahre auf dem Kreuzzug ins Glück** (something about a 125-year crusade for fortune) is a double-album whose cover painting is a *Les Misérables* tableau that depicts the corpses of Jimi Hendrix, Elvis Presley and Sid Vicious strewn in the snow. Besides a stack of typically catchy and rugged originals (including a new mix of the first album's title track), the mature album significantly contains a version of "New Guitar in Town" (a 1980 Lurkers song on which Honest John Plain of the Boys originally guested) to which Plain—in the flesh—contributes a genuine London accent and his six-string imprimatur.

From small things, baby . . . For its next trick (the first to receive an American release), Die Toten Hosen broke what would shortly become common ground, choosing a knowing selection of British and American punk classics and prevailing upon representatives of the original bands to join them in the recording studio. With Joey Ramone singing "Blitzkrieg Bop" (ha-ha), Captain Sensible singing the Damned's "Smash It Up," Jimmy Pursey singing Sham 69's "If the Kids Are United," Wreckless Eric doing his own "Whole Wide World" and Johnny Thunders (in what proved to be his final session) joining ex–Dead Boy Cheetah Chrome and ex-Dictator Handsome Dick Manitoba to vent "Born to Lose" (plus a dozen more by/with the Boys, 999, Radio Stars, Flys, Vibrators, Eddie and the Hot Rods, etc.), the excellently performed and impressively reverent **Learning English** is less a tribute than a precise re-creation. The inclusion of instruction-record bits, one genuine ringer (the Rockafellas' "Do You Remember") and an original Pistols soundalike, "Carnival in Rio (Punk Was)" sung by Ronnie Biggs ("Punk was a piss-up, punk was a punch-up/Picking your nose and chucking your lunch up") stretches the concept slightly, but the album's educational essence remains in place. The two American editions differ in cover art and content: the '94 rerelease replaces the Lurkers' "Just Thirteen" and Chelsea's "Right to Work" with **125 Jahre**'s "New Guitar in Town" and "Diary of a Lover," retrieved from a Johnny Thunders tribute album.

Back home, Die Toten Hosen made **Kauf MICH!** ("Buy ME!"), a diverse, mainstream effort that moves the band closer to the sound of early-'70s glam-rock. By solidifying stronger tom-tom beats and lightening the rhythm-guitar density, the brisk rock'n'roll of "Rambo-Dance" and such irresistible singalongs as "Drunter, Drauf & Drüber" and "Katastrophen-Kommando" become delicious memories of British bubblegum. The album is recommended to anyone—regardless of linguistic abilities—who still rues the day Mud vanished from the charts.

"Diary of a Lover" also crops up on **Love, Peace & Money,** Die Toten Hosen's first (almost) all-English album of (otherwise) originals. There's a trace of accent in Campino's ferocious singing, but not enough to really notice amid Breiti and Kuddel's big, loud guitars. A solid and invigorating album that crosses an old-school punk sound and Slade-like singalongs (with a few exceptions: the anti-fascist "My Land" is largely acoustic) for a hybrid that works on several intelligence levels. Proof that middle-finger attitude can be made cuddly without getting soft, the album ends with the anthemically inclusive "Chaos Bros." Making like a Pistol-packing Bay City Rollers, the merry *menschen* declare that "every day for us is like a Saturday night" and announce their populist credo: "We belong to you!" [i]

DIFFORD & TILBROOK

See *Squeeze.*

ANI DIFRANCO

Ani DiFranco (Righteous Babe) 1990
Not So Soft (Righteous Babe) 1991
Imperfectly (Righteous Babe) 1992
Puddle Dive (Righteous Babe) 1993
Like I Said (Songs 1990–91) (Righteous Babe) 1993
Out of Range (Righteous Babe) 1994
Not a Pretty Girl (Righteous Babe) 1995
Dilate (Righteous Babe) 1996

Here's a woman who's really *doing* something for the revolution. Taking acoustic folk as her form, resolute DIY as her ethos, empowerment as her mission and punk as her style, Buffalo-born singer/songwriter Ani DiFranco has to be admired as much for the achievement of her self-propelled stardom as for the excellence of her tartly observed, personality-filled songs. A skilled guitar plucker with an athletic voice, an infectious laugh, appealing melodies and the lyrical acuity to (usually) resist the sophomoric preciousness that afflicts other sensitive young singer/songwriters, DiFranco ambles easily on the creative waters that have drowned so many in crocodile tears. To her large and growing audience, she is a confident big sister, a plucky pal, a gutsy feminist, an unplugged rock-'n'roller; on top of it all, she's the owner and operator of a successful independent record label run as a family affair. It's tempting to revere DiFranco sound unheard, or identify her by the teenaged worshipers who attend her shows, but her outspoken albums are too substantial and determined for that.

Sketching out a characteristic map between the conversational ("Talk to Me Now"), the sexual/romantic ("Both Hands"), the observed ("Pale Purple," "Dog Coffee") and the topical (crossing picket lines to get an abortion in "Lost Woman Song"), **Ani DiFranco** gets the story going simply and handsomely with one voice and one guitar. In a Suzanne Vega timbre, the nineteen-year-old announces herself as a soft center with a hard shell who has learned how to survive in her adopted home of New York City: "I have to act as strong as I can/Just to preserve a place/Where I can be who I am." She tells off guys who harass her in the street, pushes out an undesired visitor ("Out of Habit," which contains the attention-getting "My cunt is built like a wound that won't heal") and suffers the traumatic aftershocks of a failed relationship ("Letting the Telephone Ring"), all with a mixture of sober reflection and ebullient release, relishing her power while keeping an eye on the door.

DiFranco's second album, **Not So Soft,** is true to its title. Besides adding some conga drum and overdubs, she replaces the pretty folk singing of the debut with a forceful, vibrato-curled blues-rock voice and attacks her guitar with the percussive vigor of someone who has played to many noisy crowds without an amplifier. The lyrics are also bolder, shot harder and faster from the hip. The spoken title track takes an ambitious swipe at integrating a world critique; DiFranco gets off some personal good lines ("I always wanted to be commander in chief of my one-woman army") but doesn't grab hold of anything more universal. Still on big issues, "On Every Corner" asks "How will they define our generation in the coming decades?"; DiFranco uses that concern to challenge her listeners into personal accountability. Taking the risk of sharing too much, DiFranco enunciates her humanist code in "Looking for Holes": "We can't afford to do anyone harm/Because we owe them our lives/Every breath is recycled from someone else's lungs." But revelation is on her mind: in "The Whole Night," she comfortably considers making love to a woman. Overall, though, too many songs overreach and bellyflop in mushy ground. **Not So Soft** is her least engaging album.

Imperfectly ("everything depicted herein is real, any similarity to fictitious characters or events is completely coincidental") adds drummer Andy Stochansky, an occasional bassist, bits of mandolin, trumpet and, on "Served Faithfully," Mary Ramsey of 10,000 Maniacs on viola. Making a great leap forward in both presentation and content, a newly urgent-sounding DiFranco fires on all fronts: "What If No One's Watching" tries on atheism with pin-prick sense ("What if when we're dead we are just dead?"—take that, Joan Osborne!), "Every State Line" tells a politically informed road story, "Make Them Apologize" dissects male domination in love, music and politics, "The Waiting Song" deflates the hypocrisy of rock stardom and "Good, Bad, Ugly" fishes around the difficulties of romance. "Coming Up" is a two-tracked poem that doesn't work the way it's supposed to. But the song on which **Imperfectly** pivots is "In or Out," a memorable tune that turns ambivalence into a proud statement of why-not inclusion and has become her de facto anthem. Announcing "I owe my life to the people that I love," she provocatively calls herself "Mr. DiFranco" and says, "Some days the line I walk turns out to be straight/Other days the line tends to deviate/I've got no criteria for sex or race."

What were tentative band experiments on **Imperfectly** become the rule on **Puddle Dive;** although DiFranco does several songs on her own (slapping her acoustic guitar with a rhythm-keeping intensity that obviates the need for accompaniment), the rich, playful album is marbled with tasteful instrumental contributions that fill in the tracks but stay out of the star's way. Ever more confident in her ability to equal the lyrical challenges she sets herself, DiFranco steps out on various limbs—inverting racist stereotypes in "Names and Dates and Times," tearing into the club world's peer-group competition in the devastating "Egos Like Hairdos," recounting a menstrual mishap in "Blood in the Boardroom"—and, with one exception (the trite Andy Rooney nonsense of "Pick Yer Nose"), climbs back safely. If the report of "Used to You" is accurate, her emotional bungee-jumping also brings her back in one piece. The song begins by calling her an "asshole" and concludes "I could love you/Yeah I've entertained the thought/But I could never like you/So I guess I better not."

The intent of **Like I Said** was to bring fifteen songs from the first two albums up to date by rerecording them with Stochansky and a few other sympathetic musicians. Ironically, the album succeeds at something else entirely: DiFranco's growth as a thoughtful, expressive singer informs the delicate, intimate reconsiderations. The effect is subtle but marvelous. **Like I Said** gives an entirely wrong first impression with a furiously mannered remake of "Anticipate," but quickly settles into an understated beauty reminiscent of early Joni Mitchell records. "Rockabye" is sweet and low;

cello shapes "Work Your Way Out"; subliminal bagpipes underpin "She Says"; the irritated sexual refusal of "Gratitude" becomes gracefully eloquent; a brisk spin through "The Whole Night" makes the song dance like a light heart.

Out of Range is DiFranco's masterpiece, a fully primed band (and solo) effort that delivers her into the real world with an established and presentably commercial sound, a clear artistic vision and a secure sense of place. Able to place herself into the mind of a woman who sells sex, and cleverly view life as a B-movie ("It's stupid and it's strange/It's a directionless story/And the dialogue is lame"), she remains close enough to her listeners to berate them for their passivity. Over pumping accordion in the pungent "Face Up and Sing," DiFranco allows her fatigue and irritation to show, but turns it into a positive call to action. "Some chick says thank you for saying all the things I never do/I say you know the thanks I get is to take all the shit for you/It's nice that you listen/It'd be nicer if you joined in." The shy romantic desire of "The Diner" ties DiFranco back to the winsome uncertainties of youth, but most of the album makes maturity seem like a state of grace worth reaching.

DiFranco sounds like a mainstream careerist for the first time on the proud and mighty **Not a Pretty Girl,** but the fleshed-out (self-)production, occasionally overbearing singing and a radio-ready sound converging on a stylemeld of Tracy Chapman, Suzanne Vega and Melissa Etheridge don't compromise her forthrightness or ability to tease exorbitant beauty out of a simple idea. The narrator of the spoken "Tiptoe" prepares for an abortion by walking through piers of used condoms "with a fetus holding court in my gut"; "Shy" spies men pissing in doorways. Switching easily from the personal to the public, she apologizes tenderly to a faded love ("Sorry I Am") and considers unjust incarceration ("Crime for Crime"), describes her romantic ideal ("Asking Too Much") and again rejects the record industry's advances ("The Million You Never Made"). A certain familiarity is creeping into her subject matter, though (literally in one case: a remake of **Imperfectly**'s "Coming Up"). And the depth charge she loads into a confession of infidelity ("Light of Some Kind") is kind of a cheap shot: "I still think of you as my boyfriend / I don't think this is the end of the world/Maybe you should follow my example/And go meet yourself a really nice girl." (In concert, that bit of bi-sexual bravado invariably elicits howls of approval.) Still, quiet dignity remains her real forte, and "Hour Follows Hour" is six minutes of exquisite romantic tenderness. At the height of her power, DiFranco cuts a formidable figure here, the queen of a universe she has drawn around herself. As commendable as her dedication to autonomy is, the danger of solipsistic narrowmindedness is rising. It may be time for this staunch and talented independent to make some new friends.

The opening song on **Dilate,** an ambitiously self-produced album that uses keyboards, bass and drums to expand on the guitar core, sure won't do that: "Untouchable Face" quietly leads up to a catchy chorus of "Fuck you!"—a self-indulgent and unsophisticated way to satisfy an audience's pan-animus needs. While stretching some personal musical borders here (the electric "Outta Me, Onto You," the funky beat and treated vocal of "Going Down," the pretentious trip-hop art-concept version of "Amazing Grace"), DiFranco seems to be withdrawing deeper into a private world, skillfully singing to herself more than ever. "Napoleon," yet another scornful treatise on major-label stardom, is one protest too many on the subject. "I care less and less what people think," she sings in "Dilate" before confessing to being in love; it's hard to tell which sentiment comes closer to her soul. The album has many of DiFranco's usual virtues and the added appeal of studio aplomb and varied three-dimensional instrumental presentation, but the ultimate message of **Dilate** is individualism and remoteness rather than community and intimacy. That's a change she probably didn't mean to make. [i]

DIG

Runt EP (Wasteland) 1992
Dig (Wasteland) 1993
Soft Pretzel EP (Radioactive) 1994
Defenders of the Universe (Radioactive) 1996

With the mass-market success of grunge peaking in 1993, Los Angeles' Dig fit right in, with distorted, aggressive guitar riffs, insidiously catchy melodies and rough-voiced singer Scott Hackwith. Fortunately, the quintet's self-titled album, produced by Dave Jerden, isn't some hastily thrown-together copycat shuck: the dozen tracks are uniformly well-written. Commercially, of course, Dig entered the fray a couple of beats too late, when the audience for this stuff was already too jaded to give much consideration even to a good act worthy of a little attention. (Under different circumstances, there's no doubt the soaring "Believe" or the raging "Feet Don't Touch the Ground" could have become well-deserved hit singles.) Those not suffering from grunge overload and willing to sacrifice surprises for solid songwriting, however, may find **Dig** truly likable.

Ex-Weirdos guitarist Dix Denney replaced Johnny Cornwell in time for **Defenders of the Universe,** a less stylized and more genially engaging rock record written and produced by singer Hackwith. [ky/i]

DIGABLE PLANETS

Reachin' (A New Refutation of Time and Space) (Pendulum/Elektra) 1993
Blowout Comb (Pendulum/EMI) 1994

Talk about timing. New York's Digable Planets happened along at the exact moment when many in hip-hop—newcomers and veterans alike—were seeking ways to integrate aspects of jazz into the mix. The trio of Doodlebug (Craig Irving), Butterfly (Ishmael Butler) and Ladybug (Mary Ann Vieira) met as students in Washington, DC, and began collaborating on rhymes and poetry in 1991. At that time, jazz was generations away from hip-hop; some rappers paid lip service to Miles Davis and other giants but few knew how to make their music emulate jazz's looseness, its natural feel.

One little song, built on a sample of Art Blakey and the Jazz Messengers' "Stretchin'," would change all that. A positive, laid-back statement of purpose, "Rebirth of Slick (Cool Like Dat)" became the catalyst for the jazz-hop movement. With its crisp horns, coy patter and streetwise imagery, the track also became one of 1993's biggest singles and brought Digable Planets a Grammy. The rest of **Reachin'** follows a similar script:

ethereal narratives advocating community and consciousness, supported by gently funky beats and tastefully deployed samples. Sometimes the raps stretch the limits of plausibility, but the magic's in the feel. After years of rap's in-your-face agitation, such easygoing grooves poured down like a cool, refreshing shower.

Blowout Comb hardly takes giant steps forward. Despite a militantly activist stance in the booklet and an impressive roster of guests—Jeru the Damaja, Guru, D'Influence's Sarah Webb—the tracks suffer from inertia. Backbeats that had been buoyant seem labored. Digable Planets is dabbling in more aggressive funk workouts, and the trio's growing social awareness gives its lyrics a sharper edge, but even when talking about black culture's need to resist mainstreaming—a theme pertinent to everything since turn-of-the-century jazz and Delta blues—the group never gets aboard musical vehicles powerful enough to drive those points home. [tm]

STEVE DIGGLE

See *Buzzcocks.*

DIGITAL UNDERGROUND

Sex Packets (TNT/Tommy Boy) 1990
This Is an E.P. Release EP (TNT/Tommy Boy) 1990
Sons of the P (TNT/Tommy Boy) 1991
The "Body-Hat" Syndrome (TNT/Tommy Boy) 1993

RAW FUSION

Live From the Styleetron (Hollywood/BASIC) 1992
Hoochiefied Funk (Hollywood/BASIC) 1994

SAAFIR

Boxcar Sessions (Qwest/Reprise) 1994

If George Clinton's Parliafunkadeliment Thang served as the musical basis for an overwhelming number of hip-hop releases in the late '80s and '90s, nobody in hip-hop took P-Funk's high-concept, African collectivism, democratic method and loony attitude more seriously than Digital Underground. Skilled Berkeley multi-instrumentalist Shock G (Greg Jacobs) was the group's inventive overlord, orchestrating complex song and performance structures that would allow for maximum rump-shaking individualist anarchy. When it worked, Digital Underground threw a peerless kind of conscious party, sharing more with the big funk bands of the '70s and contemporary punk-funkers like Fishbone than any hip-hop peers. When it didn't, they merely seemed weird.

Digital Underground made its first mark in 1988 with a couple of funny (ha-ha, not funny peculiar) independent singles: "Your Life's a Cartoon" and "Doowutchyalike." By 1990, they were signed to Tommy Boy and ready to unload a sack of conceptual metaphors. As an appropriate vehicle to disclose and liberate America's uptightness, the group invented (and fashioned its debut album around) the fiction of "sex packets," concentrated doses of orgasm more seductive than Prince and more addictive than crack—but safer than sex. On **Sex Packets,** alongside the imaginative fun, the Underground take a more direct approach in the irresistible nastiness of "Freaks of the Industry," the Hendrixy "The Way We Swing" and the aquaboogie of "Underwater Rimes." Aiming to create the ideal space where everyone could safely locate their own funk, they achieved it on the ridiculously bumping "Humpty Dance" (introducing Shock G's brilliant Groucho Marx–styled comic alter ego, the nerdy and congested Humpty Hump) and "Doowutchyalike." A monumental and mad-fun debut.

The six-song **This Is an E.P. Release** keeps the joint jumping with less concept and more hilarity and muscular musicality. "Nuttin' Nis Funky" showcases DJ Fuze working two copies of Miles Davis' "Back Seat Betty" while the crew lights up the microphones. And "Same Song" (plus an augmented remix of "The Way We Swing") introduced the world to Digital denizen Tupac Shakur.

The free-floating Underground expanded—no less than eighteen rhymers appear on **Sons of the P**—and attempted to consolidate itself as the rightful heirs of Clinton's throne on its second album. Unfortunately, **Sons of the P** lacks an idea as engaging or any grooves as grand as those on **Sex Packets.** Only the super-stupid "No Nose Job" (in which Humpty frantically resists Michael Jackson–like surgery) and the sublimely spare title track, in which George Clinton himself passes the torch to his spiritual children, reaches the debut's heights.

In the intervening two years before the release of **The "Body-Hat" Syndrome,** members of the Underground went on to varying degrees of artistic and commercial success. The charismatic Tupac Shakur started on his way to stardom with Shock G–produced singles like "I Get Around." Meanwhile, Raw Fusion—a long-standing duo of DJ Fuze (David Elliot) and the Underground's number-two rapper, Money B (Ron Brooks), that returned for the mothership's next flight—cut a forgettable, uneven debut, **Live From the Styleetron.** (**Hoochiefied Funk** is no better, a dull slow-groove sex collection with none of the Underground's wit or character.)

At seventy-five minutes, the CD version of **The "Body-Hat" Syndrome** is essentially a double album. Musically, Digital Underground is back at the top of its game, but conceptually the group is sounding the retreat. Where "Sex Packets" liberated, "Body Hats" insulates the crew, condom-like, from the world's evils. The seven-and-a-half-minute "Doo Woo You" is a subtle diss directed at the record label, which turned down two versions of the album. "The Humpty Dance Awards" takes a swipe at pop copyists. On the other hand, Humpty Hump's manic "The Return of the Crazy One," the insinuating "Digital Lover" (in which Humpty argues "You need a Biblical brother!"), the gorgeous "Wussup wit the Luv" and all the appearances of young Oakland rhymer Saafir the Saucee Nomad are standout moments in a massive undertaking.

Saafir's own album, which appeared the following year, has promisingly jazz-flecked beats and a pleasant flow, but the rapper's lyrics are hollow, crude and obnoxious. "Worship the dick"? Oh grow up. [jzc/i]

See also *2Pac; TPRG.*

DILLON FENCE

Dillon Fence EP (NoCar) 1989 (Mammoth) 1993
Christmas EP (Mammoth) 1991
Rosemary (Mammoth) 1992
Daylight EP (Mammoth) 1992
Outside In (Mammoth) 1993
Any Other Way EP (Mammoth) 1993
[Living Room Scene] (Mammoth) 1994

Formed at college in Chapel Hill, North Carolina, Dillon Fence started out as earnest as a country pastor and just as culturally stimulating. Although impressively accomplished in a vein indisposed toward crummy playing and singing, the clear, polite and bland guitar pop/soul of the quartet's self-released six-song debut makes it easy to appreciate the fact that Hootie and the Blowfish opened for Dillon Fence in those days. (The future platinum-minters actually get thanked on **Rosemary.**) Variable-voiced guitarist Greg Humphreys seems to have spent too much time studying the singing styles of Sting, Ali Campbell, Morrissey and Paul Young, but his trick of flattening notes at the end of lines is at least distinctive.

Exchanging drummers, Dillon Fence stabilized its lineup in time for **Christmas** (a three-song seasonal release): Humphreys, guitarist Kent Alphin, bassist Chris Goode and drummer Scott Carle. On the full-length **Rosemary,** a re-recording of **Dillon Fence**'s "Something for You" matches the album's tone by cranking the guitars into a genial roar. That approach works wonders on "Daylight," but Dillon Fence is still finding its feet here, and—with the high-fiber moralism of "Sad Inheritance," the disillusioned grumpiness of "Summer" and the aw-shucks insecurity of "Guilty"—the album is pasty-faced and nice-guy noxious. The **Daylight** EP gets its soaring title track and "Hey Mockingbird" from the LP, adding an acoustic (with flute and violin) improvement on "Sad Inheritance," the otherwise unissued funk-junk of "Sugarcane" and a rushed cover of Blondie's "Dreaming."

Producer Lou Giordano pushes Dillon Fence to new heights of wimp-distortion on **Outside In,** letting Humphreys and Alphin foam up sensual acres of pop fuzzage that provide an excellent bed for their voices. A little alterna tonic bolsters Humphreys' singing: his quiet cooing and bursts of enthusiasm make fine ingredients in these gently sizzling pop clouds. Burying the lyrics is also a good idea; whatever he's on about in "Collapsis" is rendered too elusive to interfere with the seductive undertow coming out of the amps. The album's consistently appealing surface belies its diversity: Alphin's "One Bad Habit" ably apes the Lemonheads, "Any Other Way" does white-soul with woozy confidence, "Headache" socks a Joan Jett crunch to glorious Beatlesque production pop and "Black Eyed Susan" lays on the harmonies like vintage Association. Without turning into postgraduate delinquents, Dillon Fence make magical mudpies here. (In a dubious career move, "Any Other Way" was chosen as the single from **Outside In;** the EP contains a terrible live version of a second album track, a frisky cowpunk cover and a sweet non-LP original.)

Having expanded the guitar end of its sonic spectrum, the group buttresses the bottom on **[Living Room Scene],** a harder-hitting rock album with more bottle and a shade less charm than its immediate predecessor. Humphreys exercises a raspy Rod Stewart voice (which he intimated on **Outside In**) and a fat '70s Gibson SG tone on the title track, then downplays both in the cushy electric soul folds of "Laughs" and the squalling harmony pop of "Queen of the In-Between." For the rest of the record, the band shifts among loud and soft rock-soul-pop poles in a pinball carom further complicated by letting Alphin sing his two compositions and Goode his one. If Dillon Fence shows no signs of integrating its elements into a single sound, the corners that contain it aren't being stretched any further apart. And with a steady flow of memorable songs able to withstand whatever type of arrangement comes up on the spinner, **[Living Room Scene]** sounds like the final warmup for a truly great record. Unfortunately, Alphin then left to form Granger. [i]

DIMITRI & THE SUPREME 5000

Everything Is Naked (Fierce Records USA) 1994

The paradox of rock critics who cross the write/play line lies in the jaundiced analytic vision needed to review pop for a living. Making music takes belief in one's instincts and imagination, a trait pretty much ruined by the ability to deconstruct creative efforts into their components and coldly trace them back to their sources. Writers usually have the good sense (or cowardice) not to suck in public—there's too much honor at stake and too many indefensible slag-offs in the closet to live down—but that doesn't mean many possess the talent to surpass the mediocrity they're so quick to deride in others.

All of which is by way of acknowledging the impressive quality of New York journalist Dimitri Ehrlich's self-released album. Well-played and solidly written, **Everything Is Naked** is a slick, handsomely arranged production whose diverse stylings (soft funk, rich pop, soul-flecked rock) circle around a central core of early Joe Jackson. Possessing a certain vocal resemblance, the singer/guitarist seems to have followed it to Jackson's structural doorstep. The album has a few silly songs ("Big Dreams") and a couple of overly emotional ones ("I Wanna Be Your Lover," "Eira I Tried"), but "You Let Me Down Easy (You Never See Me Again)," a saga of love spurned, is a poignant gem. "Once I was the man of your dreams/ Now I'm just a phone call you don't wanna return," Ehrlich complains, going on to lay out the situation's existential terror: "What if I was born to love only you/And what if I die that way, too?" Such anxiety over lost opportunities undoubtedly motivates a lot of would-be musicians as well; if his love life doesn't work out, Ehrlich can at least be satisfied on one score here. [i]

DIM STARS

Dim Stars EP7 (Ecstatic Peace!) 1991 [CD] (Caroline) 1992
Dim Stars (Caroline) 1992

RICHARD HELL & THE VOIDOIDS

Blank Generation (Sire) 1977 (Sire/Warner Bros.) 1990
Destiny Street (Red Star) 1982 (Razor & Tie) 1995
Funhunt (ROIR) 1990

RICHARD HELL

R.I.P. (ROIR) 1984 (ROIR/Important) 1990
Go Now (Tim/Kerr) 1995

VARIOUS ARTISTS

Who the Hell: A Tribute to Richard Hell (Cred Factory) 1995

Judging by this alternately indulgent and incendiary onetime summit of post-punk hipster demi-gods, it's probably safe to say that every subculture gets the supergroup it deserves. As befits a batch of collector scum idols—including Richard Hell, Don Fleming, Thurston Moore and Steve Shelley—Dim Stars initially released its work in an extremely small edition as a set of three 7-inch EPs, a format that, despite some aesthetic advantages, wasn't exactly conducive to repeated play. That self-defeating approach was prudently remedied by letting a larger label release it as a CD EP. The group then recorded a full album.

The full-length, no-overlap **Dim Stars** is clearly a vehicle for the long-inactive Hell, and he takes the wheel with the aplomb of a NASCAR veteran, slipping lithely into the cut-up lyrical style he worked in the '70s with the Voidoids (whose Robert Quine guests on five tracks). Even though long stretches of the album degenerate into skronky improvisation, "All My Witches Come True" and "The Night Is Coming On" jerk and skitter with the strung-out energy of Hell's heyday. The company even—after a fashion—explores roots you probably never knew the musicians had, covering Howlin' Wolf's "Natchez Burning" and desecrating '60s iconography in "Incense Is the Essence" (a collaboration with situationist noisemonger Tom Smith of Peach of Immortality and To Live & Shave in L.A.). **Dim Stars:** more than a curio, less than an essential item for non-fanatics.

Although Hell hasn't added any other significant musical achievements to his canon of late, his slender back catalogue—two studio albums (**Blank Generation** and **Destiny Street**) plus an odds-and-sods anthology (**R.I.P.**)—has been reissued, with a live compilation (**Funhunt**) and a spoken word disc (**Go Now,** verbalized from his '96 novel and accompanied by Robert Quine) augmenting his legacy a little. In 1995, a tiny North Carolina label assembled a delightful limited-edition fundraiser in tribute to him; the best-known of the thirteen Carolina bands is Vanilla Trainwreck, who make credibly enthusiastic work of "Love Comes in Spurts." Whiskey Town's country cover of "Blank Generation" is likewise unassumingly nifty. [dss/i]

See also *Gumball, Sonic Youth.*

DINK

Dink EP (Dink) 1993
Dink (Capitol) 1994

While Dink would no doubt like to be seen as slightly more aggro heirs to the experimental mantle of such Buckeye antecedents as Pere Ubu and Devo, the Ohio quintet actually has more in common with prehistoric Kent homeboys the James Gang, since its output is basic bar-band boogie retooled for the industrial age. Several years spent trawling in midwestern clubs built Dink enough of a reputation to propel its self-released EP to regional hit status, which the group with a good word on their behalf from Trent Reznor—swiftly parlayed into a major-label deal. The self-titled album reprises several of the EP's better tracks, including the swirling, synth-heavy "Green Mind," but, for the bulk of the eleven-song set, guitarists Sean Carlin and Jer Herring simply run basic hard rock riffs through enough effects to give them a fleeting illusion of modernity. Still, **Dink** has its moments: "Water" overlays an espresso-soaked canvas of bongos and bass with singer Rob Lightbody's beatnik jive, while "Get on It" gives up the funk in unexpectedly convincing fashion. [dss]

DINOSAUR JR

Dinosaur (Homestead) 1985
You're Living all Over Me (SST) 1987
Bug (SST) 1988
Fossils (SST) 1991
Green Mind (Blanco y Negro/Sire/Warner Bros.) 1991
Whatever's Cool With Me (Blanco y Negro/Sire/Warner Bros.) 1991
Where You Been (Blanco y Negro/Sire/Warner Bros.) 1993
Without a Sound (Blanco y Negro/Sire/Warner Bros.) 1994

J MASCIS

Martin + Me (Baked Goods/Reprise) 1996

SWISH

Supermax (Instant Mayhem) 1996

VARIOUS ARTISTS

Gas Food Lodging (Mute) 1992

One of the great diplomatic challenges facing underground rockers in the mid-'80s was how to repeal the punk era's edict against guitar heroics (which actually did nothing to undercut the instrument's hegemony, except to shelve it for a brief synth-pop sabbatical) without raising suspicions of cultural revisionism or unseemly nostalgia. In a gambit that proved useful for other iconoclast conundrums of burning desire for things deemed uncool (like major-label funding or vast commercial success), Amherst, Massachusetts, drummer-cum-guitarist and singer J (Joseph) Mascis hit upon a solution. (In the shadow of Sonic Youth, themselves wrapped in a curtain of radical anti-rock experimentalism, he wasn't the only or even the first one. But he did become the famous and influential archetype that explained if not excused all the subsequent claimants.) Mascis, a genuine introvert and slacker at heart, simply turned the toddler's I-didn't-do-it denial into an indolent I-didn't-know-I-was-doin'-nothin' shrug, sending up woolly clouds of stun volume and careless distortion that couldn't possibly indicate any personal effort or conscious responsibility. That he's neither a traditional nor a good lead guitarist (he's actually a hopeless Neil Young wannabe) and that he can't sing for shit above an enervated mumble/whine backs up the implicit contention of amateurism run amok. That he's kept his process slow and steady, helps out cool bands and is capable of sputtering out a monumental pop song now and then has sustained Mascis as a primo indie-rock god for more than a decade, a prominent lead guitarist in a genre that doesn't generally need or tolerate such overt wankery.

Mascis formed Dinosaur as a trio with bassist Lou Barlow (they'd been in a band called Deep Wound together) and drummer Murph (Patrick Murphy) in 1984; the Jr was appended after the objections of a group of rock geezers working on the West Coast as the Dinosaurs. Briefly issued under the original name and then given its Jr for full-scale release, **You're Living All Over Me** (the CD of which contains a tone-deaf version of Peter Frampton's "Show Me the Way," proof that any cultural atrocity is admissible so long as it's accorded full disrespect) and the superior **Bug** (which raised the band's profile significantly with an ace pop single, the boisterous but airy, Lemonhead-flavored "Freak Scene") established a style while exhausting the mileage meter of the original lineup, which collapsed when Barlow left to lead his side project, Sebadoh, full-time. (SST gathered up the band's A- and B-sides for the label and issued the eight-song **Fossils,** which is actually a useful compendium of the early years' most colorful souvenirs: "Freak Scene," "Show Me the Way," a cover of the Cure's "Just Like Heaven," **Living**'s "Little Fury Things.")

When Mascis returned nearly three years later, he was signed to a major label and, also like Evan Dando, recording essentially as a solo artist but using a group name. The clear-sounding **Green Mind** has a surprising measure of propulsive energy and acoustic-guitar diversity (which underscores the Neil Young resemblance), and sets Dinosaur Jr tradition by kicking off with a great single, "The Wagon." The pickings after that, however, are slim. "Water" and "Green Mind" are the only genuinely memorable items in a lackluster bunch; Mascis seems to have expended all his creative energy in learning the syncopated beat of "Muck" and inflating the leaky atmospheric tire that supports "Thumb." More than a lazy sound, **Green Mind** is the sound of laziness.

Accurately billed as "one new single and 7 B sides," **Whatever's Cool With Me** again starts out fine, with the engaging titular ode to apathy, sung in a just-woke-up croak at a relatively rousing tempo. With one exception, the rest is expendable sliding right on through to awful. Long concert versions of "Thumb" and the older "Keep the Glove" are sloppy and boring; the non-LP studio tracks—all cut strictly solo, four of them previously used on the British 12-inch of "The Wagon"—are slapdash and sung in various states of tuneless disrepair. Only the brisk and tight "Not You Again," in which Mascis marvels woefully at "the mess I made again . . . how do I do it?," displays the kind of small effort it takes to elevate slack rubbish into slacker art.

The same minimal exertion describes Mascis' fifteen minutes' worth of generic contributions to the score of *Gas Food Lodging:* short, pleasant, simple and restrained song-sketch exercises on acoustic and electric guitar, piano, bass and drums. The rest of the album (co-credited to Barry Adamson, but featuring tracks by Victoria Williams, Nick Cave, Renegade Soundwave and the Velvet Monkeys) is far more accomplished.

Whether Mascis' resumption of the recording process as a collective band effort (with bassist Mike Johnson and Murph) explains the great leap forward of **Where You Been** or is merely coincidental with a sudden upturn in his creative ambition, the bottom line is that it's the first Dinosaur Jr album that doesn't hinge on sensory overload as its primary selling point. Initiative elevates and articulates material that, in the past, might have been left to moulder under a burial pyre of thoughtless distortion. There's still plenty of fuzzed-out squalling, but that's only one facet of a more rounded effort. The ten-track campaign is characterized by concerted craft, solid songwriting (the standouts are "Start Choppin," "On the Way" and "Get Me," none of them in the pole position) and credible (if creaky) singing. A winsome falsetto, string quartet, piano and tympani increases the Neil Young resemblance of "Not the Same"; the vocal arrangement, acoustic picking and organ bed of "Goin' Home" and the violins on "What Else Is New" are all useful innovative touches. Although Dinosaur Jr remains an odd diversion demanding tolerance and indulgence, **Where You Been** extends itself as Mascis never before has.

And may never again. **Without a Sound,** recorded as a duo with Johnson, demonstrates that making peace with old bugbears like accurate singing and considered instrumental complexity is no substitute for inspiration, which seems to have gone missing. Imperceptibly easing off the accelerator, Mascis allows the creative tension to go slack, allowing nearly good songs to pass by like gray-suited paraders with hangovers. The sheepish recriminations of "Yeah Right" (with Thalia Zedek of Come singing along) head past repetition to the ledge of self-parody. Acoustic-based arrangements frame "Outta Hand" and "Seemed Like the Thing to Do" to good effect, but only the latter, a simple refrain repeated endlessly, manages to scratch an irritatingly gentle message into the mental bark. "I feel the pain of everyone/Later I feel nothing," Mascis sings in the leadoff "Feel the Pain" (which has half a hook leading into the chorus and nothing else to recommend it). Point taken. Having completely mastered the art of surging guitar-powered backdrops for his twinned lazy/high vocals, Mascis makes a consistently friendly noise whose pleasing effect doesn't last as long as the album. No gain, no pain.

Considering that Mascis is unlikely to ever be mistaken for a singer, it's worrisome to hear what a crummy guitarist he is when you can hear what he's actually playing. Recorded on a '95 solo acoustic tour, **Martin + Me** runs through a dubious assortment of Dinosaur Jr oldies ("Get Me" and "Not You Again," but also "Thumb," "Goin' Home," "Drawerings" and other minor album cuts) and a quartet of diverse covers (of songs by the Smiths, Wipers, Carly Simon and Lynyrd Skynyrd) with the nimble fingers of a frostbite victim. Strumming badly with a wavering sense of rhythm, picking fills like a three-lesson amateur who forgot to practice and generally showing less than no care or concern, Mascis could just as well be any no-talent singing these songs—but he's not. There's a lesson about fame and flimsiness in here someplace but it would be too much work to try and think what it might be.

Swish is Murph's trio with singer/bassist Lori Martin and Amherst guitarist Joe Boyle. Led by Martin's flexible voice and personal, provocative songs, **Supermax** (produced and released by Don Fleming) is a strong, tuneful and diverse seven-song debut, in line with various northeastern bands—other than Murph's alma pater. [i]

See also *Buffalo Tom, GobbleHoof, Mike Johnson, Sebadoh; TPRG.*

DIRTY THREE

Sad & Dangerous (Poon Village/Forced Exposure) 1994 + 1995
Dirty Three (Aus. Torn & Frayed/Shock) 1994 (Torn & Frayed/Touch and Go) 1995
Horse Stories (Touch and Go) 1996

It's not just the Dirty Three's unusual lineup—violin, guitar and drums—that makes the Melbourne trio special. The group's rumbling, kinetic sound bypasses the pure pleasure of surf instrumentals and even the heavier reality of Australia's fine swamp-rock tradition for something altogether more dynamic. Led by violin player Warren Ellis (a sometime Robert Forster sideman whose breathless rants during live shows add a further dimension), the Dirty Three fold into their burly rhythms and squalls of guitar noise a force rife with pain and possibilities.

Recorded as a demo, **Sad & Dangerous** was first released in the US in 1994 on vinyl, in a beautiful, hand-screened package that housed a subtle but delicious introduction to the Dirty Three's atypical sound. The lead track, a spooky cover of "Kim's Dirt" by former Scientist Kim Salmon, hints at a connection between the Dirty Three and their Australian forebears, a kinship that would later become more overt. The album's first half has a tense, low-key atmosphere, as Jim White's sympathetic percussion and equally attuned guitar from ex-Moodist Mick Turner (who also produced the album) flesh out Ellis' violin leads. The second half heads all over the place: "Devil in the Hole" is light on drama and heavy on decorative twists, "Jim's Dog" dips into jazzy waters and "Short Break" is a roadrunner-paced jam. "You Were a Bum Dream" forecasts Ellis' flourishing, descriptive style and ability to set and maintain a tone. While the album reveals many of the group's effective tricks, it doesn't have the coherence of the trio's next release. (The 1995 CD issue, whose initial run featured equally impressive silk-screened artwork, adds three cuts.)

Dirty Three is a much fuller exploration of the group's rich potential. The lava-like flow of the opening "Indian Love Song" doesn't relent throughout the disc's seven tracks, one of which is a more feverish and muscular version of "Kim's Dirt." The track puts a spotlight on the group's love for sonic drama, led by Ellis' supple playing (it's not surprising that he's toured with another drama-loving Australian: Nick Cave). Occasionally, his violin takes on a rootsy, vaguely Celtic tone, as on "Better Go Home Now" and the revealingly poignant "Everything's Fucked"; a lonesome-sounding accordion on "Odd Couple" further broadens the scope. Without a vocalist, the Dirty Three are able to say more about bruised hearts, drunk minds and late-night tragedies than most bands relying on easy verbal cues. [la]

DISCO INFERNO

Open Doors Closed Windows (UK Ché) 1991
Science EP (UK Ché) 1991
In Debt (UK Ché) 1992 (Carrot Top) 1995
The Last Dance EP (UK Rough Trade) 1993
D.I. Go Pop (UK Rough Trade) 1994 (Bar/None) 1994
Second Language EP (Rough Trade) 1994

Ian Crause's Disco Inferno started out in the late '80s, blending 4AD-style atmospherics with the side of New Order that *wasn't* dance music, taking as its starting point Crause's meticulous, chiming, echoing guitar sound. As the East London band grew, it discovered sequencing, electronic triggers and MIDI devices, and found its voice making almost-conventional guitar-pop songs out of unconventional sonic materials.

Disco Inferno's first three records—the single "Entertainment," the album **Open Doors Closed Windows** and the EP **Science** (all of which were later compiled, with an extra song, as **In Debt**)—reveal a band with a very big collection of Joy Division records and a very large suitcase full of effects pedals. (It's tempting to think they should have called themselves We've Got a Digital Delay Box and We're Gonna Use It.) You can practically sing either "Ceremony" or "In a Lonely Place" to half the songs, but some of them are powerfully expansive ("Set Sail" has an especially rich sound), and others, like "Freethought," find the band already experimenting with layers of sampled noise. The EP's "Waking Up" introduces another one of D.I.'s favorite tricks: letting a graceful treble-range bass guitar carry a song by itself.

The lineup for the "Summer's Last Sound" single was Crause singing and playing guitars and samples, bassist Paul Wilmot, Robert Whatley ("drum triggers and bass patterns") and studio engineer Charlie McIntosh. This last position was clearly essential to D.I.'s designs; think of engineer Gary Langan, who was counted as a full member of the Art of Noise. McIntosh is the only person named on 1993's "From the Devil to the Deep Blue Sky" single (whose noisy, nearly abstract ten-minute "B-side," "A Rock to Cling To," was the first indication of the direction the band was about to take); he also produced **D.I. Go Pop** and half of **The Last Dance,** while different producers and engineers are named on other records.

The Last Dance, a four-track EP, includes two versions of the title song (on which Crause's vocal recalls Daniel Treacy of the Television Personalities) as well as "D.I. Go Pop" (a guitar-and-MIDI barrage whose meter suggests an off-center 45) and the lengthy "Scattered Showers," which is nearly consumed in an avalanche of sound effects.

The **D.I. Go Pop** album doesn't contain the song of the same name; it also doesn't really have anything that's recognizable as pop. Crause's guitar (if that is indeed his triggering device of choice) is almost always electronically transformed into something else: a horde of whining camera-shutters on "Starbound: All Burnt Out & Nowhere to Go," a piano in the middle of a demolition derby on "A Crash at Every Speed." The bass provides the only real melodic content, and Crause desperately shouts unwieldy lyrics that can't quite be made out. It's a hard record to adjust to, but it's also unique and sometimes very refreshing, even pretty.

The album was followed by another EP, **Second Language,** which brought back the guitar while keeping the sound effects, though the epiphanic moment in the title track isn't the sampled intrusions but Crause's attack on his whammy bar near the end. "The Atheist's Burden" has a drum machine that might even make it danceable if not for the wobble-toned instruments surrounding it. The real prize from this period (and the final of four releases, beginning with **The Last Dance,** unified by complementary waveform graphics), however, is the non-album single "It's a Kid's World," a peculiarly calm assemblage of amorphous, atonal noises, sweetly ringing guitar and Crause's buried-in-the-mix vocals, set against a slowed-down sample of the walloping drums that open Iggy Pop's "Lust for Life." Bizarre, but highly effective. [ddw]

DISH

Mabel Sagittarius EP (Engine) 1994
Boneyard Beach (Interscope/Atlantic) 1995

MOTOCASTER

Acid Rock EP (Fistpuppet) 1994
Stay Loaded (Interscope/Atlantic) 1994

BLACKGIRLS

Speechless EP (Tom Tom/Black Park) 1987
Procedure (Mammoth) 1989
Happy (Mammoth) 1991

EIGHT OR NINE FEET

Flint [tape] (no label) 1989
Resolution (Reverie) 1990

Although Raleigh, North Carolina's Dish and Motocaster share singer/guitarist Bo Taylor, neither band is a side project. Motocaster, a noisy trio formerly known as Motorolla, serves as the outlet for Taylor's ruder self, while in Dish he plays a strong second banana to singer/pianist Dana Kletter, tempering her chamber-pop tendencies with a ragged, soulful edge.

Co-produced with power-pop godfather Mitch Easter, Motocaster's **Stay Loaded** is a whole lot of fun, although it's sometimes hard to tell if there are any real songs underneath the confusion. Falling somewhere between Sugar (without the terminal angst) and early Cheap Trick (without the killer hooks), Taylor and the rhythm section offer a smart person's version of heavy metal, echoing Jimi Hendrix on "Motorolla Blues," mixing big noise and Beatles inflections on "Farah" and ripping through a sleek boogie groove for "Uranus." Easter's Let's Active (whose onetime bassist Jon Heames drums and plays mellotron in Motocaster) probably would've sounded like this if he'd been less civilized.

Dish's **Boneyard Beach** is a whole 'nother thing, offering elegant, haunting melodies with nary a hint of excess sugar. Kletter's passionate yet polished singing—she contributed backing vocals to Hole's **Live Through This**—brings high drama to original tunes like the hypnotic "Wading" and "Headlights," which could have been lifted from Procol Harum's repertoire. Just in case anyone's tempted to use this accomplished work as background music, the quietly bitter "How Could Anyone" unleashes an extra-harsh put-down as Kletter sighs, through gritted teeth, "I see you barely polite to the people who are kind to you . . . I don't know anyone who could be what you are." Taylor's input surfaces in the twangy "Sad Figure" and a stunning, rip-roaring cover of the Dylan/Band tune "Tears of Rage," where he and Kletter blend their sweet'n'sour voices with thrilling results, much the way John Doe and Exene Cervenka do in X.

Before finding her voice in Dish, Kletter was one-third of Blackgirls, whose self-conscious, affected art-pop failed to find many admirers, despite the patronage of estimable folk-rock producer Joe Boyd. Taylor, a onetime member of nifty North Carolina R.E.M.-pop quartet Eight or Nine Feet (with future Motocaster bassist Brian Sliwa), first crossed professional paths with Kletter when he served briefly as Blackgirls' road manager. [jy]

See also *TPRG*.

DISJECTA

See *Seefeel*.

DISPOSABLE HEROES OF HIPHOPRISY

See *Spearhead*.

DISTORTED PONY

Work Makes Freedom EP (Bomp!) 1991
Punishment Room (Bomp!) 1993
Instant Winner (Trance Syndicate) 1994

The incessant ranting and lurching rhythms of Distorted Pony could throw even the most seasoned noise rider. Topped with tortured vocals, plus a Cop Shoot Cop–like assault on metal sheets and trashcans, the Los Angeles band spit a paralyzing quart of venom with every note. The focal point of Distorted Pony (which formed in 1986 and called it quits in '93) was Dora Jahr's seething bass and the mix of screeching guitars from David U and Robert Hammer, creating a din that most resembled the Big Black caterwaul of sound. Not surprisingly, Steve Albini was behind the production board on both Pony albums.

After a debut 7-inch, the group unleashed an ear-numbing barrage on the **Work Makes Freedom** EP. Despite the use of calculated grooves from a drum machine, each song bristles with angst and anguish, and each has its own approach to that end: the curdling haunt of "Forensic Interest," the pensive mood of "Blare" and the lightning speed of "Sinners Prayer," taken at twice the pace of most of Distorted Pony's deliberate rhythms.

Punishment Room was recorded as a quintet, with drummer London May (formerly of Dag Nasty and Samhain) adding an even more menacing force to the sound. Lyrics are as lewd as Dora's basslines: "Down Where the Dirt Collects," "Death in the Turnstile," "Castration Anxiety" are some of the indicative titles. The staccato rhythms become repetitive, but the band ventures melodies on a few tunes ("Krank," "Powerless"). Although a couple of tracks employ a slower, winding rhythm that's easier on the ears, they're no less heavy in tone than the pounding cuts.

Distorted Pony was already history by the time **Instant Winner** was released, but with proper live-fast-die-young spirit the album leaves one hell of an impressive corpse—it's easily the most potent of the three records. "Lamb Stink" and "Big Sprawling Corrupt" bring together all the band's strongest elements: chunky, churning grooves with a squeal of guitars and distraught vocals. The lyrics are as dense and bleak as ever. "Sparkle" offers "can't breathe or move my fingers/The wind won't blow in a roomful of windows . . . I see a smile and I see blood on your teeth/I see a sun and it's going to drown me." That call of distress proved to be the band's own eulogy. [mg]

DIVINATION

See *Bill Laswell*.

DJ KRUSH

Krush (Japan. Chance/Columbia) 1994
Strictly Turntablized (UK Mo Wax) 1994
Krush (Shadow/Instinct) 1995
Meiso (UK Mo Wax) 1995 (Mo Wax/ffrr) 1996

After forming the Krush Posse in 1987, Tokyo's DJ Krush made a name for himself in Japan as a solo artist with a number of jazz-based hip-hop singles, soundtrack remixes and compilation tracks. In the US, his imports helped inspire Guru's Jazzmatazz fusion; **Krush** and **Strictly Turntablized** make it clear his mix of turntable scratching and electronic sequencing with live instrumentation outstrips the efforts of other jazz/hip-hop hybridizers. Rather than simply juxtaposing horns with beats, Krush brings together the most adventurous aspects of hip-hop with the free-spiritedness of avant-garde jazz.

The American edition of **Krush** is a milestone, a dizzying collision of genres. The DJ improvises in a variety of jazz modes with trumpet players Kazufumi Kodama and Nobutaka Kuwabara, saxophonist Koichiro Samukawa, bassists Takeharu Hayakawa and Osamu Marumoto and pianist Ken Shima. "Roll & Tumble" begins with a hypnotic hip-hop beat and deep bass before stopping on a dime, then erupts into a trickling piano solo. "On the Dub-ble" adds dub bass to its mix of beats, scratching and muted Miles Davis–styled trumpet. "Into the Water" takes the Miles-like psychedelic influence even further into the mystic. The few vocal tracks—featuring Monday Michiru and Sonya Vallet—are reminiscent of Sade's cool, jazzy pop, but with more adventurous instrumentation. DJ Krush's potential impact on the future of electronic and DJ-based music cannot be overstated.

With much less of an explicit jazz element, **Meiso** involves such American notables as C.L. Smooth, Guru and the Roots to rap over the late-night beats. Still, it's Krush's show all the way. Whether behind them or on their own, his sensuous grooves—which calmly fold together Eastern and Western elements—are far more potent than any of the rhymes, opening the doors to further fascinating intercultural exploration of the space between foursquare hip-hop and floating ambient techno. [mrk/i]

DM3

See *Someloves.*

D.O.A.

Disco Sucks EP7 (Can. Sudden Death) 1978 (Can. Quintessence) 1978
Triumph of the Ignoroids EP (Can. Friend's) 1979
Something Better Change (Can. Friend's) 1980
Hardcore 81 (Can. Friend's) 1981
War on 45 (Alternative Tentacles) 1982
Bloodied but Unbowed (CD Presents) 1984 (Restless) 1992
Don't Turn Yer Back (on Desperate Times) EP (Alternative Tentacles) 1985
Let's Wreck the Party (Alternative Tentacles) 1985
True (North) Strong & Free (Rock Hotel/Profile) 1987
Murder (Restless) 1990
Talk Minus Action Equals Zero (Restless) 1990
The Dawning of a New Error (Alternative Tentacles) 1991
13 Flavours of Doom (Alternative Tentacles) 1992
It's Not Unusual . . . But It Sure Is Ugly! EP (Alternative Tentacles) 1993
Loggerheads (Alternative Tentacles) 1993
The Black Spot (Can. Essential Noise/Virgin) 1993

If the order of election to the punk-rock hall of fame were decided on the basis of unwavering dedication to both the elemental sound and the positive rebel spirit of loud-fast-rules, no band would have a right to stand ahead of Vancouver's D.O.A. in the induction ceremony. For the better part of two decades, singer/guitarist Joey (Shithead) Keithley (consistently spelled Keighley on early records) has led the band with a dedicated work ethic and a level head, ignoring all the stylistic detours that have tempted lesser men and rebuffing the creative exhaustion that comes from endless years of touring. That he has been rewarded for his efforts with little more than the respect of those in the know says a lot about the fact that punk-rock is, by definition, a marginal occupation, and that those who make millions from it aren't doing it right. Meanwhile, the D.O.A. family has suffered more than its share of personal tragedies, which underscores the obvious—that no amount of three-chord rip-and-run can slow the progress of real life, and that punk's uneasy adulthood is, after all, something of a willful illusion.

Formed in '77 as a trio of Shithead, drummer Chuck Biscuits and bassist Randy Rampage, D.O.A. (which has since seen many members come and go) took its cues from English and American punk archetypes, blasting away at a host of targets with simple, sneering energy. Although always clear and cogent in its potent aggression, D.O.A. didn't demonstrate any other distinctive features (employing the usual topics, familiar chord patterns), which makes the first records satisfying but unspectacular. **Bloodied but Unbowed** *(The Damage to Date: 1978–1983)* recapitulates that era in an exhilarating rush of shooting-gallery entertainment and rude fun; the '92 CD reissue tacks on all eight songs from the notably stronger and better-produced **War on 45.**

Two of the four Peel session tracks that compose the brief **Don't Turn Yer Back** EP reappear on **Let's Wreck the Party,** a great-sounding album that breaks ranks with a few slower tempos. (**The Dawning of a New Error** reissues that record, augmented with the rest of **Don't Turn Yer Back** and a bunch of early singles—thirty-three tracks in all.) **True (North) Strong & Free** lets a little more variety, humor and maturity into D.O.A.'s barbed-wire summer camp. "Lumberjack City," "51st State" and a cover of Bachman-Turner Overdrive's "Takin' Care of Business" balance out the harsher topics; for historical resonance, the quartet remakes "Nazi Training Camp," a song from its 1978 debut EP.

The politically charged but musically uninspired **Murder** finds a new guitarist (Chris Prohom) in place of stalwart Dave Gregg; otherwise, the most notable aspect of this high-octane/mid-tempo business-as-usual is the acknowledgment of Nelson Mandela's release (in a sore-throat rewrite of "The Midnight Special"). D.O.A. then moved to adjourn; a live album of the band's farewell show at a Vancouver club was released as **Talk Minus Action Equals Zero.** Keithley went so far as to form another group, the short-lived Joey Keithley's Instinct, but was soon back at the helm of D.O.A., joined by old bassist/singer Brian Roy Goble (ex-Subhumans) and new drummer Ken Jensen.

Produced by NoMeansNo's John Wright, **13 Flavours of Doom** relocates the spunk and inspiration absent from its slack predecessor. Leaving out the jokiness, Keithley takes his lyrical responsibilities seriously here. Thundering away with firm rhythm-guitar power (and some effective slide work) that favors the Dictators more than the Dead Boys, Keithley and Goble bellow and growl about governmental and economic injustice ("Death Machine," "Legalized Theft"), public health concerns ("Hole in the Sky," the safe-sex "Use Your Raincoat") and crud culture ("Beatin' Rock-'n'Roll to Death"). The guitarist even manages a sensitive acknowledgment of his own imperfections in "I Played the Fool." Wotta guy.

Back on the lighthearted side of the street, **It's Not Unusual** is an uneven five-song EP that merrily romps through the titular Tom Jones chestnut and follows it with "Dead Men Tell No Tales," a roaring but unintimidating vendetta against those who've crossed the band.

Although the booklet photo of D.O.A. (and a moosehead) in full-on Canuck regalia suggests producer Wright's mischievous influence might be affecting the band's course, **Loggerheads** stays on track with songs about North America's trade imbalance ("Logjam"), religious hypocrisy ("I See Your Cross"), conformity ("That Turbulent Uneasy Feeling"), welfare cheats ("Witch Hunt"), environmentalism (the intricate "The Only Thing Green") and urban decay ("I Can't Take Much More"). The absurdist society ball ("Cocktail Time in Hell") comes out of nowhere, but Keithley and co-writer Wright use it to get in digs at a long list of celebs. In line with the album's moderately elevated musical ambitions (and its producer's twisted sensibilities), the band caps it all with a mind-boggling, feedback-soaked, Melvins-speed Johnny Cash cover, "Folsom Prison Dirge," which is equally unprecedented.

Drummer Ken Jensen died in a fire at home in January '95; **The Black Spot**—recorded by Keithley, Goble and new guitarist/keyboardist Ford Pier with Wright sitting in on drums—is dedicated to his memory. Compounding the album's morbid gloom in the liner notes, Keithley eulogizes five other past bandmates (including drummer Ken Montgomery, better known as Dimwit) and associates who died in the '90s. Ironically (or maybe not), **The Black Spot** is the tautest, most precise and hard-edged of D.O.A.'s career. Spewing amplified energy, tight-formation fills, overdrive rhythms and anthemic punk choruses, the band wants only for conceptual focus in the songs. Three of Goble's songs describe a wacky perimeter: "Big Guys Like D.O.A." is a goofy ode to the band's fans, "Worries" obsesses over various anxieties and "Running Out of Time" delves deep into existential prognostication. Keithley's "Kill Ya Later" damns drug dealers, "Blind Men" bigots and "Je Declare" customs agents. "Marijuana Motherfucker" is a totally pointless David Peel joke, but a cowpunk cover of the Woody Guthrie–popularized "Bound for Glory" (the first of three linked songs—including the saw-wielding death-metal bluster of "Unchained Melody"—dubbed "The Nutwrencher Suite"), while used as a protest against reactionaries, sounds like nothing so much as a proud reaffirmation of the band's unflagging spirit. [i/jg]

See also *Jello Biafra, NoMeansNo; TPRG.*

DR. DRE

The Chronic (Death Row/Priority/Interscope) 1992
Concrete Roots (Hitman Music/Triple X) 1994

The auteur of one of the 1990s' most influential hip-hop albums, Dr. Dre (Andre Young) started out in the early '80s as a house-party/club DJ in South Central Los Angeles. He first attracted national attention as a rapper and producer in N.W.A, the group that introduced West Coast hardcore rap to America's mass market. Most listeners got their first taste of gangsta rap's profound nihilism on 1988's **Straight Outta Compton,** which contains "(Fuck) tha Police," N.W.A's most prescient and inflammatory moment: a tale of police brutality and civilian revolt that prefigured Rodney King, the city's riots and the nation's sudden awareness of the LAPD's racist habits.

In N.W.A, DJ Yella laid the foundation of punch-drunk backbeats and nearly forgotten funk samples; Ice Cube, MC Ren and the late Eazy-E looked at the streets around them and called it as they saw it. Dre provided the war-zone background noise—dicing and splicing sirens, gunshots and sinister keyboard creeps to intensify the tracks' grim realities.

N.W.A disbanded in 1990, freeing Dr. Dre to retreat behind the lines and pursue his career as a producer of such posse members as chanteuse Michel'le and rapper The D.O.C., as well as join forces with ex-UNLV football star Marion "Suge" Knight in the start-up of Death Row Records. Dre reemerged as an artist in 1991 on "Deep Cover," rapping with his young protégé, Snoop Doggy Dogg, on the movie soundtrack single. The song's languid edginess, driven by a compulsive piano loop and Snoop's nasal bite of police slang, offered a preview of the album that would follow a year later.

If N.W.A took gangsta rap off the streets and put it into the hands of record buyers, **The Chronic** took it to the next level—onto MTV and mainstream radio. Dre named his sound "G-funk," paying homage to George Clinton's P-Funk, which **The Chronic** liberally sampled. Sneakily menacing synth and loping rhythms snake under alternately sing-songy and hardcore raps—delivered by Dre, Snoop, The D.O.C. and a large crew of extras—in supremely insidious grooves. "Nuthin' but a 'G' Thang," "—— Wit Dre Day" and "Let Me Ride," are as danceable as they are complexly crafted, but all of Dre's production wizardry can't mask the nasty misogyny that is essential to his mythos. Dre lays it all bare on **The Chronic**'s unlisted finale, "Bitches Ain't Shit but Hoes and Tricks." (His no-contest plea to the 1991 beating charge of *Pump It Up* hostess Dee Barnes gave the lie to Dre's insistence that his gangsta persona is nothing but a pose created to sell his art.)

The Chronic's success exposed Dre to more than just scrutiny of his public misconduct; it also caused an exhumation of certain past accomplishments he would probably rather forget. **Concrete Roots** compiles some of his '80s work. With the exception of Michel'le's smooth kiss-off "No More Lies," the mostly sub–B-side cuts are a weak mix of filler and watered-down, post-disco rap from Dre and Yella's pre-N.W.A outfit, the oft-ridiculed and ridiculously attired World Class Wreckin' Cru'. Keep your money: there's good reason Dre didn't want you to know about this stuff. [nds]

See also *Eazy-E, N.W.A, Snoop Doggy Dogg.*

JOHN DOE

See *X.*

DOGBOWL & KRAMER

See *Kramer.*

DOME

See *Wire.*

DON CABALLERO

For Respect (Touch and Go) 1993
Don Caballero 2 (Touch and Go) 1995

Given indie-rock's need to scream, its reliance on simplicity and accessibility, its proponents' burning itch to express personalities, perambulate through obsessions and point fingers at various targets, instrumental music has rarely been the sound choice of the new generation. Outside the sphere of surf-rock nostalgists and space-rock prog noisemakers, the census of groups who make music that *could* support lyrics but choose not is growing but small. But it does include this Pittsburgh quartet named after Guy Caballero, the sleazy station owner Joe Flaherty played on SCTV.

Formed in '91 and artistically aligned with the rugged guitar aggression of bands like the Jesus Lizard, Helmet and Fugazi, but capable of great delicacy and restraint, Don Caballero—guitarists Ian Williams and Mike Banfield, drummer Damon Che (Fitzgerald, also the guitarist in The(e) Speaking Canaries) and a series of bassists—use ingenuity, muscle and a precise sense of rhythmic possibilities to easily sustain excitement for all thirty-eight nearly wordless minutes of **For Respect,** a bracing record produced—although you couldn't possibly know this from a visual inspection of the CD—by Steve Albini. Dynamic, driving, distorted and entirely free of indulgent improvisation, the eleven tracks—from the Melvins-like title cut to the ambling spareness of "Subdued Confections" and the frenzied vectors of "Belted Sweater"—underscore the value of talent in producing rugged instrumental music that's really saying something.

With a new bassist, a different producer (Al Sutton) and clearly expanded ambitions (four of the eight songs on the double album/single CD are around ten minutes long), Don Caballero cranked itself nearly off the meter; the second album is harsher, more chromatically and texturally challenging. Still tightly structured ("Repeat Defender" reveals serious King Crimson tendencies) but more open to daring discordance, sonic experimentation and meltdown cacophony, **Don Caballero 2** rewrites the book with enthusiastic determination. A good portion of "please tokio, please THIS IS TOKIO" is given over to a grinding, unyielding drone accented by what sounds like a power tool planing the guitar strings; "Dick Suffers Is Furious With You" builds on repetitive, honking animal imitations. But Don Caballero hasn't completely sacrificed its softer side to the gods of skronk, and the meditative "Cold Knees (in April)" suggests the sound of several thumb pianos, arranged by Philip Glass and fingered by Einstürzende Neubauten. [i]

See also *The(e) Speaking Canaries.*

DOO RAG

Chuncked and Muddled (Bloat) 1994
What We Do (Dependability) 1996

This Arizona duo plays electrified—and sometimes electrifying—Delta blues along the lines of modern-primitive roots duos Flat Duo Jets and the Chickasaw Mud Puppies. Featuring the virtuoso slide work of Bob Log (who sounds like Mississippi Fred McDowell after a few too many cups of coffee), the band updates its raw, vintage sound with Log's frenetic strumming and Thermos Malling's manic thrashing of his busker-style gut bucket and cardboard box percussion. Doo Rag also knows a thing or two about marketing: the debut album's enigmatic packaging, with no band photos or credits, only amplifies the false impression of poor white blues prodigies who've been locked up in an abandoned juke joint just a little too long.

With Log's authentic-sounding twangy hollering apparently funneled through a cheap bullhorn, **Chuncked and Muddled** runs down frantic takes on material associated with McDowell ("Train I Ride"), Sleepy John Estes ("Drop Down Baby") and Muddy Waters ("Can't Be Satisfied"), as well as a host of other reworked and retitled traditionals. The duo's lack of dynamic variation can get a bit tedious—especially on the CD, which has four extra tracks recorded "Live on Radio" (no further explanation given). But for the most part, Doo Rag excels at stripping some powerful music down to its primal essence, then blasting off on furious riff tangents that rock like a lifeboat in a hurricane. Pass the white lightning, please. [ma]

DOPES

Dawn of the Dopes (Unique) 1994

Kramer produced this rawly entertaining slab of energetic New York brat-rock that has its sonic roots in the raucous glory days of the Dead Boys, Pistols and Heartbreakers—and, intriguingly, the New York Dolls. The Dopes—a quintet plus utility infielder—sling hash like "Skeet Girl," "Copsucker," "W.D.O.P." ("White Dopes on Punk") and "Turnip Blue" with rude, merry abandon, backing their surly attitude with equally churlish smears of guitar aggro (by Pollen Dope and Toastie McDope) and the vocal posturing of singer Trick Fall. A couple of the tunes come dangerously close to aping '70s canon classics (and, in the case of "Amsterdam," the Jesus and Mary Chain), but the Dopes mess around too much to be efficient thieves, and the result is an enjoyably stupid jukebox that keeps mixing up the sounds of old records. [i]

DOUBLEHAPPYS

See *Straitjacket Fits.*

DOUBTING THOMAS

See *Skinny Puppy.*

DOWN

See *Pantera.*

DOWNY MILDEW

Downy Mildew EP (Texas Hotel) 1986
Broomtree (Texas Hotel) 1987 (High Street) 1993
Mincing Steps (Texas Hotel) 1988 (High Street) 1993
An Oncoming Train (High Street) 1992
Elevator EP (High Street) 1992
Slow Sky (High Street) 1994

Downy Mildew is one of those bands whose name approximates its sound, a sound that remains forever tied to a particular place and time: post-paisley underground Los Angeles in the R.E.M.-jangled '80s. To that basic psychedelifolk construction, the group adds large helpings of 4ADism, arriving at a drenched, delicate and beauteously murky brand of California goth-pop.

For a bunch of musicians so enamored of whispers, echoes and atmospheres, Downy Mildew is at its best stripped down. The oceanic wash of distorted guitar blasts, tensile lead lines and slow-building rhythmic crashes provides darkness and depth—but only when the songwriting is solid. On both **Broomtree** and **Mincing Steps,** that usually occurs when co-vocalist and guitarist Charlie Baldonado steps to the front. His skeletal acoustic-driven rockers ("Sally Pt. III," "Burnt

Bridges," "Tangled Ladders") offer a dash of verve and hookery amidst the crystalline instrumentation, while guitarist Jenny Homer's dreamy vocal support completes the band's hallmark yin/yang effect. Things get more tangled when the roles are reversed: Homer's best material ("The Kitchen," "Good Dream," both on **Broomtree**) stirs nicely, with a light and languid melodicism, but she also gets lost in abstract sonority and wandering introspection. Downy Mildew's lyrics are rarely an issue, since sonic ambience takes precedence over the wistful, naturalistic imagery. **Broomtree** is the better of the first two albums, and the High Street CD tacks on the four-song debut. **Mincing Steps** features strings (by the incoming Salvador Garza), a harder drummer (ex–Leaving Train John Hofer) and a more subdued art-folk feel, but the songwriting is not as strong.

Ending a gap interrupted only by one 7-inch for the punk label Triple X (produced by Andy Gill, of all people), the quintet reemerged on High Street, the singer/songwriter–oriented subsidiary of Windham Hill. Triple A (Album Adult Alternative) radio hadn't quite exploded yet, but that's the kind of niche both band and label must have been eyeing, and rightfully so. Unfortunately—or perhaps inevitably—**An Oncoming Train** has the impact of anything but. There's not a snappy song to be found, and the band's once-entrancing palette has been drained of its complexity and oddness. What's left are airy slow-tempo ditties (mostly sung by Homer) and plain-vanilla jangling and chirping. The **Elevator** EP culls one of the better album tracks and the A-side of the Triple X 45 ("Cool Nights") with two fine covers: a faithful, breathily choral take on Brian Wilson's "'Til I Die" and a wiry live version of Gil Scott-Heron's "Lady Day and John Coltrane."

Slow Sky, then, ranks as a full-on comeback. Perhaps the band was re-energized by its new rhythm section: bassist Janine Cooper, who came aboard when founding member Nancy McCoy was finally lost to motherhood, and drummer Rob Jacobs, who'd taken over from Hofer somewhere in the middle of the previous record. Or perhaps it's just the lilting songs, which, while still as precious as can be, are satisfyingly dramatic, with precise arrangements of ringing guitars, complementary vocals and somber strings (four additional players join violinist Garza). "Machine" is both ominous and shamelessly poppy, while slow tunes like "A Polka Dot-Scarved Woman" trade in opacity for bleakly gorgeous minimalism. Other standouts are Baldonado's haunting (and lyrically striking) "A Liar Needs a Good Memory" and Homer's first toe-tapper, the strumming and playful "Left Foot Down." [jc]

DRAIN

See *Butthole Surfers.*

DRAMARAMA

Comedy EP (Questionmark) 1984
Cinéma Vérité (Fr. New Rose) 1985
Box Office Bomb (Questionmark) 1987
Stuck in Wonderamaland (Chameleon) 1990
Live at the China Club EP (Chameleon) 1990
Vinyl (Chameleon/Elektra) 1991
The Days of Wayne and Roses (The Trash Tapes) (no label) 1992
Hi-Fi Sci-Fi (Chameleon/Elektra) 1993
Cinéma Vérité . . . Plus (Rhino) 1995
Box Office Bomb . . . Plus (Rhino) 1995
18 Big Ones: The Best Of (Elektra/Rhino) 1996

BENT-BACKED TULIPS

Looking Through . . . (Fr. New Rose) 1989 (eggBERT) 1995

Grounded in the timeless twin aesthetics of pop art and power-pop, Dramarama was nevertheless a star-crossed combo, out of synch with both the mainstream rock audience and the music business throughout its career. Formed in the basement of a collectors' record shop in Wayne, New Jersey, at the turn of the '80s, the band applied the brash energy of '70s punk and glitter-rock to the glamorous propulsion and romantic irony of David Bowie and the Velvet Underground. With the exception of the 1985 track "Anything, Anything (I'll Give You)," a modern-rock radio fave in LA for years, Dramarama never escaped the critical-acclaim ghetto. But it is a tribute to a potent sound and enthusiastic vision that Dramarama still sounds as fresh and sharp now as when it first emerged during the corporate-rock bloat of the mid-'80s.

Produced by bassist Chris Carter and singer/ songwriter John Easdale, **Cinéma Vérité** is an album of drawn-out vintage. Five tracks originally appeared on the **Comedy** EP, issued in 1984 on the band's own Questionmark label. One of those five numbers, a beautiful-loser's reading of the Velvets' "Femme Fatale," had first surfaced on Dramarama's '83 independent debut single. The other six songs were recorded after the French label New Rose commissioned a full-length album. For all its mixed parentage, though, **Cinéma Vérité** is an assured statement of refined style and desperate purpose. While Easdale's burnt-heart romanticism in songs like "Some Crazy Dame" and "Questions?" suggest Jonathan Richman by way of Raymond Chandler, the Britpop gleam and Jersey bar-band crackle in the guitars of Peter Wood and Mark Englert (aka Mr. E Boy) evoke the power-chord thrills of Mott the Hoople and the New York Dolls. And in "Anything, Anything (I'll Give You)," Dramarama bottle that contagious tension with car-radio finesse. (The 1995 Rhino reissue adds eight bonus tracks: demos and the two originals, "You Drive Me" and "A Fine Example," that appeared on the 1983 single.)

Dramarama's identification with the beautiful and the doomed intensifies on the prophetically titled **Box Office Bomb,** recorded after a move to Los Angeles. The cover model is actress Jayne Mansfield (on **Cinéma Vérité,** pride of place went to Warhol starlet Edie Sedgwick), "Spare Change" is lovingly modeled on the Stooges' kamikaze anthem "Search and Destroy" and the suffocating smog of broken promises and glittery jive in LA is perfectly captured with sunshine hooks and dark humor in "It's Still Warm." While **Box Office Bomb** suffers slightly from pressed-for-time-and-money production, "Modesty Personified" still has plenty of Blondiesque bite, and the sextet invigorates Easdale's vengeful frustration in "Whenever I'm With Her" ("Sorry I bit her . . .") with hothouse guitar drama. (**Box Office Bomb . . . Plus** has six bonus tracks: three demos, a B-side, a European track and an alternate version of "It's Still Warm.")

A spinning-wheel feeling characterizes **Stuck in Wonderamaland,** right from the opening sardonic strum'n'moan of "Wonderamaland." Note the literal echoes of Bob Dylan's acrid "It's Alright, Ma (I'm Only Bleeding)." Dramarama cranks up "Last Cigarette" with the bohemian garage-band attitude of **Cinéma Vérité;** Easdale nails his sense of stasis in grungy microcosm with an ode to late-night reruns, "70's TV." Too bad the album's engineer and co-producer Val Garay (Ringo Starr, the Motels) felt it necessary to streamline the life out of much of the material—good songs, cool cover choice (Mott's "I Wish I Was Your Mother"), but not enough grit to draw blood. The spitfire performances on the mini-album **Live at the China Club** (originally a promo disc entitled **Live in Wonderamaland**) show how the album might have sounded with its rough edges intact.

Dramarama recorded **Vinyl** under trying circumstances, temporarily replacing departed drummer Jesse (no surname) with Brian Macleod of Wire Train and session vet Jim Keltner. Midway through the sessions, the band's label declared bankruptcy (a distribution deal with Elektra saved the day). But Dramarama's dry wit and love of pop iconography remained intact. They welcomed the CD age with a record named after a vanishing species, 12-inch wax, and recruited former Rolling Stone Mick Taylor to play lead and slide guitar on the acerbic "Classic Rot." Spikier and more consistent than **Wonderamaland, Vinyl** juxtaposes sweet-'n'sour Beatle-isms ("What Are We Gonna Do?") with high-stepping paranoia ("I've Got Spies") and edgy psychedelia ("Tiny Candles").

The band broke up a year after the release of **Hi-Fi Sci-Fi,** but Dramarama went down fighting, with new drummer Clem Burke (ex-Blondie) jacking up the backbeat. **Hi-Fi Sci-Fi** is, in fact, Dramarama's tightest and hardest-rocking album. The toll of a decade's worth of bum luck and near-misses come to a boil on "Work for Food" and the slam-bam wakeup call "Don't Feel Like Doing Drugs"; even jangly melancholia like "Incredible" packs a subtle but memorable sting.

For a group that had so much trouble getting—and keeping—a major-label deal, Dramarama produced a high volume of worthy ephemera. **The Days of Wayne and Roses** is a fan-club CD of early demos and hip covers dating back to 1981; one song was actually cut in the basement of that Wayne, New Jersey, record store! (Eight of those tracks wound up among the bonuses appended to the two 1995 Rhino reissues.) The Bent-Backed Tulips release is a pseudonymous 1989 album, originally issued in Europe, containing eleven orphan tracks from the **Wonderamaland** era. The eggBERT CD version is fattened with nine additional cuts and there isn't a bummer in the whole bunch. File next to other worthy odds'n'sods classics like Elvis Costello's **Taking Liberties** and **The Great Lost Kinks Album.** [df]

DRINK ME

Drink Me (Bar/None) 1992
NYC EP (Hello Recording Club) 1994
Sleep (Bar/None) 1995

Toting a suitcase full of vaudevillian tricks and the endorsement of They Might Be Giants, Brooklyn's Drink Me indulges in the charm of animated ditties about singing clams, vocalizing trees, Grant's Tomb, barnacle-encrusted whales and comforting cups of coffee on its self-titled debut. Cherishing fragile creatures and passing moments of beauty ("St. Monday" simply recounts a daydream; "The Women" is a brief, tropical ode to femalekind), the duo—gangly Mark Amft (vocals, accordion, bass, slide guitar, ukulele) and guitarist Wynne Evans, joined on a few tracks by horn players—have an appropriately light, folky/jazzy coffeehouse touch that suits the simple songs but prevents the record from ever touching the ground.

With only accordionist Will Holshouser helping out, the urban-themed five-song EP (available only to subscribers of the Hello Recording Club) brings a tad more instrumental invention and vocal passion to Drink Me's recipe. "NYC" is a high-lonesome paean to the small pleasures of the band's hometown; the folky "Penthouse to Pavement," which convincingly sounds like a Depression-era original, takes life's elevator down in a cautionary tale; "42nd St." provides a jovial tour of the Deuce. Drink Me's timelessness is its best feature, and the group dislocates itself here in the best possible way.

The understated duo also fares well on **Sleep,** a vividly entertaining set of intimate chanteys for breakfast and fireside. Pairing sparse jugband doo-dads and autoharp with Evans' acoustic guitar, Amft casts himself in the role of whimsical sad sack for "Ladies Underwear" and "Tiny Saxophone," flexing his rubber voice to coo and yelp the role impeccably. Bluesy ballads like "Sugar Lump-Lump" (also on **NYC**) tug at the heartstrings as Amft's tender personification of a barfly enlivens a lovely hard-luck lullaby. A subtle and silly turnaround of James Brown's "I Got You (I Feel Good)" blends in beautifully, proving Drink Me's semi-antiquated act to be airtight. [i/ic]

DRIP TANK

Slake (Headhunter/Cargo) 1992
Sprawl (Headhunter/Cargo 1994

While this San Diego quartet might be best known around Southern California for initiating a live tour of 7-Eleven stores, the band's got no other gimmicks (unless breaking up counts: Drip Tank called it quits in 1995). As one contributor to the city's early-'90s renaissance, the group followed a series of singles and compilation appearances with **Slake,** an invigorating if uneven debut. The dozen songs' strength includes solid pop dynamics and excellent dual-guitar work by Julie D. and Joel Nowak, but **Slake,** for all its fun, lacks focus and rambles stylistically. In its best moments, Drip Tank delivers angular punk-pop reminiscent of the Fastbacks and, not surprisingly, local mates like aMINIATURE (whose John Lee assisted in **Slake**'s recording).

Drip Tank burned through a handful of drummers between records, but still managed to prepare an improved, confident effort for **Sprawl.** On this darker, deeper collection of better-written material, Julie and Nowak deliver more complex moods with their sly, sinewy guitar interplay. Drive Like Jehu drummer Mark Trombino's engineering helps—instead of sounding offhand, Drip Tank sounds intense and brooding. The record title was inspired in part by a Sonic Youth song of the same name, and Drip Tank reflects the influence of that group and such related phenomena as Live Skull and Band of Susans. Julie D. left in 1995 to join a promising all-female quartet, Chinchilla, and Drip Tank broke up. [mww]

DRIVE LIKE JEHU

See *Rocket From the Crypt.*

DRIVIN' N' CRYIN'

Scarred but Smarter (688) 1986 (Island) 1989
Whisper Tames the Lion (Island) 1988
Mystery Road (Island) 1989
Fly Me Courageous (Island) 1991
Live on Fire EP (Island) 1991
Build a Fire EP (UK Island) 1991
Smoke (Island) 1993
Wrapped in Sky (DGC) 1995

KEVN KINNEY/FRANK FRENCH

Everything Looks Better in the Dark (Twilight) 1987

KEVN KINNEY

MacDougal Blues (Island) 1990
Down Out Law (Mammoth) 1994

KATHLEEN TURNER OVERDRIVE

Kathleen Turner Overdrive (Booger's Banquet) 1994

TOENUT

Information (Mute) 1994

Atlanta's Drivin' n' Cryin' (also Drivin-N-Cryin) isn't an easy band to classify. The group delves into folk and bluegrass as easily as it kicks out gritty guitar rock. It's Lynyrd Skynyrd and Hank Williams, R.E.M. and Bob Dylan. It's Lollapalooza *and* H.O.R.D.E. It's eclectic—in other words, a marketing mess, which is why the group has wallowed on modern rock's second tier, never fully embraced by any particular audience despite a succession of engaging records.

The first three albums are exploratory ventures—stylistically and sonically—building up gradually from the lo-fi demo ambience of **Scarred but Smarter. Fly Me Courageous** became the band's moment of near universal appeal, and with good reason. The band expanded from a trio to a quartet (singer/guitarist Kevn Kinney, bassist Tim Nielsen, drummer Jeff Sullivan and new guitarist Buren Fowler) on **Mystery Road,** and **Fly Me Courageous** pulls together all of the sonic strings explored on the previous releases. The result is mostly raging hard rock—"Lost in the Shuffle," "Around the Block Again," "Rush Hour," "Chain Reaction," the foot-stompin' "Build a Fire" and the endlessly riffing title track, which became a battle anthem for pilots in the Persian Gulf War. **Fly Me Courageous** isn't all crank, though; "For You" is gentle, chiming folk, while the country gait of "Let's Go Dancing" echoes Tom Petty's solo work. The **Live on Fire** EP is an equally spirited affair, featuring the album track and hot performances of three older songs.

Reaction was so strong to the harder edge of **Fly Me Courageous** that Drivin' n' Cryin' mistakenly threw itself almost wholly in that direction on **Smoke.** Ironically, the album's best tracks are its few toned-down interludes: the one-guitar "What's the Difference," the spare bits of the ruinous "Patron Lady Beautiful" and the bluesy acoustic "When You Come Back." Otherwise, **Smoke** is an anonymous, undistinctive arena rock outing.

The group then took a break, lost Fowler and regrouped on a new label for **Wrapped in Sky.** The trio shoots wide this time out, capturing its broad stylistic ambitions better than on any other album. "Pura Vida," "Light" and the dramatic "Silence of Me" maintain the rock quotient in one late-album swoop, but they're counterbalanced by the jazzy gentleness of the title track, the acoustic chime of "Indian Song" and "Telling Stories," the easygoing twang of "Leader the Follow" and the Latin flavor of "Señorita Louise." Adjunct keyboardist Joey Huffman's textures are a valuable new contribution, and Kinney mines the group's new soundscape for thoughtful ruminations about Native Americans ("Indian Song"), self-determination ("Saving Grace," "Light," "Leader the Follow") and the loss of virginity ("Silence of Me").

Kinney is the group's most prolific solo artist, though none of his three outings are as satisfying as any of the band's. **Everything Looks Better in the Dark** is essentially a 1985 demo tape, remixed for release after the group began its ascent. **MacDougal Blues** has the best songs and benefits from R.E.M. guitarist Peter Buck's sympathetic production and accompaniment; **Down Out Law** is also quiet and acoustic, an almost desperate reaction to **Smoke**'s heaviness. (Most ingenuous song title: "A Beatnik Haight Street Kerouacian Ripoff in E.") Bassist Tim Nielsen and drummer Jeff Sullivan are players rather than leaders in their non-Drivin' projects: the brilliantly named Kathleen Turner Overdrive (in which Nielsen served for a time) plays fiery, energetic punk, while Toenut (Sullivan's hobby) favors an artier kind of noise that blends dense ambience with screeching vocals. [gg]

See also *TPRG.*

PETE DROGE

Necktie Second (American) 1994

PETE DROGE & THE SINNERS

Find a Door (American) 1996

After honing his chops playing punk in Seattle's March of Crimes (which also contained future Soundgarden bassist Ben Shepherd), singer/guitarist/pianist Pete Droge relocated to Portland, Oregon, where he became one of the better finds in the '90s A&R scrounge for neo-folk artists. Entering the fray as a northwestern troubadour who could easily be mistaken for Tom Petty's bastard son, Droge tips a retrospective nod to '70s boy-rock on **Necktie Second,** updating the genre with a bit of humor on "If You Don't Love Me (I'll Kill Myself)" and reviving the decade's songwriting heyday with the slick folk-pop of "Northern Bound Train." "Straylin Street" follows the same easy-flowing and catchy vibe. "Two Steppin Monkey" takes on corporate culture (although Droge's sniping lacks venom), while "Dog on a Chain" stretches out languorously. Fleshed out by producer/organist Brendan O'Brien and a couple of pals, **Necktie Second** is a quiet, smart backdrop for adult cocktail parties. [vg]

DROP ACID

See *7Seconds.*

DROP NINETEENS

Delaware (Caroline) 1992
Your Aquarium EP (Caroline) 1993
National Coma (Caroline) 1993

HOT ROD

Speed Danger Death (Caroline) 1993

As originally constituted, Boston's Drop Nineteens was able to explore and expound on many forms of indie-rock beauty. With three guitarists (Paula Kelley,

Greg Ackell and Motohiro Yasue) and two lead vocalists (Kelley and Ackell) on hand for **Delaware,** the quintet demonstrates real facility for ragged shoegazer woozenoise pop ("Reberrymemberer," the lengthy instrumental-plus-recitation "Kick the Tragedy") as well as breezy acoustic love-rock ("My Aquarium," "Baby Wonder's Gone"), mid-range Dinosaur Youth aggression ("Winona," "Delaware") and harmony-strung distortion atmospherics ("Happen"). Throughout, finely wrought melodies, airy vocals and a deft feel for textures and dynamics make every moment as disquietingly fetching as the pistol-packing waif pictured on the album cover. Topping off their alluring first-time-out achievement, the Nineteens manage a wry grin (rocking out Madonna's "Angel" and stringing together Edie Van titles for "Ease It Halen"), pricking a good-sized hole in the velvet firewall of detached seriousness shielding many groups that let their distortion pedals do the talking.

The EP contains two versions of "My Aquarium," a casually crummy cover of Barry Manilow's "Mandy" and two new originals: the evocatively undulating "Nausea" and Ackell's surprisingly thin "Movie."

When next heard from, the Drop Nineteens was an almost completely different band. With Kelley gone off to lead her own Hot Rod and the other two just gone, only Ackell and bassist Steve Zimmerman remain. Producing themselves and drafting three replacements to fill the leavers' instrumental roles (including neophyte guitarist/singer Megan Gilbert as the new Kelley), the pair made **National Coma,** an indistinct indie-rock drag that exhibits substantial effort in the writing of offbeat lyrics but doesn't try hard enough to shape the music into any particular or compelling style. Gone are the expansive distortion paintings and the acoustic schoolyard exercises; the electric guitar aggression is snarlier, used to scratch out jagged edges rather than heap on mounds of cotton wool. **National Coma** would have been a promising debut; as a sophomore album, it's a disappointing setback. And that was enough: Ackell and drummer Pete Koeplin went on to form a new trio, Fidel.

Surprisingly, Hot Rod's **Speed Danger Death** is a Juliana Hatfield soundalike. Joined by a drummer, bassist and guitarist, Kelley copies the other's melodic habits and coquettish vocal mannerisms on conceptually kindred songs like "Liar's Lady," "Candy Star" and "Perplexed," delivered in alternately gentle and fervid electro-pop arrangements. Taken on its own terms, **Speed Danger Death** is a perfectly pleasing blend of sweet and salty—a quintessential rush of modern New England power-pop, but it's hard to hear it without flashing on **Hey Babe,** and that takes some of the fun out of the ride. [i]

DROWN

Hold on to the Hollow (Elektra) 1994

The short scoop on this Southern California quartet's freshman effort is **Pretty Hate Machine**–era Nine Inch Nails fronted by Henry Rollins. **Hold on to the Hollow,** which was produced by Dave Ogilvie, is so chock full of imitation it should come with a list of ingredients. In fairness, there are some tiny twists. The opening track, "I Owe You," is peppered with just a tad of eastern folk influence; in fact, the song almost works until singer Lauren Boquette abandons his advisedly low-key intro for an unforgivable Rollins-like rant. From there on, the floodgates are open, and the Henry roast begins. "What It Is to Burn" is so miserable that one wishes Boquette would change the song's refrain "I know I wasn't ready" to "I'm a liar" and just get it the hell over with. There's a ray of hope in "Longing," but the slightly engaging piece of ambience is nearly destroyed by Boquette's sloppy, insincere attempt to expose his inner pain. Wipe the singer off "Lost" and emasculate the song's Metallica-like transitional guitar work, and there might be something reparable left. Trash the rest. [icm]

DRUGSTORE

Drugstore (Honey/Go! Discs/London) 1995

Drugstore kicks off its debut album with "Speaker 12," a letter-and-attitude-perfect imitation (but for the breathy enthusiasm of Brazilian-born bassist Isabel Monteiro's singing) of old three-chord Jesus and Mary Chain singles, but then has a struggle to better the seductive charm of that track on the thirteen that follow. (Although the sizzling stutter of "Fader" comes close.) The London trio brings a bit more to the counter than just a familiar prescription, but the dance beats, wispy melodies and sudden landslides of Daron Robinson's guitar distortion make it hard to hear much originality here. Monteiro's songs occasionally venture beyond the sound of re-Reidings, or, at least, the arrangements do: the gentle piano tinkles of "If," the surly Cramps kick of "Devil," the Liz Phair–like spareness of "Saturday Sunset" and the building drama of "Baby Astrolab" are good cases in point. Still, Drugstore keeps returning to the reliable J&M home remedy. Things could be worse. [i]

DRYWALL

See *Stan Ridgway.*

DUB NARCOTIC SOUND SYSTEM

Hands on the Dial [tape] (Punk in My Vitamins?) 1994
Industrial Breakdown EP (Soul Static Sound/K) 1995
Rhythm Record Vol. One: Echoes From the Scene Control Room (K) 1995
Ridin' Shotgun EP (K) 1995
Boot Party (K) 1996
Ship to Shore EP (K) 1996

DEAD PRESIDENTS

Spread Butter EP (K) 1995

With Beat Happening on hiatus in the mid-'90s, melodica master Calvin Johnson apparently developed a consuming interest in dub. His Dub Narcotic Sound System made its first appearances on a series of "disco plates," singles that took dub's idea of on-the-cheap, one-take production—toasting over a prefabricated but funky backing track and a disassembled dub version slapped on the B-side—and applied them to rock, or at least something distinctly not reggae. (Dubmeister Johnson has also given the treatment to tracks by the Make-Up, the Jon Spencer Blues Explosion and his own Halo Benders, among others.) The six-track **Hands on the Dial** cassette is almost entirely dub-plus-toast versions of the first few singles, including a couple of variations on the "Fuck Shit Up" groove called "Sock the Monkey," "Boot the Monkey" and so forth. Enjoyable, if not necessary.

The **Industrial Breakdown** EP couples two versions of the title track ("We've got the tools to reclaim the sound," Johnson intones) with a couple of instrumental dubs and "Typecast Sanction," a variation on the new segment Dub Narcotic added to its remix of the Blues Explosion's "Soul Typecast." **Echoes From the Scene Control Room,** Dub Narc's first full-length release, is—of course—available only on vinyl, in a great fake old-time-dub sleeve. It's mostly instrumental (including cool melodica showcases) and again confines itself mostly to backing tracks the group has already used elsewhere—why mess with a durable groove? "Bite Attack" drops the vocal out of the single "Bite," leaving virtually nothing but a stark drum pattern, and the brilliant "Respirator Version" slows "Industrial Breakdown" down to half-speed and overlays it with somebody breathing through a respirator. **Ridin' Shotgun** is Dub Narcotic's only weak record so far: three fairly dull grooves recorded in Memphis, each in vocal and instrumental versions.

Turning down the echo and laying off the controls for whole spells of the album, the relaxed and joyously sweet **Boot Party** is, overall, less dubby and more funky. When not delving deep into the usual sorts of ambient studio trickery, the songs hit a '60s R&B stride, bathing in the stoned soul picnic ambience with uplifting spirit. "Monkey Hips and Rice" and the extended "Shake-a-Puddin' " are absolute charmers. Lois Maffeo contributes guest vocals. Her role in the venture was subsequently increased; the seductive and surprisingly slick '96 **Ship to Shore** EP grants Lois featured billing and pictures her on its cover.

For Dub Narcotic tours, Johnson has used members of the Dead Presidents, a bi-racial hip-hop crew (with a live band) from Washington. Despite a few great throwaway lines (like one about "bell hooks and Gwendolyn Brooks," and the hook that goes "the only good president is a dead one"), the **Spread Butter** 12-inch—two songs, nine mixes, including a couple of hep Johnson dubs—is by-the-numbers '93-style hip-hop in the vein of Brand Nubian or lesser Black Sheep. [ddw/i]

See also *Beat Happening, Halo Benders.*

DUDE OF LIFE WITH PHISH

See *Phish.*

ANNE DUDLEY AND JAZ COLEMAN

See *Killing Joke.*

DUET EMMO

See *Wire.*

DUH

See *Steel Pole Bath Tub.*

DUKES OF STRATOSPHEAR

See *XTC.*

DUMP

See *Yo La Tengo.*

JOHN DUNBAR

See *A Confederacy of Dunces.*

SLIM DUNLAP

The Old New Me (Medium Cool/Twin\Tone) 1993
Times Like This (Medium Cool/Restless) 1996

Minneapolis guitarist Slim Dunlap was always a square peg in the Replacements. Arriving in 1987 to replace wildman Bob Stinson (who died in early '95), Dunlap was quiet, shy and reliable, a steady instrumental hand, not a raver. To all appearances, he contributed little beyond sideman skill to the group as it slouched toward Paul Westerberg's solo career. So it's a surprise to hear him rise to the occasion of his post-Mats debut with plenty of personality and a full-on collection of original rock songs.

Singing **Exile**-era Stones melodies in a pleasantly artless voice that could pass for Keith Richards on a good night, Dunlap chugs back raunch-a-roll energy with earnest effort and an invigorating dose of retro flair. Lyrically, he wavers between good-ol'-boy journeyman mundanity ("Rockin Here Tonight," "Just for the Hell of It," "The Ballad of the Opening Band"), roughed-up reflection ("Taken on the Chin," "Partners in Crime") and back-of-the-bar social navigation ("Ain't Exactly Good," which critiques a pal's musical efforts with poorly disguised disdain). Making no effort to claim any glory from his old group (although Westerberg does guest), Dunlap keeps things simple, modest and real, closing the door with an atmospheric thirty-year-old James Burton guitar instrumental, "Love Lost." More please. [i]

DURAN DURAN

Duran Duran (Harvest) 1981 (Capitol) 1983
Rio (Harvest) 1982
Seven and the Ragged Tiger (Capitol) 1983
Arena (Capitol) 1984
Notorious (Capitol) 1986
Big Thing (Capitol) 1988
Decade (Capitol) 1989
Liberty (Capitol) 1990
Duran Duran (Capitol) 1993
Thank You (Capitol) 1995

The **Decade** singles compilation should have capped it for the glamour boys of England's new romantic pop—after all, the Birmingham quintet's fabled hybrid of the Sex Pistols and Chic had lost its flavor and elasticity by the third album, and the group had to coast through the decade on weenybop fame and jetset notoriety.

Nonetheless, Simon Le Bon, Nick Rhodes and John Taylor kept at it, joined by replacement guitarist Warren Cuccurullo and drummer Sterling Campbell (later of Soul Asylum). A mishmash of funk, soul, rock, disco and found-sound sampling by the confused new lineup, **Liberty** is easy on the ears but completely vapid (and that's saying something for Duran Duran), as mentally stimulating as a sixty-cycle hum. If ever a record sounded like a group had gone past its extinct-by date, this is it.

For three years, that was that. Then, in '93, Duran Duran (minus Campbell) reappeared on the runway with **Duran Duran** (unofficially known as **The Wedding Album** for its nuptial cover art, not any John'n'Yoko references), a pretentious topical travesty that, despite its obvious awfulness, rehabilitated the group's commercial fortunes. Another shallow display of mindless eclecticism, the album shuttles wearily among Duran's old dreamy swish ("Ordinary

World"), faux-rap techno-slam ("Drowning Man"), soulful British dance-rock ("Come Undone"), Madonna gospel disco ("None of the Above") and Princely funk ("UMF," "Shelter"). At its most outrageous, Simon Le Bon duets with Brazilian singer Milton Nascimento ("Breath After Breath"), staking a thoroughly bogus claim to multi-culturalism. Likewise, the lyrics stick Duran's nose in some unlikely places: "Sin of the City" is a surprisingly literal attack on the landlords of New York's Happyland social club (where eighty-seven people died in a 1990 fire), expressing enough outrage to suggest a personal stake in the tragedy. "Too Much Information," however, takes on a more obvious issue for the video-savvy media slaves: "Destroyed by MTV/I hate to bite the hand that feeds me so much information." The band's rendition of "Femme Fatale" is overheated, but Lou Reed's song is evidently indestructible.

Not content to leave it at that, Duran jumped whole hog onto the covers-album bandwagon, recording **Thank You,** one of the worst such endeavors released by name-brand artists during the mid-'90s vogue for such things. When not attempting to copycat classic-rock originals like the Doors' "The Crystal Ship," and Led Zeppelin's "Thank You," the quartet (aided by every spare drummer on the planet) demonstrates its arrogant misapprehension of rap (besides Public Enemy's "911 Is a Joke," they take a crack at Grandmaster Melle Mel's "White Lines," a raucously rocked-up extravaganza on which the rapper redoes his own rhyme, with Grandmaster Flash scratching and other members of the Furious Five adding backing vocals). Duran Duran also makes a point of proving its lack of soul (Sly Stone's "I Wanna Take You Higher," the Temptations' "Ball of Confusion") and inadequacy for reinventing the work of real songwriters (Elvis Costello's "Watching the Detectives," Bob Dylan's "Lay Lady Lay"). [i]

See also *TPRG.*

DUST BROTHERS

See *Chemical Brothers.*

DWARVES

Horror Stories (Voxx) 1986
Toolin' for a Warm Teabag (Nasty Gash) 1988
Astro Boy EP7 (Sub Pop) 1990
Blood Guts & Pussy (Sub Pop) 1990
Lucifer's Crank EP7 (No. 6) 1991
Thank Heaven for Little Girls (Sub Pop) 1991
Sugarfix (Sub Pop) 1993

SUBURBAN NIGHTMARE

A Hard Day's Nightmare (Midnight) 1985

SPECULA

Erupt (Scat) 1995

BLAG DAHLIA

Venus With Arms EP (Atavistic) 1995

Proponents of an extremist wing of the less-is-more school of thought, the Dwarves have wreaked much underground havoc with highly confrontational (often blood-soaked) live sets that are over in ten minutes and "longplayers" of acute political incorrectness that don't last even twice that. If there weren't so much action here—imagine watching *The Evil Dead* on fast-forward—these San-Francisco-via-Chicago neo-punks might be just another bunch of exhibitionists.

The Dwarves downplay the existence of **Horror Stories,** which, all things considered, is solid reasoning. Captured in transition from teen Zappaphiles (originally known as Suburban Nightmare) to circus-freak speedballers, the quartet strains against the flower-power leash, but never manages to break free. What followed, however, is a metamorphosis as ungodly as any in the annals of rock'n'roll. **Toolin' for a Warm Teabag** lasts but nine minutes, but that's enough time for the Dwarves to slash through seven post-hardcore incantations ("Free Cocaine," "Let's Get Pregnant" and so forth) that effectively exorcise any prior embarrassments.

You might think that **Blood Guts & Pussy**'s title (along with the calculated offense of a cover that depicts two lithe young women and a rabbit-toting male dwarf, all nude and drenched in type-O claret) tells you all you need to know about the disc. Think again. Unexpectedly tight and musicianly (especially guitarist He Who Cannot Be Named), the Dwarves reveal themselves as informed pop students. Pushed along by the yammering vocals of Blag Jesus (aka Julius Seizure), these eleven tracks (fifteen minutes this time) are constantly on the verge of falling apart, but that somehow translates into immensely powerful forward propulsion. The CD includes two non-LP tracks from the 7-inch **Astro Boy.** The **Lucifer's Crank** 7-inch compiles seven alternate takes of songs from the past three records, plus a devolved obliteration of Red Crayola's "Hurricane Fighter Plane."

The water-treading **Thank Heaven for Little Girls** (which mercifully bypasses the potential sleeve transgressions offered by the title, settling for a tattooed tyke) comes as a bit of a disappointment: by trading the funnycar frenzy for a more lucid metal-punk sound, the band loses half the battle. **Sugarfix** cedes the war. Newly-pseudonymized Blag Dahlia pauses to offend only rarely (although "Smack City" is pretty funny), while the band chugs along at barely over the speed limit. The inner-sleeve art memorializes the wrestling-mask-wearing He Who Cannot Be Named, who was alleged to have been stabbed to death in Philadelphia earlier that year. It turned out to be a particularly intricate publicity stunt, and the end of the line for the band, which was dropped by an embarrassed and incensed Sub Pop in its aftermath.

Specula teams ex-Dwarves drummer Sigh Moan with the equally dopily named Specter Spec for a Big Black–inspired assault on classic rock structure. On **Erupt,** the gonzo duo splinters hard rock into jigsaw-puzzle-size shards, reassembling it on a bed of genetically altered drum loops. Whether grinding out Alice Cooper–tinged glam ("Desolation Nightmare") or fashioning stoner ballads ("Hello Pain"), Specula keep as firm a grip on irony as on their bongs. [dss]

See also *TPRG.*

DYLANS

Godlike EP (Beggars Banquet/RCA) 1991
The Dylans (Beggars Banquet/RCA) 1991
Grudge EP (UK Beggars Banquet) 1994
Spirit Finger (Beggars Banquet/Atlantic) 1994

The Dylans' flower-power pop offers little clue to the point of the group's name; all they share with

Robert Zimmerman is the undefined spirit of the '60s. Formed in Sheffield, England, in 1988, the quintet, led by singer/guitarist/bassist Colin Gregory and guitarist Jim Rodger, took the blueprint of groups like the Soft Boys and The Teardrop Explodes and used it to build an acid house with a strong song foundation. Unfortunately, the Dylans were caught in an unreceptive era between their precursors and the later commercial breakthrough of Oasis, Blur and Supergrass.

The four-track **Godlike** EP introduces the band in a beckoning swirl of Moody Blues harmonies, Byrdsy guitars and subtle grooves. The densely produced songs have busy arrangements but boast a certain liquidity. "My Hands Are Tied" has a nicely ascending chorus, but the other songs blur together.

Having dropped their musical acid, the Dylans needed to get moving on their trip, which they did on **The Dylans.** The harmonies sparkle like psychedelic Stones, and songs like the opening "She Drops Bombs" have the melodic sinew to justify the Dylans' nostalgia. "Planet Love" boasts seamless, echoed vocals and an unfolding hook; even a tune like "Sad Rush on Sunday," with its cock-rock chord changes, does something undeniably fresh and catchy.

Produced by Pascal Gabriel, **Spirit Finger** achieves a remarkable synthesis of power-pop and psychedelia, an early herald of Britain's imminent '60s-pop revival. Combining fuzzy guitars, stinging choruses and effects-laden vocals, the sextet proves that psychedelic bubblegum still hasn't lost its flavor. The album recalls the Soft Boys, Dukes of Stratosphear, The Teardrop Explodes—even early Pink Floyd. "Smarter Than You" begins with a slight concession to American alternarock, then leaves its grunge cocoon to becomes a pop butterfly of amazing sonic color. "Hell No" isn't only a frank response to a lover's insatiable demands—in the Dylans' resin-stained vision, it becomes druggy power pop. "Get It Together" and "Live in the Now" further serve to lace the band's benign nostalgia with a potent sprinkling of '60s truisms; "Two Tomorrows" doubles the psychedelic dosage of vintage John Lennon and "Kill Rave" shows the group's disdain for the trendy dance subculture.

The EP contains **Spirit Finger**'s "Grudge" and "Wise Bird," adding a pair of self-produced new tunes: "Nerve Hutch" and "Particle Ranch." Although they're overlooked now, it's likely that someday people will be looking for the new Dylans. [jo]

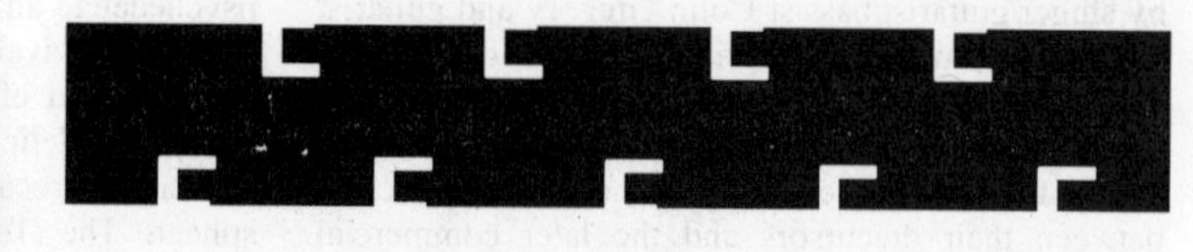

MARK E

See *Unrest.*

EARTH

Extra-Capsular Extraction (Sub Pop) 1991
Earth 2 Special Low Frequency Version (Sub Pop) 1993
Phase 3: Thrones and Dominions (Sub Pop) 1995
Pentastar: In the Style of Demons (Sub Pop) 1996

Although Earth's Dylan Carlson gained some degree of infamy for his role in arming longtime pal Kurt Cobain, the Washingtonian deserves far more credit for his efforts in dismantling rock music. Carlson's blueprint seems to have been (a) remove the rock and then (b) remove the music. Everything that's left went into the making of Earth, a "band" that expends more effort redefining notions of time and space than it does working out anything as trivial as songs or chords. Suddenly, the brown acid seems like a pretty good idea after all.

If you use it as incidental music (which it actually can serve as), the three-song, thirty-five-minute **Extra-Capsular Extraction** could pass for a particularly amorphous Melvins outing, replete with warily circling riffs and grinding, uni-directional riffs that operate at two speeds—glacial and stationary. Cobain makes a cameo (as do Melvins' then-bassist Joe Preston and Dickless/Teen Angels singer Kelly Canary), and the wordless, textural wails he discharges into the maelstrom hammered out by Carlson and bassist Dave Harwell resound eerily and tenuously beneath the grind.

Earth 2 denudes the musical beast even further. The three pieces—totaling nearly seventy-five minutes—spread horizontally rather than building vertically, taking on a character not unlike La Monte Young's protracted pieces. To that end, the individual listener can take an active role in altering exactly what he or she hears with only minor mental exertion, delving into (or totally ignoring) the multiple, constantly shifting overtones that lie beneath what seems like an undifferentiated throb on "Like Gold and Faceted," which does with low-frequency guitar tones what Tibetan throat-singers do with their voices. The comparison isn't so far-fetched: despite the intensity in the grooves, **Earth 2** is actually quite soothing—ambient, even—for those willing to surrender to it.

After that, the most rational progression for Earth would have been the creation of a single woofer-annihilating tone. Unfortunately, logic lost out: Harwell departed and Carlson devolved, surrounding himself with rock musicians in order to make rock records. Yawn. [dss]

EARWIG

See *Insides.*

EASTER MONKEYS

See *Pere Ubu.*

EAST RIVER PIPE

Point of Memory [tape] (Hell Gate) 1990
I Used to Be Kid Colgate [tape] (Hell Gate) 1991
Goodbye California (UK Sarah) 1993
Poor Fricky (UK Sarah) 1994 (Merge) 1995
Shining Hours in a Can (Ajax) 1994
Mel (Merge) 1996

Fred M. Cornog, who records under the *nom de 8-track* East River Pipe, is a lo-fi auteur by dint of circumstance alone. Despite its low-budget setting, his opulent pop is more in line with Brian Wilson's isolationist period—or even Phil Spector's monomania—than any contemporary bedsit poet. Not that he isn't given over to personal catharsis: Cornog's tortured adolescence was scarring enough that rather than lead him to more typical grad-school enmity, it dropped him to rock bottom. Homeless and alcoholic, he ended up living in the Hoboken train station at one point—an experience he never explicitly addresses as East River Pipe, but that colors much of Cornog's work.

The fifteen-song **Shining Hours in a Can,** which collects several years' worth of singles released on Hell Gate, a label operated out of an Astoria, Queens, apartment by Cornog and his companion, Barbara Powers, can be seen as either an unbroken wash of melancholy beauty or an elaborate construct of pop impressions, each more soul-stirring than the one before. The autumnal "Make a Deal With the City" (1993) exudes eloquent resignation; "Axl or Iggy" (1991) brings genuine pathos to the notion of pursuing the rock-star myth. Considering that Cornog crafted these songs alone in a "studio" that takes up one corner of his living room, they're invested with a remarkable lushness. **Poor Fricky** stays the course both in medium (that home studio again) and message (there's beauty to be found in the most unanticipated places). From the pastel-dyed pony depicted on the cover to the beaten-but-not-broken tone that seeps from the dreamy "Bring on the Loser" and "Here We Go," Cornog will make you think twice about the things (and people) that fall between the cracks. [dss]

EAT

Sell Me a God (Fiction) 1989
Epicure (UK Fiction) 1993 (Fiction/November) 1994

Sell Me a God, this grossly underappreciated London quintet's first album, is a collection of spaghetti western metal and bluesy funk that pegged them as swamp rockers with an unstoppable groove. But misfortune frowned upon Eat, and the group collapsed in 1990, the twin victim of lineup defections and singer Ange Dolittle's debilitating heroin habit. Three years later, a recharged Dolittle re-emerged—with the same rhythm section (drummer Pete Howard and bassist Tim Sewell), two new guitarists (Jem Moorshead, Max Lavilla) and the remarkably assured **Epicure.** Replacing **Sell Me a God**'s bayou atmospherics with a dozen glossy, vaguely psychedelic pop gems, this is one of the decade's greatest rock albums that no one's heard. An obvious bid for commercial superstardom, the disc abounds in oblique yet lyrical references to Dolittle's addiction ("Tranquilliser," "Golden Egg," "Fecund") set to churning anthems with soaring choruses. A meaner R.E.M.? More like an INXS that matters.

Dolittle threw in the towel during an aborted US tour (Eat's first) that found this extraordinary live act playing to empty rooms. He soon bounced back, fronting We Know Where You Live (most of the Wonder Stuff, minus singer Miles Hunt). In a bizarre development, a post-Eat Pete Howard (a member of **Cut the Crap**–era Clash) hooked up with Hunt, Senseless Things bassist Morgan Nicholls and (briefly) ex-Cult guitarist Billy Duffy in Vent, playing steely yet anonymous Therapy?-style hard pop. [db]

See also *Senseless Things, Wonder Stuff; TPRG.*

EAZY-E

Eazy-Duz-It (Ruthless/Priority) 1988
5150 Home 4 tha Sick EP (Ruthless/Priority) 1992
It's on (Dr. Dre) 187um Killa (Ruthless) 1993
Eternal E (Ruthless/Priority) 1995
Str8 off tha Streetz of Muthaphuckin' Compton (Ruthless) 1996

Many read either the effects of a decade of callous social policies or the bankrupt morality of an entire generation into the story of young Compton hustler Eric Wright's rise to become one of America's most controversial stars. But it is also fascinating how much of the persona of Eazy-E—ruthless gangsta, unrepentant misogynist, unscrupulous entrepreneur, airhead Republican and hardcore rapper—was improvised. When Wright decided to move from drug-selling to the relatively legitimate world of record-making, he never planned to rap, simply to bankroll and promote. But at Ice Cube's coaxing and coaching, as part of the N.W.A posse, Eazy cut "Boyz-n-the-Hood" and "8 Ball" (both included on **N.W.A and the Posse**) in 1987 and became a contender on the live side of the microphone. While Cube's lyrics vividly captured the daily, often deadly, motions and rhythms of the inner city in a way that flattered ghetto youth and intrigued suburban thrill-seekers, Eazy's deadpan sing-song evinced a super-masculine stoic cool. The over-tweaked bass and hyperactive bells of the single helped establish a distinctive West Coast sound.

Swept along by N.W.A's ascent, Eazy-E released his first solo album, **Eazy-Duz-It,** in 1988, just before the arrival of **Straight Outta Compton.** "Radio," a hilarious tribute to seminal Los Angeles rap station KDAY, and the Bootsy Collins–inspired "We Want Eazy" showed promise, but the album is a difficult listen—not for the sharp Stax and P-Funk–styled production (by bandmates Dr. Dre and Yella) or even for Eazy's nasal nursery-rhyme whine, but for lunkheaded lyrics like "I might be a woman-beater but I'm not a pussy-eater."

N.W.A was over when Eazy made **5150 Home 4 tha Sick,** an insubstantial EP, despite writing and production by Naughty by Nature, Above the Law, Solid Productions and Threat. Complete with a Christmas (!) tune, the record fails to project any coherent personality. A long-simmering legal feud with Dr. Dre, however, gave Eazy something to focus on. Answering Dre's harsh assault (**The Chronic**'s "—— Wit Dre Day"), Eazy pursues the vendetta with dedicated passion on the eight-track **It's on (Dr. Dre) 187um Killa.** Ironically (or not, if one views Eazy's pragmatic career with enough cynicism), the businessman rapper was reinvigorated by Dre's chart success, tapping his moody sound while referring to the onetime glam-rapper as a "bitch" and lambasting him as a phony in "Real Muthaphuckkin Gs" and "It's On." (The booklet gives prominent play to an annotated—and already embarrassing—corny old publicity photo of Dre.)

Eazy spent most of '94 consolidating (or rebuilding) his empire, introducing the world to such hardcore acts as the wildly successful Cleveland crew Bone Thugs-n-Harmony. He launched his own local radio show, which set the stage for a reconciliation with Ice Cube, with whom he was planning an N.W.A reunion record when he died of complications from AIDS in March 1995. In choosing to disclose his disease, Wright became a hero even to some former detractors in his last days. In death, after all, he was courageous and dignified.

Eternal E, a fourteen-cut posthumous hits anthology (including N.W.A showcases but omitting the anti-Dre attacks), serves as both fitting tribute and fair sampler for the uninitiated, containing "Eazy-Duz-It," "Boyz-n-the-Hood," "Radio," "8 Ball" and "Only If You Want It." Eazy had been working on an ambitious new album at the time of his death; nearly a year later, **Str8 off tha Streetz of Muthaphuckin' Compton** appeared as an epilogue to his career. The album presents some of his best ("Just tah Let U Know") and worst ("My Baby's Mama") material ever. Mostly, he just sounds derivative. Eazy's genius was never in pushing the creative edge; when he rejoins MC Ren and Yella for a partial N.W.A reunion on "The Mutha——in Real," they sound like Comptons Most Wanted. [jzc]

See also *Dr. Dre, N.W.A.*

ECHOBELLY

Bellyache EP (UK Pandemonium) 1993
Everyone's Got One (Rhythm King) 1994
On (Fauve/Rhythm King/550 Music) 1995

Many Britpop bands of the mid-'90s can trace their sonic roots back to various new wavers of the not-so-distant past; in that case, Echobelly is the result of a marriage between Blondie and the Smiths. Less self-conscious and more pop-oriented than Elastica but just as modishly tight, the smart, kicky London quintet delivers bite-size hits of melodic rock. No bland teabag Britons, the group boasts a multicultural lineup of plucky Anglo-Indian singer Sonya Aurora Madan and dynamite guitar work from Swedish-born songwriter Glenn Johansson and black lesbian Debbie Smith, late of Curve.

With two songs recut from the prior EP, **Everyone's Got One** (knowingly referred to as **EGO**) begins with three brilliant tracks highlighted by Madan's memorable lyrics: the soaring, sociological "Today Tomorrow Sometime Never," a personal attack on prearranged marriages ("Father, Ruler, King, Computer"—

"Don't pin me down with vows and flowers") and the feminist anthem "Give Her a Gun." Andy Henderson's propulsive drumming and the well-timed power chords drive again and again into big-payoff choruses, nailed by Madan's clear, cheeky voice. The stunning single "Insomniac" is another LP highlight.

Even more consistent and vibrantly produced (by Boston's Fort Apache team of Sean Slade and Paul Kolderie), **On** again leads off with a trio of terrific tunes. The dreamy and driving "Car Fiction" is as good, as effortlessly catchy, as anything on, say, **Parallel Lines;** "King of the Kerb" is equally ace, with molten melody lines; "Great Things" sums up Madan's inspirational credo: "I wanna do great things/I don't wanna compromise/I wanna know what life is/I wanna know everything." Not that the disc slacks off afterward. "Four Letter Word," "In the Year" and "Go Away" are luscious hard pop, while the Suede-like epic "Dark Therapy" proves Echobelly equally adept at longer, more complex arrangements. A sleazy dead Brit politico is playfully tackled in "Pantyhose and Roses," but the glammy, sexual "Nobody Likes You" ("let me climb inside you, caress your fevered tongue") shows Madan can even make erotica seem righteous. [gef]

See also *Curve.*

E. COLI

See *Ethyl Meatplow.*

ED HALL

Albert (Boner) 1988
Love Poke Here (Boner) 1990
Gloryhole (Trance Syndicate) 1992
Motherscratcher (Trance Syndicate) 1993
La La Land (Trance Syndicate) 1995

Although many towns claim pollutants in the water as the cause of local eccentricities, Austin's resident heirs to the Butthole Surfers' weird-rock crown say it's actually the pollen that keeps the city's music scene so, um, vibrant. Ragweed and sagebrush or not, it's unlikely that Ed Hall's dense, theatrical *rock concrète* could have manifested itself anywhere else.

Both **Albert** and **Love Poke Here** find a rock band grappling with the tenets of noise, although the squalling psychosis of **Albert**'s bagpipe-driven "Cracked" and **Love Poke Here**'s funkily assaultive "Gilbert" show the trio ill at ease simply making amusing head-cleaning music. However, by the time Ed Hall hooked up with Butthole Surfer King Coffey and his Trance Syndicate label to record **Gloryhole,** something had most definitely transpired. Maybe it was the endless gigging that accompanied the first two albums (and, by the way, you haven't seen blacklight and strobes used well until you've seen Ed Hall play a small club), maybe it was their star turn in *Slacker,* maybe it was being able to record in Butch Vig's Smart Studios in Wisconsin. In any case, **Gloryhole** (with a memorable cartoon cover) turned out to be a magnificently pummeling album. The swirling mass of sound conjured up by guitarist/vocalist Gary Chester, bassist/vocalist Larry Strub and drummer Lyman Hardy is truly a beast to behold: see scary tracks like the instrumental "Bernie Sticky" and the artistic thud of "Roger Mexico."

Holding steady on **Motherscratcher,** Ed Hall made another stunning showing on **La La Land,** which was not so much a change in direction (how many different places can you go with three apeshit guys playing extraordinarily noisy punk-rock?) but a further solidification of the sound. Not for the meek, to be sure, Ed Hall manages to make those airborne irritants seem just a little more sinister. [jf]

EDITH GROVE

Edith Grove (Avalanche) 1993

MICHAEL ASTON

Why Me Why This Why Now (Triple X) 1995

Wales-to-Los-Angeles transplant Michael Aston cited the usual "creative differences" when he quit the glammy, likable-but-mindless Gene Loves Jezebel in 1990, leaving fans to wonder what musical direction the singer would follow in his new project, a quartet called Edith Grove: back to his gothic roots? Maybe a move into less stylized territory? Nah, the slick, mainstream rock on **Edith Grove** is almost indistinguishable from the two albums GLJ made after Aston departed. Only the funk-beat suavity of "Under Your Spell" comes close to standing tall, but it's hauled under by insipid lyrics and a swelling anthem vein. Even Aston's singing is less exuberant and emotive than usual. Edith Grove didn't last, and Aston moved on to a solo career.

Following such a highly produced commercial effort, the pretty, folksy **Why Me Why This Why Now** is truly refreshing. With Edith Grove's bassist and a very tasteful drummer as support, the acoustic guitar structures (played by Mick Rossi, ex–Slaughter and the Dogs) are variously embellished by sparing amounts of violin, cello, piano and flute. Aston sounds relaxed for the first time in years, letting his tenor lilt and soar effortlessly through the melodies. He reveals a previously unknown talent for writing serious, reflective lyrics with depth and grace. In the leadoff "Avalon SW10," he pauses to "wonder what I did with my life." The clever collision of family and politics in the gentle "Trade Winds" is affecting, and "Notre Dame de la Fleur" has a gentle solemnity that suggests Leonard Cohen, although the song's religious pro-life stance may be an impediment to those of different outlooks. **Why Me Why This Why Now** sounds like the work of a man who's finally grown up and discovered himself. [ky]

See also *Gene Loves Jezebel.*

DAVE EDMUNDS

Rockpile (MAM) 1972
Subtle as a Flying Mallet (RCA) 1975
Dave Edmunds, Rocker: Early Works 1968–1972 (Fr. Parlophone/EMI) 1977
Get It (Swan Song) 1977
Tracks on Wax 4 (Swan Song) 1978
Repeat When Necessary (Swan Song) 1979
Dave Edmunds & Love Sculpture Singles A's & B's (UK See for Miles) 1980
Twangin . . . (Swan Song) 1981
The Best of Dave Edmunds (Swan Song) 1981
D.E. 7th (Columbia) 1982
Information (Columbia) 1983
Riff Raff (Columbia) 1984
The Dave Edmunds Band Live: I Hear You Rockin' (Columbia) 1987
Closer to the Flame (Capitol) 1990

The Early Edmunds (UK EMI) 1991
The Dave Edmunds Anthology (1968–90) (Rhino) 1993
Plugged In (Pyramid) 1994

VARIOUS ARTISTS

Stardust (Arista) 1974
Porky's Revenge (Columbia) 1985

ROCKPILE

Seconds of Pleasure (Columbia) 1980

Despite his image as a retro revivalist, Welshman Dave Edmunds is less a hidebound purist than a knowledgeable stylist—with impeccable taste in classic American rock'n'roll, pop and country styles—who happens to do his best work in these traditional idioms. As a singer, guitarist and producer, he has generally invested even his most derivative output with a good deal of his own energy, and has never fallen back on mere genre-mongering. While his recording career has had its share of artistic ups and downs, Edmunds has consistently demonstrated a solid grasp of the fundamental emotional appeal of the styles he emulates.

Following his late-'60s tenure leading the psychedelic-blues trio Love Sculpture, Edmunds flexed his stylistic know-how and studio technique with a pair of patchy but enjoyable solo albums, **Rockpile** and **Subtle as a Flying Mallet.** With the artist acting largely as a one-man studio band, the albums encompass Chuck Berry-esque rock'n'roll (a style at which he would continue to excel), rockabilly and blues. Edmunds also recorded several oldies covers for the 1974 rock movie *Stardust;* ironically, the band in the film, to which six of his seven tracks on the soundtrack album are credited, was named the Stray Cats—an odd coincidence, since Edmunds would produce the unrelated American trio in the '80s.

The Early Edmunds compiles both Love Sculpture albums (including long and short versions of the band's freak UK hit with Khachaturian's "Sabre Dance") and the solo **Rockpile,** plus a rare single by the pre–Love Sculpture Human Beans, in a convenient two-CD package. The same period is also covered by **Dave Edmunds, Rocker: Early Works 1968–1972** and **Dave Edmunds & Love Sculpture Singles A's & B's.**

Between 1977 and 1981, Edmunds worked productively with bassist/singer Nick Lowe, guitarist Billy Bremner and drummer Terry Williams in the multi-purpose live/studio outfit dubbed Rockpile. The arrangement was ideal, giving Edmunds—never the most prolific or distinctive songwriter—access to a sympathetic and witty writing partner (Lowe) as well as a crack band. That period yielded three of Edmunds' best albums, **Get It, Tracks on Wax 4** and **Repeat When Necessary,** as well as most of the less-inspired **Twangin . . . ,** a pair of Nick Lowe LPs and the one actually made under the Rockpile name. **The Best of Dave Edmunds** (1981) is an adequate sampler of his Swan Song years.

In the years since Rockpile's dissolution, Edmunds has cast about fitfully, trying out various directions with mixed results. **D.E. 7th** finds him bouncing back handily with a new band and a snappy set of rollicking rockers (none of which he had a hand in writing), including a custom-fitted Bruce Springsteen composition, "From Small Things (Big Things One Day Come)," an energetic cover of NRBQ's "Me and the Boys" and the well-chosen Chuck Berry obscurity "Dear Dad."

After that encouraging effort, Edmunds inexplicably put himself in the hands of machine-pop mastermind Jeff Lynne, whose wholly inappropriate production and songwriting contributions make for baffling listening on **Information** and **Riff Raff.** Though neither album is as dreadful as Edmunds devotees would have you believe (each actually contains a couple of memorable tracks), they're symptomatic of the malaise that dogged Edmunds' recording career for much of the '80s. **Closer to the Flame** is a distinct improvement over the Lynne discs, with rousing stabs at R&B and rockabilly, but still not the decisive comeback fans might have hoped for.

Oddly enough, Edmunds did some of his best post-Rockpile work on the soundtrack for an obnoxious teen-flick sequel, *Porky's Revenge:* he contributed three new tunes and produced and played on tracks by George Harrison, Jeff Beck, Clarence Clemons and Robert Plant. A semi-greatest-hits rundown drawn from several different shows, **I Hear You Rockin'** is a spirited live effort featuring Edmunds' estimable post-Rockpile '80s band with ex–Love Sculpture bassist John David (Williams) and pub-rock vets Mickey Gee (guitar) and Geraint Watkins (keyboards), a company whose talents were rather ill-served on the Lynne albums.

After **Closer to the Flame** (which has a spry title track to recommend it) failed to reignite Edmunds' career, he took another extended hiatus from record-making before re-emerging four years later with the surprisingly spry **Plugged In,** a return to his claustrophobic but cost-effective one-man-studio-band approach. This time, Edmunds manages to get engaging music out of the mechanical rhythms that weighed down his Jeff Lynne collaborations. The self-penned "I Love Music" sets the tone for an amiable set encompassing chirpy pop ("Chutes & Ladders"), Cajun-flavored rock'n'roll ("It Doesn't Really Matter"), swoony balladry (Al Anderson's "Better Word for Love"), a well-executed Brian Wilson pastiche ("Beach Boy Blood"), a cleverly reworked Otis Redding cover ("I Got the Will"), a flashy showcase for Edmunds' nimble guitar picking (Jerry Reed's "The Claw") and even a souped-up remake of "Sabre Dance."

Except for the odd foible of including a UK (not US) discography in the booklet, Rhino's two-CD, forty-one-track **Dave Edmunds Anthology** does an exemplary job of encapsulating Edmunds' career, from Love Sculpture through **Closer to the Flame.** [ss]

See also *TPRG.*

E-40

Federal (Sick Wid It) 1992 (Sick Wid It/Jive) 1995
The Mail Man (Sick Wid It) 1994 (Sick Wid It/Jive) 1994
In a Major Way (Sick Wid It/Jive) 1995

CLICK

Let's Side EP (Sick Wid It) 1990
Down and Dirty (Sick Wid It) 1993 (Sick Wid It/Jive) 1995
Game Related (Sick Wid It/Jive) 1995

SUGA T.

Paper Chasin' (4Eva Hustlin') (Sick Wid It/Jive) 1996

Armed with promotion and distribution strategies borrowed from original DIY rapper Too $hort and the local hustling game, the Click—brothers and sisters from the Stevens family of Northern California—hit the streets of Vallejo and sold tapes direct, building a reputation that resulted in six-figure sales for their full-length releases. The group's success was subsequently duplicated by other bootstrappers in the Bay Area and elsewhere, ushering in a groundswell of independent rap labels. It does need to be noted that the Click ultimately hooked itself up to a major label, which might seem discouraging to those in favor of Afrocentric self-determination. But grand issues of nationalism were never the concern of these business-sharp operators. Their success resulted from shrinking the distance between performers and fans, capturing around-the-way themes for local audiences—partying and parlaying, often pimping, but rarely polemicizing—over nostalgic early-'80s funk riffs. As a result, the "product" itself is often less interesting than the story behind it.

The Click got busy in 1990, and the irrepressibly earthy E-40 (Earl Stevens) quickly stood out. **Federal** introduced his clunky synthfunk and oddly cadenced raps, as well as his topical range—drinking wine ("Carlos Rossi"), ducking cops ("Outsmart the Po-Pos") and making money ("Federal"). The Click's **Down and Dirty** followed, with improved production values; E-40's eccentricity blossoms into genuine fun on tracks like "Mr. Flamboyant." Other members of the group—Suga T., D-Shot and B-Legit—have all released less engaging solo releases; D-Shot eventually branched out into A&R, assembling the wildly popular **Boss Ballin'** compilation of Bay Area artists.

The Mail Man (eight songs, including a remix) is excellent. From the on-point clowning of "Practice Looking Hard" ("I got a mirror in my pocket and I practice looking hard!") to the antics of the sensitive '90s male hero ("Captain Save-a-Ho"), E-40 proves a unique lyrical stylist and a cheeky rap comic. **In a Major Way** continues his ascent, sparked by the duet with Suga T. ("Sprinkle Me") and the dead homies tribute "1-Luv." Spice 1 and 2Pac join E-40 for "Dusted 'n' Disgusted." Meanwhile, back in the band, a bigger budget helped **Game Related** produce a hilarious ode to fortified wine ("Hurricane") and E-40's socio-biographical "World Went Crazy," a sympathetic chronicle of '80s East Bay ghetto life. [jzc]

EGGS

Bruiser (TeenBeat) 1993
Exploder (TeenBeat) 1994
How Do You Like Your Lobster (TeenBeat) 1995

VIVA SATELLITE!

Nishma (TeenBeat) 1996

Although certainly affected by the presence in their backyard of one of the most vibrant punk (and post-punk) scenes in America, Washington DC's Eggs were clearly more impressed by the bucolic prog-jazz-folk musings of English cult heroes like Soft Machine and National Health. Admittedly more prone to dissonant digressions than either of those bands, the instrument-swapping trio nevertheless demonstrated a marked tendency toward winsome displays of pataphysical verve that wouldn't have been out of place at a stoned soul picnic, circa 1972.

Unlike its initial barrage of swoony singles, Eggs' first album is a tentative affair, imbued with plenty of charm by the members' unabashedly effervescent interplay. By and large, however, **Bruiser** falls victim to a hyper-indie sense of self-consciousness that sees the band so bent on going unnoticed that it does everything but apologize to the listener for having to sit through the thing. The trio actually tenders that apology on the superior **Exploder**—in a liner note that mumbles "we realize this is a long album and we apologize in advance for any discomfort it may cause you." The disc is, in fact, a bit padded by Evan Shurak's whimsical instrumental interludes and extended silences (designed to mimic the dead air between sides of a vinyl record), but those affectations are offset by disarming ditties like "Why Am I So Tired All of the Time?" (buoyed by Rob Christiansen's comely trombone line) and the jittery Feelies-like "Ampellang" (a showcase for guitarist Andrew Beaujon).

The post-breakup **How Do You Like Your Lobster** compiles odds and ends culled from a number of TeenBeat compilations, as well as three pre-**Bruiser** singles. After the band's split, Christiansen, who had been moonlighting in Grenadine, formed Viva Satellite!, a wacked-out trio that debuted with what is probably the first twink-pop opera, performed in the classical style, complete with Greek chorus. The basic plot is laid out in the opening track, "The Legend of How Salt Water Taffy Came to Be," and continues—with Christiansen, Lauren Feldsher and Dan Morrissey playing a variety of parts—through interludes about love, lust and Israel–Palestine relations. School plays should all be so much fun! [dss]

See also *Grenadine.*

EGOMANIACS

See *Kramer.*

18TH DYE

Done (Ger. Cloudland) 1992 (Matador) 1994
Crayon EP (Ger. Cloudland) 1993 (Matador) 1994
Tribute to a Bus (Matador) 1995

Based in Berlin and consisting of a German (singer/guitarist Sebastian Büttrich), a Dane (drummer Piet Bendtsen) and a Danish-German (singer/bassist Heike Rädeker), 18th Dye produces music that is far from the Teutonic sort of non-rock its heritage would imply. Rather, the trio warmly embraces American indie-pop stylings, framing them in the unique European context of their surroundings. **Done,** co-produced by Chicago industrialist Iain Burgess, casts a hazy, drugged-up spell, rousing itself only to chug through the one-chord wonder of "Whole Wide World," the rocking "Can You Wink?" and the noisy, near-instrumental groove of "Girls Boots." Elsewhere, especially on the marble-mouthed "9 Out of 10," 18th Dye achieves a sort of guitar-drenched stasis, loping through its fuzzed-out pop as if in dire need of caffeine. The effect is, in a word, magical, and the way that 18th Dye embrace some clichés (droney, one-note guitar lines) while redefining others (the dull, heavy-lidded vocal monotone here isn't a symbol of slack, it's simply the right accompaniment to the music) is refreshing.

The six-song **Crayon,** self-produced with a bare minimum of button-pushing design, is a transitional document; variously rushing and loud ("Aug."), gently motionless ("16 Ink," "Crank") and nicely modulated in the middle (the delerious "Ray," "Nuit N."), the songs mainly uphold the first album's enchanting effect but offer an indication of the band's future direction.

With Steve Albini recording, **Tribute to a Bus** shifts the dynamic to focus on a noisier, more melodic sound. Seldom lapsing into the somnolent grooves of **Done, Tribute to a Bus** is a far more complicated album, and even a deceptively lazy song like "Play w/ You" finds itself decompressed into a noised-out rocker. The delicately rhythmic "Poolhouse Blue," the squally, frenetic "Only Burn" and the downhearted "Label" (which, by the way, contains a classic romantic line: "You always sound as if you're crying when you come") seem like straightforward pop songs, countered by structurally deprived numbers like the vast "Go!Song" and the sprawling, **Bad Moon Rising**–esque "No Time/11 (Spectators)."

18th Dye broke up in 1996. [jf]

EIGHT OR NINE FEET

See *Dish.*

EINSTÜRZENDE NEUBAUTEN

Schwarz EP (Ger. Zick Zack) 1981
Kollaps (Ger. Zick Zack) 1981
Drawings of Patient O.T. (UK Some Bizzare) 1983 (ZE/PVC) 1985 (Thirsty Ear) 1995
80–83 Strategies Against Architecture (UK Mute) 1984 (Homestead) 1986 (Mute) 1994
2 X 4 (ROIR) 1984
1/2 Mensch (Some Bizzare/Rough Trade) 1985 (Thirsty Ear) 1995
Fuenf auf der Nach Oben Offenen Richterskala (Some Bizzare/Relativity) 1987 (Thirsty Ear) 1995
Haus der Luege (Some Bizzare/Rough Trade) 1989 (Thirsty Ear) 1995
Strategies Against Architecture II (Mute) 1991
Die Hamletmaschine (Ger. Ego/Our Choice/Rough Trade) 1991
Tabula Rasa (Mute) 1993
Malediction EP (UK Mute) 1993
Faustmusik (Mute) 1996

EINSTÜRZENDE NEUBAUTEN/LYDIA LUNCH/ROWLAND S. HOWARD

Thirsty Animal EP (Ger. GEMA) 1982

F. M. EINHEIT

Stein (Ger. Our Choice/Rough Trade) 1990
Prometheus/Lear (Ger. Ego/Our Choice/Rough Trade) 1993

STEIN

Steinzeit (Ger. Our Choice/Rough Trade) 1992
Königzucker (Ger. Our Choice/Rough Trade) 1994

F. M. EINHEIT/ANDREAS AMMER

Radio Inferno (Ger. Ego/Our Choice/Rough Trade) 1993
Apocalypse Live (Ger. Ego/Our Choice/Rough Trade) 1995

F. M. EINHEIT/CASPAR BRÖTZMANN

Merry Christmas (Thirsty Ear) 1995

ALEXANDER HACKE

Filmarbeiten (Ger. Our Choice/Rough Trade) 1995

JEVER MOUNTAIN BOYS

Bury the Bottle With Me (Ger. Blue Million Miles) 1994

BLIXA BARGELD

Auftragsmusik/Commissioned Music (Ger. Ego/Our Choice/Rough Trade) 1995

Part deadly earnest post-musical composers, part boys-with-toys goofballs whipping up a ruckus for the pure joy of making noise, Berlin's Einstürzende Neubauten (Collapsing New Buildings) have built a distinctive, challenging and extremely imaginative sonic career out of implements generally intended for other utilitarian purposes: power drills, humming power lines, water towers, air-conditioning ducts, plate steel, glass, boulders and various large metal objects beaten with sledgehammers, pipes, wrenches and axes. Even traditional tools receive similarly brutal mistreatment—Blixa Bargeld's pained vocals and guitar are often blurred to the point of abstraction. While Einstürzende Neubauten occasionally veers into song form with intriguing, even attractive, results, the group's output more typically resembles a bunch of highly amplified (or, in some cases, barely audible) industrial sound-effects records being played at each other with little concern for anything but the raising of blood pressure and artistic hackles. Good shit.

The five-man troupe roared into action on the German avant-garde underground scene around 1980, reaching escape velocity from nearly random chaos on the carefully produced, dynamically textured **Drawings of Patient O.T.** and the artistic breakthrough of the group's career high-point, **1/2 Mensch** (aka **Halber Mensch,** or **Half Man**). In between, the **Strategies Against Architecture** compilation offered a catch-up on their prior work, including tracks from **Kollaps** and previously unissued live efforts. (For more live material, **2 X 4,** recorded over the band's first few years of touring activity, is an admirable attempt to capture the storm of Neubauten on stage.) Despite its earthquake-noting title, **Fuenf auf der Nach Oben Offenen Richterskala (Five on the Open-Ended Richter Scale)** is a shockingly restrained undertaking, one in which noises and strings are used to accent the verbals, not render them inaudible. Ultimately, the effect suggests a hypothetical soundtrack for a Marxist vampire movie. **Haus der Luege** ups the intensity level and delivers on the constant threat of sonic violence often enough to deny any emotional benefits in the generally lowered aggression.

Einstürzende Neubauten's intermittent group exertions were further curtailed in the '90s, largely as a result of numerous side and solo projects. Bargeld is the primary member of Nick Cave's Bad Seeds, which he joined in 1984; the guitarist's 1995 album, **Auftragsmusik/Commissioned Music,** was released on Ego, a label Einstürzende set up for their scoring endeavors in theater and film. (The group's own issue on the imprint include **Die Hamletmaschine,** composed for a staging of Heinrich Müller, and **Faustmusik.**) Percussionist F. M. Einheit has made albums under his own name, with German guitarist Caspar Brötzmann (**Merry Christmas**), with writer Andreas Ammer (**Radio Inferno** is an adaptation of Dante's poetry that also involves Bargeld, Brötzmann and British DJ John Peel) and as a member of Stein, a group with Ulrike Haage and Katharina Franck of the Rainbirds. Guitarist Alexander Hacke has also done film music and leads the Jever Mountain Boys, a country (!) group with Roland Wolf of the Bad Seeds and Die Haut guitarist Jochen Arbeit.

Still, there was plenty of material clattering around to fill **Strategies Against Architecture II,** an annotated two-CD compilation (1984–90) that picks up where the first one left off. As on that record, only some of the cuts come from the period's albums; live matter and previously unreleased recordings flesh out the typically bizarre and far-reaching program. There's a clanging, snarling, dramatic version of "Haus der Lüge" (long before it became the title track of an album) from a 1984 Los Angeles concert at which the band accidentally set fire to the stage, a delightfully bent but respectful 1985 rendition of Lee Hazlewood's "Sand," the ominous mystery of 1989's "Armenia II," "Ich Bin's" (an edgy 1987 chant accompanied by drumming on a plastic garbage can) and the truly daft "Bildbeschreibung," a droning, creaking piece—complete with electric shopping cart—done to accompany a dramatic reading on German radio. And that's without mentioning the group's jingle for Jordache jeans.

Tabula Rasa is, as billed, the quintet's blank-slate new beginning, a fully realized and refined song cycle about the reunification of Germany in which the group's metallic clangor and witty noises affect, rather than dominate, the musical designs. Drawing against **Fuenf auf der Nach Oben Offenen Richterskala** as if it were a sketch-pad for this work, Bargeld's melodic singing and a few of the rhythmic arrangements resemble Peter Gabriel's German translations; the central committee of instruments does a convincing imitation of "normal"—until something starts buzzing, or having the shit whacked out of it. The fifteen-minute "Headcleaner" unleashes an old-fashioned barrage of feedback, screams and banging, but—between occasional bursts of riveting mechanics—the folky "Zebulon" actually has a catchy, Velvet Undergrounded chorus. The lovely "Blume," wanly sung in English by Cave associate Anita Lane, doesn't register more than a quiet, baroque breeze. With the band's ability to make garish noise so fully developed, its inverted music-first blueprint is a stupendous revelation, a gripping blend of stately seduction and brutality that sounds like the masterpiece Einstürzende Neubauten was born to make. [i]

See also *Caspar Brötzmann Massaker, Nick Cave and the Bad Seeds; TPRG.*

MARK EITZEL

See *American Music Club.*

ELASTICA

Line Up EP (UK Deceptive) 1994
Connection EP (UK Deceptive) 1994
Stutter EP (DGC) 1994
Elastica (DGC) 1995

Like a stylish cat burglar whose cunning audacity is matched by a discriminating notion of what's worth taking, London's Elastica can easily be forgiven (at least after all debts were paid) for the indiscretions of its esoteric class-of-'77 appropriations. As the quartet's debut album gathered commercial momentum in England, a hornet's nest of legal trouble was stirred into action as rights holders for songs by Wire (compare Elastica's "Connection" to "Three Girl Rhumba," from that group's 1977 debut LP) and the Stranglers ("Waking Up" clearly recycles the chord structure of "No More Heroes") raised plagiarism claims against Elastica's most overtly derivative numbers. Given the Knack traces, Flying Lizards beats, Wire hooks and other familiar elements teasingly littered throughout the album, Elastica could probably have settled for being a new wave cover band, but **Elastica**'s value goes deeper than simple influence-peddling.

Along with drummer Justin Welch, singer/guitarist Justine Frischmann formed the group after an early stint playing guitar in Suede. Her authoritative, self-amused voice and the grunting throb of Annie Holland's rubbery bass are Elastica's most distinctive markings. (Guitarist Donna Matthews was reportedly attracted by a *Melody Maker* ad that specifically named the Stranglers and Wire, as well as the as-yet-inaudible Fall). Throughout the sixteen deceptively luxurious three-minute songs on **Elastica,** Frischmann gets firm and robust support from her bandmates, who help wrap her playful lyrics—often as not forthright commentaries on the joy of sex (or the desire for it, or groupies who trade in it, or products that aid in it, or boys who can't do it—you get the idea)—in bracingly tuneful and jagged rock, a mobile mass laced up tight with cool studio tricks. Highlights of a diverse and highly impressive debut: "Line Up" (complete with a rhythmic retch sample), the wiggly *and* thuggish techno-meets-noise-rock "Connection" (in which Frischmann executes a credible female Hugh Cornwell impression), the sleepy and slithery "Hold Me Now" and the merry Buzzcockian punk-pop of "All-Nighter."

Released as Elastica's introduction to America following a series of highly touted British singles and EPs, **Stutter** surrounds the album track—a sexual challenge to a drunk non-performer and the song that unveiled the band to Britain in late '93—with radio-session versions of the album's "Annie" and "2:1," plus the understandably discarded "Rockunroll." [i]

See also *Suede.*

ELASTIC PUREJOY

See *Low Pop Suicide.*

ELECTRAFIXION

Zephyr EP (UK Spacejunk/WEA) 1994
Burned (Spacejunk/Sire) 1995

When Ian McCulloch walked away from Echo and the Bunnymen to go solo in 1988, the singer's presumption about the Liverpool band's lack of a future without him wasn't precisely accurate. Mixing a sour cocktail of defiance, spite and stubbornness, guitarist Will Sergeant and bassist Les Pattinson drafted a singer, keyboardist and drummer to eke out one needless album, 1990's **Reverberation.** (Sergeant subsequently joined the rest of the music world in characterizing his Bunnymen postscript as "an embarrassment.")

Four years later, in one of those turnarounds that give mudslinging a bad name, McCulloch and Sergeant made up and formed a new quartet dubbed Electrafixion. The premature **Zephyr,** however, made a poor calling card: four tracks of thickly textured (and terribly recorded) dance-rock. The fuzzy wash of buzzing, distorted guitar and indistinct beats—a bit like second-era Stone Roses, but nowhere near as good—renders McCulloch's heavily reverbed voice (displaying none of its usual commanding presence) almost unrecognizable. If this was a new beginning, the end of the story was pretty easy to reckon.

Another surprise twist in the saga. **Burned,** which cleans up and preserves two **Zephyr** tracks (not, however, the one called "Burned"), sorts Electrafixion out, finding a purpose by siphoning off the essence of Echo to fuel a charged-up '90s attack. As if the old band had just emerged from a time machine, desperate to release mega-watts of pent-up energy (and maybe rave a little on the dancefloor, too), Electrafixion sheds Echo's lofty glamour by shifting the stylistic weight onto guitar, and the thickly textured album—by turns murky and clear—is largely Sergeant's. While McCulloch sings in an unmannered, surprisingly vehement voice, the guitarist has a field day, throwing off layered washes of rock guitar energy: overlapping planes of rhythm, lead, distortion, effects and ostinatos. **Burned**'s rush of disorienting mayhem could have proven unstable, but bassist Leon De Sylva and drummer Tony McGuigan nail it down with firm tactical support, giving McCulloch an anchor for lyrics—especially in "Feel My Pulse," "Who's Been Sleeping in My Head?," "Lowdown" (co-written by Johnny Marr) and "Bed of Nails"—that are stripped back and self-consciously vague but full of catchy hook lines. Electrafixion takes a little getting used to, but **Burned**—which grandly sidesteps any current fads to keep its own creative counsel—proves a near-perfect union. [i]

See also *Ian McCulloch.*

ELECTRIC BLOOD

See *Bats.*

ELECTRONIC

See *New Order.*

ELEVENTH DREAM DAY

Eleventh Dream Day EP (Amoeba) 1987
Prairie School Freakout (Amoeba) 1988
Beet (Atlantic) 1989
Lived to Tell (Atlantic) 1991
Two Sweeties EP (Ger. City Slang) 1992
El Moodio (Atlantic) 1993
Ursa Major (City Slang/Atavistic) 1994
Flutter EP (Atavistic) 1995

By the measure of popular acceptance and record company balance sheets, Eleventh Dream Day's place in the alt-rock annals is among the most frustrating could've-beens. But to a healthy assortment of fans and critics, the Chicago band is a class act all the way, an underrated and reliable font of powerful, expressive rock'n'roll. Formed by eventual spouses Rick Rizzo (guitar, vocals) and Janet Beveridge Bean (drums, vocals), plus bassist Douglas McCombs and guitarist Baird Figi, Eleventh Dream Day grew considerably over the years, although their heritage—the sonic family tree that includes the Velvets, Neil Young and Television, with added touches of Detroit noise, backwater blues, midwestern garage-pop and hillbilly ache—remained fairly constant. The evolution began immediately after the first EP, a well-written set of compact guitar-rockers that merely infers the group's live blue-flame intensity. **Prairie School Freakout,** recorded in all of six hours, brings that to the fore, with raw production (fueled by an unfixable amp buzz), epically moody songs and a dazzling array of six-string shootouts.

Enter Atlantic Records. **Beet** and **Lived to Tell** both burst with swell material, the band proving to be equally adroit with terse, hooky anthems, gorgeously tarnished ballads, skittish melodic romps and alternately cerebral/skronky jamming. The songs are just as robust as the pyrotechnics, and the lyrics—sketches and stories, imbued with life details and a frenzied sense of wanderlust—don't take a backseat either. Significantly, Bean proves to be more of a factor, moving beyond her usual soaring harmonies to write and sing lead more frequently (she'd also been recording—and continues to do so—in the country duo Freakwater with a fellow Kentucky native).

By 1992, Eleventh Dream Day had a nice little body of work and a phonebook-sized press file, but not much else. The uncertain future and shitty road existence drove Baird Figi back to a normal life. (Rizzo and Bean managed one of those, too—they had a child together—but kept the band going.) As of **El Moodio,** Figi's slot was filled by Kentucky homeboy Matthew "Wink" O'Bannon (also of Bodeco, with a solo disc to his credit as well), which made a difference, albeit one that has as much to do with Rizzo's songwriting as the guitar playing. Bean's co-writing contributes a couple of relentlessly memorable raveups ("Makin' Like a Rug" and "After This Time Is Gone"), but the record's overall tone is brooding and reflective, with results that vary from thrillingly pretty ("Motherland") and subtly mind-bending ("The Raft") to extra long ("Honeyslide," which is lovely nonetheless) and overly Youngian ("Rubberband").

That was enough for Atlantic, and the band turned to European/indie connections (which came to include overseas gigs with Yo La Tengo's Ira Kaplan sitting in). **Ursa Major** was mixed and recorded, respectively, by subterranean Chicago knob-twirlers Brad Wood and John McEntire, the latter of whom plays in Tortoise, the decidedly avant band co-founded by McCombs. An arty record that picks up from its predecessor's most meandering tendencies, **Ursa Major**—which is imbued by feelings of both adventure and exhaustion—suffers greatly from a deliberate lack of pop songcraft, though it delivers on a series of textured, slowly unfolding axe workouts. (Atavistic also released a CD EP of the album's "Flutter.")

With O'Bannon gone to concentrate on Bodeco, Eleventh Dream Day began recording an album in 1996. [jc]

See also *Bodeco, Freakwater, Green, Tortoise; TPRG.*

ELVIS BROTHERS

Movin' Up (Portrait) 1983 (Recession) 1995
Adventure Time (Portrait) 1985
Now Dig This (Recession) 1992

Losing their major-label contract and spending the better part of a decade playing Chicago-area clubs without making a record didn't blow any of the fizz out of the pseudonymous brothers Elvis: Brad (drums), Graham (bass/vocals) and Rob (guitar/vocals). The entertaining, colorful Illinois power-pop trio was a bright spot in the mid-'80s, adding the secret ingredient—a contagious fear of seriousness—to a meld of Beatles pop, Cheap Trick rock and Carl Perkins 'billy.

Now available on a single CD under the debut's title, the E-Bros' first two albums (especially the Adrian Belew–produced **Adventure Time**) are megadoses of catchy fun—delightful, witty tunes played and sung with flair and chops. **Now Dig This** emerges from the same wellspring of spirited tunefulness. There's little evidence of the trio's silly streak (always more of a live attribute), but the best songs here are otherwise as appealing as any in the band's past. "Valentine," "Strangelove," "Dreamland" and "Next Time I Fall in Love" all recall aspects of the 1965 Beatles, but with crisp modern energy and midwestern flair. Meanwhile, "I've Got Skies for Her" and "Peace of Mind" try on a psychedelic rock frock. [i]

See also *TPRG*.

EMERGENCY BROADCAST NETWORK

Telecommunications Breakdown (TVT) 1995

Beware multi-media organizations bearing cultural artifacts. Emergency Broadcast Network may very well mount exciting performance happenings, and the three videos on the trio's full-length debut package, which contains a CD-ROM and a floppy disc "interactive booklet," might be mind-blowing to those with the technology to watch 'em, but the record's audio collages are strictly any-monkey-with-a-sampler-and-a-beat-box ordinary. Originally organized by Joshua Pearson and Gardner Post at the Rhode Island School of Design in the mid-'80s, EBN specializes in topical hip-hop pastiches and high-concept put-ons that load up the sonic details without much concern for the basics; you either join the chaotic fun in progress or wait in vain for something comprehensible to catch your ear. The audio portion of **Telecommunication Breakdown** has one potent item ("Shoot the Mac-10," with guest rapper Melle Mel), but otherwise rattles and hums like a five-year-old let loose in the tape library. This is progress? [i]

EMF

Schubert Dip (EMI) 1991
Unexplained EP (EMI) 1992
Stigma (EMI) 1992
Cha Cha Cha (UK EMI) 1995

One of the archetypal pan-flashes of the early '90s, England's small-town-reared EMF—the name is an acronym for Ecstasy MotherFuckers, a tribute to the recreational drug of choice among the British rave crowd at the time—combined teen-idol looks with the faddishly popular dance beats of Stone Roses and Happy Mondays. "Unbelievable," the signature song from EMF's debut album, **Schubert Dip,** became one of the era's most ubiquitous pop smashes, mixing elements of dance music, rock and rap into a giddy techno-bubblegum confection that brought the hallucinogenic high spirits of the rave scene to the masses. The clever use of samples—a new gimmick to most rock fans—and lead singer James Atkin's coy, white-boy rapping style added to the band's enormous appeal in both the UK and America. In fairness to the quintet, and especially its songwriter, guitarist Ian Dench, EMF did write infectiously catchy riffs and **Schubert Dip** managed to spin off several other hit singles, including "Children" and "I Believe."

But if **Schubert Dip** represented the zenith of rave culture's ecstatic pop indulgence, **Unexplained** came as the morning after's ugly hangover. Gone are the frothy techno dance beats and slick pop production. The four songs are nervous and edgy, with Dench's sinuous, sinister guitar leads and Atkin's breathy, overwrought vocals. On the entirely inappropriate cover of the Stooges' "Search and Destroy" that ends the EP, his wimpy, affected singing style borders on self-parody.

The band's second full-length album, **Stigma,** is even darker and gloomier than the downbeat vibe of **Unexplained.** EMF's young fans wanted to dance, not explore the band's existential angst, and stayed away in droves. Moreover, success had left the boys bloated and bleary-eyed; they weren't fresh-faced pinups from the Forest of Dean, just over-the-hill rock stars without any new hits.

Flashes of EMF's early techno-pop sound surface in "Bleeding You Dry," by far the most listenable track on 1995's **Cha Cha Cha.** Almost every other cut on this would-be comeback, however, finds the band groping—unsuccessfully—for some new musical direction. Tracks like "La Plage" and "Secrets" bury Atkin's vocals under dense layers of psychedelicized noise, including such '60s retro stylings as flute, woodblock and wah-wah. A pair of dreary power ballads segue into "Slouch," a burst of explosive live-in-the-studio hardcore thrash; the album ends with "Glass Smash Jack," a feisty Who-like character piece about an aging alcoholic. The album proved to be a commercial failure in England, and didn't even get a shot in the US. [jt]

EN ESCH

See *KMFDM*.

ENGINE 88

See *Counting Crows*.

ENGINE KID

Astronaut EP (C/Z) 1993
Bear Catching Fish (C/Z) 1993
Angel Wings (Revelation) 1995

ICEBURN/ENGINE KID

Iceburn/Engine Kid EP (Revelation) 1994

A lot of bands heard Slint's **Spiderland,** saw the light and decided to make the same kind of music, but few were as shameless about it as Seattle's Engine Kid. The five-song debut EP by the trio of Greg Anderson (vocals, guitars), Brian Kraft (bass) and Chris Vandebrooke (drums) pays homage to Slint to the point of claim-jumping. There's that very quiet—VERY LOUD—very quiet/weird time signatures dynamic (all over); there's the inaudible-story-with-instrumental-accompaniment thing ("Furnace"); there's a Neil Young cover, just like Slint used to do live (Engine Kid's choice is "The Needle and the Damage Done"); there's something very much like the riff from "Nosferatu Man" (in "Astronaut"). It's all perfectly competent, but the hidden noise piece at the end (yes, another one of those) is the only thing that Slint hadn't already done better.

Matters improve a bit on **Bear Catching Fish** (recorded in "the basement of some guy's brick house" in Chicago—wonder whose?), which reprises "Treasure Chest" from the EP. They've still got the same slow tempos and dramatic volume shifts, but their relationship with Slint has been transformed to influence rather than impersonation. Unfortunately, they don't have much else: the only song that's especially notable is an improbable cover of John Denver's "Rocky Mountain High."

The band then replaced Vandebrooke with Jade Devitt, toured a lot and got a hell of a lot better. Instead of the big shifts in dynamics, **Angel Wings** delivers a titanic, punishing wall-of-oomph. Possibly as a result of contact with labelmates Iceburn, a Salt Lake City group fusing jazz, classical and punk, Engine Kid also seems to have discovered jazz: one track is called "Herbie Hancock," and the album ends with a twelve-minute-plus cover of John Coltrane's "Olé," abetted by a couple of members of Silkworm on horns. And they've learned they can play fast—the album's high point is a pummeling seventy-eight-second instrumental, "Nailgun." Following even more roadwork and a couple of compilation tracks, Engine Kid split up. [ddw]

JEREMY ENIGK

See *Sunny Day Real Estate.*

BRIAN ENO

Here Come the Warm Jets (Island) 1973 (EG) 1982
Taking Tiger Mountain (By Strategy) (Island) 1974 (EG) 1982
Another Green World (Island) 1975 (EG) 1982
Discreet Music (Antilles) 1975 (EG) 1982
Before and After Science (Island) 1977 (EG) 1982
Music for Films (Antilles) 1978 (Editions EG) 1982
Ambient 1: Music for Airports (Ambient/EG/PVC) 1979 (EG) 1982
Ambient 4: On Land (EG) 1982 (Editions EG) 1986
Music for Films Volume 2 (EG) 1983
Working Backwards 1983–1973 (EG) 1983
Thursday Afternoon (EG) 1985
More Blank Than Frank (EG) 1986
Desert Island Selection (EG) 1989
Boxed Set (UK EG) 1989
The Shutov Assembly (Opal/Warner Bros.) 1992
Nerve Net (Opal/Warner Bros.) 1992
Neroli (All Saints/Gyroscope) 1993
Brian Eno II: Vocal (Virgin) 1993
Brian Eno I: Instrumental (Virgin) 1994

FRIPP & ENO

(No Pussyfooting) (Antilles) 1973 (EG) 1981
Evening Star (Antilles) 1975 (EG) 1981

KEVIN AYERS/JOHN CALE/ENO/NICO

June 1, 1974 (Island) 1974

CLUSTER & ENO

Cluster and Eno (Ger. Sky) 1977
Old Land (Relativity) 1985

ENO WITH MOEBIUS AND ROEDELIUS

After the Heat (Ger. Sky) 1978

JON HASSELL/BRIAN ENO

Fourth World Vol. 1: Possible Musics (Editions EG) 1980
Power Spot (Ger. ECM) 1986

HAROLD BUDD/BRIAN ENO

Ambient 2: The Plateaux of Mirror (EG) 1980
The Pearl (Editions EG) 1984

DAVID BYRNE AND BRIAN ENO

My Life in the Bush of Ghosts (Sire) 1981

BRIAN ENO WITH DANIEL LANOIS & ROGER ENO

Apollo Atmospheres & Soundtracks (EG) 1983

ENO/CALE

Wrong Way Up (Opal/Warner Bros.) 1990

ENO/WOBBLE

Spinner (All Saints/Gyroscope) 1995

VARIOUS ARTISTS

No New York (Antilles) 1978
Music for Films III (Opal) 1988

Face it. The complexities and ironies of Brian Eno's prolific procession along his self-declared uncertainty principle ("oblique strategies") are unfathomable. Put simply, how did the most obscurely gifted of the glam-clad gang of non-musicians who revolutionized '70s rock as Roxy Music become, in turn, a bizarrely thrilling rock auteur, the fairy godmother of no wave nihilism, the successful prophet of amorphous ambient sound, a consummate foil for David Bowie and David Byrne, an adjunct member of Talking Heads and, for two decades, an in-demand record producer—as such, the indispensable ally of the world's most ambitious stadium band, U2? Or, conversely, how did someone so demonstrably ingenious at tearing at the fringes of pop become such a pompous art prat prostituting his highbrow egghead pretensions on big-bucks bombast while plying nonsense theories and making countless unlistenable albums of seemingly random drivel in dilettantish collaborations with wally progressos from several lands?

The answer, alas, isn't conveniently discernible from the new pair of sumptuous three-CD box sets that summarize the Englishman's voluminous recorded output, neatly divided into **Instrumental** and **Vocal** categories, an approach that deserves to be completed by a **Productions** collection. (Actually, the titles are a mystery. The numerals that appear on the cases are not repeated anywhere else, and while the booklets are entitled **Webs** and **One,** the latter is a component of **II,** which was, naturally, released first.) What is evident, however, is what an original and engaging method Eno brings to pop music—when he deigns to slum in such common pursuits. The **Vocal** box wisely includes (nearly in their entirety on two discs) the four essential albums with which the post–Roxy Musician staked out his esoteric personal territory in the art-rock wars. Although the infusion of subdued experimentation and subtle atmospherics as essential components increasingly tempered the wry, frenzied genius that makes the amazing **Here Come the Warm Jets** such a landmark, **Taking Tiger Mountain (By Strategy), Another Green World** and **Before and After Science** all display aspects of Eno's maturing ideas about how he would express himself in song. (For those on a limited budget, the cassette/vinyl **More Blank Than Frank** is Eno's idiosyncratic condensation of the same four albums. With some repertoire fiddling, **Desert Island Selection** is the CD edition.)

The third disc of **Vocal** is an eclectic sampler, including three tracks each from his influential world-music-plus-found-vocal samples album with David Byrne and his 1990 collaboration with John Cale (the wonderful **Wrong Way Up,** a deft subversion of Top 40 formulae which brought Eno back to singing after a long silence), a pair of **Nerve Net**'s rarefied dance-music expeditions (on which Eno's vocals are, at most, minor) and five gentle, electronic-sounding **Wrong Way Up**–like items from the modest and engaging (but unreleased) **My Squelchy Life** album, recorded in

1991. Finally, the disc offers one-song samples from Eno's 1978 single with Snatch (Patti Palladin and Judy Nylon), Cale's Eno-produced **Words for the Dying** and **After the Heat,** the second of Eno's two albums with the German duo Cluster (Moebius and Roedelius). (**Old Land** is a compilation.)

The **Instrumental** entourage is both more complex in its non-chronological (not that it matters) organization and intrinsically harder to assess, as Eno moves from the exploratory wordless band essays included on his '70s vocal albums to the conceptually provocative, sonically lulling **Music for Films,** a series of four albums of hypothetical soundtrack elements. (Besides the three commercially available volumes compiled on Disc One, there's also a sampling of the "directors edition," evidently circulated privately in 1976.) Mostly recorded alone on electronic keyboards, the brief, incidental mood-setters are lovely and graceful, and occasionally a bit more biting than that, but often seem to ebb and flow from a continuous stream rather than individually considered constructions. Considering how flimsy ambient music ("sonic wallpaper" to those not so inclined) became in others' hands—at least until the techno crowd emerged to slap on a beat—Eno's pioneering efforts in the field are handsome and mellifluously substantial.

Collaborators make the second disc in the **Instrumental** box its most compelling: "Warszawa" and "Moss Garden" from, respectively, Bowie's **Low** and **Heroes** albums have a charged drama not found in Eno's solo creations. Jon Hassell adds an avant-garde edge to their work together, and Harold Budd is presumably responsible for the lovely piano on his two joint tracks. A lengthy co-composition with Daniel Lanois from **Apollo Atmospheres & Soundtracks** adequately summarizes that space voyage; an edit from **Evening Star** provides a sense of Eno's very early ethereal guitar/tape drone tail-eating exercises with Robert Fripp.

Jumping around solo projects from the '70s to the '90s, the final disc of **Instrumental** touches on the intentionally becalming **Music for Airports,** Eno's first "environmental music" release (slower **Music for Films** with less going on); **Discreet Music** (a haunting minimalist experiment using classical structures as the basis for tape loops and manipulations); the intricately realized and expressive sound paintings of **On Land** (an album of regional ruminations with subtle contributions from Hassell, guitarist Michael Brook, bassist Bill Laswell and synthesist Michael Beinhorn); **Thursday Afternoon** (an *extremely* gauzy and motionless hour-long composition—mostly tinkly piano bits and endlessly held string-like keyboard strains—created to accompany a video-art piece); **The Shutov Assembly** (ten colorful ambient floats, some with an Eastern accent and several with bird sounds, recorded during the second half of the '80s); and **Neroli** (self-importantly subtitled *Thinking Music Part IV,* it's another hour of very nearly nothing, explained in extraordinarily pompous liner notes by one C.S.J. Bofop).

After his most excellent return to pop with Cale in 1990, Eno pushed his luck with the rhythmic invigoration of **Nerve Net,** in which vocals play a small role among the (mostly) danceable beats and lively atmospheres. Joined by more people than he's had on an album of his own in many years—in the eclectic and illustrious company are Fripp, John Paul Jones, Benmont Tench, Robert Quine and Jamie West-Oram, late of the Fixx—Eno demonstrates a facility for clubbable propulsion but doesn't exude anything like the authority of his ambient work. The elephantine and tuba-shaped "Pierre in Mist" is a marvel of oddly bent noises. "The Roil, The Choke" has a handsomely overdubbed chorus of Enos. Fripp tears the roof off "Distributed Being," and "My Squelchy Life" uses a raft of (human) speakers to expound on its title. But too many of the tracks daydream through drive time, backsliding fearlessly toward lands Eno has previously tilled.

Spinner is an oddity, but a worthy adventure. Having finished a score for Derek Jarman's posthumously exhibited 1994 film, *Glitterbug,* the meticulous master of treatments and processes gave it to Jah Wobble and let him have a go at the tracks. Serving as remixer, ad hoc rhythm section (with other musicians occasionally adding guitar, percussion, keyboards and vocals) and co-composer on a couple of total overhauls, Wobble—erstwhile Public Image Ltd. bassist/co-director and one of punk's earliest and most devoted dub proponents—pumped trippy energy and mind-altering weirdness into the project, converting Eno's cerebral mood music into febrile grooves of artistic integrity and organic strength. Wobble's seesawing pans and fader fluctuations get gimmicky and distracting by the time "Left Where It Fell" drops the curtain, but most of the music finds a very happy medium between Eno's stiff-upper-lip artiness and Wobble's let-it-throb funk.

Working Backwards 1983–1973 is an eleven-disc boxed set of vinyl containing all of his solo albums through **Music for Films Volume 2,** plus an otherwise unavailable 12-inch EP of **Rarities,** featuring "Seven Deadly Finns" and "The Lion Sleeps Tonight" (both of which also appear on **Vocal**) and three ambient pieces that resurface on **Instrumental.** The inexplicable **Boxed Set** simply packages together **Another Green World, Before and After Science** and **Apollo Atmospheres and Soundtracks.** [i]

See also *David Bowie, David Byrne, John Cale, Roger Eno, James, U2, Jah Wobble's Invaders of the Heart; TPRG.*

ROGER ENO

Voices (EG) 1985
Between Tides (Opal) 1988
Lost in Translation (All Saints/Gyroscope) 1994

ROGER ENO WITH KATE ST. JOHN

The Familiar (All Saints/Gyroscope) 1993

CHANNEL LIGHT VESSEL

Automatic (All Saints/Gyroscope) 1994
Excellent Spirits (All Saints/Gyroscope) 1996

KATE ST. JOHN

Indescribable Night (All Saints/Gyroscope) 1995

LARAAJI/ROGER ENO

Islands (UK Sine) 1995

Composer/pianist/etc. Roger Eno has aided his brother Brian on many of the latter's ambient projects, collaborating most substantially on the space-shooting **Apollo Atmospheres & Soundtracks,** for which he and Daniel Lanois both received cover credit. In turn, Brian helped out with **Voices** and released its successor on his label.

Having devoted himself to instrumental music, Roger might be seen as following his sibling's creative path too closely, but he seems far more like flesh and blood; his work is warm and earthly, not remote or vague, and rooted in classical composition, not avant-garde experimentation. Finally, the acoustic instrumentation of **Between Tides** marks the point at which their designs clearly diverge. With a more traditional bent (and presumably more formal training as a musician) than Brian, Roger makes no effort to sound especially modern or preciously arty; his music for films (and television) actually gets used in things people see. Performed on piano, strings, clarinet, flute and percussion, the sonorous pieces on **Between Tides** shift between favoring venerable English idioms—"Ringinglow," "Prelude for Saint Joan"—and invoking American styles—"Dust at Dawn (The Last Cowboy in the West)". Either way, the patient music moves with the delicate refinement of characters in a Jane Austen story.

Shifting his creative orientation a little, Eno made **The Familiar** in cahoots with Kate St. John—once of the Dream Academy, now a high-profile soundtrack composer and sessioneer (for Van Morrison, Tears for Fears, Julian Cope, the Coal Porters and many others) and low-profile solo artist—on oboe and cor anglais, with ex–Be-Bop Deluxe guitarist Bill Nelson serving as co-producer and guest instrumentalist on several tracks. Thanks to the predominance of strings and piano, the album is more chamber than pop, but it does lean in the latter direction with firmly stated themes, accessibly defined structures and, thanks to St. John's lyrics and voice, five actual songs. Her nature-loving poetry and wispy soprano provide an appealing if mild contrast to Eno's solemn, placid compositions, some of which (understandably, since the album was partly recorded in St. Petersburg) have a distinct Eastern European flavor. For all its finely wrought virtues, however, **The Familiar** never unifies into a coherent whole and sounds more like a sampler of separate undertakings.

Eno, St. John and Nelson subsequently formalized their assembly as Channel Light Vessel (crediting percussionist Laraaji and cellist Mayumi Tachibana as adjunct members), setting sail with 1994's **Automatic,** a crafty cakewalk between new age's worship of the mellifluous waft, the trendy impulse toward dance rhythms and world music and whatever residual vocal pop sensibilities might be cobbled together from St. John's background and Nelson's rock campaigns. Despite the horn solos, Nelson's e-bow peregrinations and the percolating beats, the album circumvents both ambient pallor and Kenny G noxiousness, but doesn't substitute anything much more compelling than loveliness. A few of the tracks reach their evocative plateaus, but **Automatic** could have used a tad more manual labor.

Back on a more academic plane, Eno's **Lost in Translation** is an obscurely inspired but accessibly ambitious work, a handsome set of chamber-music pieces (several with vocals) based on the writings of arcane medieval heretic Walthius Van Vlaanderen. (Oh yeah, him.) Working only with guitarist Michael Brook and percussionist David Coulter, Eno demonstrates his interdisciplinary designs. Following rock's self-reliant ethos, he does something few modern composers of music this intricate would bother to do: perform it.

"Pastoral" would be too harsh a description for St. John's alluring solo album, a set of abundantly Romantic originals rendered as chamber pop, olde-school folk, suave boulevardier ballads and cocktail jazz. Both her voice and her primary instruments (oboe, piano, cor anglais) immediately convey gentleness and grace; her ability to mold such soft clay into firm, curvaceous shapes—abetted by various collaborators, including (minorly) Roger Eno and former Ravishing Beauties bandmate Virginia Astley—is impressive. The only sour note in this entire lovely enterprise is "Green Park Blues," a duet with English jazz-pop great Georgie Fame (Van Morrison's longtime bandleader), who doesn't sing it at all well. [i]

See also *Brian Eno, Nicky Holland, Bill Nelson.*

EPMD

Strictly Business (Fresh) 1988
Unfinished Business (Fresh) 1989
Business as Usual (Def Jam/RAL/Columbia) 1991
Business Never Personal (Def Jam/RAL/Chaos/Columbia) 1992

ERICK SERMON

No Pressure (Def Jam/RAL/Chaos/Columbia) 1993
Double or Nothing (Def Jam/RAL) 1995

PMD

Shadē Business (RCA) 1994

VARIOUS ARTISTS

Insomnia: The Erick Sermon Compilation Album (Bandit/Interscope) 1996

Despite his mush-mouthed voice, lazy delivery, conventional beats and tediously routine subject matter, Long Island's Erick Sermon became a bigtime rap star as the vocal half of EPMD. Wisely, though, he's put a lot of effort into outside endeavors, and he's built himself a major studio career writing and producing both hardcore hip-hop and funky R&B crossovers. Besides his collection of gold-certified EPMD and solo albums, Sermon can hang metal-plated music by Redman, Keith Murray, Shaquille O'Neal, Supercat, Jodeci, Heavy D and others on his wall. Not to mention an ad campaign for Coca-Cola Classic. Go figure.

Strictly Business bites standard old-school samples (Steve Miller, Bob Marley and so forth) with scant imagination; except for the title track's anti-drug message and a dance called "The Steve Martin," it's unprepossessing and amateurish. Likewise, the rudimentary self-production of **Unfinished Business** is its most engaging asset: Sermon and his largely silent partner Parrish Smith (the band's acronym stands for Erick and Parrish Making Dollars) sound like a couple of kids fooling around in mom's basement, rapping about nothing, singing a line or two, making cut-in jokes with some favorite records and generally amusing themselves while the tape runs. But other than a jokey and commendable condemnation of drunk driving ("You Had Too Much to Drink"), the winsomely autobiographical "Please Listen to My Demo" and a second installment of the first album's "Jane" sex saga, **Unfinished Business** is lame.

Business as Usual is anything but: mindful of the roughneck revolution fueling gangsta rap, EPMD turns up the heat with a newly aggressive stance and smoothly charged bustling soul beats. Sermon's rapping is significantly improved (not good, just better), helpfully augmented by occasional bursts of verbal aggression from Smith (especially on "Manslaughter") and guest appearances by Redman ("Hardcore," "Brothers on My Jock") and LL Cool J ("Rampage"), whose energetic, articulate flow wakes up the album, cutting through the vocal fuzz like a machete. Using violent language and drug references for standard sucker-MC put-downs, boasts, sex tales ("Mr. Bozack," "Jane 3") and a bad-marriage grumble ("Gold Digger"), the young veterans get with a new generation while staying true to the innocuous essence of their past work.

It's only on **Business Never Personal,** the duo's final album together, that Sermon and Smith at last hit their stride as a rap/production team, rocking solo and tandem vocals rifled for gangsta gun power over solidly modern and motivated high-pressure music that shares a feel with Public Enemy's Bomb Squad. Cutting the tension, the album is littered with lighthearted references: "I got more dick than Van Dyke . . . scream loud as hell like Sam Kiniston [*sic*] . . . Ya wanna buy the cassette? Stop by Sam Goody . . ." Pulling unprecedented inspiration from god knows where, EPMD launch a principled (if, for Sermon, ultimately hypocritical) and amusing attack, complete with vocoderized examples, on artists who attempt a "Crossover," wrap up their sonic serial in an effective little crime mystery ("Who Killed Jane"), make violins wax funky in "Chill" and get protégés Das EFX in for "Cummin' at Cha," a deftly rapped track that speeds history along by sampling Cypress Hill.

With EPMD consigned to history, Sermon—"The Green Eyed Bandit"—gets up to his old nothing-going-on-but-the-rent slackness to cruise lazily through **No Pressure,** a dull no-effort dose of stripped-down bass/snare funk that brings in ringers (Keith Murray, Kam, Ice Cube, Redman, Shadz of Lingo, others) to help on half the overly familiar, repetitive tracks. The titles say it all: "Imma Gitz Mine," "Safe Sex," "Stay Real" and (snore) "Erick Sermon," in which he reaches for the sky and winds up face down in the sewer. "I have a dream like Martin Luther King/That one day, yo, I could do away with the pitiful, and the critical wack MCs/Separate the ocean and throw 'em in between/Grab my nuts, hold 'em, because they're golden . . ." Pathetic.

The woozy, scratchy, blunted and downright weird **Double or Nothing** is even more of a collaboration, with Redman and Keith Murray rhyming, co-writing or co-producing a third of the cuts; others also help take the onerous load of making a record off the star's broad shoulders. Getting Redman substantially involved was a smart move: the colorful mindbender hijacks enough of the sprawling **Double or Nothing** to make it another of his strange rambles on the funky darkside. (Although not a Redman trip, the acoustic twelve-bar guitar blues of "Live in the Backyard" is one of the most surprising things ever included on a major-label rap record, and that's saying something.) Murray and a thoroughly unskilled relative, Roslyn Noble, stumble through a litany of loopy pseudo-intelligence in "Tell 'Em"; after Sermon also sits out the studio skit that follows, it's easy to forget whose record this is supposed to be. Erick does hold his own in the entertaining "Boy Meets World," but otherwise mainly contributes to the deadly ennui that creeps in soon after.

Billing himself as PMD (no commercial anxiety there, hunh?), Smith produced himself a very cool-sounding, positive-minded but ultimately self-defeating solo debut. Using uncommon samples to summon up slow rumbles from the ambient sub-basement, he vigorously and repeatedly pledges to keep his shit hard and raw, dissing those who would feed hip-hop to R&B: "Seen MCs come and seen some MCs go/Why they choose the crossover 'cause they're blind and don't know." But that's as far as Smith's ideas extend. (He does, however, namecheck virtually every hit EPMD ever had and makes a couple of veiled references to his erstwhile partner.) Occasionally borrowing the odd rollercoaster phrasing from Das EFX (who guest here), Smith expends a lot of energy making the simple sound difficult, spewing wordy boasts and celebrity similes inna old-school style. (Pushing that front, "Swing Your Own Thing" is the most shamelessly old-fashioned party jam to appear on a '90s album yet.) Coming into his own, Smith has a sturdy voice but needs a strong creative foil to really set him off on the right track next time.

Insomnia is a showcase-cum-trial-balloon of new Sermon-produced tracks by various artists, including Redman ("Funkorama"), Keith Murray ("It's That Hit") and the man himself ("Reign"), as well as a bunch of unknowns (Jamal & Calif, Duo, Domo, the Wixtons) testing the commercial waters. [i]

See also *Das EFX, Keith Murray, Redman.*

ERASURE

Wonderland (Mute/Sire) 1986
It Doesn't Have to Be EP (UK Mute) 1987
The Circus (Mute/Sire) 1987
The Two Ring Circus (Mute/Sire) 1987
The Innocents (Mute/Sire/Reprise) 1988
Crackers International EP (Mute/Sire/Reprise) 1988
Wild! (Mute/Sire/Reprise) 1989
Chorus (Mute/Sire/Reprise) 1991
Abba-esque EP (Mute/Elektra) 1992
Pop! The First 20 Hits (Mute/Sire/Reprise) 1992
I Say I Say I Say (Mute/Elektra) 1994
Erasure (Mute/Elektra) 1995

English synth-pop duo Erasure—keyboardist/songwriter Vince Clarke (ex–Depeche Mode, Assembly) and vocalist/lyricist Andy Bell—nearly cornered the market on romantic new wave expression in the late '80s. While other electronic contemporaries were building escapist flights out of their angst and depression, Erasure was joyfully reveling in such misery. Songs like "Oh L'Amour," "Blue Savannah" and "Chains of Love" work because Bell's anguish and masochistically hopeful words—carried aloft by his soaring, often delicate, voice—are of universal constitution, while Clarke's unforgettable melodic hooks support his partner's pronouncements with complementary ease.

Erasure broke into the new decade with **Chorus,** a heady album that expands on **Wild!**'s experimentation while solidifying the duo's melodic skill. Clarke's synth strains show more subtlety and depth, making many of the songs ("Joan," even the '80s throwback "Love to Hate You") more enticing; Bell's singing is likewise improved. His progressive scale-climbing on "Am I Right?" and stunning overdubbed backup work (the act's oft-overlooked ace-in-the-hole) on the title track help make **Chorus** one of Erasure's best.

The sole redeeming aspect of the forgettable **Abba-esque,** an EP of four campy covers, was the carnival-like theater tour undertaken to promote it. Clarke's zippy Synth-mobile that raced about the stage and Bell's homoerotic ringleader routine made up for the fluff of songs like "Voulez Vous" and "S.O.S." That same year saw the release of **Pop! The First 20 Hits,** an exhaustive singles roundup.

Bell's lyrics are the star of **I Say I Say I Say;** the album displays unprecedented happiness and optimism ("Like a knight in shining armor, you came over to save me") and spirit (the uncharacteristic spontaneity of "Run to the Sun"). A church choir buoys "So the Story Goes" and "Miracle"; "Always," a poignant and infectious ode to a lost lover, brought Erasure a return to the American singles chart.

Erasure reveals Clark's emergent fascination with Pink Floyd's flightier works—see "Rescue Me," "Fingers & Thumbs (Cold Summer's Day)" and the endless introduction to "Rock Me Gently"—which occasionally clashes with Bell's words of longing and ache. The lyrics' straight-for-the-heart effect do retain their magic, however, even moving past simple romantic themes on "Grace," a plea for simple human consideration toward all. [tja]

See also *Depeche Mode.*

ROKY ERICKSON AND THE ALIENS

Roky Erickson and the Aliens (UK CBS) 1980
The Evil One (415) 1981 (Pink Dust/Restless) 1987
I Think of Demons (UK Edsel) 1987

ROKY ERICKSON

Mine Mine Mind EP (Fr. Sponge) 1977
Clear Night for Love EP (Fr. New Rose) 1985 (UK Fundamental) 1988
Don't Slander Me (Pink Dust) 1986
Gremlins Have Pictures (Pink Dust) 1986 (UK Demon) 1990
The Holiday Inn Tapes (Fr. Fan Club) 1987
Live at the Ritz 1987 (Fr. Fan Club) 1988
Click Your Fingers Applauding the Play (Fr. New Rose) 1990
Reverend of Karmic Youth (Skyclad) 1990
You're Gonna Miss Me: The Best of Roky Erickson (Restless) 1991
Mad Dog (UK Swordfish) 1992
Love to See You Bleed (UK Swordfish) 1992
Demon Angel (Ger. Texas Recordings) 1994
All That May Do My Rhyme (Trance Syndicate) 1995

ROKY ERICKSON AND THE EXPLOSIVES

Casting the Runes (UK Five Hours Back) 1987

ROKY ERICKSON AND THE RESURRECTIONISTS

Beauty and the Beast (Sympathy for the Record Industry) 1987

ROKY ERICKSON BAND

Two Headed Dog EP (Fr. Fan Club) 1988

ROKY ERICKSON AND THE NERVEBREAKERS

Live Dallas 1979 (Fr. Fan Club) 1992

ROKY ERICKSON & EVIL HOOK WILDLIFE E.T.

Roky Erickson & Evil Hook Wildlife E.T. (Sympathy for the Record Industry) 1996

VARIOUS ARTISTS

Where the Pyramid Meets the Eye: A Tribute to Roky Erickson (Sire/Warner Bros.) 1990

As lead singer of Texas' 13th Floor Elevators—one of rock's earliest and greatest psychedelic bands—Roky Erickson explored the far reaches of musical and personal extremes. The Elevators' first two albums (**Psychedelic Sounds of the 13th Floor Elevators** and **Easter Everywhere,** released, respectively, in 1966 and '67) are essential classics whose far-reaching influence transcends genre boundaries. Following a nightmarish '70s mental-hospital stint that reportedly had a devastating long-term effect on his mental health, Erickson's subsequent work revealed a singularly brilliant songwriter and performer whose talent was no less impressive for the fact that he was singing about zombies, vampires and aliens. Indeed, the demons that abound in Roky's songs are all-too-real reflections of his own troubled psyche, and the combination of the artist's oddly poetic lyrical constructions and his bracing banshee wail makes it clear, as it wasn't always, that he's not kidding.

The 1980 CBS UK album and its subsequent variants, **The Evil One** and **I Think of Demons,** stem from sessions produced by ex–Creedence Clearwater Revival bassist Stu Cook and feature many of Roky's essential songs, given blazing if somewhat overmanicured readings by a consistently hot band. The Pink Dust CD of **The Evil One** is the best available representation of this period, containing all fifteen of Roky's Cook-produced tracks. A second album, recorded for and rejected by CBS, was later released as **Don't Slander Me.** Though not quite up to its predecessor's standards, it contains much of worth, including versions of three bona fide classics: "Bermuda," the Buddy Hollyesque "Starry Eyes" and the savage title track. Those last two were rerecorded in Austin for the five-song **Clear Night for Love,** which preceded a decade-long recording hiatus.

By 1990, Roky's demons had got the best of him, and he was temporarily reinstitutionalized after being arrested in a bizarre mail-fraud mix-up. Those tribulations inspired the production of **Where the Pyramid Meets the Eye,** a tribute/benefit disc featuring nineteen artists (twenty-two on the cassette) taking trips from the Erickson songbook. Although it neglects several important items in the repertoire, the album neatly demonstrates the enduring strength and melodic accessibility of his remarkable songwriting, which stands up to interpretations by artists as diverse as R.E.M., ZZ Top, Doug Sahm, Jesus and Mary Chain, Julian Cope and the Butthole Surfers.

Though the tribute record helped raise the reclusive artist's public profile, Erickson was in no condition to take advantage. Instead, his increased notoriety helped feed the steady stream of reissues, repackagings, bootlegs and "authorized" live recordings (with various backing combos) that had begun appearing in the mid-'80s. **Gremlins Have Pictures** is an odds-and-ends collection that contains plenty of fine moments, including an incendiary live rendition of Lou Reed's "Heroin." **Click Your Fingers Applauding the Play** combines the contents of **Two Headed Dog** (itself a reissue of the four-song **Mine Mine Mind,** with early versions of "Red Temple Prayer" and "Mine Mine Mind") and **Clear Night for Love** with the considerably less essential **Holiday Inn Tapes** (lo-fi stream-of-consciousness acoustic performances). **You're Gonna Miss Me** offers a decent selection of tracks from **The Evil One, Don't Slander Me** and **Gremlins Have Pictures,** along with a few minor rarities.

Mad Dog is an excellent collection of late-'70s demos and live tracks, including alternate versions of various **Evil One** and **Don't Slander Me** numbers, many of which cut the "official" versions. **Love to See You Bleed** draws from the same pool of material, with less worthwhile music but more bizarre archival curios. **Demon Angel** offers a solid live acoustic performance, while **Reverend of Karmic Youth** mixes solo acoustic and live band tracks. As for the concert discs, **Live Dallas 1979** has good sound quality, while **Beauty and the Beast** includes a couple of hard-to-find songs. Best of the lot, though, is **Live at the Ritz 1987,** which, despite its bootleggish fidelity, boasts a ferocious performance. The CD edition includes an absolutely incredible sixteen-minute radio interview that's worth the price of admission on its own. The **Evil Hook Wildlife E.T.** album combines some savage mid-'80s live numbers with a pair of incendiary studio tracks and brief interview snippets.

After an extended period of inactivity, Roky was coaxed out of retirement to record five new, generally demon-free songs (and a version of "Starry Eyes" featuring blues-rock vocalist Lou Ann Barton), which were added to **Clear Night for Love** to construct **All That May Do My Rhyme.** The result is surprisingly cohesive, with the new material showing Erickson still capable of writing fetchingly elliptical pop tunes ("We Are Never Talking") and reflecting compellingly on his own travails ("Please Judge"). Also included is an unlisted bonus track, the 1965 single "We Sell Soul," by Erickson's pre-Elevators band, the Spades. The album was released in conjunction with the publication of a handsome, illustrated book of Roky's lyrics, *Openers II.* [ss]

See also *TPRG.*

ERIC'S TRIP

Eric's Trip [tape] (Can. no label) 1990
Catapillars [tape] (Can. no label) 1991
Drowning EP [tape] (Can. no label) 1991
Warm Girl [tape] (Can. no label) 1992 EP7 (Can. Derivative) 1993
Belong EP7 (Can. NIM) 1992
Peter EP (Can. Murderecords) 1993
Songs About Chris EP (Sub Pop) 1993
Julie and the Porthole to Dimentia EP7 (Can. Sappy) 1993
Love Tara (Sub Pop) 1993
The Gordon Street Haunting EP (Sub Pop) 1994
Forever Again (Sub Pop) 1994
Purple Blue (Sub Pop) 1996

Indie-rock's open invitation, even to those possessing limited skill and talent, is, unfortunately, a siren song to mediocrity. Openness is fundamental to the scene's character and development, but it sometimes gives a free ride to hitchhikers on the underground highway—those who sport the right clothes, a friendly smile and the right minimalist attitude rather than discernible talent.

Named for a Sonic Youth song, Eric's Trip—a sweet noisy/quiet pop quartet from Moncton, New Brunswick (due east of Maine)—has released a gargantuan amount of sketchy music since forming in 1990. Some of it is pleasant, although the band's full-length debut (1993's **Love Tara**) is a sloppy, half-baked indulgence with precious few songs that actually amount to anything. That album followed a total of thirty-three self-released cassette tracks, the seventeen songs contained on the **Belong, Peter** and **Songs About Chris** EPs plus the four items that compose **Julie and the Porthole to Dimentia.** (And don't forget the side projects: Elevator to Hell, Broken Girl, Moon Socket and Purple Knight, the band from which drummer Mark Gaudet was "borrowed" in 1991.)

Forever Again is a lot better, but still as sloppy, vague and aimless as a fluffy cloud in a spring breeze. Bassist Julie Doiron takes a greater singing role alongside soft-voiced guitarist Rick White; the songwriting tightens some of the eighteen selections into shapely forms, most noticeably when acoustic lightness is the chosen timbre. The group's lyrical themes—winsome vulnerability, passing sadness and bemused confusion—get a lot of exercise, but the record moves along briskly enough so nobody has to dwell morbidly on life's disappointments. Typical of the band's cursory designs, "About You" consists of Doiron's admission "I haven't even told my brother/I just finished telling my mother—she took it OK/I always wondered what they'd do / When I told them about you." That's either a brilliant display of musical Cubism or a song fragment. Take your pick.

The release of a third full-length album, **Purple Blue,** was discolored by the group's (quickly rescinded) decision to disband several weeks later. By way of implicit explanation, White clearly announces his exhaustion—albeit in a romantic setting—in the excitable "Sun Coming Up": "I'm sick of writing love-gone-wrong songs/Sick of even trying sometimes." An assured slip of a record that favors full-on distorted rocketry over airy folk-pop and dinky minimalism, **Purple Blue** merely lacks the tunes that would defer tedium. ("Now a Friend," a difficult post-breakup rapprochement, is a notable exception.) The short songs' near-random designs seem be based on nothing more than a simple downcast lyrical idea and whatever melody and chords come to mind; longtime producer Bob Weston gets them on tape without any signs of structuring or editing. For all the sensitivity and reflection, such thoughtlessness is hard to fathom. [i]

ALEJANDRO ESCOVEDO

Gravity (Watermelon) 1992
Thirteen Years (Watermelon) 1993
With These Hands (Rykodisc) 1996

TRUE BELIEVERS

True Believers (Rounder/EMI) 1986
Hard Road (Rykodisc) 1994

A one-man travelogue of places, eras and styles, Texas native Alejandro Escovedo first surfaced in the late '70s, playing chilly punk in San Francisco's Nuns, which he had instigated as a college film project. He moved to New York and worked with no wave art-rocker Judy Nylon, co-founded the cowpunk quartet Rank and File (appearing on its 1982 debut album following a relocation to Austin) with the Kinman brothers and then undertook his first leadership/major songwriting role in True Believers. The singer/guitarist launched the eclectic rock quintet with his brother Javier (ex-Zeros) in 1983 and cut a pair of albums, the second of which got caught in a record company shuffle and remained unreleased until 1994, when it was included on **Hard Road,** a retitled reissue of the Jim Dickinson–produced debut. Both contain strong and sensitive southwestern rock heated to various energy levels (the second is far stronger and more commercial, a gritty rock album with only the faintest Texas T), but the band never found its focus, and a shortage of stylistic conviction consigned it to generic defeat in 1987.

In Austin, Escovedo formed a floating rock "orchestra" with strings ("I Wanna Be Your Dog" a specialty), a short-lived rock band, named Buick McKane after a T. Rex song, and built a local base without benefit of any new record releases for more than five years. Then, emotionally shattered by the end of a long marriage and his ex-wife's subsequent suicide in 1991, he began his career in earnest with a wake: the redemptive, mournful **Gravity.** In the clarified artistic vision of a mature musician with a broken heart, a spiritual sense of his place in the world and a rich, resonant voice, Escovedo devised an electric folk idiom—part Townes Van Zandt, part Band, part Rolling Stones—powerfully suited to the poetic hair shirt he donned. From the somber album's very first verse ("Did you get your invitation?/There's gonna be a public hanging/And the bodies will swing side by side/And it's just I and I"), **Gravity** pulls Escovedo down, graveward, even while the stately eloquence of its sound provides him with a graceful escape route. Inconsolable grief stains his voice in the bitter "Five Hearts Breaking," memories overtake him in "She Doesn't Live Here Anymore" and a bleak barrenness descends over "The Last to Know." But "Gravity/Falling Down Again," which ends the album, has the last laugh—literally—with a "La la la/Ha ha ha" chorus as grimly devastating as any scream of pure agony.

The more artfully composed **Thirteen Years** recasts Escovedo's enduring sense of loss, using strings (partly arranged and played by Poi Dog Pondering violinist Susan Voelz, among others) and the recurring "Thirteen Years Theme" to connect the songs. Built around the title track's haunted autobiography, a narrative ballad that benefits from the elegant drawing-room setting, the album—a testament to patience and virtue—is a marvel of presentation more than content. "Ballad of the Sun and Moon" is a buoyant opener, and "She Towers Above" and "Baby's Got New Plans" wind things down with grave elegance, but the conversational "Try, Try, Try" is awkward and "Losing Your Touch," with guest guitarist Charlie Sexton, sounds an awful lot like a Replacements outtake.

Simply getting Willie Nelson and Jennifer Warnes in to sing duets with him moves Escovedo onto a new plateau, but **With These Hands** is no unseemly commercial bid, just further evidence of his broad and inclusive talent. Although the diverse collection contains some of the strongest rock he's put on tape since True Believers (the opening "Put You Down," the bluesy harmonica-wailing "Little Bottles" and the rollicking "Guilty" are surging standouts), Escovedo also essays classical-folk balladry (the Nelson-equipped "Nickel and a Spoon"), a gorgeous small-combo acoustic piano elegy ("Tired Skin") and a zesty Latin-percussion throwdown (with niece Sheila E. and a bunch of other Escovedos guesting) on the title track. The album ends with "Tugboat," an atmospheric tribute to Sterling Morrison. [i]

See also *Silos.*

ESG

ESG EP (99) 1981
ESG Says Dance to the Beat of Moody EP (99) 1982
Come Away With ESG (99) 1983
ESG (Pow Wow) 1991
Sample Credits Don't Pay Our Bills EP (Nega Fulo) 1992
ESG Live! CD (Nega Fulo) 1995

ESG is an anomaly. Renee, Valerie and Marie Scroggins—sisters from the South Bronx who all sing and play percussion in the group (which also contains bassist Leroy Glover)—are outsiders to the main musical community that appreciates them. While most contemporary dance music, rap and funk relies on machines and samples, the Scroggins have the real thing down cold, live. Accenting their tight-but-loose adept polyrhythms with a light guitar and sturdy, loping bass, they have a stark, wonderful power.

As they try to work it and earn it in the '90s, the low-profile group is making a few concessions to popular style, exhibiting more awareness of current musical trends. Unfortunately, the newer material tries too hard in comparison to the easy, unique tracks that made them darlings of the downtown crowd a decade earlier. Both **ESG** and **ESG Live!** include the sparse and spacey "UFO" and "Moody," studio tracks originally produced for the band's 99 records by Englishman Martin Hannett.

The self-titled 1991 album pulls together bits from the previous releases, including "Erase You," a spiral of staggered rhythms, with someone barking like a dog, that tells the engaging story of a guy gone bad. The five-song **Sample Credits Don't Pay Our Bills** 12-inch returns the group to longer dance tracks, with the same echoey percussion and vocals neatly placed under a soft layer of new wavish guitar. (The title refers to the long line of artists—TLC, Beastie Boys, Big Daddy Kane, Wu-Tang Clan, even indie-rockers Unrest—who have used ESG's loose loops, and the group's occasional compensation problems.)

Recorded at New York's Club USA and New Jersey's WFMU, **ESG Live!** draws attention to Renee Scroggins' voice, which goes from a cool, insistent meow to warm, soulful and beat-aware within individual songs. But the record includes some bad new material. A slick guitar solo by David Miles dominates "You and Me"; "A New Day" is awkward contemporary R&B where the beats don't match up with the singing. The lone new studio track, "Dance a Lick," includes a dreadful rap that no amount of the sisters' stupendous playing can redeem. [rxe]

ESP-BEETLES/ESP-FAMILY/ ESP-SUMMER

See *His Name Is Alive.*

MAGGIE ESTEP

No More Mr. Nice Girl (NuYo/Imago) 1994

The spoken-word glut may have given verbally oriented artists outside hip-hop a foot in the door of '90s youth culture but, confronted with the prospect of committing their work to tape, even the most serious proponents of the nouveau coffeehouse have reached for such old-fashioned rock'n'roll implements as loud guitars and steady 4/4 beats. Maggie Estep, a longtime fixture on New York's poetry/performance art scene, is no exception. Even though her solo performances seethe with a star-quality combination of charisma and content that should make such crutches superfluous, Estep's album, **No More Mr. Nice Girl** (which incorporates material from her similarly named one-woman show), finds her so bent on coloring within the lines of rock song structure that she sacrifices her usual slashing intensity for mere melodicism. (Her accompaniment on the record comes from a trio called I Love Everybody, which includes Bush Tetras guitarist Pat Place.)

It's hard to find fault with Estep's verse, rife as it is with rib-tickling one-liners and painfully precise social detailing. From the pungent sexuality that permeates "Fuck Me" to the Grand Guignol carnage that drips from "My Life of Gardening," Estep's imagery is such a sensual delight that it's almost—but not quite—possible to forgive her tentative, generic "singing." But only when Estep bobs and weaves through the closing "Bad Day at the Beauty Salon" (the album's only full-length spoken piece), attacking the lines with true gusto, are her true strengths revealed. [dss]

MELISSA ETHERIDGE

Melissa Etheridge (Island) 1988
Brave and Crazy (Island) 1989
Never Enough (Island) 1992
Yes I Am (Island) 1993
Your Little Secret (Island) 1995

Given rock'n'roll's sexual essence, it's inevitable that the private lives and public styles of people who create popular music become a pivotal issue to some of those who consume it. Fans of all but the most distant performers see themselves or their desires reflected in their icons, scattered through a shattered prism of social pressures, lyrical messages, contrived images and personal realities. Before young women began significantly integrating rock's male preserve in the last decade, the simplistic formulation that prevailed was that boys wanted to be their heroes and girls wanted to sleep with them. That thesis suffered gamely through several confusing phases (the cross-dressing and camp of glam rockers and the new romantics, bi-sexuality's trendiness, the willful asexuality of punk), surviving into the arena-rocking late '80s, thanks to manly men like Jon Bon Jovi, Bruce Springsteen and Sting. Then came uncloseted (and closeted) lesbians and gays, and it was back to the role-model drawing board.

Given the permutations of male/female straight/gay fans and performers (for non-math types, that's sixteen possible matchups), the erasure of old presumptions creates a whorl of new cross-currents. Boys want to be them, and girls want to sleep with them? Boys want to sleep with them and girls want to be them? Straight girls wish they were cool enough to be lesbians so they could be better fans? Gay people don't care if the music's good so long as it specifically addresses or includes them? Straight people think the music's cool but can't deal with (or don't ask and don't want to know about) the performer's orientation? As Ray Davies once observed, it's a mixed-up, muddled-up, shook-up world, and—in a self-obsessed inversion of pop music's onetime role as a generation's defining culture—sectarian identity politics have become an aesthetic factor of '90s rock life.

It took Melissa Etheridge years to find the commercial courage to clarify the sex of her obscure objects of desire; as a platinum-selling star, her 1993 acknowledgment of what everyone apparently already knew was a total non-event. Interestingly, her lyrics haven't changed much since the revelation. On her early albums, while wielding romance-novel ultra-passions like a sweat-drenched gladiator, the rough-voiced Kansas singer/guitarist played it coy only in terms of who she was addressing in her clenched-fist epics of jealousy, recrimination and lust. No one has ever gotten further relying on the word "you," leaving the rest to listeners' imaginations. Coming out hasn't appreciably altered that formulation.

Melissa Etheridge is a transition from folkie to rocker, using the semi-acoustic format to shape songs Etheridge overheats to a blood-curdling boil. She roars her most insignificant musings like a mortally wounded female Springsteen. The album is a ludicrous bodice-ripper, in which emotions are writ across the sky in letters that soar a thousand feet high. Aches ache, thirsts can't be quenched—even in nights of "shaking lust and fire." "I guess I'm just addicted to the pain of delight," she sings in "Occasionally," offering an enigmatic view on the joy of sex. Intemperate in extremis, Etheridge isn't afraid to make her unbridled furies seem utterly ridiculous: in "Like I Do," what she needs to know is does The Other "inject you seduce you and affect you"? The related "Similar Features" has subtler lyrics, but still heaves and lurches in its melodramatic turmoil. Powerful feelings are a great asset in art, but Etheridge hasn't got a clue how to focus her intensity into anything better than a public display of rejection.

Adding guitarist Bernie Larsen to the first album's Kevin McCormick (bass, co-production) and new drummer Mauricio Fritz Lewak, **Brave and Crazy** tones down and shifts the arrangements a notch up the evolutionary scale, but the songs (other than the tender "You Can Sleep While I Drive") fall short, as do Etheridge's uneasy efforts to locate a workable folk-rock style for herself. Either she got too much off her chest the first time, or she was reconsidering ways to express the heat of her ardor. In any case, **Brave and Crazy** is repetitive and dull.

Never Enough suffers from the same half-baked malady. The debut's rampant extroversion hangs like the ghost of lost youth on this glossy attempt at sounding grown-up and radio friendly (not to mention blonde) by sublimating Etheridge's raw fury into sessioneer-aided studio concoctions and random rhythmic variety. "It's for You" reaches back for its rousing chorus, but the verses are standard MOR mush; "Must Be Crazy for Me" tries to boil up a Meters-like gumbo but only gets the canned stew lukewarm; "Meet Me in the Back" alternates between a brisk Latin-tinged chorus and a lightly jazzified vamp verse. Although her self-produced stylistic grappling is subtly managed, it's obvious Etheridge hasn't got a clue what works for her. For all the first record's abject wretchedness, it's a model of stylistic integrity compared to this futile exertion. One could read psycho-sexual resonance into the defensive process of seeking a popularly acceptable identity, but why bother?

One has to know the right question to ask for **Yes I Am** to be the courageous personal declaration many mistook it to be. (The line's actual use in the title track is to answer "Am I your passion, your promise, your end?") Otherwise, Etheridge's lyrics conduct business as usual (even "Talking to My Angel" obfuscates: "he said that it's alright") on her breakthrough record, co-produced for maximum Bryan Adams–style anthemic arena power by Hugh Padgham. Cutting the crap, the album sets Etheridge firmly where she belongs—in the elementary wind tunnel of stadium rock with easy, bonfire songs that can be bellowed by one and all: "I'm the Only One," "Come to My Window," "All American Girl" (a dreadful attempt at topical commentary that barely deserves John Mellencamp, whom she obviously seeks to emulate in it). As Etheridge's lyrical emotions run the gamut from intense to intenser, fiddling with their presentation is pointless. Songs build from folky/arty introductions to surging electric choruses, which suits her fine. But with the quieter efforts seeming to evaporate and the songwriting very uneven, what could have been an important mainstream record collapses into a couple of hits and a bunch of filler.

Reuniting with Padgham but hiring different sidemen, Etheridge clears away the final impediments to pure commercial pop-rock on **Your Little Secret,** an efficient and unambitious followup to **Yes I Am.** Having gained some skill as a singer, she settles into a harmonious balance with the electric music's shiny appointments, getting more emotional mileage from less gut-busting intensity. Like other veteran stars with no burning creative agenda, she mines her songwriting formula reliably, bringing traces of outside styles (like the country twang of "All the Way to Heaven" and the elegiac artiness of "This War Is Over") to her rather than stretching in their direction. Meanwhile, she has fun winking at the double entendres in her lyrics. "I Really Like You" promises "I'll buy you mangos baby . . . I'll shave everything," while the title track strains not to come out and finally reveal something (which, by this point, was a secret only to those lacking access to a television, library or newsstand): "Before your cover's blown . . . You make it hard . . . I will not lie." By album's end, she can "take off my shield . . . I won't need it anymore." Phew! [i]

ETHYL MEATPLOW

Happy Days, Sweetheart (Dali/Chameleon) 1993

GERALDINE FIBBERS

Get Thee Gone EP10 (Sympathy for the Record Industry) 1994

Geraldine Fibbers EP (UK Hut) 1995

Lost Somewhere Between the Earth and My Home (Virgin) 1995

BUCCINATOR

The Great Painter Rafael (Basura!/Priority) 1994

E. COLI

To Drool (Triple X) 1996

Strong personalities searching for efficient means of expression often take the path of least resistance, and that's what sleepy-voiced singer Carla Bozulich evidently did in Ethyl Meatplow. Making a notable point of upfront sexuality, **Happy Days, Sweetheart,** the offbeat and inconsistent Los Angeles trio's one album—co-produced with typical anything-goes openness (including wacky horns and strings) by Barry Adamson—skips ambiguously from industrialized Beasties-style hip-hop to aimless noisemaking to ambient techno crooning to bouncy pop bop that sounds suspiciously like the B-52's. (John Napier, going by the name Harold Barefoot Sanders III here, has a voice evidently pawned by Fred Schneider.) A lot of the record is good fun, a lot of it isn't—"Devil's Johnson" is a bit of both, and the knowledge of bad words Bozulich demonstrates in "Queenie" is neither—but the effort's attempt to overwhelm is ultimately too successful for its own good.

Switching her allegiance to a side project convened casually with members of a punk band called Glue, Bozulich became the mouthpiece of the Geraldine Fibbers, a confused quintet as tangentially committed to the exploitation of country music as Ethyl Meatplow was to rap. **Lost Somewhere Between the Earth and My Home** uses lyrics of rustic sentimentality and devastation, Jessy Green's sawed violin and viola and somebody's warped idea of backwoods melodicism by way of Patti Smith to occasionally signify rural dignity amid Daniel Keenan's craggy guitar distortion and straightahead post-punk rock drive. (Letting it all rip in "Dusted" and "The Small Song," the Fibbers give Hole a good run for their money.) Bozulich, who alternates between venomous power and cozy restraint here, has a lot to unload, and unload she does in "Dragon Lady," which tears down and rebuilds a female ego in a pointed attack on oppression, "A Song About Walls" and "Richard," both of which portray women as relationship victims for whom violence is the only recourse. That's a potent, provocative theme, but the album's dissolute stylistic meanderings and pretensions ill-serve the songs' angry underdogs. (**Geraldine Fibbers** is a UK compilation of the band's four-song debut EP and a subsequent 7-inch single, also from '94.)

For his part, singer/guitarist Napier (whose long LA band résumé includes Fourwaycross and Chris D's Stone by Stone) launched the Basura! label and formed Buccinator, a loosely convened collective of pals that includes Jon Wahl of Clawhammer, Dave Gomez of Beck's band and Amery Smith of the Beastie Boys' touring crew. Buccinator's debut, **The Great Painter Rafael,** pores around the grubby distortions of silly guitar rock, as the quartet carefully prevents any of its instruments from actually sounding like God (or Leo Fender) meant them to. That said, it's an entertaining exercise—part Pixies, part small-scale Buttholian fashion, with similar nutjob lyrics ("Jippy," "El Tweeko")—revealing a certain internal logic and adequate flashes of thought in the slow-moving fray. At its very best, the album lays out a gristly gris gris like "Discipline the Fireman" which hypothesizes Dr. John reborn as a skronk rocker.

Donning a natty business suit, Napier subsequently launched E. Coli with bassist Johnny Baker and drummer Denis Fleps. **To Drool** is unchallenging pop punk/rock—more like an indie translation of Cheap Trick than an older Green Day—with songs that rarely surpass okay, given bonus doses of guitar and Napier's oddly effortless vocals. [i]

ÉTOILE DE DAKAR

See *Youssou N'Dour.*

EUGENIUS

Oomalama (Fire/Atlantic) 1992
Mary Queen of Scots (Atlantic) 1994

CAPTAIN AMERICA

Wow! EP (UK Paperhouse) 1991
Flame on EP (UK Paperhouse) 1992

VASELINES

Dying for It EP (UK 53rd & 3rd) 1988
Dum Dum (UK 53rd & 3rd) 1989 (UK Avalanche) 1991
All the Stuff and More (UK Avalanche) 1992
The Way of the Vaselines: A Complete History (Sub Pop) 1992

Glasgow singer/guitarist Eugene Kelly, a onetime Pastel and BMX Bandit, broke into the international pop underground as half of the Vaselines, Scotland's ramshackle brilliant noisy love-pop minimalists. (Frances McKee was Kelly's partner; the group also used a rhythm section and other musicians at times.) The band's brief recording career in the late '80s was facilitated and partly produced by scene patriarch Stephen Pastel and later received a helpful thumbs-up from Nirvana, who were fans enough to cover "Molly's Lips," "Son of a Gun" and "Jesus Wants Me for a Sunbeam." (Although the song turned up on **MTV Unplugged in New York** as "Jesus Doesn't Want Me for a Sunbeam.") The originals of those—plus everything else the group ever completed—are on **The Way of the Vaselines** (aka **All the Stuff and More**), a handy and frequently delightful nineteen-track collection.

After the Vaselines, Kelly formed Captain America, which, following two ace singles, abandoned its moniker under threat of legal action from Marvel Comics and adopted his nickname, Eugenius, instead. Released in the stylistic wake of Teenage Fanclub's **Bandwagonesque** and not that far removed from the way of the Vaselines (except for the production, a thickly laid-on spread of guitar and harmony vocals), **Oomalama** introduces a quartet firmly under Kelly's loopy direction and sharp pop instincts. Calmly applying his Robyn Hitchcocky voice to stellar songs that roll even music (a raucous catchy pop rush somewhere between the Byrds and Stooges) and odd lyrics, Kelly and his three bandmates make a merry mess that is as sensually satisfying as it is delightful. The wonderfully anthemic title track consists solely of the nonsense title and the phrase "I am alive and back again"; "Breakfast" is insistent on the point that "sometimes I can't help falling down"; "Bed-In" begins by observing, "I've watched so much TV my head's gone square." There's not a bad tune in the bunch, and highlights like "Flame On" and "Buttermilk" abound. The American edition expands the original Paperhouse UK issue with three tracks, including a gorgeous cover—with strings—of Beat Happening's "Indian Summer."

In light of such a brilliant debut, Eugenius' next album was likely to fall short, and **Mary Queen of Scots** doesn't stint on the disappointment. Craig Leon's blandly efficient production tightens up the band's sonic act to the detriment of songs that are already vastly inferior to **Oomalama**'s joy-filled gems. The shortage of inspiration in both writing and performing is obvious, blanketing the whole half-hearted effort like an overcast day. The tuneful "Blue Above the Rooftops" and the robust "Love, Bread and Beers" partially share the prior set's virtues; the album's other obvious standout, "Let's Hibernate," contains some of its few interesting lyrics, especially a couplet that might easily be used to describe what's gone wrong: "You're ugly and rational now/You've really got no point to make." [i]

See also *BMX Bandits, Pastels.*

EURYTHMICS

See *Annie Lennox, Dave Stewart.*

EVERCLEAR

Nervous & Weird EP (Tim/Kerr) 1993
World of Noise (Tim/Kerr) 1994 (Tim/Kerr/Capitol) 1994
Fire Maple Song EP (Tim/Kerr/Capitol) 1994
Sparkle and Fade (Tim/Kerr/Capitol) 1995

During the extended post-**Nevermind** bender that befogged the music business for a good portion of the early '90s—to the benefit of travel agents across the Pacific Northwest—nary a major label could fight the temptation to procure (or invent) its own angst-ridden (but user-friendly), noisy (but pop-savvy) post-grunge gaggle. At first glance, Everclear would seem to have all the markings of the Nirvana-be: singer/guitarist Art Alexakis (formerly of San Francisco's Colorfinger) wraps his frayed vocal cords around tales of self-doubt and self-hatred, straying only rarely from the tense-verse/cathartic-chorus pattern that Kurt Cobain had such a masterful way with, but the band proves more authentic than most.

While **World of Noise** (a basement recording the Portland, Oregon, trio initially released on the city's leading indie) is mostly unremarkable, Alexakis does invest some of his lyrics (especially the seething "Pennsylvania Is . . .") with the sort of white-trash sincerity that marked the Replacements' more sober moments. The **Fire Maple Song** EP uses two versions of the gentle title track to bookend four non-LP songs (highlighted by the surf-punk "Pacific Wonderland") that benefit from the fluid playing of new drummer Greg Eklund.

Sparkle and Fade (recorded at Butch Vig's Smart Studios, but not with the famed producer at the controls) is an altogether more mature, more distinctive effort on which Alexakis is encouragingly disposed to flex a pop sensibility he previously held in abeyance. His subjects still get the short end of the stick—be it the dying addict of "Heroin Girl" or the tormented interracial lovers of "Heartspark Dollarsign"—but the sheer radiance of songs like "Santa Monica" (which demands repeated listens) adds to the luster of this unexpected gem. [dss]

EVERLAST

See *House of Pain.*

EVERYTHING BUT THE GIRL

Eden (UK Blanco y Negro) 1984
Everything but the Girl (Blanco y Negro/Sire) 1984 (Blanco y Negro/Sire/Warner Archives) 1995
Love Not Money (Blanco y Negro/Sire) 1985 (Blanco y Negro/Sire/Warner Archives) 1995

Baby, the Stars Shine Bright (Blanco y Negro/Sire) 1986
(Blanco y Negro/Sire/Warner Archives) 1995
Idlewild (Blanco y Negro/Sire) 1988
The Language of Life (Atlantic) 1990
Worldwide (Atlantic) 1991
Covers EP (UK Warner Music) 1991
Acoustic (Atlantic) 1992
Essence & Rare–82–92 (Japan. Toy's Factory) 1992
Home Movies: The Best of Everything but the Girl (UK Blanco y Negro) 1993
Amplified Heart (Atlantic) 1994
Walking Wounded (Atlantic) 1996

Whether you consider them innovative anti-rockists or middle-of-the-road fuddyduddies, it's hard not to have a certain admiration for Everything but the Girl. As prime movers in the lite-jazz demi-movement that once included Swing Out Sister, Weekend and the Style Council, the group—Ben Watt and Tracey Thorn—has made impressive brushes with chart success while attracting an exceedingly loyal following that has held fast through phases of bedsit musing, lounge jazz and even slick fern-bar pop.

When Thorn (formerly of the drizzly spare gloom-pop Marine Girls) began working with proto-prog guitarist Ben Watt in their native Hull in 1982, the two didn't so much merge those aforementioned aesthetics as stew them until the mélange took on unexpected, utterly unrecognizable flavors. On **Eden,** the duo's full-length bow, Watt's contributions are low-key enough to be imperceptible, while Thorn's vocals—often multi-tracked in the best '60s la-la-la pop tradition—are positively beguiling. Imagine Astrud Gilberto imbued with British diffidence, and you'll begin to get the picture. The subsequent self-titled American album reprises about half of **Eden,** adding a half-dozen new tracks that don't tweak the formula appreciably.

Watt tables his more overtly jazzy riffs for **Love Not Money,** but the breezy ambience remains intact. Songs like "Heaven Help Me" suggest that if Thorn had been born a few years earlier, she could've given Petula Clark a run for her money as swinging London's fave songbird. **Baby, the Stars Shine Bright** isn't quite as fetching, since the added string and horn sections frequently overwhelm Watt's delicate arrangements. Likewise, the intermittent use of backing vocals is a detriment to a singer with a voice as winsomely appealing as Thorn's. Fortunately, the orchestral experiment proved short-lived: for **Idlewild,** the couple employed a bassist and a sensitive, pared-down horn section that served to underscore the album's pervasive melancholy. In songs like "Oxford Street" and (on the UK edition only) an altogether devastating version of Danny Whitten's "I Don't Want to Talk About It," the effect is as engrossing as watching waves crash against a storm-tossed beach.

The Language of Life is a trickier read. On one hand, it's a virtually complete surrender to the pressures of the commercial market, as evidenced by the degree to which the duo turns the reins over to producer Tommy LiPuma (perhaps best known for his work with George Benson). On the other hand, the songs fit neatly into a classic supper-club mold, awash in sophisticated arrangements and smoky atmosphere. While some of LiPuma's notions—like calling in saxophonist Stan Getz to play on "The Road"—are insightful, his fondness for glitz too often forces Thorn into broad gestures that sap her distinctiveness.

EBTG's ever-changing moods see them swing the pendulum back to more intimate (though still glossy) environs for **Worldwide.** Watt sculpts the sound a bit more authoritatively than he has in the past, emphasizing salable-sounding electronic keyboards on songs like "Old Friends" and "Talk to Me Like the Sea" (which sees him turn in a surprisingly effective vocal performance). Thorn again shines as both singer and lyricist, as borne out by "Understanding" and "British Summertime," either of which could elicit a sigh from the hardest of hearts.

For those who'd grown edgy about Everything but the Girl's continuing infatuation with studio gewgaws, **Acoustic** (a full-length expansion of the surprisingly successful **Covers** EP) was the perfect tonic. In the sparest of settings, Watt and Thorn essay a handful of covers (Cyndi Lauper's "Time After Time," Mickey & Sylvia's "Love Is Strange," Elvis Costello's "Alison," Bruce Springsteen's "Tougher Than the Rest") and reprise some of their best, most tender material. It's a strikingly well-considered move, one that not only presages the wealth of subsequent "unplugged" sets, but far outstrips most in terms of execution. Songs like **The Language of Life**'s "Driving" and a reworking of **Worldwide**'s "One Place" aren't merely quieter replicas but exhaustively refashioned works in their own right. Thorn benefits most from the climate, slipping easily into a sensuous simmer on the live "Apron Strings," but Watt gets into the spirit as well, eking some serious emotion out of his rendition of Tom Waits' "Downtown Train."

Watt was hospitalized for three months in mid-'92, suffering from a rare auto-immune system disease. He recovered the following year and the group continued, recording two new songs with producer Phil Ramone for the British-only greatest-hits collection.

More than two years elapsed between **Acoustic** and **Amplified Heart,** yet the hushed timbres and largely downcast moods remain the same. Deeply confessional in tone, the songs almost uniformly address lost loves with the desperate directness of diary entries: against slowly unfolding, gentle backing, Thorn pours out what sound like stream-of-consciousness pleas alternately written on her own (the twice-shy "Troubled Mind") and by Watt (the achingly solitary "Rollercoaster"). Instrumentally, Watt turns back to accentuating his deft, Joe Pass–derived guitar playing (particularly effective on the uncharacteristically cloudless "We Walk the Same Line") and crafting vintage-soul arrangements (the Philly-styled "Missing"). There may be better music for crying in your beer, but as far as weeping into your martini, there's no topping Everything but the Girl.

In 1994, Thorn guested on Massive Attack's **Protection;** she and Watt used the experience to springboard their group into a new creative era. Setting aside all past commitments to guitar, jazz-pop and orchestration, **Walking Wounded** drops EBTG gently into the programmed electronic slipstream of ultra-modern dance idioms: "Before Today" is a most delicate jungle expedition, while the title track (presented in two mixes) walks a trip-hop line around jungle's skittery rhythms. A strange development, but done with the band's impeccable good taste and sonic sophistication. [dss/i]

See also *Massive Attack; TPRG.*

EVE'S PLUM

Envy (550 Music/Epic) 1993
Cherry Alive (550 Music/Epic) 1995

Boasting a cool Generation-X moniker—arcane to the masses, but hip to young cognoscenti—this New York band plays a hard-to-define blend of rock, pop and grunge lite. With nods at dance music, new wave and au courant punk, **Envy** reflects the musical climate of its year of release, only the hooks are minimal and the quartet sounds as if it's learning songwriting on the fly. What sinks the experiment are the faux-Seattle guitars and the awful affected singing by Colleen Fitzpatrick (a former dancer and actress who previously appeared in John Waters' *Hairspray*), as she veers from a wicked-witch screech to Debbie Harry aplomb.

Eve's Plum drops the corrosive angst on the lean and less mean **Cherry Alive,** opting instead for clean pop songwriting and svelte rock guitars. Fred Maher's production brings out the cream in Fitzpatrick's voice; bolstered by a giant leap in songwriting and intraband cohesion, "Wishing the Day Away," "Want You Bad" and "Fairy Princess" soar like Blondie and the Darling Buds. Likewise, the title track synergizes hand claps, creative guitar playing and a cool chorus. [jo]

See also *Madder Rose.*

EVIL STIG

See *Gits, Joan Jett.*

EX

Disturbing Domestic Peace (Hol. Verrecords) 1980 (Hol. Ex) 1995
History Is What's Happening (Hol. More DPM) 1982 (Hol. Ex) 1995
Dignity of Labour (Hol. VGZ) 1983 (Hol. Ex) 1995
Tumult (Hol. FAI) 1983 (Fist Puppet) 1994
Gonna Rob the Spermbank EP (Hol. Sneeelleeer) 1983
Blueprints for a Blackout (Hol. Pig Brother Productions) 1983 (Fist Puppet) 1994
Pokkeherrie (Hol. Pockabilly) 1985 (Hol. Ex) 1995
1936 (The Spanish Revolution) EP (Hol. Ron Johnson) 1985
Too Many Cowboys (Mordam) 1987 (Fist Puppet) 1994
Live in Wroclaw [tape] (Hol. Red) 1987
Hands Up! You're Free (Hol. Ex) 1988
Aural Guerrilla (Hol. Ex) 1988 (Homestead) 1989
Joggers and Smoggers (Hol. Ex) 1989 (Fist Puppet) 1994
Dead Fish EP (Hol. Ex) 1990
Mudbird Shivers (Hol. Ex/RecRec) 1995 (Crosstalk/Ex/RecRec) 1996

EX/DOG FACED HERMANS

Treat [tape] (Demon Radge) 1990

EX + TOM CORA

Scrabbling at the Lock (Hol. Ex) 1991 (Fist Puppet) 1993
And the Weathermen Shrug Their Shoulders (Fist Puppet) 1993

EX & GUESTS

Instant (Hol. Ex) 1995

By 1990's **Dead Fish** EP, which lambasted the music industry the Ex had always scrupulously avoided, the Dutch punk anarchists had been around for ten years and had come close to the end of their artistic tether. Their work was all good, but they'd bumped up against the limits of their (considerable) musical skills and their records were sounding similar to each other. (Glorious exception: the machine-gun single "Stonestampers Song," the Ex's first collaboration with Dog Faced Hermans, with whom the band subsequently shared a live cassette, **Treat,** and a guitarist.)

So the Ex expanded its sonic vocabulary with two major undertakings. The first was the **6** series: six singles, released in 1991 and 1992 and later sold as a set, with sleeves modeled after a famous Russian poster. They were, respectively, "Slimy Toad" (straight-up skitter-punk), "Millîtan" (a collaboration with Kurdish folk musician Brader), "Hidegen Fujnak a Szelek" (a strikingly beautiful Muzsikas cover sung by drummer Katrin), a double-7-inch excerpting a live performance (with guest appearances by the Hermans and master free-improv drummer Han Bennink), a joke number ("This Song Is in English," performed with cartoonists Kamagurka and Herr Seele) and "Euroconfusion," a dance 12-inch with sampled percussion. It's almost all great, and you can tell how much fun they're having.

Scrabbling at the Lock, a collaboration with New York avant-garde cellist Tom Cora (who had played with Curlew and Skeleton Crew and made a handful of excellent solo records) in early 1991, is the Ex's first genuinely great album. The combination seems peculiar on paper, but it's a match made in heaven. Dedicated to taking advantage of its full range of sonic capabilities, Cora is the closest thing the cello has to a Jimi Hendrix, and the Ex were expanding how a punk band could sound by exploring improvisation and traditional music. The results are adventurous, fresh and lovely—and also rock like a house on fire. Highlights include an even better version of "Hidegen Fujnak a Szelek," the six-minute juggernaut "State of Shock" and "Batium," a whiplash-rhythm arrangement of a piece by the late Turkish composer Ismet Siral.

The Ex toured the world with Cora and subsequently recorded **And the Weathermen Shrug Their Shoulders,** which suffers only in comparison to **Scrabbling at the Lock.** Cora takes the lead less often on this denser, darker album; although not as immediate, it has its share of great songs, particularly "Dere Geliyor Dere" (another Siral piece) and two excuses for singer G. W. Sok to run off at the mouth and sound good doing it: "What's the Story" (with lyrics taken from an interview with film director Sam Fuller) and the hilarious fake materialist manifesto, "Everything & Me." It's also got "War OD," the climax of many of the Ex's shows with Cora, and one of the sharpest songs they've ever written, politically and musically.

In 1995, the Ex—minus Cora, but plus a new member, extra vocalist Han Buhrs, who ended up singing on most of the album—reappeared with **Mudbird Shivers.** Buhrs, as it turns out, is practically a vocal twin for Captain Beefheart. That's fine: he's got the range for it, and provides a useful counterpart to Sok's one-note bellow (they duet on a few tracks). "Embarrassment" has a great lyric and a great riff that don't really belong together; otherwise, the album is superb, abrasive, daring and full of unexpected kicks, including a slow, bulbous cover of the traditional "House Carpenter."

The Dutch term for free improvisation translates literally as "instant composition"—hence the title of **Instant,** a thirty-two-improv, double-CD set that finds the Ex's instrumentalists (Sok not among them, but including Buhrs on "toffee-tin bass" and harmonica) joined for duos and trios by a party's worth of guests: Han Bennink, Tristan Honsinger, Ab Baars, Michael

Vatcher and others. Hence, also, its aesthetic. A lot of these ad lib tracks could pass for composition-type compositions, or even for rock ("Karremans' Last Measure," "If the Hat Fits the Suit"). Nicely annotated, bravely executed and totally cool.

Seven early Ex albums (and the 7-inch boxed set **Dignity of Labour**) were reissued in the mid-'90s, the first time most had ever appeared on CD. **History Is What's Happening,** in particular, is worth checking out for the dead-on Gang of Four riposte "E.M. Why?" [ddw]

See also *TPRG.*

EXCESSIVE FORCE

See *KMFDM.*

EXCUSE 17

See *Heavens to Betsy.*

EXECUTIVE SLACKS

See *Tubalcain.*

EXPERIMENTAL AUDIO RESEARCH

See *Spacemen 3.*

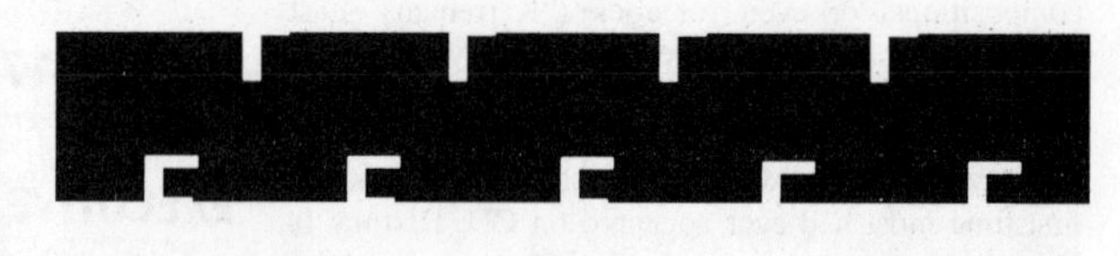

FABULON

All Girls Are Pretty. Volume I (Chrysalis) 1993

Just as not all popular albums are wonderful, not all wonderful albums are popular. Proving the latter point is Fabulon's **All Girls Are Pretty,** a record that came nowhere near the Top 200 but sounds like a collection of wall-to-wall pop-funk chartbusters. Fabulon (Kevin Macbeth, a veteran of such Miami bands as Reagan's Dream and Sleep of Reason) plays most of the instruments on his studio-intensive debut, relying as much on guitars as synths, drum machines and samples. The songs artfully contrast simple and true romantic crises ("Yesterday I left you/Today I want you back") with unabashedly catchy-sweet melodies and danceable backing tracks, a case in point being the joyous opening number, "In a Mood," which quotes both "Venus" and "My Boyfriend's Back." The allusions don't stop there—"Wonderbus" samples "A Summer Place," "Crazy Little Girl" works in a little "Soul Man" and a rich vein of '70s AM pop (from Chicago to 10cc to the Spinners) runs all through the album. (And that's not counting a cover of the Association's "Cherish.") On the delectable "Say Anything," "A Walk Through the Desert"—indeed on virtually every song here—Fabulon grafts a fan's awareness of classic pop sensibilities onto music that's unmistakably rooted in club culture; besides a deep Princely streak, **All Girls Are Pretty** owes as much to house music as it does to the Beatles.

An album so titled (and so absolutely fabulous) leaves only one question: When do we get **Volume II**? As Fabulon was dropped by Chrsysalis after one try, perhaps not for a while. [ma]

FACE TO FACE

Don't Turn Away (Dr. Strange) 1991 (Fat Wreck Chords) 1992
Over It (Victory) 1994
Big Choice (Victory) 1995
Face to Face (A&M) 1996

When punk-pop is played competently, it's as immediately appealing as power-pop—invasive hooks driven in deep by the charged playing. When it's done well, as this quartet from Victorville in Southern California demonstrates on its second full album, **Big Choice,** the rush of hooks and energy can reach into the heart of rock'n'roll and tap a little of its essence. (Incidentally, there's no connection to the Boston new wave/hip-hop Face to Face that made three albums in the mid-'80s.)

Recorded as a trio and rereleased on NOFX's label, **Don't Turn Away** is a stirring and exciting debut undercut only slightly by its overt stylistic debt to Hüsker Dü and Social Distortion (the latter in guitarist Trevor Keith's ragged-glory voice and the anthemic melodies co-written with bassist Matt Riddle). Like Northern California brethren Rancid, however, Face to Face faces east here, taking some of its useful sonic cues from late-'70s Britpunks. Kicking it strong and memorable, with taut, coherent aggression, Keith sings the spirited (but sensitive) slogans of songs like "I'm Trying," "I'm Not Afraid," "You've Done Nothing" and "No Authority."

Welcoming the group to its new major-marketed label, the seven-song **Over It** lifts three of the best numbers off the first album and catches up on some of the prolific band's early singles, including "A-OK," a song recut for the second.

In the meantime, Face to Face had added a second guitarist, Chad Yaro, and outgrown its obvious reference points. With veteran producer Thom Wilson capturing a respectably commercial sound, **Big Choice** is nothing but high-grade intelligent purified punk-pop. A smoother character to Keith's voice (frequently doubled or tripled by his bandmates) shakes off the Distortion, and the all-American melodies and adrenalized rhythms erase any foreign influence. As morally upright as Bad Religion but with a pop sensibility that's closer to Weezer, **Big Choice** benefits from the band's deft sense of song structure, knowing to release the singalong choruses at the precise moment they're needed, and then not driving them into the ground with endless repetition. Likewise, the arrangements have enough variety to keep things moving. Although odd sequencing gets the album off to a slow start, "It's Not Over," "Velocity," "Debt" and "Late" bring it to a delirious boil by the end, followed by two bonuses: a remake of **Don't Turn Away**'s "Disconnected" and a cover of the Descendents' "Bikeage." Very cool. [i]

FAILURE

Comfort (Slash) 1992
Magnified (Slash) 1994
Fantastic Planet (Slash/Warner Bros.) 1996

REPLICANTS

Replicants (Zoo) 1995

Like most premature debuts, **Comfort** captures Failure, a young trio, learning how to make cool sounds together without benefit of worthwhile songs or an established personality. Veteran engineer Steve Albini opens the doors to a crisp, cloudless sky, which Los Angeles singer-guitarist Ken Andrews, bassist Greg Edwards and the first of several drummers wisely don't attempt to fill. "Submission" and "Swallow" do play follow the leader with Big Black and their acidly antagonistic ilk, but "Something" and "Muffled Snaps" allow an alluring melodicism and whispery vocals to temper the skeletal aggression. **Comfort** contains some worthwhile lessons, but the band's term paper on the subject surely didn't need to be published.

Against booming bass and snappy drumming, the

self-produced **Magnified** is a major improvement, but not a thorough success. The mature Failure paints senseless coats of alternative guitar (a stylistic trademark, not a cultural valuation) over tuneful material that might actually be enticing if not for the underbrush. In a voice that, at times, sounds like John Linnell of They Might Be Giants, Andrews sings about "frogs . . . leaping off my brainstem" and "warm winds calling me a coward." The rocking title track and the mainstreamed epic "Wonderful Life" get the balance close, but this giant step toward a viable, worthwhile identity doesn't get there.

The Replicants side-project compounds Failure (Andrews singing and playing bass and guitar; Edwards on drums, guitar and keyboards) with a Tool (guitarist Paul D'Amour) and keyboardist Chris Pitman. The album's ingenious concept was to record, y'know, other people's old songs—I guess you could call 'em covers—in a modern idiom. (Of course, the idea of forming a group to do this pushes **Replicants** closer to K-Tel vapidity than the usual bigtimer we-do-'em-our-way processing plant.) Punching up the jukebox for new wave nuggets (Missing Persons' "Destination Unknown," Gary Numan's "Are Friends Electric?"), classic rock tracks (Neil Young's "Cinnamon Girl," John Lennon's "How Do You Sleep") and others from T. Rex, David Bowie, Steely Dan and Syd Barrett, the ad hoc wedding band evinces a few bright ideas—slowing Paul McCartney's "Silly Love Songs" (sung by guest star Maynard Keenan of Tool) to a tuneless crawl, de-gearing the Cars' "Just What I Needed" into a constantly downshifting modulation joke—but most of the renditions are more faithful, reconfiguring the instrumentation and pounding the oldies into currency without expending much creative effort. [i]

See also *Tool.*

JAD FAIR

See *Half Japanese.*

FAITH & THE MUSE

Elyria (Tess) 1994

Although Faith & the Muse is a relatively new arrival on the Southern California goth scene, **Elyria** proves it worthy of a more careful listen than most of the band's black-shrouded peers. Founders Monica Richards (ex–Strange Boutique) and William Faith (who has played in such leading acts as Christian Death and Sex Gang Children) skillfully combine haunting romanticism with Celtic melodies and loads of airy atmospherics—an amazingly intoxicating mix. Richards has a powerful mezzo-soprano, which she uses to sound otherworldly and mythical one moment ("Mercyground") and mischievous and slightly dangerous the next ("Vervain"). Faith's one vocal showcase, "The Trauma Coil," is a thundering song creepy and shadowy enough to be a holdover from his Christian Death years. Pretty instrumentals (especially "Interlude: Annabell," a meandering, mesmerizing acoustic guitar track) help make **Elyria** seem even more distant and misty. [ky]

See also *Christian Death.*

FAITH NO MORE

We Care a Lot (Mordam) 1985 + 1987
Introduce Yourself (Slash) 1987
The Real Thing (Slash/Reprise) 1989
You Fat Bastards: Live at the Brixton Academy (UK Slash/London) 1990
Angel Dust (Slash/Reprise) 1992
Easy EP (Slash/Reprise) 1993
King for a Day, Fool for a Lifetime (Slash/Reprise) 1995

MR. BUNGLE

Mr. Bungle (Warner Bros.) 1991
Disco Volante (Warner Bros.) 1995

MIKE PATTON

Adult Themes (Tzadik) 1996

A catchy song ("Epic") and a striking video (that goldfish suffocating memorably on a polished floor) made a platinum seller of Faith No More's idiosyncratic mix of heavy metal guitars, half-rapped vocals, waves of bright keyboards and powerhouse rhythm section. The 1990 success of **The Real Thing,** however, proved difficult to re-create, and the multifarious personalities that accounted for the San Francisco quintet's distinctive sound began to splinter apart.

The friction resulted in an uncomfortable followup, **Angel Dust.** On the positive side, vocalist Mike Patton (who had only joined the band in time for **The Real Thing,** replacing original singer Chuck Mosley) asserts himself more, developing a style further removed from Anthony Kiedis–like yattering and closer to the barking he does in his sideband, Mr. Bungle. The problem is that guitarist Jim Martin, whose metallic riffing gave the music such bite in the past, seems less sharp, and that throws the whole equation off. The most Faith No More–like songs on the record are its most disappointing; the best tracks are those (like "A Small Victory," which seems to run *Madame Butterfly* through Metallica and Nile Rodgers) that reveal a developing facility for combining unlikely elements into startlingly original concoctions.

Indication that the group's sense of humor might be getting the better of it, the **Easy** EP features a shockingly straight-faced cover of the Commodores' soft-soap "Easy" (and a shockingly rude picture of humping rhinos), plus **Angel Dust**'s "Midnight Cowboy," an unreleased original polka (sung in German, or what at least sounds like German, complete with sound effects) entitled "Das Schutzenfest" and the Dead Kennedys' "Let's Lynch the Landlord," crooned as if it were rockabilly over accordion, spare drumming and twangy bits of guitar.

Not surprisingly, changes were imminent. The inchoate rage of **Angel Dust** comes home to roost on **King for a Day, Fool for a Lifetime,** which starts off with the scathing "Get Out," ostensibly a kiss-off to the departed Martin. With guitar duties handled by the more flexible Trey Spruance of Mr. Bungle (a fill-in who was replaced after the album by former keyboard roadie Dean Menta), the jarring shifts in style and strange combinations of elements begin to make more sense. The jump from the mid-tempo soul ballad "Evidence" through the punkmetal grind of "The Gentle Art of Making Enemies," into which only Faith No More could successfully cram a hummable chorus, to the odd hardcore samba of "Star A.D." shows a band that is still omnivorous, but better able to chew its food. Each song its own violent squall, **King for Day** is relentlessly fascinating.

Faith No More fans who picked up **Mr. Bungle** on a whim to see what Patton's other band, a pseudonymous sextet, was like found themselves in possession of one of the most ambitiously random, fractious records in recent memory. Filled with sampled absurdities, sucker-punch time changes and contortionist (and cartoonish) vocal operatics, the album owes a debt to co-producer John Zorn's Naked City, the Boredoms and ultra-violent Japanese animation. This constant flurry of contrasting noise is jarring, as Patton vents his spleen and various other organs on the proceedings. Among the inexplicable inventions are "Travolta," "My Ass Is on Fire" and "The Girls of Porn." If that description sounds unappealing, that this is one of the finest records of its kind won't make it any more likable.

Perhaps Patton exorcised too much on **King for a Day,** or the Japanese Nintendo-core Mr. Bungle emulates grew too formidable, because **Disco Volante** is a disappointment. With the chaos not nearly as well orchestrated as on the debut, it amounts to so much undifferentiated tissue. [sf/i]

See also *Brujeria, Imperial Teen, Zip Code Rapists, John Zorn; TPRG.*

FAKES

See *Bikini Kill.*

FALL

Live at the Witch Trials (Step Forward/IRS) 1979
Dragnet (UK Step Forward) 1979
Totale's Turns (It's Now or Never) (UK Rough Trade) 1980 (UK Dojo) 1992
Grotesque (After the Gramme) (Rough Trade) 1980 (UK Castle Classics) 1993
Early Years 77–79 (Faulty Products) 1981
Slates EP (Rough Trade) 1981
Live in London, 1980 [tape] (UK Chaos) 1982
Hex Enduction Hour (UK Kamera) 1982
Room to Live (UK Kamera) 1982
A Part of America Therein, 1981 (Cottage) 1982
Perverted by Language (UK Rough Trade) 1983
Kicker Conspiracy EP (UK Rough Trade) 1983
Fall in a Hole (NZ Flying Nun) 1983
The Wonderful and Frightening World of the Fall (Beggars Banquet/PVC) 1984
Call for Escape Route EP (UK Beggars Banquet) 1984
Hip Priest and Kamerads (UK Situation Two) 1985 (Beggars Banquet) 1995
This Nation's Saving Grace (Beggars Banquet/PVC) 1985
The Fall EP (PVC) 1986
Bend Sinister (UK Beggars Banquet) 1986
Domesday Pay-Off (Big Time) 1987
There's a Ghost in My House EP (UK Beggars Banquet) 1987
The Peel Sessions EP (UK Strange Fruit) 1987
The Fall In: Palace of Swords Reversed (Cog Sinister/Rough Trade) 1987
The Frenz Experiment (Big Time) 1988
Victoria EP (UK Beggars Banquet) 1988
I Am Kurious Oranj (Beggars Banquet/RCA) 1988
Jerusalem EP (UK Beggars Banquet) 1988
Cab It Up/Dead Beat Descendant EP (UK Beggars Banquet) 1989
Seminal Live (Beggars Banquet/RCA) 1989
Dredger EP (UK Cog Sinister/Phonogram) 1990
458489 A Sides (Beggars Banquet/RCA) 1990
458489 B Sides (UK Beggars Banquet) 1990 (Beggars Banquet) 1995
Extricate (Cog Sinister/Fontana) 1990
Shift-work (UK Cog Sinister/Fontana) 1991
Free Range EP (UK Cog Sinister/Fontana) 1992
Code: Selfish (UK Cog Sinister/Fontana) 1992
Ed's Babe EP (UK Cog Sinister/Fontana) 1992
Slates/A Part of America Therein, 1981 (UK Dojo) 1992
The Collection (UK Castle Communications) 1993
Why Are People Grudgeful? EP (Matador) 1993
Kimble EP (Strange Fruit/Dutch East India Trading) 1993
The Infotainment Scan (Matador/Atlantic) 1993
BBC Radio 1 Live in Concert (Windsong) 1993
Middle Class Revolt (Matador) 1994
Cerebral Caustic (UK Permanent) 1995
The Twenty-Seven Points (UK Permanent) 1995
The Legendary Chaos Tape (Ger. Scout/Rough Trade) 1995
Sinister Waltz (UK Receiver) 1996
Fiend With a Violin (UK Receiver) 1996
Oswald Defence Lawyer (UK Receiver) 1996
Light Users Syndrome (UK Jet) 1996

Some people think chief Fall guy Mark E. Smith does the same thing over and over again, but he's such an original that the observation hardly rings as criticism. Indeed, on the Manchester band's first single, back in 1978, Smith presented his manifesto: "Repetition in the music and we're never gonna lose it." Turning subtle but powerful changes on a basic but endlessly fascinating form, Smith and the Fall have created influential music through three decades, leaving their mark on hipsters like Pavement, Girls Against Boys, the Sugarcubes and Sonic Youth while helping to ignite the rediscovery of German avantists like Can, Neu! and Faust.

Smith's signature Mancunian drawl is far more than an act of defiant regionalism (an attitude noted and emulated by some of the more astute minds of the American indie scene)—it's also the perfect medium for his half-sung poetry, which both revels in and reviles modern language and its humorous/ominous rhythms and constructions. Paired with stalwart guitarist Craig Scanlon, bassist Stephen Hanley, drummer Karl Burns and/or Simon Wolstencroft and a shifting cast of other musicians pounding out the band's cantankerous, skiffle-from-hell beats, the simple result is that the Fall isn't like any other band.

The best introduction to the Fall's early-'80s peak is the **Palace of Swords Reversed** compilation, with essentials like "Prole Art Threat" and "Kicker Conspiracy." **The Collection,** released on a British budget label in 1993, mostly samples from the same period (also including the classic singles "Totally Wired" and "How I Wrote 'Elastic Man'") and throws in a version of "Hip Priest" from the astonishing but hopelessly rare **Fall in a Hole** live album, plus a useless unreleased track and an even more useless cover of the Beatles' "A Day in the Life." However, sound quality and sequencing leave a lot to be desired; for similar territory, the twofer CD that pairs the **Slates** EP (the Fall as white-hot studio prestidigitators) and the live album **A Part of America Therein** (Smith as ranting prophet) is a much better deal.

The all-meat '84–89 A-sides collection is a fine introduction to the Fall's next period—a flirtation with pop stardom, aided by American guitarist Brix Smith, who spent those years married to Mark. On such "hits" as "Hey! Luciani," "Cruisers Creek," "Big New Prinz" and some fourteen others, the band is in perfect control of its lurching swing, Smith is at the top of his lyrical game and some primitively catchy melodies help it all go down. The liner notes contain a very helpful discography and personnel time-line. The B-sides collection is very nearly as good, with a generous helping—thirty-one slices—of prime-time Fall spread over two CDs.

Brix Smith divorced both Mark E. and the band in 1989; the sound of her absence quickly underscored the crucial contribution she made—sing-song hooks that turn his abstruse sloganeering downright catchy. The Fall rebounded somewhat tentatively with **Extricate,** on which her replacement turned out to be Martin Bramah, a Fall co-founder who had left the band roughly a decade before to form the Blue Orchids. While the bilious "Black Monk Theme Part I" (a rebuilt cover of the Monks' 1966 "I Hate You," in which Smith coughs up a stuttering heap of invective: "I hate you baby . . . you make me hate you baby . . . you maladjusted little monkey," and, no, it's not about any ex-relatives, thanks for asking) proves that Brix hadn't taken *all* the band's ammo with her, half the album does fall in a hole. Production by Smith, Craig Leon, dub master Adrian Sherwood and acid house technocrats Coldcut (who co-wrote "Telephone Thing," another highlight) is only intermittently successful. **Dredger,** a four-song EP from the same period, is basically a quickie cover of "White Lightning" (which subsequently showed up on **Shift-work**) plus some filler—"Zagreb" is pieced together from two different not-quite-ripe songs.

It's rumored that Smith and Bramah wrote an album's worth of songs together after **Extricate.** Bramah left the band in 1990, however, and only one of those songs (the uncharacteristically pretty "Rose") shows up on **Shift-work.** The album is ostensibly divided into two sections, "Earth's Impossible Day" and "Notebooks Out Plagiarists," but there's no discernible difference between them, or indeed between most of the songs. The band generally sounds like it's on autopilot. Listen closely, though, and a couple of terrific songs pop out, especially "Edinburgh Man" and "The Book of Lies," which sports organ, handclaps and a great, nagging vocal hook.

Things seemed to be looking up with the **Free Range** EP: four tough, hooky tracks in the great Fall riff-and-repeat mold. The title song, in particular, incorporates techno into its arrangement more powerfully than the group had ever quite managed before. Unfortunately, those four numbers are the only high points of **Code: Selfish** (except for maybe Smith sneering the title of "The Birmingham School of Business School"). Mark E. sounds almost sedated, and the veteran core band of Scanlon/Hanley/Wolstencroft locks mechanically into its grooves.

Ed's Babe is another perplexing 'tweener EP. The title track is a stylistic departure (slick pop) that this Fall incarnation hadn't tried before and really isn't very good at. Then there's a fantastic remix of "Free Range" and two near-instrumental experiments, one of which falls on its face and the other of which ("The Knight, the Devil and Death") is one of the most powerful pieces of music the Fall has ever produced. You never can tell.

The **Kimble** EP consists of four tracks, selected seemingly at random from the billion or so sessions the Fall has recorded for John Peel's radio show. A 1992 cover of Lee "Scratch" Perry's "Kimble" is a bit slack, but "Gut of the Quantifier" and "Spoilt Victorian Child" from 1985 have a classic, abrasive Fall edge, full of the incantatory repetition that is Smith's avowed modus operandi. The nine-minute, one-chord "Words of Expectation" (produced by Factory Records chief Tony Wilson) from 1983 is for fans only—which is not to say it isn't brilliant. The British vinyl version and the American 7-inch of "Kimble" include 1981's "C 'n' C Hassle Schmuk," which hilariously grafts the early live standard "Cash 'n' Carry" onto "Do the Huckle-Buck."

Also dating from the '80s (1987) and done for British broadcasting, **BBC Radio 1 Live in Concert** (only thirty-two minutes long, despite what the back cover says) finds the Fall in fine form, nailing a headlong groove on the opener "Australians in Europe," winding up with a veritable rockabilly raveup on "Lucifer Over Lancashire" and overall doing the voodoo they do so well on the intervening tracks. Brix turns in some perky Farfisa work on "Shoulder Pads" and a hoppin' "Fiery Jack"; for the punters, there are a couple of hits—Holland-Dozier-Holland's "There's a Ghost in My House" and "Hey! Luciani."

The four-song **Why Are People Grudgeful?** EP (named after its lead track, another Perry cover) includes three numbers from **The Infotainment Scan,** but the price of admission is justified by a brilliant bit at the end of "The Re-Mixer" (naturally, a new version of **Shift-work**'s "The Mixer"): Smith talking into a Walkman, reading from a computer manual and then the fire escape instructions on the back of his hotel room door.

With **The Infotainment Scan,** the Fall brought guitars back to the fore, as in the jittery syncopations of "Ladybird." But the real point of the album is the band's ginger exploration of different musical feels. "Why Are People Grudgeful?" touches on ska; the version of Chic's disco-era "Lost in Music" is almost reverent; the chug-trancey "It's a Curse" displays a serious Neu! influence. While the apparently autobiographical "Paranoia Man in Cheap Sh*t Room" emulates the sound of the largely deplorable turn-of-the-decade Madchester scene, the Fall invests it with far more urgency than any of the form's E-addled proponents. A remix of "The League of Bald-Headed Men" echoes techno, but "A Past Gone Mad" is far more successful.

On **Middle Class Revolt,** keyboards burble at the periphery of tracks such as "15 Ways" and "The Reckoning" (which berates "some hippy halfwit who thinks he's Mr. Mark Smith"). Although Smith is mellowing his approach, stretching out his words and not spitting out reams of verbiage, "Behind the Counter" and "M5#1" boast some of the most flat-out-rocking the Fall has done in years. "Shut Up!" is the group's third Monks cover, there's a tremendous rewrite of Henry Cow/Slapp Happy's "War" and the album's peak is provided by the battering "Hey! Student"—which the Fall was playing back in '77 as "Hey! Fascist."

Co-produced by Smith for better and for worse, the resolutely lo-fi, virtually synthless **Cerebral Caustic** easily overcomes its dinky sound. The high catchiness factor is surely due to the return of Brix, who toured with the band in '94 and co-wrote five tunes, including a ferocious duet, "Don't Call Me Darling." (She also gets to have some fun on a remake of **Dredger**'s "Life Just Bounces.") Meanwhile, the album features some fascinating innovations—not the least of which is an idiosyncratic cover of Frank Zappa's "I'm Not Satisfied." The utterly psychedelic "Bonkers in Phoenix" is amazing, while another standout, "North West Fashion," is just a mesmeric backing track and snippets of recorded conversation. The rest is prime-slice Fall in all its caustic, cerebral glory. Rich with barbed hook-lines and canny catch-phrases from a band that continues to refine its deliciously jagged edge, **Cerebral Caustic** is the best Fall album in years and a good omen for the future.

The Twenty-Seven Points isn't exactly a live album in the conventional sense—it's more of a scrapbook of what the band was doing in the first half of the '90s. Composed of live tracks, rough demos and random interpolations from Glasgow, London, Manchester, New York, Prague and Tel Aviv, the twenty-eight-track, two-CD set is frustratingly uneven but ultimately captures the Fall live experience, complete with onstage disasters ("Idiot Joy Showland" collapses and Smith yells "Right! Back in two minutes!"). The tinny, wavering sound quality would make a bootlegger sneer with derision; "Glam Racket/Star" has a *very* audible splice from a few verses of its original version to a later arrangement featuring additional vocals by Brix. Still, tracks on Disc One ("Return," "Hi-Tension Line" and "Big New Prinz") cook, with the mechanistic thrust of the band's instrumental core coming through loud and clear; the spoken-word "Ten Points" is a real treat. The second disc is much weirder, with a couple of techno experiments and Brix vocals (a rewrite of "Middle Class Revolt") and, uh, other people (what sounds like a plastered roadie on "Life Just Bounces"); it also sports a kick-ass cover of the Sonics' "Strychnine."

The first of a series of three collections of alternate versions and rarities, **Sinister Waltz** is a stone disaster: badly mastered demos from **Shift-work** and **Extricate,** atrociously recorded live versions (including a "Wings" that fades in on the third verse) and a cover of Jeff Lynne's "Birthday." The gem at the end—a version of "Edinburgh Man" even nicer than the original—doesn't really warrant slogging through the rest.

Sinister Waltz was followed, a month later, by **Fiend With a Violin,** another barrel-scraping compilation. The highlight is a weird, throbbing remix of "The Man Whose Head Expanded." The lowlight, though, that's a tough one—could it be the utterly unclamored-for instrumental version of "Ed's Babe"? The live recordings of third-rate songs from **Code: Selfish?** No, for sheer marketing dishonesty, it would have to be the "never heard before" title track, which is simply a retitled, chopped-up instrumental demo for "2x4." Another month later came the third in the series: **Oswald Defence Lawyer,** which appears to be a board tape from a live show circa 1989. Nine of its twelve tracks appear in studio versions on **Kurious Oranj** or **The Frenz Experiment;** the sound is sub-optimal if not terrible, and the same is true of the performances. Only a taut, prickly version of "Bombast" is really top-notch Fall.

The Legendary Chaos Tape brings the slightly less than legendary (though still very good) **Live in London** (Acklam Hall) cassette, recorded in 1980, to compact disc. Now if only somebody would release **Fall in a Hole**—not to mention the brilliant singles on **Early Years 77–79,** which have been out of print for over a decade. [ma/ddw]

See also *TPRG.*

FALLING JOYS

Wish List (Nettwerk/IRS) 1990
Psychohum (Nettwerk/IRS) 1992

Australia's Falling Joys will (generally) lift your spirits. Suzie Higgie's pretty vocals are the perfect complement to, alternately, the quartet's guitar spaciness and rocking normalcy. **Wish List** is all over the place, but somehow congeals as a cohesive piece of work. "Lock It" has cotton-candy ABBA harmonies; "Tunnel Vision" is modern art-rock; "Dream Hangover" has a vaguely Beatlesque melody; "Jennifer" evokes the Bangles. Other tracks range from Cocteau Twins airiness to Church-like jangle. "You're in a Mess"—recorded, mixed and produced separately from the rest of the album—has a catchy chorus, making it the obvious choice for a single.

Produced by Jessica Corcoran (who's worked with Ned's Atomic Dustbin), the heavier and darker followup is equally rife with obvious hooks. "Incinerator" reheats the classic girl-group sound without burning it alive; "God in a Dustbin" is at least reverent toward the immaculate conception of melody; the power pop of "Natural Scene" and the emotional release of "Parachute" are bonuses. Thinking-person's pop. [jo]

FALL-OUTS

See *Mudhoney.*

FALLSTAFF

See *Shrimp Boat.*

MICK FARREN

(Mona) The Carnivorous Circus (UK Transatlantic) 1970 (UK Psycho) 1984
Vampires Stole My Lunch Money (UK Logo) 1978

DEVIANTS

Human Garbage (UK Psycho) 1984

MICK FARREN & WAYNE KRAMER

Who Shot You Dutch? EP (Can. Spectre) 1987

WAYNE KRAMER

Death Tongue (Progressive/Curio) 1991

MICK FARREN'S TIJUANA BIBLE

Gringo Madness (UK Big Beat) 1993

MICK FARREN & JACK LANCASTER

The Deathray Tapes (Alive!) 1995

Mick Farren—music journalist, science fiction novelist, singer, founding member of the (Social) Deviants and Pink Fairies, Motörhead songwriter—cut his first solo album with a nascent version of the Fairies immediately upon leaving the Deviants in 1969. Nearly a decade later, the Englishman dived into the punk wave with the harrowing **Vampires Stole My Lunch Money** and showed the junior nihilists just how grim, serious and personal rock could get.

After relocating to New York, Farren pursued a number of musical endeavors with ex-MC5 guitarist Wayne Kramer. In February 1984, joined by ex-Fairies Larry Wallis and Duncan Sanderson and a drummer, the pair (billed as the Deviants) did a loose-limbed London gig that was recorded and released as **Human Garbage.** Farren and Kramer then worked on an "R&B musical" based on the death-bed ramblings of prohibition-era gangster Dutch Schultz; three songs from the production were vinylized and released as **Who Shot You Dutch?**

Death Tongue, a sloppy transitional album made with Kramer, veteran New York singer/guitarist John Collins and drummer Ed Steinberg, was released under Kramer's name even though it includes **Who Shot You Dutch**'s Don Was–produced title track and a dramatic Farren recitation on "Death Tongue," as well as collaborative originals. From there, Farren continued with Collins and fellow **Dutch** alumnus Henry Beck as Tijuana Bible. **Gringo Madness** proffers skeletal music—spare guitar diddles with the occasional infiltration of a mariachi cliché or sax for variety—over which Farren sings and recites his fervid day-of-the-dead poetry. Conflating pop culture iconography, hallucinatory alcohol visions, various minuets with Satan and the enervated desperation of a dying man sliding down the side of a mountain on his face, Farren upbeats the Beats and de-rocks the rockers. Between his bandmate's rants, Collins sings some acoustic ballads; for reasons wholly unclear, the whole shooting match winds up in a dramatic reading of "Riot in Cell Block #9." Not well suited for casual or multiple listenings, **Gringo Madness** would make an entertaining companion for that steamy dog-day night when sleep is out of the question.

Living in Hollywood in the '90s, Farren corraled another expatriate—hornman Jack Lancaster, the Rahsaan Roland Kirk of British rock, best known for his twin-sax work in the late-'60s Jethro Tull jazz-blues spinoff Blodwyn Pig—into a partnership. **The Deathray Tapes,** recorded live in front of an invited Santa Monica club audience, pulls Farren further into the spoken-word realm, as he recites trenchant, engaging tales (one reclaimed from **Gringo Madness**) over a rumpled musical bed laid on by Lancaster's treated horn flights, a rhythm section and guests. (Upping the oddity ante, actor Brad Dourif plays didgeridoo on one song; Wayne Kramer increases the release on three.) Bizarre, bracing, original and invigorating, **The Deathray Tapes** is reminiscent of '60s acid-freak festival freeforming, but Farren's sensibility—witness "Disgruntled Employee" and "Gunfire in the Night"—isn't rooted in anything but his own gristly view of reality. [i]

See also *Wayne Kramer; TPRG.*

DIONNE FARRIS

Wild Seed–Wild Flower (Columbia) 1994

Marking her departure from the crowded barnyard of Arrested Development shortly after the success of the band's first album, New Jersey native Dionne Yvette Farris' solo debut strikes out on a jazzy, forward-thinking and rock-informed R&B path. Bouncy slide guitar propels both mixes of the infectious and uncommon "I Know" (a hit in '95) as Farris' vocal swoops make the song a dazzler. Alternately sassy, introspective and resolute in her lyrics, the singer/songwriter takes on the roles of a drug to be avoided in "Stop to Think" (music written by Lenny Kravitz) and advocate for a victim of physical abuse in "Don't Ever Touch Me (Again)." Tory Ruffin's heavy, near-grunge guitar chords turn the chorus of hot-and-bothered rhapsody "Passion" upside down. Farris' circular philosophizing in "Reality" ("If we are here, then where is there?/And if in fact we're here then why aren't we there?") is couched in cozy funk; musings about the self are wrapped in violin and cello on "Food for Thought." Harmonizing with herself over main collaborator David Harris' jazzy acoustic guitar and a little appropriate percussion, Farris breathes new life into the Beatles' "Blackbird." Going even further into vocalese, Farris pulls off a Bobby McFerrin–ish exercise in her own anti-sectarian "Human." The only bit of this fine album that doesn't make clear, compelling sense is the presence of actor David Alan Grier in two pointless little skits. [re]

See also *Arrested Development.*

FARSIDE

Rochambeau (Revelation) 1992
Rigged (Revelation) 1994
Farside EP (Revelation) 1995

This Orange County, California, hardcore quartet prides itself on solid, anthemic songwriting and good instincts. While he didn't stick around to record with the group, Rage Against the Machine's Zack de la Rocha was one of its original guitarists.

Singer/guitarist Popeye (Michael Vogelsang, also heard in such bands as Triggerman, Borderline and Game Face) wears his teenage-turning-adult heart on his sleeve on **Rochambeau**—for better ("Future Days," "Hero," "Smarter Than Ever") and worse ("Constant Reminder," the overwrought title track). Sample, if slightly out-of-context, lyric: "It's boiling over I've dried my/eyes, now let's start moving." Acoustic guitar underpinnings give the record additional instrumental and emotional depth, as **Rochambeau** introduces an earnest, focused group with a good grasp on dynamics and a crisp delivery on themes like self-awareness, unity and the personal as political.

More first-person lyrics, less acoustic leavening (signaled by the Marshall stacks on the CD sleeve) and a new guitarist (Kevin Murphy, replacing Rob Haworth) mark **Rigged,** a ten-song outing that bolsters Farside's sound and approach. Twin guitars gnarl forcefully, and the quartet's songwriting is decidedly improved, with stronger melodies and riffs reminiscent of Hüsker Dü. The emo quotient is still high—Popeye and the band place a premium on friendship, loyalty, and idealism—but cynicism occasionally creeps in. Ultimately, Farside values the vivid sting of emotional pain much more than the pallor of despair, and that charges the group's batteries plenty.

Farside, a six-song EP, includes a mediocre cover of the Hüskers' "Hardly Getting Over It," but Murphy gets in the songwriting act with the solid "Lollapalooza." [mww]

FASTBACKS

Play Five of Their Favorites EP (No Threes) 1982
Every Day Is Saturday EP (No Threes) 1984
. . . and His Orchestra (PopLlama Products) 1987
Bike-Toy-Clock-Gift [tape] (Bus Stop) 1988
Very, Very Powerful Motor (PopLlama Products) 1990
In America, Live in Seattle 1988 (Ger. Lost and Found) 1991
Never Fails, Never Works (UK Blaster) 1991
The Question Is No. (Sub Pop) 1992
Zücker (Sub Pop) 1993
Gone to the Moon EP (Ger. Sub Pop) 1993
Answer the Phone, Dummy (Sub Pop) 1994
New Mansions in Sound (Sub Pop) 1996

With Kurt Bloch providing the kicky pop songs and formidable rock'n'roll guitar power, Seattle's Fastbacks—formed in 1979 and, like many bands of that time and place, able to claim future Guns n' Roses bassist Duff McKagan as its onetime drummer—made irregular contributions to the world of recorded music throughout the '80s, turning up on numerous compilations and occasionally issuing records of its own. Always good and never trendy, the band is a beloved and reliable fixture in a city that has seen lots of spectacular rises and falls.

Guitarist Lulu Gargiulo and bassist Kim Warnick play hit-and-miss with the melodies on the casually unpretentious **. . . and His Orchestra,** but everyone winds up sharing a fine time anyway. (For reasons too frightening to contemplate, Bloch takes no part in the band's vocal exercises.) Besides Bloch's charming pop-rock ditties, drummer Richard Stuverud chips in with one number, and the group does an impressive if incongruous cover of Sweet's "Set Me Free." The CD of **. . . and His Orchestra** also appends the nine songs from **Play Five of Their Favorites** and **Every Day Is Saturday.** The contents of those 12-inch EPs, plus a three-song single, were also separately compiled in England as **Never Fails, Never Works. Bike-Toy-Clock-Gift,** a cassette-only concert album, was later re-released in Germany as **In America, Live in Seattle 1988.**

Recorded as a trio of Bloch (who by then had joined the Young Fresh Fellows and was living a double-band life, not counting Sick Man of Europe, a Cheap Trick cover group with Sub Pop co-owner Jonathan Poneman), Warnick and new drummer Nate Johnson (moonlighting from Flop), **Very, Very Powerful Motor** gives Bloch's pop-rooted songs powerhouse rock arrangements that occasionally overwhelm them. In her rougher vocal moments, Warnick sounds like a more melodically astute Joan Jett. Although she sat out this record, Gargiulo nonetheless puts in several supporting vocal appearances. Cool cover: the Pointed Sticks' "Apologies."

The Question Is No. is an anthology of fourteen songs drawn from various singles, compilations and unreleased sessions between 1980 and 1992. Drummers come and go (Stuverud, Johnson, McKagan, Rusty Willoughby, who is actually the guitarist of Flop, even Bloch in a pinch) as the front line roars along in a hyperactive mess of sloppy punk-pop spunk dedicated only to getting from one end to the other of Bloch's songs. Highlights: "Everything I Don't Need" (a different version from the one on the **Very, Very Powerful Motor** CD), "Impatience," "I Never Knew," "Don't Eat That It's Poison" and the instrumental "Breakup Theme." Strict melodic adherence is out of the question, but so is arrogance, preciousness or self-importance. The vintage band pix are also excellent.

With Gargiulo back to full-time membership and Willoughby pounding the traps, **Zücker** contains the band's least punky pop, some of it downright wimpy. While Bloch works overtime on his fretwork, Warnick and Gargiulo singly and collectively manage the best-ever Fastbacks singing—none of which alters the group's underlying lack of gravity. And the songs are good, too, especially "Gone to the Moon," the new wavey "Never Heard of Him," the galloping instrumental "Bill Challenger," the harmonized hardness of "Parts," "Kind of Game"—hell, they're all good, even the cover of the Bee Gees' 1967 "Please Read Me." (The vintage picture of Rusty is also worth pulling over to the side of the road for.)

Answer the Phone, Dummy mines the same basic vein as **Zücker** with another sturdy set of Bloch tunes (pick hit: "On the Wall") that are surprising only in their reflective seriousness. The unrestrained energy with which "I Found the Star" delivers its unsettling lyric ("I've not done anything at all since I last saw you/And I haven't had a thing to eat for a day or two/I found the star that led me to the planet where you are") belies the unsteady personality the song reveals. Ditto the merry-sounding "I'm Cold": "And I'm bored of everything in front of me/I'm cold, I'm home, I'm all alone/I feel worse than I've ever known." In the folk-rocky "Meet the Author," Bloch wonders how much better things would be "if we didn't have to sleep" and "if nothing was pretty." Between the ganged-up female vocals and the raggedy, surging electric sound, the Fastbacks here resemble a looser-limbed Breeders. Besides such guests as Kim Shattuck of the Muffs, the drummer roster numbers six, with revolving percussionists on loan from Mudhoney, Love Battery, the Posies and Flop. (It seems as if a permanent drum hire would totally queer the Fastbacks' dynamic.) Alas, no vintage pictures. [i]

See also *Flop, Young Fresh Fellows.*

FASTBALL

Make Your Mama Proud (Hollywood) 1996

Fastball doesn't seem to know or care where it comes from. The Austin trio, formerly known as Magneto USA, marries a loud version of '60s Anglopop with midwestern (think vintage Replacements) raucous melody crunch, New York Kiss rock and California tunepunk on its engaging debut. Diversity works to the band's benefit, though, because the songwriting and dedication to timeless singalong virtues are consistent. Guitarist Miles Zuniga has a workable bawl of a voice; bassist Tony Scalzo (who writes half the songs) is a plainer vocalist, but not by enough to matter much. Driving with the urgency of an anxious dad on the way to the maternity ward, Fastball never sacrifices melody to haste, and the results bounce with nifty, cheek-poking ease. [i]

FATIMA MANSIONS

Against Nature (UK Kitchenware) 1989
Blues for Ceaucescu EP (UK Kitchenware) 1990
Viva Dead Ponies (UK Kitchenware) 1990 (Radioactive) 1991
Hive EP (UK Kitchenware) 1991
You're a Rose EP (UK Kitchenware) 1991
Bertie's Brochures (UK Radioactive/Kitchenware) 1991
Come Back My Children (UK Kitchenware) 1992
Valhalla Avenue (UK Radioactive/Kitchenware) 1992
Evil Man EP (UK Radioactive/Kitchenware) 1992
1000% EP (UK Radioactive/Kitchenware) 1992
Tíma Mansió Dumps the Dead (Radioactive) 1992
Lost in the Former West (Radioactive) 1994
The Loyaliser EP (UK Radioactive/Kitchenware) 1994
Nite Flights EP (UK Radioactive/Kitchenware) 1994
Popemobile EP (Radioactive) 1994

BUBONIQUE

20 Golden Showers (UK Kitchenware) 1993
Trance Arse Vol. 3 (UK Kitchenware) 1995

Whether drawing on some aspect of his Irish heritage or the feistiness identified with his adopted hometown of Newcastle, Cathal Coughlan usually sounds like a churl—or one on his best behavior—and that is part of his uniqueness: the Cork native is at the top of his form when he's the kind of utterly loutish rebel you love to hate, or wish you were, or both. The effect is especially striking—even stunning—when it belies the style or sentiment of a song, as with "The Door-to-Door Inspector" (from **Viva Dead Ponies**), a pretty ballad about a pitiless yet pitiful enforcer of Big Brotherism. However, Coughlan's in-your-face intensity can degenerate into mere gall or, through gross overstatement, turn trivial, as it does with his jokey side group, Bubonique. The struggle to find a balance was the story of Coughlan's '80s band, Microdisney, and it continues to be a mission for Fatima Mansions.

In his past life, Coughlan never seemed to get comfortable enough with himself or Microdisney to evolve steadily, and Fatima Mansions threatens to duplicate that flow chart. The rage that (at least on record) was somewhat balanced by Sean O'Hagan (now of High Llamas) is here complemented by a shifting cast of bandmates. (Only guitarist Andrías O'Gruama and drummer Nick Allum lasted from **Against Nature** to **Lost in the Former West.**) They give great color and scope to his visions, but provide less of a counterbalance than O'Hagan did; aside from covers, Coughlan writes all the material himself.

The eight-song **Against Nature** mini-album mainly features intriguing, keyboard-dominated ballads like "The Day I Lost Everything" and "You Won't Get Me Home," forerunners of "The Door-to-Door Inspector" with attractive melodies carrying despairing, almost nightmarish lyrics. Two notable exceptions are "Valley of the Dead Cars" and the potent "Only Losers Take the Bus," both propelled by high-speed staccato beats. (In three different mixes, the latter appears repeatedly throughout Fatima's international catalogue.)

In stark contrast, the band's next move was to cut the ass-kicking six-minute Stranglers-like single (and subsequent EP title track), "Blues for Ceaucescu," a suitably vicious farewell to the Romanian dictator. With the release of **Viva Dead Ponies,** it became apparent that Coughlan and company had found a dynamic way of conveying passionate sentiments that was as engaging as it was (often) harsh. The lead-off "Angel's Delight" alternates between soft ballad and heavy rock modes to portray hard-hearted urban violence (and call for the murder of cops, a deliberate provocation that failed to get Coughlan in as much trouble as Ice-T). Brief, evocative organ/synth links interlacing songs like the crunchy first-person thuggery of "Look What I Stole for Us, Darling" and "A Pack of Lies" (a beaten woman ascends to heaven where "Holy God is there to greet her and batter her into her place"). In the title track, a sour Jesus is alive and working as an acerbic shopkeeper. The album's US version is even better, losing little of consequence and integrating "Only Losers Take the Bus" and "Blues for Ceaucescu." (Curiously, those two songs were made B-sides of the UK **You're a Rose** EP, built on the album's most accessible yet least credible number.)

Besides the title cut, the high-energy **Hive** EP contains a version of Ministry's "Stigmata" that lives, breathes and *rocks* better than the original, the sneering "Holy Mugger" and the punky class warfare of "Chemical Cosh." Minus that last song, **Hive** appears on **Come Back My Children,** a compilation that also includes all of **Against Nature,** "Blues for Ceaucescu," a couple of B-sides ("What?" and "On Suicide Bridge") and an otherwise unreleased hip-hop/disco interpretation of the Velvet Underground's "Lady Godiva's Operation."

Bertie's Brochures, another eight songs, is a mixed bag of stuff that evidently didn't fit elsewhere; its tone is low-key, sad and rueful. R.E.M.'s "Shiny Happy People" becomes a snide hip-hop diatribe against the British government ("go g-go g-go go fuck yourself"), but the condemnation of career terrorism in "Smiling" is anything but frantic, leaving room for a little grief to breathe amid the bile. The title song is a touching little number about a curiously misguided life. Plus, it's all sandwiched between three simple, strong, straightforward songs about the vagaries of (gasp) romance: Coughlan's own "Behind the Moon," Scott Walker's "Long About Now" and Richard Thompson's "The Great Valerio." While not a representative record, **Bertie's Brochures** is Fatima Mansions' most broadly appealing work.

The American-only **Tíma Mansió Dumps the Dead** catch-up collection contains "Shiny Happy People," "Behind the Moon," "Bertie's Brochures," two mixes of "Only Losers Take the Bus," "Hive," "Chemical Cosh," "Stigmata" and two others.

In the liner notes to **Valhalla Avenue,** Coughlan reflects on a rugged year and thanks those whose help "kept me on the planet . . . long enough to see this record completed." He then proceeds to stroll listeners down a sordid street, itemizing his own, and the world's, wretched stories. The catchy verse and the middle eight of the opening "Evil Man" belie its declaration of denial, hypocrisy and alienation. Save for the jarring riff after the chorus, "Something Bad" rocks jauntily despite its thorough sense of disgust, somehow linking a loathsome sexual encounter with the persistence of needless militarism. The syncopated keyboard-laden rhythm of the title tune takes a light-handed approach directly counter to the song's subjects ("You put the world on hold and let despair tear you apart"). "1000%" sports a jolly, almost singalong chorus and escalates into a hard-rocking affirmation of desolation. The rest of the music isn't as memorable as those first four tracks—save the rocking "Go Home Bible Mike" (which includes yet another appalling carnal skirmish) and the more pensive anti-war "Perfumes of Paradise"—but lyrically Coughlan doesn't let up, barely pausing to sneer. The album fittingly ends with a faux dance-rock ditty urging "Be Dead." ("Evil Man" was issued as a 12-inch and as two variant CDs, both with "Evil Man 2" and remixes of previously released items. "1000%" also came out on two different EPs, one with a remix of the song and the non-LP "Paper Thin Hotel," the other with live versions of "Evil Man," "Behind the Moon" and **Viva Dead Ponies'** "White Knuckle Express.")

Lyrically, **Lost in the Former West** picks up where **Valhalla Avenue** ends: "Belong Nowhere" opens the proceedings with cheery declarations like "You're dirt, dirt/Always know your worth/As you roam the mirthless earth." In an effort toward accessibility, Coughlan gave the production reins to Gil Norton for two tracks and Jerry Harrison the rest. The net effect is to tone down the keyboards and beef up the guitars, the better to coat the brutal words in well-played, forceful but fairly conventional hard rock. Oddly, that makes it even more difficult to come to grips with; even at its catchiest—as in the Zep-like gallop of "Popemobile to Paraguay"—the music seems divorced from the issues and the deep passions. Even after repeated listens, when all the tracks have kicked in (which they eventually do), the record's appeal is intellectual, not visceral. As the previous album was not issued in the US, two of the best "rock" tracks from **Valhalla Avenue** ("Something Bad" and "Go Home Bible Mike") are included here.

One exception to that gulf on **Lost in the Former West** is the oddly calm recrimination of "Walk Yr Way," the lovely chorus chords of which contribute to its emotional complexity. Another is the commercial-sounding rock version of "Nite Flights," the tunefully doomy title tune of one of the Walker Brothers' '70s reunion records, wherein Coughlan harmonizes with imself on the choruses. That track spearheads an EP, which also features Coughlan's bleakly compelling "As I Washed the Blood Off," a version of Suicide's "Diamonds, Fur Coat, Champagne" and "It's So Cold . . . I Think," which puts a phrase from "Nite Flites" into a new context. For some reason, the album's nearly tuneless "The Loyaliser" was chosen as the lead track on an EP with the catchy if indecipherable "Gary Numan's Porsche" and "Arnie's 5," the CD and 12-inch of which also contain a greatly extended (*and* sped-up) dance mix of "The Loyaliser." The **Popemobile** EP includes "Popemobile to Paraguay," "Evil Man," "Gary Numan's Porsche" and two otherwise unreleased items: "Sleep of the Just" and a needless six-minute swipe at Bryan Adams' "(Everything I Do) I Do It for You."

A similar lack of restraint and judgment is the problem with Bubonique. Hiding behind silly pseudonyms, Coughlan and friends (including comedian Sean Hughes) have made two albums of self-indulgent bilge that boggles the mind for all the wrong reasons. None of it is radical or shocking, just unfunny and overlong. To call this work masturbatory would be wrong, since the bandmembers never seem to achieve the seconds of pleasure such activity is meant to achieve—jacking off shouldn't be this lacking in relief. The debut, **20 Golden Showers,** is unbearably torturous, since the twenty-three listed tracks actually compose one fifty-six-minute number. **Trance Arse** is a bit more listenable, but not a lot funnier. Amid potshots at Lynyrd Skynyrd and George Michael, the most noteworthy number accuses *Q* magazine of causing Kurt Cobain's death (and of being satanic, or something). Droll is *not* the word for it. Once you've heard the name of the band, you've heard the best of Bubonique. [jg]

See also *TPRG*.

SHANE FAUBERT

See *Cheepskates*.

FAUST

Faust (UK Polydor) 1971 (UK Recommended) 1979
So Far (UK Polydor) 1972 (UK Recommended) 1979
The Faust Tapes (UK Virgin) 1973 (UK ReR) 1979 (Cuneiform) 1990
IV (UK Virgin) 1973
Munic and Elsewhere (UK Recommended) 1986
The Last LP (UK Recommended) 1988
71 Minutes of . . . (Recommended) 1990
The Faust Concerts: Vol. 1 (Table of the Elements) 1994
The Faust Concerts: Vol. II (Table of the Elements) 1994
Rien (Table of the Elements) 1995

TONY CONRAD WITH FAUST

Outside the Dream Syndicate (UK Caroline) 1974 (Table of the Elements) 1993

TONY CONRAD

Slapping Pythagoras (Table of the Elements) 1995

Active in the early '70s, Germany's Faust played a mix of jazz, folk, minimalism, rock, noise, pop and modern classical that refused to be defined. In doing so, its music managed to become allied with a number of ground-breaking styles. Industrial noisemakers trace their roots back to Faust as one of the first groups to approach rock as electronic studio music. Faust's eclectic psychedelia also pigeonholed them as one of the most important German progressive rock bands; albums range from songs (**IV**) to inventive scraps (**The Faust Tapes**). The original band lasted from 1970 to 1975, though lost studio tapes continue to be released. The latest, **71 Minutes of . . .**, is a whimsical but listenable album of bits and pieces that combines the **Munic and Elsewhere** record, a lost album that was to be called **Faust Party Three** and two unreleased songs.

In its heyday, Faust was invisible to its audience, rarely touring or submitting to photographs. But in 1990, the band re-formed, initially just to play several concerts. It was a mistake to show their faces, because in concert Faust simply seemed like hippies with shock tactics and a brutal back-to-nature agenda. Joined by a few stand-ins, original members Werner Diermaier and Jean-Herve Peron smashed television sets with sledgehammers, carried a live goat over their heads, stripped naked and played with paint and chainsaws and held up a goldfish bowl and chanted for the audience to "listen to the fish."

Knowing this is important when listening to the two subsequently released CDs that document a 1990 performance in Hamburg (**The Faust Concerts: Vol. 1**) and a 1992 show in England (**The Faust Concerts: Vol. II**). The chainsaws make an appearance on the first volume's "Legendere Gleichgultickeit"; on the second, jackhammers crash through "Axel Goes Straight." Unlike the posthumously assembled studio albums, these two records of complete songs and noise collages hold together. The liner notes are painstaking transcriptions of each recording (including "unintelligible crowd expressions" and stage lines like "my amplifier is burning, Klaus"). The albums mix new compositions and butchered versions of past Faust butcheries, like "It's a Rainy Day, Sunshine Girl" on **Vol. 1.** At times, the recordings are dark ambient music, but mostly they sound like you-hadda-be-there performance art.

In 1995, Faust returned to the studio for the first

time in twenty years and recorded **Rien,** modeled after the diverse bricolâge of its most innovative album, **The Faust Tapes,** and produced by Chicago guitarist Jim O'Rourke. The album cover, back and six-page booklet all consist of blank silver pages; the credits can only be found recited in German and English as the album's seventh and final track. **Rien** is more a return to form than **The Faust Concerts,** with droning violins, pounding industrial synthesizers, odd sound effects, trumpet improvisations and, of course, power tools combining in an experimental haze. You'll get no points for guessing the lyrics to the song in which the title consists of a drawing of an ear with an arrow pointing to a drawing of a fish.

In 1973, Faust's Uwe Nettlebeck collaborated with Tony Conrad, an avant-garde film-maker and minimalist musician best known for his work with the composer La Monte Young and for playing in an early incarnation of the Velvet Underground. Twenty years later, Table of the Elements reissued their long out-of-print double-album of an entrancing seventy-three-minute violin-and-percussion drone, **Outside the Dream Syndicate,** as well as a 7-inch single of studio outtakes ("The Pyre of Angus Was in Kathmandu" b/w "The Death of the Composer Was in 1962"). The label then brought Conrad back into the studio to collaborate with Gastr del Sol, the Chicago duo of O'Rourke and David Grubbs. A rebellion against the tonality of Western music, which has its roots in the writings and theorems of Pythagoras, **Slapping Pythagoras** explores microtones (the notes between standard intervals of a scale) and new frequency relationships. To the less musically inclined, the album works as a chilling, torpid landscape of slowly bowed violin and steady-thumping drums. [ns]

See also *Gastr del Sol, Jim O'Rourke; TPRG.*

FEAR

The Record (Slash) 1982
More Beer (Restless) 1985
Live . . . for the Record (Restless) 1991
Have Another Beer With Fear (Sector 2) 1995

VARIOUS ARTISTS

The Decline of Western Civilization (Slash) 1980

The cartoon nihilism proffered by this first-wave Southern California (Reseda, to be exact) punk quartet was so over-the-top that most folks didn't bother sticking around long enough to discover that Fear could play circles around the vast majority of its pogo-friendly peers. (And those who did were generally too caught up in frontman Lee Ving's facetiously contemptuous buffoonery to tell the difference anyway.) Ving, whose second-tier acting career has had its prosperous moments over the years, has made a livelihood of putting forth an anti-woman, anti-homosexual persona that, even at its most shocking, is more akin to Don Rickles than it is to David Duke.

The Record could well be the fiercest, most scabrous spawn of LA's original punk scene, thanks in large part to the human-being lawnmower scree loosed by guitarist Philo Cramer. For his part, Ving barks through a litany of misanthropic one-liners that heap abuse on . . . well, just about everything: "Let's Have a War" suggests mass conflagration as a means for population control (as a self-consciously provincial West Coaster, the Philadelphia-born singer insists New Jersey would make an ideal ground zero); "New York's Alright if You Like Saxophones" makes a hilarious supremacist case for the cultural superiority of Fear's hometown; "I Don't Care About You" spews vitriol on anyone who doesn't happen to be in one of the myriad special-interest groups who get theirs on the rest of the album. Truly inspired stuff. (The 1991 CD issue adds Fear's typically merry seasonal contribution, the forty-four-second "Fuck Christmas.")

Fear shifted gears entirely on **More Beer,** performing acoustic renditions of songs drawn from the Pete Seeger catalogue. Yeah, right! Songs like "Bomb the Russians" and "The Mouth Don't Stop (The Trouble With Women Is)" belch forth a hops-drenched worldview that could only offend the most humorless knee-jerk liberal—plenty of whom had infiltrated the hardcore movement by the time of the album's release. Properly chastised, Fear took its leave from the scene—but not before bequeathing a whole new interpretation of the phrase "scat-rock" to future generations. (A 1992 CD adds both tracks from the band's first 45, "I Love Living in the City" b/w "Now You're Dead.")

Live . . . for the Record took more than five years to get from a radio broadcast to the record racks, but the posthumous document gives a hint of how stupid fresh (or maybe just stupid) Fear's concert shtick could be—complete with half-finished jokes, flagrant belching and side-splitting mid-song moodswings. Backed by a thoroughly plugged Cramer and drummer Spit Six (original bassist Derf Scratch, coiner of the immortal phrase "Eat my fuck," had already departed), Ving bellows through nineteen songs drawn from the first two albums—notably a wild rendition of "Camarillo," an ode to California's largest state-run mental hospital—as well as an FCC-defying rendition of "Fuck Christmas" with a wrath that borders on the rhapsodic.

After several years in limbo, Ving re-formed Fear—without any other original members—from his adopted Texas home base, and recorded **Have Another Beer With Fear.** The change of scenery seems to have had an uplifting effect, since rather than waste energy waylaying random targets, Ving concentrates on life's truly important things—beer and . . . er, beer. Orgiastic numbers like "I Believe I'll Have Another Beer" and "Beerfight" set the tone, while "Legalize Drugs" and "Public Hangings" reaffirm that old right-wing/libertarian political subtext. Although none of his new mates can muster the fluidity of the originals, Ving still woofs with gusto; heck, he's even picked up a little local color, as evidenced by the hooting "Fuck You Let's Rodeo." [dss]

See also *TPRG.*

MELISSA FERRICK

Massive Blur (Atlantic) 1993
Willing to Wait (Atlantic) 1995

Amid the sudden surge of serious young women solo artists that gripped the record industry in the early '90s, Melissa Ferrick was hardly ignored, but her gripping and honest music was unjustly overlooked. Classically trained (she was a violin prodigy and later attended the Berklee School of Music on a trumpet scholarship), Ferrick took up guitar in college and got her big break in 1991, when she was invited to open for

Morrissey at a Boston date. Although she was a total unknown outside the local club scene, Morrissey liked her so much he took Ferrick along for the rest of the tour, including a stop at New York's Madison Square Garden that had contract-toting label execs tripping over themselves to get backstage first.

Produced by Gavin MacKillop, **Massive Blur** showcases Ferrick's powerful, dramatic voice and a broad stylistic reach. Her songs are pensive and rocking, direct and oblique, often about relationships but not strictly romantic ones. "Hello Dad," a harrowing portrait of an undemonstrative, alcoholic father (who Ferrick said was fictional), is heartbreaking ("You can't fool me/Because I know/I know that you still love me"). But she's capable of humor as well. After the album failed to ignite commercially, Ferrick wrote, performed and even recorded (for a promo single) "The Juliana Hatfield Song," a good-natured lament about her lack of commercial success in comparison to that of her labelmate and pal.

Ferrick came out upon the release of **Willing to Wait,** and her sophomore effort is a vastly different album. Stripped down and gentler, it's much closer to her Boston coffeehouse roots than **Massive Blur.** Still, "Willing to Wait" blends a Crazy Horse–style stomp with the tortured Celtic warble of Sinéad O'Connor, while the upbeat "Falling on Fists" and "I Am Done" also have plenty of kick. Most of Ferrick's songs are directed at lovers who have done her wrong, but her album-opening declaration that "I want to be/Better than I am" sets a tone that prevents even the album's darkest moments from sinking into desolation. [gg]

BRYAN FERRY

These Foolish Things (Atlantic) 1973 (Reprise) 1990
Another Time, Another Place (Atlantic) 1974 (Reprise) 1990
Let's Stick Together (Atlantic) 1976 (Reprise) 1990
In Your Mind (Atlantic) 1977 (Reprise) 1990
The Bride Stripped Bare (Atlantic) 1978 (Reprise) 1990
Boys and Girls (Warner Bros.) 1985
Bête Noire (EG/Reprise) 1987
Bryan Ferry (UK EG) 1989
Taxi (Reprise) 1993
Mamouna (Virgin) 1994

BRYAN FERRY/ROXY MUSIC

Street Life (UK EG) 1986 (Reprise) 1989
The Thrill of It All (UK Virgin) 1995

The unmistakable voice of Roxy Music began his solo career as an irregular sideline after the group's second album, converting it to his vocation as the pioneering band he co-founded in 1971 faded out of existence in the early '80s. Once a courageous groundbreaker, Ferry long ago stopped taking creative chances (if not the occasional pratfall), but has had far-reaching stylistic influence. Countless modern singers have modeled themselves after one aspect or another of Ferry's archly suave style.

A brilliantly conceived shockwave against Roxy Music's unprecedented glam-rock inventions (and, alongside Bowie's virtually simultaneous **Pin Ups,** an early example of the now-commonplace star covers album), **These Foolish Things** (and the similar **Another Time, Another Place**) had the audacity to offer the rich irony of Ferry's grandly pompous, glamorously adult interpretations of songs by people like Bob Dylan, the Beatles, the Rolling Stones, Beach Boys and Kris Kristofferson. For **Let's Stick Together,** the crooner checked out some more covers but also revisited five Roxy Music songs—either recutting the vocals, substituting alternate versions or simply remixing the original tracks.

In Your Mind, produced during a period of Roxy inactivity, is the first Ferry album on which all of the material is original and new; in a significant indication of things to come, it's bland and short of good tunes. After that fiasco, Ferry split **The Bride Stripped Bare**—a heartbroken outpouring following his breakup with Jerry Hall—between new originals and relevant revivals and produced a mixed success that doesn't simply follow structural lines.

Ferry then devoted himself to the revived Roxy Music, not making another solo record until the mid-'80s, by which time the group had come to its final rest. Ferry's 1985 **Boys and Girls** doesn't sound that different from Roxy Music's 1982 swan song, **Avalon:** elegant singing and flawless production of impossibly refined romantic songs that barely have a pulse. Given the obvious care, thought and effort behind its creation, **Boys and Girls** is hard to dismiss, but its total lack of extremism or subversion goes against everything Ferry once promoted. The wan essences of "Slave to Love" and "Don't Stop the Dance" have nonetheless proven to be enduring hallmarks of Ferry's post-Roxy existence. The similarly restrained **Bête Noire** confirms his commitment to innocuous sophistication. That wonderful voice is his sole asset: what he's singing is all but irrelevant. The coolly danceable "Kiss and Tell" is about as good it gets.

Two decades after confounding fans with **These Foolish Things,** Ferry pulled the same trick on a new generation of listeners. Recorded quickly as a stopgap when he found himself unable to finish the record that ultimately became **Mamouna, Taxi** (repeating the configuration of **Another Time, Another Place,** placing a solitary original at album's end) is another eclectic jukebox of oldies, done up to a glossy studio sheen. Lacking the context of anything stylistically contrary in his current oeuvre, however, **Taxi** is just a covers album, with no resonance beyond any other collection of finely wrought interpretations. The open pop architecture of Goffin/King's "Will You Love Me Tomorrow" and Lou Reed's "All Tomorrow's Parties" benefits from Ferry's tender ministrations, but Screamin' Jay Hawkins' "I Put a Spell on You" and "Amazing Grace" (given an unseemly syncopated snare kick) don't, and the contrived synth effects on "Rescue Me" are no excuse for Ferry's soul-free mishandling of the Fontella Bass classic. (Carleen Anderson, the Houston expatriate who made her name singing with England's Young Disciples, is the subtly featured backup vocalist on all but two tracks of **Taxi;** her **Mamouna** role is even greater. Ferry, however, is nowhere to be found on **True Spirit,** her 1994 solo album.)

The enormous expense, time and effort it took Ferry to bring **Mamouna** home is nowhere evident in this especially tiresome yupfunk exercise that could easily have been titled **More Boys and Girls.** "Too fast to live, too young to die," he sings in the opening couplet of "Your Painted Smile," and that's sadly typical of the writing's invention. "You and me, we're just like night and day," he cannily observes in the title track—

which at least has a catchy two-word chorus. Without even hinting at the sound of a reunion, erstwhile Roxy Music bandmates Phil Manzanera, Andy Mackay and even Brian Eno add touches of atmosphere to this relaxing champagne bath, but the record's overwhelmingly soporific temper prevents their eccentric contributions from disturbing its placid surface.

Street Life is a poorly annotated twenty-song retrospective of Roxy Music as well as Ferry's early solo releases, "Virginia Plain" to "Slave to Love." The import-only **Bryan Ferry** is a 1989 boxed set of **These Foolish Things, Let's Stick Together** and **Boys and Girls.** [i]

See also *Young Disciples; TPRG.*

FERTILE CRESCENT

The Fertile Crescent (Knitting Factory Works) 1992

Compounding XTC's dryly bent complexity with the unintimidating boho adventurism of its own instrumental virtuosity, New York's Fertile Crescent—Staten Island native Erik Sanko (vocals/bass), Danny Blume (guitar/vocals) and Ben Perowsky (drums/vocals)—gives melodic art-pop an intelligent, friendly poke on **The Fertile Crescent.** It's a good try, but the individually impressive ingredients never quite add up to a fully integrated and focused band. Sanko's lyrics fold a bit of whimsy into literate observations and reflections without defining a clear persona; Blume unleashes a dash of Adrian Belew–like gut-busting now and again but otherwise stays out of the spotlight; Perowsky's delicacy suits some passages better than others. The pieces fall in place for "Where on Earth," "I've Seen" and "Leave Me Alone," but otherwise **The Fertile Crescent** doesn't sound quite ready for harvesting.

In late '94, Sanko—also an in-demand sideman—formed a new group named after his music publishing company, Skeleton Key. Rounded out by guitarist Chris Maxwell, drummer Stephen Calhoon and scrap metal percussionist Rick Lee, the quartet quickly became a hot club attraction and the object of a 1995 major-label bidding war. The group's self-titled debut EP appeared the following year. [i]

FFWD

See *Orb.*

ANTON FIER

See *Golden Palominos.*

FIFTH COLUMN

Fifth Column EP (Can. Hide) 1985
To Sir With Hate (Can. Hide) 1986
Work [tape] (Can. Hide) 1988
All-Time Queen of the World (Can. Hide) 1990
36C (K) 1994

This Toronto combo, which formed in 1983 and presaged the riot grrrl movement by quite a few years, is notable not only for its incisive political edge (a heady combination of feminist and lesbian-rights activism) but also for its grasp of the pop side of the agit-pop equation. While there's no mistaking the anger seething beneath the surface of the group's music, the spoonful of sugar Fifth Column secretes in the nooks and crannies helps its medicine go down in the most pogoably delightful way.

On **To Sir With Hate,** the band flutters between Slits-styled minimalism and primitive Farfisa-saturated garage-pop—even going so far as to throw in a few flamenco licks on the insistent "Kangaroo Court." While unfailingly thought-provoking—particularly on drummer-cum-guitarist (and noted film-maker) Gloria Berlin Jones' darker compositions—the album ultimately falls victim to overly antiseptic production that blunts its punch considerably.

By the time the reconfigured lineup—which saw stalwarts Jones, guitarist Charlotte Briede and vocalist Caroline Azar augmented by bassist Beverly Breckenridge—recorded **All-Time Queen of the World,** they'd sussed out a more appropriate energy level. Although still alinear enough to weave cowpunk riffing, roller-rink organ and massed drill-team chants into (mostly) coherent songs, the quartet waxes punkier than before on raucous tracts like "She Goes Boom." But what really sets Fifth Column apart is the ease with which it imparts a beguiling bubblegum tang to innocently sexy songs like the breezy "It's Science Friction."

At first, the mixture of doe-eyed eroticism and guerrilla-art screeds that imbues **36C** (recorded as a Briede-less trio, with guest guitarist Michelle Breslin and Torry Colichio of Kickstand drumming on four songs) makes for a bit of cognitive dissonance. But it only takes a few listens to reconcile the powerful anti-patriarchal sentiments of songs like "Don't" with the equally emphatic lustiness of "Donna" (a paean to longtime compadre Donna Dresch of Team Dresch, who plays on the LP). As a lyricist, Azar addresses some important issues—"M.O.V.E.," for instance, decries the loss of sisterhood that accompanies "growing up." But unlike some of her more po-faced peers, she laces her allegories with a healthy amount of biting humor, as evidenced by the sneering, anthemic "All Women are Bitches: Repeat!" Who says the sexual revolution is over? [dss]

See also *Kickstand, Team Dresch.*

FIG DISH

That's What Love Songs Often Do (Atlas) 1995

More Lemonheads than Urge Overkill, less Smoking Popes than Social Distortion, Chicago's Fig Dish drives fat-chords alternapop out of the Midwest under the speed limit, displaying basic skill rather than self-conscious style. Producer Lou Giordano attaches **That's What Love Songs Often Do** to the same sort of sizzling forcefield he erected for **A Boy Named Goo,** and the quartet—singer/guitarists Rick Ness and Blake Smith, bassist Mike Wilson and drummer Andrew Hamilton—fills it out with catchy, dynamic songs. Able to conjure up a potent haze of slacker sloth and then obliterate it with a fierce rock assault (see "It's Your Ceiling" for a concise demonstration), Fig Dish keeps attitude out of the effort, concentrating on simply effective tunes like "Rollover, Please" (remade from a '93 indie single), the angrily measured "Weak and Mean" and the very Dando-esque "Quiet Storm King," which even has an uncredited female voice joining in on the chorus. Good nourishing fare. [i]

FIGGS

Ginger [tape] (no label) 1992
Ready, Steady, Stoned [tape] (no label) 1993
Low-Fi at Society High (Imago) 1994
Hi-Fi Drop-Outs EP (Imago) 1994
Banda Macho (Capitol) 1996

The Figgs, from Saratoga Springs, New York, formed in the late '80s and, after changing their name from the Sonic Undertones, debuted with a pair of cassette albums. Punkier than their later recordings, the raucous pop tunes are playful, full of turbulent choruses and broad guitar hooks. Songs like "Sleaze" and "Bitch Theme" (from **Ginger**) reveal the good-natured band's middle-finger attitude.

Produced by Don Gehman, **Low-Fi at Society High** is rollicking power-pop, drunk with melody—imagine the early Kinks mixed with Hunter/Ronson and a swig of pub-rock. Songwriters Mike Gent (guitar/vocals) and Pete Donnelly (bass/backing vocals) know how to get a song moving; the instrumental sloppiness is merely a facade. Beneath the loose-as-a-goose frolic, the Figgs' music is actually tighter than army buddies—a dense and seamless compendium of influences and elements. Catchy riffs mixed with typically homely vocals put a wrinkle in "Favorite Shirt," and the riff-crazed "Bus" picks up momentum along the way. The back cover—a subtle allusion to **Get the Knack**'s—clarifies the Figgs' hard-to-pinpoint allegiances.

Hi-Fi Drop-Outs is a five-song EP, pairing the album's "Favorite Shirt" and "Chevy Nova" with three non-LP tracks, including a picturesque cover of the Kinks' "Village Green."

Switching labels, the Figgs returned two years later with **Banda Macho,** an album of jokey and obvious songs. Whatever sparkle was present before seems to have gone missing, leaving numbly generic pop-rock of no real distinction. [jo/i]

FILTER

Short Bus (Reprise) 1995

If this Cleveland-bred band hadn't managed a gold record with its debut, it could probably have made a nice living working the tribute circuit under a name like Eight Inch Nails. It should come as no surprise that the specter of Trent Reznor looms large over **Short Bus**—after all, Filter mastermind Richard Patrick played in an early touring version of NIN. But the slavish manner in which he and programmer/guitarist Brian Liesegang strive to replicate his precursor's industrial angst is downright embarrassing.

While Patrick puts abundant energy into his attempts to shock, his targets are yawn-worthy in their obviousness: "Hey Man Nice Shot" (the single of which includes Dust Brothers remixes) revisits not Kurt Cobain's self-destruction (as many presumed) but the inadvertently televised suicide that inspired Rapeman's far more ominous "Budd" seven years earlier. **Short Bus** seldom gets more clever than that: like most post-industrial auteurs, Patrick exploits the weaknesses of society's less fortunate, naming the album in "solidarity" with the handicapped children who ride specially equipped coaches and using "Gerbil" and "Spent" as chances to sample the rantings of a fairly damaged individual. Artistic license should not exempt Filter from charges of Gingrich-esque heartlessness. [dss]

See also *Nine Inch Nails.*

FINAL

See *Godflesh*.

FINGER

Finger EP7 (Moist) 1991
Finger (UK Shakedown) 1992
Finger (Skyclad) 1992

VARIOUS ARTISTS

Fish Hips and Turkey Lips (UK Shakedown) 1992

Had Raleigh, North Carolina's Finger managed to break free of the anonymity it endured throughout a three-year career, the quartet would undoubtedly have stood tall in the sea of dreck. **Finger** (the American album reprises five cuts from the British seven-songer) is worth searching for, worth owning and doubly worth preserving. Led by singer/guitarist Brad Rice, the band demonstrates an uncanny ability to shift comfortably into and out of a number of musical styles without losing any of its identity as a sharp, learned and elastic-tight 4x4 rock'n'roll band. The opening "Alice" sounds a bit like the pre-punk sloppiness of the New York Dolls melded with the refinement of Hanoi Rocks. On "Daddy-Oh," Finger's reference point is the sort of slovenly southern college rock associated with Athens, Georgia. From there, songs like "Drive By" and "Vessel" head into the kind of straight-on, sincere and unfettered bash'n'crash bands like the Goo Goo Dolls hie to. Two years in the (sporadic) making, **Finger** is a near-perfect blend of tremendous songwriting and a gritty, muddy recording quality that keeps everything honest.

Finger contributed three numbers ("You Can Have It All" and "Out of Focus," plus a superb remake of the album's "Vessel") to the UK **Fish Hips and Turkey Lips** compilation, which also features regional peers Small and Motorolla (later known as Motocaster). The sound is crisper than on **Finger,** but again the band eschews studio trickery to stay as lifelike as possible. The EP includes the toss-off instrumental "Hey Benny," a tribute to a seemingly endless series of prank telephone calls made to a crusty southern auto salesman in the early '80s. [icm]

(TIM) FINN (BROTHERS)

See *Crowded House.*

FIREHOSE

See *Mike Watt.*

FIREMAN

See *Killing Joke.*

FISHBONE

Fishbone EP (Columbia) 1985
In Your Face (Columbia) 1986
It's a Wonderful Life (Gonna Have a Good Time) EP (Columbia) 1987
Truth and Soul (Columbia) 1988
Bonin' in the Boneyard EP (Columbia) 1990
The Reality of My Surroundings (Columbia) 1991
Give a Monkey a Brain . . . and He'll Swear He's the Center of the Universe (Columbia) 1993
Singles (Japan. Sony) 1993
Chim Chim's Badass Revenge (Rowdy) 1996

When they were just high-school students riding the desegregation bus from South Central Los Angeles to the San Fernando Valley, the members of Fishbone were collectively hooked by the Funkadelic song

"Who Says a Funk Band Can't Play Rock" and the bold endorsement of musical genre-blending the title implies. It became their manifesto; early on, some would label Fishbone a ska group incorporating other styles, but the band's stew of funk, soul, punk, metal, jazz, reggae and seemingly everything else musical is far more distinctive—and exciting—than simple categorization allows. As Fishbone tried to explain in one of its songs, the group set out to create a "brand new nutmeg."

Produced by David Kahne, the brilliant **Truth and Soul** *should* have been Fishbone's breakthrough, but it wound up being a glorious loss. Typical of the band's impossible diversity, it contains a scorching metallic cover of Curtis Mayfield's "Freddie's Dead," the delirious party anthem "Bonin' in the Boneyard," the scalding anti-racist "Slow Bus Movin' (Howard Beach Party)," the punky "Subliminal Fascism," soulful "Ghetto Soundwave" and an acoustic ballad, "Change."

An album-related EP released nearly two years later, **Bonin' in the Boneyard** is strictly filler, two remixes (one of which would make Larry Flynt blush) of the title track and three inconsequential new songs. But it was merely the set-up for Fishbone's masterpiece. **The Reality of My Surroundings** refines and advances the promise of **Truth and Soul.** It's powerful and exciting, shucking off all stylistic barriers and mastering virtually every sound the septet lays its hands on. "Sunless Saturday" is a blitz of '70s-style album-rock à la Yes and Rush, while "Everyday Sunshine" takes a slice of Sly and the Family Stone. "Naz-Tee May'en" is frenetic funk that could stand the Chili Peppers on their ears; "Pray to the Junkiemaker" and "Pressure" are typically authoritative forays into, respectively, reggae and ska. Fishbone's uncompromising social agenda is more clearly stated than ever: the spoken prelude "Junkies Prayer" and "Pray to the Junkiemaker" send as frightening an anti-drug message as rock has ever produced ("Grim reaper has cashed my life savings check/Thy rocketh and thy pipeth restoreth me"); "Sunless Saturday" chronicles the plight of the hungry and poor; "Housework" looks at the lives of latchkey children; "Fight the Youth" decries racism and "mental slavery."

Give a Monkey a Brain is as eclectic as **The Reality of My Surroundings,** but Fishbone here commingles styles rather than hopping from one to the other. The result, unfortunately, is not as satisfying; the music is more mannered, never quite catching the furious zeal Fishbone previously tapped. The album's best moments are still powerful: Pantera would kill for the lumbering hard-rock monster groove of "Swim," Branford Marsalis blows freestyle sax on "Drunk Skitzo" and Billy Bass of Funkadelic works out with Fishbone on "Lemon Meringue." The messages are still potent—"Black Flowers" is about the African-American community's lack of leadership, "Servitude" questions true accountability—but there's a pervading sense that Fishbone's eye is on the prized alternative nation, and the band, which played Lollapalooza that summer, is compromising its instincts in that quest.

The Japanese **Singles** album is hardly a perfect retrospective: "Sunless Saturday" is one of the many essential tracks not included. But it's not a bad sampler, and the live versions of "Freddie's Dead," "Those Days Are Gone" and "Fight the Youth" provide a taste of the group's wonderful concert performances.

Returning to active duty in 1996 as a quintet, Fishbone made **Chim Chim's Badass Revenge,** a genially bitter and somehow positive broadside about the band's past record company experiences, bluntly characterized here as slavery. The album was produced by Atlanta R&B wunderkind Dallas Austin and includes guest shots by Joi and Busta Rhymes. [gg]

See also *TPRG*.

STEVE FISK

See *Pell Mell.*

FITZ OF DEPRESSION

Fitz of Depression EP7 (Mumble Something) 1989
Fitz of Depression (Meat) 1993
Let's Give It a Twist (K) 1994
Pigs Are People Too (Negative Feedback) 1994
Swing (K) 1996

Combining the construction-zone screech-metal sound favored by the more caffeinated members of Olympia, Washington's underground community with the deconstructionist philosophy of hired assassins on the trail of rock cliché, this trio resounds with a mightily unsettling force. Not quite as single-minded as, say, the Melvins or Karp, Fitz of Depression surrounds listeners with similar endurance-test parameters—with the additional dimension of a perplexing allegiance to new wave singer/songwriter pop.

The band's early singles (including an eight-song 7-inch debut) gave rise to a lot of knowing looks, given the Fitz's propensity for covering songs like Tommy Tutone's "867-5309/Jenny" and Elvis Costello's "Red Shoes"—in layers of feedback, that is. But even amid the radical revisions, there was precious little animosity in these outings. As evinced by 1993's all-original **Fitz of Depression** (another eight songs, this time on a 10-inch), any hatred inherent is probably self-directed. Singer/guitarist Mikey Dees (Mike Nelson)—who possesses the most potent mumble/roar combination since Blue Cheer packed it in—propels misanthropic screeds like "H" and "Raw Sewage" into the midst of a boggling bass/drums tangle. Sometimes, he can't be bothered to do even that, so a fair number of the songs turn out to be instrumental—most notably the mocking "Think of Words." Unremittingly ugly—and that's high praise indeed!

On **Let's Give It a Twist,** Nelson wipes some of the sludge from the crevices of the Fitzmobile, enabling a faster zero-to-sixty acceleration, but tempering some of the neck-snapping lurches in the process. New bassist Brian Sparhawk (who replaced the more monolithic Justin Warren) is a catalyst in moving things along, particularly on heads-down Britpunk smashers like "Sitting in a Room" and "Power Shack." Not quite as forbidding as its predecessor, but magnetic nonetheless. The non-stop fusillade of singles that followed exposed Nelson's skinny-tie fetish to the hilt: not only did Fitz release versions of two different Costello tunes ("Miracle Man" and "Welcome to the Working Week"), the band went so far as to B-side the latter on a cover of Joe Jackson's "I'm the Man," wrapped in a copycat picture sleeve. As usual, the band puts on a more surly face for the larger-scale **Pigs Are People Too,** which reprises the metal-punk sound of **Let's Give It a Twist,** but with enough nihil-delic heft to resurrect remembrances of Poison Idea past. Husky as they wanna be.

Swing shifts a dozen new songs, including "No Movie Tonight," "Shimmy" and "Connect the Dot." [dss]

DAVID FIUCZYNSKI JOHN MEDESKI

See *Medeski, Martin and Wood.*

5 CHINESE BROTHERS

Singer Songwriter Beggarman Thief (1-800-PRIME-CD) 1993
Stone Soup (1-800-PRIME-CD) 1995

The census count of these mild-mannered New York roots-poppers is spot-on, but the ethnic identity and familial ties of 5 Chinese Brothers don't match the title of the children's story for which the band is named. A level-headed bunch that prizes crisp musical clarity, a solid slice of urban country and a nice bit of accordion, 5 Chinese Brothers display the mature, humble charm of nice guys who can poke fun at themselves without making it sting too much.

First formed as the Special Guests at Columbia University in 1983, the group possesses two separate but equal songwriters: Baltimore-born singer/guitarist Tom Meltzer is a witty obsessive who translates his insecurities into comical appreciations of baseball, women, Brooklyn, Cubism, family and Neil Young. Bassist Paul Foglino plays the sensitive sad sack who dreams big and sometimes wins at love, putting it all into heartfelt, honest testimonials. If the two men's lyrics occasionally succumb to gawkiness or mawkishness (there's only one They Might Be Giants, and true Nashville sap doesn't run north), the quintet's handsome records are otherwise appealing and entertaining.

Originally the title of a cassette sold at shows, the widely released **Singer Songwriter Beggarman Thief** contains some of the same songs in remixed or rerecorded form. Betraying a measure of diffidence and a stylistic personality still being firmed up (the folk influence is notably stronger than it would ultimately become), the CD boasts such essentials of the canon as "She's a Waitress (And I'm in Love)," "Paul Cezanne," "My Dad's Face" and "If I Ain't Falling." **Stone Soup** benefits from the arrival of guitarist Stephen B. Antonakos, a tasteful picker who puts a pungent twang into some of the better-developed (but less overtly humorous) numbers; an increased accordion role for keyboardist Neil Thomas adds a bit of Cajun seasoning. Also, the production is richer and the playing more confident. Meltzer, who had the lion's share of memorable tunes on the first album, comes through here with "The Avalanche Song" ("And I wish we were married/So we could get divorced/Get over this loving stuff/Let nature take its course") and "Mr. Williams," a wild faith healer's pitch. But it's Foglino who has the presence of mind to celebrate the real-life "Amazing Delores," refine his romantic sensitivity (in the lovely "Nothing but Time" and "A Lot of Nights") and make the philosophical point of "You Are Where You Want to Be." Unfortunately, both writers disclose creative indiscretions. Meltzer's vituperative "Walk Away" is a churlish mood-buster, "My Friend" is a sorry gift for Neil Young and "Faith in Something Bigger" ends the album in a happyface state of personal grace. Meantime, Foglino gives in to his sentimentality: he isn't very nice to the woeful characters he creates for "Couldn't Fall in Love" and the irony of "Trust Me" protests far too much. [i]

FIVE-EIGHT

I Learned Shut Up (Sky) 1992
The Angriest Man (Sky) 1993
Weirdo (Sky) 1994

Five-Eight initially emerged from the Athens/Atlanta scene largely on the strength of singer/guitarist Mike Mantione's "Looking Up," originally a 7-inch single, then the first (and best) track on the trio's full-length debut. The song was said to be based on Mantione's recollection of studying the ceiling during electroshock therapy, though the fun he's had with the press guarantees that the story is apocryphal. Still, the singer-on-the-edge-of-a-nervous-breakdown persona has sustained the band for three solid releases.

The trio arrived at **I Learned Shut Up** with its sound already well in place: Mantione's high, sometimes querulous vocals propelled by the bash and pop of bassist Dan Horowitz and drummer Patrick Ferguson. Five-Eight became a quartet with the addition of second guitarist Sean Dunn for the eight-song **The Angriest Man,** another record in which the best number opens the show (in this case, "My Sister Is So Strange"). The music—if not the lyrics—is slightly less frantic, and the extra guitar contributes to a richer and more varied texture.

Weirdo makes it clear that Five-Eight rises or falls on strengths it has already revealed. Mantione's voice will never be a gorgeous thing, but it fits his songs well, and those—notably the opener, "Mystery James," and the obligatory psycho number, "Behead Myself"—continue to hold out the promise that he may yet knock one over the fences into immortality. [ga]

5.6.7.8'S

Can't Help It! (Gasatanka/Rockville) 1993
The 5.6.7.8's (Aus. Au-go-go) 1993

These three tough chicks from Japan filter the primal energy of early American rock'n'roll through their own likably cartoonish sensibility, making up in femme fatale swagger what they lack in technical finesse. Compiling tracks from various Japanese singles and EPs, **Can't Help It!** combines uninhibited readings of "Wooly Bully," "Wild Thing" and the Elvis Presley (by way of Wanda Jackson) "Let's Have a Party" with appropriately trashy originals like "I Was a Teenage Cave Woman," "Edie Is a Sweet Candy" and "Motor Cycle Go-Go-Go!" The Australian release, also a stitch-job, is similar in execution, with personalized covers of "Tallahassee Lassie," "Long Tall Sally" and (!) "Harlem Nocturne." [ss]

FLAMING LIPS

The Flaming Lips (Lovely Sorts of Death) 1985 (Restless) 1987
Hear It Is (Pink Dust) 1986
Oh My Gawd!!! . . . the Flaming Lips (Restless) 1987
Telepathic Surgery (Restless) 1988
Live [tape] (Lovely Sorts of Death) 1989
In a Priest Driven Ambulance (Restless) 1990
Unconsciously Screamin' EP (Atavistic) 1990
Hit to Death in the Future Head (Warner Bros.) 1992
Transmissions From the Satellite Heart (Warner Bros.) 1993

Turn It On EP (Warner Bros.) 1994
Providing Needles for Your Balloons (Warner Bros.) 1995
Clouds Taste Metallic (Warner Bros.) 1995

Loud, wild and funny, the Flaming Lips play in the same pen of cartoon-psychedelia imagery used by others, but these disenfranchised Oklahomans, led by songwriter/guitarist/singer Wayne Coyne, possess wit and ingenuity most of the acid-addled competition lacks. After two entertaining bouts of getting itself together (both contained on a single Restless CD, with a bonus of "Summertime Blues"), the group roared to real life on the inventively self-produced **Oh My Gawd!!!,** a mature and confident work with more consistent material and performances that transcends the Lips' wacky-cult-band reputation.

Lacking the necessary manic unpredictability, however, **Telepathic Surgery** is surprisingly ordinary, although one of the CD bonus tracks sees to that: "Hell's Angel's Cracker Factory" is a mind-melting twenty-three-minute jam that would do Hawkwind proud. Fortunately, **In a Priest Driven Ambulance** is an impressive return to form, with stronger material, committed performances and imaginative production. Coyne's development into a skillful enough songwriter to draw deep emotional truths out of his cartoonish (and sporadically religion-obsessed) lyrical imagery without sacrificing his sense of humor is especially impressive. Similarly, the retooled band (a quartet again, with a new drummer and an added second guitarist) demonstrates new-found finesse, lifting such ravers as "Unconsciously Screamin'" and "Mountain Side" into the stratosphere and adding an audible sense of discovery to introspective items like "Stand in Line" and "Five Stop Mother Superior Rain." (The limited-edition **Unconsciously Screamin'** EP teams the title track with three outtakes from the **Ambulance** sessions.)

Signing to Warner Bros. did not dim the Flaming Lips' lysergic sense of pop mischief. The extra, uncredited track on **Hit to Death in the Future Head** is an epic twenty-nine minutes of static (and distant rolling thunder) ping-ponging between the speakers—hardly "bonus" music, but true to Lips' form. The band applies a more focused kind of madness to the album's ten actual songs. "Halloween on the Barbary Coast" opens with a rubbery guitar line that sounds like a woozy cousin of the riff in Status Quo's "Pictures of Matchstick Men" and then heads into a Middle Eastern haze, a crude but effective avant-garage evocation of Led Zeppelin's "Kashmir." The lonely whine'n'strum of "You Have to Be Joking (Autopsy of the Devil's Brain)" features a dash of harrowing orchestration sampled from the soundtrack of *Brazil.* Without stinting on the guitar weirdness or wry melodrama (the big drum rolls and cymbal crashes in "Hold Your Head"), the Lips showcase their songwriting smarts to good effect.

As post-punk novelty singles go, "She Don't Use Jelly" from **Transmissions From the Satellite Heart** is grade-A whimsy, with Coyne's wobbly singing the perfect complement to the band's loose-limbed rumble. It's also typical of the album's drift away from amorphous sonic swirl to a more defined (at least by Lips standards) pop stance. For all of its bursts of distortion and messy feedback, "Be My Head" is tight, addictive bubblegum; in both the lumbering, psychedelic ballad "Oh My Pregnant Head" and the brisk, pulse-driven "When Yer Twenty Two," the manic sound effects provide punctuation rather than propulsion. **Turn It On** is a three-song EP; **Providing Needles for Your Balloons** is an eight-song limited-edition mishmash of unreleased studio items, the musical evidence of an in-store appearance and "Slow Nerve Action," from an Oklahoma City radio broadcast.

Clouds Taste Metallic is one long manic-pop thrill, more musically coherent than **Hit to Death** and enriched with surprisingly tight, bright harmonies that suggest a landlocked stoner version of the Beach Boys. The titles are tabloid-headline mouthfuls, but "Psychiatric Explorations of the Fetus With Needles" and "Guy Who Got a Headache and Accidentally Saves the World" are great, serrated ear candy. If **Transmissions** is more fun than unforgettable, the juxtaposition of dense instrumental constructions and simple vocal hooks on **Clouds Taste Metallic** makes it both ingenious and irresistible. You'd never have guessed it from those wild, early records, but the Flaming Lips have grown into a first-class—if still somewhat bent—pop band. [ss/df]

See also *Mercury Rev, Radial Spangle; TPRG.*

FLAMIN GROOVIES

Sneakers EP (Snazz) 1968
Supersnazz (Epic) 1969 (CBS Special Products) 1990
Flamingo (Kama Sutra) 1970 (UK Big Beat) 1990
Teenage Head (Kama Sutra) 1971 (UK Dojo) 1990
Shake Some Action (Sire) 1976
Still Shakin (Buddah) 1976
Flamin' Groovies Now (Sire) 1978
Jumpin' in the Night (Sire) 1979
Flamin' Groovies '68 (Fr. Eva) 1983
Flamin' Groovies '70 (Fr. Eva) 1983
Bucketful of Brains (Voxx) 1983
Slow Death, Live! (Fr. Lolita) 1983
The Gold Star Tapes (Fr. Skydog) 1984
Live at the Whisky A Go-Go '79 (Fr. Lolita) 1985
Roadhouse (UK Edsel) 1986
One Night Stand (UK ABC) 1987
Groovies' Greatest Grooves (Sire) 1989
The Rockfield Sessions (Aus. Aim) 1989
Rock Juice (National) 1992

VARIOUS ARTISTS

Framin' Gloovies: A Tribute to the Flamin Groovies (Chunk) 1995

By the mid-'80s, the recording saga of San Francisco's pioneering Flamin Groovies—which began in 1968 with the self-released **Sneakers** EP but had largely ceased activity by the end of the '70s—had become an intricate and moldering morass into which countless reissues, imports, repackages, long-lost session outtakes, ancient concert documents and the occasional live-down-under-somewhere disc would blurp up to grab the attention and cash of those who continued to worship guitarist/music fan Cyril Jordan's timeless labor of rock love. Even the band's new "studio" album, 1987's likably insignificant **One Night Stand,** was done virtually live in a single day (two, if you count mixdown) and consists of oldies from the Groovies ("Shake Some Action," "Slow Death," "Teenage Head") and others (Paul Revere and the Raiders, the Who).

A safe bet for neophytes (but by no means an exhaustive career overview) is **Groovies' Greatest**

Grooves, the twenty-four-song compilation that contains most of the original material from the band's three '70s albums for Sire as well as five covers from earlier Groovies greats. Cartoons by Jordan (who has long earned his living as a commercial artist) make it a nifty package; detailed liner notes by Michael Goldberg and Michael Snyder put the music in context.

Goldberg then took a more active role in the Flamin Groovies' existence: he saw to the release of the band's first real studio album in thirteen years. Crediting only Jordan and charter bassist George Alexander (while thanking the guitarist and drummer who played with them on **One Night Stand**), **Rock Juice** is perfectly pleasant Byrds-Beatles power-pop. The bulk of the songs are new Jordan lost-love originals. "Hold on Me" is a sparkling keeper; "I'm Only What You Want Me to Be" layers on the stylistic dust for a convincing time-warp to early-'60s sap balladry; the Lennon tribute, "Thanks John," is sweet in spite of its obviousness. To round things off and provide some vintage variety, the Groovies dig through the record collection to cover Bryan Hyland's "Sealed With a Kiss," the Modern Folk Quartet's Phil Spector–penned "This Could Be the Night" and Billy Riley's "Flyin' Saucers Rock'n'Roll." [i]

See also *Roy Loney and the Phantom Movers; TPRG.*

FLAT DUO JETS

In Stereo EP [tape] (Dolphin) 1985 (Sky) 1992
Flat Duo Jets (Dog Gone) 1990 (Sky) 1990
Go Go Harlem Baby (Sky) 1991
White Trees (Sky) 1993
Safari (Norton) 1993
Introducing the Flat Duo Jets (Norton) 1995
Red Tango (Norton) 1996

DEXTER ROMWEBER

Folk Songs (Permanent) 1996

That's no greasy middle-aged man, that's Dexter Romweber, a greasy younger cat from Chapel Hill, North Carolina, whose hillbilly guitar and soulful pipes recapture the primitive off-the-cuff brilliance of early rockabilly (as in Jerry Lee Lewis, not the Stray Cats). While other fans of the old stuff simply try to replicate the past, Flat Duo Jets—usually just Dex and drummer Crow—somehow become the real thing, displaying nary a hint of nostalgia.

The six appealingly shabby tracks of **In Stereo** cover the Coasters, Bo Diddley, Buddy Holly et al., but the first full album is unalloyed brilliance. Wailin', hootin' and generally acting like a country boy headed straight for hell, Romweber runs on pure forward momentum through mindless rockers like "Wild Wild Lover" and "Please Please Baby," then becomes a backwoods Romeo for wonderfully oily ballads like "Baby" and "Dreams Don't Cost a Thing."

Teaming with noted renegade producer Jim Dickinson (a champion of studio spontaneity) for **Go Go Harlem Baby** makes sense on paper, but the album is probably *too* undisciplined. The ultra-live sound of the speedballs renders some of them generic, although Romweber continues to excel on the slower cuts, offering an atmospheric reading of the instrumental classic "Harlem Nocturne" and crooning with aplomb on the Duprees' "You Belong to Me" and "Apple Blossom Time."

Produced by Caleb Southern, **White Trees** is the Jets' second masterpiece, proof that Romweber can diversify without losing his frisky urgency. Sticking exclusively to originals, the boy spews out everything from boogie woogie ("Old Soul") to funky rock ("Daughter of the Jungle") to cornball country ("Husband of a Country Singing Star") to spooky mood pieces ("Rabbit Foot Blues"). Holy moly!

Introducing is another ripsnorting winner, mixing a handful of apt cover choices (including Otis Redding's "I've Been Loving You Too Long," which gets tender, sensitive treatment, and Bo Diddley's "Pretty Thing," which rattles like a jalopy going downhill with a busted axle as Crow attempts to demonstrate a three-handed version of Bo's signature beat) and a full supply of Dexter's originals. Recorded in Brooklyn by Norton co-owner (and ex–A-Bones singer) Billy Miller, **Introducing** is compelling evidence that it's nothing in the water that makes these boys act so crazy.

A good'n'greasy delight, **Red Tango** finds Dex and Crow pulling back slightly from the psychotronic abandon of **Introducing**—yet retaining their hellbent charm. While the frantic rockers are swell, especially "Baby Are You Hiding From Me" and Ray Harris' "Lonely Wolf," the quieter mood pieces achieve a haunting resonance equal to the Flat Duo Jets' very best. In other words, "Don't Ask Me Why" and "Sea of Flames" may well frighten the overly sensitive, while the wistfully sloppy "I Wish I Was Eighteen Again," once recorded by none other than the late George Burns, will bring a tear to the most jaded eye. Lordy!

Safari is the inevitable for-collectors-only grab bag, thirty-four (!) previously unreleased tracks—almost all covers—recorded live, in various studios and at home between 1984 and '87. Although the sound is often painfully lo-fi, the magical spirit is undeniable. [jy/i]

FLATLANDERS

See *Jimmie Dale Gilmore.*

FLATLINERZ

U.S.A. (Def Jam) 1994

A prominent corpse of the buried-in-six-months horror-rap genre, New York's pseudonymous Flatlinerz—Redrum, Tempest and Gravedigger—make an inner-city joke of ghoulish violence in flamboyant hip-hop variations on *Chiller Theater* themes: "Graveyard Nightmare," "Good Day to Die," "Rivaz of Red," "Takin' Em Underground." Unrelated to any high-stakes fiction, "Satanic Verses" rhapsodizes about decapitation, spirits rising from the dead, burning flesh and "bodies entwined, being hung by barbed wire." As an innocuous antidote to the realistic brutality of gangsta rap, Flatlinerz' thick old-school beats, trivial skits and theatrical delivery are entertaining enough but, like any novelty exercise, scarcely encourage repeated listening. [i]

DON FLEMING

See *Gumball.*

FLESHTONES

Up-Front EP (IRS) 1980
Roman Gods (IRS) 1981
Blast Off [tape] (ROIR) 1982
Hexbreaker! (IRS) 1983

Speed Connection (Fr. IRS) 1985
Speed Connection II (IRS) 1985
Fleshtones vs. Reality (Emergo) 1987
Living Legends Series (IRS) 1989
Soul Madrid (Sp. Impossible) 1989
Powerstance! (Naked Language) 1992
Beautiful Light (Naked Language) 1993
Forever Fleshtones (Fr. Danceteria) 1993
Angry Years 84–86 (Sp. Impossible) 1994
Laboratory of Sound (Ichiban International) 1995

VARIOUS ARTISTS

Time Bomb! The Big Bang Theory (Skyclad) 1988

Time has always stood still for the Fleshtones. Old-fashioned in sound when they began plying their "super-rock" trade in New York's skankiest night clubs in 1976, the Queens group's determined mediums—singer Peter Zaremba, guitarist Keith Streng and drummer Bill Milhizer—have never stopped channeling the spirit of every great rock'n'roll party band that ever stepped to it, from the Coasters to the Kingsmen, the Raiders to the Kinks. Two decades later, they're still going strong, making great entrances and stylish exits and pouring it all out in uplifting sets of smart and sassy uptight bliss in between. Amazingly, Streng and Zaremba's aged-in-the-studio songwriting hasn't lost its colorful zest, which means that most of the group's '90s albums are as wide-eyed and wonderful as their first blasts of serious fun. Somewhere along the way, self-conscious re-creation became subconscious reality for the Fleshtones. Thus recharged, the Fleshtones look well-equipped to blast into the next century.

Living Legends provides a quick brush-up run through the band's first decade for those still taking off their coats and looking for the punchbowl. Adding a few nifty rarities (like the superlative "American Beat '84" done for the *Bachelor Party* soundtrack) to an unfairly stingy selection of tracks from **Up-Front** ("Theme From 'The Vindicators,'" a fictional guitar-organ-sax theme), **Roman Gods** ("I've Gotta Change My Life," the Lee Dorsey hit "Ride Your Pony") and the garage-rock classic **Hexbreaker!** ("Right Side of a Good Thing," "Screaming Skull").

The Fleshtones' other '80s artifacts include three live albums (the stupendous **Speed Connection II** and the import-only **Speed Connection** and **Soul Madrid**). **Fleshtones vs. Reality** is an uneven studio LP, bolstered by the snarling prehistoric Kinksy guitars of "Way Up Here," the raise-the-dead soul fervor of "Whatever Makes You Happy" and a swift remake of Cornelius Brothers and Sister Rose's "Treat Her Like a Lady." **Angry Years 84–86** is a belated but presentable collection of unissued tracks and demos from an unsigned era (which sounds a lot like the '60s from here, especially when the Fleshtones barrel through the Serpent Power's 1967 FM-radio classic "Endless Tunnel" for the song's full thirteen-minute length). In addition, the group undertook a couple of solo projects: Streng's Full Time Men (with R.E.M. guitarist Peter Buck) and Zaremba's Love Delegation. **Time Bomb!** features those groups amid other permutations of Fleshtones and their pals, along with non-LP tracks, including "I Was a Teenage Zombie," the Fleshtones' killer theme song for the movie of the same name.

Five years out of the American record market did nothing to dampen the Fleshtones' spirits on **Powerstance!** With Andy Shernoff of the Dictators standing in on bass (Ken Fox, ex–Jason and the Scorchers, makes his entrance to full-time membership on one song), producer Dave Faulkner of the Hoodoo Gurus strikes an agreeable compromise between the band's raw slop and commercial rock sensibilities, making the Fleshtones resemble his band as much as the inverse was earlier true. But while the album incorporates amusing citations from the Yardbirds to Gary Glitter and Slade, stokes the fire with horns and delivers some long-term tunes ("Armed and Dangerous," "Let It Rip," "Mod Teepee" and the caveman instrumental stomp "Candy Ass," which tests the studio's phasing equipment and finds it fully operational), the Fleshtones mete out the energetic music too carefully, sacrificing the urgent elbow grease that ignites their best work.

Produced in Athens by Peter Buck, the less-upward-looking **Beautiful Light** takes a few slim chances and comes up a rootsy winner. "Mushroom Cloud" reconnects the band to the organ-powered psychedlia that has served it well in the past; "Take a Walk With the Fleshtones" powers a smart stroll through the East Village with Streng's bracing Kinks chord chunk; "Whistling Past the Grave" elevates the band's melodic ambitions with Yardbirdsy atmosphere; "Pocketful of Change" takes the quartet on a tuneful western detour; strong horn charts on "Outcast" and "Pickin' Pickin'" fire Zaremba's soulful testimony into tuneful orbit. All's right on the Fleshtones front. (**Forever Fleshtones** is the identical album with the front and back cover artwork flopped and the first song likewise shifted to the caboose position.)

Laboratory of Sound, however, is one experiment the Fleshtones probably shouldn't have tried. It's tempting to blame the letdown on "engineer" Steve Albini, but other than razorblading Streng's guitar tone with his patented anti-lapidary trebling action and organizing inappropriately harsh and thin sound, he doesn't appear to be at fault. Nor does the hedonistic ethos expressed in "High on Drugs" seem responsible. No, it's Zaremba's generally ineffectual songwriting and distressingly sharp singing that keep the album from matching the easy appeal of its immediate predecessor. Streng's "Hold You" is the album's only great contribution to the collection, although Zaremba's "Accelerated Emotion" comes close; the jointly penned "We'll Never Forget" revisits old structural ground without incident. Otherwise, the monochromatic rock performances of constricted melodies leaves **Laboratory**—the casualty of inadequate preparation and overly casual execution—a disappointing write-off. Come back for the make-up. (In a fun-with-technology coda, the band sticks a honkingly fine unlisted garage version of Jim Hendrix's "I Don't Live Today" on track sixty-nine of the CD.) [i]

See also *TPRG*.

FLIPPER

Generic Flipper (Subterranean) 1982 (Def American) 1992
Blow'n Chunks (ROIR) 1984 (ROIR/Important) 1990
Gone Fishin' (Subterranean) 1984
Public Flipper Limited Live 1980–1985 (Subterranean) 1986
Sex Bomb Baby! (Subterranean) 1988 (Infinite Zero) 1995
American Grafishy (Def American) 1992

In its prime, San Francisco's Flipper was a magnificent, fascinating entity, playing what might have been typical hardcore music at an unsettlingly slow speed. As if staggered by the weight of reality but determined to plod forward anyway, leaders Bruce Lose and Will Shatter (both usually on bass and vocals) groaned and howled while Ted Falconi's clangorous guitars sputtered and wheezed. Flipper's cathartic noise—sort of a foul-smelling castor oil for the ears—was more than a gimmick, though. With repeated listenings, the songs' inner beauty emerged, delivering messages of hope and compassion.

Generic Flipper remains the definitive work, containing such bent epics as "Sex Bomb" and "Life" ("the only thing worth living for"). The live **Blow'n Chunks,** recorded in New York, adds an extra dash of entropy to the tumult—not that the quartet's studio stuff is polished in the first place. **Gone Fishin',** Flipper's second studio outing, introduces new ingredients like clavinet, sax and piano, revealing a desire to evolve from their original perfection. Interesting, but not as swell.

On the other hand, the two-record **Public Flipper Limited Live 1980–1985** is a fine, gloriously messy collection of onstage brilliance. The package itself is almost as amusing: the title is a tit-for-tat parody of Public Image (who copped the **Generic** concept), while the sleeve folds out into a poster-plus-game. Shatter died of a heroin overdose in 1987, apparently bringing the band to an end. The posthumous **Sex Bomb Baby!** is a must-hear retrospective that collects singles, compilation contributions and other important odds and ends. The Infinite Zero reissue adds three tracks.

The 1991 return of a reconstituted Flipper—fronted by Bruce (no longer Lose, and not playing bass) Loose and featuring original bandmates Ted Falconi and Steve DePace (killer drums), plus new bassist John Dougherty—was one of the most unexpected comebacks ever. Although the sense of exploring new territory, not to mention the dadaist absurdity, are inevitably somewhat faded on **American Grafishy,** mind-twisting displays like "Fucked Up Once Again" and "Flipper Twist" (right on!) prove the band's patented approach to noise still packs a punch. [jy]

See also *TPRG*.

FLOP

Somehow EP7 (Lucky) 1990
Flop & the Fall of the Mopsqueezer! (Frontier) 1992
Whenever You're Ready (Frontier/550 Music/Epic) 1993
World of Today (Frontier) 1995

By 1992, grunge had been exported from Seattle to the department stores of America's malls, and the pop-punk buried beneath the city's fuzz pedals finally found room to shine forth. Among others (notably the long-lived, crucial Fastbacks), Flop exploded with noise-pop, sporting a mod-influenced edge, loud, sunny guitars and bittersweet underpinnings. Produced by Kurt Bloch, **Flop & the Fall of the Mopsqueezer!** is one of the '90s' finest debuts. Packed with singer/guitarist Rusty Willoughby's crisp, gifted songwriting, the disc offers wry humor, buoyance and flashes of brilliance. The Kinks cover ("Big Sky") doesn't hurt, but following it immediately with the gorgeous, anthemic "Hello" ("The seed of a hesitating sun/Has given birth to the woman that you will become") clinches Willoughby's gift for both sweet juxtapositions and moving harmonies. While **Mopsqueezer** is drenched in kinetic, powerful rock ("Anne," "Entropy," the ferociously catchy "Ugly Girl Lover," "Asthenia," the nearly reckless "Parasite"), the record's depth comes from its wonderful mood changes. The shimmering "You Would Be Right" gets a waltzy treatment that places it neatly in between the Left Banke and the Who; the soulful "Sister Smile" mines doo-wop for influence; the psychedelic "Morton the Venereologist" provides weight rather than mere indulgence.

The association with a major label didn't hurt Flop so much as toughen the task facing the band in trying to better its stunning debut. **Whenever You're Ready** is a tad overproduced, with a Big Rock sound (credit Martin Rushent's mix?), but the basic elements are all there—Willoughby's engaging writing and wonderfully delicate voice, his interplay with outstanding co-guitarist Bill Campbell, the sturdy rhythms of drummer Nate Johnson and bassist Paul Schurr. If the presentation obscures some of the debut's coy charm, Flop still does well in its two- and three-minute song format. A Beatles fixation comes through clearly on the Lennonesque "A Fixed Point," while "The Great Valediction," "Port Angels," "A. Wylie," "Eat" and "Woolworth" reprise the craftiest, hookiest moments from **Mopsqueezer.** The instrumental "Z^2+C," "Need Retrograde Orbit" and the cerebral "Parts I & II" (with a nice cello arrangement) prove Flop hasn't lost its imaginative touch. Though avoiding the sophomore jinx, **Whenever You're Ready** still lacks its predecessor's immediacy.

Unveiling a new lineup with Dave Fox (ex-Posies) on bass, **World of Today** returns the band to form, as well as to producer Bloch (of the Fastbacks and Young Fresh Fellows), who renders a friendlier, more straight-ahead recording. With fewer studio embellishments, Willoughby's songwriting sounds tougher, more lively. Then, with a lyric like, "You'll get more disillusioned with age" (from "April Ate Our World"), maybe he simply *is* tougher. No matter. Bolstered by a winning cover of the Move's "Yellow Rainbow," Willoughby exposes his wounds (he has consistently displayed an intriguing disease fetish) and makes a swirling musical wonder of it all. The simple synth horns on "Vancouver Door Company" succeed far better than **When You're Ready**'s overindulgences. "Of Today" mines "Taxman" in an homage similar to the Jam's "Start!"; "Eggs and Ash" turns mellifluous and tender with a knockout backward guitar solo, and "Around" sounds like the best song Frank Black never wrote. Despite the inclusion of more long songs, Flop still sounds economical and intelligent on its impressive, exciting third record. Johnson, who has moonlighted as the Fastbacks' drummer (as has Willoughby), subsequently quit Flop. [mww]

See also *Fastbacks*.

FLOUR

Flour (Touch and Go) 1988
Luv 713 (Touch and Go) 1990
Machinery Hill (Touch and Go) 1991
Fourth and Final (Touch and Go) 1994

As bassist for two of the finest post-punk/guitar noise bands of their era, Breaking Circus and Rifle Sport (the latter also contained Todd Trainer, later of

Brick Layer Cake and Shellac), Pete "Flour" Conway had a hand in shaping both the harsh Chicago sound of the mid-'80s and its more loosely defined Minneapolis counterpart. He also released four consistently good solo albums of claustrophobic noise, of which **Fourth and Final** is, as the title suggests, the last. With only incidental instrumental assistance and driven by an overtaxed drum machine, the record is less atmospheric and more aggressive than Flour's earlier releases, closer in sound to the Chicago skronk of bands like Big Black and Bastro. Flour has a poppier sensibility, however, and he tempers the factory floor pounding with small, surprisingly delicate melodies ("Godiva") and some new wavey flourishes ("Cyannized"). [sf]

See also *Pigface; TPRG.*

FLOWER

See *Versus.*

FLOWERED UP

A Life With Brian (London) 1991

Under a banner of contrary cleverness, this London rock quintet grows its garden with a smidge of Happy Mondays' danceable stutter-beat bottom, lots of energetic guitar, sporadic trumpet bleats and singer Liam Maher's strongly accented comments on Ecstasy worship in songs like "Sunshine" and "Mr Happy Reveller." Like a watched pop, **A Life With Brian** is slow to develop, but when it does—in the pulsing party grooves of "Silver Pan" and "Phobia" and the atmospheric keyboard washes of "Doris . . . Is a Little Bit Partial"—it's worth the wait. One J. Strummer is credited with "additional lyrics" in "Take It," but the sodden mix discourages any serious consideration of his contribution. [tr]

FLOWERHEAD

Turmoil in the Toybox EP [tape] (no label) 1990
. . . ka-BLOOM! (Zoo) 1992
The People's Fuzz (Zoo) 1995

The six long songs on the self-released **Turmoil in the Toybox** find this Austin quartet toiling through the same bleary guitar-slog as retro bashers like Thee Hypnotics, only with no sense of style or evident enthusiasm for the form beyond its option of velvet-trousered indulgence, as well as a weak but obvious U2 imitation ("Star-Crossed Days"). Singer/bassist Eric Faust has the kind of voice designed to be heard from the 155th row, which makes the indie format a bit incongruous.

The band's major-league debut, **. . . ka-BLOOM!,** isn't any better. Replete with too many long songs—most of them of the sterile, neo-psychedelia-cum-'70s-stadium-shaker variety—**. . . ka-BLOOM!** is background music for the indiscriminate stoner, as common-sounding as a car horn. (The final line Faust utters in "Sunflower," the album's closing track: "Praise the Lord, and pass the goddamn bong.") The record contains exactly two decent tracks: "Snagglepuss" flows in a pleasant vintage pop vein, while "Everything Is Beautiful" is a determined, slightly grungified post-punk rip poisoned slightly by simplistic lyrics. Elsewhere, attempting to create vast aural landscapes within seven or eight minutes of recording time like some of its '70s idols, the slackjawed Flowerhead comes up with cliché-burdened tracks like "Oh Shane," "Acid Reign" (remade from **Turmoil**) and "Thunderjeff" to no real positive effect.

The People's Fuzz is even more overblown and pretentious. Where **. . . ka-BLOOM!** was at least endurable, this bubbles the tritest, safest and most predictable late-'60s and early-'70s formulae into seventy-three minutes of unmitigated boredom (a third of it devoted to an untitled bonus track of Martian rainforest sound effects) that can't decide from one verse to the next whether to ape the Beatles, Flaming Lips, Bad Company, Marshall Tucker, Blue Cheer or Styx. The songs are shorter this time, but the band remains mired in its witless regression. [icm]

FLUF

Mangravy (Headhunter/Cargo) 1992
Wasting Seed (Headhunter/Cargo) 1992
Shooting Putty at the Moon [tape] (Headhunter/Cargo) 1992
Home Improvements (Headhunter/Cargo) 1994
Whitey on the Moon (Headhunter/Cargo) 1994
Stocking the Lake With Brown Trout [tape] (Headhunter/Cargo) 1994
The Classic Years (Headhunter/Cargo) 1995

OLIVELAWN

Sap (Nemesis/Cargo) 1990
Sophomore Jinx (Headhunter/Cargo) 1991

Otis Barthoulameu, who chooses to be known simply as O., was the renaissance man of the early '90s San Diego scene. Besides fronting fluf and playing guitar in Olivelawn, the hefty singer/guitarist has been a roadie (for the Muffs), oft-published skateboarding photographer, record producer (for further, among others), van driver, stagehand (Ministry's **Psalm 69** tour), 7-inch single manufacturer (Rocket From the Crypt, Tanner) and a T-shirt hawker at his own shows—all in the name of no-bullshit rawk'n'roll, the music to which he's zealously dedicated.

Olivelawn's two albums are, for the most part, forgettable exercises in coming-of-age, post-punk riffage. Lifting MC5, Sabbath, Iggy Pop and even ZZ Top licks (the Texas trio's "Heard It on the X," covered on the Jack Endino–produced **Sophomore Jinx,** is an homage to San Diego's alternative-radio station 91X), the short-lived band was important mostly for including O. and bassist Jonny Donhowe, who formed two-thirds of the far superior fluf.

Fluf's strength lies in its to-the-point songwriting, namely O.'s gift for combining ultra-heavy hooks and tender pop strains ("happenin' melodies with friggin' raw, heavy guitar," is how he describes it). And it's a good thing the songs are so damn catchy, because the sound is often derivative. **Mangravy**'s Hüsker Dü–like Soundgarden tribute, "Kim Thayils Paw," and a version of Bob Marley's "Redemption Song" which somehow sounds like a dead-on Social Distortion cover make up in unpretentious fancy what they lack in originality. (On cassette, the album is titled **Shooting Putty at the Moon; Wasting Seed** is a 10-inch vinyl abridgment of it.)

Home Improvement (issued on vinyl with an extra track as **Whitey on the Moon** and on cassette as **Stocking the Lake With Brown Trout**) moves beyond the debut's limitations with subtlety and nuance. "Sticky Bun" has a hook you could snare a sperm whale with, while "RK Wins," an odd, spastic Rodney

King homage, lightly confronts racism. Recorded live in the studio, the album bulldozes away a clearing while erecting memorable structures. "Mark Andrea," a shameless Neil Young theft, and "Page 3+1" (which nicks a Pavement beat) are, in context, forgivable sins. "Rooked," which somehow combines Bob Mould and Jimmy Page, is a more indictable offense.

With the band being courted by major labels, **The Classic Years** was assembled to round up most of fluf's indie singles. The big deal never came, but the twelve-song compilation (there's a bonus track on the vinyl) did. While omitting "Garbage Truck" (fluf's first released song) and including some previously unissued material, the set does include such must-haves as the roller-coaster "24–7 Years" (dedicated to Kurt Cobain), the high-octane slammer "Skyrocket" and a riotous, if ironically faithful, take on PJ Harvey's "Sheela-Na-Gig." The line "gonna wash that man right outta my hair" was never funnier. [tja]

FLY ASHTRAY

Nothing Left to Spill [tape] (self-released) 1990
Extended Outlook EP7 (See Eye) 1990
Clumps Takes a Ride (See Eye/Shimmy-Disc) 1991
Let's Have Some Crate (UK Hemiola) 1992
Tone Sensations of the Wonder-Men (Shimmy-Disc) 1993
Flummoxed EP (Dark Beloved Cloud/Hemiola) 1996
Stop the Zakkos EP (Fifth Beetle) 1996

PHOAMING EDISON

Sold to the Highest Grady (Dark Beloved Cloud) 1995
Sold to the Second Highest Grady (Dark Beloved Cloud) 1996

One of New York's least glamorous and most under-publicized bands is also one of its most musically adventurous and rewarding. Although properly included on ROIR's **New York Scum Rock** compilation, Fly Ashtray are not prickly post-punkers but friendly purveyors of a warped noodle fuzz. Formed at Fordham University in the Bronx by guitarist/singer/bassist John Beekman, guitarist Chris Thomas and bassist/guitarist Mike Anzalone, the band's first release (a 1987 single, "The Day I Turned Into Jim Morrison") was as a quintet with guitarist/keyboardist/bassist/singer James Kavoussi and drummer Eric Thomas, Chris' younger brother.

Nothing Left to Spill is a compilation of early tracks that captures a British Invasion bent and the snazzy off-kilter maturation from Fall/Television-inspired rock to underground brain treasure. The songs range from giddy psychedelia to eclectic country; "To the People Who Fold Clothes, Thank You for Folding Clothes" typifies the band's odd view of the universe. Around this time, Eric Thomas moved to Japan and was replaced by Glenn Luttman; Anzalone also exited the band, though continued playing with Kavoussi in Uncle Wiggly.

The 7-inch **Extended Outlook** contains one song each by Kavoussi, Beekman, Thomas and Luttman. In a lot of ways, this EP and the three-song single (containing "Soap," "Bip" and "Feather") that followed it in 1991 are prototypes for '90s sensibilities, with plenty of sonic mayhem, nonsensical diagrams and immutably classic songs buried under piles of purposeful mis-mixing.

Released on Shimmy-Disc, **Clumps Takes a Ride** is a catalytic mash of catchy guitar excursions. Like Fly Ashtray's previous releases, **Clumps** is less a distinct dot on the band's timeline than a well-conceived cluster of material from as far back as 1988. Anzalone's "Ostrich Atmosphere" is a fanciful pop highlight. The band is a fountain of inspiration, pouring out strange dreams, like "Dolphin Brain" and "Anyway," that seem musically inevitable. If not for Fly Ashtray, someone in Pavement or the Thinking Fellers would have eventually penned these tracks.

The 10-inch, eleven-song **Let's Have Some Crate** blurs all boundaries, slipping tons of out-of-phase vocal and guitar tracks in to create a swampy swarm of sweet confusion. Where Fly Ashtray usually tucks its eccentricities into faithful song arrangements, the band pushes away from tradition on this one. The more demanding approach weighs on the band's ability to deal with heavy issues without being direly serious, but it doesn't scrape their adventurous brilliance.

Retreating from the vortex, Fly Ashtray made its most concise release yet, the Kramer-produced **Tone Sensations of the Wonder-Men.** Spilling sound everywhere in a bouncy Ashtray-groove, the eighteen-track album kicks off with the bossy "The Big 1-2-3-4," and songs pile up in rapid succession from there. Exotic nuggets like "The Girl From the Chinese Restaurant" are insanely catchy on first listen and complex enough to withstand the rigors of multiple plays. Kavoussi's forlorn and wistful "Morale Polyp" burns time away with its languid lament "How do I / get out / of this . . . wish I / never."

Phoaming Edison is a murky-psych nom-de-solo for Kavoussi, a musician-engineer who has recorded scads of New York indie albums. His first album of sonic gunk is low on structure but high on charming, confident and well-mannered mind-shifting sound experiments. With all the clanging arrhythmia and incidental sound, the **Grady** records are a peek into the gunky, confusing guts of Fly Ashtray's extraordinary machine. [ic]

See also *Uncle Wiggly.*

FLYING SAUCER ATTACK

Flying Saucer Attack (UK FSA) 1993 (VHF) 1994
Distance (VHF) 1994
Further (Drag City) 1995
Chorus (Drag City) 1995

There must be something about the landscape around Bristol, England, that incites its denizens to travel ever deeper inward in order to find inspiration for their art. Not at all dissimilar to the contemporaneous trip-hop scene that flourishes at its doorstep, Flying Saucer Attack creates a trance-like, decidedly cerebral sound—albeit without the vaguest insinuation of danceability. There's an eerie, elusive bliss in the collaborations between home-recording wizes Rachel Brook and David Pearce—kind of like an elongation of that sensorily unbound moment when wakefulness is about to give way to sleep.

The duo's self-titled debut is an amorphous compendium of loopy (literally) sonic explorations, dense and feedback-studded one moment, rapturously pastoral the next. Unfortunately, there's not nearly enough of the latter element (other than a transfiguring number called "Popol Vuh 1," which bears a passing spiritual resemblance to the prog-rock band of the same name) to merit more than a cursory listen. On **Distance,**

Pearce and Brook wield similar tools, but build a considerably more stimulating series of structures. Acoustic instrumentation (including an alluring oboe line that wafts through "Instrumental Wish") improves things, but even the more rock-tempered tracks (like the Can soundalike "Standing Stone") project a sensation of preternatural calm.

One side effect of the upswing in digital technology is the lack of good headphone records, but **Further** is a doozy in the lie-back-and-enjoy-it category. Moments here bear passing resemblance to My Bloody Valentine ("Rainstorm Blues") and the Jesus and Mary Chain (the attentively manipulated feedback patterns of "Come and Close My Eyes"); still, the reticent use of vocals (they're buried deep enough to survive an H-bomb blast) and avoidance of rock accouterments lends a more elusive vibe to this set of remarkably intimate songs. **Chorus** ventures a bit further into technological overload, employing an impressive array of proudly synthetic computer fuzz on "Feedback Song" and the wee-hour traipse "There but Not There." An inner sleeve note cautions that **Chorus** "marks the end of FSA phase one . . . when we return with phase two, who knows where the wind blows." You couldn't ask for a more appropriately ambiguous farewell—if that's what it is.

For further study: Brook and a woman named Kate play as Movietone and released a self-titled album in the UK in 1995. Matt Elliot, who has added percussion and clarinet to a number of FSA records and joins the group for its rare live appearances, is the Third Eye Foundation, with a couple of British albums to his credit. True aficionados may also know of Linda's Strange Vacation, an unrecorded early-'90s assembly of Brook, Elliot, Kate and, occasionally, Pearce. [dss]

FOETUS

YOU'VE GOT FOETUS ON YOUR BREATH

Deaf (UK Self Immolation) 1981
Ache (UK Self Immolation) 1982

SCRAPING FOETUS OFF THE WHEEL

Hole (UK Self Immolation) 1984 (Self Immolation/ZE/PVC) 1985 (Thirsty Ear) 1995
Nail (Self Immolation/Some Bizzare/Homestead) 1985 (Thirsty Ear) 1995

FOETUS ALL-NUDE REVIEW

Bedrock EP (Self Immolation/Some Bizzare/Relativity) 1987

FOETUS INTERRUPTUS

Thaw (UK Self Immolation/Some Bizzare) 1988 (Thirsty Ear) 1995

FOETUS CORRUPTUS

Rife (no label) 1989

FOETUS INC

Sink (Self Immolation/Wax Trax!) 1989 (Thirsty Ear) 1995

FOETUS IN EXCELSIS CORRUPTUS DELUXE

Male (Big Cat) 1993

FOETUS

Gash (Columbia) 1995
Null EP (Columbia) 1995

CHROME CRANKS/FOETUS

Vice Squad Dick EP (PCP) 1994

WISEBLOOD

Dirtdish (K.422/Some Bizzare/Relativity) 1986 (Thirsty Ear) 1995

CLINT RUIN/LYDIA LUNCH

Stinkfist EP (Widowspeak) 1988
Don't Fear the Reaper EP (UK Big Cat) 1991

STEROID MAXIMUS

Quilombo (UK Big Cat) 1991
Gondwanaland (UK Big Cat) 1992

Thanks to modern technology, any chump with a studio can now open up the bomb bays and drop sonic megatonnage. That's the easy part. Nailing targets and causing serious devastation, however, is a job for professionals, and no one in modern rock wrecks shit with a sharper balance of artistic control and unmitigated power than J. G. (Jim) Thirlwell, whose unmatched skill in sculpting audio thunder into theatrical monuments of bludgeoning agility is positively Zeus-like. His records—issued under endless insignificant variations on the Foetus name (as well as Clint Ruin)—are stunning in their intensity and fascinating in their impenetrable density. Few musicians can guide a record through a horrorhouse of galloping cacophony with as firm and delicate a hand. Over the course of his first fifteen years of art terrorism, a career whose only watchword is extremism, Foetus has introduced many intriguing elements (big-band swing only the most unexpectedly amusing among them) into the basic cauldron of boiling noise without seriously rethinking his approach. With fewer hummable songs than a Milli Vanilli compilation, Foetus' lie-back-and-enjoy-it-or-die records are pure expositions of sensual overload. Suffice to say, Ministry, Nine Inch Nails, Cop Shoot Cop and all those who sail on such roiling waters owe this courageous innovator their first-born in recompense for the violent audio lessons of his vinyl teachins.

The Australian expatriate spent years living in London before settling in New York toward the end of the '80s; his music took a while to reach these shores as well. The only thing to do with **Hole,** Foetus' first American release (1985), is to jump in and pray for survival. The LP has a little of everything: industrial cacophony ("Clothes Hoist"), high political drama ("I'll Meet You in Poland Baby"), spare crypto-blues ("Sick Man"), demented surf music "(Satan Place"), something ugly built on a swing beat ("Water Torture"), Neal Hefti's *Batman* theme and lots more, all played at a confusion level that makes Christmas Eve at K-Mart seem placid. (Although the first US edition added a bonus 12-inch EP of songs from 1985 singles by You've Got Foetus on Your Breath and Foetus Über Frisco, the 1995 CD omits the added material, some of which had already turned up on the **Sink** anthology.)

Nail is another strange voyage into Foetus' fevered world. From the soundtrack-styled opening ("Theme from Pigdom Come"), through a generally cinematized concept collection of high-octane rants, Foetus layers sound on sound, injury on insult. "!" is the album's existential high point, but such vehement audio orgies as "The Throne of Agony" and the '40s-jazzy "Descent Into the Inferno" provide plenty of clever lyrical invention.

Included in two mixes (one with horns and a backing chorus), the title track of **Bedrock** (most assuredly not about Fred and Wilma's hometown) is a vituperative and deliciously vulgar rap sneered over swinging acoustic bass and bongos, with an industrial-strength rusty-door guitar solo for extra heat. Two of the other tracks—"Diabolus in Musica" and "Shut"—are one slow-starting instrumental that revs up to noise concrète (complete with machine guns, metallic clangs and animal sounds) strong enough to peel layers off a boulder at a hundred paces.

Broiling up an explosive sonic smorgasbord in a free-fire zone, Foetus outdoes himself on **Thaw,** an album so intense that it makes the previous platters seem like knuckle-cracking tuneups. His arsenal here includes automatic weapons, clanging metallic percussion, a symphony orchestra and virulent lyrics about suitably violent subject matter spewed out in a voice so shredded it would give Freddy Krueger the willies. For dynamic tension, Foetus suddenly drops back amid the onslaught to whisper a verse or two over acoustic piano and string bass (in one case, sitar and tabla). Oppressive in the most rewarding fashion imaginable, **Thaw**—which concludes with the charming "A Prayer for My Death"—is the fantasy score to an unimaginable film no one should ever have to see. Bravo!

Following **Thaw**'s release, Thirlwell formed Foetus Corruptus—borrowing Raymond Watts from the like-minded Pig, plus members of Prong and the Swans—for a European tour, documented on the double-LP authorized bootleg, **Rife.** Expanding the group (and giving it the even more glamorous name Foetus in Excelsis Corruptus), he recorded the more readily available **Male** at CBGB in November '90. The double-CD extravaganza features violinist/guitarist Hahn Rowe (ex–Hugo Largo), guitarist Norman Westberg (Swans), bassist Algis Kizys (Swans) and drummer Vinnie Signorelli (Unsane). If the show sounded anything like the record does, it's amazing how convincingly Foetus can re-create his studio density and intensity on stage. Highlights include four Wiseblood numbers (the instrumental "Death Rape 2000" and the elephant-noises "Stumbo," "Someone Drowned in My Pool" and "Honey I'm Home"), "Free James Brown (So He Can Run Me Down)" and "I'll Meet You in Poland Baby," held aloft by Rowe's skillful scraping and Nazi samples provided by David Ouimet of Motherhead Bug. Applause hardly seems like the appropriate response, but there it is.

Pursuing **Thaw**'s cinematic byway, Steroid Maximus is Thirlwell's instrumental project of would-be film scores. The brassy, garishly atmospheric music on **Quilombo** and **Gondwanaland** (which have a couple of tracks in common) is stunning in its mischievous diversion of traditional concepts, from the ominously brilliant titles ("Phantom Miscarriage," "Ogro," "The Trojan Hearse," "The Smother Brother") to the nervy instrumental invention. Employing a slightly more restrained dynamic range than usual, Thirlwell delves into Wagnerian orchestration, exotic ethnic elements, blaring big-band swing, continental drift and found-sound constructions to deliver extraordinarily convincing and resonant accompaniments to whatever he's seeing in his grotesque imagination. First rate. Both records feature Lucy Hamilton, Raymond Watts and Voivod drummer Michael "Away" Langevin. **Quilombo** also employs Spoiler's Lin Culbertson and Hahn Rowe, while **Gondwanaland** finds equally unspecified uses for Roli Mosimann and Don Fleming.

The **Sink** compilation digs all the way back to the very beginning (1981's "OKFM," by the nascent Foetus Under Glass): twenty tracks from all phases of his glorious career. While the set contains some rarities and loads of great music, dubious selection logic reproduces nearly all of **Bedrock** and both sides of Foetus Art Terrorism's 1984 single "Calamity Crush" b/w "Catastrophe Crunch," the flip of which is merely an instrumental scratch remix. No home should be without it, although it's safe to say that any dose of Foetus is an equally good starting place for neophytes: he's extremely consistent (either a major shortcoming or exactly the opposite) in both standards and practices.

Finally swept into major-label clutches in '95, Foetus spewed up **Gash,** a magnificent chopper of industrial gruesomeness, vintage horn jazz (check the eleven-minute extravaganza "Slung" for snappy music your grandparents would not condone), sly samples and what can only be described as the string-laden lullaby of hell. Presumably working with the first big studio budget of his career, Foetus gets it all in the grooves, lashing together an eclectic collection as advanced and ambitious as anything he's done. The lyrics—non sequitur fever-dreams that rattle around politics, violence, current events, geography and religion—never display enough logical cohesion to imply conviction. Under the jokey title "Verklemmt," he heaves out ideas willy nilly: "By day I strangle chickens/And field your dirty looks/Investigate your chimney/There's a Chernobyl rain." (Given three remixes and joined by three other tracks, the song was issued as **Null.**) Occasionally, however, this full-service institution—eager to offend in word as well as deed—sticks his finger in the socket and pulls out a most dubious turnip like "Mighty Whity (Bring Me the Head Of . . .)," which posits a violent encounter from the perspective of a black murderer. Unique.

Wiseblood is a duo of Clint Ruin and Roli Mosimann, assisted on **Dirtdish** by Robert Quine, Hahn Rowe, Norman Westberg and Phoebe Legere. While the core pair shares the writing, Foetus' vocals guarantee the usual growled litany of sexually charged insanity (see "The Fudge Punch"). If the album lacks a full load of explosive Foetus audio dynamite, it still packs enough ugliness and venom to corrupt a monastery. The reissue adds four 12-inch tracks. [i]

See also *Chrome Cranks, Lydia Lunch, Voivod.*

BEN FOLDS FIVE

Ben Folds Five (Passenger) 1995

The '90s answer to Lee Michaels or indie-rock's very own Elton John? A piano-pumping wildman from Chapel Hill, North Carolina, Ben Folds is a keyboard virtuoso with an artlessly sincere voice and a knack for well-constructed songs that flirt convincingly with mainstream pop and soul sensibilities. Palatable and just this side of obvious, Folds' goodtime creations repeatedly display an offbeat individuality that puts him in the realm of early Todd Rundgren and Joe Jackson rather than Billy Joel.

Piano is such a distinctive rock instrument (and, for obvious reasons of do-it-yourself touring, almost unknown in alternaland) that Folds is typecast the minute he sits down to play, but **Ben Folds Five** matches mature music to a bratty sensibility. If Folds' melodic sense and ivory-tinkling are strictly traditional, the pluck of his just-past-nerdy lyrics and the fuzzed-up punch of his rhythm section (the careful observer will note that Ben Folds Five is, in fact, a trio) leads him into a world hipper than most sitdown rockers ever know. Whether describing a girl as an Axl Rose look-alike, ribbing underground pretensions, conflating "Sports & Wine" or doing the "Best Imitation of Myself," Folds is an ebullient and engaging force, supplying, as he puts it, "punk rock for sissies." [i]

FOLK IMPLOSION

See *Sebadoh.*

FOLLOW FOR NOW

Follow for Now (Chrysalis) 1991

Early emissaries of Atlanta's '90s musical uprising and the city's most impressive band to miss the commercial nerve, the eclectic Follow for Now nailed a shred-guitar sound (hence the Living Colour comparisons) to a contagious warm spirit and discreetly political lyrics (prefiguring Arrested Development to a degree). The group moved along a modern continuum from rock to funk with an adaptable rhythmic sense and an unpredictable mix-and-match stylistic menu (giving rise to a little Fishbone flavor). The quintet has no trouble following a kick-ass rock cover of Public Enemy's "She Watch Channel Zero" with a shmeary piano-cum-power ballad ("Time"), tripping into a lazy late-night funk groove ("Fire 'n Snakes," a bizarre traveling tribute to music's black founding fathers) and then pulling out the stops for a tunefully driving rocker ("Evil Wheel"). Other moves on the surprise-packed, open-minded and entertaining **Follow for Now** include Hendrixisms ("Ms. Fortune"), metallic ska (the anti-racist "White Hood") and rapped thrash ("Milkbone," which announces, "In a minute we'll groove you/Now we'd like to mosh"). [i]

FOO FIGHTERS

Foo Fighters (Roswell/Capitol) 1995

"I don't owe you anything" screams Dave Grohl over and over in "I'll Stick Around," and it sounds at once like a desperate chant against evil thoughts, a bitter testimonial to history and the needed disposal of some traumatic baggage. "I want out/I'm alone and I'm an easy target," he worries two songs later.

The spotlight is hardly an ideal hiding place, but maybe the former Nirvana drummer (whose career began in Washington, DC, in Dischord punk band Scream and such lesser luminaries as Dain Bramage) is just facing his fears. Stepping out from behind the relative safety of his monstrously battered kit, Grohl writes, plays guitar and sings in the Foo Fighters, an ambitious return to active duty following Nirvana's sudden death in 1994.

Recorded before the band's actual formation, **Foo Fighters** is entirely Grohl's doing save for a bit of guitar playing by Afghan Whigs frontman Greg Dulli. (The quartet's final lineup, pictured but not named on the record, includes guitarist Pat Smear, originally of Los Angeles' legendary Germs, a solo artist and, most recently, a touring member of Nirvana, plus the former rhythm section of Seattle's Sunny Day Real Estate: bassist Nate Mendel and drummer William Goldsmith.) On record and in concert, Grohl emerges as a potent frontpunk with a limited vocal range, good songs, ample enthusiasm and too much imagination to simply replicate the signature sound of the band that made him famous.

Roaring with guitar distortion like a fission furnace threatening imminent disaster and underpinned by a seismically massive bottom, **Foo Fighters** clearly takes some of its stylistic cues from Nirvana. The lunging bass, oblong chord progression, abrupt time shift and vocal style of "Alone+Easy Target" are unmistakable; "This Is a Call" and "I'll Stick Around," both written in the wake of Cobain's suicide, manifest his influence on Grohl's music. But other songs—the quiet, harmony-tinged "Big Me," the lightly sung verses of "Good Grief," the distorto-pop reverie of "Floaty," the overload frenzy of "Weenie Beenie," the swinging bop of "For All the Cows," the metallic riff rip of "Wattershed"—push the album beyond Grohl's past, outlining a more diverse approach Foo Fighters has yet to fully realize. The rock-solid delivery of the simple tunes, which have sketchily significant lyrics and catchy hooks, makes them seem like more than they are, and that won't wash twice. Having made a successful lift-off, Foo Fighters still has to find and reach an ultimate target. [i]

See also *Nirvana, Pat RuthenSmear, Sunny Day Real Estate, Wool.*

FOR AGAINST

Echelons (Independent Project) 1987
December (Independent Project) 1988
In the Marshes EP (Independent Project) 1990
Aperture (Rainbow Quartz/Independent Project) 1993
Mason's California Lunchroom (Rainbow/Independent Project) 1995

Despite scant acknowledgment of their fabulous work, these heartlanders from Lincoln, Nebraska, have stubbornly persisted. Few trios survive the defection of two members—guitarist Harry Dingman III and Stewart Copeland–clone drummer Greg Hill left to form the Millions after the release of **December**—much less continue to prosper artistically, yet after one false start with a new lineup, bassist/singer Jeffrey Runnings replaced his flashy ex-bandmates with a more modest (but no less solid and powerful) pair: guitarist Steven "Mave" Hinrichs and drummer Paul Engelhard.

Aperture doesn't forgo the effects-laden, atmospheric, guitar-dominated pop that distinguished the band's prior work, but uses that sound in a more mature way, supporting the riffs rather than stealing the show. With Runnings making a switch to guitar, he helps Hinrichs' low-key shimmer, warmer tones and a glimmering, troubling tease/tickle replace Dingman's soloist blitz. The resultant mood suits Runnings' lyrics of loneliness ("Today, Today" is as forlorn and heartbroken—downright glum—as alternarock gets), longing, cheated desire, frustration and cynicism—all of it belied by his sweet, boyish voice. It's not easy to make melancholy sparkle so, but **Aperture** is absolutely touching.

With **Aperture**'s bassist gone, Runnings returned to his original instrument. Otherwise, **Mason's California Lunchroom** doesn't so much change the formula as toughen it, with faster tempos and a harder edge. On the gasket-blowing "Tagalong" and "Coursing," Engelhard's lightning-quick blasting around the toms adds chops and spark, while Hinrichs employs distortion and flangers. The poignantly fragile "Hindsight" returns the group to more familiar realms of regret and sorrow, an emotional onslaught held together by the penetrating melody and Runnings' harrowing sincerity. Spellbinding. [jr]

See also *TPRG.*

FOR LOVE NOT LISA

See *Chainsaw Kittens.*

FOR SQUIRRELS

Bay Path Road (no label) 1994
Plymouth EP (Y&T) 1994
Example (550 Music/Epic) 1995

Jerry Garcia's death may have been the most discussed passing of 1995, but the tale of For Squirrels was surely the most tragic. On September 8, the group was headed home from New York City to Gainesville, Florida, after playing a triumphant showcase. In Georgia, a van tire blew out, singer Jack Vigliatura, who was driving, lost control and the vehicle flipped over, killing him, bassist Bill White and tour manager Tim Bender; guitarist Travis Tooke and drummer Jack Griego were injured. Vigliatura had just married his high-school sweetheart; the group's major-label debut was due out in a month.

Example was released anyway, and listening to it only compounds the sorrow. For Squirrels had transcended the very R.E.M.-ish jangle of its earlier work—**Plymouth**'s five songs were drawn from the self-released **Bay Path Road**—to show that it was a vibrant musical force with a fully realized sound and a knack for explosive, out-of-the-ordinary dynamics. For Squirrels did wear its influences on its sonic sleeve—the drama of Live, the punk-propelled pop fury of Soul Asylum and, of course, R.E.M. But the quartet's songs tend to twist and turn enough to make those bands sound more like reference points than direct musical models. For Squirrels' breadth was impressive, encompassing thrashing guitar rock ("8:02 PM," "Long Live the King"), stomping anthems ("Superstar"), power-pop ("Under Smithville," "Mighty K.C.") and dreamy, ambient pastiche ("Disenchanted").

Some of **Example**'s lyrics are creepy in light of the accident; "Send me off to the morgue/I'm ready to be buried," Vigliatura sings in "Mighty K.C.," But when he urges "Please don't give it up now" in "Stark Pretty," it's almost prescient. It's gratifying that **Example** was able to get the hearing it deserved; Tooke and Griego vowed to soldier on, but clearly—and sadly—it can never be the same. [gg]

ROBERT FORSTER

Danger in the Past (UK Beggars Banquet) 1990 (Beggars Banquet/RCA) 1991
Calling From a Country Phone (UK Beggars Banquet) 1993
I Had a New York Girlfriend (Beggars Banquet) 1994
2541 EP (UK Beggars Banquet) 1994
Warm Nights (Beggars Banquet) 1996

After he and fellow singer/songwriter/guitarist Grant McLennan dissolved the much-loved Go-Betweens, Robert Forster—the dour, more reflective half of that band's creative core—recorded the affectingly bittersweet **Danger in the Past** in Berlin, with fellow Australian Mick Harvey (of Nick Cave's Bad Seeds and Crime and the City Solution) producing and playing various instruments and two other Bad Seeds in tow. Forster's acute lyrics, lilting melodies and ironically distanced vocal delivery aren't all that different from the work he did with his former band, but Harvey's production lends "The River People," "Leave Here Satisfied" and the title track an intriguingly uneasy ambience.

The self-produced **Calling From a Country Phone** is closer in execution to the Go-Betweens—and the better for it, with a brighter, folk-rocky sound that makes the rueful insights of songs like "Atlanta Lie Low" and "Falling Star" go down more smoothly, suggesting a somewhat more practical long-term approach than its predecessor.

After two such lyrically challenging efforts, **I Had a New York Girlfriend**—an all-covers collection from an artist not generally known for his interpretive skills—seems a rather odd move. Still, Forster's choices—including items from the catalogues of the Monkees, Bill Anderson, Spirit, Heart and Martha and the Muffins—are quirky enough to maintain a distinctly confessional quality. His fine rendition of Grant Hart's "2541" was also released on a four-track CD single that includes two non-album tracks. [ss]

See also *G. W. McLennan.*

FOSSIL

Crumb EP (Sire/Warner Bros.) 1994
Fossil (Sire/Warner Bros.) 1995

Pictured variously on their records as sooty '40s laborers, a quartet of cardigan-wrapped frat rats beaming around the Xmas bush and a foppish table of swells tucking into champagne and cake under an ornate candelabrum, the New Jersey–spawned Fossil generates an equally ambivalent message with its music: eager to please, anxious to impress and unafraid to come off as sentimental weenies without so much as a knowing wink. Grandiose electric popsters on one hand and ready-to-rock indie club coolers on the other, Fossil owe their handsome glossy polish to co-producer Ivan Ivan, who did similar-sounding work for Figures on a Beach in the mid-'80s.

Crumb introduces the group with four songs, two of which don't reappear on **Fossil.** In a complex procession of harmonically rich guitar chords and leads, singer/co-producer Bob O'Gureck's echoed vocals and lyrics attempt to deflate Hallmark love sentiments while indulging in them. "Moon" is breathtaking in its lush energy. Meanwhile, the complete text of "Tim," which weaves a touch of feedback into its U2-like guitar folds and swoony Beatle harmonies, is "Lullaby/You're so tired/Please shut your eyes/Goodnight." Pretty daring stuff for credibility-seekers in the mid-'90s. (Even stranger, Fossil's next artifact was **Snow Day,** a promotional-only green-vinyl 10-inch of two cloying seasonal originals, an instrumental and "Moon.")

Starting off with "Moon" and "Tim," the full-length **Fossil** finally reveals O'Gureck's lyrical imagination in "Martyr's Wife," a bizarre fantasy in the words of Jesus Christ's girlfriend ("He talks in metaphors/He is a public nuisance"); "Josephine

Baker," a posthumous crush song that takes after "Pictures of Lily"; "Molly," a futile love plea delivered as a semi-acoustic breeze; and "Fiancée," a cinematic disappearance mystery. With none of the diverse tracks packing anything near the visceral thrill of "Moon," **Fossil** conveys the uncomfortable feel of a graduate-school project, an investigation of sonic and lyrical modes to test theories of music market conquest or something. Too offbeat to be mainstream accessible and too mushy for left-of-the-dial respectability, **Fossil** is a weird and pretty rock whose origins are hard to discern. [i]

KIM FOWLEY AND BEN VAUGHN

See *Ben Vaughn Combo.*

OPAL FOXX QUARTET

See *Smoke.*

FRAMPTON BROTHERS

I Am Curious (George) (Bogus) 1991
Don't Fall Asleep . . . Horrible Things Will Happen (Bogus) 1993
Frampton Brothers Hate You EP (Bolt Remover) 1994

The Frampton Brothers don't mean anything by the smart-aleck name: the Pittsburgh quartet's good-natured roots pop doesn't betray a trace of voice-tube guitar or '70s nostalgia. Singer/guitarist Ed Masley—whose wavery warble suggests Gordon Gano after successful therapy—is a skilled, unpretentious songwriter with a battered post-adolescent outlook but a resilient spirit. On **I Am Curious (George)**, produced by Charlie Chesterman, he complains mildly about the "Big Stoopid World," notes that "She Won't Talk to Me" and promises "to find my place in the sand." He and Sean Lally pour sprightly guitar all over the modest and engaging record, giving an instrumental shoutout to "Leonard Zelig," covering Peter Holsapple's indignant "Why'd You Sleep With My Girlfriend?" and wondering about the personal relevance of what "Brian Wilson Said." Best rhyme: "Lyin' in his bed with an 8-track cartridge/Dreamin' of the secret life of Keith Partridge."

Don't Fall Asleep, also mainly produced by Chesterman, is a bit tougher in its rock resolve (the addition of garagey organ contributes to the revised feel), but that doesn't undercut the sharp wit of Masley's culture-maven commentary in "Like an Oliver Stone" ("you took the '60s and you made 'em your own") or the winsome charm of "I'm in Love With the Label Rep" and "(I Wanna Be Your) Furniture." Meanwhile, "You Didn't Have to Listen," a plea for teen rejection of parental bigotry, reveals reassuring real-world awareness.

With no significant diminution in appeal, the six-song **Frampton Brothers Hate You** finds the group, rocking harder and faster than ever, in the throes of losing its sense of humor, replacing bemused observation with sardonic disillusion going on unreserved anger: "Overly Optimistic Blues" ("there's no happy ending in sight"), "Touch of Shit" ("you can save your happy endings"), "Ain't No Parade" ("I guess if it's not raining, darling, ain't no parade"). Young Fresh Fellow Scott McCaughey co-produced with Conrad Uno and guested on one track. [i]

JOHN FRANKOVIC

Under the Water Lily (Midnight) 1993

On his solo album, the bassist of Milwaukee psychedelic retro rockers Plasticland eschews both electric guitar and drums for sitar, bouzouki, trombone and organ, exploring a more meditative realm of consciousness-altering music in six brief compositions and one extravagant failure (the thirty-one-minute title track). With incidental contributions from three associates, "Your Telling Me" doesn't veer far from the band's '60s trip-pop essence, but other songs (notably the instrumental "On a Full Moon Night" and the sepulchral "Amen the End") delve deeper into stylized, droney fantasyland. "Under the Water Lily," however, is a total time-waster, a frontward/backward tape collage with noodly elements coming and going in a protoplasmic format too thin to hold any shape or move in any direction. [i]

FREAKWATER

Freakwater (Amoeba) 1989
Dancing Underwater (Amoeba) 1991
Feels Like the Third Time (Thrill Jockey) 1993
Old Paint (Thrill Jockey) 1995

This Carter Family–inspired duo began as a side project for Eleventh Dream Day drummer/vocalist Janet Beveridge Bean and childhood friend (and fellow Kentucky native) Catherine Irwin, a songwriter who'd done cover art for Dream Day albums. By the early '90s, Freakwater had helped spark a revived interest among some of the pair's indie-rock contemporaries in early country, folk and bluegrass music. Bean and Irwin's tasteful devotion to rural music on Freakwater's first two albums encouraged post-punk artists from Bad Livers to Uncle Tupelo to experiment, tongues not in cheeks, with mixing contemporary concerns and traditional country styles.

Though Bean is nominally the duo's star, it's Irwin's lyrics and husky croon that ground most of the tunes on **Freakwater;** Bean's higher, slightly off-key harmonies flutter above the weepy acoustic foundations, giving the songs an edgy tension. Although the opening track, "Miner's Song," has a clear political bent, the album is filled mostly with heartache and tragedy. From the slow-paced "Lonesome Sound" (a Bean lead vocal) to the beer-stained "Family Tradition," **Freakwater** is often difficult but always rewarding.

The mood isn't much different on **Dancing Underwater** (later combined with the first album on CD). If anything, Irwin is even more of a grievous angel, penning titles like "Your Goddamn Mouth," "No, That Can Never Be" and "A Song You Could Cry For" ("Desperately seeking more and more confusion/You sink your nails into the back of an illusion"). With slightly better production and improved musicianship by some of the same people who played on the debut—Jon Alexander Spiegel (Dobro, pedal steel, banjo), Dave Gay (upright bass)—and newcomer John Rice on fiddle, mandolin and pedal steel, **Dancing Underwater** is more satisfying than **Freakwater.** And the cover choices—from such traditionals as "Rank Strangers" and "Selfishness in Man" to Billy Sherrill's gorgeous "Wild and Blue," Bill Monroe's allegorical "The Little Girl and the Dreadful Snake" and Merle Travis' coal-mining standard, "Dark as a Dungeon"—are impeccable.

Feels Like the Third Time gets a boost in audio clarity, courtesy of Liz Phair producer Brad Wood. In addition to the richer sound, Irwin and Bean seem more confident with their material. Replacing Spiegel and Rice with fiddler/mandolin player Lisa Marsicek and adding guitarist Brian Dunn, the two women (and Gay, now an official member of the trio) find themselves in a first-rate country-folk band. Save for the charmingly wavering vocals, the album trades the primitivist feel of old Carter Family recordings for a more contemporary non-Nashville country sound. From Irwin's tragic originals ("Drunk Friend") and Bean's improved work ("Sleeping on Hold") to great cover choices—from Nick Lowe's "You Make Me" to Woody Guthrie's "Little Shoes" to a hilariously subtle feminist update of Conway Twitty's "You've Never Been This Far Before"—this fine album holds out much promise for Freakwater's brand of acoustic country.

Old Paint fulfills that promise in spades. Again produced by Wood, the songs are better, the performances stronger and the harmonies more natural sounding than ever. Where once it seemed as though the women might be using old-timey naïveté to cover up for vocal insecurities, it's clear here that they have strong musical identities of their own. Irwin puts her entire being into songs like "Smoking Daddy" with Bean wailing the accompanying vocals and hitting every note—though not with such precision that it sounds clinical. In fact, there's nothing clinical about a line like "there's nothing so sure as a razor blade above your wrist," which comes behind the cry of pedal steel in "Gone to Stay," an exquisitely plaintive song about the futility of all aspects of salvation. Whether singing high harmonies ("White Rose") or lead vocals ("Out of This World"), Bean's voice has taken on a delicate, Emmylou Harris–like purity. Irwin again wrote most of the songs, and this time the cool cover choices simply add spice to an already very satisfying original recipe. [mrk]

See also *Eleventh Dream Day, Green.*

FREE KITTEN

Call Now (Ecstatic Peace!) 1993
Unboxed (UK Wiiija) 1994
Nice Ass (Kill Rock Stars) 1995

KITTEN

Straight Up EP (Aus. Pearl Necklace) 1993

A buswoman's holiday for noise-rock scenesters—most prominently Sonic Youth bassist/singer Kim Gordon (playing guitar) and ex–Pussy Galore guitarist/singer Julia Cafritz—Free Kitten (née Kitten) gussies up its thinly sliced wryness with ephemeral R&B and hip-hop flourishes, neither of which lend the vaguest degree of soulfulness to the proceedings. That studied coolness goes hand-in-hand with a perspective so dependent on transitory pop culture references and in-jokes that the songs are in danger of fresh-date expiration by the time they reach the market.

Call Now, recorded alone by Gordon and Cafritz, appropriates quite a bit from B-boy culture—including a passel of incredibly pretentious sleeve photos casting the duo as hip-hop fashion plates—but it's hard to concede much street cred to a disc that grants "stylist" principal status, credit-wise. Then again, with songs as half-baked as "Platinumb" and "Skinny Butt," perhaps deflecting some of the attention from the audio portion of the program is a good idea. **Nice Ass** holds together a bit more coherently, thanks in part to the presence of fellow travelers Mark Ibold (Pavement; bass) and Yoshimi P-Wee (Boredoms; drums and trumpet). It also helps that the band has discovered its roots *don't* lead back to the boogie-down Bronx. "Harvest Spoon," carried by Cafritz's raspy shout, slams along with one-chord authority, while slightly more fractured tracks ("What's Fair" and the mumbled-but-explicit "Revlon Liberation Orchestra") provide some worthwhile gray matter calisthenics. Still, too many of the album's fifteen tracks—most egregiously "Proper Band" and "Greener Pastures"—are steeped in the sort of self-glorifying silliness that killed arena rock the first time around. Narcissism is most assuredly *not* go. [dss]

See also *Action Swingers, Sonic Youth, Jon Spencer Blues Explosion.*

FREESTYLE FELLOWSHIP

To Whom It May Concern (Sun) 1991
Innercity Griots (4th & B'way) 1993

ACEYALONE

All Balls Don't Bounce (Capitol) 1995

While Southern California–based G-funk hip-hop was making its crossover moves in the early '90s, a singularly different collective of rhymers dedicated to experimenting with jazz-based poetics and musical complexity gravitated toward the Good Life, a café in South Central Los Angeles. There, in now-legendary open-mic sessions, dozens of rappers proved their mettle and pushed the envelope. By 1991, a loosely configured federation of Good Life alumni dubbed the Freestyle Fellowship committed itself to wax on **To Whom It May Concern.**

The agenda is nothing if not audacious. The group declares it will reinvent LA hip-hop: "We will not tolerate fear!" Along with the charged manifestos of J-Sumbi on "Legal Alien" and "Sunshine Men," the record introduces the studied jazz sensibilities of Mikah Nine (dubbed Microphone Mike on the "Seventh Seal," "5 O'Clock Follies" and "Convolutions"), the off-center word experiments of Self-Jupiter ("Jupiter's Journey") and the Langston Hughes B-boy rebel style of Aceyalone ("My Fantasy," "Here I Am").

Joined by newcomer Mtulazaji (aka Peace), Self-Jupiter, Aceyalone and Mikah Nine cut **Innercity Griots** as a pared-down version of the Freestyle Fellowship. If the first album declared war, **Innercity Griots**' continued attack on commercialism suggests a stylistic revolution, alluding vocally and musically to Louis Armstrong, Eddie Jefferson, Art Blakey's Jazz Messengers, John Coltrane and Rakim. Mikah's scat-inflected vocals on "Inner City Boundaries" (with Daddy-O) and "Hot Potato" are astonishing, sometimes slaying with a sweet melody, other times rapid-firing up and down the scales over grand canyon–sized Bernard Purdie snare snaps and booming 808 drops. Aceyalone's African whimsicality, evidenced particularly on the poetic "Cornbread," is equally engaging.

Aceyalone's **All Balls Don't Bounce** finds him mining the same territory with baritone-voiced partner Abstract Rude. The moments of brilliance—"Knownots," the engaging beat politics of "Headaches and Woes," the spraycan rhythms of "Arhythmaticulas," the deadpan delivery of "I Think"—are very hopeful signs of a hip-hop alternative. [jzc]

FRENCH

See *Versus.*

JOHN FRENCH/FRED FRITH/HENRY KAISER/RICHARD THOMPSON

See *Richard Thompson.*

FRENTE!

Labour of Love (Aus. Mushroom) 1993 (Mammoth) 1994
Marvin the Album (Mammoth/Atlantic) 1994
Shape (White/Mammoth/Atlantic) 1996

This sunny wisp of a band wafted over from Melbourne, Australia, trailing a candy-colored jetstream of bubblegum-jazz and an uncommonly winsome temperament, both of which radiate largely from singer Angie Hart, a coquettish-voiced Tasmanian angel (she spent her formative years living in a religious community on that isolated Antipodean island). Although the band's sweetly swinging sound—heavy (so to speak) on brushed snares and gentle, Joe Pass–styled guitar picking—couldn't be more naked, no souls were bared in the making of any of Frente!'s records.

The seven-song **Labour of Love,** which served as an appetizer for the quartet's full-length American debut, yielded a minor hit in the form of a folk-pop rendition of New Order's "Bizarre Love Triangle" that was virtually unrecognizable—except to those who'd heard Devine & Statton's almost identical version four years before. Of the five originals, only the pleading title cut (a flute-tinged trifle reprised on **Marvin the Album**) is more than a melodic sketch; still, **Labour of Love** is worth seeking out for the otherwise unavailable cover of Chris Knox's lovestruck "Not Given Lightly."

Marvin the Album emits a similar post-campfire glow, one that never threatens to ignite. Guitarist Simon Austin insinuates notes more often than he actually articulates them, which adds a disarming tone to "Accidently Kelly Street," but hamstrings the mundane "Lonely" (which does vivify when Hart slips into Barry White's "Can't Get Enough of Your Love Babe"). File under: Roxette for hipsters.

Shape, Frente!'s second full-length album, is considerably less ethereal, thanks to a newfound reliance on percussive frills (bongos and the like) and the more aggressive playing of new bassist Bill McDonald. Hart's cheeriness seems to have abated as well, judging by the anti-romantic imagery she drapes across the languid melodies of "Air" and "Goodbye Goodguy." Sometimes even bubblegummers get the blues. [dss]

FRETBLANKET

Twisted EP (Atlas) 1994
Junkfuel (Atlas) 1994

William Copley's angry, raw-throated vocals and Clive Powell's grunge-guitar attack mark Fretblanket as one of the first British groups to reflect the worldwide influence of Nirvana's **Nevermind.** But **Junkfuel,** with its rampaging hardcore rhythms and pop hooks, owes at least as much to Jawbreaker and the Descendents, and Powell's lyrics showcase a bright new talent with ideas of his own. Like Fretblanket's American cousins, much of the Stourbridge (near Birmingham) quartet's oeuvre reflects the angst of a befuddled generation: "She just wanted someone who's free," Copley roars in "Twisted," but adds, "How could that be me?" When his raspy howl transforms the hooky chorus of "Song in B" ("We don't seem that happy now") into a slacker anthem, the whole affair does begin to smell like "Teen Spirit," but Fretblanket redeems itself with the high-energy punk attack of "Direct Approach" and the introspective sadness of "Curtainsville." [jt]

GAVIN FRIDAY AND THE MAN SEEZER

Each Man Kills the Thing He Loves (Island) 1989

GAVIN FRIDAY

Adam'n'Eve (Island) 1992
Shag Tobacco (UK Island) 1995 (Island) 1996

More so than any other performer associated even tangentially with the lineage of goth, Dublin's Gavin Friday (born Fionán Hanvey in 1959), the driving force behind the infamous Virgin Prunes, has evolved aesthetically to a level far beyond the white-face-and-candles shtick of his contemporaries. Like Leiber/Stoller or Bacharach/David, Friday and his keyboard-playing partner Maurice Seezer splice art song and pop music together seamlessly.

Drawing on everyone from Jacques Brel ("Next") and Bob Dylan (an inspired reading of "Death Is Not the End") to Oscar Wilde (whose words were used for the title cut), Friday and Seezer create an evocative cabaret of twilights and lowlifes on **Each Man Kills the Thing He Loves.** Producer Hal Willner (whose résumé includes albums by Tom Waits and Marianne Faithfull and tributes to Kurt Weill and others) understands Friday's vision perfectly, framing his warm, smoky baritone with such expert session players as bassist Fernando Saunders and guitarists Bill Frisell and Marc Ribot.

If **Each Man** errs on the arty side, **Adam'n'Eve** swings in the opposite direction, aiming for the charts with dexterous aplomb. "King of Trash" is a bump-and-grind homage to Marc Bolan, while "I Want to Live" and "Falling off the Edge of the World" are everything a pop song should be: big, grand, emotional and, in the latter case, political. Those two numbers also benefit from backing vocals by Friday's Dublin neighbor, Maria McKee. With the exception of the last few cuts, the eleven tracks are infused with a sense of glee that borders on dementia. Willner, Flood and Dave Bascombe share production duties, leaving just enough room in Seezer's over-the-top arrangements for Friday's growls and whoops.

Friday spent much of '93 and '94 writing music for films, including "A Thousand Years" for Annie Ross to sing in Robert Altman's *Short Cuts.* (Friday's rendition of the tune surfaced in '95, on the single of "Angel," a song from **Shag Tobacco.**) The theme song for *In the Name of the Father,* a duet with longtime pal Bono—who some feel lifted his more theatrical trappings from Friday—garnered him an Oscar nomination; more important, it introduced him to producer/artist Tim Simenon (aka Bomb the Bass). The two extended their relationship to **Shag Tobacco** (while also contributing three tracks to model Naomi Campbell's recording debut), which Simenon produced. Brilliantly tempering each other's aesthetics, they strike a disturbing balance at the intersection of the extreme tendencies of all parties involved. Friday's fascination with changing sexual mores surfaces repeatedly on "Little Black Dress," "Dolls" and "Mr. Pussy," but his own sordid background elevates the subject matter beyond cheap sensationalism. From the whispered menace of the title tune through the instrumental closer ("Le Roi D'Amour"), the twelve tracks (including a cover of T. Rex's "The Slider") simmer with delicious tension. [kbr]

See also *TPRG.*

FRIENDS OF DEAN MARTINEZ

The Shadow of Your Smile (Sub Pop) 1995

Originally the Friends of Dean Martin, this Tucson side project shuffles together John Convertino and Joey Burns of Giant Sand with Van Christian and Tom Larkins of Naked Prey (the quintet's other member, steel guitarist Bill Elm, *was* in Naked Prey) for a consciously landlocked take on the instrumental combo concept. Southwestern through and through, **The Shadow of Your Smile** (on which Giant Sand leader Howe Gelb drops by to play a little piano and organ) owes a little something to both the solemn slide swoon of Santo and Johnny (Elm's speciality) and a mood-samba sound ideal for sipping tequila by the pool (credit Convertino's handy vibework and marimba tickling). A lot of main writer Burns' originals have the jivey cool of an Angelo Badalamenti score, but the group's most potent and useful ability is to conjure up romantic visions of the desert at twilight, which it does on—of all things—Thelonious Monk's "Ugly Beauty" as well as the traditional "All the Pretty Horses" and Christian's "House of Pies." [i]

See also *Giant Sand.*

FRIGGS

America's Only Rock'n'Roll Magazine Parody EP10 (Sympathy for the Record Industry) 1994

This all-female New York–area quartet (including guitarist Palmyra Delran, late of Pink Slip Daddy) plays an appealing brand of surfy garage-pop that isn't really done justice by their Ben Vaughn-produced four-song 10-inch, which suffers from thin playing but does feature neat cover art paying tribute to *Creem* magazine. Though an obscure Kim Fowley cover and the instrumental "Conestoga Nova" are not without charm, the Friggs' virtues are far better represented by singles on such labels as Telstar and Feralette. [ss]

ROBERT FRIPP AND THE LEAGUE OF CRAFTY GUITARISTS

See *King Crimson.*

FROGS

The Frogs (Frogs) 1988
It's Only Right and Natural (Homestead) 1989
Racially Yours (unreleased)
My Daughter the Broad (Matador) 1996

Milwaukee, Wisconsin's Frogs are about as important as an alternative band could be, given that they rarely release any records. The duo's insane 1989 faux-gay-power-folk album **It's Only Right and Natural** became something of a cult classic. Nirvana and Pearl Jam had it played over PA systems before performances; the Blake Babies named their EP **Rosy Jack World** after a song on it, and were known to cover "I Don't Care If You Disrespect Me (Just So You Love Me)" as an encore; the Smashing Pumpkins' Billy Corgan and James Iha have joined the Frogs on stage at their rare, mindblowing live appearances.

It's Only Right and Natural also generated some ferocious controversy, played out in any number of public forums. Were the Frogs actually gay or were they homophobes? Were they making fun of homophobia? Were they making fun of political correctness? Was this argument even relevant? Dennis and Jimmy answered at least one of these questions, and upped the ante, when they reappeared in 1991 with a new (unreleased) recording, **Racially Yours,** and a new concept. This time, they weren't gay any more. One of them was in blackface and the other was in whiteface and they did songs about racial tension. Later tours' repertoires dipped into both albums, and added songs aimed to offend bandwagoneering musicians ("In the Year of Our Lord Grunge") and, well, absolutely everybody ("Fuck Off").

In the meantime, the Frogs kept recording tape after tape of their "Made Up Songs," distributed to anybody who happened to chance onto their mailing list. A boxed set (!) of their best songs was planned for release on Homestead in the early '90s; when the label changed managers, it was called off. A live album recorded at CBGB on the **Right and Natural** tour, featuring an over-the-top medley of "Free Bird," "The Pretender" and "Luka," was readied in 1992 for Collision Time, but the label folded before it could be released. And **Racially Yours** was too much of a hot potato for any label to handle. For a while in 1994, El Recordo planned to put it out, but that fell through.

A few Frogs recordings have snuck out here and there, though. The mediocre "Smack Goes the Dragon" appeared on the 7-inch boxed set compilation **Bruce Lee, Heroin and the Punk Scene** (on the San Francisco label Massacre at Central Hi); in '94, Matador released a single with heartfelt, distorted live versions of the gay-period "Adam + Steve" and the race-period "Now You Know You're Black." In one of the strangest incidents in recent musical history, the Frogs appeared on the B-side of Pearl Jam's "Immortality" single, straight-facedly covering that band's "Rearviewmirror." In '96, two Frogs records were released on Matador: a five-years-delayed single entitled "Here Comes Santa's Pussy" and a compilation of "Made Up Songs" called **My Daughter the Broad.** [ddw]

FRONT 242

Geography (Bel. RRE) 1982 (Wax Trax!) 1987 (RRE/Epic) 1992
No Comment EP (Wax Trax!) 1987 (RRE/Epic) 1992
Official Version (Wax Trax!) 1987 (RRE/Epic) 1992
Backcatalogue (Wax Trax!) 1987 (RRE/Epic) 1992
Front by Front (Wax Trax!) 1988 (RRE/Epic) 1992
Tyranny (for You) (RRE/Epic) 1991
06:21:03:11 Up Evil (RRE/Epic) 1993
05:22:09:12 Off (RRE/Epic) 1993

Formed in Brussels by synthesists Daniel Bressanutti and Patrick Codenys with vocalist Jean-Luc De Meyer in 1982, Belgian industrialists Front 242 (later joined by a second singer, Richard 23, aka Richard JK) pioneered the mesh of harsh, mechanized instrumentation to militantly funky beats and held the Eurotrash dancefloor in its grip during the late '80s, when the band expressed its fervent political convictions by generally railing against the system. Debuting with the now-classic (but somewhat dinky-sounding in its gloomy variation on OMD/Gary Numan/Kraftwerk synth-pop) **Geography,** the group peaked on **Front by Front,** a post-modern dancefloor explosion epitomized by "Headhunter," whose macabre theme—humans as game—is matched only by the track's vicious BPMs.

After a long stint releasing its records via Chicago industrial independent Wax Trax!, Front 242 made the corporate move to Epic. Concurrent with reissues of its entire back catalogue (including **Backcatalogue,** a 1981–85 compilation containing live tracks, **Geography** and **No Comment** selections and assorted rarities), the band produced **Tyranny (for You),** upholding its formula and adding little to the usual harsh rhythms and synthesizers but surprisingly emotional vocals.

Of Front 242's two 1983 releases, **06:21:03:11 Up Evil** (the title is coded to the order of letters in the alphabet) is the more diverse in style and rhythm—which isn't necessarily a good thing. Variation costs the band its essential driving force; the album is strong but not striking. "Religion" still carries the one-sided ideology that originally drove Front 242's passion, but not many other tracks stand up to the heritage of this once-great industrial collective. The songs on **05:22:09:12 Off** work better because Front 242 is willing to expand on its formula, seemingly inspired by those groups who regard them as genre godfathers. "GenEcide" is a sulky mid-tempo groove that puts the vocals through a whispery processor and makes them complement the swooping keyboards. With its increased use of samples and abrupt rhythm changes, the album became a techno cornerstone. [mf]

See also *Revolting Cocks; TPRG.*

FROST

See *Kid Frost.*

FROSTED

See *Go-Go's.*

JOHN FRUSCIANTE

Niandra Lades and Usually Just a T-Shirt (American) 1994

Having dropped out of the Red Hot Chili Peppers in the middle of a '92 Japanese tour, guitarist John Frusciante withdrew further, but did manage to home-record an album called **Niandra Lades,** which went unreleased until it became half of this twenty-four-track CD, preceding a dozen untitled numbers collected under the title **Usually Just a T-Shirt.** Despite the detached Syd Barrett trappings, Frusciante's ramblings are not only surprisingly listenable but stand right up there with 1994's best lo-fi recordings, although possibly the only such indulgence released on a major label.

Sung in a wavery falsetto over a couple of guitar tracks or piano, **Niandra Lades**' sketchy demo-quality material is flighty and stream-of-consciousness-driven, variously wistful (the Bad Brains' "Big Takeover," with mandolin and what sounds like tabla; "Been Insane"), hair-raising ("Blood on My Neck From Success") and nothing but weird ("Head (Beach Arab)," "Ten to Butter Blood Voodoo," "Your Pussy's Glued to a Building on Fire"). Sample lyric, from "Curtains": "You've all been always there/Your head shaped like a pear/You search through the lights/Instead of jumped in the pie/Of life that you sliced/Till it's just right." But "Mascara" is a semi-eloquent ballad, and Frusciante's compositional skill is deft and soulful in its own singular way. The album's other half, however, is more compelling. Frusciante seldom lets lyrics clutter the musical, er, vision, and lots of gorgeous, backward guitar pours forth. Many of these tracks are gentler and more atmospheric and, more than **Niandra Lades,** slip effortlessly between lucidity and madness, reaffirming the sometimes-tragic, real and slender line between the two. [mww]

See also *Red Hot Chili Peppers.*

FUDGE TUNNEL

The Fudge Tunnel EP EP7 (UK Pigboy) 1989
The Sweet Sound of Excess EP (UK Pigboy) 1990
Hate Songs in E Minor (Earache/Relativity) 1991
Fudgecake (Pigboy/Cargo) 1992
Teeth EP (Earache) 1992
Creep Diets (Earache/Columbia) 1993
The Complicated Futility of Ignorance (Earache) 1994
In a Word (Earache) 1995

Claiming divine inspiration (actually, it was Big Black they named in interviews), this trio from Nottingham, England, cranked up an infernal roar of brutal Chicago-style razor-riff punk overdrive and then refined it into a mighty metal machine. Subtle as a flying hacksaw and twice as rude (who would actually want to be in a band known as Fudge Tunnel?), the group fires off bolts of raucous energy in the first two EPs (later packaged together as **Fudgecake**). Led by Alex Newport's exploding guitar and raw shouts, the band can barely keep up with itself in calamitous performances held together by collective desperation. Rather than pose any actual threat, songs like "Leprosy," "Best Friends Wife" and "Shit for Brains" illuminate the make-believe viciousness.

Pulled tighter by co-producer Colin Richardson, **Hate Songs in E Minor** (the spine of which reads **Fudge Tunnel's First Movement**) ratchets the meaningless fury up a few harsh notches. Distortion on Newport's voice and the close-formation bludgeoning make a grindcore connection; if Fudge Tunnel ("the sphincter triplets") played much faster, there'd be real sonic hell to pay. Thundering to a close with a pair of quizzical covers—Cream's "Sunshine of Your Love" and Ted Nugent's "Cat Scratch Fever," both played like Black Sabbath songs in need of fresh coats of battery acid—**Hate Songs** smiles right through the blisters.

But enough fun, and Fudge Tunnel subsequently moved into heavier metal. Even when Newport's production of **Creep Diets** doesn't bury the music in maniacal sheets of distorted cacophony, the now-humorless trio's carefully directed ferocity and chanted lyrics point nowhere just as clearly. There is one half-temperate pop song ("Don't Have Time for You") and a quiet instrumental ("Hot Salad") to interrupt the onslaught, but **Creep Diets** is a crashing bore. All muscle and no audible brain, Fudge Tunnel—well on its way toward the violence of speed metal—turns songs into military exercises, sucking the joy of volume away in crack displays of stop-on-a-plectrum efficiency. Helmet may dance around this kind of thing, but Fudge Tunnel steps deep in it.

"Escape to nowhere/The joy of irony/Take exit 15/There you'll find me." Seekers of enlightenment—and students of irony—won't find many rewards in **The Complicated Futility of Ignorance.** The first Fudge Tunnel album to print its lyrics is revealed to be the trio's heaviest, grimmest and surliest. As a refined dose of pure musical aggression that grabs, holds and savages, however, it's the band's most effective. Having brought the presence of Adrian Parkin's drums and David Ryley's bass up to match his woolly guitar din, Newport consolidates it all with authoritarian discipline and navigates the band like a well-tuned tiger, launching agile assaults and then dropping down low for an ominous prowl until unleashing the next explosion of fury. At over an hour (including an unlisted bonus track), this is too much of a good thing, and the pretentious packaging and disgusted lyrics are warning signs for what may be ahead, but this movement of Fudge Tunnel is a stinger.

In a Word doesn't provide any answers: it's a compilation of raging 1990–93 radio broadcast sessions, intense concert rips and bludgeoning studio covers of Black Sabbath ("Changes") and late-'60s heavy trio May Blitz ("For Madmen Only"). Very 'eavy, very 'umble and a perfect stocking stuffer for the bad little kid in the family. [i]

FUGAZI

Fugazi (Dischord) 1988
Margin Walker EP (Dischord) 1989
13 Songs (Dischord) 1990
Repeater (Dischord) 1990
Steady Diet of Nothing (Dischord) 1991
In on the Killtaker (Dischord) 1993
Red Medicine (Dischord) 1995

Even the most suspicious observer would have to admit that integrity is not entirely unknown in rock-'n'roll. The ability to maintain a principled posture toward the business of making music for any appreciable length of time, however, presents a challenge that few bands have ever proven equal to. Yet those are the shoes in which Fugazi has stood now for the better part of a decade, producing pure, high-intensity punk-rock of rare intelligence and artistry without any concession to the tug of commercialism or the internal tensions that usually cause such high-minded organizations to implode. Staunch vocal opponents of violence, exploitation, alienation, stardom and conformity, the modest but explosive Fugazi is a knuckle sandwich made with nine-grain bread, building strong minds and bodies with rattling guitar power. The quartet's achievement is a marvel to behold—and even better to hear.

As the longstanding figurehead and moral conscience of Washington DC's punk scene, singer/guitarist Ian MacKaye has led the Teen Idols, Minor Threat, Egg Hunt and Embrace; the flagship of the mighty Dischord label (which he co-founded), Fugazi is the culmination of it all. The band's impressive debut, a seven-song 12-inch, blends a classic DC-core sensibility with a mature, objective outlook and crisply produced mid-tempo songs that are dynamic, aggressive and accessible. "Waiting Room," an especially catchy shoutalong, employs a call-and-response vocal arrangement that has scant punk precedent. Both MacKaye and former Rites of Spring vocalist Guy Picciotto trade raw emotionalism for an introspective, almost poetic vision, using abstractions in strongly structured compositions like "Bulldog Front" and "Give Me the Cure," a contemplation on death. MacKaye's and Picciotto's combined abilities give the quartet a rare strength; the two singer/songwriters complement each other perfectly.

Margin Walker illustrates just how far Fugazi's four have come since their hardcore beginnings. The bracing EP oozes confidence—in MacKaye's melodic guitar work, in the tight, fluid rhythms of drummer Brendan Canty and bassist Joe Lally, in the incisive lyrics and the sharply arranged vocal exchanges. The songs are great, from the raging title track to the funky Gang of Four–ish verses and poppy chorus of "And the Same" to the thickly chorded "Lockdown." Developing ideas he introduced in Minor Threat, MacKaye even manages to make the expletives in the vigorously monotonal "Promises" sound somewhat eloquent.

Fugazi put the relatively slick sound of **Margin Walker** up on blocks and stripped it down to the bare essentials for the group's first full-length LP. **Repeater** is a blueprint for the post-hardcore world, a stunning and adventurous new stage in Fugazi's growth. The title track, which is indicative of the album, offers a more powerful three-minute burst than anything on the first two records: a dizzying bassline, speedy, powerful drumming and a repetitive squeal that is barely recognizable as guitar. **Repeater**'s only disappointment is its weak lyrics; both MacKaye and Picciotto do a lot of finger-pointing at Joe Average. Still, the overzealous pontification doesn't distract overly from what is otherwise an amazing album. (**13 Songs** combines **Fugazi** and **Margin Walker** on one CD; the disc of **Repeater** adds the **3 Songs** 7-inch from 1990.)

Opening in a wobbly haze of feedback and then shifting to a temperate rock groove, **Steady Diet of Nothing** sets up a dichotomy between razorblade ferocity and methodical determination; pulling firmly with one hand and jabbing angrily with the other, Fugazi opens the door to a world of mixed emotions and conflicting impulses. The pressure instilled by the band's ability to hold itself to an economical beat and escaping shards of tense guitar is barely relieved by the stormy whorls of flat-out aggression into which they typically feed. (The instrumental "Steady Diet" whips the latter into a dangerous froth.) Armed with a unique guitar sound—a loose-stringed jangle like an electrified fence being plucked—and the urgent power of singing that makes excellent use of ordinary voices, Picciotto and MacKaye address pointed lyrical concerns from oblique angles, throwing enigmatic surprises into songs to confound easy comprehension. "Latin Roots," for instance, which appears simply enough to be about a sexual encounter, makes a dramatic issue of parents: "It's time to meet your makers." Fugazi's avoidance of obvious topics (except for the sketchy breakup of "Long Division" and "Dear Justice Letter," which is addressed directly to the Supreme Court's William Brennan) gives its songs depth and timelessness. Unlike most punk anthems, the haiku-like lyrics of "Exit Only" will probably still convey the same meaning twenty years from now.

Harsher in tone and less controlled in the body and

in the mind, **In on the Killtaker** drops the dynamic reins to unleash the furies in forcefields like "Facet Squared," "Rend It," "Great Cop" and "Smallpox Champion." Relying on less ambitiously structured songs and giving too little thought to how they're presented, Fugazi ironically proves that more is less. By paying too little attention to the low-energy levels at which the band so eminently functions, the roaring waves of scrabbly rock lose their stinging impact. The feedback squeals and rumbles that end "23 Beats Off" could be anybody's, and that's a dishonor for this band. Thanks to the biographical "Cassavetes," the album isn't a total disappointment: in a spectacular and ominous convocation of stuttering beats squeezed between ascendant guitar sweeps and falling bolts of metallic lightning, the song has everything—tension, contrast, imagination—its neighbors lack.

Red Medicine is an entirely different animal. Making punk aggression only one of several stylistic elements while fighting to free itself from the simple constraints of song form, Fugazi brings unprecedented dynamic range, four-letter words and previously unimagined elements—clattering musique concrète on "Do You Like Me," muso guitar twitterings on "Latest Disgrace," piano and sound effects on the stringy "Birthday Pony," murky dub and lancing sax in "Version," the loose-limbed jammy funk of "Combination Lock"—into an ambitious, experimental format that raises more stylistic questions than it answers. Although the album hardly supports its assertion, "Target" gets into what may be bugging the band: the song holds the proliferation of predatory commercial generation-rockers responsible for exploiting innocents and generally spoiling things. "I realize I hate the sound of guitars/A thousand grudging young millionaires/Forcing silence sucking sound." That's a tricky position for a rock band to take, and Fugazi wisely doesn't dwell on it. For all its attempted adventurism, however, the album comes across with strong songs anyway: "Bed for the Scraping," the monstrous feedback power of "By You," the demi-pop of "Forensic Scene," the hardcore intensity of "Downed City" and the near balladry of "Fell, Destroyed." **Red Medicine** is quizzical, uneven and therapeutic, a clear dividing line between the old Fugazi and . . . [icm/i]

See also *Girls Against Boys.*

FUGEES (TRANZLATOR CREW)

Blunted on Reality (Ruffhouse/Columbia) 1994

FUGEES (REFUGEES CAMP)

The Score (Ruffhouse/Columbia) 1996

The three members of the New York–area Fugees (as in Refugees, reflecting the Haitian-rooted band's pointed outsider stance) import poetic seriousness and political awareness to the snappy hip-hop of their strong, deep and diverse debut. Rappers Wyclef Jean (who also plays guitar and bass), his cousin Prakazrel "Pras" Michel and sometime actress Lauryn Hill (whose clipped, rhythmic thrust resembles MC Lyte's here) weave their involving rhymes—undoctrinaire discussions of religion, heroes, urban static, black nationalism and other related topics—together over the mostly self-produced melodic tracks on the way-too-long **Blunted on Reality.** Tucking old-school party clichés and pop culture references into modern, substantial concerns, Fugees join the familiar fun and then ratchet it up, moving the very engaging music around from driving funk to dancehall bop (with help from toaster Mad Spider) to boisterous soul to brisk ska. The trio's opinion of marijuana is hard to discern—the album title conveys a more existential sense of high-ness and the "Blunted Interlude" skit at least sounds like it's poking fun at the enervated paranoia of obsessive smokers—but Fugees' energetic, devoted consciousness and informed opinions make them sound as sober as Sunday school teachers.

Whatever further lessons the trio needed to learn sure got learned: the second album lived up to its name in the commercial sense, landing at the top of the pop charts on the strength of "Fu-Gee-La," a lackluster pre-LP single that appears on **The Score** CD in three mixes, and a bizarrely straightforward update of "Killing Me Softly With His Song," the Gimble/Fox ode to sensitive singing that was first sent to No. 1 in 1973 by Roberta Flack. Rolling along on cool, subtle beats that touch on dub and reggae but generally go their own atmospheric way with more consistency than on the debut, this complex album spreads a wide and confident net, calmly critiquing culture, economics, science and politics in daring, pointed raps that elevate the level of debate by bringing the volume and tension levels down. (Only the group's bewildering anal fixation—"defecating on your microphone" is the most unpleasant of several citations—repeatedly spoils the mood.)

Covering "Killing Me Softly," singing Bob Marley's "No Woman, No Cry" with new lyrics and prominently sampling the Flamingos' "I Only Have Eyes for You" as the basis of "Zealots" give the record instant familiarity, but Fugees' goal isn't easy pleasure. With Jean and Hill matching the fine quality of their production work on the mic, the Fugees aim barbs at the black community ("And even after all my logic and my theory/I add a 'muthafucka' so you ign'ant niggas hear me"), question other samplers' musical originality and refute a magazine's reported suggestion that "the girl shoulda went solo, the guy should stop rappin'." At **The Score**'s most unsettling point, a weird and ambiguously comical Chinese restaurant confrontation skit serves as coda to the police condemnation of "The Beast." [i]

FUN-DA-MENTAL

Seize the Time (UK Nation/Beggars Banquet) 1994
(Beggars Banquet/Mammoth/Atlantic) 1995
With Intent to Pervert the Cause of Injustice! (UK Mantra/Beggars Banquet) 1995

In the parade of American musical forms appropriated and creatively reconfigured by British groups, no genre has been more troubling or ill-served than hip-hop. Despite the two countries' social parallels, modern England has brought a fatal stiff upper lip to rap, producing lily-livered copies that may get the superficialities down but still reek of condescending pretension. Propa-Gandhi (Pakistani immigrant Aki Nawaz Qureshi, who began his music career as the drummer of the short-lived Southern Death Cult, which he co-founded with Ian Astbury) leads London's phenomenal Fun-Da-Mental, a loosely organized group that makes being different the perfect antidote to being redundant. While there are a few moments of British provincialism on **Seize the Time,** the long, convoluted album is a powerhouse, jabbing ethnic politics and culture into rap's rich vein. Along with its principled social outrage, Fun-Da-Mental overloads its careening tracks in the pulse-quickening style of vintage Public Enemy; organically integrated instrumentation like sitar, didgeridoo and tabla gives the album its distinctive sound. Besides touching on African-American activists from Huey P. Newton ("Seize the time" was a Black Panther party credo) to Minister Farrakhan, the lyrics attest to English realities (as in the solidarity statement of "Dog-Tribe"), imperialism ("White Gold Burger") and a global consciousness (as in "Mother India," a thoughtful feminist polemic written and recited by poet Subi Shah). Approaching a related faith from a very different angle than Black Muslim rappers, Fun-Da-Mental's religious loyalty (in "President Propaganda" and "Mera Mazab") gives Islamic fundamentalism an entirely new meaning.

Other than a brief recitation at the end, **With Intent to Pervert the Cause of Injustice!** consists of retitled and wordless versions of first-album tracks including "Mr. Bubbleman," "Dog-Tribe," "Seize the Time" and "White Gold Burger," as well as other instrumental jams. In this context, the pieces all drone together in a tiresome instant-cliché paste of one syncopated dance beat, sampled Middle Eastern chanting and various elements of Indian music. The individual cuts are potent and flavorful, but the net effect is ruined by the overly generous helping. [i]

FURTHER

Grip Tape (Christmas) 1992
Super Griptape (UK Ball Product/Creation) 1993
Surfing Pointers EP7 (Christmas) 1993
Sometimes Chimes (Christmas) 1993
Grimes Golden (Fingerpaint) 1994
Distance EP7 (UK Lissy's) 1995
Next Time West Coast (Japan. 100 Guitarmania) 1996

SHADOWLAND

Shadowland EP (Geffen) 1989
The Beauty of Escaping (Geffen) 1990

The next time anyone starts getting all precious about their indie-rock cred, remind 'em of further. Before becoming a prolific '90s underground sensation groovy enough to release 7-inches on Bong Load, play their hometown's cubbyhole of cool, Jabberjaw, get a UK deal with Creation and have Lee Ranaldo guest on their debut album, the Los Angeles trio was (with one additional member) known as Shadowland, whose lone album is an embarrassingly obvious attempt to jumpstart a pretty-boy arena career with a misbegotten and overheated mash of Tom Petty, the Waterboys, U2 and Sunset Strip glam-metal. (Like everyone else owning such a damningly skeleton-equipped closet, further now condemns the band's music, laying the blame on producer Pat Moran and going so far as to put "The Death of an A&R Man" on **Grip Tape** as a belated attack on then-Geffen staffer Tom Zutaut. Of course, no one made these poseurs write songs with lyrics like "Hey there Mrs. Polka-dot/Come and lay your love on my street/Hey there Mrs. Yesterday/You just crush your will beneath my feet." Best bio quotation: "We don't pretend to be anything we aren't.") Those looking for clues to Shadowland's future stylistic development need look no further than the absurd "Heroin Eyes": "Her cigarette burns in my soul like the *pavement* keeps burning through this hole in my shoe."

Adding untainted guitarist/drummer Josh Schwartz to their merry cabal, Florida-born brothers Darren (vocals, guitar, etc.) and Brent Rademaker (bass, vocals, etc.) and drummer Kevin Fitzgerald reinvented themselves as the murky lower-case childish-print first-names-only further, greasing their downward rehabilitation with a monstrous lo-fi noise-pop onslaught. (So much for the exaggerated faith people have in alternagod talent. As obvious as it's always been to some, here's irrefutable proof that any bozo with a fuzzbox and a pair of earplugs can be J Mascis or Stephen Malkmus.)

Grip Tape, recorded as badly as possible by New York scene veteran Wharton Tiers, is a riot of distortion and croaky off-key singing, straggling happily through its peppy and tuneful pop-song bits to reach the chewy center of slack squall jams each contains. More energetic than Dinosaur Jr, more melodically sensitive than Sonic Youth and less abstruse than Pavement, further cherrypicks those bands' sounds and still manages not to reek of beer-soaked carpetbaggery. (**Super Griptape** is an expanded version, with four added songs to the hour.)

Having demonstrated a superior facility for wrecking shop in high chaos mode, further tried on minimalism's simple housedress as well—a far more dubious enterprise for such a demonstrably skilled combo. (C'mon guys, we *know* you own guitar tuners.) The overlong twenty-five-song **Sometimes Chimes** paraphrases Beck, covers Unrest (nicely pruning "Isabel" into an acoustic folk song), sketches out songs like Sebadoh on a rushed schedule and occasionally noodles around as clumsily as a bunch of ten-year-olds locked in the K Records warehouse. Actually, the album gets off to a fine start with a brace of extremely catchy pop creations cut with onslaughts of happy aggression: "Generic 7," "Duck Pond," "Phase Out," "J.O.2" and especially "She Lives by the Castle 2" are all sublime mixtures of breezy allure and jagged styling that brush against British fuzzbusters like Jesus and Mary Chain, Verve and My Bloody Valentine without resorting to out-and-out replication. Basically, the first half of **Sometimes Chimes** would have made a solid album, but further makes like the Energizer bunny and—as it proceeds to approximate Ween, Sleepyhead, Dinosaur Jr, Half Japanese and so forth—sends the ratio of quality to futile slackery plummeting.

With Fitzgerald out of the group, Schwartz, the Rademakers and a drum machine made the nine-song **Grimes Golden,** a pure crystal dose of slop-pop cooked up in a busted rec-room crockpot that puts the group's bounciest ideas in a confined space and lets them ricochet around. With a charge of Neil Young winsomeness and a few Beach Boys vocal fillips, sweet little ditties like "Artificial Freedom," "Quiet Riot Grrrl" and "California Bummer" don't try to move hell and earth with guitar amplification or fall apart on contact, and the resultant rudimentary intimacy is an elixir for both songs and band. Neat.

The double 7-inch **Distance** gives each member a two-song side of his own, with a slapdash four-song rendezvous bringing up the rear. Darren's pair sounds most like the band, only scaled down in sound and style. Brent's melodic sense is stronger, as is the charged assault of his guitars and the willfulness of his ineptitude (the terrible drumming on "Spheres of Influence" and the crummy punk singing on "LHS '79'"). Josh pours it on even harder, glorying in the hapless bluster of his deep well explorations, the first of which ("Wett Katt") is unendurably tuneless.

The eight songs on the Japanese-only **Next Time West Coast** mark a giant step in further's approach to a point that balances genuine skill and pretensions of rank amateurism. While still occasionally drifting into static meltdown and at no point even suggesting slick, the generally restrained and carefully recorded songs display more craft and chops than anything in further's past. (So much for commitment.) However they got here, though, it would make an excellent place to rest awhile: "Be That as It May" adopts a rangy Neil Young folk-rock sound that works wonders, and "Grandview Skyline" is an amusing dose of humming psychedelia. The others fall in related regions between those poles. But all this progress may be headed for danger: beneath the scowls of feedback, "You're Just Dead Skin to Me" bears a frightening resemblance to a certain shadowy band of the not-so-distant past . . .

More further: the group also has chucked out singles and compilation tracks for a variety of labels, formed a festival's worth of side bands (Summer Hits, Tugboat: 3001, Yak, Rusty Troller) and contributed a track ("Insight") to the Joy Division tribute album **A Means to an End.** [i]

FUTURE SOUND OF LONDON

Accelerator (UK Jumpin' & Pumpin') 1992 (Hypnotic/Cleopatra) 1996
Lifeforms (Astralwerks) 1994
"Lifeforms" (Astralwerks) 1994
ISDN (Astralwerks/Caroline) 1995

AMORPHOUS ANDROGYNOUS

Tales of Ephidrina (Astralwerks) 1994

Under various group names, former electrical engineering students Gary Cobain and Brian Dougans have been allied with nearly every electronic dance-music trend that has swept through England since 1986. In those years, the two have also moved from recording music representative of a specific genre to transcending any single style. Their first hit, 1988's "Stakker Humanoid" (credited to the group Humanoid), showed their skill at riding a bandwagon. With blowing whistles, fast machine beats, a robotic voice repeating the word "humanoid" and wobbling, pitch-shifted synthesizer sounds, "Stakker Humanoid" quickly became a classic in England's pre-techno acid-house scene. The song might not have required a lot of imagination but it does reveal the duo's affinity for sound arrangement.

The pair used this gift to ride dance music through its next wave of trends, recording variants of techno and house (with additional influences in the electro-industrial music of bands like Cabaret Voltaire) under such names as Art Science Technology, Mental Cube, Intelligent Communication, Smart Systems, Semi-Real, Indo Tribe and Yage. But it wasn't until the duo settled down as Future Sound of London and began de-emphasizing rhythm in favor of atmospheric sounds and samples that it began to develop its reputation as one of ambient dance music's most respected innovators.

FSOL's first single, "Papua New Guinea," takes elements of techno, house, dub reggae and world music to create a spacey, haunting sound collage. Pianos tinkle, electronics bubble, an ethereal voice floats in and out of the mix and a polyrhythmic beat thumps away hypnotically. The song is included on **Accelerator,** one of the first techno albums that holds up as more than just a collection of singles. Though **Accelerator** is essentially a dance album ("Expander" and "Pulse State" are especially entrancing), the band pays particular attention to arranging the moody electronics and sound effects in the introductions and breaks of each song.

On **Lifeforms,** the band concentrates even more on continuity, taking the sounds it previously isolated in song introductions and breaks and extending them for two full CDs. With each song flowing into the next and certain sound effects recurring throughout the whole album, the meticulously arranged **Lifeforms** works best as a single piece of music listened to while lying down in the dark instead of dancing in a club. Toni Halliday of Curve adds ethereal vocalizations to "Cerebral"; Robert Fripp's light guitar textures provide a foundation for the whirring, laughing sounds of "Flak." With the sounds of rushing water, flapping bird wings, bamboo flutes, windswept chimes and acoustic guitar rubbing up against percolating synthesizers and all kinds of heavily processed electronic sounds, **Lifeforms** is thinking-person's new age. (The "Lifeforms" single takes apart the album's title track, adds new vocals by Liz Fraser of the Cocteau Twins and divides it into seven sections stretched across a total of thirty-eight minutes.)

With **Lifeforms,** Future Sound of London took the technology of dance music and freed themselves from the genre. On **Tales of Ephidrina,** recorded as Amorphous Androgynous, the band takes one last, loving look at dance music, alternating atmospheric tracks with hard-hitting dance numbers, all mixed together with a disk jockey's sense of unity. In even the simplest drum-and-keyboard rave number, the band makes sure it keeps listeners' ears occupied with a constant barrage of strange, twittering sounds buried beneath the surface.

Throughout its career, Future Sound of London has made innovative computer-animated videos for its songs, most capturing the band's sense of musical flow by depicting objects continuously morphing into new shapes. This led to the group reinventing itself as a forward-looking collective of multi-media renegades. Instead of performing in person, they began broadcasting live audio-visual concerts from their London studio to clubs and Internet users around the world. **ISDN,** an acronym for Integrated Services Digital Network, captures one such performance. Although originally released and deleted on the same day (a gimmick also employed regularly by the Orb and others), **ISDN** was later reissued as a regular release.

Where **Lifeforms** is pretty, **ISDN** is quirky. Instead of trying to create a fluid, tranquil environment, the band jumps from funk-jazz grooves to pure electronic noise. Songs like "Appendage" have moments of serenity, where a synthesizer drones over rushing water sounds, but background noises like metallic clanging give this version of ambience a dark edge. In "Egypt," FSOL returns to its roots in techno-industrial music, but for most of the album the band extends its talent for sound collage to a palette in which dance music is just one small element. [ns]

FUZZY

Fuzzy EP (Aus. Half a Cow) 1993
Fuzzy (Seed) 1994
Electric Juices (Tag/Atlantic) 1996

For an industry that lacks corporate clout or the potential for economies of scale, the *samizdat* internationalism of indie-pop style is a marvel of efficient communications and stylistic cross-pollination. A pretty-noise Boston quartet that formed on a whim, Fuzzy—thanks to a Lemonhead rhythm section connection—had its practice tape released as a six-song EP in another hemisphere even before it got up the confidence to begin playing in the shadow of Fenway Park. (Half a Cow is the label run by Nic Dalton, the ex-Lemonheads bassist who leads Godstar, in which members of Fuzzy have played.)

Before the recording of the full-length **Fuzzy** (as cleaned-up demos), drummer David Ryan found himself free of Evan Dando's employ and joined up, providing a bedrock motor for singer/guitarists Chris Toppin and Hilken Mancini, whose airy sopranos and sustained distortion leads float the band into mid-Atlantic geographic uncertainty. With a folky strain and passing resemblances to Juliana Hatfield, Velvet Crush, Veruca Salt and Elastica, **Fuzzy** is a lightweight, familiar pleasure, all kicky tunes ("Sports" and "4 Wheel Friend," both sung by Mancini, jump out), personal lyrics and peppy enthusiasm.

Electric Juices is better on all counts: songs, harmony singing, performances and production (half-and-half by Tim O'Heir and Paul Q. Kolderie). Having located a sound for itself—nothing original, but a consistent stylistic approach that guides the new wavey pop effort—the band smartly applies it to super-catchy songs both original ("Glad Again," "It Started Today" and the very Breeders-like "One Request" are highlights) and borrowed (Brian Wilson's "Girl Don't Tell Me," initially revived by the Smithereens). Sweetly engaging and as freshly cut as a suburban lawn on Sunday afternoon, **Electric Juices** is Fuzzy perfection. [i]

See also *Godstar, Lemonheads.*

G

WARREN G

Regulate . . . G Funk Era (Violator/RAL) 1994

Smooth, sexy gangsta rap provides a feast for the ears on the first album from Dr. Dre's step-brother, Warren Griffin. Much like comrade-in-arms Snoop Doggy Dogg, the Long Beach, California, MC/producer favors an appealingly lazy, conversational delivery; his wistful tone adds a seductive element of vulnerability to the groovin' hits "This D.J." and "Regulate." Typical of Warren's easy soul styling, "Regulate"—a duet with Nate Dogg originally recorded for the soundtrack of *Above the Rim*—was built on a sample of Michael McDonald's 1982 Top 5 single "I Keep Forgettin'." (The song's non-LP "Jamming Mix" actually preserves the song's original vocal refrain, making for an intriguing blend of old and new, pop and rap.) But once his sound is set in gear, Warren doesn't let the content on **Regulate . . . G Funk Era** deviate much from formula, as tracks like " '94 Ho Draft" and "This Is the Shack" demonstrate. Still, the cushiony beats and the tasty synth riffs are hard to resist. [jy/i]

PETER GABRIEL

Peter Gabriel (Atco) 1977
Peter Gabriel (Atlantic) 1978
Peter Gabriel (Mercury) 1980
Ein Deutsches Album (Ger. Charisma) 1980 (UK Virgin) 1987
Peter Gabriel (Security) (Geffen) 1982
Deutsches Album (Ger. Charisma) 1982 (UK Virgin) 1987
Plays Live (Geffen) 1983
Music From the Film *Birdy* (Geffen) 1985
So (Geffen) 1986
Passion: Music for *The Last Temptation of Christ* (Geffen) 1989
Shaking the Tree: Sixteen Golden Greats (Geffen) 1990
Us (Geffen) 1992
Revisited (Atlantic) 1992
Secret World Live (Geffen) 1994

VARIOUS ARTISTS

Passion–Sources (Real World/Virgin) 1989

From outlandishly costumed art-pop singer to world music pilgrim, human rights activist to video-savvy platinum dance-rocker, Peter Gabriel is the very model of a major modern highbrow music star: intellectual, involved, entrepreneurial, creatively adventurous, technologically au courant. That he's enjoyed massive commercial success along the way seems almost incidental to his personal global village; the relaxed pace of his recording career in no way bespeaks an absence of enthusiasm. He's just got too many other things to do. Not quite as pompous as Sting or as hidebound as Paul Simon, less of a chameleon than Bowie but more artistically committed than Madonna, Gabriel is a unique figure, and his occasional records have never succumbed to predictability, overbearing pretension or lazy plainness. It's risible to recall that, twenty years ago, Phil Collins took over for him in Genesis.

Gabriel's first four solo albums after leaving Genesis were identically titled with his name, which appears in the same typeface and position on each. As reprised on **Revisited,** a needless and not-quite-complete condensation of the first two, songs like "Solsbury Hill," "Modern Love," "On the Air," "D.I.Y." and "Here Comes the Flood" map out a complex, panoramic and dramatic playing field—at times symphonic, occasionally riveted into packets of spare energy. Beyond such concise, affecting songs as "And Through the Wire" and "I Don't Remember," the third album announced Gabriel's interest in politics and electronic tones: "Games Without Frontiers" and "Biko" brought him into the real world with a poetic vengeance; producer Steve Lillywhite and a bunch of highly skilled instrumentalists helped create a marvelous and distinctive sonic tableau. Dubbed **Security** by Geffen, the fourth **Peter Gabriel** draws further on exotic rhythms (from Africa, Asia and America) with a musique concrète technique made possible by the Fairlight synthesizer. "Shock the Monkey," "I Have the Touch" and "Kiss of Life" are among the best things Gabriel has ever done, combining all of his strengths—lyrical, melodic, structural and experimental—into bracing, original pop music with a solid footing. (**Peter Gabriel** numbers three and four were also each issued as **Deutsches Album,** with Gabriel singing all the lyrics in German.)

The two-disc **Plays Live,** recorded in America in 1982, features a good recap of his solo career to that point. In the mid-'80s, Gabriel tried his hand at film scores; for *Birdy,* he wrote new material and adapted previous recordings, meeting a major challenge with admirable style and character.

So is another adventurous, varied and striking record, with alternately self-reflective and meaningless lyrics, some of them clearly demarking a past-present-future boundary. Delving into funk ("Sledgehammer"), evanescent balladry ("Don't Give Up," with prominent vocals by Kate Bush), folk ("In Your Eyes," with vocal backing by Jim Kerr and others) and catchy dance-rock ("Big Time," featuring ex-Police man Stewart Copeland on drums), Gabriel assembled a commercial powerhouse, and the album sold in the millions without seriously compromising his artistry.

Beginning in 1982 with his pivotal role in the WOMAD festival and organization, Gabriel has made world music his business. Using his advanced studio and the Real World label, he has brought out records by artists from a wide variety of cultures, and his own music has become increasingly intertwined with traditional styles well outside Western forms. In creating the soundtrack for Martin Scorsese's *The Last Temptation of Christ,* Gabriel first made field recordings (a selection of which are compiled on **Passion—Sources**) from musicians in Turkey, Senegal, Egypt and Morocco. Those provided the inspiration (and, in some cases, actual material) for his compositions on the two-record **Passion.** This extraordinary mating of ancient and modern music unifies an enormous geographical spread into a vaguely Middle Eastern feel that is utterly engrossing in its multitudinous use of instruments. Gabriel's deft manipulation of atmospheric sounds yields narrative music of exceptional beauty and drama.

The sixteen-track **Shaking the Tree** offers an edited précis of Gabriel's catalogue, the slanted result of either insurmountable inter-label politics or the artist's unease with his early work. "Solsbury Hill" is the only track from the first album preserved intact; "Here Comes the Flood" gets a brand-new acoustic piano rendition. The second **Peter Gabriel** is overlooked completely; other than tokens from **Passion** and his work with Youssou N'Dour ("Shaking the Tree," from the Senegalese star's 1989 album, **The Lion**), the material comes entirely from **So** and **Peter Gabriel** numbers three and four. For all that, the compilation covers most of the essentials, with only "Contact," "Kiss of Life" and "D.I.Y." standing out as serious omissions.

Gabriel's two most recent records are a studio album and its attendant tour document. Like **So,** co-produced by Daniel Lanois, **Us** sets out to confront a great topic (romance) from a higher artistic plane than any of his previous records. More like abstract sound paintings with vocals and drums than sharply drawn song-type things, the dreamy soundscapes drift along on languid clouds of electronic coloration, engaging the senses with enough international accents (from bagpipes to Mexican flute, *djembe* to Senegalese shakers) to preclude Anglo-American mundanity. Sung in a husky, scratchy voice, Gabriel's lyrics explore a failed relationship (with actress Rosanna Arquette, who receives guilty liner-note thanks) in the reserved resignation of a caricature Englishman: his disappointments and inwardly aimed regrets (especially on paper) are retentive, nearly constipated, and too prosaically stiff-upper-lip for words. While ruminating on his loss with disappointing simplicity, Gabriel conveys more in the pallor of his passion than in any of his prudently scripted lines. Still, "Kiss That Frog" (rendered as a gloomy house track) offers an unattractive self-portrait; "I knew all the time I should shut up and listen," he admits in "Only Us." It's hard not to sympathize, although not for the obvious reasons. Amid the folky allure and exotic effects, the album makes two stylistic exceptions: "Washing of the Water," a Tom Waitsy piano ballad sung with aching directness, is a finely wrought digression, while "Steam" and "Digging in the Dirt" are obnoxiously transparent attempts to reprise the big-dollar dancefloor bump of **So**'s "Sledgehammer" and "Big Time."

The two CDs of **Secret World Live** come from a pair of '93 shows in Italy. Typical of Gabriel's artistic precision, it's no warts'n'all get-it-on-tape-sling-it-out job, but the finely tuned result of extensive post-production, enough evidently to carry the straight-faced quip that it's "based on an original concert by Peter Gabriel." The bulk of **Us** makes up about half the fifteen-song program; a solid dose of **So,** "Solsbury Hill," "Shaking the Tree" and a couple of non-LP items complete the bill. Significantly, some of the songs get expansive new concert arrangements: although singer Paula Cole makes a poor Bush substitute, "Don't Give Up" sprawls theatrically past seven minutes; an exciting vocal assist from Zairean soukous great Papa Wemba helps elongate the deliriously uplifting finale of "In Your Eyes" into double digits without losing drive or focus. With intense vocal performances from Gabriel and robust, detailed accompaniment by bassist Tony Levin, drummer Manu Katche, guitarist David Rhodes, violinist Shankar and others, the great-sounding **Secret World Live** is nearly as enfolding an aural experience as the studio worlds it brings to (controlled) life. [i]

See also *Youssou N'Dour; TPRG.*

DIAMANDA GALÁS

The Litanies of Satan (Y) 1982 (Mute/Restless) 1988
Diamanda Galás (Metalanguage) 1984
The Divine Punishment (UK Mute) 1986 (Mute/Restless) 1989
Saint of the Pit (UK Mute) 1986 (Mute/Restless) 1989
The Divine Punishment & Saint of the Pit (Mute/Restless) 1988
You Must Be Certain of the Devil (Mute/Restless) 1988
Masque of the Red Death (Mute/Restless) 1989 (Mute) 1993
Plague Mass (Mute) 1991
The Singer (Mute) 1992
Vena Cava (Mute) 1993

DIAMANDA GALÁS WITH JOHN PAUL JONES

The Sporting Life (Mute) 1994

After completing her **Masque of the Red Death** trilogy, a strident but striking response to AIDS, caterwauling post-opera vocalist, keyboardist, composer and political activist Diamanda Galás saw to the collective repackaging of all three harrowing albums of shriek (**The Divine Punishment, Saint of the Pit** and **You Must Be Certain of the Devil**) as a limited-edition double-CD in 1989. She then recorded a sepulchral, breathtakingly dramatic and, in the best possible sense, *appalling* live album (**Plague Mass**) at New York's Cathedral of St. John the Divine and began laying the groundwork for a new creative phase in the '90s.

The Singer finds Galás, a Greek-American born in San Diego, injecting herself into the rootsy fringes of popular music via some of the same spirituals ("Let My People Go," "Swing Low Sweet Chariot," "Were You There When They Crucified My Lord?") she incorporated into the trilogy. Following the traditional pathway of gospel into the blues, she reworks classic material of long-forgotten authorship ("See That My Grave Is Kept Clean," which gets a fairly straightforward reading over skittish churchlike organ) as well as more recent creations by Willie Dixon ("Insane Asylum"), Mike Bloomfield ("Reap What You Sow") and, in a provocative creative leap, Screamin' Jay Hawkins. Accompanying herself on skilled stride piano, she attacks "I Put a Spell on You" like a jazzwoman possessed, tearing it apart, reassembling pieces to her own ear-curdling specifications and generally casting off demons in furious flights of vocal invention. Launching her high-wire act from once-familiar terrain makes Galás' work more accessible; the singer is still a highly challenging prospect (we're not talking some Ella Fitzgerald wannabe on a creative bender here), but **The Singer** occasionally brings her into a less eccentric orbit.

Don't take the admonition to play **Vena Cava** "at maximum volume only" seriously—the a cappella undertaking can be plenty stressful at minimal sound pressures. Speaking, singing spirituals (a nervously vibrating but lovely "Amazing Grace"), seasonals ("Santa Claus Is Coming to Town") and even the polka classic "In Heaven There Is No Beer," rambling, reciting, trying on southern accents, choking, preaching and occasionally (especially in one piece's room-clearing opener) launching aerial missiles of unredeemed screeching, Galás makes Courtney Love's worst excesses on **Live Through This** sound like a tender lullaby. There's fine art at the heart of this album (like the trilogy, largely inspired by the life and death of her brother, Philip-Dimitri Galás) but getting to it through the razor-tipped underbrush can be too daunting a challenge.

Fortunately for pretentious wimps desperate to find a Diamanda Galás album they could honestly claim to have made it all the way through, she made it easy (well, easier) with **The Sporting Life.** In a shockingly productive collaboration with ex–Led Zeppelin bassist John Paul Jones (who, for a smidge of out-there shooting practice, produced a Butthole Surfers album the previous year), she sets her wildwoman voices, throat-grabbing lyrics and some sublime organ playing in the context of a rock-solid rhythm section (Pete Thomas of the Attractions does drum duties). The bottom-heavy setting renders Galás' birdcage squalling more palatable and gives her safe passage for a unique approach to street-level considerations. Whether reining herself in for the dramatic "Do You Take This Man?" and the barrelhouse balladry of "Baby's Insane," spewing sinuous melodies in "Tony," finding a potent reformulation for Dan Penn's back-door soul classic "Dark End of the Street" or making a riotous B-movie out of threatened girl-gang violence ("The Sporting Life"), Galás—who is a mighty, if bizarre, blues singer when she set her gears to it—balances unfettered expression with the intrinsically rowdy power of swinging electric music to produce her most stimulating and broadly appealing work yet. [i]

See also *TPRG*.

ALASTAIR GALBRAITH

Gaudylight EP7 (Siltbreeze) 1991
Morse (Siltbreeze) 1992
Seely Girn (Feel Good All Over) 1993
Cluster EP7 (Ger. Raffmond) 1994
Intro Version EP7 (Roof Bolt) 1994
Talisman (NZ no label) 1995
Morse and Gaudylight (Emperor Jones/Trance Syndicate) 1996

RIP

A Timeless Peace EP (NZ Flying Nun) 1983
Stormed Port EP (NZ Flying Nun) 1987

PLAGAL GRIND

Plagal Grind EP (NZ Xpressway) 1990

An accomplished painter, singer, songwriter, violinist and guitarist, New Zealand's Alastair Galbraith has brought all those talents to bear on a diverse body of work dating back to the mid-'80s. He has led the exceptional groups Plagal Grind and the Rip, recorded extensively under his own name, and collaborated with the Dead C's Bruce Russell in the experimental noise project A Handful of Dust. This last excursion notwithstanding, nearly all of Galbraith's work displays his knack for crafting beautiful pop nuggets infused with striking, often abstract lyrical imagery. Like most of the world-class talents in his homeland, he is an under-appreciated diamond in the rough.

Galbraith's skills were first showcased in the Rip, which released two EPs in the mid-1980s. The second, **Stormed Port,** is particularly fine, and features several elements that recur throughout Galbraith's subsequent recordings: a penchant for milking maximum emotional mileage out of a slow chord change; angular, almost modal, violin work (which accents several of the guitar-based songs quite nicely) and doubletracked vocals that give most of his tunes a beautiful ethereal quality.

Galbraith's best work is on the self-titled EP by Plagal Grind, the lone recording issued by a band whose ranks also included Peter Jefferies (originally of This Kind of Punishment, more recently a member of Cyclops and 2 Foot Flame and the architect of a strong solo career), David Mitchell (who had previously served in the Exploding Budgies and the excellent Goblin Mix, and would later co-found the 3Ds) and Robbie Muir (who had played with Galbraith in the Rip). While the Rip's recordings were almost folky, **Plagal Grind** ups the sonic ante with richly textured electric guitars and loads of reverb, resulting in a shimmering, mystical sound perfectly suited to Galbraith-penned songs like "Yes Jazz Cactus," "Marquesite Lace" and the majestic "Receivership." One of the high-water marks for New Zealand rock.

Morse and **Seely Girn** are superb anthologies of Galbraith's work, each featuring a wide assortment of old and new material. The albums overlap considerably but not entirely, with a number of standout tracks unique to each collection. **Seely Girn** offers the better career overview, with tracks from **Plagal Grind,** the Rip's **Stormed Port** EP and assorted hard-to-find singles and cassettes, while **Morse** is a tad stronger on a cut-by-cut basis. Obvious conclusion: get both.

The 7-inch **Cluster** EP, released in 1994, features some of the strongest material of Galbraith's career, including the slow, gorgeous "Raining Here" and the biting "Stalemate." The **Intro Version** EP is Galbraith's first serious misstep, relying more on tuneless, unformed snippets than full-fledged songs.

This random-sound approach is taken further with Galbraith's self-released **Talisman** CD, a meandering, scattershot affair that displays little evidence of his former songwriting acumen. It remains to be seen whether these latest efforts signal a new direction or just a stylistic deviation, but Galbraith's previous output remains unassailable. [pl]

See also *Peter Jefferies, Mountain Goats, 3Ds.*

GALLIANO

In Pursuit of the 13th Note (UK Talkin' Loud) 1991
A Joyful Noise Unto the Creator (UK Talkin' Loud) 1992
What Colour Our Flag (Mercury) 1994
The Plot Thickens (Talkin' Loud/Mercury) 1994

Rob Gallagher was one of a handful of London DJs creating a club phenomenon out of the residue of acid house and the beginnings of British soul (Soul II Soul et al.) when Gilles Peterson and Eddie Pillar signed him as the first artist on their new Talkin' Loud label. The project developed into a loosely formed collective of musicians (sometimes including Roy Ayers) bearing his liqueured nickname; the release of "Frederick Lies Still" (a twist on Curtis Mayfield's "Freddy's Dead") as a British single in 1989 made the group official.

With the addition of two live tracks, the domestic **What Colour Our Flag** takes the best tracks from **In Pursuit of the 13th Note** and **A Joyful Noise Unto the Creator,** avoiding their pitfalls by taking only Galliano's best songs rather than the quasi-rap spoken-word incantations and extended conga jams. Gallagher's poetic raps are an important part of the music (and what earned the group acclaim in Britain), but the majority of the fourteen tracks on **What Colour Our Flag** couch the musings within more fully formed soul grooves. The best of them (like the title song and "Prince of Peace") feature singer Auntie Val (Etienne), whose worldly alto adds an emotional counterpoint. (The core lineup also includes ex–Style Council keyboardist Mick Talbot.)

The Plot Thickens more skillfully integrates the rich multi-cultural vibe into an original, complete style. In the past—and this is true for much of what goes under the acid-jazz umbrella—reggae rhythms, world beat percussion or soul flourishes stand as cultural signifiers, fashion accessories appended to whatever groove the band is working as proof of good taste or fine intentions. Here, the various influences come together as complete songs, and the flavor is identifiably Galliano. And because the fit is tighter, the sound is also funkier, as with the thoughtful reworking of Crosby, Stills and Nash's "Long Time Gone." The album also includes another version of "What Colour Our Flag." [sf]

GALLON DRUNK

Tonite . . . the Singles Bar (UK Clawfist) 1991 (Rykodisc) 1992
You, the Night . . . and the Music (UK Clawfist) 1991 (Rykodisc) 1992
From the Heart of Town (Sire/Reprise) 1993

GALLON DRUNK/BREED

Clawfist–The Peel Sessions (Strange Fruit/Dutch East India Trading) 1992

A product of London's seedy underbelly (or, more likely, its smoky, velvet-wallpapered pubs), Gallon Drunk rose to prominence in Britain through a series of highly touted 7-inch singles and some ferocious live performances. The quartet's rumbling, expansive sound sweeps up chunks of rock and pop history—notably a primal beat and nerve from the Cramps, Bo Diddley and Scientists and a theatrical presence by way of the Birthday Party and Tom Waits—and pulverizes them into a corrosive, irresistible mess, colored by a cheap girlie/horror film aesthetic. Charismatic frontman James Johnston (vocals, guitar and organ) threatens to overwhelm the band's torrential shower of sound with his guttural, Nick Cave–inspired howling, but Gallon Drunk's lumbering rhythm section (including a full-time maracas player!) makes it an even match.

Minus one A-side ("Some Fool's Mess"), **Tonite . . . the Singles Bar** collects Gallon Drunk's first five small-pressing singles in all their raw, underproduced glory. The first, 1988's self-released "Snakepit," is sparse and chaotic, but eventually locates a groove, while "Ruby" (written by banjo-picker Cousin Emmy but later done by late-'60s New York electro-rock duo Silver Apples, whom Gallon Drunk credits), riddled by both angry organ stomps and Johnston's snarling shouts, finds an ensnaring target almost immediately. "Draggin' Along" is almost all rhythm—and an unrelenting one at that—with Johnston's vocal and guitar screeches crashing through. While also propelled by the burly power of drummer Nick Coombes and bassist Michael Delanian, "The Last Gasp (Safty)" gains cohesion from his punchy organ activity.

Released within a few months of the compilation, **You, the Night . . . and the Music**—Gallon Drunk's first real album—has a different drummer and clearer, more uniform sound. The band has developed its melodic side; many of the songs are draped in Johnston's dark piano playing. But the brimstone igniting the songs remains firmly on high. After an instrumental intro (which actually begins with the sound of a car revving up), the album launches right into a new version of "Some Fool's Mess," one of Gallon Drunk's greatest moments. The band injects a melodic hook—short and repetitive as it is—into the throbbing rhythmic pull, and Johnston, as usual, is all over the place, screaming at the edge of incomprehensibility in graphic detail about a cheating lover. The album also includes a fuller version of "Gallon Drunk" (the original 45 of which is on **Tonite**) and a very campy, Crampsy lament called "Eye of the Storm," naturally followed by "The Tornado," another wallop of dirge with some nice slide guitar.

Having traded in its grimy, off-the-streets angst for more seasoned, world-weary angst, Gallon Drunk broadened the scope of its thick, mired sound on **From the Heart of Town.** While a somewhat less heady brew than its predecessors, the album reveals the band growing within its framework, adding new sounds to the mix and settling into the studio atmosphere (aided by an actual producer, Phil Wright). "Jake on the Make," Cave-like in both its title and its lurch'n'grind, introduces banjo; "You Should Be Ashamed" and the ferocious "Bedlam" fuel the fire with squonking horns played by Terry Edwards of Tindersticks; "Loving Alone" is an outright ballad, with backing vocals by Stereolab's Laetitia Sadier.

Clawfist—The Peel Sessions, a joint album also containing tracks by Liverpool's Breed, has four numbers Gallon Drunk recorded for a '91 radio broadcast: loose takes on "Ruby," "Some Fool's Mess" and "Two Wings Mambo" (from **You, the Night**) and a previously unreleased instrumental, "Drag '91." [la]

GANG OF FOUR

Entertainment! (Warner Bros.) 1979 (Infinite Zero) 1995
Gang of Four EP (Warner Bros.) 1980
Solid Gold (Warner Bros.) 1981 (Infinite Zero) 1995
Another Day/Another Dollar EP (Warner Bros.) 1982
Songs of the Free (Warner Bros.) 1982 (Infinite Zero) 1996
Hard (Warner Bros.) 1983
At the Palace (UK Phonogram) 1984
The Peel Sessions EP (UK Strange Fruit) 1986

The Peel Sessions (Strange Fruit/Dutch East India Trading) 1990
A Brief History of the Twentieth Century (Warner Bros.) 1990
Mall (Polydor) 1991
Shrinkwrapped (Castle) 1995

With such bands as Fugazi, Red Hot Chili Peppers and Rage Against the Machine all boasting a clear Gang of Four influence, and the Henry Rollins/Rick Rubin label reissuing the Britons' absolutely essential masterpiece of a debut, Gang of Four's legacy has lasted well into the '90s. The anthology, **A Brief History of the Twentieth Century,** offers ample (seventy-seven minutes' worth, to be exact) evidence of why the Leeds quartet was one of the greatest of all the post-punk groups and a mighty rock'n'roll band by any measure. It wasn't just Dave Allen's dizzyingly propulsive basslines, Hugo Burnham's madly inventive drumming, Jon King's ominous yelp or guitarist Andy Gill's death-defying rhythmic leaps and breathtaking bursts of staccato noise. Besides the ability to build astonishing levels of tension and then release them in tidal waves of exhilarating noise and fury, the original Gang of Four had an uncanny grasp of the relationship between form and content—by subverting James Brown riffs, dub reggae and the skeletal rockitecture of Free, the band produced music that perfectly conveyed the subversive, neo-Marxist ideas of the lyrics.

Besides selected EP tracks, **A Brief History** wisely leans heavily on the incendiary **Entertainment!** for such classics as "At Home He's a Tourist," "Anthrax" and "Damaged Goods." **Solid Gold** provides the hair-raising "Paralysed," while the same album's "What We All Want" appears in a pounding '81 live version. The underrated **Songs of the Free** yields "I Love a Man in Uniform," "Call Me Up" and "We Live as We Die, Alone." Amazingly, the music has lost none of its sting over time, and the lyrics—mainly concerned with the way capitalism has infiltrated every aspect of our lives—are more relevant than ever. (As an extra, the illuminating and insightful liner notes are by number-one Gang of Four fan Greil Marcus.) Only the back end of the loosely chronological collection is slickly unsatisfying, as **A Brief History**'s four-year span culminates in a couple of meager tokens from **Hard,** the band's abysmal farewell album. (The reissues on Infinite Zero all add tracks. The **Entertainment!** CD contains the untitled four-song EP of collected single sides from 1980. **Solid Gold** is augmented by **Another Day/Another Dollar:** three tracks from 45s plus two live cuts.)

But King and Gill didn't know when to call it quits. Undaunted by the prospect of matching the ferocity captured on the **Entertainment!**-era segments of the eleven-track **Peel Sessions** compilation released in 1990, the two regrouped the following year for **Mall.** Even though the album displays glimmers of the old magic, the enterprise wants desperately for the nonpareil rhythm team of Allen and Burnham. Interestingly, the quieter tracks are the best: the eerie "Everybody Wants to Come," the pretty "Satellite" and a touching take on Bob Marley's "Soul Rebel." Elsewhere, Gill and King clearly have some serious things left to say about the intrusion of arbitrary economic systems into the most private nooks and crannies of personal life, but the chemistry is simply not there. The slick, synth-heavy/radio-ready production and lock-step drum tracks have the distinct whiff of sell-out.

Undeterred, Gill and King tried again on **Shrinkwrapped,** which never overcomes the disappointment of hearing such former iconoclasts flaunt fairly conventional music, lyrics and (courtesy of Gill) production values. The songs are a catalogue of bleak character sketches, sometimes with a creepy sexuality ("Unburden" and its related commentary, "Unburden Unbound"), making the band's usual points about the tyranny of capitalism with a subtler line than usual. In "The Dark Ride," the mentally ill narrator curses the very elements of consumer culture that were damned in **Entertainment!;** it's one of several spooky, cryptic cuts, like "I Absolve You" and "Something 99," which set the album's tone. Bolstered by an improved rhythm section, Gill lets fly with frustratingly brief bursts of the old noisy glory on "I Parade Myself," "Better Him Than Me" and "Unburden," then finally stretches out on the otherwise weak "Showtime, Valentine." While it's a distinct improvement over **Mall, Shrinkwrapped** still doesn't make a compelling case for the continued existence of the Gang of Four. [ma]

See also *Low Pop Suicide; TPRG.*

GANG STARR

No More Mr. Nice Guy (Wild Pitch) 1989
Step in the Arena (Chrysalis) 1990
Daily Operation (Chrysalis) 1992
Hard to Earn (Chrysalis) 1994

GURU

Jazzmatazz Volume 1: An Experimental Fusion of Hip-Hop and Jazz (Chrysalis) 1993
Jazzmatazz Volume II: The New Reality (Chrysalis) 1995

Rap groups that manage to be both tough and smart are rare, but Brooklyn's Gang Starr is both. Rapper Guru (Keith Elam) and DJ Premier (Chris Martin) are both perfectionists, with scholars' dedication to the study and lifestyle of hip-hop. Although both have successfully pursued other projects—Guru has released two albums under the Jazzmatazz aegis, while Premier clocks dollars producing records for every other hip-hop artist—together they make genre-defining music.

The duo didn't start all that auspiciously, however; **No More Mr. Nice Guy** finds Guru (Gifted Unlimited Rhymes Universal) Keithy E struggling to define his rap style and lyrical focus; while he touches on the topics that he would nail cold in future records, he sounds amateurish and hackneyed here. DJ Premier provides samples, beats and rhythms that are perfectly adequate, if not up to his future level. Most significantly, "Jazz Music" announces the duo's interest in getting busy with a different idiom.

Step in the Arena is a mind-blowing breakthrough; it's clear that Guru (no longer using the "Keithy E" handle) and Premier have recognized their mission. The record is hard, intricate, forceful and represents. The samples are particularly stunning, with Premier drawing on sources well outside the norm. "Execution of a Chump" and "Check the Technique" are just two of the outstanding tracks from this dense, complex record.

Daily Operation maintains the high quality, although it doesn't come as much of a surprise. Guru continues to boast about himself, his group and his borough ("Come to Brooklyn frontin'/And you'll get mushed quick"), to speak out about the oppression of the black man ("Conspiracy") and then boast about himself again. "Take It Personal" is a sludgy mix of beats and a catchy riff laid under Guru's confident, sexy voice, delivering a warning to someone who betrayed him ("When I pay you back I'll be hurting you") and then explaining it as a musical beef ("Rap is an art/You can't own no loops/It's how you hook 'em up and the rhyme style").

Hard to Earn doesn't do anything wrong, but it isn't remarkably different from the previous two. Jeru the Damaja and Big Shug (who also appears on both **Jazzmatazz** records) make guest appearances. The single, "Mass Appeal," is just a boast about how rap groups trying to gain commercial success can't compare to Gang Starr; "I'm so real to them it's scary," Guru says.

On his first **Jazzmatazz** album, Guru works on the blend he undertook on the **Mo' Better Blues** soundtrack ("Jazz Thing" with Branford Marsalis, although Dizzy Gillespie does *not* play the sax, as Guru repeats ad nauseam), bringing such jazz legends as trumpeter Donald Byrd, guitarist Ronny Jordan, pianist Lonnie Liston Smith and vibraphonist Roy Ayers into the studio to add flavor and style to his music. He also spotlights French rapper MC Solaar, Brand New Heavies singer N'Dea Davenport (the sexiest tracks are their duets) and Carleen Anderson. Guru's theory, which he goes into at length and proves by example, is that both hip-hop and jazz are "musical cultural expression(s) based on reality," so the two have much more in common than some might think. With his overwhelming enthusiasm and excellent songwriting (most of the rhymes are spontaneous freestyles), **Jazzmatazz Volume 1** is a classic record that bends genres together to create new ones.

Volume II: The New Reality is much less intriguing. Although there are moments—the duet with Chaka Khan ("Watch What You Say") and tracks produced by the Solsonics ("New Reality Style," "Defining Purpose," "Maintaining Focus")—the record suffers from Guru's excessive pride, already duly documented on Gang Starr records, at having achieved his mission on the debut. The combination of styles is far less seamless, and the songs—less hip-hop/jazz melds than hip-hop/R&B-flavored jazz blends—take fewer risks. Buying his own hype, Guru seems willing to bask in, rather than build on, his accomplishments. [mf]

See also *Brand New Heavies.*

GARBAGE

Garbage (Almo Sounds) 1995

ANGELFISH

Suffocate Me EP (Wasteland) 1993
Angelfish (Radioactive) 1994

GOODBYE MR. MACKENZIE

Good Deeds and Dirty Rags (Echo Chamber/Capitol) 1989

In one of the most felicitous international musical marriages in memory, Edinburgh singer/guitarist Shirley Manson shelved the go-nowhere Angelfish and reluctantly joined an unpretentious trio of Wisconsin-based studio rats led by ex-Spooner drummer (and producer of a new generation: Killdozer, Sonic Youth, Nirvana, Soul Asylum, Smashing Pumpkins) Butch Vig. Together, they became Garbage, a frighteningly good band with an A Team's worth of complementary skills. Sounding like a diverse stack of 1994 hits by a half-dozen bands, **Garbage** is a casebook of sharply constructed and propulsive songs, gimmicky and brilliant noir production, overcharged guitar-and-electronics rock and domineering, trenchantly provocative lyrics. In synch with the pointedly borrowed sonic signatures, the words flip a friendly finger at the Jesus and Mary Chain ("Only Happy When It Rains"), Nine Inch Nails ("As Heaven Is Wide," "Not My Idea"), Hole ("Vow"), the Breeders ("Dog New Tricks"), Adrian Belew ("Queer"), My Bloody Valentine ("Supervixen," which fits an attention-grabbing total dropout three seconds into the album) and other could-be Lollapaloozers.

Like the first Sloan album, **Garbage**'s effortlessly eclectic citations owe so much to so many that the issue of influences becomes a joke: of course that's what they're doing, and what of it? Hard-hitting, intelligent rock of intrinsic strength and witty presentation is its own reward; Manson's singing is decisively original, and such memorable lines as "I'm riding high upon a deep depression" or "If God's my witness, God must be blind" make fine additions to the grumpy bon mot compendium. A virtual sampler of uncommon imagination, **Garbage** is as good as or better than the work of most of the bands it acknowledges.

Ironically, Angelfish's first longplayer fails for the very reason **Garbage** succeeds. Having extracted itself as a quartet from the pompous Goodbye Mr. MacKenzie (a six-strong Simple Minds/Echo and the Bunnymen wannabe serious and intemperate enough to script and sing lyrics for God)—moving Manson from a supporting role to center stage in the process—the Scottish group can't seem to decide who *it* wants to be on **Angelfish:** Siouxsie and the Banshees? Cheap Trick? Blondie? The Pretenders? Holly and the Italians? (Although one of the album's best songs was written by Holly Vincent, it's not the track that sounds the most like her old band.) Glibly enabling production by ex–Talking Heads Chris Frantz and Tina Weymouth exacerbates the confusion, leaving Manson's strong vocal presence to idle in this skillful but diffident wheel-spinner. [i]

GAS HUFFER

Ethyl EP7 (Black) 1991
Janitors of Tomorrow (eMpTy) 1991
Integrity Technology and Service (eMpTy) 1992
One Inch Masters (Epitaph) 1994
The Inhuman Ordeal of Special Agent Gas Huffer (Epitaph) 1996

Perhaps the garage-band tradition is better entrenched in the Pacific Northwest than anywhere else in America because the region's perpetual precipitation encourages folks to while away their days cranking amps in their own carports or searching for Sonics singles in their neighbors'. Gas Huffer, unlike more historically minded peers, seem to have divided the above pursuits properly—spending about 90 percent of their time at the former, using the latter as little more than coasters for those ever-present tallboys.

The quartet was formed at the turn of the decade by

guitarist Tom Price (formerly the prime mover in the U-Men, a heavy, gnarled band that presaged—and outstripped—the ghosts of grunge future) and quickly garnered a rep as the apogee of Seattle's party-rock sector. Swathed in a tastelessly absurd comic-book largely drawn by drummer Joe Newton, **Janitors of Tomorrow** ambles through familiar psychobilly territory, but Price's left-field flourishes and singer Matt Wright's defeatist blue-collar humor cast the scenery in a slightly different light.

It'd be a stretch to say **Integrity Technology and Service** is any more serious than its predecessor, but the album *does* sound a whole lot more coherent. The spot-on call-and-response vocals that propel "George Washington" ("What do you think of this song? / We think it's going on too long") and Don Blackstone's crypto-surf basslines (on "Bad Vibes") are uncannily professional—but then again, "I.T.S. Credo" reaffirms the band-held view of rock as hard manual labor. Moving to Epitaph, **One Inch Masters** dispenses with the nine-to-five shtick (did the recession hit home or something?), but Gas Huffer still manages to self-reference with the best of 'em, as evidenced by the overdriven club-tour anthem "Stay in Your House." Although the presence of harmonies, middle eights and such (no doubt the influence of producer Kurt Bloch) might give primitivists pause, there's no disputing the outright dopiness of songs like "Chicken Foot" and the mock-doomy "Appendix Gone." It's not all super-premium, but the fumes will keep you going for a while. **The Inhuman Ordeal of Special Agent Gas Huffer** was also produced by Bloch and offers an attendant comic/lyric book available by mail. [dss]

See also *Mudhoney.*

GASTR DEL SOL

The Serpentine Similar EP (TeenBeat) 1993
Crookt, Crackt, or Fly (Drag City) 1994
Mirror Repair EP (Drag City) 1994
The Harp Factory on Lake Street EP (Table of the Elements) 1995
Upgrade & Afterlife (Drag City) 1996

By the time Louisville, Kentucky's Bastro disbanded in the early '90s, singer/guitarist/pianist David Grubbs (who had played in Slint and Squirrel Bait, among others) was much less interested in being in a conventional rock band than in creating and manipulating complex tone patterns. (For evidence of the transition, track down Bastro's side of its 1991 split single with Codeine or its track on the **TeenBeat 50** compilation.) **The Serpentine Similar** EP was recorded with the old lineup (bassist Bundy K. Brown and, making a few cameo appearances, drummer John McEntire) and using an old song ("Sketch for Sleepy," rewritten as "A Jar of Fat")—but under a new name, Gastr del Sol. That's fair, because this was an entirely new thing: rockless, usually percussionless, wildly exploratory and sometimes even successful. Grubbs' songs-without-tunes approach on "Easy Company" and elsewhere recalls Mayo Thompson (whose Red Krayola he subsequently joined); the instrumentals, though, demand the attention it takes to follow their interbraided melodies.

The subsequent "20 Songs Less" single introduced guitarist, composer and avant-gardist-about-town Jim O'Rourke to the mix, literally—one of his specialties is tape manipulation. Then Brown left, and Gastr del Sol became the catchall name for Grubbs and O'Rourke's collaborations, though McEntire has continued to assist them.

Crookt, Crackt, or Fly is much more mysterious than **The Serpentine Similar**—almost all acoustic, drumless, enhanced by subtle tape work and eschewing traditional tonalities, with a few unexpected leaps into full-bore rock. The focus is more on Grubbs and O'Rourke's unconventional guitar virtuosity—check out the spectacular "Every Five Miles," which sounds like John Fahey in hyperspace. Grubbs' lyrics suggest "language poetry," though "Thos. Dudley Ah! Old Must Dye" appears to be a setting of an eighteenth-century anagram-poem. Weird stuff, but often very lovely.

The five-track **Mirror Repair** is in the same vein, almost a distillation of **Crookt.** Like the album, it has a performance by bass clarinetist Gene Coleman on one piece, very short and very long tracks, surprises in the form of unexpected tape splices on top of a simple ground figure (like the woodwind squall that erupts near the end of "Eight Corners"), peculiar tonalities (the title track) and a few brief, battering passages that remind the listener that, yes, Gastr Del Sol *did* evolve out of a rock band. **The Harp Factory on Lake Street** is a single, seventeen-minute piece for a small orchestral ensemble. [ddw]

See also *Codeine, Faust, Jim O'Rourke, Red Crayola, Seam, Shrimp Boat, Slint, Tortoise.*

GATE

See *Dead C.*

GAUNT

Whitey the Man EP10 (Thrill Jockey) 1993
Sob Story EP (Thrill Jockey) 1994
I Can See Your Mom From Here (Thrill Jockey) 1995
Yeah, Me Too (Amphetamine Reptile) 1995
Kryptonite (Thrill Jockey) 1996

Probably the most prolific band to emerge from Columbus, Ohio's alcohol-fueled aggro-rock scene, Gaunt—like homeboys New Bomb Turks and Thomas Jefferson Slave Apartments—never met a punk they didn't like. Borrowing bits and pieces from frenzifiers as historically diverse as Screamin' Jay Hawkins and the Necros, the quartet nevertheless makes up its own set of loud-fast rules.

After releasing a profusion of small-pressing singles, Gaunt moved up the size ladder one notch with the 10-inch **Whitey the Man.** Swathed in a snarky bowling alley sleeve and rife with redneck-baiting numbers like "Jim Motherfucker" (a reprise of an earlier single track), the provocative disc casts frontman Jerry Wick as a subversive mole in the belly of the know-nothing suburban beast. **Sob Story,** a collection of outtakes, may be moderately—okay, severely—fidelity-challenged, but between Wick's George Jones-on-methamphetamine whine and Jovan Karcic's no-frills strumming, songs like "Frustration" and "Each and Every Side Effect" show Gaunt developing a uniquely belligerent strain of jukebox-ready beer-jerkers.

The foursome left home to record **I Can See Your**

Mom From Here (paid for, if the sleeve notes are to be believed, in car parts), which retains the reflexive spuzziness of previous releases, but boosts just enough recording quality to stave off those constant checks for stereo malfunctions. Wick really hits his stride on sneering hate-seeking missives like "Ohio" (an original that embraces one verse of the Neil Young song). Even though some of the targets and solutions are fairly obvious—"Rich Kid" (they deserve to die); "Revolution to Spite Your Face" (better to just stay home)—the album is a roaring success.

Yeah, Me Too is notable not only for incorporating shifts out of overdrive (on the uncharacteristically poppy title track and "Now"), but for containing some of the band's most fully realized songwriting to date. Somebody should send Dwight Yoakam a copy of "Justine" and wait for the royalties to roll in.

Given the presence of songs like "Hand in Pants" and "Savior Breath," it might be disingenuous to call **Kryptonite** Gaunt's attempt to get in touch with their collective sensitive side. Still, Wick's more measured delivery (heightened by the decision to unearth his gruff-but-touching vocals) and the more soulful structures (including some Dolls-styled R&B augmentations) impart an accessibility that goes mighty well with the foursome's regular-joe constitution. In '96, the industrious Wick began releasing thinly disguised solo records under the moniker Cocaine Sniffing Triumph. [dss]

GEGGY TAH

Grand Opening (Luaka Bop/Warner Bros.) 1994
Sacred Cow (Luaka Bop/Warner Bros.) 1996

Los Angeles studio hounds Greg Kurstin and Tommy Jordan (Geggy Tah comes from baby-sister pronunciations of their names) thrive on patchwork eclecticism. **Grand Opening** is an inventive first record, a multi-culti implosion that sucks in all manner of styles and instruments—in their hands, steel drums, melodica, glass bottles and piano sound as natural a combination as guitar, bass and drums—and reworks them in ways that turn out far better than reasonable expectations might suggest. At times, the two get tangled up in their own ideas, but the proliferation of ironic juxtapositions ("Last Word (The One for Her)" cuts the wedding march with a funeral dirge) and an utterly convincing P-Funk throwdown ("L.A. Lujah") make it easy to forgive.

Sacred Cow continues the duo's tactful progression towards a modern version of Steely Dan–dom. Other than a weakness for stretching songwriting ideas too thin, Kurstin and Jordan make a convincing case for themselves, ably adopting and shucking elements of style with cavalier conviction. [sf/i]

HOWE GELB

See *Giant Sand.*

BOB GELDOF

Deep in the Heart of Nowhere (Atlantic) 1986
The Vegetarians of Love (Atlantic) 1990
The Happy Club (Polydor) 1993

In mid-1986, after making enormous efforts on behalf of others, ex–Boomtown Rat Bob Geldof took a few steps in his own behalf, writing an autobiography (*Is That It?*) and signing a solo record deal. **Deep in the Heart of Nowhere** bears the onerous marks of Rupert Hine's tritely commercial overproduction, but contains both swell tunes and true wretchedness. Returning various favors, the album's cast includes Dave Stewart, Annie Lennox, Midge Ure, Brian Setzer, Eric Clapton and Alison Moyet.

With Hine again producing and ex-Rat Pete Briquette on bass, Geldof adopted a jolly and appealing neo-folk approach for **The Vegetarians of Love,** a casual and light, mostly acoustic, album that gains a mild Irish accent from violin, accordion and pennywhistle. But while the sensitively played music sounds lighthearted, Bob hasn't changed his outspoken and pointed lyrical ways. After ironically listing all the things he doesn't care about in "The Great Song of Indifference," Geldof spends the rest of the album airing his philosophical and emotional angst. "I'm thinking big things," he sings, waxing existential in "Thinking Voyager 2 Type Things," "I'm thinking about mortality / I'm thinking it's a cheap price that we pay for existence."

Working with most of the **Vegetarians** crew (but joined by World Party's Karl Wallinger), **The Happy Club** finds him enjoying the rustic surroundings even more—for the first few minutes. The album has an ebullience rarely heard in his work ("Room 19" makes teasing musical reference to the Monkees, and the stomping "Yeah, Definitely" pumps old soul into a delightfully Dylanesque vocal), but Geldof is one earthling who can never escape gravity. The brutal social critique of "Attitude Chicken" and the angry "Song of the Emergent Nationalist" are only warmups for the gorgeous, nostalgic spoken reminiscence "The House at the Top of the World," the religious accusation of "Too Late God" and the changing European politics of "Roads of Germany." A thoughtful, engaging album of genuine personal conviction. [i]

See also *TPRG.*

GEM

See *Cobra Verde.*

GENE

Olympian (Polydor) 1995
Olympian EP (UK Costemonger) 1995
For the Dead EP (UK Costemonger) 1996
To See the Lights (UK Polydor) 1996

Never mind the fact that, yes, Gene does bear a marked resemblance to the Smiths. The British foursome has a similar approach to UK guitar pop—a love of joyous songcraft composed of equal parts intelligent words, cheeky melodies and a sense of grandiose melodrama. But where Morrissey basks in his miserabilia, Gene singer/lyricist Martin Rossiter kicks against his grim London world, finding solace, community and redemption in his band's music. Despite the often dreary subject matter (which ranges from homophobia to gang violence to premature death), **Olympian** retains an exuberant spirit that never gets mopey or maudlin. Rossiter's songs are witty and articulate, often fraught with an epic temperament ("Sleep Well Tonight," or the bracing "To the City"), even when capturing the minutiae of urban life and love ("Truth, Rest Your Head"). On such soulful and electric anthems as "Haunted By You" or tender-but-tough ballads like "Your Love, It Lies," Gene conjures up echoes of the Faces, the Jam—even Queen. Guitarist Steve Mason is a wonder, whether he's getting orchestral on the majestic title track or peeling the proverbial hot licks all over "A Car That Sped." In the end, **Olympian** is so good Rossiter can be forgiven his occasional Mozzer-like growl; Gene's touching and terrific tuneage is enough. (The A-sides of the band's first two singles, "For the Dead" and the splendid "Be My Light, Be My Guide," were left off the British release but added to the US edition as bonus tracks.)

The **Olympian** EP features a different mix of "Olympian" (retooled for UK pop radio with the piano up and the guitars down), as well as two UK non-LP tunes and a fine BBC radio version of the Beatles' "Don't Let Me Down." **For the Dead** reprises the band's first 45 with producer Phil Vinall's remix of the title cut and the original B-side ("Child's Body"), plus live takes of "Sick, Sober and Sorry" and "Truth, Rest Your Head."

To See the Lights, the group's odds'n'sods (or is that more like hatful of hollow?) compilation, collects all of Gene's consistently excellent B-sides, which include the way-Smithsy "I Can't Decide If She Really Loves Me," the ripping title cut and yet another fine Rossiter romantic lament, "How Much for Love." There are also some fab radio sessions (like the amazing, bare-boned "A Car That Sped"), such live thingies as the shambolic take on the Bacharach/David standard "I Say a Little Prayer" (recorded at Glastonbury '95), plus "For the Dead" and "Be My Light, Be My Guide." [mgk]

GENE LOVES JEZEBEL

Promise (UK Situation Two) 1983 (Geffen) 1987
Immigrant (UK Beggars Banquet) 1984 (Situation Two/Relativity) 1985
Discover (Beggars Banquet/Geffen) 1986
The House of Dolls (Beggars Banquet/Geffen) 1987
Kiss of Life (Beggars Banquet/Geffen) 1990
Heavenly Bodies (Savage) 1992
Some of the Best of Gene Loves Jezebel: From the Mouths of Babes (Avalanche) 1995

Formed in London in the early '80s by Welsh identical twins Michael and Jay Aston, Gene Loves Jezebel flaunted a daring, alluring combination of new wave's melodic energy and gothic rock's dark sensuality. The band further differentiated itself from the pack with the brothers' unconventional singing style (a bizarre mixture of yelps, screams, howls and hiccups interspersed liberally throughout the coy lyrics) and glammy androgynous appearance. The quintet's entertaining sound is admirably captured on **Promise** and **Immigrant. Discover,** however, adopts a decidedly more commercial tone, and **The House of Dolls** completely abandons the original style in a calculated stab at a breakthrough. It worked to an extent, and the old Gene Loves Jezebel gave up the ghost forever.

Michael Aston quit after **The House of Dolls;** without his iconoclastic influence, **Kiss of Life** is slick and streamlined, all spiffed up and ready to take on the charts with a vengeance. The angular "Jealous" comes off fairly well, as does the easygoing title track, but the remaining songs lack the preening self-confidence so prominent on all previous releases. Left to sing alone, Jay tones down his flamboyant style considerably, further diminishing GLJ's dazzle.

The Jezebels regained their equilibrium for **Heavenly Bodies.** The songs are still unabashedly calculated, but they're also catchy and brimming with the assurance absent from **Kiss of Life.** The undulating "American Dreamer" and the jaunty "Rosary" are quite impressive, as is the serene "Heavenly Body." "Josephina" evolves from an edgy intro into a well-crafted combination of mid-tempo hard rock melodies and spacious atmospherics. Jay Aston no longer seems overwhelmed by his role as bandleader, and the occasional vocal embellishment indicates he's even enjoying it. Indicating a previously unknown talent for expressing deep emotions, his gentle, wistful vocals on the dusky "In a Lonely Place" make the song quietly powerful and lovely.

Some of the Best of Gene Loves Jezebel is true to its title; it contains only *some* of the band's best work. **Immigrant** isn't represented at all; nor is **Heavenly Bodies.** "Suspicion," from **The House of Dolls,** is in place, but that album's biggest single, "The Motion of Love," isn't. The raucous "Desire" and the dizzying "Heartache" from **Discover** make the cut, as does "Jealous" from **Kiss of Life.** A few lesser-known album tracks sweeten the pot, but the two new songs don't add much. [ky]

See also *Edith Grove; TPRG.*

GENERAL PUBLIC

. . . All the Rage (IRS) 1984
Hand to Mouth (IRS) 1986
Rub It Better (Epic) 1995

RANKING ROGER

Radical Departure (IRS) 1988

DAVE WAKELING

No Warning (IRS) 1991

INTERNATIONAL BEAT

The Hitting Line (Triple X) 1991

VARIOUS ARTISTS

The Beat Goes On (IRS) 1991

When Birmingham's brilliant ska-popping (English) Beat—the smartest and most effective pop soldiers in the 2-Tone uprising—collapsed in 1983, singer/guitarist Dave Wakeling and toaster Ranking Roger (Charlery) stuck together to form General Public, a less-focused but equally productive outfit that lasted only two albums. (The first, a rich sampler of styles and effervescent creative enthusiasm, is the keeper.)

In 1987, with their long partnership at an end, Roger and Wakeling each set out on solo careers. Adding semi-melodic singing to his vocal repertoire, Roger got so far as making **Radical Departure,** a socially conscious but duff album of pop and dance-rock originals, before succumbing to the oldies touring route in a never-say-die mob of 2-Tone veterans dubbed Special Beat. He also co-produced and guested on **The Hitting Line,** a likable if uninspired imitation of the mothership's stylings by the International Beat, a septet (unrelated to Beats International) boasting only the original band's saxophonist (Saxa) and drummer (Everett Morton).

For his part, Wakeling whipped out the sprightly title track to John Hughes' 1988 film *She's Having a Baby,* and then turned to a career in Greenpeace while dithering with a solo album for three years. In 1991, he finally released **No Warning** (originally announced in 1989 as **The Happiest Man in the World**). The lack of musician credits, the presence of canned drumming, the prevalence of piano and the liner-note references to "additional recording and mixing by" all suggest an inorganic creative process, and the record—despite typical intelligence, perspective, sensitivity, politics and a shot of soul—is drowsy and dull. (Even "Sex With You" is a snore.) But it does lead off with the wry and wonderful anti-materialist ode "I Want More," a worthy successor to Wakeling's all-time Beat classic, "Save It for Later."

That might have been all she wrote, record-wise, had Roger and Wakeling not been coaxed into a one-off reunion ("I'll Take You There," the Staple Singers number they covered for the *Threesome* soundtrack) in '94. They assembled a band, enlisted such old associates as Saxa and Mick Jones and cut General Public's belated but worth the wait third album, the modern and lively **Rub It Better.** "Never get nowhere on the fence / Maybe we all need something we can push against," sings Wakeling in the leadoff "It Must Be Tough," and that may explain a lot here. (While it promises to, the ambiguously aimed "Friends Again" sure doesn't.) Under Jerry Harrison's vibrant production, the reinvigorated rockers collaboratively unload a thrilling and powerfully positive rush of contemporary rock, dancehall, hip-hop, soul, pop and political ideas. Their skills and divergent cultural interests mix and mate with rewarding results. Even Ranking Roger's "Rainy Days," which starts with inclement weather and somehow reaches the abolition of apartheid, is giddily upbeat. Not all the tracks land squarely: Roger's autobiographical "Punk," which calls the '70s movement "original boombastic," is just too silly a novelty, the citations of Kurt Cobain and Morrissey in the crotchety "Blowhard" are self-defeating and a bouncy cover of Van Morrison's "Warm Love" is pointless. But the ones that do ("It Must Be Tough," "Rainy Days," "Big Bed," "It's Weird," "Never Not Alone") are a gift from a riven partnership that once seemed gone for good.

A handy audio digest, **The Beat Goes On** gathers up some (not enough) highlights of the Beat and follows its members' subsequent ventures: the first incarnation of General Public, Fine Young Cannibals, International Beat, Special Beat (an otherwise unreleased Prince Buster cover) and the solo records. [i]

See also *TPRG.*

GENIUS/GZA

See *Wu-Tang Clan.*

GERALDINE FIBBERS

See *Ethyl Meatplow.*

LISA GERMANO

On the Way Down From the Moon Palace (Major Bill) 1991
Happiness (Capitol) 1993 (4AD) 1994
Inconsiderate Bitch EP (4AD) 1994
Geek the Girl (4AD) 1994
Cry Wolf EP (4AD) 1995
Excerpts From a Love Circus (4AD) 1996

Self-billed as "The Emotional Wench," Indiana native Lisa Germano first surfaced as the fiddler with John Cougar Mellencamp's band, but her own work is light years away from the heartland swagger of her erstwhile employer. The self-released **On the Way Down From the Moon Palace** showcases country-tinged folk-pop with mandolin and accordion augmenting guitars and a tastefully deployed drum machine (although three tracks gain extra oomph from ex-bandmate Kenny Aronoff's drumming). Punctuated by contemplative, exquisite instrumentals, songs like "Bye Bye Little Doggie" and the Dylanesque blues "Dig My Own Grave" dispense world-weary wisdom about disintegrating relationships and bad, bad boys, while the almost Enya-esque "The Other One" suggests her future stylistic direction. Germano's papery, intimate vocals and expressive violin hooks suffuse the music with a melancholy that would only increase on her next two albums.

Produced by Daniel Lanois cohort Malcolm Burn, the brilliant **Happiness** drops most of the country flavor and incorporates a bleak, rootsy twist on the English shoegazer sound. The album is an extended meditation on depression, a suite of consistently excellent songs documenting the sarcasm and cynicism that snowball until life itself seems like a shallow, pointless joke. Within this realistic mix of vulnerability and strength, optimism and despair, candor is the reason that **Happiness** is ultimately uplifting. "Give it up, try again / Give it up, try again," Germano sings on the title track, "Ain't life fun?"

Germano did try again. **Inconsiderate Bitch** contains remixes of five **Happiness** songs, none of which appear on the second version of the album—released after Germano left Capitol for 4AD. Resequenced and partly remixed by Burn and Germano, the reworked **Happiness** amplifies the ethereal 4AD sound that lurked in the original, drops the instrumental "Breathe Acrost Texas" and a superfluous cover of "These Boots Are Made for Walkin'" and adds two fine new songs, "Destroy the Flower" and "The Earth." The effort focuses and magnifies the album's moody impact, rendering it even more atmospheric and intimate than the original—if that's possible. Not just an excellent 3:00 A.M. my-lover-just-walked-out-the-door record, but a moving and inspiring document of one person's struggle with depression. Essential listening for anyone who's had a dark day or two.

The stark, almost unnervingly candid **Geek the Girl** is not an album one listens to lightly. Produced by Germano and Burn, it's a seething, intense and relentlessly dark record whose terror is loudest in its most hushed spaces—and there are a lot of them, as Germano's whispered delivery and skeletal, home-recorded arrangements delve deeply into fear, insecurity and anxiety. Her liner notes say it's the story of a girl who gets taken advantage of sexually but still believes in the redemptive power of beauty and the love of a man—"ha ha ha what a geek!" Germano, who has been plagued by a stalker for years, lets it all go in the harrowing ". . . A Psychopath," which incorporates a genuine recording of a terror-stricken woman making a 911 call as an intruder breaks into her home. "Cry Wolf" is a searing analysis of date rape dispensed with *Twin Peaks*–like eeriness, while the dirgey instrumental "Phantom Love" says just as much as any of the songs with words. Although not as tuneful as **Happiness, Geek the Girl** is substantially more gripping.

Besides an edit of the title track, **Cry Wolf** features

remixes of **Geek the Girl**'s "Cancer of Everything" and "Sexy Little Girl Princess," an edit of "Cry Wolf" and the hitherto unreleased "The Mirror Is Gone," a trenchant gem left over from the **Happiness** sessions. [ma]

GERMS

See *Pat RuthenSmear.*

LISA GERRARD

See *Dead Can Dance.*

GETO BOYS

Making Trouble (Rap-a-Lot) 1988
Grip It! On That Other Level (Rap-a-Lot) 1989
The Geto Boys (Rap-a-Lot/Def American) 1990
We Can't Be Stopped (Rap-a-Lot/Priority) 1991
Uncut Dope: Geto Boys Best (Rap-a-Lot) 1992
Till Death Do Us Part (Rap-a-Lot) 1993
The Resurrection (Rap-a-Lot/Noo Trybe) 1996

WILLIE DEE

Controversy (Rap-a-Lot) 1989
I'm Goin' Out Like a Soldier (Rap-a-Lot) 1992
Play Witcha Mama (Wize-Up/Wrap) 1994

(MR.) SCARFACE

Mr. Scarface Is Back (Rap-a-Lot) 1991
The World Is Yours (Rap-a-Lot/Priority) 1993
The Diary (Rap-a-Lot/Noo Trybe) 1994

BUSHWICK BILL

Little Big Man (Rap-a-Lot) 1992
Phantom of the Rapra (Rap-a-Lot/Noo Trybe) 1995

BIG MIKE

Something Serious (Rap-a-Lot) 1994

CONVICTS

1-900-Dial-a-Crook (Rap-a-Lot) 1991

Anyone who comes to Geto Boys records for anything other than entertainment needs to have his head examined. The Houston rap group presents a vision so brilliantly overdone that many will never fully accept that it is just as valid as the righteous rage proffered by such would-be prophets as Public Enemy or KRS-One. Though they never achieve PE's defined production or density of sound, Geto Boys' records remain the equal of any well-done horror flick you'd care to name—full of gratuitous violence, unfeeling sex and endless exaggerations designed to split your sides in the way only the best non-family entertainment can. These guys are really sick.

Initially formed as the Ghetto Boys in the mid-'80s, the band began with only a hint of the overload they would ultimately unleash. **Making Trouble**'s sleeve prominently pictures Bushwick Bill, but the psychotic midget who would become the Geto Boys' greatest selling point is only featured talking on the album's final track, "The Problem." The rest of the record is essentially lame, as can be seen from the obvious Run–DMC image—gold chains and ugly sporting gear—and the rudimentary beats. While Geto Boys' other main players had yet to arrive on the scene, DJ Ready Red and Johnny C. are on the job, engaging in plenty of the kind of hoarse shouting that would become their trademark.

Grip It! On That Other Level is a bit better. Scarface (listed as D.J. Akshun; the rapper's real name is Brad Jordan) and Willie D(ee) join Red and Bill (New York–raised Richard Shaw) to create the blueprint for the band's nationwide major-label debut, where a bigger studio budget would allow for the kind of production values these guys deserve. Although Bushwick isn't cited as a songwriter, the members' identities are beginning to take shape. Scarface is serious and mentally unhinged; Bushwick is sociopathic in a corny way; Willie D, studly and full of himself, suffers from the sort of diction problems that would sideline most wannabe rappers. "Do It Like a G.O." makes its second appearance (the first was on Willie D's first solo album) in a much-improved version, while "Gangster of Love" (not listed on the album sleeve) is aired complete with the Steve Miller sample prudently excised from the band's major-label bow.

The Geto Boys (the article appearing for the first and only time) is the group's definitive statement. The gruesome crew comes out swinging with their sickest material to date: the insanely angry "Fuck 'Em," the hilarious "Mind of a Lunatic" (which forms the musical basis for the next album's "Mind Playing Tricks on Me" and contains the immortal couplet "Had sex with the corpse before I left her / And drew my name on the wall like Helter Skelter") and Bushwick Bill's personal statement of purpose, "Size Ain't Shit" ("First of all I laugh / Then what? / Smack their ass like a goddamned car crash"). One cannot rationalize this stuff, but there's no need to. What gives the album its power is that there is no way to make peace with this music. If you've grown up wanting music to express the most extreme feelings and ideas possible, these records go a long way toward fulfilling that goal.

The cover of **We Can't Be Stopped** features a grisly 1991 snapshot of Bushwick Bill on a hospital gurney after having been shot in the eye (which he lost as a result) by a girlfriend he begged to kill him. (That he's got a cell phone to his ear only ups the absurd horror of the situation.) Despite that graphic harshness, **We Can't Be Stopped** is actually a more introspective album. With DJ Ready Red gone, John Bido emerges as producer, and his sampling digs into soul music rather than the harder, rock-oriented bites of the band's past. Only two of the tracks are ensemble pieces; the rest are solo vamps. With an Isaac Hayes sample downbeat enough to indicate all the nights of drugging and running were finally catching up with them, "Mind Playing Tricks on Me" became a hit. "Gota Let Your Nuts Hang," however, is classic GB, with Scarface recommending lower cocaine prices as a way to bring peace to the 'hood. **Uncut Dope** is a compilation.

Till Death Do Us Part, like most hip-hop albums of the era, was influenced by Dr. Dre's **The Chronic** (on which Bushwick guested). With Willie D gone, the record introduces Big Mike (previously of Convicts), whose smoother rap style mixes with the sort of subtle keyboard shadings that would have been unthinkable just a few records back. Bushwick's raps are particularly flat, while Scarface maintains on cuts like "G.E.T.O." and "It Ain't Shit." Though the mock-newspaper album cover suggests they've succumbed to self-parody, it's been pretty clear from the beginning Geto Boys are firmly aware of what their group stands for—or, rather, stood for. At that point, amidst a flurry of solo activity, Geto Boys called it a day, having spread enough bad faith and ill vibes to finally rest in peace.

The array of solo releases show mixed results, only occasionally achieving the sort of brilliance expected from Geto Boys proper. First up was Willie Dee, whose tedious **Controversy** (recorded with the **Making Trouble** lineup) is filled with dull misogynist rants like "Bald Headed Hoes," "Welfare Bitch" and "I Need Some Pussy" (not to mention the "political" missive "Fuck the KKK"). The album is most notable for featuring "Do It Like a G.O.," a song that gets a far superior treatment on the second Geto Boys album.

I'm Goin' Out Like a Soldier musters even less punch as the music loops into infinity without ever reaching any sort of catharsis. Not only do Willie's raps have little entertainment value and a confused point of view, his diction is incredibly shoddy, full of unintelligible mumbling. By the time of **Play Witcha Mama,** he'd given up being angry and decided to appeal to the ladies with an older, more "mature" sound. The title track is a duet with Ice Cube.

Scarface is the real surprise. As effective as his work in the band was, he's even angrier when he gets to hog the mic. **Mr. Scarface Is Back** substitutes humor for horror, and sprinkles liberal amounts of blowhard self-aggrandizement. He's up to the task sample-wise as well: "Your Ass Got Took" brings Robin Trower to the gangsta world. **The World Is Yours** isn't quite so exciting. His music hasn't got any clear vision here; only "Comin' Agg" and "I'm Black," an effective song about police harassment, pack any true bite. **The Diary** is equally jumbled. The production (more of it Scarface's own work than ever) is more radio-friendly and features a thoroughly unsuccessful update ("Mind Playin' Tricks 94") and a duet with Ice Cube on "Hand of the Dead Body." "I Seen a Man Die," however, is an undeniably gripping account of just that. Broadening his success, Scarface contributed the title track to *The Walking Dead* and also did a track ("Friday Night") for Ice Cube's movie, *Friday.*

Bushwick Bill entered the solo arena a bit late. "Ever So Clear," the centerpiece of **Little Big Man,** alludes to the reason why, as it recounts how he got shot. His short-guy complex is in full force throughout the album and seems a bit sad for it. It isn't until **Phantom of the Rapra** that Bushwick puts it all together. He begins the album with a dull explanation of how rap is like street opera ("Phantom's Theme"), but is quick to drop the conceit and get down with ominous grooves and paranoiac ranting. While "Wha Cha Gonna Do?" and "Ex-Girlfriend" are unrepentant, full-force braggadocio, "Only God Knows" openly admits that underneath all the boasting resides a man who confronts his mortality every day. On the album's second half, Bushwick's sound echoes that of Dr. Dre and Ice Cube's "Natural Born Killaz." It's effective stuff and not so easily dismissed.

Big Mike's own album is smooth rap; as for Convicts, only diehards need apply.

In early '96, Bushwick Bill, Scarface and Willie D. reunited for **The Resurrection,** a slickly produced but characteristic album that isn't as big a cultural event as the participants—whose divergent styles don't really blend at all here—might hope it to be. War's "The World Is a Ghetto" provides the basis for one of the most entertaining tracks; the luxurious soul-grooving "Geto Fantasy," Bill's sardonic "I Just Wanna Die" and the funky "Still" cover familiar ground. [roc]

GHOSTFACE KILLAH

See *Wu-Tang Clan.*

GIANT MUMS

See *Airlines.*

GIANT SAND

Valley of Rain (Enigma) 1985
Ballad of a Thin Line Man (UK Zippo) 1986
Storm (What Goes On) 1988
The Love Songs (Homestead) 1988
Long Stem Rant (Homestead) 1989
Giant Songs: The Best of Giant Sand (UK Demon) 1989
Giant Sandwich (Homestead) 1989
Swerve (Amazing Black Sand) 1990 (Amazing Black Sand/Restless) 1993
Ramp (Amazing Black Sand) 1992 (Amazing Black Sand/Restless) 1993
Center of the Universe (Ger. Amazing Black Sand/Brake Out) 1992 (Amazing Black Sand/Restless) 1993
Purge & Slouch (Amazing Black Sand/Restless) 1993
Stromausfall (Ger. Return to Sender/Normal) 1993
Glum (Imago) 1994
Giant Songs Two: The Best of Giant Sand Volume Two (UK Demon) 1995
Backyard Barbecue Broadcast (Koch) 1995

BAND OF BLACKY RANCHETTE

The Band of Blacky Ranchette (Fr. New Rose) 1985
Heartland (UK Zippo) 1986
Sage Advice (UK Demon) 1990 (Amazing Black Sand/Restless) 1993

HOWE GELB

Dreaded Brown Recluse (Ger. Amazing Black Sand/Houses in Motion) 1991 (Amazing Black Sand/Restless) 1993

SPOKE

Spoke (Ger. Hausmusik) 1996

There are few bands extant today that approach music with the utter guilelessness of Giant Sand. Not to imply that the Tucson-based trio ever lapses into savantry—the members know exactly what they're doing—but under the direction of singer/guitarist Howe Gelb, Giant Sand espouses a play-free-or-die aesthetic that straddles hippiedom and punk (which, aside from the clothes, aren't all that different when you come right down to it). At times, the band variously resembles a roadhouse incarnation of Sun Ra's Arkestra or a rudimentary Grateful Dead, but whatever the mood, there's an implicit guarantee of astral projection in everything Giant Sand does.

After a brief stint in New York, where he led an unrelated combo called Giant Sandworms (which released one EP, **Will Wallow and Roam After the Ruin**), the Pennsylvania-born Gelb moved to the more sympathetic environs of Tucson, Arizona, where his cosmic cowboy wanderings adapted magnificently. Augmented by bassist Scott Garber and two drummers (playing on different cuts), Gelb recorded **Valley of Rain,** as thorny an outcropping of southwestern ambience as anything this side of Townes Van Zandt. Gelb manages to integrate elements from the western side of C&W without sounding condescending—particularly since his animated vocals always resonate, but never twang unnecessarily. Green on Red's Chris Cacavas adds piano to one song.

Ballad of a Thin Line Man brought singer/guitarist Paula Jean Brown (who had served a short tenure as Jane Wiedlin's replacement in the Go-Go's) into the fold. Her rich harmonies add considerable emotion to the acoustic songs, while Gelb shines on the ringing, Neil Young–inspired rockers. Guests on the LP include Falling James (Leaving Trains), who co-wrote and sings "Last Legs," a smoky piano ballad with an atmospheric '30s feel.

The crisp production on **Storm** plays up Gelb's wiry, minimal guitar, an invigorating contrast in we-gotta-get-outta-this-place plaints like "Town With Little or No Pity" and "Town Where No Town Belongs." A distinctive and invigorating album. The fractious scat-singing of "Almost the Politician's Wife" and the shambling beatnik prose of "Fingernail Moon, Barracuda and Me" are about the only streams-of-outré-consciousness to trickle over the sides of **The Love Songs**' solid, Band-like dam of chunky riffs and churning organ. The restraint only intensifies the wallop packed by Gelb's lyrics. On the down side, a misguided Teutonic cover of Leiber and Stoller's "Is That All There Is?" suggests that Gelb has spent entirely too much time in Europe.

Long Stem Rant finds both its greatest strength (a contagious, breathless spontaneity) and its greatest weakness (a surfeit of tangled loose ends) in the circumstances of its creation—a sleepless, cathartic one-weekend spurt of near-total improv that followed hot on the heels of Gelb and Brown's divorce. That helps account for the raw emotion that pours from Gelb on "Loving Cup," but the electric intensity that he and drummer John Convertino (the entire band here) generate can only be traced to more supernatural sources.

Swerve mates the best elements of the previous two releases, tempering **Long Stem Rant**'s scalding emotionalism with more strictly implemented structure. There's a blurry, almost numb feel to the matter-of-fact fatalism of "Can't Find Love" and the mumbling "Sisters & Brothers"; the mercurial jamfests appear to have been hacked from a single piece of rough cloth. The cover of Dylan's "Every Grain of Sand" features backing by Poi Dog Pondering; other guests include Juliana Hatfield, Falling James, Steve Wynn and Chris Cacavas.

With **Ramp,** Gelb seems to have found a way to propel himself at will into a deconstruction zone where boogie can mutate into pre-rock vocal harmony ("Warm Storm") and Sun Ra can be construed as a lounge lizard (the slurry "Jazzer Snipe"). The band takes a more aggressive tack than it has for a long while, with the volume turned up past bedtime levels for most of the set—and clear into call-the-cops territory on the gnarled "Romance of Falling," with counterpoint vocals by Victoria Williams. Lovers of polar opposites should relish the touching version of "Welcome to My World" by septuagenarian spiritual adviser Pappy Allen, a desert denizen who offered much aid and comfort to the band. The heads-down rockism of the loud'n'proud **Center of the Universe** is clearly descended from Crazy Horse, particularly when Convertino and bassist Joey Burns lock into a groove as primordial as the one that propels the harsh "Seeded (Tween Bone and Bark)." Gelb doles out more guitar freakouts than he has in some time, with uniformly cranium-expanding results—most notably on the harrowing "Loretta and the Insect World." But for the most part, he eschews indulgent side trips and works them into reasonably structured rock songs, ranging from the Quicksilver-styled "Year of the Dog" to the frothy Cal-pop of "Milkshake Girl." A wise idea indeed.

The same can't be said of **Purge & Slouch,** a collection of songs and (mostly) fragments that practically has "contractual obligation fulfilled" stamped on its cover. Much jam-session tomfoolery ensues, with the sole reward being a chance to hear Arizona legend Al Perry scrabble out some proto-garage licks on "Slander." Gelb certainly has some ability as a johnny-on-the-spot improviser, but formless pieces like "Santana, Castanada & You" don't show it off. The album is almost saved by the presence of the dispirited, incontestably brilliant "Elevator Music," which chronicles thirty-plus years of rock de-evolution with such precision that it deserves an exhibit all its own if anyone gets around to opening a parallel-universe Anti–Rock'n'Roll Hall of Fame. The live, limited-edition **Stromausfall** was sold by mail-order only.

The murmured, tentative tones of **Glum** befit the album's title. Part of the moodiness can no doubt be blamed on the enervating experience of major-label linkage (and partly on the death of Allen, who closes the album with a tear-jerking rendition of "I'm So Lonesome I Could Cry"). Gelb's quietly shamanistic attributes manifest themselves to best effect on the mercurial title track and the uncommonly confrontational "Yer Ropes" (which is veined with slide guitar, courtesy Peter Holsapple), but his unilateral rejection of form can get a bit tiring, especially when the meandering "Frontage Rd." runs smack into the stoner fusion of "1Helvakowboy Song." Live, some of these antics can be enthralling; on record, the feeling is more like being three hours into your pal's drunken revelry after you've agreed to be the designated driver. **Backyard Barbecue Broadcast** (aka **BBQ**), culled from a pair of live radio broadcasts, remedies that situation: the down-home, mostly acoustic performances, while marked by the same waywardness, practically resound with giddiness (notably the twenty-two-minute "BBQ Suite," which fuses five of the band's live staples into a Dead-like trance-mission). Sometime member Bill Elm (who also plays in Friends of Dean Martinez) adds a decidedly back-porch feel with judiciously underplayed steel guitar.

Folks wanting to test these, er, waters can dip into two equally worthy pools. **Giant Songs** draws pretty evenly from the first four Giant Sand discs, adding three tracks from Blacky Ranchette's **Heartland.** The **Giant Sandwich** CD is a particularly good choice, as it nearly doubles the LP's number of what Gelb's notes call "shy" (read: hard-to-find) songs and steps rather confidently forward with some previously unheard material, like the very early "Artists." Without overlapping **Giant Songs** at all, **Giant Songs Two** compiles tracks from all the proper albums, **Valley of Rain** through **Swerve,** including **Heartland** and **Sage Advice.**

The Band of Blacky Ranchette is a parallel Gelb outfit in which he indulges a passion for Hank Williams and Jimmie Rodgers. Though seldom unauthentic (Gelb's Appalachian roots break the soil of every track), Blacky's eponymous bow is only marginally distinct from Giant Sand. Covers of Willie Dixon's "Evil" (with manic slide guitar sawing by Rainer Ptacek) and Neil Young's "Revolution Blues" diverge only in Gelb's drawling delivery. **Heartland** is more unusual—only the angst-ridden "Roof's on Fire" is the least bit Sand-y—and emphasizes the western facet in its high lonesome duskiness. Gelb's weary, weathered croon gives an empathetic kick to the wistful title track and "Moon Over Memphis"; he proves himself a solid roadhouse piano player as well.

Recorded piecemeal over several sessions in '89 and '90, **Sage Advice** further westernizes the sound—a rending version of Waylon Jennings' "Trouble Man" underscores the outlaw feel—by generously slathering Gelb's spooky desert ballads with Dobro and pedal steel. Blacky sneaks back onto Sand territory again, as well—reinventing **Long Stem Rant**'s "Loving Cup" as a western swing two-step and again, retitled "Blanket of Stars," as a mournful, Williams-esque croon.

Many of the fifteen songs on Gelb's **Dreaded Brown Recluse** can be found—albeit in radically different form—on Giant Sand albums, but digressions like the acoustic (but still dissonant) treatment of "Loretta & the Insect World" are pleasant in a manner familiar to anyone who has ever pored over sketchbooks by a favorite artist. Gelb also revisits some older favorites to good effect (especially the epic "Bible Black, Book II"). He may come across as purposefully obscure—or even downright dotty at times—but there's no disputing the genuine, life-affirming spirit Howe Gelb brings to his music. Long may he rant.

Spoke is a side project of Burns and Convertino, who also moonlighted together in Friends of Dean Martinez until mid-'96, when they departed that instrumental organization (which has since continued on without them) and formed yet another group, Calexico. [dss]

See also *Friends of Dean Martinez, Nothing Painted Blue; TPRG.*

GIBSON BROS

Build a Raft [tape] (Old Age) 1986
Big Pine Boogie (OKra) 1988 (Homestead) 1988
Dedicated Fool (Homestead) 1989
The Man Who Loved Couch Dancing (Homestead) 1991
Memphis Sol Today! (Sympathy for the Record Industry) 1993

BASSHOLES

Blue Roots (In the Red) 1992
Haunted Hill (In the Red) 1994

GIBSON BROS/WORKDOGS

Punk Rock Truck Drivin' Song of a Gun (Homestead) 1990

WORKDOGS

Roberta (OKra) 1988 (Sympathy for the Record Industry) 1994
Workdogs in Hell (Sympathy for the Record Industry) 1993
Old (Sympathy for the Record Industry) 1994

The Gibson Bros came howling out of Columbus, Ohio, with a reckless, feckless brand of semi-competent minimalist American roots revisionism, twisting blues, hillbilly and gospel gems—as well as their own already bent tunes—into dementedly passionate, loosely played music that never stooped to gimmicks or camp. **Build a Raft, Big Pine Boogie** and the more forceful and rocking **Dedicated Fool** all capture the band banging away with primitive, hit-and-miss passion. After that, however, the quartet splintered, with guitarist (and OKra Records founder) Dan Dow and drummer Ellen Hoover leaving singer/guitarists Jeff Evans and Don Howland (ex–Great Plains) to carry on the family name.

The Man Who Loved Couch Dancing finds Evans and Howland exploring some unlikely new approaches while maintaining the Gibson Bros' tradition of good-natured obnoxiousness. The first half consists of home recordings made with Memphis guitarist Brent Stokesberry and drummer Ross Johnson, punctuated with a wacky assortment of samples and spoken-word tomfoolery; the music is even more casual than usual but has its moments. Side Two consists of sporadically absorbing live tracks recorded by a short-lived foursome with Pussy Galore/Boss Hog twins Jon Spencer (guitar) and Cristina Martinez (drums).

Howland and Evans (who'd moved to Memphis in 1990) recorded the enjoyable if only sporadically inspired **Memphis Sol Today!** at the legendary Sun studio. In contrast to the authentically unhinged **The Man Who Loved Couch Dancing,** it's a relatively straightforward—and, by Gibsons standards, well-recorded—session concentrating largely on the band's demented idea of rockabilly, with Evans and Howland joined by Jon Spencer (guitar, vocals and organ) and drummer Rich Lillash. **Couch Dancing** drummer Ross Johnson drops by to sing his own "Naked Party."

Evans and Howland subsequently parted ways. The former convened '68 Comeback, a five-piece with Peggy O'Neill of the Gories on drums, and set about releasing a burbling stream of lo-fi/all-fun singles. ("Willie and the Hand Jive" b/w "16 Tons," billed importantly as **Great Million Sellers Volume 1,** is typical.) Howland, meanwhile, formed the Bassholes.

The last stand of the original Gibson Bros lineup was on 1990's **Punk Rock Truck Drivin' Song of a Gun,** a casually well-executed collaboration with kindred spirits Workdogs, the New York duo of bassist/singer Rob Kennedy and drummer Scott Jarvis (who'd previously worked on their own and with Half Japanese, the Velvet Monkeys, Tav Falco's Panther Burns and Purple Geezus), whose rhythmic skills manage to make the Gibsons sound almost professional for the first (and only) time in their existence.

Left to their own devices, the Workdogs—importing a colorful assortment of guests—play a largely improvised, uncategorizably peculiar style of mutant gutter-roots music, anchored to a solid clock. Along with its epic title suite, a desolate sixteen-and-a-half-minute murder ballad, **Roberta** has such lighthearted shorter tracks as the ironically jaunty "Rob K's Money Crazy Boogie" and the unlikely feminist anthem "A Woman Is More Than a Box We Come In."

The self-described "blues opera" **Workdogs in Hell,** which comes complete with liner notes proclaiming the band's supposed demise, is actually an entertaining pastiche for which Kennedy and Jarvis invited an array of musician friends (including Moe Tucker, Jad Fair, Jim Foetus, Lydia Lunch and Jeff Evans) to mail in vocal and instrumental contributions, which the twosome then added to their formidable rhythm tracks.

The result is surprisingly cohesive, a nightmarish journey through all manner of sin and degradation, culminating in a wholly appropriate rendition of the Louvin Brothers' "Satan Is Real."

Without a central conceptual gimmick to hang its greasy hat on, **Old** is the Workdogs' most conventional and accessible effort to date. Despite its title, the album (with Jon Spencer, Railroad Jerk's Marcellus Hall and Chrome Cranks' Jerry Teel among its guest guitarists) is an ironically upbeat effort that balances the darker implications of songs like "Back in the Days," "Painting the Devil's Office Again" and "Robert Kennedy Blues" with a playfully humorous edge. [ss]

See also *Gories; TPRG.*

GIGOLO AUNTS

Everybody Happy (Coyote) 1988
Tales From the Vinegar Side (Sp. Impossible) 1990
Gigolo Aunts EP (UK Fire) 1992
Gun EP (UK Fire) 1993
Full-On Bloom EP (Alias) 1993
Flippin' Out (Summerville/Fire/RCA) 1994
Where I Find My Heaven EP (UK Fire) 1995

Fresh-faced power-poppers raised on Cheap Trick, the Raspberries, Kiss and new wave in upstate Potsdam, New York, the four Gigolo Aunts (named for a Syd Barrett song by singer/guitarist Dave Gibbs' *father*) relocated to Boston, made a sprightly but wimpy and amateurish debut album (different from the rare Spanish **Tales From the Vinegar Side**) and then faded back into the New England club scene. Gibbs resurfaced as Velvet Crush's second guitarist in the early '90s, but returned full-time to his own group as its career began heating up abroad.

The smart and surging '92 British EP (a four-songer built around "Bloom" and "Cope," previously self-released as a domestic single) displays a much tougher and more confident pop-rock sound than the first LP. While the ebulliently catchy hooks and stirring harmony vocals hark back shamelessly to the '60s, Phil Hurley's guitar tempests and Paul Brouwer's hyperactive drumming give the songs stylistic currency. The **Gun** EP added another essential number (the sardonic title track) to the slowly expanding canon and furthered the sense (in Britain, at least) that the Aunts were an American answer to Teenage Fanclub. It didn't hurt that the bands shared a UK label, or that the group had made "Serious Drugs," a song by the Fanclub-family BMX Bandits, a live staple.

The transatlantic release hopscotch continued when California's Alias label remixed "Bloom," adding two B-sides from the **Gun** EP, one from **Gigolo Aunts,** a dreamy studio recording of "Serious Drugs" and the instrumental "Little Carl" to create **Full-On Bloom,** something of a premature greatest hits. But even that evidently wasn't enough use for the lead song, which appears yet again (along with "Cope" and "Gun") on **Flippin' Out.** Compared to the smoothly produced fizz that charges the exemplary Byrdsy "Where I Find My Heaven" (another fine original)—and such fair new tunes as "Lullaby," "Mrs. Washington" and "Pin Cushion"—the two-year-old tracks sound weakly underproduced and more than a wee bit tired.

Adding to the discographical overlap, "Where I Find My Heaven" was borrowed from the album for the **Dumb and Dumber** soundtrack, then used—along with two lesser **Flippin' Out** songs and "Serious Drugs"—as the title track of a British EP. Time for some new tunes, guys. [i]

BRUCE GILBERT

See *Wire.*

JIMMIE DALE GILMORE

Fair and Square (Hightone) 1988
Jimmie Dale Gilmore (Hightone) 1989
After Awhile (Elektra Nonesuch) 1991
Spinning Around the Sun (Elektra) 1993
Braver Newer World (Elektra) 1996

JIMMIE DALE GILMORE/BUTCH HANCOCK

Two Roads–Live in Australia (Aus. Virgin) 1990

FLATLANDERS

More a Legend Than a Band (Plantation) 1972 (UK Charly) 1980 (Rounder) 1990

MUDHONEY/JIMMIE DALE GILMORE

Mudhoney/Jimmie Dale Gilmore EP (Sub Pop) 1994

Long before the various capitals of alternarock chic were being anointed throughout the '80s and '90s (Athens, Seattle, Chicago, Raleigh, San Diego, ad nauseum), Lubbock, Texas, was home to some of the strangest records and most idiosyncratic individualists in music. Exhibit A is **The Flatlanders,** a collaboration of Lubbock's Holy Trinity—Jimmie Dale Gilmore, Joe Ely and Butch Hancock—that still sounds weird more than two decades after its release (on 8-track cartridge no less; the reissues are in more accessible formats). Gilmore's tremulous tenor duels a musical saw for space at the top of the mix, and the whole affair has an eerie, otherworldly vibe that sends chills. Opening with "Dallas," his classic tale of alienation at twenty thousand feet, Gilmore redefined the high-and-lonesome vocabulary of Hank Williams.

While Nashville wanted nothing to do with this warped brand of country (which also incorporated a good portion of blues, bluegrass, folk and even rock), the punk and new-music scenes eventually picked up on the Flatlanders' iconoclastic artistry. Ely was the first to be adopted, as he toured and recorded with the Clash. More than a decade later, Hancock picked up the Health and Happiness Show as a backing band (with Richard Lloyd on guitar); Gilmore cut a Sub Pop EP with Mudhoney.

While Ely and Hancock recorded and performed steadily through the '70s and '80s, Gilmore dropped out of music to study metaphysics and meditation, and was not heard from again until 1988. Surrounded by his Austin-by-way-of-Lubbock gang (including Ely as producer), his solo debut, **Fair and Square,** is a warm, relatively brisk and surprisingly traditional comeback. A superb but far from prolific songwriter, Gilmore includes only two of his own songs, while running through a who's who of post-modern Texas country tunesmiths, including Townes Van Zandt's "White Freight Liner Blues," Ely's "Honky Tonk Masquerade" and David Halley's stunning "Rain Just Falls."

With slightly greater emphasis on originals, **Jimmie Dale Gilmore** revisits roughly the same terrain, in a similarly neo-traditional setting anchored by Lloyd Maines' pedal steel guitar. Besides a remake of "Dallas," the other key performance is the singer's "Deep Eddy Blues," a two-step in which the beauty of the performance cannot mask the devastation unfolding in the lyric.

It wasn't until **After Awhile,** however, that Gilmore's unique style became fully apparent. For the first time, the breadth of his writing is on display; while "Tonight I Think I'm Gonna Go Downtown," "Treat Me Like a Saturday Night" and "Midnight Train" are clearly rooted in honkytonk, folk and blues—and the singer's voice steeped in mountain balladry—he guides these traditions into terrain more closely associated with Leonard Cohen, Stephen Sondheim and Bob Dylan. For all the high-minded aspirations in the music, Gilmore never turns into a cosmic cowboy; not for nothing is he fond of quoting Ezra Pound's maxim that "The poem fails when it strays too far from the song and the song fails when it strays too far from the dance." The music on **After Awhile** embodies that synergy between heart, intellect and groove.

With **Spinning Around the Sun,** Gilmore's skills as an interpreter are given a broader context than on the Hightone discs. Gilmore treats the American songbook as a continuum, blurring the boundaries between country, blues, soul and rock'n'roll with the effortlessness of some of the 1950s pioneers: Presley, Cash, Lewis. Gilmore is no match for the early Elvis—his cover of "I Was the One" is the sole disappointment—but his dirge-tempo version of Hank Williams' "I'm So Lonesome I Could Cry" does the master justice. And his readings of contributions from his West Texas pals, including Al Strehli, ex-wife Jo Carol Pierce and Hancock, are definitive—particularly Butch's "Just a Wave."

Two Roads catches two old pals teaming up for an acoustic career retrospective while on a tour of Australia. Hancock's craggy no-nonsense croak is offset by Gilmore's soaring warble, and the material is mostly first-rate Hancock, a treasure chest of metaphysical longing and introspection.

The aptly titled **Braver Newer World** completely severs whatever tenuous ties Gilmore had left to the world of country music. Producer T-Bone Burnett inventively frames the singer's singular voice in a richly atmospheric mix, with a potpourri of percussion, pedal-steel drones, Vox organ, lowing horns and chunky baritone guitar. Even as the disc veers across a century of music, from the spectral longing of Portishead (suggested in a cover of singer Sam Phillips' "Where Is Love") to the raw sexuality of Blind Lemon Jefferson ("Black Snake Moan"), Gilmore sounds utterly in control, both relaxed and urgent. Just as Los Lobos' **Kiko** and PJ Harvey's **To Bring You My Love** embrace both experimentation and tradition, **Braver Newer World** perfects Gilmore's career-long synthesis of the two impulses. [gk]

See also *Mudhoney.*

GIN BLOSSOMS

Dusted (San Jacinto) 1989
Up and Crumbling EP (A&M) 1991
New Miserable Experience (A&M) 1992
Congratulations I'm Sorry (A&M) 1996

Fate's cruel taste for the irony of artistic success and personal failure, of abject misery arising from commercial triumph, found an easy target in Arizona guitarist/songwriter Doug Hopkins. On December 4, 1993, Hopkins shot himself into the rock'n'roll graveyard, an alcoholic depressive no longer able to watch the band he built—and had already been thrown out of—break big with two of his misleadingly chipper songs of pain and guilt.

The distinctive ingredient and tortured soul of a skilled but otherwise whitebread modern pop group taking cues from early R.E.M. (Byrdsy harmonies and chiming guitars), Tom Petty (Beatlish melodies and measured rock rhythms), the Smithereens (sizzling guitars and potent hooks) and Gram Parsons (that old faux-country twang), Hopkins brought the conviction and reality to make the Gin Blossoms something special. Unfortunately, that reality was a bleak, sardonic, self-lacerating desperation, which the Tempe quintet turned into deceptively upbeat pop. (Presumably with his approval: Hopkins was sacked after the album's completion, replaced by guitarist Scott Johnson. Although he did not contribute to **New Miserable Experience,** Johnson was listed on it as a bandmember.)

The deeply conflicted **New Miserable Experience** (released twice by A&M with entirely different CD booklets and labels) is an energetic, tuneful and resonant pop album wrongly—to its benefit and detriment—tagged as "alternative." When Hopkins isn't kicking himself for being such a fuckup ("If you don't expect too much from me / You might not be let down," he offers in the hard-to-shake "Hey Jealousy"), he either lashes out (in "Found Out About You") or shrugs it off: "Cheatin'," a country honk co-written by guitarist Jesse Valenzuela, takes the low road with the claim that "You can't call it cheatin' cause she reminds me of you." Meanwhile, Valenzuela's own tunes offer lightweight disappointments ("Cajun Song") and guarded optimism ("Mrs. Rita," "Hands Are Tied"), while singer Robin Wilson keeps his hopes high ("Allison Road"). Taken as a finished artifact, the record is a tequila sunrise laced with battery acid; heard as the soap opera it must have been to make, Hopkins' despondency cries out all alone, an alien wavelength channeled blithely by Wilson as if he didn't quite comprehend the lyrics.

The locally released **Dusted** contains renditions—casually produced, carelessly sung but similarly arranged, if dispatched at hotfoot velocity—of four tunes ("Cajun Song," "Hey Jealousy," "Found Out About You" and "Lost Horizons," another abject Hopkins drinking song) that found their way onto **New Miserable Experience.** (Two others—"Angels Tonight" and the pointedly personal "Keli Richards," which contains a morbidly foreboding gun reference—joined "Mrs. Rita" and "Allison Road" on the five-track **Up and Crumbling** EP.) Otherwise, "I Can Sleep" is a nifty harmony demonstration, but the tunes that never made it off **Dusted** are mainly Gin Blossoms average, and earned their obscurity.

In the fall of '95, "Til I Hear It From You," a song composed with Marshall Crenshaw for the soundtrack of the loved-the-album-was-there-also-a-film? *Empire Records,* became a hit single. The song doesn't appear on **Congratulations I'm Sorry,** which sounds enough like the Gin Blossoms ("Follow You Down," "My Car," "Not Only Numb") to satisfy expectations while adding nothing new to what was once an artistically promising career. Marbled with oblique references to the past (in a nice touch, the long-time-coming album fades in slowly, as if returning to life in the studio) and careful not to be too happy, the record ably relaunches the Gin Blossoms as a reliable pop commodity, coloring joy with an abiding sense of loss. [i]

M. GIRA

See *Swans.*

GIRLS AGAINST BOYS

Nineties vs. Eighties EP (Adult Swim) 1992
Tropic of Scorpio (Adult Swim) 1992
Venus Luxure No. 1 Baby (Touch and Go) 1993
Sexy Sam/I'm From France EP (Touch and Go) 1994
Cruise Yourself (Touch and Go) 1994
House of GVSB (Touch and-Go) 1996

NEW WET KOJAK

New Wet Kojak (Touch and Go) 1995

Girls Against Boys began as a studio lark for keyboardist Eli Janney (now also a busy record producer) and Fugazi drummer Brendan Canty, both regulars on the Washington, DC, punk scene. They were joined by Scott McCloud, singer/guitarist in the city's Soulside, for the industrial disco that would make up the "Eighties" portion of **Nineties vs. Eighties.** With the arrival of two more Soulsiders—Johnny Temple joining on bass and Alexis Fleisig replacing Canty—the second half of the six-song EP paints a more accurate portrait of the newly christened Girls Against Boys' future direction. On "Jamie" and "Kitty-yo," the more straightforward punk aggression is cut with a dose of sleaze, as McCloud's voice flirts with a decadent croon.

Tropic of Scorpio expands the lounge-singer-on-'ludes motif with the fluttering trumpet and jazzy atmospherics of "Everything I Do Seems to Cost Me $20" and "Everywhere I Go I Seem to Spend $20," but also rocks savagely on "Wow Wow Wow," staggers drunkenly on "Wasting Away" and pushes the distortion envelope on "Plush."

Venus Luxure No. 1 Baby is where all the flailing around starts to gel. The spin-cycle churn of Fleisig's drums, augmented by the grind of twin bassists Temple and Janney (aka Mr. Silas Greene), brings to mind the electro-trance rhythms of Kraftwerk, and songs like "In Like Flynn," "Learned It" and "Bulletproof Cupid" roar straight down the Autobahn. McCloud also finds inspiration in Times Square squalor (the band having relocated to New York City) in the eerie "Get Down" and "Satin Down," which pleads, "Taint your everything / Taint my everything."

In its CD configuration, the inter-album single of "Sexy Sam" and "I'm From France" also contains four tracks "lifted" from the three preceding releases.

McCloud's bleary nightcrawler persona becomes a shtick on **Cruise Yourself,** as he pays homage to "My Martini," snickers, "I'd invite you all back for a drink at my place, but I don't got a place," and advises "Kill the singer" on "Kill the Sexplayer." The singer's not the problem, though, it's the songs. The rockers sound tepid next to the **Venus** juggernaut, and the decadence card is overplayed on the more atmospheric tunes.

The creepiness on **House of GVSB** sounds earned instead of put-on, in large part because the twin-bass attack is so ferocious, the grooves full of such menace—especially on the pummeling funk of "Disco Six Six Six" and the white-noise boogie of "TheKindaMzkYouLike." A handful of appropriately seedy post-punk references complements McCloud's strung-out lyrical visions, particularly the way "Vera Cruz" roughs up Soft Cell's minimalist synth-pop and "Crash 17 (X-Rated Car)" takes Joy Division for a spin 'round the disco floor.

New Wet Kojak is a side project for McCloud and Temple. Joined by a variety of DC pals, including Geoff Turner (Gray Matter) and Nathan Larson (Shudder to Think), the Kojaks explore the more atmospheric outer edge of the GVSB sound. McCloud mutters instead of sings, while dance-music and dub-reggae rhythms clatter and percolate underneath murky clouds of guitar, trumpet and keyboard. An indulgence at best. [gk]

GIRL TROUBLE

Hit It or Quit It (K/Sub-Pop) 1988
Stomp and Shout and Work It on Out!!!! (Dionysus) 1990
Thrillsphere (PopLlama Products) 1990
Girl Trouble Plays Elvis Movie Themes EP7 (Sympathy for the Record Industry) 1992
New American Shame (eMpTy) 1993
Girl Trouble (eMpTy) 1995

Had the Cramps grown up in Tacoma, Washington, at the time when the Sonics and the Wailers (not those Wailers) regularly played high-school dances, they might have become Girl Trouble. As it happened, Girl Trouble was a lounge act way before cocktail rehabilitation struck; the members met not at a high-school dance but in a Tacoma bar shaped like a coffee pot. Once the foursome had taught one another to play their instruments and began gigging, the Java Jive also provided Girl Trouble with a venue and a mascot of sorts in the person of an eightysomething go-go dancer named Granny.

Girl Trouble's full-time cast has been virtually constant throughout the band's first dozen years together: lanky singer K. P. (Kurt) Kendall (briefly replaced by Dave Duet early on), guitarist Bill "Kahuna" Henderson, his sister/drummer Bon Henderson and bassist Dale Phillips. They'd been together three or four years before Olympia's K Records label finally released the band's first two singles and the initial version of **Hit It or Quit It,** thus beginning Girl Trouble's odyssey through northwestern indie labels. (The band also releases singles on its own Wigout label, published the *Wig Out!* fanzine and has contributed tracks to a frightening array of compilations.)

As is often the case with garage bands, Girl Trouble records don't vary widely one from another, although some have a thematic bent. **Stomp and Shout and Work It on Out!!!!** is a collection of covers meant as an homage to their Northwest predecessors; **Girl Trouble Plays Elvis Movie Themes** is a double 7-inch of movie themes from the first E-male, notably "Girls, Girls, Girls."

Produced by Steve Fisk, **Thrillsphere** is the band's most effective attempt at capturing its ramshackle joy in a studio. **New American Shame** presents such stare-at-the-wall quandaries as the winsome "How Can I Be Out When I Ain't Been In" and "To Tame a Woman" ("You had better be tough / Cause she'll look in your good eye / And she'll call your bluff"). **Girl Trouble** is a live album. [ga]

GITS

Frenching the Bully (C/Z) 1992
Enter: The Conquering Chicken (C/Z) 1994

DANCING FRENCH LIBERALS OF '48

Scream Clown Scream EP (Broken Rekids/Revenge) 1994
Powerline (Broken Rekids/Revenge) 1995

VARIOUS ARTISTS

Home Alive: The Art of Self Defense (Epic) 1996

Reaction to death in the rock world is often glib (if well-articulated), but the 1993 murder of Gits vocalist Mia Zapata brought Seattle's underground community together in a shared sense of tragedy, fear, sadness, horror and anger. (As of late '96, Zapata's killer has not been identified or arrested.) Zapata was special, and those lucky enough to have seen the Gits live can testify to the vocalist's gritty, raucous performances. With her ragged vocals, Zapata sounded like a punk Janis Joplin, spitting soulful tales of desperation, hard living, drinking and pain.

Frenching the Bully bears out her spirit and charisma. The music is basic, punchy and jagged—part hardcore, part hooks, all heart—and Zapata is searing and powerful. "Another Shot of Whiskey," "Second Skin," "Absynthe," "Insecurities" and "Kings and Queens" rock fiercely, but the more dynamic and darkly sultry "It All Dies Anyway" might be the record's best track.

The posthumously released **Enter: The Conquering Chicken** builds on the group's punk roots, expanding into more-developed territory on "Bob (Cousin O.)," "Guilt Within Your Head," "Seaweed," the emotional "Precious Blood" and a beautiful cover of Sam Cooke's "A Change Is Gonna Come." "Drunks," while delineating a band philosophy, is hedonistic good fun; "Beauty of the Rose" recaptures the debut's hard-hitting fury. The album was incomplete at the time of Zapata's death, so the Gits chose to flesh it out with credible filler items: her solo performance of "Social Love" and a compilation contribution, "Drinking Song," which poignantly functions as a farewell from the late singer ("So with this pint I toast to you / To all my friends—keep healthy and good").

Zapata's surviving bandmates—guitarist Andy Joe Spleen, drummer Steve Moriarty and bassist Matthew Dresdner—mounted fundraising efforts to support the criminal investigation and continued playing music together. With Spleen taking over lead vocals and guitarist Julian Gibson joining, the Gits became Dancing French Liberals of '48.

Produced by Jack Endino, **Scream Clown Scream** is a raw sloppy blast of barely premeditated punk aggression and personal turmoil. Addressing both the past and the present, the five songs are fairly captured by titles like "Scream Clown Scream," "Bottom of Our Career" and "Off the Deep End." Potent stuff.

Powerline is a healing sonic adventure, a chance for the Liberals—who audibly miss Zapata's vocals and lyrics here—to release a host of complicated emotions on one charged disc. "New Drinking Song" honors the late singer as "the Queen of Table Waters"; "Spit in Your Eye" addresses anger; "Total Seclusio" envisions a dying person's last moments. "Daily Bread" is purportedly the last song Zapata ever wrote. Despite the circumstances, there's a surprising buoyancy to **Powerline.** Joan Jett, who sings backup on "In a Past Life" (the only song remade from **Scream Clown Scream**) later joined forces with the group to tour and record as Evil Stig.

Album tracks by the Gits, Liberals and Zapata—as well as otherwise unissued contributions from Evil Stig, Pearl Jam, Nirvana, Soundgarden, 7 Year Bitch and nearly forty other artists—fill the two discs of **Home Alive,** a fundraiser arranged by and benefiting a Seattle-based organization opposing violence and abuse. The album is dedicated to Zapata, whose murder inspired the Home Alive collective into existence. [mww/i]

See also *Joan Jett.*

GLANDS OF EXTERNAL SECRETION

See *Barbara Manning.*

G. LOVE AND SPECIAL SAUCE

G. Love and Special Sauce (OKeh/Epic) 1994
Coast to Coast Motel (OKeh/Epic) 1995

The bio reads like something out of Frank Capra: a young white kid from Center City Philadelphia plays blues guitar on street corners, gets exposed to hip-hop and begins to write rambling narratives that somehow combine the earthy knowledge of the urban streets with the more timeless knowledge proffered by his heroes, blues legends like Howlin' Wolf and Blind Lemon Jefferson. G. Love (not to be confused with the rapper G Love E, who had a 1990 LP on Chrysalis) hooks up with a rhythm section from Boston; as a trio they become the first act signed to the revitalized rhythm-and-blues-oriented OKeh imprint.

Somehow, Garrett Dutton, drummer Jeffrey Clemens and string bassist Jimmy Prescott manage to form a fairly sturdy bridge between disparate worlds. The group's eponymous debut celebrates kid stuff ("Shooting Hoops," "Cold Beverage") without pandering, while introducing a trio that can slip and sway as though the musicians had been playing New Orleans after-hours joints for two decades.

That groove undergoes serious refinement on **Coast to Coast Motel,** produced by Memphis legend Jim Dickinson. Concentrating less on a hip-hop–accessible pulse and more on the blues-vamping roots, the trio establishes an easy mastery of understated rhythm and harmonic economy, aping Fats Domino one minute and Muddy Waters the next. Meanwhile, G. Love—a sketchy guitarist the first time out—demonstrates some real confidence as a guitar and harmonica soloist; he's living proof that constant touring does pay off. Dickinson keeps everything backroads simple (but does enlist the help of Rebirth Brass Band for one track); G. Love moves away from his accustomed blues shout to sing a defiant anti-oppression work song, "Chains #3," and an inclusionary folk number, "Everybody." Both are gems. [tm]

GOATS

Tricks of the Shade (Ruffhouse/Columbia) 1992
No Goats, No Glory (Ruffhouse/Columbia) 1994

A good idea for one album, the Goats became an out-of-control lesson in rap excess on the tours and album that followed it. Two of the group's three rappers—Madd and Swayzack—met while working as street vendors in Philadelphia. After trading rhymes for a while, they began to make appearances at local hiphop throwdowns, ran across white rapper OaTiekato and wound up in the offices of then-embryonic Ruffhouse Records, where producer Joe (The Butcher) Nicolo set out to capture their hard-hitting activist rap on tape.

Tricks of the Shade is a concept album, a series of liberal treatises on the welfare state stitched together with brief (and often not funny) skits involving an orphan child wandering through a carnival in search of his "Uncle Scam." Performing with a live band, the three rappers earned a reputation for haywire energy—as memorable as the punkish rant "Typical American" and the anti-racism chant "Not Not Bad" were on record, the live renditions of these songs could become funkified, George Clinton–style marathons.

Following an extended season of touring, Oatee—the Goats' most activist-minded member—left the group. The others pressed on, but downplayed the political rhetoric in favor of gangsta-style agitation. The new approach yielded a less-challenging, more run-of-the-mill sound—**No Goats, No Glory** is an all-too-familiar peek into the lives of crazy cut-up rappers, and a faint echo of earlier Goats glory. The group disbanded in 1995. [tm]

GOBBLEHOOF

GobbleHoof EP (New Alliance) 1990
Freezer Burn (New Alliance) 1992

The fact that J Mascis (Dinosaur Jr) was the drummer on GobbleHoof's six-song debut ensured a measure of fanzine-level interest for the Amherst, Massachusetts, group. However, the person who really makes **GobbleHoof** worth hearing is Charlie Nakajima (who was in the pre-Dinosaur Deep Wound with Mascis and Lou Barlow), less a singer than a dramatic speaker with a commanding presence. His credit for "narration" rather than vocals is apt. As guitarist Tim Aaron reels off competent grunge noise (complete with wah-wah and all the trimmings), Nakajima recounts his lyrics in a weary, resonant deep voice, only occasionally reaching out to catch passing melody notes.

Mascis produced the full-length **Freezer Burn,** on which the even-more-imposing-sounding Nakajima and Aaron, plus a bassist, drummer and spare axe-wielder, repeat the EP's basic formula with increased intensity and imagination. A bracing blend of ominous storytelling ("Embryo," "Sadist," the sepulchral "Shotgun"), furious singing, precise desert-storm guitar and pinpoint dynamic control (acoustic guitar finds a brief home), **Freezer Burn** opens the door to a roaring dimension that might at various times have been occupied by the Doors, Alice Cooper, David Lynch, Danzig, Nick Cave and Black Sabbath. Far less ponderous than it might seem on paper, GobbleHoof butts heads like a dark-hearted metal band, but never bludgeons its targets without good reason. [i]

See also *Dinosaur Jr.*

GOD

Breach Birth EP (UK Situation Two) 1990
Loco (Ger. Permis de Construire Deutschland) 1991
Possession (UK Venture/Virgin) 1992 (Venture/Caroline) 1992
Consumed (UK Sentrax) 1993
The Anatomy of Addiction (Big Cat) 1994
Appeal to Human Greed EP (Big Cat) 1995

TECHNO ANIMAL

Techno-Animal (Pathological/Revolver) 1991
Re-Entry (UK Virgin) 1995
Babylon Seeker EP (UK Blue Angel) 1996

ICE

Under the Skin (Pathological/Revolver) 1994

God has a face, and it looks like Kevin Martin. Although the band so named has had a fairly stable multi-member lineup, it is just one of many outlets for this British noise technician's twisted creativity. Working at a point where hardcore, experimental jazz and electronic music can be made to meet, Martin's God mines a vein similar to the likes of Scorn, Naked City, Godflesh and some of Bill Laswell's more abrasive undertakings. At one time or another, Martin has collaborated with those artists as well as Sonic Boom (Spacemen 3/Spectrum), Kevin Shields (My Bloody Valentine) and avant-garde drummer Eddie Prevost in the fittingly named Experimental Audio Research. Martin also runs the Pathological label, which has released a dozen or so equally unsettling releases, and compiled the **Ambient 4: Isolationism** and **Macro Dub Infection Volume One** albums for Virgin. (This particular God is British and is not to be confused with the more orthodox Australian outfit bearing the same name.)

After debuting in '87 with a track on Mark E. Smith's **Disparate Cognoscenti** compilation, God came forth with **Breach Birth,** a screeching, fiercely distorted deconstruction of metal that remains the most "rock" thing Martin has ever released. Sailing quickly into more experimental waters, he recruited several likeminded sonic extremists—among them members or ex-members of Henry Cow, Skullflower, A.R.Kane, AMM, Head of David, Slab and Godflesh—to form the cacophonous eleven-headed monster (with two bassists, two drummers and two saxophonists) that God has essentially been ever since. The live **Loco** (produced by Godflesh frontal lobe/God guitarist Justin Broadrick) is full of clattering percussion, thunderous basses, hyper-distorted riffs and Martin's elephant-stampede saxophone and roaring vocals. The approach on **Possession** is similar, but with almost symphonically bombastic production not unlike mid-period Swans; John Zorn guests on one track. **Consumed** is another turbulent and confrontational live outing.

The Anatomy of Addiction carries on in suitably anarchic fashion, an increasing influx of ambient and dub further adding to the planned insanity. **Appeal to Human Greed** is that album's remix collection, containing radical reshapes by such perpetrators as Laswell, Shields, Broadrick and the Lumberjacks (aka Brooklyn rappers New Kingdom).

Techno Animal finds Martin and Broadrick getting ambient well before the rest of the pack, creating profoundly unsettling atmospherics not worlds away from the soundtrack to *The Shining.* The intimidating double-CD **Re-Entry** finds them building down even further into amphetamine-addled white noise, at times employing the services of art-trumpeter Jon Hassell.

Ice is a trance-dub excursion also including Broadrick, ex-Head of David bassist Dave Cochrane and reedsman Alex Buess. [ja]

See also *Godflesh, Napalm Death, Spacemen 3.*

GODFLESH

Godflesh (UK Swordfish) 1988 (UK Earache) 1990 (Earache) 1995
Streetcleaner (UK Earache) 1989 (Earache/Combat) 1990
Slavestate (Earache/Relativity) 1991 (Earache) 1995
Pure (Earache/Relativity) 1992
Merciless EP (Earache/Columbia) 1994
Selfless (Earache/Columbia) 1994
Songs of Love and Hate (Earache) 1996

SWEET TOOTH

Soft White Underbelly EP (UK Staindrop/Earache) 1990

FINAL

One (Subharmonic) 1995

JUSTIN K. BROADRICK/ANDY HAWKINS

Skinner's Black Laboratories/Azonic (Sub Rosa/Subsonic) 1995

An ever-mutating adventure into a brutal ultraworld, Birmingham-spawned Godflesh was formed in 1988 by ex–Napalm Death guitarist Justin Broadrick (who'd just finished a stint as Head of David's drummer) and bassist G. Christian ("Benny") Green. **Godflesh** is a sonic bulldozer, its ultra-low tunings and distant, disembodied vocals (not unlike **Pornography**-era Cure) creating a bass-heavy lava flow of sound that fuses early Swans with a half-speed Sabbath. Using a numbingly precise drum machine, tornado guitar, bass from another dimension and a mind-melting array of tape loops and effects, the band projects almost no mid-range—high frequencies skitter well above the bottom-feeding throb. Heaviness raised to a singular mission.

Streetcleaner is more industrial, cluttered and even more powerful and destructive than the debut. Sounds attack from all angles (some cuts include guitarist Paul Neville, who'd played with Broadrick and Green in the pre–Napalm Death Fall of Because); seemingly unrelated elements frequently run simultaneously. But with the exception of the pulsing "Dead Head," the album jolts where its predecessor grooved.

Godflesh's next phase—incorporating a strong influence from the burgeoning techno movement—emerged on **Slavestate,** concurrent compilation tracks and bonus cuts. The debut's 1990 reissue includes two new tracks, one of which is the staggering "Wounds," a twelve-minute sci-fi shooting gallery of beats and effects so hard it hurts. The **Slavestate** mini-album (with distorted remixes and "Wound '91," the CD totals nine tracks and runs nearly an hour) catches the band thrashing onto the (dance) floor, giving **Streetcleaner**'s lurch-and-crunch the twist of a clunky rhythmic basis and winding up in a harsh and forbidding realm where Foetus might be found fronting Einstürzende Neubauten with Al Jourgensen mixing the sound.

Neville left to pursue his band, Cable Regime, full-time and was replaced on **Pure** by ex-Loop guitarist Robert Hampson. (A year earlier, Loop and Godflesh had covered each other's songs—alternately credited to Fleshloop and Loopflesh—on a split 7-inch.) Although the album is a straightforward compromise between grindcore (slow, bludgeoning riffs, shouted, raw vocals, slathering solos that neither begin nor quite end) and industrial thrash (impersonal electronic beats, endless, aimless repetition of elementary ideas, monstrous sonic density heaped on to the point of impossibility), the incongruous element is the swing of the thing. Songs like "Spite," "Mothra" and "Don't Bring Me Flowers" have a definite groove along with the rocket in the band's pocket. Other tracks (such as "Baby Blue Eyes") reshoulder a trusty jackhammer, but the standouts truly stand out. As a bonus (and further confounding those expecting one thing or another from Godflesh), the CD contains "Pure II," a twenty-minute feedback treat for ambience addicts.

Hampson's stint with the band lasted only a matter of months before he plunged full-time into Main; he was not replaced. Alone with their machines, Broadrick and Green made the thuggish, monotonous four-song **Merciless** EP—blame a lack of conceptual friction for its failings. That unlikely major-label debut paved the way for **Selfless,** reportedly inspired by the John Coltrane song of the same name (although Blue Note fans are well advised to steer clear). Institutionalizing another set of stylistic precepts—dropping the techno inclinations for slow-motion Melvins meltdown surrealism and variations on Chicago skronk ratchetry—the album shares the EP's tendency toward tedium, but doesn't succumb to it. Some tracks do devolve into thundering riff loops that are numbing in their glacial progress, but "Empyreal," the screaming "Crush My Soul," "Heartless" and the semi-restrained "Mantra" all demonstrate an incipient sense of melody and dynamics beneath all the radioactive grunge. (Following **Pure**'s plan, the CD concludes with a generous bonus: the twenty-four-minute "Go Spread Your Wings.")

Godflesh's members have indulged in a mind-boggling array of side projects; there are probably more than have reached our ears. Final is the group's ambient alter ego (released in America on Bill Laswell's Subharmonic label) and resembles Godflesh's more atmospheric album tracks. Green has played on an album by Swedish avant-jazz masters 16.17, as well as Main's **Motion Pool.** Broadrick has produced records for Terminal Power Company and Cable Regime, played remixer-for-hire (Pantera, Murder Inc. and others) and done several projects with British noise impresario Kevin Martin: touring and recording with God, recording as Techno Animal and trance dub ensemble Ice. He also works with Cochrane and drummer Scott Kiehl (aka SDK of England's Slab) in Sweet Tooth. Finally, Broadrick's solo LP contains several neo-ambient "guitar manipulations," paired with a separate album from Laswell associate Andy Hawkins. Somehow, Broadrick finds the time to run his own label, Head Dirt. [ja/i]

See also *God, Main, Napalm Death; TPRG.*

GODHEADSILO

Thee Friendship Village E.P. EP7 (Kill Rock Stars) 1993
The Scientific Supercake L.P. (Kill Rock Stars) 1994
Elephantitus of the Night (Kill Rock Stars) 1995
Skyward in Triumph (Sub Pop) 1996

Bass . . . how low can you go? The question may have been posed in the hip-hop arena, but the answer has been furnished most definitively by this monomaniacal North Dakota bass/drums (plus distorted screaming) duo. Employing outsized amplifiers and monstrously scaled kettle and bass drums—snares are strictly for lightweights—Mike and Dan create the most filling-loosening experience this side of that scrapped Go Two Rounds With Mike Tyson theme-park ride.

Following a sonically unprepossessing (and technically unsuitable) introductory blast on the 7-inch **Thee Friendship Village** four-songer, **The Scientific Supercake** does a pretty nifty job of testing, if not ravaging, the low-end response of any stereo system you'd care to try it out on. (In any case, home alone is no match for the duo's grueling live show.) Surprisingly enough, the album also reveals a sly sense of humor at play in the anti-music GodheadSilo (and producer/ex-Melvin Joe Preston) stamps into the grooves. "Songs" like "Two Peanuts Are Walking Down the Street" and "I Love U . . . nicorns" bring to mind the audio experimentations of visual artists like Kurt Schwitters—if he were a skate-punk, of course.

Elephantitus of the Night doesn't flow quite as well, largely because half of it comes from compilations and earlier singles (including all of **Friendship Village,** which gets its points across far more forcefully here). Nevertheless, the collection has its moments: "Multiple Organic" boasts a cheesy techno sheen that would do Kraftwerk proud, while the sample-loaded "Master of Balance" lopes along almost amiably. It doesn't get any lower than this.

Skyward in Triumph trades the duo's attack-dog assault for lap-dog friendliness and, surprisingly enough, makes the transition without sacrificing much of its personality. At first listen, the sound is as jarring as ever, but the shiny happy structures that reveal themselves on subsequent spins cast GodheadSilo as a pair of goofily precocious popsmiths who could pass for a (slightly) evil twin to the Spinanes. Calvin Johnson of Beat Happening sings on the title track. [dss]

GOD IS MY CO-PILOT

God Is My Co-Pilot EP (The Making of Americans) 1991
On a Wing & a Prayer EP (Funky Mushroom) 1992
I Am Not This Body (The Making of Americans) 1992
Gender Is as Gender Does EP (Funky Mushroom) 1992
How I Got Over EP (Ajax) 1992
Pissing and Hooting EP (The Making of Americans/Seze) 1993
Speed Yr Trip (The Making of Americans) 1993
When This You See Remember Me EP (Dark Beloved Cloud) 1993
Getting Out of Boring Time Biting Into Boring Pie EP10 (Quinnah) 1993
My Sinister Hidden Agenda EP (Blackout) 1993 (The Making of Americans) 1995
What Doctors Don't Tell You [tape] (Shrimper) 1993
Straight Not (Outpunk) 1993
Tight Like Fist: Live Recording (Knitting Factory Works) 1993
Sharon Quite Fancies Jo EP7 (UK Soul Static Sound) 1994
This Is No Time to Be Frail! EP7 (UK Rough Trade) 1994
How to Be (The Making of Americans) 1994
Kittybait EP (Ajax) 1994
Mir Shlufn Nisht (Japan. Avant) 1994
Sex Is for Making Babies (Fr. Les Disques du Soleil et de L'Acier) 1995
An Appeal to Reason EP (It. Runt) 1995
No Fi (The Making of Americans) 1995
Ootko Sa Poika Vai Tytto? EP (Fin. Trash Can) 1995
Puss 02 (Dark Beloved Cloud/The Making of Americans) 1995
The History of Music, Vol. 1 (Japan. Meldac) 1995
The History of Music, Vol. 2 (Japan. Meldac) 1995

At times, it seems as if this New York band exists solely to fulfill a mission from Guinness—the Book of World Records, that is. But even though God Is My Co-Pilot's record-of-the-week club shtick can grow a bit tiresome, the material—a mélange of no wave fractiousness, pan-ethnic junketeering and gay themes that incorporate both strident politics and explosive eroticism—has grown dramatically in scope over the years. Yes, GodCo can be dogmatic, but the taintless passion with which masterminds Craig Flanagin and Sharon Topper approach the creative process itself is unassailable.

On the thirty-four-song **I Am Not This Body,** Topper and Flanagin—augmented by a variety of percussionists—re-create the breathless intensity of densely packed archetypes like **Pink Flag,** but terse song lengths are hardly the whole story. The album is bursting with dizzying thematic juxtapositions—Topper can intone the gnostic gospel excerpt "Thunder, Perfect Mind" mere moments after purring the lustful fist-fucking celebration "List"—and rife with stylistic shifts that take in angular post-funk ("Angels in the Air"), back-porch country-soul ("Greasy Gizzard") and even X-styled punk ("Said & Done"). What's even more impressive is the range of references the band throws into its dada pastiches—songs are sprinkled with quotations from sources as varied as John Donne, Joseph Conrad and Little Anthony and the Imperials (whose "Shimmy Shimmy Ko Ko Bop" spins at the core of "Very Very"). A masterful, multi-layered debut.

It's worker's playtime again on **How I Got Over,** which presents six anarcho-art volleys that resemble a Mayo Thompson–run Romper Room. Figuring out exactly what the band is up to as it ricochets from neo-Sondheim incidental music to Middle Eastern jump-rope chants can be a bit like trying to divide seventeen by fire engine red, but the satisfaction elicited from the eventual solution is quite a reward all the same. **Gender Is as Gender Does** (Elliott Sharp makes a cameo on "Lonesome Elliott") is a bit more narrowcast into jazz-punk squawking, but Topper's throaty purr carries the ubiquitous libidinous subtext with the ease of a schooled porter. The fan-club-only **Pissing and Hooting** furthers both the avant-sexual and avant-noise agendas on songs like "I Hate Girls" and "Submissive," stitched together in a self-sampling frenzy.

Speed Yr Trip, on which the fixed core quintet is augmented by guests like Jad Fair and John Zorn (who blows a mean roadhouse sax on "Lo Mas Sabrosa") is no less capricious. Slithery second-line New Orleans rhythms (employed on the cutting "Anyone but You") bleed into formless noise belches ("Fat") that give way to airy Gallic melodies ("C'Etait une J. Fille"). Topper explores the lesbian libido joyfully on pieces like "They Often Look Fr.," which, like the overwhelming majority of the band's originals, was written by Flanagin, to whom she is married. Confusion *is* sex!

As evidenced by the short sharp songs that dot **When This You See Remember Me,** Flanagin's scrabbling (on guitar and bass) is hardly unschooled noise: tracks like "Jackalope Hunting" telescope bits of African high-life and Cage-ian air manipulation into fragments of utter enchantment. The snazzily packaged 10-inch EP **Getting Out of Boring Time Biting into Boring Pie** (which includes a workable cardboard model airplane) gathers fourteen blink-and-you-missed-'em stacks o' fractiousness, ranging from the heated "Starch & Chafe" to a manically splayed rendition of Thelonious Monk's "Well You Needn't." The overly dry **My Sinister Hidden Agenda** EP quickly flattens out due to a poor balance between medium and message.

Although **Straight Not** was released on the gay Outpunk label, it's one of GodCo's least obviously "out" recordings—in terms of sexuality, that is. There's no disputing the stylistic adventuring that marks tracks like the Ella-Fitzgerald-meets-Wu-Tang scat-hop of "We Signify" (or, for that matter, the giddy naïf-pop stylings of "Girl in a Car Singing Along With the Radio"). Unlike philosophical (and sonic) precursors the Minutemen, the band shows no sign of abandoning the ultra-minimalist aesthetic—even after releasing more than a hundred sub–three-minute tunes. Compiled from a handful of performances at New York's Knitting Factory, the thirty-nine-song concert document **Tight Like Fist** emphasizes the visceral edge sometimes missing in GodCo's theoretically skewed studio stuff. Topper's infectiously playful persona comes through vividly on tracks like the skipping rendition of the traditional folk song "Handsome Molly" and "Iko" (a truncated version of "Iko Iko"), while guests come and go, inserting and deleting manifold layers of skronk with every shift.

Sharon Quite Fancies Jo features another "Iko" (as well as a mostly unsuccessful extrapolation of Charles Mingus' "Better Get It in Your Soul"). While **This Is No Time to Be Frail!** is more intriguing, it too suffers from self-conscious attempts at pushing the stylistic envelope ("Childhood Dreams of Abduction and Mutilation" uses samples of Topper's voice as both rhythm and melody). Like watching paint dry—on a Pollock canvas.

In a blatant foretelling of impending slackerdom, **How to Be** contains a mere twenty-three songs (including the recorded unveiling of the chugging "Madly They Did Ride," the band's first-ever composition) but GodCo connects at better than its usual average. Sexy sonnets like "Kittybait" and "Get In" are unfailingly engaging, even if more political screeds don't quite cut it. Fans of unabashed scree should take particular note of Siobhan Duffy's wonderfully unhinged sax playing on tracks such as "Take One."

God Is My Co-Pilot has long taken part in John Zorn's Radical Jewish Culture series, which no doubt helped in the conceptualization of **Mir Shlufn Nisht,** most of which is given over to traditional Hebrew and Yiddish songs. Topper's facility with the material is pretty extraordinary, and the respectful tone (which includes adherence to the Orthodox directive that the word "God" not be written, thus making the band's name G–d Is My Co-Pilot) is refreshing indeed. Additionally, the album contains a handful of Finnish-language folk songs—largely gleaned from the repertoire of Värttinä—some of which would be reprised on **Ootko Sa Poika Vai Tytto?**

Sex Is for Making Babies (sung entirely in English for a change) is one of the most bracing GodCo records, rife as it is with slash-and-burn attacks on conventional sexual mores (see "Sissy Dog" and the ominous "Interrogation"). Since it grew out of jam sessions rather than studio time per se, it's even looser than usual, as borne out by comparatively sweet-tempered tracks like "Be Nice to Yr. Parents," but the seat-of-their-pants approach only adds to the intensity.

Puss 02 is the closest thing the band has produced to a party record. Kicking off with the ESG-styled groove "Dance," the album settles into a zone right at pelvis level, where it remains through songs as varied as the go-go-tinged "Pocketful of Sugar" (with an enticing Alex Klein bassline) and the strobing "Jackie 60." Cameos abound, with the most notable being Boredoms' drummer Yoshimi P-Wee, who squalls an adorable cover of Growing Up Skipper's "Teenage Boyfriend."

The two volumes of **The History of Music** compile virtually all of God Is My Co-Pilot's singles and EPs plus a goodly array of previously unreleased material—eighty-five songs in all. [dss]

GODRAYS

See *Small Factory.*

GOD'S FAVORITE BAND

Shacknasty (Twin\Tone) 1991
In Through the Out House (Twin\Tone) 1992
Down to the Filter (Twin\Tone) 1994

Jim Crego and Chris Benson both sing, write and play guitar and bass in God's Favorite Band. (Drummer Andy Wolf completes the Minneapolis trio.) Crego is the poppier of the pair; Benson is partial to the sensual pleasures of heavy midwestern noise-rock. Although **Shacknasty** nearly sags under the rippling punky power-trio weight of it all, Crego's excellent songs (all co-written with someone outside the band) surge with a burly melodicism that owes something to Kiss on one hand ("Die Trying") and the Magnolias on the other ("Shirtjack," "The Knot," the superb "Something to Cry About"). For his numbers, Benson tests a slow-rolling roar ("Seven Days"), screaming riffology ("Two Bit Compromise") and a quiet surprise ("Cosmic Blue Stem"). Offering listeners a choice works to GFB's benefit; if the right one doesn't get you, the left one will. And if neither does the trick, the album's bonus track nails **Shacknasty** closed with twenty-five minutes of unvarying guitar distortion.

Displaying a more creative sense of humor, **In Through the Out House** is packaged in careful tribute to Led Zeppelin's **In Through the Out Door,** complete with sepia-tinted bar-photo cover and rubber-stamped brown bag wrapper. That, of course, is where the resemblance ends. Both Benson and Crego are shifting toward a midpoint compromise in their songwriting (Benson's adjustment is dramatic), converging on a taut, economical rock style with both tunes *and* riffs. Benson does the album's adventuring, essaying the speed-country sound of "Chunky Sentence," the acoustic balladry of "Delilah," the Westerbergian restraint of "Ghost Town" and the hard pop of "Angel in the Dust." Crego simply delivers the album's standout, the uptight and self-critical "Who's Kiddin' Who?" Typical of the improved creativity and judgment that characterize the entire undertaking, the brief bonus track is perfectly harmless.

On the straightforward and serious **Down to the Filter** the differences between Crego's and Benson's contributions are more emotional than stylistic. The former's songs are disillusioned and regretful, while the latter is just depressed and lonely. This is not a happy band, but the two men manage to channel their problems into affecting music. Collectively light years ahead of what it was on **Shacknasty,** GFB now has enough musical breadth to incorporate keyboards (played by guest pianist/organist Steve Olson) and sophisticated guitar interplay in the arrangements. A substantial, accomplished and exciting album. [i]

GODSTAR

The Brightest Star in the World EP (Aus. Half a Cow) 1992 (Bus Stop) 1993
Chemcraze (Aus. Half a Cow) 1993
Sleeper (Aus. Half a Cow) 1993 (Taang!) 1993
Lie Down Forever EP (Aus. Half a Cow) 1993 (Taang!) 1994
Glasgow EP7 (UK Rugger Bugger) 1994
Four Seventy EP7 (Bus Stop) 1994
Way Out Jim (Japan. 100 Guitar Mania) 1994
Single EP (Taang!) 1994
Coastal (Aus. Half a Cow) 1995
Table for One EP (Aus. Half a Cow) 1995

SNEEZE

Sneeze EP7 (Aus. Half a Cow) 1993

Although widely unknown until the early 1990s, Nic Dalton has been releasing records under various names since 1985. While still going through his primary musical education as a member of Australian punk band the Plunderers, Dalton began to write songs that he felt were inappropriate for such use. In time, he found the friends to bring his creations to life, and in doing so launched a singular musical organization. Conceiving of it as a creative commune, Dalton (vocals, guitar, bass, etc.) dubbed the revolving, evolving band Godstar after a 1986 single by Psychic TV. Thanks to the internationalization of the independent underground, Dalton has been able to bring together diverse musicians from several continents, yet each release retains some stylistic continuity. Besides leading Godstar and Sneeze and running the Half a Cow label, Dalton has done time as a member of the Lemonheads, Love Positions and Hummingbirds. He's most prominently featured on 1993's **Come on Feel the Lemonheads** and has toured extensively with the band.

Dalton recorded **Sleeper** in Boston with Evan Dando and Tom Morgan and Alison Galloway (both of Smudge; Morgan wrote lyrics for the Lemonheads' **It's a Shame About Ray,** to which Dalton also contributed a song), former Hummingbirds/Love Positions bassist Robyn St. Clare, Rachael King of the Cakekitchen and Bob Weston of Shellac. With chiming guitars and charming vocals, most of the sixteen jangly pop confections ("Bad Implications," "Everything You Give Me Breaks," "Something Unplanned") sound like the work of such British "C86" groups as the Razorcuts, Pooh Sticks and Flatmates. Standing apart from the other tracks are two solo drone poems ("Forgotten Night" and "Every Now & Again"), which highlight Dalton's fascination with the Velvet Underground.

"The Brightest Star in the World," which was rerecorded for **Sleeper,** also serves as the spirited, immediate title track of an EP with three non-LP tracks. In turn, **Sleeper**'s "Lie Down Forever" became the lead item on an EP of otherwise unreleased material (including a number called "Sleeper") recorded at various times between '90 and '93 with Morgan, Galloway, St. Clare and ex-Lemonheads bassist Jesse Peretz. Despite the disparate circumstances and styles, the six songs on **Lie Down Forever** all bear Godstar's discernible mark. "Sleeper" betrays an affinity for early Jesus and Mary Chain, with a strong melody line engulfed in fuzz; "Lie Down Forever" and the haunting "Dead Sad Night" raise Dalton's debt to the Velvets. The **Glasgow** EP was recorded during a 1993 Lemonheads UK tour; with none of his regular cohorts in attendance, Dalton assigned the bass and drum parts to local Scottish studio musicians, but got singer/guitarist Eugene Kelly of Eugenius in to give the release that special Godstar flair. The title track of the **Single** EP also comes from **Sleeper.**

Dalton tried out democracy as a concept for the **Four Seventy** EP. Each song was written and sung by a different member of the ensemble; significantly, they all sound like Godstar. Morgan and Galloway, respectively, take the lead on "Love & Trucks" and "Sunshower," while Dalton does his quirky pop best on "Mr. Austin." St. Clare easily wins the hand with the soul-searching "Load."

With Boston's Fuzzy serving as a backing group on several songs, the magnum opus **Coastal**—recorded over the course of a year with the usual suspects—gets an extra kick on "Friend of a Friend" and the title song, which suggest how Godstar might sound if it were a proper band. Elsewhere, Dalton mounts both feisty pop songs and clearly produced sound collages inspired by Brian Wilson.

"Table for One" (from the EP of the same name) brings Godstar onto the dancefloor and sounds like something from Primal Scream's **Come Together** or the Soup Dragons' **Lovegod.** The EP also includes Dalton's tepid crack at George McCrae's disco classic "Rock Your Baby." The other three songs are more familiar Godstar terrain: "High Anxiety" is a speedy pop leftover from **Coastal.**

Sneeze is a way for Dalton and Morgan to clear out songs too "goofy" to put on albums and too good to throw away. With no song checking in over two minutes, **Sneeze** condenses twenty of 'em on two 7-inches. While almost everybody in the Godstar universe can be found on at least one track, Sneeze also includes various members of Swirl and Ratcat. Of special note here is Hummingbirds singer/guitarist Alannah Russack (via Tom Morgan's lyrics) taking a swipe at the Lemonheads on "Shaky Ground," and the final recordings by the Lemonheads' **Lovey** lineup (Dando, Peretz and David Ryan) on "Autumnal Eyes" and "Trouble in School." The most entertaining numbers are the most frivolous, like "Ripped Jeans" (a tribute to the Ramones) and "Don't Go Girlie." [mk/i]

See also *Fuzzy, Lemonheads, Smudge.*

GOD STREET WINE

Live at the 712 Club [tape] (no label) 1990
bag. (Cundalini) 1992 (Ripe & Ready) 1992

Who's Driving? (Ripe & Ready) 1993
$1.99 Romances (Eleven/Geffen) 1994
Red (no label) 1995 (Mercury) 1996

There came a point in the 1960s when the general presumption that everyone with long hair was cool, liked the same kind of music and probably shared leftist political views was revealed to be utterly baseless. The same sort of disillusionment occurred in the next decade, when stupid punks stopped pogoing and panhandling and began acting like genuine thugs. For those who lived through both sobering eras, nothing is as hard to fathom as the recent rise of jam bands, groups that—against all previous versions of acceptable youth behavior (which, in itself, supplies all the sociological explanation needed)—consciously emulate the glory days of '70s rock festivals where good vibes counted more than good music and bigger was always better. Whether specifically updating the Grateful Dead (Phish), switching instruments (Blues Traveler's John Popper blows scales on the harmonica with roughly the same impressive and pointless velocity that Alvin Lee of Ten Years After brought to the guitar; Primus leads with Les Claypool's hyperkinetic bass), looking past Santana and John McLaughlin for fusion-happy world music visions (the Dave Matthews Band, Rusted Root) or sucking too bad to count at all (Big Head Todd and the Monsters, Spin Doctors), a new generation has provided college-aged concert-goers—especially those plugged into the Internet, where buzzes are passed along at the speed of light—with an alternative to tie-dye's never-say-die (until the main one actually did) god-daddys.

Crawling into the ditch left by the Allman Brothers' endless tour bus with organ (Jon Bevo), twin guitarists (Lo Faber and Aaron Maxwell) and an adenoidal vocal resemblance to whichever one of the Doobie Brothers it was who sang, God Street Wine periodically leaves its home base in upstate Ossining, New York, to thrill audiences at perennially sold-out gigs all over Universityville, America. Wisely, the quintet first went the live route in committing its music to tape; the sold-at-gigs debut was a double-cassette recorded onstage in New York City, where the group started in 1988.

Getting a studio record together presented a more complicated challenge. Attempting to give fair play to their genial R&B, pop and funk songs *and* showcase their instrumental proficiency, **bag.** splits the difference and winds up shortchanging both. At its best (the Allmanny "Goodnight Gretchen," the New Riders–like "Borderline," the Steely Dan–ish "Waiting for the Tide"), **bag.** is the modern equivalent of that mildew-stained obscurity you took a chance on for a buck at the Salvation Army—and didn't care for enough to keep.

Who's Driving? culls shows from '92 and '93 for a jam-packed jam that shows what good memories (of Elizabeth Reed) Faber and Maxwell have. Using funky beats to start a little War (twenty-three total minutes of "Feel the Pressure" and "Hellfire," twice their combined length on **bag.**), jazzy chord patterns ("Imogene") and what sounds an awful lot like a Glen Campbell impersonation ("Stranger"), the album is well-played, unfailingly good-natured, absurdly dated and boring beyond belief.

God Street Wine's first major-label album, **$1.99 Romances** (produced in a Memphis studio by Jim Dickinson), is necessarily more concise than its live recordings. The fourteen songs average a hair less than five minutes each, which is the blink of a tuneup for this band. If that discourages long-spool solos ("Crazy Head" winds up for what promises to be an extended digression, but quickly cuts it off), the pressure of a ticking clock doesn't compromise the band's spirited cohesion, or force significantly more enthralling songcraft. Without the crutch of instrumental exposition, Faber's compositions are functionally tuneful and not-quite-clever (the unctuous "Wendy" is fandom reduced to mawkish witlessness) in various dated idioms. "Mile by Mile" manages a convincing Steely Dan impression; "The Ballroom" does a brisk reggae shuffle; the studio version of "Imogene" could be a Doobie Brothers or Boz Scaggs cover. Adding little to the good-time musics on which its muse guzzles, God Street Wine is like a top-drawer wedding band taking the liberty of showcasing some songs of its own devising while the chopped liver is being served.

After being dropped by Geffen, God Street Wine retreated to its home studio, stuck its thumb in and pulled out a new and improved studio album. **Red** was initially sold only via neo-grassroots channels (telephone sales and the World Wide Web) to fans before being licensed to a major label for retail distribution. Diehard Winos expecting another sprawling skein of old-timey funk-rock improv are likely to be shocked by the band's sudden axis shift. Disconnecting from the usual vintage allusions (specifically blotting out all the Allman comparisons), **Red** warms the plate with a couple inna old style ("Get on the Train," the soulful falsetto of "RU4 Real?") but spends more time indulging different conceits: atmospheric pop (the Beatlesque "Girl on Fire," the piano-based "Maybe," which slides amusingly from Carole King reserve to fevered symphonic gimmickry), chorus/organ gospel ("Untitled Take Two"), Dylan-imagining acoustic rusticity ("Red & Milky White"), bouncy barrelhouse blues ("Chop!"), tropical reggae ("When the White Sun Turns to Red") and measured, skeletal rock ("Which Way Will She Go?," easily the strangest thing these guys have ever done). Whether the group was finally ready to move itself forward or the corporate divorce sparked a leap of creative development, **Red** is the first God Street Wine record worth owning. [i]

GO-GO'S

Beauty and the Beat (IRS) 1981
Vacation (IRS) 1982
Talk Show (IRS) 1984
Go-Go's Greatest (IRS) 1990
Return to the Valley of the Go-Go's (IRS) 1994

JANE WIEDLIN

Jane Wiedlin (IRS) 1985
Fur (EMI Manhattan) 1988
Tangled (EMI) 1990
From Cool Places to Worlds on Fire: The Very Best of Jane Wiedlin (EMI) 1993

FROSTED

Cold (DCG) 1996

BELINDA CARLISLE

Belinda (IRS) 1986
Heaven on Earth (MCA) 1987
Runaway Horses (MCA) 1989
Live Your Life Be Free (MCA) 1991

Her Greatest Hits (MCA) 1992
Real (Virgin) 1993

Released long after the end of the Go-Go's as a going concern and right before the LA band's gummy interment as a colorful cartoon memory of '80s nostalgia, **Go-Go's Greatest** recapitulated the charming quintet's three-album recording career, the enduring highlights of which scarcely demand an entire CD. Belinda Carlisle (vocals), Jane Wiedlin (guitar/vocals), Gina Schock (drums), Kathy Valentine (bass) and Charlotte Caffey (guitar) earned their historical bragging rights as the victorious pioneer women of American new wave, but their success ultimately meant more to those who followed in their wake than it did to the quality level of rock'n'roll in the early '80s. Beyond the certified hits ("Our Lips Are Sealed," "We Got the Beat," "Vacation," "Head Over Heels" and "Turn to You," which are great enough to stand behind), "This Town," "Lust to Love," "How Much More" and maybe "Skidmarks on My Heart" are all the Go-Go's anyone needs to remember. Nevertheless, **Greatest** (which omits "Skidmarks") lays on some second-tier album tracks and a wretched new recording of "Cool Jerk," the Capitols' dance oldie.

The dysfunctional group reunited for a short '90 tour and then retreated to neutral corners, where Carlisle resumed her solo career and Wiedlin didn't. Instead, her label put together a very generous compilation of **Jane Wiedlin, Fur** and **Tangled,** augmented by "Cool Places" (her percolating 1983 collaboration with Sparks) and a spartan acoustic remake of "Our Lips Are Sealed," which Wiedlin had written with then-Specials singer Terry Hall. Despite some swell tracks ("Blue Kiss," "Tangled," "Give!"), the prime value of **From Cool Places** is Wiedlin's liner notes and the extensive discography.

After the Go-Go's' brief encore, Carlisle returned to the safety of her posh solo career, doubling its catalogue with **Live Your Life Be Free,** another big mess of overproduced song-factory pop, heavy on the light Madonna syrup (producer Rick Nowels' "You're Nothing Without Me" comes closest, although the emotional abandon of "I Plead Insanity" is strictly a male fantasy), a greatest hits collection (besting her group with six Top 40 singles—"Mad About You," "Heaven Is a Place on Earth," "I Get Weak" and the rest—plus filler) and the mold-breaking **Real.**

With Charlotte Caffey as her creative partner, prestardom pals from Redd Kross and the Germs on hand and past Svengali Nowels nowhere to be found, Carlisle brought herself back to earth, shouldering some of the songwriting responsibilities for the first time and directing **Real** toward a relatively straightforward rock-pop sound. Pat Smear, Steven and Jeff McDonald and Vicki Peterson are wasted in a record free of sharp corners or irony, but some of the romantic angst songs (the worst of which, "Lay Down Your Arms," points up Carlisle's continuing Madonna aspirations) aren't bad. Carlisle sings with all the conviction missing from all her other records—and then some. Against the pretty backdrop of Bangles-like harmonies, she emotes herself to the point of overbearing frenzy on the edgy "Tell Me," "Windows of the World" and "Here Comes My Baby," erasing years of careful composure in an amateurish lack of control.

The Go-Go's were seemingly frozen in the memory banks between A Flock of Seagulls and Men Without Hats when the fivesome unexpectedly gathered to help assemble the music and artwork for **Return to the Valley of the Go-Go's.** Part self-parodying scrapbook, part outtake anthology and part serious history, the thirty-six-track double-CD starts with rehearsal sessions and live performances from 1979, includes most of the essential items from **Greatest** in their original form and ends with a souvenir from the '90 tour and three new songs written and recorded for the occasion. A lurid, unruly history that repeatedly goes out of its way to show the group in a less-than-flattering light—and is therefore a most illuminating and impressive document—**Return to the Valley of the Go-Go's** boasts such car-wreck charmers as the punk racket of the long-forgotten "Party Pose" and "Fashion Seekers," a sloppy live "Johnny Are You Queer?" (written for, but never released by, the Go-Go's; Josie Cotton got it instead), a ripping live rendition of Wanda Jackson's "Let's Have a Party" and a high-intensity outtake of "Lust to Love" produced by Paul Wexler. "Surfing and Spying," a Caffey instrumental, and the beat-rocking "Speeding"—both reclaimed from early B-sides—are typical of the gems unearthed here. The live stuff doesn't improve the group's mediocre standing in that realm, and "The Whole World Lost Its Head" is the only new creation truly worth the bother (although "Beautiful" has a catchy enough chorus), but emptying closets to find buried treasure has its risks. This is one the band did well to undertake.

The Go-Go's toured to promote the compilation and threatened to stick together long enough to record a new album, but soon retreated to their neutral corners. When last heard from, Carlisle was solo again, Wiedlin had formed a loud power-pop group called froSTed, Valentine was busy fronting the Delphines and Caffey was in Astrid's Mother. [i]

See also *TPRG.*

GOLDEN CLAW MUSICS

See *Pop Will Eat Itself.*

GOLDEN PALOMINOS

The Golden Palominos (OAO/Celluloid) 1983
Visions of Excess (Celluloid) 1985
Blast of Silence (Celluloid) 1986
A Dead Horse (Celluloid) 1989
Drunk With Passion (Nation/Charisma) 1991
A History (1982–1985) (Metrotone/Restless) 1992
A History (1986–1989) (Metrotone/Restless) 1992
This Is How It Feels (Restless) 1993
Pure (Restless) 1994
The Pure Remix EP (Restless) 1995
Dead Inside (Restless) 1996

ANTON FIER

Dreamspeed (Japan. Avant) 1993

LORI CARSON

Shelter (DGC) 1990
Where It Goes (Restless) 1995

A vehicle for New York drummer/producer Anton Fier's restless musical talent, the Golden Palominos have, over the years, evolved from edgy downtown supergroup into a band whose art-funk amalgam has firmly defined its restrained, elegant grooves. The Palominos' diverse sound (this is one band that has never warranted accusations of repeating itself) arises from the different sets of musicians assembled for each record.

With guitarists Arto Lindsay and Fred Frith, bassist Bill Laswell and reedman John Zorn on hand, the debut sounds like a more aggressive version of Material. Some of the more avant touches (the rhythm section's off-center funk, the angular guitar and, for the time, adventurous rock use of turntables and other hip-hop techniques) now sound dated, but "Monday Night" and "I.D." are still fresh. That album (minus one track, "Clean Plate") was subsequently repackaged on **A History (1982–1985),** which also contains, in its entirety, the poppier **Visions of Excess,** where the nucleus of Fier, Laswell, guitarist Jody Harris and keyboardist Bernie Worrell is augmented by guitarist Richard Thompson and singers Michael Stipe, John Lydon and Syd Straw for a surprisingly effective collection of post-punk pop with an experimental edge. Stipe is unexpectedly passionate on a cover of Moby Grape's "Omaha" and Lydon typically vitriolic on "The Animal Speaks," but it's newcomer Straw who makes the strongest impression here. Her vocals on "(Kind of) True" and "Buenos Aires" are the first examples of what would become a Palominos' staple: striking female singing.

Straw is also featured on **Blast of Silence,** which (omitting "Brides of Jesus") is contained on **A History (1986–1989).** With such folks as Peter Blegvad, T-Bone Burnett and Matthew Sweet on hand, the Palominos here move from pop into rarefied versions of country, folk and blues. The songs assay their styles while subverting them with unexpected touches—the hand drum on the countryish "I've Been the One," guitarist Nicky Skopelitis' searing wah-wah coda on the folky "Something Becomes Nothing," the poppy acoustic guitars underpinning the bluesy "(Something Else Is) Working Harder." The rest of **A History (1986–1989)** is devoted to all but one song ("Over") from **A Dead Horse,** the first Palominos record to employ a consistent track-by-track lineup (Fier, Laswell, Skopelitis, guitarist/vocalist Robert Kidney and vocalist Amanda Kramer, ex–Information Society). The band's weakest album is tasteful and restrained to the point of blandness, with the exception of Kramer's moody "Darklands."

This Is How It Feels feels much better. Loosely based on Graham Greene's *The End of the Road,* the album moves the Palominos into a sound focused on hypnotically elegant grooves. New singer Lori Carson's breathy voice, pinned between eroticism and ennui, captures Greene's ambivalent relationship to temptations of both the flesh and earth. The album also features Amanda Kramer fronting a fine version of "These Days" that owes more to Nico (who once recorded it) than to its author, Jackson Browne.

With two monster bassists in the house (Laswell and Bootsy Collins), **Pure** enters a realm of unbridled sensuality. There's a post-coital languor to Carson's singing on "Little Suicides" and the title track. The lushly atmospheric guitars (mostly by Skopelitis and Knox Chandler) swaddle the grooves and vocals in a rich, druggy haze. **Pure** can be heard as post-modern makeout music, and could certainly be packaged with candles and a bottle of wine. The remix EP contains six **Pure**-ities reconfigured by Bill Laswell, Bandulu and New York ambient auteur Terre Thaemlitz.

Carson's two solo albums—bracketing her two with the Palominos—are quite different from each other. Produced by Hal Willner, **Shelter** is singer/songwriter fluff that can't choose between Edie Brickell breeziness and Tori Amos preciousness; the far more appealing **Where It Goes,** produced by Fier, is grave and serious, sung with aching intensity and arranged with drawing-room sophistication. [sm/i]

See also *Peter Blegvad, Bill Laswell, Chris Stamey, John Zorn; TPRG.*

GOLDEN SMOG

On Golden Smog EP (Crackpot) 1992 (Rykodisc) 1996
Down by the Old Mainstream (Rykodisc) 1996

On its debut, an EP of five items taken down from the '60s/'70s covers cupboard, midwestern supergroup Golden Smog pseudonymously included Minneapolitans Dan Murphy (Soul Asylum), Chris Mars (ex-Replacements), Gary Louris and Marc Perlman (Jayhawks) and Kraig Johnson (Run Westy Run). Imparting an acoustic/electric country-rock tilt in skillfully played arrangements, the part-time quintet offers unironic renditions of Thin Lizzy's "Cowboy Song," the Stones' "Backstreet Girl" (the disc's folky highlight), "Easy to Be Hard" (from *Hair*), the mysterious "Son (We've Kept the Room Just the Way You Left It)" and Bad Company's "Shooting Star" (sung by guest Smogger Dave "Tony James" Pirner). (Trivia buffs note: the musicians' made-up surnames derive from the streets on which they were born: Murphy, for instance, is David Spear-Way; Louris is Michael Macklyn-Drive.)

Beyond a deeper professional commitment, the replacement of Mars by drummer Noah Levy (Honeydogs) and the new chair pulled up around the fireplace for singer/guitarist Jeff Tweedy of Wilco, what makes the sextet's second coming an entirely different proposition is that all but two of the fourteen songs are originals. Suffused with a comfy pals-on-a-porch feel, **Down by the Old Mainstream** doesn't so much meld or showcase the various personalities as heap them all into a versatile "no depression" group any one of them could lead. All the voices sound like facets of the same person, and the songs (with the notable exception of Johnson's nonsensical "He's a Dick" and, to a lesser degree, a cover of Bobby Paterson's clumsy "She Don't Have to See You") fit together like pieces of a nicely worn puzzle. The electric numbers (like Murphy's "Ill Fated" and Ronnie Lane's "Glad & Sorry") are better than the acoustic ones (although Tweedy's "Pecan Pie" is pretty inviting), and the Pirner-sung ballad "Nowhere Bound" works best of all, but this modest, heartfelt album is one on which the musicians' pleasure at singing and playing arrives intact and affecting. [i]

See also *Honeydogs, Jayhawks, Chris Mars, Soul Asylum, Uncle Tupelo.*

GOLDFINGER

Goldfinger (Mojo) 1996

Armed with a cool name, solidly adrenalized pop-punk (with a side of horn-punched ska) and a helpful eye for offhand lyrics ("My Girlfriend's Shower Sucks," the infectious "Here in Your Bedroom," the trendo-scene antagonism of "The City With Two Faces," the sexual humiliation of "Mable"), this lively and colorful Los Angeles quartet got itself elected next big thing by arbiters of such things in early '96. Flashing bits of the Clash, Selecter and Social Distortion, the album is easily entertaining without shaking any tar out of the pits. There are, however, signs of superior skill, determination and personality in the grooves. Driven by the hasty rhythm section of Dangerous Darrin Pfeiffer and Simon Williams, singer/guitarist John Feldmann's voice favors conviction over melodious skill but he hits his marks and makes his points. Doubled by guitarist Charlie Paulson, he erects a rich rhythm roar that hurries the melodies—both flimsy and soaring—along without spilling a drop. [i]

GOLDIE

Timeless (ffrr) 1995

No year would be complete without another underground style fad coming out of Great Britain, and the world-shaking development to reach critical international mass in 1995 was jungle. The next tiny step in techno proceeds from the same impulse as ambient music—that the rhythmic component of club music can be deemed, if not completely expendable, subject to a highly flexible calculus. Conveniently and aptly described as dance music you can't dance to, jungle uses whatever beat-box switches create madly skittering percussion—imagine a swarm of angry insects *and* a hard rain hitting a tin roof in brisk, shifting winds—and injects the ever-changing results around, not in, the center of alternately dreamy and pro forma trip-hop soul.

A native of Wolverhampton (a city famous in glam-rock history as Slade's hometown), Goldie is jungle's crossover avatar, the first producer/artist to make an aboveground bid for commercial radio play and home stereo access. On **Timeless,** he and studio partner Rob Playford succeed in their improbable adventure by placing extremely ordinary sentimental ballads ("State of Mind," "Angel," "You & Me") at the core of several tracks, letting smooth female voices provide an alluring entry point to their manic electronic gearshifting. The album's centerpiece is the twenty-one-minute, three-part title track, which initially combines slowly undulating waves of string-like sounds with Diane Charlemagne's voice, clattering rushes of seemingly superfluous percussion and sampled sound effects. The science-fiction tension in what seems like a familiar realm is most intriguing. Elsewhere, Goldie eliminates any trace of propulsion and then flips the switches, dub style, to remove everything but the effects or the paradiddles. At its best, **Timeless** is a hypnotic suggestion that keeps you on the edge of your seat. If that's the law of (the) jungle, it's an exciting sound of music. [i]

GOODBYE MR. MACKENZIE

See *Garbage.*

GOO GOO DOLLS

Goo Goo Dolls (Mercenary/Celluloid) 1987 (Metal Blade) 1994
Jed (Death/Enigma) 1989
Hold Me Up (Metal Blade/Warner Bros.) 1990
SuperstarCarWash (Metal Blade/Warner Bros.) 1993
A Boy Named Goo (Metal Blade/Warner Bros.) 1995

Like vintage Replacements (their most obvious influence), an outback Dictators or the blue-collar spawn of early Cheap Trick, the Goo Goo Dolls brandish power-punk riffpop that just keeps getting better. Although recorded two years apart, the Buffalo, New York, trio's first two albums are virtual carbon copies of each other, flashes of brilliance ("I'm Addicted," the acoustic "James Dean") shining amid silly covers and scrawny adolescent yapping about such standard things as "Messed Up" and "Up Yours." The debut has breathless rips through Blue Öyster Cult's "(Don't Fear) The Reaper" and Cream's "Sunshine of Your Love"; **Jed** boasts a ferocious version of the Stones' "Gimme Shelter" and a crunching pisstake of Creedence's "Down on the Corner" sung by Buffalo lounge crooner Lance Diamond.

As the Goo Goo Dolls tightened up their act, the trio tamed its arena-metal tendencies and slid right into the raucous stylistic space abandoned by the 'Mats. The effervescent **Hold Me Up** really delivers the goods, focusing a variety of hard-rocking/good-humored impulses into a solid, distinctive sound. Alternating lead vocals in the band-credited songs, guitarist John Rzeznik (a harsh-voiced cynic) and bassist Robby Takac (the band's sweet-sounding optimistic popster) ride an exhilarating rollercoaster of Ramonesy riffs and insistent hooks. Besides proffering such great originals as "Just the Way You Are" and "There You Are," the Goos make good use of the Plimsouls' "A Million Miles Away" and give Prince's "I Could Never Take the Place of Your Man" the groovy soul-man treatment with more guest vocals by Diamond.

It was imprudent if irresistible to have Paul Westerberg contribute the lyrics for **SuperstarCarWash**'s centerpiece, "We Are the Normal" (apparently not a tribute to the Bonzo Dog Band's "We Are Normal"), an anthem trussed up with strings'n'things. The choice of Gavin MacKillop as the album's producer didn't entirely aid the effort, either: the sound is lively and electric throughout, but the performances occasionally lack fire and focus, which blunts the impact of some songs while improving the standing of others. "Don't Worry," "Stop the World," "Already There" and "So Far Away" are just the kind of catchy power-pop numbers to benefit from a bit of restraint, but the angry cries meant to balance them don't hit as hard as they should. Only "String of Lies," rushed along by drummer George Tutuska's unrelenting hammering, has the lyrical power to overcome any deficiency in its rendering.

With the right producer (Lou Giordano) and a terrific batch of new songs, **A Boy Named Goo** puts everything right. (Except for the lineup: Tutuska left shortly after the album was completed, occasioning the deletion of "Stand Alone," a song he had written, and the inclusion of two covers—"Disconnected" by Buffalo's Enemies and "Slave Girl" by Australia's Lime Spiders—before its release.) Emerging as prole intellectuals with tautly efficient energy to burn, the Goos rock harder—and softer—than ever, perfectly balancing their stylistic poles in an album that is as sturdy as a brick shithouse and as delicate as it has to be. **A Boy Named Goo,** which became the group's million-selling breakthrough, reaches a new creative level with trenchant lyrics of uncommon insight and resonance. "Flat Top" takes on a favorite Rzeznik theme, attacking media influence: "A television war between the cynics and the saints / Flip the dial and that's the side you're on." Paraphrasing Joe Strummer, he continues, "A visionary coward says that anger can be power / As long as there's a victim on TV." In the surging, majestic "Ain't That Unusual," he damns it all with philosophical abandon: "All we are is what we're told and most of that's been lies / It's like a made-for-TV movie and I just blew my lines." Takac's songs, although they present an entirely different worldview, are just as good and no less serious. In "Impersonality," following a descending riff with bracing slabs of rhythm guitar dollying the sweetly evocative childhood memory, he sings, "When I was three feet tall, I loved them all and lived life for myself / Falling down for laughs, your photograph, some puppets made of felt." The acoustic alienation ode, "Name," is simply gorgeous, while the searing "Only One" confronts musician self-destruction (pointedly *not* about anyone well-known) from inside and out with equally blinding disgust: "Fucking up takes practice / I feel I'm well rehearsed / Because the past is a bully and the future's even worse." **A Boy Named Goo** is the child of genius. [ja/i]

GORIES

House Rockin' (Wanghead) 1989 (Crypt) 1994
I Know You Fine, but How You Doin' (Wanghead) 1990 (Crypt) 1994
Outta Here (Ger. Crypt) 1992 (Crypt) 1994
I Know You Be House Rockin' (Crypt) 1994

Poured from a deep vein of raw garage-rock sewage with a John Lee Hooker chaser, this Detroit trio (which, like New York's kindred A-Bones, has a woman beating its skins) makes no pretense of instrumental skill or audio fidelity on its records. (The group does, however, go in for annotation. The first album's insert offers such inspiring song explanations as this, by way of "Boogie Chillun": "This was one of the first songs we ever learned, because it only has three notes. When we first started, any songs with more than nine notes in it was usually too complicated for us.") Intuitive geniuses plugged in but still making their way in the dark, guided only by pure and knowledgeable rock-'n'roll spirit, the unabashed Gories—Mick (vocals, lead guitar), Dan Kroha (vocals, rhythm guitar) and Peggy O'Neill (drums)—are both (and equally) horrible and great, their elemental wretchedness pure and unvarnished. Those who expect anything approaching professionalism should stay away, but if the words "bad" and "junk" are words of praise in your vocabulary, then dig right into the Gories. No refunds allowed.

House Rockin' is a ground-zero learning experience (for the band, that is) with tinny, gruelly, echoey sound, one-take/no-overdubs performances and Mick's growly vocals. **I Know You Fine,** produced in Memphis by Alex Chilton (who did a similar favor for the Cramps fifteen years earlier), has more sonic body and emotional booty, revving into sleazy innerspace with fiercely determined playing and singing that captures the feel of a three-day houseparty about to be raided. Given the raving enthusiasm the trio brings to items like Hooker's "Let Your Daddy Ride," Suicide's "Ghostrider" and the semi-original "Hey Hey, We're the Gories," trivialities like the untuned decimation of the aptly named original "Detroit Breakdown" are no impediment to blister-popping fun. (**I Know You Be House Rockin'** combines the first two albums into one double-length delusional nightmare on CD.)

Outta Here is marginally more accomplished, but not enough to clean up the mess. Songs like "Can't Catch Up With You," the instrumental "Omologato" and "Telepathic" (not to mention the cover of Earl King's "Trick Bag" that demonstrates the band's enthusiasm for mistreating vintage soul tunes as well as R&B classics) slop along with undiminished fervor, as wild-eyed and chaotic as ever. [i]

See also *Gibson Bros.*

GORILLA

Deal With It (Thrill Jockey) 1993

Formed by two Washington medical students (and dissolved after singer/organist/pianist Drew McRoberts and bassist Dan Merrick became doctors), Gorilla filled its one album with manic garage raving that, in its nostalgia-free intensity, resembles either a northwestern Stranglers (thanks to McRoberts' hyperactive fingers) or a punkier Fleshtones. Drawing on their region's deep roots in the genre (after all, the Kingsmen were from Portland and the Sonics came straight outta Tacoma), the quartet gathers up all the voltage lurking in their carport's electric sockets and matches it with burly, scratched-larynx vocals and frenzied playing. There isn't a molecule of spare air on **Deal With It** until the spoken-word/solo piano exercise ("Drew's Exit") that ends it; the breathless rush that begins with "Stuck on You" and blows through "This Shit's for You" and "Zero Street" is hellhound bound and as compelling as an electromagnet in a junkyard. [i]

GORILLA BISCUITS

See *CIV.*

GO SAILOR

See *Tiger Trap.*

GO TO BLAZES

Go to Blazes (Skyclad) 1988
Love, Lust & Trouble (Fr. Sky Ranch) 1991 (East Side Digital) 1995
Any Time . . . Anywhere (East Side Digital) 1994
. . . And Other Crimes (Ger. Glitterhouse) 1995
Waiting Around for the Crash (East Side Digital) 1996

Philadelphia four-piece Go to Blazes specializes in roadhouse rock'n'roll—whiskey-kissed shuffles and sour blues and Stones-influenced stomps that have a way of making everyday sorrows seem heroic. Known drinking buddies of Eric "Roscoe" Ambel (producer of their recent recordings), Go to Blazes belongs to that loose confederation of roots rockers determined to preserve the rough edges of the music, the country twangs and beer-guzzling stomps. That they haven't been heard much beyond the northeastern corridor can only be blamed on geography: since forming in Washington, DC, in 1987, Go to Blazes has followed such like-minded bands as the Bottle Rockets up and down the club circuit between New England and Virginia.

The quartet's two early albums, riddled with country knockoffs, are notable mainly for the musicianship of guitarist Tom Heyman, an adroit post-blues improviser influenced by Danny Gatton, Muddy Waters and Keith Richards. Beginning in 1992, Go to Blazes appeared on a series of singles from New York's Diesel

Only label—their contributions to the romance-of-the-highways canon include "Why I Drink" and "Messed Up Again."

The Ambel-produced **Any Time . . . Anywhere** captures Go to Blazes in peak form. The rhythm section is assured, guitarist Ted Warren's vocals are no longer self-conscious, and the songs, particularly the blistering "Between the Eyes" and a tribute to Sam Peckinpah ("Bloody Sam"), exhibit more narrative depth. The first thousand copies of the album came with a terrific bonus EP, **Live at the Mercury Lounge;** among its delights are a delirious cover of X's "Because I Do."

After years of hard-rocking, the band finally unplugged in 1995 with **. . . And Other Crimes,** for the German Glitterhouse label. This live-in-the-studio date is filled with smarter-than-bar-band covers, each one given a half-reverent, half-sneering spin. And if rollicking, slide-guitar-tinged treatments of Gene Clark's "Out on the Side" or Kinky Friedman's "Sold American" aren't twisted enough, check the downwardly mobile originals "Got It Made" and "Waste of Time" to hear just how closely the band's sense of rebellion mirrors that of anti-heroes Hank Williams Jr. and Lee Hazlewood.

The squalling guitar power of "Talk About Me" is only the most amplified demonstration of GTB's unreconstructed electric core on **Waiting Around for the Crash,** again produced by Ambel. The dozen new numbers (written separately by Heyman and Warren, with one from guest guitarist Bruce Langfeld) hit all of the band's diverse stylistic bases, from Skynyrdized southern rock ("Independence Day"), Stonesiness ("Nervous Type") and roots-punk ("What You've Made") to rustic folk ("Typhoid Mary") and twangy country blues ("Lost as Me"). Also included is a remake of Warren's "Why I Drink," originally served up on a Diesel Only 45. [tm/i]

GRAND MAL

See *St. Johnny.*

GRAND PUBA

See *Brand Nubian.*

GRANT LEE BUFFALO

Fuzzy (Slash) 1993
America Snoring EP (UK Slash/London) 1993
Fuzzy EP (UK Slash/London) 1993
Buffalondon EP (UK Slash/London) 1993
Mighty Joe Moon (Slash/Reprise) 1994
Mockingbirds #1 EP (UK Slash/London) 1994
Mockingbirds #2 EP (UK Slash/London) 1994
Honey Don't Think EP (Slash/Warner Bros.) 1995
Lone Star Song EP (UK Slash/London) 1995
Copperopolis (Slash/Reprise) 1996

SHIVA BURLESQUE

Shiva Burlesque (Nate Starkman & Son) 1987
Mercury Blues (Fundamental Music) 1990

The roots of Los Angeles' Grant Lee Buffalo stretch back to 1985 when former film student Grant Lee Phillips and Jeffrey Clark started Shiva Burlesque. (They'd earlier been in a band called the Torn Boys.) Phillips specialized in "psychedelic acoustic 12-string," feedback included, while Clark's Jim Morrison–influenced vocals were the stuff of high sweeping drama. They added upright bassist James Brenner and drummer/marimba player Joey Peters; by '87, the band's self-titled debut on Nate Starkman & Son (home to numerous other California eccentrics) was in the bins.

Shiva Burlesque screams "art-rock" from its colorful gatefold sleeve iconography (a reproduction of a painting by Deborah Lawrence). The music itself is an ambitious mélange of styles and moods. There's atmospheric, Echo and the Bunnymen–style pop with self-conscious poetry subbing for rock lyrics ("The Lonesome Death of Shadow Morton"), buoyant, shimmering folk-rock using Phillips' twelve-string as its signature ("Indian Summer")—even the occasional foray into stream-of-consciousness, post-punk freneticism (the trumpet-flecked "Train Mystery"). The inevitable press comparisons to the Doors aside, it's an impressive debut.

The second Shiva album, **Mercury Blues** (which suffered indie-label crib death anyway), lacks the subtle majesty of its predecessor's production. While the material is energetic enough—pointing the band in a more straightforward rock direction (Phillips' guitar is far more prominent, and Clark's vocals adopt an almost Tim Buckley–like fervor)—the overall impact is undermined by the flat sound. Shiva Burlesque broke up shortly thereafter. (An unauthorized reissue of **Shiva Burlesque** appeared in the UK in 1995; there's a chance of a proper American reissue for both on the horizon.)

Phillips busied himself writing songs and recording a solo album that was never released. By '92, he and Peters, along with bassist/pianist Paul Kimble, were rehearsing as Grant Lee Buffalo. The trio's debut, **Fuzzy,** produced by Kimble and partially recorded in his 16-track garage studio, packs a startling one-two punch. Its rich, three-dimensional production manages to locate the trio all over the listening space in almost orchestral fashion, with Phillips' combination of acoustic twelve-string strums and snaky, Frippish electric leads lending particular melodic/textural depth. It also signals the emergence of a major new songwriting talent, as Phillips spins evocative tales (frequently in a swooping falsetto) involving outlaws on the run, lovers lost amid the cultural debris of New Orleans and the East Village and the Closing of the American Dream as narrated by Pocahontas, the Lone Ranger ("Grace"), Red Riding Hood and the Big Bad Wolf ("Soft Wolf Tread").

As picturesque as **Fuzzy** is, **Mighty Joe Moon** is a cinematic revelation, brimming with stylistic atmosphere and sheer musical invention. Once again, Phillips is cast as a shamanistic storyteller: "Lady Godiva and Me," "Last Days of Tecumseh." Wordsmithery aside, it's easy to get wrapped up in the record's sonic wizardry—kudos again to producer Kimble—since each new spin of the disc is like tilting a painting at a different angle in order to pick up on the artist's brush stroke variations. The waltz-like "Sing Along" is initially a heavy, feedback-strewn rocker; listen closely and discern delicate percussion and keyboard touches and choirlike vocal harmonies deep in the mix. Similarly, "Mockingbirds" is a textural masterpiece offering a wealth of guitar tones, an ancient pump organ, cello and multi-tracked vocals (in places, a falsetto duet!). A rare disc whose creators are clearly under the spells once cast by Phil Spector, George Martin, Brian Wilson and Jack Nitzsche.

In England, Grant Lee Buffalo's albums have received star treatment, promoted via numerous EPs loaded with non-album material. Several tracks recorded live in London during an October '94 tour appear on the American six-song **Honey Don't Think** EP. These tunes amply demonstrate that the band is no studio fluke, as it easily reinvents its sound for the stage in slightly tougher but no less intoxicating terms.

Late '95 saw the release of a "soundtrack" tie-in for TV's *Friends;* it includes a cover of the Beach Boys' "In My Room" that showcases Grant Lee Buffalo's dead-on massed vocal harmonies in tribute to Brian Wilson. Then, in mid-'96, the band released its third album, **Copperopolis,** named for a tiny town in California's Sierra Nevada foothills. Again produced by Kimble and including guests Ralph Carney (sax, clarinet) and Greg Leisz (pedal steel), the record confirms Phillips as a pop auteur in his own right. Every song is a miniature epic recalling—but not mimicking—such greats as John Lennon ("The Bridge"), Robbie Robertson ("Even the Oxen"), Tom Petty ("Homespun"), even Tim Buckley ("All That I Have"). In fact, the album is quieter and more folk-oriented than its two predecessors, the instrumental flourishes no less enticing but definitely subordinate to Phillips' vocals. The literal and emotional centerpiece is "Bethlehem Steel," which tackles traditional Guthrie/Dylan/Springsteen subject matter and, with its surging string arrangement and Phillips' impossible falsetto, is as grandly uplifting as a film's feel-good finale. [fm]

See also *Scenic.*

GRAVEDIGGAZ

6 Feet Deep (Gee Street) 1994

Although a provocative and promising concept in principle, horror rap—an extension and institutionalization of Geto Boys' sickest fantasies—fizzled in 1994. None of its leading practitioners (the most hyped of which were the Flatlinerz and Gravediggaz, but the Insane Clown Posse and others joined in the fun) had the concentration or vision to follow either likely course to its grisly conclusion: totally cinematic cartoons or social commentary using living death, casual mayhem and demonic possession as resonant metaphors for urban desperation.

A supergroup composed of the RZA from Wu-Tang Clan, Fruitkwan and Prince Paul (who served as the project's lead producer) of the late, great Stetsasonic and Poetic of the Brothers Grimm, the Gravediggaz set off down both alleys on **6 Feet Deep,** following neither through to a full-blown concept. Before digging into the programmed gruesomeness of melodramas like "2 Cups of Blood," "Diary of a Madman" (which employs the splatter-film convention of a boy witnessing his father's murder) and "Graveyard Chamber," the group offers this couplet: "Critics say go to hell, I go yeah? / Stupid motherfucker I'm already there." Despite a hefty amount of ketchup and great green gobs of greasy grimy gopher guts (not to mention numerous hip-hop guests), **6 Feet Deep** ultimately sinks, a well-produced shaggy dog campfire story in which too much chronic gets smoked and the batteries on the chin-level flashlight run out too soon. Not scary, not enlightening and only sporadically clever (quoting Martha and the Vandellas *and* Jim Croce should count for something), **6 Feet Deep** is a good idea that lacks the inspiration or nerve to come to death. Living Colour guitarist Vernon Reid guests, as do MC Serch, Biz Markie and Masta Ace. [i]

See also *De La Soul, Wu-Tang Clan.*

GRAVEL

Halfway EP7 (Knw-Yr-Own/K) 1990
Break-a-Bone (Estrus) 1992
No Stone Unturned (Estrus) 1993

POUNDING SERFS

Pounding Serfs (K) 1988

Anacortes, Washington, where Gravel comes from, isn't a lot different from Aberdeen (where Nirvana, Melvins and Metal Church all began); both are cloistered, working-class towns that face the Pacific Ocean from remote corners of the rugged Olympic Peninsula. Singer/guitarist Bryan Elliott and bassist Dale Robinson were originally in the near-acoustic Pounding Serfs. Augmented by guitarist Rich Papritz, the Serfs pounded their rock into Gravel (sorry) with the addition of Bobby Vaux on drums.

Break-a-Bone is a remarkable debut, nine gloomy, glorious songs that suggest nothing so much as Crazy Horse fronted by an animated Mark Lanegan. Gravel aren't quite the garage-rock revivalists Estrus usually provides a home for, but the group does play with a similar brutish fervor (and never mind that Robinson is wheelchair-bound). **Break-a-Bone** is a crisp and poignant cry from the middle of nowhere; songs like "Bucket of Blood" (reclaimed from the preceding four-song EP) and "Stone Yard" have the same lonely edge as the best blues, though given a different voice.

No Stone Unturned presents a sometimes louder, sometimes lethargic but altogether less melodic variation on the same themes. The approach works for Patti Smith's "Pissing in a River" and Gravel's own "Yesterday," but for the most part the new songs seem slightly out of focus. In any event, the band toured a little and then ceased to exist. [ga]

DAVID GRAY

A Century Ends (Hut/Caroline) 1993
Flesh (Hut USA/Vernon Yard) 1994
Sell Sell Sell (EMI) 1996

Since the '70s at least, the British breed of singer/songwriter has been hardier than America's—more pub-minded than coffee-housed, comfortable in the form's solitude, less obliged to its pure acoustic trappings and closer in spirit to the wandering minstrels of past centuries. Crew-cut Welsh ex-punk David Gray sings with the chilly gusto of an autumn wind blowing on his first album, **A Century Ends.** Whether trying to rustle himself up an afternoon's "Debauchery" or watching a romance fade in "Shine," taking solace in "the light that shines through the windows of your soul" ("Gathering Dust") or losing patience as he stares out a train window ("Wisdom"), Gray sings with equal parts sensitivity and vitality, emotional attributes that underscore the Van Morrison qualities of his tenor.

A handful of sympathetic sidemen (including Neill MacColl of the Bible and Liberty Horses) back up his simple strumming and husky, accented voice with tastefully energetic encouragement. Excellent.

MacColl leads the informal band into semi-electric ladyland on **Flesh,** using grander arrangements that, thanks to an excess of extroversion in the overall effort, turn the Gaelic aspect of Gray's music dismayingly toward the Waterboys. A couple of quiet songs performed alone ("Falling Free" on piano, "Lullaby" on guitar) and the all-acoustic "Mystery of Love" do a lot to ameliorate the zeal displayed elsewhere, but the damage is done, and the album is a disappointment. "When I hear you laugh / I got a sword to stem the rivers / And cut the moon in half." Big dreams, big songs, bad idea. [i]

GRAYS

See *Jellyfish.*

GREEN

Green (Gang Green) 1986 (Hol. Megadisc) 1989
Elaine MacKenzie (Pravda) 1988 (Hol. Pravda/Megadisc) 1989
White Soul (Hol. Megadisc) 1989
Bittersweet EP (Bel. Megadisc/Play It Again Sam) 1991
EP10 (Rokchik) 1991
White Soul & Bittersweet (Widely Distributed) 1991
The Pop Tarts (Futurist) 1992
Pathétique EP (Widely Distributed) 1993

JEFF AND JANET

Jesus Built a Ship to Sing a Song To (KokoPop) 1994

LILACS

The Lilacs Love You! EP7 (Widely Distributed/Pravda) 1991
Rise Above the Filth (Widely Distributed) 1992

Drawing his initial inspiration from an eclectic quartet of influences—the Kinks, Prince, Small Faces and Motown—Chicago singer/guitarist Jeff Lescher has led the group Green through a number of lineups since the mid-'80s. An ace pop songwriter with an unpretentious knack for assessing the ups and downs of romance without malice, he possesses a phenomenal voice that can shift between stirring pop-rock singing, an ear-pinning shriek and a gospelly falsetto.

Green is an inadequately produced but brilliant collection of weirdly derivative originals played with spirit and power; **Elaine MacKenzie** improves the ambition and results on all fronts and sports a neat cover painting by Lescher. Most unpromising title for an exquisite song: "Don't Ever Fall in Love With Someone When You're Already in Love With Someone Else." (The European CD adds both sides of a 1988 single entitled **REM** in response to R.E.M.'s **Green** album.) The more mature-sounding **White Soul,** which ironically downplays Lescher's R&B side, is better still and benefits from bassist Ken Kurson's boppy "My Sister Jane," a delightful pop-punk vestige of his hardcore past.

Kurson (now a business writer) was replaced by Clay Tomasek (ex–Slammin' Watusis) in time for the **Bittersweet** EP, five fine new songs that consolidate Lescher's stylistic impulses. The '60s-soul title track gambles with lush strings and horns but laces it all up in a spectacular vocal; the brutish hard-rock guitars and punky backing cheers of "Maybe You're Right" are strangely topped off with an inveigling Kinksy melody and techno-synth. The most affecting item on the album is "The Record Company Song," a wry and disheartening torrent of Lescher's professional frustrations that culminates in "I'll do anything you ask / My will is broke and I'm tired and sad." (The belated American release of **White Soul** adds **Bittersweet** in its entirety.)

At that point, the indie-label stalwarts—Lescher, Tomasek and drummer Mark Mosher (all of whom inexplicably dressed in drag for the cover snaps)—hooked up with a bigger small record company and made **The Pop Tarts** with Chicago studio hound Iain Burgess, a keyboard-playing guest and a horn duo. The uneven effort fares well on several fronts: the simple soul of "Broken Promises" handsomely introduces the Zombies and Style Council to Antonio Carlos Jobim, "Hear What You Want to Hear" expands a snippet of Elvis Costello melody into fully formed brisk British Invasion pop and "Marga-Marguerite" deftly appropriates the high-toned sweetness of Curtis Mayfield. But other than Tomasek's goofy "Make Believe," the harder-rocking songs aren't so appealing, and Lescher sings "Long Distance Telephone," "Hot Lava Love" and "B.I.T.C.H." in a horrible shrill falsetto, making those songs unlistenable interruptions in what would otherwise be a pretty good record.

After **The Pop Tarts** failed to move the band's career onto the alternative freeway, Green returned to Widely Distributed and made the dispirited but winning **Pathétique** EP, a diverse triad of new songs, including the surprise country swing of "If You Love Me (Part II)."

Having revealed that heretofore undocumented stylistic interest, Lescher pursued it, lowering Green's profile while he teamed with Janet Beveridge Bean (Eleventh Dream Day, Freakwater) to make a wonderfully touching Gram Parsons tribute album. (For the record, neither musician appears on **Conmemorativo,** a 1993 tribute collection on Rhino.) A dozen selections either written or simply recorded by Parsons, **Jesus Built a Ship to Sing a Song To** benefits enormously from the modesty of the just-right arrangements, which are reverent *and* original, as much as the careful passion of the singing. Lescher and Bean alternate verses on "Brand New Heartache," join on the choruses of "Return of the Grievous Angel" and meld their oddly harmonious voices for the entirety of "Sin City," "You're Still on My Mind" and "Hearts on Fire." Lescher makes the most of his somber solo readings of "Love Hurts" and a bluesy all-piano "Hot Burrito #1," while Bean solos on a fast-paced "Luxury Liner" and a warbly, slow "She," letting the flaws in her delivery intensify the conviction in her voice.

The Lilacs, a quartet in which ex-Green bassist Ken Kurson played guitar and sang, debuted in '91 with a four-song 7-inch of his witty post-adolescent rock and pop originals, produced by Jim Ellison of Material Issue. Displaying the careless zeal of a high schooler on graduation day, the band suffers from a puppy-like incapability to keep its enthusiasm in check, which occasionally leads things astray on the album, ineffectually produced by Brad Wood. Still, the spunky and unpretentious **Rise Above the Filth** contains attractive examples of Kurson's sprightly '70s-styled youth-pop that compares favorably to Green's early work. Highlights: the automotive "Hop in the Stanza," "Jennifer," "Roller Derby Queen" and a country-pop oddity, "Choking/DiamondDisgrace." [i]

See also *Blow Pops, Eleventh Dream Day, Freakwater; TPRG.*

GREEN APPLE QUICK STEP

Wonderful Virus (Medicine) 1993
Reloaded (Medicine) 1995

For all the weight given to it, geography doesn't always causally influence the sound of music. So when a band makes that daring thirty-mile migration from Tacoma to Seattle in the year punk central threw its garage doors open to the world, and then makes an album that steps right into the city's then-current stylistic cliché, it's safe to assume that factors other than water supply or scenery are at stake. Novel for the genus only in that bassist/backup singer Mari Anne Braeden isn't a flannel-wearing boy, the loosely named Green Apple Quick Step displays nothing on **Wonderful Virus** any competent quintet couldn't learn from a set of Alice in Chains, Candlebox and Pearl Jam songbooks. Ty Willman is an inoffensively functional vocalist and the lyrics use more big words than Eddie Vedder, but anyone looking for originality or effective musical excitement would do better turning up other rocks.

The second album is a completely different story. Displaying some real initiative on **Reloaded,** GAQS wisely opts not to compete head-on with Pearl Jam. (The two bands share management.) Instead, the group co-opted Stone Gossard as co-producer and spread its surprisingly useful stylistic wings. After trundling through a thick soup of gloomy atmospherics ("Hotel Wisconsin") and a crunchy demonstration of wah-wah technique ("Ed #5"), the album suddenly comes alive with Braeden's lead vocal on the don't-care punk onrush of "No Favors." Her high harmonies with Willman on the poppy "T.V. Girl" and the pretty "Alligator" fan the fun. A loopy cocktail lounge instrumental ("Space C*cksucker") and an acoustic bonus track put a frothy head on the shaken-not-stirred music. Even when the lever swings back to Big Rock, the quintet still pulls something better out of its bag of tricks: the bleary-eyed gambol through "Los Vargos." Pairing up the two voices, forcing songs toward places maybe they didn't mean to go and generally not settling for the obvious when there's another idea to try, **Reloaded** gets a lot closer to nirvana. [i]

DAVID GREENBERGER AND TERRY ADAMS

The Duplex Planet Hour (East Side Digital) 1993
The Duplex Planet Halloween Special EP (Hello Recording Club) 1993

VARIOUS ARTISTS

Lyrics by Ernest Noyes Brookings Volume One (Shimmy-Disc) 1989
Place of General Happiness: Lyrics by Ernest Noyes Brookings, Vol. 2 (East Side Digital) 1991
Delicacy & Nourishment: Lyrics by Ernest Noyes Brookings, Vol. 3 (East Side Digital) 1992
Outstandingly Ignited: Lyrics by Ernest Noyes Brookings, Vol. Four (East Side Digital) 1995

The Duplex Planet, one of the best and longest-running fanzines in America, features transcripts of the sad, funny, brilliant, inane, remarkable, irrelevant and ingenious things said by the elderly residents of Boston's now-defunct Duplex Nursing Home during interviews and conversations with editor David Greenberger. It's a fantastic concept that consistently yields revelatory results, providing a completely different view of the aged for a society that generally treats its eldest citizens with cynical neglect at best and scorn at worst.

The Duplex Planet has proven so successful that Greenberger (a member of the 1980s band Men & Volts) has spun off a wide range of ancillary *Duplex* projects, including a book anthology, a comic, live performances and the extraordinary **Duplex Planet Hour** CD, a collaboration with NRBQ pianist Terry Adams. As a monologist, Greenberger reads some of the choicest material from his zine's archives, assuming the voices of his elderly charges. Adams, meanwhile, provides music in between and sometimes over Greenberger's readings. His compositions draw upon jazz, swing, Dixieland, Broadway and Tin Pan Alley, providing an ideal backdrop for the soliloquies. The combination of music and voice is almost seamless, making this one of the few spoken-word albums that never gets tiresome. Of course, Greenberger has the advantage that his material is unfailingly first-rate. Many of the pronouncements made by his aging associates are profound ("Ask not *what?,* but *what for?*"; "The idea is, when it gets too hot, get the hell outta the sun!"), others hilariously silly ("That salad is worse than Delaware!"; "I keep smokin', but what I really want to do is drive around in a stick-shift car"), but almost all provide some sort of epiphany. A wonderful and important album.

Greenberger has also put together four discs of songs based on poetry by the late Ernest Noyes Brookings, who was a resident of the nursing home. With his idiosyncratic, far-ranging recollections and observations as their rhythmically challenging starting points, groups as diverse as Yo La Tengo and XTC, the Young Fresh Fellows, Morphine, the Amazing Delores, Madder Rose and Evan Johns have written and recorded original songs based on them. "President Truman body medium size / His residence the many room outstanding White House / In competition normally wins competitive prize / In his bed there was never a thin louse." [pl/i]

GREENBERRY WOODS

Rapple Dapple (Sire/Reprise) 1994
Big Money Item (Sire) 1995

SPLITSVILLE

Splitsville U.S.A. (Big Deal) 1996

Benefiting from three equally talented singer/songwriters (Ira Katz and twin brothers Matt and Brandt Huseman), Baltimore's Greenberry Woods push all the right power-pop buttons on **Rapple Dapple,** co-produced by Andy Paley. The bouncy "Trampoline" kicks things off in fine fashion and sets the stage for what follows: piles of gutsy guitar, sweet harmonies and more hooks than the NBA all-star team. Lyrics are hit and miss, though; for every dull observation ("Waiting for Dawn to turn me on"), there are bull's-eyes: "I used to play love tongue-in-cheek / now I wish I'd kept my tongue in check." But when the melodies are as delicious as they are on "I'll Send a Message," "That's What She Said" and the slightly punkified "Nowhere to Go," such lyrical transgressions are easily overlooked.

The eighteen-song **Big Money Item** (produced by Paley) delivers more of the same manic pop thrills, although the Greenberry Woods' influences are easier to spot this time around. They borrow from Air Supply (!), the Beach Boys (you'll have a hard time believing that's not Carl Wilson singing lead on the swell "Go Without You"), the Beatles and Monkees simultaneously (the insistent "Back Seat Driver") and Big Star (the **Sister Lovers**–styled ballad "Invisible Threads"). Superb stuff, but docked for being overly derivative.

Splitsville, a pseudonymous trio of the Huseman brothers (here dubbed Captain Dusty and Messiah Kari) and singing drummer Johnny Immaculate, goes for pop-punk laughs on its maiden voyage. With song titles like "Come Back to the 5 and Dime, Larry Storch, Larry Storch," "I Was a Teenage Frankenstein" and "Gremlin With Mags," it's pretty evident how seriously this is all meant. Still, **Splitsville U.S.A.** is often hooky enough—in a Buzzcocks/Redd Kross–ish fashion—to hang in there. [jmb]

GREEN DAY

1,000 Hours EP (Lookout) 1989
39/Smooth (Lookout) 1990
Slappy EP (Lookout) 1990
Sweet Children EP7 (Skene!) 1990
1,039/Smoothed Out Slappy Hours (Lookout) 1991
Kerplunk! (Lookout) 1992
Dookie (Reprise) 1994
Insomniac (Reprise) 1995

PINHEAD GUNPOWDER

Carry the Banner (Lookout!) 1995

Who knew? One day, punk was thundering along, minding its own business, comfortable in a seemingly permanent role of rocking to the converted. Stuck in the past and digging it, the hellions of hardcore could wallow merrily in their noisy state of mindless grace without any need to peer over the edge of the commercial gutter. There was, everyone knew, nothing beyond. So far as punk was concerned, Nirvana's success had ultimately led nowhere; even Fugazi's hard-won popularity wasn't spreading to other bands.

Then came **Dookie.** The album's bratty cartoon cover—a fighter jet dropping shit bombs, with matching brown CD tray—should have limited its appeal to the crudest adolescent elements of snotnosed society, but it didn't. Young enough to be naïve and smart enough to be cynical, California's Green Day—an East Bay trio loaded up on irreverent, vulgar humor, catchy pop tunes, aggressive guitar power and harmlessly obnoxious slackertude—made a third album that differed substantially from its second only in that it sold nine million copies and opened the floodgates to loud/fast/pushy guitar bands. All of a sudden, a sound that had been around at least since the Ramones first counted off a song in the mid-'70s was good as, well, gold-plated dookie.

The teenagers' first outing was **1,000 Hours,** a buzzsaw guitar roar with songs of little note. It's impossible to conceive of Green Day now finding any use for a lyric like "Starlit night / The moon is shining bright" ("1,000 Hours"), but the imaginary video could be pretty funny. The subsequent album didn't set Green Day on destiny's course, either: **39/Smooth** (later repackaged on CD, with the contents of the surrounding EPs and a compilation contribution, as **1,039/Smoothed Out Slappy Hours**) is a relatively tame power-pop affair. Although plucky and brash, the music is too timid to even flirt with punk intensity levels. Singer/guitarist Billie Joe Armstrong's well-mannered lyrics—hopeful, uncertain, self-conscious—manage only mild psychic discomfort ("I feel forgotten.") and romantic tension rather than any rebellious insurgence; the music never even threatens to overpower such adolescent winsomeness as "I throw away my past mistakes and contemplate my future / That's when I say . . . What the hey!?!" ("Going to Pasalacqua") or the teen horniness of "Can we find a way / So that you can stay / I think I'm gonna pop" ("The Judge's Daughter"). Bassist Mike Dirnt and a competent drummer named John move the songs along, and Billie Joe sings them earnestly, without the contrived English accent he would later affect. A very tentative start.

The trio's sound and stance began to coalesce a bit more clearly on **Slappy,** specifically in the song "409 in Your Coffeemaker," which hits harder and louder and employs such essential vocabulary as "daze," "lazy" and "wasted." The EP is also notable for containing "Knowledge," a good-natured Operation Ivy cover that became (and remained) a Green Day concert staple.

With Tré Cool (Frank Wright III) smashing away as the band's new drummer, Dirnt asserting his equal place in the arrangements and Billie Joe toying with his inflection, **Kerplunk** reintroduces Green Day as pop-punks, plundering the past for chord changes and their own lives for lyrical concepts. "Welcome to Paradise," a Clash-y song (whose chorus melody owes a debt to the 1968 *Wild in the Streets* soundtrack song, "The Shape of Things to Come") of mixed feelings about moving out of the house for the first time, is the pivot connecting the band to its future; "80" introduces the anxious paranoia and suspicion of mental instability that developed into "Basket Case" on **Dookie;** "2000 Light Years Away" charges the sound but blows the vision thing. Elsewhere, **Kerplunk** falls back to the softhearted romantic pleasantries and loneliness of **39/Smooth** (except for Cool's juvenile novelty, the country-fried "Dominated Love Slave"). The CD adds the prior **Sweet Children** EP: the title track's huggable punk, two buzzing soundalike originals and a lame cover of the Who's "My Generation," marked mainly by a transient drummer's tin-can clatter.

Turning the rhythm section into a massive powerhouse and Billie Joe's guitar into a surging wall of post-Spector sound, **Dookie** (produced by Rob Cavallo and the band) crystallizes post-adolescent disgust into a give-a-shit soundtrack for useless losers who hate everything but can't be bothered to do anything about it. "I'm not growing up, I'm just burning out," Billie Joe sings in the first track. Halfhearted animosity and slacker inertia rule here. "I locked the door to my own cell and I lost the key" ("Longview") sums up the album's dispirited outlook, which is completely contradicted by the music's joyous release. A remake of "Welcome to Paradise," the unsettled "Basket Case" ("Sometimes I give myself the creeps"), "She" and the magnificent "When I Come Around" ("I'm a loser and a user so I don't need no accuser to slag me because I know I'm right") round out the fun, which easily overcomes the mutts ("Coming Clean," "Emenius Sleepus," "In the End") left yapping in the back of the kennel.

Wily enough not to fall for stardom's stupidity, Green Day still sold itself short on **Insomniac.** An evident attempt to not seem overly worried by **Dookie**'s impossible challenge, **Insomniac** *sounds* enough like its predecessor, but the familiar hand-me-ups have a careless air; many lack proper endings and just run out at unsatisfying points. The album doesn't really get off the ground until halfway in, when Green Day brings something new to the table: a riveting two-minute instrumental buildup to "Panic Song."

Returning as a grown-up-quick adult, Billie Joe acknowledges the problem without exactly confronting it, substituting rancid self-loathing, exhaustion and neurotic despair for **Dookie**'s safer targets. His change of perspective reframes the band, making it harder for fans to identify with the alienation of songs that announce "I'm a loner in a catastrophic mind / Elected the rejected / I perfected the science of the idiot" ("Armatage Shanks"). With the comforting announcement that "I've got a knack for fucking everything up" ("Bab's Uvula Who?"), he describes himself as a "Walking Contradiction" (in a song that borrows from the Kinks' "She's Got Everything"), "Brat" and "Jaded" ("I found my place in nowhere / I'm taking one step sideways"). He offers an enthusiastically ambivalent view of methedrine in "Geek Stink Breath," complains of physical meltdown in "Brain Stew" and concludes "No culture's worth a stream of piss / Or a bullet in my face" ("No Pride"). Having come to that conclusion, Green Day's next stop could be anywhere.

Pinhead Gunpowder was a two-day 1994 Armstrong side project with some local California punk brats; **Carry the Banner** runs through its program of eight originals and a pumped-up rock cover of Diana Ross' "Mahogany" inside of fifteen minutes. The semi-fast, semi-tuneful popcore sound falls between Green Day and Rancid; numbers Billie Joe sings ("Walkin' Catastrophe," "Find My Place," "Mahogany") could pass for his band's slashed-off B-sides. A useful reminder of how close Green Day remains to sub-commercial punk, this good-natured, above-average rip benefits from, but scarcely hinges on, its star power. [i]

GREEN JELLŸ

Cereal Killer Soundtrack (Zoo) 1993
333 (Zoo) 1994

For mindless, directionless energy in service less seriously of music than cheerful mass-market multimedia-twiddling, Green Jellÿ (formerly Green Jellö) takes the Twinkie. Led by Bill Manspeaker (aka Moronic Dicktator), the colorful band of Buffalo expatriates, which has often been described as Gwar for the kiddie-set, is a mere approximation of that far-funnier band's over-the-top lyrical antics and satirical heavy metal.

Cereal Killer Soundtrack, released first as a poorly animated longform claymation video and then as a belated CD under the band's original name (changed in a flash of the legal and fiscal terrors after General Foods threatened a lawsuit), purports to tell some kind of comic-book story, but that's all part of the limited effect of Green Jellÿ's joke. There's no story here, and very little substance to speak of. A piece of the film was used as the video for "Three Little Pigs" in 1993, and the clip accurately captures the flavor of the full-length album. Green Jellÿ displays a remarkable knack for blowing opportunities for incisive, lasting humor and true burlesque, resorting instead to references to breakfast food, cartoons and pooh-pooh jokes. Many popular artists are ridiculed: "Electric Harley House (of Love)" lifts its bridge from Metallica's "Enter Sandman," while "Trippin' on XTC" roasts the Red Hot Chili Peppers. There's also a limp cover of "Anarchy in the UK," this one set in the Bedrock of *Flintstones* lore—but it would appear to be a rip on the vacuous versions of that song released by Mötley Crüe and Megadeth. Is there anything to recommend here? Yes. "Obey the Cowgod" has a nifty punk wallop in its riffs and song structure; some enterprising young band would do well to steal them.

Same goes for "Carnage Rules," the song that opens **333.** Steal the song, write new lyrics, record it, make some bucks and throw your Green Jellÿ disc away. The second album is virtually indistinguishable from the first, save for some improved production values and a bit of sophistication in the lyrical mix (see "Piñata Head," a round condemnation of Green Jellÿ's own fan base). Sadistica, a female addition to the outfit, shows impressive lung power on "Fixation," and the band's rendition of "The Bear Song" (kindergarten classic "The Bear Went Over the Mountain") may evoke a snort or the odd snicker, but Green Jellÿ needs to learn the value of follow-through. [icm]

CLIVE GREGSON & CHRISTINE COLLISTER

Home and Away (UK Eleventh Hour) 1986 (Cooking Vinyl/Flying Fish) 1987
Mischief (UK Special Delivery) 1987 (Rhino) 1988
A Change in the Weather (UK Special Delivery) 1989 (Rhino) 1990
Love Is a Strange Hotel (Rhino New Artists) 1990
The Last Word (Rhino New Artists) 1992

CLIVE GREGSON

Strange Persuasions (UK Demon) 1985 (Compass) 1995
Welcome to the Workhouse (UK Special Delivery) 1990 (Compass) 1996
Carousel of Noise (Flypaper) 1994
People & Places (Compass) 1995
I Love This Town (Compass) 1996

CHRISTINE COLLISTER

Live (Green Linnet) 1995

One of those couples unfortunately obliged to do their parting in public, folky English singer/guitarist Clive Gregson (ex–Any Trouble/Richard Thompson band) and singer Christine Collister (also a Thompson associate) ended their personal and professional partnership with dignity on **The Last Word,** allowing only a few glimmers of anger and hurt to slip into the tender album's abiding sadness. The fact that he wrote all the songs loads the deck of sympathy cards, but it's not that simple. Without making it clear whose heart is being opened, Gregson—prone to vicious self-deprecation and gutsy revelation at the best of times—gives Collister lines to sing that acknowledge dishonesty, desperation, new love and various bad feelings; in his own voice, he admits cheating, lying and drinking until closing time. Finally, the two join voices and resolve to disagree with abiding regret in "I Don't Want to Lose You," a searing country lament that wets the eyes and dots the tears. "You called my bluff, you called my friends / But you never called to make amends / You wore me like a worn out shoe / But I don't want to lose you."

Nevertheless, Gregson and Collister went their separate ways, leaving behind a total of five albums of brilliantly sung sensitive music. The acoustic **Home and Away,** recorded mostly at gigs, handsomely blends Collister's deep, strong voice with Gregson's gorgeous tenor on originals and oldies (Merle Haggard's "Mama Tried," Carl Perkins' "Matchbox"). **Mischief** fits the same heartfelt songwriting and rich singing into full-blown arrangements, many of them tastefully rocked up. Gregson's striking melodies and deeply incisive lyrics are more than adequate to the stronger environment; the duo's voices rise to the occasion as well.

With elevated ambitions and widened stylistic reach, more intricate harmonies and complex material hallmark **A Change in the Weather,** a record without a single mediocre or ineffectual track. Soaring through poignant essays on wife abuse and mortality, Gregson and Collister leaven the mood with the witty and personal rock'n'roll of "(Don't Step in) My Blue Suede Shoes." On the other hand, **Love Is a Strange Hotel** is a wan acoustic covers album: a fine program performed without much spunk.

A decade after starting it with the powerful **Strange Persuasions,** Gregson—who relocated to Nashville, Tennessee, in '93—resumed his solo career with **People & Places.** A typically finespun (if mainstreamed) convocation of memorable writing, sterling musicianship and expressive singing, the economically arranged album demonstrates how easy it would be for Gregson to slide into the new country field. Instead, he folds the multiple folk and rock personalities of his past into an uncharacterizable blend, even steering clear of the adult alternative (AAA) drain. "My Eyes Gave the Game Away," a self-excoriation addressed to a former lover, could be for Collister but offers no specific clues; the love tales of "Camden Town" and "Lily of the Valley" are clearly about other people.

Welcome to the Workhouse is a collection of early-'80s demos and outtakes, simply done with various musicians in Gregson's circle. The all-acoustic and equally excellent **Carousel of Noise,** sold primarily by mail-order, is a fascinating seventeen-track footnote assembled from two '94 solo shows and contemporaneous home recordings; among the highlights are a remake of Any Trouble's "Second Choice," the expatriate's meteorological lament of "The Queen's Head," a Boo Hewerdine collaboration entitled "Dead Man's Shoes" and Buddy Holly's "Learning the Game," sung without a trace of Lubbock pop bounce.

The inevitable "Starting All Over" is the only song Collister wrote alone for her solo debut, which is otherwise filled by an eclectic set of downcast borrowings from Joni Mitchell, Rickie Lee Jones, Randy Newman, k.d. lang, Leiber and Stoller, Elvis Presley and Willie Dixon. Recorded in concert on her native Isle of Man with a second acoustic guitarist and a fretless bassist, **Live**—notable for Collister's distinctive voice and moving interpretations—is a small pleasure fans should definitely seek out. [i]

See also *TPRG.*

GRENADINE

Goya (Simple Machines/TeenBeat/Shimmy-Disc) 1993
Nopalitos (Simple Machines/TeenBeat) 1994

As indie-pop supergroups go, Washington DC's Grenadine is right up there on the talent meter, containing as it does singer/guitarists Mark Robinson (Unrest/Air Miami) and Jenny Toomey (Tsunami) and trombonist/guitarist Robert Christiansen (Eggs). With a fixation on los productos Goya (pictured on the covers of both albums) and a dynamic level of guitar strumming, spare drumming (by Christiansen) and gentle vocals that hovers around early Association records, the shimmering trio makes very pretty music together.

Despite hijacked liner notes that misleadingly promise an album of '40s pop standards, **Goya**—produced with disarming airiness and clarity (if gallons too much echo) by Kramer—includes only one known cover, the Flamingos' "I Only Have Eyes for You," which Toomey sings in an arrangement that owes a little something to Art Garfunkel. In keeping with the campy dress-up nostalgia of the entire enterprise, the breezy originals have titles like "Philco" and "Decca." Although the froth of Grenadine's jangly frappé occasionally slides from light to cloying, **Goya** generally succeeds in blending three compatible ingredients into a flavorful cocktail. (The unlisted bonus spoken/sung tape pastiche that follows "Decca Reprise" gets the bizarre aftertaste of this Shirley Temple out of the way even before the record ends.)

In much the same way Unrest could combine the same set of components into delectable treats that were just a little off, the second shot of Grenadine is one too many. A joint release on Robinson's TeenBeat label and Toomey's Simple Machines (the spine lists a serial number for each), **Nopalitos** was produced by Warren Defever (His Name Is Alive, Elvis Hitler), who loosens the spigot enough to allow thicker rock to color several songs. The problem with **Nopalitos** is its conflicted purpose. Hamstrung between the silliness of Robinson's whimsical excursions (the vo-de-oh-de vaudeville of "Hell Over Hickory Dew" and "Roundabout on a Tuesday," the clip-clop instruction of "What on Earth Has Happened to Today's Youth?") and the clammy seriousness of Toomey songs like "Steely Daniel" and "Drama Club," the album shares only one significant feature—a kindred oldie—with **Goya.** This time, "This Girl's in Love With You" gets a cruddy, cavalier reading by Toomey. [i]

See also *Eggs, Tsunami, Unrest.*

GRIFTERS

Disfigurehead EP7 (Doink) 1990
The Kingdom of Jones EP7 (Doink) 1991
So Happy Together (Sonic Noise) 1992
One Sock Missing (Shangri-La) 1993
Crappin' You Negative (Shangri-La) 1994
Eureka EP (Shangri-La) 1995
Ain't My Lookout (Sub Pop) 1996

A BAND CALLED BUD

Dad [tape] (no label) 1989

HOT MONKEY

Lazy EP10 (Shangri-La) 1994
Lion (Personal Favorite) 1995

Maybe it's something in the water (or the barbecue sauce), but Memphis has made a habit of spawning folks—from Alex Chilton to this wry foursome—with a metaphysically skewed notion of what makes pop really, well, *pop.* Like Guided by Voices, the Grifters portend the graying of indie-rock. Weaned on '60s Top 40, sustained by the punk revolution of the '70s and allowed to flourish in the lo-fi environs of the '90s, the Grifters have enough historical perspective to pirate the spoils from the good ship classic rock while leaving the fool's gold behind.

Initially known as A Band Called Bud (a name they eventually hypothesized might cause a lawsuit on the behalf of the Clydesdale-borne brewmasters), the group issued a cassette and, as the Grifters, a pair of undistinguished EPs marked by ardent Sonic Youth worship and a hazy grasp of song form. But after further seclusion in their flower-shop practice space—perhaps the best use of a cooler since Ed Gein—they re-emerged, covered in tape hiss and prepared to apprise the world about the trials and tribulations of the over-educated, under-employed Dixie intellectual.

So Happy Together, which does exactly that, is a bit overbearing in its negativity, but songs like the droning "Hate" (a litany of antipathies that basks in self-loathing) glean their subtext from the stirring interplay between guitarists Dave Shouse and Scott Taylor. Although the Grifters go out of their way to underscore the artifice of recording—dropping in audible tape splices and count-offs, thereby upping the pretense level plenty—there's enough emancipating squall on pieces like "Love Explosion" to make up for that. The band lowers the octane level a degree on **One Sock Missing,** focusing on the underlying lo-fi "charm" of its agreeably shambling soft-focus songs and burying the pulsing bass of Tripp Lamkins, which is the crux of the band's best material. It's not an altogether misguided approach, but Shouse and Taylor (who split vocals) often slip into a laconic saunter that's a little too close for comfort to Pavement frontman Stephen Malkmus' slacker slump.

While that likeness is again audible on stretches of **Crappin' You Negative,** the Grifters manifest their southern roots more clearly in dark, inscrutable parcels of Americana like "Skin Man Palace" (which is kicked into high gear by the bug-eyed shout with which Taylor proclaims himself "the Mambo King") as well as the hyperventilating spazz-blues "Holmes." Yes, quirkiness does factor into the equation on wheel-spinning digressions like "Get Outta That Spaceship & Fight Like a Man," but the bulk of **Crappin' You Negative** sounds like the product of some sort of bizarro-world psychic union between Jerry Lee Lewis and Flannery O'Connor. The **Eureka** EP furthers the band's survey of Dixiana: although they never inject more than a molecule or two of identifiably "country" content into their sound, songs like "Whatever Happened to Felix Cole?" and "Founder's Day Parade" crawl along the underside of the psyche with the uniquely southern persistence of kudzu vines.

The thoroughly engrossing **Ain't My Lookout** continues that thread, even going so far as to excavate the customarily buried drumming of Stanley Gallimore—which adds a firewater boost to most of the better-recorded songs. The positive effect of the tension between Shouse's more warped meditations (the scenester-phobic "Boho/Alt") and Taylor's more immediately infectious compositions (the doo-wop dadafest "Mysterious Friends") is palpable, but not distracting. Each gauntlet a member lays down gets picked up and carried to new realms, making **Ain't My Lookout** as much fun to hear as it clearly was to make.

Hot Monkey is Taylor's nom de doodle; the friendly **Lion** is a full no-fi dose of his late-'80s home-brew noises and loosely transcribed songs, some of which (at least "Arizona") wound up full-fledged (er . . .) Griftertunes. [dss]

GRIP WEEDS

See *Rooks.*

JACK GRISHAM/MIKE ROCHE/ RON EMORY/TODD BARNES

See *True Sounds of Liberty.*

GROOVE COLLECTIVE

Groove Collective (Giant Step/Reprise) 1994
We the People (Groove Collective/GRP) 1996

REPERCUSSIONS

Earth and Heaven (Warner Bros.) 1995

Born out of weekly sessions at New York's influential floating acid-jazz club Giant Step, Groove Collective is a ten-member combo that successfully bridges the often-explored gap between hip-hop and bebop. Whereas most fusions of the disparate forms feebly hew closer to one side or another with only empty stylistic nods justifying the blend, the Groove Collective's debut (produced by Steely Dan knob-twirler Gary Katz) masterfully tackles the middle ground. Over heavy funk and hip-hop rhythms (both looped and live, along with turntables and a bed of sumptuous percussion) first-rate jazzers like trombonist Josh Roseman, trumpeter Fabio Morgera, vibist Bill Ware and saxophonist Jay Rodriguez deliver concise but meaty solos, smartly accenting the beats whether live and flexible or sampled and rigid. Dollops of post-bop, '70s soul jazz and Afro-Caribbean styles intermingle with modern street beats; the combinations never sound forced. Percussionist Gordon "Nappy G" Clay and members of the hip-hop group the Aliens rap on a few tracks, but **Groove Collective** is, for the most part, instrumental.

Much of the Groove Collective's extensive rhythm section—Clay, bassist Jonathan Maron and drummer Genji Siraisi—join guitarist Andy Faranda and conga player Daniel Wyatt to back soul diva Nicole Willis in Repercussions. Although a different horn section appears on several cuts, by and large **Earth and Heaven** lacks the muscle, grit and energy of the Groove Collective album; it's not much more than an ordinary retro-'70s soul record. [pm]

GROTUS

Brown (Spirit) 1991
Luddite EP (Spirit) 1992
Slow Motion Apocalypse (Alternative Tentacles) 1993
Opiate of the Masses EP (Alternative Tentacles) 1994
Handjob EP (London) 1995
Mass (London) 1996

Fatalists who believe the end of the world and the turn of the millennium are somehow connected should consider booking Grotus for their end-of-the-century New Year's Eve bash. The San Francisco quartet's lyrics read like a countdown to Armageddon, while their Test Dept.–like primal rhythms (especially in later releases) head toward a spirit world holding a hint of salvation. The mirror Grotus holds up to Western society acknowledges an epidemic of cultural ills. Though the band's delivery is generally subtler, the subject matter runs along politically, socially and environmentally correct lines similar to those inscribed by Consolidated, Meat Beat Manifesto and even Skinny Puppy. In Grotus' portrait, a nation of robots addicted to drugs, television and sugar run the risk of overdosing on the barrage of information pumped into them.

The band—John Carson (bass, samples), Lars Fox (vocals, samples, percussion) and Adam Tanner (guitar, bass, samples); drummer Bruce Boyd joined in '91—contributes to that onslaught of images by using video projections during live shows. **Brown** employs as many spoken samples as a Negativland album: a recurring fundamentalist-style "I'm a god and you're a god" speech on "Malthusela," which equates the obsession with looking young and staying healthy to a sick religion. Another sampled piece, "City of the Dead," aptly prefaces "Las Vegas Power Grid," an extreme example of people shutting off reality that weaves in samples of people explaining the basics of gambling games. In "Full Metal Grotus (we need so much)," America is a society of excesses; the song details a genetically engineered lifestyle, a theme that pops up on later releases. Meanwhile, the music on **Brown** could be a score for a *Blade Runner* sequel. Grotus' blend of techno-industrial constructions and a gothic eeriness evokes a metallic chill on a par with Foetus or Nine Inch Nails.

Luddite has more varied musical constructions than **Brown,** which makes the band's message even more potent. The title track is an immediate grabber, with pounding rhythms, a heavy metal crunch and Napalm Death–style vocals. Other cuts have more seductive grooves, but the message doesn't vary. "What in the World" observes "We talk like we're in a movie / Best entertainment value for the buck / Just push rewind and put in the next tape." "Shelf Life," another complaint against genetically altered food, even repeats a line from **Brown**'s "Valhalla's Celtic Robbie," a protest against animal testing. A remake of the first album's "Brown" omits the original's spoken samples, but the music is much more cohesive, with dance rhythms as a sign of Grotus' tightening focus.

Slow Motion Apocalypse mixes the alluring music of **Luddite** and a judicious bit of the sampling activity of **Brown.** Over what sounds like a brassy '70s TV theme, "Good Evening," about the bombardment of television news headlines, jumps from serious references about AIDS and neo-Nazis to ridiculous snippets ("a piece of Madonna's underwear"). "Up Rose the Mountain" is a reminder of life's tenuousness; "Sleepwalking" again throws daggers at how most people waste the time they do have. More prominent here than in the past are Hindu references and chants, as well as a Middle Eastern flavor that conjures images of an armor-plated belly dancer. That impulse comes to the fore on "Shivayanama," where Fox's heavy vocals are enveloped by an overpowering bass. Both "Sleepwalking" and "Kali Yuga" also tap into that lilting Eastern influence. (The CD contains an unlisted version of "Brown.")

Opiate of the Masses consists of five tracks mixed-and-matched from pieces of "Shivayanama," "Sleepwalking" and "Kali Yuga." Although much of the EP tends toward tranciness ("Rasa Bliss Mix" and "Afterglow Tantra" use soothing chants and spacy electronics), "Visnu Fulfillment" is a high-energy techno-dance number colored with low-level primal scream sounds.

Grotus continues on the techno/tribal trail with the even more polished **Handjob** EP. ("T'Ain't Nobody's Bizness If I Do" even fits spoken samples to smooth funk.) Although just as determined in topical intent, the lyrics don't leave as heavy an imprint in the context of this less-crunching music. "A Bad Itch" considers the ease with which racist attitudes infiltrate society, while "Ebola Reston," presented in three mixes, warns that the disease should not be seen as an exclusively Third World problem. The original "Ebola" mix is like a techno version of Sisters of Mercy; the others, by Jack Dangers of Meat Beat Manifesto and Sasha Konietzko of KMFDM, are upbeat house tracks, providing a strange sonic contrast to the heavy-handed lyrics.

The full-length **Mass** supplants the stop-gap preview that was **Handjob,** repeating all three of its songs (though restricting "Ebola Reston" to a single incident) and adding critical portraits of a mass murderer ("Collect 'Em All"), a cable-TV addict ("Wild Bill") and a slacker ("Hand to Mouth," done as a sloppy Beck-like blues) that remain widely accessible and smartly appealing no matter how hard they rock. [mg/i]

GROVER

My Wild Life (Zero Hour) 1995 (Zero Hour/Universal) 1996

Several years after the end of Let's Active, guitarist/singer Angie Carlson formed Grover, with ex-bandmate/husband Mitch Easter on bass. Although he subsequently bowed out of the Chapel Hill trio, Easter stuck around long enough to play on and produce some of Grover's debut album, which was otherwise overseen by Kevin Salem. **My Wild Life** is roaring pop, a deceptively simple and upbeat record in which emotional turmoil blows up as affecting clouds of tuneful power. On the surface, Carlson's catchy songs are carefree releases of distortion and feedback; at the album's heaviest, Grover favors the Breeders a bit. Although she sings with little expressiveness in an ordinary voice, Carlson's relationship lyrics concede reluctance ("Yeah, I'm Dumb"), diffidence ("Hole in My Eye"), disillusion ("I'm Dreaming"), farewell ("Sweet Thing"), regret ("Heavy Past"), recrimination ("Damaged Girl") and disdain ("Superhero"). Oddly, "Pretty Machine," the album's only enthusiastically positive number, is also its clumsiest. Some people only rain when it's happy. [i]

GUIDED BY VOICES

Forever Since Breakfast (I Wanna) 1986
Devil Between My Toes (E) 1987 (Ger. Get Happy!!) 1993
Sandbox (Halo) 1987
Self-Inflicted Aerial Nostalgia (Halo) 1989
Same Place the Fly Got Smashed (Rocket #9) 1990
Propeller (Rockathon) 1992
An Earful O'Wax (Ger. Get Happy!!) 1993
Vampire on Titus (Scat) 1993
Clown Prince of the Menthol Trailer EP (UK Domino) 1994
Fast Japanese Spin Cycle EP (Engine) 1994
Get Out of My Stations EP7 (Siltbreeze) 1994
Bee Thousand (Scat/Matador) 1994
The Grand Hour EP (Scat) 1994
Crying Your Knife Away (Lo-Fi) 1994
I Am a Scientist EP (Scat) 1994
Box (Scat/Matador) 1995
Alien Lanes (Matador) 1995
The Official Ironmen Rally Song EP (Matador) 1996
Under the Bushes Under the Stars (Matador) 1996

The adage about ten-year overnight sensations has never rung more true than when applied to this Dayton, Ohio, combo, which spent the better part of a decade toiling in sub-basement obscurity before its sudden adoption by the Amerindie hipoisie. Guided by Voices major-domo Robert Pollard, a thirtysomething elementary-school teacher with a knack for knocking off as many as a dozen songs in a single day—he estimates he's written more than twenty-five hundred in his life—has perfected an oddly insistent fusion of Anglo-pop melody, arena-rock scope and lo-fi aesthetic, all of which combine to give the band its signature sound.

That signature wasn't quite so legible on the band's earliest work, wherein Pollard's regard for the jangle-pop sound of R.E.M. and Brit-popsters like the Postcard Records contingent bordered on the tributary. On the seven-song **Forever Since Breakfast,** released, as were the next four GBV records, in a vinyl-only edition of five hundred copies, Pollard and his pals (guitarist Paul Comstock, bassist Mitch Mitchell and drummer Peyton Eric) choogle along in inoffensively indie manner, set apart ever so slightly from the pack by intricate harmonies keyed by the frontman's agreeably faux-Brit accent. Still, it's nothing to write home about. There's a bit more personality evident on **Devil Between My Toes,** most of which reveals itself in little details like the martial drumbeat that anchors "Cyclops" and the skewed round-style vocal treatment afforded "Hank's Little Fingers." The term lo-fi hadn't really come into widespread use in 1987, so the few people who actually heard the album upon its original release likely just deemed the recording . . . well . . . *bad.* Nevertheless, the addled neo-psych tone of songs like "A Portrait Destroyed By Fire" goes a long way toward overcoming the project's technical limitations.

In comparison, **Sandbox** is positively slick, from the full-color packaging to occasional guitarist Steve Wilbur's relatively clean 8-track production. Pollard has begun to pare down his songwriting—nearly half the songs clock in at under two minutes—as well as introducing some embryonic wordplay (most evident in "Trapsouldoor" and "The Drinking Jim Crow"). While the band is still prone to bouts of pantomime ("Adverse Wind" is particularly Stipe-striped), guitarist Jim Pollard's increasingly edgy mini-solos and Mitchell's aggro-fied bass pounding hint at distinctiveness to come.

Self-Inflicted Aerial Nostalgia is the first release to begin to communicate the band's bizarro-world musical lexicon. Fractured fairy tales like "The Future Is in Eggs" and "The Great Blake St. Canoe Race" manifest Pollard's maturing flair for spare-yet-enigmatic lyrical forays (as well as his incremental retreat from verse-chorus-verse structure). While it's increasingly clear that GBV is Pollard's show, densely packed melodies like "Navigating Flood Regions" and "An Earful O'Wax" (which would later become the title of a German "hits" compilation) suggest that the other members somehow got themselves locked into a shared post-hypnotic suggestion that allows them to Osterize mid-period Who, Josef K B-sides and the Blue Öyster Cult into a palatable, potent concoction.

Since it was recorded in a single day, it shouldn't be too surprising that the fourteen-song, thirty-two-minute **Same Place the Fly Got Smashed** seems to pour forth in one stream-of-consciousness gush. It may be the band's darkest release, both in the doomy, distant sound (dominated in the mix by Greg Demos' slurry bass playing) and in the unusually angst-ridden delivery Pollard uses in bellowing out songs like "Airshow '88" and "Order for the New Slave Trade." The singer/guitarist gets even more somber when let loose alone—as on the bleary-eyed "Drinker's Peace," which introduces the recurring alcohol theme to GBV lore. Compelling—and more than a little disturbing.

Propeller ushers in the band's pure-pop (well . . .) era, wherein utter imperviousness to matters of fidelity and scrutability don't detract a whit from the preposterous catchiness of songs like "Quality of Armor," "14 Cheerleader Coldfront" and the Moody-Blues-via-ESP-Records "Mesh Gear Fox" (which will have you singing along without having a clue what's actually coming out of your mouth). The network of guitar lines—coming in from three directions with the full-time recruitment of perennial collaborator Tobin Sprout—is astounding, given the primitive recording quality, but the most striking aspect of the album is the band's coincident mockery of and yearning for the days when rock was BIG and its stars were bigger. The amount of inherent irony varies quite a bit as you move from the stadium-sized "G-B-V" chant that opens the album into the Laserium-ready strains of "Weed King," but the sense of wonder never abates.

When Cleveland's Scat Records—a virtual major in comparison to the band's series of self-created labels—issued **Vampire on Titus,** these reclusive rockers (who hadn't even performed live in several years) were suddenly, and somewhat bizarrely, thrust into the limelight as the world finally caught up with GBV's lo-fi, hi-NRG aesthetic. The timing couldn't have been better, as the band reached a creative zenith on songs like the surreal Beach Boys frug "Jar of Cardinals" and the baleful "#2 in the Model Home Series" (which turns eerier and eerier when Pollard clamps down on the line ". . . and now the fun begins" with the feral terror of an animal trying to chew free a limb from a trap). Elsewhere, finely wrought psychedelia wafts up enticingly in the form of "Perhaps Now the Vultures" and the melodica-driven "Marchers in Orange," both of which could pass for Incredible String Band outtakes. Simply superb. (On CD, **Propeller** and **Vampire on Titus** are jimmied onto one disc with the latter's artwork as the front cover.)

Pollard and his cohorts—particularly guitarists

Mitch Mitchell (having switched from bass) and Tobin Sprout—tighten things up even more on the bright 'n'shiny **Bee Thousand.** The album's twenty condensed songs—most of which last less than two minutes—could pass for anything from **White Album** outtakes ("Kicker of Elves") to scaled-down arena rock ("Buzzards and Dreadful Crows") to Zappa-esque prank-pulling ("Hot Freaks"). Titles like "The Goldheart Mountaintop Queen Directory" notwithstanding, the genre-jumping seldom sounds premeditated—and Pollard's voice has never sounded better. While undeniably erratic, Guided by Voices never sacrifices hummability to practice art-for-art's sake.

You'd think the rapid release rate—and dense packing of songs—would exhaust the band's considerable backlog, but you'd be wrong, judging by the number of between-LP slabs they've disgorged. **Fast Japanese Spin Cycle,** eight songs in twelve minutes, reprises a couple of previously released ditties but more than makes up for that small sin by leading with the classic-in-waiting "My Impression Now." **The Grand Hour,** a six-pack highlighted by the dizzy "Break Even," is just as fine. The band limits itself to four outbursts on **I Am a Scientist,** but two of those—the wide-eyed title track (an Andy Shernoff–"reduced" live version of the **Bee Thousand** selection) and the contorted, Soft Boys–styled "Do the Earth"—are positively indispensable.

Crying Your Knife Away, a vinyl-head's dream, is a haphazardly playful official bootleg that captures the blink-and-you-missed-it nature of GBV's live shows—although the added visual benefit of Pollard's incessant beer chugging and Daltrey-esque pirouetting will have to wait for the concert film.

In its vinyl version, **Box** combines the band's first five albums (**Devil Between My Toes** through **Propeller**), paying special attention to maintaining the homemade quality of the early packaging and artwork. A bonus disc, **King Shit & the Golden Boys,** contains nineteen previously unreleased songs spanning a five-year period. (The CD edition omits **Propeller.**) While completists will no doubt covet the rare stuff, most of it could have remained in the vaults without any great outcry.

Alien Lanes, which exudes a curiously unfinished, vaguely disinterested attitude, sacrifices a good bit of the band's skewed pop savvy—except on the Mersey-bop "Game of Pricks"—in favor of fragmentary sketches that don't really go anywhere. Pollard's rec-room haikus (like "Striped White Jets" and "Big Chief Chinese Restaurant") still gush forth with addled aplomb, but they seem to have been balanced at random atop relatively tuneless lo-fi blueprints, rather than woven into actual songs. The breach might have something to do with the unusually indistinct lineup—no fewer than eight official members, including new bassist Jim Greer, a former *Spin* magazine editor and a veteran of New York quirk-rock combo Rude Buddha, are credited—but it's becoming obvious that the band needs to take a refresher course in self-editing.

Under the Bushes Under the Stars finds GBV getting back into gear, and, for the first time, taking the step up to state-of-the-art studio recording (with a few interludes). Fortunately, they don't act like kids let loose in a candy store: apart from the addition of a few simple frills (like the acoustic detail on the glammy "To Remake the Young Flyer," one of four tracks written by Sprout), there's little shift in the sense of economy. Pollard seems to have tired of tilling Brit-psych terrain, aside from a brief dip on the swirly "Underwater Explosions." Instead, he concentrates on extra-crunchy guitar rock, characterized by the pulsing car-radio strains of "Man Called Aerodynamics" and "The Official Ironmen Rally Song." The latter is also, along with three non-LP tracks, on an EP of the same name.

In '96, Pollard and Sprout both released solo albums. [dss]

GUILD OF TEMPORAL ADVENTURERS

See *Kendra Smith.*

GUMBALL

Gumball EP (UK Paperhouse) 1990
Special Kiss (Primo Scree) 1991
Light Shines Through (UK Paperhouse) 1991
Wisconsin Hayride EP (Columbia) 1992
Super Tasty (Columbia) 1993
Revolution on Ice . . . (Columbia) 1994

DON FLEMING

Because Tomorrow Comes EP (Instant Mayhem) 1996

Formed as a result of the bitter split of B.A.L.L., Gumball allowed singer/guitarist/producer Don Fleming and drummer Jay Spiegel to jettison the calculated-sloppiness shtick and smug trashing of '60s icons that were that band's obsessive specialties. **Special Kiss,** recorded as a trio with new bassist Eric Vermillion, is actually closer in spirit and execution to the tart garage-rock sound of Fleming and Spiegel's earlier band, Washington DC's Velvet Monkeys, albeit with a higher quotient of slashing post–no wave guitar. In fact, the album—a locomotive blur of abrasive pop and gnarly guitar psychosis—sounds like a close relative of Sonic Youth's **Goo.** (Thurston Moore even plays keyboards on one number.) "You Know," in particular, recalls the singalong corrosion of Teenage Fanclub, a sense amplified by the appearance of all four Fanclubbers on the track. Having been previewed abroad with the four-song **Gumball** EP, **Special Kiss** was followed in the UK by **Light Shines Through:** three album tracks (one an alternate take) and four non-LP numbers.

To mark time before their full-length Columbia debut and show off their catholic musical taste, Gumball went the covers route on the five-song **Wisconsin Hayride.** Besides Foetus, Black Flag and Small Faces material, "New Rose" is a frisky carbon of the Damned's debut single with extra guitar by J Mascis, but the version of the Mahavishnu Orchestra's "Awakening" is a messy, ill-advised gag, a cheap shot at '70s fusion without chops or wit.

Super Tasty is exactly that, a snappy commercial effort produced by Butch Vig with the polished hum'n'snarl of classic '70s pop-punk clatter by Cheap Trick and Blue Öyster Cult. Gumball's attack is, if anything, a little too slick for the times, but Fleming's boyish tenor and the chrome-torpedo riffing guards the manifest kick of discontent in "The Damage Done" (neatly disguised with an exuberant intro of guitar-drums clamor and bright, wheezing harmonica) and the bittersweet ballad corn of "Marilyn." A bit more bite would not have gone amiss; much of Fleming's lyric irony sounds more weary than wired. Still, **Super**

Tasty is a buzzin' good time, if only for its wonderfully retro sonic glitz.

Revolution on Ice . . . makes Fleming's cynicism more explicit. The title and cartoon artwork are a combined blast at the corporate co-opting of the alternative-rock revolt; songs like "Revolution on the Rocks" and "Nights on Fire" bristle with embittered surrender and accusatory rage. The album's open-wound air, however, makes it Gumball's strongest effort to date. Less superficial than **Super Tasty, Revolution on Ice . . .** crackles with a dark, seductive intensity, heightened by the extra guitars and keyboards of new recruit Malcolm Riviera (an old Velvet Monkeys crony). The BÖC connection gets reinforced by a letter-perfect rendition of "She's as Beautiful as a Foot," complete with guest vocals by that band's original drummer, Albert Bouchard (more recently of the Brain Surgeons).

Inaugurating his Instant Mayhem label in early '96, Fleming released **Because Tomorrow Comes:** two tracks of solo "Donaldtronic" meanderings on guitar, theremin, mellotron, fuzz bass, keyboards and tapes that sound like backstage tuneup time at the Fillmore East, circa 1968, and the title song, an acoustic folk-pop strummer with a Moody Blues undercurrent. [df/i]

See also *Dim Stars, Half Japanese.*

GUMBO!

See *Arrested Development.*

GUN CLUB

Fire of Love (Ruby) 1981 (Slash) 1993
Miami (Animal) 1982 (Animal/IRS) 1990
Death Party EP (UK Animal) 1983
The Las Vegas Story (Animal) 1984 (Animal/IRS) 1990
The Birth the Death the Ghost (UK ABC) 1984 (Revolver) 1990
Sex Beat 81 (Fr. Lolita) 1984
Two Sides of the Beast (UK Dojo) 1985
A Love Supreme (UK Offence) 1985
Danse Kalinda Boom: Live in Pandora's Box (UK Dojo) 1985 (Triple X) 1994
Mother Juno (Fundamental) 1987 (2.13.61/Thirsty Ear) 1996
Pastoral Hide & Seek (UK Fire) 1990
Divinity (Fr. New Rose) 1991
In Exile (Triple X) 1992
The Gun Club Live in Europe (Triple X) 1992
Lucky Jim (Triple X) 1993

JEFFREY LEE PIERCE

Flamingo EP (UK Statik) 1985
Wildweed (UK Statik) 1985 (Triple X) 1994

RAMBLIN' JEFFREY LEE

Ramblin' Jeffrey Lee & Cyprus Grove with Willie Love (Triple X) 1992

Jeffrey Lee Pierce, for all intents and purposes, *was* the Gun Club. From his days as a peroxided, Debbie Harry–fixated Los Angeles teen-punk, through a lengthy era when he seemed convinced he could channel the spirit of Robert Johnson, to a more recent probe of the seedier side of continental balladry, Pierce—who died of a cerebral blood clot in Utah at the end of March 1996—always presented a highly individual, albeit sometimes dazed'n'confused, vision of a soul in torment.

On Gun Club's cathartic debut, Pierce's unschooled, high-lonesome howl often evokes the hell-hound-on-his-tail imagery he's trying to project. The band isn't terribly successful when it tries to preserve the letter of the blues (as on a cover of Johnson's "Preaching the Blues"), but transposing the genre's spirit to a snarled punk framework ("She Is Like Heroin to Me," the gripping "Fire Spirit") proves the Gun Club's purity of essence. **Miami,** which gave Pierce the chance to live the dream of singing with Harry, is both jumbled and dispirited. A good bit of that can be blamed on Chris Stein's sterile production, which cleanses Ward Dotson's slide guitar of its grit and pushes Pierce's vocals preposterously far in front of the mix.

The stormy period that followed—characterized by some exceedingly edgy tours—is suitably reflected on the **Death Party** EP, recorded with a Gotham-based lineup that includes drummer Dee Pop (Bush Tetras) and guitarist Jim Duckworth (who played in Tav Falco's Panther Burns). It's worth seeking out for the stately goth-rock ballad "The House on Highland Avenue." Pierce took a reconstituted Gun Club—including original guitarist Brian Tristan (aka Kid Congo Powers), who had served in the Cramps in the interim—into the studio for **The Las Vegas Story,** an odd survey of the wrong side of countless sets of tracks. His swamp-rock originals aren't quite up to snuff (particularly when he tries to wax blue-collar like John Fogerty), but his wail communicates all the urgency ingrained in Gershwin's "My Man's Gone Now" (from *Porgy and Bess*).

The Gun Club collapsed at this point, although a flurry of live releases went a long way toward obscuring that fact. Neither **Sex Beat 81** (a listless, cassette-quality document of the first recording lineup, which included bassist Rob Ritter of 45 Grave) nor **The Birth the Death the Ghost** (a catch-as-catch-can compendium of more recent material) betrays the slightest hint that Pierce is a compelling, powerful live performer. While the Dutch-origin **Danse Kalinda Boom,** dating from 1983, likewise sounds as if it could've been recorded from the parking lot, both Pierce and Kid Congo sound positively adrenalized, particularly on the feral "Sleeping in Blood City."

After a two-year hiatus, Pierce and the Kid joined forces again for **Mother Juno,** a polished album that's both sobering and sober. On songs like "The Breaking Hands," producer Robin Guthrie of the Cocteau Twins spins a delicately layered web of sound; more straightforward songs like the shimmying "Thunderhead" recast the old energy in slightly more linear terms, although guest Blixa Bargeld does his best to tilt "Yellow Eyes" on its axis. The lineup (rounded out by bassist Romi Mori and drummer Nick Sanderson) remains intact for **Pastoral Hide & Seek,** an album that lays open the first flowerings of Pierce's creeping Euro-style (not surprising, given its nascence in the city of Brussels). Pierce is still able to concoct scenarios (like "Emily's Changed") that make slipping through society's safety net seem almost inevitable. More important, he's rediscovered a dormant sense of dynamics, as evidenced by poignant interludes like the country-tinged "I Hear Your Heart Singing."

Divinity is certainly the artiest Gun Club album ever, replete with byzantine song structures and jarringly dissonant tunings on the part of both Pierce and Kid Congo. That's strange, given the directness of songs like "Keys to the Kingdom" (a straightforward New Testament reading set to a Bo Diddley beat) and "Richard Speck" (a serial killer paean). **In Exile** compiles seventeen songs from the three preceding long-players, adding the heretofore unreleased "Pastoral, Hide and Seek" (recorded during the sessions for the album of the same name). Congo's on-again/off-again involvement was off again by the time the band reconvened to record **Lucky Jim,** an eerily austere record that displays the more spectral side of Pierce's voice, particularly on the dejected title track and "Cry to Me," which gathers some Bayou musk from Bart Van Poppel's muggy Hammond organ washes. The lack of a truly heated counterpoint allows Pierce to coast a bit too easily through some of the tracks, but the manner in which he replaces post-adolescent rage with full-blown adult emptiness is mighty impressive.

Pierce's intermittent solo career was not nearly as distinguished as his work in the Gun Club. The erratic **Wildweed** is crisp but devoid of much in the way of distinctive flavor: striving to be Iceberg Slim, he delivers iceberg lettuce. The **Ramblin' Jeffrey Lee** record is slightly more palatable, if only for Pierce's indisputable gift for emulating the slurry phrasing and pig-foot playing of the country bluesmen he venerates. [dss]

See also *Nick Cave and the Bad Seeds, Congo Norvell, Cramps, Liquor Giants; TPRG.*

GUNS N' ROSES

Live ?!*@ Like a Suicide EP (Uzi Suicide) 1986
Appetite for Destruction (Uzi Suicide/Geffen) 1987
Guns n' Roses EP (Japan. Geffen) 1988
G n' R Lies (Uzi Suicide/Geffen) 1988
Use Your Illusion I (Uzi Suicide/Geffen) 1991
Use Your Illusion II (Uzi Suicide/Geffen) 1991
The Spaghetti Incident? (Uzi Suicide/Geffen) 1993

IZZY STRADLIN AND THE JU JU HOUNDS

Izzy Stradlin and the Ju Ju Hounds (Geffen) 1992

DUFF MCKAGAN

Believe in Me (Uzi Suicide/Geffen) 1993

GILBY CLARKE

Pawnshop Guitars (Virgin) 1994

SLASH'S SNAKEPIT

It's Five O'Clock Somewhere (Geffen) 1995

KILL FOR THRILLS

Dynamite From Nightmareland (MCA) 1990

NEUROTIC OUTSIDERS

Neurotic Outsiders (Maverick) 1996

Hard as it may be to believe, Guns n' Roses was once a cool and somewhat threatening rock band, bringing genuine raunch to a pathetically pouffy era before turning into a real-life Spinal Tap. Formed in 1985 by five Hollywood misfits (two locals, two Indiana refugees and a Seattle scene veteran), the quintet quickly won local raves with gritty performances and low-lifestyle imaging: early flyers proclaimed the group "Fresh from detox." Worshiping at the twin altars of Aerosmith and AC/DC, the band debuted with the first-ever fake indie buzz-building release: the limited-edition **Live ?!*@ Like a Suicide.** In fact released by Geffen (albeit with no mention of the conglomerate name), the 12-inch contains two tepid originals and two covers that, as later revealed, most likely weren't even recorded live.

Appetite for Destruction is another story. Combining an incisive pop sensibility with a fist-pumping classic-rock stance, **Appetite** was probably the first *real* rock album that a lot of teen metalheads had ever heard; if W. Axl Rose's Joplinesque screech became too grating, Slash's fiery and melodic guitar work made the songs sparkle. The sound was fleshed out with doses of '70s denim that drew in an older audience, and with songs like "Sweet Child o' Mine," "Paradise City" and "Welcome to the Jungle," **Appetite for Destruction** went on to sell many millions of copies. It also turned some of the bandmembers into hitherto-unimagined rock-star morons.

The cash-in **G n' R Lies** pairs the **Live ?!*@ Like a Suicide** EP with four semi-acoustic tracks. While the sappy "Patience" revealed a latent ballad streak, some of the other songs' racist and sexist lyrics fueled such massive media overkill that self-parody became a foregone conclusion.

Released some four years after the debut, the sprawling **Use Your Illusion**—two separate albums with matching artwork and no seeming logic to their division of thirty songs, over two and a half hours in all—contains about half an hour of music that lives up to its absurdly grandiose ambitions. The band impresses on the ambitious "Coma" and "Civil War," and rocks through several energetic no-brainers, but the albums are burdened alternately by ludicrous excess (full orchestras and choirs) and many throwaway tracks; oddly, some of the most overblown songs date back to the band's first demos.

Recorded mostly during the **Use Your Illusion** sessions, **The Spaghetti Incident?** is a back-to-the-roots–styled album of covers that contains some reasonably intriguing tracks (from the Skyliners, Stooges, Nazareth, even Soundgarden) along with several abominations. As a nominal collection of influences, the gallery hangs up the work of the Dead Boys, T.Rex, New York Dolls, UK Subs, Misfits, Fear and the Damned with the pretentious tastefulness of nouveau riche art patrons.

The two years of staggering stadium-rock excess that followed left the band's future somewhat hazy. **It's Five O'Clock Somewhere,** the first solo album from Slash (Saul Hudson), contains potential G n' R songs Rose reportedly rejected. With ex-Jellyfish member Eric Dover doing a lame Axl impersonation and Alice in Chains bassist Mike Inez in the Snakepit lineup, the album claims a couple of decent rockers but is very repetitive. Slash has also made countless guest appearances/collaborations, most notably with Iggy Pop, Michael Jackson, Carole King (!) and, best of all, high-school chum Lenny Kravitz on **Mama Said.**

Made upon his exit from the band after **Use Your Illusion, Izzy Stradlin and the Ju Ju Hounds**—despite the star's middling vocals—is a surprisingly strong album that dramatically shows the rootsy sensibility he brought to G n' R. It sounds like a good Keith Richards solo album (and is actually much better than the album Richards released around the same time).

Stradlin replacement Gilby Clarke, previously with Raspberries-inspired power popsters Candy and pop-metal quartet Kill for Thrills, released his mediocre **Pawnshop Guitars** shortly before being booted from the band; he's a featured participant on Slash's album. Bassist Duff (Michael) McKagan—who played drums or bass in such Seattle bands as the Fartz, Fastbacks, Vains, 10 Minute Warning and the DTs—made his ill-advised singing debut on **Use Your Illusion II** and took the mic for a handful of **The Spaghetti Incident?** His own album, with help from Clarke, Slash, Jeff Beck, Lenny Kravitz and Sebastian Bach, isn't much better.

There are countless bonus tracks available on Guns n' Roses' imports, most containing live material. Recommended is the self-titled Japanese EP, a convenient collection of early live tracks and (apparently mistakenly) an outtake from the **Suicide** sessions—with crowd noise added, natch.

While waiting for Axl and Slash to get their shit together for a new Guns n' Roses album, Duff (playing guitar and singing) and drummer Matt Sorum hooked up with guitarist/singer Steve Jones (just before he headed off to reunite the Sex Pistols) and bassist John Taylor (between Duran Duran obligations) to form the Neurotic Outsiders, a Hollywood jam session that became an actual group. Produced by Jerry Harrison, the band—which sounds pretty much like the slow-witted sum of its constituent hard rocking parts—has the historical cheek to include a brisk cover of the Clash's "Janie Jones" alongside the less incendiary Jones and Taylor originals on **Neurotic Outsiders.** [ja/tr]

See also *Fastbacks.*

GURU

See *Gang Starr.*

GUTTERBALL

Gutterball (Mute) 1993
Weasel (Brake Out/Enemy) 1995
Turnyor Hedinkov (Ger. Return to Sender/Normal) 1995

Post-punk Americana probably didn't need its own version of the Traveling Wilburys, but that pretty much describes Gutterball, an offhand fusion of Steve Wynn, the House of Freaks (Bryan Harvey and Johnny Hott), occasional HoF touring bassist (and ex-Silo) Bob Rupe and former Long Ryder Stephen McCarthy. As with any impromptu not-quite-supergroup, Gutterball gets by on ease and charm when the members hit their mark and feels like something less than the sum of its parts when they don't.

In contrast to the carefully constructed burnish of Wynn's early solo records and House of Freaks' major-label excursions, **Gutterball** came to be over a single weekend of playing and writing at a Virginia farmhouse. Wynn is more or less in charge, co-writing (with Harvey) eight of the twelve songs as well as three on his own (the other one is McCarthy's). Things are fairly loose, with the band's three guitars in a perpetual state of ringing Crazy Horse overdrive, but the unavoidable competence of the veteran musicians (and a cleanup mix job by Joe Chiccarelli) ultimately results in a record that's not as rough as it wants (or needs) to be. Nevertheless, the songs are sturdy and generally satisfying, especially the laconic din of "Lester Young," the poignantly thrumming "Motorcycle Boy" and the zinging romanticism of "When You Make Up Your Mind."

Weasel is much better, a more raucous and wholly collaborative effort (with Love Tractor's Armistead Wellford replacing Rupe) that captures a genuine after-hours, alcohol-and-broken-glass vibe. The record is a happily sprawling fifteen-song mess, a hit-or-miss collision of bluesy vibrato, piercing tossed-off leads and hooky bits of hard-luck noir. Both the songcraft and the guitar workouts connect with more effective violence this time, and Harvey and McCarthy capably take on additional writing weight.

The band's discography is rounded out by the limited-edition **Turnyor Hedinkov.** An odds-and-sods compilation from an odds-and-sods band couldn't be more appropriate, and the outtakes, live tracks and European radio sessions featured are gnarly, intense and illuminating. [jc]

See also *Coal Porters, Cracker, House of Freaks, Silos, Steve Wynn.*

GWAR

Hell-O (Shimmy-Disc) 1988
Scumdogs of the Universe (Metal Blade) 1990
The Road Behind EP (Priority) 1992
America Must Be Destroyed (Metal Blade) 1993
This Toilet Earth (Metal Blade) 1994

KEPONE

Ugly Dance (Quarterstick) 1994
Skin (Quarterstick) 1995

This sludge-metal performance-art troupe has made its mark by staging cartoonish Grand Guignol spectacles that split the difference between the Muppet Show and Survival Research Laboratories, adding a soundtrack that recalls (as if it matters) a Venom bootleg tape looped through the gears of a garbage disposal. The Gwar legend—something to do with pestilent aliens who've made their home beneath the Antarctic ice cap—was born of a project the members cooked up at art school in Virginia. It sure would be interesting to see those transcripts . . .

Despite some occasionally funny lyrics (and legitimately knee-slapping liner notes), **Hell-O** may well go down in history as the only listening experience more painful than those bootleg Sam Kinison sex tapes. Utterly tuneless "singing" by frontman Oderus Urungus and aimless guitar flailing—it sounds as if the musicians were wearing their papier-mâché gear in the studio—combine to make the disc an utter mess. But the dull-as-dishwater **Scumdogs of the Universe** actually makes one pine for such incompetence, since all it really has to offer is thrash-by-numbers playing over which Oderus belches childish paeans to all that's profane.

There's not much to be said for **The Road Behind,** either: the time-filling EP matches three tedious studio tracks ("highlighted" by the goofily ostentatious "Overture in N Minor") with three live tracks. Of the concert pieces, "Captain Crunch" might earn a few laughs from those prone to spending Saturday mornings in front of the TV and behind the bong. **America Must Be Destroyed,** a concept album of sorts, finds Oderus proclaiming revolution in the streets with all the slapstick conviction of Gallagher in Last Poets' drag. Unlike previous Gwar releases, it actually holds up for one complete listen, but until CD rental shops come into vogue, you'd be advised to keep your distance.

Somehow, the band convinced a smattering of session musicians to lend a hand in the cinemascoping of Gwar on the epic **This Toilet Earth.** Not that trombones alone can save flatulent outbursts like "Pocket Pool" and "Penis I See" (dedicated to the three-foot phallus that often, er, pops up onstage). Again, brief flashes of lowbrow wit surface (in the goofy "Saddam A Go-Go"), but the notion of parodying pomp-rock (see "The Insidious Soliloquy of Skullface") is far too much like carrying coals to Newcastle. Gwar was nominated for its first Grammy in 1995.

Beefcake the Mighty (also known as Mike Bishop) abandoned the Gwarship in order to pursue a career in music with Kepone, an old-fashioned power trio with just enough post–Birthday Party accessorizing to hold the interest of skronk-mongers hither and yon. Guitarist Tim Harriss juggles funk riffs and D. Boon–styled scrabbling with admirable dexterity on **Ugly Dance** standouts like "Loud" and "Leadbreath," but whinging vocals and clever arrangements (like those on "Dickie Boys") often drag the band down to the level of the chin-wagging dilettantes in Primus. Good marks for form, but very little in the way of function. **Skin** follows much the same pattern, although Bishop and new drummer Ed Trask (ex–Holy Rollers) forgo some of the thrust-and-parry nonsense in favor of heads-down, no-nonsense boogie, à la Killdozer. It's a start. [dss]

See also *Holy Rollers.*

ALEXANDER HACKE

See *Einstürzende Neubauten.*

HAGFISH

Buick Men (Dragon Street) 1993
. . . Rocks Your Lame Ass (London) 1995

It might be unfair to characterize this caffeinated combo as Dallas' entrants in the Green Day 500—after all, Hagfish had made its impact on plenty of impressionable Lone Star minds long before **Dookie**-mania gripped the land. Nevertheless, the band's speedy, snotty bashing is clearly derived from the same set of sources, with a slightly stronger dose of Ramones damage. Hagfish gained its first national notoriety as part of a CD that accompanied George Gimarc's book, *Punk Diary 1970–1979*—an anachronistic context that makes perfect sense given the gabba gabba giddiness with which ebullient frontman George Stroud Reagan III (!) barrels through the pulsing guitars.

On **Buick Men,** Hagfish sets broad locker-room humor against cuddly (if raucous) power-pop riffing. Since they're as willing to mock themselves (see "New Punk Rock Song") as the outside things they lampoon, it's hard to hold the dopiness of, say, "Lesbian Girl" against Hagfish. Seven of the album's nineteen songs were reprised on the subsequent major-label debut.

Although **Hagfish . . . Rocks Your Lame Ass** is an asking-for-trouble title, the well-dressed quartet nearly succeeds in living up to it, stringing together fourteen kinetic pogo-punk ditties that uniformly recoil when the three-minute mark approaches. (Bill Stevenson and Stephen Egerton of All produced.) Reagan's flair for blending no-holds barred humor ("Stamp" offers crude advice on trading sexual favors for nightclub admittance) and sardonic political observation (the anti-racist tract "White Food") is impressive enough, and guitarist Zach Blair readily passes the barre (chord), but the band needs to develop some eccentricities if it wants to survive punk's next death. [dss]

HAIR & SKIN TRADING CO.

Ground Zero EP (UK Beggars Banquet) 1992
Jo in Nine G Hell (UK Situation Two/Beggars Banquet) 1992 (Beggars Banquet) 1993
Go Round EP (Beggars Banquet) 1993
Over Valence (UK Beggars Banquet) 1993 (Beggars Banquet) 1994
Psychedelische Musique (Lava Surf Kunst) (UK Freek) 1995

With its pursuit of maximal volume and minimal motion, Loop was one of the earliest figureheads of England's '80s drone-rock movement, but those two extremes proved too difficult to reconcile. When the band split at the turn of the decade, frontman Robert Hampson and guitarist Scott Dowson chose to trance out totally in Main, while singer/bassist Neil Mackay and drummer John Wills (augmented by ex-Savage Opera guitarist Nigel Webb) cribbed this unsavory moniker from an old warehouse in London and persisted in their efforts to rephrase **Metal Machine Music** as power-rock.

Actually, **Jo in Nine G Hell** is a bit more conservative than that. The album's methodically building tracks reflect a post-goth sensibility reminiscent of both early My Bloody Valentine and, oddly enough, the Skids. The trio makes the mistake of enabling listeners to draw breath through the cracks of songs like "Flat Truck" and "Elevenate" (both delivered with Mark E. Smith–styled scorn). Plenty of sound, but precious little vision.

The **Go Round** EP teeters between amorphic tones and structured sound. The title cut is a Joy Division–like swirl; "Amine" and "Cymbals" weave together spacy textures and abstract noises reminiscent of Nurse With Wound. Even the more rock-based "Deeps" begins and ends with formless, meandering soundscapes.

Thanks in part to the efforts of producer Ott (of Th Faith Healers), the sonic fissures are mostly mortared over on **Over Valence.** Webb's playing is more contentious and abstract—particularly on tracks like the throbbing "On Again Off Again" and the lathe-like "K-Funk"—which confers a gripping dislocation, but the album's dominant characteristic is the promethean size of the riffs that roll forth.

Psychedelische Musique (Lava Surf Kunst) virtually dispenses with grounding elements entirely—to the point that only a few of its songs bear titles (the rest are marked off by letters or symbols). Fittingly, the attendant work is largely atmospheric, mostly instrumental and redolent of head-music forebears like Faust. When vocals are figured into the mix (as on "*"), they're flanged and distorted to the point where they could pass for just another channel of synthesizer. Wills' intricate drumming proves especially effective in this setting, maintaining a *motorik* pulse on "Kinetic" and imparting a machine-shop impersonality to "S." Alternately horrifying and riveting, **Psychedelische Musique** shows up "industrial" celebutantes like Al Jourgensen as the bubblegummers they really are. [dss/mg]

See also *Main.*

DEKOBOKO HAJIME/ YAMANTAKA EYE

See *John Zorn.*

HASSAN HAKMOUN AND ZAHAR

See *Zahar.*

HALF JAPANESE

Calling All Girls EP7 (50 Skidillion Watts) 1977
1/2 Gentlemen/Not Beasts (UK Armageddon) 1980 (T.E.C. Tones) 1993
Loud (UK Armageddon) 1981
Horrible EP (Press) 1982
Our Solar System (Iridescence) 1984
Sing No Evil (Iridescence) 1984
Music to Strip By (50 Skidillion Watts) 1987 (UK Paperhouse) 1993
U.S. Teens Are Spoiled Bums EP (50 Skidillion Watts) 1987
Charmed Life (50 Skidillion Watts) 1988 (UK Paperhouse) 1993
The Band That Would Be King (50 Skidillion Watts) 1989 (UK Paperhouse) 1993
We Are They Who Ache With Amorous Love (T.E.C. Tones/Ralph) 1990
Fire in the Sky (UK Paperhouse) 1992 (Safe House) 1993
Boo! Live in Europe 1992 (T.E.C. Tones) 1993
Greatest Hits (Safe House) 1995
Hot (Safe House) 1995

HALF JAPANESE/VELVET MONKEYS

Big Big Sun [tape] (K) 1986

JAD FAIR

The Zombies of Mora-Tau EP7 (UK Armageddon) 1980 (Press) 1982
Everyone Knew . . . But Me (Press) 1982
Monarchs (Iridescence) 1984
Best Wishes (Iridescence) 1987
Great Expectations (Ger. Bad Alchemy) 1989
Greater Expectations (Psycho Acoustic Sounds/T.E.C. Tones) 1991
I Like It When You Smile (UK Paperhouse) 1992

BETWEEN MEALS

Oh No I Just Knocked Over a Cup of Coffee (Iridescence) 1983

JAD FAIR AND KRAMER

Roll out the Barrel (Shimmy-Disc) 1988

JAD FAIR AND DANIEL JOHNSTON

Jad Fair and Daniel Johnston (50 Skidillion Watts) 1989
It's Spooky (UK Paperhouse) 1993

JAD FAIR AND THE PASTELS

This Could Be the Night EP (UK Paperhouse) 1991
No. 2: Jad Fair and the Pastels EP (UK Paperhouse) 1992

JAD FAIR/JASON WILLETT/ GILLES RIEDER

Jad Fair/Jason Willett/Gilles Rieder (Megaphone) 1992

JAD AND NAO

Half Robot (UK Paperhouse) 1993

MOSQUITO

Time Was (ERL/Smells Like) 1993 (Aus. Au-go-go) 1993
UFO Catcher (Japan. Time Bomb) 1993
Oh No Not Another Mosquito My House Is Full of Them! (Psycho Acoustic Sounds) 1993
Cupid's Fist (Hol. Red Note) 1994

COO COO ROCKIN TIME

Coo Coo Party Time (50 Skidillion Watts) 1990

JAD FAIR & PHONO-COMB

Monsters, Lullabies . . . and the Occasional Flying Saucer (Can. Shake) 1996

JAD FAIR AND THE SHAPIR-O'-RAMA

We Are the Rage (Japan. Avant) 1996

JAD FAIR AND DAVID FAIR

Best Friends (UK Vesuvius) 1996

Rock'n'roll started as a medium in which the three-chord song reigned supreme—until, of course, some wise guys got the idea that four chords, then five (and so on) would make it even better. It took years of such high-falutin' thought before a pair of Maryland-via-Michigan brothers emerged with just the opposite notion, paring rock'n'roll down to *no* chords—and promptly announcing their excitement over this development by issuing a three-record box set as their debut album. In the two decades since Half Japanese—still helmed by Jad Fair, one-half of that brotherly tandem—took shape, it's still not entirely clear that "real" chords have ever really entered the picture. In fact, brother David, who has contributed sporadically to the band over the years, has been quoted as advising would-be guitarists not to feel encumbered by any rules at all, insisting, "It's your guitar, after all."

Half Japanese was indisputably at its most unsettling when the Fairs had no outside input. The **Calling All Girls** EP crammed together nine id-bursts (like "Dream Date" and "Shy Around Girls") that rank among rock's most uninhibited expressions of sex as cause for terror, topped off with a title track that does pretty much what it promises—an extended salutation to Kate Smith, Ronee Blakely and Paloma Picasso (among dozens of others). But even the unfiltered nature of that fusillade was no preparation for **1/2 Gentlemen/Not Beasts,** a fifty-song portrait of the artist as a young man clawing to get back into the womb. As he rolls around on the rickety post-Shaggs bed of guitar and drums that comprises "Hurt So Bad" and "No Direct Line From My Brain to My Heart," Jad inflicts as much self-abuse as Iggy did with broken glass a decade before. Not that these are nihilistic manifestos. Quite the contrary: on songs like "I Love Oriental Girls" and "Ann Arbor, MI.," Jad comes across as the archetypal man who loves too much, a trait he parlays into stalker-like obsession on the tenaciously bent "Patti Smith." Although dotted with a goodly number of virtually unrecognizable covers (Dylan's "Tangled Up in Blue," Springsteen's "10th Avenue Freeze Out"), **1/2 Gentlemen/Not Beasts** sounds absolutely like nothing that came before it—and little that's come since.

Although incrementally less rudimentary (thanks in part to the aid of four additional musicians), **Loud** is in no way more conventional. The Albert Ayler–like sax squonking and discordant percussive splashes add an appropriately improvisational free-jazz vibe to stream-of-consciousness songs like "I Know How It Feels . . . Bad." **Horrible** makes a fine companion piece: Lana Zabko's blurting saxophone (and wordless backing screams) help elevate psychodramas like "Thing With a Hook" from horror-rock to just plain horror. Don't look in the basement.

Charmed Life, the release of which was delayed several years by Iridescence's failure, is a guileless burst of optimism that mutes the shriller frequencies considerably, replacing them with an unaffected, exuberant guitar/harmonica backdrop. You'd need a hard heart indeed to keep a poker face when Jad gushes about "Love at First Sight" or launches into a laundry list of his blessings on the instantly memorable title track—an utter classic. The CD and cassette versions add ten (count 'em!) bonus tracks.

David Fair doesn't appear on **Music to Strip By,** which affords Jad the license to spiral even further inward. Surprisingly, he avoids the temptation and turns in somewhat emotionally restrained performances of party standards ("La Bamba") and freshly penned originals ("My Sordid Past," "Stripping for Cash") that indicate he's spent a bit too much time scouring supermarket tabloids. Still, you have to give the guy credit for making it to his tenth anniversary in "the biz" without acknowledging the concept of singing in tune. **U.S. Teens Are Spoiled Bums** expropriates the album's best track (a preemptive strike on the incipient Gen-X mindset), adding three songs. The British CD reissue of **Music to Strip By** contains thirty-six songs—fourteen more than on the original LP.

The Band That Would Be King (later the title of a delightful, if overly earnest, 1993 documentary about Half Japanese's career, directed by Jeff Feuerzeig of Kickstand) starts with what seems like a good idea on paper—augmenting the Fairs' genuine naïveté with the studied amateurism of avant-skronkers like John Zorn and Fred Frith—and ends up losing it in a sea of sloppy pseudoimprovised glop. Jad's goofy observations (like "Ventriloquism Made Easy") sound strangely rote, while his usually exuberant and tuneless vocals are merely tuneless. The UK CD issue adds fifteen cuts to the album's original vinyl incarnation.

At first listen, **We Are They Who Ache With Amorous Love** is just as muddled, but that old Fair spirit seems to have returned. Songs like Don Fleming's "Everything Is Right" don't tickle as playfully as they might have a few years back, yet reveal more of an emotional investment on the artist's part. Still, some of the more impulsive tracks (mostly covers, like a transistor-radio–quality recording of "Gloria") should have stayed in the garage. Even though the hit-to-miss ratio on the live-in-Europe **Boo!** (the touring group includes drummer Gilles Rieder and guitarists John Sluggett and Tim Foljahn) isn't all that much better, the good songs—like the acrid "Big Mistake"—are among Jad's best in years. Bizarro-world burlesque house grind segues into credible art-doo-wop with a precision rarely seen in the band's past, but the simple-heartedness remains unblunted.

Fire in the Sky might be the closest thing to a rock record Half Japanese has yet produced. With the help of frequent collaborators like Fleming (the Gumball leader who's been an ancillary Japanese since **Charmed Life**) and former Velvet Underground drummer Maureen Tucker (who trades cameo appearances on Fair's discs for his guest spots on hers), Jad works up a head of punk-rock steam that allows him to zoom manically through hi-energy blasts like "U.F.O. Expert" and Daniel Johnston's "Tears Stupid Tears." Yips, yaws and other emotional tics are still the rule—as evidenced by the devil-taunting "Eye of the Hurricane" and the Disney-fixated "Magic Kingdom"—but even thoroughly stable folk should be able to "get" the Tucker-enhanced cover of the Velvets' "I Heard Her Call My Name." At first it seems like **Hot** takes the approach one step too far—both "Dark Night" and the opening "Drum Straight" are pointless exercises in ugliness—but the five-piece lineup (including Rieder and Jason Willett, with whom Fair later cut a trio record) hits its stride on chugging rockers that approach normalcy. One bit of advice to Jad's bandmates: wait until he's not looking and then run over that silly megaphone with the van.

Laid end to end, the sixty-nine (!) tracks compiled on **Greatest Hits** make it clear that, for all the lo-fi trappings, Half Japanese is first and foremost a good-time band. Its atmosphere is colored in bright, spangly hues by Jad's eternal optimism—a commodity that's all too rare in a cultural sub-underground where misery and irony are the currencies of choice. If not the ideal selection for diehards—**Greatest Hits** contains just four previously unreleased tracks, including a stuttering backwoodsy rendition of "T for Texas"—it's an ideal introduction for the easily intimidated.

If anything, Jad's solo records offer an even tighter closeup of the darker corners of his psyche. The twenty-seven originals (accompanied by two James Brown covers) on **Everyone Knew . . . But Me** allow him to vent about twenty-seven girls who won't give him the time of day. Or maybe it's twenty-seven rants about one girl—either way, it's tough to slog through. **Best Wishes** dispenses with the existential angst by eliminating vocals altogether on a compendium of forty-two songs, alternately titled "O.K." or "A.O.K." Some of the spasmodic guitar emissions are gripping, but most are off-putting. Dyed-in-the-wool fans probably can't live without it.

To call Jad's non-solo/non-band efforts "collaborations" would be misleading. He simply proceeds, blinders on, to do his thing while his partner du jour scurries to keep up. For his part, Kramer contributes plenty of atmosphere but little needed direction to **Roll Out the Barrel.** Its twenty-four tracks take in steep peaks and deep valleys, with many of the former coming in the form of condensed covers like a rendition of "Subterranean Homesick Blues" as B-movie jungle hunt score. Fair and Kramer recorded a followup (**The Sound of Music**) which fell victim to a financial dispute between the partners and was never released. The Daniel Johnston disc (which really ought to be subtitled *Dueling Neuroses* but was renamed **It's Spooky** in the UK) is actually quite gripping, if occasionally painful to endure. The toy piano and detuned guitar provide suitably child-like accompaniment for Johnston's hyperactively excited songs (like the giddy "I Met Roky Erickson"), but the most affecting moment may be the duo's take on Phil Ochs' "Chords of Fame," which has rarely rung truer.

Oh No I Just Knocked Over a Cup of Coffee, credited to Between Meals—the one-off name fixes its recording span in a Cambridge studio after breakfast and before lunch one 1981 day—was recorded by Jad with Erik Lindgren (Birdsongs of the Mesozoic), David Greenberger (*Duplex Planet*), Phil Milstein and Andy Paley. (Maureen Tucker dubbed drum parts on afterward.) Among the eight numbers chewed over are covers ("Route 66," "Matchbox," "What'd I Say?") and originals (including Jad's "Do You Have a Friend" and "How Will I Know.")

More recently, Fair has looked internationally for people to play with. Teaming with Scottish popsters the Pastels and their friends on a pair of three-song EPs might have sounded like a nifty concept in theory, but brought to fruition the partnership is all but fruitless. Nominally, both parties appreciate life's unsophisticated pleasures, but Stephen Pastel's artless pop and Jad's popless art mix like oil and water. Closer to home, the Phono-Comb album involves ex-members of Canada's Shadowy Men on a Shadowy Planet.

Oh No Not Another Mosquito My House Is Full of Them! by Mosquito (Jad, Half Japanese guitarist Tim Foljahn and Sonic Youth drummer Steve Shelley) is extraordinarily arduous. The record is a seven-song thirteen-minute sub-fi weenie roast of one-handed traps, trace guitar and incomprehensibly distorted (but appropriately buzzing!) screeches from Sir Fair. Ouch! Although the liner-note information is less than encouraging ("Shat out at snacktime in Hoboken"), the twenty-two-song **Cupid's Fist** is a different insect, a sometimes listener-friendly escapade that stops screwing around often enough to perform a handful of folk and folk-rock numbers. When he's not shrieking wildly, Jad sings over acoustic guitar, banjo and percussion, sounding distinctly like Peter Stampfel. There's another singer (check the electric cover of Townes Van Zandt's "Kathleen"), but the absence of last names and credits leaves the identity question open. Mosquito has other records out as well, and Foljahn and Shelley also play behind singer Chan Marshall in her group, Cat Power, which has released CDs on Smells Like and Matador.

Coo Coo Rockin Time is David Fair's solo project; the group's one album is a goodtime '50s rock'n'roll romp containing pleas for better music on the radio and vinyl records in record stores. In 1996, the Fair brothers made an album together, sweetly titling it **Best Friends.** [dss]

See also *Gumball, Daniel Johnston, Kramer, Pastels, Sonic Youth, Stinky Puffs, Maureen Tucker, When People Were Shorter and Lived Near the Water; TPRG.*

JAMES HALL

My Love, Sex and Spirit (Daemon) 1993
Pleasure Club (Geffen) 1996

MARY MY HOPE

Museum (Silvertone/RCA) 1989
Suicide Kings EP (Silvertone/RCA) 1990

As frontman for Mary My Hope, James Hall displayed the same mysterious, androgynous qualities as Bowie's Thin White Duke. The Atlanta group had a good deal more angst and melancholia swirled into the mix, though—its EP wasn't named **Suicide Kings** for nothing. Mary My Hope's edgy, unbalanced style would later be unknowingly repeated, to great commercial success, by Smashing Pumpkins; in the late '80s, people were just scared off by it. Hall, who was born in Houston and raised in Nashville, left the band and kept heading south, to New Orleans, where his dark, brooding tendencies could bloom into a solo career. (Mary My Hope guitarist Clinton Steele, meanwhile, played on World of Skin's **Ten Songs for Another World.**)

My Love, Sex and Spirit invokes a sensual, often lovely world where anger and sadness boil and hiss beneath a smoldering surface. The music bears some resemblance to Mary My Hope's melodic guitar drive, though Hall's trio (guitarist Lynn Wright, bassist Grant W. Curry and drummer Mark Brill) never indulges in his former group's arena rock tendencies. Eclectic, shifting tempos and arrangements, bold trumpet blares and Hall's singing—which veers from howling fury ("Spade") to slithering sexuality ("Sinster")—create a mesmerizing hybrid of rock, goth and jazz. Hall still often slips into Bowie mode (especially on the deeply theatrical, tension-filled strumming of "So Precious"), but there are plenty of Jim Morrison and Peter Murphy influences lurking about, too. The cryptic, oddly poetic musings are simultaneously cocky and consumed with self-doubt, a dichotomy Hall exploits in "Spade" when he maniacally growls, "I'm a rockstar—*cracking.*"

Though Hall celebrated his major-label debut by moving back to Atlanta, leaving sultry New Orleans behind did little to alter his music. If anything, he delves deeper into his frankly sexual persona on **Pleasure Club,** becoming even more darkly alluring and dangerous. The title track features a sinewy verse, followed by a seething, intensely erotic chorus. "Spade" reappears here, slowed *way* down and retitled "Black Is Black." The spindly "I'm Needy" and the soulful "Illingness" are amazingly strong, as is "Heatwave Radio." Hall's singing is more ragged and urgent; he's finally developed a distinctive vocal style of his own. Few can match Hall's charismatic delivery; like a mythological siren, he draws listeners into his clutches. [ky]

JOHN S. HALL & KRAMER

See *King Missile, Kramer.*

MICHAEL HALL

Quarter to Three (Record Collect) 1990
Love Is Murder (Safe House) 1993
Adequate Desire (Dejadisc) 1994
Frank Slade's 29th Dream EP (Dejadisc) 1995
Day (Dejadisc) 1996

After completing three albums as the leader of Austin's crafty and intelligent Wild Seeds, North Carolina–born singer/guitarist/keyboardist (and former music journalist) Michael Hall moved into a similarly wise and winning solo career, also distinguished by exemplary, incisive songwriting and easygoing musical charisma. Co-produced by Walter Salas-Humara of the Silos (with whom Hall and Alejandro Escovedo later formed the Setters), **Quarter to Three** is a restrained, resigned and largely acoustic showcase for Hall's good songs (especially "Congratulations" and "Roll Around Heaven This Way") and conversationally plain singing. The deck-clearing **Love Is Murder,** which both rocks and twangs harder than the debut, was assembled from various '91/'92 sessions in Texas and Europe (one with former Wild Seeds bandmate Kris McKay singing lead). Unstable enough to contain such eccentric outcroppings as the Daniel Johnston–styled "Let's Take Some Drugs and Drive Around" ("I'd rather get beat up than sit around all night"), the Dylanesque goofiness of "Put Down That Pig," the jocular JFK idea of "What Did They Do With the President's Brain?" and an unrecognizable acoustic cover of Led Zeppelin's "Trampled Underfoot," the album generally heads down the crooked white line of romantic difficulties, guided by the seven-minute title track, a compelling high-wire act of fatal balladry.

The alternately stirring and somber **Adequate Desire** confronts birth, life, love and death in handsomely rounded songs that don't pretend to possess answers to anything. "Every Little Thing" greets a baby with the news that it's "a great big world, that's your curse"; between surging lead guitar jousts, "I Just Do" admits the inexplicability of attraction. Even when he's succumbing to a bittersweet memory, as in "Under the Rainbow With You," Hall tempers the wistfulness with a chorus so gorgeous and uplifting that it can't possibly be regret he's feeling. But regret isn't all he's feeling in "Hello, Mr. Death," a solemn if surprisingly ineffectual tribute to Manny Verzosa, the singer/guitarist who died in a 1993 road accident while on tour with the Silos. Hall holds his sardonic wit before him like a shield but leaves his cutting edge in its scabbard: "Hello, Mr. Death / That was a dirty trick, I'm impressed . . . It's a good day to die, I guess."

There are only three songs on **Frank Slade's 29th Dream** and two of them come from **Adequate Desire,** but the title track is an album-length piece (the lyrics of which appear in full on the tray card of **Adequate Desire**) that undertakes a great mission—and fails completely. Throughout this slowly building thirty-eight-minute processional of piano, lap steel, cello, drums and distorted tape hysteria, Hall maddeningly invokes the phrase "Life is alright for the time being" as punctuation for every one of the song's enigmatic couplets. Water torture would be a relief.

Fortunately, **Day**—recorded after Hall's relocation to Chicago—is a complete return to form. A classy rock record that employs Mekons drummer Steve Goulding and frames Hall's casual singing in handsome, inventive settings of guitars, trumpet and violin, **Day** contains typically thoughtful songs of normal lengths—and extreme emotions. "Ghosts" shrugs at the prospect of oblivion; "Sweet Train" indicts religion, saying "The prince of peace is a man of war." "Las Vegas" is a soldier's story; "The Museum of Giant Puppets, PA" paints a dead end in which "the truth is like the teeth of a corpse" and "the red beast and the fat, naked dancer are rolling in blood, vomit and excrement." The symbolism of Hall's concerns can be too opaque for quick appraisal, but his imagery is invariably compelling in its raw intensity. Life, he seems to be saying, is not alright for the time being. [i]

See also *Silos; TPRG.*

TONI HALLIDAY

See *Curve.*

H.A.L.O.

See *Wire.*

HALO BENDERS

God Dont Make No Junk (K) 1994
Don't Tell Me Now (K) 1996

The side-project collaboration between Calvin Johnson (Beat Happening) and Doug Martsch (Built to Spill)—with keyboardist Steve Fisk and others helping out—is as good as anything either northwestern odd-pop icon has ever done. More complex and full-on rocking than Beat Happening and more consistently whimsical than Built to Spill, the Halo Benders combines Johnson's sonorous deep voice and pixilated lyrical ideas with Martsch's contrasting weedy tenor (he often sings entirely different lyrics here, creating what amount to rounds) and unpretentious guitar skill, realizing nifty songs in casually oblong arrangements. A sampler of extraordinary diversity, the ten tunes on **God Dont Make No Junk** hopscotch from the surf-twang goofiness of "Dont Touch My Bikini," to the dramatic Traffic sweep of "Freedom Rider," the hauntingly wistful "Will Work for Food," the overdrive punk pop of "Canned Oxygen," the skittering organ and tick-tock tempo of "Big Rock Candy Mountain" and the brief dub dose of "Sit on It." The lengthy "I Cant Believe Its True" shoulders too big a task for these hit-and-run tunesmiths, but otherwise the album is a stack of strange gems. Having spent years stripping rock down in the spartan Beat Happening, Johnson proves himself equal to far more ambitious musical adventures.

The equally wonderful **Don't Tell Me Now** reduces the eclecticism but not the kinetic invention. "Halo Bender" is a charmingly pointless theme song ("You think you're heaven-sent / Gonna get your halo bent . . . It's the halo bender / a real career ender . . . The Halo Benders / washing all your dreams away"); the lovely "Mercury Blues," gentle and pretty, is no more readily comprehensible. Calvin intones "Bomb Shelter Part 2" in a deadpan Homer Simpson voice, offering a confusing tribute to draft dodgers, military deserters and conscientious objectors. "I'm not gonna suggest you shouldn't register for the draft—that wouldn't be legal. But why not take a cue from my buddy Sam and register 10 times, 50 times, 100 times. There's no law agin' it." It's exactly that why-not imagination that makes the Halo Benders great. [i]

See also *Beat Happening, Built to Spill, Dub Narcotic Sound System, Treepeople.*

HAMMERHEAD

Ethereal Killer (Amphetamine Reptile) 1993
Evil Twin (Amphetamine Reptile) 1993
Into the Vortex (Amphetamine Reptile) 1994
Duh, the Big City (Amphetamine Reptile) 1996

Emerging from the Midwest (Minneapolis via Fargo, North Dakota, to be exact) with a brittle, pop-culture–inspired worldview, Hammerhead once told a journalist that Robert DeNiro's *Taxi Driver* character, Travis Bickle, was the "spirit of the band." Paul Sanders (guitar, vocals), Paul Erickson (bass, vocals) and Jeff Mooridian Jr. (drums) sure play as if his spirit has collectively possessed the trio. While **Ethereal Killer** isn't strictly a concept album, it's no Sunday drive through the park, either. Hammerhead plows a claustrophobic, minimalist soundfield with terrifyingly riveting precision, sharing—among the few decipherable lyrics—tales of child abuse ("Tuffskins"), murder (the title track, for one) and psychosis ("American Rampage"). On "Moleboy," Hammerhead resembles equal parts Unsane, Didjits, Wire, Helmet and Hüsker Dü in a savage, darkly melodic pummeling any of the aforementioned bands would've been pleased to pen. Hell no, it's not "fun"—it's a proficient, relentless beast.

The seven-song **Evil Twin** supplies the same throttling energy, as the trio builds a dynamic assault with one solid instrumental ("Anvil"), the sudden fury of "Washout," the sweeping aggression of "Peep" and the lumbering "Load King." The more sharply honed—refined, even—**Into the Vortex** spirals satisfyingly into a thicket of dense sound, with lyrics that are more intelligible and less obsessed with violence (although "Somebody should clean this dirty world / Someone should save all the pretty girls," from "All This Is

Yours," sounds suspiciously Travis Bickle–like). While some songs convey alienation and discord, there's a sci-fi thread running through "The Starline Locomotive," "Journey to the Center of Tetnus 4" and the instrumental "Galaxy 66."

More experimental than previous efforts, **Duh, the Big City** redefines Hammerhead's sonic heaviness with a dark melodicism underlying such sci-fi inventions as "Earth (I Won't Miss)" and "Mission: Illogical." Especially unrelenting: "Meanderthal" and the terrifying noise abstract "Mr. Bizmuth." Mysteriously hummable: "I Don't Know . . . Texas." Both: "Monkey Mountain," "Mune." After recording the album, Paul Sanders left and was replaced by Craig Klaus (ex–Crown Roast). [mww]

HANDSOME FAMILY

Odessa (Carrot Top) 1994
Milk and Scissors (Carrot Top) 1996

When Chicago guitarist Brett Sparks decided to get a band together, he avoided all the hassle of finding and auditioning musicians by recruiting his wife Rennie and best friend Mike Werner and teaching them to play, respectively, bass and drums. Thus was born the Handsome Family. With Brett writing the music and Rennie contributing lyrics, the trio plays a noisy, urbanized version of country that resembles the rural side of the Mekons. **Odessa** finds the trio just getting ahold of its sound, at times clumsily, as ideas outstrip ability. Songs on **Odessa** deal with the problems of city living ("Moving Furniture Around"), modern relationships (the wittily titled "She Awoke With a Jerk," "Everything That Rises Must Converge") and lost innocence ("Pony"). The Sparks' voices meld together in slightly off-key harmonies that are never less than affecting. If **Odessa** has a fault, it's lyrics that are sometimes too coyly knowing, tossing off pop cultural references to no real effect. But even on the worst offender ("Gorilla"), the Handsome Family's music retains its charm.

Milk and Scissors expands the trio's lyrical grasp, offering such fables as "The King Who Wouldn't Smile," "Amelia Earhart vs. the Dancing Bear" and "Emily Shore 1819–1839." [sm]

HANG UPS

He's After Me (Clean) 1993
Comin' Through EP (Clean) 1993

The Hang Ups' airy vocals suggest various three-letter bands like the dB's and La's, but rude bursts of guitar keep the Minneapolis quartet's pop precariously impolite. Songwriter/guitarist/vocalist Brian Tighe has a good grip on classic pop, but seems reluctant to put down the intrusively stark guitars. Co-produced by Ed Ackerson (27 Various/Polara), **He's After Me** gets off to a breezy start with "Waiting," a catchier, benign version of Morrissey's yodel-flirting. The Byrds-inspired "50,000 Ft." rises to the level of some of the band's other influences—Big Star and the Dangtrippers. "Waltz," an effective curiosity, borrows the melody of its verse from "Somewhere Over the Rainbow." The five-song **Comin' Through** borrows the brisk folk-rocker "Runway" from the album, adding three non-LP songs and a lysergic version of "Eight Miles High" (reclaimed from **Dü Hüskers: The Twin Cities Replay Zen Arcade** tribute album). The title track kicks in with tired but agreeable Velvets-like guitars, then falls into a pillow of Simon and Garfunkel harmonies. "This Is the Hand" has pleasant country and Lovin' Spoonful overtones, letting the guitars actually weave some texture. [jo]

HANSON BROTHERS

See *NoMeansNo.*

HAPPY MONDAYS

Squirrel and G-Man Twenty Four Hour Party People Plastic Face Carnt Smile (White Out) (UK Factory) 1987
Bummed (UK Factory) 1988 (Elektra) 1989
Madchester, Rave On (UK Factory) 1989
Hallelujah EP (Elektra) 1989
Peel Session EP (UK Strange Fruit) 1990 (Strange Fruit/Dutch East India Trading) 1991
Pills'n Thrills and Bellyaches (Elektra) 1990
Live (Factory/Elektra) 1991
The Peel Sessions EP (UK Strange Fruit) 1991 (Strange Fruit/Dutch East India Trading) 1992
. . . Yes, Please! (Elektra) 1992
Double Easy: The U.S. Singles (Elektra) 1993
Loads/Loads More (UK Factory) 1995

BLACK GRAPE

It's Great When You're Straight . . . Yeah (Radioactive) 1995

Way back in the hazy winter of the late '80s, the northern English city of Manchester became known as a debauched clubland for the disenfranchised Thatcher generation, famed for baggy rhythms and endless Ecstasy. Coming from a working-class universe of soft prospects, hard chemicals and even harder house beats, Happy Mondays became the kingpins of the scene dubbed "Madchester." Led by heroin addict and all-around bad sort Shaun Ryder, this gang of hooligans defined the low-rent highlife with notoriously over-the-top hijinks and, more important, an addictive cocktail of northern soul, Detroit acid house, football chants and trad British pop. With his cortex-addled chronicles of Mancunian thug life, Ryder was a rapping gangsta long before there was a name for it. And the Mondays' ranks included the one and only Bez (Mark Berry), an utterly deranged friend of the band whose sole role was to supply the spastic fantastic dancing that remains the scene's most enduring image.

The band's John Cale–produced debut, the inexplicably titled **Squirrel and G-Man Twenty Four Hour Party People Plastic Face Carnt Smile (White Out),** includes its first hit, the swinging "24 Hour Party People." For the most part, though, the album is unimaginative—often unlistenable—acid funk. Producer Martin Hannett (a Factory legend thanks to his work with Joy Division) was brought in to spin the dials on **Bummed,** where the Mondays' lysergic electro-funk began to resemble the residual vibrations of a painfully bad trip. A dark mélange of trippy soul, dancefloor groove and edgy rock, **Bummed** features the first truly great Happy Mondays tunes: "Mad Cyril," "Lazy Itis" and the anthemic dynamite of "Wrote for Luck." (The CD release adds Vince Clarke's "Wrote for Luck" remix, "W.F.L.")

The American space between new albums was filled with the **Hallelujah** EP (a lengthened version of the **Madchester, Rave On** EP), which found Happy Mondays diving head-first into the dance-music pool with a handful of nifty housed-up remixes. Best is "Hallelujah (MacColl Mix)," which pumps up guest chanteuse Kirsty MacColl's splendid harmony vox.

Pills'n Thrills and Bellyaches stands as the Mondays' high-water mark, the definitive baggy record, all loping, rollicking rhythms and daft psychoactive imagery. Producers Steve Osborne and famed club DJ Paul Oakenfold cast some dusty sunshine into the Mondays' previously bleak sound, moving the group even further from the difficult death disco of **Bummed.** The accepted picture of Ryder as a drooling hoodlum also disappeared, as he suddenly became a gifted satirist whose gruff singing accentuated his wonderful comic voice. Ryder spins stories of a picaresque Manchester where "God rains his E's down on me," an opiated dream world reeking of "fine smelling" dope, populated by evangelical hypocrites ("God's Cop"), wacked-out family members ("Grandbag's Funeral") and Ecstatic orgy participants ("Bob's Yer Uncle"). In addition, "Holiday" is a mordantly funny memoir of the Mondays' adventures ("I'm here to harass you / I want your pills and your grass you / You don't look first class you / Let me look up your ass you"), not to mention a hilarious riff on the importance of oversize trousers ("Loose Fit"). Not just the most masterful document of Madchester, **Pills'n Thrills and Bellyaches** is a terrific record of delightfully intoxicating charms.

Live, the stopgap souvenir of the **Pills'n Thrills** tour, was recorded on the pitch at Leeds' United Football Ground—and sounds it. For their next real record, the Mondays were sent to Barbados with producers Tina Weymouth and Chris Frantz. While the island sessions were designed to keep Shaun and Bez away from the demon dope, they made a new friend there in crack. As a result, Ryder's lyrics on **Yes, Please!** are garbled, free-form and just plain nutty ("Digger's mother switch on the cooker / Get the hillbillies down / Set out to bugger / Sweet freak / Pen and ink / How do you make a bulldog think?" from "Total Ringo"). Ironically, this improvisational breakthrough accompanied the Mondays' further dip into the musical mainstream, as the album turns the arsequake pop of **Pills'n Thrills** into a generic tropicalismo funk-lite. Because of the growing separation between Ryder and the rest of the Mondays, the record often feels like a document of a band at odds with itself—the sprightly dance tracks clash with Shaun's deeply bent mindfuck wordiness. **Yes, Please!** has been unjustly vilified as a full-on disaster, but fans will be rewarded by the reams of Ryder's fascinating nervous breakdown verse as well as the handful of fine, if lightweight, songs ("Stinkin Thinkin," "Sunshine & Love," the crack-wracked "Angel").

It came as no surprise when, following the dismal commercial/critical response to **Yes, Please!,** Happy Mondays called it quits. Megastardom had hit the Manchester bands hard, and this particular group had taken full advantage of the situation. While Stone Roses were busy flinging paint on record company walls and preparing for a five-year hibernation, the Mondays were out spewing racist, homophobic nonsense in the press and pissing away hundreds of thousands of Factory Records' pounds. In short, they had become the archetypal rock'n'roll ruffians with money to burn. The rise and fall of the Mondays mirrored the success and collapse of the smiley-face scene. A number of E-related deaths and rampant criminal activity befell Manchester, and the city became known more for its violence than its vibes. A contract-filler released after the bust-up, the handy **Double Easy** compilation proves just how swell the Happy Mondays really were, with a bevy of hits, remixes and bonus tracks—like the delicious version of John Kongos' "Tokoloshe Man" recorded for Elektra's **Rubáiyát** fortieth anniversary collection.

Additionally, the Mondays' catalogue includes a pair of Peel Session EPs. The first, recorded in 1989, contains "Tart Tart," "Mad Cyril" and "Do It Better." The second to be released actually dates from 1986 and includes "Kuff Dam," "Freaky Dancin'," "Olive Oil" and "Cob 20."

Despite a short-lived collaboration with the experimental dance-pop collective Interstella, Ryder was written off as a casualty of the Madchester mentality. But as Mondays-influenced bands like Oasis were busting out all over, Shaun and Bez returned in league with Brit-hop rapper Kermit (late of Ruthless Rap Assassins) as Black Grape. It's hard to tell whether the "Yeah" of the album title is meant as emphasis or sarcasm, though one would have to assume the latter, for the Grape are in no way the picture of sobriety. The UK's first real answer to the Beastie Boys, Black Grape pumps out heavy whiteboy hip-hop infused with a dizzying array of rhythm-heavy musics—dub, jungle, techno, ragamuffin—armed with hard-enough swagger and multitudinous pop culture references (among those namechecked are Bruce Wayne, Neil Armstrong, Planet Reebok, Dirty Harry and "the great smell of Brut"). Sonically masterminded by producers Danny Saber and Stephen Lironi (a one-time guitarist in Altered Images!), **It's Great When You're Straight** packs a big-time wallop, a tumultuous soundscape fraught with sirens, church bells and careening, blast-off sound F/X. As for Ryder, he's in fine form, dueling his sacrilegious raps ("Reverend Black Grape," "In the Name of the Father") with Kermit's aggro-toasting. Between the blunt beats and dangerous demeanor, Black Grape is a broken bottle in the face of jangly Britpopmania, not to mention a surprisingly valid vehicle for Ryder's unexpected resurrection.

After Black Grape's success, Factory attempted to cash in their chips (and maybe make back some of the moolah spent on **Yes, Please!**) with **Loads,** a pretty basic Mondays primer, the first ten thousand copies of which appended the remix compilation companion, **Loads More**. [mgk]

See also *TPRG.*

JOHN WESLEY HARDING

It Happened One Night (UK Demon) 1988 (Rhino) 1991
God Made Me Do It: The Christmas EP (Sire/Reprise) 1989
Here Comes the Groom (Sire/Reprise) 1990
The Name Above the Title (Sire/Reprise) 1991
Why We Fight (Sire/Reprise) 1992
Pett Levels: The Summer EP (Sire/Reprise) 1993
John Wesley Harding's New Deal (Forward) 1996
Dynablob (Mod Lang) 1996

Sometimes disparaged for his striking vocal similarity to Elvis Costello—who has himself expressed displeasure with the uncanny likeness—Wesley Harding Stace boasts many appealing virtues that belong to him alone. A witty but more straightforward wordsmith than Mr. C, he pens concise, catchy tunes, fancies himself a renegade folk musician rather than a pop artist and never takes himself too seriously.

It Happened One Night is a callow yet winning solo live set recorded in '88. Armed only with an acoustic guitar and plenty of pep, Harding celebrates his inspirations in "Phil Ochs, Bob Dylan, Steve Goodman, David Blue & Me" (and elsewhere salutes Joan Baez), delivers a hilariously scathing commentary on Live Aid in "July 13th 1985" and generally sparkles. **God Made Me Do It,** however, sets the course for Harding's career. This nifty EP contains four songs produced by power-pop ace Andy Paley, including the fizzy "Here Comes the Groom" and a deconstructed version of labelmate Madonna's "Like a Prayer." The free-associative ramble with former Bonzo Dog Band wag Viv Stanshall is a unique bonus.

Here Comes the Groom, Harding's first studio LP, is a stellar affair that reprises some songs from the live set. Among the good stuff: the edgy, right-on "Scared of Guns," the irreverent "The Devil in Me" and more soulful tunes like "You're No Good" and "When the Sun Comes Out." Folks who penalize Wes, as he calls himself, for echoing Elvis won't be dissuaded by the presence of Attractions Pete Thomas (drums) and Bruce Thomas (bass) on many tracks. Paley again produced, returning for the next one, too.

Had it preceded **Groom, The Name Above the Title** might have seemed fresher. Though most of the tunes, including "I Can Tell (When You're Telling Lies)" and "The World (And All Its Problems)," possess the expected zing, Paley's smart, detail-oriented production works against Harding's folkie-with-attitude cheek. The cover of Tommy James' "Crystal Blue Persuasion" that closes the album belongs on somebody else's disc (maybe Paley's); it's got nothing to do with Wes.

Switching to Los Lobos saxman Steve Berlin as the producer on **Why We Fight,** Harding opts for earthier, less contrived grooves and cuts down (though hardly eliminates) the Costello echoes. Billed as *An experiment in Folk Noir,* the album shines on "Where the Bodies Are," a scathing indictment of the justice system that presaged the O. J. Simpson case, the blithely cynical "Kill the Messenger" and the delicate and touching "The Original Miss Jesus." Harding also strives to ruffle feathers on a breezy fantasy entitled "Hitler's Tears." All in all, swell.

Pett Levels, an odds-and-ends EP, is Harding's final release on Sire, the label that tried to find him an audience and failed. The delightful "Summer Single" has a vaguely Beach Boys feel and proves Wes can still be a dead ringer for Costello unless supervised closely.

Happily, **New Deal** finds Harding in prime artistic health after an extended absence from the scene. Featuring the boy and his guitar with minimal accompaniment—a steel guitar here, a fiddle there—this triumphant return is a relatively subdued yet consistently witty affair. Harding again tries on the mantle of Phil Ochs for "The Triumph of Trash," a tart broadside against greed and mindless nostalgia, then turns sweetly wistful for "In Paradise," a gentle sequel to the Kinks' "Waterloo Sunset." On "Heart Without a Home," "Infinite Combinations" and others, he sounds down but never out, saved from self-indulgence by keen intelligence and crisp melodies.

Dynablob, an intriguing fan club release available only by mail-order, collects scraps ranging from 1986 to 1994, mostly the remnants of rejected studio sessions. Highlights include a countryfied version of "The Devil in (Little Ol') Me," the wonderfully jaunty "Talking Return of the Great Folk Scare Blues," "The Celestial Shuttle" (verbose and overlong at eight minutes, yet still arresting) and the striking "Eating Each Other's Babies," all enhanced by the clever, typically self-deprecating liner notes. (And don't miss the groovy faux-Dylan cover art.) Not for beginners, but essential for hardcore fans. [jy]

See also *TPRG.*

CHRIS HARFORD AND THE FIRST RAYS OF THE NEW RISING SUN

Be Headed (Elektra) 1992
Comet (Black Shepherd) 1996

Neil Young demonstrated that sensitive singer/songwriters and roaring, distorted guitars could mess around and make beautiful music together; Princeton, New Jersey's Chris Harford (ex–Three Colors) is one happy result of that union. On his exceptional solo debut—a handsome quilt of gentle country rock, simple acoustic soliloquies and raging noise-rock storms (occasionally mixing approaches within a song)—the well-connected guitarist with the hoarse whisper receives assistance from such eclectic guests as Richard Thompson, Ween, the Proclaimers, Loudon Wainwright III, Matt Sweeney (ex-Skunk, pre-Chavez) and the Rollins Band rhythm section. But what really distinguishes **Be Headed** is Harford's finely crafted writing and the emotion-laden resonance of his delivery. Collectively, "Unsaid Things," "You Know Me the Best," "Living End," "My Little Sadness," "Road With You" and "Sing, Breathe and Be Merry" richly portray the artist as an incisive empath with as strong a sense of self as of song structure. Whether ripping into a meltdown guitar solo or barely breathing a lyric into the silence, Harford is a singular voice, and **Be Headed** captures all of his facets and subtleties.

Harford made a second album, but it ran into label resistance and never appeared. In early '96, he self-released some of it, along with a handful of 8-track demos for other tunes, all recorded between 1989 and 1994, as **Comet.** The absence of marquee names and the occasionally skeletal arrangements have no adverse effect on the nine tasteful, incisive songs, simply performed with help from longtime associates Kevin Salem (guitar), Dave Dunton (piano), Claude Coleman Jr. (drums) and others. Forged in Harford's artistic furnace, quiet numbers like "Dying to Be Free," "Second Guessing" (with an explosive Salem solo) and "Long Time Friend Gone" are the easy equals to **Be Headed**'s best. [i]

See also *Kevin Salem.*

HARMONY ROCKETS

See *Mercury Rev.*

BEN HARPER

Welcome to the Cruel World (Virgin) 1994
Fight for Your Mind (Virgin) 1995

Ben Harper grew up in California's Inland Empire, interested in the acoustic guitar and Dobro rather than the harder-edged sounds that influenced many of his contemporaries. Thus, on his debut, Harper expresses his anger with the world—and his desire for a better one—with a mellow mixture of blues and soul. The results are beautiful, sometimes even uplifting, especially on funkier numbers like "Mama's Got a Girlfriend Now" and "Like a King." The trouble is that while the former is a playful double entendre worthy of an old blues tune, the latter seriously juxtaposes Kings Rodney and Martin Luther. Harper's versatility is as impressive as his songwriting, but more grit would help.

Harper doesn't find that grit on **Fight for Your Mind,** which is just as mellow. But he does flesh out his songs a bit more—especially rhythmically—and projects the confidence that comes with experience. His soulful, yearning vocals give the album an appealing warmth, even though the lyrics to songs like "Oppression" come across a bit heavy-handed. If Harper sometimes fall short, it's mostly because he's so ambitious; his best work is probably ahead of him. [rl]

TIM HARRINGTON

See *Masters of Reality.*

DEBBIE HARRY

KooKoo (Chrysalis) 1981
Rockbird (Geffen) 1986
Def, Dumb & Blonde (Sire/Reprise) 1989
Debravation (Sire/Reprise) 1993

DEBBIE HARRY/BLONDIE

Once More Into the Bleach (Chrysalis) 1988
The Complete Picture: The Very Best of Deborah Harry and Blondie (UK Chrysalis) 1991

JAZZ PASSENGERS

In Love (High Street) 1994

Scant though they might seem, the four albums credited to singer/actress Debbie (Deborah on the latter two) Harry are plenty, thank you. For all the wonderful pop the New Yorker made with Blondie in the late '70s, and despite enthusiastic support from collaborators like Nile Rodgers, Chris Stein and Mike Chapman, her frustrating search for a second conducive musical environment on which to found a solo career has yielded precious little of memorable substance.

Produced in Blondie's waning days by Chic (a typical trailblazing move by Harry and then-partner Stein), **KooKoo** finds Harry out of her depth, straining to meet their rhythmic music halfway; at best, maybe a third of the record is moderately successful infectious funk-pop. **Rockbird,** nicely organized, only with too much tinkly synthesizer, by J. Geils Band keyboardist/songwriter Seth Justman, paves a pop path Harry can navigate, but the material is weak. "French Kissin," which recalls Blondie's playful charm, and the effervescent "I Want You" are the only keepers. Likewise, **Def, Dumb & Blonde** offers one handy reminder of Blondie's surging '60s guitar pop ("Maybe for Sure," produced for old time's sake by Mike Chapman) and one kicky love song ("I Want That Man," produced by the Thompson Twins), but not much else worthy of its clever title.

Between the transparent Madonna pretensions, dance thrust and myriad of overseers, **Debravation** is a fast ride to nowhere. Harry's singing is more assured and comfortable than ever, but the record has no destination, hopping around stylistic cubicles in tribute to the sounds that made Blondie famous: there's peppy techno-bop (Arthur Baker's "I Can See Clearly"), a rappy throwdown (Stein's "Stability"), mushy elegance (Anne Dudley's "Strike Me Pink"), rock-disco ("Rain"), noirish cinematography ("The Fugitive") and punky guitar pop ("Standing in My Way"). Grabbing at genres like a rich kid filling bags in the candy store, **Debravation** can't keep its hands off anything. "Communion" has a spirited "Like a Prayer" chorus; "My Last Dance (With You)" is a country oldie played here by R.E.M.; "Tear Drops" is straight-up doo-wop. Track by track, the amusement percentage is surprisingly high, but the album's net effect is neutralized by its random eclecticism.

After serving (along with Freedy Johnston, Jeff Buckley, Mavis Staples and others) as a vocal guest on the Jazz Passengers' **In Love** (singing "Dog in Sand"), Harry has kept herself visible by performing with the group.

Once More Into the Bleach is a compilation of danceable remixes that differ significantly from the originals. Besides an assortment of Blondie hits, it features Harry's solo "Rush Rush" (from the *Scarface* soundtrack) plus a handful of tracks from **KooKoo** and **Rockbird. The Complete Picture** is another compilation. [i]

See also *TPRG.*

HARVEST MINISTERS

Little Dark Mansion (UK Sarah) 1993 (Widely Distributed) 1994
A Feeling Mission (Setanta/Bar/None) 1995

The gentleness of acoustic music gives it a certain emotional harmony with twinky pop, which partly explains how this folky Dublin sextet wound up first on England's Sarah and then on two different American indie-pop labels. Sidestepping preciousness and sublimating Gaelic influences in favor of an eloquently pure lyricism that's more Neil Young than Van Morrison, the group led by singer/songwriter/guitarist William Merriman is faceless in the best possible way: the handsome music is the star, not the diversely arranged performances or the retiring individual personalities. That brings it in line with Amerindie's country minimalists (Palace, Scud Mountain Boys) on one hand and pop pastoralists like Speed the Plough on the other. As a bonus, the Harvest Ministers serve as a reminder why travesties like the Waterboys *really* had no business hanging about Ireland.

That said, the warmhearted, occasionally wry **Little Dark Mansion** is a little *too* plain—underwhelming, even—but there are bright flashes amid the careful musicianship. "Fictitious Christmas" is lively, thanks to Aingeala de Burca's fiddling and Gerardette Bailey's singing; the piano-driven "Railroaded" has the elegiac majesty of Shane MacGowan at his sentimental best and a vocal performance that recalls Ian Hunter singing "Ballad of Mott the Hoople." (The US edition adds three tracks from pre-LP UK singles, including the ironically ebullient "If It Kills Me and It Will.")

A Feeling Mission is the real deal, a snappy, assured and organic record with starch in the songs and fresh roses stuck smartly in their lapels. Cycling comfortably through rustic quaintness, atmospheric chamber pop and mild jazz-lite swing, the revised lineup (introducing fair-voiced singer Maeve Roche and giving more play to multi-instrumentalist Padraig McCaul) makes fine handiwork of Merriman's oddly canted compositions, especially "That Won't Wash," "Cleaning Out the Store," "The Only Seat of Power," "An Inopportune Girl" and "Modernising the New You." Singular in both word and sound, **A Feeling Mission** is exquisite and substantial. Fans of Aztec Camera, Go-Betweens, Everything but the Girl and the Jayhawks may find this album very much to their taste. [i]

PJ HARVEY

Dry (Too Pure/Indigo) 1992
Rid of Me (Island) 1993
4-Track Demos (Island) 1993
To Bring You My Love (Island) 1995

JOHN PARISH & POLLY JEAN HARVEY

Dance Hall at Louse Point (Island) 1996

VARIOUS ARTISTS

Too Pure–The Peel Sessions (Strange Fruit/Dutch East India Trading) 1992

England's Polly Jean Harvey—distinct from the group PJ Harvey—came to public attention in 1992 with **Dry,** a startlingly scabrous and extremely dramatic portrait of a woman on the verge of total emotional collapse. While Harvey would later downplay its trenchancy and focus, it's important to note how explicit and abject **Dry**'s worldview was: on the opening track ("Oh My Lover"), the singer begs for merely the opportunity to share her lover with another woman; ten songs later, the tightly wound "Water" (as in "walking on") ends the album with a gulp. And in the album's ferocious centerpiece, "Sheela-Na-Gig," Harvey revels in the figure of a fertility goddess presenting her privates for servicing, only to have them met with derision. Backed by bassist Stephen Vaughan and drummer Robert Ellis (who made a '96 UK LP as Spleen), the singer/guitarist set these uncomfortable emotional tone poems to loping slide-marked settings that range from the whirlwind that is "Sheela-Na-Gig" to sparer, more open landscapes of tremulous bass and serrated guitar. The album is a corrosive—but somehow beautiful—portrayal of female trouble on a scale infrequently seen attached to musical forces so controlled.

Dry's dramatic power disguised something Harvey already understood: that the somewhat received bleakness of its analysis of sex was a dead end. Harvey retrenched. Her work, she said repeatedly in interviews, wasn't so serious: it was constructed, she said, through two key inspirational axes—the blues and humor. Why weren't people getting the joke? But neither of these are much in evidence in **Dry,** or, truth be told, **Rid of Me.** "Recorded" by Steve Albini, the second album is problematic. The musical impassivity of **Dry** turns utterly unforgiving here, all of its beauty and grandeur banished. The resulting harshness—emotionally and aurally—is authentically transgressive, but with an ideological purity that pushes the album to the edges of the impersonal on one side and the cartoony on the other. Harvey's idea of humor comes out as sardonicism, and her ideas devolve into slogans. Some are pretty provocative—"Rub 'Til It Bleeds," for example—but others ("Douse hair with gasoline") fall flat. Matters aren't helped by Harvey's consistently over-the-top vocalizing, which includes wailing, whispering, distorted growling and so forth; it all serves to distance the singer from her songs. Even a cover of Dylan's "Highway 61 Revisited"—whose themes nicely foreshadow the almost biblical tales of love and horror Harvey would offer on her third studio album—seems somehow off.

During **Dry**'s ascendance, tapes of Harvey's demos for the record circulated: they're not so much revelatory as a striking testimony to how fully the then-twenty-one-year-old had conceptualized her debut. Shortly after **Rid of Me** she offered the second album's home version, including a few unreleased songs, as **4-Track Demos.** Even throwaways like "Driving" show an easy fluency with rock forms, but the stripped-down recordings also expose the slightness of some songs.

On **To Bring You My Love** (produced by Harvey, Flood and John Parish with a new collective of backing musicians), she reaches at least part of the elemental balance she's sought. While this is definitely not a comedy record, the blues, particularly, seep out of the record's pores, from the growled vocal litanies and crawling bass to the abrasively carnal expostulations that give the album its thrills and chills. With a great deal of violence and no little aplomb, she settles the issue of sex through the simple expedient of expropriating male terminology—and its rampant libido—whole. The result is an album-length genderfuck of no little punch—lines like "You oughta hear my long snake moan" are designed with that in mind. Harvey's not trying to plead a case, make a point or convert believers: she's just clearing territory, and it turns out that such personal *lebensraum* is necessary just on the basis of the title song, as epic and menacing a statement of sexual potency as has ever been heard in rock or any of its source genres—and, yes, that is saying something.

What Harvey will do next is up for grabs. Her attempts to distance herself from the perfervid early-'90s female star-making machinery has ranged from the glamourless nudity on her record covers to the joyless party dress she adopted for **Rid of Me**–period shows. For the artwork of **To Bring You My Love** and its subsequent tour, she reinvented herself as a garish chanteuse, all slinky dresses, high heels and exaggerated eyelashes, and went on the road backed with a peerless group of avant-garde sessionmen, including Tom Waits henchman Joe Gore and Pere Ubu's Eric Drew Feldman. At points on the record and during these shows there's a bit of evidence that Harvey is an art-rocker, with all the potential for disaster the tag has unfortunately come to imply. Harvey may yet turn into a figure of David Bowie–like pretentiousness, but for now she's displaying an imposing union of ambition and ability that few contemporary recording artists can touch.

Harvey's collaboration with John Parish finds her writing lyrics to his music, although **Dance Hall at Louse Point** also includes a cover of the Leiber/Stoller-penned 1969 Peggy Lee hit "Is That All There Is?" [bw]

See also *Moonshake.*

CHRIS HASKETT

See *Rollins Band.*

UMAR BIN HASSAN

See *Last Poets.*

HATER

See *Soundgarden.*

JULIANA HATFIELD

Hey Babe (Mammoth) 1992
Forever Baby EP (Mammoth) 1992
I See You EP (Mammoth) 1992
Only Everything (Mammoth/Atlantic) 1995

JULIANA HATFIELD THREE

Become What You Are (Mammoth/Atlantic) 1993

BLAKE BABIES

Nicely, Nicely (Chew-bud) 1987 (Mammoth) 1994
Slow Learners (UK Utility) 1989
Earwig (Mammoth) 1989
Sunburn (Mammoth) 1990
Rosy Jack World EP (Mammoth) 1991
Innocence and Experience (Mammoth) 1993

Just as the trio was hitting its stride with its best album, 1990's **Sunburn,** the Blake Babies greeted the new decade by breaking up. Singer/bassist Juliana Hatfield lit out for the big time, picking up a guitar and staking out turf as the *Sassy*-generation spokeswoman for adolescent angst—a niche particularly well-suited to the girlish quality of her singing voice. Along the way she also became something of a gossip subject, thanks to an ambiguous long-term relationship with Lemonheads leader Evan Dando and her 1993 claim/admission that she was still a virgin. Discriminating listeners, meanwhile, argued about whether she was better as a Blake Baby.

There's no real consensus on that issue, although it's poseur-fashionable to diss Hatfield's albums *just because.* With Gary Smith producing and studio contributions from Dando, Mike Watt and John Wesley Harding, **Hey Babe** is a solid solo debut, filled with jangly guitar, a textbook's worth of hooks and lots of singalong melodies. Throughout, Hatfield sings about unrequited love and a debilitating lack of confidence that's hard to take seriously; on "Ugly," she delivers "I'm ugly, with a capital U" with so much infectious exuberance you can practically hear hallways full of high-school girls joining in. But a song like "Everybody Loves Me but You" outlines the kind of precious arrogance some find so off-putting. **Forever Baby** is a five-song EP: three album tracks and two new ones, including a song written by J Mascis. **I See You** borrows two more from **Hey Babe** and adds three from a late-'92 session produced by Lou Giordano.

Hatfield re-embraced a group vibe—kind of—for **Become What You Are:** bassist Dean Fisher and ex-Bullet LaVolta drummer Todd Philips muscle up the sound, but it's still Hatfield's show. She again taps into the teen zeitgeist ("Spin the Bottle," "I Got No Idols"), but this time explores more complex, ambivalent emotions. "Supermodel" takes resentful aim at those who are marketed for their beauty ("The highest paid piece of ass / You know it's not going to last / Those magazines end up in the trash") but also views their stardom from the point of view of a mate. The necessarily fictionalized "My Sister" concerns love / hate sibling relationships—until Hatfield changes tense ("I miss my sister / Why'd she go?"). Name-checking groups such as the Violent Femmes and the Del Fuegos, Hatfield cruises through another batch of songs that play easy on the ears—and, more often than not, stick in them.

Hatfield cranks it up on **Only Everything** without losing her instinctive pop charms or her treatises on what she describes as "white, middle-class angst." (Blessedly, nobody asked about her sexual experience this time around.) Dense layers of punky guitar fury propel "What a Life" and the all-French "Fleur de Lys," while "OK OK" and "Congratulations" lean more toward power-pop. "Simplicity Is Beautiful" mines a prettier end of the spectrum; the boisterous "Dumb Fun" lives up to its title. The album's most striking track—and its semi-hit single—"Universal Heart-Beat" uses a riveting electric piano lick to bridge its bright verses and hard-rocking choruses. The song's key line, "A heart that hurts / Is a heart that works," provides a manifesto that applies to every song of Hatfield's solo output.

In retrospect, the Blake Babies' sound had a lot more in common with the first stage of Hatfield's solo career than it seemed to at the time. (And not just because she reclaimed her song "Nirvana" from the **Rosy Jack World** odds'n'sods EP and recut it for her first album, or recast **Earwig**'s "Boiled Potato" as "Feed Me" and stuck it on the **I See You** EP.) The lesson of **Innocence and Experience**—a careful, illustrative anthology that follows the Boston trio from its first steps in 1986 to its final chapter five years later, including a few remixes, unreleased demos and a live Neil Young cover—is how fully formed the core of Hatfield's musical persona was from the very beginning. Even songs written or co-written by guitarist John Strohm ("Cesspool," "Lament," the impassioned "Star") fit cleanly into the mold, although Hatfield's sweetly served disdain is pointier when she's left to her own creative devices, as in "I'm Not Your Mother" and "You Don't Give Up." [gg/i]

See also *Antenna, Helium, Lemonheads; TPRG.*

SOPHIE B. HAWKINS

Tongues and Tails (Columbia) 1992
Whaler (Columbia) 1994

On her debut album, Sophie Ballantine Hawkins commands "Let's fill the world with desire." On her second, she proclaims herself "the wild woman at your door." Consider her a kind of boho Madonna; Hawkins was raised in a sophisticated Manhattan household and began pursuing music in earnest as an adolescent. She studied jazz, as well as percussion with the Nigerian master Babatunde Olatunji; her bands played everywhere from the Catskills to CBGB. She did a brief stint in Bryan Ferry's band and logged time as an actor and a performance artist.

When she finally emerged with **Tongues and Tails,** Hawkins' music and image were fully formed. Willing to include a nude photo of herself in the CD booklet, she claimed in interviews to be "omnisexual," upping a titillation factor already used to great effect by Prince and Madonna. It's a shame that such media manipulation obscured the album's music, which offers a fresh and inventive blend of rock, dance music, rap, jazz touches and world music styles that bring an exotic touch to the unbridled and unabashed lust of Hawkins' lyrics. Co-produced by Rick Chertoff and former Todd Rundgren sideman Ralph Shuckett, the album boasts terrific players (bassist Mark Egan, drummer Omar Hakim) and Hawkins' advanced sense of arrangements, which marry polyrhythmic dance grooves and droning ambient synthesizers. The album opens with its best shot, the sultry Top 5 smash "Damn I Wish I Was Your Lover," and backs it up with "California Here I Come," "Mysteries We Understand," "Before I Walk on Fire" and "Live and Let Love"—each a solid, memorable composition. **Tongues and Tails** has only a couple of missteps: "Saviour Child," which sounds like a *Flashdance* soundtrack leftover, and a lumbering, slowed-down cover of Bob Dylan's "I Want You," whose rambling wordiness doesn't fit Hawkins' more clipped, direct style.

In the wake of **Tongues and Tails'** adventurous spirit, **Whaler** is a surprising turnabout, a slick, synthesizer-driven collection of upbeat pop tunes whose chart ambitions are as naked as Hawkins' carnal desires: Janet Jackson or Paula Abdul could have recorded "As I Lay Me Down," the song that broke **Whaler** in North America nearly a year after its release. Fortunately, Hawkins hasn't abandoned her knack for intriguing instrumental touches—the Middle Eastern synthesizer squiggle of "Right Beside You," the polyrhythmic underbelly of "Did We Not Choose Each Other," the bongo attack of "Sometimes I See," the layered vocal harmonies at the end of "Don't Don't Tell Me No," the bouncy texture of "Swing From Limb to Limb." [gg]

TED HAWKINS

Watch Your Step (Rounder) 1982
Happy Hour (Rounder) 1986
On the Boardwalk: The Venice Beach Tapes [tape] (no label) 1986
Dock of the Bay: The Venice Beach Tapes [tape] (no label) 1987
The Best of the Venice Beach Tapes (Hol. Munich) 1989
I Love You Too (UK P.T.) 1989
The Next Hundred Years (DGC) 1994
The Kershaw Sessions (UK Strange Roots) 1995

If not for the wonderful quality of his voice—an older, harshened, less urbane Sam Cooke—and the extraordinary breadth of his catalogue, both original and otherwise, it would be impossible to connect the dots of Ted Hawkins' tale. His death from a stroke at the beginning of 1995, less than a year after getting the break of his life, is the sort of cosmic irony few novelists would have the gall to will on a fictional character.

Like a latter-day Leadbelly, the Mississippi-born (in 1937) folksinger did time on a chain gang as a young man; he was in his thirties (and not clear of the law for another couple of decades) by the time he found his way to Los Angeles, where he became a fixture on the boardwalk in Venice Beach and Santa Monica, bellowing out songs while brusquely strumming an open-tuned guitar. Hawkins began recording in the '70s under the auspices of producer Bruce Bromberg, but it wasn't until 1982 that an album finally appeared under his name. The wonderful **Watch Your Step** indulges the vintage soul inherent in Hawkins' voice with a couple of rousing full-on showband arrangements (the title track, "Who's Got My Natural Comb?"), but otherwise presents his earthy power without complications. Teaching a mighty acoustic lesson in roots music, Hawkins inhabits that secular place just outside the churchyard where gospel, folk and soul meet.

Bromberg keeps a similar template on **Happy Hour**: a couple of spare electric numbers (the rock-'n'rolly "My Last Goodbye," the countryfied "Happy Hour," the two-guitar blues of "You Pushed My Head Away") amid the solo performances in a mix of styles that all take flight in Hawkins' sturdy emotional delivery. The songwriting isn't as engagingly diverse as on the debut—Hawkins (reassuringly getting harmony assistance from his wife, Elizabeth, on three numbers) uses romance's ups and downs as a stand-in for any more pointed comments about his life. There are a couple of ill-conceived duds ("California Song" was produced in evident tribute to the worst end of '60s folk-rock), but moving numbers like "Cold & Bitter Tears" and "Ain't That Pretty" keep the album grounded in the spirit.

Following a couple of cassettes sold personally by the busker, Hawkins emigrated to England, where he enjoyed the same kind of appreciation American blues greats once met there. (**The Kershaw Sessions** documents his stay abroad with radio broadcasts from the late '80s.) He returned to California in '90, where he was "discovered" (now *there's* a dada "readymade" concept) by a big-league A&R man and converted from itinerant street singer to major-label priority project. The subtext to all this is frightening to consider. The people behind the project undoubtedly proceeded from genuine appreciation of Hawkins' talent, but—given rock'n'roll's bottomless ability to exploit—it's hard not to imagine marketing executives considering the rich House of Blues–style hypability of a charismatic middle-aged black man plucked from the clutches of poverty and despair (an archetype ripe for condescension and historical self-delusion) and delivered to the ready arms of a white audience, an easy one-hour fix for guilt about homelessness and racism.

Carefully, if at times conspicuously, produced with top sessioneers (and, in spots, a calculated Nashville accent) by Tony Berg, **The Next Hundred Years** hauls Hawkins into the digital age, surrounding his husky voice with more instrumentation than it needs yet still not cutting into Hawkins' art or personality. "Afraid," "There Stands the Glass" (a drinking song popularized by Webb Pierce) and Jesse Winchester's "Biloxi" all pray a little too hard toward central Tennessee, but they're among the album's strongest songs. Hawkins' own sparely rendered "Ladder of Success" sounds closer to his heart, as he expresses the homely spiritualism of his abiding faith: "This is a message to all those who been trying to reach the top of the hill . . . no matter how great you are, you got to know somebody that knows somebody who will lend you a helping hand." [i]

HAZEL

Toreador of Love (Sub Pop) 1993 + 1995
Are You Going to Eat That (Sub Pop) 1995

Hazel emerged in the first batch of Portland, Oregon, bands (Crackerbash, Heatmiser, Pond, Sprinkler) that seemed to flower spontaneously just as nearby Seattle was in the throes of grunge overkill. From the first, Hazel was a bit of an oddity, a trio of young musicians accompanied by a much older dancer, Fred Nemo, whose role is roughly comparable to that of Bez in Happy Mondays. **Toreador of Love** (initially entitled **Lucky Dog**) features a handful of bouncing songs like "She's Supersonic" and "Everybody's Best Friend" that retain some of emo-core's rhythm (a penchant for starting and stopping chaotically) but not at the expense of pop songsmithing. Drummer Jody Bleyle adds tart supporting vocals to guitarist Peter Krebs' leads, while Brady Smith's bass remains unobtrusive.

By **Are You Going to Eat That,** Hazel's future was clouded by Bleyle's role in Team Dresch (whose Donna Dresch co-produced the album) and her co-ownership of the Candy-Ass label; Krebs had begun playing the odd solo acoustic show. Bleyle's vocals are more prominent and the band's recorded sound is fuller, but there's little real improvement between discs. If anything, Hazel's pop penchant has been de-emphasized in favor of the miasma of indie-rock. The album's most striking songs—"Crowned" and "Ringing in My Ears"—are all but acoustic. [ga]

See also *Team Dresch.*

JOWE HEAD

See *Television Personalities.*

HEALTH & HAPPINESS SHOW

Tonic (Bar/None) 1993
Instant Living (Bar/None) 1995

Hoboken, New Jersey's reputation for homey country music largely post-dated the Bongos' early-'80s heyday, so singer/guitarist James Mastro, who joined that trio in progress way back when, could be making up for lost time in his new group, the name (if not exactly the music) of which pays homage to Hank Williams. **Tonic** presents the Health & Happiness Show as an ebullient outfit with a catholic approach, using mandolin, fiddle, accordion, lap steel and electric instruments to weave a warm and winning skein of styles: stately Band-like waltzes ("I Do"), frisky folk-rockers ("Drunk-Eyed Waltz"), skillet-licking blues ("Engine Engine"), Gram Parsons country ("We Are Here") and Celt-rock ("The Man Who Married the Moon," "River of Stars"). The craft-conscious quintet invests each original song with dignity and devotion, reinventing itself while leaving a distinct overall imprint.

Instant Living is another fine—but completely different—record. Showing an all-electric backbone in lieu of the debut's rustic trappings, the group brings its stylistic adventures home to a more organic, consistent sound that encompasses slide-happy Little Feat, elements of Neil Young and Bob Dylan. Although the feedback-laden roots rock of "Sugar in Your Eyes," the crisp desire of "You Is Fine" and the noir howls of "On Your Way" set the tone, there's still room for variety. The fiddles and stirring beat of "Tossed Like a Stone" summon up **Tonic**'s Gaelic ambience, "Anytime" has a peaceful, easy feeling and "Many Kindnesses" suggests R.E.M.'s old folk-rock side. [i]

HEART THROBS

Cleopatra Grip (Elektra) 1990
Jubilee Twist (A&M) 1991
Vertical Smile (UK One Little Indian) 1993

Although fronted by women, Reading's Heart Throbs were distinct from the so-called "blonde" pop bands of the day (Darling Buds, Primitives). Making sweet-girl sounds, the English quintet had a darker, menacing tone that got stronger with each of its albums, all of whose titles are euphemisms for female genitalia. Singer/guitarist Rose Carlotti and bassist Rachael DeFreitas—both sisters of late Echo and the Bunnymen drummer Pete DeFreitas—were the band's focal points; on **Cleopatra Grip,** co-produced by Gil Norton (Bunnymen, Pixies), Carlotti lends a breathy coo to the psychedelically charged, slightly dancey guitar rock. While songs like "I Wonder Why" and "Slip & Slide" rely a bit too heavily on easy choruses, the positively haunting "In Vain" and "Dreamtime" display melodic mastery of post-punk atmospherics.

DeFreitas and drummer Mark Side left after the subsequent tour; with their replacements, the Heart Throbs self-produced **Jubilee Twist.** Though the album is superficially not much of a departure from the debut, Carlotti sounds more forceful, especially on the lovely "Winter Came Too Soon" and the churning "The Girl Became the Stairs." Note the Siouxsie echoes of "Too Late."

Vertical Smile finds the group toting yet another rhythm section and headed in a much harder direction. With Alan Borgia's guitar way raunchier and up front, Carlotti stretches herself a bit thin, often coming off as a Kate Bush wannabe on such tracks as "Perry Said," though PJ Harvey would probably do well with the angry "Apple Pie"—which speaks volumes about the talent at work here. [db]

See also *Pale Saints.*

HEARTWORMS

See *Velocity Girl.*

REVEREND HORTON HEAT

Smoke 'Em If You Got 'Em (Sub Pop) 1990
The Full-Custom Gospel Sounds of the Reverend Horton Heat (Sub Pop) 1993
Liquor in the Front (Sub Pop/Interscope/Atlantic) 1994
It's Martini Time (Interscope) 1996

TENDERLOIN

Let It Leak (Qwest/Warner Bros.) 1994
Bullseye (Qwest/Warner Bros.) 1995

Not that it necessarily means much, but Dallas rockabilly wildman Jim Heath (Horton Heat to record buyers, the Rev to his fans) sports a shit-eating grin and a hideous striped jacket on the first album, clenched eyes and a white clerical robe on the second, a screaming mouth and an AC/DC T-shirt on the third. More to the point, while his trio's debut was produced by nobody, Gibby Haynes and Al Jourgensen, respectively, manned the studio helm on the next two.

By modern standards, **Smoke 'Em If You Got 'Em** is fresh but mild; although Heat sings "I'm Mad" and promises a "Psychobilly Freakout," the skilled guitar picker and his trusty rhythm section (slap bassist Jimbo Wallace and drummer Patrick "Taz" Bentley) never really cut loose. Despite the album's vintage atmospherics, songs like "Marijuana" and "Eat Steak" make it clear they're not reverent revivalists, either. By this evidence, Jerry Lee could pin these wusses to a wall with one hand in his pants.

Fortunately, that was just the opening gambit in Heat's musical negotiations with the devil. Egged on by the twisted genius of their personal Butthole Surfer savior and pushing songs with real moxie, shape and wit, the boys sound truly possessed (at least by the spirit of Mojo Nixon) on **The Full-Custom Gospel Sounds.** This downright fine drunken blast is played with gear-stripping power and captured with loads of audio hot sauce. From the salacious raunch of "Wiggle Stick" through "Livin' on the Edge (of Houston)," played at lickety-split velocity, to the thoroughly dissolute funhouse mirror collapse of "Gin and Tonic Blues," which wraps things up (Heath has admitted to actually passing out during the song's recording), the album is an all-out ride toward twisted neo-'billy righteousness.

Hitching up to the major-label feeding trough and throwing in with the Ministry maestro, Team Heat loses its stylistic head on **Liquor in the Front.** The band's twangy hysterics still set the basic course, but the songwriting is corny and conservative, and Jourgensen has the temerity to play industrial dress-up in a few spots: a relentless downbeat on "Baddest of the Bad," the clattery synth drums on "Yeah, Right" and the strident, tinny tone (especially on "I Can't Surf") all draw connections to a genre for which the band has no rational use. Heat attempts a Jerry Lee imitation on the uncluttered "I Could Get Used to It," "Rockin' Dog" hits a jivey Stray Cats groove and "Cruisin' for a Bruisin'" is top-notch chrome 'billy business, but nothing here is as wickedly unkempt as **The Full-Custom Gospel Sounds.** And it hardly helps that this weak album ends on a lame joke: Taz's ridiculously sloppy rendition (on piano, no less, accompanied by barnyard noises and belches) of Scott Joplin's "The Entertainer."

Taking guitar tech Kirk St. James along with him, Bentley bolted the Reverend's entourage in '94 to join Tenderloin, a Kansas-to-Dallas quartet that had toured as their opening act that year. St. James and Bentley (who also co-produced) both appear on the band's **Bullseye** LP, putting a hair more gleeful maniac jizz into the jagged-up but futile blues-rock boogie bluster of **Let It Leak.** Covers of Dr. Feelgood ("Milk & Alcohol") and ZZ Top ("Heard It on the X") give 'Loin leader Ernie Locke stuff to sing, but then so do band originals like the moody "Inseminator" and the hell-bent "Dip Your Body in Ink."

In '96, Heat—joined by Wallace and new drummer Scott Churilla—declared **It's Martini Time,** an eclectic and sophisticated album that ended the procession of wackball producers by putting Thom Panuzio at the studio controls. Adopting a suave entertainer pose for some tunes and a more familiar rockin' daddy stance for the rest, Heat whips around his colorful track with the focus, drive and efficiency of a champion racer. [i]

HEATMISER

The Music of Heatmiser [tape] (no label) 1992
Dead Air (Frontier) 1993
Yellow No. 5 EP (Frontier) 1994
Cop and Speeder (Frontier) 1994

ELLIOTT SMITH

Roman Candle (Cavity Search) 1994
Elliott Smith (Kill Rock Stars) 1995

Portland, Oregon's Heatmiser features the melodic-abrasive formula that made the Northwest famous, but with a lyrical twist—the band's Neil Gust is an openly gay songwriter. And Elliott Smith, Heatmiser's other singer/songwriter, has emerged as a force on his own.

Firing off fourteen songs in thirty-seven minutes, **Dead Air** is laced with hints of Fugazi, Hüsker Dü and Helmet, although the record is not nearly as distinctive as any of those bands. With its crisp drum bash, big, distorted guitars and Gust and Smith's hoarse vocals submerged just enough to muffle the lyrics (stray audible lines and their delivery make it clear we're listening to some angry/sensitive young men here), it's a textbook example of the strengths and weaknesses of early '90s indie hard rock. Particularly on "Stray," "Still" and "Lowlife," the energy and urgency are enough to rescue the music from the merely generic. But just barely.

Yellow No. 5 offers up five more quick slices, this time with a bit more personality and varied approaches. The punky attack of the hyperactive lead-off track ("Wake") and the frantic "The Corner Seat" alternates with the subtly skewed rock of "Fortune 500" and "Idler," which works up to a modest majesty, propelled by a grand whammy-bar hook. Most listeners missed the gay content of **Dead Air,** but there's a lyric sheet this time.

Striking out on his own, Smith became a minor hipster sensation in '94 with the brittle, brooding and impressively consistent (albeit thirty-minute-long) **Roman Candle.** A far cry from Heatmiser's aggro attack, the album features hushed, folky tunes with lightly brushed drums, acoustic twelve-string guitars and some pretty fingerpicking by Smith, whose hoarse whisper tells tales of disintegrating relationships sketched in elliptical yet pungent terms, like diary entries. Especially on the title track, "Condor Ave." and "No Name #3," Smith radiates palpable hurt and bitterness without once raising his voice.

Smith's extracurricular activities only strengthened the band—Heatmiser attains a powerful sense of mood on **Cop and Speeder,** especially in "Flame!" and "Antonio Carlos Jobim." Thanks to improved songwriting, the album finds the band beginning to emerge from its flat monochrome tones. The lyric sheet is unnecessary this time—the vocals are way up front. Except when he sounds like a ringer for Sebadoh's Lou Barlow, Gust is developing a more original vocal approach, while Smith has figured out how to integrate his seething whisper into a full-tilt rock band (even if he is saving his best tunes for his solo albums). Lashing out at a succession of failed loves (or is it just one?), the band purges with vehemence and a dark confessional candor that's not always attractive but undeniably honest, nailing it most effectively on "Busted Lip."

The second solo album improves greatly on the recipe. **Elliott Smith**'s songs, melodies, arrangements and production are all stronger and more fully realized than those on **Roman Candle,** although the record covers the same thematic territory—substance abuse, disappointment and his uniquely resigned defiance. Bleak, almost uncomfortably unsparing and yet tragically beautiful, "Needle in the Hay," "Coming Up Roses," "Southern Belle"—and virtually every other track here—make Smith something of a Nick Drake for the indie-rock cognoscenti. [ma]

HEAVENLY

Heavenly vs. Satan (UK Sarah) 1991
Le Jardin de Heavenly (K) 1992
P.U.N.K. Girl EP (K) 1993
The Decline and Fall of Heavenly (K) 1994
Operation Heavenly (K) 1996

TALULAH GOSH

Steaming Train EP (UK 53rd & 3rd) 1987
Where's the Cougar Matey EP (UK 53rd & 3rd) 1988
Rock Legends: Volume 69 Talulah Mania (Ger. Constrictor) 1989 (UK Avalanche) 1991
They Scoffed the Lot (UK Sarah) 1992
Backwash (K) 1996

Innocence is so inimical to the basic principles of rock'n'roll—the very term is a sexy refutation of unspoiled youth—that bands who hie to it as their creative calling must face an over-under shotgun of culture and nature in their willful resistance to musical and emotional progress. Clinging to a coy, joyful time of sexless crushes and whimsical obsessions—of peppy AM radio melodies and soaring folk harmonies—as an adult artistic lifestyle raises more questions about emotional development than retro bands merely stuck in, say, an homage to the surf-guitar '60s.

Youth culture's obsession with infantilism has lately become a source of mild concern for sociologists (if not marketers). In truth, though, the legions of barrette-sporting love-rock fans toting Hello Kitty and Keroppi accessories are not attempting a return to the womb but merely affecting a style—albeit one that seems cloyingly cutesypoo and pathetically wet to those of more serious mien. That same dissonance attaches to the uncomplicated music favored by the hipper segments of this populace: many find the adorable stick-figure music of Shonen Knife, Tiger Trap, Softies, Beat Happening, the Pastels, Cub, Cannanes, Heavenly and their giddy ilk insufferably precious.

Which, from a mainstream perspective, it probably is. And of course the pretension of innocence is, by definition, an impossibility. But the music that has come from these possessors of power-pop's softest hearts can be delightful, uplifting, charming and altogether refreshing, an echo of times gone by in both life and art. Wistful at its core and winsome to its sweet marrow, tweepop (which reached cultural mass in England as "shambling" around 1986 and has lately acquired the more derisive "cuddlecore" handle) offers a cotton-candy alternative, a knowing effort to build a community in which adulthood is made abstract and real life is returned to the playground—which brings it back to the raw essence of what rock'n'roll was about in the first place.

Talulah Gosh was at the forefront of English tweepop in the late '80s; the Oxford quintet (which ended, ironically enough, so its education-minded members could pursue their university studies) crafted light blasts of pure spun pop on such handy subjects as "My Best Friend," "Beatnik Boy," "Testcard Girl," "Pastels Badge," "In Love for the Very First Time" and "Steaming Train." The mild-mannered songs collected on the posthumous **Rock Legends** singles retrospective skitter along with brisk precision, buoyed by accomplished singing in high, girlish voices.

Unlike many revelers in the genre, Talulah Gosh introduced structural complexity to the party: "Talulah Gosh" ("was a film star for a day") shifts easily from a major-key verse to a minor-key bridge and a giddy sped-up chorus. Likewise, "Bringing Up Baby" fits a syncopated beat and evanescent harmonies into the program; the group may have been dedicated to creating light-headed moods, but Talulah Gosh understood how trying a chore that can be. **They Scoffed the Lot** consists of the band's two British radio sessions, from 1986 and 1988—the first and last things the group ever recorded. The twenty-five-track **Backwash** contains both albums, a 1986 flexi tune and live versions of two otherwise unrecorded numbers.

After the group ended—creating a family tree of Oxford popsters that has continued to spread its genealogical limbs through such groups as Saturn 5, Carousel, Razorcuts and Bugbear—singer Amelia Fletcher (who has also sung on records by the Pooh Sticks and Wedding Present) released an uncharacteristic techno-pop dance single ("Can You Keep a Secret?," sort of mid-period Bananarama with fewer trimmings) and then formed Heavenly with two former bandmates, guitarist Peter Momtchiloff and drummer/brother Mathew Fletcher; bassist Rob Pursey, who had been in Talulah Gosh briefly at its start, came along as well. Proceeding down a more rocking version of the old group's course, Heavenly debuted with the eight-song **Heavenly vs. Satan.** Titles resemble the old band's ("Cool Guitar Boy," "Lemonhead Boy"), and the catchy guitar music is likewise sprightly and good-natured, even when it shifts into a minor key to follow lyrics into demure romantic confrontation: "Shallow," "Stop Before You Say It," "Wish Me Gone."

Le Jardin de Heavenly brings the group (a quintet with the addition of keyboard-playing second vocalist Cathy Rogers) to a new level of achievement in the arrangements, pointillist marvels of detailed delicacy. Wandering easily into a sound strongly reminiscent of the most artful '60s folk-rock, harmony-packed songs like "Starshy," "And the Birds Aren't Singing" and "So Little Deserve" coexist easily with the brasher punk italics of "Tool" and "Sort of Mine." The album ultimately suffers from the wanness of its writing, but the centerpiece is absolutely brilliant: "C Is the Heavenly Option," an ingenious duet between Amelia and Calvin Johnson (Beat Happening), offers interactive sets of romantic choices, the results of which are "get chucked and end up unhappy" or "love will bowl you over."

Heavenly continues to play word games on the ebullient title track of **P.U.N.K. Girl,** but the five-song EP sobers up quickly, souring the fantasy affair of "Hearts & Crosses" with date rape, underpinning "Atta Girl" with dance-rhythm drive and wrapping it in prickly lyrics ("I don't have to be cute . . . Can't you concentrate on something other than me?"), leveling accusations in "Dig Your Own Grave" and bluntly deflating someone's romantic illusions in the nervy a cappella "So?" Like an unexpected slap in the middle of an evening that seemed to be going well, this stinging record makes it seem as if Heavenly had grown up overnight—and was none too pleased about it.

While the EP's primary changes were lyrical, the brief but substantial **The Decline and Fall of Heavenly** rethinks the music a bit as well, expanding the stylistic repertoire to include deracinated R&B, noise and other elements. Among the disillusioned distortions of "Me and My Madness" are feedback and raw guitar power; "Modestic" opens with a spot of brass; between the cowbell hits, "Skipjack" employs vibes and a minimum of guitar to spread a new kind of ambience; "Sacramento" is a boldly noirish instrumental. Emblematic of Heavenly's new state of the union, "Sperm Meets Egg, So What?" skips through grown-up concerns with a shrug and a wrinkled nose; if only life were so simple.

As Heavenly was completing its new album, Mathew Fletcher took his own life in June 1996. [i]

See also *Pooh Sticks.*

HEAVENS TO BETSY

These Monsters Are Real EP7 (Kill Rock Stars) 1992
Calculated (Kill Rock Stars) 1993
Direction . . . EP7 (Chainsaw) 1994

SLEATER-KINNEY

Sleater-Kinney (Chainsaw) 1995 (Villa Villakula) 1995
Call the Doctor (Chainsaw) 1996

EXCUSE 17

Excuse 17 (Chainsaw) 1994
Such Friends Are Dangerous (Kill Rock Stars) 1995

Forget Paris in the springtime: Olympia, Washington, was a better place to experience life as a young grrrl in the early '90s. Singer/guitarist Corin Tucker and drummer/bassist Tracy Sawyer—collectively known as Heavens to Betsy—were right in the thick of the city's productive and empowering scene, succinctly reflecting its emotions in their music. **Calculated,** the duo's only full-length release, demonstrates an ability to articulate more than just anger ("Terrorist," "Nothing Can Stop Me," the anti-racist "White Girl"); the album's range of emotions includes fear, confusion and vulnerability. Despite the pair's rudimentary instrumental skills, the songs are well-formed, and their contrasting vocal styles (Tucker's warbly fortitude versus Sawyer's spine-chilling screams) create a mighty tension. (**Direction,** like **These Monsters Are Real,** is a four-song EP; though in the same vein, it's more consistently inflamed than the album. Pick hit: "Driving Song.")

After H2B parted ways, Tucker—the more melodic of the two—formed a new trio, Sleater-Kinney (named after a local road), with singer/guitarist Carrie Brownstein and drummer Lora Macfarlane, replaced after the second album by Toni Gogin. (Brownstein, aka Carrie Kinney, was still in Excuse 17 when that trio made **Such Friends Are Dangerous,** a seriously good album that doesn't sacrifice musical competence to a burning punk sound and prickly lyrics.)

Tucker's captivating vocal style provides a heightened sense of urgency on Sleater-Kinney's ten-song debut (CD on Chainsaw, 10-inch vinyl on Villa Villakula); her angry songs ("Dont Think You Wanna," "A Real Man") are filled with repeated breaking points, making her lost-love plaints ("Slow Song") even more heartbreaking. **Call the Doctor** is significantly better, the work of stronger individuals meshed into a more cohesive band. The addition of Brownstein's harmonies to Tucker's songs yields something like the Indigo Grrrls. Tucker's vibrato can be disconcerting at times, especially on the more energetic numbers ("My Stuff," "Anonymous"). Best song title: "I Wanna Be Your Joey Ramone." [dps]

HEAVY VEGETABLE

A Bunch of Stuff EP7 (The Way Out Sound) 1993
The Amazing Undersea Adventures of Aqua Kitty and Friends (Headhunter/Cargo) 1994
Frisbie (Headhunter/Cargo) 1995

LESSER/ROB CROW

1995 Lesser Rob Crow Split CD (Vinyl Communications) 1995

ROB CROW

Lactose Adept (Earth Music/Cargo) 1996

California's Heavy Vegetable was a close group of friends—the Encinitas addresses listed in **Frisbie** locate guitarist/singer/songwriter Rob Crow and singer Eléa Tenuta living together, bass player Travis Nelson in the apartment next door and drummer Manuel Turner a stone's throw away.

The band's first recorded appearance, a split single with Powerdresser, sounds very much like Slint. The four-song EP, **A Bunch of Stuff,** however, sounds like a great first single by four different bands, none of which resembles Slint at all: it goes from gorgeous airy harmonies to high-speed precision pounding to acoustic playfulness in the blink of an eye.

The Amazing Undersea Adventures of Aqua Kitty and Friends is more stylistically homogeneous—a high-speed rush of seventeen racing, pounding, slightly geeky, rhythmically twisted tunes (including a much faster electric take on **A Bunch of Stuff**'s "Doesn't Mean Shit") with a few acoustic interludes. Clever vocal arrangements, weird time signatures and terrific musicianship are the order of the day. The terrifying, hardcore-velocity hospital death fantasy "Black Suit" is the highlight, though there's some wonderful lyrical or instrumental detail in almost every song. Best title: "Listen to This Song, Kill Pigs, and Try to Sue Me."

Crow's half of his split CD with Lesser consists of twenty-five short, mostly acoustic home recordings, including three punkish tracks recorded with Fantasy Mission Force. Pleasant, but nothing to write home about.

The cover of **Frisbie** again features a domestic pet out of its element—a dog in mid-air (**Aqua Kitty** Photoshopped the titular feline into a seal tank)—and adds a few songs by Nelson to the mix. Heavy Vegetable's compression paradigm is operating at top efficiency here: the album's first twenty-six songs (plus the six-second "Tune Travis Tune") are over with in less than forty minutes. They're followed by the majestic six-minute "Going Steady With the Limes," a slow polyrhythm that builds into an unforgettable three-part vocal arrangement. Song topics include friends in the band, Wesley Willis (notably the hum-along eighty-one-second "Song for Wesley"), Crow's stolen guitar ("Spatula") and whatever else came to mind ("It's so fucking hard to find a job / when you don't drive / I don't even fucking know how / My rent is *way* overdue"). It's a wonderful album; unfortunately, the band split in the middle of a subsequent tour.

In '96, New Jersey native Crow released **Lactose Adept,** a thirty-song solo album recorded on borrowed tape machines, while launching a new band, Thingy (named for the lead-off song on the first Heavy Veg LP), with Tenuta. [ddw]

HELIUM

Pirate Prude EP (Matador) 1994
The Dirt of Luck (Matador) 1995
Superball+ EP (Matador) 1995

AUTOCLAVE

I'll Take You Down EP7 (K/Dischord) 1992
Autoclave EP10 (Mira/Dischord) 1992

TACKLE BOX

On! (Rockville) 1993
Grand Hotel (Rockville) 1993

Part brainy guitar pop, part Dramamine evaluation tool, Boston's Helium serves as a vehicle for the fascinating lyrical perspective and detuned, lurching guitar expression of Mary Timony. Her playing, by far the band's most distinctive feature, nibbles at the edges of post–My Bloody Valentine soundwall, but her string-bending and note refraction incorporate elements of guitar-dependent world music as diverse as Hawaiian slack key and African highlife.

Helium pulls out all the dimension-rending stops on the debut EP: Timony's wavering guitar shimmers and undulates across the surface of "XXX" and "OOO," songs that are every bit as distinct as those titles would indicate. When the trio does maintain a degree of linearity, the menace is palpable, as evidenced by the severe "I'll Get You, I Mean It." The overall effect is adrenalizing and sense-testing—kind of like being forced to walk on a Saran Wrap membrane stretched over a piranha tank.

Timony revamped Helium's lineup—replacing bassist Brian Dunton (who, like drummer Shawn King Devlin, had been moonlighting from Dumptruck while also playing in Tackle Box) with Ash Bowie of Polvo—for **The Dirt of Luck,** but her own basic m.o. remains blissfully unchanged. The doubled vocals—usually one track of sweet, childlike lilt undercut with an ominously distorted counterpart—impart a dizzyingly inscrutable character to the proto-Wiccan lyrics of "Silver Angel" and "Medusa," both of which are furrowed with the scythe-like guitar leads that trail in her wake. Best of all is the opener, "Pat's Trick," a distorted, percussive exercise in sexual obsession made riveting by Timony's fluttering-yet-powerful delivery. The **Superball+** EP reprises an album track that surrounds Timony's wispy vocals with an offbeat pennywhistle-driven melody, adding four otherwise unavailable songs that range from the ridiculous (the Fall-plundering "What Institution Are You From?") to the sublime (the suitably succubus-like "I Am a Witch").

Before forming Helium, Timony led Autoclave, a Washington, DC, quartet that mined much the same territory, although Timony had yet to learn the restraint she displays in Helium.

Tackle Box was the brainchild of singer/guitarist/songwriter Greg Kendall; the quartet was completed by Michael Leahy, Juliana Hatfield's guitarist on **Hey Babe. On!** is a marvelous pop record, full of strong melodies, crisp playing and witty reference points like "Mark Lindsay's Ponytail." Considering hotel life, "Check-Out Time" touches on the transience of existence, but makes a joke of the experience as well. The more diverse and ambitious **Grand Hotel,** which has no such residential concerns beyond the plangent "Moon Villa," stops off both on guitar distortion floors ("Grand Hotel") and on inveigling intimate landings ("Whiskey Jag"), delivering the same kind of sturdy material with higher fuzzbox settings and an elevated energy level. [dss/i]

See also *Polvo, Shudder to Think, Slant 6.*

RICHARD HELL

See *Dim Stars.*

HELMET

Strap It On (Amphetamine Reptile) 1990 (Interscope) 1992
Meantime (Interscope) 1992
Born Annoying EP (Amphetamine Reptile) 1993
Betty (Amphetamine Reptile/Interscope/Atlantic) 1994
Born Annoying (Amphetamine Reptile) 1995

While contemporaries were mucking about in swamps of feedback and messy sludge-rock power chords, this New York quartet formulated a metal-bore sound so clean, crisp and martial that some wags adopted Teutonic accents when discussing "das precision rock sound." Guitarist/singer Page Hamilton mastered the art of discipline as a foot soldier in Glenn Branca's guitar army (he was also, briefly, in Band of Susans) and found a remarkably astute way to recast some similarly avant-garde playing for the moshpit set.

Strap It On instigated a furious record company bidding war. It may take a little imagination to envision volume-intensive, minimal meditations like "Sinatra" and "Bad Mood" as fist-pumping anthems, but Hamilton's drill-instructor bark and ambivalent lyrical soundbites have an undeniable visceral appeal. The burnished veneer is broken occasionally by the wiry, slightly less restrained leads of Australian guitarist Peter Mengede. An auspicious debut.

The group took a qualitative leap forward with **Meantime,** an album that earned Helmet the approval of commentators no less shrewd than Beavis and Butt-head. "Unsung" and "In the Meantime" both reveal a bit of development in the frontman's Ozzy-like vocal intonations, but it's still the immediacy of the riffs Hamilton and Mengede mete out—albeit clinically—that drives this juggernaut. Hamilton also seems inclined to allow more insight into his terse lyrical observations. "Unsung" derides easy outs for those with flawed egos: "to die young is far too boring these days." Beneath the guitar sparring, bassist Henry Bogdan (who played in an embryonic version of Poison Idea) and drummer John Stanier maintain a chilly, lock-groove rhythm that changes precious little from track to track—which actually works to the songs' advantage. Although slightly more user-friendly, **Meantime** still owes more to La Monte than Angus (Young).

Mengede left Helmet after **Meantime**'s release (and now leads the burly fuzz quartet Handsome with ex-Quicksand guitarist Tom Capone), but he can be heard on both releases that bear the name **Born Annoying.** The EP reissues both sides of the band's 1989 debut single (including the title track), adding two songs from its first demo tape. The full-length appends six tracks, including the previously unreleased (and mighty impressive) "Geisha to Go."

On **Betty,** reconstituted by the arrival of guitarist Rob Echeverria (formerly of New York hardcore pummelers Rest in Pieces), Helmet made a conscious—and not entirely well-advised—decision to advance beyond the primary colors of the past. Throwaways like the delta-shronk "Sam Hell" and the deconstructionist take on the jazz standard "Beautiful Love" are the most gratuitous offenders, but there's equally little to recommend in the standard-issue metal grooves of "Wilma's Rainbow" (the title of which takes the *Flintstones* fixation one step too far). The gnashing "Milquetoast" and a few others possess some of the old vigor, but **Betty,** by and large, crumbles into rubble. [dss]

See also *Band of Susans, Sick of It All.*

KARL HENDRICKS TRIO

Buick Elektra (Peas Kor) 1992 (Grass) 1994
Some Girls Like Cigarettes (Big Ten Rex) 1993 (Merge) 1995
The Karl Hendricks Trio Sings About Misery and Women (Fiasco) 1993
A Gesture of Kindness (Fiasco) 1995
For a While, It was Funny (Merge) 1996

Neurotic and noisy, this Pittsburgh trio pins Violent Femmes–styled coitus-pining to spiraling guitar sallies that are strongly reminiscent of Dinosaur Jr, a combination that allows singer/guitarist Karl Hendricks to divest himself of his surplus anxiety in half the time. **Buick Elektra** was recorded shortly after Hendricks split his old band, Sludgehammer—the name pretty much tells the whole story—and consequently suffers from a surplus of extraneous skronk. That's a drag, since a few of the tracks (notably the argumentative "Dumber Than I Look") reveal him to be an unusually self-aware writer. As evidenced by the deconstruction of the Rolling Stones' "She Was Hot," he's also saddled with an intrinsically indie-rock penchant for machine-gunning sitting ducks. (The Grass reissue adds "I Hate This Party" from a '91 7-inch.)

There's a lot less smirking on **Some Girls Like Cigarettes,** which seems to move from one shade of gray to the next as Hendricks rambles from lamenting his lack of action ("Pittsburgh's Hottest Babes") to reliving the kind of pre-adolescent loneliness that never fully recedes (the touching "Baseball Cards"). Bassist Tim Parker and drummer Tom Hoffman stay out of the way of guitar lines that flutter erratically and—at least on the album-closing "How's the Cat?"—engagingly. True to its title, **The Karl Hendricks Trio Sings About Misery and Women** concentrates on tunes concerning those two subjects—and a considerable area of overlap that seems to have enmeshed Hendricks. He's not too given to metaphor, as evidenced by gushings that range from maudlin self-pity ("Do You Like to Watch Me Sob?") to self-aware indignation ("You're a Bigger Jerk Than Me"). This time around, however, the trio stifles its all-noise all-the-time posturing enough to allow delicate melodies like the piano-laced "Flowers Avenue" to shine through.

Maybe the full-throttle playing he's asked to contribute to The(e) Speaking Canaries (in which he serves as bassist) has given Hendricks enough of an opportunity to pump up the volume, since **A Gesture of Kindness** is markedly more refined than its predecessors. It's not exactly mellow—check the raveup ending of "Breathtaking First Novel"—but the album makes it explicit that Hendricks isn't as afraid to grow up as the bulk of his bermuda-shorted peers. [dss]

See also *The(e) Speaking Canaries.*

JOE HENRY

Talk of Heaven (Profile) 1986
Murder of Crows (Coyote/A&M) 1989 (Coyote/Mammoth/A&M) 1993
Shuffletown (Coyote/A&M) 1990 (Coyote/Mammoth/A&M) 1993
Short Man's Room (Mammoth) 1992
Kindness of the World (Mammoth) 1993
Fireman's Wedding EP (Mammoth) 1994
Trampoline (Mammoth/Atlantic) 1996

After singer/songwriter Joe Henry signed to Mammoth Records in the early '90s, the label reissued the well-crafted but characterless **Murder of Crows** (produced by Anton Fier) and the confidently poetic **Shuffletown,** an acoustic collection that recalls prime Van Morrison. With rustic backing from the Jayhawks, Henry maintains his stately charm on the handsome **Short Man's Room,** walking a tradition-respecting bluegrass-strewn line between Dylan's artfulness and Morrison's emotionalism, with vivid side trips into sentimental storytelling. The country stylings are occasionally too self-conscious, and the title track sounds like a moldy Steve Goodman song, but "Last One Out," an observant bar-room waltz, is gorgeous, as are the heartbreaking "A Friend to You," the fiddle-accented "Best to Believe" and "One Shoe On," an evocative ballad about death.

Kindness of the World demonstrates Henry's disinclination to settle for a single way to present his songs. Backed by a pair of Jayhawks and several other acoustic instrumentalists, Henry heads down from the hills and aims toward the heart of old Nashville, surrounding a Tom T. Hall cover with similarly heart-tugging original ballads like "She Always Goes," "This Close to You" (both of which sound like should-be standards) and "Kindness of the World," done as a pedal steel–tinged duet with Victoria Williams. "Dead to the World," however, is a solid rocker, and the simple arrangement of "Who Would Know" is built around piano and Dobro guitar. The songs are so fine that such eclecticism doesn't call attention to itself; **Kindness of the World** sounds completely organic and thought-out.

The very-country **Fireman's Wedding** gangs up the titular album track (from **Kindness of the World**), a pair of live recordings and two freshly cut studio covers, including an outstanding rendition of Merle Travis' coal-mining classic "Dark as a Dungeon" with backing vocals by Billy Bragg.

Trampoline launches Henry into an entirely different orbit. Although some of the nine songs quietly revisit the solemn country and folk terrain of his past efforts, the extraordinary album has the idiosyncratic broadmindedness to employ Helmet's Page Hamilton as its electric guitarist, cover Sly Stone's "Let Me Have It All" as a fuzzy roots groove and set an opera singer loose in the background of "Flower Girl." The record's opening lines—"There's something caught in my teeth / And a cricket that won't let me sleep" (from "Bob & Ray")—instantly set its unsettled tone, while short-story songs like "Ohio Air Show Plane Crash," with the grim certitude in fate of Nathanael West, tacks the '40s/noir mood down so it can't curl up around the edges. The wondrous Dylanesque title track announces "The floor will have its way, it seems . . . but this time I'm not coming down," while "Medicine" promises "I'm straighter than a razor / Well anyway, I will be soon" in between patches of noise-guitar aggression. Through it all, Henry keeps his head and sings his heart. A great record of depth and imagination. [i]

See also *Jayhawks; TPRG*.

KRISTEN HERSH

See *Throwing Muses*.

HE SAID

See *Wire*.

RICHARD X. HEYMAN

Actual Size EP (N.R. World) 1986
Living Room!! (N.R. World) 1988 (Cypress) 1990
Hey Man! (Sire/Warner Bros.) 1991

With some minor assistance, multi-talented New York power-popper Heyman does it all—vocals, guitars, keyboards, drums, etc.—on his six-song EP and sparkling debut album, an impressively accomplished 8-track home brew that was remixed and minorly resequenced for reissue inside a new cover. On **Living Room!!,** Heyman realizes an undated collection of tuneful styles in shapely songs that favor subtlety rather than eccentricity.

Co-produced by Andy Paley, **Hey Man!** accomplishes the same audacious one-man-band feat, taking advantage of a real studio situation to multiply the arranging details (including multi-tracked vocal harmonies) without succumbing to pointless doodling or numbing slickness. What the winning album does indulge a little is Heyman's ability to summon up the sound of archetypes, which he does in the precise Beatlisms of "Loud," the baroque Left Banke intricacy of "To Whiskey Flats" and the Byrdsy harmonies of the Dylanesque "In the Scheme of Things." If he sometimes gets a little too close to the flame of the past, Heyman elsewhere makes fine use of his knowledge of past pop lore, channeling it into delightful originals like "Caught in a Lie," "Falling Away" and "Back to You." The best tunes pair magical melodies with substantial lyrics that reveal a strong individual personality after all. The faint military metaphors that march through Heyman's love songs are finally explained near the end of **Hey Man!** in the revealing "Civil War Buff." [i]

See also *TPRG*.

JOHN HIATT

Hangin' Around the Observatory (Epic) 1974
Overcoats (Epic) 1975
Slug Line (MCA) 1979
Two Bit Monsters (MCA) 1980
All of a Sudden (Geffen) 1982
Riding With the King (Geffen) 1983
Warming Up to the Ice Age (Geffen) 1985
Bring the Family (A&M) 1987
Slow Turning (A&M) 1988
Y'All Caught? The Ones That Got Away 1979–1985 (Geffen) 1989
Stolen Moments (A&M) 1990
Perfectly Good Guitar (A&M) 1993
Walk On (Capitol) 1995

JOHN HIATT AND THE GUILTY DOGS

Hiatt Comes Alive at Budokan? (A&M) 1994

LITTLE VILLAGE

Little Village (Reprise) 1992

VARIOUS ARTISTS

Love Gets Strange: The Songs of John Hiatt (Rhino) 1993

Not every rocker needs to be Dorian Gray; some manage to find satisfaction in lives and music that proceed along a natural path toward, and through, middle age. Few have portrayed maturity's arc with more unbridled enthusiasm than John Hiatt, the Indianapolis-born singer/songwriter whose adventures in the lost and found department of life have produced a singularly artful musical diary of an eventful existence. If the short version is that Hiatt morphed from Elvis Costello into Andy Griffith—a rootsy young idealist who survived bouts with belligerence and self-destruction only to emerge as a corny family man raising horses and kids on a Tennessee farm—that perception entirely overlooks the imagination and individuality that has informed every aspect of a real fine career.

After two albums of unsteady exploration—**Overcoats** variously favors Dr. John, Elton John and Tim Hardin—Hiatt made **Slug Line,** a fierce bolt of compassionate new wave rancor, and the similar (but less often likely to draw blood) **Two Bit Monsters.** The Geffen era—nicely recapitulated, plus tracks from the two MCA LPs, on **Y'All Caught?**—is a hit-and-miss mess, as various producers woefully attempted to buy hits for an artist whose songs have always done the trick for others. (Bonnie Raitt is by no means the only satisfied customer on a long list of clients.)

Hiatt's career got a strong second wind with **Bring the Family,** an album of uncommon simplicity and candor cut in four very productive days with Nick Lowe, guitarist Ry Cooder (in whose band Hiatt has played), veteran session drummer Jim Keltner and a hands-off producer. In a heartfelt outpouring as complex and contradictory as life itself, the songs blend desperation and loss, tentative optimism and true love.

Following what appears to be a pattern, **Slow Turning**—a more upbeat vision of family and faith—is similar but a notch less striking. It does, however, contain some classics, including the title tune, "Drive South" and "Feels Like Rain." **Stolen Moments** is a full-fledged good'un, boasting a sunny disposition, a marked Bob Dylan influence and some of Hiatt's most beautiful compositions: "Through Your Hands," "Real Fine Love," "Thirty Years of Tears."

Having passed forty, with familial stability threatening to dull the sharpness of his vision, Hiatt engaged producer Matt Wallace to make the remedial and rewarding **Perfectly Good Guitar,** an amped-up exercise that drives a superior collection of typically handsome and sensitive tunes onto the front lawn of Neil Young's eternal-youth noise farm. The ecstatic "Something Wild" is just that, and "Buffalo River Home" finds a place for sweet distortion in a tender reverie.

But the title track, another storm of guitar fury, is a curmudgeonly and condescending attack on musicians who would dare demolish an instrument. The song makes him out to be the worst kind of intolerant, uncomprehending old fart, but if that's where Hiatt has to go to unearth a heartbreaking jewel like "Blue Telescope," then what the hell.

Rock therapy was good for Hiatt; despite its embarrassing cover art, the live album of his '94 tour has a calm, settled authority underpinning the acoustic/electric performances. With six numbers from **Slow Turning** and five upbeat choices from **Bring the Family, Hiatt Comes Alive at Budokan?** is a pretty chipper set, and a righteous reflection of an enthusiastic and engaging concert-giver.

Traces of **Perfectly Good Guitar**'s axe frenzy appear on **Walk On,** but only as incidental coloration. Otherwise, the album calmy returns Hiatt to the rustic folk-roots sound of his most natural habitat, with mixed but generally positive results. Recorded with the Guilty Dogs' rhythm section (Cracker bassist Davey Faragher and drummer Michael Urbano) and David Immerglück (Monks of Doom/Ophelias) on guitar and mandolin, **Walk On** is one of Hiatt's least personal albums—the songs are more external than reflective. But a writer of his caliber rarely strikes out, and a skilled craftsman (witness "Cry Love" and "You Must Go") doesn't always require deep inspiration. "The River Knows Your Name" is a lovely, serene prayer to nature (that gets away with rhyming "name" and a mispronounced "Seine"), "Your Love Is My Rest" is a convincing romantic ode, and "Mile High"—an unlisted '40s-styled jazz-pop ballad that makes bizarre reference to "all of the smack in Manhattan"—is as tender as it is uncommon. But other songs take a more conceptual route, like the short narrative of the rocking "Good as She Could Be," the bizarre David Lynch–style mystery set to funky feedback-accented noir music of "Wrote It Down and Burned It" and the contrived nonsense of "Ethylene." If Hiatt had seemed to be settling down, this album opens a trapdoor that he doesn't quite fall through.

Based on the experience of **Bring the Family,** Little Village should have been cool, but the reunion of Hiatt, Lowe, Cooder and Keltner—co-writing a batch of songs and cutting 'em with the three singers taking turns on lead vocals—turned out to be far less than the sum of its parts the second time. Despite the abundance of compatible talent, **Little Village** betrays no organic sense of collaboration and is a best-forgotten blunder. Rather than enhance one another's creative efforts, the four men manage to blunt their individual personalities into a band of undistinguished bores. "Don't Think About Her When You're Trying to Drive" (a song far more graceful than its title) is an exception, but Hiatt's showcases—which fill half the record—are surprisingly dull and, for the most part, sound like his castoffs ("Solar Sex Panel"?). Lowe phones in his two spotlight dances like an uneasy house guest, and Cooder's contributions further dessicate the atmosphere of this cheerless party.

Love Gets Strange, compiling previously issued covers, bears witness not only to the greatness of Hiatt's songs but to the rarefied echelon of those who choose to interpret them. Leaving Bonnie Raitt out of the mix, folks like Johnny Adams, Rosanne Cash, Katty Moffat, Marshall Crenshaw, Kelly Willis, Nick Lowe, Emmylou Harris and Jeff Healey all make excellent use of a wide-ranging collection of Hiatt classics. [i]

See also *Cracker, Nick Lowe; TPRG.*

HIGH BACK CHAIRS

Of Two Minds (Dischord) 1991
Curiosity and Relief EP (Dischord) 1992

Despite the first-rate power-pop attack led by fine singer/guitarist Peter Hayes, Washington DC's High Back Chairs is probably best remembered as the final stop in Jeff Nelson's career as a drummer (besides Minor Threat, the co-owner of Dischord Records spent quality time in Teen Idles, Grand Union, Egg Hunt, 3 and Senator Flux), and as the first group home of Velocity Girl drummer Jim Spellman, who played guitar in the quartet alongside Hayes and bassist Charles Steck (ex–Velvet Monkeys).

Of Two Minds' eight songs are polished but gripping, hard and mean. Benefiting from Ted Nicely's production, the record—underneath the usual great melodic wall of guitars—is one of Dischord's first excursions into roots-rock pop. "Miles to Inches" and "Doldrums" have the reports of a small cannon and hooks so clean and big they're as grabby as a little kid in a shopping cart. The mix of spirited earnestness and streamlined rock power is enormously appealing.

Also produced by Nicely, **Curiosity and Relief** is no departure. Crisp guitars again rule the day, with more sing-song pop choruses, heavy bass and drums, lulling backing vocals and a '60s-meets-'80s feel. The outstanding "Share" is representative of the half-dozen selections, but the band also tries some quieter moments, such as "Unending," which approaches prettiness without pulling up lame. Coming out at a time when grunge held a lot of sway in Amerindie land, this breezy, supremely melodic, gutsy rock seemed almost noble. Replacements were enlisted when Nelson decided to retire from playing and Spellman pledged his troth to his other band (selling his Les Paul in the process), but two original Chairs missing soon meant no chairs at all, and the band folded. [jr]

See also *Velocity Girl.*

HIGH LLAMAS

Apricots EP (UK Plastic) 1991
Santa Barbara (Fr. Vogue) 1992
Gideon Gaye (UK Target) 1994 (Delmore) 1994 (Alpaca Park/Epic) 1995
Hawaii (UK Alpaca Park) 1996

SEAN O'HAGAN

High Llamas (UK Demon) 1990

Onetime *New Musical Express* journalist Sean O'Hagan was half of the creative core of the Irish combo Microdisney, which at its best mixed lush melodicism with biting, politically charged lyrical venom. While ex-partner Cathal Coughlan went on to explore aggression and chaos with Fatima Mansions, O'Hagan opted to luxuriate in melody, first as a solo artist on **High Llamas** and then with the band bearing that album's name.

The charmingly whimsical **High Llamas** is lightweight and pleasant, with intriguing lyrics but an underdeveloped musical personality. By the time O'Hagan and his cohorts (keyboardist Marcus Holdaway, bassist John Fell, drummer Rob Allum) recorded the mini–magnum opus **Gideon Gaye,** they'd arrived at a distinctive approach, informed by **Smile**-era Beach Boys and **Sgt. Pepper**–vintage Britpop. The result is a homespun, heartfelt art-pop masterpiece, with airy arrangements and gorgeous melodies in richly detailed tunes—"The Dutchman," "Checking In, Checking Out," "The Goat Looks On" and the fourteen-minute "Track Goes By"—that liberally quote Brian Wilson's lost classic without sacrificing O'Hagan's purposefully playful point of view. (**Apricots,** the British EP on which the High Llamas made their debut, was expanded to full length and issued in France as **Santa Barbara.** The Delmore and Epic issues of **Gideon Gaye** are identical save for the artwork.)

The seventy-seven-minute, twenty-nine-track **Hawaii** is a gentle, leisurely mood piece that's simultaneously expansive and intimate, packing in even more vintage Brian Wilson references (not only in the subtly imaginative arrangements but also in the title and cover art) while simultaneously carving out a distinctive melodic and lyrical identity of its own. Though the songs are less obviously catchy than those on **Gideon Gaye,** O'Hagan's inventively derivative method really emerges as a cohesive (if sprawling) personal voice.

O'Hagan has lately split his musical efforts between leading the High Llamas and working as an auxiliary member of Stereolab. [ss]

See also *Palace Brothers, Stereolab*.

HIGH RISK GROUP

See *Kustomized*.

DEVIN HILL

Stars (Big Deal) 1994
Wayout Lane (Big Deal) 1995

DANGTRIPPERS

Days Between Stations (Dog Gone) 1989 (Sky) 1990

Devin Hill was the linchpin of Iowa's Dangtrippers; five years after that exemplary power-pop quartet's sole album, he resurfaced in Minneapolis, offering up an even more appealing solo record. With the help of five musicians (including the Dangtrippers' other singer/guitarist, Doug Roberson), Hill adds Byrdsy country flavoring to the purified essence of melodic rock in a sterling set of songs, some of which stash lyrical razors in the candy apples. **Stars**' title song offers chin-up romantic encouragement in a classic Big Star frame, but its next-track neighbor, "Pretty Baby," is a murderous stalker's threat, misleadingly sung with relaxed affection and no shortage of charm: "Your heart beats now, but it won't beat for long." That's followed by "Run Like Hell" (not the Pink Floyd song), which employs sweet Everly Brothers harmonies and mandolin to announce Hill's revulsion for the song's subject. The R.E.M.-ish "Lovers Again" can't escape its unhappy context; the Shoesy "19th" evinces ambiguous motives for revisiting old memories. With pristine musicianship and an unsettling vibe, the too-brief **Stars** brings troubled emotions to pop's amusement park.

In synch with indie-pop's mid-'90s rural current, the high-lonesome singer turns countryward on **Wayout Lane,** letting acoustic guitars, twangy leads and dusty/pretty harmony blends (plus organ) shape such songs as "Old Armed Robbery" and "Meet Me at Home." "Wish You Luck" upholds Anglo-pop purity (check the recent Colin Blunstone compilation for reference points), but Hill consistently infuses the album with American elements that grant it adequate stylistic unity. Except for "Popping My Balloon," Hill works with a different set of musicians here, and consigns them to a smaller role, doing more himself. "Last to Learn," "It's Coming 'Round" and "To Get to You" are fine, mostly because the vocal arrangements are so good; other songs float by without leaving much of a trace. [i]

See also *TPRG*.

HILT

See *Skinny Puppy*.

HINDU LOVE GODS

See *R.E.M.*

HIP CLUB GROOVE

Trailer Park Hip Hop (Can. Murderecords) 1994

Just what the world needs: a teenaged rap trio from the sticks of Nova Scotia. Actually, the blunted lyrical visions of MacKenzie and Cheklove Shakil and the scratch-happy turntable activities of DJ Moves (Brian Higgins) are enjoyably all right for what they are. Hooked on product names, B-boy slang, recent movies and food metaphors, derivative of old Beasties and A Tribe Called Quest (but down with the '90s enough to make an informed lyrical reference to Fu-Schnickens) and charmingly casual ("Shure Shots" collapses in a tongue-tied "blahblahblahsumpinsumpinsumpin" breakdown and no one seems to care), the members of Hip Club Groove don't pretend to be anything they're not, and they have the imagination, personality and skills to bring off a credible variation on the theme. Adjusting the beats from an energetic old-school snap (as in the geographical pun of "Bay Oh Fun-Day") to woozy jazz-soul ("Jizz," which pokes fun at Tom Petty along the sexy way), the trio keeps it real in what is likely a chilly musical environment. Bringing a whimsical indie-rock sensibility to mild-mannered hip-hop, the laddies make it sound right at home. [i]

HIP DEEP TRILOGY

Cannibal Smile (Widely Distributed) 1993

Chicago punk pioneer Lorna Donley—the bassist/singer/poet who led the group Da in the early '80s when the city's indie scene was first taking shape—returns with this trio, a harsh cage for her feral vocals and Joe Callahan's buzzing guitar. Although Donley tucks smart, detailed small-scale personal dramas into songs like "The Story of the I" and "Train Wreck," the lunging musical aggression and lurid B-movie ideology that laces through **Cannibal Smile** too often sacrifices those intellectual gifts to the angry gods of rock thunder. [i]

HIS NAME IS ALIVE

Livonia (UK 4AD) 1990 (4AD/Rykodisc) 1992
Home Is in Your Head (UK 4AD) 1991 (4AD/Rykodisc) 1992
The Dirt Eaters EP (UK 4AD) 1992
Mouth by Mouth (4AD) 1993
King of Sweet (Perdition Plastics) 1994

Sound of Mexico [tape] (Time Stereo) 1995
Stars on E.S.P. (4AD) 1996

BONE MACHINE

Decapasaurus (A.U.D.) 1988

PRINCESS DRAGONMOM

The Real Folk Blues [tape] (Japan. G.R.O.S.S.) 1994
Honey Moon [tape] (Square D) 1995
Slow Poke (Insignificant) 1995

ESP-SUMMER

ESP-Summer (Time Stereo) 1994 (Perdition Plastics) 1996
ESP-Summer EP10 (Farrago) 1995

ESP-BEETLES

With The [tape] (Time Stereo) 1994
Live ESP [tape] (Time Stereo) 1995

ESP-FAMILY

ESP-Family [tape] (Time Stereo) 1994

S. VAN GELDER

No Credit [tape] (Time Stereo) 1995

MYSTIC MOOG ORCHESTRA

Mystic Moog Orchestra (Tantalus) 1995

CONTROL PANEL

Technological [tape] (Time Stereo) 1995

Apparently unfamiliar with the rule that proclaims all rock musicians in their twenties to be lazy, Warren Defever has managed to find more than a little bit of truth in the adage "music is my life." Although His Name Is Alive is ostensibly his main project, this resident of Livonia, Michigan (a suburb of Detroit), has made quite a reputation for himself as both a producer and a collaborator, creating or helping to create an astonishing amount of quality music.

Upon its first appearance, **Livonia** was justifiably regarded as yet another sojourn into 4AD atmospherics: in its moody, ethereal translucence, coupled with femme vox and a seeming lack of direction, the album seemed doomed to exist in the label's pretty-but-insubstantial ghetto. That it was recorded by Defever, then sent off in pieces to be mixed and reconstructed by 4AD head Ivo Watts-Russell added fuel to that suspicion. However, the sweeping dissonance of tracks like "Some and I" and "Reincarnation" and the sparse instrumentation of something like the title track (a bonus cut added to the Rykodisc reissue) point toward Defever's non-pretty tendencies and decidedly unique take on composition, which would later be revealed more fully.

The twenty-three-track **Home Is in Your Head** shattered any notions that HNIA was simply another pleasant blip on the 4AD radar. Neither abrasive nor halcyon, the album paints quick song-portraits wrapped around Defever's stop-start guitar, mysterious drone loops and Karin Oliver's throaty, beatific voice. Momentary blasts of haunting chaos ("Put Your Finger in Your Eye," "Chances Are We Are Mad") rest neatly next to sections of pastoral bliss ("Why People Disappear," "Mescalina"), resulting in a work that, though spotty when considered track by track, makes a collective masterpiece. The five-track **Dirt Eaters** EP (appended to the Rykodisc version of **Home Is in Your Head**) contains a different version of the album's "Are We Still Married?," a cover of Rainbow's (yes, Ritchie Blackmore's Rainbow) "Man on the Silver Mountain" and three previously unreleased originals.

Mouth by Mouth marks an abrupt shift in Defever's compositional process. Gone are the bits of songs couched in spacious sound, replaced by more fully thought-out songs that, if not always successful, are always interesting. Defever's guitar playing is considerably more up-front this time; from the opening percussive blast of "Baby Fish Mouth," an excellent cover of Big Star's "Blue Moon" and the stunningly distorted "Drink, Dress, and Ink"—through the ethereal psychobilly of "Jack Rabbits" and the simplistic, poignant "Ear"—**Mouth by Mouth** comes very close to being a "normal" rock record. Defever's scattered attention span continually keeps things from becoming mundane; though **Mouth by Mouth** isn't perfect, it's certainly far from average.

After **Mouth by Mouth,** Defever found himself increasingly engaged in extracurricular activities and plunged into a number of projects that would probably scare the facepaint off your average 4AD trainspotter. Although His Name Is Alive was conceived while Defever was still involved in Elvis Hitler (and Snake-Out, and the more stylistically reasonable late-'80s dream-pop of Bone Machine—whose lone album contains a very early version of **Home Is in Your Head**'s "There's Something Between Us and He's Changing My Words"), the rash of activity that has followed **Mouth by Mouth** is truly staggering. In addition to making all this music, Defever releases most of it through his own Time Stereo cassette label.

If neither is a necessary addition to the oeuvre, His Name Is Alive's first two post–**Mouth by Mouth** records have their own pointedly individual charms. **King of Sweet** reveals the large, expansive instrumental pieces that were severely pared down on **Home Is in Your Head** in their full form (although "Are You Comin' Down This Weekend?" appears no fewer than five times). Seamlessly mixed, they provide an hour of sleepy background music—but don't doze through Defever's stomping "Out of the Blue, Into the Black" riff rippage near the end. **Sound of Mexico** is culled from two HNIA Mexican appearances and has collaborations with Jorge Reyes, as well as soundcheck noises, lengthy improvisational pieces and snippets of Mexican TV. Entertaining, but only once.

Princess Dragonmom (like the scantily recorded live antics of, um, His Name Is Arrive) is Defever's answer to the Japanese noise explosion. The group's three releases are true endurance tests; the creepy noise/tape-loop mischief of ESP-Beetles follows a similar tack.

ESP-Summer, a collaboration with ex–Pale Saints bassist/vocalist Ian Masters, is a surprisingly forthright adventure in which Defever provides acoustic accompaniment to Masters' lilting falsetto. The Farrago 10-inch contains remixed versions of the originals found on the Time Stereo/Perdition Plastics edition. ESP-Family is, in Defever's words, "Communist folk songs," but the stunning music contained on the band's lone release sounds like a surprisingly accomplished field recording. **Mystic Moog Orchestra** documents Defever and fifteen friends all playing Moog synthesizers at their most obnoxious settings. With its gurgling, spacious keyboard sounds, the Control Panel release seems to be his nod to the ambient movement. [jf]

See also *Elvis Hitler, Pale Saints, Tsunami.*

ROBYN HITCHCOCK

Black Snake Diamond Röle (UK Armageddon) 1981 (Glass Fish/Relativity) 1986 (Rhino) 1995
Groovy Decay (UK Albion) 1982
I Often Dream of Trains (UK Midnight Music) 1984 (Glass Fish/Relativity) 1986 (Rhino) 1995
Groovy Decoy (Glass Fish/Relativity) 1985
Exploding in Silence EP (Relativity) 1986
Invisible Hitchcock (Glass Fish/Relativity) 1986 (Rhino) 1995
Eye (Twin\Tone) 1990 (Rhino) 1995
Perspex Island (A&M) 1991
Gravy Deco (Rhino) 1995
You & Oblivion (Rhino) 1995
Mossy Liquor (Outtakes and Prototypes) (Warner Bros.) 1996
Moss Elixir (Warner Bros.) 1996

ROBYN HITCHCOCK AND THE EGYPTIANS

Fegmania! (Slash) 1985 (Rhino) 1995
Gotta Let This Hen Out! (Relativity) 1985 (Rhino) 1995
Element of Light (Glass Fish/Relativity) 1986 (Rhino) 1995
Globe of Frogs (A&M) 1988
Queen Elvis (A&M) 1989
Respect (A&M) 1993
Greatest Hits (A&M) 1996

Robyn Hitchcock is one of pop's great surrealists, an artist whose work has the appearance of familiarity yet none of its reassurance. While he often gets compared to poor old Syd Barrett (an acknowledged influence), this London native has closer relations outside the music world: Rene Magritte (logic-defying juxtapositions), Marcel Duchamp (dada absurdity), Edward Lear (whimsical, grotesque fabrications), Charles Addams (gloomy, cartoonish venom). Displaying a keen sense of irony as well as a dry, put-on (and put-*upon*) wit, Hitchcock's creations—in song, story, graphics and film—erect puzzling layers of incredibility that stymie presumptions about motivation or meaning. When his penchant for self-amusement runs away with him, as it sometimes does, Hitchcock can be far too self-conscious in his version of eccentricity, making nonsense seem both glib and random. At his best, however, he wields bizarre imagery brilliantly to make stealth runs at life's most challenging problems, elevating the mundane to provocative art.

Not truly a rock musician and too arch to be a folkie, Hitchcock has recorded both solo and with a group ever since dissolving the influential and offbeat new wave band the Soft Boys in 1980. (That group's three "official" albums—**A Can of Bees, Underwater Moonlight** and **Invisible Hits**—were reissued in 1992 by Rykodisc, followed the next year by a two-CD classics/rarities collection, **The Soft Boys 1976–81.**)

Using his ex-bandmates for backing, **Black Snake Diamond Röle** gets Hitchcock's second career off to a good start, beginning pointedly with the jaunty "The Man Who Invented Himself" and then taking a bewildering (but catchy) turn with "Brenda's Iron Sledge" and the edgy, theatrical "Do Policeman Sing?" The 1995 reissue (part of Rhino's nine-disc program to rehabilitate and consolidate Hitchcock's back catalogue) adds three tracks from later singles and two outtakes: a thuggish alternate version of the album's unnerving admission of obsession, "I Watch the Cars," and the proto–hip-hop of "Grooving on a Inner Plane."

Hitchcock's second album wasn't such a smooth ride. Hoping to get away from a standard guitar-based sound, he got Steve Hillage (ex-Gong) to produce. The result was the overambitious, rhythm-driven **Groovy Decay** (which employs, among other session hands, future Waterboy Anthony Thistlethwaite on sax and ex–Gang of Four bassist Sara Lee), a nondescript album that stretched the songs so far from Hitchcock's desires that he subsequently issued the idiosyncratic demos as **Groovy Decoy.** (Putting a cap on the whole episode a decade later, Rhino assembled both into **Gravy Deco,** adding a laughable disco mix of "Night Ride to Trinidad" and "Kingdom of Love.")

Burned by that misadventure, Hitchcock didn't go near a studio for two years. When he did, it was to record the mostly acoustic **I Often Dream of Trains** with a minimum of help. The spare piano and guitar arrangements make memories of Barrett's solo albums inevitable, but Hitchcock's fantasies are strictly his own: "Sometimes I Wish I Was a Pretty Girl" ("so I could look at myself in the shower"), "I Often Dream of Trains," "Sounds Great When You're Dead," the a cappella "Uncorrected Personality Traits." Besides the exercises in neurotica, however, he delivers gorgeous, aching melodicism in "Cathedral" and "Flavour of Night." The expanded Rhino version inserts the five bonus tracks from an intervening CD edition into the middle, adding a pair of songs from a contemporaneous 12-inch and five album demos. An oddity, to be sure, but one of Hitchcock's most involving and unguarded outings.

Through a fateful series of circumstances, Hitchcock convened old Soft Boys pals Morris Windsor (drums) and Andy Metcalfe (bass) as the Egyptians and cut **Fegmania!,** establishing the shimmering, inconspicuous electro-pop sound that would become his benchmark. The material is both imaginative and confidently grounded, equal to morbid merriment in "My Wife & My Dead Wife," metaphoric silliness in "The Man With the Lightbulb Head" ("I turn myself on in the dark") and serious contemplation in "Glass." The reissue adds three EP tracks (including a charming take on "Bells of Rhymney" that underscores the Byrdsy element in his work), three demos, a live track and a ten-minute instrumental, "The Pit of Souls Parts I–IV."

With keyboardist Roger Jackson becoming an official Egyptian, **Gotta Let This Hen Out!** is an essential live album—and career retrospective—recorded in London in 1985. The reissue adds three tracks from the same gig, left off the original album but previously available on the miscredited **Exploding in Silence** EP.

Element of Light is another fine record, highlighted by the descending rock drama of "If You Were a Priest," the arcing delicacy of "Winchester" and "Airscape," the moody restraint of "Raymond Chandler Evening" and two eerie John Lennon–like apparitions: "Somewhere Apart" and the gay romance of "Ted, Woody and Junior." Led by co-producer Metcalfe's fretless bass luxuries, the Egyptians perfectly complement Hitchcock's finely modulated writing and singing. Twice as long as the original, the reissue adds ten B-sides, prior CD bonus tracks, demos and a live number.

Long before Rhino began gathering up the leftovers, Hitchcock did it himself on **Invisible Hitch-**

cock, a compilation of simply recorded items from 1980 to '85. A few had already become manifest in different versions, but most of the songs were aired for the first time here. The '95 edition has six extras, the neatest of which is the B-side version of "Listening to the Higsons"—which begins with a wok (!) solo.

While clearing the vaults with one hand, Hitchcock was busy filling them with the other. **You & Oblivion** consists of twenty-two otherwise unreleased solo songs—mainly dating from the mid-'80s, but several older than that—and the first half of a short story, *The Professor,* he co-wrote with James Fletcher. (It concludes in the **Invisible Hitchcock** booklet.) Although the material is not first-rate, it's by no means barrel-scrapings, and the album is a softly lined treasure trove of comely also-rans given rudimentary acoustic performances. "Victorian Squid" is evidence of an overly self-amused intellectual disposition and "Keeping Still" is coy sex advice, but "Birdshead," "August Hair," "Polly on the Shore" and "You & Me" are all outstanding.

Signed to a major American label for the first time, Hitchcock tried too hard and missed the target on **Globe of Frogs.** Busy production—including guitar contributions from Peter Buck—doesn't impede the catchy melodies ("Balloon Man," "Flesh Number One (Beatle Dennis)," "Vibrating," "Chinese Bones"), but neither does it mask the lyrics, which draw dangerously close to self-caricature. The dull **Queen Elvis** continues the downward slide with less appealing tunes and more forced ideas.

Wisely repeating the retreat/retrench tactic that proved so helpful once before, Hitchcock next stripped down for another acoustic solo record on an indie label. Resounding with honest, nearly unguarded emotionalism, the romantically minded **Eye** is a visionary thing of simple, graceful beauty. "Linctus House" offers a gorgeous meditation on flagging love; "Executioner" teases the entrails of another failed affair ("I know how Judas felt / But he got paid"); "Transparent Lover" limns the elusiveness and danger of devotion. Even "Queen Elvis"—a song not included on the album of the same name—is lovely and meaningful. The reissue appends three demos that aren't very different in sound from the album versions.

Given his prior bad experience, Hitchcock's decision to use an outside producer couldn't have been an easy one. The capable Paul Fox was a safe choice (he's proven to be a mindful collaborator for XTC, Sugarcubes, 10,000 Maniacs and other tricky auteurs), but the very idea of a strong, if conservative, studio influence carries an element of risk. **Perspex Island,** which occasionally ignores the author's emotional state to soar into delightful flights of psychedelic sprightliness, doesn't always sound like much of anything. (Not much like Hitchcock, leastways.) Still, moved by heartbreak, Hitchcock's songs are forceful and vivid; again steadied on solid ground, his lyrics have rarely been more direct or touching. Free of the past don't-I-odd? affliction, the sardonic "So You Think You're in Love," the lonely "Birds in Perspex," the desperate "If You Go Away" and the sadly resigned "She Doesn't Exist" (for which Michael Stipe joins his bandmate Buck in the album's guest book) are all poignantly top-notch.

Thus emboldened, Hitchcock recklessly made **Respect** with another XTC production alumnus, John Leckie. The gamble mostly paid off in a febrile high-tech album unlike anything in Hitchcock's background. With Windsor and Metcalfe adding loads of lush vocal harmonies and using digital drums, keyboards and computers, many of the arrangements downplay guitar for an artificial sound that works once you get used to it. Leckie smartly picks up on both sides of a divided set of songs, modestly respecting the serious/solemn ones ("Arms of Love," "Serpent at the Gates of Wisdom," "Then You're Dust") and letting the madcap reins out for Hitchcock's entertaining return to hallucinatory wordplay ("The Yip Song," "Railway Shoes," "The Wreck of the Arthur Lee," "When I Was Dead," the utterly ridiculous "Wafflehead"). Not a good place to start and not an album for narrowminded fans, **Respect** is a tight squeeze through a narrow passage that leads Hitchcock safely out of one realm and into the grander possibilities of another.

In '95, Hitchcock took a surprising dip back into the indie world, releasing a pungently informal three-song solo 7-inch ("I Something You" and "Zipper in My Spine" b/w "Man With a Womans Shadow") on K Records. The following summer, delivered from the netherworld of tiny labels, Hitchcock borrowed one of their tactics, releasing the vinyl-only **Mossy Liquor** a few weeks before **Moss Elixir.** While the two related but distinct albums have half their songs in common (including "Sinister but She Was Happy," "Heliotrope," "The Devil's Radio" and "De Chirico Street"), the versions are all different. Overlapping the discography a shade further back, **Moss Elixir** retrieves the B-side of the K 45. [i]

See also *R.E.M.; TPRG.*

ELVIS HITLER

Disgraceland (Wanghead) 1987 (Restless) 1988
Hellbilly (Restless) 1989
Supersadomasochisticexpialidocious (Restless) 1992

SPLATTER

. . . From Hell to Eternity (Sector 2) 1994

Singer/guitarist Jim Leedy is the fiery Michigan rocker who calls himself Elvis Hitler; joined by the Defever brothers—guitarist John and bassist Warren, whose primary musical enterprise is His Name Is Alive—and a drummer, he roars through familiar-sounding originals that inbreed the Cramps, Mojo Nixon and the Stray Cats. **Disgraceland** has such convincingly obvious anthems to delinquency as "Hot Rod to Hell" and "Live Fast, Die Young," a few numbers about another feller named Elvis and "Green Haze (Pt. I & II)," a bit of inspired dementia in which Hitler sings the *Green Acres* theme over "Purple Haze."

Hellbilly is louder and harder, a less stylized but still exciting dish of overamped guitars, raw vocals and drummer Damian Lang's swampy backbeat. Besides covering "Ballad of the Green Berets" and borrowing "(Ghost) Riders in the Sky" (for "Showdown"), Elvis pokes fun at glam-rockers ("Hang 'Em High") and car nuts ("Gear Jammin' Hero," "Crush, Kill, Destroy"), saving his least judgmental sentiments for vampires and other horror-movie monsters.

Supersadomasochisticexpialidocious (a title sure to be found atrocious) retools the band to play plain hard rhythm-guitar rock somewhere between '70s lunkpunk and Brownsville Station, with a passing stylistic nod to Social Distortion. The lone 'billy bop—

"Shove That Sax" ("up your ass")—and the hep instrumental "Dickweed" sound stranded on the wrong album. Otherwise, lurid lyrics like "Bury the Hatchet" ("right in your skull"), "Shotgun Shell," "Bloody Bride" and "Ghouls" are entirely too obvious, as is the double bludgeoning of bubblegum standard "Yummy Yummy Yummy." The only à la carte entree on this boring blue-plate menu is a surprising (not good, just surprising) cover of Danielle Dax's "Cathouse."

Concocting a bizarre cover story, Elvis Hitler was finally laid to rest, freeing Leedy, John Defever and drummer Todd Glass to make a pit stop and re-emerge as Splatter. Pumping out a sizzling and massive rock sound, **. . . From Hell to Eternity** suffers a little from Leedy's punny lyrical conceits ("If you were me / You'd be the way I am") but hits the highway in a frenzy of white-line fever, cranking through souped-up twangin' ravers like "I'm Dropping Out," "Truck Driver," "21st Century" and "Hard Rockin' Daddy" with nary a backward glance. [i]

See also *His Name Is Alive.*

HITSVILLE HOUSE BAND

See *Wreckless Eric.*

KELLY HOGAN

See *Jody Grind.*

HOLE

Rat Bastard EP7 (Sympathy for the Record Industry) 1990
Pretty on the Inside (Caroline) 1991
Live Through This (Geffen) 1994
Ask for It EP (Caroline) 1995
Softer, Softest EP (Aus. Geffen) 1995

When held up against the monumental public art installation that is Courtney Love, Hole's records seem like measly artifacts. No other modern musician has bumrushed stardom with as vehement or desperate a sense of personal destiny. Against reason and the odds, La Love has managed to make her group the sine qua non of rising-up-angry female alternarock, in the process forcing **Live Through This** to become a vital necessity in the well-versed '90s culture sack.

Pretty on the Inside, a surly milkshake of broken rock shards, calculated shock lyrics and highly personalized punk animus, introduces an LA quartet consisting of Love (screeching vocals/roaring guitar), Eric Erlandson (sloppy noise guitar), drummer Caroline Rue and bassist Jill Emery (ex–Super Heroines). Harsh on the ears but actually no rougher than a lot of other groups aiming rusty knives at unsuspecting sonic poke holes around the same time, the album was produced with craggy abandon by a hip-world tag team of Don Fleming and Kim Gordon; their obvious attempt to make a Sonic Youth record doesn't quash the original impulses Love and Erlandson brought to the studio. Against the relentless barrage of grungy rock noise, Love screams her vicious disease-and-sex lyrics (see "Teenage Whore," "Babydoll," "Mrs. Jones" and "Pretty on the Inside" for the primary liturgy of rottendeathsmacksuckvirusfleshscars) as if she were a demented Joan Jett fan counting on being heard in another galaxy. Impressive in its need to outrage, the ferocious (except for "Starbelly," which consists of a wordless "Cinnamon Girl" plus a phone message and a Fleetwood Mac extract) **Pretty on the Inside** has aged well, and now sounds like a very modern and decisive statement of purpose.

Released several years later sporting a grisly slit-wrists cover photo, the scantily valuable **Ask for It** displays the post-debut Hole from several angles: live in early '92 (rubbishing the Velvets' "Pale Blue Eyes" like a careening bar band), in the studio around the same time (covering the Wipers' "Over the Edge" without any evidence of **Pretty on the Inside**'s brutality) and, for the BBC in late '91, previewing the second album's "Doll Parts" (acoustic and off-key) and "Violet" (pretty much as it wound up), plus the otherwise unreleased "Drown Soda" and a Germs/Beat Happening medley.

Live Through This, which presents the full flowering of Hole-ness (and a new rhythm section: drummer Patty Schemel, formerly of Seattle's Kill Sybil, and bassist Kristen Pfaff, whose subsequent drug OD brought Montreal's Melissa Auf der Maur into the lineup), has, like the debut, proven to be far more consequential—for its own merits, not the attendant hubbub—than it might have initially seemed. Released in a tragic bad-timing coincidence a week after the suicide of Love's husband, Kurt Cobain, the death-obsessed album is harrowingly prescient and loaded with regrettable lyrical allusions that, ironically, gave her career valuable emotional momentum.

What seemed like the lurid imaginings of a provocative showoff crying for attention on the first album here become a stirring cry of freedom and individuality from an unstoppable life force with the guts to bare herself and face the consequences. "Live Through This," written and recorded well before she had a proper tragedy to fix on, includes lines like "Someday you will ache like I ache." The most unfortunate couplet in "Jennifer's Body" offers "With a bullet, number one / Kill the family, save the son." Germane in a similarly convoluted sense is the oath in "Asking for It" that promises to no one in particular, "If you live through this with me / I swear that I will die for you." But Love's vow in "Miss World"—"I made my bed I'll lie in it / I made my bed I'll die in it"—sends as profound a message of taking responsibility in the age of victimhood as any of her extra-musical actions.

Making a fetish of the loud/soft dialectic borrowed from Nirvana, Love (buttressed by "additional vocals" by Dana Kletter of Dish) switches between a sturdy quiet voice that sounds like Holly Vincent and a harridan holler (something Nina Hagen pioneered a decade earlier); capably guided by Fort Apache producers Sean Slade and Paul Q. Kolderie (but partly mixed by J Mascis and Scott Litt), the band handles the abrupt shifts from peppy acoustics to smoothed-out full-blare raunch with poise. Hole remains Love's vehicle top to bottom, but even while making the first true post-Nirvana album—thanks to timing, it's virtually the sound of the spirit leaving Cobain's corpse—**Live Through This** has the strength of character to make that a respectable designation.

The import EP for **Live Through This**' "Softer, Softest" appends four non-LP tracks: a flat acoustic rendition of "He Hit Me (It Felt Like a Kiss)," the Crystals' appalling Goffin/King–penned ode to physical abuse, done strictly for effect (witness Love's introduction) at Hole's *MTV Unplugged* taping, plus three ragingly electric concert items ("Miss World," "Teenage Whore" and a bear-like cover of Duran Duran's "Hungry Like the Wolf") recorded in Melbourne in January 1995. [i]

See also *Babes in Toyland, Christian Death, Janitor Joe, Kill Sibyl.*

NICKY HOLLAND

Nicky Holland (Epic Associated) 1992

Keyboard player, songwriter and arranger Nicky Holland—whose extensive credits begin in 1981 with the Ravishing Beauties, a band with Virginia Astley and Kate St. John, and include The Teardrop Explodes, Fun Boy Three, Jill Sobule, Lloyd Cole, Ryuichi Sakamoto and many others—eventually became a crucial Tears for Fears adjunct, touring with the group in 1985 and co-writing more than half the songs for **The Seeds of Love.** Holland's first solo album is a dignified affair. Singing her graceful pop reflections (plus a stylish cover of the Grateful Dead's "Box of Rain") in a reedy alto—a deeper-voiced Joni Mitchell channeling Carole King—she makes adulthood sound like a reasonable place to be. [i]

See also *Tears for Fears.*

HOLLY AND THE ITALIANS

See *Holly Vincent.*

HOLLYFAITH

Chameleon (Large Orange) 1991
Purrrr (Epic) 1993

By the time **Chameleon** came out, Atlanta's Hollyfaith was one of the most beloved acts on the southern touring circuit, thanks to gritty, oversized guitar riffs, hyperactive rhythms and singer Rob Aldridge's distinctive, Jägermeister-saturated growl. The quartet neatly binds these elements together with seemingly inexhaustible energy, swaggering melodies and a healthy dose of arrogance on the album's woozy "Voodoo Doll," the scrambled, fun "Birdie" and the petulant, sassy "Whatsamatta."

The Hollyfaith buzz reached major labels, and the band signed to Epic, which released the disastrous **Purrrr.** Aldridge sounds bored instead of dangerously sensual; drummer Jeff Warncke and bassist David Franklin—usually a fiery rhythm section—seem subdued. Even guitarist Kevin Morrison can't bring his normal intensity to the effort. The slightly menacing "Color of Blood" and the swooning power balladry of "Needs" come across well enough, but new versions of "Whatsamatta" and "Voodoo Doll" have little of the spark they displayed on **Chameleon.** Maybe the band was overwhelmed by commercial pressures, maybe producer Don Fleming steered them wrong. In any case, **Purrrr** is a big letdown for anyone aware of Hollyfaith's once-riveting presence. [ky]

PETER HOLSAPPLE & CHRIS STAMEY

See *Chris Stamey.*

HOLY BARBARIANS

See *Cult.*

HOLY ROLLERS

As Is (Dischord) 1990
Fabuley (Dischord) 1991
Holy Rollers (Dischord) 1993

For all the stylistic presumptions that have arisen about the sound of their scene, some of the bands on Washington DC's Dischord Records would sooner experiment than go along with the generic core. In the case of the Holy Rollers, this proved to be a worthwhile endeavor. The trio's first album, **As Is,** can't be characterized so much by individual tracks as by the band's enthusiasm for punk-rock variety. Guitarist Marc Lambiotte, bassist Joe Aronstamn and drummer Maria Jones display a remarkable range of musical knowledge that adequately supplements their limited musical abilities. Jones' vocals on "Head On" recall the sort of stripped-down, anti-art influence of New York's no wave movement, stirred with a bit of early LA hardcore, while the straightahead punk stylings of "Dahlia" echo early TSOL or Bad Religion. Holy Rollers are quick to cover social issues—air quality in "Poison Lung," racial injustice in "Ode to Sabine County"—but the choppy lyrics and disjointed thoughts belie their good intentions.

The more diverse **Fabuley** is hindered by some of the same weaknesses as **As Is,** but the trio's lack of polished musical ability ultimately comes off more charming than deadly. Experiments with vocal interplay on "What You Said" and "Skin Deep Guilt" (engaging songs that both hint at '60s pop) and the bluesy intro to "Addiction" can't disguise the fact that none of the three can sing a lick. Holy Rollers know how things *should* sound, if not how to actually make them sound that way. Fugazi's Ian MacKaye makes a guest appearance on the powerful "Perfect Sleeper"; like "Cross the Line," it decries the precarious financial situation of many who live in the District, or on the District's streets. The jazzy, atmospheric spookiness of "Moment Before Impact" also makes for a memorable listen.

Dischord combined the vinyl-only **As Is** and **Fabuley** on one CD bearing the latter name in late 1991. The Rollers spent the next year and a half lying low and dealing with the departure of Jones (replaced by Ed Trask) and the addition of bassist C. Maynard Bopst, which allowed Aronstamn to move to guitar. The new lineup's **Holy Rollers** suffers from the changes. The material and craftsmanship are strong, but the band seems to have narrowed its vision, opting to stick with tried and true DC rock variations while cutting back on the vocal intricacy and the thematic diversity of individual songs. Aronstamn is the primary lead singer, and his compositions have turned more personal and angry: "Set Up" is a blistering damnation of a former friend for some betrayal. "Gold," a neat stream-of-consciousness musical discussion, introspectively considers personal identity, trust and insecurity; the disjointed "Killing Alley" again addresses life on the streets of DC. The disc has its quieter moments: "House of Fetish" builds into a crescendo not unlike those produced by Girls Against Boys. [icm]

See also *Gwar.*

HOME

IX (Relativity) 1995
Elf::Gulf Bore Waltz (Jetset) 1996
X (Emperor Jones/Trance Syndicate) 1996

With a sensibility that falls somewhere between the Residents and Can, this determinedly loopy Florida quartet likes nothing better than a good beer-bong-fueled jam session—the results of which they capture in real time, letting the audience handle the editing process later on its own. The title of the band's "official" recorded bow isn't an affectation—Home actually did record eight albums in the two years before its release, all issued on the Screw Music Forever label in tiny editions of nth-generation cassette dubs that could be purchased only at a couple of record stores around their Tampa home base. When intently focused, Home can squeeze an agreeably synthetic, Devo-esque pop-tone (like "Make It Right") from its gizmos. More often, though, Home lapses into wildly freeform freak-outs (like "Atomique") that combine electronic noise, found sound and even a bit of spoken word (if you can call snippets of surreptitiously recorded automobile conversation "spoken word"). Those endowed with short attention spans will no doubt have the easiest time making it all the way through **IX.** [dss]

HONCHO OVERLOAD

See *Hum.*

HONEYBUNCH

See *Velvet Crush.*

HONEYDOGS

The Honeydogs (October) 1995
Everything, I Bet You (October) 1996

"It hardly takes a genius / Just a human with a penis / That's me." Adam Levy, the human in question, doesn't give himself enough credit. "I hear you like 'em tough as nails, well I break like a twig / I'm good at feeling sorry for myself, I'm lazy as a pig." Actually, the singer/guitarist is nothing of the sort, and his Minneapolis band—initially a trio with drummer/brother Noah (lately of Golden Smog as well) and bassist Trent Norton—demonstrates the kind of casual midwestern overachievement that leaves earnest strivers wondering where they were when the talent rations got handed out. Amalgamating the region's recent stylistic schools (wistful reflection, Stonesy rock'n'roll, rustic folksiness—in short, the Replacements crossed with the Jayhawks), the Honeydogs add a Beatlesy pop element, a warm soul stream and a bit of Hendrix to their first album, overdoing the variety a hair but generally nailing one track after another with wry sincerity and casually brilliant songcraft. Besides "That's Me," highlights include the zippy show-starter "What I Want," the Mellencamped "I Miss You," the spare electric country of "Put Me to Bed" and "Like a Fortress," which reimagines "The Wind Cries Mary" as an Otis Redding song.

Recorded as a quartet with second guitarist Tommy Borschied, **Everything, I Bet You** glazes the Honeydogs' leanings with more of everything: the country numbers have the formality of pedal steel, the dispirited ballads are more deeply emotional and purposefully produced, the rock has a tougher edge. The only element not amplified is the songwriting. Although still solid, and occasionally—"Moth," "Your Blue Door," the tender "Miriam" and the bouncy "Busy Man"—even better than that, the material lacks the fine consistency of the debut. [i]

See also *Golden Smog, Martin Zellar.*

HOODOO GURUS

Stoneage Romeos (Big Time/A&M) 1983
Mars Needs Guitars! (Big Time/Elektra) 1985
Blow Your Cool! (Big Time/Elektra) 1987
Magnum Cum Louder (RCA) 1989
Kinky (RCA) 1991
Electric Soup (Aus. RCA) 1992
Gorilla Bisquit (Aus. RCA) 1992
Crank (Zoo) 1994
Blue Cave (Zoo) 1996

For four albums in the '80s (try **Magnum Cum Louder** for the peak experience), this international-minded quartet from Sydney, Australia, perfected a rollicking, genre-bending blend of kitschy garage-rock, power-pop, psychedelia, surf and winsome balladry that made it one of the most entertaining modern rock bands. Going against the early-'90s wave of angst and despair that swept away feel-good nostalgia, however, the band lost sight of its strengths and began making records that didn't do its talent justice.

Kinky reveals a confident, thoroughly proficient band with a batch of excellent songs and no new ideas. "Head in the Sand" starts things off on a poundingly aggressive note, while the ultra-pretty "Castles in the Air" has one of those chill-inducing hooks so rarely found in contemporary pop. Despite the album's meaningless title and the self-explanatory "Miss Freelove '69" (on which the group gamely indulges in retro flower-power shtick), **Kinky** is an innocuous delight.

But apparently not delightful enough to keep them signed. Singer/guitarist Dave Faulkner took advantage of the band's recording hiatus to produce the Fleshtones' **Powerstance!** (thereby validating long-held perceptions of the Gurus' stylistic debt to the New York crew). In the meantime, two similar-looking Australian releases appeared. **Electric Soup** collects the singles-oriented band's best-known songs, wisely omitting the weaker tracks that plagued its early albums. **Gorilla Bisquit,** a twenty-strong compilation of B-sides, live tracks and rarities, is nearly as good. Among the highlights: a terrific live cover of the Flamin Groovies' "Teenage Head," the wave-riding instrumental "Little Drummer Boy (Up the Khyber)," the Booker T. tribute "Lover for a Friend" and the revelatory "The Wedding Song," as lovely a ceremonial as you're likely to hear.

For the first four songs (including the passionate "Crossed Wires"), **Crank** sounds like the work of a revitalized band with something to prove. But then the rest of the album plods by. Mediocre and surprisingly gimmicky, **Crank** includes both an odd, whiny parody of Boston ("Less Than a Feeling") and a lame "Louie Louie" rip (*c'mon,* guys). Add Ed Stasium's lead-footed production and you've got the least imaginative Gurus album yet. If only they'd return to the Hoodoo they do so well.

Blue Cave has moments in which the giddy thrill of tuneful wit charged by enthusiastic playing takes hold, but the sense that the group is grasping at ill-fitting, unfashionable styles loads the album with wet sand and prevents it from soaring much above the predictability of songs such as "Waking Up Tired" and "Always Something." [db/i]

See also *TPRG.*

WILLIAM HOOKER

. . . Is Eternal Life (Reality Unit Concepts) 1978
Brighter Lights (Reality Unit Concepts) 1982
Lifeline (Silkheart) 1989
Colour Circle (Cadence) 1989
The Firmament/Fury (Silkheart) 1992
Subconscious (Ecstatic Peace!) 1992
Shamballa: Duets With Thurston Moore and Elliott Sharp (Knitting Factory Works) 1993
Radiation (Homestead) 1994
Armageddon (Homestead) 1995

WILLIAM HOOKER/LEE RANALDO

Envisioning (Knitting Factory Works) 1995

This New York–based drummer has played a large part in forging a bond between the city's free-jazz and downtown rock scenes while—and this is the tricky part—refusing to compromise the purity of essence that's pervaded his music for nearly two decades. Hooker plays with enough power to steer combos suffused with post-punk guitar scree, while maintaining a terpsichorean grace (reminiscent of Rashied Ali, a John Coltrane sideman who has had ephemeral involvement with the avant-rock scene as well) that effortlessly demonstrates the limits of most "rock" percussion.

Hooker's work is steeped in new age philosophy—**. . . Is Eternal Life** resounds with intricate patterns that bring to mind aural recreations of Druid stone circles—but the burning intensity of something like the side-long duet with reedman David Murray would no doubt provoke convulsions among Windham Hill devotees who claimed the term as accepted nomenclature for their brand of Holiday Inn jazz. **Brighter Lights** further explores the ancient. Hooker's rolling, imperceptibly shifting patterns—crafted almost exclusively on floor toms and bass drum, a tactic that adds considerable loam to spirit-world forays like "Others (Unknowing)"—betray little cognizance of the presence of pianist Mark Hennen and Alan Braufman, whose unfettered flute work nevertheless makes its mark. Through it all, Hooker plays with the passion—and dervish-like viscerality—of a shaman.

The six extended phrases that make up **The Firmament/Fury** offer more variation—in part because of the shifting lineup, and in part because Hooker's own improvisations tend to develop in less linear fashion. The album touches on the subtle, organic textures of his earlier work (as on "For the Spirit of the Earth," a duet with serene alto player Claude Lawrence) but spends more time exploring a more menacing head, particularly on the tracks like "Pralaya," where Hooker takes up the acidic challenge of Borbetomagus guitarist Donald Miller. Feeling your way through its textures is like exploring a bas-relief map of the soul.

The live **Subconscious** lets Hooker exhibit his range as a bandleader—no mean feat for a guy who's "just" a drummer—as he guides a copacetic sextet through the terrain's intricate rhythmic paths, quietly asserting himself without once overplaying. **Shamballa** alternates duets with bassist/guitarist Elliott Sharp and guitarist Thurston Moore: Sharp's contributions lend an unusual sensuality to the proceedings, while Moore acquits himself admirably as a heat-of-the-moment improviser with a minimum of electro-shtick. Even so, **Envisioning,** Lee Ranaldo's long-simmering collaboration with Hooker, strikes more deeply into the subconscious, since the other Sonic Youth guitarist seems less self-conscious about surrendering himself to the drummer's flow.

Radiation, culled from a pair of live dates, may be the furthest "outside" of Hooker's recordings, insofar as his collaborators (Miller again, along with electronics wiz Brian Doherty, reedman Charles Comp and trombonist Masahiko Kono) do their utmost to avoid so much as a single standard progression. It's up to Hooker to act as captain, navigator and engine-stoker—and deeply moving songs like "Green" and the two halves of the "Darkness" suite prove him up to the task. Pure exhilaration. In comparison, the studio-spawned **Armageddon** sounds almost mellow—aside from the spine-tingling "State Secrets," which showcases Black Rock Coalition co-founder Jesse Henry's shattering guitar work. An attempt to integrate post-hip-hop turntable work gives "Time (Within)" an air of gimmickry, but elsewhere, Hooker's playing is as free of space and time constraints as ever. [dss]

See also *Borbetomagus, Elliott Sharp, Sonic Youth.*

HOOTERS

Amore (Antenna) 1983
Nervous Night (Columbia) 1985
One Way Home (Columbia) 1987
Zig Zag (Columbia) 1989
Out of Body (MCA) 1993
Hooterization: A Retrospective (Columbia/Legacy) 1996

Not since the glory days of Booker T. and the MGs has a group more assuredly suited to back others tried so hard to be an autonomous hit machine. Hard on the heels of **Amore,** Philadelphia's Hooters—led by singer/guitarist/mandolinist Eric Bazilian and singer/keyboardist Rob Hyman, neither of whom is the kind of strong frontman required by a band hoping not to be Toto—embarked on what has proven to be a commercially fruitful sideline as creative midwives, most effectively for Cyndi Lauper and Joan Osborne, especially when produced by Rick Chertoff, whose involvement with the pair dates back to their days in the Hooters' '70s precursor, Baby Grand.

The Hooters' easy facility in many stylistic genres (reggae, the main impulse on **Amore,** remains in the repertoire, along with glossed-up heartland rock versed in folk traditionalism) matches an inability to pin down any clear-cut personality; intelligent, effective songwriting (sometimes topical and recently displaying a spiritual bent) is accompanied by unstable and often dubious artistic discretion. Knowing when to tone it down or let it go are not among the band's most reliable assets.

The three Columbia albums are hit-and-miss grab-bags. **Nervous Night** sounds like the work of an overly enthusiastic John Mellencamp cover band: "And We Danced" and "Blood From a Stone" (later given a real dose of energy by Red Rockers) are all right, but the residual reggae groove of "All You Zombies" leads the band into absurd melodrama. **One Way Home** adds a Gaelic dance-band inflection and nudges the electricity up a few notches; the anthemic presentation of songs like "Satellite," "Karla With a K" and "Fightin' on the Same Side" overstates their arguable cases. The title track is an even worse insult to reggae than "All You Zombies." While **Zig Zag** gets its musical character from restrained performances and largely acoustic instrumentation, the clumsy protest lyrics come from newspaper headlines: the campfire classic "500 Miles" (with guest credibility provided by Peter, Paul and Mary) gets a noxiously slick reggaefied arrangement and an update to cover events in Tiananmen Square, while John Lee Hooker's "Boom Boom" is transformed into something about Russia entitled "Mr. Big Baboon." Pushing the sentimentality arrow deep into the red, "Beat Up Guitar" is a mushy ode to the band's hometown.

Even more than the previous albums, **Out of Body** is an everywhere-at-once hodgepodge that truly reflects the band's lack of a reliable personality. "Twenty-Five Hours a Day" is overzealous kitchen-sink bombast that sounds like Simple Minds; Cyndi Lauper adds her voice to "Boys Will Be Boys," an ebullient number that could have gone on *her* first album; chamber strings inflect the religious rock of "Shadow of Jesus"; sitar kicks off the middle-aged nostalgia of "Great Big American Car." Typical of the Hooters' habitual sly borrowing, they introduce "Boys Will Be Boys" with an irrelevant chorus from the old Irish folk song "Wild Mountain Thyme" as a red herring and then base their song's melody on the doo-wop chestnut "Glory of Love." Likewise, they touch on the beginning of "(What's So Funny 'Bout) Peace, Love and Understanding" in the rocking "Dancing on the Edge" and then scamper away, purloined cookie crumbs trailing behind them. As usual, it takes somebody outside the group to get the Hooters' juices flowing. [i]

See also *Cyndi Lauper, Joan Osborne Band; TPRG.*

HOOTIE & THE BLOWFISH

Hootie & the Blowfish EP [tape] (no label) 1990
Time EP [tape] (no label) 1991
Kootchypop EP (no label) 1993
cracked rear view (Atlantic) 1994
Fairweather Johnson (Atlantic) 1996

On first blush, the major-label debut by this South Carolina bar band (the beginnings of which were a mid-'80s acoustic duo called the Wolf Brothers) is a thoroughly bland rehash of Woodstock pop values. On second blush, too. Beyond culturally inclusive wholesomeness, the quartet's prime asset is singer Darius (don't call him Hootie) Rucker, whose resonant, husky bear of a baritone gives the band's otherwise generic '70s-accented pop-folk songwriting its soupçon of soul and crypto-spiritual uplift. Offensive only to those who demand obscurity, an edge or some ballast in their music, Hootie offers economically played and harmless singalong radio fare for the many millions on the fringes of rock, especially those of a certain age, who hear the siren song of the southern '70s in the band's grooves. As familiar as the face in a mirror, **cracked rear view** is just about as deep.

Although most bands in Hootie's enviable position would be fatally blinded in the platinum headlights, rooted to the creative two-lane until the next unstoppable force came along to deliver a flattening blow, the quintet sounds utterly unperturbed by the pressure on **Fairweather Johnson.** (Merely releasing a followup before its mega-selling predecessor had completely run its course is an act of courage in this era of overly strategized micro-marketing.) Other than the casual sports goof of the title track (not to mention the rude colloquial possibilities of the title itself), the album carefully respects its predecessor's safe virtues, adding a gloomy lyrical cast and more organ but little else. The fact that "Old Man & Me" is a band oldie can be seen as a genial nose-thumb to those who would level unwarranted accusations of corporate style-calibration. In Hootieland, it was ever thus.

The two early EPs are cassettes sold by the group at shows; the first (five songs) contains an early version of "Hold My Hand," while the second (four songs) boasts another future hit, "Let Her Cry." The five-song **Kootchypop**—a thoroughly professional effort which is 95 percent of the way toward the sound that made the band millionaires—features a second recording of "Hold My Hand" (**cracked rear view** actually features the third) as well as "Running From an Angel," "Only Wanna Be With You" and "Old Man & Me," which was recut for **Fairweather Johnson.** [i]

JAMIE HOOVER

See *Spongetones.*

RICH HOPKINS

See *Sidewinders.*

HUGH HOPPER & KRAMER

See *Kramer.*

HOT MONKEY

See *Grifters.*

HOT ROD

See *Drop Nineteens.*

HOUSE OF FREAKS

Monkey on a Chain Gang (Rhino) 1987
Tantilla (Rhino) 1989
All My Friends EP (Rhino) 1989
Cakewalk (Giant/Reprise) 1991
Invisible Jewel (Brake Out/Enemy) 1994

The creative leap that brought House of Freaks to life in Richmond, Virginia, as a duo of guitar/vocals (Bryan Harvey) and drums (Johnny Hott) has become an article of faith for the group. Intelligence, urgency and creative use of guest musicians far outweigh any structural doubt about what properly constitutes a rock combo. Related by scope and approach to the Violent Femmes and redolent of cultural history in much the same way as the early Band, House of Freaks covers a rich and evocative American musical landscape.

Harvey and Hott demonstrated and explored their immediate surroundings in **Monkey on a Chain Gang** and **Tantilla,** resonant albums of southern lore and heritage. The latter, handsomely produced by Englishman John Leckie and aided only by a keyboardist, contains the core and the acme of the band's creativity. Over memorably original music that smolders with repressed passion and explodes in gloriously liberated choruses, Harvey castigates the memory of Jim Crow racism ("White Folk's Blood"), summons up the Civil

War ("Big Houses"), questions religious faith ("The Righteous Will Fall") and ruminates on his roots ("Family Tree").

The six-song **All My Friends** brings horn players and other instrumentalists along to test out a jazz-inflected urban variation on the band's theme. "This Old Town" is acoustic folk, and "Ten More Minutes to Live" (an intriguing hypothetical contemplation) follows in **Tantilla**'s footsteps, but "Meet Your Heroes," a dig at fame, does the rhumba, "You Can't Change the World Anymore" comps along with cool nightclub élan and "You'll Never See the Light of Day" jitters like a tiny Spike Jones extravaganza with bullfighting accents and jaw harp.

Cakewalk, the band's lone shot at the commercial bigtime, is something of an extravaganza. Among the two dozen people credited with "musical help and inspiration" are ex–Long Ryders guitarist Stephen McCarthy, ex-Silos bassist/guitarist Bob Rupe, **Tantilla** organist Marty McCavitt and producer Dennis Herring. The diverse, often busy (but occasionally spare, as in the offhand acoustics of "Magpie Wing") arrangements could have dandified even plain material, but the pair's writing, notwithstanding a lyrical shift to more personal reflections, is right on track—expansively original, vital and surprisingly poppy. "I Got Happy" and "This Is It" do the band's trademark sound proud, but the Beatlesque "Honor Among Lovers," the rockifying Marshall Crenshaw soundalike "Never" and the doo-woppy "A Good Man" all explore unknown stylistic crannies in the Freaks' house. The creepy "Ants," however, would have better been left in the basement from where it seems to have been excavated.

In '92, Harvey and Hott wrote and recorded the serendipitous **Gutterball** with McCarthy, Rupe and Steve Wynn, forming a part-time band in the process. Between Gutterball projects, they have continued as House of Freaks, recording **Invisible Jewel** in Richmond with **All My Friends** producer Bruce Olsen and no acknowledged helpmates. If the album title doesn't quite convey the extent of the band's defeated depression, perhaps these detail the mood: "It's a Fucked Up World," "Whipping Boy," "Stupid Things," "I'll Treat You Right Someday," "Awholelottanothingoingon." Opening romantic wounds, rediscovering the mundane details of their hometown and switching back to raw, no-frills rock music effectively stripped of life (but deeply ingrained with "Working Class Hero"–era Lennonism and '60s Beatleshness), Harvey and Hott barely bother to pick up the pieces of what sound like broken lives. The despair of "Lonely" circles back on itself: "I don't miss you / But I'll tell you one more time / While you were crushing dreams / I was filling all of mine / Now I'm lonely." "Motorbike" plants a surprising melodic gem in all this tear-stained grit; "Fat Boy Tom" is just a furious drum solo. **Invisible Jewel** is a tough, honest and compellingly sad (though not quite for the right reasons) chapter in an otherwise artful career. [i]

See also *Gutterball; TPRG.*

HOUSE OF LOVE

The House of Love (Creation/Relativity) 1988
The House of Love (Ger. Creation/Rough Trade) 1988
The House of Love (Fontana/PolyGram) 1990
A Spy in the House of Love (UK Fontana) 1990 (Fontana/Mercury) 1991
Babe Rainbow (Fontana/Mercury) 1992
Audience With the Mind (Fontana/Mercury) 1993

Between the Smiths/Echo and the Bunnymen and the Britpop resurgence, this London quartet briefly caught England's late-'80s imagination on the strength of stunning early singles, leader Guy Chadwick's forceful, smart persona, lead guitarist Terry Bickers' array of powerful, echoed sounds and the sustained promise of importance and (or) greatness. House of Love was an archetypal case of could have, should have, why didn't they?

The first self-titled LP (the cover pictures two band members) shows real flashes of this inspiration, especially on the Jesus-and-Mary-Chain-meets-Left-Banke wall-of-three-chord-pop single "Christine" (often regarded as the band's classic moment), the nifty "Road," and the achingly beautiful "Love in a Car." The second eponymous effort (butterfly cover), which induced Bickers to depart and form Levitation, is less flashy and exciting, but better-crafted and more consistently shimmering, ranging from the crackling "Hannah" to the slithery menace of "Shine On," remade from the group's first single.

Two collections of non-LP material also document this early period. The German album compiles the band's first two 12-inch singles, most notably the ebullient "Nothing to Me." The other, **A Spy in the House of Love,** is a less important but good-value smattering of second-album outtakes and B-sides.

Despite the release of four strong singles from the album, House of Love mysteriously lost its longstanding UK popularity with **Babe Rainbow.** If not as dramatic or sweeping as its predecessors, **Babe Rainbow** is no less ambitious and even more lovely. Perhaps the quieter, more contemplative guitar tone of "Feel," "Crush Me" and the outrageously pretty "Girl With the Loneliest Eyes" was out of fashion in the wake of shoegazing's rise, but Chadwick's continued ability to pen dripping choruses and tickling, lithe riffs make this graceful charmer an underrated masterwork.

The same cannot be said of the band's finale, **Audience With the Mind.** The decision to write, record and release an LP quickly seemed a refreshing approach after two epic recordings, but Chadwick's songs have no bite. Sounding more like a collection of B-sides than **A Spy in the House of Love,** this is the sound of a band just getting by. The group still leaves behind some bright moments: the slimy, cold-hearted gravel dirge of "Erosion," the moody "Corridors," the wistful "Shining On," the uncanny calm of "Hollow" and "Into the Tunnel." Even half-baked and shoddily written, House of Love could routinely extract a tension, drama and resignation rarely found in modern pop. [jr]

See also *Levitation; TPRG.*

HOUSE OF PAIN

House of Pain (Tommy Boy) 1992
Same as It Ever Was (Tommy Boy) 1994

EVERLAST

Forever Everlasting (Warner Bros.) 1990

A few months before quick-melting Florida conehead Vanilla Ice made his arrival on the scene, Los Angeles' Everlast (Erik Schrody) made a spirited if ineffectual longplaying debut as a self-styled boxer/rapper on **Forever Everlasting.** Produced under the auspices of Ice-T's Rhyme Syndicate, the album did nothing but raise some narrowminded eyebrows, and Everlast left the ring, an overeager, under-prepared palooka ready for the showers.

The story would have ended there if not for his inspired embrace of a different sort of ethnic profiteering and a hookup with producer DJ Muggs of Cypress Hill. Joined by rapper Danny Boy O'Connor and producer DJ Lethal, Everlast opened House of Pain as the first Gaelic hip-hop group, draping it carelessly in Irish imagery more as a marketing scheme than a cultural identity. A three-leafed logo, orange and green colors, topical references (scattered through tracks like "Shamrocks and Shenanigans" and "Top of the Morning to Ya"), a couple of lines of "Danny Boy" and a vocal dedication to pub life are hardly the alpha-omega of Irish reality; the crude band's careful avoidance of politics has kept it that way.

Actually, it wouldn't matter if the flag flying on the cover of **House of Pain** were Venusian; the only track that matters is "Jump Around," a great, boisterous party single produced by Muggs with an aggravating whistle and an irresistible chorus. The rest of the album is fine for what it is—medium-weight old-school-quoting boasts over simple, woozy beats—but nothing more. **Same as It Ever Was,** which adds "On Point" (a number that mentions Schrody's '93 gun bust) to the repertoire, maintains House of Pain's functional mediocrity without significantly falling off or wising up. [i]

See also *Cypress Hill.*

PENELOPE HOUSTON

Birdboys (Subterranean) 1987
The Whole World (Heyday) 1993
Silk Purse (From a Sow's Ear) (Ger. Return to Sender/Normal) 1994
Karmal Apple (Ger. Normal) 1995
Cut You (Reprise) 1996

PENELOPE HOUSTON AND PAT JOHNSON

Crazy Baby (Ger. Return to Sender/Normal) 1994

All punk-rockers grow up eventually, but few have done so as gracefully as Penelope Houston. In her solo career, the one-time teenage Avenger treads a softer, often folk-oriented path, successfully avoiding the enervating trap of generic roots ennui. The reasons are simple enough. Over the years, the Californian's songwriting has become sharp and well-developed; her arrangements (fashioned with a steady core of backing musicians) are skillful and unorthodox. Then there's that voice—a sweet, sinewy instrument of wide-ranging expressiveness and utter clarity.

After a post-punk hiatus that lasted four years, Houston reemerged in 1986 with a minimal single released under the name -30-, made with such collaborators as Howard Devoto and Alex Gibson. That record's two tracks are included on **Birdboys,** a melodic and sometimes spirited album that is, finally, mediocre. In retrospect, Houston just wasn't ready to do commanding work in a softer context—the jangling music is minor and some of the material is downright chirpy.

Six years of writing, playing and traveling later, everything fell into place. **The Whole World** is a gorgeous, odd and uniformly thrilling record. Houston's phrasing is controlled and masterful, the songs are witty, well-sketched and tinged with bittersweet urgency. The acoustic band—Mel Peppas (mandolin, guitar), Steven Strauss (bass), Eliot Nemzer (guitar) and Kevin Mummey (drums)—is an intriguing chamber-folk combo, led by Houston's autoharp and melodica; instrumentation also includes *bandonéon, dumbek,* clarinet and french horn. Every song is a joy, from the torchy "Behind Your Eyes" and the ominous "Sugarburn" to the straightforward pop swing of "On Borrowed Time" and the no-nonsense feminism of "Glad I'm a Girl." A virtually perfect record, with one of the best displays of pure vocal gifts the "alternative" universe will ever hear.

The Whole World found its warmest reception overseas, where Houston was dubbed the Queen of New Folk in various languages. Whatever the value of such an appellation, it did enable her to crank out a bounty of material for the German Normal label. **Karmal Apple,** the only formal album of the bunch, is neither as ornate nor as captivatingly unique as its predecessor, but it's still a fine effort that replaces quirkiness with vivacity and eclecticism with solidity. Standouts include the sprightly "Everybody's Little Dream," the tough pop of "Fall Back," the melodramatic "Flourish" and, best of all, the string-laden balladic beauty of "Water Wheel" and "Make Me."

Return to Sender is Normal's limited-edition, generally off-the-cuff, series of American music. As the title would suggest, **Silk Purse (From a Sow's Ear)** fits right into that notion, with a handful of charming live tracks and outtakes, including a darkly pretty cover of Alex Chilton's "Take Care." Houston shares the credit on **Crazy Baby** with Patrick Johnson, a frequent songwriting partner. The record's primary attraction is the chance to hear Houston singing in an ultra-minimal context, as nine of Johnson's songs (plus one he cowrote and another by Mary O'Neil, another songwriter Houston regularly favors) are presented in spare arrangements. Both records offer good stuff as far as these things go, and are definitely essential for fans.

All of Houston's prior releases are fairly hard to find, so maybe it's not such a bad thing that **Cut You,** her major-label debut, consists almost entirely of new recordings of previously issued songs. (Houston is not exactly a prolific composer.) Fortunately, **Cut You** does not suffer from any flashy revisionism. Longtime listeners may prefer the original renditions—it is odd to notice an electric guitar that wasn't there before, or a french horn that's MIA—but the record offers a solid cross-section of her material, the playing and recording quality are absolutely vibrant and Houston sings as wonderfully as ever. New versions of "Harry Dean" and "Waiting Room" (both on **Birdboys**) are definite improvements, while the all-new "Pull" is an out-and-out scorcher, with speedy circular guitar licks and no-nonsense vocals. The album also includes the two best items from **The Whole World:** the beautiful, wistfully defiant "Sweetheart" and the brilliant "Qualities of Mercy," a wise, impeccably structured and soul-tugging song with the bonus of a clever Gerry and the Pacemakers pun. [jc]

See also *TPRG.*

ROWLAND S. HOWARD

See *Lydia Lunch, These Immortal Souls.*

DANIELLE HOWLE

See *Lay Quiet Awhile.*

H. P. ZINKER

. . . And There Was Light EP (Matador) 1989 (UK Roughneck) 1991
I Don't Know What's Going On EP (UK Roughneck) 1990
Beyond It All (Roughneck/Fire) 1990
The Sunshine CD EP (Roughneck) 1991
Hovering (UK Roughneck) 1991
Mysterious Girl EP (UK Roughneck) 1992
Perseverance (Roughneck/Thrill Jockey) 1992
The Reason EP (UK Roughneck) 1992
Staying Loose: A Compilation (Energy) 1993
Mountains of Madness (Energy) 1995

Raised and originally based in Innsbruck, Austria, singer/guitarist Hans Platzgumer and bassist/singer Frank Puempel had toured Europe with several bands (and managed prolific recording careers as precocious teens) before relocating to New York in 1989 as H. P. Zinker. Recorded with a drum machine, the six-song **. . . And There Was Light**—the first-ever release on Matador Records—opens with a cover of Led Zeppelin's "Dancing Days." From there, the weird original material fuses metal with classical, punk, jazz, folk and noise. The rumblin' rockers and intricate, intriguing soundscapes would be a lot easier to take seriously in a voice that didn't so unmistakably recall Elmer Fudd; still, the songwriting and imagination resonate long after the laughter subsides.

Beyond It All adds American drummer Dave (The Waz) Wasik and shows dramatic improvement on all fronts. The power-trio format enables Zinker to create looming, pristine riffs (not unlike Dinosaur Jr) amid the neo-classicism, shades of Sabbath and balls-out rock. Lengthy instrumental passages make for some startling updates on early-'70s progressivism but, unlike the icons of that genre, Zinker seldom wanders into excess or incoherence. Platzgumer no longer sounds like a cartoon, and the lyrics are likewise no joke.

After the dandy charms of **The Sunshine CD** EP (five songs, including a remake of the first EP's "Sunshine," Evan Dando as lead singer on the lovely "To One in Paradise" and a trio version of Dave Brubeck's "Take Five"), the challenging ambition of **Hovering** contains the usual array of ideas and styles—from the sprawling "Das Testament" epic to the five taut minutes of Helmet-meets-the-Fall in "Our Precious Love" and the modest gentility of the wordless "Flug Nach Alpha Centauri." Puempel then left Zinker to Platzgumer, who, with Wasik in tow, proceeded unimpeded into the '90s.

Adding them to a pair of '91 leftovers, the duo recorded the title track of the skippable **Mysterious Girl** and an overly serious cover (except for Hans' hairy guitar-solo coda) of Alice Cooper's "Billion Dollar Babies" with a temporary bassist, then got ex-Skunk guitarist Stephan Apicella (dubbed Stevie Apathetic) to fill the slot on **Perseverance.** If Zinker's third album is something of a retrenchment, it's a successful one, setting the group on its own timeless island, where Creamy wah-wah, Dr. John's funky gris gris swamp, spaghetti western weirdness and folk-rock—in both pompy and slackish variations—can all happily coexist. The inclusion of the EP's "Mysterious Girl" provides a useful vintage pop element. Meanwhile, the happy reassurance of "Soulmate" balances some of tension that grips the breezy "Now That You're Gone" (bad-news romance), "Warzone City" (urban crime) and "A Million Sparks Riding My Mind" (creative workaholism). The words' emotional resonance with the music is nil, but that's all right. When Platzgumer lobs lines like "I see the world through two eyes and they're stoned" (which concludes "Should I explain the words of this song / You anyway won't get the meaning"), how he opts to frame them is his business.

Although the trio's bassist (Uvey Batruel) is new, the sound and concept of **Mountains of Madness** are old: the title track's lyrics come from H. P. Lovecraft. (Rudimentary Peni devoted a 1988 album to the late English horror novelist; his name was borrowed by a '60s Chicago group; the Vaselines eulogized him in song.) Likewise, the hard-rock album expends all its stylistic energy in the cool packaging, leaving behind track-by-track eccentricity for a full-frontal Woodstock-zone guitar assault that favors the Mountain part of the title a whole lot more than the Madness. Not funny enough to be a joke and too silly/dated to be earnest, this is one forgotten time capsule item that could stand to be buried for a few more decades. Later that same year, Zinker buried itself and broke up.

The eighteen-track **Staying Loose** assembles tracks from the first three albums and four of the EPs (excluding the first, although half of its songs appear in versions from other releases anyway). A varied sampler with most of the band's high points, it's the most illustrative and accessible Zinker release to be had. [ja/i]

See also *Chavez.*

HUGGY BEAR

Rubbing the Impossible to Burst EP7 (UK Wiiija) 1992
Kiss Curl for the Kid's Lib Guerrillas EP7 (UK Wiiija) 1992
Her Jazz EP7 (UK Catcall/Wiiija) 1993
Don't Die EP7 (UK Wiiija) 1993
Taking the Rough With the Smooch (Kill Rock Stars) 1993
Long Distance Lovers EP7 (Gravity) 1994
Main Squeeze EP7 (UK Famous Monsters of Filmland/Rugger Bugger) 1994
Weaponry Listens to Love (Kill Rock Stars) 1995

HUGGY BEAR/BIKINI KILL

Our Troubled Youth/Yeah Yeah Yeah Yeah (Catcall/Kill Rock Stars) 1993

VARIOUS ARTISTS

Shimmies in Super-8 EP7 (UK Duophonic) 1993

BLOOD SAUSAGE

Happy Little Bullshit Boy (UK Wiiija) 1993

When Huggy Bear's first EP came out, there was an instant buzz about the English group in the international pop underground—they were "boy/girl revolutionaries" (translation: a credible riot grrrl band with a boy singing most of the time), they covered their record packages with political manifestos that didn't make very much sense, they refused to be interviewed or photographed, they didn't reveal their actual identities and they were young and irrepressibly energetic. **Rubbing the Impossible to Burst** doesn't exactly have any decent songs beneath the bluster, but Huggy Bear sure was promising.

Kiss Curl for the Kid's Lib Guerrillas and **Her Jazz** consolidated the band's positions with some pretty good (if hookless) songs, a couple of odd tape recordings and an awful lot of energy flying off in all directions. (The band's side of the split LP with Bikini Kill is pretty much of a piece with these EPs.) **Don't Die** is better, with the still-anonymous male vocalist screaming his throat off on "Dissthentic Penetration" and "Pansy Twist," and a short, explosive boy/girl chant called "No Sleep." (Released almost simultaneously, the twelve-song **Taking the Rough With the Smooch** collects singles two, three and four.) The double-7-inch **Shimmies in Super-8,** a various-artists release on Stereolab's label, devotes a side to four tracks from an early Huggy Bear tape: one quiet song, a couple of found-sound pieces and somebody's attempt to sing "Foolish Little Girl" into a Walkman. It's tossed off, but tremendously affecting and unusual.

Then Huggy Bear disappeared for a year, and something happened. The dreadfully recorded **Long Distance Lovers** is so dull and awkwardly played that it's hard to believe it's the same band; a couple of horn players fail to liven things up. **Main Squeeze** is more of the same: muddy, unimaginative riffs that go nowhere. By its final recording and only real album, **Weaponry Listens to Love,** Huggy Bear is a complete disaster, a stunningly dull band grinding away behind an incomprehensible sloganeer who won't shut up. He still sounds passionate, but what he's saying makes no sense at all, and it's frankly not worth the effort to try to figure out. [ddw]

See also *Bikini Kill.*

HUM

Fillet Show (12 Inch/Cargo) 1991
Electra 2000 (12 Inch/Cargo) 1993
You'd Prefer an Astronaut (RCA) 1995

HONCHO OVERLOAD

Smiles Everybody (Mud) 1993

You don't need to send for Sherlock Holmes to discern the resemblance between the sound of Hum and the overpowering buzz-pop of the Poster Children. The bands come from the same town (Champaign, Illinois), Hum bassist Jeff Dimpsey played guitar on the Poster Children's **Daisy Chain Reaction;** they've toured together; Hum's first two albums were released on the Kids' indie label.

Dimpsey (who also plays in Honcho Overload—a more straight-rock band that includes Hum singer/guitarist Matt Talbott and had its album produced by power-popper Adam Schmitt) wasn't in the lineup that made **Fillet Show,** but he joined in time for the second album, as did guitarist Tim Lash, completing a quartet with drummer Bryan St. Pere. Produced in Chicago by Brad Wood, **Electra 2000** is bracingly loud but generically obvious in its attack: simple melodies kicked along with a brisk backbeat and covered in sizzling, sensual guitar aggression. Turning down does wonders for "Double Dip," but the inoffensive Hum is really just one of a hundred bands that want to be the next Superchunk. (For the obligatory incongruous exception, the unlisted bonus track, which follows "Winder," is a jaunty if endless organ instrumental.)

A couple of items on **You'd Prefer an Astronaut** cut the speed in half and double the distortion, thereby shifting archetypes toward a mid-Atlantic Dinosaur Jr. The rest redefine the group's basic sound with greater dynamic variety, spaciousness and understatement, as well as much-improved songwriting. Too much quiet doesn't suit the group, either (see "Why I Like the Robins," "I Hate It Too" and the Schmitt-produced "The Very Old Man"), but "Stars" and "Suicide Machine" make excellent use of noise's allure, and "I'd Like Your Hair Long" is a roaring tune that works. More misses than hits, but a step in the right direction. [i]

See also *Poster Children.*

CHARLIE HUNTER TRIO

Charlie Hunter Trio (Prawn Song/Mammoth) 1993
Bing! Bing! Bing! (Blue Note) 1995

CHARLIE HUNTER QUARTET

Ready, Set, Shango! (Blue Note) 1996

Charlie Hunter is one of a handful of musicians spearheading the "grits-and-gravy" renaissance, a return to the greasy grooves and organ-centered riffage popular in jazz clubs of the late '50s and '60s. But he's no mere revivalist: he's a youngster whose first guitar teacher was Joe Satriani. He grew up listening to Eric Clapton and the usual blues-rockers, as well as Charlie Christian and Charles Mingus. He favors an eight-string guitar that allows him to play basslines and makes him sound like he has three demented hands.

Hunter first surfaced as the guitarist in Disposable Heroes of Hiphoprisy, supporting rapper Michael Franti's neo-psychedelic flights of political fancy. As a side project, Hunter, drummer Jay Lane and saxophonist Dave Ellis began gigging around San Francisco's fertile jazz-roots-world scene, where they were discovered by Les Claypool. Produced by the Primus bassist, **Charlie Hunter Trio** was recorded on an 8-track tape machine for one hundred dollars. Though deceptively clean, its diffuse, fusiony compositions don't fully convey the group's sass and spirit—only "Dance of the Jazz Fascists" (aided by a couple of guest percussionists and trumpeter Scott Jensen) comes close.

But that spirit nearly overwhelms **Bing! Bing! Bing!,** a thoroughly refreshing mélange of understated guitar melodicism and fat backbeats. Produced by jazzbo Lee Townsend (Bill Frisell, John Scofield), **Bing! Bing! Bing!** is the sound of a young man who wishes he was old enough to have hung out in clubs where that dirty, take-no-prisoners swing went down—he's a bit wistful but anxious to prove he can burn. Alternating between hard shuffles and airy ballads, Hunter covers more terrain than a Manhattan bike messenger, yet never sounds overextended. His blues ("Greasy Granny") are the real thing, his bepop swings effortlessly and his rethinking of Nirvana's "Come as You Are" (in 5/4!) is that rare cover strong enough to enrich appreciation of the original. [tm]

See also *Spearhead.*

GEORGE HUNTLEY

See *Connells.*

HURRICANE

See *Beastie Boys.*

LIDA HUSIK

Bozo (Shimmy-Disc) 1991
Your Bag (Shimmy-Disc) 1992
The Return of Red Emma (Shimmy-Disc) 1993
Joyride (Caroline) 1995

LIDA HUSIK/BEAUMONT HANNANT

Evening at the Grange EP (Astralwerks) 1994

HUSIKESQUE

Green Blue Fire (Astralwerks) 1996

Washington, DC, native Lida Husik began writing songs in high school; she first played drums in a punk band. After moves to San Francisco and Hoboken, she ended up back in the capital area, where she met scenester Don Fleming. He passed her tape to Shimmy-Disc, whose owner, producer/artist Kramer, clearly heard a kindred spirit in Husik's psychedelically laced songs. He provided a sympathetic workshop in which she could develop and produced her first three albums.

A dozen concise numbers, including the Nico-like "Hateful Hippy Girls," **Bozo** offers simple but nifty new wave pop with an echoey, ethereal presence. Accompanying herself gently on piano and guitar with only occasional assistance (on drums, mainly) and sparing found-sound samples, Husik sings in an alluringly enervated voice—actually several of them—like a *Twin Peaks* lounge act.

Issued less than a year later, **Your Bag** contains half as many songs. Two of them run seven minutes each; "Marcel" and "The Match From Mars" are longer than that. Brimming with the excitement of textural experimentation, Husik—joined by percussionist Jamie Harley—draws elongated instrumental portraits using elementary ingredients. Dreamy, relaxed and occasionally tedious, **Your Bag** layers a mighty soft bed and then lies in it as if there were nothing else in the world to do. Even the heavy guitars of "Toy Surprise" are as cushiony as a down comforter.

Husik's final Shimmy-Disc outing, **The Return of Red Emma** (a name she also recorded under in DC, before any label affiliation), brings her back to a baker's dozen tunes, but the swirling moods seem less to spring mysteriously from the songs themselves—as they do on **Bozo**—than to be draped over them. It sounds oddly unsettled and tired at the same time.

With greater sonic clarity helping to reveal her progress, Husik tries a few new things on **Joyride** without abandoning the skills she's already demonstrated. As usual, she plays most of the instruments except drums herself. Despite three producers (including British ambient/techno musician Beaumont Hannant), the gorgeous album maintains a consistent accessibility throughout. Although it gains rock momentum toward the end, the first half of "Mother Richard" makes explicit a '60s folk-rock element abiding in the previous records (if Mazzy Star ever needs a new vocalist, Husik should definitely be short-listed); "Glorious" flirts with the suave harmony gentility of pop's neo-jazz stylists; a cover of the Dentists' "Strawberries Are Growing in My Garden (And It's Wintertime)," with vocals by that group's Mick Murphy, is extraordinary pastel-colored psychedelia. Between the intricate vocal arrangements, the endless, attractive music and Husik's inventive playing, **Joyride** is the pinnacle of her pop art.

Husik then undertook a full-time collaboration with Hannant. Recorded in England, **Evening at the Grange** features her vocals and guitar floating in and about the architecture of his electronic landscapes. The EP emphasizes pop song structure over sheer ambience and succeeds in that it warms the blank coolness that usually characterizes Hannant's genre.

Billing themselves as Husikesque, the duo treats, bolsters and coats his programmed beats and electronic music with her atmospheric melodies on **Green Blue Fire.** Husik's frequent use of a first-person vantage point in the lyrics also has the effect of presenting a real human being amid all the technology. Built on the foundation of their EP, **Green Blue Fire** is by turns stark, still and catchy. [dbg/i]

HÜSKER DÜ

See *Sugar.*

ICE

See *God.*

ICE CUBE

AmeriKKKa's Most Wanted (Priority) 1990
Kill at Will (Priority) 1990
Death Certificate (Priority) 1991
The Predator (Lench Mob/Priority) 1992
Check Yo Self EP (Lench Mob/Priority) 1993
Lethal Injection (Lench Mob/Priority) 1993
Bootlegs & B-Sides (Lench Mob/Priority) 1994

DA LENCH MOB

Guerillas in tha Mist (Street Knowledge/EastWest) 1992
Planet of da Apes (Street Knowledge/Priority) 1994

Quitting N.W.A following a management dispute, South Central superstar Ice Cube (O'Shea Jackson)—a music veteran at twenty-one—went solo, temporarily suspending his coastal allegiance to hook up with Public Enemy and the Bomb Squad (keeping his own extended family, the hometown Lench Mob, in the mix as well) for **AmeriKKKa's Most Wanted.** The producers' hyperactive energy provides a springy canvas for the surly chaos of the commanding rapper's explosive persona. Declaring himself "The Nigga Ya Love to Hate" and leading the trademark "Fuck you, Ice Cube!" cheer from the first bell, Cube keeps hammering away, swinging wildly with his eyes closed; anger provides the only directional cues for this rebel with many causes. Too wound up to consider any issues carefully and say something responsible about them, Cube gets little but a high-tension power charge from "Endangered Species (Tales from the Darkside)," his duet with Chuck D. He finds a better adversary in "It's a Man's World," a sexist tract in which newcomer Yo Yo cleans his clock but good. The album is indefensible in its galling violence and misogyny: "What I need to do is kick the bitch in the tummy," Cube's remedy for an unwanted pregnancy in "You Can't Fade Me," can be taken as immature peer pressure stupidity or pathological sexism, either of which is cold comfort. If in no way a cogent political manifesto, **AmeriKKKa's Most Wanted** is nonetheless a hip-hop landmark, a dynamic and riveting bridge between the scattered spray of N.W.A's group grope and the machined barrel of '90s gangsta rap.

Kill at Will consists of two **AmeriKKKa** remixes and five new tracks. One continues the album's trivial blurt from the Lench Mob's J-Dee and another is just shoutouts, but a couple do count for something: the lighthearted "Jackin' for Beats" (which bites EPMD, PE, Digital Underground, LL Cool J and others) and the devastating "Dead Homiez," in which he solemnly contemplates the murder of a friend over an evocative mix of horn, guitar and piano.

With its spoken-word dialogue introductions, **Death Certificate** demonstrates Cube's increasingly cinematic sense of drama (good)—as well as his fondness for taking pains to stir up senseless controversy (not so good). At the sprawling album's best, "A Bird in the Hand" presents the deadly working-vs.-hustling paradox in down-to-earth terms that make it real and powerful. But whether Cube means what he says or not, the unabashedly racist "Black Korea" fuels anti-Asian hostility, and the notorious "No Vaseline," a harsh, threatening attack on former bandmates Dr. Dre, MC Ren and Eazy-E, litters anti-Semitism ("you let a Jew break up my crew . . . get rid of that devil real simple/Put a bullet in his temple . . . 'cause you can't be a nigga-for-life crew/With a white Jew telling you what to do") amid other name-calling.

That same year, Ice Cube got his film career going with a starring role in *Boyz n the Hood* (its title taken from an N.W.A rap he wrote). He makes reference to his media move in "When Will They Shoot?," the song that opens **The Predator.** Peppering the album with spoken-word collages about fear, racism and riots, Cube drifts further into pulp fiction, providing a sequel to **AmeriKKKa**'s "A Gangsta Fairytale," making unnerving light of random murder in "Now I Gotta Wet 'Cha" and effectively describing an uncommonly calm 'hood in the slowly rolling "It Was a Good Day." Mostly laying off the gratuitous crudeness and cruelty, Cube pops the top and shows the strength of his intelligence in low-riding songs that, like "Check Yo Self," a collaboration with Das EFX, make excellent use of old soul records. (Credit producer DJ Pooh of King Tee fame, DJ Muggs of Cypress Hill and others.) The subsequent EP, which gives Das EFX cover billing, contains two non-LP mixes each of "Check Yo Self" and "It Was a Good Day," plus "24 With a L."

Kicking **Lethal Injection** off with another creepy fatal pun vignette, Cube's self-production recalculates his trajectory all over the place. He stretches his stylings to swing lazy G-funk grooves for the father-loving rhymes of "Down for Whatever" (a prelude to his 1995 family reminiscence film, *Friday*), uses Marvin Gaye's "Inner City Blues" to set a restrained mood for the Nation of Islam preaching of "When I Get to Heaven" and firms up the beats for "Really Doe." Reverting to his old shit-stirring, Cube whips up a particularly nasty cocktail of racism and misogyny in "Cave Bitch" and then attempts to counteract it with the warm party funk of "Bop Gun" (an "interpolation" of P-Funk's "One Nation Under a Groove"). Nice try; no dice.

Bootlegs & B-Sides is a quizzical anthology that heaps together remixes (four tracks from **Lethal Injection,** two from **The Predator**), rarities, outtakes and the efficient "D'Voidofpopniggafiedmegamix," which stitches snatches of fourteen Cubisms into a seamless five-minute retrospective. Although a solid enough representation of the rhymer's peerless skills, the album's choice of songs is off; the non-LP items are scarcely essential ("2 n the Morning," for instance, is totally routine sexplay). Most of the remixes are equally mundane, but the remake of "Check Yo Self" substitutes the beats from "The Message" for what was on **The Predator,** and "It Was a Good Day" replaces the original track with the Staple Singers' light, upbeat "Let's Do It Again," completely chasing away the hit's somber feel. Doing it again, at least in these few cases, was worth the effort.

In '92, three Lench Mob–sters declared themselves Da Lench Mob and made a tough, angry album that Cube produced, co-wrote and made a substantial vocal appearance on. Although none can shine Cube's skills, T-Bone, J-Dee and Shorty are all strong and effective rappers, and the violent racial wrath of **Guerillas in tha Mist** outweighs any flaws in their vocal presence. The group repeatedly refers to white people as "tha devil," slagging off Madonna ("you motherfuckin' slut"), the Beatles, Elvis Presley ("never been caught for the songs he stole"), Marilyn Monroe and George Washington ("maggot/He wore a wig like a faggot") in "You & Your Heroes," a track which tacitly acknowledges its debt to Public Enemy's "Fight the Power" by biting a bit off it. J-Dee narrates a rugged tale of criminal injustice ("Lost in tha System") and the crew revels in genial animosity ("All on My Nut Sac"), but Ice Cube gets the last word (as it were) with "Inside tha Head of a Black Man," a collage of gruesome sound effects. Chilling—and *not* like Bob Dylan.

Old-school-styling Maulkie (formerly of the duo Yomo & Maulkie, who had a Yella-produced album on Ruthless/Atlantic in '91) replaced J-Dee for the second Lench Mob album, shifting the sound's orbit further from planet Ice Cube, who executive-produced but let others do most of the actual track work. His "Cut Throats" and the trio's "Trapped" are as malevolently ferocious as anything on **Guerillas,** but Maulkie takes a lead role in bringing the P-funk and softening the debut's rage on "Chocolate City" and "Mellow Madness." Stripping the gears with too much arbitrary tone-shifting, **Planet of da Apes** is no match for its predecessor's focused fury. In early 1995, T-Bone (Terry Gray) was acquitted of murder charges stemming from a fatal shooting in a Los Angeles bowling alley. [i]

See also *Mack 10, N.W.A.*

ICE-T

Rhyme Pays (Sire) 1987
Power (Sire) 1988
The Iceberg/Freedom of Speech . . . Just Watch What You Say (Sire/Warner Bros.) 1989
O.G. Original Gangster (Sire/Warner Bros.) 1991
Home Invasion (Rhyme Syndicate/Priority) 1993
The Classic Collection (Excello/Rhino) 1993
VI: Return of the Real (Rhyme Syndicate/Priority) 1996

BODY COUNT

Body Count (Sire/Warner Bros.) 1992 + 1992
Born Dead (Virgin) 1994

Ice-T entered the 1990s with a bang—literally. First, the Los Angeles rapper released **O.G. Original Gangster,** the double-length album that remains the artistic peak of his career. A year later, he ignited one of the decade's hottest controversies when his thrash-metal side band, Body Count, raised the hackles of police officers nationwide with the song "Cop Killer." Ice-T's brassy vocal delivery informed the West Coast rap style of artists ranging from Ice Cube to Coolio, but he has a better narrative sense than any of his competition. Moreover, Body Count bridged the gap between angry white suburban youth and inner-city blacks far more naturally than the previous (and often aesthetically superior) rock-rap collaborations of Run–D.M.C. and Aerosmith ("Walk This Way") or Public Enemy and Anthrax ("Bring the Noise").

If Ice-T's '80s work sometimes seemed cheesy in its wishy-washy imitation of East Coast rap, by the time of **The Iceberg,** he and producer Afrika Islam had come up with a sound of their own. He, Islam, D. J. Aladdin and other members of the Rhyme Syndicate team perfected that sound on **O.G.,** the magnum opus on which the rapper chucked the free-speech sermonizing of the previous disc for a seamless collection of riveting tales of ghetto life tempered by big dollops of humor. On earlier albums, Ice-T had presented the old aural vérité argument that graphic gunfire and misogyny simply reflect ghetto realities, but **O.G.** paints a more three-dimensional picture of early '90s South Central LA; along with the violence and sexism, he offers solutions. Beginning with "Home of the Bodybag," which describes the environment in which the young Ice-T (Tracy Marrow) was raised, the album careens through the 'hood, offering a dubious rationalization of sexist language ("Bitches 2"), a laundry list of respected fellow MCs set to a beat ("M.V.P.s") and an intentionally romanticized tale of rappers who gain fame ("Lifestyles of the Rich and Infamous"). The Rhyme Syndicate's cool, subtle samples, beats and smooth bass power Ice-T's eminently listenable tunes. And tunes they are: from "Straight Up Nigga" to the metal anthem "Body Count" (which introduced the band Ice-T formed with a high-school friend, Ernie C), each track of **O.G.** makes an indelible mark. Gangsta rap has since spiraled downward, but **O.G.** remains a classic of the genre.

There was no way Ice-T could keep that momentum going after the controversy surrounding "Cop Killer" led to the end of his major-label record deal. (The track was ultimately deleted from **Body Count** and the album reissued with a Hendrixized remix of **The Iceberg**'s "Freedom of Speech" in its place.) Released on an independent label, his subsequent solo rap album, **Home Invasion,** is an uneven attempt at recreating the confident power of its predecessor. Ice-T, whose forte is spinning gritty tales that verge on poetry, had regressed to overly dramatizing his public relations fiascoes. Though **Home Invasion** is not a total throwaway, the good songs are few and far between.

The Body Count albums are spotty affairs. Ice-T and his band—guitarists Ernie C and D-Roc, bassist Mooseman and drummer Beatmaster "V"—understand the conventions of thrash-metal, but often go cartoonishly overboard with their lurching rhythms, chunky riffs and squalling guitar solos. Body Count's metal isn't as gratuitous or clueless as the Red Hot Chili Peppers' funk, but it's close. Like the Chili Peppers, Body Count cares about its chosen genre—even Ice-T's first rap album sampled a Black Sabbath riff for its title song—and **Body Count** (which has a remake of the band's eponymous song) does contain some hilariously taboo moments from the master of ceremonies.

In "KKK Bitch," Ice-T envisions doing the nasty with the daughter of a white supremacist; in "Evil Dick," he describes what everyone knows but won't admit—that the average male of our species is motivated not by his brain but by his gonads. The anger in Ice-T's account of white reaction to black integration in "There Goes the Neighborhood" comes off entirely genuine, as do the reality scenarios of "Bowels of the Devil," which puts your average death-metal band satanic obsessions to shame. But the embarrassingly slick lead guitar instrumental "C Note" is, at best, a bad Eddie Hazel imitation. As for "Cop Killer," it's a piece of ugly fiction ("I got my twelve-gauge sawed off/I got my headlights turned off/I'm 'bout to bust some shots off/I'm 'bout to dust some cops off") that frightened those whose abiding prejudices made them take it as a direct threat.

Born Dead repeats every lick, line and move of its predecessor—but with far less of Ice-T's engaging humor. It could be a sophomore slump. Or it could be that Ice-T is best when he injects metal into his rap, not the other way around. What's clear is that Ice-T, like his namesake (ghetto poet Iceberg Slim) is an intelligent storyteller with a lot to say. At his laziest, he reverts to tired locker-room humor; at his best, he provokes amped-up anger like nobody since the MC5.

The mid-'80s tracks on **The Classic Collection** find a whiny young rapper in search of a voice. The mixes are funkier, and producer Lee "D. J. Flash" Johnson relies more on straight turntable scratching than multi-tracking. Several of the selections ("6 In the Mornin'," "Killers," "Body Rock") are among the cuts that first brought Ice-T to the public eye. A few are good if extremely dated-sounding, but nothing stands out in light of what would ultimately come from Los Angeles' Original Gangster. [mrk]

See also *TPRG.*

IDA

Tales of Brave Ida (Simple Machines) 1994
I Know About You (Simple Machines) 1996

In the 1960s, groups like Brooklyn's Ida would be strumming their acoustic guitars in coffeehouses, hoping that Melanie or Tom Paxton or David Geffen would come along and notice something—the fineness of their harmonies, the insights of their songs, the gentleness of their souls, the cut of their sandals—and give them a boost up the ladder of mass-market love. Phew! Although the only firewall that's been truly breached is the fact that Daniel Littleton and Elizabeth Mitchell don't mind singing over the din of distortion-aided electronic strums now and again, the fact that their first record sounds like shoegazy dream-pop with all the extraneous instruments mixed out (or run backward, as in "Vacation"), and that they record for a highly credible indie label, ensures that nobody here gets mistaken for Indigo Girl and Boy or Peter, Paul Is Dead and Mary. This ain't your dad's folk music.

On **Tales of Brave Ida,** Mitchell (whose first group was a Brown University duo with Lisa Loeb; Ida is actually on "Stay" somewhere), does most of the singing in a fluty, reassuringly inexact soprano. Littleton, a former punk in Maryland's highly rated Hated (and now concurrently Jenny Toomey's partner in Liquorice, the successor to a project called Slack), either joins her helpfully or takes the lead ("Coupons," "Accidents," "Looking Through the Glass") often enough to keep the textures variable and engaging. With a string bassist and cellist making occasional additions to the calm melodic processions, the song styles shift around, never settling into a standard format—but never quite escaping its sensitive borders, either. "Nick Drake" is a floating, nearly ambient piano/guitar instrumental and "Temping" has the wispy cool of jazz-pop, but "F. Boyfriend" slowly builds to a soaring, loud climax. In "Shotgun," Mitchell doubles her voice prettily over crisp electric guitar suggestions; when Littleton adds his, it's clear that Ida knows how to make minimal resources do a lot more than meets the ear.

Having added drummer Michael Littleton, Ida is unveiled as a trio on **I Know About You,** but percussion is not the crucial missing ingredient that explains the great leap forward of the band's second album. Sticking to a gentle, understated but fully inhabited dynamic range and handsomely abetted by guest strings and bass (Rose Thomson of Babe the Blue OX), Mitchell's cool, confident voice is more than agreeable; the subtle songs are as powerful for their sound as for their thought content. [i]

See also *Tsunami.*

IDAHO

The Palms EP (Caroline) 1993
Year After Year (Caroline) 1993
This Way Out (Caroline) 1994
The Bayonet EP (Fingerpaint) 1995
Three Sheets to the Wind (Caroline) 1996

Perhaps one can trace the proliferation of what's been dubbed sadcore to the imminence of the millennium, the bleak consensus that the twentysomething generation is destined to be worse off than its predecessors or the technology-accelerated breakdown in interpersonal communication. More likely, this oh-so-Caucasian progeny of the blues has found its niche because the only thing that feels better than complaining about your lot in life is hearing someone else grieve about the things that make his or her existence even worse than that.

The unmitigated gloom that permeates the worldview of Idaho leader Jeff Martin is considerably more existential than that of the bulk of his peers. Yes, the Los Angeles band's dirge-like tempi clock in right between kindred spirits like Low and Red House Painters on rock's radar gun, but Martin doesn't offer the pastoral interludes that alleviate the darkness of those bands' work. On **Year After Year,** one of the more morose compendiums in recent memory, Martin and partner John Berry (son of sitcom perennial Ken Berry) fluctuate between whisper-soft meditations and shattering primal screams. Despite some dangerously goth-like undertones, the latter satisfy more fully, particularly the feedback-punctuated "Gone" and "Here to Go," which plumbs the lowest depths of Martin's gravelly baritone. Released as a preamble to the album, **The Palms** contains "Gone," adding two unstimulating non-LP variations on the basic Idaho theme and "Creep," an ill-advised fling at rocking out.

Martin and Berry parted ways before the recording of **This Way Out,** an entirely solo set that, when it breaks open, emits the unmistakable air of a hermetically sealed room. Accompanying himself on four-string guitar (his usual instrument of choice), Martin sounds a bit less like a man whose idea of a party game is bobbing for barbiturates: admittedly, songs like "Crawling Out," "Still" and "Glow" won't be filling dancefloors any time soon, but the album does offer a bit of release to go with its tension.

For **The Bayonet** EP, Martin reinvented Idaho as a full-fledged band, even going so far as to allow for some collaborative songwriting on two of its four tracks. One of those group efforts ("The Worm") is a startlingly visceral shard of Joy Division–styled gloom-metal driven by Terrence Borden's pulsing bass. **Three Sheets to the Wind** retains the same four-piece lineup, allowing for a mingling of voices quite unlike any of Idaho's previous releases: Mark Lewis' brushed drumming gives "If You Dare" a nearly jazzy feel, while "Catapult" ventures onto classic rock turf, with Martin's baritone sacrificing some of its monochromatic intensity in favor of a gritty virility. A stimulating turn of events. [dss]

IDHA

Melody Inn (Creation/TriStar Music) 1994

Born in Stockholm, based in Oxford, England, and devoted to vintage American country rock (specifically Bobbie Gentry and Gram Parsons), singer/songwriter Idha Ovelius is a serious artist only in the unique Creation Records sense: while her pleasant music is camp, anachronistic, derivative and absurd, Idha's ingenuous sincerity is nearly enough of a reason to believe in **Melody Inn.** Singing in clear, whispery English with a Scandinavian accent, Idha renders her own simple—OK, thoroughly feeble ("My heart is aching/For the land where I was born/My soul is crying/Lord, I feel so forlorn")—originals over spare Anglo-country-rock backing by keyboardist Ian McLagan, pedal steeler Gerry Hogan and Ride guitarist (and Idha spouse) Andy Bell, among others. The album is wisely fleshed out with covers: "Red Balloon" (Tim Hardin), "From Me to You" (Janis Ian), "Hickory Wind" (Gram Parsons) and "I'm Losing More Than I'll Ever Have" (Primal Scream, and not the fabled Tennessee bluegrass group either, but her very own UK labelmates). Flimsy and listenable if you tune out the lyrics, **Melody Inn** is perfectly pointless, except for its chic anti-chic chic. Or something like that. [i]

IDLE WILDS

Big Hit Records EP (no label) 1993
Dumb, Gifted and Beautiful (Ardent) 1995

Pennsylvania's Idle Wilds play gorgeous pop music that draws a time line directly from the Beatles to Big Star—and in doing so, the band draws attention to itself. The melodies on the **Big Hit Records** EP reveal singer/songwriter David Gray to be a pop imagist on a par with Tommy Keene or Marshall Crenshaw—though his themes wallow more in dark self-pity than giddy optimism. "Freakin'" is a hooky Matthew Sweet–style tune; "All the Wrong Reasons" locates its melody and arrangement on the Left Banke; "You're Cool" evokes classic Illinois melody-makers like Pezband and Off Broadway. All the songs are near-perfect, and **Big Hit Records** is not to be missed by even casual fans of power-pop.

The quartet's full-length debut, **Dumb, Gifted and Beautiful,** mixes a slew of fresh originals and new versions of some of the EP's best songs. Repeats include the chorus-pushing "Crying on the Inside" and the heartstring-pulling "Surrounded," as well as "Freakin'." Excessive use of guitar feedback sometimes shrouds the hooks, but **Dumb, Gifted and Beautiful**—recorded at Ardent Studios and produced by John Hampton—is generally as good as earthy pop music gets. [jo]

BILLY IDOL

Don't Stop EP (Chrysalis) 1981
Billy Idol (Chrysalis) 1982
Rebel Yell (Chrysalis) 1983
Whiplash Smile (Chrysalis) 1986
Vital Idol (UK Chrysalis) 1986 (Chrysalis) 1987
Idol Songs: 11 of the Best (UK Chrysalis) 1988
Charmed Life (Chrysalis) 1990
Cyberpunk (Chrysalis) 1993

Whatever else Billy Idol—London punk-pop pioneer in Generation X, new wave rock video pioneer on MTV—got up to in the first half of the '90s (and that list would have to include recovering from a motorcycle crash, facing criminal charges, making like a Hollywood celebrity and reading William Gibson novels), the one thing he neglected to do was make a record anyone needed to hear. Pretentiously wired into technology and fantasy trends about which Idol appears to have only the most superficial passing knowledge, **Cyberpunk** is third-rate self-parody (cue the synthesizers, samplers and sequencers, tell the guitar players to come back on Thursday) that trusses him up in sci-fi lingo and futurist mumbo jumbo. (Exactly how a cover of Lou Reed's "Heroin" fits in all this is unclear.) The spoken-word segments, chanting monks, sound bites, treated voices and hypermarketing appurtenances might be forgivable if the music were any good, but songs that fixate on a single line and batter it senseless are as stimulating as a flying-toaster screen saver. "I'm out of control/I think I'm goin' crazy/I'm out of my mind/You can see it in my eyes." Sorry, Bill, that's just the reflection of boredom in your contacts. [i]

See also *TPRG*.

I LOVE YOU

Live EP (Medusa) 1989
I Love You (Geffen) 1991
All of Us (Geffen) 1994

I Love You was an ill-fated LA blues-rock band with far more promise than luck. The quartet's stoner vibe and stripped-down guitar riffage led to its post–Guns n' Roses major-label deal just before the release of the indie **Live,** recorded at Raji's in Hollywood. With numerous obvious nods to Eric Clapton and Cream—including a brazen cover of Cream's "SWLABR"—the five songs offer little of creative note and serve only as a warmup.

I Love You features the band's ultimate (and best) lineup: singer Christopher Palmer, guitarist Jeff Nolan (who, in late 1995, joined Screaming Trees), bassist Mike Kossler and drummer Tom Sweet. The album bears an unexpected, often irritating metal hue—credit producer Geoff Workman—but has enough solid songwriting and boss fretwork to hold its own.

Produced by Chris Goss of Masters of Reality, **All of Us** reveals a cosmic side and improvisatory designs in psychedelic, jam-session–hatched tunes about smoking weed, spiritual awakening and loving your fellow man—all part of I Love You's positive message.

And just like Goss' own band and the criminally neglected Kyuss, the record was a commercial flop. I Love You was subsequently dropped and broke up. [tja]

IMMERSION

See *Wire.*

IMPERIAL TEEN

Seasick (Slash/London) 1996

SISTER DOUBLE HAPPINESS

Sister Double Happiness (SST) 1988
Heart and Mind (Reprise) 1991
Uncut (Dutch East India Trading) 1992
Horsey Water (Ger. Sub Pop/EFA) 1994

Faith No More keyboard mainstay Roddy Bottum and Lynn Perko, formerly the drummer in Sister Double Happiness (the disappointing emo-rock band led by singer Gary Floyd and Perko on and off since Texas' punk-rocking Dicks split in the mid-'80s), are the prominent half of San Francisco's Imperial Teen, a quartet that sounds nothing like their other bands. In this intimate, casual and engaging small-pop setting, Bottum plays guitar and sings; Perko drums, sings and spells Jone Stebbens (who was Perko's bandmate in Reno's Wrecks) on bass. Lest the catchy tunes and sweet, simple indie-styled arrangements (that occasionally blow up in brief punk storms) be taken too literally, this subversive bunch sets mildly provocative sexual lyrics to its inviting music. That makes **Seasick** (co-produced by Steven McDonald of Redd Kross) something of a disorienting ride: the easy appeal of "Imperial Teen," "Butch" and "You're One" is in no way impeded by passing references to cross-dressing, bondage and S&M, but they do alter the impression the songs leave behind. Near the end of the album, "Luxury" musters a Nirvana-like roar to deliver an angry critique that could be about Kurt and Courtney (an early member of Faith No More). That's the thought that resonates after the music stops. [i]

See also *TPRG.*

INBREDS

Darn Fool Dog [tape] (Can. Proboscis Funkstone) 1992
The Let's Get Together EP (Can. PF) 1992
Egrog EP (Can. PF) 1993
Hilario (Can. PF) 1993
Kombinator (Can. PF) 1994 (PF/Tag) 1995

Not to be confused with Th'Inbred (an '80s quartet from West Virginia), Kingston, Ontario's poppy Inbreds forswear rock's essential implement and sound no worse for it. Although Mike O'Neill (bass/vocals) and Dave Ullrich (drums) can thus claim membership in two trendy '90s movements—the two-piece (the Spinanes, Local H, Mecca Normal, Kicking Giant and so forth) and the no-guitars (Morphine, GodheadSilo and so forth)—the duo makes nothing of its gimmick and instead concentrates on strong songwriting. O'Neill allows guitar into two songs on **Kombinator** (the band's first American issue following a series of tapes and records self-released in Canada), but otherwise he gets the melodic job done by sticking to thin strings, trebly amplification and distortion pedals, all of which serve to render his bass playing close enough to sound like guitar in a full band. Thanks to his comfortable, adolescent voice and casual harmonies, the group's simple three-minute kernels—brisk and tuneful observations of interpersonal relationships that aren't going so well—have a vulnerable sweetness that makes them stick. The thoughtful lyrics make them worth chewing over. In the course of two brief verses, "Link" switches from "If you were a dog, I'd put you down/Tired of your moping around/Aren't you so glad to be alive" to "Pushing the swing for my sister's child/Told me she loved me but she wouldn't say why/What could she know she's only five."

Illustrating the Inbreds' precocious nascence, **Hilario** is a twenty-one-track compilation taken from the first three PF-label releases and a subsequent split single. Although it's clear the two had the architecture of their simple sound down from the very beginning, it took their songwriting a few months to shed a weakness for conceptual gimmickry ("Granpa's Heater," "T. S. Eliot") and find a reliable perch from which to fly. As an amusing footnote, the generous, uneven disc contains "Farmboy" (1989), the pair's first recording together, as well as some experimental efforts that break the band's mold. [i]

INDICATE

See *Main.*

INDIGO GIRLS

Indigo Girls EP (Indigo) 1986
Strange Fire (Indigo) 1987 (Epic) 1989
Indigo Girls (Epic) 1989
Nomads*Indians*Saints (Epic) 1990
Indigo Girls Live: Back on the Bus, Y'All (Epic) 1991
Rites of Passage (Epic) 1992
Swamp Ophelia (Epic) 1994
1200 Curfews (Epic) 1995

Harmony is one of nature's great mysteries, but the sound of perfectly blended voices—even regardless of individual qualities—is irrefutable, a force able to surmount almost any musical obstacle thrown in its path. As a credible explanation for the early success of the Indigo Girls—when harmony was the only useful weapon they could wave at horrifically prosaic lyrics and overbearing emotionalism—it'll have to suffice. Until the Georgia duo of Amy Ray and Emily Saliers (who was actually born in Connecticut) gained enough of a creative foothold to explore subtler, more sophisticated areas, they got by on nothing more than the elemental allure of their interwoven singing.

Without any significant adjustment in the coffeehouse crooning of their nascence, Ray and Saliers segued from hometown folkies to chart stars in 1989, long before they were any good. Ready in a pole position thanks to two indie records and a major-label contract when Tracy Chapman's debut album opened the floodgates in 1988, the Indigo Girls were swept up in acoustic pop's commercial resurgence. Arriving on the national scene at just around the same time as Melissa Etheridge (who could probably have replaced the rough-voiced Ray in those days), they provided a gentler, less torrid—and, yes, more harmonious—sonic alternative, a measure of button-down restraint that Ray later attempted to redress.

The first three records describe the pair's casual transition from amateur folk to lightly electrified, accomplished folk-rock, raising the stylistic flag of '60s singer/songwriters, only with preposterous lyrics. Although influenced by such greats as Bob Dylan and Tim Hardin, Ray and Saliers (writing separately, as they have continued to do) land neck deep in the clunky self-searching pathos of a later time, unmediated by any artful sensibility. Most notably, the **Indigo Girls** album contains Saliers' ebullient signature tune "Closer to Fine," a melodic winner that has to navigate such choppy academic waters as "I went to see the doctor of philosophy/With a poster of Rasputin and a beard down to his knee/He never did marry or see a B-grade movie/He graded my performance, he said he could see through me." This is not what "college radio" was supposed to mean.

"Hammer and a Nail," which opens **Nomads∗Indians∗Saints,** has the kind of rousing jingle chorus that excuses all sorts of sins—if you can hear it through the gales of laughter sure to accompany couplets like "I look a lot like Narcissus/A dark abyss of an emptiness." (Mary Chapin Carpenter sings on the track; Peter Holsapple plays accordion. The album, like **Indigo Girls,** was produced by frequent R.E.M. studio collaborator Scott Litt.) The stylistic gulf between Saliers (alluring, joyous folk optimism, with bookish lyrics and sometimes a country twist) and Ray (downcast melodrama with an incipient rock edge and a gristly Springsteen fixation) gapes wide here, and that makes for a diminution—literally and thematically—in the album's, er, harmony.

Back on the Bus, Y'All is a brief and not especially well-sung live record containing six originals, Ray's wretched mugging of "All Along the Watchtower" and the **Nomads∗Indians∗Saints** not-live version of the overwrought "1 2 3." Four years later, the duo filled two CDs with an assortment of live performances, radio broadcasts and ephemera (including one new studio recording and a basement tape from 1982) and issued them as **1200 Curfews.**

Peter Collins produced **Rites of Passage**, erasing the folk patina to reveal a crystalline mainstream pop center around the snappy, subtle rhythms of bassist Sara Lee and drummer Jerry Marotta; guest appearances by the Roches, Jackson Browne and David Crosby signify the group's stature and modern aspirations. Complicating the sound is good: full-bodied arrangements soften (or at least disguise) Ray's hard edges and give Saliers an ambitious plateau to explore. "You know me I take everything so seriously," she sings, and dadgone it, she's right, upping the album's literacy quotient with songs about "Galileo" and "Virginia Woolf." (The one entitled "Romeo and Juliet" belongs to Mark Knopfler, however.)

Collins' goal for the stripped-down **Swamp Ophelia,** however, appears to be a modern analogue to Carole King's **Tapestry.** With more intricate vocal designs, piano and light, breezy arrangements (Marotta is positively zen in his subdued touch; Lisa Germano adds an extra acoustic trimming, either violin or mandolin, to half the songs), the songs reclaim the Indigos' roots without shedding the pop sensibility they've gained along the way. While Saliers (who breaks the rules with a solo rendition of "Fare Thee Well") isn't at her best, recycling an old melody for "Least Complicated" and generally succumbing to a wistful, dispirited tone, Ray has stopped overpowering every song for a change. Although her anguished "Fugitive" *is* typically zealous, the craggy "This Train Revised," an original about the Holocaust that borrows phrases from Woody Guthrie and Peter Gabriel, nearly merits the Patti Smith–styled delivery.

Outside her group responsibilities, Amy Ray owns and operates Daemon Records, a cool indie label in Georgia. [i]

See also *TPRG.*

INFECTIOUS GROOVES

See *Suicidal Tendencies.*

INSIDES

Euphoria (Guernica/4AD) 1993
Clear Skin (UK Guernica/4AD) 1993

EARWIG

Past (UK La-di-da) 1992
Under My Skin I Am Laughing (UK La-di-da) 1992 (La-di-da America) 1994

Less R&B-influenced than the similarly moody Portishead, the Brighton duo Insides recalls an older stratum of offbeat, melodically simple semi-electronic music. On **Euphoria** songs like "Walking in Straight Lines," "Distractions" and the intriguingly titled (but unrelated) "Carly Simon," it's hard to decide which is lovelier, Julian Sergei Tardo's sonic backdrop (the hypnotic, circular synth patterns and gently ticking beats of Kraftwerk; deep New Order basslines; limpid, echoing guitar reminiscent of Durutti Column reverberator Vini Reilly) or Kirsty Yates' haunting, breathy vocals. The overall effect is entrancing, a combination as timeless and tranquil as Young Marble Giants or Chris and Cosey. The adjunct **Clear Skin** consists of one wan thirty-eight-minute track of wordless instrumental gentility that suggests Insides own a well-worn copy of **Tubular Bells.** Good soundtrack for soaking.

Before their contraction into Insides, Yates and Tardo had, along with Dimitri Voulis, been Earwig, a trio that pursued a more guitar-oriented path akin to Cranes or Slowdive. The group's first three 12-inch singles (1990–91) were collected on 1992's **Past.** By the time Earwig's proper debut album, **Under My Skin I Am Laughing,** was issued later that year, the sound—as on the (included) fourth single "Every Day Shines"—was wafting closer to **Euphoria**'s unknown electronic pleasures. [gef]

INSPIRAL CARPETS

The Peel Sessions EP (UK Strange Fruit) 1989 (Strange Fruit/Dutch East India Trading) 1991
Cool as **** EP (Cow/Rough Trade) 1990
Life (Mute/Elektra) 1990
The Beast Inside (Cow/Mute/Elektra) 1991
Revenge of the Goldfish (Cow/Mute/Elektra) 1992
Devil Hopping (Cow/Mute/Elektra) 1994
The Singles (Cow/Mute) 1995

Friendly neighbors of the end-of-the-'80s Manchester rave scene alongside Happy Mondays and Stone Roses, Oldham's better-behaved Inspiral Carpets raised the retro-pop stutter-groove stakes with the distinctive chortle of Clint Boon's vintage Farfisa beat. Adding that garagey '60s ingredient to the swirling whorls of carefully formed psychedelic and Tom Hingley's strong, pleasant voice brought the quintet major chart action at home. (**The Singles,** which doubles as a career-spanning album sampler, provides a handy overview of the group's UK successes.) It also provided adequate creative momentum to keep the Inspirals more durably productive—if not consistently good—than most of their peers.

Gathering up five tracks from the band's late-'80s UK singles, **Cool as ****** (the title sanitizes the band's Cow label T-shirt parody of a British milk-ad slogan) provided a weak introduction to America; the four-song Peel EP notably contains the memorable "Directing Traffic," and the group's rendition of "Gimme Shelter." The debut album (US and UK editions of **Life** differ) is too much of an occasionally good thing that contains such essentials as the sturdily melodic "This Is How It Feels," the poppy "Move" and a new, unimproved version "Directing Traffik."

Adding no memorable songs to the Carpets' catalogue, **The Beast Inside** is a misbegotten attempt at formula-tinkering that broadens the band's dynamic net but doesn't pull anything worthwhile in. "Grip" builds a funky fire, and "Please Be Cruel" boils it up good and slow; Hingley whispers the verses of "Sleep Well Tonight" and "Niagara" over delicate instrumental washes; "Beast Inside" wanes gothic, with carillon intro and foot-dragging tempo. "Dreams Are All We Have" is a graceful soundtrack-like instrumental that couldn't be less psychedelic if it was wearing a bowler.

Evidently reconsidering diversity as a strategy, Inspiral Carpets returned to the straight and narrow for **Revenge of the Goldfish,** laying down consistently brisk beats and a thick instrumental shag on which the organ-pumping ghosts of Steppenwolf and Arthur Brown do the funky monkey. Material-wise, the record is hit-and-miss. "Dragging Me Down" and the surly "Irresistible Force" get the blood pumping, but the cheek to name a pop original "Bitches Brew" doesn't yield a song worth provoking the ghost of Miles Davis for. The Carpets do better with "Fire," honoring an earlier English tune by the same name with a rousing chorus and dramatic swelling flourishes. Elsewhere, nonsensical lyrics ("Smoking Her Clothes," "A Little Disappeared," "Here Comes the Flood") and routine sounds make **Revenge of the Goldfish** a hollow victory.

An incorrigibly mature album that siphons off most of the band's remaining personality in favor of various stripes of ordinary (like a very sorry imitation of the Animals and a surely unintended recollection of the forgotten Fischer-Z), **Devil Hopping**—produced, like **Revenge of the Goldfish,** by Pascal Gabriel—is an object lesson in the evil of banality. The nearly lifeless music is at best self-parodic; the lyrics are hopelessly trite. How is "It's a funny old world/It's a funny old human race . . . Knowing you're just a rolling stone/And you're never gonna gather no moss" for blinding invention and insight? Ironically, **Devil**'s best moment—a version of the leadoff "I Want You" with Mark E. Smith of the Fall jabbing his wry interjections all over Hingley's singing, which suddenly resembles mid-'80s Paul Weller—isn't even on it. You'll need **The Singles** for that one. [i]

See also *TPRG*.

INTERNATIONAL BEAT

See *General Public.*

INTO PARADISE

Under the Water (UK Setanta) 1990
Into Paradise (Ensign/Chrysalis) 1990
Churchtown (Ensign/Chrysalis) 1991
Down All the Days (UK Setanta) 1992
For No One (UK Setanta) 1993

Lucky for this brooding, gentle Dublin group, singer/guitarist David Long has one of those spot-on whines that manages to add the sense of emotional fragility—heft even—his clichéd words don't necessarily deserve. The tunes themselves are a different, and often glorious, story. Produced by Adrian Borland (of the late, great Sound), **Under the Water** (released in the US as **Into Paradise,** with a few tracks replaced) is slow-moving, simple, guitar-driven post-punk with faint echoes of Echo and the Bunnymen (a connection made explicit on "Red Light"). Pretty—not to mention pretty depressing—melodies ("The Pleasure Is Over," "Going Home") more than compensate for Long's earnestly dreary and angsty lyrics, which occasionally sink into dreaded fire-and-desire couplets. But the worst offense is the fact that drummer Ronan Clarke's name is misspelled on the US edition's booklet. Tough break.

The soaring, anthemic "Rain Comes Down" opens the much-improved, negligibly brighter **Churchtown,** which exhibits all of the debut's strengths and few of its weaknesses. While much of the material is as downbeat as that of any gaggle of goths, the elegant, ringing guitars make even the most funereal tracks (especially "I'm Still Waiting") sound absolutely lovely. Cure and Echo fans should pounce.

The eight-song, thirty-three-minute **Down All the Days** is by far Into Paradise's best and most consistent effort. The tighter format is a big plus, letting the quartet avoid the filler that dotted its first two releases. "Sleep," the invitingly atmospheric centerpiece, continues the band's tradition of hooking plaintively beautiful tunes to the direst of lyrics—in this case, Long's self-doubt over a hopeless affair. The seven-track **For No One** covers no new ground, but the samey song titles ("Letting Go," "Don't Let Me Down," "Move Over," "Move Up, Move Out") indicate that Long could use a good thesaurus. The disc's other distinction is the churning "All of These" about—what else?—a spent love affair, and the most rocking tune the group has ever attempted. [db]

INXS

INXS (Aus. Deluxe) 1980 (Atco) 1984
Underneath the Colours (Aus. Deluxe) 1981 (Atco) 1984
Shabooh Shoobah (Atco) 1982
Inxsive (Aus. Deluxe) 1982
Dekadance EP (Atco) 1983
The Swing (Atco) 1984
Listen Like Thieves (Atlantic) 1985
Kick (Atlantic) 1987
X (Atlantic) 1990
Live Baby Live (Atlantic) 1991
Welcome to Wherever You Are (Atlantic) 1992
Full Moon, Dirty Hearts (Atlantic) 1993
The Greatest Hits (Atlantic) 1994

MAX Q

Max Q (Atlantic) 1989

For all its studio efficiency and tight-knit personal cohesion, INXS—the Sydney-born sextet that hasn't changed its lineup in fifteen years—often sounds like a group of tourists unable to decide between visiting the zoo or having a late lunch. Although singer Michael Hutchence has always written the bulk of the material with keyboardist Andrew Farriss (one of three brothers in the band), they've rarely seemed to be in stylistic synch with the band. As the world's only Jagger-Pop-Bono-Morrison hybrid, Hutchence fancies himself an old-fashioned rock idol, a fringey stadium shaman and a trendy young groover pushing the envelope. The others, meanwhile, sometimes rise to the occasion but are more often perfectly content to churn out rote rock-funk that isn't going to win any pioneer awards on the hipitude circuit. At times, INXS lurches to life with sudden bursts of stylistic ambition; when it does, the resulting records can be exciting and original. But a needle drop through the sixteen-track **Greatest Hits** reveals precious few such moments: a dismaying majority of the band's moneymakers hit their marks and nothing more.

After three exceedingly dull albums that, with the exception of **Shabooh Shoobah**'s "The One Thing," failed to provide any evidence of what was allegedly an exciting live phenomenon back home in Australia, INXS moved onto the modern dancefloor with **The Swing** and got the party started. Thanks especially to the album's Nile Rodgers–produced "Original Sin," INXS shook off their provincial marginalism and got in the mid-'80s slipstream, with solid beats, dramatic vocals and a safe harbor in the forward port of mainstream dance-rock. The following year, Chris Thomas produced **Listen Like Thieves,** consolidating the sextet's commercial breakthrough with crisp, lively sound, dollops of aggressive guitar work and as little vocal posturing as Hutchence seems capable of. The title tune and "What You Need" have solid melodies, seductive atmospheres, strong rhythms and decisive hooks.

With Hutchence emerging as a would-be actor and a pin-up star, INXS went on auto-pilot for **Kick,** an album of vapid video-disco with incongruous political lyrics on a couple of songs, pretentious posturing and laughable soul pretensions on others. Other than the spare and snappy "New Sensation," this is one of those not uncommon cases when a million fans *can* be wrong. "We all have wings/But some of us don't know why"—now *that's* heavy. The band then took a three-year recording rest while Hutchence did a side-project album (**Max Q**) with Australian underground rock legend Ollie Olsen. That indulgence over, INXS got back to business for the even more dire **X.** Weak hooks jammed roughly into weaker (and obviously self-derivative) songs, dead-end melodies, vacuous lyrics and the Billy Idol–like digressive spoken-funk-groove-and-harmonica single ("Suicide Blonde")—those are **X**'s good points. It was as if the group were aping everything that flashed by on MTV.

Although INXS issued a live-on-tour compilation, the best-of and two studio albums in the first half of the '90s, the sextet seems to have faded from commercial reliability and front-line prominence. If so, it's not for want of trying. The intriguingly good **Welcome to Wherever You Are** shuffles the deck with samples, world music accents and surprising conceptual inversions, striking a mindful balance between ambition and common sense; the results are uneven but sometimes genuinely rewarding. "Communication" uses the studio to excellent effect, fitting the pieces together with catchy guitar work and a Hutchence vocal that serves the song, not the other way around. "Back on Line" heads down a sinuous keyboard path that suggests where U2 might have headed if the Edge had taken piano lessons as a child. And instead of letting the orchestra on "Baby Don't Cry" provide background shading as is traditional for such endeavors, INXS and their co-producer Mark Opitz push it to the front of the mix, forcing the rock instruments to compete, which makes for one hot-blooded arrangement.

Full Moon, Dirty Hearts (which, unlike **X,** *is* the band's tenth album) retreats disappointingly to the safety of familiar routines—and the wishful U2 aura that has frequently attended the band. The recycled rock-funk repetition ("Make Your Peace," "I'm Only Looking") and Hutchence's un-hunh? duets with Ray Charles, the Stonesy "Please (You Got That . . .)," and Chrissie Hynde (the sensuous "Full Moon Dirty Hearts") are one thing. But the panels of thick mechanical guitar distortion, fuzzed bass and weird-snare veneer on "The Gift," "Days of Rust," "Time" and the spoken "Viking Juice (The End of Rock & Roll)" could justify a letter of protest from U2's embassy. [i]

See also *TPRG*.

IRIS

See *Philistines Jr.*

IRON PROSTATE

Loud, Fast, and Aging Rapidly (Skreamin' Skull/Skyclad) 1991

Most rock bands would prefer to turn a blind eye to the subject of getting older, but Iron Prostate looks middle age in the face and laughs. Determined to grow up gracelessly, this band of (mostly) fortyish punk enthusiasts—including veteran rock critic Charles M. Young on bass—proudly displays its influences (Dead Boys, Ramones) on **Loud, Fast, and Aging Rapidly.** On songs like "Rock'n'Roll Nursing Home," singer Scott Weiss (formerly of Ed Gein's Car) envisions a rock obsessive's waning years, barking out lyrics like "I've got my Ramones albums/And my blue-gray hair" while the band pumps out vintage class-of-'77 riffs. Fun songs ("Pumpkinhead") and bad puns ("Hell Toupee") abound on an album likely to appeal to punk junkies of all ages.

Though Iron Prostate seemed to have some even funnier songs for its followup ("Bring Me the Head of Jerry Garcia," which was released as a single in '92), the group dissolved in the midst of sessions with, of all people, Meat Loaf producer Jim Steinman. Guitarist George Tabb went on to form Furious George. [ts]

IVY

Lately EP (Seed) 1994
Realistic (Seed) 1995

Dreamy French pop hasn't washed up on American shores for some time now, but it's shaping up as a mid-'90s mini-mode. Although formed and based in New York City, Ivy has a Paris-born singer, Dominique Durand, to give the trio a legitimate claim to the accent.

Thanks to her cooing charm and the beguiling sonic reverie crafted by husband/guitarist Andy Chase and drummer/bassist Adam Schlesinger, Ivy's gentle potion has charmed its way into the pop underground.

The self-produced five-song **Lately** boasts a semi-acoustic cover of the Orange Juice's "I Guess I'm Just a Little Too Sensitive" (pronounced, of course, *lee-dul*) and an original (the wah-wahing "I Hate December") actually recorded in the City of Lights. "Get Enough," first issued as the band's debut 7-inch single, also gets a spot on **Realistic;** Durand's airy, petal-soft lilt and the music's toned-down pop bounce make it forever Ivy. Produced by Ultra Vivid Scene's Kurt Ralske, the rest of **Realistic** strays little from that path. *Très agréable.*

In 1996, without relinquishing his role in Ivy, Schlesinger unveiled a new band, Fountains of Wayne, and recorded—with singer/guitarist Chris Collingwood—an eponymous debut album that is a marvel of exceptional electric pop ingenuity. (After it was released, the pair formed a quartet with ex-Belltower guitarist Jody Porter and drummer Brian Young of the Posies.) Schlesinger also added to his creative achievements the same summer by writing the catchy title song for Tom Hanks' retro-rock movie, *That Thing You Do.* [vg/i]

JACK FROST

See *G. W. McLennan.*

JACKOFFICERS

See *Butthole Surfers.*

JACKONUTS

Jackonuts EP (Radial/Matador) 1992
On You (Radial/Matador) 1994

Along with several compilation appearances and a couple of singles (one contains a surprising B-side cover of Algebra Suicide's "True Romance at the World's Fair," another leads with the incomprehensible "Tracy Chapman's Lips"), the five-song **Jackonuts** and the eight-song **On You** are the entire recorded history of the explosive Jackonuts (aka Jack'O'Nuts, aka Jack-o-nuts) thus far. While the quartet is still active—guitarist Brooks Carter did double duty in David Barbe's Buzz Hungry—its output hardly bespeaks a saga that dates back to 1989.

Think of the band as Athens, Georgia's answer to Scratch Acid or Jesus Lizard; think of vocalist Laura Carter (ex–Bar-B-Q Killers, no relation to Brooks) as David Yow with XX chromosomes. While she, like he, revels in scatology and both front groups creating unnerving, snaky sonics based in part on the Birthday Party, Jackonuts do have an identity of their own.

Compared to the relatively straightforward and nearly tame (well, maybe songs like "Head Full of Shit" are hard to shoehorn into that description) **Jackonuts** EP, **On You** heads right for the edge. Produced half-and-half by Barbe and Steve Albini, the record finds the Georgians going for the dirge, loping low into raw, physical rhythms punctuated by Brooks' wiry, cat-skinning guitar style. The lyrics can be wildly surreal. In "Hook," Laura Carter goes from the abstract cooking symbolism of "I'm the yogurt on the vindaloo" to random threats ("If my fangs were big enough I'd kill you") to vehement social critique ("Hate the halo of P. C. clone")—all phrased with the eccentric timing of a bag lady. While it's hard to fathom the context of the band's anger at times, it's easy to be drawn in by the record's taut, sinister nuances. [mww/i]

See also *Sugar.*

JACKSHIT

See *7Seconds.*

JOE JACKSON

Look Sharp! (A&M) 1979
I'm the Man (A&M) 1979
Beat Crazy (A&M) 1980
Jumpin' Jive (A&M) 1981
Night and Day (A&M) 1982
Mike's Murder (A&M) 1983
Body and Soul (A&M) 1984
Big World (A&M) 1986
Will Power (A&M) 1987
Live 1980/86 (A&M) 1988
Tucker (A&M) 1988
Blaze of Glory (A&M) 1989
Stepping Out: The Very Best of Joe Jackson (UK A&M) 1990
Laughter & Lust (Virgin) 1991
Night Music (Virgin) 1994

Ending a decade-long association with A&M Records—during which he exchanged youthful rock excitement for conceptual excursions into big-band jump blues (**Jumpin' Jive**), Latin-jazz (**Night and Day, Body and Soul**), film scores (**Mike's Murder, Tucker**), small combo jazz-pop (**Big World**), orchestral composition (**Will Power**) and rocking retrospection (**Blaze of Glory**)—Joe Jackson arrived at his new label in 1991 a confident, accomplished pop auteur ready for whatever challenges he could envision.

The overwhelmed consumer indecision of "It's All Too Much" ("They say that choice is freedom/I'm so free it drives me to the brink") sets the tone on **Laughter & Lust.** "Only love can be stranger than fiction," he sings, expressing bewilderment in aisles outside the supermarket. Smiling through the tears, Jackson elaborates on the confounded romantic theme in "Goin' Downtown," "Drowning" and "Jamie G.," while expressing unhappy certainty in the difficulties of "When You're Not Around" and "The Other Me." Pictured on the cover in prison stripes toting a ball and chain, Jackson soft-pedals the wry adventures of an Englishman living in New York, keeping his stylistic ambitions to himself. The lyrics do the heavy lifting; backed by longtime musicians Graham Maby (bass), Sue Hadjopolous (percussion) and others, the singer/keyboardist keeps to a straight, sophisticated middle rock-pop road that is suitable but uncharacteristic after so many genre explorations. The current-events commentary of "Obvious Songs" is a sore thumb, and "Hit Single" breaks the thoughtful mood with a novelty conceit, but otherwise **Laughter & Lust** is an affecting, reflective album. Given its threatening, self-appraising tone, Jackson's close copy of Peter Green's Fleetwood Mac classic "Oh Well" fits in quite well.

Night Music returns Jackson to the realm of high concepts, although exactly what the tranquil album's concept might be—beyond an intricately futile attempt to conjure up the sound of dreams—is hard to divine between four nocturnes (played variously on piano and by string quartet) and such weirdly melodic lyrical contraptions as "Flying" and "The Man Who Wrote Danny Boy" (a duet of sorts with Clannad's Máire Brennan). "The older I get the more stupid I feel," Jackson sings. Stupidity isn't the problem here, musical self-consciousness is. Mixing a little Tin Pan Alley, some Gaelic folk flute, a spot of classical singing and chamber arrangements, **Night Music** is a torpid fever fantasy that scarcely suggests the peaceful imaginings of sleep. [i]

See also *TPRG*.

KATE JACOBS

Safe as Houses EP [tape] (Small Pond) 1990
Pure Science EP [tape] (Small Pond) 1991
The Calm Comes After (Small Pond) 1992 (Bar/None) 1993
(What About Regret) (Bar/None) 1995
A Sister EP (Bar/None) 1996

Kate Jacobs—Hoboken, New Jersey's indie-label answer to the folk/country compromise popularized by Mary Chapin Carpenter and Shawn Colvin—has a clear, plucky soprano, a firm melodic sense and an excellent instrumental compatriot in guitarist Dave Schramm.

Lyrics are the Virginia native's strong suit. A sentimental romantic with a sensitive touch, she writes down-to-earth small tales—almost all of her songs contain dialogue—that consider relationships as comfortably and credibly as they contemplate great truths and search for deep meanings. On **The Calm Comes After** (self-released one year and expanded, resequenced, repackaged and reissued the next), Jacobs shifts topical gears without ever lurching. She mulls over "a cosmic kind of ache" in "Destiny's Darling" and announces herself "Easy to Steal"—"even though I kind of wish he'd lock me up inside his heart." She helps expel existential dolor in "Sadness Rises" and pays a sweet visit to an old friend in the magical "Talk to Me." She raves about a friend from Kansas in "Iris Has Faith" and has the nerve to begin "Definitely Not Romance" by asking "What is the meaning of life, anyway?" The courageous family tragedy of "Now They're Here" is the only compelling addition to the album's Bar/None edition; otherwise, the improvements are just window dressing.

Although Jacobs recorded **(What About Regret)** with the same trio as her first album, the results are quite different. Exchanging sprightly lightheartedness for a mild melancholy and warm country stylings for music of wider ambition, Jacobs raises her sights to a higher, more literary plane. In this realm, characters are having harder times living with their blues ("My Old Haunts," "Be Brave"). They face fears ("Oh Vagabond"), disappointments ("A Sister") and loneliness ("Made My Bed")—and don't emerge unscathed. The songs' powerful poignancy and rustic reality make Jacobs resemble Victoria Williams at times, as do her impressively improved storytelling skills. The pot-farming saga of "3 Years in Nebraska" is a charmer; the sparsely furnished "No Question," a story worthy of Colette (but apparently based on the creator of *The Story of O*), concerns a woman who daily writes a chapter of a compelling novel to keep her married lover from leaving her and becomes a famous author in the process. A moderately demanding emotional experience, **(What About Regret)** rewards careful listening with details and empathy, like a series of personal letters from close friends.

Released to coincide with the publication of Jacobs' children's book, *A Sister's Wish,* the 1996 EP joins the memorable **Regret** song of the title (on which the book is based) with four characterstically fine new tunes. The sweet "Shallow" has a sharp Schramm solo; the guitarist co-wrote and duets quietly with Jacobs on "The Heart of the Matter." "You Sleep, I'll Drive" lifts the tempo while attempting to settle some emotional disharmony, and ends **A Sister** with the reassurance that music is a potent palliative for the bumps in life's road. [i]

See also *Schramms*.

JACOB'S MOUSE

The Dot EP (UK Liverish) 1991
No Fish Shop Parking (UK Blithering Idiot) 1991 (Frontier) 1992
I'm Scared (Frontier) 1993
Wryly Smilers (UK Wiiija) 1994
Rubber Room (UK Wiiija) 1995

Jacob's Mouse nibbled at a smorgasbord of genres but never really sank their teeth into any one. One minute, the trio from Bury St. Edmunds cranked out a dub groove; the next, they were doing ninety in a school zone leaving a cloud of burnt rubber, skid marks and hundreds of frightened kids. But every second, the Mouse breathed a frenetic intensity and ingenuity reminiscent of early Pixies. Formed in '87 (when the three childhood friends were all of sixteen), Jacob's Mouse boasts one of the most adept singing drummers on record. Sam Marsh can pound out intricate fills and instigate time changes while spurting out **Raw Power**–esque vocals. Bassist Jebb Boothby completes an impeccable rhythm section, while Jebb's twin brother, Hugo, serves up an equally potent platter of fat, '70s guitar licks and Seattlized distortion. Together they produce a mesh of sinuous Fugazi-type grooves, Mudhoney-style tattered pop and Captain Beefheart–like quirky surprises—an unlikely combination for rural Britons.

Despite their tender age, the threesome dabbles in a mosaic of musical styles on **The Dot** EP. "Enterprise" is as ragged and raucous as the MC5. "Hey Dip Sugar" is a frenzied spiral of energy, and the band keeps that puissance tightly wound on "Ho-Hum." In just five songs, the Mouse establishes itself with striking maturity and magnetic force. **No Fish Shop Parking** taps into the same elements as **The Dot,** but tests out an even more diverse, unabashed scramble of musical modes—all in just thirty minutes. At the root is a heavy rock influence (à la Sabbath and other '70s rock dinosaurs), but Jacob's Mouse tosses trippy echoes onto the vocals of "Tumbleswan," a rockabilly beat on "Caphony" and a frantic blitz on "Justice." A hint of Fugazi funk also surfaces on "Carfish," presaging a sound that grew more prominent on subsequent records. The highlight is "Company News," the band's poppiest venture, complete with handclaps and an almost danceable beat. The lyrics (when audible) aren't always exactly uplifting: "A Place to Go To" is about death, and "She Is Dead" makes a mantra of the title.

Although **I'm Scared** kicks off with straightahead groove-based rock, it's quickly evident (on the third track, "This Room") that a few more musical textures have slipped into the mix. The cut brings together psychedelic synth sounds and rhythms heavy enough for a booming system; then guitars cut in and Sam sings about the sickness of mind and body. To the band's credit, all the seemingly disparate pieces fit together. The Mouse also toys with reggae and hip-hop rhythms ("Body Shop") and even dips into tribal drum grooves on "Coalmine Dig." Still, the majority of the album is as charged as a pile of firecrackers in a lightning storm. The CD also features all three tracks from **Ton Up,** a single released shortly before **I'm Scared.**

Wryly Smilers, a compilation of singles that followed **I'm Scared,** further accentuates the trio's divergent tastes. "Biz Marmite" is an odd montage of whispers and hushed sounds; a distorted guitar whir and hammering bass power "Fandango Widewheels"; a sampled British woman speaks through the musical din on "Sag Bag." Again, the emphasis is on razor-edged rock—there's even a trace of White Zombie on "Group of 7."

The band's final release, **Rubber Room,** again ventures into new territory. The first track, "Kuff Prang," fuses cool jazz with puncturing rock; the synth sound on "Foam Face" recalls Suicide. Jacob's Mouse digs one of its deepest funk grooves on "Public Oven," but also offers the introspective "Domestic," which jumps abruptly from acoustic quiet to a wall of noise—an extremely abridged Metallica epic of sorts. Although more disjointed than **I'm Scared,** the album is no less powerful, further proof that Jacob's Mouse—a band that split up in its prime—could master any genre and give it a distinct twist. [mg]

JALE

Dreamcake (Sub Pop) 1994
14 08 93 EP (Ger. Sub Pop) 1994
Closed EP (Can. Murderecords) 1995
So Wound (Sub Pop) 1996

First heard adding an ethereal voice to her Sloan pals' **Smeared** album, Halifax singer/guitarist Jennifer Pierce brought her own everyone-writes/everyone-sings quartet out to play a couple of years later with the smart and strong **Dreamcake,** recorded (as opposed to produced) by Liz Phair collaborator Brad Wood. A diverse collection of contemporary electric indie-pop styles (some audibly influenced by Sloan) from a palette of appealing melodies, gentle harmony singing and buzzing guitar power, the casual-sounding record articulates the longings and frustrations of mindful young women who know when to draw the line and walk away from a bad scene. Although "3 Days" clearly announces "I want you to touch me," the slowly simmering "I'm Sorry" turns desire on its heel in stark language: "I despise the way you make me feel/I'm not a bad person/My heart is good . . . You bring out only the worst in me." The quid pro quo romantic vow of "Promise" ("Never leave me guessing, always be proud of me . . . Let me make you happy and take you to the country, always stay with me . . . And if you do this for me . . . I will never go away") nicely balances the salvage effort of "To Be Your Friend," the reconciliation attempt of "Mend" and the loneliness of "Love Letter." Although the product of four personalities, **Dreamcake** ultimately seems like one individual patiently enduring romance's vagaries.

The German **14 08 93** EP contains the album's "Not Happy," an alternate version of "3 Days" produced by Paul Kolderie, a remix of "Love Letter" and the non-LP "I Lied." **Closed** adds five fine new studio recordings to the Jale stack. Guitarist Eve Hartling's "Jesus Loves Me" and bassist Laura Stein's punky "Double Edge" represent the band's rocking side; Pierce's "Nine Years Now" and "Long Way Home" take a lighter approach with lovely harmonies; drummer Alyson MacLeod's brisk "Wash My Hands" leans firmly in both directions. Although it demonstrates how distinct each member of Jale's music is, the EP again displays the band's common purpose.

Jale introduces its lighthanded new drummer, Mike Belitsky, on **So Wound,** which was co-produced by Brad Wood in Chicago. Appreciably elevating the band's skill and confidence levels from indie-pop cuteness to real contention (while upholding the lyrical fortitude), the album is a taut, purposeful marvel of great pop songs in a number of cohesively connected modes. "Tumble" sounds like someone's been taking singing lessons from Liz Phair and the harmonies of "All Ready" call to mind the Bangles, but "Ali," "Over You," "Hey Hey," the punky "Mosquito" and "Despite" (with Belitsky's backing vocals for a nice contrast) are pure—and great—in their Jale-ness. [i]

See also *Sloan.*

JAM

See *Paul Weller.*

JAMES

Stutter (Blanco y Negro/Sire) 1986
Strip-mine (Blanco y Negro/Sire) 1988
One Man Clapping (UK One Man/Rough Trade) 1989
Gold Mother (Fontana) 1990
James (Fontana) 1991
Seven (Fontana/Mercury) 1992
Laid (Mercury) 1993
Wah Wah (Mercury) 1994

The name James must mean "flux" in Manchester parlance: the English group has been changing and evolving along an unpredictable course ever since making its debut as a folky new wave quartet in 1983. Surviving several stages of the city's pace-setting musical development, James has followed a unique agenda, expanding its ambitions wider and deeper—if not always for the better—with each discontinuous album.

Produced by Lenny Kaye, **Stutter** is rustic folk-rock, energetic and busy (à la Violent Femmes), handsomely neo-traditional in its musical spirit (like the Proclaimers) and pompously silly in Tim Booth's lyrics and vocals. Hugh Jones' more ambitious production helps the band move into sparkling folk pop—like something Johnny Marr might have done outside the Smiths around the same time—on **Strip-mine,** a charmingly modest entertainment whose highlights include the horn-spiked "Charlie Dance" and "Stripmining." The live **One Man Clapping** is ruined by Booth's suddenly insufferable Morrissey pretensions, but that was the end of that.

Gold Mother introduces the new James—a grandiosely dramatic seven-piece complete with trumpeter and violinist playing long, instrumentally overloaded poetic rock epics akin to early Waterboys. Booth's lyrics are also serious and self-important, revering childbirth in the title track, damning religious exploiters in "God Only Knows," attacking the establishment in "Government Walls" and grappling with issues great and small in "Hang On," "Walking the

Ghost," "Come Home" and "How Was It for You." **Gold Mother** made the group stars in England, but America still wasn't buying, so the band's new label tried it again, deleting "Crescendo" and "Hang On" in favor of "Sit Down" and "Lose Control" and reissuing it as **James.** No takers.

Seven refashions the septet into an English Simple Minds, spreading its wings across a grand polyrhythmic tableau in which everyone plays at once and nobody gets hurt. Against a surging model of dynamic textures in tautly controlled arrangements that employ the members' skills to the fullest, Booth keeps his singing dramatic but eloquent—more Liam Neeson than Charlton Heston, which serves to sharpen the vibrant music's focus. Whether topical ("Bring a Gun") or romantic ("Don't Wait That Long"), the lyrics are more considered and set lower in the mix, but the music's invigorating force is what makes the buoyant **Seven** James' first fully satisfying album.

Trumpeter Andy Diagram got off the bus as the other six teamed with Brian Eno (thereby encouraging the U2 **Joshua Tree** component of James' thinking) to make not one but two albums: the subdued, largely acoustic and folk-inflected **Laid** and **Wah Wah,** a compilation of improvisational sketches for it. Putting unprecedented weight on Booth's vocals (which rise to the occasion, despite habitual repetition of tag lines in simple songs which seem under-written as a result), **Laid** tucks the band into quiet instrumental beds, fluffed up with space and air rather than demonstrative personality. The only thing that rouses the band to all-together-now enthusiasm is the tasteless sex talk of the title track. Although pretty in its fussed-over gentility and alluring in small doses, the enervated **Laid** is a stylish bore.

In a typically Eno-esque conceptual experiment that could imaginably have been planned for his U2 charges, **Wah Wah** was processed, edited and pieced together (in tribute to Eno's days in Roxy Music, the credits have it "remade-remodeled") from days of studio improvisation (they don't call it jamming anymore). Engineer/mixer Markus Dravs shaped the results into twenty-three distinct chunks diverse enough to float like audio wallpaper one minute, hit a heavy dance groove the next, trail off into world music adventures and then come back with a nearly formed song. A lively ambient album unique in the process of its creation, **Wah Wah** is credibly listenable and, in its way, more intriguing than the album that byproduced it. [i]

See also *TPRG.*

WENDY JAMES

Now Ain't the Time for Your Tears (DGC) 1993

In her futile bid for artistic credibility, former Transvision Vamp chart tart James begged Elvis Costello to write a song for her. Rather than pen her a single single, however, Elvis took it upon himself—with help from his missus, Cait O'Riordan—to spend a weekend cutting ten pungent tunes from the bolt of curt, sharp-tongued cloth that typified his early work with the Attractions. (His demo sessions with Pete Thomas, who wound up playing on James' LP, had something to do with the group's **Brutal Youth** reunion.)

The tragedy of James' unappealing voice and incompetent singing is ameliorated by Thomas' typically superb drumming and occasionally nullified by the casual brilliance of Costello's hasty retrofits. A few of the tunes are gimmicks (the soundalike Clash citations of "London's Brilliant," the orchestral humphering of "I Want to Stand Forever") or uncharacteristically trite ("Fill in the Blanks," a prostitute's monologue, trips over clumsy lyrics; the chord progression in the stately waltz "Do You Know What I'm Saying?" has an infuriating stall), but "This Is a Test," "Basement Kiss," "Earthbound," "We Despise You" and "Puppet Girl" are all fine belated additions to Costello's early canon. Still, the suspicion that Costello (who ultimately derided the Chris Kimsey production) aimed his conceptual darts at James' ambitions rather than the subjects of his songs leaves the album—inexplicably titled after a Bob Dylan lyric in "The Lonesome Death of Hattie Carroll"—feeling like a practical joke at her expense. [i]

See also *Elvis Costello.*

JAMIROQUAI

Emergency on Planet Earth (Orenda/Columbia) 1993
The Return of the Space Cowboy (Orenda/Work) 1995

While all involved will insist that it is a band, Jamiroquai is, for all intents and purposes, Jason Kaye, a skinny Mancunian with a '70s soul jones, one goofy hat (that's him in silhouette on the cover of both records) and a knack for replicating the sound of Stevie Wonder. **Emergency on Planet Earth** is an audacious debut, a solid set of soul grooves that are charmingly retro but not so reverent that Kaye doesn't take a few original liberties—who would have thought didgeridoo could be so funky? Jamiroquai is less a product of the British acid-jazz scene than his own little world, one that plainly revolves around American soul. Not a bad thing at all.

With **Return of the Space Cowboy,** Jamiroquai turns away from railing against incipient environmental collapse and the injustices faced by native peoples, instead considering simpler pleasures, like the joys of marijuana. That change of focus not surprisingly results in a looser record. His m.o. is the same, but a little more refined, as Kaye settles into an increasingly personal style. The laid-back groove of "Space Cowboy" is a classic of the genre, regardless of the year in which it was recorded. Ultimately, Jamiroquai's biggest obstacle in being regarded as a major new voice in soul music may well be the uncanny resemblance of his voice to Wonder's. [sf]

JANE'S ADDICTION

See *Porno for Pyros.*

JANITOR JOE

Big Metal Birds (Amphetamine Reptile) 1993
Lucky (Amphetamine Reptile) 1994

This workmanlike Minneapolis trio—perhaps best known as the first recording project of the late Kristen Pfaff, who left Janitor Joe to accept the bass slot in Hole—is appropriately named, given the blue-collar manner in which it rakes through grit-mottled riffs, fashioning a burnished, no-frills end product likely to pique the curiosity of those prone to solicit ear perforation. On **Big Metal Birds,** Pfaff and guitarist/primary vocalist Joachim Breuer (a former member of the Bastards) share songwriting duties. Both operate within easy reach of the line separating punishment and reward: Pfaff's contributions (the surly "Boys in Blue") tend to be slightly more spacious, while Breuer's ("One Eye," for instance) stipulate that drummer Matt Entsminger maintain perpetual motion.

After Pfaff's departure, the remaining Joes recruited bassist Wayne Davis, a slightly less aggressive player than Pfaff, who is missed on tracks, like "Piss Corner," that would benefit from her take-no-prisoners style. Still, Breuer's menacing rasp and abstract-but-ornery prose keep tension levels at or above the minimum daily requirement, most notably on the dismissive "Pest" and "No Smokes for Wave." [dss]

See also *Hole*.

JARBOE

See *Swans*.

DUANE JARVIS

D. J.'s Front Porch (Medium Cool/Twin\Tone) 1994

Portland, Oregon, singer/guitarist Duane Jarvis walked a long mile through all sorts of musical affiliations (serving with Marvin Etzioni, Divinyls, Dwight Yoakam, Lucinda Williams, John Prine and others) before settling down on his front porch—actually, a Venice, California, recording studio—with a stack of affecting, low-key originals burnished by a sincere roustabout's voice of experience and a few pointed references to drinking. The Kinks' "This Is Where I Belong" makes as good a theme song as any for this roots-and-beyond solo album, which finds D. J. backed simply by his brother Kevin on drums and bassist Bobby McDonald, with pianist Rick Solem and viola/violin contributions from Tammy Rogers. The trio modulates its attack from nearly nothing (the jazzy brush strokes and jazz fiddle of "I Can Hardly Wait") to nearly raucous (the cold feet of "Good on Paper"), with a moany Tom Petty country stroll ("A Little Bit of Hurt"). In the vintage-toned middle ground, "She's Like a Drink" and "Darlinghurst Road" take equal parts Stonesy raunch and the kind of R&B and rockabilly rock that once resounded in Sun's tiny room. Throughout, Duane and the boys move things along with generous helpings of swamp spirit and the kind of skilled playing that neither ducks out nor calls attention to itself. Good enough. [i]

JASON AND THE NASHVILLE SCORCHERS

Reckless Country Soul EP7 (Praxis) 1982
(Praxis/Mammoth) 1996

JASON AND THE SCORCHERS

Fervor EP (Praxis) 1983 (EMI America) 1984
Lost & Found (EMI America) 1985
Still Standing (EMI America) 1986
Thunder and Fire (A&M) 1989
Essential Jason and the Scorchers, Volume One: Are You Ready for the Country (EMI) 1992
A Blazing Grace (Mammoth) 1995
Clear Impetuous Morning (Mammoth/Atlantic) 1996

JASON

One Foot in the Honky Tonk (Liberty) 1992

Hillbilly cats with a serious punk streak, Jason and the Scorchers were—in their early days—about as un-Nashville as any Nashville-based band could be. Fronted by tightly wound Illinois farm boy Jason Ringenberg, ably abetted by flame-throwing guitarist Warner Hodges and the crack rhythm section of bassist Jeff Johnson and drummer Perry Baggs, the group set out to blend incompatible elements and succeeded well beyond their expectations, mixing dirty roots rock, nihilistic, energy-crazed hardcore and traditional cornball country, spiked with dashes of blues and gospel. It may ultimately be little different from what Jerry Lee Lewis did, but few artists can presume to approach the Killer's outlaw majesty the way the Scorchers do when everything clicks.

The original **Reckless Country Soul**—a Hank Williams classic, a Jimmie Rodgers number and a pair of originals, all recorded live to 4-track and issued on a modest 7-inch—was clearly a formative work. The reissue—augmented by a leftover from the band's first session, five outtakes from studio time later in '82 and an unlisted bonus—is an entertaining snapshot of the boys rooting around for a style to call their own. In a wild and randy cover of Carl Perkins' "Gone Gone Gone" and the ripsnorting medley of Kostas' "I'd Rather Die Young" and George Morgan's "Candy Kisses," they stumble right into it.

While the **Fervor** EP kicked the renamed band into high gear (the disc's major-label rerelease brought the track count up to seven with a barn-burning cover of Bob Dylan's "Absolutely Sweet Marie"), **Lost & Found** is a sizzler from start to finish. In these lower-fi, post-'80s times, Terry Manning's clean, echoey production seems a bit sterile, but there's no denying the band's righteous fury. Red-hot originals like "White Lies" and "Last Time Around" (not to mention soulful covers of moldy oldies "Lost Highway" and "I Really Don't Want to Know") render discussions of genre bending, or blending, moot: Here, the Scorchers are simply excitement personified. (The aptly, if optimistically, titled **Essential Volume One** compiles **Fervor** and **Lost & Found** in their entirety, plus four odds and ends.)

Maintaining that breathtaking intensity was probably impossible—not even the best band can deliver a killer live show every single night. In any case, the two subsequent albums define a downward curve on which the band spins out its eager-to-please freshness. **Still Standing** is fine enough, despite the presence of clever-yet-crass producer Tom Werman (Cheap Trick, Mötley Crüe). Highlights include "Shotgun Blues," "Crashin' Down" and a ripping cover of the Stones' "19th Nervous Breakdown," but it all sounds a tad forced. **Thunder and Fire,** by contrast, is simply a dud. Jason and company strain for effect, and the material seems shopworn. No wonder they disbanded soon after.

Ringenberg's 1992 solo album, dubiously credited to "Jason," was a misguided attempt to infiltrate the country mainstream. A host of Music City reliables—from producer Jerry Crutchfield to slick session players to trusty songwriters like Dennis Linde, Paul Kennerley and Kevin Welch—are on hand, but the feeling's all wrong. The contrast between Jason's insistent drawl—he couldn't relax if his life depended on it—and his glib colleagues suggests two records playing at once.

A few years later, all the original members reunited to fire up Jason and the Scorchers again; the quartet's electrifying 1995 reunion album is the best thing they've done in a decade. There's nothing new here, just plenty of slashing, go-for-broke rock'n'roll like "Cry by Night Operator," "One More Day of Weekend" and "American Legion Party," all of which are about as intellectual as they sound. The wicked cover of George Jones' "Why Baby Why" almost stands up to the original, but the standout may be, believe it or not, an atomic version of John Denver's "Take Me Home, Country Roads." God bless these hillbilly punks. [jy/i]

See also *TPRG.*

JASPER & THE PRODIGAL SUNS

People Get Ready EP (CherryDisc) 1995
Everything Is Everything (Geffen) 1995

Having led one version of the group in Atlanta, singer/guitarist Jasper moved to Boston in 1992 and formed a new quintet there, providing hip-hop with an invigorating jolt of kitchen-sink ethics. The combination of live beats, guitar, steel drums, bass and saxophone yield results that are funky, frenetic and diverse: Rastafarianism, hip-hop, jazz (free and bop), calypso, blues and soul influences drive a danceable, spiritual message to both the brain and the booty.

While occasionally suggesting a blend of such contemporaries as G Love (a close friend whose guitar style Jasper's resembles), Soul Coughing (a quartet that uses samples where the Prodigal Suns prefer sax and Trinidadian percussion), Ben Harper and San Francisco new-jazz progenitors like Broun Fellinis, Jasper & the Prodigal Suns ultimately possess a singular sound. Before making the six-song **People Get Ready** EP, saxophonist Jim Hobbs, drummer D'jango Corranza and bassist Timo Shanko—seasoned as street musicians—had already been playing regularly on the Boston scene as the Fully Celebrated Orchestra; percussionist Mackie Burnett, a sixty-two-year-old native of Trinidad, was Corranza's drum teacher. Jasper's a natural frontman; with his righteous confidence ("Tough Guy"), declarations ("The Free Style") and personal reflections ("Sincerely Jasper"), the debut is razor sharp and an excellent companion to the full-length followup.

Everything Is Everything unleashes major grooves immediately, as Corranza and Shanko lock in on the beats bolstering "Peace & One Love." Burnett's percussive energy bubbles along with the rhythm section as Hobbs leads the five-piece into bursts of mid-tempo improv on "Word to the Mother," Jasper's ode to Africa. The singer drops knowledge on identity ("All Brothers Ain't Brothers") and tries a different, more soulful version of "Sincerely Jasper." Complete with samples and antic instrumentation (Burnett and Hobbs are fired up), "Give Me a Bomb" is the ultimate companion to Disposable Heroes of Hiphoprisy's "Television (Drug of a Nation)." The tender "Without You," the vivid "Babylon Is Falling," the Rastacentric "Thanks & Praise" and the party flavor of the autobiographical "Only in the South" give **Everything Is Everything** a well-rounded confidence and a warm, familial quality. One of 1995's best new bands. [mww]

JAWBOX

Jawbox EP7 (DeSoto/Dischord) 1990
Grippe (Dischord) 1991
Novelty (Dischord) 1992
Savory+3 EP (Atlantic) 1994
For Your Own Special Sweetheart (Atlantic) 1994
Jawbox (Tag/Atlantic) 1996

JAWBOX/LEATHERFACE

Your Choice Live Series (Ger. Your Choice) 1995

Formed in 1989 by ex–Government Issue bassist J. (Jay) Robbins, Jawbox went a long way toward stretching the boundaries of the formulaic call-and-response thrash of the DC/Dischord sound. With Robbins as singer, guitarist and songwriter, **Grippe** (recorded as a three-piece) is a rich, varied, polyrhythmic tour de force that still bears repeated listening. Every lyric is a free-verse poem, open to interpretation, although lines like "You woke from a dream of a blank page/Unwritten story of six years sleeping" suggest a search for identity, which Robbins certainly established after years as an overlooked backup player. It's odd that Kim Coletta's bass, such a forceful presence in the band's live performances, is mixed so low here; odder still to hear a Dischord band cover a Joy Division song ("Something Must Break").

Shortly after recording **Grippe,** Jawbox added second guitarist Bill Barbot, who makes his debut on **Novelty.** Robbins' writing is even more eclectic on this sophomore effort, soaking up influences from other bands like a sponge. Some songs reflect the dissonant, erotic harmonies of labelmates Shudder to Think; the pounding, percussive anger of other tracks smacks of Helmet. But **Novelty** is a disappointment, despite its inventiveness and undeniable intensity. The mushy mix wastes the dual guitars, and Robbins' vocals frequently seem dreary and monochromatic.

Jawbox's decision to leave the insular and fiercely independent protectorate of Dischord for Atlantic Records raised quite a few eyebrows and suspicions in and around the highly principled DC punk scene. But **Savory+3,** Jawbox's major-label debut, only takes Robbins' cerebral songcraft to a higher level. With Zachary Barocas replacing Adam Wade on drums, the EP has a brighter, crisper sound than anything the band had previously recorded. "Savory," an uneasy love song sung to an angel (real or metaphoric, it's impossible to tell), welds a mesmerizing melody to an enigmatic hook—"one hand will wash the other." Effortlessly switching gears from a hushed whisper to an explosive climax, "68" showcases the band's dynamic command. The four-song EP concludes with a cover of the Big Boys' "Sound on Sound," perhaps meant to reaffirm the band's DIY/underground commitment.

Also co-produced by Ted Nicely, **For Your Own Special Sweetheart** rocks even harder than the EP, with electrifying tracks like "FF=66," "LS/MFT" and "Chicago Piano" recalling the angry percussive hardcore of Fugazi. Robbins continues to weave beauty and discord into each song; grating, dissonant guitars dissolve into cascading, harmonic vocals, propelled by Barocas' rock-solid drums and Coletta's thumping, melodic basslines. The lyrics rarely make linear sense, so each song's meaning tends to be communicated by the timbre of the music and the emotional quality of his vocals—seething with anger on "Breathe" and "Jackpot Plus!," yearning and wistful on "Savory" and "Reel." Still, most tracks manage to incorporate a range of emotions and dynamics, leaving listeners to discern their own interpretations. **For Your Own Special Sweetheart** is not an easy album to like—there are no cuddly cartoon images or instantly hummable pop melodies—but it's there to be appreciated for those willing to invest the effort.

Co-produced by John Agnello, **Jawbox** finds the group doggedly sticking to the same formula of melodic dissonance and off-kilter rhythms without appreciably expanding its musical vocabulary (or potential appeal). The songs range from disconsolate balladry to frenetic hardcore-tempo shouting matches between Robbins and Barbot, all driven by the former's obsessive search for grace within musical and emotional anarchy. Moody, driven and downbeat (save for the occasional sanguine moment, like the rousing "Excandescent"), **Jawbox** is a work of integrity and passion from a pop band that refuses to write pop songs.

The German live album which the quartet shares with Leatherface documents Jawbox in action at Chicago's Lounge Ax in October 1994. [jt]

JAWBREAKER

Unfun (Shredder) 1990
Chesterfield King EP (Tupelo/Communion) 1992
Bivouac (Tupelo/Communion) 1992
24 Hour Revenge Therapy (Tupelo/Communion) 1994
Dear You (DGC) 1995

Although identified as a product of Berkeley's East Bay punk scene, Jawbreaker first came together in the late '80s in New York City, where its three members were attending New York University. Jawbreaker's 1990 debut, **Unfun,** was recorded over a week-long school break. With its rollercoaster riffs, lurching rhythms and guitarist Blake Schwarzenbach's sore-throat vocals, **Unfun** offers a rousing alternative to the testosterone-fueled thrash of '80s hardcore, proving that catchy pop-punk could provide the same intensity of feeling and spirit. Bassist Chris Bauermeister and drummer Adam Pfahler, borrowing the power-trio dynamics of Hüsker Dü, anchor Schwarzenbach's Modern Lit lyrics on infectiously upbeat cuts like "Busy" and "Down." In what would become a running theme, Schwarzenbach addresses several songs to the punk scene around him: "Sorry we ain't hard enough to piss your parents off," he croaks on "Incomplete," adding, "Hatred's not our policy, we tried that game and lost." (The CD of the album includes the band's 1989 **Whack & Blite** single.)

The self-abuse Schwarzenbach wreaked with his gravelly singing style eventually led to painful throat problems, which accounts for the aggravated hoarseness on **Bivouac,** recorded in 1992 after the post-graduation trio had settled in San Francisco. Although it lacks the playful brightness of **Unfun, Bivouac** repeats the trio's formula of literate, well-crafted pop songs filled with unpredictable breaks and changes. "Seven hundred miles to play to fifteen angry men/I need some sleep/They hate the songs," Schwarzenbach sings on "Tour Song," one of the most perfect summaries of life in the all-ages punk-rock underground. "Two cool people came/They're hiding by the door, eyes wide with fright/A guy, a girl, in love with the whole world/It almost makes it right." Produced with loud, loose reins by Steve Albini, **24 Hour Revenge Therapy** continues the Jawbreaker tradition of aggressive guitars, half-screamed vocals and witty, literate (and often self-referential) lyrics. "The Boat Dreams From the Hill" ("I wanna be a boat/I wanna learn to swim/Then I'll learn to float/Then begin again") and others have the chunky rhythm guitar chord shapes that bring Jawbreaker in synch with the rise of the East Bay's pop-punk scene. Faced with the choice between a potentially viable career in major-label music and the sectarian style hypocrisy of the local bands around them, Schwarzenbach responded with the pithy "Boxcar": "You're not punk and I'm telling everyone/Save your breath, I never was one." On "Indictment," he champions the band's style of catchy pop-punk—"I just wrote the dumbest song/It's gonna be a singalong/All our friends will clap and sing/Our enemies will laugh and be pointing."

After the runaway success of **Dookie** in late 1994, Jawbreaker signed to DGC Records for its fourth album. Sadly, **Dear You** has all the earmarks of a classic major-label sellout: with almost none of his customary raspiness, Schwarzenbach sings rather than shouts, while the production (Green Day star Rob Cavallo and the band) crafts a much glossier, more radio-friendly sound. Most of **Dear You** is given over to dysfunctional love songs, filled with confused emotions, self-loathing and complicated, twisted metaphors. The closest **Dear You** comes to the old Jawbreaker is the anthemic "Save Your Generation," in which Schwarzenbach admonishes his peers to seize life and stop slacking off: "I have a present: it is the present," he sings, "I have a message—save your generation, we're killing ourselves by sleeping in."

Jawbreaker dissolved amicably the following summer. [jt]

JAYHAWKS

The Jayhawks (Bunkhouse) 1986
Blue Earth (Twin\Tone) 1989
Hollywood Town Hall (Def American) 1992
Tomorrow the Green Grass (American) 1995

At their best, Minneapolis' Jayhawks played a heartfelt breed of countryfied roots-rock that was intimate yet epic, a sound built around the earth-and-sky interplay of singer/guitarists Mark Olson and Gary Louris and the band's balance of stately sensitivity and electric kick. **The Jayhawks** is an impressive debut, staking out an essentially derivative style with enough energy and personality to make it sound consistently fresh. The first record's material is generally uptempo and lighthearted in comparison with the weightier tone of **Blue Earth,** on which main writer Olson unveils a resonant, gracefully melancholy lyrical vision.

Hollywood Town Hall, the Jayhawks' major-label bow (produced by George Drakoulias), so consistently emphasizes the quartet's bittersweet mid-tempo material that it resembles a concept album. Despite—or because of—this relatively narrow view, the record attains a rough-hewn, holistic state of grace that is as impressive as any of the band's myriad influences. The hook-inclined Louris is considerably more prominent here, co-writing all of the songs with Olson and singing lead or co-lead on many of them, including "Waiting for the Sun" and "Settled Down Like Rain." Olson's somewhat darker vision and rougher-hewn voice don't really make a major impression until the album's final three numbers: "Wichita," "Nevada, California" and "Martin's Song" (which, like "Two Angels," was rerecorded from **Blue Earth**). Though **Hollywood Town Hall**'s conceptual focus is a bit too limited to really do the band justice, it's hard to argue with an album this beautifully written, played and sung.

In contrast, **Tomorrow the Green Grass**—which uses a session drummer (Don Heffington, ex–Lone Justice) and adds keyboardist Karen Grotberg to the longstanding core of Olson, Louris and bassist Marc Perlman—broadens its predecessor's stylistic base but generally lacks its emotional cohesion. There's much to admire and enjoy here, from high-lonesome balladry ("Blue") to romantic pop ("I'd Run Away") to fatalistic musings ("See Him on the Street")—even a sunny ode to Olson's wife, Victoria Williams ("Miss Williams' Guitar"). As its title suggests, **Tomorrow the Green Grass** ultimately seems like a transitional effort of a group with the potential for greatness. Alas, the Jayhawks' destiny seems likely to go unfulfilled. Olson quit in late 1995, after which the remaining members announced their intention to continue under a new name. [ss]

See also *Golden Smog, Joe Henry; TPRG.*

JAZZ BUTCHER

A Bath in Bacon (UK Glass) 1982
A Scandal in Bohemia (UK Glass) 1984
The Gift of Music (UK Glass) 1984
Sex and Travel (UK Glass) 1985
Hamburg (UK Rebel/Glass) 1985
Hard EP (UK Glass) 1986
Conspiracy EP (UK Glass) 1986
Distressed Gentlefolk (Big Time) 1986
Bloody Nonsense (Big Time) 1986
Big Questions (The Gift of Music Vol. 2) (UK Glass) 1987
Fishcotheque (Creation/Relativity) 1988
Spooky (Can. Creation/Mercury) 1988
Big Planet Scarey Planet (Genius) 1989
Cult of the Basement (Rough Trade) 1990
Edward's Closet (UK Creation) 1991
Condition Blue (Sky) 1991
Western Family (UK Creation) 1993
Waiting for the Love Bus (UK Creation) 1993
(Creation/TriStar Music) 1994
Illuminate (UK Creation) 1995

Though you wouldn't expect it from his ever-fluctuating lineup of merry sidemen (alternately and seemingly randomly known as the Jazz Butcher, the Jazz Butcher Conspiracy and the Jazz Butcher and his Sikkorskis From Hell), Oxford philosophy graduate Pat Fish has consistently recorded some of the cleverest genre-bouncing pop of the past fifteen years. It doesn't hurt that he leavens intelligent, smart-alecky lyrics and wickedly parodic songs with a rapturously effective heart—a condition he continues to mine well into the '90s.

Condition Blue announces his inspired lyrical lunacy immediately on the opening raveup, "She's a Yo-Yo." The downtrodden "Honey" is not the Bobby Goldsboro tune, but could be—if Goldsboro nodded out over pints of bitter at a wood-paneled pub. And the disc's standout, the upbeat "Shirley MacLaine" (as in "I've had a thing about Shirley MacLaine since I was so high"), is emblematic of all the things great about the Jazz Butcher. (**Western Family** is a **Condition Blue**–heavy live album recorded at North American dates.)

Over the course of **Waiting for the Love Bus**' fifteen tracks (thirteen in the UK), Fish runs through everything from captivating love songs ("Whaddya?") to muscular rockers ("Bakersfield") to torchy ballads ("Baltic") to hypnotic whimsy ("Penguins"). This is Fish at his most seductive and romantic, and it makes for his greatest achievement. Appended to the American edition, two imaginative covers—a reverb-coated "Everybody's Talking" and "Do You Wanna Dance?" (which sounds like very early Human League fooling with a music box)—add a sense of inspiration to this outlandish original. In all, the perfect Jazz Butcher recording, one that would be hard to top for sheer entertainment value.

Illuminate, subtitled "The Difficult Tenth" (but, really, who's counting?) doesn't quite reach those heights, but it's a perfectly welcome addition to the inventory. With songs jokingly calling for the privatization of everything, praising Brian Eno's vocal prowess and criticizing a woman's "Joan Collins boots," the record boasts some of Fish's sharpest witticisms. Production by recurrent co-conspirator (and Love and Rockets bassist) David J is perhaps a bit too airy, often letting the songs meander, but even an average cut of Butcher beats the prime of lesser mortals. [db]

See also *TPRG.*

JEAN PAUL SARTRE EXPERIENCE

Jean Paul Sartre Experience EP (NZ Flying Nun) 1986
Love Songs (NZ Flying Nun) 1987 (Communion) 1988
The Size of Food (Communion) 1989
Elemental/Flex EP (Communion) 1990
Precious EP (NZ Flying Nun) 1992
Breathe EP (NZ Flying Nun) 1993
Jean Paul Sartre Experience (NZ Flying Nun) 1995

JPS EXPERIENCE

Bleeding Star (Matador) 1993

Pop's rocky road is strewn with innumerable tattered gig flyers and dented band buttons. What would an alien traveler think if he picked up a scrap of debris bearing the words "Jean Paul Sartre Experience"? "So poetic, so perfectly evocative . . . but of what?" his musings would no doubt begin. Upon hearing the actual music, he might even fire off a missive to the late French existentialist's estate and chide them for forcing the New Zealand quartet to switch to the ineffectual "JPS Experience"—or, in a fashion similar to that sardonic Pink Floyd lyric, he might simply wonder, "Which one's Sartre?"

Prodded by the anxieties of teen boredom and inspired by the financial comfort of the dole, JPSE formed in the suburbs of Christchurch in late '84 (the name was inspired by a member's housemate who consumed magic mushrooms to excess and earned the nickname "The Existential Experience"). In '85, the band's reputation brought them a slot at the Flying Nun Records Christmas bash, and by next summer the label was ready to commit the JPSE demo tape to vinyl. The quartet—early recordings list their soundman as a fifth member—would relocate to Auckland on the northern island in '89, but, before that, three proper JPSE recordings were issued.

The self-titled debut is a rare, mysterious gem. Neither as saccharine as the Chills nor as moody as the Verlaines (two other Flying Nun bands of the time to which JPSE was often compared), the record twitches and shudders un-self-consciously between the gaps opened by Quicksilver, the Velvets and R.E.M. without ever committing to any one style. The chiming/modal guitars, exotic rhythm section murmurs, meditative vocals and guest trumpet (!) of "Walking Wild in Your Firetime" are sufficient to earn the five-song 12-inch "classic" status.

Love Songs was completed under stress; one member had temporarily defected, mid-sessions, to England. Still, the album—while more mannered and therefore less immediate than its predecessor—is a remarkably mature recording that showcases quite a breadth of styles. Notable are the piano/guitar noir blues of "Jabberwocky," the insanely funky "Let That Good Thing Grow" and the hypnotic love ballad "Grey Parade." Communion brought JPSE to the attention of Stateside listeners via its own version (totally different artwork) of **Love Songs,** which combines four album tracks with the entire first EP (wise move); the CD version adds two more cuts from the New Zealand edition of **Love Songs.** Just to confuse fans everywhere, Communion would see fit in 1990 to release a five-song CD EP, **Elemental/Flex,** containing three more **Love Songs** tunes not originally found on the American issue, plus (again) "Flex" from the **Jean Paul Sartre Experience** EP and "Elemental" from **The Size of Food.** In early '95, Flying Nun issued the first EP and the first album together as **Jean Paul Sartre Experience,** tagging on an early 45 ("I Like Rain" b/w "Bo Diddley") for good measure.

With the band roster back to normal, JPSE released **The Size of Food** simultaneously in New Zealand and America. Critical opinions tend to diverge regarding the album. While it has its share of Kiwi brilliance—the serpentine wallop of "Slip" is pure Velvets, while "Thrills" is a wailing slab of cracked pop-psych worthy of Robyn Hitchcock—it also contains some distracting experiments that find the band flirting needlessly with art-rock and dance motifs. Meanwhile, other songs (the lush, Church-like "Elemental" and "Inside & Out") seem to point in yet another direction.

Sure enough, the **Precious** and **Breathe** EPs continue in that vein; the former's title track is a catchy, groove-oriented number, while "Breathe" would fool a blindfold test subject into thinking a new Steve Kilbey track had surfaced. The tune's glamorous ennui helps sets the mood for **Bleeding Star,** where it also appears. An immaculate big-budget production, the album (credited to JPS Experience) unveils a new commercial face for the band. "Modus Vivendi" is all Jesus and Mary Chain feedback'n'buzz; the multiple guitar overdubs and simple melody of "Into You" define the term "pop anthem"; the fat drum sound, thick reverbed axes and yearning vocal harmonies that course through "Ray of Shine" create a towering wall of modern psychedelia.

Access to technology was long overdue for JPSE, as **Bleeding Star** was both the band's sonic tour de force and its swan song. JPSE broke up in 1994, leaving behind some of the finest New Zealand records ever. And one of the greatest band names, period. [fm]

JEFF AND JANET

See *Green.*

GRAEME JEFFERIES

See *Cakekitchen, Peter Jefferies.*

PETER JEFFERIES

The Last Great Challenge in a Dull World (NZ Xpressway) 1990 (Ajax) 1992 + 1995
Electricity (Ajax) 1994
A Chorus of Interludes (Ajax) 1996

PETER JEFFERIES/JONO LONIE

At Swim 2 Birds (NZ Flying Nun) 1986 (NZ Xpressway) 1990

PETER JEFFERIES/ROBBIE MUIR

Swerve EP7 (Ajax) 1992

CYCLOPS

Goat Volume (NZ IMD) 1994

NOCTURNAL PROJECTIONS

Another Year EP (NZ Hit Singles) 1982
Understanding Another Year in Darkness EP (NZ Hit Singles) 1983
Nerve Ends in Power Lines (Ger. Raffmond) 1996

Although he's never cultivated as high a profile as some of his contemporaries, Peter Jefferies can be found dangling from just about every important branch of New Zealand's post-punk family tree. Over the course of a decade and a half, he's wended his way from fronting the aggro-punk Nocturnal Projections to co-starring (with brother Graeme) in the dour This Kind of Punishment to his role as in-house tape-manipulator at the Xpressway label. It's on his solo records—and the collaborations in which he's allowed to take the reins—that the expansive sweep of Jefferies' vision can best be appreciated.

The tone of **The Last Great Challenge in a Dull World** is unremittingly bleak, but Jefferies can invest that base mood with either anger or defeat, which puts him that much further ahead of most emotional one-trick ponies. On the songs where he flies solo—like the drizzly "On an Unknown Beach"—his elegant piano shadings and flat, firm vocals are reminiscent of John Cale at his most severe. Elsewhere, members of the Dead C and Look Blue Go Purple make cameos that add a brittle rock edge—especially evident on the astringent "Cold View." The basement fidelity doesn't restrict Jefferies: on the contrary, the paucity of production draws you in close enough that you can practically feel him breathing down your neck.

Electricity proceeds in much the same manner, wending its way from introspective observations like "By Small Degrees" and "Quality" (a stately march that recalls "All Tomorrow's Parties") through nerve-jangling tape-loop experiments like "Next." Fortunately, Jefferies concentrates on the more melodious (if somber) end of things for most of the record, an approach that crystallizes beautifully on an album-ending cover of Barbara Manning's "Scissors." **A Chorus of Interludes** collects much of Jefferies' harder-to-find material, including the entire **Swerve** double 7-inch and his stirring (separate) collaborations with scene stalwart Stephen Kilroy and Straitjacket Fits' leader Shayne Carter, whose "Knocked Out or Thereabouts" is a pleasantly abrasive surprise. Cyclops is another collaborative effort, this time with Look Blue Go Purple's Kathy Bull: the duo has issued numerous singles, as well as the drunk, acid-flecked **Goat Volume** LP, all of which cleave to the essential ethos "noise annoys . . . and we dig it." [dss]

See also *Cakekitchen, Mecca Normal, Straitjacket Fits.*

JELLYFISH

Bellybutton (Charisma) 1990
Spilt Milk (Charisma) 1993

BEATNIK BEATCH

At the Zula Pool (Industrial) 1987
Beatnik Beatch (Atlantic) 1988

GRAYS

Ro Sham Bo (Atlantic) 1994

At the very dawn of the '90s, a semi-successful (if misguided) marketing approach led to brief retro-psychedelic notoriety for Jellyfish, a quirky San Francisco quartet led by multi-instrumentalists Andy Sturmer (mainly vocals and drums) and Roger Manning (mainly keyboards). While the eye-popping cover art and the band's absurdly whimsical wardrobe pushed the Summer of Love style, there's nothing remotely psychedelic about the music within. The disparity was unfortunate, because **Bellybutton** is a fine debut, a pleasant—occasionally wonderful ("The Man I Used to Be," "Now She Knows She's Wrong," the silky "Bedspring Kiss")—pastiche of pop icons from the Beatles to Squeeze via 10cc, the Beach Boys and Badfinger, smoothly produced by Jack Joseph Puig and Albhy Galuten.

A three-year hiatus resulted in half the band jumping ship, but also helped germinate a stunning new crop of Sturmer/Manning tunes. Completely wiping away any lingering whiff of psych hype, **Spilt Milk** is sharper and far more vibrant than its predecessor, with clever hooks galore. Masterfully recorded, arranged and sequenced (Sturmer and Manning joined Puig and Galuten for a four-man production committee), the disc is sophisticated enough to engender Queen comparisons. Cushioned by creamy harmonies, "New Mistake" brilliantly swirls and soars like aural tiramisu. "Joining a Fan Club" and "The Ghost at Number One" have as much spinning melodic punch as any Raspberries or Cheap Trick gem; the crisply edited "All Is Forgiven" is built around a thunderous rhythm track, while "Russian Hill" spins a more pensive, acoustic web. In a frustrating development, just as Jellyfish hit its lush apex, a simmering rift between Sturmer and Manning led to the group's dissolution late in '93.

Before Jellyfish, Sturmer and Manning had managed a first call-up to the big leagues in the generic pop foursome Beatnik Beatch. Though '87 indie effort **At the Zula Pool** was nothing to kick sand in the lifeguard's face about, it was reissued on a major a year later, with five weaklings replaced by four stronger new cuts, and still promptly sank from view.

While Sturmer and Manning have remained quiet since the breakup, **Bellybutton** guitarist Jason Falkner hooked up with **Spilt Milk** session guitarist Jon Brion (who'd toured with 'Til Tuesday, and co-produced Aimee Mann's **Whatever** album in '93), singer Buddy Judge and ex–Lloyd Cole drummer Dan McCarroll to form the Grays. Falkner's "Very Best Years," which opens this decent debut disc, sounds exactly like his old band; adding to the sense of déjà entendu, Puig produced. Although three songwriters ensure a certain degree of variety ("Not Long for This World" rocks like a punchier Church; "Friend of Mine" lopes with the haze of early Neil Young), the album is still bland, and **Ro Sham Bo** simply doesn't scale the heights of either Jellyfish record. Falkner released a solo album, **Author Unknown** (Elektra), in 1996. [gef]

See also *Aimee Mann; TPRG.*

JENNIFERS

See *Supergrass.*

JENNYANYKIND

etc . . . (No. 6) 1994
Blues of the Afflicted EP (No. 6) 1994
Mythic (No. 6) 1995

Though the group hails from the indie-rock breeding ground of North Carolina, Jennyanykind stands apart from its statemates with a sound that doesn't particularly lend itself to 7-inch singles, pogo dancing or triple-bills with Superchunk and the Archers of Loaf. Instead, the trio of bassist Tom Royal and the Holland brothers, Michael (vocals/guitar) and Mark (drums), mucks about in more psychedelic waters, spewing out the sort of trippy acid-pop skronk the early Flaming Lips excelled in, though it obviously goes back further, to antecedents like Pink Floyd, Hendrix and Quicksilver Messenger Service.

etc . . . also fits in fairly well as an American version of England's post–My Bloody Valentine space-pop. The record is both rumbling and dreamy, with most of the tension coming from Michael Holland, whose enervated vocals constantly clash with his hotwired guitar workouts; the rhythm section rolls along behind him both delicately and rudely. It's a good sound that can also be (as with most of the UK shoegazers) wan and generic. Fortunately, Jennyanykind renders the aesthetic with deftness and energy. There are murky moments, but the band generally has the chops and song strength—most notably, the riff-happy "Windchimes," the lovely "Shiny, Shiny" and the rolling "Long"—to pull it off.

Blues of the Afflicted is, as its title suggests, darker, rockist and groovy, though the somber tone is tempered somewhat by childlike touches of calliope rhythms and freaky falsetto backing vocals. Holland leans hard on his wah-wah pedal while brother Mark whacks the skins with newfound heaviosity, giving the epic riffs, slashing solos and thundering bottom end definite power. But with the exception of the whimsical "She's So Sinful," the songs aren't as good; in fact, they're barely songs.

Mythic pumps up the volume even more; the light, melodic qualities Jennyanykind had when it started are but a memory now—even the vocals are mannered and ominous. The din is of a more experimental nature, with skewed song structures, dissonant guitar tones, vaguely funky rhythm work and an overall feel of Tom Waits–style cabaret-rock strangeness. "Jellyfish" is an angst-ridden art ditty, while "The Tale of the Cigarette King" shuffles along nervously beside a tugging organ and a skittish guitar line. In two short years Jennyanykind has become both more intriguing and innovative and less likable. The band has since signed to Elektra. [jc]

JERU THE DAMAJA

The Sun Rises in the East. (ffrr/PayDay) 1994

Straight-edge Brooklyn rapper Jeru the Damaja (Kendrick Davis) puts forth "pugilistic linguistics," "verbal gymnastics," "vocabulary calisthenics," "scientifical powers" and "Mind Spray" with dry, forceful articulation on his first album, but the imaginative production by D. J. Premier of Gang Starr runs circles around his uninspired writing. A marvel of uncommon elements shaped into atmospheric tableaus (like the edgy cinematics of "You Can't Stop the Prophet" and the aptly titled "Statik"), the tracks give Jeru a fascinating and diverse playground. He strives to match the sonic diversity with an essay on cultural heritage ("Jungle Music"), a scorecard on the prevalence of evil ("Ain't the Devil Happy") and a treatise on sexual politics (the trumpet-flayed "Da Bichez," in which he divides women into opposing camps of sisters/young ladies/queens and greedy exploiters). But for too much of **The Sun Rises in the East.**, the Damaja is a drag, an average old-school boaster wearing '90s colors. The album's biggest disappointment is "Come Clean," an extraordinary offbeat construction of simple drums and echoing electronic plunks, wasted on a boring sucker-MCs rhyme that is ironically stymied by the track's elusive rhythms. [i]

JESSAMINE

Jessamine (Kranky) 1995

The neo-futurist school of drone-rock has produced a goodly number of bands able to make a fine racket, but few with the gumption to buckle down and apply their theorizing to bona fide songs. While now based in Seattle, this quartet initially formed in Galion, Ohio, a college town near the Buckeye state's center, a geographical fact that probably helps explain the decidedly Pere Ubu–styled electronics that bleat at the margins of Jessamine's electro-garage tunes. Anyone prone to involuntary episodes of astral projection should get quite a kick out of the madly oscillating, strobing sounds emitted by Rex Ritter's array of vintage gizmos—not to mention the undulating vocals by Ritter and bassist Dawn Smithson. The dynamic swoops that underscore the memorable melodies of "Ordinary Sleep" and "You Have Ugly Talents, Martha" impart a feel that's not unlike a more assertive version of Stereolab, but Jessamine's emphatically mercurial approach defies easy capture. [dss]

See also *Spacemen 3*.

JESUS AND MARY CHAIN

Psychocandy (Reprise) 1985
Darklands (Blanco y Negro/Warner Bros.) 1987
Barbed Wire Kisses (B Sides and More) (Blanco y Negro/Warner Bros.) 1988
Automatic (Blanco y Negro/Warner Bros.) 1989
Rollercoaster EP (UK Blanco y Negro) 1990
The Peel Sessions EP (UK Strange Fruit) 1991
Honey's Dead (Blanco y Negro/Def American) 1992
Almost Gold EP (UK Blanco y Negro) 1992
The Peel Sessions (Strange Fruit/Dutch East India Trading) 1992
The Sound of Speed (UK Blanco y Negro) 1993
Stoned & Dethroned (Blanco y Negro/American) 1994
Sometimes Always EP (UK Blanco y Negro) 1994
Come On EP (UK Blanco y Negro) 1994
I Hate Rock 'n' Roll EP (UK Blanco y Negro) 1995
The Jesus and Mary Chain Hate Rock 'n' Roll (Blanco y Negro/American) 1995

Fusing obvious power-pop melodies with industrial-strength guitar distortion, stuttering drum beats and caricatured lyrical perversity in a cauldron of echo and attitude, the Jesus and Mary Chain—Scottish brothers Jim (mainly vocals) and William (mainly guitar) Reid—created a modern sound so far over the top of all other "Sister Ray" jumpstarters that it became as directly influential on subsequent bands as the Velvet Underground itself. An absolutely brilliant singles band stuck behind an unflinchingly enervated and insular pose, the narrowminded duo (plus as many as three other players for live purposes) has made inconsequential creative progress over the course of a decade, raising and lowering the sonic chaos drawbridge without damage while keeping its songwriting remarkably consistent (some might say repetitive). One great idea is plenty.

Awash in feedback and fuzz, tunes and drones, wit and crude ugliness, **Psychocandy**—harsh, tense, claustrophobic, joyful—is the must-own starting point; easy-listening Brillo for troubled teens. An early demonstration of the Reids' determined anti-conformism, **Darklands** all but eliminates the sonic violence, leaving skeletal guitar-pop songs—menacingly restrained and hosed down in echo—colored only occasionally with familiar washes of woolly fuzz guitar. **Barbed Wire Kisses,** an uneven compilation of 1985–88 B-sides, live tracks, rarities, acoustic demos, remixes, outtakes and other ephemera, offers a helpful recapitulation of what the young group did in its spare time.

The lazy but entertaining **Automatic** was recorded with no assistance other than a live drummer on one song. (The clattering synth-drums are a significant problem.) No longer in search of—or shying away from—the ultimate in guitar noise, the Reids inhabit a down-the-middle loudness over which Jim can sing what have become fairly predictable lyrics. As cynical and plastic as the approach is, the brothers' incisive pop sense redeems "Blues From a Gun," the Lou Reed–ish "Halfway to Crazy" and "Head On," which borrows a venerable rock'n'roll riff and allows a bit of warped positivism into the band's perverse fantasies of self-degradation: "I'm taking myself to the dirty part of town/Where all my troubles can't be found."

The six-song **Peel Sessions** EP is notable for its first half: a February 1985 document of **Psychocandy** songs played by the short-lived quartet (with future Primal Scream leader Bobby Gillespie on drums) that originally recorded them. The rest of the live-in-the-studio disc is from November 1986 and mixes a preview of **Darklands'** "Fall" with the non-LP "Happy Place" and "In the Rain."

Beginning with the dauntingly vicious sneer—"I wanna die just like Jesus Christ"—of the jangly dance drone "Reverence," **Honey's Dead** fires a pile of great tunes down a wind tunnel of sensual guitar aggression. Sharing the vocal responsibilities sixty-forty for the first time, Jim and William kick out the venal jams like an inspired '90s T.Rex, altering the proportion of a few familiar ingredients to differentiate such winning blasts of grimy beauty as "Far Gone and Out," "Catchfire," "Rollercoaster" (retrieved from a 1990 EP), "Sugar Ray," "Teenage Lust" and the semi-gentle "Good for My Soul" and "Almost Gold." (That last song was made into an EP with three live tracks.) Able to navigate loud and soft with unwavering allure, whispery menace and irresistible pop power, the Reids demonstrate their mastery of studio dynamics on an album that almost rivals **Psychocandy** as a statement of renewed purpose. Only now they've developed a sense of humor: "Frequency" ends the album by interleaving "Reverence" and the Modern Lovers' "Roadrunner," a song of notable influence on them.

The Sound of Speed is a second B-sides compilation (covering 1989–93) from the format fetishists, whose vinyl, cassettes and CDs inevitably have substantial content differences. The twenty electric and acoustic tracks include variant versions of "Reverence," "Sidewalking" and "Teenage Lust," the band's contribution to *The Crow* soundtrack ("Snakedriver") and an assortment of other reasonably good second-shelf originals. "Something I Can't Have" and the techno-sequenced "Penetration" are entirely album-worthy; "Why'd You Want Me," plucked off the "Far Gone and Out" single, is excellent. The mellow folk-rocker has bowed string bass and refreshingly candid lyrics: "Why did you let me in?/I've got no shoes/I've always got the blues/I gave myself to drink and drugs and filth." Like **Barbed Wire Kisses, The Sound of Speed** contains typically revealing and idiosyncratic cover versions. The Temptations' "My Girl" receives touching respect in a quietly simple rendition, while Leonard Cohen's "Tower of Song" gets the full Chain-rattling treatment and Willie Dixon's "Little Red Rooster" is pulverized in a crunching all-out noise pedal festival. The 13th Floor Elevators' "Reverberation" almost comes out sounding like one of their songs, but a solid, reverent rip leaves Jerry Reed's twangy "Guitar Man" standing in Atlanta.

Letting the sonic pressure off as never before, the Reids made **Stoned & Dethroned** nearly safe for the entire family. For those familiar with the band's audio violence, the threat alone is enough; it's possible to hear these lightly delivered pop tunes, some edged in attenuated savagery, as explosions-in-waiting. That tension gives the record an effective emotional undertow. (Ignorance of the overload circuitry waiting in vain to be switched on will cause an incomplete appreciation of what otherwise appears to be a restrained batch of pop tunes.) The album's stylistic cohesion survives a bunch of studio musicians, an annotated division of labor that credits each Reid for his own songs (occasionally relegating Jim to an incidental role) and two guest vocalists: Shane MacGowan on "God Help Me" and Mazzy Star's Hope Sandoval on "Sometimes Always," a Sonny and Cher–like duet with Jim (also issued as an all-quiet-on-the-studio-front EP with two non-album tracks and a pretty remake of **Automatic**'s "Drop"). More unsettling than the album's light folk-rocky touch, however, is the sporadically upbeat mood (yeuch!) and the weakness of its material. There simply aren't enough memorable variations on the band's three-chord theme here. Four are really good ("Sometimes Always," "Never Saw It Coming," "Between Us" and "She") and a couple more are passable, but the rest of the tunes simply evaporate. The lack of songwriting spunk is fatal to such indifferent performances.

Perhaps that's why **The Jesus and Mary Chain Hate Rock 'n' Roll.** The album is yet *another* rarities compilation: four new tracks (trivial except for the title tune and the raw noise of the Stones-quoting "33 1/3") from a '95 British EP, the cinematic "Snakedriver" again, a lewd dance mix of "Teenage Lust," "Penetration" and "Something I Can't Have" (both in better-mastered versions than appear on **The Sound of Speed**) and five recent B-sides, one written by **Stoned & Dethroned** bassist Ben Lurie. Alternately acoustic and blisteringly electric, short and far from sweet, the strong set pivots on William's venomous and deliciously masochistic titular kamikaze spew, which reaches an existential breakthrough in the line "I hate rock'n'roll hates me." Other notable tracks are his fingerpicking blues "New York City," Jim's "The Perfect Crime" (from the **Sometimes Always** EP) and an almost-collapsing bash wryly entitled "I'm in With the Out Crowd." You have to know where you belong in life, and the Reids most assuredly do. [i]

See also *Primal Scream; TPRG.*

JESUS JONES

Liquidizer (UK Food) 1989 (Food/SBK) 1990
Live EP (Food/SBK) 1990
Right Here, Right Now EP (UK Food) 1990
Doubt (Food/SBK) 1991
Perverse (Food/SBK) 1993

History will record Jesus Jones as a one-hit wonder (1991's "Right Here, Right Now"), a shoe-in for the inevitable '90s retrospectives to come. The truth is that the London quintet started in an interesting place and went downhill from there, ultimately buried by frontman Mike Edwards' over-reaching sonic ambitions.

Liquidizer was an ear-catching start, however. Infatuated with American hip-hop, New York guitar noise and British dance music, Jesus Jones—named following a Spanish vacation during which natives referred to all of the musicians as Jones (the Jesus is supposed to be pronounced *Hay*-zeus)—blended all their influences into the album's busy, sample-heavy sound. The band's superior melodic intent to stylistic soulmates Pop Will Eat Itself resulted in a jacked-up blend that worked for both the ears and the feet, particularly on "Move Mountains," "Info Freako," "Bring It on Down" and "What Would You Know?" The **Live** EP, recorded in Chicago, shows the group isn't quite as good onstage—not surprising considering the amount of machinery deployed for **Liquidizer.**

Doubt doesn't have the bursting freshness of its predecessor, but it was Jesus Jones' moment in the mainstream sun. The optimistic "Right Here, Right Now," inspired by the fall of communism in the Soviet Union and other international events, is a deserving pop hit, snaking Edwards' infectious melody over a subtle but subversive hip-hop beat. "International Bright Young Thing" is another winner, but the rest of the album lacks **Liquidizer**'s propulsive joys.

Then there's **Perverse,** which enjoys the historical distinction of being the first album recorded entirely (except for Edwards' vocals) on computer. For all its sonically dense, in-your-face attack, this is one floppy-disc fusillade that flops. Form takes precedent over substance, and Edwards and producer Warne Livesey pump up the electronic fuzz tones and industrial guitar riffs at the expense of songs' character. Occasionally the tunes will out: the hushed quality of "Yellow Brown" is effective, and a firm, unfettered groove buoys "The Right Decision"; clean production and a powerful arrangement make "Idiot Stare" the album's best track. Beyond that, however, **Perverse** makes sonic rubble of Jesus Jones' already slight virtues. [gg]

See also *TPRG.*

JESUS LIZARD

Pure EP (Touch and Go) 1989
Head (Touch and Go) 1990
Goat (Touch and Go) 1991
Liar (Touch and Go) 1992
Lash EP (Touch and Go) 1993
Show (Collision Arts/Giant) 1994
Down (Touch and Go) 1994
Shot (Capitol) 1996

DENISON/KIMBALL TRIO

Walls in the City (Skin Graft) 1994
Soul Machine (Skin Graft) 1995

Few bands have sustained a sense of genuine danger for as long as this formidably malevolent Chicago foursome. Seemingly intent on crafting a soundtrack for society's collapse—or at least the world's worst bout of bedspins—the Jesus Lizard runs like a perpetual friction machine, drawing spark after spark from the conflict between the instrumentalists' tightly wound, coolly forceful approach and frontman David Yow's utterly blotto psychic suckerpunches. The band has benefited greatly from its association with Steve Albini, whose brittle, audio vérité recordings are tailor-made to capture—and exacerbate—that tension. Even more important, Yow is gifted with one of the most atonal, animalistic voices to have ever hit the rock stage: even a passing listen proves him to be living testament to the notion that hate is a many-splendored thing.

On its debut (recorded as a trio with a drum machine), the Jesus Lizard (which reuninted Texas native Yow with bassist and former Scratch Acid bandmate David Wm. Sims, following the latter's tenure in Albini's Rapeman) musters plenty of sound and fury, but only intermittently strikes sheer adrenal gold. When it does—as on a stygian revamp of Neil Sedaka's "Breakin' Up Is Hard to Do"—the queasy feeling is hard to shake. **Head** delves even deeper into the heart of weirdness, with Yow giving voice to ugly but hilarious nightmare imagery like the babble that runs through "If You Had Lips." The more unhinged his delivery gets, the cooler his bandmates play it, particularly newly arrived drummer Mac McNeilly (ex–Phantom 309, in which he played bass), whose self-possessed demeanor is reminiscent of Charlie Watts at his most implacable. The instrumental "Tight and Shiny" became a concert staple, giving Yow the chance to demonstrate his unique mastery of the testicle solo—a microphone maneuver most performers would never have the (sorry) balls to attempt. (The **Head** CD includes **Pure** as a bonus.)

On **Goat,** the quartet sinks elbow-deep into the bowels of the American nightmare, turning up all sorts of unpleasant parasites that pass unnoticed among us. Yow's disjointed couplets—at times he sounds like a preacher speaking in tongues—bounce off targets both subtle ("Rodeo in Joliet") and freakish (the antagonistic "Then Comes Dudley"). Guitarist Duane Denison no longer wields his guitar like a lawnmower, so, instead of flying sonic mulch, he comes forth with identifiably blues-based riffing that's twisted enough to underscore the music's edge but linear enough to maintain the perception that these really are slices of everyday life.

Liar substantiates its title within the first five seconds of the opener, "Boilermaker," as Yow blurts "I'm calm now . . . I've calmed down." The exceptionally violent lurches that mark the album's songs—driven by Sims' pulsing bass, which often acts as lead instrument—are made all the more formidable by the control with which they're orchestrated. Yow, on the other hand . . . well, let's just say he's intent on making his otolaryngologist a wealthy person. The wordless shrieks that punctuate tracks like "Gladiator" and "Slave Ship" hardly seem affected—on the latter, they provide a convincing counterpoint to his rantings of blistered hands, torn-off fingernails and emotional breakdown. The singer has never been more darkly humorous either, as proven by the adrena-waltz "The Art of Self-Defense," wherein he ponders the plight of a "sad, sad, sad, sad, sad pygmy" on a killing spree.

The **Lash** EP supplements a pair of studio recordings—including the shuddering "Glamorous," in which Yow froths about being pursued by "homosexual gangsters," among other emo-spasms—with four live songs that don't quite capture the intensity of the Jesus Lizard in concert. Although the performances aren't bad (other than "Bloody Mary," they're not all that great, either), the record has an off-putting sterility.

Although the Jesus Lizard once shunned major-label interest so vigorously that it's alleged they countered one potential suitor with a demand of a one-record, one-million-dollar contract (which the exec supposedly considered), the band agreed to a one-off deal for the release of **Show,** a bracing live disc recorded in December '93 during the CBGB twentieth anniversary festival in New York. Experienced on an "on" night—like this one—the quartet musters as much might as any band extant: see the ferocious one-two punch of the speed-crazed "Deaf as a Bat" and "Sea Sick." With the stage-diving Yow spending as much time flailing in mid-audience as onstage, Denison is left to fill the space with barbed-wire–wrapped Keith Richards–styled riffing (on a cover of the Dicks' "Wheelchair Epidemic" and "Puss," previously available on a 1992 single split with Nirvana) and some good'n'greasy slide playing (on "Nub"). Not that Yow cedes his ringmaster role: between offering dedications to his parents and paeans to his penis, he leaves the crowd in stitches every time.

Down explores a rather more subdued side of the band. Oh, sure, Yow still paces between riffs like a trapped animal as he yammers out his tales of emotional incarceration ("Fly on the Wall," one of three **Down** songs previewed on **Show**) and utter contempt for humanity (like the privileged-baiting "Countless Backs of Sad Losers" and the thoroughly misanthropic "50¢"). But the amount of space his bandmates give him blunts the impact noticeably. Denison's playing is both more florid and more minimal, riddled with sharp, disconnected leads (as on "Mistletoe") that supplant the claustrophobic riffing of previous releases. Although the songs, when dissected, are just as disquieting as anything the band has ever done, **Down** is the first Jesus Lizard album that could conceivably serve as background music.

After years of playing hard-to-get, the Liz took a final step off the short pier of indie-label sanctity. Following a stint on the '95 Lollapalooza, the group consummated its flirtation with major labeldom with **Shot.** Ending a career-long streak of recordings with Steve Albini, the band called upon GGGarth Richardson, who imparts a slightly glossier sound that emphasizes Sims' bass throb. Songs like "Thumbscrews" and "Skull of a German" prove Yow hasn't lost anything in terms of horror-storytelling, but his stab at "singing" (much in the manner he employed in his Scratch Acid days) is ill-advised.

The mathematically inaccurate Dennison/Kimball Trio teams the guitarist with former Laughing Hyenas/Mule drummer Jim Kimball. Together, they craft curiously tension-free improvisations that blend West Coast cool jazz and movie score atmospherics. Kimball's terpsichorean brushings prop up most of the short pieces on **Walls in the City** (particularly the snazzy "Walk Away"), since Denison seldom manages to make his note flurries coalesce. **Soul Machine** is a dramatic improvement. While still emphatically non-rock, the album reflects a willingness to wallow in the pleasures of a swinging groove. As such, pieces like the title track and a version of Ornette Coleman's "Lonely Woman" succeed in drawing the listener in, rather than eliciting coolly distant admiration. [dss]

See also *Laughing Hyenas, Mule, Pigface; TPRG.*

JOAN JETT

Joan Jett (Blackheart) 1980
Bad Reputation (Boardwalk) 1981 (Blackheart) 1992
The Hit List (Blackheart/CBS Associated) 1990

JOAN JETT AND THE BLACKHEARTS

I Love Rock-n-Roll (Boardwalk) 1981 (Blackheart) 1992
Album (Blackheart/MCA) 1983 (Blackheart) 1992
Glorious Results of a Misspent Youth (Blackheart/MCA) 1984 (Blackheart) 1992
Good Music (Blackheart/Epic Associated) 1986
Up Your Alley (Blackheart/CBS Associated) 1988
Notorious (Blackheart/Epic Associated) 1991
Flashback (Blackheart) 1993
Pure and Simple (Blackheart/Warner Bros.) 1994

EVIL STIG

Evil Stig (Blackheart/Warner Bros.) 1995

Generation gaps evidently mean nothing to Joan Jett. Following the comical but not insignificant late-'70s existence of the fake-rebel Runaways, Joan Jett was ushered into her solo career by an older generation of radical rockers—two of the tracks on **Joan Jett** (retitled **Bad Reputation** for its major-label relaunch in 1981) were produced and performed by ex-Pistols Steve Jones and Paul Cook. A dozen years later, following a hugely successful mainstream career that set her on a fast track toward middle age, the Baltimore-born singer/guitarist was rejuvenated by her welcome into a younger cadre of musical upstarts who view her as a feminist role model. These days, she seems younger than ever. The newest numbers on **Flashback,** a highly selective twenty-two-song odds'n'ends retrospective, are a live '92 performance with L7 of the Runaways' "Cherry Bomb" and 1993's "Activity Grrrl," a song Jett was inspired to write by Bikini Kill, a band she also produced. Otherwise, **Flashback** offers such intriguing items as the scrapped Pistols-backed version of "I Love Rock 'n Roll" and Jett's personalized version of the Pistols "EMI" ("MCA").

Always a contradiction of commercial accommodation and left-of-the-dial aspiration, Jett sounds unfazed by the incongruity of songwriting collaborations with both Paul Westerberg *and* Desmond Child on the slickly run-of-the-mill **Notorious.** Likewise, Jett's covers album, **The Hit List,** includes her renditions of "Pretty Vacant" and "Roadrunner" alongside AC/DC's "Dirty Deeds Done Dirt Cheap" and the Kinks' "Celluloid Heroes." Like the good Orioles fan she is, Jett keeps her eye on the ball.

Even on **Pure and Simple,** the most ambitiously uncommon album of her career, Jett can't simplify her life. While moved to unprecedented levels of boisterous energy by her obstreperous disciples—Kathleen Hanna (Bikini Kill), Kat Bjelland (Babes in Toyland), Donita Sparks and Jennifer Finch (L7) all stop by to write and play with her—she still employs the same old song-factory pros. (In one of rock's oddest culture clashes, Hanna, Child and Jett all share songwriting credit for the tunelessly hostile "You Got a Problem.") Still, a renewed sense of purpose and Hanna's random antagonism help Jett survive a daunting stack of big-league producers, and **Pure and Simple** is a punchy, no-frills collection of chunky electric guitar chords, 4/4 beats and melodically shouted choruses as catchy and cool as any in her past. Searching for a sense of place, Jett spends the album trying to deny her self-consciousness: "As I Am," "Wonderin'," "Spinster" and "Insecure" all acknowledge uncertainty and plead for acceptance—if not understanding. Her tributes to new pals ("Activity Grrrl") and murdered Gits singer Mia Zapata ("Go Home") are too oblique and awkward to convey much, but the point of her concern is well taken. Whether she is a riot grrrl or just plays one in the studio, Jett has never been better. Even her handlers might have learned something from this one. (The album, CD and cassette contain different sets of songs that suggest a careful bit of demographic calculation. Bjelland's "Here to Stay" and Sparks' "Hostility" appear on vinyl but not CD; the reverse is true for Child's shmaltz-slathered "Brighter Day" and onetime Bryan Adams songwriter Jim Vallance's wonderful "Wonderin'.")

Jett subsequently deepened her involvement in the indie-rock world and her commitment to the memory of Mia Zapata by performing three early-'95 benefit shows fronting a band with the former Gits, who had already regrouped as Dancing French Liberals of '48. **Evil Stig,** the pro temp quartet's semi-live album (the proceeds of which were marked for a fund to find Zapata's killer) consists largely of Gits songs—half of them from the 1994 **Enter: The Conquering Chicken** album—but also contains **Pure and Simple**'s "You Got a Problem" and "Activity Grrrl" (not "Go Home," *that* went to the **Home Alive** compilation), a needless remake of Tommy James' "Crimson & Clover" (the song was a hit for Jett in 1982) and a poppy Evil Stig original, "Last to Know." It's weird the way the album doesn't differentiate between the freewheeling stage work and overproduced studio efforts, but that's always been typical of Jett's not-quite-in-tune career. No matter. This gutsy, hoarse and rousing record that strikes a workable balance between the veteran's arena experience and the young'uns' raucous punk animation is an important and impressive step in Joan Jett's creative rehabilitation. [i]

See also *Gits.*

JEVER MOUNTAIN BOYS

See *Einstürzende Neubauten.*

JEWEL

Pieces of You (Atlantic) 1995

Jewel Kilcher's voice—a strong, twangy alto with a soaring high end and a coquettish wiggle in its walk—is the audible product of the young singer/guitarist's fascinating boho background. (So is her yodeling.) Raised on a rural Alaskan homestead, she shared stages with her musician parents by the age of six, attended high school at a Michigan arts academy (paying most of her own way) and followed her mother to San Diego where she became a surfer and lived by herself in a van.

Unfortunately, the story of Jewel's life is more intriguing than the painfully earnest lyrics of her songs, innocent observations that take pointed, poetically rendered stands against prejudice, sexism, religion, romantic injustice, cynicism, cruelty and the cold. (**Pieces of You** contains, agonizingly enough, a song called "I'm Sensitive.") Produced by Neil Young associate Ben Keith, recorded both in the studio and in performance at a San Diego coffeehouse, the mostly acoustic album is pretty, affecting and occasionally overbearing. [i]

JODY GRIND

One Man's Trash Is Another Man's Treasure (Safety Net/DB) 1990
Lefty's Deceiver (DB) 1992

ROCK*A*TEENS

The Rock*A*Teens (Daemon) 1996

KELLY HOGAN

The Whistle Only Dogs Can Hear (Long Play) 1996

With the potent, pliant vocals of Kelly Hogan leaping over slap bass, brush-stick drumming and acoustic guitar, the Jody Grind brought rocked-up energy and attitude to a pre–rock-era sound. The Atlanta trio's debut, **One Man's Trash Is Another Man's Treasure,** is steeped in a bebop, swing and jump blues vibe, with credible interpretations of a wide range of twentieth-century non-rock tunes: Henry Mancini's "Peter Gunn," Duke Ellington's "Mood Indigo," the Gershwins' "It Ain't Necessarily So." Even the band's originals, ranging from the hard-swinging "Eight-Ball" to the jug-band blues "My Darlin'," wouldn't have sounded out of place in a 1940s speakeasy. Fortunately, Hogan has enough vocal gusto and the band plays with enough snap and humor to make this more than just gimmicky revivalism—but just barely.

The Jody Grind expanded to a quartet for **Lefty's Deceiver,** adding bassist Robert Hayes to the original lineup of Hogan, Bill Taft (guitar) and Walter Brewer (drums). The moodier, slightly darker and more textured sound—fleshed out with pedal steel, mandolin (played by R.E.M.'s Peter Buck) and additional percussion by producer Michael Blair—makes the debut seem quaint by comparison. Such superb originals as the atmospheric "3rd of July" constitute the bulk of the album, and the band successfully attempts straight-ahead rock for the first time on "Hands of June" and "Superhero"; "Lounge Ax" blends power chords with jazzy rhythms. Hogan's agile singing again makes the biggest impression, but it's the title of a swinging little instrumental, "Blues for the Living," that underlines the band's determined transition into the now.

Just as the Jody Grind should have been celebrating this triumph, the band was shattered by the deaths of Hayes and new drummer Robert Clayton in a car crash in April 1992. Taft wound up joining Smoke; Hogan next turned up playing spelunker guitar and doing crazed out-back vocals in the Rock*A*Teens, a souped-up reverb-guzzling jalopy fronted by yelping singer/guitarist Chris Lopez (ex–Opal Foxx Quartet). The quartet's eponymous album, produced by David Barbe with singleminded purpose—using echo as a blurring tool the way other bands rely on distortion—is spring-delayed into a different time zone. If that leaves cool tunes like "Down With People," "Picks Her Teeth" and "Who Killed Bobby Fuller?" lagging behind the sonic frenzy, the swampy tension thus created gives the album a powerful hallucinatory dimension.

On her own, Hogan wears a less distracting habit: **The Whistle Only Dogs Can Hear** is a casual and sincere record that presents her as a versatile, confident, personable singer and (with help from Taft) songwriter. Rather than fix on a single style here, Hogan uses her light stylistic touch, strong voice, sensitive band support and some smart, arcane covers to tap into country ("Lucky Nights"), acoustic folk (Vic Chesnutt's "Soft Picasso"), swanky blues (Dairy Queen Empire's "Do Right"), chamber pop ("Map"), New Orleans soul ("Nothing Takes the Place of You," a song by Toussaint McCall included on the **Hairspray** soundtrack) and ragged indie-rock ("Feel Good Hit")—all without seeming indecisive. Good one. [gk/i]

See also *Smoke.*

JOHN AND MARY

See *10,000 Maniacs.*

JOHNBOY

CalYx EP7 (Undone) 1992
pistolswing (Trance Syndicate) 1993
claim dedications (Trance Syndicate) 1994

Johnboy were briefly Austin's most promising underground mayhem-makers, having caught the ear of Butthole Surfer King Coffey (who signed the band to his Trance Syndicate label) as well as the favor of then–newly arrived local hero Bob Mould. But the trio self-destructed just before the release of its second album, leaving artistic promises unfulfilled and missing out on a slot as Sugar's opening band.

Working within the same dirgey, dynamic, ear-splitting vein as some of their labelmates (as well as certain Amphetamine Reptile and Touch and Go kindred spirits), johnboy excelled at threatening aural apocalypses that are equal parts punk and art-rock, slowcore and industrial. **Pistolswing** calls to mind Big Black, or great forgotten Homestead din-mongers like Phantom Tollbooth and Honor Role. The noise produced by guitarist Barry Stone, bassist Tony Bice and drummer Jason Meade is intricately structured and even uplifting at times, achieving an imposing and chaotic beauty on songs like the snapping "pistol swing" and the well-paced, almost-catchy "sourmouth."

There's little room for friendly things like grooves or hooks amid the heaviness, and if you assume the band might have found a place for them by the second album, you'd be wrong. **Claim dedications** is a far more precise excursion, however, with sleeker guitar tones and even more intimidating metronomic force. Both albums offer the sort of pounding, spectacular construction-site guitar sludge that would be better off if the instrumental textures weren't marred by nondescript, spoken/shouted punk-rock vocals, though the impressionistic lyrics are occasionally adroit.

Since the end of johnboy, Stone and Bice have resurfaced in another Trance Syndicate band, Desifinado. [jc]

EVAN JOHNS AND THE H-BOMBS

See *Eugene Chadbourne With Evan Johns and the H-Bombs.*

MIKE JOHNSON

Where Am I? (Up) 1994
Year of Mondays (Tag/Atlantic) 1996

Where Am I? proves that there's more to Mike Johnson than his role as bassist for Dinosaur Jr. While remaining part of the Mascis fold, Johnson has always pursued his own vision—first as a member of the defunct Oregon punk combo Snakepit and, later, as the arranger, co-producer and guitarist on Screaming Trees singer Mark Lanegan's solo records. On his quietly mournful debut, Johnson follows Lanegan's lead, proffering sparse, darkly saturated songs of intimate allure. His rambling, whiskey-soaked baritone pinpoints Leonard Cohen and Kevin Ayers as equally clear influences; his selection of songwriters to cover (Townes Van Zandt, Lee Hazlewood, Gene Clark) displays an eclectic ear. Along with Barrett Martin of Screaming Trees (who serves as bassist, cellist, pianist and percussionist on **Where Am I?**) and David Krueger (violin), the guitar-playing Johnson is an understated frontman. The debut's baleful, folky sullenness suits Johnson's vocal delivery well; "100% Off," which first appeared as a 45 (added to the CD as one of two bonus tracks), finds him taking a more aggressive stance. **Where Am I?** wallows in dejection ("Save Today" and "Separation" thrive on miserable sentiments), but Johnson turns wretchedness into a positive gesture.

The same cast returns for the intermittently rocking but consistently more richly realized **Year of Mondays,** joined by J Mascis (on drums), Dana Kletter of Dish and members of Juned, whose first album Johnson produced and whose bassist Leslie Hardy is Johnson's wife. The suave calm in his voice is here illuminated by a pale dawn, broadening the appeal of an assured, gorgeous album. A bridge between adult consequence and youthful abandon, **Year of Mondays**—dedicated to Charlie Rich—is a treat for glumsters of all ages. [vg/i]

See also *Dinosaur Jr, Screaming Trees.*

DANIEL JOHNSTON

Songs of Pain [tape] (no label) 1981 (Stress) 1988
Don't Be Scared [tape] (no label) 1982 (Stress) 1989
The What of Whom [tape] (no label) 1982 (Stress) 1989
More Songs of Pain [tape] (no label) 1983 (Stress) 1988
Yip/Jump Music [tape] (no label) 1983 (Stress) 1986 (Homestead) 1989
Hi, How Are You [tape] (no label) 1983 (Stress) 1986 (Homestead) 1988
Retired Boxer [tape] (no label) 1984 (Stress) 1987
Respect [tape] (no label) 1985 (Stress) 1987 (Sp. Ay Carramba Rekkids/Munster) 1993
Continued Story [tape] (no label) 1985 (Stress) 1987 (Homestead) 1991
Live at SXSW [tape] (Stress) 1990
1990 (Shimmy-Disc) 1990
The Lost Recordings I [tape] (Stress) 1991
Lost Recordings II [tape] (Stress) 1991
Big Big World EP (UK Seminal Twang) 1991
Laurie EP (UK Seminal Twang) 1992
Happy Time EP7 (Seed) 1994
Fun (Atlantic) 1994

DANIEL JOHNSTON AND EYE BAND

Artistic Vice (Shimmy-Disc) 1991

JAD FAIR AND DANIEL JOHNSTON

Jad Fair and Daniel Johnston (50 Skidillion Watts) 1989
It's Spooky (UK Paperhouse) 1993

VARIOUS ARTISTS

A Tribute to Daniel Johnston Vol. 1–4 EP7 (Ger. Little Teddy) 1995

Between institutional stays for manic depression, pop savant Daniel Johnston has recorded a vast and remarkable body of inimitably ingenuous songs, using whatever resources were at hand: a dinky cassette machine or a 48-track studio, playing piano or guitar and singing in a boyishly vulnerable tremble. Equally disturbing in its weirdness and beautiful in its Beatlesque melodicism and loopy invention, Johnston's music is an extraordinary mixture of art and madness. But the fringe-weird product of a pitiable genius carries with it an uneasy air of freakshow exploitation. As difficult as it is to resist his innocent charms, it's no easier to view Johnston's cult-figure prominence and recent major-label contract without some concern.

Born in California and raised in West Virginia, Johnston wound up in Austin, Texas, where he began recording and giving away homemade tapes at the beginning of the '80s; the local Stress label later distributed them as inexpensive cassettes with photocopied covers of his cartoons. The collections are wildly uneven: **Songs of Pain** is lucid and stunningly incisive, casually cogent and artistically invigorating. On the other hand, **Don't Be Scared** is disjointed, a muddy transliteration of some fine songs. As musically accomplished and clear as **Songs of Pain,** the quietly harrowing and confessional **The What of Whom** rivetingly sets plaintive cries for help to tender melodies. **More Songs of Pain,** performed forthrightly on piano and voice (except for the sound of a TV announcer and a sixty-cycle hum that occasionally find their way to tape), fits a sweet version of Johnston's beloved Beatles' "I Will" amid intensely winsome originals and a jaunty instrumental. Dating from the same time but unreleased for nearly a decade, **The Lost Recordings I** is a hissy, badly edited and haphazard effort that could have easily remained out of circulation.

Johnston first reached vinyl with Homestead's 1988 reissue of **Hi, How Are You.** Despite the muffled sound and toy instruments, there's no mistaking the inspired wit and riveting honesty. "Big Business Monkey" attacks an employer with venom and clever rhymes; "I'll Never Marry," the now-classic "Walking the Cow" and "She Called Pest Control" allude to romantic problems. While "Hey Joe" rewrites "Hey Jude," the anguished autobiographical complaints of

"Keep Punching Joe" is simply sung over a big-band swing record.

The two-record **Yip/Jump Music** is more consistent in sound and style, less angry and performed almost entirely on cheap chord organ. The lyrics offer enthusiastic elegies to "The Beatles," "God" and "Casper the Friendly Ghost," while exploring personal issues in "Sorry Entertainer" and "I Live for Love." The album's standout is "King Kong," an extended and erudite a cappella plot summary and analysis.

Back in the tape-only world, **Retired Boxer** is of generally high quality, with exemplary piano playing, a reminiscence about Daniel by an unidentified acquaintance, a Christmas greeting and the moving "I'll Do Anything but Break Dance for Ya, Darling." The eighteen-song **Respect** (available in Spain on 10-inch vinyl) is also brilliant, loaded with the remorseful "An Angel Cry," a solemn cover of "A Little Bit of Soap," a grimly offbeat interpretation of "Heartbreak Hotel" and the sharply worded "Just Like a Widow."

Recorded as badly as possible, Austin's Texas Instruments give Johnston electric support on five **Continued Story** tracks (including a "Cadillac Ranch" parody entitled "Funeral Home"). Played on two guitars, "Ain't No Woman Gonna Make a George Jones Outta Me" is a left-field winner, as are Johnston's measured piano version of "I Saw Her Standing There," the rocking "Ghost of Our Love" and "Girls." There's more chaff than usual, but not enough to outweigh the good stuff. (The contents of **Continued Story** are included on the CD of **Hi, How Are You.**) The bootleg-quality **Live at SXSW** finds Daniel and his acoustic guitar enthusiastically performing his songs (a couple of them twice) at three Austin venues.

Following a joint venture with Jad Fair (who, in comparison, seems about as offbeat as an insurance salesman), Daniel released **1990:** four 1988 live tracks and a half-dozen professional studio recordings, one with instrumental assists from drummer Steve Shelley and guitarist Lee Ranaldo of Sonic Youth. (Producer Kramer plays on the magnificent "Some Things Last a Long Time," a bewitching song co-written with Fair.) Clear sound, well-recorded piano and a touch of echo on the vocals don't damage Johnston's basic virtues, but neither do they make these songs—most strongly religious—any better than they would have been on a two-dollar cassette.

During an early-'90s stretch back in West Virginia, Johnston made the wonderful and accessible **Artistic Vice** with a six-piece band, including four guitarists besides the star (who apparently had no access to a piano at Chuck Picklesimer's house, where Kramer came down to produce). The ebullient blast of lo-fi electric garage-rock begins by declaring—with conviction—"My Life Is Starting Over" and includes such enthusiastically upbeat declarations as "I Feel So High," "Hoping" ("there is a God"), "Happy Soul," "I Killed the Monster" and "It's Got to Be Good." An especially unsettling homage to his cartoon friend ("I Know Caspar"), the Rorschach recitations of "A Ghost Story" and "The Startling Facts" and several more miserable episodes in Johnston's series of obsessive love odes to the unrequited love of his life quash any illusions of mental health, but the glimmers of deliverance make this cogent album as encouraging as it is enjoyable.

Johnston might not top the short list of rock-'n'rollers least likely to be invited into the corporate boardroom, but he's definitely up there. Nonetheless, in an industry stampeded by the rise of "alternative rock," the signing of a genuine underground cult icon proved irresistible, and, after much toing and froing, Johnston wound up with an Atlantic Records contract and made **Fun** with producer Paul Leary of the Butthole Surfers. Not too surprisingly, Johnston's fragile music wilts in an atmosphere of organization, pristine sound and occasionally ambitious arrangements ("Life in Vain," "Happy Time" and "Lousy Weekend," which employ strings, are the exceptions to an otherwise spare instrumental rule). Themes and subjects that previously prompted radiant songs of broken glass from Johnston here fail to spark anything memorable ("Love Wheel" and "Silly Love" come close, though, and Leary's manic guitar storms shock "Psycho Nightmare" to life). Ignoring the butterfly-on-a-wheel circumstances of its creation, there's nothing identifiably wrong with the record, but **Fun** is—fittingly or not—the most forgettable album in Johnston's catalogue. **Happy Time,** a red-vinyl 7-inch preview of **Fun,** contains two tracks from it, an unreleased original ("Come See Me Tonight") and a wavery rendition of the Beatles' "Love Me Do."

Big Big World is a British EP containing '86 recordings: the title track, "I Stand Horrified," "December Blues" plus, on CD only, "Hard Time." The '89-vintage **Laurie** EP (a name that will register nervously with fans) also contains "The Monster Inside of Me," "Whiz Kid" and "The Lennon Song." **It's Spooky** is the belated UK issue, with bonus tracks, of **Jad Fair and Daniel Johnston.**

In addition to Texan Kathy McCarty's extraordinary 1994 tribute album, **Dead Dog's Eyeball,** there's a German-label series of four-song, four-band EPs on which assorted indie rockers do Daniel's music. **Vol. 1** features the Television Personalities and Bartlebees. **Vol. 2** stars the McTells and some lesser-knowns. **Vol. 3** has Half Japanese and the Bedlam Rovers. **Vol. 4** includes tracks by Kickstand (with Luna's Dean Wareham helping out) and the Mad Scene. [i]

See also *Half Japanese, K. McCarty, Texas Instruments; TPRG.*

FREEDY JOHNSTON

The Trouble Tree (Bar/None) 1990
Can You Fly (Bar/None) 1992
Unlucky EP (Bar/None) 1993
This Perfect World (Elektra) 1994
Freedy Johnston EP (Hello Recording Club) 1995

Freedy Johnston writes epic songs of loss and heartbreak and sings them with unassuming earnestness, as though apologizing for intruding on a private moment. He charmed his way into the hearts of rock critics with the opening line from **Can You Fly**'s "Trying to Tell You I Don't Know": "Well I sold the dirt to feed the band." Turned out this was a true story. When his first album, **The Trouble Tree,** garnered encouraging notices, the Kansas native sold his inherited family farm in order to finance the recording of a followup. He moved to New York, gathered an incredible supporting cast and recorded **Can You Fly,** an album that stands as one of the most plaintive singer/songwriter statements of the '90s—marked by gentle tempos, snake-like melodies and finely wrought observations of personal crises.

The Trouble Tree barely hints at such depth. It captures Johnston's wheedling and whiny voice in extreme close-up, forcing listeners to seek refuge in overextended wordplay and spare guitar-based arrangements. Johnston tries too hard to be clever and the effort is audible: only "Down on the Moon #1" and "Fun Ride" stand up to repeated scrutiny.

With **Can You Fly,** however, Johnston finds a way to be dramatic *and* musical. Replacing the raw angst-matter of his earlier work with a storyteller's penchant for detail, he writes of despair, the end of a relationship ("Tearing Down This Place"), love with a mortician's daughter and the metaphysics of flight, all with a wide-eyed enthusiasm. Even the simple act of dedicating a song, as captured in "In the New Sunshine," can be an occasion for discovery. This ability to transform the familiar serves Johnston musically as well: his wrenching lyrics are framed by simple guitar counterpoint and haunting, austere, extremely grounded instrumental tracks.

Johnston was snapped up by Elektra after the release of the six-song **Unlucky** EP, which includes a **Can You Fly** single ("The Lucky One," also presented in its demo form) and a surprisingly prairie-minded treatment of "Wichita Lineman." **This Perfect World,** Johnston's Butch Vig–produced major-label debut, lacks some of its predecessor's punch but nonetheless shows plenty of poetic growth. He sounds downright comfortable singing in non-rock contexts: the mournful title track, one of several concerned with suicide, is built around acoustic guitar and cello, while "Gone Like The Water" exhibits the easy affability of a country picnic. The ballad-heavy album's single, a medium-tempo confession entitled "Bad Reputation," stands as a classic pop hit that wasn't. [tm]

HOWARD JONES

Human's Lib (Elektra) 1984
The 12-Inch Album (UK WEA) 1984
Dream Into Action (Elektra) 1985
Action Replay EP (Elektra) 1986
One to One (Elektra) 1986
Cross That Line (Elektra) 1989
In the Running (Elektra) 1992
Working in the Backroom (UK Dtox) 1993
The Best of Howard Jones (Elektra) 1993

English new wave techno-pixie Howard Jones assembled his massively popular career from humanist philosophy, chart smarts and electronic keyboards. Using instruments that, in the mid-'80s, were generally favored for their mechanical anonymity, the Southampton native created bouncy, warmhearted missives of personal encouragement and general goodwill. This likable ex-hippie may very well have been the new age's first pinup popster.

Human's Lib ("New Song," "What Is Love?") and **Dream Into Action** ("Things Can Only Get Better," "Like to Get to Know You Well") are the essentials of the canon. (**The 12-Inch Album** assembles hits in their remixed form; **Action Replay** collects alternate versions and remixes.) **One to One,** produced by Arif Mardin with a full complement of backup musicians, and the melancholy, overly ambitious **Cross That Line** are both dispensable. All four of Jones' '80s albums are fairly represented on the exhaustive 1993 retrospective, as is **In the Running,** a fussed-over years-in-the-making tribute to Jackson Browne (or Tears for Fears; it's hard to tell). Using loads of live musicians to load up the panoramic production, Jones—who remains a solidly appealing songwriter through it all—comes up with a bland mainstream record that sounds far more artificial than his rudimentary old synth-pop efforts.

Jones' most intriguing project of recent years is **Working in the Backroom,** self-released and sold at his shows. The liner notes explain the modest, home-made album as a compilation of technically imperfect demos—of course, his proficiency is such that this stuff is equal to most Top 40 artists' highly polished perfection. Still, the absence of studio intricacy allows the typically well-crafted originals to breathe as they haven't in ages. Beyond the pleasure of hearing a major star rediscovering the joyful essence of his art, some of these optimistic songs are as ingenuously winning as the old standards. (Incidentally, for those who still have their old scrapbooks, Jed—the terpischorean with whom Jones performed early in his career—now teaches dance in England.) [i]

JOYKILLER

See *True Sounds of Liberty.*

JPS EXPERIENCE

See *Jean Paul Sartre Experience.*

JUICY

For the Ladies (Slow River) 1994
Olive Juicy (Slow River) 1996

Without making a big political issue out of it, New York/Boston's Juicy wades right into the charged world of enlightened relationships on its sparkly guitar-pop debut. Thanking "all of our super-talented rocker friends and ex-boyfriends for the inspiration," Juicy—guitarist/singer Kendall Meade, guitarist/singer Lisa Marafioti, bassist Jen Levin and drummer Meggean Ward—plays simple, alluring love-rock that sounds alternately like a female Pooh Sticks working without a producer and a four-piece Beat Happening. Plainspoken and puckish on the brief **For the Ladies,** Juicy reclaims some dignity in the wake of being dumped ("Fuck You I'm Cool"), gripes about the embarrassing behavior of a friend's "Psycho Ex-Boyfriend," ruminates atmospherically about being "Sad," attributes a sexual encounter to being "High" and gets an unexpected thrill from the itinerant "Rocketboy." Juicy isn't about to resolve any of the great issues in the war between the sexes, but getting these melodic shots in is to the benefit of all.

Olive Juicy, produced by Wharton Tiers, finds Juicy slimmed down to a one-guitar three-piece (minus Marafioti) but unwavering in its conceptual dedication: "True Love Tomorrow?" and "Sourheart" are just two of the new dozen. There's also a wry cover of Don Henley's "The Boys of Summer" for good measure. [i]

JUNED

See *Kill Sybil.*

JUNE OF 44

See *Rodan.*

JUNGLE BROTHERS

Straight out the Jungle (Idlers/Warlock/Gee Street) 1988
Done by the Forces of Nature (Warner Bros.) 1989
JBeez wit the Remedy (Warner Bros.) 1993

"Educated man from the Motherland," begins Afrika Baby Bambaataa on the Jungle Brothers' debut album, putting these charter members of the Native Tongues posse on the Afrocentric tip way before it was cool. Expanding on Grandmaster Flash's concept of the inner city as a jungle (sometimes), New Yorkers Mike G, Uncle Sam and Baby Bambaataa turned it into a defining metaphor.

Straight out the Jungle contains a few landmarks—the house riff of the groundbreaking club hit "I'll House You" bravely defied rap's prevailing homophobia, while "Jimbrowski," a droll exercise in phallic idolatry, almost singlehandedly popularized the term. But despite strong entries like "Because I Got It Like That" and "Sounds of the Safari," several duff tracks diminish the album, while the vestigial old-school beats and rapping style leave the rest sounding dated.

Not so on the group's artistic breakthrough, **Done by the Forces of Nature.** Armed with a fatter, denser sound, the JB's lose the drum machine and move on to funky sample loops, their rampant creativity making for highly musical hip-hop. Proud, smart, playful and just plain good-hearted, the album radiates an upbeat spirituality, continuing on the righteous Afrocentric tip with jams like "Acknowledge Your Own History," "Black Woman" and the densely polyrhythmic manifesto "Tribe Vibes." The sampling of the funk canon is consistently ingenious, drawing on African music and a miscellany of other sources as well; there's endless rhythmic invention in the irresistible beats *and* rhymes that quote everyone from George Clinton to Jesus. The group continues to incorporate outré sounds like disco ("What 'U' Waitin' '4'?"), while the title track and the hilarious "Kool Accordin '2' a Jungle Brother" prefigure the jazz-rap trend by several years. The funky "Good Newz Comin" strings together everything from gospel choirs to Blue Swede, then gives way to a joyous *soukous*-style breakdown. Largely overlooked, **Done by the Forces of Nature** is one of rap's finest hours.

After a long spell away from the studio (except for some film soundtrack work), the Jungle Brothers reemerged with the disappointing **JBeez wit the Remedy.** With its harder and more aggressive sound, the album simply doesn't have the creative spark or infectiously happy-go-lucky vibe that distinguished **Done by the Forces of Nature.** Instead, there's sampled gunfire and talk of "niggas" and "not trustin' nobody." It's hard to believe this is the same group that declared (on **Straight out the Jungle**) that "the Jungle Brothers are about surviving. And helping others to survive." Apparently, when such an outlook became passé, the Jungle Brothers succumbed to fashion. And that's a damn shame. [ma]

K

PAUL K (AND THE WEATHERMEN)

Patriots (Shrunken Stomach) 1988
The Big Nowhere (Hol. Cool Tunes/SilenZ) 1992
The Killer in the Rain (Hol. SilenZ) 1992
The Blue Sun (Homestead) 1993
Blues for Charlie Lucky (Hol. SilenZ) 1993
Garden of Forking Paths (SilenZ) 1994
Corpus [tape] (Shrimper) 1995
Coin of the Realm (Fiasco) 1995
Achilles Heel (Thirsty Ear) 1995
Now and at the Hour of Our Death, Amen (Ger. Glitterhouse) 1996

Paul K is one of the post-punk generation's first bona fide bluesmen, a guy whose tales from the darkside are drawn from his own experiences as a reformed junkie and small-time criminal with the jailhouse record to prove it. Throughout the mid-'80s, the Louisville, Kentucky, native (né Kopasz) released dozens of home recorded cassette albums, but the one-time winner of a debating scholarship hamstrung his own progress by living a lifestyle sufficiently shadowy that he ended up a New York squatter pulling small-time stickups to make ends meet. That was then.

Whatever his personal predicament, Paul K's paradoxically world-weary and mystically sanguine mindset—a fusion not all that different from unambiguous influences like Townes Van Zandt—seldom wavered. Although the alternately temperate and wired **Patriots'** dizzyingly moodswings—from the rootsy working-man's lament "Landfill Blues" to the side-filling seventeen-minute title track—make for difficult sledding when taken in one sitting, the individual elements signal good things to come.

And come they do on **The Big Nowhere,** a mostly acoustic set recorded without his on-again/off-again backing band, the Weathermen (no relation to the techno group of the same name): drawing considerably from literary sources (most tangibly on the stealthy, ghost-in-the-machine saga "Robespierre"), K spins yarns as detailed as they are venomous. In the process of indicting slumlords ("The Arson Biz") and sociopathic social climbers ("Too Many Yakking Passengers"), he moves from observer to frontline soldier in a class war he knows is hopeless, but feels compelled to fight anyway. Gut-wrenching stuff.

The presence of a full complement of Weathermen isn't the only thing that makes **The Killer in the Rain**—a title that, like its predecessor, points up the inspiration Paul K takes from the dark detective fiction of writers like Raymond Chandler and Jim Thompson—such a visceral release. A clenched-teeth sense of desperation practically grabs you by the lapels from the onset of the opening "The Third Day Is the Worst," not only in the form of K's stiletto-sharp guttersnipe observations, but also in the acutely wracking post-Hendrix guitar scree he strews across the hardscrabble rhythms of songs like "Highway Zero." But in exemplary bluesman fashion, he ducks away from the hellhounds on his tail long enough to beg absolution on the outlaw hymn "Sacred Mud."

The Blue Sun, culled from K's cassette archives, resounds with an even greater urgency than his "proper" albums. By alternating incendiary pieces like the title track (as rending an approximation of withdrawal—emotional or pharmacological—as you're likely to hear) with ghostly quiet tracks like "Haunt Me 'Til I'm Gone," K is able to take listeners on an emotional rollercoaster ride that's utterly depleting. **Blues for Charlie Lucky,** another solo recording, is even darker than its antecedents, thanks in large part to the almost rakish manner in which the singer/guitarist struts through catastrophic tales like "Black and Blues" and the downright hysterical "Nicotine Psychos Blues." Few players can wring the sort of distortion displayed on the suicidal "Stop the Film" from an acoustic guitar without losing a foothold in folk tradition, a tradition Paul pays respects to by performing "John Riley"—and twists by annexing William Blake's mystical epic "Jerusalem."

There's a steely dignity at the core of **Garden of Forking Paths,** a disposition that's all but nonexistent in these post–post-modern times. Greeting the onset of maturity with decorum rather than nails dug into the last shreds of adolescence, K splits his time between acknowledging past failures (the album-opening "Stone in My Shoe" begins by conceding "We failed/We fucked up/Now it's time/To live our lives more quietly") and reaffirming his mistrust of the system (as on the unruffled "To Win Is to Fail"). The Christian subtext of previous releases is more overt this time, as evidenced by the ecstatic "7 Gates to the City" and a cover of David Olney's recovered-cynic allegory "Jerusalem Tomorrow"—but the searing guitar work that rends the latter song is a guaranteed restorative, whatever your faith.

Judging by **Coin of the Realm**'s tone, Paul K seems to have come to a personal peace. Not that its seven songs betray a great deal of happiness per se: it's just that he's concentrating less on private demons than on the universal ones addressed in the sneering, render-unto-Caesar title track and the seething "Pillar of Salt." That timbre carries over to **Achilles Heel,** on which the current Weathermen lineup stays at a gritty simmer from end to end. Paul's populist philosophies—detailed in both "Roses for the Rich" and "Internet Worm"—are typically trenchant and nicely set off by the corrosive black humor that emanates from tracks like the anti-ironist rant "Rerun." He also pays tribute to Van Zandt, eking every last drop of emotion from that writer's fallen-angel lament "Tecumseh Valley."

He may not be a boxcar-riding troubadour, but Paul K is just about the only credible proponent of the drifter's-eye-view of the world we have left. For that alone, he is to be treasured.

Now and at the Hour of Our Death, Amen is a live album—half solo acoustic, half with a band—recorded in Lexington in February '96 and released the following month (!) in Germany. [dss]

BRENDA KAHN

Goldfish Don't Talk Back (Community 3) 1989
Epiphany in Brooklyn (Chaos/Columbia) 1992

New Jersey–born singer/songwriter Kahn begins her first album with nothing more than brushed drums and a wise insight—"I don't know nothing 'bout singing the blues/I got no holes in my pockets, rips in my shoes/But I got a heart that's heavy." That striking introduction leads to an otherwise inconsistent collection of clever topical anti-folk and folky-rock originals. Kahn's voice works best in gentle, jazzier settings; challenged with string bass, light drumming and her own hearty guitar strumming, a loss of control obscures the nicer qualities of her singing.

Those nicer qualities are largely absent from **Epiphany in Brooklyn,** an album so melodramatically oversung that Kahn could be auditioning for the Ethel Merman part in some Broadway-does-folksingers production. Even the tender and intimate "My Lover" and "Lost" get out of hand at pivotal junctures, revealing not just Kahn's indelicacy but her unstable pitch. Producer David Kahne does little to improve or obscure the elemental guitar/voice delivery: a little cello here, some mandolin there, an economical rhythm section to give several songs a little drive. The onetime mixologist pours a lot of her personal observations in bars, making a blend of the scuzzy and artistic that rivets reality to her like an old coat. But it all sounds like demos, offhand efforts of a moderate talent lacking the tools to adequately deliver her finely observed thoughts. [i]

KARP

Mustaches Wild (K) 1994
Suplex (K) 1995

Having little more than geographical proximity and the overdrive settings on their amplifiers in common with the Melvins, Karp—a trio from Tumwater, Washington—has nonetheless repeatedly been compared to Buzz's clique by dint of its unmitigated squalling. **Mustaches Wild** lets rip with fast, assailing shitstorms of guitar noise, frantic screaming and flailing percussion—ugly, shapeless and poorly recorded. "Valley of the Kings" effectively breaks the gruesome mold with an atmospherically refined instrumental intro and a segment of wispy, quiet vocals before the cruelty begins, but that's as good as it gets.

Suplex is a different story. Not only does the album extend the courtesy of printed lyrics—revealing some imagination in the tales of consumerism ("Pic," "Treats to the Soul") and roller derby history ("Connect 5"), as well as random collections of epigrams ("Shotzie," "Absolutely Fibulous" and "Lorch-Miller," which takes two-and-a-half minutes to reach the first vocal line)—the band's ungodly power surges have been channeled into effectively semi-tight riff exercises. Between the amplitude modulation, pummeling songs that occasionally do more than start and stop the semi-understandable singing, **Suplex** takes a giant step in the right direction. [i]

KATHLEEN TURNER OVERDRIVE

See *Drivin' n' Cryin'*.

MATT KEATING

Tell It to Yourself (Alias) 1993
Satan Sings EP (Alias) 1993
Scaryarea (Alias) 1994

Keating can easily be pigeonholed in that neo-singer/songwriter slot alongside Matthew Sweet and Freedy Johnston, among others; at a glance, his '90s twentysomethingness is almost archetypal. (His voice works against him too, somewhat stiff and nasal, like a young Jackson Browne.) What makes him worth watching is that, while continuously complaining, he finds ways to be engaging about it, either by sheer quality or by virtue of an intriguing (lyrical or musical) spin. **Tell It to Yourself** tilts toward the former ("Sanity in the Asylum" and "Show Me How" are instant grabbers). The album contains the pick of the songs he amassed after leaving Boston and his former group, Circle Sky, to follow his songwriting muse to New York, and was cut with the help of guitarist Kevin Salem and Circle Sky's old drummer, John Sharples.

Scaryarea takes a step backward and a step forward: less accessible tunes more forcefully presented. The backing tends less to blandness and more to bandness than on the debut: Keating (guitar, co-production), Adam Lasus (bass, co-production) and Joel Stone (drums) form a tight unit that can musically match the frequently jarring lyrical woes, as on "(I Thought I heard My) Head Exploding" and "Your Other Face." (For color, Chris Murphy adds fiddle or mandolin to five tracks, and lap steel guitarist Eric DelaPenna and Salem stop by, too.) Keating's pursuit of ambitious lyrical ideas and rhyming schemes is erratic, though the hits (viz. the dyspeptic, dopey brilliance of "McHappiness": "a quarter life with cheese") are largely worth enduring the misses. If he sticks around long enough, he just might transcend any facile bracketing completely.

The EP contains the LP version of "Sanity," a demo of a second LP track and three live acoustic guitar renditions of songs from the first album. [jg]

TOMMY KEENE

Strange Alliance (Avenue) 1982
Back again (Try . . .) EP (Dolphin) 1984
Places That Are Gone EP (Dolphin) 1984
Songs from the Film (Geffen) 1986
Run Now EP (Geffen) 1986
Based on Happy Times (Geffen) 1989
Sleeping on a Roller Coaster EP (Matador) 1992
The Real Underground (Alias) 1993
Ten Years After (Matador) 1996

Like so many other talented American power-pop energizers, Tommy Keene has neither lost faith in the magic of brash/sensitive tuneful music nor enjoyed any appreciable commercial success from it. A versatile guitarist, gifted songwriter and appealing singer, the Bethesda, Maryland, native graduated from Washington DC's new wave Razz (which also contained bassist

Ted Nicely, who was a stalwart sideman to Keene while becoming an eminent producer on his own). He went solo at the start of the '80s and has been releasing sterling records on and off ever since. An underappreciated member of the southeastern fraternity that includes Matthew Sweet, Chris Stamey, Don Dixon, Tim Lee and Mitch Easter, Keene spent some '90s time on the road in Velvet Crush, but returned to his own career in mid-decade with **Ten Years After,** the first new full-length to bear his name since the end of a major-label fling in 1989.

For those who haven't been following the story from the beginning, **The Real Underground** looks like a Keene best-of but isn't. The album draws from only two previous records, and is predominantly made up of otherwise unreleased tunes. In addition to all six songs on **Places That Are Gone** and the two studio numbers on **Back Again (Try . . .),** the twenty-three-song collection includes top-quality leftovers of various vintages, including outtakes from the five-song **Sleeping on a Roller Coaster.** (The informative and enthusiastic liner notes don't precisely detail the material's sources, but given Keene's modest and steady approach over the years, it hardly matters.) Highlights include "Places That Are Gone," "The Real Underground," "Mr. Roland," "Dull Afternoon," "Hey Man," the Who's "Tattoo" (sung over solo guitar) and a precise full band re-creation of the Flamin Groovies' "Shake Some Action."

Taking tips from the louder, punkier pop enthusiasts who have come of age since he was young, Keene replaces guitar jangle with a lush fuzz roar on **Ten Years After,** recorded as a trio by Adam Schmitt. Armed with original songs that are as winningly tuneful and incisive as ever (and an unlisted Who cover at the end), Keene manages the calculated and potentially hazardous sound shift confidently, raising the energy level of his singing without blowing his top. A timely and tasteful update of Keene's reliable skills, **Ten Years After** handily cleans the clocks of those who know the style but can't deliver such high-quality substance to it. [i]

See also *TPRG.*

KATELL KEINEG

O Seasons O Castles (Elektra) 1994

VARIOUS ARTISTS

Straight Outta Ireland (Scotti Bros.) 1992

Welsh-born, Scottish-bred and currently living in Ireland, Katell Keineg somehow reflects each of those landing points (and a few American ones besides) in her hauntingly textured, wildly emotional music. She's a singer/songwriter by trade—**O Seasons O Castles** has its share of relationship-disintegration songs, including the pelting "Franklin" and the more metaphysical "The Gulf of Araby"—but she's also a bit of a musicologist, and her interest in Irish folksong and jazz-vocal phrasing give the Fred Maher–co-produced album surprising depth. Keineg was signed after two songs ("Hestia" and "Destiny's Darling") circulated on the **Straight Outta Ireland** compilation; she chose not to rerecord those tracks for **O Seasons O Castles.** [tm]

SEAN KELLY

See *Samples.*

SCOTT KEMPNER

Tenement Angels (Razor & Tie) 1992

Between the end of the Del-Lords in 1990 and the formation of the Little Kings with rock'n'roll great Dion DiMucci in 1995, Bronx-born singer/guitarist Scott ("Top Ten") Kempner maintained his membership in the sporadic Dictators, toured with the big-in-Europe Brandos and made **Tenement Angels,** a thin but appealing solo album, with the instrumental/production aid of Missouri's Skeletons. Consistent with his work in the Del-Lords, the album has an easy-going urban roots-rock sound— '60s AM radio given a heartland kick, a taste of country and a little musical poetry. That approach goes a ways toward keeping the hard emotional times potently described in "Bad Intent," "Livin' With Her, Livin' With Me," "Lonesome Train" and "Love Among the Ruins" from dragging the album down too much. Likewise, a cover of the Reflections' optimistic 1964 hit "(Just Like) Romeo and Juliet" and a couple of goodtime originals further cut the tension, allowing Kempner to burn in the flame of love and escape with nothing more than a few singed feathers. [i]

STEPHEN KENT

See *Trance Mission.*

KEPONE

See *Gwar.*

KEROSENE

Arrhythmia (Sire/Warner Bros.) 1993

Another entrant in the British export parade of would-be chart bands like Ned's Atomic Dustbin and EMF, this Manchester quintet formerly known as Collision erects a sheer roaring-guitar firewall on its first album (produced for post-Nirvana America by Dinosaur Jr pal John Agnello) and uses it to hang up moral-compass lyrics like "Shame," "Worthless" and "Mercy." Singer Paul Taylor has a plain, adequate rock voice that doesn't provide much contrast to the audio backdrop, but songs thoughtfully geared for group singing (especially "Excess" and "Everybody's Icon," a Carter the Unstoppable Sex Machine–like satire on superstar egos: "If I didn't exist/Who would they look up to?/I'm bigger, I'm better, I'm stronger, I'm faster than them") go a long way toward making **Arrhythmia** better than the average modern pop wildebeest. [i]

TARA KEY

See *Antietam.*

KICKING GIANT

January [tape] (Loose Leaf) 1989
Boyfriend Girlfriend [tape] (Loose Leaf) 1990
Secret Teenage Summer [tape] (Loose Leaf) 1991
Present [tape] (Loose Leaf) 1992
Halo (Spartadisc) 1993
Alien i.D. (K) 1994

It is one of the odd ironies of minimalist indie-pop that bands that make the simplest, most unpretentious music often package it with maximum complication and obscurity, as if they still had something to hide (or dress up) after exposing themselves so haphazardly on tape. Formed at art school in New York but relocated in mid-career to Olympia, Washington, Kicking Giant—guitarist/singer Tae Won Yu and drummer/singer Rachel Carns—occupies a place of honor in the fanzine pop underground as talented and confirmed DIY diehards who issued the bulk of their work on homemade cassettes and compilations (much humbler than vinyl) before ever putting out a CD.

Folded inside a foot-square red-and-black credits sheet packed in a six-inch clear plastic sleeve with a tiny loose lyric booklet (too big for the CD shelf and too small to file safely among singles), the laser-ready **Halo** draws most of its material from the pair's prior tapes. Like other underpopulated combos, Kicking Giant occasionally falls into the noisemaking trap, filling space with undirected energy, as on the chaotic "Go Girl (Riot)" and the muffled "Throw." But more often than not, **Halo** is a charmer, lo-fi pop in which imaginative playing sketches out highly appealing songs that don't sound wanting for additional density. Carns is an adequate beat-keeper who knows when to keep her hands to herself; Yu maneuvers his guitar between foursquare power ("Satellite"), punky abstraction ("Fuck the Rules"), feedback sculpture ("13.13.13."), delicate pointillism ("If Not You") and all of the above ("This Sex"). Their singing is strictly casual love-rock adorable, but missed notes don't injure the spirited catchiness of kicky declarations *d'amour* like "Halo," the nicely harmonized "Rocket" and "Wierd."

Alien i.D., essentially Kicking Giant's first real album, comes in a regular CD jewel box with an unreadable hash of typography. Relatively consistent med-fi sound and far more expansive musical ambitions allow the group to explore audio effects (the skeletal "A Blonde's Blonde"), droney fingerpainting ("Inside Out Flower"), sharp-edged art-rock ("The Town Idiot," narrated by guest vocalist Sue P. Fox) and flat-out roaring noise devastation ("Serrated Edge"). The straightforward pop songs are actually more of a problem: the pretty "Appetite" and the harsh "Drownings" are fine, but others leave the feeling that bits are missing. Kicking Giant is not going quietly into the real world. [i]

KICKSTAND

On Training Wheels [tape] (no label) 1991
Wheelie [tape] (no label) 1992
Kickstand (Queenie) 1994

FLYING SAUCER

Real EP7 (TeenBeat) 1991
A Place EP7 (Homestead) 1992

Grasping the judicious logic that minimalist pop singing is most safely showcased at minimal volume levels, Hoboken's Kickstand plays it Sunday-morning gentle on **Kickstand,** a tonedeaf but actually delightful twenty-three-track opus that includes nine songs from the prior (and incrementally punkier) cassettes and one from a Clean tribute EP. Skillfully weaving together hushed guitar strums (Jeff Feuerzeig, in real life a film director responsible for the excellent Half Japanese documentary, *The Band That Would Be King*), subliminal bass plunks (Tammi Colichio, who has designed artwork for records by many cool bands, including Codeine, the Breeders and Gumball) and brush-tapped drums (Torry Colichio, who, like her twin sister, doubles on one-finger Casio), the trio is hindered only by the Colichios' key-bending vocals. The Undertones' "Teenage Kicks" proves surprisingly well-suited to a spare shimmerpop rendition (complete with lead guitar by Jad Fair here), but it's hard to appreciate that insight between ear-tingling melody cringes; original numbers (and a cover of Young Marble Giants' "Colossal Youth," with organ by Caroline Azar of Fifth Column; ex–Flying Saucer Torry has drummed in Fifth Column as well) fare much better but still present a challenge to pitch-sensitive listeners. Meanwhile, on his occasional spotlights, Feuerzeig manages an impressively collected imitation of Beat Happening's Calvin Johnson. Strolling calmly through the forest of twee with a consistent sense of stylistic purpose and diverse arranging ideas, Kickstand is never cloyingly coy or precious; the group grips and pushes its delicate inventions with helpful confidence. Despite a bad habit of letting simple wisps of genuine songcraft drone on for three or four minutes, the delectable melodics of "How to Make a Girl Cry," "Magic," "Wish Upon a Star," "Full Moon" and "Take the Highway" make such breath-holding pleasurable. [i]

See also *Fifth Column.*

KID FROST

Hispanic Causing Panic (Virgin) 1990
East Side Story (Virgin) 1992

LATIN ALLIANCE

Latin Alliance (Virgin) 1991

FROST

Smile Now, Die Later (Ruthless/Relativity) 1995

King of the low-riding rhymers, Los Angeleno Kid Frost (Arturo Molina, Jr.) brought hip-hop home to Mexican-Americans in 1990 with a potent single, "La Raza." That coolly devastating declaration of ethnic pride—rapped in a dead-serious bilingual whisper over a groovalicious late-night sax track—leads off and closes **Hispanic Causing Panic,** a likable album that just doesn't contain enough other numbers like it. "Come Together" has the cool sound and positive unity lyrics, "Homicide" goes halfway and "Ya Estuvo," sparked by rollicking harmonica wails, teaches a lesson by translating Spanish verses into English to satisfy a curious onlooker. The rest of the album, while easy enough to roll through, reveals Frost's alter-ego voice—ordinary and unaccented—and says nothing that hasn't been on a hundred other records.

Latin Alliance, the soundalike work of a Frost-led collective of local Hispanic hip-hoppers (A.L.T., Markski, Lyrical Engineer), is a topical album that peaks with his inevitable rapped-up cover of War's "Low Rider" but also includes appealing rhymes about identity, undocumented aliens, community unity and social dangers. Other than the fast-flowing Hip Hop Astronaut, who drops an invigorating breakout jam over busy conga drums in "Valla en Paz (Go in Peace)," the Kid's preeminence goes unchallenged here.

Frost pops the conceptual clutch for **East Side Story,** sketching out a loosely told saga—in slang-packed raps, old soul songs and audio drama scenes—of a Chicano victim of police racism who winds up in jail and slips deeper into "Mi Vida Loca." (The fact that the MC switches from first to third person doesn't make it any more cohesive, but the idea is plain enough.) While several producers surround him with compelling busy-bass music, Frost reverts to his best *c'mere-lemme-get-wit'-you* voice, interpreting himself for an out-of-town trip in "These Stories Have to Be Told" and "Another Firme Rola (Bad Cause I'm Brown)," adapting Bill Withers' "Ain't No Sunshine." talking over the Persuaders' "Thin Line Between Love and Hate," even jousting across the cultural divide with a dancehall toaster in "Home Boyz." More musically than dramatically compelling, **East Side Story**—hip-hop with a bright mind, a good heart and a stylistic difference—is the one to hear.

So it's doubly dismaying to hear Frost make like a dumbass gangsta on **Smile Now, Die Later,** a truly mixed-up, muddled-up mess recorded with maximum pretension for Eazy-E's label. Rapping slang in a voice that quotes 2Pac and alternately apes Ice-T and Warren G, Frost (with production by A.L.T., Cold 187um from Above the Law and others) tries a bit of everything—except what made **East Side Story** cool. There are swoony female soul vocals and G-funk boomin' beats, a guest appearance by Rick James (!) and flamenco guitar, lurid crime melodrama and "La Raza Part II." "You Ain't Right," rhymed over "You're No Good," paints grim first-person portraits of various ne'er-do-wells without comment and then slags off drive-by gang-bangers; "How Many Ways Can You Lose a Body" makes a joke of corpse disposal. Bury this one with it. [i]

DAVID KILGOUR

Here Come the Cars (NZ Flying Nun) 1992
Spiritual Gas Station EP (NZ Flying Nun) 1994
Sugar Mouth (NZ Flying Nun) 1994
First Steps and False Alarms (Ajax) 1995

STEPHEN

Dumb EP (NZ Flying Nun) 1990
Radar of Small Dogs (NZ Flying Nun) 1993

If David Kilgour had done nothing more than co-lead the brilliant New Zealand pop band the Clean, his legacy would already have been assured. Throw in his collaboration with brother (and fellow Clean-mate) Hamish in the underrated Great Unwashed, his brief stewardship of the short-lived but excellent group Stephen and his membership in the great one-off cover group the Pop Art Toasters, and his career looks even more impressive. And that's even before you get to his solo work.

Kilgour's first album under his own name, the gorgeous **Here Come the Cars,** proceeds logically from prior endeavors. Employing the rhythm section from the Strange Loves, he delivers a baker's dozen tunes without a single stinker in the bunch. Predictably, many of the songs recall Kilgour's straight-ahead guitar-pop work with the Clean ("Fine," "Spins You Round"), but others, particularly the crystalline title track, show a slower, more contemplative side that he'd previously kept under wraps. Catchy, multi-textured and thoughtful all the way through.

Spiritual Gas Station is an unnecessary EP that includes two tracks from **Here Come the Cars** and three more from his then-forthcoming **Sugar Mouth,** which rendered **Spiritual Gas Station** redundant when it appeared a few months later. **Sugar Mouth** offers more of the same pop finery displayed on **Here Come the Cars** and seems almost effortless in the process. You don't have to be a jangle-rock fan to appreciate the craftsmanship evident in great songs like "Fallaway," "1987" and the extremely Clean-like "Crazy," all of them loaded with beautifully impressionistic little guitar touches. This is the work of a clear-eyed pro with all his skills at their peak.

First Steps and False Alarms consists of twenty demos Kilgour recorded between 1987 and 1992, a few of which he later fleshed out with Stephen and on **Here Come the Cars.** The relaxed, loosely structured feel of the proceedings invites comparisons to his work in the Great Unwashed, and the album is generally far stronger than most similar odds'n'sods collections. While Kilgour's solid but unspectacular lyrics have never ventured too far beyond the fairly rote confines of love and alienation, his devotion to superior songcraft makes him a major talent. [pl]

See also *Clean.*

KILLDOZER

Intellectuals Are the Shoeshine Boys of the Ruling Elite (Bone Air) 1984 (Bone Air/Touch and Go) 1989
Snakeboy (Touch and Go) 1985
Burl EP (Touch and Go) 1986
Little Baby Buntin' (Touch and Go) 1987
12 Point Buck (Touch and Go) 1988
For Ladies Only (Touch and Go) 1989 + 1990
Uncompromising War on Art Under the Dictatorship of the Proletariat (Touch and Go) 1994
God Hears Pleas of the Innocent (Touch and Go) 1995

When they first appeared on the scene, this Madison, Wisconsin, trio wanted folks to believe they were moonshine-swillin', small-mammal–torturin' dudes who did a lot more than just *kiss* their cousins. They validated those impressions with a sound reminiscent of the most primitive country blues imaginable impaled on shards of Birthday Party distortion. Having exhausted that shtick, however, Killdozer returned to exhume their *real* roots—on the wrong side of the tracks in one of the few American burgs to have fallen under socialist rule this half-century. Whether quoting from *The Communist Manifesto* or *John Wayne Gacy's Big Book o' Fun,* Killdozer never sheds its smirk.

Breaking a lengthy silence with the agitprop-sleeved **Uncompromising War on Art Under the Dictatorship of the Proletariat,** Killdozer displays a lineup change (guitarist Paul Zagoras having supplanted Bill Hobson, whose brother Dan still holds court from the drum throne) and a philosophical shift as well. Such concerns as police-community relations (the crux of the blistering "The Pig Was Cool") usurp unadorned pigfuckery as the band's main theme, although Killdozer can still deliver a punchline (like the cover of Humble Pie's "Hot 'n' Nasty") with the best of 'em. (The CD includes **Burl.**)

Steve Albini's recording lends a dry, audio vérité quality to the discomfiting slices of life that make up **God Hears Pleas of the Innocent.** Singer Michael Gerald so totally immerses himself in the protagonists of "Porky's Dad" (a farmer on the verge of losing the family spread) and "A Mother Has a Hard Road" (matriarch appraising her dysfunctional brood) you'd swear he was playing host to itinerant spirits. Technophobes take note: you and yours will chortle heartily at the snarky instrumental "Paul Doesn't Understand Jazz." (Killdozer disbanded in '96.) [dss]

See also *TPRG.*

KILLER SHREWS

See *Gary Lucas.*

KILLING JOKE

Almost Red EP (UK Malicious Damage) 1979 (UK Island) 1981 (EG) 1990
Killing Joke (Malicious Damage/EG) 1980
what's THIS for . . . ! (Malicious Damage/EG) 1981
Revelations (Malicious Damage/EG) 1982
Ha EP10 (Malicious Damage/EG) 1982
Fire Dances (EG) 1983
Night Time (EG/Polydor) 1985
Brighter Than a Thousand Suns (EG/Virgin) 1986
Outside the Gate (EG/Virgin) 1988
The Courtald Talks (Invisible) 1989
An Incomplete Collection (EG) 1990
Extremities, Dirt & Various Repressed Emotions (Noise International/RCA) 1990
Laugh? I Nearly Bought One! (EG/Caroline) 1992
Pandemonium (Big Life/Zoo) 1994
BBC in Concert (UK Windsong) 1995
Willful Days (Blue Plate) 1995
Democracy (Zoo) 1996

ANNE DUDLEY AND JAZ COLEMAN

Songs From the Victorious City (China/TVT) 1991

MURDER INC.

Murder Inc. (Invisible) 1992 (Futurist/Mechanic) 1993
Corpuscule EP (Invisible) 1992

FIREMAN

Strawberries Oceans Ships Forest (UK Parlophone) 1993 (Capitol/EMI) 1994

US AND THEM

Symphonic Pink Floyd (Point Music) 1995

Emerging at the tail end of '70s punk, a time when bands like Wire, the Fall, Public Image and Gang of Four were experimenting with the very structure of rock, British nihilists Killing Joke went a step further, adding noisy synthesizers to the overpoweringly brutal attack. Clearly prefiguring industrial rock of the late '80s, the Joke spat out an ominously energetic melding of the organic and mechanical: Geordie Walker's hypnotically dissonant guitar patterns melded with synth washes and trance-like rhythms informed by tribalism, funk and dub reggae. Atop it all sat the savagely strident vocals of neo-pagan jester Jaz Coleman, spouting images of technological decay and paranoia.

Following the unrefined **Almost Red** EP, the band's eponymous debut—a convincing depiction of audio apocalypse—is chock full of viciously intense anthems like "Wardance," "Requiem" and the dance-floor missile "Change." The followup, **what's THIS for . . . !,** is nearly as terrific, emphasizing drummer Paul Ferguson's insistent, implacable beats on "Follow the Leader" and "Tension."

While quite a few individual numbers on **Revelations** shine ("Empire Song," "The Hum"), taken as a whole, the album suffers from an uninvolving lethargy; Conny Plank's monochromatic production doesn't help. Their Armageddon paranoia reaching its apogee, Jaz and Geordie fled to Iceland before the record's release, and bassist Youth (Martin Glover) left to pursue production projects (he ended up becoming one of the decade's most prolific remixers), effectively ending the band's first era.

Presaged by the jaunty "Birds of a Feather" non-LP single and the convincing 10-inch live EP **Ha,** a brighter, more joyous fervor caught the superb **Fire Dances,** as Walker's complex chordings and catchy fills cascade through songs like "Let's All Go (To the Fire Dances)" and the ferocious "Frenzy." The upward spiral continued two years later with **Night Time,** a superior effort—smart and sonically sophisticated—which includes two incredible singles: the lush, spacious, danceable yet torrid "Love Like Blood" and the stomping "Eighties," later the basis of a tiff with Nirvana, who nicked its ominous bass riff for "Come as You Are."

Brighter Than a Thousand Suns moves further in the "Love Like Blood" direction, muting the guitar thrum and tribal rhythms in favor of moody electro-beats laden with swelling synth washes and elegiac vocals. Not classic Joke, but quite enjoyable. **Outside the Gate,** however, is an abominable and obvious attempt at slick commercialism. Gaudy keyboard arrangements swamp the atypically anemic guitar, the band's energy is nonexistent and Coleman's lyrical frothings on bombast like "America" seem forced. Killing Joke wisely broke up. **BBC in Concert** documents parts of two live shows (from '85 and '86) by the quartet; the set list includes "Love Like Blood," "Requiem," and "Tension."

Perhaps inspired by all the new industrial bands aping their early style, Killing Joke re-formed for a tour, demonstrating new resolve to recapture the old formula. The addition of drummer Martin Atkins (Public Image/Brian Brain/Ministry/Pigface) helped; he provided the group with a visceral punch. Bassist Paul Raven, who'd replaced Youth after **Revelations,** rejoined just in time for the recording of **Extremities, Dirt & Various Repressed Emotions.** The album has all the intoxicating intensity and righteous fury missing from **Outside the Gate** mated to a more timely Ministry-like feel. The throbbing juggernaut "Money Is Not Our God" and the scalding pound of "The Beautiful Dead" are primed by Atkins' powerful drum work and Walker's scorchingly obtuse riffs, though the relentless metallic roar eventually proves numbing.

The Killing Joke name was retired again, as Walker, Raven, Atkins and Ferguson went on to work as Murder Inc., with John Bechdel on keyboards and a laconic-sounding Chris Connelly taking Jaz's spot on vocals. Recorded by Joke fan Steve Albini and released on Atkins' label, the sextet's viscous drones on **Murder Inc.**—"Last of the Urgents," "Hole in the Wall"—are at least comparable to Killing Joke (particularly Walker's pernicious guitar), if nowhere near as memorable. The album was later reworked and reissued by Mechanic, deleting "Mrs. Whiskey Name" and adding two new tracks. The EP contains Foetus remixes. Several Murder Inc. participants have recorded with Atkins' main project, Pigface; Raven later joined Prong.

For his part, Coleman conducted classical symphonies from his home base of New Zealand and recorded an ambitious Middle Eastern orchestral record with composer (and former Art of Noise keyboardist) Anne Dudley. Based on the duo's impressions of Cairo, **Songs From the Victorious City** has Jaz playing violin, "cobra pipe" and flute, conducting a large assemblage of traditional Egyptian musicians on pieces ("Minarets and Memories," "Ziggarats of Cinnamon") that owe equal structural debts to Arabic and Western classical traditions, buttressed by electronic pop beats and snatches of vocals.

Among his countless projects (one of which, Brilliant, inadvertently gave rise to the KLF), Youth made **Strawberries Oceans Ships Forest,** an anonymous (literally and figuratively) record of lightweight ambient techno sound collages with Paul McCartney, as the Fireman. Youth and Coleman later teamed up (the former as producer, the latter as arranger) to confront another classic rock dinosaur, Pink Floyd. Using the London Philharmonic Orchestra as their paintbrush and **Dark Side of the Moon** and **The Wall** as their gouache, the reformed rebels turn psychedelic headphone trips into bombastic elevator music, a quintessential exercise in baby boom marketing, complete with uproariously self-important liner notes by both guilty parties. (According to Jaz, the "solo peasant violin [in 'Money' is] to remind us of a forgotten quality of life.")

Amazingly, Killing Joke—Jaz and Geordie—reformed yet again in 1994, this time reclaiming the group's rhythmic roots through the return of original bassist Youth. (Only drummer John Dunsmore is new.) Led by the engrossing minor hit "Millennium," **Pandemonium** is a significant upgrade from **Extremities, Dirt & Various Repressed Emotions.** It really sounds as if Youth had never left—his cyborg bass throb fits like an iron glove around the stable core: Walker's blindingly dissonant chord shapes and Coleman's tyrannical shouts and doomsday themes. The crunching title track illustrates how Coleman's affection for Middle Eastern scales yields a Zeppelin-like rock result; those elements meld regally with Tangerine Dream–state synthesizer on "Labyrinth," while the exhilarating techno-drive of "Whiteout" shows their acolytes how a Joke is properly told.

This time, the reunion took hold long enough to yield a second album with the same four-piece lineup. The vigorous-sounding **Democracy,** however, is the wrong kind of joke—either Midnight Oil with a raspy singer or James Hetfield attempting to hijack U2—complete with inane lyrics about "Prozac People," "Intellect" and "Another Bloody Election." Vote with your feet.

Laugh? I Nearly Bought One! is a commendable overview of the band's first decade, with some notable omissions: a few obscure tracks take the rightful place of more essential choices, and **Fire Dances** isn't represented at all. **An Incomplete Collection** is simply a boxed set of the first five full albums; **The Courtald Talks** is an interview disc. The most recent Killing Joke anthology, **Willful Days,** assembles a baker's dozen 12-inch mixes, B-sides, rarities and otherwise unavailable material. [gef/i]

See also *Chris Connelly, Crush, Ministry, Pigface, Prong; TPRG.*

KILL SYBIL

Fairlane EP7 (eMpTy) 1992
Kill Sybil (eMpTy) 1993

JUNED

Juned (Up) 1994
Every Night for You (Up) 1996

As a historical note, Seattle quintet Kill Sybil—initially just Sybil, the name under which the group issued a 1991 single—once had future Hole batterer Patty Schemel sitting on its drum throne. (Her brother Larry Schemel was one of the band's two guitarists.) Her drumming on two tracks, however, is not the best feature of the band's lone album. **Kill Sybil** boasts impressive three-dimensional sound and tempers the rage of punk hormones with bright pop tunes that could have been snatched from tweepoppers like Tiger Trap. Frequently resembling Hole's **Live Through This** (which it predates) in presence if not temper, **Kill Sybil** is better than good in every department other than Tammy Watson's unsteady lead vocals. And even that problem is successfully addressed with overdubbing. Additionally, Stevescott Schmaljohn of Treepeople joins his moonlighting bandmate, drummer Eric Akre, to sing "Broken Back," and guitarist Dale Balenseifen takes the mic for "Something to Tell." Except for a brief blurt of in-concert incoherence, the songs have shape, substance and dynamic variety ("Best" even waxes gently atmospheric before unleashing its power); the guitarists' furious strumming layers unconventional chords into intriguing textures and then punctures them with noisy solos. Best of all, there's more diverse melodicism than should be expected from such an energetically clamorous band. Even when the music is jumping around wildly, Kill Sybil keeps its feet on solid ground.

Balenseifen subsequently formed Juned (the name is allegedly skatepunk slang for getting fucked over and learning something from it, a process that undoubtedly fed into songs here like "Leeches," "Sick Smile," "Shallow" and "Deserve It"). Though unafraid of rocking out when need be, the all-female quartet—which, in an odd small-world coincidence, includes bassist Leslie Hardy, who was briefly in Hole directly before Kristen Pfaff—is more purely pop-minded and even-keeled than Kill Sybil, and the better for it. In its darker hues, the record summons up a powerful early-'80s UK new wave vibe, like Echo and the Bunnymen or early Cure. But the jazz/folk allure in Balenseifen's voice (with occasional harmonies by ex–My Diva guitarist Claudia Groom and drummer Lenny Rennalls) nicely counterweights the thoughtfully determined electric strumming, a bristly, pretty rush of mildly unconventional chord patterns and abruptly changing rhythms. Dinosaur Jr bassist Mike Johnson co-produced and plays guitar on two songs.

Every Night for You is a startling improvement, a finely played and sung album of alluring textures that would be hard to peg for its indie (not to mention punk) roots strictly on its sound. Coming on like the Cranberries with the Edge as lead guitarist, Juned and Johnson don't so much explore the parameters of their soft new surroundings as luxuriate in them. Though the dreamy singing and rich (but firmly propulsive—these women are no shoegazers) guitar arrangements are irresistible, the songs are frustratingly two-dimensional, revealing little beyond their fine surfaces. The breezy "Hearts to Bleed," "Kyuss" and "Possum" are notably superior, but things like "Titanic," "Evynd's Lullaby" and the prog-rock instrumental "Sisters of the Red Sun" never expand on their initial impressions. A great leap forward, but Juned still has some room to grow. [i/ja]

See also *Hole, Mike Johnson, Treepeople.*

KING BUZZO

See *Melvins.*

KING CRIMSON

Discipline (Warner Bros.) 1981
Beat (Warner Bros.) 1982
Three of a Perfect Pair (Warner Bros.) 1984
The Compact King Crimson (EG) 1987
Frame by Frame: The Essential King Crimson (EG/Caroline) 1991
The Abbreviated King Crimson: Heartbeat (EG/Caroline) 1991
The Great Deceiver (Live 1973–1974) (EG/Caroline) 1992
The Concise King Crimson (EG/Caroline) 1993
The First Three (EG/Caroline) 1994
Vrooom EP (Discipline) 1994
Thrak (Discipline) 1994

ROBERT FRIPP AND THE LEAGUE OF CRAFTY GUITARISTS

Live! (Editions EG) 1986
Show of Hands (Editions EG) 1991

TOYAH & FRIPP

The Lady or the Tiger (Editions EG) 1986

SUNDAY ALL OVER THE WORLD

Kneeling at the Shrine (EG) 1991

ROBERT FRIPP

1999 Soundscapes Live in Argentina (Discipline) 1994

A quarter-century after first introducing the world to the highbrow art-rock of King Crimson, and a decade after disbanding the group for the *second* time, English guitarist Robert Fripp unretired it (he'd been active with other things) as a double trio with three returning sidemen (guitarist/singer Adrian Belew, Stick player/bassist Tony Levin, drummer Bill Bruford), drummer Pat Mastelotto (ex–Mr. Mister) and Stick player Trey Gunn, the last two of whom had been in the band Fripp and David Sylvian took on tour in '93.

A gutsy half-hour document of the new Crimson's first fortnight of rehearsals, **Vrooom** is an impressively accomplished work in progress: the descending instrumental theme for which the EP is titled is fully formed, gripping in its complex rhythmic drive and hair-raising in its dynamic twin-guitar details. (A distractingly delayed snare that surfaces a few minutes in was later rethought, but the piece's content proceeded undisturbed in any noticeable ways.) Likewise, the Belew-verbalized "Sex Sleep Eat Drink Dream" and the tropical "One Time" are most of the way there and don't sound very different from the **Thrak** tracks. Some adjustments were subsequently made to "Thrak," another wordless extravaganza, and the dramatically mounting (but never quite ending) instrumental wryly titled "When I Say Stop, Continue" is just a rough sketch for the album's "B'Boom." Any other band with Crimson's aspirations would die to make an album this amazing; for Fripp, it's just a warmup.

In its ultimate form, **Thrak** is an absolute monster, a cerebral sextet adventure stunning in its precisely controlled rock power. The numbers Belew sings (the Beatlesque "Dinosaur," "Walking on Air," "People," the two previewed on **Vrooom** and two others) move things along and provide accessible oases, but the album is really about the group's stupendous instrumental workouts. Fripp's role (at least as it appeared on the group's subsequent tour) is extremely low-key, leaving the melodic heavy lifting to MIDI-man Belew and the two Stick players. Still, it's the flawless egghead complexity of the entire company—dipping toes into chromatic jazz but clinging to the eccentric rock core that has always centered King Crimson, making it all sound improvised (which it most assuredly is not)—that gives **Thrak** its fervent, ferocious majesty. Among modern musicians, Fripp has a unique concept of how to pique listeners' intelligence; the dichotomy of bludgeoning, tonally and rhythmically challenging volume exercises and fussy exactitude, of ideas lovingly framed and then brutally detonated, makes the new old King Crimson one of the liveliest and most provocative outfits of the '90s.

For some back-catalogue history, **Frame by Frame** is a lavish and thorough boxed retrospective (dwarfing 1987's skimpy **Compact King Crimson**): three chronologically grouped discs of studio material and a fourth of live tracks. **The Abbreviated** and **The Concise** are, respectively, a pointless sampler-plus-medley and a futile fourteen-cut précis of the box. **The Great Deceiver** is a second four-disc set, this one of tracks recorded live by the early-'70s band. **The First Three** merely boxes the band's initial longplayers: **In the Court of the Crimson King** (1969), **In the Wake of Poseidon** (1970) and **Lizard** (1970).

Gunn, who has also made solo albums, was evidently a favorite pupil at Fripp's guitar school in West Virginia; he appears on **Show of Hands,** the second of Fripp's student-played albums. Unlike the mid-'80s **Live!,** the intricate massed acoustic-guitar compositions—all of which strive to emulate the maestro's nitpicky inventions anyway—are primarily the disciples' own. Gunn also shares the rhythm section chores in Sunday all Over the World, a quartet with Fripp and his wife, English rock singer Toyah Willcox. **Kneeling at the Shrine,** a belated followup to **The Lady or the Tiger,** is a typically careful but ultimately unhappy ménage of Fripp's rarefied guitar excursions, a stylishly spacious Japan-like bottom and Willcox's alternately soulful and Kate Bush–y vocals. Not jazz, not pop and not fine art, it's a load of good intentions and exquisite performances in search of a focal point. [i]

See also *Adrian Belew, Brian Eno, Orb, David Sylvian; TPRG.*

KING KONG

Old Man on the Bridge (Homestead) 1991
Funny Farm (Drag City) 1993
Me Hungry (Drag City) 1995

If simplicity is a virtue, then Ethan Buckler must be a saint. The Louisville native (and Slint alumnus) has clearly pored over the gospel according to Jonathan Richman, but the manner in which he evolved from nascent noise-rock demigod to prince of the sort of pop that would be as comfortable in a preschool or nursing home as a smoky bar room is truly unique.

When Buckler formed King Kong in the late '80s, his objective was to get back to rock's true roots—which he perceived as the blues. As a result, **Old Man**

on the Bridge seldom strays from traditional blues structures or subject matter—aside from pillaging the Stones' catalogue for a serviceable rendition of "I'm Free." When Buckler and his cohorts (bassist Darren Rappa and drummer Rich Schuler) grind out their own take on the music, it's a friendly, front-porch version redolent of the bluegrass country surrounding their home base: "Lifesaver Blues" breezes along with nary a hint of strife, but "Business Man" gives off just enough "Yankee go home" reticence to ring true.

King Kong then underwent a rethink as drastic as anything since the Modern Lover swapped tales of psychotic co-eds for evaluations of what really *does* make the ice cream man tick. With its herky-jerky rhythms and kitschy organ flourishes (by newcomer Britt Walford, the drummer of Slint), **Funny Farm** bears more than a passing resemblance to the B-52's' early days—an analogy furthered by the decidedly Cindy Wilson–ized vocal harmonies Amy George drizzles over "Island Paradise" and the frankly touching "Dirty City, Rainy Day." It's Buckler who really steals the show, however, with his deadpan delivery of such *Rain Man*–worthy sketches as "Uh-Oh" and a title track that rings uncomfortably authentic.

Me Hungry regresses even further. A concept album that seeks to explore the inner caveman in all of us finds Buckler stripping down his communicative abilities to little more than grunts and monosyllabic prattle ("Me scared, me excited . . . must climb tree"), while Amy Greenwood (née George) provides a real-time aural libretto. The shtick can get tiresome, but when the backing tracks groove (as on "Animal" and the agreeably goofy "Beastie Bear"), it's possible to suspend disbelief. Still, if you've seen *Clan of the Cave Bear,* there's probably little need to climb into this wayback machine. [dss]

See also *Slint.*

KING MISSILE (DOG FLY RELIGION)

Fluting on the Hump (Shimmy-Disc) 1987
They (Shimmy-Disc) 1988

KING MISSILE

Mystical Shit (Shimmy-Disc) 1990
The Way to Salvation (Atlantic) 1991
Happy Hour (Atlantic) 1992
King Missile (Atlantic) 1994

JOHN S. HALL & KRAMER

Real Men (Shimmy-Disc) 1991

In the '60s, college professors attempted to prove that the best rock'n'roll lyrics were, in fact, poetry. In the '90s, self-declared poets gamely attempted to prove that they could be rock'n'rollers. Rather than attempt to prove either right or wrong, the most prudent course is to declare victory and withdraw from the battleground.

John S. Hall deserves a good chunk of the credit/blame for spearheading New York's electric poetry movement. After parting company with guitarist Dogbowl (his musical partner on **Fluting on the Hump** and **They**), Hall shifted the emphasis of his work from wimpy indie-pop singing to the wry, offhand shaggy-dog pieces he had word-tested on tracks like **They**'s "Fish" and **Fluting**'s "At Dave's." He hooked up with guitarist Dave Rick (Phantom Tollbooth/Bongwater/B.A.L.L.) and keyboardist/bassist Chris Xefos (When People Were Shorter and Lived Near the Water); with the band's moniker trimmed short for **Mystical Shit,** Hall makes do with fewer melodies while demonstrating an omnivorous taste for prurience ("Gary & Melissa," which details a couple's sexual explorations) and religion ("Jesus Was Way Cool").

In a quizzical pre-Nirvana bout of major-label alternaweird enthusiasm, Atlantic signed King Missile, who made **The Way to Salvation** as a quartet (using drummer Dave Ramirez, on loan from Hypnolovewheel) with strong musical ideas caroming between Rick and Xefos. Their inventions—propulsive, but shaped as much for loosely structured soundtrackery as verse/chorus song form—are custom built for Hall, whose singing and talking are equally rooted in dry self-amusement at nothing in particular. His prose is less poetry than truncated and smugly pointless short stories; amusing but ill-suited for repeated spins. The closest the album comes to pop transcendence is "My Heart Is a Flower," a thick guitar'n'organ summer-of-love psychedelidrone that Hall recites as if he were auditioning for an off-Broadway play. (Incidentally, the randiness suggested by the title of "Sex With You" is a joke, which Hall erodes by adding to his short list of primal needs over Rick's wah-wah wailing.)

Happy Hour nails it. In songs like "Detachable Penis," "The Evil Children," the comically exaggerated film fandom of "Martin Scorsese" ("I wanna chew his fucking lips off and grab his head and suck out one of his eyes and chew on it and spit it out in his face and say thank you for *all of your fucking films*") and the let's-have-a-riot whaddayagot? anomie of "It's Saturday," Hall's surreal accounts have the vivid sense of purpose previously absent; he's not aiming at eliciting wan smiles, he's trying to provoke intelligent thought. Meanwhile, the band (drummer Roger Murdock is that new face in the booklet photo) locks into diverse rock grooves that would be worth hearing even without the vocals. Excellent.

Losing sight of the line between nonsense and rubbish, Hall indulges in elliptical word games on **King Missile** and—thanks to his imploring whine, bored condescension and forced contrivances—winds up sounding like Jerry Seinfeld fronting They Might Be Giants. The music is unassailable (Rick does his part with several hair-raising noise-fuzz-wah-guitar solos), but—with the exception of "The Dishwasher," an extraordinary multi-leveled evocation of the post–stress syndrome crime-fearing urbanites endure daily—the album draws close to self-parody. Aiming to scuff away the vocals/music division and reintegrate a regular wiseass rock group from the pieces, King Missile shoots a hole in its soul. [i]

See also *Kramer, When People Were Shorter and Lived Near the Water; TPRG.*

KING'S X

Out of the Silent Planet (Megaforce/Atlantic) 1988
Gretchen Goes to Nebraska (Megaforce/Atlantic) 1989
Faith Hope Love (Megaforce/Atlantic) 1990
King's X (Atlantic) 1992
Dogman (Atlantic) 1994
Ear Candy (Atlantic) 1996

It's an oversimplification to say this distinctive trio's music took five steps to go from trumpeting the "Power of Love" in near-anthemic terms to ranting

"Go to Hell" in unprintable ones—but not by that much. Along the way, King's X established a voice, virtually lost it and then partially regained it, evidently by getting pissed off that they'd lost it in the first place.

Formed in 1980 in Springfield, Missouri, as the Edge, the trio moved in '85 to Houston, where former ZZ Top associate Sam Taylor became their manager, inked them to the alternametal Megaforce label and began co-producing their records. One factor that set them apart from run-of-the-mill hard-rock/metalers—and apparently made it tough to procure a major-label deal—is that bassist/lead vocalist Doug Pinnick is black. What's more, many of his lyrics are written from a clearly Christian perspective (a stance endorsed by guitarist Ty Tabor and drummer Jerry Gaskill). Actually, most of the words aren't specifically religious, seldom preach and are frequently thoughtful, evocative—even sensitive. (**Out of the Silent Planet,** and the song of the same name on **Gretchen Goes to Nebraska,** were titled in honor of the Christian sci-fi novel of that title by C. S. Lewis.) Add the unusual blend of influences—Hendrix, Metallica and Free, but also the Beatles, British prog-rock, black gospel—and you have a potent plan for eluding a mainstream pigeonhole.

The trio's first two LPs did just that, although it was the mainstream's loss: strong bass counterpoints powerful drums, guitars slash, crunch, chime and wail, high-harmony vocals surround the confined yet sincere soulfulness of Pinnick's voice—all of which (and more) might happen in a single song: "In the New Age" and "Wonder" on **Out of the Silent Planet** and "I'll Never Be the Same" and "Send a Message" on **Gretchen Goes to Nebraska.** On both albums, melodies are often derived from, or embellished by, great slithering riffs, creating a tantalizing contrast, tension even, between their precision and the guitar and vocal passion. The debut is simpler and a tad more ponderous, the second (with better sound) is ambitious enough to blend in elements like pipe organ (played by Taylor) and Tabor's sitar, dulcimer and wooden flute. Both albums grow in stature with repeated listening.

Problems crop up on **Faith Hope Love**—unnecessary codas and sonic extras (recorder, cellos, french horn, additional backing vox) that come across as overkill rather than clever adornments. The lyrics are more ham-handed, even pushy. Generally, the killer riffs and bluesy chords are harder to find. The harmonies sound less like the Fab Four and more like blanded-out Crosby, Stills and Nash. Some may have been dismayed by the anti-abortion sentiments of "Legal Kill"; "Mr Wilson" appears to be an oblique statement against capital punishment. "Its Love" finally garnered the group airplay (and not undeservedly), but it's clearly a trivialization of the group's virtues.

King's X finds the band off Megaforce, with Taylor getting co-writing credit on all songs and acting as sole producer. Though less bloated than **Faith Hope Love,** it's even more trivial; the only standouts, "Lost in Germany" and "Black Flag" (not about the band), would have been minor treats on either of the first two albums.

The trio signaled its new beginning—Sam Taylor had been sent packing—by kicking **Dogman** off with the title track, an aggressively ugly, crunching blues. The disc isn't quite the step up that *should* have followed **Gretchen:** the songs take too long to kick in, and producer Brendan O'Brien's live-in-the-studio approach yields sub-par sound, not particularly crisp and lacking a solid bottom. But the lyrics are back to early quality levels, if almost unremittingly negative: "The just and the unjust all walk side by side . . . is it a blessed thing to live? . . . sometimes I think the pain blows my mind." That doesn't even include "Go to Hell," a minute of catchily cathartic punk rant with electronically muddied vocals and no printed lyrics. The standout, tucked between the grindcore-meets-the-blues of "Black the Sky" and "Don't Care" (which sounds like a surly outtake from **Silent Planet**), is the stunning "Fool You." The band's bitter disappointment is given vivid, dimensional life by the anthemic, brilliantly arranged music. Varying the tone somewhat are the knowing escapism of "Pretend" and the self-mocking humor of "Complain." "If I could find my magazine this bug would die."

Dogman must have purged the band's bile, because **Ear Candy** is, hands down, the most consistently "pretty" album King's X has made. It's wreathed in gorgeously plangent guitars and full vocal harmonies. The band's reorientation doesn't sacrifice energy or presence, though; even on such a laid-back album, the trio still kicks ass, as on the adrenalized opener, "The Train." The lyrics are hardly fluff, either. Beyond the wistful reminiscences (Tabor's "Mississippi Moon") and hard-earned lessons ("A Box"), the songs crystallize new, mature stances. Received religious "wisdom" gets the treatment in "Lies in the Sand (the ballad of . . .)" and "Run." The punchy yet touching "Picture," about Pinnick's rapprochement with his father, and "Life Going By," which subtly shifts from simple memories to implications of empowerment and responsibility, affirmatively close out an album that may be as close to **Gretchen** as they can now get. [jg]

KEVN KINNEY

See *Drivin' n' Cryin'*.

KITCHENS OF DISTINCTION

Elephantine EP (UK One Little Indian) 1989
Love Is Hell (UK One Little Indian) 1989 (One Little Indian/Rough Trade) 1990
Strange Free World (One Little Indian/A&M) 1991
The Death of Cool (One Little Indian/A&M) 1992
Cowboys and Aliens (UK One Little Indian) 1994 (One Little Indian/A&M) 1995

If not actually in the stylistic company of such dream-pop bands as Lush and Ride (no My Bloody Valentine influence here), South London's Kitchens of Distinction at least traffics in a similar aesthetic, thanks to the delayed, swirling, lost-in-space playing by the king of effects, guitarist Julian Swales. Led by singer/bassist Patrick Fitzgerald (no relation to the similarly named '70s English anti-folkie), the trio's majestic sound seems to vibrate and ooze—particularly at wall-shaking volumes, as evidenced by some killer live B-sides.

Love Is Hell is a naïve start but, at its best, a minor knockout. "In a Cave" showcases Swales—twinkling, glistening, ravishing—as do "Prize" and the punchier "The 3rd Time We Opened the Capsule." But it's on **Strange Free World,** the trio's masterpiece, that its sonic vision is fully realized. Producer Hugh Jones is the perfect partner, as his skill at capturing ferocious guitar sound catches Swales shimmering and sliding from all corners of the room. Such sweeping tunes as "Quick as Rainbows" and the manic dance propulsion of "Drive That Fast" are filled with lofty beauty and quiet passion. The sweet horns on the closing "Under the Sky, Inside the Sea" add a smart new wrinkle.

Although Jones does another exciting production job on **Death of Cool,** the formula is beginning to wear a little thin. (Few would have noticed if this had been released as the second half of **Strange Free World.**) But what it lacks in stylistic variety and consistent songwriting (a couple of dull eight-minute epics meander aimlessly), it makes up for with some of the band's finest compositions. The paralyzing "4 Men," underpinned by a dense layer of shivering Swales fabric, indulges Fitzgerald's homoerotics (the singer is openly gay; "Breathing Fear" tackles gay-bashing). The opening horror-of-romance-lost "What Happens Now" batters forcefully, powered along by drummer Dan Goodwin; the Swales-sung "Can't Trust the Waves" has a lovely, starlight-kissed glow.

The self-produced **Cowboys and Aliens** reveals the group losing its songwriting touch. While Fitzgerald continues to sketch poignant breakup feelings ("Now It's Time to Say Goodbye," the adrenaline-rushing title track), the shortage of hooks makes this the least of their fine albums. [jr]

KITTEN

See *Free Kitten.*

KLŌVER

Feel Lucky Punk (Mercury) 1995

For rockers looking to bag a major-label record contract in the first months of **Dookie**-time (that's 1994 by the regular calendar), a c.v. with a credible punk past was as good as gold. Active 'core vets who had developed their pop sensibilities rather than drug habits, metal aspirations or tattoo collections stood a good chance of being swept through the Green (Day) door and getting to take a swing at ringing the chart bell with powerful tunes and historical grit.

Klōver has its roots planted in the mighty tradition of Boston's Bud-guzzling skatepunks, Gang Green, in guitarist Chris Doherty and drummer Brian Betzger. (Geography might explain the quartet's choice of cover song on the reasonably good **Feel Lucky Punk:** the Real Kids' sturdy "All Kindsa Girls.") Mohawked singer/guitarist Mike Stone has a Mike Ness–like presence, offering the same kind of simpleminded populism and rebel anger that initially fueled Social Distortion's rockets. In the Clashy "Our Way," he identifies the target group: "We're the radiation generation/When I was born I wish I'd known/Mom and dad got the meat . . . and we got the bone." Likewise, "I Wanna Be" makes the standard demand for self-determination, but "YRU (Still Here)" redirects the animosity from parental/social to peer/personal. Served up as charged rhythm-guitar rock anthems, "Our Way," "Beginning to End," "Sandbag" and "I Wanna Be" let the punk-pop flag fly, unaffected by its long stay in storage. Jimmy Pursey would have been proud. As of early '96, however, Klōver had folded and Gang Green was back in action. (Incidentally, another veteran of Gang Green—guitarist Chuck Stilphen—currently leads the band Scratch with his bass-playing brother Glen.) [i]

KMFDM

What Do You Know, Deutschland? (Ger. Skysaw) 1986 (Wax Trax!) 1990 (Wax Trax!/TVT) 1993
Don't Blow Your Top (Wax Trax!) 1988 (Wax Trax!/TVT) 1993
UAIOE (Wax Trax!) 1989 (Wax Trax!/TVT) 1993
Naïve (Wax Trax!) 1992 (Wax Trax!/TVT) 1993
Money (Wax Trax!) 1992 (Wax Trax!) 1993
Angst (Wax Trax!/TVT) 1993
Naïve—Hell to Go (Wax Trax!/TVT) 1994
Nihil (Wax Trax!/TVT) 1995
Juke Joint Jezebel: The Giorgio Moroder Mixes EP (Wax Trax!/TVT) 1995
Xtort (Wax Trax!/TVT) 1996

KMFDM V. PIG

Sin Sex & Salvation EP (Wax Trax!/TVT) 1995

EXCESSIVE FORCE

Conquer Your World (Wax Trax!) 1991 (Wax Trax!/TVT) 1993
Gentle Death (Wax Trax!/TVT) 1993

EN ESCH

Cheesy (TVT) 1993

Germany's KMFDM began as a quartet of low-tech living-room musicians in Hamburg who unintentionally found themselves in synch with Chicago's Wax Trax! label, where groups like Ministry were attempting the first fusions of the strident noise of industrial music with the electronic dance rhythms of disco. The mix of sampled speeches, mechanical funk beats, sound collages and growling, distorted vocals on **What Do You Know, Deutschland?** still sounds aggressive and innovative—and the song "Positive" may be one of rock's first statements on the AIDS virus.

Making the obvious leap to Wax Trax!, KMFDM magnified its beats on **Don't Blow Your Top** and tried to write more cohesive songs on **UAIOE.** The band (whose name is, among other things, an acronym for *Kleine Mitleid Für Das Mehrheit*—"no pity for the majority," the punchline to a German joke that doesn't translate) entered the '90s with only two of its original members remaining: En Esch (vocals, drums, guitar) and leader Sascha Konietzko (electronics, vocals).

KMFDM began adding more guitars and personal (as opposed to political) angst to its music on **Naïve.** As the striking propaganda-style graphics (by the artist Brute!) that decorate most of KMFDM's album covers suggest, bluntness is the band's favorite mode of expression. "If I had a shotgun, I'd blow myself to hell," they sing through electronic effects on "Piggybank." A lawsuit over a sample forced the album's deletion in 1993; KMFDM remade five of the songs and reissued it as **Naïve—Hell to Go.** With venomous remixes like "Leibesleid (Infringement Mix)" and "Go to Hell (Fuck MTV Mix)," Konietzko and pals don't seem too pleased about the compromise.

More open to new influences than many electro-industrial peers, KMFDM mixed the tag-team raps of the Beastie Boys with grand orchestral samples to come up with the catchy title track to **Money,** a wandering concept album about baby boomers, fundamentalists and others battling for the minds of the younger generation. A lonesome steel guitar rings over the Nietzsche-goes-disco chants of female backing singers on "Help Us/Save Us/Take Us Away." Though half the **Money** songs are throwaways that pound away far too long, the album marks the beginning of KMFDM's transition into pure aggression, with ceaseless rhythms and plenty of grinding guitars. This enabled the group to pick up bored heavy metal fans looking for a release in more alternative bands like Ministry and Nine Inch Nails. (Konietzko actually remixed songs for Megadeth and White Zombie.)

Angst is the fulfillment of **Money**'s promise, a meld of pop choruses, metal guitar riffs and industrial machine-beats that accompanied the band's relocation to the United States. The lyrics to the infectious manifestos are KMFDM's love letter to itself: "Light" describes the band's music as a "frontal assault on the seven senses" and "deified Dada, hard but true." The album's best verbal exhibition is "Sucks," the antithesis of "Light." "Our music is sampled, totally fake/It's done by machines 'cause they don't make mistakes," Konietzko screams before listing pop stars that share some of KMFDM's initials (Kylie Minogue, Depeche Mode).

Sin Sex & Salvation, a collaboration between Konietzko and Englishman Raymond Watts (an early KMFDM member who left to make Foetus-ized industrial music under the name Pig), comes off as a hasty, regressive experiment. Except for two mixes of "Secret Skin," a second-rate industrial anthem, the five-track EP's songs go nowhere and seem to have been made by a random punching of synthesizer and sampler buttons.

As Konietzko returned to industrial's formless roots with Watts, En Esch (the band's baldest member, and the one most prone to cross-dressing) explored KMFDM's other main influence—German electro-pop—on his solo album. The underrated **Cheesy** is low-tech disco performed with a sense of humor and experimentation. "Love me like an animal," coos falsetto-voiced Liisa Vihma on "Cum." The introduction to the twelve-minute "Daktari" has Dean Ween (yes, of Ween) scraping his guitar strings as En Esch drops the electronics for a harmonica (yes, a harmonica) solo.

Watts stuck around when the band regrouped on **Nihil,** a faster, angrier and less accessible album than **Angst;** it features up to four guitars flailing away at once. "Juke Joint Jezebel," later remixed into a great pop single by Giorgio Moroder, matches Watts' deep-voiced musings on sex and religion with looped guitar riffs and electro-funk beats. So overwrought that one can only hope they're intended as parody, lyrics range from scenes of self-torture ("These eyes are twitching like a cup of squirming flies" in "Flesh") to clichéd student politics ("Terror," an original entitled "Search & Destroy"). There's even a guilty ode about masturbation ("Disobedience").

At its best, Excessive Force, the band's side project, is KMFDM lite, with house-music rhythms, samples and pianos softening the sound. At its worst, Excessive Force is KMFDM lazy. On **Conquer Your World,** Konietzko teams up with Buzz McCoy of My Life With the Thrill Kill Kult for a collection of uneven song scraps, of which "Conquer Your House II," full of soulful diva vocals and clubby beats, is the only keeper. **Gentle Death** stars house singer Liz Torres as a dominatrix caught in Excessive Force's electronic dungeon. Though the band employs a broader palette on the album, using shards of techno music, the theme from "Hall of the Mountain King" and recordings of a Chicago cab driver, **Gentle Death** nonetheless plays like a half-finished KMFDM album. [ns]

See also *Pigface.*

KNAPSACK

Silver Sweepstakes (Alias) 1995

Pavement's spiritual connection to Northern California isn't entirely lost on this loud young quartet from Davis, but it's certainly trivialized. Habitual hastiness, the guitars' unwavering sizzle-roar and singer Blair Shehan's unfortunate ability to bellow in eerie imitation of Perry Farrell leaves Knapsack pissing on the wrong tree. Gearing down (as in "Effortless" and "Centennial") lets a better side emerge, but the album is dismayingly determined to wrong all rights. Inside the nifty silverfoil CD cover, songs like "Addressee" lead nowhere at all. [i]

CHERI KNIGHT

See *Blood Oranges.*

KNITTERS

See *X.*

CHRIS KNOX

Songs for Cleaning Guppies (NZ Flying Nun) 1983
AD 1987 [tape] (NZ Walking Monk) 1987
Seizure (NZ Flying Nun) 1989 + 1990
Not Given Lightly/Guppiplus (NZ Flying Nun) 1989
Song for 1990 + Other Songs EP10 (NZ Flying Nun) 1990
Croaker (NZ Flying Nun) 1991
Polyfoto, Duck Shaped Pain & "Gum" (NZ Flying Nun) 1993
Meat (Communion) 1993
Not Given Lightly EP10 (Communion) 1994
One Fell Swoop & Undubbed EP (NZ Flying Nun) 1995
Songs of You & Me (Caroline) 1995
Songs From 1990 EP7 (Caroline) 1996

TALL DWARFS

Three Songs EP (NZ Furtive) 1981 (NZ Flying Nun) 1985
Louis Likes His Daily Dip EP (NZ Flying Nun) 1982
Canned Music EP (NZ Flying Nun) 1983
Slugbuckethairybreathmonster EP (NZ Flying Nun) 1984
That's the Short and Long of It (NZ Flying Nun) 1985
Throw a Sickie EP (NZ Flying Nun) 1986
Hello Cruel World (NZ Flying Nun) 1987 (Homestead) 1988
Dogma EP (NZ Flying Nun) 1987
Weeville (NZ Flying Nun) 1991 (Homestead) 1992
Fork Songs (NZ Flying Nun) 1992
The Short and Sick of It (NZ Flying Nun) 1992
3 EPs (NZ Flying Nun) 1994

TOY LOVE

Toy Love (NZ WEA) 1980

Chris Knox is the godfather of the New Zealand alternative-music scene—if Iggy Pop, Joan Jett, Robyn Hitchcock and Lou Reed were all the same person, that's how important he is to Kiwi pop. The Enemy, Knox's unrecorded early group, was by all reports New Zealand's first great punk band; its successor, the coulda-been-a-contender Toy Love, made one pretty good album and some more-than-pretty-good singles; the group even flirted with mainstream Antipodean success. After Toy Love broke up, bassist Paul Kean joined the Bats; Knox and guitarist Alec Bathgate formed a still-going experimental duo, Tall Dwarfs. Then there's his lengthy solo career, his engineering of many important early New Zealand pop records, his legendary half-improvised live performances (somewhere between music and standup comedy), his championing of the Omnichord (one of the silliest instruments ever played onstage) and his generous nurturing of the international pop scene. It also doesn't hurt that he's a first-rate songwriter.

Knox sings in Tall Dwarfs most of the time, but the group is a full-fledged collaboration with Bathgate; their records are very different from Knox's solo records, with ultra-weird arrangements (often dominated by their signature loops of deeply unconventional percussion) and subtler, trickier songs. The duo's first four EPs are collected on the essential **Hello Cruel World.**

The Short and Sick of It compiles two less crucial records: **That's the Short and Long of It** (an album-of-sorts with some outtakes and live stuff, three tracks recorded with Mike Dooley of the Enemy and Toy Love, including the Enemy's "Gone to the Worms" and two remakes of **Three Songs'** "Nothing's Going To Happen" recorded with a twenty-two-piece lineup, as Wall of Dwarfs) and **Throw a Sickie,** an EP mostly recorded through illness (it shows).

Weeville, Tall Dwarfs' first proper album, is unpretentious but insidiously great. Instead of the Dwarfs' earlier berserk arrangements, most of the songs slowly work their way under your skin on the strength of melody alone. Highlight: "Mr. Brocolli," a joyful Bathgate-sung ditty with a clarinet solo.

Fork Songs, Tall Dwarfs' tenth-anniversary album, is their most low-key record and their most despairing. Bathgate steals the show again with the twelve-string–driven "Life Is Strange" and its killer chorus; elsewhere, Knox savages groupie-fucking rock stars ("Boys"), small-town hypocrisy ("Lowlands"—"We need you but we hate you/Spend your cash then get out") and anyone who's ever tried to do anything ("Skirl"). The CD appends **Dogma,** the single best Tall Dwarfs record whose six songs adroitly convey the duo's inventiveness, tunefulness and smart, bitter cynicism.

Despite the title, **3 EPs** is not a compilation but rather eighteen new songs, divided into three six-song "EP" sections, each with its own individual lyric sheet: *A Question of Medical Ethics, Up the Down Staircase* and *Sam's Spaniel.* Whatever. Pavement's Spiral Stairs and Bob Nastanovich put in appearances on "Senile Dementia" and the heavy-handed U2 joke "Postmodern Deconstructivist Blues." Most of the rest is in a by-now-familiar vein—breaking no new ground (apart from the seven-minute drone "Neusyland"), but still not like anything else around. Great Alec moment: "Bee to Honey." Great Chris joke: "Two Dozen Lousy Hours" ("are all it takes to make one lousy fucking day").

Knox's first solo album was the ultra-limited **Songs for Cleaning Guppies,** aptly subtitled *Chris Knox Ego Gratification Album.* With **Seizure,** though, he came through in a big way. It's a brilliant record, with one marvel of wit, melody and DIY production after another—including two songs a lot of songwriters would give their careers for: "The Face of Fashion," later ruined by Marshall Crenshaw, and "Not Given Lightly," a heartstopping declaration of love for his children's mother that's still often the climax of his live performances. A 12-inch remix of "Not Given Lightly" appeared backed by ten songs collectively called **Guppiplus** (basically the good bits from **Songs for Cleaning Guppies**).

Song for 1990 + Other Songs is a quickie 10-inch, split between the title track (a fuzzed-out, sarcastic critique of New Zealand politics) and five fleeting, delicate, late-night, acoustic songs on the other side. (The latter reappear on the domestic **Songs From 1990.)**

Croaker couldn't help but suffer from following **Seizure,** and indeed the songwriting turns a little lugubrious in its second half; also, Knox overuses several structures. There's still some terrific stuff here, though. The first fifteen minutes are unstoppable, with the exquisite "Light" and "Lapse," a song that's about either a drug experience or eating citrus, and "Dunno Much About Life but I Know How to Breathe." The narrator of "Liberal Backlash Angst (The Excuse)" is such a convincing asshole ("Fuck the forests, rip 'em down and paint 'em blue / Fuck the virus, take yer condoms off and screw") that a few dimwits didn't realize Knox was kidding.

Meat, Knox's first domestic release, collects most of **Seizure** and a good-sized chunk of **Croaker;** the accompanying **Not Given Lightly** 10-inch includes the remix of its title song and most of the **Seizure** and **Croaker** songs that didn't make it onto **Meat.**

Exploiting compact discs' capacity for holding lots and lots of music, **Polyfoto, Duck Shaped Pain & "Gum"** is effectively three different things: *Polyfoto* is a short introductory medley of bits of demos, *Duck Shaped Pain* is the album proper and *"Gum"* is a five-song guitar/vocal EP. It's actually Knox throwing a bunch of songs at the wall and seeing what sticks. What sticks are the hilarious anti–new age rant "[& to think it all started with] Trim Milk" (kazoo solo!), the date-rape revenge fantasy "Not a Victim," the vaguely Arabic-sounding "Under the Influence" (rerecorded as a single) and an endlessly tuneful attack on people who deny personal responsibility, "View From the Bridge" (whose bridge goes "Let's go to the bridge and then drown"). Much of the album otherwise finds Knox and his Omnichord cruising on autopilot, but aside from the feel-my-pain "Intensive Care," it's never less than pleasant. Or much more.

Continuing the value-packing trend, **Songs of You & Me** effectively contains two complete albums on one CD: *Hanging Out for Time to Cure Birth* is the subtitle for eleven songs about other people, while *A Stranger's Iron Shore* is ten songs Knox wrote about himself. (To avoid burnout, don't listen to both of them in the same sitting.) It's a return to form. Knox's unique weirdness is back ("Lament of the Gastropod," "Chemicals Are Our Friends"), his social-conscience lyrics are on the mark and rarely heavy-handed, his words have never been cleverer (check out the frenetic babble of "A Song to Welcome the Onset of Maturity"), his gift for simple, flawless melodies has never gone away. **One Fell Swoop & Undubbed,** released more or less simultaneously with the album, contains a remix of **You & Me**'s title song and live-to-8-track versions of two other numbers from it, plus ABBA's "SOS" (played for laughs) and John Lennon's "Mother." [ddw]

KOOL G RAP & DJ POLO

Road to the Riches (Cold Chillin'/Warner Bros.) 1989
Wanted Dead or Alive (Cold Chillin'/Warner Bros.) 1991
Live and Let Die (Cold Chillin') 1992
Killer Kuts (Cold Chillin') 1993
Rated XXX (Cold Chillin') 1996

KOOL G RAP

4, 5, 6 (Cold Chillin'/Epic) 1995

Introduced to the world by pioneering producer/DJ Marley Marl, Kool G Rap and DJ Polo remain among the less-celebrated alumni of the legendary Queens-based Juice Crew (which included Big Daddy Kane, Roxanne Shanté, Master Ace, Craig G., MC Shan and Biz Markie). But Kool G Rap's street-corner documentary thematics and raw, lispy, word-dense delivery were crucial to the development of East Coast hardcore; artists from the Wu-Tang Clan to Nas owe him.

The duo debuted in 1986 with the Marl-produced single "It's a Demo" b/w "I'm Fly," a record that sounds like an LL Cool J outtake. A remixed version of "It's a Demo" appears on **Road to the Riches;** while the title track (based on a Billy Joel sample), "Truly Yours" and "Poison" are solid offerings, the rest of the tracks are as dated-on-arrival as the gold ropes around their necks on the back cover. **Wanted Dead or Alive,** in contrast, is an album of considerable style. The slowed-down tempos (provided mostly by Large Professor) give Kool G the space to drop more striking imagery and change up his delivery; "Talk Like Sex" showcases him at his bawdy best; the sharply detailed "Streets of New York" is stunning, "The Message" updated with a '90s photojournalistic detachment. Only Biz Markie's horrible singing on "Erase Racism" mars the album.

In a hoped-for merger of West and Southwest with East Coast gangsta rap, **Live and Let Die** pairs Kool G Rap with producer Sir Jinx (Ice Cube, Del tha Funkee Homosapien), features guest appearances from Ice Cube and Geto Boys Scarface and Bushwick Bill on "Two to the Head" and generally raises the crime quotient. A tantalizing piano-and-guitar hook cements the *Goodfellas*-styled tale of "Ill Street Blues"; "Letters" punches poetic on every line, even revealing the rapper to be a De La Soul fan. Jinx's thick funk suits Kool G well, but many tracks ("Go for Your Guns," "Still Wanted Dead or Alive") are way too obvious. (**Killer Kuts** anthologizes cuts from the duo's three records, plus a remix of "On the Run." The track selection is hard to quibble over, but G Rap was never a singles artist.)

Following the dissolution of the partnership, Kool G Rap (Nathaniel Wilson) returned with **4, 5, 6** (the title signifies the winning combination at celo, the street dice game). The contemporary mix of hardcore rhymes and slick soul fits him like a glove; the album hits its peak on "Fast Life" (with Nas guesting), "For da Brothaz" and both mixes of "It's a Shame." [jzc]

KORN

Korn (Immortal/Epic) 1994
Life Is Peachy (Immortal/Epic) 1996

Far beyond its own success, Pearl Jam opened the doors to countless smart but thuggish guitar bands that could claim alt-rock cachet while playing music otherwise likely to be shoved in metal slots and ignored by trend-conscious Lollapaloozers. California's Korn, a quintet from Huntington Beach, has a grip on the thrash-hop of bands like Rage Against the Machine as well as the raw rock aggression of northwestern powerhouses and the theatrical rap of Cypress Hill. Put all together under the guidance of producer Ross Robinson, Korn's multiple personalities unite to form a fiery ball of teeth-gritting anxiety that refuses to relinquish its anger. Singer Jonathan Davis (who also contributes bagpipes to the intro of nursery-rhyming "Shoots and Ladders"; the album's other stylistic lark is the Gregorian chant that begins "Daddy") is an unrepentant howler in the great grindcore tradition—his nominal voice is harshly grating, his frantic bellows are real window-rattlers. Bassist Fieldy uses a gated mechanical sound that helps articulate the rhythm/riff roar of two *loud* guitars; drummer David Silveria (who's done moonlight time in Infectious Grooves) hammers it all home with authoritarian control. Most of the lyrics on **Korn** are generic animosity, and blow by without incident—except for "Faget." Following a seething verse that ends with "You got this pretty boy feeling like I'm enslaved/to a world that never appreciated shit/you can suck my dick and fucking like it!," Davis finished the song with repeated screams of "I'm just a faggot!" If nothing else about **Korn** gets a rise from a jaded rocked-out world, that line is certainly a traffic stopper. [i]

See also *Suicidal Tendencies.*

KOSTARS

See *Luscious Jackson.*

KRAMER

The Guilt Trip (Shimmy-Disc) 1993
The Secret of Comedy (Shimmy-Disc) 1994
Music for Crying (Japan. Creativeman Disc) 1995

CARNEY-HILD-KRAMER

Happiness Finally Came to Them (Shimmy-Disc) 1987
(Hol. Shimmy-Disc Europe) 1990
Black Power (Shimmy-Disc) 1994

JAD FAIR & KRAMER

Roll Out the Barrel (Shimmy-Disc) 1989

JOHN S. HALL & KRAMER

Real Men (Shimmy-Disc) 1991

DAEVID ALLEN & KRAMER

Who's Afraid? (Shimmy-Disc) 1992

DOGBOWL & KRAMER

Hot Day in Waco (Shimmy-Disc) 1993
Gunsmoke (Shimmy-Disc) 1995

EGOMANIACS

Fahy-Harley-Kramer (Shimmy-Disc) 1993

HUGH HOPPER & KRAMER

A Remark Hugh Made (Shimmy-Disc) 1994

CAPTAIN HOWDY

Tattoo of Blood (Shimmy-Disc) 1995

Mark Kramer stopped using his first name long before Jerry Seinfeld's not altogether dissimilar, if less musical, neighbor became part of the cultural vernacular. Joining Eugene Chadbourne in the Chadbournes, he played bass and "cheap organ"; with the addition of drummer David Licht, that group became Shockabilly. A rapid, voluminous output resulted before they splintered apart in the mid-'80s. Kramer then turned his attention to his studio, Noise New York (later relocated to become the larger and more remote Noise New Jersey), and label, Shimmy-Disc, which he quickly filled with the endless stream of projects he produces—as well as the output of his own '80s bands, B.A.L.L. (which became Gumball upon his departure) and Bongwater (a duo with actress/performance artist Ann Magnuson).

Kramer's first proper solo album came on the heels of the dissolution of both of those groups (in, respectively, '90 and '91). **The Guilt Trip** is a monumental feat. Recorded with Licht and guitarist Randolph Hudson III, the three-record set (also issued on two CDs) is structured with a complete understanding on the pacing of six sides of music. Sonically, Kramer layers on an array of hot-wired psychedelia, some of it grafted to simple pop song structures, some of it to grand instrumental overtures. Lyrically, it's a highly personal work that throws love, devotion, forgiveness and atonement into the mix. Although Kramer announced the release as the first of three such tripleheaders attending a film project, what followed was **The Secret of Comedy,** a conventional-length single album. Although similar in sound, it's ironically less focused than its enormous predecessor, a dark work laced with Kramer's catchy songs and brimming with surprises. The Japanese **Music for Crying** compiles nineteen songs (recorded between '85 and '94) from Kramer's solo and collaborative albums.

Carney-Hild-Kramer is a trio with Ralph Carney (Tin Huey, Tom Waits and so forth) and Daved Hild (the Girls); other players from inside and outside the Shimmy compound also contribute. The group seems to exult in the process of composing in the studio—improvising, seeing what comes up and then building on it. Despite the high indulgence factor potential in such an enterprise, Carney and Kramer have the instrumental skills and Hild the cliché-free lyrics to make the effort pay off. The European CD of **Happiness Finally Came to Them** adds one song; the **Black Power** CD incorporates eleven of the first album's eighteen cuts as a bonus.

Jad Fair came into contact with Kramer when the latter produced two Half Japanese albums. Guests on their joint effort include Penn Jillette (who duets with Jad on "Subterranean Homesick Blues") and John Zorn, but it's Jad's lyrics of romance and hope and Kramer's layered instrumental tracks that unify the diverse, sometimes experimental, set of short songs. A second album was begun but scrapped after the two men had a financial falling out; most of the completed instrumental tracks surfaced on the final Bongwater album.

As producer, arranger, instrumentalist and label magnate, Kramer played an essential role in the career of King Missile (Dog Fly Religion); he subsequently made albums with both of that group's original principals. Kramer provides an aural setting for John S. Hall's drolly comic monologues on **Real Men.** Using his own compositions, samples and a barrage of sound effects, Kramer succeeds in upping the ironic ante of Hall's surreal metaphysics without stepping into the cliché-ridden quagmire of poetic noodling. Officially teamed as a duo, Kramer and Dogbowl (Stephen Tunny) made **Hot Day in Waco** and **Gunsmoke,** the solidest musical offerings in the Dogbowl canon (which also numbers four solo albums). Either one is a perfect entry point into the singer/guitarist's idiosyncratic but friendly songs.

The rotating lineup of Australian-born progresso Daevid Allen's Gong included Kramer in the late '70s; **Who's Afraid?,** a far-ranging excursion from folk to psychedelia, features Allen's lyrics and guitar playing, Kramer's music and production and David Licht's superb drumming.

Tracing Allen's career back even further, to the late-'60s jazz/prog-rock Soft Machine (whose sound and approach may well be close to the center of Kramer's sensibility), Kramer made a record with that band's bassist, Hugh Hopper. **A Remark Hugh Made** is by turns forceful and dreamily atmospheric. One-time Hopper bandmate Robert Wyatt makes a vocal cameo on "Free Will & Testament"; Gary Windo's tenor saxophone playing is among the final recordings he made before his death in 1993. (The album credits cite its recording date as 1994, which is obviously incorrect. Many Shimmy-Disc releases bear copyright dates a year earlier than the actual release.)

Captain Howdy is Kramer's band with Penn Jillette (of Penn and Teller), a much more serious outing than Penn's prior joke band, Bongos, Bass & Bob. **Tattoo of Blood** features Deborah Harry, guitarist Billy West (the voice of *Ren & Stimpy,* among many others), drummer Bill Bacon (replacing Licht, who left to play klezmer, as the Shimmy-Disc house drummer) and a title song written by Lou Reed. Kramer manages to find effective musical means to support, surround and propel Jillette's limited singing voice; "Dino's Head" is, in fact, a monologue set on a painstakingly sculpted musical bed. If that sounds like the Bongwater approach, it is, and in this case it's also used as an opportunity for publicly continuing the battle over money being waged between Kramer and Ann Magnuson.

Egomaniacs is a trio with drummer Jamie Harley and singer/guitarist Kim Fahy (leader of the Mabuses, who have a Shimmy-Disc album of their own; the two Britons previously played together in the Assassins). The songs are largely Fahy's, but Kramer's swirling production and arrangement touches, as well as his always-inventive bass playing, are equally key to their propulsively hypnotic sound. [tr]

See also *Damon and Naomi, Half Japanese; TPRG.*

WAYNE KRAMER & MICK FARREN

Who Shot You Dutch? EP (Can. Spectre) 1987

WAYNE KRAMER

Death Tongue (Curio/Progressive International) 1991
The Hard Stuff (Epitaph) 1995
Dangerous Madness (Epitaph) 1996

JOHNNY THUNDERS & WAYNE KRAMER

Gang War (Zodiac/DeMilo) 1990

As one component of the legendary MC5, guitarist Wayne Karmer helped create the soundtrack for a revolution that never came—but not for lack of trying. With its proto-metal-cum-free-jazz-scree rock'n'roll, the Five gave voice to the dope, guns and fucking in the streets discourse that exploded from Detroit, home base of the radical White Panther organization for which they served as de facto house band. When the MC5 sank into a morass of drug abuse and lethargy after adviser John Sinclair was sent to prison on drug possession charges (a predicament that befell the guitarist a decade or so later), Kramer went into semi-retirement.

The counter-counterculture agitator re-emerged around 1980 to join Johnny Thunders in the execrable Gang War, a dead-end partnership documented only on a ten-years-after album of live tracks and studio scraps. Collaboration with writer/ex-Deviant Mick Farren proved far more successful. Following a mid-'80s live album as the resurrected Deviants, the pair created "an R&B musical," **Who Shot You Dutch?,** which flourished in live performance in New York for a good while; musically, the songs documented on the 12-inch hold up today.

With Farren and New York scene vet John Collins (guitar/vocals) billed and pictured on the cover, **Death Tongue** is a literal continuation of that project. "Who Shot You Dutch?" appears on the ten-track CD, along with a ludicrous put-on version of "MacArthur Park" and originals written by various permutations of the trio. Cheap production and dime-store drumming keep **Death Tongue** in the margins, but the down-in-the-mouth rockers ("Spend the Rent"), resistible come-ons ("Take Your Clothes Off"), angry missives ("Negative Girls"), poignant reflection ("The Scars Never Show") and the cheery MC5-like riptide of "Fun in the Final Days" do limber Kramer up for his next major campaign. (Farren and Collins, meanwhile, continued as Tijuana Bible.)

It took another punk revolution—the third? fourth?—to coax the guitarist back into full-throttle amp-damage with **The Hard Stuff,** which careens from free-jazz–backed spoken word to bug-eyed metal in a manner every bit as fierce and feral as Kramer's golden age. His mastery of controlled feedback and mutated Chuck-Berry-via-Sonny-Sharrock riffs colors songs like "Edge of the Switchblade" and "Sharkskin Suit," while members of Los Angeles' Clawhammer, providing backing on several cuts, act as catalysts of chaos, accentuating the desperate tone of "Hope for Sale" and "Crack in the Universe." Ironically, it's the still-revolutionary-after-all-these-years lyrics by Farren—especially the coolly horrific depictions of societal malignancy in "Pillar of Fire" and "Bad Seed"—that really resurrect the MC5's firepower, but Kramer himself proves lyrically incisive on the spoken "Incident on Stock Island," a slice of trailer park noir worthy of Charles Bukowski (whom the guitarist eulogizes with an untitled, album-ending monologue).

Dangerous Madness stokes the flames of sedition with just as much zeal, but some of Kramer's targets—like the "People Who Died"–styled litany he trots out on the title track—are perilously close to being sitting ducks. It's difficult to find fault with his playing, however: between the proto-punk harmonics he lashes around the sentimental "Wild America" and the furiously avant squeals that pierce "The Rats of Illusion," he asserts his claim to the dissonance throne with utterly irrefutable power. Likewise, sullen spoken pieces like "A Dead Man's Vest" glisten with a coat of freshly spilled blood that would do Jim Thompson proud. He may not be quite as far ahead of his time now as he was two decades ago, but Wayne Kramer is still more dangerous than the vast majority of today's cable-ready punks [dss/i]

See also *Clawhammer, Mick Farren; TPRG.*

PHIL KRAUTH

See *Unrest.*

LENNY KRAVITZ

Let Love Rule (Virgin) 1989
Mama Said (Virgin) 1991
Are You Gonna Go My Way (Virgin) 1993
Circus (Virgin) 1995

The old fart's cry—that youth is wasted on the young—got a new twist in the hands of Lenny Kravitz, a sprout who reckons that history shouldn't be left to its ghosts. Reaching back to the era that ended with Woodstock, the multi-talented singer/instrumentalist borrows from the Beatles, Jimi Hendrix and Sly Stone in a dedicated attempt to re-create not just the sound of their records but the tenor of their times. The son of NBC producer Sy Kravitz and TV actress Roxie Roker, Kravitz grew up bi-coastal, learning drums, guitar and piano while developing his voice as a member of the California Boys Choir and the Metropolitan Opera (!). All that training went into making the self-produced and largely solo-played **Let Love Rule.** While the album has its guilty pleasures—the title track's funky gristle and anthemic climax, for one—Kravitz's false memories wear thin after repeated listens. Low points are "Mr. Cab Driver" (an understandable but ungainly complaint about urban racism) and "I Built This Garden for Us," a mawkish love ballad done up as baroque Paul McCartney psychedelia, complete with fat organ, "Eleanor Rigby" strings and a vintage-fuzzed guitar solo. The crazy quilt time-capsule album is an impressive achievement with a sometimes engaging soulful vibe, but the fashion-conscious Kravitz mainly succeeds in proving that image can be (nearly) everything.

Kravitz subsequently grew more sophisticated and R&B-geared in his appropriations, playing up his Princely falsetto and cozy soul grooves. The no-less-retro-minded but less rococo **Mama Said** doesn't show as much slavish devotion to its sources, instead mixing various stops on the wayback organ to mildly original effect, limited mainly by the plainness of Kravitz's songwriting. Even the dissolution of his marriage yields trite phrases that are more painfully outdated than his music. "There are so many rainbows that we were to climb . . . we've got to get our heads untangled and free our state of mind" ("The Difference Is Why"). Amid the album's broadening, "Stop Draggin' Around" is a pale Hendrix imitation and "All I Ever Wanted," which Sean Ono Lennon co-wrote and plays piano on, is an homage to John Lennon that even includes Kravitz's weak stab at primal screaming. "Stand by My Woman" also borrows Lennon's signature echo-delayed vocals/piano signature for its verses, but shifts into lush harmony soul for the chorus. Slash co-wrote and plays guitar on "Always on the Run." All told, **Mama Said** is a dull sidestep that neither builds on nor refutes the designs of the debut.

Kicking off with the exciting rock-funk sizzle of the Hendrixy "Are You Gonna Go My Way" (the *has*-to-be-intentional duff solo makes it clear this young turk knows his place in history), Kravitz's third album strikes a truly productive balance between style and substance. While he's still appropriating Beatlisms, making like Prince, aping Led Zeppelin and touching other obvious reference points, Kravitz adds more than enough of himself—a diehard romantic with a split lip and a busted heart—in the Zeppy "Is There Any Love in Your Heart," the soulful ballad "Black Girl" and the discofied "Sugar" to sublimate the stylistic kleptomania. In the touching acoustic "Sister," Kravitz gives himself a good talking to on behalf of the woman who has left him: "Did you have to fall in love/With a man/That never was/Up to no good." As never before, such earnestness and devotion sound sincere rather than just part of the disguise, and it's hard not to be drawn to the unguarded persona pulling off all these musical parlor tricks.

Though the title of **Circus'** curtain-raiser—"Rock and Roll Is Dead"—might indicate some epiphany in Kravitz's creative outlook, the song is simply the first of three sequential vehicles for his utterly pointless tribute to Led Zeppelin. (If it's dead, rock'n'roll's ancient spirit seems to have found a willing corpse to inhabit.) Worse, the lyrics switch at the end from a dig at hollow stardom to a plea for icon understanding, which makes the reborn rocker seem equally lost in place *and* time. Despite the funk bump of "Tunnel Vision," the generic balladry of "Can't Get You Off My Mind" and the Prince-styling old-school affectations of "Don't Go and Put a Bullet in Your Head," **Circus** is Kravitz's most rocking record and, with only occasional assists on guitar, bass and keyboards, also his simplest and most direct. If he were a compelling songwriter, such an unguarded approach might be beneficial, but it turns out that Lenny is only as good as his window dressing. [vg/i]

KRIS KROSS

Totally Krossed Out (Ruffhouse/Columbia) 1992
Da Bomb (Ruffhouse/Columbia) 1993
Young, Ri¢h & Dangerou$ (Ruffhouse/Columbia) 1996

Beyond the cootchie-coo freakshow aspect of kiddie bands, it's rare that pre-teens get their strings pulled by credible enough backliners to make records of substantial merit. While Kris Kross' unbelievable success—more than four million copies of the Atlanta duo's **Totally Krossed Out** crossed retail counters in 1992—and goofy reverse oversize fashions are now little more than a memory (the second album, an unseemly attempt to go hardcore, did a fraction of the business), the debut fulfills nineteen-year-old producer Jermaine Dupri's dreams with highly entertaining results.

Dupri and engineer/mixer Joe "The Butcher" Nicolo work both sides of the chronological fence on **Totally Krossed Out,** treating spunky and skillfully burbling rappers Chris Kelly (aka Mack Daddy) and Chris Smith (aka Daddy Mack)—born, respectively, in 1978 and 1979—like kids without repressing their need to act older. "I Missed the Bus" faces school without complaint, while "Party" accepts the pair's age impairment with good-natured frustration. "Lil' Boys in the Hood," "A Real Bad Dream" and "It's a Shame," however, unflinchingly face up to the reality of drugs and violence as adults, implicitly making a dismal point about the impossibility of protecting kids from the dangers of urban existence. Still, all that was overshadowed by two picture-perfect pop exercises—the Jackson 5–sampling "Jump" and the equally danceable "Warm It Up"—that ate up the charts. Age and gimmicks may have contributed to the records' successes, but such potent singles craft didn't need the help.

Where the debut makes effective sport of rap's macho posturing by keeping sight of the rappers' tender years, the stingy **Da Bomb**—thanks to the pair's deeper voices, popularity and hardening attitude—has a fuzzier time defining where they're at on life's maturity elevator. The modest, fan-praising "Alright" is as wholesome as oatmeal but the title track, which begins as harmless rote bravado, turns ugly (or at least rashly exploitative) with a detailed discussion of firearms. "Sound of My Hood" is a non-judgmental observation about gunplay. Other than an infusion of dancehall styling, **Da Bomb** sacrifices targeted efficiency for tonnage and fails to detonate.

Defying the odds, the prematurely adult Kris Kross (still working with Dupri) ended 1995 with a stylish new rap/R&B single ("Tonight's tha Night") in Billboard's Top 40, and released their third album in early '96. The skimpy effort barely makes it past the half-hour mark and includes one remix, three filler chat intervals ("It's a Group Thang" is a sleazy invitation to a three-way; "Interview" draws journalist dream hampton into a credibility-queering spot of collusion), other time-wasters and a bunch of guests to take the vocal load off the young playboys. With soft, soulful grooves and grown-up raps styled like a junior tag team of Snoop and 2Pac, **Young, Ri¢h, & Dangerou$** is as miserable as it was inevitable. [i]

KRS-ONE

See *Boogie Down Productions.*

ED KUEPPER

Electrical Storm (Aus. Hot) 1986
Rooms of the Magnificent (UK Hot) 1987
Not a Soul Around EP (UK Hot) 1987
Everybody's Got To (True Tone/Capitol) 1988
Today Wonder (Ger. Rattlesnake) 1990
Honey Steel's Gold (UK Hot) 1992 (Restless) 1995
Black Ticket Day (Aus. Hot) 1992
Real Wild Life EP (Aus. Hot) 1992
Serene Machine (Aus. Hot) 1993 (Restless) 1994
Character Assassination (Restless) 1994
The Butterfly Net (Restless) 1994
Legendary Bully (UK Castle Communications) 1994
A King in the Kindness Room (Aus. Hot) 1995
Sings His Greatest Hits for You (Aus. Hot) 1995 (Hot/TRG) 1996
I Was a Mail Order Bridegroom (Aus. Hot) 1995
Exotic Mail Order Moods (Aus. Hot) 1995

AINTS

S.L.S.Q. Live (Aus. Hot) 1991
Ascension (UK UFO/Hot) 1991
Autocannibalism (Aus. Hot) 1992
Afterlife (Aus. Hot) 1993
Shelf Life Unlimited!!—Hotter Than Blazing Pistols (Restless) 1995

Although deservedly a legend in his native Australia, Ed Kuepper is virtually unknown in North America. What little awareness of him there is resulted from the lanky guitarist's beginnings as a teenager in Brisbane, where he formed the band that would become the Saints in 1973 with singer Chris Bailey and launched an international punk sensation. No genre retrospective is complete without the Saints' classic Kuepper-penned singles: "(I'm) Stranded," "This Perfect Day" and "Know Your Product."

The group split in 1978 after three brilliant albums (although Bailey again used the name in the '80s) and Kuepper formed the equally uncompromising, eclectic and jazzy Laughing Clowns before going solo in 1986 with the sparse, sprightly **Electrical Storm.** Though (like the Saints and Laughing Clowns) this formative effort features sterling horn work, the title track and "Car Headlights" herald a pleasant retreat to the folkish rock that's been Kuepper's forte ever since.

Rooms of the Magnificent is no departure, but employs deeper production touches and boasts one of Kuepper's best tracks (with his best horn use since "Know Your Product"), "Also Sprach the King of Eurodisco." The guitarist deftly mixes Laughing Clowns' edgy stubbornness and skewered, rhythmic force with more accessible hooks. **Not a Soul Around** contains three songs from the first two albums, including an edited version of "Also Sprach the King of Eurodisco," and the title track's preview of the third.

Everybody's Got To, Kuepper's only solo LP for a major label, is even better. Self-production with a more commercial sensibility enhances rather than blunts such numbers (both released as singles) as "Burned My Fingers" and "When There's This Party." The blistering brass that punctuates "Not a Soul Around" is a quintessential Kuepper moment; the album has the Australian's single most inspired set of songs.

Jettisoning three-fourths of the quartet that backed him on **Everybody's Got To** (retaining only drummer Mark Dawson), Kuepper went on a tear, recording no fewer than twelve albums in the first six years of the '90s (plus greatest hits packages). **Today Wonder,** which started the wrecking ball rolling, is a low-key acoustic outing, with covers of Tim Hardin, Donovan, the Animals and Skip James showing Kuepper's artistic breadth. His originals (including a sharp reworking of the Clowns' "Eternally Yours") maintain the quality level.

Kuepper formed the Aints with Celibate Rifles guitarist Kent Steedman to play his old Saints songs for two gigs, one of which was recorded and released as **S.L.S.Q. Live.** There's no quibbling with the stunning material, but the album is strictly a hadda-be-there souvenir: this rag-tag bunch are horribly outclassed by the old Saints' live documents found on such compilations as **Live at the Hope and Anchor** or **Scarce Saints.** Still, the gigs inspired Kuepper to form a "real" Aints with new players (exit Steedman). For the superheated "It's Still Nowhere" alone, the fiery **Ascension** is a hell of a record; one imagines mixing-board needles melted into the red. A treat for fans of Hendrix, Cream and the Who more than narrowminded punks. **Autocannibilism** is much the same, only it's not as well-produced (actually, it's quite murky) and the material isn't as convincing.

Returning to his solo work and enlarging on the melancholic acoustic base, **Honey Steel's Gold** is Kuepper's most brooding, reflective LP, its simple character belied by the lush timbre of the piano, acoustic guitars and his bluesy voice. Like refugees from the Saints' **Prehistoric Sounds,** "King of Vice" and "The Way I Made You Feel" (another Kuepper classic) display a veteran master at his sharpest. The US release also tacks on the four B-sides of the **Real Wild Life** EP, including covers of the Kinks (a lackluster version—Kuepper does this inspired choice way better live—of **Village Green**'s "Last of the Steam-Powered Trains"), Paul Revere and the Raiders and Willie Dixon.

Black Ticket Day is effectively part two of **Honey Steel's Gold.** The mixture of the acoustics and the lower registers of Kuepper's voice combine for unique moods, as on "There's Nothing Natural" (redone from **Today Wonder**'s more stripped-down version) and "It's Lunacy." Though uneven, this weaker work still has plenty of great moments.

There's still not much change on **Serene Machine,** but Kuepper is starting to claw more, with a harsher bite on such dramatic songs as "When She's Down" and "Sleepy Head (Serene Machine)," which employs surprising gospel-ish backing vocals on the choruses to dramatic (as opposed to clichéd) effect.

Character Assassination is Kuepper's best '90s LP yet, a confidently etched and unnerving work. The violins throughout are dazzling, especially on "Little Fiddle (And the Ghost of Xmas Past)" and "By the Way"; the acoustic guitar is so well recorded it's like he's playing in your room. Kuepper even deftly reinserts tasteful Stax-style horns on such numbers as the fuming "My Best Interests at Heart." (Johnny Cash's "Ring of Fire" sounds great with trumpets, too!) It's amazing how Kuepper can use such carefully constructed backgrounds and an acrimonious voice to stir up the same tension and intensity that once required much louder music. The **Butterfly Net** best-of is proof of how long and how well he's managed this trick. This perfectly chosen overview is both made to order as a sparkling introduction and a testament to the songwriter's best gifts. (**Legendary Bully** is another compilation.)

Having accomplished so much, **A King in the Kindness Room** finds Kuepper searching for a new direction. An ambitious mish-mash and a lot weirder and more experimental than his other records, this wobbly album includes a few out-and-out duds. But it also contains a few gems. No Saints fan will be unhappy to learn that "Messin' Pt. II" (an update of 1977's "Messin' With the Kid") makes great reuse of that timeless blues riff. Or that "Pissed Off" is a pop single with a harsh dance beat that belongs on any Kuepper best-of. (He also reinvents Gordon Lightfoot's "Sundown" and AC/DC's "Highway to Hell" in bizarre covers.)

Sings His Greatest Hits for You, the Australian best-of, covers the same period as the American **Butterfly Net,** only far less comprehensively. Likewise, **Shelf Life Unlimited,** the Aints anthology, can be neglected in favor of **Ascension,** which outclasses the other two LPs to the point of being a virtual best-of all by itself.

Only Kuepper's most rabid supporters are likely to be aware of the surprisingly essential **I Was a Mail Order Bridegroom.** (The title refers to the fact that Kuepper didn't want this LP of unplugged versions of his best songs commercially released, and thus it was sold only by mail.) This rare album is well worth obtaining, however. All sixteen tracks were recorded live in the studio with a big, ringing sound. Kuepper attacks the strings as if it were still 1977 and likewise hits every period of his career. The highlights include the Saints' "Messin' With the Kid" (originally sung by Bailey) and a cover of Who's "The Seeker." Despite its obscurity, this is one of Kuepper's best albums. **Exotic Mail Order Moods** is another non-retail album. [jr]

See also *TPRG.*

KUSTOMIZED

The Mystery of Kustomized EP (Matador) 1994
The Battle for Space (Matador) 1995
At the Vanishing Point (Matador) 1996

HIGH RISK GROUP

Running Among the Sevens EP (UK Blaster) 1991

With the once-mighty Boston art-noise scene threatening to recede from the world's consciousness, ex–Mission of Burma/Volcano Suns drummer Peter Prescott launched this fun-spirited ass-biting quartet in which he sings and plays wiry guitar. Kustomized's drummer, Kurt Davis, sang in Bullet LaVolta (where he was known as Yukki Gipe); guitarist Ed Yazijian and bassist Bob Moses complete the loose-fitting lineup. Keeping it all in the family, former Volcano Suns bassist Bob Weston, now of Shellac, produced the first two records, honing a serrated Chicago edge onto the band's casual stylings.

If Steve Albini hadn't actually produced a Fleshtones album, some of the six shitty-sounding tracks that compose **The Mystery of Kustomized** would at least give some indication of how that pairing might work out. "Big Trick" and a cover of Joy Division's "Dead Souls" are strictly windswept exercises in venomous guitar slashing, but the racing "Overnight Namedrop," "Nothing. Not One," "It Lives!" and the goofy "Full" have rock'n'roll hearts ticking beneath the band's burly aggression.

While twenty-two minutes of adrenalized slop is no hardship post, a full-length album of Kustomized's loud nonsense is a lot to sit through. Elaborating on the EP's vintage garage-rock essence, **The Battle for Space** benefits from sharper studio fidelity and a fatter rhythmic core, winding up shifting a latter-day New York Dolls through '90s equipment. Still, Kustomized's work habits—dazed fuzzbusters on a high-speed chase under the watchful eye of a critical noise expert—don't do any favors to songs ("The Day I Had Some Fun," "Puff Piece," "33 1/3" and the unlisted bonus cut appended to the final track) that would have benefited greatly from being put up on blocks and stripped down.

With Malcolm Travis—recently freed of his rhythmic obligations to Bob Mould in Sugar—taking over from Davis and Weston out of the picture, Kustomized shifted gears for the better on **At the Vanishing Point.** Diverse in tone, less prone to self-defeating indulgence and equipped with more generally reliable material, the album reveals the quartet's stylish side in "The One That Got Away," economically driven by two-fingered organ until a flamethrower guitar break, a properly noirish version of "Harlem Nocturne" and the opening instrumental, "Handcuffs." Elsewhere, Kustomized joyfully overkills simple tunes like a cover of Government Issue's "Bored to Death" with delirious power. So much for suave bachelor pad music—this brings it all back home to the crash pad floor.

Before Kustomized, Ed Yazijian played lead violin (!) in Boston's excellent but little-known High Risk Group. **Running Among the Sevens** contains the five songs from two late-'80s singles released in the US on Harriet and adds an extra track, "Dull Stare." A third single, "Pulsed," was produced by Come's Thalia Zedek, whose voice has a lot in common with HRG guitarist Debbie Nadolney's low-pitched rasp. Come's sound, in fact, has a lot in common with the droning, muscular throb that characterized High Risk Group. [i/ddw]

See also *Shellac.*

KYUSS

Wretch (Dali) 1991
Blues for the Red Sun (Dali/Elektra) 1992
Kyuss (Chameleon/Elektra) 1994
Demon Cleaner EP #1 EP (Ger. Elektra) 1994
Demon Cleaner EP #2 EP (Ger. Elektra) 1994
. . . And the Circus Leaves Town (Elektra) 1995
One Inch Man EP (UK Elektra) 1995

Kyuss was spawned on the wrong side of the tracks in the country club oasis of Palm Desert, California; lacking anything resembling a club scene, the band honed its chops playing "generator parties" in the desert (presumably scattering gila monsters for miles around), emerging with a parched and blistering sound at the vortex where Black Flag, Black Sabbath and the Misfits meet. It's hard to discuss Kyuss without exhausting the permutations of the words "hot" and "dry," but song titles like "Molten Universe," "Caterpillar March," "Demon Cleaner" and "Asteroid" are aptly evocative.

Wretch (which followed an extremely rare 1990 release, **Sons of Kyuss**) contains the band's demos and sounds like it, creeping at times into a sort of grunge-Danzig realm. The album does surge with energy, however; guitarist Josh Homme's ultra-distorted, oddly tuned riffs and John Garcia's menacingly melodic vocals are full of the promise that bloomed on the band's next album.

Kyuss found itself through the agency of Chris Goss, the Masters of Reality vocalist whose affinity for droning fuzz-riffs, floorboard-rattling bass and skull-shattering cymbals proved a perfect fit on the three Kyuss albums he produced. On **Blues for the Red Sun,** Goss tapped into Kyuss' hidden reserve of nitrous oxide, resulting in a sound that's like speed-metal only without the speed, summoning visions of a flared tailpipe spewing exhaust fumes. The ferocious "Thumb" and the droning instrumental "Apothecaries' Weight" show Kyuss equally potent at playing hard and soft; though the album does drag a bit toward the end, it's one of the most gratifying blasts of volume this decade has yet produced.

Delayed for nearly a year by the collapse of Chameleon Records, the monolithic **Kyuss** (informally known as **Welcome to Sky Valley** for the road sign pictured on its cover) picks up right where its predecessor left off, verging into (tongue-in-cheek) ultra-pretentiousness by dividing the album into three roman-numeral "movements" and indulging in some of the most over-the-top instrumental work since the demise of Mountain. New bassist Scott Reeder (ex-Obsessed, but also a Palm Desert native) adds considerable Rickenbacker girth to an already fearsome rhythm section; the quartet branches out instrumentally with the trippy, acoustic "Space Cadet" and the calmer "Whitewater." The rest of it, however, is pure, brilliant brute force.

Kyuss had reached the end of that particular stylistic tether, however. **. . . And the Circus Leaves Town** finds the band seeking a new direction with limited success. Following another personnel change (Alfredo Hernández of Palm Desert's Yawningman—whose "Catamaran" is covered here—replaced original drummer Brant Bjork), the songs are shorter, more concise and more deliberately melodic than in the past. But there's really not much here the group hadn't done before. The **One Inch Man** EP contains three self-produced tracks that stake out punkier, rawer sonic terrain and seem to hint at a promising new stylistic vein—unfortunately, they turned out to be the last songs Kyuss recorded. The band threw in the towel in late '95. Guitarist Josh Homme subsequently formed Gamma Ray and toured in Screaming Trees. [ja]

See also *Masters of Reality.*

LABRADFORD

Prazision LP (Kranky) 1993
A Stable Reference (Kranky) 1995
Labradford (Kranky) 1996

You don't need to be a card-carrying krautrock connoisseur to plunge headfirst into the placid-looking waters that pool up beneath Labradford's vintage analog synthesizers and electronic gizmos—but it couldn't hurt. With an equal affinity for ambient soundscapes and Neu!-inflected *mekkanik*-rock, the Richmond, Virginia, duo of Carter Brown and Mark Nelson manages to draw listeners off into an nth dimension where sound takes on cross-sensory attributes. Initial exposure is a bewildering, befogging experience—kinda like being relocated on a planet where the atmosphere is pure ether—but once you get used to breathing the stuff, ordinary air seems so . . . well, *ordinary.*

Prazision LP is sequenced with splendid alacrity: pieces like "Listening in Depth" and "Skyward With Motion" start as static washes but develop almost imperceptibly, with layers of synth and found sound that ebb and flow, creating frequency oscillations that seem to shift as you move around within them. The duo breaks the ambient mood with a handful of more conventionally structured songs (like the engrossing "Accelerating on a Smoother Road") that give the honey-throated Nelson the opportunity to murmur abstract but subconsciously uplifting lyrics over spangled backgrounds worthy of Spacemen 3.

Arriving bassist Robert Donne positions himself squarely in the center of **A Stable Reference,** adding a solid floor that presents a slight impediment to out-and-out astral projecting. Oddly, the addition of a member results in the subtraction of several sonic layers on songs like the stark "El Lago" (which is marked by Donne's cybernetic timekeeping and a cathedral-like organ wash loosed by Brown). A penchant for psychic drift still exists—witness "Eero" and "Balanced on Its Own Flame"—but Labradford's paths seem a little more clear-cut the second time around. [dss]

LAIKA

See *Moonshake.*

LAIKA & THE COSMONAUTS

C'mon Do the Laika! (UK Dojo) 1988
Surfs You Right (UK Dojo) 1990
Instruments of Terror (Texicalli) 1993 (Upstart) 1994
The Amazing Colossal Band (Upstart) 1995
Zero Gravity (Upstart) 1996

Laika and the Cosmonauts (bassist Tom Nyman, guitarist Mikko Lankinen, guitarist/organist Matti Pitsinki and drummer Janne Haavisto) are Finland's entry into the global surf revival. With a rave review from Dick Dale on the back cover of **Instruments of Terror** ("Listening to Laika and the Cosmonauts' new CD makes me feel that I'm standing toes over on that endless wave in the midst of a tropical sunset"), they gained mucho credibility for mostly original feel-good retro epics that combine the usual influences: Dale's surf twang, '60s spy flicks and TV themes, the Ventures and Tornadoes, Bernard Hermann soundtracks. Everything on the album is high-energy fun, but the group's only stroke of true genius is "Psyko," a medly of the themes from *Psycho* and *Vertigo.* **Colossal Band** also has moments of charm—the moody twang of "The Downwinders" and the twang bar soul of "Aztec Two-Step" and "The A-Treatment"—but it's not a good sign that the best moments are again soundtrack covers—"The Avengers" and John Barry's "The Ipcress File."

In '96, Laika and the Cosmonauts were asked to contribute four tunes to the *Flipper* soundtrack. The group also released **Zero Gravity,** a compilation of its first two European albums, **C'mon Do the Laika!** and **Surfs You Right,** as a tie-in for an American tour. Highlights include a Johnny and the Hurricanes take on Dizzy Gillespie's "Night in Tunisia," "Surfs You Right" (a Dale-influenced stomp) and "Oahu Luau," a faux Hawaiian cha-cha. [jp]

LAMBCHOP

I Hope You're Sitting Down (Merge) 1994
How I Quit Smoking (Merge) 1996

It's rare for a band manned by musicians raised on avant-gardery to pursue pre-rock forms without first donning a specious cloak of irony, but this Nashville-based ten-piece has staked its claim to the title of America's first post-punk jugband without the slightest hint of dress-up pretense or faux-hayseed hooting. While the band is wed to old-time instrumentation—banjo, mandolin, lap steel, trombone—Lambchop doesn't underscore its primitivism with overtly Appalachian ephemera. Instead, frontman Kurt Wagner (whose '20s-vintage Gibson L-3 is the music's most important element) crafts a passel of subtle, detailed songs that, for the most part, could pass as products of any of the past seven decades. In a clear voice surprisingly reminiscent of Glen Campbell's, Wagner sticks to topics familiar to any country fan—from skid-row death ("Soaky in the Pooper") to everyman's appreciation of life's little pleasures ("Under the Same Moon")—on **I Hope You're Sitting Down,** which also goes by the spine name **Jack's Tulips.** To his credit, Wagner doesn't feign guilelessness: his characters worry about the Holocaust and crashing their Volkswagens far more often than they do the state of their crops. In other words, Lambchop would have knocked 'em dead at Woodstock—the first one, that is.

Wagner pumps down the volume even further on

How I Quit Smoking, a collection of songs that spiral in on themselves with agoraphobic insularity. Evidenced by songs like "The Man Who Loved Beer" and the "The Scary Caroler," the obsessions are roughly the same; Wagner's chin-stroking delivery gives him the air of a dotty old uncle who's about to give his brood nightmares for weeks to come. [dss]

ANITA LANE

See *Nick Cave and the Bad Seeds.*

MARK LANEGAN

See *Screaming Trees.*

K.D. LANG AND THE RECLINES

A Truly Western Experience (Can. Bumstead) 1984
Angel With a Lariat (Sire) 1987
Shadowland (Sire) 1988
Absolute Torch and Twang (Sire) 1989

K.D. LANG

Ingénue (Sire/Warner Bros.) 1992
Even Cowgirls Get the Blues (Sire/Warner Bros.) 1993
Lifted by Love EP (Sire/Warner Bros.) 1993
All You Can Eat (Warner Bros.) 1995

It's not uncommon for a performer to gain creative momentum after leaving the starting gate, but few modern singers have developed their art at the exponential rate of Canada's k.d. lang. Over the course of her first seven albums, Alberta native Kathryn Dawn Lang has ably followed an arc from cowgirl country-western rock'n'roll to the lush synthesizer ambience of modern balladry, growing as a vocalist from a Patsy Cline–idolizing belter to a controlled, sophisticated chanteuse, revealing a stunning instrument along the way. Factor in that lang walks the commercial walk without sacrificing her dignity and that she is one of the first open lesbians to ever crack the Top 10, and she transcends simple pop stardom as a boundary-busting heroine.

A Truly Western Experience is a good-natured debut (sincere down to its cover pic of Patsy) that can't decide where it's headed. There's feverish rockabilly ("Bopalena"), weepy aspiring Nashville country ("Pine and Stew"), smoky blues ("Busy Being Blue"), western swing ("Up to Me"), rustic singer/songwriterdom ("Tickled Pink") and, naturally, a Cline hand-me-down ("Stop, Look and Listen"). lang can certainly sing here, but it's an equivocal introduction, to say the least.

After hooking up with guitarist/mandolinist/fiddler Ben Mink (who has been her writing/recording/production partner ever since), lang made her major-label debut, **Angel With a Lariat.** Produced by Dave Edmunds and including a cover of Joe South's "Rose Garden" (a hit for Lynn Anderson), the album is a weird rock'n'roll interpolation of barn-dance country, with lang overzealously playing the part of rambunctious barker and Edmunds still suffering the adverse after-effects of his time spent being produced by Jeff Lynne. lang's singing is sure and strong but, other than the straightforward country balladry of her own "Diet of Strange Places" and the melancholy oldie "Three Cigarettes in an Ashtray," the songs suffer from two-step predictability and the futile attempt to mix oil and water.

Though she's filed under "country" in many minds, k.d. lang has always operated outside the Nashville establishment. But for one shining moment in 1988, she went from pressing her nose against the glass to the heart of the country-western world, recording **Shadowland** in Tennessee with Owen Bradley, the veteran producer who had supervised the studio career of Patsy Cline thirty years earlier. lang maintains her individuality on this album of standards, even in the daunting presence of legends like Kitty Wells, Loretta Lynn and Brenda Lee, all of whom put in guest appearances. Cooing through nightclub numbers like Peggy Lee's "Black Coffee," quavering through yearnfests like "Shadowland," she forges a distinct identity somewhere between swaggering country boy and angelic girl crooner. Whether she comfortably inhabits the songs or not, the enormously subtletly and skill in her singing is unmistakable.

Absolute Torch and Twang wheels back and forth between genteel and rollicking neo-country. The "torch" is in achy-breaky ballads ("Nowhere to Stand," "Pullin' Back the Reins"), while the "twang" is in funny do-si-dos like "Full Moon Full of Love" and "Big Boned Gal." But as hard as lang tries to be sincere, she can't seem to dislodge the tongue from her cheek. That doesn't necessarily take her out of the country music tradition; she's just chosen to identify with the genre's campy, humorous elements.

Switching gears in 1992, lang made **Ingénue,** a cathartic flood of dreamy ballads to wash clean her heart, obviously poisoned by an unquenched romantic obsession. The album captures lang's musical and emotional struggle between succumbing to, and breaking free from, her pain. The opening lines say it all: "Save me/Save me from you/But pave me/The way to you." More important, **Ingénue** signals a shift toward a more unbounded, luxurious and contemporary approach to songwriting. There are precious few hints of country here, just the honey-drip of "Constant Craving" and the saucy pop of "Miss Chatelaine."

Even Cowgirls Get the Blues, the soundtrack to Gus Van Sant's movie, keeps running with that shift, sculpting a lush ambience that's part piano bar, part sagebrush plain. "Keep Me Moving" is a Sylvester-style disco raveup, complete with flute and horns, while "Hush Sweet Lover" is a slinky lounge ballad blooming with strings and "Cowgirl Pride" is a from-the-hip, by-the-book bluegrass stomp. Sandwiched between the songs are semi-jazzy piano instrumentals—nice but far less intriguing than titles like "Kundalini Yoga Waltz," "Don't Be a Lemming Polka" and "Virtual Vortex" might imply. **Lifted by Love** contains three remixes of two album songs, a remix of "Miss Chatelaine" from the previous LP and "No More Tears (Enough Is Enough)," a duet with Erasure's Andy Bell recorded for the *Coneheads* soundtrack.

Following her life-sapping obsession on **Ingénue** and her behind-the-scenes role on **Even Cowgirls Get the Blues,** lang retakes center stage with **All You Can Eat.** On the cover, she's standing tall, hands proudly on her hips, having located her self-confident swagger and set it to a totally different sound. Nearly a dance record, **All You Can Eat** is driven by languid syncopation and lang's formidable pipes and mystical rhapsodizing. On "Sexuality," she addresses the issue head on for the first time: "How bad could it be/If you would fall in love with me?" Listening to the voluptuousness of lang's alto, the answer is obvious. [nds/i]

JONBOY LANGFORD AND THE PINE VALLEY COSMONAUTS

See *Mekons.*

DANIEL LANOIS

Acadie (Opal/Warner Bros.) 1989
For the Beauty of Wynona (Warner Bros.) 1993

When not otherwise occupied making exquisitely detailed and supremely tasteful records with the Neville Brothers, Emmylou Harris, Peter Gabriel, Robbie Robertson and U2, Quebec-born producer/guitarist Daniel Lanois has found the time to put two dozen of his own compositions on a scintillating pair of albums. With studio contributions from the Nevilles, U2, Brian Eno (his U2 production partner) and primary collaborator Malcolm Burn on keyboards and guitar, **Acadie** is the kind of album the Band might have made if their studio had been an urban art gallery rather than a rustic Woodstock homestead. Rhythms shush with eloquent restraint as Lanois sings (partly in French) his spiritually informed romantic perceptions of nature ("Fisherman's Daughter," "Under a Stormy Sky," "Ice," "Still Water") in an engaging, comfortable voice. Through the intricate delicacy of their varied arrangements, Lanois' songs allude to R&B, pop and folk without actually committing themselves; if that sometimes holds **Acadie** at a distance, it's a testament to Lanois' mature artistry (or perhaps fussy technique) that his cerebrally emotional music defies easy categorization. Capped off by a quiet but overly meddlesome production of Aaron Neville singing "Amazing Grace" (ohh, that Eno!), the translucent **Acadie** is a lovely and thoughtful tapestry.

The hearty passions that fire up **For the Beauty of Wynona** engorge it with the visceral presence completely lacking in the first album. Backed by a stable quartet led by Burn rather than a collection of marquee guests, Lanois takes a less punctilious approach, trading increased accessibility for diminished depth. He drops the coy guise and cozies up to acoustic folk music ("The Collection of Marie Claire"), unleashes New Orleans swamp gas ("The Messenger," "Brother L.A."), lays on energized atmospherics ("Waiting" and the title track, both of which can be traced back to U2 and make a clunky fit with the rest of Lanois' designs here), tries an echo-chambered interpolation of doo-wop ("Death of a Train"), bizarrely ethnic dance-funk ("Indian Red") and husky singer/songwriter pop ("The Unbreakable Chain," the Dylanesque "Lotta Love to Give" and "Sleeping in the Devil's Bed").

The lesson of these two albums is that Lanois' true gift is for arcane studio manipulation, not unadorned music-making. The fine, wan watercolors of **Acadie** will continue to prick the imagination long after the thicker primaries of **For the Beauty of Wynona** have worn away. [i]

See also *Brian Eno.*

LARD

See *Jello Biafra.*

AL LARSEN

See *Some Velvet Sidewalk.*

LA'S

The La's (UK Go! Discs) 1990 (Go! Discs/London) 1991

CAST

All Change (Polydor) 1996

The La's were one of the decade's few new Britpop groups to take cues from '60s beat, rather than psychedelia, new wave or punk. On its lone album, the distinctive Liverpool quartet—which favored acoustic guitars and folky harmonies but delivered taut electric rock as well—echoes groups like the Hollies, Searchers and Beatles. Lee Mavers writes profoundly tuneful songs with thoughtful words and sings them with a skilled mixture of pop allure ("There She Goes" is an absolute gem) and pub-band sturdiness ("Failure" is an odd bit of garage-punk). Beyond melodic assets, the La's make good, independent-minded use of rhythm as well. "Liberty Ship" has the seafaring tempo to match its lyrical metaphor, while "Way Out" pairs a measured drum/rhythm-guitar beat with double-time lead figures; "Freedom Song" uses the oompah swing of a Kurt Weill number.

But that was all the troubled band could manage. Bassist John Power left the La's at the end of 1991, picked up a guitar and spent the next three years assembling Cast, a four-piece that lit up London beginning in 1995 and even had Oasis' truculent Noel Gallagher singing its praises. **All Change,** which followed a couple of singles, shows what all the fuss was about. Cast slams forth with a combination of Merseybeat bop and American garage-rock drive—Freddie & the Dreamers meet the Seeds, if you can imagine that. With a refreshingly angst-free outlook, the John Leckie–produced album of bright, optimistic and irresistibly tuneful pop is neither silly nor simpy. A couple of songs ("Sandstorm," "Walkaway") tread a bit too close to Oasis' sonic terrain, but that doesn't stop Cast from being a formidable new soldier in the mid-'90s British reinvasion. [i/gg]

LAST EXIT

Last Exit (Enemy) 1986
The Noise of Trouble: Live in Tokyo (Enemy) 1986
Cassette Recordings '87 (Celluloid) 1988
Iron Path (Virgin) 1988
From the Board (Ger. Enemy) 1989 (Enemy) 1996
Köln (Ger. ITM) 1990
Headfirst Into the Flames: Live in Europe (Muworks) 1993

BILL LASWELL AND PETER BRÖTZMANN

Lowlife (Celluloid) 1987

Last Exit, a four-piece avant-garde jazz supergroup, brought to their improvisations a fondness for volume and violence that makes most rock bands sound tame. In the late Sonny Sharrock, Last Exit boasted a guitar pioneer whose volcanic work in the '60s New York free-jazz scene remains a profound influence on virtually every rock soloist who has experimented with noise, from Jimi Hendrix to Thurston Moore. In Germany's Peter Brötzmann, it showcased perhaps the premier exponent of energy playing among modern saxophonists; his ferocity would later be echoed by the sheets-of-sound rock-trio recordings made by his son, guitarist Caspar Brötzmann. In Ronald Shannon Jackson, it had a drummer who combined the bluesiness of his Texas heritage with African polyrhythms and the take-no-prisoners approach of

Ornette Coleman's 1970s groups, of which Jackson was a vital member. And in Bill Laswell, it had a producer and organizer with close ties to the rock community, as well as a bassist capable of holding down the musical center in a musical maelstrom.

All but one of the Last Exit discs are live performances culled from the group's formative tours in 1986 and '87. On **Last Exit,** the sound is as unrelenting and incendiary as a blast-furnace, epitomized by the hyper-speed metal of "Enemy Within." While blues riffs crop up as occasional reference points and an out-of-breath Jackson indulges in a bit of spoken-word whimsy on "Voice of a Skin Hanger," the overall impression is one of supernatural intensity, the agitated instrumental voicings of Sharrock and Brötzmann suggesting human cries.

Although released late in the story, **Köln** was actually among the group's first performances together, recorded four days before the 1986 Paris date documented on **Last Exit.** Sharrock has said he first met Jackson on the way to the group's first concert a few days before, and the lack of rehearsal brings spontaneity, energy and a palpable tension to the group interaction. The nineteen minutes of "Hard School" are as harrowing as they are unrelenting, with Brötzmann, goaded by Jackson, coming out screaming and later inciting Sharrock to join in the carnage. The call-and-response patterns break down into a frenzied free-for-all in the aptly titled "Taking a Beating"; Brötzmann and Sharrock play hide and shriek in "Last Call."

On **The Noise of Trouble: Live in Tokyo,** the restless quartet flies from traditional blues motifs to high-energy skronk and back again with dexterity and daring. "Panzer Be-Bop" is typical of the manic thrust, opening as a drum tour de force for Jackson, then mutating into a boogie, before Brötzmann blows everything into orbit. On "Blind Willie," a nod to blues great Blind Willie Johnson, Brötzmann and Sharrock turn into heavyweights slugging each other silly, while Sharrock's intro to "Pig Cheese" is enough to leave any guitar aficionado slack-jawed. The disc is also the only Last Exit release to feature outside musicians: pianist Herbie Hancock and reedman Akira Sakata. **Cassette Recordings '87** (also issued as **From the Board**) offers another tumultuous extended piece, "Line of Fire," and disembowels Jimmy Reed's "Big Boss Man." But it's apparent that the group is nearing the end of its creative tether with the blow-your-brains-out approach.

Last Exit's sole studio recording, **Iron Path,** introduces a less frantic direction, with more value placed on the space between notes. The compositions impose a thin veneer of structure: the recurring slide-guitar phrase in "Devil's Rain," the Oriental motif of the title track. Some of the more textured pieces at times suggest King Crimson at its most venturesome, while "Prayer" employs a majestic Sharrock riff for Jackson to scurry under, and "Cut and Run" hints at surf-metal.

Headfirst Into the Flames, culled from 1989 European dates, has a more refined sense of interplay. While cutthroat power is still very much part of the group's repertoire, the emphasis is more on give-and-take. On "So Small, So Weak, This Bloody Sweat of Loving," Sharrock sculpts feedback before a swaggering tempo is introduced by Jackson, a more successful "rock" excursion than anything on **Iron Path.** "A Knight of Ghosts and Shadows" engages in evocative shadowplay before erupting, and "Jesus! What Gorgeous Monkeys We Are" simmers rather than boils for all of its eleven minutes, a four-way conversation of the type rarely heard on the earlier albums. [gk]

See also *Caspar Brötzmann Massaker, Bill Laswell.*

LAST POETS

Last Poets (Douglas) 1970 (Metrotone/Restless) 1992
This Is Madness (Douglas) 1971 (Metrotone/Restless) 1992
Chastisement (Blue Thumb) 1972 (Celluloid) 1992
At Last (Blue Thumb) 1973
Delights of the Garden (Casablanca) 1975 (Celluloid) 1985
Oh My People (Celluloid) 1985
Freedom Express (Celluloid) 1991
Retro Fit (Celluloid) 1992
Holy Terror (Black Arc/Rykodisc) 1995
The Best of the Prime Time Rhyme of the Last Poets (UK On the One) 1995

LIGHTNIN' ROD

Hustlers Convention (Casablanca) 1975 (Celluloid) 1985

UMAR BIN HASSAN

Be Bop or Be Dead (Axiom) 1993

JALALUDDIN MANSUR NURIDDIN WITH SULIEMAN EL-HADI

Scatterap/Home (Bond Age) 1994

ABIODUN OYEWOLE

25 Years (Black Arc/Rykodisc) 1996

There was nothing even remotely like the Last Poets when the trio of New York wordsmiths (Umar Bin Hassan, Abiodun Oyewole and Jalaluddin Mansur Nuriddin) and their percussionist (Nilaja) burst on the scene in 1970. For the first time, here was an outfit that understood African chanting and free-jazz dissonance; with the accompaniment of just hand drums, the group was able to express the message of black nationalism in frenetic howls and galvanizing taunts, using images so true to the streets they could not be denied.

The first two Last Poets recordings—1970's eponymous debut and 1971's **This Is Madness**—formed the blueprint for what's now called spoken word, and provided the essential inspiration for most message-oriented rap. The records addressed the black community using taboo confrontational language—in rants, such as "Niggers Are Scared of Revolution," designed to wake up and provoke a black audience—and insisted on a hearing for grievances long swept under the rug. (Compare that track from the Last Poets' debut to Ice Cube's "Scared Lil' Nigga" insert on Da Lench Mob's **Planet of da Apes** for a quick reminder of the group's enduring influence.) After the racial conflicts and progressive socio-politics of the late '60s, the Last Poets' turbulent delivery was a clear reminder that change was still a long way away.

There was, inevitably, an artistic decline. Following a few key personnel changes—Oyewole left in 1971 before **This Is Madness,** Hassan left afterward—the Poets began to sound like a cartoon version of their former greatness. The group recorded for a few more years, but never regained the sense of mission that informed its early work.

Along the way, however, the Poets have offered

some interesting solo projects. Nuriddin transformed himself into the sharp-tongued Lightnin' Rod for **Hustlers Convention,** a wry mid-'70s concept album commentary on blaxploitation. A decade later, producer Bill Laswell coaxed Nuriddin and Sulieman El-Hadi into the studio for a trivial, repetitive dance album, **Oh My People,** that borrows little but the name from the Last Poets.

With Laswell's help, Hassan cut timely updates of "This Is Madness" and "Niggers Are Scared of Revolution" for his acidic, jazz-centric solo project, **Be Bop or Be Dead.** The remainder of the album is filled with riffs on jazz legends and autobiographical notes on the successes and failures of black nationalism, with contributions from Oyewole, Bootsy Collins, Bernie Worrell, Buddy Miles and Amina Claudine Myers.

Two rival Last Poets have cropped up in the last few years. Nuriddin and El-Hadi issued the dismal **Scatterap/Home** under the Last Poets name in 1994. Hassan and Oyewole collaborated on **Holy Terror,** another Laswell project released in 1995, and Oyewole's **25 Years** (also produced by Laswell) the following year. Supported by the usual jazz-funk luminaries, Hassan and Oyewole summon a little of the old spark, but rarely deliver the strident message that was once their calling card. [tm]

BILL LASWELL

Baselines (Celluloid/Elektra Musician) 1983
Hear No Evil (Venture/Virgin) 1988
Deconstruction: The Celluloid Recordings (Metrotone/Restless) 1993
Sacred System: Chapter One (Book of Entrance) (ROIR) 1996

MATERIAL

Temporary Music 1 EP (Zu) 1979
Temporary Music 2 EP (UK Red Music) 1981
Temporary Music (Fr. Celluloid) 1981 (Restless) 1993
American Songs EP (Hol. Red Music) 1981
Busting Out EP (ZE/Island) 1981
Memory Serves (Celluloid/Elektra Musician) 1981 (Metrotone/Restless) 1992
One Down (Celluloid/Elektra) 1982 (Metrotone/Restless) 1992
Red Tracks (Red) 1986
Seven Souls (Virgin) 1989
The Third Power (Axiom) 1991
Live in Japan (Restless) 1994
Hallucination Engine (Axiom) 1994

MASSACRE

Killing Time (OAO/Celluloid) 1982

PRAXIS

Praxis EP (Celluloid) 1984
Transmutation (Mutatis Mutandis) (Axiom) 1992
Sacrifist (Subharmonic) 1994

BILL LASWELL AND PETER BRÖTZMANN

Lowlife (Celluloid) 1987

VARIOUS ARTISTS

Axiom Collection: Illuminations (Axiom) 1991
Axiom Collection II: Manifestation (Axiom) 1993

AXIOM AMBIENT

Lost in the Translation (Axiom) 1994

AXIOM FUNK

Funkcronomicon (Axiom) 1995

ALTERED BEATS

Assassin Knowledges of the Remanipulated (Axiom) 1996

DIVINATION

Ambient Dub Volume 1 (Subharmonic) 1993
Ambient Dub Volume Two: Dead Slow (Subharmonic) 1994
Akasha (Subharmonic) 1995
Distill (Sub Meta) 1996

CHAOS FACE

Doom Ride (Subharmonic) 1994

JONAH SHARP/BILL LASWELL

Visitation (Subharmonic) 1994

BILL LASWELL/PETE NAMLOOK

Psychonavigation (Subharmonic) 1994

KLAUS SCHULZE/BILL LASWELL/ PETE NAMLOOK

Dark Side of the Moog IV (Ger. Fax) 1996

BILL LASWELL/TETSU INOUE

Cymatic Scan (Subharmonic) 1994

YOSUKE YAMASHITA/BILL LASWELL/ RYUICHI SAKAMOTO

Asian Games (Verve) 1994

M. J. HARRIS/BILL LASWELL

Somnific Flux (Subharmonic) 1995

BILL LASWELL/NICHOLAS JAMES BULLEN

Bass Terror (Bel. Sub Rosa) 1995

AUTOMATON

Jihad (Strata) 1994

WEB

Web (Subharmonic) 1995

Straddling genres, roles and responsibilities like a veritable Atlas of the bass, Bill Laswell is an insanely prolific everywhere-at-once figure in modern music, contributing to funk, art-rock, ambient, hip-hop, world music, spoken word, dub, reggae, jazz, noise and rock as a producer, player, composer and multiple-label entrepreneur. If there's no easy way to join the dots of his career into the audible consensus of an identifiable sound (*you* find the common ground between the Ramones, Herbie Hancock, Ryuichi Sakamoto, Motörhead, Yellowman and the Last Poets), it's safe to say that Laswell has facilitated the meeting and greeting of music and musicians as much as anyone. With his enormous grasp and promethean productivity—the majority of it accomplished in his Brooklyn bunker—Laswell continually brings together ideas few others have attempted to integrate.

Of course, giving the man his career props doesn't mean anyone has to plow through all of his records. His discography is impossibly large and scattered, filled with solid achievements, nice tries and dubious missteps. He presents a sonic department store: there for browsing and selective consumption, not wholesale acquisition. Finally, Laswell's oeuvre is indicative of an exceptionally broad artist unbound by conventional concerns—of any sort. The only area for which he hasn't shown any enthusiasm is the sound of his own voice.

The Illinois native's emergence on the New York scene came in the late '70s via the group Material, an adaptable experimental rhythm section with drummer Fred Maher and keyboardist Michael Beinhorn. Making an open-ended connection between progressive rock, contemporary funk and modern jazz, Material became both a bedrock and a testing ground, open to collaborative input from guitarists Fred Frith, Robert Quine, Nile Rodgers, Nicky Skopelitis and Sonny Sharrock, saxophonists Archie Shepp, Henry Threadgill and Oliver Lake and vocalists Nona Hendryx and Bernard Fowler. Material faded out as an entity with the departure of Maher and Beinhorn (both for production careers), but Laswell has maintained both the model and the name. His subsequent endeavors are as much matchmaking as musicmaking.

The early '80s were a boom time for Laswell. With Material underway, he, Maher and Frith consolidated themselves into a side band, Massacre. He began making solo records under his own name, adding a hip-hop EP to the catalogue as Praxis. At the same time, Material became a versatile production/playing unit for hire: the group's co-production of Herbie Hancock's genre-crossing "Rockit" (1983) remains one of Laswell's hallmark achievements. It doesn't include that track, but the two-CD **Deconstruction** does anthologize Laswell's outstanding work from this era. Culling records by Material, Massacre, Time Zone, Fab Five Freddy, Touré Kunda, the Last Poets, Manu Dibango and Fela Kuti—as well as Laswell's LP collaboration with Last Exit's Peter Brötzmann (playing bass saxophone here)—the set offers a relatively concise introduction to the early proliferation of Laswell's tendrils.

As the group's only steady member, Laswell has invoked the Material name sporadically over the years. **Red Tracks** is a reissue of the band's initial EPs, but **Seven Souls** is all new, a release of energetic world music beat calisthenics with stalwart guitarist Skopelitis, reggae drummer Sly Dunbar, violinists Simon Shaheen and Shankar, and vocals by, most prominently, author William S. Burroughs. **The Third Power** focuses on the development of African-American music, with contributions from Herbie Hancock, Maceo Parker, the Jungle Brothers, Last Poets and Bootsy Collins. The results are disappointingly dull, but **Hallucination Engine** attempts to combine the designs (as well as the rosters) of its two predecessors for an international throwdown that shifts among low-key fusion jazz behind saxophonist Wayne Shorter, clubbable Indian violin droning by Shankar and funky philosophizing by Burroughs.

Praxis has also come a long way in Laswell's thinking since the early days: quite unlike the modest electro-boogie beats and scratches of the 1984 EP (which credits no musicians whatsoever), **Transmutation (Mutatis Mutandis)** involves Laswell only as a supervisor: the group is formulated as a quintet of hyper-speed freak guitarist Buckethead, keyboardist Bernie Worrell, bassist Bootsy Collins, a drummer and a turntable/mix man. The album is insane in the best possible way: a frenctic rollercoaster of stop-on-a-dime rock, soul and hip-hop conniptions tightly wound around a solid funk core. When the frantic instrumental assault needs a breather, Bootsy semi-sings over the jam groove of "Animal Behavior."

The recent Material and the second Praxis albums were all released on the Axiom label, which Laswell launched in 1990, effectively converting his undefined band concept into a full-fledged record company. As well as churning out titles by Skopelitis, Shaheen, Threadgill, Shankar, Mandingo, Ginger Baker and Umar Bin Hassan of the Last Poets, Laswell has put together a label sampler (**Illuminations**) and a dub collection (**Manifestation**). He has also convoked three star-packed repertory extravaganzas devoted to specific genre indulgence. Axiom Ambient's two-disc **Lost in the Translation** uses such non-ambient exemplars as Sonny Sharrock, the late Eddie Hazel, Ginger Baker and Pharaoh Sanders to enter that realm. Axiom Funk's two-disc **Funkcronomicon** is more straightforward: Laswell assembles P-Funk alumni from George Clinton on down (including some of Hazel's final guitar mania), Sly Stone, Maceo Parker and other erstwhile JB's, Sly and Robbie, Buckethead, Anton Fier and others for a fluid and feverishly fresh ride on the Mothership's orbital module. Be sure to check Bootsy's cover of Hendrix's "If 6 Was 9," baby. That track also provides a portion of the basis for the album by the hip-hop–centric Altered Beats: both Prince Paul and DXT (known as Grand Mixer D.ST back in the Celluloid day) have at it in decidedly different remixes. Otherwise, **Assassin Knowledges of the Remanipulated**—a loosely flowing and tedious album that has more of an old-school sensibility than befits a 1996 production (not to mention an unwound atmosphere more in keeping with ambient music)—features various DJs, from Tokyo's Krush to San Francisco's Q-Bert, as well as Jah Wobble, New Kingdom and Chinese vocalist Liu Sola.

In '94, Laswell added the Black Arc imprint to his portfolio, producing funk and rock LPs by Bootsy, Buddy Miles Express, Slavemaster and assorted P-Funk folk. That same year, launching Meta Records, Laswell began making albums of spoken word (over his music) with Paul Bowles, William S. Burroughs and others. Subharmonic (now Sub Meta) concentrates on experimental trance and ambient projects.

Divination is a continuing ambient umbrella; on **Akasha,** his bandmates are Fier, DXT, Mick Harris (the ex–Napalm Death drummer who records as Scorn and Lull and plays with Laswell in Painkiller) and Japanese bassist/producer Haruomi Hosono (ex–Yellow Magic Orchestra). It's difficult to envision what role that collective played in producing this uneventful double-disc album of soporific sound effects and wan music by the yard.

Besides his solo career (Chaos Face is a nom de bass, while **Sacred System** is an ambient/dub exercise made with Fier's assistance), Laswell has lately been whipping out collaborative albums as quickly as his temporary partners—drawn from the worlds of post-grindcore atmospherics and elsewhere—can get into and out of his Greenpoint studio. Both Harris and his one-time bass-playing bandmate in Scorn, Nicholas James Bullen, have made records with Laswell, although the latter's **Bass Terror**—which incorporates jungle and dub stylings—consists of three separate instrumental solo pieces. Keyboardist Tetsu Inoue has recorded with Laswell individually and as part of Automaton, a quartet with Skopelitis and violinist Lili Hayden.

Extending his ambient outreach to more audibly established masters of the field, Laswell has done discs with both Pete Namlook and Jonah Sharp (Spacetime Continuum). Web pairs the bassist with New York experimental ambient DJ/producer Terre Thaemlitz for another minimalist reverie, this one using rattling, scraping, walking and similarly dramatic noises to disturb the dramatic keyboard strains. [i]

See also *Brian Eno, Golden Palominos, Last Exit, Last Poets, Napalm Death, Painkiller, Scorn, Spacetime Continuum, James Blood Ulmer, John Zorn; TPRG.*

LATIMER

World's Portable EP (World Domination) 1994
LP Title (World Domination) 1995

This Philadelphia quartet shows a wonderful talent for intertwined guitar riffs (Sonic Youth meets Television), neck-snapping rhythmic oomph and dynamic songwriting. The five-song **World's Portable** barely suffers from its 8-track recording. "Wants" unleashes a barrage of twin-guitar workouts (Geoff Doring and Rich Fravel); "Good for Motion" harnesses those jagged guitar battles in a whirl of feedback and fury; "Dirgesque" and "Stringbeñder" are as good as the titles imply—the former is emotive, with drop-D guitar tunings, while the latter is punishing, leaving the track awash in interplanetary noise.

The full-length, recorded in Memphis at Easley (by 1995, the studio of choice for Sonic Youth, Jon Spencer Blues Explosion and Guided by Voices), effectively proves Latimer's debut was no fluke. Recording "Carolida," "Stringbender" and "Dirgesque" from the debut was well worth the effort—this is how these songs were meant to be heard. "Stringbender" is particularly transcendent, a calisthenic exercise in sonic abandon. The rest of **LP Title** works on the same principle—the self-assured group's guitars tangle and snarl loudly in the mix (you can recognize the Spencer sound in the Easley equipment) as the vocals (by Doring and Fravel) crackle. Latimer packs nine more bristling winners onto the record, including the angry "Kiss 120," the eccentric "Cold Front Killer" and the straight-ahead "Hold Down." Guesting on two cuts, World Dom honcho/ex–Gang of Four bassist Dave Allen acquits himself well. Fravel left after the album and Latimer continued as a trio. [mww]

LATIN ALLIANCE

See *Kid Frost.*

LATIN PLAYBOYS

See *Los Lobos.*

LAUGHING HYENAS

Stain [tape] (no label) 1986
Come Down to the Merry Go Round EP (Touch and Go) 1987 + 1995
You Can't Pray a Lie (Touch and Go) 1989
Life of Crime (Touch and Go) 1990
Crawl EP (Touch and Go) 1992
Hard Times (Touch and Go) 1995

Unlike labelmates Die Kreuzen and Scratch Acid—who were merely abrasive and unsettling—Detroit's Laughing Hyenas were, at the outset anyway, an actively threatening outgrowth of midwestern hardcore. Banshee John Brannon (ex–Negative Approach) rolled his eyes back in his head and smashed mics into his teeth; dressed in bad-luck tattoos, the scowling Kevin Strickland wrestled his bass; Jim Kimball menaced his drums like a criminal. Larissa Strickland (ex-L7) was the only member with a smile, but her chilling, isolated guitar playing was an equally intimidating part of the group's violent makeup.

With **Life of Crime,** the Hyenas' muscular, lurching version of the blues finds a precision and concision lacking on dirgier early releases. The album is a dynamo of bad vibes, the entire band hitting angrily as one tough fist of coordinated animosity. Larissa, who began playing guitar only six months before joining the Hyenas, is a cunning self-made stylist, combining limber melodic flashes with soaring, crying chords. Brannon still seems an inexhaustible well of rage, and Kimball and Kevin knock out deep, repeating grooves like cavemen suckerpunching mastodons. (The **Life of Crime** CD includes **You Can't Pray a Lie** in its entirety.)

The rhythm section left in 1992 to form the disappointing Mule; **Crawl** shows the remaining half also worse for the split. Brannon and Larissa are in howling fine form on "Living in Darkness" and the violent "Girl," but the basically excellent, accessible four-song effort lacks the electricity to inspire all-out panic. Even rebuilt with bassist Kevin Reis (soon replaced by Ron Sakowski) and drummer Todd Swalla of the Necros, the Hyenas' momentum is clearly shaken.

Coming five years after **Life of Crime, Hard Times**—seven long songs—is the sound of all-out weariness. Plenty of straight-ahead sludge rock stays true to the Stooges, the Stones and AC/DC, but the band's steel nerves have gone to pot. Straight-ahead beats and repetitious material run down what energy is left, and no one sounds like they care. The 1995 CD reissue of the Birthday Party–like **Merry Go Round** (originally six songs on vinyl and seven on cassette; the new edition adds four early tracks, including a cover of Alice Cooper's "Public Animal #9" from a Sub Pop single and a live version of "Dedications to the One I Love") would seem to be either a red flag or a eulogy, as this debut portrays the Hyenas as a most volatile and ambitious adventure. [ic]

See also *Jesus Lizard, Mule; TPRG.*

PETER LAUGHNER

See *Pere Ubu.*

CYNDI LAUPER

She's So Unusual (Portrait) 1984
True Colors (Portrait) 1986
A Night to Remember (Epic) 1989
Hat Full of Stars (Epic) 1993
Twelve Deadly Cyns . . . and Then Some (UK Epic) 1994 (Epic) 1995

Rock-star comeuppance can be a sweetly satisfying dessert for churlish observers of fluke careers that explode and collapse, but there's no joy whatsoever in witnessing the difficult struggle of Cyndi Lauper's second act. The '90s have been heartlessly indifferent to the plucky and sensitive '80s darling, and that's a crying shame.

Through a lucky strike of talent (a stupendous voice that can do more tricks than a trained seal), tunes (a bizarre but superlative convocation of new wave and pop originals and covers, sparked by Robert Hazard's seemingly innocuous "Girls Just Want to Have Fun") and timing (just reaching its stride and household penetration, the two-and-a-half-year-old MTV was desperately seeking colorful characters for mutually satisfying liaisons), the New York native's first solo album, released in January '84, was positively unstoppable, spawning five remarkably dissimilar hit singles (from ebullient to somber, giddy to bitter) before relinquishing its grabby hold on the era's imagination.

The second album has three equally delightful tunes ("Maybe He'll Know," "True Colors" and "Change of Heart"), but otherwise falls on its face. Other than the touching "I Drove All Night," **A Night to Remember** sinks even lower. It's downright depressing to hear such a gifted singer turn her natural abilities into a costume parade of no-two-the-same vocal guises in service of mediocre, often bizarre, material by various hits-for-hire types.

Lauper's life followed her career for a while; divorce and illness (followed, more auspiciously, by a new marriage) kept her from making a new album for four years. When she did, Lauper had the good sense to co-write all of the autobiographical songs on **Hat Full of Stars,** collaborating with such empathetic pals as Allee Willis, Mary Chapin Carpenter, Nicky Holland and Rob Hyman and Eric Bazilian of the Hooters. But putting house-music hotshot Junior Vasquez in the mix as co-producer wasn't such a great notion (especially if he's responsible for the awful synth-drum sound that afflicts "That's What I Think," "Feels Like Christmas" and several others), and parading players from Carlos Alomar to Hugh Masekela through the studio dissipates any organic feeling she might have sought. The same stylistic insecurity that made **A Night to Remember** so forgettable afflicts this far-better album; the record works often enough on a track-by-track basis but has no overall cohesion. When Lauper doesn't strain to sing herself up various species of tree, **Hat Full of Stars** has a plain, honest grace. "Sally's Pigeons," despite its prosaic memory, is lovely; the soul-tinged '60s-isms of "Who Let in the Rain" and the title track, an unaffected Carole King–like reflection ("I'm trying to live in the present but I keep tripping on the past"), provide needed balance to the exertions that elsewhere mar the album.

A decade after her success, Lauper finally gave in to history's tug, and forestalled the crisis of another album with a greatest-hits package. Although salted with three new cuts, **Twelve Deadly Cyns** is pointedly aimed at springboarding a second life from "Girls Just Want to Have Fun." Pinning the song to a slow reggae-funk groove and tacking on the refrain from Redbone's "Come and Get Your Love," Lauper succeeds in reinvigorating her signature number—which inadvertently makes its original version and such first-album compatriots as "Money Changes Everything" and "She Bop" (all remastered to accentuate what never sounded like harsh, shitty and artificial production before) seem antiquated. A post-AIDS remake of Barry Mann/Cynthia Weill's "I'm Gonna Be Strong" (originally done by Blue Angel, though it's not the song for which Lauper's first band was known) and a previously unwaxed reggae original ("Come on Home") bookend the oldies. The US edition of **Twelve Deadly Cyns** eliminates one of three **Hat Full of Stars** selections (too bad) and a ballad from the soundtrack of *Tycoon* (good idea). [i]

See also *Hooters; TPRG.*

LAY QUIET AWHILE

Delicate Wire (Daemon) 1993

DANIELLE HOWLE

Live at McKissick Museum (Mill) 1995 (Mill/Daemon) 1996
About to Burst (Simple Machines) 1996

Formed by bassist/violinist/DC hardcore refugee Dan Cook and his guitar-toting brother Phil, South Carolina's intriguing Lay Quiet Awhile eventually (after a pair of EPs) came to be fronted by colorful and talented local singer/songwriter Danielle Howle.

Delicate Wire, the quartet's sole album, is an eclectic, tasteful blend of folk-pop and electric art-rock filtered through a decorous indie sensibility. Howle's ingratiating voice alludes to much but never gives her secrets away; diverse, finely played arrangements turn the literate reflections and stories of life's little excitements—a robbery, a cracked skull, a first plane ride, the veins of a leaf—into enchanting miniatures. Howle is a sturdy singer, and her bandmates match her enthusiasm and precision.

On her own in Columbia after Lay Quiet Awhile dissolved in the midst of preparing for a second album, Howle made a 1994 single for Simple Machines and then began working on a solo record (with accompaniment by her electric trio, the Tantrums) for the label. In the meantime, using a lot of the same material, she cut and self-released **Live at McKissick Museum,** an engaging acoustic album that showcases her husky singing and clever tunes. "Big Puffy Girl Handwriting" and "Frog Song" favor her whimsical side; "I Held the Satchel" (also on **About to Burst**) and "Back of Your Mind" take a more solemn look at love and life. What's more, the live disc preserves the irrepressible comic commentary with which she introduces each number. The infectious mood of this modest record makes it hard not to laugh and applaud along with the small audience. [i]

LAZY

Some Assembly Required (Roadrunner) 1994
Revolutions per Minute (Roadtrip) 1995
The Lazy Music Group (Roadrunner) 1996

The elimination of restrictive sex roles from rock has, not surprisingly, done very little to close the real-life gulf between men and women. One can only imagine the band discussions that might have preceded the decision to have guitarist Steve Schmoll, the only male member (er . . .) of Lazy, sing the garagey "Pussy Strut" on the Cincinnati trio's first album. (Actually, the song is a Cramps-ian cat pun made literal by a refrain of meows, so there was probably no thought given to it at all.) A collection of extraordinarily catchy songs informed by '70s new wave (in the vein of Richard Hell and Television) but shaped into modern indie-pop derivatives from sweet minimalism to juvie punk to organ/fuzzy retro rock, **Some Assembly Required** is hindered only by inept singing: Schmoll is artless and barely adequate, while wispy-voiced bassist Suzann Lynch carries tunes like a vertiginous waitress. If memorable originals like "Crush," "St. Christopher," "I Tried to Tell You," "Candy Kiss" and "Come Down" weren't so intrinsically appealing, their frustrating performances would be no big deal, but the songs truly deserve better.

The eight-song, 10-inch **Revolutions per Minute** divides the band's sound into its component parts: genial twee (two girl-centric originals sung with a bit more success by Lynch) and easygoing garage-pop (sung by Schmoll, who's up to the simple task). "Favorite Song" has a trace of Pooh Sticks flavor, but the resemblance of the catchy "Thea's Really Happening" to the Lemonheads ends with its title. The record's small-pleasure highlight, however, is a cover of Cupid Car Club's "Grape Juice Plus."

Obviously not operating on the same stylistic wavelength as her bandmate, Lynch left after that record. Schmoll and drummer Meghan Haas drafted Kari Murphy and set about making a new album in '96. [i]

LAZY COWGIRLS

Lazy Cowgirls (Restless) 1985
Tapping the Source (Bomp!) 1987
Third Time's the Charm EP (Aus. Grown Up Wrong) 1988
Radio Cowgirl (Sympathy for the Record Industry) 1989
How It Looks–How It Is (Sympathy for the Record Industry) 1990 + 1991
Ragged Soul (Crypt) 1995

How many great rock'n'rollers come from Indiana? Folks with aboveground vision might cite Guns n' Roses' Axl Rose and Izzy Stradlin, the late Shannon Hoon or scrappy little bastard John Mellencamp; art-pop fans might point to the Vulgar Boatmen, Antenna and Lisa Germano. Those with a nose for hard, fast, punky raveups, however, should know that the Lazy Cowgirls have been making some of the coolest, most soulful noise around for the last decade, without receiving anywhere near the acclaim they deserve. Led by balding, insistent shouter Pat Todd and blast-furnace guitarist D. D. Weekday, these anything-but-lazy boys brilliantly capture the frustrations resulting from liquor, sex and other everyday perils in their twisted anthems, suggesting a funkier Ramones or a hellish cross between Johnny Rotten and Bruce Springsteen.

The self-titled debut finds the group putting down generic roots with vigor if not much distinction, but the Cowgirls hit their stride with a vengeance on **Tapping the Source.** Never mind the covers of oldies like "Justine" and "Yakety Yak," which were sufficiently raunchy in their original '50s versions. Furious fist-in-the-air originals like "Can't You Do Anything Right" and "Goddam Bottle," a desperate testimonial to the destructive power of same—not to mention an anguished, hyped-up version of country crooner Jim Reeves' "Heartache"—capture the group's thrilling emotional fire at white heat.

Radio Cowgirl is a nicely overwrought live set, highlighted by such tasteful originals as "Meat Shop" and disheveled covers of the Ramones ("Carbona Not Glue"), Larry Williams ("Slow Down"), the Saints ("Know Your Product") and the 13th Floor Elevators ("You're Gonna Miss Me"). The CD release adds eight studio tracks, including songs by the New York Dolls ("Who Are the Mystery Girls") and Kinks ("This Is Where I Belong").

How It Looks—How It Is finds Todd and company still choking on their own bile in stylish fashion, spewing bad attitude in all directions on "Alienation Maybe," "D.I.E. in Indiana," "Cheap Shit" and other testimonials to the desperate life. The subsequent CD edition adds a remixed version of the Australian **Third Time's the Charm** EP, minus the interview that originally accompanied the five tracks. The sound on **Third Time's the Charm** is inferior to the band's other stuff, but completists won't care.

Resurfacing a half-decade later with a second guitarist and a new rhythm section, the Cowgirls unexpectedly deliver their masterpiece—and best shot at commercial success—with **Ragged Soul.** Co-produced by Earle Mankey, this wonderful blast boasts cleaner, more dynamic sound without sacrificing any of the rough'n'ready urgency. Angst eruptions like "I Can't Be Satisfied," "Frustration, Tragedy & Lies" and the almost radio-friendly "Who You Callin' a Slut?" are simply magnificent, with new drummer Ed "Stewball" Huerta making a deft, explosive contribution. Long may they ride. [jy]

See also *TPRG.*

LEADERS OF THE NEW SCHOOL

A Future Without a Past . . . (Elektra) 1991
T.I.M.E.: The Inner Mind's Eye, The Endless Dispute With Reality (Elektra) 1993

BUSTA RHYMES

The Coming (Elektra) 1996

Stomping forth from Long Island in 1991, these young protégés of Public Enemy's Bomb Squad hit with subtle Afrocentric politics coated in tasty upbeat rhymes. "Case of the P.T.A." and "Teachers, Don't Teach Us Nonsense!!" are original schoolboy pranks and light protests propelled by the sharp breakbeats of Cut Monitor Milo and the fine vocal contrasts between the ragga-edged Busta Rhymes, the exuberant Charlie Brown and the straight-ahead Dinco D. Turning the high-school experience into a concept album (albeit a none-too-weighty one) divided into *Homeroom, Lunchroom* and *Afterschool* sessions, **A Future Without a Past** is highly amiable, at its wittiest on "The International Zone Coaster" and "Sobb Story." Others subsequently took different combinations of the Leaders' formula—Busta's raspiness, the revivalist old-school routines, infectious high-energy choruses—to greater commercial success.

The Leaders of the New School made all the right moves between albums (check out their cameos on A Tribe Called Quest's "Scenario"; members also appeared in a couple of movies) and were poised to break out. **T.I.M.E.: The Inner Mind's Eye** is thus all the more disappointing. Seemingly trying to play catchup with the West Coast freestylers, **T.I.M.E.** never really takes off; only the singles "Connections," "What's Next?" and "Spontaneous (13 MC's Deep!)" manage small pleasures. The group subsequently disbanded, freeing Busta Rhymes to get his explosive solo career underway. [jzc]

PAUL LEARY

See *Butthole Surfers.*

LEATHERFACE

Cherry Knowle (UK Meantime) 1989 (Ger. Bitzcore) 1994
Beerpig EP7 (UK Meantime) 1989
Fill Your Boots (UK Roughneck) 1990

Smokey Joe EP (UK Roughneck) 1991
Mush (Seed) 1992
Compact and Bijou EP (UK Roughneck) 1992
Do the Right Thing EP (UK Roughneck) 1993
Minx (UK Roughneck) 1993
The Last (UK Domino) 1994
Live in Oslo (UK Rugger Bugger) 1995

LEATHERFACE/JAWBOX

Your Choice Live Series (Ger. Your Choice) 1995

By far England's finest, most exciting punk band of the '90s began up north in Sunderland as a pretty-good/nothing-special thrash quartet that suddenly caught fire for its third album, the band's only US release. Those who thought real punk was passé missed out on the overwhelming passion, sincerity and smarts of singer/guitarist/lyricist Frankie Stubbs. With a Lemmy-like Frankenstein monster growl, Stubbs' intellect and desire burn all over **Mush, Minx** and **The Last;** the band is equally red-hot, a finely tuned, post-Ruts pummeling unit.

Cherry Knowle and **Fill Your Boots** are dispensable; both are fine hardcore records but add nothing especially exciting to the genre. Nevertheless, the seeds of Leatherface's later work are there in the debut's "Colorado Joe/Leningrad Vlad," "Discipline" and "Cabbage Case," and the second album's "Razor Blades and Aspirin" and "New York State."

Mush, however, is a knockout. Led by a ferocious guitar attack (Stubbs and co-writer Dickie Hammond) at more manageable fast tempos—the rhythm section's work is much improved—the fifteen-song fireball has awesome throat-grabbing drive and thoughtful lyrics. Following such great tracks as "Dead Industrial Atmosphere" and the anthemic "I Want the Moon," the album ends with an eye-opening detonation of "Message in a Bottle" as if it were written by the **Give 'Em Enough Rope** Clash instead of the Police. **Mush** is a shake-you-up, make-you-angry, get-your-ya-ya's-out experience.

Minx was bound to be in **Mush**'s shadow, and it is. Stubbs' grotesquely rough voice still pours out the fury and Leatherface remains an unreservedly mighty force, but there are fewer places where the tuneful roar goes over the deep edge. The album starts off cracklin' (especially the low, fast and thoughtfully violent "Fat, Earthy, Flirt" and the old-time smasher "Books"), but fails to sustain the pace, as the songwriting lacks dramatic edge. The closing "Pale Moonlight," however, blows away the acoustic version found on an earlier EP.

If **Mush** is the punishing punk classic, **The Last** is the mature masterpiece. Recorded but a few weeks before the group split up onstage, the LP finds Leatherface broadening into more varied styles and making use of outstanding production—without sacrificing the massive muscle and precision. "Little White God" is the song of the band's career (and recalls the final days of the Ruts before heroin finished off singer Malcolm Owen). Using a huge-sounding punk/reggae beat for the verses, with Stubbs' gruff, tormented voice bellowing about the consequences of cocaine addiction ("He's in love with the little white god/He's so in love, he's forgotten about being a mod"), this dramatic single was an incredible send-off for an inspired group. Elsewhere, "In My Life" sways back and forth like a drunken rummy, and a few tracks hearken back to older days, but "Shipyards" is a curveball (a boozy, bluesy Stubbs backed mainly by piano and drums) and the closing "Ba Ba Ba Ba Boo" is an obvious tribute to Louis Armstrong.

In the wake of Leatherface's dissolution, Hammond formed Doctor Bison and Stubbs unveiled Pope, whose album, **Pope John Paul George Ringo,** was shelved when the band split up. Meanwhile, the posthumous **Live in Oslo** appeared, to prove that Leatherface was even more bloodthirsty live than on record. [jr]

LEATHERWOODS

Topeka Oratorio (Medium Cool/Twin\Tone) 1992

TODD NEWMAN

Too Sad for Words EP (Bus Stop) 1995

The Leatherwoods were a loose duo composed of Kansas-to-Minneapolis transplants Todd Newman and Tim O'Reagan, with assistance from utility man "Pablo Louseorama" (aka Paul Westerberg, who co-wrote two songs while contributing guitar, bass and keyboards). **Topeka Oratorio** is a lost classic that skirts the edges between exuberant power-pop and mournful folk-rock, a record that's all the more lovable because it's so utterly minor. The well-observed songs are mostly small-town sketches and bittersweet, overly romanticized romances: imagine Mark Eitzel's world-view fused with the deft musical drive of (early) Marshall Crenshaw and you'd have the lilt of gems like "She's Probably Gonna Lie," "Wastin All My Time," the bubblegummy "Jamboree" and the outright rocker "Don't Go Down." "Lost dogs don't ever have their day," Newman notes on "Happy Ain't Coming Home," one of several wrenchingly gorgeous ballads, and so it was with the Leatherwoods.

O'Reagan went on to play drums with Joe Henry and the Jayhawks, and began piecing together a solo album. Newman returned to Kansas, leaving behind an embittered, only half-humorous ditty called "The Twin Tone Years" ("all I got is this lousy T-shirt"). That's one of the six songs on **Too Sad for Words,** a record that lacks the esprit of its predecessor but essentially offers more of the same: acoustic garage-pop with jaunty melodies, aching vocals and a generally downbeat demeanor. [jc]

LEAVING TRAINS

Well Down Blue Highway (Bemisbrain/Enigma) 1984
Kill Tunes (SST) 1986
Fuck (SST) 1987
Transportational D. Vices (SST) 1989
Sleeping Underwater Survivors (SST) 1991
Loser Illusion Pt. 0 EP (SST) 1991
The Lump in My Forehead (SST) 1993
The Big Jinx (SST) 1994
Drowned and Dragged EP (SST) 1995

Falling James (Moreland) is one of the rock underground's most fascinating denizens—and not solely because he married Courtney Love and lived to tell the tale. He's a gifted high-octane songwriter who often obscures his best songs under cloaks of obscenity and shoddy recording, an incisive political thinker with an equally strong bent for slapstick and—for the last few years, at least—a low-budget successor to pre-surgery Wayne County, given his propensity for performing spiffed up in fishnets, cocktail dresses and full makeup. James' long strange trips have exhausted a slew of lapsed bandmembers (not to mention a seemingly dwindling audience) but, after more than a decade, the Leaving Trains remain one of the most vital agents of chaos in indie-rock.

That said, the Los Angeles band's debut, **Well Down Blue Highway,** is actually the picture of restraint: James' quietly desperate delivery suits subtly seething songs like "Creeping Coastline of Lights" and "I Am in a World Crash With You" marvelously, and when the clock registers rage-time, guitarist Manfred Hofer responds with some totally wired riffing. **Kill Tunes** sacrifices some of that reserve in favor of an old-school pub-punk approach that will remind some of the Saints (whose "Private Affair" gets a lusty run-through here). The frontman displays his boozehound-next-door humor for the first time on "A Drunker Version of You," and it provides a welcome respite from the vitriol sprayed elsewhere.

As you'd expect from an album entitled **Fuck,** James has pretty much mothballed his sensitive side. Backed by an all-new lineup—one that slows down only enough to draw a better bead on the targets it's intent on running down—he howls through blast after blast of the kind of rancorous nihil-punk that made Los Angeles (in)famous in the '70s. Blistering, but kind of numbing after a while. **Transportational D. Vices** pours more kerosene on the same fire, with James' rasp adding a fitting frenzy to tracks like "Cement." Now and again, the band turns down and James takes the opportunity to really bare his soul—an action that proves utterly forbidding on the self-loathing dirge "Everybody Loves a Clown."

Sleeping Underwater Survivors exploits James' ability to unchain that sort of nightmare-state self-awareness even more fully. On the hypnotic "Relapse, Recover" and "Room at the Bottom," he divests himself of some ugly demons indeed. New guitarist Bobby Belltower goes a long way toward establishing a heady atmosphere as well, with his stealthily oppressive sound washes. James really begins to unglue on **Loser Illusion Pt. 0,** a quickie EP that sees him rant through both bizarro-world conspiracy theories ("Rock'n'Roll Murder" seems to blame "the man" for the death of every musician this side of Jim Croce) and societal death knells ("Bleach in the Fishtank") with wounded-beast urgency.

Belltower's departure signaled a return to stylistic ground zero, where a transmuted lineup—which saw James split frontman duties with bassist Chris "Whitey" Sims, whose mediocre bass playing can't make up for his abysmal singing—recorded **The Lump in My Forehead.** While mottled with some remarkably inscrutable songs ("Bob Hope," for instance, traces all the world's infirmities back to the comedian), the album essentially gives anarchy a bad name. Historical note: James turns in his most heartfelt performance on "Women Are Evil," which reads like an open letter to ex-wife Love.

In comparison, **The Big Jinx** is practically a party album, concentrated as it is with loud/fast crunchers like "Sex War" (a duet with scene stalwart Annette Zilinskas) and "Ice Cream Truck." James even manages to slip out of horror-show character long enough to deliver one of his patented confessionals, the lovely "A Woman's Clouds."

At some point in the 1989 recording session that produced the archival **Drowned and Dragged,** it's likely that someone uttered the phrase "hey, you got ephedrine in my coffee!" Not that that's a bad thing: "Die" and "Dream Until You're Sore" are as exhilarating as they are exhausting. [dss]

See also *TPRG.*

BEN LEE

See *Noise Addict.*

TIM LEE

See *Windbreakers.*

LEE HARVEY OSWALD BAND

The Lee Harvey Oswald Band EP (Touch and Go) 1989
A Taste of Prison (Touch and Go) 1994
Blastronaut (Touch and Go) 1996

A lovely name, a tied-off, nude and unconscious nubile on the cover, pix of cross-dressing slobs with guitars, liner notes in Japanese, a phony band history that claims two decades of existence and a fully functional slab of goodtimes garage-punk—yep, that sounds like **A Taste of Prison** all right. Bowie-accented singer/guitarist Zowie Fenderblast, bassist/singer Dredge and drummer Jimmy Meat shoot for the wild-eyed manginess of freakazoids like the Butthole Surfers or Mummies, but their evident playing ability, '60s/'70s reference points and a seemingly wholesome core make the Minneapolis trio sound more like Urge Overkill practicing to be an MC5 cover band.

The EP's six songs (all included on the album's CD) match the grungey musical effort with super-trashy recording quality; a supposed live-in-Germany item could have been taped through a backstage pay phone. More purposefully, "When the Satans Come Marching In" plays an ancient medical speech about LSD over a noisy instrumental psychout. The medium-fi album itself has a strong air of Spinal Tap put-on, although the covers (Little Eva's "Loco-Motion," Wings' "Junior's Farm") are convincingly performed, and originals like "Jesus Never Lived on Mars," "Roadside Full of Tammy" ('70s crud-rock nostalgia) and the distorted "Van Gogh and the Chemical Haze" are big fun whatever the band's stupid motives.

In mid-'96, the Oswalds took another shot with **Blastronaut,** a clearly produced and wittily original tribute to Ziggyfied glam. With Fenderblast confidently cruising in his shtickshift, the trio pounds it out in tuneful slabs of sizzling silliness, covering the Move's "Brontosaurus" in heavyweight garbage, duffing up the Amboy Dukes' "You Talk Sunshine . . . I Breathe Fire," contributing such neat originals as "Easy Amplification" and beating Sigue Sigue Sputnik at its own game with "Rocket 69." Cool deal. [i]

LEMONHEADS

Hate Your Friends (Taang!) 1987
Creator (Taang!) 1988
Lick (Taang!) 1989
Create Your Friends (Taang!) 1989
Lovey (Atlantic) 1990
Favorite Spanish Dishes EP (UK Atlantic) 1990 (Atlantic) 1991
Patience and Prudence EP (UK Atlantic) 1991

It's a Shame About Ray (Atlantic) 1992 + 1992
My Drug Buddy EP (Atlantic) 1993
Come on Feel the Lemonheads (Atlantic) 1993
car button cloth (Tag/Atlantic) 1996

Major-label success found a select number of underground rockers in the early '90s, and Boston's Lemonheads certainly benefited from the *glasnost* that revealed irreverent youth pop to be as commercially viable in the new world as anything the grown-up song factories could generate. But the real achievement of onetime Blake Babies bassist Evan Dando was to demonstrate that a scenester as determinedly unmainstream as he could, via the cute-boy network of *Sassy* magazine and MTV, be made into a genuine pinup idol—Peter Tork for Generation Slack. To be sure, stranger things have happened—witness the world of Morrissey—but as a Walter Mittyesque success story, Dando's ascension from indie-rock's trenches rates a notation in the inspirational record book.

By decade's turn, the Lemonheads had become nothing more than a name and a touring vehicle for Dando. Original bassist Jesse Peretz was on his way to success as a video director; Ben Deily had also left, replaced by drummer David Ryan. The group's three albums (the first two combined on a single CD as **Create Your Friends**) had brought the Lemonheads a growing measure of fanzine/college success, especially for **Lick**'s boppy cover of Suzanne Vega's "Luka." That was enough to get the band on Atlantic in time to make **Lovey.**

Although shapeless, uninvolving, indulgent and trivial, the well-sung mid-tempo rock of **Lovey**—which, beyond a Gram Parsons cover ("Brass Buttons") and two collaborative compositions, Dando wrote by himself (and reportedly performed most of instrumentally as well)—proved the corporate transition wouldn't squeeze the pulp out of his offbeat talent. But it was another cover, this time of Mike Nesmith's Linda Ronstadt–sung "Different Drum," that brought the Lemonheads their next British chart success, served up in 1990 on **Favorite Spanish Dishes** along with an acoustic rendition of **Lovey**'s "Ride With Me" and Dando's non-LP "Paint." America's **Favorite Spanish Dishes** adds covers of the Misfits' "Skulls" and New Kids on the Block's "Step by Step."

Cutely titled for the band that originally did its cover song, the British **Patience and Prudence** EP offers "Half the Time" and "Stove" (enough with the thumb-sucking winsomeness already) from **Lovey,** plus a non-LP original and 1957's "Gonna Get Along Without Ya Now."

The credits list Juliana Hatfield (bass, backing vocals), David Ryan (drums) and Dando (guitars, vocals), and that's pretty much what you get for your money on **It's a Shame About Ray.** The simple, unambitious and nearly unvarying (except for the pedal steel on "Hannah & Gabi") album of low-key folk-rock pop—the Ramones channeled by Simon and Garfunkel—is distinctive only for the colorless enervation of Dando's singing. The dishwater tedium is broken only by a couple of neat melodies and one unnerving lyric. The breezy "Alison's Starting to Happen," "Bit Part" ("in your life") and the woolly "Ceiling Fan in My Spoon" contain all the brash energy the album can muster and are actually good enough, while the downcast title track taps out the emotionalism in Dando's reserve. Otherwise, the humalongs are strictly no-stick nothings. What's memorable is "My Drug Buddy," a musically nondescript duet with Hatfield that offers a first-person account of scoring. In the just-say-no era, Dando's casual enthusiasm is shocking, but his inability to express anything clearly or firmly makes the song just another hazy shade of enigma.

The inescapability of the Lemonheads' cover connection was reinforced when a version of "Mrs. Robinson" recorded for *The Graduate*'s twenty-fifth anniversary video relaunch got a solid MTV push and was subsequently added to a rerelease of the album, for which the powers that be took the opportunity to primly trim the title of "My Drug Buddy" back to just "Buddy." Nonetheless, both of those attention-getters were combined on the five-song **My Drug Buddy** EP, which also contains two songs from the next album and the otherwise non-LP "Shaky Ground."

Compared to **It's a Shame About Ray**'s concise, low-key consistency, the sprawling **Come on Feel the Lemonheads** (the title is presumably a '70s rock-fan wink at Slade's "Cum on Feel the Noize") virtually brims with stylistic initiative and Dando's revelatory lyrics about the hollow feelings attending adulation. Not that he has much to say about it, but the fact of his response gives the record a personal reality previous albums managed to avoid. At its fringes, the album offers fifteen bizarre minutes of sonic indulgence ("The Jello Fund") and a jarring juxtaposition of the cheese-eating country cutesiness of "Being Around" ("If I was a booger would you blow your nose?") with the faux funk of "Rick James Style" (the album's second version of "Style," an unsettling but insightful drug equivocation, this one with guest vocals by the titular star). In the center, Dando manages to vary the ratio of strong rock, acoustic singer/songwriter pop and semi-electric country without incident. Hatfield sings lots of backup without picking up a bass (Australian Nic Dalton, of Godstar, joins Ryan in the rhythm section); Belinda Carlisle guest vocalizes on the peppy and defiant "I'll Do It Anyway." Like the album's changes in attitude, the material is uneven and unpredictable, with too many wan melodies and drifting nothings that might have been developed into something if serious effort were on the agenda. Even the countryfied "Big Gay Heart" fails in its attempt to be provocative. "It's About Time" (Hatfield's showcase) has the album's loveliest melody and lots of clangy guitar noise to go along with the rueful lyrics; "Into Your Arms" is tenderly romantic. Somewhere between a discombobulated mess and an unevenly good showing by an artist in turmoil, **Come on Feel the Lemonheads** essentially clears Dando's decks, leaving the Lemonheads' future completely up in the air, where it remained until the release of **car button cloth** three years later. [i]

See also *Fuzzy, Godstar, Juliana Hatfield, Smudge; TPRG.*

LEN BRIGHT COMBO

See *Wreckless Eric.*

ANNIE LENNOX

Diva (Arista) 1992
Medusa (Arista) 1995

EURYTHMICS

In the Garden (UK RCA) 1981 (RCA) 1993
Sweet Dreams (Are Made of This) (RCA) 1983

Touch (RCA) 1983
Touch Dance (RCA) 1984
1984 (For the Love of Big Brother) (RCA) 1984
Be Yourself Tonight (RCA) 1985
Revenge (RCA) 1986
Savage (RCA) 1987
We Too Are One (Arista) 1989
Greatest Hits (Arista) 1991
Live 1983–1989 (Arista) 1993

In the '70s, she was one of five Tourists, singing lame new wave retreads with little creative control. In the '80s, she gave a face and voice to Eurythmics, an inventive and open-ended partnership with Dave Stewart in which she dared to be great in any number of stylistic settings. In the '90s, she undertook a solo career that proved that, as Harry Nilsson noted in song, one is the loneliest number.

The Scottish native's immediate prehistory is aptly covered in Eurythmics' **Greatest Hits,** an unannotated stack of chart singles that omits only "Right by Your Side" from the duo's inventory of American Top 40s. That it wholly sidesteps the disputed **1984** soundtrack is a shame, but the album otherwise collects the songs that made Eurythmics famous.

As a studio-centric experiment untroubled by a stable lineup in its early days of touring, Eurythmics never offered more than an adequate concert experience and, at times, a lot less than that. The first half of the semi-chronological double-disc live compilation, drawn from various European and American shows in the mid-'80s, is downright dire, but the later chronicles—especially "Thorn in My Side," "Missionary Man" and "The Last Time"—partly redeem the effort with energetic, skilled playing and remodeled arrangements.

Two years after parting ways with Stewart in 1990, Lennox carefully delineated the new nature of her career by abandoning the easy action of Eurythmics rock to wrap her estimable pipes around pop music of a more sophisticated stripe. Recorded with a trio of keyboard programmers and a batch of guests, **Diva** doesn't entirely eschew beats or volume, but still lays its antiseptic egg on a plush satin cushion. Lennox has the voice and artistry to sing anything she chooses, but autonomy casts her adrift in a sea of mature restraint with no creative wind blowing. She hedges her bets with the full-blooded (and magnificent) "Walking on Broken Glass," the funk-line "Precious" and the pulsing "Little Bird," but the heart of **Diva** is in lush, romantic vocal showcases like "Cold," "Primitive," the glacial "The Gift" and the stops-out grandeur of "Stay by Me." The CD bonus track—a real you-shouldn't-have-bothered joke—is "Keep Young and Beautiful," a 1933 show tune (from *Roman Scandals*) obviously selected for its anachronistic sexism and recorded with smug fish-in-a-barrel patronization and scratchy mock-Victrola sound.

Perhaps mindful of her limitations as a songwriter, Lennox joined the flood of established artists (Duran Duran, Elvis Costello, Luther Vandross, Ramones, Guns n' Roses, Gloria Estefan) resorting to albums of covers in the mid-'90s. Choosing obvious K-Tel memories and skimming their surfaces to fashion willfully wrongheaded milquetoast yuppie scum interpretations, Lennox fills **Medusa** with wan, deracinated renditions of rock, soul and singer/songwriter classics. Among the victims of this insulting mistreatment: Procol Harum's "A Whiter Shade of Pale," Al Green's "Take Me to the River," the Temptations' "I Can't Get Next to You" (done to a garish disco turn), the Persuaders' "Thin Line Between Love and Hate," Paul Simon's "Something So Right" and Neil Young's "Don't Let It Bring You Down"—what, no Carly Simon numbers on the jukebox the night this thing was conceived? The few surprise selections on **Medusa** fare even worse. Lennox and producer Stephen Lipson pulp the Clash's "Train in Vain" into laughable cream cheese jazz and bake Bob Marley's "Waiting in Vain" into a sugary acoustic soufflé. The only song here that benefits from her ministrations is "No More 'I Love You's,'" a minor 1986 hit from Britain's otherwise forgotten The Lover Speaks, and that's only by dint of the original's obscurity. [i]

LEONARDS

The Leonards (Rock Ranch) 1988
Blister (Red Planet) 1993

CUSTOMERS

Green Bottle Thursday (Vapor) 1996

Fans of fiery, unpretentious modern garage-rock with more spit than polish may want to check out the two seven-song mini-albums by the LA-based, Detroit-rooted Leonards. The 1988 debut is a bit tamer than **Blister,** recorded five years and a couple of personnel changes later, with namesake guitarist Lenny Grasso handling lead vocals in place of the departed John Pozza. His singing is rough, but there's a convincing bite and a desperation that, if occasionally annoying, can also be effective—as on "Sheep," a song about sticking to your guns in the face of what's hot at the moment. That song cuts right to what the Leonards seem to have been about. Not everything always gels, but every song has some good moments, and the guitar interplay between Grasso and Mark Slocum is often incendiary.

Calling himself Sloke, the ex-Leonard resurfaced in the Customers, notable only for being the first group to release an album on Neil Young's Vapor Records. The guitarist formed the quartet—a none-too-clever amalgam of the Replacements and Crazy Horse—with Minnesota expatriate Ryan Sexton (vocals/guitar) and an Atlanta-bred rhythm section. [ds/i]

LETTERS TO CLEO

Aurora Gory Alice (CherryDisc) 1993 (CherryDisc/Giant) 1994
Wholesale Meats and Fish (CherryDisc/Giant) 1995

If this Boston quintet goes down as a '90s one-hit wonder for the Top 10 "Here & Now," it won't be for lack of effort. Originally released by the independent CherryDisc, **Aurora Gory Alice** was a respectable local seller when Giant reissued it in 1994 (with a fancier booklet but no major changes); aided by exposure on MTV's Buzz Bin and inclusion on the *Melrose Place* soundtrack album, "Here & Now" broke big a year after the album's original release. The record's airy sonics, Kay Hanley's soaring vocals and the band's smart pop-rock songwriting make for a solid, if not especially challenging, effort. "Get on With It" typifies Cleo's approach—big swathes of guitar swirl set off by pretty singing—but "Rim Shak" features some aggressive riffing that could've come from a Soundgarden session, the sunny guitars of "I See" evoke timeless pop imagery and the unplugged "Step Back" offers pleasant pop minimalism.

While the production (again by Mike Denneen) is less intimate and organic on **Wholesale Meats and Fish,** the band's second album is the better one, featuring grittier songs, stronger performances and more stylistic diversity. Sure, "Fast Way" sounds like the Pixies, but it's a cool track, bolstered by Greg McKenna's and Michael Eisenstein's buzzing guitars and Hanley's yearning vocals. "Awake," a playful breakup winner, benefits from a percussive groove (check the handclaps and shakers!). Hanley's kittenish coo on "Laudanum" is convincingly sexy, and the clever lyrics ("I want you to be like me/It would be so easy if you'd just agree") help, too. The album's highlight, "Little Rosa," is '60s-influenced jangle-pop genius. "Do What You Want, Yeah" is a discordant, throwaway genre exercise, and "He's Got an Answer" packs some misdirected hooks that backfire, but "Acid Jed" successfully attacks neo-psychedelia. [mww]

LEVELLERS

Carry Me EP (UK Hag) 1989
Outside Inside EP (UK Hag) 1989
A Weapon Called the Word (UK Musidisc) 1990
Levelling the Land (UK China) 1991 (China/Elektra) 1992
Fifteen Years EP (UK China) 1992
See Nothing, Hear Nothing, Do Something (UK China) 1993
Levellers (UK China) 1993 (China/Elektra) 1994
Zeitgeist (UK China) 1995 (China/Elektra) 1996

Although derided as the pied pipers of the crusties (Britain's raggletaggle hippie resurgents around the turn of the decade), Brighton's self-reliant Levellers, named for a seventeenth-century egalitarian movement, proffer an undeniably stirring mix of Celtic folk, punky rock and politically charged anthems. Not so much folk-rock as modern rock out of old-time folk, the Levellers give intimate music long consigned to the margins of the pop world a jolt of mass-appeal bigness without entirely sacrificing its essence.

"One Way," a UK hit single that also serves as the opening track of **Levelling the Land,** heralds the freedom train by announcing "There's only one way of life—and that's your own." Powered by rich, fiery arrangements of rocking (guitar, bass and drums) and acoustic (mandolin and violin) instruments that give a mostly English spin to the hybrid sound of the Pogues (or, alternately, inject honesty and a rock spine into the Waterboys), such sentiments ring as resonant echoes of an ageless cultural populism. The group's weakness is letting its poetic agitprop go overboard (protesting the human cost of the Falklands War on **Levelling the Land,** "Another Man's Cause" offers nothing that hadn't already been covered far more eloquently by Phil Ochs and Bob Dylan a quarter-century earlier). But the Levellers often strike a match of memorable folk melodies and thoughtful intelligence. Objectionable on principle only to those allergic to positivist sincerity in their pop music, the Levellers—whoever their audience might be—display an enthusiasm and energy level wholly antithetical to slack hippie aesthetics.

Levelling the Land, the quintet's first American release, follows the inspiring "One Way" with the rugged pioneer fantasy of "The Boatman," a couple of rocking reels, several pungent slices of autobiography and the angry state-of-1991 report, "Sell Out." Guitarist Mark Chadwick's strong, direct voice and dramatic delivery make the catchy songs sound important even when they're not; fiddler Jon Sevink saws away with the feverish abandon of a country traditionalist, leaving the responsibility for contemporary rock stylings primarily to drummer Charlie Heather and guitarist/vocalist Simon Friend.

Following a singles compilation (**See Nothing, Hear Nothing, Do Something**), the group made **Levellers,** a harder-rocking, less distinctive and personable album. The disastrous "This Garden" slaps didgeridoo onto dance rhythms and an attempted rap vocal; "The Player" has the bland pop sound of singer/songwriter rubbish. Although the songs concern similar current-events topics, the knee-jerk protest either falls flat or is inflated and demeaned with prosaic artistry to create cardboard characters like "Julie" (living in a council flat, a young woman is made redundant and rejected by social services) and "Dirty Davey" (persecuted by the police, a poor black squatter hangs himself in prison). Other than "100 Years of Solitude" (a swipe at the apathy of "This walkman generation/In search of sweet sedation") and the scattershot "Broken Circle," **Levellers** blows it.

Zietgeist gets the group back on the right track, although the train now runs through some stylish and uneven environs. Prone to a glistening mainstream folk-rock sound (the galling "Hope St." is truly one of Ralph McTell's "Streets of London"), the band has to keep reminding itself to be righteous in sound and word. The result is an inconsistent album that waffles a little (make that a lot) but sidesteps lyrical potholes and comes across with enough pulse-quickening passion to nullify the occasional Stealers Wheel sheen. The merry jugband stomp of "Just the One" is just a grandstand play, but the sharpest rockers—"4.am," "Leave This Town" and the catchy, Clash-quoting "Fantasy" (the first two supercharged with Sevink's fiddle-on-fire solos)—are as potent as any in the band's repertoire. For all the dismaying detours, the Levellers still know which way to glory.

For a mild antidote to the Levellers' seriousness, try to find the snide 1992 novelty single, "Crusty Girl (Solstice Ritual Folksong)," by England's parodic and pseudonymous Dishevellers—Pig, Frig, Stig, Wig, Dig and Slapper. [i]

LEVITATION

Coppelia EP (UK Ultimate) 1991
The After Ever E.P. EP (UK Ultimate) 1991
Coterie (Capitol) 1991
Need for Not (Capitol) 1992

The quintet formed by guitarist Terry Bickers after his exit from House of Love severed his stylistic ties to that band, making its first impact on Britain via a pair of highly rated EPs. **Coppelia**'s "Smile" has the graceful restraint and tasteful texturing of prime Echo and the Bunnymen; Bickers' relaxed deadpan shifts the focus a little, as does the production (slap-back echo on Dave Francolini's snare, sitar effects). "Paid in Kind" sets the same sort of majestic pop structure to a more insistent beat and trebles the distortion-guitar layering, but "Rosemary Jones" is a loose-limbed ramble through gentle psychedelia.

The three-song **After Ever** follows a related

course, droning a little (the echoey "Attached"), popping a little ("Firefly") and tripping a little (the stunning ten-minute "Bedlam" matches the fader control and samples of ambient techno to maniacal feedback extrusion and the ethereal placidity of dream-pop). Levitation's songwriting is calmly handsome, but it's the band's imaginative instrumental deployment (and the uncommon balance of the mixes) that gives the records their most striking qualities.

Coterie reprises four numbers from **Coppelia** and two from **After Ever,** although half of the old songs are presented in live, sometimes feedback-soaked, renditions that sail between de-rhythmed raviness and scaled-down U2. Otherwise, the album adds two new tunes (the brisk and sinuous "Squirrel" and the floating, Pink Floyd–like "It's Time") and offers a well-rounded sense of the group's intentions.

Levitation's first real album, **Need for Not,** is at once more ambitious and less adventurous. Applying its considerable weaving skills to songs that wind up sounding like '70s progressive art-rock updated with modern trimmings, the group ebbs and flows, rushes and relaxes, roars and feints with delicately controlled power, sidling up to mainstream accessibility through the familiarity of its mellotron sound, buttery basslines, howling guitars and elongated constructions should hold for baby-boomers raised on free-form radio. Next ride on the wayback machine starts in ten minutes. The line forms to your left. [i]

See also *House of Love.*

LIBERTY HORSES

Joyland (Gramavision) 1993

For his epilogue to the Bible, London singer/guitarist Neill MacColl (half-brother to Kirsty, son of folksinger Ewan and the nephew of American folk great Pete Seeger) brought along that band's bassist Leroy Lendor, drafted his guitarist/singer brother Calum and hired American session drummer Robert Bond. Liberty Horses' lone album fell victim to various business calamities, moved through several labels and was repeatedly delayed. Rough Trade/Capitol announced it for late '92, but canceled the release. In any case, **Joyland** is pristine pop from the Ralph McTell/Gerry Rafferty/Blue Nile school. Neill's husky voice has a lot of personality; the band's songs are earnest and attractive—even when the overweening lyrical sap is rising in the elevator-smooth arrangements. [i]

ALAN LICHT

See *Love Child.*

LIFERS GROUP

Lifers Group EP (Solid Productions/Hollywood BASIC) 1991
Living Proof (Solid Productions/Hollywood BASIC) 1993

Former Hollywood BASIC president and hip-hop visionary Dave "Funken" Klein had lots of good ideas; the concept of making a record out of the *Scared Straight* anti-crime program was one. Formed by Rahway Prison (New Jersey) inmate Maxwell Melvins and consisting of real life-sentence convicts, the Lifers Group represented a small effort to reverse some negative trends. Klein and Melvins saw a hard-hitting album recorded inside the prison as a way of broadening the Lifers Group's message.

The first EP has only four proper songs but is filled out with edits, remixes and bonus beats. The centerpiece of **Lifers Group,** "The Real Deal," is chilling material. Although most of the themes had already been covered, sometimes more adeptly, by Public Enemy and N.W.A, authenticity lends an undeniable edge to the lyrics. Knowledge Born Allah recalls Kool G Rap at his finest, while Rocky D and Chuck X also contribute hard verses; the European duo Solid Productions provides appropriately direct, angular funk.

Living Proof trades intensity for a showcase of Rahway's considerable lyrical/musical talents. "Freestyle 1" is just that. The problem is not in the message or the sound—as on-point as ever—but in the very anonymity of the performers. Ironically, with record labels marketing the "realism" of so-called gangstas, the Lifers Group's inside story could barely compete. [jzc]

LIFE, SEX & DEATH

The Silent Majority (Reprise) 1992

Rarely has a manufactured hype backfired on a scale as massive as the one that blew up in the face of this Chicago-to-Los-Angeles circus-metal act and the label that shelled out what was mooted to be a record-setting advance in order to sign it. Exploitive on levels even Malcolm McLaren would never have dreamed of, Life, Sex & Death was a sub–Jane's Addiction ensemble with a very dubious gimmick—a singer named Stanley, who (depending on which story you believe) was either a well-schooled poseur pretending to be a filth-encrusted, mentally unbalanced derelict plucked from the streets of his hometown or an authentic example of same. (This topic was actually hotly debated in the letters pages of several Los Angeles publications.)

Either way, the quartet proved so utterly sickening in action that its audio component didn't get much attention —**The Silent Majority** doesn't do much to encourage further exploration. The gravel-voiced Stanley (who was later revealed to be a well-traveled glam-metal singer named Chris Stann) alternates between fried stream-of-consciousness rants (like "Tank" and "Train") and puerile phallocentric limericks ("Big Black Bush" and "Wet Your Lips") while guitarist/mastermind Alex Cain regurgitates an endless stream of lackluster riffs retrieved from Dave Navarro's dustbin. For once, P. T. Barnum's pet axiom about underestimating the intelligence of the American people was proved wrong: **The Silent Majority,** followed logically by Life, Sex & Death, sank without a trace. [dss]

LIGHTNING SEEDS

Cloudcuckooland (UK Ghetto) 1989 (MCA) 1990
Sense (MCA) 1992
Jollification (Trauma) 1994
Pure Lightning Seeds (UK Virgin) 1996

As a member of Big in Japan, guitarist Ian Broudie was a participant in the late-'70s Liverpool new wave scene that spawned Echo and the Bunnymen and The Teardrop Explodes. He found far greater success as a producer, however, and became an architect for one wing of England's modern pop hangover in the '80s. But Broudie evidently had it in his heart to be a musician, and the start of a new decade found him launching the Lightning Seeds, essentially as a solo endeavor.

Looking the part of a bespectacled technerd on the **Cloudcuckooland** cover, Broudie admits minor contributions from such local pals as Ian McNabb (of Icicle Works), Henry Priestman (Yachts/Christians) and Andy McCluskey (Orchestral Manoeuvres in the Dark) but otherwise mixes his high-tech power-pop and Pet Shop metaphors without outside assistance. With glorious choruses like the one on "Pure," the album is eminently agreeable, but strictly the sum of its sources. Broudie rewrites both the Rolling Stones and Righteous Brothers on "All I Want," croons an evanescent '60s falsetto in "Sweet Dreams" and strings up a Troggsy folk-rock feel underpinned by modern dance beats for "Fools." His lyrics are equally run-of-the-romantic-mill, but no less appealing for it.

Broudie made a studio partner of synth programmer Simon Rogers (an '80s member of the Fall) and songwriter collaborators of Ian McNabb and Terry Hall (Specials/Fun Boy Three/Colourfield) on **Sense.** If Broudie used his vocal resemblance to Neil Tennant as an intriguing gimmick on the debut, he seems determined to transform Lightning Seeds into Pet Shop Little Brothers at a couple of points (most obviously "The Life of Riley" and "Blowing Bubbles") on this disgruntled production extravaganza. As he shifts rhythms and arrangement styles across the spectrum of contemporary techno-pop, every filligreed touch seems borrowed from somebody, whether Elvis Costello and Julian Cope ("A Cool Place"), Nick Lowe and Spandau Ballet ("Sense") or Stone Roses and the The ("Where Flowers Fade"). A strange achievement and not an altogether unpleasant one.

While continuing with Rogers and **Sense**'s other intimates, adding vocalists Alison Moyet and Marina Van Rooy to the team for one song each on **Jollification.** Broudie wrote and sings "Change," its best song, all by his lonesome. Wisely taking pains to not simply ape others here, he uses fewer dance beats and comes up with better results. Still, Broudie needs the right sort of goal, like modernizing the Beatles in "Perfect" or upending Depeche Mode's bleak electronic hustle in "Marvellous," to engage his gears. If true originality continues to elude the Lightning Seeds, at least Broudie's radar is scanning an ever-widening horizon for inspiration.

Pure Lightning Seeds is a British compilation of the first two albums. [i]

See also *TPRG.*

LIGHTNIN' ROD

See *Last Poets.*

LILACS

See *Green.*

LILYS

In the Presence of Nothing (Slumberland/spinART) 1992
A Brief History of Amazing Letdowns EP (spinART) 1994
Eccsame the Photon Band (spinART) 1995
Better Can't Make Your Life Better (Ché/Sire) 1996

The Lilys' first single, 1991's "February 14th," channels My Bloody Valentine pretty intensely, although there's a touch of Dinosaur Jr in Kurt Heasley's croak as well. The next year's **In the Presence of Nothing** (a jab at Velvet Crush), on which the lineup included members of Velocity Girl and Suddenly, Tammy!, is even more a product of hero-worship. Songs like "There's No Such Thing as Black Orchids" and "Tone Bender" could have come straight off **Loveless,** from the guitar effects to the weird conjunction of chords to the breathy androgyny of Heasley's vocals. The album also includes a glacial twelve-minute instrumental, "The Way Snowflakes Fall," and an unlabeled appearance of "Threw a Day" from the first single.

Almost two years passed before the next Lilys release, as the roving East Coast band went through a handful of relocations and a flurry of lineup changes. Sometimes Heasley—the only permanent member—would appear onstage with a six-piece band; sometimes, it would just be him and a drummer. The five-song-plus-noise-doodle EP **A Brief History of Amazing Letdowns** ditches MBV as a reference point; the band has rediscovered pleasant, straightforward guitar pop. "Any Place I've Lived" is the best melody Heasley's written to date; "Jenny, Andrew, and Me" (a Tsunami reference?) has a clever strummed solo over knotty chords.

Eccsame the Photon Band is a much crazier record, and a much quieter one. Recorded mostly as a duo with Heasley and Harold Evans (of Poole), it consists largely of long, slow, spare songs, with titles like "FBI and Their Toronto Transmitters" and "The Turtle Which Died Before Knowing," built around spaces and silences—minutes can go by in a track before anything significant happens. Listen carefully, though, and you'll hear some elegantly twisted superstructures, especially on the album's centerpiece, the impossibly deliberate "Overlit Canyon (The Obscured Wingtip Memoir)." There are also a couple of not-too-weird pop songs ("The Hermit Crab" and "Radiotricity") as well as a lovely fakeout ending to the album. [ddw]

See also *Monsterland, Suddenly, Tammy!, Velocity Girl.*

LIMBOMANIACS

See *M.I.R.V.*

JOHN LINNELL

See *They Might Be Giants.*

LIQUOR GIANTS

You're Always Welcome (Lucky) 1992
Here (East Side Digital) 1994
Liquor Giants (Matador) 1996

PONTIAC BROTHERS

Big Black River (Fr. Lolita) 1985 (Sympathy for the Record Industry) 1993
Doll Hut (Frontier) 1985 + 1992
Fiesta en la Biblioteca (Frontier) 1986 + 1992
Be Married Song EP (Frontier) 1987
Johnson (Frontier) 1988
Fuzzy Little Piece of the World (Frontier) 1992

After playing mutant swamp-blues-rockabilly guitar with the Gun Club in the early '80s, Ward Dotson embarked on a less contrived musical course as guitarist, main writer and de facto leader of the Orange County–based Pontiac Brothers, a quartet of unlikely heroes whose Stonesy tunes featured ambivalently introspective lyrics that grew increasingly insightful until the band's late-'80s breakup.

Dotson is the sole charter member of Liquor Giants, a bicoastal band that operates in a similar vein, the main difference being his lead vocals, which are technically limited but actually a bit more expressive than those of Pontiacs frontman Matt Simon. **You're Always Welcome** is a dynamic debut, with crunchy, hook-filled tunes like "Over the Hill," "Greatest Hit" and "I Wanna Get Drunk With You" exploring young-adult angst with barbed, fatalistic humor. **Here** is nearly as good, with one of many highlights provided by "Everybody's a Genius," a tart commentary on indie-scene backbiting from someone who's obviously been there.

On the Liquor Giants' eponymous Matador album, Dotson once again addresses a litany of letdowns and fuck-ups with an unsparing lyrical eye and an awesome mastery of trad rock'n'roll dynamics. Snappy pop-rockers like "Chocolate Clown" and "Jerked Around" and more restrained tunes like "Here" and "Hideous Pleasure" show him melding garage crunch, pure-pop pleasure and hard-won lyrical insight as deftly as ever.

In between the first two Liquor Giants discs, Dotson (who'd moved for a while to New York, where he'd also recorded with the Pussywillows and the Hello Strangers) reconvened the Pontiac Brothers to make **Fuzzy Little Piece of the World.** Though apparently conceived as a casual one-off, the album retains the balance of beery abandon and wounded introspection that originally made the band special, while maintaining the requisite level of tunefulness on numbers like "Cry" and "Clowns Join the Circus." Around the same time, Frontier paired up **Doll Hut** and **Fiesta en la Biblioteca** and reissued them on a single CD. [ss]

See also *Gun Club; TPRG.*

LIQUORICE

See *Tsunami.*

LITTLE VILLAGE

See *John Hiatt.*

LIVE

Four Songs EP (Radioactive) 1991
Mental Jewelry (Radioactive) 1991
Throwing Copper (Radioactive) 1994

Between the increasingly smug, ironic stance of most post-modern entertainment and the generally diminished expectations of a generation resigned to also-ran status, it's somewhat surprising that a band like this quartet from York, Pennsylvania, materialized at all, much less took up residence at the apex of the pop charts. With an affinity for oversized, passionate anthems and guileless expressions of morality, in both the implicitly Christian and devoutly humanist sense, Live recalls nothing so much as a Stateside U2: armed and ready for spiritual battle at all times. Trouble is, their musical weapons are loaded with blanks.

The group had been together for several years—since junior high school, actually—by the time it evolved into the Amish-rock juggernaut of **Mental Jewelry,** produced by Jerry Harrison. That description isn't as far-fetched as it might first seem—deadly earnest frontman Ed Kowalczyk is so suspicious of all things corporeal that he does everything but don a hair-shirt for band photos. The band's breast-beating breakthrough single, "Operation Spirit" (also the lead track of the accurately titled **Four Songs** EP, which boasts two non-LP cuts), preaches self-denial as a way of life.

Bassist Patrick Dahlheimer and drummer Chad Gracey may worship at the shrine of Our Lady of Perpetual Motion, but their disjointed cadences seldom coalesce into tenable rhythms. Similarly, Kowalczyk's resonant baritone musters plenty of bluster, but little in the way of tunefulness—which only accentuates the self-importance of the proceedings. It's one thing to keep the faith, but Live's insistence on anointing themselves post-modern saviors (see the self-important "Take My Anthem") is remarkably off-putting.

It took Live three years to follow the success of their debut, and the ensuing time did help the young band's worldview evolve. While every bit as intense as its predecessor, **Throwing Copper** is markedly less starry-eyed. Not so much cynical as world-weary, the bulk of the tracks gnash and wail dolefully enough to cast Live as a less muscular little brother to Pearl Jam. Having pondered the spirit world, Kowalczyk seems more interested in tactile matters this time: not surprisingly, he doesn't like what he sees. "The Dam at Otter Creek" details a backwoods murder; the undeniably gripping "White, Discussion" provides a millennialist's up-close-and-personal look at Armageddon; both feature clever guitar embellishment by Chad Taylor.

It's hard to argue with the sort of personal politics Kowalczyk and Live espouse in songs like "Selling the Drama"—and that lack of conflict is precisely what makes them so prosaic: does the band think that its audience needs to be told that racism, world hunger and nuclear war are bad things? Let's see them get into topics that really pit brother against brother—like which of the Stooges was cooler, Iggy or Shemp? After all, as Bono learned, it's better to laugh at yourself before others do it for you. [dss]

LIVING COLOUR

Vivid (Epic) 1988
Time's Up (Epic) 1990
Biscuits EP (Epic) 1991
Stain (Epic) 1993
Dread (Japan. Epic/Sony) 1993
Pride (Epic) 1995

VERNON REID

Mistaken Identity (550 Music/Epic) 1996

At the turn of the decade, Living Colour was poised to spearhead the first trend of the '90s. The New York quartet's debut, **Vivid,** was a two-million seller that kicked open the door for black bands to enter the hard-rock mainstream. Touring with the Rolling Stones in 1989 helped. And thanks to MTV, the revolution was being televised. Unfortunately, the movement never really caught fire, and by mid-decade Living Colour had sputtered along with it.

Not for lack of trying, though. **Time's Up** is a worthy successor to **Vivid** and the best of Living Colour's albums, a stylistically broad effort that delivers a pointed Afrocentric treatise ("Pride," "New Jack Theme," "Elvis Is Dead") while employing guest cameos from Little Richard, Queen Latifah and ex–James Brown saxman Maceo Parker. The title track pays homage to mentors Bad Brains, while "Pride,"

"Type" and "Information Overload" keep the group's headbanger credentials intact; they also bolster Vernon Reid's guitar-god status, as he twists together jazzy modals and punky, staccato riffs—though he also displays a deft touch with African high-life rhythms on the hypnotically buoyant "Solace of You." Singer Corey Glover, meanwhile, gets to showcase on the desperate blues of "Love Rears Its Ugly Head" and the spare, lusty funk of "Under Cover of Darkness."

Biscuits is a filler EP containing two outtakes from **Time's Up** and four live tracks from '89 and '91. The covers of James Brown, Al Green and Talking Heads provide a road map through Living Colour's influences; Reid's treatment of Jimi Hendrix's "Burning of the Midnight Lamp" is a highlight of his recording career.

Bassist Muzz Skillings split before **Stain**, irreparably altering the focus and chemistry of the original foursome. Doug Wimbish proved a fine fill-in, but he was still finding his way into the band when **Stain** was recorded. That's not to say the album's a bomb: "Ausländer" and "Postman" show that Reid still leads a fierce rock outfit; "Nothingness" is dense, ambient funk that lets Glover roll over a fluid Wimbish bass vamp. Topical as ever, Living Colour offers a post–Rodney King rail against police ("This Little Pig") and makes its case for sexual tolerance on the clever "Bi," about a couple who cheat on each other—with the same woman. Still, **Stain** is off-kilter, the work of a group trying to heal itself and get back on course.

Living Colour never achieved either, breaking up during 1994 and sending Glover to a VJ seat on VH1 and Reid to myriad musical projects. The Japanese **Dread** is the best of the live souvenirs released in other countries; the group's playing is solid, brilliant at times, and it includes an acoustic version of "Nothingness" and a take on Prince's "17 Days." Ironically, four new songs recorded in 1994—which crop up on the **Pride** retrospective—form what could have been the core of another compelling Living Colour album. "Release the Pressure" and "Sacred Ground" are molten rockers, "Visions" treads more ambient soul terrain—an American Seal with testosterone—and "These Are Happy Times" is convincing, stomping funk. Too late to save the group, these souvenirs at least provide an assurance that Living Colour never suffered for ideas.

In 1996, Reid returned with his first solo album, intriguingly co-produced by Prince Paul and Teo Macero. [gg]

See also *Gravediggaz, Public Enemy; TPRG.*

LL COOL J

Radio (Def Jam/Columbia) 1985
Bigger and Deffer (Def Jam/Columbia) 1987
Walking With a Panther (Def Jam/Columbia) 1989
Mama Said Knock You Out (Def Jam/Columbia) 1990
14 Shots to the Dome (Def Jam/Columbia) 1993
Mr. Smith (Def Jam) 1995

The constant changing of the guard is essential to pop music's timetable, but the consumers of hip-hop have made career longevity as rare as beats in a ballet. No matter how talented or successful a new artist may be, the delicate balance of subjects and sounds that makes a star one day can seem awfully dated and defensive a year later; with the dominant role of producers and the singles-driven nature of the industry, very few rappers have proven to be long-term bankable investments.

Old-schoolers have especially suffered from the commercial fade. Although many of New York's '80s pioneers have continued to make records, their very endurance paints them negatively as oldtimers; efforts at attaining currency through the employment of hot studio names (a far more effective tactic in rap than rock, where the creation of music generally remains outside the purview of the producer) usually fail on principle, caught between the past and a hard place.

So who told LL Cool J he could go and score credible Top 5 pop hits off his *sixth* million-selling album in a row? (The irony of the situation is that James Todd Smith, a Queens high schooler when he began his recording career, was all of twenty-seven upon the release of **Mr. Smith.**) Well-hedged as an actor with his own TV sitcom (*In the House*), LL Cool J remains a pure entertainer (no pretense of shoot-'em-up malevolence here) and, at heart, a rap traditionalist—the very thing that has doomed virtually all of his original peers to the commercial past tense.

From the very beginning, LL came to play with a catchy pop instinct, an exuberant good nature and sharp, straight confidence on the mic. One of the earliest full-length rap albums to be issued (it was Def Jam's first longplayer), **Radio** remains a primary classic of hip-hop's original commercial surge. After that, however, a conflicting set of impulses began complicating the effort. The uneven **Bigger and Deffer** introduces mushy soul crooning, a hint of LL's extensive crossover ambitions. Equally lightweight but more imaginative, **Walking With a Panther** locates catchy hooks and sound ideas ("Jingling Baby," "I'm That Type of Guy") as well as wholesome rudeness ("Big Ole Butt") that make it an unusual charmer.

LL answered the not-unwarranted charge that he was getting soft and dated with **Mama Said Knock You Out,** a lyrically aggressive album with harder jeep-beat production by Marley Marl. Still, the three hits taken from it describe an equivocal set of impulses: the unforgettable tough-talking title track swings like a cornered titan looking to inflict serious damage, while "The Boomin' System" is a carefully calibrated nod to street-level tastemakers and "Around the Way Girl" details his romantic ideal in a genial, low-pressure jam. A funkier remix of "Jingling Baby" and the bitter "Cheesy Rat Blues" flesh out an impressive return to form.

After a three-year gap, LL dropped back in with **14 Shots to the Dome,** attempting to cover himself with references to guns, blunts and 40s in "Buckin' Em Down," "Ain't No Stoppin' This" and "How I'm Comin'," which adapts the female hook from "Jingling Baby." The efforts to push LL closer to the front of the gangsta class are unconvincing; the dancehall guest shot by Lt. Stitchie ("Straight From Queens") is all too predictable. "Back Seat" and "Stand by Your Man" (not a cover) both address "the ladies" with the same mushy unctuousness of his past passes; "A Little Somethin'" pushes an easygoing party vibe and "Cross-roads" is a bizarre but intriguing monstrosity. Most positively, on the amazing and detailed "Funkadelic Relic," LL replays his career with the avowed awareness of his strange position as an active rap antique.

Having failed to renew his hardcore credentials,

Mr. Smith turned them in on **Mr. Smith.** (Despite the previous LP's title, this is the album where LL finally unveils his hat-shielded dome.) Puffing up gauzy quiet storms of designer soul with producer Jean Claude "Poke" Olivier and others, LL plays the masterful, patient romantic, imagining a crush leading to marriage ("Hey Lover"), crowing about his stature ("Mr. Smith") and swearing allegiance to the music he used to make ("Hip Hop"). Rashad Smith heats up the funk on an explicit safe-sex session ("Doin It") and the related "Loungin"; Keith Murray guests on "I Shot Ya." Given **Mr. Smith**'s choice of sappy and crude, the **Panther** remains the best option. [i]

See also *TPRG.*

BILL LLOYD

Feeling the Elephant (Throbbing Lobster) 1987 (DB) 1990 (East Side Digital) 1996
Set to Pop (East Side Digital) 1994
Confidence Is High EP (Swed. Sound Asleep) 1995

Although his original claim to fame was as a country songwriter (and half of the hip country duo Foster and Lloyd, who recorded for RCA in the '80s), Bill Lloyd has always been a true popster at heart. His solo recordings are influenced equally by early Big Star, Anglo-pop and Everly Brothers–styled country; in addition to the requisite big, ringing guitars, Lloyd helps sets himself apart from the jangling crowd with humorous, often sardonic, lyrics.

Feeling the Elephant, which was remastered and issued on CD by DB in '90 and then given a third life (with bonus tracks) in '96 on ESD, is a super-strong collection of highly accomplished demos (most recorded on 8-track between '83 and '86) that showcases Lloyd's songwriting versatility and clear, expressive voice. Highlights include the full-throttle rocker "All at Once You Unzipped" and the insanely infectious "Nothing Comes Close." With songs like "Lisa Anne" (which contains the immortal line, "I've got a hole in my heart the size of your jacuzzi"), **Feeling the Elephant** is a must-hear for power-pop fans.

After Foster and Lloyd split, Lloyd released the aptly titled **Set to Pop,** getting a little help from such friends as Marshall Crenshaw, Al Kooper, Big Star drummer Jody Stephens, E Street Band bassist Garry Tallent and Poco's Rusty Young. A smidgen more country-influenced than **Feeling the Elephant, Set to Pop** is truly an embarrassment of hook-filled riches. There's nary a false step among the fifteen tracks, with the devastating post-breakup "I Know What You're Thinkin'," the hilarious "Channeling the King" (Elvis speaks with Bill from beyond the grave) and the plaintive "A Beautiful Lie" leading the way. Great, great songs that deserve a wider audience.

Confidence Is High is a solid five-songer (one of them co-written by Marvin Etzioni) that Lloyd recorded—solo, except for some overdubbed drums—in his Nashville home studio. [jmb]

RICHARD LLOYD

See *Television.*

LMNOP

LMNOP [tape] (Baby Sue) 1982
LMNOP LMNOP [tape] (Baby Sue) 1984
LMNO3 [tape] (Baby Sue) 1985
Elemen Opee Elpee (Baby Sue) 1986
Pony (Baby Sue) 1988 (Fr. New Rose) 1988
Numbles (Fr. New Rose) 1989 [tape] (Baby Sue) 1990
Mnemonic [tape] (Baby Sue) 1993
The Tiny Cupcake Dilemma [tape] (Baby Sue) 1994
Camera-Sized Life (Baby Sue) 1995
Pound (Baby Sue) 1996
LMNOP EP (UK Fierce) 1996

Stephen Fievet *is* LMNOP. Drawing from a consistent and seemingly bottomless well of neat melodies, memorable hooks and substantial personal lyrics, the one-man power-pop auteur from Georgia loads each perky studio arrangement with rich layers of guitar, harmony vocals and whatever else his febrile invention may contrive to add. Except for occasional descents into corny puns or gratuitous vulgarity (**LMNO3**'s "Sitting on Uranus" lands an early hit in both departments), Fievet creates ingenuous indie-pop, packed with intelligence and enthusiasm.

LMNOP's darker side (no secret to readers of the deeply disconcerting and outrageously crude *Baby Sue* comic Fievet draws and publishes as Dr. Don W. Seven) began to surface in the lyrics of the excellent **Numbles.** In a delightful voice, Fievet sings such unsettling hummables as "You're getting headaches so much of the time / Your memory has run dry and darkness is all you feel." With nine of the best tracks from **Pony** and **Elemen Opee Elpee** added as a bonus, the French **Numbles** CD is an essential introduction to Fievet's bent world of wonder.

After two further cassette-only releases—the full-length, all-new **Mnemonic** and the live solo acoustic retrospective, **The Tiny Cupcake Dilemma**—LMNOP issued its first domestic CD, the thirty-song, seventy-minute **Camera-Sized Life,** which reclaims one song from each of those two tapes. Pouring out new tunes by the bushel, Fievet never falters stylistically: with small adjustments in approach, each nugget has a full apportionment of melody, sprightly guitar, firm drumming and light, energetic, multi-tracked singing. But the even confidence of the performances belies the turmoil of the lyrics, which sail from simply enigmatic through discomforting to flat-out scary. "Stranger's Son" ends by sweetly calling its object "a scum-faced fuck," hoping "your car gets crushed." "Goodbye" starts out "Used to be a fag / I used to be a bum / I used to be a vandal / Now I'm not one." "Ush" moralizes "There can be no peace without penalty" and offers such grotesque images as "cut into my brain like knives . . . I can hear the scratch of rat claws." "Taking Off" announces "I wanna crawl up inside you and never go away." The charged-up "Torn Lining" recalls that "Imagination led me right to my death." A repeat offender from **Mnemonic,** "Fix My Wagon" jovially invites mayhem: "Kill me, please / I want to be your victim / Don't bother me / Unless you can hurt me." Only the howling feedback and somber tone of "MFSB" ("My father has lost his mind / My brother has lost his soul") suits the gothic horror of Fievet's imaginings, which no longer display the flip charm of his early work. In the voice of Daniel Johnston or Trent Reznor, such nervy sentiments would be delivered with clues to how they are meant to be taken, but LMNOP serves them still bleeding on a context-free plate with a friendly smile. Now, that's truly frightening.

Pound is forty-song CD of new material (except for four numbers from **Mnemonic**): the selections include "Unnatural Interest in Excretory Functions," "The Beauty of Death," "Retarded Fucker," "KKK Crown" and "I Don't Want to Be a Member of Your Fan Club Anymore." LMNOP continues. [i]

See also *TPRG*.

LOCAL H

Ham Fisted (Island) 1995
As Good as Dead (Island) 1996

Joining the Spinanes, House of Freaks and others in the underpopulated guitarist-and-drummer corps—but doubling those bands' aggression to a roaring grunge assault and adding bitter, funny lyrics—this Zion, Illinois, twosome (the remnants of a quartet formed in 1990) covers its bottom through Scott Lucas' specially outfitted axe and an octave splitter. Technically true to the first album's claim of basslessness, Lucas (who plays bass notes on his low strings while slashing away at chords *and* strain-singing in a raw voice) and hard-hammering Joe Daniels manage to sound like a full-spectrum band—and a 140-proof one at that. Tucking a few Cheap Trick textures and hooks into the mid-tempo punk roar (shades of the frenzied Couch Flambeau), the duo rips through numbers like "Mayonnaise and Malaise" and "Chicago Fanphair '93" with intense conviction, fortifying average songwriting with stirring performances. (The stylistic exception is the album-closing "Grrrlfriend," a brief, quiet pop ballad: "I'm in love with a riot grrrl / I'm a boy and I know that that's bad.") Although far more impressive live, when Lucas' gimmicky feat is plainly visible, **Ham Fisted** still offers an entertaining haymaker of cranked-up, stripped-down '95 noise.

As Good as Dead keeps the rock hard while bringing sturdier material to the effort, which only serves to underscore the band's creative debt to **Nevermind**-era Nirvana. Not that it really matters; Local H's songs are catchy and abrasive in the best possible way. If Presidents of the United States of America's record can capture the public imagination, this album has many of the same sonic virtues, plus the extra sleeve-tugger of sizzling aggression. "High-Fiving Motherfucker" is a hysterical put-down ("Got no taste in music / And you really love our band / Your haircut is atrocious / Been the same since '83"), while the acoustic half of "No Problem" saws away more quietly yet still draws blood. Despite the slam promised by the lob title of "Eddie Vedder," the angry song only goes as far as wondering "If I was Eddie Vedder / Would you like me any better?" It's a start . . . [i]

LISA LOEB

Lisa Loeb [tape] (no label) 1992

LISA LOEB & NINE STORIES

Tails (Geffen) 1995

In the summer of '94, a smart, sensitive take on modern relationship travails popped off the *Reality Bites* soundtrack to become the first single by an unsigned artist to ever top the *Billboard* chart. With the success of "Stay (I Missed You)," New York singer/songwriter Lisa Loeb became a hot property with a pretty voice, horn-rimmed glasses and a millstone around her neck. Beginning your career at the top leaves little room for missteps.

Far from an arriviste sensation, Loeb had been performing with her unstable band, Nine Stories (so named in collegiate tribute to J. D. Salinger), in local clubs since 1990. Long before her lucky break, the result of a friendship with actor Ethan Hawke, the Texas émigré had committed ten songs to tape and sold an untitled cassette of them at gigs. Straightforward acoustic-guitar renderings of material both ingratiatingly lovely ("Snow Day," "Hurricane," "Guessing Game," "Do You Sleep") and irritatingly precious ("This," "Airplanes," "Train Song"), the cassette—which does not include "Stay" in any form—suggests the sensitive seriousness of a young Paul Simon. But while the songs demonstrate Loeb's impressive compositional imagination, they also reveal her blind spot to lyrical clumsiness. Several fine numbers ("It's Over," "Come Back Home") stumble over language offenses: words like "stultify" and "muse," and references to Hadrian's Wall are not indicative of acute artistic judgment.

Produced slowly by Loeb and boyfriend Juan Patiño (who also recorded her debut) under the glowering cloud of commercial expectations, **Tails** is a painstaking translation of Loeb's music into mainstream presentability. And, to a degree, it succeeds in moving her past The Big Hit, which is wisely saved for the album's final slot. Conveniently, that also puts it as far as possible from "It's Over," a song that shares its melody.

Modulating the presentation to portray Loeb in three dimensions, **Tails**—which recycles four songs from the cassette—employs solo simplicity ("Sandalwood"), punchy rock ("Taffy," "Garden of Delights," "Alone"), surging power-pop (the Bangles-like "Waiting for Wednesday"), baroque folk-pop with strings ("It's Over," "Hurricane"), even something like country ("Lisa Listen"). Intensely tuneful but prone to repetition of choruses whose content merits one pass through, **Tails** is a considered and respectable account by a gifted artist with plenty of room to grow. Still, at the first inkling of the guitar introduction to "Stay," all of the effort and quality preceding it flies out the window. **Tails** meets the challenge of giving Loeb a clear shot at credibility, confirming that she's capable of much more than a hit single, but the exquisite "Stay" remains the song on which her career hinges. [i]

See also *Ida*.

JACK LOGAN

Bulk (Medium Cool/Twin\Tone) 1994
Bulk 101 (Medium Cool/Twin\Tone) 1994
Out of Whack EP (Guilt Ridden Pop) 1995
Mood Elevator (Medium Cool/Restless) 1996

Jack Logan and a loose confederation of drinking buddies spent more than a decade writing songs and recording them in various garages, working more or less for their own amusement, never trying to land a record contract. All had day jobs: Logan and his best friend Kelly Keneipp repaired swimming-pool motors. After amassing over six hundred songs on tapes of varying quality, Logan sent them to Peter Jesperson, the Minneapolis producer known for discovering and nurturing the Replacements. Jesperson went through the collected works and sorted out the forty-two songs of the two-CD **Bulk**—some cry-in-your-beer country ballads, some uptempo rockers, some lugubrious narratives about death.

Logan, who lives in Winder, Georgia, is a raconteur in the southern style. His characters wear their humanity proudly, and their circumstances update the southern gothic morality of Flannery O'Connor to include the current society of the trailer park and the long-haul trucker. **Bulk** is so diffuse it's impossible to pick just a few highlights. The rock anthems include the reverent "Female Jesus" and the tale of a sad end, "Floating Cowboy." Country sendups include the self-explanatory "New Used Car and a Plate of Bar-B-Que." The album's gorgeously understated ballads, which glance at Chris Isaak and Richard Thompson, ponder the timeless questions of love and longing in genuinely new ways; Logan wonders if, after acquiring the car and house and woman that once seemed unattainable, "Would I Be Happy Then?" The promotional **Bulk 101** is an eleven-song "highlights" sampler from **Bulk; Out of Whack** is a typically homegrown four-song EP that finds Logan's sardonic wit in rare form.

Mood Elevator, credited to Logan and his four-piece band, Liquor Cabinet (in which Keneipp plays guitar and keyboards), is a more traditional studio effort—just seventeen songs, most of them under three minutes. The discipline extends to the songs themselves, which are tightly focused yet still infused with Logan's novelistic imagery and ear for the memorable—but hardly gratuitous—melody line. "Ladies and Gentleman" is nothing more than the account of a man stepping up to address an assembled crowd; the somber "My New Town" collects the dejected musings of a man alienated by his new environment. Guitarist Dave Phillips underlines Logan's pain with graceful, elegant solos that are usually constructed from just one or two notes, and the band, which supported Logan on much of **Bulk,** has acquired the good sense to know when to roar and when to lay back. [tm]

LOIS

Butterfly Kiss (K) 1992
Strumpet (K) 1993
Lowrider [tape] (SlabCo) 1994
Shy Town EP (K) 1995
Bet the Sky (K) 1995
Snapshot Radio EP (K) 1996
Infinity Plus (K) 1996

An Arizona native who wound up in Olympia, Washington, as a result of attending nearby Evergreen State College, singer/songwriter Lois Maffeo had been a scene fixture there before starting the band that bears her name. (It really is a band—she's been known to refer to it as "The Lois.") She'd sung on the Go Team's "My Head Hurts" with Calvin Johnson, done a girl-punk radio show on KAOS-FM, been in a short-lived band called the Cradle Robbers with future Spinane Rebecca Gates and, most notably, been half of a group called Courtney Love, a name she made up with a one-time Portland, Oregon, roommate who also found a use for it. Maffeo's duo with drummer Pat Maley (who now runs Olympia's Yo Yo studio and label) recorded three charming 7-inch singles. Even after a move to Washington, DC, Lois remains a guiding force in the northwestern love-rock world.

The first Lois album, **Butterfly Kiss,** is very much in the Courtney Love mode, with Maffeo strumming an acoustic guitar and singing in her lilting near-lisp, backed by drummer Molly Neuman (borrowed from Bratmobile) and, occasionally, bassist/producer Stuart Moxham of Young Marble Giants fame. The songs are simple but lovely. "Valentine" has become something of an indie-pop standard; the single "Press Play and Record" is charming and sassy ("I'm the most terrifically bored girl the world has yet to see").

Strumpet introduces electricity to Lois' guitar, and has a few more guest stars on bass: Donna Dresch (Team Dresch) and Codeine's Stephen Immerwahr, who duets with Maffeo on "Wet Eyes." The record is dreamier than **Butterfly Kiss,** with at least two Lois classics: the blithely witty title track ("You say I'm walking around like I own the whole place / Well I do") and "The Trouble With Me" ("is that I'm trouble"). The highlight, though, is the final track, an a cappella cover of the Zombies' "The Way I Feel Inside"—perfectly heartbreaking and perfectly adorable.

The cassette-only **Lowrider** contains live performances from a couple of San Francisco shows. In addition to songs from the first two albums, Maffeo resurrects Courtney Love's "Uncrushworthy" and "Highlights" and "Long Time Gone" (the B-side of "Press Play and Record"), joins the Spinanes for their "Hawaiian Baby" and offers another a cappella cover: the Smiths' "Girlfriend in a Coma"!

Sometime around 1994, Lois toured with Amy Farina, a drummer under the only occasionally fortuitous impression that she was John Bonham. The **Shy Town** EP couples the title track (from **Bet the Sky**) with four Ian MacKaye–produced songs recorded by the rock-out lineup (relatively speaking) of Maffeo, Farina and bassist Juan Carrera: two new ones, plus the former B-side "Page Two" and Courtney Love's "Hey! Antoinette."

Bet the Sky is a welcome return to acoustic wimpiness, featuring another new drummer, Heather Dunn (ex–Tiger Trap), and Fugazi's Brendan Canty playing a little guitar, harmonica and organ. Though it contains fewer instantly memorable songs than Lois' other records, the album does have some of Maffeo's best lyrics (the hook of "Charles Atlas" recalls "I loved the boy who kicked the sand / Long before the arms made the man") and some beautiful, assured singing. [ddw]

See also *Dub Narcotic Sound System, Tiger Trap.*

LONDON SUEDE

See *Suede.*

ROY LONEY AND THE PHANTOM MOVERS

Out After Dark (Solid Smoke) 1979
Phantom Tracks (Solid Smoke) 1980
Contents Under Pressure (War Bride) 1981
Having a Rock'n'Roll Party (War Bride) 1982
Fast & Loose (Double Dare) 1983
The Scientific Bombs Away!!! (Aus. Aim) 1988 (Norton) 1989
Action Shots! (Marilyn) 1993

ROY LONEY AND THE LONGSHOTS

Full Grown Head (Can. Shake) 1994

Singer/guitarist Loney was frontman for the Flamin Groovies during that band's original rockabilly/R&B-inspired incarnation, and he's continued in a similar vein in his solo career, rock'n'rolling with the devotion of a true believer. After leaving the Groovies in 1975, Loney assembled the Phantom Movers (which originally included ex-Groovies James Ferrell and Danny Mihm) and maintained the rootsy spirit he had brought to the band, emphasizing raw, unpretentious American grit immune to the whims of popular taste.

Emerging from a five-year recording hiatus with the energetic but unfocused **Scientific Bombs Away!!!** and, another half-decade along, the spirited but sonically ragged live **Action Shots!,** Loney better serves his talents on **Full Grown Head,** which teams him with Young Fresh Fellows Scott McCaughey, Jim Sangster and Tad Hutchinson and Joey Kline of the Squirrels for a lively set of appropriately frantic originals as well as McCaughey's "Just My Kind," "Tobacco Road" and the umpteenth version of "Slow Death." On the evidence of **Full Grown Head,** this three-decade vet still has what it takes to make vital, timeless rock'n'roll; there are plenty of younger enthusiasts who could stand to take a few hints from his example. [ss]

See also *Flamin Groovies, Young Fresh Fellows; TPRG.*

LONG RYDERS

See *Coal Porters.*

MARY LOU LORD

Mary Lou Lord (Kill Rock Stars) 1995

As difficult as it was for a time to hear over the din of Lord's notoriety as the face on Courtney Love's dartboard, the Boston folksinger—a busker and cofounder of the band that became Helium—renders the infamy irrelevant on her debut mini-album, an affecting acoustic gem that is alternately sad, funny, malicious and tender. Using a whiskery soprano that can only paraphrase the harsher emotions in the lyrics and a guitar captured in all her rhythmic imperfection, Lord mixes and matches an exquisite selection of songs from the Bevis Frond (including "Lights Are Changing," the only one of the eight to be rocked up, complete with Juliana Hatfield on backing vox), Daniel Johnston ("Speeding Motorcycle") and Matt Keating (whose "That Kind of Girl," with its vindictive lyrics about "smashing pumpkins," is supposedly *not* about the Hole star). But it's Lord's three compositions that make the sharpest impression here: the wistful absence-makes-the-heart-uncomfortable "Helsinki," the smartly comical Tom Lehrer–like band iteration of "His Indie World" ("What's the story? He says, Butterglory/I say what's the news? He says, the Silver Jews") and "The Bridge," a searing, poignant entreaty presumably directed at Kurt Cobain. By making her words suit the intimacy of her voice (or the other way around), Mary Lou Lord tears deep into the soft pulp of the universal heart. [i]

TRACI LORDS

1000 Fires (Radioactive) 1995

Following in the awful tradition of English t&a star Samantha Fox, actress Traci Lords throws her voice into the dance-music ring with this album of pumping house beats. Taking able writing/production help from such styling studio gurus as Ben Watkins, Babble, Juno Reactor and Mike Edwards of Jesus Jones, Lords manages to coo and whisper her way through innocuous tagline lyrics ("I Want You," "Fallen Angel," "Say Something," "Good-n-Evil," "Okey Dokey") notable mainly for their chaste imagery and language. The only erotic content (and convincing proof of Lords' creative involvement) on **1000 Fires** is "Father's Field," a disturbing childhood rape recollection recited melodramatically over ambient Babble beats. [tr]

LORDS OF ACID

Lust (Caroline) 1991
Voodoo-U (Whte Lbls/Antler Subway/American) 1994

Lords of Acid were the only band to successfully make the transition from Belgium's new beat movement—a slow-pounding late-'80s precursor to techno—to techno itself. The group first emerged in 1988 as a collective of ubiquitous new beat musicians and producers (Praga Khan, Jade 4 U, Olivier Adams) fronted by Nathalie Delaet, who gave the band its identity by delivering salacious come-ons over churning keyboards and a drum-machine groove.

Lords of Acid's first single, 1989's "I Sit on Acid," remains the group's best mock-libidinous anthem, particularly the remix, which begins as a parody of Front 242's industrial dance-club hit "Welcome to Paradise." Both versions are included on **Lust,** which is basically a collection of singles plus filler. With lyrics that aren't much more than intermittently repeated song titles ("Rough Sex," "Pump My Body to the Top" and "I Must Increase My Bust"), **Lust** plays itself out quickly.

Three years, three singles and one new frontwoman later (England's Ruth McArdle took Delaet's place), Lords of Acid diversified their music and their subject matter on **Voodoo-U.** Providing songs for films like *Bad Lieutenant* and *Mortal Kombat* helped the band bring its techno out of the underground (which had never really embraced it anyway) and into the mainstream. Behind a fast flurry of drums, bass and guitar—in addition to the usual panoply of electronics—McArdle doesn't just play blow-up doll in songs like "Young Boys" (the lyrics of which caused some major corporate anxiety at American Records' distributor) and "Drink My Honey"; she raps in "The Crab Louse" and sings in "Do What You Wanna Do." However, other than the ambitious wailing and sampling of "Out Comes the Evil," the appeal of **Voodoo-U** depends on how much one likes Andrew Dice Clay, 2 Live Crew and others who find naughty words intrinsically funny. [ns]

LORDS OF THE UNDERGROUND

Here Come the Lords (Pendulum/Elektra) 1993
Keepers of the Funk (Pendulum) 1994

Like other hardcore musicians, hip-hoppers are generally presumed to come from America's teeming underclass; between the harsh language, rough stylings and streetwise sensibility, it's hard for casual observers to imagine mic-checking products of the environment to be by way of stable families, comfortable circumstances and college educations. Though rarely discussed, class does play a role in shaping rap style; without correlating thousands of musicians' personal histories and the contents of their records, the anecdotal evidence suggests that rappers favoring lighthearted whimsy and trippy examinations of pop culture's frivolities in their work aren't people whose real lives have been a daily struggle to survive. (The converse, thanks to self-proclaimed gangstas, is by no means reliably true, however.)

Formed at Shaw University in North Carolina,

Lords of the Underground—Doitall (Dupré Kelly), Mr. Funky (Al-Terik Wardrick) and DJ Lord Jazz (Bruce Colston)—returned home to Newark, New Jersey (Colston is actually from Cleveland), and launched their career via producer Marley Marl, who happened to be their first manager's cousin. Smoothly entertaining, loaded with diverting references, nearly wholesome and just loopy enough to make a lasting impression, **Here Come the Lords** walks a cagey line between straight-up hardcore and a slightly removed pop version of it. (The bonus track, "What's Goin' On," takes a step back to offer a bemused, indignant observation that "Everybody and their momma got a rap song . . . What used to be noise is now making a killing.") Marl's beats are, as usual, effective, imaginative and inconspicuous, setting the Lords on a solid platform from which to rhyme. The trio's claims to underground credibility are belied by the album's easy accessibility—even "Grave Digga" is no threat to public safety—but the Lords manage a deft verbal dance across prejudicial barriers with tough talk *and* friendly charm.

The solid success of their debut lit a flame of mercantile desire; merry dreams of metallic rewards and chart rankings dance through their heads on **Keepers of the Funk.** Besides razzing human beatboxery ("shooting spit in your face"), "What I'm After" specifies "the gold and, after that, the platinum . . . a stack of those plaques" as the goal; thanks to the trio's good-humored intelligence, however, the Lords come off more motivated than greedy. Too often, the MCs lock into tiresome repetition of taglines rather than substantial verses here, but when their pens get busy (as on the old-schooly "Tic Toc"), the sophomore jams are as much fun as the debut's. George Clinton even drops by to offer his words of encouragement on the title track. [i]

LOS LOBOS

Los Lobos del Este de Los Angeles: Just Another Band From East L.A. (New Vista) 1978
. . . and a time to dance (Slash) 1983
How Will the Wolf Survive? (Slash/Warner Bros.) 1984
By the Light of the Moon (Slash/Warner Bros.) 1987
La Pistola y el Corazón (Slash/Warner Bros.) 1988
The Neighborhood (Slash/Warner Bros.) 1990
Kiko (Slash/Warner Bros.) 1992
Just Another Band From East L.A.: A Collection (Slash/Warner Bros.) 1993
Colossal Head (Warner Bros.) 1996

VARIOUS ARTISTS

La Bamba (Slash/Warner Bros.) 1987

LOS LOBOS WITH LALO GUERRERO

Papa's Dream (Music for Little People) 1995

LATIN PLAYBOYS

Latin Playboys (Slash/Warner Bros.) 1994

In 1987, a bio-pic soundtrack cover of Ritchie Valens' eternal Mexican-American party song elevated Los Lobos from solid popularity and lofty critical regard (for the groundbreaking **. . . and a time to dance** and **How Will the Wolf Survive?**) to a cultural institution with the potential of becoming a freeze-dried cliché. While putting the Southern California quintet on the fast track, "La Bamba" nearly drove them (Cesar Rosas, Louie Pérez, Conrad R. Lozano, David Hidalgo and Steve Berlin) into a narrow and unwarranted oldies rut. But anyone who presumed Los Lobos would accept a vapid sinecure as a Spanish-singing Beach Boys had sorely underestimated them. Los Lobos' mission, it turned out, was to become a living repository of soulful American music as it has taken root in New Orleans, Chicago, Memphis, California and elsewhere. If that makes them something of a reincarnation of Little Feat, so be it.

Rather than fade into lazy oblivion, the group refreshed itself with a dignified and satisfying retreat into acoustic Mexican traditionalism (**La Pistola y el Corazón**) and then landed on its creative feet with the thrilling, all-American blues-rock diversity of 1990's **The Neighborhood.**

From there, Los Lobos delivered **Kiko,** a handsome but diffident gumbo-spiced album of disappointingly weak material, followed by a deep and valuable career compilation. The former, a predominately acoustic outing that recalls the Band in its artfully dull dotage, rises to atmospheric heights in the vivid and moving "Kiko and the Lavendar Moon" but otherwise settles for studio presentation over solid content: the bluesy swagger of "That Train Don't Stop Here," the bluegrass inflections of "Two Janes," the flagrant distortions of "Wicked Rain," the jazzy piano inventions of "Just a Man" and the Dixieland brass band of "Rio de Tenampa."

The two-disc, two-and-a-half-hour, forty-one-cut **Just Another Band From East L.A.: A Collection**—not to be confused with the long-lost indie record of *boleros* and *rancheras* with which the band made its folky debut in 1978 (although three tracks from that record are included here for history's sake)—fills in the gaps and amplifies the creative breadth of Los Lobos' astonishingly eclectic oeuvre. The selection of album cuts is basically right on, except for the miscalculation that short-sells **The Neighborhood,** omitting the ferocious snake boogie of "I Walk Alone," Jimmy McCracklin's twist-mad "Georgia Slop" and the tender acoustic pathos of "Little John of God." Otherwise, there are a couple of outtakes, the essential soundtrack contributions (the treatment of **La Bamba** is noteworthy: only two of the band's eight tracks appear here) and a handful of live numbers, including a vintage-sounding replay of Cream's "Politician," a subtle and sensitive '92 reading of Marvin Gaye's "What's Going On" and a version of the Grateful Dead's "Bertha" (from the same tour) that suggests a dismaying element in the band's current mindset.

During the long gap between albums, singer/guitarist Hidalgo and drummer/singer Pérez—the band's primary songwriters—convened the Latin Playboys, a studio quartet with Tchad Blake and Mitchell Froom, producers/musicians making instrumental contributions. The group's lone album is so fully realized that it sounds like the work of an actual band. (In a way, it is. Froom produced **Kiko** and **Colossal Head;** Blake engineered them.) On **Latin Playboys,** the foursome explores the off-kilter sonic territory Los Lobos ventured into on **Kiko.** If the Playboys lack the raw roots-rock energy of Los Lobos, the album has a loose, experimental feel, and its Latin-tinged avant-garde soundscapes are just as powerful in a more subtle way. Unclassifiable and unbelievably beautiful.

An entirely different side of Los Lobos emerges on **Papa's Dream.** Lalo Guerrero and his little friends tell and act out a delightful kids' story, with music by Los

Lobos. The mix of Mexican folk songs and American rock'n'roll tunes ("La Bamba" is rendered twice, in its traditional form and an electric variation) is utterly engaging, and helps propel the heartwarming tale of a blimp ride to Mexico. Educational and entertaining for children of all ages.

Barely overdue according to Los Lobos' unhurried recording timetable, the modest, lazy and good-natured **Colossal Head** arrived nearly four years after **Kiko.** Maintaining that album's range of sounds (and not just in Froom's prominent and unmistakable drum tones) as well as its slipshod songwriting, **Colossal Head** sets **Kiko**'s artiness (like the vintage-styled Latin dance jazz of "Maricela" and the wah-wah atmosphere of "Little Japan") against echoes of **The Neighborhood**'s let-it-rip raucousness: the live-sounding "Mas y Mas" is pretty much an excuse to crank up a bucketload of guitar soloing. (The album-ending instrumental, "Buddy Ebsen Loves the Night Time," further contributes to the filler feel.) This time, though, the diverse stylistic menu shifts in and around a core having to do with the acceptance of middle age. (And beyond: "Manny's Bones" offers a conciliatory view of death.) "Too tired, too tired sister, to hold my fist so high"—the resignation of "Revolution" matches the serene groove in which the album's opening number conducts its business. Meanwhile, over the steady sound of a ride cymbal that has to be about a yard across, the lethargic, party-vibing "Life Is Good" announces the band's personal satisfaction with such eminent conviction that you have to wonder where to sign up for some of whatever they're having. Mining simple pleasures, **Colossal Head** nearly makes standing still sound like progress. [i/rl]

See also *TPRG*.

LOS STRAITJACKETS

The Utterly Fantastic and Totally Unbelievable Sound of Los Straitjackets (Upstart) 1995

No matter how many groups have gone out to play in the past and never returned, surf is always up for a few twang-crazed instrumental quartets dead set on revisiting the mythical beach to recreate the crisp, bracing sounds of early '60s string-slingers like Dick Dale, Duane Eddy and the Ventures. Hidden behind garish wrestling masks and a linguistically misleading name, this Nashville quartet is powered by guitarists/songwriters Eddie Angel and Danny Amis. Amis' lengthy career shooting the rock'n'roll curl began in Minneapolis, where he led the Overtones for one great vocal 45, "Red Checker Wagon," and wound its way, in the early '80s, through New York's Raybeats, whose "The Calhoun Surf" gets covered here, and a 1983 solo EP (**Whiplash!**) before making that big turn south.

On a scale of one to kowabunga, Los Straitjackets are mighty nifty, playing salty reverb-drenched originals with colorful titles like "Gatecrusher," "Jetty Motel," "Caveman" and "Tailspin." If Los Straitjackets add nothing new to the genre (though Angel's memorable "University Blvd." has the makings of a twang repertoire standard), they uphold its great traditions in jubilantly timeless fashion. [i]

LOTION

Lotion EP (KokoPop) 1992
Lotion EP (KokoPop) 1993
Full Isaac (SpinART) 1994
The Agnew Funeral E.P. EP (spinART) 1995
Nobody's Cool (spinART) 1996

As the popularity of indie-rock burgeoned in the '90s, cities that hadn't been producing much in the way of original bands discovered themselves flooded with groups that, if not actually novel, were at least in workable synch with the sounds of the times and could contribute incrementally to the fun by making minor adjustments in the finest formulae. Such was the case with New York, where clubs were suddenly inundated by young outfits raised on '80s college radio.

Lotion, a Manhattan quartet formed in '91 by brothers Bill (bass) and Jim (guitar) Ferguson, singer Tony Zajkowski and drummer Rob Youngberg, took its early cues from a transatlantic delegation of R.E.M., Hüsker Dü, Happy Mondays and Echo and the Bunnymen. "Tear," the song that—in different versions (edgy/fierce and smooth/majestic)—leads off both the four-song '93 **Lotion** EP and **Full Isaac,** crossbreeds the ringing guitars of Manchester power-pop with a Stipe-like melody and a Mouldy vocal. While the **Lotion** EP, produced and released by Kramer, gladly lays bare the band's stylistic sources (and becomes trivial as a result), the *Putney Swope*–quoting **Full Isaac,** produced by Kurt Ralske ("a prince"), garbs them in surprisingly diverse and pretty arrangements. The brisk and tuneful "She Is Weird City" (a song recycled from the three-song '92 EP, also untitled) could be a Stone Roses outtake, but cellos (courtesy of the New York group Rasputina) and layered harmonies give the coda of the driving "Around" a baroque Moody Blues feel; tremolo guitar and Babe the Blue OX's "rumpus" (?!) pack the pulsing "Dock Ellis"; tabla, finger cymbals and droney strumming paints "Long" into another musical galaxy. But Lotion's songwriting isn't yet strong enough to connect the dots of this eclectic canvas, and Zajkowski lacks the vocal presence to hold the pieces together. As nice as the parts are, **Full Isaac** scatters at the mildest breeze.

Taking its title from another bit of *Putney Swope* business, **The Agnew Funeral** maladroitly previews the brilliant **Nobody's Cool** with the unmemorably pleasant "Switch" and surrounds it with a gorgeous cover of the Left Banke's "Walk Away Renee," the perplexing "Marijuana Vietnam," "Famous Redheads" (five minutes of pretty pop with billowing distortion and power drumming), "Treat Me," a noisy window-steamer that also rises and falls in an impressive display of dynamic control, and—twenty-one minutes later—an unlisted bonus version of it.

In a stroke of extraordinary collegiate luck, reclusive novelist Thomas Pynchon took a shine to Lotion, and wound up visiting the studio and writing the liner notes to **Nobody's Cool.** To the band's inestimable credit, his three paragraphs of prosaic musing is the record's least imaginative and involving component. Produced by Jim Rondinelli, the exhilarating album folds great gushing storms of friendly guitar noise into casually (but clearly) sung songs equipped with strong melodies and potent lyrical character. Substantial content underpins the pure thrall of sound here: beyond the breathless rush of "Dear Sir" and the shapely enigma of "The New Timmy," "Sandra"—which ends coyly with the tinkle of toy piano—avoids sensationalism despite taking the disconsolate vantage point of a man kept at restraining order's length. "Rock Chick" strikes that peculiar balance of vulnerably farcical serious irony well known to Pavement fans; "Precious Tiny" turns familial affection into ten minutes of droney feedback extravagance and still comes off tender. (For those Robert Downey aficionados with exceptionally discriminating ears, there's a chunk of dialogue from *Putney Swope* inaudibly sunk into the song's noise coda.) [i]

LOUD FAMILY

Plants and Birds and Rocks and Things (Alias) 1993
Slouching Towards Liverpool EP (Alias) 1993
The Tape of Only Linda (Alias) 1994
Interbabe Concern (Alias) 1996

The Loud Family by any other name would sound just as poppy, post-modern, kaleidoscopic and nasty/sweet. In other words, it would sound like Game Theory. Loud Family singer, songwriter and guitarist Scott was the driving force in that California band for much of the '80s; at the end, the group's ever-revolving lineup had gone all the way 'round to include original drummer Jozef Becker (who spent the intervening years in Thin White Rope) and longstanding cohort Michael Quercio (ex–Three O'Clock). When Quercio formed Permanent Green Light in Los Angeles, Miller and Becker stayed in San Francisco, taking on three musicians who'd done some Game Theory session work and also had their own band, This Very Window.

Game Theory was always Miller and whomever, so the new name was essentially a symbolic gesture. Brilliantly produced (as was Game Theory) by Mitch Easter, **Plants and Birds and Rocks and Things** kicks off with a collage of Miller-familiar sound effects and music samples. Having copped his record title from America's "Horse With No Name," Miller opens it with "He Do the Police in Different Voices," a song that quotes lines from "Come Together," "Crystal Blue Persuasion," the Pixies' "Debaser," Alex Chilton's "Bangkok" and Television's "Venus." Over the course of this nineteen-tune compendium of moody meandering, razor-edge power-pop, cracked psychedelic introspection and weirder-than-weird ear candy, it's clear that Miller is back in a big way. As usual, he surrounds rich veins of classic Big Star–style melodicism and new wavey keyboard pop with a minefield of processed vocals, techno squiggles, cut-and-paste soundscapes and recurring spoken motifs. It's either the madness of a borderline visionary or the indulgence of a studio/computer geek (Miller has an esoteric programming day job), but either way it works, adding depth, thematic unity and overall sonic craziness to songs that are already uncommonly strong. See the driving, rabidly infectious "Idiot Son," the propulsive "Sword Swallower" and the disquietingly memorable "Last Honest Face."

Slouching Towards Liverpool is a between-records stopgap. A must for completists and fans, it features one LP cut, a track from the band's brief Quercio period, an unapologetic (and perfectly swell) cover of Big Star's "Back of a Car" and three live tracks, including Game Theory's "Erica's Word."

Democracy ill-serves **The Tape of Only Linda:** it's one thing to let the other guys chip in with a few fair-to-middling tunes, but almost all of the songs are group collaborations and they just aren't as good as Miller's lone-genius work. The problem with this concise record (ten songs, no tangents!) is not so much the absence of whimsy as it is the weak material. The sound is sharp, and the quintet rocks out with an epic mélange of amped-up guitars, odd rhythms and insinuating keyboard riffs, but the disappointing end result is neither particularly inventive nor especially tuneful. (Despite Miller's denials, the title clearly seems to be a reference to a notorious bootleg tape of an isolated Linda McCartney.) [jc]

See also *Permanent Green Light.*

LOUDHOUSE

See *Sponge.*

LOUD LUCY

Breathe (DGC) 1995

The major-label feeding frenzy that descended on Chicago in the wake of the Smashing Pumpkins, Liz Phair and Veruca Salt catapulted this young trio into the mainstream after only a few live gigs and a single 7-inch on a DIY label. Loud Lucy singer/guitarist/songwriter Christian Lane struggles valiantly to establish some sort of identity on **Breathe** (produced by Brad Wood, natch), but the combination of big guitar chords and sensitive indie-rocker lyrics—exemplified by would-be anthems like "Not Here" and "On the Table"—never gels. Because Lane can't decide whether he wants to be in Cheap Trick or Pavement, Loud Lucy winds up sounding like Nirvana—or rather, any one of dozens of "alternative rock" Nirvana wannabes: soft verses, loud choruses and not an original idea in hearing range. [jt]

MONIE LOVE

Down to Earth (Eternal/Warner Bros.) 1990
In a Word or 2 (Warner Bros.) 1993

Following spotlight-grabbing cameos with Queen Latifah, De La Soul, the Jungle Brothers and Fine Young Cannibals, London-born New York rapper Monie Love (Simone Johnson) leapfrogged to the front of the female MC class with the brilliant **Down to Earth.** Like Latifah's early records, **Down to Earth** mixes up soul, hip-hop and house in a delightful musical tumult bound together by staunchly independent—and charmingly blunt—feminist lyrics. Love's prickly charisma and sharp wit fills "Monie in the Middle" (a catchy, hook-filled put-down tale of high-school romance) and the autobiographical "Don't Funk wid the Mo." Mistreatment of women is a recurrent theme: "Pups Lickin' Bone," "It's a Shame (My Sister)," "R U Single," "I Do as I Please" and "Just Don't Give a Damn" all assert women's rights and the need for self-respect in a hostile environment. Except for a rabid attack on pork ("Swiney Swiney") and the irritable tone that occasionally creeps into Monie's sing-song delivery, **Down to Earth** is a spectacular debut.

Love the second time, however, wasn't so nice. Marley Marl, who co-wrote and produced most of **In a Word or 2,** strands Love's increasingly bellicose relationship narratives in go-nowhere tracks—lazy assemblies of bass, snappy snare and jazzy accents that dig grooves and just lie in them. Untempered by repeated proud testaments to her motherhood, Love's get-out-my-face antagonism and Marl's slo-mo blandness cancel out the lively pop charm and uplifting righteousness of **Down to Earth.** Two numbers produced by Prince—the sappy title track and the empowering "Born 2 B.R.E.E.D. (Build Relationships Where Education and Enlightenment Dominate)"—aren't much better. Only "There's a Better Way," a cautionary story about HIV, hits the right mix of music and mind. [i]

See also *TPRG.*

LOVE AND ROCKETS

Seventh Dream of Teenage Heaven (UK Beggars Banquet) 1985 (Beggars Banquet/RCA) 1988
Express (Beggars Banquet/Big Time) 1986
Earth•Sun•Moon (Beggars Banquet/Big Time) 1987
Love and Rockets (Beggars Banquet/RCA) 1989
Hot Trip to Heaven (American) 1994
This Heaven EP (UK Beggars Banquet) 1995
Body and Soul EP (American) 1995
The Glittering Darkness EP (UK Beggars Banquet) 1996
Sweet F.A. (American) 1996

DANIEL ASH

Coming Down (Beggars Banquet/RCA) 1991
Foolish Thing Desire (Beggars Banquet/Columbia) 1992

DAVID J

Etiquette of Violence (UK Situation Two) 1983
Crocodile Tears and the Velvet Cosh (UK Glass) 1985
David J on Glass (UK Glass) 1986
Songs From Another Season (Beggars Banquet/RCA) 1990
Urban Urbane (MCA) 1992

Few bands ever return from a five-year sabbatical, and fewer still come back to create something vital and new after such an extended hibernation. By the early 1990s, it appeared Love and Rockets had splintered irrevocably into solo careers, but the three Englishmen (David J, Daniel Ash and drummer Kevin Haskins) weren't quitters, having shown similar survival instincts when they initially salvaged the fledgling Rockets (minus frontman Peter Murphy) from the ashes of gothic godfathers Bauhaus. Beyond the simple surprise of resurrection, Love and Rockets' **Hot Trip to Heaven** is a radical rethink, opening the trio's sound to admit ambient and electronic influences. "Body and Soul," the Orb-like opener—clocking in at fourteen-plus hypnotic minutes—signals the change with pulsing cycles of electrotones and whispered vocals, then reaches an endless, chiming main phase of repetitive psychedelic melodies that pay homage to two long-standing Love and Rockets touchstones, Brian Eno and the Beatles. The band's penchant for diversity works hand in hand with its fresh, creative ideas, from the mysterious chugging dancebeat of "Ugly" to the torchy, sitar-laden "No Worries" and the Bolan-meets-Seal atmospherics of "Trip and Glide" (gilded with wordless vocals by Natacha Atlas on loan from Transglobal Underground). Adorned with arousing samples and a distorted rap, "This Heaven" flirts with Stereo MCs–style alternahouse, while the brooding bassline and tingling keys of "Voodoo Baby" strongly recall David Lynch composer Angelo Badalamenti. With a vocal by bassist David J that is both wiry and wry, "Be the Revolution" circles itself mesmerizingly. Not until the title track, halfway through the album, does Daniel Ash even unholster his signature fuzz guitar (actually fuzz bass).

Directly preceded by a five-song 1996 EP—which includes, among other things, a Bauhaus tribute (the title track), an outtake from the band's long-lost 1988 "Swing Sessions" ("Bad Monkey") and an eighteen-minute improvisation ("Ritual Radio") salvaged after a studio fire—**Sweet F.A.** is a return to such standard Rockets formulae as delicate acousticisms ("Pearl," the title cut) and a revival of their Jesus and Mary Chain fetish (the dark drone "Use Me," with its honeyed vocal melodies); the ambient/techno vein that ran through **Hot Trip to Heaven** is nowhere to be found. That said, it's a fine album. "Here Come the Comedown" and the music-biz rumination "Shelf Life" give off Portisheady trip-hop vibes; "Natacha" (Atlas?) is alternately raw and expansive. Ash's axe is back in the power saddle, too, spiking "Judgement Day" as well as the nicely tart "Sweet Lover Hangover," which surprisingly gave Ash, Jay and Haskins another hit single.

As with **Coming Down,** Ash's solo debut (which first employed Atlas), **Foolish Thing Desire** is an enjoyable grab-bag of atmospheric post-mod rock, if less quirky and fragmented than its predecessor (and also without any of the Jesus and Mary Chain fuzz that fascinated him on **Coming Down** and **Love and Rockets**). The title track works as the sort of romantic Bowiefied ballad the Psychedelic Furs used to do so well; "Get Out of Control" and "The Hedonist" rock a bit harder, wielding muscular, noisy riffs. With its engine-revving effects and Spectorian jingle, "Roll On"—the disc's best song—continues to flaunt Ash's obsession with two-wheelers (previously noted on Love and Rockets' rumbling 1988 single "Motorcycle"), powered by a tireless Velvet Underground drive.

Like Ash's albums, the eclectic solo efforts by David J (Haskins; he and Kevin are brothers) rarely ascend to the level the two achieve when paired. After a four-year layoff, the bassist restarted his extracurricular sideline in 1990 with **Songs From Another Season.** (He also continues to moonlight with the Jazz Butcher, whose associate, Max Eider, contributes to J's endeavors.) The album follows nicely from **Crocodile Tears** with accomplished and attractive light folky pop somewhere around Lloyd Cole or the Waterboys. **Urban Urbane** occasionally leaves behind the earnest acoustics of his prior releases for an edgier, more, well, urbane approach. The funky traction, punch horns and female soul vocal accents of "Some Big City" recall the Higsons or APB, while "A Man of Influential Taste" successfully shoots for an opaque late-night jazz aura. The album sags badly in the center—the slight "Space Cowboy" only proves Ash isn't the only Rocket with a JAMC jones; "Tinseltown" and the countryfied "Serial Killer Blues" aren't much solider—but several subsequent tracks ("Bouquets, Wreaths and Laurels" and the elegant "Hoagy Carmichael Never Went to New Orleans") in his more familiar neo-folk vein save the day. Old cohort Peter Murphy puts in a guest vocal appearance on "Candy on the Cross." [gef]

See also *Jazz Butcher, Transglobal Underground; TPRG.*

LOVE AS LAUGHTER

See *Lync.*

LOVE BATTERY

Between the Eyes EP10 (Aus. Sub Pop/Waterfront) 1990 (Sub Pop) 1991
Dayglo (Sub Pop) 1992

Far Gone (Sub Pop) 1993
Nehru Jacket EP (Atlas) 1994
Straight Freak Ticket (Atlas) 1995

If at times it seems rock'n'roll has become little more than a big money-sucking organism, this Seattle quartet has managed to get pretty far fueled on nothing but cheap equipment and cheap pot. Splitting the difference between metallic thud and garage-fuzz, Love Battery ambled straight down the double yellow line that divided the two main camps in Sub Pop's early-'90s dominion—and, to their credit, emerged relatively free of treadmarks.

Formed by singer/guitarist Ron Nine and drummer Jason Finn (veterans of local warhorses Room Nine and Skin Yard, respectively), Love Battery had a mighty impressive unveiling in the form of the classic 1989 single "Between the Eyes," later expanded as the lead track of a six-song Australian EP that was subsequently released domestically as well. Nothing on **Dayglo** approaches the headbang-necessitating riffery of that song, but the superfuzzed overkill that guitarist Kevin Whitworth wrings from songs like "Out of Focus" brings on wooziness faster than a liquid light show. Likewise, "Damaged" (not the Black Flag song) runs through a laundry list of psychologically fractured pals in appropriately cautionary "People Who Died" fashion.

Love Battery was poised in the on-deck circle to take a swing at "next big thing" fortune, but legal wrangling delayed the release of the largely ignored **Far Gone** long enough to leave a sour taste in the mouth of all concerned. Too bad, since the band (by this time including bassist Bruce Fairweather, best known as the guy from Mother Love Bone who *didn't* join Pearl Jam) had furthered its dynamic skills noticeably: the drunken ramble "Searching for Rose" slurs with appropriate unsteadiness thanks to Fairweather's mercurial basslines, while "Head of Ringo" chugs along on a melody that reflects the balmy distress of Nine's decapitated-drummer nightmare.

The four-song **Nehru Jacket,** meant only as a teaser for the **Straight Freak Ticket** album, turned out to be much stronger in its own right. Short, sharp and to the point (not to mention fitted with a charming cover of the Telescopes' acid-pop "Please, Before You Go"), it might be Love Battery's essential discharge. The subsequent album (released after Fairweather's departure and containing only two of the EP's tracks) falls victim to over-styling: "Fuzz Factory" and the bellicose "Straight Freak Show" (a tribute to journalist Hunter S. Thompson) have snap and crackle, but the pop never materializes. Having divided his employment loyalties for months, drummer Jason Finn left the band after **Straight Freak Ticket** to join the Presidents of the United States of America, who promptly went on to mass-market success. [dss]

See also *Mother Love Bone, Presidents of the United States of America.*

LOVE CAMP 7

Love Camp 7 EP (Bowlmor) 1990
Where the Green Ends (Ger. Houses in Motion) 1992 (Bowlmor) 1993
Conspiracy of the Flowers (Ger. Houses in Motion) 1994
Live in Vegas (Bowlmor) 1996

This literate Brooklyn group, named for a trashy 1968 sex flick, came together in the late '80s. Guitarist Dann Baker, bassist Bruce Hathaway and drummer Dave Campbell (sometimes with a fourth member, on guitar or sax) have a keenly developed sense of interplay, and the collaborative material could have been arrived at in no other manner. With all three core members singing—often in carefully arranged harmonies—Love Camp 7 presents a friendly sheen that stands in contrast to the quirky turns in the music and the peculiar lyrics. They can rock out when they want to, and they want to on most songs—but only for a little while, then they abruptly change direction. They're like a big funny guy who unexpectedly asks to borrow your eyeglasses. Confidently loopy without being comical and arty without being arch, Love Camp 7 comes up with either the oddest hooks or the hookiest oddities. And they occasionally turn the guitars up real loud.

Following the five-song EP and a pair of singles, LC7 began making albums. **Where the Green Ends** and **Conspiracy of the Flowers** are pretty much interchangeable. The former has such eccentric inventions as "A Million Martha Grahams," "My Love Is Measured in Inches" and "Dinah Shore (Is the Lesbian Next Door)." The band only misses the mark when it takes on covers: **Conspiracy of the Flowers'** version of Phil Spector's "Then I Kissed Her" (done as "Then She Kissed Me") shows that the group's idiosyncrasies don't translate to other people's songs.

Live in Vegas isn't. [dbg]

LOVE CHILD

Love Child EP7 (Trash Flow) 1990
Love Child Play Moondog EP7 (Forced Exposure) 1990
Okay? (Homestead) 1991
Witchcraft (Homestead) 1992

ALAN LICHT

Sink the Aging Process (Siltbreeze) 1994

9-IRON

Movie Tonight? EP7 (Feedbag) 1993
9-Iron (Safe House) 1993
The Make Out King (Safe House) 1995

ODES

Me and My Big Mouth (Merge) 1996

From a genesis as the mascots of New York's art-hipster scene, this Vassar College–spawned trio built itself a reputation as one of Gotham's most mercurial bands, able to leap from twee pop tunes to galvanizing skronkadelic constructs in a single bound. Part of that chameleon-like nature derived from the complex creative tension between bassist/singer Rebecca Odes, drummer/guitarist/singer Will Baum and guitarist/singer/drummer Alan Licht, who joined the other two in progress.

Love Child's debut EP didn't allow for much in the way of digression; its six songs chug in a palatable (if derivative) early-Velvets manner, with only the amiable "Sofa" making much of an impression. On the followup, which actually postdates **Okay?** and does not involve Baum, Licht and Odes tackle four songs (most provocatively, the droning "All Is Loneliness") from the repertoire of legendary New York street singer Moondog. **Okay?,** which reprises several songs from the Trash Flow record, can be seen as an exercise in guileless solipsism—an oxymoron that nevertheless fits the disc's twenty-one brief tunes. Odes' opalescent ditties run the gamut from faux-naïf ("He's So Sensitive") to faux-decadent ("Church of Satan"), while Licht uses his center-stage turns mostly as frames for some breathtaking (if abridged) solos. Baum, who wrote and sings over half of **Okay?,** opted out of Love Child between the album's recording in February 1990 and its release late the following year; the band's drum duties were taken over by Brendan O'Malley, freeing Licht to dedicate himself to guitar.

Licht gets a chance to stretch out a bit more on **Witchcraft;** while his expansive sorties dexterously fuse free-improv atonality and hammer-down rockism, the songs' connective tissue is a bit too frail to sustain the recurrent tension. Love Child broke up soon after its release. Licht's solo album betrays his more academic side, with protracted experiments in color and tone taking the place of rock *qua* rock structure. Fascinating in doses (a taster can be found on the pre-LP single "Calvin Johnson Has Ruined Music for an Entire Generation," an Olympia-directed salvo dripping with New York–intellectual chutzpah), **Sink the Aging Process** will fit neatly next to **Metal Machine Music** in your arsenal of, um, party platters.

The Los Angeles–based 9-Iron is Baum's dubious attempt to channel the wide-eyed wonder of Jonathan Richman into willfully prosaic indie-pop songs about meeting girls, talking to girls, deflowering girls and so on. The far-too-precious **9-Iron,** recorded as a trio with that dog drummer Tony Maxwell (contributing guitar, vocals and bass) and Love Jones drummer Ben Daughtrey (spelled on one song by Walt Mink's Joey Waronker), has a creepy smug streak that crosses out the songs' kick-me-hard winsomeness and makes it hard to side with the vocalist of complaints like "The Girl Won't Listen" and "She Hasn't Called." **The Make Out King** shifts Maxwell to drums and imports bassist John Goldman to little notable effect. "(She's So) Impatient (With Me)," "Theoretical Mind," "Trophy Girl" and "Is There Fuchsia in Your Future, Felicia" make 9-Iron seem like a blind date who's adorable until he gets to the doorway.

Odes' **Me and My Big Mouth** is an eight-song album recorded with Love Child alumnus O'Malley and Sammy guitarist Jesse Hartman. [dss]

See also *Run On, that dog.*

LOVED ONES

Boom Boom (Out Goes the Lights) EP7 (Get Hip) 1992
The Price for Love (Hightone) 1993
Better Do Right (Hightone) 1994

While the Loved Ones physically call Northern California's Bay Area home, spiritually, their musical domain is Chicago by way of London's Marquee Club. By the time the foursome united their bowl cuts in 1991, most of the rhythm and beat groups that littered the West Coast in the '80s had faded away, but that didn't stop them from declaring their stylistic allegiance to those who paid tribute to the Yardbirds, Pretty Things, Animals and Them.

Beyond its vintage graphic conceits, the debut EP exudes sharp Carnaby Street style on Little Walter's "Boom Boom (Out Goes the Lights)," Jesse Turner's "Sticks & Stones" and two originals: the Otis Redding–influenced "Hold On," written by Van Morrison soundalike singer Bart Davenport, and guitarist Nicolas Rossi's "Crying in the Morning."

Rossi and bassist Michael Ducasse split, replaced by bass-strumming songwriter Mike Therieau. With lead guitarist Xan McCurdy and a solid rhythm section completed by drummer John Kent, the quartet was able to step up to the next level on **The Price for Love,** produced by Scott Mathews and Bruce Bromberg. Highlights of this mostly original collection include Davenport's harmonica work on the instrumental label tribute "Hightone Hop" as well as the stomping "None of Your Business." With Mathews adding Otis Spann–style piano, the Loved Ones muster a convincing Chess Records sound on "I Told the Truth."

Following the lead of other revivalists (like the Chesterfield Kings) who've changed stylistic obsessions in mid-career, **Better Do Right** swaps the first album's upbeat blues charge for the laid-back groove-oriented soul sound of Stax and Muscle Shoals in the late '60s. Davenport's "What Is Love?" wouldn't sound out of place on a Rufus Thomas or Otis Redding platter. The Loved Ones have since broken up, with McCurdy and Davenport forming a band called the Supernaturals. [mk]

LOVE INTEREST

See *Pigface.*

LOVE JONES

Here's to the Losers (Zoo) 1994
Powerful Pain Relief (Zoo) 1995

Despite Love Jones' smarmy shtick—playing the '90s "Cocktail Nation" revival to the hilt, even if from the periphery—it's hard not to fall for the band's sassy, wry pastiche. Call it nuevo-retro or whatever: the five Louisville gentlemen mine vintage Earth, Wind & Fire licks, sing sweet soul harmonies and spice things up with Latin percussion and swing.

And former Squirrel Bait drummer Ben Daughtrey plays in this outfit? Uh, yep—he's the sarcastic co-frontman/conga player extraordinaire. With bassist Barry Thomas, vocalist Jonathan Palmer, guitarist Chris Hawpe and drummer Stuart Johnson, Love Jones trips back through disco, blaxploitation film soundtracks and *Love American Style* reruns to deliver tight, if disposable, blue-eyed funk with more than its share of winks.

Here's to the Losers sways into the title track in real lounge-revival style, and then paints a clever urban portrait with "Central Avenue." The rest of the debut offers percolating, excessively smooth samba-soul-funk, with smirking lyrical anecdotes of mundanity ("Li'l Black Book," "Custom Van," "Drive-In," "Ohio River") and truly tender ballads ("Warming Trend," "Fragile") that, in this context, seem more ironic than romantic.

Love Jones is more musically suave if not more enduring on **Powerful Pain Relief,** co-produced by Paul du Gré. Better songwriting and fatter arrangements carry the ebullient opener, "The Thing," into sly cuts like "Vigilante" and the solipsistic "Me." The ample Isaac Hayes appropriations here don't hurt, either. While **Powerful Pain Relief** is perhaps more fully realized than its predecessor, Love Jones sometimes sounds (is it the modern technology or something else?) more like Chicago than the **Wild and Peaceful**–era Kool and the Gang. A case of misplaced aspirations? [mww]

See also *Love Child.*

LOVE 666

Love 666 (This Record Is Not on a Label) 1994
American Revolution (Amphetamine Reptile) 1995

There's nothing exactly wrong with the slew of bands that take the fuzzed-out mayhem of the MC5 out of context . . . until you hear one like this DC trio apply it to its original revolutionary function. Get a load of Love 666's post–White Panther manifestos—a boundless array of screeds that are pro-drug, pro-violence and anti–just about everything else—and you may find yourself on the frontlines of the class war the band seems so intent on fomenting.

Guitarist Joe Johnson's emphatic string-wrestling imbues the band's self-titled debut with the sort of metallized Sun Ra spaciness that characterized **Kick Out the Jams,** a texture underscored by Dave Unger's distorted sine-wave keyboards. It's an extremely oppressive combination, but then again, you wouldn't expect breezy beer-commercial backing when a foam-flecked maniac is egging you on with words of wisdom like "fuck the man and fuck his plan . . . if you want to thank him for all that he's done / Blow his fucking head off with your right to own a gun." This *really* ain't no party, no disco, no foolin' around.

American Revolution doesn't back off the agenda for a moment. While the songs are a bit more likely to follow verse-chorus-verse structures, those frameworks are mined with verbiage every bit as explosive—most notably the martial "National" and the strobing, synapse-sundering "MDMA." So which side are *you* on? [dss]

LOVE SPIT LOVE

Love Spit Love (Imago) 1994

PSYCHEDELIC FURS

The Psychedelic Furs (Columbia) 1980
Talk Talk Talk (Columbia) 1981
Forever Now (Columbia) 1982
Mirror Moves (Columbia) 1984
Midnight to Midnight (Columbia) 1987
All of This and Nothing (Columbia) 1988
Book of Days (Columbia) 1989
Crucial Music: The Psychedelic Furs Collection (CBS Special Products/Relativity) 1989
World Outside (Columbia) 1991
Here Came the Psychedelic Furs: B-Sides & Lost Grooves (Columbia/Legacy) 1994

Throughout the '80s, English singer Richard Butler, his bass-playing younger brother Tim and guitarist John Ashton led the Psychedelic Furs, a group that evolved from derivative late arrival in the arty-poetic dissipation realm of the new wave to a pungent and stylish powerhouse in the genre's transition toward the viability of "alternative." Produced by Steve Lillywhite, **Talk Talk Talk** (which contains "Pretty in Pink," a John Hughes soundtrack hit and a great, characteristic tune) smartly set the Furs on their distinctive track: intelligently provocative modern rock songs delivered in Butler's unmistakable raspy wheeze, a languorous blend of inertia and down-turning eloquence.

Mirror Moves brought the Furs to an unrepeatable zenith of commercial/creative achievement; the rest of their career was an anti-climax. **World Outside,** colorfully co-produced by Stephen Street, recovers some of the artistic dignity and momentum the band notably lost on **Book of Days** (the pulsing and melodic "In My Head" and the grandiose "Sometimes" are especially heartening), but it was too late to keep the Furs from finally running to ground. **All of This and Nothing** is a useful summary of the band's best years; **Crucial Music** is a more haphazard but no less entertaining anthology. **B-Sides & Lost Grooves** scours the singles collection for fifteen non-album songs, remixes and a couple of live tracks. Among the treats are a version of "Mack the Knife" from 1987, a live "President Gas" from 1983 and an eight-minute extension of 1987's "Heartbreak Beat."

Living in New York in the wake of the band's dissolution, Tim Butler helped Richard relaunch himself in Love Spit Love, a quartet (unfortunately) named after an art exhibit of copulating couples. An admitted Jane's Addiction fan, the singer/lyricist applies a sense of that group's experimental neo–hard rock to his new band's debut. The overall sound is unmistakably Furry but with an even slicker, harder edge, courtesy of ex–Pale Divine guitarist Richard Fortus and producer Dave Jerden (Jane's Addiction, natch). But the disc doesn't lack for variety: witness the British music hall twinkling on "Jigsaw" and the Zeppelinesque orchestration of "Green." On the pummeling rocker "Change in the Weather" and the goose-pimply reverse lullaby "Wake Up," Butler has never sounded better—his nicotine-coated growl has over the years mellowed into a powerful scratchy croon that shimmers on his most accessible record since the Furs' glory days. [i/db]

LYLE LOVETT

Lyle Lovett (Curb/MCA) 1986
Pontiac (Curb/MCA) 1987
Lyle Lovett and His Large Band (Curb/MCA) 1989
Joshua Judges Ruth (Curb/MCA) 1992
I Love Everybody (Curb/MCA) 1994
The Road to Ensenada (Curb/MCA) 1996

You've heard of the country music outlaw? Lyle Lovett is the music's reigning white-collar criminal—and, like many of his counterparts in the real world, he's enjoyed little of the social ostracism his profession deserves. Instead, he's living in luxury, his victims not even aware they've been had. The Texan's first record produced three country hits; while he's never had huge mainstream success, he's one of the most respected songwriters in America. He tours with his crack Large Band as a classy, top-dollar theater act; he acts credibly in movies; his surprising marriage to Julia Roberts made him a household name and fodder for the tabloids. And through it all, Lovett's assault on everything modern country music holds dear—its superficiality and gimmickry, falseness and bad taste—has been unrelenting. Why is Lyle Lovett walking around a free man?

The eponymous debut is a striking if ultimately unsuccessful affair. If he was trying to create a subversive album of truly contemporary country he was almost too successful—there's even a Garth Brooks–ian arena rocker ("You Can't Resist It") half a decade too early. Aside from "An Acceptable Level of Ecstasy (The Wedding Song)," a big-band–flecked epic of racial, musical and romantic entanglements, you have to pay close attention to catch the savagery beneath the record's sheen. "Closing Time" is a brutal run at the "Piano Man" genre of romanticized barflies; in other songs, lines like "If I were the man that you wanted / I would not be the man that I am" at once mock old-fashioned country wordplay and dig a little bit deeper. In one pointed couplet, he asks in decidedly unrhetorical fashion who can forgive a lover's infidelities: "God will / But I won't," he sings flatly. "And that's the difference between God and me."

Such elegant contempt for the opposite sex has left a lingering aroma of the misogynist around Lovett's head. Pop lore has it that the bitterness stems from a lack of romantic success—not hard to comprehend for someone with his crinkly face, dishpan mouth and sarcasm as involuntary as a stutter. But this interpretation overlooks Lovett's unconventional but palpable charisma *and* that he hasn't much use for the male of the species either. His next two records are impeccably designed, sui generis exercises in hyperintellectual eclecticism. Touches of country, pop, gospel, folk, jazz, bluegrass and rock elbow for prominence over the course of bitter nursery rhymes (**Pontiac**'s touching "If I Had a Boat"), gender fun (**Pontiac**'s "She's No Lady"), this or that bit of classic country tunesmithery and complex jokes, like a rapturous run at "Stand by Your Man" on **Lyle Lovett and His Large Band.** The star of these two records, however, is the care with which Lovett constructs his songs. There are no throwaway lines, no empty rhymes, no clichés, no vacant effects; while the tunes don't all work, not one is worthless. In rock'n'roll's forty disreputable years only Randy Newman has produced such adult music, or brought such irreproachable aesthetics to the task of charting moral sleight of hand.

Joshua Judges Ruth (the title a biblical punning swipe at his misogyny rep) begins with a wan essay on relationships: "I love a woman," Lovett sings. "What I don't know." (The crack would later serve as a grim epitaph for his short-lived marriage.) The rest of the record is just more faultlessly conceived and executed bravura songwriting, much of it savage love poetry—titles like "She's Already Made Up Her Mind" and "She's Leaving Me Because She Really Wants To" tell the story. A bit more self-confident, he sometimes lapses into over-seriousness, and the album seems a bit slow musically. But his nasty streak saves him: lest things drag, Lovett brings in a deeply irreligious song like "Church" or tosses in a death in the family. Lovett enjoys a good funeral: they're good for a joke or two, and they make him feel alive.

In late 1994 Lovett released a collection of early and rejected songs. The original title—the upbeat **Creeps Like Me**—was changed to the rather more ominous **I Love Everybody.** Panned or ignored on release, the record actually bears some scrutiny. It's divided into three nice parts: a group of offbeat song workouts, a sequence of almost nonsense-based curiosities and then a closing suite of love songs. The full complement of eighteen tunes is a little overlong, but as a curio it serves its purpose well. [bw]

LOW

I Could Live in Hope (Vernon Yard) 1994
Long Division (Vernon Yard) 1995
Transmission EP (Vernon Yard) 1996
The Curtain Hits the Cast (Vernon Yard) 1996

It's been said that writing isn't so much what you put in as what you leave out: from the minimal, translucent sounds that waft out of this Duluth, Minnesota, trio, it's clear that Low feels the same holds true for music. Although Low employs a standard guitar-bass-drums lineup (okay, Mimi Parker's kit consists of a snare and a hi-hat), the group manages to draw less from those instruments than any combo in recent memory—and that's most assuredly a plaudit.

I Could Live in Hope lies just this side of Mennonite in its asceticism. Songs like "Slide," "Cut" and "Words" (in which guitarist Alan Sparhawk's mumbled "too many words" lament sounds fairly ironic) are taciturn to the point of being monosyllabic, which imparts a certain weight to lyrics that hang heavily over the gray sonic vistas. Kramer's thin, brittle production style makes him a perfect match for the band, particularly on the slightly less monochromatic songs sung and written by Parker. The ambience of **Long Division** is just a whit warmer (not to imply that it won't still leave you searching for a jacket)—credit that either to the slightly more outgoing presence of new bassist Zak Sally (the only member of the band able to tear his eyes from his feet in live performance) or to the washes of reverb Sparhawk daubs onto tracks like "Shame" and "Swingin'." A bleakly beautiful perspective on life beneath the permafrost.

The five-song **Transmission** EP, recorded separately with Kramer and Steve Albini, features Low's solemn rendition of the Joy Division song for which it's named. Besides that number (done for 1995's **A Means to an End** tribute album), the EP contains a remake of **Long Division**'s "Caroline" and a cover of the Supreme Dicks' "Jack Smith." [dss]

NICK LOWE

Jesus of Cool (UK Radar) 1978 (UK Demon) 1989
Pure Pop for Now People (Columbia) 1978
Labour of Lust (Columbia) 1979
Nick the Knife (Columbia) 1982
The Abominable Showman (Columbia) 1983
16 All-Time Lowes (UK Demon) 1984
Nick Lowe and His Cowboy Outfit (Columbia) 1984
The Rose of England (Columbia) 1985
Nicks Knack (UK Demon) 1986
Pinker and Prouder Than Previous (Columbia) 1988
Basher: The Best of Nick Lowe (Columbia) 1989
Party of One (Reprise) 1990 (Upstart) 1995
The Impossible Bird (Upstart) 1994

NICK LOWE & THE IMPOSSIBLE BIRDS

Live! On the Battlefield EP (Upstart) 1995

ROCKPILE

Seconds of Pleasure (Columbia) 1980

Britain's pub-rock movement, the unpretentious early-'70s scene that played such a crucial role in the run-up to do-it-yourself punk, was based on English admiration for earthy Americana: country, R&B, rockabilly, western swing. Which provides an easy (if incomplete) explanation for how Nick Lowe could emerge from the mild-mannered Brinsley Schwarz to become the co-founder, house producer and debut artist of the viciously independent Stiff Records (home to Elvis Costello, the Damned, Wreckless Eric and Madness, among many others), rock his way through a decade of geezer wave rock and wind up, in the mid-'90s, highlighting an eloquently understated and surprisingly sober album with a stark country ballad he wrote for Johnny Cash.

After a pair of wryly brilliant piss-takers (**Pure Pop for Now People,** the American equivalent to **Jesus of Cool,** and **Labour of Lust**) that paired sprightly pop and a savage lyrical wit, the singing bassist and guitarist put down his cutting sword and moved into a rootsier room of rock's house. Starting with Rockpile, a rocky but exhilarating quartet he led with guitarist Dave Edmunds, Lowe added a short-lived marriage to Carlene Carter (which made Cash his step-father-in-law), countless exemplary production jobs, a series of good-going-on-great solo records (**The Rose of England** and **Pinker and Prouder Than Previous** being the high points), John Hiatt's **Bring the Family** and Little Village to his résumé.

The Impossible Bird brings Lowe to a new stage in his stylistic progress, a restrained run at rock from a country angle rather than the other way 'round. The quiet grace of this handsome, affecting, lovelorn record is outside Lowe's familiar realm, but he seems to have reached it naturally, ready to make the most of a little understatement. With American guitarist Bill Kirchen (of Commander Cody fame) providing the authentic twang and British pub vet Geraint Watkins laying down a carpet of soulful organ, Lowe stashes his comedy outside and gets down to the serious business of sharing tender thoughts like "Lover Don't Go," the sweetly amorous "Shelley My Love," the gospelly "I Live on a Battlefield," the acoustic "Withered on the Vine" and "The Beast in Me," which Lowe gave Johnny Cash for **American Recordings.** Compared to the Man in Black's rendition, the author takes the menace out of the song, crooning it quietly over simple acoustic guitar. Covers of Buck Owens' "True Love Travels on a Gravel Road" and Ray Price's "I'll Be There" add resonance to Lowe's sensitive originals, which form his single best batch in ages.

An American tour in support of **The Impossible Bird** yielded three nifty concert recordings (**Pure Pop**'s "36 Inches High," **Labour of Lust**'s "Without Love" and "Dream Girl"); an LP cut and Lowe's tribute-album rendition of Arthur Alexander's "In the Middle of It All" flesh out **Live! On the Battlefield.** In the midst of all this Lowe life, Upstart reissued the thin, Edmunds-produced **Party of One** with the bonus addition of two uneventful outtakes from the sessions. [i]

See also *Dave Edmunds, John Hiatt; TPRG.*

LOW POP SUICIDE

The Disengagement EP (World Domination) 1992
On the Cross of Commerce (World Domination) 1993
The Death of Excellence (World Domination) 1995

SHRIEKBACK

Care (Warner Bros.) 1983
Jam Science (UK Arista) 1984
The Best of Shriekback: The Infinite (UK Kaz) 1985
Oil and Gold (Island) 1985
Big Night Music (Island) 1986
The Best of Shriekback Volume Two: Evolution (UK Kaz) 1988
Go Bang! (Island) 1988
The Dancing Years (Island) 1990
Sacred City (World Domination) 1992

ELASTIC PUREJOY

The Elastic Purejoy (World Domination) 1994

Attempting to reclaim a position of authority within the jagged guitar lines of the industrial infrastructure that perhaps owes its essential architecture to the Gang of Four, bassist Dave Allen (who had spent the '80s giving his old band's skeletal funk a wider panorama in Shriekback, then King Swamp) formed Low Pop Suicide as a trio with guitarist/singer Rick Boston (ex–Hand of Fate) and Ministry/Revolting Cocks drummer Jeff Ward. Set to serrate rock with ominously controlled bass-powered ferocity, Low Pop Suicide looked like a cohesive unit (or at least Allen's vehicle) at the outset, but Ward left after recording **On the Cross of Commerce;** Allen, and Ward's replacement, followed suit before **The Death of Excellence.** For a trio with only three records, this group has gone through an awful lot of changes.

The exploratory EP, four songs co-written and co-produced by Allen and Boston, has some of Shriekback's febrile density, but none of Barry Andrews' wanton invention; Boston sings "Disengaged" and the driving "Turn of the Screw" with semi-Reznorized drama and scads of slash'n'pedal guitar as Ward and Allen underpin him with not unreasonable rhythmic force.

The sonic aggression level is appreciably higher on the full-length debut, which was recorded with Ward in early 1992 but names the incoming Melle Steagal as the band's drummer. (Ward killed himself in 1993.) Even before suffering its first personnel adjustment, the band sounds different—and not for the better—on the new material. ("Disengaged" and "Crush" were picked up from the EP.) Roaring or whispering inanely simple lyrics in a foolishly curdled voice and playing like a frustrated metal thug without an idea in his head, Boston hacks away with zero creative energy, stripping songs like "Kiss Your Lips" ("There was nothing that I liked better than to kiss your lips"), the hopefully ironic "Gimme, Gimme" and "Your God Can't Feel My Pain" of all possible color and texture. There isn't even any pain—just unconvincing drama and a sad case of arena envy. "All in Death Is Sweet," a dreamy instrumental, demonstrates that shutting Boston up is one idea that works.

Perhaps the problem was Allen's divided attention. Besides his responsibilities running the World Domination label, the bassist/businessman had to work on Shriekback's reunion album in London at the same time Low Pop Suicide was making **On the Cross of Commerce** in Los Angeles. Although his throbbing bass tones are essential to Shriekback's low'n'slow creep, Allen could have phoned his parts in, as keyboardist/singer/co-producer Barry Andrews continues to fix the group's vision, shaping its smoky-velvet wallop on **Sacred City.** Made as a trio with original drummer Martyn Barker (with guest contributions from ex-Damned/Public Image guitarist Lu Edmonds, guitarist Karl Hyde of the Underworld and a didgeridoo player) after four years apart, the quietly energetic album is lyrically themed as an urban love offering: "(Open Up Your) Filthy Heart (To Me)" is typical of the artful band's ambivalent feelings, while "Beatles Zebra Crossing" is an intriguing and uncommon Fab Four memorialization.

Back in Low Pop land, Boston and the returning Steagal, joined by new bassist Mark Leonard and a couple of spare drummers, reinvented the band for **The Death of Excellence,** an album that trades in the venomous posturing of its predecessor for a more diverse rock menu not notably beholden to any specific model. In "Zombie," Boston wonders "How I ever got so far away from things that really matter"—an apt thought for an album that rediscovers stuff like melody, dynamics and variety. Spilling harsh guitar sparingly makes it a more effective tool here (especially in "Philo's Snag," where it rustles quietly in the background), but Boston's writing isn't equal to the numerous settings (pseudo-Beat rhyming, Neil Youngian stomp, semi-acoustic restraint and so forth). **The Death of Excellence** is crap, but a better brand of crap. Clearing away the endlessly exploding Sheetrock at least takes the rattle out of the ride.

Owning a record label ensures Allen an outlet and exposure for whatever projects he undertakes; his next stop after Low Pop Suicide and Shriekback was *singing* in the Elastic Purejoy, a quartet with drummer Scott Petersen, ex–Sky Cries Mary bassist Joseph E. Howard and Sage guitarist Marc Olsen (who also served briefly in Sky Cries Mary). Allen claims literary inspiration for some of his originals on **The Elastic Purejoy,** which helps explain the pretentious lyrics. (Beyond unfortunate bits like "blood runs thicker than the sperm and spittle of worn-out lovers," "If Samuel Beckett Had Met Lenny Bruce" is, fortunately, the worst of it.) Finding use for both Sebadoh's "Soul and Fire" and Brian Eno's "Stiff," the band serves a random stylistic master here, proceeding from plain rock, woozy fuzz-pop and unaffected folkishness to tautly executed sonic adventures that set wanton noise against carefully measured temperance. Driving feedback stakes into the heart of acoustic songs is a good gambit, but it's not the only workable idea here; the group disassembles a stuck-in-the-funk dance groove with interplanetary freakout visitations in "You Are My PFM" and lets buzzing guitars lurk beneath the radar of enervated Pink Floyd drama in "Witness." Confounding sonic predictability (and revealing Allen to be a functional singer), **The Elastic Purejoy** is occasionally engrossing, a disorienting late-night hallucination that might be all too real. Boston guests on several tracks, as does this generation's Natalie Wood, a guitarist who has done the same for Low Pop Suicide. It's a small (World Domination) world after all . . . [i]

See also *Gang of Four, Sage, Sky Cries Mary; TPRG.*

L7

L7 (Epitaph) 1988
Smell the Magic EP (Sub Pop) 1990
Bricks Are Heavy (Slash) 1992
Pretend We're Dead (Japan. Polydor) 1992
Hungry for Stink (Slash/Reprise) 1994

Like Lunachicks and Babes in Toyland, L7 emerged from rock's pre–riot-grrrl wing, seeking not to steamroller or dismantle the male mosh society but rather to join it. Girls just wanna bang heads, as it were. That's a feminist stance in its own right, but in time L7's four members would show they had plenty on their minds—along with bad humor-tinged attitude to spare. Not for nothing did director Oliver Stone choose their song "Shitlist" as Mallory Knox's theme in his *Natural Born Killers.*

Before L7, bassist Jennifer Finch was in Sugar Baby Doll with Courtney Love and Babes in Toyland's Kat Bjelland; guitarist Suzi Gardner fronted Los Angeles outfit the Debbies. With shouts of "Let's Rock" and—gasp!—a boy by the name of Roy Koutsky in the drum seat, the **L7** album is a heady but largely inconsequential introduction; it's all brute force and speed, grunge as a sheer sonic description. **Smell the Magic** is where things start to get interesting. Moving to Sub Pop and enlisting drummer Dee (Demetra) Plakas (ex–Problem Dogs: for a good chuckle, find the quartet's dinky 1983 new wave single, "City Hall"), L7 still brings the noise, but with a melodicism that isn't as evident on the first album. Their songs are more pointed, too, railing against conformity, corporate-fed definitions of beauty and, in the flip-off anthem "Shove," society in general.

Bricks Are Heavy, the Los Angeles quartet's best to date, delivers. Without taming the quartet's attack, co-producer Butch Vig adds definition and dynamics to L7's sound; Suzi Gardner and Donita Sparks finally sound like a guitar tandem instead of a pair of thrashers, while Finch and Plakas form a piledriver rhythm section. A strong batch of songs also helps the cause, from the fury of "Everglade" and the biting anti-military rant "Wargasm" to the slow grind of "One More Thing," the hyper surf wave of "Mr. Integrity" and the radio-ready groove of "Pretend We're Dead." The Japanese **Pretend We're Dead** EP is worth searching out; it bolsters **Bricks'** strengths with some unreleased numbers, including an ironic take on Guns n' Roses "Used to Love Her (Him)," and five hot live cuts.

Hungry for Stink doesn't hit **Bricks Are Heavy**'s highs for a simple reason: the songs aren't as good. L7 still plays the hell out of them, and there are moments—the wonderfully lusty and snot-nosed "Andres," for one. But even if it doesn't exactly stink, **Hungry** is still a letdown.

Finch quit in the summer of '96, reportedly to attend college. [gg/vg]

LUCAS

To Rap My World Around You (Uptown) 1991
<<Lucacentric>> (Big Beat/Atlantic) 1994

Lucas Secon would seem to be the very model of the modern alternarapper, given his ability to leap from Rakim to Roland Barthes in a single verbal bound and his flair for mutating classic jazz phrasing—a trait no doubt facilitated by having a composer father who wrote for the Mills Brothers back in the day. The Scandinavian-American MC has never thrown many street-cred shapes—never had it, most likely never will—but the giddy wordplay he pirouettes through on **<<Lucacentric>>** is every bit as freeing as the rhymes proclaim themselves to be. The album's hit, "Lucas With the Lid Off," makes it clear that when Lucas crows about size, he's talking about above-the-neck attributes. Although the jazz-reggae hybrid that bubbles beneath most of the tracks does grow repetitive after a while, there are twists like "Spin the Globe," a rapid-fire torch-pass between Lucas and multi-lingual rappers Al Agami and Jam that's elevated above novelty status by the sheer zest the performers pour into it.

Earlier in his career, Lucas made **To Rap My World Around You,** an ill-advised attempt to position himself as the thinking girl's Vanilla Ice. [dss]

GARY LUCAS

Skeleton at the Feast (Enemy) 1992
Gods and Monsters (Enemy) 1992
Bad Boys of the Arctic (Enemy) 1994

KILLER SHREWS

The Killer Shrews (Enemy) 1993

Gary Lucas has toured Europe with Leonard Bernstein playing his Mass and was a member of Captain Beefheart's Magic Band in its final recording lineup (on **Ice Cream for Crow,** after a cameo on the previous **Doc at the Radar Station**). He has produced albums for eclecticist Peter Gordon and jazz saxist Tim Berne and is a mainstay of Manhattan's downtown avant-rock scene. He also joined Joan Osborne on her **Relish** album and co-wrote songs that appeared on Jeff Buckley's **Grace.** Most of which efforts manifest the salient fact here: he's one mutha of a guitarist.

What makes Lucas so terrific is not just his technique, of which he has loads, but also his imagination, his openness to different musical forms (and ability to meld them) and his sense of humor. (In the notes to **Skeleton at the Feast,** Lucas calls Wyndham Lewis' witticism that "laughter is the mind sneezing" a good description of his music.) Imagine a combination of John Fahey, Jeff Beck, Robert Johnson, Jimi Hendrix and James Williamson—sounds potentially disgusting, actually, but it's as if Lucas has somehow gleaned all their best bits in simpatico fashion.

Skeleton at the Feast is Lucas live in a solo mode: on electric, National Steel and twelve-string, both unadulterated and channeled through a maze of effects boxes, playing mostly his own blues-based ("Robert's Johnson") compositions, but also a medley of "Little Drummer Boy" and "Are You Experienced?" and "Hitchcocked," which interprets/interpolates Bernard Herrmann's themes from *Vertigo* and *Psycho.* The last half-hour of the album is a live recording of a superbly evocative score for the 1921 German silent film *The Golem,* which he composed with Walter Horn, who plays keyboards.

Gods and Monsters is the name of Lucas' second album as well as his ever-changing band. That widely varying fluidity is the source of its—and **Bad Boys of the Arctic**'s—strengths (when he is enhanced by his collaborators) and weaknesses (when their presence dominates or seems forced). **Gods and Monsters** features ex-Woodentops leader Rolo McGinty as well as cameos by Mekon Jon Langford, ex–Pere Ubu bassist Tony Maimone and Tackhead drummer Keith LeBlanc. It may be the best introduction to Lucas because it's the most eclectic: some acoustic material, a clutch of tracks rooted in (but looking past) folk-blues, a flirtation with rap and splendid interpretations of Pink Floyd's "Astronomy Domine" and, linked, Miles Davis' "Jack Johnson" and Suicide's "Ghostrider."

Bad Boys of the Arctic is more of a Gods and Monsters band record (there's even a live track from one of their gigs), but the cast of contributors is as extensive as before. Singing (which Lucas does on four tracks) is not his, er, strong suit, but he gets welcome lead vocals from Dina Emerson (bohemian siren) and Sonya Cohen (wistful young thing) on five tracks. Again, his exuberance carries the day; covers this time are radical reworkings of the late avant-cellist/vocalist Arthur Russell's "Let's Go Swimming" and Percy Grainger's "Children's March."

The Killer Shrews is his collaboration with Langford and Maimone. Much rockier than any of Lucas' albums, more esoteric than the Mekons and with greater funkified rhythmic drive than either, it's a pleasant surprise for this kind of super-session. The verbiage ranges from smart ("Handfull of Gimme (And a Mouth Fulla Much Obliged)") to just plain silly ("Bring Me the Fat in California"), but the riffs (even—gasp!—tunes) are generally catchy, and there's gobs of enjoyably indulgent show-off guitaring by Lucas. The rip-roaring take on "The Brain From the Planet Eros" is a step up from the lo-fi version on **Gods and Monsters.** The vocalizing, mostly Langford's, is homely but tolerable; Barbara Manning guest sings on two tracks. [jg]

See also *Mekons.*

LUCY'S FUR COAT

Jaundice (Relativity) 1994

Five suburban guys from San Diego get together to play catchy blue-collar rock. Fusing a little influence from neighbors Rocket From the Crypt and employing manic frontman Charlie Ware, Lucy's Fur Coat moves from an average local band to a solid songwriting force in just a couple of years, signs to Relativity, releases **Jaundice** and then breaks up a year later. So it goes. Electrified by great dual-guitar energy and melodies (Mike Santos and Tony Sanfilippo) and bubbling rhythms (drummer Scott Bauer and bassist Rob Brown), **Jaundice** veers from antic, radio-friendly pop ("Treasure Hands") to mid-'80s rock ("Easy" sounds like it belongs on a Screaming Trees disc). "Southern Cookin'," "Falling Out" and "Sensor" sum up the guitar's critical role in the San Diego scene—Sanfilippo and Santos deliver buoyant, driving riffs and infectious, hooky fills. Meanwhile, "Super" connects with an anthemic, joyous attack. A solid mix of hard rock and indie ethics. [mww]

LULL

See *Scorn.*

LUNA[2]

Lunapark (Elektra) 1992

LUNA

Slide EP (Elektra) 1993
Bewitched (Elektra) 1994
Bonnie and Clyde EP (UK Beggars Banquet) 1995
Penthouse (Elektra) 1995
Luna EP (No. 6) 1996

Continuing to ply his quiet, creative tribute to the Velvet Underground after the end of Galaxie 500, New Zealand–born singer/guitarist Dean Wareham formed

Luna in New York with a fellow disciple—ex-Feelies drummer Stanley Demeski—and bassist Justin Harwood, late of the Chills. (Guitarist Sean Eden joined right after the first album.) Taking understatement as its essential ethos, the artfully laconic trio plays simple, relaxed guitar pop with a firm rhythmic spine, positing Wareham's conversational singing and judicious lead guitar distortion against Demeski's exacting time-keeping and Harwood's lyrical bass work. Appealing melodies and lyrics sprinkled with attention-getting oddities (**Lunapark**'s opening line—"You can never give the finger to the blind"—is a typical eyebrow-raiser) complete the Luna formula, which started out strong but lately seems to be running low on inspiration.

Initially forced to add a superfluous superscript to mollify a singer with a prior claim on the name, Luna introduced itself on **Lunapark,** an album of graceful economy produced with pristine elegance by Fred Maher. The band exudes a cool, collected late-night atmosphere, even on such relatively demonstrative outpourings as "Slash Your Tires," the danceably bustling "Smile" and the quick-paced "I Can't Wait." Despite one egregious lapse in originality—hijacking the chords and melody of Bob Dylan's "Queen Jane Approximately" for "I Want Everything"—and a couple of overly drowsy numbers, **Lunapark** is a dream that stays with you long after the dawn.

The six-song **Slide** EP gets its title track from **Lunapark** and adds a demo of the album's "Hey Sister," the surprisingly aggressive "Rollercoaster," spare, languorous covers of Beat Happening's "Indian Summer" and the Velvets' "Ride Into the Sun" and a bracing rendition of Steve Wynn's "That's What You Always Say."

Bewitched expands the quartet's reach, increasing the energy and dynamics while incorporating spots of trumpet, clarinet, organ, vibes and a visit from VU guitarist Sterling Morrison. With one foot in the artful restraint of **Lunapark** and the other setting off for more ambitious parts, the album builds its sandcastles on a bed of solid tunes: the catchy "Tiger Lily," the Feelies-like "Friendly Advice" (which obsesses on a pair of chords for more than six mesmerizing minutes), "This Time Around," "Going Home" and the gently grand condescension of "I Know You Tried."

Though it *sounds* like a Luna record, **Penthouse** sags as the band merely goes through the motions. (The glum booklet photo matches, if not explains, the music's tepid enthusiasm level.) The melodies and emotionally limited arrangements—which include traces of theremin, mellotron, strings and guest star Tom Verlaine—are at best adequately plain and frequently less than that. (Aping the Feelies' rising and falling monomania—which Luna does on "Freakin' and Peakin'"—hardly flatters a band that should have long ago moved beyond such temptations.) Whether the result of inadequate effort, willful apathy or both, Wareham's singing is careless, his lyrics pedestrian going on awful. Considering the band could once claim songwriting as its most striking asset, it's telling that the two most memorable items here are Verlaine's guitar solo on "23 Minutes in Brussels" and the jamming coda of "Kalamazoo." For those who make it to the end, **Penthouse** contains, as a bizarre unlisted bonus, "Bonnie and Clyde," a duet (recorded originally by Serge Gainsbourg and Brigitte Bardot) sung in French by Wareham and Stereolab's Laetitia Sadier. [i]

LUNACHICKS

Lunachicks EP (UK Blast First/Mute) 1989
Babysitters on Acid (Blast First) 1990
Binge and Purge (Safe House) 1992
Jerk of All Trades (Go-Kart) 1995

The Lunachicks must have missed the how-to-be-a-sweet-young-lady symposium in finishing school (actually, singer Theo Kogan, bassist Squid and guitarist Gina Volpe met at New York's High School of Performing Arts): they roar and swill in the punk-polluted cesspool of garbage rock with the wanton enthusiasm of characters disgorged from a bleary Robert Williams cartoon. As innocuously hard on the ears as they strive to be on the eyes, the quintet has a merry sense of lurid junk-culture fun, a good-natured feminist spirit and unfailing enthusiasm for exuding sonic grief from every pore.

Stepping into the ring with a four-song EP issued on two 7-inch singles in a gatefold sleeve and later repackaged on CD, the Lunachicks strut their overdrive guitar noise in such gorgon sloptunes as "Sugar Luv," "Jan Brady" and "Makin' It (With Other Species)." Guitar-wringers Sindi B. and Gina lead the zealous attack, and the rabid thrash isn't half bad, but Theo's vocals are much worse than that. **Babysitters on Acid** reuses those three songs, hurling nine more crudities (like "Octopussy," "Pin Eye Woman 665," the autobiographical "Born 2B Mild" and the title "tune") into the fetid stew.

Binge and Purge, which contains sharply ironic songs about women's self-image concerns, is the Lunachicks' great leap forward. Besides an overall tightening of the band's musical wig, Theo's tempered singing is much more musical (that she's low in the mix doesn't hurt, either). Still delivered in overdrive, songs like "Apathetic," the antagonistic pop-punk of "C.I.L.L." and the rootsabilly statement of purpose "This Is Serious" are sturdy and catchy. "We're not sweet, but we might be sour / Born in the days of flower power / Give us all your money and your credit cards too . . . too much of us is dangerous."

With hard-hitting new drummer Chip in the lineup, the Lunachicks rev up an edgy punkmetal sound on **Jerk of All Trades,** using the rigid aggression to convey crudely scatological/sexual lyrics like "Fingerful," the dyslexic "F.D.S. (Shit Finger Dick)" and "Buttplug." Inoffensive songs of varying seriousness about pets, dolls, adolescent pranks and reproductive rights ("Fallopian Rhapsody") give the album a conceptual variety thoroughly blunted by the stultifying sameness of the music, a relentless barrage that furiously digs itself down a boring hole. Only "Why Me" and the title track—a wry and wailing dissection of women's roles that uses a guest trumpeter to paraphrase Rossini—display the inventive colors of **Binge and Purge.** [i]

LYDIA LUNCH

Queen of Siam (ZE) 1980 (Widowspeak) 1985 (Triple X) 1991
13.13 (Ruby) 1982 (Widowspeak) 1988
The Agony Is the Ecstacy EP (UK 4AD) 1982
In Limbo EP (UK Doublevision) 1984 (Widowspeak) 1986
The Uncensored Lydia Lunch [tape] (Widowspeak) 1985
Hysterie (UK Widowspeak) 1986 (CD Presents) 1986
Honeymoon in Red (Widowspeak) 1987 (Atavistic) 1996

Drowning in Limbo (Widowspeak) 1989 (Atavistic) 1995
Oral Fixation (Widowspeak) 1989
Conspiracy of Women (Widowspeak) 1990
Crimes Against Nature (Triple X) 1993
Universal Infiltrators (Atavistic) 1995
Transmutation/Shotgun Wedding: Live (Aus. Insipid Vinyl) 1996

LYDIA LUNCH/MICHAEL GIRA

Hard Rock [tape] (Ecstatic Peace!) 1984

LYDIA LUNCH AND LUCY HAMILTON

The Drowning of Lucy Hamilton EP (Widowspeak) 1985

LYDIA LUNCH/THURSTON MOORE

The Crumb EP (Widowspeak) 1988

CLINT RUIN/LYDIA LUNCH

Stinkfist EP (Widowspeak) 1988
Don't Fear the Reaper EP (UK Big Cat) 1991

LYDIA LUNCH/ROWLAND S. HOWARD

Shotgun Wedding (Triple X) 1991

HARRY CREWS

Naked in Garden Hills (Widowspeak) 1989

LYDIA LUNCH/HENRY ROLLINS/ HUBERT SELBY JR./DON BAJEMA

Our Fathers Who Aren't in Heaven (Widowspeak) 1990

LYDIA LUNCH/EXENE CERVENKA

Rude Hieroglyphics (Rykodisc) 1995

After a prolific decade in fearless soul-baring multi-media art terrorism, producing records, films, poetry and even a comic book (*Bloodsucker,* drawn by Bob Fingerman), Lydia Lunch—who first caught the attention of thrill-seekers as the young vocalist of Teenage Jesus and the Jerks, progenitors of New York's no wave ugly minimalism scene in the late '70s—spent the first half of the '90s taking it easy, so to speak. (For a compelling ten-year recap of her garishly decadent confrontationalism, try **Hysterie,** a career retrospective that covers Teenage Jesus, 8 Eyed Spy and the little-known Beirut Slump, as well as several subsequent one-offs.) While continuing her spoken-word activities apace, Lunch put in guest appearances with Thrill Kill Kult and Lab Report, but cut back on her collaborative musical projects. Still, she made a full-length album with guitarist Rowland S. Howard (ex–Birthday Party/These Immortal Souls) and an EP with Clint Ruin (aka Jim "Foetus" Thirlwell).

Lunch first crossed paths with Howard in the early '80s when she shared a live album (**Drunk on the Pope's Blood/The Agony Is the Ecstacy**) with the Birthday Party; that led to **Honeymoon in Red,** on which the uncredited group plays a major role. On **Shotgun Wedding,** which was produced by Thirlwell employing a rhythm section and a second guitarist, Howard and Lunch go after gloomy atmospheres more than rock grit, casually messing up Led Zeppelin's "In My Time of Dying" and breathing clammy life into Alice Cooper's "Black Juju" (props to drummer Brent Newman) while also pulling together dreamy, occasionally rip-roaring originals (Lunch's lyrics, Howard's music). Casual, raspy, well-played and at its best when Lunch exhales her husky words rather than makes to sing them, **Shotgun Wedding** manages to set and keep an effective end-of-the-road mood with lots of pulsing circulation and invasive exploration but a minimum of bloodshed. Neatly done.

Memorable mainly for its dirty cover snap, **Stinkfist**—Lunch's first documented date with Clint Ruin—is the primally percussive end result of a convoluted and protracted recording/performance process involving Cliff Martinez (ex–Red Hot Chili Peppers), D.J. Bonebrake (X), Roli Mosimann and others. What actually made it onto vinyl is the clattering all-but-instrumental title track (plus a bonus-beats version, "Son of Stink") and the three-part "Meltdown Oratorio," a Lunch recitation and sexy moaning session over rhythmic Ruin-ous noise adventures. A party on the precipice of perdition. (**Stinkfist** was later combined on CD with **The Crumb,** her noisy squonk party with Sonic Youth guitarist Thurston Moore, Bush Tetras guitarist Pat Place, pianist Kristian Hoffman, drummer Richard Edson and sax torturer Jim Sclavunos.)

The four-song **Don't Fear the Reaper** contains two originals (the total overload insanity of "Clinch" and the jazzily appealing "Serpentine"), a rough'n'-tumble but essentially respectful version of the titular Blue Öyster Cult hit and a demolition derby version of the Beatles' "Why Don't We Do It in the Road." Inconclusive but intermittently entertaining.

Other than those efforts, Lunch has been concentrating on non-musical expression. Having begun a taboo-busting spoken-word career in 1984, her growing catalogue, which dates back to **The Uncensored Lydia Lunch** cassette, now includes **Hard Rock, Oral Fixation** (the CD of which includes **The Uncensored**), **Conspiracy of Women, Universal Infiltrators** and a three-CD box, **Crimes Against Nature.** In addition, Lunch fills one side of **Our Fathers Who Aren't in Heaven,** a double studio album she shares with Henry Rollins, author Hubert Selby Jr. and San Francisco writer Don Bajema.

Of course, Lunch can be equally frustrating and irritating with or without notes and noises. **Rude Hieroglyphics** finds her onstage in Florida with Exene Cervenka, the X singer with whom she had previously published a volume of poetry (*Adulterer's Anonymous*). Working in tandem and encouraging each other's worst excesses, the two tick off sneering, indignant, self-righteous opinions about O. J. Simpson, women, welfare, abortion, the surgeon general, reproductive rights, parenthood (something to which Lunch is violently opposed), the Catholic church (ditto), masturbation (very much in favor), the information highway (against), Courtney Love (against), museums (for), germ warfare, Nazi doctors, yadda yadda yadda. As current-events art, this is a total waste, a boring double-barreled harangue only occasionally broken when Cervenka stops to read an actual piece of prose. Lacking the appealing self-effacement of Henry Rollins or the standup wit of Jello Biafra (two rockers active in spoken word), **Rude Hieroglyphics** is bad lecture night at the poli-sci club. [i]

See also *Foetus, Sonic Youth, These Immortal Souls, X; TPRG.*

LUSCIOUS JACKSON

In Search of Manny (Grand Royal) 1992 (Grand Royal/Capitol) 1993
Natural Ingredients (Grand Royal/Capitol) 1994
Fever in Fever Out (Grand Royal/Capitol) 1996

KOSTARS

Klassics with a "K" (Grand Royal) 1996

The contentious issue of cultural appropriation—

which might have dogged any other hip-hop–rock quartet formed by two grown-up club kids and an ex-Beastie girl—is no match for the contact-high sensibility of lines like "I got pretty little feet they're so petite / I got shiny little legs so nice and neat / My bellybutton—Q-tip it clean," as Luscious Jackson details in "Let Yourself Get Down," the infectiously funky groove that opens the seven-track **In Search of Manny.** The band's graffiti-tag logo pretty much sums up the local pride and color that roots these New York women and their smart, catchy music.

Gabby Glaser (guitar, vocals) and Jill Cunniff (vocals, bass), friends since the two twelve-year-old protopunks started hanging out together in the East Village around 1980, formed Luscious Jackson a little more than a decade later in a basement studio, rapping their offbeat adventures ("She Be Wantin It More," "Daughters of the Kaos") and aggravations ("Life of Leisure," a rip at mooching slacker boys) over extra-cool loops that owe something to ESG. As the group evolved toward the stage, drummer Kate Schellenbach (another longtime Village pal, she was in the original punk incarnation of the Beastie Boys and played on the band's 1982 **Polly Wog Stew**) joined, as did keyboardist Vivian Trimble. Although the all-fun **In Search of Manny,** released originally on the Beastie Boys' indie label and then again via Capitol, was essentially recorded as a duo, the full band appears on two tracks, including "Bam-Bam," a kitschy and gleeful party groove that became a showstopper.

Ironically, as Luscious Jackson grew into a mighty live act, its studio work—played on real instruments, with samples reduced to an incidental role—suffered, cutting back on the giddy carnival panic that moved **Manny** into high gear. The self-produced **Natural Ingredients** begins with "Citysong," a right-on metropolitan manifesto, and then shifts nicely through the trance-poppy "Deep Shag" and the ominous wah-wah strut of "Angel," but ultimately bogs down in repetitive time-wasters. Despite the cultural aphrodisiac of campy '70s funk and soul ambience (complete with pops and scratches), the album is gripping only in fits and starts. Weak numbers fall flat and the good ones are worked to the bone. "Strongman" sends a stirring feminist message ("It takes a strong man to stand by a strong woman"), but the song's weak melody fails it; "Energy Sucker" is defeated by the sketchy, lumbering dub track; "Here" is good disco fun that dances itself into a hole. **Natural Ingredients** may look good on paper, but sometimes a more artificial menu is better for the body.

The side-project Kostars are Cunniff and Trimble (although Schellenbach is their album's beat-keeper and Glaser plays guitar on "Hey Cowboy"). Produced by Josephine Wiggs of the Breeders, the duo's lite cocktail thing sounds like a genially relaxed Luscious Jackson relieved of its funky drummer. More agreeable than consistently compelling, **Klassics With a "K"** breezes along on Trimble's keyboards and gentle rhythms: "Red Umbrella" is almost a bossa nova, while "Don't Know Why" (guest-starring Ween) is wistful acoustic folk-pop, and "Jolene on the Freeway" (complete with automotive effects) finds a mellow groove and rides it with a bare-bones arrangement of synthesized percussion and melodic fillips. More than nice, but no substitute for the mother band's best. [i]

See also *Beastie Boys.*

LUSH

Scar EP (UK 4AD) 1989
Mad Love EP (UK 4AD) 1990
Sweetness and Light EP (UK 4AD) 1990
Gala (4AD/Reprise) 1990
Black Spring EP (UK 4AD) 1991
Spooky (4AD/Reprise) 1992
Split (4AD/Reprise) 1994
Lovelife (4AD/Reprise) 1996

Lush has often sounded like a more pop-based Cocteau Twins, with hints of My Bloody Valentine's noise sheets. A gushing, twin-guitar overdrive with forward surges serves the shapely melodies; guitarists Miki Berenyi and Emma Anderson, who write the band's songs separately, add distinctive harmonies to every number. (**Mad Love** was produced by the Cocteaus' Robin Guthrie, which furthers Lush's comparisons to that band.)

Gala compiles the London quartet's first three British EPs, adding two new tracks, one of which is a surprisingly effective rendition of "Hey Hey Helen," an ABBA obscurity co-written by an unrelated Andersson. Though an inconsistent collection (blame the uneven material), "De-Luxe" (from **Mad Love**) and the whooshing "Breeze" (from the Tim Friese-Greene–produced **Sweetness and Light**) are among the band's best efforts.

Spooky, then, is Lush's first proper LP, recorded in one stretch in one place (and with a transitional bassist, the original one having left). Strangely, this more refined effort—again produced by Guthrie—seems just as disjointed and haphazard as **Gala.** The second half is stronger than the first, highlighted by Berenyi's "For Love." Piling one hook on just as another recedes, moving from scintillating verse to hot chorus with a stunning bridge, this cynical take on those obsessed with *being* in love is a knockout. Anderson's distortion-marbled "Superblast!" is well-titled; her "Monochrome" provides an introspective close to the album. Despite its flaws, **Spooky** is still beguiling.

While employing more diverse tempos and styles than usual, **Split** doesn't reformulate Lush (now containing Phil King as permanent bassist) so much as toughen the sound and bring the band into more disciplined focus. In addition, both songwriters have made great lyrical strides. Co-producer Mike Hedges tightens and pushes the group in a way Guthrie didn't, but Lush retains its playful charm in sunnier numbers like "Lovelife." Lifted by dramatic, cinematic strings and accented by what sound like tuned glasses being struck, Berenyi's gorgeous "Light From a Dead Star" opens the album with the most tearing, sad track of Lush's career, a song of adult hurt at being left behind by wandering hearts. Throughout the album (two-thirds written by Anderson, although Berenyi's songs are stronger), frank expressions of bitterness, heartbreak, spite and regret give the band emotional ballast previously missing. Singing over thick layers of fuzz-guitar pop, Miki rips into a supposed friend for a romantic transgression in "Hypocrite," but allows herself to be tagged by anger's whiplash. "I'm sure you think it's OK / What you've done to me / 'Cause I'm so bad to him . . . I dish it out but I can't take it / I know you think it's wrong / And maybe you're right but this is my song."

Lush switched gears on **Lovelife,** toning down the woolly guitar rush and applying themselves to the fashionable mid-'90s Britpop sound that incorporates both '60s influences and large doses of '70s punk/new wave. The peppy "Single Girl" and "Ladykillers" could have been recorded by Elastica, Sleeper or even Echobelly. (In fairness, Lush displayed this sort of direct edge in its early EPs, when those groups didn't even exist.) Lush's lyrics are again sharp and insightful; both of those songs (and others on **Lovelife**) attack immature, self-obsessed men who take women for a ride. The album's funniest number is "Ciao!," a hilarious continental sendup of male/female duets in which Berenyi and guest vocalist Jarvis Cocker of Pulp share a vitriolic view of their ended affair. Meanwhile, strings and horns (as on Anderson's "Tra La La" and the airy and sophisticated folk-pop of her album-ending "Olympia") extend an olive branch to fans of the band's older obsessions.

Drummer Chris Acland committed suicide in October 1996. [jr]

See also *Pale Saints; TPRG.*

LYNC

These Are Not Fall Colors (K) 1994

LOVE AS LAUGHTER

The Greks Bring Gifts (K) 1996

As a small city with a handful of important indie labels and a tightly knit scene describing a relatively narrow stylistic realm, Olympia, Washington, has unearthed far more backyard talent than sociological statistics would suggest possible. Lync was one such band, a raucous local trio whose one album strikes a workable truce between the lazy sloping melodics of Pavement, the harsh rhythmic attack of Fugazi, the fun-with-noise indulgence of Sonic Youth and the gooey nuclear tweemelt of Superchunk. A lot of good ideas thrown around willy-nilly, **These Are Not Fall Colors**—not really good, but far from bad—is the kind of slackadaisical debut that raises more questions about the band's intentions and abilities than it answers.

Adding little of use to the investigation, singer/guitarist Sam Jayne and Lync bassist James Bertram played on Beck's **One Foot in the Grave** album just before recording their own. Lync broke up at the end of '94, leaving its mysteries unsolved and unexplained. Jayne, however, devoted himself to Love as Laughter, a cute, modest basement lo-fi solo project in which songs rather than big, scary sounds are the point. On **The Greks Bring Gifts,** a cheap synth, occasionally fuzzy/occasionally tuned electric guitar, sporadic drumming and Jayne's twinkiest power-pop voice give vent to winsomeness and weirdness in a venture that's equal parts Ween and Philistines Jr. "Keep Your Shade" and "The Youth Are Plastic" have the slapdash charm of an adolescent Jesus and Mary Chain cover band; "Uninvited Trumpets" is a catchy song pumped along by one-finger sequencer; "High Noon" could be a lost Buddy Holly number finally ricocheting back from Pluto. Other items are equally haphazard and amusing. You have been warned. [i]

LYRES

The Lyres EP (Ace of Hearts) 1981
On Fyre (Ace of Hearts) 1984
Someone Who'll Treat You Right Now EP (Fr. New Rose) 1985
The Box Set (Fr. New Rose) 1986
Lyres Lyres (Ace of Hearts) 1986
Live at Cantones! (Pryct) 1987
A Promise Is a Promise (Ace of Hearts) 1988
Live (Sp. Impossible) 1989
Live 1983: Let's Have a Party!! (Pryct) 1989
Nobody but Lyres EP (Taang!) 1992
Happy Now . . . (Taang!) 1993
Some Lyres (Taang!) 1994
Those Lyres (Norton) 1995

Mercurial singer/organist Jeff "Monoman" Conolly—once of late-'70s retro-punksters DMZ—has led Boston's Lyres through a decade and a half's worth of malice, moodswings and abrupt personnel shakeups without ever wavering in his devotion to the band's singleminded musical mission. Leaving such effete concepts as introspection and artistic progress to rock critics, the Lyres remain the flagship band of the garage-rock pack, churning out tough, gritty R&B-based workouts that are authentic enough in vintage sound and spirit that Conolly has eclipsed most of the one-hit (or no-hit) wonders he originally set out to emulate.

The Lyres' '90s output is a confusing tangle of recycled tracks, rerecorded songs and 7-inch singles on various indie labels. The six-song **Nobody but Lyres** is a typically mixed bag that's made obsolete by **Happy Now . . .** and **Some Lyres,** each of which recycles three of the EP's six cuts. **Happy Now . . .** finds the foursome rocking as fiercely and infectiously as ever; though it contains only two original compositions, the covers—other than the Isley Brothers/Human Beinz anthem "Nobody but Me," Bo Diddley's "I Can Tell" and a pair of ancient Rolling Stones numbers ("Stoned" and "Now I've Got a Witness")—are obscure enough to render such distinctions meaningless. **Some Lyres** is a consistently groovy anthology of Ace of Hearts–era album tracks and rarities that includes both sides of the band's 1979 debut single and clever cover art spoofing the Rolling Stones' **Some Girls. Those Lyres** collects eleven recent singles sides—most of them quite good—and adds a spirited '93 live set recorded in Oslo. [ss]

See also *TPRG.*

M  M M M M M M M M M

KIRSTY MACCOLL

Desperate Character (UK Polydor) 1981
Kite (UK Virgin) 1989 (Charisma) 1990 (IRS) 1994
Electric Landlady (Charisma) 1991 (IRS) 1994
Titanic Days (IRS) 1993
Galore (IRS) 1995

The essence of Kirsty MacColl's career, which flashes brilliantly on the **Galore** retrospective, is difficult to glean from simply going through her four actual albums. One of the most alluring and technically proficient harmony pop singers England has ever produced, Kirsty MacColl (daughter of the late folksinger Ewan MacColl) has cut a stack of wonderful recordings since making her go-nowhere solo debut, a delightful Stiff new wave 45 of "They Don't Know" b/w "Turn My Motor On," in 1979. Nothing about MacColl's progress has ever been that simple again. A novelty hit ("There's a Guy Works Down the Chip Shop Swears He's Elvis") and a modestly winning rock-country-pub-pop album (**Desperate Character**) followed two years later, but another was scrapped and no more longplayers were forthcoming. With a lavish Billy Bragg cover ("A New England") in mid-decade to keep her name afloat, MacColl spent the '80s writing hits for Tracey Ullman, raising a family with producer Steve Lillywhite and racking up session credits singing on records by everyone from Talking Heads to the Smiths to the Rolling Stones.

In 1987, MacColl duetted with Shane MacGowan on the Pogues' rambunctious and profane "Fairytale of New York" and had her biggest chart success ever. Then she made **Kite,** co-writing and recording with guitarists Johnny Marr (ex-Smiths) and Pete Glenister (ex-Hitmen). This sturdy, provocative collection mixes full-bodied pop styles ("Free World") with some country ("Don't Come the Cowboy With Me Sonny Jim!"), adding a film noir story sung in French, a pair of wonderful covers (the Kinks' "Days" and the Smiths' "You Just Haven't Earned It Yet Baby") and pointed lyrical assaults on both Margaret Thatcher and shallow pop stars. A most encouraging second start for MacColl.

Musically inspired by some time spent in New York City, MacColl brought an international rhythmic thrust to **Electric Landlady,** resulting in the uneasy hip-hop bed of "Walking Down Madison," the U2-ish snap of "Lying Down," the salsa-inflected "My Affair" and the mariachi horn accents of "My Way Home." While Lillywhite's production is consistently tasteful enough to downplay the sense that MacColl is dabbling, the album keeps veering off on distracting tangents that undercut her jaundiced romantic writing. Not a bad record, but hard to embrace in toto. (**Galore,** however, gives the album short shrift by omitting the pure pop delight of "All I Ever Wanted.")

Following a split with her husband/producer, MacColl got another crew in to work on the solemn, sorrowful **Titanic Days,** which Lillywhite mixed after all. Touring band member Mark E. Nevin (ex–Fairground Attraction) co-wrote seven of the clearly personal songs and played guitar on the entire album; Glenister, bassist Gary Tibbs (ex-Vibrators/Roxy Music) and keyboardist Steve Nieve (Attractions) are also on hand. Sounding confident but too disheartened for full-scale inspiration, MacColl mixes stylistic metaphors on this disjointed, distant outing. The evanescent "Angel" has a bustling club beat and pizzicato violin plucks; the title track is lushly dramatic; "Last Day of Summer" is breezy folk-pop; "Can't Stop Killing You," co-written by Marr, sounds like an Anglofied Carly Simon classic. Though easy to admire and enjoy from time to time, **Titanic Days** is not an album to cherish with the fervor of **Kite.**

Besides most of the essential tracks from those four records, **Galore** includes MacColl's two Pogues collaborations (the other, a Cole Porter cover, was done for a compilation) and a pair of new recordings: a robust original (the romantic triangle of "Caroline") and a ponderous duet on Lou Reed's "Perfect Day" with Evan Dando of the Lemonheads. [i]

See also *TPRG.*

SHANE MACGOWAN AND THE POPES

See *Pogues.*

MACHINES OF LOVING GRACE

Machines of Loving Grace (Mammoth) 1991
Concentration (Mammoth/Atlantic) 1993
Gilt (Mammoth/Atlantic) 1995

Industrial rock from the lite side: the technological rhythmotics of **Machines of Loving Grace** spring from the same middlebrow collegiate conformism reflected in the Tucson, Arizona, band's Richard Brautigan–derived moniker. Programming its tiny gears in the direction of Ministry, Foetus and Nine Inch Nails, the group led by growly singer Scott Benzel and keyboardist Mike Fisher samples and regurgitates reality in mild-mannered celebrity percolations like "Cicciolina" and "Burn Like Brilliant Trash (At Jackie's Funeral)" on its harmless homemade debut, adding the generic apocalyptics of "Terminal City" and the South Africa–citing "X-Insurrection." Dismal and redundant.

Veteran noise sculptor Roli Mosimann hits the accelerator as the producer of **Concentration,** an album that embraces all the form's standard attributes—distorted vocals, malevolent whispers, chanted slogans, pummeling layers of instrumental overdrive and walloping beats—and none of the frantic desperation, genuine aggression or invention that can make it all exciting. The group's intelligence works against its sonic desires: complex lyrics indicative of recent book learning and historical awareness don't mesh with the grind. The screamed profanity of "Albert Speer" lacks conviction, while the sexuality of "Perfect Tan (Bikini Atoll)" is too cerebral to work up a sweat; the glancing politics of "Cheap" are totally trivial. Although Benzel repeatedly claims (in the driving "Shake") that "I lost my mind," his conscientious delivery makes cavalier behavior unthinkable.

Replacing its rhythm section and adding second guitarist Tom Coffeen, Machines of Loving Grace gets closer to the center of the lava spew with **Gilt,** a garish noise-powered album less tiresomely dependent on keyboards than the first two. Producer Sylvia Massy (who did a similar-sounding job for Tool) encourages lots of grinding, gnashing, howling strings and bomb-weight drumming, but muscling up the eggheads doesn't improve the memorability of their songwriting enough. Attempting to feed what appear to be substantial lyrical ideas into a genre that has trouble supporting any more complexity than someone shrieking "I wanna fuck you like an animal," the Machines are beached on their own ambitions. Without the musical imagination to rewrite the rules, the band can't command careful attention, even to songs with titles as promising as "Richest Junkie Still Alive," "Kiss Destroyer" and "Serpico." [i]

CRAIG MACK

Project: Funk da World (Bad Boy/Arista) 1994

A major player in the mid-'90s resurgence of New York hip-hop, Brentwood, Long Island, MC Craig Mack endured his share of ups and downs—cutting a single at seventeen, descending into thug life and snagging a last-ditch job as a gofer for EPMD—before making the lucky career connection with producer/Bad Boy Records entrepreneur Sean "Puffy" Combs outside a Manhattan club. Combs arranged for Mack to rap to Mary J. Blige on her second LP and then oversaw **Project: Funk da World,** a likable blend of non-gangsta words and unloaded modern grooves buoyed by the late-summer success of "Flava in Ya Ear," an upbeat anthem vague enough to suit a broad range of funk fans.

Uneven but ingratiating, **Project: Funk da World** has good-natured old-school rhymes (the chanting repetition of "Get Down," "Judgement Day" and the scratchy "Funk Wit da Style" all stop short of anything much heavier than MC competition), easygoing beats and the star's husky, marble-mouthed voice, which resembles, in turn, Biz Markie, 2Pac and Erick Sermon. Mack is a natural entertainer; the party follows him even when he doesn't have a lot to say. And when he does have something on his mind—notably the religious fervor of "When God Comes"—he's a sharp, economical commentator. While representing a broad program of social responsibility (which includes a misplaced attack on women), Mack warns, "You can't get strapped for when God comes." [i]

MACK 10

Mack 10 (Priority) 1995

Declaring crime pays in "10 Million Ways," Ice Cube protégé Mack 10 attempts to enumerate how in a grisly gangsta record that begins with a brutal hold-up skit—and then turns *seriously* ugly in an exaggerated cesspool of predatory sex, murder and pigeons (!). Cube did production duties on half the tracks by his soundalike Inglewood pal and takes the mic (in "Westside Slaughterhouse") to share a bloody joke or two. For his part, the scowly Mack 10 declares himself "Armed & Dangerous" and the "Chicken Hawk," chronicling nefarious actions in slang that is all but incomprehensible to law-abiding listeners, even with the inexact libretto provided: "Herd this nigga had the chickens/36 zones in each sack to be exac/Got 50 G's or more in street value worth of crack/As he put it down out of control with the cavey got benzos on the ground twistin front and back cadeys." Say *wha?* To his small credit, Mack 10 is not without wit in his chosen argot: "Me shoot straight/Never hesitate/Fools cooperate/Or I dragum, tagum, body bagum with my magnum." Party on, Garth. [i]

MADDER ROSE

Bring It Down (Seed) 1993
Swim EP (Seed) 1993
Panic On (Seed/Atlantic) 1994
The Love You Save EP (Seed) 1995

SPEEDBALL BABY

Speedball Baby (PCP/Matador) 1994
Get Straight for the Last Supper EP (PCP) 1995
Cinéma! (Fort Apache/MCA) 1996

Madder Rose is a quintessential Lower East Side rock band, complete with sullen thirtysomething postgraduates of the Manhattan club scene, fuzzed-out guitars, even the obligatory aura of decadence. Guitarist Mary Lorson's vocals key the allure—breathy and childlike, she combines the sultry hippie appeal of Natalie Merchant with the winsome, hipper charms of Juliana Hatfield. Most of the material, written by either Lorson or guitarist Billy Coté, is typical New York post-punk fare, with a bleary-eyed torpor providing a local variant on the generational angst of Seattle grunge.

With its sludgy, distorted guitars, mid-tempo pace and abstract lyrics, **Bring It Down** (produced by Kevin Salem) suggests the druggy languor of a heroin high, which inspired the British music press to trumpet Madder Rose as the second coming of the Velvet Underground—a hyperbolic but not altogether inappropriate benediction. The lurching, woozy tempo makes "Swim" sound as if the quartet were paddling against the beat in a bowl of oatmeal; "Lay Down Low" borrows its syncopated rhythm from the Velvets' "Foggy Notion." But Coté's stinging riffs and brisk, fluid solos—along with Lorson's coy and emotive vocals—suggest a much wider range of influences at work as well.

The six-song **Swim** EP packs up a remix of the album track with three new originals, an oldie and a cover of Jonathan Richman's "I Wanna Sleep in Your Arms" (the Iggy Pop writing credit of which acknowledges the song's appropriation of a Stooges riff, not a heretofore unknown collaboration). This version of "Swim" accentuates the vocals and, if anything, cuts the murk and haze of the original, but the rest of the EP revels in Madder Rose's reputation as a baby VU: Lorson's "Z" offers an ethereal melody over a swirl of densely distorted guitars, while Coté's "Amnesia" and "Baby Gets High" (retrieved from the flipside of the band's 1992 debut 45) are trippy paeans to altered states of consciousness. Even the frenetic, amphetaminized Richman tune has the band panting "I wanna sleep in your arms" as if they're all on the verge of passing out.

Panic On wakes Madder Rose up and moves the group forward in several directions: Lorson's distinctive vocals still take center stage, but Coté's guitar provides a much fuller and more eclectic foil. The debut's seedy, bohemian quality gives way to a much lighter touch, like the Roy Orbison twang Coté brings to "Car Song," the gentle country lilt of "What Holly Sees" and the bouncy, Feelies-like perkiness of "Drop a Bomb." Notwithstanding the leadoff song's avowal—"I could just sleep forever"—**Panic On** is helpfully alert and engaged. Four long tracks—running between four and nearly six minutes each—end the album on a note of wistful romanticism, as Lorson's evocative vocals conjure images of lost love and dark city streets.

The delightful **The Love You Save** EP slows the titular Jackson 5 song down to a spare, mid-tempo ballad, allowing Lorson to caress the lovely melody lost in the original's hyperactive bubblegum arrangement. (The track also gives the band a chance to showcase its new bassist, Matt Giammalvo, late of Eve's Plumb.) In contrast, the other tracks—"No Avail," "Diane" and Allen Toussaint's "Ruler of My Heart" (recorded with original bassist Matt Verta-Ray)—continue in the direction suggested by the romantic mood of **Panic On**'s closing tracks—restrained pop music with the tart, adult tang of a dry martini.

Decamping for the usual "artistic differences," Verta-Ray went on to form Speedball Baby. The group's eponymous debut—retro-rockabilly skronk that sounds like warmed-over Cramps covers—doesn't offer much in the way of originality, but it does explain why Verta-Ray felt uncomfortable in the increasingly dainty, mainstream and accessible Madder Rose. **Get Straight for the Last Supper** doesn't differ appreciably from the band's debut, aside from singer Ron Ward's (formerly the drummer for the far more sedate Blood Oranges) surprisingly credible, wailing rendition of Van Morrison's "T.B. Sheets." A tempest in a beer glass. [jt/dss]

See also *Crush, Sr.*

MADONNA

Madonna (Sire) 1983
Like a Virgin (Sire) 1985
True Blue (Sire) 1986
Who's That Girl (Sire) 1987
You Can Dance (Sire) 1987
Like a Prayer (Sire) 1989
I'm Breathless (Sire) 1990
The Immaculate Collection (Sire) 1990
Erotica (Maverick/Sire/Warner Bros.) 1992
Bedtime Stories (Maverick/Sire/Warner Bros.) 1994
Something to Remember (Maverick/Warner Bros.) 1995

"Alternative" seems a strange description for a pop superstar who has achieved the status and global name recognition of a demi-goddess. But through seven albums and three compilations (**Who's That Girl** is a various-artists movie soundtrack on which she has four songs), from "Holiday" to "Bedtime Story," the shoe has continued to fit Madonna, not least because the fashions she's worn have varied so spectacularly. Since releasing her first single in 1983, Madonna has dodged the conventional industry wisdom of a fixed image plucked from a stable of stereotypes. Instead of choosing diva, tomboy, sultry chanteuse or fluffy kitten, Madonna decided to be them all, eschewing only the role of guitar-slinging rocker. Over the last decade, she's reinvented herself in song and video countless times, providing listeners with an alternative to the usual pop replicants. Her steady transformation—from bejeweled, soiled ingénue to sleek sophisticate, with detours into peep shows, strip clubs and drag—has been as dramatic as her ascension from New York club kid to international industry.

Though she's firmly ensconced in the pop mainstream, from MTV to the charts, the cultural artifacts that inspire Madonna separate her from the pop-product pack and earn her a firm, if contested, perch in the safe end of the avant-garde. She's turned to—and exploited—the cultural margins to enrich her work and pique the interest of fans since her earliest days, parsing everything from the dancefloor rhythms of urban gay clubs to the visuals of bondage leather fetishists. Madonna's "alternativeness" has insured her success. She's never come to the table without bringing something new.

House music and the rough iconography of '90s sexuality are the clear influences on **Erotica,** the release of which coincided with that of the photo book *Sex,* Madonna's collaborative effort with fashion photographer Steven Meisel. Through an alter ego, Dita, Madonna explores her version of the less pop-friendly faces of desire. "Once you put your hand in the flame/You can never be the same," sings "Dita" on the title track. "There's a certain satisfaction/In a little bit of pain." **Erotica**'s insistent, consistent rhythm creates a comfortable but kinetic ambience for Madonna's vocal and lyrical whims, and Shep Pettibone's production is squeaky clean. But a certain laziness is **Erotica**'s weakness. Too often the rhythm tracks and mixing board soundbites that are the building blocks of club music stand in for genuine songwriting. For every intricate funhouse like "Secret Garden," there's a bland, by-the-numbers stinker like her version of the classic "Fever."

Bedtime Stories cashes **Erotica**'s check. Where **Erotica** was overly digital, **Bedtime Stories** explores the soulful side of club music—perhaps a result of Madonna's admiration of New York club DJ Junior Vasquez, who, like Miss M, was a devotee of New York's famous Paradise Garage, where richer, vocals-driven mixing was the rule. **Bedtime Stories**' lush compositions balance melodious storytelling and dancefloor drive; the album's producers (among them Babyface, Nellee Hooper, Dallas Austin and Madonna herself) can fit more instrumental layers on the head of a pin than most DJs could mix into an entire set. The emotional depth here is also unprecedented for her. Previously, even when Madonna reached for lyrical complexity, she wound up with simplified pap. But "Inside of Me," which at first appears to be a plain old love song, turns out to be a lonely ode to someone irrevocably gone. "Take a Bow," in the same guise, could easily be Madonna singing to herself: "You're one lucky star/You don't know who you are."

Madonna again turned to the clubs for ideas in 1995, when she hooked up with Massive Attack and Nellee Hooper on an intriguing sorrowful remake of Marvin Gaye's "I Want You." The track is one of three new recordings on **Something to Remember,** a compilation sifting through the ballads (including "Live to Tell," "This Used to Be My Playground," "Crazy for You" and "I'll Remember," all coincidentally from soundtracks) in Madonna's oeuvre. Though somewhat illuminating to historians, the retrospective is most useful for the void it highlights. It proves just how bland Madonna can be when not stimulated by the right people. [nds]

See also *TPRG.*

MAD SCENE

Falling Over, Spilling Over EP7 (Homestead) 1992
A Trip Thru Monsterland (NZ Flying Nun) 1993
The Greatest Time! EP7 (Merge) 1995
Sealight (Merge) 1995
Chinese Honey (Merge) 1996

Hamish Kilgour was always the most unassuming member of New Zealand's Clean, which may help explain why his latest band, the Mad Scene, has received less attention than his brother David's solo outings or Robert Scott's Bats. In any event, the Mad Scene, which also includes Lisa Siegel on guitar and vocals and, in its most recent incarnation, former Go-Betweens bassist Robert Vickers, is a solid and occasionally spectacular pop band that has shown steady improvement throughout its recorded career.

The Mad Scene debuted in 1992 with the 7-inch **Falling Over, Spilling Over** EP, three songs from which also appear on **A Trip Thru Monsterland.** Recorded at various times during 1991 in New York and New Zealand and released on Flying Nun (Kilgour, despite having relocated to New York, was without an American record deal at this point), the album finds the group reaching to come to terms with a sort of textural guitar-pop that sounds, unsurprisingly, much like the Clean. Some of the efforts—like "Paper Plane," "People to Talk To," "Whole World" and "Bee"—are exemplary, although "Eye" and the badly misconceived "What's Going On" are less successful. A worthwhile and promising beginning.

A few personnel changes later, the group reappeared in '95 with another 7-inch, **The Greatest Time!** Anchored by "Balloon," a slow, haunting song that stands among Kilgour's finest, the three-song single was soon followed by **Sealight,** a superior album and easily the band's best work. Siegel (spelled Seagul), whose previous turns at the microphone had ranged from amateurish to shy, sounds more confident (though no less disarmingly childlike), and her songwriting has advanced to the point where she now lays claim to the lion's share of the band's top work: her "Spilled Oranges," "Birthday Party" and "Transatlantic Telephone Conversation" are as good as anything Hamish has ever come up with. For his part, Kilgour makes some fine contributions as well ("You Wear Funny Clothes," "Marching Song"), but Vickers weighs in with the record's strongest track (sung by Siegel), "Here Goes Nothing." A great record from a band coming into its own.

The seven-song **Chinese Honey** marks time with two excellent drone-oriented tracks that find the band in top shape ("The Big Setup," "Waiting for the Rain"), a pleasant but inconsequential '60s-pop genre exercise from Siegel ("I Met You in My Dreams") and a few middling tracks of filler. Not the Mad Scene's strongest work, but enough to encourage investigation of any subsequent releases. [pl]

See also *Clean, Run On.*

MAD SEASON

See *Alice in Chains.*

MAGIC HOUR

No Excess Is Absurd (Twisted Village) 1994
Will They Turn You on or Will They Turn on You (Twisted Village) 1995
Secession '96 (Twisted Village) 1996

CRYSTALIZED MOVEMENTS

Mind Disaster (Twisted Village) 1983 + 1996
Dog. Tree. Satellite Seers . . . (Twisted Village) 1987 (Forced Exposure) 1988
This Wideness Comes (Twisted Village) 1989 (No. 6) 1990
Damaged Lights (Twisted Village) 1991
Revelations From Pandemonium (Twisted Village) 1992

B.O.R.B.

Trailer Full of Smoke (Twisted Village) 1992
Blast off With B.O.R.B. (Twisted Village) 1993
B.O.R.B. in Orbit (Twisted Village) 1993

WAYNE ROGERS

Ego River (Twisted Village) 1992
The Seven Arms of the Sun (Twisted Village) 1993
Absent Sounds (Twisted Village) 1993
All Good Works (Twisted Village) 1995

VERMONSTER

Spirit of Yma (Twisted Village) 1990
Instinctively Inhuman (Twisted Village) 1991
The Holy Sound of American Pipe (Twisted Village) 1992

VARIOUS ARTISTS

Deep Funnels of Entry (A Twisted Village Compilation) (UK Shock) 1993

Since the waning of the original psychedelic era, folks have proven all too willing to use the p-word to describe music marked by the merest hint of trippiness, rather than conserve it for sonic outbursts designed to truly alter mind states, acting as conduits into another dimension. Connecticut's Wayne Rogers, who acts as the (admittedly undulating) axis for this entire series of bands, is most assuredly a proponent of the latter form, as he's proven over a decade's worth of hallucinogenic guitar excursions that seem custom-designed for astral projection.

Magic Hour, which teams Rogers and longtime partner Kate Biggar (guitar) with ex–Galaxie 500 constituents Damon Krukowski and Naomi Yang (who record on their own as Damon and Naomi), is unequivocally the most graspable of the lot—which means the band's space-rock sculptures maintain shapes for up to thirty seconds at a time. The general vibe exuded is that of a dank-hued rejoinder to a new generation of post-hippie revivalists, a Velvet Underground to Phish's Grateful Dead. While hardly nihilistic, **No Excess Is Absurd** reflects a certain affinity for decay, both in the slowly unraveling melodies of feedback-dosed tracks like "Isn't a Way" and "Heads Down #2" and a pervasive lassitude that recalls the earliest output of Pere Ubu.

On **Will They Turn You on or Will They Turn on You,** the quartet sails right past "slowcore" and "psychedelic." Krukowski and Yang assert themselves a bit more extensively on this outing, lending a propitiatory placidity to deliberately paced songs like "Chance Was" and "When I Remembered." The impassive rhythms frame Rogers' pensive vocals nicely, but twenty-plus minutes of the relentless "Passing Words"—with extended improvisational do-si-dos—provide the album's strongest magic. A similar sensibility invested the increasingly inflamed live sets that led up to the recording of the idyllic improv track (yes, just one) that constitutes the breathtaking **Secession '96.**

For many years, Rogers led Crystalized Movements, a fluid aggregation with such a sporadic recording/performance schedule that some folks thought the prefix "the shadowy," so often appended to mentions of the group, was actually part of its name. **Mind Disaster** is, for all intents and purposes, a manifestation of Rogers' most elusive dream states. Accompanied by drummer Ed Boyden, he wends through elongated jams—which gel into song form only by coincidence—trailing a hypnotically glimmering thread of distortion, fuzz and the odd garage-prog riff. Spectacular, if overly dependent on acidic enhancement for full enjoyment. Also dating from this early-'80s period, the belatedly released **Damaged Lights** is a collection of direct-to-boombox outtakes, ranging from the medicated post-Yardbirds blues of "Here Comes the Train" to such wild feedback excursions as "I Am the Only Guitarist in the World and I'm Bleeding."

Rogers put a "real" band together before recording **Dog. Tree. Satellite Seers . . . ,** an album that, while slightly less unhinged than its predecessors, would likely fade the paisley of faux-lysergic posers at a hundred paces. The addition of second guitarist Eric Arn seems to have encouraged Rogers to focus on structure (not to mention vocals) a bit more meticulously: the two engage in a handful of scintillating duels based in chord progressions that press forward rather than spiral endlessly. Biggar joined upon Arn's departure, cementing the band's final lineup and nudging the sound ever so slightly out of its druggy torpor on **This Wideness Comes.** While guitar experiments like "Third Half" are still the order of the day, the more tightly arranged tracks (like the forbidding "The Second a Siren") radiate a confidence that borders on belligerence, a nice change from the insular ambience of past releases. Rogers' vocals—excavated by the use of a studio with contemporary equipment—impart a sense of anxiety that contributes plenty to the overall mood.

Revelations From Pandemonium, which proved to be Crystalized Movements' finale, is far and away the group's most successful intermingling of concentrated drug-bazaar rapture and post-modern sonic mischief-making—thanks in part to judicious use of vaporous keyboard fillips. If at times redolent of **Sister**-era Sonic Youth, the album—particularly open-ended spine-gnawers like "This Dimming Today"—establishes the Rogers/Biggar tandem as a force to be reckoned with.

Since the end of Crystalized Movements, Rogers and Biggar—abetted by a wide variety of fellow travelers stoked on a combination of imported psych bootlegs and homegrown combustibles—have crafted some of the headier improv-rock of the '90s. B.O.R.B. (an acronym, logically enough, for Bongloads Of Righteous Boo) is a hit-and-miss proposition thanks to its exceedingly crude, minimal set-up (the two guitarists are joined by St. Johnny's Tom Leonard on organ) and live-to-two-track recordings. Still, there are moments of pure transcendence, such as **Blast Off**'s nearly album-long "I Was a Beautiful Swan."

Where B.O.R.B. sometimes come off as sonic archaeologists reassembling the skeletons of eras past, the considerably rawer Vermonster sounds like a primitive tribe intent on digging the marrow out of those bones by any means necessary. The ranks of the guitar army are bolstered by the addition of *Forced Exposure* publisher Jimmy Johnson, whose sustained, fuzzy tones add an nth dimension to the pair of free-form freakouts that make up **Instinctively Inhuman.** Vermonster really hits its stride, however, on the double-disc **The Holy Sound of American Pipe,** which backs up such narcocentric titles as "Return to the Apex of High" and "Ecstatic State of Human Elevation" with twisted, raga drones that serve to disorient even as they delight. [dss]

See also *Damon and Naomi, St. Johnny.*

MAGICK HEADS

See *Bats.*

MAGNAPOP

Sugarland EP (Bel. Play It Again Sam) 1991
Magnapop (Play It Again Sam USA/Caroline) 1992
Kiss My Mouth EP (Bel. Play It Again Sam) 1993
Hot Boxing (Play It Again Sam/Priority) 1994
Fire All Your Guns at Once EP (Bel. Play It Again Sam) 1996
Rubbing Doesn't Help (Play It Again Sam/Priority) 1996

The recorded output of this Atlanta popcore foursome gives truth to the old saw that great live bands often make mediocre records. On stage, Magnapop is electric and alive with garage-rock simplicity, punk dynamics and classic new wave songwriting, sealed by Linda Hopper's molasses-sweet trill and, most important, the action-packed axe antics of genuine guitar heroine Ruthie Morris. But on record . . .

The **Sugarland** EP consists of early demos; those five songs, along with six later ones, make up Magnapop's eponymous debut. Of the tunes produced by the band, the best are the driving "Garden" and a feedback 'n' power chord role reversal of Big Star's "13." ("Ear" has lyrics by *Duplex Planet* poet Ernest Noyes Brookings). The record's other high points were recorded with Michael Stipe. (Hopper and drummer David McNair were in the early-'80s Athens primitive pop combo Oh-OK, which also included Matthew Sweet and Stipe sibling Lynda.) The dizzying "Merry" and the jangly, skanky "Favorite Writer" overcome Stipe's slight production values by virtue of their incandescent hooks. **Magnapop** suggests the possibility of great pop things to come.

Ted Niceley produced Magnapop's first serious studio effort, **Kiss My Mouth,** striking the right balance of slick and spontaneous on the four exceedingly perky songs, especially "Texas" and the lissome "Lay It Down." But Bob Mould's production of **Hot Boxing** doesn't sound all that different from their demos. The performances and songwriting are clearly more confident, but the studio accentuates the band's—especially

Morris'—hardcore punk swagger, neglecting to add the pop sparkle their best stuff demands. Rerecorded versions of "Texas," "Lay It Down" and **Magnapop**'s "Skinburns" pale compared to the original models; though "Idiot Song" and "Here It Comes" are energetic, the record never quite hits the heights suggested by their more primitive material. With the charm (and crutch) of lo-fi ingenuousness gone, **Hot Boxing** reduces Magnapop to generic, if good, '90s girlpunk.

The four new songs of **Fire All Your Guns at Once,** produced by California punk veteran Geza X, bring Magnapop to a surprisingly modern point, like a punchy early-'80s new wave band given an enticing and subtle update. The real problem is the dichotomy between the music's genial aggression and the lyrics' vehemence: singing "You can't fuck with me" (in "Voice Without a Sound") as if it were a moon/June refrain leaves a strange aftertaste, as does the restrained arrangement of the angry "Down on Me." [mgk/i]

MAGNETIC FIELDS

Distant Plastic Trees (UK Red Flame) 1991 (Merge) 1995
The Wayward Bus (PoPuP) 1992 (Merge) 1995
The House of Tomorrow EP7 (Feel Good All Over) 1993
[CD] (Feel Good All Over) 1996
Holiday (Feel Good All Over) 1994
The Charm of the Highway Strip (Merge) 1994
Get Lost (Merge) 1995

6THS

Wasps' Nests (London) 1995

Stephin Merritt is a contradictory character: an avowed ABBA aficionado with a monumental misanthropic streak, a recondite home recorder with Spectorscope ambitions, an incurable romantic afflicted with jadedness that borders on the terminal. In short, the reclusive mastermind of the continually transmuting Magnetic Fields is the quintessential pop eccentric, dispatching universally touching songs to a world he'd just as soon have no contact with.

The Boston native had spent some time on New York's embryonic club-kid scene before returning to his hometown in order to distill what would become the Magnetic Fields formula—a combination of saccharine synth-pop plinking and doleful narratives delivered in deadpan voices so uninvolved you'd swear the singers were reading a foreign language phonetically. At first, Merritt relied on singer Susan Anway (whose voice, at its best, recalls a pooped Tracey Thorn) to channel his tales of lost—or generally unconsummated—love. On **Distant Plastic Trees,** they're explicit both in terms of lust ("Railroad Boy") and self-loathing ("Falling in Love With the Wolfboy"). The baroque pop structures of songs like "Smoke Signals" are redolent of the classics Merritt clearly holds dear, but his impressionistic wordplay—which often alights on bracing, upsetting images—seldom settles into simple cliché. He's more prone to string together non sequiturs that start out absurdist but end up eviscerating, most notably in "100,000 Fireflies" (later covered by Superchunk), which kicks off with the confession "I've got a mandolin/I play it all night long/It makes me want to kill myself."

While every bit as synthetic, **The Wayward Bus** is considerably more twee. Merritt again puts words in Anway's mouth; she bills and coos over skeletal backing that directs attention to the most self-involved depresso tales this side of Morrissey. The singer does an admirable job of negotiating the seas of cheese that comprise "Tokyo á Go-Go" and the Gallic "Suddenly There Is a Tidal Wave"—which concludes with a wish to be reincarnated as Pippi Longstocking (!). There's a certain amount of charm here, but keep the insulin handy. (In a bout of discographical confusion, the import-only **Distant Plastic Trees** was quietly included in the PoPuP CD of **The Wayward Bus;** minus one track, the albums were subsequently reissued as an official co-billed twofer by Merge.)

At this point, Merritt decided he no longer needed a mouthpiece and began singing his own songs in a splendid baritone croon. On **The House of Tomorrow**—as close to "rock" as the Magnetic Fields is likely to get—he actually bears a passing vocal resemblance to Morrissey in the earliest days of the Smiths, particularly on the swooning "Love Goes Home to Paris in the Spring." What's still most striking, however, is Merritt's seemingly inexhaustible supply of oddball rejoinders, including references to a lover who can look "like a Swiss army knife with wings, dance like a Hindu deity" *and* be "best friends with Timothy Leary." What was that about the brown acid again?

Holiday, which, like most Magnetic Fields records, accessorizes Merritt's Casio structures with the unconventional bookends of Johny Blood's tuba and Sam Davol's cello, is an airily low-key effort. Merritt's droopy-lidded delivery not only suits the nonchalant air of regret that imbues songs like "Deep Sea Diving Suit," it adds a charming vulnerability to the openly gay singer's boy-crazy anticipation on "Desert Island" and "Take Ecstasy With Me." The album is equally saturated with innocence and decadence, but the balance is likely to seem right only to those who can imagine the latent beauty of a landscape like the one Merritt conjures in "Strange Powers": "On the ferris wheel, looking out on Coney Island/Under more stars than there are prostitutes in Thailand . . ."

Although you have to admire Merritt's ability to weave his synthetic fabrics into gossamer threads, there are certain places where only the real thing will do, as evidenced by the ill-advised synth-country foray of **The Charm of the Highway Strip.** Rather than revel in the Casio artifice at which he excels, Merritt seems too eager to duplicate authentic instrumentation, blunting the impact of songs like "Lonely Highway," which appropriates snatches of Lee Hazlewood's "Jackson." Likewise, the knowing attitude that can be charming in his pure pop ditties sounds unpleasantly smug in "Two Characters in Search of a Country Song." There are moments (like "Born on a Train") that simulate a fortuitous stretch of radio crosstalk projecting Scott Walker into the middle of the Grand Ole Opry, but for the most part, **The Charm of the Highway Strip** is hardly a fantastic voyage.

Fortunately, Merritt returns to his laboratory on **Get Lost.** More intricately layered than most of the band's work—new accouterments include ukulele (played by longtime drummer/manager Claudia Gonson), banjo, even bass guitar—songs like "The Desperate Things You Made Me Do" and "You and Me and the Moon" betray a dancey new wave sensibility that was previously only hinted at. That coincides with a marked downturn in the cynicism quotient: "Why I Cry" and "The Dreaming Moon," while delivered as frigidly as ever, force Merritt to reveal a lovable side in spite of himself.

The 6ths is the first of Merritt's myriad side projects (the Gothic Archies and Future Bible Heroes are others) to see the light of day—on a major label, no less—and it's appropriately enigmatic. **Wasps' Nests** allows him to fully cultivate the Phil Spector/Joe Meek side of his personality by putting fourteen different singers through the paces of his original creations with a rigor evident in the precise dispassion used by each. Sebadoh's Lou Barlow mumbles through a downcast "In the City in the Rain" without losing his slacker cool, while Unrest frontman Mark Robinson turns in a credible approximation of Merritt's own style on the bossa nova–styled "Puerto Rico Way." Since Merritt has constantly pointed to ABBA as an inspiration, it's appropriate that he should be most successful in spinning confections around sweetly impassive female voices: here, he links gloriously with Heavenly's Amelia Fletcher on "Looking for Love (In the Hall of Mirrors)," Yo La Tengo's Georgia Hubley for "Movies in My Head" and Helium's Mary Timony on "All Dressed Up in Dreams." Think of it as bubblegum that bites back. [dss]

MAGNOLIAS

Concrete Pillbox (Twin\Tone) 1986
For Rent (Twin\Tone) 1988
Dime Store Dream (Twin\Tone) 1989
Off the Hook (Alias) 1992
Hung Up On . . . EP (Alias) 1992
Street Date Tuesday (TRG) 1996

Formed in the towering shadow of Hüsker Dü and the Replacements and a few years behind Soul Asylum, the Magnolias seemed doomed to be Minneapolis' scruffy also-rans, the band that got left behind when everyone else graduated to the big leagues. And while the revolving-lineup group has never developed a national profile anywhere near the scale of those other bands, singer/guitarist John Freeman has persevered, finally making an album to prove his band's worth.

Concrete Pillbox, co-produced by Grant Hart, is like an anthology of mid-'80s Minneapolis punk style. Shedding such imitation (save an abiding Buzzcocks influence) for a loud, textured pop-punk personality of their own, the Mags came back with **For Rent,** a hard-driving and catchy collection sparked by strong songs like "Walk a Circle" and "Goodbye for Now." **Dime Store Dream,** recorded in Prince's Paisley Park Studios by producer Jim Rondinelli, has a raging guitar sound, hyper drumming and more cool songs ("Flowin' Thru," "In My Nightmare," "Don't See That Girl" and the Replacements-like "Coming on Too Strong").

That trio of records, however, was just a warmup for **Off the Hook.** Played with taut, scrabbly precision by returning drummer Tom Cook, super bassist Caleb Palmiter and guitarist Kent Militzer, the best songs of Freeman's life portray a dispirited romantic avoiding anger and bitterness by discharging his emotional burdens into sensitive, tuneful, speedy rock'n'roll. Rarely has punk sounded such a winsome note. For an artless singer, Freeman's voice is incredibly expressive; carried along on bracing rhythm-guitar riffs woven with pretty lead figures, his wry lyrics and catchy hooks help **Off the Hook** rabbit-punch back at disappointment with a poker face and the certainty of a better day coming. "When you ask me how I'm doing/Do you really want to know?/And I'm lying when I tell you I'm fine/I'm really kinda low/But I put on a smile/If only for a while/But when I'm not up to giving/And when I'm not up to living/I think of tomorrow." Freeman's world here is fraught with ambivalence. "Hello or Goodbye" attempts to resolve a relationship one way or another; in "Matter of Time," a lover is heading out west, and Freeman balances his disdain for the smog and sure-to-break dreams of Los Angeles with cocky hope for her return. Chalking up eleven fine originals and a bristling cover of Chris Osgood's perplexed "Complicated Fun"—all inside forty minutes—**Off the Hook** is everything a punk-pop record should be.

Hung Up On . . . piles together the album version of "When I'm Not," a needless remix of "Hello or Goodbye," a goofy Hanna-Barbera cartoon song ("Way Out") and three live numbers, including "Last Train to Clarksville" and "Fathers and Sins," a cruel attack on Hank Williams, Jr., given a reprise from **Dime Store Dream.**

Street Date Tuesday brings a new set of Mags back to the racks with no diminution (or much change of any sort) in the power of Freeman's terse, vulnerable spirit. The album's extra-feisty sound is occasionally matched by lyrics of angry frustration ("Dropping Blood and Names," "Bullet for a Badman"), but the strongest and most stirring tunes again allow hope to get a foothold ("Hello Belinda," "Weather Couldn't Get Any Better," "Even Without You"). And the deliberate "Polecat Creek" is downright poetic in its affecting connection of private and public places. If not quite the equal of **Off the Hook, Street Date Tuesday** still flies the Mags' flag high and loud. [i]

See also *TPRG.*

MAIDS OF GRAVITY

See *Medicine.*

MAIN

Hydra EP (UK Situation Two) 1991
Calm EP (UK Situation Two) 1992
Hydra-Calm (UK Situation Two) 1992 (Beggars Banquet) 1995
Dry Stone Feed (UK Beggars Banquet) 1992
Firmament (UK Beggars Banquet) 1993
Motion Pool (Beggars Banquet) 1994
Ligature (UK Beggars Banquet) 1994 + 1995
Firmament II (Beggars Banquet) 1994
Corona EP (UK Beggars Banquet) 1995
Terminus EP (UK Beggars Banquet) 1995
Maser EP (UK Beggars Banquet) 1995
Haloform EP (UK Beggars Banquet) 1995
Kaon EP (UK Beggars Banquet) 1995
Neper EP (UK Beggars Banquet) 1995
Hertz (Beggars Banquet) 1996

INDICATE

Whelm (UK Touch) 1995

After exorcising his rock'n'roll demons and splitting up Loop at the turn of the decade, guitarist Robert Hampson (concurrent with a short stay in Godflesh) devoted himself to a campaign to promote inertia by any means necessary. Under the guise of Main, Hampson and his collaborator, guitarist Scott Dowson, explore ambient structures that edge imperceptibly from tranquility to clamor, manifesting as stealthy a progression as one of Brian Eno's abstract film scores. Main has a bit of common ground with ambient techno—largely a shiatsu-like body consciousness—but the group's edifices allow for the introduction of more *real* ambient sound than most.

Main is at its most aggressive on **Hydra** and **Calm** (compiled with a bonus track, "Thirst," as **Hydra-Calm**), leaning hard into the array of flangers and phasers that provide the elegant dislocation of bass-heavy tracks like "Flametracer" and "There Is Only Light." It would be misleading to insinuate that the band was playing "rock" at this stage, but only a few of these pieces (notably the opalescent twenty-minute "Thirst") luxuriate in languor to the fullest. While **Firmament** operates within the realm of songform, the influences are clearly more diffuse—a bit of 23 Skidoo–styled percussive wankery used to underpin an array of primitive electronics that seem to have been appropriated from Cabaret Voltaire's Sheffield basement. Abrasive, but not much more.

A note on the back of **Motion Pool** heralds a push into "drumless space," a Jello-floored realm that's actually quite soothing to infiltrate. The album's pieces are distinct and compact—if considerably more formless than what had come before. Hampson's vision is not yet fully realized: the self-conscious "VII" might as well have been lifted whole from one of those old sound effects records that clutter thrift-store bins. But when the pieces connect (or more precisely, when they hang just the right distance apart), there's a sense of indigenous menace—particularly palpable on "Rail" and "Crater Scar"—that's positively enthralling.

Firmament II ushers in a new era, wherein all of the rock (and most of the music) is removed from Main's sphere of influence. The disc consists of a single piece, mottled with subtle clattering, that refuses any sort of personal connection. Oddly enough, the album makes for compelling enough ancillary listening to provoke sequential spins—it sure beats those white-noise generators when it comes to drowning out the outside world.

The half-dozen EPs that emanated from the Main camp in 1995 are to be taken as a piece—as evidenced by their subsequent compiling in the minimal-yet-luxurious **Hertz** box. If experienced with too much of a time lag, the records tend to blend together, but immersion accentuates the subtle differences between, say, the Terry Riley-esque harmonic drones that dominate **Corona** (two long, incrementally intensifying pieces) and the more strident Reich-isms consolidated in the three movements of **Terminus.** When Hampson strives for industrial audio vérité (as on sections of the fragmented **Maser**), he fails to provide a trenchant format for the urban sounds he so lovingly re-creates. But when he transfigures those same factory scenes into three-dimensional form (as on the icily beautiful **Haloform**), Hampson makes a case for atmosphere as an end in itself. [dss]

See also *Godflesh, Hair & Skin Trading Co., Jim O'Rourke.*

MAIN SOURCE

Breaking Atoms (Wild Pitch) 1991

Main Source was led by upstate New York rapper/producer Large Professor and featured K-Cut and Sir Scratch, brothers from Toronto, on the turntables. After a well-received indie 12-inch single, "Watch Roger Do His Thing," the group signed to Wild Pitch and cut the superb **Breaking Atoms.** "Looking at the Front Door" demonstrates Large Professor's crisp, direct rhyme storytelling; "Just a Friendly Game of Baseball" is an extraordinary extended metaphor and a cutting examination of race relations. "Live at the Barbeque" (which introduced the world to up-and-coming New York rapper Nas) is one of the best posse sessions ever cut. But Main Source also pushes the limits of the musical form with "Peace Is Not the Word to Play," illustrating the dynamic possibilities of the two-DJ format. Before the group could expand on that promising debut, however, Large Professor left for a highly successful production career. He signed a solo recording deal in late 1995. Meanwhile, the two brothers kept the name, picked up old-school rapper Mikey D and continued, releasing one dull single before being dropped by their label. [jzc]

MAJESTY CRUSH

Fan EP (Vulva) 1992
Love 15 (Vulva/Dali) 1993
Sans Muscles EP (Vulva) 1994

Detroit's Majesty Crush specialized in lush, dreamy guitar rock of the Galaxie 500/shoegaze variety, but gave it a nasty twist: a fascination with pornography and stalkers. The four-piece band (with inaudible connections to the city's techno scene) suffered from singer David Stroughter's habit of restraining melodies to one or two notes, but the rhythm section of bassist Hobey Echlin and drummer Odell Nails III (both ex–Spahn Ranch) was surprisingly powerful, and Michael Segal's guitar kept everything shimmery and lovely—no matter how dark the lyrical vision.

The **Fan** EP starts off with Majesty Crush's nominal anthem, "No. 1 Fan," a love song of the sort that inspires restraining orders; in the chorus, Stroughter breathily intones, "I'd kill the President for your love." The four other songs are slow, whooshy and of a piece, including a rerecording of the band's first single, "Sunny Pie," an ode to a check-out clerk at an X-rated bookstore.

Love 15 reprises "No. 1 Fan," "Horse" and "Penny for Love" from the EP and also contains remakes of three songs from early singles, with nicer production all around. The stalker theme continues in the new "Uma" and "Seles," plus "Boyfriend," which appears to be an offer to win somebody's love by torturing and killing her significant other. Creepy.

Dali Records went out of business almost immediately upon the release of **Love 15,** so the band released **Sans Muscles** on its own Vulva label (so named after a hoax, in the fanzine *You Can't Hide Your Love Forever,* involving an all-black female speed-metal band). The production is relatively on the cheap again, but the band is tougher and tighter than ever. It wouldn't be a Majesty Crush record without rerecordings, so "Uma" reappears under the name "Bestower of Blessings." The highlight, though, is "If JFA Were Still Together," whose lyric proceeds from the assumption that JFA was not a hardcore band but an actual army devoted to protecting John Hinckley's favorite young actress. [ddw]

MAKE-UP

See *Nation of Ulysses.*

MALFORMED EARTHBORN

See *Brutal Truth.*

MALFUNKSHUN

See *Mother Love Bone.*

MANIC STREET PREACHERS

Stay Beautiful EP (Columbia) 1991
Generation Terrorists (Columbia) 1992
Little Baby Nothing EP (UK Columbia) 1992
Gold Against the Soul (Columbia) 1993
The Holy Bible (UK Epic) 1994
Everything Must Go (Epic) 1996

For all their deliberate effort to antagonize and shock, the Manic Street Preachers came at the British charts in the early '90s with a strongly traditional pop sound—which they quickly outgrew. If the band got a lot of bat-biting mileage out of an early episode in which rhythm guitarist Richey James razored "4Real" into his arm in bloody response to a rock critic's impertinent question about the band's sincerity, that was nothing to compare to the cliffhanger with which he bowed out of the rat race—and likely off this mortal coil—several years later.

Initially, the mascara-lined Welsh glam quartet essentially hijacked the old new wave and dressed it up with nouveau arena-rock cynicism. Right before the UK was overrun by copyists, revivalists and dated attitude-mongers, the Manic Street Preachers made it their mission to update the great rock'n'roll swindle for a clientele that considered the Clash and Sex Pistols golden oldtimers. In fact, there's nothing on **Generation Terrorists** that Generation X (and, once removed, Mott the Hoople or Slade) hadn't done with greater élan more than a decade earlier. Admittedly, Billy Idol never thought of dissing American music institutions in his song titles, as the Manics did with "Motown Junk," one of the five UK single sides compiled as **Stay Beautiful.**

Less terrorists than cat bandits, the Manics are so concerned with cutting dashing figures that the loot nearly gets left at the job. Still, the debut album gets by on chunky singalong rock anthems (melodies by singer/guitarist James Dean Bradfield and drummer Sean Moore) and credibly sharp topical lyrics (written by James and bassist Nicky Wire). The songs concern consumerism ("Slash n' Burn"), exploitation of models ("Little Baby Nothing," with sections sung by Traci Lords), youth culture (the particularly insightful "Stay Beautiful"), drugs ("Another Invented Disease") and politics ("Democracy Coma," "You Love Us"). "Condemned to Rock'n'Roll," one of the record's most metallic numbers, offers a most uncontemporary vision of history: "The past is so beautiful/The future like a corpse in snow." (The original British edition omits "Democracy Coma" but contains five songs excised from the US release, including "Spectators of Suicide," "So Dead" and the provocative "Methadone Pretty," all of which fall short musically but stress the complicated—or is that just confused?—intelligence of the band's soapbox.) The **Little Baby Nothing** EP uses the song's single version and adds lame live takes of "You Love Us" and two other songs, recorded in a Japanese club in mid-'92.

Wisely moving forward from its self-conscious sourcing (but erroneously choosing to indulge the Sunset Strip glam-metal side of its heritage), the quartet returned a year later sounding like a British Guns n' Roses on **Gold Against the Soul.** Luckily, Bradfield's no Axl, although roses are used both in the cover art and as the lyrical motif of the dismally depressed "Roses in the Hospital." The blasting Americanized riff-rock record wallows in misery ("From Despair to Where") and self-abuse ("Drug Drug Druggy"), with random acts of violence against—get this—those caught looking backward ("Nostalgic Pushead"). The sardonically sympathetic treatises on childbirth ("Life Becoming a Landslide") and those afflicted with a rare and bizarre disease ("Symphony of Tourette") are even harder to reckon. Making grim and pretentious use of music that betrays no imagination at all, the Manic Street Preachers come off a lot like their name: unfocused, didactic and too lost in their own world to convince anyone of anything.

The Holy Bible is an entirely different story. The music is back to straightforward glam-pop rock, only without melodic distinction. (Mark Freegard's fadeaway mix gives a clear field to the vocals by tightening the instrumental attack into a compressed electric force field that's appealing but indistinct.) The lyrics, however, are some of the most articulate, upsetting and brutally decadent in pop memory. With unidentified spoken-word soundbites used as introductions, the band tackles anorexia (the first-person "4st. 71b."), political correctness ("P.C.P."), impermanence ("Die in the Summertime"), genocide ("The Intense Humming of Evil"), sex for sale ("Yes"), assassination ("Archives of Pain") and radical politics ("Ifwhiteamericatoldthetruthforonedayit'sworldwouldfallapart," "Revol"). Some of the hallucinatory revulsions defy categorization: "I am idiot drug hive, the virgin, the tattered and the torn/Life is for the cold made warm and they are just lizards." For all the fever burning on paper, the album's music is completely out of synch, creating a tragic dissonance between incendiary words and hit-parade sounds that squanders the worth of both. At no point do the intensity levels come within spitting distance of each other, which does irreparable damage to the entire effort. As probably befits its title, **The Holy Bible** can be absorbed without a word being actually understood.

On February 1, 1995, Richey James (Richard J. Edwards)—who had been institutionalized the previous summer to treat a long history of alcohol abuse, depression and anorexia—left a London hotel, drove to his apartment in Cardiff and vanished, leaving behind his passport, Prozac and credit cards. His car was later found abandoned at the Severn Bridge, a popular suicide spot near Bristol. Although he was initially declared missing, the police search was eventually called off and James was presumed dead. Later that year, the three remaining Manics decided to continue and began working on **Everything Must Go,** an unfortunate Journeymanlike postscript to the band's tragedy. Despite Mike Hedges' feverish overproduction (nice harp arpeggios, dude), this needless epilogue, which employs some vestigial James lyrics for morbid measure, is sorely deficient in spirit, imagination and adventure. [i]

AIMEE MANN

Whatever (Imago) 1993 (Geffen) 1995
I'm With Stupid (UK Geffen) 1995 (DGC) 1996

Several years after the breakup of 'Til Tuesday, the Boston new wave band that scored big with "Voices Carry" in 1985, vocalist Aimee Mann launched her unhurried solo career with the mightily impressive **Whatever.** Receiving assistance from producer/multi-instrumentalist Jon Brion (of the Grays), as well as Roger McGuinn and drummer Jim Keltner, Mann moves easily between tough (musically *and* lyrically) rockers like the angry "I Should've Known," the sprightly pop-rock of "Could've Been Anyone" and the tender balladry of "Mr. Harris," which expertly details a May/December romance. Many of the songs allegedly concern Mann's bitter breakup with singer/songwriter Jules Shear (who shares writing credit on one tune here with Mann and Marty Willson-Piper of the Church). Regardless, she was certainly able to channel her emotions into a piece of work that's both highly personal and easy on the ears.

After protracted record company miseries that saw a completed second album change labels before its release, **I'm With Stupid** finally appeared in America in early 1996. Again recorded with substantial help from Jon Brion, **I'm With Stupid** is a stripped-down and more aggressive record than its predecessor, with growling guitars as the backdrop for Mann's alternately sweet and accusatory, slightly jazzy vocals. Squeeze's Chris Difford and Glenn Tilbrook lend their distinctive voices to "Frankenstein" and "That's Just What You Are"; Juliana Hatfield harmonizes on two tunes; Michael Penn lets rip with a few white-hot guitar solos; former Suede guitarist Bernard Butler adds his six-string stylings to "Sugarcoated," which he co-wrote. Inspired somewhat by less-mainstream artists like Beck and Liz Phair (Mann tosses off the f-word more than once here), **I'm With Stupid** deftly straddles the line between minimalism and grandeur while maintaining the keen lyrical sense that distinguished **Whatever.** [jmb]

See also *Jellyfish.*

BARBARA MANNING

Lately I Keep Scissors (Heyday) 1988
One Perfect Green Blanket (Heyday) 1991
Barbara Manning Sings With the Original Artists (Feel Good All Over) 1995

28TH DAY

28th Day (Restless) 1985 (Skyclad) 1992 [tape] (Devil in the Woods) 1992

WORLD OF POOH

The Land of Thirst (Nuf Sed) 1989
A Trip to Your Tonsils EP (Nuf Sed) 1993

SF SEALS

Baseball Trilogy EP (Matador) 1993
Nowhere (Matador) 1994
Truth Walks in Sleepy Shadows (Matador) 1995

GLANDS OF EXTERNAL SECRETION

Northern Exposure Will Be Right Back (Starlight Furniture Company) 1995

SNOWMEN

Soundproof (Ger. Normal) 1995
In Orbit (Double Play) 1996

Barbara Manning is far from a prolific writer of songs—in ten years of recording, she's released only a few dozen of her own—but she's a great one, with subtle, unforgettable melodies and lyrics that cut to the heart of personalities and relationships. She's also got a gift for interpreting other people's songs (many of which have been written specifically for her clear Californian twang) and an intriguing taste for combining straightforward singing and guitar playing with much more experimental sounds.

28th Day, a pretty good guitar-pop band of the kind that was so common in the mid-'80s, released a single seven-song mini-album in the US during its existence. The group's main significance, as the packaging of the 1992 edition makes clear, was as Manning's first band (she played bass; guitarist Cole Marquis wrote most of the songs but drummer Michael Cloward co-wrote a couple). While managing to make some fine music, the trio never captured the richness and power of its live sound in the studio. The expanded Skyclad CD contains thirteen songs (one is called "Instrumental #1"); Cloward's Devil in the Woods label subsequently offered a cassette version that appended live material and other things to the CD's contents. The best songs are Manning's "Burnsite" and "Stones of Judgement," though "Dead Sinner" and a reworking of the folk song "This Train" are noteworthy, too.

After 28th Day broke up, Manning joined singer/guitarist Brandan Kearney's noise project World of Pooh and turned it into a rock band. The group's sole album, **The Land of Thirst,** commands high prices from collectors, and with good reason: it's a magnificent record. The terrible tensions within the band are hidden by wan melodies, but come out in the *brutal* lyrics: "Stay away, your flesh disgusts me / Your attentions are an ugly parody of things I've always wanted" (from Kearney's "Mr. Coffee-Nerves"). Almost every song is a killer, but the best are Manning's "Scissors" (covered by everyone from Peter Jefferies to Yo La Tengo), Kearney's "Playing One's Own Piano" and their collaboration, the simple, tragic "I'm on the Wrong Side." Secret weapon: drummer Jay Paget, who later joined Thinking Fellers Union Local 282. A subsequent World of Pooh single was notable for Manning's "Someone Wants You Dead"; the long-delayed **A Trip to Your Tonsils** EP rounded up most of the band's remaining recordings, including another version of "Stones of Judgement" and a cover of Les Paul and Mary Ford's "Blow the Smoke Away."

Around the same time that she got involved in World of Pooh, Manning made her first solo album, **Lately I Keep Scissors.** Marquis, Kearney, producer Greg Freeman, drummer Melanie Clarin and Manning's sister Terri all play on the record, which includes different versions of World of Pooh's "Scissors" and "Somewhere Soon." Aside from "Breathe Lies" (co-written with Lindsey Thrasher of Vomit Launch, who covered Manning's "Every Pretty Girl") and a cover of Marquis' "Prophecy Written," all the songs are her own; they reveal a songwriter of tremendous lyrical power and breadth of sonic vision—"Make It Go Away" almost sounds like My Bloody Valentine.

The eight-song **One Perfect Green Blanket,** on the other hand, has the vague scent of filler. There's a remake of "Someone Wants You Dead," an extra track from a foreign pressing of **Scissors,** a nice Bats cover ("Smoking Her Wings") and another Marquis song done for a compilation. That leaves three new songs, one of which ("Sympathy Wreath," a farewell to World of Pooh) appears twice. The CD appends all of **Scissors.**

After an exquisite solo single (the live staple "Haze Is Free (Mounting a Broken Ladder)" and a cover of Wings' "Don't Let It Bring You Down") and a pair of 7-inchers done in collaboration with *Bananafish* magazine editor Seymour Glass (one under the name the Glands of External Secretion), Manning reappeared with her new band, the SF Seals (named after a baseball team; the title and artwork of **One Perfect Green Blanket** also reflect an interest in minor-league ball). The group started with a lineup of Manning, Clarin, bassist/singer Michelle Cernuto (who wrote a handful of their early songs) and guitarist Lincoln Allen, though it gradually evolved into Manning and whoever happened to be onstage or in the studio with her at the time. The **Baseball Trilogy** EP presents three songs about diamond greats: covers of Les Brown's "Joltin' Joe DiMaggio" (with a neat little-big-band arrangement) and Mad V. Dog's "The Ballad of Denny McLain" and Manning's own "Dock Ellis," about the man who pitched a no-hitter while tripping on acid.

The Seals' first full-length, **Nowhere,** is a disappointment: lukewarm songwriting, a weak remake of the seductive Manning/Glass single "8's," a couple of okay covers, a dreadful noise piece and too many songs that dissolve into protracted feedback or sound-collage endings. It's not without its great moments, but they're best experienced by going for the single, which pairs "Still?" with a punchy cover of Faine Jade's '60s psych obscurity, "Don't Underestimate Me."

Barbara Manning Sings With the Original Artists is a peculiar but mostly successful album. With Manning employed primarily for her interpretive skills, backing is provided by a cast of Feel Good All Over label regulars, including the Mekons' Jon Langford, the Coctails' John Upchurch and ex–Young Marble Giant Stuart Moxham (whose '90s band is named the Original Artists). The ten-song repertoire consists of a pair by Langford (including "Big Eye," heard in a different version on the Killer Shrews' album), five by Moxham, one by Manning (the outstanding "Optimism Is Its Own Reward") and covers of "Cry Me a River" and Lora Logic's "Martian Man." Everybody involved gets poppy and cuts loose a little, especially Moxham, whose "Daddy Bully" has go-go checks all over it. It's probably the most fun record Manning's made.

The second SF Seals album, **Truth Walks in Sleepy Shadows,** boasts eleven musicians, including a core group of Manning, Clarin, guitarist Brently Pusser (of Three Day Stubble) and bassist Margaret Murray (of U.S. Saucer). Unlike earlier records, it's clearly Manning's show this time, and the album is better for it. The production is lovely—the vibraphones on "Ladies of the Sea" and calliope on "Kid's Pirate Ship" are especially nice—and Manning's songs are simple and sweet (though "Pulp" has disturbing undertones of domestic violence). As usual, the cover choices are unexpected and fine: this time, the band essays songs by the Pretty Things, Faust and John Cale.

Northern Exposure Will Be Right Back, the first full-length Glands Of External Secretion record, is a self-indulgent mess: tape collages of recorded moments in the lives of Manning and Seymour Glass (radio shows, malfunctioning refrigerators, birthday parties, unwell cats). It's also completely charming and engaging, an audio scrapbook of their friendship and their love for peculiar sounds. Almost every track has some kind of organized instrumental component, though only a few are recognizable as songs—most delightfully, a version of the Bee Gees' "Run to Me" recorded by Manning and her sister when they were teenagers. The Dead C's Michael Morley makes a guest appearance on a couple of the sequences that were recorded live.

In '92, singer/guitarist/songwriter Cole Marquis returned from a period out of music and unveiled the Snowmen, his quartet with guitarist Rich Avella; the group has so far issued albums in Germany and the US. [ddw]

See also *Gary Lucas, Mekons, Stuart Moxham, Thinking Fellers Union Local 282, Three Day Stubble, U.S. Saucer.*

MAN OR ASTRO-MAN?

Is It . . . Man or *Astro*-Man? (Estrus) 1993
Destroy All Astromen! (Estrus) 1994
Your Weight on the Moon (UK One Louder) 1994
Live Transmissions From Uranus! (Homo-Habilis) 1995
Project Infinity (Estrus) 1995
Intravenous Television Continuum (UK One Louder) 1995
What Remains Inside a Black Hole. (Aus. Au-go-go) 1995
Deluxe Men in Space EP (Touch and Go) 1996
Experiment Zero (Touch and Go) 1996

Considering how many garage bands have been formed by those whose heads were shrunk by spending their youth glued to the TV watching monster movies, it stands to reason that trashy science-fiction would have polluted its share of minds as well. Taking a few obvious cues from Devo but going far deeper into the land of cheap and dodgy, the four men of Alabama's prolific Man or Astro-Man? (whose names, naturally, are Coco the Electronic Monkey Wizard, Dexter X (aka Dr. Deleto and His Invisible Vaportron), Star Crunch and Birdstuff—*Birdstuff?*) play reverbed whammybar guitar instrumentals, faster and looser but not unrelated to the usual surf-flavored twang, and dress them up with comical bits of film dialogue, instruction records and various intrusions of pseudo-technology on a budget—the kind of thing that would have made Ed Wood proud. When they open their mouths to sing (as they do from time to time), the lyrics are strictly of a piece with the spectacular packaging.

Since 1992, MOAM has issued something like two dozen singles and more than a half-dozen full-length albums; their rambunctious pure-fun emissions are a can't-miss proposition for those of a mind to tune in. **Destroy All Astromen!** comes to Earth with a couple of relevant Ventures covers, the guest organ–ized "Landlocked" and the delightfully sung "Mystery Science Theater 3000 Love Theme." **Project Infinity** is a singles compilation with some new tracks; **Live Transmissions From Uranus!** documents a Florida concert from late '94. **Deluxe Men in Space** previews **Experiment Zero** with "Maximum Radiation Level" but its other five tracks (including a couple of covers) are non-LP. [tr]

JONO MANSON BAND

See *Blues Traveler.*

MARILYN MANSON

Portrait of an American Family (nothing/Interscope) 1994
Smells Like Children (nothing/Interscope) 1995
Antichrist Superstar (nothing/Interscope) 1996

There's nothing as lamely pitiful as contrived outrage, and no band around fails to shock with as much concerted effort as Marilyn Manson. The Ft. Lauderdale protégés of Trent Reznor (who signed the garishly named and appointed quintet to his label and co-produced their albums) bring a serial-killer trading card mentality to a sound that drops an Alice Cooper olive into a vat-sized White Zombie cocktail. Presenting themselves as depravity-loving social commentators *and* bad-natured comedians, Marilyn Manson step into the slimy sonic caldron left unattended lately by the Butthole Surfers. They want so desperately to seem like jerks that maybe it's best to let them have their way.

The moronic mad-libbing of the group's murder-is-fun culture icon names (like the namesake vocalist and such male compatriots as Madonna Wayne Gacy, Daisy Berkowitz and Twiggy Ramirez) is only one facet for which the sprites of originality seem not to have been present; the profanity-laced lyrics are equally obvious and dumb. The virile, mid-speed rock has Reznor's sonic footprints (that is, things *he* picked up from Ministry and Foetus) all over it, but the effect inverts Nine Inch Nails' intimate malevolence writ large; the main distinctions of Marilyn Manson's music are largely extraneous—haunted-house sound effects and annoying samples. (**Portrait of an American Family** ends with seven minutes of a faintly ringing phone.) While some of the songs move around with enthusiastic ferocity and there *are* glimmers of wit (Arthur Brown's "I bring you" shout from "Fire" that kicks off "Lunchbox," Manson's Elmer Fudd voice on "My Monkey"), the album's self-conscious gimmickry and rote vulgarity take the fun out.

Wielding the same big shtick on **Smells Like Children,** the band works overtime like Santa's baddest elves in a valiant effort to offend somebody—*anybody.* Trundling through industrial noise, sample manipulation and various effects in "Diary of a Dope Fiend" and "Scabs, Guns and Peanut Butter," the album goes outside of songdom for cut-up sex sounds ("F*** Frankie") and "May Cause Discoloration of the Urine or Feces," a ridiculous but evidently serious four-minute medical phone conversation with a bewildered blood pressure patient. Not exactly the band's second album (but not exactly not, either), the grab-bag includes a remix of the debut's "Dope Hat" and plodding covers of Eurythmics' "Sweet Dreams (Are Made of This)" (evidently chosen for its passing reference to "abuse"), Screamin' Jay Hawkins' "I Put a Spell on You" (shock-rock's very own "Johnny B. Goode") and a charged rendition of Patti Smith's "Rock'n'Roll Nigger" that reveal nothing beyond Manson's transparent desperation to impress rock's impressionables. [i]

APRIL MARCH

April March EP (KokoPop) 1993
Chick Habit (Sympathy for the Record Industry) 1995

PUSSYWILLOWS

Spring Fever! (Telstar) 1988

VICTOR BANANA

Split (Splat Co) 1989
Like a Velvet Glove Cast in Iron (Jenkins/Peabody) 1993

NEIL SMYTHE

Refrains (Jenkins/Peabody) 1995

With her wavery Nancy Sinatra voice and pedal-pusher persona, the pseudonymous April March (in reality Elinor Blake, formerly of New York's Pussywillows) conjures up the kicky spirit of a late-'50s dippity-do teenager on her kitschy five-song solo debut. Written, produced and accordion-packed in vintage Los Angeles style by the pseudonymous Vic Hazlenut and His Orchestra, which includes drummer Carlo Nuccio of the Continental Drifters, the whole affair is over in nine minutes, but that's enough to contain "Stay Away From Robert Mitchum," "Kooky" and "How to Land a Man," smart slices of cultural ephemera from the mildew-soaked bins of an imaginary junk store.

March ups the scale (eight songs, twenty minutes) and relocates her stylistic environs on **Chick Habit,** latching on to the suddenly chic realm of '60s Gallic pop as crafted by Serge Gainsbourg and the like. Singing old songs in serviceable French (except for a translated second version of the title track), she receives appropriately dated super-stylized backing from a small studio company headed by Andy Paley. Jonathan Richman strums guitar on "Le Temps de L'Amour." *Formidable!*

March's shadowy collaborator, Vic Hazlenut, is actually one Tim Hensley, who has released albums of his own under other pseudonyms. As Victor Banana, the young auteur made his debut with the incredibly mature **Split:** twenty-one songs, each a finely wrought piece of literate songcraft populated by pirates, dancers, monsters and doctors. Shunning any unnecessary electricity, Hensley (vocals, guitar, accordion) employs only a viola player, bassist and drummer. Music for a quirky and literate cabaret.

It makes perfect sense that comic artist Dan Clowes has drawn all the Banana/Smythe covers; Hensley's music is the aural equivalent of *Eightball.* The second Victor Banana album is a "soundtrack" to Clowes' graphic novel, *Like a Velvet Glove Cast in Iron.* Between album and book, no movie ever need be made. Invitingly creepy.

The material proffered by Neil Smythe (an anagram of Tim Hensley) on **Refrains** is not all that different from his other alter ego. The arrangements, though, draw from a broad spectrum, pulling in flute, oboe, clarinet, vibraphone, banjo and more. Quietly slick and cynical, the album's songs either come from, or are aimed at, Mars' version of Las Vegas. [i/dbg]

See also *TPRG.*

ZIGGY MARLEY AND THE MELODY MAKERS

Play the Game Right (EMI) 1985
Hey World! (EMI) 1986
Conscious Party (Virgin) 1987
Time Has Come: The Best of Ziggy Marley and the Melody Makers (EMI Manhattan) 1988
One Bright Day (Virgin) 1989
Jahmekya (Virgin) 1991
Joy and Blues (Virgin) 1993
Free Like We Want 2 B (Elektra) 1995

Although no one actually imagines Ziggy (David) Marley will ever replace his late father as the international icon of reggae music, the resemblance in their voices and the junior Marley's firm dedication to his heritage make it easy to hear more than a talented young man finding his way as a pop warrior in the conscious world.

Joined vocally in the Melody Makers by his younger brother Stephen and elder sisters Cedella and Sharon Marley Prendergast, Ziggy was all of sixteen when he made the Grammy-nominated **Play the Game Right** firmly in the Wailers' tradition. From there, the group matured and expanded its stylistic ambitions on the wonderful **Hey World!** and the thoroughly modern **Conscious Party,** which was produced by Talking Heads Chris Frantz and Tina Weymouth and employed a superb crew of international backup musicians. Giving up their rootsiness, the Melody Makers forged a fresh, appealing and sincere substitute.

Ziggy's talents really blossomed on **One Bright Day.** Downplaying Rasta culture even more than before, the freedom-minded album uses the band's catchiest melodies to promote music's universal power. With explicit lyrics and stylistic demonstrations, the Melody Makers express their solidarity with the South African struggle and African-American culture.

The course charted by the Melody Makers in the '90s has taken the group further from the stylistic essence of reggae, with no single idiom emerging to replace it. **Jahmekya,** which notably grants an increased role to Stephen Marley (he sings lead on two songs and wrote or co-wrote six; his distinctive reedy voice gives the album its most intriguing sonic ingredient) and employs an all-Jamaican backing band, includes the straight-up syncopation of Bob Marley's "Rainbow Country" and the powerful African commentary of "Namibia." Otherwise, the group tries on hip-hop beats, rock beats, disco beats and techno beats in a vain and uninspired costume play that leaves the band overdressed with nowhere to go. The Melody Makers' desire to keep growing—and the freedom to be whatever they want to be—is commendable, but change for its own sake is no substitute for decisive action.

Evidently through with random experimentation, the band followed that mess with **Joy and Blues,** a comfortable and cohesive album of nothing but reggae riddims, embellished with typical Melody Makers creativity, from one end to the other. Rather than dick around, Ziggy drinks deep of rich musical streams and gets down to business as usual. Whether it's the familiarity of the sound, the concentration of energy or the band's congenital fluency in their father's tongue, the album is a solid winner. Amid lyrics that venture no new insights on equally predictable topics, the romantic disillusionment of Bob Marley's "There She Goes" provides a different perspective. Stephen again provides a contrasting voice, singing his own "Rebel in Disguise" and Richie Havens' "African Herbsman" with a creaky, comical intonation that sounds faintly like Marc Bolan.

Ziggy's picture alone is on the cover of **Free Like We Want 2 B,** but it's Stephen who's moving on up in the Melody Makers' universe. As the band handsomely stretches the elastic boundaries of reggae (only tearing through once, in the acoustic reverie of "Beautiful Mother Nature"), Ziggy comes across with the uplifting "Power to Move Ya," "Live It Up" and the funky "Today" (which sounds disconcertingly like the Police), but his themes are routine, his topical lyrics tired. ("G7" hits a new tedium point in socio-economic theory.) Meanwhile, Stephen steps out of his brother's happyface shadow with a sound and ideas of his own, rubbing salt in old political scars with the enervated resentment of "Bygones." Elsewhere, his "Tipsy Dazy," "Keep On" and the powerhouse fraternal collaborations of "Water and Oil" and "Hand to Mouth" add mightily to the band's most affecting and memorable collection. [i]

See also *TPRG.*

CHRIS MARS

Horseshoes and Hand Grenades (Smash) 1992
75% Less Fat (Smash) 1993
Tenterhooks (Bar/None) 1995
Anonymous Botch (Bar/None) 1996

Oddly enough, the most prolific artist to rise out of the ashes of Minneapolis' self-destructive Replacements has been drummer Chris Mars. The unfailing rhythmic glue that held the 'Mats together through the wild digressions of its early days, Mars became so dissatisfied with Paul Westerberg's intentions on 1990's **All Shook Down** that his outspoken opinions eventually led to his departure. That was a bad omen for the band, which never made another record. Relying on his artwork (and unemployment checks) for funds, Mars first signed up with the part-time Golden Smog, a local supergroup that took to the Twin Cities bar scene as an offbeat cover band. Then he got a solo career underway.

Mars sings, drums and plays guitar and keyboards on **Horseshoes and Hand Grenades,** enlisting bassist J. D. Foster as his sideman. (Dave Pirner and Dan Murphy of Soul Asylum make contributions to three tracks as well.) The results sound nothing like the Replacements. Filled with bitter tirades against the privileged ("Reverse Status") and scenesters ("Popular Creeps"), the set also reveals Mars' sentimental side on "Before It Began." On this surprising, impressive record, Mars falters only with his hoarse, tuneless vocals.

75% Less Fat, recorded solely with Foster, contains another dose of biting reflection: "Stuck in Rewind" fixes a piercing stare on barflies, "Public Opinion" slags the politically correct and "Whining Horse" shows no pity for complainers. But it's the instrumental sidetrack of "Nightcap," a soft jazz-pop number, that suggests Mars has more on his mind than rock. **75% Less Fat** may not push the envelope, but it cements an image of Mars as a serious musician with his own vision.

After leaving the majors, Mars spent some time creating album covers and showing his accomplished grotesqueries at art galleries before moving to Bar/None and releasing **Tenterhooks.** Fans of Mars' first two albums may be disappointed by his newfound fascination with an odd amalgamation of styles that run from rap and jazz to disco and midwestern surf-rock—complete with kettledrums, strings and found sounds. Recorded in Mars' living room with guitarist Chuck Whitney and trumpeter Doug deGrood (in real life, respectively, a computer technician and ad copywriter), **Tenterhooks'** scattershot approach is more self-indulgent than intriguing. The disc's diversity proves that Mars is best off sticking to what he does best: rock. "White Patty Rap" takes on Caucasian musicians who help themselves to African-American music, but it's a confusing turn. And while Mars reaches for touching balladry on "Mary," his vocals are still too rough to carry it off. Mars refuses to go on the road, so Syracuse's Wallmen toured behind **Tenterhooks,** covering the material for him—joined center stage by a cardboard Mars standup. [vg/dss]

See also *Golden Smog.*

MARVIN

The Mandolin Man (Regional/Restless) 1992
Bone (Regional/Restless) 1992
Weapons of the Spirit (Restless) 1994

After playing bass in Lone Justice, New York–born Marvin Etzioni shouldered his mandolin and Telecaster, stashed his surname and set off on a tasteful, intelligent and inconsistent solo career. A folky humanist with a homely voice, the singer/songwriter brings a little of Tom Waits' artful majesty and Leonard Cohen's poetic gravity to intimate-sounding creations of love, faith and family. Arranged with plenty of acoustic variety (thanks to contributors' accordion, clarinet, cello, strings and piano), **The Mandolin Man** is a handsome and tender debut—nothing more than an honest craftsman revealing his better qualities in sensitive songs like "Wings of Night" and "How Great Is the Ocean." Etzioni is surprisingly able to make the religious inspiration that drives "God Be With Us" and others be of a piece with the album's secular creations. Marquee-name assists come from Benmont Tench, former Lone Justice drummer Don Heffington, Peter Case and Victoria Williams, who has since done far better by the album's heartbroken "Can't Cry Hard Enough" than its co-author.

Bone, however, is disappointing and self-amused, a dry, dull, offhand Stonesy rock album that drops the veil of virtue and brings out the worst in Marvin's singing and some of the weakness in his songwriting. "Hope You're Happy," "The Naked Truth" and "Boy Meets Devil" (co-written with Radney Foster) are the only genuinely good tunes, and they're hardly peak achievements. The rest (discounting a fair try by his four-year-old son) are a sorry bunch.

Weapons of the Spirit returns wholeheartedly to Marvin's belief in love and Lord and gets back to more carefully considered three-dimensional music-making with some of the same people who helped out on the first record (plus Maria McKee, Sam Phillips, bassist Jerry Scheff, Nashville viola player Tammy Rogers and Toad the Wet Sprocket). Victoria Williams duets on "Daughter of the Rainbow"; McKee loads up the romantic promises of "Temple & Shrine" with a chorus of backing voices. If the devotional lyrics weigh heavy after a while and Marvin's singing waxes too zealous in its passionate declarations, the songs have real musical character and the performances are loaded with bright colors and memorable flavors. The gospel cradle never rocked so sweetly. [i]

MARXMAN

33 Revolutions per Minute (UK Talkin Loud) 1993 (Talkin Loud/A&M) 1994

Politics, like most perishables, doesn't travel particularly well. By the time it crosses an ocean, practically all its flavor disappears, a difficulty that better agit-poppers ameliorate by simply, well, kicking out the jams. This strident UK-based Anglo-Irish-Caribbean hip-hop quartet, however, can muster neither the requisite energy nor the slightest innovation needed to get its arduously wordy missives into gear—a decided detriment when it comes to reaching listeners who could give a toss about the monarchy.

Since we live in an age of diminished expectations, it's not too surprising Marxman lowers the titular ante from spiritual forefathers Stiff Little Fingers' mandate for "78 Revolutions a Minute." Still, the heavy-handedness with which the foursome addresses issues like Northern Irish home rule ("Sad Affair") and colonialism in general ("Ship Ahoy," with a cameo by Sinéad O'Connor) negates the moderately interesting trad-folk flourishes that accompany the de rigueur funky drummer beats. And while it's certainly encouraging to hear rappers actively decry misogyny—as Marxman do on the seething "All About Eve"—it would be even more tenable if the screed were invested with even a whit of that old Hyde Park Speakers Corner soapbox passion. As it stands, *The Communist Manifesto* offers more succinct ideas, even if you can't dance to it. (The UK and US editions differ only in the completely redone artwork.) [dss]

MARY MY HOPE

See *James Hall.*

J MASCIS

See *Dinosaur Jr.*

MASSIVE ATTACK

Blue Lines (Virgin) 1991
Protection (UK Circa) 1994 (Virgin) 1995

MASSIVE ATTACK V MAD PROFESSOR

No Protection (UK Circa) 1995 (Gyroscope) 1996

SHARA NELSON

What Silence Knows (UK Cooltempo) 1993 (Chrysalis) 1994
Friendly Fire (UK Cooltempo) 1995

Born and raised in Bristol, England, the Massive Attack collective is responsible for summoning up the spooky, clubby and groovy sound made most popular by another Bristol band, Portishead. Spawned in 1987 from the Wild Bunch, a group of musicians—including Neneh Cherry and Nellee Hooper (who spun his side of the coin into Soul II Soul)—who assembled in the early '80s, Massive Attack takes languorous reggae/dub rhythms and adds synthesizers, vocalists and luscious soul stylings to make a potion that gets to the essence of cool.

Blue Lines' songs dabble in several different veins but retain the same rhythmic backbone: a slow, hypnotic beat and reggae's traditional one-three emphasis. Singer Shara Nelson (a former member of Adrian Sherwood's On-U Sound posse) has a delicate yet strong soul voice; other vocalists on the album include reggae veteran Horace Andy (who shines on "Hymn of the Big Wheel"). Other members of the amorphous group—most significantly the soon-to-be-a-star Tricky—contribute an understated Brit-rap component. Despite the various voices and styles, the record is remarkably cohesive, covering William DeVaughn's 1974 hit "Be Thankful for What You've Got" and James Brown's "Blue Lines" while relying on the strength of Nelson and Andy's vocals to define and maintain its direction. Because of the group's sonic signature and clear confidence behind a soundboard, Massive Attack spent a good portion of the next few years doing outside remix and production work.

Many other bands had discovered the Massive Attack recipe by the time Nellee Hooper co-produced **Protection** with the group, so the elegant innovators had changed course. With four of the first album's seven gone (including Shara Nelson and Tricky, both off to their respective solo careers), the group needed another powerful singer to lead the melody from their clubby drone, and got Tracey Thorn (Everything but the Girl) to add her silky, poignant vocals to the title track and "Better Things." Tricky returns as a guest (on "Euro Child" and "Karmacoma"), as does Horace Andy (for "Spying Glass" and a cover of the Doors' "Light My Fire"). Newcomer Nicolette, who sings on two tracks, sounds like Eartha Kitt—the same annoying nasal emphasis and pronunciation. **Protection**'s lack of cohesion means that what remains from the original is the beautiful, intoxicating rhythm tracks and the pristine production qualities. What it lacks is the soul.

A promising idea in principle, the Mad Professor (Neil Fraser) cut a dub version of **Protection,** turning "Spying Glass" into "I Spy," "Heat Miser" into "Backward Sucking," "Better Things" into "Moving Dub" and so on. While the veteran English studio pro's radical reorientations certainly relieve the album of its glib surfaces and occasionally manage to tease out a seductive undertow that wasn't originally there (see "Trinity Dub," remixed from "Three," and "Cool Monsoon," drawn from "Weather Storm"), the rhythmic and sonic tumult he wreaks on the immaculate tracks often leaves a shapeless mess.

Shara Nelson's disappointing solo debut (she also appears on Guru's **Jazzmatazz Volume II**) puts the spotlight on the Londoner's throaty, dynamic voice, but the songs—engaging mid-tempo soul workouts which she co-wrote—aren't as strong or mysterious as what she sang with the group. [mf/i]

See also *Tricky.*

MASTERS OF CEREMONY

See *Brand Nubian.*

MASTERS OF REALITY

Masters of Reality (Def American) 1988 (Delicious Vinyl) 1990
Sunrise on the Sufferbus (Chrysalis) 1993

BOGEYMEN

There's No Such Thing As . . . (Delicious Vinyl) 1991

TIM HARRINGTON

Master Frequency and His Deepness (Triple X) 1996
Shinola (Delicious Vinyl) 1996

Hailing from the upstate college town of Syracuse, New York, Masters of Reality began in the early '80s as a semi-electronic duo of vocalist Chris Goss and guitarist Tim Harrington; the name is evidence that the band has always taken a certain delight in being defiantly out of step with the times. By its first album, the group had transmogrified into a phantasmagoric blues-metal quartet, driven by Harrington's raunchy and dexterous riffs, Goss' Cream-flavored voice and Vinnie Ludovico's devastatingly solid drumming. One of the most innovative hard-rock outings of its era, the album (also known as **The Blue Garden**) was given a powerful but overly melodramatic mix by producer Rick Rubin and bears some distinct tags of physical graffiti. Veering between crunch, twang, jangle, pop-riff-rock ("The Candy Song") and near-prog-rock ("Kill the King"), the album is near-brilliant but almost too diverse, and a quasi-mystical conceptual angle certainly didn't make it any easier to swallow.

Times caught up with the band quickly enough: the Dust Brothers bought the rights to the album for their Delicious Vinyl label. (Rap producers' puzzling fascination with the band may come down to its drummer.) Adding one song (the haunting "Doraldina's Prophecies"), the team remixed, resequenced, repackaged and reissued the album eighteen months after its initial release. Given a new context, **Masters of Reality** makes a lot more sense, as the focus stays on the songs instead of the baffling concept.

Shortly before the rerelease, however, Harrington and Ludovico threw a wrench into the marketing plan by splitting to form the Bogeymen. Goss and bassist Googe kept the Masters flag blasting with guitarist/producer Daniel Rey and—astonishingly—ex-Cream/Blind Faith drummer Ginger Baker. The reconstituted group toured behind the album and entered the studio to begin recording a followup for yet another label. **Sunrise on the Sufferbus** is stripped-down, bare-bones blues-rock with melodies as simple, memorable and, at times, annoying as bubblegum pop. While generally satisfying, Rey and Goss (who share the guitar duties) have little of Harrington's finesse, and the songs' starkness often gives an impression that something's missing.

The Bogeymen's **There's No Such Thing As . . .** is perhaps a more fitting second Masters of Reality album, displaying greater diversity in songwriting and arrangements. Harrington's fretwork is superb throughout, although his vocals are merely adequate and don't do the songs full justice.

In 1994, with ex–Redd Kross drummer Victor Indrizzo in tow, the Masters of Reality signed with their fourth record company (Epic) and completed an intriguing if patchy album called **The Ballad of Jody Frosty.** It went unreleased, and the band was dropped. Goss has also been working as a producer, most notably on three Kyuss albums. Indrizzo joined the Magnificent Bastards (the side group belonging to Stone Temple Pilots singer Weiland) and Samiam.

Harrington re-emerged in '96 with not one but two solo albums, the experimental **Master Frequency and His Deepness** and the comparatively commercial **Shinola.** While "getting into electronics" has long since lost its conceptual novelty, Harrington, as usual, provides his own unique twists on **Master Frequency:** dusting off possibly the very same drum machines that the Masters abandoned in the mid-'80s, much of the album pits mechanized rhythms against Foghat-sized raunch-riffs (and, on the Tom Waits–ian "Material Outcast," a string bass). The remainder of the album is even weirder, veering between Beefheart-esque tone poems and the tripped-out "Backward Prayer," which sounds like a **Satanic Majesties** outtake. If it's not meant to be taken *too* seriously, **Master Frequency** finds the old Master comfortable in a new setting. [ja]

See also *Kyuss; TPRG.*

MATERIAL

See *Bill Laswell.*

MATERIAL ISSUE

Material Issue EP (Big Block/Landmind) 1987
International Pop Overthrow (Mercury) 1991
Destination Universe (Mercury) 1992
Freak City Soundtrack (Mercury) 1994
Goin' Through Your Purse (Mercury) 1994

Fans of Chicago's Material Issue cite late singer/guitarist Jim Ellison's seemingly effortless knack for writing brisk, unforgettable hard-pop tunes. Detractors point to his annoyingly affected British accent and that his songs (while enjoyable) can seem a bit too calculated. There's something to be said for both arguments, but there's no doubt that, at its best, Material Issue was responsible for some of the decade's juiciest power-pop.

The **Material Issue** EP (produced by Jeff Murphy of Shoes) is a great beginning, six songs filled with punky energy, enthusiastic performances (by Ellison, bassist Ted Ansani and drummer Mike Zelenko, who would go on to pound the skins on a few Shoes discs) and hooks up the wazoo. "She's Going Through My Head," the riff-happy "A Very Good Thing" and "Chance of a Lifetime" are standouts.

Released by a major label willing to believe the band's brand of old-style pop music could actually be made popular, **International Pop Overthrow** was lauded by genre partisans as a de facto triumph for the power-pop underground. It didn't hurt that the album contains such tuneful confections as "Valerie Loves Me" (a radio hit), "Renee Remains the Same," "Crazy" and "Diane." But while there are some great tracks, way too many are simply ordinary. (Issued to radio around the same time was the promo-only **11 Supersonic Hit Explosions,** which features a lovely acoustic version of "Diane" and the otherwise unavailable "The Girl Who Never Falls in Love," along with covers of Paul Simon's "The Boxer," Thin Lizzy's "Cowboy Song" and Sweet's "Blockbuster.")

The sophomore jinx bit Ellison on **Destination Universe** (co-produced, as was **International Pop Overthrow,** by Shoes' Jeff Murphy), which suffers from a serious lack of strong tunes. The number that received the most attention—the silly "What Girls Want" ("a man with lips just like Mick Jagger/Rod Stewart's hair and Keith Richards' stagger")—sounds a little like Tommy Roe's "Dizzy" rocked up a bit. Just to hammer home his familiarity with '60s/'70s AM radio, Ellison acknowledges the riff from the Edison Lighthouse's "Love Grows (Where My Rosemary Goes)" in his own "When I Get This Way (Over You)." Another bad sign: Ellison rewriting the first album's "Crazy" and calling it "Girl From Out of This World." Only the sweetly affecting "Next Big Thing" and the powerfully poppy "Whole Lotta You" stand between **Destination Universe** and creative oblivion.

The trio then came back strong with its finest album, **Freak City Soundtrack,** produced by glam/bubblepop guru Mike Chapman. New versions of the debut EP's "She's Goin' Thru My Head" and "A Very Good Thing" are the cornerstones of the disc, which also features a cool cover of the Green Pajamas' late-'80s pearl "Kim the Waitress" and such nifty Ellison originals as the hyper "Goin' Through Your Purse" and the manic "Help Me Land"—two minutes of slashing power chords, a frenzied vocal and Zelenko's totally out-of-control drumming. **Freak City Soundtrack** is an unqualified triumph.

The live (and longer than listed) **Goin' Through Your Purse** is very nearly a Material Issue best-of, containing as it does sweaty performances of "Valerie Loves Me," "Kim the Waitress," "Diane," "What Girls Want" and five more, all recorded in front of a rabid hometown crowd. You can almost hear the beer being spilled.

Ellison killed himself in a Chicago garage in June 1996. [jmb]

DAVE MATTHEWS BAND

Remember Two Things (Bama Rags) 1993
Recently EP (Bama Rags) 1993
Under the Table and Dreaming (RCA) 1994
Crash (RCA) 1996

The Dave Matthews Band stands apart from the myriad neo-hippie jamsters populating rock'n'roll's H.O.R.D.E. wing. Unlike most of its spiritual compatriots, the DMB doesn't center its sound on blues licks or electric guitar workouts. Matthews, a South African expatriate who spent time in New York before moving to Charlottesville, Virginia, set out to make acoustic rock—not folk—and mined the city's club scene for sympathetic bandmates to go south with him. Bassist Stefan Lessard and drummer Carter Beauford are a supple rhythm section steeped in jazz sensibilities, while saxophonist Leroi Moore and violinist Boyd Tinsley are distinctive soloists who bring an exotic, world music flavor to the music. On top of all that is Matthews' reedy singing (which has drawn comparisons to Sting) and his fluid popcraft—a solid songwriting base from which the improvisations stem.

Because the DMB established itself as a live act, it's appropriate that its first independent releases are performance-based. **Remember Two Things** is burdened by modest sound and production—as well as meandering jams—but it's still easy to find the fresh, lively center of "Tripping Billies" and "Recently." Eight of the ten tracks are live: the others, "Seek Up" and "Minarets," mark the band's concert chops as more advanced than its studio prowess. The five-song mail-order-only **Recently** EP remixes the title track, adding acoustic demos of two tunes slated for the next album and a pair of live numbers, including "All Along the Watchtower."

Under the Table and Dreaming vaults the Dave Matthews Band—already in possession of strong grassroots popularity and a mighty merchandising machine—into the major leagues, sonically and commercially. Steve Lillywhite's production brightens and muscles up the quintet's sound, homing in on Matthews' melodies and grooves while retaining just enough soloing not to betray the band's spirit. "Ants Marching," one of two songs repeated from **Remember Two Things,** is now a bouncy pop hit; the new "What Would You Say" and "Typical Situation" are just as catchy. "Jimi Thing" is a unique Hendrix tribute, a homage not to his guitar flash but to his spirituality ("Sometimes a Jimi thing slides my way/And keeps me swingin'"). As a lyricist, Matthews forwards a populist world view, sometimes poetic and occasionally oblique. The truth is, the Dave Matthews Band's primary appeal is musical, and Matthews' troupe gives every indication that it's tapped into a pretty deep and diverse font of inspiration.

The group didn't tinker with its creative process much in following up that breakthrough. Lillywhite is back on board; the DMB's Celtic-flavored jauntiness remains intact on "Too Much" and the aptly named "Two Step." **Crash** is hardly a replay of **Under the Table and Dreaming,** however; the band employs a variety of new instruments (flute, baritone sax, six-string bass, electric guitar) to create darker or heavier textures and tones. Moore leans closer to R&B as well, bringing a honking King Curtis sensibility to bear on the sound. "41," meanwhile, is an arresting simulation of the group's onstage improvisational voodoo. [gg]

ERIC MATTHEWS

See *Cardinal.*

MAZZY STAR

She Hangs Brightly (Rough Trade) 1990 (Capitol) 1991
So Tonight That I Might See (Capitol) 1993
Among My Swan (Capitol) 1996

Artfully and delicately proceeding from Velvet Underground drone and folk-rock strum, California's Mazzy Star makes music that can be either spellbinding or soporific. As a member of the Rain Parade, guitarist David Roback was a central figure in the "paisley underground," a loose community of Los Angeles bands that gave psychedelia a post-punk revival in the early '80s. After folding the group, he formed the short-lived Clay Allison with ex–Dream Syndicate bassist Kendra Smith. That band evolved into Opal, which combined textural folk and spacy feedback on 1987's moody **Happy Nightmare Baby.**

Smith left Opal in mid-tour to retire (she later returned to action as a solo artist), and Roback began playing with sullen-sounding Los Angeles singer Hope Sandoval as Mazzy Star. Sandoval's voice is chillier than Smith's—chillier than just about anybody's, actually—but Roback's neo-psychedelic style remains largely the same as it was in Opal. Still, most of **She Hangs Brightly** is absolutely haunting. On melodic songs like "Blue Flower" and "Ride It On," Sandoval's eerie voice draws the listener into Roback's gentle swirl of feedback. But the news isn't all good: on some tunes, things slow to the point of lifelessness. (The band is officially a duo, but Opal's drummer, Keith Mitchell, is among the album's cast of musicians.)

Unfortunately, much of the uneven **So Tonight That I Might See** drones along at that same aural crawl. The album does have some real gems, though, including the transcendent "Fade Into You," which became an improbable hit. That song, "Five String Serenade" and a few others redeem the record, but also make the rest seem weaker by comparison. At worst, Sandoval doesn't sound haunting so much as plain old uninterested, and Roback's guitar playing is so languid it seems to fade into nothingness. Mazzy Star makes a compelling case for the idea that quiet psychedelia has a place in the music of the '90s, but the duo also shows how quickly the style can become tired. [rl]

See also *Kendra Smith; TPRG.*

MCALMONT & BUTLER

See *Suede.*

MCCARTHY

See *Stereolab.*

K. MCCARTY

Dead Dog's Eyeball: Songs of Daniel Johnston (Bar/None) 1994

KATHY MCCARTY

Sorry Entertainer (Bar/None) 1995

Bob Dylan had the Byrds, Laura Nyro had the Fifth Dimension and John Hiatt has Bonnie Raitt, but no songwriter ever had a more imaginative or beneficial interpreter than Daniel Johnston enjoys in Kathy McCarty. On **Dead Dog's Eyeball,** her revelatory album in tribute to him, the former singer/guitarist of Austin's Glass Eye (joined by that band's rhythm section and a handful of pals adding piano, horns and strings) takes an incisive selection of songs from Johnston's homemade cassettes and recasts them in diverse, original settings as if she were unlocking implicit mysteries scrutable only to her. Even in the face of the songs' mounting eccentricity, McCarty and co-producer/bassist Brian Beattie honor them by truly respecting Johnston's melodies and lyrics in their reimaginings.

A tick-tock beat, jagged guitar interjections and cellos provide an effectively edgy underpinning to McCarty's clear-voiced delivery of the absurd "Walking the Cow"; semi-tonal harmonies, Munchkin chorus and stutter drumming make "Rocket Ship" a magnificent bout of weirdness; simple acoustic guitar supports the first half of a sensitive folky rendition of "Living Life." Very few of Johnston's songs fail to bloom in McCarty's magic garden, and most are models of efficient ingeniousness: the bouncy piano, bumping bass and banjo of "Like a Monkey in a Zoo," the metronome percussion of the spartan "I Am a Baby (In My Universe)," the detuned Residential guitars on the distortion-heavy "Sorry Entertainer," the stately piano melancholy of "Going Down," the rock power of "Wild West Virginia," the dynamically dramatic Beatles paraphrasing of "Oh No!" and the cocktail jazz swoon of "Desperate Man Blues." A sublimely empathetic coincidence of writer and performer, **Dead Dog's Eyeball** is a brilliant feather in the caps of both.

The seven-song **Sorry Entertainer** plucks two tracks from the album, offers a rhythmically superior remake of "The Creature," three previously unissued Johnston covers ("Worried Shoes" is amazing; "Love Wheel" is merely great) and one vintage Glass Eye original. [i]

See also *Daniel Johnston.*

SCOTT MCCAUGHEY

See *Young Fresh Fellows.*

BRUCE MCCULLOCH

See *Bob Wiseman.*

IAN MCCULLOCH

Candleland (Sire/Reprise) 1989
Faith & Healing EP (UK WEA) 1989
Candleland (The Second Coming) EP (UK EastWest) 1990
Mysterio (Sire/Reprise) 1992

Walking away from Liverpool's Echo and the Bunnymen in mid-'88, singer Ian McCulloch picked up a guitar, reflected deeply on his turbulent professional and personal life and wrote the songs for his first solo album. (Actually, at least "Proud to Fall" was composed before leaving the band.) The alluring **Candleland,** atmospherically produced by Ray Shulman, somberly distills the dreamy rock sound of 1987's **Echo & the Bunnymen** to give Mac's musical life a brilliant second chapter. Sweeping melodies, expressive vocals, surprisingly good guitar playing and resonantly emotional lyrics (the haunting "Start Again" bids farewell to his late father as well as Bunnymen drummer Pete De Freitas, who died in a 1989 auto accident, and another friend) make such excellent new songs as "Flickering Wall," "White Hotel" and "Proud to Fall" immediately familiar. Varied arrangements make style-breakers of "Faith and Healing," "The Cape" and the waltz-time "I Know You Well," proffering them as everything from orchestrated balladry to New Orderized dance-pop. With only one serious flaw—the songs' elementary chord patterns—**Candleland** is a major, magnificent record.

Besides a remix of the title song, the **Faith & Healing** EP offers a trio of non-LP tracks performed with McCulloch's hard-rocking tour band, the Prodigal Sons. Although two of the new tunes are lame, "Rocket Ship" is a keeper. The **Candleland** EP adds three more good'uns to a sturdier, elongated version of the album's evanescent title track, again featuring vocals by Cocteau Twin Elizabeth Fraser.

It took three separate producers on **Mysterio** (including Cocteau Twin Robin Guthrie and onetime Yacht Henry Priestman) and the four Prodigal Sons (no longer billed as such) to undo the aching ambience of **Candleland,** replacing it with various flavors of harder/louder/more danceable ordinary. Nowhere near as careful or moody this time around, McCulloch's downcast songwriting makes **Mysterio** a fair followup, but the stirring presentation works against the promising material's emotional impact. The very Echo-like "Magical World" gets things off to a promising start and "Honeydrip" hooks loosely onto the Jesus and Mary Chain with entertaining results, but the rest of the album (which includes an almost-there version of Leonard Cohen's "Lover Lover Lover" and "Vibor Blue," a hapless techno/slide-acoustic hybrid twelve-bar) rarely connects the way **Candleland** does. [i]

See also *Electrafixion; TPRG.*

MC EIHT FEATURING CMW

See *Comptons Most Wanted.*

DUFF MCKAGAN

See *Guns n' Roses.*

MARIA MCKEE

Maria McKee (Geffen) 1989
You Gotta Sin to Get Saved (Geffen) 1993
Life Is Sweet (Geffen) 1996

Maria McKee's voice and songwriting are stronger and more mature on her first solo album than they ever were in Lone Justice, the Los Angeles country-rock group that made its second and final album in 1986. McKee sings out like she's got one night onstage in a two-bit bar to prove herself. But her lyrics don't reveal any clear artistic mission and Mitchell Froom's over-stylized production (the strings and horns are a bit much) drowns or drains her personality out of the album, leaving characterless elegance instead of a strong statement. McKee's efforts, however, are not entirely negated. "Am I the Only One (Who's Ever Felt This Way?)" is a rousing country ballad Linda Ronstadt might have sung. "Panic Beach" is a dramatic narrative vividly told with literary precision; twangy stomps like "Drinkin' in My Sunday Dress" are simply irresistible. Richard Thompson, whose "Has She [He] Got a Friend for Me?" McKee covers here, guests on guitar and mandolin.

Exchanging the pre-Raphaelite blonde washout cover photos of **Maria McKee** for a darker, more urban image, the singer/songwriter made **You Gotta Sin to Get Saved** with a studio band consisting of Lone Justice alums (mandolin demon Marvin Etzioni, drummer Don Heffington, onetime Patti Smith keyboardist Bruce Brody), Benmont Tench and the Jayhawks' two guitarists. The altered lineup and look, however, offer scant indication of the album's shocking musical change. With but a passing nod to country ("Only Once," a pretty weeper, and the acoustic "Precious Time"), McKee abandons subtle reflection to emerge as a passionately robust rocker, covering Van Morrison ("My Lonely Sad Eyes," "The Way Young Lovers Do") and Carole King/Gerry Goffin ("I Can't Make It Alone") just for starters. Belting her way through a thicket sprouting from '60s rock and vintage white soul (Rita Coolidge and Bonnie Bramlett come to mind in spots), McKee explores romance and reminiscences in surging originals like the lyrically resigned (but vocally torrid) "I Forgive You," a Spectoresque gospel rouser, and "Why Wasn't I More Grateful (When Life Was Sweet)," a souled-out torch song that sounds like an old Ike and Tina hit. Saving the best for last, McKee lets it all hang out in the infectious title track, a rollicking admission of roving eye unease that goes out walking like Fats Domino and comes back with a masterful Ronnie Spector impression. Like much of this amazing, unexpected album, McKee splits her convictions between the music and the words, sinning and saving herself in a fission explosion that blasts into the spirit of rock'n'roll.

After that tricky victory, McKee made a complete mess of her next record. Starting with a promising central theme—childhood, both her own and others'—**Life Is Sweet** goes straight over the top in a bewildering styleless hodgepodge of bad production ideas, bizarre gimmicks (paraphrasing melodies and rhythm guitar sounds from **Ziggy Stardust**?), uneven writing and singing so mindlessly zealous in spots that McKee can't possibly be hearing herself. Angry electric guitars and string arrangements fight to be heard in the poorly balanced confusion; at no point does it sound as if anyone is in charge. There are lovely bits strewn about, but there's always a spoiler lurking nearby, whether a lyric like "And I pray for the stigmata stain" (in the otherwise alluring "Carried"), a needless explosion of volume (in the initially spare and appealing title track) or the weird instrumental mix (brushed drums, scraggy and dissonant guitar distortion imitating Mick Ronson, electric bass, dramatic strings) of "Smarter." [i]

See also *TPRG.*

SARAH MCLACHLAN

Touch (Can. Nettwerk) 1988 (Arista) 1989
Solace (Nettwerk/Arista) 1991
Live (Can. Nettwerk) 1992
Fumbling Towards Ecstasy (Nettwerk/Arista) 1994
The Freedom Sessions (Nettwerk/Arista) 1995

Discovered in her teens fronting a new wave band in Halifax, Sarah McLachlan (who subsequently relocated to Vancouver, on Canada's other coast) quickly evolved into one of the most captivating voices in pop music, yet another vital figure in Canada's rich legacy of innovative singer/songwriters. Equally adept on piano and guitar (credit years of classical training on both), McLachlan's primary instrument on **Touch** is her sweet, reedy voice, reminiscent of Sinéad O'Connor but unfamiliar with stridency. Although she was only twenty at the time, the album shows her to be a songwriter of promising lyrical insight. Only the haunting "Ben's Song" and the single "Vox" (included on CD in original and extended remix form) boast the compelling hooks that distinguish her subsequent work, but **Touch** is an impressive debut.

The album made McLachlan a star in Canada; not surprisingly, the transitional **Solace** reflects a mood of lost innocence. "Black," "Mercy" and "Lost" are as melancholy as their titles suggest, and only a lighthearted cover of Donovan's "Wear Your Love Like Heaven" injects any cheerfulness. Atmospherically framed by producer Pierre Marchand (who would repeat the role on her next two studio albums), **Solace** is graced with thoughtful arrangements, sensitive playing and, most important, melodies that equal McLachlan's sharpening skills as a lyricist. The first four cuts—"Drawn to the Rhythm," "Into the Fire," "The Path of Thorns (Terms)" and "I Will Not Forget You"—are outstanding. (The limited-edition seven-song **Live,** containing concert versions of material from **Solace** and **Touch** as well as "Back Door Man," was released only in Canada.)

Even the cover of **Fumbling Towards Ecstasy**—a photo of the artist gazing happily into the camera, where previously she had averted her eyes—signals McLachlan's growing confidence and aesthetic maturation. After touring for over a year, McLachlan had visited Cambodia and Thailand to narrate a video documentary. Exploring the emotions generated by those experiences, the twelve songs of **Fumbling Towards Ecstasy** are less self-indulgent, boasting a new sense of objectivity that increases the emotional impact. "All the fear has left me now/I'm not afraid anymore" she announces on the title track. "Hold On" confronts a love's mortality, while "Ice" meditates on addiction. The jazzy "Ice Cream" balances the pervasive darkness with light.

In addition to an extensive CD-ROM scrapbook track, **The Freedom Sessions** presents stripped-down versions—in arrangements ranging from solo piano and voice to full semi-acoustic band workouts to feedback-laced electric rock duo—of seven **Fumbling Towards Ecstasy** songs, including "Hold On," "Elsewhere," "Plenty" and "Good Enough." The record ends with a loose, boozy band cover of Tom Waits' "Ol' 55," followed by an unlisted and extraordinary second rendition (on acoustic guitar, bass and brushed drums) of "Hold On" that turns the searing ballad into a soft, soulful moan. Aside from showcasing her increasing vocal dexterity (particularly on a bluesy version of "Ice Cream"), the minimalist approaches of **The Freedom Sessions** underscore McLachlan's fundamental talent as a songwriter. [kbr]

MALCOLM MCLAREN

Duck Rock (Island) 1983
Fans (Island) 1984
Swamp Thing (Island) 1985
Paris (No!/Vogue/Gee Street/Island) 1995

MALCOLM MCLAREN AND THE BOOTZILLA ORCHESTRA

Waltz Darling (Epic) 1989

MALCOLM MCLAREN PRESENTS THE WORLD FAMOUS SUPREME TEAM SHOW

Round the Outside! Round the Outside! (Virgin) 1990

Most people, if they get the chance, have to settle for one great achievement in the cultural arena. For Malcolm McLaren, however, being the manager of the notorious Sex Pistols was just a chapter in his fascinating and capricious multi-media career. A brilliant carpetbagger whose precise talents—beyond aestheticism and the canny ability to peg influential trends in a wide panorama (fashion, retail, politics, music, art, film, literature) early enough to exploit them as a pioneer rather than a bandwagon-jumper—are difficult to pin down, McLaren has made himself the star of his own entrepreneurial undertakings. Despite the odds stacked against his mounting a successful recording career (that he's not exactly a musician is high on the problems list), McLaren has crafted a bizarrely significant oeuvre of high-concept adventures.

The Londoner's first vinyl forays were into the field of hip-hop: **Duck Rock,** which famously collated rap and Appalachian music, actually had stylistic impact on the urban mix via "Buffalo Gals," a square dance call set to a kinetic scratch track. His next venture was exponentially more improbable. Feeding classic opera into a hip-hop blender, McLaren came up with the surprisingly entertaining **Fans.** With Bootsy Collins and Jeff Beck on hand, **Waltz Darling** hooks an orchestra to muscular rock-funk for what sounds like an electrified version of Gilbert and Sullivan but often amounts to little more than lushly generic club music. The retrospective (or scraped-together, as the case may be) **Swamp Thing** arises from various early-'80s sessions and includes drastic (per)versions of "Wild Thing," "Duck Rock," "Buffalo Gals" and Bow Wow Wow's "Eiffel Tower." Aggravating but fascinating.

Wrapping up the decade with another backward/forward sidestep, McLaren reunited with the World Famous Supreme Team—his B-boy compadres on **Duck Rock**—for the hip-house stew of **Round the Outside! Round the Outside!,** which samples (intellectually, not electronically) both Shakespeare and opera and includes an updated remix of "Buffalo Gals."

McLaren then stayed out of the record racks for five years, returning in 1995 with **Paris,** a high-style travelogue that turns Serge Gainsbourg's heavy-breathing classic ("Je T'Aime . . . Moi Non Plus," which McLaren has the temerity to cover here—in English, no less) into a full-blown epic of erotic geography. Over diverse and frequently alluring strains of dance, pop, jazz, African and movie soundtrack music, McLaren unwisely sings a bit, but mostly recites theatrical poetry in obvious homage to William Burroughs' sense of grimy wonder, navigating his namedropping reminiscences and impressions in and around such local landmarks as Catherine Deneuve, Françoise Hardy and Sonia Rykiel—all of whom add their voices to the effort. Absurd on the surface ("Walking With Satie," "Miles and Miles of Miles Davis," "Jazz Is Paris"), the album manages a seductive appeal in the monomania of its pretensions; if McLaren is a crappy poet, his devotion to the subject is touching, and even the worst photographer's snapshots show *something.* The CD contains a second disc entitled **The Largest Movie House in Paris,** which reprises much of the album in instrumental remixes. [i]

See also *TPRG.*

G. W. MCLENNAN

Watershed (Beggars Banquet/RCA) 1991
Fireboy (UK Beggars Banquet) 1993 (Beggars Banquet) 1994

GRANT MCLENNAN

Horsebreaker Star (Beggars Banquet/Atlantic) 1995

JACK FROST

Jack Frost (Arista) 1991
Snow Job (UK Beggars Banquet) 1996

As the sunnier, poppier half of the Go-Betweens' singer/songwriter team, Brisbane native Grant McLennan established himself as an incisive lyricist and a crafty melodicist. In his solo career, he's maintained, and in some instances surpassed, the standards he set with his former band.

Before striking out completely on his own, McLennan followed the Go-Betweens with Jack Frost, a collaboration with Steve Kilbey of the Church. **Jack Frost** reflects the salient qualities of both men's prior work while maintaining a distinctive sound and attitude of its own, working in styles ranging from dark, uneasy gloom-rock ("Every Hour God Sends," "Number Eleven") to lighter acoustic-based fare ("Civil War Lament," "Thought That I Was Over You").

Watershed shows McLennan's lyrical acuity to be intact, but is relatively short on hooks, unwisely downplaying his pop instincts in favor of a more singer/songwriterly air. **Fireboy,** on the other hand, offers a near-perfect convergence of observant, passionate words and jangly, surging tunes: "Lighting Fires," "One Million Miles From Here," "Whose Side Are You On?"

Horsebreaker Star, the relaxed, richly organic magnum opus, is something of a left turn—but very much in the right direction. Recorded in Athens, Georgia, with R.E.M. pal John Keane and a cast of local players (plus guest vocalist Syd Straw), it's a masterful quilt of warmly haunting songcraft ("Ice in Heaven," "All Her Songs"), nervy jangle-rock ("Dropping You," "Put You Down") and quiet turbulence ("I'll Call You Wild," "Horsebreaker Star"). Released overseas as a twenty-four-track double CD, the album's US edition deletes—without major damage—six tracks (including a nice cover of the Byrds' "Ballad of Easy Rider") but adds **Fireboy**'s "Lighting Fires." In either incarnation, **Horsebreaker Star** is a gem all the way through. [ss]

See also *Robert Forster.*

JAMES MCMURTRY

Too Long in the Wasteland (Columbia) 1989
Candyland (Columbia) 1992
Where'd You Hide the Body (Columbia) 1995

John Mellencamp "discovered" James McMurtry; besides a backing band, both men have shared the nagging feeling that something's rotten in Peoria. McMurtry's lyrics read as riveting poetry, but they're that much more powerful when heard in the company of a modest hook and a heartland backbeat. Sung in a flat deadpan, the songs tell tales too fully formed and evocative to be called sketches—they're more like short story collections, blessed with the laconic concision of Raymond Carver.

Mellencamp produced **Too Long in the Wasteland,** using most of his band to back up the Texas-born singer/guitarist, who displays a Lou Reed–like sense of melody—minimal but catchy. In this wasteland, poor, alienated characters roam the four-lane highways, reform schools, gas stations and strip malls that form a gray backdrop for heartbreaking tales of disintegration. The beauty is in the details—the styrofoam cup of coffee, the sink full of dishes, the bullet holes in the mailbox. In typically specific terms, "Painting by Numbers" bitterly rails at the numbing conformity and mediocrity of Middle America; there's genuine poignancy and stinging bitterness in tunes like "Terry," "Outskirts" and the title track.

The Mellencamp mafia returns to back McMurtry on **Candyland,** which actually manages to improve on **Wasteland**'s winning formula: the songs stand out more as hummable tunes. With Mellencamp sideman Michael Wanchic behind the board, it's a compelling assortment of small-town tragedies of lost love, lost youth and lost ideals that exposes unpleasant aspects of an America most people would prefer to deny. In "Where's Johnny," a local BMOC loses the thread and becomes a reclusive loser; "Safe Side" describes the ugly socio-economic line that divides San Antonio; the acerbic litany of "Good Life" assails empty comforts, materialism and complacency. In the catchy title tune, a pot-smoking ice cream man rolls through the streets of suburbia—mundane and yet deeply telling, it's indicative of the unsparing power of McMurtry's poetic eye.

On **Where'd You Hide the Body,** McMurtry profiles the same inexorable heartland heartbreak as before, but switches from third person to first, *becoming* characters instead of describing them. With producer Don Dixon on bass, keyboards and guitar, McMurtry branches out musically, adding horns, organ and wah-wah guitar for a more developed melodic sound. McMurtry appears to have mellowed, that animating bitterness abated, the still piercing observations dissolving into a softer focus. It doesn't always work to his advantage, but after the definitive triumph of **Candyland,** it's a necessary progression. [ma]

MC 900 FT JESUS WITH DJ ZERO

Too Bad EP (Can. Nettwerk) 1989
Hell With the Lid Off (Nettwerk/IRS) 1990

MC 900 FT JESUS

Welcome to My Dream (Nettwerk/IRS) 1991
One Step Ahead of the Spider (American) 1994

The places musicians begin, the places they end up and how they get from there to here defy logic so often that predictability no longer has much of a stake in the equation. Mark Griffin was a conservatory-trained classical trumpeter doing sessions and toiling in a Dallas record store when he tried his hand at cutting some hip-hop beats and layering on samples and his voice; in a mixmaster minute, he was MC 900 Ft Jesus (name courtesy Oral Roberts), well on his way to a fascinating career as a beatbox raconteur and imaginative sonic architect.

As documented on the four-song 1989 EP and the following year's album (which repeats "Too Bad" and a less caustic mix of "Shut Up"), Griffin's early work isn't rap or techno, although the MC, working with turntable maestro DJ Zero (at least on the road), certainly employs elements of both. Looped grooves with uncommon elements are the starting point for simple but inventive audio collages and distorted lyrical inventions with more forward propulsion than industrialists and less verbal action than rhymers. Both records are tentative and experimental, but album tracks like "UFO's Are Real," "Truth Is Out of Style" and the first-person sci-fi narrative of "Spaceman" introduce a distinctive and intelligent being searching for—and occasionally finding—offbeat ways to express his offbeat ideas.

Welcome to My Dream releases Griffin from his growth-stunting reliance on technology, using a complement of competent live musicians to erect a rhythmically intricate, stylistically varied podium—noir jazz, percolating funk and jumped-up hip-hop are the fundamental struts—on which he recounts his troubled character studies. (Sidemen provide drums, bass, horns, percussion and turntables; the star handles guitar, keyboards and trumpet.) Griffin has a melodramatic flair for evocative art-film detail: "Adventures in Failure," "Killer Inside Me," "The City Sleeps" and "Hearing Voices in One's Head" describe human time bombs slinking through the urban jungle like characters in a particularly grim cartoon strip. Griffin isn't yet a master of his verbal delivery or music, though; the best beats far outstrip the ones that just toodle along. Likewise, his fables are less engrossing on record than on paper. Lots of promise, but this channel is not quite tuned in yet.

A new label, a full band (with Indian percussion contrasting the horns) and a one-song guest shot by guitarist Vernon Reid help elevate MC 900 Ft Jesus' creative stature on **One Step Ahead of the Spider.** The refinement of a vivid vocal style is matched by a vast improvement in the propellers devised to convey the lyrics. Griffin's connection to hip-hop is gone: the music of "New Moon" and "Tiptoe Through the Inferno" is free-flowing jazz in which voice serves as just one of the instruments. "But If You Go" bubbles lightly with electronic techno-funk and sweet backing vocals; "Gracías Pepé" ripples on a light ambient bed; "New Year's Eve" (the album's highlight, a character study inspired by, and evocative of, *A Confederacy of Dunces*) glides over a gentle percussion breakdown. At the record's odd extremes, Griffin nearly sings Curtis Mayfield's "Stare and Stare" over Reid's spare wah-wah soul, while "Bill's Dream" is a quiet instrumental that gives the star a chance to rest his voice and toot his horn. Although Griffin's coordination of words and music has never been so sympathetic or original, there's still an ungainly clumsiness to his work. Another couple of months in the studio should get him where he's going. [i]

MC REN

Kizz My . . . Black Azz EP (Ruthless/Priority) 1992
Shock of the Hour (Ruthless) 1993
The Villain in Black (Ruthless) 1996

An unheralded force in N.W.A, MC Ren (Lorenzo Patterson) actually co-wrote "(Fuck) tha Police" and "Straight Outta Compton." His first solo record, a six-song EP released shortly after the band's last album, showcases a strong, grumpy rapper with a straight-talking natural flow and a mean streak. The sex scene of "Behind the Scenes" goes the extra mile to be distasteful, as does the violence of "Right Up My Alley." In "Final Frontier," the MC evenly announces, "Kick a little ass in my spare time/To keep myself occupied when I'm not busting up a rhyme." Ren is not, it appears, a very nice man. But the record ends on a surprising note: the hip-hop orthodoxy of "Kizz My Black Azz," which decries stage costumes and live instrumentalists at rap concerts: "Save the shit for parades . . . people don't go to rap shows so they can hear a band/It's like a man trying to fuck a man/It defeats the whole purpose."

Although the back cover of the EP announces "From the upcomin' album 'Life Sentence,'" that didn't happen. Ren dropped the all-new **Shock of the Hour** instead. Moving away from the blunt, N.W.A-grade beats of **Black Azz,** these tracks slump down into the cushiony deconstructions of Dr. Dre's G-funk era. As the album grooves along like a low-slung sports car crawling the streets with blacked-out windows, Ren clears his throat with six tracks of the "Same Old Shit," holding his dick and a 40, looking for ho's and sucka MCs to vanquish. He raises his target sights much higher on the album's second half, delivering fiery promises of racial Armageddon: the Public Enemy–styled "Mayday on the Front Line" only warms the plate for the violent and threatening "Attack on Babylon," "Do You Believe" (which uses a sampled Farrakhan phrase to set off an entire Muslim-inflected racist diatribe) and the similarly themed payback vendetta of the title track. [i]

See also *N.W.A.*

MC SERCH

See *3rd Bass.*

MC SOLAAR

Qui Seme le Vent Recolte le Tempo (Fr. Polydor) 1991
Prose Combat (Cohiba) 1994

MC Solaar is the biggest hip-hop star in France. That may not sound like much of a distinction, but his translations (both musical and linguistic) of hip-hop have been instrumental in internationalizing the form, and his recordings—including guest spots on other artists' albums—have given him substantial cachet among America's rap cognoscenti.

Born Claude M'Barali in Dakar, Senegal, the Paris-based Solaar won acclaim as the first rapper *en français* after the release of his "Bouge de La" single in 1990. That song, along with two subsequent French radio hits, is included on **Qui Seme le Vent Recolte le Tempo,** an album on which his fluid phrasing vies with what—in this country—would be the best samples money could buy, rendering it unreleasable here. Still, the title track found its way to Tommy Boy's **Planet Rap** compilation, and "Caroline" was included on the first volume of 4th & B'way's **The Rebirth of Cool** series. The groundswell of US street notoriety culminated on Guru's first **Jazzmatazz** album, to which Solaar contributed "Le Bien, le Mal."

With all samples cleared, **Prose Combat** was released just as hip-hop's taste for jazz was passing its peak. Still, it's a stylistically assured, sophisticated record on a par with any issued that year. Solaar has skills—his slick, swiftly delivered rhymes merit comparison to the storied likes of Rakim and Big Daddy Kane—and, more important, presence. Because his French is even more impenetrable than hip-hop slang, you can't help but focus on the rhythm of Solaar's phrasing; when combined with the richly textured jazz cool unspooled by DJ Jimmy Jay, the result is like great scat singing. [sf]

MCTELLS

The McTells [tape] (UK Bi-Joopiter) 1986
Expecting Joe [tape] (UK Bi-Joopiter) 1988
Jesse Man Rae EP (UK Frank) 1988
Wind Up EP (UK Bi-Joopiter) 1989
Cut Up (UK Bi-Joopiter) 1990
Buffalo EP (UK Frank) 1992
Everything EP (Ger. Little Teddy) 1992
What Happens Next (UK Vinyl Japan) 1994
Smash Up (Ger. Little Teddy) 1994
Cut Up/Smash Up (Slumberland) 1996

The McTells are the most significant (and prolific) band on the International Pop Underground affiliate Bi-Joopiter. Granted, that's not saying much, but the English trio does what it does well. The band's early work holds a British mirror up to Australia's Cannanes, minus the anguish. Delivered as light pop, the songs are punctuated (well, dominated) by "bop bops" and "whoo-oos," and concerned mostly with losing girls and lackadaisical wanderings.

The first side of the plaintively happy **Cut Up** pairs singer Paul Nixon's nasal melodies to chattering, nervous, mod-ish pop. Side Two adds a sprightly organ and animated character to the already lively bass, creating an even more captivating sound that is, impossibly, smooth and awkward at the same time. **What Happens Next,** an oddly sequenced career-retrospective-cum-singles-compilation, has the bonus of some previously unreleased material. The six newly recorded songs—glossier productions, with a washy guitar sound copped from the legions of My Bloody Valentine imitators—are scattered amidst the band's rustic pop bits from the 1980s. And even though the collection includes numbers from every period, it's not an impressive bunch—the short, bobbing singles, overall, exemplify the band's methodical nature, but don't make a lasting impression. Nixon creates some tension, however, by scrawling the phrasing and scowling the happy lyrics.

Smash Up, McTells' second real full-length, has a little more muscle, a little more push, but it's just as whiny as ever. The band doesn't let its three-chord energy flag, but it does retrace steps. Nixon's voice barely holds up, and there's a dreadful Daniel Johnston cover ("Museum of Love"). Cuteness abounds, however, in a lower-key way. Two instrumentals have neat touches: "West Pier" incorporates bells, and "In a Vacuum" has an actual noisy, static-y vacuum picking up dust through the whole song. **Cut Up** and **Smash Up** are scheduled for American release on a single CD in 1996. [rxe]

MEATHOOK SEED

See *Napalm Death.*

MEAT PUPPETS

In a Car EP7 (World Imitation) 1981 (SST) 1985
Meat Puppets (Thermidor/SST) 1982
Meat Puppets II (SST) 1983
Up on the Sun (SST) 1985
Out My Way EP (SST) 1986
Mirage (SST) 1987
Huevos (SST) 1987
Monsters (SST) 1989
No Strings Attached (SST) 1990
Forbidden Places (London) 1991
Too High to Die (London) 1994
No Joke! (London) 1995

Their eccentricities notwithstanding, the Meat Puppets were perhaps the most major-label-ready act on the SST roster. Fueled by acid, endless roadwork and a mystical sense of music's role in desert ecology, the Phoenix, Arizona, trio of brothers Curt (guitar/vocals) and Cris (bass/vocals) Kirkwood and drummer Derrick Bostrom traveled from elementary punk thrash up to a cerebral and often dizzying high-wire stretched between desert country punk and old-school psychedelic improvisation, ignited by Curt's stunning instrumental virtuosity. That the group occasionally chose to do the ZZ Top choogle or play jazz up there didn't really change the course of their history. The generously endowed **No Strings Attached** recapitulates the Meat Puppets' career to date with two dozen chronological selections, from the 1981 EP debut through **Monsters.**

That said, **Forbidden Places** is an unfortunate big-league debut, a surprising misreading of the group's strengths—the earthy introspection underscoring even their most twisted songwriting; their fluid power-trio drive—by producer Pete Anderson. Best known for the down-home cool of his work with Dwight Yoakam, Anderson focuses too much on the back-porch promise of Curt's acid-cowboy whine and sands down the band's rowdy charm to an overfine crust. There's a heavy streak of trippy paranoia in Curt's lyrics—like the attack of the "little red tongues" and "fat ripe rats" in "Open Wide"—but the guitar twang is too clean, the distortion too polite to suggest menace or fear.

Forbidden Places is actually a double bummer, a so-so record that arrived just as grunge-mania broke wide open. A new generation of ruffian bands, many of them raised on the Puppets' SST classics, raced past them into the charts. Then, in late '93, Kurt Cobain invited the Kirkwoods to join him on camera for three Puppets songs (all taken from the band's second LP) performed during Nirvana's *MTV Unplugged* appearance. It was an impressive gesture of artistic respect and punk-rock fraternity that did wonders for the Puppets' mainstream profile. "Oh, Me," "Plateau" and "Lake of Fire" became highlights of Nirvana's resultant acoustic album, particularly "Lake of Fire," which

Cobain sings with a vivid, desperate ache in his voice that now sounds eerily prophetic.

Cobain also lent his name to **Too High to Die,** contributing a celebrity quotation ("I owe so much to them") stickered on the cover. More important, **Too High to Die** benefits from the surprisingly commercial touch of the Butthole Surfers' Paul Leary, who co-produced it. Without muting the prairie pothead quality of the band's sound or Curt Kirkwood's free-associative imagery, Leary and the Puppets establish a warm, cohesive feel even between strange bedfellows like "Never to Be Found" (tangled hyper-strum), "We Don't Exist" (hooky speed pop) and "Severed Goddess Hand" (an almost R.E.M.-ish hymn, despite the weirdo title). "Backwater" actually became a hit, a post-modern take on '70s Dixie rock (its coltish kick bears a disarming resemblance to Lynyrd Skynyrd's "Sweet Home Alabama") with a feisty guitar sound that belies the blood and ennui in the lyrics.

No Joke! is made of even darker stuff, a mixed litany of comic bad-trip metaphors and outright nihilism produced by Leary and the Puppets with grim potency. (In the case of "Head," all it takes is piano, cello and tense electric jangle.) There's a brutish, heavy metal quality to the guitar fuzz deployed on most of the songs: the gambit practically dares you to hang in there for the good hooks carried by the Kirkwoods' distinctive vocal drone. That may have accounted for the record's dim chart showing, and the Puppets' return—at least for the time being—to cult status. [df]

See also *Nirvana; TPRG.*

MECCA NORMAL

Mecca Normal/The First LP (Can. Smarten Up!) 1986 (K) 1995
Calico Kills the Cat (K) 1988
Water Cuts My Hands (K/Matador) 1991
Dovetail (K) 1992
Flood Plain (K) 1993
Jarred Up (K) 1993
Sitting on Snaps (Matador) 1995
The Eagle & the Poodle (Matador) 1996

2 FOOT FLAME

2 Foot Flame (Matador) 1995

Vancouver's Mecca Normal is a singular group, one that draws only minimally from the past and that couldn't possibly have sprung from any other individuals than poet/vocalist Jean Smith and guitarist David Lester. Though the duo's sometimes strident music can be more admired than enjoyed, its strong vision and determined individuality richly reward those willing to invest in it. Mecca Normal's arresting sound pairs Smith's piercing tones and riveting lyrical juxtapositions with Lester's fiery playing. Despite the large discography, Mecca Normal owes its reputation primarily to intense live performances: Smith taunts the audience, weaving through onlookers, microphone in hand, staring them down and charging them to reexamine and take responsibility for the world they live in. Meanwhile, Lester throws himself at his instrument, filling up the silence, drenching it with passion and sweat. When Smith belts out "Man thinks woman when he talks to me/Something not quite right" as Lester's guitar extrusions crash down around her, it's hard not to consider the implications of her words.

Mecca Normal's first album, initially released on its own label and sold at shows, offers an early glimpse of the band's nascent sound. Recorded on a cassette 4-track, the songs are captured with a raw authenticity that renders some of them very difficult to listen to. (In this setting, Smith's voice can be quite sharp.) It took Smith and Lester a while to find their aptest means of expression—"Tolerate Me," for example, sounds like a rant—but the album does offer two songs that have remained in the group's live set: the fierce "Are You Hungry Joe?" and "I Walk Alone," an affirmation of women's pride. As with all Mecca Normal albums, Smith's art adorns the cover.

Calico Kills the Cat finds Smith and Lester in a studio more amenable to the lower registers of her voice, so it's not quite so shrill. Her words and expression, however, are unwaveringly confrontational, while Lester's passion-filled guitar slashes are stronger, more expressive and curling around tough melodies. "Blue TV" and "Richard" are the seeds of Mecca Normal's future.

The changes between **Calico Kills the Cat** and **Water Cuts My Hands,** which was recorded in Olympia, Washington, with Calvin Johnson and Patrick Maley, are harder to trace. Smith's new focus on the nuances and malleability of words (the way she croons "mushroom water" on the title song, for example) has become a hallmark of her singing, and Lester heightens the dramatic nature of his guitar playing, dancing in and out of Smith's iron-edged words. (The two albums are contained on a single CD.)

Dovetail, also recorded with Johnson and Maley in Olympia, sees Lester developing the delicate, melodic side of his playing—always there but never at the forefront—which, in turn, strengthens the melodic pull of Mecca Normal's songs. Smith, meanwhile, has shifted toward sensitive, artistic emotional observation more than politically conscious challenges. "Throw Silver" is a beautiful, melancholy ballad with sweet guitar; "This Machine" lashes out in both sound and angry but abstract poetry ("I am wanting / I am wishing for wind / To knock this stillness out / Making it anything"). Using her work as a spoken-word artist to inform her singing, Smith displays increasing control as a vocalist.

Flood Plain builds upon **Dovetail**'s stylistic accomplishments without specifically broadening them; on the whole, the songs aren't as memorable. Smith's vocals and Lester's playing are in closer synch than ever, however; like a couple who finish each other's sentences, the two dip and slide around each other, building intrigue and mystery on "Ribbon" and "Museum of Open Windows," a protest against the cost of medical care. Making increasingly good use of the studio, the band layers Smith's vocals ("Current of Agreement") and vibrantly contrasting guitar parts ("Greater Beauty") to enhance the sound and effect.

Many of the missing links between Mecca Normal's albums are found on **Jarred Up** (the title comes from a lyric in **Dovetail**'s "This Machine"), a compilation of the many singles the group released between 1987 and 1993. Among the twenty-two songs are some of the duo's most potent: the gender-conscious "Strong White Male" and "Man Thinks Woman," the powerful humanistic plea of "It's Important," the inspirational sing-song "This Is Different," the angry "Broken Flowers." Of all the Mecca Normal albums, **Jarred Up** best captures the group's fascination with the dichotomies of anger and beauty, feeling and thought, man and woman.

Mecca Normal rethought its stylistic approach after **Flood Plain;** what the duo came up with was **Sitting on Snaps,** which lets in a few outside contributors (including New Zealander Peter Jefferies, who became Mecca Normal's first drummer after the album's release) and casts a wider sonic net than ever before. When Smith sings "This is not what it's supposed to be" on the album's first song ("Vacant Night Sky," one of two colored in dark gray hues by Jefferies' emotive piano playing), she is, as usual, quite serious. Lester evinces a more experimental ear ("Frozen Rain," the dirgey "Only Heat"), while leaving room for some really lovely songs ("Trapped Inside Your Heart") and Smith's confident expressions ("Pamela Makes Waves").

The Eagle & the Poodle sounds like the logical next step after **Sitting on Snaps.** On the surface, it's surprising how little having drummer Jefferies as a third member alters Mecca Normal's overall aural recipe, but it's not quite so startling given Smith and Lester's strong musical personalities. In fact, it's notable how well Jefferies (who appears on seven of the thirteen cuts) integrates himself into the fold; on "Drive At," for example, his aggressive rhythms don't overshadow the dynamic between vocals and guitar, instead following Lester's turbulent waves. Even so, the guitarist has less space to sprawl out and make noise. Smith shifts between empathetic lyrics and singing ("Her Ambition") and scathing howls ("Prize Arm"), but she is equally compelling in both modes. One thing remains unchanged: Mecca Normal rejects the status quo, even its own version.

Smith's side band, 2 Foot Flame, is a trio with Jefferies and Michael Morley of the Dead C. All three bring a taste for unconventional structures, with an emphasis on the nuances of sound. The songs on **2 Foot Flame** are denser and heavier than Mecca Normal's, drenching Smith's potent vocals in a sea of complicated noise: Morley's moaning synth and shards of guitar, the rhythmic undertow of Jefferies' drumming, the gloomy plodding of his piano playing. While "Lindauer" and "The Arbitrator" wrap tightly around wiry song structures, others sprawl in a static wash ("To the Sea," the ten-minute "Cordoned Off").

Among her other endeavors, Smith has published a novel, *I Can Hear Me Fine,* which is as difficult and engaging as her music. [la]

See also *Dead C, Peter Jefferies.*

MEDESKI, MARTIN AND WOOD

Notes From the Underground (hap-Jones) 1992 (Accurate) 1995
It's a Jungle in Here (Gramavision) 1993
Friday Afternoon in the Universe (Gramavision) 1995
Shack-man (Gramavision) 1996

DAVID FIUCZYNSKI/JOHN MEDESKI

Lunar Crush (Gramavision) 1994

Medeski, Martin and Wood have built an improbable following composed of dyed-in-the-wool jazz fans, hip acid jazz kids and (go figure) a loyal legion of Phish fans. Now a bold, revisionist organ trio with Chris Wood's upright bass taking the traditional electric guitar role and a wide array of non-traditional sources—from New Orleans second-line rhythms to hard-hitting funk—supplanting the usual greasy sanctified sounds, the band's auspicious debut revealed a piano trio (although various tracks employ horn players).

Drummer Billy Martin (who's worked with John Lurie and Ned Rothenberg) injects copious backbeat accents, propulsive fills and generally funks up the proceedings while Wood (who's served with Marc Ribot, Elliott Sharp and the new music ensemble Rough Assemblage) exploits his fat, woody tone to deliver furious ostinatos and gorgeously tensile solo statements and anchor the adventurous musings of pianist John Medeski, a veteran of the Either/Orchestra and groups led by John Zorn, Oren Bloedow and David Byrne. Whether deconstructing Duke Ellington's "Caravan" with a chunky, rollicking groove, exploring accessibly free terrain on an original such as "Querencia" or sculpting fat acoustic funk on "Uncle Chubb," **Notes From the Underground** established Medeski, Martin and Wood as a distinctive if somewhat unfocused entity.

In order to accommodate the trio's desire to tour incessantly (most clubs don't have a decent piano and they're a bitch to lug around), Medeski switched to a Hammond B-3 and a Wurlitzer. The charged-up sounds that emerge on the group's second album, **It's a Jungle in Here,** prove the new instrumentation perfectly suited to the trio's highly rhythmic concept. Most organ trios rely on foot pedals for basslines, but Medeski, Martin and Wood have the flexible bottom of Wood, which—in concert with Martin's increasingly complex but still funky playing—elevates the music well above mere organ grinding. The trio's stylistic tendencies are more expansive as well. A medley of Thelonious Monk's "Bemsha Swing" and Bob Marley's "Lively Up Yourself" eschews the pairing's potential novelty factor in favor of focusing on the rhythmic overlap. With equal acuity, the trio transports King Sunny Adé's "Moti Mo" into a languorous sprawl cleverly accented by Soweto Township–like horns, summons the spirit of the Meters on "Wiggly's Way" and burns down the joint on the scorching "Beeah."

Emboldened by incendiary gigs, the group undertook a healthy measure of experimentation on **Friday Afternoon in the Universe,** which complements the expected funk with Medeski's Sun Ra–inspired keyboard flights. Short, rough-hewn vignettes like "Paper Bass" and "Tea" are pure improvisation, instantaneous explorations building into massive, irresistible grooves. On other tunes, the heavy wah-wah organ and clavinet machinations of '70s-era Herbie Hancock and Miles Davis ride atop streamlined rhythmic beds, combining a shivering spaciness with sober, economical undergirding. The trio's boundless energy and loud attack have naturally attracted plenty of rock fans, many of them following the recommendation of Phish in the group's fan newsletter. Without compromise, Medeski, Martin and Wood have crafted a delirious amalgam of sounds and styles with surprisingly broad appeal, while at the same time taking bolder chances with each new album.

Medeski's collaboration with guitarist David Fiuczynski, who's worked with Me'Shell Ndegéocello and various Black Rock Coalition groups, delivers a slicker, more contemporary blend of funk, hip-hop, rock and blaring '70s jazz fusion. Fiuczynski's extroverted playing exploits loads of post-metal effects, but the album's terrific knack for devising danceable yet intelligent rhythmic patterns (courtesy of drummers Gene Lake and Jojo Mayer) offsets the potential for snoozy heroics. Outside his band, Medeski gets to explore less restrained playing, masterfully serving up huge slabs of sound by way of piercing clusters, lightning-fast runs, groovy wah-wah vamps and dense, textured soundscapes. The eccentric vocals by Michelle Johnson and Gloria Tropp tend to be a little overindulgent, but it's not bad for a modern fusion album, and it provides a different context in which to appreciate Medeski's vast talents. [pm]

See also *Phish.*

MEDICINE

Shot Forth Self Living (Def American) 1992
The Buried Life (American) 1993
Sounds of Medicine EP (American) 1994
Her Highness (American) 1995

MAIDS OF GRAVITY

Maids of Gravity (Vernon Yard) 1995

When one uses the word "interesting" to describe an experience, it's not always immediately clear if it's a tribute or a backhanded slag—which makes it the ideal term to describe this alternately fascinating and pretentious Los Angeles outfit. Before forming Medicine in early 1991, guitarist/vocalist Brad Laner was a late-'80s member of Savage Republic, a band that fused modern-classical-cum-industrial-rock electronic drones with exotic ethnic components.

Shot Forth Self Living is an exceedingly uneasy marriage of unequivocally horrible noise and dreamy drone-pop, and the two elements wrangle in virtually every one of its songs. "Aruca" begins with thirty seconds (although grouches might tab it as closer to a week) of garbage-disposal roar that gives way to feedback-enhanced dance-pop layered with beckoning, submerged vocals by Beth Thompson (ex-Fourwaycross). The layering process is even more prominent in "One More," a breathtakingly loud nine-minute exploration of guitar texture that encloses a core of ethereal post–My Bloody Valentine pop. An auspicious debut.

Medicine pared down from a quintet to a trio (Laner, Thompson and drummer Jim Goodall) shortly before recording **The Buried Life,** leaving Laner as sole guitarist. Although the effect isn't dramatic, the album *is* less identifiably rock. Both "Slut" and "The Pink" are cut from the same dance-noise cloth as parts of **Shot Forth Self Living,** but simply lack the edge of earlier material. Goodall adds some clever tape effects to several songs, but Laner seems content to coast, trotting out a few of his showier axe-manipulation tricks without bothering to find them tenable contexts. "Never Click" is a bracing splash of Jesus and Mary Chain–styled fuzz-rock, though. Van Dyke Parks arranged and plays piano on "Live It Down."

Sounds of Medicine (subtitled *Stripped and Reformed Sounds*) is the band's answer to the now-obligatory remake/remodel collection. Medicine's twist? Have producers like Billy Corgan and Cocteau Twins' Robin Guthrie simplify the band's often dizzying sonic infrastructures—a task Guthrie fudges by calling in bandmate Liz Fraser to provide backing vocals on "Time Baby 3." "Little Miss Drugstore" and "Little Slut" are merely slivers of songs that appeared, respectively, on the first and second albums. There's a new song ("Zelzah") and, as a bonus for true discordophiles, "Lime 6," sixteen live minutes of pealing feedback skronk.

Her Highness begins with Laner refracting some lustrous guitar rays at the onset of "All Good Things," but that encouraging invocation soon gives way to a mishmash of listless psychedelia ("A Fractured Smile") and sub-Siouxsie pop trifles ("Candy Candy"). Those of a charitable disposition might call **Her Highness** the sound of a band treading water, but its overall feel is so lifeless that there seems to be no disputing the fact that Medicine has already gone down. The group broke up in early '96.

Ed Ruscha and Jim Putnam, the bassist and guitarist who bailed out of Medicine after the first album, picked up the thread of an old home-recording group they once had and launched Maids of Gravity with drummer Craig "Irwin" Levitz. The group's unassuming debut—which seems a little anonymous but is actually quite enticing once you get to know it—disassembles shoegazer pop into a dreamy slo-blo excursion that floats lazily through a quiet "Cowgirl in the Sand" canyon but occasionally erupts in glorious flaming balls of Crazy Horse distortion and drive. [dss]

See also *Permanent Green Light.*

MEGA CITY FOUR

Tranzophobia (UK Decoy) 1989
There Goes My Happy Marriage EP (UK Decoy) 1990
Who Cares Wins (UK Decoy) 1990
Terribly Sorry Bob (UK Decoy) 1991
Sebastopol Rd. (Big Life/Caroline) 1992
Inspiringly Titled the Live Album (UK Big Life) 1992
Magic Bullets (UK Big Life) 1993
The Peel Sessions (Strange Fruit/Dutch East India Trading) 1993
Soulscraper (UK Fire) 1995

Mega City Four singer/guitarist Wiz must sit around between meals, thinking up rousing choruses. After five studio albums and a dozen non-LP singles and EPs, he hasn't run short of them. Though the young quartet from Farnborough, a nowhere English farm town, was too smart to accept any "punk" tag thrown at them, the band's earliest works are high-octane blasts of melodic pop, with loud, clean, heavy guitars and a souped-up rhythm section. The more recent mature work, though tempered by comparison, is even more immediately convincing and satisfying.

The usually reliable Iain Burgess' production on **Tranzophobia** is way too muddy, and the band's chunky sound is a little rag-tag sloppy in places, but the hooks are so ringing and the lyrics so first-rate, that, like the early Descendents, the record overcomes such troubles. Although none of the eight hot tracks from the band's first four 7-inch singles is on the album (*some* bands believe in value for money), **Tranzophobia** sounds like the MC4's own **Singles Going Steady** anyway, with one catchy tune after another. Don't miss "Severe Attack of the Truth" and "Things I Never Said."

Burgess failed a second time on **Who Cares Wins**—again, the mix is murkier than it should be, and the long record sounds as if it were pressed on cardboard—but the band's work is dramatically improved. Coinciding with more manageable tempos and tightened ensemble work, Wiz's writing displays more breadth and breath. The hooks are more deceptive but just as deep, and the harmonies on "Messenger," "Who Cares?" and the ripping backbeat blast of "Me Not You" are a plus. Typically, none of the four songs from the intervening **There Goes My Happy Marriage** EP are repeated on the album.

With Mega City Four signed to Big Life, the band's former label released the twelve-song **Terribly Sorry Bob,** a compilation of all its non-LP tracks to date. The best document of the group's early period, it piles one should-have-been-a-hit amphetamine rush onto the next, culminating in the beautiful charm of "Finish" (from **There Goes My Happy Marriage**). A resounding riposte to anyone who believed, before the success of Green Day, that fast tempos, aggressive buzz guitars, simplicity and cheerful intelligence were dead.

That done, the Megas metamorphized magnificently on **Sebastopol Rd.** The transformation mirrors that of the young Replacements, whose mid-period work (down to a blatant lift of the "I Will Dare" riff for "Anne Bancroft") seems to have inspired this album of dense pop songs with deep, jagged edges. The knowing frustration/heartbreak of "Prague" and the glorious "Scared of Cats" ("Begging for the truth, and then wishing I was told a lie") run counter to the euphoric, confident sweetness of the twin-guitar noise. Acoustic strums also abound, over which the singer vents optimism, experience and, most of all, poignant disillusionment. A rough-edged pop classic, **Sebastopol Rd.** garnered the group its first UK Top 40 ("Stop") and became its only US studio album release.

Inspiringly Titled the Live Album adequately documents the **Sebastopol Rd.** tour, but its main value is less the five songs from the album than the ten older ones, which benefit from the band's sharpened knives (the fierce-sounding MC4 was known to play two hundred gigs a year) and enormous improvement as a unit. The album closes with a smoking version of Hüsker Dü's "Don't Want to Know If You Are Lonely."

The quartet's brush with UK fame was brief. A falling-out with the record company consigned **Magic Bullets**—which fails to match **Sebastopol Rd.**'s end-to-end excellence—to relative obscurity. Still, it's far from a failure. "Perfect Circle" jump-starts the album, the single "Iron Sky" is a lacerating, fresh gem, "Enemy Skies" recalls the whomp and whack of the band's early days and "Speck" closes things on a somber note. Best of all, the melodies still stick to you like a dog in a thunderstorm.

After being dropped by Big Life, the band took two years before striking a new deal with Fire Records, during which interval **The Peel Sessions** appeared. The two sessions included are from five years apart ('88 and '93): with five **Tranzophobia**-era recordings followed by four songs recorded after the fourth album, the stylistic jump is startling. The nine-track record is notable mostly for the two unreleased songs, "Stay Dead" and "Slow Down," written in preparation for **Soulscraper.** [jr]

MEGADETH

Killing Is My Business . . . and Business Is Good! (Combat) 1985
Peace Sells . . . but Who's Buying? (Combat/Capitol) 1986
So Far, So Good . . . So What! (Capitol) 1988
Rust in Peace (Combat/Capitol) 1990
Countdown to Extinction (Combat/Capitol) 1992
Youthanasia (Capitol) 1994
Hidden Treasures (Capitol) 1995

A founding member of Metallica, Megadeth leader Dave Mustaine hails from a generation of headbangers unafraid to list the Sex Pistols and the Dead Boys as influences alongside Black Sabbath and Iron Maiden. When he was booted out of Metallica—over power struggles and a growing drug problem—the singer/guitarist hooked up with bassist David Ellefson and took his rock'n'roll vision a step further. With an outspoken political orientation (the group name comes from the military term for nuclear war casualties), Megadeth attacks speed metal with abundant chops, intricate arrangements, tricky time signatures, on-a-dime tempo pivots, explosive dynamics and bold tonal experiments. The group also has an intriguing taste in covers, tackling Nancy Sinatra's "These Boots Are Made for Walkin'," Willie Dixon's "I Ain't Superstitious" and the Pistols' "Anarchy in the U.K." (with laughably wrong phonetic lyrics) on its first three albums. If Megadeth sounds like just another technically accomplished thrash band to the non-discerning listener, there is, in fact, more going on here.

That said, Megadeth's albums are relatively interchangeable; only metal fanatics and guitar gearheads will appreciate the subtle differences between them. **So Far, So Good** is the best of Megadeth's first phase. The quartet took a great stride forward with 1990's **Rust in Peace,** overhauling its lineup to bring in guitarist Marty Friedman, a capable foil for the newly clean and sober Mustaine, and jazz-schooled drummer Nick Menza, the son of saxophonist Don Menza. **Rust in Peace** and **Countdown to Extinction** are solid and fresh-sounding, incorporating even trickier instrumental twists without sacrificing the band's headbanging crunch. **Youthanasia** moves Megadeth to a more centrist, mainstream-friendly position, employing polished production and more conventional song structures. "Train of Consequences" and "Elysian Fields" are killer songs by any measure, metal or otherwise.

Hidden Treasures, an eight-song roundup of Megadeth's contributions to soundtracks and compilations, includes cover versions of Alice Cooper's "No More Mr. Nice Guy," Black Sabbath's "Paranoid" and a previously unissued version of the Sex Pistols' "Problems." Among the originals are "Angry Again" (from *Last Action Hero*), "Go to Hell" (from *Bill & Ted's Bogus Journey*) and "99 Ways to Die" (from **The Beavis and Butt-head Experience**). [gg]

See also *Metallica; TPRG.*

MEICES

Not Funny Ha Ha EP7 (Two Car Garage) 1991
Meices [tape] (Two Car Garage) 1991
Greatest Bible Stories Ever Told (eMpTy) 1993
Tastes Like Chicken (London) 1994
Dirty Bird (London) 1996

MICE

Who Cut the Cheese (Waffle) 1988

Grunge was Sub Pop's lucky marketing term and helped carry some of the label's early groups (Soundgarden) to commercial success and others (Mudhoney) to critical acknowledgment. It's all rock'n'roll when the day's over, but if the loosely defined noise-pop genre had to have a typical representative, it might as well be San Francisco's Meices, a scrappy, loud, fun-loving garage-rocking trio led by singer/guitarist Joe Reineke. (The group, which formed in Florida and migrated to the West Coast, losing its original drummer and bassist in the process, was originally called the Mice, and released an obscure album under that name.)

Greatest Bible Stories Ever Told ain't even close to a theological tract, as Reineke and company storm through eleven hooky paeans to party tricks ("Pissin' in the Sink"), shoplifting (the speedy "Alex Put Something in His Pocket") and Los Angeles ("La La Land"). In between the hijinks and ear-piercing feedback, Reineke delivers one or two genuinely pretty/scruffy tunes ("This Way," "Didn't Wanna"), a three-chord raveup ("Don't Let the Soap Run Out"), a condescending anthem for snot-noses ("Hey Little Punker": "They look funny, but they're fun to party with") and a solid package of tuneful, muscular rock.

The Meices signed with London and brought friend Kurt Bloch of the Fastbacks in to record **Tastes Like Chicken.** Like its predecessor, the album has its share of silly, energetic charmers ("The Big Shitburger"), but Reineke offers introspection along with his sloppy guitars and three-minute-plus pop songs. Proving there's more to the Meices than just juvenile posturing, "Daddy's Gone to California" bridges the gap between **Bible Stories'** thrashy ethos and **Chicken**'s more dynamic material. Reineke's warbly vocals sometimes resemble Tom Petty's, and cuts like "Hopin' for a Ride," "Slide" and "Now" reveal a nice bittersweetness developing in the band's style.

Given the Meices' background and sharpening writing/playing skills, it's not surprising that **Dirty Bird,** co-written by Reineke and bassist Steve Borgerding and produced by Gil Norton, fits nicely alongside those Goo Goo Dolls albums on the shelf. Expressing more emotion than usual in his voice, Reineke packs dense guitar chunk and wry, sensitive lyrics into "Wow" (complete with horns and surf leads), "Disenchanted Eyes," "Hey Fella" and "Rosies on the Dole." The yelping "Hold It" reconnects the band to its sloppier past, while the semi-acoustic "Uncool" suggests just how uncomfortable the Meices will sound when they get around to making that long-awaited *MTV Unplugged* appearance. [mww/i]

MEKONS

The Quality of Mercy Is Not Strnen (UK Virgin) 1979 (Blue Plate) 1990
Devils Rats and Piggies a Special Message from Godzilla (UK Red Rhino) 1980
It Falleth Like Gentle Rain from Heaven—The Mekons Story (UK CNT Productions) 1982 (Feel Good All Over) 1993
The English Dancing Master EP (UK CNT Productions) 1983
Fear and Whiskey (UK Sin) 1985
Crime and Punishment EP (UK Sin) 1985
The Edge of the World (UK Sin) 1986 (Quarterstick) 1996
Slightly South of the Border EP (UK Sin) 1986
Honky Tonkin' (Sin/Twin\Tone) 1987
New York [tape] (ROIR) 1987 [CD] (ROIR/Important) 1990
So Good It Hurts (Twin\Tone) 1988
Original Sin (Sin/Twin\Tone) 1989
The Dream and Lie of . . . EP (UK Blast First) 1989
The Mekons Rock'n'Roll (Twin\Tone/A&M) 1990
F.U.N. '90 EP (Twin\Tone/A&M) 1990
The Curse of the Mekons (UK Blast First) 1991
Wicked Midnite/All I Want EP (Loud Music) 1992
I ♥ Mekons (Quarterstick) 1993
Millionaire EP (Quarterstick) 1993
Retreat From Memphis (Quarterstick) 1994
Mekons United (Touch and Go) 1996

MEKONS/KATHY ACKER

Pussy, King of the Pirates (Quarterstick) 1996

SALLY TIMMS (AND THE DRIFTING COWGIRLS)

This House Is a House of Trouble EP (UK T.I.M.) 1987
Butcher's Boy EP (UK T.I.M.) 1987
Somebody's Rocking My Dreamboat (UK T.I.M.) 1988
To the Land of Milk and Honey (Feel Good All Over) 1995
It Says Here EP (Feel Good All Over) 1995

JONBOY LANGFORD AND THE PINE VALLEY COSMONAUTS

Explore the Dark and Lonely World of Johnny Cash: Misery Loves Company (Scout/Feel Good All Over) 1995

VARIOUS ARTISTS

'Til Things Are Brighter . . . (Red Rhino/Fundamental) 1988

Punk's reigning contrarians, the Mekons were formed in Leeds, England, in 1977 by art students Jon Langford and Tom Greenhalgh. Their first single, "Never Been in a Riot," took dead aim at one of punk's sacred cows, the Clash's "White Riot," and the Mekons have gladly been outsiders ever since. The group has survived countless personnel changes, miserable fortune with record companies and a constant state of near-poverty by adapting to the times, its music expanding beyond punk to embrace twisted versions of country, reggae and electronica. And singer/guitarist Langford has become a pivotal figure in the underground rock and art scenes, as a producer, songwriter, bandleader, sideman, cartoonist, painter, writer, critic and all-around instigator. All the while, the Mekons have continued to put out records of bewildering variety, erratic musical quality and enormous heart. These function almost without exception as critiques of power and the abuse of power—whether in government, the record industry or, less frequently, the bedroom.

The early albums are significant for their socialist bent and utter disregard for Britpunk fashion, a chapter closed by 1982's **The Mekons Story.** Among two-chord screeds, avant-garde rumblings, folkish musings and the sound of one man shouting above the din of his own foot stomping on a floorboard, a voice slurs and giggles as it reads the band's contract with Virgin Records. More than just denouncing how art is inevitably reduced to commerce, the Mekons poke fun at themselves: put a price on this bilge, sucker.

After several years of near-silence, **Fear and Whiskey** and **The Edge of the World** established the Mekons in North America. Mutant country records haunted by the long shadow of the Reagan-Thatcher era (as epitomized by singer/guitarist Greenhalgh's cry that "It's hard to be human again"), both albums and two companion EPs (**Crime and Punishment** and **Slightly South of the Border**) collect bleary-eyed waltzes, ballads and mid-tempo mood pieces. For spice, there's the occasional stomper. **Fear and Whiskey** wins in that realm with "Flitcraft" and a blow-out-the-burners version of Hank Williams' "Lost Highway." The music is mostly first-rate, economical melodies lifted by rustic **Basement Tapes**–style intimacy and instrumentation: fiddle, piano and harmonica fleshing out guitars, drums and bass. On **The Edge of the World,** Sally Timms joins full-time as the band's third principal vocalist, her crystalline tone providing just the right touch of unflinching world-weariness between Greenhalgh's going-down-slow croon and Langford's beery bawl.

Original Sin provides a fine overview of this period, combining the entire **Fear and Whiskey** with all but one song off the two EPs and a track each from **Edge of the World** and the earlier **The English Dancing Master** EP.

Honky Tonkin' offers more scrappy folk and country tunes and an absurdly detailed bibliography that inspired their creation. The by-now-routine left-wing attitude is more explicit, with "If They Hang You" paying homage to author Dashiell Hammett for refusing to name names in the McCarthy-era Communist witch-hunt and "The Trimdon Grange Explosion" recounting a nineteenth-century mining disaster.

So Good It Hurts is a more polished, pop-friendly production, with Timms' beautiful but unforgiving voice showcased on a cover of the Rolling Stones' "Heart of Stone" and "Ghosts of American Astronauts," a surreal portrait of imperialism. Greenhalgh draws a poignant parallel between his band and another guy who bucked the system in "(Sometimes I Feel Like) Fletcher Christian."

New York is an audio vérité diary of the band's 1986–87 tour through the "soft, gross underbelly of America." Interspersed through the sixteen songs are bits of dialogue that document almost too well the band's road-weariness, twisted humor and fondness for a drink (or seven). A reckless run through the Band's "The Shape I'm In" qualifies it as the disc's unofficial theme song.

The band's sole major-label album, **The Mekons Rock'n'Roll,** is titled as though it were a genre unto itself, and it just might be. Elvis Costello once threatened, "I want to bite the hand that feeds me," but the Mekons tear away an entire limb with this withering indictment of Rock'n'Roll Inc. Ushered in by the Motörhead-like roar of "Memphis, Egypt," the disc's mission statement is delivered with a Doberman's snarl: "We know the devil and we have shaken him by the hand / Embraced him and thought his foul breath was fine perfume / Just like rock'n'roll." While the disc has its share of murky self-indulgences, the best moments—among them swipes at the "Dublin messiah" Bono in "Blow Your Tuneless Trumpet" and the grim excesses of "Cocaine Lil"—more than live up to the implications of the album title. Issued as a four-song preview of **Rock'n'Roll, The Dream and Lie** EP notably includes "Heaven and Back," one of two tracks left off the album's American edition.

F.U.N. '90 finds the band thumbing its nose at a record-label executive who suggested they not take things so seriously. The offbeat four-song EP is swathed in acid-house beats and includes both a cover of Robbie Robertson's "Makes No Difference" and a collaboration with the late rock critic Lester Bangs, "One Horse Town."

The Curse of the Mekons compiles the ravings of a rock'n'roll Lazarus, a band too stubborn or too dumb to quit, even with its A&M deal down the tubes and no American distributor in sight. (The album still has not been released in the US.) "Call it intuition, call it luck / We're right in all we distrust," Greenhalgh sings, a Mekons manifesto if there ever was one. Despite the back-against-the-wall scenario, the album is among the Mekons' most accomplished, blending the reggae washes of "Sorcerer," the Stonesy assault of "The Curse" and the mandolin-driven country of John Anderson's "Wild and Blue." The **Wicked Midnite/All I Want** EP is the sole remnant of an aborted deal with a fly-by-night California label: two songs from the then-forthcoming **I ♥ Mekons** album and '91 live versions of "The Curse," "Waltz" and "Amnesia."

With the group reduced to a quartet—Langford, Greenhalgh, Timms and violinist Susie Honeyman—**I ♥ Mekons** is built on a thrift-shop foundation of hip-hop loops, dub rhythms and assaultive polkas. But the resilient melodies and resonant vocals make it a minor triumph. A barbed-wire valentine for an era confronting AIDS and dabbling in virtual sex, the disc is the work of skeptics who refuse to cave in to cynicism. They see the "narrow snake . . . solid and defined" in the grass ("Dear Sausage") and yet plead with a lover to "lead me into temptation" on the album's finale, Lonesome Bob's "Point of No Return." Like the narrator in that song, the band has crawled from the wreckage enough times to know the risk of trying again, but refuses to turn away. The title song of **Millionaire** is the melodically irresistible Timms showcase from **I ♥ Mekons.** The EP is fleshed out with a track from **The Mekons Story** and live versions of "All I Want," "Blow Your Tuneless Trumpet" and "(Sometimes I Feel Like) Fletcher Christian."

The band regains its rock'n'roll gusto on **Retreat From Memphis,** the drum machine replaced by a newly recruited rhythm section. Like **The Mekons Rock'n'Roll,** the album was recorded immediately after many of the songs had been road-tested on tour and represents the studio Mekons at their most visceral. Thematically, **Retreat From Memphis** also works as a sequel to **Rock'n'Roll,** a meditation on power (the record industry) by the powerless (a lowly indie-rock band) in such songs as "Do I Know You?" and "Insignificance."

Pussy, King of the Pirates is a bawdy collaboration between the Mekons and author Kathy Acker, who provides between-songs narration from her novel of the same name. Timms, in particular, attacks the explicitly sexual lyrics with relish, her voice breaking into an uncharacteristic rasp. The music ranges from the ghostly Caribbean atmospherics of "The Song of the Dogs" to the disco bounce of "Antigone Speaks About Herself" to the industrial grind of "Into the Strange."

Mekons United packages a full-length CD of new material with a two-hundred-page book containing the band's novel-in-progress, full-color illustrations of paintings, film stills and written contributions from various associates.

Timms' solo albums are well worth seeking out, as they showcase a voice that, while not especially agile or well-suited to uptempo material, has a bell-like clarity that can be both seductive and subversive. **Somebody's Rocking My Dreamboat** is closer to mainstream pop than anything the Mekons have recorded, but that's not a criticism. While "Horses" and the countryish "Chained to the Anchor of Love" would have fit on a Mekons album, the electronic framework for the lilting "Mombassa" and the dramatic reading of Dolly Parton's "Down From Dover" are winning stylistic departures.

To the Land of Milk and Honey, recorded, like its predecessor, with heavy involvement from Langford and now part-time Mekons drummer Steve Goulding, is full of pretty—if stoic and unsentimental—ballads. The originals co-written by Timms and Langford are solid, notably the cabaret-style anti-torch song "Round Up" and "Longing, Madness & Lust," a bilious commentary on unchecked desire. Four well-chosen covers, ranging from John Cale's "Half Past France" to Procol Harum's "Homburg," round out a strong collection. Timms' album version of Stuart Moxham's "It Says Here" is the lead track of an EP of otherwise unreleased material: two studio originals and live acoustic covers of tunes by Dolly Parton and Tim Hardin recorded in New York.

In '88, Langford (with Goulding on the traps) executive produced and performed on **'Til Things Are Brighter,** a tribute album to Johnny Cash with vocal contributions from Marc Almond, Michelle Shocked, Steve Mack of That Petrol Emotion and Cathal Coughlan of Fatima Mansions. In 1995, he did it again, without the guest stars. Using members of his side band, the Waco Brothers—as well as Timms, singer Jane Baxter Miller and others—Langford pays a sincere, sloppy rustic return visit to the shrine of Cash on **Misery Loves Company.** He gives somber, underworld country-rock readings to some of the Man in Black's bleakest compositions ("What Is Truth?," "I Still Miss Someone," "Home of the Blues," "Busted"), adding some of his favorite covers in the same realm ("Cocaine Blues," Kris Kristofferson's "Sunday Morning Coming Down"), adding effective original touches but occasionally letting the songs do too much of the work. [gk]

See also *Gary Lucas, Barbara Manning, Waco Brothers; TPRG.*

MELTING HOPEFULS

Prune Juice EP [tape] (no label) 1991
Magnet for Stains EP [tape] (no label) 1992
Heal Back Harder EP [tape] (no label) 1993
Space Flyer (bigPoP/Shanachie) 1994
Viva la Void (bigPoP) 1995

Although they could easily veer off into art-rock pretensions, Melting Hopefuls somehow skewer the lines between pretty pop, rambunctious noise, precious poetry and generic post-punk just enough to stay out of trouble. The quintet records in its rehearsal/recording space in suburban New Jersey; as a result, the records have a touch of homespun intensity that suggests music in a constant experimental state. Meanwhile, singer/lyricist Reneé LoBue shifts between extroverted commentary and more private thoughts. (The 1994 album's "Pulling an Allnighter on Myself," released as a single and then remixed and included on **Viva la Void,** received a bit of notoriety for being about catching one's date in the act of masturbation.) Highlighted by that song and "Turn on the Turn-Off," the eight-song **Viva la Void** is stronger than the thirteen-track **Space Flyer.** The playing is sharper and the overall feel—though definitely post-Pavement—catches the pioneer spirit of indie-rock while steering clear of its dead ends. [roc]

MELVINS

Melvins EP7 (C/Z) 1986
Gluey Porch Treatments (Alchemy) 1987
Ozma (Boner) 1989
Bullhead (Boner) 1990
Eggnog EP (Boner) 1991
10 Songs (C/Z) 1991
Melvins (Boner/Tupelo) 1992
Your Choice Live Series (Ger. Your Choice) 1993
Houdini (Atlantic) 1993
Stoner Witch (Atlantic) 1994
Live (X-mas) 1996
Stag (Mammoth/Atlantic) 1996

SNIVLEM

Prick (Amphetamine Reptile) 1994

KING BUZZO

King Buzzo EP (Boner/Tupelo) 1992

DALE CROVER

Dale Crover EP (Boner/Tupelo) 1992

JOE PRESTON

Joe Preston EP (Boner/Tupelo) 1992

Being true to yourself in rock'n'roll works as a commercial gambit only if who you are is at least partly in synch with what the world is ready or waiting for. For every big name doing something that at least seems original, there's invariably a more radical, more iconoclastic, more intemperate out-there version of same, someone whose idealism (or incapacity, as you like) keeps the masses at bay. In the case of Kurt Cobain, that someone was (and is) Aberdeen homeboy Buzz Osborne, singer/guitarist of the Melvins, inimitable steamrolling overlords of the slow-flowing magma.

The trio has being going since the mid-'80s. Osborne, mainstay drummer Dale Crover and a procession of bassists (a pre-Mudhoney Matt Lukin and Lori Black, the punk-rock daughter of Shirley Temple, among others) have produced a steady stream of the sludgiest, heaviest downer music this side of Henryk Górecki. Weaned on Black Sabbath, Black Flag, Kiss, Motörhead and the Nuge, Osborne (who prefers to be called King Buzzo) upends silly old notions of stability, melody and structure in a growling, ominous arena-scorning punk/metal meltdown that stops, starts, speeds up, unwinds, curves, collapses and explodes on an uncharted course. Osborne's incalculable imagination and bent wit mark him as a singular composer, one who bellows creepy lyrics in short bursts of anti-dirge drama. Oppressive in the best possible sense, the Melvins produce richly sensual, stunningly ugly music that gives the feeling of being crushed by a friendly fat guy tripping his brains out. When the band is truly in its glory, the Melvins replay the sinking of the Titanic, invoking the grinding inexorability of an implacable iceberg tearing apart the hull of a great vessel inch by grueling inch. It is a wonder to behold.

Following a debut 7-inch EP (later expanded by three songs and reissued on CD as **10 Songs**) and album, Osborne and Crover relocated to San Francisco in 1988, got Black in the band and made **Ozma,** an outpouring of overweight weirdness cut into short slices like "Let God Be Your Gardener," "Cranky Messiah," "Creepy Smell" and "Raise a Paw." (The cassette includes an extra song; the CD appends all of **Gluey Porch Treatments.**) With Black renamed Lorax, the trio cut the more expansive **Bullhead**—longer tracks played more slowly, and with more downward pressure. Between the groaning syncopated plod of "Boris"—beat, beat, beat, bend, beat, beat, beat, beat, bend—and the relative brisk organization and feedback of "Cow," **Bullhead** is the clearest exposition of Melvin-dom to that point, and the blueprint for much of what was to follow. (The well-recorded January 1991 concert—presumably in Germany, considering the label and the opening stage remark about *Hogan's Heroes*—consists of material from the first three albums played with surehanded power by the San Francisco lineup. The rendition of **Bullhead**'s "Anaconda" is especially impressive.)

The twenty-minute **Eggnog** is a mixed drink; of the three exceptionally fast-paced tracks that fill its first half, only "Antitoxidote" (a cheer of "Pigs don't let it!" set to a racing boogie rumble) is the only one that sounds like an actual song rather than a fragment extended by ear-splitting jams. The rest of the record is given over to "Charmicarmicat," an awesome slo-mo monument of riveting enervation that seems to breathe between notes as Crover counts off downstrokes in increments of ten.

By the time the Melvins got back into the studio, the group had been cited as a primary influence and favorite band by their old pal in the suddenly ascendant Nirvana. Notoriety was encouragement to indulge itself, and the band's next project was a high-concept tribute to Kiss: three simultaneously issued solo albums with consistent Kiss-parodying artwork and come-ons to join the nonexistent Melvins Army. Black had been packed off to some private hell and did not get to make a solo record; one-album bassist Joe Preston, however, was around and did. His off-the-wall contribution to this undertaking consists of found-sound tapes, some chaotic crypto-metal noise played by people called Denial Fiend and Salty Green; Preston's only credit is for vocals and co-writing, although neither activity yields anything audibly attributable (unless something unexpected transpires more than halfway through the twenty-three-minute "Hands First Flower").

King Buzzo's four-songer is an exposition of opposites, recorded as a two-man army with one Dale Nixon (a name Greg Ginn once used in Black Flag): "Annum" is tense pop, quietly sung and delicately played, while "Porg" is a sonic collage that sounds nothing like the Melvins and "Skeeter" fires an instrumental salvo straight down the band's speed alley while someone named Dave recites a shaggy sex story. Crover's disc is more surprising and entertaining: joined only by bassist Debbi Shane, he sings and plays original songs that build muzzy heavy-pop structures evolving from Melvins rhythms. "Hex Me" is the best of the four tracks, but the whole disc reveals an entertaining soft spot in the band's rugged demeanor.

Melvins (an album announced as **Lysol** but released without any indicated title after the spray's manufacturer got wind of it), the only longplaying document of the Osborne-Crover-Preston lineup, registers only one track on the CD display, but there are in fact a full-stop pause and several song changes in the unidentified thirty-minute monster. The first half is a big gulp of guitar distortion that the rhythm section weighs in to from time to time; at the twelve-minute mark, the arrival of a steady beat and vocals shape it into a bone-crushing mother of a song. After the brief intermission, the trio gets right back into it, shifting gears from sludge to a martial drum exhibition to a complete rendition of Alice Cooper's creepy "Ballad of Dwight Fry," ending the program with a concise original. Weird and wonderful.

Cobain's clout got the Melvins (who had parted company with Preston and reclaimed Black for a brief spell) signed to Atlantic; for good measure, he co-produced half **Houdini**'s tracks and played guitar on one. (Too bad he didn't bring them along to *MTV Unplugged* instead of the Meat Puppets.) Faithful to the band's basic principles but open to suggestion and appreciably accelerated and tightened from its baseline, **Houdini** is a wild-eyed humdinger, teetering between the Melvins' traditional fuck-you stance and an it's-here-if-you-can-take-it posture. "Hooch," "Copache," a thoroughly devolved cover of Kiss' "Going Blind" and the glacial-paced "Hag Me" blast away with typical bummed-in fervor. The self-produced "Honey Bucket" explores the stylistic link with Nirvana, but new ideas appear here as well: "Spread Eagle Beagle" is a cranky percussion solo, "Pearl Bomb" ticks away to a fast electronic beat and the spry "Sky Pup" comes from some heretofore unknown corner of the Melvins' universe.

Before assenting to make its second major-label album, the mischievous Melvins (with bassist Mark Deutrom) adopted a clever nomenclatural disguise—Snivlem—and cut **Prick** for the Amphetamine Reptile label. Perhaps reasoning that it's not the Melvins so it doesn't have to be good, King B and the boys fucked around, slopped a bunch of dull, mind-numbing dreck onto a platter and deemed it an album. It isn't. Among the eleven formless tracks are newsreel interviews, acoustic and demi-electric jams that go until the tape runs out, ambient noise, church bells and anything else left lying around an English studio. A total obnoxious time-waster that only makes a great band look bad—and, worse, ineffectual.

Stoner Witch gets back to serious business, but without much inspiration. Sharing the load around (Crover and Deutrom both play some of the guitar and co-wrote most of the songs; Buzz gets credit for bass as well as his usuals), the Melvins weigh in somewhere between Ministry, Motörhead and a Moog orchestra, mainly playing terse, mobile songs that bear a fair resemblance to days of old but are motivated and propulsive in ways the Melvins never used to be. Crover especially sounds like a changed man, thundering away in rhythms that drive songs along rather than poke idly at their progress like a cat standing on a mouse's tail (except on the quiet noir swing of "Goose Freight Train" and the pure-noise first half of "Magic Pig Detective"). Osborne's desire not to be restricted to the structural limits of music he's been playing steadily for a decade is certainly understandable; the album can be seen as a transitional effort to widen the group's possibilities, to identify areas for further study. That doesn't make it a keeper. As a slab of determined rock force, **Stoner Witch** certainly kicks butt, but it lacks too much of the special everything that makes the Melvins unique.

The X-mas release is a spectacularly packaged hard-cover album of four 7-inches; if a collection of vinyl 45s is the worst imaginable format for a live record by a band prone to elongated workouts and a technology-challenging dynamic range, the use of maddening lock grooves brings the whole concept in line with the band's genial perversity and makes it an artistic coup of some sort. Recorded on the Melvins' '95 Tora Tora Tora Tour and sprinkled with such comical offbeatitude as radio ads and call-in shows, official arena announcements and loopy stage patter, **Live** is an essential condiment to the band's more substantial (if unpredictably uneven) main courses.

The lively and entertaining **Stag** remedies the failings of **Stoner Witch** by bringing the spunk back and leavening the behemoth metal snarling with variety and humor: the inaugural sitar, the odd sonic effects and wailing trombone on "Bar-X-The Rocking M," the unabashed pop vigor of "Black Bock," the munchkin gimmickry of "Skin Horse" and the shocking acoustic blues of "Cottonmouth." No longer confined to a single design, the Melvins spread their wings and drop a fat sky patty all over rock's ugly landscape. [i]

See also *Mudhoney*.

MENSTER PHIP AND THE PHIPSTERS

Phip City! (Telstar) 1993

This humble, almost-lost classic offers conclusive proof that you don't need a budget—or even much talent—to make timelessly great rock'n'roll. In their parents' basement in suburban Fairlawn, New Jersey, during the early '60s, Kenny Collins, his brother Richie and various friends and relatives pounded out rudimentary but undeniably infectious rock with their loosely constructed "band," Menster Phip and the Phipsters, recording delirious originals ("Daddy Wants a Cold Beer," "Sing a Song All Day Long"), surreal-to-the-point-of-unrecognizability covers ("Land of 1,000 Dances," "I Saw Her Standing There") and even a bogus commercial for Great Shakes (remember them?) on a two-track reel-to-reel deck for their own amusement. Though the group never performed publicly or released any recordings in its lifetime, tapes eventually found their way to Hoboken's Telstar label, which redressed history's injustice by releasing a twenty-song collection as **Phip City!** While Collins and friends show little in the way of conventional musical ability, their abundant spirit more than compensates, making these genuine basement tapes a triumph of enthusiasm over technique. [ss]

MENSWE@R

Nuisance (Laurel/London) 1995

Although the need for a post-punk version of Duran Duran hasn't exactly been established, this young suburban London quintet came strutting into the UK press headlines proudly proclaiming themselves precisely that. Unflaggingly attentive to fashion and generally capable of pouting through big-lipped, big-riffed glam-pop confections with attitude to spare, Menswe@r does its best to make precursors like Suede look like the Grateful Dead. It would be easier to dismiss them if frontman Johnny Dean didn't have such an innate comprehension of what makes a pop singer into a pop *star:* the sneered asides that punctuate the Wire-damaged "Daydreamer" and the melodramatic sweep that blankets "Being Brave" positively radiate charisma. His bandmates capture the limelight on occasion—guitarists Chris Gentry and Simon White toss off a fair Richards/Taylor counterfeit on the cheeky "Stardust"—but only Dean has the potential to catapult this otherwise ordinary band to teendream status. [dss]

ME PHI ME

One (RCA) 1992

Frat-rapper/poet Me Phi Me promotes individuality, political progress and a positive outlook in his low-key rhymes and whispery singing on **One;** producer Chris Cuben-Tatum (CeeCeeTee) spreads out a richly woven hip-pop-soul-blues carpet with live musicians (heavy on acoustic guitar, some of it played by MPM) and cushiony backing vocals. An ingratiating, uplifting trip with some of PM Dawn's spacy imagination, a bit of the sunny disposition that would later inspire Spearhead and something of the introspective new age mindset adopted by Des'ree, Me Phi Me is a charming self-helper who knows his way around the kitchen sink: "Row Row Row Your Boat," Sly Stone, Johnny Nash, Djivan Gasparyan and guest vocalist Michael Franks all find uses here. MPM's philosophical uplift becomes heavy ballast pulling down the entertainment factor after a while, but the music floats along on its variety and originality regardless. [i]

MEPHISTO WALZ

Terra Regina (Cleopatra) 1993
The Eternal Deep (Cleopatra) 1994
Thalia (Cleopatra) 1995

Barry Galvin (aka Bari-Bari; guitars, bass, keyboards), David Glass (drums) and Johann Schumann (bass) played in Christian Death in the first half of the '80s (Glass even longer); in the following decade, enlisting a vocalist aptly named Christianna, they formed Mephisto Walz, a band that has little in common with their past gothic lives. The material on **Terra Regina** is ambient and almost new agey, something along the lines of what might happen if Enya wrote an album while feeling really moody. The pretty, languid sound of tracks like "Umbrea" and "The Starveling" quickly turns ponderous when applied to weaker songs like "A Gathering of Elementals" and "Am Sonntag." The faster-paced "In the Room That Love Exists" and "Protecteur" (in which Christianna sounds remarkably like Berlin's Terri Nunn) inject some much-needed energy into the routine, preventing **Terra Regina** from sinking under its own murky layers.

The Eternal Deep's material is far more structured, as well as more animated. No aimless experimentation bogs things down until the very last track, the weirdly pulsating "Aborigine Requiem." The band goes a little overboard with this newfound zeal on "Der Sack," but **The Eternal Deep** marks a promising turn toward better songwriting. Meanwhile, covers of the Stooges' "I Wanna Be Your Dog" and the Rolling Stones' "Paint It, Black" are distorted nearly beyond recognition.

Thalia strikes an uneven compromise between the debut's lavish meanderings and **The Eternal Deep**'s fervent excitability. The intriguing woozy lilt of "Mephisto Walz" makes it fit to be played at a ghostly masquerade ball. The quivering and skipping "No Way Out" is another standout, as is an echo-laden cover of Jefferson Airplane's "White Rabbit." On the other hand, there's the inexcusable self-indulgence of noodly instrumentals like "A Precession of the Equinoxes" and the amelodic "Aglaia at Auroras." [ky]

See also *Christian Death.*

NATALIE MERCHANT

Tigerlily (Elektra) 1995

The reflective melancholy singer Natalie Merchant brought to 10,000 Maniacs was often buoyed by the band's uplifting music and her own occasional bursts of lyrical joy. After severing her ties to the band in 1993, she dropped the veil of smiles and put her disconsolate passions into a glass menagerie case that does little to leaven the mood. On her mesmerizing solo debut, recorded with three demure sidepersons (the rhythm section had been in the Wallflowers) and a handful of guests, Merchant applies her inimitable alto with a cool evenness that scarcely betrays the songs' powerful emotions.

Merchant wades deep into her private sea of discontent on **Tigerlily.** There's alienation ("Carnival"), destruction ("San Andreas Fault") and loss ("Beloved Wife," the breezy-sounding "River" [Phoenix]). In affairs of the heart, she offers dismay ("Jealousy," in which—quite unlike Alanis Morissette's coarse calculus—Merchant's concern over her replacement extends to the woman's reading habits), disappointment ("Cowboy Romance") and disgust (the exquisite and haunting "Seven Years"). When she metes out glimmers of hope, it's like dangerously potent medicine. "How I'll often treasure moments that we knew, the precious, the few," she sings over solo piano in "The Letter," and it characterizes the album's tenor as well. A master of mood as well as musical expression, Merchant has a rare understanding of harmony, especially the unique ways her heart and mind can work together. [i]

See also *10,000 Maniacs.*

MERCURY REV

Yerself Is Steam (Rough Trade) 1991 (UK Mint Films/ Jungle/Beggars Banquet) 1992 (Columbia) 1992
The Hum Is Coming From Her EP10 (Columbia) 1993
Boces (Columbia) 1993
Something for Joey EP (Columbia) 1993
Everlasting Arm EP (Big Cat) 1994
See You on the Other Side (Work) 1995

HARMONY ROCKETS

Paralyzed Mind of the Archangel Void (Big Cat) 1995

SHADY

World (Beggars Banquet) 1994

Plenty of bands advocate anarchy, but few have practiced it with the single-minded determination of Mercury Rev, a psychedelically inclined sextet given over to every-man-for-himself excursions as open-ended as "pop" music has seen in many a year. While analogous in some ways to the Flaming Lips (a band that guitarist Jonathan "Dingus" Donahue played with for one album, **In a Priest Driven Ambulance,** in 1990; Rev bassist David Fridmann co-produced that LP), Mercury Rev possesses neither the Lips' pop savvy nor the user-friendliness. The free-form freakouts, however, are there in full force.

On **Yerself Is Steam** (go on, say it aloud), the band—which formed in Buffalo in the '80s—layers the sonic effluvia on so thick you'd swear they were counting on the sheets of sound as protection against a long lake effect snowstorm. Donahue and primary vocalist David Baker occasionally poke their heads out to recite inscrutable verses like those of "Chasing a Bee" and "Coney Island Cyclone" (the disc's most linear—and Lips-like—tune), but the most compelling songs, like the sumptuous "Sweet Oddysee of a Cancer Cell t' th' Center of Yer Heart," aggressively challenge listeners to cull individual kernels of sound from the pandemonium. (The British edition included a bonus record, **Lego My Ego,** containing single sides, radio sessions, live material and the score for a short film.) Besides a bracing six-theremin assault on the title track, **The Hum Is Coming From Her** teams the band with avant-garde poet Robert Creeley, who reads his "So There" over skewed big-band backing.

Boces (which takes its name from a New York State program designed to train the unskilled labor force of the future) asserts the band's everything-including-the-kitchen-sink aesthetic from the first notes of the dizzying "Meth of a Rockette's Kick"—a ten-minute mélange of piercing feedback, doo-wop harmonies and Suzanne Thorpe's tranquil flute playing. Every so often, Mercury Rev manages to coerce all the elements it tosses up to hang there in mid-air, defying gravity (as on the opalescent "Something for Joey"); more frequently, kismet fails to do its part, rendering tracks like "Trickle Down" and "Downs Are Feminine Balloons" simply slipshod and shapeless. Besides the LP track of its title, **Something for Joey** gives an American release to the Creeley collaboration "So There," includes two '93 live tracks (**Boces'** "Boys Peel Out" and thirteen minutes of "Very Sleepy Rivers"), plus a phone interview with porn actor Ron Jeremy, who appeared in the "Something for Joey" video.

Baker left the group in 1994, citing the usual irreconcilable differences—but judging by the affinity between the parties' subsequent output, those conflicts were probably the intra-band equivalent of squabbles over what color to paint the guest bathroom. Admittedly, the title track of the **Everlasting Arm** EP (reprised on **See You on the Other Side**) is a fairly straightforward wisp of **Smile**-like pop, but ancillary pieces like "Dead Man" (written and read by Suicide legend Alan Vega) and thirty-odd minutes of surreptitiously recorded family-room chatter indicate that all the kinks haven't been ironed out. **See You on the Other Side** establishes Donahue's role as unchallenged leader, but other than an appreciable sludge-removal effort, he does little to tamper with the ingrained formula. "Empire State (Son House in Excelsis)" and "Sudden Ray of Hope" are augmented with some surprisingly punchy, direct brass lines, but there's no mistaking the scattered bliss-pop undertow that permeates "Young Man's Stride." The trip is still long and strange; it's just marked by fewer stopovers.

The Harmony Rockets pseudonym allows Mercury Rev ample room for digression: **Paralyzed Mind of the Archangel Void** consists of a single undulating forty-minute piece that recalls some of the late '60s' more arcane trance-rock meditations.

Shady, essentially Baker's solo project (with cameos by St. Johnny's Bill Whitten and ex–Rollerskate

Skinny guitarist Jimi Shields), lets him serve up slightly more reasonable portions of the same sonic eccentricity he brought to Mercury Rev. He's just as likely to play depth-perception parlor tricks—layers of harmonies and guitar noise ebb and flow through songs like "Hey Yeah!" and "Soul of Things to Come"—but **World** reveals a heretofore unseen sentimental side in the shape of the lovely "Narcotic Candy" (co-written by Seam's Sooyoung Park) and a cover of Gene Clark's "Life's Greatest Fool." Sweetly addictive. [dss]

See also *Flaming Lips, St. Johnny.*

MERCYLAND

See *Sugar.*

MERCY RULE

100 MPH EP7 (Pravda) 1992
God Protects Fools (Caulfield) 1993 (Caulfield/Relativity) 1994
Providence (Relativity) 1994

THIRTEEN NIGHTMARES

Shitride (Pravda) 1989

On the powerful and provocative **Shitride,** Thirteen Nightmares—an insidious left-wing quartet from Lincoln, Nebraska, led by singer/guitarist Greggory-David Cosgrove—demonstrates an extraordinary balance of rawness and subtlety. The band's bracing slam-dance of midwest rock generations—the MC5, Cheap Trick and Soul Asylum are the record's spiritual forefathers—is hindered only by a distorted take on radical politics that undercuts the music's fist-in-face power.

In **Shitride**'s wake, Thirteen Nightmares bassist/singer Heidi Ore and guitarist Jonathan Taylor bade farewell to Cosgrove and formed Mercy Rule with new drummer Ron Albertson. Following a 7-inch with four songs (none of which have since resurfaced on album), the band made the ferocious **God Protects Fools.** The raucously oblique "My Mouth"—with a catchy hook, nagging guitar lick and Ore's raggedy Chrissie Hynde–like vocals—is a killer kickoff. If nothing else on the album achieves that level of immediacy or impact (though the similar-sounding "Summer," with an eleven-word text, comes close), the claustrophobic meltdown buzz, plastered with Ore's righteously inflamed singing of intriguing lyrical sketches about personal achievement ("We Know") and romantic discord ("Dare Me," "Pale," "Time of Day"), adds up to a rewarding nerve-rattler.

The creative progress of **Providence** fine-tunes Mercy Rule's assault, coordinating the guitar, bass and drums into a driving engine of well-shaped aggression. The measure of musical sophistication, expedited by producer Brian Paulson's cleaner, better balanced mix, however, has the unfortunate effect of revealing the monochromatic inadequacies of Ore's voice. When the band runs its dynamic meter at medium, she can be artlessly effective, but she overpowers the folky "Which Road" with soulful bravado. Conversely, in high gear, her husky caterwauling—more like the frantic side of Janis Joplin than anything else—is too much of a distraction. Oddly, Mercy Rule also shows the mark of the '70s rock beast, countering the modernism of punk belligerence with the implicit nostalgia of dated reference points. [i]

MERMEN

Krill Slippin' (Kelptone) 1989
Food for Other Fish (Kelptone) 1994
Live at the Haunted House (Shittone) 1994
A Glorious Lethal Euphoria (Toadophile) 1995 (Mesa) 1995
Songs of the Cows EP (Mesa) 1996

Now here's a band that's actually *doing* something for the revolution. Granted, the radical movement in question—instrumental twang rock—is headed back in time and out to sea, but San Francisco's long-running Mermen have the distinction of being the genre's most ambitious revisionists. Led by monster guitarist (and surfer) Jim Thomas, the trio rides the wild surf as if Jimi Hendrix had come back to be a rodeo star.

On **A Glorious Lethal Euphoria,** the band's first national release, Thomas lassos bucking broncos of feedback with soft hands. Equally capable of settling down to precise figures of reverbed/tremoloed modesty, he whips the luridly titled originals ("Scalp Salad," "Pulpin' Line," "The Drowning Man Knows His God") into stormy seas of aggressive rock virulence and sends soft breezes to caress placid lilypads, never settling for generic methodology. Bassist Allen Whitman and drummer Martyn Jones do a lot more than merely back Thomas up, however; their contribution to the campaign is equally intricate and motile. Finishing the aptly titled album off with a Brahms movement, the Mermen leave an old, rarely challenged medium much better off than they found it.

The brief **Songs of the Cows** is even better, a virtual symphony of trio improvisation as close in dynamic achievement—not style, 'cause this sure ain't no blues—to Cream at its zenith. Exciting, varied and engaging in ways the jam bands (whose audience will likely embrace the Mermen, who don't waste time with lyrics or pop structures at all—what a concept!) can't possibly touch, this febrile, visceral rock is performed with exceptional intelligence and flair. Untainted by cerebral haughtiness and careful to avoid anus-climbing delusions, the Mermen take the best feature of surf music—the pure riff—and sail away with it. Magical. [i]

METAL FLAKE MOTHER

See *Squirrel Nut Zippers.*

METALLICA

Kill 'Em All (Megaforce) 1983 (Elektra) 1987
Ride the Lightning (Megaforce) 1984 (Megaforce/Elektra) 1984
Whiplash EP (Megaforce) 1985
Master of Puppets (Elektra) 1986
The $5.98 E.P. Garage Days Re-Revisited EP (Elektra) 1987
. . . And Justice for All (Elektra) 1988
Metallica (Elektra) 1991
Live Shit: Binge & Purge (Elektra) 1993
Load (Elektra) 1996

DIE KRUPPS

A Tribute to Metallica EP (Ger. Rough Trade) 1992 (Hollywood) 1993

One of the most important and influential new rock bands to emerge in the 1980s, California's uncompromising Metallica rose from humble origins to affect the attitudes of a generation, its bone-crunching grooves and punkish fuck-that-shit ideology providing the backdrop to contemporary teenage wasteland. Although the once-magnificent quartet has since settled into stadium-rock routine—a semi-ossified state of stardom when an album takes as many years as it does millions to make—the Sex Pistols of metal have aged pretty gracefully, even if they now have more in common with Van Halen.

Formed in 1981 by Danish drummer/tennis pro Lars Ulrich and skatepunk guitarist James Hetfield, Metallica originally included guitarist Dave Mustaine, who split to form Megadeth just days before **Kill 'Em All** was recorded in mid-'83. Combining Ulrich's love for Eurometal (everything from Motörhead to Jethro Tull) with Hetfield's Misfits worship, the album shrugs off many of metal's traditional sonic clichés, retaining only the power, velocity and blazing guitars. Bracingly unusual (although hardly radical), **Kill 'Em All** is a raw but explosive classic that paved the way for literally hundreds of similar bands, even though—like so many classics—it all sounds a bit tame in retrospect. The 1987 reissue adds a bruising pair of then-obscure metal covers—dubbed "Garage Days Revisited"—from the European B-side of "Creeping Death."

The band's sound takes on a life of its own with **Ride the Lightning.** Hetfield's lyrics and strained vocals are scarcely improved, but the pulverizing crunch-grooves unleash primal instincts and are essential lessons in the science of the riff. Despite mainstream radio's general boycott of uncommercial metal, **Master of Puppets,** universally acknowledged as the band's creative peak, roared into the Top 30 on the strength of constant touring and a rabid underground buzz. Multi-tracked harmony solos by lead guitarist Kirk Hammett, tautly controlled rhythms and simple vocal arrangements make songs about insanity, the futility of war and cocaine addiction burn white-hot with excitement.

In September 1986, a bus crash in Sweden killed bassist Cliff Burton, but the band recruited Jason Newsted as his replacement and returned in late '87 with **The $5.98 E.P. Garage Days Re-Revisited,** a slapdash package of five covers (including songs by Diamond Head, Killing Joke and a neat Misfits medley) recorded in LA during rehearsal jams.

The sprawling **. . . And Justice for All** runs over sixty-five minutes, which, considering the contents, is about twenty-five too many. An ultra-dry mix and endless directionless riffage make it cold and static; although "Blackened" and "Dyers Eve" are relatively concise blasts of speed, and the chilling "One" (basically a third rewrite of **Ride the Lightning**'s "Fade to Black") became an unlikely hit single, metal's most underground band had grown perilously bloated.

Self-consciously attempting to take it to the next level and make a mature, commercial rock album, the group enlisted Aerosmith/Mötley Crüe producer Bob Rock. **Metallica** has a comparatively stripped-down, simpler sound: four- to five-minute songs, basic tempos and a greater emphasis on melody. (Hammett's lead guitar is pure Thin Lizzy throughout.) Despite the potential for disaster, **Metallica** is a welcome change, and the band even survived the "Beth" syndrome, successfully employing strings on the power ballad "Nothing Else Matters" (essentially "Fade to Black" part four). Although the album kicks off with the stunning "Enter Sandman" and "Sad but True," it gradually loses focus and interest before finishing with the bruising "The Struggle Within." (Several concurrent single releases contained demo versions of album tracks as well as the usual obscure covers—most prominently the Anti-Nowhere League's remarkably profane "So What.")

Grueling is too unkind a word to describe Metallica's three-hour live sets, but it certainly applies to the exhaustive and exhausting **Live Shit: Binge & Purge.** Boxed in a toaster-sized mock equipment flight case—one of the most lavish retail packages ever produced—it presents no less than three entire live shows on three CDs and three videos; it also contains a fascinating seventy-two-page scrapbook that reveals the labrynthine logistics of keeping a trans-global rock machine on tour for three years. (The CDs stitch together a complete set from five Mexico City shows in early '93. The videos hail from two nights in Seattle '89 and two in San Diego '92.) A more thoroughly retrospective live set might have been more invigorating, but concision and conservatism have never been Metallica watchwords.

Bob Rock returned to help the newly shorn Metallica produce **Load,** its second studio album of the '90s.

Long-running Düsseldorf industrialists Die Krupps put a genuine Saxon bootprint on seven of the band's songs in **A Tribute to Metallica.** (The American edition adds "One" and a wacky Dave Ogilvie remix of "Enter Sandman" to the German six-track.) Krupp-meister Jürgen Engler makes a good point by demonstrating the proximity of techno rhythms to the band's mechanical precision, but he also employs guitars and a harsh, distorted voice to keep the renditions of "For Whom the Bell Tolls," "Nothing Matters" and others recognizably close to the originals. [ja/i]

See also *Megadeth; TPRG.*

METAL MIKE

Plays the Hits of the 90's EP (Triple X) 1991
Ted Nugent Is Not My Dad! EP (Triple X) 1992
My Girlfriend Is a Rock EP (Triple X) 1993
Next Stop Nowhere: The EP Collection (Triple X) 1994

ANGRY SAMOANS

The Unboxed Set (Triple X) 1995

Onetime rock critic Mike Saunders, whose claim to posterity (and the explanation for his nom de rock) is having coined the phrase "heavy metal," spent (wasted?) the entire '80s playing in LA's rude, stupid and rarely funny punk joke Angry Samoans. Amazingly but efficiently, **The Unboxed Set** recapitulates the band's entire studio catalogue—forty-three songs in all—on a single seventy-six-minute CD, complete with properly grumpy liner notes by the band's other main man, guitarist Gregg Turner. Anyone with a hankering to hear the original versions of "My Old Man's a Fatso," "Get Off the Air" or "They Saved Hitler's Cock" can now indulge with lubricated ease.

Anyhow, Saunders went solo in the '90s and made better use of his time. Forming a new band in the same modest punk-pop style but with a marginally less lethal sense of humor, the singer/guitarist issued a series of good-natured mini-albums: **Plays the Hits of the 90's, Ted Nugent Is Not My Dad!** and **My Girlfriend Is a Rock.** Those records are all collected (along with five tracks from two singles) on the twenty-two-cut **Next Stop Nowhere.** Although Saunders' originals ("Let's Burn the Flag," "High on Drugs," "I Don't Like This World Anymore") are passable, he reserves his real enthusiasm for lovingly rendered covers chosen from various revealing fan/collector compartments: obscure punk (the Nervebreakers' "My Girlfriend Is a Rock," the Dictators' "Next Big Thing," pre–Redd Kross Red Cross' "S&M Party"), '70s glam (Sweet's "Wig Wam Bam"), '70s trash (two by Lobo!), British pop rarities (Dave Davies' "This Man He Weeps Tonight") and country (Merle Haggard's "I'm a Lonesome Fugitive"). Years of effort have turned Saunders into a more than adequate artless singer, and the band's playing skill matches the complexity of the material. This lightweight romp is easily enjoyable if less than significant. Come back Mike, nowhere's too far for a punk-rock baby. [i]

METHOD MAN

See *Wu-Tang Clan.*

MIDNIGHT OIL

Midnight Oil (Aus. Powderworks) 1978 (Columbia) 1990
Head Injuries (Aus. Powderworks) 1979 (Columbia) 1990
Bird Noises EP (Aus. Powderworks) 1980 (Columbia) 1990
Place Without a Postcard (Aus. CBS) 1981 (Columbia) 1990
10,9,8,7,6,5,4,3,2,1 (Columbia) 1983
Red Sails in the Sunset (Columbia) 1985
Species Deceases EP (Aus. CBS) 1985 (Columbia) 1990
Diesel and Dust (Columbia) 1987
Blue Sky Mining (Columbia) 1990
Scream in Blue Live (Columbia) 1992
Earth and Sun and Moon (Columbia) 1993
Breathe (Work) 1996

The advantages of a Midnight Oil live album over a Midnight Oil concert are obvious: you get all the anthemic passion and none of the distraction—specifically, the spastic calisthenics of gangly singer Peter Garrett. **Scream in Blue Live** recaps the righteous Australian rockers' twenty-year career with a dozen performances of their rousing best, dating back to 1982 and ranging geographically from a theater in Sydney to a flat-bed truck in midtown Manhattan. Time has generally been good to the Oils, as the group has learned—both on record and onstage—to present its political anger as confident grand drama rather than desperate zeal. Smartly sequenced to flow like a single show and buttress the least compelling songs with the sturdiest, the album gives good play to such artful fist-wavers as "Read About It" (from **10,9,8,7,6,5,4,3,2,1** the quintet's masterwork), "Beds Are Burning" (a stirring call to return land to the Aborigines from **Diesel and Dust,** another top-rank album), "Stars of Warburton" (one of the few songs to hit the mark cleanly on **Blue Sky Mining**) and the anti-nuclear/pro-activism "Hercules" (from the four-song **Species Deceases**). A fine introduction to an invigorating if occasionally overbearing band.

Maturity has significantly improved the Oils' methodology, but it's been accompanied by a distinct decline in the group's creativity. Following the arc of **Diesel and Dust** and **Blue Sky Mining, Earth and Sun and Moon** continues the slow slide that began in the mid-'80s; although the bottom has yet to fall out, Midnight Oil just doesn't write 'em like they used to. Co-producer Nick Launay settles the band into a sonic easy chair as Garrett sings lazy, routine lyrics like an outdated codger passing the torch. "Renaissance man are you ready/See what a world that you can make," is his most optimistic view, mirror-imaged by "The world is crashing down on me tonight . . . I know this is the end of the beginning of the outbreak of love." "God knows it's been fun," he opines in the memoir-like appraisal of "Feeding Frenzy." Even the topicals (the environmental title track, the monarchy-attacking "Truganinni") lack the usual bite. Only the folky family history of "In the Valley" has the kind of stand-up-and-be-counted chorus on which the group's reputation rests, and it's tucked away near the end of the album. Going, going . . . [i]

See also *TPRG.*

MIGHTY LEMON DROPS

Happy Head (Sire) 1986
Out of Hand (Sire) 1987
Janice Long Session EP (UK Nighttracks/Strange Fruit) 1987
World Without End (Sire/Reprise) 1988
Laughter (Sire/Reprise) 1989
Sound . . . (Sire/Reprise) 1991
Ricochet (Sire) 1992
All the Way (UK Overground) 1993

It took the Mighty Lemon Drops (initially the Sherbert Monsters) three albums to fully outgrow its original fixation on Echo and the Bunnymen. While hardly a disqualifying attribute in itself, the sonic resemblance on **Happy Head** and **Out of Hand** (later combined on a single CD) make it hard to take the enjoyable young quartet from Wolverhampton seriously. **World Without End,** warmly produced by Tim Palmer, is a more mature, sophisticated and individualized effort, but Paul Marsh still sings as if he's trying to impress either Ian McCulloch or Jim Morrison.

The departure of original bassist/co-writer Tony Linehan in the early stages of **Laughter** left guitarist David Newton to come up with nearly all the material on his own. He did, and that was all it took to finally disconnect the band from its original impulses; the accent on **Laughter** is in line with the psychedelically tinged pop joy of Stone Roses' debut, released in the same year. Intricately overdubbed vocal arrangements, excellent guitar playing and impossibly catchy choruses make every long song a rich, cleverly sustained delight. "Into the Heart of Love," "Where Do We Go From Heaven," "Second Time Around" and "The Real World" (more likely a nod to Peter Gabriel's studio, where the album was recorded, than the not-yet-created MTV show) are not so much standouts as simply the most instantly memorable items of an altogether great album that remains by far the band's best.

Sound . . . finds the Mighty Lemon Drops blowing in the stylistic breeze to drift uncertainly down a rockier, semi-danceable cobblestone path. (It may be worth noting, if there's a thesis to be mounted here, that Newton came up with half the songs himself and the rest in collaboration with various permutations of the group and producer Andy Paley; his unaided creations tend to be more purely pop-directed.) Stumbling through faint stabs at blues, beat-era rock'n'roll and ravedelia, the group sounds lost and bored, a plight exacerbated by the dire production, which is not only flat and sloppy but inconsistent at that. The album comes to life in fits and starts—coughing up "Big Surprise," "Annabelle" and "Unkind" as a cruel reminder of **Laughter**'s virtues—but is otherwise a cheerless drag.

The solemn faces pictured, and the Newtonian songwriting credits listed, on **Ricochet** suggest a chastened combo determined not to botch another album. What's in the grooves confirms a safe, solid return—to the careful, clearly detailed sound of Manchester acid-pop. Atmospheric layers of echoey vocals and distorted guitars invigorate nicely shaped songs—alternately lazy and soaring—that make do without **Laughter**'s wide-eyed innocence yet still manage an encouraging romanticism. Dreamy guest vocals by Susie Hug on "Nothing" and "Falling Deep" (which she co-wrote with Newton) are a big plus, as are the occasional keyboard intrusions by sessioneer John Barry Douce. Nice one.

All the Way is a strange appendix: a 1990 live recording from Cincinnati mixed with a handful of 1986 demos. [i]

See also *TPRG.*

MIGHTY MIGHTY BOSSTONES

Devils Night Out (Taang!) 1990
The Mighty Mighty Bosstones EP (Taang!) 1991
More Noise & Other Disturbances (Taang!) 1992
Ska-Core, the Devil and More (Mercury) 1993
Don't Know How to Party (Mercury) 1993
Question the Answers (Mercury) 1994

There's surely a book to be written on the mysterious historical adhesion of ska and punk. The inexplicable solidarity of faintly related (by virtue of velocity) musics and distantly removed cultures somehow traveled through several generations of English skins to spark the early-'80s uprising of 2-Tone bands like the Specials, Madness and the Selecter. A few years later, with ska fully isolated from its Jamaican roots and its leading revivalists moving on to other pop rhythms, the phenomenon alit in Boston, where the Mighty Mighty Bosstones picked up the hybrid's banner. As the most visible major-label proponents of America's resilient and flourishing grassroots ska scene, the group competes for young goodtime fun-seekers with hippie jam bands, yet offers a distinctive and febrile enough alternative to get invited onto 1995's Lollapalooza (whatever that proves).

Recorded as a scruffy six-piece, **Devils Night Out** is a strong and confident debut. The common hazard with bands that graft forms together is that fans never know how much of each component they're going to get, and the Bosstones, on record anyway, have frequently shown more devotion to bludgeoning hard rock than bluebeat. (Live, they make like an early Madness tribute band.) **Devils Night Out** is a some-of-this-and-some-of-that joint free of the stylistic ambition that has since messed up their focus. A couple of minutes into the opening track's grubby hardcore, the band suddenly shifts into a brisk pick-it-up beat, and that's about the size of it, although there are some out-and-out punk numbers that don't change direction and "The Cave" stays away from the rock channel. Dicky Barrett's gargly lead vocals are punkily gruesome, but tight, imaginative rock-hard arrangements (with guest trombonist Davey Holmes joining the lone on-board horn man, saxophonist Tim Burton) and boisterous, nearly humorous lyrics ("Hope I Never Lose My Wallet," "A Little Bit Ugly," "Do Somethin' Crazy," "The Bartender's Song") keep the spirited jam moving.

Before making their second album (again co-produced by Paul Q. Kolderie), the Bosstones wacked out an untitled EP (referred to as **Where'd You Go?** because of that song's pole position) of two originals and three rock covers: Aerosmith's "Sweet Emotion" (which ends up sounding like the Dictators), a roaringly reverent rendition of Metallica's "Enter Sandman" and Van Halen's "Ain't Talkin' 'Bout Love," complete with Nate Albert's bargain-bin Eddie V licks.

Signed to Mercury as a better-dressed octet with three full-time brass-blowers, the Bosstones equivocate heavily on the self-produced seven-song mini-album, **Ska-Core, the Devil and More.** Covering Minor Threat, SSD and the Angry Samoans (all inside five minutes), they're flat-out speedpunks with horn breaks; digging into Bob Marley's pre-reggae catalogue, they do a jazzy bluebeat job on "Simmer Down," letting second vocalist Ben Carr spell Barrett (who only sounds right bellowing punk) on a few lines. They also take a live run at two tracks and deliver their mightiest original yet, "Someday I Suppose," a catchy and well-integrated rock-ska ode to uncertainty.

Metal veteran Tony Platt produced the misbegotten **Don't Know How to Party,** gaining the plaid-clad band a devastating guitar and drum sound while reducing ska's role to a stylistic accent—a rhythmic variation that gives the horns something to do. "What Was Over," the most concerted effort in that direction, is half-hearted and quickly abandoned. Encouraging the band's rock mainstreaming might have worked out if the charge had been applied to equally high-voltage songwriting. Except for "Holy Smoke," Stiff Little Fingers' "Tin Soldiers" and an inferior remake of "Someday I Suppose," the turgid songs are like dead bodies being plugged in to make them twitch.

Getting Kolderie back for the bulk of **Question the Answers** (the Butcher Brothers did three tracks) was a smart move: he helped pave the band's way home to an organic blend of its better impulses on what is by far the Bosstones' best album. The group skates comfortably around a pit of pure ska-pop, funk and unmitigated thrash (frequently piling the pieces together with seamless skill), scooping horn charts into the unlikeliest places and pressing it all into service of thoughtful, well-crafted singalongs. "A Sad Silence," "Hell of a Hat," "Pictures to Prove It," "Toxic Toast" and "Bronzing the Garbage" are among the blaring highlights. [i]

MIKE & RICH

See *Aphex Twin.*

MILES DETHMUFFEN

Nine-Volt Grape (Presto) 1990
Clutter (Rainbow Quartz) 1994
Miles Dethmuffen EP (Summerville) 1995

Boston's underappreciated Miles Dethmuffen proudly wear their skinny-tie new wave influences on their sleeves, to the point of declaring on one song that they "believe in the '80s." Indeed, the four bandmembers are unwavering in their love of happy hooks, jangling melodies and clever wordplay. Produced by Paul Q. Kolderie, the terrific **Nine-Volt Grape** positively snaps and crackles with no-frills guitar-pop energy, kicking off with the ridiculously upbeat "In Clover." Bassist Linda Bean P. serves as the passionate honest heart to guitarist Ad Frank's terminal wiseacre, as the two swap lead vocals and engage in classic boy/girl-group harmonies. Though it's almost impossible to choose among the record's many witty and pointedly charming songs, standouts include Frank's puckish feminist rallying cry (of sorts), "The Wandering Sexist Rogue Meets Miles Dethmuffen's Fabulous Hammered Dulcimer," the wallflower's lament of "Mike Foley's All Night Party" and the bittersweet relationship-in-crisis melodrama, "Cohabitants."

The years following **Nine-Volt Grape** yielded just one single, 1992's very wonderful "Mouth of Hell" b/w "Painting the Bridge." The band's long-time-coming sophomore LP, **Clutter,** however, is somewhat of a misstep. While not bad by any stretch, **Clutter** has a darker demeanor; the once-sprightly sound suffers from John C. Wood's monochromatic rock production. Still, the album features some of the shiniest jewels in the Dethmuffen crown: Linda's anthemic "Loveman, We Love You" and the perky-but-sad "Sleeping Bag" (both dating from '92 Kolderie sessions), as well as Ad's plaintive "Hope I Don't Spend All My Money on Liquor."

The eponymous '95 EP is a definite return to form. Wood remains behind the board, only this time the church bells chime, the guitars glimmer and the choruses are deliciously catchy. With swell pop delights like Frank's heartwrenched arena ballad "White After Labor Day" and Bean P.'s jittery "Dying to Hear From You," the six-track disc is an ideal representation of Miles Dethmuffen's brainy Beantown power pop. [mgk]

MILK CULT

See *Steel Pole Bath Tub.*

MILLA

The Divine Comedy (SBK) 1994

On the pecking order of likely prospects to make the worst vanity-project album imaginable, waifish teenage fashion models fall somewhere between stars' drug dealers and relatives of Bill Gates. Kiev native Milla Jovovich's desire to make a record is a mild surprise; that she had the nerve to write all of the lyrics and some of the music would seem to be a major risk. But the crowning shocker of **The Divine Comedy**—a folky and grown-up pop tapestry sung in a fine, skilled voice—is that it's genuinely good. No, *really.* Not just good for an eighteen-year-old model, but good for anyone—a record album by a talented young woman possessing all the prerequisite aptitudes to make credible record albums.

Like some medieval princess delivered into a modern recording studio, Milla displays classical romantic sensibilities, describing a timeless kingdom of pale lips, burning fires, falling skies and breaking hearts. (That the only actual folk song here is in Russian doesn't deter Milla's penchant for Anglo-Saxon stylings.) Set into handsome arrangements of strings, pennywhistle, acoustic guitar, dulcimer, harmonium, mandolin and piano played by Anglo-American studio pros like Eric Bazilian of the Hooters, Rupert Hine, Ethan James and Phil Palmer, words like "pavement" ("The Alien Song") and "freak" ("Charlie") provide the only lyrical clues that Milla is not a devout traditionalist. **The Divine Comedy** is a throwback to English art-rock like Renaissance, Traffic's **John Barleycorn Must Die** and Jethro Tull's **Minstrel in the Gallery.** (Comparisons to Steeleye Span or Fairport Convention would be misleading, as this is too glibly modern a production to make any convincing folk pretense.) Highly enjoyable for what it is and stunning for what it isn't (namely awful), **The Divine Comedy** achieves the unthinkable: it makes the possibility of a sequel welcome. [i]

DONALD MILLER

See *Borbetomagus.*

MINDFUNK

Mind Funk (Epic) 1991
Dropped (Megaforce) 1993

Guitarist Jason Everman, a onetime member of both Nirvana and Soundgarden (not that his role in either amounted to anything), is the calling card of this misleadingly named big-rocking quintet, though you wouldn't have known it on **Mind Funk,** the band's Spinal Tapped lunk-o-metal debut, which bills him as Jason Coppola. (Is that a dig at Nicolas Cage?)

Everman dropped the pseudonym after the band parted ways with Epic, so it's not clear which led to the title of **Dropped,** a competent and tasteful but undistinguished second album produced in generic northwest style by Terry Date. Making good use of spacious dynamic variety and respecting the songs rather than attempting to cover them over, Everman and Louis Svitek whip up smartly modulated guitar noise, bolstered by a strong, slightly stiff rhythm section and functional tunes. The weak link (besides the lyrics) is singer Patrick Dubar—he's adequate but not powerful or distinctive enough to drive it all home. Willing to settle for trying popular sounds rather than seek a compelling personality, Mindfunk has a ways to go before becoming more than a historical footnote. [i]

See also *Nirvana, Soundgarden.*

MIND SCIENCE OF THE MIND

See *Shudder to Think.*

MINISTRY

With Sympathy (Arista) 1983
'Twitch' (Sire) 1986
Twelve Inch Singles 1981–1984 (Wax Trax!) 1987
The Land of Rape and Honey (Sire) 1988
The Mind Is a Terrible Thing to Taste (Sire) 1989
In Case You Didn't Feel Like Showing Up (Live) EP (Sire) 1990
Psalm 69 (Sire/Warner Bros.) 1992
Filth Pig (Warner Bros.) 1996

Although Cuban-born Alain Jourgensen launched Ministry in Chicago as an obnoxiously collegiate modern-dance alliance, he didn't stop there and wound up becoming a leading pioneer of industrial noise, ripping up rock's floorboards with a maniacally harsh intensity rarely heard outside sheetmetal factories. It took a while for him to move from point A to point B, but once Jourgensen reached meltdown potential, there was no restraining Ministry. The group became a beehive of spinoff activity (issuing forth Revolting Cocks, Pigface, Lard, Pailhead, 1000 Homo DJs and many other bands) and a crucial source of stylistic inspiration. It's safe to assume that Nine Inch Nails would never have gotten where it is had Jourgensen not gone out on the sonic limb first.

Since repudiated by Jourgensen as the product of label coercion, **With Sympathy** is sophomoric yuppie-funk: brutish singing and scanty, derivative ideas overstretched by numbing repetition. Most heinously, "I Wanted to Tell Her" chants the title lyric like a litany, as does "Work for Love," which adds moronic lyrics to the numbing two-chord vamp. Fortunately, that was the end of Ministry's polite attempts at dancefloor accessibility. Produced by Adrian Sherwood, the transitional **'Twitch'** takes the first steps into a murky swamp that subsumes Jourgensen's distorted, nearly spoken vocals within a pounding onslaught of electronic rhythms, found-sound tape bits and scratch-mix noise effects.

Ministry's triumphant emergence in **The Land of Rape and Honey** is heralded by "Stigmata," a queasy synth riff and a blood-curdling shriek. Co-produced by Jourgensen (calling himself Hypo Luxa) and bassist/keyboardist Paul Barker (Hermes Pan)—Ministry's two official members—the album steps off the ledge of rock convention for an unnervingly powerful assault. William Rieflin's thundering drums underpin burning layers of sound, leaving Jourgensen's deranged vocals fighting frantically to be heard. **The Land of Rape and Honey** is a spectacular monument to man's capacity for ugliness.

The Mind Is a Terrible Thing to Taste compresses that explosive energy into a tightly wound punk-guitar attack that constantly threatens an explosive catastrophe. If less chaotically unpredictable than its predecessor, the album is no less obsessive in its diabolical power. When Jourgensen chant-roars the title of "Breathe" over and over, obedience seems like the safest course. Chris Connelly (of Fini Tribe and the Revolting Cocks) sings lead on "Cannibal Song" and "Never Believe."

Six songs with a running time exceeding forty minutes, **In Case You Didn't Feel Like Showing Up (Live)** is a speaker-shredding souvenir of Ministry's 1989–90 North American tour, a memorable extravaganza that saw as many as nine musicians—including drummer Martin Atkins and Skinny Puppy's Nivek Ogre—onstage. Storming through a devastating précis of the two previous LPs, this incarnation of Ministry is a punishing beast, furiously thrashing to a runaway piledriver beat.

As other bands (and horror movies) began to catch up with and even surpass the brutality of Ministry's overkill, the duo stuck to its guns, ignoring the potential for self-parody, redundancy and the gravitational pull of speed metal with a sensual racket of an album whose title appears only in hand-written Greek. (Officially, it's known as **Psalm 69,** with an unlisted and unexplained subtitle of *The Way to Succeed and the Way to Suck Eggs.*) Amid the shred guitar, jackhammer drums (Ministry has made a virtual religion of unaccented rhythms), samples and cruelly torn vocals of such nihilist outbursts as "Just One Fix," "N.W.O.," "Hero" and "Corrosion," one-song guest Gibby Haynes of the Butthole Surfers makes an inspired choice of collaborator. On a samey album that upholds the band's creative convictions rather than advance any new ideas, Haynes raises the ante appreciably on "Jesus Built My Hotrod," which he co-wrote and sings.

The long layoff between albums—accompanied by a temporary change of locale to Austin—didn't recharge Jourgensen, it aged him. Meanwhile, the competition had consolidated its power, leaving Ministry sounding rattled and unsteady on its feet. **Filth Pig** has some of the old bark, but the bite is mainly a memory. Sounding more like Suicidal Tendencies or Rollins Band in the thrash-rappy "Dead Guys" and "Crumbs," Ministry (getting its last work from Bill Rieflin, who was replaced mid-project by Rey Washam, most recently of the Didjits) goes through its paces—the chanted antagonism of "Useless," the blunt instrument riff moving "Lava" along—like a slow-witted fighter, displaying none of the old heart or fervor. The pointless exercise of covering Dylan's "Lay Lady Lay" as reverently as possible further undercuts the band's personality and credibility; "Brick Window" is a good enough song to end with, but the performance allows the final bell to ring without landing any solid blows. [i]

See also *Jello Biafra, Blohole, Chris Connelly, Pigface, Revolting Cocks, Skinny Puppy, Supersuckers; TPRG.*

MINK DEVILLE

See *Willy DeVille.*

MINUS 5

See *Young Fresh Fellows.*

MIRANDA SEX GARDEN

Madra (Mute) 1991
Iris EP (Mute) 1992
Suspiria (Mute) 1992
Fairytales of Slavery (Mute) 1994

Discovered by Barry Adamson singing madrigals for shillings on Portobello Road and used in his *Delusion* soundtrack, London's Miranda Sex Garden didn't have to change their tune when the rarely backward-looking Mute Records signed the three young women to inject a little old-fashioned Art into the business of modern music. Armed with an attractive look, an adequately hip attitude, a provocative name—it's hard to imagine the home of Einstürzende Neubauten, Wire and Depeche Mode showing as much interest in a blandly titled bunch of middle-aged enthusiasts from some jerkwater church group—and a sheaf of seventeenth-century English songs, music students Jocelyn West, Kelly McCusker and Katharine Blake first held forth on **Madra,** a collection of reverent a cappella renditions of such ancient oldies as "It Was a Lover and His Lass," "Though My Carriage Be but Careless" and "Away, Thou Shalt Not Love Me."

After that offbeat start, the group began developing toward contemporary rock. West left and was replaced by singer/violist Donna McKevitt; guitarist/organist Ben Golomstock and drummer Trevor Sharpe joined; McCusker and Blake brought out their violins, and the group collectively wrote four of the five songs that compose the exploratory **Iris.** The group's muse wasn't quite ready to be set free, however: the lyrics are precious little poems that could have been punched out by some Romantic madlib computer, the melodies merely a trellis on which to weave the intricate harmonies. Efforts to mount a pop-group sound (as in "Fear") are too rarefied to breathe, while the pointillist exercise "Falling" and the all-atmosphere "Blue Light" pluck hovering cascades of voices and instruments out of the air without benefit of forward momentum. Unbearable.

The quintet got its bearings, however, and emerged on **Suspiria** as an intriguing, challenging art felon dancing eccentrically near the fringes of goth. Reconfiguring itself for each song, MSG shifts comfortably between string-driven rock and more exotic mixtures, allowing the three soaring sopranos—who are capable of summoning up memories of both '70s progressives Renaissance and a sedated Diamanda Galás—to dominate regardless. Now capable of revving up a blustery cloud of edgy energy, the group also has a firm grip on silence: Nick Cave's nicotined fingers seem to be riding the narcoleptic controls of "My Funny Valentine." (The album's other cover is a song from *Eraserhead.*)

McCusker was the next to go. As if to compensate for her departure, MSG rented a bass guitarist and got Neubauten's Alex Hacke to produce **Fairytales of Slavery.** The confident, adventurous and *loud* rock record sets Blake's ethereal voice against lumbering rhythms, sonic pattycake and driving electric textures. (Hacke's industrial bandmate, F. M. Einheit, plays guest "drill" on one song, and "stones" on another.) Blake's lyrics still don't amount to much—for all the album's titular and graphic provocation, "A Fairytale About Slavery" is an idle and innocuous six-line inquiry, while the wordless vocals of "The Monk Song" are more suggestive and gripping than any literal singing here—but the sensual power of the Mirandas' fervent music is fantastic. [i]

See also *Barry Adamson.*

M.I.R.V.

Cosmodrome (Prawn Song/Mammoth) 1994

LIMBOMANIACS

Stinky Grooves (In Effect) 1990

Co-produced, engineered, played on and issued by Les Claypool, the album by Primus pal M.I.R.V. (Mark Haggard, formerly a guitarist in the Limboniacs, an efficient but obnoxious funk/rap joke whose **Stinky Grooves** is fairly summarized by its title) is a ridiculous smoking-cornsilk concept album with the same sort of Zappa-meets-the-Firesign-Theater sniggering and hallucinatory dislocation that afflicts Primus, but with a bit less virtuoso bluster. Spoken parts and phone calls in goofy voices by assorted characters, sound effects, jazzy instrumental interludes and a few actual songs add up to the kind of stupid amusement good for a few well-baked chuckles in the college dorm. Once. Maybe. [i]

See also *Primus.*

MISS ALANS

Smack the Horse (Genius/Rough Trade) 1990
All Hail Discordia (Duck Butter Music) 1991
Blusher (Zoo) 1994
Big Sun EP10 (Mach) 1995
Ledger (World Domination) 1996

The Miss Alans formed at Fresno State University, majoring in dreamy pop with minors in R.E.M. jangle and lightweight psychedelia. **Smack the Horse** is a more apt representation of the band's technique than **All Hail Discordia,** which was recorded and mixed live to 2-track in a club and has a rushed, uneven quality to both the performances and production. Both albums highlight Miss Alans' strengths, though: rhythm guitarist Scott Oliver's wavery, hickoid vocals, Manny Diez's piercing guitar leads, delicately crafted pop tunes and a subtle fascination with music's cosmic edges. Plus, **All Hail Discordia** has the group turning Ted Nugent's macho-rock "Great White Buffalo" into a trippy power-pop stream with gnawing slide guitar and a gullible vocal.

Blusher is a major improvement, a calm clarification and expansion of the quartet's sound—credit maturity, experience, adequate studio time and producer Tracy Chisholm, who's worked with Belly. Oliver's singing is far stronger and more assured, able to focus a simple electric pop song like "Mag Wheel" or the acoustic "Blurry Doll" to fine effect. But the gentle thrust of the album is in its blissed-out soft guitar washes—think British shoegazers like Spiritualized in a quiet phase—which provide laconic accompaniment to the tear-stained, often bitter but sometimes sanguine lyrics. Appealing and atmospheric numbers like "State of Grace," the low-key "Supercharged" and "Winona" paint Miss Alans in pretty pastels with an emotional undertow; "Patti Smith Fan Club" and "The Sad Last Days of Elvis Aron Presley" adjoin celebrities to broader topics with poetic intelligence.

After parting ways with Zoo, the Miss Alans made a four-song 10-inch for an independent label and then signed with World Domination, which released **Ledger** the following summer. [vg]

MR. BUNGLE

See *Faith No More.*

MR. HAGEMAN

See *Thinking Fellers Union Local 282.*

MR. RIGHT & MR. WRONG

See *NoMeansNo.*

MR. T EXPERIENCE

Everybody's Entitled to Their Own Opinion (Disorder) 1986 (Lookout!) 1995
Night Shift at the Thrill Factory (6th Int'l/Rough Trade) 1987 (Lookout!) 1996
Big Black Bugs Bleed Blue Blood (Rough Trade) 1989
Making Things With Light (Lookout!) 1990
Milk Milk Lemonade (Lookout!) 1992
Gun Crazy EP7 (Lookout!) 1993
Our Bodies Our Selves (Lookout!) 1994
The Mr T Experience! . . . and the Women Who Love Them (Lookout!) 1995
Alternative Is Here to Stay EP (Lookout!) 1995
Love Is Dead (Lookout!) 1996

Talk about your unsung heroes. Northern California's Operation Ivy may get the textbook credit for shaping impressionable Berkeley/East Bay minds, but the Mr. T Experience (aka MTX and, lately, MTX "Starship") was cranking out a premium grade of grabby pop-punk on the now-legendary Gilman Street scene (even singing about the club by name) well before Green Day started playing there. After an on-off decade of jokey pop-culture celebrations, wistful romantic complications, political satire, grand schemes and stupid ideas, singer/guitarist Dr. Frank (Portman) is still at it, older and wiser but keeping his musical scalpel sharp and wielding it with uncompromised enthusiasm.

The self-released first album (recorded and mixed in a single July day) is sloppy mid-tempo punk that leaves tunefulness a goal more than an actual quality. "Danny Partridge" (a song about Danny Bonaduce's drug bust), "I'm in Love With Paula Pierce" (a Kinksy mash note to a Pandora), a cover of the Monkees' "Pleasant Valley Sunday" and the toe-curling hyper-instrumental "Surfin' Cows" are easy highlights of an entertaining but not fully baked debut.

Changing drummers and getting Kent Steedman of the Celibate Rifles in to produce, the quartet cut the faster, harder and more love-minded seventeen-song **Night Shift at the Thrill Factory,** adding "Skatin' Cows" to the wordless repertoire and such sensitive reflections as "Now We Are Twenty-One," "Dick With Ears" and "(Cause I Love You and I) Don't Know What I'll Do If You Don't (Love Me Too)." Showboating his education to a manic rock'n'roll beat, Dr. Frank rams through "The History of the Concept of the Soul" (complete with footnotes) and the more simply existential "A Zillion Years" with the un-self-conscious abandon of a smart guy who doesn't care if people think he's a geek. Besides the ode to "Gilman Street," the seven-song **Big Black Bugs Bleed Blue Blood** addresses an obvious influence ("End of the Ramones") and indulges the Doc's gentler side in "Song About a Girl Who Went Shopping."

Concurrent with a label switch to the band's long-term group home, **Making Things With Light** finally brings Dr. Frank's melodic designs to fruition: from the wonderful leadoff "What Went Wrong," producer Kevin Army (who has worked on all of the band's day-shift albums) pushes the vocals to the fore, compressing the roaring rhythm guitars to a loud, clear supporting role. But while the music is appreciably stronger and smarter than usual, Dr. Frank has abandoned topicality, writing a little about himself ("I'm Breaking Out," "I Don't Get It") and a lot about sick relationships ("She's No Rocket Scientist," "Parasite," "So Long, Sucker," "Psycho Girl"). The multilingual "Pig Latin" and the cameo portrait of "The Girl Who Still Lives at Home" are the only truly characteristic songs, although rhythm guitarist Jon von does contribute the rote-punk grievances of "Zero."

Moving a giant step forward in instrumental complexity, **Milk Milk Lemonade** intertwines guitars and voices with more care, skill and diversity than the band has ever previously displayed. Departing from standard pop-punk, "Two-Minute Itch" is rootsabilly raunch; "Christine Bactine" riffs its way into hard rock. Elsewhere, Dr. Frank invests heavily in simple, effective melodies (check the catchy surf-twisting "Last Time I Listened to You" and the Dickiesesque "I Love You but You're Standing on My Foot") and expresses intriguing lyrical concepts economically. "Ready Set Go" matter-of-factly describes "the normal progression / Starts with love and affection / Goes on to sick obsession"; "Make Up," "What Do You Want?" and "See It Now" deal deftly with hard interpersonal issues. The Smiths' "What Difference Does It Make?" both deserves and survives the rough handling it gets here.

After that high point of intricacy and stylistic ambition, MTX broke up, regrouped without co-founder Jon von (who went on to record with the masked Rip Offs) and cranked out an EP and album before dissolving again. Wisely opting not to overcompensate with too much of everything, the trio can't duplicate **Milk Milk Lemonade**'s relatively fancy arrangements on **Our Bodies Our Selves** (although the intricate "Personality Seminar" comes close), and instead focuses on solidly melodic songs that keep the energy and genial aggression at manageable levels. Surprisingly, there's a pair of solo acoustic numbers, including "Even Hitler Had a Girlfriend," a comic plaint of loneliness that sounds like a whinge John Otway would write. If the record suffers a bit for the band's shakiness, Dr. Frank's creative momentum and consistently improving songwriting—see "The Dustbin of History," "More Than Toast" and "Game Over"—carry him through. In a heartwarming nod to MTX tradition, there's even a nifty instrumental ("Bridge to Taribithia") and a Ramoned version of Donna Summer's "I Feel Love."

After further personnel shifts, MTX settled more comfortably into the six-legged format and essentially relaunched itself as a pure pop-punk outfit. Billed as MTX "Starship" for **. . . And the Women Who Love Them,** the group mounts a sizzling and streamlined three-chord rhythm guitar attack on the six touching electric songs of self-flagellation and heartbreak. (The seventh, "Now That You Are Gone," is another one-man, one-guitar moan.) At this point in the band's development, presentation doesn't make that much nevermind: the material is good enough to shine without any instrumental buffing. "My Stupid Life," "All My Promises" and the positively winsome "Tapin' Up My Heart" highlight this winning case of loss.

Perhaps emboldened by the mersh success of East Bay rock (or at least positively irritated by it, as evidenced by the deadpan anthem "Alternative Is Here to Stay" that appears twice on the four-track EP of the same name), Dr. Frank and a half-new rhythm section fill **Love Is Dead** with nothing but loud, catchy and lovable singalongs, roaringly produced by Army as if he were erecting the sonic safety barrier around a particularly dangerous radioactive dumpsite. Sturdily supported by the unbreachable wall o'rock, the sardonic "Dumb Little Band," an incisive and unglamorous why-we-rock self-portrait, admits failure but not defeat: "Our friends are busy with their own affairs becoming punk rock millionaires / They're taping their live album at the Hollywood Bowl / We're taping our flyers to the telephone pole." That grimsmirk spirit infects the whole wonderful album, which mates spunk, hooks and insightful intelligence as if inventing a new musical form. Dr. Frank may not be doing any better with women than he is with the band (witness the teenaged frustration of "I'm Like Yeah, but She's All No"), but the competing forces in his life make for one hell of an album. "I don't want to get screwed over by just anyone—you're the only one I want to get screwed over by." Likewise, I'm sure. [i]

See also *TPRG*.

MOBERLYS

Jim Basnight and the Moberlys (Safety First) 1980
Jim Basnight and the Moberlys EP (Precedent) 1984

First Album (Precedent) 1995
Sexteen (Ger. ATM) 1995

JIM BASNIGHT

Pop Top (Precedent) 1993
Retro [tape] (no label) 1993
B-Sides [tape] (no label) 1994
Total Shit [tape] (no label) 1994

ROCKINGHAMS

Rockinghams Roughs EP [tape] (Precedent) 1994
Monsters of Rock [tape] (Precedent) 1995
Monsters of Rock EP (Precedent) 1996

Seattle power-pop pioneer Jim Basnight led the Moberlys visibly in the late '70s and nearly out of sight for another decade; the original quartet was over by the time its album of sparkling mid-tempo tunes was assembled and released. In the mid-'90s, while the singer/guitarist was recording and performing solo and with the Rockinghams, Basnight repackaged eight tracks from the Moberlys' album with six others (ignoring the intervening EP) and issued them as **First Album.** Not surprisingly, the delightfully surf-boppin' "Live in the Sun" moves up to lead off the CD, which is a catchy and illustrative document of the Northwest's musical past. Expanded for German release with nicer packaging, the twenty-three-track **Sexteen** adds back two more from the old album and digs seven more out of the vaults to assemble the most complete Moberlys collection ever.

Miles from the Moberlys' elementary adolescent exuberance, Basnight's **Pop Top** is an accomplished adult record—albeit an unevenly eclectic and commercial-minded one that runs a gamut from pretty pop to smarmy radio rock. His songwriting has developed in a number of different directions, and parts of the skillful album don't sound that different from a smarter indie analogue of Tom Petty, Bob Seger, John Mellencamp or Bon Jovi. Perhaps exchanging one era's stars for another's is inevitable, but **Pop Top** isn't very much fun. Four unpretentious guitar-rockers produced by Peter Buck of R.E.M. are easily the album's best: the echo-drenched simplicity of "Hello Mary Jane," "Evil Touch" and the magnificently melodic "Restless Night" connect Basnight to his past without having to relive it.

Randomly constructed and meaninglessly titled, the solo cassettes (sold by mail if no other way) don't offer any information about their sources or intent. Each album-length tape contains unfamiliar, presumably new, material (the best is **Total Shit**'s "Bare My Soul," with nervy, defensive lyrics) along with old tracks from the first Moberlys album; **Retro** includes an extra-big helping of those, plus all four songs from the Moberlys' 1984 EP and an early version of the Rockinghams' "Uncertain." In any case, all of the music keeps to the same pop-rock straight and narrow, so it doesn't much matter what came from where.

The Rockinghams, Basnight's trio with bassist Jack Hanan and ex-Muffs drummer Criss Crass, is spunkier and less obviously eager to join the mainstream—and that's good. In a typically inexplicable sequence of record releases, the twelve-song **Monsters of Rock** tape (which supplants the six-song **Roughs** tape and contains all five songs drawn off for the **Monsters of Rock** CD EP, which has identical artwork in addition to the same title—not *too* confusing) starts off with traditional electric pop (shades of the Plimsouls) but quickly moves into smeary glam-rock (debt to the Dolls), surging boogie ("Uncertain") and chunky riff power ("Hello Mary Jane," a song also on **Pop Top**). Nothing new, but not bad.

In '95 the multifarious Basnight co-wrote the songs for *Little Rock*, a civil-rights musical staged by the Seattle Children's Theatre. [i]

See also *Muffs*.

MOBY

Go Remixes EP (Instinct) 1991
Moby (Instinct) 1992
Early Underground (Instinct) 1993
Ambient (Instinct) 1993
Move EP (Elektra) 1993
Everything Is Wrong (Elektra) 1995
Disc EP (Elektra) 1995
Everything Is Wrong (DJ Mix Album) (UK Mute) 1996
Rare: The Collected B-Sides (Instinct) 1996

Richard Melville Hall wears many different brightly colored hats; a list of his characteristics reads like outlandish fiction. This born-again Christian vegan who doesn't even kill the cockroaches in his New York City loft creates amazing techno, soul and jungle music. But he began his musical career as a hardcore punk in Connecticut's Vatican Commandos and performs live as a guitar-wielding or keyboard-pounding rocker, not a rarefied electronics controller. Like Richard James (Aphex Twin) or Michael Paradinas (*μ*-Ziq), Moby is a true innovator, making the mold even as he's breaking it. Although nominally a "techno artist," Moby dabbles in a wide panoply of musical styles.

Moby's first 12-inch vinyl releases ("Next Is the E," "Drop a Beat," "Go") were released on the New York dance independent Instinct, which later collected them on three CDs: **Moby, Early Underground** and **Rare.** The first contains "Go," which sets Angelo Badalamenti's *Twin Peaks* theme swooping softly against a rhythm track. (The **Go Remixes** EP features several different takes on "Go," most of which differ substantially from each other.) These early songs are primarily fast-paced dance tracks, using samples and synthesizers to carry the distinctively plentiful melodies. **Moby** begins with the hammering repetition of "Drop a Beat," which is classic techno: fast, fast, fast, with whistles and a repeated sample. Although most of the tracks don't break away from standard formulae, his compositional flair shines through. **Ambient** demonstrates Moby's vision of ambient music to be as innovative as on his rhythmic music, but the record isn't as engrossing as his other work.

The six-track **Move** EP contains two dissimilar mixes (one heavy on piano) of the title track, a bubbling and mobile high-energy dance pulse with vocals by Carole Sylvan and Rozz Morehead, as well as the techno gospel of "All That I Need Is to Be Loved" (the EP gives thanks to Jesus Christ), the percussion-driven "Morning Dove," the atmospheric jungle mania of "Unloved Symphony" (which uses an orchestral passage for its bridge) and the nearly subliminal piano/ambience background of "The Rain Falls and the Sky Shudders."

Everything Is Wrong, Moby's astonishing major-label debut, reveals even more facets to his music: although there's plenty to dance to, "Hymn" is delicately beautiful, "What Love" wraps its rock center in skeletal electric-guitar blues and "All That I Need Is to Be Loved" (completely remade from the EP version) is stark hardcore industrial thrash. Even Moby's techno sounds different; "Feeling So Real" and "Everytime You Touch Me" set female diva and male dancehall vocals against massive jungle rhythms. "Bring Back My Happiness" is an infectiously catchy (and incredibly fast) dance workout. Mimi Goese (ex–Hugo Largo) sings on "Into the Blue" and "When It's Cold I'd Like to Die"; her light, airy voice fills the languidly elegant songs with mournful emotion. And Moby's passion isn't restricted to **Everything Is Wrong**'s tunes: the booklet contains a list of "Facts That I've Collected" (about such issues as meat production, pollution, fur and animal testing) and includes two essays, one of which explains the record's title and another that begins "The Christian right is neither. God is angry, I think." (The following year, Mute issued a two-CD album of remixes in the UK.)

On the technological surface, **Disc** offers only the album's "Everytime You Touch Me," a remix of "Feeling So Real" and the previously unreleased "Shining." Tap into **Disc**'s CD-ROM portion, however, and there are two more album tracks and the title cut of **Move** as well as the visuals. [mf/i]

MODERN ART

See *Sundial*.

MODERN LOVERS

See *Jonathan Richman (and the Modern Lovers)*.

MOIST

Silver (Chrysalis/EMI) 1994

Although the hot-wired guitars, dramatic tension and balls-to-the-great-unknown lyrics paint Vancouver's Moist as a big-rocking modern quartet praying to a city to the southeast, David Usher's weedy voice and a carefully controlled loud-pop sensibility suggest the spineless quintet might owe equal loyalty to the arena-kings of Toronto, Rush. Moist was able to get itself chosen for the bottom of the bill (under Hole and Metallica) at Molson's summer-of-'95 festival inside the Arctic Circle; making an album better than this turgid heap of poorly executed and derivative mediocrity, however, is evidently out of the band's reach. [i]

MOJAVE 3

See *Slowdive*.

MOLES

See *Cardinal*.

MOLLY HALF HEAD

Sulk (UK Playtime) 1993 (Columbia) 1994
Dunce (UK Columbia) 1995

This Manchester quartet, whose complex arrangements and skewed pseudo-poetry have roots in the members' avant-noise origins, produce an intricate and original post-punk roar. But despite superior instrumental chops, it's singer Paul Bardsley who remains front and center. Second only to Mark E. Smith in the Potentially Annoying Vocal Affectation Pantheon, Bardsley is fond of pronouncing almost all of his consonants as z's. That idiosyncrasy aside, **Sulk** is a revelation. Moody yet muscular, it manages to blend the tuneful dynamics of grunge with Bardsley's Smith-like inscrutable dada-esque scribblings ("Green hits a hole that just about buries me/Peeling spuds was taking five/Sad therapy? No"). The domestic blisters of "Barny" and the scarily obsessive "Taste of You" highlight a stunningly assured debut filled with songs that try to say something in a way only some listeners are likely to understand.

The more challenging sophomore effort, co-produced by Craig Leon, rocks harder as Bardsley waxes even less intelligible (imagine a drunken Zima pitchman singing the lines "In grimstitch snortel form you can't be nursed/It's time to learn to take your soup with fork"). Here's one band for whom enclosed lyric sheets are mandatory, if all but useless. [db]

MONEY MARK

See *Beastie Boys*.

MONKEYWRENCH

See *Mudhoney*.

MONKS OF DOOM

Soundtrack to the Film: "Breakfast on the Beach of Deception" (Pitch-a-Tent/Rough Trade) 1988 (IRS) 1993
The Cosmodemonic Telegraph Company (Pitch-a-Tent/Rough Trade) 1989 (IRS) 1993
Meridian (Baited Breath/Moist) 1991
The Insect God EP (C/Z) 1992
Forgery (IRS) 1992

At its peak in the mid-'80s, Northern California's Camper Van Beethoven was a strikingly precocious ensemble unable (despite regular releases) to contain the disparate enthusiasms of its members. The Monks of Doom was one of several side projects to emerge, giving a forum to bassist Victor Krummenacher, guitarist Greg Lisher, drummer Chris Pedersen and Ophelias guitarist David Immerglück (who later joined Camper). The band's first two longplayers—mildly psychedelic improvisational guitar rock, with occasional forays into jazzy ethnicity (the more song-oriented **Cosmodemonic Telegraph Company** is a big improvement; the first is mostly instrumental and has a less-distinct personality)—appeared on Camper's label, only to vanish in the miasma of distributor Rough Trade's demise.

The quartet next landed on the roster of Chapel Hill's ill-fated Baited Breath/Moist. **Meridian** does a fair job of rendering the schisms that had developed within Camper. Multi-instrumentalist Jonathan Segel brings a whimsical collection of sounds to the mix, David Lowery displays a strong country/pop songwriter's sense and Victor Krummenacher—in many ways the principal Monk—is revealed as the band's serious intellectual. **Meridian** is a curious flavor of indie prog-rock—imagine if the Grateful Dead had drifted in that direction in the early '70s. The songs don't reveal flashy instrumental skills, but are quite ambitious, almost theatrical, in construction.

Seattle's C/Z Records got the consolation prize in the Monks' post–Rough Trade sweepstakes, a five-song EP entitled **The Insect God.** Although it draws direct inspiration from Edward Gorey's book of the same title ("an admonitory tale of temptation, hapless greed, abduction and unspeakable ritualistic practices"), **The Insect God** is in many ways a lighter, not to mention more concise, outing. It also details the band's frames of reference, with covers of Syd Barrett's "Let's Split" and Frank Zappa's "Who Are the Brain Police?" for clues.

Made for yet another label, IRS (which reissued the first two albums for good measure), **Forgery** audibly benefits from a bigger recording budget. The Zappa influence is consequently more apparent. It's a tight and cleanly played record but, as with the Monks' entire oeuvre, the literate songs and sounds come too often from the head and too rarely from the heart. Or lower. [ga/ss]

See also *Counting Crows, Cracker; TPRG.*

MONO MEN

Stop Draggin' Me Down (Estrus) 1990
Booze EP (Estrus) 1991
Wrecker! (Estrus) 1992
Bent Pages (Estrus) 1993
Shut Up! EP (Estrus) 1993
Sin & Tonic (Estrus) 1994
Live at Tom's Strip n' Bowl (Estrus) 1995
Ten Cool Ones (Scat) 1996

ROOFDOGS

Pound Bound [tape] (Estrus) 1987
Having a Rave-Up With the Roofdogs EP (Estrus) 1990

Even though they're not the most primitive or "authentic" of modern-day garage bands—there's nary a single one-chord song or bowl haircut among their assets—Bellingham, Washington's Mono Men are pretty much unparalleled for sheer scope of know-how. Equally proficient in proto-punk, surf and likkered-up R&B, the quartet plays party-rock the old-fashioned way—loud, hard and until four in the morning. NRBQ, eat your hearts out!

While the Men are heard at their best on singles—if you need proof, check out one of the three dozen (!) or so they've released—there's enough dynamic sense in the band's bag of tricks to sustain an album without ramalama burnout. **Stop Draggin' Me Down** divulges that straightaway, with guitarist David Crider (who also runs Estrus, one of the '90s' pre-eminent garage labels) marshaling riffs into formations that can churn (as on the pissed-off title track) as well as tickle (the twangling "That's Her"). CD pressings append three extra tracks, including the incendiary (no pun intended) "Burning Bush" from the band's 1989 debut single. The subsequent **Booze** EP—swathed in a cover treatment that pays graphic homage to the Sonics' **Boom**—sticks to standard northwestern garage fare, but Crider and John Mortensen bang out guitar riffs with both power and clarity, a novelty in this scuzzier-than-thou genre.

Wrecker! explores the darker fringes of the genus thuddus, recalling precursors like the Music Machine in minor-chord-driven, paranoia-tinged tunes like "Took That Thing." A newfound appreciation for stereophonic sound brings out the beefy flavor imparted by the tghtasths rhythm section of Ledge Mortenson and Aaron Roeder (who slips some head-turning drum maneuvers between spates of head-down 4/4 pounding). That trend continues on **Bent Pages,** which—despite covers of both the Sonics ("Boss Hoss") and Billy Childish ("Catalina")—might be the band's most, er, mature record: the swirling "Away" sounds a lot like the Doors' pop-conscious material, while the album-closing version of the Wipers' "Over the Edge" burns with an intensity that no structure as rickety as a garage could possibly contain.

The band apparently needed a psychic breather after that, since it seems like the darkest ingredient to go into making the all-instrumental **Shut Up!** was the odd imported beer. Split evenly between originals (Crider's tremolo-crazed "Phantom on Lane 12") and covers (a wicked version of Link Wray's "Rumble"), the set goes a long way toward reclaiming non-vocal rock from the prog-hounds on the left and the lounge lizards on the right. Underground illustrator Art Chantry, who cooks up the majority of the quartet's cheesecake sleeves, turns in a particularly snazzy Irving Klaw–styled number this time around. As befits its title, **Sin & Tonic** is rife with songs of praise for the things twelve-step groups were invented to exorcise. Not that it's a party album per se: "Mystery Girl" and "Scotch" seethe more than they explode, with edgy guitar leads snaking in and out of the rhythm section's hip-waggle. The tension does give way to release on the punkabilly "Waste o' Time" and the menacing "Hexed," both of which provide hundred-proof purgatives for the soul. The live album preserves a particularly in-the-pocket set (allegedly recorded at Illinois' favorite strip joint/bowling alley) for which the Mono Men deserve extra credit, given the intensity of the band-wide obsession with both burlesque and ten-pins.

The Roofdogs, who pre-dated the Mono Men, were responsible for the first Estrus release—the **Pound Bound** cassette, which trickled out in the waning days of '87. With the four future Mono Men augmented by Farfisa organist Josie P. Cat, the 'Dogs energetically saunter through the six surf-leaning ditties on **Having a Rave-Up,** which borrows the title and clones the sleeve art of the classic Yardbirds LP. [dss]

MONO PUFF

See *They Might Be Giants.*

MONSTERLAND

Loser Friendly EP (spinART) 1992
Destroy What You Love (Seed) 1993
At One With Time EP (Seed) 1994

Danbury, Connecticut's Monsterland knew enough about feedback *and* harmonically alluring indie-pop craft to jumble the pieces together and produce a jangly rush of soft airborne thistles whose impact is entirely pleasurable. The shabbily produced **Loser Friendly** is a semi-good introduction, all soaring tunes, skittering guitar exuberance, self-conscious lyrics ("Magazine" resorts to the Cynthia Heimel book title, *Get Your Tongue Out of My Mouth I'm Kissing You Goodbye*) and badge-sporting reference points, most notably a modest punk-pop cover of Blondie's "(I'm Always Touched by Your) Presence Dear." Bassist Thom Monahan's voice is nothing special, but in tandem with resourceful guitarist Greg Vegas, the trio's singing is both adequate and beside the point.

From such dinky beginnings, Monsterland made a sound-breaking trip to the majors without untoward incident. On **Destroy What You Love,** reliable producer Ted Nicely triples the amplitude and density of the band's music, replacing small-scale youthfulness with a thick blast of real-world power, mustering a fast-paced tribute to My Bloody Valentine that retains its all-American focus. Monsterland rises to the challenge by redoubling its melodic grip, harnessing the added energy to strengthen the music, not obliterate its charms. "Lobsterhead," "Rid of You," a cover of Bailter Space's "Fish Eye" and "At One With Time" (remade from a 1990 45) are all juicy morsels set on cool fire by endless layers of bristly guitar. Forcing Monahan to sing harder is actually beneficial; Todd Cronin's zealous drumming also falls in comfortably with the bold rock surge.

Recycling "At One With Time" from the album, recalling the careening "Blank" from a single and the comic "Girlfriend on Drugs" from a Danbury compilation, Monsterland only had to come up with three new numbers to fill out the '94 EP, which is a backpedaling blunder for a band that seemed to be making strong forward progress. "Jane Wiedlin Used to Be a Go-Go as Far as We Know" is a brilliant title—too bad the lyrics couldn't find any use for it in an altogether forgettable song. Monsterland broke up later in '94. Vegas formed a new band and Monahan joined the Lilys. [i]

MONSTER MAGNET

Forget About Life, I'm High on Dope [tape] (Cool Beans) 1989
I'm High, What Are You Gonna Do About It [tape] (Cool Beans) 1990
Monster Magnet (Ger. Glitterhouse) 1990
Spine of God (Primo Scree/Caroline) 1992
25............tab (Caroline) 1993
Superjudge (A&M) 1993
Dopes to Infinity (A&M) 1995
I Talk to Planets (A&M) 1995

DAISYCUTTER

Shithammer Deluxe (Pond Scum/Rockville) 1992

Although the term one-dimensional usually carries negative connotations, some artists are possessed with an ability to render that single dimension utterly mesmerizing. Take Monster Magnet mastermind Dave Wyndorf, a guy who has built a veritable sonic church upon a stoner's creed that venerates a holy trinity comprising the inventory of Robitussin, the director of *I Spit on Your Grave* and that thrift store with the stockpile of dirt-cheap *Famous Monsters* back issues—with a clear preference given to the first member of that troika.

Up through the mid-'80s, Wyndorf was the singer in New York's Shrapnel, the junior punk-pop-metal quintet led by future Ramones (and others) producer Daniel Rey. After his discharge from that band, the New Jersey native was bent on letting his freak flag fly—a goal Monster Magnet's self-released, cannabis-overloaded cassettes clearly achieved. Extended Hawkwind-styled jams like "Needle Freak" and "Lizard Johnny" (which sound as if they were recorded on a cassette machine positioned at the far end of a vacuum cleaner hose) reflect Wyndorf's strobing universe as assiduously as flea-market Doors mirrors glued to the inside of his eyelids.

From there, Monster Magnet merely intensified its idiosyncrasies, adding more reverb to the guitars and Wyndorf's already incomprehensible vocals. Not that far removed from the heyday of Blue Cheer, **Spine of God** is an exercise in sonic overkill that leaves the paraquat-free listener wondering "how can brains so small move fingers so fast?" The band lays its cards on the table with the flanged drumbeat that introduces the opening "Pill Shovel," the grand marshal of a narco-procession that encompasses "Medicine" and the virulent "Nod Scene." Since Wyndorf and John McBain splay a formidable array of distorto-guitar over everything (including an appropriately mangy cover of Grand Funk Railroad's "Sin's a Good Man's Brother"), numbness sets in early . . . but it's a *good* numbness. The four-track **25............tab** adds a bit of Teutonic drone to the psychoactive cocktail, but the overall effect is not noticeably different—although thirty-two head-swimming minutes of "Tab . . ." should elate true believers.

Given Wyndorf's predisposition to mind-travel, it was probably just a matter of time before he discovered the kind of honest-to-Tolkein hobbit-rock that mottles **Superjudge,** an album at once heavier and less substantial than the band's previous work. New guitarist Ed Mundell (formerly of Daisycutter, a band organized by ex–Monster Magnet man Tim Cronin) speaks a more standard metal dialect, as borne out by his contributions to "Cyclops Revisited" and "Elephant Bell." Wyndorf seems to have specters of stadium stages dancing in his head throughout. Other than an exquisitely excessive rendition of Hawkwind's "Brainstorm," the fates would probably turn thumbs down on **Superjudge.** Monster Magnet did an abrupt about-face on the followup, however, investing **Dopes to Infinity** with a much-missed sense of self-directed humor (evident in the deadpan posturing of "Ego, the Living Planet") and even a break in the wall of wail (in the form of the Farfisa-driven garage-pop "Dead Christmas"). Sometimes nothing succeeds like excess.

I Talk to Planets is a CD-ROM containing eight songs from **Dopes** and two from **Superjudge** as well as a heap of visuals. [dss]

COUNTRY DICK MONTANA

See *Beat Farmers.*

MOONPOOLS & CATERPILLARS

Lucky Dumpling (EastWest) 1995

Although the inclusion of a song entitled "Sundays" on the absolutely wonderful **Lucky Dumpling** at least acknowledges the resemblance, any characterization of this spunky and smart Los Angeles (Glendale, to be precise) quartet as America's new wave rocking reply to the Sundays barely gets the week started. Behind Utah native Kimi Encarnacion's strong, careening vocals—a sweetheart of falsetto yodels, yelps, nonsense syllables, whoops and delicate caresses—subtle power guitarist Jay Jay Encarnacion (her husband) and the rhythm section timewarp four decades of electric pop for an individualized set of enticing flavors. If Blondie had been flash-frozen in the late '70s and then thawed out in time to hear some of the late-'80s British bands they inspired, Moonpools & Caterpillars would be right there, joining in the giddy, tuneful fun.

Moonpools' engaging melodicism perfectly suits the songs' heartening lyrics, which express deep appreciation for nature and life, offer homespun philosophy and rave about cars, childhood, travel and romance. In "Hear," Kimi sings, "The day I find myself I'll be so very proud . . . Simply doing what you feel is the best way not to go wrong." In the wrong hands, such stuff could be insufferably precious, but set to music so breathlessly ingenuous, it reaches out like a revelation. "Colossal Youth" (which has nothing really to do with Young Marble Giants beyond its title) vents at harmful parental judgmentalism with compelling anger. But in "Crazy Old World," she turns to a greater power and prays, "Mother wind, whisper to me, tell me all I need to know/Warm my skin, don't let me worry." While the words go off on semi-spiritual retreats, the music remains solidly grounded. "Summertime" quotes the harmonica line from War's "Low Rider"; odd bits of calypso and an aura of theatrical grandeur add breadth to this uncommonly inspiring debut. Rendered with rich, exacting, textured gusto by producers Richard Gottehrer and Jeffrey Lesser, **Lucky Dumpling** is one joyful treat. [i]

MOONSHAKE

First EP (UK Creation) 1991
Secondhand Clothes EP (UK Too Pure) 1992
Eva Luna (UK Too Pure) 1992 (Too Pure/Matador/Atlantic) 1993
Big Good Angel EP (UK Too Pure) 1993 (Too Pure/Matador) 1994
The Sound Your Eyes Can Follow (UK Too Pure) 1994 (Too Pure/American) 1995
Dirty & Divine (C/Z) 1996

LAIKA

Antenna EP (UK Too Pure) 1994
Silver Apples of the Moon (UK Too Pure) 1994 (Too Pure/American) 1995

A textbook example of how very different musicians can work together—and sometimes can't—Moonshake (named after a Can song) was built on a tension that briefly made it one of the most exciting bands in England before causing it to splinter. Of the band's two frontpeople, American expatriate Margaret Fiedler favored tranced-out grooves, odd sampled timbres and mystical, sensual incantations, while Dave Callahan (ex-Wolfhounds) demonically enunciated tales of moral disintegration and urban squalor. Both built their songs on crashing, atonal samples; that's about all they had in common. Add a gifted dub bassist (John Frenett), a rock drummer (Mig) deft enough to get around the bizarre rhythms constructed by Fiedler and Callahan and, as an unofficial fifth member, engineer Guy Fixsen (who'd done the same for My Bloody Valentine, among others) and you have one spicy, confusing gumbo.

On the **First** EP, it's clear that the band had been impressed by MBV's **Glider**—all four songs are focused on wobbling, warping keyboard-and-guitar textures. Their songwriting is better, though, especially Fiedler's "Coward," whose form suggests an old English ballad and which she delivers with murderous calm. Fiedler also sings some of Callahan's songs here—the only time she ever did. (The CD appends a remix of "Coward.")

The three-song **Secondhand Clothes** also includes some front-and-center guitar (including an actual big riff in the title track), but the focus is shifted to pitting disorienting keyboard sounds against the rock-steady rhythm section and the two singers' distinctive vocal and lyrical approaches. The original lineup's only album, **Eva Luna** (whose American release appends **Secondhand Clothes**), also includes the whomping single "Beautiful Pigeon." The album kicks off with Callahan's best song, a cancerous dub-rock slither called "City Poison," and thereafter pretty much alternates between the two writers' tracks. Callahan bellows and sneers through his songs, and Fiedler nearly whispers through hers, but the music is always big, weird and unnerving.

Callahan's three songs on **Big Good Angel** are pretty excellent on their own, especially "Seance." Unfortunately for him, they're up against a bunch of killers from Fiedler—sexy, scary and rhythmically fascinating. "Two Trains" is an unstoppable, shimmery recasting of the idea of female hysteria; "Flow" explodes into two frenetic, clattering bridges; and "Girly Loop" features the brilliant hook "she knows what God gave her eyelashes for."

It was clear, by this point, Moonshake was essentially two bands; shortly thereafter, that's what it became. Fiedler and Frenett departed with Fixsen to form Laika (named after the first dog in space); Callahan and Mig stuck around as Moonshake and made the "guaranteed guitar-free" album **The Sound Your Eyes Can Follow** with a host of guest musicians, including a couple of Too Pure labelmates—Polly Harvey (who sings on half the album's tracks) and Stereolab's Katharine Gifford. Built mostly on creepy sampled loops, it's Moonshake's darkest record; highlights include the prostitute's diary "Just a Working Girl" and the nihilistic one-two punch that closes the album, "The Grind" and "Into Deep Neutral."

Laika's splendid **Silver Apples of the Moon** was recorded almost entirely at home by Fiedler and Fixsen with some help from Frenett and percussionist Lou Ciccotelli (joined onstage by ex–PJ Harvey drummer Rob Ellis). Vocally, it's Fiedler's show, except for one number sung by Fixsen and a couple of cool instrumentals. The album's light, shimmering surface belies the gorgeous density of its sound and the occasional menace of its lyrics, as on the hip-hop–flavored "44 Robbers" and the booth-dancer monologue "Coming Down Glass." **Silver Apples**' best track, the fluid, erotic groove (in 7/8 time!) "Marimba Song," is previewed on **Antenna** in two versions, along with an adorable dueling-samplers instrumental, "Squeaky," and one other song. [ddw]

REBECCA MOORE

Admiral Charcoal's Song (Knitting Factory Works) 1995

Armed with a keening, dramatic voice that immediately calls to mind Dolores O'Riordan of the Cranberries, New York singer/guitarist/pianist Rebecca Moore nonetheless brings refined experimental artistry to her darkly whimsical and impressionist debut. Moore upends the visions of Edward Lear and Lewis Carroll here, backed in her family nostalgia by bassist Reuben Radding (a onetime bandmate of drummer Dave Grohl in the pre-Nirvana Dain Bramage), cellist Jane Scarpantoni, trumpeter Steven Bernstein, vocalist Larry Miller and, playing six-string bass on "If You Please Me," guest star Jeff Buckley. At her most intriguing and appealing, Moore grapples with ominously surreal wordplay: in "Twisty Lullag'bye," she sings "Beware the mighty forks of despair!/Dragging their tines along my spine/Beware the mighty spoons shaking their caved-in heads." An open-ended artist willing to abandon safe structuralism for freely meandering adventures, Moore conducts a rarefied tour through a bizarre imagination, painting herself as an eccentric, personal artist well worth examining. [i]

R. STEVIE MOORE

Roger Ferguson and Ethos EP7 (Basic Sounds) 1973
Phonography (Vital) 1976 (HP Music) 1978
Four From Phonography EP7 (HP Music) 1978
Stance EP (HP Music) 1978
Delicate Tension (HP Music) 1978
Everything You Always Wanted to Know About R. Stevie Moore but Were Afraid to Ask (Fr. New Rose) 1984
What's the Point?!! (Cuneiform) 1984
Verve (UK Hamster) 1985
Glad Music (Fr. New Rose) 1986
R. Stevie Moore (1952–19??) (UK Cordelia) 1987
Teenage Spectacular (Fr. New Rose) 1987
Warning: R. Stevie Moore (Fr. New Rose) 1988
Has-Beens and Never-Weres (UK Heliotrope) 1990
Greatesttits (Fr. Fan Club) 1990
Contact Risk (Fruit of the Tune) 1993

The son of top Nashville session bassist Bob Moore, R. Stevie Moore began doing his own one-man home recordings as a teenager. Over the course of two decades spent perfecting his technical, musical, lyrical and conceptual skills, Moore's omnivorous, individualistic pop blender has dug into his awesome—and seemingly bottomless—well of talent and produced, since 1981, several hundred (!!!) tapes of his original work, self-released and sold exclusively via mail-order from the author's home studio in New Jersey. Since the early '80s, his scattered stream of vinyl and CD releases (all but two are imports) have nearly all been assembled, with little overlap, from his cassette-club tapes. Suffice to say, aficionados of fertile pop imagination, resourceful home studio technique and more stylistic diversity than most record stores can offer are highly recommended to get with Stevie. Start anywhere, and be assured that if you like what you hear on any of the discs, there are countless hours more of equal quality where that came from. (To not overstate the case, it should be acknowledged that the albums favor the cream of the cassette crop, omitting the more esoteric ramblings, personal indulgences, sonic experiments and radio-show elements that find their way into Moore's handmade missives.) "Unsung hero" only touches on the injustice of obscurity for this wry, heartfelt artist whose limber genius, vitality and productivity make him a far more profound cultural asset than any number of next-big-things with maybe two good albums in 'em. Why no major label has ever signed him is one of the modern era's mysteries.

Moore's unveiling to the music world came via **Phonography,** a rudimentary but obviously brilliant overture. **Stance** is a much-improved three-song 12-inch; **Delicate Tension** is astonishing in its varied expositions of Moore's idiosyncratic perceptions of life and smooth, versatile voice. There are hints of Zappa, Rundgren, Townshend, McCartney, Wilson, Chilton, Stanshall and countless others. With that, Moore began concentrating on making cassettes and didn't record another full studio LP for commercial release for the better part of a decade.

Everything You Always Wanted to Know is a disjointed two-record compilation sampling a decade's worth of back catalogue with originals, covers (of Slade and the Big Bopper), strange experiments and sublime successes. The more concise and better conceived **What's the Point?!!** is an ideal introduction, containing such gems as "Part of the Problem," "Puttin' Up the Groceries," "Bloody Knuckles" and "World's Fair," the last three of which are also on **Everything;** the erratic but gem-strewn **Verve** is a compilation of early-'80s tracks.

Glad Music, a proper studio album recorded in 1985, reprises "Part of the Problem" and adds a dozen more examples of Moore at the top of his creative powers. There's real C&W played with mock-seriousness ("I Love You So Much It Hurts"), an unnervingly precise synth-flavored version of the Association's "Along Comes Mary" and witty, hand-clapping rock'n'roll ("Shakin' in the Sixties"). Yet another anthology, **(1952–19??)** assembles twenty-one tracks recorded between 1973 and 1986, including such Moore classics as "Delicate Tension," "Goodbye Piano" and "Satisfaction." Some of the items are tossed-off fragments, others excellent achievements with full-fledged arrangements. The punky "Jesus Rocks" and the reflectively acoustic "Back in Time" are among the previously unvinylized treasures.

Teenage Spectacular includes covers of Dr. Hook and Dr. Dylan amidst original pop musings, witty balladeering and brief mind-altering tape experiments. The simple musical constructions on guitars, keyboards and drums reveal traces of Moore's many influences and a sense of his monumental creative grasp. **Warning,** containing tracks of 1986–87 vintage, includes remakes of RSM oldies ("Manufacturers") as well as the Beatles' "Getting Better." **Has-Beens and Never-Weres,** which samples a decade of Moore music going back to the mid-'70s, includes a tribute to the Residents and a song entitled, with typical industry-taunting wit, "Bonus Track (LP Only)." Despite the dumb humor of the title, **Greatesttits** is an important twenty-four-track CD retrospective of Moore's most appealing originals and covers—another brilliant doorway to his wonderful world.

Moore's output has slowed in recent years; cassette titles like **Unpopular Singer** (which contains "Why Do You Hate Me So Much?" and "Fuckin' Idiots Everywhere") and the despairing liner note in the **Contact Risk** compilation ("If you don't like this, I quit") allude to why. Cult stardom can evidently be a lonely and frustrating state. Although it was assembled in 1993, there's nothing more current than two band tracks from the fall of '90 on **Contact Risk;** amazingly, except for a hissy, weird dose of 1968 pathos, the 1975–87 material sounds relatively contemporary and would be impossible to audibly segregate by decade without the artist's detailed production information. A typically spectacular hodgepodge, the set caroms around perfect popcraft ("Under the Light," "Play Myself Some Music"), bizarre poetry (three installments of "I Could Be Your Lover"), goofy country ("Elation Damnation"), sultry loveman funk ("Times Have Changed"), radio fund-raising ("Pledge Your Money"), kinetic falsetto gimcrackery ("You Can't Write a Song") and echoey acoustic folk ("Hours of Delight"). For all the inconsistency in audio quality, Moore's melodic powers never falter, and the hour floats and swoops by with the delightful, unpredictable grace of a kite. [i]

See also *TPRG*.

THURSTON MOORE

See *Sonic Youth.*

ALANIS MORISSETTE

Jagged Little Pill (Maverick/Reprise) 1995

ALANIS

Alanis (Can. MCA) 1991
Now Is the Time (Can. MCA) 1992

Either an astute bandwagon jumper with exquisite timing, the sharp-tongued mouthpiece for calculating commercial interests or a maturing young artist clumsily finding her creative purpose after two premature hack jobs (or all three), Ottawa-born singer Alanis Morissette helped define the mid-'90s by downloading all the ethernet enthusiasms music-buyers had developed for stand-up women like Chrissie Hynde, Madonna, Sophie B. Hawkins, Liz Phair and Courtney Love (if not Adina Howard, Ani DiFranco and Gillette) and, with **Jagged Little Pill,** galvanizing it. At just the right cultural moment, putting a slickly commercialized spin on the trendiness of youthful angst, Morissette made herself the lightning rod for polar sympathies, offering a potent but misleading combination of cheap fantasy thrills and the illusion of female empowerment. Basically, Morissette—who sings in a piercing yet throaty warble that some find unendurable—owes her stardom to the supposed shock/titillation value of "You Oughta Know," a petulant post-breakup song that crudely asks "Would she go down on you in a theater?" and "Are you thinking of me when you fuck her?" It's amazing how little it takes to get people off these days.

The Canadian began her career as a ten-year-old TV star on *You Can't Do That on Television*; turning to music, billed under her first name, she made **Alanis** at sixteen. Formulaic electronic dance tripe co-written by the precocious singer and produced by Leslie Howe ("for Ghetto Records") in obvious imitation of Paula Abdul and Janet Jackson, the debut does actually presage Morissette's future in the independence of "On My Own," the determination of "Too Hot" ("You gotta go for gold and you'll make it baby") and the o.p.p. provocation of "Jealousy" ("Jealousy—some girls have it rough oh baby").

The second album musters a smarter breed of dance music, leaving the Tiffany young-adult section of the style library to borrow ideas from Madonna. Quaint in its obviousness but not altogether horrible, **Now Is the Time** (also produced by Howe) begins with the announcement, "We play the game with determination/We don't give a damn 'bout our reputation" and includes such pointed songs as "No Apologies," "Give What You Got" and "Big Bad Love," in which Morissette ineptly muses on the incomprehensible ("I wonder why I am so unrelentless") and loses herself in block-that-metaphor confusion ("I don't believe your blood is bad to the bone"). The sexual bravado of "The Time of Your Life" clues into the aggrieved, mildly politicized, self-examining persona Morissette rode to fame: "In a world that does not recognize women are victimized/What does that symbolize/Why do I want the things I usually criticize/It may be self-destructiveness, or maybe it's the emptiness inside."

None of that, of course, amounts to anything more than a couple of mildly embarrassing outfits left hanging in a teenager's closet when she moved out and entered the adult world. The twenty-year-old who made the multi-platinum **Jagged Little Pill** in collaboration with producer/songwriter/instrumentalist Glen Ballard (the studio hand behind Wilson Phillips' hits and a one-time Michael Jackson songwriter) is a distinctly different creature, a cocky deep thinker determined to be the most mannered singer since Eartha Kitt. On crafty pop-rock songs that make deft use of contemporary trends in sound, she cycles haphazardly through a display case of borrowed voices—all of them reeking of the self-righteousness that drives her clunky, jammed-in lyrics—with a freewheeling sense of pitch and ever-varying timbre. When she isn't spitting out the lyrics to "You Oughta Know," she's keening like Sinéad in "Hand in My Pocket," cooing "Perfect," deadpanning like a wan artiste in "All I Really Want" or making like a new-fangled folkie in "Right Through You." At least she knows what she's doing, as "You Learn" acknowledges: "I recommend biting off more than you can chew . . . I recommend sticking your foot in your mouth at any time . . . You live you learn." Although inexplicably hailed as a role model by those incapable of independent thought, Morissette is, in fact, a paradigm for our time: ninety-six channels on and nothing but angry me-me-me talk shows. [i]

MORPHINE

Good (Accurate/Distortion) 1992 (Rykodisc) 1994
Cure for Pain (Rykodisc) 1993
Yes (Rykodisc) 1995
Super Sex EP (Rykodisc) 1995

TREAT HER RIGHT

Treat Her Right (Soul Selects) 1986 (RCA) 1988
Tied to the Tracks (RCA) 1989
What's Good for You (Rounder) 1991

"She told me things about her life/She never told me she was someone's wife," sings a deadpan Mark Sandman on the first song on Treat Her Right's first album. The "low guitar"–player's pulp-fiction narratives, with appropriately sinister and smoky musical accompaniment, would later flourish with Morphine, but in Treat Her Right he had to share time with the more conventional, blues-derived offerings of guitarist David Champagne. The Massachusetts quartet was distinguished less by its songs than by its exotic taste in offbeat covers (the debut album concludes with James Blood Ulmer's "Where Did All the Girls Come From?," the second tackles Captain Beefheart's "Hit a Man") and sparse instrumentation: slide guitar, a second guitar doubling as a bass, bare-bones drums and harmonica. While the group occasionally veered toward finger-snapping pop (as on Sandman's "Marie," from **Tied to the Tracks**), they preferred to play variations on Canned Heat's swamp-blues, typified by such "On the Road Again" knockoffs such as Champagne's "Big Medicine," also on the second LP. **What's Good for You,** the band's post-majors third album, leans heavily on an eclectic range of covers, giving the band's oddball treatment to songs by Bob Dylan, Buck Owens, John Lee Hooker and the Rolling Stones.

After Treat Her Right dissolved (sending harmonicat Jim Fitting off to play with, among others, the The), Sandman formed Morphine with saxophonist Dana Colley and drummer Jerome Deupree, replaced during the recording of **Good** by Treat Her Right's Billy Conway. With Sandman's two-string slide bass and baritone voice—singing in much the same range as Colley's baritone saxophone—Morphine immediately established a minimalist, low-end sound that could have easily become a gimmick: a "power trio" not built around the sound of an electric guitar. Instead, with sly intelligence, Morphine has expanded its offbeat vocabulary on each album.

Good establishes the goods, excavating a slippery, sultry groove that suggests blues and bebop without becoming either by providing ample room in the spacious mix for two evocative voices: Sandman, with his smoldering-cigarette vignettes, and Colley, who veers from staccato riffing and hot-rod honks to Albert Ayler squeals. In "You Speak My Language" and "You Look Like Rain," the treated vocals and dissonant soundscapes push the noise envelope.

Cure for Pain refines the sound and Sandman's terse, hard-boiled lyricism: "Thursday" could have been taken straight out of a Jim Thompson novel, a tawdry met-her-at-the-poolhall scenario in which violence lurks in the not-too-distant future. "A Head With Wings" and "Buena" both rock more ferociously than anything on **Good.**

With **Yes,** the band creates its most effortless blend of noir moodiness, experimental skronk and full-bore ravers. "If I am guilty so are you . . . It was March 4, 1982," Sandman sings on "Radar," a typically delicious collision of the mundane and the malevolent. In Sandman's world, all the characters have something to hide as they flit among paranoia, fear and temptation. The group mines ferocious neo-funk on "Honey White," trolls avant-garde waters in "Sharks," offers a sunny respite in "All Your Way" and even delivers an acoustic kissoff, "Gone for Good." (Drawn from the album as a single, "Super Sex" became an EP with the addition of live takes on "Birthday Cake" and "Have a Lucky Day" and the instrumental "Sundayafternoonweightlessness.") Having initially drawn attention for its novel attributes, Morphine has developed into a terrific band for the most traditional of reasons: its songs.

Sandman has since released a nifty solo single ("Swing It Low" b/w "Bought Myself a Steak") under the name Like Swimming. He also resumed Supergroup, an informal trio he had with Chris Ballew (whose two-string bass style was inspired by Sandman) before the latter went off to form Presidents of the United States of America, long enough to cut a naff live 45 ("It's Not Like That Anymore" b/w "Telepathic Cathy"). [gk/i]

See also *Presidents of the United States of America; TPRG.*

MORRISSEY

Viva Hate (Sire/Reprise) 1988
Bona Drag (Sire/Reprise) 1990
Kill Uncle (Sire/Reprise) 1991
Morrissey Live at KROQ EP (Sire/Reprise) 1991
Your Arsenal (Sire/Reprise) 1992
Beethoven Was Deaf (UK HMV) 1993
Vauxhall and I (Sire/Reprise) 1994
World of Morrissey (Sire/Reprise) 1995
Southpaw Grammar (Reprise) 1995

Johnny Marr discovered Morrissey in 1982, sometime after, one assumes, Steven Morrissey invented himself. Wags asserted that not since the Who had so formidable a talent been married to such an embarrassing, nay pitiful, lead singer. With the demise of the Smiths five years later, hastened by Marr's inability to cope with the stardom his monstrous partner exulted in, the road ahead was plain: Marr, master of a powerfully recombinant style of rhythm guitar playing—indeed, perhaps the most focused such player in England since Keith Richards—would go on to greatness, and his morose Mancunian sidekick would take his place at the end of a very long list of English eccentrics of interest to no one but themselves. Yet here we are nearly a decade on; Marr is a sideman to other artists and Morrissey, well, Morrissey is a yawping demi-star and a serious wit, still despised and still rather laughable but with curiously persuasive pretensions to substance.

That substance rests on a somewhat warped appeal to a certain sensitive segment of disaffected middle-class youth. Too gentle for grunge, too questioning for pop pabulum, they hear in their love-wounded icon some echo of their own uncategorizable sadness. Morrissey is ostentatiously proud of this connection—he speaks about it earnestly in interviews and makes an extraordinary meet-and-greet effort, letting fans hug him with amazing forbearance. Such showboating, however, only serves to disguise the central metaphor of his work. Well, not disguise, really, for Morrissey's rampant homoeroticism marks everything the man does, from the cheesecakey album covers and his carefully made-over sidemen to song title after song title ("I Am Hated for Loving," "Certain People I Know," "Will Never Marry," "The End of the Family Line"). Morrissey claims to be a celibate and may even be telling the truth, but that's a metaphor, too: for the connection that can never really be consummated between fan and star.

His solo work has, naturally enough, been on the English model: occasional albums confused with a blizzard of multi-track and multi-format singles irregularly collected into patchwork albums. After briefly attempting to continue the Smiths without Marr, he began collaborating with the group's engineer-cum-producer, Stephen Street. The resulting **Viva Hate** is neither Morrissey embarrassed nor Morrissey bereft, but it is not quite a serious work, either. With Durutti Columnist Vini Reilly taking on the primary guitar responsibilities, this morose affair is filled with Morrissey's trademark weepy asides, extravagances, posturing and unabashed self-pity. "Late Night, Maudlin Street" is just that, with little of the self-deprecating humor or compositional élan of Smiths tracks like "Half a Person." But the album also gets serious—notably on the savage if unsubtle political attack that is "Margaret on the Guillotine"—and, just to throw everyone off, Morrissey and Street manage to conjure up two thoroughly sublime singles. The effervescent "Suedehead" is as melodically propulsive as anything Marr had provided the singer; "Everyday Is Like Sunday," by contrast, is a shimmering, molten truth attack on the very concept of vacation. (Thatcher, the beach—Morrissey can get worked up about anything.) Those who had imagined Morrissey would be adrift without Marr were obviously mistaken.

Bona Drag is a surprisingly enjoyable collection of singles ("Suedehead" and "Everyday Is Like Sunday" among them) and new tracks; in much sharper relief than on **Viva Hate** is the solo Morrissey maelstrom of imagined grievances, waspish quips and genuine petulance, all coming out on album as a sort of emotional air guitar played at stadium intensity. In this fashion he swoons to be a crippled child ("November Spawned a Monster"), aches to be a gangster ("The Last of the Famous International Playboys") and is given his walking papers even by the spirits above him ("Ouija Board, Ouija Board"). Too many of the other songs are less rewarding, but the album ends in an astonishing moment of recorded intelligence. "Disappointed" shivers and shakes with a tremoloed riff so cleverly reminiscent of Marr's epochal "How Soon Is Now?" assault that it's hard not to take the song as the singer's comment on the breakup. "I'm truly disappointed," smirks Morrissey, and closes the track off with a very funny couplet—"This is the last song I will ever sing/No I've changed my mind again," complete with respective cheers and groans from an imaginary audience—that lampoons his own excesses better than any of his critics. Yet the track also captures the tragedy of his emotional insularity: to truly appreciate the song's multi-dimensionality you have to be more interested in Morrissey than is perhaps healthful. It would be easier to persuade the curious to make the effort if the artist worked at a consistently high level, but his albums have been erratic since then.

Produced by Clive Langer and Alan Winstanley, **Kill Uncle**—mostly co-written with new collaborator and guitarist Mark E. Nevin, late of Fairground Attraction—seems indistinct, though it does contain "Sing Your Life," "Driving Your Girlfriend Home" and "There's a Place in Hell for Me and My Friends." **Your Arsenal,** largely written with guitarist Alain Whyte and produced by the late Mick Ronson, is a bit more sparkly, with any number of sweet tunes, among them the irresistible "You're the One for Me, Fatty," whose splendid mix of love and cruelty comes as close as any Morrissey song to capturing the singer's fey take on romance. **Beethoven Was Deaf** is an okay live album released in the UK, heavy on the hits and without so much as a nod or a wink to the Smiths.

Strange things happen on 1994's more ambitious **Vauxhall and I,** written half with Whyte, half with **Your Arsenal**'s other returning guitarist, Boz Boorer, who supplies the album's strongest songs. The opening "Now My Heart Is Full," with characters trotted out from Graham Greene's portrait of aimless pre-war youth, *Brighton Rock,* is dramatic and funny. "Tell all of my friends," begins the grandiose chorus, but the singer immediately drowns in a sea of digressions: "Don't have too many/Just some raincoated lovers' puny brothers." "The More You Ignore Me, the Closer I Get" is an amusing and catchy essay on romantic obsession, containing the wry couplet, "I bear more grudges/Than lonely high court judges." This album also has a killer closing track, the histrionic and thunderous "Speedway," which takes his emotional excesses to psychotic, almost *Sunset Boulevard* levels.

World of Morrissey is a **Bona Drag**–type collection, including some live piffle from **Beethoven Was Deaf,** a long and bloodless run at "Moon River" from a UK single and the plangent "Boxers," with its memorable portrait of a fighter "losing in front of your home crowd." **Southpaw Grammar,** like **Vauxhall and I,** produced by Steve Lillywhite and played and written by Whyte and Boorer, continues Morrissey's ring fixation—the title, he says, is a reference to "the school of hard knocks"—but ventures like the eleven-minute opening track ("The Teachers Are Afraid of the Pupils") show the pop pugilist not up to his game. (Incidentally, the "Dagenham Dave" here is unrelated to the old Stranglers song of the same title.)

Accompanying such pallid recent stuff is Morrissey's dedication to becoming recognized as a world-class eccentric, canceling shows, interviews and video shoots without warning. He hasn't managed a coherent series of appearances in the States in years. [bw]

See also *TPRG.*

MOSQUITO

See *Half Japanese.*

MOTHERHEAD BUG

See *Cop Shoot Cop.*

MOTHER LOVE BONE

Shine EP (Stardog) 1989
Apple (Polydor) 1990
Mother Love Bone (Stardog/Mercury) 1992

MALFUNKSHUN

Return to Olympus (Loosegroove/550 Music/Epic) 1995

TEMPLE OF THE DOG

Temple of the Dog (A&M) 1991

With one pair of Green River veterans off to form Mudhoney, another two ex-members of that Seattle roots-of-punk combo—guitarist Stone Gossard and bassist Jeff Ament—launched a hoary-sounding '70s hard-rock band, Mother Love Bone. With second guitarist Bruce Fairweather, drummer Greg Gilmore and singer Andrew Wood (formerly the singer/bassist in Malfunkshun), Mother Love Bone made its debut on **Shine,** an EP whose four tracks shrug off Zeppelin and motorsludge—both common regional tendencies in the late '80s—in favor of a crisp rip that favors Free, Aerosmith and other blues-based bands of the early '70s. To its credit, the quintet demonstrates noteworthy songwriting facility and the wisdom to tone things down and open the sound up, giving a genuine three-dimensionality to its creation.

With major-label success looming on the horizon (Stardog being a PolyGram pseudo-indie imprint, named for a song of the band's) and the northwestern scene nearing critical mass, Wood died of a heroin overdose in March '90, making the posthumous release of the band's completed album, **Apple,** a hollow and meaningless roar. Still, **Apple** focuses all of Mother Love Bone's assets into a potent rock rush, like contemporaneous Guns n' Roses, only with better vocals and worse guitar. When the pain of the tragedy eased and MLB's legend had grown as a result of subsequent developments, the album and EP were combined on a single disc and reissued as **Mother Love Bone,** with a bonus CD containing a **Shine** outtake version of "Capricorn Sister" and the unreleased "Lady Godiva Blues."

Later in 1990, working on weekends as they developed a new project with guitarist Mike McCready (ex-Shadow), Gossard and Ament—joined by vocalist Chris Cornell and drummer Matt Cameron of Soundgarden—recorded an album in tribute to Wood. Most of the songs on **Temple of the Dog** are Cornell's; two ("Say Hello 2 Heaven" and "Reach Down," eleven minutes of grinding gospel carried by a McCready/Gossard guitar slalom) address his late friend directly.

Between such sentimentality, the grim drug reality of "Times of Trouble" and the faith-testing religiosity of "Your Saviour" and "Wooden Jesus," the album is a powerhouse, with more evocative intensity than either Soundgarden or Mother Love Bone had ever demonstrated. McCready and Gossard play up a furious storm of guitar when needed; Eddie Vedder, who had just arrived in Seattle from California to join their new band, renamed Pearl Jam, sings backup on three songs and shares lead with Cornell on "Hunger Strike."

Digging back to the scene's prehistory, a full album's worth of studio recordings by the Kiss-loving Malfunkshun—Andrew Wood, drummer Regan Hagar (later of Brad and Satchel) and Andrew's brother, Kevin (who now plays guitar in Devilhead)—dating from 1986 to 1987 were belatedly dredged up and issued as **Return to Olympus.** Other than the surprising and bizarre "Enter Landrew," which throws serious riffology against a credibly fey vocal imitation of Marc Bolan, the Zepped-out trio makes obvious, retrograde rock noise ("Jezebel Woman"), even going so far as to cover Ted Nugent's "Wang Dang Sweet Poontang." But at least one song in this pile—"Luxury Bed (The Rocketship Chair)"—has a rhythmic component that has since become very familiar to fans of northwestern rock. [i]

See also *Brad, Devilhead, Love Battery, Pearl Jam, Soundgarden; TPRG.*

MOTHERS OF INVENTION

See *Frank Zappa.*

MOTOCASTER

See *Dish.*

MOTORCYCLE BOY

See *Pillbox (NYC).*

BOB MOULD

See *Sugar.*

MOUNTAIN GOATS

Songs for Petronius EP7 (Shrimper) 1992
Chile de Arbol EP7 (Ajax) 1993
Philyra EP7 (UK Theme Park) 1994
Beautiful Rat Sunset (Shrimper) 1994
Zopilote Machine (Ajax) 1994
Orange Raja, Blood Royal EP7 (Walt) 1995
Nine Black Poppies (Emperor Jones/Trance Syndicate) 1995
Sweden (Shrimper) 1995
Nothing for Juice (Ajax) 1996

For an expanding horde of cassette-cuddling sub-undergrounders, home taping isn't killing music, it's about the only thing keeping it alive. Those folks have long held this shadowy Claremont, California, "group" (essentially singer/guitarist John Darnielle, plus whichever of his pals happens to have some free time and a spare Maxell) in high esteem. That's due not only to the Goats' unflagging dedication to budgetless recording, but on account of Darnielle's inordinately guileless appreciation of life's simple pleasures—and his palpable dismay over its equally basic disappointments.

Beyond what's listed above and a couple of singles, the Mountain Goats have released five full albums only on tape. That's fair, since the bulk of the material is gleaned from Darnielle's direct-to-boombox recording (take that, all you 4-track "minimalists"). Yes, it's a bit snobbish to insist that every bit of extraneous noise and equipment hum be conserved, but it's Darnielle's party and he'll buzz if he wants to. The early EPs are hamstrung a bit by the academic's polysyllabic excesses (**Songs for Petronius** betrays his fascination with mythology; **Chile de Arbol**'s sleeve boasts a Chaucer quotation—in Middle English, no less). Once you master the lingo, however, they make for fascinating listening, particularly the latter EP's "Fresh Berries for You," a starry-eyed prophecy of the coming of . . . the Easter Bunny!

The eight-song **Beautiful Rat Sunset** kicks off with yet another paean to a rabbit endowed with mystical powers, but the madrigal-like stateliness of "Itzcuintli-Totzli Days" makes it clear that Darnielle isn't just playing the quirkiness card: his affably alinear, vaguely acid-tinged ditties borrow randomly from history texts ("Song for Cleomenes") and cookbooks ("Seeing Daylight") alike, but he can drop the printed-word smarts for heart-rending recollections of lost-love night-sweats with a memory vivid enough to recall time (to the minute), place (to the exact address) and weather (particularly a moment when "the humidity climbed into numbers I don't care to repeat"). Utterly charming.

Despite their fragmentary nature, Darnielle's songs are much better suited to the longplaying format, as borne out by the rollercoaster emotional ride of **Zopilote Machine.** His artless strumming is about the only constant in a miasma of love songs ("Alpha Incipiens"), medieval minstrelsy ("Azo the Nelli in Thalticpac?") and crypto-Aztec ruminations ("Quetzalcoatl Is Born"). It's a whole lot—well, a little—less pretentious than it sounds, thanks to a delivery heartfelt enough to make Darnielle sound like he's leading a revival meeting rather than a grad school seminar. To ratify the Mountain Goats' status as a group, there's even a harmony vocal (from either Rosanne, Rachel, Amy or Saarah) on "Sinaloan Milk Snake Song." A little learnin' never hurt anyone.

Nine Black Poppies is marked by a more standard adherence to song structure/timing and an unmistakable (if cryptic) comic bent. The latter element runs throughout "Cubs in Five" (a litany of implausibilities, such as "Bill Gates will singlehandedly spearhead the Heaven 17 revival"), but it's the former that makes the album more accessible than Darnielle's previous output. Sure, his yammerings often make the thesaurus a more likely accompaniment than air guitar, but when at his romantic best (like "Stars Fell on Alabama"), Darnielle is a troubadour par excellence—one who gives a whole new meaning to the phrase "getting medieval on your ass."

The four-song **Orange Raja, Blood Royal** is notable for having violin parts overdubbed by New Zealand's Alastair Galbraith. [dss]

MOUNT SHASTA

Put the Creep On (Skin Graft) 1994
Who's the Hottie (Skin Graft) 1995

SHAKUHACHI SURPRISE

Space Streakings Over Mount Shasta (Skin Graft) 1996

Dirt and Phantom 309 co-founder John Forbes fled the simmering Atlanta underground in the early '90s for harsher midwestern (Chicago) turf, forming this scorching four-piece scuzz-skronk ensemble. Although the group's peers include Cows, Butthole Surfers and other pigfuck leaders, Mount Shasta certainly goes to extremes others don't.

Put the Creep On is a good example of extreme. Live and *loud* (and ostensibly recorded in under two hours), the eleven-track debut is a dissonant deluge of disaffected sonics, although it's anybody's guess what the hell Forbes is ranting about. Could be scatological (see "Edible Tuber"), but regardless of lyrical context (content?!), the scruffy quintet cranks, twists and pummels out a worthy and palpable din that at its best perverts Beefheart (through a Clawhammer filter) and at its worst gets unwanted houseguests out of the living room pronto. Hunting for buried melodicism? Keep looking—maybe behind that yowling over there.

Dirt alum Chris Lopez joins the relentless romping on **Who's the Hottie,** recorded with Sugar/Buzz Hungry's David Barbe, who doesn't exactly reel Mount Shasta in. The band piledrives with hallucinogenic (brown acid, natch) frenzy, fractured rhythmic countenance and all the menace of a mean drunk—if not the same abandon that fuels the predecessor. For "subtlety," dig "Rusty Shovle Wrinkled Skin," a psychedelic, spag-western foray into slide-guitar expanse and eccentric tunings. As jagged as a broken beer bottle. Both discs come with great cartoon sleeves, featuring band mascot Gumballhead the Cat, by Rob Syers. In 1996, Mount Shasta joined up with Japanese labelmates Space Streakings for a one-off release as Shakuhachi Surprise. [mww]

See also *Space Streakings.*

MOUSE ON MARS

Frosch EP (UK Too Pure) 1994
Vulvaland (UK Too Pure) 1994 (Too Pure/American) 1995
Iaora Tahiti (Too Pure/American) 1995

So sterotypically German as to be almost comical, the Düsseldorf duo of Jan St. Werner and Andi Toma supposedly met at a death-metal show and began collaborating on expansive electronic music under the *nom de tech* of Mouse on Mars. The pair's music, while unabashedly rooted in such krautrock forebears as Kraftwerk and Neu!, wholeheartedly embraces the mindswelling possibilities of modern electronica.

Debuting with the stunning "Frosch" single—a dubby ride through fuzzy, phase-drenched patterns—Mouse on Mars knocked unsuspecting listeners on their ears with **Vulvaland.** Opening with "Frosch" and continuing through such like-minded sub-grooves as the beautifully washed-out vocals of "Chagrin," the alarming "Future Dub" and the truly epic "Katang," **Vulvaland** offers womb-like comfort through distant echoes of warm, distorted sound.

For their second album, St. Werner and Toma expand the parameters of Mouse on Mars beyond any reasonable hopes and expectations. Although on **Vulvaland** they paid tribute to the soul of a studio genius with "Die Seele Von Brian Wilson," they proudly proclaim on **Iaora Tahiti** that "this record does not sound in mono" and then set off on a stereophonic journey that uses the debut's trippy dub as a jumping-off point. The album employs such decidedly non-electronic tools as live drums and pedal steel on several tracks, but **Iaora Tahiti** is far from being a rock record. Still, with several songs clocking in well below five minutes (only the nearly thirteen-minute "Die Innere Orange" approaches the grand scope of **Vulvaland**'s pieces), MOM tinkers with its sound in a number of different ways. Gauzy Casiotones ("Kompod"), aboriginal drone ("Papa, Antoine"), the ethereal krautrock nod of "Hallo" and the ambient pop (is that possible?) of "Gocard" all showcase a group completely unafraid to carry the torch of their land's experimental heritage. [jf]

STUART MOXHAM & THE ORIGINAL ARTISTS

Signal Path (Feel Good All Over) 1992
Random Rules (Fr. Peak) 1993
Cars in the Grass (Feel Good All Over) 1994

STUART MOXHAM

Fine Tuning (Feel Good All Over) 1995

Revisionists might dub Welsh guitarist/keyboardist/singer Stuart Moxham the godfather of love-rock, but when he, his brother Philip and singer Alison Statton—the Young Marble Giants—first foisted their doomy beatnik jazz-pop on an unsuspecting post-punk audience at the dawn of the '80s, the mood they sought to convey was anything but innocent. Despite the sometimes timorous tones, the Giants proved to be a touchstone for neo-minimalists as philosophically diverse (to say the least) as the Olympia brat-pack, Galaxie 500 and Hole leader Courtney Love (who covered "Credit in the Straight World"). After the group's premature split, the Cardiff native went on to lead the Gist—an equally minimal, but slightly less pastoral, combo that had an equally brief existence, releasing a lone album in 1983.

Nearly a decade passed before Moxham—who had gone on to pursue more conventional grown-up activities like animation—would return to public airing of his music. **Signal Path** indicates that the ensuing years did little to change the spirit of his work, but they certainly nudged his delivery toward the middle of the road. That's not necessarily a bad thing: songs like "Her Shoes (Are Right)" and "Over the Sea" have a mellow lilt redolent of mid-'60s adult pop, complete with brushed drums and sunny harmonica that subtly shade Moxham's gentle (if slightly flat) voice. He's quite a bit less successful when he strays off the pop path bounded by Burt Bacharach and Brian Wilson and attempts to tackle pseudo-jump blues ("No One Road") and reggae (the downright embarrassing "Yeah X 3"). Fortunately, such detours are infrequent, and those able to endure them are compensated by the exquisite "Knives (Always Fall)," a duet with Statton.

Cars in the Grass covers much the same ground, with the added benefit of Moxham finding a slightly more secure footing as a vocalist. The Original Artists (who include his brother Andrew on drums) provide accompaniment that varies from spare to superfluous. For **Fine Tuning,** Moxham forgoes their backing altogether, opting to record a passel of his older material (plus the previously unreleased "I Wish" and "One of These Days") with just his acoustic guitar for company. He goes back as far as the Young Marble Giants (for "Nita," "Final Day" and a still-moving reprise of "Credit in the Straight World") and the Gist ("This Is Love"), but neither the years nor the occasional muffed note can tarnish the simple brilliance of his songs. [dss]

See also *Barbara Manning, Alison Statton & Spike.*

MOXY FRÜVOUS

Moxy Früvous EP [tape] (Can. no label) 1992
Bargainville (Can. WEA) 1993 (Atlantic) 1994
Wood (Can. WEA) 1995

The whimsical intelligence of Tom Lehrer, the Smothers Brothers and other jokey troubadours of '60s folk found a brief resting place in this acoustic Toronto quartet. Formed at university and initially highbrow a cappella street buskers, Moxy Früvous followed the career lead of the city's Barenaked Ladies, debuting with a self-released cassette that made them the toast of lighthearted Canada. But while both groups have a folky underpinning, an occasional resemblance to the harmony-pop side of Squeeze and the temerity to write completely ridiculous songs, the resemblance ends there, as Moxy Früvous is not inclined to the other's pandering stupidity and, for one album anyway, did a better job avoiding sappy inward reflection.

With several of them remakes from the cassette, the deftly structured songs on **Bargainville** are often overbearingly cute ("Stuck in the 90's," which stoops to the pitiful rhyme "Join the parade, wave the flag, tell the world it's your lackey/Abbie Hoffman was wacky") or sensitive ("Gulf War Song"), but just as frequently compulsively clever and thoroughly charming (see "Video Bargainville," "My Baby Loves a Bunch of Authors" and "King of Spain," which explains how the fallen monarch wound up working in a Pizza Pizza). Guitarist Mike Ford, bassist Murray Foster, drummer Jean Ghomeshi and guitarist/accordionist David Matheson arrange their pleasant voices in wonderful harmonies, elevating the music with genial spirit.

Wood chucks all of that out by the barn, reinventing the band as serious folk-pop mush-kateers, a latter-day acoustic America (perhaps they'll change the now-cumbersome Moxy moniker to Canada). The sweet singing and a hint of wit faintly echo **Bargainville,** but you'd never recognize the quaint old place in the slick shopping mall built on its foundation. [i]

MUDHONEY

Superfuzz Bigmuff EP (Sub Pop) 1988
Mudhoney (Sub Pop) 1989
Boiled Beef & Rotting Teeth EP (UK Sub Pop/Tupelo) 1990
Superfuzz Bigmuff and Early Singles (Sub Pop) 1991
Every Good Boy Deserves Fudge . . . (Sub Pop) 1991
Let It Slide EP (Sub Pop) 1991
Hate the Police EP (Aus. Au-go-go) 1991
Piece of Cake (Reprise) 1993
Five Dollar Bob's Mock Cooter Stew (Reprise) 1993
My Brother the Cow (Reprise) 1995

MUDHONEY/JIMMIE DALE GILMORE

Mudhoney/Jimmie Dale Gilmore EP (Sub Pop) 1994

MONKEYWRENCH

Clean as a Broke-Dick Dog (Sub Pop) 1992

FALL-OUTS

The Fall-Outs (Super Electro) 1992 + 1995
Here I Come and Other Hits (Estrus) 1993
Sleep (Super Electro) 1994

BLOODLOSS

Human Skin Suit (Aus. Greasy Pop) 1988
The Truth Is Marching In (Aus. Aberrant) 1990
In-a-Gadda-da-Change (Sympathy for the Record Industry) 1993
Misty (Aus. Au-go-go) 1995
Live My Way (Reprise) 1995

THROWN-UPS

Felch EP (Amphetamine Reptile) 1987
Smiling Panties EP (Amphetamine Reptile) 1987
Eat My Dump EP (Amphetamine Reptile) 1988
Melancholy Girlhole Box (Amphetamine Reptile) 1990
Thrown-Ups (Ger. Glitterhouse) 1990

It would come as no great surprise to discover that the members of this Seattle Bigfoot-rock progenitor were sent home from school with report cards covered with comments about laziness and unfulfilled potential. Although possessed of the ability to toss off staggeringly galvanizing anthems—early singles, like the legendary debut "Touch Me I'm Sick" could easily have propelled them to the stature Nirvana later achieved—Mudhoney's endemic smugness and creative inertia has kept them shackled at a middling career point where they're generally less known for their output than for their historical standing as the guys from Green River who *didn't* join Pearl Jam.

Superfuzz Bigmuff (named in honor of the vintage guitar distortion pedals Mark Arm and Steve Turner, respectively, used to chisel out the sludge-punk sound later dubbed grunge) makes it clear that Mudhoney, in the grand tradition of earlier Pacific Northwest rock, intends to let a smirk be its umbrella. Songs like "In 'n Out of Grace" allow singer Arm (a Green River alum, as is Turner) ample room to wheedle in classic garage-punk fashion. The 1991 reissue adds six early songs—like the creepy "Sweet Young Thing (Ain't Sweet No More)," a 45 track also on the import-only **Boiled Beef** EP—that rank with their best work ever. The full-length **Mudhoney** is a big letdown, relying on Turner's wah-wah wash to mask the lack of ideas. (It doesn't.) Other than the seething "This Gift," there's little to differentiate this sort of posturing from the metal-boy variety it was meant to supplant.

Every Good Boy Deserves Fudge extends the period of coasting. Producer Conrad Uno's dry 8-track production sharpens Mudhoney's garage-rock edge—evident in Arm's fuzzed-out vocals and a shared fondness for second-hand blues progressions—enough to stand apart from the watered-down metal of most flannel merchants, but they don't go anywhere with it. As usual, there are a handful of riffs that make you go "hmmmmm"—notably the ones running through "Let It Slide" and "Check-Out Time," both of which revisit Arm's death-is-cool fixation. All too often, however, the quartet displays a pre-pubescent infatuation with its own slop, which oozes from half-baked songs like "Fuzzgun '91" and "Don't Fade IV." The subsequent EP (untitled, though known as **Let It Slide** for the song with which it begins) augments a pair of **EGBDF** tracks with three previously unreleased tracks, including a cover of "The Money Will Roll Right In," from the catalogue of Bay Area hardcore pioneers Fang.

Even though those smirks haven't faded, **Piece of Cake** indicates that Mudhoney has practiced more than just lip action: Arm's pissed-off diatribes about his own dissatisfaction ("No End in Sight") and his antipathy toward those who don't share it ("Suck You Dry") bounce off a revamped set of fuzzed-out riffs. A deft mix helps bring out the volatile rhythms laid down by drummer Dan Peters and bassist Matt Lukin (ex-Melvins). Sure, there's still some filler (including a passel of untitled instrumental interludes that drip with disdain), but the genuine fire that flares up in "Ritzville" (an evil twin to R.E.M.'s "Rockville" that turns on a shrugged "it's as good a place as any to go and die") is heartening. The effort must have taken a lot out of the band, considering the lackluster heave it gives the seven-track **Five Dollar Bob's Mock Cooter Stew,** a dull, dopey mishmash of suburban-boy backwoodsiness and rote garage aping (although "Between Me & You Kid" does eke a few more miles out of the well-worn "Psychotic Reaction" riff).

Though largely ignored by a waning public, **My Brother the Cow** fulfills the promise made way back when. Arm's verge-of-hysteria shriek—best showcased on lurching, feedback-drenched songs like "Execution Style" and "Judgment, Rage, Retribution and Thyme"—is Mudhoney's signature, but when the singer drops the intensity just a notch, his lyrical incisiveness cuts with stiletto precision. The wry icon-bashing of "Generation Spokesmodel" ("listen to my songs, I guarantee you'll relate/look at me, recognize your face") might mask the taste of venom with the sugar-coating of snappy punchlines, but there's no missing the bracingly acrid aftertaste. Nowhere is that used to better effect than on "Into Yer Shtik," a pointed open letter to Seattle's most famous rock widow, which ends its reading of the riot act with the suggestion "why don't you blow your brains out too?" The topper, however, is the epic closing track, "1995." Picking up where the Stooges' "1969" left off—complete with a similarly squawking free-jazz-as-concealed-weapon sax line—Arm and the band agonize dissolutely over the vast emptiness of existence and then shrug, deciding the whole shebang is only half-vast after all. And who can argue with that?

The joint EP with Jimmie Dale Gilmore is a nifty sidestep, an improbable collaboration that actually kills several birds with one shiny platter. If not quite faithful, Mudhoney's modest but spiny two-stepping cover of Gilmore's "Tonight I Think I'm Gonna Go Downtown" proves the group *can* actually muster a convincing measure of cultural respect, while the Texan's stirring version of **Piece of Cake**'s bluesy "Blinding Sun" extols the cowboy ballad's intrinsic virtues. If nothing else, the Gilmore/Mudhoney rendition of Townes Van Zandt's "Buckskin Stallion Blues" demonstrates the band's ability to play it straight and keep their 'tude to themselves. (Rounding out this fascinating oddity are the artists' original versions of the two swap-meet numbers.)

In the Monkeywrench, Arm and Turner join with members of Poison 13, Gas Huffer and Lubricated Goat in order to lovingly deconstruct (read: cluelessly bash through) the maximum R&B side of mid-'60s Britrock. If the sounds stacked up to the high-concept packaging, **Clean as a Broke-Dick Dog** would be terrific fun. (Of course, if cat spit tasted just a little bit better, it would provide an inexpensive alternative to Guinness Stout.) Turner approaches the same beast with a bit more regard (if no more sobriety) in the Fall-Outs, a longstanding garage band he joined on bass in the early '90s. On **The Fall-Outs,** the trio's fondness for circa-'63 Stones speed-blues is as clear as vodka: songs like "The Life for Me" and "Ambition" (an ode to lack of same) stop well shy of the two-minute mark, but the sheer energy exerted in those seconds could carry most bands through an entire set. Authenticity, rather than freshness, is definitely the point on **Here I Come,** but again, the Fall-Outs get over on enthusiasm—along with the rising snot level that accompanies these more Sonics-like proto-punk bashes.

Through the agency of drummer Martin Bland, an Australian member of the Monkeywrench, Arm joined forces with his foreboding—if often silly—Aussie combo Bloodloss (a loose, long-running group that includes former members of Lubricated Goat) shortly after the release of the trashily involving **The Truth is Marching In.** Rather than pour forth the viscous sludge one might expect, Bloodloss churns up a dour, post-Cave blend of gutter-blues and garage-rock that's most effectively captured on **In-a-Gadda-da-Change,** well-marbled with Arm's smoky organ lines. **Misty** appends several singles (including the demented "Hair of the Future") to that album for Australian release. **Live My Way,** the band's American major-label unveiling, tones down the sonic ugliness a tad—focusing attention on Renestair EJ's boozy sax playing and the punkified Tom Waits arrangements—but the self-loathing vibe of songs like "Hated in My House" and "Face Down in Mud" remains unabated.

Arm and Turner were once half of the Thrown-Ups, a much funnier—and scarier—sludgehammer of a band with a fixation on body parts and bodily fluids and a fondness for what sounds like perfectly good guitars being jammed neck-first into garbage disposals. The EPs don't have much, er, subtext, but Turner's equipment eviscerating is captivating enough in its own right. The twelve-song **Melancholy Girlhole Box** (eponymously retitled for German release) may well be the most willfully inept *object de f'art* ever knowingly committed to tape. Even GG Allin would be green with envy (or for some other reason) after slogging through no-fi transgressions like "Sloppy Pud Love" and "Hairy Crater Man." Heck, there's even some vision of the future in the form of "Stock Boy." Testimony to the notion that sometimes art is 99 percent desecration and 1 percent inspiration. [dss]

See also *Jimmie Dale Gilmore, Melvins, Mother Love Bone; TPRG.*

MUFFS

The Muffs (Warner Bros.) 1993
Blonder and Blonder (Reprise) 1995

Los Angeles will always find a place in its heart for those who believe fun is everything—and stoopid fun is the best fun of all. That's the best way to account for the Southern California herodom granted this thrashy, thrashy bubblepunk band fronted by Kim Shattuck, once a member of the kickier Pandoras. There's nothing terribly wrong with the Muffs—aside from Shattuck's sometimes wince-inducing screech, that is—but try as they may, the band's obsessively obtuse tunes don't so much carry the Ramones' torch as tag along in its shadow hoping to make something from its fallen ashes.

On the quartet's full-length debut (which was preceded by a handful of sharp, memorable singles), the Muffs display abundant old-school pop savvy—"Saying Goodbye" is the kind of deadpan-sweet kiss-off tune that could've made Blondie a success *sans* disco beats—but curiously meager energy levels. The vast majority of the sixteen tracks fall into a desultory mid-tempo rut, which is a drag—either "From Your Girl" or "Every Single Thing" would have made a touching power ballad in less clumsy hands. Shattuck's guitar leads do sparkle on several tracks, however, so much so that they made second guitarist Melanie Vammen (another ex-Pandora) expendable. (Rob Cavallo, who would become a lot better known for a Green Day album he worked on the following year, co-produced.)

Both Vammen and drummer Criss Crass departed during the two years between Muffs releases; the latter (who moved back to Seattle and joined the Rockinghams) was replaced by Roy McDonald. Thus reconstituted, the trio (again employing Cavallo) recorded **Blonder and Blonder,** a considerably more dynamic restatement of purpose. Less fussy than its predecessor, the album gives Shattuck a chance to accentuate her flair for sparkling melodies both goofy and melancholy (as evidenced by "Funny Face" and "Laying on a Bed of Roses"). On the other hand, the sparser backing draws more attention to her numbing caterwaul and rote lyric tosses—see "On and On" and "End It All." [dss]

See also *Moberlys.*

MULE

Mule (Quarterstick) 1992
Wrung EP (Quarterstick) 1994
If I Don't Six (Quarterstick) 1994

After leading the band Wig in Detroit, singer/guitarist Preston Cleveland renamed himself P. W. Long (aka P-Bone) and formed Mule with bassist Kevin Strickland (renamed Kevin Munro) and drummer Jim Kimball. (The rhythm section had previously played in Ann Arbor's Laughing Hyenas, a band led by Cleveland's older brother, John Brannon, who was in an early version of Mule as well. Got all that?) Together, they lumbered into rock's ugly-noise battleground, braiding a twisted southern sensibility into midwestern aggression.

Mule contains an entertaining but uninformative comic book (*The Story of Mule*) and one acoustic old-timey ballad ("Now I Truly Understand") that walks a rocky road between condescension and sincerity. Otherwise, the band unloads nasty, harsh tunelessness of a species near and dear to Steve Albini (engineering here as Lenard Johns). A passing whiff of Lynyrd Skynyrd in "Mississippi Breaks" and Long's bogus backwoods hollerin' on "Mama's Reason to Cry" add an irrelevant accent to the proceedings; "What Every White Nigger Knows" contributes a bolt of arrogant stupidity.

Kimball left to form the Dennison-Kimball Trio, replaced by Daniel Jacob Wilson. Wisely dropping the 'billy club and folk pretensions, **Wrung** turns Mule toward Nick Cave's Birthday Party armageddon visions, using Long's bellowing vocals and trebly guitar abrasion to drive the four songs ("The Rope and the Cuckold" among them) into a fierce sick headache.

As if following Cave's progress from a distance, Mule tones it down—and even swings, after a fashion—in "The Beauteous" and "Nowhere's Back" on **If I Don't Six;** the latter song imports a very useful bit of organ. Most of the other seven tracks on the record (which begins enticingly enough with the orgasmic panting of guest Laura Borealis) also displays a little extra thought, restraint and musicality, as well as a workable rapprochement with raw country desires ("Obion," "A Hundred Years"). The album is still as hard and dangerous as rusty nails to a blind carpenter, but the careful hammering makes the music reach in deeper, with fewer splinters and busted thumbs. [i]

See also *Jesus Lizard, Laughing Hyenas, Wig.*

MUMMIES

Never Been Caught (Telstar) 1992
Fuck CDs, It's the Mummies (UK Hangman) 1992
The Mummies Play Their Own Records (Estrus) 1992
Party at Steve's House (Pin Up) 1994
The Mummies (no label) 1994

Beyond their inspired low-budget visual gimmickry—they drive around in an old hearse and perform wrapped head to toe in gauze bandages—San Francisco's Mummies play lo-fi garage-rock with a convincingly reckless spirit and a frantic R&B edge.

Pretty much summing up everything you need to know about the Mummies, **Never Been Caught** (whose wonderfully trashy cover art depicts the stylishly draped men cavorting in a variety of activities) fields seventeen tunes, divided between in-yer-face originals by mastermind Trent Ruane and well-chosen vintage covers. English kindred spirit Billy Childish was so taken with the foursome that he released **Fuck CDs, It's the Mummies**—similar to, though shorter than, **Never Been Caught**—on his Hangman imprint.

The Mummies Play Their Own Records compiles the band's non-album singles up to that point, adding four new tracks. **Party at Steve's House**—ostensibly recorded live in the titular domicile—takes a somewhat jollier frat-rockish direction, with the emphasis on slyly moronic originals ("Don Gallucci's Balls" is a tribute to the Kingsmen member and Stooges producer) whose formal mastery is so complete that they might as well be covers. The sleeve art includes photos of two band members swinging from nooses.

In keeping with the band's staunchly anti-digital stance, all of the Mummies' official releases were vinyl-only, helping to ensure their obscurity outside of the indie and garage-rock underground. Nevertheless, some enterprising (if underhanded) soul released an unauthorized CD—packaged with a rubber-stamped plain white sleeve—composed largely of sub-par tracks recorded (with ex–Raunch Hand Mike Mariconda, himself the subject of a song on **Never Been Caught,** producing) for an unissued album for the Crypt label. [ss]

MURDER INC.

See *Killing Joke.*

MURMURS

The Murmurs (MCA) 1994

The New York–based singing-songwriting-busking Murmurs—Florida native Heather Grody and Nebraska expatriate Leisha Hailey—display lovely, harmonious voices and serviceable folk-pop melodies on their debut album, but that's the last of their good news. Trouble hits halfway through the first track ("Bad Mood") with this irritating bit of irritation: "Nothing seems to go my god damn way." Beware of neophytes who make a bid for sympathy before properly introducing themselves—especially ones who wear wings in their album art. "Ticket to Zen" finds its own sweet relief, but the record's demi-hit, "You Suck," squeezes a dose of self-absorbing pus from some deep romantic wound, a gratuitous gripefest as welcome as an unprompted harangue from the guy sitting next to you on the subway. [i]

PETER MURPHY

Should the World Fail to Fall Apart (UK Beggars Banquet) 1986 (Beggars Banquet) 1996
Love Hysteria (Beggars Banquet/RCA) 1988 (Beggars Banquet/Atlantic) 1995
Deep (Beggars Banquet/RCA) 1990 (Beggars Banquet/Atlantic) 1995
Holy Smoke (Beggars Banquet/RCA) 1992 (Beggars Banquet/Atlantic) 1995
You're So Close EP (Beggars Banquet/RCA) 1992
The Scarlet Thing in You EP (Beggars Banquet/Atlantic) 1995
Cascade (Beggars Banquet/Atlantic) 1995

By the time the late '80s rolled around, Peter Murphy had worked hard to rid himself of the gothic image the Englishman (from Northampton, actually) had earned as the brooding, vampiric singer of Bauhaus. After that band broke up in '84, Murphy did a short stint in Dalis Car, a weirdly atmospheric group he formed with ex-Japan bassist Mick Karn, before setting out on a determinedly non-goth solo career. But, try as he might to smother it, even his most blatantly commercial writing always contains more than a hint of the darkly sensual sound that made Bauhaus an archetype.

Should the World Fail to Fall Apart is a dreamy, mildly experimental effort that turns modest understatement to Murphy's benefit. Even at low volume and languorous tempo, he can't shake the old theatrics out of his voice. The covers of Magazine's "The Light Pours Out of Me" and Pere Ubu's "Final Solution" are intriguing but ungainly. **Love Hysteria** sets Murphy's commanding baritone against brittle, airy music built on a dual fixation with **Lodger**-era Bowie and the group Japan.

Murphy finally got the balance right on **Deep,** smoothly blending his usual moody eloquence, abiding Bowie obsession and newfound mainstream impulses into one exhilarating musical vision. Murphy's mysterious persona is commanding on quietly atmospheric songs ("A Strange Kind of Love," "Marlene Dietrich's Favourite Poem") as well as on intricately worked pop tracks ("Seven Veils," the ominous, syncopated "Roll Call"). Released as a single, the peppy rock danceability of "Cuts You Up" even gained Murphy a measure of American commercial success.

Murphy apparently spent all his songwriting reserves on **Deep. Holy Smoke** is thoroughly uninspired, an album of, at best, halfhearted clichés and, at worst, risible stupidity. In "The Sweetest Drop," a belated tribute to Duran Duran attempting to sound like Bryan Ferry, he strives to describe sex as if it were an eighteenth-century museum exhibit: "Concur and swallow me/Explode, secrete your tender . . . give me what I thirst . . . press towards the burst." Although he elsewhere has the temerity to use the title "Hit Song," at least the tune's lyrics concern nothing at all. The fleeting sparks of life here—the suavely laid-back throb of "Keep Me From Harm" and the gritty "Low Room"—are not nearly enough to salvage this mess. The **You're So Close** EP is worth seeking out for its live versions of songs from **Deep** (a ferocious "Line Between the Devil's Teeth," a shimmery extended take on "Cuts You Up") and **Love Hysteria** ("All Night Long").

Following a personal relocation to Turkey, Murphy made the much-improved **Cascade.** If not as awe-inspiring as **Deep,** the album is mercifully free of **Holy Smoke**'s obvious commercial ambitions. "The Scarlet Thing in You" (also the title track of a four-song EP containing a live version of "Dragnet Drag" and an album outtake) does aim at the Top 40, but with honest exuberance and a real melody. "Huuvola," a gorgeous, drifting ballad, surrounds Murphy with an aura of romance and mystery, as does the more surreal, unstructured title track. Pascal Gabriel (EMF, Inspiral Carpets) produced; Michael Brook contributes "infinite guitar." [ky/i]

See also *TPRG.*

KEITH MURRAY

The Most Beautifullest Thing in This World (Jive) 1994
Enigma (Jive) 1996

Like Craig Mack, rapper Keith Murray is a Long Islander who got a helping hand from EPMD: Erick Sermon co-wrote, produced and guests on his debut album. An articulate, upbeat MC genially surrounded by scratchy, slow-rolling beats, Murray keeps his clever rhymes moving, dropping culture references and his "sychosymatic" lingo. A benign rapper in the old-school tradition, Murray keeps cursing, sexuality and violence at bay, instead spending his time praising weed and juice ("Herb Is Pumpin'," "Get Lifted," the Redman-produced sci-fi pot fantasy of "Escapism"). At his warmest and fuzziest, Murray fills the title track (presented in two mixes) with gentle bragging. All of the album's unpleasantry is relegated to "Bom Bom Zee," with guest vulgarity from Hurricane Gee. But drop-ins don't all bring heavy manners: with Sermon and Redman (as well as a sample of "The Show") in the mix, the good-natured "How's That" boosts the energy level in a virtuoso free-for-all of shoutouts and shutouts. [i]

MUSIC REVELATION ENSEMBLE

See *James Blood Ulmer.*

MUTTS

The Mutts EP (Shanghai) 1985
Stinko's Ranch (Loud Music) 1992

The Mutts' 1985 EP introduces a mildly amusing hooks'n'humor guitar band, yet only hints at how good the Los Angeles quintet would get at it. By the '92 LP, the core of that group—guitarist Kevin Grover and bassist Eddy Sill—had re-emerged as lead singers of an otherwise new quartet, with novice Mutt Billy Murrell on guitar. The band's songwriting is miles better, too: the album kicks off with the instantly winning melodies of "Cricket" and (sigh) "Emilyn." The Mutts go on to mock—oh so melodically—how clueless they (as Everymen) really are on "John Hughes Movie (Not Quite Like A)," "I Live With a Cat" and "Just What I Was Afraid Of" ("You're just what I wanted . . . needed . . . was afraid of"), with new drummer Paul Legaspi kicking butt behind 'em all the while. [jg]

See also *TPRG.*

MX-80

See *Bruce Anderson.*

MY BLOODY VALENTINE

This Is Your Bloody Valentine EP (UK Tycoon) 1985 (Ger. Dossier) 1988
Geek EP (UK Fever) 1986
The New Record by My Bloody Valentine EP (UK Kaleidoscope Sound) 1986
Sunny Sundae Smile EP (UK Lazy) 1987
Strawberry Wine EP (UK Lazy) 1987
Ecstasy EP (UK Lazy) 1987
Isn't Anything (Creation/Relativity) 1988 (Creation/ Sire/Warner Bros.) 1994
Feed Me With Your Kiss EP (UK Creation) 1988
You Made Me Realise EP (UK Creation) 1988
Ecstasy and Wine (UK Lazy) 1989
Glider EP (UK Creation) 1989 (Sire) 1990
Tremolo EP (UK Creation) 1990 (Sire/Warner Bros.) 1991
Loveless (Creation/Sire/Warner Bros.) 1991

This Dublin-born band didn't take long to establish itself as the cornerstone of a loose, largely media-built coalition of bands playing aggressive (and aggressively opaque) pop music that stood in direct opposition to both rockism and the twee bedsit romanticism of the pallid anti-rockists. But while most of the embryonic shoegazers maintained a tacit connection with pop tradition, My Bloody Valentine gradually transformed its lexicon via radical addition-by-subtraction: by the dawn of the '90s, the band had reinvented itself as a herald of sound as sacrament.

The early records capture a group in step with the times, but perhaps a bit too eager to get into the studio. On **This Is Your Bloody Valentine** (recorded, incidentally, in Berlin) the band betrays some awkward Batcave-ish roots as it "progresses" from campy Doors mimicry to spelunking in Nick's Cave. The only thing missing is originality. **Geek** is pretty much a carbon copy, largely because of David Conway's basso profundo (occasionally *ridiculoso*) croon, but **The New Record** uses a broader palette: the breathy "Lovelee Sweet Darlene" is outright childlike in its innocence.

By this time, My Bloody Valentine had begun construction on a wall of sound/noise (depending on your aesthetic values) that's often likened to the Jesus and Mary Chain's. But where the Reids sequester themselves in a forbidding cage of hardened steel, MBV beckon from behind a glistening, almost transparent curtain of the thinnest gold leaf. This approach became all the more tantalizing when Conway left after **Sunny Sundae Smile** (notable for the silliest song ever about blow-up-doll love) and took most of the stormclouds with him. **Strawberry Wine** replaces the gloom with lush West Coast psychedelia that owes a fair amount to Arthur Lee.

Ecstasy (later paired with **Strawberry Wine** as **Ecstasy and Wine**) ups the dissonance factor a bit, and greatly de-emphasizes the shared vocals of new member Bilinda Butcher and Kevin Shields (both also play guitar), presaging a Creation trademark-in-the-making tendency to elevate sound over song. There are certainly several of the latter on the band's first bona fide longplayer, **Isn't Anything.** Most, it seems, revolve around, er, non-mainstream sexuality (check out "Cigarette in Your Bed"—only on the British edition—for some strange kicks); all ride waves of languid "glide guitar" (the band's phrase) to almost narcotic effect. Trivia buffs should note My Bloody Valentine's appropriation of Public Enemy's "Security of the First World" riff—a full two years before Madonna's "Justify My Love."

Feed Me With Your Kiss (a single from **Isn't Anything**) and **You Made Me Realise** (not its real name: the four-song 12-inch that features that tune actually has no title) favor more conventional structures—to the point of curiosity on "You Made Me Realise," which strips down to skeletal riff-rock basics for an X-like hootenanny. **Glider,** on the other hand, is a wholehearted embrace of stasis—not at all a bad thing, given the band's extraordinary ability to arrive without traveling. The best track, "Soon," all but dispenses with frills like choruses and chord progressions, opting instead for seven minutes of mesmerizing swells and contractions. That futurist-styled transmutation of motion set the stage for the further surrender of pop convention that marks the aptly titled **Tremolo,** four new songs whose buoyancy is largely owed to the constant sweeping motions with which Shields wields his whammy bar. In his hands, the oft-abused axe appendage becomes a magic wand.

The quartet spent nearly three years (and nearly a half-million dollars) recording **Loveless,** a glorious and singular album that stands as one of the decade's most important audio statements. **Loveless** is pop shredded through the looking glass and painstakingly reassembled on the other side—with each piece set just far enough off-kilter that your senses never regain their balance. Part **Pet Sounds** and part **Metal Machine Music,** the album buffs elements of pure noise until the whole is enticing, shimmering—and, on gauzy tracks like "I Only Said" and "When You Sleep"—nearly perfect bubblegum. The deliberate lurching and pitching of songs like the epic "To Here Knows When" seem designed to approximate inner-ear dysfunction, with the clincher being "Touched," a quease-courting ninety-second sample loop that will sorely test your faith in technology.

It was on several tours in support of **Loveless** that My Bloody Valentine *really* served notice of its intent to challenge audience endurance: sets that began at earplug-oxidizing volume escalated precipitously, culminating in an epic dissertation on a single chord—a D to be precise—that often passed the twenty-minute mark. The limit-pushing evidently took a lot out of My Bloody Valentine: although a third full album has been rumored to be near completion several times, nothing has been heard from the trailblazing band since it began a studio stint that, as of early 1996, had already seen four years come and go. [dss]

See also *Spacemen 3; TPRG.*

MY DAD IS DEAD

My Dad Is Dead . . . and He's Not Gonna Take It Anymore (St. Valentine) 1986 (Ger. Houses in Motion) 1990

Peace, Love and Murder (Birth) 1987 (Ger. Houses in Motion) 1991
Let's Skip the Details (Homestead) 1988
The Best Defense (Homestead) 1988
The Taller You Are, the Shorter You Get (Homestead) 1989
Shine EP7 (Scat) 1990
Chopping Down the Family Tree (Scat) 1991
Out of Sight, Out of Mind (Scat) 1993
Hello EP (Hello Recording Club) 1995
For Richer, for Poorer (Emperor Jones/Trance Syndicate) 1995
Shine(r) (Emperor Jones/Trance Syndicate) 1996

Actually the work of a person rather than a band, My Dad Is Dead's voluminous output has plainly explored the troubled waters of the soul, both personal and philosophical, for nearly a decade. Ohioan Mark Edwards writes, plays and sings his material with instrumental and vocal help from a floating gene pool of fellow Cleveland musicians (Prisonshake's Chris Burgess has also produced the bulk of his recordings).

My Dad Is Dead, largely inspired by Edwards' paternal loss, is a compelling, hypnotic debut that ranges from thrashy aggression to supple melodicism to industrial gloom, all unified by the downbeat lyrics. The album's weak link is Edwards' flat singing (which has since improved). **Peace, Love and Murder** and **Let's Skip the Details** show considerable growth; **The Best Defense,** which assembles outtakes and 4-track home recordings, is unessential but contains some fine moments, including three surprisingly harmonious instrumentals. **The Taller You Are, the Shorter You Get** (a double LP) brings Edwards to a new plateau of ambition and accessibility. His lyrics have grown less morose and more philosophical, and he sings them with newfound expressiveness.

Leaving the Homestead label, Edwards released an impressive eight-song double-7-inch, **Shine** (later expanded by a dozen previously unreleased tracks from the same sessions and elsewhere and reissued as **Shine(r)** by Emperor Jones/Trance Syndicate), and then his first full-length on local indie Scat. Packaged in a magnificent die-cut sleeve (on both LP and CD issues), **Chopping Down the Family Tree** boasts its fair share of Edwards' familiar lyrics and dense, metallic instrumentation, but the fog hovering over his head has lifted a little further. The album's first half revels in gritty guitar sounds and biting lyrics (the title cut proclaims "The strength of the family can be an illusion when built on control and based on collusion"), while the second blooms under the first's dark waters, reaching a tentative cheerfulness, both lyrical and musical, on "Without a Doubt" and "Shine" (a song not featured on the EP of that name).

The terse, plodding sound of **Out of Sight, Out of Mind** (credited to MDID rather than My Dad Is Dead, and recorded as a trio with bassist Matt Swanson and Prisonshake drummer Scott Pickering) regresses into gloomy self-awareness, and Edwards' lyrics match the shift: the protagonist in "She's in Love" faces dangerous consequences for indulging herself in that way, "Razor Strap" reveals an abused child and "The Prisoner" proves Edwards knows exactly where he stands. His guitar buzzes angrily throughout, acting as the album's blood supply, while thundering drumbeats are its heartbeat. The only ray of sunshine is the closer, the chiming, nearly anthemic "You Are the One," one of his strongest songs, where once again Edwards' lyrical and musical sides are effectively synchronized.

Although he plays with the same musicians on **For Richer, for Poorer** (absent Burgess' production), Edwards' eighth album casts an altogether sunnier glow than **Out of Sight, Out of Mind.** The grating guitar sounds and throbbing rhythms are in less evidence, replaced by carefully fashioned guitar hooks and gentler beats. There's still plenty of stylistic variation, and Edwards even broadens the range and delivery of his deadpan vocals ("Way Too Wise"). Largely because he's pushing his well-defined sound in new directions, **For Richer, for Poorer** stands alongside **The Taller You Are** and **Chopping Down the Family Tree** among MDID's strongest albums. Edwards spells it all out on "Heirloom": "I tore myself apart, and picked up all the pieces, and from them fashioned a heart."

The five tracks on My Dad Is Dead's entry in the Hello CD of the Month subscription-only series are otherwise unavailable outtakes. [ss/la]

See also *Cobra Verde, Prisonshake; TPRG.*

MY HEAD

See *Suicidal Tendencies.*

MY LIFE WITH THE THRILL KILL KULT

I See Good Spirits and I See Bad Spirits (Wax Trax!) 1988
Kooler Than Jesus (Wax Trax!) 1990
Confessions of a Knife . . . (Wax Trax!) 1990
Sexplosion! (Wax Trax!) 1991 (Interscope/Atlantic) 1992
13 Above the Night (Interscope/Atlantic) 1993
Hit & Run Holiday (Interscope) 1995

Longtime Chicago disco scenester Frank Nardiello had dabbled in various art-punk bands when in 1987 he met kindred spirit Marston Daley, who had just moved to Chicago from Boston. Nardiello and Daley rechristened themselves Groovie Mann and Buzz McCoy, and enlisted keyboardist Thomas "Buck Ryder" Lockyear, "go-go butt" dancer Jacky Blacque and an ever-changing array of local nightcrawlers, dubbed the Bomb Gang Girlz, to create My Life With the Thrill Kill Kult. Less a band than a lurid low-brow art project, Thrill Kill Kult initially began as a movie, then evolved into a continuing electro-disco soundtrack for an imaginary series of sex-Satan-and-gore flicks.

Emerging amid a flock of hard-edged and essentially humorless industrial bands on the Wax Trax! label, Thrill Kill Kult strove to set themselves apart with tabloid-magazine outrageousness. But **I See Good Spirits and I See Bad Spirits** isn't nearly bombastic enough; the dreary mix of electronic atmospherics, vaguely ominous chants, disco beats and B-movie samples aspires to sleaziness but never breaks (out in) a sweat.

The seven-song **Kooler Than Jesus** collects the contents of two early 12-inches and adds two numbers. The title track, originally a 1989 single, is a dance groove sturdy enough to warrant a remix on **Confessions of a Knife.** A sendup of all things gothic, **Knife** is bathed in fake blood and thriller-chiller mockery. "Christian zombie vampire" goes the nursery rhyme chant in "The Days of Swine and Roses." The tales of the occult, mental illness and murder are framed by metal guitars, warbling world music vocalists and rubbery basslines, which serve to make the Kult's high-concept kitsch listenable enough.

Vampires are replaced by dominatrixes on **Sexplosion!**, a campy romp that evokes myriad James Bond ripoffs, both in lyrical content and in the swagger of the John Barry–like instrumental accompaniment—particularly "The International Sin Set." With its deliciously decadent chorus of "Uber baby!" and grinding guitar, "Sex on Wheelz" is the Kult's peak moment on record, while "Mystery Babylon" dabbles in a Latin groove, "A Martini Built for 2" swanks it up with airport-lounge organ and "Princess of the Queens (The Lost Generation)" tinkers with rap. (Other than tinkered artwork, a deleted remix of the album's "Dream Baby" and a different bonus edit of "Sex on Wheelz," the record's major-label reissue is identical to the indie original.)

Wrapped in brilliantly colored psychedelic artwork, **13 Above the Night** is a denser, more elaborately produced record, with snatches of gospelized call-and-response vocals, chicken-scratch funk guitar and bass percolating in a neo-psychedelic mix. But the cheap-thrill lyrics now come dressed up in literary pretensions, with such babblings as "She speaks of life's Eternal scrolls/In Ancient Splendor we will roam," from "Dimentia 66 (The Ballad of Lucy Western)."

The black-and-white **Hit & Run Holiday** gets the Kult back on the low road where it belongs, with tales of drag-strip lust and hot-rod heartbreak. Horns pad out the disco rhythms, and "Glamour Is a Rocky Road"—with its cheesy keyboards, twangy guitar and gum-smacking female chorus—evokes the bubblegum surf-rock of the early B-52's. The Kult also accurately critiques its limitations on "Mission: Stardust": "Glamour is my only weapon." [gk]

See also *TPRG*.

MY SISTER'S MACHINE

Diva (Caroline) 1992
Wallflower (Chameleon/Elektra) 1993

Seattle singer Nick Pollock can claim genealogical props for membership in an unrecorded version of the nascent Alice in Chains, but that's not much to build a career on. Not surprisingly, his more recent quartet—formed with the guitarist (Owen Wright) and bassist (Chris Ivanovich) of another local band, Mistrust—skillfully hits many of the same bellowing not-quite-metal hard-rock marks with more conscious stylistic variety and decidedly less inspiration. If Kiss or Black Sabbath ever need a backup vocalist, Pollock's number should be on their shortlist. [tr]

MYSTERIES OF LIFE

See *Antenna.*

MYSTIC FUGU ORCHESTRA

See *John Zorn.*

MYSTIC MOOG ORCHESTRA

See *His Name Is Alive.*

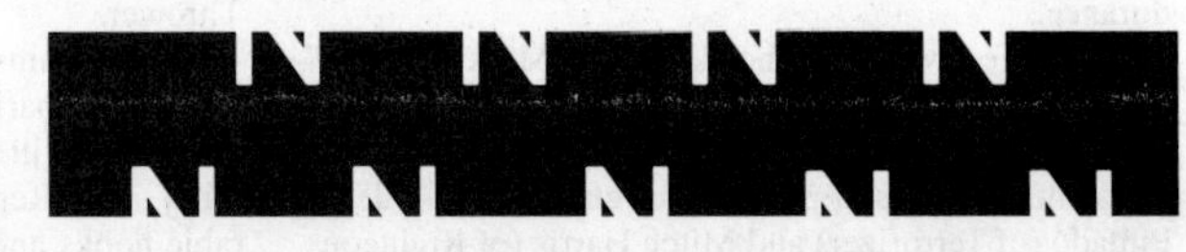

NAKED CITY

Torture Garden (Shimmy-Disc) 1990
Heretic, Jeux des Dames Cruelles (Japan. Avant) 1992
Grand Guignol (Japan. Avant) 1992
Leng Tch'e (Japan. Toy's Factory) 1992
Radio (Japan. Avant) 1993
Absinthe (Japan. Avant) 1993

JOHN ZORN

Naked City (Nonesuch) 1989

While this semi-fluid aggregation wasn't leader John Zorn's first attempt at a fusion (so to speak) of improv-jazz and free-rock elements, it has without a doubt been the hornman's most extreme. Drawing equally from the random viscera spew of hardcore punk (highlighted by the presence of Boredoms singer Eye Yamatsuka) and the intellectually challenging tonal experiments of modern classical composers like Charles Ives, Naked City creates a constantly shifting sonic environment that's tricky to navigate no matter what survival tools the listener brings along.

On **Naked City** (which is actually credited to Zorn as a solo artist), the band sets the tone for things to come by jimmying no less than twenty-five brief bursts of deceptively well-ordered noise onto a disc adorned with a gruesome post-execution photograph. Egged on by Zorn's saxophone, guitarist Fred Frith and precise drummer Joey Baron let their usual tight reins out to wax playful on pieces like "N.Y. Flat Top Box" and "Speedball." What's most striking, however, is the cinematic quality of such noir soundbites as "The Sicilian Clan" and "Latin Quarter," both of which illustrate their title subjects magnificently—albeit in an entirely unconventional manner.

Torture Garden is a bit less exhilarating, in part because the group swings its pendulum too far into rock territory, and in part because Zorn doesn't control the arrangements with the same exactitude as on the debut. As such, it could pass for any number of post-Minutemen art-punk combos having a go at jazzbo miscegenation—with a facelessness that's unforgivable, given the unique styles of the participants. Yamatsuka asserts himself more strongly on **Heretic,** a film score dedicated to (and clearly influenced by) avant director Harry Smith. Over the course of two dozen rough-edged pieces—most of which sound hewn from longer improvs—the group seldom downshifts from warp speed (or warped objective) long enough to allow breathing room for artists or audience.

Grand Guignol is a forty-one-"song," sixty-minute dissertation on deconstructionist theory that mixes Monk, Messiaen and Madball with an alternately compelling and disconcerting lack of cultural ranking. Since it was recorded at a handful of sessions (from 1989 through '91) with minor shifts in lineup (most including Zorn and guitarist Bill Frisell), **Grand Guignol** doesn't cohere particularly well—but if you like your musique concrète smashed into window-aimed bricks, it might be your cuppa meat.

On **Radio,** Naked City revisits the darkened movie theaters that provided spiritual succor for the band's initial recordings, with a particular spotlight on keyboardist Wayne Horvitz, whose elusive, chattering runs often got short shrift on earlier Naked City releases. Horvitz is pushed even further to the fore on the strictly instrumental **Absinthe,** which suffers greatly from the absence of Yamatsuka. Zorn disbanded Naked City in 1993, choosing to concentrate his energies on Masada, the linchpin project of his Radical Jewish Culture collective. [dss]

See also *Boredoms, Painkiller, John Zorn.*

NAPALM DEATH

Scum (Earache) 1986
From Enslavement to Obliteration (Earache) 1988
The Peel Sessions EP (UK Strange Fruit) 1989
Napalm Death EP (UK Rise Above) 1989
Mentally Murdered EP (UK Earache) 1989
Harmony Corruption (Earache/Combat) 1990
Live Corruption (UK Earache) 1990
Suffer the Children EP (UK Earache) 1990
The Peel Sessions (Strange Fruit/Dutch East India Trading) 1991
Mass Appeal Madness EP (Earache/Relativity) 1991
Death by Manipulation (Earache/Relativity) 1991
Utopia Banished (Earache/Relativity) 1992
The World Keeps Turning EP (Earache) 1992
Nazi Punks Fuck Off EP7 (Earache) 1993
Fear, Emptiness, Despair (Earache/Columbia) 1994
Greed Killing EP (Earache) 1995
Diatribes (Earache) 1996

BLOOD FROM THE SOUL

To Spite the Gland That Breeds (Earache) 1993

MEATHOOK SEED

Embedded (Earache) 1993

The first two albums by Napalm Death set a lasting high-water mark for musical extremism with blinding unpredictable speed and noise. The worldwide race for faster/louder effectively ended in the twenty-eight frenzied bursts of **Scum,** so the contentious crew of trailblazers from Birmingham, England, turned to industrial dirges—à la early Swans—for **From Enslavement to Obliteration.** Napalm Death became heroes to underground tape-traders, inspiring innumerable scabby imitators while fathering a host of bands from its own ranks to fill the Earache roster to the bloody gills. Grotesque vocalist Lee Dorrian (who later founded Cathedral), guitarist Justin Broadrick (who went on to Head of David and Godflesh), quickly replaced by guitarist Bill Steer of Carcass, were the integral early members of Napalm Death, the band with ten-second songs and lineups of equally brief endurance.

Restaffed with metalhead vocalist Mark "Barney" Greenway in 1990, Napalm Death (otherwise bassist Shane Embury and drummer Mick Harris) recruited two American poison-pen pals for guitar duties—Jesse Pintado (of Terrorizer) and Mitch Harris (of Righteous Pigs)—thus arriving at its first semblance of internal stability. In an attempt to conform with the thriving world of death metal, **Harmony Corruption** is Napalm Death's most disappointing moment. Predictable thrash tracks like "Unfit Earth" and "Vision Conquest" owe too much to influential but monotonous punk-metal bands like Death and Repulsion. Curious onlookers must have wondered what all the fuss was about.

The thirteen-song **Death by Manipulation** collects the **Mentally Murdered, Suffer the Children** and **Mass Appeal Madness** EPs and more ferocious grindcore. Raw production serves the band's intensity well, as the blend embraces wicked minor-key metal and wild moments of hyperactive abandon. A European version includes tracks from a 1987 split EP with influential Japanese blurcore group S.O.B. For collectors, Earache also issued the limited-edition **Live Corruption** and the deluxe boxed **Live at Salisbury.**

Volatile drummer and key personality Mick Harris left Napalm Death in 1992 to pursue computer music in Scorn and play the part of avant-garde enfant terrible in projects with John Zorn and Bill Laswell. **Utopia Banished** shows a slight improvement in the band's situation, thanks to the unrestrained drumming of Californian Danny Herrera and the introduction of atmospheric elements on "Contemptuous." Lyrically, the song "Aryanisms" takes a strong stand against the fascist tendencies brewing among the genre's adherents: "Challenge the sordid claims to purify," bellows Greenway in his usual voice from the cesspool of hell. "I cannot begin to comprehend how you wear such shame with vigour/Homophobic race antagonist/Harmony can only flourish with mutual regard."

With only Embury remaining from the early lineups, Napalm Death began to evolve beyond its legacy, touring Russia, the Middle East, Asia and other regions hungry for Western decadence. Released after a trip to South Africa, **Nazi Punks Fuck Off** includes three versions of the Dead Kennedys song, musically unremarkable but significant as a further indication of leftist sentiment—a courageous stand as such contemporaries as Morbid Angel and Deicide were irresponsibly preaching quite the opposite.

Fear, Emptiness, Despair, Napalm Death's major-label experiment, shows the same lineup binding bleak English punk roots with the progressive metal aggression of its three-fifths American membership. As the whirlwind thrashes forward on "Retching on the Dirt," a guitar or an extra beat is always riffing back in tense counterpoint. The band's dissonance becomes a conscious effect, not a side benefit of chaos, and the marriage of intense anger and calculation yields a near-masterpiece of passionate negative realism.

Released after an uncharacteristically long silence, **Greed Killing** points the way toward further change, combining two Napalm-style attempts at accessibility with a few short blasters and one live track (**Fear, Emptiness, Despair**'s "Plague Rages"). Something is up, as the band's massive presence has been transliterated into sonic terms more familiar to Björk than Bolt Thrower.

With drums coming down in constant flurries and Greenway roaring his brains (or at least his uvula) out, **Diatribes** still manages to slow the pace and sound fairly airy. Repetitive discordant guitars find memorable hooks and create heavy, haunting background as intricate rhythms pile up on each other in a well-orchestrated onslaught. Whether metal fans or the pop scene are prepared for radio-ready grindcore, "Just Rewards" and "Glimpse Into Genocide" are relatively mainstream rock songs, an indication that Napalm Death's long-term achievement may not be as idiomatic exemplars, but as genre-destroying innovators.

On their own, guitarist Mitch Harris and bassist Shane Embury have taken advantage of corporate backing to record with their friends and drum machines. Embury and vocalist Lou Koller of Sick of It All present a harshly digitized vision of hardcore as Blood From the Soul: **To Spite the Gland That Breeds** is anger taken to the point of exhaustion. (Most biologically dubious lyric: "Tendons on a nerve edge/Spasms uncontrolled.") There's more breathing room in Harris' Meathook Seed, Skinny Puppy–style metal psychedelia executed with the help of Embury and two members of Obituary. [ic]

See also *Brutal Truth, Cathedral, God, Godflesh, Bill Laswell, Painkiller, Scorn, Sick of It All; TPRG.*

NAS

Illmatic (Columbia) 1994
It Was Written (Columbia) 1996

A thoughtful rapper from New York City's Queensbridge projects, twenty-year-old Nasir Jones—briefly known as Nasty Nas—calmly piles on the internal rhymes in the fast-flowing but brief **Illmatic,** an uncommon and impressive debut that flashes intelligence, pot, civic pride—and bits of anti-Semitism and homophobia. In "N.Y. State of Mind" (not the Billy Joel anthem), Nas evenly chronicles a gunplay incident; he claims a hustler past in "Life's a Bitch." In the same song, he offers up this irrefutable bit of pragmatic philosophy: "Life's a bitch and then you die/That's why we get high/'Cause you never know when you're gonna go." The MC's imaginative tracks were produced by some of New York's finest: DJ Premier, Q-Tip, Pete Rock and the Large Professor (who gave Nas his first break, having him rap on Main Source's "Live at the Barbeque"). **Illmatic** dresses a solid rhythmic backbone in fascinating embellishments: piano arpeggios running through "The World Is Yours," horns blurting all over "Halftime," Hammond organ in "Memory Lane (Sittin' in da Park)," xylophone and string bass in "One Love" (no Marley connection here), the ghostly vocals and subliminal brass in "It Ain't Hard to Tell." Nasty? Nah. Nas.

For all the critical acclaim and street cred earned by **Illmatic,** the debut offered no clear indication that Nas was poised on the brink of major stardom. Released in July '96, **It Was Written**—boasting a notable bi-coastal collaboration with Dr. Dre and contributions from Lauryn Hill of the Fugees and others—exploded out of the proverbial box and bombed in at the top of the pop album charts. [i]

See also *Main Source.*

NATION OF ULYSSES

13-Point Program to Destroy America (Dischord) 1991
Plays Pretty for Baby (Dischord) 1992

CUPID CAR CLUB

Join Our Club EP7 (K) 1993

MAKE-UP

Destination: Love (Live! At Cold Rule) (Dischord) 1996

Dressed to kill in matching, mod-ish business suits (and hairnets), wrapping themselves in teen-mutiny mythology complete with an intricate double-talk manifesto and album acknowledgments to fellow punk bands (Bikini Kill) and Latin American guerrillas (the Shining Path), the Nation of Ulysses was certainly the most colorful of the straight-edge hardcore insurrectionists on the Dischord roster. But underneath the elaborate shtick and the impressive pompadours, the Washington, DC, group made a high-speed racket devoted to the timeless revolutionary spirit in all the best rock'n'roll. "It's illicit, cool and out of tune," they sing on the 1991 single "The Sound of Young America," a "My Generation" for the Fugazi generation.

With tongue only partly in cheek, the quintet refers to its sonic attack in the liner notes of **13-Point Program** as "Soul Music." There's plenty of the roughhouse, twin-guitar variety in such high-velocity bursts of angry-young-man attitude as "A Kid Who Tells on Another Kid Is a Dead Kid," "Cool Senior High School (Fight Song)" and "Hot Chocolate City." Singer Ian Svenonius (who doubles on occasional bleating trumpet) has a deeper, throaty quality to his delivery than most DC-style barkers—not quite a Stax/Volt Rollins but a striking combination of ardor and menace that elevates his breathless rage above mere harangue. (The CD edition of **13-Point Program** includes the "3-point remedial program"—that is, the three tracks from the "Sound of Young America" 7-inch.)

Plays Pretty for Baby opens with another bright, brusque call to arms, "N-Sub Ulysses": "I'm not talking about a Beatles' song, written 100 years before I was born . . . who's got the real anti-parent culture sound?" Again produced by Fugazi's Ian MacKaye, **Plays Pretty for Baby** is even meaner and leaner than **13-Point Program,** shaking with a desperation echoed by the back-cover photo of five Nation of Ulysses dolls going up in flames. In "The Hickey Underworld," Svenonius sounds like he's tearing his throat inside out; Steven Kroner and Tim Green's guitars in "50,000 Watts of Goodwill" and "Maniac Dragstrip" grind and wail like factory machinery. The Nation of Ulysses dissolved before changing the world, but these two albums are an incendiary epitaph. Svenonius and some of his former bandmates subsequently regrouped, first as Cupid Car Club then as the Make-Up. [df]

NAUGHTY BY NATURE

Naughty by Nature (Tommy Boy) 1991
19 Naughty III (Tommy Boy) 1993
Poverty's Paradise (Tommy Boy) 1995

On one hand, Naughty by Nature's mixed message pushes rock-hard ghetto rhymes, shoot-'em-up skits and violent symbology (the machete toted on the debut's cover; the ominously hoisted chainsaw pictured on the second; the band's baseball bat logo). At the same time, the East Orange, New Jersey, trio has popped out a couple of catchy hit singles that disarm the gangsta pose with a clever, easygoing vibe and samples that don't all come off the standard hip-hop shelf. Brought to market under the benevolent Flavor Unit wing of Queen Latifah, the self-produced group—led by MC Treach, as in "treacherous" (his real name is Anthony Criss; the other members are Vinnie and DJ KG)—raps with take-no-prisoners intensity on the serious rhymes but can also manage a genial community spirit when the mood strikes.

The first album contains both "Ghetto Bastard" (a stirring, angry autobiography Treach blurts over a loop of Bob Marley's "No Woman No Cry"—performed by German disco-joke Boney M, using the "everything's gonna be alright" refrain for calming reassurance) and "O.P.P.," a call-and-response charmer about infidelity that summons up a stuttering, rhythmic flow and isolates the piano figure and a squeaky Michael interjection from the Jackson 5's "ABC." Naughty by Nature was off to a great start, full of promise as a band that could be expected to kick some great singles *and* pump some fresh ideas into roughneck rap.

19 Naughty III takes the trio sideways, adding the not-as-good testimonial "Hip Hop Hooray" to the Naughty by Nature hit list, referring to "O.P.P." and otherwise mixmastering down a narrowing corridor of toughness ("Take It to Ya Face," "Knock Em Out da Box") and solidarity ("The Hood Comes First," "Sleepin' on Jersey"). This time, though, the rhymes blur the line between pride and anger. Unlike the first album's clear differentiation, the group integrates a nearly consistent middle ground, undercutting its own threat while also harshing its mellow.

Firmly established as major players, Naughty by Nature pushed into adulthood on **Poverty's Paradise.** The thoughtful militancy of "Chain Remains" and "World Goes Round" is an excellent development, as is the cozy soulful slide of the X-rated "Sunshine." Additionally, the descending chord changes and catchy chorus of "Feel Me Flow" uphold the band's impulse toward appealing pop accessibility, but a lot of this long, complex and musically restrained album is surprisingly tedious. With a boisterous party spirit substituting for content, dragging down a bunch of tracks ("Clap Yo Hands," the dice-playing "City of Ci-Lo," the geographical shout-out "Craziest"), **Paradise** moves closer to the parking lot. [i]

ME'SHELL NDEGÉOCELLO

Plantation Lullabies (Maverick/Sire/Reprise) 1993
Peace Beyond Passion (Maverick/Reprise) 1996

If Me'Shell Ndegéocello's phenomenal debut didn't singlehandedly reinvigorate '90s funk on the hip-hop side, it wasn't for lack of effort. A dust-clearing blast of imagination and richly realized vision, the highly charged album unveiled an intricate, intelligent black woman with a lot on her mind and ample talent to express herself. A political, sexual and cultural manifesto that eschews dogma for a more instinctual outpouring, **Plantation Lullabies** introduces a conscious, self-contained universe still in the process of sorting itself out.

The bass-playing singer/songwriter (who was born a Johnson in Berlin and raised in Washington, DC, before relocating to New York in the early '90s; her adopted surname is Swahili for "free like a bird") conflates culture, romance, nostalgia and politics in the percolating "I'm Diggin' You (Like an Old Soul Record)" and reveals a ruthless competitive streak in "If That's Your Boyfriend (He Wasn't Last Night)." She walks an edgy personal line in lacerating the politics and suicide of dope ("Shoot'n' Up and Gett'n High"), rips apart sexual and aesthetic racism in "Soul on Ice" and lets her soft romantic heart bleed in "Outside Your Door." A bravura collection of contradictory impulses delivered on platters of simmering, subtle grooves and rapped in a variety of engaging voices, **Plantation Lullabies** puts a provocative mind to music that mainly means to move the feet.

Having received more critical acclaim than commercial success for her best shot, Ndegéocello found backdoor fame the following year when her duet with John Mellencamp on Van Morrison's "Wild Night" became a Top 5 single.

Dispensing with rap (although she does talk her way through the Freudian self-analysis in a free adaptation of Marvin Gaye's "Inner City Blues") and adding an arty pop sheen, Ndegéocello comes on like a livelier, more provocative Des'ree on **Peace Beyond Passion,** a religiously themed reflection that *sounds* like an old soul record. There's a certain dissonance between the music's alluring tug and the rough lyrics of "Deuteronomy: Niggerman" ("My view of self was that of a divine ho") and "Leviticus: Faggot," but the playing—by a team of Oliver Lake (drums), David Fiuczynski (guitar) and Wendy Melvoin (guitar), with guest shots by organist Billy Preston, saxophonist Joshua Redman and guitarist Wah Wah Watson—gives the singer a handsome vintage bed on which to lay her thorny roses. [i]

YOUSSOU N'DOUR

Immigrés (Fr. Celluloid) 1984 (Earthworks/Virgin) 1988
Nelson Mandela (Fr. Polydor) 1985 (Polydor) 1986
Inédits '84–'85 (Celluloid) 1985
The Lion (Virgin) 1989
Set (Virgin) 1990
Eyes Open (40 Acres and a Mule/Columbia) 1992
The Guide (Wommat) (Chaos/Columbia) 1994

ÉTOILE DE DAKAR

Absa Gueye (Stern's) 1993
Thiapathioly (Stern's) 1994

Youssou N'Dour was born in Senegal to musician parents; he began performing at circumcisions and baptisms while still a child. His first single, "M'ba," was released when he was thirteen; he became a radio star. By sixteen, with a high, sweet tenor that can cut to the bone, N'Dour was the featured vocalist with the Star Band de Dakar. In 1977, he led a walkout and formed Étoile de Dakar; playing an Africanized version of Cuban music, the new group developed into one of Senegal's most influential dance bands. Étoile's first album, **Xalis,** was a major hit, and the band moved to Paris, where it was reborn as the Super Étoile de Dakar in 1979. The new band based its sound on a Senegalese rhythmic style called *mbalax,* and electrified the audience at London's African Nights festival in 1984. After seeing a Touré Kunda concert, N'Dour decided to take a stab at the pop market by using international rhythms, including rock and reggae. Peter Gabriel told the press that N'Dour's **Immigrés** got him hooked on African rhythm, and had N'Dour sing on "In Your Eyes," a track on his '86 album, **So.** (That same year, N'Dour also played drums on Paul Simon's **Graceland** project.) N'Dour's opening sets on Gabriel's subsequent tour drew raves, as did their joint rendition of "In Your Eyes," which became the climax of Gabriel's set.

All of that gave a big boost to the release of N'Dour's Anglo-American debut. **Nelson Mandela** is packed with solid *mbalax* jams like "N'Dobine," "Samayaye," "Wareff" and the title tune, all highlighted by exciting vocals that are supported by rippling layers of percussion, sharp horn charts and a propulsive bassline. The percussion break on "Nelson Mandela" is a particular standout. At the time, the cover of the Spinners' "The Rubberband Man" sounded as if it had been tacked onto the disc by the accounting department, but N'Dour's subsequent crossover moves leave room for doubt.

Recorded a year earlier but released after **Nelson Mandela** in the US, **Immigrés** is less polished, but also more exciting. The short disc's densely layered arrangements show off the combination of the Cuban, Arabic and African elements that make Senegalese music so unique. Even on "Pitche Mi," the album's sole ballad, the percussion sizzles.

On **The Lion,** N'Dour dips heavily into the pop sounds that plague his recent records. The title track sounds like *mbalax* meets the Go-Go's, while "Old Tucson," a song about the museums N'Dour has visited on his world travels, is merely puzzling. Tracks like "Kocc Barma" and the moody "Macoy" are balanced by funk-heavy tunes like "The Truth" and "Shakin' the Tree," another duet with Gabriel. The song became a hit and a live staple for both artists; Gabriel also included the track, with redone vocals, on his anthology album, which he even named for the song.

N'Dour puts out at least three cassettes of new material a year for the Senegalese home market, items his British and American fans have to track down in specialty shops or mail-order catalogues. (Music piracy also plays a part; an artist has to keep releasing material to keep ahead of those who produce cheap duplications of every cassette.) **Set,** which mixes traditional acoustic instruments, inspired drumming, driving electric bass and sharp, staccato horn lines, was recorded for local release; after it became a huge hit in Senegal, Virgin released it to the world—albeit with a bit of pop sweetening. In any case, **Set** is one of the best Afropop albums ever. The title song, driven by talking drums and timbales, extols brotherhood and international peace and became an anthem for disaffected Senegalese youth. "Sabar" and "Sinebar" show off the band's relentless percussive chops; "Miyoko" has a slight reggae lilt, and "Xale (Our Young People)" mixes a cappella Senegalese singing with a European classical string section to good effect.

With **Eyes Open** (released on Spike Lee's label), N'Dour began his crossover moves. Most tunes include refrains in English or French; the percussion is downplayed in favor of swooping fretless bass and rock-influenced guitars. Standout tracks include "No More" (a subtle acoustic ballad to Africa's former colonial masters sung in English), "Live Television" (with a loping, almost ska beat), "Country Boy" (a funky African lament that's a distant cousin to Stevie Wonder's "Living for the City") and the album's two token African rhythm tracks, "Marie-Madeline La Saint-Louisienne" and "The Same," a tribute to the continent's influence on the world's music.

The Guide finds N'Dour balancing on a tightrope between Africa and MTV. The preponderance of ballads would indicate that this is clearly aimed at Western ears, but the percussion (when it's used) is more prominent. It's slightly less patronizing than **Eyes Open,** but "7 Seconds," N'Dour's duet with dancefloor diva Neneh Cherry, the African hip-hop of "How You Are" and a cover of Bob Dylan's "Chimes of Freedom" will make purists long for the days of **Set** and **Immigrés.** Recommendations: "Leaving (Dem)," a smooth African dance track; "Without a Smile (Same)," a jazzy ballad with sax by Branford Marsalis and a percussion track that suggests Brazilian *afoxe* rhythms; "Mame Bamba," one of the few tracks with the kind of percussive energy that made N'Dour's reputation; and "Tourista," a tune that could have been written for the Drifters—had they been Senegalese.

Those dismayed by N'Dour's crossover dreams will rejoice over Stern's' reissues of the best of Étoile de Dakar. The original recordings weren't made under the best conditions, but the band's fiery drumming and pounding basslines and N'Dour's youthful, unrestrained vocals will curl your hair. The band was just finding its own voice when these tunes were laid down and their excitement infuses every note. Their rumba is a lot harder than the smooth *soukous* of Zaire; the drummers sound like they're trying to drive the rhythm into the center of the earth, the singers wail with an almost religious ecstasy and the balance of Cuban and African elements is sublime. The percussive salvo that opens "Dom Sou Nare Bakh" on **Absa Gueye** will drop you in your tracks. The smooth calypso beat of "Tu Veras" sets up Badou N'Diate's rippling guitar solo; by "Baye Wali," you can hear the band beginning to find its own voice, the sound that was to become *mbalax* ("rhythm" in Wolof). On **Thiapathioly,** tracks originally recorded in 1980, Senegalese percussion slowly overwhelms the Cuban rhythms, creating a sound Dakar found irresistible. The title tune opens the disc with frantic talking drums set against the more Caribbean sound of the congas, and every subsequent track ups the rhythmic ante. By this time El Hadji Faye had joined N'Dour in the band's front line; their vocal competition adds a whole other dimension to the sound. [jp]

See also *Peter Gabriel.*

NEARLY GOD

See *Tricky.*

NED'S ATOMIC DUSTBIN

The Ingredients EP (UK Chapter 22) 1988
Bite (UK Chapter 22) 1990
God Fodder (furtive/Columbia) 1991
Grey Cell Green EP (furtive/Columbia) 1991
Are You Normal? (furtive/Chaos/Columbia) 1992
0.522 (UK furtive) 1994
Brainbloodvolume (furtive/Work) 1995

Although not the first rock band to field two bassists, Ned's Atomic Dustbin—formed with quickly abandoned goth intent in England's West Midlands in the late '80s—got the furthest commercially with such a lineup, riding along the same wave of colorful/dopey Angloslack dance-punk as the Wonder Stuff, EMF and Jesus Jones. The chucked cobblestone sloganeering of "Kill Your Television" (first included on **Bite**) gets **God Fodder** off to a strong, provocative start, and the quintet carries through with catchy melodies (the memorable "Grey Cell Green," remade from **The Ingredients**), pulsing adrenaline beats and a wool-covered wall of fuzzy pop noise on which able singer Jonn Penney pastes challenging personal lyrics. Derivative to the core, the Neds pinch bits from a random selection of English bands (Wedding Present, Icicle Works, New Order and so forth), but they do so with such breathless enthusiasm that it suits the good-natured cheesiness of the whole endeavor. The **Grey Cell Green** EP surrounds the **God Fodder** standout with a horribly recorded live version of the album's "Until You Find Out" and three studio cuts from a 1991 UK single (the soft/loud "Titch" is a keeper). For further Neds B-side study, **0.522** collects most of 'em.

Whether it's the flat songwriting, dumb samples or Andy Wallace's otherwise tidy production, **Are You Normal?** drains the fun out of Ned's Atomic Dustbin, leaving only cloddish conceits (songs like "Not Sleeping Around," verses like "My childhood obsession/It's my record collection/So what makes us so squeaky clean?/If we're food for worms that's not my scene") timed to generic stutter beats and sunk by uninspired music. "A Legend in His Own Boots" and "Spring" prove that the band hasn't completely lost its knack, but the bulk of the album is a tiring waste.

Following a long studio layoff, the Neds returned with **Brainbloodvolume** (wasn't that a Red Hot Chili Peppers' title?), an altogether happier effort. The five-some seems confident and relaxed enough to enjoy the work; the songs appear to be the result of actual wood-shedding, not last-minute whip-ups. Getting it all down in a clear mix of bristling, textured power and slick commercialism, producer Tim Palmer ably follows the group's minor stylistic perambulations, which display a bit of wit ("Floote" has a jammy flute winding through the pop-hop song; the four-minute finale is entitled "Song Eleven Could Take Forever") while juggling modern dance beats, driving rock, pinging atmospherics, found-sound silliness and glossy mid-tempo pop. If not as serious and significant as the self-important band would have it, **Brainbloodvolume** has no shortage of well-crafted tunes and intriguing lyrics, all wrapped up with the élan of skilled and mature chart hogs. [i]

NEGATIVLAND

Negativland (Seeland) 1980
Points (Seeland) 1981
A Big 10-8 Place (Seeland) 1983
Over the Edge Vol. 1: JamCon '84 (SST) 1985 (Seeland) 1994
Escape From Noise (SST) 1987
Helter Stupid (SST) 1989
Over the Edge Vol. 2: Pastor Dick [tape] (SST) 1990
Over the Edge Vol. 3: The Weatherman [tape] (SST) 1990
Over the Edge Vol. 4: Dick Vaughn: Moribund Music of the 70's [tape] (SST) 1990
U2 EP (SST) 1991
Guns EP (SST) 1992
Free (Seeland) 1993
Over the Edge Vol. 5: Crosley Bendix: The Radio Reviews (Seeland) 1993

Over the Edge Vol. 6: The Willsaphone Stupid Show (Seeland) 1994
Over the Edge Vol. 7: Time Zones Exchange Project (Seeland) 1994
Over the Edge Vol. 1½: The Starting Line (Seeland) 1995

The dearly learned moral of Negativland's story is simple: those who test gas leaks with lit matches encounter a lot of bad smells and occasionally blow themselves to kingdom come. The albums documenting *Over the Edge,* the absurdist San Francisco Bay Area troupe's KPFA radio show (imagine *Prairie Home Companion* as envisioned by twisted urban culture snots and executive produced by prankster Alan Abel), are generally obnoxious, exhausting and cloying proof of why tape recorders and microphones shouldn't be allowed to fall into the hands of multi-media hicknerd wiseacres with access to the airwaves. Drop the laser needle (or the tape head) anywhere and you get a collage of found sounds, put-on phone calls, dryly offbeat sketches (shades of *The Goon Show* filtered by the Firesign Theater) featuring regular characters, old records, in-jokes and whatever else can be plucked from the supermarket shelves of America's vast sonic wasteland. On early albums like **Escape From Noise** and **Points,** there's even original music in the mix.

Since Negativland's real stock in trade is conceptualization, not execution, implicit in the group's bunker ambitions is a grander vision of its potential activist role in pop culture. Having constructed a self-willed alternate reality (the media analogue of a child's cardboard box house) on the radio, Negativland moved, late in the '80s, to expand its surreal conceits beyond the simple limits of album tracks. (The early cassettes are straight dubs of the radio shows; the first of these to be released was later divided into a pair of CDs: **Jam-Con '84,** with previously unissued material, and **The Starting Line.**)

As inspired propagandists coming to terms with an ability to manipulate the truth, Negativland shifted their mindfuck campaign to a higher plane with **Helter Stupid,** turning **Escape From Noise**'s "Christianity Is Stupid" (which consists of that slogan, and others like "Communism is good!" repeated in a JFK-like voice over plodding martial metal) into a full-fledged prank that backfired into a success beyond their wildest dreams. Wielding a hoax press release as its weapon, Negativland implied that the song *might* have been responsible for inspiring the murder of a Minnesota family, and that was all it took. The media fell for it like a stock crash, as the group's fatal role was accepted as truth and explored incompetently by various news organizations. The liner notes of **Helter Stupid** detail the stunt's chronology and aftermath, clearly acknowledging the "electronic environment of factual fictions" of their undertaking.

Their power as cage rattlers thus amply proven, the cunning stunt team—basically Richard Lyons and Mark Hosler, joined by various permutations of David Wills, Don Joyce, Ian Allen, Peter Dayton, Chris Grigg and others—began to rationalize its role as cultural empiricists, searching for buttons that, if pushed, might produce Negativland's unique brand of public performance art. (Exactly how this differs from, say, covering a street in petroleum and then smashing a department store window to see what might happen when the police arrive is unclear. Therein lies the crux of Negativland's creative flaw.) They evidently didn't have far to look. Following three more volumes of radio show transcriptions, Negativland released their pièce de resistance—although whether they had any clue as to what they were getting into, legally, culturally or personally, is subject to extremely unsteady hindsight. There's actually a documentary film, *Sonic Outlaws,* on the subject.

Packaged as a masterpiece of disinformation, the **U2** CD, to all intents and purposes, looks like a U2 single entitled "Negativland." Inside, on the brilliant "Special Edit Radio Mix" (the "A Cappella Mix" is comparatively dull), Negativland crosses U2's "I Still Haven't Found What I'm Looking For" (played stupidly on kazoo and synthesizer) with various angry voices and a profanity-laced studio tantrum thrown by swell-guy radio star Casey Kasem ("That's the letter U and the number 2 . . . these guys are from England [*sic*] and who gives a shit? . . . names that don't mean *diddleyshit*"). The track is a sublime cut-up editing job that makes no point but has a wonderful time doing it, a good yuk by some merry pranksters thumbing their noses at a couple of cultural institutions. Ooops.

What seemed like a harmless if nasty joke quickly called down a shitstorm of legal trouble—from U2's record company and music publisher and SST Records—on the band. Buried in a flurry of lawsuits, financial battles and personal imprecations, the band and the labels agreed to a settlement by which the record was recalled and destroyed; the copyrights of its contents were reassigned and damages paid. Meanwhile, the bloodied but wry Negativland portrayed the whole fiasco as both an outrageous attack on free speech, a revealing display of corporate greed and a semi-intentional dissection of intellectual property rights (or something like that). The resemblance to I-meant-to-do-that excuse-making *and* Marcel Duchamp's readymade tactic of putting a credit next to a manufactured object and claiming it as a piece of art should not go unremarked.

Negativland took on something safer than U2 in its identically designed next release: **Guns.** Dedicating the two dull tracks of western movie sound collage to "the members of our favorite Irish rock band, their record label, and their attorneys" might have been taken the wrong way, but Negativland got no mileage of any sort out of this dud, and the group—having published a book about their personal culture wars—went back to issuing radio escapades without further incident. [i]

See also *TPRG.*

NELORIES

Plasticky EP (Japan. iPor supuesto!) 1991
Banana EP (Japan. iPor supuesto!) 1992
Mellow Yellow Fellow Nelories (Japan. iPor supuesto!) 1992
Waiting EP (Hello Recording Club) 1993
Indie Pop Car Baby EP (Japan. Suite supuesto) 1993
Daisy (Japan. Suite supuesto) 1993
Starboogie (Japan. Suite supuesto) 1994
An Ordinary Miracle EP (Japan. Suite supuesto) 1995

The Japanese independent scene has evolved through a multitude of different forms over the last decade, ranging from the psychotic sonic excursions of Boredoms and Fushitsusha and the noise brutality of Zeni Geva to the garage rock of Teengenerate, the pop-punk of Shonen Knife and the twisted disco of Pizzicato Five. Somewhere on the outskirts of all this lies Nelories. Led by Jun Kurihara (vocals, accordion) and Kazmi Kubo (guitars), Nelories match a left-field naïveté with the arty cabaret style epitomized in the '80s by England's Monochrome Set. Also of influence on Nelories is the French style of *yeye* bubblegum pop.

Although not fully bilingual, Kurihara insists on writing all of her lyrics in English, the result of which is songs that are, at best, abstract. "The Chestnutfield Family" (from the **Plasticky** EP) includes such lyrics as "Father get up at 5:30 every Sundays/Then he drives to Golden Valley to play golf/He grins with Louis Vuitton bag in hand/Saying 'Todays a good day I'd like to go out for eat.'"

The Nelories' debut album, **Mellow Yellow Fellow Nelories,** consists of two of **Plasticky**'s four tracks, three of **Banana**'s four and five other songs. One theme popping up in many Nelories songs is Kurihara's obsession with high fashion; in addition to that Vuitton citation, she namedrops designers Lacroix and Versace in "Emerald." Nelories go so far as giving Gaultier his own theme song in "J.P.G." Each and every song is a joyful romp.

Nelories' sole American release so far is the four-song **Waiting** EP, issued by the subscription-only Hello Recording CD-of-the-month club. "Waiting," "Banana" and "Plastic Sky" all come from the group's Japanese records; "Bubbly" had previously appeared only on a British single.

Recording in London, the group augmented their sound on **Daisy** with the help of Monochrome Set's frontman Bid as producer and occasional second guitarist. "A Girl in a Checkered Dress" reveals a strong understanding of Everything but the Girl; "Eyes & Shoes" finds Nelories moving into their own vision of smoky nightclubs and torch singing. The highlight, however, is "Garlic," which could have been lifted from an early-'80s Monochrome Set record.

On **Starboogie,** the duo tries out a number of new styles. As improbable and incongruous as it sounds, Nelories leapfrog successfully from the Velocity Girl–like alternapop of "Service Area" to the electro dance of "Popstars" to the gently swaying "So Anyway I Sing" to (if only Nelson Riddle had done the arrangement) "The Shooting Pictures." Some songs, like "White Volkswagen," simply don't make any sense; at the album's funniest point, "Blue Flower" vacillates between elevator music and brassy bombast. [mk]

BILL NELSON

The Strangest Things Sampler (Cocteau/Enigma) 1989
Blue Moons & Laughing Guitars (Venture) 1992
Practically Wired (All Saints/Gyroscope) 1995
After the Satellite Sings (Resurgence/Gyroscope) 1996

Bill Nelson released such a glut of sleepy-time guitar'n'synth music in the '80s that even the most diehard fans of his prodigious instrumental technique, sophisticated art pretensions or his '70s rock band, Be-Bop Deluxe, could be found comatose, buried under the pressed-plastic mountain and befogged by all the gentle (or not-so-gentle) atmospheres. By 1989, a ten-year wallpapering effort had produced a discography of at least two dozen albums, including a four-CD boxed set (with T-shirt, no less). Enigma Records, which gamely attempted to keep up with the Englishman's Cocteau-label issue for a while, piled together some of the period's significant results and a lot more into **The Strangest Things** and then got on with other corporate endeavors, like going out of business.

In '92, Nelson returned to the real world (relatively speaking) with **Blue Moons & Laughing Guitars.** The following year, Nelson made a tentative overture to the real world, helping Roger Eno and Kate St. John on their collaborative album, **The Familiar.** The threesome then formed a trio, Channel Light Vessel, whose **Automatic** brings him a few leagues closer to music that doesn't simply drift along prettily. Meanwhile, his smooth one-man voyage continues: **Practically Wired** (*or how I became . . . Guitarboy!*) is a spry, graceful instrumental work that spans a wide dynamic range, using keyboards and samples to enliven a typically finespun set of guitar-based mood pieces. The piss 'n'vinegar techno trip of the opener, "Roses and Rocketships," demonstrates Nelson's currency (imagine King Crimson doing jungle music) and shows a lot more zest than one has come to expect from him; of course, the album soon succumbs to the swoon. But it remains sonically diverse, and returns often enough with a pulse to stay reasonably invigorating. Welcome back, pilot of the future. [i]

See also *Roger Eno; TPRG.*

LOEY NELSON

See *Carnival Strippers.*

SHARA NELSON

See *Massive Attack.*

NEUROTIC OUTSIDERS

See *Guns n' Roses.*

NEW BOMB TURKS

So Cool, So Clean, So Sparkling Clear EP7 (Datapanik) 1992
!!Destroy-Oh-Boy!! (Crypt) 1992
Drunk on Cock EP (Engine) 1993
Information Highway Revisited (Crypt) 1994
Pissing Out the Poison (Crypt) 1995
Scared Straight (Epitaph) 1996

Bad taste—and attitude—is timeless. That's a tacit understanding in the ranks of this Columbus, Ohio, quartet, which was weaned on the nectar of late-model midwestern punk before moving on to solid sustenance like Johnny Thunders bootlegs, garage-rock obscurities and *Deliverance*-primitive rockabilly tumult. Like all of its influences, the New Bomb Turks is unequivocally a singles band (as borne out by the twenty-odd 7-inchers they've loosed on trash culture vultures worldwide), but the band's more sustained salvos betray plenty of stamina in the bloodline as well.

Like many of his predecessors, peripatetic Turks screamer Eric Davidson plays hide'n'seek with his keen wit, dotting some songs with clever cultural references—both high- and low-brow—and stomping through others with neanderthal thickness. **So Cool, So Clean, So Sparkling Clear,** the 7-inch wisenheimer debut, hits with the economic bluntness of a blackjack swipe, both in its covers (Radio Birdman's "Do the Pop" and the Nervous Eaters' "Just Head") and in the ramalama originals (both of which are reprised on the band's first album). Over the course of **!!Destroy-Oh-Boy!!**'s sixteen cuts, the Turks exhibit an innate mastery of rock'n'roll's truly important gestures—the flipped bird, the dropped trou, the beer-stein hoist—not to mention a devotion to the hallowed three-chords-and-a-cloud-of-phlegm formulation that dates back to the '50s. While "Tail Crush" evokes the no-fi frat-stomp of the Sonics and "Long Gone Sister" injects a megadose of caffeine into a rockabilly romp, the Turks seem most drawn to the fanboy-as-theorist-as-degenerate-rocker spirit of the Dictators, who would likely nod in approval at the cagey "Born Toulouse-Lautrec" and "Let's Dress Up the Naked Truth."

Drunk on Cock is more single-minded in its adherence to the loud-fast rules, but a righteously rockin' tribute to kindred spirits ("American Soul Spiders," which celebrates the Japanese trash-rock combo of the same name) and a maddeningly memorable anti-anthem ("This Place Sucks") stay with you like a White Castle belly bomb. Its title aside, there's nothing remotely *moderne* about the decidedly Detroit-inspired meltdown **Information Highway Revisited:** guitarist Jim Weber just about empties his James Williamson bag of tricks on tracks like "Id Slips In" and "Bullish on Bullshit" (an opaque rewrite of the Stooges' "Sick of You"). Davidson waxes atypically reflective on "Brother Orson Welles" (an ominous art-versus-commerce rant) but there's no shortage of broad humor—as documented on the jeering "Apocalyptic Dipstick," a perfect antidote for anyone in danger of a politico-punk overdose.

Pissing Out the Poison drains the quartet's reservoir of rarities, most of which bear the all-in-good-fun sonic bruises common to on-the-fly recordings. Besides exhibiting the Turks' proficiency as a gutter-rat bar band (on such covers as the Modern Lovers' "I Wanna Sleep in Your Arms" and Hawkwind's "Ejection"), the fully-loaded twenty-six-song collection gives some nifty in-progress looks at catalogue staples: the first EP/LP's "Cryin' in the Beer of a Drunk Man" (also revamped here as "Croonin' in the Beer of a Drunk Man") and "Girl Can Help It." More fun than a slingshot loaded with rotten eggs. [dss]

NEW DUNCAN IMPERIALS

Feelin' Sexy! EP7 (Pravda) 1990
Hanky Panky Parley Voo! (Pravda) 1990
The Hymns of Bucksnort (Pravda) 1991
Live, Rare, and Bad (Pravda) 1992
Loserville (Pravda) 1993
We're in a Band EP (Pravda) 1993
The New Duncan Imperials Live! (Pravda) 1995

Launched as the humorous alter ego to Chicago's more serious (and now more defunct) Service, the pseudonymous New Duncan Imperials (singer/guitarist Pigtail Dick, drummer Goodtime and bassist Skipper, aka Kenn Goodman, owner of the Pravda label) cobble together a woolly mixture of country rock, midwestern power-pop and similar energetic guitar vehicles, all in the hopes of acting silly and getting away with it. The rambunctious twenty-three-song **Hanky Panky Parley Voo!** offers cheap jokes like "I'm Schizophrenic (No I'm Not)," scattershot satire ("Jimi Page Loves Country"), covers of Buck Owens, Hank Williams *and* Hasil Adkins, trashy romance ("6-Pack of Love") and celebrations of essential consumer products ("Jägermeister" and "Velour!").

Like the debut, **The Hymns of Bucksnort** is good, silly party fun—only the jokes are thin, the mud-wallowing targets entirely too predictable. With gimmicky genre digressions, the sophomoric sophomore album yoyos between cornpone country and mild punk, from a cruel cover of the Webb Pierce–popularized "There Stands the Glass" to the twelve-second softcore puzzle of "Wing Dosso." Rooting around the scrapheap of society, the trio goofs on food ("Chef of the Future," "Baloney," "Chili Pie," "Gizzards, Scrapple & Tripe"), shelter ("Home Sweet Mobile Home"), work ("$65 an Hour"), entertainment ("White Trash Boogie," "Throw Up Waltz") and romance ("Mystery Date," "Has Anybody Seen My Gal?") in numbers that are exactly as entertaining as their titles.

Originally cassette-only but ultimately slapped on CD as well, **Live, Rare, and Bad** is an assemblage of concert tunes, radio interviews, an unaired 7-Eleven commercial and so forth.

Loserville gathers the Duncans into a more concerted, ambitious outfit, farting around with more maturity (although "Turkey Neck" has a certain Ween-y air to it . . .), focusing mostly on rock and setting its eye-poking vocals less conspicuously into fast dink-metal punk-pop and related stylings. "Tilt-a-Whirl" is a genuinely good song; "If I Liked You" could pass for same if not for rude lyrics and such lowbrow neighbors as "Ugly Stick," "Clock in My Pocket" and "Shitload of Kissin'." Although the hick-pop of "Running With a Fork in My Mouth" and the adolescent anxieties of "Haircut and New Shoes" sound like **Bucksnort** leftovers, borrowing Tom Jones' "It's Not Unusual" for a garish horn-wearing cover gives **Loserville** an undeniable sexual undertow.

Probably inspired by their participation in Pravda's goofy K-Tel tribute series (**20 Explosive Dynamic Super Smash Hit Explosions!, Super Fantastic Mega Smash Hits** and so forth), the Duncs cut **We're in a Band,** a theme-night covers EP containing the trio's renditions of Grand Funk's "We're an American Band," Boston's "Rock & Roll Band," Creedence's "Travelin' Band," Wings' "Band on the Run" and the Moody Blues' "I'm Just a Singer (in a Rock and Roll Band)." Must have been a boring summer in Chicago . . .

The live album was recorded at a show in late '93 and contains renditions of fifteen NDI numbers, including "Home Sweet Mobile Home," "Running With a Fork in My Mouth" and "Rock & Roll Band." [i]

See also *TPRG*.

MARTIN NEWELL

The Greatest Living Englishman (UK Humbug) 1993
(Pipeline) 1993 (Ger. Pink Lemon) 1995
Let's Kiosk! EP (UK Humbug) 1995

CLEANERS FROM VENUS

Blow Away Your Troubles [tape] (self-released) 1981
On Any Normal Monday [tape] (self-released) 1982
Midnight Cleaners [tape] (self-released) 1982
In the Golden Autumn [tape] (self-released) 1983
Under Wartime Conditions [tape] (UK Acid Tapes) 1984
(Ger. Modell) 1986
Songs for a Fallow Land [tape] (self-released) 1985
Living With Victoria Grey [tape] (self-released) 1986
Going to England (UK Ammunition) 1987
The Brotherhood of Lizards [tape] (self-released) 1988

Town and Country (Ger. RCA) 1988
Golden Cleaners (UK Tangerine) 1993
Back From the Cleaners: Best of the Cleaners From Venus Vol II (UK Tangerine) 1995

BROTHERHOOD OF LIZARDS

Lizardland (UK Deltic) 1989 (Long Play) 1995

As the Cleaners from Venus, English retro-pop auteur Martin Newell (a onetime member of the pre-Clash/Gen X London SS) and assorted collaborators began issuing charming, offbeat cassettes of his kitschy and clever originals in 1981. Later in the decade, with a stack of tapes, three vinyl/CD albums under the name (and a bunch of reissues to come, like the useful rarities-sprinkled pair released on CD by Tangerine), Newell retired the Cleaners moniker and transmogrified into the Brotherhood of Lizards, a duo with bassist/drummer (and |t future New Model Army conscript) Peter Nelson.

Lizardland, the only album credited to the Brotherhood, is melodic and clever without fuss, a dozen melodic and modestly poetic vignettes ("Market Day," "The World Strikes One," "Love the Anglian Way," "Dear Anya") of life in these British Isles. The bubbly '60s psychedelipop of "She Dreamed She Could Fly," the catchy chorus of "It Could Have Been Cheryl" and the Turtlesque refrain of "The Happening Guy" are positively brilliant; the remainder is merely splendid. With improved cover art and a pair of bonus tracks recalled from the relatedly titled Cleaners' last tape, **Lizardland** even received a belated American release.

Besides publishing books of his poetry, Newell's radical next step was to launch a solo career, with help from some old pals. Produced and drummed on by XTC's Andy Partridge (the album's American cover nonsensically trumpets "Featuring the New Improved Andy Partridge" in type as large as the artist's name), **The Greatest Living Englishman** is another absolute delight, a seamless, sensitive blend of XTC, the Beatles and all those who have pledged their fealty to one or the other. Alternately rustic, pop-accomplished and mildly psychedelic, each song is a distinct-sounding gem of tuneful delectability and country town lyrical resonance. The "Home Counties Boy" enjoys "Christmas in Suburbia," promises "We'll Build a House" (but can't say when) and looks back on it all as "The Greatest Living Englishman." Newell is a skilled singer, an excellent songwriter and a dab keyboard hand; Partridge gilds his efforts with countless deft touches (toy piano, Starr-y drumming, XTC soundalikes, effects) and dewy clarity that removes all sense of time for a pure treat. (A limited-edition version of the English release included a bonus spoken-word CD.) **Let's Kiosk!** is a four-song EP of the album's rousingly catchy "The Jangling Man" plus three otherwise unreleased numbers.

At presstime, Newell had a new record, **The Off-white Album,** in the can for a 1996 release. [i]

See also *New Model Army; TPRG.*

NEW FAST AUTOMATIC DAFFODILS

Pigeonhole (Bel. Play It Again Sam) 1990 (Mute) 1991
The Peel Sessions (Strange Fruit/Dutch East India Trading) 1991
Bong EP (Mute/Elektra) 1992
Body Exit Mind (UK Mute) 1992 (Mute/Elektra) 1993

Manchester's New Fast Automatic Daffodils (the New FADS, for short) rode the early '90s rave wave, gathering inspiration from the same Northern (Britain) and American soul as Happy Mondays. More than Ecstasy and baggy pants, however, the FADS are musical descendants of A Certain Ratio and the Fall. The quintet's disjointed funk—which combines serious rhythm and a disgruntled indie attitude (witness a 1989 12-inch entitled "Music Is Shit")—echoes various bands that hail from the region.

Pigeonhole (the American CD of which adds the title track as a bonus) is a collection of sloppily funky songs characterized by Dolan Hewison's strummy new wave guitar and Andy Spearpoint's uncompromisingly deep singing, which is similar in tone to the Wedding Present's Dave Gedge. The lyrics are not nearly as important as percussion, bass and the overall groove of the song; like James Brown, Spearpoint is happy to riff on a particular theme to the point of nonsense. (See "Fishes Eyes" and "Penguins.") "I Found Myself in Another Room," another domestic add-on, is a throw-down jam in which blasts of rhythm pepper the flailing guitar and the careening vocals.

The Peel Sessions consists of two BBC studio appearances, from '89 and '90: Jimi Hendrix's "Purple Haze," the album's "Big," "Part 4" and "Get Better" and three more. **Bong** combines the first two tracks ("Bong" and "It's Not What You Know") from the second album with three non-LP tracks, none of which are strikingly different.

Produced by Craig Leon, **Body Exit Mind** is similarly grooved to **Pigeonhole,** but the music is more focused and the lyrics more pointed, the inevitable progression of a band determined to make improvements. The guitar sound has gained stridency, although the band's percussive aspects remain unchanged. Unlike **Pigeonhole,** however, the songs are cohesive and distinct rather than shapely jams; the band's new direction is clearly displayed in the passionate guitar line of "Stockholm" and the lyrics of "It's Not What You Know" ("I could get a good job if I tried/But what's the point?"). [mf]

COLIN NEWMAN

See *Wire.*

TODD NEWMAN

See *Leatherwoods.*

NEW MODEL ARMY

Vengeance (UK Abstract) 1984
No Rest for the Wicked (Capitol) 1985
The Ghost of Cain (Capitol) 1986
New Model Army (Capitol) 1987
Vengeance/The Independent Story (UK Abstract) 1987 (JCI) 1988
Radio Sessions 83–84 (UK Abstract) 1988
Thunder and Consolation (Capitol) 1989
Impurity (UK EMI) 1990
Raw Melody Men (UK EMI) 1991
The Love of Hopeless Causes (Epic) 1993

The Love of Hopeless Causes, New Model Army's first American release in four years (and perhaps last), musters up another cache of spirited, gutsy material: classic British rock reminiscent of the Clash, Who, Jam and Billy Bragg.

After a string of terrific albums capped by the panoramic majesty of **Thunder and Consolation,** the Bradford trio led by Justin Sullivan (vocals, guitar, keyboards) and Robert Heaton (drums) with bassist Peter Nelson (formerly of the Brotherhood of Lizards) regrouped with the tough, economical **Impurity** and an excellent double-live album, **Raw Melody Men** (the title is an anagram for New Model Army), which distilled the fire burning inside sixteen of their gritty modern-day folk/punk songs.

Perhaps taking a cue from the concert record's invigorating sound, **The Love of Hopeless Causes** was waxed live in the studio with Niko Bolas and then mixed by veteran producer Bob Clearmountain, achieving a fine compromise between clarity and rawness. The blasting single "Here Comes the War" alternates between anxious verses and the intense power-chord-fueled chorus, "Put out the lights on the age of reason." A distorted synth-bass riff rolls through the laconic ballad "Living in the Rose," while "These Words" is the latest in the band's line of intimate acoustic creations ("sometimes your hunger for life seems like desperation"). New Model Army's biggest strength has always been Sullivan's songwriting and bullshit-immune moral fervor, and traditionally styled Army tunes (minor-key bittersweet anthems all) like "Believe It," "White Light" and "Bad Old World" are heavily armed with melody, heart and hooks. Filled with self-questioning and regret, the last of those is an especially well-written and personal observation on friends who have chosen to drop out of urban society and head off for the simple life. [gef]

See also *Martin Newell; TPRG.*

NEW ORDER

Movement (Factory) 1981
1981–1982 EP (Factory) 1982
Power, Corruption and Lies (Factory) 1983 (Qwest) 1985
Low-life (Qwest) 1985
Brotherhood (Qwest) 1986
Substance (Qwest) 1987
Technique (Qwest) 1989
The Peel Sessions Album (UK Strange Fruit) 1990
Republic© (Qwest/Warner Bros.) 1993
(the best of) New Order (Qwest/Warner Bros.) 1995
(the rest of) New Order (UK London) 1995

REVENGE

One True Passion (Capitol) 1990
Gun World Porn EP (Capitol) 1992

ELECTRONIC

Electronic (Warner Bros.) 1991
Raise the Pressure (Warner Bros.) 1996

OTHER TWO

The Other Two & You. (Qwest/Reprise) 1993

In its first decade, New Order gathered itself up from the funeral of Joy Division to wield profound influence on electronic-aided dance-rock via a half-dozen unevenly extraordinary albums of catchy, invigorating, emotionally remote and deceptively stupid songs. The Manchester band's essential items are **Power, Corruption and Lies** and **Low-Life,** followed by the Eurostyled **Technique; Brotherhood** contains the brilliant "Bizarre Love Triangle" and nothing equally memorable; **Substance** is a lengthy compendium of 12-inch singles. After **Technique,** rock history's only recorded souvenir of the momentary Ibizan Balearic beat pseudo-fad, singer/guitarist Bernard Sumner, bassist Peter Hook, keyboardist/guitarist Gillian Gilbert and drummer Stephen Morris put the group on hold and set off in different directions to do other things.

Hook assembled a trio called Revenge and whipped out the wretched **One True Passion.** (The title enthusiasm apparently refers to buxom leather-and-chain-clad women.) Restyling New Order's formula with a thicker, warmer sound and second-rate vocals, the oversexed Revenge could almost be a clumsy tribute band. New Order's flimsy lyrics are one thing, but Hook's macho black leather bluster is aggressively dumb. (Song titles include "Surf Nazi," "Kiss the Chrome" and "Fag Hag.") No prizes for solving witless lyrical conundrums like "Kiss the chrome/Why am I alone?" **Gun World Porn,** unveiling a reconfigured group in which Hook doesn't play bass, adds four murky new songs—still sounding like New Order's thuggish alter ego, with a side order of Nine Inch Nails—to Revenge's worthless oeuvre, tacking on three remixes and a phone message to fill the time.

Sumner and ex-Smiths guitarist Johnny Marr, initially in collaboration with Pet Shop Boy Neil Tennant, formed Electronic, which issued a single in 1990 and an album in mid-'91. **Electronic** is a strange but entertaining meld of electro-pop dance music with guitar, blipping sequencers and a strong Tennant vocal/keyboards influence. (He sings two cuts.) With Marr's creative role not strikingly evident, Electronic also sounds like New Order (especially due to Sumner's distinctive voice and rhythmic patterns), only taking a breather in a parallel universe ruled by the Pet Shop Boys. Five years later, Sumner and Marr reactivated Electronic for **Raise the Pressure,** an album with all the sprightly melodic pep no longer guaranteed by New Order. The duo occasionally descends to formulaic dance drive or deficient simplemindedness here, but more often their marriage of styles and sensibilities is uncannily productive, filling one another's voids to strike a smart balance between guitar warmth and techno coolness, between pop heads and moving feet.

That leaves the other two—real-life couple Gilbert and Morris, who dubbed themselves the Other Two and got some jobs doing soundtrack music for film and television. (One of their clients is *America's Most Wanted.*) On **The Other Two & You.,** Gilbert sings the direct lyrics of their percolating dance-pop originals in a sweet, breathy air-pop voice over layers of lush/stuttering keyboards, busy rhythms and minimal bits of guitar. As Stephen Hague co-produced, it's a fair companion piece to New Order's contemporaneous **Republic©,** underpinning an equally appealing surface with greater variety and marginally more creative depth.

Republic©, the only new New Order album of the last seven years, is pleasantly diverting and lightly inflected techno-pop. (Credit co-producer/co-writer Hague for both attributes.) Taking unspecified assistance from guest instrumentalists, the record gets off to a great start with the richly guitar textured "Regret" and the peppy, vocally active "World." The songs don't remake the New Order sound so much as add useful stylistic ideas and instruments to the mix, bringing out the essential tunefulness with deliriously seductive results. Other than those two and "Special," however, the record is prosaic, flat and dull. With Sumner still caught in Tennant's thrall but lacking the garish musical determination to make anything original (or even vivid) from the influence, the band winds up sounding half-hearted and misguided, hamstrung by flimsy songs, derivative stylings and wan arrangements.

Evidently unwilling to move forward, New Order returned to its past for further retrospective releases in 1995. The seventeen songs assembled under the arguable **(the best of)** title don't overly overlap **Substance,** and therein lies the problem. While omitting early essentials like "Ceremony" and "Everything's Gone Green," the indulgent anthology finds room for the first album's Hook-sung "Dreams Never End," three **Republic©** songs (enough to obviate any but a true fan's need to own that album), "Touched by the Hand of God" (from the *Salvation* soundtrack) and "World in Motion," an absurdly sincere 1990 English World Cup team theme. "Blue Monday," "True Faith" and "1963" all appear in versions different from those on **Substance;** the vocal rendition of "Let's Go (Nothing for Me)" was co-written and co-produced specifically for the record by Arthur Baker. If not an especially useful package, **(the best of)** still packs such gems as the folk-styled ballad "Love Vigilantes," "Age of Consent" and "Bizarre Love Triangle," allowing it to serve as a handy highlights reel for newcomers.

Typical of the band's recycling efficiency, a third compilation was issued in the UK: **(the rest of)** spins further afield to offer alternate mixes of such songs as "Confusion," "Blue Monday" and "Touched by the Hand of God." [i]

See also *Pet Shop Boys; TPRG.*

NEW RADIANT STORM KING

My Little Bastard Soul (Axis/Cargo) 1992
Rival Time (Homestead) 1993
August Revital (Grass) 1994
Hurricane Necklace (Grass) 1996

College brought this trio together in Amherst, Massachusetts, a supportive academic community close enough to New York and Boston to provide a solid base for a fledgling indie-pop/rock band in its developmental stages. The group comes off a little derivative and amateurish on **My Little Bastard Soul,** but the record shows New Radiant Storm King's emerging songwriting skills. The musicianship is shaky and shuffling at times—they might have edited this record to a shorter length—but the debut is braver, more interesting and more fulfilling than efforts from lots of similar combos that didn't post careers nearly as long. Drummer Elizabeth Sharp, bassist/vocalist Peyton Pinkerton and guitarist/vocalist Matt Hunter wield influences as varied as their geographical backgrounds (Washington, DC, New York and Phoenix, respectively).

Those influences take stronger shape with **Rival Time,** and the group sounds more relaxed in the studio. Hunter and Pinkerton play off each other better, Sharp's more solid and the three produce edgy lo-fi tension and swirling, nuanced noise-pop. The shadows of Mission of Burma, early Cure, Gang of Four and Sonic Youth (as well as Sleepyhead and Small Factory) loom large here, and while New Radiant Storm King occasionally substitutes geeky recklessness for strong dynamics, **Rival Time** is just as often brooding and mysterious.

There are still some awkward, unsatisfying moments ("Go Back and Start" and, ironically, "Misdirected Energy") on **August Revital,** but the group has shaped and streamlined its snaky, enchanting style to a convincing peak. Hunter and Pinkerton work magic making hummable melodies from discordant riffs, while the whole band moves as one effortlessly from sweeping power to delicate fluidity. Throughout its records, New Radiant Storm King successfully typifies indie-rock ethics, embodying the struggle to make meaningful sound from a deeply personal vision. [mww]

NEW WET KOJAK

See *Girls Against Boys.*

NICE

See *Cannanes.*

NIGHTBLOOMS

Butterfly Girl EP (UK Fierce) 1992
The Nightblooms (UK Fierce/Paperhouse) 1992 (Fire/Seed) 1993
24 Days at Catastrofe Café (Fire/Seed) 1993

In the course of just a few years, this Dutch quartet underwent a nearly complete transformation of sound, even though its two-man/two-woman lineup (they all lived together) remained fixed. (That Steve Gregory, the mysterious Svengali/auteur behind the Pooh Sticks and Fierce Records, produced the band couldn't possibly have anything to do with that, now could it?) "Crystal Eyes," a 1990 single, cakes singer Esther Sprikkelman's lovely little melody in a thick crust of howling guitars (including a spectacular whammy-bar solo by Harry Otten), amp noise and general mayhem; the noise level on its flip side, "Never Dream at All," is so extreme that it's hard to notice the fragile tune at all.

The title track of the **Butterfly Girl** EP, on the other hand, demonstrates the Nightblooms' ability to *not* exert its power—for most of the song, the band lets Sprikkelman and bassist Petra van Tongeren sing with scant accompaniment, if any, though the constant low-level feedback hints at what happens when the Nightblooms do let loose. The EP also reprises "Crystal Eyes" and throws in a straightforward rocker and a live noise-fest.

The centerpiece of **The Nightblooms** is an eight-minute version of "Butterfly Girl" with some ghostly tape loops at the beginning. Most of the album sets Sprikkelman and van Tongeren's clear, unaffected harmonies over fairly conventional shoegazey rock, though usually to exceptionally beautiful effect. The band also plays with some weird song structures ("A Thousand Years") and the kind of subtle dynamic variation few can pull off.

The first half of **24 Days at Catastrofe Café** is enough of an about-face that—if not for Sprikkelman's breathy lisp—it's nearly impossible to believe it's the same band. The record starts with seven short, crunchy riff-rock numbers with handclaps and all the fixings, including a rerecording of "Never Dream at All" that could pass for a long-lost sibling of "We Will Rock You," followed by the lighter-waving "Everyone Loves You" (including a five-minute, stadium-pleasing guitar solo). The two remaining songs get back onto more familiar territory, with a ten-minute epic called "Shatterhand" that distills and amplifies everything that was noteworthy about the first album and—also like **The Nightblooms**—a short, drumless, gorgeous coda ("Sweet Rescue"). [ddw]

NINE INCH NAILS

Pretty Hate Machine (TVT) 1989
Broken EP (nothing/TVT/Interscope/Atlantic) 1992
Fixed EP (nothing/TVT/Interscope/Atlantic) 1992
The Downward Spiral (nothing/TVT/Interscope/Atlantic) 1994
Further Down the Spiral (nothing/TVT/Interscope/Atlantic) 1995

If, as John Lydon once wailed, anger is an energy, Trent Reznor could power a pretty good-sized city all by himself. The Pennsylvania farmboy turned Cleveland industrial auteur virtually perfected the tantrum-rock genus, spewing lyrical vitriol at an astounding array of targets (not the least of which being himself) and obsessively sequestering himself, Macintosh at the ready, to craft the caustic isolationist anthems that made him the anti-hero to a blanker-than-blank generation of young devotees. Despite revisionist attempts to make him seem like one, Reznor wasn't exactly a novice when he recorded **Pretty Hate Machine:** he'd released singles with a number of Cleveland and Erie, Pennsylvania, bands, including the synth-pop Exotic Birds (wherein Reznor's intricate coif was but one of the Flock of Seagulls influences), the pomp-pop Innocence and dance act Slam Bam Boo (a gig that helped land him a brief role in the Joan Jett/Michael J. Fox film *Light of Day*).

But, like Ministry's Al Jourgensen—his most direct progenitor alongside Jim "Foetus" Thirlwell—Reznor had some demons that needed exorcising, and exorcise them he did on **Pretty Hate Machine.** The album initially seemed to be little more than an overly derivative compendium of industrial-pop clichés—albeit one with impeccable presentation—but proved to be a turning point in the genre's development. In "Head Like a Hole" and other songs, Reznor synopsized all of its indigenous themes—authority is very bad, sado-masochistic sex is quite good—with uncommon vigor. With a nod to David Bowie (and another to confrontational performance troupe Survival Research Laboratories), Reznor subsequently synthesized a stage persona unrivaled in its turbulence (keyboard banks and hired musicians alike risked damage when the singer hit his, er, "stride" in performance).

Angered by what he saw as antagonistic management, Reznor spent the next three years on a very vocal strike against his record label—a label that declined to return his volleys, since **Pretty Hate Machine** spent most of that time on the pop charts. Eventually, a non-amicable divorce was hashed out, and Reznor was able to set up his nothing label and begin draining the reservoirs of psychic pus that had built up. The first lancing loosed **Broken,** a quickly recorded, unequivocally venomous collection of songs that portray the performer as more than just a dilettante. Yes, the martial "Last" resounds with all the banality of a Hellmark greeting card, but the EP's more straightforward pieces (like the gradually intensifying hairshirt anthem "Wish") betray more than a few tangible psychological afflictions at play. Unfortunately, more attention was paid to the Grand Guignol, pseudo-snuff videoclip that accompanied "Happiness in Slavery" (not to mention the hidden-track cover of Adam Ant's "Physical") than to **Broken**'s more human virtues.

For **Fixed,** a limited-pressing companion piece, control freak Reznor ceded jurisdiction over his songs to a battery of industrial sound-sculptors. The head Nail does stick his hand in here and there (as on "Screaming Slave," a gnarled reconfiguration of "Happiness in Slavery"), but the results are more intriguing when Reznor goes out for a smoke. The Coil remix of "Gave Up" refracts the song in funhouse-mirror style with sparks of sound and snippets of voice growing less recognizable with every gyration. Thirlwell demolishes the superstructure of "Wish," leaving only the kettledrums that pound out the tribal foundation. Interesting, but of limited use, unless you have access to the sort of dance-club–scaled sound system required to exact full response from the disc.

According to Reznor, the often-delayed, twice-aborted **The Downward Spiral** came to fruition when he realized "I've done everything I've ever wanted to and I'm still pretty miserable." Whiny? A bit. Self-important? Certainly. Fascinating? You bet! Even though he's still taken enough with his own carefully cultivated image to make a point of noting that parts of the album were recorded in his home studio—in the same home (yawn) the Manson family murdered Sharon Tate—Reznor manages to impart enough real substance to accommodate non-adolescents this time around. The significant increase of diversity on **The Downward Spiral** arises from Reznor's crafting some serious (read: hook-free) industrial music (such as the suicidally void title track) and a fair number of comparatively tranquil pieces. Like, say, Bowie's **Low, The Downward Spiral** generates plenty of tension in its quieter moments. "A Warm Place" is actually quite touching in its surrogate-womb quest; the bleak "I Do Not Want This" worrisome in its self-loathing. Even though the album's hues seldom moderate past deepest indigo, the few escape valves—like the INXS-esque sexfest "Closer" (which contains the memorable couplet "I want to fuck you like an animal/I want to feel you from the inside")—make Reznor seem more corporeal, less like a character in his own Oz-like fantasy world. With the tinkering done by Rick Rubin, the Aphex Twin, Foetus, Coil and Reznor, the superfluous eleven-track **Further Down the Spiral** deconstructs a half-dozen songs from its companion album. Demand the originals. [dss]

See also *Filter, Pigface.*

9-IRON

See *Love Child.*

NINE POUND HAMMER

The Mud, the Blood, and the Beers (Wanghead) 1989 (Crypt) 1991
Smokin' Taters! (Crypt) 1991
Hayseed Timebomb (Crypt) 1994

Blindly driving an old scrapheap with a stuck accelerator, fueled by potent trailer-park hootch and heading straight for hell, Nine Pound Hammer roared out of Lexington, Kentucky, belching mother-humping bourbon-soaked rock'n'roll and a sardonic swig of southern culture that makes Jason and the Scorchers sound like a Sunday afternoon tea society and the

Cramps like fussy stylists. Between the relentless butt-kicking Blaine Cartwright gives his guitar and the manic hyperbole of Scott Luallen's careening vocals (not to mention the pair's bugeyed songwriting), Nine Pound Hammer jabs the raw force of Jerry Lee Lewis and the pure electricity of punk into a fever blister that gushes forth with septic fun.

The thinly produced **The Mud, the Blood, and the Beers** (which is included, in its entirety, on the **Smokin' Taters!** CD) is a Ramonesy debut containing such statements of cultural purpose as "Redneck Romance," "Gear Head," "Drive-In" and "Barefoot County." If the Hammer makes like a four-headed Mojo Nixon here, it bears noting that the band beat him to the Eagles-murdering punch by two years with "Bye Bye, Glen Frey."

The second album (with new bassist Matt Bartholomy joining drummer Rob Hulsman in the rhythm section) smokes out of the speakers with redoubled purpose and fluid, road-tested rockabilly punk. When not messing around with classics like "Folsom Prison Blues" or acknowledging the miscegenated existence of "Surfabilly," the relentless group thrashes around its own time and place, admitting to certain family secrets ("Feelin' Kinda Froggy"), personal weaknesses ("Turned Traitor for a Piece of Tail"), episodes of drunk driving ("Don't Get No"—the rest of the thought is "better than this") and bouts of employment ("Headbangin' Stock-Boy"). Kinda takes your breath away, don't it?

Louder, faster and fully tanked up on wickedly clever admiration for life's losers, Nine Pound Hammer rips into **Hayseed Timebomb** like the proverbial one-eyed cat heading for the seafood store during a three-day catnip bender. The album's trash-filled swamp of beer, No-Doz, junk food, sloppy sex and rifles blurs the us-them culture line in a hyped-up wail of droll debauchery. Changing the other back wheel this time (adding drummer Bill Waldron to the lineup), the Hammer spews such colorful plumes as the queasy culinary litany of "Run Fat Boy Run," the go-nowhere hero of "Shotgun in a Chevy," the autobiographical "Stranded Outside Tater Knob," the departing "Outta the Way, Pigfuckers" and, best of all, the title song's violent nutjob. "He's headin' into town, riding on a derailed train/The devil's playing skeeball deep inside his brain/People in this town will never forget his name." Nine Pound Hammer's derailed train just keeps gathering momentum as it rolls on into the night. [i]

NIRVANA

Bleach (Sub Pop) 1989 + 1992
Blew EP (Ger. Sub Pop/Glitterhouse) 1989
Sliver EP (Sub Pop) 1990
Nevermind (Sub Pop/DGC) 1991
Hormoaning EP (Japan. DGC) 1992
Incesticide (Sub Pop/DGC) 1992
In Utero (Sub Pop/DGC) 1993
MTV Unplugged in New York (DGC) 1994
Singles (UK Geffen) 1995
From the Muddy Banks of the Wishkah (DGC) 1996

The teen spirit that is always a component of the ether can hover for years without coalescing into anything more than a haze—that vague, uneasy, something-in-the-air feeling rising like swamp gas as a byproduct of living young and unsteady in a hostile world that hasn't yet made its intentions clear. But it can also go off with a spectacular atmospheric bang. The catalysts that ignite such cultural explosions rarely survive the experience, and the havoc they instigate is invariably all out of proportion to their efforts. But the changes so wrought can be vast, leveling the land and ushering in an era to which old rules no longer apply.

That said, **Bleach** is not quite the sound of music's past being sent to its belated grave. Despite traces of catchy melodicism ("About a Girl"), a versatile screamer and a superior grip on dynamics to temper the thick, molten aggression (learned from dark '70s metallurgists via the Melvins), Nirvana's debut is a punk album of its time, class and place. This late-'80s aftershock of indie rock's dare-to-be-ugly thuggery and meaninglessness was grounded in a hope-free slacker/lumpenproletariat lifestyle and forged too far from any influential music capitals to bother with pretenses of cool or the need to be self-conscious about sounding like Golden Earring (something the group does on "Love Buzz" before unleashing a furious feedback raveup). Faced with the option of hate-you/hate-me lyrics, Aberdeen-born singer/guitarist Kurdt Kobain (as he chose to misspell his name on the cover) opted for the latter, declaring himself a "Negative Creep" and seeing his worthlessness reflected in someone else's eyes ("Scoff"). Otherwise, the songs are nothing special; neither is the guitar playing. The rhythm section of bassist Chris Novoselic and drummer Chad Channing (Melvins drummer Dale Crover plays on "Floyd the Barber" and "Paper Cuts," both recorded as a demo nearly two years earlier but not appreciably different in approach) puts up a powerful struggle, but Jack Endino's on-the-cheap production keeps its pounding presence from being clearly felt. Guitarist Jason Everman, although listed as a member of Nirvana, is not on the album; "Love Buzz," rather than the declaration of devotion to Melvins leader Buzz Osborne some took it to be, is a cover of a silly obscurity by Holland's Shocking Blue—probably the only group ever touched by the hand of Nirvana to get no career boost from it.

The trio that made **Nevermind** two years later had a lot more to show and say for itself. Bolstered by the 1990 arrival of Thor-like hammerer Dave Grohl, the band had spent enough time working the club circuit to become a popular and respected underground attraction, prized for its calamitous brink-of-chaos guitar-smashing performances and ear-splitting sonic brimstone. Cobain had developed prodigiously as a songwriter, and had located the lull'em/slaughter'em power switch, which became Nirvana's most influential signature. His haphazard lyrics—often disconnected fragments strung together at random, as much a social statement in structure as in content—were like an alphabet slate, ideal for disaffected youth to adopt, interpret and take as personally as they needed to.

Signed by an open-minded label that could wave the Sonic Youth flag in its sales pitch, Nirvana wound up in the studio with producer Butch Vig. Exhibiting the talent that would define the sound of his own Garbage album four years later, Vig's uncanny sense of placement—putting an effect here, a seemingly unthinkable twist there, pairing vocal lines with other elements and pulling incongruous concepts down off shelves to fulfill visions the band wasn't even having—helped shape **Nevermind** in the most extraordinary way. What could have been just a better brand of **Bleach** became the Rosetta Stone of '90s punk-rock. Together, the four (plus mixmaster Andy Wallace, who did major post-production surgery, including samples and effects, on the results) made a prismatic album that has it all: anger, humor, tunes, power, subtlety, venom, pity, slickness, slackness, stupidity, screams, whispers, insight, allure, repulsion, clarity, confusion—and an uncredited Youngbloods fragment sung by Novoselic at the head of "Territorial Pissings."

Blasting away in huge power-chord slabs sheep-dogged by Novoselic's potent bass figures and super-charged by Grohl's rhythmic might, the songs don't reinvent the wheel, but they do send it careening down a modern highway without a care in the world. Rejecting the most holy of values in "Stay Away," Cobain sings "I don't know why I'd rather be dead than cool," and that's a liberating breakthrough in itself. The group's rejection of standard post-adolescent anxieties (meanwhile defining life itself as the era's new miserable experience) invigorates every note, making strong emotions even stronger and sending the rock meter through the roof. Showing a complete lack of regard for the fear of being exactly what his songs claimed him to be—a confused loner, bored and disconsolate, unwilling to make any effort on his own behalf—Cobain transcended the common role of sensitive stoner hero. Punks had been talking the talk for years, but few ever slouched the slouch with as much genuine conviction.

An intricate and convoluted mesh of ideas and influences wrapped around a brick going through a window, **Nevermind** is the subconscious of a troubled mind given a monumental and compelling airing. The dozen songs (thirteen, counting the seven-minute unlisted vamp known as "Endless, Nameless" that belatedly follows the last track on all but the first fifty thousand copies of the album and quickly became a rote alternarock gimmick) accumulate into a barreling boulder. But they also exist in individual vacuum-packed universes, and many don't bear up to close scrutiny. For all its perception and celebration as an anthem, "Smells Like Teen Spirit"—a four-chord sizzle-fest loaded with quizzical tributes to alienation and anomie—is ill-suited to the office. It has a less grabby chorus than "In Bloom" (an arrogant and condescending attack on the kind of fan who "likes all our pretty songs . . . but he don't know what it means") or even "Drain You," which reconfigures the "Teen Spirit" chord structure to much better effect. Between the general Scratch Acid screech, the Killing Joke menace of "Come as You Are" and the slithery Melvins bottom distortion of "Breed," Nirvana might be seen here as the bristling sum of its record collection, but the raw power and the originality of "Polly" (an unnerving and ironic rape fantasy based on an actual event), the gorgeous, cello-haunted "Something in the Way," the drum-rolling "Stay Away" and the swinging, light-footed "Lounge Act" truly come from within. Ultimately, though, it's not really the track-by-track merits of **Nevermind** that matter.

By whatever confluence of circumstances, strategies, talent and luck aligned in the fall of 1991, **Nevermind**—defying all expectations—became a multi-million-selling phenomenon, indisputable proof that kids would buy music that moved them even if it came with all the fuck-the-mainstream characteristics that always defined punk out of broad acceptance. Like the '77 new wave explosion without the inevitable wipeout, **Nevermind** turned the '90s—for better and *much* worse—into the "alternative" decade, a time when no musical exponent was presumed too outlandish for commercial consideration. That Nirvana—in fact, **Nevermind**—was a one-off explains why so much of what floated in with the subsequent backwash is so bad; that's what floodgates are for in the first place. Still, as a sweeping colonic, the album became—alongside "That's All Right," "Maybellene," **The Times They Are a-Changin',** "I Want to Hold Your Hand" and "Anarchy in the UK"—one of the most epochal pieces of plastic in rock'n'roll history.

Hormoaning, issued in Japan and Australia to promote a Pacific Rim tour in early '92, consists of six tracks, none of which had been on LP at the time. The covers of songs by Devo ("Turnaround"), the Wipers ("D-7") and the Vaselines ("Molly's Lips" and "Son of a Gun") come from a 1990 John Peel session. The band's own "Aneurysm" and "Even in His Youth" were lifted from the "Smells Like Teen Spirit" CD single.

Most of **Hormoaning** wound up on **Incesticide,** the rarities compilation released in lieu of a **Nevermind** followup in '92. The fifteen-track set contains a B-side from the **Blew** EP ("Stain") and both studio tracks from the **Sliver** EP ("Sliver" and "Dive"); there's a different version of "Aneurysm," a fast, electric "(New Wave) Polly" and "Been a Son" from a second BBC radio session, previous compilation tracks ("Beeswax" and "Mexican Seafood") and vault excavations. Except for "Sliver" (an early indication of the burgeoning catchiness in Cobain's writing) and the charms of the two Vaselines tunes, the music is pretty consistently second-rate—and wholly unimproved by the appalling rock-star hubris of Cobain's liner notes. "A big 'fuck you' to those of you who have the audacity to claim that I'm so naive and stupid that I would allow myself to be taken advantage of and manipulated. . . . If any of you in any way hate homosexuals, people of different color, or women, please do this one favor for us—leave us the fuck alone! Don't come to our shows and don't buy our records."

In Utero captures the group in a downward spiral of confusion and instability. (A couplet from "Territorial Pissings"—"Just because you're paranoid/Don't mean they're not after you"—aptly describes the self-absolving principle driving the process.) Unlike **Nevermind**'s relative un-self-consciousness, a jittery sense of being caught by jailbreak floodlights afflicts nearly every track, starting with the overt acknowledgment of "Teen Spirit" in "Rape Me." Concern for coolness is the likely explanation for the selection of producer Steve Albini; the album's harsh Jesus Lizard–strength abrasion and scorched-throat singing dares the band's converts to maintain their enthusiasm. The corrosive sound is no cosmetic skin-peel: the songs' content is equally rough and damaging. The predictable flagellant's shame of "Serve the Servants" ("Teenage angst has paid off well/Now I'm bored and old") is only the beginning. "Dumb" ("I think I'm dumb/Or maybe just happy"), "Rape Me" ("Hate me/Do it and do it again"), "Milk It" ("I am my own parasite") and "All Apologies" ("Everything's my fault/I'll take all the blame") all open ragged and bloody wounds of self-loathing.

Musically, the record is likable in fits and starts.

"Serve the Servants," "Heart-Shaped Box," the horrific "Rape Me," the stunning "All Apologies" and the feedback-splayed "Frances Farmer Will Have Her Revenge on Seattle" muster reliably appealing structures. But driller-killers like "Scentless Apprentice," "Very Ape," "Milk It," "Tourette's" and "Radio Friendly Unit Shifter" are explosions of malignant sound rather than vision. The album ends in a round refrain of "All in all is all we are"—a suitably enigmatic (or meaningless, take your pick) coda to what would prove to be the band's studio finale.

Singles is a British box containing all six UK CD singles from **Nevermind** and **In Utero.**

Two months after the release of **In Utero,** Nirvana taped an episode of *MTV Unplugged.* Having frightened off some of its fans with holy-terror noise, the group must have relished the thought of rattling punk traditionalists—at least those who had already forgotten the sound of **Nevermind**'s "Something in the Way"—with its antithesis. (Paying back the media agency of their initial stardom probably wasn't a bad hedge, either, especially after **In Utero**'s predictable sales shortfall.) A year later, by which time it was obliged to serve as Nirvana's epitaph, the show's soundtrack was released as **MTV Unplugged in New York.**

Taking advantage of the opportunity, the trio—augmented by guitarist Pat Smear (the ex-Germ punk veteran who had joined Nirvana as a touring member in 1993), cellist Lori Goldston and two-thirds of the Meat Puppets—used it to publicly explore other facets of its creative desires. Cobain's singing is frequently stretched to the breaking point, which only underscores the unguarded atmosphere of this daring triumph. A gentle infusion of air, delicacy and baronial grace illuminates appropriate selections from all three preceding albums ("About a Girl" and "All Apologies" yes, "Teen Spirit" no). Meanwhile, covers of songs by David Bowie ("The Man Who Sold the World"), the Meat Puppets (a trilogy of evidently unsingable tunes from the Arizona band's **II** album), Vaselines ("Jesus Doesn't Want Me for a Sunbeam") and Leadbelly ("Where Did You Sleep Last Night," a folk standard also known as "In the Pines") extend the band's stylistic reach well beyond the constipated brutality of punk. Nirvana had bootstrapped itself to a new plain.

Kurt Cobain died from a self-inflicted shotgun blast at home in Seattle in early April 1994. The following year, Dave Grohl recorded an album by himself and then, with Pat Smear, formed a quartet called Foo Fighters around it. Krist Novoselic (who reclaimed the spelling of his given name for **In Utero**) became involved in anti-censorship political action and convened a trio called Sweet 75. In addition to the success of her group, Hole, Courtney Love—Cobain's widow—has become famous as the widow of Kurt Cobain.

The yang to **Unplugged**'s yin, **From the Muddy Banks of the Wishkah** is a raging full-on live compilation of tracks recorded on various stages in America and Europe between 1989 and 1994 and assembled by Grohl and Novoselic. The versions of "Polly" and "Breed" predate Grohl and so feature drummer Chad Channing; among the surprise songs are "Spank Thru," a forgotten Sub Pop compilation item from 1988, and "Sliver." [i]

See also *Earth, Foo Fighters, Meat Puppets, Mindfunk, Pat RuthenSmear, Wool; TPRG.*

MOJO NIXON

Otis (Enigma) 1990 (IRS) 1991
Whereabouts Unknown (Blutarski/Ripe & Ready) 1995

MOJO NIXON & THE TOADLIQUORS

Horny Holidays! (Triple Nixxxon/Triple X) 1992

PLEASURE BARONS

Live in Las Vegas (Hightone) 1993

JELLO BIAFRA & MOJO NIXON

Will the Fetus Be Aborted? EP (Alternative Tentacles) 1993
Prairie Home Invasion (Alternative Tentacles) 1994

MOJO NIXON AND SKID ROPER

Mojo Nixon and Skid Roper (RBI/Enigma) 1985 (IRS) 1991
Frenzy (Restless) 1986 (IRS) 1991
Get Out of My Way! (Restless) 1986 (IRS) 1991
Bo-Day-Shus!!! (Enigma) 1987 (IRS) 1991
Root Hog or Die (Enigma) 1989 (IRS) 1991

After five albums with partner Skid Roper in the '80s, Mojo Nixon got with producer Jim Dickinson and assembled the ultimate trailer-park-rock studio band for his solo debut. John Doe (X bassist), Country Dick Montana (Beat Farmers singer/drummer), Bill Davis (Dash Rip Rock guitarist) and Eric Ambel (Roscoe's Gang guitarist) help launch **Otis** into a solidly musical orbit. Adjusting himself to such skilled company, Mojo straddles their sonic missile to rant and rave about the legal profession ("Destroy All Lawyers"), ex-Eagles ("Don Henley Must Die"), politics (the funky "Put a Sex Mo-Sheen in the White House") and celebrity teeth ("Shane's Dentist"). With the exception of an unironic ballad bad enough, one hopes, to discourage any such missteps in the future, **Otis** is maximum Mojo.

For his next trick, **Horny Holidays!** puts a big wet Nixon pucker on seasonal songs, drawing material—classics, doggerel and originals—from diverse sources (Dr. Seuss to Chuck Berry, "Jingle Bells" to James Brown's "Santa Claus Go Straight to the Ghetto"). Backed by a tight bar-room trio, raunchy of voice, suggestive of lyric whenever possible (check Jimmy Butler's "Trim Yo' Tree" and his own "It's Christmas Time," which could easy pass for the J. Geils Band) and as ruthlessly casual as can be, Mojo gives the holiday season a spirited and playful squeeze of the butt cheeks. Phil Spector would be . . . mortified.

Never the most insular rock'n'roller around, Mojo then spent some time making records with illustrious pals. Dragging the Toadliquors along to meet the elder statesman of San Francisco punk, he cut **Prairie Home Invasion,** a rousingly good political country-rock album, and an EP with Jello Biafra. He also teamed up with more traditional cronies—Country Dick Montana and ex-Blaster Dave Alvin—to form the pro tem Pleasure Barons, a thirteen-piece extravaganza complete with horns and "choir." **Live in Las Vegas,** which doesn't bother to identify which Las Vegas stage (if any) actually withstood the revue's revelry, gives equal time to all three principals. Alvin does his usual button-down rootsabilly work on such vintage jukebox memories as "Games People Play" and "Closing Time," even working up a sprawling, bigtime "Gangster of Love." Montana wraps his resonant pipes and boisterous spirit around "Take a Letter Maria," "Who Do You Love?," Nancy Sinatra's "Jackson" and the two-song "Definitive Tom Jones Medley." Mojo trots out three of the best numbers from his private stash and, with Alvin's lead guitar as endorsement, effortlessly hijacks the show with careening, elongated performances of "Louisiana Lip Lock," "Debbie Gibson Is Pregnant With My Two Headed Love Child" and the geographically resonant "Elvis Is Everywhere." (If not Las Vegas, then pray tell where?)

Looking after its own bizness for a change, the Mojo World Empire finally spewed out the long-awaited followup to **Otis,** the Eric Ambel–produced **Whereabouts Unknown.** With keyboard player Pete Gordon the only remnant of the Toadliquors (among the other musicians are ex-dB's drummer Will Rigby and guitarist Simon Chardiet of the Bar Sinisters), the playing is crisp and perfunctory country rock; instrumental accuracy is thoroughly wasted on (if not toxic to) a vocalist this instinctual. Fortunately, Mojo is in credibly foul form, and has enough solidly entertaining originals to make his own party happen: the penis-enlargement fantasy of "Gotta Be Free" ("This is the greatest country on earth / Cause, honey, now I got girth!"), the swingin' Gulf War protest of "My Free Will Just Ain't Willin'," the lowdown boogie of "Don't Ask Me Why I Drink" and the woman-loving inconsideration of "Not as Much as Football." "You Can't Kill Me" is a six-minute barrelhouse epic of slide-guitaring all over the melody of "Amazing Grace" which Mojo uses as a podium for a litany of personal preaching, rabble-rousing and politicking. (He has, after all, been hanging around with Biafra.) For good measure, **Whereabouts Unknown** includes a sweet, sloppy solo acoustic rendition of the obscure oldie "If I Can Dream," the uproarious "Tie My Pecker to My Leg" (co-written by Montana) and a properly obnoxious cover of Morrissey's "Girlfriend in a Coma" that includes a sneak attack on the song's author. Like Mojo says, you can't kill rock'n'roll—no matter how hard he tries. [i]

See also *Dave Alvin, Beat Farmers, Jello Biafra; TPRG.*

NOCTURNAL PROJECTIONS

See *Cakekitchen, Peter Jefferies.*

NOEL COWARD'S GHOST

Peyote Marching Songs, Vol. 1 (Shzoid) 1995

Burdened only by its perplexing nomenclature, this amazing solo creation by New Yorker Lane Steinberg (aka Cheepskates collaborator Lane Hollend)—who led the nifty Wind through three tuneful records in the mid-'80s—seems to have blown in from a parallel pop universe. Endlessly inventive, intricately crafted and burnished with gorgeous harmonies, this homemade stunner variously sounds like XTC ("Excuses"), the Left Banke ("The Lovely Maiden Voygle"), the Beach Boys ("Timon of Athens," "A Ghost in Wexford Terrace"), **Sell Out**–era Who ("Spanish Birthday Across the Miles"), Syd Barrett ("Benzaline") and nobody in particular ("Sad Lions"). Most of the songs gaily mix stylistic metaphors as Steinberg realizes his fantasies, using countless skillfully played instruments. But as the oblique lyrics don't provide much of a clue, **Peyote Marching Songs, Vol. 1**'s intentions are as enigmatic as the choice of its title. [i]

See also *Cheepskates.*

NOFX

Liberal Animation (Fat Wreck Chords) 1988 (Epitaph) 1991
S&M Airlines (Epitaph) 1989
Ribbed (Epitaph) 1991
The Longest Line EP (Fat Wreck Chords) 1992
White Trash, Two Heebs and a Bean (Epitaph) 1992
Punk in Drublic (Epitaph) 1994
I Heard They Suck Live (Fat Wreck Chords) 1995
Heavy Petting Zoo (Epitaph) 1996

NOFX fuses I-got-the-world-up-my-ass (think Circle Jerks) attitude, British punk-era political cynicism and a snotty vocal tenor wedged somewhere between Dead Milkmen bratcore and an air of early Social Distortion disillusion. The Hollywood-formed foursome jabs at the ill-effects of capitalist society—repression, prejudice, the poor—all with an underlying sense of paranoia. But rather than stand on a soapbox, vocalist/bassist Fat Mike and crew opt for sarcasm and humor, producing a one-two punch that, on the early releases, helped distract from the music's monotony and continues to set the band apart from the power-punk pack. In recent years—NOFX has been going more than a decade, though Fat Mike and guitarist Eric Melvin are the only remaining original members—the group has, to the disappointment of punk purists, become more pop-friendly.

Expressing blatant distaste for '80s just-say-no conservatism, NOFX debuted with a 7-inch "The PMRC Can Suck on This," released on Fat Mike's own Fat Wreck Chords label. Soon after, the band put out **Liberal Animation,** a generally straightforward punk-paced collection with a few reggae rhythms and "Here Comes the Neighborhood," which mixes a slow, introspective intro and hard-rock guitar solos. The songs are a bit sloppy, but one look at the lyric sheet and cover illustration (three cows, one sporting a Dead Milkmen T-shirt, sitting at the dinner table partaking of roast human) makes it apparent the band's not very serious about its agit-prop. There are silly songs ("On the Rag," "Beer Song," "Truck Stop Blues" and "A200 Club," about crabs) and digs at non-carnivores. "Vegetarian Mumbo Jumbo" asks "Why should I be sad about cows getting hit in the head . . . It's survival of the fittest and we're winning." The band does offer up a bit more insight with the anti-politics stance of "Free Dumb" and the focus on hypocrisy in the lifestyle of peace punks in "Piece." The main feat here is that Fat Mike pulls off stupid and sarcastic equally well.

S&M Airlines maintains the breakneck speed but expands the band's stylistic repertoire with more prominent guitar solos and ska/dub grooves. Parts of the amusing "Professional Crastination" recall the beginning of Iggy's "The Passenger," though the song quickly jumps to hyperspeed and then back to the reggaefied breaks; "Life O'Riley" also toggles between ska and fast punk. Many of the lyrics again poke fun at American society—"Jaundiced Eye" supports minority pride—but the band is no less prone to spouting un-PC humor. "You Drink, You Drive, You Spill" puts a twist on the statistic that thirty-five percent of auto deaths are alcohol-related. "The other 65% are not alcohol-related / What does this tell us about the drunk drivers / They seem to have a better record than the sober team."

Ribbed continues the lyrical levity in "Moron Brothers," "Food, Sex and Ewe" and "Shower Days." "New Boobs" is a funny take on silicone society and an example of the band's broadening style: the song devolves into a Sha Na Na–like '50s parody. NOFX even offers up its first ballad, "Together in the Sand," penned by short-term guitarist Izzy Drew Lynn. Mike doesn't alter his bratty delivery, but the record's increased use of harmonies would become permanent.

It's on **The Longest Line**—which introduces new guitarist, singer and trumpet-player El Hefe—that the NOFX sound really comes together and spreads apart. On "Kill All the White Man," NOFX takes its affinity for reggae one stop further by imitating the form's vocal style. Though the band is serious about its anti-racist stance on that cut, the "Batman"-like chorus of "white man" lightens the touch. On the title track, you can taste their soured view of life; "The Death of John Smith" offers further commentary on the void in middle-class America.

White Trash, Two Heebs and a Bean adds poppier melodies, softening the edge but not the attitude. A guide to creating formulaic hits ("Please Play This Song on the Radio") sticks in a slew of curses just to mess with DJs. Tracks that dive into untested waters serve to break up the more predictable fare: a jazzed-up cover of Minor Threat's "Straight Edge" complete with Louis Armstrong–style vocals, the Al Jolson–era ditty "Buggley Eyes," the "Oi!" chants and ska beats of "Bob."

There's not much change in **Punk in Drublic.** The pace is still brisk; most of the songs hold to the standard Offspring/Green Day style. The highlights are the jokes: "The Brews" is a takeoff on typical Oi skinhead sound with lyrics that would make a rabbi proud, "My Heart Is Yearning" is an operatic vocal parody. As far as that Top 40 punk style, the sound works best on "The Quass," "Don't Call Me White" and "Punk Guy," where the band brings back some of the old British flavor.

Announcing that "NOFX are: same as last album but older and fatter," **Heavy Petting Zoo** continues the band's crude and catchy socio-political-sexual analysis in Weezer-tight pop blurts like "Hobophobic (Scared of Bums)," "Bleeding Heart Disease" and the weight-conscious "Hot Dog in a Hallway." Fat Mike revels in his Howard Stern–like sensibilities: "The Black and White" attempts to settle the feminist anti-pornography movement with the predictable "I think they need a good hard fuck," "Freedom Lika Shopping Cart" accuses the homeless of chronic irresponsibility and "Release the Hostages" tastefully praises Johnnie Walker Red for "keep[ing] my insides warm like a cunt." Musically unassailable and lyrically unforgivable (but with an impressively principled printed nose-thumb at TV, major labels and commercial radio), **Heavy Petting Zoo** is a punk album in spirit if not always in sound.

The brilliantly titled **I Heard They Suck Live,** recorded in early '95 at a Hollywood club, contains solid, straightforward live versions of songs from each of the band's prior releases plus a cover of Rudimentary Peni's "Nothing but a Nightmare." [mg/i]

NOISE ADDICT

The Taste in My Eyes EP (Aus. Fellaheen) 1994
Young & Jaded EP10 (Grand Royal) 1994
Def EP10 (Ecstatic Peace!) 1994
Noise Addict Vs. Silver Chair EP (Aus. Fellaheen) 1995
Meet the Real You (Aus. Fellaheen) 1995 (Grand Royal) 1996

BEN LEE

Grandpaw Would (Fellaheen/Grand Royal) 1995
Away With the Pixies EP (Aus. Fellaheen) 1995

Australia's Ben Lee made his recording debut at fourteen with a startlingly great home-recorded three-chord single, "I Wish I Was Him," about envying Evan Dando ("He's got six different flannel shirts, Airwalks not thongs/He even understands the words to Pavement songs"). The song was discovered by Thurston Moore and Mike D. of the Beastie Boys (mentioned in its lyrics), both of whose labels put out EPs of Lee's band, Noise Addict. ("I Wish I Was Him" was subsequently covered by Bikini Kill's Kathleen Hanna and reportedly performed by Dando himself.)

The Taste in My Eyes (later reissued as **Noise Addict Vs. Silver Chair,** which the *other* band of Australian teenagers has nothing to do with beyond the title) is a piss-poor five-song quickie with a full electric band. "I Wish I Was Him" appears in a dull, rocked-up remake (the joke was funnier when Lee didn't announce it). Ominous chorus (from "Baby Shoes"): "I wish I could grow back down."

Noise Addict's American debut came via **Young & Jaded,** a much better set of early recordings that includes the original version of "I Wish I Was Him" as well as a cover of Jonathan Richman's "Back in Your Life" and four new Lee originals, notably the anti-carnivore anthem "Meat." The other two members of Noise Addict are mercifully scarce—the rudimentary recording and Lee's not-quite-tuned guitar make the going tough enough. Still, Lee's incipient songwriting talent is very much in evidence. The same, however, isn't true of **Def**—seven weak numbers (including a remake of **Taste in My Eyes**' "Phone Remedy") disastrously recorded and featuring some of the worst drumming ever committed to record. The band's pubescence may be an excuse, but that doesn't make the record any more fun to hear.

Lee recorded his solo album in America with producer Brad Wood, who made it sound very much like an earlier production of his, Liz Phair's **Exile in Guyville.** Decent production, as it turned out, makes all the difference in the world. **Grandpaw Would** is a joy: one wonderful, catchy little pop song after another, including fleshed-out remakes of **Young & Jaded**'s "Pop Queen" (with backing vocals by Rebecca Gates of the Spinanes) and "Don't Leave," as well as the melancholy "Away With the Pixies," the hook of which is sung by Phair. The lyrics show that Lee's been studying his vocabulary lists ("I don't think that's a suitable metaphor," "be a bit more ductile like me"—that kind of thing) and that he understands relationships better than most songwriters twice his age ("Trying to Sneeze"). And he's not even in college yet.

The Australian **Away With the Pixies** EP includes its title track in the **Grandpaw Would** version, a not-as-good demo of "Ductile" and six extra 4-track-recorded songs, only one of which ("Shirtless") is really worth hearing. It's a little redundant to refer to one of Lee's records as juvenilia, but that's basically what this is.

On Noise Addict's first full album, **Meet the Real You,** the band (an altered four-piece lineup) has learned to play well enough for Wood's production to make up for whatever's lacking; the remake of "Poison 1080" (from **Def**) is much improved. Unfortunately, Lee may be getting too cocky from all this early attention. The album contains both a brief joke called "Contractual Obligation" and a song in which he disses a woman for only hanging out with him because he can get her into shows; he reportedly wrote most of the album in the studio, a sloppy practice that's usually the province of much older, lazier bands. Oh, Ben. He knows perfectly well what time it is ("16" is a great song about his ambivalence), but the clock *is* running. [ddw]

NOMEANSNO

Betrayal, Fear, Anger, Hatred EP7 (Can. Wrong) 1981
Mama (Can. Wrong) 1982
Look! Here Come the Wormies! (Can. Wrong) 1984
You Kill Me EP (Can. Undergrowth) 1985 (Alternative Tentacles) 1991
Sex Mad (Can. Psyche Industry) 1986 (Psyche Industry/Alternative Tentacles) 1987
The Day Everything Became Nothing EP (Alternative Tentacles) 1988
Small Parts Isolated and Destroyed (Alternative Tentacles) 1988
The Day Everything Became Isolated and Destroyed (Alternative Tentacles) 1988
Wrong (Wrong/Alternative Tentacles) 1989
Live + Cuddly (Wrong/Alternative Tentacles) 1991
0+2=1 (Alternative Tentacles) 1991
Why Do They Call Me Mr. Happy? (Alternative Tentacles) 1993
The Worldhood of the World (As Such) (Alternative Tentacles) 1995

HANSON BROTHERS

Gross Misconduct (Alternative Tentacles) 1992

MR. RIGHT & MR. WRONG

One Down and Two to Go (Can. Wrong) 1994

Emerging from their basement laboratory in Victoria, British Columbia, in the early part of the 1980s, the latter-day Wright Brothers—Rob (bass, vocals, guitar) and John (drums, vocals, keyboards)—first revealed the fruits of their disquieting musical recombination experiments on the 7-inch **Betrayal, Fear, Anger, Hatred** statement of purpose and the full-length **Mama,** an accomplished and impressive display of taut and direct lock-formation bass/drums/etc. simplicity (think of Devo on a jazz tip, Motörhead after art school or Wire on psychotic steroids) and pointedly warped lyrics.

But that was just the beginning. The five-song **You Kill Me** abuses Jimi Hendrix (a tuneless "Manic Depression"), nervously rips open the schematic "Body Bag" and includes a cartoon poster of a drug shooter. Alternative Tentacles later paired that record on a tape and CD with **Sex Mad,** a full-length set of obsessions ("Love Thang," "Revenge," "Dad") which pours out punky collegiate weirdness and slash'n'burn egghead energy.

The Day Everything Became Nothing, a six-song 12-inch, offers more dada invention with concertedly intense music. The unstructured prose of the title track is supported by pounding drums alternating with bursts of guitar noise; "Beauty and the Beast" syncopates the rhythms for a disorienting effect that impressively manages to suggest funk and negate it in the same line.

Small Parts Isolated and Destroyed focuses the insular band's alienation into fairly presentable form, modulating the carefully arranged muscular rock and punk into a tense knot of energy with fewer jagged points and rough edges. Ably punctuated by unsettling rhythm shifts, Rob's noisy guitar solos provide most of the record's appeal. (**Small Parts** later joined its immediate predecessor on a power-packed CD entitled **The Day Everything Became Isolated and Destroyed.**)

Wrong puts an angry amphetamine charge into **Small Parts**' precision, sending NoMeansNo into clamorous, roaring overdrive that, in its most highly evolved organization, suggests King Crimson's Clockwork Orange–reared offspring. As self-amused and often enraged lyricists, the Wrights don't bother with longwinded expressions of sensitive emotions: the complete screamed libretto of "Brainless Wonder" is "I need lunch / Feed me now / I need lunch / Where's my break?!!!" Occasional descents into mere punk are disappointingly plain, but bracingly original tracks like "The End of All Things" and "Big Dick" are utterly invigorating.

If by no means cuddly, the live disc recorded in Europe the previous year proves the gale-force ferocity of NoMeansNo—convened here as a trio in which the guitarist remains unidentified—in concert. The Wrights play with the coordinated fury of linked threshers; the buzzing guitar noise and Rob's singing leap out through the dense rhythm assault to administer a firm sonic throttle to the Wire-like "Two Lips, Two Lungs and One Tongue" (from **Wrong**), "Body Bag" (**You Kill Me**) and "Teresa, Give Me That Knife" (**Small Parts**). Teetering thrillingly on the brink of meltdown, NoMeansNo whips it good.

L'amour seems to have entered the Wrights' world on **0+2=1,** a restrained and reflective—even poetically sensitive—album that makes an unconvincing stab at establishing a new stylistic beachhead. "Now" begins the album with acoustic guitar, a mild two-step and lyrics about "the things I have heard you whisper in the dark"; "Mary (The Last)" uses a funk tempo. Ultimately, however, the group returns to an attenuated version of its toxic shock formulation and salvages the album with effective Devo-esque riffology in "The Fall," the horror-show creepiness of "Everyday I Start to Ooze" and the brutal industrialism of "I Think You Know."

Why Do They Call Me Mr. Happy? bares more of the duo's inner adult with better results, relegating willful offensiveness ("Kill Everyone Now") and unrestrained anomie ("Madness and Death") to a minor supporting role; even "Cats, Sex and Nazis," with its lyrics about flesh-eating zombies, is essentially a love song. Generally maintaining a consistent, controlled blare (except for the sweetly popped parts of "Slowly Melting" and the "Dancing in the Streets" takeoff of "Lullaby"), NoMeansNo waxes eloquent, contradicting the music's free extroversion with thoughtful considerations of loneliness, devotion, emotional need and the meaning of life. "I woke up dreaming that I was dead . . ."

Taking a great leap forward in overall presentation, **The Worldhood of the World (As Such)** is as rough and grubby an album as the band has thrown off in years. Sounding thuggishly comfortable in their sonic element, the Wrights turn outward again, addressing violence ("I've Got a Gun"), social Darwinism ("Predators") and life's castoffs ("Victim's Choice," "He Learned How to Bleed") with surprising compassion and concerted musicianship cranked up high and hard. A couple of songs—"The Jungle," "Lost," "My Politics," "State of Grace"—continue to explore the provocative self-analysis that has become a significant element of NMN's work, but the organic integration of mind and body makes this a satisfying, nearly profound, expression of a mature, sophisticated band—no longer geared just for cult adulation—that hasn't lost its taste for blood or gristle.

When they're not being NoMeansNo, the Wrights and a couple of pals masquerade as the Ramones-cloning comic pop-punk Hanson Brothers (guitarist Tommy, singer Johnny, bassist Robbie and drummer Kenny). If the hockey-rockers don't try very hard to make music that resembles their purported idols, at least the quartet shouts its song countdowns and has the imitation graphics end together. "Comatose" is something of a soundalike, and the beer-guzzling "Blitzkrieg Hops" ("Hey! You! / Let's brew! . . . Tastes like an import / Crack another cold quart") does rewrite the similarly titled original, but most of **Gross Misconduct** sounds no more like the Ramones than any other speedy group with a dumb sense of humor. Sample lyric: "I saw her driving the Zamboni / I asked her out for some spumoni."

The magazine-concept release cryptically credited to Mr. Right & Mr. Wrong is a rabid, irresponsible and stylistic diverse sampler of new NMN tracks (like the delicate indelicacy of "This Wound Will Never Heal," the raging "Who Fucked Who?," the spoken meta-mechanics of "Widget"), a couple of solo blues numbers by Mr. Wrong (Rob Wright), the Hanson Brothers' rewritten cover of the Kinks' "Victoria," a song by Swell prod. and some delightfully bizarre-lite Wright Brothers leftovers from '79–80. For convenience and amusement, the back cover offers alternate CD programming strategies—by song type, chronology and alphabetical order. [i]

See also *Jello Biafra, D.O.A.; TPRG.*

NO SAFETY

See *Zeena Parkins.*

NÖSFERÄTU

Rise (Cleopatra) 1993
Legend (Cleopatra) 1994
The Prophecy (Cleopatra) 1995

England's Nösferätu is, bar none, the most theatrically goth outfit ever assembled; the band is so devoted to its pretensions that it drives to gigs in a hearse. Unlike the members of Sisters of Mercy, Bauhaus, Christian Death and other genre giants, vocalist Louis DeWray, guitarist Damian Deville and bassist Vladimir Janicek are completely sincere; no tongue-in-cheek Screaming Lord Sutch moments ever lighten *their* moody world. **Rise** is rife with vampire lyrics, creepy synth sound effects, slithering guitar and frilly harpsichord flourishes. Through songs like "Vampyres Cry," "Dark Angel," "Lament" and "Alone," DeWray makes sinister old Andrew Eldritch seem like a nursery-rhyme-crooning kindergarten teacher. For the enthusiast, **Rise** is orgasmic. For everyone else, the album is simply dress-up silliness.

Legend, a back-catalogue CD collection, features early versions of "Vampyres Cry" and "Dark Angel," along with 12-inch remixes and tracks from singles and compilations. The album seethes and hisses with all the fury and sensuality of a newly inducted child of the night. Snicker all you like, there's never been a band that so perfectly—and enthusiastically—embodies the goth stereotype. The material suffers from poor production, but some of the songs shine through the murk. DeWray's darkly melodramatic charisma gets full exposure on the excellent, pulse-quickening "Abominations," the horror-eroticism of "Pictures of Betrayal" and the Middle Eastern–facing "Arabian Heat."

Unfortunately, DeWray left Nösferätu after **Legend**'s release, replaced by the inexcusably awful Niall Murphy, whose frail, quavery vocals make him sound like he'd be more comfortable fronting a new wave band. On **The Prophecy,** it becomes painfully obvious that it was only DeWray's emotional vocals that prevented Nösferätu from seeming idiotic. The band still strives to be the universe's spookiest attraction with songs like "Requiem," "Thrill Killer," "Shadowmaker" and "Grave Desires," but the shiver-inducing magic is irretrievably gone. Talk about your living dead. [ky]

NOTHING PAINTED BLUE

A Baby, a Blanket, a Packet of Seeds (Jupa) 1990
Power Trips Down Lover's Lane (KokoPop) 1993
Placeholders (Scat) 1994
The Future of Communications EP (Scat) 1995

FRANKLIN BRUNO

A Bedroom Community (Simple Machines) 1995

Led by bespectacled philosophy student Franklin Bruno, the prolific Nothing Painted Blue purveys fine, nervous aggro-pop, much of which has earned the band a reputation as logorrheic eggheads (for one thing, the obviously self-aware trio named one of its limited-edition cassettes **Logorrhea**). But though ØPB—the preferred abbreviation, natch—are certainly brainy sorts, the music they make is decidedly intra-disciplinary, boasting the verbosity and imagistic flair of an English major, the hyperactive drive of a physics prodigy, the formulaic precision of a math wiz and the big-picture skepticism of a Marx-loving epistemologist. (Yep, they also have a song called "Epistemophilia.")

Singer/guitarist Bruno and drummer Kyle Brodie were high-school classmates who formally began the group in 1987, when Bruno and bassist Michael Neelon were attending Pomona College. Los Angeles was just a freeway drive away, but the band has always stuck to its suburban roots (the so-called Inland Empire), a commitment that eventually bore fruit in the form of other bands (Refrigerator, Diskothi-Q, Mountain Goats) and labels (most notably Shrimper). ØPB's own imprint, Jupa, was responsible for **A Baby, a Blanket, a Packet of Seeds,** a promising sixteen-track medium-fi album that nods in the direction of Flying Nun for its perky melodicism and bands like Slovenly, or maybe even the Pop Group, for its skewed, skeletal energy.

Power Trips Down Lover's Lane pays off on the

debut's promise. Though the band has said Shimmy boss Kramer's shiny production doesn't quite capture their murkier side, the album is a thoroughly infectious rollercoaster of herky-jerky riffs and memorable melodies, helped along by snaky violin parts and the supple touch of new bassist Joey Burns (also of Giant Sand). Songs like "Peace Dividend," "Block Colors," "Campaign Song" and "Storefronts" all burst with perfect pacing, pointed emotion and lazy beauty, as does a Go-Betweens cover, "Rock and Roll Friend." Bruno is at his best lyrically here, offering a dense, brain-tickling batch of clever couplets and finely wrought scenarios that manage to be linguistically punch-drunk, substantively pointed and overwhelmingly evocative all at once. "She's cherubic / She's seraphic / She's omniscient when it comes to traffic," he sings of "Officer Angel," a tribute to a real-life cop-turned-traffic-reporter. "Register," a witty critique of love and consumption, plays with every definition of the title word.

The self-produced **Placeholders** brings out that elusive murky side. It accents the music over the lyrics, then puts a further emphasis on distorted guitar crud and a harder (though sometimes slower) rhythmic attack. It's a good-not-great effort—the lack of sprightliness makes the hooks less endearing and the words less affecting, although "Weak," "Rightful Heir" and "Spread Your Poison" do deliver in both of those departments. There's simply too much rock-damage and too much art-damage. And compared to Bruno's best, the lyrics of the otherwise lively "Career Day" and the plodding "Houseguest" are mundane and unrealized. Personnel notes: on this record Peter Hughes (of Diskothi-Q) took over from Burns (who left to concentrate on Giant Sand), while subsequent live shows saw Neelon returning, this time on violin and second guitar.

If the followup EP, **The Future of Communications,** is a step up in pop quality, that's probably because it's a step back chronologically: it leads off with an old single—the great, giddy "Sorely Tempted"—and tacks on one radio track and three other recordings, plus the titular "song," a fifteen-minute spoken treatise on life, school, work and, yeah, the future of communications, as conceived by the band's pal Scott Banks. Anyone who listens to it more than once is either a terminal grad student or one of the people featured on it—which happens to be the same thing.

Bruno's solo album, which arrived between **Placeholders** and **The Future of Communications,** finds him playing nearly all the instruments on thirteen ornate, highly personal tracks that are more folk-rock than one-man indie weirdness. The songs, supported mostly by piano and acoustic guitar leads, have a certain hushed momentum, but the thin vocals and robust lyrics seem a little out of place without the punch of a full band.

Nothing Painted Blue (and Franklin Bruno solo) have also spewed out a healthy number of cassettes, EPs and 7-inches for the Jupa, Shrimper, Scat, Simple Machines, Anyway and Car in Car labels. As of mid-1996, Scat was preparing to gather much of that output on a Nothing Painted Blue compilation CD called **Emotional Discipline Harmonies,** while Bruno was said to be collaborating with Tsunami/Liquorice/Simple Machines queen Jenny Toomey on an "indie-rock musical." [jc]

See also *Giant Sand.*

NOTORIOUS B.I.G.

Ready to Die (Bad Boy/Arista) 1994

"Things Done Changed," observes the Notorious B.I.G., a burly Brooklynite who swapped his own doomed life as a street hustler for the fat success of a powerhouse album in 1994. But his gloomy track isn't about his personal salvation. "Back in the day, our parents used to take care of us," he raps darkly. "Look at 'em now, they even fuckin' scared of us." Opening the abundantly grim **Ready to Die** with a dramatic collage that proceeds from physical birth to jail-release rebirth inside of three minutes, Biggy—the product of an environment that stylistically includes 2Pac, Ice Cube and EPMD—pushes his way purposefully and nonjudgmentally through a high-stress land of stickups ("Gimme the Loot"), vigilant self-defense ("Warning") and the constant threat of sudden oblivion ("Ready to Die"). Following a transitional oasis of hip-hop reminiscence ("Juicy"), however, the album shifts gears, setting aside the hard, spare beats and lyrical violence for lush soul tracks and crude rhymes about sex ("Me & My Bitch," "Big Poppa," "Friend of Mine"). Finally, the Notorious B.I.G. embraces the conflicting impulses of his record (and mindstate) in "Suicidal Thoughts," a touchingly poignant personal contemplation on his life—and beyond. "When I die, fuck it, I wanna go to hell / Cause I'm a piece of shit it ain't hard to fuckin' tell . . . Crime after crime, from drugs to extortion / I know my mother wish she got a fuckin' abortion . . . I wonder if I died would tears come to her eyes?" All the sound-effect blasts and imprecations couldn't possibly deliver a harsher, more desolate message than that. [i]

NO USE FOR A NAME

No Use for a Name EP (Woodpecker) 1989
Let Em Out EP (Slap a Ham) 1990
Incognito (New Red Archives) 1990
Don't Miss the Train (New Red Archives) 1992
The Daily Grind (Fat Wreck Chords) 1993
Leche Con Carne (Fat Wreck Chords) 1995

As the walls that separate punk and pop continue to crumble, bands that can teeter on the edge, like No Use for a Name, are suddenly, well . . . making names for themselves. No Use's home state of California is at the hub of this crossover trend, as bands like Offspring, Rancid, Bad Religion and Green Day crawl out of the woodwork and onto commercial radio and MTV like termites from a brush fire. In No Use's case, the move has been gradual, spanning four albums, some eight years and about a half-dozen lead guitarists. What's remained constant is the unabashed energy infused by drummer Rory Koff and bassist Steve Papoutsis, as well as attendance at the Bad Religion school of socially aware lyrics and melodic harmonies. No Use is occasionally plagued by overblown vocals—the result of Tony Sly making the switch from hardcore-style rants to real singing—but that hasn't significantly slowed the band's marked musical progression.

An early formation featured Chris Dodge and Sly on vocals, with Sly also on lead guitar. The quartet's self-titled debut EP rings with basic mid-'80s hardcore (à la Black Flag) or, in more melodic moments, early Descendents (parts of "Shotgun," for instance). Though the four songs are not unique, No Use at least spits 'em out on target. (The in-your-face "NoItAll" also appears on the first album.)

One year and four songs later, No Use throw a few curves in with the traditional speedballs on **Let Em Out.** The EP starts with a scream on "It Won't Happen Again"—which also pops up on the debut album—as its tempo changes stir a hornet's nest of tension. The solid hardcore of "Pacific Bell" and "Born to Hate" incorporate chants.

Incognito comes off the blocks at a scorching clip and rarely lets up. Dramatic rhythm shifts on "Puppet Show" and elsewhere prove No Use's crisp musicianship. But the songs are too often predictable in structure—breakneck speeds mixed with slow, exaggerated mosh parts. Sly does refrain from forcing his voice on most of **Incognito,** keeping it where it's most potent, raspy and aggressive. He's especially effective using the spoken vocal approach on "Record Thieves" (originally on **Let Em Out**) and "Weirdo," where his offhand delivery recalls Black Flag's "TV Party." As a portent of things to come, No Use provides "Truth Hits Everybody" with a Police-like chorus that actually works.

The momentum established with **Incognito** dissipates on the followup, the transitional **Don't Miss the Train.** It's not the pace so much as the focus that's lost: metal-edged lead guitar and poppier harmonies seem out of place alongside the hardcore pace and lyrical bent. The album does have a few tracks where it all comes together, though: "Punk Points" and "Get Out of This Town" recall the first album's ripping sound. Sly keeps it under control for those songs, unlike the strained vocals of "Tollbridge" and "Thorn in My Ride." As for the band's commercial impulse, it's hit and miss. The music of "Death Doesn't Care," an allusion to the pointlessness of killing for your country, complements the tension of the lyrics. But other tracks on **Don't Miss the Train** sound as if the band is waiting at the wrong station.

Improved songwriting elevates **The Daily Grind,** although the tempos flow so well together that it's difficult to differentiate among the tracks. Dynamic variety would have helped, but the precision drumming and sharp fingerings of the latest lead guitarist are a boon. There's also a big difference in Sly's vocals, which generally fit the music better. Lyrically, the band casts a cynical eye on society. As "Countdown" observes, "Another wall is built between color and race / Another wrong decision about peace is made / Another chemical is dumped into the sea . . . Another day, another pain, another misery."

Two years and yet another guitarist later, the accessible **Leche Con Carne** uses hooks, dynamics and diversity to effectively straddle the punk-pop line. Along with the commercial-inroading "Soulmate," tracks like "Leave It Behind" sport catchy riffs. While the lyrics again dwell on social ills, from wife-beating ("Justified Black Eye") to the fiasco in Waco, Texas ("51 Days"), Sly finally proves himself as a singer without faltering. The unlisted bonus track—a covers medley of '70s classics that includes snips of Berlin's "Metro," the Knack's "My Sharona" and Toni Basil's "Mickey"—offers an indication of the specific sources of the band's burgeoning pop sensibility. [mg]

C. C. NOVA

See *Steel Pole Bath Tub.*

HEATHER NOVA

Spirit in You EP (UK Butterfly/Big Life) 1993
Glow Stars (UK Butterfly/Big Life) 1993
Blow (UK Butterfly/Big Cat) 1993 (Big Cat) 1994
Live From the Milky Way EP (Big Cat/Work) 1995
Oyster (Big Cat/Work) 1995

Born in Bermuda, educated at the Rhode Island School of Design and career-launched in London, Heather Nova (née Frith) conjures up powerful atmospheres in her baroque musical dramas. Throwing her strong, wavery voice into thick, swelling clouds of artful guitar-and-cello rock, Nova marries Patti Smith's thrusting rhythmic aggression with breathless swoons of fluttering expressiveness (Kate Bush on spanish fly) in a mannered but robust full-body press of stirring melodies and sensual obsessions. That she exhibits an obnoxiously coy Beavis and Butt-head idea of lyrical sexuality ("She said 'come' and 'cock' and 'go down' and 'touch myself,' *heh-heh, heh-heh*") is a disappointment given the self-possession and intrinsic tug of her work.

The singer/guitarist/songwriter made her recording debut in 1990 with **These Walls,** a four-song UK 12-inch under her real name; as Heather Nova, she returned several years later with **Spirit in You** and her first album, **Glow Stars,** which reprises all four of **Spirit**'s tunes.

The live-in-London **Blow**—released initially as a six-song EP and then expanded with three more from a different (but, if the audible clap-o-meter is an accurate gauge, no better attended) gig, **Blow** presents Nova and her quartet as a formidable musical force, giving her originals vivid, expansive band arrangements of a sort unheard since the mid-'70s glory days of Steve Harley and Cockney Rebel. Possessing an endless array of engaging vocal gimmicks (including a bunch from Björk), Nova blows each song into an intricate epic, caressing verses like a folkie and attacking choruses with the unbridled enthusiasm of a musical Jackson Pollock. "Maybe an Angel," "Sugar," "Doubled Up" and "Light Years"—none of which are on **Glow Stars** and all of which were recorded for Nova's American studio debut—receive gloriously over-the-top renditions full of winding instrumental inventions and delirious vocals.

Live From the Milky Way documents a slightly bigger-sounding Amsterdam club date: simpler, more electrifying versions of three **Blow** songs and three quieter new numbers, one of which ("Verona") is unfortunately archetypal of lyrics that make her out to be a demurely pretentious college-poet pornographer: "It gets inside you like the sun / It makes you wet just like the rain / It makes you sound so sentimental / It's a lovely kind of pain."

In that pursuit, Nova gets **Oyster,** her first American studio album, off to a dismally calculated start with "Walk This World," the point of which appears to be the phone sex sleaze of its chorus tag: "I want you to come . . . [pregnant pause] . . . walk this world with me." Lines like "I'm not touched but I'm aching to be" hammer home the do-me theme; "And I'm sucked in by the wonder and I'm fucked up the lies" provides the obligatory four-letter thrill. Nova doesn't have room on her plate for much besides thinking about nookie (and watery geography—this island girl takes to rivers and oceans the way Bruce Springsteen hits the nighttime highways), but **Oyster** finds far more elegant ways to slouch around the bedroom. "Blue Black" alludes to a variety of sexual transgressions ("You made me a victim . . . I gave it away, whore for a day . . . and was it familiar when you touched my sister"). "Heal" offers a general view of water's restorative inspiration, but the metaphysical romantic metaphor of the power ballad "Maybe an Angel" (which could very well lead to an inadvertent case of mistaken identity with Alanis Morissette) hits harder than either. [i]

KAZUYUKI K. NULL/JIM O'ROURKE

See *Jim O'Rourke.*

TERRI NUNN

See *Big F.*

JALALUDDIN MANSUR NURIDDIN WITH SULIEMAN EL-HADI

See *Last Poets.*

NUTLEY BRASS

The Nutley Brass Plays the Greatest Hits of Shimmy-Disc! (Shimmy-Boot) 1995
Ramones Songbook as Played by the Nutley Brass EP7 (Vital Music) 1995
Beat on the Brass (UK Nectar Masters) 1996

The loungecore happy hour—truly one of the most pointless form-over-function musical affectations in recent memory—is largely the refuge of those with one simple, silly idea. Led by Sam Elwitt (also of the Sea Monkeys), the Nutley Brass—New Jersey's own goofy easy-listening marching band—at least pours some conceptual imagination into the cocktail mix. **The Nutley Brass Plays the Greatest Hits of Shimmy-Disc!,** true to its title, contains deadpan loopy instrumental renditions of tunes by Fly Ashtray, Uncle Wiggly, Daniel Johnston, King Missile, Lida Husik and seven other bands from the roster. That few listeners are likely to recognize the original songs only makes the joke funnier. Elevator goooooing . . . sideways!

Likewise, the **Ramones Songbook** 7-inch offers jaunty strike-up-the-band/'60s sitcom renditions of "Gimme Gimme Shock Treatment," "Beat on the Brat," "Havana Affair" and, with wonderfully ludicrous "ooh!" "aah!" contributions by the David Abramson Singers, "Chinese Rocks." Taking a broader view, **Beat on the Brass** turns the band's unwanted attentions to a stack of punk/new wave classics. [i]

N.W.A

N.W.A. and the Posse (Macola) 1987
Straight Outta Compton (Ruthless/Priority) 1988
100 Miles and Runnin' EP (Ruthless/Priority) 1990
Efil4zaggin (Ruthless/Priority) 1991
Greatest Hits (Ruthless/Priority) 1996

Ice Cube calls it "reality rap"; everyone else settles for the simplistic and misleading gangsta tag. In any case, N.W.A (Niggaz With Attitude) came straight out of Compton with an unpoliticized expression of urban alienation, autobiographical rage and action-movie fantasies. By feeding a vast audience of disaffected young people a profoundly negative glamorization of brutal street life, N.W.A—the rap Mayflower that carried Ice Cube, Dr. Dre, the late Eazy-E, MC Ren and others from a loose agglomeration of South Central Los Angeles neighborhood pals to enormous and influential solo stardom—managed to put their city and their sound on the international map, sell loads of powerful records, provoke governmental concern and raise disturbing issues about the context and import of rhymes that describe violence, misogyny and sociopathic behavior.

N.W.A. and the Posse is a loose and funky warmup, a showcase for various permutations of the sprawling young crew (some of whom fell away when shit got serious) to rap about cars, girls, drugs and booze over Dre's on-the-money Cali tracks. Although much of the record is strictly for fun ("Drink It Up" is a goofy party number sung to the tune of "Twist and Shout"; "Fat Girl" tells a dumb story about an overzealous, overweight woman), the autobiographical "Boyz-n-the Hood" (written by Ice Cube, rapped by Eazy-E) and Cube's non-judgmental "Dope Man" aptly demonstrate the group's tougher side.

Shifting into high gear, with Yella joining Dre behind the board, the group made the blistering and genre-defining **Straight Outta Compton,** a shocking and fearless roughneck explosion that demands respect and threatens violence at every turn. "Do I look like a motherfucking role model?" Cube asks in "Gangsta Gangsta": "To a kid looking up to me life ain't nothin' but bitches and money," he observes, but doesn't take heed of such responsibilities. (Alongside a remix of the first album's "Dopeman," Cube's nearly upstanding "Express Yourself" typifies the ambivalence that continues to describe his work.) The controversial "(Fuck) tha Police," a mock trial of Los Angeles' cops, promises armed resistance to unwarranted hassles, underscoring the point with the sound of gunshots. Whether this hyper-drama is meant to be taken seriously or not, the distinction—created by first-person delivery of realistic tales that shift without blinking from hustling women at parties to shooting people for fun—was obviously lost on some listeners, especially in the hair-trigger minds of official power.

Exploiting their notoriety as FBI-certified troublemakers, N.W.A—with Ice Cube gone, pretty much the preserve of Eazy, Dre and Yella—rap a high-tension action adventure on the title track of **100 Miles and Runnin',** which also includes "Sa Prize (Part 2)," a crudely theatrical continuation of "(Fuck) tha Police." But any hope of a political consciousness taking hold is dashed by "Just Don't Bite It," a detailed discussion of fellatio.

"Why do I call myself a nigga ya ask me / Well it's because motherfuckers wanna blast me . . . Back when I was young, getting a job was murder / Fuck flipping burgers, 'cos I deserve a 9-to-5 I could be proud of" puts social analysis into the opening minutes of **Efil4zaggin,** the final salvo from the group that would soon collapse under the vindictive antagonism that arose between Dre and Eazy. Otherwise, the wretched album (which gives lots of songwriting credit to The D.O.C., who sat out the previous record and didn't do much of note on **Compton**) slides back into the sleaze for an obnoxiously adolescent and ugly sex trip: "Findum, Fuckum & Flee" and "She Swallowed It" are merely typical of the album's stupidity. Even worse but not unrelated, "To Kill a Hooker" is an appalling short story. For a crew that once stood for something (granted, it was never easy to know exactly what), this record is a sorry end. [i]

See also *Dr. Dre, Eazy-E, Ice Cube, MC Ren.*

NYACK

11 Track Player (UK Echo) 1995

AENONE

Saints & Razors EP (KokoPop) 1993

As Aenone, Craig Sterns (vocals/guitar) and Kim Collister (guitar)—childhood pals from suburban Nyack, New York—played exquisite storm-pop. The quartet's four-song EP is a translucent curtain of woolly distortion against which Sterns sings gently flowing melodies in a wispy high register that belies the skill of his technique and the quality of his voice. The brisk and breathtaking "Saints & Razors" is the catchiest song My Bloody Valentine neglected to write; Aenone attenuates the sonic attack on "Gaze" without undercutting its shapely appeal. The record's only bum note is sounded—literally—on the out-of-tune "Celestia."

Two years on, Sterns, Collister and Aenone bassist Bill Stair resurfaced in London as three-fourths of Nyack, a neat Teenage-Fanclub-meets-the-Jesus-and-Mary-Chain electric-pop band—still noise-friendly but lighter in atmosphere and standing less heavily on their distortion pedals. Sterns' voice doesn't have quite the same allure on **11 Track Player** (which sports a red and green variation on the cover of Zipgun's 1992 album, **8 Track Player**), but the delicate consistency of his distinctive tunes—some of them ("I'm Your Star," "Sunrise in My Head" and "Knumb," formerly "Numb") retrieved from the Aenone repertoire, if not the EP—carries the album, which on enhanced CD contains a nifty Nyack video scrapbook. [i]

EVA O

See *Christian Death.*

OASIS

Supersonic EP (UK Creation) 1994
Shakermaker EP (UK Creation) 1994
Live Forever EP (UK Creation) 1994
Definitely Maybe (Creation/Epic) 1994
Cigarettes & Alcohol EP (UK Creation) 1994
Whatever EP (UK Creation) 1994
Some Might Say EP (UK Creation) 1995
(What's the Story) Morning Glory? (Epic) 1995

The debut album by the brashest brats Britain has produced in a decade sloshes cocky rock-star attitude all over sensually loud rhythm-guitar pop, one-upping elders like Stone Roses and the Jesus and Mary Chain by swiping their best features and adding a heavy dose of unfashionable Beatles worship. Landing squarely in familiar post-punk mud, the young working-class Manchester quintet wastes nothing on false modesty, instead thrashing about with the confident assurance that it was poured there just for them.

On **Definitely Maybe,** Oasis navigates a precarious path between eager-to-please enthusiasm, derivative redundancy and pure obnoxiousness, making its roaringly tuneful way on the inescapable hooks and cockeyed lyrics written by guitarist Noel Gallagher and the deadpan sneer and profound inertia of his singing brother Liam. Challenging each other with blistering layers of guitar and piled-on vocals (with these fraternal antagonists fighting to get their hands on the board, the mixdown sessions must have been a living hell), the Gallaghers set up a complete package of guileless guts and attention-grabbing hubris. **Definitely Maybe** rolls out one brilliant song after another: "Shakermaker" (whose unsanctioned use of the New Seekers' old cola jingle was resolved with some changes to the purloined lyrics), the idealistic "Live Forever," the George Harrison–esque "Up in the Sky," "Columbia" ("I can't tell you the way I feel / 'Cos the way I feel is oh so new to me"), the trippy "Supersonic," the T. Rexy "Cigarettes & Alcohol," "Slide Away," the acoustic kissoff "Married With Children." With lines like "I hate the books you read and all your friends / Your music's shite, it keeps me up all night," Oasis makes rudeness and arrogance part of their how-did-I-get-here naïve wonder. How else to explain a debut album that opens with a self-fulfilling original entitled "Rock 'n' Roll Star"?

A bunch of EPs and couple of million records later, Oasis announced its second coming with the help of Gary Glitter (all samples cleared this time) in "Hello," the number that opens **(What's the Story) Morning Glory?** by immediately acknowledging "It's never gonna be the same." No argument there. With new drummer Alan White in place, Oasis follows its template part of the time, but also reins in the megapower noise, adding harmonica and such muso fripperies as mellotron. While Noel does a credible job as co-producer, his new songs aren't as grabby, snide, direct or obvious as the first album's; the reference points are buried, the constructions more intricate. The dreamy "Wonderwall" is rendered with complex understatement (acoustic guitar, cello, piano, musical drumming) that would have been unthinkable on the debut; the monumental "Don't Look Back in Anger" is almost theatrical in its singalong sweep. Meanwhile, "Some Might Say" offers a surprisingly positive (or is that droll irony?) homily; "She's Electric" is like Kinksy folk-rock. Ironically, now that Oasis has earned its bragging rights, there's nothing like "Rock 'n' Roll Star" to deal with the band's self-willed ascension. Even "Champagne Supernova," a majestic seven-minutes-plus closer fitted out with the record's best melody, says a lot less than it promises. **(What's the Story) Morning Glory?** is an underwhelming followup to a stellar debut, but the record's degree of difficulty reveals that Oasis' ambition is as great as its self-esteem. [i]

MATTHEW O'BANNON

See *Bodeco.*

OBLIVIOUS

See *Holly Vincent.*

RIC OCASEK

Beatitude (Geffen) 1982
This Side of Paradise (Geffen) 1986
Fireball Zone (Reprise) 1991
Quick Change World (Reprise) 1993

CARS

The Cars Anthology: Just What I Needed (Elektra/Rhino) 1995

Singer/guitarist/keyboardist Ric Ocasek made his first two solo albums while still leading the Cars; on both, bandmates and friends from groups he's produced or just palled around with help him restyle and exfoliate the Cars' clear-cut sound with more substantial lyrics and ambitions. **Beatitude** employs Jules Shear, Stephen Hague and Darryl Jenifer from the Bad Brains, letting synthesizers prevail in a richly textured and often languid popscape. Ocasek found work for guitarists Steve Stevens, Tom Verlaine, Roland Orzabal and G.E. Smith on **This Side of Paradise,** an album that brought him solo chart success for the single "Emotion in Motion."

Ocasek didn't bother with his usual celebrity casting call for **Fireball Zone,** which Nile Rodgers co-produced and played guitar on. A warmer, softer progression from the exacting, clinical pop of the Cars (which quietly closed down in the late '80s), the album straddles a pleasing middle ground between the strict rhythms and fey singing of Ocasek's instinctual designs and Rodgers' rein-loosening funk. So while the backbeat snaps with firm, clocklike precision through the standard keyboard washes, other pieces in the sonic puzzle move at a more relaxed pace, oiled by smoochy soul backing vocals. Still, hearing the former chilly new wave auteur sincerely sing "Keep That Dream" ("get your disposition out of the rain") and an original entitled "All You Need Is Love" is mighty unsettling. Although "Flowers of Evil" strikes a more appropriate post-punk chord, the song only gives Ocasek "the slicker city blues."

That engaging side trip done, Ocasek zigzagged back across the road and climbed back into the sleek lines of his old ways on **Quick Change World,** reuniting with ex-Cars keyboardist Greg Hawkes for an economical excursion in a familiar vehicle. Nearly dispensing with the previous album's pollyanna philosophizing (he does wonder "why can't we try to live in peace?" in "Help Me Find America"), Ocasek wastes little effort on complex lyrics. If not quite to the Cars' schematic level, he strips the prose down to complain mildly about "Hard Times" while admitting to various measures of anxiety. "When I try to sit tight I get nervous and confused," he notes in "Come Alive," an agitated number (complete with skid marks) which also offers this characterization of official might: "They scream until their neck bleeds / And jack off in the wind."

That Ocasek can still manage a perfectly accurate remake/remodel of the Cars design a decade on is a pyrrhic achievement at best: if he's not stalled in creative neutral, then he's forced by an unmanageable musical personality or blinkered vision to follow a stylistic vector he can't redirect. Either way, the Cars' original remains a more compelling expression of Ocasek's urges (and influences: Roxy Music, Jonathan Richman, Lou Reed, John Cale) than anything on his '90s solo records. **Just What I Needed** completely trumps the band's 1985 **Greatest Hits** with forty selections, stopping at all of the roadmarks in the Cars' career and proceeding from there. The sparklingly packaged set includes three B-sides, an outtake version of **Candy-O**'s "Night Spots" and seven previously unissued demos, among them a clumsy cover of the Nightcrawlers' venerable "Little Black Egg." A broad swipe of '80s nostalgia that holds up fairly well track by track but wears thin over the course of two jam-packed CDs, **Just What I Needed** (over)does it once and for all. [i]

See also *TPRG.*

OCEAN BLUE

The Ocean Blue (Sire/Reprise) 1989
Cerulean (Sire/Reprise) 1991
Beneath the Rhythm and Sound (Sire/Reprise) 1993
Peace and Light EP (Sire/Reprise) 1994

Formed in Hershey, Pennsylvania, by high-school friends with a shared fondness for new wave and post-punk, the Ocean Blue fused their influences—the Smiths, the Teardrop Explodes, R.E.M.—into a likable debut. The college-radio hit "Between Something and Nothing" (which smacks of "Lips Like Sugar"–era Echo and the Bunnymen) sets the tone for the whole affair: twelve pleasant tracks just inspired enough. With polished production by Mark Opitz (except for two tracks handled by John Porter, who also did the Smiths' debut), tunes like "Drifting, Falling" and the chugging "Vanity Fair," all with lyrics by singer/guitarist David Schelzel, are very if-you-like-then-try. . . . Perfectly pleasant, but no great shakes.

Cerulean benefits from meatier sound and stronger, if inconsistent, songwriting. The coloring-book imagery of "Marigold" seems better suited to Book of Love; "Questions of Travel," with its repeated refrain of "Americans dreaming" (of various exotic locales), comes off way too precious. But memorable tracks—the swirling "Ballerina Out of Control," "Breezing Up," the sweeping title cut—outweigh the mediocre ones. The LP is a marked improvement.

The self-produced **Beneath the Rhythm and Sound** lacks the outside opinion it clearly needed; a more seasoned set of hands could've brought "Sublime" (which pleads for multi-tracked backing vocals) and "Either/Or" (which suggests the band had been living with a copy of the Chills' **Submarine Bells**) to much fuller fruition. With fewer hooks than on the second album, Schelzel's increasingly opaque, simplistic lyrics dominate the forefront, setting his consistently flat singing (never a noticeable problem before) front and center throughout, except on "Bliss Is Unaware," where he takes a backseat to keyboardist Steve Lau's Haircut One Hundred–style sax riff.

Peace and Light is a four-song EP of new/old live/studio cuts, and the band's last release for Sire. After his decision to come out of the closet generated friction with his outspokenly Christian bandmates, Lau left the quartet, eventually becoming a record company executive. With his replacement, Oeddie Ronne, the Ocean Blue signed a new deal and began work on a fourth album. [kbr]

SINÉAD O'CONNOR

The Lion and the Cobra. (Ensign/Chrysalis) 1987
I Do Not Want What I Haven't Got. (Ensign/Chrysalis) 1990
Am I Not Your Girl? (Ensign/Chrysalis) 1992
Universal Mother (Ensign/ Chrysalis) 1994

As grand an artistic and commercial success as her unprecedented 1987 debut, **The Lion and the Cobra.,** was, it turned out that O'Connor—only twenty at the time of its release—was just warming up. **I Do Not Want What I Haven't Got.,** again self-produced, dwarfs its predecessor in terms of creative ambition and achievement. Amazingly, this harrowingly personal testament to the tumult in her life sold two million copies in a month, largely on the strength of a memorable video for her version of Prince's "Nothing Compares 2 U." Refusing to be typecast, O'Connor makes a warm orchestral bed for "Three Babies," delivers the otherwise a cappella "I Am Stretched on Your Grave" over a clattering hip-hop beat, gathers thickly chugging electric guitars for "Jump in the River" and sings "Black Boys on Mopeds"—a topical indictment of English hypocrisy—as acoustic folk. But such haphazard diversity is no impediment to the album's overall impact. Unified by the razor-sharp intensity of her lyrics and the staggering power of her vocals, **I Do Not**

Want What I Haven't Got. is an absolute masterpiece.

Having gotten it, however, O'Connor demonstrated just how much she didn't want it. Her subsequent career has been a blur of miscalculation, misbehavior, confusion, confession and obfuscation, a troubled time with more miseries than victories. In the midst of absurd public controversies that mingled politics, religion and personal eccentricities into a fever blister of animosity (culminating in her being booed offstage at a 1992 Bob Dylan tribute concert in the wake of her televised papal picture shredding), O'Connor dropped a real bombshell: **Am I Not Your Girl?** A straight-faced big-band collection of pop, jazz and other standards O'Connor explains as "the songs that made me want to be a singer," the surprising sidestep showcases her basic vocal skills more than any interpretive artistry. Although she turns in credible enough performances (except maybe on "Don't Cry for Me Argentina," which wasn't a good idea on any level), O'Connor brings no real panache or imagination to the effort. "Bewitched, Bothered and Bewildered," "Why Don't You Do Right?" and "I Want to Be Loved by You" have all been sung better numerous times; regardless of the song's likely significance to the vocalist's similarly troubled life, O'Connor's delicate rendering of "Success Has Made a Failure of Our Home" (a Loretta Lynn song previously essayed by Elvis Costello) pales against the garish arrangement and is eventually overcome by her far more passionate delivery of the appended "Am I not your girl?" coda. The only track that truly soars is "Scarlet Ribbons," hauntingly sung against nothing but a tin whistle and uileann pipes. If only the album had stopped there. But the band immediately strikes up a jolly instrumental encore of "Argentina," a sure sign of artistic insolence. That time-waster leads somewhere even worse, into a quiet anti-clerical rant, a bizarre speech in which the oddly hinged star announces "So, yeah, I am angry, but I'm not full of hate; I'm full of love."

Calling **Universal Mother** "a prayer from Ireland," O'Connor opens her fourth album with a fragment from a 1970 speech against patriarchy by Germaine Greer and includes her own loopy theorizing, spoken over a snappy jazz-hop track, about what she believes to be the damage caused by Ireland's lost history. Little else in this largely acoustic and wholly poetic statement about God, womanhood and her native culture is quite so direct. In this handsome and uncomforting quilt, a one-guitar folk rendition of Nirvana's "All Apologies" joins a lullaby ("My Darling Child") written by Irish music veteran Phil Coulter, an a cappella snippet ("Am I a Human?") sung by O'Connor's young son and an unprepossessing batch of originals. **Universal Mother** has the anxious enthusiasm of a high-school notebook: besides touching numerous topical signposts in the grooves, O'Connor fills the booklet with poetry, dedications and endless expressions of appreciation to all and sundry. Obsessed with her inspirations, O'Connor hasn't got much left to say about her actual obsessions in the songs. So while "Red Football" issues a prickly veiled protest against Ireland's anti-abortion laws, she mostly professes love, gratitude and grief, blames God for everything under the sun (in the techno-grooved "Fire on Babylon") and then announces (in "All Babies") that "All babies are crying/For no-one remembers God's name." That's a lot to ponder and not enough to enjoy. [i]

See also *TPRG*.

ODES

See *Love Child.*

OFFBEATS

See *Prisonshake.*

OFFSPRING

Offspring (Nemesis) 1989 (Nitro) 1995
Baghdad EP (Nemesis) 1990
Ignition (Epitaph) 1992
Smash (Epitaph) 1994

When everyone else is moving backward, the man who refuses to budge an inch can sometimes find his way to the front of the pack—just ask this stridently unchanging Orange County surf-punk band. For the first several years of its career (which actually began with a self-released 1987 single), the Offspring didn't make much of an impact on the second—or third, depending on who's doing the counting—generation of similarly minded suburbanites moshing through Southern California clubland with the distant ring of patriarchs like Agent Orange and TSOL resounding in the distance. But with revivalist punk rendered boffo box office in the mid-'90s, the quartet's derivative-but-catchy riffage propelled it to multi-platinum status and the distinction of being the biggest-selling indie-label rock band ever.

On **Offspring**—which barely sold out its three-thousand-copy pressing upon initial release—the group displays a knack for crunchy, repetitive songs that suffer from frequent charges into thrash territory led by overwrought guitarist Kevin "Noodles" Wasserman. There's nothing particularly eventful in the songs themselves; frontman Bryan "Dexter" Holland throws all the right socio-political shapes, but his libertarian "insights" into subjects like Middle Eastern politics (a subject he beats into the ground on "Teheran" and "Beheaded") are strictly out of *Ayn Rand for Dummies.* When Holland looks in his own backyard, he doesn't show that much more acumen: "Elders" and "Blackball" (the latter reprised from that first single) are little more than rote expressions of lingering-adolescent angst. **Baghdad** (again with the Persian Gulf?) sees the band slam through three identikit originals, appending a version of "Hey Joe" that sacrifices all of the song's inherent tension for a transient power-chord rush.

That speed-is-everything aesthetic isn't as pervasive on **Ignition,** but the continued reliance on superfluous dynamic shifts and proto-metal textures is positively grating. There's no denying the band's ability to craft a mindlessly catchy hook—the call-and-response chorus of "Kick Him When He's Down" is guaranteed to stick in your head for a good while after the album is shelved—but those moments are far outweighed by the scenery-chewing that plagues songs like "Take It Like a Man" and the nebulous call-to-arms "We Are One." Holland is the worst offender, lapsing again and again into a rangeless bellow that suggests nothing so much as testosterock precursors like Rob Halford or Ronnie James Dio scaled down to a lower octave. Wasserman (who does inject some compelling surf leads into "Dirty Magic") and drummer Ron Welty are just as likely to overreach, however, wrecking some fairly canny song structures with extraneous eruptions.

Although the foursome had raised its profile a mite by the time **Smash** was released, there was little reason to assume the Offspring would reach beyond the skatepunk set: after all, the stiff surf-thrash sound that ricochets from the album's grooves is almost identical to that of the band's previous releases. However, the Offspring succumbed to the lure of novelty, tagging a Latino-rap catchphrase onto the chorus of an otherwise undistinguished moshfest and—presto!—scaled the charts with "Come Out and Play." That Epitaph could muster the financial resources to hire the same radio promotion people employed by the big boys didn't hurt, but more than anything, the Offspring gets over on a combination of lowest common denominator angst (see the Henry-Rollins-meets-Dick-Dale self-help groaner "Self Esteem") and aggro dance-party fluff (like the ska-tinged "What Happened to You?"). What's most striking in the end is the band's utter inconsequentiality: if Green Day turns out to be the new punk's pop-savvy Beatles and Rancid its street-smart Stones, the Offspring have earned the distinction of being the new Herman's Hermits—look for Dexter Holland on the Tahoe supper club circuit a few years after the turn of the century. [dss]

SEAN O'HAGAN

See *High Llamas.*

OL' DIRTY BASTARD

See *Wu-Tang Clan.*

OLD 97'S

Hitchhike to Rhome (Big Iron) 1994
Wreck Your Life (Bloodshot) 1995

Much as self-respecting power-pop groups understand that their records are never going to join their idols' in the hit parade, country-rockers like Dallas' Old 97's know damn well that wiseacre underground sensibilities never got anyone a warm welcome on Music Row. Good for them. The energetic quartet, with ties to Killbilly and roots in a Denton outfit called Smeg Wentfields and Dallas' Peyote Cowboys, is cool and catholic enough to get both Texas honkytonk titan Don Walser and head Mekon Jon Langford to make guest appearances on its second album, which includes the latter's "Over the Cliff"—as well as Bill Monroe's "My Sweet Blue-Eyed Darlin'."

Hitchhike to Rhome has tight, crisp Telecaster sound, an easygoing backbeat and affably unconvincingly high-lonesome vocals by acoustic strummer Rhett Miller and bassist Murry Hammond. Neither traditionalists nor reverent Gram Parsons fusionists, Old 97's don't waste much elbow grease on seriousness, but their efforts in the direction of silliness won't strain any funnybones, either. The middle ground they inhabit is fine: the music do-si-dos with lyrics that are reliably good-humored even when they're not overly clever. ("If my heart was a car/You would have stripped it a long time ago" locates the median strip pretty accurately.) Those who stick around to album's end will be rewarded with "Ken's Polka Thing," a slack accordion instrumental by lead guitarist Ken Bethea, and a little something extra.

Wreck Your Life puts a little more meaty ham on the wry, bolstering the twangy rig-rock with rattlesnake venom while playing up the lyrics' she-done-me-wrong/I'm-a-bad-boy sardonicism in memorable numbers like "Victoria," "Doreen" and "W-I-F-E." In lazy waltz time, Miller worries "I'm gonna die someday staring at the dressing room wall." Explaining his source of desperation, he opines "I stopped believing in true love when Reagan was king," concluding, "Punk rock'll get you if the government don't get you first." Words to inscribe in nightclub bathrooms everywhere. [i]

O-LEVEL

See *Ed Ball.*

OLIVELAWN

See *fluf.*

OLYMPIC DEATH SQUAD

See *Unrest.*

OLYMPIC WORLD

See *Pastels.*

O-MATIC

See *Braniac.*

ONE DOVE

Morning Dove White (ffrr) 1993

One Dove brings a sense of trad pop tunecraft into the ever-mutable sound of late-'80s UK club culture, that no-limits stir fry of techno, acid-house, ambient, hip-hop and just about every other musical thing up to—and often including—the kitchen sink. The Glasgow trio of Ian Carmichael (keyboards), Jim McKinven (onetime guitarist in Altered Images) and chanteuse Dot Allison throw their romantic Bacharach-esque ballads and glittery dance-pop ditties into the mix, resulting in smashing post-Madchester bubblegum reminiscent of a less kitschadelic Saint Etienne. Allison's breathy voice, as sweet and wispy as candyfloss, has the added kick of a little Scottish C&W twang, which adds personality and color to the hummable hooks and twinkling melodies of songs like the terrific "White Love." **Morning Dove White** is largely the handiwork of UK mixmaster general Andrew Weatherall. With the aid of his Sabres of Paradise and Boy's Own Productions cadres of musical manipulators, Weatherall—best known for reconfiguring an iffy Primal Scream song into the groundbreaking "Loaded"—takes One Dove's shimmering songs and uses them as a canvas. This supernatural mélange of spooky dub F/X, '60s spy-movie symphonics and pulsating, off-rhythm house beats provides a deep groove that contrasts and accentuates One Dove's lighter nature. The record also boasts cameo contributions from Primal Scream guitarist Andrew Innes (donating an acoustic strum to "Breakdown") and dub bass god Jah Wobble (on "There Goes the Cure"). Though plainly designed as a crossover into the pop realm, **Morning Dove White** is still a new-fangled kind of pop record, one that bears evidence of clubland's remix-remake-remodel mentality. In addition to fine tracks like the lustrous "Fallen," it includes three versions of "White Love" and two of "Breakdown." Stephen Hague's "radio mixes" are deliciously futuristic delights, as perfect for the Barcalounger listener as for those aiming at dancefloor hipsway. [mgk]

YOKO ONO

Approximately Infinite Universe (Apple) 1973
Season of Glass (Ono Music/Geffen) 1981
It's Alright (I See Rainbows) (Ono Music/Polydor) 1982
Starpeace (Polydor) 1985
Onobox (Rykodisc) 1992
Walking on Thin Ice (Rykodisc) 1992

YOKO ONO/IMA

Rising (Capitol) 1995
Rising Mixes EP (Capitol) 1996

JOHN LENNON/YOKO ONO

Unfinished Music No. 1: Two Virgins (Apple) 1968
Unfinished Music No. 2: Life With the Lions (Zapple) 1969
Wedding Album (Apple) 1969
Some Time in New York City (Apple/Capitol) 1972
Double Fantasy (Lenono Music/Geffen) 1980
Heart Play (Unfinished Dialogue) (Ono Music/Polydor) 1983
Milk and Honey (Ono Music/Polydor) 1984

PLASTIC ONO BAND

Live Peace in Toronto 1969 (Apple) 1969 (Capitol) 1989 + 1995

JOHN LENNON/PLASTIC ONO BAND

John Lennon/Plastic Ono Band (Apple) 1970

YOKO ONO/PLASTIC ONO BAND

Yoko Ono/Plastic Ono Band (Apple) 1970
Fly (Apple) 1971
Feeling the Space (Apple) 1973

VARIOUS ARTISTS

Every Man Has a Woman (Polydor) 1984
New York Rock: Original Cast Recording (Capitol) 1995

Most listeners, if they have come across Yoko Ono's music at all, remember the squeals of her "bag" music on Side Two of **Live Peace in Toronto 1969,** the intense B-sides found on early-'70s John Lennon singles or as Lennon's equal partner on **Some Time in New York City** and **Double Fantasy.** (Although the former suffers from excessive sloganeering, some of her music—"We're All Water," "Sisters, O Sisters"—stands up; sixteen years and a tragedy later, while Lennon's half of **Double Fantasy** sounds treacly and soft, songs like "Kiss Kiss Kiss" feel utterly contemporary.) Still, Ono's solo albums of the early '70s were taken quite seriously by many musicians who have since incorporated some of her ideas into more commercially accepted work.

Ono came to her marriage with Lennon a fully formed artist and composer, a member of the Fluxus group who had collaborated with John Cage, La Monte Young, Ornette Coleman and Charlie Haden. Yet, until recently, Ono has never received due consideration as a musician. In the popular imagination, she has been variously portrayed as John Lennon's Weird Girlfriend, the Woman Who Broke Up the Beatles and Famous Rock Widow. But it is possible to argue that it was her fame—and her connection with the Beatles, in effect—that kept Yoko Ono from becoming a serious modern composer.

If that's overstating the case, there's no denying the sheer power of **Yoko Ono/Plastic Ono Band** (released simultaneously with **John Lennon/Plastic Ono Band), Fly, Approximately Infinite Universe** and **Feeling the Space.** Usually produced as adjuncts to John's albums, often drawing from the same pool of musicians and working as variations on the themes in each other's work, these albums were profoundly influential. Beyond the new wave bands that took notice at the time, echoes of Ono's attitudes, vocal styles and bluntly honest, self-referential lyrics can still be heard in the music of such artists as Tori Amos, the Boredoms, Sonic Youth, Cibo Matto and Courtney Love, another famous rock widow, who has somehow managed to find commercial success while learning nothing from Ono about dignity.

Those albums and her post-1980 solo work (**Season of Glass, It's Alright** and **Starpeace**) are out of print, but the six-CD **Onobox** contains most of their music. The exemplary package, compiled by the artist herself, is comprehensive, well-organized, extensively annotated (with a thoughtful essay by Robert Palmer) and beautifully designed (the back covers of the individual CDs can be arranged to form a portrait of Ono, just like the old Beatles trading cards). Listening through it in a sitting instills new respect for Ono's career. (**Walking on Thin Ice** is a single-disc distillation of the box set that provides a well-chosen flyover for those lacking the time, money or inclination to suffer the full set.)

The first disc, **London Jam,** contains her most compelling and avant-garde work, the music detractors usually think of when discussing Ono. And it *is* strong stuff—dense, uncompromising and emotionally unguarded. Like many composers of the '60s, Ono disdained "written" music; her interest was in ideas—totally improvised, fearlessly exploratory—rather than songs. With bassist Klaus Voormann and Ringo Starr providing a solid yet supple bottom, Lennon and Ono (with occasional help from Eric Clapton, Jim Keltner and Bobby Keyes) move through the music, endlessly trying new ideas. The vocals are wordless or use simple, repeated phrases like a solo instrument, finding unexpected melodic or harmonic lines, closer in effect to Ornette Coleman or Albert Ayler than a pop singer. To Beatle fans who picked up either volume of **Unfinished Music** or **Fly,** they probably sounded unfathomably strange, but to the contemporary listener they sound amazingly of a piece, on a par with Beefheart, Can and Public Image. The exploded song forms anticipate techno and rock music's interest in dub production techniques ("Mind Train") and the music of Nusrat Fateh Ali Khan. Yet, "Midsummer New York" and "Is Winter Here to Stay?"—either of which would sound at home on a Fall or Sonic Youth album—show that Ono can nail a twisty rocker.

If Ono appears to back off from the implications of **Fly,** the tracks on **New York Rock** and **Run, Run, Run** (Discs Two and Three of **Onobox**) drawn from **Approximately Infinite Universe** and **Feeling the Space** show her working in a more song-oriented format. Using Elephant's Memory and a coterie of studio musicians, she is still capable of making compelling music. Both albums chronicle the Ono/Lennon relationship and travails with unstinting honesty and a feminist perspective. The personal, self-absorbed lyrics of "Death of Samantha" bring Tori Amos and Liz Phair to mind, while the pain and doubt and anger of "What Did I Do!" and "What a Bastard the World Is" ("Oh, don't go / I didn't mean it / I'm just in pain") could serve as a blueprint for the whole school of self-abnegation rock attended by the likes of Hole, Sebadoh and Pearl Jam. Ono also shows a talent for pastiche, matching the loving, almost submissive lyrics of "I Want My Love to Rest Tonight" to a '50s girl-group chord pattern and arrangement, and the aggressive "She Hits Back" to a grinding blues. There are also snatches of the old sonic fire on "It's Been Very Hard": her trademark glissandos, trills, moans and screams float over the top of a smoky cocktail quartet.

Ono's best-known songs show up on Disc Four (**Kiss, Kiss, Kiss**). These are the songs that appear alongside Lennon's on **Double Fantasy** and the posthumous **Milk and Honey.** More groove-oriented than her previous work, the edgy, cautionary "Walking on Thin Ice" and the frankly erotic "Kiss, Kiss, Kiss" were popular at new wave danceclubs. The loving "Beautiful Boys" musically hearkens back to her Japanese heritage, while a later attempt at pastiche, the jaunty "Yes, I'm Your Angel" led the publishers of "Makin' Whoopie" to sue Ono for plagiarism. (She eventually paid to settle the suit.) Today, "Hard Times Are Over" and "Don't Be Scared" teem with an irony that must have been painful for Ono to contemplate. It's a testament to her passion and commitment to facing hard emotional truths that she included them on **Onobox.**

That commitment runs below the surface on Disc Five (**No, No, No**). These songs, written and recorded in the period following Lennon's murder in December 1980, confront her reaction to his death head-on. At the time, **Season of Glass** and **It's Alright,** with shots ringing out and screams of obvious pain, seemed to pick at open wounds most listeners wanted healed. In the context of **Onobox,** it becomes obvious that, for Ono, this *was* the healing process. Like Lou Reed's most confessional albums, Ono's post-Lennon songs can concentrate on lyrics to the detriment of the music. But the quiescent "Silver Horse," the corrosive "No, No, No" and the hauntingly dissonant "Never Say Goodbye" stand out. There's no denying their power as unsparing documents of memory, mourning and faith. The songs from the anti–Star Wars **Starpeace** return lyrically to Ono's early-'70s activism. Her heart may have been in the right place politically, but the results are as heavyhanded as the title; the songs tend toward tepid new wave agitpop.

Onobox also includes as its final disc the previously unreleased **A Story,** a meditation on love and loneliness written and recorded in 1974 during her separation from Lennon. **A Story** contains some of the warmest and most subdued music of her career. From the rueful bossa nova of "Dogtown" to the low-key funk of "Yes, I'm a Witch" and the optimistic pop of "Yume O Moto," Ono made the perfect VH1 album two decades before VH1.

Rising is Ono's only album of the '90s so far. While some of the songs (written for a play about Hiroshima) are OK and try for a modern, grungey sound ("Warzone" sounds like Nine Inch Nails, and "New York Woman" bashes along like 7 Year Bitch), the best that can be said about IMA (the trio led by her son, Sean Ono Lennon) is that it's no Elephant's Memory. The six-track **Rising Mixes** gives four songs from the album an amusing going-over at the hands of Tricky, Ween (!), Cibo Matto and Thurston Moore.

With her idiosyncratic vocals, difficult melodies and personal lyrics, it's not surprising that few have attempted to cover Ono's songs. Two albums have tried to very different effect. **New York Rock** is a collection of Ono's songs (among them "Midsummer New York," "What a Bastard the World Is" and "We're All Water") used as the score for an off-Broadway production written by Ono; singing her work, these trained voices sound at sea. A tribute album, **Every Man Has a Woman** is a little more successful, with Elvis Costello's version of "Walking on Thin Ice" and Harry Nilsson's take on "Loneliness" leading a roster that also includes Rosanne Cash, Roberta Flack and Eddie Money. [sm]

ONYX

Bacdafucup (JML/RAL/Chaos/Columbia) 1992
All We Got Iz Us (JML/RAL/Def Jam) 1995

Bald heads, bad attitudes, cool jams and words you can't say on television are the hardcore hallmarks of Onyx, the extreme Brooklyn/Queens crew that takes roughneck gangstarism straight over the top. Signed and smartly produced by Run–DMC's Jam Master Jay (whose entrepreneurial instincts frequently lead him toward caricatures, like the put-on Afros), Onyx gleefully mines crime, violence and sex for bludgeoning shock potential with such vehemence that it ascends to a grim joke. Beyond sheer malevolence (the title track, "Bust dat Ass" and "Bichasniguz"), **Bacdafucup** arms the old-school party wave in "Throw Ya Gunz" (". . . in the air / Buc buc like you just don't care"), gives lust a torpedo-like charm in "Blac Vagina Finda," makes a mugging career mundane in "Stik'n'-Muve" and mingles in skits (including "Bichasbootleguz," with an Asian-accented offender) that all end in brutal blasts. For all its superficial offensiveness, though, the album (which went platinum, giving new meaning to the phrase "number one with a bullet") is hard to dismiss: the powerful quartet boasts several compelling rappers, Jay's simple beats are atmospherically effective and "Slam" has an irresistible gang chorus *and* a shattering freestyle from Sticky Fingaz (whose fast guttural growl sounds like a cross between Method Man and Ol' Dirty Bastard).

Stripped back to a trio of Fredro Starr (now calling himself Never), Sticky Fingaz and DJ Suavé Sonny Caesar (billed as Sonee Seeza), Onyx took over the production for **All We Got Iz Us,** an evil-minded followup that strives hard to make **Bacdafucup** sound like spring break at Sunday school. The album begins with a demonic voice pushing a victim to suicide (Sticky Fingaz, who announces in the liner notes that "I ain't got no love for nobody, 'cept my Moms," later offers to do himself in, " 'cept they might not sell weed in hell"). It gets worse. Declaring themselves "young, black and just don't give a fuck," Onyx rationalizes drug dealing ("killing my own people . . . they gonna get it from somebody, I'd rather it be me") and makes music about theft ("Purse Snatchaz"), violence ("Betta Off Dead") and murder ("Shout"). If the topics of Onyx's charged rhymes weren't so disastrous for so many, the album would be sensationalist sport, but the proximity of reality and the relentlessness of the band's nihilism takes all the fun out. [i]

OPAL

See *Kendra Smith.*

OPERATION IVY

See *Rancid.*

ORACLE

See *Wire.*

ORB

"Kiss" (UK Wau! Mr. Modo) 1989
"A Huge Ever Growing Pulsating Brain That Rules From the Centre of the Ultraworld" (UK Wau! Mr. Modo) 1989 (UK Wau! Mr. Modo/Big Life) 1991
"Little Fluffy Clouds" (UK Big Life) 1990 (Wau! Mr. Modo/Big Life/Mercury) 1991
The Orb's Adventures Beyond the Ultraworld (Wau! Mr. Modo/Big Life/Mercury) 1991 (Island Red) 1994
Peel Sessions (Strange Fruit/Dutch East India Trading) 1991
Aubrey Mixes: The Ultraworld Excursions (UK Wau! Mr. Modo/Big Life) 1991 (Caroline) 1992
"Blue Room" (Wau! Mr. Modo/Big Life/Mercury) 1992
U.F.Orb (Wau Mr. Modo/Big Life/Mercury) 1992 (Island Red) 1994
Adventures Beyond the Ultraworld: Patterns & Textures Version (UK Wau! Mr. Modo/Big Life) 1992
Live 93 (UK Inter-Modo/Island) 1993 (Island Red) 1994
Pomme Fritz EP (Inter-Modo/Island Red) 1994
Orbvs Terrarvm (Island) 1995
Peel Sessions 92–95 (UK Strange Fruit) 1996

SPACE

Space (UK Space/KLF Comm.) 1990

FFWD

FFWD (UK Inter-Modo/Discipline) 1994

VARIOUS ARTISTS

Auntie Aubrey's Excursions Beyond the Call of Duty: The Orb Remix Project (UK Deviant) 1996

Richard Hell may have seen his as the blank generation, but it was Dr. Alex Paterson who assumed the mission of transforming his into the blankest generation with the ambient house soundscapes of the Orb. After roadying for Killing Joke, Paterson found his way into an A&R position at Brian Eno's EG Records, where he somehow wound up merging Eno's ambient systems with his own punk ideals and firm grasp of the burgeoning UK electronic movement to create—with the help of KLF-er Jimmy Cauty and an old Minnie Riperton record—a twenty-three-minute genre-defining single, "A Huge Ever Growing Pulsating Brain That Rules From the Centre of the Ultraworld." With that, "ambient house"—as the single was cover-billed—was born. A seemingly lazy blend of Eno's sound-as-wallpaper tactic, KLF's frenzied sample theft, prog-rock's meandering expansiveness and the effective dance grooves of the acid-house scene, the Orb singlehandedly helped usher in a new, and surprisingly popular, way of thinking about music.

The partnership between Cauty and Paterson ended after the "Ever Growing" single (remnants of the collaboration with Paterson's parts deleted—were released by Cauty on the **Space** LP), yet Paterson carried the ideas of the Orb forward with **Adventures Beyond the Ultraworld,** a double-disc set created with the help of Thomas Fehlman (Sun Electric), Youth (Killing Joke and others), Steve Hillage and Miquette Giraudy (ex-Gong, System 7) and Thrash (aka Kris Weston, the closest thing to a full-time collaborator Paterson has had in the Orb). Containing the surprising smash hit "Little Fluffy Clouds" (little more than a beat with Rickie Lee Jones prattling on about youth in the desert: the song is also available on a six-mix CD EP) and the very house-oriented "Perpetual Dawn," the two-hour set is filled with the sort of found sounds and homeopathic trippiness that had previously been the sole domain of new agers. Injecting danceable bits and electronic rhythms, Paterson's creation became an entirely new beast. And, in keeping with the themes of sonic excess put forth on **Ultraworld** (ten songs in two hours), the album was followed by a pair of limited-edition reconfigurations, the most successful being **Patterns & Textures,** a CD that accompanied a live video of the same name.

Further upping the ante, Paterson (this time with help from Thrash, Jah Wobble, Hillage and Giraudy) released the mind-bending electronic space-rock of "Blue Room," which, at 39:58, is the longest single to ever reach the top spot on the UK charts, and possibly the most amelodic song ever to chart anywhere. **U.F.Orb** continues on the course laid out by **Adventures,** containing both "Blue Room" and the stunning "Towers of Dub." Although a live album may not seem like the most logical course for a techno artist to take, the four-LP, two-CD **Live 93** is an amazing piece of work, showcasing Paterson's remarkable hippie versatility and demonstrating that electronic music need not solely be the domain of pasty-faced computer programmers.

In 1994, Paterson abandoned the genre with both **Pomme Fritz** (subtitled *The Orb's Little Album*) and **FFWD** (a collaboration between Paterson, Thrash, Fehlmann and Robert Fripp). The impenetrable gloom of the six vaguely angry **Pomme Fritz** tracks—all modifications of a central motif—and the modular systems-sounds of **FFWD** are neither danceable nor dreamable, and it is glaringly obvious that Paterson had grown weary of the music that he helped to codify. With the release of the nearly eighty-minute **Orbvs Terrarvm,** the hippie electronica of early Orb seems to have given way to the onetime punk's prior tendencies. All murky bottom end and sinister undertones, tracks like the piano-based prog swirl of "Oxbow Lakes" and the painfully psychedelic "Slug Dub" are merciless to casual listeners and certainly test the faith of even stalwart electro-experimentalists. And, even though **Orbvs Terrarvm** may not be the easiest ambient to listen to, it's certainly refreshing to see the genre's founder not content to simply rehash the same snooziness. [jf]

See also *TPRG.*

ORBITAL

Orbital (ffrr) 1992
Halcyon EP (ffrr) 1992
Orbital 2 (ffrr) 1993
Diversions EP (ffrr) 1994

Snivilisation (ffrr) 1994
In Sides (ffrr/London) 1996

With one foot hopping on the dancefloor and the other spiraling through the stratosphere, bedroom boffins Phil and Paul Hartnoll burst into the public consciousness during the heyday of the UK rave scene; amidst a stream of brilliant electronic singles from the duo, the shimmering polyrhythms of "Chime" hit the British Top 20 in April 1990. The first Orbital album (informally dubbed **Orbital Green** because of the cover) compiles ten of the best of those tracks, including "Belfast," "Choice" and a Moby remix of "Speed Freak."

The five-track **Halcyon** finds the brothers engaged in further experiments to construct epics out of recognizable samples, folded and layered to break down any sense of linear progression within the tracks. The eleven-minute title cut is built around a vocal snippet from Opus III's popular cover of Jane and Barton's "It's a Fine Day"; "The Naked and the Dead" and "The Naked and the Dub" effortlessly spin unimaginable mileage from a bit of Scott Walker's version of Jacques Brel's "Next." "Sunday" and a short radio edit of the eight-minute "Chime" round out the satisfying EP.

The second album (known as **Orbital Brown:** the numerical designation appears only on the spine) stretches the duo's aesthetic across an entire album conceived as such. From the Terry Riley–esque out-of-synch opening loops "Time Becomes," the Orbitals twist beats and melodies into a musical moebius band; the expansive "Lush 3-1" and "Lush 3-2" are the best representation of this. "Impact (The Earth Is Burning)" brings things back to this planet by injecting an ecological theme, while "Halcyon + On + On" reinvents the title cut from the previous EP. As on previous releases, the individual tracks are blissful experiments in disorientation, but this album functions best listened to as a cohesive, transcendental whole.

Diversions is an apt title for an EP that includes three worthwhile interpretations of "Lush" (by C. J. Bolland, Psychick Warriors ov Gaia and Underworld) that had previously appeared on a UK single. Yet another version of "Lush" (from a John Peel Session) segued into "Walk About," the non-LP "Semi-Detached" and a longer version of "Impact" ("Impact USA") complete the record.

Decidedly more earthbound than its predecessors, **Snivilisation** is a slower, eclectic affair. As titles like "Science Friction" and "I Wish I Had Duck Feet" (and the goofy illustrations) all suggest, the ten tracks capitalize on the band's sense of humor via clever samples and juxtaposition of disparate musical elements in the playful arrangements. "Sad but True" and "Are We Here?" incorporate vocals by Alison Goldfrapp basically for their timbre, thereby sidestepping the trap of imposing a linear agenda on their swirling polyrhythms; the latter cut also shows that the duo has been paying attention to the emergence of jungle/drum and bass culture. A tricky album to digest, **Snivilisation** bears up well to the repeated listenings required to grab hold of it. [kbr]

ORCHESTRAL MANOEUVRES IN THE DARK

Orchestral Manoeuvres in the Dark (UK DinDisc) 1980 (Virgin) 1987
Organisation (UK DinDisc) 1980 (Virgin) 1987
O.M.D. (Virgin/Epic) 1981
Architecture & Morality (Virgin/Epic) 1981 (Virgin) 1994
Dazzle Ships (Virgin/Epic) 1983
Junk Culture (Virgin/A&M) 1984
Crush (Virgin/A&M) 1985
The Pacific Age (Virgin/A&M) 1986
The Best of OMD (Virgin/A&M) 1988
Sugar Tax (Virgin) 1991
Liberator (Virgin) 1993

The Best of OMD recapitulates the brilliant beginning, impressive progress and sorry decline of a band that helped spearhead the '80s techno-pop movement in England. Orchestral Manoeuvres in the Dark played an important role in the music's development, proving early on that electronics were capable of interacting comfortably with regular rock instruments and not chilling the mood or forcing it into machine-like precision. Founded and led for a decade by Liverpool singer/bassist Andy McCluskey and keyboard player Paul Humphreys, OMD crafted some of the genre's sprightliest singles ("Electricity" and "Enola Gay," divided, respectively, between the first two albums but united on the American consolidation, **O.M.D.**) as well as its most evanescent ("Souvenir," the high point of **Architecture & Morality**). Proceeding into more ambitious extra-pop realms, OMD worked out the kinks on the gimmicky **Dazzle Ships** and then peaked with **Junk Culture,** which is represented on the anthology by "Tesla Girls," "Locomotion" and "Talking Loud and Clear." But the mainstreamed **Crush** reveals McCluskey's highbrow lyrical pretensions to be without intellectual foundation, a revelation that helped explain the group's American Top 5 hit, "If You Leave," a dull ballad from the **Pretty in Pink** soundtrack. Although the offending song was excluded from OMD's next album, that didn't prevent **The Pacific Age** from being a ponderous drag all the same.

Toward the end of the '80s, the low-profile Humphreys vanished, leaving the brand name to his more outgoing partner. OMD/McCluskey pressed on with **Sugar Tax,** a confident album consistent with the band's recent work. For all the synthetic-sounding keyboards and halfhearted forays into various unchallenging stylistic realms (mainly designer soul and energetic club beats), the melodramatic edge in McCluskey's voice and the stability in his prosaic songwriting deliver it all back to OMD's doorstep. The album is simply another ordinary, mediocre record from a once-captivating band.

Liberator heads straight for the dancefloor, taking two different routes. While "Dollar Girl," "Agnus Dei" and "Love and Hate You" run through the house, "Everyday" and "Dream of Me" (which explicitly acknowledges its obvious debt to "Loves [*sic*] Theme") are more than a little touched by the hand of Barry White. While it's hard to imagine many rock artists less inclined to have a Love Unlimited or Village People epiphany, both genres find a skilled transducer in McCluskey. All those years spent in the company of keyboards evidently left him fully able to make convincing percolating rhythms and layers of faux violins, and both get good use on what is a pretty stupid but diverting exercise. **Liberator** is most agreeable if you can forget who's behind it—not that covering the Velvet Underground's "Sunday Morning" as if it were 1981 all over again and dropping in vintage OMD citations elsewhere make that any easier. [i]

See also *TPRG*.

ORGANIZED KONFUSION

Organized Konfusion (Hollywood BASIC) 1991
Stress: The Extinction Agenda (Hollywood BASIC) 1994

New York's Organized Konfusion got started as a duo of Queens high-school friends concerned just as much with graffiti art, comic books and science fiction as with urban survival, black family life and fly beats and rhymes. Prince Poetry and Pharoahe Monche had formidable mentors—among them the late hip-hop producer Paul C. and the Ultramagnetic MCs—but they added up to much more than the sum of their influences. "Releasing Hypnotical Gases," on the band's debut, begins with an obscure break from Weather Report and then shifts uptempo into a riveting apocalypse narrative. That the track also worked as an extended scatological joke, a comic-book fanatic's trivia test and one of most complex set of battle rhymes ever written shows how weird, funny and virtuosic Organized Konfusion could be. At the same time, though, they offered vivid snapshots of black life—reminiscing on the family on "Who Stole My Last Piece of Chicken?" and relaxing with friends on "Fudge Pudge."

After three years of disillusioning experiences in the record industry, Poetry and Monche turned in the none-too-subtly named **Stress: The Extinction Agenda.** "Black Sunday," sort of an autobiographical sequel to "Who Stole My Last Piece of Chicken?," lacks that earlier track's lightness and nostalgia, replacing it with bluesy ennui and anti-corporate rage. The final track is simply entitled "Maintain." But if the album catches the duo in a stalemate with larger forces (Disney, the parent company of their record label, to be exact), its sound is often gripping. The duo's counterpoint to the unrestrained gunplay of hardcore rap, a jarring barrel's-eye view on "Stray Bullet," is absolutely compelling. **Stress: The Extinction Agenda** also finds its groove more consistently than the first LP, moving lithely from the thick jazz textures of "The Extinction Agenda" to the stark colors of "Stress" to the easy funk of "3-2-1." [jzc]

ORIGINAL SINS

Big Soul (Bar/None) 1987 + 1994
The Hardest Way (Psonik) 1989
Self Destruct (Psonik/Skyclad) 1990
Party's Over (Aus. Psonik/Dog Meat) 1990
Eat This EP (Psonik/Skyclad) 1991
Move (Psonik/Skyclad) 1991
Out There (Psonik/Skyclad) 1992
Sally Kirkland EP (Psonik/Skyclad) 1992
Acidbubblepunk (Psonik) 1994
Turn You On (Bedlam) 1995
Bethlehem (Bar/None) 1996

BROTHER JT

Descent (Twisted Village) 1991
Meshes of the Afternoon (Twisted Village) 1992
Vibrolux (Bedlam) 1994
Holy Ghost Stories (Bedlam) 1994
Music for the Other Head (Siltbreeze) 1996
Rainy Day Fun (Drunken Fish) 1996

The rocking Bethlehem, Pennsylvania, garage that incubated and continues to house the Original Sins hasn't had a new coat of paint or even a serious spring cleaning in ages. Led by diminutive howler/guitarist J.T. (John Terlesky), the quartet—which underwent only one drummer change between its 1987 debut and 1996's **Bethlehem**—has stayed true to its chosen era, re-creating the down and dirty organ-fueled excitement and atmosphere of '60s punk bands like the Standells and Seeds. Synthesizing convincing originals from standard ingredients, the Sins have been remarkably consistent in their quality control, trying new vintages now and then but keeping stylistic ambition from overtaking them (like the Chesterfield Kings) while steering clear of the sense that they've done it all before (like the Lyres).

Big Soul is an instant classic, slyly simple contemporary grunge stripped of nostalgia and ready to pop. (The 1994 CD reissue adds a half-dozen tracks—including covers of "Sugar Sugar" and a brief bit of "Route 66"—not on the original vinyl.) Likewise, **The Hardest Way** (which kicks off with the self-conscious "Heard It All Before") seems like the logical result of an anachronistic environment. J.T.'s storming guitar roar and Dan McKinney's chunky Korg organ provide a tersely exciting bed for lyrics that—other than a few happy love songs—resound with alienation and negativity.

After those modest, concise garage freakouts, **Self Destruct** delivers a surprising level of domineering intensity, beginning with the cover photo of J.T. holding a pistol to his head with a grin on his face. The new-sound Sins here are a snarling psychedelic powerhouse, a thickly seething cauldron of hyperactive feedback and wah-wah, rabid vocals, galloping rhythms and lyrics about drugs and sex. Some of the longer songs (the teetering-on-the-brink "Black Hole" runs past eight minutes) spend too much time on instrumental workouts, but **Self Destruct** captures acid-rock's disorienting chaos with a visceral impact few other bands can touch.

Four of the eight songs on the Australian **Party's Over,** issued a month after **Self Destruct,** are first-rate bonus tracks from **The Hardest Way** CD and cassette; three more are developmentally significant outtakes from the same sessions.

Doubtless aided by producer Peter Buck, the group regained its composure on **Move,** leaving psychedelia behind for a poppier sound (think Paul Revere and the Raiders and the Knickerbockers) and a giddy, upbeat mood that J.T. acknowledges (by way of a possible explanation) in the album-opening "She's on My Side." In a masterful display of greatness, the two dozen three-minute tracks (all J.T. originals!) vary the emotional and stylistic temperature more than ever: "Devil's Music," "It's a Good Life" and "Like an Animal" (like roughly half of the songs) churn and burn with classic fervor, while "Getting the Feeling" hits a Rascally soul groove, "Move" sounds a lot like Steppenwolf, "I Never Dreamed" is a shockingly quiet ballad and the winsome "I Surrender" and "Not Today" are essentially folk-rock. **Move** does just that, and in a bunch of perfectly good directions. If the Sins can try out new old things without blowing their cool, more power to 'em.

Settling down in one place again, **Out There** is an unrestrained, feedback-flaring Fleshtones party groove and another trip down to the lyrical dumps. Reclaiming the no-messing-about purity of their garage-fueled essence, J.T. and the boys rip through a cover of Tommy Roe's "Dizzy" and such originals as the you're-nowhere surf-rock diss of "Wipe Out," the defiantly dispirited "One Good Reason" and "Killing Time" and the icon-worshiping "Sally Kirkland." The fully charged music writhes like a snake charmer with a case of the hives, but you gotta worry about J.T.'s mood swings.

Covered with a snapshot of Ms. K and Joe Franklin, **Sally Kirkland** recycles that song and the wah-wah enthusiasm of "Get Into It" from **Out There** (including long/short versions of each) and adds bristling covers of the Saints' "Erotic Neurotic," Bob Dylan's "Can You Please Crawl Out Your Window," the Velvet Underground's "Head Held High" and the Stooges' "1969." Hot shit.

The uncharacteristically crummy artwork on **Acid-bubblepunk** is worse than the halfhearted music inside, but the whole thing is a disappointing drop in the Sins' standards. The self-production is colorless and flat, the pop is noncommittal (see "Drivin' Round") and plain; the rock numbers are mostly boring songs given low-octane performances. The album ends with a nearly eight-minute hippie-seduction tale recited by J.T. over the barest slide guitar and bass accompaniment. As he observes elsewhere, "(It's Really Not So) Groovy (Anymore)."

Happily, the great-leap-forward **Bethlehem** sets the Sins back to rights with impressively recharged creative energy.

Although he's not identified as such anywhere on the packages, Terlesky is the shadowy Brother JT, feedback evangelist and thorn in the side of the establishment. On these solo releases, he unskeins jagged reels of Hendrix-styled feedback and some surprisingly pretty improv as well. The druggy atmosphere—particularly on the cascading **Descent**—is a far cry from the Original Sins' frat-house revelry, but its air is every bit as charged. Fuzzface (**Bad Thoughts;** Aus. Dog Meat, 1993) is another J.T. side project of sub-Stooges/MC5 raving. [jy/tr]

JIM O'ROURKE

Some Kind of Pagan [tape] (Sound of Pig) 1989
It Takes Time to Do Nothing [tape] (Audiofile) 1990
The Ground Below Our Heads (Ger. Entenpfuhl) 1991
Tamper (Aus. Extreme) 1991
Secure on the Loose Rim [tape] (Sound of Pig) 1991
Disengage (Staaltape) 1992
Scend (Divided) 1992
Rules of Reduction EP3 (Fr. Metamkine) 1994
Remove the Need (Extreme/Cargo) 1993
Use [tape] (Soleilmoon) 1994
Terminal Pharmacy (Tzadik) 1995

JIM O'ROURKE AND HENRY KAISER

Tomorrow Knows Where You Live (Can. Les Disques Victo) 1992

JIM O'ROURKE/HENRY KAISER/ JOHN OSWALD/MARI KIMURA

Acoustics (Can. Les Disques Victo) 1994

KAZUYUKI K. NULL/JIM O'ROURKE

Neuro Eco Media [tape] (Nux Organization) 1992
New Kind of Water (Charnel House) 1993

EDDIE PREVOST/JIM O'ROURKE

Third Straight Day Made Public (Complacency) 1994

JIM O'ROURKE AND GÜNTER MÜLLER

Slow Motion (Sw. For 4 Ears) 1995

INDICATE

Whelm (UK Touch) 1995

BRISE-GLACE

When in Vanitas . . . (Skin Graft) 1994

YONA-KIT

Yona-Kit (Skin Graft/Nux Organization) 1995

Prolific Chicago guitar improviser, keyboardist, tape manipulator, composer and producer Jim O'Rourke is most conveniently identified in rock terms as a core member of Gastr del Sol, but he has also recorded solo, served in Red Krayola, written for the Kronos Quartet, produced Faust, collaborated with Henry Kaiser and K. K. Null and done numerous other projects. The admitted workaholic, who operates just as comfortably in the low fringes of underground skronk as in more technique-conscious realms and experimental processes, also forms and records transient groups of likeminded adventurers as a matter of creative habit.

O'Rourke started out, like many other experimenters, making home tapes and sending them to people whose work he admired. Some of them took notice, and he began working with renowned avant-garde composers and players at a relatively young age. O'Rourke's aesthetic *is* definable, even though the quantity and range of his releases militates against that.

Some Kind of Pagan unveils O'Rourke's skill at expanding the potential of the electric guitar without pedals or processors. Bombastic to pretty, the solemn gonging and deep ringing sounds, tempered with squeaking and scratching, are remarkably difficult to identify as guitar. But beyond that realm, O'Rourke also plays with found sounds, tape—and the patience of his audience. **Scend** makes audio atmospheres from field recordings of nature and water, a playground and trucks. Both of the album's long pieces build from absolute quiet to occasional peaks of volume. There's so much space that it blurs the line between listening to his piece and listening to the ambient noise of the space in which you hear it—and that may be part of his point.

Tamper moves into more classical territory, at least in terms of instrumentation. The album meshes strings, winds and voice into what's become the dark landscape of O'Rourke's music. In moving subtly from stark quiet to loud, visceral masses of sound, the pieces take on—in some sense—the role of very slow-moving horror-movie background music.

Released as a 3-inch CD, **Rules of Reduction** is an engaging seventeen-minute musique concrète piece that returns to the ideas used in **Scend,** only more concise and sophisticated. Part of a series of film-like sound tableaux, O'Rourke's entry is a mesh of city street noise augmented by saxophone, piano and waves of circus-like accordion, interspersed with faint, placid interludes that include gull sounds and soft piano. Lovely, and not jarring except when it means to be.

Remove the Need is a quartet of unaccompanied live improvs, one of them a half-hour long, recorded in Chicago and Zurich. Using carefully controlled feedback and some sort of bowing technique to produce his primary sounds, the guitarist never audibly strikes a string; the edgy but not unpleasant music drifts and tolls in thin, narrow and high streams of uninterrupted tone that undulate slowly, like the dramatic accompaniment to a tense psychological thriller in which nothing ever happens.

Created over the course of two years, **Terminal Pharmacy**'s two pieces, "Cede" and "Terminal Pharmacy," invert the typical modern process of endless addition: the former, which credits a clarinetist, a bass trombonist and drummer John McEntire (it's unstated and undiscernible what O'Rourke's instrumental role, if any, is), is instead the final result of reduction, as it shifts between subliminal and nearly inaudible. Gentle rattles, footsteps and the sounds of a car door opening occasionally break the near-silence of wavery sustained notes far off in the distance, but that's about all that happens for the first twenty-five minutes. (A few things transpire in the quarter-hour that follows, but not enough to change the overall sensation of staring at a blank screen waiting for the movie to begin.) The suspicion of fakery is not dissipated by the deadpan put-on of O'Rourke's liner notes: "Finding out what the material 'meant' in a more articulated way required going over it again and again, until it was exhausted (cf. Grand Funk Railroad's own theatre of eternal music, 'I'm Your Captain')." The shorter "Terminal Pharmacy" employs a half-dozen cellists, two accordionists and four flute players to make some atonal scrapy, honky noises, but again not enough occurs to encourage the feeling that a piece of music is actually being performed.

O'Rourke's collaborative improvisational recordings can blur together; the differences between them depend entirely on his choice of partner. For instance, Henry Kaiser's frenetic proficiency is nicely dulled in their collaboration. The best and most accessible pieces on **Tomorrow Knows Where You Live** overlay both players to produce the sound of eight classical guitarists delicately fingering all at once. On other tracks, O'Rourke contributes his usual ethereal tonescapes with shuddering bits.

On the other hand, Kazuyuki K. Null of Japan's Zeni Geva dominates **New Kind of Water.** His forceful guitar wringing rides right over O'Rourke's, churning and gurgling in what is, much like the title, an angular, chopped, rocky version of the sounds of water.

The more recent **Slow Motion** strikes a better balance. O'Rourke and Swiss percussionist Günter Müller both have an intricate sense of construction that starts where jazz (even free jazz) ends. Müller never really gets around to hitting his drums—he more often brushes, rubs, vibrates and creates squeaks with his entire kit. O'Rourke counters with an echoey sound space that envelops Müller's miniatures; overall the pieces resemble a big, clanky digestive system of strings and metal.

Brise-Glace brings O'Rourke together with bassist Darin Gray of St. Louis' Dazzling Killmen, free-minded drummer Thymme Jones of Cheer-Accident and Illusion of Safety, guitarist Dylan Posa (Cheer-Accident, the Flying Luttenbachers) and such guests as Kaiser and David Grubbs. Engineered by Steve Albini, **When in Vanitas . . .** consists of five loosely structured instrumentals that make essential use of sixty-cycle hum, ebbing and flowing in sparely strummed tangles that are often little more than meandering doodles but occasionally (the percussion-shaped and distortion-riddled "Restrained From Do and Will Not (Leave)," for instance) light on something more substantial.

Yona-Kit, with Gray, Jones and singer/guitarist K. K. Null, is a tauter, ruggedly played song-rock proposition also recorded by Albini, who achieves a more characteristically raw sound here than on the Brise-Glace disc. Nonchalantly aggressive with Null's typical nods to both Big Black and Foetus, songs like the vituperative "Franken-Bitch," the walloping "Skeleton King," the intricate "Disembody" (which sets an alternately slow/fast beat under a nagging, busy guitar lick) and "Slice of Life," a maddeningly repetitive twenty-three-minute instrumental, scratch at the eardrums like a rabid cat fighting for its life before the tranquilizers knock it over.

O'Rourke played and recorded with Illusion of Safety early in his career; the relationship eventually ebbed to the point where the group would merely mix in samples of his guitar improvisations. Organum (David Jackman) has used his work in this way as well. O'Rourke eventually recorded **Use,** a DAT tape meant not as an actual album but as sampling fodder for other musicians.

O'Rourke has recorded with Tatsu Aoki, Trance, Eddie Prevost, Untitled, Smog, Mats Gustafsson, the Elvis Messiahs, Mimir, Philip Gelb and Robert Hampson of Main (as Indicate). He's also produced or remixed pieces for Oval, Tortoise, Labradford, Main, U.S. Maple, Melt Banana and This Heat. [i/rxe]

See also *Faust, Gastr del Sol, Main, Red Crayola, Zeni Geva.*

JOAN OSBORNE BAND

Soul Show: Live at Delta 88 (Womanly Hips) 1991

JOAN OSBORNE

Blue Million Miles EP (Womanly Hips) 1993
Relish (Blue Gorilla/Mercury) 1995

While studying film at New York University in the '80s, Kentucky émigré Joan Osborne began haunting Manhattan's clubs, finding and taking any opportunity to sing in public. With a strong if unsteady voice, she went through phases of dedication to the blues, R&B and Janis Joplin hippie rock—all of which are exhibited in **Soul Show,** a self-released live album recorded clearly with a rocking quartet before an enthusiastic New York house. Other than wobbly pitch, a dubious set of covers, too much coquettish vampery and the crazed miasmic overemoting would-be belters typically mistake for genuine conviction, Osborne does herself proud in a showcase that foreshadows her pop future: she overcooks "Son of a Preacher Man" until the pot turns black, never gets a hoarse handle on her brisk run at Sonny Boy Williamson's "Help Me" and absurdly attempts to turn "Lady Madonna" into a roadhouse standard. Osborne fares best as a soulful singer/songwriter on two strong originals: "Crazy Baby," which she redid on her studio album, and the ready-for-Raitt "Match Burn Twice" extract from, rather than attempt to swallow whole, her influences.

Still not on her final approach to stardom liftoff, Osborne cut a three-song CD single named for her properly bizarre studio cover of Captain Beefheart's offbeat "His Eyes Are a Blue Million Miles."

Then came **Relish,** the album that made Osborne a textbook overnight sensation in 1995. With help from some canny pop formalists, she swept out of the post–Bonnie Raitt breezeway—that Sheryl Crow inversion of the progression from folk into rock—to emerge as a sturdy, forthright all-American singer able to bring the trappings of rustic blues (complete with the raunchy big mama sexuality white men find so seductive when it comes from hip, attractive white women) to the video era. The original Cyndi Lauper team—producer Rick Chertoff and the Hooters' core of keyboardist Rob Hyman and guitarist Eric Bazilian—co-wrote, performed and produced **Relish,** a bionic simulation of flesh and blood.

Using her husky alto in a variety of intonations but occasionally getting mighty careless with those pesky notes, Osborne manages an agile balance of mainstream juice, arty pretension ("Spider Web" is a coy Lyle Lovett–styled fantasy about Ray Charles) and touchstone tradition (again making lame work of Sonny Boy Williamson's "Help Me," with Gary Lucas on guitar and Osborne doing her best to sound completely wasted). Subject-wise, she juggles sex (the woozy "Let's Just Get Naked" and "Right Hand Man," which credits a Beefheart sample) and spirituality ("St. Teresa") just as so many conflicted greats have. "One of Us," a smartly crafted Bazilian original that inexplicably begins with an unrelated field recording (similar to a gimmick Lauper once employed), wittily wonders "What if God was one of us? / Just a slob like one of us / Just a stranger on the bus." The song musters the devastatingly blasé sentiment that "An' yeah, yeah, God is great" but then can't resist unfurling a few extra bolts of theological cuteness: "Nobody calling on the phone / 'Cept for the Pope maybe in Rome." **Relish** is nice on top, but the album's main course is already a little off. [i]

See also *Hooters.*

OTHER TWO

See *New Order.*

OTTOMAN EMPIRE

Lester Square (DB) 1993
Ottoman Gold (Casino) 1994

COOLIES

dig . . ? (DB) 1986
Doug (DB) 1988
Take That You Bastards! (Casino) 1995

ANNE RICHMOND BOSTON

The Big House of Time (DB) 1990

One of the better families of entertaining Atlanta indie-rock swims in and out of the corpse of the Coolies, a group of high-concept jokers (and cover-song boys) led in the '80s by singer Clay Harper and guitarist Rob Gal. Besides forming the Ottoman Empire as his primary musical venture this decade, Harper opened the Casino label, which recently reissued the Coolies' two-album catalogue as the two-CD **Take That You Bastards!,** complete with three previously unreleased cuts.

Lester Square is a rustic epilogue to the Coolies: joined by a different set of instrumental associates, Harper and Gal downplay (if not eliminate) their past silliness for lighthearted personal sincerity in an easy and engaging semi-acoustic folk/pop mode. The better songs here—"Train," "Ol Duke," "Do You Know What You Like?"—are unprepossessing but mighty sweet.

Gal is only the fill-in bassist on **Ottoman Gold,** which pairs Harper instead with (Wreckless) Eric Goulden; the English veteran co-wrote three songs, produced the album (in mono) and sings and plays on it. (In turn, Harper co-wrote a song for and released Eric's own '94 album, **12 O'Clock Stereo,** on Casino.) A rocking pop slab, **Ottoman Gold** subliminally interlaces the Coolies' old zig with Eric's old zag to frolic with vintage garage zest, fired up to a delightful club sweat that never loses sight of the tuneful songs. The repeated references to England are strange given Harper's drawly southern voice, but it's all in keeping with the, well, recklessness, of the venture.

Anne Richmond Boston, one of the two singers in Atlanta's Swimming Pool Q's, and possessor of a most remarkable voice, was at one time married to Rob Gal. In the group, Boston evinced an aching yet stately emotional purity that recalled British folkie Sandy Denny but was unmistakably American in tone. Three years after leaving the Q's, Boston made her impressive reemergence with the exquisite **The Big House of Time,** a graceful adult gem that resonates with understated passion and plain old common sense. The original songs (by Boston and Gal, who also produced and played on the album) are consistently fine; well-chosen material by John Hiatt, John Sebastian, Neil Young and former Q's bandmate Jeff Calder provides a brilliant showcase for Boston's sharp interpretive powers. [i/ss]

See also *Wreckless Eric; TPRG.*

JOHN OTWAY & WILD WILLY BARRETT

John Otway & Wild Willy Barrett (UK Extracked) 1977 (UK Polydor) 1977
Deep & Meaningless (UK Polydor) 1978
Way & Bar (UK Polydor) 1980
I Did It Otway EP (Stiff America) 1981
Gone With the Bin: The Best of Otway & Barrett (UK Polydor) 1981

JOHN OTWAY

Where Did I Go Right? (UK Polydor) 1979
Deep Thought (Stiff) 1980
All Balls & No Willy (UK Empire) 1982
John Otway's Greatest Hits (UK Strike Back) 1986
Cor Baby, That's Really Me! (UK Strike Back) 1990
Under the Covers and Over the Top (UK Otway) 1992
Premature Adulation (UK Amazing Feet) 1995

ATTILA & OTWAY

Cheryl: A Rock Opera (UK Strike Back) 1991

JOHN OTWAY AND THE BIG BAND

Live! (UK Amazing Feet) 1993

Deep into his third decade of charmingly madcap music-making, the irrepressible nutter of Aylesbury (forty miles northwest of London) shows no signs of slowing down. In willful disregard of commercial realities and with no evident concern for anything else that might be transpiring in the world of popular music, Otway continues to follow his own eccentric muse with touching (or is that touched?) dedication. Shortly after inaugurating the '90s with **Cor Baby, That's Really Me!,** a spectacular twenty-one-track retrospective issued in conjunction with an autobiography of the same name, Otway produced a rock opera, a freshly cut collection of covers and a live album—all on different small labels. (The unplugged set, the CD-ROM and the duets disc are probably in the works.)

Unpredictable, ingenious, inconsistent, un-self-conscious, emotionally unguarded, totally reckless about public displays of foolishness and enormously lovable, Otway is capable of dizzying quality and style swings. **Cor Baby,** for instance, has stomping Ot-rock classics like "Really Free" and "Beware of the Flowers 'Cause

I'm Sure They're Going to Get You Yeh," sentimental ballads ("Geneve" comes shmeared in Richard Harris–style orchestration), Pete Townshend–produced British bluegrass ("Misty Mountain"), tender love missives ("Montreal," "Middle of Winter"), self-abusive stupidity ("Headbutts") and folk songs ("Jerusalem").

In a mind-boggling leap of conceptual invention, Otway and performance poet Attila the Stockbroker (John Baine) managed to spring an entire theatrical entertainment from "Cheryl's Goin' Home," the 1965 Bob Lind B-side that has been in Otway's repertoire from the very start of his career. Creating a convoluted and calamitous saga of star-crossed romance, railroad fetishists and randy goats told from conflicting perspectives in narration (Attila) and song (Otway), the pair staged *Cheryl* in England and then recorded it. Owing more to Attila's wickedly peevish rhymes than to Otway's fairly functional songs, **Cheryl: A Rock Opera** is a hysterical slash of radio-play silliness (à la Frank Sidebottom) about a gullible sap in love with a drug-addicted prostitute who finds yuppie success as a Conservative party direct-mail marketing executive (or something like that). A couple of nasal rap interludes (by "MC Trainspotter and the Platform 2 Live Crew") are intrusively cloddish, but otherwise **Cheryl** is in the running as this generation's truly off-Broadway *Tommy.*

Although Otway has always made good if irreverent use of other people's songs—"Green Green Grass of Home" and "The Man Who Shot Liberty Valance" are among his best numbers ever—he chose a whole new batch for **Under the Covers and Over the Top.** (OK, he had already cut "You Ain't Seen Nothing Yet," but that's the only one, and it didn't have a simultaneous translation into German the first time.) Recorded with various accompanists, the album includes ludicrously sincere but laughable (per)versions, more spoken than sung, of "I Am the Walrus," "Woodstock," "I Will Survive" (done Bob Dylan–style), Bobby Goldsboro's "Honey," "Billy Don't Be a Hero" (live) and David Bowie's "Space Oddity" rendered in a Scottish brogue against a three-dozen-member brass band. Big fun. (Just for the record, Sidebottom was the first oddball to think of mating Serge Gainsbourg's sexy "Je T'Aime . . . Moi Non Plus" and "Wild Thing.")

Recorded in London with the grandly named Big Band (a standard electric rock quartet, natch), Otway's live album is relatively straightforward, a career-spanner of originals and covers ("House of the Rising Sun" is a new one) given earnest treatment. The scanty measure of inter-song remarks is a minor disappointment, but the skillful rock energy and Otway's sheepdog appeal make the music enough by itself. [i]

See also *TPRG.*

OUTNUMBERED

See *Pansy Division.*

OVARIAN TROLLEY

Pofus [tape] (self-released) 1992
Crocodile Tears (Shimmy-Disc) 1994

Indiana natives relocated to San Francisco, sisters Laurie (bass/vocals) and Jennifer (drums/vocals) Hall played in a band called Glorious Clitoris before forming Ovarian Trolley with guitarist Buck Bito; the trio debuted in '92 with a self-released cassette and made its big push two years later with the Kramer-produced **Crocodile Tears.** Taking their harmonic cues from a weird combination of X and the Jefferson Airplane, the Halls wail/sing together not *entirely* unpleasantly over scraggly electric ugliness propelled by firm (except when they slip) beats. Some of the songs ("Crocodile Tears," "Lost Girls") are nearly pretty, displaying the melodic assurance and dynamics to shore up the Trolley's good side; others ("Puppy," "Coin Op.") merely establish a noisy groove and stone it into submission with shouted lyrics. The album's real achievement, however, is "Senorita," a cackling, moaning anti-harassment opus with Latin percussion and an appropriately unctuous and insinuating guitar figure. [i]

OVERPASS

Overpass (New Alliance) 1993
Manhattan (Beach) (Smells Like) 1995

SLOVENLY

Even So EP (New Alliance) 1984
After the Original Style (New Alliance) 1985
Thinking of Empire (SST) 1986
Riposte (SST) 1987
We Shoot for the Moon (SST) 1988
Highway to Hanno's (SST) 1992

When the eclectic semi-avant San Francisco rock quintet Slovenly ended its long run in 1992, three of the band's mainstays headed back to Southern California and regrouped. As Overpass, guitarist/singer Tom Watson (also a current member of Red Krayola), bassist Scott Ziegler (whose other band, Dingle, issued **Red Dog** on New Alliance in 1994) and drummer Rob Holzman (a first-album member of Saccharine Trust) take the freewheeling tradition-busting they've explored in the past and apply it to crafty songs whose clear-eyed focus benefits from the trio's ability to take the scenic route and still not get lost.

Overpass has its jazzy side, especially when the band hits the accelerator in tight formation displays of wiggly whatsit, or when guest Lynn Johnson of Cruel Frederick blows a little bass clarinet into the improvisations. But it's steadfastly a smart and humorous rock album, one with a lot more to offer than, say, Primus. When they present themselves, the clearly delineated songs balance helpful verse/chorus attributes with bizarre lyrics, hairpin melodic turns, craggy (and sometimes Neil Youngy) guitar interjections and don't-try-these-at-home obstacle-course rhythms. Free advice: start with "R.C Kola," "Craze," "Boniak Harvest" or the Zappa–esque "Rubber Nipple" to avoid the sense of cerebral dryness conveyed by the album's first few numbers.

Manhattan (Beach) pulls in the experimental reins for a tighter, more disciplined version of the first album's complicated songhood. Diminished risk-taking doesn't make Overpass a safer bet, however. Having played together for so many years, the three seem able to think as one; whatever spark—and rhythmic depth—seems absent here may be attributable to a lack of tension in the creative process. Even with Watson's plain voice (which resembles Lou Reed when he still sang) helping calm the sometimes turbulent, sometimes showy instrumental waters, the songs don't flow as easily, and stylistic ingredients that aided the effort the first time out are more like distractions here.

Right before mutating into Overpass, Slovenly (which also included singer Steve Anderson and guitarist Tim Plowman, whose collaboratively pretentious lyrics were always the band's albatross) concluded a four-year album hiatus on **Highway to Hanno's.** With guest horns and violin upping the textural variety and the band playing at the peak of its cohesive abilities, the music (other than the free-jazz blowing of "Hamster Wheel," the chaos of "Benny's Jam" and the collage weirdness of "Thank You Purple Jesus") is an easily met challenge, both intricate *and* accessible. But Anderson's self-important singing is another matter, especially in light of the more likable Watson's subsequent demonstration of skill in that department. While ushering Slovenly out in style, **Highway to Hanno's** also explains why it had to end. [i]

See also *Red Crayola; TPRG.*

OVERWHELMING COLORFAST

Overwhelming Colorfast (Relativity) 1992
Two Words (Relativity) 1994
Moonlight and Castanets (Headhunter) 1996

As Jerry Lewis is to France, Bob Mould is to San Diego, California. At least that's the feeling one gets from mulling over the output of Padres-land bands like fluf and, most conspicuously, this quartet (which actually hails from the suburban outback of Antioch). Singer/guitarist Bob Reed clearly used late-period Hüsker Dü albums like **Candy Apple Grey** and **Flip Your Wig** as the soundtrack to numerous air guitar practice sessions: he's appropriated a goodly number of Mould's phrasing tricks (it's safe to assume the raw-throated rasp comes naturally) as well as his tendency to cast gorgeous psychedelic leads adrift in a sea of amp-fuzz.

On the quartet's self-titled (and Butch Vig–produced) debut, Reed manages to take those old, borrowed things (most in evidence on the poppy-but-cathartic "It's Tomorrow" and "Arrows") and fuse them with something new and something blue (like the heart-on-his-sleeve "Totally Gorgeous Foreign Chick"). A weakness for sappy sentiment gets the best of him more often than one would expect from a skater dude, but there's enough ballast (like the garage-rock stomp "Try") to keep the band grounded. While **Two Words,** produced by Kurt Bloch, is less derivative, it's more a regression than a progression, laden as it is with funny-punk detours like "Winky Dinky Dog" and unreconstructed AOR rewrites—"How Ya Doin" could pass unnoticed on one of those **Best of Southern Rock** cassettes you can find at truckstops nationwide. Reed deserves some credit, however, for presaging Weezer's "Buddy Holly" with a sweet little trifle called "Roy Orbison." [dss]

OWT

See *Zeena Parkins.*

ABIODUN OYEWOLE

See *Last Poets.*

P

See *Butthole Surfers.*

PAINKILLER

The Guts of a Virgin (Earache/Relativity) 1991
Buried Secrets (Earache/Relativity) 1993
Execution Ground (Subharmonic) 1994 (Japan. Toy's Factory) 1995
Rituals: Live in Japan Featuring Keiji Haino (Japan. Toy's Factory) 1995

M. J. HARRIS/BILL LASWELL

Somnific Flux (Subharmonic) 1995

Bassist/producer Bill Laswell and alto sax abuser John Zorn are bosses of the New York vanguard, with long careers built on adventurous collaborations and cultural adaptations. So maybe it shouldn't have come as a surprise that when they finally got together, it was with Mick Harris, drum demon of Napalm Death, to conjure an excited new hybrid of jazz and grindcore. If such an auspicious commotion sounds too good to be true, it isn't: Painkiller's extremes combust in a creative boom larger than the sum of its parts.

The Guts of a Virgin is an abbreviated (twenty-four minutes) exposition of versatile thrash jazz. Each instrument occupies its own sonic terrain, combining in a sprawl of unanticipated death metal. The shell-shocked preamble "Scud Attack" sets the tone for an uncalculated frenzy that frees Zorn from the academic distance of his usual work. Laswell rips into his bass like an adrenalized teenager, and Mick Harris pummels the drums mercilessly, holding back here and there to preserve atmosphere. The wailing "Damage to the Mask" foreshadows the melodic terror that became the band's forte.

The ten tracks of **Buried Secrets** include incipient ambience sprouting amidst the breakneck rampage. After plenty of ferocious squeal and bombast, "Blackhole Dub" opens a passage to the urban space jazz that will probably be Painkiller's gift to the future. Justin Broadrick and Benny Green of Godflesh sit in for two songs, tying the spaciness and the spazziness to monolithic pounding akin to early Swans. Killing off a few skeletons, the twenty-two-second "The Ladder" and the fifty-four-second "Skinned" pay blasting homage to the Boredoms. Painkiller seems to be developing into a more organic version of Zorn's prolific and acclaimed Naked City.

Conjuring a free-form sprawl that transcends the group's earlier efforts, **Execution Ground** is an experimental adventure mixed like dance music. The piercing sax is coated in reverb, while the bass and drums are equalized to their deepest frequencies. Harris disproves the jungle DJ precept that there are certain beats only a drum machine can handle. Laswell's playing is at its funky best, while Zorn's horn recalls the crying tones of Miles Davis on **Bitches Brew.** Two of the trancey thudding tracks on Disc One ("Pashupatinath" and "Parish of Tama") are revisited in ambient form on Disc Two, allowing Zorn to show off his softer side and Harris to display some patchworks of computer samples.

Lest these serial collaborators seem too close-knit, the trio is joined by kinky avant-garde guitarist Keiji Haino for the Japanese live CD **Rituals.** The Japanese edition of **Execution Ground** adds an extra disc, a 1994 live set accompanied by versatile screamer Yamatsuka Eye of the Boredoms.

Somnific Flux is a spare ambient album by Laswell and Harris, part of a flurry of similar atmospheric releases on Laswell's Subharmonic label. Both lengthy cuts, "Distal Sonority" and "Capacious," are extended examples of pure presence, offering wavering electronic moods that differ from Harris' solo Lull recordings in that original sound sources are unrecognizable. Somewhere between Harris' home base in Birmingham, England, and Laswell's homestead in Greenpoint, Brooklyn, the two summon the presence of a slick wet dungeon straight out of the *Doom II* video game. [ic]

See also *Boredoms, Bill Laswell, Naked City, Napalm Death, Scorn, John Zorn.*

PAIN TEENS

Pain Teens (Anomie) 1988
Case Histories (Anomie) 1989 (Trance Syndicate) 1990
Born in Blood (Trance Syndicate) 1990
Stimulation Festival (Trance Syndicate) 1992
Destroy Me, Lover (Trance Syndicate) 1993
Beast of Dreams (Trance Syndicate) 1995

One of the first bands to till the not-inconsiderable territory where industrial and goth intermingle, Houston's Pain Teens forged a signifier-heavy composite that harvested every cliché in both books but still managed to engross more often than it repelled. Maybe that had something to do with the sirenic presence of frontwoman Bliss Blood, who isn't shy about exploiting her physical charms—it's not hyperbolic to see her breathy, come-hither incantations as a sort of malicious, industrial-strength analogue to Traci Lords.

The gothic attributes are less obtrusive on the band's early records. **Case Histories,** compiled from prior cassette releases (and appended to the CD edition of its successor), follows chaos theory to the letter. Although most of the songs lob spitballs at the twin titans of church and state, Blood hits a pair of bullseyes: "Preppy Killer," which extrapolates from an infamous NYC murder case, and "New Woman," a solemn meditation on sexual mores. The overwrought **Born in Blood**'s virtually centerless collages of creep-sound coalesce briefly when Scott Ayers' ambulance-siren guitar rises above the miasma of loops and samples, but the album doesn't take long to reveal itself as nothing but an extended hissy fit. At the end, we know that Blood probably doesn't care too much for whiskers on kittens or warm furry mittens, but tracks like "The Secret Is Sickness" and "Christo" divulge little else.

Most of the increasingly goth-flavored **Stimulation Festival** sticks to tried-and-true topics: there's tiresome sacrilege ("God Told Me" sees Blood moaning about the dark side of organized religion; "The Poured Out Blood" splices televangelist samples to illustrate the same point) and human suffering ("Hangman's Rope") to spare. When the quartet allows for some abstraction, as on the sinuous "Indiscreet Jewels" and a subdued cover of the Birthday Party's "Wild World," the Pain Teens merit attention. Those interludes are sporadic, however.

Destroy Me, Lover (swathed in a pulp paperback sleeve) is a bit more substantial. Blood revisits old haunts on tracks like "Sexual Anorexia," but fortunately, she's more prone to digressions like "RU 486," a jarringly poppy paean to the so-called abortion pill, complete with shimmering girl-group harmonies. Ayers and Blood divested themselves of the band's rhythm section for **Beast of Dreams** (though Ayers leaps into the instrumental breach), a smoky collection of pan-ethnic mood sketches that are uniformly redolent of the abattoir.

After the Pain Teens called it quits in 1995, Blood relocated to New York and began playing in a number of groups, among them Emma Peel. [dss]

PALACE BROTHERS

There Is No One What Will Take Care of You (Drag City) 1992
Days in the Wake (Drag City) 1993
An Arrow Through the Bitch EP (UK Domino) 1994

PALACE SONGS

Hope EP (Drag City) 1994
The Mountain EP (UK Domino) 1994

PALACE MUSIC

Viva Last Blues (Drag City) 1995

PALACE

Arise Therefore (Drag City) 1996

Although the recent crop of indie-rock Appalachiana—bands that've turned to rustic, backporch forms of expression as a reflexive escape from the leviathan moshpit that has all but enveloped the genre formerly known as alternative rock—is as rife with charlatans as any clique, Palace frontman Will Oldham appears to be the real thing. With his roots firmly planted in the bluegrass country of Kentucky (okay, he's from a tony Louisville family, but at least he ain't no Yankee interloper) and a preternatural command of trad-folk source material, Oldham doesn't just unplug, he tunes out the last several decades entirely, tapping into a sound (and vision) that harks back to the troubadours of another century.

With its brittle recording and acoustic, banjo-dominated instrumentation, **There Is No One What Will Take Care of You** is a surprisingly authentic re-creation of Depression-era country à la Jimmie Rodgers in his more profane moments or the Louvin Brothers: Oldham's high, parched tenor is strongly reminiscent of Ira Louvin's. (As if to further prove his rural mettle, Oldham even engages in a modern variation on chicken-stealing, neglecting to credit '20s bluesman Washington Phillips as the author of "I Had a Good Mother and Father.") But all of this isn't mere stylistic affectation: he calls forth fire and brimstone in songs like "Idle Hands Are the Devil's Playthings" and "(I Was Drunk at the) Pulpit" with a sincerity that seems related to his 1987 role as a preacher in John Sayles' *Matewan.* Oldham really elicits chills, however, when he crosses over to the dark side of the soul in songs like "Riding," an epic first-person account of incestuous lust. A dark and troubling album of time spent at the crossroads.

The second album—which was self-titled upon its initial release, but soon renamed **Days in the Wake**—maintains much the same tone, but improves the sonic quality from field-recording level to mere lo-fi. Oldham's songs resonate with an extraordinary sense of emptiness that has little to do with the facile angst of his peers. The clouds of gloom that loom during the opening seconds of "You Will Miss Me When I Burn" (which begins with the revelation "when you have no one, no one can hurt you") abate ever-so-slightly when Oldham is able to fantasize his way off the corporeal plane (in "No More Workhorse Blues," he envisions himself as a free-running thoroughbred). There's a hint of artifice in the too-cute "I Send My Love to You," but by the time Oldham is finished with the litany of death, disease and debauchery that festoons the other nine tracks, it's long forgotten. Combining the contents of two Drag City singles, **An Arrow Through the Bitch** augments three originals (including the morbid "Trudy Dies") with a cover of the Mekons' "Horses"—yet another testament to Oldham's abiding preoccupation with the ponies.

Oldham renamed the band for **Hope** (and, for the first time, identified his collaborators, who here include ex-Royal Trux drummer Rian Murphy and High Llamas/Stereolab keyboardist/guitarist Sean O'Hagan). While still spare and high-lonesome, the six-song EP is clearly a contemporary artifact—Oldham goes so far as to cover Leonard Cohen's "Winter Lady"—which diminishes (but doesn't eliminate) the metaphysical weirdness of his vision. The fuller tone of these songs, colored to a great degree by Liam Hayes' Hammond organ, is reminiscent of Dylan's initial Nashville forays—particularly the hypnotic "Agnes, Queen of Sorrow."

Hayes makes his presence felt even more expansively on **Viva Last Blues,** which sees another change of name (this time in order to pay tribute to Palace Music, the sire of superstar racehorse Cigar). With more reliance on organ, piano and what sounds like analog synth (although none is credited), songs like "Tonight's Decision (and Thereafter)" and "New Partner" advance a bit too far into country-rock territory, but there are enough moments of utter obsession (like the ecstatic "Old Jerusalem") to satisfy unreconstructured Luddites.

Oldham returns to his roots on **Arise Therefore,** which could be a backporch recording if it weren't primitive enough to make one doubt whether there was a porch there at all. The instrumental backing—mostly banjo, acoustic guitar and cardboard-box percussion—is most assuredly subordinate to the cracked-voice renderings of Pentecostal fury and sordid behavior. When he's in Sunday-morning mood, he sounds positively angelic (as on the hymnlike "The Sun Highlights the Lack in Each"). But when he gets a taste of those stygian waters, he turns positively malignant (as in the disturbing medieval allegory "A Sucker's Evening," wherein he evenly proposes that a cohort help him subjugate a rival: "I'll hold his arms, you fuck him/The fuck, he deserves it"). That internal struggle between God and the devil has been crucial to southern music from Robert Johnson to Jerry Lee Lewis, and it's clear that Will Oldham sees his soul as prime tug-o'-war material. Some copies of the album were packaged with a bonus EP containing twenty minutes of music performed by Palace/Oldham for the film *The Broken Giant.* [dss]

See also *High Llamas, Royal Trux.*

PALEFACE

Paleface (Polydor) 1991
Raw (Shimmy-Disc) 1995
Get Off (Sire/Elektra) 1996

Hailing from New York's Lower East Side, durable anti-folk bard Paleface served up a brilliant self-titled debut in 1991. With a booming acoustic guitar and a bit of country twang, Paleface is a punk rocker reborn as urban homesteader. His plaintive voice hustles brash strumming through a cleverly worded outpouring of ruminations on sidewalks, heartbreak and disillusionment in America. Produced with an excess of echo by Kramer, moody bits of prose like "Constant Misunderstandings" and "World Full of Cops" are passionate protests for the individual in a land of too many police chiefs. Given a full-band arrangement (including banjo!), "Burn and Rob" brings the collusion of rock-'n'roll records and slackerhood to a logical criminal conclusion in a sardonic style very nearly borrowed from Phil Ochs.

The major-label world wasn't ready for Paleface: the mainstream ignored him, while indieville, which should have provided his prime audience, never knew he existed. Sent packing before the release of his second album, Paleface worked as a barback while former roommate Beck took large chunks of his Beat ramble and guitar shuffle to the bank. Paleface resurfaced on **Raw,** a record consisting of five new studio tracks augmented by lo-fi live and home tapes from his cassette releases. Lacking the dignity of the debut, **Raw** is basically a collection of unassuming one-takes by a slightly pissy singer/songwriter. Mature cuts like "Reflections" and "Better Friends Than Most" cross paths with sarcastic throwaways like "Some Stupid Love Song" and the monotonous "Hair of the Dog." The Kramer-produced album does, however, include "With a Girl Like You," Paleface's contribution to Shimmy-Disc's Rutles tribute.

Paleface has packaged and sold numerous homemade cassettes in limited editions; among these **Burn and Rob** is infamous for including umpteen versions of the punky title track.

Get Off, Paleface's third album, was produced by Andy Paley without undermining the singer/songwriter's raw passion or loopy sensibilities. (In other words, it still doesn't sound ready for prime time, but *is* organized and listenable.) Using a band, occasionally honking away on harmonica and sometimes roaring like a man possessed, Paleface fills the brief but diverse record with his own brand of urban blues—serious ("G.G.F.U."), silly ("Your Commercial Sucks," "Oh the Pain, Ouch!") and solemn (the Tom Waitsy "I'll Be Right Back," performed on piano)—as well as punk ("Don't You Understand?") and poppy folk ("My Fault"). Fascinating. [ic/i]

PALE SAINTS

The Comforts of Madness (UK 4AD) 1990
Half-Life EP (UK 4AD) 1990
Flesh Balloon EP (UK 4AD) 1991
In Ribbons (4AD) 1992
Throwing Back the Apple (UK 4AD) 1992
Slow Buildings (4AD) 1994

SPOONFED HYBRID

Spoonfed Hybrid (UK Guernica) 1993

ESP-SUMMER

ESP-Summer (Time Stereo) 1994 (Perdition Plastics) 1996
ESP-Summer EP10 (Farrago) 1995

Signing to 4AD around the same time as Lush, this Leeds trio's first LP marries the label's traditional etherealism (such songs as "A Deep Sleep for Steven" approximate the Cocteau Twins' trancescapes) and long, languid instrumental passages, with more pop-oriented hooks and an odd mix of piston power and floating vocals from bassist/leader Ian Masters. Highlighted by an inspired cover of the pre–Mazzy Star Opal's "Fell From the Sun," this is an extremely strong, ear-catching debut.

Thus, it's remarkable how much better **In Ribbons** is. Credit likely belongs to the newfound guitar interplay brought on by the addition of second guitarist (and original Lush singer) Meriel Barham, who also takes over a third of the vocal duties, and much-improved production by the venerable Hugh Jones, but **In Ribbons** works on many higher planes. Jones' sonic beauty is particularly scintillating, making the work by Gil Norton and John Fryer (separately) on the first LP seem like a grubby, energetic pre-wash. Fierce tunes ("Throwing Back the Apple," "Baby Maker") offset the LP's more sinewy moods, keeping it cogent and convincing. The lush, haunting "Hunted" and the closing "A Thousand Stars Burst Open" are lovely and deeply felt; even the most hardened listener would have to acknowledge their appeal. **In Ribbons** is alluring and attractive, rich in complexity and raw emotion.

Slow Buildings' complete failure to scale those heights is the direct result of the experiment-prone Masters' departure in 1993. Rather than call it a day, the remaining three regrouped with new bassist Colleen Browne (late of the Heart Throbs), letting Barham assume complete control of the vocals. Not only is Masters' sweet voice missed, but the band lacks able enough songwriting. Hugh Jones' glistening production sound can't make up for the shortage of hooks, especially on the album's weak second half. If not held up against the infinitely superior Masters era, however, the new Pale Saints still have much to offer: "Fine Friend" is almost as entrancing and pretty as Mazzy Star's "Fade Into You," which it resembles, as does "One Blue Hill." Best of all is the opening instrumental "King Fade," proof that the ensemble can still whip up a dazzlingly disjointed and off-kilter sea of sound.

Masters' Spoonfed Hybrid, a collaboration with Chris Trout (ex–A.C. Temple), seems like a more worthy heir to the Pale Saints' legacy. The band's self-titled debut (which, incidentally, appeared before and completely betters **Slow Buildings**)—electronic backing and weirder, more stripped-down construction—is a slight departure for Masters, but his voice provides the familiar eerie/pretty element. The opening "Heaven's Knot" is particularly juicy. From there, Masters keeps things quieter, mixing intriguing bits of piano, organ, light strings and long fragments of brooding silence on "1936" and other tracks. A splendid and refreshing odd little album.

Masters completed another gem before 1994 ended, this time in a Michigan basement with His Name Is Alive maestro Warren Defever as ESP-Summer. The even-simpler acoustic approach makes Masters' boyish singing all the more pronounced and striking. [jr]

See also *Heart Throbs, His Name Is Alive; TPRG.*

PALM FABRIC ORCHESTRA

See *Poi Dog Pondering.*

PANSY DIVISION

Smells Like Queer Spirit EP7 (Lookout!) 1992
Undressed (Lookout!) 1993
The Nine Inch Males E.P. EP7 (Lookout!) 1994
Deflowered (Lookout!) 1994
Pile Up (Lookout!) 1995
Wish I'd Taken Pictures (Lookout!) 1996

OUTNUMBERED

Why Are All the Good People Going Crazy (Homestead) 1985
Holding the Grenade Too Long (Homestead) 1986

The limited potential of special-interest rock seemed certain until Green Day took Pansy Division on tour with them in late 1994. The sight of barely teenaged throngs mindlessly singing "Bunnies" ("And we get our bodies all hot and sweaty and runny/Then we fuck like . . .") along with the concupiscent San Francisco queercore trio gave punk's subversive ability to provide common ground for divergent values a huge goosing. Pansy Division's gift to mankind is an ability to invite inclusion regardless of orientation.

The basic rock produced by Jon Ginoli (vocals/guitar), Chris Freeman (bass) and a chain of drummers is serviceably mild-mannered and utilitarian—no threat to the established musical order there. The horny band's genially explicit lyrics, however, cut right to the chase. Besides "Bunnies," **Undressed** contains the sexstruck "Fem in a Black Leather Jacket," the phallic peculiarity of "Curvature," the straight-boy frustrations of "The Story So Far" and the explanatory dissertation of "Versatile" ("Our roles are not cast in stone/We trade off getting boned").

Ginoli's melodic constructs are appreciably better on **Deflowered;** a raunchier guitar sound gives the improved second album more punk body. The Buzzcocks aura that permeates "Reciprocate" is underscored by the album's cover of Pete Shelley's "Homosapien"; meanwhile, the band illustrates one source of its winsome mock-innocence in a sex-switched rendition of Jonathan Richman's "A Song of Remembrance for Old Girlfriends." Otherwise, the band reviles Los Angeles in "Fluffy City," enthuses about "James Bondage" and "Groovy Underwear," bitches out a "Negative Queen" ("He thinks he's Oscar Wilde, but he's Paul Lynde") and marvels at penis size in "Beercan Boy." But the laughter ends in the lonely "Deep Water" and "Denny," a bittersweet depiction of an AIDS casualty.

Pile Up, a twenty-cut collection of singles and compilation tracks, is heavy on covers that seem to have been chosen for their direct or double entendre lyrical value. Songs come from Beat Happening, Liz Phair, Velvet Underground ("He's a femme fatale"), Spinal Tap, Nancy Sinatra, Hüsker Dü, Joe Jackson, Roxy Music, Prince and Nirvana (the ribald parody of "Smells Like Queer Spirit"). The album also includes such 7-inch Pansy Division originals as "Touch My Joe Camel," "Ring of Joy," "Bill & Ted's Homosexual Adventure" and "Homo Christmas." There are undoubtedly those who will be mortified by the songs' bluntness, but it's hard to resist the sprightly enthusiasm of Pansy Division's desire.

"Woke up with a morning woody/But no one's here to share the goodies." **Wish I'd Taken Pictures** gives the Pansys' good-natured zipper-busting a sharper Ramonesy rhythm charge. The upbeat rock slop still doesn't quench the band's spirited and joyous taste for breathless lust ("Dick of Death"), comical dilemmas ("Pee Shy," "Expiration Date") or jealous romance ("Pillow Talk"). Ginoli's singing is especially improved—he's becoming a regular Modern Lover of sodomy. In a turnaround on the abiding hetero terror of orientation betrayal, "I Really Wanted You" glumly faces up to the impending straight marriage of an erotic object.

Prior to coming out, moving out west and forming Pansy Division, a young Ginoli made two mid-'80s albums as the front man of the Outnumbered in Champaign, Illinois. [i]

PANTERA

Metal Magic (Metal Magic) 1983
Projects in the Jungle (Metal Magic) 1984
I Am the Night (Metal Magic) 1985
Power Metal (Metal Magic) 1988
Cowboys From Hell (Atco) 1990
Vulgar Display of Power (Atco) 1992
Far Beyond Driven (EastWest) 1994
Driven Downunder Tour '94 Souvenir Collection (Aus. EastWest) 1994
The Great Southern Trendkill (EastWest) 1996

DOWN

Nola (EastWest) 1995

The concerted coverup of Pantera's early glam-metal albums is one of hard rock's best in-jokes. The band is said to grow belligerent at their mere mention, all but denying the records' existence amid threats and obscenities. (As the albums were released on a label owned by the Abbott brothers—later known as guitarist Diamond, later Dimebag, Darrell and drummer Vinnie Paul—they've been easy to suppress, although bootleg CDs do seem to be available.) The first three, which feature original singer/guitarist Terry Lee Glaze, got the Texas quartet started in the realm of pouffy hair and ridiculous rock, praying to Kiss and Aerosmith in exclamatory songs like "Rock Out!," "Heavy Metal Rules!" and "Onward We Rock!" Singer Philip Anselmo arrived in time for **Power Metal,** the record that contains "Proud to Be Loud" and Darrell's only recorded Pantera vocal, on "P*S*T*88," a song also known as "Pussy Tight."

The only connection to those bleached career roots

discernible on **Cowboys From Hell** is the group's publishing company (Power Metal Music) and the incongruous antique saloon photograph on the cover; what's inside the record is brain-rattling. Pantera's "power-groove" style relies not on all-out speed, but on a persistent bottom-heavy rhythm. The quartet plays punky heavy metal as vicious and menacing as it was meant to be; "Cemetery Gates" (not the Smiths song) and the anthemic title track soon became the mosh pit's state of the art. No wonder the band buried its past in a shallow grave and moved on.

The seemingly perpetual tour that followed **Cowboys From Hell** made for a long wait between albums, but it was time well spent. All swagger and brutality (you thought "Fucking Hostile" was perhaps a lullaby?), **Vulgar Display of Power** is one of the boldest signatures ever stamped on hard rock. The guitar and bass stay so close in the groove they cross like high-tension wires; Anselmo's bellicose roar grows ever more frighteningly believable. His best work is often in the margins of the songs, growling "Is there no standard anymore?" ("Walk") and "I'd kill myself for you; I'd kill you for myself" ("This Love") as a precursor to the chorus' embittered refrain.

Far Beyond Driven, Pantera's next set of odes to sociopathy, doesn't quite take the stylistic leap forward of the previous two, but it is a formidable slab of music nonetheless. The only refinements to the quartet's style are the abrupt industrial squeals with which Darrell punctuates his riffs and an even-larger Terry Date–produced wall of sound. A musical embodiment of blind, blunt rage, Pantera is the zen of ugly rock noise.

Driven Downunder Tour '94 Souvenir Collection is a snazzy Australian set containing a special booklet and CDs of **Far Beyond Driven** (with a bonus track, "The Badge"), a live EP (**Alive and Hostile**) and a Japanese EP of **Vulgar Display**'s "Walk.'

Anselmo's Down, which began as a drunken jam session with guitarist Pepper Keenan of Corrosion of Conformity, drummer Jimmy Brower of Eye Hate God and guitarist Kirk Windstein and bassist Todd Strange of Crowbar, evolved into more of an official side project when tapes of the session began circulating through the metal underground with Grateful Dead–like efficiency. **Nola** is an influenced-by-bands-influenced-by-Black-Sabbath romp that lacks the channeled aggression of Pantera, but swings a lot more, thanks to the lazy snare slap Brower drops in just behind the beat. Not essential, but a pleasant diversion. [sf]

PAPA'S CULTURE

Papa's Culture, but . . . (Elektra) 1993

Somewhere between a greased-gears Steely Dan and a pleasantly sedated They Might Be Giants, this ingenious Northern California duo—a bassist/composer raised on Count Basie and a post-punk folkie/toaster guitarist with wry funnybone—belies its members' roots to create a warm, jazzy, reggaefied funk-pop laced with charmingly odd lyrics. Laying down infectious rhythms reminiscent of the early Beat, and playful soul stylings that would do Sly Stone proud, Harley White (bass, music) and Blake Davis (guitar, vocals, words) make memorable songs like "Swim," "It's Me" and the Zappa-esque "Muffin Man" effortlessly enjoyable while describing a world of their own fantastic imagination. The album can barely contain the band's hyper-invention: tracks burble over with adroitly applied instrumental variety (horns, strings, reeds, harmonica, sitar), samples (Charles Mingus *and* Carl Reiner) and lyrics that mingle Jacques Cousteau, Brian Wilson, mom, grandpa, Bob Marley and Black Uhuru without ever getting bogged down in topicality or random referencing. Still, the relaxed grooves and sophisticated studio craft move it along with smooth ease. [i]

PAPAS FRITAS

Passion Play EP (Minty Fresh) 1995
Papas Fritas (Minty Fresh) 1995

They must be offering accelerated courses in indie-pop adorability at Ivy League schools—how else to explain the seeming ease with which this trio, formed at Tufts University in Massachusetts in '93, was ready for the closeup of its wonderful self-produced debut album inside of two years? Sounding as fresh and youthful as an after-school milk commercial—notwithstanding guitarist/pianist Tony Goddess' occasional tendency to affect a lazy J Mascis/pothead creak in his singing—the group turns extraordinarily fetching pop concoctions like "Lame to Be," "TV Movies," "Possibilities" and "Smash This World" into disarmingly sophisticated and diverse small-scale charmers with abundant skill and no evidence of effort. Crossing a strong aroma of '60s time-capsule folk-rock (imparted by acoustic guitar, simple piano and simple harmony-vocal arrangements, plus a little chamber quartet action on "Passion Play") with a post-modern sense of onrushing fuzz-guitar whimsy, Papas Fritas come off like a crisp and focused Beat Happening on one hand and a Brian Wilson–obsessed Modern Lovers on the other. Drummer Shivika Asthana provides a delightful vocal foil for Goddess; if they're not quite Sonny and Cher for the practice-amp set, Papas Fritas is still a reason to believe in the value of higher education.

Besides the exquisite title track, the introductory **Passion Play** EP is nearly a waste: its three long non-LP songs are a watery Jonathan Richman indulgence ("Means"), the junk-rock nonsense of "Radio Days" and the catchy but minor "Howl." [i]

PARIS

The Devil Made Me Do It (Scarface/Tommy Boy) 1990
Sleeping With the Enemy (Scarface) 1992
Guerrilla Funk (Scarface/Priority) 1994

CONSCIOUS DAUGHTERS

Ear to the Street (Scarface/Priority) 1993

While much of the hip-hop community headed one way in the early '90s, Paris (Oscar Jackson) picked up the lyrical gun for another purpose. Influenced by both the Black Panther party and the Nation of Islam (which at one time would have been a difficult dialectic to resolve), the tough-voiced but college-educated California rapper has upheld the political heritage of the Bay Area by devoting himself to militant politics. Over diverse, imaginative and burningly intense self-produced tracks on **The Devil Made Me Do It,** Paris expounds on revolutionary nationalism ("Brutal," a non-vinyl bonus track, offers a concise history of the African-American struggle) and Muslim faith with archival soundbites and carefully detailed written descriptions of pivotal historical figures, from Nat Turner to Huey P. Newton.

The peak of Paris' creative power, **Sleeping With**

the Enemy advances his musical stylings into the '90s and pumps up the intelligence of his righteous anger. "I'm madder than a motherfucker," he announces in "Guerrillas in the Mist," the album's bustling centerpiece. "I see the community need work/Black power mean more than a T-shirt." Good ideas and good sense are not the same thing, however. "Bush Killa," offered in two mixes, falls into the trap of fantasizing about presidential assassination. In tandem with the cop-killing "Coffee, Donuts & Death," the song led to the album's rejection by the Time Warner–owned Tommy Boy, leaving Paris to issue it on his own Scarface label. Quoting classic rap joints along with anachronistic slang like "pigs," Paris fills his songs with informed references to current events, self-criticism and potent motivation that make the record a valuable learning experience. A deft juggler of lyrical drama, history, payback violence, newsreel samples and commentary who never descends to preaching or dry pedantry, Paris stands alone in an important field that could use a few more good men.

Paris raises the didactic level on **Guerrilla Funk,** using the wordy CD booklet to recommend Afrocentric books, speakers and stores, discuss religion, media and education and photographically urge the shooting of police. (What once seemed like a faint echo of Jello Biafra's agit-prop culture approach seems to have bloomed.) The tracks, however, don't park as much articulate energy as before, employing irony ("40 Ounces and a Fool") and nostalgia ("Back in the Days") more than overt calls to rouse the rabble. Taking his cues from the loping, melodic G-funk sound of the Long Beach gangstas, Paris likewise tones down the rhetorical spray in the rhymes, rolling the same ideas with slow, easy aplomb instead of uptight agitation. "Outta My Life," for instance, does the "Dead Homiez" drill in an intriguing stylistic blend of Ice Cube, 2Pac and Warren G. While stand-in raps by the Conscious Daughters (especially on "Bring It to Ya") don't really affect the tone, soulful vocal stylings by Da Old Skool further soften the album's blunt force, making it an equivocal, unthreatening and overly derivative spaceholder.

Besides releasing it on his label, Paris wrote the diverse music, played it with engineer Eric Valentine and produced the busy-beat debut by the Conscious Daughters, a young Oakland tag team (Carla Green, Karryl Smith) possessing average skills, big attitudes and no pretense of political awareness. Songs include "Wife of a Gangsta," "Princess of Poetry" and "Crazybitchmadness." [i]

GRAHAM PARKER (AND THE RUMOUR)

Howlin Wind (Mercury) 1976
Heat Treatment (Mercury) 1976
Stick to Me (Mercury) 1977
The Parkerilla (Mercury) 1978
Squeezing Out Sparks (Arista) 1979 + 1996
The Up Escalator (Stiff/Arista) 1980 (Razor & Tie) 1991
High Times (Can. Vertigo) 1980
The Best of Graham Parker and the Rumour (UK Vertigo) 1980 + 1992
Another Grey Area (Arista) 1982 (Razor & Tie) 1991
The Real Macaw (Arista) 1983 (Razor & Tie) 1991
It Don't Mean a Thing If It Ain't Got That Swing (UK Vertigo) 1984
Anger: Classic Performances (Arista) 1985
Pourin' It All Out: The Mercury Years (Mercury) 1986
The Mona Lisa's Sister (RCA) 1988
Live! Alone in America (RCA) 1989
Human Soul (RCA) 1990
The Kid With the Butterfly Net EP (UK Demon) 1991
Struck by Lightning (RCA) 1991
The Best of Graham Parker 1988–1991 (RCA) 1992
Burning Questions (Capitol) 1992
Live Alone! Discovering Japan (UK Demon) 1993
Passion Is No Ordinary Word: The Graham Parker Anthology 1976–1991 (Rhino) 1993
Live on the Test (UK Windsong International) 1994
Christmas Cracker EP (Dakota Arts) 1994
12 Haunted Episodes (Razor & Tie) 1995
BBC Live in Concert (UK Windsong International) 1996
Acid Bubblegum (Razor & Tie) 1996

GRAHAM PARKER AND THE SHOT

Steady Nerves (Elektra) 1985

GP + THE EPISODES

Live From New York, NY (Classic) 1996 (Rock the House/Razor & Tie) 1996

VARIOUS ARTISTS

Piss & Vinegar (Buy or Die) 1996

A crabby pug whose bark is every bit as ferocious as his talent, Graham Parker comes on like an arrogant bantam with the world's bone up his butt—and then delivers the musical goods that justify his conceit and erase the ill-will he so enthusiastically spreads. Remote and defensive in one song, Parker can drop his guard and be selflessly frank and incisive the next. And while he's proven himself capable of truly obnoxious haughtiness, the self-appraisal that appears as a preface to his monumental 1993 career retrospective is unfairly harsh.

It's never been clear what really motivates Parker's strong-minded songwriting, but one of the buttons clearly marked DO NOT PUSH is attached to recording contracts. Over the course of twenty years, he's issued original albums via half a dozen American companies (not counting an abortive liaison with Atlantic in the mid-'80s that ended without any audible result), half of whom have waved goodbye with compilations. **Pourin' It All Out, Anger** and **The Best of Graham Parker 1988–1991** document his work on, respectively, Mercury, Arista and RCA. **It Don't Mean a Thing** and **The Best Of** (greatly expanded in its 1992 reissue edition) are British collections of his early years. All are useful but, short of owning the essential albums, the two-CD **Passion Is No Ordinary Word** will certainly suffice as a well-annotated if minorly incomplete introduction to the first fifteen years of Parker's howlin' wind.

Arriving on the mid-'70s London scene as a rough'n'ready product of the pub-rock era—an R&B-loving Nick Lowe with a sharper, more ambitious pen, as it were—Parker predated Elvis Costello and Joe Jackson, both of whom would second his illustration that the singer/songwriter idiom could be recharged, giving intelligent rock fans an excitable and energetic alternative to (slightly) older guardsmen like Bob Dylan, Neil Young, Randy Newman and Van Morrison. Backed by the Rumour—a crack team of pub alumni containing guitarist Brinsley Schwarz, keyboardist Bob Andrews (both ex-members, as was producer Lowe, of the band Brinsley Schwarz), guitarist Martin

Belmont (ex–Ducks Deluxe), drummer Stephen Goulding and bassist Andrew Bodnar (both ex–Bontemps Roulez)—Parker poured it all out on the great **Howlin Wind** and **Heat Treatment,** stumbled a bit on the overzealous **Stick to Me** and then fulfilled one contractual obligation with a live album, **The Parkerilla.**

Parker entered a new creative realm with **Squeezing Out Sparks,** a tough, lean, sophisticated album that, for the first time, sounds carefully arranged rather than banged out. Loaded with some of his most powerful songs ("Passion Is No Ordinary Word," the nettlesome and ambiguously anti-abortion unwanted-pregnancy ode "You Can't Be Too Strong," "Discovering Japan" and "Local Girls"), the album stands as Parker's career high, a peak dividing intuitive youth from self-conscious maturity. In 1996, Arista repackaged **Squeezing Out Sparks** with the addition of **Live Sparks,** a 1979 promo release that replicates the complete album, in correct sequence, live.

With that triumph as encouragement, Parker went into a protracted period of weakened resolve and diminished inspiration, further damaged by his uncalled-for posturing as a hothouse flower. **The Up Escalator** has the intense, driven sound of **Squeezing Out Sparks** but vastly inferior material. (The 1991 CD adds "Women in Charge," the B-side of 1980's "Stupefaction.") Made without the Rumour, **Another Grey Area** is incrementally better, but equally forgettable. (The CD reissue adds "Mercury Poisoning," Parker's 1979 frag attack at his first label.) David Kershenbaum's drippy production on **The Real Macaw** exacerbates the problem: Parker needs to be provoked, not muted in tasteful understatement. Getting Schwarz back in the fold was a wise move, however. (With no chronological logic, the reissue tacks on Parker's 1979 B-side rendition of the Jackson 5's "I Want You Back.")

Billed to Graham Parker and the Shot, **Steady Nerves** rights the balance, toughening the band attack for a bracing series of characteristically pithy performances. **The Mona Lisa's Sister** gets Parker further down the road to full recovery of his creative vigor, as his sharp tongue and sketchy melodicism attack another collection of polished songs that has its ups ("OK Hieronymus") and downs ("Get Started, Start a Fire").

Not quite finished sabotaging himself, Parker recorded the solo **Live! Alone in America** onstage in Philadelphia, evidently to demonstrate how crucial accompaniment is to putting his songs across. Naked renditions of classics ("White Honey," "Gypsy Blood," "Back to Schooldays," "You Can't Be Too Strong") are blunt but lifeless; of the provocative new songs, only the blistering "Soul Corruption" is strong enough to rise above the demo-like presentation. (**Live Alone! Discovering Japan** takes a similar tack in another land. **Live From New York, NY,** initially released by an audiophile label, is also contemporary. **Live on the Test** and **BBC Live in Concert,** however, delve back to vintage electric sets with the Rumour.)

Human Soul is much, much better. Fronting a band composed of Schwarz, Bodnar and ex-Attractions Steve Nieve and Pete Thomas, Parker bounces back with renewed enthusiasm and ambition. With nods to ska, brassy soul and swinging rock, he waxes romantic ("My Love's Strong"), sexy ("Call Me Your Doctor") and familial ("Big Man on Paper"); the songs all reveal newfound gravity and sensitivity. Distorted only in concept, the "surreal side" of the record addresses topics familiar (imperialism, the record industry's torment of a certain self-important genius), unexpected (AIDS misinformation) and downright oblique ("Sugar Gives You Energy").

Swinging back into the other lane of the stylistic highway, **Struck by Lightning** is rustic and mostly acoustic. "She Wants So Many Things," the six-minute rant that opens the sprawling album, paints Parker in the worst possible light—he's the jerk in the aisle seat who launches into a creepy tirade about a tormentor you don't know—but the song is merely misplaced, and the record quickly finds more solid footing. Although Parker devotes his attention to intimate, personal lyrics rather than intricate music here, the tunes are sturdy and graceful. As usual, GP leads with his chin, blurting out lines that either miss by a mile (try to find the music in a refrain that goes "Pull your skin like wrapping paper round my heart") or hit their mark with heat-seeking accuracy ("Some believe in a heaven up above/With a God that forgives all with His great love/Well I forgive you if you forgive me hey!/Who needs the third party anyway?").

Fighting his way back to a comfortable studio medium on **Burning Questions,** Parker uses crisp, unobtrusive soul, folk and rock backing as a platform for affectingly expressed heartfelt thoughts that cut the unease with warmth and poison the love with doubt. The fond and knowingly detailed "Just Like Joe Meek's Blues" is not so much about the late British producer as about the pointlessness of "waiting breathlessly for the Joe Meek revival/But it didn't stand any chance of survival." "Mr. Tender," he says, "is something I'm not . . . I rave and rant," but he resolves, in the name of love, to "smooth the edges from my roughness and lose the venom in my toughness." The subtlety of Parker's vision, and the various levels on which he can appraise himself and his world, make **Burning Questions** justify its title. Excellent.

Parker's seasonal record is a between-labels one-off: three originals (including the appropriately jaundiced "Christmas Is for Mugs") proffered in needless demo versions and merry full arrangements starring a New York crew led by producer/guitarist Jon Tiven. Jimmy Destri (ex-Blondie) plays keyboards, Gary Lucas adds mandolin and banjo, Crispin Cioe blows sax; Nona Hendryx shares lead vocals with Parker on "Soul Christmas," a namechecking tribute to R&B greats.

"People think I'm filled with hate/They've got it wrong/That's out of date," Parker declares helpfully in an otherwise ludicrous song of lust entitled "Pollinate" (a botanical successor to "Sexual Healing"). He proceeds to spend most of the ominously titled **12 Haunted Episodes** reiterating the good humor behind his discouraging exterior. A humble, unpretentious production on which a drummer and organist are the singer/guitarist/bassist's only collaborators, the Dylanesque album contains a few intentional sideswipes ("Disney's America," "See Yourself," the ego-scraping "Cruel Stage") but is basically a drive in the country of undying love: "Partner for Life," "Next Phase," "Loverman" all pledge that troth with evident devotion. The music is, at times, lackluster; if Parker's upbeat mood is scarcely infectious, the tight connection to his heart pours out a foundation of humanity that's both sturdy and inviting.

Acid Bubblegum is a new studio album. **Piss & Vinegar** is the now-inevitable tribute effort. [tr]

See also *TPRG*.

ZEENA PARKINS

Something Out There (No Man's Land) 1987
Ursa's Door (Can. Les Disques Victo) 1992
Nightmare Alley (Table of the Elements) 1993
Isabelle (Japan. Avant) 1995

ELLIOT SHARP/ZEENA PARKINS

Psycho Acoustic (Can. Les Disques Victo) 1995

NO SAFETY

This Lost Leg (Sw. Rec Rec) 1989
Spill (Knitting Factory Works) 1992
Live at the Knitting Factory (Knitting Factory Works) 1993

OWT

Good as Gold (Homestead) 1989

A pillar of New York's hybrid art/jazz/rock universe, the prolific Zeena Parkins has appeared on dozens of albums with Tom Cora, Fred Frith, Elliott Sharp and John Zorn. She and Cora jointly invented the electric harp, an amplified tension machine that became her trademark as a member of the unconventional Skeleton Crew. In 1986, Parkins and singer/guitarist Chris Cochrane formed No Safety, a high-energy quintet with the emotional power to reach beyond the collegial walls of the Knitting Factory.

The group's smart debut, **This Lost Leg,** is a trim exercise of the best of '80s brain sounds: Skeleton Crew, the Art Bears and Etron Fou Leloublan. The rhythm section of Curlew—Ann Rupel (bass) and Pippin Barnett (drums)—punctuate a record that is as limber and physical as it is heady. No Safety are effective songmakers without relying on established blues-based ways of doing things. Their offbeat tonal math is as invigorating on its simplest level as when analyzed to the nth degree.

Spill, the foot-dragging American debut (for which Barnett was replaced by Tim Spelios of Chunk), reflects the mediocre art-rock malaise that seemed to dampen the downtown scene's spirit with the onset of respectability. Primary vocalist Cochrane imparts the unfortunate specter of Sting on middling fusion-rockers like "Summer Dress," while the group's instrumental aptitude too often digresses into jammy white funk.

All of No Safety's best assets are recaptured for the fiery **Live at the Knitting Factory,** on which Parkins and Cochrane alternate vocals on sixteen new songs that tackle topical subjects ("Ms. Quoted") and personal matters ("Take Me") without really drawing a distinction. The Rupel-penned "Balm" is a transcendent high point. Guitar and harp gristle agitate the creative flow, wresting a danceable cacophony that makes great organic sense. "Eight Year Old With an Uzi" voices complicated feelings eloquently, shifting between dissonance and fluidity like the Meat Puppets riding with Jazz Passengers. Parkins sparks the proceedings with excitement, while Cochrane's angry character comes across like Neil Young dipped in the fountain of youth.

Before No Safety and outside Skeleton Crew (which she joined in the mid-'80s), Parkins launched a solo career. **Something Out There** is a collection of duets with cellist Cora, percussionist Ikue Mori, turntable manipulator Christian Marclay and others. **Good as Gold** showcases a project with ex-Branca drummer David Linton. **Ursa's Door** consists of a long title track (with Cochrane, cellist Margaret Parkins, violinist Sara Parkins and percussionist David Shea), plus a fifteen-minute piano solo. Her contribution to the Table of the Elements series is an eclectic fifteen-part meditation on electric and acoustic harps.

The meat of **Isabelle** is a ten-part suite inspired by Isabelle Eberhardt, a nineteenth-century Swiss adventuress and Sufi convert. Joined by pianist Lisa Crowder and the two string-players from **Ursa's Door,** Parkins twists modern chamber music with Middle Eastern vocal samples and serpentine harp arpeggios. The CD also packs **Hup!,** a set of five duets with Mori in which Parkins shows her most animated and peculiar musical personality. [ic]

See also *Dead C, Elliott Sharp.*

ANDY PARTRIDGE/HAROLD BUDD

See *XTC.*

PASSENGERS

See *U2.*

PASTELS

Up for a Bit With the Pastels (Glass/Big Time) 1987 (UK Paperhouse) 1991
Comin' Through EP (UK Glass) 1987
Suck on the Pastels (UK Creation) 1988 (Rockville) 1990 (Creation/TriStar Music) 1994
Sittin' Pretty (Homestead) 1989
Songs for Children EP7 (UK Overground) 1990
Speeding Motorcycle EP (UK Paperhouse) 1991
Thru' Your Heart EP (UK Paperhouse) 1991
A Bit on the Side (UK Kids Playtime) 1992
1986–1993 Truckload of Trouble (Seed) 1993
Mobile Safari (UK Domino) 1995 (Up) 1996
Worlds of Possibility EP (UK Domino) 1995

JAD FAIR AND THE PASTELS

This Could Be the Night EP (UK Paperhouse) 1991
No. 2: Jad Fair and the Pastels EP (UK Paperhouse) 1992

OLYMPIC WORLD

Hot Wheels EP (UK Domino) 1994

SANDY DIRT

Sandy Dirt EP (UK Domino) 1995 (K) 1996

Formed in the early '80s by singer/guitarist Stephen Pastel (McRobbie), Glasgow's still-active Pastels was among the first indie-pop bands to mount a do-it-yourself aesthetic based on a wide-eyed, almost childlike view of the world but grounded in a '60s-revering love for sweet melodies and beholden to "a rejection of orthodox pathways," as Stephen spells it out in the notes to the **Truckload of Trouble** compilation. That ethos threw the band in line with punk, at least ideologically; musically, the Pastels' avoidance of such accepted premises as singing on key made the group pop rebels to some, a hard-to-acquire taste for others. But like their American cousins Beat Happening, the Pastels' effusive charm elevates the artistic reach of their endeavors, yielding a number of wonderfully memorable songs.

By the end of the '80s, the Pastels had two albums, two compilations, (**Suck on the Pastels** and the semi-legit **A Bit on the Side**) and numerous singles and EPs under its belt. The '90s began with more singles, most of which are reprised (some in remixed form, or with minor alterations) on **Truckload of Trouble.** The far-ranging eighteen-track set dips further back for a previously unreleased version of the first album's sweet, sexy, psychedelic "Baby Honey" (one of the group's finest moments) and the jaunty singles "Truck Train Tractor," "Crawl Babies" (also from the debut LP) and "Comin' Through," the lead track of a 1987 EP on which future Vaselines/Eugenius leader Eugene Kelly is noted as a member. The album also contains two of the five tracks from **Thru' Your Heart** (the title tune and "Firebell Ringing," steered by longtime Pastel Aggi Wright's creaky vocals) and a couple of cover versions: a winsome, banjo-driven take on Mike Nesmith's "Different Drum" (originally released as a K single) and a bouncy, orchestrated (glockenspiel, toy clarinet and so forth) rendition of Daniel Johnston's "Speeding Motorcycle." **Truckload of Trouble** includes just one ("Dark Side of Your World") of the six single sides the Pastels recorded with Jad Fair. Many tracks here feature contributions from Teenage Fanclub guitarist Norman Blake. Not simply a useful introduction to the Pastels, it's also a handy seven-year stack of nifty 45s by a casually exceptional singles band.

Mobile Safari, only the Pastels' third studio album in nearly fifteen years of existence, solidifies the group's '90s lineup: Stephen, Aggi and Katrina Mitchell form the group's core, with help from guitarists David Keegan (ex-Shop Assistants) and Fanclub bassist Gerard Love. The album builds upon the Pastels' oft-copied shambling pop sound, but rounds off some of the songs' rough edges with fleshed-out arrangements and sensitive, clear production. The threesome's vocals remain cheerfully off-key as **Mobile Safari** takes them through the sultry "Exploration Team" ("Everyone should have a friend, to lead and to follow/To open up to and to lose control/Someone to explore," croons Stephen), the billowy pop of "Yoga" and the finger-snapping "Worlds of Possibility" (featuring nifty brass work), on which the trio's songwriting styles gel nicely. Dean Wareham of Luna adds some lovely, soft-hued guitar color to the album. The CD single of "Worlds of Possibility" offers an alternate version of the song—de-emphasizing the horns in favor of a nice Wareham solo—along with two more originals and a cover of bubblegum-era obscurity "Love It's Getting Better."

In 1995, Katrina (who also has a side-project band called Melody Dog; Olympic World is another Pastels offshoot), Stephen and Aggi recorded an EP with Some Velvet Sidewalk's Al Larsen (while he was an artist-in-residence at the Glasgow School of Art) under the name Sandy Dirt. All five songs (including a take on Van Morrison's "Slim Slow Slider," in which Larsen recites, rather than sings, the words) represent an even amalgam of the Pastels' casual pop and SVS's nervy, angst-renting songs. [la]

See also *Eugenius, Half Japanese, Some Velvet Sidewalk, Teenage Fanclub; TPRG.*

MIKE PATTON

See *Faith No More.*

PAVEMENT

Slay Tracks 1933–1969 EP7 (Treble Kicker) 1989
Demolition Plot J-7 EP7 (Drag City) 1990
Perfect Sound Forever EP10 (Drag City) 1991
Slanted and Enchanted (Matador) 1992
Exact Wording of Threat EP (Matador) 1992
Watery, Domestic EP (Matador) 1992
Westing (by Musket and Sextant) (Drag City) 1993
Crooked Rain, Crooked Rain (Matador) 1994
Gold Soundz EP (Matador) 1994
Range Life EP (Matador) 1994
Rattled by la Rush EP (Matador) 1995
Wowee Zowee (Matador) 1995
Pacific Trim EP (Matador) 1996

GARY YOUNG

Hospital (Big Cat) 1995

While ambivalently shoddy production values have been part and parcel of independent recording since the dawn of the 4-track, Pavement was the first band to explicitly equate the medium with the message, thereby precipitating the lo-fi revolution that agitated the indie world in the early '90s. Yes, cellar-dwelling auteurs existed before these Stockton, California, savants jerry-rigged their first distortion boxes, but few waved their Luddite flags so proudly as to list items like "would-be sonorous SG tripe" among their inventory of instruments

Using the shadowy pseudonyms S. M. and Spiral Stairs, pals Stephen Malkmus and Scott Kannberg recorded and released the striking, scree-encrusted **Slay Tracks 1933–1969** on a whim. Although only a scant handful of copies were pressed, a striking number fell into the right hands, including those of influential British DJ John Peel and at least one member of the Wedding Present, who had a minor British hit with a cover of the EP's most accessible song, the high-lonesome "Box Elder." By the time the pair reconvened to record the blatantly Swell Maps–inspired **Demolition Plot J-7,** they'd been persuaded to let Gary Young (a fortysomething New Yorker who ran the local studio they favored) contribute drum tracks to songs like "Perfect Depth," dispatching them on the perilous path to "real" bandhood. Although still relatively amorphous, the two members' individual proclivities—Kannberg is a diehard Fall worshiper, Malkmus a covert bubblegum buff who hides his sweets under a blanket of feedback—are starting to emerge.

Like its predecessors, **Perfect Sound Forever** was built in a day (making those comments about Rome seem pretty silly in retrospect), but even so, this seven-song 10-inch can't be described more aptly than in its flippant title. A sort of holy grail for the indie-rock underground's true believers, **Perfect Sound Forever** concentrates years of over-education, outcast status and record-collecting geekdom into one remarkably heady quaff of brew. Even as it sets up its own rules, though, the disc succeeds on mainstream terms: it's got the mock-heroic instrumental intro ("Heckler Spray"), the chantalong crowd unifier ("From Now On") and the epic ("Angel Carver Blues/Mellow Jazz Docent"). You'd be hard pressed to find a single molecule of **Perfect Sound Forever** that hasn't been cloned by some aspiring noise-pop band in the '90s. All three of the above releases—along with a handful of subsequent compilation tracks, including the spunky "Baptiss Blacktick" and the 1991 7-inch of "Summer Babe"—are compiled on **Westing (by Musket and Sextant).**

By this time, Malkmus and Kannberg had recruited a few friends to flesh out a live incarnation of Pavement. Besides the aforementioned Young (whose onstage antics—like handstands, audience baiting and formidable vodka drinking—became as important as his drumming), the bi-coastal band now included bassist Mark Ibold (plucked from the ranks of New York's Dustdevils) and percussionist Bob Nastanovich (coaxed away from Kentucky's horse-racing circuit). **Slanted and Enchanted,** the quintet's first recording, revealed the indie world's secret to the larger universe: from the initial notes of "Summer Babe" (which introduced the band's patent-worthy cotton-candy harmonies into the mix for the first time), it was evident that the times were a-changin'. Oh sure, songs like "Trigger Cut" and "Zurich Is Stained" make more sense if you're at least moderately grounded in semiotics, but even elliptical lyrics can't hamper enjoyment of a melody as naggingly insistent (if off-kilter) as "Chesley's Little Wrists." A must-own.

While Pavement is nothing if not prolific, the band's deep slacker vibe makes for some downright lazy releases—like the time-filling **Watery, Domestic.** Cleverly ensconced in a graffiti-scratched rooster sleeve taken directly from a thriftstore perennial, the four songs inside are decidedly half-baked, as are the "bonus" tracks that accompany "Summer Babe" on **Exact Wording of Threat.** Young's semi-acrimonious departure kept the band in limbo for a while; eventually, transplanted Virginian Steve West was named as his replacement.

True to form, Pavement rebounded with **Crooked Rain, Crooked Rain,** a pointedly self-referential album that often seems to address nothing other than itself, as evidenced by the cradle-to-the-oldies-circuit allegory "Cut Your Hair," which follows Anyband from musician wanted ads ("no big hair!") to the big time ("tension and fear . . . a career"). The countryfied "Range Life" is a little more pointed in its rock-as-rock-criticism, deflating blustery targets like Smashing Pumpkins and Stone Temple Pilots with deadpan precision. Malkmus keeps a snug hold on the reins, ceding Kannberg only the Mark E. Smith soundalike "Hit the Plane Down." But with its languid humor ("5–4=Unity" rewrites Dave Brubeck's "Take Five") and easygoing melodicism (in full effect on such instant charmers as "Silence Kid" and "Gold Soundz"), **Crooked Rain, Crooked Rain** makes a damn fine case for dictatorship. The **Gold Soundz** and **Range Life** EPs (as well as the following year's **Rattled by la Rush,** built around a **Wowee Zowee** item) append their respective title tracks with a passel of vague non-LP songs (aside from **Gold Soundz**' intriguing "Strings of Nashville") meant only for completists.

Wowee Zowee, completed with unusual dispatch, seems like a bit of a rush job. Despite some uncommonly clear-cut playing—songs like "Motion Suggests" and the jazzy "Grave Architecture" go from point A to point B without so much as a stopover at point Z—there's a palpable lack of enthusiasm. "Fight This Generation," a wannabe anthem (or parody thereof?), falls as flat as any of the boneheads lampooned on the band's previous releases; even Kannberg seems detached when squalling through "Brinx Job." A recharge had better be in the offing.

After his firing, Young returned to the studio and conceived the righteously freaky—and fittingly titled—**Hospital,** which is also the name of his band. Reminiscent of nothing so much as the work of the legendary Wild Man Fischer, the album finds Young unraveling stream-of-consciousness yarns in an altogether unlistenable voice. It's good-natured enough—his songs rarely address anything more contentious than the wacky characters buzzing around his cranium—but in no way essential. [dss]

See also *Silver Jews.*

PAW

Dragline (A&M) 1993
Death to Traitors (A&M) 1995

There was a brief window of time when record executives thought they could achieve instant nirvana by unearthing, well, instant Nirvana—and bands in burgs big and small sought to position themselves under just enough of a grunge layer to at least give off a Seattle aroma. To be fair, this Lawrence, Kansas, quartet developed its angst-ridden proto-metal sound far enough in advance of **Nevermind**'s arrival (and far enough removed from hipster ground zero to walk around sporting old-fashioned beards instead of de rigueur goatees) that they can't really be called cash-in artists. Unfortunately, from the titanic triteness that permeates their records, they can't exactly be called trailblazers, either.

Paw's debut gives a wide berth to vocalist Mark Hennessy's raw-rubbed rasp, an instrument that proves most effective in putting across the high-plains drift of squalid tales like "Gasoline" and "Pansy." His credibility as a backwoodsman isn't all that high—unless you view the University of Kansas as being on a par with Leavenworth in terms of its hardening quality. Much of the quartet's sonic heft emanates from the formidable drum-pounding of Peter Fitch, whose brother Grant hammers out echo-drenched guitar riffs that revisit a limited number of arena-rock clichés with alarming frequency.

Death to Traitors curbs the metallic agitation to a large degree: that's both its greatest strength and its biggest failing. With the intensity turned down a notch, Hennessy has more room to maneuver vocally, which endows "Hope I Die Tonight" with a good deal of passion. In the process, however, Paw surrenders the anthemic attributes that helped mask the emptiness beneath the cavernous shells of their songs—proof that bigger isn't always better. [dss]

PEACH COBBLER

See *Run On.*

PEARL JAM

Ten (Epic Associated) 1991
Vs. (Epic Associated) 1993
Vitalogy (Epic) 1994
No Code (Epic) 1996

THREE FISH

Three Fish (Epic) 1996

It has been aptly noted that Eddie Vedder's true talent is for being a rock star. His passionate singing is special not for any merits of its tremulous roar but for seeming like the voice of a very troubled deep thinker whose every grunt bespeaks imponderable existential calamities and supernatural power. His humorless lyrics rarely make much sense, yet they invariably convey just how troubled and desperate his feelings must be. As a public figure, though, the Chicago-born jut-jawed Kirk Douglas of alt.rock alienation burns with larger-than-life rebel fire, and it's impossible not to admire both his excruciating sensitivity and his incorrigibly principled and virulently conflicted sense of self. Music has little to do with why so many young people of the '90s have looked up to Vedder as a worthy and humble god who truly understands and deeply cares for them. (You do have to give the man his props on another front: he knows his old Who records.)

In turn, Pearl Jam—a hard rock combo that would be crushed into the dirt in a battle of the bands with, say, the generation-older Aerosmith, yet whose rhythm section's muscular movements have been more widely imitated than Beavis' snicker—has been able to cast itself as a paragon of integrity, taking a leadership role as virtuous crusaders by challenging big bad business on behalf of the common fan. None of which says anything about the merits of their megaselling records. Ultimately, Pearl Jam's achievement is ennobling thuggish electric rock without dressing it up, turning the lunkheaded leftovers of two decades back into an impressive and respectable '90s banquet. It's rare that an arena band has shown such skill at communicating rock's profound majesty without pomposity. Who else could release an ode to vinyl ("Spin the Black Circle") on CD and not look like total chumps in the process?

Pulled together in Seattle at the start of the '90s by ex–Green River punks and Mother Love Bone rockers Jeff Ament (bass) and Stone Gossard (guitar), Pearl Jam—with Vedder, lead guitarist Mike McCready and Dave Krusen, the first of several drummers, completing the lineup—made its debut on **Ten,** an effectively somber loud/soft Big Rock record shaped by McCready's Joe Perry riffs and elevated by the vocalist's self-willed charisma. With his straining, barely contained intensity and profound unease, Vedder inflates the trivial lyrics of "Even Flow" and "Porch" into sweeping melodic anthems, holds himself back in "Black" and turns traumatic souvenirs of a troubled adolescence into the grown-up obsessions of "Alive" and "Jeremy." "Once upon a time I could control myself" Vedder avers in "Once," clearly implying that the expiration date has since passed. Nothing about the album bears out that effective, threatening gimmick, but his conviction makes it hard to ignore.

Other than new collaborator Brendan O'Brien's significant production improvements—he fine-tunes Ament's chunky rubberband bass into a bigfoot behemoth thundering just ahead of new arrival Dave Abbruzzese's whacking snare drive and fries Gossard's rhythm guitar chording into an incinerating structural wall—**Vs.** doesn't suggest the existence of any vast well of creative imagination to be tapped in Pearl Jam's backyard. (Album packaging, however, is something else entirely.) A few new musical ideas crop up—acoustic guitar in "Daughter," chukkachukka wah-wah in "Blood," hand drums in "W.M.A.," a different sort of hook in "Glorified G," a moody minor-key progression in "Rearviewmirror," organ on "Indifference"—but the band's central equation already seems set in stone. Vedder's lyrics, meanwhile, are receding deeper into schematic elusiveness. If "Glorified G" is meant to be a statement against firearms, its ironic message fails to even register an unambiguous vote on the issue; "Elderly Woman Behind the Counter in a Small Town" boils down to a thin aphorism ("Hearts and thoughts they fade away"); the anti-police "W.M.A." (white male American) brings the protest song to a nadir of communication skill. The bellowing "Leash" comes as close as the album gets to crystallizing a statement of purpose, and it's a highbrow doozy: "We are young/ Drop the leash/Get out of my fucking face." For the youth of today, zen master ideas like that may be hard to resist, but it's really not much to go on. **Vs.** is a substantially better album than **Ten,** but no less maddeningly vague in its ambitions and content.

On **Vitalogy,** Vedder tones down his anomie in favor of lyrics about insects, albums, romance and aging, but he still fills the record with vein-popping vocalizing of catchphrases with the odious potential to become guiding principles in high-school corridors. "All that's sacred comes from youth," he sings in "Not for You" (the guitar figure of which comes from Neil Young's "Mr. Soul"). Otherwise, the group's third album delivers the standard dose of blustery exertions ("Last Exit," "Tremor Christ," "Whipping," "Immortality" and the tuneless frenzy of "Spin the Black Circle") and several songs of more intriguing merit. "Satan's Bed" (aka "Already in Love") tries out organ-driven garage-rock; the chunky, countryfied "Corduroy" compares favorably to Soul Asylum. On the other end of this uneven album, the seven-minute "Hey Foxymophandlemama, That's Me" unveils a surprising weakness for nonsensical tape collage. Ultimately, **Vitalogy** comes down to "Nothingman," a slow and tender minor-key waltz eulogizing a splintered romance. Displaying the restraint and sublety so absent elsewhere, the group handsomely frames a fraught Vedder performance to achieve atmospheric folk-rock magnificence. By resisting its instinctive bump and grind, Pearl Jam is revealed to be far more profound in the impact of a whisper than a scream.

In June '96, Ament unveiled a hippiesque side band, Three Fish, with singer/guitarist Robbi Robb of Tribe After Tribe and Seattle drummer Richard Stuverud. Two months later, Pearl Jam released **No Code.** [i]

See also *Alice in Chains, Brad, Frogs, Mother Love Bone, Neil Young.*

PEGBOY

Three Chord Monte EP (Quarterstick) 1990
Strong Reaction (Quarterstick) 1991
Fore EP (Quarterstick) 1993
Earwig (Quarterstick) 1994

Pegboy is a throwback to the golden age of Chicago's punk scene, and with good reason. Founding guitarist John Haggerty was a key member of Naked Raygun, whose brawny, brainy sound defined the city's underground for the better part of the 1980s. Like Raygun, Pegboy has little patience for anything but terse, crunchy melodies that surge into big, singalong choruses, and Haggerty's economical guitar style is perfectly suited to this no-frills approach, underpinned by the walloping drumming of brother Joe Haggerty and the nothing-fancy bass playing of Steve Saylors. If there's a weak link, it's the gruff but colorless vocals of Larry Damore, like Saylors, a former member of Chicago hardcorites Bhopal Stiffs.

The quartet comes out blistering on **Three Chord Monte** with four alienation anthems that ruminate on missed opportunities, including "My Youth," which acknowledges the group's pushing-thirty status more honestly than many of its peers. The towering lead cut, "Through My Fingers," stands as Pegboy's finest moment on record. **Strong Reaction** lives up to the EP's promise without really expanding upon it. Quibbles about the occasionally melodramatic lyrics, in which the passage into adulthood dissolves into tragedy, are obliterated by the ferocious attack.

Steve Albini joined the band briefly as bassist after Saylors' departure, and is heard on **Fore.** While retaining Pegboy's melodic songwriting, the rivet-gun noise-rock of "Never a Question" and the metal foreplay and treated vocals of "Jesus Christ," which quotes a certain rock opera, suggest a willingness to tinker with the formula.

Earwig is respectable if hardly revelatory, with another Raygun alumni, Pierre Kezdy, joining on bass. Again, the pleasure comes in hearing the Haggerty brothers interact; John sounds like he's trying to drill holes in the wall of the percussion Joe throws up on "Gordo." And in "Sinner Inside" and "Sideshow," Damore and the band take their downcast anthems to a new level of introspection. [gk]

PELL MELL

Rhyming Guitars EP (Indoor) 1982 (SST) 1990
The Live Cassette [tape] (no label) 1982
For Years We Stood Clearly as One Thing [tape] (K) 1985
The Bumper Crop (SST) 1988
Flow (SST) 1992
Interstate (DGC) 1995

STEVE FISK

Kiss This Day Goodbye [tape] (A.R.P.H.) 1982
'Til the Night Closes In [tape] (K) 1986
448 Deathless Days (SST) 1987
One More Valley [tape] (K) 1988
Over and Thru the Night: A 10-Year Retrospective 1980–1987 (K) 1993

Pell Mell has often been compared to such early rock instrumental figures as Link Wray and Duane Eddy, even though the band's shimmering keyboards and guitar sound owe little stylistic allegiance to such supposed forebears. In one respect, however, the comparison is apt: while most modern- or prog-rock instrumental groups favor abstract composition over articulated songwriting, Pell Mell's best material—like that of Wray and Eddy—sounds like genuine *songs,* songs that swing and move, songs that build, peak and fall, songs that just happen to not have lyrics or vocals.

Since the group first coalesced in Portland, Oregon, around 1980, Pell Mell's members—the most nationally prominent of whom is keyboard player Steve Fisk, who joined in 1983—have come and gone over the years, with most of the lineups scattered around various northwestern and California cities. (Founding drummer Bob Beerman and bassist Greg Freeman have been in place the longest; both they and Fisk are on **The Bumper Crop,** a collection of tracks from '83 and '84 that overlaps, song-wise, **For Years We Stood Clearly as One Thing.**) Geographical impediment has led the group to write its songs by mail—someone will get an idea, lay it down on tape and mail the tape to a bandmate, who in turn overdubs his ideas and so on, until the tune is completed. When enough material has been compiled in this manner, Pell Mell convenes, finishes the songs and records them.

Pell Mell's 1980s sound, interesting but inconsistent, received a bit of a makeover when guitarist Dave Spalding joined the band in time for 1992's **Flow** album. Spalding not only recharged the group's songwriting batteries (he's credited with seven of the album's eleven tunes), he also redirected their instrumental focus from keyboards to guitars. The result is an album full of songs that are crisp and sharp where some previous Pell Mell efforts had meandered and dragged. Highly recommended.

The success of **Flow** helped make Pell Mell one of the more intriguing major-label signings of the 1990s—who could have imagined Geffen being interested in an all-instrumental group? The resulting album, 1995's **Interstate,** is a solid continuation of **Flow**'s sound, although it has less consistently stellar material.

Beyond the intermittent confines of Pell Mell, the Louisiana-born, Los Angeles–bred and Seattle-based Fisk has had an enormous, influential and inconspicuous career. His long list of credits includes production of records by Soundgarden, Screaming Trees, Beat Happening and many others, scores for independent films, the music for Steven Jesse Bernstein's album, the band Pigeonhed and collaborations with early Pell Mell guitarist Bill Owen (as Duck Hunt), Negativland and Greg Ginn.

The retrospective **Over and Thru the Night,** a meandering collection of small-scale weirdness compiled from Fisk's cassette albums, displays several hinged sides of his studio mind: layers of cinematic and political found-sound loops, effects, music, electronic beats, tape manipulation, uncleared song samples (A Flock of Seagulls' "I Ran" on 1981's "X Mass," the Beatles' "Taxman" on 1986's "Taxman," Creedence's "Keep on Chooglin'" on 1987's "You Used Me"). Intriguing, occasionally amusing and good for use in answering-machine and party tapes, this short decade is not exactly an artistic achievement for the ages. [pl/i]

See also *Steven Jesse Bernstein, Brad.*

PENELOPES

In a Big Golden Cage (Japan. ¡Por supuesto!) 1993
Touch the Ground (Japan. ¡Por supuesto!/Rail) 1994

As formative influences, musical antecedents can be limiting or liberating, a formula to follow or a fertile field to nurture and see what might come up. In the case of Hyogo-based singer/guitarist Tatsuhiko Watanabe, mastermind of the Penelopes, what he's heard—and it's evident from the band's two albums that he's traveled widely in pop style circles, from Merseybeat, Monkees, the Who, Roy Orbison and Neil Diamond to the Style Council, Elvis Costello, Edwyn Collins and the Smiths—is simply essential creative nutrition, the raw materials to be processed and recombined for his sweetly rendered social and political commentaries.

In Watanabe, Japan has its first great Western indie-pop auteur, an eccentric as capable of conjuring up '60s AM radio delectability as serious '90s alternapop. Contrary to the prevailing noise/kitsch/garage/punk genre winds blowing across the Pacific, the Penelopes strike up breezy guitar strums at easy tempos, arranging catchy melodies into lush harmonies (the vocals are in English, with a perceptible but unobtrusive accent); keyboards top it all off, shaping Watanabe's easy travels through numerous Anglo-American idioms.

In a Big Golden Cage (which followed a series of self-released cassettes) navigates various realms of semi-acoustic retro guitar pop as if to the manor born. Watanabe matches the brisk clarity of early Johnny Marr songs while singing in a pretty voice. But if the sounds are echoes of the past, the lyrics take a modern course, cagily expressing frustration at the strictures and consumer obsessions of Japanese life in veiled, seemingly romantic terms. The horn-charged "Love Without Radar," "Paper Tiger in Me" and the lush "Evergreen" are especially delectable treats, but the whole album is wonderful in its exotic familiarity.

The more forthright, diverse and accomplished **Touch the Ground** favors synthetic horns and the roller-rink organ pep of early Attractions in the pursuit of "My Own Soul Music" and "Good Music," an autobiographical ode that credits good music for helping him escape "the teenage wasteland." In keeping with the general increase in spunk, Watanabe makes his desires and opinions explicit here, both in cheerful sonic citations and lyrics like "Stand Up, Change Your World" and "The King Half-Undressed," which he sings in a confident, handsome voice. A wonderful, uncommon record whose geographical circumstances truly add to its extraordinary resonance. [i]

PENNYWISE

A Word From the Wise EP (Theologian) 1989
Pennywise (Epitaph) 1991
Wildcard EP (Theologian) 1992
Wildcard/A Word From the Wise (Theologian) 1992
Unknown Road (Epitaph) 1993
About Time (Epitaph) 1995

As a skatepunk answer to Bad Religion, Pennywise's eponymous debut weds driving, warp-speed punk-rock to intelligent, positive-thinking lyrics. The clean production, tight vocal harmonies and crisp ensemble playing provide a fine showcase for the Hermosa Beach, California, band's high-energy odes to self-reliance and camaraderie. Jim Lindberg's husky, rapid-fire vocals have the commanding presence of Bad Religion's Greg Graffin, although the dude-friendly lyrics eschew the latter's daunting vocabulary and cocked-eyebrow cynicism for more robust, adolescent zeal. In fact, with the exception of "Homeless"—which urges the government to aid disenfranchised Americans before squandering dollars overseas—the lyrics read like a handbook on how to survive high school. "Rules," "Living for Today" and "The Secret" offer advice on repelling peer pressure and defying conformity ("the only rules you should play by? . . . rules made up by you"), while "Come Out Fighting" and the anthemic "Side One" address the standard theme of scene unity ("come together, fight together, unite together as one!").

With little support from radio or video, **Pennywise** found an appreciable audience in the aggro punk-rock demi-monde of surfers, skaters and snowboarders—enough to encourage a repackaging of two 1989 EPs (**Wildcard** was released three years after being recorded) on compact disc. This look at the infant Pennywise isn't pretty; the songs are juvenile, generic hardcore bordering on frat-rock. Lindberg's vocals all but mimic Kevin Seconds of 7 Seconds on the punk-rock tunes, the lyrics of which are painfully clichéd. Two of the eight tracks are stabs at Chili Pepper–styled funk in which Lindberg awkwardly raps the lyrics. The album closes with a silly, sped-up cover of Ben E. King's "Stand by Me."

Pennywise's influences still loom large on **Unknown Road**—the title tune and the stirring "Homesick" both bear Bad Religion's thumbprint, and Lindberg's vocals frequently recall those of Graffin and Seconds—but there are signs the band is developing its own identity. Randy Bradbury subs for missing-in-action bassist Jason Thirsk (who shot himself to death in July 1996) on all but two tracks; he and drummer Bryon McMackin provide a throbbing bottom to the machine-gun tempos. Experimenting with feedback and other effects, guitarist Fletcher Dragge finds a much wider repertoire of riffs to flesh out the arrangements. The lyrics, while still primarily earnest pep talks for sullen adolescents, are likewise fuller and more richly drawn, filled with metaphor and poetry. "City Is Burning," about the Los Angeles riots, is a case in point, its anger directed not at the rioters but at the complacent suburban know-nothings who "sit back and watch TV while the problems grow outside."

In the wake of the Offspring's commercial success, the beefier, ballsier and more radio-friendly tone of **About Time** sounds great. With Epitaph chief Brett Gurewitz co-producing, Pennywise escapes the tinny, thin-sounding dynamics of its first two albums and adds a driving, metallish bottom to the guitar and bass. It's probably no coincidence that Lindberg's vocals (on cuts like "Searching" and "Perfect People") have a booming pop-metal swagger reminiscent of the Offspring's Dexter Holland. While still preaching positive thinking to impressionable teens, the lyrics are no longer as simplistic as slogans spray-painted on a schoolyard wall. The band even finds a few new ideas to explore, as on "Freebase" (a cautionary drug tale, told from the point of view of a crack dealer) and the delightfully self-deprecating "Perfect People," in which the band actually betrays a sense of humor. [jt]

PERE UBU

The Modern Dance (Blank) 1978 (Rough Trade) 1981 (UK Fontana) 1987
Datapanik in the Year Zero EP (UK Radar) 1978
Dub Housing (Chrysalis) 1978 (Rough Trade) 1989
U-Men Live at Interstate Mall (TriCity) 1979
New Picnic Time (UK Chrysalis) 1979 (Rough Trade) 1989
The Art of Walking (Rough Trade) 1980 + 1989
390 Degrees of Simulated Stereo (Rough Trade) 1981 + 1989
Song of the Bailing Man (Rough Trade) 1982 + 1989
Terminal Tower: An Archival Collection (Twin\Tone) 1985 (Rough Trade) 1989
The Tenement Year (Enigma) 1988
One Man Drives While the Other Man Screams (Rough Trade) 1989
Cloudland (Fontana) 1989
Worlds in Collision (Fontana) 1991
Story of My Life (Imago) 1993
The Hearpen Singles EP7 (Tim/Kerr) 1995
Ray Gun Suitcase (Tim/Kerr) 1995
Folly of Youth See Dee + EP (Tim/Kerr) 1995
Datapanik in the Year Zero (DGC) 1996

PETER LAUGHNER

Peter Laughner (Koolie) 1982
Take the Guitar Player for a Ride (Tim/Kerr) 1994

ROCKET FROM THE TOMBS
Life Stinks (Jack Slack) 1990
EASTER MONKEYS
The Splendor of Sorrow (Hit & Run) 1992

Although New York and London are generally credited with spawning what came to be known as punk-rock, a contingent from Cleveland has a fairly good claim to planting many of its seeds in the early '70s. Born from the ashes of Rocket From the Tombs (a band that also produced the Dead Boys), the nascent six-piece Pere Ubu began tinkering with its avant-garage sound—a polyhedral hybrid of Detroit-styled guitar squall, kraut-rock drone and, perhaps most important, the death knells of Cleveland's collapsing industrial infrastructure—in the summer of 1975, self-releasing "30 Seconds Over Tokyo," one of the first indie singles of the punk era, by year's end.

With its debut album, **The Modern Dance,** Pere Ubu engineered a dauntingly seamless coupling of arty introspection and old-school garage-rock squall. Frontman David Thomas (alternately known as Crocus Behemoth) used his bizarro-world warble to yelp out fusillades of angst ("Life Stinks") and spin dream-world visions ("Sentimental Journey") that ultimately proved far darker and more challenging than any three-chord ranter operating at the time. **Datapanik in the Year Zero** repackages five songs culled from singles released on the band's own Hearthan (aka Hearpen) label, including the Seeds-gone-dada "Cloud 149."

The spectacular **Dub Housing** accentuates the more amorphous qualities of the band's sound, drawing heavily on synthesizer player Allen Ravenstine's utterly original soundscaping ability. Songs like "Codex," "Caligari's Mirror" and the ominous title track conjure up images straight out of art-house psychological horror films like *Carnival of Souls.* Simply one of the most important post-punk recordings. **New Picnic Time** is significantly less riveting: guitarist Tom Herman, who was largely responsible for the foreboding atmospherics of the band's earlier albums, strafes against the whimsical, lighthearted structures of songs like "The Fabulous Sequel" and "Small Was Fast," while Thomas' increasingly eschatological observations (reflecting his longtime faith as a Jehovah's Witness) grow more and more unsettling. The lack of communication between members was reflected in Herman's subsequent departure (to form the more aggro Tripod Jimmie) and the recruitment of dada-minded instigator Mayo Thompson (with whose Red Crayola a few Ubu-ites had recorded) as a replacement.

It didn't take Thomas and Thompson long to develop a common language, as evidenced by the ditzy-but-compelling aura of **The Art of Walking,** rife as it is with hymns of praise to life's mundane moments. Like a fourth-dimensional doppelgänger for Jonathan Richman, Thomas warbles his thoughts on "Birdies" and "Arabia" (with hastily scribbled lyrics appended to what was originally intended to be an instrumental), while Thompson paints the landscapes in dazzlingly shiny—if occasionally unnatural—colors. The live **390 Degrees of Simulated Stereo** doesn't document this lineup—it dates mostly from the band's earliest days and features spellbinding, brutal versions of classics like "The Modern Dance" and "My Dark Ages."

Drummer Scott Krauss, er, bailed before the release of **Song of the Bailing Man,** and his replacement, Anton Fier (the Cleveland native had briefly played in an early incarnation of Ubu, concurrent with his tenure in confrontational art combo X-Blank-X). Fier's lighter, jazzier playing sets the tone for an album that, for all its Euro-prog inconoclasm, never quite ignites. After a disastrous US tour, the band fell apart, with Krauss and bassist Tony Maimone focusing their energies on Home and Garden (a studio aggregation, led by the unfortunately named guitarist Jim Jones, that was invested with rustic Anglophilia) and Thomas actively embarked on a solo career. The first chapter in the Ubu story is neatly summarized on **Terminal Tower,** an annotated collection of eleven essential tracks, highlighted by the hard-to-find "Lonesome Cowboy Dave" and "Untitled" (an alternate take on "The Modern Dance").

The final incarnation of the Wooden Birds (Thomas' backing band) evolved back into Pere Ubu at the end of a 1987 European tour, when Krauss was appended to a lineup including Maimone, Ravenstine, Jones and second drummer/prog-rock stalwart Chris Cutler. Sounding vital—and as futuristic as ever—the new Ubu recorded **The Tenement Year,** a surprisingly edgy set that integrates Thomas' loopy digressions into a noise-pop context not all that far from the band's original concept. Although Krauss and Cutler occasionally trip over one another in mixes that tend toward muddle, tracks like the pulsing "George Had a Hat" and the cyber-romantic "We Have the Technology" resonate with the still-potent clatter of Ubu's avant-garage. Recorded in 1978, '80 and '81, **One Man Drives While the Other Man Screams** (its title taken from a grocery-store jingle that penetrated the collective Cleveland consciousness for years) makes a fine companion piece to the prior Ubu live set, reprising some of the finer moments from the **Dub Housing** era, as well as a rare rendition of the gorgeous single track "Heaven."

While admittedly label-imposed, the stab at metamorphosis that manifests itself throughout the glossy **Cloudland** is actually quite persuasive. Producer Stephen Hague (known for his work with the Pet Shop Boys and New Order) brings a heretofore unimaginable sense of sonic harmony to the handful of songs he worked on, and while his wholesale deletion of the band's more anarchic ancillary noise might disturb purists, the overall effect is mighty compelling—particularly on the contagious "Waiting for Mary." Longtime cohort Paul Hamann takes the helm for some more typical Ubu-isms (like the loopy "Nevada!," which incorporates a chunk of "Sloop John B"), but taken as a whole, **Cloudland** stands proudly as Pere Ubu's pop masterwork.

The band underwent another sea change before the release of **Worlds in Collision:** Ravenstine left to pursue a career in aviation and was replaced by former Captain Beefheart sideman Eric Drew Feldman. Cutler also departed, and Ubu decided one drummer would suffice. Produced by Gil Norton, **Worlds in Collision** furthers the pop propensities of **Cloudland** with such unabashed singalongs as "I Hear They Smoke the Barbecue" (a single of which was actually released under the alias the Modern Solution in order to circumvent Ubu's art-house vibe). Although wistfully pretty tracks like "Oh Catherine" impart an old-fashioned charm to the album, the less-than-inspired rock numbers show the band to be in desperate need of a recharge.

There's considerably more creative juice flowing through **Story of My Life,** the most stripped-down Pere Ubu album to date. With the departure of Feldman (who joined Frank Black's band), Jones, doing double duty on guitar and keyboards, assumes the role of primary soundscaper. He plays the part masterfully on classically disorienting songs like "Heartbreak Garage" and "Louisiana Train Wreck," on which his serpentine, stinging guitar leads are totally enrapturing. Thomas sounds rejuvenated as well, as he navigates the whimsical waters of songs like "Postcard" (a surreal world tour taken in three-by-five snapshots). Midway through a tour supporting the album, Maimone left (to join They Might Be Giants, among other things) and was replaced by Michele Temple, a member of Cleveland's Vivians who had played with Krauss and Jones in Home and Garden.

As Pere Ubu reached its twentieth anniversary as a band—a feat in itself, given Thomas' assertion that the band initially planned to split up after recording just one single—it returned to indie-dom for the release of **Ray Gun Suitcase,** a wildly eclectic, captivatingly meandering set that harks back to its early '80s incarnation. That has something to do with the synth and theremin playing of Robert Wheeler, whose futuroswirl approach is most evident on songs like "Red Sky" and the furious "My Friend Is a Stooge for the Media Priests," not to mention Thomas' most visceral performances in years. With the departure of Krauss—the new drummer is Cleveland stalwart Scott Benedict—Pere Ubu may appear to bear little resemblance to the band of old, but the spirit most assuredly remains willing. **Folly of Youth See Dee +** is a CD-ROM: besides the visuals, the disc contains **Ray Gun Suitcase**'s "Folly of Youth," demos for two other songs from it and a "jam" entitled "Ball n Chain."

In a substantial expansion from the EP format, the second Ubu release to be titled **Datapanik in the Year Zero** is a deluxe five-CD box of the first coming of Ubu, containing **The Modern Dance, Dub Housing, New Picnic Time, The Art of Walking** and **Song of the Bailing Man,** plus an hour of previously unreleased live recordings and an entire disc of Ubu-related rarities.

As chronicler of—and prime mover in—the groundbreaking Cleveland scene in the early '70s, Peter Laughner (who died in 1977 at the age of twenty-four) ranks as one of underground rock's true unsung heroes. Though Lou Reed was undeniably his major influence (particularly as a vocalist), Laughner's work can scarcely be narrowcast as mere tribute. The self-titled album, gleaned from a brace of demos and live recordings, reveals his folkier side, with nods to Ramblin' Jack Elliott ("Rag Baby") and Richard Thompson (on the melancholy "Baudelaire"). The two-record **Take the Guitar Player for a Ride** is much more exhaustive (and exhausting): from the sorrowful epic "Amphetamine" (a line from which gives the album its title) to a hushed version of Robert Johnson's "Me and the Devil Blues" (recorded the night before his death), it's a detailed map of a one-way route down to the crossroads. The CD has three fewer songs than the vinyl.

Rocket From the Tombs, alternately "led" by Laughner, Thomas and Stiv Bators (then merely the ex–lead singer of Youngstown glitter bozos Mother Goose), kept the flames of midwestern stun-rock raging through the early '70s. **Life Stinks,** taken from a local radio broadcast, showcases the band at its best, melding searing shock guitar (by Laughner and Gene O'Connor, who later copped the nom de punque Cheetah Chrome and became a Dead Boy) with spaced-out Germanic doodle on tracks like "30 Seconds Over Tokyo," "Life Stinks" (both Laughner compositions that would grace the Ubu catalogue) and "Ain't It Fun" (a future Dead Boys staple). The lovingly, exhaustively annotated set (which comes with a bonus 7-inch featuring "Transfusion" co-written by Laughner and his ex-wife, Cleveland poet/musician Charlotte Pressler) also includes a bevy of lesser-known tracks that attest to the band's intuitive futurism. Anyone attempting to divine the roots of punk will certainly have his or her rod set awhirl here.

Before his stint in Ubu, Jones played with a number of seminal bands, ranging from the psychedelically inclined Mirrors (which survived from 1974 well into the '90s, although Jones split in the first decade) to the aforementioned Home and Garden. The most inspirational, however, might have been the Easter Monkeys, a foursome that laid post–Birthday Party dementia atop gnarled midwestern spazz-rock rhythms. The posthumous **Splendor of Sorrow**—released several years after the band's implosion—is highlighted by frontman Chris Yarmock's unhinged rants on songs like "Take Another Pill" and "Monkey See, Monkey Do." The id's all right. [dss]

See also *Frank Black, Red Crayola, They Might Be Giants; TPRG.*

PERMANENT GREEN LIGHT

Permanent Green Light (Gasatanka/Rockville) 1992
Against Nature (Gasatanka/Rockville) 1993

After LA power-pop combo Three O'Clock punched out with 1988's **Vermillion,** singer/bassist Michael Quercio joined San Francisco's Game Theory (with which he'd previously played and produced numerous tracks). He and that group's Scott Miller meant to form a new group altogether, but Quercio chose to stay in LA, where he formed a new trio, christened Permanent Green Light after a watercolor hue immortalized in a song title by '60s kooks the Godz.

The self-titled, self-produced (with a couple of buddies) mini-album is a lot like a (largely) keyboardless version of the Three O'Clock: an appealing high-energy pastiche of American- and English-style power-pop featuring Quercio's high, wry Angloid vocals and, occasionally, the somewhat sweeter voice of guitarist Matt Devine. The first four cuts are just swell, if lyrically odd ("We could just die / Like martyrs on a hillside"). The last three tracks are much less impressive, but include a reference to the band's hard-to-figure infatuation (led by drummer-cum-Keith-Moon-fan Chris Bruckner) with J. K. Huysmans' classic novel of fin de siècle decadence, *Against Nature.*

That book also supplied the title for the band's next album, not to mention its artwork and some lyrical inspiration, notably on the Devine-penned "Portmanteau." The first half of the album, starting with the hard-charging, Sweet-ish "Honestly," is enjoyably diverse fare—but then come variations that didn't work even in the heydey of prog-rock. One terrific return to form, "(You & I Are the) Summertime," and one successful deviation, Quercio's acoustic trance-ish "Fireman" (shades of Alex Chilton's "Holocaust"), alternate with lesser cuts to fill out the disc. Overall, it's an entertaining enough effort, with noteworthy melodic and vocal harmony influence by the Raspberries and (notwithstanding Permanent Green Light's guitar-dominated sound) the Left Banke and Stories.

Devine departed in mid-'95, joining Medicine as second guitarist for what turned out to be that band's final tour. By a weird coincidence—Medicine is nothing like PGL, especially onstage—Devine's replacement, Bernard Yin (ex-Spindle), had also previously toured as second guitarist with Medicine. A late-'95 7-inch ("Together" b/w "Queen of Market Street") and other demos cut with Yin (but written solely by Quercio) suggest the album planned for '96 will be the band's most assured and consistent. [jg]

See also *Loud Family, Medicine.*

PET SHOP BOYS

Please (EMI America) 1986
Disco (EMI America) 1986
Actually (EMI Manhattan) 1987 + 1988
Introspective (EMI Manhattan) 1988
Behavior (EMI) 1990
Discography: The Complete Singles Collection (EMI) 1991
Very (EMI) 1993
Disco 2 (EMI) 1994
Alternative (EMI) 1995
Bilingual (Atlantic) 1996

LIZA MINNELLI

Results (Epic) 1989

What might well have been a short-lived novelty bash, Pet Shop Boys—the droll, all-electronic London duo of ex–*Smash Hits* journalist Neil Tennant (vocals) and Chris Lowe (programming)—instead developed into one of the most influential and era-defining overground dance-music groups to emerge in England during the 1980s. Savvy pop sense, lushly inventive production and Tennant's deadpan pronouncements have kept the duo's unmistakable records popular; the replacement of glibly acerbic jokes with more serious, reflective lyrics has prevented the creative stagnation that has sandbagged so many of their peers.

Smart young pleasure-seeking suburbanites dreaming of the joys wealth and fame might bring, the Pet Shop Boys initially sounded like smug stockbrokers investing in a growth industry. **Please** has the ingredients of the band's formula: shapely, powerful beats given co-billing but not real pre-eminence, covered by extended strains of fake strings and Tennant's Al Stewart (as archly scripted by Martin Amis) voice. But it's all been left out in the rain with too many loose ends and a tragic lack of subtlety and soul. Tennant's haughty lyrics scatter in-jokes and self-amused esoterica throughout "West End Girls" and the wry "Opportunities (Let's Make Lots of Money)." **Disco** is a remix album, employing an assortment of American dubmen (Shep Pettibone, Arthur Baker, the Latin Rascals and others) for extended versions of those two songs, plus "In the Night" (the B-side of "Opportunities") and other savories from **Please.**

As Tennant would later opine (in **Behavior**'s "Being Boring"), "I never dreamt that I would get to be/The creature that I always meant to be." Nonetheless, he did, and the Pet Shop Boys refined their skills and dropped some of their pretensions to become, not just the stylish musical realization of the sort of contented affluence relatively unknown in England, but—in the singer's lyrics—a chronicle of life as a maturing homosexual, of love's mundane details and AIDS' profound devastation. If not quite British pop's ultimate yuppies, Pet Shop Boys occupy a significant sociological spot in the charts. In a very loose sense of style, pose and effect, the Pet Shop Boys are the Roxy Music of their generation.

Like the cynical fiction of writers like Jay McInerney and Bret Easton Ellis that became popular around the same time, **Actually** trades the attitudinal incoherence of **Please** for a decisive formula on a crafty album of greedy materialism (and a scathing indictment thereof) with songs like "Shopping" and "Rent" serving as incisive social satire likely to be mistaken by those hoping to have their arrogance certified. The duo's melodic sense is far stronger, and the well-arranged record (entirely programmed on Fairlight synthesizer) draws as much from **Abbey Road** as from Kraftwerk. Tennant's voice has lost none of its creepy unctuousness, but "It's a Sin" has a brilliant refrain, and Dusty Springfield's guest vocal on "What Have I Done to Deserve This?" handily salvages the tune. (The following year, the Pet Shop Boys wrote and recorded the magnificent "Nothing Has Been Proved" for Springfield to sing on the *Scandal* soundtrack. The pair played much the same Svengali role on the ungodly **Results,** wherein Liza Minnelli emotes absurdly over coy and starkly inappropriate songs.)

The boring and redundant **Introspective** jams six songs (four of them also issued as singles) into forty-eight minutes, largely dispensing with such needless formalities as melody in favor of protracted pre-mixed dance grooves. "Always on My Mind" (popularized by Willie Nelson and, in England at least, Elvis Presley) receives a nine-minute house version; "Left to My Own Devices," which employs an orchestra, is another of Tennant's insufferable diary entries; "Domino Dancing" deftly inserts a salsa breakdown into the middle of a standard mid-tempo concoction.

Where **Introspective** revealed absolutely nothing about the men behind the music, "Being Boring"—the song that leads off the superior **Behavior**—is downright generous in its reflective view of the band's shifting existence *and* the decimation wrought by AIDS. Co-produced by Harold Faltermeyer, **Behavior** returns to the lush and tuneful musicality of **Actually,** with Tennant *singing* substantial and affecting lyrics that seem to come from the heart, not the calculating mind. While "How You Can Expect to Be Taken Seriously?" tweaks an unnamed pop star, "Jealousy" and "So Hard"—both touching breakup songs—and the new-love "Nervously" explore emotional depths Tennant's lyrical elevator never previously stopped at.

Packed in a brilliant embossed opaque orange jewel box, **Very** is another musical peak. Sounding more comfortable, confident and good-natured than ever, Tennant and Lowe gather up a steaming dance brew—generalized disco as reinvented for another time and place with elements of trip-hop, house, jungle and other contemporary developments, including the Carter the Unstoppable Sex Machine–styling "Yesterday, When I Was Mad"—that is as potent in its way as any overproduced ABBA hit. Punching holes in the quiet dusky afternoon gloom that frequently pervades their records, Tennant plays it lighthearted and a little light-headed, humbling himself mildly in "I Wouldn't Normally Do This Kind of Thing," detailing his pickup routine in "To Speak Is a Sin," indulging a regal tabloid fantasy in "Dreaming of the Queen" and paying grand tribute to the fans of drama in "The Theatre." Even the ominously titled "Liberation" is simply about the power of love. Lowe matches his partner's sunnier disposition with a genial whirlwind of engaging, frequently exciting music that mixes its cagey reference points (a lot of '70s soul touches, but also courtly horns and, in "The Theatre" sensibly enough, showy fanfares) to excellent effect.

The Pet Shop Boys' discography is heavy with remix records and compilations. The annotated **Discography** batches together eighteen A-sides from the pair's first six years, from "West End Girls" through "Suburbia" (a rerecording of the **Please** track), "It's a Sin," "Always on My Mind," "Being Boring" and an absurd 1991 hi-NRG cover medley of U2's "Where the Streets Have No Name" and Frankie Valli's "Can't Take My Eyes Off You," plus the new "DJ Culture" (boring, housey) and "Was It Worth It?" (peppy and romantic neo-disco).

An apparent attempt to up their cred in heavier dance circles, **Disco 2** contains remixes by David Morales, Jam & Spoon, Junior Vasquez and others of **Very**'s "Go West" (a cover of the Village People oldie), "Liberation," "Can You Forgive Her?," "Yesterday, When I Was Mad" and "I Wouldn't Normally Do This Kind of Thing," as well as **Behavior**'s "So Hard," the 1990 B-side "We All Feel Better in the Dark" and the fragment "Absolutely Fabulous," all edited into one endless, cliché-packed, exhausting megamix that has its moments but too often clubs good songs into shapeless corpses of endless repetition.

Casting around for something else to anthologize, the singles-oriented Pet Shop Boys gathered up their B-sides and format leftovers and filled the two discs of **Alternative** with thirty also-rans, an uneven but ultimately illuminating collection that goes back, recording-wise, to 1983, includes three Lowe vocals, a Stephen Sondheim song cut as a demo for Minnelli and compositions by Brecht/Weill and Noel Coward. The lengthy booklet interview by Jon Savage gives the contents the intriguing context impossible to glean from the far less fascinating task of listening to all of it. (Tennant's explanations of the sources of titles—an aspect of tiny impact on the final result—are extraordinary.) A treat for fans, this stylistic hodgepodge is a courageous showcase for a big band's smaller efforts. [i]

See also *New Order; TPRG.*

LIZ PHAIR

Girly Sound [tape] (Girly Sound) 1991
Second Tape [tape] (Girly Sound) 1992
Exile in Guyville (Matador) 1993
Whip-smart (Matador/Atlantic) 1994
Juvenilia (Matador) 1995

Punk-rock and hip-hop (if not John "Working Class Hero" Lennon) brought four-letter words into the music mainstream, but it was Liz Phair who reclaimed "fuck" as active verb for the undersexed indie-rock generation. Arriving in the cute and coy wake of Juliana Hatfield, the soft-willed infantilists and a million wimpy boy bands fearful of letting their testosterone leak out, singer/guitarist Phair emerged from a Chicago bedroom to bare her knuckles and some portion of her soul in melodically seductive and lyrically blunt eyewitness accounts of the war between the sexes. Whether Phair *is* the daring, desirous and disgusted woman of her songs or a provocatively imaginative nose-thumber, the gap between her creations and her self led directly into a maze of fantasies, controversies and contradictions for fans and detractors alike. A singer who announces herself as "your blow-job queen" and promises "everything you ever wanted . . . I'll fuck you 'til your dick is blue" (to quote the oft-cited "Flower" on **Exile in Guyville**) raises issues that can't properly be settled in a two-minute song. As illuminating and resonant as her impudent declarations of independence may be, she's also been seen as a titillating cockteaser or a willing victim with a cute butt. And that's not accounting for suspicions that she's a big phony.

Ultimately, it doesn't matter where the truth and illusion in all this lies: Phair cuts a potent figure in modern rock by stepping outside the boundaries against which such female pioneers as Chrissie Hynde, Holly Vincent, Joan Jett and Nina Hagen had to strain. By changing the terms of the struggle, Phair helped add a crucial why-not option to the creative menu for girls with guitars. At worst, it's hard to imagine Alanis Morissette making **Jagged Little Pill** without **Exile in Guyville** as encouragement.

Before signing with Matador, Phair had a reputation on the groovy fanzine circuit owing to her homemade Girly Sound cassettes, actual samples of which can be heard on the **Juvenilia** mini-album. (She also remade songs from both for the LPs.) But the attention and adulation that met **Exile in Guyville** was earned strictly on the album's considerable merits. Phair's avowed conceptual device of writing and recording an analogue to the Rolling Stones' **Exile on Main St** produced audible echoes of that record here and there but amounted to a red herring, a pirate's map for academically minded critics who wasted endless hours in scrutiny and debate. How Phair (and co-producer Brad Wood) approached the construction of her eighteen-track extravaganza doesn't matter. It's the individual songs, not their unfathomable totality, that makes **Guyville** (the title a wryly critical nickname for Chicago's incestuous underground rock scene) so great. The spare arrangements feature Phair strumming oddly shaped guitar chords and singing in a soft, unsteady voice, as Wood and engineer Casey Rice add lean portions of drums, guitar, bass and organ to fashion a fascinating variety of sounds. "Fuck and Run," "6'1"," "Divorce Song" and "Never Said" march to brisk rock strength. "Explain It to Me" and "Gunshy" lose themselves in woozy tremolo swirls. "Glory" is an acoustic whisper; "Soap Star Joe" a bluesy raunch. In truth, presentation matters little to Phair, whose ingenious gift for tartly expressive lyrics and memorable melodies fills the album with songs that express strong ideas in a most alluring fashion. Opening a wardrobe of dramatis personae that includes sexual bully ("Flower"), simpering victim ("Divorce Song"), romantic skeptic ("6'1""), self-critical pushover ("Fuck and Run"), housebound hostage ("Help Me Mary") and defensive punk ("Never Said"), Phair reflects the uncertainty of real life, caulking brash outspokenness about her personal experiences with fears and irrationalities anyone can understand.

Returning with **Whip-smart,** Phair is still the ideal '90s woman: smart, sexy, charming, crude, autonomous. Upping the ante in diversity, ambition and emotional maturity, Phair amplifies her strengths, complicates her character and reveals no heretofore overlooked flaws. If no songs here are as singularly devastating as "Fuck and Run," **Whip-smart**'s fuller arrangements and consistent quality are a satisfactory trade-off. Sidestepping the trap of writing about career calculus, Phair continues her mine-strewn journey through carnality, relationships and self-discovery. Though riddled with geographical references and vehicular motion, the album sits still long enough to resume the debut's hapless, low-expectations grappling. In the conspicuous first verse of the album-opening "Chopsticks," over a suitably naïve two-finger piano figure, she meets a man who likes "to do it backwards." That suits her fine. Replying with a hooker's withering suckerpunch, the narrator has her own angle on the position. "That way we can fuck and watch TV." Point, set. Meanwhile, other songs map out new terrain. In "Go West," one of several that pose seemingly serious personal reflections in an ambiguous blur of pronouns and romantic reports, Phair announces, "I've got to tear my life apart . . . It feels like I've got something to prove, but in some ways it's just something to do." The real love creeping up on her in the catchy "Cinco de Mayo" and the soulful, Pretenders-like ballad "Nashville" outlines a future free of self-satisfying disdain and the ironic toxins of "Jealousy" ("I can't believe you had a life before me/I can't believe they let you run around free"); the title track goes so far as to conceive wisdom-filled parenthood. But while she seems happy to embrace hope, Phair isn't ready to relinquish her diffidence: the dreamy, low-key "Shane" ends with a mantra that commands "You gotta have fear in your heart."

The sketchy presentation of the five rudimentary Girly Sound artifacts—crudely recorded with one electric guitar and doubletracked vocals—on **Juvenilia** isn't what makes them insignificant. As for these formative efforts, Phair's melodic skills are in a more advanced state than her lyrics, which only hint at the focused invention to come. ("California" and "South Dakota," which prefigure the geographical obsessions of **Whip-smart,** both make joking reference to fucking cows.) The sullen "Easy" is the only song strong enough to have potentially found a home in **Guyville;** the others are strictly for the archives. Otherwise, this interim release contains the second album's "Jealousy," the previously unissued piano-backed "Animal Girl" and a pointless cover of the Vapors' new wave nugget, "Turning Japanese," hastened along breathlessly by Material Issue, whose Jim Ellison does half the singing. [i]

PHARCYDE

Bizarre Ride II the Pharcyde (Delicious Vinyl) 1993
(Delicious Vinyl/Capitol) 1995
LabCabinCalifornia (Delicious Vinyl/Capitol) 1995

Dennis the Menace didn't die in that go-cart crack-up, he went underground and spent the next few years in South Central Los Angeles, recuperating in Pharcyde Manor, listening to P-Funk records with his breakdancing homies Imani Wilcox, Booty Brown (Romye Robinson), Slim Kid (Tre Hardson) and Fat Lip (Derrick Stewart)—aka the Pharcyde. D the M eventually got himself straightened out and went into Republican politics; his pals, meanwhile, took what they had learned from the mega-brat and rode their boards down to the studio to make a loopy and extraordinarily entertaining alternate-reality debut album. Inhibitions get dropped faster than the warm'n'funky soul-jazz grooves on **Bizarre Ride II the Pharcyde,** a record cut with live musicians and samples of Jimi Hendrix, the Lovin' Spoonful, Donovan, Herbie Mann and Slick Rick. While these sophomoric jokesters aren't as crude or simple as Biz Markie, the clever, verbally agile rhymers don't mind talking about masturbation ("On the DL"), busting on moms ("Ya Mama"), making a major sex miscalculation ("Oh Shit"), getting into a painful sexual jam ("4 Better or 4 Worse") or copping to romantic ineptitude ("Passing Me By"). The group is obviously having a ball horsing around, and the record conveys that with infectious delight.

Having relocated to a middle-class section of the city, the older-wiser quartet moves past comedy for sober adult intelligence on its second album. The Pharcyde summarizes its newfound ambition in song as "I gotta kick somethin' that means somethin'," but **LabCabinCalifornia** merely recasts the group as love men who croon ("Runnin'," "She Said," "Hey You," "Y?") as well as they rap. The music is smoothed out, tightened up and generally cooled off into a cushioned, darkened living room, where relationships and other topics can be discussed quietly over a spliff and a glass of wine. Maturity hasn't cost the group its inveigling hip intimacy, but there's far less colorful business to connect with. Songs like "Groupie Therapy" (upstanding, despite the title) and "Devil Music" (an autobiographical complaint about the alienation of labor) are easy enough on the ears, but—outside of the wacked-out nostalgia trip of "The Hustle"—the low-key album lacks the energy, imagination and memorability of a truly bizarre ride. [i]

JOEL R. L. PHELPS

See *Silkworm.*

PHILISTINES JR.

Greenwich, CT EP (Tarquin) 1991 (dot dot dash) 1996
The Continuing Struggle of . . . the Philistines Jr. EP (Tarquin) 1993
The Sinking of the S.S. Danehower (Tarquin/dot dot dash) 1995

IRIS

After School Special (Bubble Core) 1996

ZAMBONIS

100% Hockey (dot dot dash) 1995

"Hey, what are you guys doing down there?" "Oh nothing, mom, just recording one of the sweetest, most adorable and sublimely accomplished dinkypop albums of 1995." Connecticut brothers Peter (vocals, guitar, organ, drums) and Tarquin (bass, vocals) Katis are, with drummer Adam Pierce, Philistines Jr. Their stock in trade is simple, gentle songs of surreal whimsy that spin tunefully like Brian Wilson's mildest dreams while evincing the outlandish basement-brewed conceptual wizardry of pioneering British producer Joe Meek. All of this is accomplished in voices with the fresh-scrubbed wholesomeness of 4-H Clubbers. Rudimentary, perhaps, but hardly naïve.

Unlike most pop auteurs aiming to whip up confectionery masterpieces, the Philistines Jr. neatly balance guitar and rudimentary organ for an irresistible, joyful pop sound that is neither raw jangle nor synthesizer flash. Using toy piano as an accent and strikingly clear sound as an asset, **The Sinking of the S.S. Danehower** (perhaps inspired by the underwater photo of young musicians Paul and Dave Danehower that graces the back cover) is a small masterpiece, wandering in and out of the story/theme advanced in "We Will All Go Down Together" and "Wo Ist Das Unterseeboot?" with a lovely cover of "Moon River," the VCR adventure of "N," the enthusiastic welcome back of "It's Paul & Dave!" and "The Sci-Fi Song," a thoughtful (if noisy) consideration of being in a band that tours in outer space. Even the instrumentals are memorable.

With equally sparkling music, the five-song **Continuing Struggle** is delightfully direct, offering engaging random-access autobiographical lyrics as a bonus. The title track begins to recount the band's tangential A&R experience and then trails off; "My Short-Lived Career as a Professional Athlete" skates into a broken leg on the hockey rink; "The Army Song" promotes the draft for personal reasons ("Mandatory conscription would be Adam's friend and be my friend . . . I could take orders from someone other than my older brother"). Mom and Dad Katis get in the act for "145 Old Mill Road" (the family's address in Greenwich); the latter parental unit points out that it's not too late for the brothers to apply for medical school. One hopes they haven't taken his advice.

The Philistines' rhythm section also serves in the not entirely dissimilar Iris, a tighter, rockier quartet led by sweet-voiced singer John Meyer and guitarist Kan Nawaday. (The Katis brothers also play in the hockey-themed Zambonis.) Engineered by Peter Katis, **After School Special** is charming but less whimsical and invigorating than the other band's records. Dynamic bouts of My Bloody Valentine bent-guitar exorcism and a wispy approximation of Haircut One Hundred add character, but the material—some of which is downright delightful—could be more consistent. [i]

SAM PHILLIPS

The Indescribable Wow (Virgin) 1988
Cruel Inventions (Virgin) 1991
Martinis & Bikinis (Virgin) 1994
Omnipop (It's Only a Flesh Wound Lambchop) (Virgin) 1996

LESLIE PHILLIPS

Beyond Saturday Night (Word) 1982
Dancing With Danger (Word) 1985
Black and White in a Grey World (Word) 1986
The Turning (Word) 1987
Recollection (Myrrh) 1987

In the late '80s, fine-voiced singer/songwriter Leslie Phillips turned her back on a successful career as a contemporary Christian artist in order to make more personally fulfilling music under her historically resonant nickname, Sam. (**The Turning** was quite audibly produced by her husband and fellow Christian subversive, T-Bone Burnett; **Beyond Saturday Night** was produced by future Jellyfish associate Jack Joseph Puig. **Recollection** is a smart sampler, with a couple of previously unreleased songs and a home demo.) If Phillips' gospel discs were a cut above the shallow, preachy tracts that dominate that genre, her pop work—produced and occasionally co-written by Burnett—is a revelation, consistently addressing difficult questions rather than offering simplistic answers.

The Indescribable Wow is an impressive if somewhat tentative debut. Most of the songs are thoughtful ballads with ornate, acoustic-based art-pop arrangements, but it's on the album's two rockers, "Holding on to the Earth" and "What You Don't Want to Hear," that Phillips' vision comes across most forcefully. **Cruel Inventions** is more assured and distinctive, both musically and lyrically, with songs like "Go Down," "Raised on Promises" and "Where the Colors Don't Go" effortlessly demonstrating the strength of her vision.

Martinis & Bikinis makes good use of a more driving, psychedelicized sound; with Phillips' strongest lyrics yet, it's her best and bravest effort. The Beatlesque "Baby, I Can't Please You" pointedly addresses doctrinaire fundamentalism in pop terms; "I Need Love," "Circle of Fire," "Strawberry Road" and "Same Rain" all illuminate thorny spiritual issues while showcasing an increasingly incisive melodic ability. [ss]

PHISH

Junta (no label) 1988 (Elektra) 1992
Lawn Boy (Absolute A Go Go) 1990 (Elektra) 1992
A Picture of Nectar (Elektra) 1992
Rift (Elektra) 1993
(Hoist) (Elektra) 1994
A Live One (Elektra) 1995
Billy Breathes (Elektra) 1996

DUDE OF LIFE WITH PHISH

Crimes of the Mind (Elektra) 1994

SURRENDER TO THE AIR

Surrender to the Air (Elektra) 1996

When Jerry Garcia passed away in 1995, the smart money in the New Dead lottery was on Phish—but then it had already been so for those aware of the band. Formed in 1983 at the University of Vermont, the quartet was among the first-born children of the Dead, heavy on improvisation and eclecticism and self-marketed via a grassroots stew of constant touring on the college circuit, a mailing list, hotlines and, later, Internet sites. By the mid-'90s, with practically no airplay, Phish had quietly hooked one of the largest and most devoted followings of any such band.

The Dead tag is both a compliment and an albatross—and not quite fair to Phish. Frank Zappa and Sun Ra are equally valid touchstones for the group. Like them, Phish draws from a broad musical palette (rock, jazz, bluegrass and country, just for a start). Like them, Phish uses clever and sometimes arcane humor as part of the mix. And, like those forebears, Phish's music can be brilliant one moment, ponderous the next. The four musicians truly live to jam; they even practice improvisation via round-robin-style drills. But outside performance settings, Phish can phlounder as easily as it can phloat.

Junta, initially a cassette sold at shows, is a not-ready-for-prime-time event. The musicianship is clearly outstanding: guitarist Trey Anastasio and keyboardist Page McConnell are inventive soloists, while bassist Mike Gordon and drummer Jon Fishman form a supple, versatile rhythm section. Their songwriting skills are not as finely developed at this point, however, and the group resorts to looooong, solo-filled pieces—eleven minutes of "David Bowie," twelve minutes of "Fluff's Travels," more than twenty-five of "Union Federal." **Lawn Boy** is a marked improvement, more cohesive even given the band's tendency to ramble and to favor style (solos) over substance (songs). Nevertheless, there are some good yuks in the title track, "Bathtub Gin" and "Run Like an Antelope." Two particularly strong numbers—"Bouncing Around the Room" and "The Squirming Coil"—have remained concert favorites and appear on the live album.

A Picture of Nectar is Phish's best album, as well as its most varied. It wouldn't be accurate to call them tunesmiths yet, but there's a greater dedication to letting the songs dictate when and where the extended instrumental passages are appropriate, Phish infuses "The Landlady" and "Stash" with samba and other Latin ingredients, takes a cocktail jazz path on "Magilla" and does a bit of country two-stepping on "Poor Heart." But many of the album's best moments come when Phish gets funky, as McConnell's rich organ licks work in tandem with Anastasio's guitar attack on "Llama," "Cavern" and "Guelah Papyrus." **A Picture of Nectar** also contains two versions of "Tweezer"—one funky, the other rocking—which is as close to a signature song as Phish has.

Rift and **(Hoist)** represent two problematic attempts to follow up **A Picture of Nectar**'s progress. Where **Nectar** stayed mostly to one style per song, **Rift** tries to blend them together; the title track, for instance, interweaves country and rock elements. Produced by veteran Muscle Shoals keyboardist Barry Beckett, the album has its highlights—particularly the subtle dynamics employed in "Maze" and "Horn"—but many of the songs are either too cutesy ("Weigh") or too convoluted ("Mound," "It's Ice").

Produced by Paul Fox, **(Hoist)** finds Phish out of water; it's the first album constructed entirely out of newly written material rather than road-tested songs. Consequently, the record feels unusually stiff and mannered, the antithesis of Phish's aesthetic. A handful of numbers stand out—"Julius," "Sample in a Jar," "Scent of a Mule"—and the guest shots from Alison Krauss, Béla Fleck and the Tower of Power Horns add some new sonic dimensions, but the album lacks the material to really make the most of them.

A Live One puts Phish back in its element in all its stretched-out, indulgent glory. Spreading just a dozen songs over two CDs, Phish mixes fan favorites with an equal number of new tracks to make **A Live One** essential even to the tape-traders. "Tweezer" is the album's epic, a thirty-one-minute workout that bounces from the original arrangement into Hendrixy psychedelia, Return to Forever jazz fusion and bits that sound like outtakes from Jethro Tull's **Thick as a Brick.** The album also contains strong renditions of "The Squirming Coil," "Harry Hood" and "Stash"; the standout among the new tunes is "Simple," a strong, winding rocker with appealingly silly lyrics ("We've got a saxophone/'Coz we've got a band/And we've got a saxophone in the band").

Crimes of the Mind is the belated release of a 1991 session with the Dude of Life—singer/songwriter Steve Pollak, a Phish phriend from New York who occasionally pops up at the band's shows. The Dude is given to the same philosophical whimsy as Phish ("Life is a TV show/It should've been canceled long ago"), and the music is a bit tighter than the group's—but only a bit. Surrender to the Air is a horn-powered instrumental ensemble assembled and led by Anastasio; among the players on the partly improvised **Surrender to the Air** are guitarist Marc Ribot, keyboardist John Medeski and Phish drummer Jon Fishman. [gg]

PHOAMING EDISON

See *Fly Ashtray.*

PHRANC

Folksinger (Rhino) 1985 (Island) 1990
I Enjoy Being a Girl (Island) 1989
Positively Phranc (Island) 1991
Goofyfoot EP (Kill Rock Stars) 1995

Hipsters rarely eat their young, but elders are a tastier kettle of worms. Those busy being reborn don't usually find it in their hearts to lend a respectful hand to those who took the giant steps before anyone knew enough to admire them for it. In the mid-'80s, buzz-cut Californian Phranc (Susan Gottlieb) brought lesbian folksinging out of the coffeehouses and near the indie-scene fringes of punk. (As an ex-member of such bands as Nervous Gender and Catholic Discipline—with whom she can be seen performing in *The Decline of Western Civilization,* sporting a Rickenbacker and a porkpie hat—Phranc is a lot more than she appears to be.) At the time, the powers of punk (never mind the rest of music) weren't exactly out searching for new gender markets or ways to unplug rock. But a decade later, with homocore bands and acoustic artists both commonplace and credible, Phranc found a welcoming home among riot grrrls and the estimable Kill Rock Stars label; the perpetuation of her entertaining, illuminating and inclusive career is not just right but natural.

Phranc's first two albums are spirited one-woman topical modern folk. On the debut, she sings about "Female Mudwrestling" and Los Angeles' celebrity coroner, Thomas Noguchi. On **I Enjoy Being a Girl,** white guilt, family, pets, stupid emblem-wearing and a favorite tennis pro all get spinkled with her good-natured ironic wit. The brief **Positively Phranc** intermittently brings tasteful electric accompaniment into the picture while narrowing the lyrical focus to mostly concentrate on romance (a concept that here involves, as it so often does, cars and girls). The AIDS lamentation "Outta Here" is cast as the end of love, while "Hitchcock," co-written with Dave Alvin, uses the director's films to suffer over a woman who resembles Kim Novak (in *Vertigo,* Phranc cleverly notes, "both of her look so much like you"). Upholding her topical responsibilities, Phranc tenderly eulogizes masquerading jazz pianist Billy Tipton and rails against identity strictures (a little late for that one . . .). With typical aplomb, she rewrites Jonathan Richman's "Pablo Picasso" as "Gertrude Stein" ("girls could not resist her stare") and sings Brian Wilson's "Surfer Girl" as a gorgeous a cappella double entendre.

In the summer of 1991, shortly after **Positively**'s release, Phranc's brother was murdered, and her recording career took a back seat to other concerns for several years. She toured a campy Neil Diamond tribute show for a while, and in '94 released a single on KRS. The following year, she made **Goofyfoot,** a spry surfing-obsessed EP with backing from bassist Donna Dresch (Team Dresch), drummer Patty Schemel (Hole) and drummer Tobi Vail (Bikini Kill). The three originals are "Surferdyke Pal," the reverb-splattering beach-twangin' instrumental title track and "Bulldagger Swagger," which was the A-side of the prior 7-inch. Elsewhere, Phranc proves herself a dab hand on ukulele in a nifty cover of "Mrs. Brown You've Got a Lovely Daughter" and a stylish southern crooner on "Ode to Billy Joe." [i]

See also *Bikini Kill, Hole, Kill Sybil, Team Dresch; TPRG.*

PICASSO TRIGGER

Plutonium EP7 (Jettison) 1992
¡Fire in the Hole! (Alias) 1994
T'ain't EP (Alias) 1994
Bipolar Cowboy (Alias) 1995

When Raleigh, North Carolina's Picasso Trigger broke up in 1995, everyone wondered what had taken them so long—fronted by a walking tantrum named Kathy Poindexter, they'd always been a volatile crew, seemingly devoted to pissing off and confusing as many people as possible. The musical core of the band (which was named after Andy Sidaris' boobs-and-bombs action flick) was Lisa Cooper, a cocky left-handed guitarist with a thin but brutal sound and a serious taste for sour barre chords, and bassist Samuel Mintu, whose occasional lead vocals were just this side of a seizure; Picasso Trigger went through more drummers than any band since Spinal Tap.

The quartet is still figuring out what it's doing on the four-song **Plutonium**—and consequently comes as close to indie-rock normalcy as it ever would. (Mintu's "Love Pot 69," however, is menacing, weird and very original). Poindexter's voice is double-tracked and treated to disguise its limitations; by **¡Fire in the Hole!** (produced by Sugar's Dave Barbe), she's starting to catch on that its limitations could also be its strengths. Following the barre chords as her guide to a melody, Poindexter whines, sneers and hollers her way through the album (which includes a rawer rerecording of the earlier single "Valentine") while Cooper, Mintu and drummer Jon McClain grind away behind her. The peak is an over-the-top rant called "Queenie"—when Poindexter screams "one two *fuck you!*" right before the last chorus, she sounds as if she's just come up with it and is very pleased with herself.

The six-song, twelve-minute **T'ain't** is a small breakthrough for the band. Looser, nastier and funnier than before, they blast through pissy little stomps with titles like "Red Headed Retard" and "Lo-Fi Tennessee Mountain Angel." Poindexter cops a major 'tude here, pretending to lose her voice on "Anti'd" and swaggering around with a trumpet on "Kiss Me Where It Counts."

Recorded in three frantic days, **Bipolar Cowboy** is less a final bow than a parting shot (the last song is "Buckshot Goodbyes"). The recording quality is pretty much pure tin, but that only adds to the fun: everybody's feeding back, everybody sounds like they're out of their minds with caffeine and hate, everybody's barging ahead with the song whether the rest of the band is ready or not and *nobody* gives a shit. Mintu gets in his finest vocal moment (the self-explanatory "Riot Girrrls Taste Like Chicken"), Cooper's bizarre guitar parts keep everything off balance (she actually takes a couple of solos) and Poindexter is flat-out rabid, hissing "You can *suck my ass*" ("Serve This") and laying into a "stupid whore" on "City Slut Slander." The perfect album for a really bad mood. [ddw]

JEFFREY LEE PIERCE

See *Gun Club.*

PIGEONHED

See *Brad.*

PIGFACE

Spoon Breakfast EP (Invisible) 1990
Gub (Invisible) 1990
Welcome to Mexico . . . Asshole (Invisible) 1991
Fook (Invisible) 1992
Washingmachine Mouth (Invisible) 1992
Truth Will Out (Invisible) 1993
Notes From Thee Underground (Invisible) 1994
Feels Like Heaven . . . Sounds Like Shit! (Invisible) 1995

BIZARR SEX TRIO

Bizarr Sex Trio EP (Invisible) 1990
Careless Use of Knives EP (Invisible) 1992

LOVE INTEREST

"Bedazzled" (Invisible) 1993

Coventry-born drummer Martin Atkins segued from looking at the back of John Lydon's head in Public Image Ltd. to pursuing a flaky '80s pop-to-hip-hop solo career as Brian Brain. Then he joined Killing Joke and later took to the road with Ministry. The everyone-in-the-pool talent roster Atkins encountered in that last endeavor became the template for Pigface, a floating industrial crap game to which the adopted Chicagoan has devoted himself (and the resources of his Invisible Records label) in the '90s.

Regularly drawing on some of the same co-conspirators but featuring an ever-widening cast of guests, each Pigface release is a recombination lab super-session of intriguing possibilities, voluminous contractual permissions and godawful caterwauling racket. If often a victim of concept over content, Pigface does spew up a thrill or two often enough to make its records more than post-industrial curiosities.

Spoon Breakfast and **Gub** (conveniently combined on the latter's CD issue) announce Atkins and Ministry drummer William Rieflin as the band's nucleus (a partnership that promptly ended); participants include Trent Reznor (Nine Inch Nails), Paul Barker (Ministry), Nivek Ogre (Skinny Puppy), Chris Connelly (Revolting Cocks), En Esch (KMFDM) and David Yow (Jesus Lizard). Steve Albini, who "engineered" this freewheeling calamity, plays guitar, bass and oscillators. For all its unabashed self-indulgent awfulness, the record does contain some promising items, like Reznor's guitar-and-keyboards-free "Suck" and Connelly's song-like "Point Blank" and "Little Sisters" (especially the "Tonight's the Night" remix). Otherwise, Pigface offers lazy, pointless and horribly recorded percussion breakdowns—worse than sitting through a drummer's (no, make that *two* drummers') soundcheck.

Welcome to Mexico . . . Asshole is an atrocious live album that sounds like it was recorded by audience members on broken cassette recorders. (Some **Gub** material is actually damaged in the process.) A version of "Stowaway," a song from Connelly's first solo album, is well played but too crudely recorded to be worth hearing; without Reznor singing, "Suck" does. Two thumbs down.

Fook gets the Pigface juggernaut back to the safety of a studio hangar with a sense of creative mission and a stellar cast: besides Connelly, En Esch and Ogre, there's Andrew Weiss and Chris Haskett from Rollins Band, Flour, Jesus Lizard bassist David Sims, Mary Byker of Gaye Bykers on Acid, Paul Raven of Killing Joke, Lesley Rankine from Silverfish and others. Pigface's first proper effort is an excellent synthesis of ideas and influences; the collaborative songwriting and shifting permutations of players produce everything from harsh industrial charges ("Alles Ist Mine," "Seven Words") and bone-crushing heaviness ("Auto Hag") to sound collages ("Insemination") and dramatic cello-burnished rock restraint ("Ten Ground and Down"). Silverfish's "Hips Tits Lips Power!" (pulled from a song originally entitled "Big Bad Baby Pig Squeal") is potently jizzed up with two bassists, electronic effects and samples. If by no means consistently good, **Fook** is surprisingly cohesive through all the tumult, and an indication that Pigface might not be such a bad idea after all.

Washingmachine Mouth is a sample-heavy remix record that drastically unlaces some of **Fook.** The walloping, distorted "I'm Still Alive," for example, eliminates nearly everything but the titular vocal sample and becomes the light, trancey, traffic-passing "Flowers Are Evil"; other overhauls, like the seven-minute "Satellite—Needle in the Groove (No Damage Done)," are far denser. The seven-track disc also includes a couple of leftovers, like the rocking "Cutting Face."

Truth Will Out is another live album, recorded clearly at two shows in late '92 and early '93 with Genesis P-Orridge (Psychic TV), Ogre, Esch, Weiss, Hope Nicholls (ex–Fetchin Bones, more recently of Sugarsmack) and Jim Marcus (Die Warzau) among the notables. P-Orridge's tape-library contributions provide color, but this incarnation—lacking Connelly and Rankine, for two—hasn't got a suitable vocalist or a strong stylistic director. (It *does,* however, contain an overabundance of seasonal bonhomie and political satire that gets in the way of doing the songs.) Drawing freely from previous work ("Suck" yet again; "7 Words," "Hips, Tits, Lips, Power," "Point Blank"), finding a place in its porcine heart for a brief a cappella "Jingle Bells" and building an entire song around a sample from *Henry: Portrait of a Serial Killer,* Pigface squanders perfectly good recording technology on rarely worth-it performances.

Shonen Knife, Flea, Jello Biafra and Michael Gira (Swans) compose the freshman class on **Notes From Thee Underground,** a P-Orridge–influenced outing that knocks down the industrial walls to explore droney pop ("Chikasaw"), chop-suey funk ("Hagseed"), crazed backwoods rock ("Magazine"), rock-hop ("Fuck It Up") and sample-damaged Led Zeppisms ("Think"). In something of a Brian Brain flashback, Atkins takes a rare vocal turn and plays piano (as well as "orchestra") on the theatrical "Psalm Springs Eternal." Organizing the company's complementary skills track by track, this is easily Pigface's most accessible and rewarding barbecue. Soowee!

Notes From Thee Underground was followed by another remix collection, the truly uneven thirteen-track **Feels Like Heaven.** If you can get past the ringer—a hysterical new recording of Reznor's "Suck" sung with gutless pop conviction by Taime Down (of Faster Pussycat) over ambient psychedelic sitar backing—there are other memories to be either amusingly distorted or stultifyingly repeated. Rankine's "Chikasaw" gets thrice deconstructed (including a loopy hey-where'd-the-song-go? interpolation by Youth); the incalculable overkill of "Steamroller" comes back twice, once covered in electronic blips and mechanoman voices. Among the rest, a few are, if not improvements, at least credible extensions, but too much of **Feels Like Heaven** is tedious and redundant.

Atkins has also occasionally worked solo among samplers and synthesizers as Bizarr Sex Trio. The eponymous five-song debut (originally issued in an edition of seven hundred as a 12-inch with hand-screened covers but subsequently made available on CD and cassette) is typical Chicago industro-dance nonsense: electronic beats, looped found-sound phrases, keyboard strains and random noises. **Careless Use of Knives,** another five tracks stretched over a half-hour, is sillier and more inventive, but comes no closer to having real applicability in any field other than acid-trip stimulation or answering-machine filling. For all the promise of its title, "Your Pregnancy Begins Now" merely hammers home phrases like "Sometimes we need to see a doctor" and "careless use of knives." Oh well.

The Love Interest is a one-off date comprising Atkins, Connelly, Sims and singer Mary Lynn Bowling; "Bedazzled" is a four-mix single of the Dudley Moore composition for the 1968 movie of the same name, given a big beat, a pop vocal and sample seasoning. The basic performance is stylish enough, but it could have been an album track. One version is plenty. [i]

See also *Jello Biafra, Chris Connelly, Dead Voices on Air, Flour, Jesus Lizard, Killing Joke, KMFDM, Ministry, Nine Inch Nails, Revolting Cocks, Rollins Band, Shonen Knife, Silverfish, Skinny Puppy, Sugarsmack.*

PILLBOX (NYC)

Jimbo's Clown Room (Circumstantial) 1993
Pillbox EP10 (Feralette) 1995

MOTORCYCLE BOY

Popsicle (Triple X) 1991

The snarly glam-punk spirit of the Stooges, New York Dolls and Dead Boys lived for a time in the skinnyassed tattooed bodies of Pillbox, a New York quartet that offered a skankier, more menacing and less theatrical alternative to the likeminded and better-known D Generation. In capturing the lost-boys sound and tawdry ambience of their idols without overdoing it, the energetic **Jimbo's Clown Room** drives down a power alley of sharp, memorable songs on twin hotrods, guided by guitarist Ratboy's slithery Johnny Thunders/Steve Jones raunch and ex–39 Steps singer Chris Barry's wavering, whiny conviction. The catchy plea to a drug dealer ("Come Up Heroin") is pitiful *and* obnoxious, but "What She Wants," "Sister Caroline" and the amphetaminized "Nowhereland" wrap the line between inspiration and imitation around history's neck to fine effect.

The Pillbox on the flatly recorded followup EP has a new bassist and a different singer/lyricist. Although he clearly wouldn't have suited the sound of **Jimbo's Clown Room,** the plain-voiced Mark Phelan is also the wrong man for the band's newly slicked-back guitar rock, a poppier and not specifically retro-minded rethink. As Pillbox's sonic architect, Ratboy (Gilbert Avondet) reveals himself capable of writing and playing more complicated and subtle music—the atmospheric drug epic "Red Bag/Blue Bag" dedicates delicate piano, feedback and acres of space to a strongly melodic chorus—but **Pillbox** never latches on to any ideas as immediate or exciting as the album.

Back in Los Angeles, Ratboy was the guitarist in Motorcycle Boy, whose **Popsicle** album was thinly produced by ex-Dolls guitarist Syl Sylvain. Despite the big hair and mascara, the quartet (unrelated to the English band that came out of the Shop Assistants) plays taut, unfancy garage rock and stripped-down punkabilly, offering rudimentary songs like "Honalulu Baby," "Shak n'Bones," "Suicide" and the sax-powered "Swamp Stomp." Despite the titular similarity, **Popsicle**'s "What I Want" and **Clown Room**'s "What She Wants" have nothing in common but desire. [i]

PINHEAD GUNPOWDER

See *Green Day.*

PIPE

See *Small.*

PITCHBLENDE

Kill Atom Smasher (Fistpuppet/Cargo) 1993
Au Jus (Fistpuppet/Cargo) 1994

PITCHBLENDEQUARTET

Gygax! (Headhunter/Cargo) 1996

Part Pavement disciples, part Sonic Youth revisionists and part "math rock," Washington DC's brave Pitchblende peeled off an ambitious debut in the twenty-two-track **Kill Atom Smasher.** Abstract experimental noise fragments—titled by length, for example, "(1:05)" and "(:15)"—break up intense, dissonant songcraft. "Flax," the pick of the litter, is a tumble of jagged propulsion and sly, percussive slinkiness; "Sawed Off City" proves the quartet's knack for wonderfully off-kilter pop; and "Visceral Plane" can't help but call Sonic Youth directly to mind. If much of **Kill Atom Smasher** treads equally familiar turf, it's not just pretentious drivel. Guitarists Treiops Treyfid and A. Justin Chearno twist engaging madness from their instruments, and the record's collage-like qualities make it a rollercoaster listen.

At just eighteen songs, **Au Jus** is more streamlined (eight tracks, however, are "ambient noise," "silence" or spoken-word segues). If **Kill Atom Smasher** is Pitchblende's undergraduate term paper, **Au Jus** is a master's thesis, featuring tighter grooves, a Devo-like strut and better overall songwriting. Relatively straightforward cuts like the snaky "Nine Volt" and the taunt "Karoshi" are a nice foil to the expansive rhythmic complexity of "Cupcake Jones," "Human Lie Detector," "Short Term" and the band's odd guitar tunings.

The nomenclatural alteration on the spine of **Gygax!** appears to be of no significance; the same foursome is responsible for the continued adventures of Pitchblende within. Mapping out a febrile, complex post-punk jazz that doesn't take the self-willed freedom of expression simply as a cue for rampant noisemongery, the group's thoughtful, angular, edgy, sometimes gripping dissertations on rock sound shift in and out of song structure with confident ease and dazzling rhythmic fluidity. The vocals (everyone but Chearno sings) are incidental, except as they distract the group from its instrumental mission. The lyrics, however are indicative and intriguing, especially "Crumbs of Affection" ("love sliced in a pie graph"), "Mercator Projection" ("the cursor stares back, passively blinks"), "Pertaining to the Champ" (a sad biography of Muhammad Ali) and the oblique "Kevorkian." [mww/i]

PITCHFORK

Eucalyptus (Nemesis/Cargo) 1990

This pre–Drive Like Jehu lineup sounds pretty much like what it is—guitarists Rick Fork (né Froberg) and John Reis, with drummer Joey and bassist Nick delivering some formative scree, prepping to take over gosh knows what. Had the members of this unit simply faded into indie oblivion after its four-year (1986–90) existence, **Eucalyptus** might not count for much more than a forgotten blast of adolescent dissonance. But Pitchfork laid major groundwork for the San Diego underground. When the group disbanded, Reis and Froberg yearned to explore uncharted turf; hence the more satisfying, ahead-of-its-time flaying of Drive Like Jehu. On **Eucalyptus,** Froberg's yowling isn't as deranged and developed as in Jehu, but the map is made, and their dual-guitar work holds up well compared with the supersonic mania the two have compiled in their current outfit. [mww]

See also *Rocket From the Crypt.*

PIXIES

Come on Pilgrim (UK 4AD) 1987 (4AD/Rough Trade) 1988 (4AD/Elektra) 1992
Surfer Rosa (4AD/Rough Trade) 1988 (4AD/Elektra) 1992
Doolittle (4AD/Elektra) 1989
Bossanova (4AD/Elektra) 1990
Trompe le Monde (4AD/Elektra) 1991

As the rock underground slouched toward mainstream acceptance in the late '80s—well before the Nirvana earthquake made such baby steps seem trivial—the Pixies fired a much-needed salvo of strident aggression and willful nonconformity across the bow of left-field music. Although the Boston-area quartet became the influential darlings of college radio, the Pixies proved to be less hallowed institution than prep school, readying its two principal figures—singer/guitarist Black Francis and bassist/singer Kim Deal (billed on the early records as Mrs. John Murphy)—for not always bigger and not always better things.

Following neighbors Throwing Muses onto the British 4AD label, the Pixies debuted with the eight-song **Come on Pilgrim,** an anarchic pop explosion of gritty art passion sung and shrieked in English and Spanish over rhythms that race, rest and drift. Steve Albini's production of **Surfer Rosa** gives the Pixies a virulent, slashing guitar sound perfect for songs like "Bone Machine" and Deal's "Gigantic." (The **Surfer Rosa** CD includes **Come on Pilgrim.**)

Doolittle is the apotheosis of the Pixies' art, a tension-filled blend of abrasion and balm that shifts uneasily between the freakout horror of "Debaser," the catchy pop of "Here Comes Your Man," the punky roar of "Crackity Jones," the melodic surf-noise of "Wave of Mutilation" and the unnerving calm of "Monkey Gone to Heaven." Gil Norton's production helps rein in Francis' excessive tendencies (not that he doesn't still manage some merciless shrieking) and harnesses Joey Santiago's guitar to striking effect.

Though also produced by Norton, **Bossanova** is poorly mixed and displays little variety or invention outside the CD booklet's art direction. (The lyrics are especially trivial.) The best tracks—"Velouria," "The Happening," "Blown Away," "Allison"—would have been fine inclusions on **Doolittle** but are inadequate to carry an album by themselves.

The Pixies—sounding more and more like the Black Francis Experience (except on the Deal-sung "The Navajo Know")—relocate their truculent energy but not their capacity for memorable (even dynamic) songwriting on the thin-sounding **Trompe le Monde.** A taut cover of the Jesus and Mary Chain's "Head On" mainly succeeds in calling attention to the material issue. Except for a couple of opaque relationship numbers ("Subbacultcha," "Letter to Memphis"), the gulf between what the band's lyrics evidently concern and what the enigmatic phrases actually convey has never been wider; even what appear to be clear-cut topicals like "U-Mass," "Alec Eiffel" and "The Sad Punk" make only tangential reference to their nominal subjects. The faint traces of stylistic imagination ("Lovely Day" starts off in Motown and winds up among the New York Dolls) only amplify the vacuum where the group's inspiration once burned.

Two albums too late, the Pixies gave up the ghost of a once-glorious career, releasing its members to follow their divergent creative paths. Black Francis inverted his name to Frank Black and went solo; Deal switched to guitar and made a full-time go of her side project, the Breeders. Adopting a lower profile, Joey Santiago and drummer David Lovering formed a new quartet, the Martinis. [i]

See also *Frank Black, Breeders; TPRG.*

PIZZICATO FIVE

Pizzicato Mania (Japan. Non Standard) 1987
Couples (Japan. CBS/Sony) 1987
Bellissima! (Japan. CBS/Sony) 1988
On Her Majesty's Request (Japan. CBS/Sony) 1988
Soft Landing on the Moon (Japan. CBS/Sony) 1990
Hi Guys! Let Me Teach You (Japan. Seven Gods/Columbia) 1991
This Year's Model (Japan. Seven Gods/Columbia) 1991
London-Paris-Tokyo EP (Japan. Seven Gods/Columbia) 1991
Readymade Recordings EP (Japan. Seven Gods/Columbia) 1991
This Year's Girl (Japan. Seven Gods/Columbia) 1991
Sweet Pizzicato Five (Japan. Triad/Columbia) 1992
Pizzicato Free Soul (Japan. Triad/Columbia) 1992
Instant Replay (Japan. Triad/Columbia) 1993
Bossa Nova 2001 (Japan. Triad/Columbia) 1993
Souvenir 2001 (Japan. Triad/Columbia) 1993
Expo 2001 (Japan. Triad/Columbia) 1993
Free Soul 2001 (Japan. Triad/Columbia) 1993
A Television Workshop (Japan. Triad/Columbia) 1994
A Children's Workshop EP [tape] (Japan. Triad/Columbia) 1994
Five by Five EP (Matador) 1994
Made in USA (Triad/Matador) 1994
Overdose (Japan. Triad/Columbia) 1994
Big Hits and Jet Lags 1991–1995 (Japan. Triad/Columbia) 1995
Quickie EP (Matador) 1995
Unzipped EP (Triad/Matador/Atlantic) 1995
The Sound of Music by Pizzicato Five (Triad/Matador/Atlantic) 1995
Romantique '96 (Japan. Triad/Columbia) 1995
Antique '96 (Japan. Sony) 1995
Non Standard Years: Pizzicato Five 1985–1986 (Japan. Non Standard) 1995
A Quiet Couple (Japan. Sony) 1995
Combinaison Spaciale: Pizzicato Five in Dub EP (Japan. Triad/Columbia) 1996
Sister Freedom Tapes EP (Japan. Triad/Columbia) 1996

There is a persistent stereotype in America that Japanese bands simply attempt to replicate American and British pop, and that the charm of the music is in how they get it wrong or unwittingly fall into the culture gap. At first listen, that may seem to be true of Pizzicato Five. But the Tokyo group, which was formed in 1984 by Yasuharu Konishi, a Tokyo college student consumed with '50s, '60s and '70s pop, soul and television theme music, is much more than the sum of its kitschy Western influences. Its songs are rich nuggets of pop-art irony, created in the belief that mass-produced consumables have replaced art and, therefore, art can no longer be a serious pursuit.

Unlike other contemporary Japanese bands that have achieved some notoriety in America (like Shonen Knife), Pizzicato Five are practically superstars at home. And you'd have to scour the globe to find anyone who can challenge the prolific group's productivity, which has yielded nearly two dozen cleverly designed and packaged albums in the first half of the '90s alone. Then there are Konishi's many side projects, including Tokyo's Coolest Combo (lounge instrumentals); Girl Girl Girl (an eclectic trio) and several solo albums, including a mock spaghetti western soundtrack and tribute compilations to Burt Bacharach and Serge Gainsbourg.

Following two singles, "Audrey Hepburn Complex" and "In Action" (collected, along with other early tracks, on **Non Standard Years**) and an electro-pop album, **Pizzicato Mania**, the group made its bow on a surprisingly sophisticated major-label debut. Full of syrupy Bacharach-style arrangements and song titles like "Odd Couple and the Others" and "The Apartment," **Couples** often sounds like the soundtrack to a very corny '70s TV series, complete with tinkling bells, punchy brass and, of course, pizzicato strings. Except for a few words in the chorus of the bossa nova "Magical Connection," the album is sung entirely in Japanese by a soft-voiced male/female tag-team. An instrumental version of the album was later released as **A Quiet Couple; Antique '96** is a collection of the era's odds and ends.

Bellissima! takes a detour to Motown, dedicating the album to Alberto Moravia and Smokey Robinson. Like a Japanese Style Council, the band plays mannered soul music, relying on falsetto harmonies, dinner-jazz rhythm sections, funky basslines, even steel drums to propel its songs. Though all the right ingredients are present and "Temptation Talk" and "World Standard" have their moments, the album is too methodical and mechanical to be effective. The vocals especially sound stiff.

The band returned to form on the fast-paced **On Her Majesty's Request,** jumbling up spy music, mod rock, smoky jazz, synth-pop and sweeping orchestral arrangements. Each of the nineteen songs appropriates something different, from the Simon and Garfunkel parody of "Homesick Blues" to the frenetic chase music of "Feint Operation" to the funky turntable tricks of "Her Majesty au Go Go."

Soft Landing on the Moon unveiled the tactic that makes P5's discography so extensive and confusing: recycling and repetition. The album revisits songs from its three predecessors, updating the material with new arrangements, remixes, vocals by newcomer Maki Nomiya—even a poem or interview excerpt. Temporarily abandoning its string-and-brass lounge-pop, Pizzicato Five relies on '80s-styled synthesizers and drum machines.

With **Hi Guys! Let Me Teach You,** Pizzicato Five launched a series of five records released in consecutive months. Supposedly the soundtrack to a television show, **Hi Guys!** is composed mainly of slick instrumentals, like the hypnotic harmonica-meets-strings groove of "Memories of Schooldays" and the terrific electronic bachelor pad music of "Spacemen on the Schoolyard." As on the band's past recordings, **Hi Guys!** contains spoken-word sections that sound so tantalizing one longs for English translations.

Number two in the series, **This Year's Model,** elevated Nomiya to full band membership; her sweet, spoiled diva vocals and homemade costumes helped Pizzicato Five congeal its ironic retro-pop. With Nomiya writing lyrics in addition to Konishi, the band also increased the amount of Japanese singing and conversation in its songs, making them harder for the linguistically impaired to penetrate. For what it's worth, most are either naïve hippie love songs or material-girl fashion songs, a fusion of selfless '60s idealism and '90s selfishness that adds yet another facetious layer to the band's work.

This Year's Model opens with the freewheeling, fast-paced "Brigitte Bardot T.N.T.," followed by a question-and-answer session in Japanese ("This Year's Girl #1") in which Nomiya is grilled on her likes and dislikes. The following EPs—**London-Paris-Tokyo** and **Readymade Recordings**—contain less distinct versions of the same songs and more Japanese dialogue. At this point, developing into a multi-media performance group, Pizzicato Five began releasing videos, with Nomiya's flamboyant homemade outfits and Konishi's gift for film collages and slogans (like "very famous in Japan" and "beauty is only skin deep") contributing to giddy spectacles that blur the line between tribute and parody.

With Nomiya's voice unifying **This Year's Girl** and dance beats running throughout the record (the fifth in the series), Pizzicato Five sounds for the first time like a band instead of a concept. "Twiggy Twiggy," a blaring song full of samples from *Hawaii Five-O* and Lalo Schifrin soundtracks, could easily fit into a cabaret scene in a James Bond film. The album's highlight, however, is "Baby Love Child," which mixes turntable scratching, soft acoustic guitar, Nomiya's innocent vocals and a melody echoing "I Got You Babe."

Sweet Pizzicato Five pushes the band's tacky love songs closer to disco, with live instruments and '50s/'60s influences fading to the background. Instead, there are stronger, simpler beats, techno keyboards and cheesy choruses (like the Beatles-borrowed "beep-beep, beep-beep, yeah" in "Tout Va Bien"). Though "Catchy" isn't so catchy, most of the album is, particularly "Funky Lovechild," a sitar-enhanced rewrite of "Baby Love Child."

Further conditioning its audience not to expect too much originality from an organization that sees pop as a process of duplication and mass production, Pizzicato Five began what it called a "world series of remixes." **Pizzicato Free Soul,** a double-album available only on vinyl, is a danced-up remix of the entire **Sweet Pizzicato Five.** The rawer live album, **Instant Replay,** is something of a joke, given the group's heavy concert reliance on backing tapes. Though the versions of "Action Painting," "Twiggy Twiggy" and "Brigitte Bardot T.N.T." aren't great, **Instant Replay** is the first Pizzicato Five album on which, in some songs, electric guitar is a dominant presence.

Pizzicato Five outdoes itself with kitsch culture on **Bossa Nova 2001.** Nomiya delivers a "hare hare" chant in the light, bouncy "Hallelujah Hare Krishna," riffs on Sly and the Family Stone's "Dance to the Music" in "Sweet Soul Revue" and adds a "cha-cha-cha" to "Magic Carpet Ride." (As with many Pizzicato Five songs, "Magic Carpet Ride" borrows only its title from an American hit.) Though songs like "Groovy Is My Name" are sickeningly sweet, **Bossa Nova 2001** is a career highlight. The band reaches back to its first records for the Bacharach arrangements without ever losing sight of the dance drive of its later records. It also hits new heights in irony with "Sophisticated Catchy," a song that includes only the lyric "catchy"—repeated often.

Expo 2001 (and its double-album vinyl equivalent, **Free Soul 2001**) also ranks among P5's best, with extended dance remixes of past songs (most from **Sweet Pizzicato Five** and **Bossa Nova 2001**) by Saint Etienne, Towa Tei of Deee-Lite, Telex and others. Though nearly identical, the albums are just different enough to force hardcore collectors to get both. (**Free Soul** has three songs **Expo** doesn't; the CD has one song the vinyl doesn't.)

It must be a lot of work for Pizzicato Five to prove that it can crank out disposable pop the same way Andy Warhol manufactured serigraphs. Though the band's songs sometimes veer towards homogeneity, its musical and production standards and its gift for appropriating cultural styles regardless of popular meaning rarely falter. **A Children's Workshop** EP (the cassette edition of **A Television Workshop**), ostensibly the soundtrack to a Japanese television show (*Ugo Ugo-Ihuga*), features light, jovial dance-pop numbers like "The Night Is Still Young" and Bacharach/David's "Me, Japanese Boy."

For all that, Pizzicato Five was still all but unknown in the United States, but the **Five by Five** EP remedied that. Culled from the band's albums with Nomiya, it includes an "English Mix" of "Baby Love Child" and an English-language version of "This Year's Girl." It's well worth the wait to find out what Nomiya is actually saying in the long, endearing interview: "What food don't you like?" "Food that makes me fat." "What do you wear when you sleep?" "Pajamas."

The Japanese-language version of "This Year's Girl" appears on the band's second American album, **Made in USA,** half of which comes from **Bossa Nova 2001** ("Magic Carpet Ride," "Sweet Soul Revue," "Go Go Dancer," "Peace Music") and the rest from previous P5 albums, with a focus on tracks that include words in English. (Selections from the album, extended and remixed, compose the four-song **Quickie** EP.) As a "greatest-hits" package, the only advantages the Japanese equivalent, **Big Hits and Jet Lags 1991–1995,** has over **Made in USA** are the Pizzicato Five luggage tags included with the album and the adorable "We Love Pizzicato Five" song chanted by American schoolchildren—both evidence of Pizzicato Five's megalomania and global ambitions, prerequisites for any band lampooning the star-making machinery of the '90s.

Pizzicato Five gets even more international on **Overdose,** with vocals in French, a cover photo taken from the Brooklyn Bridge and mastermind Konishi being taught how to say "a new stereophonic sound spectacular" by an American woman. **Overdose** is a lush, slick album that gracefully combines the band's glossy orchestrations with its high-energy disco. In all but a few songs, Pizzicato Five shines with pop polish, particularly in the upbeat dance gem "Happy Sad" and "If I Were a Groupie," with its English and Japanese soundbites of conversations with groupies.

These songs are included on both of Pizzicato's following American releases, the **Unzipped** EP (named after the documentary film about designer Isaac Mizrahi, which incorporates "Happy Sad") and **The Sound of Music by Pizzicato Five.** On both CDs, a running translation of the Japanese "Groupie" soundbites are provided in the right channel of the mix. **The Sound of Music** includes an AmEx-styled plastic fan club card, the Beatles-echoing "We Love Pizzicato Five" chant ("When you're not mean to us we're blue/Oh, P5 we love you"), six more songs from **Bossa Nova 2001** and four from **Overdose.** In addition, there's an English remake of **Sweet Pizzicato Five**'s house-music love song to a disc jockey, "CDJ," but, tellingly, the American vocalist is unable to capture Nomiya's pampered sense of detachment. [ns]

PLAGAL GRIND

See *Alastair Galbraith.*

PLAINFIELD

See *Jello Biafra.*

PLASTIC ONO BAND

See *Yoko Ono.*

PLASTIC THEATRE ART BAND

Live at Luna Park (Plastic Echo) 1995

In 1966, young trumpeter Tommy Peltier cut an LP (recently reissued) of his compositions as leader of the Jazz Corps, which at the time featured multi-reed jazz titan Roland Kirk. Nearly thirty years later, Peltier reinvented himself as an elfin singer/songwriter/synth-guitarist . . . and it works, with an oddly dignified grandiosity, counterpoising airy-fairy songs about "Angel Feathers" with earthy images of Louisiana. Blending precious pop, classical, jazz, New Orleans R&B and a dollop of gospel, Peltier's leaps from arch (almost British-sounding) baritone to startling falsetto are matched with Lynn Fanelli's more conventional (but darned soulful) warbling, propelled/embellished by Peltier's quasi-orchestral (if somewhat undermixed) synth-guitar, Louie Spears' stand-up bass (plucked and bowed) and Timm Boatman's percussion (more evocative than many a full set of traps). [jg]

PLASTIKMAN

Sheet One (NovaMute) 1993
Recycled Plastik EP (NovaMute) 1993
Musik (NovaMute) 1994

Windsor, Ontario, native Richie Hawtin, aka Plastikman, got his start DJing in such Detroit clubs as the Shelter and the Music Institute. Influenced equally by local hardcore, ambient and house, the sound of Plastikman is that of acid-house's most sparse intensity, and it's just as effective on an early-morning dancefloor as it is on a couch. Certainly aware that the best dance music is the kind that shakes your ass as well as your brainpan, Hawtin's style blends mindless bleeps and grooves with a depth and thoughtfulness that eclipses the majority of his faceless counterparts. As a writer, remixer and producer, Hawtin's style has infected dozens of artists, from Lords of Acid and Kenny Larkin to LFO and Robotman.

Containing such tracks as "Plasticity" and "Smak," **Sheet One**—Hawtin's debut as Plastikman—is decidedly ambient in texture, and the perforated blotter-sheet cover art provides a clear intimation of the record's utility. Still, "Helikopter" ups the ante with mind-numbing beats that require no pharmacological assistance to be effective. The four-track **Recycled Plastik** reprises two non-album singles ("Krakpot," "Spastik"), adding the otherwise unreleased "Spaz" and "Naturalistik."

Musik finds Hawtin's trademark TB-303 in a remarkably different frame of mind, largely abandoning by-the-book techno in favor of expansive, groove-heavy jams that, at times ("Konception," "Ethnik") border on the beautiful. As Hawtin points out in the liner notes, "just because you like chocolate cake doesn't mean you eat it every day," and **Musik** finds the auteur extensively updating his menu. There are typical minimalist thumps ("Fuk") and serious hardcore numbers ("Goo"), but on the mindblowing "Plastique" and the undeniably funky "Marbles," it's apparent that Hawtin, having helped create the beast that is acid-house, is ready to move on to more challenging experiments.

Also in Hawtin's extensive catalogue are Plastikman singles and remix discs, plus records as FUSE, States of Mind and Cybersonik, many of them released on the Plus8 label he operates with sometime musical collaborator John Acquaviva. [jf]

PLEASURE BARONS

See *Mojo Nixon.*

PMD

See *EPMD.*

P.M. DAWN

Of the Heart, of the Soul and of the Cross: The Utopian Experience (Gee Street/Island) 1991
The Bliss Album . . . ? (Vibrations of Love and Anger and the Ponderance of Life and Existence) (Gee Street/Island) 1993
Jesus Wept (Gee Street/Island)1995

Although Jersey City, New Jersey's P.M. Dawn arrived on a trancey pop carpet of soft-spoken rap, the duo quickly shook off the constraints of any particular musical style and made itself sui generis. While they initially shared a less aggressive attitude and knowledge of history with Arrested Development, the Cordes brothers—Attrell (aka Prince Be, aka the Nocturnal, aka Reasons) and Jarrett (aka DJ Minutemix, aka J.C./The Eternal)—have always been about forging dreamier, lusher grooves. With Brian Wilson, the Beatles and jazz in the mix and a grandiose spiritual sense unmatched since the days when Prince was Prince, P.M. Dawn plies a sound that has its head in the clouds and its feet planted firmly on the dancefloor.

Of the group's first three albums, **Of the Heart, of the Soul and of the Cross** sticks the closest to rap's fundamentals, yet still contains enough surprises and new ideas to announce a unique post–hip-hop style. Intricate backing vocals and psychedelic instrumentals set a luxurious table for Prince Be's gently proffered introspection. "Reality Used to Be a Friend of Mine" drifts away on a cloud of sanguine confidence, yet real life—and the afterlife—remain a source of concern. In "Even After I Die," an insecure love letter to his father, Be admits, "I think I'll still be scared even after I die." Recorded in England (where the group was originally signed and found its initial success) and mixed by Killing Joke bassist-cum-ambient-producer Youth, the album quotes the Beatles' "Baby You're a Rich Man" and fields an eclectic array of samples—from Hugh Masekela to the Doobie Brothers to Spandau Ballet's sappy "True," the basis of P.M. Dawn's ethereal "Set Adrift on Memory Bliss."

The Bliss Album . . . ? is as expansive as its full title, **Vibrations of Love and Anger and the Ponderance of Life and Existence.** The fleet-tongued "Plastic" sums up the anger (which appears to be inspired by Be's onstage altercation with KRS-One); "Filthy Rich (I Don't Wanna Be)" and "When Midnight Sighs" do ponder life and existence, while "To Love Me More," "More Than Likely" (with guest vocals by Boy George) and "I'd Die Without You" address love in a style that could easily fit in on albums like **Abbey Road** or **Sexual Healing.** Among the album's other intriguing appointments are a cover of the Beatles' "Norwegian Wood (This Bird Has Flown)" and samples of George Michael and Joni Mitchell.

P.M. Dawn discards any remaining vestiges of rap on **Jesus Wept,** an album on which the personal, the political and the religious are intertwined into a rich musical reverie. The record ends with an ecstatic medley entitled "Fantasia's Confidential Ghetto," a place where Prince ("1999"), Talking Heads ("Once in a Lifetime") and Harry Nilsson ("Coconut") not only coexist but sound wonderful together—as close to a musical definition of utopia as you'd want to hear. [sm]

P'O

See *Wire.*

POE

Hello (Modern/Atlantic) 1995

Armed with quirky, smart lyrics and a light, rising voice punched up from the Edie Brickell vending machine, New-York-to-LA (by way of the world) singer/songwriter Poe runs through a garish wardrobe of styles on her promising but not exactly good debut, which is au courant enough to use a disconnected modem as a human metaphor. Aided by eight songwriting partners and three producers, she strides purposefully through atmospheric club pop ("Hello" and "Another World"), continental glitz ("Fingertips"), scraggly guitar funk-rock ("Choking the Cherry"), string bass chamber pop ("That Day"), mainstream gloss ("Angry Johnny"), piano balladry ("Fly Away") and acoustic guitar simplicity ("Beautiful Girl"). In the album's most striking song, Poe describes a run-in with a motorpsycho nightmare in "Trigger Happy Jack (Drive by a Go-Go)." Poe has enough personality to keep the pleasant and occasionally intriguing album her own, but not enough to make it a strong statement. [i]

POGUES

Red Roses for Me (UK Stiff) 1984 (Stiff/Enigma) 1986
Rum Sodomy & the Lash (Stiff/MCA) 1985
Poguetry in Motion EP (Stiff/MCA) 1986
If I Should Fall From Grace With God (Island) 1988
Peace and Love (Island) 1989
Hell's Ditch (Island) 1990
Essential Pogues (Island) 1991
The Best of the Pogues (UK Warner Music) 1991
The Rest of the Best (UK Warner Music) 1992
Waiting for Herb (Chameleon/Elektra) 1993 (Elektra) 1993
Pogue Mahone (UK Warner Music) 1995 (Mesa) 1996

NICK CAVE & SHANE MACGOWAN

"What a Wonderful World" (Mute/Elektra) 1992

SHANE MACGOWAN AND THE POPES

The Snake (UK ZTT) 1994 (ZTT/Warner Bros.) 1995

VARIOUS ARTISTS

Straight to Hell (Hell/Enigma) 1987

As the Anglo-Irish octet's singer, colorful public persona and primary songwriter, Shane MacGowan was always the man to see about the Pogues, from the band's early days as punk's idea of an Irish folk group through its adventurous maturity as lusty world music dilettantes. But alcohol and other bad habits made MacGowan increasingly erratic, and for a while the London-based band's figurehead threatened to plow its prow into a figurative, if not a literal, tree.

The Pogues managed to make five albums—none of which are bad, and two of which (**If I Should Fall from Grace With God** and **Peace and Love**) are extraordinary examples of literate traditionalism feeding contemporary invention—before taking the gutsy cure-or-die (for both bodies) step of chucking MacGowan out in the fall of 1991, replacing him for road work with ex-Clashman Joe Strummer, the producer of **Hell's Ditch.** (For his part, MacGowan claimed to have left under his own power, dubiously complaining the group had grown too progressive.) While the Pogues figured out how to proceed, the band's label bought some woodshedding time by releasing two British compilations and the American **Essential Pogues,** a fair dozen tracks from the preceding three albums augmented by the long version of "Yeah, Yeah, Yeah, Yeah, Yeah" and a cover of the Stones' "Honky Tonk Women." Both of those songs are also on the not-entirely-bottom-scraping **Rest of the Best,** along with fourteen more, from the first album's "Dark Streets of London" to the high points of **Hell's Ditch,** "The Sunnyside of the Street" and "Summer in Siam." **Essential** has some overlap with the more consistent fourteen-song **Best of the Pogues,** but not as much as might be imagined: "Fairytale of New York" (which features Kirsty MacColl), "Misty Morning, Albert Bridge" and a few others.

As MacGowan sloped pitifully around the perimeter of a career, managing little more than a duet on "What a Wonderful World" with Nick Cave (the three-song CD single also packs Nick's version of Shane's "Rainy Night in Soho" and *his* take on Cave's "Lucy"), the courageous but chastened Pogues returned to action. **Waiting for Herb,** a modest back-to-the-roots record that could have been much worse, unveils tin whistler and occasional vocalist Spider Stacy as the band's new singer. (As if to reinforce the choice's inexorable logic, bouzouki/concertina/cittern/mandolin player Terry Woods wraps *his* ungainly voice around "Haunting" early on. 'Nuff sung.) Had MacGowan still been at the helm, the album's diffident stylistic retrenchment and lyrical tepidity would have been seen as a creative collapse; without him, **Waiting for Herb** introduces a corporeal ghost of the band that does its memory no serious harm. After Stacy's "Tuesday Morning" and accordionist James Fearnley's "Drunken Boat," guitarist/banjo player Jem Finer contributes the record's best songs ("Smell of Petroleum," "Once Upon a Time," the collaborative "Sitting on Top of the World"), but nothing here has the fervid imagination or riveting poetic imagery of MacGowan's finest worksongs.

The second post-Shane album is a bit more troublesome. The septet's membership has even less in common with the old band: Stacy, Finer and the rhythm section of Andrew Ranken and Darryl Hunt (who replaced founding bassist Cait O'Riordan after she ran off with Elvis Costello, the producer of the band's second LP) are the only holdovers from **Herb,** joined by newcomers in the slots left by James Fearnley (off to join the Low & Sweet Orchestra), Terry Woods (a solo career) and Phil Chevron (illness). A resultant shortage of songs that are more than workably agreeable and a complete lack of edge in their performances leaves the harmless album sounding like the work of a skilled and spirited but bog-ordinary Irish pub band (never more so than in the fine but inexplicable cover of Bob Dylan's "When the Ship Comes In"). That makes the LP title seem doubly unwarranted, as Pogue Mahone (Gaelic for "kiss my ass") was the rude name for a defiant band that shortened it to the Pogues. This **Pogue Mahone** goes down without a fight or a sneer.

Back in the MacGowan camp, the man who was in no shape to make a Pogues record managed to pull his own out of a hat as if by wizardry. Decorated with depressing photos of the dental disaster in various poses of appalling dissipation (including one where the flame of his lighter hovers a half-inch to the left of the cigarette he's attempting to light), **The Snake** introduces the enfeebled star's ironically named sextet, a rock-oriented outfit that can also mix up a convincing Gaelic-flavored bustle. The Pogues never invoked the memory of Mott the Hoople (with a nod to the Clash) the way this lot does on "Victoria," but on traditional ballads like "Roddy McCorley," "Nancy Whiskey" and "The Rising of the Moon," the Popes reclaim enough of the older band's sound for the transition to hardly matter. (Of course, the lengthy list of guests, which runs from Johnny Depp to members of the Pogues and Dubliners, might have something to do with the Popes' evident stylistic breadth.) Anything **The Snake** gives up in the way of subtlety or stylistic invention it more than gets back in the consistent excellence of MacGowan's songwriting, which is as sweeping, foul and fully realized as anything in the Pogues catalogue. The profanity of "Donegal Express" sounds as natural as breathing, but so does the cinematic fable of "A Mexican Funeral in Paris," which MacGowan growls against crisp horn blares. "That Woman's Got Me Drinking" is a careening doozy on an all-too-familiar theme, but the touchingly sincere "The Song With No Name" is a gorgeous pledge of romantic troth and "Haunted" is a campy but seductive Sonny and Cher duet with Sinéad O'Connor. **The Snake** is a shockingly good record from a cat with nine lives. [i]

See also *Circle Jerks; TPRG.*

POI DOG PONDERING

Poi Dog Pondering EP (Texas Hotel) 1988
Circle Around the Sun EP (Texas Hotel) 1989
Poi Dog Pondering (Texas Hotel/Columbia) 1989
Wishing Like a Mountain and Thinking Like the Sea (Texas Hotel/Columbia) 1990
Fruitless EP (Texas Hotel/Columbia) 1990
Jack Ass Ginger EP (Texas Hotel/Columbia) 1991
Volo Volo (Columbia) 1992
Pomegranate (Pomegranate) 1995 (Pomegranate/Bar/None) 1995
Electrique Plummagram (Platetectonic/Bar/None) 1996

PALM FABRIC ORCHESTRA

Vague Gropings in the Slipstream (Carrot Top) 1994

Sometimes, being poised on the verge of success can be the most enlightening—and embittering—place for a rock band. For Poi Dog Pondering, the large and amorphous Chicago-via-Austin (but originally from Waikiki) ensemble led by singer/guitarist Frank Orrall, that's one place they are unlikely to either be willing or welcome to visit again. On the strength of two breezy, folk-tinged debut EPs, Poi Dog was snatched from its road-happy ways (the group's early touring schedule of North America puts the comparatively lazy antics of Phish to shame) and enlisted by the Major Label to make some Alternative Music. (If only they had come along a few years later and been able to take advantage of the rise of neo-hippiedom.) After Columbia repackaged the two EPs together as the band's eponymous full-length debut, Poi Dog set about making a proper album. Whether owing to Orrall's faulty effort or to the blinding glare of impending stardom, **Wishing Like a Mountain and Thinking Like the Sea** betrays the band's whimsically beautiful music with a slick, hippified mélange of overarching "global musics" and dry, by-the-book folk. Gone, for the most part, is Poi Dog's gleefully reckless musical abandon, replaced with a studied effort to solidify a sound. The **Fruitless** EP (two live tracks, a **Wishing** remix and studio covers of Canned Heat, New Order and Roky Erickson), **Jack**

Ass Ginger (two edits of the titular preview of the forthcoming album, a collaboration with the Dirty Dozen Brass Band and two more non-LP tunes) and **Volo Volo** (which bears an occasional disconcerting resemblance to smart UK popsters like the Smiths, Wedding Present and Waterboys) continue the sad trend. When it was all over, the presumption was that this extraordinarily promising group had come to an end.

Despite appearances, Poi Dog didn't simply disappear after **Volo Volo.** Relocating to Chicago in 1992, Orrall enforced a creative hiatus on the band; meanwhile, he put together his funkily exotic Palm Fabric Orchestra's **Vague Gropings in the Slipstream,** a masterpiece of instrumental nonchalance. Violinist Susan Voelz took the time to record the first of her two stunning solo albums.

The hiatus proved worthwhile, for when Poi Dog reemerged in 1995 with **Pomegranate,** the band had not only gotten better, but had also become more conscious of its original intentions. A collection of groovy, danceable numbers propelled by Orrall's dramatic voice and overly poetic lyricism, **Pomegranate** manages to recapture both the fun-loving spirit and accomplished musicianship that made Poi Dog such a delight at the start. **Electrique Plummagram** takes Poi Dog cross-culturing further down a Chicago dance alley, offering clubby remixes of three **Pomegranate** songs and four new tracks, including a version of Frankie Knuckles' "Hard Sometimes." [jf]

See also *Susan Voelz; TPRG.*

POISON IDEA

Pick Your King EP (Fatal Erection) 1983 (Taang!) 1992
Record Collectors Are Pretentious Assholes EP (Fatal Erection) 1985 (Taang!) 1992
Kings of Punk (Pusmort) 1986 (Taang!) 1992
War All the Time (Alchemy) 1987 (Tim/Kerr) 1994
Filthkick EP (Shitfool) 1988
Darby Crash Rides Again EP (American Leather) 1989
Ian MacKaye EP (In Your Face) 1989
Feel the Darkness (American Leather) 1990 (Tim/Kerr) 1994
Official Bootleg EP (American Leather) 1991
Live in Vienna EP (American Leather) 1991
Dutch Courage (Bitzcore) 1991
Blank Blackout Vacant (Taang!) 1992
Pajama Party (Tim/Kerr) 1993
We Must Burn (Tim/Kerr) 1993
Religion & Politics Parts 1 & 2 EP (Tim/Kerr) 1994
Your Choice Live Series (Ger. Your Choice) 1994
The Early Years (Tim/Kerr) 1994
Dysfunctional Songs for Co-Dependent Addicts (Tim/Kerr) 1994
Pig's Last Stand (Sub Pop) 1996

JEFF DAHL AND POISON IDEA

Jeff Dahl . . . Poison Idea (Triple X) 1993

It's easy to self-destruct in a hurry—the sheer number of live-fast/die-young bozos can attest to that. But to really experience nihilism seriously and sink into the innermost circle of hell through the quicksand one mouthful at a time . . . now *that* takes guts. If any band stands as testament to such temerity, it's Poison Idea. The Portland, Oregon, quartet maintained an appetite for self-destruction—by means of drugs, alcohol and a dietary intake that elevated the mean weight of band members well past the three-hundred-pound mark—for a decade and a half, making sure to suckerpunch any arbiter of good sense on its way down.

When Poison Idea formed, the band espoused relatively traditional hardcore values: the main goal was to cause, as the title of a later album put it, war all the time. The earliest material is available on **The Early Years,** a twenty-two-track CD of singles and the like, which features three separate—and equally invigorating—versions of the anthem "This Thing Called Progress."

Pick Your King, wrapped in an appropriately sacrilegious sleeve, positioned the foursome as true keepers of the faith, what with guitarist Tom Roberts' Angeleno-styled ampheta-strum attack (especially reckless on "Cult Band" and "Castration") and the blink-and-you-missed-it jimmying of thirteen songs into just over fifteen minutes. If there's anything they *don't* hate, you wouldn't know it from listening to this. **Record Collectors Are Pretentious Assholes** backs off from that extremism long enough for frontman Jerry A. to profess his undying love for what made Milwaukee famous on "A.A.," (which closes with an entirely believable salutation "trembling hands / bloodshot eyes / propose a toast to my demise"). While most of the group's peers are lucid long enough that you can imagine them handling day jobs, the blind rage of songs like "Die on Your Knees" and "Don't Like It Here" (wherein Jerry views making it to the toilet as a victory in itself) is as formidable as pre-domestication Iggy.

By the time **Kings of Punk** was released in 1986, Roberts had rechristened himself Pig Champion—a fitting moniker, since he had ballooned over the 450-pound mark—and the band's psyche had grown considerably uglier. The cover photo of Jerry A., his chest still bleeding from the band's logo he'd gouged with a razor blade, is a mighty compelling measure of the local barometric pressure. Drawn out to conventional lengths, songs like "God Not God" and the pro-death missive "Subtract" are even more discomfiting than the sixty-second explosions of yore—the elongation makes their sincerity all the more graphic. **War All the Time** weighs down (no pun intended) the band's sound with more conventional metal dynamics, from the incredibly monolithic drumming of new recruit Thee Slayer Hippy and the thick rhythm riffing of second guitarist Eric "Vegetable" Olsen. The viscera you feel may be your own—being pulled straight through your ribcage on "Romantic Self-Destruction" (a scumbag's-eye-view of the absurdity of that juxtaposition) and the pro-death (what, again?!) "Push the Button." This is truly the sound of cockroaches ruling the earth after mankind's demise.

Darby Crash Rides Again (which pays loving tribute to the Germs' deceased frontman) and **Ian MacKaye** (which treats the Fugazi guitarist to a venom bath that's every bit as sincere) are two sides of the same coin, replete with a herald of a forthcoming "Drug Revival" and a rather touching transsexual appreciation ("Ballad of a Pre-Op"). While the band's needs are, shall we say, basic, Jerry A. is surprisingly articulate within the limited contexts. The increasingly locked-in rhythm section—Myrtle Tickner (a male) had joined on bass—feed the plague ever more effectively. That's particularly explicit in a live setting—as evidenced by the half-dozen in-concert bonus tracks appended to **Ian MacKaye** when it was reissued as **Dysfunctional Songs for Co-Dependent Addicts.**

Although Poison Idea had begun to chase its own tail, **Feel the Darkness** demonstrates that the band was willing to bite down—hard—when it caught that pesky appendage in its teeth. Jerry's forthright self-loathing breaks the surface of Champion's riffstreams with unsettling precision on "Gone for Good" and "Death of an Idiot Blues." His eyes-rolled-back onslaught even gives "The Badge" (perhaps the most chilling cop-killing missive this side of Compton) a sense of authenticity. **Dutch Courage,** recorded live in Europe, oozes a downright bizarre mixture of professionalism and contempt. Champion and new partner Mondo are capable of stop-on-a-dime time changes (see songs like "Plastic Bomb" and "Getting the Fear"), but the hate-hate crowd relationship is reminiscent of that evidenced on the Stooges' **Metallic K.O.,** peaking on an incendiary rendition of "Hangover Heartattack" which extols the idea of cholesterol death.

Blank Blackout Vacant (which, in typically explicit fashion, adorns its sleeve with a dictionary definition of "nihilism") wastes no time in adding its own variations for Webster's delectation. "Icepicks at Dawn" (with sampled fistfight sound effects) and "Smack Attack" are prototypical PI rants, but there's evidence of some technical progression: "Star of Baghdad" is shot through with aggro-surf guitar soloing, and a cover of "Vietnamese Baby" struts with the glammy cheekiness of the New York Dolls' original.

The awesome **Pajama Party** confirms the band's ability to pass for a party band on a River Styx cruise line. Its thirteen covers—culled mostly from singles and compilations—range from the faithful (the Damned's "New Rose") to the unrecognizable (Jimmy Cliff's "The Harder They Come") and from the ridiculous (the Go-Go's' "We Got the Beat") to the sublime (the MC5's "Kick Out the Jams"). In a related vein, the joint mini-album with Jeff Dahl includes the collaboration's two-cover tribute to the late Stiv Bator(s) and three of PI's own tunes as well as some of Dahl's.

The six-song **Religion & Politics** begins with nearly a minute of acoustic guitar picking—and if that's not scary enough, the title track actually suggests there might be some point to life after all. That kind of abstract progression didn't bode well: Champion split soon thereafter, and the four-piece that recorded the European live album (as per Your Choice's policy, part of its royalties were donated to an animal-rights organization) simply had no spark at all. Poison Idea broke up in 1994. [dss]

See also *Jeff Dahl.*

POLARA

See *27 Various.*

POLVO

Can I Ride EP7 (Kitchen Puff) 1991
Cor-Crane Secret (Merge) 1992
Today's Active Lifestyles (Merge) 1993
Celebrate the New Dark Age (Merge) 1994
This Eclipse EP (Merge) 1995
Exploded Drawing (Touch and Go) 1996

Practitioners of a particularly slide-rule-dependent brand of modern-day prog-rock, this North Carolinian quartet can, depending on one's point of view, hypnotize or anesthetize. Polvo's lengthy, enigmatic songs have far more in common with Gentle Giant and ELP (on a budget, of course) than anything contemporary, and its disavowal of hooks is all but complete. Of course, to tech-heads and those of a cerebral orientation, those traits are nothing to grouse about.

After a self-released double-7-inch, the Chapel Hill denizens recorded **Cor-Crane Secret,** a debut that quickly laid down the clinical gauntlet. The opening "Vibracobra" buries a provocative, vaguely Middle Eastern guitar line beneath an oscillating storm of chord changes; "Kalgon" simply removes the former element, leaving guitarists Ash Bowie and Dave Brylawski to see-saw madly without progressing so much as an inch. Bowie's unsteady vocals are generally submerged, but the unusually clear-cut "Can I Ride" reveals that decision to be a good one.

Today's Active Lifestyles furthers Polvo's search for the lost chord, and you have to give the band credit for running through just about every permutation a fretboard has to offer. Trouble is, the arrangements seem almost random. "Thermal Treasure" splinters under the pressure applied by its stop-start structure. Placed in the pole position, the evidently angry song (mutterings about the misdeeds of some unnamed "motherfucker" are occasionally audible) sets the album's tone. The detuned and woozy "Lazy Comet" has some seductive powers, but the band's overweening interest in flexing its instrumental muscle soon breaks the spell.

The energy level is a bit higher on the seven-song **Celebrate the New Dark Age,** but Bowie and Brylawski still noodle with virtually absolute tunnel vision. The fact that both concentrate on fractured chord disseminations ("progressions" is a bit too linear a description) rather than offer up any tangible leads can create a sort of eustachial whiplash, as evinced by the ornate "Fractured (Like Chandeliers)." The band is beginning to show flashes of proficiency at structuring songs, however. The throbbing "City Spirit" pushes Steve Popson's bass to the fore, underscoring the tension between Bowie's watery vocal and Eastern guitar tone. That a similarly Asian tone imbues "Solitary Set" and "Old Lystra" is more consistency than one usually expects from these guys. (The mini-album was issued, besides CD and cassette, as a double 7-inch.)

With Bowie moonlighting on bass in Helium, the five-song **This Eclipse** reclaims form(lessness) to a large degree, but benefits from the clearest production—by Brian Paulson—Polvo has ever received. The separation afforded the guitarists' never-twining parts lends some logic to "Batradar" and "Titanup," but it's hard not to ruminate about what the band might be capable of if someone made them walk a straight line just once.

No such intercession is forthcoming on the sprawling **Exploded Drawing,** but Polvo does make a few minor modifications to its sound—such as parting the sonic curtain enough to allow Eddie Watkins' tom-tom-heavy drumming to carry songs like "Fast Canoe." But even though Polvo has grown more adept at translating its work for the mathematically impaired, the band's guitar calculus hasn't acquired the slightest degree of warmth. [dss]

See also *Helium.*

POLYGON WINDOW

See *Aphex Twin.*

POND

Pond (Sub Pop) 1993
The Practice of Joy Before Death (Sub Pop) 1995

Shortly after Seattle first *happened,* the Oregon city three hours to the south—where the Wipers, Poison Idea and Dead Moon had been knocking about in honorable obscurity for years—began to produce a fresh crop of its own bands. Portland's class of '92 included Sprinkler, Heatmiser, Hazel and Pond. The fledgling Pond's Charlie Campbell (guitars/vocals) and Chris Brady (bass/vocals) were really from Juneau—they ended up in Portland because Alaska's liquor laws kept the underage Campbell from playing in bars. A year after arriving, they plucked drummer Dave Triebwasser from the ashes of Thrillhammer and began to polish their pop act. Spotted opening for (and recommended by) Sprinkler, they were signed to Sub Pop after a '92 7-inch.

Pond was rather more of a pop band than Seattle's grunge label was then known for. **Pond** is an unusually polished debut, which begins with the sprightly drone of "Young Splendor" and moves easily along to songs like "Agatha" (about being a scared child) and "Foamy," about a messianic hooker. In part, the record owes its sound to the production by Jonathan Auer of the Posies; still, the songs revel in a post-punk pop glory, and carry a guarded exuberance.

The Practice of Joy Before Death is a less certain undertaking. Largely repudiating pop, the trio promote Adam Kaspar from engineer to producer and head toward the emo-core of bands like Polvo and Sunny Day Real Estate. The songs aren't so much *about* things as they are about a stumbling expression of feelings. Which unfortunately means they're less about being *songs.* [ga]

PONTIAC BROTHERS

See *Liquor Giants.*

PONY

14" EP7 (Ah.Um Fidelity) 1993
Cosmovalidator (Homestead) 1994

During its short lifespan, Pony showed lots of potential. Plainly enamored of the dissonant force of punk, the New York trio had some good songs and a charismatic (if somewhat somber) frontman in Dallas Crowe. On the right night, Pony was magnificent live. All the band lacked was the cohesion that would allow its contradictory impulses to co-exist. The down-to-earth concerns of drummer Jimmy James and bassist M. Kitty Dubois clashed with Crowe's art-rock pretensions. Onstage, not only did the threesome rarely look at each other, they always seemed on the verge of a fight.

The four-song **14"** (a double 7-inch) barely hints at the band's power. Badly recorded, with muffled, demo-like sound, the record has only songwriting to set it apart. Like many bands formed in the wake of Nirvana, Pony built on the soft verse/loud chorus paradigm, but added a terse angularity reminiscent of Wire or the Minutemen in off-kilter structures influenced by The Scene Is Now and Mission of Burma. In the tradition of the Replacements and Pavement, Pony's best songs concern the travails of being an "alternative" band. "Driving Ms. Danger," which describes a couple's move to New York, starts with a throttled guitar riff, then changes vocalist and narrator as it moves into an all-out attack; in "Michael," a descending chord change leads into an arcing, pleading vocal line. Both songs show up on **Cosmovalidator,** but are overshadowed by the brooding "Prizefighter," which starts out like Wire but ends in a flurry of noisy guitar, and the thrashy, shadowy "Grand Hotel."

Pony broke up in late 1994. Crowe moved to Seattle, while James and Dubois have been performing and releasing singles under the Speed King name. [sm]

POOH STICKS

Alan McGee EP (UK Fierce) 1988
The Pooh Sticks EP (UK Fierce) 1988
Orgasm (UK 53rd & 3rd) 1988
Multiple Orgasm (UK Fierce) 1989
Trade Mark of Quality (UK Fierce) 1989
Formula One Generation (Sympathy for the Record Industry) 1990
The Pooh Sticks (UK Overground) 1991
The Great White Wonder (Sweet Virginia/Sympathy for the Record Industry) 1991 (Fierce/Zoo) 1992
Million Seller (Zoo) 1993
Optimistic Fool (Seed) 1995

Less a group than a garishly mounted but sublimely subversive pop put-on, Wales' Pooh Sticks—formed in Swansea in 1987 by Steve Gregory (manager, songwriter, producer, Fierce label owner and all-around string-puller) and singer Hue Williams—have fashioned an amazing career in '70s camp with equal measures of deadpan parody and ingeniously derivative craft. Whipped into a mysteriously fictional froth of cartoon characters, make-believe history and, in the early days, bizarrely configured record releases, the group is like the Archies in reverse, a false front created to carry out the schemes of those responsible, not to further an illusion in which the creators don't matter. As high-concept rock'n'roll swindlers, the Pooh Sticks are an impressively sustained contrivance. Andy Kaufman would have been proud.

Using anonymous pickup musicians, stealing song titles and taking teen-obsessed lyrical potshots at the indie-pop world and the Frampton years, the group has managed to package delightful bubblegum that can be taken on very different levels: as irony-dripping kitsch, witty cultural comment, plagiarized rubbish or just pure pop fun. This highly amusing joke with no punchline proves only that none was needed.

Alan McGee is a boxed set of one-sided singles, four songs from which subsequently turned up on 1988's **Pooh Sticks,** a one-sided 12-inch. (The flipside contains scratched-on stick figures.) After that came a deluge of singles, picture discs and flexis on Gregory's unpredictable Fierce label. (Among the company's most extraordinary vinyl achievements is **Riot!,** a 7-inch documenting the unruly aftermath of an abortive 1985 Jesus and Mary Chain gig.) **Orgasm** is a tight, clean-sounding record—ostensibly "recorded live . . . in Trudi Tangerine's basement"—that includes such essential self-conscious originals as "Indiepop Ain't Noise Pollution," "On Tape" and the classic mouthful of "I Know Someone Who Knows Someone Who Knows Alan McGee Quite Well." The **Multiple Orgasm** CD combines **Orgasm** with ten avowedly studio tracks that actually sound sloppier and less clear than the album's "live" portion.

Judging by Hue's horrifically tuneless singing, the half-hour **Trade Mark of Quality** *is* believably live. (The bootleg styling of its title and original mail-order-only release, however, are defeated by Gregory's liner notes and the Fierce logo.) In any case, the roaringly slapdash rhythm-guitar-rock from a pair of English club gigs in March '89 delivers raw versions of such excellent songs as "Young People," "Heroes and Villains" and a cover of the Vaselines' "Dying for It" (also included in a studio rendition). Good messy fun, but not the ideal place to first meet the Pooh Sticks. (The eponymous nine-song 1991 Overground release compiles BBC radio sessions from 1988 and 1989.)

Formula One Generation—the Poohs' first proper studio album—is self-indulgent ("Tonight" takes forever to gather itself into an actual song) and uneven, but the lack of sonic luster can't spoil such cool tunes as "Susan Sleepwalking," "Radio Ready," "Dare True Kiss Promise," "Soft Bed, Hard Battles." (The inclusion of yet another version of "Dying for It" doesn't hurt, either.) But there's an especially hasty quality to the performances, which leaves them mildly lacking that certain esprit de pooh.

Nothing whatever is lacking from **The Great White Wonder.** (The title is another vintage bootleg reference; the end of "I'm in You" tacks on a historic Dylan moment for good measure.) This giddy rock-pop masterpiece refines and focuses the band's strengths—adding the alluring voice of Heavenly singer Amelia Fletcher (who also toured with the group) for good measure—on a wonderful collection of songs with shamelessly recycled titles. (With the liner notes quick to point out the sources, "Sweet Baby James," "Desperado," "I'm in You" and "The Wild One, Forever" have nothing else in common with anything by, respectively, James Taylor, the Eagles, Peter Frampton or Tom Petty.) With surging fuzz-guitar power, Hue's engagingly wan voice and a conscientiously dippy tone, the group portrays a closed universe of boys, girls and rock'n'roll music. "Young people—they turn me on," sings Hue; a character listening to the radio "turns into someone else"; another has her "hips swaying to the radio beat." As a piano pounds under the slabby chords of Lou Reed's "Rock'n'Roll," "Desperado" outlines a plan for future stardom, promising "I'll take to the lifestyle like a fish takes to water . . . this is the only life I know," as if saying it made it so. In a not-so-subtle tribute to a bygone era, the album's centerpiece, "I'm in You," is a glorious seventeen-minute monstrosity that gets a couple of trivial verses out of the way quickly and then settles in for a magnificently epic Neil Young–style guitar solo. (Collectors' alert: the Zoo reissue omits some of the more potentially actionable bits of familiar '70s rock originally incorporated on the album.)

The title track of the equally great **Million Seller** follows the thread of "Desperado"; in it, Hue acknowledges the romantic hazard of the hit he's sure he's about to create: "If the tune strikes a chord / And people know every word / Might as well say goodbye / When I tell her / Gonna write a million-seller." Reflected in the album-ending "That Was the Greatest Song," **Million Seller** sets the agenda for another easy winner, one that recalibrates the rock/pop ratio in a democratic embrace of firm rock and mushy pop. (The thanked but uncredited Kevin Salem is responsible for the album's guitar power, added to some of the largely acoustic tracks as an afterthought.) A sparkling remake of "Susan Sleepwalking" that obliterates the **Formula One Generation** version and "I Saw the Light" (title only borrowed from Todd Rundgren) are briskly electric; at the other stylistic extreme, "When the Girl Wants to Be Free" oozes piano-ballad sap. With Fletcher's voice sweetly balancing Hue's, "Let the Good Times Roll" and "The World Is Turning On" are fabulous confections, candypop mountains of ABBA-rock production and witty/silly lyrics.

Those two albums may have to suffice for a while. Even the liner notes of **Optimistic Fool** are disappointing. The generally medium-strength guitar rock, while adequate, is obvious and unambitious—even in its expected lack of ambition. The brisk tunes, while intermittently memorable, revisit familiar ground: "Opening Night," "First of a Million Love Songs," "Song Cycle" and "Prayer for My Demo" (unrelated, save for title and the fact of an uncommon skittering club rhythm, to a number on the first Urban Dance Squad album). That sound you hear is the line between self-amusement and self-obsession being scratched away. Hue's female vocal foil (not Fletcher, who would have been a notable asset here) pales behind him; the drums sound like shit. Even deliberate junk needs to live up to certain standards. [i]

See also *Heavenly, Kevin Salem.*

POOKA

Pooka (Elektra) 1993

The malignant Irish sprite that gave Manchester's Natasha Jones and Sharon Lewis their band name also describes the mischievous heart that lurks within the English duo's sweet-voiced acoustic folk. Looking like frecklefaced Druid urchins on the album's back cover portrait, the not-so-innocents threaten to spit on annoying people, dream of "taking your breath," inform a flower of its impending death and offer themselves up to some object of desire as, variously, a little girl, a little man, a woman and a mouse. In the daintily vulgar "Between My Knees," they "want to treat you cruel." Harmonizing beautifully in wan pre-Raphaelite voices, Jones and Lewis surround themselves in arrangements that shift seamlessly from one-guitar blues (the opening "City Sick") to a swelling shroud of piano and strings (the coda of "Bluebell") and suddenly erupt in raucous slide-guitar rock ("Rolling Stone"). Slender, sensuous, seductive, occasionally precious, **Pooka** opens a window into a looking-glass world with wonder and mystery. [i]

IGGY POP

The Idiot (RCA) 1977 (Virgin) 1990
Lust for Life (RCA) 1977 (Virgin) 1990
TV Eye Live (RCA) 1978 (Virgin) 1994
Kill City (Bomp!) 1978
New Values (Arista) 1979
Soldier (Arista) 1980
Party (Arista) 1981
Zombie Birdhouse (Animal) 1982 (IRS) 1991
I Got a Right (Invasion) 1983 (Enigma) 1985
Choice Cuts (RCA) 1984
Blah-Blah-Blah (A&M) 1986
Instinct (A&M) 1988
Brick by Brick (Virgin) 1990

American Caesar (Virgin) 1993
Naughty Little Doggie (Virgin) 1996

Noble philosopher and drooling idiot, transcendent shaman and earthbound sucker, Iggy Pop is in many ways the ultimate embodiment of rock'n'roll. While a similar claim can be made for artists from the Stones to the Clash to the Ramones to Half Japanese, the former James Jewel Osterberg is a walking, talking one-man melodrama, reflecting both the scary, stupid extremes of rock and its fearless, indomitable spirit. From his early drug-fueled days fronting the Stooges through his surprising reincarnation as a solo artist in the late '70s, to his continuing search for fulfillment up to the present day, Iggy has maintained the blend of restless intellect and animal hunger that gives his music—no matter how presented or configured—its raw vitality.

Reemerging from the ashes of the Stooges during the punk explosion—appropriately, since he was one of the movement's godfathers—Iggy's first two solo albums benefit from the production and writing collaboration of pal David Bowie (who'd been responsible, and reviled by purists, for his controversial mix of **Raw Power,** the Stooges' third and final LP). Though the relatively low-key outing features such enduring material as "Funtime" and "China Girl" (later rerecorded and turned into a hit by Bowie himself), **The Idiot,** with its techno undertones, mainly serves as proof the Ig is alive and well. The more raucous and flat-out wonderful **Lust for Life** defines Iggy as the relentless searcher, pondering the meaning of it all in the title track and laughing at convention in "Success." (Highlights from the two albums—a side of each—were later combined for the **Choice Cuts** compilation.)

The masterful **Lust for Life** was followed by a shoddy live album. Recorded in '77 with two different bands (one with Bowie) underpinned by the rhythm section of Hunt and Tony Sales, **TV Eye Live** (named after a Stooges song) offers no new insights into the old and more recent material and is mighty difficult to sit through.

Signing to Arista, Iggy got off to a strong start, reuniting with Stooges guitarist James Williamson (also his partner on the warmed-over **Kill City**) for **New Values.** This confident display restates his desire to find truth (in the title track), offers the sick-joke complaint of a little man ("Five Foot One") and flirts with vertigo on the dizzying "Don't Look Down." Again, **Soldier** and **Party** dissipated his artistic momentum with less consistent material and performances. Both boast a few scattered thrills, notably the former's "Knocking 'Em Down (in the City)," but are for serious fans only. (The international band on **Soldier** is pretty fascinating, though: Glen Matlock and Steve New of the Rich Kids, Barry Andrews of XTC/Shriekback, Ivan Kral of the Patti Smith Group.)

Jumping ship, Iggy teamed up with buddy-producer (and deputized bassist) Chris Stein from Blondie for **Zombie Birdhouse,** released on Stein's Animal Records. The respectful production is a bit too respectful, with rock'n'roll often ignored in the interest of celebrating Iggy the deep thinker. Provocative stuff, but not as much fun as it should have been.

Iggy returned to trusty comrade Bowie for **Blah-Blah-Blah,** his debut on yet another label. The Thin White Duke doesn't fail his client, turning in a slick, surprisingly commercial album that features the radio-friendly "Cry for Love" (co-written by Sex Pistols guitarist Steve Jones) and a delightful cover of the '50s Australian classic "Real Wild Child (Wild One)." In typical rollercoaster fashion, however, Iggy followed that with the disappointing **Instinct,** produced by Bill Laswell and featuring a grinding no-name hard rock band led by Jones. Anyone searching for high points should catch the title track and "Cold Metal."

Happily, Iggy in the '90s has been a focused and exciting, if not overly prolific, presence. Produced by the commercially savvy Don Was, **Brick by Brick** includes everything but the kitchen sink, employing proficient Los Angeles studio vets and degenerate rock stars alike as Iggy shows off his skills as a crooner ("Moonlight Lady") and, as always, a take-no-prisoners noisemonger ("Butt Town"). The album even brought the legend his first honest-to-goodness Top 40 hit single in the form of "Candy," a sweet duet with Kate Pierson of the B-52's.

As if to acknowledge his new mainstream visibility, **American Caesar** presents itself as Iggy 101, laying out his credo for beginners. Printed right on the disc, the forty-six-year-old singer writes, "I tried to make this album as good as I could, with no imitations of other people and no formula shit. This is individual expression." And so it is. Produced by Malcolm Burn, this sixteen-track extravaganza features the acoustic "Jealousy" (a resentful meditation on pampered rock gods: "When he acts like an ass / He's treated like a rogue"), the anguished, painfully honest "Fuckin' Alone," a tuneful celebration of racial harmony ("Mixin' the Colors") and, of course, some blistering rockers, including the absurdist "Boogie Boy," wherein he confesses, "I like to make a dumb-ass noise." The album also has a few missteps, including the pretentious "Caesar" finale, a cover of "Louie, Louie" spoiled by too much social commentary and "Beside You," a pleasant but obvious attempt to duplicate the success of "Candy." Regardless, Iggy still has plenty to say and still deserves to be heard.

Perhaps realizing he'd spread himself too thin on **American Caesar,** Iggy made a more coherent statement with **Naughty Little Doggie.** Reveling in his noble bad-boy persona, the punk godfather emphasizes gritty, driving rockers like "I Wanna Live" and "Heart Is Saved"; this time, slower songs, such as the anguished "Outta My Head," seem like true confessions of the soul rather than calculated overtures to the mainstream. While Iggy doesn't try to break new ground, his unflinching candor in discussing sexual obsession—in "Shoeshine Girl," "Keep on Believing" and the cheerfully obscene "Pussy Walk"—is reassuringly sure to upset those who deserve to be shaken up. At the other extreme, "Look Away" offers a touching memoir of the decadent old days and such luminaries as the ill-fated Johnny Thunders and groupie Sable Starr. Eloquent and direct as ever, Iggy sings, "I went straight / And serious too / There wasn't much else / That I could do." [jy]

See also *TPRG.*

POP ART TOASTERS

See *Chills.*

POP WILL EAT ITSELF

Poppiecock EP (UK Chapter 22) 1986
Poppiecock (UK Chapter 22) 1986

The Covers EP (UK Chapter 22) 1987
Box Frenzy (Chapter 22/Rough Trade) 1987
Now for a Feast! (Chapter 22/Rough Trade) 1988
Can U Dig It EP (RCA) 1989
This Is the Day . . . This Is the Hour . . . This Is This! (RCA) 1989
Cure for Sanity (RCA) 1990
The Looks or the Lifestyle (RCA) 1992
There Is No Love Between Us Anymore (UK Chapter 22) 1992
Weird's Bar and Grill (UK RCA) 1993
16 Different Flavours of Hell (UK RCA) 1993
Go Box Frenzy/Now for a Feast! (UK Chapter 22) 1993
Amalgamation EP (nothing/Interscope/Atlantic) 1994
Dos Dedos Mis Amigos (nothing/Interscope/Atlantic) 1994
Two Fingers, My Friends (UK Infectious) 1995

GOLDEN CLAW MUSICS

All Blue Revue (UK Infectious) 1994

What a wrong, strange trip it's been. Hailing from the boondocks of Stourbridge, England, Pop Will Eat Itself began as a buzzy Buzzcocks wannabe (documented on the exhilarating **Now for a Feast!,** which combines the **Poppiecock** album and some early singles). The sample-crazed **Box Frenzy** showcased their transformation into juvenile but clever parodic rappers, while the rich and funny **This Is the Day . . . This Is the Hour . . . This Is This!**—on which the boys embraced techno, rap, industrial, dance, ambient—set the course for the band's future. Unfortunately, that future was a devolution into utter formula, complete with bullhorn-assisted apocalyptic sloganeering, tiresome metallic riffs and fit-inducing bpm exercises.

Cure for Sanity marks the beginning of the artistic end, as subsequent Poppies albums became sonically dense, soulless adventures in irrelevancy—dance music that became increasingly difficult to dance to. The quartet replaced its beatbox with a live human drummer to no avail on **The Looks or the Lifestyle;** the album still sounds factory-built, underwritten and overproduced. Even "Karmadrome," the lone highlight, manages to eighty-six a throbbing, frantic dance track with an awful bridge.

Dropped by RCA after **Lifestyle,** the Poppies were snatched up by fan Trent Reznor for his fledgling nothing label. Before the group could get a new full-length album out, however, a spate of British releases of varying quality appeared. **There Is No Love Between Us Anymore** compiles eight pre-irritation-era songs, including the great Buzzcocks-inspired title track (a 1987 single also on **Box Frenzy**). The live **Weird's Bar and Grill** documents a '92 performance from London's Brixton Academy. RCA's so-there compilation, **16 Different Flavours of Hell,** can hardly be called a greatest-hits album, as it disregards all of the band's superior early material—but it also leaves out a lot of crap. **Go Box Frenzy/Now for a Feast!** is a British double-CD reissue of those two records. Including a couple of remixes, the seven-track **Amalgamation** offered a foretaste of the band's nothing debut.

Perhaps owing to Reznor's patronage, the Poppies turn up the guitars on **Dos Dedos Mis Amigos** and rock harder than ever. The "songs," however, are every bit as unmemorable as those on **The Looks or the Lifestyle,** save for the growling "Cape Connection," which sounds awfully like Killing Joke. **Two Fingers, My Friends** is the remix companion to **Dos Dedos,** with studio intrusions by the likes of Foetus and Renegade Soundwave. Graham Crabb (originally the Poppies' drummer, then co-vocalist and lyricist with guitarist Clint Mansell) left PWEI after **Dos Dedos** to concentrate on his Golden Claw solo project. [db]

See also *TPRG.*

PORK

Fresh EP7 (Subpar/Worthless) 1992
Strip (No. 6) 1994
Slop (Emperor Jones/Trance Syndicate) 1996

Between a couple of raw, raucous Ramonesy singles in '92 and '93 ("Wanna Ride" on the four-song **Fresh** is a must-hear) and a successfully skirted major-label flirtation in '95, the brilliantly slapdash Austin trio of guitarist/singer Dana Smith, drummer Edith Casimir and bassist/singer Mary Hattman wanged out **Strip,** a magnificent din donut of a debut. Barely produced by Smith's husband, Alejandro Escovedo, the half-hour album flays off the skill and technology that made punk hidebound and boring in the '80s and drives straight back to the unpolished atavism of joyful '77 amateurs. Gutsy three-chord songwriting ("Bum Magnet," "Go Away," "UHF," "Bad Bad Bad") and two boss covers (a recklessly crude rip through Leiber/Stoller's "I'm a Hog for You Baby" and a heartfelt swipe at Escovedo's "Gravity") set Pork on the right course, and un-self-conscious rocking brings it home.

Signing to an Austin indie, Pork let ex-Dumptrucker Seth Tiven clean up their sonic act a bit (the band's concert experience and improved instrumental skills are also likely explanations) on the purified punk goo of **Slop.** With a welcome remake of "Wanna Ride" joining a tall stack of catchy new originals, the girls cut to the chase in winningly wanton assertions like "Tell You No Lies," "Fun," "Regret" and "Liked It." No fooling. [i]

PORNO FOR PYROS

Porno for Pyros (Warner Bros.) 1993
Sadness EP (Warner Bros.) 1994
Good God's Urge (Warner Bros.) 1996

JANE'S ADDICTION

Jane's Addiction (Triple X) 1987
Nothing's Shocking (Warner Bros.) 1988
Ritual de lo Habitual (Warner Bros.) 1990
Then She Did EP (Warner Bros.) 1991

PSI COM

Worktape 1 [tape] (Right Brain) 1984
Psi-Com EP (Mohini) 1985 (Triple X) 1993

Through his creation and supervision of Lollapalooza, Los Angeles' notorious Perry Farrell (originally Queens' own nobody, Perry Bernstein) has had a substantial impact on '90s rock. No question about it. But that achievement does nothing to improve the shittiness of Farrell's recorded work, unmistakable for his keening doubletracked shriek and contrived-to-offend lyrics. While widely admired and frequently imitated, his bands are pretentious, tasteless and blatantly self-indulgent. If Michael Bolton had less hair, an even more obnoxious ego and a fetishistic taste for life's seamy side, he'd be the insufferable Perry Farrell.

In a fit of typical grandiose melodrama, the kick-me-hard provocateur dissolved Jane's Addiction, three albums young, shortly after having the group headline the first Lollapalooza in 1991. Bassist Eric Avery and guitarist David Navarro formed Deconstruction and made an album; Navarro then decamped to the Red Hot Chili Peppers, where he has thrived. Meanwhile, Farrell and drummer Stephen Perkins stuck together and launched Porno for Pyros with bassist Martyn LeNoble (ex–Thelonious Monster) and guitarist Pete DiStefano, whose obvious inferiority to Navarro is pretty much the crucial factor in **Porno for Pyros'** turgid weakness. Of course, the relentless stupidity of Farrell's wishfully scandalous dilettantism—"Ever since the riots / All I really wanted was a black girlfriend . . . it's so exciting and foreign"—adds to the misery, but that's old news for him. Essentially Jane's Relapse minus the stylistic imagination and feverish intensity, **Porno for Pyros** struggles along with melody-impaired material (the catchiest hook, in "Cursed Male," isn't very different from the old "Jane Says") and lyrics that predictably concern sex ("Orgasm"), drugs ("Bad Shit"), violence ("Packin' .25") and generic outrage ("Blood Rag"). In "Sadness," Farrell proudly declares "I've got the devil in me," but **Porno for Pyros** proves that he's full of something else.

The subsequent EP of "Sadness" includes a remake of the song ("A Little Sadness") and three acoustic live tracks (one about cooking and another describing a Christmas cancer miracle, both seemingly improvised on the spot) not from the debut album.

While he helpfully turns the attack down to an alluringly cool semi-acoustic breeze on parts of **Good God's Urge,** Farrell's obnoxious personality remains unchanged, which leaves the album another love-it/hate-it proposition. Among the band's guests are bassist Mike Watt (who subsequently toured as a Pyro), Dave Navarro and, on "Porpoise Head," all of Love and Rockets.

The 1993 reissue of the **Psi-Com** EP makes widely available the amusing sound of a young Perry Farrell attempting to channel the voice of Siouxsie Sioux in a transparent effort to catch the British new (goth) wave. [i]

See also *Deconstruction, Red Hot Chili Peppers, Suicidal Tendencies; TPRG.*

PORTASTATIC

See *Superchunk.*

PORTISHEAD

Dummy (Go! Discs/London) 1994
Sour Times (Nobody Loves Me) EP (Go! Discs/London) 1994

This ambient-dance-cum-lounge-pop band stationed itself on the frontlines of the Bristol, England–generated trip-hop revolution, which could be considered the Newtonian equal-and-opposite-reaction to an increasingly strident, frenzied techno scene. Deploying an electro-torch sound that skirts genres as varied as spaghetti western film scores, '80s new wave and modern hip-hop, Portishead (the name comes from the blue-collar coastal town where producer/mixmaster Geoff Barrow spent his youth) is no less bleak than its more obstreperous peers; the group simply refines its anger into elegant resignation.

On **Dummy,** singer/lyricist Beth Gibbons—whose crystalline yet downbeat voice provides a perfect medium to transport the monochromatic emotions into the system—beckons listeners into a landscape that's at once surreal and poignant. Beneath her quavering soprano, Barrow (who has produced and remixed artists as varied as Depeche Mode, Paul Weller and Gravediggaz) scatters melodic lines sampled from sources like old War albums and *Mission: Impossible,* but those oft-used hip-hop elements are transfigured, realizing film noir elegance in this context. The oh-so-chilled beats that made a left-field hit out of the unipolar lament "Sour Times (Nobody Loves Me)" are also represented in songs like "It Could Be Sweet" (a nonchalant lustfest that's a study in cognitive dissonance) and "Glory Box" (a mournful dissertation on the tribulations of womanhood). Gibbons proves even more effective when unshackled from the rhythms. She fluctuates from a rickety-but-purposeful quaver to a Sade-like husk on "Numb" and the *Cabaret*-styled "Wandering Star"—songs that are all but motionless. Let's hear it for inertia!

Recorded around the same time as **Dummy** and included on the six-track CD single of "Sour Times (Nobody Loves Me)" is the soundtrack music for *To Kill a Dead Man,* a black-and-white short film that Portishead used as its support "act" on tour. Although persuasive mood-setters in their own right, the songs—more like sketches—don't benefit from their excision for an audio-only release. [dss]

POSIES

Failure (23 Records) 1988 (PopLlama Products) 1988
Dear 23 (DGC) 1990
Frosting on the Beater (DGC) 1993
Amazing Disgrace (DGC) 1996

Before helping Alex Chilton and Jody Stephens restart Big Star in 1993, Jon Auer and Ken Stringfellow were merely the Posies, Seattle's bravest contribution to the power-pop lineage that flows from '60s Britain through '70s Memphis. The two multi-instrumentalists are superlative students and proponents of the form, most notable for an uncanny ability—which they now seem to have stashed away—to conjure up the joyful sound of the Hollies in their vocal harmonies.

The duo's homemade (and initially self-released, on cassette) debut is a nifty morsel of neo-Merseybeat with oddly quotidian lyrical concerns. The subsequent **Dear 23,** produced by John Leckie with a rhythm section on hand, is simply marvelous: confident, catchy, uncommon and as original as the pair's chosen style allows. The melodies are irresistible, the singing delightful and surging electric guitar power (notably in the extravagant finale, "Flood of Sunshine") cuts the sweetness just enough to give the record rock bite.

Teethmarks of sonic aggression are all over **Frosting on the Beater,** a Don Fleming–produced escape from tweeness that suspends the Posies' innate tunefulness in a stronger solution. Although making the music louder and rougher undercuts the band's distinctiveness (one Matthew Sweet is plenty, thanks), it doesn't affect the Posies' vocals other than to obscure their specific Holliesque aspect. But neither does it especially benefit them: the record's allure owes little to the resulting contrast and everything to the sturdy melodies of the songwriting. Wisely declining the temptations of shoegazing, psychedelia and other trendy designs, the Posies crank up their pure pop without changing its basic attributes. No wonder it tastes so good.

Returning from their Big Star adventure (Auer and Stringfellow joined Chilton and Stephens in the '93 revival of that fabled group), the Posies made **Amazing Disgrace.** Whoever puked on their breakfast cereal ("Everybody Is a Fucking Liar," "Hate Song," "Broken Record," "Daily Mutilation," the "who gives a shit?" refrain of "Ontario") sure didn't spoil the Posies' dedication to joyous pop uplift: the album's sound strikes a relentlessly positive mix of the roaring enthusiasms of **Frosting on the Beater,** the retro propriety of **Dear 23** and such new/old elements as the '80s punk rush of "Grant Hart" and the '80s rock clout of Cheap Trick (two of whom guest on "Hate Song"). Great. [i]

See also *Big Star, Sky Cries Mary, Young Fresh Fellows; TPRG*

POSSUM DIXON

Music for a One Bedroom Apartment EP7 (Surf Detective) 1991
Apartment Music [tape] (Surf Detective) 1992
Possum Dixon (Surf Detective/Interscope/Atlantic) 1993
Sunshine or Noir? EP (Surf Detective) 1995
Star Maps (Surf Detective/Interscope) 1996

Formed around 1990 and named after a suspected murderer mentioned on *America's Most Wanted,* this Los Angeles quartet chronicles slacker life in its hometown with driving edgy pop-rock that updates new wave bands like the Attractions, Yachts and Wall of Voodoo. The self-released **Apartment Music** cassette sets the tone for things to come, matching singer/songwriter/standup bassist Rob Zabrecky's offbeat, literate lyrics about heartbreak and job woes with music that sometimes sounds like it's about to boil over from pure tension. (Four of the tape's seven songs were redone for **Possum Dixon.**)

Co-produced by Earle Mankey, **Possum Dixon** doesn't stretch any musical boundaries, but the band's songwriting skill and raw energy make up for that. Against the tight playing of drummer Richard Treuel and guitarists Robert O'Sullivan and Celso Chavez, Zabrecky projects both frustration and an odd sort of vulnerability when singing irresistible songs like "Watch the Girl Destroy Me." And though he sometimes takes his twentysomething angst too seriously, "Nerves" and other numbers do a fair job of capturing what it's like to be young, poor and alienated in the City of Angels. **Sunshine or Noir?** contains four new tracks (two of which appear on the next album) and an energetic live version of **Possum Dixon**'s "In Buildings."

Recorded as a trio with revolving drummers, **Star Maps** is a more mature effort than **Possum Dixon,** but lacks some of its predecessor's raw energy. Rather than continue to churn out three-chord raveups, the band expands a bit stylistically—with mixed results. "Personals," a haunting number about newspaper ads, packs a subtle if powerful punch, but "Reds" and others lack the earlier work's bite. Though the stylistic expansion is admirable, Possum Dixon can't disguise the fact that its basic strength remains stripped-down art-punk. [rl]

POSTER CHILDREN

Toreador Squat [tape] (Poster Children) 1988
Flower Plower (Limited Potential) 1990 (Limited Potential/ Frontier) 1991
Daisychain Reaction (Twin\Tone) 1991 (Twin\Tone/ Sire/Reprise) 1992
Tool of the Man (Twin\Tone/Sire/Reprise) 1992
Just Like You EP (Twin\Tone/Sire/Reprise) 1994
Junior Citizen (Twin\Tone/Sire/Reprise) 1995

Formed in 1987 at the University of Illinois at Champaign-Urbana by guitarist Rick Valentin and bassist Rose Marshack, Poster Children have sifted through almost as many styles of post-punk guitar rock as they have drummers (six, as of **Junior Citizen**'s Howie Kantoff).

Recording as a trio with producer Iain Burgess in 1988, Poster Children tried on various guises, from "Non-Reggae Song," which parodies Joe Jackson in his ska phase, to the John Lydon–isms of "Modern Art." A few month later, with Steve Albini as engineer, they conjured up a Dinosaur Jr–style guitar hurricane with muffled, deadpan vocals. The tracks from both sessions are collected on **Flower Plower.**

Poster Children is a quartet on the Albini-engineered **Daisychain Reaction,** with a second guitarist (Jeff Dimpsey, on loan from Hum) thickening the sound. The band's increasing mastery of dynamics—soft-to-loud, slow-to-fast and back again—is evident in the rudely titled "If You See Kay," where it especially complements Valentin's psychotic vocals. "Space Gun" and "Chain Reaction" explore a spacier, neo-psychedelic guitar sound, and the more spacious arrangements and oddball tempos give Bob Rising, one of a string of good to excellent drummers, plenty of room to swing.

Tool of the Man, a sarcastic acknowledgment of the band's arrival in the major-label world, brings in another drumming dynamo, Johnny Machine, and a permanent second guitarist, Jim Valentin (Rick's brother). Far from acting like tools of the man, Poster Children opt for an even less homogenized approach: sugar-free rockers mixed with knottier, more experimental mood pieces. "Redline," "Three Bullets" and "In My Way" explore the quieter fringes of the band's sound, while "Blatant Dis" hums along on taut guitars, which uncoil into a spaced-out midsection before regaining their galvanizing stride.

With the graphically matched **Just Like You** and **Junior Citizen,** both produced by Brian Anderson at Smart Studios in Madison, Wisconsin, Poster Children dabble in disco and the most straightforward pop tunes of their career. The six-song **Just Like You** introduces a touch of bombast missing from the band's previously self-effacing records, as well as keyboards and samplers. Valentin declares "I'm sick of it all" and "I'm not like you" with increasing agitation and more than a touch of sarcasm, as though kissing off the band's past. On **Junior Citizen,** Valentin's vocals have never been more pronounced, the rhythms never more insistent (or rigid), the tunes never punchier or more melodic. Keyboards encourage a richer, more varied sound, by turns brighter and stranger. The title track works as a double-edged commentary on Generation X self-pity and self-doubt, and forces a reassessment of a band that heretofore had seemed a likable but unremarkable example of underground earnestness. [gk]

See also *Hum, Seam, Tortoise; TPRG.*

POUNDING SERFS

See *Gravel.*

PRAM

Gash EP (UK Howl) 1992
Iron Lung EP (UK Too Pure) 1993
The Stars Are So Big, the Earth Is So Small . . . Stay as You Are (UK Too Pure) 1993
Helium (UK Too Pure) 1994 (Too Pure/American) 1995
Sargasso Sea (Too Pure/American) 1995

Some people sit around whining about the limitations of standard rock instrumentation—others do something about it. Firm believers in pure DIY aesthetics, London's Pram fabricated a thoroughly original, if not universally palatable, sound based on a framework of homemade theremin and assorted electronic widgets, topped off with the ominous little-girl-lost vocals of Rosie Cuckston.

On the group's earliest records, Pram's bare-bones electro-drone brings back fond memories of vanguard '60s noisemakers—like Silver Apples and Fifty Foot Hose—who jerry-rigged gizmos that made watching the itinerary get laid out as much fun as actually taking the trip. **Gash** doesn't hold up particularly well to repeated listens, since its four tracks offer little more than affirmation they'd bought that krautrock program card for the old synthesizer. **Iron Lung** is more interesting, if only for the inexhaustible enthusiasm with which the group approaches sound: "Cumulus" finds Pram maddeningly fixated on the tone of a pennywhistle; "Water Toy" could be just that. (The group has a serious fetish for kiddie trinkets.) Good, clean—if bleary—fun.

Pram grew up (and how!) during the making of the full-length **The Stars Are So Big, the Earth Is So Small . . . Stay as You Are.** While stretches of the record are friendly enough—the *mekkanik* rhythms rumble pleasantly beneath Cuckston's distracted trill—some decidedly menacing shapes are thrown by tracks like the gradually cresting title cut and "Radio Freak in a Storm." By the latter's crescendo (the song clocks in at nearly eleven minutes), cold sweats will be the least of your worries. Only marginally more linear, **Helium** provides more restful listening: the theremin swirls that emanate from "Gravity" (which, unlike a lot of the band's output, actually allows the listener the luxury of experiencing the titular state) and "Dancing on a Star" verge on the sanguine. In the meantime, Cuckston honed her delivery to a deadpan recitation, all the better to transmit crypto-beatnik cyber-madrigals like "Things Left on the Pavement." **Sargasso Sea** stays the course, embellishing tracks like the apocalypto-tango "Loose Threads" with muted, lounge-jazz horns. Even Mr. Sinatra might approve—provided he doesn't listen too closely. [dss]

PRAXIS

See *Bill Laswell.*

PREMATURE EJACULATION

See *Christian Death.*

PRESIDENTS OF THE UNITED STATES OF AMERICA

The Presidents of the United States of America (PopLlama Products) 1995 (PopLlama Products/Columbia) 1995

Two bass strings, three guitar strings, two fuzzboxes, a three-piece drum kit, an unwieldy name, rudimentary production of songs about peaches, stray cats, boll weevils and lumps, a cover of the MC5's ineffectual call to arms, "Kick Out the Jams," and a carefree goofball attitude—that sure sounds like the recipe for a million-selling album, doesn't it? Not merely Seattle's most improbable success story of '95, this unprepossessing novelty trio scored one of the whole decade's leftest-field home runs. Singer/demi-bassist Chris Ballew (a former Beck sideman and Boston resident who acknowledges the instrumental inspiration of Morphine's similarly equipped Mark Sandman, a one-time roommate with whom he has an intermittent band called Supergroup), half-guitarist Dave Dederer and ex–Love Battery drummer Jason Finn could not be more intrinsically indie if they had the PopLlama logo tattooed on their foreheads. Nonetheless, the college-kid mainstream welcomed their debut album like the local pot dealer. So exactly where does that leave "We Are Not Going to Make It," a number borrowed from a defunct Brooklyn band called Traci Lords' Ex-Lovers? A rewrite of the Monkees' theme, the song predicts failure, explaining "There's a million better bands with a million better songs / Drummers who can drum / Singers who can sing." Is it prescient irony? A preemptive credibility hedge in the event of major-label failure? A fib?

Grasping the essence of pop singledom, the Presidents make their songs chewy, stupid, disposable, diverse and imaginative. Like the winsome "little bag o'bones" loved and hated in the leadoff "Kitty," **The Presidents of the United States of America** is instantly ingratiating and massively irritating, the kind of record you love for a week and then trade in for one you can actually live with. A mixture of the Spin Doctors' grub funk and They Might Be Giants' dada whimsicality stripped down and rushed along as simply as possible, the album is full of catchy tunes and smart, loopy nonsense (sprinkled with such surprises as the John Lennon paraphrase that ends "Feather Pluckin") perfect for rowdy singalongs. [i]

See also *Love Battery, Morphine.*

JOE PRESTON

See *Melvins.*

PRETENDERS

Pretenders (Real/Sire) 1980
Extended Play EP (Real/Sire) 1981
Pretenders II (Real/Sire) 1981
Learning to Crawl (Real/Sire) 1984
Get Close (Real/Sire) 1986
The Singles (Real/Sire) 1987
Packed! (Sire) 1990
Last of the Independents (Sire) 1994
The Isle of View (Warner Bros.) 1995

It was Hank Williams who sang "I'll never get out of this world alive," but it was the Pretenders who went out of their way to determine just how much tragedy a group could endure without actually giving up. In 1980, Ohio expat Chrissie Hynde was the mind, muscle and heart of a superlative London quartet that married her forthright sexuality and independence to inarguably great music, vaporizing stereotypes rock women had been expected to accept. Bursting with a truly original sound, a marvelously distinctive singer and great, tough pop songs—"Tattooed Love Boys,"

"Mystery Achievement," "Kid," "Brass in Pocket"—the first album is an absolute classic. **Pretenders II** suffered from a shortage of material, but still came across with "Message of Love" and "Talk of the Town." Then things started going very wrong. Guitarist James Honeyman Scott died of a drug overdose in 1982, bassist Pete Farndon left and subsequently followed Scott's fatal lead. Hynde had a kid; the band hit the skids.

Learning to Crawl brought the reconstituted group—Hynde, drummer Martin Chambers and two newcomers—back to form but not stability. **Get Close,** recorded largely with session players (including drummer Blair Cunningham, late of Haircut One Hundred), has very little beyond "Don't Get Me Wrong" and "My Baby" to recommend it. Those songs also appear on **The Singles,** an essential career retrospective containing all of the band's English A-sides from 1979 to 1986, plus Hynde's winning duet with UB40 on a reggae rendition of "I Got You Babe."

Subtle production and keyboards by Mitchell Froom on **Packed!** free Hynde to give her most emotionally mature songs the full benefit of that inimitable voice, and she does manage to breathe a little life into the Pretenders' stiffening body. But many of the melodies are rewrites; worse, the lyrics lack focus and intensity.

Following another long gap, **Last of the Independents**—with Chambers back in the fold after most of a decade—gamely puts in for a recharge, but the haphazard mix of punchdrunk rockers, glossy power ballads (the obvious and sappy "I'll Stand by You") and a handsome cover of Bob Dylan's "Forever Young" (parental lullaby? misguided pretension? self-amused irony?) isn't the ticket home. Dealing with the hired-gun devils of California factory songwriting may help pay the mortgage, but it's no way to regain creative momentum. And with unsettling lyrics like the notorious "He hit me with his belt / His tears were all I felt" ("977"), "Bring on the revolution / I wanna die for something" ("Revolution") and an ode to "Tequila," Hynde sounds like she's sliding off an emotional cliff with no brakes. She even makes a hash of feminism: both the overheated "I'm a Mother" and "Money Talk" proclaim that power flows from the barrel of her sex organs. Now *that's* progress.

An acoustic career retrospective from a veteran band going nowhere is a dead cert indicator of a creative gas gauge aimed at empty, yet the Pretenders actually get good mileage from the form. Recorded live and seated before an invited audience in a London studio with the **Last of the Independents** band (Chambers, guitarist Adam Seymour, bassist Andy Hobson), a string quartet and a percussionist, **The Isle of View** benefits from both the songs' familiarity and their refreshing rearrangements. Wisely restricting the last two studio records to a quota of one song each and **Get Close** to two, Hynde runs through some of her very best, drawing most heavily from **The Pretenders.** As comfortable as Hynde has always been with rock's power, turning down the heat allows her to reach a new vocal peak. "Back on the Chain Gang," "Lovers of Today," a semi-electric "2000 Miles," a harmonium-accompanied reading of Meg Keene's stunning "Hymn to Her" and a stately rendition of "Kid" are especially affecting. Even **Packed!**'s "Sense of Purpose" is a joy. Hynde also does a sensitive turn on Ray Davies' "I Go to Sleep," but amateur-hour piano by Blur's Damon Albarn chops(ticks) the dreamy song into little pieces. And given the oblong lyrical cadences of "Private Life" and "The Phone Call," opening them up in this way only serves to reveal their structural potholes. [i]

See also *TPRG.*

PRETTY & TWISTED

See *Concrete Blonde.*

PRIMAL SCREAM

Sonic Flower Groove (UK Elevation) 1987
Primal Scream (UK Creation) 1989
Come Together EP (Sire/Warner Bros.) 1990
Screamadelica (Sire/Warner Bros.) 1991
Dixie Narco EP (UK Creation) 1992
Give Out but Don't Give Up (Creation/Sire/Warner Bros.) 1994
(I'm Gonna) Cry Myself Blind EP (UK Creation) 1994

Glasgow's Primal Scream made its public debut in October '84, the show at which vocalist/superfan Bobby Gillespie also made his first appearance as the Jesus and Mary Chain's style-over-competence drummer. The group released a pair of singles on Creation over the next two years, but took a back seat to Gillespie's other career until he left the Reids' employ in early '86.

The brightest light of the Primals' early days is the oft-compiled B-side "Velocity Girl," a ninety-second blast of densely echoed Rickenbacker bliss that is a defining moment of Britain's short-lived C86/anorak pop era. It took several years and wardrobe changes for Primal Scream to equal that moment.

The first two albums parade the group's influences so obviously that it's hard to spot an original thought. **Sonic Flower Groove** was recorded twice (first with Smiths producer Stephen Street, then with Red Crayola kingpin Mayo Thompson). The latter version won out, but the album is so Swinging London '60s-obsessed there's even a song entitled "Aftermath." For **Primal Scream,** the band squeezed into leather gear and fast-forwarded to 1969; the album is so Detroit-obsessed that there's even a song called "Gimme Gimme Teenage Head." But the record did lead to something completely different.

As psychedelic drugs (re)conquered England, the C86 crowd began infiltrating the burgeoning rave scene, and the bowl haircuts and Rickenbackers were replaced by baggy pants and sampling equipment practically overnight. Primal Scream seized the moment brilliantly—if inadvertently. DJ friend Andrew Weatherall (who'd never been in a recording studio before) had a go at remixing "I'm Losing More Than I'll Ever Have," a track from **Primal Scream.** He chopped out most of the original song, threw in a groove and loads of samples (including Peter Fonda dialogue from *The Wild Angels*) and emerged with the awesome "Loaded."

"Loaded" primed the works for the dazzling **Screamadelica,** a dance album with a rock album's accessibility. Primal Scream found itself reborn as an avatar of pop/ambient/house. Although the technicolor sound was basically masterminded by Weatherall and programmer Hugo Nicholson (apart from Gillespie, the actual band seems to appear on less than half of its own album), Primal Scream's flagrant derivativeness works beautifully to its advantage in this format: MC5 quotations and guitar solos appear in the middle of tripped-out dance grooves, and the group spans three generations of British beat by collaborating with Jimmy Miller, Jah Wobble and the Orb on a single disc. A truly inspired fusion of pop, rock and dance, **Screamadelica** brought new respectability to the word "influence," and even won the prestigious British Mercury Award.

Expanded from a three-song British 12-inch, the American **Come Together** EP contains "I'm Losing More Than I'll Ever Have," three mixes of "Loaded," two of "Come Together" (a single from the then-forthcoming third album) and a live version of "Ramblin' Rose." The **Dixie Narco** EP combines remixes with a bluesy ballad B-side; the album spawned four additional British singles that are of remix-spotter interest only.

Three long and unproductive years after **Screamadelica,** out came **Give Out but Don't Give Up,** bearing a neon Confederate flag on its front and a picture of late Funkadelic guitarist Eddie Hazel on its back—disproving the axiom that you can't tell a book by its cover. Much to the chagrin of the band's dance audience, Primal Scream had pawned its samplers, gone to Memphis and given their libidos full sway, producing what is essentially a fair-to-middling Black Crowes album. (That band's producer, George Drakoulias, contributed heavily.) Despite a few interesting riffs and a collaboration with George Clinton, **Give Out but Don't Give Up** is about as funky as *Bill* Clinton's sax playing, and left the band right back where it was five years earlier. Now if they'd only give it to a clever novice to remix . . . [jg/ja]

See also *Jesus and Mary Chain; TPRG.*

PRIME MINISTER PETE NICE & DADDY RICH

See *3rd Bass.*

PRIMUS

Suck on This (Prawn Song) 1989 (Caroline) 1990
Frizzle Fry (Caroline) 1990
Sailing the Seas of Cheese (Interscope/EastWest) 1991
Miscellaneous Debris EP (Interscope/Atlantic) 1992
Pork Soda (Interscope/Atlantic) 1993
Tales From the Punchbowl (Interscope/Atlantic) 1995 (Prawn Song/Interscope) 1996

SAUSAGE

Riddles Are Abound Tonight (Prawn Song/Interscope/Atlantic) 1994

PORCH

Porch (Prawn Song/Mammoth) 1994

LES CLAYPOOL AND THE HOLY MACKEREL

Highball With the Devil (Prawn Song/Interscope) 1996

Bay Area power trio Primus is living proof that punk music did not succeed in killing off progressive rock; if anything, in Primus' hands, the two mesh pretty well. Once described as Rush on crack, the band invigorates the musicianly ambitions and literary pretensions of '70s art-metal with an intricate instrumental frenzy closer to Metallica (for whom singer/bassist Les Claypool once auditioned) or late-period Black Flag than the Mahavishnu Orchestra and a cutting, streetwise lyric attitude distinguished by Claypool's Zappa-esque wordplay. The searing quality of Primus' early club shows is ably captured on **Suck on This,** initially issued on Claypool's own Prawn Song label. There are moments, like the breakneck finish of "Frizzle Fry," when Primus sounds like a crowd-surfer's King Crimson (circa **Red**) fueled by thumb-slapping Funkadelic bass. Raw but promising stuff.

Claypool's idiosyncratic singing and trebly, bullish bass dominate the group's attack on **Frizzle Fry,** which reprises five songs from the live record. But the studio debut also effectively showcases drummer Tim "Herb" Alexander's tight, frenetic technique and guitarist Larry LaLonde's aggro-fusion chops. Cleaner sound and extra production touches (a few guitar overdubs, some neat vocal trickery) also enhance the abrasive kinetics of the songs. Meanwhile, Claypool gives good wordplay—lively metaphor-hopping laced with prickly social complaint—in his stream-of-consciousness stoner's blues "Spegetti Western" and "Harold of the Rocks" and the droll protest of "Too Many Puppies" and "Pudding Time."

Primus actually gets leaner and meaner in both sound and worldview on **Sailing the Seas of Cheese.** Claypool's rubbery, agitated basslines underpin the dark argument of paranoiac warnings like "Here Come the Bastards" and "Sgt. Baker" ("I will rape your personality . . . Strip you of your self-integrity"), while LaLonde's riffing is shaved down to a corrosive, hand-drill whine. Comic relief is provided in the a cappella shower song "Grandad's Little Ditty" and Tom Waits' vocal cameo on "Tommy the Cat," a gravelly, motor-mouthed rap in which he sounds like a psychotic auctioneer with tuberculosis. But a thick air of betrayal and impending violence hangs heavy over the songs and the group's tense playing. As corporate rock of the early '90s goes, this record is deep, grim and anything but cheesy.

The holding-pattern EP **Miscellaneous Debris** is aptly named, a five-song collection of covers running the gamut from a brittle, overaccelerated remake of XTC's "Making Plans for Nigel" to a quick stab at an old Meters instrumental and a rough excavation of Pink Floyd's "Have a Cigar." It's all very amusing if you're a serious Primus fan; otherwise, this is the sort of thing best left to concert encores. Notable exception: a nifty rendition of the Residents' spookhouse rhumba "Sinister Exaggerator."

Pork Soda actually debuted in the Billboard Top 10, a remarkable achievement for such an idiosyncratic combo. On "Welcome to This World," the hyper-funk rattle and dizzying velocity of Claypool's bass part suggest a homicidal cross between Bootsy Collins and Jaco Pastorius. Ironically, a slight predictability has crept into Primus' winning, weirdo ways on this album. Claypool's melodramatic yelping sometimes blurs the shades of black humor in his lyrics, leaving one extended gag. Also, while LaLonde's guitar playing is more full-bodied than on **Sailing the Seas of Cheese,** the power-trio format has its tonal limitations. For all the inspired complexity, the herky-jerky time and tempo changes don't always provide enough variety. Still, there *is* a contagious energy to the hectic interplay on "DMV" and "Nature Boy." Meanwhile, the eerie, low-key dramatization of suicide in "Bob" shows that Primus realizes that not everything worth doing is worth overdoing.

During an extended working vacation from

Primus, Claypool reactivated the Prawn Song label and cut a side project under the name Sausage featuring original Primus guitarist Todd Huth (whom LaLonde replaced in '89, and who has more recently been leading Porch). With drummer Jay Lane, Claypool and Huth resurrected some of their early, unrecorded material for **Riddles Are Abound Tonight.** For an ad hoc reunion, it's really good, with an emphasis on brisk, fluid jamming and less of the jokey vocals that dominate Primus records. If **Sailing the Seas of Cheese** is Primus' moshpit variation on the Mothers of Invention's **We're Only in It for the Money,** the Sausage album is kind of Claypool's **Hot Rats.** (Other Prawn Song releases have included albums by the Charlie Hunter Trio, Alphabet Soup, Eskimo and Laundry, a band featuring Tim Alexander.)

Produced and engineered by Primus at Claypool's home studio for a reported five thousand dollars, **Tales From the Punchbowl** (also issued as a visually enhanced CD) is a mixed cocktail. The first track, "Professor Nutbutter's House of Treats," is a lot better than its title suggests—a seven-minute wigout of bulldozer rhythm and sizzling Robert Fripp–style guitar. But the extent to which Primus are prisoners of their own mischief is evident in "Wynona's Big Brown Beaver," a ripsnorting rocker with some greasy countryfied guitar; it became a novelty hit mostly because of the allusion (intended or otherwise) to a certain actress' genitalia. As funny and pointed as the band can be in song, there are times when you can't help but wish that Primus was just an instrumental combo.

In 1996, Claypool released a solo album, **Highball With the Devil,** and Tim Alexander left Primus. [df]

See also *M.I.R.V.; TPRG.*

PRINCE

For You (Warner Bros.) 1978
Prince (Warner Bros.) 1979
Dirty Mind (Warner Bros.) 1980
Controversy (Warner Bros.) 1981
1999 (Warner Bros.) 1982
Sign "o" the Times (Paisley Park) 1987
The Black Album (unreleased) 1987 (Warner Bros.) 1994
Lovesexy (Paisley Park) 1988
Batman (Warner Bros.) 1989
Graffiti Bridge (Paisley Park/Warner Bros.) 1990
The Hits/The B-Sides (Paisley Park/Warner Bros.) 1993
The Hits 1 (Paisley Park/Warner Bros.) 1993
The Hits 2 (Paisley Park/Warner Bros.) 1993
Come (Warner Bros.) 1994
Purple Medley EP (Warner Bros.) 1995

PRINCE AND THE REVOLUTION

Purple Rain (Warner Bros.) 1984
Around the World in a Day (Paisley Park) 1985
Parade (Paisley Park) 1986

PRINCE AND THE NEW POWER GENERATION

Diamonds and Pearls (Paisley Park/Warner Bros.) 1991
[symbol] (Paisley Park/Warner Bros.) 1992
Music From the Motion Picture Girl 6 (Warner Bros.) 1996

[symbol]

The Beautiful Experience EP (NPG) 1994
The Gold Experience (NPG/Warner Bros.) 1995
Chaos and Disorder (Warner Bros.) 1996

VARIOUS ARTISTS

1-800-NEW-FUNK (NPG) 1994

As the young general of the purple side, Minneapolis' one-man musical army won the war hands down in the '80s. Setting his own shameless high/low standards and then sticking to them through thick and thin—thereby defining the baseline quality of his records in terms of his unbelievable talent, rather than the other way around—Prince singlehandedly revitalized, diversified and reshaped the sound of funk. He sent a crosscut saw through race-based genre divisions, put more unabashed sexuality into music than Blowfly in bed with Madonna and shepherded a stable of talent to public attention with writing and production contributions under a panoply of pseudonyms.

A whirlwind of self-propelled creativity, Prince began as a lubricious wunderkind (the self-produced **For You** is a mighty assured debut for a teenaged R&B auteur) and accelerated from there, hitting his pan-stylistic stride on **Dirty Mind** (the unnerving "When You Were Mine," later covered by Cindi Lauper, is a quintessential new wave pop song) before powering on through **1999** and **Purple Rain.** Although uneven, both of those albums contain so many classic tracks in diverse, original molds (the former boasts "1999," "Little Red Corvette," "Delirious" and "Automatic"; the latter, his first recording with a band, has "Let's Go Crazy," "When Doves Cry," "Purple Rain" and "I Would Die 4 U") that they are defining chapters in the decade's music.

By the middle of the '80s, Prince had starred in and scored two goofy films (*Purple Rain* and *Under the Cherry Moon,* soundtracked as **Parade**), launched his own label (Paisley Park, which eventually became home to George Clinton, Mavis Staples and others) and bestowed hits on Sheena Easton and the Bangles. But he had also dissolved the Revolution and withdrawn from touring.

The excellent **Sign "o" the Times** reiterated the unbounded autonomy of his music, pingponging from the ultra-spare title track to the sex-rocking "U Got the Look I Like" to the aching soul ballad "I Could Never Take the Place of Your Man." But the double-album also marked the end of the innocence—such as it was. Later that same year, a hard, dirty and funky record bearing no official title but known informally as **The Black Album** was either withdrawn by Prince or rejected by his label (though enough illicit copies circulated that it probably could have charted had it been given a bootleg bar code). Seven years later, at a point when Prince's relationship with Warner Bros. had completely soured, the record finally received an official release, stylishly dressed in basic information-free black and lauded on a cover sticker as "legendary."

At the time, however, what appeared was the lyrically (if not visually) modest **Lovesexy,** an expansion of Prince's idyllic views on religion and love, followed by the ludicrously overdone **Batman** soundtrack and the uninspired **Graffiti Bridge,** the album of his third vanity film, which brought Tevin Campbell to market and features Princely collaborations with George Clinton and the Time.

With his creative momentum slowing, Prince arrived in the '90s on a downward spiral. His label wasn't doing well, his movies were not being taken seriously and his albums no longer arrived as major events. With rap a dominant force in the marketplace, that Prince was no MC was a notable commercial impediment. Worse, the eccentricities of Prince's obsessive personality seemed to be compromising, rather than compelling, his work. His ratio of mind-boggling surprises to predictable fixations—monomania doesn't begin to describe Prince's devotion to carnality—had fallen, and it wasn't clear he could get it back up.

Resorting to the same share-the-mic approach that got him over **Graffiti Bridge,** Prince made **Diamonds and Pearls** with the New Power Generation, a multifarious mod squad—complete with rapper and a more businesslike female foil than Prince's usual slinky playthings—geared not so much to support the star as to complement him. Although facile and frivolous on the surface, the album is deceptively strong, with self-amused tributes like the Sly-styling "Daddy Pop" (in which the phrase "sock it to me" gets aired for what must be the first time since Nixon resigned) and the mock movie musical number "Strollin'" displaying more ingenuity than borrowed influence. Meanwhile, the outrageous sex vamps ("Get Off" and "Cream") go well into the red zone, tempered by the luxurious romance of the titular ballad and the falsetto delicacy of "Willing and Able," which loads up the style cart with high-life guitar flow, a guest gospel group *and* mellow NPG rhyme-buster Tony M—yet never even threatens to tip over.

With such a solid carriage, it took some conscious effort for Prince to drive himself off the rails, but he did it on his next album, titled with the unpronounceable logo he subsequently adopted as his personal designation. (Ironically, he gets the record off with the definitive "My Name Is Prince.") Despite nods to reggae, rap and techno, the insubstantial album mainly consists of familiar funk, pop and soul ballad designs. Belatedly attempting to claim a place in hardcore hip-hop, he sidles up to the sound of jeep beats in the first track and then goes for the throat in the unconvincing and self-consciously rude "Sexy M.F.," which drops the coquettish charm of his best come-ons for blunt, witless profanity. Throughout this overlong album, Prince lets signifying intent take precedence over content. His repeated digs at journalists serve only to expose a glass jaw; the attempts to explain himself here are far more confusing than anything one might imagine about his values or motives.

Following a stupendous hits/flips career retrospective—available as a fifty-six-song triple-CD and as two single discs of eighteen A-sides each—Prince became The Artist Formerly Known as Prince (or Glyph or Symbol as the wags had it). He formalized the affectation on **The Beautiful Experience,** an impressively chameleonic five-version (pick a style, any style) single of "The Most Beautiful Girl in the World," an ordinary falsetto ballad used to mount an extraordinary are-you-she? marketing campaign.

Further confusing trivial matters, **Come** is credited to "Prince 1958–1993." Declaring the "dawning of a new spiritual revolution," ol' whatsisname plays a human sundial here, watching the female world revolve lazily around his dick. From the crashing surf (a familiar metaphor to fans of Russ Meyer movies) that opens the album to the whimpering female orgasm that ends it, Prince makes no bones (er . . .) about his fleshly desires, although he still finds time to attack racism in "Race" and evil parents in "Papa." The latter's locked-in-the-closet story winds up with an unexpected and unsettling coda—"Don't abuse children or else they turn out like me"—that raises some curious questions about the artist's own upbringing. In fact, the album is no more sex-obsessed than usual, but the explicit bookends (the eleven-minute "Come" and the much shorter "Orgasm"—there should be a bonus track called "Smoke") are nasty enough to color the whole album beet-red. The taut, economical and effective bed of simple funk and soul stands little chance of drawing attention away from the bedroom.

The Paisley Park label folded in '94, stranding a bunch of artists. The former entrepreneur saw to the release of **1-800-NEW-FUNK,** a roster sampler he helped write, perform and produce for George Clinton, Madhouse, NPG, Nona Gaye and Mavis Staples. Meanwhile, Warner Bros. whipped up **Purple Medley,** which reprises the highlights of Prince oeuvre in eleven efficient minutes.

Perhaps the name change and shedding of corporate responsibilities lifted some weight off the diminutive diva's shoulders, for **The Gold Experience** spins out from the multi-colored designs of **Diamonds and Pearls** with stronger rock and loftier pop ambitions, rectifying the bad ideas of **Come** and **[symbol]** by relocating the essential Prince-ness of their intentions. After a bracing introduction, "Shhh" settles in for a quiet storm, then, accompanied by the line "You say you want a slow jam," opens the door to a blistering rock guitar solo. The sleekly gorgeous "Dolphin" is miles and away the best pop song in the Minneapolitan's catalogue since "Raspberry Beret." And rather than attempt to join the roughneck pose, the determined veteran makes an end run around it here. Prostrating himself at the vaginal altar in the hysterical falsetto/rap delirium of "P Control," "your captain with no name" works up a mighty testosterone sweat exalting the sexuality of womankind and then slaps down those who don't share his terrible awe. "Don't you *think* about calling her a 'ho,' you juvenile delinquent," he warns no one in particular. "Best sit yo' ass down—talkin' about pussy control." This man is one willing slave to love. A reappearance of "The Most Beautiful Girl in the World" speaks to his respect for the female species—at least as a pleasurable physical manifestation—but his mercurial mood turns over in "Billy Jack Bitch" and "I Hate U." Consistently stimulating, surprising and sparkling, **The Gold Experience** is an instant refresher course in why Prince—or whoever—earns his egotism every day.

Just when the name thing seemed to have been settled once and for all, director Spike Lee prevailed upon the man from Minneapolis to create a soundtrack album for his phone-sex film *Girl 6*—and to do so under the marketable Prince rubric. Lee's humiliating liner note is positively prostrate in its grateful acquiescence to form: "Many thanks 2 The Artist Formerly Known As Prince. U made a great sacrifice to make this happen. I love U and U will see the dawn." **Girl 6** feeds a couple of new (at least previously unreleased) songs into an album of such oldies as "Pink Cashmere," "Hot Thing," "Erotic City," "Girls & Boys" and "How Come You Don't Call Me Anymore." Besides nine Prince cuts, there's a Vanity track, two by the New Power Generation and one by the Family.

The funk-rocking **Chaos and Disorder**—"originally intended 4 private use only"—is a compilation of studio leftovers cobbled together by ♀ as a final bird-flip farewell to his longtime label. Backed by the New Power Generation, the undatable music and singing are loose and lively. Some of the melodies are well-crafted, the overall tone is refreshingly warm and buttery and there's lots of boss lead guitar work. That said, the half-baked lyrics of "Dinner With Delores," "I Rock, Therefore I Am" and "Dig U Better Dead," plus an incongruous rap, mess up what might have been a fine old time. [i]

See also *George Clinton; TPRG.*

PRINCESS DRAGONMOM

See *His Name Is Alive.*

PRISONSHAKE

Singles 87–89 EP7 (Scat) 1989
I'm Really Fucked Now (Scat) 1990
A Girl Called Yes (Aus. Rubber) 1990
Della Street EP (Scat) 1991
The Roaring Third (Scat) 1993

OFFBEATS

Why Do You Hang Out EP (Oops!) 1983
I Can See Your House From Here EP (St. Valentine) 1984
Evolution of the Stickman (Relativity) 1986

SPIKE IN VAIN

Disease Is Relative (Trans Dada) 1984

Like so many bands spawned in Cleveland's post-industrial shadows, Prisonshake walks a fine line between—or, more to the point, refuses to recognize the incongruity of melding—old-school rock songwriting and avant-spuzz structure-demolition. As the years have progressed, the decreasingly prolific quartet (which relocated to St. Louis in 1995) has phased out some of its more quarrelsome habits, settling into an altogether galvanizing groove that harks back to the days when "rocking out" was a universal aspiration, not an ironist's refuge.

The singles collection—actually a box of 7-inch discs reprising Prisonshake's first four 45s—is a meticulously packaged set, reflecting guitarist/Scat majordomo Robert Griffin's venturesome design sensibilities. It's no mere curio, though: the post-punk power balladry of "Deanna" and the caustic "Fairfield Avenue Serenade" seethe with the sort of gut-corroding tension that drives characters in Jim Thompson novels to drink or kill . . . or possibly both.

In a ballsy move—one not seen since Half Japanese's 1980 debut—Prisonshake chose to release a full-blown box set as its first "album." Composed of one CD, one vinyl record, one cassette and a 7-inch single (with no overlap), **I'm Really Fucked Now** deluges listeners with about three hours' worth of short, sharp songs, ineffectual in-jokes and plenty of fragmented material in between. The CD (most of which is reprised on **A Girl Called Yes**) introduces a more expansive side—evident on the simmering "By the Side of the Road"—not to mention the flair for post-Replacements melancholia (propelled by a self-negating Doug Enkler vocal) aired on "Bedtime Beats You Senseless." The vinyl disc remixes several tracks from the singles, while the cassette (aside from Griffin's gripping "Then She Prayed") would best be recycled to tape one of the band's incendiary live shows.

The unexpectedly tender **Della Street** volunteers love songs, (almost) nothing but love songs, giving Enkler a chance to exhibit his suave side and affording the dauntingly versatile rhythm section of Chris Burgess and Scott Pickering the opportunity to ply their tricks in more challenging contexts. That said, the EP's most compelling track—a sprawling "Stuck in St. Louis"—reverts to Prisonshake's improvisatory bar band best.

Produced by Andy Shernoff of the Dictators, **The Roaring Third** consolidates Griffin and Enkler's decidedly diffuse approaches masterfully, with the former tangled up in the blues-punk strains of "Carthage Burns!" and "2 Sisters" and the latter wringing out rustic-sounding ballads, like "Always Almost There" and "Cigarette Day," that could easily provide chart fodder for John Mellencamp if he ever gets around to doing that covers set.

Before playing in Prisonshake, Enkler pulled a stint in the Offbeats, a good-natured if lightweight funnypunk quartet that had a considerable local following. Concurrently, Griffin played with Spike in Vain, a harrowing Birthday Party/Flipper-styled quartet whose excursions into barely controlled chaos are well-documented on **Disease Is Relative.** [dss]

See also *Cobra Verde, My Dad is Dead.*

PROCLAIMERS

This Is the Story (Chrysalis) 1987
Sunshine on Leith (Chrysalis) 1988
King of the Road EP (UK Chrysalis) 1990
Hit the Highway (Chrysalis) 1994

Talk about second chances. For all the wit and charm of their two neo–Everly Brothers albums in the late '80s, the folky Proclaimers—not too surprisingly—failed to incite much Stateside enthusiasm. The American market for Scottish twins with thick accents strumming acoustic guitars and tapping on bongos had yet to be developed; after five years had passed, history seemed ready to pass Craig and Charlie Reid by for good. Then "I'm Gonna Be (500 Miles)," the brothers' catchy second-album avowal of abject devotion, was tucked into the Johnny Depp film *Benny & Joon* (the soundtrack of which contains no other pop songs) and became a hit. Faster than you could say haggis and neeps, the bespectacled Glaswegians were shooting their way to sudden—if substantially belated—stardom.

Wisely, the Reids accepted the ironies of their career without making it an issue on their third album, which simply picks up where **Sunshine on Leith** left off. **Hit the Highway** gives their unreconstructed brogues and bristling enthusiasm—for love of women, life and God—a conducive, full-blooded instrumental setting, and they sing up a storm. Pete Wingfield's unfussy Nick Lowe–styled production hits a series of fine folk-soul-rockabilly-country-rock grooves, and the pair's plainly sung real-life originals of romance ("Let's Get Married," "Shout Shout"), toil ("Follow the Money") and faith ("The More I Believe," "The Light") do them proud, but America's enthusiasm for these latter-day Lonnie Donegans evidently ran out at 500 miles. [i]

See also *TPRG.*

PROFESSOR AND MARYANN

Fairy Tale (Bar/None) 1994
Lead Us Not Into Penn Station (Bar/None) 1996

Transplant the prairie skirt rock of the Innocence Mission to the cruel urban metropolis and there stands this acoustic duo from Staten Island, New York. The degree of Professor and Maryann's appeal hinges on one's penchant not for *Gilligan's Island* reruns but for hearts-and-flowers romance; the unbroken sincerity of Ken Rockwood's songwriting on **Fairy Tale** could benefit from a shot or two of cynicism and wit. Likewise, the babywoman vocals of partner Danielle Brancaccio—equal parts Clare Grogan (Altered Images) and Claudine Longet (including the poor enunciation of both)—slather too much cutesypoo icing over sentimental bon-bons like "You Can't Use a Broken Heart." To his credit, real-life academic Rockwood writes likable tunes and possesses a conversational tenor; Fernando Kral's clean, crisp production flatters his simple guitar playing. The faux-hipster vibe of "The Only Cool Spot in Town" and "Dog Tired" suggest that he may mature into an amusing storyteller.

The punning title of **Lead Us Not Into Penn Station** is just the first indication that the milk of human kindness has begun to sour for the duo, and not a moment too soon. "House by the Water" implies that Rockwood would love to blow the big city, but the song's non-stop energy colors his writing for the better; "Flea Circus," "Cadillac (I'm Still in Love With You)" and especially the resigned "Stumbling Home" all demonstrate the interplay of light and dark missing from the debut. More important, Brancaccio has shaved that extra perkiness from her delivery, yielding infinitely more charismatic results, particularly on "Tropical Rain." A most promising followup. [kbr]

PROFESSOR GRIFF (AND THE LAST ASIATIC DISCIPLES)

See *Public Enemy.*

PROLAPSE

Crate EP (UK Cherry Red) 1994
Pull Thru' Barker EP (UK Cherry Red) 1994
Doorstop Rhythmic Bloc EP (UK Cherry Red) 1994
Pointless Walks to Dismal Places (UK Cherry Red) 1994
Backsaturday (UK Lissy's) 1995 (Jetset/Big Cat) 1996

The year 1993 might not have seemed an auspicious time for new initiatives in post–Sonic Youth noise-pop. A motley gaggle of archaeology students and practitioners of experimental drama might not have seemed the people for the job, and English sleaze-rock backwater Leicester was definitely not the place. Somehow, Prolapse made this kind of activity fun again. As unappealing as the prospect of droning guitar, grinding bass riffs and pounding drums—garnished with the destruction of whatever discarded household appliances might be gleaned from the streets in the vicinity of the show—sounds, Prolapse stands apart from the art bores with its liveliness, submerged humor and preference for driving rhythmic grooves over self-indulgent fretwank. The most arresting part of the sextet's performance (often unsettling even for the initiated) is the unpredictable and generally tempestuous interaction between the two vocalists: sensitive souls in the audience tremble as the huge, hairy Scot Mick Derrick attacks the diminutive Linda Steelyard verbally and physically—yet it is generally the larger contender who takes away the more serious injuries.

Ten of Prolapse's best tunes appeared on three 1994 EPs, which proved that the group could be enjoyed as pop music in the security of one's own home; eight more followed on the band's first album at the end of that year. This was not the grim listening experience that the title **Pointless Walks to Dismal Places** or the listing of such titles as "Headless in a Beat Motel" or "Hungarian Suicide Song" might portend.

Perhaps disappointed that these offerings failed to bring them to a less discerning audience, though, Prolapse was not as prolific in 1995, releasing only a couple of singles and **Backsaturday,** an "interesting" second album recorded in a couple of days without the precaution of writing songs before rolling the tape. Beyond the occasional melody (see "TCR," one of the two American edition add-ons, which makes good use of counterpoint singing) and flashes of dynamic variety ("Framen Fr. Cesar"), the lock grooves and loosely declaimed vocals suggest the Fall with a different accent. [pnm]

PRONG

Primitive Origins (UK Spigot) 1987
Force Fed (UK Spigot) 1988 (In-Effect) 1989
Beg to Differ (Epic) 1990
The Peel Sessions EP (UK Strange Fruit) 1990 (Strange Fruit/Dutch East India Trading) 1991
Prove You Wrong (Epic) 1991
Whose Fist Is This Anyway? EP (Epic) 1992
Cleansing (Epic) 1994
Rude Awakening (Epic) 1996

Whether they're metal or not, this underground-spawned, speedcore-trained New York trio produces some of the most brutally assaultive power-rock around. Formed by singer/guitarist Tommy Victor and his CBGB co-worker Mike Kirkland (bass/vocals) with drummer Ted Parsons of the Swans, Prong debuted with **Primitive Origins,** a record whose annoying reliance on change-on-a-dime tempos keeps the lyrical street-smarts from sinking in. **Force Fed** is a far less hysterical showcase for the group's considerable chops. The control displayed on "Look Up at the Sun" and (on the US version) the grinding "Bought and Sold" is heartening. A pair of creepy-crawly instrumentals that are equal parts muscle-flex and mind-control set the stage for Prong's major-label bow.

Oddly enough, **Beg to Differ** is a lot more radical than either of Prong's indie discs. Delivering violent minimalist lyrics in a drill-sergeant bark over stark backdrops, the LP has the feel of a post-nuke documentary. The pointillist precision of Parsons' drumming leaves plenty of room for Victor and Kirkland's shared death dance. (The CD adds a nice live version of Chrome's "Third From the Sun" retrieved from a British 12-inch.)

Kirkland was replaced by Troy Gregory just before the recording of **Prove You Wrong,** a change of little sonic or compositional consequence, although it does leave Victor the sole lead vocalist. While the trio's devotion to precisely lurching rhythms keeps the songs choppy—a clenched fist twitching spasmodically as it prepares to deliver a haymaker—this dull record makes that attribute part of a tentative shift toward industrial anti-musicality. Basically, blunt-instrument originals like "Unconditional," "Hell If I Could" and "Positively Blind" walk a sloppy line parallel to Helmet; meanwhile, a tuneless cover of the Stranglers' "(Get a) Grip (on Yourself)" is harsher than the original but nowhere near as threatening. (The six-track **Whose Fist Is This Anyway?** is **Prove You Wrong**'s remix EP. Foetus and Killing Joke bassist Paul Raven are the ones tampering with "Grip," "Hell If I Could" and two others here.)

Raven subsequently joined Prong, taking over from Gregory and bringing sampler John Bechdel from Murder Inc. along with him. Seared by Terry Date's sharp-edged co-production, **Cleansing** doesn't venture too far from the band's stripped-down raunch, but does embrace tempos that are easier to follow and hoarse vocals that are harder to bear. The samples are fairly incidental, and the power is sharp and efficiently focused. Ultimately, **Cleansing** finds Prong in its favorite position: straddling styles and driving down its own power alley.

Recorded in January 1989, the Peel EP offers commanding high-voltage renditions of "Defiant," "Decay," "Senseless Abuse" and "In My Veins." [dss/i]

See also *Killing Joke, Swans; TPRG.*

CHUCK PROPHET

Brother Aldo (Fire) 1990
Balinese Dancer (China/Dutch East India Trading) 1993
Feast of Hearts (UK China) 1995

For years, Chuck Prophet did his talking with his fingers, playing the lone guitar-slinger to Danny Stuart's downbeat raconteur in the core of Green on Red. So it was a pleasant surprise when the San Francisco native finally opened up his mouth and his songbook, revealing a deft, brooding and fully formed singer/songwriter. **Brother Aldo** introduces what is actually a duo: on most songs, Prophet is joined by singer/accordionist Stephanie Finch, whose forlorn soprano provides ethereal counterpoint to his dark, gravelly tone. The other key bandmember is Chris Isaak bassist Roly Salley; pianist Spooner Oldham, Dan Penn's songwriting partner, also shows up on two tracks. There's plenty of Prophet's greasy string-bending to be found, set in a sepia-colored semi-acoustic context that includes catchy twang-pop ("Face to the Wall" and the title track), circus-barker cabaret ("Step Right This Way") and heavenly harmony-driven melodicism ("Tune of an Evening"). There's also "Look Both Ways," a song written with Chris Cacavas and Steve Wynn that later turned up on one of Wynn's records.

In a typical dumb-luck music biz move, Prophet got himself a decent European record deal—only to end up licensing his second effort to the same US indie that manufactured and distributed his first one. Its commercial viability notwithstanding, **Balinese Dancer** finds Prophet with the blues—and playing them too. Song titles like "Baton Rouge" and "Savannah" speak to the record's rootsy southern feel, though the smoking swamp-rock is augmented by grandiose pop touches and an assortment of organs, Latin percussion and folky stringed things. Highlights include the raucous, party-ready title track, the glittering melancholia of "One Last Dance" and the plaintive, loping "Who Am I Foolin." Finch takes on more of a subordinate role here, which is unfortunate; among the other contributors are Salley, David Grisman, Al Kooper, drummer Kenneth Blevins (John Hiatt, Sonny Landreth) and steel guitar ace Greg Leisz.

By this point, Prophet's solo career was a full-time gig, as he and Stuart brought Green on Red to a close in 1994. On the Steve Berlin–produced **Feast of Hearts,** he hooks up with the well-traveled Cracker rhythm section of Michael Urbano and Davey Faragher. (Coincidentally, former Camper Van Beethoven-ite David Immerglück plays mandolin and steel guitar on a few songs, though Greg Leisz is back as well.) Several numbers were co-written with Jules Shear. Not surprisingly, the result is more polished and energetic, with reverberant production that's not quite a deficit but definitely comes at the expense of Prophet's roughhewn individualism. Still, within the jaunty rock'n'roll competence lies some of his most sustained and eloquent playing. When he's not rolling through grooving burners like "Hungry Town," Prophet demonstrates newfound melodic prowess on jewels like the quietly breezy "Oh Mary" and the elegiac "Battered and Bruised." [jc]

See also *TPRG.*

PSI COM

See *Porno for Pyros.*

PSYCHEDELIC FURS

See *Love Spit Love.*

PUBLIC ENEMY

Yo! Bum Rush the Show (Def Jam/Columbia) 1987
It Takes a Nation of Millions to Hold Us Back (Def Jam/Columbia) 1988
Fear of a Black Planet (Def Jam/Columbia) 1990
Apocalypse 91 . . . The Enemy Strikes Black (Def Jam/Columbia) 1991
Greatest Misses (Def Jam/Chaos) 1992
Muse Sick-n-Hour Mess Age (Def Jam) 1994

PROFESSOR GRIFF (AND THE LAST ASIATIC DISCIPLES)

Pawns in the Game (Skywalker) 1990 (Luke) 1991
Kao's II Wiz*7*Dome (Luke/Atlantic) 1991

TERMINATOR X

Terminator X & the Valley of the Jeep Beets (P.R.O. Division/RAL/Columbia) 1991
Super Bad (P.R.O. Division/RAL) 1994

CHUCK D

Autobiography of Mistachuck (Mercury) 1996

It doesn't sound like a revolutionary idea at this point, but the leap-of-faith recognition of rap as a political medium in the mid-'80s had little more than "The Message" and the Last Poets to go on. Yet that was enough for Carlton Ridenhour, an Adelphi College student and disc jockey. As Chuck D, the self-styled "lyrical terrorist," he joined forces with comic foil Flavor Flav (William Drayton) and DJ Terminator X (Norman Rogers). Adopting a dramatic military pose and linking up with a spectacular new production team, the three formed Public Enemy as Chuck's militant bullhorn with a blasting beat.

Loaded with the bracing, bustling sound (by Hank Shocklee, Bill Stephney and others) that would become PE's trademark as much as Chuck's commanding delivery, **Yo! Bum Rush the Show** is a brilliant combination of hard-edged guitar (largely supplied by Vernon Reid) and off-kilter samples of all descriptions, topped with in-your-face raps by Chuck and Flav. But for a record that seemed to shake the firmament upon its release, surprisingly few tracks are political—even "Public Enemy No. 1" and "Miuzi Weighs a Ton" are standard MC boasts, and "You're Gonna Get Yours" is about a car. But amid such wheel-spinning, "Rightstarter (Message to a Black Man)" and "Timebomb" reveal the stirrings of an incisive thinker with something far more potent on his mind.

The blistering **It Takes a Nation of Millions to Hold Us Back** pays off on the debut's promise with topical classics like "Don't Believe the Hype," "Bring the Noise" and "Prophets of Rage." Making masterful use of knowledge and language, Chuck fires off salvos in a dozen directions, dropping names from Marcus Garvey to Minister Farrakhan, J. Edgar Hoover to Margaret Thatcher. While the music's titanic power is undeniable, the album's polarizing content makes it one of the first pop records to turn politics into an aesthetic criterion.

Before PE could make another album, a very public ruckus broke out over crude anti-Semitic assertions made by Professor Griff (Richard Griffin), the group's minister of ignorance, in a newspaper interview. Attempting to salvage the situation, Chuck D cut Griff loose in June of '89, then briefly dissolved the group. The following January, a couple of provocative lines in a pointed new single about the band's troubles ("Welcome to the Terrordome") fanned the embers back into flames, and set the stage for **Fear of a Black Planet.**

Produced by Shocklee's peerless Bomb Squad, PE's third album is a masterpiece of art and articulation, a roaring subway train of rhythmic noise over which Chuck and Flav (aided, news-style, by relevant spoken-word bites and guests) deliver harangues flowing from a haphazard but rising Afrocentric consciousness. Beyond "Fight the Power"—a spectacular call to arms initially recorded for Spike Lee's *Do the Right Thing*—**Black Planet**'s power is trained on racism in the movies ("Burn Hollywood Burn"), racism in emergency services ("911 Is a Joke") and black sexism ("Pollywanacraka").

Apocalypse 91 . . . the Enemy Strikes Black has the careening energy and topical juice of its predecessor, but Public Enemy is showing its vulnerability. Rather than handle the production personally, the Bomb Squad oversees a small group of newcomers, who leave a few weak spots. Five years after Run–DMC paired off with Aerosmith, the metallic remake of "Bring tha Noize" with Anthrax doesn't mesh and smacks of crossover anxiety; Flav's personal "A Letter to the New York Post" and "How to Kill a Radio Consultant" take the group further down a narrow solipsistic alley, fighting the power of the big historical picture Chuck marshals so effectively in "Can't Truss It" and "By the Time I Get to Arizona," a slam at the state's refusal to celebrate Martin Luther King Day. Even worse, "More News at 11" displays a bunker mentality, raising and dismissing significant questions about the group's future. The album does uphold PE's righteous opposition to oppression, regardless of source—"I Don't Wanna Be Called Yo Niga," "1 Million Bottlebags," "Get the F--- Outta Dodge"—but the group had passed peak power. Its turf chopped up by success, competition, internal troubles and inertia, Public Enemy was beginning to show erosion of its vitality and sense of mission.

In the face of gangstarism and rap's loss of political consciousness, PE issued **Greatest Misses,** an uneven collection of six substantial remixes (an enigmatic stack o' tracks that betrays nothing in terms of artistic intent), a live version of **Apocalypse 91**'s "Shut Em Down" and a half-dozen new creations, interspersed with comical or self-serving soundbites that turn the record into a scrapbook more than a retrospective. Chuck's tragic sports fable "Air Hoodlum" is the strongest of the previously unissued numbers, and Flav's bouncy "Get off My Back" is all right, but the others lack passion and punch. Of the remixes, Chuck Chillout's sketchy edition of "How to Kill a Radio Consultant" and Sir Jinx's boisterous "Who Stole the Soul?" make the most difference.

A subject of great critical concern before its release and the object of disdain afterward, **Muse Sick-n-Hour Mess Age** is another sprawling, boisterous, courageous missive that is hardly the creative disaster detractors described. Chuck's vituperative pre-emptive "I Stand Accused" ("They say I'm fallin' off / Yeah, they better call it off . . . Sick and tired of critics / But I can take a hit") and Flav's real-life problems with drugs, guns and the law don't set an especially inviting table. But even though **Muse Sick-n-Hour Mess Age** regrettably abandons the Bomb Squad's densely packed tumult in favor of a varied, less distinctive patchwork, Chuck D remains rap's sharpest, deepest thinker and music's most riveting orator. Keeping his wide-ranging eye open to destruction from within and without, he connects social and political oppression with its effects on cultural achievement. He accuses the historical white power structure in "Thin Line Between Law & Rape" ("took the rest / We ain't got jazz, rock and roll . . . a few fat ladies left singin' da blues"). "So Whatcha Gone Do Now?" slams real gangstas and, obliquely, the rappers who praise them; "Give It Up," "Live and Undrugged" and "They Used to Call It Dope" disdain drug use. An accusation against the World Health Organization ("Race Against Time") comes off nutty, and "Hitler Day" gets far too exercised about the racism of national holidays, but otherwise the album's buttonholers discourse with sharp ideas and solid reason. And repeatedly answer the question of PE's contemporary relevance—to hip-hop and the world at large. Still, Chuck's next move was to release a solo LP in '96.

After bouncing out of Public Enemy for the second and last time, Professor Griff made a pair of solo albums that move beyond the group's articulate anger with the esoteric imaginings and didactic conviction of his chosen sector of Muslim faith. Although its strong rhythm tracks are gripping enough, the baldly proselytic **Pawns in the Game** isn't about entertainment. In one typical example of Griff's outlandish beliefs about science, history and world events, he describes the UPC bar code as "an anti-Christ mechanism." Also brought to market by Luther Campbell, **Kao's II Wiz*7*Dome** pulls Griff (billed alone) closer to reality, with flaming nationalism and self-righteous victimhood rather than crackpot theories. But this time, over beats that are boring (with a disconcerting near-subliminal layer of bass), Griff articulates little, even in "My Ideology."

Terminator X has also cut a pair of solo albums.

Like Marley Marl, the DJ writes and produces his records, using guest rhymers to verbalize the songs. **The Valley of the Jeep Beets** features little-known artists (except for Chuck D and Sister Souljah on "Buck Whylin'") with average skills; the Terminator's beats are likewise less than monumental. **Super Bad** is a much more ambitious and successful project. Rallying the Godfathers of Threatt—old-school stars including Whodini, Grandmaster Flash, DJ Kool Herc and the Cold Crush Brothers, plus some of **Jeep Beets'** cast—Terminator X leads a good-natured A-to-the-Z romp through rap's early history. Tripping from Jamaica to the Bronx and back, the diverse album is kinetic, jazzy, soulful, cinematic and absurdly entertaining. [i]

See also *Sister Souljah; TPRG.*

PUBLIC IMAGE LTD.

Public Image (UK Virgin) 1978
Metal Box (UK Virgin) 1979
Second Edition (Island) 1980
Paris au Printemps (UK Virgin) 1980
The Flowers of Romance (Warner Bros.) 1981
Live in Tokyo (UK Virgin) 1983 (Elektra) 1986
This Is What You Want . . . This Is What You Get (Elektra) 1984
Commercial Zone (PiL) 1984
Album (Elektra) 1986
Cassette [tape] (Elektra) 1986
Compact Disc [CD] (Elektra) 1986
Happy? (Virgin) 1987
9 (Virgin) 1989
The Greatest Hits, So Far (Virgin) 1990
That What Is Not (Virgin) 1992

Opening Public Image's superb 1990 career compilation with the eponymous song that introduced the band to the world, John Lydon (no longer calling himself Johnny Rotten, as he did in the Sex Pistols) vehemently casts every bit of baggage overboard and then climbs onto the rail to follow it: "I'm not the same as when I began . . . the public image belongs to me . . . it's my entrance, my own creation, my grand finale, my goodbye." From that encouraging beginning, **The Greatest Hits, So Far** proceeds through the adventures of a band born in opposition, maintained in flux and fueled by Lydon's animus toward everything that tampers with his acute intelligence. Although a single disc is inadequate to fully ventilate PiL's claustrophobic closet, the fourteen songs—five of them remixed, one of them new (the useless environmentalism of "Don't Ask Me")—sketch its four walls of warped disco, caterwauling post-punk, ingenious anti-pop and worldbeat cacophony with enough detail to guide further investigation by intrigued parties.

PiL's first new album since the brilliant commercial advance of **9, That What Is Not** is a thorough comedown. Less notable for its musical contents than for the dare-you-to-see-vulgarity joke of its furry-triangle cover, the record's halfhearted stab at commercial acceptance steps squarely in the traps its predecessor smartly avoided. Produced with scant personality by Dave Jerden, the mix occasionally leaves Lydon (who sounds like a self-parody anyway) to compete for attention amidst thick clouds of guitar, drums and such unfathomable ephemera as the Tower of Power horns, a harmonica player and backing singer Bonnie Sheridan. Stabbing at some version of rock-pop normalcy, the songs display either a loss of conviction, an absence of inspiration or a grave lack of effort. Although Lydon has a few things on his agenda (deities, drug abuse, soldiers), he can't make anything of them, and his quixotic humor doesn't exactly help: There is no discernible purpose in his quoting "God Save the Queen" at the end of "Acid Drops."

Besides publishing his autobiography in 1994, Lydon has been promising a solo album for several years, but the Sex Pistols reunion in 1996 further postponed that eventuality.

Discographical asides for latecomers: The debut album is also known informally as **First Issue. Second Edition** is the American version of **Metal Box. Commercial Zone** is an abandoned version of **This Is What You Want** issued by (and featuring, as the one on Elektra does not) founding guitarist Keith Levene, who left PiL during the album's production. The generically packaged 1986 release has three format-specific titles. [i]

See also *Golden Palominos, Jah Wobble's Invaders of the Heart; TPRG.*

PULP

It (UK Red Rhino) 1983 (UK Fire) 1994
Little Girl EP (UK Fire) 1985
Dogs Are Everywhere EP (UK Fire) 1986
Freaks (UK Fire) 1986 + 1993
Separations (UK Fire) 1992 (Razor & Tie) 1995
Pulpintro: The Gift Recordings (UK Island) 1993
His 'n' Hers (Island) 1994
The Sisters EP (UK Island) 1994
Masters of the Universe: Pulp on Fire 1985–86 (UK Fire) 1995
Different Class (UK Island) 1995 (Island) 1996
Countdown: 1992–1983 (UK Nectar Masters) 1996
Simply Fuss Free (UK Island) 1996

Pulp proves that old saw about perseverance. It took ages, but singer/auteur Jarvis Cocker has grown to become a star, recognized as British pop's most astonishing storyteller and acerbic social commentator, beloved by those with a taste for wit, fashion and panache. But in Pulp's earliest incarnation, it sounds as if Cocker's goal was to be the Edwyn Collins of Sheffield. The mini-album **It** is sparse C86 folk, all wispy melodies and wimpy vocals, with "My Lighthouse" (co-written with Simon Hinkler, later of the Mission, and reprised from Pulp's 7-inch debut) being the best.

Freaks finds Cocker beginning to compose his tales of *Power, Claustrophobia, Suffocation and Holding Hands,* as the LP's subtitle has it. The band indulges in Bad Seeds–like cabaret and angular keyboard-based pop, but Cocker's lyrical genius and musical ambition are as yet unformed. The long-term lineup—bassist Steve Mackey, guitarist/violinist Russell Senior, keyboardist Candida Doyle and drummer Nick Banks—coalesced in 1988, and though there are moments (like "My Legendary Girlfriend") that hint at the Pulp to come, **Separations**—released three years after it was recorded—is still mediocre.

Just as **Separations** was finally hitting the shops, Pulp reinvented itself with the three self-released singles later collected on **Pulpintro.** The cultish tweepop gave way to a futuristic torchy theatricality, with

Cocker's deft touch for moving—and often perverse—lyrical reminiscence providing a seductive poignancy and charm. For the soundtrack to Cocker's plangent narratives, Pulp began concocting a piss-elegant mélange of glam, indie, electro-pop and '70s dance music, alive with sleazy glitter synths and pomp romanticism. Lyrically, Cocker had at last found his voice, exposing himself in such confessional scenarios of hometown Sheffield (proclaimed here "Sex City") as "Razzmatazz" and "Babies," a startling and irresistible musical short story that tells of how young Jarvis developed his voyeuristic tendencies by peeping his best (girl) friend's older sister in the act.

The bottled-up sexuality that is such a distinct part of the British personality is the theme of **His 'n' Hers.** Cocker's cracked-actor croon, fraught with appropriately timed hard breaths and deep sighs, gives life to brutally frank bedsit melodramas in which Our Jarvis peers through suburban blinds and screen doors. There he witnesses England's middle class at desperate play, with illicit teatime trysts ("Acrylic Afternoons") and wretched attempts at erotic restoration ("Pink Glove"). Along with the now-trademark stylized Stylophone symphonics, the Ed Buller–produced album is awash in terrific guitar-twinkling pop ditties ("Lipgloss" and "Do You Remember the First Time?") and strictly-ballroom disco operettas ("She's a Lady," which plucks a hook from Gloria Gaynor's "I Will Survive"). "Babies" is also included, while "Razzmatazz" appears as an unlisted bonus track. A wonderful record.

With the Britpop explosion beginning to bloom, Pulp gave "Babies" another go at chart success with the four-song **The Sisters** EP, which also includes "Your Sister's Clothes" (the sisters from "Babies" four years on). Like most sequels, it fails to recapture the delightfulness of the original. The EP's high point is the splendid "His 'n' Hers," a surprising omission from the album that took its name. For its part, Fire Records capitalized on Pulp's growing success with **Masters of the Universe,** a compilation of the band's post-**It,** pre-**Freaks** singles. With the exception of the spooky "Dogs Are Everywhere," most of the material is pretty weak. Not the same Pulp that folks were coming to love.

In 1996, after a decade-and-a-half's existence, Pulp had its British breakthrough with "Common People," a stunningly catchy, masterfully sardonic paean to upper-class slumming that made the thirty-three-year-old Cocker one of the most popular voices of Britain's teenybop generation. In addition, the Chris Thomas–produced **Different Class** boasts a fistful of classic (in the UK, at least) singles: the freaks' call to arms of "Mis-Shapes," the wistful bubblegum folk ditty "Something Changed," and the magnificent "Disco 2000," which quotes another dancefloor anthem, this time the guitar riff from Laura Branigan's "Gloria." Throughout the record, Cocker points his poison lens and impeccably dissects class warfare and sexual politics through snapshots of beautifully drawn characters, both real and imagined. There are superlative swoony ballads ("Underwear," "Live Bed Show"), snatches of ska ("Monday Morning") and jungle ("F.E.E.L.I.N.G. C.A.L.L.E.D.L.O.V.E."). "Sorted for E's & Wizz" chronicles Cocker's lost weekend at a late-'80s rave, nailing that disconcerting sense of loneliness that can occur when you're out of your head among twenty thousand people: "This hollow feeling grows and grows and grows and grows / And you want to phone your mother and say / Mother, I can never come home again / 'Cause I seem to have left an important part of my brain somewhere / Somewhere in a field in Hampshire / Alright." (**Simply Fuss Free** is a boxed set of six CD singles from **Different Class.)**

The two-disc **Countdown** compilation was dumped onto an unsuspecting public (without the band's approval) after **Different Class** catapulted Cocker and the band into the limelight. The set collects the best of Pulp's dodgy years, and therefore is not really very good at all. [mgk]

PURPLE OUTSIDE

See *Screaming Trees*

PUSSY GALORE

See *Jon Spencer Blues Explosion.*

QUEEN LATIFAH

All Hail the Queen (Tommy Boy) 1989
Nature of a Sista' (Tommy Boy) 1991
Black Reign (Motown) 1993

Although *Living Single* made her far better known in 1993 as a sitcom star than she ever was as a rapper, Queen Latifah is a musician first and foremost: she even found time to cut her third album that same year. An influential and inspiring figure of wisdom and serenely forceful skills, Latifah (Newark-born Dana Owens) began her recording career with the feminist positivity and old-school sound of the generally wonderful **All Hail the Queen.** The communally spirited debut contains "Ladies First" featuring Monie Love, "Mama Gave Birth to the Soul Children" featuring De La Soul and "The Pros" featuring Stetsasonic star Daddy-O.

Nature of a Sista' is overly ambitious and wildly uneven, largely due to a disorganized troop of studio guides. While Naughty by Nature, Luis Vega and K-Cut modernize her hip-hop, respectively, on "Latifah's Had It Up 2 Here" (which isn't as belligerent as all that), the busy, intense title track and the dancehall bop of "Sexy Fancy," SoulShock and CutFather lamely attempt to remake her as a full-service R&B performer. Tracks on which she delivers messages of unity, romance and hip-hop theory as semi-ept soul singing are so heinous and unsuitable that they sully the genuinely fine tracks. (The star doesn't help at all with the self-produced sextasy shmaltz of "How Do I Love Thee.") Although Latifah rides it all out with articulate passion and dignity—the "doo-doo stain" put-down of "Sexy Fancy" is uncharacteristically immature—**Nature of a Sista'** is not a feather in her crown.

Latifah doesn't cut back on the melodic ambitions for **Black Reign**—if anything, her third is more eclectic and style-conscious—but she gets a firmer grip on the artistic challenge and turns in a stronger, more confident-sounding record. Adding crypto-gangsta hardcore coarseness to her verbal repertoire (with guest shots by Treach, KRS-One and Heavy D, who used to be vocally averse to bad words), Latifah rhymes over bottom-booming jeep beats and sings to sweet soul, dancehall and, in the case of "Winki's Theme," a song for her late brother, a live jazz quartet. Although the bulk of the raps concern love and sex, "Just Another Day..." is a violent 'hood portrait, and "U.N.I.T.Y." takes a strong stand against women being called demeaning names. Latifah's shouldering roughneck style is a disappointing concession (especially now that she's a TV titan: would Mayim Bialik call herself a "gangsta bitch"?), but **Black Reign** is a fine recovery. [i]

QUEEN SARAH SATURDAY

Queen Sarah Saturday EP (Thirsty Ear) 1993
Weave (Thirsty Ear) 1993
June German EP (Sound Proof) 1995

Ten seconds into "Lift," the leadoff song on Queen Sarah Saturday's longplaying debut, someone whips out the hoariest fast-break guitar cliché in the how-to-grimace-and-get-chicks playbook. A minute later, the unspecified offender is back at the trough for a refill. In the meantime, vocalist/guitarist Johnny Irion has managed to demonstrate just how challenging the intricacies of generic alterna-rock melodics can be to a non-singer. There are moments on **Weave** where the young Durham, North Carolina, quartet doesn't quite sound like a bunch of no-talents ineffectually attempting to ape the latest sounds in northwestern grungery—but not many. Irion and Ryan Pickett do whip up a competent frenzy of honking guitar squall on "Dreamer" and elsewhere (they also nervously muster a bit of southern twin-leads on the gentle introduction to "Water"), but that's not much to hang an album on. (The pre-LP **Queen Sarah Saturday** EP contains a live version of "Lift" as well as three casually recorded non-LP songs. Thanks to the band's diffidence and seeming studio inexperience, "Gigi" and the eight-minute "ACD-C" almost come out all right.)

After parting company with its label, the band cut, and got some North Carolina friends to release, a winningly modest five-song EP displaying all the invention, taste and personality absent from the album. The diverse and all-too-brief **June German** leads off with "Robert DeNiro," an energetic Midwest-styled pop-punk rave with mad-crazy bass and cool lyrics ("Oh my goodness, he knows a thing about a thing or two / Robert DeNiro on a train, and your ass is on the tracks stuck with Super Glue"), and backs it up with the flower-powered "Sugar Momma" and the pretty, low-key and weird "Mr. Magic Teeth." Come back boys, all is forgiven. [i]

QUEERS

Love Me EP7 (Doheny) 1982
Kicked Out of the Webelos EP7 (Doheny) 1984
Grow Up (UK Shakin' Street) 1990 (Lookout!) 1994
A Proud Tradition EP7 (Doheny) 1992 (Selfless) 1993
Too Dumb to Quit EP7 (Doheny) 1993 (Selfless) 1993
Love Songs for the Retarded (Lookout!) 1993
Look Ma, No Flannel EP7 (Clearview) 1994
Beat Off (Lookout) 1994
Surf Goddess EP (Lookout) 1994
Rocket to Russia (Selfless) 1994
Shout at the Queers (Selfless) 1994
Suck This (Clearview) 1994 + 1996

The Queers Move Back Home (Lookout!) 1995
My Old Man's a Fatso EP7 (Wound Up) 1995
A Day Late and a Dollar Short (Lookout!) 1996
Bubblegum Dreams EP7 (Lookout) 1996
Don't Back Down (Lookout!) 1996

When a fork in punk's gutter offered the choice of obno/angry or obno/funny, bawling New Hampshire singer/guitarist Joe Queer (King) is one leather-jacketed road warrior who had no trouble deciding which way to head. (Do the titles "Kicked Out of the Webelos," "Ursula Finally Has Tits" and "I Can't Stop Farting" point the way?) Joined by stalwart bassist B-Face, drummer Hugh O'Neill and various second guitarists, the faithful Ramones fanatic—whose devotion runs deep enough that the Queers frequently play the band's songs in concert and rerecorded the entire **Rocket to Russia** album, in order, released in a tiny edition packaged with parody artwork—stands for all that is fun about loud-fast-rules rock, and his band flies the popcore banner with glorious conviction. Derivative enough to play surf rock, recycle familiar melodies and bandy buzzwords like "cretin" about, the Queers nonetheless put their own New England dirtbag stamp on loud, sloppy three-chord pop and have hacked up more than their share of catchy fist-pumping sing-alongs, dumb/brilliant ideas, great tunes and raucous energy, filling a long stream of records with countless minutes of good stupid entertainment.

Despite the name, the Queers are gay-neutral—they're not, and they don't care. Still, there's a fair amount of good-natured, avowedly tongue-in-cheek name-calling ("Fagtown") in the prolific band's early-'80s singles—most of which feature original singer Wimpy Rutherford—compiled on the thin-sounding but illuminating and funny as shit **A Day Late and a Dollar Short.** Track thirty-four is a twenty-minute reunion of the old lineup doing a live-in-the-studio WFMU broadcast in the early '90s.

Grow Up, the debut album that contains "Junk Freak" ("We're not as famous as the Pixies or the Bags / Hey, we may be the Queers but we ain't no fags") also announces (in "Gay Boy," remade from a single) "It's perfectly acceptable to be a gay boy." (As the liner notes admit, "We know some of these lyrics are pretty insensitive but we didn't write these songs to hurt anybody's feelings.") Joe does have strong objections to other things, some of which he shares on **Love Songs for the Retarded:** white-power skins ("You're Tripping"), certain green vegetables ("I Hate Everything") and hippies ("Granola-Head," which contains the immortal couplet "I'd rather be at home / Listening to the Ramones"). But when he sings "Fuck the World," it's only because he wants to spend the night hanging out with a girlfriend. And while his **Beat Off** harangue about "Ben Weasel" repeats other people's complaints about the writer/Screeching Weasel rocker (also the album's producer), Joe can't muster any harsher indictment than "He don't like Nirvana / I know he don't like Prong / And I'll bet you five bucks that he don't like this song." He manages a much stronger attack on rock'n'roll uniform wearers in "Drop the Attitude Fucker."

For a while, the band's studio albums were fairly consistent, navigating a narrow stylistic realm, each adding a few Queers qlassics to the qanon. **Love Songs for the Retarded** has the strongest material and the fullest sound. **Beat Off** boasts "Voodoo Doll," "Too Many Twinkies" and a ripping cover of Tommy James' "Mirage." The shitty-sounding **Grow Up** has "I Met Her at the Rat," "Burger King Queen," "Goodbye California" and the winsome "I'll Be True to You"; the sizzling, upbeat and pop-conscious **Move Back Home** soars with such sensitive character studies as "If You Only Had a Brain," "High School Psychopath II" and "She's a Cretin."

After years of such solid achievement, the Queers accelerated to genuine pop-punk-surfcore brilliance. The four-song 7-inch **Bubblegum Dreams** inaugurates the trio's new pop era with the irresistible "Punk Rock Girls" ("Me and Dr. Frank have both decided that we love them more than toast," Joe sings, implicating his Mr. T Experience–leading labelmate in the post-adolescent lechery) and three other tunes, including a diabolical falsetto-spiked cover of the Beach Boys' "Little Honda," and a solid swipe at the Muffs' "End It All." The full-length **Don't Back Down,** also produced by JJ Rassler (ex-DMZ) and engineer Mass Giorgini, takes off from there, showcasing another Brian Wilson tune (the anthemic hodad ode of the title track), a version of the same-vintage Hondells B-side, "Little Sidewalk Surfer Girl" and a killer cavalcade of super-catchy melodic originals: "Janelle, Janelle," "I Can't Get Over You," "I Only Drink Bud" and "Born to Do Dishes." Without abandoning crudely funny sexism ("No Tit," "Brush Your Teeth") and smiley-face animosity ("I'm OK, You're Fucked"), the Queers catch a wave and shoot the tube, taking pop-punk out for another exhilarating ride as if it were a brand new toy.

Although presented as a live album, the limited-edition (and vinyl-only) **Shout at the Queers** was, like **Suck This,** recorded before a small crowd in a South Carolina studio. Both capture the breathless rush of a Queers set with enthusiastic abandon. The former has an alternate drummer in place of O'Neill; the latter features Vapid and Panic from Screeching Weasel in the lineup. [i]

See also *Screeching Weasel.*

QUICKSAND

Quicksand EP (Revelation) 1990
Slip (Polydor) 1993
Manic Compression (Island) 1995

The members of this New York quartet grew up on the stridently philosophical side of the tracks of the mid-'80s punk scene in Gotham, having cut their teeth in zealous combos like Youth of Today, Gorilla Biscuits and Absolution. By the time Quicksand formed in 1989, they'd outgrown the one-dimensional sonic attack of that era, but not the militant—and occasionally sanctimonious—outlook.

A self-titled EP (released on a label that also became ground zero for New York's intriguing Krishna-core movement) vaunted both the band's best and worst instincts: guitarist Tom Capone's muscular, cliché-free riffing, serving up a blue-collar rejoinder to the art-Sabbath crunch concurrently conjured by Helmet's Page Hamilton, is catalytic enough to provoke involuntary locomotion, but frontman Walter Schreifels' strained proselytizing capsizes songs like the brotherhood paean "Omission." The spacious instrumental closer, "Hypno Jam With Dan" (featuring Dan Doolin on trumpet), is thoroughly impressive, however.

There's not a whole lot of breathing room to be found on **Slip,** an album that sees the quartet swerve from the path it had scoped out—roughly parallel to the trail blazed by Fugazi—for more commercial pursuits. **Slip** is hardly a sell-out, more like a U2-ization, right down to the vocal swoops Schreifels flaunts in shirt-rending tunes like "Head to Wall" and "Unfulfilled." Even Capone seems prone to a few Edge-styled harmonic tangents, which saps some of the raw power—a shortage that's particularly evident on a rerecording of "Omission."

Manic Compression is quite a bit more direct—the martial overtones of "Delusional" are downright ominous. Producers Wharton Tiers (who also worked on the band's debut) and Don Fury condense the sonics considerably on tracks like the writhing "Divorce" and the brittle "Thorn in My Side" (both of which indicate Schreifels should ease up on the Jane's Addiction listening). Quicksand split up in late 1995, but Schreifels—who went on to form the four-piece World's Fastest Car—reached the charts anyway, as co-producer of "Can't Wait One Minute More," a '95 hit for longtime cohorts CIV. [dss]

See also *CIV.*

RACHEL'S

Handwriting (Quarterstick) 1995
Music for Egon Schiele (Quarterstick) 1996
The Sea and the Bells (Quarterstick) 1996

This unique music and design project based in Louisville, Kentucky, centers on the core of Jason Noble (ex-Rodan), namesake Rachel Grimes and Juilliard student Christian Frederickson. Somewhere between meticulous and improvisational, the Rachel's blurs the genres of classical and experimental music to deliver sublime, intelligent, occasionally haunting compositions. In the indie-rock world with which these composers are associated—through Noble's background, the Quarterstick label and musicians on the first album—Rachel's is quite an anomaly.

Recorded at various times and places beginning in 1991, **Handwriting** unites an unlikely collection of players, as members of Rodan, the Coctails and Shellac join members of two symphony orchestras and other musicians in an intriguing seven-song recording. Frederickson plays viola, Grimes piano and Noble electric bass, guitar and tapes. The supporting cast provides strings, percussion and woodwinds. Using vibes, winds and traps, "M. Daguerre" is the closest to jazz the ensemble gets, but the song's main theme gives way to effective, unsettling improv, as well as delicate passages led by Grimes' piano and a string section. Other selections (the title track, "Southbound to Marion," "Saccharin," "Seratonin" and Grimes' solo piano composition, "Frida Kahlo") are contemporary classical pieces; while they're good listening, they don't "rock" in any conventional sense. Finally, Noble seems to be in charge of "Full on Night," a fourteen-minute avant-abstraction with guitar, piano, tape loops and percussion that wouldn't sound too out of place on a Slint record or the *Eraserhead* soundtrack. The limited-edition CD comes in a handsome letterpress paper sleeve with an equally stylish booklet.

The Rachel's also became involved in scoring for stage productions and film. **Music for Egon Schiele,** performed by Grimes, Frederickson and cellist Wendy Doyle and packaged even more ornately, is a Grimes composition for a dance/theater production based on the life of the Viennese painter. [mww]

See also *Coctails, Rodan, Shellac.*

RADIAL SPANGLE

Raze EP (UK Mint Industries/Beggars Banquet) 1993
Ice Cream Headache (Mint Industries/Beggars Banquet) 1993
Birthday EP (UK Mint Industries/Beggars Banquet) 1993
Syrup Macrame (Mint Industries/Beggars Banquet) 1994

Some rock bands are born of the rustbelts and heartlands; the members of Radial Spangle, however, had either the misfortune or the good grace (take your pick) to be stuck in Norman, Oklahoma. Unlike fellow Normans the Flaming Lips (an early influence), Radial Spangle opted not to tour, instead digging in and writing songs that reflected both an isolationist naïveté and a warped, mind-expansionist aesthetic. As with America's small-town homegrown psychedelic warriors of the '60s, geographical limitations bred grand stylistic permutations. Mercury Rev's Jonathan Donahue took a liking to the band; he put in a good word to his English label, and Radial Spangle—despite never having played outside the city limits—found itself with a recording contract in 1992, just months after forming.

Ice Cream Headache was engineered by Rev's David Fridmann but essentially self-produced by the band, whose creative core consists of guitarist Alan Laird and bassist April Tippens (Richard English, ex–Flaming Lips, did the drumming but was replaced shortly after the album's release by Kelsey Kennedy). Imperfect but entertaining, the record is equal parts abrasive, assaultive skronk (the opening "Raze" features neo-metallic guitar distorto-riffing and a pounding drum pattern, while "Drip" owes an obvious debt to the Lips), dreamily atmospheric pop-swoon ("Canopy and Shoe," "Snow") and experimental weirdness (a disjointed, nine-minute, psychedelic jam called "Copper"). One connecting feature throughout is Laird and Tippens' quirky, sweet-but-sour boy/girl harmonies. Another is Laird's wah-wah and effects box fetish, which he rarely fails to put on display, even during the quieter songs.

After **Birthday,** which includes three songs from a John Peel session, Laird and Fridmann again teamed up to produce **Syrup Macrame.** While less in-your-face, the album displays a lighter touch that suggests a songwriting talent eager to branch out. Each tune is enigmatically designated as either "countrysong" or "citysong," and there does seem to be a stylistic division. "Marble" is gentle and pastoral, with shimmery/echoey guitar lines and a contemplative Laird vocal; it's a countrysong. "Special Love" is more spasmodic, serving up clipped, dissonant guitar notes over a martial beat; this citysong sounds a lot like Wire or the Fall. Several lapses in musical judgment mar the disc's overall quality: "Busy Hole" is a pointless percussion/vocal rant, while "Patio Furniture" inexplicably attempts country banjo/singalong hoedown shtick. Also, the album doesn't employ the Laird/Tippens harmonies prominently enough. Still, the band's knack for gorgeous melodies is profound, and the Radial Spangle pop-psych sensibility, while in transition, remains rooted in the anything-goes ideal that has always fueled small-town rockers. [fm]

See also *Flaming Lips.*

RADIOHEAD

Drill EP (UK Parlophone) 1992
Pablo Honey (Capitol) 1993

My Iron Lung EP (UK Parlophone) 1994
The Bends (Capitol) 1995

It's usually safe as milk to assume that bands that make splashy entrances—as England's Radiohead did, with a gimmicky self-deprecating US debut ("Creep") that slyly "fuck"ed its way up the charts—have no place to go but down. That makes the enormous creative growth between **Pablo Honey** and **The Bends** all the more admirable.

The Oxford quintet has one bad habit (trying to sound like a young English U2) and several good ideas on **Pablo Honey,** although "Creep" is not chief among them. The single's comforting admission of worthlessness ("I wish I was special, so fucking special, but I'm a creep") predates Beck's "Loser" by a year, but Thom Yorke's vocals are too self-consciously drab to be convincing. Johnny Greenwood's choking guitar explosions are far more corrosive, but they're not what the song is about. The fervent, nearly spiritual view of alienated ambition stated in the rousing and catchy "Anyone Can Play Guitar" cuts much closer to the bone and seems truer to the band's actual desires. "Destiny protect me from the world . . . I wanna be Jim Morrison." In a similar musical vein, "Ripcord" uses a twin-guitar roar and Yorke's impassioned singing (sometimes layered into Byrdsy harmonies) to good effect, lashing out at the quiet melodic lines with aggressive, edgy noise assaults. While other tracks exploit that dynamic tension ("Blow Out" detonates the first half's jazzy daintiness with Greenwood's howling wind-tunnel noise demonstration and Phil Selway's Keith Moon drum bursts), a few remove the electroshock therapy completely. The acoustic "Thinking About You" is a fine, sensitive love song that suggests a solemn intelligence beneath the media-conscious bluster.

The five noncommittal new tracks on **My Iron Lung** deconstruct the first album's ingredients, leaving a simpler, less evidently contrived and casually produced sound. That's progress of a sort, though only "The Trickster" and "Permanent Daylight" have the compositional clarity to take advantage. The Beatlesy title track is an intriguing digression, but the lyrics ("This is our new song / Just like the last one / A total waste of time") only reinforce the structural resemblance to Radiohead's previous bout of ego failure.

"Am I really sinking this low? . . . I wish it was the '60s / I wish I could be happy / I wish I wish I wish that something would happen," sings Yorke in the disconsolate title track of **The Bends.** He then proceeds to savagely yawn and moan his way through such vague miseries for the entirety of this provocative testament to faded glamour and crepuscular youth. Produced, as was the EP, with a minimum of fuss by John Leckie, **The Bends** constantly undersells itself, which makes Yorke's expressions of acceptable angst all the more dismally seductive. Everything here is fake or broken; Yorke is cynical, vulnerable and exhausted. His response to pain is chemical anesthesia; he dreams of being "Bullet Proof" and chooses unconsciousness over confrontation. (Reprised in this context, "My Iron Lung" makes perfect sense: "We're too young to fall asleep / Too cynical to speak / We're losing it can't you tell?") Meanwhile, guitarists Greenwood and Ed O'Brien tickle and rattle with a staggering array of clever instrumental approaches, building a complex web of energy and anger, frustration and hopelessness—all in the guise of accessible pop songs. Now *that's* special. [i]

RAEKWON

See *Wu-Tang Clan.*

RAGE AGAINST THE MACHINE

Rage Against the Machine [tape] (no label) 1992
Rage Against the Machine (Epic Associated) 1992
Evil Empire (Epic) 1996

Based in Southern California, this multi-ethnic thrash/rap quartet takes a revolutionary stance behind former Orange County straight-edge vocalist Zack de la Rocha (formerly of New York's Inside Out and California's Farside) and his incendiary lyrics. Blasting away at cultural imperialism, the politics of greed, Eurocentricism and injustice, Rage Against the Machine unleashes an inspired and inspirational clamor that raises awareness as well as neck hairs. (The group practices what it preaches, battling censorship and protesting on behalf of Native American prisoner Leonard Peltier. In 1995, de la Rocha helped organize relief missions to Chiapas, Mexico, to aid the indigenous rebels there in their struggle with the government.)

Musically, Rage Against the Machine creates an awesome pastiche of hardcore's fury, hip-hop's journalistic lyricism, metal's rhythmic crunch and reggae's righteousness. Guitarist Tom Morello plays an innovative mix of crunching distortion and sirening feedback. (New York City native and Harvard honors graduate Morello was in LA's Lock Up, which made an album entitled **Something Bitchin' This Way Comes** for Geffen in 1990.)

The blueprint for the group's major-label album was laid on the twelve-song self-released cassette, the cover image of which is stock-market indexes with a single match taped to the inlay card. While the tape's version of "Bullet in the Head" was transferred intact to the subsequent album, the potent "Darkness of Greed" wasn't; others ("Auto Logic," "The Narrows," the perfunctory raga-rock of "Mindset's a Threat") were more understandably left behind. And while "Clear the Lane" showcases Morello's def(t) instrumental gifts, the song doesn't pack much lyrical weight.

On its full-fledged debut (with an even more provocative image, of a Buddhist monk's self-immolation), the band turns the revolutionary power up full blast, as bassist Timmy C. and drummer Brad Wilk anchor the proceedings with belligerent rhythms. Juxtaposing South Central LA and South Africa on "Township Rebellion," de la Rocha looms metaphysically large, especially backed by the ferocity of the band's musical attack. When he whispers, "Anger is a gift" on "Freedom," his seething is entirely believable. De la Rocha may turn to hooky sloganeering on his choruses, but he backs it up with substantial verses. Lines like "If we don't take action now / We settle for nothing later" ("Settle for Nothing") and "We gotta take the power back" ("Take the Power Back") signal urgency while the surrounding verses detail why. And though the group is too traditionally macho to include feminism in its radical platform, **Rage Against the Machine** is still one of the most empowering records of the '90s.

Rage constructs another savage soundtrack on **Evil Empire**—Morello's guitar yields an array of aggressive sounds, and Wilk and Timmy (renamed Tim Bob) are even more forceful. Still inflammatory but more subtle, de la Rocha pursues his political involvement with references to Mexico and persons of color ("Without a Face," "People of the Sun," "Wind Below," among others). Barking his revenge fantasies at the privileged in "Down Rodeo," de la Rocha also makes an attempt to bring women into the fold with "Year of tha Boomerang" and "Revolver," a tale of domestic violence. While just as furious as its predecessor, **Evil Empire** lacks the immediacy that made it so explosive. [mww]

See also *Farside.*

RAILROAD JERK

Railroad Jerk (Matador) 1990
Raise the Plow (Matador) 1992
Milk the Cow EP7 (PCP) 1993
We Understand EP (Matador) 1993
One Track Mind (Matador) 1995
Bang the Drum EP (Matador) 1995

Basically, there are three things you can do on bottleneck guitar—tease out sliding melody lines like some would-be Delta jazzman (see Duane Allman), focus on hard, simply effective licks (the Elmore James approach) or slash at it casually for the raucous uncertainty of chords that never stop to articulate notes but smother them in rusty disrepair, instantly evoking trouble and desperation. New York's Railroad Jerk, of course, dives straight into the sonic garbage can option on its first album, a northern punk distortion of southern rural blues that's disarming in its reverence and bracing in its free-minded chaos alteration of stock structures.

Railroad Jerk, harshly recorded in a two-day blast with Wharton Tiers, pits Minnesota native Marcellus Hall's voice, electric guitar and harmonica against a lurching rhythm section in which guitarist Chris Mueller complicates, rather than passes over, the intentionally awkward tempos. Scavenging classic country blues records for whatever bits they find useful, the quartet reassembles them with their eyes clenched shut, ensuring plenty of loose ends, calamitous collisions and raw scrapes along the way. "Old Mill Stream" and "Talking RR Jerk Blues" (which casually quotes lines from various '60s rock'n'roll hits) and "Ninety-Nine Miles" will never be added to the Delta Blues Museum's permanent collection, but the band's enthusiasm and structural integrity—reminiscent of the Stones' early records—make the songs compelling on their own terms. Rather than make a big condescending deal out of its reference points, Railroad Jerk simply gets on with original music that acknowledges its debts.

Hall and bassist Tony Lee are the only survivors of the debut's lineup on **Raise the Plow;** drummer Steven Cerio and various guests, including Uncle Wiggly guitarist William Berger, join them for a more sophisticated, refined exploration of broader terrain and influences. Having partly exorcised its need to kick against the pricks, Railroad Jerk can manage the poise to make a psycheDylanesque run at the blues in the mounting cataclysm of Bukka White's all-but-unrecognizable "Fixin' to Die" (the droning "You Can't Go Back" drops a second Dylan reference), throw Creedence Clearwater against a wall in "Call Me the Son," goof on a country two-step in "Yes Baby" and summon up visions of Gary Lucas' cerebral guitar work for Captain Beefheart in the edgy "During the War." Not an entirely satisfying album—the band's many ideas too often run a few steps ahead of their execution—but an encouraging leap forward.

Following the **Milk the Cow** double-7-inch, the placeholding **We Understand** EP finds Hall and Lee joined by guitarist Alec Stephen (who joined in time to be pictured but not included on **Raise the Plow**) and drummer Dave Varenka, casually mucking out some of the same artistically appointed stalls with more determination and familiarity. At times, Railroad Jerk sounds like four unrelated musicians randomly in search of a parallel finish line, but the group has its own unique gravity and holds together to keep from going off the tracks in different directions. Although the band isn't quite ready to be pinned down and mounted, the four songs ("Halfway Across" and "Grandstand Blackout" are the keepers) triangulate a raunchy, melodic rusticism that incorporates elements of Tom Waits, Television, the Mekons and Fall—without drawing a bead on any of them.

With an intriguing declaration—"Well I'm hi-fi and I'm low-brow / I'm history but you know I'll make it somehow"—Hall kicks the band (amazingly, the same lineup) into gear on **One Track Mind,** a dandy album that can't decide whether it wants to be loved, hated, feared or simply ignored. Coming on like a post-punk resurrection of the Band or a scum-rock **Beggars Banquet** but too singular and erratic to characterize, the record uses Hall's acidly ironic intelligence and gritty singing as an accessible spindle in "Gun Problem," "The Ballad of Railroad Jerk," "Home=Hang," "Zero Blues" and other tracks. But the music won't toe the line. Indulging the band's craggy abstruseness, "Bang the Drum" is a Beck-style "Maggie's Farm" rap variation; "You Better Go Now" is a maddening syncopated firewall of nearly unrelated scales and solos; "Riverboat" rolls Tom Verlaine in an alley and dumps him and his weird guitar playing in a swamp. At a potent high point, "Forty Minutes" bleakly faces impending doom with only acoustic guitar, a death rattle, a bit of harmonica and a sardonic la-la-la chorus for accompaniment to Hall's last will and testament. "Who will the world revolve around now?" he wonders, wry to the very end.

Bang the Drum contains the titular album track, a hideous alternate version of "Home=Hang," an outtake and three live acoustic radio-studio scraps, including a properly cavalier cover of the Beatles' "Why Don't We Do It in the Road?" and **Railroad Jerk**'s "In My Face (Pretty Flower)." [i]

See also *Smack Dab.*

RAINCOATS

The Raincoats (UK Rough Trade) 1979 (DGC) 1993
Odyshape (Rough Trade) 1981 (DGC) 1994
The Kitchen Tapes [tape] (ROIR) 1983
Animal Rhapsody EP (UK Rough Trade) 1983
Moving (UK Rough Trade) 1984 (DGC) 1994
Extended Play EP (Smells Like) 1994
Fairytales (Tim/Kerr) 1995
Looking in the Shadows (DGC) 1996

Somehow, the Raincoats' old records have gotten better since they were made. After Kurt Cobain repeatedly cited the neglected English post-punk band as an inspiration (and other bands, from Sonic Youth to the Voodoo Queens, chimed in), his band's record label reissued the London quartet's three studio albums with nice liner notes. The vinyl-only **Fairytales** samples all three albums, though rather unevenly: eight songs from the first, three from the second, two from the third.

Invited to open for Nirvana on their 1994 tour, the decade-gone Raincoats re-formed, with original members Gina Birch (bass/vocals) and Ana da Silva (guitar/vocals) joined by new violinist Anne Wood and guest drummer Steve Shelley of Sonic Youth. Cobain's suicide ended those plans, but the band went on a triumphant American tour anyway, playing a lot of classics, a few new originals and a cover of Alternative TV's "Love Lies Limp." A John Peel session from April 1994 (two new songs, "No One's Little Girl" from **Moving** and "Shouting Out Loud" from **Odyshape**) was released on Shelley's label as **Extended Play.**

On **Looking in the Shadows,** the first new Raincoats album in a dozen years, Birch, da Silva, Wood and American drummer Heather Dunn (ex–Tiger Trap, Lois) present a hair-raising variety of stylistic approaches. The first half favors calm, cute, occasionally craggy pop that thaws out a vintage new wave sound: "Only Tonight" and "Forgotten Words" resemble the deadpan neo-cool of Angel Corpus Christi, while the disconcerting "Babydog" (a droll fantasy alternative to fertility), the willfully insipid "Pretty" and the noisy avant-continental "Don't Be Mean" (unveiled on the EP) take slipperier turns through the band's past. The second half has a tougher, less alluring punk edge and fewer instances of coquetry. The slickness—credit years of experience, maturity, the reunion's recharge and producer Ed Buller, known for his work with Pulp and Suede—draws a clear line between the Raincoats then and now. While longtime fans may perceive it as an abandonment of ideals, this bewitching record stands proud against the sounds of today. [ddw/i]

See also *Tiger Trap; TPRG.*

RAIN TREE CROW

See *David Sylvian.*

RAKE'S PROGRESS

Cheese Food Prostitute EP (hifi) 1994
Altitude (Almo Sounds) 1995

Art school has been the petri dish for more great English bands than that nation's unemployment line. Though America's education system doesn't provide quite the same refuge for creative teenagers trying to avoid a career, it's not uncommon for dreamy rockers studying painting or graphic design to coalesce around audio projects. While that process can yield Talking Heads, it is also responsible for the Rake's Progress. Westchester-born guitarist Gregg Lapkin and singer Tim Cloherty, the core of the New York–based quintet, met at Parsons School of Design in the late-'80s; the others brought along impressive credits studying and performing classical music, a genre that might have served them better than the band's uninspired middle-of-the-road alternapop and rock.

The inexplicably titled six-song EP starts (and might as well have ended) with the mildly rendered "You Must Be on Drugs," mainly an excuse for the invigorating, questionably unironic singalong chorus: "Sell me something, get me high / Make me perfect, make me blind / Squeeze my head to milk my mind." The Banana Splits said it better. **Altitude** adds a few more catchy bits while toughening the attack into a generic nothing that could be Toad the NRBQ Sprocket or somebody equally faceless. Songs about cross-dressing ("Howard Is a Drag"), drinking ("Man Overboard," "2 Eggs Any Style"), romantic collapse ("Whatever," "Looks Like This Could Be the End"), suicide (the mawkish semi-acoustic "I Hope You Miss Me"), geography ("Port au Prince Tourist Information") and urban paranoia ("I'll Talk My Way Out of This One," reprised from the EP) evince a certain rakish intelligence, but the band's overriding blandness keeps the album from leaving any permanent marks. Even the occasional bout of stupidity ("Heart Full of Stuff" works over the word "fuck" like a six-year-old who has just been punished for saying it) is incidental. [i]

RAMBLIN' JEFFREY LEE

See *Gun Club.*

RAMONES

Ramones (Sire) 1976
Leave Home (Sire) 1977
Rocket to Russia (Sire) 1977
Road to Ruin (Sire) 1978
It's Alive (UK Sire) 1979 (Sire/Warner Archives) 1995
End of the Century (Sire) 1980
Pleasant Dreams (Sire) 1981
Subterranean Jungle (Sire) 1983
Too Tough to Die (Sire) 1984
Animal Boy (Sire) 1986
Halfway to Sanity (Sire) 1987
Ramones Mania (Sire) 1988
Brain Drain (Sire) 1989
End of the Decade (UK Beggars Banquet) 1990
All the Stuff (And More) Volume One (Sire/Warner Bros.) 1990
All the Stuff (And More) Volume Two (Sire/Warner Bros.) 1991
Loco Live (Sire/Warner Bros.) 1992
Mondo Bizarro (Radioactive) 1992
Acid Eaters (Radioactive) 1994
¡Adios Amigos! (Radioactive) 1995
Greatest Hits Live (Radioactive) 1996

DEE DEE KING

Standing in the Spotlight (Sire) 1989

VARIOUS ARTISTS

Rock'n'Roll High School (Sire) 1979
Gabba Gabba Hey: A Tribute to the Ramones (Triple X) 1991

Although it took the Ramones two decades to decide they'd had enough—the band retired after doing Lollapalooza as a farewell tour in 1996—the group will always owe its enduring legacy to the first three albums of a prolific and frequently great career. The undisputed punk-pop classics that form the group's must-own triptych are the collective blueprint for a distinct and sublimely original rock'n'roll sound and vision that have been copied endlessly (sometimes literally) since the albums were released in the 1970s.

But perfection—even moronic three-chord cartoon

perfection—is unsustainable. Coincident to its first lineup change (the departure of drummer/co-producer Tommy Erdelyi), **Road to Ruin** led the New York quartet off the tracks it had so brilliantly laid. Through two determined but uneven subsequent decades, singer Joey Ramone (Jeff Hyman), guitarist Johnny Ramone (John Cummings), bassist Dee Dee Ramone (Douglas Colvin, later replaced by Christopher "C.J." Ward) and either Marky Ramone (Marc Bell) or Richie Ramone (Reinhardt) on drums have attempted to reclaim, revitalize, revise or reinvent the spirited joy of those primary masterstrokes.

The Ramones spent the '80s making up-and-down albums with an amazing array of producers in a number of divergent (but related) styles. **End of the Century,** with the intimidating presence of the legendary Phil Spector, is good; the polish and (relative) wordiness of the songs show the band outgrowing punk's limits. Dubious bonus: Joey warbling "Baby, I Love You." Graham Gouldman of 10cc produced **Pleasant Dreams,** edging the Ramones from minimalism toward heavy metal while admitting their careerist frustration in "We Want the Airwaves."

The underrated **Subterranean Jungle** (produced by Ritchie Cordell and Glen Kolotkin) eases off the breakneck tempos but otherwise puts the Ramones back to where they once belonged: crummy '60s pop brought into alignment with modern rock taste. That means not only a couple of acid-age oldies ("Time Has Come Today," "Little Bit o' Soul") but originals with mental problems ("Psycho Therapy") and boys hung up on girls and themselves.

On **Too Tough to Die**—with Richie taking over from Marky and Erdelyi returning to co-produce with Ed Stasium (the same tag-team as on **Road to Ruin**)—the Ramones get serious about stealing back some thunder from the scene they'd inspired. The sound is more ferocious than ever, and the quick-hit lengths of some songs fly the old-school flag. (Ironically, the album's best track is "Howling at the Moon," a slick pop number produced by David A. Stewart.) But on **Animal Boy,** produced by ex-Plasmatic Jean Beauvoir, the Ramones resemble a straight rock band as never before, giving a commercial kick to some very cool songs, including "Something to Believe In" and "My Brain Is Hanging Upside Down (Bonzo Goes to Bitburg)," a topical doozy about then-president Reagan.

The years of stylistic foundering ended temporarily on **Halfway to Sanity,** a confident dose of Ramones fundamentalism co-produced by guitarist Daniel Rey. The mix of gutsy rock and effervescent pop has some of the most intriguingly thoughtful lyrics of the band's career. Upon the album's release, Richie quit over a salary dispute and Marky reclaimed his drummer's seat.

Produced with no special character by Bill Laswell, **Brain Drain** is Dee Dee's swan song. The Ramones' unease makes them sound aimless and diffuse on all but a few tracks. So while it sinks to the grumbly "Don't Bust My Chops," the album rises to deliver the anthemic inspirational message of "I Believe in Miracles," the clumsy but convincing "Pet Sematary" (created as the theme song for the Stephen King horror film) and the poignant if unseasonal "Merry Christmas (I Don't Want to Fight Tonight)."

With that equivocal gesture, the Ramones ceased to record for Sire, which unloaded **Loco Live,** a flat thirty-two-song Barcelona concert (1991) document. Debbie Harry's liner notes are a nice touch, and it *is* the recorded debut by new bassist/singer C.J. (who also plays in Los Gusanos, a non-punk rock quartet from Long Island that debuted in '93 with a 7-inch of "Quick to Cut" b/w "Ride" on Vital Music).

The three years that elapsed between **Brain Drain** and **Mondo Bizarro** signaled major changes in the rock environment as well as the band's internal alignment. Although gone from the lineup, Dee Dee, always a crucial contributor to the Ramones aesthetic, co-wrote three songs; in a harbinger of his expanding role, C.J. got to sing two numbers. But whatever might have been taking place in Seattle or Chicago—an indirect result of what the Ramones did more than a decade earlier—producer Ed Stasium protects against any evidence of it sneaking in here. An ordinary-sounding big-punk album that gets most of its character from Joey's vocals (newly bolstered and deepened; at one point, he resembles Iggy Pop) and most of its inner strength from outside songwriters (Daniel Rey, Dee Dee and Andy Shernoff), **Mondo Bizarro** reaches for old-fashioned values like silly lyrics ("Heidi Is a Headcase"), topical protest ("Censorshit") and urban reality ("Cabbies on Crack"), but succeeds best in the sensitive genericism of "Poison Heart," "Strength to Endure" and "I Won't Let It Happen," a folk-rocker whose chorus was unceremoniously lifted from Slade's "I Won't Let It 'Appen Agen."

Other people's pop tunes have always been fodder for the Ramones; going back to the first album's 1:51 distillation of Chris Montez's "Let's Dance," the quartet has fed all manner of originals into its trash compactor to prove they could all come out sounding the same. That's one problem with **Acid Eaters,** an entertaining but thin album of apt '60s oldies. The Amboy Dukes' "Journey to the Center of the Mind" (sung by C.J.), Jan and Dean's "Surf City," Love's "7 and 7 Is" and the Seeds' "Can't Seem to Make You Mine" are effective Ramones source material and come out cool, but the Who's "Substitute" (notwithstanding Pete Townshend's inaudible backing vocals) and the Jefferson Airplane's "Somebody to Love" have entirely wrong attributes for them; the clumsy renditions are plain and inadequate. Creedence's "Have You Ever Seen the Rain" nicely survives the roughhousing, but C.J.'s punk emission of Dylan's "My Back Pages" ends in a draw, as does Joey's gentle rendition of the Stones' "Out of Time."

Titled to be the band's parting bow, **¡Adios Amigos!** begins with a fitting cover—Tom Waits' "I Don't Want to Grow Up," charged with enough brisk punk energy to bring its wistful wish within cosmic reach—and dives headlong into the band's familiar moshpit with a marvelously unambitious rhythm-guitar sound. Produced by Daniel Rey, the album is lean, hard and basic; as disconcerting as it is to hear C.J. spell Joey as lead vocalist on a third of the songs, the record holds together, and his artlessness actually serves to extend a hand toward the Green Day generation. Joey's sixteen-word "Life's a Gas," C.J.'s nine-word "Got Alot to Say" ("I can't remember now" and a personal pronoun complete the concordance) and the clichéd concern of Dee Dee/Rey's "Cretin Family" are downright nostalgic; Joey's "She Talks to Rainbows" is one of his most accomplished and appealing songs ever. Bolstering the effort, the band borrows "The Crusher" from Dee

Dee's 1989 solo album and reclaims its cover of the Heartbreakers' "I Love You" from a Johnny Thunders tribute record. Recorded before a final decision about the band's termination had been made, the Ramones sound glad to be doing what they do; **¡Adios Amigos!** is ironically as lively and encouraging a record as they've made since the mid-'80s. Next stop (as soon as they're eligible, in 2001): The Rock and Roll Hall of Fame.

Rock'n'Roll High School is the various-artists soundtrack to the band's brilliant B-movie; it contains two new songs and an eleven-minute live medley. **It's Alive,** a London concert recording with Tommy drumming, reprises most of the first three albums; long available only as a double-album import, it was packaged as a single CD for its belated US issue. **Greatest Hits Live** captures a nifty New York show from February '96: if not exactly what the title promises, the sixteen tunes (augmented by a pair of leftover studio numbers) are a nostalgic stroll through the band's back pages, zipping from "Beat on the Brat" to "Pet Sematary" and juxtaposing oldies like "I Wanna Be Sedated" with the group's recent swipe at the "Spiderman" theme.

Despite several dubious selections, **Ramones Mania** is a basic career primer: thirty cuts (something from each preceding album except the live one, plus a handful of rarities) in non-chronological order, with detailed annotation and voluminous liner notes by Billy Altman. **End of the Decade** is a limited-edition boxed set containing six UK 12-inches from the mid-'80s. The two volumes of **All the Stuff (And More)** are single-disc repackages of **Ramones/Leave Home** and **Rocket to Russia/Road to Ruin** with a fair allotment of bonus tracks, including demos, B-sides and live numbers.

The Ramones tribute album (not to be confused with the remakes of their first three albums by, respectively, Screeching Weasel, Vindictives and the Queers) is an exercise in futility. The brudders' sound is so clearly etched and, to a certain degree, easily copied that the strategic decision—flat-out imitation versus creative revision—is doomed to either fall short or sound wrong. Tracks by the West Coast punk bands featured on **Gabba Gabba Hey** are either redundant (L7, White Flag, Electric Ferrets, Badtown Boys) or awful (Agnews, Bad Religion, Pigmy Love Circus, Bulimia Banquet, Buglamp featuring Keith Morris), leaving only the hardcore acceleration of Flower Leperds, Creamers and Rigor Mortis, and the incomparable Mojo Nixon ("Rockaway Beach") to simultaneously uphold and alter the originals. Also on hand: Motorcycle Boy, Flesheaters, Jeff Dahl, D.I. and Chemical People. [i]

See also *NoMeansNo, Nutley Brass, Queers, Riverdales, Screeching Weasel, Stop; TPRG.*

LEE RANALDO

See *Sonic Youth.*

RANCID

Rancid (Epitaph) 1993
Let's Go (Epitaph) 1994
. . . And Out Come the Wolves (Epitaph) 1995

OPERATION IVY

Hectic EP (Lookout!) 1988
Energy (Lookout!) 1989

Cynics may dismiss this Bay Area quartet as "not the Clash, but an incredible simulation!" On the other hand, hyperbole-prone supporters might call them the Stones to Green Day's Beatles. (Which, if you were wondering, makes Offspring the new Herman's Hermits.) The truth about Rancid lies somewhere in between. Yes, they spend too much time playing dress-up and excavating riffs that are two decades old—which is especially ironic, given their forebears' assertion "no Elvis, Beatles or the Rolling Stones in 1977"—but the street-smart, guttersnipe outlook that invests their short, sharp songs is seldom short of exhilarating.

From 1987 to 1989, bassist Matt Freeman and singer/guitarist Tim Armstrong were in Oakland's Operation Ivy, the East Bay scene-setting quartet that blended hardcore's aggression with ska's joviality; Operation Ivy broke up after releasing an album in 1989. The pair subsequently hooked up with drummer Brett Reed and launched Rancid. **Rancid** unveils the pugnacious sound of a band wearing its influences—which range from Joe Strummer to Mick Jones—on the sleeves of its torn T-shirts. A few songs in, however, it's easy to find yourself caught up in the surge of Ricochet Rabbit energy with which Armstrong bounces aggro note clusters off Freeman's pulsing bass (which, often as not, carries the songs' melody lines). The class-conscious snottiness of "Rats in the Hallway" is more realistic coming from kids with the certifiable prole credentials of these guys, who were raised in the drab factory towns that surround San Francisco, not the big city itself. Most of these sentiments (like those espoused in "Unwritten Rules") were clichés by the time the band was in kindergarten, but a few spins through "Hyena" and "Whirlwind" leave little doubt that they mean it, maaaaan.

Other than the arrival of ex–UK Subs guitarist Lars Frederiksen to complete the four-man lineup, **Let's Go** doesn't add much to the equation—if anything, it's something of a regression, from the identikit bashing of short-but-formless thrashers like "Burn" and the utterly idiotic "Nihilism" to Freeman's shabby affected British accent. It's encouraging to note the better-integrated use of ska elements, a style that Rancid deploys in much the same way the Clash did reggae: only occasionally does the quartet dive headlong into bluebeat—more often, the skanking is limited to isolated breaks and middle eights (as in the nostalgic "Radio," co-written by Green Day's Billie Joe Armstrong). The odd clever twist is a paltry payoff, however, for having to endure a stream of assembly-line constructions—like the wannabe yobbo anthem "The Ballad of Jimmy & Johnny" and the strangely saccharine preachfest "Dope Sick Girl." Perhaps they misunderstood what the Sham in Sham 69 stood for.

. . . And Out Come the Wolves is more fully formed than its predecessors, but there's still no denying the kleptomaniacal glee with which Rancid treats its Clash (and, by extension, Mott the Hoople) collection. This time around, the most blatantly paraphrased riffs turn up in "The 11th Hour" and "Maxwell Murder," which appropriates a good bit from "London's Burning" (including a "dial 999" reference that makes little sense in 911-equipped America). Even so, Rancid's songs provide a pretty nifty stars'n'stripes rejoinder to the working-class punk of British bands. As "Lock, Step & Gone" and the piercingly memorable "Olympia WA." prove, the quartet's members are well versed in the three B's of downmarket culture: beer, bus rides and boredom. These songs differ from their previously generic punk plaints, thanks in large part to the subtle lyrical detailing (folks as diverse as East Bay junkies and ska great Desmond Dekker get regular namechecks) and the still-rudeboy-after-all-these-years ska beats that burble through "Time Bomb" and "Ruby Soho." They might have been punk's Sha Na Na at one point, but **. . . And Out Come the Wolves** casts Rancid in an utterly natural light. [dss]

See also *Dance Hall Crashers.*

MICHAEL RANK

See *Snatches of Pink.*

RANKING ROGER

See *General Public.*

RAW FUSION

See *Digital Underground.*

EDDI READER WITH THE PATRON SAINTS OF IMPERFECTION

Mirmama (UK RCA) 1992

EDDI READER

Eddi Reader (Blanco y Negro/Reprise) 1994
Candyfloss and Medicine (UK Blanco y Negro) 1996

In the late '80s, former session singer Eddi Reader provided the bubbly Scottish voice for the alluring jazz-pop of Fairground Attraction ("Perfect" being that outfit's most enduring song). The band never was on solid ground, though, and she prudently moved on to a solo career after one neat album. (Guitarist Mark Nevin also did well for himself following the group's dissolution: he became an important collaborator for Kirsty MacColl and Morrissey.)

Reader's solo debut has the gossamer translucence of morning dew. Moving on organically from Fairground Attraction, the acoustic Patron Saints (guitarist Neill MacColl, double-bassist Phil Sterioulos, drummer Roy Dodd and sit-in pianist Jools Holland) provide unhurried, fat-free arrangements—gentle, lovely, pristine—to which Reader sparingly applies her voice. Rather than pin down a vocal style, she breezes around Fred Neil's "Dolphins" and "That's Fair" like Harriet Wheeler of the Sundays, sweeps like Joni Mitchell through an imaginative recasting of the traditional "The Blacksmith," invests John Prine's nauseating "Hello in There" with idiosyncratic phrasing (getting louder at the end of each line) borrowed from Rickie Lee Jones and sounds a quiet country note in Steve Earle's "My Old Friend the Blues." A fascinating hybrid of folk tradition, contemporary stylishness and Shaker simplicity.

Her second album tightens the stylistic focus and ups the commercial stakes, locating a midpoint between old Joni Mitchell records and the glib sentimental veneer of new country—sacrificing **Mirmama**'s abundant charm in the process. Reader remains an extraordinary singer, comfortably familiar with her abilities, but the album is a victim of the material's intemperate emotional outpourings. Old associate Mark Nevin wrote the bulk of the songs and plays guitar; k.d. lang associate Greg Penny produced, using bassist David Piltch from the Canadian's company. Nevin's "The Right Place" puts some nice touches on a post-breakup rebirth and Boo Hewerdine's sardonic "Joke (I'm Laughing)" seethes with quiet disdain, but what possible need is there for another literal "Dear John" song? The best numbers are those in which Reader has a compositional hand: "Wonderful Lie," a collaboration with Hewerdine, finds an easy groove and fills it with a dreamy reminiscence. **Eddi Reader** is pretty and fine, but Eddi Reader needs more songs worth singing. [i]

RECOIL

See *Depeche Mode.*

RED AUNTS

Drag (Sympathy for the Record Industry) 1993
Bad Motherfucken 40 O-Z (Sympathy for the Record Industry) 1994
#1 Chicken (Epitaph) 1995
Saltbox (Epitaph) 1996

An evening spent with the Red Aunts is about as soothing as a soak in a tub of raw sewage. The Southern California band's brand of unfiltered music is toxic, especially when the vocals hit the piercing pitch of a three-year-old throwing a tempter tantrum. Obvious and valid comparisons include L7, the Lunachicks and Babes in Toyland, but this foursome takes a sharp claw to every riot grrrl/foxcore cliché it can shred. Starting with the old one-chord-wonder punk credo, the Aunts add a progression or two, smother it with distortion and top it off with din-singing by either bassist E. Z. Wider (Debbi Dip, aka Connie Champagne) or one of the guitarists, Angel and Sapphire (Terri Wahl and Kerry Davis, aka Louise Lee Outlaw and Taffy Davis). Abrasive as their mix is, the Red Aunts generate a vital energy and humor absent from many indie bands.

From the first shrieks of **Drag,** the Red Aunts shrug off female roles to give an estrogen-laced kick to such typically testosterone-fueled subjects as sex, cars, booze and vengeful violence. Songs like "Built for a Barstool," "Hot Rod" and "Lonely Beer Drops" sound like someone's tonsils are being shaved with shards of glass. There is another side to the band, however, and the Red Aunts do interject a few well-sung tunes: "Lethal Lolita" is a playful tease, while the humorous "Sleeping in the Wet Spot" is inspiring enough for a hum-along. The Aunts best merge their gruff and feminine styles on the powerful "Teach Me to Kill."

As the title implies, **Bad Motherfucken 40 O-Z,** produced by then–Bad Religion guitarist Brett Gurewitz, is even tougher, with songs like "Die Baby" and "Monster Fucker Mother Trucker." Although the band is a bit tighter, there's no substantial change from **Drag.** Propelled by hard-hitting drummer Cougar (Leslie Ishino, aka Ishino Destroyer), the Aunts careen through their songs, although the bluesy "Ice Tea" almost lets you catch your breath and "Batman a Go-Go," the band's catchiest tune, introduces a new wave beat to the atonal crunch.

Mr. Brett again grabs the production reins on **#1 Chicken,** released on his Epitaph label. The move coincides with the band's heightened musical prowess, as evidenced on "Rollerderby Queen," which involves more musical changes than most Red Aunts songs, plus a proper guitar solo and fat, pounding bass. But the band is clearly true to its original tenets: the cover even boasts that the Aunts rip through fourteen songs in twenty-three minutes. And the sentiments are also the same, with tracks like "When Sugar Turns to Shit," "Hate" and "Satan," and lines like "Hit you with my hammer / Hit you till you're dead / Then I'm gonna cut off / Your motherfucken head" ("Detroit Valentine"). Even when they profess "I've got a crush on you" ("Krush"), it's so shrill you've got to figure they're concealing more than one lethal weapon. **#1 Chicken** leaves no doubt that these Aunts can bite with a vengeance, but they'd be even more potent with a little less squawking. [mg]

RED CRAYOLA (RED KRAYOLA)

The Parable of Arable Land (International Artists) 1967 (UK Radar) 1978 (Collectables) 1993
God Bless the Red Krayola and All Who Sail With It. (International Artists) 1968 (UK Radar) 1979 (Collectables) 1993
Soldier-Talk (UK Radar) 1979
Three Songs on a Trip to the United States (UK Recommended) 1984
Malefactor, Ade (UK Glass) 1989
The Red Krayola (Drag City) 1994
Amor and Language (Drag City) 1995
Coconut Hotel (Drag City) 1995
Hazel (Drag City) 1996

ART & LANGUAGE AND THE RED CRAYOLA

Corrected Slogans (Music Language) 1976 (UK Recommended) 1982
Kangaroo? (Rough Trade) 1981 (Drag City) 1995
Black Snakes (Sw. Rec-Rec/Ger. Pure Freude) 1983

MAYO THOMPSON

Corky's Debt to His Father (Texas Revolution) 1970 (UK Glass) 1988 (Drag City) 1994

Rock is a young person's game, but extreme literate weirdness is best left to those who've been around the block enough times to know where the real bizarre shit can be dug up. Returning from a five-year studio absence, barbecued Texas original Mayo Thompson—who began recording his truly distorted "Free Form Freak-Outs" as the singer/guitarist/leader of the psychedelic Red Crayola in 1967—encountered simpatico members of the '90s generation (specifically members of Gastr del Sol, Tortoise and Overpass, plus Chicago's fearless Drag City label) and entered the most audibly productive phase of his career, issuing two new albums plus two arcane oldies inside two years.

Recorded by a collective of seven (including guitarists David Grubbs, Jim O'Rourke and Tom Watson, drummer John McEntire and German synthesist Albert Oehlen), **The Red Krayola** is a potent modern exposition of Thompson's Beefheart-ian musical inventions and wickedly offbeat lyrics. For all its idiosyncratic juxtapositions, the album is a relatively straightforward electric affair—alternately engaging and patience-testing—that sends antagonistic elements (noisy guitar, catatonic electronic blips, contrary rhythms, Thompson's ever-changing vocal affectations) out to disrupt the calmly logical organization of restrained, tuneful inventions like the waltz-time "Jimmy Silk/Supper Be Ready Medley," "Pride," "Book of Kings" (which paraphrases Carly Simon *and* quotes children's verse), the courtly, Roxy Music–like "Miss X," the chromatic "Art-Dog" and "Suddenly," crooned as a sweet harmony vocal exercise. Traditionally cavalier in his appreciation of song structures, Thompson fleshes out the album with "Rapspierre" (another of his accelerated Marxist theory courses, this one containing sing-song doggerel about monkeys, random keyboard noises and turntable scratches), the ripping drive-gear "People Get Ready (The Train's Not Coming)" near-instrumental and the catchy mantra "I Knew It." Provocative and, for the most part, highly entertaining.

Nine more new songs can be found on the brief, wispy and unambitious **Amor and Language,** the work of numerous musicians, although the undifferentiated list of participants includes sexy cover model Rachel Williams. Unlike the cagey complexities of **The Red Krayola** (and despite the admonition to "play extremely loud"), "The Ballad of Younis and Sofía" and "Luster"—which use only skeletal bits of guitar and organ for accompaniment—are typical. Actually, the mild-mannered approach is appealing and accessible, giving Thompson's penchant for eccentric lyrical terrain a clear field. Adding to the bizarre historical recitation of "A-A-Allegories" and the frozen waste matter falling from the sky in "Stil de Grain Brun," the detailed geometric romance of "T(I,II)" is intriguing enough, doubling the pleasure as the sonic doodles suddenly give way to a normal-sounding (with squiggly synth) rock band instrumental. Some people try to sing the periodic table of the elements and get called asshole; this never happened to Mayo Thompson.

Coconut Hotel, however, is pushing it. The all-improvised doodles on various real (guitar, horns, bass, piano, organ) and found instruments (mainly splashing water, handy clangables, shakeables and chalkboard-pleasant scrapeables) was recorded in 1967 by the original Red Crayola (Thompson, Steve Cunningham and Frederick Barthelme) and understandably rejected by International Artists as the followup to **The Parable of Arable Land.** The trio's photo on the back cover is no less unnerving or off-putting than the random contents, which could only serve as a fatal test for hypertension or the soundtrack to something far more squirm-inducing than *Eraserhead.*

Between the '60s Red Crayola (thanks to prompt objections from the manufacturer, the name was quickly changed, in America at least, to Red Krayola)—whose groundbreaking influence was not lost on bands as diverse as Galaxie 500 and Spacemen 3—and his recent resurgence, Thompson's career charted a spotty course between a mutually productive relationship with Pere Ubu (after the group guested on **Soldier-Talk,** Thompson turned around and joined the band), work with the loose and not especially useful Art & Language combine and the occasional solo record masquerading as a Red Krayola project, like the half-live album-length **Three Songs on a Trip to the United States,** made as a trio with drummer Jesse Chamberlain and Ubu synthesist Allen Ravenstine.

In 1970, Thompson actually did record a solo album, **Corky's Debt to His Father,** which got an obscure local-label issue at the time in Texas, was revived in England years later and was finally introduced to American CD racks through the good offices of Drag City. A left-field version of a blues and neo-vaudeville album—played mostly acoustic on slide guitar, piano, bass and elementary traps, with some horns and electricity—**Corky's Debt** doesn't sound much closer to any mainstream in 1995 than it would have done a quarter-century earlier. The fairly titled "Good Brisk Blues" might have come from a Dylan bootleg, and "Venus in the Morning" does suggest a functional knowledge of barrelhouse music, but the lyrics ("they cover her politely from all indelicate eyes") are from a completely different realm. A self-conscious embrace of abnormality in all its glorious dislocation. [i]

See also *Gastr del Sol, Overpass, Pere Ubu, Jim O'Rourke; TPRG.*

REDD KROSS (RED CROSS)

Red Cross EP (Posh Boy) 1980 + 1987
Born Innocent (Smoke 7) 1982 (Frontier) 1986
Teen Babes From Monsanto (Gasatanka) 1984
Neurotica (Big Time) 1987
Third Eye (Atlantic) 1990
Phaseshifter (This Way Up/Mercury) 1993
2500 Redd Kross Fans Can't Be Wrong EP10 (Sympathy for the Record Industry) 1994

VARIOUS ARTISTS

Desperate Teenage Lovedolls (Gasatanka) 1984
Lovedolls Superstar (SST) 1986

Only Southern California (Hawthorne, actually) could have bred kitsch-pop brothers Steven (bass/vocals) and Jeffrey (vocals/guitar) McDonald, who drove onto the LA punk scene as adolescents in 1980 singing merry jingles about culture icons and local clothing stores. Moving through a series of lineups (the first had future Black Flag member Ron Reyes and future Circle Jerk Greg Hetson), Red Cross (renamed Redd Kross after **Born Innocent** to mollify a certain unamused charitable organization) has released only four full albums in a decade and a half; none completely captures the McDonalds' giddy and informed dedication to '70s schlock, although each contains some chewy delights.

With muddy sound and sloppy, uninspired playing, **Born Innocent** celebrates such anti-idols as "Linda Blair," "Charlie" (Manson) and Patty Hearst; although unmentioned on the sleeve and label (for fear he would get out of jail and come after them for royalties) the LP actually includes a cover of Manson's "Cease to Exist." The brief but excellent **Teen Babes From Monsanto** runs strictly on wicked irreverence, painting a loud and convincing garage brand on Kiss' "Deuce," the Rolling Stones' "Citadel," the Stooges' "Ann," David Bowie's "Saviour Machine" and two others, leaving "Linda Blair 1984" the sole original.

With Redd Kross providing most of the music, the McDonalds appeared in *Desperate Teenage Lovedolls,* a no-budget Z-movie made by area scenesters, and on its soundtrack album, alongside Black Flag, White Flag and others. Redd Kross also appear on the soundtrack of the sequel, *Lovedolls Superstar,* contributing a brilliant rendition of the Brady Bunch's "Sunshine Day."

The nearly adult **Neurotica** reclaims "Ballad of a Love Doll" from the first film's score and adds such fuzzed-out folk-pop acid trips as "Peach Kelli Pop" and "Janus, Jeanie, and George Harrison." With harmony-heavy arrangements, the band has never sounded better. But Big Time collapsed and Redd Kross was temporarily prevented from making another album under its own name. The McDonalds stayed busy with side projects, releasing records as the Tater Totz and Anarchy 6.

Third Eye is a partially successful attempt to go straight (or at least as straight as an album with mock-Keane back-cover portraits could be) for mass-market consumption. Much of the band's trademark wackiness is gone, replaced by disciplined musicianship, streamlined songwriting and radio-savvy production. **Third Eye**'s accessible lighthearted pop-rock (like "Bubblegum Factory" and "Love Is Not Love") is pretty good, while scattered attempts to fuse the new sobriety with the humor of earlier efforts ("Elephant Flares," "Shonen Knife" and "1976," which revisits the dreaded decade with incisive passing tributes to Kiss, Cheap Trick and Elton John) seem forced. That last song also appears on the mostly oldies soundtrack for *The Spirit of 76,* a 1991 cinematic kitschfest that features the McDonalds in a cast headed by David Cassidy.

Introducing a brash five-piece band that can rock way loud without obscuring the catchy melodies, the self-produced **Phaseshifter** consolidates **Third Eye**'s progress toward a serious pop-rock amalgam somewhere between late Beatles (credit Jeffrey's Lennon-like singing and the harmonies) and early Cheap Trick (blame it on the roaring guitars and flattened melodies). With the comic relief in the songs kept out of the spotlight—a passing Axl Rose lyrical reference, a few whimsical topics ("Jimmy's Fantasy," "After School Special," "Saragon"), a brief Hollies paraphrase in "Monolith"—it's possible to overlook the McDonalds' colorful personalities in the lighthearted songs, hearing only the catchy tunes, the Big Noise and the skilled musicianship. Keyboardist Gere Fennelly gets an especially prominent role, detailing many of the arrangements and lending the album a theatrical tone in spots; new guitarist Edward Kurdziel and drummer Brian Reitzell galvanize the energetic attack. For all the evident Redd Kross sound and spirit in **Phaseshifter,** the album shifts those distinctive attributes into music others could have made.

The band's most recent issue, **2500 Redd Kross Fans Can't Be Wrong,** contains a new song ("Any Hour, Every Day") and a handful of overseas tracks from '91 and '92. [i]

See also *TPRG.*

RED HOT CHILI PEPPERS

The Red Hot Chili Peppers (Enigma/EMI America) 1984
Freaky Styley (Enigma/EMI America) 1985
The Uplift Mofo Party Plan (EMI Manhattan) 1987
Mother's Milk (EMI) 1989
Blood Sugar Sex Magik (Warner Bros.) 1991
What Hits!? (EMI) 1992
Out in L.A. (EMI) 1994
One Hot Minute (Warner Bros.) 1995

Like many veteran bands that suddenly break on through to the mainstream side, the Red Hot Chili Peppers—depending on the observer's perspective and principles—either scored when they were good and ready or snatched the gold ring at a point when their initial inspiration had already burned away, and mediocrity became the Los Angeles quartet's secret sauce for chart success. Ultimately, it comes down to whether one views a shift from credible and crazy punk funk—hard-hitting wiseguy party music heavy on the George Clinton downstroke—to sensitive wimpo ballads like "Under the Bridge" (the solemn wet willie that sent

1991's **Blood Sugar Sex Magik** into triple-platinum orbit) as progress or not.

At one time, the quartet led by singer Anthony Kiedis and monster bassist Flea (Michael Balzary) was the only notable blender regularly feeding in thrash, rap, funk and rock and spitting out a hybrid that has since become common. Highlighted by the enigmatic density of "True Men Don't Kill Coyotes," **Red Hot Chili Peppers** is a thoroughly entertaining mutation of George Clinton, Sly Stone, Kurtis Blow and Sonic Youth, an original blast of serious fun that didn't find many takers in the racially retarded rock underground.

Founding guitarist Hillel Slovak, having sat out the first LP, returned for the raunch-minded **Freaky Styley,** produced by the grandmaster of P-Funk hisself, George C. Although the ass-moving music is rock hard, the songs are more weird than wonderful, and the record is like a madcap teenaged exorcism.

Busy and casual sounding, **The Uplift Mofo Party Plan** divides rock and funk down the middle, with the catchy "Behind the Sun" (co-written with producer Michael Beinhorn) at its soft center. On guitar-heavy tracks like "Me & My Friends" and "Fight Like a Brave," Flea's popping bass is the sole connection to the group's old sound; elsewhere, repetitive rhythm grooves reaffirm the Peppers' twin commitments to sex and the dancefloor (if not sex *on* the dancefloor).

Sobered by Slovak's fatal OD in June 1988, the Chili Peppers regrouped with guitarist John Frusciante and drummer Chad Smith to make **Mother's Milk,** a phenomenal whipping dedicated to their late guitarist and friend. The band's relentless intensity, solid funk chops and angry loss compel the strong anti-drug messages of "Knock Me Down" and "Taste the Pain" (both reportedly wishful thinking for Kiedis, who is said to have first-hand knowledge of such problems) to meld with the wanton sexuality of "Sexy Mexican Maid" and such whimsy as a high-speed rap cheer for "Magic Johnson." In the album's best meeting of form and function, Flea's mindfuck bass work slamdunks Stevie Wonder's "Higher Ground." A promising growth stock in the Chili Peppers' portfolio, **Mother's Milk** nurtured the band for bigger, if not necessarily better, things.

Most of the aforementioned songs and a stack more from the first four albums (plus "Show Me Your Soul," the group's contribution to the *Pretty Woman* score) compose **What Hits!?,** a useful if incomplete retrospective wanged together after the Chili Peppers left EMI. Through what must have been some impressive lawyering, the album includes "Under the Bridge," a Top 5 hit from the band's Warner Bros. debut.

Rick Rubin, whose career-launching interest in hip-hop had not been exercised in years, produced **Blood Sugar Sex Magik,** attempting to help the Peppers find a modern use for what were by then old-hat funk obsessions. No dice. Peppering his vocabulary with four- and twelve-letter words, Kiedis spends "The Power of Equality," "If You Have to Ask," "The Righteous & the Wicked" and "Sir Psycho Sexy" trying to rap without really trying to sound like a rapper (or demonstrating any of the self-conscious goofing that buoyed his early efforts in this direction); elsewhere, the sprawling album clings to syncopated beats as if wandering in a zombie fog. With the minor exception of "Give It Away" (which at least has a cogent vocal and airtight playing) and the hyped-up "The Greeting Song," the material is shapeless and nearly useless. Kiedis stretches simple lyrical gimmicks across tuneless vamps that lack drive, destination and colorful scenery to watch along the way. Frusciante blares on his axe now and then to wake the band and keep it from drifting off the road, but even that doesn't hasten the impatient waits for tracks to end. Amid all this tedium, the light pop digressions—"Breaking the Girl," "Under the Bridge," "I Could Have Lied"—provide a welcome respite and stand out without actually having much to recommend them (like, for instance, a really good vocalist). Throughout, the Chili Peppers go through the motions with none of the early days' raw energy or zany invention. For an otherwise unavailable taste of that era, **Out in L.A.** stacks up remixes, demos of lesser tracks from the first two albums, fragmentary outtakes that deserved to remain that way and crummy live renditions of **Mofo**'s "Special Secret Song Inside" (aka "Party on Your Pussy"), Jimi Hendrix's "Castles Made of Sand" and a brief, rude jazz incident, "F.U.," credited to Thelonious Monk. Of possible value to scholars of the band, **Out in L.A.** is way too uneven to be of serious concern to anyone else.

Frusciante left abruptly in '92 and was succeeded by two other guitarists before the band finally settled on Dave Navarro, late of Jane's Addiction and Deconstruction and clearly the most talented musician other than Flea ever to don the Chili Peppers' light bulb. Taking a front seat in the studio and playing like a man possessed, Navarro binds, tilts the balance and essentially directs the sound of **One Hot Minute,** which was produced by Rubin as if the previous album had never happened. Exciting and busy where its predecessor was a lazy drag, **One Hot Minute** kicks a thick, hot rock tone and puts up songs that go at least one step beyond the minimum requirements of a tempo and a key. (Why some of them pointedly echo old songs—"One Big Mob" recalls "True Men Don't Kill Coyotes"—is hard to imagine; it sure can't be a cure for commercial insecurity.) In this tougher, richer context, restrained acoustic ballads and warm soul grooves no longer arrive with LOOK! DIFFERENT! sirens blaring, but rather slot into an organic whole where emotional compression and explosive power become symbiotic dynamic forces and make it all work in ways previously beyond the band's grasp.

For all the musical integrity of **One Hot Minute,** words are its most notable element. Kiedis has his lyrical act together better than ever before, focusing on drug addiction and death not as lurid headline disasters but as ambivalent and personal emotional dilemmas. "My tendency for dependency / Is offending me . . . I'm pretending see / To be strong and free / From my dependency," he admits in "Warped," acknowledging, in "Aeroplane," that "I like pleasure spiked with pain" and remarking, in the dismal "My Friends," "Imagine me taught by tragedy / Release is peace." "Transcending" describes "friends near death" and muses you "never know when the gods will come and take you." Amid all this angst, he grasps love (not sex for a change) and devotion as essence and salvation; "Falling Into Grace," "Coffee Shop" and "Deep Kick" glow with hope and enthusiasm against the gloom. Taking angry potshots at the church ("Shallow Be Thy Game"), stardom's lure ("Transcending," about River Phoenix) and an unnamed "homophobic redneck dick" ("Pea"), the album offers much food for thought. Meanwhile, the music, despite its risk-taking ambition, never falters or fails to keep the jam moving on the good foot. [i]

See also *Deconstruction, John Frusciante, Porno for Pyros; TPRG.*

RED HOUSE PAINTERS

Down Colorful Hill (4AD) 1992
Red House Painters (4AD) 1993
Red House Painters (4AD) 1993
Shock Me EP (4AD) 1994
Ocean Beach (4AD) 1995
Songs for a Blue Guitar (Supreme/Island) 1996

As much an exercise in self-flagellation as a working band, Red House Painters afforded Ohio-bred, San Francisco–based singer/songwriter Mark Kozelek the latitude to—to paraphrase Mick Jagger's false offer—take his heart in his hand and pour it all over the stage. Without using the safety net provided by metaphor, Kozelek, a self-possessed agoraphobic with a ghostly voice reminiscent of Tim Buckley's, airs myriad insecurities and emotional inconstancies over his quartet's skeletal backing.

Kozelek has frequent—you might even say obsessive—thoughts of childhood. He pines for the days when he was free to cavort on swings and rollercoasters (references to which crop up on almost every record). In keeping with that, **Down Colorful Hill** commences with "24," a hymn mourning having reached what he apparently considers senior citizen status. For most of the record's duration, Kozelek swings between musings about his own psychic pain ("Medicine Bottle" seems to address an ex-girlfriend who struggled to gain entry into his private world) and that of comrades with even greater difficulties ("Michael" expresses his feelings about a friend suffering from mental illness). Heavy going, particularly when most of the six songs, all recorded as demos, approach or pass the ten-minute mark.

The next year brought two distinct albums, both eponymous and shawled in sepia-tone sleeves, both rendingly confessional and mesmerizingly minimal. The first (which carries a photo of a dilapidated rollercoaster on its cover) offers more emotional contrast than any of the other Red House Painters albums, even opening with the vaguely sanguine "Grace Cathedral Park," an autumnal melody that recalls Brit baroque-popsters Eyeless in Gaza. Of course, old demons don't die easy, as evidenced by the wistful "Things Mean a Lot" (Kozelek's dismay at the transience of relationships) and the anguished "Katy Song" (an epic that fades out on several minutes of wordless wails, à la Buckley). Guitarist Gordon Mack, bassist Jerry Vessel and drummer Anthony Koutsos periodically muster a restrained jazzy groove, but for the most part, spartanism still prevails.

The second **Red House Painters** (distinguished by its sleeve photo of a rural footbridge) returns to the epic song length and sketchy sonic infrastructure of the debut; Kozelek likewise reverts to a more monochromatic outlook. "Evil" is a shuddering, dead-of-night assessment of a relationship turned poisonous; "New Jersey" reprises a song from the second album, adding a more palpable sense of friction. An unironic rendition of Simon & Garfunkel's "I Am a Rock," however, is distracting, and a dirge-like album-ending version of "Star-Spangled Banner" is downright baffling.

The four-song **Shock Me** EP extends what's rapidly becoming a tradition, bookended as it is by *two* versions of the title cut, originally brought to you by . . . Kiss. **Ocean Beach** lets the emotional and sonic pendulum swing a little more readily, allowing the band to wander as far afield as country-tinged instrumentals ("Cabezon") and romantic, Iberian digressions ("San Geronimo"). Admittedly, there's nothing remotely perky here, but **Ocean Beach** does portend a sunrise on the RHP horizon.

Kozelek's outlook is not appreciably brighter on the primarily acoustic (but occasionally roaring) **Songs for a Blue Guitar**, which typically lacks credits but thanks, among others, the Cracker rhythm section and makes fine use of pedal steel guitar in several songs. Amid the beguiling originals are bemusing but pleasant covers of Yes' "Long Distance Runaround" and the Cars' "All Mixed Up," as well as eleven minutes of "Silly Love Songs," a billowing Crazy Horse electric jam leading into a gracefully slow reduction of Wings' hit. [dss]

REDMAN

Whut? Thee Album (RAL/Chaos/Columbia) 1992
Dare Iz a Darkside (RAL) 1994

Hopped up on funk, skunkweed, horror movies and the urban siege, Newark, New Jersey's Reggie Noble become Redman and—under the production wing of rap's very own King Midas, Erick Sermon—made his full-length premiere in '92 with **Whut? Thee Album,** a darkly weird old-school adventure that steps off reality into a bizarre fantasy world. "Snapped the neck on Michael Myers then I freaked it / Cause it was August and he was talkin' this trick-or-treat shit," Redman brags in the comically belligerent "Rated 'R,'" which also contains the admission, "I beat up the devil with a shovel so he dropped me a level." Rolled as thick and pungent as a major spliff (detailed free-verse instructions for which are provided in "How to Roll a Blunt"), **Whut?** buzzes from subject to subject—sex, drugs, violence, daydreams, bragging, superheroes, hell, insanity, money—like a remote control with a fused switch. The tracks and skits are entertaining on their own, but the bustling, soulful album gains eccentric momentum as it rolls along.

Picking up where the first album left off—literally, with a slight return of the **Whut?**-ending "Encore"—the red-cased **Dare Iz a Darkside** is so hoochified that it's a wonder Noble could find the mic between puffs. "A Million and 1 Buddah Spots" details the geographical extent of his sedative obsessions; "Green Island" blames his sinus problems on the same hobby. Far-off bass throbs in through a cloud of incidental sound that occasionally uses altered voices (as in "Dr. Trevis" and "Rockafella"); except when a snare drum snaps to attention, there's no focus to the music. And that's precisely the fuzzy point. But while Redman's delivery amazingly remains unimpaired, the album's vagueness pollutes his rhymes ("Cosmic Slop" is a disappointingly descriptive title), which display less of the debut's zany invention and contribute to **Darkside**'s debilitating fatigue factor. [i]

See also *EPMD.*

RED RED MEAT

Red Red Meat (Perishable) 1992
Jimmywine Majestic (Sub Pop) 1994
Bunny Gets Paid (Sub Pop) 1995

Despite the sanitization it's received in recent years through the efforts of high-profile technicians like Stevie Ray Vaughan, Eric Clapton and Robert Cray, the blues was meant to be a squalid, severe thing. Red Red Meat may not hit enough blue notes to convince purists that they play the *blues,* but there's no doubting this Chicago aggregation lives it—with the hellhound teethmarks to prove it.

The self-released debut is awash in the same sort of bad vibes that saturated precursors like **Let It Bleed** and **Tonight's the Night** (Neil Young's tenuous lead guitar style being a clear influence on frontman Tim Rutili), but the band's considerable vitriol remains unchanneled; its ideas drift away on the narcotic breeze that blows through virtually every groove. Bassist/cofounder Glynnis Johnson (Rutili's longtime girlfriend) died of complications from AIDS in 1992, marking the end of this edition of the band.

When Red Red Meat resurfaced, the bass slot was held by Tim Hurley (a six-foot-five ex-lawyer who provides a nice bookend for six-foot-nine guitarist Glenn Girard), and Rutili had written a suite of songs that—even when not explicitly addressing the loss of Johnson—absolutely resound with regretful passion, while Girard's slippery slide runs grease the path for the disjointed, uncomfortably numb lyrics he scatters across "Braindead" and "Rusted Water." Far more focused musically, **Jimmywine Majestic** opens with a gnarled Stones riff (in the seething "Flank"), dragging the listener on a trip that takes in all the usually hidden scenery the wrong side of the psychic tracks have to offer.

Following Girard's departure, **Bunny Gets Paid** manages to open the door enough for other instruments—notably Moog synthesizer and viola—without allowing a whiff of air to enter the hermetic atmosphere. The sparse, delirious "Carpet of Horses" is certainly the closest thing to a bona fide blues song in the reconfigured quintet's repertoire, while the remarkably tense "Rosewood, Wax, Voltz & Glitter" verges on hostage-situation melodrama. Placing yourself in the midst of the proceedings is not unlike enjoying a closeup look at the implosion of a fully occupied building. [dss]

REDUCERS

The Reducers (Rave On) 1984
Let's Go! (Rave On) 1984
Cruise to Nowhere (Rave On) 1985
Redux (Rave On) 1991
Shinola (Rave On) 1995

A local fixture in New London, Connecticut, the Reducers soak up influences—Chuck Berry, Anglopop, glam, roots rock, punk and more—and reconfigure them into punchy, catchy tunes fed by blazing guitars at speedy tempos. On the politely energetic debut, the everyone-sings-everyone-writes quartet offers social critique and consumer culture in the worshipful "Black Plastic Shoes," the bitter "Life in the Neighborhood" and the politically paranoid "Scared of Cops." The title track of the better-produced **Let's Go!** is a great traveling number with a catchy, urgent chorus; the rest of the LP is enthusiastic and lyrically acute. Over a churning R&B vamp on "Bums I Used to Know," the band chides itself for "this honky imitation of the blues."

Redux contains all of those songs and two dozen (!) more in a substantial one-disc career summary. The all-new **Shinola** finds the reliable Reducers—conviction, enthusiasm and middlebrow craft unflagging more than a decade after self-releasing their first album—pretty much where they began. In light of the youthful aspirations of "Let's Go!," the abiding ambition of "Real Gone"—an adult version of the same runaway dream—is truly poignant. Otherwise, the band—Peter Detmold (guitar), Hugh Birdsall (guitar), Tom Trombley (drums) and Steve Kaika (bass)—is increasingly a collection of its individual impulses: sizzling boogie ("Don't Make Mad" is proof that a little spice can invigorate even the hoariest rock leftover), old-school power-pop ("Some Other Time"), an obsession with violence ("The Witness," "The Power of the Gun") and a variation on British roots rock ("Medium Cool"). Flashes of such vintage influences as Wreckless Eric, 999, the Records, Cheap Trick and the Clash mark these guys as record collectors tied to a lost era, but the album's real sign of time passing is "Baby, You're Gonna Lose," a badly sung acoustic harmony warning addressed to a wayward teenager. Staring into the eye of the generation gap, the parental protagonist remonstrates, "If you keep it up girl you could wind up on the end of a gun," admitting, in the next breath, "Don't know what to do because I'd be the same if I was you." [i]

LOU REED

Lou Reed (RCA) 1972
Transformer (RCA) 1972
Berlin (RCA) 1973
Rock n Roll Animal (RCA) 1974
Sally Can't Dance (RCA) 1974
Lou Reed Live (RCA) 1975
Metal Machine Music: The Amine β Ring (RCA) 1975
Coney Island Baby (RCA) 1976
Rock and Roll Heart (Arista) 1976
Walk on the Wild Side: The Best of Lou Reed (RCA) 1977
Street Hassle (Arista) 1978
Live Take No Prisoners (Arista) 1978
The Bells (Arista) 1979
Growing Up in Public (Arista) 1980
Rock and Roll Diary 1967–1980 (Arista) 1980
The Blue Mask (RCA) 1982
I Can't Stand It (UK RCA) 1982
Legendary Hearts (RCA) 1983
Live in Italy (UK RCA) 1984
New Sensations (RCA) 1984
City Lights (Arista) 1985
Mistrial (RCA) 1986
New York (Sire) 1989
Retro (UK RCA) 1989
Magic and Loss (Sire) 1992
Between Thought and Expression: The Lou Reed Anthology (RCA) 1992
Set the Twilight Reeling (Warner Bros.) 1996
Different Times: Lou Reed in the '70s (RCA) 1996

LOU REED/JOHN CALE

Songs for Drella (Sire/Warner Bros.) 1990

Those who found the young Lou Reed—a deadpan chronicler of heroin's rush, adventures in peculiar sexuality and suicide's bloody razor—a daunting purveyor of unseemly nastiness disguised as art may be nonplused by his middle-aged existence. After years of joking about (and testing) ways to die, Reed was properly introduced to mortality in the deaths of several close friends and joined the literary club of those addressing life's great issues, only to discover how little he has to add on the subject. From a malevolent, self-obsessed delinquent, Reed became a sensitive and universal-minded rabbi, crafting solemn music whose plain-spoken directness has all the lightness and charm of *Schindler's List.* Somehow, whatever Reed takes on comes out difficult.

During the '80s, having already explored glam rock, effete decadence, thuggish metal, radical noise indulgence, put-down comedy and idiosyncratic ideas of pop and mainstream rock on his '70s solo albums, Reed settled into adulthood with an elementary recipe of expertly recorded guitar, bass and drums designed primarily to serve as an inconspicuous, nearly style-free bed for his increasingly speech-like vocalizing. Meanwhile, he traded away the lurid obsessions that had long driven his lyrics for a more reflective, observational tone, informed by current events, loving feelings, nesting instincts—even the onset of self-conscious spirituality—among other personal experiences one doesn't encounter walking on the fabled wild side. **Between Thought and Expression,** a confused and unsatisfactory three-CD box, anthologizes his work between the 1972 solo debut, **Lou Reed,** and 1986's **Mistrial,** hitting the most obvious essentials ("Walk on the Wild Side," "Caroline Says," "Street Hassle," "Waves of Fear") but otherwise culling fifteen studio and live albums without any clear aesthetic logic and adding little unreleased or obscure material of real significance. "Little Sister," from the soundtrack of the little-known *Get Crazy* (in which Reed plays a befuddled rock star with incisive wit), and a bizarre 1980 rendition of "The Star-Spangled Banner" are cool, but Reed must have bucketloads of more intriguing outtakes in the can. While the gripe window is open, ninety-two seconds of **Metal Machine Music** can't fully convey the stunning affront of Reed's fun-with-oscillators experiment. And *where* is that shameless pinnacle of offense, "I Wanna Be Black"?

After **Mistrial,** Reed spent a couple of years reading the daily papers, then reared back and fired his most ambitious verbal salvo. Coalescing years of simmering outrage and frustration, he spewed out **New York,** a tumultuous and frequently stunning comment on the state of life in the big city—and beyond. For an hour, drummer Fred Maher, second guitarist Mike Rathke and bassist Rob Wasserman eloquently follow Reed as he talk-sings about crack addicts, child abusers, welfare hotels, racism, AIDS and much more, finishing things off with a gentle remembrance of the late Andy Warhol ("Dime Story Mystery"). As clunky as some of its modest songs and ambitious lyrics may be, this unlikely-sounding masterpiece is among Reed's strongest, most durable albums.

With Warhol's death still very much on his mind, Reed next undertook a sentimental collaboration with old Velvet Underground bandmate John Cale. Presented as a chronological progression of fictionalized biographical (and autobiographical) songs, **Songs for Drella** contains fascinating personal reminiscences, but has almost no merits as an album of music. Neither Cale nor Reed can make anything listenable out of the stiff, arrhythmic prose; the dashed-off backing on a guitar, keyboards and viola is equally artless. Rather than attempt to make a record, Cale and Reed would have done better to write *A Book for Drella.* (For collectors, the record was initially available as a limited-edition CD with a velvet cover and an insert book.)

Magic and Loss is further evidence of Reed's fundamental difficulty in getting deep, honest and affecting ideas to function as the text of music. Writing after the deaths of songwriter Doc Pomus and a close female friend, Reed searches for existential solace from the unfairness of it all. A few of the tracks (the recollective "Dreamin'/Escape," "Cremation/Ashes to Ashes") are haunting in their spare beauty, but with nothing evidently standing between his thoughts and their expression, most of the work comes out unmeditated and clunky—heartfelt but no more entertaining than a grim conversation with a thoughtful commentator. The fact that Reed pronounces his desolation in a voice as sympathetic but detached as that of the receptionist in a funeral parlor doesn't help. Neither do the occasional medical details. "I saw two isotopes introduced into his lungs / Trying to stop the cancerous spread," Reed reports in "Power and Glory/The Situation," a track given its edgy strangeness by Jimmy Scott's otherworldly guest vocals. "They're trying a new treatment to get you out of bed / But radiation kills both bad and good / It can not differentiate," he explains to no one in particular in "Sword of Damocles/Externally," which then goes on to matter-of-factly claim an absurd present-tense pharmaceutical cool that blows the whole thing: "That mix of morphine and dexedrine / We use it on the street." (Reed can't possibly be so out of the loop to think anyone still imagines him waiting for the man, can he?) For all the good intentions, projects like this make it very difficult to gauge the line between a creative genius bending words to suit his purposes and a slack underachiever coasting on his rep and attempting to hide behind the pretense of free verse. As someone who generally leaves it completely open which he's doing (since he's certainly done both), Reed remains, in his own way, as courageous, furious and fraudulent as he's always been. Good for him.

Although memorial nostalgia is a standing theme of Reed's songwriting—after all, that's what "Walk on the Wild Side" is, and **Songs for Drella** and **Magic and Loss**—the song that opens **Set the Twilight Reeling** sounds like the onset of senility. "Egg Cream," which offers a lip-smacking recipe for a childhood delight ("Some U Bet's chocolate syrup, seltzer water mixed with milk / Stirred up into a heady fro'—tasted just like silk") is more deserving of the late Ernest Noyes Brookings than the author of some of rock-'n'roll's most terrifying creations, no matter how old or peaceful he's grown. The rest of the album (recorded as a trio with bassist Fernando Saunders and drummer Tony Smith) isn't so lame, though "NYC Man" and "HookyWooky" come close. On the other hand, "Trade In," backed up by the equally attractive "Hang on to Your Emotions," is a pretty, memorable love song that Reed actually sings. The charged current-events grousing of the anti-Republican "Sex With Your Parents Part II (Motherfucker)," recorded live, summons up the ghost of **New York,** while "Adventurer" is a long, involving description of someone and "Riptide" contains some of his cagiest, most inflamed guitar wanging in years. Ultimately, Reed brings it all together in the title track, which closes the album. Shifting easily from graceful acoustic reflection to impassioned electric flagrancy, he throws a net around the various corners of his world and makes it clear he's far from finished.

Walk on the Wild Side, Rock and Roll Diary, I Can't Stand It, City Lights and **Retro** are all compilations. [i]

See also *John Cale, Maureen Tucker, Velvet Underground; TPRG.*

REEGS

Return of the Sea Monkeys (UK Imaginary) 1991
Rock the Magic Rock (UK Imaginary) 1992

This Manchester combo formed by guitarists Dave Fielding and Reg Smithies after their bandmates in the Chameleons went off to launch the Sun and the Moon in 1987 mixes a droney semi-psychedelic attack and a strong melodic sensibility with partial success. Though a few memorable numbers like "Blind Denial" (from **Rock the Magic Rock**) yield a nice power pop/art rock hybrid that recalls some of the Church's finer moments, the Reegs' tendency to overuse technical frills—like the stiff programmed drumming that dominates too many of their tunes—works against the band's better interests. Indeed, it's on quieter, more acoustically based efforts, like "Goodbye World" and "Running to a Standstill" (both from **Rock the Magic Rock**) that the band shines most brightly. **Return of the Sea Monkeys** was assembled from two prior EPs and the band's contributions to various Imaginary Records tribute albums. [ss]

See also *Mark Burgess and the Sons of God.*

VERNON REID

See *Living Colour.*

REIN SANCTION

Broc's Cabin (Sub Pop) 1991
Mariposa (Sub Pop) 1992

Years after Dinosaur Jr's J Mascis introduced his pedal-driven, melancholic noise-guitar histrionics to indie-rock, Rein Sanction's Mark Gentry emerged from his Jacksonville, Florida, basement with drummer/brother Brannon and bassist Ian Chase. Although hamstrung by the Dinosaur Jr comparisons, the trio nonetheless created two powerful albums.

Broc's Cabin, produced by Shimmy-Disc honcho Kramer, revels in dense psychedelia, abundantly frenzied guitar and at least one song title—"Sasquatch"—that aptly describes the band's style. Mark Gentry's liberal use of wah-wah, distortion and envelope filter could also draw some comparisons to early Meat Puppets, but the blueprint here seems effectively Dinosaur-esque—pretty, sludgy and pretty sludgy.

Jack Endino twisted the knobs and slid the faders for **Mariposa,** but the band's initial sound is roughly duplicated all the same. Mark's voice is more plaintive here, even as the caterwauling trio drowns what few vocals exist. (Rein Sanction's strength lies in its sprawling jams and expansive instrumental energy.) He's not much of a vocalist and doesn't have to be—his languid, overpowering guitar really sings, as the throwaway title "B-F#" might suggest. (The song itself, an acoustic-based jam with fluttering backward guitar riffs, is simple and a strong diversion from the group's usual overdrive.) Despite such efforts at diversification and strong tracks like "Loaded Decision," "Blow" and "Railway," the inclusion of a live cover—Hendrix's "Ain't No Tellin"—possibly indicates Rein Sanction's shortage of its own ideas. [mww]

R.E.M.

Chronic Town EP (IRS) 1982
Murmur (IRS) 1983
Reckoning (IRS) 1984
Fables of the Reconstruction (IRS) 1985
Lifes Rich Pageant (IRS) 1986
Dead Letter Office (IRS) 1987
Document (IRS) 1987
Eponymous (IRS) 1988
Green (Warner Bros.) 1988
Out of Time (Warner Bros.) 1991
The Best of R.E.M. (UK IRS) 1991
Automatic for the People (Warner Bros.) 1992
Monster (Warner Bros.) 1994
New Adventures in Hi-Fi (Warner Bros.) 1996

HINDU LOVE GODS

Hindu Love Gods (Giant/Reprise) 1990

TROGGS

Athens Andover (Rhino) 1992

R.E.M. didn't reinvent the wheel or demolish any stylistic barriers when the quartet popped its curly little head up from the collegiate fields of Athens, Georgia, at the beginning of the 1980s; the power-pop underground already had other Byrdsian bands with jangly guitars and mumbly singers. Of course, no other band had a mumbly singer with the potent artistic vision or charisma of Michael Stipe, or the unique brains/brawn extrovert/introvert art/rock chemistry of R.E.M.—two of the reasons why the group rose steadily through an uneven series of '80s albums to stand as one of the world's biggest and best-loved rock'n'roll combos. Unlike Nirvana, whose success largely defined an era, the equally inscrutable R.E.M. (and their transatlantic cousins, U2) worked their way into household namedom without setting off any revolutionary times-they-are-a-changin' alarms. True, plenty of imitators followed, and the group's breakthrough proved highly beneficial for others whose humble/indie beginnings would no longer be looked on with commercial skepticism. R.E.M. also helped prove that rock didn't have to be callow, cynical and calculated to resonate with large population segments, but the world after **Document** sold a million copies wasn't significantly different than it had been.

Chronic Town and the masterful **Murmur** introduced a band with style, content, imagination and dedication. All it took was a lot of hard work and bad videos—appealingly tethered to integrity, considerate public behavior and vocal indie-scene solidarity—to build a massive following among America's young intelligentsia. The hard part for R.E.M.—Stipe, guitarist Peter Buck, bassist Mike Mills and drummer Bill Berry—was figuring out what to do, musically speaking, with its fame.

R.E.M.'s first era came to an end with **Document,** the final album it made for IRS. The tally included the bracing five-song **Chronic Town** (with "1,000,000" and "Wolves, Lower"), a breathtaking full-length debut (**Murmur,** containing "Catapult," "Moral Kiosk," "Talk About the Passion" and "Radio Free Europe," rerecorded from a 1981 indie single) and the refined and fine **Reckoning:** "Harborcoat," "So. Central Rain (I'm Sorry)," "(Don't Go Back to) Rockville," "Pretty Persuasion." Then came an uncomfortable period of recalibration, during which R.E.M. groped around for a new approach that it didn't find in time to salvage the vague, colorless and dull **Fables of the Reconstruction** (aka **Reconstruction of the Fables**) or the overly restrained and political **Lifes Rich Pageant.** The latter does contain a totally ace cover of the Clique's psychedelic obscurity "Superman," sung in a delicious near-whine by Mills, and the affectingly languid "Fall on Me," but otherwise fails to connect.

With Stipe opting for a brave new world of enunciation on **Document,** Scott Litt's dynamic co-production pushes the songs back into the world of the living, with a bright, loud sound and an infusion of much-needed rock energy. Without sacrificing sensitivity, Buck plays up a storm, pushed into high gear by Berry's walloping big beat. The entire first half is brilliant, from the maniacally intense "Finest Worksong" to the stomping horn-flecked nostalgia of "Exhuming McCarthy," a goofball cover of Wire's "Strange" and the name-dropping nonsense of "It's the End of the World as We Know It (And I Feel Fine)." The back nine is half as good, which is to say the sound is swell but the songs aren't. Nonetheless, millions misunderstood the stinging irony of "The One I Love" and made it R.E.M.'s first hit single.

Dead Letter Office, a curious and amusing B-sides/rarities collection, reveals R.E.M.'s proclivity for recording covers (by Pylon, Roger Miller, the Velvet Underground and Aerosmith) and a goofy sense of humor not often indulged on their albums. Buck's liner notes explain the origins of all fifteen outtakes, pisstakes and oddities; the CD adds the contents of **Chronic Town.** A kiss-off greatest-hits compilation, **Eponymous** omits crucial songs but has the original indie 45 version of "Radio Free Europe," an unused vocal take on "Gardening at Night" (from **Chronic Town**), an alternate mix of "Finest Worksong" and "Romance," a soundtrack contribution not previously on an R.E.M. record. It took the English office a couple of years to get around to it, but the import-only **The Best of R.E.M.** expands on **Eponymous** with added (and subtracted) tracks.

Quelling fears of sell-out lameness or overfed incapacity, **Green** is a great, mature, subtly political record with an abundance of memorable songs given surprisingly diverse and thought-out performances. Dropping its reliance on familiar jangle-pop tone and crisp tempos, the band strides boldly into the modern rock arena, testing novel rhythms (the dancey "Pop Song 89," whose old-style chorus contrasts strikingly with the new-fangled verses; the tense, piledriving "Get Up"), uncommon atmospheres (the sweaty palms and U2-ish carpet-bombing of "Orange Crush," the rough drone of "Turn You Inside Out") and unabashed chart-pop stylings ("Stand"). Jane Scarpantoni's cello adds baroque woodiness to the solemn "World Leader Pretend" ("This is my mistake / Let me make it good"). An articulate yet enigmatic reinvention that delivers the band to an artistic plane loaded with new possibilities, **Green** propels R.E.M. into the future without renouncing its past.

Adding keyboards, strings and horns to adjust the style settings even further, R.E.M. (also employing adjunct touring member Peter Holsapple, post-dB's/pre–Continental Drifters, on guitar and bass) challenged audience expectations and themselves further with the ambitious, overproduced (again by Litt and the band) and inconsistent **Out of Time.** The numbers that work—"Radio Song" (with guest rap by KRS-One), the folk-rocking "Losing My Religion," the uplifting "Shiny Happy People" (with Kate Pierson of the B-52's chiming in), the acoustic "Half a World Away," "Me in Honey"—effectively progress from (or at least uphold) **Green**'s forthright example and are almost enough to carry the weight. The other half of the album, however, drags them down with material that is either too weak to withstand gummy layers of gratuitous instrumentation or falls prey to gimmicky concept experiments. "Low," "Endgame" and "Country Feedback" are blandly negligible; the happyface pop of "Near Wild Heaven" and the sung/recited "Belong" are ineffectual in their willful incongruity. **Out of Time** has too many important songs to banish from the collection, but it's also a dismal reminder of what happens when too many people tell creative musicians how great they are.

Automatic for the People refocuses all the random initiative of the group's great leap forward into a singular vision, with a cohesive collection of brilliant songs and a profoundly moving mood of somber dignity. Whatever R.E.M. once was no longer counts in the new math being reckoned in this eloquent chamber. On the most restrained and moody of R.E.M.'s records, haunting, beautiful elegies like "Everybody Hurts," "Nightswimming," "Star Me Kitten" and the David Essex–quoting "Drive" (some of which make exquisite use of a small orchestra) suck the air away and leave the lingering sadness of a long-ago funeral. Without breaking the mostly acoustic spell, the stronger-shouldered (Who-like, in fact) "Ignoreland" turns up the energy level, giving fuller play to Buck's distorted ardor, which lurks subliminally in compressed feedback accents elsewhere. In addition to his stupendous, hyper-sensitive singing, Stipe's lyrical obsessions are more obvious and sublime than ever; his homages to Montgomery Clift ("Monty Got a Raw Deal") and Andy Kaufman ("Man on the Moon") are quizzical, indirect and loaded with other concerns. The Litt/R.E.M. production, complex and detailed as it is, invariably benefits the songs, culminating in the tightrope balance of "The Sidewinder Sleeps Tonite" and "Try Not to Breathe," which reconcile everything the band has learned with ideas it had never before explored. That's creative progress, and **Automatic for the People** is a masterpiece.

In keeping with the band's one up, one down pattern, **Monster** was doomed, and R.E.M. didn't let down those expecting to be let down. Opening with loud, snarly guitar chords that stay unnaturally high in the mix even after Stipe begins singing "What's the Frequency, Kenneth?" (title courtesy of Dan Rather's unexplained street attack), **Monster** is the quartet's raunchy Big Rock effort. Evidently unaware that turning up doesn't equal turning on, and seemingly incapable of performing hard-edged electric music with credible conviction, R.E.M. appears to have designed this stolid misfire to give Pete Buck a showcase and a chance to check out the tremolo switch on his amplifier. It sure isn't based on top-notch songs or any need for this warmed-over heat treatment. "Strange Currencies," a sweet ballad that could be an **Automatic** leftover, and "What's the Frequency, Kenneth?" are all right, but that's about it. Despite the lyrics' surprising sexual directness, "Crush With Eyeliner" and "Star 69" are clumsy nothings; others here don't even reach their modest plateaus. Stipe's vocal caricatures never get in synch with the raucous songs (in the case of the toned-down soul of "Tongue," he trots out a pitiful falsetto); he's left sounding lost in the studio. Mills and Berry trundle along at such carefully measured paces that they draw off the potential excitement in Buck's distortion slashes—busting out isn't usually done with such precise restraint. Anomalies are to be expected in the road of a band unwilling to settle for the easy solution, but this one so obviously doesn't work that it strikes an especially sour chord. Of course, it does clear the decks for another potential winner. Or, unfortunately, **New Adventures in Hi-Fi.**

Detailing the extracurricular activities of Mills, Berry, Stipe and especially Buck would fill a book (in fact, Tony Fletcher's *Remarks—The Story of R.E.M.* lists more than three dozen outside records on which they have appeared), but two albums do stand out for the primary involvement of all but Stipe. **Hindu Love Gods** is the belated issue of a 1987 studio get-together in which Buck, Mills and Berry back singer/guitarist Warren Zevon on old blues standards and a Prince song. Minus their marquee value, the threesome's playing is characterless (and not especially adept) bar-band issue, and the album is no biggie. The same is mostly true of the Troggs' **Athens Andover,** for which the great British Invasion singer Reg Presley and his current cohorts join forces with the same threesome and Holsapple in the hopes of mounting a hip comeback. It's the best appointed album of the Trogg's illustrious career, but that train's long since left the station, and songs like "Deja Vu," which resorts to the unforgivable ploy of stringing together the titles of past hits, don't make the wheels spin any faster. Even the few good tunes are too simple to present any challenge or stylistic opportunity for the players. Presley is a game vocalist but, by this point, a formulaic songwriter (who *really* should know better than to pen a song that has him repeatedly singing the phrase "it worries me" with a previously unnoticed Elmer Fudd accent). The Americans' two contributions don't help much, either. It was generous of R.E.M. to participate in an album by a musical hero, but **Athens Andover** isn't anybody's home run. [i]

See also *Vic Chesnutt, Golden Palominos, Robyn Hitchcock, Young Fresh Fellows; TPRG.*

RENTALS

See *Weezer.*

REPERCUSSIONS

See *Groove Collective.*

REPLICANTS

See *Failure.*

REPULSA

Repulsa (S.O.B.) 1994

Take a wild guess . . . Merry flower-power pop? Ambient techno? Dancehall skatepunk? Merseybeat? Nope. A testament to honest billing, Repulsa is, in fact, a California rock singer with lusty loins and a major attitude problem. The hard-hitting songs on her Matthew King Kaufman–produced album (S.O.B. actually stands for Son of Beserkley, a successor to Kaufman's pioneering label, which first brought Jonathan Richman, Greg Kihn and the Rubinoos to public attention) include such tender ministrations as "I Want You Dead," "Sex Pig," "F.T.W." and "Fuck Yourself." Truth be told, Repulsa's bellowing is an entertaining version of venomous self-righteousness—Courtney Love by way of Susan Powter and Lydia Lunch—and the thrash-metal is well-played and clearly produced. If nothing else, **Repulsa** would make a reasonable stocking stuffer for the weasely maggot masochist who lives up the street. [tr]

RESIDENTS

Meet the Residents (Ralph) 1974 (East Side Digital) 1988
The Residents Present the Third Reich 'n Roll (Ralph) 1976 (East Side Digital) 1987
Fingerprince (Ralph) 1976 (East Side Digital) 1987
The Residents Radio Special [tape] (Ralph) 1977
Not Available (Ralph) 1978 (East Side Digital) 1988
Duck Stab EP (Ralph) 1978
Duck Stab/Buster & Glen (Ralph) 1978 (East Side Digital) 1987
Babyfingers EP (Ralph) 1979
Eskimo (Ralph) 1979 (East Side Digital) 1987
Nibbles (UK Virgin) 1979
Diskomo/Goosebump EP (Ralph) 1980
The Residents Commercial Album (Ralph) 1980 (East Side Digital) 1988
Mark of the Mole (Ralph) 1981 (East Side Digital) 1988
Intermission (Ralph) 1982
The Tunes of Two Cities (Ralph) 1982 (East Side Digital) 1988
The Residents Mole Show (no label) 1983 (Ralph) 1983
Residue of the Residents (Ralph) 1983
American Composer Series–Volume 1: George & James (Ralph) 1984
Whatever Happened to Vileness Fats (Ralph) 1984 (East Side Digital) 1991
Ralph Before '84, Volume One: The Residents (UK Korova) 1984
Assorted Secrets [tape] (Ralph) 1984
Part Four of the Mole Trilogy: The Big Bubble (Black Shroud/Ralph) 1985 (East Side Digital) 1989
The Census Taker (Episode) 1985
PAL TV LP (UK Doublevision) 1985
The American Composer's Series–Volume II: Stars & Hank Forever! (Ralph) 1986
13th Anniversary Show Live in Japan! (Ralph) 1986
The 13th Anniversary Show Live in the USA (Ralph) 1986
Heaven? (Rykodisc) 1986
Hell! (Rykodisc) 1986
Hit the Road Jack EP (Ralph) 1987
Snakeywake EP (UWEB) 1987
The Mole Show Live in Holland (Hol. Torso) 1987 (East Side Digital) 1989
Santa Dog '88 EP (UWEB) 1988
God in Three Persons (Rykodisc) 1988
God in 3 Persons Soundtrack (Rykodisc) 1988
Double Shot o' My Baby's Love EP (Rykodisc) 1989
Buckaroo Blues (UWEB) 1989
Buckaroo Blues & Black Barry [tape] (Ralph Special Products) 1989

The King & Eye (Enigma) 1989
Cube E: Live in Holland (Enigma) 1990
Liver Music (UWEB) 1990
Stranger Than Supper (UWEB Special Product) 1990
Freak Show (Cryptic Official Product) 1990 (East Side Digital) 1995
Blowoff EP (Cryptic) 1992
Our Finest Flowers (Ralph/East Side Digital) 1992
Gingerbread Man (East Side Digital) 1994
Bad Day on the Midway (Inscape) 1995
Hunters: The World of Predators and Prey (Milan) 1995
Have a Bad Day (East Side Digital) 1996

RESIDENTS + RENALDO AND THE LOAF

Title in Limbo (Ralph) 1983

VARIOUS ARTISTS

Eyesore: A Stab at the Residents (Vaccination) 1996

What's a Resident? Epithets abound, but anent actual identities, anyone who knows ain't talking. Cinéastes transplanted—so the story goes—from Shreveport, Louisiana, to the San Francisco area who also dabble in musical experiments, the foursome (trio? duo?) has woven a remarkable cloak of secrecy. Aside from the avowed purpose of avoiding misleading and potentially divisive individual credits, this attention-getting mystique leaves absolutely nothing to contemplate but the music itself.

In the course of a lengthy and convoluted career that shows no signs of flagging, the Residents have produced an enormous and bewildering array of increasingly accessible high-concept records. Despite limited technical and compositional ability, the group's ample wit and unbridled imagination, in the service of works seeking to trample sacrosanct icons and rock's boundaries, have proven versatile and adaptable, as useful for ambient soundscapes as parodic musicology, electronic rock and film scores.

Close to the Residents' snickering hearts is the idea of rotating the nostalgically familiar to an angle that exposes a darker aspect that normally goes unseen or ignored. For what putatively is a musical group, that's pretty subversive if you think about it. And that is what the Residents would have you do. The group has made a career out of pushing its audience to think, rather than merely absorb; as sharp as visceral reactions can be, the what-are-they-*really*-up-to? factor has been a component of the Residents' work from the get-go.

Although they've had the benefit of considerable prowess, courtesy friends like the late guitarist Philip (Snakefinger) Lithman, the Residents have never pretended to instrumental virtuosity and have often sounded goofy, even downright silly. Yet one of their fortes is assembling seemingly simple-minded elements into mosaics of subtlety and complexity; even without benefit of the synthesizers now available, the "phonetic (re)organization" principle, an evident ability to manipulate tapes and an ornery creative vision resulted in the impressive sonic assemblages of their earliest releases—even on the debut LP, 1974's **Meet the Residents** (the CD of which includes the even earlier "Santa Dog" double 45; four attempted albums—only two completed—that preceded "Santa Dog" were never released).

Fingerprince built on the primitive execution of **Meet the Residents** by integrating synthesizers (which eventually became a trademark Residential characteristic) and expanding the group's propensity for extended or conceptual works. The songs—and the framing thereof—stepped up a notch on **Duck Stab** and reached a benchmark on **Eskimo,** the band's totally fabricated but terrifically evocative portrait of Eskimo life and culture. On the other hand, the band's truly wacky interpretive side, hinted at on **Meet the Residents** and given free rein on **Third Reich 'n Roll** (where it was used to make a controversial analogy about mindless cultural fascism), hit with sledgehammer force on the subsequent "Satisfaction" and "Beatles Play the Residents/Residents Play the Beatles" 45s (included on the **Third Reich** CD). By now it was clear—while they couldn't compete with the instrumental facility or orchestral ambitions of Frank Zappa, the Residents' relentless, compunctionless otherness could make him seem safe and normal by comparison.

The band embarked on three major projects in the '80s: the uncompleted Mole Trilogy, the open-ended American Composer Series and, in a related vein, the **Cube E** trilogy. The Mole Trilogy (**Mark of the Mole, The Tunes of Two Cities** and **The Big Bubble,** plus **Intermission,** included on the **Mark of the Mole** CD) is impressive, a parallel of the cultural relationship of African-Americans to white America in about as oblique and abstract a way as possible. Its creation catalyzed the Residents to mount a Mole Show tour in 1982–83—astonishing, considering they'd performed in public just three times in the previous ten years. The albums also raise two important Residential issues.

First, it can't be over-stressed how much effort the Residents' virtues sometimes take to discern. A prime example is **The Big Bubble,** which is one of the hardest Residents albums to recommend—especially out of context. At first, its simplistic and repetitive nature is flat-out irritating. Yet repeated listenings engender respect for the band's struggle to create and sustain the unusual emotional stance of an uprooted but partially miscegenated people attempting to assert its identity, and for the effort put into establishing a credible foreignness for the Moles, including the fictional Mohelmot language in which some of the album is sung.

Second, the Mole story was never resolved! Their first humongous flub? Or perhaps it's a statement: America hasn't resolved its partial absorption of African-Americans, so why—how—should the band? You never know with these guys, but getting folks to consider the ramifications may be the point.

The American Composers series makes no major statements, it just provides the chance to compare and contrast Residential faves in characteristically bizarre style. **George & James** (as in Gershwin and Brown) is much more entertaining than **Stars & Hank Forever** (John Philip Sousa and Hank Williams); while the latter album has its moments, the format isn't flexible enough for the task. But then there's Cube E: **Buckaroo Blues, Black Barry** and **The King and Eye** (known in performance as "The Baby King"). As a live oeuvre subtitled *The History of American Music in 3 E-Z Pieces,* it's a sensational take on the cowboy musical tradition, early African-American musics including gospel and country blues, and how rock'n'roll crawled up its own ass as illustrated by the alienated plight of Elvis Presley. (This project also generated a tour, which was as striking visually as musically.)

After twenty years, it became time for a look backward—in fact, three looks: Voyager issued an hour-long videodisc called *Twenty Twisted Questions,* featuring both released and unreleased videos and live performances and more. With **Our Finest Flowers,** the Residents themselves provided a unique alternative to a greatest-hits album (which would have been somewhat redundant, considering the **Heaven?** and **Hell!** compilations from 1986; for serious fans, there's also **Stranger Than Supper,** an assortment of live tracks, studio rarities and a self-professed "jam" on **Black Barry**'s "New Orleans") by recombining pieces of their fave tunes (including collaborations with Snakefinger and Renaldo and the Loaf) into tracks different enough that you'd swear they were newly recorded (but they were not). In '93, the leader of Uncle Willie's Eyeball Buddies (UWEB)—the Residents' appreciation society, which has issued numerous non-commercial records—wrote and compiled the not-entirely-reliable but extremely informative and entertaining *Uncle Willie's Highly Opinionated Guide to the Residents,* published by Ralph. His conclusion? "What It All Means" is . . . nothing. Ooookay. There's also **Louisiana's Lick,** a best-of sampler with misleading track attributions, done as a promotional item but available through mail-order.

More recently, the Residents have sought to enhance their visual side. As far back as the mid-'70s, they shot what they hoped would be a landmark underground film-on-videotape, *Vileness Fats* (mysteriously abandoned but later distilled into the wild half-hour *Whatever Became of Vileness Fats?* video, with a new soundtrack). Long before MTV, the Residents made some remarkable music videos, two of which are in New York's Museum of Modern Art's permanent collection. They later scored several episodes of *Peewee's Playhouse* and a number of MTV shows, and they corkscrewed musical archetypes for the soundtrack of *Saturday Night Live* alumnus Garrett Morris' 1985 film, *The Census Taker.* (That score wound up on the **Vileness Fats** CD reissue.) As the '90s unfold, the Residents move into a unique position among their ostensible peers as the pre-eminent creators of musical works explicitly created for CD-ROM.

Freak Show is a group of relatively accessible—if often unnerving—portraits of, well, freaks: a living head, a piano-playing human mole, a woman with a "living wig of worms" and so forth. It's not all despairing; "Jello Jack the Boneless Boy" hangs on by dreaming of being a bird and believing that "God is singing in his dreams at night." Not all the freaks are on display—some are the paying public. The imagery is uncomfortable, and when the lead vocals are performed by guest performers, they tend to be uncharacteristically (for the Residents) melodramatic. Still, there are more than enough lyrical twists and turns to avoid mere gross-out overkill, and the music shifts textures and tempos (the frequently used circus oompah is a touchstone) to follow suit. "Everyone comes to the Freak Show / But nobody laughs when they leave." Indeed!

Freak Show was adapted for a deluxe graphic album comic featuring top names in the cartooning world (Kyle Baker, Brian Bolland, Richard Sala and others) in a work that is interpretive rather than merely representative of the songs. (Early copies featured "Blowoff," **Freak Show**'s title tune leading into a thirteen-minute medley of music that didn't make the final CD; it's quite good, at times what the music those "alien" musical groups in the *Star Wars* movies should have sounded like. The EP has since been sold by itself via mail order.) The graphic album helped inspire the transformation of **Freak Show** into the first Residents interactive CD-ROM in '94, realized with the help of computer animator Jim Ludtke.

Gingerbread Man was created expressly for the interactive CD-ROM format, yet it uses a similar formula: the songs are portraits of aging, despairing or angry people. If anything, it's simpler and more straightforward than **Freak Show,** sounding very nearly like a "regular" band at times—well, as close as they've ever come, especially when guest Todd Rundgren voices "The Aging Musician" (who curses gun control and MTV for derailing his career). Much of the music is built around a single melodic phrase, which is somewhat limiting, but the effect is haunting rather than tiresome. An entertaining (if not major) musical work, and a transitional interactive undertaking. **Bad Day on the Midway** was created to be an interactive CD-ROM game; music based on it was released on standard CD as **Have a Bad Day.**

Meanwhile, the Residents released the **Hunters** soundtrack, from the Discovery Channel's cable series on animals in the wild. Who would ever have thought the Eyeballs would be doing educational TV? Without compromising their stylistic approach at all, the group pulls it off fairly well. Normally, the Residents are excellent at using slower tempos, muted or echoed percussion and synths that wash or drone to put across a dreamy feeling; that's what they do here for fifty-nine minutes, yet its varied tunelets and expressive textures are anything but dull.

If the Residents continually risk trivializing themselves by seeming willfully obscure rather than abstractly profound, it's obvious they don't care. It's part of the reason they can function as they do. That they have no more public identities than four bodies in tuxes with eyeball heads and top hats is more than just a cute gag. We've had only "their" word that they've been a foursome all along, and no one's ever said it's been a stable foursome; that familiar Residential vocalist (we even saw his face, albeit under heavy makeup, as Granddad in *The King and Eye* live shows) is the only certifiable thread of personnel continuity since the early albums. The passage of time has given this deliberate anonymity the stature of a genuine Statement, and despite occasional diversions and missteps—or what seem like missteps in the short run—the Residents forge on at a high and amazingly uncöopted level of achievement, eschewing the easy path. As the fictional group the Big Bubble on the album of the same name, they might as well be describing their own brand of musical brine. "Sugar melts and goes away/But vinegar lasts forever."

Eyesore: A Stab at the Residents is a thirty-track collection featuring an eclectic set of tribute-payers, from Cracker, Primus and Stan Ridgway to Heavy Vegetable, Thinking Fellers Union Local 282 and Supercollider; Snakefinger's old version of "Smelly Tongues" is wisely included as well. [jg]

See also *Cheepskates; TPRG.*

REST IN PIECES

See *Sick of It All.*

RETSIN

See *Rodan.*

REVENGE

See *New Order.*

REVERBS

See *Velvet Crush.*

REVOLTING COCKS

Big Sexy Land (Wax Trax!) 1986
You Goddamned Son of a Bitch (Wax Trax!) 1988
Beers, Steers + Queers (Wax Trax!) 1989
Linger Ficken' Good . . . and Other Barnyard Oddities (Sire/Reprise) 1993

Of all the interconnected side projects to come off the Chicago industrial factory floor in the mid-'80s, RevCo is the only one to have taken on a stable life of its own. Formed by scene majordomo Al Jourgensen (Ministry) and two Belgians—producer/musician Luc Van Acker and Richard 23 of the avant-garde dance machine Front 242—the Revolting Cocks, joined by various can-rattling friends, occasionally get together to make a little rhythmic noise in the studio and on the road.

The technological bent of the debut 12-inch ("No Devotion") and **Big Sexy Land** didn't last long. The album's synthesized club beats are left relatively unsullied by Jourgensen's usual compost-heap attack. On tracks like "We Shall Cleanse the World," "Big Sexy Land" and "T.V. Mind," vocals (when there are any) don't get in the way; spoken-word samples, bass and other elements add color and scraps of structure, but the downstrokes remain surgically clean. Although it's undoubtedly not the group's intention, a polite record like this could give the genre a good name.

With R23 returning to his European day job, RevCo established its long-term lineup of Jourgensen, Van Acker, Scottish-born singer/guitarist Chris Connelly (ex–Fini Tribe), bassist Paul Barker (Ministry) and industrial utility drummer William Rieflin. Caught bringing the noise live at a 1987 Chicago concert on the four vinyl sides of **You Goddamned Son of a Bitch,** the quintet is transformed, swapping abstruse clinical detail for a harsh, distorted dose of malevolent reality. Even though the set list includes all but one number from **Big Sexy Land** (the title track, as it happens), the live album resembles it only in passing. Rather than feebly dancing to the performance, one envisions the audience warily eyeballing exit routes in case the heaviness gets out of hand.

The same vein-popping intensity—and a few other things, like "In the Neck," an ugly number unveiled on the live album—moves into the studio for **Beers, Steers + Queers.** Although the band's concept is still distinctly less bloodthirsty than Ministry's, the interlocking personnel lists and Jourgensen's forceful leadership do make for a certain resemblance, even when Connelly's quoting both Johnny Rotten and John Otway in "(Let's Get Physical)." Awash in growl-shredding vocals and a fidgety three-note guitar solo, the thick and thundering "Get Down" leans more in that direction, but it's probably safe to assume that no one else would attempt cowboy hip-hop, as RevCo does on the amusingly bizarre rap-noise title track.

Making their first album specifically for CD (not to mention a major label) after four years off, the Revolting Cocks calmed down and stretched out, filling **Linger Ficken' Good** with lengthy, precisely calibrated beats-plus-samples-and-stuff tracks. Breaking the pattern, "Butcher Flower's Woman" rips open a raw, messy hole, "Mr. Lucky" takes another hip-hop hit and the title track puts the volume down to inject rude, funny samples and patter into a brisk and snappy jazz walk. Otherwise, most of the unwavering rhythms carry Connelly's cranky-sounding processed vocals in monotonous grooves that remove their sting. The jam only gets moving full-steam-ahead in a grinding, sleazy but safe cover of Rod Stewart's "Da Ya Think I'm Sexy?" Now what does that mean? [i]

See also *Chris Connelly, Front 242, Ministry, Pigface.*

REVOLVER

Heaven Sent an Angel EP (UK Hut) 1991
Crimson EP (UK Hut) 1992
Venice EP (UK Hut) 1992
Baby's Angry (Caroline) 1992
Cold Water Flat (Caroline) 1993

Formed in London in 1990 by two refugees from the southern English city of Winchester, Revolver—Mat Flint (vocals, guitar, keyboards), Nick Dewey (drums) and Hamish Brown (bass)—spent the first two years of its existence (chronicled on **Baby's Angry,** which consolidates all but two tracks from a pair of EPs and a maxi-single) progressing from energetic by-the-numbers shoegazing (more Lush than My Bloody Valentine) to subtly textured and distinctive pop melodicism. Expressing abject romantic devotion ("Heaven Sent an Angel," "Don't Ever Leave," "Cherish") without playing coy, Revolver is clearly more interested in songcraft than the simple sensuality of sound for its own sake. By the end of the process, the firm rhythms and pretty echo-tunnel singing add up to "Since Yesterday," a stately elegy that sends hooks flying on a captivating and complex wash of orchestra, voices, acoustic strumming and raw distortion. If the same single's "Red All Over" suggests an unnatural familiarity with the Moody Blues, it also suggests a usefully contrasting Wedding Present influence.

Cold Water Flat accommodates the trio's expanding audio ambitions with a handful of guest players adding horns, strings, percussion, didgeridoo and flute. While the jangle-poppy "I Wear Your Chain" could, without the pizzicato fiddling, be a Teenage Fanclub song, "Cradle Snatch" evolves into a six-minute psychedelic Doors jam. The dreamy smooch of "Nothing Without You" and the semi-acoustic "Coming Back" wrap the cotton wool loosely enough to be the Dream Academy or suchlike. "Makes No Difference All the Same" buries a fine-sounding song about romantic murder (?!) behind strings, scraggly guitar jabs and whatever else the band can lay its hands on. Having evolved quickly, Revolver now can't seem to harness its talent and divergent stylistic ideas into a cogent personality. Although agreeable enough, **Cold Water Flat** is far too elaborately furnished, with needless bits of musical business indiscriminately slathered everywhere. Like a posh showroom, the album is impressive rather than inviting, its overproduced surface glittering brightly to discourage discovering what might lie underneath. [i]

REX

See *Codeine.*

BUSTA RHYMES

See *Leaders of the New School.*

MARC RIBOT

Haitian Suite [tape] (Music of the World) 1988
Rootless Cosmopolitans (Antilles) 1990
Requiem for What's-His-Name (Bel. Les Disques du Crépuscule) 1992
Shrek (Japan. Avant) 1994
John Zorn: The Book of Heads (Tzadik) 1995
Don't Blame Me (Japan. DIW) 1995

MARC RIBOT/FRED FRITH

Sounds of a Distant Episode (Bel. Subsonic) 1994

Newark-born guitarist Marc Ribot is best known as a sideman: his edgy playing can be heard on albums by Tom Waits, Elvis Costello, Sam Phillips, Syd Straw, Marianne Faithfull, Foetus and others. Ribot has also been part of New York's avant-jazz scene, as a member of the Lounge Lizards and in collaborations with John Zorn, Anthony Coleman, Ikue Mori, Robert Quine, Elliott Sharp and David Shea. When he's in the driver's seat, however, Ribot explores volume, noise and his Jewish heritage. What unifies his work is an easily recognizable sound: restless, angular leads that take sharp, unexpected melodic turns and a witty intelligence that moves from dissonance into harmony, teetering between chaos and control. Playing as if the solos of free jazz saxophonist Albert Ayler were transposed to guitar, Ribot calls his style Brutal Atavistic music.

Named for Ribot's band of the time, **Rootless Cosmopolitans** (a description of Jews used by Joseph Goebbels and later appropriated for a poem by Allen Ginsberg) is a harder-edged version of the "fake jazz" he played with the Lizards, especially in his duets with clarinetist Don Byron. (An argument can be made that if you drain the intelligence and wit from this and the early Lounge Lizards albums and replace it with smarmy irony you wind up with cocktail music.) He also deconstructs rock music, with a wry take of Hendrix's "The Wind Cries Mary."

While less cohesive, **Requiem for What's-His-Name** still has its moments. The jazz side has been deemphasized, and Ribot's Captain Beefheart edges take up the slack. He also grants his gimlet-eyed humor some play, in the cracked, stiff blues of "Clever White Youths" and the appropriation of hardcore elements in the anti-anti-Semitic "Yo, I Killed Your God." But jazz comes to the fore on the album's best track, a passionate, charged reading of Duke Ellington's "Caravan."

Ribot moves even closer to rock with **Shrek.** (The name, Yiddish for shock or horror, is apt.) This intense, almost violent music unleashes a full-blown attack Boredoms fans might appreciate. From the volume pedal experiment of "Spigot" to the Eastern European–tinged march of "Hoist the Bloody Icon High," Ribot and his band (sometimes known as Shrek, it includes Soul Coughing bassist Sebastian Steinberg) play with breathtaking freedom and passion. With Chris Wood replacing Steinberg, Shrek also appears on Ribot's half of the **Sounds of a Distant Episode,** where—less song-oriented, concentrating more on the idea of pure amplified sounds—the tracks come off like a classically trained, rigorous Sonic Youth.

While he continues to use a band onstage, Ribot's recent recordings have showcased his solo playing. **The Book of Heads,** a 1978 composition by John Zorn, was written in an attempt to codify free guitar playing. It tests the virtuosity of anyone who attempts to play it, and Ribot is very much up to the task. Like much of Zorn's work from the late '70s, the series of fragments changes moods and styles abruptly. Using different implements to strike the strings (balloons, *mbira* keys, toys), it sounds at times like a six-stringed variation on John Cage's treated piano. While not easy listening by a long shot and at times infuriating, **The Book of Heads** has moments of power and beauty.

Don't Blame Me is far more accessible and altogether more satisfying: reworkings of pop and jazz standards ("Ol' Man River," "These Foolish Things," Ayler's "Ghosts," Ellington's "Solitude") that combine Ribot's melodic sense with improvisations recalling John Coltrane and Ornette Coleman. [sm]

See also *Elvis Costello, Phish, Tom Waits, John Zorn.*

JONATHAN RICHMAN (AND THE MODERN LOVERS)

Jonathan Richman & the Modern Lovers (Beserkley) 1977 (Beserkley/Rhino) 1986
Rock'n'Roll With the Modern Lovers (Beserkley) 1977 (Beserkley/Rhino) 1986
Back in Your Life (Beserkley) 1979 (Beserkley/Rhino) 1986
The Jonathan Richman Songbook (UK Beserkley) 1980
Jonathan Sings! (Sire) 1983 (Sire/Blue Horizon/Warner Bros.) 1993
Rockin' and Romance (Twin\Tone) 1985
It's Time for Jonathan Richman and the Modern Lovers (Upside) 1986
Modern Lovers 88 (Rounder) 1987
The Beserkley Years: The Best of Jonathan Richman and the Modern Lovers (Beserkley/Rhino) 1987
Jonathan Richman (Rounder) 1989
Jonathan Goes Country (Rounder) 1990
23 Great Recordings by Jonathan Richman and the Modern Lovers (UK Beserkley/Essential/Castle Communications) 1990
Having a Party With Jonathan Richman (Rounder) 1991
I, Jonathan (Rounder) 1992
¡Jonathan, Te Vas a Emocionar! (Rounder) 1994
You Must Ask the Heart (Rounder) 1995
A Plea for Tenderness (UK Nectar Masters) 1995
Surrender to Jonathan! (Vapor) 1996

MODERN LOVERS

The Modern Lovers (Beserkley) 1976 (Beserkley/Rhino) 1986
Live (Beserkley) 1977
The Original Modern Lovers (Bomp!) 1981
Live at the Long Branch Saloon (Fr. New Rose) 1992
Precise Modern Lovers Order: Live in Berkeley and Boston (Rounder) 1994

After years of nominal accompaniment by a series of sidepeople dubbed the Modern Lovers, Jonathan Richman—having long since left behind his historical role as the Velvets-channeling underground rock pioneer—made the conceptual break with his legendary group and went solo. (The early days are clearly audible on the monumental **The Modern Lovers,** the vault excavation of **The Original Modern Lovers** and the amazing early-'70s live tracks belatedly issued first on a French LP then on **Precise Modern Lovers Order;** the 1977 **Live** finds the group already in the thrall of Richman's second childhood.)

For Richman, being solo has meant different things. Following the relatively ambitious **Modern Lovers 88, Jonathan Richman** takes it literally, for an exercise in minimalism that necessitates only the artist, his guitar and percussive footstomps (although an unobtrusive rhythm section pops up on two songs). The lonely-boy act doesn't play as well on record as it does live, and the material is spotty (three out of twelve tracks are instrumental covers of pop standards like "Blue Moon," one is sung in French and another in Spanish), but **Jonathan Richman** is not without its charms. Check out "Closer," "Fender Stratocaster" and "I Eat With Gusto, Damn! You Bet," a spoken-word defense of sloppy table manners.

By contrast, **Jonathan Goes Country**—in which the singer is backed by a full band of seasoned studio pros led by producers Lou Whitney and D. Clinton Thompson (both of Morells/Skeletons fame)—is thoroughly ingratiating. The program is a mixture of well-chosen covers, reworkings of previously recorded Richman tunes and a few swell new originals. Rather than sounding like a gimmicky affectation, the album's faux-Nashville arrangements prove to be a perfect vehicle for Jojo's bucolic sincerity.

Except that some of its numbers were recorded at gigs, the **Having a Party** title doesn't literally signify anything beyond the ebullient one-man-happening spirit of the author. In a pensive frame of mind for much of the record, Richman reconsiders past times with newfound gravity. He pores over a non-relationship ("Just for Fun"), expresses remorse for "My Career as a Homewrecker," makes fun of the Modern Lovers in "Monologue About Bermuda" (a musically illustrated anecdote about his discovery of calypso) and explains his rejection of city life in a poem called "1963." Displaying his genius for offbeat observations about obvious things, he enthuses about a positive interpersonal adjustment ("The Girl Stands Up to Me Now"), worries about nomenclatural associations in "When I Say Wife" ("wife sounds like your mortgage / wife sounds like laundry"), describes "Our Swinging Pad" and speeds up "Cappuccino Bar" as the lyrics' sugar/caffeine buzz kicks in. With the barest bits of incidental accompaniment, Richman rolls another easy spare.

Ably assisted on low-tech instruments by various pals and offspring and recording in a California basement, Richman hits peak form on the casually wonderful and all-original **I, Jonathan.** With infectious enthusiasm, sloppy charm and the topical eclecticism of his best mid-'80s work, Jojo rejoices about such diverse subjects as the superiority of gay nightlife ("I Was Dancing in the Lesbian Bar"), little fishies (the electric surf instrumental "Grunion Run"), skydiving ("Tandem Jump," complete with sound effects), the changing nature of house parties ("Parties in the U.S.A.") and one rock'n'roll group he admires ("Velvet Underground"). As a bonus, **I, Jonathan** reprises 1983's wistful reminiscence "That Summer Feeling" (from **Jonathan Sings!,** itself given a second chance the following year, with the addition of the previously UK-only "The Tag Game" as a bonus track) in a sweetly floating acoustic rendition that gains resonance from the passage of another decade in Richman's life.

Jonathan had already test-driven his multi-lingual vocal skills on record; still, the singer's all-Spanish album is a happy conceptual surprise. **¡Jonathan, Te Vas a Emocionar!** includes loosely translated renditions of songs from previous J.R. albums—**I, Jonathan**'s "A Higher Power" ("Una Fuerza Allá") and "You Can't Talk to the Dude" ("No Te Oye"), **Party**'s "Just for Fun" ("No Mas por Fun") "The Neighbors" ("Los Vecinos") and "Reno" ("Reno") from **Country,** plus a reprise of **Jonathan Richman**'s Spanish trial balloon "Cerca"—as well as a couple of Mexican numbers and new originals. Emoting with gently robust romanticism over nylon-string guitar and piano, Richman is no less charming in a foreign tongue, even when he gets up to his old tricks like waxing handsomely sentimental about the Marx Brothers ("Harpo en Su Harpa"), focusing deeply on a gum wrapper ("Papel de Chicle") or recounting a Persian lovers' fable ("Shirin y Farad," first told on his '86 LP). Putting extra care into his singing, Richman wraps his instinctual nonchalance in credible conviction, even if—as he notes in the voluminous booklet of liner notes and lyrics—"Don't blame . . . the people who helped me for the way I 'stretch' the language at times. I do the same in English."

Richman brings an equal measure of ambition to his customary métier in **You Must Ask the Heart,** a deep and wide exclamation of love's power that revisits many of his musical fascinations with lightly balanced but fully formed band arrangements. Evidently incapable of organizing himself into stylistically consistent albums, Richman lays out the usual smorgasbord here, blithely following the serious personal revelations of "To Hide a Little Thought" and a handsomely rocking cover of Tom Waits' "The Heart of Saturday Night" with the abject silliness of "Vampire Girl" and the merry ethnic grumble (sung by actress Julia Sweeney) of "Just Because I'm Irish." Besides the usual rustically rendered pop, there's some country (the original title song and Amanda McBroom's "The Rose") and a relevant Spanish ballad ("Amorcito Corazón"). Elsewhere on this magnificent album, he sympathetically defends a young woman in trouble ("Let Her Go Into the Darkness"), offers an a cappella tribute to pitcher "Walter Johnson," a version of Sam Cooke's "Nothing Can Change This Love" and a personal paradox ("City Vs. Country"). Employing innocence like an instrument, Richman turns the joyfully spirited **You Must Ask the Heart** into an amazing feat. Although he's been making music his own way for a quarter of a century, Richman still sounds like he's playing with a brand-new toy.

The organ-ic **Surrender to Jonathan!,** a full-band album which was produced by Andy Paley and released on Neil Young's Vapor label, contains remakes of "Egyptian Reggae" and "I Was Dancing in the Lesbian Bar" as well as eleven new originals. **A Plea for Tenderness** is a British compilation. [ss/i]

See also *TPRG*.

RIDE

Ride EP (UK Creation) 1990
Play EP (UK Creation) 1990

Smile (Sire/Reprise) 1990
Fall EP (UK Creation) 1990
Nowhere (Sire/Reprise) 1990
Vapour Trail EP (Sire/Reprise) 1991
Going Blank Again (Sire/Reprise) 1992
Carnival of Light (Sire/Reprise) 1994
Live Light (Mutiny) 1995
• Black Nite Crash EP (UK Creation) 1996
Tarantula (Sire) 1996

Inspired by the Manchester rave scene, Oxford-to-London art-school quartet Ride—Mark Gardener (vocals/rhythm guitar), Andy Bell (vocals/lead guitar), Steve Queralt (bass) and Laurence "Loz" Colbert (drums)—began in 1988, laying washes of guitar damage and ethereal vocals over shuffling dance beats. The tentative first EP leads off with an original entitled "Chelsea Girl" and follows up with three similar long noise-pop creations, the best of which is "Close My Eyes." The more distinctive **Play** has a louder, harsher sound (converting the previous record's jagged squalls into a continuous thick gauze) and, on the exemplary "Like a Daydream," rich folk-rock harmonies. The two EPs, which contain too much filler to make it a completely safe venture, were combined as the eight-song **Smile,** Ride's awkward introduction to America.

The "recorded by Marc Waterman" credit on **Nowhere,** Ride's first proper album, seems apt for the nonchalance of the fuzzy, unfocused sound and the meandering miasma of the band's playing. While dreamy vocals in constricted melodies and gauzy pulses of guitar distortion remain consistent ingredients, the drumming shifts from rear-guard action to driving danceability without evident premeditation. Traces of various shoegazers (My Bloody Valentine and, in "Taste," Stone Roses) surface in the lazy, bland tunes; with the exception of the gentle, breezy "Vapour Trail" (maladroitly punctured by Colbert's stutter beat), **Nowhere** is really nothing.

Alan Moulder, who mixed **Nowhere,** co-produced **Going Blank Again** with Ride, and it's a night-into-day improvement. The sound is clear and bright, the songs fully formed and briskly propelled—melodies traverse a reasonable part of the scale and the arrangements (helpfully marbled with uncredited keyboards) repeal the previous album's genial chaos with the kindness of coordinated displays. Lyrics remain a weakness, but amount to a minor inadequacy on this appealing platter. Given the music's trend-riding aspect, Ride still come off like kid brothers tugging at the big bands' stylistic sleeves, but the evidence here of growing confidence and songwriting skill (check out "Leave Them All Behind," "Time of Her Time" and "Cool Your Boots," which begins, intriguingly enough, with a line of dialogue from *Withnail & I*) puts maturity within reach.

Alas, **Carnival of Light** grabs at it too firmly; the handsome album is a stylishly tepid bore. John Leckie is responsible for the mild overproduction: the school choir on "I Don't Know Where It Comes From," Beatlesque cellos and sitar effects on the instrumental "Rolling Thunder" and Deep Purple organist Jon Lord's guest extravagances are a bit much for such an essentially simple band. Significantly, the record ends Ride's reliance on guitar textures, relegating deep-pile sensuality to a part-time hobby via Bell's keyboard competence. "Birdman" gets up a good head of steam and compares favorably to the last album's best tracks, but the Lord-churned "Moonlight Medicine," at nearly seven minutes, is stretched beyond the elastic potential of such a slight composition. Ride finds its most solid groove in the Creation's 1967 classic, "How Does It Feel to Feel?," which—guided by initial producer George Drakoulias—receives the full neo-psychedelic rave-beat treatment and emerges a slow, woozy hangover of compelling sonic muzz. Otherwise, the instrumentation doesn't really serve the vocals, and several songs feel like the work of two competing factions.

Ironically, it's on the in-concert **Live Light**—a ten-song career cross-section performed before an appreciative audience—that Ride manages a truly satisfying album. Away from the studio, the quartet puts some real thought into the playing and the singing, varying the attack with power and delicacy. Songs like "Chelsea Girl," "Close My Eyes" "Seagull," "Leave Them All Behind" and "Only Now" receive the treatment they deserve, pulling the group across a thermometer full of emotional temperatures in settings that stress guitar *and* dynamics. While the older songs are improved in more capable hands, the newer songs aren't picked spare by fussy technique.

Sailing off into the career sunset, Ride ended its backward run with just the kind of direct, unpretentious and easily likable guitar-pop album it always needed to make. Displaying maximum melodies and a minimum of distractions, the sensually rich **Tarantula** strips Ride back down to its roots and winds up sounding like a young Teenage Fanclub with more ideas and a different accent. Also the title track of an otherwise non-LP British EP, "Black Nite Crash" opens a solid chunk of fuzzy punk-pop decadence ("See the girls coughing, looking underfed / When they go to sleep they dream of being dead"); other than a little rhythmic variety (the Steppenwolf chords of "The Dawn Patrol" stand on a mild dance beat) and the Doorsy electric piano of "Ride the Wind," the album is relaxed and subtle, a stark contrast to Ride's previous try-too-hard missteps. Abutting the acoustic sparsity of "Castle on the Hill" and the roaringly tuneful "Gonna Be Alright" is no hardship; for a change, both songs feel like the results of a single collected mind. With that, the band broke up. [i]

STAN RIDGWAY

The Big Heat (IRS) 1986
Mosquitos (Geffen) 1989
Partyball (Geffen) 1991

DRYWALL

Work the Dumb Oracle (IRS) 1995

Launching his solo career, **The Big Heat** turned Stan Ridgway's pulp fiction/film noir aesthetic—always an element in Wall of Voodoo, the Los Angeles band he formed in 1977 and exited in 1983—into a full-blown cinematic musical experience. The singer/songwriter's bizarre characters and tales are as vivid as any vintage Robert Mitchum movie (and twice as hummable). Changing labels, **Mosquitos** fluctuates between the expected vignettes of loners and losers ("Calling out to Carol") and tunes that sound like outtakes from the soundtrack of a southwestern sci-fi epic. Ridgway's literary penchant gets a workout on "Can't Complain," a musical short story about a couple of down-and-out construction workers, and "Peg and Pete and Me," which condenses a scenario right out of *The*

Postman Always Rings Twice into five nasty little minutes.

Ridgway describes **Partyball** as a "party record"; if so, it's a soirée no one in his or her right mind would want to be invited to. "Jack Talked (Like a Man on Fire)" is another tale of insanity and alienation, while the rest of the album serves up odes to trigger-happy cops, hopeless love, Harry Truman and the atom bomb, otherworldly chain gangs and plague-ridden dystopias, interrupted by odd instrumental interludes that continue Ridgway's fascination with soundtrack music for invisible movies.

After those great solo records, Ridgway returned to a group format for **Work the Dumb Oracle.** Along with keyboardist/singer Pietra Wexstun (who provided backing vocals on **Mosquitos** and **Partyball**) and drummer Ivan Knight, he turns in another brooding body of work that views the City of Angels in a jaundiced light that makes Tom Waits and Charles Bukowski look like optimists. The modus operandi is familiar: ghostly harmonica, spooky carnival keyboards, guitars fuzzier than a slab of bacon left out in the desert sun, cholesterol-thick basslines that pound your chest like a coronary and Ridgway's unique voice, the sound of a rusty nail being pulled out of an old gray plank. The punks, hoods and perverts who people Ridgway's universe are still out in force, and the music is as chillingly eclectic as ever, with "My Exclusive Sex Club" notably serving up an odd combination of Latin and Arabic licks. [jp]

See also *TPRG.*

AMY RIGBY

See *Shams.*

RIP

See *Alastair Galbraith.*

RIVERDALES

Riverdales (Lookout) 1995

Though it could certainly be seen as an affront to the real thing, a generation landslide of devoted Ramones clone bands has emerged in the '90s, each replicating the divine roar and joyful idiocy of the brudders' late-'70s punk-pop to the extent of the members' ardent ability and interpretive songwriting acumen. Oddly, several of them are side projects of other bands, which makes the tribute all the more implicitly condescending. The Hanson Brothers are NoMeansNo's hockey interpolation of the concept; Chicago's Riverdales are three alumni of the temporarily defunct Screeching Weasel (who once recorded a version of the Ramones' first album in its entirety). Benefiting here from the mixdown mettle of Green Day's Billie Joe Armstrong, the trio has the surging rhythm-guitar roar down cold, applying it enthusiastically to a dozen original songs that pull close enough to classic Ramones vehicles to chance a scrape. While using nothing but road-tested chord patterns, the Riverdales add a few lyrical ideas ("Not Over Me" and "She's Gonna Break Your Heart" visit an old romantic pop tradition alien to the Ramones; "I Think About You During the Commercials" is couch tater genius). Still, bassist/singer Dan Schafer (Danny Vapid in SW), guitarist/singer Ben Foster (aka fanzine scrawler Ben Weasel) and drummer Dan Sullivan (SW's Dan Panic) make a point of using the reserved girl's name (Judy) and the secret word ("lobotomy")—both in the same song—and recycling such standard topics as mental health ("Wanna Be Alright"). When all is said and done—and it only takes a hair over a half-hour to sing it and do it—the Riverdales swallow their pride and pay generous homage that rocks like crazy. Gabba gabba!

As of early '96, the Riverdales had taken a back seat to a relaunched Screeching Weasel. [i]

See also *Queers, Screeching Weasel.*

TOM ROBINSON

North by Northwest (IRS) 1982
Cabaret '79 (UK Panic) 1982
Hope and Glory (Geffen) 1984
Still Loving You (UK Castaway) 1986
Midnight at the Fridge (UK Dojo) 1987
The Collection 1977–1987 (UK EMI) 1987
Back in the Old Country (UK Connoisseur Collection) 1989
Last Tango (Ger. Line) 1989
Living in a Boom Time (UK Cooking Vinyl) 1992
Love Over Rage (Rhythm Safari/Priority) 1994
Having It Both Ways (Cooking Vinyl) 1996

TOM ROBINSON & JAKKO M. JAKSZYK

We Never Had It So Good (Fr. Musidisc) 1990

TOM ROBINSON BAND

Power in the Darkness (Harvest) 1978 (Razor & Tie) 1993
TRB Two (Harvest) 1979 (Razor & Tie) 1993

SECTOR 27

Sector 27 (IRS) 1980

Tom Robinson wasn't the first openly gay recording artist, but the Tom Robinson Band was the first group led by a proudly uncloseted rocker to really make an impact on mainstream Anglo/American pop fans. Robinson's saga began in Finchton Manor, a home for "maladjusted" boys, where he came out and met future lead guitarist Danny Kustow. Robinson's first group, Cafe Society, was signed to the Kinks' Konk label and released one forgettable album. After a long legal and personal battle with Ray Davies, the singing bassist was released from his contract and set about forming the Tom Robinson Band. Kustow resurfaced, and after recruiting young keyboard wizard Mark Ambler and drummer Brian "Dolphin" Taylor, they were ready to go. EMI, fresh from their debacle with the Sex Pistols, signed the band, whose first single, the rousing non-political road anthem "2-4-6-8 Motorway," was a Top 10 hit in England. The band collapsed after two albums, and Robinson launched the short-lived Sector 27 before going solo in the early '80s.

Robinson looks like a slightly dazed everyman on the cover of **North by Northwest,** but the tunes, many co-written with Peter Gabriel, are uniformly strong. The music is dark and moody, with synth-heaving arrangements, but it has a low-key charm that's more personal than political, lightened by more danceable new wave and reggae beats. "Atmospherics (Listen to the Radio)" is one of the gloomiest rock tunes ever written, and another Robinson classic.

Having lost his appeal for the record industry, Robinson recorded and released "War Baby," a number that sounds like a Steely Dan outtake, on his own. It became a major British hit in 1983, and revitalized his career. On the cover of **Hope and Glory,** Robinson wears a red star on his chest, but inside he sounds like any other middle-of-the-road rock artiste. With the exception of "Cabin Boy," a bouncy bit of gay double entendre, the best tracks are tunes redone from **Sector 27.** "War Baby" and a cover of Steely Dan's "Rikki Don't Lose That Number" got him some US notice as well, but the album mainly sounds like product.

Most of Robinson's musical output over the following decade was live documents (adding **Midnight at the Fridge, Last Tango** and the acoustic **Living in a Boom Time** to **Cabaret '79**) and compilations, although the collaboration with Level 42 guitarist Jakko Jakszyk and **Still Loving You** are new studio efforts. As of the early '90s, Robinson had returned to the Quaker faith of his childhood and had a wife and child; he was also hosting *The Locker Room,* a BBC Radio forum for sensitive new age Britons.

His first American album release in ten years, **Love Over Rage** is the strongest thing Robinson has committed to wax since **Power in the Darkness.** It rocks as hard as that legendary album and combines the political concerns of the early work with the more personal touch of Robinson's middle career. "Roaring" opens the set with a thumping, two-fisted rocker that laments the folly of youth while tempering its nostalgia with hard-won realism. "Loved" is sweetly touching romance with a reggae beat. "Green" blasts corporate polluters who wrap themselves in "green" rhetoric, while "Hard" talks about problems of the common man vis-à-vis sexism and sensitivity without getting wimpy or self-conscious about it. "Silence" is a shriek of pain that'll pound your brain like a bad headache, and "Chance" ends the album with an implicit journey from darkness to light, and from gay sex to married life. Robinson can still sound preachy, but overall this is a stunningly mature work. [jp]

PETE ROCK & C.L. SMOOTH

All Souled Out EP (Elektra) 1991
Mecca and the Soul Brother (Elektra) 1992
The Main Ingredient (Elektra) 1994

Hailing from Mount Vernon, the same New York suburb that produced Heavy D. and the Untouchables production crew, the teenaged Pete Rock (Phillips) came into prominence as a backup DJ for hip-hop producer Marley Marl. His recording career began with a series of fairly routine remix jobs for a number of new jack swing crossover artists, but took off when he and rapper C.L. Smooth (Corey Penn) dropped the stunning debut EP **All Souled Out.** Rock's already mature musical sense merges the tunesmithing craft of his R&B productions with the sound pastiche of his hip-hop background. Smooth's laid-back delivery and keen social gaze complement the songs well, as on the wonderful "Good Life," where southern funk horns punctuate the cutting look at middle-class African-America.

Mecca and the Soul Brother rises on the incredible "They Reminisce Over You (T.R.O.Y.)," meant as a tribute to the late Heavy D. dancer Trouble T-Roy. In it C.L. Smooth waxes autobiographical, revealing heart-rending tragicomedies of his own family. "Ghettos of the Mind," "Anger in the Nation" and "Straighten It Out" take on the serious task of nation-building; Pete Rock's turn on the mic ("For Pete's Sake") and a mic-passing session with Grand Puba ("Skinz") lighten the mood. Between tracks, Rock teases listeners with samples of rare sides that lesser producers would have turned (and often did turn) into entire songs.

The duo sounds to be running out of steam on **The Main Ingredient.** Pushed toward commercial R&B by the minor success of the first album's "Lots of Lovin," **The Main Ingredient** detours into unimaginative singles like the embarrassing "Searching" and the only slightly more tolerable "Take You There." Nonetheless, the sublime "All the Places" (built on Donald Byrd's "Places and Spaces") proves they still have it. Partly undercut by the commercial embrace of gun-toting hardcore rap, the duo called it quits in 1995. [jzc]

ROCK*A*TEENS

See *Jody Grind.*

LEE ROCKER'S BIG BLUE

Lee Rocker's Big Blue (Black Top) 1994

LEE ROCKER & BIG BLUE

Atomic Boogie Hour (Black Top) 1995

Professing himself a blues boy at heart, ex–Stray Cats bassist Lee Rocker (Drucker) thumped his tea chest and sang in this combo—a likable, sharp blues trio with California guitarist Mike Eldred and drummer Henree DeBaun (aka Henree DeLuxe, once a new wave rocker in Unit III With Venus). Sparely recorded in Memphis with the Memphis Horns, as well as guest shots by local guitar god Scotty Moore and English keyboard great Ian McLagen, the distressed originals and genuine antiques (Jimmy Reed's "Shame Shame Shame," Paul Williams' "The Hucklebuck") on **Lee Rocker's Big Blue** receive a less-stylized Chicago blues treatment than the Stray Cats' rockabilly revitalization—and achieve concomitantly blander results. Though Rocker's artless singing is adequate, and his skilled cohorts work up a good club-sized sweat (ironically sounding at times like rockabilly cats playing urban blues, as the Stray Cats used to do on occasion), the album never shakes off the air of an ambitious outsider trying to be something he ain't.

Atomic Boogie Hour, made in Texas with the Memphis Horns (again) and a keyboard sessioneer, is a whole lot better. Limiting the covers to Chuck Berry's "Beautiful Delilah" and Howlin' Wolf's "Call Me the Rocker (Good Rockin' Daddy)," the album tightens the band's sound into Chicago coffee—freshly ground and firmly packed. Eldred kicks out impressive junior Stevie Ray Vaughan guitar panache, and Rocker sings in a comfortable voice that gets the job done. There's little chance anyone will mistake this for the real thing, but blue-eyed blues boys have done a whole lot worse by uptown Saturday night music. [i]

ROCKET FROM THE CRYPT

Paint as a Fragrance (Headhunter) 1991
Circa: Now! (Headhunter) 1992 (Interscope/Atlantic) 1993
All Systems Go! (Japan. Toy's Factory) 1993 (Headhunter) 1993
The State of Art Is on Fire EP10 (Sympathy for the Record Industry) 1995
Hot Charity (Perfect Sound) 1995
Scream, Dracula, Scream! (Interscope) 1995

DRIVE LIKE JEHU

Drive Like Jehu (Headhunter) 1992
Yank Crime (Cargo/Interscope/Atlantic) 1994 (Headhunter) 1994

Most rock history/record collector geeks could easily pass for science club presidents—just replace the pocket slide rule with a copy of some beat-up album price guide. But for John "Speedo" Reis, the skipper of San Diego's Rocket From the Crypt (and Drive Like Jehu's first mate), the pursuit of rock obscurity doesn't translate into impenetrably cerebral wankery; Reis and his bandmates hit the boards as if wired from the ingestion of the collective essence of Iggy, Jerry Lee Lewis and Roky Erickson. Top that off with a tacit understanding of the importance of flash—the band takes the stage in spiffy matching threads and encourages its fans to obtain Rocket-logo tattoos—and you've got what might be the first great punk-rock show band.

Paint as a Fragrance (lodged in one of the era's yuckiest sleeves) isn't nearly as representative of the quintet's capabilities as a bevy of concurrent singles. While the album does boast a surfeit of energy, the band often feints when it should jab, backing off intensely memorable riffs while dragging uneventful throbs to the point of tedium. Released after the band had built up an impressive head of steam on a half-dozen 7-inches (the best of which, a one-sided issue on Drunken Fish, finds them gamboling neck-deep in the frenzied riffage of an unreleased MC5 track, "Gold"), **Circa: Now!** resolves that problem tout de suite: Reis' concise lyrics (almost soundbites, really) adhere to the gray matter instantly, while guitarist N.D. metes out crunching, repetitive riffs redolent of CBGB circa 1979. Highlights include the ridiculously catchy "Hippy Dippy Do" and "Sturdy Wrists," not to mention the stein-waving beerhall singalong "Ditch Digger."

After signing one of those increasingly common bank-busting deals—one which ensured both Rocket and the more esoteric Jehu the chance to be offered up for mass consumption—the band emptied its archive into the compilation **All Systems Go!,** a jam-packed collection (with some variation in its Japanese and American editions) of singles and rarities, including the goony "Pigeon Eater" (from a '92 Merge 45) and the pointed "Where Are the Fuckers?" (a truly timeless question), from a '92 Sub Pop 45. Two vinyl-only releases—**The State of Art Is on Fire,** a remarkably primitive 2-track recording that recalls contemporary Detroit (goo-goo) muckmasters the Gories, as well as prehistoric Cleveland punkers the Pagans, and **Hot Charity**—helped flush the group's system of a bilious backlog. The nine-song **Hot Charity,** a boozy, invective-laced triumph that fuses the band's garage-rock sensibility with soul revue horns (a hybrid that's most striking on the swaggering "Cloud Over Branson" and "Guilt Free," wherein Reis repeatedly warns his subject that "we'll be strong, you'll be dead"), really cries out to be found and heard.

On **Scream, Dracula, Scream!,** the sextet (now augmented by trumpet player JC 2000) compresses blistering punk, swivel-hipped rockabilly and hot buttered soul like some unholy alliance of the Dictators and the E Street Band. But while the members' defiant trashiness implies the only culture they know is the one that prompted that last free clinic visit, these fourteen songs betray a voracious knowledge of lowbrow iconography, from the Egypto-fuzz riffs that give "On a Rope" its Mancini-meets-MC5 swing to the sleighball-sated Spector-sound rush of "Young Livers." Reis' raging river of vitriol splashes some unusually worthy targets this time around—see "Suit City" (which borrows from Wire more effectively than, say, Elastica) and the chugging "Ball Lightning," which asks Gen X *in toto* the $64,000 question, "You want some cheese with your whine?"

Reis is "only" the guitarist in Drive Like Jehu—a more fractured prog-punk foursome with a propensity for extended, yammering jams—but that's kind of like saying Diana Ross was *only* the lead singer of the Supremes. Although the band's self-titled debut isn't exactly fastidious, it gels when Reis' above-the-fretboard plinking tails frenzied singer/guitarist Rick Froberg around in increasingly constricting circles on "Caress," and even more when the two come to an uneasy standoff in the uptight "Good Luck in Jail." The more viscerally fractious **Yank Crime** (CD on Interscope; vinyl on Headhunter) is a good deal more compelling: "Here Come the Rome Plows" and the disorienting "Luau" find Froberg sounding like a man pleading for help as the guitar undertow pulls him down for the third and final time. Even so, those crashing waves make the breakers look mighty inviting.

Although rumors of an impending double-LP release by Back Off Cupids, John Reis's minimalist-styled solo project, persist, only two singles and a compilation track have appeared in recorded form. [dss]

See also *Pitchfork, Wool.*

ROCKET FROM THE TOMBS

See *Pere Ubu.*

ROCKINGHAMS

See *Moberlys.*

RODAN

Rusty (Quarterstick) 1994

JUNE OF 44

Engine Takes to the Water (Quarterstick) 1995
Tropics and Meridians (Quarterstick) 1996

RETSIN

Salt Lick (Simple Machines) 1995
Egg Fusion (Simple Machines) 1996

SONORA PINE

The Sonora Pine (Quarterstick) 1996

As an influential indie-rock landmark, Slint's second album, **Spiderland,** helped chart new directions for abstract guitar skronk. While the quartet's tenure was short, Slint left its mark most palpably at ground zero: the exciting and close-knit Louisville underground scene.

Though it would be unfair to call Rodan—guitarists Jason B. Noble and Jeffery Mueller, bassist Tara Jane O'Neil and drummer Kevin Coultas—Slint Jr., comparisons are inevitable. Both bands use haunting speak-sing vocals, rely on propulsive, start-stop/quiet-loud rhythm dynamics and create noisy, sweeping music. In many ways, **Rusty** sounds like what Slint might've evolved into. The record's wiry energy might also fit the loosely defined "math rock" category, coined to describe bands that play complicated music more akin to theorems than just sound (kind of like **Ozma**-era Melvins married to a more atmospheric art-core interpretation of Big Black). Sometimes breathtaking, sometimes indulgent, **Rusty**'s expansive songs include the mysterious, twelve-minute opus "The Everyday World of Bodies," the ghostly "Bible Silver Corner," the ferocious "Shiner" and the singular, ethereal "Tooth Fairy Retribution Manifesto."

June of 44 melds guitarist/vocalist Mueller with three East Coasters: guitarist/vocalist Sean Meadows, bassist/trumpeter Fred Erskine (ex-Hoover) and drummer Doug Scharin (ex-Codeine). An essay in angular rock dynamics, **Engine Takes to the Water** blends surrealistic lyrics with improvisatory skronk ("Pale Horse Sailor"), evokes a fragile, wandering edginess ("I Get My Kicks for You"), weaves unconventional melodies ("Mooch," "Have a Safe Trip, Dear") and forcefully tackles fluid, loping rhythmic structures ("Take It With a Grain of Salt"). With Mueller and Erskine's vocals showing similarities to Slint's Brian McMahan, June of 44—a little more straight-ahead than Rodan—carries the torch well, making salient revisions as necessary. **Tropics and Meridians** expands on the first album's notions: six lengthy tracks showcase the group's navigational skill, cohesive organization and dramatic guitar designs.

Retsin is O'Neil's post-Rodan band with Cynthia Nelson of New York's Ruby Falls; both contribute vocals, guitar and bass to the cause. The group, which uses various drummers in the studio and a rhythm section onstage, came into being when the women met as actors in the film *Half Cocked;* their union resulted first in a song on the soundtrack and then in **Salt Lick.** Treading a casual line between southern rusticity and urban indie-pop that occasionally suggests a looser Spinanes, the eight-song record is angular and intriguing, with personal lyrics of unsettled emotions and experiences.

Moving up a notch to medium-fi, **Egg Fusion** adjusts the stylistic balance to strike a more abstractly countryfied tone, making good use of the singers' wavery emotionalism and shuffling back-porch rhythms. The lyrics are more confident and striking as well. The singsongy unraveling of "Kangaroo" seethes with intimations of real life: "I love how you listen when I left you were glistening / Sorry but so full of peace / I like you better than those rock & roll pucker boys that you wrote me about." Members of Antietam help out.

The simultaneous Sonora Pine folds some of Rodan's branches back on itself: the band includes O'Neil (guitar/bass/organ/vocals), Coultas (drums/percussion/tapes) and Meadows (guitar/organ/vocals), plus violinist Samara Lubelski; Rachel Grimes of Rachel's plays piano on "The Hook." **The Sonora Pine** is a quizzical and disorienting blend of riveting sharp-edged guitar rock and elegant violin-shaped balladry, with minor bouts of dreamy found-sound ambience and antique organ drone. Inconsistently fine on a track-by-track basis (among the gentler songs, "The Gin Mills," "Ooltewah" and the spare "One Ring Machine" flow the most alluringly), the album is too disjointed for its own good; not knowing the band's purpose is too disquieting for this kind of music. [mww/i]

See also *Codeine, Come, Rachel's.*

WAYNE ROGERS

See *Magic Hour.*

ROLLERSKATE SKINNY

Novice EP10 (UK Showbiz) 1992
Trophy EP10 (UK Placebo) 1993
Shoulder Voices (UK Placebo) 1993 (Beggars Banquet) 1994
Threshold EP (UK Placebo) 1994
Horsedrawn Wishes (Warner Bros.) 1996

Formed in Dublin in 1992, Rollerskate Skinny recorded its first album as a quartet, with Jimi Shields (brother of My Bloody Valentine resident genius Kevin Shields) bringing guitar, voice and drums to the manifold abilities of unrelated founders Ken Griffin (vocals/guitar/keyboards), Ger Griffin (guitar) and Stephen Murray (bass/guitar). A bit like Sloan's **Smeared** in its derivative variety, **Shoulder Voices** is a fascinating and delightful debut that jumps easily from intimate indie tunefulness (the vocals sound like Pavement) to free-fire pop noise, with plenty of wild and wonderful textures along the continuum. The constant gear-shifting makes it nigh on impossible to get a handle on the group's intentions, but the balance of strong, engaging songwriting (see especially "Bow Hitch-Hiker," "Bella" and the Beach Boys–ish "Shallow Thunder"), alluring atmospheres ("Miss Leader," "Violence to Violence") and raw sensual abandon (just about every song has some liberating blast of distortion, but the Robyn Hitchcock–like "Some Give Birth" bears a resemblance to MBV) obviates the need for such concerns. A great, imaginative beginning.

Shields didn't stick around (or get asked back) for the followup, but **Horsedrawn Wishes** (recorded with a hired drummer and a major reliance on keyboards and "orchestration") is no less impressive in its riot of excellent ideas supporting, not disguising, worthy songs. If anything, the madly ambitious production raises the band's creative vision higher, making Rollerskate Skinny that much more considerable in its achievement. If the Beatles had reached psychedelic cruising altitude around 1995, this might be their kind of album: vivid, self-confident, innovative, too involuted to easily master and thoroughly entertaining. Very well done. [i]

See also *Mercury Rev.*

ROLLINS BAND

Life Time (Texas Hotel) 1988
Do It (Texas Hotel) 1989
Hard Volume (Texas Hotel) 1989
Turned On (Quarterstick) 1990
The End of Silence (Imago) 1992
Weight (Imago) 1994

HENRY ROLLINS

Hot Animal Machine (Texas Hotel) 1987
Big Ugly Mouth (Texas Hotel) 1987 (Quarterstick) 1992
Sweatbox (Texas Hotel) 1989 (Quarterstick) 1992
Live at McCabe's (Texas Hotel) 1990 (Quarterstick) 1992
Human Butt (2.13.61/Quarterstick) 1992
The Boxed Life (Imago) 1993
Get in the Van (2.13.61/Time Warner Audio Books) 1994
In Conversation (UK Tabak) 1995
Everything (2.13.61/Thirsty Ear) 1996

LYDIA LUNCH/HENRY ROLLINS/ HUBERT SELBY JR./DON BAJEMA

Our Fathers Who Aren't in Heaven (UK Widowspeak) 1992

HENRIETTA COLLINS AND THE WIFEBEATING CHILDHATERS

Drive by Shooting EP (Texas Hotel) 1987

HENRY ROLLINS/GORE

Live (Hol. Eksakt) 1987

CHRIS HASKETT

Language (213CD) 1995 (2.13.61/Thirsty Ear) 1996

Before stabilizing his musical career as the gut-wrenching vocalist of Rollins Band and bringing his unmitigated personal unease to the masses through a major-label hookup, Henry Rollins kept riding the countercultural independent/underground path he had learned in Black Flag (chronicled in the book *Get in the Van,* also available in a Grammy-winning CD/cassette audio version read by the author). His first two solo records, one of which was released under the enigmatic Henrietta Collins pseudonym, are intense but indulgent, and calibrated not to be acceptable in polite society as it stood in 1987. Times have, of course, changed; by concentrating his efforts and shaking off the self-defeating aspects of rock in rebellion, the self-disciplined Washington, DC, native has emerged as a potent figurehead to those who need loathing—for self, for enemies, for the world—in their stun-power music. That many see this angry rock god as a constipated musclebound knot of neuroses bellowing about his inner problems has only fed Rollins' need to, well, bellow about his inner problems.

Mingling his amusing spoken-word releases (the two-discs-each **Sweatbox, Boxed Life** and **Human Butt,** as well as the shorter **Big Ugly Mouth** and **Live at McCabe's,** were all recorded live on tour; there's also an obscure Swiss-only release and the intimate **In Conversation; Everything** is a reading with musical accompaniment by saxophonist Charles Gayle and drummer Rashied Ali) with rock records by Rollins Band, the former Henry Garfield has become the personification of the hardcore punk as a sensitive, super-energetic and fucked-up adult.

Loaded with doubt but sure of his devils, Rollins—joined by the brilliant, strong ensemble of guitarist Chris Haskett, bassist Andrew Weiss (as of **Weight,** Melvin Gibbs), drummer Sim Cain and soundman Theo Van Rock—fine-tunes the line between angst and anger, swinging his rage inward and outward like a weather vane. Playing music that bulks up the simplicity of raw power into a complex, jazz-oriented storm of driving sonic rain, the amazing Rollins Band has, at its best, come close to upstaging its namesake, even with his obsessions and principled pronouncements. Rollins doesn't rap and the band doesn't play punk (more a jazzy, thrashy, swing take on the many moods of Jimi Hendrix), but what they do together has the strengths of both. The group's loud guitar rock with a strong, inventive rhythmic clock borrows only the better attributes of metal, ensuring that noise is never a substitute for purpose.

Alienation is the unifying theme on **Life Time:** "What Am I Doing Here?" and "There's Nothing Like Finding Someone When You're Lonely to Make You Want to Be All Alone" get to the meat of Hank's solitude. (Typically winsome lyric: "I hate the world that I think hates me . . . I feel dark and cold and alone . . . Wish someone would come and touch me.") **Do It** contains six live tracks (recorded in '87 in Holland) and three killer studio covers, including the Pink Fairies' titular classic, produced by Ian MacKaye. Rollins sinks into an existential funk on the seven-song **Hard Volume,** announcing (in "What Have I Got") that "I've got a wantless need . . . I am a clenched fist / Looking for a wall to kiss." Oddly, the rest of the band seems unaffected by his moods, and the music—a well-organized rock juggernaut—thunders along happily. **Turned On** catches a November '89 show in Vienna, a lengthy set that includes material from **Hot Animal Machine** up through **Hard Volume.** Rollins is his usual balls-to-the-wall self, and Haskett is in rare form, spewing out sizzling solos.

A pivotal event in Rollins' life occurred in December 1991, when he witnessed the murder of his best friend, Joe Cole. No specific mention of that traumatic event emerges from the despair and animosity on **The End of Silence,** although the primal rage therapy of the titanic "Just Like You" could be a response of one sort, and phrases here and there allude to abiding pain, sorrow and guilt. The band's electric cudgel is armed with unprecedented sonic clarity on its first bigtime album, separating the instruments into cleanly articulated weapons divebombing the singer's burly musings. Cain's precision, Weiss' busy aggression and Haskett's non-stop metallisms coalesce as a gargantuan attack, hampered only by Rollins' careless melodic grip and unwavering lyrical concerns. "Low Self Opinion" is posed as an observation of someone else, yet it's hard not to read Rollins' anti-ego in thoughts like "You sleep alone at night / You never wonder why / All this bitterness wells up inside you." The music doesn't have much melodic shape—at worst, the sludgy twelve-minute "Blues Jam" (not hardly) comes close to being filler and the nine-minute "Obscene" has the guitars trailing Cain's battering beat—but "Tearing," a dysfunctional (what else?) relationship song, hits a mighty groove that gives the refrain a potent kick. **The End of Silence** finds Rollins Band fully armed but not quite loaded.

Weight supplies much of what was missing in stronger, better-written songs ("Step Back," "Fool" and "Liar") and the growing artfulness of Rollins' vituperation. "Icon" scorns the weight of stardom from both ends: "It doesn't matter what you say / Because they'll always find some meaning in it anyway" counterpoises "All eyes turned up to the hero / Strung out self-abusive circus freak." "Wrong Man" and "Divine Object of Hatred" both tear at the same illusory elevation (the latter's description of fan frenzy is unmistakable: "So much hatred, so much violence / They love me / Oh they'd kill to have me / They'd have to kill me") but generalize the victimization and misunderstanding to more personal relationships. "I'm not all men / I'm just one man / I'm not that man / I'm not all men," Rollins sings in the chorus of "Wrong Man," equating the difficulty of forming an honest bond with thousands in a stadium with the challenge of getting square in private with a single person; "Liar" comes at the same problem from a different angle. "Civilized" issues a stern message to a gun-toting murderer, although it's not clear whether he's addressing a gangsta rapper or the person who killed Cole. The most striking song, however, is the noir *Taxi Driver* spareness of "Tired," in which Rollins can barely whisper out his emotional exhaustion: "I'm so tired of looking inside myself." Now *that's* tired. [i]

See also *Pigface, Ween; TPRG.*

DEXTER ROMWEBER

See *Flat Duo Jets.*

ROOFDOGS

See *Mono Men.*

ROOKS

The Rooks (Guardian) 1993
Chimes EP (Not Lame) 1995

THE ROOKS/TWENTY CENT CRUSH

A Double Dose of Pop (Not Lame) 1995

GRIP WEEDS

House of Vibes (Ground Up) 1994

There have been countless Beatles imitators over the years, but few artists have demonstrated the ability to build on the group's tuneful legacy with enough originality to add their own twists and shouts. New York's Rooks, led by the immensely talented Michael Mazzarella, is one of the rare exceptions.

The Connecticut-born writer/singer/guitarist/producer gets able assistance on **The Rooks** from bandmates Kristin Pinell (lead guitar/vocals, the same role she fills in the Grip Weeds), Annmarie Gatti (bass) and Jim Riley (drums), as well as guests like the Grip Weeds' Kurt Reil, Richard X. Heyman and drummer Patrick Yourell (who had previously played with Mazzarella in the Broken Hearts). **The Rooks**' bright, '60s-influenced pop packs a real wallop, both musically and lyrically. Easy faves are the stately ballad "Steeplechase," the unashamedly Beatlesque "Night Writer" and the swirling "Reasons."

The Rooks steal the spotlight from Twenty Cent Crush on the **Double Dose of Pop** CD, offering up three remixes from **The Rooks** and six new songs. The presence of a new rhythm section—Gatti and Riley are gone, replaced by deputy bassist Nancy Leigh and drummer Yourell—does nothing to alter the Rooks' pleasing signature sound, which takes an introspective turn on the sweetly nostalgic "Music Sound Sensation" (with former Car Elliot Easton adding some acoustic twelve-string) and the hopeful "In a Pinwheel Spin."

Dedicated to Mickey Mantle, the **Chimes** EP (with new bassist Anne Benkovitz in the fold) finds Mazzarella continuing to wax introspective, with such melancholy pop songs as "It's a Crying Shame" and "War." But the record also contains the playful "Friends of Mine" and a typically ethereal Christmas tune ("Christmas").

The four Grip Weeds (so named for John Lennon's character in the film *How I Won the War*) offer up a dozen tasty, upbeat psych-pop morsels on their debut disc, which features the singing and songwriting talents of guitarist Rick Reil, drummer Kurt Reil and bassist Mick Hargraves, along with late arrival Pinell's amazingly expressive and fluid lead guitar runs. **House of Vibes** is definitely a stimulating dwelling, with all dozen songs keeping one foot in the '60s (without coming off as stale or retro) and the other in the here and now. Impressive. [jmb]

ROOTS

Organix (Ger. Remedy) 1993
Do You Want More?!!!??! (DGC) 1995
Illadelph Halflife (DGC) 1996

The next time someone grumbles that hip-hop artists have no business messing with jazz, send them to the Roots. The Philadelphia outfit (initially formed as a performing arts high-school duo called Square Roots in the late '80s), which built a reputation busking in the city's South Street shopping district, proves it is possible to integrate elements of jazz without turning rap into a variety show—or trivializing one of America's most essential art forms.

The Roots—lyricists/vocalists Black Thought (Tariq Trotter) and Malik Abdul-Basit, drummer B.R.O. the R. ? (Ahmir-Khalib Thompson) and bassist Hub (Leonard Nelson Hubbard)—manage this by approaching their craft the way jazzers do, allowing the music to change and breathe and move, relying on interplay between musicians for much of the spark. (Notably, the group rarely employs sampling in its work.) Built around a cushiony and ever-present Fender Rhodes electric piano, "Mellow My Man" and other selections on **Do You Want More?!!!??!** link the airy openness of exploratory jazz with the fat bottom of the streets. Hub establishes a wickedly firm foundation with his bass, and the other musicians slowly turn up the heat, until a simple vamp begins to boil. But things never get real wild: keeping the music at a constant simmer, Black Thought and Malik B. create an uncluttered, silky-smooth foreplay zone in which their carefully syncopated wordology is supported (but never overshadowed) by calm, complementary solos. On this medium-tempo-heavy album, the Roots aim high—dropping in bagpipe solos and Steve Coleman's saxophone, pitting their skills against those of agile jazz-pop singer Cassandra Wilson. The Roots may not always wind up with a masterpiece, but they do get sparks to fly—something that has eluded many of their fusion-minded peers. [tm]

ROSETTA STONE

Adrenaline (Cleopatra) 1992
Epitome EP (Cleopatra) 1993
Foundation Stones (Cleopatra) 1993
The Tyranny of Inaction (Cleopatra) 1995

Liverpool's Rosetta Stone gained widespread popularity in the gothic scene with a highly melodic, danceable interpretation of gloom. Singer/guitarist Porl King, guitarist Porl Young, bassist Karl North and the trio's drum machine maintain classic goth's darkly mysterious and sensual qualities, but deliver the music with an unorthodox upbeat spirit. **Adrenaline**'s ten tracks feature strong, memorable melodies and King's provocative-but-aloof vocals. To his credit, he never delves into the deep/creepy warbling that makes so many of the genre's vocalists a joke. In particular, "Come Hell or High Water," "An Eye for the Main Chance" and "Subterfuge" are atmospheric, evocative and club-ready. **Epitome** features three versions each of the album's "The Witch" and "Adrenaline," plus a dizzying cover of Eurythmics' "Sisters Are Doin' It for Themselves." Given such daring originality, Rosetta Stone came to be regarded as the saviors of goth, destined to rescue the genre from its backward-looking traditions.

Foundation Stones contains 1990 demos of eight songs that didn't make it onto the first album, as well as four live tracks recorded during the **Adrenaline** English tour. The studio work sounds remarkably like early Sisters of Mercy material, but the strong, flowing melodies more than make up for this lack of originality. In particular, the evocative, tightly woven "Chapter and Verse" and "Cimmerian" provide a tantalizing preview of the confident, skilled songwriting abilities that elevate **Adrenaline.**

With all that going for them, goth's would-be saviors mercilessly abandoned their flock with the pointless, dull **Tyranny of Inaction.** Young's departure after **Adrenaline** left King and North free to create frigid bits of industrial-influenced shrapnel that effectively tear Rosetta's former fluid sound to shreds. "Nothing," and "Never" are decent, though neither possesses the powerful, exhilarating qualities previously found in Rosetta Stone. The rest of **Tyranny** is a dismal, distorted, directionless mess. [ky]

See also *Wake.*

ROYAL TRUX

Royal Trux (Royal) 1988 (Drag City) 1993
Royal Trux EP7 (Vertical) 1990
Twin Infinitives (Drag City) 1990
Royal Trux (Drag City) 1992
Cats and Dogs (Drag City) 1993
Dogs of Love EP (UK Domino) 1993
Thank You (Virgin) 1995

When the peripatetic Royal Trux—a revolving cast of musicians who orbit around Pussy Galore expatriate Neil Hagerty and junkie-priestess-turned-Calvin-Klein-model Jennifer Herrema—talks about wanting to emulate the Rolling Stones, they're not articulating a desire to pantomime an nth-generation version of **Exile on Main St.** They're doing their level best to fashion a reprobate hybrid of Altamont evil and Marrakesh mind-fog. And more often than not, they succeed.

The duo's earliest work presented them as a sort of a narcoleptic Sonny and Cher, disseminating the doctrine of "better" living through chemistry on a scale that would earn a twenty-one-gun salute from Bill Burroughs. The self-titled debut is so staggeringly disjointed that you want to give Hagerty and Herrema the benefit of the doubt and presume they were trying to capture a musical form of cut-up creativity wherein they recorded "songs" and then snipped the master tapes apart, allowing fate to decide how the slivers would be reassembled. Although most of the album's pieces build a carpet of lumpy, arrhythmic percussion, absolutely nothing else lingers long enough to give listeners even a momentary foothold: "Bad Blood" bristles briefly with spikes of guitar invective before nestling in a cocoon of distracted acoustic noodling. "Jesse James" juxtaposes random hollers that could well have been captured by dangling a microphone out a tenement window. Whether **Royal Trux** is an elaborate joke or an art-brut monument is in the ear of the beholder.

That said, the epic **Twin Infinitives** (initially a double-vinyl release) makes its predecessor sound like a product of a crack (no pun intended) Brill Building songwriting team. While reminiscent of **Trout Mask Replica** in its apparent real-time recording and off-the-cuff melodic lexicon (a feature hammered home by Herrema's slurry, somnolent delivery—she's at her spookiest on "Ice Cream" and the fractious "Jet Pet"), an array of cheap synths is used to mimic the sensory overload of a strip-mall video arcade ("Solid Gold Tooth"). But that's just the half of it: tape-speed manipulations, toy-store instrumentation, blues harp and pornographic moans fade in and out, colliding head-on during the relentless fourteen-minute opus "(Edge of the) Ape Oven." **Twin Infinitives** is one of those rare albums that will sound as utterly damaged and as wholly out of place a decade from now as it did the day of its release.

The coherence with which Hagerty picks out the opening chords of "Air," the hazily psychedelic opener of the band's second untitled album (no doubt less an affectation than a genuine product of the memory loss surrounding the recording of the first one) marks a sea change in the realm of Royal Trux. The 1992 album is studded with enough bona fide rock songs (like the choogling "Move") to make it seem as if Royal Trux had inverted the '60s blueprint by getting its bloated rock operas out of the way *before* venturing into commerciality. Hagerty delivers the disc's most affecting moment in the squatter-blues hymn "Junkie Nurse," but the collective weight of Herrema's seductive, languid vocals (a perfect complement to her slo-mo stage stalking) mark her as a star in the making. **Cats and Dogs** brings additional musicians into the picture for the first time (in the conventional sense, that is; calling **Twin Infinitives'** guests "musicians" would be stretching things), and the forced fraternization helps bring out some heretofore concealed—if rudimentary—social skills. Both "Teeth" and the agreeably tough-talking "Let's Get Lost" sound as if their notation is carved, if not in stone, at least in something a bit more fixed than oatmeal. Heck, "Skywood Greenback Mantra" could almost pass for a biker-bar jukebox rave.

That raunchy flavor permeates the band's major-label debut, **Thank You**—one of the last productions by the late David Briggs, a veteran of many Neil Young sessions—which positively oozes unreconstructed rock-star hoodoo. A marked southern rock skew is evident on songs like "(Have You Met) Horror James?" and the no-nonsense boogie of "You're Gonna Lose," a turn of events that stems in part from the presence of drummer Chris Pyle (whose dad Artimus was a member of Lynyrd Skynyrd), and even more from Herrema's increasingly Joplinesque rasp. Although the band's new course can be stultifying (the repetitious "Ray O Vac" is one exercise in self-flagellation that doesn't bear waiting out), Royal Trux has carved a profoundly gritty niche on whatever planet it is they're transmitting from. [dss]

See also *Palace Brothers, Jon Spencer Blues Explosion.*

SPOOKEY RUBEN

Modes of Transportation Vol. 1 (TVT) 1995

Toronto's Spookey Ruben (a Virginia native who once led a DC thrash band called Transilence) is another of those inexplicable autonomous studio-pop auteurs who crop up every year, armed with the manifold instrumental aptitude of a music school, the vitality of a well-rested basketball forward and enough novel ideas to shame a team of TV writers. A visually oriented sprout from the Brian Wilson/Todd Rundgren/R. Stevie Moore garden of idiosyncratic production pop, Spookey skips merrily through his garishly dressed solo album, strewing evidence of skilled ingenuity and far-ranging imagination without obscuring the sturdy essence of his accessible songwriting. Just as "Welcome to the House of Food" isn't nearly as loopy as the title suggests ("Wendy McDonald," the second of his fast-food hallucinations, is), **Modes of Transportation Vol. 1**—recorded with only incidental assistance on a few tracks—is less dense and disorienting than its packaging. Instead, the eminently likable album makes its insidious weirdness a pleasant surprise, whimsical bits that compete gently with Spookey's flexible voice. "When you're holding on to something / You're holding on to nothing / When you're holding on to nothing / You're holding on to something." Whatever. [i]

RUBY

See *Silverfish.*

RUMP

Hating Brenda (Caroline) 1993

One of the silliest culture micro-fads of the early '90s was a self-consciously ridiculous obsession with hating Brenda Walsh, the baby bitch of the original *Beverly Hills 90210.* This particular whimsical animosity (which led to copycats' taking potshots at Evan Dando and other pop stars) got a lot of mileage in 1993, thanks to Kerin Morataya and Darby Romeo, the visionary editors of influential Los Angeles zine *Ben Is Dead,* who gave free run to their pique, producing one nationally circulated (and widely publicized) issue of the deliciously evil *I Hate Brenda Newsletter.* The duo subsequently fed the same concept into a musical effort, producing this dubious bit of ephemera with a batch of their friends. Complete with a prudent, self-deflating manifesto ("as the line between TV and reality disintegrates, we feel it necessary to admit that we hate Brenda only as much as one can hate a fictional television character"), Rump's eight-song mini-album keeps a clear focus on the target of its surprisingly mild (at least until the long, unidentified epilogue to the final song) enmity: "Brenda Can't Dance to This," "Every Day Is Brenda Day," "Who *Is* Brenda?" "Dylan's Choice." But if the message is constant, the medium isn't. Rump spreads its styles—techno-pop, power-pop, deep dance dub, Chili funk, house, noisy skronk—all over the dial. Which blunts the conceptual impact, leaving this one for the time capsule, not the CD player. [i]

RUN–DMC

Run–DMC (Profile) 1984
King of Rock (Profile) 1985
Raising Hell (Profile) 1986
Tougher Than Leather (Profile) 1988
Back From Hell (Profile) 1990
Together Forever: Greatest Hits 1983–1991 (Profile) 1991
Down With the King (Profile) 1993

"Two years ago a friend of mine / Asked me to say some MC rhymes." With those humble words on a 1983 12-inch entitled "Sucker M.C.'s (Krush Groove 1)," eighteen-year-old Joseph "Run" Simmons launched the career of rap's most enduring group—and set alight a cultural revolution. By any measure the undisputed New York champions of old-school rap, Run–DMC weren't the first (or even the best) rappers around, but superb rhyming skills, diverse subject matter, artistic integrity and unprecedented stylistic imagination made the Hollis crew—Run, DMC (Darryl McDaniels) and DJ Jam Master Jay (Jason Mizell)—early, enduring and essential leaders of '80s rap, a potent singles group of wide appeal. The group's importation of electric guitar leads into "Rock Box" and "King of Rock" led directly to the trailblazing 1986 crossover monstrosity, "Walk This Way," with Joe Perry and Steven Tyler of Aerosmith (and similar efforts by others); the "My Sharona" riff used for "It's Tricky" furthered the outreach program. What's more, no other hip-hop group was as quick to incorporate reggae into its music. The Beastie Boys certainly owe the interjectory vocal arrangements of their rap records to Run and DMC. Countless other debts to the trio could be enumerated.

But that doesn't mean the group has been able to take its primacy for granted; **Back From Hell** finds the maturing trio fighting to hold its turf and reclaim its standing by coming on a lot tougher than usual and not sounding entirely happy about it. Still, the album is a fairly effective update that doesn't quite renounce the group's more temperate origins.

Few hip-hop acts have stuck around long enough to justify, much less release, greatest-hits albums while still active, and no one else save Public Enemy, Ice Cube and LL Cool J have enough essential tracks in the can to fill a collection as firmly packed with high-grade hits as Run–DMC's. A nostalgic trip through several eras of beat-box music—from the minimal voice/drums simplicity of "Sucker M.C.'s" through the pumped-up hubbub of "Pause" and "The Ave." to "Rock Box," "My Adidas" and "Walk This Way"—**Together Forever** gathers eighteen almost all-prime cuts that cover the story in ample detail. It's not only the best Run–DMC collection on the market, it's an essential rap classic.

In light of the next album, that compilation marked a pivotal point in Run–DMC's lives. More significant than the shaved heads pictured on the cover of **Down With the King** is the religious fervor announced within. Coming off a troubled three-year layoff, the three inaugurate their second decade by revisiting their birthplace: before exalting the heavenly ruler, the title track repeats the couplet that opens "Sucker M.C.'s." Besides heaping praise on the Lord ("Can I Get It, Yo" invokes the old "Run's House" as "God's house"; the album scatters minor references to both the band's history and its new devotion throughout), the other item on the **King**'s hardcore agenda is to get the respected veterans back into what has become a very different young man's game. Without diving off into gangsta pandering (as **Back From Hell** very nearly did) or making too much of this funky God thing, the concerted catch-up employs a cross-section of early-'90s studio hipsters (Jermaine Dupri, EPMD, Q-Tip, Pete Rock, the Bomb Squad, Kay Gee) and guest stars (Onyx, Mad Cobra, KRS-One and Tom Morello of Rage Against the Machine) to modernize, diversify and commercialize the group's determinedly East Coast sound. For all the activity surrounding them, however, Run and DMC still dominate with their distinctive flow. (Jay's scratches also help keep the present tense at bay.) What Run–DMC doesn't dominate, unfortunately, is the record's artistic vision. Evidently unwilling to devote an album to God and suddenly lacking anything else they can fully get behind, the MCs say rhymes that circle around very little (and thereby make a stronger old-school statement than the choice of beats ever could) in uncohesive settings. Despite some fine music and its announced purpose, **Down With the King** is an unsteady and deeply uninspired drag. [i]

See also *TPRG.*

RUN ON

On/Off EP (Matador) 1995
Start Packing (Matador) 1996

PEACH COBBLER

Georgia Peach (Ajax) 1995

New York's Run On is an underground supergroup of sorts, teaming Fish & Roses/Information/V-Effect/Les Batteries drummer Rick Brown, Last Roundup/Fish & Roses/Shams/Six Layer Cake singer/bassist Sue Garner, Love Child guitarist Alan Licht and multi-instrumentalist/college-radio broadcasting vet David Newgarden (who has also played in the Mad Scene and the Moles) in a combo that juggles a disparate and seemingly unreconcilable array of elements into a compelling avant-rock hybrid that never seems less than organic.

The five songs that compose **On/Off** take as many distinctly different approaches—from the playful aggression of "Into the Attic" to the hushed balladry of "Pretty Note"—yet the EP is surprisingly cohesive, managing a nice balance of rock and avant-garde impulses. The foursome stakes out a more consistent and distinctive style on the full-length **Start Packing,** achieving a vibrantly unpredictable balance of adventurousness and melodicism. The first half is winsomely melodic, while a more abrasively experimental (but still accessible) sonic approach dominates the latter portion. Brown and Licht each take credible turns at the mic, but it's Garner's unaffectedly assertive vocals that come close to stealing the show on tightly crafted tunes like "Tried," "Go There" and "Tell Me."

Peach Cobbler teams Brown and Garner with French-born Dominique Grimaud and Monique Alba; **Georgia Peach** consists of twenty-one short tracks recorded separately in the principals' respective hometowns: stream-of-consciousness acoustic ditties, refurbished Delta blues, tape collage experiments, sound effects and audio-vérité snippets. Not surprisingly, it's scattershot, but the album's more synergistic juxtapositions have an undeniable charm. [ss]

See also *Antietam, Love Child, Mad Scene, Shams.*

RUST

Rust (Atlantic) 1994
Bar Chord Ritual (Atlantic) 1996

CREEDLE

Half Man, Half Pie!! (Headhunter/Cargo) 1992
Silent Weapons for Quiet Wars (Headhunter/Cargo) 1994
When the Wind Blows (Headhunter/Cargo) 1996

Fed to the major-label mainstream as part of the trendy San Diego scene (along with Rocket From the Crypt, Drive Like Jehu and others), Rust is nothing more than Stone Temple Pilots with an ineffectually nerdy singer (John Brinton). The quartet's seven-song **Rust** mini-album, clearly recorded by Wharton Tiers, is appallingly stupid, proffering the lamest clichés without a hint of embarrassment. ("Is this the way the world ends? / Not with bombs but with our friends / We'll see the forest for the trees / We'll wreck it with our disease." Sheesh.) The full-length **Bar Chord Ritual,** overseen by a more commercial producer (Dave Jerden), is concomitantly more presentable. Guitarist Czar Michael Suzick makes a good, bracing row, but Brinton—who writes the lyrics, natch—is such a phony-sounding dud that none of the generic Lollapalooza thunder matters. Whether he's moaning about getting up in the morning ("Five More Minutes"), examining society's ills ("Someone You Know"), contemplating existential dilemmas ("Perhaps?") or detailing the subtleties of romance ("A Nights Comedy," "Song for a Wedding,"), he misses the mark equally in words and deed. Maybe those dreams of the Buzz Bin and the Second Stage are too daunting.

Suzick and drummer Pat Hogan also play in a local band called Red Truck; bassist Timothy Blankenship (ex–Liquid Sunshine) moonlights in the Rust-outstripping Creedle. Done up in especially lurid comic-book artwork, **Half Man, Half Pie!!** combines guitar rock—alternately scraggly, angular, noisy, melodic and jazzy—with such found-sound spoken passages as the blandly rendered confession of a murderer, the desperate cries of an accident victim, commercials and phone calls. Imagine a band rehearsing in the rec room with the TV on way too loud, and that's the beginning of this end. (Typical of San Diego scene in-breeding, there's a song named for Drive Like Jehu drummer Mark Trombino.)

It seems Creedle was only cracking its knuckles the first time: like the debut only *way* more so, the long, weird, intricate and madly inventive **Silent Weapons for Quiet Wars** (subtitled *The secret teachings of all ages: an encyclopedic outline of Masonic, Hermetic, Cabbalistic and Rosicrucuan Symbolical Philosophy*) is absolutely captivating. Ultimately a down-to-earth surreal joke, this art-damned approximation of Monks of Doom gone grunge-o-punk is jampacked with samples, processed vocals and all sorts of zany musical maneuvers. There's a disturbing intelligence buried beneath all the silliness, and it's probably safest left there. [i]

RUSTED ROOT

Cruel Sun (Blue Duck) 1992
When I Woke (Mercury) 1994
Remember (Mercury) 1996

The popularity of the neo-hippie H.O.R.D.E. caravan gave rise to MOR hacks like Dave Matthews and Blues Traveler, but those two are Dylan and the Dead in comparison to Pittsburgh's Rusted Root. The seven-person troupe of raggle-taggle patchouli-soaked minstrels is like a multi-culti Cowsills sharing a commune with 10,000 Maniacs and a percussion collective. The lineup includes three—count 'em—three drummers, not to mention flute, guitar, bass, banjo, marimba and "on and off planet energies, etc. and endless possibilities." Like, wow, man!

Despite the assistance of assorted sprites and faeries, Rusted Root's rhythmic world music–influenced drivel is better suited for a Pringles commercial than a tribal gathering. The self-produced indie debut, **Cruel Sun,** was a success on the northeastern college frathouse circuit, so the inevitable major-label release, **When I Woke** (produced by Bill Bottrell, of Sheryl Crow fame), soon followed. A veritable cacophony of cockamamie claptrap, **When I Woke** is the type of record that thirtysomething middle-management types listen to and think they're hip because they've finally put away their Eric Clapton **Unplugged** CD and are getting into "alternative rock." In a buttclenching caterwaul, guru/guitarist Michael Glabicki spouts specious new age gobbledygook about peace, love and the environment (with about as much impact as a "Save the Whales" bumper sticker on the back of a BMW) over sticky-sweet drumboogie jams with titles like "Beautiful People," "Back to the Earth" and "Infinite Tamboura." While it's one thing to have a cult following in Pittsburgh, Rusted Root somehow scored a hit with the abysmal "Send Me on My Way," notable only for its yodeling campfire chorus. [mgk]

RUSTY

Rusty EP (Can. Handsome Boy) 1995
Fluke (Tag) 1995

Formed in '94 by ex-members of the Doughboys and One Free Fall, Toronto's Rusty debuted with an eponymous EP, the five songs of which gave the punky quartet a leg up on its album, which sees the first bid with a like number of new tracks. A noisy, pointless screaming nothing with atrocious sound on Mitch Perkins' drums and the vocals mixed down to the point of total incomprehensibility, Rusty (in the epiglottal person of vocalist Ken MacNeil) sings about "Punk," "California" and "kd lang" on **Fluke.** "Wake Me" makes amusing use of a Creedence-like choogle amid the post-Replacements bluster, but that's as good as it gets. Rubbish. [i]

PAT RUTHENSMEAR

Pat RuthenSmear (SST) 1988

PAT SMEAR

So You Fell in Love With a Musician . . . (SST) 1992

DEATH FOLK

Deathfolk (New Alliance) 1990
Deathfolk II (New Alliance) 1992

GERMS

Germs (MIA): The Complete Anthology (Slash) 1993

VARIOUS ARTISTS

Live From the Masque 1978 Volume One (Flipside) 1995 (Year One) 1996
Germs (Tribute): A Small Circle of Friends (Gasatanka/Grass) 1996

A decade after smearing himself with punk glory as the unskilled guitarist contributing to the nullifying legend that was the Germs—see **(MIA),** a definitive thirty-song career summation, and the twelve bawling minutes of live Germhood on the **Masque** disc for recent evidence—and just before his resurgence as the hired hand in Nirvana's final year, Pat Smear made two solo albums and another pair as half of the Death Folk. While all four records have their moments, Smear—a likable character who can't really sing and doesn't bring much to the songwriting table (on the 1988 record, his lyrical role is limited to two co-writing credits, and one of those is just additions to "Golden Boys," the words of which are by late Germs singer Darby Crash)—is clearly better off as part of something bigger.

Making **Pat RuthenSmear** with keyboardist Paul Roessler, a drummer and several guests, the lisping singer/versatile guitarist (whose real name is George Ruthenberg) takes an enjoyably weird if indulgent romp through various non-punk pop and rock styles as if he were trying to boil down everything Rodney had played on the ROQ over the prior fifteen years. Showcasing instrumental skill and scenery-chewing vocal stylings, Smear flips the idiosyncratic tracks toward Redd Kross giddiness, acoustic restraint, dance thwack, experimental nonsense and whatever else comes into his studio-bound head. The kind of album only friends could love, **Pat RuthenSmear** nonetheless has stuff others might also find amusing.

So You Fell in Love With a Musician . . . employs Death Folk bandmate Gary Jacoby (otherwise of Celebrity Skin) on drums; Pat plays almost everything else. His singing is far more assured and presentable—his explosive yells give the record a bit of Hole's melodrama and suggest a stylistic affinity with Nirvana. His rock chops are likewise in higher, tighter gear; he detonates exciting guitar bursts all over "Creep Street" and demonstrates cool tone and firm lead control in "Holy Bulsara." (Those who fail to note the Brian May/Queen touchstones in Smear's music should note that Freddie Mercury was born Frederick Bulsara.) The album is uneven enough to include "Ever Alone With Thee" (an ineffectually camp faux-gospel, complete with harp solo) and the torchy sap of "Love Your Friends"; in spots, it's as axe-wanky indulgent as a hair metal record. Still, Smear's goofy enthusiasm, cool playing and the whole thing's casual, underproduced quality give it a crummy, ass-backward sort of charm.

Pat (guitar, vocals, keyboards, bass) and Gary (vocals, guitar, tuba) go the Chad & Jeremy acoustic route on **Deathfolk,** jointly singing and strumming their amusing admixture of adolescent humor ("Monkey Brains," "Rad Man"), rude sex ("Yellow 1," "Typical Girl") and a stylistically suitable Queen cover, "'39." The album's final numbers (the loud punk of "Jack," a jokey pirate rendition of Jacques Brel's "Amsterdam" and "Work!," a bass'n'drums generator with haunted-house vocals) ruin the mood, but the rest is good for a tuneful laugh or two. **Deathfolk II** drops the first album's conceptual pretense for unabashed power-pop, mutant metal and brash rock, occasionally slamming into punk ("Jojo Luv"), anarcho-country ("Azrael") and electric piano balladry (the comical "Medeley" of rubbish-rock covers). Joining a long line of teen-dreaming Los Angeles bands (echoes of Sparks, the Pop, Redd Kross and the Quick abound), the duo melodically describes "Scary Girl," "Romeo Bob," "Baby Hugh" and "LuLu Bell" (a version of which Pat put on his solo album the same year) capping the whole thing off with a rollercoaster rendition of the Go-Go's' "Automatic." [i]

See also *Foo Fighters, Nirvana; TPRG.*

SAAFIR

See *Digital Underground.*

SAGE

Forked (Will) 1993
7th Standard Rd. (Will) 1995

Bookending his 1994 stint in the Elastic Purejoy, Seattle guitarist/singer Marc Olsen (*not* the Jayhawks guy) made a couple of albums with Sage, a trio containing bassist/singer Guy Davis and drummer Mike Williamson. The rangy little combo forgoes fancy furnishings and vocal exactitude in its loose-limbed muso rock explorations: the elusive lyrics (**Forked**'s politically charged "Snow" is partly sung in Spanish) don't interfere with the unpretentiously accomplished instrumental work, which seems to be the band's real purpose. The first album demonstrates Sage's well-honed internal mechanism, an intelligent and organic blend of busy drumming, rubbery bass and inventive guitar incursions—jazzy leads, dreamy chords and abrasive punky jabs. Occasionally as dryly cerebral as the Minutemen, **Forked** could have benefited from fleshier, clearer production. As it stands, the brief album still offers plenty to chew on.

Improved studio facilities and producer Steve Fisk brought **7th Standard Rd.** up to bracing sonic snuff, and Sage's formidable chops take tense advantage of the clarity and presence. The album is much more song-oriented than the debut, leaving the fierce, complex arrangements to fend for themselves in breaks between the verbal foreplay. Mostly sung in an echo-drenched dramatic whisper, traumatic childhood images ("Monkey Bars," "Doll Factory," "Teat") share space with grim narratives of angry silence ("Buzz Saw"), a death in the family ("Nothing to Say"), vague miseries ("Slip Jig") and ecology ("Buried Water"). "Compadré," meanwhile, supplies the album's Spanish-language component. An uncommon, adventurous and gripping record from a band with a lot weighing on its collective mind. (Cinematic footnote: Olsen performs onscreen in 1995's *Georgia.*) [i]

See also *Low Pop Suicide.*

GREG SAGE

See *Wipers.*

SAINT ETIENNE

Foxbase Alpha (UK Heavenly) 1991 (Warner Bros.) 1992
So Tough (Warner Bros.) 1993
You Need a Mess of Help to Stand Alone (UK Heavenly) 1993
Xmas '93 EP (UK Heavenly) 1993
Tiger Bay (Warner Bros.) 1994
Too Young to Die (UK Heavenly) 1995

Saint Etienne's music embraces soaring house rhythms, Petula Clark young sophisticate nightingale vocals and a healthy aesthetic appetite that gives the three Britons license to borrow bits of whatever strikes their fancy. These sonic confectioners tastily mix soulful dance-pop and abstract samples in an unusually creamy electronic base, resulting in breezy modern songs of multi-layered richness.

Foxbase Alpha, the 1991 debut by Sarah Cracknell (vocals) and Croydon masterminds Bob Stanley (keyboards) and Peter Wiggs (keyboards), pricked up ears with a lilting cover of Neil Young's "Only Love Can Break Your Heart." Otherwise, it offers sleek girl-groupisms ("Carn't Sleep," "Kiss and Make Up" and Spring") and universal groove anthems ("People Get Real" and "Etienne Gonna Die," which borrows a chunk of dialogue from David Mamet's *House of Games*).

So Tough opens with an invitation to pull up a chair at "Mario's Cafe" as the band sketches out a London scene ("Rainy cafe Kentish Town Tuesday/Joking around still digging that sound/Everyone's dreaming of all they've got to live for"). Grooving manifestoes ("Join Our Club" and "Junk the Morgue") fit in snugly alongside the percolating "Conchita Martinez" (which samples the spiraling guitar licks of Rush's "Spirit of the Radio") and the dubby "Railway Jam" and "Calico." "You're in a Bad Way" arrays Cracknell's glossiest vocals in a classic Supremes setting.

You Need a Mess of Help to Stand Alone is an ephemera collection containing B-sides, compilation items and the like. The holiday EP bears the exuberant "I Was Born on Christmas Day" and a cover of Billy Fury's "My Christmas Prayer."

"Urban Clearway," the pulsating panorama that begins **Tiger Bay,** approximates a hybrid of Donna Summer's "I Feel Love" and the theme from TV's *Hart to Hart.* Each atmospheric track on this most cinematic of Saint Etienne's albums sounds like an outline for an imaginary film. Cracknell's gliding ingénue vocals give "Hug My Soul" (included in two versions) the feel of a big Vincente Minnelli dance number. "Like a Motorway" is a wistful, end-of-a-relationship narrative; "Former Lover" is evanescently gentle and hymn-like.

Too Young to Die is a comprehensive retrospective of Saint Etienne's singles portfolio, with one new track ("He's on the Phone") and remixes by Aphex Twin, Sure Is Pure and the Chemical Brothers. Initial copies came as a two-disc set. [re]

KATE ST. JOHN

See *Roger Eno.*

ST. JOHNNY

Four Songs EP7 (Asthma) 1992
Go to Sleep EP7 (Ajax) 1992

High as a Kite (UK Rough Trade) 1993 (Caroline) 1993
Speed Is Dreaming (DGC) 1994
Early Live Recordings EP7 (Twisted Village) 1994
Let It Come Down (DGC) 1995

GRAND MAL

Grand Mal EP (No. 6) 1996

This determinedly indolent Connecticut combo incorporated the best and worst elements of post–Sonic Youth guitar rock into its fuzzy, feedback-encrusted worldview. The quartet's undeniable cleverness and occasional virtuosity could prompt a pleasant buzz, but St. Johnny's overwhelming lethargy too often prevented those rudimentary ideas/riffs from maturing into the kind of songs that last longer than a quick contact high.

The band's initial EP releases are less encumbered by slackness, if only because the 7-inch format forces a slightly tighter focus. The self-released debut is a gauze-filtered look at suburbia from singer/guitarist Bill Whitten's modern stoner point of view—which essentially means that his proclamations about not caring about anything are less nihilistic than they are just plain bored. On **Go to Sleep,** Whitten's lope is a little less languorous, but he's still possessed with a remarkably hermetic attitude that allows him (on the instantly catchy title track) to recognize "I know we're in trouble . . . I know we're in deep," only to come to the conclusion that a nap is the answer to all his problems. **High as a Kite** compiles the EPs; the US edition adds three previously unreleased tracks.

Luddites might disagree, but St. Johnny was wise to skulk out of its basement bunker and record **Speed Is Dreaming** in a proper studio, as it allows Tom Leonard's controlled, methodical guitar sculpting to be appreciated on its own plentiful merits. Leonard tends to rely heavily on one trick—adding layer upon layer, only to pull the whole pile out at once—but that stratagem truly accentuates Whitten's disconnected murmurings. As made manifest in songs like "I Give Up," "You Can't Win" and "Down the Drain," Whitten inhabits a space where defeat is victory and ambivalence conquers all. He strings together phrases lackadaisically enough that you never forget just how jaded he is about the process—just in case you do, there's a song called "I Hate Rock and Roll"—but as borne out by thrown-away lines like "as the streets creep by/as usual I'm appalled," he's got his finger on the (fading) pulse of America the Bored.

Although Leonard's departure (he was replaced by Jim Roberts) didn't change the band's direction per se, the sound of **Let It Come Down**—almost unrecognizable as St. Johnny—isn't nearly as suitable a vehicle for transporting Whitten's ennui. As a matter of fact, the album is the aural equivalent of trying to cross the Atlantic in a Volvo. Laden with Pavement-lite shambling ("Bluebird") and hip-hop/skronk hybrids so lame even Sonic Youth wouldn't touch 'em ("Scuba Diving"), the album quickly passes laid-back on its way to the obnoxiously slapdash stage. The instrumental presence of tangent-seeking pals like Mercury Rev's Grasshopper and Dave Fridmann (who engineered and co-produced with Whitten) doesn't help matters.

After St. Johnny broke up at the end of 1995, Whitten recorded a mostly solo fuzz-rock EP under the Grand Mal moniker. The tone of the self-titled six-song EP is encouragingly aggressive, thanks to Whitten's rediscovery of the power of punctuating disjointed feedback bursts and a few forays into dance culture (à la Primal Scream) buoyed by the soulful belting of Carmen Quinones. [dss]

See also *Magic Hour, Mercury Rev.*

SAINTS

See *Chris Bailey.*

WALTER SALAS-HUMARA

See *Silos.*

KEVIN SALEM

Soma City (Roadrunner) 1994
Glimmer (Roadrunner) 1996

Since his stint in Dumptruck, Pennsylvania-born guitarist/singer Kevin Salem has had his hands full producing (Madder Rose, Scarce, Grover), playing with friends (Roscoe's Gang, Freedy Johnston, Yo La Tengo, Chris Harford, Miracle Legion) and doing session work (Pooh Sticks)—not to mention a debilitating bout with lyme disease. The New York resident also writes songs and fronts his own band, a quintet that has included former Dumptruck/Chris Harford associate Dave Dunton on keyboards and Keith Levreault (ex–Blood Oranges and Roscoe's Gang) on drums. **Soma City** is less a reality-alleviating elixir than a cathartic venture with forceful guitar lines ("Lighthouse Keeper") wedged alongside rough-hewn pop ("Remain," "Will"). Produced by Niko Bolas, **Soma City** distinguishes its meatier rock with a good dosage of dramatic flourish. Butch Vig co-wrote "Forever Gone," a painful breakup song, with Salem; Syd Straw drapes her graceful, ethereal vocals into the background on four tracks. Salem's ragged and sometimes desperate voice serves these slices of self-conscious introspection and world-weary resignation very well. [vg]

See also *Eric Ambel, Chris Harford and the First Rays of the New Rising Sun, Freedy Johnston, Pooh Sticks.*

SALT

Bluster EP (Island Independent) 1995
Auscultate (Island) 1996

After decades of softening the center of commerce-pop without a thought of kicking out the jams, mid-'90s Sweden has been swimming in the hip end of the rock pool. Salt, the Stockholm art-school trio of singer/guitarist Nina Ramsby, bassist Daniel Ewerman and drummer Jim Tegman, sounds like Elastica, but with a pronounced American rock bent and rawer production. Ramsby is a controlled, forceful singer with no perceptible accent, a complicated persona (the sketchy lyrics say a lot) and emotion to burn. On the LP, she savors the sensuality of "Obsession" ("I've got your name on my lips/I've got your face in my eyes/I've got your breath in my mouth/I've got your smell on my body"), delivers the sleepy invitation of "Lids" like a caress and lashes into the fantasy sexuality of "Undressed" with searing passion. Hindered a bit by inept sequencing, **Auscultate** has the material and dynamic gear-switches to make a pungent first impression. [i]

SALT-N-PEPA

Hot, Cool & Vicious (Next Plateau) 1986
A Salt With a Deadly Pepa (Next Plateau) 1988
Blacks' Magic (Next Plateau) 1990
A Blitz of Salt-n-Pepa Hits: The Hits Remixed (Next Plateau) 1991
Very Necessary (Next Plateau/London) 1993

Who'd have thought Salt-n-Pepa—the groundbreaking female Queens-based hip-hop group responsible for 1988's sassy club hit "Push It"—would become one of the biggest rap acts of the '90s? The group entered the decade taking their frank banter about male-female power struggles into the Top 20 with "Let's Talk About Sex"; by 1995, they'd rerecorded the single as "Let's Talk About AIDS," produced several button-pushing videos (including one for a compilation single, "Ain't Nuthin but a She Thing") and had three platinum albums under their belts. Though rarely credited for it among more rockist musical circles, Salt-n-Pepa are *the* original riot grrrls of rap.

After a powerful debut produced by manager Hurby "Luv Bug" Azor and a slight sophomore slump, Salt-n-Pepa hit their stride at the turn of the decade with **Blacks' Magic,** a sort-of concept album held together by its recurring theme of self-empowerment—sexual, racial and otherwise. On it, Salt (Cheryl James), Pepa (Sandy Denton) and Spinderella (De De Roper) spice up the minimalism of such late-'80s singles as "Push It" and "Tramp" (from **Hot, Cool & Vicious**) with a slicker, more commercial sound, delicious pop hooks, sung refrains and brighter dynamics. The added sweetness appealed to a larger audience without sacrificing the edge of Salt's sassy lead raps, Pepa's husky responses and the group's confrontational lyrics. The women also got more involved in the technical aspects of their music. DJ Roper (the group's second Spinderella) co-produced the title track, and James produced three other songs, including the Top 40 hit "Expression." On the album cover, the three women are surrounded by ghost-like images of such late, great African-American musicians as Jimi Hendrix and Billie Holiday. **Blacks' Magic** glides from uplifting raps focusing on self-respect ("Expression," "Independent") to black- and feminist-themed songs ("Negro Wit' an Ego," the title track) and invocations to open discussion ("Let's Talk About Sex"). Although some complained that the group had sold out with the newer, slicker sound, such fans had apparently been paying more attention to chart positions than the artful subtlety in the grooves.

A Blitz of Hits is a collection of mostly unfortunate remixes. Why, for example, UK producer Shuv'd felt a need to clutter up such a powerful song as "Push It" with unnecessary techno blips and horn-like sounds—replacing the original version's simple, brutal percussion, synth bass and keyboard lines with an aimlessly wavering imitation—is a mystery. Moreover, Blacksmith's ill-conceived update of "Expression" adds nothing to Salt's own stripped-down original. Only DJ Mark the 45 King works an improvement, pulling away a few layers to create a funky update of the first album's "My Mic Sounds Nice." Beyond that, Azor's re-edit of "Shake Your Thang" (the band's collaboration with go-go kings E.U.) is not different enough from his own original production of it on **A Salt With a Deadly Pepa** to even include.

In 1993, after moving to a major record label, Salt-n-Pepa hit new commercial and artistic peaks with the fun and sassy **Very Necessary,** a stunning album that is the most confident and consistent of the band's career. Adding pinches of dancehall and smooth R&B, tighter rhymes, tougher and more self-assured vocals (plus collaborations with such crooners as vocal group En Vogue), Salt-n-Pepa deliver the funky "Shoop," the proudly feminist "None of Your Business" and the eminently hummable "Whatta Man." [mrk]

SAMMY

Debut Album (Smells Like) 1994
Hi Fi Killers EP (UK Fire) 1994
Kings of the Inland Empire EP (Smells Like) 1995
Majik Man EP (UK Fire) 1995
Leopard Skin Swatch EP (Sp. Radiation) 1996
Tales of Great Neck Glory (DGC) 1996

Sammy's first longplayer sounds so much like Pavement that the resemblance hits like a yard of concrete. That's not really such a bad thing, though; the duo of guitarist/bassist Luke Wood (a former member of Washington DC's Soulside who *didn't* join Girls Against Boys) and singer/guitarist/pianist Jesse Hartman shares that band's musical adventurousness as well as its particular post-punk musical style. Sammy buries a catchy melody beneath the surface dissonance of "Hi Fi Killers," and "Rudy" is an off-kilter punk song complete with slightly pinched vocals and a sense of sonic drama. The rest of **Debut Album** is similarly derivative, but few who hear the appealingly fractured pop will be able to muster serious objections.

Kings of the Inland Empire offers more of the same. On "Inland Empire," Sammy mixes chugging, buzzing guitars with world-weary vocals; "Cracked Up" also evokes Pavement's style. If not quite as strong as the first album, the EP is good enough, and "Teen Tour" offers some hints about where this band is going.

Sammy then signed to DGC (Wood is an executive at the company) and recorded **Tales of Great Neck Glory,** a more distinctive effort, using three different drummers in the studio. Reference points are all over the punk map—from the Velvet Underground to Sonic Youth—but the musical voice here is Sammy's own. And on atmospheric songs like "Blue Oyster Bay" and the quiet "Anything," the band expands its emotional range without leaving behind the art-damaged take on pop that makes its first album effective. Powerful and loads of fun. [rl]

See also *Girls Against Boys, Love Child.*

SAMPLES

The Samples (Arista) 1989 (What Are Records?) 1993
Underwater People (What Are Records?) 1991
No Room (What Are Records?) 1992
The Last Drag (What Are Records?) 1993
Autopilot (What Are Records?) 1994
Outpost (MCA) 1996

SEAN KELLY

Light House Rocket (What Are Records?) 1995

Sean Kelly, the frontman and chief songwriter of this Boulder, Colorado, group, has a high-pitched, plaintive voice that recalls Sting. For better or worse, it's made the Police a stylistic touchstone the Samples haven't been able to shake; the early albums' frequent excursions into Caribbean rhythms only lend credence to the comparisons. There are far worse saddles to carry, and some of the Samples' other influences—particularly touches of jazz and Celtic folk—give the band's sound a bit of distinction. The Samples have won their audience on the grassroots level, via heavy touring concentrated on college campuses. Although a favorite of the H.O.R.D.E. crowd, the band hasn't made the same impact as Phish or Blues Traveler.

The Samples, which found the group on a major label for about a minute, is filled with gentle, pleasant melodies that make the most of Kelly's vocals, his harmonies with bassist Andy Sheldon and the ringing interplay of Kelly's lead guitar with Charles Hambleton's acoustic guitar, mandolin and banjo. Keyboardist Al Laughlin generates a haunting flute sound for "Close to the Fires" (the Samples' homage to the American Indian), while "African Ivory" is the most subtle kind of protest song. "My Town" and "Waited Up" mine exotic sources—Jamaica and West Africa, respectively—but nothing on the Samples' debut really takes off with the energy of the band's live shows.

Perhaps that's why **Underwater People,** with its five live tracks (plus three previously unreleased studio numbers), works better. "After the Rain" and "My Town" are so superior to their studio counterparts that they practically sound like different songs. Branford Marsalis' guest solo on "Giants" is revelatory, while the acoustic version of the first album's "Feel Us Shaking" reveals just how much Kelly's vision leads the band at this point. (Hambleton left after the debut and only appears on a couple of the second album's tracks. He wasn't replaced, and the Samples have remained a quartet since.)

No Room begins a prolific period of three albums in as many years. The sound remains organic, but it's also more expansive, mixing reggae tracks ("Did You Ever Look So Nice") with more atmospheric pieces ("Nothing Lasts for Long"). "When It's Raining" is a standout, a shimmering melody surfing on a wiggly groove, finally capturing in the studio some of what the Samples transmit onstage.

The ominously titled **The Last Drag** is even more ambitious—musically and lyrically—but also less consistent. Kelly's angst-filled worries about the environment, his love life and our general state of being have lost their subtlety. (His mood seems to be contagious: his "Darkside" is matched by Sheldon's "Prophet of Doom" and drummer Jeep MacNichol's "Misery.") Beyond the lyrics, though, all four Samples have a hand in writing the music, which yields a greater dynamic range and a new infusion of ideas. "Taxi" blends jazz and rock touches, "Nitrous Fall" has a gaseous ambience and "Darkside" alternates boppy verses and menacing choruses.

The democratic approach is more fully realized on **Autopilot,** even though Kelly finishes the album with three solo compositions. The rhythmic "Weight of the World" manages to ruminate on Kurt Cobain's suicide and media hype without turning cloying, while Kelly turns from observation to action on "Dinosaur Bones" as he sings "I'm gonna find the secret/And then I'll find just what went wrong." "Madmen" is one of the hardest rockers the Samples have put on record; "Buffalo Herds and Windmills" displays a country influence. Sheldon's "The Hunt," a quiet guitar and flute piece, makes a nice change of pace. But even four albums on, there's still that Sting/Police thing: "Dinosaur Bones" could have appeared on **Synchronicity,** while "As Tears Fall" sounds like a slowed-down version of "If You Love Somebody Set Them Free."

The Samples took a break from touring in 1995, and Kelly took the opportunity to go solo. **Light House Rocket** is a ruminative affair, close to the band's sound but even quieter—kind of like a focused demo session. This time he's looking inward (one song is titled "Me Myself and I"), chewing over thoughts of loss and love on "Mary" and "On the Losing End of Distance." A reworking of the Samples' "Could It Be Another Change" and a fresh take on "Amazing Grace" are the album's most notable moments. [gg]

SAND RUBIES

See *Sidewinders.*

SANDY DIRT

See *Pastels, Some Velvet Sidewalk.*

OUMOU SANGARÉ

Moussolou (Women) (World Circuit) 1991
Ko Sira (Marriage Today) (World Circuit) 1993

Oumou Sangaré, from the Wassolou region of Southern Mali, is not one of those world music cheerleaders who exhort listeners to get up and dance. Backed by violin, the lute-like *kamelengoni* and minimal percussion, she creates processional chants and arresting call-and-response episodes from regal, serpentine melodies. More important, she's an activist. Her songs champion the cause of women in Mali, speaking out against the still-common practice of polygamy, decrying the edicts of the "wise men" who rule many provinces there. This lyrical stance has made Sangaré a celebrity in West Africa: months after her first cassette, **Moussolou,** was released in 1990, her blend of traditional musical signatures and revolutionary themes became an electrifying force in Malian cultural politics.

Moussolou, which was released in Europe and the US in 1991, shows why. It's a thoroughly mature opening statement, a gloriously original alternative to the rhythm emphasis of West African pop. Its spare instrumentation gives the improvisation-minded singer a wide berth: on "Diya Gneba," her voice dives and shimmies and moans, sometimes insisting on the spotlight but just as often recoiling from it. Leading her supporting vocalists through tricky phrases that suggest ritual chants, Sangaré is, at twenty-three, supremely assured about her powers. She's a vocalist who, in the griot tradition, does more than merely entertain. She educates.

Ko Sira (Marriage Today) exhibits further refinement. Sangaré shouts less, and is more inclined to let her nimble, rhythmically exacting musicians fill in the spaces between pronouncements—there are more solos than on **Moussolou,** and each is magnetic. Her songs pay homage to spirits, offer advice to a new bride, discuss the homesickness of touring and warn of the tricks of womanizers. But none feel preachy: because she's passionate about her message and firm in her beliefs, Sangaré makes everything she sings sound like an epic battle for the soul, and leaves no doubt about which side she's on. [tm]

SATCHEL

See *Brad.*

MICHIHIRO SATO AND JOHN ZORN

See *John Zorn.*

SAUSAGE

See *Primus.*

JIM SAUTER/DON DIETRICH/ THURSTON MOORE

See *Borbetomagus.*

SCARFACE

See *Geto Boys.*

SCENIC

Incident at Cima (Independent Project) 1995
Acquatica (Independent Project/World Domination) 1996

The cold wind that blows through the East Mojave desert in Arizona and California blows through this whole album. The first new band formed after a long layoff by Savage Republic leader/guitarist Bruce Licher, with bassist James Brenner from the underrated Shiva Burlesque (which mutated into Grant Lee Buffalo) and drummer Brock Wirtz, Scenic plays nothing but instrumentals inspired by the lonely beauty of that desert. The group reflects the land not only in its music, but also in the lush, tinted photos of the characteristically gorgeous Independent Project CD package. With its spindly guitar and harsh rhythms, **Incident at Cima** is an important rock recording rather than mere ambient soundtrack, yet it still manages to capture the Mojave's spacious, barren landscapes perfectly. "The Kelso Run" features chilling, tumbleweed-blowing harmonica, while "On the Dune" splendidly evokes the majestic side of this rocky terrain. One can all but glimpse the endless mountains that run through the region. Other cuts are as methodically slow as the dusty trail of the Old West. Like the desert, the unique **Incident at Cima** is soulfully alone—quiet, thoughtful and timeless. [jr]

See also *Grant Lee Buffalo.*

ADAM SCHMITT

World So Bright (Reprise) 1991
Illiterature (Reprise) 1992

After warming up as a member of such Champaign, Illinois–area combos as Pop the Balloon (with future Velvet Crush–er Ric Menck), the Farmboys and the Elvis Brothers, Adam Schmitt very nearly crafted the perfect pure pop album on his first try with **World So Bright.** Getting assistance from a couple of drummers (one of them Kenny Aronoff), violinist Lisa Germano and guitarist Jay Bennett from Titanic Love Affair, Schmitt is a DIY pop guy in the grand tradition of artists like Emmitt Rhodes (and more recently, Richard X. Heyman). His well-crafted songs are mega-tuneful guitar-driven gems with hooks galore and lyrics that rise above the prosaic "boy meets girl/boy loses girl/boy misses girl/boy goes looking for another girl" fodder. In the dense and electric "River Black," for example, the protagonist drowns a woman who refuses to give him the time of day. More conventional winners are the acoustic (with strings) harmony exercise "Elizabeth Einstein," the somber ballad "Lost," the shimmering "Scarlet Street" and the hit-in-a-perfect-world "Can't Get You on My Mind." Schmitt's winningly boyish voice and the smooth, radio-friendly production are the sweet icing on a delicious cake.

The harder-rocking tone of **Illiterature** is something of a shock, not only because Schmitt throws some (gasp!) grungier numbers into the mix, but because some of the song lengths ominously pass the six-minute mark. Beyond the initial blow of hearing Schmitt scream (think John Lennon on "Twist and Shout") over distorted guitars on the Cheap Trick–ish opener, "Just Listen," however, **Illiterature** is a strong sophomore success. It's certainly moodier than **World So Bright;** some of the tunes—like "Thanks for Showing," a supremely bitter kiss-off to a broken relationship, and the downright cranky title track—find Schmitt uncharacteristically agitated. But while turning the amps up and penning lyrics like "We got no chance to change the world/It's dumped on us to save it" may smack of pandering to a Gen-X audience, Schmitt's unerring melodic skill helps keep **Illiterature** from going off the tracks. Although he hasn't released an album since, Schmitt has been active as a producer for Tommy Keene, Honcho Overload, Hum, Titanic Love Affair and others. [jmb]

FRED SCHNEIDER

See *B-52's.*

SCHOOLLY D

Schoolly-D (Schoolly-D) 1986
Saturday Night!—The Album (Schoolly-D) 1987 (Jive) 1987
The Adventures of Schoolly-D (Rykodisc) 1987
Smoke Some Kill (Jive) 1988
Am I Black Enough for You? (Jive/RCA) 1989
How a Blackman Feels (Capitol) 1991
Welcome to America (Ruffhouse/Columbia) 1994
The Jive Collection Series Vol. 3 (Jive/RCA) 1995
Reservoir Dog (Contract/PSK) 1995

The original architect of gangsta rap, West Philadelphia's Schoolly D (Jesse Weaver, Jr.) has made a career as the rhyming reporter of violence, drugs, gangs and other grim aspects of modern urban reality. Whether he's a detached observer, a fictional stand-in or an amoral exploiter (corners of a triangle that aren't very far apart), Schoolly is a potent rapper with a deromanticized tell-it-like-it-is style. And while his native locale has worked against him—the cold-blooded art he pioneered found a better commercial berth in California and Texas—Schoolly and his loyal DJ, Code Money, have stuck it out in the city of brotherly love.

After two self-released shots right into the bow (the essentials of which are compiled as **The Adventures of Schoolly-D**), Schoolly lost his gangsta concentration on the disappointing major-label debut, **Smoke Some Kill.** His followup, however, switched its focus from street crime to black power and got back in the groove. **Am I Black Enough for You?** is a loud and proud album that uses spoken-word bites (political speeches, *Star Trek* dialogue, Richard Pryor crack-horror routines) to increase the consciousness. If the record doesn't wind up saying much of anything, the inspirational chant of "Get Off Your Ass and Get Involved" and the Afrocentricity of "Black Jesus" are a whole lot more positive and encouraging than "It's Krak" or "Mr. Big Dick." (The 1995 Jive compilation draws equally from the first three albums, adding one jam from **Am I Black Enough for You?** and the previously non-LP "Code's Megamix.")

Despite those inklings of political savvy, the titular report of **How a Black Man Feels** is neither illuminating nor impressive ("We're fucking up the nation/ Think about it if you doubt it/Crack cocaine, we'll do without it/Some are up and some are down/Some muthafuckas can't be found"). "Original Gangster," a Caribbean-inflected track mixed by KRS-One, offers equally useless thoughts on a substantial topic. In fact, other than the unfashionable stripped-down beats (complete with Run–DMC samples), Schoolly's ugly and all-too-common gangsta threats ("Die Nigger Die" is unfortunately typical) sound like a sorry-ass imitation jackin' for bucks.

Shifting to his third major label in three albums (and mislaying an "l" from his name in the process), Schoolly made an important hookup with Philly's Ruffhouse organization, whose Joe "The Butcher" Nicolo executive-produced and helped mix **Welcome to America.** Working with the label's house band (including bassist Chuck Treece and drummer Mary Harris, who later joined Spearhead) and assorted DJs and MCs, Schoolly got himself a hardcore record that *sounds* miles better than any others he's made, strapped with psychedelic guitar, thundering bass grooves, tense rhythms, bits of horn, piano and sound effects. Rhyme-wise, the self-declared "No Good Nigga" is still fronting big-time, putting himself in the picture at the center of the action: killing, robbing, smoking sens, drinking 40s, pulling gats on every muthafucka he sees (including, in the title track, the president, since "He ain't nothin' but a bitch, I figure") and waving his dick around. Except for the perceptively autobiographical "Another Sign," the lyrics of **Welcome to America** are witless and insulting, a thuggish grunt without imagination or insight. Shame about all that good music going to waste.

Schoolly came back to his senses on the self-released and almost singlehanded **Reservoir Dog,** a homey, stripped-down session of scratchy samples and simply effective keyboard/drum machine inventions (and a badly recorded live track). Despite the intentional vintage-style P-Funk packaging and presentation, other than having soulful singer Tamika Vines on a bunch of these tracks, this R-Dog hasn't learned any new tricks ("Big Fat Bytches," "Hustler Life" and "Date With Death" come down the usual sex and guns chutes), but tones the songs down to tolerable vulgarity levels and sparks them with some better ideas. "Nigger Entertainment" actually adds another chapter to his slim volume of cultural/political insights, "Ghetto-funkstylistic" does a look-around with typically lurid vision, "If You See My Little Brother" offers thoughtful advice to the hip-hop community and "Eternity" (giving credit for conception to director Abel Ferrara) dabbles ineffectually in metaphysical zombie cinema: "I'll bite your neck/Treat you with no respect." [i]

SCHRAMMS

Walk to Delphi (OKra) 1990 (East Side Digital) 1995
Rock Paper Scissors Dynamite (Ger. OKra/Normal) 1992 (East Side Digital) 1995
Little Apocalypse (East Side Digital) 1994
The Schramms EP (Matador) 1994

DAVE SCHRAMM

Folk und die Folgen (Ger. Return to Sender/Normal) 1994

Although he stayed in Yo La Tengo long enough to play on that band's 1986 debut album and has since come to be known around East Coast indie circles as the guitarist to send for when superb Nashville-style picking or pedal-steeling is needed, Long Island native Dave Schramm has pledged his musical troth to the band that bears his name, a sterling country-pop-rock quartet that manages to not compromise its humble lack of pretense with a literary bent that regularly looks to Emily Dickinson for song lyrics.

The robust and handsome **Walk to Delphi** unveils the group, in which Schramm—joined by bassist Al Greller, organist Terry Karydes and ex–Human Switchboard drummer Ron Metz—makes the Dylanesque most of his woody, knockabout voice. Avoiding the standard templates (no Gram Parsons or George Jones tunes, thanks just the same; the only cover here is Tom Paxton's "Everytime"), Schramm doesn't so much play country as reclaim its folky aspects to shape his singer/songwriter rock. The band does other things as well: "Big Stink" and "Gusano Verde" are original southwestern instrumentals. If Schramm's melodies are attractive without being memorable, the whole enterprise is so cozy and good-spirited that it's hard not to pull up a chair and enjoy the warmth. (The '95 reissue improves the artwork and replaces the calamitous electric "Gusano Verde" with a much nicer acoustic "sketch." It also restores the Dickinson lyrics of "Number Nineteen," which were on the original vinyl and cassette issue but replaced on the OKra CD when a publisher belatedly denied the group permission to adapt the poem.)

Schramm's singing and writing are notably more assured on **Rock Paper Scissors Dynamite:** "Talking to Me Poor" sounds like the great lost outtake from **The Byrds Play Dylan.** The group's range gets a good workout here: the peppy rock arrangement of "Her Darkness" energizes a nice tune, while smoothing the burrs off the Saints' "In the Mirror" leaves a lonely pop ballad; the country style of "Nine Years" serves the wistful solemnity of the confessional lyrics. A sharp, often moving, record. (The belated US issue adds a song, "Sorrow on Sorrow.")

The careful centrism of **Little Apocalypse** is too much of a good thing. With Karydes gone (replaced by George Usher), Schramm sets off down a semi-electric country-rock road, a development that's not entirely for the better. While stability gives him room to stretch out and showcase his excellent instrumental skills, it puts too consistent a stamp on the fine songs, obscuring the ample merits of "Where Were You," "A Woman's Name," "Heart Not Within" and Lucinda Williams' "Side of the Road." A pair of instrumentals—the slide-driven "Duck Hunting in Hell" and the acoustic "Little American Hymn"—stand out for their stylistic variance, an attribute that doesn't flatter the rest of the album.

Schramm's solo record, released in a tiny edition in Germany, is, ironically, the best of the bunch. Making do without a rhythm section on this intimate, mostly acoustic outing resolves the stylistic quandary of **Little**

Apocalypse; as if to make that perfectly clear, **Folk und die Folgen** begins with a gorgeous rendition of "A Woman's Name." Deftly arranging acoustic guitar and sparing measures of lap steel, organ, piano and harmony vocals into watercolors shimmering with melodic light, Schramm barely disturbs the air—the performances nearly come to a standstill between words—yet still conveys an enormous breadth of feeling in his sure, delicate delivery. The version here of "Talking to Me Poor" is equal to the band's but very different in feel. The spare cover of David Blue's "Sister Rose" is even finer than the Schramms' version on the Matador single, which also includes **Little Apocalypse**'s "Heart Not Within" and the previously unreleased "What I Knew Today." [i]

See also *Kate Jacobs, Yo La Tengo.*

SCORN

Vae Solis (Earache/Relativity) 1992
Lick Forever Dog EP (Earache/Relativity) 1992
Deliverance EP (Earache) 1992
White Irises Blind EP (Earache) 1993
Colossus (Earache) 1994
Evanescence (Earache) 1994
Ellipsis (Earache) 1995
Gyral (Earache) 1995
Logghi Barogghi (Earache) 1996

LULL

Cold Summer (Subharmonic) 1994

Napalm Death drummer Mick "Human Tornado" Harris started toying with computers around the same time as some former bandmates, but the results—in Scorn—are more at odds with his physically overpowering tenure as an indefatigable one-man battery squad. Recorded after Harris had already joined Bill Laswell and John Zorn in Painkiller, the first Scorn releases are less imposing than Justin Broadrick's sludgy Godflesh, but Harris developed the group until it became his point of departure from rock music.

Broadrick and American Pat McCahan of Candiru rotated through guitar spots on the first releases, wherein Harris and fellow Napalm Death refugee Nick Bullen (bass/vocals) are caught struggling to innovate. **Vae Solis** seems to be the natural outcome of calculated grindcore, picking up the detached threads of late Swans and Einstürzende Neubauten. **Lick Forever Dog** (remixes of tracks from **Vae Solis**) and the following two 12-inches are similar Anglo-Saxon angst, of interest mainly to eager metal collectors who had never heard **Holy Money.** An intense electronic metal band was still an idea whose time had yet to come.

Harris and Bullen back away from overkill on **Colossus,** loading on moody synth and distressing vocal samples to create an ominous modernist sound similar to God and Ice. **Evanescence,** a topsy-turvy stew of confusion and emotion, practically severs the members' final ties to grindcore. With James Plotkin of Old taking over on guitar, the threesome create a dark digital domain where fancy danceable beats pop under thick clouds of textured samples, deep bass and minimal muted vocals. Where the economics of experimental music seem to dictate that artists run a small number of ideas over a repetitive string of spin-off releases, **Evanescence** is a dense moment of grandeur. Though probably important in introducing Scorn to the emergent ambient dub community, the remix collection **Ellipsis** only serves to make the band appear more ordinary. A better record would have been Harris and Bullen's unique take on original tracks by Bill Laswell, Scanner, Autechre, Coil and Meat Beat Manifesto, instead of vice versa.

Bullen withdrew from Scorn in early 1995 after a violent nightclub incident, leaving Harris to go it alone. Distinct from his Lull project, which focuses on introspective incidental noise and samples, the subdued **Gyral** takes Scorn into club music, capturing a sophisticated suite of atmospheric dub that tempers the confusing musical ambition of **Evanescence.** Minus Bullen, Scorn scales down to the solemn sound of one quiet man working late at night in England's loneliest dancehall. Tracks are based mostly on ghostly loops, with guitars and vocals done away with entirely. In ten years, Mick Harris has grown about as far beyond his animalistic early output as possible. [ic]

See also *Bill Laswell, Napalm Death, Painkiller.*

CASEY SCOTT

Creep City (Signal/Capitol) 1993

"If this song was a book, it would be fifteen pages long, have a fake gold binding and big, bold easy-reader type face." And it would be on a third-rate Patti Smith tribute record, like almost everything else on Scott's dismally derivative album. Underscoring the enormous influence Bob Dylan had on her idol, the New York–based singer/poet/guitarist (backed by three sidemen dubbed the Creeps) heists the prolix rush of tripped-out imagery from the one and the sneering, jut-jaw declamatory passion from the other, omitting only a musical personality of her own. The hopeless opening couplet of the spare, simple album—"The maggot king sits fast asleep upon his well-lit throne/The queen is in the parlor with her ear pressed to the phone"—says it all, but Scott puts a fine point on her solipsistic arrogance in "Ryan": "the kind of girl that I was . . . a post-punk psycho from a whitebread nightmare . . . the kind of girl who messes with your head and you'd follow her anywhere." Wrong. [i]

MIKE SCOTT

See *Waterboys.*

SCRAPING FOETUS OFF THE WHEEL

See *Foetus.*

SCRAWL

Plus, Also, Too (No Other) 1987 (Rough Trade) 1989
He's Drunk (Rough Trade) 1988
Smallmouth (Rough Trade) 1990
Bloodsucker (Feel Good All Over) 1991 (Simple Machines) 1993
Velvet Hammer (Simple Machines) 1993
Travel On, Rider (Elektra) 1996

Before the media-savvy riot grrrls came of age and put a cool name to being young, female and punk, there was nothing glamorous or trendy about having the guts to flip the sexual script and muck about in the mire of America's indie-rock world. Columbus, Ohio's Scrawl, a trio of tough chicks with no specific agenda and—at the outset—a lot more enthusiasm than skill, began rocking out in 1985, initially as Skull. On the first record (later paired on CD with the second, as well as being reissued on its own), guitarist Marcy Mays, joined in disharmony by bassist Sue Harshe, mount an attack with aggressive music and really bad vocals.

While both singers show improvement on the more proficient and varied **He's Drunk,** their voices still didn't blend well enough not to notice. Only when producer Gary Smith reined in the discordant excesses on the mild-mannered and poppy **Smallmouth** did the group finally deliver its sturdy melodies via presentably confident vocals. The sketchy lyrics touch on real-life encounters and personal problems with engaging near-the-surface intimacy; the music is a bit brasher than that but not by much. While some of the songs are clearly punk-derived ("Rot," "Absolute Torture"), the band's '70s rock roots get to showing in "Charles," a rewrite of Kiss' "Beth," which leaves a message for a lover waiting on a rocker. Mays' sweet piano cover of Eurythmics' bitterly sarcastic "I Need You" ends the album on a handsome, smartly feminist note.

The Scrawl on the seven-song **Bloodsucker** (issued twice with adjusted artwork) is harder, in both its rock edge and its emotional stance. Evidently embittered by bad experiences in the record industry (Rough Trade's collapse undoubtedly among their woes) and relationships, Mays and Harshe sing and play with renewed fervor, which works to their advantage in dispirited songs like "Love's Insecticide," the depressed "Please Have Everything" and the powerfully edgy "Clock Song," a Gang of Four–like call and response that sets miserable lines ("Don't want to get out of bed . . . Don't want to look at myself") against an encouraging chorus of "Go, girl, go!" Scrawl's ripping cover of Cheap Trick's "High Roller"—stripped-down and businesslike—isn't as good in the execution as the conception, but makes its point all the same.

Dana Marshall replaced original drummer Carolyn O'Leary in 1992; the following year, Scrawl recorded **Velvet Hammer,** a great-sounding modern-rock record (credit uncredited engineer Steve Albini) delivered straight from the jaws of hell. "Drunken Fool," "Your Mother Wants to Know," "Tell Me Now, Boy," "Take a Swing" and "Prize" are only some of the blunt, raw, conversational songs of first-person failings and ruined romance. Singing in an unsure voice that aptly reflects the mood of this poignant and unnerving album, Mays (effectively harmonized, and spelled with little emotional improvement on "See" and part of "Remember That Day," by Harshe) rips herself apart, wishing only for the relief of release: "I know you're sick of me not acting my age . . . I want to be strong but I don't put up a fight . . . All my friends look at me like a stooge, look at me I'm a loser . . . You ask me not to drink so I passed out in a different bed . . . I can almost feel myself evaporating." Hard to enjoy in light of the obvious pain, but a terribly potent bloodletting of misery into art. [i]

See also *Afghan Whigs; TPRG.*

SCREAMING TREES

Other Worlds EP (Velvetone/K) 1985 (SST) 1988
Clairvoyance (Velvetone) 1986
Even If and Especially When (SST) 1987
Invisible Lantern (SST) 1988
Buzz Factory (SST) 1989
Change Has Come EP (Sub Pop) 1989
Something About Today EP (Epic) 1990
Uncle Anesthesia (Epic) 1991
Anthology: SST Years 1985–1989 (SST) 1991
Sweet Oblivion (Epic) 1992
Nearly Lost You EP (UK Epic) 1992
Dust (Epic) 1996

BEAT HAPPENING/SCREAMING TREES

Beat Happening/Screaming Trees EP (K/Homestead) 1988

MARK LANEGAN

The Winding Sheet (Sub Pop) 1990
Whiskey for the Holy Ghost (Sub Pop) 1994

PURPLE OUTSIDE

Mystery Lane (New Alliance) 1990

SOLOMON GRUNDY

Solomon Grundy (New Alliance) 1990

A melodic mixture of psychedelia and '60s garage-rock has made the Screaming Trees, spawned in remote Ellensburg, Washington, one of the most influential, atypical and under-rated bands to spring from the Northwest. Highlighted by Mark Lanegan's deep, mournful voice and Gary Lee Conner's snarling guitar work, the Trees conjure reverent but never derivative visions of the Seeds, Stooges, 13th Floor Elevators and even the Amboy Dukes. Unlike most of their peers, the Trees have improved steadily with each album, moving in a remarkably linear and consistent curve toward the almost classic-rock grace of **Sweet Oblivion** and the awesomely ambitious **Dust.** Perhaps most impressive has been Lanegan's progress from a good singer into a truly great one.

Other Worlds (recorded before the band had played a gig) and **Clairvoyance** both have flashes but are formative efforts that find the young musicians trying to rise above their influences. **Even If and Especially When**'s "Transfiguration" is the proverbial quantum leap where the band discovered its voice. Dropping the baby fat (well, some of it) without compromising the trademark garagey roar, the band hit on a sound it would gradually refine on each successive release. **Even If** sounds like an album made by guys who had just turned twenty—which they actually had.

Invisible Lantern ups the ante even more as the Trees' pop streak matures with "Smokerings" and especially the marvelous "Night Comes Creeping." Bassist Van Conner (Gary Lee's brother) left for several months in '88 and was replaced by Donna Dresch (later of Team Dresch). That lineup recorded a lost-to-the-ages disc with Painted Willie guitarist Vic Makauskas, all tapes of which vanished when his studio was sold. (Another great lost Trees album—the reportedly rejected followup to **Sweet Oblivion**—was recorded in early '94 with producer Don Fleming.)

Buzz Factory completes the SST era in a slightly gnarlier sonic setting courtesy of grunge domo Jack Endino (Steve Fisk had produced all of the band's prior dates). Highlights include "Where the Twain Shall Meet," "Flower Web" and "Black Sun Morning." All of the aforementioned tracks (but nothing from **Clairvoyance**) appear on the Trees' twenty-one-cut volume of SST's **Anthology** series, but the three post-puberty albums are all well worth owning. The **Change Has Come** double-7-inch seems to be an outtakes collection but features the dazzling "Days"; the CD and 12-inch include an ultra-psychedelic bonus track.

Uncle Anesthesia, co-produced by Soundgarden's

Chris Cornell and northwestern metal kingpin Terry Date, suffers from some major-label-debut stiffness but generally finds the band benefiting from the sonic upgrade. "Something About Today" and "Bed of Roses" show the group's songwriting reaching new heights, and the only dip in quality comes on the blatant Doors tribute "Before We Arise." The four-song **Something About Today** features the excellent "Who Lies in Darkness," a mutant version of the title track and two album previews. Founding drummer Mark Pickerel left shortly after recording **Uncle Anesthesia** (he currently serves in Truly) and was replaced by hard-hitting Skin Yard alumnus Barrett Martin.

Screaming Trees' fortunes rose as "Nearly Lost You" dwarfed almost every other song on the **Singles** soundtrack, parting the waters for **Sweet Oblivion.** Boasting a comparatively arena-sized punch (courtesy Don Fleming behind the board), the album fairly screams "maturity," dispensing with the wah-wah pedals and allowing a latent classic-rock side to shine more brightly than ever. (The band even bases the guitar parts of "No One Knows" on a piece of the Who's "Naked Eye.")

Although it hasn't been compiled yet, there's an album's worth of B-sides and compilation tracks (including Small Faces, Jethro Tull, Black Sabbath and Youngbloods covers) from the band's Epic years. None is great, but "E.S.K." and the acoustic version of "Winter Song" (both on the British **Nearly Lost You** EP) are worth tracking down. The quartet has also contributed to Sonics, Velvet Underground and John Lennon tribute albums; Lanegan did a song for the **Twisted Willie** (Nelson) collection.

The **Beat Happening/Screaming Trees** EP is almost entirely the former's show, although the one Lanegan-sung track ("Polly Pereguin") is pretty great.

Lanegan's two solo albums are marvelous and easily rank with the Trees' best work. Providing a fascinating portrait of his role in the band, the albums sound distinctively like *him,* yet nothing like them. Moody and ominous, they alternate between slow, twanging rockers and stark, yearning laments; both feature a Lee Hazlewood–styled acoustic menace encouraged by the substantial role of longtime friend/Dinosaur Jr bassist Mike Johnson. **The Winding Sheet** features "Where Did You Sleep Last Night," the sole track to surface from a planned Leadbelly tribute EP by "a botched side-project with some guys in another band" (Kurt Cobain and Krist Novoselic of Nirvana, who subsequently made good use of the song and Lanegan's vocal approach to it). Mark Pickerel plays drums on the album; Jack Endino and Steve Fisk also contribute.

The masterful **Whiskey for the Holy Ghost** (take that, Nick Cave) dramatically one-ups its predecessor, although it took so long to finish that it became a running joke on the Sub Pop release schedule. With guest spots by everyone from Dan Peters of Mudhoney to J Mascis, the album uses acoustic guitars to almost symphonic effect, and the songs find Lanegan pouring misery onto tape in his finest fashion yet.

The Purple Outside is Gary Lee Conner playing everything except drums; it basically sounds like the Trees without Lanegan singing. Solomon Grundy is Van's side band, whose album rocks aplenty but is a bit thin in the songwriting department. Van also depped for **Green Mind**–era Dinosaur Jr before Mike Johnson joined the band; Lanegan and Martin appear on albums by Johnson and Mad Season; Lanegan and Gary Lee appear on Mike Watt's alternative rock-royalty slumber party **Ball-Hog or Tugboat?** [ja]

See also *Alice in Chains, Beat Happening, Mike Johnson, Team Dresch, Truly; TPRG.*

SCREECHING WEASEL

Screeching Weasel (Underdog) 1987
Boogadaboogadaboogada! (Roadkill) 1988 (Lookout!) 1992
Punkhouse EP7 (Limited Potential) 1989 (Selfless) 1993
My Brain Hurts (Lookout!) 1991
Pervo-Devo EP7 (Shred of Dignity) 1991 (Outpunk) 1992
Wiggle (Lookout!) 1992
Ramones (Selfless) 1992
Anthem for a New Tomorrow (Lookout!) 1993
How to Make Enemies and Irritate People (Lookout!) 1995
Kill the Musicians (Lookout!) 1995

SLUDGEWORTH

What's This? (Johann's Face) 1991
Losers of the Year (Lookout!) 1995

As bored teenagers growing up on the outskirts of Chicago, the first incarnation of Screeching Weasel (1986) jerry-rigged a simple, raw punk sound out of borrowed parts, meshing the snotty suburban attitude of New Jersey's Adrenalin O.D. to the high-speed sonic assault of the early Ramones. The band also borrowed the Ramones' convention of adopting punk-rock surnames, christening themselves Ben Weasel (vocals), Johnny Jughead (guitar), Vinnie Bovine (bass) and Steve Cheese (drums).

Whipping through twenty-seven songs in under thirty-five minutes, the debut suffers from its no-budget one-day production, generic hardcore rants ("California Sucks," "Leave Me Alone") and an often puerile sense of humor. But there are a few keepers, including the deliciously misanthropic (and wonderfully catchy) "Murder in the Brady House" and the anthemic "Experience the Ozzfish," a salute to Chicago scenester Warren Ozzfish.

Boogadaboogadaboogada!, some copies of which included a poster of the band bowling in the nude, offers another blast of rapid-fire hardcore punk. With a new bassist named Fish (none other than the infamous Warren Ozzfish!), **Boogada**'s punk snarl is crisper and more accomplished; the songwriting is much sharper, teeming with funny, bouncy, singalong tunes like "I Hate Led-Zeppelin," "I Wanna Be Naked" and "Hey Suburbia." The **Punkhouse** EP's grainy production and lackluster songwriting make it a disposable footnote, except that it marks the only non-compilation recording with drummer Brian Vermin and the debut of longtime bassist and guitarist Dan Vapid, who appears under the name Sewercap.

Internal squabbles led to the group's breakup and an eighteen-month hiatus, although Weasel and Jughead continued to perform in a new band variously called the Gore Gore Girls and Wiggle. At the urging of Lookout Records' Lawrence Livermore, Screeching Weasel re-formed in '91 and recorded its finest album, **My Brain Hurts.** Fast, funny and brimming with lively melodies, it inaugurates the band's stable lineup with whipcrack drummer Danny Panic, bassist Dave Naked and the versatile Dan Vapid on guitar and backup vocals. While Weasel's nasty anti-everything diatribes (like "Fathead" and "What We Hate") still take center stage, head-bobbing pop/punk tunes like "Cindy's on Methadone," "Guest List" and "Teenage Freak Show" turn the band's jaundiced eye back on the punk scene itself with wry and savvy results.

For its throwaway Patsy Cline cover and dumb song about creepy girls, the **Pervo-Devo** EP still merits mention for its gay-porn picture sleeve and the song "I Wanna Be a Homosexual," a silly but nonetheless courageous poke in the eye at the ingrained homophobia of the hardcore scene.

Wiggle trades Dave Naked for bassist John Personality of Chicago's Vindictives and sounds much better than the band's prior releases. Unfortunately, the songwriting just isn't up to snuff, with too many one-joke Ramones ripoffs (Vapid's "I Was a High School Psychopath") and a lot of unnecessary guitar doodling. The album does boast one of Weasel's best girl songs ("Jeannie's Got a Problem With Her Uterus") and a touching love song co-written by fanzine poobah Aaron Cometbus.

Part joke, part homage, **Ramones** (a complete SW rendition of the first Ramones album) was recorded as part of a series (the Queers and Vindictives later covered **Go Home** and **Rocket to Russia,** respectively) and, given Screeching Weasel's obvious debt to the boys from Queens, probably seemed like a good idea at the time. The band (here a four-piece, with Vapid on bass and Weasel on rhythm guitar) sounds like it's having fun, but the arrangements copy the original so closely that this academic exercise does little more than prove it can be done.

You can certainly hear the Ramones' influence all the way through **Anthem for a New Tomorrow,** but Screeching Weasel has grown up. There are still girl songs, but they're not quite so silly anymore, and they're mixed in with surprisingly adult meditations on loneliness, illness, hopelessness and rage, all set to a pounding 4/4 beat and the same frantically strummed three chords.

Using labelmate Green Day's Mike Dirnt to substitute on bass for the departed Dan Vapid, Screeching Weasel recorded **How to Make Enemies and Irritate People** as its purported final album. If it's not the band's best work, it's certainly the best-sounding, with a booming bottom and textured vocals. Production aside, it's also one of the band's strongest efforts, boasting a couple of pretty good Ramones knockoffs ("Nobody Likes You," with a classically snotty lead vocal, and "Surf Goddess," co-written by Joe King of the Queers, whose own repertoire includes an original called "Ben Weasel"), two primo girl songs (with requisite singalong choruses) and the touching "I Wrote Holden Caufield."

Culled from out-of-print singles and EPs, alternate takes, compilation tracks, live recordings and the **Ramones** album, **Kill the Musicians** includes an extensive band history written by Ben Weasel (a longtime *Maximumrocknroll* columnist), some vintage photos and thirty-one tracks, arranged chronologically. As a guided tour through the band's career, it's something of a bumpy ride and far from a definitive best-of collection, but worthwhile nonetheless for rarities like the original version of "I Wanna Be a Homosexual" and the out-of-print "Punkhouse."

After Screeching Weasel's demise (which proved short-lived: the band resumed in early '96), Weasel, Panic and Vapid (using their real names—Foster, Sullivan and Schafer) continued to play together as the Riverdales. Previously, Vapid had moonlighted from Screeching Weasel (along with onetime Weasel drummer Brian Vermin) as the lead singer of Chicago's Sludgeworth. **What's This?** mixes thrashy funk-rock with upbeat, Descendents-styled pop-punk; with EP and compilation tracks added, it was reissued in 1995 as **Losers of the Year.** [jt]

See also *Queers, Riverdales.*

SCUD MOUNTAIN BOYS

Pine Box (Chunk) 1995
Dance the Night Away [CD] (Chunk) 1995
Massachusetts (Sub Pop) 1996

The Scud Mountain Boys take a Codeine-like approach to rural country music. Formed as a trio in '91, the Northampton, Massachusetts, group plays dryly amusing originals and covers on nearly subliminal energy planes. Both **Pine Box** (vinyl only) and **Dance the Night Away** (CD)—which have three songs in common—are seductively gentle, letting pretty melodies carry lyrics whose wary perspective, irony, bitterness and random threats of violence strew dirt on the sugar cookies. "Don't ask for nothing, you'll never be let down," goes the refrain of "Peter Graves' Anatomy" (one of the shared tracks), and that's the retiring band's personality in a nutshell. Recorded on 4-track in guitarist/singer Bruce Tull's kitchen, **Pine Box**'s "Down in Writing" is a model of caution, while "Silo" makes promises of destruction all the more chilling with its offhand tone. Meantime, covers of Jimmy Webb's "Wichita Lineman" and Cher's "Gypsies, Tramps and Thieves" proves that the band's subtle stylings can work on external sources as well.

Joined occasionally on **Dance the Night Away** by a drummer (either Tom Shea or Keith Levreault of Kevin Salem's band) and the Tubercular Boys Choir, the Scuds barely disturb the silence as they whisper such slightly bent inventions as "Letter to Bread" and "Television" ("send me a show/you're the only world I know"). Although able to rouse themselves to a mild roots-rock roar—as on the neurotic "(She Took His) Picture," which resembles the dB's—Tull, Stephen Desaulniers (bass/vocals) and Joe Pernice (vocals/guitar) make understatement far more engrossing.

With Shea a full-time member on drums and mandolin, the Scud Mountain Boys emerge as a shyly, slyly miserable crypto-country group on **Massachusetts.** Pushing the excellent songwriting and quietly resonant harmony singing to the fore, the album is an atmospheric marvel—fully arranged, languidly delivered and occasionally branded by artful lead-guitar electricity. Whispered with the intimate breathiness of Colin Blunstone, memorable lines about difficulties with women and alcohol pop out with easy aplomb: "Cigarette Sandwich" is a devastating self-portrait set to disarmingly pepped-up music; "I've been down before/I'm no stranger to the canvas," whispers Pernice in "Glass Jaw" with no hint of concern. In "Grudge," not quite hiding the desperation in his voice, he casually (and hopelessly) attempts to arrange a sex date with an ex: "Tonight I got nowhere to go/And I thought that I would call you and see if you were home/I'm sorry but I'm pretty stoned/I hope I didn't scare you/I hope to God you were alone." Taking a rare lead vocal, Desaulniers sings "Liquor Store," a dismal ode to drinking that sounds like a solemn Elvis Costello covering Gram Parsons. Rooting around various quadrants of rock's past country incursions, **Massachusetts** finds a new place to hang its head. [i]

SEA AND CAKE

See *Shrimp Boat.*

SEAL

Seal (ZTT/Sire/Warner Bros.) 1991
Seal (ZTT/Sire/Warner Bros.) 1994

Yuppies need good music, too. For those in need of artful, adult intelligence with a beat, Seal (Sealhenry Samuel) is a better bet than an open lunch slot at the racquetball court. Actually, the stylish London-born singer/songwriter is more substantial than his fast-track success might imply, but the remoteness of his emotionalism makes him seem shuttered even when he's disgorging his heart. Intimacy doesn't usually sound this glossy and impersonal.

Produced by Trevor Horn in tribute to Bryan Ferry's elegant mid-Atlantic aspirations, Seal calmly wraps his husky voice around slow-moving melodies in lush, soulful dance grooves appealing in conception and magnificent in execution. The first of Seal's two untitled albums (no Peter Gabriel connection should be read into that) reveals an unsettled sense of historical place, as if the otherwise modern auteur had spent the '80s listening to old Bill Withers, Stevie Wonder, Richie Havens and Joni Mitchell records. As Horn modulates the tone from house-hunting warm ("The Beginning") to atmospherically cool ("Crazy"), pop rich ("Wild") to folky spare ("Deep Water," "Whirlpool") to rock hard ("Killer"), Seal offers vague, reflective commentary on love, the environment, society and personal issues, leaving a strong sonic impression without articulating many literal ideas. If there's a lesson to be gleaned from "Miracles will happen . . . But we're never gonna survive unless we get a little crazy," it'll need some elaboration.

The second **Seal** (will there someday be a seventh **Seal?**), again produced by Horn, is a somber but lightly rendered affair that tests the singer's optimism with tear-filled lessons of pain and loss. Richer with handsome melodies, devoted to vocals and arranged more delicately than the debut, **Seal** refines the music to a rarefied realm in which sounds glisten and syllables are placed as carefully as the threads in a tapestry. "Kiss From a Rose" is the number that brought Seal to the top of the charts after it was included on the *Batman Forever* soundtrack in August '95, but it's "Prayer for the Dying"—seemingly an AIDS-related farewell to a friend—that serves as the album's centerpiece. That eloquent declaration of hope in the face of despair is followed by such relevancies as the supportive "Don't Cry," the questioning "People Asking Why" and the guardedly grateful "I'm Alive." But for all the passion sequestered in Seal's creations, **Seal** is a disturbingly distant and conflicted record in both word and feel. His need to remain private in public strips the songs of their impact, and his filigreed delivery doesn't match the life-and-death issues he's singing about. "Life is confusing and I don't know why," Seal sings in "People Asking Why." For all its solid achievement, the ambitions of **Seal** might have been a compellingly realized masterpiece if he had given that one some more thought. [i]

SEAM

Headsparks (Homestead) 1992
Kernel EP (Touch and Go) 1993
The Problem With Me (Touch and Go) 1993
Are You Driving Me Crazy? (Touch and Go) 1995

Seam began as a trio in Chapel Hill, North Carolina, with Mac McCaughan of Superchunk on drums, Lexi Mitchell playing bass and he-of-the-perpetual-whisper Sooyoung Park (ex–Bitch Magnet) leading the way on guitar and vocals. With an inspirational nod to the spare pop dreaminess of Galaxie 500 and Codeine, **Headsparks** is a somewhat awkward—but occasionally beautiful—debut. The disc's highlights generally coincide with its Park-injected lullabies ("Feather," "Granny 9x"); the most awkward battles take place when he fumbles his way through the perkier Mac-driven ditties ("Grain," "Atari").

Things changed for the better once Park and Mitchell split with McCaughan, moved to Chicago, found a friend and producer in Brad Wood (Liz Phair) and grew into a four-piece with the addition of ex-Bastro members Bundy Brown (guitar) and John McEntire (drums). The four-song **Kernel**'s best idea is a radical reworking of **Headsparks**' "Shame," which benefits significantly from a slower pace and Park's vocals (Velocity Girl's Sarah Shannon sang the original).

Seam's lineup turnstile took another spin for **The Problem With Me,** sending the Bastros on their way and replacing them, albeit briefly, with Craig White (Repulse Kava) and Bob Rising (Repulse Kava/Poster Children). The nine-song record contains some of Seam's best work: through the minimalist melodies of "Road to Madrid," "Dust and Turpentine" and the outstanding "Stage 2000," Young repeatedly hits the less-is-more button to fine effect.

Despite a complete personnel makeover, that quiet strength carries into **Are You Driving Me Crazy?,** again produced by Wood (except for two tracks produced by Casey Rice). Joining Park here are drummer Chris Manfrin (ex-Travis), bassist William Shin (ex–Poem Rocket) and guitarist Reg Shrader (ex–Circus Lupus). Though Park's songwriting skills are at their peak ("Port of Charleston," "Two Is Enough"), the band is unable to provide the same brilliant turbulence that makes **The Problem With Me** so powerful. [dps]

See also *Gastr del Sol, Poster Children, Superchunk.*

SEAWEED

Seaweed EP7 (Leopard Gecko) 1990
Seaweed (Leopard Gecko/Tupelo) 1990
Despised (Sub Pop) 1991
Weak (Sub Pop) 1992
Four (Sub Pop) 1993
Go Your Own Way EP (Sub Pop) 1993
Spanaway (Hollywood) 1995

Weaned on all-ages hardcore shows in their Tacoma, Washington, hometown, the five members of Seaweed struck out in late 1989 to emulate their heroes. The agile hook-core quintet was soon playing bars where its members were too young to drink, wowing onlookers with incessant pogoing and urgent metal-influenced riffs. Six years later, Seaweed's maturation (and punk's newfound commercial appeal) proved marketable, as the band signed on with Disney's Hollywood Records.

Seaweed compiles early singles from K and Leopard Gecko (a label run by Seaweed bassist John Atkins). Highlights include "Deertrap" (wherein vocalist Aaron Stauffer anguishes over his discovery of a dying animal and his inability to save it), "Carousel," "Stargirl" and "Just a Smirk." Even at this early stage, the band's rhythmic punk-metal effectively accompanies Stauffer's yearning confessions of confusion and doubt, and the songs show a solid grasp of the best of mid-'80s post-punk. The sound quality is bargain basement, but the group's sincerity and earnest songwriting make **Seaweed** too intense to be discounted.

Jack Endino recorded **Despised,** a six-song EP fattened by four remixed singles, bringing out the crucial rhythm work of Atkins and drummer Bob Bulgrien, heightening the tension between guitarists Clint Werner and Wade Neal. Again, the band's aggressive and brooding, yet catchy, songwriting gives Stauffer ample support for his tales of emotional struggle. ("It's not so clear to me that I was wrong, I betrayed you," he wails on "Stale.") Waning adolescence (in interviews of this period, members discussed their proclivity for masturbation) clashes with thoughtful, unique perspectives on the transition into adulthood (Neal contributes a gorgeous acoustic guitar track to the otherwise forceful "Sit in Glass").

Endino returned for the sarcastically titled **Weak.** More fully realized and powerful than anything the group had previously done, the ten songs are anything but weak. Neal and Werner boost the guitars, tangling awesome heaviness into chiming rhythmic work. Stauffer ponders more abstract concepts—in the chorus of "Taxing," he bellows, "Sit and watch the world fall down/Crumble into loss/Martyr wrote across my wall/Supervision costs." He sounds changed on "New Tools" ("I understand that I can't understand the new breed"); "Clean Slate," "Baggage," "The Way It Ends" and other tracks focus on the volatile dynamics of relationships.

A sonic architect in his own right, Werner had recorded the demos for **Weak** at his homemade 8-track studio. By 1993, Werner's basement held a complete 16-track facility, and Seaweed self-produced **Four** at home. The efforts yielded the epic "Kid Candy," the angry "One Inch Punch" (a Bruce Lee maneuver), the driving "Turn Out," the varied "In Fairness" and the throttling, hooky "Losing Skin." True to its foundations, Seaweed turns out a meaty combination of hard-hitting metallic oomph and subversive hooks.

Co-produced by the band and mixed by Andy Wallace, **Spanaway** changes little, although an increased budget and studio time enable Seaweed to deliver its best work, an inspired major-label debut. The opening "Free Drug Zone" rumbles furiously; the guitars on "Crush Us All" sound interplanetary. Stauffer turns into a friggin' poet—the tender intro to "Saturday Nitrous" includes the line, "Diving under golden skies so cherry/Blossoms clouding up my sight/Take a breath in cleansing/The nectar sweet and sticky." Sure, he's still obsessed with relationships and arguments ("Not Saying Anything," "Start With"), but other songs commune with nature (the spectacular "Magic Mountainman"), travel ("Defender") and detail visions of an apocalyptic future ("Last Humans"). Having grown up on **Spanaway,** Seaweed sews together a record that cohesively binds its past and its future. [mww]

SEBADOH

The Freed Man (Homestead) 1989
Weed Forestin (Homestead) 1990
The Freed Weed (Homestead) 1990
Asshole EP7 (Vertical Industries) 1990
Gimme Indie Rock EP7 (Homestead) 1991
Sebadoh III (Homestead) 1991
Oven Is My Friend EP7 (Siltbreeze) 1992
Rockin' the Forest (UK 20/20) 1992
Sebadoh vs. Helmet (UK 20/20) 1992
Smash Your Head on the Punk Rock (Sub Pop) 1992
Soul and Fire EP (UK Domino) 1993 (Sub Pop) 1994
Bubble & Scrape (Sub Pop) 1993
Rebound EP (UK Domino) 1993 (Sub Pop) 1995
4 Song CD (UK Domino) 1994
Bakesale (Sub Pop) 1994
In Tokyo (Japan. Bolide) 1995
Beauty of the Ride EP (UK Domino) 1996
Harmacy (Sub Pop) 1996

FOLK IMPLOSION

Folk Implosion [tape] (UK Chocolate Monk) 1994
The Electric Idiot EP (Bel. Ubik) 1994
Walk Through This World With the Folk Implosion EP (Drunken Fish) 1994
Take a Look Inside . . . . the Folk Implosion (Communion) 1995
The Folk Implosion: Lou Barlow 50/50 John Davis (Communion) 1996

FOLK IMPLOSION ET AL.

Kids Soundtrack (London) 1995

SENTRIDOH (LOU BARLOW)

Losers [tape] (Shrimper) 1991
Most of the Worst and Some of the Best [tape] (Shrimper) 1993
Losercore EP7 (Smells Like) 1993
The Mysterious Sentridoh EP EP7 (Little Brother) 1994
Louis Barlow's Acoustic Sentridoh EP7 (Fr. LoFi) 1994
Winning Losers: A Collection of Home Recordings 89–93 (Smells Like) 1994
10 Songs (Shrimper) 1995
Louis Barlow's Acoustic Sentridoh (Shrimper) 1995

LOU BARLOW AND FRIENDS

Another Collection of Home Recordings (Can. Mint) 1995

After being booted from Dinosaur Jr for what J Mascis dubbed "excessive social ineptitude" (mull *that* one over), Lou Barlow focused his energies on Sebadoh, a "band" that had existed since the mid-'80s. Propelled by the creative tension between Barlow's fractured singer/songwriter delirium and Eric Gaffney's more aggressive noise collage work, Sebadoh set the standard by which all subsequent lo-fi combos would be judged. Although often maddeningly slothful and utterly incapable of separating—or even acknowledging the difference between—the wheat and chaff of their produce, the band has enough intrinsic songcraft skill to make mighty engaging pop records when it so chooses.

Barlow and Gaffney recorded the thirty-two-song **The Freed Man** in various living rooms and bedrooms from 1986 to 1988, which doesn't seem to have been a long enough span for the duo to go back and finish more than a handful of these half-baked fragments. Although their writing styles are radically different, they share a notion that a single clever idea—as contained in "Why Do You Cut Off Your Sleeves" and "I Love Me"—is enough to justify a song's release. The frustrating part is that, when developed—like Barlow's "Healthy Sick," later covered by Bettie Serveert—those ideas often turn out to be pretty good after all. To paraphrase an old TV commercial, it sounds like **The Freed Man** was more fun to make than it is to eat.

Although sonically indistinguishable from its predecessor, **Weed Forestin** is a considerably more distinct crystallization of the Sebadoh "thing." Barlow's gift for throwing off moving heartbreak lyrics—and his penchant for submerging them under layers of off-putting noise—makes songs like "Temporary Dream" and "Take My Hand" utterly riveting. Barlow serves notice of things to come on the feedback-mottled "Brand New Love" (later covered by Superchunk), which might be the most guileless, genuine love song produced in indie-rock's post-post-modern times. **The Freed Weed** compiles forty-one tracks from the two prior releases.

The addition of Jason Loewenstein—primarily as a drummer, but also a third songwriting voice—pushes Sebadoh precariously close to professional territory on **Sebadoh III,** a mid-fi recording that betrays some real effort on the members' part. As unhip as that might sound to Sebadoh purists, it allows Barlow to vent both undiluted bile (on "The Freed Pig," a pointed jibe at Mascis) and hippie-dude hopefulness ("Total Peace") with élan. Gaffney channels his aggro more effectively, which distinguishes powerful songs like "Violet Execution" (marked by some jarringly jagged guitar lines) and "As the World Dies, the Eyes of God Grow Bigger" from his previous tantrums. The pointless deconstruction of Johnny Mathis' "Wonderful! Wonderful!" aside, it's a stellar effort.

The silliness and indulgence were obviously only in temporary remission, as evidenced by the squawk-fest **Oven Is My Friend,** which only approaches listenability on the title track, an obscure hardcore cover. The eight-song **Rockin' the Forest** has its share of pointless noise digressions as well, but they're sandwiched between some outright rock songs, rife with dynamics and sagacious observations. The latter element is especially evident on "Gimme Indie Rock," which could function as a loving tribute to or a wry dismissal of the increasingly incestuous underground scene—slipperiness being the ironist's most important tool. **Sebadoh vs. Helmet,** which overlaps **Rockin'** slightly, adds covers of Nick Drake's "Pink Moon" and David Crosby's "Everybody's Been Burned," both of which emphasize Barlow's vulnerable vocal croak and surprisingly dexterous acoustic guitar playing. **Smash Your Head on the Punk Rock** is a twelve-song best-of covering the previous two releases.

By the time **Bubble & Scrape** was released, the strain between members was palpable, what with Gaffney's numerous sabbaticals and Barlow's spending more time on his solo Sentridoh project. Despite, or perhaps because of, the evident lack of communication, the album is Sebadoh's most urgent yet, with Barlow and the increasingly confident Loewenstein crafting rough-hewn pop gems, and Gaffney kicking dirt over everything in sight (on rants like "Elixir Is Zog"). Barlow's best efforts—like "Soul and Fire" and "Two Years Two Days"—could pass for bizarro-world Brill Building derivatives; fortunately, they, along with dark, acoustic Loewenstein compositions like "Happily Divided," dominate the disc.

Gaffney left—for good this time—before the recording of **Bakesale,** a comparatively slick recording that finds Barlow compensating for the noisemaker's departure by toughening up his own approach. While "Together or Alone" and "Not a Friend" are marked by his typical loner's melancholy, Barlow positively kicks out the jams on "License to Confuse." At the same time, Loewenstein, now ensconced in the bass slot (occasional collaborator Bob Fay takes over drum duties), assumes a heftier chunk of the songwriting. His tracks, while not terribly dissimilar to Barlow's, offer needed if subtle counterpoint. (Despite its title, **4 Song** contains "Rebound" and "Careful" as a two-tune preview of **Bakesale** and eight 4-track recordings by the new lineup.)

Barlow has made no secret of his contempt for standard music biz operations, refusing high-profile gigs whenever they're offered and continually subverting Sebadoh's poppiest material with sonic red herrings—which makes the Top 40 breakthrough he achieved with the similarly abstruse Folk Implosion (for the admittedly catchy "Natural One") all the more comical. A side project he's shared with cassette-underground stalwart John Davis, the Folk Implosion is only marginally distinguishable from recent Sebadoh releases in that Barlow's introversion has given way to a sort of wry worldview that still bears a certain mistrust of the world. The twenty-four-song eponymous British cassette (parts of which are reprised on both **The Electric Idiot** and **Take a Look Inside**) is both short and sharp, with surprising fidelity for a collection of home recordings. The same can be said of the five-hundred-pressed **Electric Idiot** EP, the contents of which got a second commercial life on the seven-song **Lou Barlow 50/50 John Davis** (aka **The Folk Implosion,** along with both sides of a '95 single).

Take a Look Inside . . . . . . the Folk Implosion is more ambitious than those releases, thanks in part to minor studio tinkering (on the reverb-laden "Blossom") and in part to snappy genre juxtapositions—like the Mersey-punk title track and the Lennonish "Slap Me." Yes, pothead silliness takes its toll on the Residents-styled pastiche "Sputnik's Down," but Barlow and Davis pack the twenty-two-minute, fourteen-song disc with enough good ideas to compensate. Although the insular Barlow seems like an exceedingly odd choice to provide a soundtrack for a movie about urban youth on sex-and-drug binges, his work on the *Kids* soundtrack (which also includes equally misplaced songs by Daniel Johnston) is fairly effective, if (aside from "Natural One") less than compelling—a charmingly subtle dance-pop variation on Barlow's usual bedsit romanticism.

Sentridoh is essentially Barlow's compost heap—an outlet for him to release the type of half-finished discards most artists would tape over. **Winning Losers** contains ten acoustic numbers, four of them from a cassette entitled **Losers**—you get the self-deprecating thematic idea. The Lou Barlow and Friends disc is leftovers from collaborative efforts with Fay and others. An endless array of cassettes—most of them on California's Shrimper imprint—compile snippet after snippet of one-take acoustic muddle. As the aptly titled **Most of the Worst and Some of the Best** implies, Barlow can't be bothered to differentiate between the two—or to tune his guitar even a little—so that his refusal to play by the rules becomes the product in itself. If this is art, give me product any time. [dss]

See also *Dinosaur Jr.*

KEVIN SECONDS/5′10″

See *7Seconds.*

SEED

ling (Mechanic/Giant) 1994

These Texans began as the Dig, but were forced to yield the moniker to some other faceless young band vying for four of those all-important *120 Minutes.* Seed got theirs with a nonsensical dayglo video for "Rapture"—a sweet, sun-drenched ditty that falls somewhere between Blind Melon and Boston, with shrill harmonies and a piston rhythm guitar riff. But once you get past the vocal similarities to Brad Delp (or was that Sib Hashian?), Seed doesn't add up to much more than the quartet's calculatingly understated photographs (standard-issue flowing manes and flannel for the back cover; thrift shop Edwardian for the booklet). This is album-rock for the post-alternative universe. Singer/bassist Chadwick Salls' lyrics drip with both flowery positivism and awkwardly dark religiosity, with one song ("Kids . . . This Is Fabulon") paying hip tribute to Katherine Dunn's novel *Geek Love.* The sound is a yeoman's mish-mash of '60s effluvia, '70s genericism, '80s heartland-grunge and '90s faux-funk weirdness. But in the year after **ling**'s release lots of bands had insinuating one-hits that were no less moronic than "Rapture." So take pity on Seed. They could have been Sponge. They could have been Better Than Ezra or Deep Blue Something. Perhaps it's some consolation that the other Dig didn't fare any better. [jc]

SEEFEEL

More Like Space EP (UK Too Pure) 1993
Pure, Impure (UK Too Pure) 1993
Quique (Too Pure/Astralwerks) 1994
Polyfusia (Too Pure/Astralwerks) 1994
Starethrough EP (UK Warp) 1994
Succor (UK Warp) 1995

DISJECTA

1.0 (UK Warp) 1995
Clean Pit & Lid (UK Warp) 1996

When London's Seefeel released its first EP in 1993, the quartet was one of the few bands using guitars as a primary instrument in creating largely textural pieces, more in line with the ambient sounds of contemporary electronic bands. As the band developed, it gradually grew out of its blissed-out, post–My Bloody Valentine cocoon and into an equally fertile electronic realm. The four songs on **More Like Space** glide and glimmer at an unhurried pace; the band molds guitar lines like taffy, looping sounds with a sequencer. The songs' airy structures and production might have let them float off into mid-air if it weren't for the viscous dub-influenced basslines, which rope tracks back to the inner stratosphere. While the nearly nine-minute title song and "Blue Easy Sleep" are essentially instrumental, "Time to Find Me (Come Inside)" showcases Sarah Peacock's wispy vocals, barely-there coos that mainly add texture. "Come Alive" is the only Seefeel track to feature the vocals, however subdued, of guitarist and chief songwriter Mark Clifford.

After the release of a new three-song 12-inch (which contains "Plainsong," a much more bubbly and overt song than its predecessors), the Aphex Twin remixed two different versions of "Time to Find Me," both of which are included on **Pure, Impure,** along with "Moodswing" and "Minky Starshine" (the two B-sides of the "Plainsong" 12-inch) and another Aphex remix. **Pure, Impure** and **More Like Space** were then repackaged in toto as **Polyfusia,** bringing America up to date with this impressive developing band.

Seefeel's first proper album, the seductive **Quique,** is an hour-long expansion of the same themes, with a subtle shift toward sound over substance. As the songs grow airier and Peacock's vocals become more an element than a lightpost, the rubbery basslines and looped guitar sounds, repeated until they form melodies, become the songs' primary glue. A reappearance of "Plainsong," the most vocal-heavy track here, joins the haunting and self-explanatory "Filter Dub," plus such near-ambient excursions as "Through You" and "Signals"—hints of the band's next sonic shift.

A label switch to top British electronic label Warp (home to the Aphex Twin) signaled the band's drift away from song structure toward inviting sonic wallpaper. Seefeel isn't quite wall decoration with the **Starethrough** EP. The distance between now lead-heavy basslines and the airy snippets of Peacock's vocals is considerably thinner, however; on the title cut, the vocals and Clifford's inventive guitar permutations hang like a fog over the thick rhythms. "Spangle" stands among Seefeel's finest cuts, the same components coalescing into a compelling whole and Peacock's vocals adding a Cocteau Twins–like touch, while the barely-there "Lux 1" foreshadows the spareness of the group's next endeavor.

The vocals on **Succor,** another double-album-length project, are down to a minor element, the looped guitar sounds are stretched out over time and space (words are totally out of the picture); even the basslines are diluted. What remains are electronic rhythm patterns and subtly repeated bits of sound, which gel into an airy representation of the band's primary elements but don't achieve the same potency as the band's other CDs. "Fracture" and "Ruby-Ha" eventually emerge as memorable songs; so does "Rex," whose sharper techno beats and quicker pace set it apart.

In 1995, leaving open the question of whether Seefeel would still record together, Clifford began recording his own material under the name Disjecta, while the other three began collaborating as Scala. The **1.0** CD (also called **Looking for Snags**), which collects two instrumental 12-inch EPs, **Looking for Snags 1** and **2,** furthers Clifford's movement away from warm, guitar-generated sounds and vocals, and toward colder electronics. He's most successful when he builds repetitive refrains into subliminal hooks, as on "K-Bop" and "Skeeze," or attempts to create a mood ("Looking for Snags"), but his mastery of the techniques isn't adequate for the songs to really stick; without basslines or vocals, much of it amounts to little more than nifty background music. [la]

SELECTER

Too Much Pressure (Chrysalis) 1980
Celebrate the Bullet (Chrysalis) 1981
Selected Selecter Selections (Chrysalis) 1989

Out on the Streets: Live in London (Triple X) 1992
The Happy Album (Triple X) 1994
Hairspray (Triple X) 1995
Back Out on the Streets (Triple X) 1996

Fluked into existence by an eponymous instrumental used as the B-side of the Specials' debut single in 1979, the Selecter has proven to be a durable survivor of the Coventry-based 2-Tone scene. The original group—a predominately Caribbean-rooted septet led by English guitarist Neol Davies and fronted by vocalist Pauline Black (née Vickers)—made a brilliant debut album and a disappointing followup, then collapsed as the British ska revival's moment of glory came to an end. (The 1989 **Selected Selecter Selections** compilation draws, more or less, the nine best songs from the first LP and the five best from the second.) The members splintered into other musical ventures, with only Black (who went solo, at one point partnered with ex-Specials/Fun Boy Three Neville Staples and Lynval Golding) seemingly certain of a real career future.

But the latter-day bluebeat refuses to die, and the Selecter returned to action with a credible live album from a '91 reunion tour. The efficient quintet of Black, Davies and three new sidemen plays the old Selecter tunes with less than manic energy but credible fealty to the originals. Betraying a tinge of embarrassment amid the enthusiasm, Black introduces "Three Minute Hero" by saying "This one's for us."

The Happy Album, an all-new studio effort, introduces a reconfigured band. Davies is out, vocalist Arthur "Gaps" Hendrickson, whose verbal jousts with Black back in the day gave the Selecter a lot of its bustling excitement, is in; the core quartet contains Black (fussing over a faux-ragamuffin accent) and two holdovers from the live album: bassist Nick Welsh, who co-wrote and co-produced, and keyboard player Martin Stewart. Playing a modern-sounding mixture of new originals and reggae covers (Toots Hibbert's "Sweet and Dandy," Delroy Wilson's "I Want Justice"), the Selecter keeps ska as its boppy touchstone, although occasionally slowing it down to a reggae strut, while using samples, electronics, contemporary rhythms and broader songwriting to roughly parallel for the memory of 2-Tone what Big Audio Dynamite did for punk. Burdened by a social conscience ("California Screaming" is about, among other things, Rodney King; the anti-war "Copasetic" and "Mother Knows Best" veil their particular issues in obscure detail), **The Happy Album** is anything but, and that's to its credit.

The same mob made **Hairspray,** but you'd never know it from the catchy chorus of "My Perfect World," which leads it off, or the cornball pot-centric version of Bob Dylan's "Rainy Day Women #12 & #35" that curls up near the end. In between, the Selecter returns to a mild-mannered, occasionally silly ("Chocolate Whip") version of its roots, clinging to the familiar peppy keyboard, bass, guitar and snare syncopation of ska but adding giddy new wave power-pop elements and sunny, lightweight (save for the misery epic "Then She Did") lyrics. The sound suggests some 1980 band—the Yachts, perhaps, or the Go-Go's—that has just happened onto some old Skatalites records. A surprising step backward, to be sure, but the harmlessly bizarre blend of elements (including, on a cover of Nancy Sinatra's "Sugar Town," sessioneer B. J. Cole's pedal steel) is surprisingly delightful. **Back Out on the Streets** is a compilation, with several new items, of the band's three '90s albums [tr]

See also *TPRG.*

SENSE FIELD

Sense Field EP (Run H20) 1991
Premonitions (Run H20) 1992
Killed for Less (Revelation) 1994
Sense Field (Revelation) 1994
Building (Revelation) 1996

Although formed three thousand miles away in Southern California, Sense Field—singer Jonathan Bunch, guitarist Chris Evenson, drummer Scott McPherson, guitarist Rodney Sellars and bassist John "Slow Johnny" Stockberger—conceptually grew out of New York's '80s hardcore scene, crafting a thoughtful sound built on progressive and diverse musical ideas, superb chops and shared personal conviction. The band's songs are populated by easy-to-identify-with characters—dissatisfied romantics, reflective dreamers, challenged ideologues—whose lofty goals and impassioned thoughts add righteous majesty to the quintet's dramatic music. A variety of aural ingredients—snappy pop melodies and vocal harmonies, Pink Floyd–inspired soundscapes, sweeping AOR pomp and polish and enough hardcore edge and urgency to make it all stimulating—and an often-startling use of dynamic morphing makes the band's albums enticing and provocative.

Sense Field, released shortly after **Killed for Less,** repackages the band's two self-released EPs, adding two previously unreleased songs ("Greater Than" and "First Things First"). The pretty Lennonesque melody of "Dreams" and the reached-promised-land of "Found You" (which was rerecorded and included on **Killed for Less**) are among the highlights.

Packaged handsomely with paintings of elegant ballroom dancing scenes by Gavin Oglesby, **Killed for Less** delivers myriad influences whipped by the band's savvy inventions. Smart vocal harmonies give way to sucker-punch howls from Bunch; lulling acoustic strains are often met by fiery, anxious riffs. There's rarely a dull moment. The title track is both inspirational ("now I can move you without pushing you") and downright frightening ("heaven help me, I've killed them, killed them, killed for less"), while "Voice" (another song recut from **Sense Field**) may be the least offensive power ballad since Led Zeppelin's "D'yer Maker."

Sense Field subsequently signed with Warner Bros., thereby ending its indie career. **Building,** although initially released by Revelation, was distributed and eventually rereleased by the band's new corporate home. [tja]

SENSELESS THINGS

Postcard C. V. (UK Way Cool) 1989
Is It Too Late EP (UK Decoy) 1990
Can't Do Anything EP (UK Decoy) 1990
The First of Too Many (Epic) 1991
Empire of the Senseless (UK Epic) 1993
Peel Sessions (Strange Fruit/Dutch East India Trading) 1994

Young, fresh-faced and refreshingly unaffected, the Senseless Things bounded out of the London suburb of Twickenham in the late '80s. Mark Keds' willowy lead vocals, Ben Harding's aggressive but melodic guitar work and Cass Browne's energetic scattershot drumming (bassist Morgan Nicholls completes the quartet) provided an entertaining one-two punch, borrowing from poppy UK punk bands like the Buzzcocks as well as the grittier American punk'n'roll of the Replacements.

The group enjoyed a successful five-year run in the UK, with a ten-song debut LP, a string of hit singles and EPs (produced by Jon Langford) and regular appearances at England's big summer festivals. Senseless Things signed to Epic worldwide at the height of its popularity in 1991 but were dropped in America after only one release, the ironically titled **The First of Too Many.** The album has more than its share of bouncy melodies, sweet harmonies and hummable hooks, especially on tracks like the effervescent "Everybody's Gone," but Americans were diving headlong into grunge that year and not terribly interested in what the UK had on offer. The Sensies' lyrics were probably too British for export anyway; songs like "Got It at the Delmar" and "Fishing at Tescos" were huge hit singles at home but the lyrics made little sense to American ears.

Fans looking for a more comprehensive view of the band's career might want to check out their **Peel Sessions** disc, which chronicles three appearances on John Peel's BBC program. The first four cuts, from March 1988, capture the early, punkier Sensies, with a raw, stripped-down sound. The second session (February 1990) catches the band at its peak, brightly polished tracks like "Is It Too Late" and "Tell Me What's on Your Mind" brimming with criss-crossing harmony backup vocals and zingy power riffs. The final session, from October 1993, finds the band in a more somber mood. The songs are moodier, the tempos less manic. None of the dozen songs on the **Peel Sessions** disc appear on **The First of Too Many.** The Senseless Things' final album, **Empire of the Senseless,** was never released in the US; the group disbanded in 1995. [jt]

See also *Eat.*

SENTRIDOH

See *Sebadoh.*

ERICK SERMON

See *EPMD.*

SETTERS

See *Silos.*

BRIAN SETZER

The Knife Feels Like Justice (EMI America) 1986
Live Nude Guitars (EMI Manhattan) 1988

BRIAN SETZER ORCHESTRA

The Brian Setzer Orchestra (Hollywood) 1994
Guitar Slinger (Interscope) 1996

Having evidenced grand stylistic ambition on his two extracurricular solo albums (the first is a nifty and accomplished grab-bag; **Live Nude Guitars** is a sleazy must-to-avoid), Long Island singer/guitarist Brian Setzer put down the Stray Cats (perhaps for good) in the early '90s and let his musical dreams blossom, ambitiously reversing into a '40s future of swing, crooner pop and jump blues. Setting his wayback machine for the pre-rock era when volume was a function of orchestra size not amplification, Setzer assembled a brassy big band (the seventeen-strong company first toured, complete with monogrammed music stands, in '93) and set about recording **The Brian Setzer Orchestra,** an offbeat, entertaining album of standards and his typically seamless original recreations.

Setzer's non-parochial sensibilities allow him to navigate hairpin turns, directing the company from a Sinatra-esque creation like "September Skies" (a new song your grandmother will swear she remembers from the war) into a theatrical rendition of Vince Taylor's rocking "Brand New Cadillac," a lavish Al Jolson toe-tapper ("There's a Rainbow 'Round My Shoulder") into a jazzed-up "Route 66," without causing any calamitous damage. As Carl Perkins' "Your True Love" (1957) segues into "A Nightingale Sang in Berkeley Square" (a 1940 song also done by Bobby Darin), Setzer uses his past identity and unabashedly dated arrangements to leapfrog decades and make the transitions slide like a trombone. While Setzer is unlikely to challenge Mel Tormé in the smoothie stakes, the pompadoured tattoo canvas handles the diverse material with his usual cocky aplomb and skill and plays tons of superlative—if gratuitously flashy and sometimes ill-placed—guitar.

With Phil Ramone producing and Joe Strummer contributing the lyrics to "Ghost Radio" and "Sammy Davis City," **Guitar Slinger** improves substantially on the debut. Brassier and bolder, with fewer ballads and more of a rock'n'roll attack at its core, the album includes a version of the Stray Cats' old "Rumble in Brighton" and a not-quite-dramatic-enough take on 1962's "Town Without Pity" as well as such time-travel originals as "Hey, Louis Prima" and "The Man With the Magic Touch," a tribute to Count Basie. In the hands of an artist with less skill, knowledge or devotion to his musical ideals, this kind of endeavor could be a musty, laughable show-and-tell; with Setzer waving the magic wand, **Guitar Slinger** trains a telescope at long-gone sounds and projects them into the present with imagination and excitement. [i]

See also *TPRG.*

SEVEN MARY THREE

Churn (5 Spot) 1994
American Standard (Mammoth/Atlantic) 1995

A derivative imitation of an unoriginal group, Seven Mary Three further dilutes the tincture of generic alternative angst on its major-label debut, **American Standard.** Formed at college in Virginia but primarily based in Orlando, Florida, the quartet redoes the effective Live gimmick of mixing Pearl Jam's gutbusting ultra-passion with the tremulous folky roots literacy of early R.E.M. Behind Jason Ross, a Tom Waitsy bellower with serious Eddie Vedder pretensions, guitarist Jason Pollock shifts easily from roaring aggression to sensitive balladry; the muscular rhythm section of Casey Daniel (bass) and Giti Khalsa (drums) follows suit. The songs on **American Standard** (all but two remade from the self-released **Churn** CD) deal with relationships ("Cumbersome"), religion ("Devil Boy," the record's only memorable number), guilt ("Lame") and the rest of it ("Water's Edge," "Favorite Dog") with over-dramatic bombast, blowing every incidental adolescent emotion into a monumental cataclysm of overpowering desperation. For those caught in the time of life when too much is never enough, a flaming cocktail of this steroid awfulness is probably the perfect elixir, but that pretty much rules out **American Standard** for everyone else. [i]

7SECONDS

Socially Fucked Up [tape] (Vicious Scam) 1981
3 Chord Politics [tape] (Vicious Scam) 1981
Skin, Brains and Guts EP7 (Alternative Tentacles) 1982
Committed for Life EP7 (Squirtdown) 1983
The Crew (Better Youth Organization) 1984
Walk Together, Rock Together (Positive Force/BYO) 1985
Blasts From the Past EP7 (Positive Force) 1985
New Wind (Positive Force/BYO) 1986
Praise EP (Positive Force/BYO) 1987
Live! One Plus One (Positive Force/Giant) 1987
Ourselves (Restless) 1988
Soulforce Revolution (Restless) 1989
Old School (Headhunter/Cargo) 1991
Out the Shizzy (Headhunter/Cargo) 1993
alt.music.hardcore (Headhunter/Cargo) 1995
The Music, The Message (Immortal/Epic) 1995

JACKSHIT

Hicktown EP (Squirtdown) 1984

DROP ACID

Making God Smile (Restless) 1991
46th & Teeth E.P. EP (Headhunter/Cargo) 1992

KEVIN SECONDS/5′10″

Rodney, Reggie, Emily. (Earth Music/Cargo) 1994

Unlike most of rock's commercial explosions, the 1994 success of Green Day didn't set off a slamjump of bandwagon dancers. What did happen was that all the bands that had labored in punk-pop obscurity far longer than the East Bay bombers got a free recharge and the opportunity to throw their hats in a newly green-lined ring. Among the many reliable outfits receiving a well-deserved break in the major label goldrush was 7Seconds, the fifteen-year obsession of singer/guitarist Kevin Seconds (Marvelli), his bass-playing brother Steve Youth and (for nearly as long) drummer Troy Mowat. Formed in 1980 as a hardcor(e)dinary quartet in Reno, Nevada, 7Seconds relocated to Sacramento, California, by decade's end—by which point the group (occasionally with second guitarist Bobby Adams expanding the unstable lineup) had developed its catchy melodicism and rhythmic diversity to match the charging rock energy and high-minded straight-edge philosophy. (Jackshit was Steve Youth's Reno side band.)

The three early 7-inches (the nine-song **Skin, Brains and Guts,** the seven-song **Committed for Life** and half of the four-song **Blasts From the Past**) compiled on **alt.music.hardcore** are big on the righteousness ("Racism Sucks," "Anti-Klan," "Drug Control") but equally generic in their adolescent hardcore rush. **Old School** (a compilation of singles and other tracks recorded in the early to mid-'80s, including two other **Blasts From the Past** plus a running-speed "These Boots Are Made for Walking") is likewise blunt and direct. The part-studio/part-live (there's a fun concert cover of Nena's "99 Red Balloons" and a bunch of the EP songs) **Walk Together, Rock Together,** however, demonstrates an early interest in slowing things down and tuning them up along positive Clash/Pistols lines. Recorded at two Sacramento shows two years later, the badly mixed and thin-sounding **Live! One Plus One** contains another rendition of "99 Red Balloons" as well as such moralist boulders as "You Live and Die for Freedom" and "Regress, No Way!" Demonstrating new rhythmic variety, "The Save Ourselves" cuts a funk figure, while "Walk Together, Rock Together" gets an unexpected reggae accent. **Ourselves,** recorded as a quartet, and the three-man **Soulforce Revolution** are both state-of-the-art: intelligent lyrics of personal and political consequence, moderately powerful singing, buzzing guitars and brisk tempos.

Kevin Seconds then took a time-out in Drop Acid, a lumbering rock trio with a different rhythm section; the unappealing **Making God Smile** presents a tougher rock beast, mixing in distant peals of Seattle thunder, stutter-beat drumming, dirgey metal and arena-guitar bigness, none of which suit his voice or his songwriting. "Bluesy" and the bonus track "Knew," which could be 7Seconds numbers and are the best things here, mainly sound out of place. It took the coherent second dose, with three other sidemen, to finally reveal the limber modern rock he had in mind. The four-songs-and-some-phone-messages **46th & Teeth** doesn't play coy with its ambitions (beyond the musclebound bottom and angry lyrics, "Tiny Paws" even has the disconnected sound of a cheering crowd); truly, Kevin Seconds has as much right to be Stone Chain Danzig as anyone.

Kevin's other side project, a trio named 5'10", veers in the opposite direction. Although the rhythm guitar playing on the bass-free **Rodney, Reggie, Emily.** is loud and fuzzy, the rudimentary strumming, simple drumming (by Brent Spain, of Drop Acid at the time of **Making God Smile**) and friendly singing make the record either a peppy set of song demos or a strange cousin to the small-pop minimalism of bands like Beat Happening. The melodic material is intimate and conversational, giving oblique, engaging twists to such prosaic concerns as friends, family, grade school and orgasms. (For live appearances, 5'10" became a trio with the addition of ex–Tiger Trap bassist Jen Braun.)

Meanwhile, back at the ranch, 7Seconds ended a four-year gap in 1993 and returned to album action with the great **Out the Shizzy,** an engaging, accessible and original melodic punk-pop diversion. Although Mowat plays the vari-speed numbers like he's being paid by the stick hit, the twin-guitar attack paves it all into a smoothly buzzing ride. Occasionally dispirited or pained lyrics don't diminish the affability or pacifism of Kevin's singing; in "Weak Link," he rejects the scene's baser attitudes: "The music, its purpose/Not here to make ya hateful." A great leap forward.

With that, the band moved on to its post-alternative phase. Signed to a major label for the first time, 7Seconds retreated to a more determinedly punk sound and did its heritage proud on **The Music, The Message.** In a tight, tuneful rush, the group looks inward and outward in a mixed celebration of what it is (grown-up), how it got there and how Kevin feels about that—all at a 90 mph backbeat. His economical songs acknowledge the band's history ("I Can Remember") and enemies ("Get a Different Life," "Such & Such," "First Ya Told Us"), as well as his own maturity ("See You Tomorrow," "Punk Rock Teeth") and lifetime feelings about rock'n'roll ("The Music, The Message," "See You Tomorrow"). Maybe this is not how 7Seconds wants to be perceived, but safeguarding a timeless sound makes this stimulating, likable album positively wholesome. [i]

7 YEAR BITCH

7 Year Bitch EP10 (C/Z) 1992
Sick 'Em (C/Z) 1992
¡Viva Zapata! (C/Z) 1994
Gato Negro (Atlantic) 1996

The release of 7 Year Bitch's debut coincided both with the Seattle grunge frenzy and with one of the media's periodic women-in-rock fixations. Even so, the band's spartan punk gave voice—with remarkable force and poise—to a complicated agenda all its own. Taking sonic inspiration from the Runaways (and, by extension, Joan Jett), the quartet wrote songs of unabashed desire like "In Lust You Trust" *and* gave voice to the blunt feminism of "Dead Men Don't Rape." Along with the Gits, 7YB had been part of the Rathouse collective, which made instruments and recording facilities available. Released after the death of guitarist Stefanie Sargent by heroin misadventure, **Sick 'Em**—a complete collection of the band's singles, compilation tracks and the contents of the eponymous six-song 10-inch picture disc—is a fairly primitive and monochromatic burst of punk rage. Male musicians groused that the band's comparatively rudimentary grasp of their instruments was being ignored by critics simply because they were girls. Not quite. Even at her most tentative, vocalist Selene Vigil already had real star quality on stage; bassist Elizabeth Davis and drummer Valerie Agnew may not have been especially adroit, but they got the job done. Taken in small doses, the primitive songs are quite powerful.

Named not for the Mexican revolutionary but for Mia Zapata, the murdered lead singer of the Gits, **¡Viva Zapata!** marks the recorded arrival of Roisin Dunne on guitar. Produced by the ubiquitous Jack Endino, the album is cleaner and more polished than its predecessor. It is also a much darker—though less angry—album. Songs range from "M.I.A." and "Rock a Bye" (written to departed friends) to a cover of Jim Carroll's "It's Too Late," and the quieter post-lust "Damn Good and Well" (with the refrain "don't let your emotions get in the way of a really good time"). "Icy Blue," the best song of the set, neatly merges the band's personal and political impulses.

7 Year Bitch then found its way to the majors, though there was predictable friction about how much their sound should change for **Gato Negro.** In the end, co-producer (with the band) Billy Anderson played it straight down the middle, resulting in the group's most varied, accomplished and coherent outing. Instrumental competence is no longer open to question, and Vigil's vocals don't need brute force to convey menace. With a nifty occasional resemblance to the knotted power of Rollins Band, great songs like "24,900 Miles per Hour" and "Miss Understood" also make it plain the band's personal and political personae were not weakened in the process. [ga]

SEX CLARK FIVE

Neita Grew Up Last Night EP7 (Records to Russia) 1987
Strum & Drum! (Records to Russia) 1987 (Beehive Rebellion) 1996
Battle of Sex Clark Five (Bloodmoney/Skyclad) 1989
Ketchup If You Can EP7 (Records to Russia) 1990
Antedium (Skyclad) 1993

The totally unique (not to mention hard-to-define and often downright weird) Sex Clark Five is a quartet from Huntsville, Alabama. The strangely intoxicating **Strum & Drum!** is a catchy mélange of rapidly strummed guitars, airy, Shoesy vocals (courtesy of guitarist/songwriter James Butler and bassist Joy Johnson) and songs (twenty of 'em!) that typically clock in under two minutes. Often goofy ("If You See Her With Me Let Me Know"), sometimes straightforward ("Faith"— definitely not the George Michael tune) and always intriguing, **Strum & Drum!** is a near-classic first step. (In early 1996, Beehive Rebellion put **Strum & Drum!** on CD with fourteen bonus tracks, including the prior **Neita Grew Up Last Night** EP, as well as flexi-disc tracks and a previously unreleased cover of the Byrds' "Have You Seen Her Face."

Battle of Sex Clark Five is not quite as wonderful as the debut, mainly due to a paucity of memorable melodies. Butler's lyrics veer toward infuriating obtuseness or dull political preoccupations ("The Wermacht's Lament," "Sock Hopra"); the band often seems to be strumming and drumming aimlessly. Still, the giddy "I'm a Fool With You," the acoustic punk of "Accelerator" and the nutty, autobiographical "Ballad of Sex Clark Five" (sung by Johnson) are all stellar.

Antedium continues the SC5's slow slide, with few worthy tracks among the two dozen offered. The haunting "Old World Girl," the alluring "Cold and Gray," the garagey "Strum & Drum!" and the high-speed wackiness of "Knights of Carumba" are all fine, but some songs are simply dull ("Civil War" and the twenty-three-second "Ketchup If You Can^2," a different song from the noise-instrumental title track of the 1990 four-song red 7-inch, are prime offenders). The band does get extra points, though, for slyly appropriating the opening riff to "Helter Skelter" on "Curley Shuttle Reprise." Best song title honors: a tie between "I Got Use of My Legs" and "America Under the Mongol Yoke Prelude." [jmb]

RON SEXSMITH AND THE UNCOOL

Grand Opera Lane [tape] (Can. no label) 1991

RON SEXSMITH

Ron Sexsmith (Interscope/Atlantic) 1995

No singer/songwriter of this decade has made an album anywhere near as gorgeous as the almost-perfect debut by Canada's sublimely gifted Ron Sexsmith, who worked as a messenger in Toronto before devoting himself to music. Like Ray Davies, Sexsmith is an unpretentiously distinctive observer of life's usual things—romance, parenthood, places, seasons. And like Tim Hardin's, his lived-in voice is a deeply affecting instrument, resonating with heartbreaking tenderness. Each wavery note he sings on this gentle masterpiece conveys a wealth of emotions, to which producer Mitchell Froom, outdoing himself, adds sparing instrumentation—a subtle rhythm section, occasional keyboards and a bit of cello behind Sexsmith's skillfully picked acoustic guitar—that suits the diverse tenors of these songs. Able to accommodate crisp rock (the Kinksy "Summer Blowin' Town" and the rollicking "First Chance I Get"), Sexsmith and Froom also manage a mild bit of gumbo ("In Place of You") and swoony classic pop ("Wastin' Time").

Perhaps two of the dozen originals (joining a sterling cover of Leonard Cohen's "Heart With No Companion" and an atmospherically adjusted second version of "There's a Rhythm" produced by Daniel Lanois) could have been omitted; the rest are exquisite examples of Sexsmith's creative magic. The deliberate "Lebanon, Tennessee" playfully imagines and praises a homey place the native of a small Ontario town might like to live, while "Speaking With the Angel" brings throat-tightening compassion to the threat of interference with infancy's innocence: "Would you poison him with prejudice from the moment of his birth . . . He that never lays blame, he don't even know his name." "Secret Heart," "In Place of You" and "Words We Never Use" delve into the dark mysteries of loving and come up on the right side of a good thing; "Galbraith Street" reminisces about an old neighborhood and the price of maturity. An uncanny album of sweet tears and warm smiles, **Ron Sexsmith** is a must-hear.

The prior self-released cassette sounds very different: it's a concerted attempt to gumbo up syncopated rhythms and spark up what could fairly be described as a small-scale northern John Hiatt vibe. Here, Sexsmith is energetically backed by a piano-playing bassist and a drummer (both of whom add backing vocals), with a stack of friends—including producer Bob Wiseman—intruding on his compassionate (if melodically imprecise) voice with generous but unnecessary horns and guitars. For all the mistreatment of songs (whose jumble level seems to be in indirect proportion to compositional potency), there's plenty of evidence of what was to come, even beyond the roomy acoustic rendition of "Speaking With the Angel," the only song to be carried forward. The similarly intimate "Trains," the joyous romantic declaration of "In This Love" and the country sweetness of "Every Word of It" all shine with the raw ingredients **Ron Sexsmith** burnished to such glowing power. [i]

SF SEALS

See *Barbara Manning.*

SHADOWLAND

See *further.*

SHADOW PROJECT

See *Christian Death.*

SHADOWY MEN ON A SHADOWY PLANET

Savvy Show Stoppers (UK Glass) 1988 (Jetpac/Cargo) 1990
Dim the Lights, Chill the Ham (Jetpac/Cargo) 1991
Sport Fishin': The Lure of the Bait, The Luck of the Hook (Jetpac/Cargo) 1993

Filed a couple of discs down from the Shadows and a little closer to the Residents than might be safe for small children, Toronto's Shadowy Men on a Shadowy Planet do the instrumental guitar combo thing in a somewhat different kitchen from Britain's four-decades-young Fender twangers. The trio of Brian Connelly (guitar), Don Pyle (drums) and Reid Diamond (bass) has been cranking out cagey and catchy pieces of twisted reverb-splat invention with delightfully lurid pop culture titles since 1985, although most of the group's fame owes to its day job, making the soundtrack noises for TV's Kids in the Hall. That zesty little mock-western piece that runs under the show's credits is "Having an Average Weekend," a track from the Shadowy Men's first single, compiled along with the contents of four other self-released 7-inches on the chewy and delicious **Savvy Show Stoppers.** The long-playing debut also contains a brief and charming radio play (with music) by cartoonist Charles Burns ("Big Baby"), a rare organ interlude (the apparently live but you never can tell "You Spin Me Round '86") and "Run Chicken Run," hysterical scratchings in Link Wray's barnyard. The more organized and slightly less daft **Dim the Lights, Chill the Ham** contains "Exit From Vince Lombardi High School," "Ben Hur Picked off in a Gazebo" and "Who Painted Whistler's Mother." Incrementally more diverse in its creative ambitions, the Steve Albini–engineered **Sport Fishin'** boasts such catches as the pluckin'/chanted "Fortune Tellin' Chicken," the economical "They Don't Call Them Chihuahuas Anymore," the properly noirish "Spy School" and the scrabbly funk of "We're Not a Fucking Surf Band."

Occasionally prone to interjecting exclamatory voices to chant a title like the second album's "5 American 6 Canadian" and not above whistling or putting silliness from bargain bin vinyl finds at the beginnings of numbers, Shadowy Men mix their music (mostly original, but with a cover here and there) around enough to defy easy pigeonholing: just when the salt air threatens to become a scenery fixture, they trot out something from an inland clime, or step on the gas for a decidedly non-retro spot of acceleration. Unfailingly enjoyable, gummily consistent and as atmospheric as two weeks in a submarine, Shadowy Men are truly the instrumental kings of the Great White North.

Or were. Don Pyle and Reid Diamond, joined by guitarist Dallas Good and Fifth Column bassist Beverly Breckenridge, subsequently formed Phono-Comb in collaboration with Jad Fair and released a debut album, **Fresh Gasoline** (Touch and Go), on its own in '96. [i]

See also *B-52's, Half Japanese.*

SHADY

See *Mercury Rev.*

SHAKUHACHI SURPRISE

See Mount Shasta.

SHAMPOO

We Are Shampoo (UK Food) 1994 (Food/IRS) 1995

Britain's pop machine demands a diverse diet, but one staple of the regimen is colorful rock'n'roll bubblegum, disposable fluff that feeds on its own silliness and disappears before becoming a real bore. As if the '70s glam era were some cultural vampire in need of regular refreshment, young English blood—carefully refined to remove all traces of seriousness—is periodically offered up to feed the giddy chart maw. Some of the human sacrifices have enough chewy musical meat on their bones to justify the overbearing attitude that inevitably comes with being overnight sensations; others lack the conceptual qualities needed to avoid self-destruction.

Jacqui and Carrie, the two self-declared "megababes . . . blonde-haired teenaged terminators" of Shampoo, come on like a junior *Absolutely Fabulous,* reveling in their obnoxious wild youth as manifest destiny. Turning "who gives a fuck?" into maddeningly good entertainment, the pair sports thick London accents, colorful get-ups and more bratty who-me? hubris than Alicia Silverstone in *Clueless.* Quietly aided by songwriter Lawrence Hayward (Felt/Denim) and skilled studio handlers who truly know how to balance thick guitar power with efficient synthesizer bop, they nick sonic signatures from Bananarama, Sweet, Alice Cooper, Bryan Adams and the Troggs with impunity. Meanwhile, they slag off Whitney Houston and Mariah Carey (in "Dirty Old Love Song"), throw up kebabs (in "Shiny Black Taxi Cab") and dismiss supermodels, hippie chicks and riot grrrls with blasé indifference. They're probably wretched to be around, but from the safety of a CD it's easy to endorse the language-busting title of "Viva la Megababes." [i]

SHAMS

Quilt (Matador) 1991
Sedusia EP (Matador) 1993

BIGGEST SQUARE THING

A Square Thing's Prerogative EP7 (Butt Rag) 1989

AMY RIGBY

Diary of a Mod Housewife (Koch) 1996

The New York trio of Sue Garner, Amy McMahon Rigby and Amanda Uprichard had some beautiful songs but occasionally sold short their greatest asset: casually spectacular, country-based three-part harmonies. All the Shams really needed backing them up were Rigby and Garner's graceful, unobtrusive acoustic guitar and bass playing—their voices were the rightful stars of the show.

Quilt finds the band mostly sharing the instrumental spotlight with Robert Quine, Lenny Kaye and ex-dB's drummer Will Rigby; though the guests play tastefully, the extra instruments still sometimes get in the way of the simplicity of Amy Rigby's songs. The album's highlight is a rerecording of the first Shams single, 1989's "Only a Dream," but there are lots of other great moments; the beautifully constructed frustrated-love songs "Stuck Here on the Ground" and "Watching the Grass Grow" would be on oldies radio every eight hours if they'd only been recorded twenty years earlier. **Quilt** also has a drastic rearrangement of Richard Hell's "Time" (with Hell's old bandmate Quine adding a little lead guitar), Uprichard's pleasant "Ice Tea" and an adorable a cappella novelty, "File Clerk Blues."

The three-song **Sedusia** is something of a letdown. Garner's "Continuous Play" is lovely, but "Voices in My Head" drags on and on and the live favorite "Love Me With Your Mind" (which rhymes "thrill" with "ce-re-be-rill") gets cheesy moans, synth-drums and—shades of Bananarama—unison singing. Following **Sedusia,** the Shams began work on a second full-length album, but broke up before it could be completed.

The Biggest Square Thing, Garner's experimental duo-plus-guests with singer/guitarist Ruth Peyser, released one 7-inch: three songs that barely total five minutes. An edgy, no wave–like record that's interesting though too short to be substantial, it couldn't sound less like the Shams. Garner went on to form Run On with former Fish & Roses bandmate Rick Brown. Rigby became a solo artist, releasing an appealing album in 1996. [ddw]

See also *Run On.*

SHAPIR-O' RAMA

See *When People Were Shorter and Lived Near the Water.*

ELLIOTT SHARP

Hara (Zoar) 1977
Resonance (Zoar) 1979
Rhythms and Blues (Zoar) 1980
ISM (Zoar) 1981
I/S/M:R (Zoar) 1982
Nots (UK Glass) 1982 (Ger. Atonal) 1992
(T)here (Zoar) 1983
Live in Tokyo [tape] (Zoar) 1985
Virtual Stance (Ger. Dossier) 1986
In the Land of the Yahoos (SST) 1987
K!L!A!V! (Newport Classic) 1990
Beneath the Valley of the Ultra-Yahoos (Sulphur/Silent) 1992
Westwerk (Ger. Ear-Rational) 1993
Terraplane (Homestead) 1994
'Dyners Club (Sw. Intakt) 1994
Tectonics (Ger. Atonal) 1995
Arc 1: I/S/M 1980–1983 (Atavistic) 1996

ELLIOTT SHARP/CARBON

Carbon (Atonal) 1984
Marco Polo's Argali/Carbon: Six Songs (Ger. Dossier) 1985
Fractal (Ger. Dossier) 1986
Larynx (SST) 1988
Monster Curve (SST) 1989
Sili/Contemp/Tation (Ear-Rational) 1990
Datacide (Enemy) 1990
Tocsin (Enemy) 1992
Truthtable (Homestead) 1993
Autoboot (no label) 1993
Amusia (Atavistic) 1994
Interference (Atavistic) 1995

ELLIOTT SHARP/ORCHESTRA CARBON

Abstract Repressionism: 1990–99 (Can. Les Disques Victo) 1992

ELLIOTT SHARP AND THE SOLDIER STRING QUARTET

Tessalation Row (SST) 1987
Hammer, Anvil, Stirrup (SST) 1989
Twistmap (Ger. Ear-Rational) 1991
Cryptid Fragments (Extreme) 1993

SEMANTICS

Semantics (Rift) 1985
Bone of Contention (SST) 1987

BOOTSTRAPPERS

Bootstrappers (New Alliance) 1990
Garbage In=Garbage Out (Ger. Atonal) 1992

BACHIR ATTAR AND ELLIOTT SHARP

In New York (Enemy) 1990

BOODLERS

Boodlers (Cavity Search) 1994

ELLIOTT SHARP/ZEENA PARKINS

Psycho Acoustic (Can. Les Disques Victo) 1995

HOOSGOW

Mighty (Homestead) 1996

There aren't many musicians who need so many different band names under which to work. But Elliott Sharp has that many different ideas, sounds and styles swirling in his clean-shaven head. And, at the expense of a linear career that could earn him bigger bucks or notoriety, he has explored them all. Sharp is a composer, improviser, instrument inventor and mathematician able to play clarinet, saxophone, guitar, bass, sampler, piano, computer and instruments of his own creation—like the slab, pantar and violinoid. Since 1979, he has been based in Manhattan, making a name for himself as a freelance avant-gardist willing to collaborate with anyone, from Pere Ubu to the Kronos Quartet, and try anything, from jungle dance music to the blues to compositions based on fractals and the Fibonacci number series.

Since the start of the '90s, Sharp has put an end to a dozen side projects and started a dozen more, increasing, along the way, the political content of his music and his kinship to experimental dance music. Where Carbon was a vehicle for some of Sharp's noisiest, densest, longest experiments in the '80s, it began transforming into a sort of industrial metal band on **Datacide** and solidified, for the first time ever, its lineup (as a quintet) on **Tocsin.** (The Orchestra Carbon album **Abstract Repressionism: 1990–99,** a seven-movement, hour-long composition, offers a glimpse into the band's past.)

On the angrier **Truthtable** and **Amusia** albums, Sharp's distorted voice howls about conspiracy theories and corruption as Zeena Parkins plays her electric harp like a lead guitar and Sharp, bassist Marc Sloan and sampler-player David Weinstein grind out sheets of rhythmic, metallic noise. On **Interference** and parts of **Autoboot** (an authorized bootleg Sharp made mixing unreleased Carbon studio tracks and excerpts from live performances), Carbon focuses less on Sharp's paranoia in favor of more abstract instrumentals endowed, on some tracks, with the more atmospheric minimalism of ambient music.

One of Sharp's most accessible solo records of late is **Beneath the Valley of the Ultra-Yahoos** (a Russ Meyer–titled sequel to 1987's **In the Land of the Yahoos**). Each of the fragmented pop songs lasting two to three minutes enlists a different avant-garde musician, from Eugene Chadbourne playing piano and singing the blues on "Return of the Pharm Boys" to Sussan Deihim wailing ethereal Middle Eastern vocals on "X-Plicit."

If it wasn't for the distinctly chunky sound and warbling slides of Sharp's guitar, **Terraplane** would sound as if another musician made it. With David Hofstra on bass and Joseph Trump on drums, Sharp reinvents himself as the thinking-person's bar bluesman. The album opens with Otis Rush's "All Your Love" and continues by mixing Sharp's own, convincing twelve-bar compositions with Elmore James and Freddie King standards. On **'Dyners Club,** the composer moves forward half a century, performing with his guitar quartet. The band retunes its instruments to riff out-of-phase on "Residue" and explore Sonic Youth's cacophonous terrain on "Flowtest."

Other than **Nots,** a reissue of a 1982 album augmented by unreleased and rare material he recorded in the early '80s, Sharp's solo albums this decade aim to convert mathematical and scientific terms and theories into music. One of the best of these is **Tectonics,** a sophisticated record in which machine-driven techno rhythms and free jazz merge in an exploration of the deformities of the earth's surface (which range from songs about geology to one about Newt Gingrich).

Cryptid Fragments uses the scientific term for a creature whose existence has been documented only anecdotally (like Bigfoot) as an analogy for the instruments in its title track. Sharp created the seventeen-minute "Cryptid Fragments" by giving cellist Margaret Parkins and violinist Sara Parkins a score to play. He then spent 150 hours at the computer rearranging and processing the music until what was left was not the sound of the violin and the cello but those of virtual instruments that exist only in computer memory. "Shapeshifters," also on the album, uses a similar process to manipulate the scraping and sliding of the Soldier String Quartet.

Sharp's avant-garde jam bands have yet to approximate the chaotic beauty of his '80s group the Semantics. The Boodlers, a trio with Fred Chalenor on bass and Henry Franzoni on percussion, offers competent but uninteresting laid-back, slightly psychedelic avant-jazz and computer-processed noise. In its second incarnation, Bootstrappers—Sharp supplemented by bass (Thom Kotik) and percussion (Jan Kotik)—veers away from jazz and all-out noise in favor of industrial-sounding avant-garde funk. (The rhythm section on **Bootstrappers** was Mike Watt and George Hurley of fIREHOSE.)

Sharp's collaborations don't always work. **In New York,** an improvisation with Bachir Attar, the leader of Morocco's Master Musicians of Joujouka, is a case in point. On the album's best tracks, Attar's flutes and strings spin and soar over Sharp's electric guitar underpinning. But the intrusion of a crudely programmed drum machine and a disequilibrium between Attar's spiritual, buoyant playing and Sharp's craggy, scientific jamming make it an experiment that doesn't quite succeed. Still, like everything Sharp has done, this imaginative undertaking is better heard than ignored. [ns]

See also *William Hooker, Zeena Parkins; TPRG.*

JONAH SHARP/PETE NAMLOOK

See *Spacetime Continuum.*

SHED SEVEN

Change Giver (Polydor) 1995

One of the dozens of scrappy young hopefuls to emerge from the mid-'90s Britpop renaissance, this energetic quartet weds a simplistic rough-hewn guitar roar to drearily infantile lyrics that mostly serve to celebrate singer Rick Witter's witless narcissism. Luckily, the band puts forth quite a catchy melodic racket that oddly recalls both the Smiths ("Head and Hands," "Ocean Pie") and **Electric**-era Cult ("Casino Girl" and the terrific "Dirty Soul"). Unsubtle, inane and yet strangely appealing. [db]

SHELLAC

Shellac at Action Park (Touch and Go) 1994

BIG BLACK

Lungs EP (Ruthless) 1982 (Touch and Go) 1992
Bulldozer EP (Ruthless/Fever) 1983 (Touch and Go) 1992
Racer-X EP (Homestead) 1984 (Touch and Go) 1992

Atomizer (Homestead) 1985 (Touch and Go) 1992
The Hammer Party (Homestead) 1986 (Touch and Go) 1992
Headache EP (Touch and Go) 1987
Sound of Impact (UK Walls Have Ears) 1987
The Rich Man's Eight Track Tape (Homestead) 1987 (Touch and Go) 1992
Songs About Fucking (Touch and Go) 1987
Pigpile (Touch and Go) 1992

RAPEMAN

Budd EP (Touch and Go) 1988
Two Nuns and a Pack Mule (Touch and Go) 1989

Steve Albini has spent so much time cementing his role as viscera-rock's most quotable raconteur—sort of the George Jessel of hatecore, if you will—that it's almost possible to forget how much genuine impact the guy has had on the rock cosmos. In the '80s, as leader of Big Black and Rapeman, the Chicago singer/guitarist ushered in an era of malevolent detachment; as an extraordinarily prolific producer (or, as he insists on putting it, "recorder" or "engineer") of bands as varied as Jesus Lizard, the Pixies, Nirvana, Wedding Present, Shadowy Men on a Shadowy Planet, PJ Harvey and the Fleshtones (plus countless others less well known: more than three dozen of the bands reviewed in this book have been in the studio with him), he's honed a clean-but-assaultive aesthetic that revolutionized guitar rock; as self-appointed arbiter of indie morals, he's reaffirmed ascetic values with a verve rarely seen outside Amish country. In short, Steve Albini is not out to win any popularity contests—and he's perfectly willing to assail those who would curry his favor by nominating him in one.

Albini's long performing hiatus ended in 1993 when he formed Shellac with bassist Bob Weston (ex–Volcano Suns) and drummer Todd Trainer (formerly of Breaking Circus and Rifle Sport, but still the captain of his own Brick Layer Cake). The group debuted with a pair of 7-inch singles released in late '93 and then released a full album the following year. Not surprisingly, Albini essentially picks up where he left off when Rapeman imploded, turning confrontational in the very first line of **Shellac at Action Park**'s opener, "My Black Ass," which summarizes his attitude as an artist with remarkable precision: "You're gonna eat what I fix/I hope you choke on it." While offering nothing to ease the ingestion process, the three members of Shellac (all of whom earn their livings as recording engineers) keep the atmosphere remarkably pristine, so much so that each note, each drumbeat of the brittle instrumental "Pull the Cup" seems to hang in mid-air for eons. Purely in terms of sonics, **At Action Park** is less conventional than anything any of the members have been involved with in the past—its pulsing frequencies have more in common with the machine shop than the rock machine—but that doesn't mean you won't relish the ear canal damage it's likely to provoke.

The Big Black catalogue was consolidated and reissued in late '92, augmented by the release of **Pigpile,** a live album recorded in London during the quartet's 1987 farewell tour. (**Songs About Fucking** was released posthumously; **The Rich Man's Eight Track Tape** is a CD repackage of **Atomizer, Headache** and a single; **The Hammer Party** is a compilation of the first three EPs.) As invigorating as the sharp-edged music on **Pigpile** is, Albini's liner notes, explaining the band's operative principles and detailing the set's twelve songs, are equally aggressive and intense. [dss]

See also *Brick Layer Cake, Crush, Sr., Kustomized, Pegboy, Rachel's; TPRG.*

SHELTER

Perfection of Desire (Revelation) 1990
Quest for Certainty (Equal Vision) 1992
Attaining the Supreme (Equal Vision) 1993
Mantra (Supersoul/Roadrunner) 1995

You know culture's getting complicated when you need a working knowledge of Eastern religions to follow the lyrics of a hardcore band. Krishna-core has its leading proponent in Shelter, a hard-hitting New York foursome with excellent chops, a fair punk-pop melodic sense in the slower songs and a bright-eyed straightedge attitude toward metaphysics, existentialism, vegetables and the hypnotic power of television. Formed after a pilgrimage to an Indian *ashram* in 1989 by former Youth of Today singer Ray Cappo (who also founded and sold the Revelation label, replaced it with Supersoul, has plans to launch a line of "cruelty-free sneakers" and does spoken word in his spare time), the group—which includes ex-YOT guitarist John Porcelly—is only one of several mixing reverence with rock; others include 108 and Prema.

On **Mantra,** Cappo's lyrics tend toward important-sounding vagueness ("Empathize can I look through your eyes I'll find/Different paradigms and different minds never two of a kind . . . I have been born in the age of thoughtlessness and I too commit the crime of living in this world considering all to be mine"), but he is an articulate and principled spokesman for transcendental thought set to a tough 4/4 beat. Still, "Message of the Bhagavat" is a mouthful, a reminder that some memories of the '60s are eternal. [i]

JIM SHEPARD

See *V-3.*

SHIRK CIRCUS

Because of You, I Missed the Guess Who Concert EP7 (M.Y. Nation) 1993
Words to Say (Bar/None) 1994
March (Bar/None) 1995

New Jersey's Shirk Circus plays a curious mesh of Minneapolis-style post-punk and influence-welcoming pop. Considering that the trio's long-playing debut, **Words to Say,** was cut as first takes in an hour, the album's stylistic diversity is amazing. Only the low-budget production keeps songs like "#14 (What Would You Be If You Weren't Nothing?)" from achieving Paul Westerberg's dream of being the Raspberries and in a shitty mood at the same time.

The forward-moving **March** shows singer/guitarist/songwriter Josh Silverman in a creative growth spurt. A glorious riff rises from the guitar bluster on the title track; the tuneful punk of "I Regret Everything" takes a step back—not that the band should regret having recorded it. "Guess Who Came Home Today" is a spectacular mix of 10cc and Elvis Costello; the memorable "Where Have You Been?" is thick and rich, intricately arranged but essentially straightforward. The twin-lead break of "Roses" is a nice touch, as is the Spectoresque percussion in "Everything Beautiful in the World Is Dying." Give Shirk Circus some time—at least in the studio—and it might very well record a modern pop masterpiece. [jo]

SHIVA BURLESQUE

See *Grant Lee Buffalo.*

MICHELLE SHOCKED

The Texas Campfire Tapes (UK Cooking Vinyl) 1986 (Mercury) 1988
Short Sharp Shocked (Mercury) 1988
Captain Swing (Mercury) 1989
Arkansas Traveler (Mercury) 1992
Kind Hearted Woman (Mood Swing) 1994 (Private Music) 1996

Recorded live at a folk festival on a portable tape machine, **The Texas Campfire Tapes**—complete with the atmospheric (if unreliably natural) sound of chirping crickets—made Dallas-born Michelle Shocked (Johnston) the darling of the British folk scene. An uncertain but ambitious singer whose early style was a weave of jazz, blues and rock'n'roll as much as folk, she comes off as a talented amateur with modestly appealing songs and the hint of substantial potential. Although Shocked's disingenuous pretensions conflict with the emotional candor of her music—her chosen idioms are no place for phonies—she is a gifted character who doesn't let down her guard, even when she's letting down her guard.

Parlaying UK success into an American record deal (which led to **Campfire Tapes**' domestic issue) Shocked made **Short Sharped Shocked,** her first studio album, with guitarist Pete Anderson (Dwight Yoakam's producer). Using a bunch of session players, he provided a crisp, tasteful Nashville country bed for some of her songs. While maintaining a tenuous connection to acoustic folk with the winsome "Memories of East Texas" and Jean Ritchie's "The L+N Don't Stop Here Anymore," Shocked otherwise favors full-bodied arrangements: hence the uptight R&B sound of "If Love Was a Train" and the glib singer/songwriter pop treatment of "Anchorage," a wonderfully affecting correspondence between old friends. Shocked even rocks out punkwise, joining ex-Texas politicos MDC for an unlisted hard-rocking rendition of her first album's "Fogtown." (Could that be the first secret CD bonus track?)

As surprising a contrast as **Short Sharp Shocked** was to **The Texas Campfire Tapes,** the slick **Captain Swing** is a real shocker. Anderson leads a band with horns, piano and strings in a modern evocation of '40s jazz. As a songwriter, Shocked isn't yet equipped to pull off an entire album in this style (indeed, she has to recycle one first-album tune to make ten tracks, most of which are insubstantial love songs), and her voice isn't quite up to the challenge, either. Still, such fearless ambition is to be admired, and the album serves notice that Shocked isn't sitting still for anybody's expectations of her.

Indeed. "My early intention was to present this record with a cover photo of myself wearing blackface . . . my sincere intention was that it would provide a genuine focus on the real 'roots' of many of the tunes included; blackface minstrelsy." Without getting into Shocked's dubious musicology (or the advisability of a white woman reviving such charming American cultural memories as "Jump Jim Crow"), it's just as well for all concerned that the cover of **Arkansas Traveler** is ungarnished by paint beyond the shack'n'outhouse backdrop. The peripatetic collection was recorded in a dozen locales—including LA, Memphis, Dublin, Woodstock and Australia—with as many casts of collaborators. (Pops Staples, Hothouse Flowers, Bernie Leadon, Uncle Tupelo, Taj Mahal, the Band, Doc Watson, Alison Krauss and Clarence "Gatemouth" Brown are only some of the names here.) Musically, Shocked is in an old-timey mood; if there's swinging or rocking to be done here, it's with a full-on country accent. Obnoxious if you think too hard about the project but almost unfailingly fine if you lie back and enjoy the surprisingly cohesive sounds, **Arkansas Traveler** draws too much attention to itself for such modest music, but that doesn't make the songs—a hodgepodge of unmarked traditionals (among them "Cotton Eyed Joe," "Frankie and Johnny" and "Cripple Creek") and derivative originals—any less appealing.

Shocked subsequently parted ways with her label and released the rejected **Kind Hearted Woman** on her own, selling it at shows. [i]

See also *TPRG.*

SHOES

Un Dans Versailles (no label) 1975
Black Vinyl Shoes (Black Vinyl) 1977 (PVC) 1978 (Black Vinyl) 1992
Present Tense (Elektra) 1979
Tongue Twister (Elektra) 1981
Boomerang (Elektra) 1982 (Black Vinyl) 1990
Silhouette (UK Demon) 1984 (Black Vinyl) 1991
Shoes Best (Black Vinyl) 1987
Present Tense/Tongue Twister (Black Vinyl) 1988
Stolen Wishes (Black Vinyl) 1989
Propeller (Black Vinyl) 1994
Tore a Hole EP (Black Vinyl) 1995
Fret Buzz (Black Vinyl) 1995

Influential pop pioneers in the do-it-yourself deluge, Zion, Illinois' Shoes proved how unnecessary fancy studios and major labels were to the creation and dissemination of marvelous music and then learned, by trying the other side, just how right they were. After practicing with the privately issued **Un Dans Versailles,** Shoes made the landmark **Black Vinyl Shoes,** a self-released miracle of 4-track living-room production that got them an invitation to join the big leagues. But as many likeminded musicians have painfully discovered, pop doesn't necessarily stand for popular, and—three albums later—the quartet returned to its own studio and its Black Vinyl label. By the late '80s, songwriters Jeff Murphy (vocals/guitar), his brother, John Murphy (vocals/bass) and Gary Klebe (vocals/guitar), using hired drummers, were back in business and up to speed, putting out a best-of, reissuing their back catalogue and working on new material.

Stolen Wishes, Shoes' first new album in five years (and the inspiration for an unprecedented bicoastal tour in mid-'90), has all the band's hallmarks—thick rhythm guitars, whispery vocals, heavenly harmonies, sensitive lyrics—plus keyboards, including synthesizer dressing on several of the enormously catchy tunes. Ric Menck of Velvet Crush is the album's drummer, although the rigid, strident clatter on "Feel the Way That I Do" is surely electronic. (Ironically, mock horns add a handsome texture to the glorious guitar pop of "Let It Go," and imitation strings quietly shade in "Love Does.") The introduction of new elements into the group's sound—whose intrinsically retro styling makes it anachronistic to begin with—is overdue, but Shoes' warm songs are better served by real instruments than obviously fake simulations.

Another half-decade passed before Shoes dropped another new album, but as consistency is both the band's blessing and its curse, precious few marks of stylistic change disturb the winsome Britpop familiarity of **Propeller** (at least not after the stuttering ZZ Top chug of Klebe's memorable "Animal Attraction," which gets the record off on a novel foot). With far less of the keyboard technology that characterized **Stolen Wishes** (but a weaker set of tunes), **Propeller** turns more easily, spinning out the usual romantic ups and downs with the typical mix of comely melodicism and muted aggression. Menck drums on half the songs; highlights include John Murphy's gauzy "Don't Do This to Me" and grabby "Tore a Hole," Jeff Murphy's riff-driven "Silence Is Deadly" and Klebe's "Never Ending." An equivocal placeholder.

The subsequent EP bridges **Propeller** and the live **Fret Buzz** with both studio and concert versions of "Tore a Hole" and two otherwise unreleased tracks from the same December 1994 Chicago club gig that produced **Fret Buzz.** With drummer John Richardson laying down the beat, the rocking set draws mainly from **Propeller** and **Stolen Wishes** but digs all the way back to 1979 for **Present Tense**'s "I Don't Wanna Hear It" and includes the otherwise non-album "In Harm's Way," recorded at soundcheck. Energetically played and for the most part well-sung (without benefit of studio reverb or overdubs), **Fret Buzz** doesn't do much more than prove what these concert-shy studio hounds can do live, but that's enough. [i]

See also *Velvet Crush; TPRG.*

SHONEN KNIFE

Burning Farm (Japan. Zero) 1983 [tape] (K) 1985
Yama No Attchan (Japan. Zero) 1984
Pretty Little Baka Guy (Japan. Zero) 1986
Shonen Knife (Gasatanka/Giant) 1990
Pretty Little Baka Guy + Live in Japan! (Gasatanka/Rockville) 1990
712 (Gasatanka/Rockville) 1991
Let's Knife (Virgin) 1993
Rock Animals (UK Creation) 1993 (Virgin) 1994
Brown Mushrooms and Other Delights EP (Virgin) 1993
We Are Very Happy You Came (UK Creation) 1993
The Birds and the B-Sides (Virgin) 1996

VARIOUS ARTISTS

Every Band Has a Shonen Knife Who Loves Them (Gasatanka/Giant) 1989

Having registered a solid and satisfying blip on the Western indie-pop radar screen by firing loopy salvos of American-style pop-punk back from Japan, Shonen Knife proceeded from adorable Hello Kitty amateurishness to a more accomplished Ramonesy archetype as their international stature grew. Initially viewed as hapless wide-eyed shoppers in the great music mall, the consumer-culture-obsessed Osaka trio—Naoko Yamano (vocals/guitar), her sister Atsuko Yamano (drums/art) and Michie Nakatani (vocals/bass)—have grown into a solid band, losing a lot of their childlike grace in the process.

The colorful Knife's early records are magical treats of whimsical absurdity, ingenuous attacks of product endorsement and artless reports of mundane Japanese reality: "Ice Cream City," "I Wanna Eat Choco Bars" and "Public Bath" (all on **Pretty Little Baka Guy**) accurately describe the band's conceptual impulses. **Burning Farm** and the dinky-sounding **Yama No Attchan,** both sung almost entirely in Japanese, were packaged together for America as **Shonen Knife,** with helpful translations of such catchy Knife essentials as "A Day at the Factory," "Insect Collector," "Cycling Is Fun," "Flying Jelly Attack" and "Twist Barbie" included in the booklet. The belated American vinyl issue of **Pretty Little Baka Guy** contains five songs from a 1990 Osaka concert; the CD and cassette replace three studio tracks with formative live efforts from 1982. K's cassette-only edition of **Burning Farm** adds three songs from a Japanese compilation.

Even before the Knife started touring here in 1990, the band's growing cult following—at least in and around Los Angeles—was commemorated in a sprawling tribute album, **Every Band Has a Shonen Knife Who Loves Them** (available in single-disc and double-disc vinyl configurations, as well as CD), and a song on Redd Kross' **Third Eye** LP. The trio returned the fraternal attention on **712,** which boasts "Redd Kross," "White Flag" and "Blue Oyster Cult," a harmony explosion about food poisoning, as well as the rapped "Shonen Knife," which samples the Runaways, quotes the Monkees, mentions Jonathan Richman and offers the self-description "ultra eccentric super cult punk pop band." Redd Kross' Steven and Jeff McDonald, along with several other LA musicians, put in guest appearances, mocking up a John Lennon/Asian woman duet on "The Luck of the Irish" and helping Naoko (here billed as Nancy) through an atrocious cover of the Beatles' "Rain." Otherwise singing well—mostly in English—with improved instrumental skills, Shonen Knife adds the indolent "Lazybone" ("I don't wanna ride a crowded subway/I wanna go by car"), "Fruit Loop Dreams" and "Diet Run" to their product line.

That brought the trio to critical commercial mass, and the young women's next album was mixed by American producer Craig Leon to an approximation of the buzzing rhythm roar he achieved on **Ramones** and issued on a major label. The decision to rerecord some of the band's best songs (but failing to filter out such also-rans as "Ah, Singapore," "Black Bass" and a Buzzcocks rewrite, "Devil House") for the all-English **Let's Knife** make it something of an anti-climax for fans, but it's hard to resist clearly rendered versions of "Twist Barbie," "Riding on the Rocket," "Cycling Is Fun," "Insect Collector" and "Flying Jelly Attack." Sonic consistency and fake-sounding drums are incongruous attributes for Shonen Knife, but their plainly audible enthusiasm—and the assurance in their giddy voices—makes this de facto greatest hits worth its weight in Sanrio gift certificates.

Though it was inevitable that Shonen Knife would eventually lose its guilelessness, **Rock Animals** rips it off the threesome like stolen clothing. The album is an effort to make the group a number of things it's not. Dragging typically slender and only moderately charming song ideas out to insupportable lengths (the forty-eight-minute album contains only eleven numbers; the five-minutes-longer **Let's Knife** squeezes in seventeen), co-producer Page Porrazzo slickly shoehorns the band into the teetering high heels of inappropriate and unappealing stylings that negate Shonen Knife's personality and leave the band sounding uncomfortable, awkward and pretentious. For these guys, simplicity and naïveté aren't just assets, they're fundaments—even if it's all a self-conscious put-on. Greater subtlety and invention might have put the wrong-headed mainstreaming goals of **Rock Animals** within reach, but this clumsy mess (complete with guest appearance by guitarist Thurston Moore) throws innocence away on nothing.

We Are Very Happy You Came is a live album; **The Birds and the B-Sides** is an enticing odds-and-ends compilation of '90s matter, most of it happily light in tone and spirit, cleverly produced and previously unavailable in the US. Among the eighteen selections are five live Knife classics, nifty covers of the Carpenters, Kinks, Phil Spector, Martha and the Vandellas ("Heatwave" by way of the Who) and Brian Wilson ("Don't Hurt My Little Sister"), and such nifty original studio rarities as the exhilarating "Space Christmas" and "Strawberry Cream Puff," a number left off the American edition of **Rock Animals.** Creative rehabilitation sometimes comes in strange packages. [i]

See also *Pigface.*

SHRIEKBACK

See *Low Pop Suicide.*

SHRIMP BOAT

Some Biscuit [tape] (self-released) 1988
Daylight Savings [tape] (self-released) 1988
Speckly (Specimen Products) 1989
Volume 1 (Specimen Products) 1991
Duende (Bar/None) 1992
Small Wonder EP7 (Ajax) 1992
Cavale (Bar/None) 1993

SEA AND CAKE

The Sea and Cake (Thrill Jockey) 1994
Nassau (Thrill Jockey) 1995
The Biz (Thrill Jockey) 1995

FALSTAFF

Falstaff (Specimen Products) 1995

Over the course of two bands and seven albums' worth of work, Chicago singer/guitarist Sam Prekop has drawn from enough disparate sources to make himself admirably difficult to pin down. Is he a folkie with jazz influences? A jazzbo with a jones for Caribbean music? An art-rocker with country leanings? The labels, of course, are less important than Prekop's music, which incorporates all these elements into a consistently playful brand of cerebral rock.

Prekop first showed up fronting Shrimp Boat, whose self-released **Speckly** album features the sort of herky-jerk rhythms and warm jazz/folk intermingling (a banjo playing here while a sax plays a sharp solo line there) that have come to characterize his career. This approach—simultaneously challenging and inviting—recalls the excellent work of several like-minded bands, including Men & Volts, the Minutemen and, especially, New York's Mofungo/The Scene Is Now collective, whose Willie Klein and Chris Nelson appear to be the primary influences on Prekop's mildly yodel-ish vocal style. The overall effect is crisp and, thanks to Prekop's knack for simple melodies, addictively catchy. Despite one badly pretentious polemic (the environmentalist "An Orchid Is Not a Rose," which includes the embarrassing line, "An orchid is not a coal-burning power plant") and a sonic paradigm still in its developmental stages, **Speckly** clearly heralds the arrival of a significant talent.

When Bar/None took longer than expected to issue Shrimp Boat's second studio album, the group filled the void by releasing **Volume 1,** a collection of early recordings, live tracks and related ephemera, most of it predating **Speckly** and much of it sounding quite a bit like the more fragmented late-'60s work by the Red Krayola. Interesting but inconsequential.

Shrimp Boat takes a great leap forward with **Duende,** a beautiful, expansive album featuring fuller production and a more confident approach to incorporating the quartet's assorted musical influences into an overall sound. With the drum kit now manned by Brad Wood (later to be known as Liz Phair's producer), **Duende**'s sixteen songs are anchored in roots rhythms—sometimes leaning toward country, sometimes toward folk, but always unmistakably organic—providing a simple base for Prekop and crew to build upon. On some songs, they throw bebop elements into the mix ("Bumble Bees"); on others they reference scat ("Sunday Crawls Along"), free jazz ("Duende"), even a hint of calypso ("Malva Rosita"). Incredibly, it all works, with liberal doses of humor and good cheer all around. Essential.

Cavale, which turned out to be the group's swan song (and includes three of the four songs from the 7-inch **Small Wonder** EP), is significantly more complex in conception yet much subtler in execution. The roots-based bottom is gone. Here, Shrimp Boat builds its assorted influences into the songs' rhythmic underpinnings rather than layering them on top, and the set relies as much on technical precision as it does on conception. The delivery, however, is much more gentle and restrained, resulting in an album whose best tunes sound tailor-made for lazy afternoons or rainy Sundays.

When Shrimp Boat dissolved, Prekop and **Cavale** bassist Eric Claridge borrowed Archer Prewitt (guitar/keyboards) from the Coctails and John McIntyre (drums/keyboards) from Gastr del Sol/Tortoise to form the Sea and Cake, whose superb self-titled debut album takes **Cavale**'s ambitious compositional scope a step further and is more successful in the bargain. Any hints of folk and country are gone, leaving Prekop free to experiment with a variety of beautifully interwoven textures and rhythms, many of them taken from Caribbean and African sources. At its most pastoral, the record will have you reaching for a tropical drink; at its most bracing, even non-dancers will be hard-pressed to sit still. Highly recommended.

Nassau, the fine followup, comes flying out of the box with the dynamite "Nature Boy," Prekop's most supercharged song since **Duende,** but quickly settles back into the mid-level groove of its predecessor. With McIntyre contributing more and more overdubbed keyboard textures, the album finds the group veering closer to art-rock, an indulgence largely mitigated by Prekop's still-evident playfulness and melodic gift. The ten songs, which are crammed with enough detail to reward close attention but sufficiently pleasant to function well as background music, breeze by like a calm summer day.

The third Sea and Cake album released inside a thirteen-month span finds the group's formula wearing thin. Where most of Prekop's previous output shuffles, **The Biz** meanders; dynamic grooves give way to lazy jamming, hooks are outnumbered by pointless riffs and some of the mellower material would be right at home on a lite-rock radio station. A major disappointment.

In the wake of Shrimp Boat's demise, guitarist/vocalist Ian Schneller also formed a new band. **Falstaff,** his group's self-titled debut (packaged with a square beverage coaster in place of the traditional CD booklet), is an uneven mix of amiable, low-key tunes with strong echoes of Shrimp Boat and patience-trying songs whose over-obvious lyrics, vocals and rhythms border on novelty. [pl]

See also *Coctails, Gastr del Sol, Tortoise.*

SHUDDER TO THINK

Curse, Spells, Voodoo, Mooses (Sammich) 1989
Ten-Spot (Dischord) 1990
Funeral at the Movies EP (Dischord) 1991
Get Your Goat (Dischord) 1992
Your Choice Live Series (Ger. Your Choice) 1993
Hit Liquor EP (Epic) 1994
Pony Express Record (Epic) 1994 (Sammich) 1994

MIND SCIENCE OF THE MIND

Mind Science of the Mind (Epic) 1996

Shudder to Think is not an easy band to love, but there are rewards for those who do. The Washington, DC, quartet's most obvious distinguishing feature is singer/guitarist Craig Wedren's voice—a huge, mincing, swooping thing that declaims his wildly surreal "poetic" lyrics and beelines for a quasi-operatic vibrato at the slightest opportunity. If you can get past that, or learn to like it (it *is* mighty expressive), there's the instrumental backing: gnarly, riff-based prog-rock cunningly disguised in shiny punk and hard-rock clothes. The band has pretensions to Art, and sometimes pulls it off. In short, Shudder to Think is great if you can stand 'em.

The band's vinyl-only debut, on the Sammich label (which later released the vinyl edition of **Pony Express Record**), is one of the rarest DC-scene records. Moving to Dischord, the original lineup—Wedren, bassist Stuart Hill, drummer Mike Russell and dreadlocked guitarist Chris Matthews—made the eleven-song **Ten-Spot,** which contains a handful of promising, tricky post-hardcore songs, notably "Jade-Dust Eyes" (originally from a split single with Unrest) and "Rag," but suffers from shallow, tinny self-production.

Funeral at the Movies is a state-of-the-band EP whose highlights include a manic cover of Jimi Hendrix's "Crosstown Traffic," a pretty song called "Red House" (*not* a Hendrix cover) and a couple of live standards, "Chocolate" and "Day Ditty." There's also a ridiculously awful "surreal" recitative, "I Blew Away/Ride That Sexy Horse": sometimes arty just means pretentious. The CD version includes all of **Ten-Spot.**

The band's songwriting improves dramatically with **Get Your Goat,** getting even stranger and artier (as does Wedren's voice, which goes for the big vibrato with alarming frequency). The album incorporates tough rock riffing and schizoid dissonance. The lyrics are hit-or-miss: "Stick a fish in a tattoo gun/Watch what color ink comes out," for example, works as what Robert Bly calls "leaping poetry," but the next couplet in "Shake Your Halo Down"—"Die, gin bottle wedged in wet hand/Best at what I do, mom says"—is just plain babble. "She Wears He-Harem" opened the band's shows for years; a free-noise passage in "Shake Your Halo Down" recalls My Bloody Valentine's "You Made Me Realize"; Wedren's unaccompanied singing on "Funny" hints at German art-song. The production (by Eli Janney) still doesn't do the songs justice, but there's definitely something interesting going on.

Matthews was subsequently replaced by guitarist Nathan Larson, whose muscular hard-rock approach is more simpatico with Wedren's. **Your Choice Live Series,** despite not-great sound, is an interesting document, recorded at a German show, of the band trying to figure out how to rework its songs—"Shake Your Halo Down" becomes a show-closing raveup, Atlanta Rhythm Section's "So in to You" (which wouldn't show up in a studio version until **Pony Express Record**) a bizarre choice for a cover. The album is also notable for "I Grow Cold," available nowhere else, and "Birthday Song," which became the opening section of "No Rm. 9, Kentucky."

Debuting new drummer Adam Wade (and dedicated to Matthews and Russell), Shudder made its farewell to Dischord a career-high-point single containing two great, bizarre songs (both with long silent passages): "Hit Liquor" and "No Rm. 9, Kentucky." In 1993, an equally terrific and weird three-song demo tape ("Kissi Penny," "Gang of $" and "X-French Tee Shirt") made the rounds, and Shudder to Think built a reputation as a tremendous live band. Signed to Epic, their first recording session for the label produced live-to-two-track versions of a bunch of older songs, which showed up on various B-sides and promotional records for a while (the best is a ferocious two-minute condensation of "Shake Your Halo Down," on the "X-French Tee-Shirt" single).

Pony Express Record is Shudder to Think's Big Rock Move, with production by Ted Nicely and a blast-out-of-the-speakers mix by Andy Wallace (of **Nevermind** fame). Despite a huge promotional campaign, it stiffed commercially. Too hard-rock for the avant-gardists and *way* too weird for hard-rockers, the record alienated the band's core constituency of Dischord cultists by including (slightly inferior) rerecordings of both sides of the "Hit Liquor" single, and, more significantly, by being on a major label. It's still got some great moments: "X-French Tee-Shirt" gets almost an entire song out of a single chord, the metallic "Chakka" is built on a riff that keeps evaporating and recondensing, "9 Fingers on You" enters "Detroit Rock City" territory and "Own Me" is a cunning Larson rewrite of Lesley Gore's "You Don't Own Me." (The preceding **Hit Liquor** EP contains the recut title track, demos for the album's "Kissi Penny" and "Full Body Anchor" and live-in-the-studio alternate versions of one song each from **Ten-Spot** and **Funeral at the Movies.**)

Wedren was sidelined with Hodgkin's disease in late 1995. Larson's solo project, **Mind Science of the Mind,** finds him backed by a group including Helium's Mary Timony and the Dambuilders' Joan Wasser. If, for the most part, far milder, the songs are harmonically and rhythmically almost as out-there as Shudder to Think songs. Without Wedren's voice, though, it's just not the same. What these songs need is something with real personality to push them over the top, and Larson's perfectly reasonable singing doesn't quite do it. [ddw]

See also *Dambuilders, Helium.*

JANE SIBERRY

Jane Siberry (Can. Duke Street) 1980 (East Side Digital) 1991
No Borders Here (Duke Street/Open Air) 1983
The Speckless Sky (Duke Street/Open Air) 1985 (Duke Street/Warner Bros.) 1988
The Walking (Duke Street/Reprise) 1987
Bound by the Beauty. (Duke Street/Reprise) 1989
When I Was a Boy (Reprise) 1993
Jane Siberry: A Collection 1984–1989 (Can. Duke Street) 1994
Maria (Reprise) 1995

VARIOUS ARTISTS

Count Your Blessings (Can. Alert) 1994

A product of the Ontario coffeehouse scene, Canada's Jane Siberry was initially compared to such diverse female colleagues as Joni Mitchell, Kate Bush and Laurie Anderson. Ultimately, though, she stands as an original (and quickly proved herself as such), seamlessly melding aspects of high and low art into her music as effectively as any of her peers. Siberry's eponymous first album is a low-budget, folk-oriented affair, modest but already pointing at her potential on songs like "Marco Polo" and "Writers Are a Funny Breed."

Siberry's previous job explains "Waitress," the amusing lead cut of **No Borders Here.** Buoyed by inventive arrangements informed by the enthusiasm of new wave, Siberry rips through nine delightful, skewed narratives and observations, including "Extra Executives" and "Symmetry (The Way Things Have to Be)." Her gifts as a charismatic storyteller are more than sufficient to sustain longer pieces like the seven-plus minutes of "Mimi on the Beach." **The Speckless Sky** picks up where **No Borders Here** leaves off (both albums include tracks entitled "Map of the World"), but with an even greater scope, particularly on the expansive "One More Color" and the intimate "The Taxi Ride."

Siberry fans split into camps with **The Walking.** The epic songs ("The White Tent the Raft," "The Bird in the Gravel") are stretched to proportions likely to alienate those predisposed to linear songwriting, as Siberry switches voices and perspectives. Elsewhere, an air of lost love generates some of Siberry's most touching vignettes: "The Lobby," "The Walking (And Constantly)" and particularly the draining "Goodbye." Listeners who savored **The Walking** are apt to find **Bound by the Beauty.** a bit anemic, but those who thought the former too ambitious will cherish it, as the material is distinctly more grounded. "Everything Reminds Me of My Dog" and "The Life Is the Red Wagon" border too closely on whimsy, but are counterbalanced by darker cuts like "La Jalouse." **A Collection 1984–1989** includes two tracks each from Siberry's second and third albums and three each from her fourth and fifth—it's a fair representation of her work up to that point.

On **When I Was a Boy,** Siberry forges the most effective union of her extreme aesthetic leanings yet. With production assistance from Brian Eno on two tracks and Michael Brook on a third, Siberry serves up a dozen musical constructions that are highly complex but no less seductive for it. The rumbling "Temple," "Love Is Everything" (included in two versions), the multiple-personality "An Angel Stepped Down" (with vocal cameos by Rebecca Jenkins and Holly Cole) and "Calling All Angels" (a duet with k.d. lang, originally recorded for the Wim Wenders film *Until the End of the World*) are standouts. The album is Siberry's most coherent since **No Borders Here,** and leagues more ambitious.

Count Your Blessings is a Christmas album—featuring Siberry, Cole, Jenkins, Mary Margaret O'Hara and Victoria Williams—recorded live in concert in 1993 for a CBC broadcast. Along with some delightful ensemble numbers, Siberry contributes vocal solos on an original song, "Are You Burning Little Candle," and the traditional "In the Bleak Mid Winter."

Recorded without an outside producer, **Maria** suggests that Siberry has grasped Eno's idea that the processes of creativity can be more interesting than the creation. The musical material for these ten tracks was recorded in a single three-day session with a jazz quartet; Siberry then constructed songs from her favorite passages. Coming off like Chris Connor aspiring to the flights of Betty Carter, the normally versatile Siberry rarely asserts the vocal presence necessary to carve definite shapes from the rambling improvisations. Most of the tracks, particularly "Lovin' Cup" and "Begat Begat," are pleasant to hear but tiresome to follow; consistent lyrical themes concerning childhood lend the album a certain unity, but not enough to make it cohesive. Strangely enough, the album's most effective cut is the sprawling twenty-minute "Oh My My" (divided from the other nine cuts by a two-minute silence), which weaves quotations from "Puff the Magic Dragon" and "Mary Had a Little Lamb" into a musical tapestry that condenses the lyrical ideas explored elsewhere into an entrancing meditation on lost innocence. [kbr]

See also *TPRG.*

SIBLING RIVALRY

See *Stop.*

BOBBY SICHRAN

From a Sympathetical Hurricane (Columbia) 1994

Mixing hip-hop and blues-rock might sound like a dicey concept, but New York one-man-band guitarist Bobby Sichran (a onetime Das EFX studio hand) combines them and traces of folk so seamlessly it's hard to tell where one ends and the other begins. Best of all, Sichran's music flows so naturally that his genre-blending never sounds self-conscious. **From a Sympathetical Hurricane,** which walks a line between Beck's Delta delusions and an especially weird variation on Dylan-loving, is undeniably groovy—even if it's a bit inconsistent. Great moments include the title track (a mellow slice of hybrid hip-hop) and the funky "Real Live Wire," during which Sichran samples the Talking Heads' "Psycho Killer"; some filler toward the end of the album doesn't prevent it from being enjoyable. [rl]

See also *Das EFX.*

SICK OF IT ALL

Blood, Sweat, and No Tears (In-Effect) 1989
We Stand Alone EP (In-Effect) 1991
Just Look Around (Relativity) 1992
Scratch the Surface (EastWest) 1994

REST IN PIECES

My Rage (One Step Ahead) 1986 (Blackout) 1994
Under My Skin (Roadracer) 1990

The demise of New York hardcore is reported so often you'd think it was fallout from the local tabloids' death grip. Regardless of changing fashions or global warming trends, though, a few bands have stuck to their traditionalist guns, making the loud-fast frenzy noise for fans of true mosh power. Among the city's stalwarts are Sick of It All, formed in 1985 by singer Lou Koller and his guitar-playing brother Pete.

Other than a guest introduction by KRS-One, the explosive but tight quartet doesn't reveal any original ideas on the clearly articulated debut, but that's part of the point. Angry thrashers like "World Full of Hate," "Disillusion" and "My Revenge" state the band's case with fiery conviction.

Recorded with a new drummer and bassist standing in for the first album's Arman(d) Majidi and Rich Cipriano, Sick of It All introduces hardcore rhythms to a buzzing metallic environment on the studio side of **We Stand Alone** (issued on cassette and as a 7-inch). Besides covering Minor Threat's "Betray," speaking out against senseless violence ("What's Goin' On") and standing up to false friends ("We Stand Alone"), the band checks in with savage live performances of four songs from the debut.

Reuniting the original lineup, the self-produced **Just Look Around** (which repeats the EP's "What's Goin' On" and "We Stand Alone") holds the line on punk's hegemony, tying the unwavering aggression to distinctive mid-tempo rhythms and a sizzling guitar sound behind Lou Koller's comprehensible bellowing. An excellent hardcore record that, if not consistently accessible to mainstream rock tastes (check out the sophisticated instrumental coda of "The Pain Strikes," though), at least shows a willingness to share its righteous anger ("We Want the Truth," "Just Like Around," "Shut Me Out") with a broader audience.

Moving to a major label with a new bassist (Craig Setari), an uncompromised Sick of It All got a radioactive recharge: **Scratch the Surface** is harsher, speedier and more inflamed than **Just Look Around.** As a result of Lou's incessant fifth-gear shrieking, though, the songs' lyrical content is flooded out. "Step Down" has a catchy enough structure ("melody" would be pushing it), but the proclamation of underground integrity ("Please have more to give than fashion and images") flies by unheeded; the anti-superficiality title track and "Force My Hand," with their chanted choruses, make a stronger impression, but the album's emotional blur is pretty overwhelming. As a blast of unreconstructed hardcore in a time and a place where such a thing was once impossible to imagine, **Scratch the Surface** makes Sick of It All's principled point loud if not clear.

For a time, Majidi was also the singer in Rest in Pieces, a New York hardcore contingent notable for contributing guitarist Rob Echeverria to Helmet. [i]

See also *Helmet, Napalm Death.*

SIDEWINDERS

¡Cuacha! (San Jacinto) 1987
Witchdoctor (Mammoth/RCA) 1989
Auntie Ramos' Pool Hall (Mammoth/RCA) 1990
7 & 7 Is EP (Mammoth/RCA) 1990
Do Not Play This Disc . . . for Educational Purposes Only EP (Mammoth/RCA) 1990

SAND RUBIES

Sand Rubies (Atlas) 1993
Goodbye EP (Atlas) 1993
Sand Rubies Live (San Jacinto) 1996

RICH HOPKINS AND THE LUMINARIOS

Personality Crisis (Ger. Houses in Motion) 1992
Dirt Town (Brake Out/Enemy) 1994
Dumpster of Love (San Jacinto) 1995

RICH HOPKINS

Paraguay (San Jacinto) 1995

UNDERBELLY

Mumblypeg (Brake Out/Enemy) 1993

More than one observer of the Arizona rock scene has noted that had the Sidewinders not been derailed by legal and label problems, the Tucson quartet might've beaten neighboring Tempe's Gin Blossoms to the brass ring. Or maybe it was just a case of the too-good/too-early American band syndrome in the conservative pre-Nirvana era.

Formed in 1986 around the songwriting core of guitarist Richard Hopkins and vocalist David Slutes, the Sidewinders quickly garnered local acclaim and recorded **¡Cuacha!** for Hopkins' own San Jacinto label. (San Jacinto has released numerous regional records, including some by the Gin Blossoms.) The album has its share of jangly folk-rock moments instantly familiar to any fan of mid-'80s R.E.M. Yet its traditional feel—part psychedelic pop and part dust-bowl blues—suggests influences stretching back at least two decades.

The two Mammoth albums, however, nail down a specific identity. Hopkins' expansive "big guitar" references Neil Young and Crazy Horse; his uncomplicated melodies are as immediate and hummable as Tom Petty's. And Slutes' enigmatic lyrical concerns (the drug of love, the mystic powers of the sun and moon, the dark edges of the soul)—delivered in the best romantic baritone since Neil Diamond (there's even a cover of "Solitary Man" on **Witchdoctor**)—make for a charismatic combination. A brooding mid-tempo rocker like **Witchdoctor**'s "Bad Crazy Sun" contrasts with the full-tilt heavy guitar stomp of **Auntie Ramos'** "Doesn't Anyone Believe." The band typically swings between these two poles, knowing just when to add harmony vocals, a weeping violin or a brace of acoustic guitars.

The Sidewinders' allegiance to Arthur Lee and Love led to their covering "7 & 7 Is" on **Auntie Ramos' Pool Hall** and on two separate EPs. The version on **Educational Purposes Only** is acoustic, as are two additional Love covers ("Signed D.C.," "Singing Cowboy"); the record also contains a few Sidewinders originals.

Had the next album appeared on schedule the band's destiny might've been different. Unfortunately a North Carolina covers band called Sidewinder appeared on the horizon waving legal papers. Forced out of the public eye for two years, the Tucson group became the Sand Rubies, recorded an album and waited for contract wranglings to end. Late 1993's **Sand Rubies** and the **Goodbye** EP have the familiar panoramic Sidewinders sound, with some admirable twists courtesy four separate producers (Larry Hirsch, Waddy Wachtel, David Briggs and Mike Campbell). The mandolin/twelve-string arrangement of "Guns in the Churchyard" is breathtaking, and a cover of Neil Young's "Interstate" is ruggedly hypnotic. But all the protracted delays extracted a toll; when it came time to tour behind the record, the original rhythm section had long since departed. The Sand Rubies dissolved for good in the middle of '94. Two years later, San Jacinto issued an excellent posthumous live album that amply demonstrates that the band had balls and chops. (Since the demise of the Sand Rubies, Slutes has formed a new band, Ginger; a name change is imminent. Hopkins has been even busier, working on five full-length albums.)

The three records Hopkins issued using the Luminarios name vary in style. **Personality Crisis** is almost a Tucson compilation, with numerous guests handling lead vocals. Throughout, though, his guitar signatures are present, and he even manages to stake out a cover of "Stepping Stone" for his own. The transitional **Dirt Town** finds him trying his hand at lead vocals for the first time, with moderate success on some tracks (a blazing "Dirt Town"; a credible cover of the Animals' "When I Was Young"). The tunes are folkish in flavor, but with enough amplification and Young-ian solos to satisfy old Sidewinders fans. Ditto the brasher, more garagey **Dumpster of Love,** which introduces the Luminarios as a real band. Hopkins' singing is better, and he's growing as a lyricist too. But he'll always be a fretboard wrangler at heart. Nodding once more to a hero, he serves up a sloppy-but-searing "Powderfinger."

One pleasing anomaly in the Hopkins discography is **Paraguay,** an instrumental acoustic disc culled from recordings he made back in the early '80s while working as a Peace Corpsman in South America. Playing with several Paraguayan musicians and frequently giving them the spotlight, he delivers a convincing set of traditional, flamenco-flavored tunes and the odd cover or two (such as a Latinized version of "A Whiter Shade of Pale"). A creative and musically astute man.

Underbelly is a one-off collaboration between Hopkins and ex–Naked Prey/Woodcocks singer/guitarist David Seger. In addition to a boozy cover of Buffy Sainte-Marie's "Cod'ine," **Mumblypeg** offers a wealth of archetypal desert rock: somber minor-key chord progressions wedded to edge-of-desperation vocals, with a solid blues foundation.

Mid-'96 found Hopkins touring a version of Luminarios that included ex-MC5 bassist Michael Davis. [fm]

SILKWORM

Advantage [tape] (no label) 1988
Girl Harbrr EP [tape] (no label) 1989
Girl Harbrr Out-Takes EP [tape] (no label) 1989
L'ajre (Temporary Freedom) 1992
. . . his absence is a blessing EP (Stampede) 1993
In the West (C/Z) 1994
Libertine (El Recordo) 1994
The Marco Collins Sessions (Matador) 1995
Firewater (Matador) 1996

JOEL R. L. PHELPS

Warm Springs Night (El Recordo) 1996

Over the years, this Seattle (originally from Missoula, Montana) band has explored some of the headier reaches of post-punk, formulating a tense, austere sound—nurtured by fellow Montana expatriate Steve Albini, who has recorded most of its albums—that falls roughly halfway between the Wedding Present and Dream Syndicate. Recent releases have seen a shedding of some of the vestigial gloom of the self-distributed cassettes—put on tape not long after the band's rise from the ashes of the goth-pop combo Einheit—and a firm embrace of the more nuanced aspects of spatially challenging guitar rock.

On its "official" debut, **L'ajre,** the quartet seems to spend an undue amount of time making a list—and checking it twice—of the components it wants to include. Martial, Mission of Burma rhythms? Check. Feedback dappling? Right. Smirking observation? Double check, judging by the tongue-*through*-cheek stance of songs like "Shithead." The thing is, amidst all the cross-referencing, guitarists Andy Cohen and Joel Phelps manage to work up a noise-mongering head of steam with minimal slippage into Sonic Youth tribute. Promising, if less than distinctive.

In the West cuts down substantially on the spectrum of crib notes, letting three subtly different songwriting voices—some of the better ideas seem to come from bassist/vocalist Tim Midgett—provide a sense of anticipation for what might be lurking around the next corner. Midgett's loping basslines—one part post-funk, one part underwater wooze—give an intangible propulsion to spare tracks like "Garden City Blues" (which also draws some charm from drummer Michael Dahlquist's inexact percussive spurts). When the aggro level is raised too high (as on "Incanduce" and the overly Burma-like "Pilot"), Silkworm grows awfully shrill. But as a whole, the exquisitely spacious album's deep rhythmic caverns invite and demand casual lingering.

Although it still emphasizes snap and crackle over pop, **Libertine** is slightly more immediate than its predecessors. Midgett's beefed-up Europop and Cohen's scree-infused post-psychedelia don't exactly mesh, making for a slightly schizy feel, but it's a good thing that the Pynchon-via-(Tom)-Verlaine "There Is a Party in Warsaw Tonight" and the ether-reaching "Written on the Wind" co-exist peacefully without trying to bridge the gap for consistency's sake. Phelps left the group (amicably) at this point, and the remaining trio filled time with the four-song **The Marco Collins Sessions** EP (a radio broadcast packaged in a hilarious **Peel Sessions** parody sleeve promising other editions from bands like Zip Code Rapists, Blodwyn Pig and the Vinnie Vincent Invasion). The contents, while not nearly as interesting as that, do include a nice version of "Scruffy Tumor," a song which originally appeared on **. . . his absence is a blessing.**

The pared-down three-piece Silkworm cuts a very different figure, as evidenced by the sprawling **Firewater.** Cohen takes advantage of the spartan surroundings in order to launch some monumentally trebly, barely-in-control solos like those that riddle "Drag the River" and "Slow Hands." Oddly enough, while Phelps provided the most melancholy songs on earlier albums, **Firewater** may well be the most downbeat Silkworm set yet—particularly the achy-breaky "Tarnished Angel" and "Miracle Mile," a why-bother dismissal of modern-day rock hepcats.

Phelps' solo endeavor is a dark, melancholy-dappled set characterized by the same introspection that marked his contributions to Silkworm. While it's a bit restrained overall—he spends a good bit of the album murmuring through clenched teeth—**Warm Springs Night** should secure a spot in any insomniac's wee hours listening pile. [dss]

SILOS

About Her Steps. (Record Collect) 1985
Cuba (Record Collect) 1987 (Watermelon) 1994
Tennessee Fire EP (Record Collect) 1987
The Silos (RCA) 1990
Hasta la Victoria! (Ger. Normal) 1992 (Watermelon) 1994
Diablo (Ger. Normal) 1994
Susan Across the Ocean (Watermelon) 1994

WALTER SALAS-HUMARA

Lagartija (Record Collect) 1988
Lean (Ger. Return to Sender/Normal) 1994
Radar (Watermelon) 1995

SILOS\WALTER SALAS-HUMARA

Ask the Dust (Watermelon) 1995

TANGO PROJECT

White Rabbit (Newport Classic) 1992

SETTERS

The Setters (Ger. Blue Million Miles) 1993 (Watermelon) 1994

Conceived in Cuba, born in New York, raised in Florida and variously resident in Los Angeles, Brooklyn and thousands of road miles in between, singer/guitarist Walter Salas-Humara is a modern-day Johnny Appleseed, absorbing and spreading musical influences across the land, planting and nurturing bands and styles in various locales and returning occasionally on his endless travels to tend to them. An unflashy auteur whose roots-rock amalgam drapes country, punk, baroque stateliness and pop in an abiding sadness, the talented Salas-Humara is an unsung hero whose crucial role in one wing of Amerindie expression is hard to grasp from seeing any one corner of it.

After founding and leaving the Vulgar Boatmen in Gainesville, Salas-Humara headed north to New York, where he and singer/guitarist Bob Rupe (ex-Bobs) opened the Silos for business. Working against a tide that had not yet discovered informed urban country-rock, the Silos released three fine, modest records on Salas-Humara's own label and then, in an honorable but futile bid for major-label recognition, made one for RCA. The Silos-sounding solo **Lagartija** also speaks to the Vulgar Boatmen's origins; a third of the songs were written by members of that band, including (on the CD) "Heartbeat," a drastically reworked version of which appears on their 1995 LP. **Lagartija** and **About Her Steps** were later packaged together as **Ask the Dust.**

The Silos marked the end of the original Silos; Rupe left, and Salas-Humara proceeded with a new collective version of the band, assembling a touring company but using more than a dozen pals to record **Hasta la Victoria!,** an affecting album that firmly defines his downcast rustic semi-acoustic pop. (Although the rhythm section of the previous Silos contributed to the new album, viola/violinist Mary Rowell—whose own band, Tango Project, made a '92 LP—has proven to be the group's only other long-term era-spanner.) Salas-Humara writes simple, quiet love songs of enormous emotional intensity. Eloquent understatement makes the difficult stories implicit in his best efforts resonate deeply. "Find Someone" stands out for its untrammeled enthusiasm; the tangible sense of distance and desolation in "Miles Away," of disappointment in "Sometimes When I Come Over" and of family complications in "Try Tomorrow" are more typical of the album's somber tone. Still, Salas-Humara (with vocal accompaniment by Victoria Williams) manages to end on a hopeful note, with the energetically rocking epic "Find a Way." (The American CD contains two songs not on the original German edition.)

Besides shifting its geographical focus to Austin, Texas (home of Watermelon Records), the Silos added veteran singer/guitarist Manuel Verzosa to its lineup, giving Salas-Humara a valuable creative foil and sending the group in a more rocking direction. Verzosa was killed in an icy crash while on tour in November 1993; the album he had completed with the group was issued overseas as **Diablo,** then (with the addition of "Change the Locks" and "Fallen Angel" as a tribute) in the US as **Susan Across the Ocean.** This uneasy record that can't seem to locate its purpose (but manages a couple of exquisite songs in the search) contains such devastating originals as the delicate title track, a painful parting memory written from the perspective of a sixty-year-old. The unsettling mysteries of "The Sounds Next Door" and the resignation of "Nothing's Gonna Last" explore other emotional issues. Nearly half the songs are covers, including Austin singer/songwriter Michael Hall's recklessly restless "Let's Take Some Drugs and Drive Around," Pork's punky "Wanna Ride," Jonathan Richman's competitive "I'm Straight" (druguality, not sexuality) and Lucinda Williams' angry "Change the Locks."

Maintaining his parallel solo/group existence, Salas-Humara released an excellent acoustic live album, **Lean,** as a two-thousand-copy edition German mail-order pressing. Recorded as an Austin college-radio broadcast, the club show from the spring of 1993 features a guitarist, bassist, Verzosa on voice and percussion, singer (and ex–Wild Seed) Kris McKay and Salas-Humara's brother, Ignacio, on maracas. The dozen originals form an ideal retrospective of his best work. It's a shame the record is so hard to obtain.

Although such Silos family members as Rowell, Dave McNair, J. D. Foster and drummer Darren Hess (lately of Poi Dog Pondering) help out, Salas-Humara plays most of the instruments on **Radar,** a substantial solo digression with noisy guitar occasionally cragging up more diverse material. As much stylistic experiment as serious songwriting effort, **Radar** is a dry, edgy undertaking that lays an appealing country carpet for "I Won You Won," "Ride" and "Get Out," but otherwise veers off in various challenging offshoots. While it's easy to embrace the barbed charms of the Neil Young–ish "Be Honest With Me" and be haunted by the mournful-sounding "Rejuvenation" (written and recorded with Mary Janes singer/guitarist Janas Hoyt, an erstwhile member of Indiana's Vulgar Boatmen), **Radar** as a whole is standoffish, too demanding of patience for instant gratification.

The Setters is a part-time collaboration with labelmates Alejandro Escovedo (with whom Salas-Humara shares a deep stylistic affinity) and Michael Hall. For **The Setters,** the trio teams with producer/guitarist (and Lucinda Williams collaborator) Gurf Morlix, accordionist Lisa Mednick and ex-Giant Sand bassist Scott Garber in a relaxed, handsomely detailed and easy-on-the-ears southwestern supersession. Not bothering to write anything together, the three principals bring and sing their own tunes: Salas-Humara's offerings are "Susan Across the Ocean," "Nothing's Gonna Last," "Shaking All Over the Place" and "Hook in My Lip." Hall does "Let's Take Some Drugs and Drive Around," "Don't Love Me Wisely," "River of Love" and the pensive closer, "A Better Place"; Escovedo contributes "It's Hard," "Helpless," "Tell Me Why" and "She's Got." Mostly performed with burnished folky restraint but occasionally delivering crisp rock energy, the album's pieces fit together as seamlessly as the participants' well-matched emotional barometers. Even a spooky cover of the Stooges' "I Wanna Be Your Dog" (an Escovedo concert staple) worms its way into the disc without causing any stylistic upset. [i]

See also *Cracker, Alejandro Escovedo, Gutterball, Michael Hall, Vulgar Boatmen; TPRG.*

JIMMY SILVA

Remnants of the Empty Set (PopLlama Products) 1986

JIMMY SILVA AND THE EMPTY SET

Fly Like a Dog (PopLlama Products) 1987

JIMMY SILVA AND THE GOATS

Heidi (East Side Digital) 1991

JIMMY SILVA'S GOAT 5

Near the End of the Harvest (PopLlama Products) 1995

Seattle singer/songwriter Jimmy Silva's death at the age of forty-two, two days before Christmas 1994, deprived the pop underground of one of its finest unheralded tunesmiths, one whose wryly inventive, offhandedly insightful lyrics were brilliantly balanced by jangly, hook-intensive melodies. After a stint in Vietnam, Silva played around the Bay Area with his band the Empty Set in the early '70s, but it wasn't until the next decade that he was discovered and embraced by indie-pop fans.

Remnants of the Empty Set, with guest appearances by Smithereens drummer Dennis Diken and Beau Brummels singer Sal Valentino, salvages some swell songs from the defunct band's repertoire, with the warm-voiced Silva sharing lead vocals with a variety of pals. **Fly Like a Dog** continues in a similar vein, with the addition of kindred spirits the Young Fresh Fellows to the cast.

The consistently wonderful **Heidi** marks Silva once and for all as a master of his craft. His remarkable gifts are showcased on poignant, lovingly rendered songs like "Tin Whistle and a Wooden Drum," "From Every Doorway" and "What Makes It Hard to Be Kind?" The last is sung by the Fellows' Scott McCaughey, who joins Ken Stringfellow of the Posies and PopLlama boss Conrad Uno in the album's gallery of guest vocalists. (The CD adds the contents of **Remnants** plus two previously unreleased outtakes of similar vintage.)

The posthumously released **Near the End of the Harvest** is a moving memorial to Silva's talents, with a harder roots-rock sound than its power-poppy predecessors as well as a darker, foreboding lyrical edge manifested in songs like "Longshoreman's Hall," "Christmas Is Holy" and "Tell It to the Raven." Silva's vocals are warmer and more expressive than ever, making it all the more curious when he surrenders the leads to his bandmates on five of the album's fourteen songs. Whoever's singing, though, it's a marvelous album, as well as a bittersweet epitaph for an underappreciated artist. [ss]

See also *Young Fresh Fellows; TPRG.*

SILVERCHAIR

frogstomp (murmur/Epic) 1995

Classical music prodigies are generally admired for their ability to master and replicate the works of great men, not create their own. Originality isn't the issue, precocious virtuosity and artistry are. In rock-'n'roll, which maintains a pretense of looking forward and only intermittently places emphasis on instrumental skill, being an adolescent wizard is good for only a few novelty points unless you turn out to be Stevie Wonder, Prince or the King of Pop. Kid bands (Old Skull, Stinky Puffs, Noise Addict) are taken as exactly that, and judged accordingly, expected to be cute or bratty and nothing more. Which is why silverchair is such a logic-defying shocker. There's nothing audible on the competently derivative **frogstomp** that gives away the tender ages of this Australian threesome; their sure proficiency at dramatic Seattle-style rock thunder becomes frightening only with the knowledge that they were barely fifteen when they wrote and recorded the album.

Guitarist Daniel Johns' admitted vocal mimicry of Eddie Vedder isn't an exact match, but still mighty impressive for a kid who's still in high school. The songs he co-writes with drummer Ben Gillies have more of a '70s Bad Company mock-western feel beneath the bludgeoning power but the same kind of anguished lyrics (albeit sketchier and stupider) as Pearl Jam: "Suicidal Dream," "Pure Massacre" and the execution-inspired "Israel's Son" are especially disturbing under the chronological circumstances. Silverchair's youth has certainly been an asset in the band's rise (earning it such backbiting nicknames as Kinder-garden, Silver Highchair and Alice in Chairs), but **frogstomp** comes without any caveats, asking—and requiring—no indulgence for its creators' tender years. By the way, that gulp you hear is the sound of twentysomething strivers rethinking their career choices. [i]

SILVERFISH

Dolly Parton EP (UK Wiiija) 1989
T.F.A. EP (UK Wiiija) 1990
Cockeye (Touch and Go) 1990
Fat Axl (Wiiija/Touch and Go) 1991
Fuckin' Drivin or What EP (UK Creation) 1991
Organ Fan (UK Creation) 1992 (Creation/Chaos/Columbia) 1993
Silverfish With Scrambled Eggs EP (UK Creation) 1992
Damn Fine EP (UK Creation) 1993
Crazy EP (Creation/Chaos/Columbia) 1994

RUBY

Salt Peter (UK Creation) 1995 (Creation/Work) 1996
Salt Peter Remixed—Revenge, the Sweetest Fruit (UK Creation) 1996

A few seconds of any Silverfish song could wrench the most cast-iron gut, leaving a mess of entrails in its wake. But in the case of this London quartet, the more you bleed the better you feel. Jacked-up rhythms are smothered by an electric blanket of guitar distortion, setting the pace for Lesley Rankine's razor-toothed lyrics and penetrating screams (think *The Exorcist*'s Linda Blair on a bad day). Rankine unhinges more than a few female stereotypes as she expresses rather than represses her violent and sexual urges in vengeful gun-wielding fantasies and blatant descriptions of lubricious desires. Anthem phrases like "total fucking asshole" ("T.F.A.") and "Hips Tits Lips Power!" ("Big Bad Baby Pig Squeal") are just the steel tip of this volatile iceberg. Judging by voice alone, Rankine could slam dunk Babes in Toyland, L7 and Courtney Love all in one shot. Musically, the band hovers over basic punk, grunge and noise groupings without holding to any single path.

Even the band's formation story is a bit thorny. Bassist Chris P. and drummer Stuart, who originally played together in the Rover Girls, met guitarist Fuzz after his band, the In-Stinks, finished a gig; they recruited Rankine (ex-Grizzelders) after bouncers tossed her out of a Terminal Cheesecake show for starting a fight. Silverfish debuted in their home base of Camden in late '88 and was eventually credited for inspiring a dance dubbed the Camden Lurch.

The band's Stateside debut, **Cockeye,** consists of the **Dolly Parton** and **T.F.A.** EPs plus the outstanding "One Silver Dollar." Careening with brute force from the hearty "motherfucker" that begins the album, propelled by steadily grinding rhythms, the nine cuts pile on phasers and untamed guitar squeals to create a constant blur of noise. Belting through the thick assault with a gravelly wail that sounds more spoken than sung, Rankine is especially prominent on "T.F.A.," "On the Motorway" and "One Silver Dollar," but she occasionally drops back in the mix. "Weird Shit" breaks up the chaotic swill with some jarring grooves and occasional primate-like shouts, although the high-pitched guitar squeals are trying on the ears.

With production guidance from crunch master Steve Albini, Silverfish hammers through the more playful **Fat Axl.** While equalling **Cockeye**'s steroids dosage, the album tries out rhythmic twists and lyrical turns and ties the guitar tangents closer to the grooves. There's even a slightly funky, blown-out version of Melle Mel's "White Lines," complete with sireny guitar parts and Rankine's near-rap delivery, a sign she's experimenting with vocal ideas. The trace of black humor behind that possessed spirit leads to such pungent similes as "Like a funeral procession who've forgotten the hearse" (in "Shit Out of Luck") and this wry observation in "Spoon": "Too much sugar/Too little taste/ Got the right arse but the wrong face."

The **Fuckin' Drivin or What** three-song EP features the epochal "Big Bad Baby Pig Squeal" (also included on **Organ Fan**). It's hard to say no when Rankine asks "Are you afraid of me?"; there are a few phrases on "Texas Tea" where she sounds like a witch.

By the point of **Silverfish With Scrambled Eggs** and **Organ Fan** (the EP is included on the domestic edition of the album), Rankine had begun to sing rather than always scream; the more focused music creates an effective vehicle for her voice. "Crazy" (a number learned from the soundtrack of a 1969 Italian flick) is as close to a love song as Silverfish ever got. "This Bug" toys with harmonies, though the lyrics still acknowledge Rankine's gruff persona—"Sometimes I feel like Joan of Arc/The way I bite and spit and bark." Still, lyrics about revenge, guns and male anatomy surface (see "Mary Brown": "But I'll get a knife and a big fat wife/With a shiny shiny knife she'll cut the balls off the fuckers"). "Joos" resounds with bold and brassy Foetus-isms courtesy of Jim Thirlwell, who produced the album and plays brass in a few spots. He emphasizes Rankine's role and leads the music toward broader gestures, though there's still the wound-up "Suckin' Gas" and machine-gun beats of "Fuckin' Strange Way to Get Attention." Silverfish also does a fairly conventional version of David Essex's "Rock On" in which Rankine occasionally sounds like Joan Jett.

On the **Damn Fine** EP, also produced by Thirlwell, Rankine switches between a smoky delivery and her coarser self, blended over repetitive rhythms. The EP contains live versions, recorded in London in '92, of three **Organ Fan** tracks.

By the end of '93, the tensions expressed in the music became a reality for the band and Rankine called it quits. She relocated to Seattle, formed Ruby with multi-instrumentalist Mark Walk and shed the sexless Silverfish look for a sultry chanteuse pose. With no trace of the Silverfish howls, the mood on **Salt Peter** (which cuts a surprising line between Garbage and Portishead) is still dark, the lyrics strong—if not quite as blatant. The single "Paraffin" is filled with sexual innuendo: "trap him in my flower bed and then I'll feed him with my paraffin." Her odd lyrical timings, comparable to Björk's, match Walk's quirky arrangements. (Walk and Rankine met in Pigface. Better than traffic school . . .) Their mix works best on the edgier cuts, like the dance-heavy "Tiny Meat," which (like "Swallow Baby") veers into Luscious Jackson territory. Former Ministry drummer William Rieflin breaks through the trip-hop haze on "Pine" and "Flippin' tha Bird." The music on "Swallow Baby" doesn't ever gel, however, and Rankine sometimes pushes too hard on "Bud." Rankine has refined the pure adrenaline spunk that made Silverfish such a rush into something more sophisticated and seductive, but Ruby could still use some more polish before it goes out. [mg]

See also *Pigface.*

SILVER JEWS

Dime Map of the Reef EP7 (Drag City) 1991
The Arizona Record (Drag City) 1993
Starlite Walker (Drag City) 1994
The Natural Bridge (Drag City) 1996

When the Silver Jews debuted, the project seemed like little more than a chance for Pavement's Steve Malkmus and Bob Nastanovich to satisfy their conceptual cravings at a time when their "real" band's issue was growing respectable enough for consumption by John Q. 90210. But as the band developed, it became evident not only that the Silver Jews was a group, but that frontman David Berman had his own unique vision—that of a stoner dude who'd be just as content to jam on a Grateful Dead bootleg while cruising around smoking a spliff as hang out at a Sebadoh concert while, uh, smoking a spliff.

Berman's helpers hide behind pseudonyms like Hazel Figurine and Spill Fantauzza on the group's debut, but there's no mistaking idiosyncratic eruptions like the accidental-recordist "Canada" and the post–**Highway 61** travelogue "SVM f.t. Troops." While the songs sound like they could have been outtakes from Pavement's **Slay Tracks** sessions, that doesn't make them sound any less like outtakes. Berman takes the reins a little more willingly on **The Arizona Record,** imparting a slightly dazed, Neil Young feel to ambling songs like "Secret Knowledge of Backroads." Far too often, however, the Silver Jews seem more concerned with medium than message; the audio vérité tenacity they apply to the utterly atonal tangle "I Love the Rights" and the echo-drowned "The War in Apartment 1812" does little to enhance what might have been reasonably persuasive songs.

Starlite Walker is an altogether different beast, one that not only maintains cogent form from one end to the other but seems to display a concern with previously secondary matters like sequencing. The opener—deftly titled "Introduction II"—addresses the Jews' audience with the honest-to-1974 salutation "Hello my friends/Come on, have a seat," and progresses unambiguously forward. Berman dispenses with the low-tech crutches, extracting his agreeably twangy voice from the lower reaches of the mix, which reveals an ability to write memorable parables like "Advice to the Graduate" (which counsels its subject "on the last day of your life, don't forget to die"). While it gets laid-back enough at times to pass for a long-lost New Riders of the Purple Sage album, **Starlite Walker** possesses enough temperate charm to soothe even the most savage discordophile. [dss]

See also *Pavement.*

DESMOND SIMMONS

See *Wire.*

SIMPLE MINDS

Life in a Day (PVC) 1979 (Virgin) 1987
Real to Real Cacophony (UK Arista) 1979 (UK Virgin) 1982 (Virgin) 1988
Empires and Dance (UK Arista) 1980 (UK Virgin) 1982
Sons and Fascination/Sister Feelings Call (UK Virgin) 1981
Celebration (UK Arista) 1982 (UK Virgin) 1982
Themes for Great Cities (Stiff) 1982
New Gold Dream (81–82–83–84) (Virgin/A&M) 1982
Sparkle in the Rain (Virgin/A&M) 1984
Once Upon a Time (UK Virgin) 1985 (Virgin/A&M) 1986
Sister Feelings Call (Virgin) 1987
Live in the City of Light (Virgin/A&M) 1987
Street Fighting Years (Virgin/A&M) 1989
Themes Vol. 1: March 79–April 82 (UK Virgin) 1990
Themes Vol. 2: August 82–April 85 (UK Virgin) 1990
Themes Vol. 3: September 85–June 87 (UK Virgin) 1990
Themes Vol. 4: February 89–May 90 (UK Virgin) 1990
Real Life (Virgin/A&M) 1991
Glittering Prize–'81/'92 (UK Virgin) 1992
Good News From the Next World (Virgin) 1995

Simple Minds made steady progress after forming in Glasgow in 1978, developing from the new wave Roxy Music/Velvet Underground aspirations of **Life in a Day** to the commanding anthemic power of **New Gold Dream** inside of three years. Between Jim Kerr's distinctive throaty vocals and guitarist/keyboardist Charlie Burchill's insightful sense of music that can rock a human sea, Simple Minds (regardless of who else was in the changing lineup at the time) had the vision, passion and tools to share the enlightened mass arena with U2.

Having reached that impressive creative plateau—ably sustained on the succeeding **Sparkle in the Rain**—Simple Minds still couldn't navigate the career curve thrown its way when "Don't You (Forget About Me)," a song given the group to record for the otherwise worthless soundtrack of *The Breakfast Club,* became a chart-topping American hit in early 1985. Rattled to the rafters by phenomenal success attributable to a single number they didn't write, the group made a series of gross miscalculations, allowing its majesty to billow into bombast, its intelligence to encourage pomposity. Simple Minds attempted to become America's favorite rock band on the appallingly overheated **Once Upon a Time,** marked time with a live album and then shouldered global politics in the sanctimonious **Street Fighting Years.**

After those two debacles, the group wisely pulled in its horns, producing only one new album in the following half-decade. Although an enormous and enduring European following kept the band afloat through constant touring buoyed by flashy CD reissues of its 12-inch singles (the **Themes** sets) and a hugely popular British compilation (**Glittering Prize**), America continued its commercial yawn despite 1991's **Real Life.**

Another desperate lunge for artistic significance that relies on high-minded lyrical concerns and arty studio contrivances to embellish the band's intrinsic qualities, **Real Life** overdoes it on every front and winds up the least memorable record of Simple Minds' career. The lyrics address such grandiose topics as "Woman," "African Skies" and "Real Life," in which characters from Washington, DC, and Dublin cross paths in New York (where a gangland hit takes place on a dock and space shuttles fly above a desert as "sixteen men from a dying earth take their last dream." Or something like that). Kerr huffs and puffs with the teeth-gnashing conviction of a televangelist, which only makes things worse. Although several tracks sound like there might be usable melodies in there someplace, the arrangements nonchalantly pile on electric instruments, an orchestra, soulful backing singers and far too many keyboards (including ethnic-sounding instrumental samples); producer Stephen Lipson lets it all become a fuzzy mess. If this is real life, maybe we should see what's behind door number two.

After a lengthy rethink, Simple Minds—by this point officially reduced to Kerr and Burchill, joined in the studio and onstage by an assortment of hired hands—returned to earth with the surging guitar-powered and relatively streamlined **Good News From the Next World.** (In a double irony, the album was co-produced by the duo and Keith Forsey, onetime associate of synthesizer kingpin Giorgio Moroder and the author of Simple Minds' double-edged single.) Without reducing his intensity, Kerr focuses himself into accessible and tunefully forthright songs that depict the big issues through a personal sensibility. Two of the strongest tracks, "Hypnotised" and "She's a River," are poetic love songs; others ("Night Music," "My Life") contemplate the meaning of art. Betraying an irresistible optimism that breathes life into the music,

"And the Band Played On" and "Great Leap Forward" reawaken the vitality of vintage Simple Minds songs like "Promised You a Miracle." [i]

See also *TPRG.*

SINCOLA

Sincola EP (Rise) 1994
What the Nothinghead Said (Caroline) 1995
Crash Landing in Teen Heaven (Caroline) 1996

Sincola's take on angular post-Pixies pop—all herky-jerk hooks and jagged cadences—is made special by virtue of a pervading scent of enigmatic genderfuck. The Austin fivesome tweaks the standard boy-meets-girl pop text by imbuing its fizzy tunes with a chaotic, amorphous nature that ping-pongs between sexual notions of hetero-, homo- and bi-. On the band's eponymous debut EP, Wendell Stivers and Kris Patterson's percolating guitars bounce and battle with the vigorous rhythmic kick of bassist Chepo Peña and skins-pounder Terri Lord, but no matter how you slice it, the real star of the show is singer Rebecca Cannon. This self-described "kewpie doll bitch" whoops, snaps, hiccups and shouts as if possessed by some sort of wanton, green-eyed imp from slumber-party hell. Boasting five strong doses of deliriously off-balance bubblepunk, the EP makes a swell first sip of Sincola, with the bullet train sea chantey "Hey Artemis" and the signature tantrum that is "Bitch" the most blatant standouts.

As produced by Brian Beattie (late of Glass Eye), **What the Nothinghead Said** fine-tunes Sincola's mercurial sound, giving it just the right shades of new wave gloss and punk-rock punch. Powered by the band's perky crunch and colored by Cannon's ferocious Siouxsie snarl, the record is unerringly infectious. Roles reverse ("Girlfriend"), carnality becomes cryptic ("Hint of the Titty") and catchy, blood-boiling dynamics abound. In addition to reworked versions of "Bitch" and "Hey Artemis," the shoulda-been-hits just keep coming: the anthemic anathema of "Sedate Me," the breakdown car song "Drive" and the amazing "Amazing," which practically begs for an upraised lighter as it finishes the record off. Packed with great songs and a remarkably iconoclastic personality, the tantalizing **What the Nothinghead Said** provides a bitchin' passport into the strange and scary world of Sincola. [mgk]

See also *Stretford.*

SIOUXSIE AND THE BANSHEES

The Scream (Polydor) 1978 (Geffen) 1984
Join Hands (UK Polydor) 1979 (Geffen) 1984
Kaleidoscope (PVC) 1980 (Geffen) 1984
Juju (PVC) 1981 (Geffen) 1984
Once Upon a Time/The Singles (PVC) 1981 (Geffen) 1984
A Kiss in the Dreamhouse (UK Polydor) 1982 (Geffen) 1984
Nocturne (Wonderland/Geffen) 1983
Hyaena (Wonderland/Geffen) 1984
Tinderbox (Wonderland/Geffen) 1986
Through the Looking Glass (Wonderland/Geffen) 1987
The Peel Sessions EP (UK Strange Fruit) 1987
Peepshow (Wonderland/Geffen) 1988
The Peel Sessions EP (UK Strange Fruit) 1988
The Peel Sessions (Strange Fruit/Dutch East India Trading) 1991
Superstition (Wonderland/Geffen) 1991
Twice Upon a Time—The Singles (Wonderland/Geffen) 1992
The Rapture (Wonderland/Geffen) 1995

Formed by a group of Sex Pistols fans on the London new wave scene in 1976 and largely responsible for the spread of chilly romanticism as an appealingly remote stylistic statement, the once mighty Siouxsie and the Banshees reached the '90s in their dotage. With its punk roots and subsequent marriage of goth and world music (on early-'80s peaks **Kaleidoscope** and **Juju**) a distant memory, a band that once proudly bucked trends had grown bland, pompous, slick and stagnant. In the process, the veteran group has been wasting the talents of Budgie, one of rock's most exciting and inventive drummers.

Produced by Stephen Hague, **Superstition** begins with the fairly catchy "Kiss Them for Me," but falls off precipitously from there. Horrendously dated synth and guitar sounds and the album's overall soul-less groove underscore the weak songwriting (partially redeemed by Siouxsie Sioux's noticeably extended vocal range). Only "Shadowtime" manages to even recall some of the old spirit. (For a bracing comparison, check out **The Peel Sessions** mini-album released the same year. The two four-song blasts from '77 and '78 (previously issued on UK EPs) contain such canon classics as "Hong Kong Garden," "Metal Postcard," "Love in a Void" and "Helter Skelter" played with vision and ardor by the band's first stable lineup: singer Siouxsie Sioux, drummer Kenny Morris, bassist Steve Severin and guitarist John McKay.)

Twice Upon a Time, the band's second hits compilation, collects ten years of material, beginning with the beginning of the end, 1982. It was right about **A Kiss in the Dreamhouse** that the Banshees began to lose their edge, although they did coast respectably through the rest of the '80s. Once strong guitarists and songwriters John McGeoch and the Cure's moonlighting Robert Smith left, the band's material suffered accordingly. Singles like "Fireworks," "Slowdive" and "Melt!" (the last two from **Dreamhouse**) all have the dark, alluringly detached eroticism that was the hallmark of the band, but the magic began to ebb with the appearance of **Tinderbox**'s "Cities in Dust" and "Candyman." The cover of Iggy Pop's "The Passenger" (from the eclectic all-covers album, **Through the Looking Glass**) is fine, and so is the Devo-esque "Peek-a-Boo" (from **Peepshow**). But by the end of the eighteen-song retrospective ("Face to Face," a nondescript collaboration with soundtrack hack Danny Elfman for *Batman Returns*), all is lost.

Although short on songs, **The Rapture**—the band's first new album in four years—is elegant, stylish and mature. The five tracks produced by John Cale are scarcely distinguishable from those which the band oversaw; several numbers—notably "Not Forgotten," with its pounding drums, and even the accordion- and steel-guitar–draped "The Lonely One"—sound like throwbacks to an earlier era, as if the Banshees were staking a claim to their own formidable legacy. The eleven-minute title track, an ambitious suite that incorporates a string quartet, is the reportedly now-defunct band's best work in years. [ma]

See also *Crush; TPRG.*

SISTER DOUBLE HAPPINESS

See *Imperial Teen.*

SISTER SOULJAH

360 Degrees of Power (Epic) 1992

On her album, Bronx-born, Ivy League–educated community activist Sister Souljah raps her angry black nationalism in an articulate voice pumped up with melodramatic outrage. Simply produced in old-school style by Public Enemy studio associate Eric "Vietnam" Sadler and others, Souljah preaches "The Hate That Hate Produced," making the solipsistic proclamation that she "was not born to make white people feel comfortable . . . if my survival means your total destruction, then so be it." Souljah's militant Afrocentricity contains such positive elements as self-reliance, self-defense, entrepreneurship, unity and education, but proceeds into paranoia ("The Final Solution" is a fantasy scenario in which the US government reinstitutes slavery), syllogism ("There's no such thing as a Black racist!") and absurd sexism ("White women . . . want to sleep with your Black man . . . White feminist say that they are the sisters of Black women/Ask you to join their women's movement/And then they want to give you five hundred reasons why you should leave your Black man/And let them eat your pussy!"). Chuck D. alternates verses with Souljah on "State of Accommodation; Why Aren't You Angry"; Ice Cube's supportive appearance on "Killing Me Softly; Deadly Code of Silence" sets his calm intensity against Souljah's shrill hectoring. For all of its didactic tedium, **360 Degrees of Power** is way more compelling than the tiresome relationship exploits of Souljah's 1995 autobiography, *No Disrespect.* [i]

SIX FINGER SATELLITE

Six Finger Satellite EP (Sub Pop) 1992
The Pigeon Is the Most Popular Bird (Sub Pop) 1993
Machine Cuisine (Sub Pop) 1994
Machine Cuisine Companion [tape] (self-released) 1994
Severe Exposure (Sub Pop) 1995
Paranormalized (Sub Pop) 1996

Although 1992 brought more than enough repetitive post-hardcore records from brand-name indie labels Amphetamine Reptile and Touch and Go, Sub Pop still saw fit to sponsor this Providence-based cabal of smart boys in space suits. Emulating an amped-up and emotionally overwrought Joy Division on the four-track debut, the laddies—founders John MacLean (guitar) and Jeremiah Ryan (vocals), with drummer Richard Pelletier and a few other members coming and going—have obviously had access to a complete catalogue of Gang of Four and Mission of Burma records.

But that was only an introduction. A year later, the adjusted quintet took a giant step up the creative ladder with **The Pigeon Is the Most Popular Bird,** released on CD and on vinyl as two 12-inch EPs. Even when the album prods at previously poked topsoil, it pecks with complexity and enthusiasm. The group's cold bravado advances an acidic and adrenaline-fueled guitar ethos in songs that arrive nestled between odd, untitled instrumentals. It takes plenty of plays to find all the hooked nettles Six Finger Satellite has hidden in whirly energy flashes like "Laughing Larry" and "Neuro-Harmonic Conspiracy." The band reeks of psychosis and superiority, but the terse presentation is impeccable. (Kurt Niemand, the album's bassist, died in '95, reportedly of an overdose.)

After collapsing behind a swirl of drug rumors, the band re-entered orbit with **Machine Cuisine,** a conceptual mini-album of eight songs on 10-inch vinyl. Temporarily restaffed as a scientific guitar-free trio, 6FS plays heartless Germanic proto-techno with amoral undertones. The pulsing flow is about as warm as Ian Curtis' ashtray, but the construction is genuinely clever and dryly hilarious. Robotic vocals revisit Devo's neurotic erotica, stoking the fires of computer desire on the opening "Love (via Machine)"; catchy electro-pops like "The Magic Bus" (an original) and "The Greek Arts" modulate G-funk style synth over tight Kraftwerk rhythms and intentionally trite lyrics. (The mail-order **Machine Cuisine Companion** cassette footnotes the platter with MX-80 Sound–inspired jams, a Suicide cover and much more Moog madness.)

Severe Exposure integrates the designs of the all-synth outing with the previous brash scissor rock, flashing a guitar band confident enough to delve heavily into disco beats and dramatic vocals. With the mood so established, plenty of panicky songs about animals, gaming and translocation are gathered in the album's full-bodied silvery mercurial radiance. "Rabies (Baby's Got The)" and "Simian Fever" are animal aggressive and messy, while sharing the synthetic digitone lusts of new wave. [ic]

6THS

See *Magnetic Fields.*

SKIN

See *Swans.*

SKINNY PUPPY

Back and Forth Series 1 [tape] (Can. self-released) 1983
Remission EP (Can. Nettwerk) 1984
Bites [tape] (Can. Nettwerk) 1985
Mind: The Perpetual Intercourse (Nettwerk/Capitol) 1986
Cleanse Fold and Manipulate (Nettwerk/Capitol) 1987
Bites and Remission (Can. Nettwerk) 1987 (Nettwerk) 1990
VIVIsectVI (Nettwerk/Capitol) 1988
Rabies (Nettwerk/Capitol) 1989
Twelve Inch Anthology (Nettwerk) 1990
Too Dark Park (Nettwerk/Capitol) 1990
Last Rights (Nettwerk/Capitol) 1992
Back and Forth Series Two (Nettwerk) 1993
The Process (Subconscious/American) 1996
Brap (Back and Forth Vols. 3 & 4) (Nettwerk) 1996

TEAR GARDEN

Tired Eyes Slowly Burning (Can. Nettwerk) 1987 (Nettwerk) 1990
The Last Man to Fly (Can. Nettwerk) 1992
Sheila Liked the Rodeo (Can. Nettwerk) 1993

HILT

Call the Ambulance Before I Hurt Myself (Can. Nettwerk) 1989 (Nettwerk) 1990
Journey to the Center of the Bowl (Nettwerk) 1991

DOUBTING THOMAS

The Infidel (Wax Trax!) 1991

It took Vancouver's Skinny Puppy several years and just as many albums to evolve a distinct, if limited, voice from a simple reiteration of various pre-industrial archetypes (Cabaret Voltaire, Throbbing Gristle, Chrome), but the 1986 addition of synthesist/sampler Dwayne Goettel (replacing Wilhelm Schroeder) to the founding core of multi-instrumentalist cEVIN Key and singer Nivek Ogre (plus, until **The Process,** producer Dave "Rave" Ogilvie) gave the group the internal dynamic it needed to mount its principled (if cliché-dependent) electronic attack.

The promising **Cleanse Fold and Manipulate** warmed the scalpel for **VIVIsectVI,** a principled objection to vivisection and other forms of human brutality (ironically employing musical brutality to convey its message). Teaming up with the likeminded (if more rabid) Ministry meister, Al Jourgensen, Skinny Puppy kept up the pressure on **Rabies,** although the album's lack of variety leaves the impression that Skinny Puppy might have already reached the end of its creative leash.

The environmentally minded **Too Dark Park** overloads tracks to the point of bursting. Between the spoken- word samples, domineering synth beats and Ogre's harshly distorted vocal seethe, blunt weaponry like "Convulsion," "Tormentor" and "Spasmolytic" beat the band's point into the ground. Meanwhile, evidence of a lighter touch allows pretty bits to embroider the dramatic gloom of "Morpheus Laughing" and "Nature's Revenge," thereby drawing a useful connection between the latest industrial designs and decade-earlier English new wavers from Joy Division to Gary Numan and OMD.

With an increase in the use and diversity of samples and greater sonic and dynamic variation than in the past, **Last Rights** unwinds the sound a little to good effect. Except for Ogre's comically grubby vocals, Skinny Puppy seems to have geared itself here for soundtrack atmospheres more than dancefloor domination. But while "Killing Game," the symphonic "Riverz End" and the sketchy collage of "Lust Chance" benefit mightily from respites and reductions in the pressure and density, the European influence of extremists like Test Dept. and Einstürzende Neubauten is clearly audible in the calamitous violence of "Knowhere?" and "Scrapyard," which amusingly crushes a spot of hoedown violin under the thunder. And "Download" ends the album in a maddening blizzard of backward electronic regurgitation that will undoubtedly send listeners rushing to check the condition of their CD players.

Skinny Puppy's final proper album was completed only after three years' work with four different producers (Roli Mosimann, Martin Atkins, Greg Reely and Dave Ogilvie, who alone is credited, although Atkins is listed as a vocalist on "Death"). By the time the smoke cleared, Ogre had quit the band (June '95) and Goettel had died of a heroin overdose (August '95), thereby putting an end to Skinny Puppy before the album's release. A stripped-down stroke of stylistic ambition that vainly attempts to incorporate such shocking innovations (for these guys) as Ogre's inept melody singing and an accented 4/4 drum beat (on the dreamy "The Cult" and the weirdly effective "Amnesia"), **The Process** supposedly concerns a "psychotherapy cult" from the '60s, a notion ungleanable from simply listening to the record. Ironically, the band's change of direction would be welcome if there were a chance it could be refined and better applied in the future, but as it stands, **The Process** arrived too late for all concerned.

Skinny Puppy's early work is easily accessible thanks to the merged **Bites and Remission** repackage, the **Twelve Inch Anthology** (which assembles four singles from the latter half of the '80s) and **Back and Forth Series Two** (compiled from the band's pre-Nettwerk cassette releases, plus home demos and live cuts from the early '80s). The two-CD **Brap,** an enhanced double-CD, footnotes the band's career with two dozen live tracks and demos.

The one common thread of Skinny Puppy's side projects is that none of them involved Ogre. (No more prone to idleness, he did some time with Pigface, and has a group with Raven of Killing Joke.) The Tear Garden is Key's collaboration with singer Edward Ka-Spel of the Legendary Pink Dots. Hilt attaches Alan Nelson (a '70s punk-rock bandmate of Key's) to the non-Ogre Puppys. Doubting Thomas is simply a no-vocalist duo of Key and Goettel. The ambient techno/industrial tracks on **The Infidel** date from 1987 to 1990. [tr]

See also *Dead Voices on Air, Ministry, Pigface; TPRG.*

SKUNK

See *Chavez.*

SKY CRIES MARY

Until the Grinders Cease (Fr. Lively Art/New Rose) 1989
Don't Eat the Dirt . . . EP (Fr. Lively Art/New Rose) 1990
Exit at the Axis EP (World Domination) 1992
A Return to the Inner Experience (World Domination) 1993
This Timeless Turning (World Domination) 1994

Seattle's Sky Cries Mary didn't set out to revitalize the legend of Hawkwind and rekindle the notion of space rock (or even become a Jefferson Airplane for the '90s). Actually, the group began by making particularly nasty noises in the guise of an industrial band. SCM began as theater student Roderick Romero's senior thesis, and evolved into dadaesque cacophony. Jon Auer and Ken Stringfellow, who were simultaneously writing and recording clever pop songs as the Posies, hit things and looped tapes—think Negativland, not Ministry—while Roderick made grating noises into the microphone. Early sets were as much performance art as music, and presented as a kind of endurance test for local hipsters. The aptly titled debut, **Until the Grinders Cease** (engineered and mixed by Auer), is a comparatively moderate document of that phase. The band was much more abrasive live, though "When the Fear Stops" is a precursor to the more spiritual bent that eventually followed. The CD offers a ninth bonus track.

Don't Eat the Dirt . . . is much the same, with the addition of input from maverick producer Steve Fisk. The EP includes a Fisk remix of "When the Fear Stops," a more varied supporting cast and an unrecognizable version of Jimi Hendrix's "Spanish Castle Magic." That, along with a video also entitled **Until the Grinders Cease,** was enough to convince Dave Allen that he'd found the next great industrial band, and he signed them to his World Domination label.

And then things changed. Roderick reconnected with singer Anisa (they subsequently married), who'd had a cameo in his senior thesis. The four-song label debut, **Exit at the Axis,** introduced Anisa, as well as DJ Fallout, drummer Ben James, bassist Joe Howard (now a member of the Posies) and guitarist Ivan Kral (Patti Smith Group, Iggy Pop). The transition became complete by 1993's **A Return to the Inner Experience**, by which time Kral had departed. While the background still hides the sounds of inanimate objects being beaten, the full-length album has a decidedly Eastern—and vastly more spiritual—bent. Live shows began incorporating incense and a light show; Roderick and Anisa wrapped their voices around each other as if singing were a tantric exercise. (Maybe it is.) The result isn't so much dance music as it is trance music. Cornershop has come at the same combination of sounds from a markedly different starting point, but with much the same result.

Guitarist Michael Cozzi (ex-Shriekback) joined in time for **This Timeless Turning;** Howard was replaced by the one-named Juano. The songs are slightly more forceful, and both singers sound as if they're more comfortable with their roles. The business behind the voices continues to be dense and layered, though live it's sometimes hard to tell exactly which musician is emitting those sounds. [ga]

See also *Low Pop Suicide, Posies.*

SLACK

See *Tsunami.*

SLANT 6

Soda Pop*Rip Off (Dischord) 1994
Inzombia (Dischord) 1995

AUTOCLAVE

I'll Take You Down EP7 (K/Dischord) 1992
Autoclave EP10 (Mira/Dischord) 1992

Nicely updating the stripped-down power and acute melodic skills of Wire with a slightly charming, amateurish rhythmic attack, Washington DC's Slant 6 offered refreshing primitivism amid the increasingly prog-ish early-'90s Dischord sound. Led by guitarist/singer Christina Billotte with drummer Marge Marshall and bassist Myra Power, the combo delivers succinct but clunky punk-rock highlighted by unexpectedly strong pop hooks and occasionally odd instrumental angularities on its debut. While the rhythm section sometimes struggles to keep a steady beat, Billotte is talented enough to offset these setbacks with a rare blend of supreme confidence, breezy attitude and consistently terrific songs.

Inzombia is a major disappointment. While the trio's playing has improved, the songs are lackluster. They do take more chances—the largely rhythm-free "Click Click," the girl-group-isms of "Ladybug Superfly" and the humor in "Retro Duck"—but the tedious title track, which takes up a third of the short album, is an extended chunk of quasi-sci-fi film filler that feebly attempts to create horrific atmospheres through poorly executed pin-drop drama. The group broke up shortly after its release.

Before forming Slant 6, Billotte played bass in Autoclave with Mary Timony (pre-Helium). The quartet's eponymous six-song 10-inch showcases plenty of endlessly inventive twin-guitar counterpoint, setting languid, remarkably sophisticated pop tunes amid a sumptuous, harmonically compelling sound world. It's unfortunate Autoclave had such a short existence; years after the group's dissolution, there's still no one producing records that resemble this distinctively knotted music. [pm]

See also *Helium.*

SLAPP HAPPY

See *Peter Blegvad.*

SLAPP HAPPY HUMPHREY

Slap Happy Humphrey (Public Bath) 1995

While English and American bands struggle to make a measly millimeter of stylistic progress here and there, Japan's Slapp Happy Humphrey (the name is a meaningless overlap of Peter Blegvad's old group and wrestler Happy Humphrey) comes along with a bizarre concept that doesn't tinker with convention so much as pour gasoline on it and strike a match. What the trio does—carefully explained in the eponymous debut's liner notes by guitarist Jojo Hiroshige (which would truly be perfect if they were a complete fabrication)—is to cover songs by '70s/'80s pop singer Morita Doji, with Mineko Itakura cooing them gently over Fujiwara's implacable acoustic guitar and weepy violin. What makes it so strange is the irregular intrusions of Jojo's highly compressed but otherwise uncontrolled noise demonstrations. It's as if an overly sensitive shortwave tuner were picking up an Yma Sumac broadcast *and* the top end of a Sonic Youth practice session. The two elements never do better than occupy the same air space; any connection between them is strictly hypothetical. Incidentally, for those desperate enough to care, Jojo (who runs Alchemy Records) mentions his vocal solo project, Nishijin Saburo, and declares that since "he began the style known as 'noise' in 1979, there hasn't been any *original* music." Get back, Jo. [i]

SLASH'S SNAKEPIT

See *Guns n' Roses.*

SLAYER

Show No Mercy (Metal Blade) 1983
Hell Awaits (Metal Blade) 1985
Live Undead (Metal Blade) 1985
Reign in Blood (Def Jam) 1986
South of Heaven (Def Jam) 1988
Seasons in the Abyss (Def American) 1990
Live: Decade of Aggression (Def American) 1991
Divine Intervention (American) 1995
Undisputed Attitude (American) 1996

TSOL/SLAYER

Abolish Government EP7 (Sub Pop) 1996

"Bones and blood lie on the ground/Rotten limbs lie dead/Decapitated bodies found/On my wall: your head!" Whether you find these lyrics brilliant, hilarious, moronic, repulsive or genuinely evil (or all of the above) is a nearly foolproof barometer of how you'll feel about Slayer. A more hateful breed than homeboys Metallica or Megadeth, Slayer was formed in Orange County, California, in 1982 by singer/bassist Tom Araya and guitarists Kerry King and Jeff Hanneman.

Musically, the band combines the frenzied speed and power of hardcore with Black Sabbath's lurching riffs and ultra-graphic takes on lyrical subject matter. While rockers from Robert Johnson to Venom had flirted vaguely with the forked one down below, Slayer took the pure evil image to realms of hitherto-unimagined overkill on **Show No Mercy** and **Hell Awaits.** Although the production is hardly pristine, Slayer's first two albums are unquestionably among the most threatening music of their time. The **Show No Mercy** CD adds a three-song 1984 EP, **Haunting the Chapel; Live Undead** is a barely listenable '84 live set some claim was recorded in a rehearsal with a bunch of noisy friends.

The unlikely figure of producer Rick Rubin then entered the picture. Although known at that point only for his pioneering work in rap, Rubin had long been sampling old metal albums, and co-produced "Walk This Way," Run–DMC's duet with Aerosmith. Applying his lean, less-is-more production technique to Slayer's blistering aural apocalypse, **Reign in Blood** wields a punch, clarity and sense of doom rivaled only by Sabbath and Metallica's best. Variations on the word "death" appear in the lyrics no fewer than fifty-six times; between "Angel of Death" (a revoltingly graphic song about Joseph Mengele) and "Jesus Saves," the album manages to offend all denominations. (Public Enemy later sampled the refrain of "Angel of Death" on "She Watch Channel Zero?!" to staggering effect. In a further bit of pan–Def Jam incest, King contributed "frozen metal" guitar to the Beastie Boys' "No Sleep Till Brooklyn.") A surgically precise hit-and-run attack that lasts all of twenty-six minutes, **Reign in Blood** is almost universally regarded as the ultimate speedmetal LP.

Slayer's cover of "In-a-Gadda-Da-Vida" on the *Less Than Zero* soundtrack was an indicator of things to come. Having established a reputation as the fastest and most extreme band in the world, Slayer did the only thing possible: slow down. Produced by Rubin and the band, **South of Heaven**'s sound is even leaner, with Dave Lombardo's astonishingly innovative drumming providing an intricate framework for the sharp, angular riffs and pig-squeal leads. Most impressively, this album grooves from end to end. Araya comes into his own, lofting haunting melodic refrains as well as his trademark volatile spew. The lyrics confront such real-life topics as mass-murderers, abortion and yet more Nazis. **Seasons in the Abyss** basically fuses its two predecessors, exploring little new territory and even repeating ideas from older songs. That said, it's still a scorcher, and the title track is one of the quartet's best songs.

Coinciding (fittingly enough) with the Gulf War, the band's first arena tour was documented on the twenty-three-track **Live: Decade of Aggression,** originally released in an extremely heavy limited-edition metal case. Although it's basically a greatest-hits-live outing, the earlier material sounds great in the hands of the by-then-seasoned band, and it contains some long-absent friends like "The Anti-Christ."

For the next four years, inactivity reigned in the Slayer camp. Lombardo left and was replaced by ex-Exodus drummer Paul Bostaph, who debuted on the blistering "Disorder," a collaboration with Ice-T for the *Judgment Night* soundtrack (which united rappers and rock bands, to generally excruciating results). While not much of a traditional "song," this five-minute apocalyptic rant is one of the most exciting tracks Slayer's ever laid to wax. Unfortunately, the same cannot be said of **Divine Intervention,** which is awfully by-the-numbers considering the time it took to make. A lot of the old punch is missing (maybe because Rubin sat this one out), Araya's voice sounds tired and the band isn't doing anything drastically different from what it did in 1988. While still a powerfully aggressive band, Slayer is in danger of becoming a nostalgia act.

That threat goes unchallenged by **Undisputed Attitude,** Slayer's covers album. The choice of material—unreconstructed hardcore songs by Minor Threat, D.I., Dirty Rotten Imbeciles, Dr. Know, TSOL, Verbal Abuse—leads the band straight into old-time thrashland. Toning down the imposing grandeur of its evil empire, Slayer takes convincing small-scale breakneck rips through simple ravers like "Guilty of Being White," "Abolish Government" and "I Hate You" (plus two of Hanneman's vintage contributions to the genre, an incongruous new slow metal number, "Gemini," and an uncalled-for sexual rewrite of "I Wanna Be Your Dog"). The album is fine for what it is, but Slayer could be roasting in commercial hell if it doesn't start looking forward sometime soon. Now *that's* scary.

The high-concept '96 EP matches the Slayer album's TSOL cover medley with that band's original renditions of the same songs, "Abolish Government" and "Superficial Love." [ja/i]

See also *TPRG*.

SLEATER-KINNEY

See *Heavens to Betsy.*

SLEEPERS

See *Toiling Midgets.*

SLEEPYHEAD

Punk Rock City USA (Slumberland) 1993
Hot Stuff EP (Sp. Radiation) 1994
Starduster (Homestead) 1994
Communist Love Songs (Homestead) 1996

VARIOUS ARTISTS

Chinny Chin Chin (See Eye) 1992

Twinky pop students of Sonic Youth, New York's Sleepyhead wields noisy guitars and some of the airiest vocals on the planet. For all of the casual instrumental aggression, the trio—Michael Galinsky (bass), Chris O'Rourke (guitar/vocals/keyboards) and Rachael McNally (drums/vocals)—sings its eccentrically titled love missives with a timorous adolescent fervor. That effect amplifies the lyrics' wimp factor, maxing out the winsomosity of **Punk Rock City USA** numbers like "Riff Test" and the mostly acoustic "Different Colored Letters." (Before the debut album, Sleepyhead issued a pair of singles and contributed four songs to a '92 compilation.)

Previewed on a Spanish EP named for one of its songs, **Starduster** (which, unlike the first album, contains the hyperspeed "Punk Rock City USA") starts out by claiming adulthood at twenty-two in "What's Gonna Set You Free?" and proceeds to demonstrate an elevated state of maturity in subject matter, songwriting and arrangements. (Diminishing his vocal diffidence, O'Rourke employs a hoarse whisper for most of the record.) Concurrent with a tendency toward restrained playing is the dose of well-crafted lyrical imagination that leads to intriguing places like the tremolo-powered afterlife of "Sick of Heaven." A clear mix and the band's understatement casts **Starduster** toward subtler tastes, but Sleepyhead's gentle charms remain intact.

Co-produced by Martin Bisi, **Communist Love Songs** is an all-ways-'round improvement, an absolute charmer of alluring pop, inveigling organ strains, witty and substantial lyrics and an increased vocal role for McNally. She duets (disorientingly, given that their voices have the same helium register) with O'Rourke on "The Communist Love Song," making a romantic joke of Marxist sensibilities ("I think you love your credit card much more than you love me"). Managing everything from a sweet lilt to cagey fortitude and urgent intensity, the trio replaces the we-can't-play we're-indie-rock excuse with modest excellence; whatever their political affiliation, "My Blooz," the goofy "Ice Cream Cone," the biographical ballad "Rolling Rita" and "Forensic Studies Show" make **Communist Love Songs** an easy winner of minds and hearts. [i]

SLICK RICK

The Great Adventures of Slick Rick (Def Jam/Columbia) 1989
The Ruler's Back (Def Jam/Columbia) 1991
Behind Bars (Def Jam) 1994

Penal reform hasn't yet gotten around to offering prison inmates easy access to professional recording facilities, but the increasing incidence of jail time among active rap artists has sent associates scrambling for ways to keep their music in circulation even when they're not. As hard as it is to juggle the logistical demands and creative resources of a busy career, having to work around the judicial system must up the difficulty factor considerably. If not quite on a par with an escape from Alcatraz, getting albums out of convicted felons takes a parlor trick of ingenious bail-based/work-release scheduling.

In 1985, Doug E. Fresh and MC Ricky D earned eternal hip-hop points for the brash, nearly innocent human beat-box single "La-Di-Da-Di" (b/w "The Show"), an early, influential and endlessly quoted party rap record. As Slick Rick, however, the London-born Ricky Walters returned with the same relaxed sing-song delivery *and* lyrics of stunning misogyny and vulgarity. (While it contains some innocuous rhymes, **The Great Adventures** pivots on such charmers as "Treat Her Like a Prostitute" and the ambiguously moralized criminality of "Children's Story.")

Bringing some unintended prophecies of the album to pass, Walter wound up convicted of attempted murder for a 1990 shooting incident and had to record **The Ruler's Back** (named for a track on his debut) while waiting to be sentenced. Exhibiting surprisingly good judgment on what is his most entertaining and least offensive longplayer, Rick doesn't sink to the crudity of the first album. He doesn't make much of his legal situation, either. Instead, Rick devotes his clever storytelling prowess to a tale of sexual two-timing ("I Shouldn't Have Done It"), a cinematic dope deal ("Bond"), a romantic campaign ("Venus," complete with a sung *and* whistled interlude of the '59 Frankie Avalon hit) and a highly colloquial version of the Old Testament ("Moses"). Besides looping "La-Di-Da-Di" into several tracks, producer Vance Wright pumps up busy, exciting dance beats, pushing Rick into a faster, more invigorated flow on its way to dancehall bounce. And with that, Slick Rick began his enforced hiatus.

Several years of incarceration (and deportation battles and parole hearings) later, **Behind Bars**—actually recorded during a work-release furlough and augmented by leftovers from **The Ruler's Back** and remixes—touches on the live-from-inside chill of an Iceberg Slim novel in the title track, but otherwise doesn't mention it. Referring to prison in the opener, "Behind Bars," as "razorblade city," Walters—sounding tougher but unbroken—breathes a temporary sigh of relief at being out: "At least for now, no more accumulatin' cuts and scars behind bars." From there, relationship trouble is the order of the day. ("I'm Captive" ignores the title's obvious topical potential.)

The album is understandably fragmented; it takes awhile to settle down after the shift from Prince Paul's hard beats on "Behind Bars" to the gentle soul of "All Alone (No One to Be With)," a supportive and sympathetic portrait of a young single mother. Rick doesn't seem very connected to the music, but his complaints ring with the rancid air of preoccupation by someone with too much time to obsess about his frustrations. Beginning with the announcement that "bitches ain't no good," Rick details disastrous encounters (including the acquisition of herpes) in "A Love That's True (Part I)"; "Get a Job" accuses women of not earning their keep. The ear-pleasing "Sittin' in My Car" makes fine use of Billy Stewart's summery "Sitting in the Park," but Rick's rude rhyme about cheating on a girlfriend spoils the music's seductive power. [i]

See also *TPRG*.

SLINT

Tweez (Jennifer Hartman) 1989 (Touch and Go) 1993
Spiderland (Touch and Go) 1991
Slint EP (Touch and Go) 1994

THE FOR CARNATION

Fight Songs EP (Matador) 1995
Marshmallows EP (Matador) 1996

Formed by former Squirrel Bait members Brian McMahan (guitar) and Britt Walford (drums), Slint ruptured the impenetrably dense facade of late-'80s ugly rock. While the Louisville quartet's 1989 debut **Tweez** (actually recorded in 1987, with Steve Albini) posits a variety of then-functionless tactics, approaches and strange sonic schematics, it set the stage for what was to come on the second installment of the band's troubled existence. Extreme leaps in dynamic range—in terms of volume, density and tempo—are achieved by some alchemical grace without ever actually managing to deliver a real song anywhere on the record. Mixing a lopsided punk spirit with seemingly incongruous mathematical precision, Slint bore out a weird twist on prog-rock. By and large **Tweez** is an album of fractured but exciting ideas, loosely strewn together with garbled dialogue, random screams and weird sonic effects. Shortly after recording the album, bassist Ethan Buckler left the band, eventually forming King Kong, and was replaced by Todd Brashear.

The six lengthy songs that make up 1991's **Spiderland,** again recorded by Albini, are dramatically more developed and sophisticated than anything on the debut, beautifully transporting the flurry of vibrant ideas from **Tweez** into dizzyingly complex but transcendent tunes. While McMahan's lyrics remain hopelessly oblique and a bit precious, there is nevertheless a palpable shift from notebook scribblings toward narrative experimentation. In conjunction with this change, his vocal delivery is synchronized with the music, his hushed mumbling accompanying the quiet parts while an unrelenting scream rises to meet the loud sections. Walford's powerful drumming undergirds a complicated lattice of harmonically puzzling, contrapuntal guitar lines and thick, propulsive basslines. The band's remarkable ability to shift sonic gears—from soft to hard and spare to cluttered—contributes to the unique power of the songs, which seem concerned with the arduous journey more than the destination.

The eponymous EP features two nameless songs recorded between the band's albums that provide a useful illustration of Slint's transformation, as well as suggesting the secondary nature of lyrics. Both cuts are instrumental, but it seems as if words were meant to be inserted at a later date.

Slint's influence has proven vast and far-reaching, spawning loads of less important imitators such as Rodan and June of 44. While most of Slint's ex-members played in early incarnations of Palace Brothers, guitarist David Pajo went on to join Chicago's Tortoise, Walford drummed pseudonymously on the first Breeders album and played keyboards in King Kong. McMahan withdrew from music for several years before moving to Chicago and forming The For Carnation. On **Fight Songs,** the band's three-song debut, McMahan is joined by Pajo (since departed), drummer John Herndon and bassist Doug McCombs (both of whom play in Tortoise) to muse upon the more lyrical side of Slint. "Grace Beneath the Pines" is a lengthy and quiet solo piece with fairly ridiculous but highly personal lyrics, while the short instrumental "How I Beat the Devil" is surprisingly jaunty, exuding a marked Slovenly influence.

The For Carnation's six-song **Marshmallows** non-specifically credits McMahan, Herndon, McCombs, Brad Wood and four others. [pm]

See also *Breeders, Gastr del Sol, King Kong, Tortoise; TPRG.*

SLIPSTREAM

See *Spiritualized.*

SLOAN

Peppermint EP (Can. Murderecords) 1992
Smeared (DGC) 1993
Underwhelmed EP (DGC) 1993
Twice Removed (DGC) 1994
One Chord to Another (Can. Murderecords) 1996

Their adventures in the greater alternarock world may not have left an enormous cosmic dent anywhere else, but in Halifax, Nova Scotia—a remote maritime city previously marked as the hometown Sarah McLachlan left—Sloan is a name young people know. Through their records, their involvement in the indie Murderecords label and their stylistic influence on other bands, Sloan has not only made the great Northeast a better place in which to shake and pop but also helped haul Canadian rock into greater synch with the Anglo-American hipoisie.

The six-song **Peppermint** EP, recorded quickly, cheaply and casually at co-producer Terry Pulliam's Halifax home, demonstrates most of the quartet's best attributes in raw form: thick, noisy storms of guitar energy, gently alluring melodic vocals (with guest help from Jennifer Pierce of Jale), the self-effacing diffidence and clever wordplay of "Underwhelmed," the friendship observations of "Marcus Said," the surging melodic power of "Sugartune." All three songs, and nine others cut at the same time, were later cleaned up and edited by remixer Dave Ogilvie for inclusion on **Smeared;** the others ("Pretty Voice," "Lucky for Me," "Torn") are no less nifty for having been left behind.

When Ogilvie finished remixing the tracks that became **Smeared,** the band's sloppy, inexperienced punk enthusiasm had been decanted into sparkling, sublimely balanced punk-pop power that reveals the multiplicity of Sloan's influences. Very nearly a stylistic sampler of cool bands, the group mixes up the sounds of My Bloody Valentine, Nirvana, Sonic Youth, Dinosaur Jr, Velvet Underground, Cheap Trick and others, adding the diversity that comes from having four singers/songwriters. Sloan combines elements that should compete and cancel each other out; the resulting songs somehow become double-strength artistic achievements. The whoosh of feedback that howls through the pretty "I Am the Cancer" does nothing to untie the song's emotional connections; the nerdy dictionary exercise of "Underwhelmed" makes a failed pass sound even more unjust; the Sonic Youth guitar bed of "500 Up" only contributes to the wryness of the lyrics' trendinista jibe ("but all they really care about is cutting their hair/and letting it grow").

The album's semi-acoustic "What's There to Decide?" joins "Underwhelmed" on the subsequent EP, along with two newly recorded items. "Amped" is in the **Smeared** spirit, but the eight heavy-bottomed minutes of "Sleepover" points to a new set of influences and ambitions driving Sloan.

Recorded two-and-a-half years after **Smeared,** the mature, pensive and eclectic **Twice Removed** presents a very different picture. Gone are the dense skeins of squalling noise and specific sonic citations, replaced by carefully intertwined, spaciously electric arrangements, evanescent '60s harmonies and trickier rhythms. As on **Smeared,** Sloan (working here with producer Jim Rondinelli) treat each song as a separate undertaking, holding on to a central reserved guitar-pop tone while allowing each member's creations to assume their own shape. Although the credits specify lead singer, not author, guitarist Jay Ferguson, bassist Chris Murphy, guitarist Patrick Pentland and drummer Andrew Scott clearly take turns at the creative controls, with mixed but predominately good results. Amazingly, the album holds together—complex, subtle, rich in ideas and fascinating in its shy, sardonic unhappiness. Murphy's "Penpals" stitches together phrases from foreign fan letters ("I have only thirteen years and I am crazy of you . . . send me documents"), allowing their linguistic clumsiness to become a charm, not a joke. In "Bells On," he quietly lists a litany of trouble—"While I'm at this funeral/You're in New York/I've been divided by grieving/You're sleeping with a mutual friend"—before unleashing the dogs. "If you had a funeral/I'd be there with bells on," he sneers, and then dances on with a merry la-la-la refrain. His

"Coax Me" also deals with death, but absurdly lightens the load with orange juice and Consolidated ("It's not the band I hate, it's their fans"). "Think I've lost my sense of humor," warns Pentland in "Worried Now," suffering mightily from the high anxiety of being told not to worry. Ferguson begins the jagged guitar/fuzz-bass "Snowsuit Sound" with a bad memory—"Pushed off of the silver swings/I got my braces full of sand"—and then watches things get worse from there, allowing the song to nearly reach the halfway point before suddenly unveiling one of the most heavenly refrains Brian Wilson overlooked when he was writing music for Jan and Dean.

Evidently, the four Sloan squares were losing their gravitational center, and the group spent much of '95 playing farewell shows and pursuing outside interests (variously managing the Inbreds, drumming for Super Friendz, playing in the Sadies and working at Murderecords). After all that, however, Sloan released a new 45 ("Same Old Flame" b/w "Stood Up") late in the year and quickly recorded a third album. **One Chord to Another** shrugs off retirement with audible nonchalance and renewed spirit. A happy result of confident and mature pop artistry, the (mostly) low-key songs restate the debut's youthful innocence with refreshing stylistic simplicity, horns and gorgeous harmony arrangements underscoring the canny '60s Beach Boys/Beatles sensibility that pops in and out of the record. Welcome back! [i]

See also *Jale.*

SLOVENLY

See *Overpass.*

SLOWDIVE

Just for a Day (UK Creation) 1991 (Creation/SBK) 1992
Blue Day (Fr. Creation) 1992
Souvlaki (UK Creation) 1993 (Creation/SBK) 1994
Pygmalion (UK Creation) 1995

MOJAVE 3

Ask Me Tomorrow (4AD) 1996

Imagine if mid-period Cocteau Twins sang in recognizable English and used more conventional rock structures, with three guitarists so steeped in echo and delay it's almost dizzying. Add irresistible melodies and male/female harmony cooing. Reading quintet Slowdive never quite earned the respect they deserved—with the exception of some accolades heaped on their first three singles—but they were surprisingly one of England's most formidable bands when the tempest they whipped up was at its most swirling.

Just for a Day is up and down in material, but the songs that are solid are breathtaking, and those that aren't are at least hypnotic and slowly sensuous. "Spanish Air" and "Catch the Breeze" have perfectly windswept, otherworldly textures and a timeless, boundless beauty thanks to those oceans of guitars and Simon Scott's surprisingly aggressive drumming. The two-minute coda to "Catch the Breeze" is the band's zenith, a rapturous non-vocal passage of subconscious wonder.

Blue Day compiles the band's first three singles (minus "Catch the Breeze" and a cover of Syd Barrett's "Golden Hair"). Three of the seven songs show why the press raved: "Slowdive" sports a guitar line so memorable it sears. Likewise, "Morningrise" and "She Calls" (which has another sparkling instrumental passage to rival "Catch the Breeze") are dense lattices of splendor.

Though not as big or swirling, **Souvlaki** is more consistent in that it continues the thunderous mood music with the songwriting more to the fore. Everything is simplified, as if Brian Eno's presence on two songs—he contributes keyboards and treatments, and co-wrote one tune—hammered home the better aspects of ambient music. On the opening "Alison," the largely uplifting "When the Sun Hits" and the darkly blissful "Machine Gun," Slowdive proves it is still capable of jaw-dropping flourishes. Best of all, a mild dose of reggae propels "Souvlaki Space Station" to fascinating, trance-like heights amidst the rain of guitars. (The US edition adds four songs, including a cover of Lee Hazlewood's "Some Velvet Morning.")

Slowdive may have spent too much time with Eno: **Pygmalion** is totally out of left field. Essentially a solo ambient recording by singer/guitarist Neil Halstead that should have been released under his own name, it completely lacks all the tension, songwriting, sounds and power of the band's work, leaving only the spatial dimensions. As background mood music, Talk Talk did this better; at best, **Pygmalion** is an LP to fall asleep to. A couple of tracks approximate the band's former dream-like sound and pulse, but otherwise it's an unmitigated disappointment.

Slowdive was dropped shortly after **Pygmalion**'s release. Halstead, Rachel Goswell (Slowdive's other singer) and drummer Ian McCutcheon became Mojave 3 and signed to 4AD. With the new name and label came a complete change in direction: On **Ask Me Tomorrow,** Halstead's once-billowing cathedrals-of-sound guitar becomes a teasing whisper, plucked as delicately as if someone were sleeping nearby. (McCutcheon has to resort to brushes in order to keep from drowning him out.) But instead of snoozy background music, the album returns to the musicians' strengths, with developed compositions and pretty chords again harnessing Goswell's gentle singing to wistful, caressing music. Songs such as the Mazzy Starish opener "Love Songs on the Radio," "Tomorrow's Taken" and the biggest-sounding thing here, the closing "Mercy" (great insistent piano by Christopher Andrews) don't just tickle and tease, they tug. The mountainous sonic vistas are likely gone forever, but, in the quietest way possible, Mojave 3 remains among the most beautiful noises in all of creation. [jr]

SLUDGEWORTH

See *Screeching Weasel.*

SLUG

Swingers (Magnatone) 1993
The Out Sound (PCP) 1994
The Three Man Themes (PCP) 1995

The members of this industrial-noise-college (collage) rock band met and formed Slug in 1988 while working as DJs at KXLU, the radio station of Loyola Marymount University in Los Angeles. Drummer Tomas Palermo, bassist Damion Romero and guitarist Todd Williams kicked off Slug's illustrious career by staging a series of guerrilla performances in a campus quadrangle where the trio "entertained" fellow students with raging feedback and other Big Black–like noise assaults of guitars, boom boxes, turntables and a microphone. Within a year, Slug had added three more KXLU air personalities: singer Steve Ratter, second guitarist Rich Alvarez and second bassist Michael B. After landing some gigs in the greater LA area, Slug began releasing singles and EPs on its own Magnatone label, most of which are collected on the debut CD.

Swingers' title track opens like a Glenn Branca suite, with Ratter's wails blended into a thick, buzzing wall of guitars and basses. The rest of the music is equally influenced by the noise and avant-garde rock coming from downtown New York, as well as the DJ/collage work of artists ranging from Public Enemy's Bomb Squad to Throbbing Gristle. As powerful and abrasive as tracks like "Lockjaw" and "Face Down" are, however, Slug had not yet mastered the art of recording. As a result, songs that shake like an earthquake in a live setting fall a bit flat in the studio. Slug makes up for it with humor, interjecting samples of cartoons and preachers between the clatter.

Bassist Collin Rae (a veteran of several experimental bands, including Ultra Vivid Scene) replaced Alvarez before Slug recorded **The Out Sound.** The group's music begins moving outward in all directions here, with lengthier songs, more dynamic range and adventurous studio tinkering. In some places, the band incorporates the loud-soft dynamics of Nirvana ("Ex-Chest"); in others, they come off much like San Diego's similar (if slightly more accessible) Drive Like Jehu, with screeched vocals, wild tempo changes, a hulking drive and instrumental intensity ("Aurora F"). The album also features a hint of things to come in the gentler, spacier, dub bass and psychedelic guitar sound of "Coordinate Points."

Between **The Out Sound** and the ambitious double-length **The Three Man Themes,** drummer Palermo (host of KLXU's dub reggae show) had been busy at local clubs as trip-hop DJ Tomas, writing for the techno/dance zine *Urb* and clerking at an indie record store. Meanwhile, Ratter had begun playing keyboards. Their respective experiences made a great impact on **The Three Man Themes,** moving Slug from its original Branca/Big Black persona to ambient-dub-psychedelic punk-rock. While the album includes its quota of lurching, acid-tinged guitar squalling, drones and harmonics ("Unesque," "Resonance Man"), it also finds the band exploring Aphex Twin territory. "The Grey Man" is an extended suite of electronic ambience intermittently spiced with gurgling aquatic sounds and jingling metallic noises. There's also dub ("The Distinct Room"), a Tanzanian witchcraft song ("Kayamba Dance"), a Can cover ("Oh Yeah!") and an instrumental tribute to early Sonic Youth ("The Gentle Man"). Amazingly, it all holds together seamlessly. Whether or not Slug continues such excursions in several different directions at once, **The Three Man Themes** will likely stand as its masterwork. [mrk]

SMACK DAB

Queen Crab (Homestead) 1993
Majestic Root (Homestead) 1994

This quirky Brooklyn combo was formed at the urging of Wm. Berger (here playing drums), who recognized creative sparkle in modern dancer Linda Hagood and encouraged her to take up guitar and songwriting. The duo was joined by bassist Alec Stephens on **Queen Crab,** a wonderful collection of light, idiosyncratic material like "Big Planet," "Lucky" and "Dancing Uvula." With a cartoony southern voice so high-pitched that many reckoned it to be contrived (it's not), Hagood fits in with the love-rock of Beat Happening and the Mad Scene but shows more musical ambition. Contributions to tribute albums for the Fall and Love around this time showed Smack Dab's versatility and humor.

After Berger left to concentrate on Uncle Wiggly, newcomer J. Z. Barrell (ex–Alter Boys) brought his studio engineering prowess and instrumental versatility to the fuller, more mature **Majestic Root.** Where **Queen Crab** was a fanciful one-woman show with excellent support, **Majestic Root** shows Hagood's positive reflections on love and life in a more adult light, with subdued tones and more intricate arrangements. The agile band covers a great deal of sultry, arty and troubled ground under her indelible stylistic stamp. Stephens exited Smack Dab in 1994 for a career slinging guitar with Railroad Jerk and was suitably replaced by Kansas City's Jeffrey J. Jensen, a Jonathan Richman fanatic. [ic]

See also *Railroad Jerk, Uncle Wiggly.*

SMALL

Cakes EP (Rockville) 1993
Free T-Shirts for Spain EP (Alias) 1994
Chin Music (Alias) 1994
Silver Gleaming Death Machine (Alias) 1995

SMALL 23

True Zero Hook (Alias) 1993

PIPE

6 Days Till Bellus (Jesus Christ) 1995
International Cement (Jesus Christ) 1996

When North Carolina's Small formed in the summer of 1991, not only was the quartet unaware that a massive amount of hype was about to descend on the Chapel Hill scene (Superchunk and its Merge label being magnets), it didn't plan on duking it out, record-bin-wise, with several other similarly named combos: Rhode Island's Small Factory, Canada's Smalls and Oregon's Small. The northwesterners' threat of legal action prompted a rechristening to Small 23 for a time during the **True Zero Hook** period (advance tapes of **Chin Music** also bore the numerically augmented name), but the group reclaimed its original moniker and released its 1994 album as Small.

Small initially consisted of ex-Superchunk drummer Chuck Garrison (who also moonlights in Pipe), bassist Matt Walter and singer/guitarists Mike Kenlan and Eric Bachmann. Walter financed the band's debut 45 as well as a split single with Pipe, attracting the attention of Rockville, which issued **Cakes.** The EP betrays an obvious Dinosaur Jr/Superchunk influence, boasting a pair of solid vocalists and a twin-guitar, rev-it-up style of scruffy, melodic pop-punk—a credible document of an eager young group.

Bachmann left just before the EP's release in order to commit full-time to his other project, Archers of Loaf; he was replaced by Dave Hollinghurst. By the fall of '93, the group had released a 45 and **True Zero Hook.** That longplaying debut suffers somewhat from depthless production and unadventurous arrangements, with too many songs simply being displays of circular riffing and chorus-based singing. Still, when Small bears down here, it shines: "Makes Me High" is a wonderful, punkish update on the old Big Star pop formula, and the six-minute "Chopsocky" carefully strides up the dynamics staircase to a delirious, feedback-ridden, anthemic finale.

The quickie EP **Free T-Shirts for Spain** finds Small moving in leaner, less hurried directions. The destination, **Chin Music,** is a diverse, rewarding stew. Benefiting from a decent recording budget and the availability of numerous guitars and amps, the record's adventurous nature includes T. Rex on a power pop binge ("Mona Skips Breakfast"), Who-ish cynical rock ("My Head Is Full of Chocolate"), Replacements-style edgy punk ("Toastmaster"), even a bit of geographical exoticism (the Eastern-tinged melodies of "The Scenic Route").

Established as one of North Carolina's leading young rock bands (along with Superchunk, Polvo and Archers of Loaf), Small made **Silver Gleaming Death Machine.** Going for a bigger, rawer feel that would accurately represent its live sound, Small relied on its proven weapons: yearning, no-angst dual vocal hooks with singalong choruses, spindly, melodic riffs grafted to meaty power chords and solid drumming in the style of Keith Moon. In a sense, this worked to the band's disadvantage, as it sacrificed personality and identity for immediacy and impact. Still, the record isn't exactly a step backward. In the dynamic rush of "Do the Math," the vocalist gets worked up to the point of hoarseness while the guitars perform two-note splits and flips.

Drummer Garrison's (and for a spell, bassist Walter's) role in Pipe diluted neither combo; in fact, Pipe earned a sort of legendary underdog status around Chapel Hill. A handful of 45s trickled out, followed by **6 Days Till Bellus,** a thirteen-song/twenty-four-minute punkfest. Vital and exhilarating, it's like a more hardcore Rocket From the Crypt, particularly in the desperate, pumice-scraped vocals and the precision fretboard uproar (the latter courtesy of former Bad Checks guitarist Cliff Mann). Highlights: "You're Soaking in It," which sounds like a cross between the Sex Pistols' "God Save the Queen" and Superchunk's "Slack Motherfucker," and the dense, clanging "The Metal Bus."

International Cement perfectly balances hardcore roar ("Recliner" and "Lo Boy" could have been recorded fifteen years ago) with dragstrip/garage-shock crunch—"Inhalación de Cemento" has a cool Yardbirds raveup feel, and the swaggering cover of Billy Childish's "Hatred, Ridicule and Contempt" is equally perfect for jukeboxes, teen dance parties and the airwaves. Throughout, the band remains tightly focused—raw as hell but with no frayed edges. Credit to producer Mitch Easter for keeping a powerful formula intact. [fm]

See also *Archers of Loaf, Superchunk.*

SMALL FACTORY

I Do Not Love You (spinART) 1993
For If You Cannot Fly (Vernon Yard) 1994
The Industrial Evolution (Pop Narcotic) 1996

GODRAYS

TV Stars With No Arms EP7 (Vernon Yard) 1996
Songs for TV Stars (Vernon Yard) 1996

For better and worse, Providence, Rhode Island's Small Factory may have been the quintessential '90s indie-pop band, a textbook example of how and why it all works—and sometimes doesn't. The tuneful and talented trio of drummer Phoebe Summersquash, guitarist David Auchenbach and bassist Alex Kemp (all of whom sing and write) displayed a firm grasp of song structures as well as the ability to express a range of youth-oriented emotions, from anxiety to pleasure and back again. The group played with well-arranged skill that never seemed fussed-over or even conscientious, generating as much or as little instrumental energy—from restrained subtlety to breezy rich harmony pop to distortion-shredded feedback blowouts—as songs demanded. After a number of catchy 7-inch singles that established club-level fanzine credibility, the band came out into album society on the right sort of label—hip, connected, just big enough. Wrapping **I Do Not Love You** in bland, enigmatic illustrations of fruit, the group survived its limitations (no wholly competent singers, no clearly distinctive sound) by maintaining an easygoing, casual style varying the sonic ingredients enough to make the record seem three-dimensional. Displaying personality ("I'm Not Giving Up"), sensitivity ("All Your Reasons") and worldliness ("Junky on a Good Day") in the lyrics—and covering "Valentine" by indie icon (and scene pal) Lois Maffeo—Small Factory took its best shot at art in the form of intimate, populist bopalong communication.

The trio was subsequently wooed and signed by the cool indiesque division of a full-scale record company leviathan. Recorded without a name-brand producer (though the solidly major-label-credentialed Jim Rondinelli did mix it), the second album was carefully formed in the image and sound of its predecessor, making no visible or audible concessions to the change of corporate venue. Despite an incrementally better studio effort, the band's basic attributes remain unchanged: Kemp's high, adenoidal singing (ably embedded in the others' pretty backing) still misses notes; arrangements keep to the straight and narrow; the shapely but rarely memorable originals are joined by another hip cover: New Radiant Storm King's "Everyone's Happy for the First Time in Weeks." Having essentially made the same album for a second time and seen it released through a sympathetic powerhouse to no substantially different effect, Small Factory chose oblivion over futility and broke up in 1995. Auchenbach launched a band called Flora Street. Kemp and Summersquash formed the Godrays and moved to New York; their debut EP is a homey and neat double 7-inch of pop-plus-guitar-noise tunes that wouldn't have been outside the realm of Small Factory's possibilities. Recorded with guests contributing added guitar, bass, vocals and percussion, **Songs for TV Stars** advances the duo's designs with added flair and more intriguingly structured songs.

The Industrial Evolution footnotes Small Factory's career in a posthumous anthology of singles and compilation tracks. [i]

SMALL 23

See *Small.*

S*M*A*S*H

S*M*A*S*H EP (Hut USA/Vernon Yard) 1994
Self Abused (Hut USA/Vernon Yard) 1994

The wanton, post-dated punk-rock and slapdash artwork favored by this shy English trio can't disguise the provocative literacy and uncompromising conviction that propels its music. Singer/guitarist Ed Borrie's lyrics—which are far less rugged in construction than the songs—make offbeat sense: "Drugs Again" (one of the four single sides compiled on the EP) weighs narcotic oblivion and romantic commitment with disarming equanimity, while "Revisited No. 3" (the EP's previously unissued item) rues a friend's self-destruction, correcting an old notion (and explaining the band's name) with the line "Suicide is not painless."

Avatars of the new wave of new wave, S*M*A*S*H borrow some of the old, add some of the new—and then slam it all into a wall at 60 mph, stepping back to admire their handiwork. The brief, brash EP—which sounds a bit like uncooked Oasis crossed with a very cranky Teenage Fanclub—is depthcharged with intriguing bits, not the least of which is a 1971 Germaine Greer essay included to explain the song "Lady Love Your Cunt." Cutting out the pop center (but revisiting "Real Surreal"), **Self Abused** is much harsher, both musically and lyrically. The album blusters along on a distorted bass bottom and scaly guitar aggression. (Think the Stranglers and Gang of Four fed through a Steve Albini noise processor, although Carter the Unstoppable Sex Machine is also a relevant comparison.) For all its superficial discouragement, however, **Self Abused** is considerably better than it appears: Borrie's voice, when he isn't roaring, is light and appealing, and the songs' melodies and ideas are worth digging through. Besides dropping references to Sir David Attenborough, Michael Jackson, Bob Dylan, the starship *Enterprise* and the Brontës, the literate band works over culture politics in "Bang Bang Bang (Granta 25)" and personal challenges in "Altruism," which promises "If my dreams aren't realized/I'm a future suicide/But I'm still alive." [i]

SMASHING PUMPKINS

Gish (Caroline) 1991
Lull EP (Caroline) 1991
Peel Sessions EP (UK Strange Fruit/Hut) 1992
Siamese Dream (Virgin) 1993
Pisces Iscariot (Virgin) 1994
Mellon Collie and the Infinite Sadness (Virgin) 1995

Perfectionists haven't had it easy in the indie-rock era—just ask Billy Corgan, the much-maligned, megalomaniacal leader of Smashing Pumpkins. In a lo-fi age, Corgan feels limited by a 72-track mixing board; from a world bounded by platinum-selling regular joes and fundamentalists who coin label names like Kill Rock Stars, he seeks old-school rock stardom of the highest degree. In short, he blurs the line between genius and jerk with more enthusiasm than just about any musician of the past decade.

Corgan has never made it easy on himself. Barely out of his teens in Chicago, the diehard, Cure-worshiping goth (an influence that can still be heard in the Pumpkins' deceptively spry angst narratives) packed up his black duds and white makeup for a move to sunny Florida—hardly the place to maintain that coveted pallor. He led a band called the Marked—named in deference to the large strawberry birthmarks shared by Corgan and the band's drummer—but soon returned to Chicago, where he formed the blueprint for the Pumpkins and then the band itself, most certainly in that order.

After a couple of indie singles—and an infrequent-but-prestigious gigging schedule that leaned heavily on management's control of the Windy City's bigger alt-rock cabarets—the Pumpkins began attracting national attention. Corgan, who admitted (and later denied) that he'd assembled the lineup of Asian androgyne James Iha (guitar), bottle-blonde ice queen D'Arcy Wretzky (bass) and all-American boy Jimmy Chamberlin (drums) for "maximum visual impact," never allowed the other members to play on Pumpkins demos—a decision that seemed wise, given the unevenness of early shows. Before long, however, Corgan's vision proved prescient—the group's glimmering grunge alternative seemed to touch a note in kids who wanted to worship at the altar of Big Rock with only the mildest of assurances that they were existing on the same plane as the band.

Co-produced by Corgan and Butch Vig, the defiantly old-fashioned **Gish** propelled the Pumpkins to demi-star status. Buoyed as it is by Corgan's conspicuous displays of virtuosity and quasi-mystical crooning, the album has an undeniable, womb-like appeal: as layer after layer of dark, warm sound wafts down upon the listener, there seems to be little choice but to lie there and be enveloped. If you can fight off the lassitude Corgan tries so hard to impart, it's easy to discern that all **Gish**'s sound and fury signify nothing more than an attempt to prove punk never happened. The ostentatious riffing and glistening structures of songs like "Rhinoceros" and "Suffer" are easily traced back to '70s pomp-rock forefathers like Rush and ELP—with Chamberlin's skittery new romantic underpinnings the only concession to modernity. Corgan's neo-classicist bent is evident in details like the modal intro to the opener, "I Am One" (not to mention its patchouli-laden lyrical gyrations), while his familiarity with the Beatles' songbook reveals itself in "Siva" (a blatant "Helter Skelter" rewrite). By disc's end, you're left with the feeling that the only reason the name of the London Symphony Orchestra doesn't appear on **Gish** is that Corgan didn't have enough time to learn the bassoon player's parts—you know, just in case.

The **Lull** EP leads off with the album version of "Rhinoceros," appending two LP outtakes ("Blue" and the unusually aggressive "Slunk") and a two-year-old demo of Corgan in a solo acoustic performance ("Bye June") that's understated and actually quite lovely.

After months in the studio—a good portion of that time *sans* band—Corgan at last produced what he referred to as the first full-blown Smashing Pumpkins album, **Siamese Dream.** The mood is promptly set by the opener, "Cherub Rock," a pseudo-anthem that wastes plenty of energy mocking and upbraiding an indie-rock scene that Corgan could buy and sell without overdrawing his checking account. The complaints are mostly disingenuous—after all, the band had worked to garner a veneer of street-cred—but it's unlikely the kids who willingly climbed between the sometimes leaden strata of mellotron and tubular bells that make up "Soma" and "Mayonaise" could care: Corgan's free-floating discontent is ambiguous enough to touch something in most everyone with a gripe. While it'd be wrong to be too hard on Corgan for borrowing from his influences—who doesn't?—you'd think that all those hours of studio time would cultivate more inspired plunderings than the "American Woman" cop that provides the intro for "Hummer" or the "Immigrant Song"–derived rhythmic fusillade that props up "Geek U.S.A." Who says the me generation is dead?

Pisces Iscariot is a typical odds'n'sods collection (mostly British B-sides) in that it's easy to see why the majority of the tracks—particularly the never-before-released trifles "Whir" and "Spaced"—didn't make the cut the first time around. Although the album starts on a deceptively intimate note with "Soothe" (a gentle track Corgan allegedly recorded alone in his bedroom), it doesn't take long for the band's typical bluster to kick in on hot-air balloons such as "Starla" and the paradigmatically crabby "Pissant." Most artists use collections like this as an opportunity to let their hair down and have some fun—especially when given the chance to pay tribute to spiritual forefathers on the obligatory array of covers. Corgan manages to savor just such a moment during a BBC-radio version of the Animals' "Girl Named Sandoz" (also on the three-song **Peel Sessions** EP), although his hipoisie-defying rendition of Stevie Nicks' Fleetwood Mac superfluity "Landslide" is just plain pointless.

After a successful stint headlining Lollapalooza, the band—all of them this time—entered the studio for a protracted stay, and it wasn't long before a trickle of advance intelligence began suggesting that the project in progress would make **Siamese Dream** sound like Half Japanese. Corgan threw down the gauntlet long before the set's completion, confessing it would be a two-record concept album, one disc of "day," one of "night." And darned if he wasn't serious: **Mellon Collie and the Infinite Sadness** (which clocks in at over 140 minutes, split evenly between *Dawn to Dusk* and *Twilight to Starlight*) is dauntingly ostentatious—it begins with a Keith Emerson–styled piano instrumental and employs a full string section—but Corgan's vision, while still overwhelmingly inward-directed, has begun to come into focus. Alternating between polished ballads (the creamy "Tonight, Tonight," the breathily insinuating "Thirty-Three") and harsh, genuinely tortured expressions of angst ("Jellybelly" finds him musing that "living makes me sick, so sick I wish I'd die"), he frames a sweeping story that's reminiscent of nothing so much as Genesis' **The Lamb Lies Down on Broadway**—but in Corgan's world, no one is innocent.

Much of the album's immediacy springs from the pared-down guitar sound. The overall tone is lush and textured, but Iha and Corgan have learned the power of positive skronk ("Where Boys Fear to Tread") and the joys of a simple fuzztone (showcased in "Bullet With Butterfly Wings"). Although Corgan *is* a bit more sympathetic this time around, it's still difficult to like a guy who'll throw a tantrum as mindless as "Fuck You (An Ode to No One)" and compound that by deadpanning lines as treacly as "Cupid hath pulled back his sweetheart's bow/To cast divine arrows into her soul" (from "Cupid de Locke"). On the surface, Corgan seems to be on a never-ending quest to play all of rock's archetypal roles at once—angst-ridden naïf and swaggering guitar hero, geeky outsider and king snake, yin and yang. But often as not, he simply ends up hiding behind his wall of machinery, hoping never to be revealed as post-modernism's very own Wizard of Oz.

Jimmy Chamberlin was sacked after his longtime drug addiction became public in the wake of tour keyboardist Jonathan Melvoin's fatal heroin overdose in a New York hotel room in July of '96. The band quickly replaced him with Matt Walker of Filter and carried on. [dss]

PAT SMEAR

See *Pat RuthenSmear.*

SMEARS

Kick My Butt EP (Hell Yeah) 1993
Love Is fer Suckers (Headhunter/Cargo) 1994
Smears in the Garage EP (Headhunter/Cargo) 1995
Like Hell (Headhunter/Cargo) 1996

With local indie-rock god John Strohm co-producing, Bloomington, Indiana's Smears—three excitable young women with extremely bad attitudes—make an impressively forceful mid-tempo racket on **Love Is fer Suckers.** Taking turns at the mic, guitarist Kathleen Gregg and bassist Gretchen Holtz roar out a frightening litany of likes (crystal meth, fucking, Patty Duke's body) and hates ("Stupid Chicks With High Voices," "Vom-Sorb," "Ear Ache," you, it), parading catchy tunes with convincing irritation. An overriding sense of good-natured humor and breaks in the volumetric pressure (the winsome "No Fun," parts of "Knock Knock Joke") help the pill go down, undercutting the Hole resemblance. Best rhyme: "I'm having a panic attack and an existential crisis/I sure would like to buy that but I don't know what the price is."

The trio followed that album with **Smears in the Garage,** an EP of covers (the CD of which appends the seven songs from the early EP), then a second Strohm-produced full-lengther, **Like Hell.** Musically refined but lyrically unrepentant, these terminal grumps describe "Worst Day of My Life," complain that "The Good Old Days Sucked" and announce "I'm a Whore" and "I'm gonna cheat on my boyfriend." "Not Fucking Happy" pretty much covers the stance here, but don't let *that* put you off what is actually a friendly sounding and peppy little record. [i]

SMILE

Maquee (Headhunter/Cargo) 1994 (Headhunter/Atlantic) 1995

While it's unlikely a power trio from the vast sprawl of Orange County, California (Tustin, to be precise), can change the rock landscape one iota, you can't blame the dry-humored Smile for trying. "Before we start/I'd like to say that we're all done," winks singer/guitarist Mike Rosas on **Maquee**'s fuzzadelic first track, "Rock Anthem for the Retarded Teenage Hipster Population," before continuing, "Remember what we started for/Remember it was fun." Fun it is. The eleven-track disc (reissued intact by Atlantic) boasts frenetic post-punk gems packed with gritty swagger ("Staring at the Sun . . ."), sunny melodies ("Spud Gun," "Moosh," "Jack Shrimp," "Until (?)") and mature percussive surprises ("Picture Made Past"). Comparisons to Nirvana are not misplaced, as Rosas' crackling guitar and wry lyrics are bolstered by the substantial rhythmic talents of drummer Scott Reeder and bassist Aaron Sonnenberg. A potent debut. [mww]

CURT SMITH

See *Tears for Fears.*

ELLIOTT SMITH

See *Heatmiser.*

KENDRA SMITH

KENDRA SMITH AND DAVID ROBACK AND KEITH MITCHELL

Fell From the Sun EP (Serpent/Enigma) 1984

OPAL

Happy Nightmare Baby (SST) 1987
Early Recordings (Serpent/Rough Trade) 1989

GUILD OF TEMPORAL ADVENTURERS

Kendra Smith Presents the Guild of Temporal Adventurers EP10 (Fiasco) 1992

KENDRA SMITH

Five Ways of Disappearing (4AD) 1995

Floating serenely through the ether, Kendra Smith has inhabited many hues of psychedelia, from the primary paisley feedback scrawl of the Dream Syndicate (which the onetime bassist co-founded with Steve Wynn in 1981) to the swirly translucence of Opal (a group with ex–Rain Parade guitarist David Roback that transmuted into Mazzy Star upon her 1988 departure), the stonewashed pale Velvet folk-rock of the informal Guild of Temporal Adventurers to the shiny, thickly applied pop-art surfaces of her solo album. Although the Californian has, on more than one occasion, followed the logic of drop-out music to its ultimate conclusion and withdrawn completely, she keeps coming back, a beguiling semi-precious stone in the not-quite-here and the not-quite-now.

Smith and Roback initially formed Clay Allison with drummer Keith Mitchell (ex–Green on Red/Romans) and guitarist Juan Gomez. Gomez and the moniker lasted for one 7-inch single, after which the remaining threesome recorded two new songs to flesh out the pleasantly understated **Fell From the Sun** and then renamed themselves Opal. That group recorded a 1985 12-inch, one full album (**Happy Nightmare Baby**) and enough leftovers to fill the posthumous **Early Recordings.**

By '91, Smith seemed to have made her back-to-rustic-life hippie move permanent and was through with even gentle rocking and rolling. **The Guild of Temporal Adventurers** put paid to that assumption. Recorded as a trio of Smith, Jonah Corey and A. Phillip Uberman with four aides-de-weird, this spare and lovely 10-inch of folky electric pop wraps the persistent Nico/Velvets element of Smith's music—underscored by her adoption of pump organ as a primary instrument—around mild mysticism and a subtle intrusion of atmospheric sound effects. (To get to Smith from the sound of Nico, hold the accent and raise the room temperature about fifteen degrees in tone and passion.) Smith does most of the singing—the lullaby-like "Stars Are in Your Eyes" and the droney "Earth Same Breath" ("All the Next Day's Parties"?) are especially pretty—but co-writer Corey joins her on two of the six songs, including the Eno-esque "Wheel of the Law."

Picking up from there with real studio effort (Smith co-produced with Uberman), **Five Ways of Disappearing** is the most ambitious and successful undertaking of Smith's career. Both a strong recapitulation and a brave relaunch, the album has it all: quiet Velvety obsessions ("Get There"), cerebral songdom ("Aurelia," "Space Unadorned"), trancey rock ("Drunken Boat"), trad folk ("Maggots"), Kurt Weill's Berlin ("Bohemian Zebulon"), folk-rock ("Valley of the Morning Sun"), new wavey bubblegum ("In Your Head") and one of the best acoustic Led Zeppelin imitations in recent memory ("Bold Marauder"). No two tracks have much in common beyond Smith's enervated singing; even when she might just be aiming to sound ordinary, the record comes off appealingly offbeat. Though some songs are amiss, precious or overly derivative, as a personal sampler, **Five Ways of Disappearing** is an impressive—and colorful—achievement. [i]

See also *Mazzy Star; TPRG.*

SMITHEREENS

Girls About Town EP7 (D-Tone) 1982
Beauty and Sadness EP (Little Ricky) 1983 (Enigma) 1988
Especially for You (Enigma) 1987 (Capitol) 1991
The Smithereens Live EP (Restless) 1987
Green Thoughts (Enigma/Capitol) 1988
11 (Enigma/Capitol) 1989
Blow Up (Capitol) 1991
A Date With the Smithereens (RCA Victor) 1994
Blown to Smithereens: Best of the Smithereens (Capitol) 1995
Attack of the Smithereens (Capitol) 1995

Putting heartfelt conviction into downcast power-pop with deep, devoted roots in rock'n'roll history, the Smithereens did something previously unimaginable in the '80s. The New Jersey quartet came out of that wonderful fringe world in which updates of old-school pop notions were understood to have no mainstream commercial appeal (Dwight Twilley and the Raspberries notwithstanding)—and proved there *was* significant sales potential for fan-made music.

A long stretch on the East Coast club scene yielded a pair of incisive and charming indie EPs before the record deal that led to the simple, memorable **Especially for You.** While the music rings with sounds of the '60s British Invasion and its American response, singer/guitarist Pat DiNizio's hurts and disappointments give the songs current resonance. The album caught a film soundtrack updraft and wound up becoming the conveyor belt for a hit single, "Blood and Roses." The Smithereens were off and running. **Green Thoughts** held the stylistic course and neatly dodged the sophomore jinx with more great songs, but the terse, tuneful and towering **11**—excellently produced by Ed Stasium—is light years better, adding rock crunch to the guitar sound and erasing the Beatlesque nostalgia with contemporary power.

That album remains the Smithereens' finest hour. Another Stasium production, **Blow Up** gets off to a good start with the biting (but stolid) "Top of the Pops" (not the Kinks' song) and a souled-out detour, "Too Much Passion," but then runs out of gas somewhere in the middle of a relevantly rueful number called "Tell Me When Did Things Go So Wrong." (Short answer: when you were persuaded to hire song doctors like Diane Warren, who wrote the turgid and conspicuous "Get a Hold of My Heart" with DiNizio.) The tired material on this pallid nadir is unimproved by restrained playing and arrangements that cover the band's assets in guest keyboards, vocals, strings and saxophone. Drummer Dennis Diken lays down a crackling backbeat and Jim Babjak cranks up his guitar for the penultimate track ("It's Alright"), but it's too little too late.

A Date With the Smithereens settles the stylistic confusion by getting rid of all the outsiders (save for Don Dixon, who co-produced with the band, and Lou Reed, who plays on two tracks) and focusing on buzzing guitar raunch taken at a deliberate pace. The proximity to metal-edged arena power is mildly disconcerting, but it's DiNizio's songwriting that has truly lost its balance. Ruminating on a romantic breakup, he wanders aimlessly between the affecting pathos of dispirited pop poetry and alienated, disconsolate grumbling, making tender emotional points in one song and sounding like a miserable, self-absorbed shit in the next. (Typically, the grim "Life Is So Beautiful" squanders its entire sense of irony in the title.) "Guess what there's a black cloud inside of my head," he sings in the opening "War for My Mind," and that's an accurate emotional forecast for this hit-and-miss album, which threatens to be cutting and ferocious but instead contains a heroic paean to John Gotti and a gratuitous topical broadside ("Sick of Seattle"). While the two good tracks—"Miles From Nowhere" and "Long Way Back Again"—sound like lost **11** gems, "Afternoon Tea" ("for a party of one") fails in its bid to recapture the first album's Anglophiliac innocence. **A Date With the Smithereens** has its moments, but carries way too much baggage for it to be a fun time.

Blown to Smithereens, a well-chosen compilation drawn mainly from the first three albums (using a total of three songs to represent the last two), doesn't have any of the band's many rarities other than a cover of the Outsiders' "Time Won't Let Me" done for the soundtrack of *Time Cop.* Still, it's a great Smithereens record to have if you're only having one. But it's no match for **Attack of the Smithereens.** The album is the happy result of a big-league band of diehard rock'n'roll fanatics (among Diken's many extracurricular projects is a 1995 compilation of singles produced by Joe Meek) sticking around long enough to amass a large catalogue and yet still having the will to assemble a humbly magical résumé of its back pages. Among the outtakes, B-sides, demos and live tracks are the group's very first public appearance, stints backing Otis Blackwell, the Kinks, Graham Parker and the Beau Brummels, even an in-store appearance. An attic loaded to the rafters with super-cool covers (the Who's "The Seeker," the Beatles' "One After 909," the Kinks' "World Keeps Going 'Round," Iggy Pop's "Lust for Life," Frank and Nancy's "Something Stupid"), rudimentary and acoustic versions of classic tracks and other ungilded memories, this is the ultimate Smithereens devotees disc assembled and entertainingly annotated by the ultimate Smithereens devotees. Would that all bands had the guts and personability to give themselves a joyous going over like this. [i]

See also *Young Fresh Fellows; TPRG.*

SMOG

Macramé Gunplay [tape] (Disaster) 1988
Cow [tape] (Disaster) 1989
A Table Setting [tape] (Disaster) 1990
Tired Tape Machine [tape] (Disaster) 1990
Sewn to the Sky (Disaster) 1990 (Drag City) 1995
Floating EP7 (Drag City) 1991
Forgotten Foundation (Drag City) 1992
Julius Caesar (Drag City) 1993
Burning Kingdom EP (Drag City) 1994
Wild Love (Drag City) 1995
Kicking a Couple Around EP (Drag City) 1996
The Doctor Came at Dawn (Drag City) 1996

Consisting of the peripatetic Bill Callahan and a shifting cast of backing musicians, Smog is an unheralded pioneer of the lo-fi movement, with all the opportunity for intimate self-revelation and solipsistic self-indulgence the genre offers. The music is shot through with a pinched melancholy that more than occasionally turns bitter and veers unpredictably between almost painful candor and self-parody. And Smog appears to have been an influence on bands such as Pavement and Guided by Voices, if not for its production philosophy then at least for song titles like "Olive Drab Spectre" and "A Jar of Sand."

A one-man production recorded at "Dumpster Porta-studio," the damaged and drumless **Sewn to the Sky** echoes the Residents, Captain Beefheart and the soundtrack to *Eraserhead.* Callahan's repetitive, alien guitar riffs form bleak soundscapes, with occasional vocals deeply submerged in the distorted murk. "Garb" is just a two-note bass figure and some kooky pickup noises; on "Fruit Bats," Callahan intones something about "a symphony of fruit bats rapping on my window pane." Suffused with the vague gray atmospherics suggested by the band's name, **Sewn to the Sky** is primitive and promising.

The recording is still willfully crude and that *Eraserhead* vibe lives on, but **Forgotten Foundation** finds Callahan getting more song-oriented—more traditional arrangements, more vocals, more melody. Still, tracks like the shaggy-dog story of "Evil Tyrant" are more the rule. While he manages to attain a genuinely forlorn ambience, the sketchy approach eventually becomes tedious.

With cello, violin, acoustic guitar and banjo leading the mostly acoustic way, the spare, folky **Julius Caesar** is by far Smog's best yet. Callahan's songwriting is far more focused than ever before, even if the songs display a distinctly split personality, veering between elation ("When You Walk") and depression ("Your Wedding"), although mostly the latter. Highlights include the gleeful, brilliant "I Am Star Wars!" (based on a loop of the intro from "Honky Tonk Women"), the touching cellos on the instrumental "One Less Star" and "37 Push Ups," if only for the immortal line, "I feel like Travis Bickle/And I'm listening to 'Highway to Hell'."

The six-song **Burning Kingdom** breaks Smog's lo-fi policy with even more listenable production and fleshed-out arrangements. On "My Shell," heavy drums cut a clear path through the thicket of electric guitar and cello; Callahan's voice is a marvel of baleful alienation. There's the relentlessly minor-key psychodrama "My Family," which begins "Mother is smoking pot in the bathroom/I can hear her butt squeaking on the tub/As the water grows cold around her legs" and "The Desert," wherein Callahan intones "I'm crawling through the desert without water or love" to the accompaniment of funereal organ. Cheery stuff.

The clearly produced **Wild Love** finds Callahan in an even more morose frame of mind than usual. With a relentless, bitter pessimism that is sometimes hard to take seriously, his somber voice scuds over minor keys and drum machines, depicting an unhappy childhood ("Bathysphere," as apt a metaphor for his self-absorbed viewpoint as any), bitter romantic disappointments and the futility of life in general: "Wild love/Someone shot down my wild love," are the complete lyrics to the minute-and-a-half title track. Amid such despair, the brilliant "Prince Alone in the Studio" (yes, the Purple One), underscored by a grandiosely melancholic backing track, becomes a self-referential metaphor for the tragic art-vs.-love pathos of a hermetic existence.

Kicking a Couple Around leads off with a solo acoustic guitar performance of "Your New Friend" from a 1995 BBC broadcast; Callahan sounds like Jonathan Richman on spoiled downers as he anxiously rues a love's new circumstances. The other three whispery tracks, recorded in Chicago by Steve Albini, are no more extroverted or upbeat. Still, "The Orange Glow of a Stranger's Living Room" lets some lovely picking and piano pierce the warm gloom of his abiding displacement. [ma/i]

SMOKE

Heaven on a Popsicle Stick (Colossal/Long Play) 1994
Another Reason to Fast (Long Play) 1995

OPAL FOXX QUARTET

The Love That Won't Shut Up (Long Play) 1993

In its prime, Atlanta's Opal Foxx Quartet threatened to serve as a one-band cure for terminal jadedness. After all, who could muster an "I've seen it all before" yawn when confronted with a ten-piece beatnik-jazz-cum-performance-art troupe fronted by a rail-thin drag queen who sang about anorexia and happened to be a vocal doppelgänger for Tom Waits? Not surprisingly, the Quartet had difficulty holding shape and disbanded in 1992, but not before recording enough material (much of it produced by Michael Stipe) to cobble together the posthumous **The Love That Won't Shut Up,** released at a one-off reunion show on New Year's Eve '93. (Thoughts of further gigs were erased when drummer Allen Page died in early '94.) While Opal himself is clearly the featured attraction—just check out the mind-boggling medley of "I Don't Know How to Love Him" and "Strange Fruit" for proof—the canvas of steel guitar, cello and reeds is plenty beguiling on its own.

After the Quartet, Opal shed the dresses and the alias, returning to life as Benjamin and shaping a more manageable quintet—albeit one with some returning members and a similar flavor. Smoke's **Heaven on a Popsicle Stick** ventures into territory as varied as Balkan folk ("Hole") and sports-bar blues ("Hank Aaron") while keeping one foot grounded in *Twin Peaks*-style swing. That general sense of discombobulation—aided by both Brian Halloran's rolling cello bowing and Benjamin's fetishistic lyrical penchant ("Luke's Feet" waxes poetic about a certain *90210* star's, er, appendages)—gives this **Heaven** a decidedly Dali-esque tone.

As the bleak title indicates, the followup is an altogether darker affair. Colored by the muted cornet playing of Bill Taft (a former member of the Jody Grind who also served in Opal Foxx), **Another Reason to Fast** finds Benjamin waxing wounded about boyfriends lost, benders undertaken and other similar topics. His voice, grown even more gravelly with the passage of time and the consumption of unfiltered smokes, raises dissipation to an apex worthy of the most elegantly wasted cabaret diva. Sure to leave you shaken *and* stirred. [dss]

See also *Jody Grind.*

SMOKING POPES

Get Fired (Johann's Face) 1993
Born to Quit (Johann's Face) 1994 (Capitol) 1995

After Weezer, power-pop bands playing it simple had to be carefully examined for signs of triple-sec irony and rude condescension. The Ramones might have been exploiting a fictional persona, but the distinction between their *being* cretins and their *pretending* to be cretins never meant the brudders might be snidely laughing at their fans. The commercially calculating new breed, however, has carefully mapped and navigated the gaping hole between naïveté and the appearance of naïveté—hiding the Pope in the pizza by laying on the cheese, as it were. Does "I love my girlfriend" *really* mean that, or is it a sardonic comment on the wholesomeness of dubious sentiment and nostalgia? "Don't get cute or sarcastic," sayeth Elvis Costello. These days, a lot of bands defy both ends of that edict.

The Smoking Popes was formed in 1990 in Crystal Lake, Illinois, by two Caterer brothers, Josh (guitar, vocals) and Matt (bass), and a neighbor, drummer Mike Felumlee; guitarist Eli Caterer, the youngest of the siblings, joined the band in progress. Despite a few conflicting flashes (like the blasé "Let Them Die" and the coyly suggestive "Double Fisted Love") on **Get Fired,** the short, shoddy indie debut is so earnestly witless that it actually might be sincere. The Popes chuck awkward turns into standard pop chord progressions, fleshing out their boppy, Magnolias-recalling tunes with roaring guitars behind Josh's budding Vic Damone (by way of Morrissey) croon. Playing it rough but singing it sweet, the band puts dynamic tension into the cheerleading "Let's Hear It for Love," "Don't Be Afraid" and "That's Where I Come In" but winds up competing with itself.

Born to Quit, a twenty-eight-minute indie release reissued by a major, refines the Popes' romantic innocence while mortising up the Ramonesy guitar wall and sublimating Josh's deepening voice into a cross between Pat DiNizio and Morrissey. The production has barely graduated to second-rate, but the band's skills are much improved, and the smoothly catchy songs (especially the gimmicky "Rubella," the Beatlesque "My Lucky Day" and the amazingly Smiths-like "Need You Around") go down like gumdrops. The band's deadpan innocence is still unsettling (Brian Wilson was the last rock'n'roll songwriter to get away with anything like the sappy "Mrs. You and Me"), but sometimes a love song is just a love song. [i]

SMUDGE

Love, Lust & Lemonjuice EP (Aus. Half a Cow) 1992
Superhero EP (Aus. Half a Cow) 1993
Manilow (Can. Half a Cow/Shake/Cargo) 1993
Impractical Joke EP (Can. Half a Cow/Shake/Cargo) 1993
Tea, Toast & Turmoil (Can. Half a Cow/Shake/Cargo) 1993
The Outdoor Type EP (UK Domino) 1994
Hot Smoke and Sassafras EP (Can. Half a Cow/Shake) 1995

If Sydney, Australia's Smudge seems like one big footnote to the Lemonheads, that's unfortunate: Tom Morgan's band is a nifty little pop group in its own right. The singer/guitarist is best known for co-writing half of the songs on **Come on Feel the Lemonheads** with Evan Dando. Smudge drummer/occasional singer Alison Galloway is purportedly the subject of Dando's "Alison's Starting to Happen" (from **It's a Shame About Ray,** an album to which Morgan also contributed some lyrics). Nic Dalton, who operates the band's label, Half a Cow, played bass in the Lemonheads. (Morgan and Galloway are both regulars in Dalton's own band, Godstar; recent Smudge bassist Adam Yee works at the like-minded Fellaheen label.) It's easy to see what Dando saw in Morgan—he's a gifted songwriter with a tangy wit and a way with power-pop hooks, and he's got a similar song-connoisseur mentality.

Smudge's first two EPs are combined on **Tea, Toast & Turmoil,** along with a handful of rarities and the trio's first single, "I Don't Want to Be Grant McLennan," a brilliant two-minute joke about plagiarizing Go-Betweens records. Other delights include three very short songs about food (one of which rhymes "wuss" with "babaganouj"), a cover of "Make All Our Dreams Come True" (better known as the *Laverne & Shirley* theme) and "Divan," an offer of crash-space with a perfect little pop melody. Still, most of the record (notwithstanding an unlisted straight punk-pop rendition of John Waite's "Missing You") is more promising than actually good.

At twenty-one tracks in forty-one minutes, **Manilow** is promising *and* good. Beyond its remakes ("Divan" and "Pulp"), giggles (a three-second funk parody, the theme from *Charles in Charge,* the "Kelly Kelly Kelly" song from *Cheers,* "Scary Cassettes," about confusing Lou Barlow with Lou Reed) and Dando collaborations ("Down About It" and "Desmond"), there's some solid in-house songwriting and tight, muscular playing. "Dave the Talking Bear," "Not Here for a Haircut" and "Impractical Joke" are all cryptic but heartfelt; the last was released as a single in Australia, Europe and Canada, with four different extra tracks on each version.

The Outdoor Type includes three songs from **Manilow** (one acoustic), plus a cover of You Am I's "Berlin Chair" and the title track, Smudge's best song to date. Insanely catchy, funny and honest, it's about lying to someone to win their love and then having to live up to the lies ("I can't go away with you on a rock-climbing weekend/What if something's on TV and it's never shown again?"); it's been covered by Sharon Stoned and—of course—Dando.

The subsequent **Hot Smoke and Sassafras** is a bit of a comedown. Despite some great song titles ("I Am Not the Cosmos" and "All The Money in the World Can't Buy You a Near Death Experience"), the record relies too much on turning up the volume to compensate for absent or borrowed hooks. "Coal Surge" is the only track of the eight listed that's really up to Smudge snuff, and the "hidden track" joke is funny *once.* [ddw]

See also *Godstar, Lemonheads.*

SMUGGLERS

The Smugglers at Marineland (Can. Nardwuar the Human Serviette) 1991
Atlanta Whiskey Flats (Trade Mark of Quality/PopLlama Products) 1992
Wet Pants Club (Sp. Radiation) 1993 + 1994
In the Hall of Fame (PopLlama Products) 1993
Party . . . Party . . . Party . . . Pooper! EP7 (Can. Mint) 1994
Senor Pantsdown EP (Sp. Rock and Roll Inc.) 1995
Selling the Sizzle! (Mint/Lookout!) 1996

BEAUTICIANS

Imepriale (Can. Cheemo) 1995

Stylish Vancouver garagesters with hearts of pure rock'n'roll rubbish, the wonderful Smugglers represent the pop side of the monoxide-flavored genre in the great Northwest with flash, trash, goofball humor and self-deprecating Canuck charm. The lively quintet—which also operates Mint Records and numerous side bands—hasn't always been captured at its best on record, but when the moon is right and the mics are set just so, no one else can offer such compelling evidence that the Fleshtones have colorful Canadian spawn, raised on radioactive shellfish from the Black Lagoon. Where's a sitcom producer when you need one?

The Smugglers at Marineland was recorded in Seattle by an early lineup, back when the young band's heat-prostration stage gear consisted of wool pea jackets, toques and wading boots. Released by Vancouver DJ/journalist mentor/annotator Nardwuar the Human Serviette, the 10-inch platter sardine-jams in nine ripping songs and two futile interview bits. Between covers of the Kinks ("I Took My Baby Home"), Billy Childish ("Yardbird") and Jimmy Silva ("Is That, Rock?"), the Smugs hit the surf, B-52's style, on "Pebble Beach," go all fuzzy and mushy about "Jailbait," sing the praises of their hometown in the Trashmen-styled "Vancouver, B.C." and make the cultural observation, set to a brisk Jerry Lee Lewis beat, that "Calgarians Don't Dance." Singer Grant Lawrence's unassuming voice gives the songs all the offhand personality they require.

Precisely packaged as a vintage bootleg but actually a legitimate PopLlama product, **Atlanta Whiskey Flats** introduces a new rhythm section as well as a wider range of songwriting styles. Tempering the essential brisk racket with sprightly pop faculties (though blunted by the flat, inept mastering), the Smugglers concentrate on delivering cool songs like the upbeat likes-list of "Canadian Ambassadors," the giddy tour diary of "Fun in the USA," the winsome foiled romanticism of "What'd I Do Wrong?," the crude "She Said: Shut Up!" (sung by bassist K. Beezley) and the instrumental "Reid." At times sounding like the Star Club–era Beatles, the Smugglers accomplish their mission with maximum likability.

Billed as Los Smugglers on the Spanish-released **Wet Pants Club** (originally an eight-song vinyl issue, it became a CD with four additional songs recorded a year later), the fearless five let out the electric stops and muster some real fidelity—hot, clear and effective—for a change. The mixed program balances originals—both retro ("Paper Doll," "Time Marches On," the instrumental "Don Valley") and relatively modern ("Surrender," "Mach 1," "Amnesia")—and nifty covers (the Who's "La La La Lies," the Boys' rude "Kiss Like a Nun," Frank Zappa's surf instrumental "Pacifica Stomp"), all fired-up with tight and fuzzy garage-pop power. Boss!

In the Hall of Fame usefully compiles the best bits of **Atlanta Whiskey Flats** and **Marineland,** adding a loose 45 track from 1992 and nine previously unreleased studio cuts, two of which (including a blues-wailing harp-powered white-boy rendition of Muddy Waters' "Can't Be Satisfied") predate **Marineland** by a year. The shitty sound (even on CD) doesn't seriously impair the thrill of extra-hard-rocking numbers like the winning statement of principle, "Rock'n'Roll Was Never This Fun," a raw-voiced Sex Pistols soundalike Sid Vicious would never have condoned. Even with a measure of topicality creeping into the soup ("Alan Thicke," "My Morrissey Shirt"), the Smugglers remain global thinkers, as songs like "Your Mom's the Devil" clearly demonstrate.

The 7-inch **Party . . . Party . . . Party . . . Pooper!**, released in four different personality sleeves, contains four peppy numbers, most prominently the band's "Smuggler King" and a racing cover of Paul Collins' great Beat song, "Walking Out on Love." The four-song **Senor Pantsdown** was released only in Spain.

Introducing the group's snappy new business suits (the boots remain, however) and Mint's hookup with Lookout!, **Selling the Sizzle!** is a doozy, an intense burst of ebullience that takes its lighthearted mission ("To Serve, Protect and Entertain") very seriously. With drum-tight playing, soaring fidelity and Lawrence as the versatile mouthpiece, the Smugs step out of the slop-rock shadows as a rip-roaring '60s showband with deliciously memorable party songs that serve equally well as tribute and parody. A personalized version of Freddy Cannon's "The Dedication" tunes in kitschy teen radio memories with a stomping beat and messages from the band, but the song's title could just as easily apply to the band's winning enthusiasm.

When not engaged in their primary endeavor, guitarist Nicholas Thomas leads the Tonics (a 7-inch on Zapruder), while guitarist David Carswell is in both the Evaporators (one album on Nardwuar the Human Serviette) and Thorsen, a Nordic metal band that squeezed a single out but left its album in the can. Bassist Beez sings and plays guitar in the Beauticians, an absurdist quintet in which a violist and a violinist gracefully aid and abet a hyperactive Monty Python sense of whimsy ("Eric the Fish" may well remind some of "Eric the Half-a-Bee"). The smartly produced and sweetly harmonized **Imperiale**—which couldn't be much further removed from the Smugglers' sound—shifts styles all over the pop-folk-rock-country continuum, all in service of humorous items like "New Age Song for a Cynical Generation," "Party Girl With a Problem" and "Stockboy Jack." If a little too much at times, the album is irresistible in small doses and is recommended to restless fans of They Might Be Giants and Barenaked Ladies. [i]

NEIL SMYTHE

See *April March.*

SNATCHES OF PINK

Send in the Clowns (Dog Gone) 1987
Dead Men (Dog Gone) 1989
Bent With Prey (Caroline) 1992

MICHAEL RANK

Coral (Caroline) 1993

CLARISSA

Silver (Mammoth/Atlantic) 1996

Chapel Hill, North Carolina's Snatches of Pink played a tasty blend of Stones raunch and punk insistence, well-crafted tunes delivered with jackhammer finesse on its debut, **Send in the Clowns.** Singer Andy McMillan is a young good-ol'-boy with an aching twang stuck in his throat, spurred to spill his guts by Michael Rank's barbed guitars.

The grunge level rises dramatically on **Dead Men.** With Rank assuming lead vocal duties from McMillan (now the full-time bassist; Sara Romweber, formerly of Let's Active, is the drummer), Snatches could be a big-time boogie band debilitated by bad drugs. Caught in a thoroughly muddy mix, the performances are stirringly urgent.

Returning after a three-year gap, the trio sounds like an unwillingly sober Black Crowes on the tense, disturbing **Bent With Prey.** The emotionally charged scene-setter is built on savvy, intelligent songwriting and justifiably busy production that stops just short of being overblown. Aside from Rank's desperate, guttural exhalations (and introspective lyrics that nearly reach the point of self-abuse), the delicately layered instrumentation is lovingly crafted. "Mother Crane" epitomizes the album's subtle twists: clearly recorded twelve- and six-string acoustic guitars, glazed with solid drumming and nearly nonexistent bass. Highly recommended.

Following Rank's solo album, which he cut with Romweber and bassist Freddie Salem, the three original Snatches regrouped as Clarissa, taking a full-on flyer down the dynamically restrained path blazed on **Bent With Prey.** No less emotional in his writing but more inclined to a whisper than a scream (though the wah-wah solo in "High Horses" gets up a head of rock steam and "Slow Punch" keeps threatening to explode), Rank works to draw listeners in to him, rather than make much of an effort to go out and sell his songs. If **Silver** is underwhelming in its consciously pretty inventions as a result, an edgy undercurrent ensures that the ride, if sometimes enticing (like the soulfully southern "Butterfly"), never quite turns easy. [jy/icm/i]

See also *TPRG.*

SNEAKERS

See *Chris Stamey.*

SNEETCHES

Lights Out! With the Sneetches (UK Kaleidoscope Sound) 1988 (UK Creation) 1990
Sometimes That's All We Have (Alias) 1989
Slow (Alias) 1990
1985–1991 (Alias) 1991
Think Again (Bus Stop) 1993
Obscure Years (UK Creation) 1994
Blow Out the Sun (spinART) 1994
Starfucker (Bus Stop) 1995

CHRIS WILSON AND THE SNEETCHES

Chris Wilson and the Sneetches (Marilyn) 1993

San Francisco's Sneetches—singer/guitarists Matt Carges and Mike Levy, drummer Daniel Swan and, from **Slow** on, bassist Alejandro (Alec) Palao—is one of the most tasteful, consistently tuneful pop bands on the American scene. Echoes of the Zombies, Left Banke and Easybeats (they've covered songs by all three) abound; simple, uncluttered arrangements let their like-minded originals' substantial charms shine through.

Lights Out! (written and played entirely by Carges and Levy) is an eminently likable and fresh-faced debut that proves the Sneetches to be confident songwriters and performers. The Zombies influence rears its pretty little head on "Lorelei," while "I Don't Expect Her for You (Look at That Girl)" takes direct aim at Merseybeat. A fine first step from a band that obviously knows where it wants to go. All eight tracks of **Lights Out!** were remixed and included on the **1985–1991** CD compilation.

Sometimes That's All We Have (the CD adds a Sneetched-out version of Fred Neil's "Everybody's Talkin'" from a 1990 flexi-disc) is another groovy collection that often sounds like the Association with a severe attitude problem (witness "Another Shitty Day"). **Slow** is—and this is not a criticism—more of the same, eleven dreamily infectious numbers including the Sneetches fan favorite "Heloise" and (on the CD) a spot-on cover of the Left Banke's gorgeous "She May Call You Up Tonight."

Besides reissuing the debut, the **1985–1991** compilation ties up some loose ends by gathering three tracks from a 1989 12-inch (including a peppy reworking of the Monochrome Set's "He's Frank"), outtakes from **Slow** and **Sometimes That's All We Have,** a version of the Raspberries' "I Wanna Be With You" recorded with vocal assistance by Shoes and four new songs. Tying for top tune honors: a superb reading of the Easybeats' "Pretty Girl" and the gentle, flowing "Just Another Lonely One," which may be the best thing the Sneetches have ever recorded.

The **Think Again** mini-album collects several Bus Stop singles—it's a tad harder-edged than the earlier stuff but no less melodically stimulating. ". . . And I'm Thinking" is a **Revolver**-ish prize, the piano-based "A Good Thing" is devastatingly beautiful and the cover of the Buffalo Springfield's "Flying on the Ground Is Wrong" nearly eclipses the original. **Obscure Years** collects the seven tracks that compose **Think Again** and adds seven more outstanding cuts, including an amazingly intense run-through of Vanda/Young's "Watch Me Burn," the Monkee-ish "This Time" and the languid "Come Along With Me," which contains the inspirational couplet "You think he's funny/But he's such a dummy." (**Starfucker** separates out the seven cuts not from **Think Again.**)

The all-new **Blow Out the Sun** is a good-as-ever distillation of the Sneetches' influences, meshed into a brilliantly conceived and fully realized record. "A Light on Above" and "What I Know," in particular, come off like long-lost Lennon/McCartney/Vanda/Young/Argent/Blunstone (whew!) collaborations—yet still sound totally contemporary. Great!

The group's one-off collaboration with former Flamin Groovies singer/guitarist Chris Wilson resulted in the seven-song **Chris Wilson and the Sneetches:** three Groovies tunes ("Between the Lines," "I'll Cry Alone" and "Slow Death") performed live at the DNA Lounge (Groovies alumnus Roy Loney joins in on "Slow Death"), full-band versions of cuts from Wilson's early '90s acoustic album, **Random Centuries,** and a nice, twelve-string-drenched version of Goffin/King's "Goin' Back." [jmb]

SNEEZE

See *Godstar.*

SNIVLEM

See *Melvins.*

SNOOP DOGGY DOG

Doggystyle (Death Row/Interscope) 1993
Tha Doggfather (Death Row/Interscope) 1996

VARIOUS ARTISTS

Murder Was the Case (Death Row/Interscope) 1994

When Disney finally opens its X-rated amusement park, Snoop Doggy Dogg will surely be one of the young crowd's favorite characters, serving gin and juice, passing out blunts, rapping to big-booty women and entertaining tourists with his comical gangsta caricature and tales of jurisprudence. Arriving fully strapped with unassailable street cred and hip-hop fame—thanks to a murder indictment (for which he was subsequently tried and exonerated) and his collaborative role on Dr. Dre's **The Chronic**—the former Calvin Broadus paid off on the hype with **Doggystyle,** furthering the work begun by Dre, Ice Cube and Eazy-E in N.W.A with a distinctive landmark album that gave the West Coast a real leg up in the rap race and placed Snoop at ground zero in the subsequent political controversy over family values and the sound of music.

Working over a slow-rolling platter of Dre's finest funk, strung together as a radio broadcast and punched up with skits (the classroom bit in which a young Snoop announces his adult ambition is pretty funny), the rapper flips the script on roughneck hardcore style with a quietly inveigling sing-song, musical breadth and playful persona. Dispassionately obsessed with death, Snoop shifts easily from tales of heartless nut-busting and pot-smoking to caps-busting as if they were all of equal consequence. He issues rote threats of violence in "Who Am I (What's My Name)?" and elsewhere shoots a rival over a woman. The surrealism of Snoop-ness becomes manifest in "Murder Was the Case," which begins with a drive-by shooting that leaves the narrator in a coma, discussing the afterlife with a supreme MC. Ultimately, though, Snoop's favorite target is women, who are repeatedly treated to outrageous abuse. "Aint No Fun (If the Homies Cant Have None)"—with Warren G, Nate Dogg and Kurupt of Tha Dogg Pound taking turns being crude on the mic—describes an especially offensive communal sexual ethos. A compelling artist whose private sensibilities are impossible to gauge, Snoop Doggy Dogg plays both sides of the reality fence, inviting listeners into his house and then rubbing their noses in his shit.

Using Snoop's album track as the blueprint for a short film he directed, Dre put together **Murder Was the Case,** a full-length soundtrack album (*In beloved memory/Calvin Broadus, 1972–1994*) that starts off with a drastic remix of the original song and follows it with the appallingly violent and topical Ice Cube/Dre collaboration "Natural Born Killaz" and "21 Jumpstreet," a new Snoop tune (with Tray Dee). The rest of the record turns a sonic spotlight on other posse rhymers. Sam Sneed's intelligent "U Better Recognize" is a nostalgic dose of MC boasting, but the other blasts of violence, misogyny and vulgarity have all the charm of a crummy exploitation movie. [i]

See also *Dr. Dre, Tha Dogg Pound.*

SNOWMEN

See *Barbara Manning.*

JILL SOBULE

Things Here Are Different (MCA) 1990
Jill Sobule (Lava/Atlantic) 1995 + 1995

Early in 1995, Denver native Jill Sobule emerged as a fresh new voice on the pop scene, singing about kissing a girl. Provocative, sure, but then Sobule was no newcomer. She had kicked around the club and coffeehouse circuit for years, and had already put out one album. But few heard the Todd Rundgren–produced **Things Here Are Different,** a collection of spirited and earnest singer/songwriter material such as "Sad Beauty" and "Tell Me Your Dreams." It was an estimable debut—Sobule's voice is far more elastic and expressive than the little-girl tag usually slapped on it suggests—but it was under-promoted and commercially ignored. MCA opted to not even release her second album, which was produced by Joe Jackson.

Fortunately, that's not the end of the story. "She's gonna sing, you're gonna listen," a voice barks on **Jill Sobule,** and that's what happened, thanks to "I Kissed a Girl"—a clever, perky ditty that only hints the encounter may have gone beyond the parameters of innocence. It was a novelty hit, but the rest of the album backs it up. Sobule leads with her wit here, crafting a series of engaging characters that include "Margaret," the Catholic school goody two shoes who grows up to become a porn star, war couples from the French resistance and Bosnia in, respectively, "Resistance Song" and "Vrbana Bridge," and the straitlaced shoe store manager with a wild nocturnal alter ego in "Karen by Night." Sobule's musical palette is varied, drawing on bossa nova for "(Theme From) The Girl in the Affair," new wave rock on "Karen by Night," acoustic troubadour styles on "The Jig Is Up" and "Trains." For those who listen beyond "I Kissed a Girl," **Jill Sobule** holds rewards that should have been recognized years ago. (Later pressings of the album include "Supermodel," a song written by David Baerwald, recorded for the *Clueless* soundtrack and released as the followup to Sobule's first hit.) [gg]

SOCIAL DISTORTION

Mommy's Little Monster (13th Floor) 1983 (Triple X) 1990 (Time Bomb) 1995
Prison Bound (Restless) 1988 (Time Bomb) 1995
Social Distortion (Epic) 1990
Story of My Life . . . and Other Stories EP (Epic) 1990
Somewhere Between Heaven and Hell (Epic) 1992
Mainliner (Wreckage From the Past) (Time Bomb) 1995
White Light White Heat White Trash (550 Music/Epic) 1996

Proudly out of step with the rest of Southern California's hardcore brigade in its early days and growing further apart with time, Fullerton singer/guitarist Mike Ness has led his influential group through a fitful career of turbo-charged roots rock that was ironically vindicated when Social Distortion was recognized as the sonic template for some of the bands that broke California punk-pop into the big time in 1994. The raw evidence of the nascent group's distinctive origins is already unmistakable on the temperate mid-tempo chunk and West-Coast-country-meet-the-Clash essence of the ten 1981 singles and compilation tracks (including "1945" and "Playpen," twice each) patched together as **Mainliner,** which contains Ness' amused contemporary liner-note observation that "people were actually scared of punk being played."

While **Mommy's Little Monster** is an aggressive punk-pop classic of its era, **Prison Bound** (made and released after the hell-raising Ness had reportedly paid his debt to society and gotten clean and sober) pushes beyond the genre with acoustic guitars and a significant Johnny Cash country influence. Confounding expectations of a major-label tone-down (and despite a righteous cover of "Ring of Fire" and the rootsy "Ball and Chain"), **Social Distortion,** if anything, reorients the quartet toward the first album's furious rhythm guitar assault. The **Story of My Life** EP combines the single version of that album track with a pair of bracing 1990 live cuts ("Mommy's Little Monster" and "1945") and previously unissued studio renditions of Bo Diddley's Willie Dixon–written "Pretty Thing" and rockabilly legend Ersel Hickey's "Shame on Me."

If Dave Jerden's rock-solid production on **Somewhere Between Heaven and Hell** isn't as savagely electric as it was on **Social Distortion,** Ness and his three loyal bandmates (guitarist Dennis Danell, bassist John Maurer and drummer Christopher Reece) give up nothing in their driving melodicism. Lashing his husky voice to an unyielding (and, to its mild detriment, unvarying) wall of dynamic rhythm guitar power pushed along by Reece's relentless backbeat, Ness lays out the autobiographical original "Born to Lose," snappy, catchy winners ("Bad Luck" and "When She Begins"), rebel-without-a-clue classics ("King of Fools," "Cold Feelings," "Sometimes I Do") and tough-romance ravers ("Bye Bye Baby," "This Time Darlin'," "Making Believe"). Even when dealing with such familiar topics, Ness' unpretentious reflections have a proud poetry and occasionally make deft use of clichés without wallowing in them. Social D isn't stretching the limits of three-chord rock'n'roll any, but few such bands have as much skill or conviction.

White Light White Heat White Trash, rippingly produced by Michael Beinhorn with punk veteran Chuck Biscuits in the drummer's seat, allows Ness to wax sensitive and reflective without sacrificing an inch of the band's sturdy sonic aggression. "I Was Wrong" is an extraordinary and respectable mea culpa, and sets the tone for an album of mature consideration and searing rock power. "Through These Eyes," "Pleasure Seeker," "Gotta Know the Rules," "Untitled" and "Don't Drag Me Down" redefine the growling singer as a man of the underworld who has learned how to get along in the light. [jr/i]

See also *TPRG.*

SOFT CELL

See *Marc Almond.*

SOFTIES

See *Tiger Trap.*

SOLOMON GRUNDY

See *Screaming Trees.*

SOMELOVES

Something or Other (Aus. White Label) 1989
Sunshine's Glove EP (Aus. White Label) 1990

DM3

One Time, Two Times, Three Red Light (Aus. Citadel) 1993

Soultop EP (Aus. Citadel) 1994
Road to Rome (Aus. Citadel) 1996

Criminally underrated Australian pop king Dom Mariani first came to prominence in the '80s as a member of the garage/pop combo the Stems, whose best recordings can be found on the Australian-only **Buds** CD. After the Stems splintered (singer/guitarist Richard Lane went on to form the punk-pop Chevelles), singer/guitarist Mariani put together the Someloves with guitarist Darryl Mather. The Someloves' only full-length release is one of the great lost power-pop masterpieces of the modern era: words like "jangly," "chiming" and "hook-filled" don't even begin to do it justice. Produced by Mitch Easter, a man who knows a great pop artist when he hears one, **Something or Other** features guest shots by Easter, Angie Carlson of Grover on keyboards, as well as SpongeTone Jamie Hoover and Windbreaker Bobby Sutliff on backing vocals. Mariani has one of those perfect pop voices and can write a melody with the best of 'em, two qualities that make **Something or Other** a real revelation. The **Sunshine's Glove** EP includes two killer tracks from the album and four others of equal quality.

After Mather and Mariani parted company, the latter formed the DM3 with bassist Toni Italiano and drummer Pascal Bartolone. Recruiting Easter to mix (and add some guitar and sitar to) their debut release, Mariani and friends came up with the awkwardly titled **One Time, Two Times, Three Red Light,** another monumental achievement (or, as the back cover states, an "unashamed pop recording"). The overall sound is a bit more guitar-heavy than the Someloves, but the perky melodies have no problem coming to the fore.

Road to Rome, again produced by Easter, is more of the same: dazzling guitars, delicious melodies and hooks, hooks, hooks are the order of the day. Particularly noteworthy are the Rundgrenesque single "Something Heavy," the amazing "Soultop" (imagine a collective raveup by early Deep Purple, the Zombies and the Plimsouls) and the anti–Albert Goldman vibe of "Dead Stars." [jmb]

JIMMY SOMERVILLE

Read My Lips (UK London) 1989 (London) 1990
The Singles Collection 1984/1990 (UK London) 1990 (London) 1991
Dare to Love (London) 1995

Blessed with an extraordinary falsetto, diminutive Glaswegian Jimmy Somerville has wrapped his powerful pipes around an impressive array of original tunes and well-chosen covers since striking out on his own in 1989. His solo career neatly dovetails with the most distinctive aspects of his two previous ensembles, the strident gay politicism of Bronski Beat (a trio) and the glitzy disco show business of the two-man Communards. Though the two might seem at odds, Somerville embodies the dichotomy known to many urban gay men, for whom ecstatic dancing and AIDS activism often command equal time and energy.

Working with a mixed bag of producers (including Pascal Gabriel and Stephen Hague), **Read My Lips** is a confident, coherent solo debut. As in the Communards, the singles—covers of Sylvester's "You Make Me Feel (Mighty Real)" and Françoise Hardy's "Comment Te Dire Adieu" (a duet with June Miles Kingston, included in two mixes)—downplay the politics, but cuts like "And You Never Thought That This Could Happen to You" and the fierce "Read My Lips (Enough Is Enough)" capture the late-'80s rage of activist groups like ACT UP and Queer Nation. In "Perfect Day," "Heaven Here on Earth (With Your Love)," Somerville tempers the tone with romance.

The well-programmed eighteen-song singles collection reçapitulates Somerville's entire career, beginning with the Bronskis' groundbreaking 1984 single, "Smalltown Boy," and adding a new reggae-tinged cover of the Bee Gees' old "To Love Somebody."

Somerville recorded little over the next four years, although he did perform a lot. The few cuts he did unleash—an electro-pop "From This Moment On" (incorporating "I Feel Love," a leitmotif throughout his career) for the **Red Hot + Blue** AIDS awareness project and contributions to the soundtracks of *Orlando* and *Postcards From America*—showed the artist maturing, especially on his chest-voice rendition of Nancy Sinatra's "So Long Babe." Without straying far from proven formulae, **Dare to Love** fulfills that promise, as Somerville exhibits increased control over his instrument. The sentimental numbers outweigh the overtly political ones, but the single ("Heartbeat") is an uplifting house anthem and the covers fit the overall aesthetic (a needless reworking of the Supremes' "Someday We'll Be Together"). Tellingly, the double whammy of the erotic reverie "Alright" and the uncomfortable "Too Much of a Good Thing" suggests that Somerville, like many gay men, has begun to find the fun/fight dichotomy exhausting. [kbr]

See also *TPRG*.

SOME VELVET SIDEWALK

From Playground Til Now [tape] (AL) 1988
I Know EP7 (K) 1988
Appetite for Extinction (K/Communion) 1990
Avalanche (K) 1992
I Scream EP (K) 1993
Whirlpool (K) 1994
Shipwreck (K) 1995

AL LARSEN

The Insect Way [tape] (Pebbles) 1991

SANDY DIRT

Sandy Dirt EP (UK Domino) 1995 (K) 1996

Although this Olympia, Washington, outfit—along with fellow travelers Beat Happening—introduced the term "love-rock" into the underground lexicon, Some Velvet Sidewalk isn't all sweetness and light. Sure, frontman Al Larsen's unrelenting artlessness—evident in both his purposefully detuned, primitive playing and Jonathan Richmanesque tales of ice cream, dinosaurs and the like—borders on naïveté. But there's enough tensile strength in his presentation to keep sugar shock at bay.

Presaging the guitar/drum duo format that would become an essential segment of the indie-pop underground, Larsen and Robert Christie disturbed the peace as willfully as their proto-grunge contemporaries, first with a tape, a careening four-song EP that attempted to reduce thirty-odd years of primordial ooze into seven minutes of unhewn sound and then with the fractured, often utterly daft **Appetite for Extinction.** Larsen really lets his geek flag fly, splaying chords and almost-chords in a cadence so odd that you just *know* the stops and starts serve mostly to give him a chance to push up his glasses. Between the epic grind of "Snow" and the too-brief pop discourse of "20,000 Leagues," Some Velvet Sidewalk covers all of nerd-pop's bases, getting thrown out only when they unplug on the insufferably twee "Crayons."

In a bow to tradition, Larsen reconfigured SVS as a power trio of sorts, adding bassist Don Blair and replacing Christie with Martin Bernier. The new lineup gives **Avalanche** more magnetism in the traditional sense, prompting the odd head-wag (on the groove-oriented "Peaches") and head-bang (on the unhinged "Loch Ness," an impassioned plea to "let that monster go"). Although Larsen's nasal delivery can be one of the band's greater charms—especially when he's struggling, à la Richman, to fit in as many words per bar as possible—his ineptitude as a "singer" reveals itself again when the band turns down on "Little Wishes." Fortunately, the recording levels stay in the red throughout the **I Scream** EP, which is structured around two mixes of **Avalanche**'s "Ice Cream Overdrive," a thoroughly over-the-top, Stoogesque bash celebrating the frozen sweet. "Shame," which finds Larsen reinventing hip-hop as Jungian therapy, is tough sledding, but the bile spewed on the minimal "I Blame You" goes a long way toward greasing the skids.

Whirpool is considerably more composed than Some Velvet Sidewalk's previous work. Although Larsen's pseudo-savant lyrics still gouge at normally sheltered parts of the psyche—see the title track and "How Will I?"—producer Steve Fisk spreads the band's sound out considerably, encouraging the exploration of mid-range frequencies as opposed to just squeal and thump. On "Big City Plans," the trio even shelves the give-me-primitivism-or-give-me-death banner, adding guest trumpet and Fisk organ to very good effect.

On **Shipwreck,** which was actually recorded in 1990 but shelved as the band's second album, Larsen fills out the band with a rhythm section made up of fellow primitivists like Louise Olsen and Bikini Kill's Tobi Vail (the slightly more rock-minded Donna Dresch also guests). It's less resolute in its adherence to Richmania, thanks to primal screams that are more adult than most of Larsen's childlike purgatives. If nothing else, the crude disc should serve to prove that the Sidewalk king is extremely unlikely to go in search of the lost chord: two is plenty for him.

The side band Sandy Dirt was convened in Scotland, where Larsen recorded five songs with the Pastels. **Sandy Dirt** is a sometimes tense marriage of decidedly different perspectives on what makes pop tick. Neither Larsen nor Stephen Pastel is what you'd call a fusspot about sonics, which makes for a few flinch-worthy melodic clashes. But, overall, the EP's mélange of sweetness and bite passes the "you got chocolate in my peanut butter" test with flying colors. [dss]

SONIC YOUTH

Sonic Youth EP (Neutral) 1982 (SST) 1987
Confusion Is Sex (Neutral) 1983 (SST) 1987 (DGC) 1995
Kill Yr. Idols EP (Ger. Zensor) 1983
Sonic Death: Sonic Youth Live [tape] (Ecstatic Peace!) 1984 (SST) 1988
Bad Moon Rising (Homestead) 1985 (DGC) 1995
Death Valley 69 EP (Homestead) 1985
EVOL (SST) 1986 (DGC) 1994
Sister (SST) 1987 (DGC) 1994
Master Dik EP (SST) 1988
Daydream Nation (Blast First/Enigma) 1988 (DGC) 1993
Daydream Nation EP (Blast First/Enigma) 1988
Goo (DGC) 1990
Dirty (DGC) 1992
Experimental Jet Set, Trash and No Star (DGC) 1994
Made in USA (Rhino) 1995
Screaming Fields of Sonic Love (DGC) 1995
Washing Machine (DGC) 1995

CICCONE YOUTH

The Whitey Album EP (Blast First/Enigma) 1988
The Whitey Album (Blast First/Enigma) 1988 (DGC) 1995

SONIC YOUTH/EYE YAMATSUKA

Shit TV EP (Ecstatic Peace!) 1994

LEE RANALDO

From Here to Infinity (SST) 1987
Scriptures of the Golden Eternity (Father Yod) 1993 (Father Yod/Drunken Fish) 1995
Broken Circle/Spiral Hill EP (Starlight Furniture Company) 1994
East Jesus (Atavistic) 1995

THURSTON MOORE

Psychic ♥♥♥'s (DGC) 1995

In the '80s, Sonic Youth was bringing the noise as the creator of a new guitar vocabulary. In the '90s, the New York quartet has become a respected institution, able to have it both ways: reliably cranking out prickly albums for a major label while serving as tastemakers and mentors to a new generation of would-be musical revolutionaries.

More than just updating the noise-rock innovations of Jimi Hendrix or the Velvet Underground, Sonic Youth took them someplace fresh. The group's early live shows embodied their harmonic sense of adventure and their lust for dissonance, as guitarists Lee Ranaldo and Thurston Moore battered or bowed the innovatively tuned strings with drumsticks or tortured them with screwdrivers. The band's early records—erratic and muddy sounding as many of them are—explore a more ambient, atmospheric direction in noise, with bell-like tones that could have lulled an infant and low rumbles that one feels more than hears. While the band was capable of rocking with purpose—as on a lacerating cover of Iggy Pop's "I Wanna Be Your Dog," from **Confusion Is Sex**—the overall tone on that album and other works from the same period is one of a diffuse, hovering anxiety, a vague sense of impending doom.

The **Sonic Youth** EP is marred by the work of Richard Edson, a trumpet player and actor masquerading as a drummer; **Sonic Death** is a compilation of poorly recorded live performances. With Bob Bert on drums joining Moore, Ranaldo and bassist/singer Kim Gordon, **Confusion Is Sex** (and the related **Kill Yr. Idols,** later included on the former's CD as part of DGC's mid-'90s catalogue rehabilitation) is a record that has increased in stature over the years. Once its ghostly lattice-work of pulsing drones and shimmering feedback seemed impenetrable; now some of it sounds as contemporary as any of the ambient soundscapes concocted by the Orb or the Aphex Twin.

During this early period, Sonic Youth was intimately connected with the noisy remnants of the New York no wave scene, inspired by the dense guitar tapestries of Rhys Chatham and Glenn Branca, with whom Moore and Ranaldo had both played. **Bad Moon Rising** takes the first step out of that art ghetto, most notably on "Death Valley '69," a Moore/Lydia Lunch duet that verges on conventional rock—albeit of the most disturbing variety. The rest hovers rather than motors, exuding all the horrible beauty of a mushroom cloud on the horizon, while the lyrics dwell on the downside of Reagan's America. ("Satan Is Boring," from the **Death Valley 69** EP, is included as a bonus track on the reissue; the rest of the 12-inch came from previous SY records.)

With **EVOL,** Sonic Youth fully embraces rock and creates a near-masterpiece. A simple explanation for this transformation might be the addition of drummer Steve Shelley (a Michigander who once played in the Crucifucks), who stepped in after Bert left to play with Pussy Galore (and later form Bewitched). The propulsive rhythms turn "Death to Our Freinds" into a harrowing rollercoaster ride, and the band's increasing mastery of dynamics is apparent on "Expressway to Yr. Skull" (also listed as "Madonna, Sean and Me") and "Shadow of a Doubt." "Star Power" and a CD-bonus cover of Kim Fowley's "Bubblegum" celebrate a thorny brand of pop.

Sister has a warmer, more insular sound than its predecessor (it was recorded on vacuum-tube equipment), which gives the relatively compact songs a disturbing glow. In simultaneously hewing to rock-song form and blowing it apart, the album exploits a near-constant state of tension. Dissonant guitars barrel along with ragged force on "Tuff Gnarl" but twist snake-like through the bliss of "Cotton Crown," with rare harmony vocals by husband and wife Moore and Gordon. "Master-Dik," with flailing guest guitar by J Mascis, flirts with a looped, hip-hop rhythm, recycled on an experimental, largely self-indulgent EP.

Daydream Nation is and remains the quintessential Sonic Youth release, an ambitious work that brings together the band's varied strengths under one double-album-length roof, from the long-form "Trilogy" to the relatively compact "Kissability." The opening one-two battery of "Teen Age Riot" and "Silver Rocket" presents the band at its most melodic and accessible, while the mood piece "Providence" is SY at its most experimental.

A cooler-than-thou shtick unfortunately prevails on **Goo,** the band's major-label debut. The album loads up on terse, sharply produced rockers like "Dirty Boots" and "Kool Thing" (with guest vocals by Public Enemy's Chuck D), but is full of insufferable coyness, epitomized by "Tunic," a "tribute" to Karen Carpenter.

Dirty loses the wise-ass attitude in favor of shorter songs and more direct, charged lyrics that push Sonic Youth dangerously close to punk-rock convention. A cynic might interpret this shift as Sonic Youth's attempt to woo the Lollapalooza Nation, right down to the hiring of producer Butch Vig and mixer Andy Wallace, the **Nevermind** tag team. Whatever the intent, the disc is shot through with urgency. Shelley's drums send the songs hurtling like a dirt racer with bad shocks, while the guitars splatter the windshield with roadkill. Righteous indignation, political and otherwise, is the primary mood: Gordon mines withering, post-feminist sarcasm on "Swimsuit Issue," while "Chapel Hill" imagines a mosh pit atop Senator Jesse Helms' head and "Youth Against Fascism" gets surprisingly topical with an endorsement of Clarence Thomas accuser Anita Hill.

Experimental Jet Set, Trash and No Star is the band's most private record since **Sister,** and also its most overt exploration of the blues—not so much as a musical form but as a feeling. The use of acoustic guitar on the opening "Winner's Blues" is a first on a Sonic Youth record and establishes the disc's more intimate tone. Whereas before the band's lyrics had all the grimy flash of Lower East Side graffiti, now they carry the more personal and soul-searching perspective of adults pushing into middle age. The disc has almost an older sibling's empathy for its awkward young subjects: the SST record label junkie in "Screaming Skull," the fledgling riot grrrl in "Self-Obsessed and Sexxee," the boy who wishes he were a girl and gets mugged for it in "Androgynous Mind," the over-achiever in "Quest for the Cup" who pronounces "All my dreams come true . . . but now I have a bunch of other dreams." When Gordon splits open the languidly seductive album-closing "Sweet Shine" with her cry of "I'm comin' home, mama!" it's a rare moment of unguarded poignance. Jadedness could have set in by this late stage, but **Experimental Jet Set** paints Sonic Youth as downright compassionate.

Released several months after Sonic Youth headlined Lollapalooza, **Washing Machine** returns the band to the sprawling guitar epics that established its live reputation in the mid-'80s, this time structuring them around cyclic rhythms reminiscent of German art-rockers Neu! and Can. Musical references to the Shangri-Las, the Byrds' "Eight Miles High" (by way of John Coltrane's "India") and "Gloria" are sprinkled throughout, as Sonic Youth veers between trance-guitar experiments and more concise statements. The two impulses are spectacularly integrated on the nineteen-minute closer, "The Diamond Sea," in which a lovely melody and fanciful, Lewis Carroll–like lyrics are tucked inside pulsing waves of guitar until it all comes crashing down in a hail of distortion.

Screaming Fields of Love, a seventeen-track sampler of pre-**Goo** album tracks, was assembled to introduce newcomers to the band's reissued catalogue. The absence of rarities makes it unessential for serious consumers. The same isn't *quite* true for **Made in USA,** the stylistically unambitious (although occasionally spare and atmospheric) soundtrack of instrumentals and songs for a 1986 straight-to-video Christopher Penn/Lori Singer film.

Of the band's countless side projects, **The Whitey Album** is perhaps the most notorious. Sonic Youth's members teamed up with then-fIREHOSE bassist Mike Watt (who had guested on **EVOL**) as Ciccone Youth, an experimental group who thought it might be fun to deconstruct Top 40 tunes like Robert Palmer's "Addicted to Love" and Madonna's "Burnin' Up" and "Into the Groove," redubbed "Into the Groovey." But the joke doesn't translate, and the disc comes across as a self-indulgent mess. More recently, Moore and Shelley joined forces with Richard Hell and Don Fleming in New York underground supergroup Dim Stars. Moore and Ranaldo have each made records with free-jazz drummer William Hooker; Moore has also collaborated with Lydia Lunch and Borbetomagus. Shelley, who operates the Smells Like Records label (Blonde Redhead, Sentridoh, Sammy, etc.), participates in Mosquito, a Jad Fair diversion with guitarist Tim Foljahn (of Two Dollar Guitar and Half Japanese), Chan Marshall's Cat Power (also with Foljahn) and played on the Raincoats' reunion tour. Ecstatic Peace! is Moore's label; among many other releases, it issued the group's collaborative EP with Eye of the Boredoms.

Gordon's primary outside endeavors have been a clothing line called X-Girl and Free Kitten, a band she leads with ex–Pussy Galore guitarist Julia Cafritz. Ranaldo's solo works include **From Here to Infinity,** an experimental collection of short lock-groove compositions (most under a minute long)—some of which are included on the career overview **East Jesus,** which touches on spoken-word narrative and incorporates tape loops to underscore atmospheric, sometimes heavily processed guitar pieces.

Moore's solo debut, **Psychic ♥♥♥'s,** recorded with Shelley and Foljahn, is composed of minimalist songs that empathize with, or are inspired by, women. Most of the music is built around a single chord or riff, and in tinkering with repetition and reinvestigating the extended guitar opus (the fifteen-minute "Elegy for All the Dead Rock Stars") the album provides a natural bridge between **Experimental Jet Set, Trash and No Star** and **Washing Machine.** [gk]

See also *Bewitched, Borbetomagus, Boredoms, Dead C, Dim Stars, Free Kitten, Half Japanese, William Hooker, Lydia Lunch, Maureen Tucker, Mike Watt; TPRG.*

SONORA PINE

See *Rodan.*

SON VOLT

See *Uncle Tupelo.*

SORDID HUMOR

See *Counting Crows.*

SOUL ASYLUM

Say What You Will . . . (Twin\Tone) 1984
Made to Be Broken (Twin\Tone) 1986
Time's Incinerator [tape] (Twin\Tone) 1986
While You Were Out (Twin\Tone) 1986
Hang Time (Twin\Tone/A&M) 1988
Clam Dip & Other Delights EP (UK What Goes On) 1988 (Twin\Tone) 1989
Say What You Will, Clarence . . . Karl Sold the Truck (Twin\Tone) 1989
And the Horse They Rode in On (Twin\Tone/A&M) 1990
Grave Dancers Union (Columbia) 1992
Runaway Train EP (Columbia) 1993
Let Your Dim Light Shine (Columbia) 1995

If no other band steps forward any time soon, Soul Asylum might as well serve as the textbook example (paradigm, if you will) for the powers and pitfalls, the triumph b/w tragedy of "alternative" rock in the '90s. After spending nearly a decade making extraordinary rock'n'roll for all the best romantic reasons—to drive through snowdrifts in a drafty van, sleep on strangers' floors, make less money than a burger-flipper, drink too much beer and admit unshakable fears and abiding depression at high volume to small crowds—Soul Asylum moved to its second major label (the first having been, in truly classic post-indie fashion, an unmitigated commercial disaster) and stepped into a platinum spotlight.

Whether the quartet had to trade in its hard-won integrity or simply flash it at the door for a ticket onto the runaway escalator, the three-million-copy success of **Grave Dancers Union** shifted Soul Asylum from underdog to sitting duck, replacing the irrational confidence of obscurity with the insecurity of fame and exchanging small audiences of patiently devoted fans for teeming masses of show-us-your-hits newcomers unaware of the band's hard-fought history. That the music industry and radio should suddenly welcome—and then cold-shoulder—a band it had so enthusiastically overlooked for years inevitably invited suspicion regarding the quality of the records, but the lesson of all this is that shifting viewpoints are far more pernicious than shifting realities: most of the attributes used to explain Soul Asylum's breakthrough had always been there. But it goes further than that. The idea that a band should be great until it succeeds, and then—without making any unwarranted changes in its music—become wretched and disposable suggests that people impress their expectations on records a lot deeper than they realize.

Born into a Minneapolis scene then dominated by two great bands at the peak of their artistic powers, the young Soul Asylum (formed as Loud Fast Rules) was shaggier than the Replacements and less pop-savvy than Hüsker Dü. **Say What You Will,** produced by the latter's Bob Mould, culminates the band's hardcore slop phase and introduces an awareness of country music and a nascent aptitude for difficult rhythms and vocal interplay. Beyond the sturdy melodies and taut, '70s-informed rock energy, it intimated that hoarse singer/guitarist Dave Pirner might possess genuine talent as a hallucinatory storyteller and enigmatically confessional lyricist.

Indeed he did. The confident, emotionally compressed sound and material on the raw, fiery **Made to Be Broken** is light-years better; a decade on, it remains an essential Soul Asylum LP. Raging dual vocals and interwoven guitar work by Pirner and Dan Murphy, supported by new arrival Grant Young's precise, varied drumming, make the tuneful power of "Tied to the Tracks," "Ship of Fools," "New Feelings" and the countryish title track shatteringly original. "Never Really Been" points up an ability to convey the same wit and energy on touching (mostly) acoustic guitar ballads and contains this quintessential Pirner self-deflating shrug: "You were thinking I was distressed about some universal press/But I was just depressed about my last pinball game." The onomatopoetic "Whoa!" explodes in a breathtaking syncopated fury of incoherent shrieking and stands as one of Soul Asylum's funniest, most accomplished adventures.

Time's Incinerator is a cassette compilation of 1980–86 outtakes, covers, concert tracks and assorted nonsense. The 1989 CD reissue of **Say What You Will,** namechecking bassist Karl Mueller, adds five outtakes.

While You Were Out songs like "Closer to the Stars," "Freaks," "The Judge" and "Never Too Soon" are as good as any on **Made to Be Broken,** but the band races through hasty arrangements of them as if they couldn't afford the studio time. (Maybe making two albums in the same year wasn't such a good idea.) Whatever the group doesn't trash on its own (like the semi-country of "Passing Sad Daydream," which encapsulates Pirner's ambivalent personal philosophy: "Now if you got to hate someone/Might as well hate yourself/You'll find that you don't deserve it/No more than anyone else"), Chris Osgood's thin, messy production attends to.

Getting to the majors through their indie label, Soul Asylum made **Hang Time** with the production team of Ed Stasium (Ramones, Living Colour) and Lenny Kaye (James, Suzanne Vega). Bolstered by unprecedented sonic excellence and fully considered arrangements (but hindered by a bizarrely separated drum sound and fussiness), Soul Asylum delivered a mighty riff-rocking bang riveted with typically complex rhythmic and harmonic maneuvers. The first two tracks—"Down on Up to Me" and "Little Too Clean"—wallow in heavy '70s chunk that suggests a reverse in direction, but the record abruptly rights itself with the inspiring Clash-like pop blare of "Sometime to Return" and doesn't again falter. Highlights include the good-luck story "Ode," the theatrical "Marionette," Murphy's "Cartoon" (which contains such succinct lines as "If you're cryin' in your beer you're gonna drown"), "Beggars and Choosers," the majestically poignant "Endless Farewell" (a wistful Pirner piano lament) and the runaway intensity of "Standing in the Doorway" and "Jack of All Trades." Throughout, Soul Asylum generates unrestrained power in service of great tunes and structural surprises in a typically stripped-down genre. Substantial lyrics match equally intricate music while maintaining a casual, loose feel.

Reasserting their sense of humor, the band cut a batch of covers for the **Clam Dip** EP, whose front shot—a nude Mueller up to his waist in party food—spoofs a classic Herb Alpert (the A in A&M) sleeve. The English and American editions differ substantially: the import contains covers of Foreigner's "Juke Box Hero," Janis-Joplin-by-way-of-Slade's "Move Over" and "Chains," a terrific Minneapolis new wave obscurity by the Wad. By the time it was released Stateside, "Chains" was the only remaining cover, leaving the EP an odds-and-ends set of originals: a folk song for striking Hormel workers ("P-9"), the determined rock of "Just Plain Evil" and "Take It to the Root," a raving funkfest.

Steve Jordan (the drummer in Keith Richards' X-Pensive Winos) produced **And the Horse They Rode in On,** exchanging **Hang Time**'s punctilious studio finesse for a rawer, liver sound. (Ironically, he arranges a hollow, tin-can drum tone for Young's superb playing.) The brilliant and varied material has plenty of intrinsic appeal; delicately applied guitar effects, melodica (on Murphy's chantey-like "Gullible's Travels"), even choral bells (on Pirner's affecting piano lament, the romantic "We 3") do the rest. With a chanted refrain and anti-suicide lyrics that acknowledge Cheap Trick, "Easy Street" is an instant SA anthem; "Veil of Tears," "Be on Your Way," "Grounded" and "Nice Guys (Don't Get Paid)," a bizarre but moral crime fantasy, all further prove Pirner's songwriting genius and the band's remarkable ability to roar and sigh at the same time. A tremendous record that makes Soul Asylum sonically presentable without messing the group up.

Hard though it may be for some to hear the music on **Grave Dancers Union** through its sales figures and ill-conceived videos, the record that made Soul Asylum a hot property actually follows a reasonable and credible course from **And the Horse They Rode in On.** "Runaway Train" *is* an anomaly—an exceptionally obvious acoustic ballad, slicked up like a wet road to radio-ready one of Pirner's most programmatic down-in-the-mouth lyrics: "So many secrets I couldn't keep/Promised myself I wouldn't weep/One more promise I couldn't keep." (The EP adds live takes of "Black Gold" and "Never Really Been," a studio cover of William Bell's soul oldie "Everybody Loves a Winner" and an otherwise unissued acoustic original.) That the song became the group's breakthrough hit is ironic, but it's no indication of the nature of the album, which is otherwise not different enough from the A&M LPs to explain its disproportionate popularity or controversy.

Drawing minimal attention to his work, producer Michael Beinhorn furnished a comfortable playroom with guest musicians (organist Booker T. Jones, a string quartet, pals from Golden Smog) in which the group could do some belated growing up, and the results flow naturally from that. There are hardy melody rockers ("Somebody to Shove," "Black Gold," "Keep It Up," "April Fool"), rustic folk-rockers ("Without a Trace"), power balladry ("New World") and offbeat digressions (the thuggy noise-fest "99%," the pretty production pop of "The Sun Maid"). Pirner's verbiage takes typically playful form to convey an especially sincere and desperate burden: self-loathing, confusion and doubt permeate the album worse than ever. His uncertain career and an unsettled relationship keep colliding. In "Get on Out," he poses the soon-to-be-moot question: "Could you still make it with a guy who never made it?"

Three years and a couple of lifetimes later, Soul Asylum shaped up without Young (who, it emerged, had already been replaced on **Grave Dancers Union** by Sterling Campbell, a former member of Duran Duran, B-52's and David Bowie's band). **Let Your Dim Light Shine,** produced by Butch Vig, bellyflops off the diving board with the clumsy "Misery" ("They say misery loves company/We could start a company/And make misery") and contains one bewildering Tom Petty clone ("Bittersweetheart"), but otherwise gets down to the business of considering Soul Asylum Superstar with the usual measures of detached insight, churning guitar power and country funk. But here Pirner seems to be straining to sound like himself in the lyrics. Against uplifting power chords in "Tell Me When," he demands, "When does life begin?," only he's not thinking of conception in any biological sense. Paying tribute to early Cheap Trick in the snarly chorus, the singer has to pinch himself in the bridge of "Hopes Up": "Don't know what I was hoping for/I feel like feeling better than I ever felt before." In the closing "I Did My Best," which models its elegiac folk-rock closely on the Band's "The Weight," he pays the price for feeling so good, pleading for exculpation that could be either personal or public: "I did the best I could do/With all the mess that I've been through/What did you expect me to do?" Strange images abound—the two-headed president in "String of Pearls," the porcelain-seated outhouse of the loud/hard "Just Like Anyone," the jaded thirteen-year-old hooker of the touching "Eyes of a Child." Greeted by knee-jerk critics' sellout howls and found wanting by the devotees of "Runaway Train," the album failed to match **Grave Dancers**' chart positions. Thus was Soul

Asylum delivered to a place Pirner had already described in song: "Homesick for the home I never had." [i]

See also *Golden Smog; TPRG.*

SOUL COUGHING

Ruby Vroom (Slash) 1994
Irresistible Bliss (Slash/Warner Bros.) 1996

In theory, few musical propositions are less savory than lily-white wanna-beats "branching out" to flex a few alternarap muscles, but in practice, it can work out—provided the musicians involved carefully circumvent minstrelsy. This New York foursome recognizes that none of its personnel is from the 'hood, even as it asserts its right to use hip-hop constructs as a foundation for what frontman M. (Michael) Doughty has dubbed "deep slacker jazz." **Ruby Vroom,** an unusually well-realized debut, lives up to the jazz portion of that claim, thanks in large part to the graceful, elastic finger-popping rhythms instilled by upright bassist Sebastian Steinberg and drummer Yuval Gabay (both of whom cut their teeth on the city's experimental music scene). Those unflagging beats—along with sampler wiz M'ark de Gli Antoni's brimming quiver of musique concrète, cartoon themes and out-and-out skronk—provide a foil for Doughty's sometimes surreal, sometimes grittily noir blank verse. When he strives for humor (as on "Casiotone Nation"), the reformed rock critic has an appealingly biting wit; when he wants to hustle up some atmosphere (like the Beckett-meets-Raymond-Chandler "Screenwriter's Blues"), he can practically make you taste the bar-room floor.

On **Irresistible Bliss,** Doughty sacrifices some B-boy accouterments and plants his feet more firmly in beatnik territory in both message (a more socially conscious tone is set by songs like "White Girl") and medium (his percussive couplet lobs are, at times, straight outta Ginsberg). The band adapts to Doughty's whims with a more abstract—though still groove-based—sound that spotlights de Gli Antoni's capering, which proves most effective on "Super Bon Bon" and "Soundtrack to Mary," a rare opportunity for Doughty to actually *sing* (after a fashion). [dss]

See also *Marc Ribot, John Zorn.*

SOUL-JUNK

See *Trumans Water.*

SOUL II SOUL

Club Classics Vol. One (UK 10/Virgin) 1988
Keep on Movin' (Virgin) 1989
Vol II 1990 A New Decade (Virgin) 1990
Volume III Just Right (Ten/Virgin) 1992
Volume IV The Classic Singles 88–93 (UK Ten/Virgin) 1993
Volume V Believe (Virgin) 1995

CARON WHEELER

UK Blak (EMI) 1990
Beach of the War Goddess (EMI) 1992

When "Keep on Movin'," the lead track of Soul II Soul's 1988 debut (released in the US as **Keep on Movin'**) became a hit in 1989, it signaled a quiet revolution in soul music: lovely harmonies and a charming chorus laid over a slow, silky, electronically propelled dance groove imaginatively laced with delicate instrumental accents. Producers Jazzie B (Beresford Romeo, also the group's primary songwriter) and Nellee Hooper, the masterminds of what was never a formal group, came from the same Bristol scene that spawned Massive Attack, Portishead and Tricky, but their approach has always been more mainstream (and commerce-minded: Soul II Soul's first decisive step, in 1982, was opening a clothing/records shop in Camden; the group also produced a fashion line) than those three.

Lacking a single vocalist—the debut's star diva, Caron Wheeler, quickly left to capitalize on her success with a solo career—Soul II Soul has been unable to maintain a steady sound or level of quality. **Vol II** is genially entertaining and relatively consistent, yielding the successful singles "Get a Life" and "A Dream's a Dream." Although Wheeler returned to guest ("Take Me Higher") on **Volume III,** Hooper was already off to a successful career as an independent producer (scoring hits with Björk and Madonna, among others), leaving Jazzie B in charge of what had devolved from a groundbreaking, if creatively unreliable, soul collective to a not particularly exciting R&B act. **Volume IV The Classic Singles 88–93** is a UK-only compilation; **Volume V Believe,** containing some lovely vocal performances (including three by Wheeler) backed by very soulful music, continues Soul II Soul's transformation into a traditional British R&B combo.

Proceeding from the alluring grooves, confused feminism and cultural identity thoughts of **UK Blak,** Wheeler's second album is chock full of political and social ideology—there's even a suggested reading list, including *A Healthy Foods and Spiritual Nutrition Handbook, Marcus Garvey* and *African Holistic Health.* The songs, however, are much less memorable. Her voice is fine and the album's sound is more cohesive, but she has yet to advance her solo career beyond a footnote to Soul II Soul. [mf]

See also *TPRG.*

SOUNDGARDEN

Screaming Life EP (Sub Pop) 1987
Fopp EP (Sub Pop) 1988
Ultramega OK (SST) 1988
Louder Than Love (A&M) 1989
Screaming Life/Fopp (Sub Pop) 1990
Badmotorfinger (A&M) 1991
Superunknown (A&M) 1994
Alive in the Superunknown EP (A&M) 1995
Down on the Upside (A&M) 1996

HATER

Hater (A&M) 1993

Soundgarden spearheaded the Northwest's revival of that non-metal rock gulch between late-'60s innovation and late-'70s rebellion, years in which groups like Grand Funk, Led Zep and Mountain prevailed. Never as punk (or pop) as Nirvana or as out-and-out heavy as the Melvins, smarter than Alice in Chains but less intense than Pearl Jam, the Seattle quartet started out too early and, for a while, seemed doomed to chase grunge's commercial juggernaut. In the '90s, however, hard work and the mounting demand for thuggish guitar-rock power brought Soundgarden mainstream success, thereby eliminating any vestigial countercultural distinction between the group and the bands that originally inspired it.

Happily unspecific in its stylistic derivation, the accomplished six-song **Screaming Life** EP introduces Chris Cornell's Robert Plant–channeling vocals, Kim Thayil's turgid guitar power, Hiro Yamamoto's rubbery bass action and Matt Cameron's steady-as-she-goes drumming. The assimilation of both classic rock riffs and punk noise keeps things interesting, but Cornell's unabashed mimicry stands out as Soundgarden's essential feature. The band's two Sub Pop EPs were later joined on one ten-track CD. **Screaming Life/Fopp** contains the latter's three '88 live tracks—"Kingdom of Come," a cover of Green River's "Swallow My Pride" and the titular Ohio Players song—plus a pointless dub mix of "Fopp."

Soundgarden then became Sub Pop's first offering to the corporate ogre by signing with A&M in 1988. In what subsequently became a common major-label ploy to bolster new bands' hipness cred before turning on the hype, **Ultramega OK** was released by SST. A noticeable improvement, with less self-conscious posturing and more evidence of an emerging personality, the album finds Cornell reducing (not eliminating) his reliance on Plant clichés. For all the energetic bluster, though, an inadequate comprehension of what constitutes a song (something Soundgarden's forefathers always grasped) leaves the quartet tethered to the past, attempting to get by with touchstones rather than originality.

With its standard-issue Charles Peterson hair-photograph cover and Terry Date production, **Louder Than Love** is an inauspicious commercial unveiling, all muscle and no brains. The songs plod; Cornell roars with fringed-leather power; Thayil throws out licks haphazardly, whether they fit or not; the rhythm section does nothing more than keep the beat. Whether or not they mean to, Soundgarden could easily be America's answer to the Cult. "Uncovered," built on a variation of the descending riff from "Dazed and Confused," is the closest the record comes to finding and sticking with an idea that works; while the chords of "Big Dumb Sex" hold together, Cornell's lyrics are unendurably stupid.

Yamamoto left; he was briefly replaced by ex-Nirvana guitarist Jason Everman, who was gone before the sessions for the next album began. Ben Shepherd, *his* successor, wasted no time in making his presence known on **Badmotorfinger,** writing or co-writing four songs and fattening up the band's bottom with driving, shapely bass riffs that give both Thayil and Cornell a firmer foundation than they've ever had. (Not that either does anything especially new with it.) The speeding "Jesus Christ Pose" and "Holy Water" ("Holy Bible on the night stand/Next to me/As I'm raped by/Another monkey circus freak/Trying to take my/Indignance away from me"—*indignance? monkey circus freak?* What is Cornell *on* about?) find the singer growing into his messianic role, an apt verbal analogue for his growing rock stardom. Finally, it's Soundgarden's insistence on taking the simplest ideas and beating them into the ground with the repetitive concentration of bodybuilders that keeps the album (which went platinum in any case) from anything more involving than groundshaking sonic power. Sometimes an earthquake is just an earthquake.

The shocking development on **Superunknown**—besides the beneficial introduction of Michael Beinhorn as the band's first new studio collaborator and the fact that it went straight in at the top of the charts—is "Black Hole Sun," an honest-to-god psychedelic pop song, and a stunningly good one at that. (If Cornell could write something like this, why hadn't he ever shown any evidence of it before? Maybe the short haircut had something to do with it.) In this great creative leap forward, other numbers—"The Day I Tried to Live," "Head Down," "Spoonman," "Limo Wreck"—incorporate bridges, dynamic variation, bursts of melody and other useful bits of musical business. ("Half" goes way out on a sitar-and-tabla-like limb that could perhaps be growing from Led Zeppelin's world music adventures.) Fitted out with Cornell lyrics that thoughtfully describe what sounds like a deadly depression—witness "Let Me Drown," "Fell on Black Days," "Like Suicide"—the songs pack a wallop that is amplified by, rather than based in, the band's forceful playing. (**Alive in the Superunknown,** a video-packed CD-ROM supplement to the album, contains its title track, a live version of "Fell on Black Days," an acoustic "Like Suicide" and the previously unissued-in-the-US "She Likes Surprises.")

There's no "Black Hole Sun" on **Down on the Upside,** but the general inclination of the album is toward songs of that caliber and nonconformity. The predominance of classic riff-rock remains (this time, throwing elements of Bad Company, Free, Black Sabbath and Lynyrd Skynyrd into the Zeppitude), but simply wrought songs like "Tighter & Tighter," "Never Named," "Blow Up the Outside World" and the understated "Overfloater" expand the band's reach enough to warrant suspicions of creative effort. While Cornell is still mucking about his usual animosity/suicide/rot rut, faint glimmers of page-turning imagination, like "Ty Cobb," improve the lyrics. There may still be little discernible purpose to Soundgarden's music, but the group *is* getting closer to its home.

Typical of too many moonlit releases from Northwest stars—so much studio time, so little inspiration—the eponymous album by Hater, a five-piece starring drummer Matt Cameron and bassist Ben Shepherd (here playing guitar), is a silly waste of time. A sloppy studio bash that has to have been more fun to make than it is to hear, **Hater** has a Cat Stevens cover ("Mona Bone Jakon"), Stoogey punk ("Tot Finder"), T.Rex-by-way-of-the-Beatles rock ("Putrid") and cowpunk ("Blistered"). With exactly one solid original, Shepherd's "Circles," **Hater** is trivial and self-indulgent, unreleasable were it not for the stature of the participants. [i]

See also *Brad, Pete Droge, Mindfunk, Mother Love Bone, Truly; TPRG.*

EPIC SOUNDTRACKS

Rise Above (UK Rough Trade) 1992 (Bar/None) 1993
Sleeping Star (Bar/None) 1994
Debris (Ger. Return to Sender/Normal) 1995
Change My Life (Bar/None) 1996

Having spent his teens and early twenties as time-keeper/noisemaker with pioneering English homebrew primitivists the Swell Maps, this Birmingham native (since relocated to London) could probably have released tapes of his kitchen putterings and earned avant-garde kudos. When he decided to make his solo bow—after interim stints in the Jacobites (led by his brother, Nikki Sudden), Crime and the City Solution and These Immortal Souls—Epic Soundtracks (born Paul Godley) did something considerably more audacious: he remade himself into an utterly charming singer/songwriter, inspired by the heyday of the Brill Building and all but untouched by the hipster musical lexicon.

Rise Above drew some noise on account of cameos by J Mascis (in his ancillary role as session drummer), Rowland S. Howard, Lee Ranaldo and Kim Gordon, but those guests maintain a respectful distance from center stage. Thus, Epic is free to shine brightly on such spry odes to *l'amour* as the ecstatic "Meet Me on the Beach." It's on the more melancholy tracks, however, that clever turns of phrase give way to heartfelt intimacy: "She Sleeps Alone/Love Fucks You Up" paints a hazy, poignant pastel of a fast-lane denizen's off-hour misery. There's considerably more optimism coursing through **Sleeping Star,** which often approximates the warm, jamming feel of a vintage Band record—an impressive feat when you consider how much of the project is essentially solo. Epic's warm baritone has grown more confident; while he spends a bit too much time rhapsodizing about the liberating power of rock'n'roll (as on "Something New Under the Sun"), his enthusiasm is contagious.

He manages to retain just enough of that intimacy to overcome the rock conceits that permeate much of **Change My Life.** Much more ambitious than his previous solo efforts, the album loses momentum when Epic tries to affect a hard-guy edge. He's much better off when he's unabashedly starry-eyed, as on a no-fi CD bonus medley of Alex Chilton's "Nightime" and "Thirteen," or "Stealaway," which adds horns and tubular bells (!) to the mix and allows him to indulge his Spectorsound obsession.

Debris is a limited-edition collection of outtakes, rarities and radio session tracks. [dss]

See also *These Immortal Souls.*

SOUP DRAGONS

Hang-Ten! (Sire) 1987
This Is Our Art (Sire) 1988
Lovegod (Big Life/PolyGram) 1990
I'm Free EP (Big Life/PolyGram) 1990
Hotwired (Big Life/Mercury) 1992
Hydrophonic (Raw TV Products/Mercury) 1994

The old parental fears—matches, alcohol, a rough crowd, drugs—are passé. What seems to send UK (especially Scottish) bands spiraling over the edge of sanity and sanctity this decade is that demon dancebeat. Two years' worth of singles and EPs (collected as the **Hang-Ten!** album) had identified the Soup Dragons as Glasgow's junior Buzzcocks; that image ended with the release of **This Is Our Art,** a closet full of try-on styles: '60s garage psychedelia, hard rock, funk and more. Then the quartet abandoned any punk edge it once had and embraced young Britain's burgeoning acid rave culture with grooved pockets of electronically aided crossover pop rhythmatism. A lazy, Madchester-styled cover of the Rolling Stones' "I'm Free" (featuring guest toasting by Junior Reid) became the band's career-making hit, sparking the success of the otherwise original **Lovegod,** an effective, accessible (if ultimately tedious) trip of house-geared rhythms, semi-firm melodies and singer/guitarist/programmer Sean Dickson's obviously mind-expanded lyrics. "Dream-E-Forever" is only the most blatant Ecstasy fan letter.

Hotwired isn't as druggy or clubby as **Lovegod.** The group integrates danceable rhythms into moderate, engaging pop productions rather than using them as the album's structural building block. Dickson's commitment to hedonism and freedom ("Pleasure," "Running Wild") remains unabated, but he appears to have moved beyond simple ideas of oblivion by ingestion (searching for a way to solve someone's problems in "Absolute Heaven," he still can't find anything "to take you out of your mind"). And "Mindless" is a love song to a person, not a pill. Consistent in tone (except for the mushy strings on "Forever Yesterday") and occasionally strikingly good (the sharp, memorable "Dream-On (Solid Gone)" and the crisp, snappy "Everlasting"), **Hotwired** is the first Soup Dragons album to live up to the band's increasing potential.

But someone's ego was evidently on a steeper growth curve, and guitarist Jim McCulloch, bassist Sushil Dade and drummer Paul Quinn soon found themselves de-mobilized. Dickson recorded the awful and excessive **Hydrophonic** as a solo album under the band name, getting abundant session aid from new pals Bootsy Collins, the Scottish Chamber Orchestra, the Kick Horns, Lynval Golding, Neville Staples, Tina Weymouth and Mickey Finn. A soggy hodgepodge of lunkheaded rock, would-be hip-hop, blues, soulful backing vocals and chants, extraneous disco strings, limp, stupid songs and mechanical drumming, the self-produced (natch) **Hydrophonic** repeatedly sounds like it's either about to break into a chorus of "Brother Louie" (or "Gimme Shelter") or rebuild Pink Floyd's **Wall**—neither of which is a viable option for the salvation of this once-happening band. Flush it. [db/i]

See also *BMX Bandits, Superstar; TPRG.*

SOUTHERN CULTURE ON THE SKIDS

Voodoo Beach Party EP7 (Lloyd Street) 1985
Southern Culture on the Skids (Lloyd Street) 1985
Too Much Pork for Just One Fork (Moist) 1992
Santo! Sings EP7 (Zontar) 1992
For Lovers Only (Safe House) 1992
Girlfight EP10 (Sympathy for the Record Industry) 1993
Peckin' Party EP (Feed Bag) 1993
Ditch Diggin' (Safe House) 1994
Dirt Track Date (DGC) 1995 (Telstar) 1995

Since 1985, Chapel Hill singer/guitarist Rick Miller has been leading his merry band of North Carolina trash merchants, dressing up in hillbilly threads but playing bugeyed rock'n'roll, instrumentals, R&B and country swill with a lurid sense of humor, abundant skill and true historical dedication. The trio takes a loose and evidently well-meant minstrel-like approach to its Appalachian heritage, walking a strange line between the poles of taunting and exploiting a widely disrespected people. Southern Culture on the Skids' records do neither, but simply take what they know and bend it into a cheerful caricature of a colorful personality.

The first album (also known as **First Album**) combines refried hillbilly twang and hot-rod instrumentals with a slight nod to the Cramps: see such lo-fi wheelies as "Psycho Surfing," "Primitive Guy" and "Atom Age Trucker." It's almost touching that "Demon Death" helps itself to the *Outer Limits* theme.

Other than a single here and there, SCOTS was little heard from over the next seven years. Then came the deluge. Unveiling a lineup with bassist/singer

Mary Huff and drummer Dave Hartman, the Skids announced their return with **Too Much Pork for Just One Fork** (containing such delicacies as "Voodoo Cadillac," "Back in the Woods" and "Eight Piece Box," an ode to fried chicken) on the ill-fated Moist label, which went out of business shortly after. Demonstrating the group's versatility, "Viva Del Santo" (on the four-song **Santo! Sings**) pays tribute to the prowess of the great masked Mexican wrestler and movie star to the sounds of a mariachi surf band.

SCOTS continue their excursions into trailer park camp with **For Lovers Only,** on which they discover the perils of the "Barnyard Ballbuster," marvel at "The Man That Wrestles the Bear," offer a creepy recipe in "Biscuit Eater" and pay tribute to the Wray-man in "Link's Lung." The comical "Clyde's Lament" disgorges a lazy swampabilly moan last seen coming from Jeffrey Lee Pierce and the Gun Club back at the turn of the last decade. "Nashville Toupee" sticks a collective tongue out at men who have taken advantage of the rug trade. Standing apart from the rest of the fourteen songs here is a cover of Jo Anna and Bob Neel's "Daddy Was a Preacher but Mama Was a Go-Go Girl," on which Huff takes the lead and proves that she could easily join the pantheon of hot rockin' ladies like Wanda Jackson and Janice Martin if given half a chance.

If a good "Girlfight" is what you want, that's just what you get on the title track of the 10-inch EP. Besides the joys of hair-pulling and nail-scratching, the group take time out to tip their hat to past daddies, singing "Hey Chuck Berry" to the tune of "Hey Bo Diddley" and following that with a cover of Norman Petty's "Wheels."

Peckin' Party serves up three new studio tracks (Link Wray's "Run Chicken Run" and two originals—one a second serving of "Eight Piece Box"—that gain added instrumental depth from guest sax by Jim Spake) and three songs (including "Daddy Was a Preacher but Mama Was a Go-Go Girl") recorded live at Chicago's Lounge Ax.

Recorded in Memphis, **Ditch Diggin'** makes it clear that SCOTS has developed into a band skilled enough to get its songs played on commercial country radio—if not for the mouthful name and the congenital silliness responsible for such demented lyrics as "Put Your Teeth Up on the Window Sill" and "Tunafish Every Day." (Think of SCOTS as the snide but affectionate result of growing up with *Hee-Haw.*) Contributing to the laid-back attitude that permeates the album, co-producer Doug Easley adds lap steel; fiddler Roy Brewer and saxman Spake also play on the record. There's a Louvin Brothers song ("The Great Atomic Power") and another Link Wray cover ("Jack the Ripper, Parts 1 & 2"), but it's not enough to turn the throttle to full.

Dirt Track Date introduces Southern Culture to the deep waters of major labels (with a vinyl edition on Telstar) and pulls the group out a little worse for wear. At best ("Greenback Fly"), the album recalls George Thorogood's bar band raunch; more often, the processed vocals (see "White Trash" and the funkish "Soul City") lead down a dead-end dirt road. Only when the band revisits its own back catalogue (new versions of "Voodoo Cadillac," "8 Piece Box" and **Santo! Sings**' "Camel Walk") does **Dirt Track Date** fetch up memories of the band's wild past. Even Huff's "Nitty Gritty" comes off bland. Lacking the ebullient sense of reckless fun that filled their best work, **Dirt Track Date** runs on nothing but the fumes of shtick. [mk/i]

SPACE

See *Orb.*

SPACEHOG

Resident Alien (hifi/Sire) 1995

Pointedly copping melodies, guitar sound, vocals and a stylistic posture from glam-era David Bowie may be an odd choice two decades on, but it isn't intrinsically any more despicable than the usual pilferage that goes on in the rock world. If Spacehog—four lads from Leeds who emigrated to New York City before launching their miserable career—had a second idea of any merit, the group might be excused for such light-fingered designs, but **Resident Alien** is unmitigated rubbish, stupid and obvious. To be entirely fair, singer/bassist Royston Langdon gets off a nifty bit of tuneage in the leadoff "In the Meantime," and his guitarist/brother Antony Langdon's intentionally provocative lyrics in the libertarian "Space Is the Place" ("And just because you kiss your brother/It doesn't mean to say your [*sic*] gay/And just because you're fucking him/It doesn't mean you don't love me") are attention-grabbing, but nothing here is worth a second listen. [i]

SPACEMEN 3

Sound of Confusion (UK Glass) 1986 (UK Fire) 1989 (Fire/Taang!) 1994
Walkin' With Jesus EP (UK Glass) 1986
Transparent Radiation EP (UK Glass) 1987
The Perfect Prescription (UK Glass) 1987 (Genius) 1988 (Fire/Taang!) 1996
Performance (UK Glass) 1988 (UK Fire) 1991 (Fire/Taang!) 1994
Playing With Fire (UK Fire) 1989 (Fire/Bomp!) 1989 (Fire/Taang!) 1994
Spacemen 3 EP (UK Fire) 1989
Taking Drugs to Make Music to Take Drugs To (Father Yod Production) 1990 (Bomp!) 1994
Dreamweapon: An Evening of Contemporary Sitar Music (UK Fierce) 1990 (Sympathy for the Record Industry) 1993 (UK Space Age) 1995
Losing Touch With Your Mind (Sp. Munster) 1991
Recurring (Fire/Dedicated/RCA) 1991
Spacemen Are Go! (Bomp!) 1994
Transparent Flashbacks: The Glass Singles (UK Fire) 1995
The Singles (Fire/Taang!) 1995
Revolution or Heroin (UK Fierce) 1995
For All the Fucked Up Children of This World We Give You Spacemen 3 (Sympathy for the Record Industry) 1995
Live 1989 (UK Space Age) 1995

SONIC BOOM

Spectrum (UK Silvertone) 1990

SPECTRUM

How You Satisfy Me EP (UK Silvertone) 1991
Soul Kiss (Glide Divine) (Silvertone) 1991
True Love Will Find You in the End EP (UK Silvertone) 1992
Indian Summer EP (UK Silvertone) 1993
Spectrum EP10 (Sympathy for the Record Industry) 1993

Undo the Taboo EP (UK Silvertone) 1994
Highs, Lows and Heavenly Blows (UK Silvertone) 1994
Songs for Owsley EP (Reprise) 1996

SPECTRUM AND JESSAMINE

A Pox on You (UK Space Age) 1996

EXPERIMENTAL AUDIO RESEARCH

Mesmerised (Sympathy for the Record Industry) 1994
Beyond the Pale (Big Cat) 1996

From the general tone of his post–Spacemen 3 output, it's clear that English guitarist, keyboardist and singer Pete "Sonic Boom" Kember was the reason that band spent so much of its performance career sitting down. Kember's explorations of sonic possibilities have always been marked by nuances of shade and pitch rather than immediately recognizable "songs." Yes, he's got a certain infatuation with the spangle-pop of late '60s icons like Brian Wilson, but as time has passed, Kember has increasingly disabused himself of his more corporeal leanings, choosing instead to ascend into the ether and send down missives from above

The Sonic Boom solo album **Spectrum** is little more than a loosely connected cluster of shimmers, spangles and sparkles, reminiscent of nothing so much as Suicide (whose "Rock 'n' Roll Is Killing My Life" he covers here) on anti-depressant medication. The one-chord guitar vamps don't stray far from the more pastoral side of the Spacemen tracks, but Kember's repudiation of rock as a form is hardly ambiguous. Recorded as a quartet, **Soul Kiss (Glide Divine),** if anything, is a retrograde journey (albeit a gorgeously dappled one) backward into Summer of Love popcraft. Songs like "How You Satisfy Me" are colored in bright dayglo tones by Kember's distorted organ and Geoff Donkin's insistently exuberant drumming. Even when the mood is more dilatory (as on "Lord I Don't Even Know My Name" and the seductive "Quicksilver Glide Divine"), it's a sense of tranquility, not torpor, that prevails. (In the UK, the CD was originally packaged in a liquid-filled plastic sleeve.)

Following the **Indian Summer** EP—politely restrained three-man covers of Beat Happening, Bo Diddley, Daniel Johnston, Jan and Dean and, on the self-titled US equivalent, the 13th Floor Elevators—**Highs, Lows and Heavenly Blows** (previewed on **Undo the Taboo,** with three non-LP items) strips away most of the exoskeleton that held up the songs on the past two albums, eschewing niceties like rhythm and verse-chorus-verse structure in favor of a more Eastern sense of space and time. Each of the pieces on the album, while short and somewhat individual, sounds like it could have been hewn from a larger whole that's resonating out there to this day. Kember's Vox Starstreamer organ is an important element in preserving the radiant patina that gleams off the surface of everything in sight; his experimentation with non-standard scales is inherent in the elegant dislocation that lies beneath.

The revolving membership of Experimental Audio Research precludes classifying it as a band—it's more a loose affiliation that includes Kevin Shields of My Bloody Valentine, Kevin Martin of God and elder statesman Eddie Prevost (who, as a member of the seminal AMM, has been exploring the potential of sound sculpture for more than three decades). **Mesmerised** consists of four long pieces that ebb and flow, building circular-thinking motifs in the manner of Cluster. The appropriately titled "D.M.T. Symphony" is probably the most soothing (and at times, numbing) of the tracks, while "Guitar Feedback Manipulation" (essentially just that) tends to oscillate more earthily, though aggression never enters the picture.

Beyond the Pale finds the collective delving more into the realm of everyday electronics to create post-ambient tonal structures like the title track, which consists of fifteen or so minutes of spangled keyboard seascapes dotted with the occasional passing of sleek guitar out near the horizon line. A handful of more compressed pieces ("Dusk," "The Calm Beyond") aren't quite as profound in terms of atmosphere-altering but, experienced as an unbroken aggregate, **Beyond the Pale** is a mighty fine ablution. E.A.R. has also spawned a wide variety of perversely formatted singles—including discs ranging from five to eight to ten inches in diameter—filled with loops and drones that could be vestigial waves left ringing three decades after La Monte Young's Theatre of Eternal Music.

In its original incarnation, Spacemen 3 divined a loud, strange, shimmering beauty from the bleak landscapes surrounding its homebase in industrial Rugby. The art-schoolers' early days were marked by a narcodelic haze that permeated both the hymn-like drug anthems and the bizarrely chosen covers (Glen Campbell *and* the Stooges) on **Sound of Confusion. The Perfect Prescription** opiated the masses even more strongly, with singer/guitarists Jason Pierce and Kember constructing glissando-laden melodies with no perceptible center—a disorienting characteristic that proves most effective on a long, luxurious cover of the Red Crayola's "Transparent Radiation."

S3 sounds absolutely ecstatic on the concert recording **Performance,** which probably has more than a little to do with the fact that the gig it was taken from was in Amsterdam. Most of the material comes from extant releases, although a new song, "Come Together" (which "borrows" from the Who in much the same way Led Zeppelin "borrowed" from Willie Dixon), is probably the highest point. The self-titled 12-inch EP, containing three more live items and stage intro music from 1988, was distributed to the first two thousand buyers of the British edition of **Playing With Fire,** easily the Spacemen's studio pinnacle. More a statement of purpose than a mere official bootleg, **Taking Drugs to Make Music to Take Drugs To** injects listeners into the quartet's very fiber, presenting as it does some embryonic 1986 recordings of songs that would turn up on later albums. Just say yes!

The positively enthralling **Dreamweapon** presents the band at its most freewheeling and completely insular stage. The centerpiece, a forty-five-minute drone dream wryly entitled "An Evening of Contemporary Sitar Music," is a study in texture; the guitars (Kember, Pierce and Steve Evans) lazily enmesh and disentangle as if engaged in a Beckett-inspired game of cat's cradle. Utterly surreal. The incidental pieces aren't quite as overwhelming, although Kember's feedback-shaping solo turn on "Ecstasy in Slow Motion" restores the good name of navel-gazing as a spectator sport. (In appropriately disorienting fashion, one side of the Fierce vinyl plays from the inside out.)

Although Spacemen 3 had already split, the group was obligated to deliver one more album. **Recurring,** for which Kember and Pierce recorded their contributions separately, hangs together surprisingly well, thanks in part to the amount of fog inherent in even the most lucid Spacemen release. The gospel-blues sense of yearning that popped up now and again on earlier releases is diffused through practically every bar of songs like "Why Couldn't I See?" and "Feel So Sad," while a flair for tension-building makes a maelstrom out of Mudhoney's otherwise ineffectual "When Tomorrow Hits."

Most of the posthumous releases simply rehash the same dozen or so songs in imperceptibly discrete versions. Devoting eighty minutes to eleven tracks, **The Singles** (and the similar UK package) is a neat bundle of early material, including the entire **Transparent Radiation** EP and tracks from the "Take Me to the Other Side" and "Walkin' With Jesus" 12-inches. **Live 1989** (issued in America as **Spacemen Are Go!**) is an indifferent concert performance of the, er, hits. The band is much better served by **Revolution or Heroin** (talk about a tough choice!). Although not well recorded, the album—which ends with a meaty free-form freakout dubbed "Muzik Konkret"—captures the Spacemen aesthetic at its most aggressively blurred, with the only hints of lucidity coming from between-song tapes of vintage White Panther oratory. The Spanish **Losing Touch With Your Mind** is an authorized bootleg of alternate mixes and takes.

For All the Fucked Up Children of This World professes to contain the first-ever Spacemen 3 recording session, which is very likely the case, given the amusingly punky tone of rudimentary versions of "Things'll Never Be the Same" (which sounds like it was pulled directly from a Shadows of Knight bootleg) and "Walkin' With Jesus." About the only reason to own this artifact (besides the goofy booklet photo of the band in new romantic drag) is a bizarre drone-gospel take on "Fixin' to Die." Then again, not owning it would probably be like buying a set of encyclopedias and jettisoning the Q volume. [dss]

See also *Darkside, God, Jessamine, Spiritualized; TPRG.*

SPACE STREAKINGS

Hatsu-Koi (Nux Organization/Charnel House) 1993
7-Toku (Skin Graft) 1994

The Boredoms, Shonen Knife and Pizzicato Five may get all the media attention, but there's a lot more to contemporary Japanese rock than that. With a cast that reads like a badly translated film festival—Captain Insect (bass, programming), Karate Condor (guitar, guitar synth, vocoder), Screaming Stomach (vocals, guitar, trumpet) and Kame Bazooka (vocals, sax, guitar)—Space Streakings creates hyper-speed meltdown noise, a thick hysterical barrage of galloping electronic percussion, horns, whistles, samples and shouted Japanese vocals, achieving a disjointed level of frenzy that suggests a flooding factory full of workers scrambling for the exits in a blind panic. Far more boisterous and a lot less methodical than American industrialists, the quartet rushes in and around its tracks, layering bits on to a point of distraction in which chaos would come as a welcome relief. Kazuyuki K. Null of Zeni Geva produced **Hatsu-Koi** ("First Love"); Steve Albini attended to the studio documentation of **7-Toku.** Short-attention-span fans never had it so good, but neither album is for the easily agitated. [i]

See also *Mount Shasta.*

SPACETIME CONTINUUM

Fluresence EP (Reflective) 1993
Sea Biscuit (Astralwerks) 1994
Emit Ecaps (Astralwerks) 1996

SPACETIME CONTINUUM WITH TERENCE MCKENNA

Alien Dreamtime (Astralwerks) 1993

JONAH SHARP/PETE NAMLOOK

Alien Community (Ger. Fax) 1993
Alien Community 2 (Ger. Fax) 1994
Wechselspannung (Ger. Fax) 1994
Wechselspannung 2 (Ger. Fax) 1995

JONAH SHARP/TETSU INOUE

Electro Harmonix (Ger. Fax) 1994

JONAH SHARP/BILL LASWELL

Visitation (Subharmonic) 1994

JONAH SHARP/DAVID MOUFANG

Reagenz (Reflective) 1995

Even before his 1993 emergence with **Fluresence,** DJ, recording artist and independent label head Jonah Sharp was already well on his way to becoming a luminary in the world of electronic music. Sharp left Scotland in his teens and became immersed in London's acid jazz/rare groove scene as a drummer before being drawn to the blossoming "intelligent techno" genre. He subsequently relocated to Northern California, where he launched Spacetime Continuum.

Recorded live at a San Francisco multimedia event, **Alien Dreamtime**—a performance with author Terence McKenna and didgeridoo player Stephen Kent—only hints at Sharp's potential with unique rhythms and timbres. Penned in by the nasal drone of McKenna's prolonged lectures on psychedelic shamanism, the musicians are denied the breadth to truly explore the potential of such a collaboration. McKenna does step aside for interludes, but the time isn't sufficient for Sharp and Kent to really shine, and Sharp seems reliant on techno formulae.

With Sharp the sole composer, producer and performer of Spacetime Continuum, **Sea Biscuit** is a wholly more satisfying affair, much more in the spirit of a debut album. The seven lengthy tracks (averaging more than ten minutes each) evolve in organic spirals that suggest forms without reiterating them to the point of over-familiarity. Sharp paints shifting aural tableaux with detailed emphasis on tone color (although his selections aren't as exotic as Future Sound of London), particularly on the final "A Low Frequency Inversion Field." The beats are persistent but subtle; as soon as the Kraftwerkian pops of "Pressure" begin, the collage of pulsing noises simply folds them into the mix.

Emit Ecaps finds Sharp moving away from the intersection of ambient and techno, experimenting successfully with the rhythms of jungle/drum and bass culture. Although still perfectly suitable as listening music, this is the first Spacetime Continuum album that actually invites the listener to dance. Sharp's extensive sonic palette is undiminished, but he juggles juxtapositions of both timbre and rhythm, using light, playful breakbeats to underpin slower-moving ambient textures. "Iform" starts the ten-track collection off slowly, percolating along in a "traditional" Spacetime vibe until a funky bassline kicks in after two minutes; on "Kairo," the musical elements slither around one another like snakes in a basket: jazz bass, staccato keyboard blips, a smidgen of banjo, the fluttering of double-time programmed drums.

Sharp is also a prodigious collaborator, with projects on his own Reflective label (known for its inventive, shiny packaging), ambient guru Pete Namlook's Fax label and others. The two **Alien Community** records with Namlook are fairly similar in feel, both reminiscent of **Sea Biscuit.** The distinct styles of the individuals are a little more pronounced on the less interchangeable **Wechselspannung** albums, which find the pair experimenting with electro rhythms, among other sounds. Written and performed with the equally prolific Bill Laswell, **Visitation** is a dark, minimal work—practically space music. [kbr]

See also *Bill Laswell, Trance Mission.*

SPAHN RANCH

See *Tubalcain.*

SPAIN

The Blue Moods of Spain (Restless) 1995

The glacially paced, attention-span-taxing music that's come to be dubbed slowcore would seem an unlikely export for sunny, spontaneous Southern California, but Spain goes a long way toward proving you can't always judge a book by . . . well, its place of publication. Led by bassist/vocalist Josh Haden (a former member of the Minutemen-damaged agit-punk combo Treacherous Jaywalkers, the son of venerable free-jazz bassist Charlie Haden and brother of that dog's Haden sisters), the quartet ambles deliberately through soundscapes that evoke the windswept romance suggested by its name. While **Blue Moods** isn't exactly jazzy in sound, its minimal, extended meditations are steeped in the jazz mindset. Haden is possessed of an eerily emotionless voice, which imbues songs like "I Lied" with the proper degree of frigidity. His mantra-like repetition of brief phrases—echoed in the vibrato-laden dual guitar leads—induce a sort of cognitive white-out that makes it easy to get lost within the music's misty reaches. [dss]

SPARE SNARE

Live at Home (UK Chute) 1995
Disco Dancing (Japan. Chute/100 Guitar Mania) 1995
Spare Snare (Prospective) 1995
Smile, It's Sugar EP (UK Deceptive) 1996

Dundee, Scotland's Jan Burnett is sometimes Spare Snare all by himself. Sometimes, he records (and plays live) with multi-instrumentalists Alan Cormack, Paul Esposito and Barry James Gibson. The band's baffling discography includes a flurry of singles, flexi-discs and variant editions, but it's all worthwhile and ultra-hooky. The home-recorded songs have a uniquely sour drone-pop mood matched by nothing else, and the full-band material is solid indie-rock of the Pavement school.

Disco Dancing compiles both sides of the first three Spare Snare singles (including two very different versions of "Thorns"), adding a noisy instrumental and a second, home-recorded take on the bitter, funny "Skateboard Punk Rocker." "As a Matter of Fact," the first single, is especially great: a twisted, out-of-tune guitar whine with Burnett tunefully spitting "I know you're lying/Because that's what I've *heard.*"

The misleadingly titled ten-track **Live at Home,** recorded as a quartet, includes new, mostly rocked-up takes on all the songs from **Disco Dancing** (two more versions of "Thorns"—well, it *is* the group's best song). There's also the new "Wired for Sound," "My Better Half" (on CD only), a splendid heartbreak song called "Bugs" and, depending on which edition you get, a slow or fast version of "Call the Birds." **Spare Snare** is the American equivalent of **Live at Home,** with some more noise and tune fragments tossed in as a bonus. [ddw]

SPASM

See *Dead Voices on Air.*

SPEARHEAD

Home (Capitol) 1994

DISPOSABLE HEROES OF HIPHOPRISY

Hypocrisy Is the Greatest Luxury (4th & B'way) 1992

BEATNIGS

The Beatnigs (Alternative Tentacles) 1988

With his six-foot-six frame, Michael Franti can see the horizon better than a lot of people. But it's the little things the San Franciscan notices that make **Home** such an engaging album. Spearhead is a better-than-fine recovery from the political drudgery of his previous group, the cool-sounding but ultimately tiresome Disposable Heroes of Hiphoprisy. (Franti and Disposable percussion cohort Rono Tse had started off together in the Beatnigs, using tape collages, declamation and industrial noise to make similar—and, in the case of "Television, the Drug of the Nation," identical—points to the rap-ready **Hypocrisy Is the Greatest Luxury.**) In Spearhead, Franti rolls the rip-and-read content into a mighty George Clinton funk spliff, chucking explicit polemics in favor of a far more inviting humanist sensibility.

Where Disposable Heroes spent its album issuing grim pronouncements on immigration, media, public health and racism over rocked-up Public Enemy–styled beats, **Home** (produced to a slow, Gil Scott-Heron bubble by Franti and Joe "The Butcha" Nicolo) takes a subtler route, shining a megadose of deliriously warm sunlight to illuminate serious issues—poverty, HIV, police, suicide—as well as such cultural signifiers as food, basketball and nightlife. An intelligent, articulate poet, Franti delivers his perceptive rhymes with a philosophical glass-is-half-full/"Love Is da Shit" attitude and a healthy appetite for life's simple pleasures. Behind his mellow sing-speak, Mary Harris and toaster Ras I Zulu add busy vocal contrasts, while an instrumental quartet lays out sweetly flowing organic hip-hop, informed by the feel, not the beat, of reggae and sparked by harmonica, organ, chicken scratch guitar and horns. "I am deadly serious about us havin' fun," Franti vows in "People in the Middle." In "Piece o' Peace," a going-out-clubbing number that namechecks former Disposable bandmate Charlie Hunter (who co-wrote and plays on "Love Is da Shit" and "Positive"), Maury Povich and African Head Charge, he says, "We livin' life at the top of our lungs." But the grimmer end of Franti's agenda receives a full airing as well. "Positive," a thoughtful and provocative first-person rumination on the possible results of an HIV test, wonders "How'm I gonna live my life if I'm positive?/Is it gonna be a negative?" The mighty indictment of "Crime to Be Broke in America" enumerates enough specific information to make it resemble a Disposable number, but "Hole in the Bucket," an internal monologue about the knotty issues of giving change to a panhandler, wittily couches the dilemma in an O. Henry story, leaving a lasting impression no litany of statistics ever could. [i]

See also *Charlie Hunter Trio; TPRG.*

SPECTRUM

See *Spacemen 3.*

SPECULA

See *Dwarves.*

SPEEDBALL

Do Unto Others, Then Split (Energy) 1995

The Motor City Speedball makes motor music—it's as simple as that. The quartet's debut is filled with auto imagery, from the gearshift map printed on the CD itself to lyrics like "Live fast/Die young/Live fast/Get on your hog and ri-yi-yid" ("Hog"). Frontman and chief songwriter Chuck Burns, who began his musical life in Detroit as a drummer, formed Speedball in Los Angeles in 1992 with fellow transplants Mike Alonso (drums) and Bill Kozy (guitar) and LA native Jeff King on bass. After the 1992 riots, the foursome returned to Detroit and further refined their sound. **Do Unto Others, Then Split** puts Speedball firmly in metal territory, though its music swings a little more than most of its brethren's. There's a little Blasters in their Motörhead, which makes Speedball a comfortable fit in a number of rock styles. The songs are short, punchy and economical—a series of sharp jabs rather than prolonged bludgeonings. "All Screwed Up" boasts a rockabilly wiggle, while "Gypsy" and "Ass, Gas or Grass" are tough, punky rockers. "Piss and Moan" dresses a hooky pop song in power chords; the speedy "Sin" is so heavy and nasty you can practically hear Burns spitting into the microphone. [gg]

SPEEDBALL BABY

See *Madder Rose.*

SPEED THE PLOUGH

Speed the Plough (Coyote/Twin\Tone) 1989 (East Side Digital) 1992
Wonder Wheel (East Side Digital) 1991
Mason's Box (East Side Digital) 1993
Marina (East Side Digital) 1995

WILD CARNATION

Tricycle (Delmore) 1994

TRYPES

The Explorers Hold EP (Coyote) 1984

The Feelies are gone, but some of the fine bands that arose from their New Jersey strumming circle are still going strong, upholding some version of the same dedication to glimmering guitar-pop beauty. Speed the Plough began as the Trypes, a little-known but continuing band at one point joined by three Feelies (Glenn Mercer, Stan Demeski and Bill Million) on hiatus. Together with John Baumgartner (keyboards), Marc Francia (guitar), Toni Paruta (woodwinds) and Brenda Sauter (bass), they made **The Explorers Hold,** a placid and introspective 1984 EP. When the Feelies left (taking Sauter with them) to reactivate their band, the remaining threesome recruited new members and became Speed the Plough.

With Paruta and songwriter Baumgartner mixing it up on not-quite-there lead vocals, the eponymous debut is rough around the handsome, rustic edges; although clearly Feelies-influenced (thanks especially to Jim DeRogatis' prim and precise drumming), **Speed the Plough** is gently colored by acoustic instrumentation rather than driving guitar—more bucolic than neurotic. The album was helpfully remixed for its 1992 reissue, with "Fathers and Sons," an outtake from the original sessions, added.

Recorded by a lineup that resembles the Trypes (Sauter and Demeski are the moonlighting rhythm section), **Wonder Wheel** takes STP to a new level. Sounding like a homey group of folks who probably subscribe to the *Utne Reader* and tie up their recycling bundles just right, the sextet illuminates tuneful pop songs like "The Tide Won't Tire" and the downbeat "Final Day" with gorgeous vocal harmonies and intricate tapestries of flute, piano, light drumming, bass, banjo and guitar. The skittering "Hemlock Tree" and medieval-styled "Story of the Moon" suggest vintage Jethro Tull transplanted to Haledon, New Jersey; more often, however, Speed the Plough retains its original grip, exploring the gap between indie-rock and modern folk to good effect. Since the creative focus is so clearly elsewhere, it's surprising how often the band still hitches its wagon to a patented Feelies speed-beat, but it actually adds to the cheery mood.

Baumgartner acquires a nasty habit of repetition on **Mason's Box;** songs that don't have much to say do so ad infinitum. It's not a big problem, though. With nine players credited on the usual assortment of instruments, the album touches on rollicking folk and, in "Morro Bay" and Sauter's showcase, "Follow Your Vision," more Feeliesque pop. The real sign of progress is rearward, in delightful explorations of idyllic '60s folk-rock. "Deepest Brown" and "Oh, the Paradise" sound like something Paul Simon might have produced for a young tie-dye band around 1966, while "The Roof Is Off (The Stars Are There and It's Mighty Cold)" makes good use of "Girl from Ipanema" elements in a fluted confection that could be by Renaissance—if not from the Renaissance.

More eclectic than any previous STP record (noise guitar, tabla-punctuated psychedelia, light jazz-pop, boulevard accordion *and* an Erik Satie flute piece!), **Marina** is the group's modest masterpiece. Crafted with splendid instrumental delicacy and personal and friendly in a close, familial way, the record exudes warmth and sensitivity in creations of nearly spiritual gentleness. When the singers join voices in "Said & Done" to exult that "I reach out for your hand and I am really not alone," it's impossible not to share their joy. The gorgeous "Bayswater Lane" sets a snow-on-the-evergreens mood potent enough to induce sensual delirium. Flawed vocals remain Speed the Plough's one weakness, but music this engaging doesn't demand exactitude so much as expressiveness, and **Marina** positively glows with credible emotions.

When she's not working in Speed the Plough, Sauter gives the Feelies' racing concision a generous dose of folky ventilation in Wild Carnation, a trio with current STP bandmates Richard Barnes (guitar) and

Christopher O'Donovan (drums). Singing her wistful, nostalgic reminiscences in a low, pleasing voice that sometimes wanders away, Sauter opens **Tricycle** by proving she can do the buzzing fever-pitch pop-rock thing in "The Rising Tide." Most of the album, however, eases up on the tension and the density (while retaining the brisk tempos), allowing acoustic guitar strums and spare drumming to set the emotional tone, mirrored in rustic songs like "Shaker Tune" and "The Music Box." Elsewhere, Barnes' distortion leads and pretty jangle figures add bite. Sauter addresses her lyrical interests—the relocation of Brooklyn's baseball team, trains, airplanes, the environment and people—in straightforward terms, investing more solemnity in the words than the music. [i]

See also *Wake Ooloo; TPRG.*

SPELL

Seasons in the Sun (Mute) 1993

Of all the covers albums issued in the '90s, **Seasons in the Sun** is surely the only one consciously intended as a statement of satanic aesthetics. A collaboration between all-around bad guy Boyd Rice and English singer Rose McDowall (ex–Strawberry Switchblade), Spell is a lot safer to hear than contemplate. That's a shocking statement, considering the high noise/chaos level of Rice's previous sonic experiments; the peaceful, easy feeling of this soft, pretty folk-rock record is truly shocking. The selection of tunes is consistently ironic and offbeat: John Leyton's ethereal Joe Meek classic, "Johnny Remember Me," a couple of Nancy Sinatra/Lee Hazlewood obscurities, the Terry Jacks hit sapfest that provides the album's title, Bobby Sherman's "Free Now to Roam" and (natch) "Rosemary's Baby (Lullaby Part 1)." Disconcerting only in context, **Seasons in the Sun** grows a sweetly sick flower. [i]

SPELL

Mississippi (Island) 1994

Formed in Denver as a side project by drummer Garrett Shavlik and a pair of friends, Spell became a full-time undertaking when he left the Fluid in '93. With a heavy-bottomed rock sound and shifting vocal arrangements of Shavlik, guitarist Tim Beckman and femme bassist Chanin Floyd (none of whom can sing all that well), Spell alternately sounds like a bad Sonic Youth cover band, a well-behaved Hole or X auditioning for grunge night. "Superstar" and "4-b" have hooky melodies and a few other tracks rise above the generic roar, but this **Mississippi** isn't worth the visit. [i]

JON SPENCER BLUES EXPLOSION

A Reverse Willie Horton (Pubic Pop Can) 1992
Crypt Style (Crypt) 1992
The Jon Spencer Blues Explosion (Caroline) 1992
Extra Width (Matador) 1993
Mo' Width (Aus. Au-go-go) 1994
Orange (Matador) 1994
Experimental Remixes EP (Matador) 1995
Now I Got Worry (Matador) 1996

PUSSY GALORE

Feel Good About Your Body EP7 (Shove) 1985
Groovy Hate Fuck (Shove) 1986
Exile on Main Street [tape] (Shove) 1986
1 Yr. Live [tape] (Shove) 1986
Pussy Gold 5000 EP (Shove/Buy Our) 1987
Right Now! (Caroline) 1987
Groovy Hate Fuck (UK Vinyl Drip) 1987
Sugarshit Sharp EP (Caroline) 1988
Dial M for Motherfucker (Caroline) 1989
Historia de la Musica Rock (Caroline) 1990
Corpse Love (Hut/Caroline) 1992

Whether you perceive him as a smirking art-schooler slumming on the po' side of the music world or a primitivist prophet with an uncanny knack for devolving rock back to its crudest state, it's hard to dispute the notion that Jon Spencer does it his way. He's never been a poet or a pauper, but Spencer *has* been a record collector extraordinaire, a certified semiotics student and (judging by photos in some of Dixie's more obscure roadside shacks) a dedicated soul food aficionado. Given the amount of smoke and mirrors he employs to realize absolute simplicity, it's almost impossible to divine what makes Spencer tick—but in light of the uniform purity of his "essence," it's easy to forget the means and simply groove on the end.

For a good portion of the '80s, Spencer and fellow Brown University alum Julia Cafritz led Pussy Galore, a DC-to-NYC band that put his advanced semiotics classes to good use, deconstructing rock to the point where it needed but a handful of words (chiefly "fuck") and *no* true chords. While Pussy Galore (which variously contained ex–Sonic Youth drummer Bob Bert, Spencer's future Boss Hog partner Cristina and Royal Trux co-founder Neil Hagerty) grew slightly more conventional toward the end of its five-year run, the band's most vigorously abstract early work is collected on the twenty-eight-track **Corpse Love** retrospective, which provokes puzzlement, indignation . . . mostly, it just *provokes.* Having exhausted that particular vein, Spencer tooled around as a sideman in the Honeymoon Killers and Gibson Bros and then formed the Blues Explosion, a trio that—while seemingly just as unschooled—pauses to genuflect, rather than piss, on the graves of its inspirations.

Even though the Blues Explosion—Spencer, second guitarist Judah Bauer and ex-Honeymoon Killers drummer Russell Simins—doesn't so much play the blues as play *with* its signifiers, the group frequently falls into impressively raw approximations of such uninhibited genre forefathers as Hound Dog Taylor on embryonic releases like **Crypt Style** and **A Reverse Willie Horton.** While the bulk of the repertoire on both albums eventually appeared elsewhere, the latter disc is frenzied enough to merit pursuit. Lo-fi versions of songs like "History of Sex" far outstrip those on the self-titled Caroline disc—with their echoey mixes and cardboard drums, they sound like they could've been appropriated from scratchy 45s found in a secluded Tennessee thrift shop. A few tracks—like a reverb-heavy "Lovin' Up a Storm" and the squalling snippet "40 Lb. Block of Cheese"—appear nowhere else.

The Jon Spencer Blues Explosion—the "official" debut—maintains a good deal of the crude appeal of its low-budget neighbors. Spencer, who sounds like a man who's just mainlined melted-down copies of Hasil Adkins' entire back catalogue, hiccups and hyperventilates through the trebly commotion he and Bauer kick up on "Chicken Walk" and "Write a Song." Those tracks in particular present a sea change in Spencer's attitude. They're basic—almost ridiculously so—but it's not hard to imagine stylistic progenitors like Adkins or Screamin' Jay Hawkins (whose "Constipation Blues" might make a nice cover for the Blues Explosion to tackle) nodding in appreciation at the authenticity of Spencer's tribute.

Spencer keeps his pedal to the mettle throughout **Extra Width,** enhancing his palette with scratchy funk guitar (an innovation Simins matches with exponentially more swinging beats on "Afro") and ear-splitting blasts of theremin—admittedly an "axe" they don't have much use for in rural Mississippi. A few stretches, however, tiptoe uncomfortably close to the precipice of minstrel-show mimicry: It's more than a little worrisome when the decidedly white-bread singer's glottal hijinks cross into Soul Brother #63 territory on "History of Lies," but Spencer doesn't appear to give any more thought to that shtick than to any of the other personae he slips into. As for the songs, Spencer hasn't lost his gift for meta-rock synthesis: "Soul Typecast" and "Soul Letter" are as circular in their content as any JB's track, and the mostly instrumental "Inside the World of the Blues Explosion" conveys more biography in its single riff than any scribe could muster in a thousand words. **Mo' Width** is an Australian appendix of outtakes from the album sessions.

Orange, which elevates Spencer's beloved theremin to cover-star status, is a bit more modern—although that's a relative term. The tone is set in the unlisted intro track, rife with lush Philly-soul strings rubbing lasciviously enough against thick guitar riffs to draw a proud-poppa purr from Isaac Hayes. The recurring "Blues Explosion!" exhortation has become a sort of hoodlum mantra for Spencer, who blurts it into the face of song after song. Although "half-finished" would be overselling tracks like the fuzz-for-fuzz's-sake "Dang," there's a singleminded seductiveness at play in such hormonal outbursts as "Sweat" and "Bell-bottoms"—the raison d'être of which is clearly evident in their titles—that vaults the Blues Explosion into the ranks of rock's truly primal forces.

As if to prove his willingness to sacrifice ego for his art, Spencer allowed *himself* to be deconstructed—by studio wizards as dissimilar as Moby, Dub Narcotic Sound System and Wu-Tang Clan's the Genius—on the six-track **Experimental Remixes** EP. While the reworkings of **Orange** numbers are not all successful—Beck's buffoonery doesn't add a heck of a lot to the version of "Flavor" he and Beastie Boy Mike D spend a good deal of time revamping—the trial-and-error tone conforms to Spencer's unwavering sense of adventure. Proof that sex—even when disguised—sells for a very good reason.

Showing a bit more of a funky bottom than usual, the JSBX keep their six feet firmly planted in the mud on **Now I Got Worry,** going so far as to reflect some genuine Delta glory off labelmate R. L. Burnside (the blues-singing Mississippi oldtimer Spencer's crew backed on 1996's **A Ass Pocket of Whisky**) in the instrumental "R. L. Got Soul." [dss]

See also *Boss Hog, Cibo Matto; TPRG.*

MALKA SPIGEL

See *Wire.*

SPIKE IN VAIN

See *Prisonshake.*

SPINANES

Manos (Sub Pop) 1993
Strand (Sub Pop) 1996

Poor workmen, the old saw goes, always blame their tools. Proving the converse—that real talent renders the selection of implements immaterial—the two Spinanes employ only guitar, voice and drums on **Manos** to produce fully developed and highly distinctive indie-rock. Best, the group manages the neat trick of sounding perfectly right while breaking with long-standing tradition. Emerging from the Beat Happening/K Records orbit, Rebecca Gates (of Portland, Oregon) and Scott Plouf (of Olympia, Washington) eschew the bassist option and never miss it on the glorious **Manos,** obviating any need for a thumping bottom with her uncommonly inventive rhythm guitar work and handsome doubletracked singing and his economically sturdy and sympathetic drumming. Sometimes rustic/folky in the 10,000 Maniacs elegiac vein but loud enough in spots to resemble punk, the finely written songs soar on Gates' rich melodies and cryptic phrases, stepping out on ledges just long enough to look down and come back inside. The gorgeous "Entire" begins the album by deconstructing the band's sound down to voice and acoustic guitar, "Noel, Jonah and Me" and "Spitfire" kick it into full electric drive and **Manos** flows from there. Shifting easily from the dreamy zone of "Epiphany" to the edgy, droney aggression of the title tune to the busy pop allure of "Grand Prize," the Spinanes do more stylistic exploration than most bands with four can manage.

After a long wait, it turns out **Manos** was just a warmup. With subtler ambitions, more expansive ideas and a far surer hand in their execution, **Strand** rewrites the book on what the duo can do. Without being intrinsically different—using dietary helpings of overdubbery, Gates still sings and plays (although what she plays here includes piano, organ and mellotron; Elliott Smith is one of two backing vocal guests), and Plouf still rivets it all together with straightforward drumming—the album exists on another plane, a dreamstate rooted in studio experimentation, not live practicality. The subliminal whoosh of "Madding" introduces the record's otherworldliness, and nothing that follows—not even the quiet explosions detonating in the background of "Punch Line Loser," cutting lines like "There's no time for the boredom you inspire" ("Oceanwide") or the whiskery guitar scratches that introduce the sensuously devoted "Lines and Lines"—contravenes the pensive moodiness. Exposed more clearly by the sheerness of the sound (and undoubtedly strengthened by several years of touring), Gates' singing and lyrics are a revelation. So is the music. Other than when Plouf digs into a busy fill-'er-up beat that calls attention to itself, **Strand** erases thoughts of its creative circumstances and rises on its own terms as a tensile thing of strong but impossibly delicate beauty. [i]

See also *Team Dresch.*

SPIN DOCTORS

Up for Grabs . . . Live (Epic) 1990
Pocket Full of Kryptonite (Epic) 1991
Homebelly Groove . . . Live (Epic) 1992
Turn It Upside Down (Epic) 1994
You've Got to Believe in Something (Epic) 1996

The dark-horse success story of 1992, the Spin Doctors are an amiable jam-happy combo who became the poster boys for a growing clan of bands—including Blues Traveler, Widespread Panic and Phish—inspired by the hippie bonhomie and extended improvisations of the Grateful Dead and the Allman Brothers. The group's good-timey sound, grounded in bar-band blues, Steve Miller pop and bouncy white funk, was out of synch with most college-radio playlists, and singer Chris Barron's stage presence—like Gumby on Maui Wowie—seemed too geeky for MTV. Nevertheless, the Spin Doctors' rubbery grooves and simple, jaunty songwriting on the multi-platinum **Pocket Full of Kryptonite** became a popular alternative for mainstream rock fans unmoved by the heavy angst and fuzz-tone brutality of Seattle grunge.

Recorded in front of a highly partisan crowd at New York's Wetlands club, **Up for Grabs . . . Live** is an EP-ish (six songs, forty-five minutes) taste of the band's early stage act, complete with Barron's daffy, no doubt bong-fueled, patter. The music gives good buzz, though. Although they don't match the improvisational heights of the Allmans or the Dead, guitarist Eric Schenkman, lefty bassist Mark White and drummer Aaron Comess apply wiry muscle to their elemental grooves, and the contagious bounce of songs like "Yo Mamas a Pajama" and "Big Fat Funky Booty" is enough to excuse the sophomoric lyrics. **Homebelly Groove . . . Live** is an updated—and less satisfying—edition of **Up for Grabs,** issued as a stop-gap between the band's first two studio albums. It drops three of the original's tracks in favor of previously unissued cuts from the same '90 Wetlands date and adds '92 radio broadcast versions of three **Kryptonite** songs.

Pocket Full of Kryptonite had been out more than eight months before it took off on the back of the single (and video) "Little Miss Can't Be Wrong." In retrospect, it's hard to see why it took so long. The bright choruses and lively cadences of that song and the two hits that followed, "Two Princes" and "Jimmy Olsen's Blues," sound tailor-made for commercial radio. In between the smashes, however, the album falls a little flat as the band mistakes clever licks for good melodic ideas ("Refrigerator Car") and the mean-spirited tone of some of Barron's lyrics (especially "Little Miss Can't Be Wrong") seeps through. But, musically, the Spin Doctors go about their business with enthusiasm (that's about all Barron's thin voice has going for it); the no-frills, frat-party feel of the production suits their modest charms.

Compared to **Kryptonite, Turn It Upside Down** is almost no fun at all. The band's notion of progress is the hammy Shakespearean pastiche "Cleopatra's Cat"; its idea of gettin' down is the corny funk and lightweight rhymes of "Biscuit Head." As if to confirm their paucity of hooks, the Spin Doctors end up reprising some of their old club material, including "Big Fat Funky Booty" to no improved effect.

The flat chart performance of **Turn It Upside Down** was quickly followed by Schenkman's mid-tour resignation. The Doctors recruited Anthony Krizan to fill the guitar spot, but the band's commercial momentum continued to fizz away. Co-produced by old James Taylor cohort Danny Kortchmar, the hopefully titled **You've Got to Believe in Something** is nothing special. "She Used to Be Mine" and "Sister Sisyphus" reprise the peppy white funk of the **Kryptonite** hits without the drop-dead hooks; the other new originals are just pleasant, pale roots-pop. ("House" is an old live staple exhumed for the effort.) The album's "secret" bonus track, a thudding cover of KC and the Sunshine Band's moldy disco oldie "That's the Way (I Like It)," with Biz Markie on vocals, should have stayed hidden—in the vault. [df]

SPIRITUALIZED

Run/I Want You EP (UK Dedicated) 1991
Lazer Guided Melodies (Dedicated/RCA) 1992
Medication EP (UK Dedicated) 1992
Fucked Up Inside (UK Dedicated) 1993
Electric Mainline EP (UK Dedicated) 1933
Pure Phase (Dedicated/Arista) 1995
Let It Flow (UK Dedicated) 1995

SLIPSTREAM

Slipstream (Ché/Carrot Top) 1995
Side Effects (Ché) 1995

When Spacemen 3 called it a day around the dawn of the decade, singer/guitarist Jason Pierce was freed to expand upon his more classicist theories of dream-state drone as pure pop with Spiritualized. Only slightly less narcotic in effect than his previous band, this free-flowing aggregation has proven slightly more likely to assent to verse-chorus-verse structure (albeit an extremely distended form thereof), while preserving the spangled sonic surroundings that add such a transportive quality to his compositions. If you can imagine LaMonte Young and Brian Wilson jamming at a corner (hash) bar, you've got a pretty clear vision of the Spiritualized totality.

Lazer Guided Melodies takes full advantage of Pierce's facility for crafting songs that build slowly—majestically, even—from simple acoustic kernels to fully orchestrated euphonies. With the core quintet augmented by full horn and string sections (put to best use on "Step Into the Breeze"), the band plays with texture to the point that songs like "Angel Sigh" and the sunny, gentle "You Know It's True" take on an almost sculptural quality. That trait is accentuated by Pierce's tireless tinkering with sound *qua* sound—vocals are flanged, notes ping-pong from speaker to speaker, keyboard tones modulate madly—as well as the vinyl-oriented assemblage of tunes into four neatly configured three-song suites, culminating with "200 Bars," a whirring number that lasts precisely as long as its title indicates, with the bars quietly enumerated by keyboardist Kate Radley. More than merely psychedelic, it's positively celestial.

Fucked Up Inside is a limited-edition seven-song live release initially available only by mail order. Among the selections is a version of Spaceman 3's "Walkin' With Jesus."

Judging by the intricately layered sound of **Pure Phase** (an utterly appropriate title), it would be reasonable to assume that Pierce spent every last moment of the three years that separate Spiritualized's two long-players parked behind a mixing board. With the band stripped down to a trio of Pierce, Radley and new bassist Sean Cook (although still augmented by as many as six brass players, the Balanescu Quartet, first-album guitarist Mark Refoy plus three singers credited with "slide vocal" and "flow vocal"), he makes more use of the fissures between notes. Although a cursory listen leaves the impression that it's merely a refinement of the first album's spacy ambience, **Pure Phase** actually represents a great leap forward—or sideways, at least—into minimalist structure. In the place of **Lazer Guided Melodies**' ebb and flow, **Pure Phase** offers one long, sustained crescendo. It may vary in volume, from the placid "The Slide Song" to the wailing void-blues of "All of My Tears," but there's an amazing consistency of tone running through the album's fourteen songs, not to mention a spiritual aspect that elevates "Lay Back in the Sun" and "Let It Flow" to a gospel-like emotional pinnacle. (The English edition was released in a spectacular glow-in-the-dark embossed slide-cover case.)

Ostensibly a "single," the lavishly packaged **Let It Flow** actually stretches over three CDs, boasting three versions of the title song as well as nine other tracks—live work and radio sessions, the bulk of which are otherwise unavailable. Of the rarities, the pulsing raga "Things Will Never Be the Same" (an S3 oldie) and the heady, harpsichord-tinged "Take Your Time" are particularly substantial.

After playing in Spiritualized, guitarist Mark Refoy (also a major contributor to Spacemen 3's **Recurring** album) formed Slipstream. The quartet's two albums (which have two tracks, including a shambling cover of Kraftwerk's "Computer World," in common) center on light, appealing guitar pop with ambient/noise fringes that occasionally (especially on **Slipstream**) move from threat to domination. Refoy's voice, wan but lovely, nicely augments the relaxed tone of songs like **Side Effects**' "Hearing Voices," "Late Too Late" and "Give It Some Time" and the harder-rocking **Slipstream**'s semi-acoustic "Harmony," "One Step Ahead" and "She Passes By" (which paraphrases another Kraftwerk classic). Although the eponymous debut is more consistently alluring than **Side Effects,** which is basically a singles compilation, both are tasty treats. [dss/i]

See also *Spacemen 3*.

SPLATTER

See *Elvis Hitler*.

SPLENDORA

In the Grass (Koch) 1995

WYGALS

Honyocks in the Whithersoever (Rough Trade) 1989

If Veruca Salt were a decade older and a bit less pleased with themselves, or if the Breeders favored the Throwing Muses side of their parentage rather than the Pixies, either might sound a bit like New York's multi-faceted Splendora. In the '80s, ex-Individuals singer/guitarist Janet Wygal and her drummer brother Doug formed the Wygals, in which ex-dB Gene Holder played lead guitar. Janet's new quintet contains a different sibling (bassist/singer Tricia), cellist Cindy Brolsma, violinist Jennifer Richardson and drummer Delissa Santos.

Holder co-produced **In the Grass:** smart and engaging harmony flower-pop with a jolting rock spine and the textural benefit of strings used in various imaginative ways. The album's thin, harsh sound is discouraging, as is the paceless sequencing; once one is acclimatized, however, songs like the folk-rocky "No Place," the surging "Beautiful," the moody and keening "Rat Fink," the Salty "Pollyanna" and the feed-back-flecked "Shirt On" are satisfying and distinctive examples of a dandy band loaded with modern pop potential. [tr]

See also *TPRG*.

SPLITSVILLE

See *Greenberry Woods*.

SPOKE

See *Giant Sand*.

SPONGE

Rotting Piñata (Chaos/Columbia) 1994
Wax Ecstatic (Columbia) 1996

LOUDHOUSE

For Crying Out Loud (Virgin) 1991

Talk about a change-up. . . . Anybody who bought into the muscular popcraft of Sponge would probably blanch at an earful of its predecessor. Loudhouse was a short-lived Detroit band that tried to patch together the city's vibrant techno scene and the hard-rock heritage established in nearby Ann Arbor by the MC5 and the Stooges. The quartet's lone moment of distinction was an industrial revision of Deep Purple's "Smoke on the Water" that only homed in on the original when guitarist Mike Cross took the occasional pass at the familiar four-note riff. A bit of play on MTV's *Headbanger's Ball* and its use in the movie *Point Break* gave the song some extra promotional push, but not enough to save Loudhouse, which broke up after Virgin decided against releasing a second album. Frontman Kenny Mugwump (Greenbaum) split, and Vinnie (né Mark Dombroski, listed as Vin E.) moved up from behind the drum kit. As Sponge, he and the Cross brothers—Mike and bassist Tim—crafted guitar-oriented rock that was part Aerosmith, part MC5 and, thanks to the inventive (no blues clichés) slide approach of guitarist Joey Mazzola, fresh enough to fall within the modern parameters. Ultimately, Sponge is a song band;Vinnie appreciates the kind of catchy hooks and hummable choruses that made radio fixtures of "Plowed" and "Molly." But these are subversive pop hits, colored by murky sonic structures that layer a bit of lead around their listener-friendly cores. Elsewhere on **Rotting Piñata,** Sponge shows an affinity for density and drone—particularly in "Pennywheels" and the metallic chug of "Neenah Menasha"—while "Giants" explores tense instrumental dynamics.

After myriad soundtrack and tribute album appearances (we'll keep "Go Speed Racer Go" from 1995's **Saturday Morning: Cartoons' Greatest Hits**), Sponge came up with a few surprises on its second album. Displaying a mild fixation (two songs) with cross-dressers, **Wax Ecstatic** is markedly stripped down from the dense fury of **Rotting Piñata,** incorporating new instrumentation (piano, saxophone, cello) and working its way through such rootsy numbers as "The Drag Queens of Memphis" and the album-closing "Velveteen." Sponge still rocks hard on "I Am Anastasia," "Got to Be a Bore" and "Wax Ecstatic," but the Bowie influence ("Silence Is the Drug," "My Baby Said," "Death of a Drag Queen") is hard to miss. [gg]

SPONGEHEAD

Potted Meat Spread (Shimmy-Disc) 1989
Legitimate Beef (Hol. Community 3/Semaphore) 1991

Curb Your Dogma (Triple X) 1993
Brainwash EP (Triple X) 1994
Infinite Baffle (Triple X) 1996

Taking a long walk off rock's short pier, Spongehead—Atlanta native Doug Henderson on guitar, bass and vocals, his brother Dave on "electrocuted tenor sax-bass" and drummer/vocalist Rev. Mark E. Kirby—blows a raucous ventilation through, and gouges some big holes in, the corridors connecting free-jazz, bludgeoning skronk and garden-variety power-trio jamming. Adding a hefty dose of distracted, vulgar and sullen commentary on the world at large, the imaginative and well-informed Spongehead takes the Z train on a winding path to some of the most savvy and humorously accessible meta-rock around.

The group formed in Brooklyn in 1985 and made its first album, with Kramer producing, for Shimmy-Disc. (Spongehead also contributed to the label's fabled **20th Anniversary of the Summer of Love** compilation.) Dave Henderson's role in the rhythm section—his tenor horn runs through an octave splitter and a bass amp—is an eccentricity that connects Spongehead faintly to the surly noir drive of Morphine, but it's also an easily accepted component of an entirely more thunderous clamor.

Amid honks, roaring slabs of guitar and what sounds like hogs being slaughtered, **Legitimate Beef** contains a James Blood Ulmer cover but otherwise underscores the Hendersons' past experiences in the company of Eugene (Shockabilly) Chadbourne: the album wallows in topical name calling, dada rudeness and scatological skullduggery. Don't look for clues in the song titles, though. "Zombie Movie" is about the desolation of quotidian life, while "Fuck You (I Love You)" considers personal relations about as much as "Capitalism"—the entire lyric of which is "Capitalism is on my dick (get it off)"—explores political economy. "Plumber's Lament" is about the "river of shit" the narrator must endure. Capping the whole loopy extravagance off in dumb-ass style, "Spongehead Theme" is a latter-day answer to the Dictators' "Master Race Rock."

Curb Your Dogma, produced by Dave Sardy of Barkmarket (whose "Mirror" is among the album's songs), outgrows some of the juvenilia (not all of it: the fiercely incisive tabloid-scan "Nothing" wonders "What bitch is Donald Trump hanging his dick inside of today?"). More important, it organizes the band's sonic attack into a tightly packed wall of roiling, buzzing, bottom-feeding aggression. Doug Henderson's Tom Waitsy vocals are far stronger, too; when he growls, "This ain't the heaven I heard of in the Psalms" (in "Metal Jesus Fucker") he really means it, God. A forcefield of thoroughly brutal jollity, **Curb Your Dogma** gives prime 'head.

The trio's use of the studio is even more confident and ambitious on **Brainwash.** There's a monumentally funky/manic rendition of Sly Stone's "Don't Call Me Nigger, Whitey," a venture deep into disorienting distortion ("VR") and chunks of thunderous "Jelly." In addition to the five new songs, the EP contains two remakes of "Plumber's Lament," one (annoyingly placed at CD track ninety-nine) that halfheartedly prunes the bad words.

Infinite Baffle is really the shit. Having checked for weak spots on previous records (and giving "Brainwash" a "Migraine Mix"), Spongehead is an indestructible rock behemoth here, focusing all of its attributes into steel-girdered songs that lumber with an agility the sheer sonic pressure should preclude. The album is consistent where prior records were haphazard, hard-hitting where the others threw wild punches—even swinging after a fashion (see "1919"). **Infinite Baffle** is the most accessible and entertaining ton of bricks to land in a long time. [i]

SPONGETONES

Beat Music (Ripete) 1982
Torn Apart EP (Ripete) 1984
Where-Ever-Land (Triapore) 1987
Oh Yeah! (Black Vinyl) 1991
Beat & Torn (Black Vinyl) 1994
Textural Drone Thing (Black Vinyl) 1995

JAMIE HOOVER

Coupons, Questions and Comments (Triapore) 1990

Originally proud altar boys at the Church of the Holy Mersey, North Carolina's SpongeTones—Jamie Hoover, Patrick Walters, Rob Thorne and McCartney lookalike Steve Stoeckel—have evolved from the zesty Beatlish originals of their first two releases to producing lush, superbly crafted pop-rock that owes a debt to other British Invasion acts (Searchers, Zombies) without coming off as slavishly imitative.

Beat Music is a gas from start to finish, a collection of lovingly performed early-Beatles pastiches. Don't miss the high-octane "She Goes Out With Everybody" or the simply wonderful "A Part of Me Now," two of the greatest songs the Fab Four (and the Rutles) never wrote. The six-song **Torn Apart** is more of the same; the explosive title track is one of the SpongeTones' finest efforts. **Beat Music** and **Torn Apart** were consolidated on CD as **Beat & Torn,** with a previously hard-to-find bonus track.

Where-Ever-Land (with three tracks produced by Don Dixon) is where the SpongeTones start to expand their sound a touch, adding dabs of garagey rock ("Up in Smoke"), soulful, horn-fueled pop ("Self Sufficient Guy"), full-tilt screamers ("Forget About May") and slightly psychedelic balladeering ("Images"). The best thing here by far is the Hoover/Greg James collaboration, "Anna"—four minutes of delicious harmonies, subtle guitars and beautifully imaginative lyrics tucked inside a to-die-for melody. Two Merseybeat-flavored tracks are buried near the end of the album, almost as an afterthought.

Moving to Shoes' Black Vinyl Records, **Oh Yeah!** takes the SpongeTones ferrying back down the Mersey with often sparkling results. Stoeckel's "Stupid Heart" hearkens back to **Beatles '65,** while Hoover's "Return the Boy" is a heartfelt beat ballad. The disc's only real negative aspect is the disappointingly thin-sounding production.

Textural Drone Thing finds the SpongeTones branching out again, with splashes of breathy Zombies-like melodicism, Claptonesque guitar and instrumental variety (mandolin, saxes, dulcimer). Three songs co-written by Hoover and Bill Lloyd are as rootsy and poppy (pootsy? roppy?) as you'd expect, and there are still flashes of the SpongeTones of old, especially on Pat Walters' Lennony ravers, "Try to Please" and "Rattle My Chain." Have Mersey!

Recorded with minimal assistance (he does pretty much everything but drum here), Hoover's pleasant solo effort finds him departing slightly from the SpongeTones' sound. The main difference is the lead vocals, which are often more soulful ("Soldier") or gut-ripping ("The Box," "In the Black"); the overall presentation of **Coupons, Questions and Comments** is more in-your-face as well. His knack for winning melodies remains intact, especially on the 'Tones-like "In Shame," the sweetly simple "Jack in the Box," the kinetic "Forgive and Forget" and the downright nasty "Watching You Stumble." Two instrumentals (one cutely titled "Ignoramos and Andy") mainly showcase his beefy guitar work. Odd coincidence(?): the opening riff to Robyn Hitchcock's "So You Think You're in Love" is identical to Hoover's "Questions," which preceded it by a year. In late '95, Hoover resurrected his long-dormant solo career with the release of the "Nobody Wins This Time" single on the Swedish Sound Asleep label. [jmb]

SPOONFED HYBRID

See *Pale Saints.*

SPRINGHOUSE

Land Falls (Caroline) 1991
Eskimo EP (Caroline) 1991
Postcards From the Arctic (Caroline) 1993

The sonic resemblance of Springhouse to some of the dream-textured art-pop groups about whom drummer/journalist Jack Rabid has written extensively in his fanzine *The Big Takeover* is no coincidence, but then neither is it a criticism. Knowing that cognoscenti can discern echoes of England (Chameleons and Comsat Angels), New Zealand (Chills) and Australia (Church) in the New York trio's records is hardly enough to support charges of untoward derivation. Springhouse's most distinctive feature was its own singular invention: singer/songwriter Mitch Friedland's nylon-string guitar, played through harmonizing effects to produce a wash cycle safe for the finest gauze, driven with firm rock fortitude by Rabid's English-accented drumming and Larry Heinemann's busy bass.

Land Falls is a sweeping, exhilarating debut, containing three gorgeous songs—"Eyesore," "Layers" and "Open Your Eyes"—that are easily the equal of anything by the band's putative archetypes. Amid the imaginative chord progressions and stylishly grand arrangements, however, Friedland's voice goes awry at the top end of his range; Rabid's two turns at the mic ("Eskimo," "Alone") make an even trade of safety for allure. The trio occasionally drags its creative tail, allowing the sensual rapture of billowing atmospheres to obscure lesser material, but the album pairs solid tunes with seductive sounds often enough to make it both pleasurable and memorable. (The **Eskimo** EP surrounds that sympathetic song about winter homelessness with "Layers," two non-LP originals and a Rabid-sung cover of the Saints' "Angels.")

Produced by Joe Chiccarelli, **Postcards From the Arctic** redresses most of the debut's shortcomings with improved singing, more consistent songwriting and carefully considered instrumental designs that thoughtfully serve the material rather than overwhelm it. The trio still gets plenty of mileage from its pretty propwash, but the addition of new elements—guest violin and keyboards—and a radically expanded dynamic sense move it all up a creative notch. After several easygoing verses of "Worthless," the romance-on-the-rocks song blows open with Friedland's anguished declaration, "I feel so worthless now," before settling back on a handsome cello bed. The striking "Asphalt Angels," which uses the mournful sound of an English horn to excellent effect, funnels the Springhouse style into a gully between the Moody Blues and My Bloody Valentine, while the gentle "Time to Go" is positively Beatlesque. The discovery of an original sound in such sophisticated byways makes **Postcards From the Arctic** a sterling accomplishment; that the group couldn't image-monger effectively or affect appropriate accents (or maybe that its records didn't appear in another era entirely) proved to be insurmountable impediments to its commercial success, and Springhouse disbanded. [i]

SQUEEZE

(U.K.) Squeeze (A&M) 1978
Cool for Cats (A&M) 1979
Argybargy (A&M) 1980
East Side Story (A&M) 1981
Sweets From a Stranger (A&M) 1982
Singles—45's and Under (A&M) 1982
Cosi Fan Tutti Frutti (A&M) 1985
Babylon and On (A&M) 1987
Frank (A&M) 1989
A Round and a Bout (IRS) 1990
Play (Reprise) 1991
Greatest Hits (UK A&M) 1992
Some Fantastic Place (A&M) 1993
Ridiculous (UK A&M) 1995 (IRS) 1996
Piccadilly Collection (A&M) 1996

DIFFORD & TILBROOK

Difford & Tilbrook (A&M) 1984

Old-fashioned pop craftsmen saved from a workingman's death in English pubs by the new wave, singer/guitarists Chris Difford and Glenn Tilbrook—the core of Squeeze—found their forte/niche in setting small dramas of British life to music that can be ebullient, reflective, gay or morose. Aided along the way by tasteful rhythm sections and keyboard players both flamboyant (Jools Holland) and soulful (Paul Carrack), the duo has weathered stylistic digressions, endless lineup adjustments and the onset of maturity to become the resident bridgemen on the span between British dancehall tradition and modern tuneful ironists. It's a wobbly bridge, though, and the band's records are aggressively uneven: few groups have thrown the dice with as unpredictable results as Squeeze. If closer in tone to Paul McCartney than Ray Davies, Squeeze—even at its worst—has always produced catchy songs inhabited by real people.

The early records put the London quintet on a solidly upward trajectory. John Cale produced the eponymous debut (which billed the group as U.K. Squeeze in the US), an inconsistent album that tries too hard to be wacky; cut without him, "Take Me I'm Yours" is the easy highlight. Overall, **Cool for Cats** is substantially better. Primary vocalist Tilbrook, a sweet triller, and the gruffer Difford show greater confidence at the mic; together, they create arresting, odd harmonies to go with their bent pop tunes. Wonderful cuts abound, including "Slap & Tickle" (a sleazy synth rocker), the romping title track and the cinematic "Up the Junction," three minutes of working-class heartbreak. Squeeze truly grew up on **Argybargy,** an album of finely etched pop music: "If I Didn't Love You," "Farfisa Beat," "Pulling Mussels (From the Shell)," "Another Nail in My Heart."

With Holland's subsequent departure, Paul Carrack (ex-Ace) entered the picture. Produced by Elvis Costello and Roger Bechirian (apart from one cut by Dave Edmunds), **East Side Story**'s fourteen-song jumble is an incoherent tour de force that touches on everything from soul to country to psychedelia. Highlights include Carrack's vocal showcase "Tempted," "In Quintessence" and the winsome "Is That Love." After Don Snow replaced Carrack (who went on to do very nicely for himself in Mike and the Mechanics), Squeeze pulled its stylistic horns in partway for **Sweets From a Stranger.** "When the Hangover Strikes" conducts a leisurely trip into Cole Porter land; "I've Returned" soars on the strength of ringing guitars and an exuberant Tilbrook vocal.

As Squeeze concentrated on making albums rather than singles after **Cool for Cats, Singles—45's and Under,** a compilation released soon after the announcement of the band's dissolution, was an oddly chosen eulogy with no sense of occasion. Even "Annie Get Your Gun," the sole new track, isn't so great. Still, the LP is a handy introduction to the band's early triumphs.

After the split, Difford and Tilbrook stayed together, releasing one overproduced album that differs little from the band's worst work, except that it's funkier and more boring. Trying to get over like Hall and Oates, the English duo lacks the cynical instincts to make such a slick veneer stick.

Two years of unsatisfying divorce later, Tilbrook and Difford reconvened Squeeze with Holland, drummer Gilson Lavis and new bassist Keith Wilkinson. But things didn't fall back into place. **Cosi Fan Tutti Frutti** is afflicted by the same bland ineffectuality as **Difford & Tilbrook.** The depressed "Last Time Forever," while sonically impressive, is a regrettably somber turn for Squeeze, no longer able to manage a wry smile in the face of life's inexorable calamities.

Refitted with a second keyboardist, Andy Metcalfe (simultaneously serving as Robyn Hitchcock's bassist), a twelve-legged Squeeze righted itself on **Babylon and On,** a confident and likable return to sound and form. "Tough Love," "Footprints" and especially "The Prisoner" affirm Squeeze's aptitude for agreeable pop. Dubious stabs at soul and funk fall flat, however, and Tilbrook's sitar playing on the insipid "Some Americans" is simply absurd.

Although dismayingly overlooked, **Frank** completes Squeeze's rehabilitation, bringing the group full circle to a modernized version of jaunty pub rock. Relocating its original magic with memorably inventive material and spirited delivery, Squeeze seems exuberantly youthful, as if music-making had suddenly become fun again. From giddy celebrations of new romance ("If It's Love," "Peyton Place") to sardonic views of emotional wreckage ("Slaughtered, Gutted and Heartbroken," "Rose I Said"), the songs surge with wit and melodic energy. (And who else would write a truly sensitive song about menstruation and melancholy?) Co-produced by Tilbrook and Eric Thorngren, **Frank** has a relaxed, live-in-the-studio sound that makes it intimate and inviting. It's easily Squeeze's best since **Argybargy.**

The same enthusiasm flows in **A Round and a Bout,** recorded live at a pair of English dates in January '90. Matt Irving (keyboards, accordion) joins the Hollandaised lineup for a delightful career summary, complete with four numbers from **Frank.** The brisk, no-nonsense performances work wonders, recharging the entire program. Proof that miracles do happen: an upbeat overhaul turns **Sweets From a Stranger**'s plodding "Black Coffee in Bed" into a marvelous jolt of pop soul. Even the audience-participation "If It's Love" sounds like fun.

A dozen years after fitting a complete and satisfying soap opera into the three sprightly minutes of "Up the Junction," **Play** finds Squeeze's songwriters no longer capable of such acuity or efficiency. The simple good-love-gone-bad concept album (the booklet is a script that incorporates song lyrics) attempts a breakup in the similarly intimate "Letting Go," but can't come to the point. The song's wishy-washy tone, uncharacteristically clunky lyrics and general spinelessness typify this listless album. (Does the guest involvement of Bruce Hornsby suggest anything? To be fair, Steve Nieve is involved as well.) Things pick up near the end—"Gone to the Dogs" has some of the band's old charm, the massed chorus of "Sunday Street" essays British gospel with stirring results and "Wicked and Cruel" is venomous enough to be entertaining—but getting there is no fun at all.

Made with a new lineup (Carrack and Attractions drummer Pete Thomas joining Tilbrook, Difford and Wilkinson), the lively and unpretentious **Some Fantastic Place** partly undoes the damage of **Play**; it's a simple, warm album hindered only by poor quality control on the writing. Too many of the songs revisit overly familiar terrain of failed and failing relationships, leaving tired melodies to be spiffed up by sharply noted details: the initialed 45s left behind in "Images of Loving," an attempted rapprochement in "It's Over," a cat flap in the kitchen door that provides a dog's-eye view in "Cold Shoulder." Still, the Vandellas-like "Everything in the World" is a spunky opener, and the mellow soul of Carrack's "Loving You Tonight" does the record a heap of good. In the minor-key title track, a downcast showstopper that somehow doesn't dominate the album's mood, Tilbrook pays loving tribute to a recently deceased young woman, keeping a stiff upper lip while making no effort to hide a broken heart; even his guitar solo burns with unbridled passion.

With Squeeze reduced for the first time to a quartet (Difford, Tilbrook, bassist Keith Wilkinson and new drummer Kevin Wilkinson), the affecting **Ridiculous** displays a minimum of fuss (other than the strings contributing cinematic sweep to childhood in "Electric Trains" and desire in "I Want You"). After all this time, the band's reports from the home front have a familial intimacy; since so many of the songs instill at least the assumption of personal reality, it's hard not to think of the two writers as central characters in a long-running serial. And, though obscured by the shared credits and the sweet-voiced Tilbrook's preeminence as the band's lead singer, it does sound as if one partner is faring a lot better than the other. (The notion of two strong, autonomous auteurs going through individual adulthoods in tandem, delivering the public results to record year after year, does have a hairy *28 Up* aspect to it.) On one side of the couch are golden-colored reminiscences

("Electric Trains," "Walk Away"), rocky but resilient relationships ("Heaven Knows," "Daphne"), love rushes ("This Summer") and positive self-knowledge ("Grouch of the Day," "Long Face"). Then there's the abject guilt of "Temptation for Love," the blocked vacancy of "Lost for Words," the shame and desperation of "Great Escape" and the reluctant, dysfunctional romanticism of "Fingertips": "It's funny how I loved you like the bottle at my lips . . . You typify the things to me that I no longer do . . . You're always there right in my face but that is nothing new/I'm so in love with you." It doesn't take a psychiatric social worker to discern a pattern in there. When he's in the spotlight, Difford recites his bits as if some posh old uncle of Neil Tennant's had been heavily sedated and hauled unawares into the studio—an approach that doesn't make him out to be the happy camper here. **Ridiculous?** Not hardly.

Piccadilly Collection is as confusing as the cover-pictured London Circus: the sixteen-track retrospective works backwards from **Some Fantastic Place** to **Argybargy,** with twice as many tunes from **Difford & Tilbrook** as **East Side Story.** If not a balanced aesthetic recapitulation of any sort, the album repeats only four songs from the 1982 singles compilation, and the appearance of five non-LP items (including the B-side medley "Squabs on Forty Fab") makes it a must-have for completists. [jy/i]

See also *TPRG.*

SQUIRREL NUT ZIPPERS

The Inevitable (Mammoth) 1995
Hot (Mammoth) 1996

METAL FLAKE MOTHER

Beyond the Java Sea (Moist) 1991

Oh, why the hell not? The increasingly eclectic and eccentric Southeast—Chapel Hill, North Carolina, to pin specific geographical responsibility where it belongs—grew the Squirrel Nut Zippers, musical wackos who turn the clock back to half-past-swingtime on **The Inevitable,** a rollicking and skillful not-so-big-band platter of almost entirely original hi-de-ho, zip-a-dee-doo-dah and vo-de-oh-do. The tuxedoed septet's entertaining folly rolls down memory lane with Blossom-Dearie-meets-Billie-Holiday crooning (by banjo-strummer Katharine Whalen) and the less stylized vocal vamping of guitarists Jim Mathus and Tom Maxwell and saxophonist Ken Mosher. Vic Godard, Brian Setzer and other modern nostalgists have tiptoed through these tulips before, but none with the straight-faced charm lofted by this merry bunch of coconuts. A defiant ode to influenza ("La Grippe") is worth the price of admission. "If it's good enough for granddad, good enough for me."

Pushing a good regressive gimmick toward dedicated stylistic fetishism, the Zippers recorded **Hot** live, down to the vocals, in a New Orleans studio. They haven't covered "Winchester Cathedral," but they're getting there.

Before the Squirrel adventure, Mathus plied his trade in Metal Flake Mother, a Carrboro quartet whose **Beyond the Java Sea** sounds, on the surface, like a dull echo of Superchunk. Generic indie-pop, however, is merely the launching pad for an industriously multifarious effort. Gamely going along with the band's stylistic impulses, producer Lou Giordano documents Metal Flake Mother's skilled and confident forays into grandiose pop ("Dance for Nails"), not-so-grandiose pop ("Matador"), piano balladry ("Open a Vase"), twang-guitar instrumentals ("Moss Howl," "Squash Beetle"), continental drama (the House-of-Freaks-meets-Nick-Cave "Sutpen" and "Safer") and tuneful garage-rock ("Mr. Flavor"). [i]

SQUIRRELS

See *Young Fresh Fellows.*

CHRIS STAMEY

It's a Wonderful Life (DB) 1983
Instant Excitement EP (Coyote) 1984
It's Alright (Coyote/A&M) 1987
Fireworks (RNA) 1991
Wonderful Life (East Side Digital) 1992

CHRIS STAMEY AND FRIENDS

Christmas Time (Coyote) 1986 (East Side Digital) 1993

PETER HOLSAPPLE & CHRIS STAMEY

Mavericks (RNA) 1991

ALASKA

Alaska EP (Hello Recording Club) 1995

CHRIS STAMEY & KIRK ROSS

The Robust Beauty of Improper Linear Models in Decision Making (East Side Digital) 1995

SNEAKERS

Sneakers EP (Carnivorous) 1976
In the Red (Car) 1978
Racket (East Side Digital) 1992

DB'S

Stands for Decibels (UK Albion) 1981 (IRS) 1989
Repercussion (UK Albion) 1982 (IRS) 1989
Like This (Bearsville) 1984 (Rhino) 1988
The Sound of Music (IRS) 1987
The dB's Ride the Wild TomTom (Rhino) 1993

North Carolina singer/guitarist (and sometime trumpeter) Chris Stamey spent the late '70s and early '80s helping put the Southeast on the map as a preeminent nouveau pop zone. In a creative progression of more complex ambitions and deeper emotional expressions than most of his musical neighbors, this casually effective singer and superlative melodicist graduated from collegiate Chapel Hill power-pop legend Sneakers (a band that involved Mitch Easter) to a New York/Hoboken-based career backing Alex Chilton and forming the influential dB's. Stamey began making solo records while still in the dB's; **It's a Wonderful Life** is a moody and adventurous experiment that stretches far beyond the band's Big Star–influenced directness. Abandoning the dB's on the eve of the group's first American album in 1984, Stamey instead made the brief **Instant Excitement,** an odd, upbeat hodgepodge that includes a homely reading of John Lennon's "Instant Karma," an idyllic love song ("When We're Alone"), a frisky country-rocker and an instrumental opus. The '92 **Wonderful Life** combines both records and adds a couple of alternate versions as well as Stamey's illuminating liner-note commentary.

The musicians credited on **Instant Excitement** compose the Chris Stamey Group on the delightful **Christmas Time** mini-album; the dB's back him on the Brian Wilson–like title track. The original songs are all seasonal: "The Only Law That Santa Claus Understood," "You're What I Want (for Christmas)," "Snow Is Falling," even a new acoustic version of the unexpectedly appropriate "It's a Wonderful Life." The reissue has a different cover photo from the same session (see Chris crinkled in laughter!/see Chris betray the faintest Mona Lisa smile!) and eleven added tracks (but one deletion). Among those bringing extra presents, Alex Chilton sings Mel Tormé's "The Christmas Song" and, as Big Star with drummer Jody Stephens, his own "Jesus Christ." The dB's do Jose Feliciano's "Feliz Navidad," while that band's Peter Holsapple renders "O Holy Night." Syd Straw gets off a good pun covering Blondie's "(I'm Always Touched by Your) Presents, Dear." A warm, spirited winner—the more the merrier.

Stamey subsequently recorded (**Visions of Excess**) and toured with the Golden Palominos before settling down to make the direct and lucid **It's Alright** with a snazzy collection of friends: Chilton, Richard Lloyd, Anton Fier, Mitch Easter, Faye Hunter, Bernie Worrell and Marshall Crenshaw are among the players. The songs vary from boppy ("Cara Lee") to somber ("The Seduction") to loud ("Incredible Happiness") to idyllic ("27 Years in a Single Day"), but Stamey's dry, plaintive voice invests it all with peerless sincerity and sterling appeal.

Stamey played second guitar behind Bob Mould on the latter's first-LP tour in 1989; the next year, he teamed up with ex-bandmate Holsapple and recorded the magnificent acoustic-flavored and country-accented **Mavericks.** This major career highlight for two singer/songwriters at the peak of their powers is a heartfelt and deeply moving collection that neatly delineates their differences *and* the points of their stylistic coincidence. With filigreed instrumental assistance from guitarist Dave Schramm, cellist Jane Scarpantoni, drummer Michael Blair and others, the pair sets its sights on dissections of romantic troubles—Stamey: "I Want to Break Your Heart," "Haven't Got the Right (to Treat Me Wrong)" and "Lovers Rock," although his partner rues "She Was the One"—and satisfactions (Holsapple: "The Child in You," "Taken," "I Know You Will" and the stunning collaboration, "Angels"). Beyond the masterful performances, the record is loaded with enough heartbreaking harmonies and painterly production details to make every moment worth savoring.

Released the same year as **Mavericks, Fireworks** is a more idiosyncratic collection of electric pop songs recorded over the course of three years with various associates, including Peter Buck, Graham Maby, Schramm, Easter, Fier and Holsapple. Traveling on familiar ground, both musically and thematically, the record benefits from Stamey's advanced skill and creativity; the clear shift in perspective between a typically incisive, detailed and downcast narration of bellyflop romance like "The Newlyweds" and the intimately personal chronicles of "The Company of Light" and "Something Came Over Me" (a song that also appears in different forms on **Wonderful Life, Instant Excitement** and the original **Christmas Time**) describes the breadth of Stamey's talent. The album also draws fascinating lines from the past to the present. Although a cover of William Bell's "You Don't Miss Your Water" suffers from incongruously mechanical sound, Stamey does better by train songs in "The Brakeman's Consolation" and cleverly twists an old Kinks riff into an original homage to music's power in "On the Radio (For Ray Davies)." Even the guitar jam coda of "All the Heart's Desire/Black Orchids" shifts time frames to good effect. The circumstances of **Fireworks**' creation prevent the record from amassing momentum as it moves along, but many of the tracks are excellent.

Sprinkled throughout Stamey's records are instrumental creations ("Still Life") that are as much sonic experiments as formally constructed compositions. The 1995 collaboration with Kirk Ross (prepared guitars) fills an album with formidably fleshy, stylish and often dramatic improvisations. Yo La Tengo guitarist Ira Kaplan and percussionist Ed Butler help out, but the principals make most of the impressive noises, pastorals and handsome sound portraits themselves. Variously styling up a punk King Crimson, a less aggressive Einstürzende Neubauten and a drummerless jazz fusion group, **Robust Beauty** has pretentious titles ("Bukowski Attends His Funeral March (Suite)," "The Arsonist and the Fire Engine," "Staircase Descending a Nude" and, worst of all, "Meditation on a Theme"), but the music is far less precious and arty than they imply. Certainly a very different side of the pop auteur, but not a bad effort in this new realm.

On the other side of his personal coin, Stamey leads a North Carolina band called Alaska, a relatively traditional (for him) rock trio with bassist John Chumbris and drummer John Howie. The group's first release, a nifty six-track EP with production/playing help from Mitch Easter, was issued in mid-'95 by the subscription-only Hello Recording Club. Investing songs with varying degrees of electric power, mild to biting, Stamey writes from a pointed and ironic perspective: the irresistibly harmonized "Stupid Pop-Rock Song" casts a condescending eye at his onetime stock in trade, while "Rock Manager" puffs up a big phony to prove how evil the species is. (The bracingly loud "My Advice to You," meanwhile, makes sarcasm its own reward.) As these numbers measure the growing distance between Stamey and his past musical lives, "Yeahyeahyeah," an oblique tribute to Miles Davis (especially in light of the Kirk Ross collaboration), points up new developments in his creative taste.

An early-'90s resurgence of label interest in Stamey's back catalogue brought Sneakers' oeuvre to CD for the first time. Recasting the group's history somewhat to paint it as a revived partnership of Stamey and Easter (thereby relegating Will Rigby, Rob Slater and Robert Keely to alumni status), the rich **Racket** contains beneficial remixes, previously unissued tracks and three of the band's '70s songs rerecorded just for the occasion with ex-dB's bassist Gene Holder. An amazing example of ingenuity overcoming technical limitations, **Racket** is weird, wonderful and winsome. To celebrate, the duo played a '92 Sneakers reunion concert in a Winston-Salem record store.

Ride the Wild TomTom gives equally offbeat treatment to the dB's. Rather than a compilation of the band's four albums, the twenty-six tracks—with the exception of four songs from singles—are demos and outtakes, half of them cut in 1979 at the *New York Rocker* magazine office. ("I Read New York Rocker," however, was recorded in North Carolina. Go figure.) Holsapple's liner notes call these "home and field recordings," and they surely do have the raw, new wave enthusiasm of a young band having a blast putting its abundant ideas on tape with minimal input or interference from the real world. With that in mind, the raveup cover of the Grass Roots' "Let's Live for Today" has all sorts of resonance here. [i]

See also *Continental Drifters, Golden Palominos; TPRG.*

STANFORD PRISON EXPERIMENT

Stanford Prison Experiment (Chrome Gods/World Domination) 1994
The Gato Hunch (Chrome Gods/World Domination) 1995

A lot of bands come up with names they live to regret (Hootie and the Blowfish, Moonpools and Caterpillars, Beatles), but you'd have to search around to top the stylistic misapprehension conveyed by the handle (the title of a classic sociology investigation) attached to this at-large Los Angeles rock group. Carefully covering the Minutemen's "It's Expected I'm Gone" but otherwise playing tunefully thrusting Rage Against the Tool Jam riffrock on its debut album, the quartet racks up a big, buzzing guitar noise with intelligent excoriating anti-authority and anti-personal lyrics sung by Mario Jimenez. Co-produced by World Dom label owner (and former Gang of 4, Shriekback and Low Pop Suicide bassist) Dave Allen, songs like "Written Apology," "Sheepshit" and "Super Monkey" thunder along tightly, avoiding bluster while managing ferocious pressure. The only thing missing is any individual style.

With ace producer Ted Nicely's help, Stanford Prison Experiment hit upon a more focused plan for its second album, and set about becoming a West Coast Fugazi on **The Gato Hunch.** Guitarist Mike Starkey's clangorous feedback-edged razor burns and the Davey Latter/Mark Fraser rhythm section's steady foot-shifting power clearly set the sonic agenda, while Jimenez—tilting his voice at a familiar semi-melodic D of C angle—sings out impressionistically expressed anger at everything from God to conformists to "Hardcore Idiot." For all the derivation, **The Gato Hunch** is a much more focused and compelling album than the debut and leaves the impression that this Experiment might ultimately discover something worth knowing. [i]

STARBILLY

See *Big Wheel.*

STARLINGS

Valid (UK Anxious) 1992 (Anxious/Atlantic) 1993
Too Many Dogs (Anxious/Atlantic) 1994

Needless proof that nationality is no guarantee of talent, New Zealand expatriate Chris Sheehan is Starlings, a bland compromise between the slick Dylanesque confessionalism of Elliot Murphy and the intimate casualness of Beck. Loping along semi-tunefully with a self-conscious late-night feel and dull lyrics about scoring and addiction, **Valid** is occasionally interrupted by noise incursions ("Now Take That") or brisk guest drumming ("That's It You're in Trouble"), but the ex-junkie's pretentiously dramatic whisper never achieves artistic liftoff.

Although **Too Many Dogs** evinces more energy, rhythmic variety ("Loch AAngeles Monster" and "Other Peoples Children" strike a clubby dance groove), style and studio ambition (he's no Prince, but the record does sound like a spare rock band effort), Sheehan's tired solipsism fails to connect on any level. "Mr Wishy Washy" attempts to register an ironic social comment—but can't rouse itself to say anything worth recalling. Now *that's* wishy-washy. [i]

STATE OF PLAY

See *Curve.*

ALISON STATTON & SPIKE

Weekend in Wales EP (UK Vinyl Japan) 1993
Tidal Blues (UK Vinyl Japan) 1994
Maple Snow (UK Vinyl Japan) 1995

DEVINE & STATTON

The Prince of Wales (Bel. Les Disques du Crépuscule) 1989 (Rockville) 1990
Cardiffians (Bel. Les Disques du Crépuscule) 1990

Cardiff-born singer Alison Statton's first group, Young Marble Giants, lit and carried a bright torch for the lo-fi indie scene that would flourish in the '90s. Her subsequent group, the coolly jazz-inflected Weekend, anticipated the suave cocktail pop that Everything but the Girl, Sade and others would popularize. After the end of Weekend, Statton went back to university, but re-emerged near the end of the '80s in a duo with Manchester guitarist/songwriter Ian Devine (ex-Ludus). The pair made two albums of spare, Celtic-flecked folk-pop, covering tunes by New Order ("Bizarre Love Triangle" on **The Prince of Wales**) and Crystal Gayle ("Don't It Make My Brown Eyes Blue" on **Cardiffians**) in the process.

Moving on, Statton reunited with Weekend guitarist Spike and recorded the five-song **Weekend in Wales** in a matter of hours. While the smooth sound of "A Greater Notion" would not be out of place on lite-FM, the song has an inherent charm that sets it apart from the pabulum of that genre. Violinist Paul Sax adds a chamber-like character to the proceedings; erstwhile Young Marble Giant Philip Moxham plays percussion.

Extensive use of string bass, violin, viola and trumpet fill out the sound of the more ambitious **Tidal Blues,** which contains a new version of "A Greater Notion." The album's warm, organic nature is epitomized by the gentle sway of "Take Heart" and Statton's lush doubletracked vocals on "Lemming Time." Nico's **Chelsea Girl** makes an apt point of reference for the elegance of songs like "Hidden Combat." The only misstep comes when the duo quickens the pace on a fiddle-driven hoedown ("In This World") and loses the plain beauty of Statton's voice in the confusion.

Recorded live in Japan, **Maple Snow** recaps Statton's career with songs from both Weekend and Young Marble Giants. In place of **Tidal Blues**' string-ensemble arrangements, Statton, Spike, Philip and Stuart Moxham are joined by keyboardist Sarah McGuinness. Statton's enormous growth—both stylistically and vocally—is unmistakable in the comparison of Young Marble Giants' stark original of "Salad Days" and the splendid, full performance the song receives here. Spike's guitar fluency reaches its pinnacle on the reworking of Weekend's "Midnight Slows." [mk]

See also *Stuart Moxham; TPRG.*

STEEL POLE BATH TUB

Butterfly Love (Boner) 1989
Lurch EP (Boner) 1990

Tulip (Boner) 1991
The Miracle of Sound in Motion (Boner/Tupelo) 1993
Live in Germany (Ger. Your Choice) 1993
Some Cocktail Suggestions . . . From Steel Pole Bath Tub! EP (Boner/Tupelo) 1994
Home Is a Rope EP7 (Genius) 1995
Scars From Falling Down (Slash/London) 1995

DUH

Blowhard (Boner) 1991

TUMOR CIRCUS

Tumor Circus (Alternative Tentacles) 1991

MILK CULT

Love God (Boner/Tupelo) 1992
Burn or Bury (Basura!/Priority) 1994
Bruce Lee Marvin Gaye (ZK) 1995

C.C. NOVA

Milk Cult C.C. Nova Dispatch (Communion) 1994

Steel Pole Bath Tub, a Bay Area threesome (two of whom originally hail from Bozeman, Montana), puts a happy face (well, sorta) on industrial-strength grind rock, leavening its pitbull riffs with jaggedly humorous short stories that couldn't be further from established noise-boy motifs. On the surface, Steel Pole Bath Tub isn't all that different from a thousand other post–Big Black combos, but a plunge below the clamorous veneer reveals a clever ear for a twisted sample—not to mention a peculiarly pop-savvy way with a guitar hook.

Neither of those is especially evident on **Butterfly Love,** an album steeped deeply enough in irony ("Thru the Windshield of Love") to serve as a display in some future-world exhibition of post-modernism. Although Darren Mor-x's boot-boy drumming is guaranteed to raise cerebral welts, the album simply doesn't have a whole lot of enduring impact. The **Lurch** EP mitigates the one-dimensionality significantly, with guitarist Michael Morasky enveloping the songs in enough effects to make it clear that the title refers to the music's queasy motion, rather than the Addams Family butler—although the trio's pop culture fetishism doesn't rule out some sort of influence from the latter. For a CD compendium of the first two discs, look under the **Lurch** handle.

Before the release of the fairly impressive **Tulip,** Steel Pole began building its rep as one of America's better po-mo cover bands, slathering 7-inch singles with aggressively deconstructed versions of the Velvets' "Venus in Furs" and Jimi Hendrix's "Voodoo Chile." If nothing on **Tulip** approaches those tracks in terms of sheer inventiveness, the band's use of samples is far more cagey: in terms of sheer found-sound layering, it's hard to think of any rockers who top these guys, making for an appropriately oppressive sonic environment—given the James Ellroy–styled psychospiel that makes up most of the lyrical content. It's interesting to see the development of two distinct voices within the songwriting: Morasky tends toward self-contained audio noir stories, while bassist Dale Flattum intones ominous real-time journal entries (often precise enough to contain day and date).

The Miracle of Sound in Motion provides the most cogent crystallization of the band's sound yet, falling as it does smack in the middle of the intersection between mind-control and muscle-flex. While undeniably creepy—Flattum's approximation of a speed-freak's ranting on "Pseudophedrine Hydrochloride" is awfully spot-on—the album fully discloses the trio's workaday experimentalism. Tracks like "Train to Miami" (one of Morasky's journeys to the center of the heart of psychic darkness) and "Thumbnail" are marked by sonic lunges every bit as "out" as any number of avant-garde artistes, but Steel Pole's timbre remains decidedly rock. The album's most unexpected pleasure materializes when the band throws a curve: a thoroughly straight reading of the Pogues' "Down All the Days."

Some Cocktail Suggestions, six songs recorded by Steve Albini, appears to be a water-treading move. While aggressive enough—both "Ray" and the shivering "Hit It" pulse with angry-parolee venom—the EP doesn't sustain much in the way of forward motion. It does, however, provide a detailed bartender's guide, complete with a practical hangover remedy.

The intriguingly straightforward **Scars From Falling Down** relegates the band's battery of samples to subordinate status, a state of affairs that enhances Morasky's fractured-but-judicious riffing while doing little to protect the air of mystery that's one of Steel Pole's chief assets. Abetted on three tracks by Ed Stasium mixes, the self-produced band does its best to sound like a rock combo; still, songs like "Home Is a Rope" and "3 of Cups" (one of two numbers named after favorite cocktail lounges) plant enough random depth charges to allay the fears of diehard fans. Heady stuff indeed.

Duh (aka Death's Ugly Head) is a semi-legendary, ultra-fluid Bay Area "super"-group (anchored by Morasky and Boner label owner/ex-Fang guitarist/Star Pimp bassist Tom Flynn) that specializes in full-squall idiot-rock like "Hex" and "Hot Day for the Ice Cream Man" (the silliest invocation of Lucifer this side of Deicide). Lock Primus and Poison Idea in a closet together, and the results would probably end up sounding like this.

Milk Cult, SPBT's industrialized sideline with DJ/sample fiend C.C. Nova, is a markedly more shadowy and less song-oriented project, replete with plenty of doom-rock atmosphere, clanking percussion and walls of samples thick enough to contain the wild shrieking of whoever it is pops up to do the singing. For the easiest entry into the Cult's compound, try **Burn or Bury,** which features guest yowling by Mike Patton on "Psychoanalytwist" and a lot of twisted but accessible rock-with-samples; the ambient, random-access no-singing weirdness of **Love God,** which makes an effort to be taken as fictional film music, is a lot more daunting. C.C. Nova's demented solo collage record offers an even worse assault on the nerves, using such creative ingredients as "Bach's Flute Dance (from Badinerie of B-minor Suite) 5" yellow plastic childrens record burned with a Bic lighter played @ 16 rpm thru faulty stereo cable" and "various sound effects records looped with Scotch brand magic tape, scratched, ruined, and then returned to the SF Public Library. (Sorry)"

Tumor Circus teams the entire Steel Pole lineup with Jello Biafra for a handful of predictably "shocking" attempts to tweak middle-class kulcha: the self-titled record compiles previously released singles on the order of "Meat Hook Up My Rectum." Do you really need to know more than that? [dss]

See also *Jello Biafra.*

STEIN

See *Einstürzende Neubauten.*

STEPHEN

See *David Kilgour.*

STEREOLAB

Super Electric EP10 (UK Too Pure) 1991 (UK Duophonic) 1996
Switched On (Slumberland) 1992
Peng! (UK Too Pure) 1992 (Too Pure/American) 1995
Low Fi EP10 (UK Too Pure) 1992
The Groop Played "Space Age Batchelor Pad Music" (UK Too Pure) 1993 (Too Pure/American) 1995
Jenny Ondioline EP (UK Duophonic) 1993 (Elektra) 1993
Transient Random-Noise Bursts With Announcements (Elektra) 1993
Mars Audiac Quintet (Elektra) 1994
Refried Ectoplasm [Switched On Volume 2] (Drag City) 1995
Cybele's Reverie EP (UK Duophonic) 1996
Emperor Tomato Ketchup (Elektra) 1996

STEREOLAB/NURSE WITH WOUND

Crumb Duck EP10 (UK Clawfist) 1993
Crumb Duck (UK United Dairies) 1996

STEREOLAB WITH CHARLES LONG

Music for the Amorphous Body Study Centre (UK Duophonic) 1995

VARIOUS ARTISTS

Too Pure–The Peel Sessions (Strange Fruit/Dutch East India Trading) 1992
The Lost Weekend (UK Blast First!) 1993

MCCARTHY

Red Sleeping Beauty EP (UK Pink) 1986
Frans Hals EP (UK Pink) 1987
The Well of Loneliness EP (UK Sept) 1987
I Am a Wallet (UK Sept) 1987 (UK Midnight) 1990
A la Guillotine (UK Pink) 1988
This Nelson Rockefeller EP (UK Sept) 1988
The Enraged Will Inherit the Earth (UK Midnight) 1989
At War EP (UK Midnight) 1989
Banking, Violence and the Inner Life Today (UK Midnight) 1990
That's All Very Well but . . . The Best of McCarthy (UK Cherry Red) 1996

The clinical name chosen by this London-based sextet is somewhat appropriate, given its fondness for gene-splicing experiments in which hair-thin fibers of kraut-rock drone, Europop lilt and didactic theory are hybridized to provocative ends. But while explaining Stereolab's modus operandi requires plenty of academic discussion—mostly about matters such as semiotics and post-structuralism—the group always manages to execute its theories with a peerless brainiac charm that alternately recalls Astrud Gilberto fronting a particularly zoned version of Neu! and a parallel-universe lounge-pop Arkestra conducted by LaMonte Young.

Formed by Tim Gane (who had fronted McCarthy, perhaps the bubbliest Marxist brigade ever to hit the UK) and French-born Laetitia (Seaya) Sadier, Stereolab made its initial incursion through a series of limited-edition (some mail-order-only) singles united sonically (by the tension between Gane's scratchy guitar and Sadier's lulling vocal drone) and visually (by the recurrent cover image of a grinning, pointing cartoon). The band's first three singles are compiled on the ten-song **Switched On** collection, which seems to glide almost seamlessly from track to track, thanks in part to the controlled *motorik* drumming of Joe Dilworth (on loan from Th Faith Healers). Sadier's drowsy Francophone coo is at its most sirenic on "Changer" and "Au Grand Jour"; when she's buoyed by the harmonies of Gina Morris (who would soon depart) on songs like "The Way Will Be Opening," the magnetic field is even stronger. (That early lineup, with bassist Martin Kean, ex-Chills, is also documented on the Peel Session EP, performing four songs in July '91. The disc also contains BBC tracks by PJ Harvey and Th Faith Healers.)

Released concurrently with **Switched On, Peng!** might as well be subtitled *Everything You Always Wanted to Know About Analog Synthesizers but Were Afraid to Ask.* The love with which both Gane and Sadier navigate an array of vintage Moogs is palpable on both pastoral drones (like "Super Falling Star") and more direct Kraftwerkian plunders ("Orgiastic"). What sets Stereolab apart, however, is the way in which the group consistently re-creates the utopian worldview espoused by mid-'60s advocates of better living through science—as evidenced by the starry-eyed "Peng! 33." On the post-structuralist front, Stereolab offers up "Mellotron," the first of what would be many self-referential tributes to sound for the sake of sound.

The addition of yet another singing keyboardist, Mary Hansen, was first chronicled on the "John Cage Bubblegum" single, a title that in itself gives about the best description of Stereolab's sound extant. An even more sumptuous, opalescent approach was ushered in when second guitarist Sean O'Hagan (formerly of Microdisney, also of High Llamas) and new drummer Andy Ramsay joined for the recording of **The Groop Played "Space Age Batchelor Pad Music."** Presaging the ironic lounge music revival, Stereolab leaped feet-first into the martini-fueled Moog-music singled out in the album's title with plenty of Gane's meta-pop ideas in tow. Cheekily divided into "Easy Listening" and "New Wave" sides, the album isolates the individual components of the band's hybrid sound, concentrating its lilting minimalism on the first half (see "The Groop Play Chord X" and the consumerist anthem "Ronco Symphony") and the electro-glide pulse on the latter's "We're Not Adult Orientated (Neu Wave Live)." A sonic cocktail with an entirely different kind of twist. **The Lost Weekend,** a sampler of various bands, was available only at two London shows at which the band supported the Afghan Whigs: it includes a version of "Crest," which would later show up on **Transient Random-Noise Bursts With Announcements.**

Stereolab styled the packaging of **Transient Random-Noise Bursts With Announcements** from a test disc dating back to the days of hi-fi, complete with advisories about what each track is designed to troubleshoot. (The group also sampled the disc for one track here.) While there's no disputing the presence of a tongue-in-cheek subtext, the reverence with which the sextet assembles its sonic ramparts is impossible to miss: there's as tangible a defiance in the *mekanik* drones of "Our Trinitone Blast" (an emphatically strobing melody overlaid by Sadier's soapbox declamations) as in the purposefully MOR (in the Dionne

Warwick sense of the word) breezes of "Pack Yr Romantic Mind." The album's centerpiece, however, is the eighteen-minute "Jenny Ondioline," a blissfully chaotic, mantra-like excursion that ebbs and flows with an intensity reminiscent of "Sister Ray": Gane's automatic strum acts as a bed of nails that somehow supports the floats of vocals and synthesizers without puncturing them. Elektra also released an EP, different from the British issue, featuring a pared-down version of "Jenny Ondioline" accompanied by three tracks, including the otherwise unavailable "Fruition."

It would've been hard to top that creative burst, and **Mars Audiac Quintet** does suffer a bit in comparison. With O'Hagan taking an active but non-membership part (leaving room for the arrival of keyboardist Katharine Gifford), the band's approach isn't all that different, but there's a discernible lowering of intensity on the more overtly rockist tracks. It's still a kick to hear Sadier trill sweetly through missives like "Nihilist Assault Group"—a song that echoes the Sex Pistols saw about wanting nothing so much as to create "more bands like us." In another of Stereolab's familiar tributes to bizarro-world ancestors, "International Colouring Contest" samples a zinging bit of exotica called "Into Outer Space With Lucia Pamela" (a vintage space-age pop singer); the track is far more otherworldly than those of any of Stereolab's more determinedly shticky peers.

In some ways, that disc seems to mark the end of an era for Stereolab. As evidenced by **Emperor Tomato Ketchup**'s sexy trip-hop-styled opener, "Metronomic Underground" (which could pass for a Tricky remix), the fairly precise borders the band laid out for itself have been torn down—or at least penetrated with enough holes to allow for some cross-cultural pollination. Even the more traditionally 'Lab-ish tracks are marked by subtle twists, like the live string section that punctuates the Europop "Cybele's Reverie." Sadier's Marxist musings have grown even more pointed—songs like "Tomorrow Is Already Here" would have her walking unemployment lines alongside Dalton Trumbo back in the '50s—and her delivery is considerably more earthy.

Refried Ectoplasm, which assembles compilation cuts, outtakes and single tracks from the post–**Switched On** period, is a terrific get-acquainted visit with the band's ever-changing moods. In addition to self-explanatory mood pieces like "Harmonium" and "Farfisa," the thirteen-song set contains a previously unreleased "country" (the band's designation, not necessarily a factual description) reworking of the airy "Tone Burst."

Music for the Amorphous Body Study Centre comes from a gallery installation in which Stereolab provided the "soundtrack" for Charles Long's interactive soft sculptures. At the show, one experienced each ambient piece through headphones plugged into the individual work for which it was designed, in terms of both theme and acoustics. One of the pricey artworks might be an impractical stereo system add-on, but those headphones will enhance your appreciation of this disc, as well as the rest of the band's catalogue. [dss]

See also *High Llamas, Palace Brothers, Th Faith Healers.*

STEROID MAXIMUS

See *Foetus.*

DAVE STEWART

Lily Was Here (UK Eligible/BMG) 1989 (Arista) 1991
Greetings From the Gutter (EastWest) 1994

DAVE STEWART AND THE SPIRITUAL COWBOYS

Dave Stewart and the Spiritual Cowboys (Arista) 1990

VEGAS

Vegas (UK RCA) 1992

One of the items on Dave Stewart's agenda as a solo artist has seemed to be sorting out speculation about his talents. Sure, the former Eurythmic (and Tourist and Longdancer) can play guitar. And, yeah, he's a versatile, resourceful and chart-savvy producer, a knack he's repeatedly proven for others as David A. Stewart (the initial distinguishes him from ex-Hatfield and the North prog-rock popster Dave Stewart, who has made a number of albums and UK hits in partnership with Barbara Gaskin). His own albums certify an ability to gather and organize sound with wit and dispatch. But nothing in Stewart's past ever suggested he could sing or write lyrics. And the sorry fact is he can't.

Given Eurythmics' tall stack of hits and that Stewart and Annie Lennox split the duo's creative chores, it would be easy to assume that he possesses real songwriting aptitude, as well as the stylistic suss to retain a consistent musical personality whatever the genre being refracted. So why can't he manage a single sharp melody or intelligent lyric on his own? It turns out she wasn't the chameleon in the group, he was. Stewart hasn't got a signature of any sort: she evidently got custody of (and then promptly discarded) the band's distinctive sound. **Dave Stewart and the Spiritual Cowboys** and **Greetings From the Gutter** are both flat-out embarrassing, full of songs that never should have been written or sung. The first one is an ordinary-sounding guitar-rock record pockmarked by vindictive and unseemly slags—in the no-points-for-guessing-who "King of the Hypocrites," he sneers, "You told me you were a Christian/You told me you so were pure/But I think you're so sick inside/You're never gonna find a cure"—and moronic fantasies. "Fashion Bomb" descends to anatomically inept grade-school doggerel: "She's radio active, you can see it in her eyes/Radioactive from her hips to her thighs."

Greetings From the Gutter is a pretentious soul/rock mess recorded with a band containing Bootsy Collins and Bernie Worrell and lousy with high-profile guest stars like Laurie Anderson, Lou Reed, Lady Miss Kier and Mick Jagger. It's no big surprise that the songs all suck, but Stewart's inexplicable attempt to imitate David Bowie is a bewildering development. Besides aping the mannered voices, accent and intonation of his infinite better, Stewart loads up on material expressly designed to aid the effort. "Chelsea Lovers," complete with a coy reference to "a Ziggy cartoon," is very nearly a rewrite of "Drive-In Saturday." "St. Valentine's Day" contains a familiar line about "killing time"; "Tragedy Street" (which boasts the hauntingly clever chorus "How come you're always in the middle of a tragedy/How come you're always walking down Tragedy Street") concerns a character named Angie. For good measure, Stewart replicates Mick Ronson's ripping guitar sound and puts a sax solo by David Sanborn (who, coincidentally, played a similar part on **Young Americans**) into "Oh No, Not You Again," another crude personal attack that ends this miserable and obnoxious album. During the song's long coda, there's an atrocious tearful scene acted out by Carly Simon and Sanborn. "I'm fucking suffocating here," belches Sanborn at one point. He's not the only one.

Before getting on with his tragically vocal solo career, Stewart tried his hand at film scoring, an area he should definitely explore further. **Lily Was Here** is an excellent piece of work, a varied but carefully interwoven set of themes explored by Stewart on guitar, an orchestra of strings and Candy Dulfer on saxophone. In addition to a bunch of more-than-wallpaper instrumentals (songs, really), the album contains a finespun number ("Second Chance") delicately sung, co-written and played by Virginia Astley and a version of Eurythmics' "Here Comes the Rain Again" that places Lennox's original vocal track in an entirely new and alluring acoustic guitar and strings setting.

In between his other projects, Stewart formed Vegas in partnership with singer Terry Hall (formerly of the Specials, Fun Boy Three and Colourfield). With a skilled and recognizable vocalist again in his corner, Stewart is able to concentrate on building the lush and varied production settings for the co-written songs (and a string-driven cover of Charles Aznavour's dapper "She") on the short-lived duo's one album. [i]

STIGMATA A GO GO

Stigmata-a-Go-Go (Pow Wow) 1993
It's All True (Grass) 1994

Of all the Pavement-loving, fanzine-reading, Kinkos-working, Loisaida-living noisemakers to rear their ugly little heads in New York clubs in the '90s, Stigmata a Go Go has the distinction of being among the few in possession of enough talent to justify the mandatory urban attitude. Georgia-spawned singer/ guitarist Gary Greenblatt evidently knows from Dinosaur Jr and Sonic Youth, but he brings fresh enthusiasm and minimal posturing to intelligent songs whose tenacious melodies bear up nicely to the trio's calmly clangorous energy. Both albums (distinguishable mainly by the second's inferior sound) wrap persuasive creations in lush leis of benign barbed wire and pole-vault easily over the similar but less imaginative efforts of countless like-minded bands. "Worthy #2," "She Comes Undone" and the superlative "Half-Asleep" are the grabbers on **Stigmata-a-Go-Go;** the followup boasts "Sterno Heart" (which begins with an idle choice: "Sometimes things get so confusing/ Whether to lick your boots or kick your teeth in"), "Riotkeeper" and "D Boon," a detailed and touching tribute to the late Minutemen leader. [i]

STING

The Dream of the Blue Turtles (A&M) 1985 (A&M/Mobile Fidelity) 1990
Bring on the Night (A&M) 1986
. . . Nothing Like the Sun (A&M) 1987 (A&M/Mobile Fidelity) 1991
. . . Nada Como el Sol EP (A&M) 1988
The Soul Cages (A&M) 1991
Ten Summoner's Tales (A&M) 1993
Demolition Man EP (A&M) 1993
Fields of Gold: The Best of Sting 1984–1994 (A&M) 1994
Mercury Falling (A&M) 1996

The king of pain(ful self-consciousness), Sting has always seemed both older and younger than the music he is making. In the Police, he was a former schoolteacher trying to seem dignified while still leaping around in a blonde bleach job singing lyrics like "De do do do, de da da da." Capable of monstrous pomposity yet ultimately addicted to the humiliating showmanship and intrinsic stupidity of rock'n'roll, he is permanently a man outside his art. Unlike David Bowie, who effortlessly appears to be a mature, civil adult even at moments of extreme theatrical silliness, Sting (Gordon Sumner) can't buff up that aspect of his image the way he has pumped up his biceps; the elbow grease and sweat equity he puts into his music has created a permanent dissonance between his highbrow studio pretensions and his audience-pleasing poster-boy pandering. *What* he sings and *why* he sings it have never really been in synch.

Sting's solo career very clearly reflects his enormous creative ambition, the personal issues that drive him in real life and the burning need to be taken seriously and admired. Few artists have ever struggled so hard to have hit records that could (hypothetically speaking of course . . . right?) hang in the Louvre—and rectify some of society's ills along the way. The nakedness of his desires is touching at times, except when he's being an absolute jerk about the way he's gone about achieving them.

The four albums recapitulated on **Fields of Gold** (which contains two new items—the lugubrious and cliché-packed "When We Dance" and "This Cowboy Song"—plus an alternate version of "We'll Be Together" and eleven fairly obvious back catalogue selections) begin with 1985's **The Dream of the Blue Turtles,** on which Sting, attempting to sound older and graver than his thirty-three years, employs top-notch young American jazzers to erase memories of the Police's simpleminded pop. The auteur sounds like he's having a bloody fine time jamming with such cool cats, but the results mainly point up the narrow possibilities of his singing. In an effort to write himself a ladder down from his own chartbound tree, Sting proffers both Police couldhavebeens ("If You Love Somebody Set Them Free") and preposterous sleep-inducers ("Russians," "based on a theme by Sergei Prokofiev"). An uncertain start.

Sting then took some of the same musicians out on the road and brought back the dull-as-a-dentist's-office two-CD **Bring on the Night** (which, despite its incidence of otherwise undocumented material, goes unrepresented on the compilation). Finally alighting in Switzerland, Sting produced **Nothing Like the Sun,** one of the most self-important records on record. Even as the nouveau sophisticate sings "History Will Teach Us Nothing," his pedantic instincts and bulging ego inform the lyrics at every turn with political dilettantism, literary namedropping and prolix pseudo-profundities. In what passes for light relief (but is, in fact, outlandish pomposity), Sting fancies himself a theatrical toff, singing the culturally autobiographical "Englishman in New York" over plucked violins and tootling horns as if the nouveau dandy had acquired Noël Coward's soul on approval. (**Nada Como el Sol** consists of four songs from the internationalist's album sung in Spanish with one, "Fragile," reprised in Portuguese.)

Setting aside his guitar and global pretensions, Sting waxes more personal and reflective on **The Soul**

Cages, alternating obvious pop singles that reveal strong ties to his Police era and expansive theatrical meanderings that cry out for a context the album fails to provide. With repeated references to his late father, **The Soul Cages**—aseptically produced with Hugh Padgham—has solemn emotional resonance and a settled maturity unheard in Sting's previous work, but the contradiction between fine art and commercial demography is the album's strongest message.

Ten Summoner's Tales is the first Sting album on which he seems able to bring his music and mindset within spitting distance of each other. An oddly conceived blend of nostalgic jazz stylings ("It's Probably Me," co-written with Michael Kamen and Eric Clapton, reaches for the elegance of Cole Porter only to tip over his martini glass) and elegiac pop, the album is by no means a wall-to-wall winner (the clumsy ballad "Love Is Stronger Than Justice," the poorly sung would-be jump blues of "She's Too Good for Me" and David Foxxe's narration see to that). Still, it has a higher proportion of appealing songs than usual, and the grandiosity of their presentation is at least scaled back to manageable proportions. The jaunty bounce of "If I Ever Lose My Faith in You" actually strengthens the song's inherent desolation, bolstering the unlikelihood of the title's conditional prospect by buoying it on a melody that uplifts too sweetly to encourage such notions. The handsome folk essence of "Fields of Gold" doesn't make it original, but Sting intones the lyrics with winning solemnity; the acoustic "Shape of My Heart" crosses Antonio Carlos Jobim and Jim Croce and still winds up on the right side of a good thing. At this rate, Sting might be on his way to making a genuinely great record sometime in the next millennium.

When the title of an old Police song, "Demolition Man," was borrowed for a Stallone/Snipes futuristic action movie in 1993, Sting rerecorded the track for the soundtrack; an EP of that horrendous, lifeless remake slaps on five live cuts—"King of Pain," a fussy and badly sung rendition of the Beatles' "A Day in the Life" and three of **Ten Summoner's Tales,** all of which benefit from the staged simplicity.

Never having evinced a shred of humility in the past, Sting proudly keeps his leonine head up through the devastating romantic rejection (real or imagined) chronicled on **Mercury Falling.** He can't even offer the satisfaction of simple misery in "I'm So Happy I Can't Stop Crying," a snappy Nashville jaunt that provides the album's most direct consideration of the seeming changes in his life. "Seven weeks have passed now since she left me/She shows her face to ask me how I am/She says the kids are fine and that they miss me/Maybe I could come and baby-sit sometime." The personal cluelessness—a mix of egotism and willful self-delusion—that Sting inadvertently admits when he uses the same song to offer a generalized complaint about the role of "Sunday fathers" ("What can a father do but baby-sit sometimes?") can also be read into the casualness with which the album flits among Squeezey pop-soul ("You Still Touch Me" and "All Four Seasons," a wry but respectful love song), theatrical suavity ("The Hounds of Winter"), simple pop ("Lithium Sunset"), adult mush ("I Was Brought to My Senses," "Let Your Soul Be Your Pilot"), old-time tragic folk balladry ("I Hung My Head," a catchy put-on that causes good ol' Sting to invent a backwoods brother named Jeb) and a laughable Berlitz French accent mangle ("La Belle Dame Sans Regrets"). A glib, by-the-numbers exercise in insincerity, **Mercury Falling** barely scrapes the surface of deep feelings. Ask any mature woman how she feels about emotional forthrightness—no wonder Sting's in the doghouse. [i]

See also *TPRG*.

STINKY PUFFS

A Little Tiny Smelly Bit of . . . . . . the Stinky Puffs (Elemental) 1995
Songs and Advice for Kids Who Have Been Left Behind EP (Elemental) 1996

Born in 1984 and raised among the Residents, Simon Fair Timony—underground rock's coolest adolescent—is the singer and lyricist of the flatulently named Stinky Puffs, a shambly Hoboken, New Jersey, kitchen combo that, in its initial studio incarnation, included his mom, Sheenah Fair, on drums, stepfather Jad Fair on effects, scene dude Don Fleming on guitar and Sonic Youth scion Cody Linn Ranaldo on guitar. Singing in a confident waver, Timony offers an ingenuous child's-eye view of some pretty weighty topics on the debut: a notorious murder trial ("Menendez' Killed Their Parents," recorded with two-thirds of Sleepyhead), his personal response to a friend's suicide (the tender "I'll Love You Anyway," for Kurt Cobain) and the challenge of evaluating one's superego in a post-consumerist society ("I Am Gross!/No You're Not!"). The disc also offers the same four short songs performed live in Olympia, Washington, at 1994's YoYo a Go Go festival. Billed as the Super Stinky Puffs Band, the historic one-off features Yo La Tengo guitarist Ira Kaplan and, making their first (only?) public appearance together since the end of Nirvana, bassist Krist Novoselic and drummer Dave Grohl. To his credit, the unflappable star sounds like he's hanging out with playmates, goofing around until the pizza arrives. More than a novelty and less than the real deal, the record is both fun and touching, an unintended but obliquely wry commentary on indie-pop's childish fixations.

Working with his mom, the junior Ranaldo and some young non-celeb musicians, Fair then recorded a short, more traditionally accomplished EP entitled **Songs and Advice for Kids Who Have Been Left Behind.** Growing (literally) into his art, Timony ventures another version of "I'll Love You Anyway," a wistful song about the departure of his step-father ("I Know I Know"), an ascending list of supplements ("The Vitamin Song"), a wild slab of guitar psychedelia with dubby vocals ("Rubber Pen") and a gruesome rock cover of Gary Wright's "Dream Weaver." [i]

STONE ROSES

The Stone Roses (Silvertone) 1989 + 1989
Turns Into Stone (Silvertone) 1992
Second Coming (UK Geffen) 1994 (Geffen) 1995
The Complete Stone Roses (Silvertone) 1995

No one can ever accuse Stone Roses of letting their career get in the way of anything important. A spectacular example of poorly programmed and self-defeating chaos, the Manchester quartet, which made its debut with a 1985 single, released a grand total of two albums and a pair of overlapping compilations in its first decade. Despite a leading role in the late-'80s Madchester rave scene, the band didn't make its American concert debut until the mid-'90s.

Originally a mod combo known as English Rose (a Jam reference), Stone Roses galvanized their city's—and, by media extension, nation's—Ecstasy-driven post-punk subculture with an utterly brilliant 1989 album of chiming, atmospheric and winningly arrogant folked-up rock. Where others joined the shuffling beat dance patrol or the more explicitly psychedelicized acid-rock guitar fiesta, Stone Roses found their métier in sumptuous songwriting and announced their arrival with an embarrassment of tuneful riches. (As devoted to hubris as to melody, the band reached some sort of a religiously detailed ecstatic peak with "I Am the Resurrection.")

"I Wanna Be Adored," "She Bangs the Drums," "Elephant Stone" (a Peter Hook–produced single added, in a short version, to the album's US edition) and "Waterfall" open **The Stone Roses** with sublimely potent pop, sung with alluring, echo-drenched enervation by pinup face Ian Brown. Stylishly produced by John Leckie and dressed in a Jackson Pollock–styled splatter cover painting by guitarist John Squire, the album is a stunningly well-realized debut, a record-as-cultural-identity one-off as cataclysmic as **The Smiths** or **Ziggy Stardust.**

The album elevated Stone Roses to the head of the Manchester class, and nearly made them US stars when it hit the charts here. But the group retired into a mesh of lawsuits and other self-induced calamities. Evidently more intent on driving associates around the bend than reaping a commercial harvest, Stone Roses produced only a couple of singles (the first, "Fools Gold," was added to a second US version of the first album) during its lengthy hibernation period.

In the meantime, Silvertone (which the band was suing to get off) issued **Turns Into Stone,** an eleven-cut compilation of singles, including the two A-sides that had already found their way onto the American album. The second-tier sources (mostly B-sides) make for an uneven album, but there is enough neat stuff ("Mersey Paradise," "Standing Here," an alternate long version of "Elephant Stone") to make it more than just an obligation for fans. Following the issue of the band's belated second album (on a different label), Silvertone replaced **Turns Into Stone** with the far superior **The Complete Stone Roses.** Not quite what its title implies, the collection dispenses with the insignificant (and backward) "Simone" from the "She Bangs the Drums" CD single, but adds two illustratively formative pre-LP 45s and a half-dozen post-LP tracks. Complicating the deal, the versions of "Fools Gold," "One Love" and "Something's Burning" are all shorter than those on the first anthology.

The long-awaited and laboriously produced **Second Coming** is a strong, sober album suffused with the knowledge that life is harder than it looked from the vantage point of teenagers. (The title barbs the chronologically obvious with typical gall.) Youth and novelty no longer seem to be the watchwords; the album is strewn with self-conscious retro citations. The quartet's creative focus seems have to shifted from singer Brown to guitarist/songwriter Squire, and his '70s-rock playing is dominant, summoning up the sour air of Altamont raunch and the macho flash of Led Zeppelin. Anchored only to seductive dance rhythms and irresistibly hook-filled songwriting, the album has a weirdly unlocated sense of time and place, which makes it as great as the first for entirely different reasons. When not playing K-Tel games with classic-rock memories ("Tears" dances purposefully on "Stairway to Heaven") or stretching dance grooves into extended sonic experiments (like the eleven-minute-plus opener, "Breaking Into Heaven"), Stone Roses reclaims its folk-rock roots in the richly realized "Ten Storey Love Song" and the acoustic simplicity of "Tightrope." Taking one from each column in its stylistic arsenal, Stone Roses wraps **Second Coming** up in "Love Spreads," a snarly boogie with cushy vocals and trippy, messianic lyrics.

Reni (Alan Wren) left the band in the spring of '95 and was replaced by Rebel MC drummer Robbie J. Maddix in time for the band's first-ever American tour. [i]

STONE TEMPLE PILOTS

Core (Atlantic) 1992
Purple (Atlantic) 1994
Vasoline EP (UK Atlantic) 1994
Interstate Love Song EP (Atlantic) 1994
Tiny Music . . . Songs From the Vatican Gift Shop (Atlantic) 1996

Stone Temple Pilots arose from obscurity in San Diego (where the group was formed as Mighty Joe Young) to worldwide attention so quickly and with a sound so close to what was happening on radio via Seattle that the backlash set in before the quartet's debut album, **Core,** finished reeling off its succession of hits. Tweaked to commanding post-metal power by producer Brendan O'Brien (Black Crowes, Pearl Jam, Red Hot Chili Peppers), **Core** resonates with the sonic effects of Nirvana, Pearl Jam and Soundgarden in plain view. "Plush" and "Piece of Pie" were understandably mistaken for Pearl Jam, and Scott Weiland's dry, constricted vocals on the dramatic, semi-acoustic "Creep" ("I'm half the man I used to be") sound uncannily like Kurt Cobain. Where the northwestern groups STP were aping fought to break tired rock formulae, the Californians served up their innovations pre-digested and refined for mass consumption, writing songs catchier, more radio-friendly and less compellingly serious than their bull-headed counterparts. The bass/guitar brotherhood of Robert and Dean DeLeo makes a solid but flexible noise, and Eric Kretz drums with the hamhanded power of John Bonham, driving songs like the Nirvana-seeking "Sex Type Thing" (whose ironic idea of a crude come-on is "I'm gonna learn ya my philosophy/You wanna know about my atrocity?"), "Sin" and "Crackerman."

Again produced by O'Brien, **Purple** (a title that appears nowhere on the package) is tighter and more confident, drawing the band closer to establishing a characteristic sound but not quite getting there. Weiland possesses a strong, gritty voice and the others can certainly play, but the group can't seem to shake off its kleptomaniacal instincts. The roaringly melodic "Interstate Love Song," "Vasoline" and the "Creep"-soundalike "Big Empty" all repeat their downbeat hard rock with maximum efficiency. The odd acoustic pop of "Pretty Penny" provides an intriguing contrast to the loudness (and doesn't sound anything like Nirvana's "Polly"—well, not *too* much), but the syncopated Jane's-ish monotony of "Army Ants" is a bad sign.

So were Weiland's heroin addiction and May 1995 drug bust. Nonetheless, he and the band got themselves sorted out long enough to make a third album before remanding the singer to a medical facility for treatment of his drug dependency. Reinvented as a Lollapalooza-era Cheap Trick, down to the alluring Beatlisms amid the tuneful electric crunch, STP gives its no-stylistic-integrity all to catchy power-pop on **Tiny Music . . . Songs From the Vatican Gift Shop.** There are exceptions, like the relaxed cocktail pop of "And So I Know" and the blustery "Art School Girl," but not enough to alter the primary impression. Even "Trippin' on a Hole in a Paper Heart," a Pearl Jammy composition that could have gone in that direction, is reined in with a Robin Zanderesque vocal. The free-association lyrics are too oblique or stupid to mean much outside the group ("Adhesive Love" seems like a silly way to almost sing "Peace and Love," and "Ride the Cliché" isn't about anything at all), and the music isn't breaking any boundaries, but **Tiny Music** Tricks this dragon out in a second set of stripes. [roc/i]

STOP

Never (Smut Pedlurz/Bomp!) 1995

SIBLING RIVALRY

In a Family Way EP (Alternative Tentacles) 1994

The short-lived Sibling Rivalry paired Joey Ramone with his younger brother, guitarist/singer Mickey Leigh. The duo's three-song CD single contains a snappy, guitar-flashed rendition of Blodwyn Pig's obscure "See My Way," Leigh's neat pop original "On the Beach" (from the repertoire of his '80s band, the Rattlers) and a gritty rocker Leigh recorded with no fraternal assistance.

The rest of the time, Leigh leads Stop, a lighthearted rock trio with bassist Stephen Sane and drummer Pat Carpenter. **Never** is an entertaining hodgepodge of originals ("The Idiot Son of 007," "Ballad of Mickey Leigh," "Proud to Be Human"), collaborations (the fierce "Cake and Eat It" has lyrics and lead vocals by Handsome Dick Manitoba of the Dictators; the late Lester Bangs, who was Leigh's bandmate in 1978's Birdland, wrote the words to the old highway boogie of "Metal Eyes") and covers (Dee Dee Ramone's catchy "Outsider," Johnny Cash's "Ring of Fire"). Although lumbering a bit heavily at times, the diverse **Never** also works up vintage punk energy, a wah-wah freakout, riff grunge, late-'60s acid guitar psychedelia and sepulchral folk-rock. Stop. Cool. [i]

IZZY STRADLIN AND THE JU JU HOUNDS

See *Guns n' Roses.*

STRAITJACKET FITS

Life in One Chord EP (NZ Flying Nun) 1987
Hail (NZ Flying Nun) 1988 (Rough Trade) 1990
Melt (NZ Flying Nun) 1990 (Flying Nun/Arista) 1991
Down in Splendour EP (NZ Flying Nun) 1990
Missing From Melt EP (Flying Nun/Arista) 1991
Roller Ride EP (NZ Flying Nun) 1991
Done EP (NZ Flying Nun) 1992
Blow (Flying Nun/Arista) 1993
If I Were You EP (NZ Flying Nun) 1993
Cat Inna Can EP (NZ Flying Nun) 1993

DOUBLEHAPPYS

Cut It Out EP (NZ Flying Nun) 1985
How Much Time Left, Please? EP (NZ Xpressway) 1990 (UK Avalanche) 1991
Nerves (NZ Flying Nun) 1992

Straitjacket Fits sprang from the ashes of DoubleHappys, a trio (named after a particularly loud brand of firecracker) that formed in Dunedin, New Zealand, in the early '80s. Childhood friends Shayne Carter and Wayne Elsey (both singing, playing guitar and writing songs) and John Collie (drums) were younger than the rest of the Flying Nun mob when the group debuted with the wonderful "Others Way" b/w "Anyone Else Would" single: melancholy pop songs wrapped in charming lo-fi sound. The following **Cut It Out** EP—which actually made the Kiwi Top 20—further highlights Carter's honeyed-but-scathing voice and the contrasts in the band's sound. Sadly, that was as far as DoubleHappys got: Elsey was killed in a train accident in 1985. The six-song **How Much Time Left, Please?** captures an embryonic live set; the highly recommended **Nerves** augments most of the above with two previously unreleased practice-room tracks.

Carter and Collie, reconstituted with guitarist/singer Andrew Brough and bassist David Wood, then formed Straitjacket Fits—similarly melodic but angrier, more complex and less overtly poppy than DoubleHappys, with Carter and Brough's voices building cathedral harmonies that redefine the word "soaring." The four-song **Life in One Chord** occasionally trips over its own ambition but dazzles on the wild "Dialing a Prayer." While equally intense, **Hail** is more controlled and refined, as the bracing rush of the title track and "Life in One Chord" are balanced by Brough's "Take From the Years" and a gorgeous cover of Leonard Cohen's "So Long Marianne." (The American edition of **Hail** replaces four tracks with the contents of **Life in One Chord.)**

On **Melt,** Gavin MacKillop's ultra-lush production blankets everything in a dense, hazy sound that at times blurs the instruments and vocals into echo-drenched sonic clouds. While this approach occasionally yields mush, it also results in brilliance: a swooping, swooning, swelling, surging, soaring (and all that) rush that beautifully captures the intensity of the band's live shows. **Melt** features the Fits' best batch of songs, particularly "Bad Note for a Heart," "Missing Presumed Drowned" and Brough's lilting "Hand in Mine."

The misleadingly titled **Missing From Melt** actually includes remixes of three album tracks along with two uneventful non-LP songs. **Roller Ride** boasts three live tracks; **Down in Splendour** combines some of the extras from both EPs. However, the Fits' best non-LP track is a version of Jean Paul Sartre Experience's "Flex" on the rare **Roger Sings the Hits,** a Flying Nun tenth-anniversary compilation wherein members of the label's roster cover each other's songs.

Blow, a word that evidently has fewer negative connotations in New Zealand than America, buckles under Paul Fox's uncomfortably slick production, but he's not the only one to blame for this album's lifelessness. Andrew Brough's departure had apparently removed the creative tension that seethed throughout the band's previous work, and most of the songs are downright bland (an adjective that applies to none of their earlier material). Only "Train" and "Burn It Up" show any of the old glimmer, and they're both buried by a stifling mix and plodding rhythms. The band split up after a final tour in '93. (The **Done** EP features two non-LP tracks and different recordings of two album songs; **If I Were You** includes a remix of the title track as well as a pair of demos; **Cat Inna Can** features the non-LP "Sycamore" and a cover of the Sex Pistols' "Satellite").

Carter has recorded several tracks over the years (scattered on Xpressway and Flying Nun compilations and singles), solo and in collusion with Peter Jefferies. In '94, Carter formed a new band called Dimmer (which briefly included Jefferies) but has been plagued by lineup instability. Their debut 7-inch ("Crystallator") was released by Sub Pop in late '95. [ja]

STRAPPING FIELDHANDS

The Demiurge EP (Siltbreeze) 1992
Future Pastoral EP (Siltbreeze) 1993
Discus (Omphalos) 1994
In the Pineys EP (Siltbreeze) 1995
The Caul (The Now Sound) 1995
Wattle & Daub (Shangri-La) 1996

If you had to produce a list of the influences on American post-punk—in descending order of importance—chances are rustic British folk would rank somewhere near the end. At times, however, it seems as if that's the only music to have had any impact on Philadelphia's Strapping Fieldhands, an unabashedly Anglophile quintet weaned on the Incredible String Band's **Layers of the Onion** (with just a dusting of the Bevis Frond for flavor). Don't call 'em revivalists, though: like kindred lo-fi spirits Guided by Voices, the Fieldhands (aside from percussionist Jeff Werner) are all old enough to remember the stuff as contemporary.

Like good and evil twins separated at birth, the quintet's first two EPs thresh deeply into rural territory, sharing a "production" quality rough enough to qualify them as (no pun intended) field recordings. **The Demiurge** lies squarely on the creepier side of the tracks, with Bob Dickie's cello and bass providing a suitably gothic latticework to aid the organic growth of frontman Bob Malloy's neo-Appalachian allegories (the best of which is the porch-mystic "Poor Mr. Jesus"). **Future Pastoral** finds the band, augmented by second guitarist Jacy Webster, on a jollier bender, but on a bender nonetheless: "Stacey Donelly" and the desert moan "Ol' Jimmy Cole" (which boasts some cleverly sampled 78 rpm pops 'n' clicks) stagger with the unfettered glee of vintage Holy Modal Rounders fortified with vintage port.

Discus, the band's first full-length release, allows for a more expansive look into the Fieldhands' world, albeit one that intensifies the Anglo-fetish: Malloy's affected-but-charming faux British accent has seldom been thicker, his prose never more Merrie Olde than on "Lonnie Donegan's Mum's Tea Chest" or "Biscuits and Kippers." The heavy skiffle vibe is broken by such oddities as the pogo-folk "Boo Hoo Hoo" and the lugubrious Hawkwind doppelgänger "Luminous Bodies." Downright weird. **In the Pineys** again zigs when you'd expect it to zag, lowering the studio quality another notch (you can actually hear a telephone ringing amid the between-track background noise) and offering up an all-hands-on-deck chantalong version (CD buyers can make that two) of Melanie's Woodstock kitsch-fest "Lay Down (Candles in the Rain)." [dss]

STRETCHHEADS

Five Fingers Four Thingers a Thumb a Facelift and a New Identity (UK Moksha) 1988
Eyeball Origami Aftermath Wit Vegetarian Leg EP7 (UK Blast First) 1990
Pish in Your Sleazebag (UK Blast First) 1991
Barbed Anal Exciter EP (UK Blast First) 1991

The voice is inhuman, reminiscent of nothing so much as *Sesame Street*'s Grover with electrodes affixed to his genitals; over a mindbogglingly fast skittering racket, it's yelling "In my life/I was disappointed," then letting loose with something that sounds like a Tourette's sufferer speaking in tongues: BLBLBLB-LBLBLBLBLBLBLBLBLBLBLBLBLDZUUUUHH! The band is Glasgow, Scotland's Stretchheads, the weirdest, fastest and heaviest thing ever to come cartwheeling out of the British Isles. Bassist Mac (no last names were ever given), guitarist Andy, drummer Richie (later replaced by Jason) and the aforementioned vocalizer, who went by the handle P6, had a rather limited aesthetic, but they squeezed it until the tube begged for mercy.

The Stretchheads' first album, **Five Fingers Four Thingers,** introduces a band that's instantly diagnosable as hyperactive, hungry and completely strange. Not to mention Scottish: the country has produced an entire school of high-speed, percussion-heavy, jabbering bands, including Archbishop Kebab, Dawson, Badgewearer and the early Dog Faced Hermans (note the song title "Long Faced German"). Kylie Minogue's pop hit "I Should Be So Lucky" gets Stretchhead-ized so thoroughly that it's impossible to tell from the rest of the songs unless you're listening very closely; the originals sound of a piece at first, but eventually their scratchy, screechy rhythms resolve themselves into bizarre but smashing hooks (the best belongs to "Shape and Cleanse").

The band's greatest record is **Eyeball Origami Aftermath Wit Vegetarian Leg:** four speed-crazed songs (all but one of which they subsequently rerecorded), each one faster and crazier than the next. P6 makes some truly unbelievable vocal noises, the drums are faster than human hands can generally move; gratuitous but totally enjoyable sound-collaging and inner-groove madness add to the fun.

With **Pish in Your Sleazebag** (whatever that means, it sounds really gross), the tape-play becomes high-intensity studio trickery. A few tracks have dub-style wipeouts, and there are lots of heavily manipulated between-song interludes—maybe to make up for the shortage of an album's worth of songs. There are a couple of great new ones, though, particularly "Acid Sweeney." There's also a rerecording of **Eyeball**'s "Incontinent of Sex." As usual, the song titles are priceless: "3 Pottery Owls (With Inuendo)," "Mao Tse Tung's Meat Challenge," "HMS Average Nostril." The CD version appends **Eyeball Origami Aftermath,** a 1990 12-inch with a longer version of the album's plodding, super-heavy "Housewife Up Yer Fuckin Arse Music" and a remix of elements from the album that leads into a cut-up of the theme from *Rhoda;* it also has completely messed-up indexing (maybe the band's habit of sticking a million fake endings in every song confused a technician).

Stretchheads' final recorded bow was the six-song **Barbed Anal Exciter** EP. Compared to their earlier records, it's more barbed, just as anal and not quite as exciting. The sound is thick and friction-filled, but the band seems to have slowed down a little, and the inferior rerecording of **Eyeball**'s "New New Thing in Egypt" is unnecessary. If it were the only Stretchheads record it'd be priceless, but if you've heard another one you've heard a better one. [ddw]

STRETFORD

Target EP7 (Unclean) 1993
Zerox Love EP7 (Rise) 1993
Crossing the Line (Unclean) 1995

Austin's Stretford has often been accused of affecting its time-honored Britpunk sound a tad too efficiently, right down to the "whoa-oh" harmonies and thickly accented vocals. But the truth is Stretford major domo Carl Normal is an actual ex-pat who was at it well before the Green Day–inspired renaissance. The men and women of Stretford (named for the English town of Normal's birth) are unapologetically classicist drill-bit pop-punksters, with rolling horn charts and singularly frantic hooks that hearken back to Buzzcocks, Stiff Little Fingers and the Saints. Preceded by a pair of modest 7-inchers, **Crossing the Line** suffers from typically muted no-budget sound quality but compensates with catchy songwriting. Stuttered riffs and simple bashing rub up against sweet vocals on songs like "Wonder Girl" and "Zerox Love" (not a mistake, just a trademark necessity), while Normal shows off more refined melodic flair on the balladic "Silhouette" and the swinging, horn-laden "I Used to Know." Not earthshaking stuff, but it's more than likable. The band that made the record no longer exists, but this is a good thing, as the new lineup—with Normal switching to guitar, a new bassist replacing him and a three-piece horn section where there was once a lone trumpeter—is far better, its freewheeling, almost sumptuous live shows offering the promise of more fully realized future recordings. Austin scene trivia: Stretford's original horn player was eventual Sincola vocalist Rebecca Cannon, while one of the current trumpeters is Jennings Crawford of the Wannabes. [jc]

See also *Sincola.*

DAN STUART

Can o' Worms (Monkey Hill) 1995

As long as Green on Red kept going, there was no real reason that vocalist/songwriter Dan Stuart (unlike guitarist Chuck Prophet) should pursue a solo career. But after six records as a fully operative band and four more (plus a live LP and a best-of) with various auxiliary members, Green on Red finally fizzled out. Stuart logged a couple of depressing, dope-sodden years in Spain then reemerged, drug free and many pounds lighter, with **Can o' Worms.** Using producer/bassist J. D. Foster, guitarist extraordinaire Jon Dee Graham and ex–Poi Dog Pondering drummer Darren Hess as his backing band, Stuart runs through an eleven-song set of desert blues-pop that's both memorable and moodily transgressive. The stirring "La Pasionara" is genuine flamenco soul (complete with *guitarrón* and gypsy violin); "Who Needs More" is an ironic, roughly endearing bit of love talk, and "Waterfall" shines and shimmers along a three-guitar tremolo. The record doesn't exactly reinvent the edgy roots-rock wheel, but it's several notches better than Green on Red's final efforts. The time off and the ugly dose of real life definitely did Stuart's art some restorative good. [jc]

STYLE COUNCIL

See *Paul Weller.*

SUDDENLY, TAMMY!

Suddenly, Tammy! (spinART) 1993
(We Get There When We Do.) (Warner Bros.) 1995

Rejecting orthodoxy in rock is both commendable and modern, but defying standards does not necessarily provide a key to anything better. So while it's true this brother-sister-high-school-pal trio from Lancaster, Pennsylvania, hasn't got a guitar in its piano-based lineup (beating Ben Folds to the record racks by several years), Suddenly, Tammy! is ultimately less notable for what it is than what it's not.

The overly polite indie-label debut sidesteps the likely Carole King comparisons, mostly because the delicate melodies aren't memorable enough and Beth Sorrentino hasn't got that strong or distinctive a voice. (She is, however, a skillful pianist.) Lacking the cynical gloss of the mainstream pop to which it aspires—as well as the idealistic eccentricity of rock's underground—the self-produced **Suddenly, Tammy!** offers only the aesthetic paradox of an attractive bore.

(We Get There When We Do.) exchanges the debut's uncertain goals for a tiresome fit of arty adulthood, using delicate watercolors rather than bright fingerpaints. Ken Heitmueller's fretless bass is a tip-off of the elevated ambition borne out in the elliptical songs; produced by Warne Livesey, the album is precious in both word and sound. Wielding her soprano confidently while her bandmates take a more prominent role in the arrangements, Sorrentino places the enigmatic lyrics like a sculptor, making good use of natural imagery in "Snowman," "River, Run" and "Beautiful Dream" before stumbling into the affected realism of "I just finished braiding my hair/My head's been wet all day." Back to the showers. [i]

See also *Lilys.*

SUEDE

Suede (nude/Columbia) 1993
The Drowners EP (nude/Columbia) 1993
Stay Together EP (UK nude) 1994

LONDON SUEDE

Stay Together EP (nude/Columbia) 1994
dog man star (nude/Columbia) 1994
New Generation EP (UK nude) 1995
Trash EP (UK nude) 1996

MCALMONT & BUTLER

The Sound of . . . McAlmont & Butler (UK Virgin) 1995
(Hut/Gyroscope) 1996

In Britain's 1992–93 alternapop playing field, still full of anonymous, asexual shoegazer outfits and imported American grunge, Suede moved quickly to fill a power vacuum with spark, spunk and androgyny in the grand tradition of Bowie and the Smiths. The London quartet generated such hot and heavy hype that Suede had been on the cover of *Melody Maker* before its first single (the luscious, muscled glam-pop of "The Drowners," with its none-too-ambiguous lyrics, "We kiss in his room to a popular tune," a bit of sexual image-mongering reflected in what appears to be a gay kiss on the first album's cover) was even released.

Although some backlash was inevitable, Suede's eponymous debut deserved the enthusiasm. Brash Baudelaire-in-waiting Brett Anderson sighed and wailed with startling presence and overt emotion—Bowie, Bolan, and (Kate) Bush all wrapped in one—but what gives the record its backbone is guitarist Bernard Butler's painterly pyrotechnics, a controlled flashiness—alternating melancholic delicacy and tangy crunch—that connects the dots back between Johnny Marr and Mick Ronson. Raunchy rippers like "Animal Nitrate" and "Metal Mickey" balance the brooding balladry of "Pantomime Horse" and "Sleeping Pills."

Like no band since the Smiths, Suede saves many of its most memorable tunes for release only as extra tracks on singles. The belated US **The Drowners** EP collects four of the best of these early B-sides, most notably the legendary, exquisitely obsessive "My Insatiable One," soaring "To the Birds" and "He's Dead," shot through with Butler's searing, almost Hendrixian leads.

Before getting around to a second album, the band (credited as the London Suede in America from this point on due to the usual conflicting claims crapola, this time with a female solo artist in Washington, DC) crafted an excellent, elaborately arranged stand-alone single, "Stay Together." The US release of the same name has five B-sides, including "Dolly" and the killer ballad "High Rising."

With fickle punters' attention having shifted to even newer upstarts like Oasis and Elastica (an early incarnation of Suede featured the latter's Justine Frischmann, Anderson's erstwhile paramour), **dog man star** had to get along commercially on its considerable musical merits rather than the band's momentum. Suede offers more densely dramatic rockers—the thunderous "We Are the Pigs," the aching "Heroine" and the terrific, tawdry "This Hollywood Life"—but the arrangements and production (again by Ed Buller) are far more sophisticated, incorporating horns and strings. "Daddy's Speeding" has an orchestrated Beatles feel; the final four tracks evince substantial evolution, using spare piano motifs and acoustic guitar to underscore Anderson's vocal histrionics, peaking on the Floydian "Asphalt World" and the epic closer, "Still Life." An absolutely superb disc.

Talented but introverted, Butler quit Suede immediately before **dog man star**'s release. (The guitarist resurfaced in '95 as half of a diverse and fascinating '70s rock/soul duo with falsetto singer David McAlmont.) Riding out the near-calamity of Butler's departure, the band hired a tender seventeen-year-old—the previously unknown Richard Oakes—to fill his glittering guitar shoes. While in live performance the youngster was content to display his mastery of the Butler sound (and image—he's a dead ringer for his predecessor), his debut recordings—two new tracks, both co-written by Oakes and Anderson, on the UK "New Generation" CD single (not the EP)—bode well for Suede's flamboyant future. [gef]

See also *Elastica*.

SUFI

See *A.R.Kane*.

SUGAR

Copper Blue (Rykodisc) 1992
A Good Idea EP (Rykodisc) 1992
If I Can't Change Your Mind EP (Rykodisc) 1992
Beaster EP (Rykodisc) 1993
File Under: Easy Listening (Rykodisc) 1994
Your Favorite Thing EP (Rykodisc) 1994
Besides (Rykodisc) 1995

BOB MOULD

Workbook (Virgin) 1989
Black Sheets of Rain (Virgin) 1990
Poison Years (Virgin) 1993
Egoverride EP (Rykodisc) 1996
Bob Mould (Rykodisc) 1996

BUZZ HUNGRY

Fried Like a Man (Engine) 1994
At the Hands of Our Intercessors (Compulsiv) 1995

HÜSKER DÜ

Everything Falls Apart and More (Rhino) 1993
The Living End (Warner Bros.) 1994

DÜ HÜSKERS

The Twin Cities Replay Zen Arcade (Synapse) 1993

MERCYLAND

No Feet on the Cowling (Tupelo) 1989
Enter the Crafty Bear EP7 (Planned Obsolescence) 1991
Spillage (Rykodisc) 1994

Rock musicians have mid-life crises just like everyone else, they simply have them earlier and deal with them by unplugging and disclosing heretofore untapped sensitivity—which is certainly more credible than buying a fancy sports car and a toupee. Having weathered such a creative predicament in the wake of Hüsker Dü's 1988 implosion, Minneapolis singer/guitarist Bob Mould left town and retreated to the insularity of solo twilight on a pair of albums that revealed both his disdain for the rock merry-go-round and his profound personal misery. When he regained his bearings, Mould was, impressively, able to rejoin the fray—as leader (a term he abjures) of Sugar—at just about the spot Hüsker Dü would have reached had *that* trio continued to exist.

Both **Workbook** and **Black Sheets of Rain** are psychological trials played out in public. On the former, style-breaking, mostly acoustic album (recorded with a rhythm section and cellist Jane Scarpantoni), Mould shows little compunction about airing his personal demons, but his unfettered approach is largely stymied by the overly tasteful playing of drummer Anton Fier and bassist Tony Maimone. As a result, raw passion sometimes cooks down into singer/songwriter mush. The record works best when Mould lets a little optimism unknit his brow, or at least his musical horizon ("See a Little Light," "Heartbreak a Stranger," "Dreaming, I Am").

The disarray of **Black Sheets of Rain**—which could be an overheard session of exceedingly bellicose primal scream territory—sounds like an overly sensitive reaction to accusations of having gone soft. He's back to electric guitar—but rather than an impenetrable wall of sound, Mould hangs a thin, opaque sheet of distorted riffage, an accompaniment that proves difficult to stomach after a few soundalike tunes. Likewise, the bilious contents of songs like "Disappointed" and "Out of Your Life" would probably have better been saved for wee-hour answering machine messages. **Poison Years** compiles the highlights of both albums, appending a non-LP item and five live tracks, including an unblinking version of Richard Thompson's "Shoot Out the Lights."

After another retrenchment, Mould emerged and—abetted by bassist David Barbe (formerly of Athens local heroes Mercyland) and drummer Malcolm Travis (a veteran of such Boston combos as the Zulus and Human Sexual Response)—formed Sugar, a band that allowed his bottled-up angst to gush forth with geyser-like intensity. With **Copper Blue,** Mould reclaimed his role as exemplar of ear-splitting power-pop (or is that melodic bludgeon-rock?), tearing through an array of galvanizing love songs ("Changes," the lust-as-sacrament "A Good Idea") with audible relish. Even though the kinder, gentler Mould is capable of writing a song as achingly pretty as "If I Can't Change Your Mind" (which could easily become a hit for Wynonna Judd), he's no less likely to turn his volume knob clear to the right, and Travis' sternum-thumping beats encourage that impulse to a great degree. **Copper Blue** has but one dark interlude, but it's also the album's most powerful: "The Slim," a harrowing tale of a lover lost to AIDS, matches the emotional pain with the visceral sonic ache caused by collisions between slow-moving glaciers of dissonance.

In terms of sound, that song pointed the way to **Beaster,** a howling six-track statement of rage-through-ritual that straddles ecstatic spirituality and outright blasphemy. On songs like "J.C. Auto," Mould's crescendoing wails (both vocal and amp-derived) are thoroughly riveting; his bandmates maintain just enough structure to allow for lifejacket-free navigation, but the waters are certainly choppy. A powerful expression, and not for the squeamish. The other post–**Copper Blue** EPs augment album tracks with previously unreleased material: **If I Can't Change Your Mind** exists in no fewer than three distinct versions, each with a different trio of B-sides, the best of which includes BBC radio session versions of "The Slim" and "Where Diamonds Are Halos."

File Under: Easy Listening takes a step or two back toward pop convention. But while the mood is still predominantly ebullient, Mould is more likely to pepper his melodies with barbs: the amorous "Gift" is veined with note-bending screeches, and even the beach-blanket singalong "Your Favorite Thing" pumps up the volume to levels lovebirds might have trouble nuzzling to. There are signs of burnout, however: neither "Gee Angel" nor "Granny Cool" rise above sketchbook status, with Mould seemingly content to bash out a soaring chord progression and coast home from there. He even revisits the bedsit gloom that inundated his **Poison Years** on tracks like the brooding "Panama City Motel," which can't be a good sign. The rasp inherent in Barbe's contribution—an anti-corporate middle-finger called "Company Book"—makes for a nice contrast, though. (The four-song EP of **Your Favorite Thing** contains another Barbe tune, "Frustration.")

With rumors of an impending split on the horizon, Sugar released **Besides,** a compilation that raids the band's considerable backlog of B-sides (hence the title). While a fair number of the cuts are alternate or live versions of songs available elsewhere, the seventeen-track collection does touch on some less-traveled terrain. Mould rages with typical isolationist fury on "Mind Is an Island" and the jaggedly accusatory "And You Tell Me," while Barbe (normally the inveterate noisemonger) cools things down with a gorgeously melodic "Where Diamonds Are Halos." The capper is a titanic version of the Who's "Armenia City in the Sky" (long a staple of the band's live set), which trails a dayglo jetstream that's impossible to avoid getting swept up in. Initial pressings of the album included a bonus full-length live CD, recorded before an adoring Minneapolis crowd, that reveals Sugar's torrid intensity as well as its inability to shift gears in concert. While hard-edged songs like "Company Book" and the instrumental "Clownmaster" are rendered absolutely crushing, more subtle numbers (like "Gee Angel" and "Changes") lose all their texture and bleed into an undifferentiated roar.

Apparently soured on the craving for democracy that led him to form Sugar, Mould dissolved the band in late 1995 and picked up his solo career in pretty much the same dour spot he left it off. Many of the songs—a majority, in fact—on **Bob Mould** betray the degree to which the ever-popular tortured-artist effect has affected him. Dealing with topics like his own misunderstood genius and the sorry state of his industry ("Egoverride," "I Hate Alternative Rock") might be good therapy for Mould, but they don't do much to enlighten listeners.

While in Sugar, Barbe served concurrently as de facto frontman of Georgia's Buzz Hungry, a significantly surlier aggregation that walks a tightrope tautly stretched between the burnished Steve Albini axis and the more frayed structures common to local sound-blasters like, say, the Bar-B-Q Killers. **Fried Like a Man** wastes no time in setting up the trio's agenda, seeing as it lurches straight into "The Beer Commercial," a rancorous indictment of . . . well, just about everything modern society has to offer. Barbe's thin, arid voice works just fine in that sort of declamatory context, but when the band downshifts for a prettier tune like "When Diamonds Are Halos" (recorded in superior, rougher form by Sugar), his deficiencies as a frontman are laid bare.

At the Hands of Our Intercessors is more of a group effort; drummer Brooks Carter dots the landscape with a handful of textured instrumentals ("Vomit Ball" is a particular favorite). The tone of the disc isn't that different from its predecessor; it even kicks off with "White Sky," another list of grievances that includes "a plethora of mediocre rock bands" among our universal woes. Barbe, however, sounds a little less tightly wound, which allows him to sustain vocal melodies for more than a bar or two before launching into gut-wrenching screams. A surf-rock rewrite of the traditional "There Is a Time" benefits most from the restraint, but the most pleasant surprise comes from new bassist/guitarist Eric Sales, who checks in with the stellar Who-styled "Black Hole Soul."

Besides a tribute edition of **Zen Arcade** (in complete and correct sequence) made by two dozen Minneapolis/St. Paul bands (including Walt Mink, Arcwelder, Hammerhead, God's Favorite Band and the Blue Up?), the glorious memory of Hüsker Dü was refreshed in the '90s by **Everything Falls Apart and More,** a reissue of the band's 1982 album repackaged to include some early single tracks (like the machine-gun thrasher "Statues"), and a terrific live set, **The Living End,** recorded in 1987 on the Hüskers' final tour. Likewise, **Spillage** is a vivid and exciting requiem for Mercyland, Barbe's energetic punk-pop trio, which broke up in 1991. [dss]

See also *Jackonuts; TPRG.*

SUGARCUBES

Life's Too Good (Elektra) 1988
Here Today, Tomorrow Next Week! (Elektra) 1989
Illur Arfur! (UK One Little Indian) 1989
Box of 12-inch singles (UK One Little Indian) 1990
Box of 7-inch singles (UK One Little Indian) 1990
Box of 6 CDs [CD] (UK One Little Indian) 1990
Stick Around for Joy (Elektra) 1992
It's-It (Elektra) 1992

The shock of the new that attended the Sugarcubes' unprecedented first album launched the extraordinary Icelandic quintet into the international arena with acceleration to spare. Behind Björk Gudmundsdóttir's unmistakable vocals, the band busted stylistic moves the likes of which had never been heard; alien precepts (singer Einar Örn's trumpet among them), batty lyrics and abundant creative energy pushed it past the limits of ordinary Anglo-American rock. After **Life's Too Good, Here Today, Tomorrow Next Week!** was, inexorably, a disappointment (innovation, after all, is only innovation the first time), carrying the group sideways in an unwarranted effort to meet the rest of the world halfway. (**Illur Arfur!** is that second album sung in Icelandic. The three format-specific British collections repackage the band's early non-LP catalogue.)

The Sugarcubes continue heading the wrong way on **Stick Around for Joy,** bringing producer Paul Fox in to further polish the sound into a pleasing but unexceptional mix of guitar, keyboards and the intricate, hard-hitting rhythms that always gave the band its dance credibility. Nonetheless, Björk's singing is shapely, passionate and willfully bizarre; she carries the album pretty much on her own. (Not surprisingly, she was on the verge of launching a solo career.) Örn's accented color commentary in the lusterless "Gold," the gripping "Hetero Scum" and the angry "Leash Called Love" is mundane and extraneous to his bandmate's ecstatic invocations; she's clearly better off on her own.

As Björk readied her solo debut, the Sugarcubes iced their career as a band (a seemingly permanent situation) with **It's-It,** a radical remix retrospective of essential (and not-so-essential) songs from all three albums. More a companion collection than a proper walk down the Sugarcubes' memory lane, **It's-It** does a disservice to the debut's "Birthday" in two completely different directions, and disassembles "Blue Eyed Pop" and the second record's "Regina" to the point of total torpor. But Todd Terry does find a way to replate "Gold," and Tony Humphries tones "Leash on Love" up with merry house accessories, so **It's-It** is not a total loss. [i]

See also *Björk; TPRG.*

SUGARSMACK

Top Loader (Invisible) 1993
Spanish Riffs EP (Yesha) 1995

A couple of years after North Carolina's rugged Fetchin Bones ran out of musical hooch, raucous singer Hope Nicholls was drafted by Invisible Records owner/Pigface ringleader Martin Atkins and took part in his band's **Fook** tour, a roving calamity documented on the **Truth Will Out** album. Continuing their association, Atkins co-produced (with Mark Walk, now of Ruby) and released a record for Sugarsmack, Nicholls' quintet with former Bones guitarist Aaron Pitkin on bass and organ. **Top Loader** is a dense, evocative muzz of angry '60s/'70s psychedelic distortion that never obscures Nicholls' raspy Janis-Joplin-in-the-'80s vocals or the firmly shaped songs, some of which reek delightfully of leftover acid, from San Francisco hippiedom to Roky Erickson brainfry. While the band shifts styles like a restless channel surfer ("Freak" is a danceclub loop; the rocking "B.L.A.S.T." takes it to the factory floor), Atkins and Walk get it all down with enough subsonic consistency to make the album an invigorating, enveloping experience. "Boomerang" drives straight into the darkness with a sinuous guitar riff and Nicholls' "metaphysical highway" lyrics, while Sugarsmack grabs hold of a passing Stooges punk groove for "Pissed Off," inciting her to a thrilling show of extroversion. For contrast, the long, go-nowhere "Seven Seas" patiently absorbs attention like a public access infomercial, giving **Top Loader** the various cycles needed to complete its unstable mission. "Bring on the UFOs!"

Spinning out of Chicago's gravitational pull, Sugarsmack re-emerged on **Spanish Riffs,** five songs (plus tape-chopping "interludes") clearly produced by Caleb Southern. Singing carefully in this better-focused, more illuminated and conscious-sounding blast of mock aggression, Nicholls balances the angular but restrained atmos-pop muzz of "Acorn" with bursts of unreconstructed wildness, like the sax-tooting "Creme Horn" and the funky feedback of "Fishnet," that owe equal debts to Pylon and old Butthole Surfers. The EP's high point, "Stuff," finds her working the line "I *need* more stuff!" over in voices that shift from an urgent whisper to a delirious shriek. [i]

See also *Pigface.*

SUICIDAL TENDENCIES

Suicidal Tendencies (Frontier) 1983
Join the Army (Caroline) 1987
How Will I Laugh Tomorrow . . . When I Can't Even Smile Today (Epic) 1988
Controlled by Hatred/Feel Like Shit . . . Deja Vu (Epic) 1989
Lights . . . Camera . . . Revolution (Epic) 1990
The Art of Rebellion (Epic) 1992
Still Cyco After All These Years (Epic) 1993
Suicidal for Life (Epic) 1994

INFECTIOUS GROOVES

The Plague That Makes Your Booty Move . . . It's the Infectious Grooves (Epic) 1991
Sarsippius' Ark (Epic) 1993
Groove Family Cyco: Snapped Lika Mutha (BHG Musick/550 Music/Epic) 1994

CYCO MIKO

Lost My Brain! (Once Again) (Epic) 1996

MY HEAD

Endless Bummer (Capitol) 1996

One of the first hardcore bands to shrug off the distinction between punk and metal, Suicidal Tendencies—formed in Venice, California, in 1982 as a personal soapbox for fiery singer Mike Muir—made its intentions to not be contained by genre or expectations known early by selling scads of its first album. Muir's obvious politics ("Fascist Pig," "I Shot the Devil" [aka "I Shot Reagan"], "Memories of Tomorrow") and wily personality ("Possessed," "Won't Fall in Love Today") make **Suicidal Tendencies** a classic. "Institutionalized," a unique, devastating centerpiece, is among the era's quintessential expressions of teen dislocation, converting generation gap misunderstandings into a complete communications breakdown.

Pumped by success, Muir then led the group through a period of uneven progress that, if nothing else, upheld the intense band's energy and animosity level. The Motörhead-ish **Join the Army** straddles ominous war-pigs power and hyperspeed punk; **How Will I Laugh Tomorrow** is an articulate speedcore rocket. The 1989 **Controlled by Hatred** has two edits of the previous album's title track plus seven new songs in an unchecked metallic vein.

"I'd rather feel like shit than be full of shit," Muir roars like a wounded animal on **Lights . . . Camera . . . Revolution,** an electric storm so loud and bracing that tracks seem to echo over the silence after they end. Over the frenzy, Muir covers his standard alienation-independence-loneliness topics with typical intensity, adding vague thoughts about political action ("Give It Revolution"), the atmosphere of violence ("Disco's Out, Murder's In") and televangelism ("Send Me Your Money").

Using a session drummer to complete the otherwise fixed lineup of guitarists Rocky George and Mike Clark and bassist Robert Trujillo (following the departure of longtime hammerer R. J. Herrera), Muir shifts onto a more mainstream sizzle-rock plane—Aerosmith crossed with Danzig—for **The Art of Rebellion,** sharply produced by Peter Collins (Rush, Alice Cooper, Indigo Girls). Daring to sound more approachable and ordinary than ever before, Suicidal gallops and kicks as hard (but not as fast) as ever when called upon to, but otherwise entertains a full gamut of modern dynamic possibilities. Parts of "I'll Hate You Better" could be the Spin Doctors; "Monopoly on Sorrow" amazingly finds room for acoustic guitar, cello and carefully melodic singing; with fretless bass and harmony vocals, the T.Rexy "I Wasn't Meant to Feel This/Asleep at the Wheel" is even more restrained and intricate than that. No such messing afflicts the lyrical obsessions: Muir's personal vision ("an emptiness so full . . . screaming inside myself") remains unaffected. Typical of the album's altered orthodoxy, "Can't Stop" intentionally references the paranoia, suffering and dramatic narration of "Institutionalized" with shockingly winsome lyrics: reaching for a comparison to being "emotionally paralyzed, light-headed," Muir tries "You know, kinda like when you gotta sneeze? The relief it brings?" Impressive in its ambition, disappointing in its compromise.

Culminating a decade-long grudge against the unassailable independent label that issued **Suicidal Tendencies,** Muir moved to replace it with **Still Cyco After All These Years,** a song-for-song remake that benefits from the new band's skin-tight instrumental skill but otherwise brings nothing new or especially modernized to the (turn)table. (While at it, he covers two songs from **Join the Army** and adds the newly written "Don't Give Me Your Nothin'.") In a trade ad at the time, Muir offered this guarded explanation for the quixotic exercise: "Why did we record our first album? In the early '80s we hated everything we heard . . . **Suicidal Tendencies** was our response to the 'new music' of the '80s. Why re-record the album? Because history repeats itself."

The singer pokes fun at stylistic slumming in the opening of **Suicidal for Life:** "Invocation," a funky mush groove over which he does a radio rap, smoothly transmutes into the wildly cranking thrash of Mike Clark's "Don't Give a Fuck!" That sets the tone for a relentlessly raging explosion on which Muir seems to have discovered a dictionary of bad words and is having a blast trying 'em all in sentences. Don't expect much airplay for songs like "No Bullshit," "Fucked Up Just Right!," "No Fuck'n Problem" and "Suicyco Muthafucka." The restrained, malevolently gothic ("fucked up feelings kill") "What Else Could I Do?" relieves the charged atmosphere midway, and "Love Vs. Loneliness" takes it way down at the end, but otherwise the ferocious five (with drummer Jimmy DeGrasso in the house) stay hard and down to kill on this album, reclaiming their primacy as upholders of the hardcore faith. Closing off with a recommendation to question authority, Muir turns out the lights with the not-exactly-profound observation that "cool is only 3 letters away from fool."

Joined by Suicidal bassist Trujillo and punk-funk pals (including, on **The Plague That Makes Your Booty Move,** Jane's Addiction/Porno for Pyros drummer Stephen Perkins), Muir also leads Infectious Grooves. Rather than adhere to a clear-cut formula, the group moves it around from 'core-tinged rhythmic grooves to soulful metal to funk fusion to flat-out rock on the first album, which tucks in bits of silly dialogue and other digressions—Trujillo's acoustic slide playing on "Infectious Blues," the ska beat and piano jazz sections of "Monster Skank"—as well. Unpredictable but not so far from Muir's usual noise to be a major challenge for ST faithful, **The Plague** clears the decks of untried ideas but, other than the good-natured party lyrics, doesn't bond them into any sort of cohesive whole.

Infectious Grooves' second infection, **Sarsippius' Ark,** digs into the band's organic Fishbone stew with phenomenally entertaining relish. Pulled together from various sources (1989 demos with entirely different sidemen, first album outtakes, a '92 LA concert, new sessions) and stitched up by spoken bits from a Richard Pryor–sounding fictional music biz narrator, **Ark** is more unified and consistent than either of the Grooves' other discs. David Bowie's "Fame" and Led Zeppelin's "Immigrant Song" make perfect covers for the quintet's furious once-overs; such hot'n'funky originals as "Savor da Flavor," "Don't Stop, Spread the Jam!" and "Slo-Motion Slam" strike a blistering balance of motion and metal that's easy to catch and hard to shake.

Hooking another new drummer to **Ark**'s core foursome (with guitarists Dean Pleasants and Adam Siegel), Muir and Trujillo allow a bit of lyrical and musical backsliding into ST terrain on **Groove Family**

Cyco. Apart from the central hybrid of searing guitar punk and ultra-hard funk, the album displays the band's willingness to go the pure rock route on straight-ahead 4/4 tracks like "Frustrated Again" and "Do What I Tell Ya!" and parts of "Made It." Ideal for those frustrated by the Red Hot Chili Peppers' revisionism in the '90s, the album pumps up the jam with a functional and fun balance of popping bass, syncopated rhythms and Marshall stacks of power chords. See "Rules Go Out the Window" for the record's most clearly expressed statement of purpose. (Siegel, ex-Excel, subsequently put out a record as the leader of a new trio called My Head, whose bassist Dave Silva was in a pre–Pearl Jam band with Eddie Vedder. Nothing like the guitarist's Infectious Grooves work, **Endless Bummer** is smart and engaging alternative rock with memorable tunes and a '70s/'90s personality all its own.)

As if two recording careers weren't enough, Muir—billing himself as Cyco Miko—began 1996 with a solo album. **Lost My Brain! (Once Again)** is, of all things, an old-fashioned punk record of mid-tempo rhythm-guitar rock (ex-Pistol Steve Jones is one of three barre-chorders on hand) that has none of speedcore's double-bass-drum gallops, chrome production sheen or blazing riffery. When Jones cranks up a solo in "All Kinda Crazy," his licks are strictly from the Chuck Berry textbook; Dave Kushner's heated wah-wah exhibition in "Gonna Be Alright" is Van Halen–era rawk. Ending the album with an inclusive stump-speech song ("Cyco Miko Wants You"), Muir comes off as Mister Rogers for the disaffected generation: "If you've got a good heart/And always back up what you say/If you can set your own agenda/Then come over my way." And don't be a Don't Be. [i]

See also *Korn; TPRG.*

SULTANS OF PING F.C.

Stupid Kid EP (UK Rhythm King/Epic) 1992
U Talk Too Much EP (UK Rhythm King/Epic) 1992
Casual Sex in the Cineplex (UK Rhythm King/Epic) 1993
Teenage Punks From Planet Sexy EP (UK Rhythm King/Epic) 1993
Michiko EP (UK Rhythm King/Epic) 1993

SULTANS OF PING

Teenage Drug (UK Rhythm King/Epic) 1994

SULTANS

Good Year for Trouble (UK Rhythm King/Epic) 1996

Every decade needs its rowdy goofball gang of piss-taking cross-dressing hard-drinking prats willing to do anything to have a good musical time and a few laughs along the rock'n'roll way. (It does, doesn't it?) The leading candidate for '90s honors so far is Cork's Sultans of Ping F.C. (now just the Sultans)—not a soccer team exactly, but a garrulous Irish gang who pal around with and sing about Shonen Knife while otherwise striking a sonic posture somewhere between past contenders John Otway, Tenpole Tudor, the post-Rotten Pistols and the New York Dolls. (Plus Carter the Unstoppable Sex Machine, Billy Bragg and—until a recent Stooges push—the Waterboys or someone wimpy like that.) In other words, ludicrously brilliant.

U Talk Too Much previews the first album's best track (the rousing, disgusted and catchy "You Talk Too Much") and also boasts the giddy "Japanese Girls," "Robo Cop" and "Armitage Shanks," which predates the Green Day song that misspells the same toilet manufacturer's name by three years. **Casual Sex in the Cineplex** romps further through such silly shoutalong yobbo charmers as "Kick Me With Your Leather Boots," the viciously funny Fall parody of "Where's Me Jumper?" and the intentionally nauseating (with strings) pill-popping domesticity of "Let's Go Shopping." Dispatching another personal affront in song, the Sultans of Ping rip apart a "Stupid Kid," cheer on a favorite player ("Clitus Clarke"), offer a loopy soccer anthem in "Give Him a Ball (And a Yard of Grass)" and make a pit stop for the superficially pretty pop of "Veronica," which announces "you are what you eat" and then follows the omnivorous thought: "that means you're everything in the world/Everything edible/That means you're everything in the fridge." Damn straight. [i]

SUN CITY GIRLS

Sun City Girls (Placebo) 1984
Grotto of Miracles (Placebo) 1986
Midnight Cowboys From Ipanema (Breakfast Without Meat) 1986 (Amarillo) 1994
Horse Cock Phepner (Placebo) 1987
And So the Dead Tongue Sang EP (Pulp) 1989
Torch of the Mystics (Majora) 1990 (Tupelo) 1994
Dawn of the Devi (Majora) 1991
Live From Planet Boomerang (Majora) 1991
Three Fake Female Orgasms EP (Majora) 1992
You're Never Alone With a Cigarette EP (Majora) 1992
Eye Mohini EP (Majora) 1992
Napoleon & Josephine EP (Majora) 1992 (Can. Scratch) 1996
Instruments of Torture EP (Poon Village) 1993
Kaliflower (Abduction) 1993
Valentines From Matahari (Abduction) 1993
Piasa . . . Devourer of Men (Abduction) 1994
Jacks Creek (Abduction) 1994
Apna Desh 78 (Deep Eddy Grammaphone) 1995
Dante's Disneyland Inferno (Abduction) 1996
300,003 Cross Dressers From Beyond the Rig Veda (Abduction) 1996

EDDY DETROIT

The Philosopher's Journey (Pan) 1987

From (semi) humble beginnings in the realm of post–Butthole Surfers acid skronk, this determinedly hallucinatory Arizona trio has propelled itself, cartoon character style, against the furthest reaches of world music. Employing both real experience (members have spent a good deal of time in Southeast Asia, going so far as to gig on a cruise ship in Indonesia) and pharmaceutically aided astral projection, the Sun City Girls have staked out a singular patch of polluted ozone, all the better to rain down interstellar transmissions on the earthbound multitudes. And like other extraterrestrial phenomena, their messages arrive in random sequence, often many years after they were sent.

The trio's self-titled debut ranges from raga-rock to saxophone squawk, the fractious pieces convening into coherent groupings beneath Alan Bishop's avant-political rantings. At times utterly riveting ("Your Bible Set off My Smoke Alarm"), at times impossibly muddled ("Metaphors in a Mixmaster"), it's an imposing bow. By **Grotto of Miracles,** the trio had crept considerably closer to the edge, even as it left noise-for-noise's-sake (aside from the Arto Lindsay–damaged "Black Weather Shoes") behind. While Rick

Bishop's guitar playing is the band's most user-friendly entrance point (particularly on airy pieces like the Wes Montgomery–styled "In a Lesbian Meadow"), it's brother Alan, nominally the bass player, who proves the MVP, pitching in on a plethora of plundered ethnic instruments. (**Midnight Cowboys From Ipanema,** culled from a series of 1986 recordings and originally issued on cassette, is little more than an extended practical joke furthered by co-conspirator Gregg Turkington of Zip Code Rapists "fame." The album sandwiches ten straight-but-intentionally-incompetent covers of slough-bucket hits (like "Midnight at the Oasis" and Rush's "Fly by Night") between niblets of giddily abstruse performance art. Strictly a one-spin disc.)

Horse Cock Phepner revisits the wild-eyed skedaddling of the debut, upping the vulgarity level on the Tourette's-touched "Nancy Reagan" and dosing the proceedings with prankster politicking reminiscent of the Yippie heyday (Tuli Kupferberg's "C.I.A. Man" even gets a run-through). Unfortunately, too much of the album is given over to unsculpted blocks of found sound and purloined conversation samples stitched together with the enthusiastic schlockiness of a junior-high Howard Stern fan. A long "official" recording break (during which the band actually recorded more than a dozen cassette albums) took the Girls back to the fringe, as evidenced by the ethnodelic jazz pirouetting of **Torch of the Mystics.** Titles like "Blue Mambo" and "Esoterica of Abyssinia" may reek of Sears catalogue exotica, but the band never comes across dilettantish. Percussionist Charles Gocher is particularly dexterous with pan-cultural touches, layering African drums beneath melodies gleaned from the Aegean (and vice versa), while Alan Bishop's tarrying (and the conspiracy theories behind songs like "Radar 1941") adds an extraterrestrial dimension.

Dawn of the Devi is even more capricious, telescoping its continent-hopping into discrete patches of utterly dizzying density. "The Kissy Sting" lopes from combative tribal drumming to olde-tyme waltz elegance before disintegrating into a noise-boy hoot. There are pieces that stay on an even keel throughout—"The Court Magicians of Agartha" puts an avant twist on *kroncong* (an Indonesian form of tango music)—but, for the most part, the album's hazy insularity (perfectly captured in a sleeve photo that pictures the trio, back to its audience, lost in the throes of an improv high) doesn't kowtow to stylistic neatniks. The two-record **Live From Planet Boomerang** is less successful, in large part due to the presence of two all-but-impenetrable side-long jams. Minus those, the album is considerably better; Rick Bishop picks out a lazy, mariachi-styled melody on "Amazon One," while the entire ensemble (fleshed out with horns and keyboards) shines on a version of Duke Ellington's "The Tap Graveyard" and the strongly Sun Ra–influenced "You Could Be Making History and We're Already Forgetting You."

The six pieces on **Three Fake Female Orgasms** are less concrete, more atmospheric. Although sound-collage building supersedes actual playing on tracks like "The Reflection of a Young Boy Eating From a Can of Dog Food on a Shiny Red X-Mas Ball," the overall effect of the psychic pummel is enormous. Seemingly inspired by some combination of the **Tube Bar Tapes** and Church of the Subgenius, **Napoleon & Josephine** presents a few long stretches of Alan Bishop's roving-reporter pedestrian harangues in you-are-there style. **Instruments of Torture** consists of four improvised pieces ("Nephthys" features some lovely viola playing by Brian Hageman of Thinking Fellers Union Local 282) drawing heavily on the ambience of the Mediterranean, particularly in the blues-tango "Nites of Malta."

The bassist pushes his conspiracy theories to the fore from the beginning of **Kaliflower,** using the grating percussive backdrop of "X + Y = Fuck You" as a foundation for a jaw-dropping diaspora-rap that manages to tie together dozens of holocausts across the ages. He's also the prime mover behind the mournful Gypsy drone of "The Venerable Uncle Tompa" and the purposefully ugly, Stooges-unplugged psychedelia of "Dead Chick in the River." Bracing, to say the least. The closest the trio has come to "rock" in some time—which, truth be told, isn't all *that* close—**Valentines From Matahari** is notable for electrifying the atmosphere (as well as the instruments) on tracks like "Sev Archer," which boasts a Rick Bishop guitar melody that could pass for Dick Dale gone flamenco. The ethnic elements are still firmly in place, as evidenced by Gocher's opulent percussive foray "Black Tent" and the muezzin-like wails that punctuate "Circus Haddam," but such raw materials are most often used in building good old-fashioned walls of noise.

Jacks Creek sets the wayback machine for the mid-nineteenth century, yielding songs like the banjo-and-spoons spookfest "Useless Stillborn." The determinedly pernicious "Jazz Music of the Civil War" recombines martial snare drumming, a harmonica endlessly blowing "Dixie" and square-dance strings into a whole that makes *Deliverance* look like a picnic. The band's penchant for fractured fairy tales is indulged on "Gurnam," which couches ten minutes of UFO chatter in Gabby Hayes (*not* Gibby Haynes—ask your mom) cackling. So out it's in.

Alan Bishop served as part of the backing band for Eddy Detroit, a self-styled post-punk Rod McKuen who croons his wide-eyed psychobabble-cum-poetry over a lite-psych backing reminiscent of a Holiday Inn lounge band tripped-out for the summer of love. [dss]

See also *TPRG.*

SUNDAY ALL OVER THE WORLD

See *King Crimson.*

SUNDAYS

Reading, Writing and Arithmetic (Rough Trade/DGC) 1990
Blind (DGC) 1992

The Sundays burst on the British scene in an artful shimmer of catchy guitar folk-pop, topped off by Harriet Wheeler's enchanting, melody-melting little-girl voice. On the London-based quartet's debut album, David Gavurin builds subtle tension into wonderful tunes like "Can't Be Sure" and "Hideous Towns" by picking out beguiling demi-acoustic guitar figures in songs that ache for the release of a satisfying strum. Elsewhere, minor-key contemplations ("My Finest Hour") evoke a rainy afternoon feel with poetic skill. Unlike other bands in a related vein (the Cocteau Twins, Everything but the Girl, the impending early Cranberries), the Sundays burble with energy—exploding with uplifting sweeps of melodic joy ("Skin & Bones," "I Won"), getting faintly funky ("A Certain Someone"), even raising a cloud of mild guitar smoke now and again. The band's lyrics—bizarre fragments of opaque introspection that reveal themselves slowly in Wheeler's uncommon phrasing—only add to the record's sparkling charms.

The band's artistic growth on **Blind** isn't all for the better. While increased confidence and ambition make Wheeler's singing more technically accomplished, her development from adolescent wonder to adult aplomb deducts some of the band's gravity-defying magic. A change in co-producers from Ray Shulman to engineer Dave Anderson barters finely attenuated atmospheric detail for a richer, more often electrically charged—but less emotionally fulfilling—sound. Beyond a disappointing (in concept *and* execution) cover of the Stones' "Wild Horses," some of the songs compare favorably to the first's most alluring creations, but some crucial element—desire? innocence? invention? joy?—is in too short supply for **Blind** to meet the debut's daunting challenge. This time, the lyrics and melodies skitter off the disc like water on a hot griddle, evaporating without a trace. [i]

SUNDAY'S WELL

See *Blood Oranges.*

SUNDIAL

Other Way Out (UK Tangerine) 1990 (UK UFO) 1991 (UK Acme) 1996
Overspill EP (UK UFO) 1991
Reflecter (Dutch East India Trading) 1992
Fazer EP (UK UFO) 1992 (UFO/Dutch East India Trading) 1993
Return Journey (UK Acme) 1994
Libertine (Beggars Banquet) 1994
Going Down EP (UK Beggars Banquet) 1994
Acid Yantra (Beggars Banquet) 1995
Live Drug (UK Acme) 1996

MODERN ART

Stereoland (UK Color Discs) 1987
All Aboard the Mind Train (Ger. OOD) 1989 (UK Acme) 1994

Amid such peers as the Bevis Frond, Bristol's Seers and such Japanese exponents of new psychedelia as High Rise, Ghost and Fushitsusha, England's Gary Ramon lives in a world of mind expansion and trippy hallucinations, with one ear on today's alternative sounds and the other firmly pointing to the past. The river of music upon which Ramon rides might bring to mind such well-known outfits as Soft Machine, Pink Floyd and early King Crimson but it's bands that have been lost to obscurity—Dark, Astral Navigations, Group 1850, Savage Resurrection—that are of real significance to his work. (In the late '60s and on into the early '70s, England had a sizable population of underground psychedelic bands producing tiny private pressings of their records. Although possibly made without the groups' parents even being aware at the time, records by Tintern Abbey, Moonkyte and the like now fetch absurdly high collectors' prices.)

Modern Art's debut album, **Stereoland,** was the first of Ramon's many records. Limited to a run of three hundred copies, **Stereoland**—in a hand-painted sleeve—contains jangly '60s-influenced pop originals in line with contemporaries like the Bachelor Pad. Recorded by a quartet the following year and released in a German edition of 500, **All Aboard the Mind Train** marks the real start of Ramon's journey. Reeking of lysergic consumption, the album contains original lyrics like "Without a shadow of a doubt/We've got to take this way out/Through the backdoor of our minds/Watching out for these designs" as well as a cover of the Monkees' "Circle Sky." In 1994, Ramon remixed, remastered and re-pressed the record in an edition of five hundred for his own Acme label.

Modern Art became Sun Dial (often Sundial) at the start of the new decade; made as a trio, **Other Way Out** conjures up memories of Pink Floyd's **Piper at the Gates of Dawn** and Nice's **Thoughts of Emerlist Davjack.** Ramon's vocals scream (or whisper, as the case may be) Syd Barrett's influence; Anthony Clough's keyboards, while not bombastic, are reminiscent of the Nice's psychedelic adventures. (Clough also plays flute much in the style of Ian McDonald on King Crimson's early records.) The 1991 UFO edition adds two tracks ("Visitation" and "Other Side"); the Acme version appends three more, bringing the album to a total of eleven songs and an hour in length. Despite its belated release, **Return Journey** was also recorded in 1990; the album includes a cover of "Magic Potion," a 1969 nugget by the Open Mind, and exploratory waves of effect-filled guitar solos.

Reflecter and **Libertine** are career sidesteps. Self-produced as a quartet with guitarist Chris Dalley, bassist Nigel Carpenter and drummer John Pelech, **Reflecter** takes a contemporary Manchester detour, accenting the loudly textured guitar drones and echoey vocals in songs like "I Don't Mind" and "Easy for You" with a brisk and modern dance–influenced tone. (For comparison, check the very different versions of **Reflecter**'s "Slow Motion," "Mind Train" and "Sunstroke" that appear on **Return Journey.**) The **Fazer** EP has "I Don't Mind," a techno house remix of "Easy for You" (retitled "Easy Fazer") and two non-LP tracks.

If **Reflecter** was a minor breach of stylistic faith, though, **Libertine**—a gimmicky-sounding big-budget studio affair with electronics taking a place of honor right behind the guitars—attempts a more radical revamp, nodding toward shoegazer rock and ambient techno, with precious little of what distinguished Ramon's previous work.

Acid Yantra, however, is a fine return to form, as Ramon casts off contemporary musical life for a ride on a hallucinogenic magic carpet. With **Libertine** drummer Craig Adrienne and new bassist Jake Honeywill in tow, Ramon returns happily to the organic simplicity of analog 8-track recording. "Yeah you know what you got to find/And the searching's on your mind/Yeah you're doing fine/All your thoughts are out of line" ("Red Sky")—*these* are the true children of **Aoxomoxoa.** At points, Ramon's fluid, acid-drenched guitar recalls Funkadelic's Eddie Hazel in his "Maggot Brain" glory; elsewhere, his hands are guided by the soul of Jimi Hendrix.

Recorded in London at the band's only live show of 1995, **Live Drug** consists of songs from **Acid Yantra** as well as such earlier items as "Slow Motion," "Fireball" and "Exploding in Your Mind." [mk]

SUNNY DAY REAL ESTATE

Diary (Sub Pop) 1994
Sunny Day Real Estate (Sub Pop) 1995

JEREMY ENIGK

Return of the Frog Queen (Sub Pop) 1996

This Washington foursome, the object of an abundance of next-big-thing excitement at the outset of its brief career, wasted no time giving off contradictory signals of populist intent and elitist values. Sunny Day Real Estate's everyman side prompted the band to craft cinematic, emotionally draining anthems redolent of early U2; its obsession with obscurity begat a strident refusal to give songs "proper" titles: Instead, the series of singles that preceded the band's full-length bow were differentiated only by numerics—"Song #2," "Song #3" . . . straight through to an impressively rich pairing (on their own One Day I Stopped Breathing label) of "Song #8" and "Song #9."

With that mostly (there *are* songs called "47" and "48") out of its system, the band recorded the sweeping **Diary,** an album that's not nearly as confessional in tone as the title might indicate. Still, it's easy to get lost within guitarist Jeremy Enigk's mystic excursions: while not even remotely as gifted a singer, he frequently recalls Van Morrison in his phrasing and mantra-like repetition of key couplets (particularly on the steep trajectories of "Seven" and "Grendel"), not to mention the tangibly spiritual subject matter of tracks like "Song About an Angel." When Enigk announced his conversion to born-again Christianity, the latter aspect began to dominate his songwriting to too great an extent for the other members, and the band split shortly after **Diary** was released. The second album seems to have been cobbled together from demos and such, an (under-)production value that's particularly vexing for a band this dramatically inclined. In 1995, bassist Nate Mendel and drummer William Goldsmith joined Dave Grohl and Pat Smear in Foo Fighters.

Whatever is going on in Enigk's life, his delectable solo debut makes no obvious reference to spirituality of any sort. Following Cardinal's lead towards a rapprochement with psychedelic '60s chamber pop by using strings, horns, harpsichord and harmonies, the multifarious auteur (guitar, bass, drums, keyboards and flawed vocals) dabbles in various idioms on **Return of the Frog Queen** with abundant skill and few specific reference points. (He matches the sound with such quizzically oblique word paintings as "Shade and the Black Hat" and "Lewis Hollow.") Other than some Beatlisms, the record occasionally suggests how Syd Barrett might have sounded had he been able to mount a full-fledged production effort, but there's so much else going on here that any sense of nostalgia quickly evaporates. Magical. [dss/i]

See also *Foo Fighters.*

SUPERCHUNK

Superchunk (Matador) 1990
The Freed Seed EP7 (Merge) 1991
No Pocky for Kitty (Matador) 1991
Tossing Seeds (Singles 89–91) (Merge) 1992
Hit Self-Destruct EP (Aus. Hippy Knight) 1992
On the Mouth (Matador) 1993
Foolish (Merge) 1994
Driveway to Driveway EP (Merge) 1994
On Paper It Made Perfect Sense EP (Aus. Fellaheen) 1994
Incidental Music 1991–95 (Merge) 1995
Here's Where the Strings Come In (Merge) 1995

PORTASTATIC

I Hope Your Heart Is Not Brittle (Merge) 1994
Scrapbook EP (Merge) 1995
Slow Note From a Sinking Ship (Merge) 1995

BRICKS

Winterspring Cassette [tape] (Merge) 1989
A Microphone and a Box of Dirt (Merge) 1993

Although Superchunk has never been revolutionary, the North Carolina quartet has done more to foment the indie-pop revolution than nearly any other band extant, feeding its flames with a steady stream of releases, an incessant appetite for touring and a voracious fandom that's seen it underwrite numerous kindred spirits on its own Merge label. Like missionaries bringing the word to the outback, Superchunk ushered in an era in which ethics and avowed self-determination were just as important as artistic productivity—a stance that's probably influenced far more culturalists than the band's sound. Still, that sound, at once warmly familiar and nervily fresh, bridges old-school power-pop and hardcore, its energetic hooks inviting a pogo-dance resurrection even as the decidedly downbeat lyrics air singer/guitarist Mac McCaughan's quarrels with the world.

After issuing one 1989 single under the moniker Chunk (a name already taken by a New York–based free-improv band led by Samm Bennett), the Chapel Hill foursome embarked upon a journey to the center of the post-hardcore mind, portioning out segments of incurably contagious adrena-pop the way a doting mom doles out citrus to her pack. The first official Superchunk single, 1990's "Slack Motherfucker," proved particularly galvanizing, what with an insurgent chorus ("I'm working . . . but I'm not working for you") tethered to a trebly guitar hook powerful enough to pierce the cerebrum at a hundred paces. The song turns up again on **Superchunk,** where it's easily the best track. McCaughan's bug-eyed yelping conveys plentiful passion throughout, but other than the indie-rock call-to-arms "My Noise" ("It is my life, it is my voice, it is stupid, it is my noise"), it's hard to deduce what all the commotion is about.

No Pocky for Kitty is significantly more fully realized, not only in the surfeit of indelible hooks—the opening notes of "Skip Steps 1 & 3" set the insistent tone—but in the emergence of McCaughan's opaque yet curiously coercive lyric expression. Without actually saying much of anything concrete, he manages to effectively convey paranoia (in the stuttering "Cast Iron") and romantic obsession (the brooding "Seed Toss," which also appears, alongside a handful of Sebadoh covers, on **The Freed Seed** EP)—both gain a good deal of their urgency from the speedily springy playing of bassist Laura Ballance. McCaughan hasn't refined his top-of-the-lungs shout any further, but these songs make shouting along a more viable option than administering a dose of Ritalin. The **Tossing Seeds** compilation confirms Superchunk's status as the yardstick by which all post-punk singles bands must be judged. Free of the filler the foursome often (so to speak) tosses off in the breathless rush to fill its albums, it fills a room like a (baker's) dozen roses, some thorny (like "The Breadman" and "Fishing"), some softly aromatic (like the cover of Sebadoh's "Brand New Love"). While a handful of the tracks can also be found on attendant longplayers, **Tossing Seeds** is the only current place to find the band's defining statement of purpose, "Cool," a 1991 B-side in which Mac cops to the given that he can offer "nothing new . . . everything's borrowed, everything's used," before pulling an about-face in order to blithely insist "We're cooler than you, and you know it's true." Awesome!

The band took a full week to record **On the Mouth**—as opposed to the forty-eight-hour sessions used in the past—and the benefits are immediately apparent. Not only does producer John "Speedo" Reis make the most of new drummer Jon Wurster's emphatic thumping, he brings out the best in the band's somewhat formulaic melodic schemes, both the velocity-minded (like the cryptic "Precision Auto") and the more rhythmically resonant (like the Ballance-carried "The Question Is How Fast"). McCaughan is mostly as ambiguous as ever in doling out his lyrics, although the pessimistic countenance he presents on "New Low" and "Untied" does leave a palpable sense of disquietude. The token self-reference-cum-state-of-the-band address is even a bit gloomy this time around: the eloquent "From the Curve" finds the singer dodging a flurry of self-doubt, bemoaning being put in a position of having "so much to answer for." Probably Superchunk's finest effort.

The specter of a broken relationship—specifically that of McCaughan and Ballance—looms over **Foolish,** from its plethora of slow, brooding songs to its grim cover (which pictures a cute little bunny inside and a caricature of a woman ignoring a hanging rabbit carcass outside). On the album's uncharacteristically draggy opener, "Like a Fool," McCaughan slips into a wounded falsetto to air the full extent of his psychic pain, evoking a hopelessness that resurfaces in the teed-off "Water Wings." Oddly, the band's harmonies have never sounded more in synch, although they tend to get a bit lost when set against the increasingly complex textures of songs like "Driveway to Driveway" and "Kicked In." That hankering for intricacy gets the best of a few too many songs (especially "Why Do You Have to Put a Date on Everything"), which blunts the impact of what could have been an extremely affecting album. (**Driveway to Driveway** proffers the album track, plus acoustic renditions of it and two older songs.)

Incidental Music, a companion piece to **Tossing Seeds,** compiles eighteen uniformly cool odds and ends (B-sides, split 7-inches, imports, compilation tracks, a soundtrack item and the previously unreleased "Makeout Bench"). Of particular note are the snarling "Cadmium" and an impossibly finespun cover of Magnetic Fields' "100,000 Fireflies."

Here's Where the Strings Come In splits the difference between the wild and innocent Superchunk and the band grizzled by professional and personal experiences. McCaughan sounds as snottily declamatory as ever on the nose-thumbing "Hyper Enough," and no less prone to flights of starry-eyed reverie (as evidenced by "Sunshine State"). And while the quartet has learned to marshal some of its contemporary instrumental prowess (see the twisting "Detroit Has a Skyline," which features some nifty interplay between Mac and guitarist Jim Wilbur), they also seem to have lost the ability to paint a picture rather than use a thousand words.

Since McCaughan apparently subscribes to the adage about idle hands, he does a fair amount of solo recording under the guise of Portastatic. Generally more muted and introspective than his work with Superchunk, **I Hope Your Heart Is Not Brittle** is dominated by soft-focus melodic sketches like "Naked Pilseners" and "Beer and Chocolate Bars" (with vocals by the Bats' Kaye Woodward) and bookended by a pair of untitled instrumentals that spotlight his rudimentary but comely trumpet playing. ("Naked Pilseners" was also released as the lead item on a Matador single with a cover of Magnetic Fields' "Josephine" and another McCaughan original.) **Slow Note From a Sinking Ship** is similar in intent, but not execution: having come into possession of some old analog synths, Mac applies them to songs like "When You Crashed," which is highly reminiscent of '60s French film music (or the lighter moments of Stereolab). The presence of more collaborators (like bandmate Jon Wurster and Polvo's Ash Bowie) detracts from the intimacy a bit, but when it's just Mac and his 8-track (as on "Pastime" and "Skinny Glasses Girl"), **Slow Note** feels like it was written for you alone. **Scrapbook** rounds up five odds and ends.

Bricks was a homebrew recording project of McCaughan's while he was studying at Columbia in the late '80s. (As a teen in Chapel Hill, he'd already been in trios called Slushpuppies and Wwax, both of whom are documented on posthumous Merge releases.) On the appropriately titled **A Microphone and a Box of Dirt,** it's easy to spot the genesis of his reedy guitar technique (particularly on the Eastern-tinged "Smoking Hooch With the Flume Dude" and the oddly Beatlesque "You Shouldn't Have Smashed Your Guitar") as well as his enigmatic writing style: "The Girl With the Carrot Skin" will have you singing some embarrassingly silly couplets much longer than you'd probably like. An intriguing artifact for fans, and a diverting collection on its own merits. [dss]

See also *Seam, Small.*

SUPERCONDUCTOR

Heavy With Puppy EP (Boner/Tupelo) 1992
Hit Songs for Girls (Boner/Tupelo) 1993
Bastardsong (Boner) 1996

This Vancouver seven-to-nine-piece (four to six guitarists, two bassists, one drummer) has done its part to prove the parental belief that all rock'n'roll is really sonic mayhem. Led by co-vocalists Carl Newman (who also fronts the Bacharach-meets-Beatles quartet Zumpano) and Keith Parry (who doubles on drums), Superconductor mishmashes a love of metal, sugar-pop and Japanese noisecore together into a musical potluck. On the five-song **Heavy With Puppy** (produced by Numb's Don Gordon), "Satori Part One" and "Bushpilot" demonstrate the band's tightness and melodic leanings, while the noise-scaped instrumentals ("Riffmania" and "Clamhammer") make a strong case for the less-is-more aesthetic.

By the time of **Hit Songs for Girls,** the band seemed to have found a method to its madness, carving out space for both vocal and instrumental melodies to rise above the din. Standout tracks include the country-meets-Kurt romp "E-Z Bake Oven" (with Kevin Kane of Grapes of Wrath guesting on slide guitar) and the hummable, bracingly boisterous "There Goes Helen," which suggests a Pixiesque mentality at work.

Pulling out all the stops, the hour-long pseudo-rock-opera **Bastardsong** incorporates harmonica, antique synthesizers, *Gilligan's Island* soundbites— nothing is safe from the band's noodling. From the opening chords of "The Bastard Overture," clean, evenly mixed vocals and surprisingly tight massed guitar work make this an easier listen . . . to a point. When the electronic experimentation begins a few cuts into this nineteen-track monolith—unleashing synth-generated pops and whizzes as well as Newman's primal screams—Superconductor banishes melody to clamber through a host of unsettling time and style changes. In the rare moments of calm ("Cloud Prayer," "Mary Ann"), the group comes off as downright Nick Drake–like. For the most part, though, **Bastardsong** bridges a most unboring bridge to Boredom. [dps]

See also *Zumpano.*

SUPER DELUXE

Famous (Tim/Kerr) 1995 (Tim/Kerr/Revolution) 1996

As pop's timeline reels out ever further, those who choose to root around in its archives have grown ever more haphazard in their pickings and porings. Genres that once elicited staunch sectarian divisions are now so remote—especially to musicians born well after the last original notes had been played—that any style at hand can now be emulated or incorporated without prejudice or context. In other words, "I don't care *where* you found that—just put it in your mouth!"

On its brief, splendid debut, the young Seattle foursome Super Deluxe demonstrates a clear awareness of '90s noise but primarily brings Squeeze-like harmonic subtlety to winning originals rooted in that nonexistent netherworld between the original British Invaders and their softhearted new wave receptors. Which doesn't exclude intimations of country-rock, suggestions of Sloan or—on "Disappearing," which is surely one gimmicky video away from monster smashdom—blowzy Kurt Cobain guitar. Braden Blake writes nifty songs that make teen-adorable meters rise without sacrificing adult strength. "Flustered" manages to work in such seductive imagery as "semi-precious crystal teardrops," while there's "a monster underneath my bed" in "Johnny's Gone Fishin'." (The coincidental timing of "Holly's Dream Vacation," another song about *Breakfast at Tiffany's,* was unfortunate.) He baits the tunes with killer hooks and sings them in a suitable Mr. Softee voice. Together with second guitarist/vocalist John Kirsch, Blake fills the ten tracks with smart harmonies and the fuzzed-up/ringing rhythm guitars that say "we know it's 1995 but we've kept our record collections anyway." What more could anyone ask? [i]

SUPERDRAG

The Fabulous 8-track Sound of Superdrag (Darla) 1995
Superdrag Plays Regretfully Yours (Elektra) 1996

While common sense would lead to the assumption that the titular 8-track of Superdrag's debut mini-album is one of those full-featured studio contraptions that puts eight separate channels of music on tape—more than it took to record the entire Beatles' catalogue, it might be noted—the Knoxville quartet's "fabulous sound" would be better explained if it had been captured on a vintage cartridge player plugged into a dilapidated Chevy van's cigarette lighter. The guitars sound like they're being played through a transistor radio; there's no way to know the rhythms aren't being beaten out on shoeboxes. Fortunately, the fuzzy fortitude of singer/guitarist John Davis' Weezer-beat pop songs is righteous fuel for such lo-fi obfuscation. "I keep on breathing anyway"—a shrugged line in "Bloody Hell"—typifies the level of ambition Davis claims, although that doesn't keep him from slipping delightful melodies and clever chord changes through the haze of guitar distortion and pancake-flat sound. Armed with realistically (meaning both hopeless and a little cynical) romantic lyrics, the seven catchy songs are structured simply enough to withstand the distorted onslaught and come out grinning. The wobbly noise storms blowing through "Blown Away" only invigorate the already peppy tune; "Really Thru" has the casual aplomb of prime Jesus and Mary Chain. Easy, casual fun.

The same can't be said of **Regretfully Yours,** which adds the sound of dollar signs to the mix and loses some spunk in the process. Signed to a major label, Superdrag assents to clearer sound and more sensible arrangements at the hands of producer Tim O'Heir, who does nothing out of line except drain off *just* enough of the haphazard charm to make the tunecore commercially presentable. That Davis' vulnerably sweet and sour songwriting is in full effect is the album's saving grace, but the audible sense of what Superdrag is about has changed a lot. Naturally, the most engagingly messy tracks are shunted to the back of the disc. [i]

SUPER FRIENDZ

Mock Up, Scale Down (Can. Murderecords) 1995

Halifax power-poppers from the Sloan galaxy—not only did the Nova Scotia stars provide the young quartet with a label, they furnished a fill-in drummer for several tours—the Super Friendz bring sparkling tunefulness and invention to the unpretentiously delightful **Mock Up, Scale Down.** Informed both musically and topographically by the environment of their maritime city, Super Friendz draw romantic conundrums in watery colors ("Undertow"), hit the beach in "Come Clean," fall overboard on the Beatlesy "One Day" and explore paradoxical provincialism in the rock-idol entreaty of "Rescue Us From Boredom," an energetic rock wave amid the album's brisk breezes. Adjusting their instrumental roles for each song, guitarists Drew Yamada and Matt Murphy and bassist Charles Austin share the vocals in high, fresh voices, providing variety and fleshing out a more complex personality than most such bands can offer. [i]

SUPERGRASS

I Should Coco (Capitol) 1995
Alright/Time EP (UK Parlophone) 1995

JENNIFERS

Just Got Back Today EP (UK nude) 1992

Emerging as the brats of the Britpop movement, Oxford's irresistibly goofy trio Supergrass burst onto the scene whipping out immediate, punchy tunes with a distinctly English accent, sort of like Green Day by way of the Small Faces and Buzzcocks.

Singer/guitarist Gareth (Gaz) Coombes and drummer Danny Goffey had been teenage members of the Jennifers, a quartet whose only release, a four-track EP, is a mildly entertaining bit of energetic jangledelia. To the chagrin of no one, that band packed it in, and two years later, Gaz and Danny resurfaced with bassist Mickey Quinn as Supergrass. The band—whose moniker is British slang for a police informer—first hit with the amphetamine bubblegum 7-inch "Caught by the Fuzz," which chronicles a lad's first pot bust and deals with that situation's primary crisis: that is, Mom's gonna be pissed. That single—an acoustic version of which later appeared on a Sub Pop 45—was quickly followed by the boisterous Slade-meets-Madness stomp, "Mansize Rooster."

Both of those singles (along with their respective flipsides, "Lose It" and "Sitting Up Straight") appear on Supergrass' full-length debut, **I Should Coco,** along with a bounty of other hook-strewn ditties extolling the giddy exultation and dopey abandon of post-pubescent youth. Punky glam guitars, Keith Moon–ish drum rolls and helium harmonies abound, notably through the Carnaby Street swing of "She's So Loose" and "Alright," an utterly delightful, mostly monosyllabic, teen anthem. "We are young/We run green/Keep our teeth/Nice and clean," sings the nineteen-year-old Gaz over a barrelhouse music-hall piano. (It should be noted that his glee in young adulthood doesn't only inform his music. This is, after all, a man who is so pleased with his newfound ability to grow facial hair that he sports pop's most ridiculous muttonchops since Noddy Holder.) Being young, the 'Grass do enjoy a wank, though the spirits are so high that the sped-up silliness of "We're Not Supposed To" and the Beatlesque blues spaceout, "Sofa (of My Lethargy)" go down as easy larfs. The good-natured and curiously eccentric **I Should Coco** finds these kids to be alright indeed.

Alright/Time includes the two LP tracks for which the EP is named, a rapido-speedo take on the Kenny Rogers and the First Edition nugget "Just Dropped In (To See What Condition My Condition Was In)" and "Je Suis Votre Papa Sucre," a pointless bit of Parisian tomfoolery. [mgk]

SUPER HEROINES

See *Christian Death.*

SUPER JUNKY MONKEY

Screw Up (TriStar Music) 1995
Parasitic People (TriStar Music) 1996

A couple more exports like this and the image of Japanese women as the timid flowers of a repressively patriarchal garden will be gone forever. The young Tokyo quartet takes random elements of hip-hop, metal, thrash-funk, punk, dancehall and pure noise and loads them all into a blast furnace from which grilled guitar (by Keiko Yamaiwa), thunderous rhythms (drummer Matsudaahh! and bassist Shinobu Kawai), stop-start cheers and roaring vocals (by Mutsumi Takahashi, who also supplies most of the lyrics) emanate in discontinuous blasts of loudly aggressive this'n'that. Except for keeping the tumult and sound pressure levels high, no two songs—especially the ten-second blares "Tamage" and "Revenge"—here are really alike. (**Screw Up** is the band's second album; the first was the Japanese-only **Cabbage.**) "Buckin' the Bolts" crosses L7 with Suicidal Tendencies for a punchy shoutalong, but "Bakabatka" showcases Takahashi's trilling raggamuffin flow (in Japanese, naturally) and "Ukatousen" is a cagey rock-rap hybrid unlike anything attempted by Run–DMC or Anthrax. "Decide" funks up techno beats with guitars and urgent chants of "We must decide!"; "Where're the Good Times" puts fancy Living Colour–styled syncopation underneath slick '70s-voiced soul-rock; "We're the Mother" updates Golden Earring with gothic chanting and funky vamping and stylized rapping. Get the picture? Super Junky Monkey bring the chops and enormous flexibility to their funhouse vision of modern music, but sometimes crazy shit is just crazy shit.

Parasitic People is more of the same—which, in this band's case, means expanding farther afield on all fronts while firming up a more commercial center. Once you get through laughing at the chipmunk voices you'll start noticing how much of this seemingly random wall covering sticks. [i]

SUPERNOVA

Ages 3 and Up (Amphetamine Reptile/Atlantic) 1995

The three guys of Supernova—Art (bass), Dave (drums) and Jo (guitar)—would have you believe they came from the planet Cynot 3, landed on Earth and formed a rock band in order to capture the world's supply of tinfoil. Onstage, they dress up in Speedos and super-hero capes, shave geometric shapes into their heads like some demented basketball team and wrap themselves in, that's right, tinfoil. If Supernova sounds like a novelty act, at heart it is. But rarely has a novelty act rocked with such conviction or been so incisively funny.

On the basis of **Ages 3 and Up,** one would guess that the Cynotions (or Costa Mesans, where the California trio actually resides) heard much the same music growing up as the members of Green Day, CIV and the Offspring. The trio's songs (twenty in just under forty minutes here) are short and catchy, all buzzsaw guitars and raspy vocals. With little chance (or need) for musical or lyrical development, tunes start, make their point and sprint to the finish, flinging off satiric lyrics playing on the flotsam of media culture as they go. "Mentos" is a fantasy about being the star of a candy-mint commercial; "Vitamins" advises listeners to take 'em "two by two"; the subject of "Oreo" is, well, cookies. Great fun, but even a good joke is hard to tell twice. [sm]

SUPERSNAZZ

Superstupid! (Sub Pop) 1993
I Wanna Be Your Love EP (Lucky) 1993

Taking their band name from a Flamin Groovies album, these four Tokyo women—singer/guitarist Spike, guitarist Kanako, bassist Tomoko and drummer Skinny Minny—play their infectious garage-rock with a brutal authority that belies the submissive image of Japanese women. Both of the quartet's US releases were recorded at Seattle's Egg Studios with Fastbacks/Young Fresh Fellows guitarist Kurt Bloch producing. The full-length **Superstupid!** mixes fast-and-hard originals (including one called "Uncle Wiggly") with delirious covers of Link Wray, Holland-Dozier-Holland and the Rivingtons' "Papa-Oom-Mow-Mow." The five-song **I Wanna Be Your Love**—recorded before but released after **Superstupid!**—features a pair of Sonics songs, the Groovies' "Teenage Head" and a different, less effective take of "Papa-Oom-Mow-Mow." As often as not, it's hard to tell just what language Spike is shouting in, but execution this spirited means it hardly matters. [ss]

SUPERSTAR

Greatest Hits, Volume One EP (UK Creation) 1992
Superstar (SBK) 1994

Maybe it's something in the water (saltpeter, perhaps?), but Scotland's pop scene seems to be populated by the least macho, most willingly snuggly characters this side of the Muppets. A veteran (alongside future members of Teenage Fanclub) of such seminal Glasgow acts as the BMX Bandits, the one-single Boy Hairdressers and the Groovy Little Numbers (a boy/girl duo that released a pair of 12-inches), Superstar mastermind Joe McAlinden may well be the cuddliest of the cuddlecore icons, ambling as he does between lush Jimmy Webb–styled balladry and breezy, brass-tinged arrangements redolent of '60s Eurofilm scores. After a series of singles on Creation, McAlinden and his fluid assembly of backing musicians (headed by former Soup Dragons guitarist Jim McCulloch) recorded one of the '90s' most ethereal—and most sadly overlooked—albums. Compelling enough when experienced from afar, **Superstar** reveals true heavenliness in its details: the Spanish guitar flourishes that punctuate "Amouricity," the swelling vocals that crest on the chorus of "Feels Like Forever" and the Renaissance fair strings that frame "Don't Wanna Die." The group split up not long after its sole American tour. [dss]

See also *BMX Bandits, Teenage Fanclub.*

SUPERSUCKERS

The Songs All Sound the Same (eMpTy/Musical Tragedies) 1992
The Smoke of Hell (Sub Pop) 1992
La Mano Cornuda (Sub Pop) 1994
The Sacrilicious Sounds of the Supersuckers (Sub Pop) 1995

DIDJITS

Fizzjob (Bam Bam) 1986 (Touch and Go) 1989
Hey Judester (Touch and Go) 1988
Hornet Piñata (Touch and Go) 1990
Backstage Passout (Southern) 1990
Full Nelson Reilly (Touch and Go) 1991
Little Miss Carriage! EP (Touch and Go) 1992
Que Sirhan Sirhan (Touch and Go) 1993

As if Seattle didn't already have enough scrungy sponges guzzled to the gills on '70s and '80s Britrock, the Supersuckers arrived there from Tucson at the start of this decade and set about proving that Sabbath and Zep weren't the only malevolent forces creeping around Mr. Gates' neighborhood. On **The Songs All Sound the Same**—an entertaining compilation of three singles, plus previously unreleased covers of Madonna ("Burning Up"), the Dead Boys ("What Love Is") and Nazareth ("Razamanaz")—the unpretentious quartet demonstrates a facility for aping both Motörhead ("Sex & Outrage") and Bad Company ("Saddletramp"), fueled by good-natured enthusiasm and little else. Singer/bassist Edward Carlyle Daly III (aka Eddie Spaghetti) has a functional shout that gets the words out without making any big stink about it; guitarists Ron Heathman and Dan Bolton make enough slovenly noise to ensure that nothing else much matters.

Signing to Sub Pop and getting together with producer Jack Endino, the Supersuckers streamlined their alcohol-burning funnycar and floored the accelerator for **The Smoke of Hell,** a feckless joyride that cruises right past the manic rockabilly Caddy being driven down the same lost highway by labelmate Reverend Horton Heat. Jettisoning the transatlantic components from its sound, the band belches out such all-American exhaust fumes as "Hell City, Hell," "Hot Rod Rally," "Drink and Complain" and "Sweet 'n' Sour Jesus." None of it means nothing, but the sheer expense of tightly compressed energy is its own breathless reward. (For proof of serious creative activity behind the blur, check the B-side of the "Hell City, Hell" single, a smoking gun rhythm rock rendering of Ice Cube's "Dead Homiez.")

While the Supersuckers really get into their flannel cowboy shtick visually on **La Mano Cornuda,** the album shifts towards less-incendiary garage-pop. Half the numbers stick to the crazed skedaddle rock'n'boogie of **The Smoke of Hell** ("I Was Born Without a Spine," "She's My Bitch"), but the rest are catchy mid-tempo charmers ("On the Couch," "Creepy Jackalope Eye," "Clueless") or forcefield '77-style rockers ("How to Maximize Your Kill Count," "Glad, Damn Glad"). Conrad Uno's production doesn't raise Endino's blinding gleam, but the effect is salutary, allowing the band to indulge its naturally wanton slop-rock instincts to great hairy effect. (In a bratty indulgence, the smirking quartet cruelly patches in embarrassing phone messages from Endino and Mudhoney bassist Matt Lukin.)

The stupendous **Sacrilicious** unveils a super-charged Supersuckers, with Heathman traded for a short stay by ex-Didjits guitarist/singer Rick Sims, a forceful visionary and a sharp songwriter with a blistering sense of humor. Produced by Butthole Surfer Paul Leary, the carefree Supersuckers come on like a gangbusting Mojo Nixon fronting a young Replacements: "Bad Bad Bad," "Born With a Tail," "The 19th Most Powerful Woman in Rock," "Bad Dog," "Ozzy" and "Run Like a Motherfucker" (sung by Sims, whose thin yelling is no match for Eddie's confident on-point holler) all draw a witty, squinty-eyed bead on their targets and mow them down with shapely plumes of flamethrown pop aggression. Upping the creative ante one notch, "My Victim" manages the neat trick of plugging Otis Redding's "Try a Little Tenderness" into a runaway rock blender without shorting out either appliance. The album-closing capper is "Don't Go Blue," an acoustic blues warning to those threatened with extinction: "If cussin' and swearin' is all you're gonna do/You'll be playing the blue room, opening up for you-know-who."

The penultimate lineup of Champaign (actually, Mattoon), Illinois' Didjits—a milkshake of midwestern punk rancor and wily wiseacre irony—included ex–Scratch Acid/Rapeman drummer Rey Washam. The trio's five-song **Little Miss Carriage!** is typically fast, furious and clever: wry, sketchy lyrics about death, drugs and decapitation and a cover of Ronnie Montrose's dumbass anthem, "Rock the Nation." If only Sims had a stronger voice . . .

With Washam's brief tenure over (his next high-profile stop was Ministry), drummer Todd Cole joined Sims and bassist Doug Evans for **Que Sirhan Sirhan,** a full-frontal punk assault that comes out swinging and doesn't let up for one breathless instant. The non-stop intensity is made even more exhausting by Sims' shrill singing, but the Didjits' brainy breed of hardcore carries more than the usual six-pack of cleverness. [i]

See also *TPRG.*

SUPREME COURT

Goes Electric (DB) 1993

When Glenn Phillips met Jeff Calder in 1975, the former, late of Atlanta's Hampton Grease Band, had just released his first solo album and was playing a string of dates in Florida. Calder was assigned to write about him for a local paper. A little over a year later, Calder moved up to Atlanta intent on forming a band and immediately got in touch with Phillips. The two did some writing together and Calder was introduced to a young guitarist named Bob Elsey, who'd learned more than a thing or two from Phillips. Elsey and Calder formed the Swimming Pool Q's and produced an impressive body of work in the '80s. Some of Calder's songs reveled in literary construct, others in the voices of true loose-cannon backwoods southern characters.

In the meantime, Phillips released nine instrumental albums with his own band. (Calder appeared on 1985's **Live,** singing their two joint compositions, "Sting Ray" and "Pony to Ride.") With that ensemble making no new inroads after years of touring and the Q's at a virtual standstill, the opportunity was ripe for Calder and Phillips to join forces in a group. The impetus for undertaking an album together was inadvertently provided by Phillips' longtime bassist Bill Rea, who was due to undergo wrist surgery and faced the possibility of not being able to play again. With drummer Bob Andre, the quartet recorded **Goes Electric.** If this had been a group of unknowns, it would stand as a commendable and solid debut, but, given the two leaders' previous accomplishments, it falls short. Calder's deranged roadside prophets and gamblers feel like they're being kept back a safe distance, while Rea's impeccable fretless playing, always the perfect foil for Phillip's maniac-on-fire guitar, provides too pretty a sheen. [dbg]

SURGERY

Soul Eater EP (Circuit) 1989
Nationwide (Amphetamine Reptile) 1990
Trim, 9th Ward High Roller EP (Amphetamine Reptile) 1993
Shimmer (Atlantic) 1994

Unreconstructed adherents to the rock'n'roll lifestyle—from free-flowing recreational intoxicants to daily doses of penicillin as preventive medicine—this transplanted Syracuse quartet did its best to bring a little bit of orgiastic revelry to New York's increasingly po-faced Lower East Side post-punk scene around the turn of the decade. Blessed with a preternatural ability to make even the most abrasive skronk exploration choogle at least a little, Surgery became the party band for folks too cool to party.

The five-song debut is kind of a mess. Kramer's hollow production does little to accent Sean McDonnell's bawling, brawling voice—easily the group's most potent weapon. Too bad, since both "Stupid Chile" and "Souleater" radiate a menace reminiscent of Altamont-era Stones. **Nationwide** captures that essence far more effectively: Scott Kleber's guitar casually makes a case for the argument that Sonic Youth and Foghat aren't mutually exclusive objects of veneration, squalling and boogieing with equal aplomb on tracks like "Maliblues" and "Do It to It Dynamo." The all-too-short album's most encouraging facet is the band's disposition to draw from the often-ignored bluesier end of the Detroit rock spectrum, a prowess that springs in no small part from bassist John Lachapelle and drummer John Leamy's shared willingness and ability to swing.

Surgery's blues influence is even more pronounced on the six-song **Trim, 9th Ward High Roller.** Kleber fires machine-gun riffs into the adrenalized walking blues (would that be running blues?) of "A.K.," and drips languid, Eddie Hazel–esque leads over the expansive "Brother Remington." McDonnell stretches effectively, embracing a few hip-hop phrasing tricks and making the most of his natural-born sneer—as evidenced by the morning-after taunt ("I was hopin' you were rich, so I could sleep off this sick buzz") that opens the lurching "Kickin' Around."

On **Shimmer,** the quartet pursues its low-tech aspirations with high-tech tools; the results are mixed. Producer GGGarth Richardson cuts away some of the gristle that non-devotees might have found unsavory, but in doing so loses a good deal of the rhythm section's meat. McDonnell, however, has rarely sounded better: his drawling delivery and down'n'out lyrical perspective fuse firmly on the hazy "Shimmer" (based on little more than a rudimentary drum track) and the giddily lawless "Gulf Coast Score." A still-extant inclination to boogie takes Surgery over the (ZZ) top on "Low Cut Blues," but the hyper-hybridized sounds of the band's blues-metal/hip-hop are mostly quite intriguing.

Surgery ceased to exist after Sean McDonnell suffered a fatal asthma attack in early 1995. [dss]

SURRENDER TO THE AIR

See *Phish.*

BOBBY SUTLIFF

See *Windbreakers.*

SWALES

Heartbroke & Bummin' [tape] (Sonic Delights) 1990
Moya Krova [tape] (Sonic Delights) 1991
Nightlife EP [tape] (Sonic Delights) 1992
Pleasureland (Bar/None) 1992
What's His Name (Bar/None) 1995

The Swales came into being in 1990 when singer/guitarist Bob Carr, who'd been writing songs, decided to record some of them at home (Bloomingdale, New Jersey) with his roommate Larry Bonforte on bass. While a friend made the resulting tapes available through his DIY cassette mail-order service, the duo also sent their honest and rootsy pop to various labels. Bar/None released a single ("On Your Side" b/w "Dude Rocker") in '91; Carr and Bonforte formed a full band with drummer Eric Harris (later of Chocolate USA) and guitarist Rich Weiner. The quartet went into a proper studio with producer Gene Holder and recorded noisy new versions of songs from the tape (including "On Your Side") to create **Pleasureland,** a harsh-edged album that alternately sounds like Joy Division, Robyn Hitchcock and the Flying Burrito Brothers.

Carr cut **What's His Name** with a completely new lineup, making unpretentious country-rock the rule; Holder's smoother production serves the crisp, restrained performances. Still, the overriding character of Carr's proud and simple songs depicting the small corners of American life ("Tanqueray Tango," "Teach You to Drive") remains unchanged. There's a strong thread that runs through both albums (down to the choice of photographs), making them chapters of a continuing story; the songs generally depict humble working people hoping things will get better while they go about living. "On Your Side" even makes its third appearance; like an annual school picture, it reveals the growth that happens while you're hardly even noticing the days go by. [dbg]

See also *Chocolate USA*.

SWALLOW

Blow (4AD) 1992
Blowback (UK 4AD) 1992
Hush EP (UK Rough Trade) 1994

Although they were probably joking when they said it, the British duo of Mike Mason and Louise Trehy pretty much nailed it when, in an interview, they dubbed themselves the "Cockatoo Twins." The music on **Blow** fits rather stereotypically into the 4AD stable of cosmic, guitar-based angel rock—so much so it's almost (*almost*) possible to overlook the fact that, while beautiful, it is also stunningly derivative. Mason's churning, phasing-heavy guitar lines, supple melodies and store-bought drum patterns provide Trehy with quite a pedestal for her whispery, cherubic come-on of a voice. Though blissfully enjoyable, tracks like "Sugar Your Mind," "Cherry Stars Collide" and "Tastes Like Honey" are by-the-book 4AD.

The limited-edition **Blowback** ironically reveals the duo's strong points and ability to transcend simple allure in favor of something far more substantial. Composed of remixes and instrumental versions of **Blow** songs, the eight tracks show Trehy and Mason skilled at more than simple atmospherics. The dubby redux of "Peekaboo" and the voiceless guitar swoon of "Tastes Like Honey" are superior to the original versions, thus making **Blow** seem that much more negligible.

Swallow re-emerged without much fanfare several years later to release the four-song **Hush** EP. Although Trehy's unmistakable voice is still in full effect, Mason's gooey guitar lines are replaced with more straightforward playing and writing. A cover of Steve Miller's (?!) "Dear Mary" is probably more than indicative of where the band thinks it's heading. [jf]

SWANS

Swans EP (Labor) 1982 (Young God) 1990
Filth (Neutral) 1983 (Young God/Sky) 1989
Cop (UK K.422) 1984
Swans EP (Homestead) 1984
Greed (PVC) 1985
Holy Money (PVC) 1986
Children of God (Caroline) 1987
Feel Good Now (UK Product Inc.) 1987
"Love Will Tear Us Apart" (Caroline) 1988
The Burning World (Uni) 1989
White Light From the Mouth of Infinity (Young God) 1991
Body to Body, Job to Job (Young God) 1991
Love of Life (Young God) 1992
Omniscience (Young God/Sky) 1993
Cop/Young God (Young God/Sky) 1993
Greed/Holy Money (Young God/Sky) 1993
Celebrity Lifestyle EP (Young God/Invisible) 1994
The Great Annihilator (Young God/Invisible) 1995
Kill the Child (Atavistic) 1996
Die Tür Ist Zu (Ger. World Service/Rough Trade) 1996
Soundtracks for the Blind (Young God/Atavistic) 1996

SKIN

Blood, Women, Roses (UK Product Inc.) 1985
Shame, Humility, Revenge (UK Product Inc.) 1988
The World of Skin (Product Inc.) 1988

WORLD OF SKIN

Ten Songs for Another World (Young God) 1990

JARBOE

Thirteen Masks (Hyperium/Sky) 1992
Sacrificial Cake (Young God/Alternative Tentacles) 1995

M. GIRA

Drainland (Young God/Alternative Tentacles) 1995

BEAUTIFUL PEOPLE LTD

Beautiful People Ltd (Bel. Sub Rosa) 1993

Extreme to the max, the early releases by New York's Swans are always described in the terms of no-rules, bare-knuckle fighting: pummeling, bludgeoning, punishing. The band's 2/2 rhythms, martial pounding and minimal lyrics howling out alienation and despair—all played at bowel-loosening volume—have drawn opponents as well as devoted fans. What adherents found, especially in the '80s **Greed/Holy Money/Children of God** period, was catharsis unlike any other in music.

The diversity in instrumentation and textures that seemed such a breakthrough on **Children of God** later became the band's métier. It's the exception, rather than the rule, when **Love of Life** bursts into crushing rhythms. The primitive pounding at the center of "Her," for example, is an interlude meant to hold the acoustic balladry in relief. Determined to carry the Swans agenda of making you feel his alienation into an array of increasingly more accessible styles, leader Michael Gira mellows his basso profundo into a mournful approximation of Johnny Cash to accompany songs that range from creepy, vaguely psychotic country-folk to what sounds like a dispirited, semi-acoustic Depeche Mode. Not as stunning in its passion as the band's best work, **Love of Life** is still an often beautiful, haunting record. Recorded at various '92 shows, **Omniscience** is a nicely presented live document of this phase of the band's career. (Working backward, the concert compilation **Kill the Child** dates from '85 to '87.)

The band's early years are revisited in **Body to Body, Job to Job,** a collection of previously unavailable studio recordings, live cassette recordings and tape loops from 1982 to 1985. That the metronomic boom, boom, boom of the tape loops doesn't stand out that much from the crunch, crunch, crunch of the songs is a good indication of how far Swans' ideas on tempo changes and musical diversity had come. Still, **Body to Body** is an important document of the years when Swans included drummer (now producer) Roli Mosimann and, if only occasionally, Thurston Moore. Admirers of a band that uses abasement as a trope should find the live versions of rages like "Half Life" quite satisfying. Swans' label also took advantage of the CD format to reissue remastered versions of **Cop** and **Young God** (actually, the untitled 1984 EP that contains the title song, "Raping a Slave" and two others) on one CD, and **Greed, Holy Money** (which mark the arrival of singer Jarboe into the former male preserve) and two mid-'80s 12-inch sides on another.

Although she has moved increasingly to the forefront of the group and World of Skin (formerly Skin), her duo with Gira, Jarboe's solo work lays bare her desire to be a diva. On the highly stylized **Thirteen Masks,** she adopts different female identities (from Kate Bush–like sensitivity to a Diamanda Galás–styled confrontational glower) as sounds run from airy whispers to thumping techno, each track taking on the signature sounds of such collaborators as Jim Thirlwell, Mosimann, Gira and Tony Maimone (Pere Ubu/They Might Be Giants). If **Thirteen Masks** is a nice artistic step forward, Beautiful People Ltd—Jarboe's duo with multi-instrumentalist Lary Seven—is a further stride. Perhaps because Gira's only involvement with the record was its mix-down, Jarboe is at her freest, trilling though a collection of shimmery, off-kilter pop songs. Even the most Skin-sounding tracks, like "Liquid Bébé Psychedelia," receive gentler, lighter treatment, and all the usual pretense seems in the service of fun. Don't miss the live cover of *West Side Story*'s "I Feel Pretty."

The Gira/Jarboe conspiracy continues with **Drainland** and **Superficial Cake,** a simultaneously released pair of "solo" albums that, of course, feature each other as well. If anything, the division between the albums separates the temporal lobes of modern Swans; Gira's impossibly deep voice and leaden dirges dominate his offering, while Jarboe focuses on otherworldly instrumentation and her often pretty singing. Both are somewhat lesser versions of what the two do together in Swans or World of Skin. (The two albums were also issued together as one triple-vinyl package.)

The Great Annihilator shows Swans within reach of attaining the qualities Gira found so appealing in the band's namesake—beautiful and idyllic on the surface, but predisposed to removing a digit from those who get too close. The album also reveals, however, that the band is running out of ideas. With guitarist Norman Westberg back in the fold (he departed some time after **White Light From the Mouth of Infinity**), the record proves Swans as adept as ever at taking different musical paths to arrive at the same existential nightmare, and indeed, getting better at reconciling the more accessible side of the sound. The images are also more complex, going far into pop culture to examine what a "Celebrity Lifestyle" means, a big step for a band that uses rape as a symbol for capitalism. Still, the record is unlikely to satisfy long-term followers. A more accessible Swans may also be a less cathartic one.

No such concerns need be raised about **Die Tür Ist Zu (The Door Is Closed),** which is described in press materials as the "first statement in the final chapter of Swans." A hefty portion of the seven lengthy songs (several recorded live) is devoted to grandly dramatic mock-Wagnerian instrumental passages; other than a southern child's spoken sample, the lyrics that do crop up are in German. Ex–American Music Club guitarist Vudi is among the conspirators here. [sf]

See also *Prong, Unsane; TPRG.*

MATTHEW SWEET

Inside (Columbia) 1986
Earth (A&M) 1989
Girlfriend (Zoo) 1991
Altered Beast (Zoo) 1993
Son of Altered Beast (Zoo) 1994
100% Fun (Zoo) 1995

That Matthew Sweet can write a wonderful pop song and has great taste in guitarists is a given, but since **Girlfriend,** his 1991 breakthrough album, the Nebraska native's choice of producers has been questionable. In retrospect, **Girlfriend** appears to be a once-in-a-lifetime combination of time, musician and production. Drummer/co-producer Fred Maher, who had previously worked with Lou Reed, Lloyd Cole, Scritti Politti and the Golden Palominos, gives the album a spacious, detailed, crystalline sound. Sweet's vocals (including his multi-tracked Byrdsy harmonies) are always front and center, drummer Ric Menck (of Velvet Crush, whose first album Sweet produced) and Sweet's bass move the songs along with brisk rhythmic efficiency. The guitars—Sweet on rhythm, with Robert Quine and Richard Lloyd sharing lead duties—give his retro tendencies a modern edge. Quine's leads easily pierce the muscle of the catchy, propulsive title track and the folky acoustic strums of "I Wanted to Tell You"; Greg Leisz's pedal steel puts a country point on "Winona," "You Don't Love Me" and the lush "Your Sweet Voice." Written during Sweet's divorce, the songs have a pungent, plaintive edge, from the invocation of "Divine Intervention" to the almost gleefully misogynistic "Does She Talk?" From the cover photo of a young Tuesday Weld to the sound of a needle skipping on scratchy vinyl between tracks, **Girlfriend** is close to being a paradigm for 1990s power-pop.

Which makes the two albums that have followed it both disappointing and puzzling. On paper, Richard Dashut might have seemed like a smart choice, but **Altered Beast** is a mess. The bright, clean sound of the producer's work with Fleetwood Mac should have fit with Sweet's pop sensibility, but their collaboration yields a record that is far too busy and, in spots, viscous and sludgy. Getting contributions from Mick Fleetwood, Nicky Hopkins and Pete Thomas, as well as most of the **Girlfriend** cast, the project feels rushed, with too many competing guitars (played variously by Sweet, Quine, Lloyd, Leisz and Ivan Julian) and vocal performances that too often sound offhand. But what's truly surprising is the songwriting, which suffuses the entire album with snotty nastiness; **Altered Beast** has all the antipathy of the Stones' **Aftermath** and none of the swagger. The credible hooks of "Devil With the Green Eyes" and "Time Capsule" barely counterbalance the bitterness at the songs' heart. "The Ugly Truth" appears twice, first as a smudged, overloaded pop production and later as "Ugly Truth Rock," which the band (here Sweet, Lloyd and drummer Ron Pangborn) crashes through with unfettered joy. It's easily the best thing on the album, and an indication of what Sweet might have done with better production. **Son of Altered Beast** is a seven-track companion piece containing a B-side ("Ultrasuede"), a remix ("Devil With the Green Eyes"), live versions of **Altered Beast**'s "Someone to Pull the Trigger" and "Knowing People" and three other concert numbers, including a version of Neil Young's "Don't Cry No Tears."

Sweet's songwriting is back to form on **100% Fun,** but Brendan O'Brien is yet another dubious producer choice. His fat, distortion-laden muffle sacrifices detail for power—not bad if you're Stone Temple Pilots or Pearl Jam, but deadly for a writer like Sweet. Adding to the problems, new drummer Stuart Johnson (on loan from Love Jones) has a loose, behind-the-beat approach that allows some of the best songs here to turn flaccid. (Fortunately, the memorable melodic charms of "Giving It Back" and "Come to Love" can't be stopped.) Menck holds down the beat on five cuts, and some of the album's highlights ("Sick of Myself," "We're the Same") are among them. [sm/i]

See also *Golden Palominos, Television, Velvet Crush; TPRG.*

SWEET TOOTH

See *Godflesh.*

SWERVEDRIVER

Son of Mustang Ford EP (UK Creation) 1990
Rave Down EP (UK Creation) 1990
Sandblasted EP (UK Creation) 1991
Raise (A&M) 1991
Mezcal Head (A&M) 1993
Ejector Seat Reservation (UK Creation) 1995

It became apparent early in this Oxford, England, foursome's history that they were too knife-edged heavy to be truly grouped with the then-reigning dream-pop sound. With vague hints of the Stooges, the punkish end of metal and bits of '60s rock, this intense band straddles several fences, but never fails to kick beneath the contrast of guitarist Adam Franklin's tough-sounding but laconic vocals.

Raise is spotty—not too surprising, since a good portion of it was culled from the preceding EPs rather than sessions for a proper album. Nevertheless, the pounding "Son of Mustang Ford" establishes the group as a punishing and formidable force. Franklin's vocals sound pond deep on the whip-lashing opener "Sci-Flyer," "Sandblasted" and the vaguely psychedelic "Rave Down."

From the opening moments of "For Seeking Heat," it's obvious **Mezcal Head,** produced by Alan Moulder and the band, is twice as explosive. The two guitarists (Franklin and Jimmy Hartridge) keep up a gargantuan, monstrous feel throughout the album, enlivening the all-powerful "Blowin' Cool" and "Duel." The band is tighter and more flexible than before, but also bigger-sounding, thanks to newcomer Steve George's blasting fuzz bass, which has an edge hard enough to recall the Move. An improved sense of melody adds to an impressive effort, flawed only by the overly generous length of too many songs.

Ejector Seat Reservation has no such problem; instead, the album finds this harsh, heavy band working in a more tempered, classic-pop format. Several cuts, including "The Birds," recall the late-'60s Who (whose songs Swervedriver has covered). "Bring Me the Head of the Fortune Teller" bubbles over in gnashing electricity; Franklin's bitterness over thwarted goals spills over the crushing guitars. Likewise, the title track and "How Does It Feel to Look Like Candy" lay on the fuzz and distortion in the choruses—the latter even uses angry brass. And "Last Day on Earth" is a stunning pop masterwork. The ascending, soaring verse hook is so intense that Franklin must resort to a throaty falsetto to complete it. Without a second of filler or wasted space, **Ejector Seat Reservation** is one of the most quietly ambitious records of this decade. [jr]

SWINGIN' NECKBREAKERS

Live for Buzz (Telstar) 1993
Shake Break! (Telstar) 1995

This no-nonsense New Jersey trio embodies the best qualities of the contemporary garage-band genre, combining hook-filled songs (their own, as well as some well-chosen covers) with a pummeling instrumental attack and an all-too-rare—in this context, anyway—ability to swing. Produced by ex–Das Damen drummer and future Matador Records exec Lyle Hysen, **Live for Buzz** is a blast from start to finish, boasting consistently catchy tunes, punchy playing and an engagingly cocky attitude manifested in bassist Tom Jorgenson's vocal sneer and smart-assed lyrics. If **Shake Break!** isn't quite as consistent, it's darn close. [ss]

SWIRLIES

Swirlies Number One EP7 (100% Breakfast) 1991
What to Do About Them (Taang!) 1992
Blonder Tongue Audio Baton (Taang!) 1993
Brokedick Car EP (Taang!) 1993
Sneaky Flutes (Taang!) 1996
They Spent Their Wild Youthful Days in the Glittering World of the Salons. (Taang!) 1996

SWIRLIES/KUDGEL

Fish Dreams Red EP7 (CinderBlock/Nervous) 1992

TROLLIN WITHDRAWAL

Drumzena Drumpet Volume One EP7 (Chimp) 1993
Drumzena Drumpet Volume Two EP7 (Chimp) 1994
Shit Power! [tape] (self-released) 1994
The Magazine Apocalypso EP7 (Chimp) 1995

The Swirlies have never quite settled on an identity, and that suits them just fine—they've got one foot squarely in My Bloody Valentine territory, another in the region of home-recording tape-weirdness and a third in la-la pop land. Despite a turbulent lineup and inconsistent output, they've produced some very interesting records, though never a great one; if anything, they get tripped up by having too *many* ideas.

The initial lineup—singer/guitarists Seana Carmody and Damon Tutunjian, bassist Andy Bernick and drummer Ben Drucker—was the most popular representative of the informal Boston/Cambridge "chimp rock" scene that also encompassed Kudgel, Fat Day and a handful of other bands. Beginning with the six-song debut, the Swirlies released a handful of singles in 1991 and 1992. **Fish Dreams Red,** a split double single with Kudgel, includes two Swirlies home recordings, one of which is the awesome, nearly inaudible "Her Life of Artistic Freedom"—basically amplified surface noise with a little guitar and singing. That track also appears on **What to Do About Them,** along with all three songs from the band's first (and most straightforward) single and three new songs, one of which was recorded in a real studio.

The group spent a lot more time in the studio making **Blonder Tongue Audio Baton,** which incorporates mellotron, Moog and noise—lots and lots of noise, from shortwave radio, feedback, tapes and whatever else they could pull in. The principle for most of the album seems to be that playing a pure-pop song (with the requisite MBV chord changes and blissed-out guitarstorms) and a pure-noise recording at the same time makes both of them more interesting to hear. That's mostly true here, especially on the static-spattered "Pancake" and "Park the Car by the Side of the Road." Elsewhere, the band undermines itself with structures that scurry busily around and end up nowhere and too many tempo and texture changes within songs.

The subsequent **Brokedick Car** EP is unabashedly filler, but listenable enough. It's got a shorter version of **Blonder Tongue**'s "Wrong Tube," two home-demo quickies and two alternate mixes of "Pancake": the less-noisy "Pancake Cleaner" and a dance version entitled "House of Pancake."

The Swirlies spent several years going through lineup change after lineup change; by 1996, when the group next released a record, Carmody and Drucker had been replaced by, respectively, Christina Files and Anthony DeLuca. Still, the sound isn't very different. "Sneaky Flutes," the centerpiece of the mini-album of the same name, is a noisy rocker that subsequently appeared (as "San Cristobal de las Casas") on the full-length **They Spent Their Wild Youthful Days in the Glittering World of the Salons.** The six untitled tracks surrounding it on **Sneaky Flutes,** though, showcase the band's more experimental side, including noise blurts, found dialogue and a pointless but charming setting of an A. A. Milne poem.

Cartoonist Ron Rege was for years an unofficial fifth Swirlie, drawing the band's record covers, making between-song noise on its recordings and borrowing Tutunjian's 4-track tape deck when the band was on tour. That's where Trollin Withdrawal, a duo of Rege and a gentleman who goes by the name of Non-Robot #27, comes in. Their recordings of tunelets, raps, babbling and noise (three 7-inch EPs with seven to ten songs apiece and a cassette) have the lowest imaginable "fidelity" (like, on a Walkman in the back seat of a VW Golf); mostly, they sound like Beck's most self-indulgent moments. Rege and N.R. #27 are effectively non-musicians, and they're overly enamored of the "speed-up" setting on the tape deck. Those warnings posted, the records are a delight: totally fun, inventive, charming and sweet, and improving with multiple listenings. When the two of them chant "your dreams can come true and your prayers can be answered" on **The Magazine Apocalypso**'s "Bumping Incident," they're giggling like they're stoned out of their minds, but they also sound like they really mean it. Not for the easily annoyed, but definitely at the top of their strange class. [ddw]

SWISH

See *Dinosaur Jr.*

DAVID SYLVIAN

Brilliant Trees (UK Virgin) 1984
Alchemy–An Index of Possibilities [tape] (UK Virgin) 1985
Words With the Shaman EP (UK Virgin) 1985
Gone to Earth (Virgin) 1986
Secrets of the Beehive (Virgin) 1987
Weatherbox (Virgin) 1989
Brilliant Trees/Words With the Shaman (Blue Plate) 1991

DAVID SYLVIAN AND HOLGER CZUKAY

Plight & Premonition (Venture/Virgin) 1988
Flux + Mutability (Venture/Virgin) 1989

RAIN TREE CROW

Rain Tree Crow (Virgin) 1991

DAVID SYLVIAN & ROBERT FRIPP

The First Day (Virgin) 1993
Damage (Virgin) 1994

A restless progressive and inquisitive collaborator since the end of the extraordinary Japan in the early '80s, exquisite London-born singer David Sylvian (né Batt) spent the first stage of his solo career discharging what remained of Japan's dreamy, high-art pop explorations while infusing them with jazz and world musics on **Brilliant Trees** and paring it all down to pure ambience (on the cassette-only **Alchemy—An Index of Possibilities** and **Words With the Shaman,** the EP drawn from it). He then moved further down both roads on the ambitious **Gone to Earth,** a double-album of semi-conventional songs and languid instrumentals. Without any loss of ambition, the jazz-oriented and acoustic-based **Secrets of the Beehive** is more simply presented and accessible. Recapitulating all of that, the gorgeous **Weatherbox** is a lavishly packaged five-CD cardboard cube containing **Brilliant Trees,** an expanded **Alchemy, Gone to Earth** and **Secrets of the Beehive,** plus an extensive and detailed booklet.

Sylvian's two albums with Czukay, which feature other members of Can, consist of long, lulling instrumentals not unlike extensions of **Gone to Earth** and **Secrets of the Beehive.** The subtitles of the two pieces on **Flux + Mutability**—*A big, bright, colourful world* and *A new beginning is in the offing*—fairly reflect the music.

After that, Sylvian went back over some old ground, either in an effort to refashion his past into his future or to clear the decks for the new undertakings he would venture in the mid-'90s. First, he reunited with his old bandmates—bassist/bass clarinetist Mick Karn (Anthony Michaelides), synthesist Richard Barbieri and drummer Steve Jansen (né Batt; he and David are brothers)—but perversely declined to call the group Japan, instead settling on the enigmatic Rain Tree Crow. Improvising loose but impressively structured music in the studio (to which Sylvian added lyrics), the four easily reclaim their old sound in the ethereal spaciousness of "New Moon at Red Deer Wallow" and the smoothly flowing Bryan Ferry illusions of "Every Colour You Are," "Boat's for Burning," "Blackwater" and "Pocket Full of Change." Few "rock" musicians have ever better understood the value of *not* playing, and **Rain Tree Crow** owes its soaring beauty to the gaping holes left in its sonic net.

For his next trick, Sylvian resumed another old alliance—with guitarist Robert Fripp, who played a prominent instrumental role on **Gone to Earth.** Using a handful of musicians—including Stick player Trey Gunn (with whom Fripp would soon re-form King Crimson), drummer Jerry Marotta and co-producer David Bottrill taking the Eno-esque role of treatments and programming—the pair made **The First Day,** a fascinating and rewarding dialectic between Fripp's searing, rhythmically intense physicality and Sylvian's cerebral nonchalance. Although the elder statesman clearly gets the upper hand in setting the sonic agenda, Sylvian inserts himself productively into the process with confidence. He palliates Team Fripp's furious aggression with delicate keyboards and vocals whose shapely curves are not quite hidden behind harsh distortion. Five of the seven tracks go on too long—a contiguous point in the stars' approaches that doesn't serve the purpose of what's going on here—but **The First Day** is an engrossing, invigorating and mind-expanding adventure of sharp teeth and smooth skin.

The Sylvian/Fripp tour that followed featured Gunn, guitarist Michael Brook and drummer Pat Mastelotto (who also wound up in King Crimson). As documented on the phenomenally clear-sounding **Damage** album, this group's center of gravity is weighted toward Sylvian; Fripp calmly rips shit up as usual, but in the context of a record whose overall mood is quieter and more placid than the studio release. Expanding the majority of the material from **The First Day** with Rain Tree Crow's "Every Colour You Are," three **Gone to Earth** oldies and three otherwise unreleased songs written by Fripp, Sylvian and Gunn, the quintet brings more skilled accomplishment to live performance than most bands can manage in months of overdubbing. [i/ja]

See also *Michael Brook, King Crimson; TPRG.*

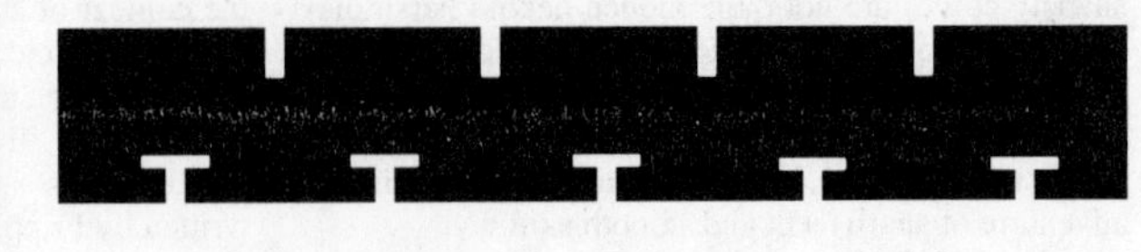

TACKLE BOX

See *Helium.*

TAD

God's Balls (Sub Pop) 1989
Salt Lick (Sub Pop) 1990
8-Way Santa (Sub Pop) 1991 + 1991
Inhaler (Mechanic/Giant) 1993
Infrared Riding Hood (Mechanic/EastWest) 1995
Live Alien Broadcasts (Futurist) 1995

Without a doubt the heaviest band on Sub Pop's embryonic roster—and that's not a gibe at sumo-sized singer/guitarist Tad Doyle's girth—this Seattle-via-Idaho foursome did its best to create an image of hinterland inbreeding, right down to exaggerations about Doyle's down-time meat-cutting pursuits. And on the impressively punishing **God's Balls,** the band more than lived up to its malignant advance billing: the riff-heavy "Behemoth," "Satan's Chainsaw" and especially the Ed Gein–inspired "Nipple Belt" hit like a succession of knees to the groin, with Doyle's rugged, sneering vocals adding insult to injury. Thanks to a typically fine Steve Albini recording, the seven-song **Salt Lick** sounds even more ominous than its predecessor, even while toning down the bass-irrigated throb. This time around, Doyle and second guitarist Gary Thorstensen don't so much strangle the songs with their strings as lay them open with jagged lashes. (The **Salt Lick** CD contains seven of ten songs from **God's Balls.**)

Produced by Butch Vig, **8-Way Santa**—which had to be withdrawn and reissued after one of its inadvertent cover stars (whose photo was found in a local thrift shop) took exception to being linked with the devil's music—reshoulders the sludgy overkill of Tad's debut. Doyle attacks the often-unnerving lyrics ("Flame Tavern," "Plague Years," "Giant Killer") with gusto, but the songs bleed into a viscous, amorphous mess. Producer J Mascis saves **Inhaler** from the same fate with a mix that gives added heft to newcomer Josh Sinder's thudding-but-sharp drumming—an alacrity that should come as no surprise given Mascis' own history behind the skins. But Doyle's increasingly abstract yarns—the best ones here are "Paregoric" and "Luminol"—have seen better days.

Although **Infrared Riding Hood** (produced for old time's sake by the debut's Jack Endino) certainly merits extra credit for clever christening, those brownie points won't help offset the penalties warranted for the sheer redundancy of skulk-fests like "Bludge" and "Thistle Suit." In a nominal nod to the digital era, the quartet stretches the album past the one-hour mark. **Live Alien Broadcasts,** recorded in a Seattle studio, recapitulates several years of Tad's history, appending four new songs. They needn't have bothered with those, since a determined reluctance to abandon its beloved sludge has long since fossilized the band. [dss]

See also *TPRG.*

TALKING HEADS

See *David Byrne and Brian Eno.*

TALL DWARFS

See *Chris Knox.*

TALULAH GOSH

See *Heavenly.*

TANGO PROJECT

See *Silos.*

TANNER

Ill Gotten Gains (Caroline) 1995

When Ryan Fox left pioneering San Diego quartet Fishwife (the first group to record for Headhunter Records), the band's three remaining members could've hung it up. Instead, they took a summer vacation, then returned as this propulsive, rhythmically taut trio.

Following a handful of strong singles, singer/guitarist Gar Wood, bassist Matt Ohlin and drummer Chris Prescott teamed with Drive Like Jehu drummer Mark Trombino to produce their impressive debut. Wood, a far less theatrical vocalist than Fox, strains his (sub)urban tales of alienation through a dry, nasal larynx that works well with Tanner's angular, dynamic songwriting. Rather than write verse-chorus-verse punk, the trio piles riffs together—sort of a "hey, this would sound great after that" style—and the almost effortless march through complex changeups is engaging, quirky and cool. "Catalogue" is a great example of this skillful approach, as are "Hey Jigsaw" (which suckers the listener in with a loping hook before delivering a fiery gear change in mid-song) and "Guard Dog," a sinister dirge about paranoia. [mww]

TAR

Handsome EP (Amphetamine Reptile) 1989
Roundhouse (Amphetamine Reptile) 1990
Jackson (Amphetamine Reptile) 1991
Clincher (Touch and Go) 1993
Toast (Touch and Go) 1993
Over and Out (Touch and Go) 1995

After a brief fling as Blatent Dissent, a fairly conventional mid-'80s punk band at Northern Illinois University in DeKalb, the members of Tar moved to Chicago and adopted a thicker, harder, more textured sound. A number of the band's discs were engineered by Steve Albini or Iain Burgess, sonic architects of the

Chicago post-punk fringe, and they capture the no-frills interplay of guitarists John Mohr and Mark Zablocki and the drill-press precision of drummer Mike Greenlees and bassist Tim Mescher (later replaced by Mike Zaluckyj).

The quartet is still working through its record collection on **Handsome;** "Same" quotes the Sex Pistols, "Seam" rewires Wire and "Downtime" regurgitates Iggy Pop's vocal mannerisms. But Tar also begins threading subversive melodies through a thick fabric of dissonance created by its custom-made aluminum guitars, particularly on the vicious tug and pull of "Mel's."

Roundhouse is a more fully realized effort, with guitars that methodically churn like threshers through a wheat field, underpinned by coldly relentless lunge-and-lurch rhythms. It's the most industrial-sounding of Tar's albums, and substantially reminiscent of then-labelmates Helmet. Mohr's monotonal vocals are effectively buried, just another layer in the band's ominous sonic grid.

Mohr begins to develop a vocal personality on **Jackson,** almost in spite of the bleak subject matter. "I don't understand how the hands of progress could be so cold," he wails on "Trauma." A refined sense of dynamics and tempo is also evident: "Walking the King" starts at a trot and than abruptly dissolves into a crawl. "On a Transfer" glides and gallops on a bed of overdriven guitars; "Dark Mark" builds relentlessly to a double-time finale.

With two live cuts and an alternate version of the 1992 single "Teetering" augmenting four new studio songs, **Clincher** introduces more pronounced melodies, particularly on "Lady Steps," which sounds like a **Zuma**-era Neil Young outtake. **Toast** expands the melodic terrain and displays even more confident vocals. The band's wry humor also emerges, most prominently on "Satritis," which posits that it's better to make fun of guitar solos than to actually play them. Indeed, Mohr and Zablocki establish a twin-guitar vocabulary so reliant on tension-building rhythms and textures that individual expressions of technique would be superfluous.

Over and Out, Tar's best and most varied album, is the aptly titled finale—a rare instance in which a band bows out before the corpse starts to decompose. The old power is there on "Known Anomalies" and "Time to Strike," while "Welk" shapes up as the band's hookiest song and "Q.V.C.," with cello-like e-bow guitar, sustains a contemplative mood. The emotional centerpiece is the tumultuous "Building Taj Mahal," which ruminates on a band's last stand: "I am familiar with the concept of filler," sings Mohr, but adds, "This one is special." He'll get no argument here. [gk]

See also *TPRG.*

TEAM DRESCH

Personal Best (Chainsaw/Candy-Ass) 1995
Captain My Captain (Chainsaw/Candy-Ass) 1996

Unlike mainstream rock musicians who've crept out of the closet timidly, delivering platitudes about why one's sexual orientation is really no big deal, the Northwest's raucously sexy Team Dresch says it loud—and frequently—they're dykes and they're proud. From the debut album's title and cover art (both borrowed from the lesbian coming-of-age film) to biographical advisories noting that "none of [the band's] members have ever had a boyfriend," the Portland/Olympia quartet (which for a time included drummer Scott Plouf of the Spinanes) is anything but coy about its sexual subtext. Fortunately, Team Dresch—named for bassist (and riot-scene godmother) Donna Dresch—realizes that bands can't live by frankness alone and takes the time to thread two-minute punk-pop outbursts like "She's Crushing My Mind" and "Hate the Christian Right!" with sharp, memorable hooks that pierce the pleasure center just as surely as the lyrics get that gray matter to stewing. There's no denying the seriousness of the underlying message delivered by singer/guitarists Kaia Kangaroo (Wilson) and Jody Coyote (Bleyle, who also holds down the drum slot in Hazel), but the joy with which they deliver it proves even riot grrrls wanna have fun.

Captain My Captain improves the assault on all levels. The playing and production (by John Goodmanson) are harder, tighter and more musically enticing; songs like "Uncle Phranc," "Don't Try Suicide," "The Council" and "Musical Fanzine" deliver important ideas with artful intelligence, cool vocals and a wry sense of irony. Hard on the heels of the band's album, Kaia (whose discography already included a '93 album with her old band, Adickdid) released her eponymous solo debut, an acoustic folk outing, via the Chainsaw/Candy-Ass consortium. [dss/i]

See also *Hazel, Phranc, Screaming Trees.*

TEAR GARDEN

See *Skinny Puppy.*

TEARS FOR FEARS

The Hurting (Mercury) 1983
Songs From the Big Chair (Mercury) 1985
The Seeds of Love (Fontana) 1989
Tears Roll Down (Greatest Hits 82–92) (Fontana/Mercury) 1992
Elemental (Mercury) 1993
Raoul and the Kings of Spain (Epic) 1995

CURT SMITH

Soul on Board (UK Mercury) 1993

OLETA ADAMS

Circle of One (Fontana) 1990
Evolution (Fontana/Mercury) 1993
Moving On (Fontana/Mercury) 1995

With **Tears Roll Down,** haughty and dour English pop pointillist Roland Orzabal closed the door on his youth, his group and his first decade of meticulous stardom. Besides compiling the essentials (and then some) from three astonishingly accomplished Tears for Fears albums—the precocious and dismally uplifting **The Hurting** ("Mad World," "Pale Shelter"), the grandly realized **Songs From the Big Chair** ("Shout," "Everybody Wants to Rule the World," "Head Over Heels") and the imposing dense delicacy of **The Seeds of Love** ("Sowing the Seeds of Love," "Woman in Chains")—the collection includes the previously unreleased "Laid So Low (Tears Roll Down)" as confirmation of Orzabal's intention to proceed without his evidently superfluous partner, Curt Smith, who was finally relieved of his duties in 1991. (The singer/bassist subsequently made **Soul on Board,** an uneventful and low-key solo album of handsomely appointed designer soul-pop that leans as much toward Paul Young as to his former group's sound. Though he adopts a chin-up stance in "Calling Out," Smith can't hide his bitterness, and he unloads his hurt in "Words.")

Retaining the group name, **Elemental** opens the second stage of Orzabal's career without major innovation—a few surprises, maybe, but no wholesale reconsiderations in the pompous sensitivity of his boundless creative ambition. The fanaticism of Orzabal's artistic imperatives and the signature sound of his echoed, textured throatiness overshadow any stylistic tinkering he and his new studio collaborators (co-writer/co-producer/guitarist/keyboardist Alan Griffiths and co-producer Tim Palmer) might have contrived. **Elemental** is substantially more involved than the first two albums but much less fussy than the absurdly over-produced third. Significantly, the Beach Boys tribute, "Brian Wilson Said," isn't nearly as involuted as the Beatles invocation of "Sowing the Seeds of Love" (although both equally indicate the distance between Orzabal's labored constructions and his idols' sheer ingenuity). The album essentially upholds Orzabal's dedication to create remarkable textures and settings for essentially ordinary pop songs sprung from his bristly, remote and self-critical personality. "Cold" acknowledges his impassiveness ("My temperature's been rated and I'm cold . . . Been excommunicated 'cos I'm cold"), while "Goodnight Song" addresses the fatigue, inadequacy and boredom of performing ("the sounds we are making are so uninspired . . . played so wrong/ Blame the crowd, they scream so loud, so long"). But the animosity of "Mr. Pessimist" is directed outward, as is the dismayingly cruel "Fish Out of Water." Taking a tuneless, needless and vindictively harsh dump on Smith, Orzabal fairly gushes condescension: "The only thing you made was that tanned look on your face . . . With all your cigarettes and fancy cars/ You ain't a clue who or what you are." Making reference to the home studio where **Elemental** was recorded, Orzabal gloats over the kicking he's crafting and heaps on the humiliation. "Now in Neptune's kitchen you will be food for killer whales." Charmed, I'm sure.

At least **Raoul and the Kings of Spain** (announced for release on one label in early '95 and then scrubbed, altered and issued by another five months later) contains no disgraceful vendettas. The topic here is family heritage; while Roland (born Raoul) seems to harbor strong, inflated opinions about his ancestors ("father was an island . . . mother was the sea . . . all mothers come from heaven . . . all fathers come from hell"), he brings a more cultured artistry—and unprecedented restraint—to bear on the great issues. Though it segues into a fervid flamenco episode, "Sketches of Pain" begins with one acoustic guitar; "Secrets" reaches the point of '80s Elton John, but goes no further; "Humdrum and Humble" switches weirdly between suave Bowiesque calm and a snakey Bo Diddley raveup; "I Choose You" and "Me and My Big Ideas" (with guest vocals by Oleta Adams) are simple, lush ballads; "Falling Down" was reportedly produced without overdubs. (Sure.) While again writing and producing with Griffiths and Palmer, Orzabal sensibly assembled a lively band (including Griffiths, bassist Gail Ann Dorsey and drummer Brian MacLeod), which gives the diverse album more breathing room than any in TefoFe's past, varying the emotional temperature and the ambience all over the place. His singing is revealed to have new facets here; the rancor-free writing is more plainspoken and imaginative—as if the need to prove himself was no longer a driving force. Lines like "These are the days of a different paradigm" are indicative of a pseud who still can't come down off his lofty plane, but the infusion of real people and the unveiling of a new Roland make **Raoul and the Kings of Spain** the most (well, first) ingratiating album of his career.

After plucking her out of a midwestern hotel lounge to feature her voice on **The Seeds of Love,** Orzabal co-produced and played on Oleta Adams' **Circle of One,** fitting her mature songs (mainstream pop-soul originals with a theatrical bent and stirring lyrics of womanly self-determination) into tasteful arrangements that highlight the rich warmth of her voice. The album made Adams a star in her own right, and she took it from there, establishing a solid place in the adult-contemporary field without further assistance from her young mentor. [i]

See also *Nicky Holland; TPRG.*

TECHNO ANIMAL

See *God.*

TEENAGE FANCLUB

A Catholic Education (Matador) 1990
God Knows It's True EP (Matador) 1990
Everything Flows EP (UK Paperhouse) 1991
The King (UK Creation) 1991
Bandwagonesque (DGC) 1991
The Concept EP (UK Creation) 1991
What You Do to Me EP (DGC) 1992
Radio EP (UK Creation) 1993
Norman 3 EP (UK Creation) 1993
Thirteen (DGC) 1993
Deep Fried Fanclub (UK Paperhouse/Fire) 1995
Grand Prix (DGC) 1995
Mellow Doubt EP (UK Creation) 1995

In the late '50s, Scotland's youth looked westward, saw American jugband music, decided it was good, and produced Lonnie Donegan, the lively superstar of skiffle. Three decades later, having witnessed stylistically self-willed homegrown inventions like Big Country and the Postcard popsters (Orange Juice et al.), Scotland's young people turned again to the colonies for inspiration and saw Big Star, the Byrds and Neil Young. Arising from the gene pool of a strong local indie-pop scene guided in the late '80s by the Pastels and Vaselines, and ultimately given their big push into the world by Creation Records (the playground of Scottish entrepreneur Alan McGee), there came a new generation of international bands, foremost among them Teenage Fanclub.

From the time it was formed as a successor to the obscure Boy Hairdressers, itself an outgrowth of the BMX Bandits, the Glasgow quartet of Norman Blake (vocals/guitar), Raymond McGinley (vocals/guitar), Gerard Love (vocals/bass) and Francis Macdonald (drums, replaced following the recording of the first album by Brendan O'Hare) has demonstrated a calmly garrulous pop sensibility, adapting (never quite aping) their sources and mirroring Amerindie irreverence with good-natured aplomb and a lilting Scottish burr.

The band's wonderfully rich blend of loud, layered guitar and raggedly handsome harmony vocals was established almost from the first: "Everything Flows," the group's winning debut from mid-'90, contains all of Teenage Fanclub's distinguishing features. (Still, among the early Paperhouse and Matador singles compiled on the tasty and reasonably solid **Deep Fried Fanclub**—which also contains a '92 K Records single and a demo of **A Catholic Education**'s "Critical Mass"—are two primeval B-sides that don't have the sound down at all.) Displaying plenty of the right spirit and attitude, TFC was instantly welcomed into the international pop underground, and has held on to its indie credibility despite grander label arrangements. Cover versions—and influences—have been flying between Olympia (Beat Happening), Memphis (Alex Chilton/Big Star), Providence (Velvet Crush) and Glasgow ever since.

Recorded in a week, the rough and relaxed **A Catholic Education** keeps the vocals offhand and the root melodies ascending; the combination of informal and uplifting presents the straightforward guitar pop in a flattering light. That leaves only the uneven songwriting to control the album's caliber; after "Everything Flows," "Critical Mass," "Eternal Light" and "Everybody's Fool" (proof that sweet sounds don't always imply a sweet disposition), slim pickings keep **A Catholic Education** from being a full course.

The four-song **God Knows It's True** (repeated in toto on **Deep Fried Fanclub**) was produced by Don Fleming in a one-day New York session and sounds it; the title track and "So Far Gone" are keepers. **Everything Flows,** another fully compiled four-songer, boasts a shaggy cover of Neil Young's "Don't Cry No Tears" and "Primary Education," a B-side demo for "Catholic Education."

The King was rumored to have been made in order to either satisfy or break TFC's contractual obligations; regardless, the hastily tossed together album is an interesting curio. Included among the nine tracks are a quizzical pair of non-originals: Madonna's "Like a Virgin," which can be seen as a response to Ciccone Youth's versions of "Burnin' Up" and "Into the Groove," and Pink Floyd's oft-covered psychedelic classic, "Interstellar Overdrive." The rest might seem disposable on first listen, but further investigation reveals a number of them—including the Bevis Frond–like guitar wank of "Opal Inquest" and the Butthole Surfers–influenced "Robot Love," complete with vocals distorted beyond recognition—to be quite interesting (as is the skronking saxophone of Superstar leader Joe McAlinden, guesting here). **The King** was reportedly deleted the day of its release, making it an instant collectors' item—a gambit the group had already used in late '90 with the one-day release of a one-sided 7-inch of "The Ballad of John and Yoko."

Bandwagonesque is the pinnacle of Teenage Fandom, a superb blend of great songs, wry inside humor and diverse, energetically relaxed performances (not to mention the chintzy fuck-us sack o' money cartoon cover). A month spent in Liverpool with Don Fleming worked clarifying wonders for the group, and **Bandwagonesque** is a modern pop classic. The highlights of this highlight include Love's harmony apocalypse "Star Sign," elegiac "Guiding Star" and "Pet Rock." Doubling the fun, Blake contributes the glammed-up "Metal Baby," the Big Star–styling, Status Quo-naming fan portrait "The Concept" and the even *more* Chilton-like "What You Do to Me." The obvious tribute being paid in no way diminishes the band's own achievement here: aping a group whose twenty-year-old records never sold is hardly a sellout strategy. If not for the pretentious trendiness of so many Big Star acolytes, this wouldn't be any sort of an eyebrow-raiser at all. The '92 **What You Do to Me** EP consists of the album track, a raveup version of it and four more leftovers, including "Like a Virgin," T.Rex's "Life's a Gas" and two Gerry Love originals. (The radio snippet that precedes "Maharishi Dug the Scene" is from an old Alex Chilton interview.) Besides the title tune, **The Concept** presents the demo of "What You Do to Me" and two non-LP numbers.

The sound is tougher and less gauzy, the songs country-inflected and a notch shy of those on **Bandwagonesque;** still, **Thirteen** is an excellent followup that moves the band along without losing its way. Self-consciously hitting back at the music press ("Song to the Cynic"), the US music biz ("Commercial Alternative"), radio ("Radio") and absolutely everything (the Gram-Parsons-by-way-of-the-Lemonheads "120 Mins"), the band finds space in its heart to express admiration for another Byrd (the Neil Youngy instrumental "Gene Clark") and one of its own ("Norman 3"). TFC also admits emotional need ("Hang On," with a Marc Bolan intro) and faces a hard breakup ("The Cabbage"). Pitched at a lower emotional key by a more accomplished outfit, **Thirteen** goes out on a limb and comes back safe and sounding good. (The CD contains six bonus tracks. Recorded simply in electric and acoustic variations, the extras are quite good—especially McGinley's "Genius Envy." The covers of Gram Parsons and Phil Ochs, however, are justly consigned to their subordinate fate.)

Without casting off its basic approach, Teenage Fanclub (now including new drummer Paul Quinn) transformed itself into a Byrdsy/Beatlesque country-rock combo on **Grand Prix.** Completing an organic progression that leaves the group just on the other side of a crucial line in the stylistic sand, the enticing album tones everything down—sounds *and* emotions. The production is occasionally conspicuous, and the record lets the energy lag in spots, but it's a largely successful course adjustment. With McGinley, Love and Blake each writing a third of the songs, the diverse album takes cues from all sorts of eras and idioms; for every strong country leaning (the **Revolver**-ish "About You," the Chiltonesque "Neil Jung," the acoustic "Say No"), there's a more familiar-sounding pop number (the swoony "I'll Make It Clear," the daring "Verisimilitude," the rousing "Don't Look Back") and something unprecedented (the piano-based "Tears," the ripping/whispering "Hardcore/Ballad"). [i/mk]

See also *BMX Bandits, Superstar.*

TEEN ANGELS

Daddy (Sub Pop) 1996

Diminutive singer/guitarist Kelly Canary (like ferocious drummer Lisa Smith, an alumna of Dickless) sounds like both her feet are being fed to hungry piranhas throughout Teen Angels' roaring **Daddy;** the speaker-shredding screams she uses to inarticulate such short ditties as "Go Away," "Fire in the Hole," "Tijuana Pavement Princess," "Sell Out" and a cover of the Supersuckers' "Jack Shit" are Teen Angels' main distinguishing feature. Jack Endino's production of the dozen tracks pulls a clear rock instrumental sound out of the punk trio's pit, but Canary's industrial-strength hollering is the take-it-or-leave-it factor in deciding whether or not to try this toe-dipping descent into sonic splattercore. [i]

TEENGENERATE

Audio Recording (Cruddy Record Dealership) 1993
Teengenerate EP10 (Sympathy for the Record Industry) 1994
Get Action! (Crypt) 1995
Smash Hits! (Estrus) 1995

Initially known as the American Soul Spiders, this Tokyo foursome (Fink, Fifi, Sammy and Suck, later replaced by Shoe) filters its love for traditional garage-punk through a lo-fi fast-and-hard aesthetic with exciting results. It's significant that the band attacks songs by the Queers ("Kicked Out of the Webelos") and Bill Haley ("Shake, Rattle & Roll") with equal spirit on the seventeen-song recorded-in-one-day **Get Action!** Meanwhile, singer/guitarist Fink's originals maintain a consistent level of enthusiasm. The same is true of **Audio Recording:** eleven numbers cut with Scott McCaughey in Seattle one Friday in June '93. Covers include "Shake a Tail Feather," Chuck Berry's "Baby Doll" and Radio Birdman's "Burn My Eye."

The best bet for new converts would have to be **Smash Hits!,** a compilation drawn from Teengenerate's prodigious indie-singles catalogue: ace versions of songs by the Zeros, Nervous Eaters and Pretty Things stand alongside the band's frantic originals. [ss]

TOWA TEI

See *Deee-Lite.*

TELEVISION

Marquee Moon (Elektra) 1977
Adventure (Elektra) 1978
The Blow-Up [tape] (ROIR) 1982 [CD] (Fr. Danceteria) 1989 + 1993
Television (Capitol) 1992

TOM VERLAINE

Tom Verlaine (Elektra) 1979
Dreamtime (Warner Bros.) 1981 (Infinite Zero) 1994
Words From the Front (Warner Bros.) 1982
Cover (Virgin/Warner Bros.) 1984
Flash Light (IRS) 1987
The Wonder (UK Fontana) 1990
Warm and Cool (Rykodisc) 1992
The Miller's Tale (UK Virgin) 1996

RICHARD LLOYD

Alchemy (Elektra) 1979
Field of Fire (Mistlur/Moving Target) 1985 (Grand Slam) 1992
Real Time (Celluloid) 1987 (Grand Slam) 1992

They came, they rewrote the book on guitar rock and then they split up, leaving only a pair of seminal new wave records behind as proof that they had ever existed at all. The brainchild of Tom Verlaine (Miller) and Richard Hell (whose crucial role in the band was actually over before its recording career got underway), Television was a revolutionary force on New York's Bowery circuit in the mid-'70s, an unprecedented amalgam of the Velvet Underground's primal scream, Bob Dylan's esoteric detachment, Roky Erickson's brain-spasm pop and John Coltrane's high-wire improvisation. Influenced by, and in turn influential on, Suicide, Talking Heads, Patti Smith and David Bowie, Television threw punk's disdain for guitar jamming back in the face of those who didn't realize that the form could still be mined for nail-biting excitement and high rock'n'roll art.

Marquee Moon and **Adventure** only tell part of the story; neither captures the band's white-hot intensity or the cavalier instrumental technique (initially pure incompetence) that vindicated all of its early pretensions. When Television was still just an underground phenomenon in New York, the band's stock in trade was un-self-conscious desperation: amid the breaking strings, wildly fluctuating rhythms and songs perennially on the brink of implosion, Verlaine would scrunch his face up, flail blindly at his Fender and spasmodically blurt out his poetic obsessions as if they were talismans against unseen evil. And work made them free. Television had resolved its contradictions by the time it finally made a full-length record. Unlike many of the other amateurs tearing gripping music from the ether in dark clubs around the same time, Television—Verlaine, bassist Fred Smith (not the MC5 great), guitarist Richard Lloyd and drummer Billy Ficca—had, for better and worse, secured full control of its art.

The group turned off before the turn of the decade; an illuminating live-in-'78 compilation, **The Blow-Up,** was released posthumously. Verlaine and Lloyd moved on to solo careers that started strong and petered out; the rhythm section scattered into various bands, remaining active but well out of the limelight. In 1992, with scarcely a word of explanation, Television—a band that many presumed was far too principled and cool to look back in pleasure, yet managed to do so in the most progressive manner possible (a lesson likely noted by Lou Reed, who got his own back-together movement going the following year)—reunited for one impressive album and a stupendous tour before returning to neutral corners.

Although the joint effort came as a complete surprise, the four members hadn't been all that estranged. Smith, who had contributed in some way to all of Verlaine's albums, was a true collaborator on the encouragingly strong **Flash Light** and the offbeat **The Wonder;** Ficca is the drummer on **Warm and Cool,** Verlaine's enigmatic collection of short and simple atmospheric guitar instrumentals that play like sketches for a work in progress. (Making a cute play on Verlaine's real name, **The Miller's Tale**—released in the UK, where he and the group were always better received than at home—is a two-disc retrospective. The first reviews his career with solo and Television tracks; the second documents a 1982 London live set.) Lloyd was the furthest out of orbit: not having made a record of his own in five years, he was recording and touring with Matthew Sweet. (Lately, the guitarist has been playing in Health and Happiness Show.)

A fascinating advance on the band's creative values after a fourteen-year hiatus, **Television** betrays no particular time frame: it is neither nostalgic nor pointedly modern. More rocking than Verlaine's '80s efforts, distinctly in keeping with the sound of the original band but not an echo of it, **Television** takes good advantage of the musicians' far-superior skills and sensitivity to underplay the attack and strike an unsettling mood of handsome surrealism. Verlaine sets the impenetrable agenda—he is credited with "songs"; the band is assigned responsibility for "music"—but Television brings his ideas to collaborative fruition with the organic intricacy of empaths. Although deceptively simple and dynamically lacking at the outset—"1880 or so," "Shane, she wrote this" and "In World" are admirable without leaving much of a mark—the album suddenly kicks into gear. Introduced by an itchy little riff, the noir detective tale of "Call Mr. Lee" opens a trapdoor into a mystery world—an alternate-universe experience familiar to witnesses of TV's first go-'round. "No Glamour for Willi" lashes a sweet, Eno-like chorus to wiggly-guitar verses and comes up a poppy charmer; "Beauty Trip," moving briskly along a Lloyd slide figure, rolls card-playing and romance together in a distinctly Dylanesque manner. The record quietly gains momentum from there: on "The Rocket," Verlaine begins spreading his wings with intense, skittering solos; by the finale, the David Lynch–like "Mars," he's really into the zone, screeching and yelping lyrics for emphasis and bouncing bedspring noises out of his guitar just like in the old days. It may not have been for long, but Television was definitely back. [i]

See also *Matthew Sweet; TPRG.*

TELEVISION PERSONALITIES

Wheres Bill Grundy Now? EP7 (UK Kings Rd) 1978 (UK Rough Trade) 1979 (UK Overground) 1992
. . . And Don't the Kids Just Love It (UK Rough Trade) 1981 (UK Fire) 1991 (Razor and Tie) 1995
Mummy Your Not Watching Me (UK Whaam!) 1982 (UK Dreamworld) 1987 (UK Fire) 1991
They Could Have Been Bigger Than the Beatles (UK Whaam!) 1982 (UK Dreamworld) 1986 (UK Fire) 1991
The Painted Word (UK Illuminated) 1985 (UK Fire) 1991
Chocolat Art (Ger. Pastell) 1985 + 1993
Salvador Dali's Garden Party EP (UK Fire) 1989
Privilege (Fire) 1990
Camping in France (UK Overground) 1991
How I Learned to Love the Bomb EP (UK Overground) 1992
Closer to God (Fire/Seed) 1992
Not Like Everybody Else EP7 (Ger. Little Teddy) 1993
You, Me and Lou Reed EP (UK Fantastic Planet) 1993
Far Away & Lost in Joy EP (UK Vinyl Japan) 1994
The Prettiest Girl in the World EP7 (UK Overground) 1994
Yes Darling, but Is It Art? (Early Singles and Rarities) (Fire/Seed) 1995
Do You Think If You Were Beautiful You'd Be Happy? EP (UK Vinyl Japan) 1995
I Was a Mod Before You Was a Mod (UK Overground) 1995
Paisley Shirts & Mini Skirts (UK no label) 1995
Top Gear (UK Overground) 1996
Made in Japan (Ger. Little Teddy) 1996

JOWE HEAD

Pincer Movement (UK Hedonics) 1981
Strawberry Deutschmark (Ger. Constrictor) 1986
The Jowe Head Personal Organiser (Ger. Hollow Planet/Constrictor) 1989
Jowe Head's Legendary EP EP7 (Ger. Get Happy!!) 1991
Unhinged (UK Overground) 1994

For some people—even those who didn't live through it—one crucial era or another remains paramount, the fountainhead to which all subsequent existence must pay tribute. London singer/guitarist Daniel Treacy evidently considers the pop-art/mod '60s all there is to life; via the Television Personalities—the eccentric, haphazard group that has lobbed his brilliant salvos of vulnerable, adenoidal, damaged genius into the pop world for two decades now—Treacy has fashioned himself the voice of a long-lost young generation. While he draws heavily on mid-'60s pop and psychedelia (to the point of covering songs by the Creation on **They Could Have Been Bigger Than the Beatles** and in concert), Treacy doesn't seek to recreate a sound so much as honor a culture. His artfully (but consciously) naïve and amateurishly played inventions are littered with cinematic and literary references ("Look Back in Anger," "A Picture of Dorian Gray," "A Good and Faithful Servant," "Privilege") and real-life icons ("I Know Where Syd Barrett Lives," "David Hockney's Diary," "Lichtenstein Painting").

A tender, detached, often wounded romantic with a mighty knowledge of his stylistic forebears, Treacy—aided by various sidemen—writes and sings with even more Britishness than Ray Davies or Damon Albarn. As wonderful as they are slapdash, the TVPs' early records are magical to those with the patience for them. The shoebox production on **Mummy Your Not Watching Me** causes a tragic mistreatment of great songs. Recorded live in Germany in 1984, the band is woefully out of tune for most of the **Chocolat Art** album (which is augmented by a spectacular far-flung twenty-two-fragment covers medley on its 1993 CD edition). Treacy turned relatively serious in the late '80s, and the two studio albums recorded after the long layoff that followed **The Painted Word** (itself not bad-sounding, and containing the superb "Someone to Share My Life With") are entirely presentable, professionally produced with no diminution in winsome power.

For a superb primer to the TVPs pioneering days—including such pivotal new wave–era singles as "14th Floor" (the group's debut), "Part Time Punks" and "Wheres Bill Grundy Now?" (both from the '78 EP, a four-song 7-inch that has been issued under both titles) and running into the mid-'80s—**Yes Darling, but Is It Art?** could hardly be bettered. The generously detailed and indispensable rarities compilation is the ideal accessory for fans of the band's albums who are unprepared to hunt down a cornucopia of obscure 45s, EPs and sampler contributions. For further historical background, **Paisley Shirts & Mini Skirts** documents the group's nominal live unveiling (May 1980, on a bill with This Heat and Essential Logic) with muffled sound, lengthy tuning misadventures, a catty dedication of "Part Time Punks" to the Monochrome Set and several songs otherwise lost to posterity.

Privilege was recorded as a trio with ex–Swell Maps bassist/singer Jowe Head and drummer Jeffrey Bloom (the same lineup as appears on **Chocolat Art** and **Camping in France,** a rough but charming live album recorded in 1985; don't miss the Jesus and Mary Chain tribute). Sounding in spots very much like Pete Shelley (especially on "Sometimes I Think You Know Me Better Than I Know Myself"), Treacy is a bad-mood guy here (witness "All My Dreams Are Dead," "This Time There's No Happy Ending" and "Sad Mona Lisa"), but he does brighten long enough for the pop-art happening of "Salvador Dali's Garden Party" (which lists all the posh celebrities in attendance). **Privilege** dresses Treacy's characteristically direct songs with just the right amount of keyboards, and his voice is as boyishly engaging as ever.

Continuing onward and upward with the same rhythm section and guest players adding violin, sax and percussion to the bright arrangements, the nineteen-song **Closer to God** is miles better and certainly the most accessible and easily appealing TVPs LP. For all the magical music he's churning out, however, Treacy himself doesn't seem to be doing very well. The album presents a jumble of neuroses and threats of emotional collapse, barely buoyed by fits of hope and declarations of love ("Little Works of Art," "Honey for the Bears," "This Heart's Not Made of Stone," "Coming Home Soon"). Though wrapped in cute and cuddly pop swaddling, songs refer to scars, doubts, depression, needle marks, razorblades and wrists, the inability to cope and exotic pharmaceuticals. "My Very First Nervous Breakdown" isn't quite as flip as he makes it out to be, and "Very Dark Today" is a frightening emotional weather report. But as Treacy is quick to point out, "It's not a shame / It's not a hard luck story . . . Don't cry for me," and the tunefulness elevates the record, if not the artist, from the trough—real or imagined—from which he's singing. And while the dramatic title track ("the ballad of a Catholic boy") recalls parochial school with bitterness, it ultimately concludes the album with a seemingly upbeat message: "Just when I thought I'd lost my way / I'm feeling closer now/Closer to God."

The TVPs didn't release more than some 45s over the next few years. **How I Learned to Love the Bomb** is a reissue of five single sides from 1986; **The Prettiest Girl in the World** gathers four rare tracks from 1987. **Not Like Everybody Else** contains four amusing covers of songs by the Kinks, Joe Meek and others. ("Whatever Gets You Through the Night"???) That Treacy is unaccompanied on **Far Away & Lost in Joy,** a quartet of boxy-sounding new songs, may help explain the reduction in output, but then so should the disheartened tone of material like "I Don't Want to Live This Life," "Do You Know What They're Saying About Me Now?" and the sardonic title track. Continuing to use the TVP name for solo work, Treacy made **Do You Think If You Were Beautiful You'd Be Happy?,** another four-track EP, for the same label; though better recorded and the first to showcase his somber skills on piano, it's equally downcast, leaving things off with the loud, minor-key hurt of "I Suppose You Think It's Funny."

Treacy plunges into far deeper personality waters on **I Was a Mod Before You Was a Mod,** as if **Closer to God** had been a jolly diving board on which he'd been dancing with his eyes closed. He calls himself "a danger to myself" in "A Stranger to Myself," and that's not the worst of it. The title track of this nearly unaccompanied (save for producer Liam Watson's drumming) album is delightful in its old-fashioned culture-mongering, but otherwise the landscape is as bleak as a Siberian winter. Suffering through such anxieties as "I Can See My Whole World Crashing Down," "Haunted," the self-loathing of "Things Have Changed Since I Was a Girl," the rugged childhood damage of "Everything She Touches Turns to Gold," the desperately, creepily personal "Evan Doesn't Ring Me Anymore" and the groveling, nearly suicidal apologies of "A Long Time Gone," he holds music—here, a strange patchwork of hasty-sounding stylistic innovations (piano, vibes, organ, a soul feel on one song) and more familiar moves—up as a protective shield with gaping holes. For all of Treacy's artistic assets—his singing, melodies and lyrical acumen remain as strong as ever—even devoted fans may find it impossible to genuinely enjoy listening to such harrowing and heartbreaking expressions of loneliness and misery. Suffering for art is one thing, but this is tragic.

After parting company with Treacy, stout-hearted multi-instrumentalist and sonorous vocalist Jowe Head resumed the intermittent low-budget solo career he began when Swell Maps ended. **Unhinged** repeats the entire contents of **Personal Organiser,** a casual and wildly eclectic 1989 German release, adding four leftovers from those sessions (including the massed "Crab Chorus," the speed-drumming goth-trombone noise of "Marzipan" and the Bonzo Dog Band–styled rendition of "Istanbul," the oldie covered to snappier effect by They Might Be Giants) and seven equally unpredictable-sounding live tracks, the oddest of which is the Fall-styling "Tarbabies." Four of the same songs make up **Jowe Head's Legendary EP.**

For Treacy's sake, it's encouraging to hear him reunited with Jowe on **Top Gear,** a long, sloppy and poignant live album (the band's fourth official concert LP; the same tour also produced the fifth, **Made in Japan**) cleanly recorded in Osaka in April 1995. With drummer Lenny Helsing on loan from the Thanes, the TVPs very nearly outnumber the "crowd": the smattering of polite applause suggests an audience of perhaps a half-dozen. Nonetheless, a composed and confident Treacy still wields his music like a flashlight, pouring his heart and his not-quite-tuned guitar into the career retrospective with a lot more evident meaning than the audience could possibly appreciate. Each of the eighteen songs is a reminder of the thin line between his art and life. He barely gets through "All My Dreams Are Dead" and makes the tenderness of "If I Could Write Poetry" and "Little Works of Art" and the confessions of "This Heart's Not Made of Stone" achingly real. The jollier songs (like "Magnificent Dreams," "I Hope You Have a Nice Day" and "Picture of Dorian Gray") buoy the mood; the emotional scorecard winds up about level. Not at all for neophytes, but a must for fans. [i]

See also *TPRG.*

TEMPLE OF THE DOG

See *Mother Love Bone.*

TENDER FURY

See *True Sounds of Liberty.*

TENDERLOIN

See *Reverend Horton Heat.*

10,000 MANIACS

Human Conflict Number Five EP (Mark) 1982 (Christian Burial/Press) 1984
Secrets of the I Ching (Christian Burial) 1983 (Christian Burial/Press) 1983
The Wishing Chair (Elektra) 1985
In My Tribe (Elektra) 1987

Blind Man's Zoo (Elektra) 1989
Hope Chest (Elektra) 1990
Our Time in Eden (Elektra) 1992
MTV Unplugged (Elektra) 1993

JOHN AND MARY

Victory Gardens (Rykodisc) 1991
The Weedkiller's Daughter (Rykodisc) 1993

Though they would eventually achieve tremendous commercial success, 10,000 Maniacs seemed unlikely candidates for mainstream stardom at the start of their recording career. The sprawlingly eclectic sextet from the remote upstate New York burg of Jamestown originally drew inspiration from an unpredictable array of influences, from folk to punk to reggae, an approach that's reflected on **Human Conflict Number Five** and **Secrets of the I Ching.** Both indie discs document the Maniacs' gently frenetic early sound, driven by the skirling guitars of Robert Buck and John Lombardo and given additional depth by Dennis Drew's subtly atmospheric keyboards. Natalie Merchant's odd, whispery vocals and fragmentary lyrics are already distinctive and intriguing. The former disc has a rather indecisive, unformed feel, but the latter begins to bring some needed focus to the band's warmly eccentric vision by concentrating on the folk-rock elements. The contents of both (minus the **Human Conflict** version of "Tension," a song the band recorded for each) are smartly assembled, in remixed and resequenced form, on **Hope Chest.**

The Wishing Chair is a compelling major-label debut, as ex–Fairport Convention producer Joe Boyd helps the group sharpen its sound without sacrificing its original organic urgency or the inquisitive wonder of Merchant's lyrics. The band's assertiveness and the singer's introspection achieve a graceful balance on picturesque numbers like "Can't Ignore the Train," "Lilydale" and "Back o' the Moon," as well as three rerecorded **Secrets of the I Ching** numbers (including the third "Tension Makes a Tangle").

In My Tribe marks a decisive turning point. The departure of John Lombardo—the band's de facto leader and most prolific composer—shifts the songwriting balance of power in Merchant's favor. Also, the band trades Boyd for the more commercially oriented Peter Asher, whose polished production smooths out much of the edge but adds a stately melodic grace that can be appealing, particularly when applied to material as heartfelt as "Don't Talk," "The Painted Desert," "A Campfire Song" (featuring a vocal cameo by Michael Stipe) and the spry, Caribbean-flavored "Like the Weather." The album also includes a competent but unnecessary remake of Cat Stevens' "Peace Train," which became an embarrassment to the band when Stevens joined other Moslems in calling for the assassination of author Salman Rushdie.

The musical simplicity that was refreshing on **In My Tribe** began to feel constricting on **Blind Man's Zoo,** which features emotionally and musically on-target material ("Eat for Two," "Headstrong") but also suffers from an increasing tendency towards well-intentioned but unfocused preachiness ("Please Forgive Us," "You Happy Puppet"). That's less of a problem on **Our Time in Eden,** the lyrics of which tend to explore more personal territory. New producer Paul Fox gives the band a sound that's frequently gorgeous but rather anonymous, underlining Merchant's increased creative dominance (more than half of the songs are her solo compositions). Still, it's hard to fault standouts like "Stockton Gala Days," "Candy Everybody Wants" and "Few and Far Between"—the last two featuring the legendary JB Horns. Rather than strip down to basics, the band expanded tastefully for **MTV Unplugged,** on which nine added musicians lend a hand on reworkings of thirteen Maniacs tunes, as well as a decent reading of Patti Smith's "Because the Night."

Merchant left the band to go solo following **MTV Unplugged.** The Maniacs regrouped by bringing John Lombardo back into the fold, along with singer/violist Mary Ramsey (who had guested on **Our Time in Eden** and **MTV Unplugged**). Replacing Merchant with Lombardo and Ramsey was an inspired move, since the two albums the pair recorded as John and Mary maintain much of the ghostly grace of the Maniacs' early work—not altogether surprising, given the presence of Maniacs Robert Buck (guitar) and Jerome Augustyniak (drums) on both discs. Ramsey's vocals are similar to—but less self-absorbed and more melodic than—Merchant's; Lombardo's songwriting continues to explore familiar themes of human memory and cosmic mystery. **Victory Gardens** is a seductive, low-key delight, while the more fully realized **The Weedkiller's Daughter** (with guest contributions by Alex Chilton, Bob Wiseman and Mary Margaret O'Hara) is even stronger. [ss]

See also *Natalie Merchant; TPRG.*

TERMINALS

Disconnect EP (NZ Flying Nun) 1988
Uncoffined (NZ Flying Nun) 1990
Disease [tape] (NZ Xpressway) 1991
Cul-de-Sac (NZ Flying Nun) 1992
Touch (Ger. Raffmond) 1992
Little Things (Ger. Raffmond) 1995

VICTOR DIMISICH BAND

Native Waiter EP (NZ Flying Nun) 1982
Mekong Delta Blues [tape] (NZ Xpressway) 1988

Terminals' origins are in the Victor Dimisich Band, a Christchurch group focused more on garage than pop. When that outfit (which never included anyone named Victor Dimisich) broke apart, several members joined Bill Direen in the Bilders, while the majority became Terminals. Creating a niche of their own within the brainy, wistful New Zealand pop sound of the Bats, Chills and others, Terminals ignored the sweetness of their compatriots' music to embrace the dark side, pointing the quartet closer in spirit to Australia's Birthday Party. The songs are like a messy emotional archaeological dig in which the excavation of pained feelings also unearths a few shining fragments.

The change in guitarist Stephen Cogle's vocals charts the transition between the band's first two recordings. Although he retains a Syd Barrett–like edginess on both, the neat warbling drawl he evinces on **Disconnect** is smoothed out on **Uncoffined.** The shift costs him some uniqueness, which he later made up for in clarity and intensity. Both records include tense, random organ mixed with brief squiggles of guitar feedback, anchored by drummer Peter Stapleton, who thuds on his small kit like mausoleum doors slamming. **Cul-de-Sac** is a CD reissue of the combined records. (In an unusual role reversal, Cogle, who writes most of the band's music, doesn't provide any of its lyrics. Stapleton, who divides his time—and a lot of the Victór Dimisich Band songs—between Terminals and a group called Scorched Earth Policy, takes care of that duty.)

The live **Disease,** recorded at various public haunts or in practice sessions, is essentially a muddy live preview of **Touch,** which contains pared-down/cleaned-up versions of nearly the same set of songs. Recorded in a real studio and on a 4-track between 1990 and 1992, **Touch** is full of garbled vocals (Cogle sings from his spleen and nerves rather than his heart or mind), Mick Elborado's twittering space organ and tea kettles boiling away in the background. Although a little slower, with the organ ringing more hollow and Cogle letting his bandmates sing more, **Little Things** doesn't vary the sound much. With less of **Touch**'s out-there experiments, however, it most closely resembles **Uncoffined.** [rxe]

TERMINATOR X

See *Public Enemy.*

TEXAS

Southside (Mercury) 1989
Mothers Heaven (Mercury) 1991
Ricks Road (Mercury) 1994

In an era when most internationally prominent Scottish bands were guzzling at the Byrds/Big Star pop bar, chugging down Stones sterno or staring vacantly at their shoes, this uncommon Glasgow quartet (whose bassist, John McElhone, formerly played it twee in Altered Images and funky in Hipsway) elected instead to pour a glossed-up mainstream Americana brew of bland radio rock flavored with folk-rock and country. Sharleen Spiteri's deep, handsome, unaccented voice sounds like the new Nashville; her bandmates' agile backing, though, is too modern-rock to be part of that world. Although the derivative, bland songs (mostly Spiteri/McElhone collaborations) on **Southside** don't pander stupidly enough to explain it, the record was a major worldwide success. (But who gets the songwriting royalties for "Everyday Now," a number that models its refrain on "I Shall Be Released"?)

Evincing more commercial desire than stylistic integrity, Texas added a keyboard player, changed drummers and lunged hard at all manner of Transeurolantic pop furnishings on **Mothers Heaven,** a varied heap of dull dung. The title track scales down Simple Minds mock-gospel grandiosity (with backing vocals by Maria McKee); "Why Believe in You" jiggers through a dramatic modern dance; "This Will All Be Mine" sinks down for atmospheric harmonica blues; "Return" is acoustic skiffle; "In My Heart" has a catchy Linda Ronstadt–type chorus. Spiteri is a fine singer, but dressing up such generic writing in so many different outfits makes Texas seem awfully desperate to find something—anything—that might stick.

The songs are still underwritten (endless repetition is a mild problem), but **Ricks Road,** produced by Paul Fox, is actually good. Integrating a retro-rocking core from bits of Delaney and Bonnie, Linda Ronstadt, the Pretenders, Annie Lennox and Bonnie Raitt, the quintet doesn't try half as hard and comes across twice as nice. Accented with, not dominated by, country, bluesy or gospel-rock fervor, Spiteri gives full voice to such memorable, straightforward songs as "You Owe It All to Me," "You've Got to Live a Little," "Listen to Me," "So Called Friend" and a credible (if oversung) cover of Al Green's "Tired of Being Alone." If Texas hasn't bagged a sound of its own yet, at least the group is finally shopping in the right aisle. [i]

TEXAS INSTRUMENTS

!More Texas Instruments! (Longhead) 1985
The Texas Instruments (Rabid Cat) 1987
Sun Tunnels (Rabid Cat) 1988 (Doctor Dream) 1993
Crammed Into Infinity (Rockville) 1991
Magnetic Home (Doctor Dream) 1993
Speed of Sound (Doctor Dream) 1994

Triumphant rock stars are a dime a dozen—or at least heavily discounted at a chainstore near you. Quietly heroic mavericks like the Texas Instruments are rarer currency. All TI ever does is grow, survive and take pleasure in the simple fact of its existence, a living testament to craft, excellence and the timeless power of populist American rock'n'roll. Over a decade-plus career, the Texas Instruments has sculpted a sustained and articulate body of work that stands in proud defiance—almost as if it were an indirectly proportional factor—of unprofitable tours, bad record company mojo and a low national profile. Even the locals are complacent: the only combo left standing among its ballyhooed Austin peers (True Believers, Zeitgeist, Glass Eye, Wild Seeds) is taken utterly for granted by most hometown clubgoers. (But there are probably people living down the block from the Louvre who've never seen the Mona Lisa, either.) Bassist Ron Marks gets recognized on the street sometimes, but only from his appearance in *Slacker.*

Unlike books, you can judge a band by its cover(s). Early on, TI—then a trio composed of El Paso buddies Marks and guitarist David Woody, plus Lubbock-bred drummer Steve Chapman—tackled songs by the Minutemen, Woody Guthrie and Bob Dylan. This de facto post-punk/folk/rock hybrid remains an accurate, if incomplete, model of the band's aesthetic. The first two records are both twangy and jammy—the Meat Puppets are a reasonable analogy—with promising songs and an affable DIY looseness. **Sun Tunnels** contains versions of Dylan's "You Ain't Going Nowhere" and Mike Watt's "Life as a Rehearsal," but also the homegrown acoustics of "Little Black Sunrise" and the boppy Dylanized observation of "Watch'n It All Go Down."

The band finally blossomed on its fourth album: the music on **Crammed Into Infinity** is more precise, while the lyrics hit hard with observant social sketches and pointed cultural muckraking. "Don't Force Me (To Force You)" smartly compares the vision of society's marginals to those who have it easy; the weary, insanely catchy title track is a nonpareil rock'n'roll song.

After **Crammed Into Infinity** was recorded (but, the indie biz being what it is, several years before it was released) TI picked up second guitarist Clay Daniel, who broadened the band's sound both melodically and rhythmically. The lyrics brim with content, care and economy of image on **Magnetic Home,** while the music is a commanding convergence of jumping rhythms, seething guitars and compact hooks, brushed with power and finesse in a palette that includes trance-inducing psychedelia, rockist country-western, toe-tapping near-funk and rubberband power-pop. "Armagideon's Child" and "Magnetic Home" are both propulsive anthems; "Vision" is lovely rumination tempered with Daniel's fierce leads.

The followup is an equally good collection of songs by a band in its artistic prime—if they were younger, or newer or somehow associated with Uncle Tupelo, the Texas Instruments would be hailed as '90s roots-rock saviors. **Speed of Sound** has an alienated, somber feel on the one hand (the woozy title track, "The King of Nothing") and a pungent sense of guitar-driven violence on the other ("Let It Shine," "Top of the Tower"). The disc is rounded out by a cover of the Small Faces' "Song of a Baker," and it's a tribute to the band that they make it sound like an original, from its garage-soul lilt right down to the capitalism-conscious-slice-of-life lyrics.

Amazingly, after years of intermittent but unrealized harassment from a certain electronics corporation, 1996 saw the Texas Instruments finally giving in to renewed legal pressure, resulting in a name change to the Instruments (still TI to fans and friends). [jc]

See also *Daniel Johnston; TPRG.*

THA DOGG POUND

Dogg Food (Death Row/Interscope) 1995

In the Death Row clan's surreal gangsta clubhouse, Dat Nigga Daz (Long Beach DJ/producer/rapper Delmar Arnaud) and Kurupt (Philadelphia-born rapper Ricardo Brown) came up as the quick-study kid brothers, helping Dr. Dre and Snoop Doggy Dogg (Arnaud's cousin) with their projects. Nobody took notice until the pair made the band name official (the whole posse is known as the Dogg Pound as well) and began preparing its own album. Opponents of gangsta rap's excesses ran for their pulpits to roundly denounce what they hadn't heard. They needn't have bothered. **Dogg Food,** which gets vocal contributions from such pound-pals as Snoop, Lady of Rage, Michel'le, Prince Ital Joe and Nate Dogg and was mixed by Dre, is a low-key, unambitious and only mildly imaginative replay of **Doggystyle,** rolling over familiar G-funk terrain with the same minimum of venom and violence. (But a lot of bad words and something else: "If We All Fuc" and the sound-effected "Some Bomb Azz Pussy" get busy with sweaty adolescent fervor.) With plenty of the wiggly bass worms and soulfully sung refrains that are the label's trademark, the album is a functionally adequate addition to the funk shelf, but tracks like "Sooo Much Style," "I Don't Like to Dream About Gettin Paid" (an involving story about an ex-hustler's problems staying straight) and the aptly titled DJ Pooh–produced "Smooth" are nothing to get freaked about. Although **Dogg Food** shouldn't be judged by what it isn't, Tha Dogg Pound's unimpressive debut doesn't leave much of a stain. (Best alt.rock.cred line, from "Reality": "I maintain/Ain't that much strain/To make me twist myself/Like Kurt Cobain.") [i]

THAT DOG

that dog (DGC) 1994
old timer EP (DGC) 1994
Totally Crushed Out! (DGC) 1995

Loitering around the fringes of noxious cutesypoo wearing the latest indie-rock garb, Los Angeles' lower-case that dog makes like a privileged pop music debutante, coyly feigning childishness that doesn't entirely disguise mature intelligence and poise. The harmonizing wispy voices belonging to guitarist Anna Waronker (sister of Walt Mink's Joey), bassist Rachel Haden and her violin-playing twin Petra (who also plays in the Weezer-related Rentals; their brother is in the band Spain and their father is jazz great Charlie Haden) stamp a folky ambience on the quartet's wan creations; even on those songs laid low with guitar distortion, the vocals breeze along paying little heed to their changing environment.

Switching between delicately strung-out chamber rock (with a guest cellist) and jellied punk-pop, **that dog** is a no-cal Shirley Temple that attempts to subsist on anorexic melodies and flavorless performances. That leaves only the wit of such self-conscious lyrics as the laundry list of inanely trivial gripes that makes up "Westside Angst," the sweetly derisive "Punk Rock Girl" and the junk-TV worship of "Paid Programming" to cling to. It's not enough. (The **old timer** EP contains the titular album track and another, plus a live version of the non-LP "Grunge Couple" and the otherwise unissued "I Invented a Head.")

Perhaps belated recognition of the debut's stylistic weakness explains the firmer textures of **Totally Crushed Out!,** a rosy-cheeked and punky power-pop album resembling Veruca Salt in spots. The band's vocal capabilities actually connect with the energized arrangements, dressing them up rather than ignoring them. The relationship- and self-obsessed lyrics still reflect a stunted high-school sensibility (or the arch representation of one) and occasionally descend into avoidable clumsiness ("When it's a day of days/I go into a craze/My head and body feel malaise"), but when the giddy ideas match the peppy music—as in the roaring "Lip Gloss"—that dog can be a pleasure to have around. [i]

See also *Love Child, Weezer.*

THAT PETROL EMOTION

Manic Pop Thrill (UK Demon) 1986
Babble (Polydor) 1987
The Peel Sessions EP (UK Strange Fruit) 1987
Live (Mansfield) 1988
End of the Millennium Psychosis Blues (Virgin) 1988
Peel Sessions Album (UK Strange Fruit) 1989 (Strange Fruit/Dutch East India Trading) 1991
Chemicrazy (Virgin) 1990
Sensitize EP (UK Virgin) 1990
Fireproof (UK Koogat) 1993 (Rykodisc) 1994

Formed in the mid-'80s by Northern Ireland's O'Neill brothers as a serious adult challenge to the teenage kicks they enjoyed (or not) in the Undertones, That Petrol Emotion brought their nationalism to the fore in a musically divergent and politically potent rock quintet. Switching over from rhythm guitar, Damian O'Neill initially played bass in the Petrols; his older brother Seán (previously known as John) and Derry homeboy Réamann Ó Gormáin (aka Raymond Gorman) played guitar; drummer Ciaran McLaughlin and Seattle singer Steve Mack completed the lineup.

The first two albums are strong, articulate and angry, vehement displays of radical commentary and scourging energy. Mack is a fine, controlled shouter in the British blues-rock tradition; the band's combination of slide guitars, Bo Diddley beats, wild harmonica wailing and raveup release recalls the early Stones, Yardbirds and Velvet Underground.

While some of the more restrained material on the stylistically scattered **End of the Millennium Psychosis Blues** (produced, as was **Babble,** by ex-Swans drummer Roli Mosimann) is underwhelming, "Sooner or Later," "Tension," "Here It Is . . . Take It!" and "Groove Check" (on which the band's Celtic funk-rock, complete with horns, is in full effect) are gripping. Seán Ó Néill subsequently chose family life over rock'n'roll and left the band. Damian returned to guitar, McLaughlin emerged as the leading songwriter and the Petrols drafted a new bassist, John Marchini, who made his debut on the Scott Litt–produced **Chemicrazy.** Given all the changes (one of which is Mack's newly mannered singing), it's surprising the album sounds anything like its predecessors, but the band's febrile guitar inventions remain firmly in place. In the absence of Seán's disconsolate moodiness and Mosimann's loud impudence, though, what remains is crisply presentable but emotionally defused, lyrically inadequate and blandly commercialized. While the slithery "Scum Surfin'" and the pop melodicism of "Sensitize" prove there is life after the end of the millennium, **Chemicrazy** is a dose of the wrong medicine.

Seemingly on the ropes after losing their record deal, the Petrols—with yet another bass player, Brendan Kelly—rebounded with the indie-released **Fireproof** (shades of the Undertones' "Tearproof"?). Proclaiming themselves the "Last of the True Believers," the Petrols reclaim the edgy roughness and intensity of **Babble,** minus the topical conflagrations—a good idea on the surface, as the Petrols' ability to wrap thorny guitars around an inviting musical stream remains impressive. But the droney, melody-deprived rockers can't get by strictly on drive, and the album's parallel attempt to advance the quintet's Beatlesque pop aspirations is also stymied: only "Speed of Light" hits the humalong target squarely. Without a striking songwriter to focus all this vigor, That Petrol Emotion is a lit fuse looking for something to detonate. **The Peel Sessions** album, given a domestic release, documents the original lineup in two four-song sets from 1985. [i]

See also *TPRG*.

THEE AMAZING COLOSSAL MEN

See *Compulsion.*

THEE HEADCOATEES

See *Billy Childish.*

THEE HEADCOATS

See *Billy Childish.*

THEE HYPNOTICS

Live'r Than God! EP (UK Situation Two) 1989
Live'r Than God! (Sub Pop) 1989
Come Down Heavy (Beggars Banquet/RCA) 1990
Soul Glitter & Sin (Beggars Banquet/RCA) 1991
The Very Crystal Speed Machine (American) 1994

Hailing from High Wycombe, a town northwest of London, Thee Hypnotics became a favorite of the fickle British music press with its first single, 1989's "Justice in Freedom." It was a stunning debut that, in both politics and volume, echoed the MC5, and by length (nearly nine minutes) hearkened back to the very early days of English metal. The quartet—singer James Jones, guitarist Ray Hanson, drummer Mark Thompson and bassist Will Pepper—followed that with the solid "Soul Trader," then released the five-song **Live'r Than God!** in-concert EP, complete with an even longer version of "Justice in Freedom." Like most young bands with vigorous live reputations—and especially a group with a penchant for extended compositions—Thee Hypnotics' live sound doesn't translate well, nor is the recording quality particularly good.

It might not have mattered, had not **Live'r Than God!** become half of the band's first US issue, a live/studio summary of work to date. For licensing reasons, the live "Justice in Freedom" was used rather than its clean and punchy studio counterpart, and the tapes sent to Sub Pop produced surprisingly tinny sounds. What had seemed full and rambunctious on English vinyl translated onto American CD as thin and more dated than it meant to be.

Though the band also encountered sound problems recording their first full-length studio album, **Come Down Heavy** (with new drummer Phil Smith) delivers what the title promises. With guest shots by Phil May and Dick Taylor of the Pretty Things (Rolling Stones contemporaries who know a thing or three about old-school grunge), Thee Hypnotics still sound like refugees from early-'70s Detroit—hard between the Stooges and Nugent—who've awoken two decades later with a bad hangover. The songs are tighter (not shorter), and Hanson plays as if he were the long-lost son of Peter Green.

Just as the cylinders seemed to be firing, Thee Hypnotics got into a car wreck while touring the States. In the aftermath, Robert Zyn was added on rhythm guitar. **Soul Glitter & Sin** (subtitled *Tales From the Sonic Underworld*) begins with the band's usual bang, but drifts into psychedelic lassitude, either heading off in too many directions at once or simply running out of ideas.

Three years later, with Zyn gone, a new label deal in hand and kindred raunch-rock revivalist Black Crowes singer Chris Robinson in the producer's seat, Thee Hypnotics made **The Very Crystal Speed Machine.** Ironically, working in a California studio with Americans (guitarist Marc Ford and keyboardist Eddie Harsch of the Crowes pitch in) leads the quartet to sound more like English antecedents (especially Free, Led Zeppelin and late-'60s Stones) than it ever has. A dubious achievement, to be sure, but the album completes Thee Hypnotics' transition from self-conscious fetishists aping a vintage sound to dedicated retroids ready to join the real things in the road-goes-ever-on trenches. And that's something to grow on. [ga/i]

See also *TPRG*.

THE(E) SPEAKING CANARIES

The Joy of Wine (Mind Cure) 1993
Songs for the Terrestrially Challenged (Mind Cure) 1995
(Scat) 1995

If you've been staying up late wondering when the indie scene would spawn its own Joe Satriani, Damon Che (Fitzgerald) is the man to—no value judgment intended—give you a good night's sleep. Che, who spends part of his time manning the drums in Pittsburgh prog-punk instrumental trio Don Caballero, uses his other trio as a conduit for technique-obsessed, sporadically riveting guitar explorations—not to mention an unhealthy fixation on the oeuvre of (no, really) Eddie Van Halen.

On its debut, The(e) Speaking Canaries demonstrates a reasonable fluency in free-form freakouts that owe a fair amount to psychedelic brethren like Crystalized Movements, but the compound fractures in both recording quality and compositional consummation result in a half-baked effort. The sprawling **Songs for the Terrestrially Challenged,** however, boasts some emphatically mesmerizing moments: Che unskeins some of the more fetching controlled feedback explorations you're likely to hear, especially "Summer's Empty Resolution" and the Middle Eastern–tinged "Famous No Space." When he and comrades Karl Hendricks (the singer/guitarist of the trio that bears his name plays bass here) and Noah Leger (also the drummer in Hurl) coalesce, they project a mightily fuzzy roar that could be called garage-rock—providing the garage in question is scaled to house an aircraft carrier. But when they resort to Van Halen covers—as they do twice on the album—you'll think you're in Hades' first Ground Round lounge. The album was recorded twice with little variation in repertoire: Scat's is the standard one, while the Mind Cure issue offers the same material in impenetrable lo-fi. [dss]

See also *Don Caballero, Karl Hendricks Trio.*

THE FOR CARNATION

See *Slint.*

THELONIOUS MONSTER

Baby . . . You're Bummin' My Life Out in a Supreme Fashion (Epitaph) 1986
Next Saturday Afternoon (Relativity) 1987
Stormy Weather (Relativity) 1989
Beautiful Mess (Signal/Capitol) 1992

After leading Los Angeles' inconsistent, unreliable, disreputable but often inspired club legend Thelonious Monster through three albums—each of which drew nearer to commercial presentability for the floating organization of up to seven (including ex-Weirdos guitarist Dix Denney, Circle Jerk Zander Schloss and 45 Grave bassist Rob Graves)—singer/self-confessed fuckup Bob Forrest let the band collapse and set about making a highly personal solo album. That record was ultimately scrapped, but parts of it were salvaged and completed by most of the **Stormy Weather** band to become the relaunched Monster's fourth—and best—album. Despite the riot of credits (it looks as if half the music world had some part in its production) and such guest stars as Tom Waits, Dan Murphy and Dave Pirner of Soul Asylum, Al Kooper, Michael Penn and Benmont Tench, **Beautiful Mess** is a lot more together than the title would suggest.

Alternately self-critical, apathetic, bitter and frightened, Forrest's lyrics have a lacerating, confessional power in which his self-destructive past feeds a new, no less jaundiced appreciation of life. "I just can't be sad," he sings after listing his assets in the folk-rocking "I Live in a Nice House," but he's clearly not convinced. The soulful "I Get So Scared" and the Faces-like "Ain't Never Been Nuthin' for Me in This World" sound more like it; the familial alienation of the stomping "Blood Is Thicker Than Water" and the dismal plea of the wah-wahing "Body and Soul?" (co-written with Kooper) cut closer still to the bone. The affecting suffering of Forrest's auto-sacrifice would be unbearably tragic (or too solipsistic) to behold were it not for the glimmers of redemption in his ability to see himself. Still, it's a rugged way to make a living. "It's like my body and soul can't take it anymore / Please somebody help me / I never wanted help before." [i]

See also *Circle Jerks; TPRG.*

THERAPIST JOHN'S ZIP CODE REVUE

See *Zip Code Rapists.*

THERAPY?

Babyteeth (UK Wiiija) 1991
Pleasure Death EP (UK Wiiija) 1992
Caucasian Psychosis (Quarterstick) 1992
Nurse (A&M) 1993
Hats off to the Insane EP (A&M) 1993
Perversionality EP (A&M) 1993
Troublegum (A&M) 1994
Infernal Love (A&M) 1995

In musical terms, the city of Belfast has never unleashed anything as beastly as Therapy?. This uncompromising (and sometimes truly vile) trio has more than earned its reputation as the capital's most notorious sonic stepchild. Something of an Irish analogue to Big Black, the group produces an incessant pounding, screeching and grinding aural assault capable of inducing a trance-like effect on one hand and an unsettling tumult of harsh images and sensations on the other.

Babyteeth owes a great deal to a handful of conventional influences, not the least of which is the sort of hardcore punk more often associated with California and Chicago than the British Isles. The seven-song record's true strength is its uncommon, sometimes otherworldly mix. Singer/guitarist Andrew Cairns' power chords, draped over beats (by ex-goth drummer Fyfe Ewing and bassist Michael McKeegan) that would find themselves at home in a New York danceclub, are augmented by production that turns it all into a nearly impenetrable wall of torturous sound. (See "Animal Bones" and "Meat Abstract" for prime examples thereof.) Despite **Babyteeth**'s powerful sound, tracks like the vacuous "Loser Cop" are better programmed out. The intro is fine, but the song quickly dissolves into an adolescent rant punctuated with nearly three minutes of the word "asshole."

Pleasure Death is difficult to distinguish from its predecessor, but the trio's fascination with the darker side of the human psyche is beginning to solidify into a style. The opening "Skinning Pit" navigates a tricky shift from dance to metal-on-metal grind—and then back again. The instrumental "D.L.C." adds a novel twist to some shopworn speedmetal clichés, while "Shitkicker" might have come from a Greg Ginn record. **Pleasure Death** is hampered by overly distorted vocals, but the disc merits a few listens. **Babyteeth** and **Pleasure Death** may lack variety, but few records sound this foreboding or nasty. **Caucasian Psychosis** combines them for American release.

Therapy? hit its zenith after signing with A&M, releasing **Nurse** at the start of '93. This unforgettable bomb blast of a record fine-tunes the atmosphere of the first two EPs by adding a little more crunch to the low end. At the same time, the vocals are treated to some mixing-board crispiness, then hauled closer to the front. The album's most intriguing aspect is its subject matter, which poses Therapy? as a self-anointed voice of the mentally ill and physically abused. The minimalist lyrics eerily convey the mindset of someone in a declined psychological state or struggling to overcome some sort of socially unacceptable abnormality. The album could well provide a professional with a bit of weekend spot diagnosis brush-up fun. "Nausea" smacks of anti-social behavior and a problem with intimacy; the techno-dancey "Teethgrinder" hints at a compulsion disorder; "Neck Freak" indicates obsessive behavior coupled with some amount of hypochondria; the dub-heavy "Deep Sleep" suggests clinical insomnia.

The six-song **Hats off to the Insane** represents a significant change for the band. Jettisoning the gargantuan, completely unnatural sounds of the first three platters in favor of clear, crisp production, the record is still bigger than life, with "Turn" and "Totally Random Man" sounding as if Metallica's **. . . And Justice for All** had run headlong into mid-'80s Killing Joke.

Troublegum, Therapy?'s second full-length studio album, founders in two areas. "Femtex" and "Stop It You're Killing Me" feature trite, predictable metallic riffs that might better have been left to Mötley Crüe. Also, the lyrics are too literal, leaving precious little to the imagination. For all of its failings, though, **Troublegum** has some intriguing high points, including the infectious pop-metal strains of "Hellbelly," the pop-punk of "Nowhere" and the two-headed "Die Laughing," which sports an Andy Summers–ish intro. (The album reprises two tracks from **Hats off to the Insane**—"Turn" and the pained adolescent anthem "Screamager"—and trots out a chilled-fire cover of Joy Division's "Isolation.")

The trio's stylistic progress toward a cranky conciliation with the mainstream continues on the noxious **Infernal Love,** a caricatured, ugly and ineffectual epistle on the disasters of love and lust. "A Moment of Clarity" begins quietly, but Therapy?'s blustery onslaught is as inevitable as Cairns' devotion to mood-darkening lyrics. That song and the cello-bottomed "Bowels of Love" paint desire as a dreadful compulsion; the latter is comical in its determined embrace of emotional ugliness. "Me Vs You," another study in hard rock vs. quiet strings, ends an affair in no uncertain terms; "Diane" (a harmony/cello exercise that resembles the work of Alejandro Escovedo) is a first-person rape-murder fiction; "30 Seconds" makes a passing reference to being "Buggered by a priest/ When you were seven years of age." Furthering the experiment, "Stories" sounds an awful lot like an angry young Police cover band testing out new lyrics to "Message in a Bottle" and "Loose" is chewy, catchy midwestern punk-pop. At the album's low point ("Bad Mother"), Cairns addresses a dying parent in the least sympathetic and most self-obsessed terms imaginable. "It's a beautiful day/But I don't see it that way . . . I'm edgy, cramped and cold/Trying to keep down the things/That you keep wanting to throw up." Lovely. [icm/i]

THESE ANIMAL MEN

Too Sussed? EP (Hut USA/Vernon Yard) 1994
Taxi for These Animal Men EP (UK Rise/Virgin) 1995
(Come on, Join) The High Society (Hut USA/Vernon Yard) 1995

The minute an English toddler caught sight of the Sex Pistols on British television and registered a subconscious thought ("that rock'n'roll swindle fing looks easy i bet i can get away wif that when i get older") somewhere between its noodle and nappy before reinserting its thumb and crawling off to do something more pressing, Britain was doomed to endure an endless series of young bands determined to top the wanton exploits and arrogant posturing of their predecessors. Self-appointed stars from the Manic Street Preachers to Primal Scream to Radiohead to Oasis have provided the United Kingdom (and parts beyond) with colorful Clockwork brats on parade, generating news stories, obnoxious interviews and, occasionally, some good—if rarely original—music.

At the start, Brighton's These Animal Men—singer/guitarist Boag, guitarist Julian "Hooligan" Hewings, bassist Patrick Murray and drummer Steve Hussey—got by on sheer attitude. Although tuneful and harmony cushioned, the band's early records spring from the same fountain of energetic rock/pop (spigots marked Mott the Hoople, David Bowie and the New York Dolls) that has nurtured bands from Generation X on down. Retrieved from a live BBC session, the speeding title track of the five-song **Too Sussed?** begins with the "Baba O'Riley" riff and then blasts along on pure adrenaline, spewing clever-sounding impending-adulthood rubbish for lyrics. The EP also contains the quartet's first two singles: "Speed King," an especially catchy automotive romantic tale that winks at methamphetamine users, and "You're Not My Babylon," an absurdly grandiose psychodrama about John Dillinger beating up his girlfriend. Despite some idiosyncrasies, the music is as programmed by history as the record's crucifixion cartoon cover.

Come the full-length album, the quartet is revealed to be the second coming of the Only Ones—and not just because Boag replicates the guitar solo from "Another Girl, Another Planet" almost note for note on "You're Always Right." Putting some fight into the fey, provocative intelligence into the words and street-level life into the anthemic melodies, These Animal Men turn their Bowie Primary School education into vintage glam-pop with a moving Romantic aesthetic undercurrent. Taut songwriting, good singing, buzzing electricity and a dynamic grasp that works piano balladry (as in the *Room at the Top* realism of the title track and "My Human Remains") into the band's plans make **(Come on, Join) The High Society** a compelling bolt of content, not posture. The assessment of fame in "Empire Building" is remarkably level-headed, and the canny self-awareness of "We Are Living" alludes to far deeper insight than young bands usually can admit: "A supercharged skinny hell-bent on his own destruction/I can't change the world only my own generation." The inclusion of "Too Sussed?" rolls back the carpet of progress for a few minutes, but otherwise **The High Society** is a fine place to rub ears. (The **Taxi** EP contains five songs from the album.) [i]

THESE IMMORTAL SOULS

Get Lost (Don't Lie!) (SST) 1987
I'm Never Gonna Die Again (Mute) 1992

Formed as a breakaway from Crime and the City Solution, These Immortal Souls was (and is, such as it may exist) led by onetime Birthday Party mainstay guitarist/singer Rowland S. Howard. Peopled by Howard's bass-playing brother Harry, drummer Epic Soundtracks and keyboardist Genevieve McGuckin, the group debuted on the **Get Lost (Don't Lie!)** mini-LP, did a tour and then wasn't heard from again for several years.

In fact, there was little recorded evidence of Howard until his 1991 **Shotgun Wedding** album with Lydia Lunch and the reunion of These Immortal Souls the following year. **I'm Never Gonna Die Again** brings the four original members back together, joined by guest Anthony Thistlethwaite (sax, slide mandolin), for another gritty, dramatic dose of loosely fraught rock. Not that far in sound or spirit from the point where the old Gun Club met Nick Cave's early solo work (although lyrical bits of the guitar tension owe something to Television as well), the album pairs Howard's lazy, artless voice with jagged, sweeping music that draws blood as it pulls its thorns across the landscape. "Welcome the kiss of sugar splinters/The sting of frozen candied kisses." Demonstrating expanded stylistic range, "So the Story Goes" treats a doo-wop structure to a shocking razor burn, while the melodic song power of "Hyperspace" mounts a serious challenge to the carefully calibrated sonic aggression. The American CD includes three bonus tracks, including a rangy live version of "My One-Eyed Daughter." [i]

See also *Lydia Lunch, Epic Soundtracks; TPRG.*

THE THE

Burning Blue Soul (UK 4AD) 1981 (4AD) 1993
Soul Mining (UK Some Bizzare) 1983 (Some Bizzare/Epic) 1984
Infected (Epic) 1986
Mind Bomb (Epic) 1989
Shades of Blue EP (UK Epic) 1991
Dusk (UK Epic) 1992 (Epic) 1993
Solitude (Epic) 1994
Hanky Panky (550 Music/Epic) 1995

For all of the ominous brooding in his dramatic music, London's Matt Johnson, aka the The, has, over the years, matured into a subtle and versatile artist. Working in styles ranging from light dance-influenced pop to mutant country, he's outgrown the fashionable despair embraced as an ultimate goal by lesser lights, creating moving testimonials to love and hope while continuing to gaze, clear-eyed, into the abyss. Johnson's seemingly dour vocals are often laced with sardonic humor and outbursts of passion, as if he were compelled to unleash pent-up emotions out of necessity rather than as part of an act.

Before his first album (**Burning Blue Soul** was released in 1981 as a Matt Johnson solo project; it was credited to the The upon its reissue more than a decade later), Johnson played guitar on an EP by the Gadgets, released a single as the The and contributed a the The track to the electro-pop scene-starting **Some Bizzare Album** compilation. Recorded with virtually no outside assistance, **Burning Blue Soul** offers little hint of what was to come. Clearly the work of someone still trying out his ideas, this sparse opus mixes simple pop and rudimentary tape-manipulated weirdness. For fans only. Though tracks from the projected followup, **The Pornography of Despair,** surfaced as B-sides and bonus cuts, the album never received a full-blown release. Still, Johnson always takes pains to include it in the discography that invariably accompanies his releases, perhaps with an eye to mystique building.

Soul Mining documents his growing comprehension of art and craft. Johnson favors a fuller band sound, and some of the gently engaging pop tunes, such as "Uncertain Smile" and "This Is the Day," are compelling portraits of inner confusion. But there's also some less satisfying confrontational noise for its own sake. **Infected,** however, finds him with a better grasp of a broad sonic range, from the subtle undertones of "Heartland" to the thumping grooves of the title track. Tackling big, timely subjects with the seriousness of a concerned social commentator, Johnson sometimes comes across excessively stern, meaning a good time is not had by all.

With former Smiths guitarist Johnny Marr joining the fold for **Mind Bomb,** Johnson relaxes his white-knuckle grip slightly without compromising his vision, resulting in the The's most palatable album to date. Continuing to tackle Serious Stuff in gripping tunes like "Armageddon Days Are Here (Again)" and "The Violence of Truth" (where he exclaims, "God is evil! God is love!"), Johnson favors warmer yet still bracing textures that supply added zing to his uneasy sagas.

Dusk consists of nothing but high points. With Marr still in the band (contributing bluesy harmonica as well as sparkling guitar), Johnson fervently stalks truth and inner peace, naturally finding neither. The tunes are concise, often catchy explorations of our need for love and fulfillment. In "Bluer Than Midnight," Johnson muses bleakly, "Why can't love touch my heart like fear does?," while he struggles to affirm the undying spirit in "Love Is Stronger than Death." Tempering the bleak content with edgy, rough-hewn music adds warmth to what could have been merely grim "entertainment."

Reaching from **Burning Blue Soul** to **Dusk, Solitude** offers live takes, remixes and deconstructions of familiar works as well three-fourths of the 1991 **Shades of Blue** EP, including the title track, a Duke Ellington tune. Interesting though hardly essential.

Hanky Panky might have sunk to self-conscious gimmickry in less perceptive hands, but Johnson makes it work beautifully. Covering eleven classics by country-music immortal Hank Williams, he finds that aching spot deep in the soul where all great art originates. The spare, no-nonsense renditions of "My Heart Would Know," "Six More Miles," "I Saw the Light," "Your Cheatin' Heart" and others capture the tension of the The's best stuff without sacrificing the sad grace of the originals. Johnson has been progressing toward something like Williams' eloquent directness his entire career—maybe this tour de force tribute will help him break through once and for all. [jy]

See also *TPRG.*

THEY MIGHT BE GIANTS

They Might Be Giants [tape] (TMB Music) 1985
They Might Be Giants (Bar/None) 1986 (East Side Digital) 1986
Don't Let's Start EP (Bar/None) 1987 (Bar/None/East Side Digital) 1987
(She Was a) Hotel Detective EP (Bar/None) 1988
Lincoln (Bar/None/Restless) 1988
They'll Need a Crane EP (Bar/None/Restless) 1989
Don't Let's Start (UK One Little Indian) 1989
Flood (Elektra) 1990
Istanbul Not Constantinople EP (Elektra) 1990
Miscellaneous T (Bar/None/Restless) 1991
Apollo 18 (Elektra) 1992
I Palindrome I EP (Elektra) 1992
The Guitar EP (Elektra) 1992
Why Does the Sun Shine? EP (Elektra) 1993
Back to Skull EP (Elektra) 1994
John Henry (Elektra) 1994
Factory Showroom (Elektra) 1996

JOHN LINNELL

State Songs EP (Hello Recording Club) 1994

MONO PUFF

Mono Puff EP (Hello Recording Club) 1995
Unsupervised (Rykodisc) 1996

The Brooklyn duo of John Flansburgh (vocals/guitar) and John Linnell (vocals/accordion/saxophone/keyboards) has proven that it can effortlessly toss off erudite, informative, humorous and absurd appreciations of topics both great and small in a constantly expanding universe of musical languages. After a decade in business, however, the challenge for They Might Be Giants is to stay strong, to remain relevant, to move ahead without abandoning the core charm of their whimsical art. Weathering two major and potentially devastating developments—commercial success and the formation of a full-fledged band—the two Johns have had to fight an uphill battle to keep their place in the '90s.

The Giants' debut album is diabolically clever and wildly eclectic, a romp of fully realized masterpieces that could not possibly fail to entertain even the fussiest, hardest-hearted idiot. (Unfortunately, the band has attracted far too many other kinds of idiots to make attending shows a completely enjoyable experience.) Literate, accomplished, bursting with ideas, hooks, puns, dadaist nonsense and other neat tricks, **They Might Be Giants** is almost too good to be true. Recast from a substantially different self-released cassette, most of the nineteen tracks are brilliant.

Lincoln maintains the Giants' baffling level of invention while raising the musical complexity, electricity, energy level and variety. Playing mix'n'match with their instruments, idioms and influences on eighteen songs, the Giants hit a few clinkers, but also come up with such enduring gems as "Ana Ng," "They'll Need a Crane" and "Kiss Me, Son of God." Plucking intricate wordplay and uncommon melodies from their own private ether, the pair magically continues to explore a part of the musical continuum no one else seems able to locate. (Subsuming the EP of the same name, which contains three delightful B-sides, the full-length **Don't Let's Start** is a British-only compilation that also contains all of **(She Was a) Hotel Detective** and all but the title track of **They'll Need a Crane.**)

Moving to a major label for **Flood** brought the Giants a vastly expanded audience as well as the predictable (and utterly undeserved) critical backlash. Another deft pogo dance on the tightrope between sense and nonsense, **Flood** is an avalanche of bizarre ideas juggled with the duo's gyroscopic sense of what makes a pop tune click. With improved production resources (Clive Langer and Alan Winstanley on four tracks; the rest are self-produced), the Giants sound better than ever. "Birdhouse in Your Soul" anthropomorphizes a nightlight; "Particle Man" is a science lesson set to an oompah beat; the Farfisa-rock "Twisting" mentions the dB's and Young Fresh Fellows in lyrics about a spiteful ex-girlfriend. The EP led by the album's uproarious geopolitical lesson, "Istanbul (Not Constantinople)"—written, in what can only be called proto-Giants style, by Jimmy Kennedy and Nat Simon in 1954—also contains a droll lecture on the presidential timber of "James K. Polk," a soul goof ("Stormy Pinkness") and a wild intercultural hip-hop mix (by Daddy-O of Stetsasonic) that turns "Istanbul" inside out.

The prolific band's leftovers—B-sides drawn from the vast archive of the Giants' Dial-a-Song phone service, plus a handful of non-LP mixes—fill **Miscellaneous T,** which is nearly an exact replica of **Don't Let's Start.** This neat if uneven appendix to the long-playing oeuvre contains such charmers as "Hey Mr. DJ, I Thought You Said We Had a Deal," "Nightgown of the Sullen Moon," "I'll Sink Manhattan," "The Famous Polka" and "We're the Replacements."

Apollo 18 launches the group into a higher orbit, structuring degree-of-difficulty songs into intricate, ambitious arrangements and going so far as to create a crude interactive exercise, "Fingertips": twenty-one discontinuous frag-rock haikus, each given its own CD track, thereby allowing for ten gazillion random-sort permutations. Otherwise, amid such typically cerebral inventions as the challenging poetic device of "I Palindrome I," the existential dilemma of "My Evil Twin" and the noir scenario of "Turn Around," the pair takes a goodfoot step in a new direction with "The Guitar," a boppy funk groove that adapts "The Lion Sleeps Tonight," using guest singer Laura Cantrell to bring the familiar melody in an ethereal voice. Despite the edgy nervousness (and tinny sound) that pervades the album, the Giants show no creative flopsweat: they continue to vacuum up familiar pop idioms and recycle them with more and better ideas than they had in the first place. (The **IPI** EP adds a surprising dancehall reorientation of the album's "She's Actual Size" and two inferior new items.)

The next EP—an exercise in wry frivolity—contains John (Mr. Science) Linnell's deadpan rendition of 1959's instructive "Why Does the Sun Shine? (The Sun Is a Mass of Incandescent Gas)," an intentionally dinky cover of the Allman Brothers' "Jessica," a bottom-of-the-well bass clarinet toodle through the Meat Puppets' "Whirlpool" and the boys' own "Spy" (later included on **John Henry**). Significantly, the record brings the Giants into a new phase—the early stages of assembling a full-fledged band with drummer Brian Doherty (Freedy Johnston, Silos).

Back to Skull furthers the process, making it official with Doherty and two bassists (the departing Graham Maby and the incoming Tony Maimone). The organic reorganization grants the Giants unprecedented freedom and breadth. "Snail Shell," a preview of **John Henry,** flows like few tracks in the repertoire, although it sounds more like a dry run than a real song. Still, the lack of inspired songs plus a joyless disco/lounge remake of "(She Was a) Hotel Detective," makes this a sorry showing.

The same shortage of inspiration on **John Henry** can be taken as either a payback for too many generous years of brilliance, creative burnout (witness "The End of the Tour") or the novelty of a new toy leading to creative impatience. Despite some good numbers, Flansburgh and Linnell spend too much of the album impressing themselves with previously impossible group exercises (like the madcap improvs of "Spy") in service of thin jokes ("O, Do Not Forsake Me," "Extra Savoir-Faire," the Alice Cooper title pastiche of "Why Must I Be Sad?") and watery stylistic conceits. "Meet James Ensor," "Subliminal" and "I Should Be Allowed to Think" all score with the band's typical high achievement standards, but too much of **John Henry** suffers from studio-bound weakness.

Both Flansburgh and Linnell have released EPs of otherwise unavailable material via the former's subscription-only Hello CD club. Linnell's contains four entries in his self-appointed Fifty State Songs project. Flansburgh's, done under the Mono Puff name, proved to be a warmup for a full-length album released the following year. Leading a trio with help from such cool pals as guitarist Jay Sherman-Godfrey, bassist Erik Sanko (Skeleton Key), actress Elena Löwensohn and vocalist Nancy Lynn Howell, Flansburgh rocks a little more than usual and doesn't try so hard to be a smart-aleck. Yet the coffee achiever can't help being himself, and manages to uphold the Giants' winning spirit in such oddities as "Unsupervised, I Hit My Head," odes to Red Sox pitcher Bill Lee ("What Bothers the Spaceman") and a dead president ("Nixon's the One"), and a seductively sedated rendition of Gary Glitter's "Hello Hello I'm Back Again." An easy line drive into the Green Monster. [i]

See also *TPRG*.

TH FAITH HEALERS (UK)

A Picture of Health EP (UK Too Pure) 1991
In Love EP (UK Too Pure) 1991
L' (Fr. Too Pure/Virgin) 1992 (Too Pure/American) 1995
Lido (Too Pure/Elektra) 1992
Don't Jones Me—and Then Some EP (Too Pure/Elektra) 1993
Imaginary Friend (UK Too Pure) 1993 (Too Pure/Elektra) 1994

VARIOUS ARTISTS

Too Pure—The Peel Sessions (Strange Fruit/Dutch East India Trading) 1992

The first group signed to England's Too Pure label (PJ Harvey, Moonshake, Stereolab), Th Faith Healers stirred up an early buzz by playing entire concerts consisting of three songs and just about as many fuzz-drenched chords. The cream of the London quartet's early non-album work is collected on the seven-song **L'**, in which trance steamroller "Delores" and the epic sludgefest "Slag" are balanced by the surprising delicacy of "Lovely." The band writes some catchy melodies, then does its best to shred them to pieces, as on "Gorgeous Blue Flower in My Garden" and the acerbic "Pop Song."

With Can's "Mother Sky" as its centerpiece, **Lido** finds guitarist Tom Cullinan, bassist Ben Hopkin and drummer Joe Dilworth cranking out hypnotic drone rock that crests with cathartic power and recedes. Whether predicting someone's imminent demise in "This Time," sending up the "Love Song" or pole-axing the resurgence of '60s counterculture in "Hippy Hole," singer Roxanne Stephen chants or screams perverse, nursery rhyme lyrics. (The resequenced American edition adds a recut version of "Reptile Smile" and "Moona-ina-Joona," a track not on the British LP.)

Imaginary Friend (for which the band picked up the America-only "UK" appendage) is another collection of cyclical mantras, climaxing with the twenty-minute "Everything, All at Once Forever," which reappears after ten minutes of dead space for an extended coda. The transcendence-through-repetition vibe is heightened by the haiku-like lyrics; Stephen works over the phrase, "See, sun, scent" in "Kevin" until the syllables stop making sense and become just another texture in the sonic whirlpool. In the same way, Cullinan works the core riffs in "Heart Fog" and "Sparklingly Chime" until they splinter into white-noise fragments. [gk]

See also *Stereolab*.

THINKING FELLERS UNION LOCAL 282

Wormed by Leonard [tape] (Thwart) 1988 [CD] (Thwart) 1995
Tangle (Thwart) 1989 (Can. Scratch) 1994
The Natural Finger EP7 (Ajax) 1991
Lovelyville (Matador) 1991
Mother of All Saints (Matador) 1992
Where's Officer Tuba? EP (UK Hemiola) 1993
Admonishing the Bishops EP (Matador) 1993
The Funeral Pudding EP (Ajax) 1994
Strangers From the Universe (Matador) 1994
Porcelain Entertainments (Ger. Return to Sender/Normal) 1995
TFUL282 (Japan. Japan Overseas) 1995
I Hope It Lands (Communion) 1996

WHITE SHARK

Muggy Bog EP10 (Nuf Sed) 1994

MR. HAGEMAN

Twin Smooth Snouts (Starlight Furniture Company) 1995

VARIOUS ARTISTS

Not All That Terrifies Harms [tape] (Nuf Sed) 1990
Not All That Terrifies Harms EP7 (Ajax) 1991
Step, Step, Steppin' on Satan's Foot (Tedium House) 1994

Thinking Fellers Union Local 282 originally emigrated from Iowa in the mid-'80s and set up shop in San Francisco. Since then, they've become one of the most original, interesting collaborative groups of musicians in rock, locating and exploring the common ground between Can, Captain Beefheart and the Carpenters. The core group of Brian Hageman (guitar, mandolin, many other instruments), Mark Davies (guitar, banjo, many more other instruments), Hugh Swarts (guitar) and Anne Eickelberg (bass) has been together since the beginning, originally with Paul Bergmann and later with Jay Paget on drums; everybody sings. Sometimes they sound like misfit kids putting on a music (and variety) show, other times like a crack orchestra of unearthly devices.

Wormed by Leonard, a self-released cassette named after Leonard Nimoy's book of poetry *Warmed by Love,* is the band's most delicate recording, showing an early folky vein. "Hell Rules" suggests a nuttier John Fahey, with its soft vocal interplay matched by the instruments. Other pieces, like the intensely overmodulated anti-convoy song "Truck Driving Man," break with *any* kind of tradition. They're taking both their aesthetic and their limitations seriously here. The CD reissue appends some compilation tracks and very early rehearsal tapes; the four best songs from the album are picked out for **The Natural Finger,** a 7-inch EP that includes "Hell Rules" and the melancholy western "Narlus Spectre."

The self-released **Tangle** includes a lot of similar songs, but with a noisier, meaner tone. The pendulous shifts in guitar sound and a complex train-chug of collective force are punctuated by any of the following: broken chords, keening choruses, accordion, trumpet and spoken bits. "Sister Hell" became something of a college radio hit.

Lovelyville is one of the Fellers' jokiest records, going so far as to include a cover of Sugarloaf's "Green-Eyed Lady." Dark and absurd, it points to the '70s childhoods of TFUL282 as an influence on their music. Hageman's vocals dominate the record; the lyrics he sings, with their visceral surrealism, are *not* enhanced by elocution. "Nothing Solid" is an epic closer to the main body of the album, as the band clusters together, chanting and tunelessly shouting the chorus. The CD includes an eight-song "sub-album," **The Crowded Diaper:** petite songs smothered by automatic writing via tape recorder.

The double-length **Mother of All Saints,** the kind of record for which the word "sprawling" was coined, documents TFUL282's meandering period. There are songs here, but they're fewer and further between than on earlier records. Thirteen of the twenty-three tracks are hypnotic instrumentals and found noises (as with **Lovelyville,** there are samples from, and allusions to, the infamous *Raymond & Peter* tapes of drunken, brawling roommates). There's a sleepy sensibility, excess everywhere and few concessions to "entertainment"—the only conventionally catchy melody comes from Hageman's viola on the instrumental "Star Trek." Lyrics move with dream-logic and hover around images of disease ("Infection"), small creatures and smothering physical entrapment ("Fish Bowl," "Hummingbird in a Cube of Ice"). The sound of the album is so dense and strange that it takes quite a few spins to get into and resists the listener almost every step of the way.

The English **Where's Officer Tuba?** EP was originally meant to come out before **Mother of All Saints,** but didn't show up until a little later. It mostly consists of tracks from the album, with the significant exception of a cover of Caroliner's (oops, Caroliner Rainbow Open Sore Chorale's) "Outhouse of the Pryeeeee," which originally appeared on a 1991 split single.

Admonishing the Bishops (a euphemism that also alludes to the Bishop brothers of the Sun City Girls, with whom TFUL282 did a national tour) is the Fellers' most straightforward record: four songs, no noise, no instrumentals, no experimental stuff. "Hurricane" is one of the best things the band has ever recorded, a six-minute piece with a confidently atonal riff and a six-line lyric about stasis that turns, briliantly, into a yodel. "Undertaker" is TFUL-ized rockabilly; "Father" is a pop variation on Caroliner's basic songwriting approach. The group's ensemble playing is on a new level: even "Million Dollars," the only song here that doesn't quite work, has some strikingly inventive passages.

The Funeral Pudding also has four new compositions (one of them an exotic spy-movie instrumental, "Flames Up"), but the resemblance ends there. It also has five improvised jams recorded at the band's rehearsal space; unfortunately, Thinking Fellers are no Can. Their strength is writing and arranging songs, like the two astonishing Eickelberg vocals here: the clinkety-clankety "Waited Too Long," on which she deftly conflates the voices of a frustrated little girl and a bitter middle-aged woman, and "Heavy Head," with lyrics that appear to be about depression and gorgeous music that appears to be about staying calm in the face of the void.

The improvisations on the subsequent full-length **Strangers From the Universe** are mercifully brief, basically just bridges between songs. And what songs! Berserk rhythms are presented with deadpan simplicity, like the sickly funk riff of "Socket" that keeps sticking a banana peel in its own path. The arrangements are unconventional and sometimes thrilling (Davies' Optigan [obscure '60s keyboard kin to the mellotron] intro to "Cup of Dreams" is particularly lovely). The lyrics have one foot in absurdity and the other in graceful poetry—check out the delirious rambling of "The Operation" or "The Piston and the Shaft," a series of vaguely upsetting metaphors for sex. And Eickelberg tops herself with "Noble Experiment," a blackly sweet waltz-time lullaby for the human race's tenure on the planet.

The limited-edition **Porcelain Entertainments** begins with six live tracks recorded in San Francisco. Four of the songs appear in superior studio versions elsewhere (including a medley from *A Fistful of Dollars,* on a contemporaneous single). The other two are a formless jam and a great two-minute instrumental, "Quacky." The album also includes four practice-space noodles of varying degrees of inconsequentiality and another set of solo pieces, of which Eickelberg's Casio-on-speed "White Box" is the best. Hageman's "52 Girlfriends" has incomprehensible lyrics by Sun City Girls' Charlie Gocher. Illustrative, but really for completists only.

I Hope It Lands, on the other hand, is for everyone. The band has the miraculous group-mind of a flock of birds, and the record *flows* like nothing they've ever done before—even the little noise-twiddles are part of the record's grand mid-air arc. So are the songs, which makes it hard to focus on individual ones. The album peaks at particular moments: the rhythmic gymnastics in the chorus of "Brains," the bit in the slow drift near the end of "Triple X" where everybody suddenly bears down at once, the high notes in "Empty Cup." Bonus points for titling one of the interludes "rampaging fuckers of anything on the crazy shitting planet of the vomit atmosphere" for no apparent reason.

The Japanese **TFUL282** compilation isn't exactly a greatest-hits—it steers clear of the band's most familiar songs in favor of album tracks that got overlooked the first time around, reassembling them in seemingly random order. It's got five tracks apiece from **Wormed** and **Lovelyville,** six from **Mother,** three from **Tangle,** one each from **Admonishing the Bishops** and **The Funeral Pudding,** two from **Strangers** and—making its fourth appearance—"Trevor."

Mr. (Brian) Hageman's solo album, **Twin Smooth Snouts,** is a little simpler than full TFUL282 music and also less accessible. He usually uses one or two contrasted or combined sounds (as opposed to the Fellers' four or five), retaining the band's loose, detuned string sound; his lyrical imagery is cryptic, thick and vaguely country-ish. He mostly sings in a monotone, and his instrumentals drag on (great titles, though: "Johnosaurus Wayne," "Shave the Gum," "Hamburger Pharmacy"). There are some nice touches, like the sound of a vibrator, *erhu,* car radio and metal rod, and creative stereo separation. "Rosa" transforms a traditional Cuban melody into a bar-room ballad.

Going under the name the White Shark, goofier, odder Feller Mark Davies (wears skirts, plays banjo) is behind the **Muggy Bog** EP. A cheerful and complex musical vision, its wry lightness is based on the oddness of ordinary beauty: the chorus of "Waiting for the Day" is "doing the dishes, scrubbing the dog, getting out of bed and going to work" (of course, the day he's waiting for is the Apocalypse). One song is sung from the point of view of mosquitoes ("We suck blood as a means to survive"); "Sodium Chloride" is a mini-musical about a man addicted to salt. There are also extraneous covers of Rod McKuen and Burt Bacharach.

The Fellers have developed an extended family in the San Francisco scene that centers on *Bananafish* magazine (run by unofficial sixth Feller Seymour Glass) and the Nuf Sed label (run by unofficial nineteenth Feller Brandan Kearney). The consistently great Nuf Sed cassette compilation **Not All That Terrifies Harms** includes a handful of tracks by TFUL282 and related bands, both celebrated (Caroliner) and unknown (the Lockhorns, whose piece is called "Eickelberg Reign O'er Me"). Six tracks from the tape were later released as the 7-inch EP of the same name, including TFUL's "Trevor" (in a slightly different version), the White Shark's horribly creepy "This Is Emergency" and "The World of Sound" by Fellers personal-band-mythology joke the Enablers. There's also a blow-out cover of the Blue Öyster Cult's "Dominance and Submission" by World of Pooh, with Kearney and a pre-Fellers Jay Paget.

A book collecting the first four issues of *Bananafish* includes a CD, **Step, Step, Steppin' on Satan's Foot,** with solo tracks by Swarts, Davies, Bergmann, Paget, Eickelberg and Hageman (among many other things). Various members of the band have also recorded singles with their side projects. The best are Job's Daughters (basically Davies and Kearney, with a seven-person chorus including Swarts: their rapturous cover of the Cowsills' "The Prophecy of Daniel and John the Divine" is something of an underground classic) and Heavenly Ten Stems, a septet also including Kearney and Davies that played covers of Asian film music and kicked up a huge cloud of tribute/minstrelsy controversy in the process. [rxe/ddw]

See also *Barbara Manning, U.S. Saucer, Zip Code Rapists.*

THIN WHITE ROPE

Exploring the Axis (Frontier) 1985
Moonhead (Frontier) 1987
Bottom Feeders EP (UK Zippo) 1987
In the Spanish Cave (Frontier) 1988
Red Sun EP (UK Demon) 1988
Sack Full of Silver (Frontier/RCA) 1990 (Frontier) 1992
Squatter's Rights EP (UK Frontier/Real Time) 1991
The Ruby Sea (Frontier) 1991
The One That Got Away 6-28-92 Gent (Frontier) 1993
When Worlds Collide (Sp. Munster) 1995
Spoor (Frontier) 1995

If David Lynch were to assemble a hard-rock band from scratch, chances are he'd come up with something that sounds a lot like Thin White Rope. The Davis, California–bred group defined its high-lonesome desert-rock with enough metallic edge to get the pulse pounding—and enough ominous surrealism to make the blood run cold. Perhaps the most twisted element in its mix was the quavering, tightly wound voice of frontman Guy Kyser.

Kyser reins in his more effusive impulses on **Exploring the Axis,** a debut that placed the band smack in the middle—rather than on the fringe, as the title might imply—of post-paisley underground West Coast rock. Kyser and Roger Kunkel are a clearly simpatico guitar tandem; they combine to issue a warm, fluid sound that parts only occasionally to allow the release of some overflow dissonance. **Moonhead** alters the modus operandi a bit, stretching song lengths and forging a provocative, embryonic bond between wiry, Television-styled guitar interplay and groove-conscious kraut-rock rhythms (held in place by Jozef Becker's incredibly focused drumming). The next time you need to win a sucker bet, dare your mark to sit through all of the feral "Crawl Piss Freeze" in the dark.

As if to prove there are times when shirt-renders just wanna have fun, too, the band allowed itself to get a little loopy on **In the Spanish Cave.** Kyser's voice—while by no means "normal"—sounds apropos in the eccentric hootenanny environs of "Mr. Limpet" and "Ahr-Skidar," but the rustic accouterments don't particularly suit the band. The six-song **Bottom Feeders** is much more effective, particularly a spine-tingling version of Jimmy Reed's "Ain't That Loving You Baby" that sounds like it could have been recorded right after a trip to the crossroads. That mood was apparently intensified by another trek—this one corporeal—behind the Iron Curtain, where Thin White Rope became the first American indie band to tour the Soviet Union. The subsequent **Red Sun** EP is fittingly grim, both in its choice of cover versions (including Gene Pitney's "Town Without Pity," Marty Robbins' "They're Hanging Me Tonight" and Lee Hazlewood's "Some Velvet Morning") and its acoustic reworking of the title track, which further darkens one of **Spanish Cave**'s bleaker numbers.

Sack Full of Silver is the first full-on studio documentation of the band's visceral improv style, rife as it is with songs (like "On the Floe") that rise and fall on crests of post-Hendrix controlled feedback. To thicken the sonic miasma even further, Kyser and new drummer Matthew Abourezk perform a long, loving do-si-do in the framework of a faithful (if rocked-up) rendition of Can's "Yoo Doo Right."

On **The Ruby Sea,** Kyser (whose vocal affectations are growing more irritating with each passing year) cements his reputation as manic sound sculptor and Americana-grounded troubadour. While he wrings some fittingly wrenching sounds from his six-string on songs like "Midwest Flower," he seems more concerned with creating atmospheres, which he does most effectively on the title track's netherworld ballet. Less edgy than its recent predecessors, **The Ruby Sea** does explore other planes: witness the neo-bluegrass "Tina and Glen" and the creepily sweet music-box tinkling that imbues "Puppet Dog."

Given Thin White Rope's stellar live reputation, it's surprising the band took eight years to release its first concert disc, but **The One That Got Away** was worth the wait. Recorded in Belgium (where the band was big), the generous two-disc set preserves the uniquely capricious experience of a TWR show, from moments of straightahead rock power ("Not Your Fault") to death-knell balladry ("Some Velvet Morning") to bulging-vein attempts to tear the roof *and* walls off the sucka (the electrifying howl "Eleven"). As ever, the band plays without the slightest awareness that it's under audience scrutiny, which helps explain how, after more than an hour of ups and downs, Thin White Rope scours its quiver and pulls out both Bob Dylan's "Outlaw Blues" and Hawkwind's "Silver Machine."

When Worlds Collide and **Spoor** were both released after the band split up so Kyser could dedicate himself to a career in botany (no joke: the guy's got a graduate degree!). The albums overlap to some extent, but both possess worthwhile individual highlights. The Spanish release is more of a career overview, collecting nineteen songs that span the first six years of TWR's existence. **Spoor** is more of a trinket for diehards, with its loving demo/remix recapitulation of favorites, including a terrific rendition of the Stooges' "Little Doll" and the primordial stomp "Ants Are Cavemen," both from a Sub Pop 7-inch. [dss]

See also *TPRG*.

3RD BASS

The Cactus Al/bum (Def Jam/Columbia) 1989
The Cactus Cee/D [CD] (Def Jam/Columbia) 1989
The Cactus Revisited (Def Jam/Columbia) 1990
Derelicts of Dialect (Def Jam/Columbia) 1991

MC SERCH

Return of the Product (Def Jam/Chaos/Columbia) 1992

PRIME MINISTER PETE NICE & DADDY RICH

Dust to Dust (Def Jam/Columbia) 1993

Between the Beastie Boys' **Licensed to Ill** rock-rap and Vanilla Ice's watered-down pop-hop, New York's 3rd Bass—MC Serch (Michael Berrin), Prime Minister Pete Nice (Nash) and DJ Richie Rich (Lawson, not to be confused with an Oakland rapper using the same double-R handle)—turned up to disprove the whites-can't-rap falsehood, a flipside to the blacks-can't-rock prejudice faced by Living Colour and others. A straight-up and original hip-hop crew capable of delivering intelligent, serious raps but addicted to classic sitcom television, crazy found-sound samples and verbal slapstick, 3rd Bass concentrated on content more than presentation. The group got too silly for its own good and worked itself into a political corner by trying too hard to be down with almost everybody: in its righteous enthusiasm, **Derelicts of Dialect**'s "No Master Plan No Master Race" moves from racial solidarity to unsupportable pretense. Overcome by the reality of shifting styles and the cliché of musical differences, the two rappers split up after two albums, leaving behind some great tracks that helped define the music's turn-of-the-decade progress.

Produced by Sam Sever, members of Public Enemy's Bomb Squad and Stetsasonic's Prince Paul, **The Cactus Al/bum** (aka **The Cactus Cee/D**) established the band's talent as well as its legitimacy. Settling the fronting question in the autobiographical "Product of the Environment," the trio makes a hysterical issue of put-downs in "The Gas Face" and packs in two other great singles: the dramatic "Steppin' to the A.M." and "Brooklyn-Queens." Rarely able to keep a stupid idea from getting play (like Serch's goofy Satchmo imitation in "Flippin' off the Wall Like Lucy Ball"), **The Cactus** is uneven but seriously enjoyable.

The Cactus Revisited, a remix record, overhauls (in one case updating) the sound or lyrics of six **Cactus** tracks (including all four of its singles) and a B-side. Rather than just recycle old material while working on a followup, the companion piece both summarizes and extends the flavor of **The Cactus.**

Unlike the generally outward-bound lyrics of **The Cactus, Derelicts of Dialect**—another sprawling, uneven hodgepodge in which Serch and Pete Nice continue to alternate verses—is more self-centered (the title track, the autobiographical "Word to the Third," "Daddy Rich in the Land of 1210"), judgmental ("Pop Goes the Weasel" details the case against phony rappers), cranky ("3 Strikes 5000") and dumb ("French Toast," "Sea Vessel Soliloquy," "Al'z A-B-Cee'z" and "Eye Jammie" are all broad joke skits). Production by the group, Prince Paul, Sam Sever and others gives the rhymes easygoing demi-funk foundations packed with amusing details. Too long by half but sprinkled with such febrile inventions as "Green Eggs and Swine" (which bites *All in the Family* and quotes Dr. Seuss), "Herbalz in Your Mouth" and "Ace in the Hole," **Derelicts of Dialect** is a credible second—and final—act for 3rd Bass. (I Don't Know.)

With 3rd Bass dissolved, Serch (already pursuing his future career as an impresario by developing such acts as KMD) made a strong and serious solo album. In a sinewy, seductive flow of political, cultural and personal opinion, Serch reasserts his ample skills, trimming away most of 3rd Bass' extraneous furnishings and comedy to kick intricate and insightful verbal barrages about racism ("Hard but True," "Social Narcotics"), programmed thinking ("Don't Have to Be"), migraines ("Hits the Head"), hip-hop theory ("Scenes From the Mind") and his own New York stories (the title track). The concise and contained **Return of the Product** makes no mention of 3rd Bass; if there was any bad blood between the former bandmates, it got left outside the studio.

Likewise, Pete Nice and Daddy Rich offer no overt animosity to Serch on their album, but then **Dust to Dust** doesn't offer much of anything. Unaided by weak comedy inserts, the bustling tracks (produced either by the duo or by the Beatnuts) are entirely ordinary, and the Prime Minister's unengaging rhymes fish around fruitlessly in tired and repetitive look-at-me-I'm-rapping eddies of boasts and insults. On this flat platter, "Blowin' Smoke" doesn't refer to Nice's stogie.

Following their career-closing solo albums, Serch moved completely behind the scenes to sign, produce and manage rappers. Nice pursued his real love—baseball—by reportedly opening a second hall of fame in Cooperstown. [i]

13 ENGINES

Before Our Time (Nocturnal) 1987
Byram Lake Blues (Nocturnal) 1989
A Blur to Me Now (SBK) 1991
Perpetual Motion Machine (EMI Music Canada/Atlantic) 1993
Conquistador (Can. EMI) 1995 (Nettwerk) 1996

This Toronto quartet started out playing loud adolescent rock-pop with greater artistic ambitions than most such bands, both in the literate lyrics and in the broadly dynamic instrumental designs. While singer John Critchley (guitar, keyboards) and Australian émigré guitarist Mike Robbins write dramatic songs that cry out for intricate wide-screen arrangements, the group's reliance on simple rock tools creates an exciting tension between grand imagination and basic execution. Fortunately, 13 Engines has the chops to keep the material from sounding shortchanged. If **Before Our Time** has a slight edge over the Neil Young–inflected **Byram Lake Blues,** it's in the debut's unself-conscious sense of exploration and discovery. But both albums (now available on one CD) are well worth hearing.

A Blur to Me Now, recorded in California by David Briggs, brought 13 Engines into major-label clutches for the first time with no appreciable damage. Critchley's production of **Perpetual Motion Machine** focuses the maturing band's considerable strengths—memorable melodies, provocative lyrics, dynamic electric-rock sizzle—as never before, revealing odd bits of influence as varied as glam-era Bowie, Robyn Hitchcock and Pete Shelley. Consistently stirring, occasionally dramatic ("More"), rippingly loud ("Unconscience") but equally able to tone it down ("Moment of Clarity" and the acoustic "What If We Don't Get What We Want?"), the unpretentiously arty album lacks only a marketing gimmick (or a transcendent single, although "Smoke & Ashes" comes mighty close) to get 13 Engines onto the alt-hit parade.

Conquistador indulges Critchley's fandom as never before: he channels the singing style of Hitchcock (occasionally switching to Shelley instead) accurately enough to force a disbelieving second look at the credits. The effect isn't unpleasant, however. The tunefully nasty songs ("Cootie Girl" offers an ambivalent character description, while "Tailpipe Blues" invites an unspecified affronter to "wrap your lips around the tailpipe of my car") don't rely on novelty, compressing an efficient power-pop sound with memorable melodies to carry the oblique lyrics. Two "wet dream" references are too many, but "Menefreghista," "Beneath My Hand" and "Vermillion" are all superior creations. [i]

THIRTEEN NIGHTMARES

See *Mercy Rule.*

THIRTY OUGHT SIX

Bosozuku (Candy-Ass) 1994
Hag Seed (Mute America) 1995

Portland, Oregon's Thirty Ought Six aren't post-punk innovators, they just do the genre proud. A power trio in the truest sense, this explosive unit has frequently (and aptly) been compared to both Hüsker Dü and Nirvana. On **Bosozuku,** bassist Sean Roberts' whisper-to-a-primal-scream singing ("Boy Wonder," "Tuckahoe") balances the emotion and power in the music. Guitarist David Blunk takes major responsibility for the rhythmic drive, while drummer Ryan Paravecchio fills the occasional din with offbeat jazz-inflected hits; Roberts favors bass chords.

Bosozuku suffers from an overdependence on instrumentals (four of twelve songs), a foible corrected on **Hag Seed,** which makes good use of Roberts' raw-boned lyrics and the highly charged music. Blunk takes over lead vocals for "Wheeler" and "Tourmaline" (a duet with soon-to-be-ex-Sunny Day Real Estate frontman Jeremy Enigk), and his gentler, subtler approach provides helpful contrast to Roberts' desperation. [dps]

THIS KIND OF PUNISHMENT

See *Cakekitchen.*

THIS MORTAL COIL

"Sixteen Days" (UK 4AD) 1983
It'll End in Tears (UK 4AD) 1984 (4AD/Valentino) 1985 (4AD) 1993
Filigree and Shadow (UK 4AD) 1986 (4AD) 1993
Blood (UK 4AD) 1991 (4AD) 1993
1983–1991 (4AD) 1993

This Mortal Coil is one of the few recording groups to give the word "pretentious" a positive meaning. A loose, studio-only entity orbiting around 4AD founder Ivo Watts-Russell and producer John Fryer, TMC was initially (despite protestations to the contrary) a 4AD house band, employing members of the Cocteau Twins, Dead Can Dance, Wolfgang Press, Colourbox and others. With a mix of ultra-hip covers and originals that practically define the word "ethereal," TMC's ultra-melancholy, virtually ambient style can be patience-trying. But when all of the elements coalesce, the group is capable of beautiful innovation.

The debut single slips a spellbinding take on Tim Buckley's "Song to the Siren"—the siren in question being Cocteau Twin vocalist Liz Fraser—between slabs of vintage new wave (featuring early 4AD cash cow Modern English) that have aged badly enough to warrant exclusion from the otherwise complete **1983–1991. It'll End in Tears** fully lives up to its name: slow, quiet and miserable, its centerpieces are "Song to the Siren," "A Single Wish" and Howard Devoto's unbelievably depressing reading of Alex Chilton's "Holocaust."

The patchy **Filigree and Shadow** is longer and more ambitious, replacing the former sparseness with so much echo that each instrument sounds like three. String sections and electronic rhythms figure heavily, and a wholly different cast of vocalists (Alison Limerick, Deirdre Rutkowski, Breathless' Dominic Appleton) add to the near-hymnal quality of the album. There are far too many instrumentals, but emeralds rising from the ether include Buckley's "Morning Glory," Colin Newman's "Alone" and a jarring take on the Talking Heads' "Drugs."

Blood, announced as the last TMC album, is easily the best. With much of the same crew as **Filigree and Shadow** on hand, the album is a more fully realized take on its style. It loses focus toward the middle (does anyone really need to hear an entire song based on a baby's googling?), but highlights include Gene Clark's "With Tomorrow," the Rain Parade's "Carolyn's Song" and a winsome duet on Chris Bell's "You and Your Sister" by Kim Deal and Tanya Donelly.

The beautifully packaged **1983–1991**—a limited-edition American-only release—includes all three albums (then issued individually) in their entirety, plus a full-length fourth disc containing most of the original versions of the cover songs. [ja]

See also *TPRG.*

THIS PICTURE

Naked Rain EP (UK Rough Trade) 1989
A Violent Impression (Dedicated/RCA) 1991
City of Sin (Dedicated/Arista) 1994

On **A Violent Impression,** This Picture, an English quartet from Bath, seems like just another U2 knock-off: an overeager band mistaking hyper-emotive delivery for true soul and feeling. While guitarist Robert Forrester and bassist Austen Rowley churn out anthemic, ultra-enthusiastic instrumentation, drummer Duncan Forrester (Robert's brother) backs everything with the same kind of pulse-quickening energy U2 employed on its **War** album. Symon Bye's insistence on pushing his sweet, almost delicate tenor into fiery, Bono-esque exclamations (circa **The Unforgettable Fire**) on nearly every song doesn't help, either. The times when things do come together perfectly—as on the bewitching, voluptuous balladry of "Death's Sweet Religion" and the adrenaline-rush excitement of "Naked Rain"—only make the other material seem more lacking in conviction.

The identity crisis continues on **City of Sin.** Again, a few outstanding tracks make the others sound uncertain, but there is some notable progress, especially in Bye's singing. He's more controlled and confident here, proving especially charismatic on the quiet, lovely "The Prophet." "Nobody cares when you're in this rut," Bye sings on "Highrise," and one is left to wonder if he's talking about his own group's frustrations over not being able to brave a leap into musical originality. [ky]

ANTHONY THISTLETHWAITE

See *Waterboys.*

PAT THOMAS

It's a Long, Long Way to Omaha, Nebraska (Heyday) 1988
Too Close to the Ground (Gr. Di-Di Music) 1990
St. Katherine (Ger. What's So Funny About) 1993
Live in Denmark, Germany and San Francisco (Ger. Strange Ways) 1994
Fresh (Ger. Strange Ways) 1995

ABSOLUTE GREY

Green House (Earring) 1984 (Midnight) 1986
What Remains (Midnight) 1986
Painted Post EP (Midnight) 1987
A Journey Through the Past (Gr. Di-Di Music) 1988
Sand Down the Moon (Gr. Di-Di Music) 1989
Broken Promise: An Absolute Grey Anthology (Ger. Strange Ways) 1995

Pat Thomas first recorded as drummer with Rochester, New York's unjustly obscure Absolute Grey, whose beautifully bleak garage-folk-pop fit nicely alongside the early work of such contemporaries as R.E.M. and 10,000 Maniacs, and whose front-woman, Beth Brown, was a few years ahead of her time in writing and singing nakedly personal lyrics in an alt-guitar-rock context. Besides a generous sampling of the band's records, the two-CD **Broken Promise** has demos, live tracks and touchingly personal liner notes.

On his own records, Thomas writes and sings semi-confessional folk-rock tunes that show an unforced '60s influence and an instinctive understanding of his sources. The **St. Katherine** CD collects eighteen songs from his first two solo efforts plus previously unreleased numbers by a short-lived duo, Minor Characters. The fondness for Van Morrison manifested in **St. Katherine**'s wry **Moondance**-tribute cover art gains resonance with an offhandedly harrowing ten-minute reading of Van Morrison's epic "T.B. Sheets" that concludes **Live in Denmark, Germany and San Francisco.** Half of that album finds Thomas backed by members of A Subtle Plague and Slovenly on lightly electric rock tunes; the rest is acoustic folk-blues with a smaller combo.

The more overtly electric **Fresh** is Thomas' most consistently satisfying solo release; he spins a variety of his own worthy compositions as well as tunes written by pals Steve Wynn and Chris Cacavas, both of whom play on the album. Initial copies included a six-song bonus disc entitled **Get Your Rocks Off:** three outtakes from the album sessions and covers of Allen Ginsberg, Bob Dylan and the Jaynetts' immortally odd "Sally, Go 'Round the Roses." [ss]

See also *TPRG.*

THOMAS JEFFERSON SLAVE APARTMENTS

Career Interruption Code EP7 (Datapanik) 1992
You Can't Kill Stupid EP (Datapanik) 1993
Bait and Switch (Onion/American) 1995

Most of the bands operating under the Luddite doctrine that's been dubbed "lo-fi" are quiet . . . sweet-tempered . . . *pussycats* even. This Columbus-spawned quartet—the brainchild of former Great Plains front-man Ron House—makes like that same pussycat injected with a goodly dose of the rabies virus, tearing apart the shabby confines of its 4-track studio with glee. The Slave Apartments (to use the shorthand preferred by the band) spent a few years releasing limited-edition singles—including one that never went on sale at all; you had to write House directly with a good reason for him to send you one for free. The edition "sold" out quickly, and from the exhausting rush of **Bait and Switch,** it's easy to see why. House's high-pitched whine gives an oddly vulnerable edge to self-deflating tracks like "My Mysterious Death (Turn It Up)" and "You Can't Kill Stupid" (which addresses the singer's early-'90s battle with cancer), while Bob Petric's splatter-punk guitar riffs action-paint the margins of pieces like the spot-on cover of "Cyclotron" (from the catalogue of Cleveland proto-punks Electric Eels) with unremittingly chaotic abandon. The topper, however, is the revolutionary screed "RnR Hall of Fame," which tosses verbal firebombs at the very concept of the Cleveland rock hall, advocating that someone "blow it up . . . before Paul Westerberg gets in." Bait and switch? Duck and cover is more like it. [dss]

MAYO THOMPSON

See *Red Crayola.*

RICHARD THOMPSON

Starring as Henry the Human Fly! (Warner Bros.) 1972 (Hannibal) 1991
(Guitar, Vocal) (UK Island) 1976 (Hannibal) 1991
Live (More or Less) (Island) 1977
Strict Tempo! (UK Elixir) 1981 (Hannibal) 1991
Hand of Kindness (Hannibal) 1983
Small Town Romance (Hannibal) 1984
Across a Crowded Room (Polydor) 1985
Daring Adventures (Polydor) 1986
The Marksman (UK BBC) 1987
Amnesia (Capitol) 1988
Rumor and Sigh (Capitol) 1991
Sweet Talker (Capitol) 1992
Watching the Dark: The History of Richard Thompson (Hannibal) 1993
Mirror Blue (Capitol) 1994
you? me? us? (Capitol) 1996

RICHARD AND LINDA THOMPSON

I Want to See the Bright Lights Tonight (UK Island) 1973 (Hannibal) 1991
Hokey Pokey (Island) 1974 (Hannibal) 1991
Pour Down Like Silver (Island) 1975 (Hannibal) 1991
First Light (Chrysalis) 1978 (Hannibal) 1991
Sunnyvista (UK Chrysalis) 1979 (Hannibal) 1991
Shoot Out the Lights (Hannibal) 1982

LINDA THOMPSON

One Clear Moment (Warner Bros.) 1985
Dreams Fly Away (Rykodisc) 1996

JOHN FRENCH/FRED FRITH/HENRY KAISER/RICHARD THOMPSON

Live, Love, Larf & Loaf (Rhino) 1987 (Shanachie) 1996
Invisible Means (Windham Hill) 1990

VARIOUS ARTISTS

Beat the Retreat (Capitol) 1994
The World Is a Wonderful Place (Green Linnet) 1993

The drizzly love affair between gloomy alternarockers and Richard Thompson has little to do with the English singer/guitarist's revisionist folkie heritage in Fairport Convention, his extraordinary instrumental skill or the generally fine solo albums he's made in recent years. No, what resonates most among the shaving-razor-and-Valium set are the songs he wrote during the difficult passage and aftermath of his marriage and musical partnership with singer Linda Thompson: "Shoot Out the Lights," "Withered and Died," "Walking on a Wire," "For Shame of Doing Wrong," "Dimming of the Day." Unlike the depressives who marble the acoustic world, however, Richard Thompson has never been the sort whose own life seems threatened by the miseries detailed in his work: even cornered on the cover of **Shoot Out the Lights,** the couple's harrowing masterpiece, he's smiling. Some abiding optimism inherent in his personality (and perhaps his Sufi Islam faith) has kept him looking past the disasters, incisively—sometimes impishly, especially when he writes and sings in the first person—chronicling the worst things people can do to each other without drawing the obvious cynical conclusions about mankind. Matched by the unpretentious sincerity of his performances, his songs are, at their best, enlightening and at the very least soul-nourishing.

Among the merchants of grim (which is only one facet of Thompson's much broader art), Thompson exhibits a rare sense of humor and sanity that, combined with his brutal emotional honesty, makes him a paradigm of underground sensibilities—in a career that is nothing of the sort. Basically, he's a troubadour who accepts sadness as a fellow-traveler in open-minded enthusiasms that have deposited him comfortably in realms as diverse as "Matty Groves" and Pere Ubu. His mid-'80s participation in the Golden Palominos and a two-album partnership with Henry Kaiser, John French and Fred Frith are as much part of Thompson's oeuvre as ballads of the eighteenth century. As a result, his songs have proven equally useful to folkies like Jo-El Sonnier, June Tabor and sometimes sideman Clive Gregson, as well as those of a more restless, rebellious nature, most notably Bob Mould, Elvis Costello and Maria McKee. (For his part, Thompson playfully does Who songs in concert.) The two tribute albums reflect that duality: **The World Is a Wonderful Place** favors homey types like Victoria Williams, Christine Collister, Peter Blegvad and Marvin Etzioni; **Beat the Retreat** holds the center with Bonnie Raitt ("When the Spell Is Broken"), Los Lobos ("Down Where the Drunkards Roll"), Beausoleil ("Valerie") and June Tabor ("Beat the Retreat"), but also opens the doors to Mould ("Turning of the Tide"), R.E.M. ("Wall of Death"), X ("Shoot Out the Lights") and Dinosaur Jr ("I Misunderstood").

Watching the Dark, a three-disc collection that stretches from late-'60s Fairports to 1992 Thompson, is not for beginners. Compiled by devotees as a fan's fantasy, half of the forty-seven songs are live or previously unreleased; it's a treat for those up to speed, but hardly the basic introduction Thompson's vast and uneven oeuvre could use. While **Rumor and Sigh** is an immediate, accessible representative of Thompson's mature art at its peak, the sharpest, most memorable jolt of where he's come from can be found in the Richard and Linda section: the subtly religious **Pour Down Like Silver, Shoot Out the Lights** and the happy loving couple's barely more upbeat **I Want to See the Bright Lights Tonight.** All three are eloquently, exceptionally beautiful and deeply affecting personal expressions. (For a different view of the era, Linda Thompson's **Dreams Fly Away** is a twenty-song career overview with unreleased material and alternate versions, some from the duo's time together.)

Thompson's solo albums of the '80s are commendable but uneven, lacking the insidious spark of his best creations. Although he'd already worked with producer Mitchell Froom on **Daring Adventures** and **Amnesia** (the best thing about which is the photo of Thompson barre-chording a chainsaw, threatening it with a Townshend-like windmill), Thompson had a third-time's-the-charm artistic epiphany on **Rumor and Sigh.** Backed with tasteful electric rustic pop arrangements (close in tone to John Hiatt's **Slow Turn-**

ing), Thompson antes up a superlative, far-ranging set of witty new tunes on topics as varied as pornography ("Read About Love"), fatal motorcycles ("1952 Vincent Black Lightning"), fragile 78s ("Don't Sit on My Jimmy Shands"), alcoholics ("God Loves a Drunk") and sociopathy ("Psycho Street"). The love songs, too, are anything but ordinary and predictable. The payoff to the title of "I Feel So Good" is "I'm going to break somebody's heart tonight." Facing a failure to communicate in "I Misunderstood," Thompson slices and dices himself with surgical aplomb: "I thought she was saying good luck, she was saying goodbye."

Sweet Talker is the pleasant but minor soundtrack to an instantly forgotten film. Thompson wrote the music and sings three of the four vocal songs (the rocking "To Hang a Dream On" is the keeper); otherwise, he and a company of cronies, both old and new, perform handsome instrumentals in various inflections and idioms, using accordion to invoke zydeco in "Roll Up," tin whistle and *bodhran* to dance an Irish jig in the first half of "Conviction," keyboards to achieve an elegant sitting-room grace in "Sweet Talker" and so on. (Thompson had previously essayed instrumental music, devoting **Strict Tempo!** to the task. He also had scored before, for a couple of BBC-TV series, 1987's *The Marksman* and 1990's *Hard Cash.*)

Although created under similar circumstances, **Mirror Blue** doesn't have quite the fervent imagination or gusto of **Rumor and Sigh.** Froom goes a little overboard in the arrangements, bringing back a bit more from his Elvis Costello projects than just drummer Pete Thomas and a hollow snare sound. But audio fingerpainting is not the real problem: few of the songs are as lively or melodically stirring as those on the previous record. Thompson partially compensates by playing a whole lot more guitar, both acoustic and electric. The mighty solo that moans organically out of "The Way That It Shows" is thrilling; and his rock-'n'rolling on "Shane and Dixie" is good, exciting fun. But a second song about vintage motors ("MGB-GT") is one too many, and the lyrics of strong compositions like "Easy There, Steady Now," "King of Bohemia" and the nearly maudlin "Taking My Business Elsewhere"—sung with a shade too much theatrical flourish—fall too easily into predictable rhymes.

Everything that's wrong with **Mirror Blue** is worse on **you? me? us?,** beginning with the intemperate overabundance of songs. Trotting out eighteen new numbers (too few of which are unexpected or even notably fine ideas), Thompson is entirely too generous, sacrificing full development and consistent quality for a surplus of half-baked goods. (Dividing the two discs into *voltage enhanced* (mildly electric) and *nude* (richly acoustic) doesn't help. The two versions of "Razor Dance" aren't exactly black and white in tone and typify the album's miscalculated sense of discretion. The melodramatic "Dark Hand Over My Heart" and "Hide It Away" are typical lovelorn plaints; "The Ghost of You Walks" isn't very different from "I Misunderstood"; "Cold Kisses" is the token creep song in which the narrator rifles through a girlfriend's old photographs to check out past lovers. "She Cut off Her Long Silken Hair" is an exquisite folk song, and others have the reliable attributes to pass muster, but it's a chore fishing through the mediocre many to reach the proud few. Thompson sings like an anxious drama student attempting to impress a fussy elocution teacher, and the production by Froom and Tchad Blake seems to be a replay of their last record with Los Lobos. [i]

See also *Golden Palominos.*

THOMPSON TWINS

See *Babble.*

THOUSAND YARD STARE

Weatherwatching EP (UK Stifled Aardvark) 1990
Keepsake (UK Stifled Aardvark) 1991
Hands On (Polydor) 1992

Call it poetic justice, but this English quintet from Slough—whose name refers to the look in the eyes of shell-shocked Vietnam veterans—didn't have an original idea in its head. That's not to say **Hands On,** produced by Stephen Street, isn't any good. The album's money shot, the loping, trance-like six-minute-plus "Comeuppance," merges a "Guns of Brixton" bassline with the sound of early Tears for Fears. Elsewhere, the band resembles a less fuzzy Ned's Atomic Dustbin, especially on "0–0 a.e.t. (no score after extra time)," and—thanks to guest fiddler Martin Bell—a junior Wonder Stuff. All told, **Hands On** is a perfectly okay album from a band that has not been heard from since. [db]

THREE DAY STUBBLE

Friendly Park Survivors [tape] (Nerd Rock) 1981
Nerd Rock [8-track] (Cool Beans) 1982
Monster (Fartblossom) 1987
Wafer of Darkness (Nerd Rock) 1991
Festival of the Wedding of the Sea Goat (Nerd Rock) 1993

On a long-term mission to confront, confuse and ultimately comfort its battle-scarred audience, Three Day Stubble combines the most eccentric extremes of Houston (the band's birthplace) and San Francisco (its adopted home). Dressed in garish, clashing polyester plaids, the group's self-actualization campaign has sometimes been hindered by the false impression that its music is a joke. In the long run, Stubble's aggressive lack of ego is more radically unsettling than all the razor blades and spiked dog collars in punkdom.

The **Friendly Park Survivors** cassette is one of Stubble's more prescient moments. Contained on a small scale, the bustling psychedelia and exotic inclinations are cohesively integrated on "Beli & Bali," "Boogin' Around" and "Hurly Whurly Mama." Stream-of-consciousness vocalist Donald the Nut, Brently Pusser and Wilma combine the best of '70s psychedelia and '80s no wave with fiercely expressive self-invented guitar and home sounds. Viewed from a 1995 home-taping perspective, the cassette is dazzling and way ahead of its time—in every way (except self-importance) the equal of Stereolab and Tortoise.

Issued as an honest-to-god 8-track tape, **Nerd Rock** compiles eight tracks, most of which resemble a stoned hybrid of Texas blues and the Master Musicians of Jajouka. After a successful West Coast tour in 1983, Stubble relocated to California, where it became a hit on the experimental underground. The group at this time was a tilt-a-whirl of outside collaborators, notably Brad Laner, who later founded Medicine.

Monster is a tuneless, rambling epoch of self-justification, meaning it fits right in with the prevalent DIY punk records of the day. Like a spaced-out Half

Japanese, the band vamps through "Turbulance of Motion," the anti-hardcore spoof "Nick the Dick" and nine other ventures in search of the almighty positive mental attitude. Pusser shines as a wigged-out guitar hero; his reassuring riffs anchor the rhythmic and vocal flakiness. Still, hanging through linear jams for the full hour can be psychically exhausting.

The late '80s saw a great deal of personal turmoil for Three Day Stubble, with periods of inactivity that left co-founder Wilma back in Houston. A 1987 Texas jaunt produced a permanent second guitarist, and **Wafer of Darkness** put Stubble back on track. Newcomer Mr. Hungry joins Pusser for an awesome, discombobulating dual guitar attack, enabling the bouncy polynote riffing of "Mind Over Matter." Deeply affecting revelations from maturing man-child-prophet Donald find him at odds with an alienating modern world in "Look Experience" and "Teckaknowlegy." The title track is a nerdy white-soul take (complete with catchy falsetto refrain) on James Brown.

Festival of the Wedding of the Sea Goat follows the band's hit-or-experiment quality, with convoluted boogie numbers like "Stone Lizard Angina" mixing it up amongst a cappella improv from Donald (fresh from performing his personal art form avi for Mr. T on *The Gong Show*). New bassist Murder'r Bob (ex–Tragic Mulatto) replaced ten-year stalwart Capt. Dan Man mid-recording. Comparisons to Captain Beefheart persist, though Stubble still does not seem at its core to be a rock band. If there's a Residents influence to be noted, it seems to hail from **Eskimo,** not **Duck Stab.** Frenetic as the band can be, there are no sharp edges—Stubble proves enthusiastically that music can soothe shattered nerves without sounding like aural anesthesia.

Three Day Stubble tightened up its musical act in 1993 with the addition of drummer Don Bolles (ex-Germs/45 Grave), replacing Dave "Spumoni" Cameron, a former Roky Erickson associate who commuted to Stubble rehearsals from Austin. Marking the persuasive flair of Stubble-mania on the rise, the Boredoms were inspired to dress in nerd gear; Stubble prepared a greatest-hits-live CD for Japan release in 1996. Pusser concurrently became a regular member of Barbara Manning's SF Seals. [ic]

See also *Barbara Manning, Medicine.*

THREE DOCTOR'S BAND

See *Zip Code Rapists.*

3DS

Fish Tales (NZ Flying Nun) 1990
Swarthy Songs for Swabs EP (NZ Flying Nun) 1991
Fish Tales/Swarthy Songs for Swabs (Flying Nun/First Warning) 1991
Hellzapoppin (Flying Nun/First Warning) 1992
The Venus Trail (Merge) 1994
Caterwauling EP (NZ Flying Nun) 1995
Strange News From the Angels (Flying Nun) 1996

With members drawn from other notable New Zealand groups (Look Blue Go Purple, Exploding Budgies, Bird Nest Roys, Goblin Mix), the 3Ds have achieved a nearly perfect amalgam: brash, head-butting guitar lines that shape themselves around irresistible hooks and colorful song structures supported by burly rhythms. The band (named for founders David Saunders, Denise Roughan and Dominic Stones, although fourth member David Mitchell fits right in) fashions these elements into both buoyantly poppy and incessantly grinding songs. Maintaining a high quality level, the quartet's music resounds with ingenuity and passion.

Both Saunders and Mitchell (whose creepy artwork adorns many NZ records) play aggressive, melodic guitar lines with a dizzying and dynamic array of hooks driving all seven songs on **Fish Tales:** the crunchy, snarling "First Church," the more contemplative "Fish Tails," the playful "Evocation of W.C. Fields." Saunders, Mitchell and bassist Roughan alternate vocals on all of the 3Ds' recordings; while none has a "nice" voice, they're all distinctive singers, adding another layer of intrigue to an already engaging mess of sound. **Fish Tales** makes it gleefully apparent that these four have more than their share of musical ideas and the gutsy energy to make something of them.

The six-song **Swarthy Songs for Swabs** begins with the aptly named exuberant "Sing-song," one of the band's finest moments. "Ritual Tragick" suggests the 3Ds' closest Northern Hemisphere counterpart, Pavement; although there are no traces of Pavement's lazy "Range Life" vibe here, the 3Ds' facility for hooks and their deft incorporation into compact song structures certainly equals that of their more famous brethren. The CD containing both vinyl EPs is rounded out by two leftovers recorded on a Portastudio with bassist Rachael King of the Cakekitchen.

With such a promising introduction, **Hellzapoppin,** the 3Ds' first full-length, gets off to a delicious start. Overstuffed with the Davids' punchy guitar lines and fervently chased by their sing-songy vocal shouts, "Outer Space" perfectly captures the group's spastic energy and crisp melodicism. Though thoroughly enjoyable, the other poppy songs here ("Hellzapoppin," "Hairs") don't equal "Outer Space," but the group's range is never limited to such confines. Roughan carries the surly "Sunken Head" through dark, choppy waters, "Ugly Day" rides the ferocious waves of a beefed-up guitar sound and "Leave the Dogs to Play" employs a thick lurching melody and distorted vocals.

The Venus Trail can't match **Hellzapoppin**'s amazing gusts of energy—not even with the angry, two-minute sock in the face "Hey Seuss"—yet it attains nearly the same level of accomplishment in the expanded range of sounds. "Beautiful Things" applies a quieter setting to a familiar 3Ds song structure, highlighting Roughan's firm ability to lead the band, while the duets on the mellow, electric "The Young and the Restless" and the somber, acoustic "Spooky" erect a new tangent on which the group will certainly build in the future. [la]

See also *Cakekitchen.*

THREE FISH

See *Pearl Jam.*

3 LB. THRILL

See *Uncle Green.*

THRONEBERRY

Sangría (Alias) 1994
Trot Out the Encores (Alias) 1996

Having named themselves after the 1962 NY Mets' infamously hapless first baseman, "Marvelous" Marv

Throneberry, these Cincinnati pals of the Afghan Whigs might well be your standard-issue indie-rock dweebs with low self-esteem. Instead, **Sangría** opens with singer/guitarist Jason Arbenz informing the world that "I've been touched / The hand of greatness has selected me." You've got to admire a first album that begins with such a cocky announcement. Produced by big Whig Greg Dulli at his bandmate John Curley's Ultrasuede Studio, the record comes close to validating Arbenz's god complex. **Sangría** captures the band's Big Rock dynamics (oh-so-similar to the Whigs' brand of punk-soul); blended with Arbenz's raspy voice and bleary-eyed heart of darkness, the result is stirring songs like "Green Goddess" and the half-drunk-at-4:00-A.M. innuendo of "Shellac the Bozak." Throneberry might not be ready to part the Red Sea just yet, but **Sangría** is a damn fine invocation.

Extensive touring and bouts with illness kept Throneberry out of the studio for a while, save for a cool version of "Here Comes My Girl" that appeared on 1994's **You Got Lucky,** the otherwise awful Tom Petty tribute album. Finally, early '96 yielded the heartbreak of **Trot Out the Encores.** Murky and indistinct production that is clearly someone's idea of modern rock radio-friendly (producer Joe Chiccarelli?) quashes the simple sparse emotionalism found on **Sangría.** Arbenz's boozy tongue-in-cheek wit is in evidence, and there are a handful of good songs (notably "Drops of Moxie" and the lounge-crawling "Hooray for Everything!"), but, in the end, **Trot Out the Encores** is pretty much a swing and a miss. [mgk]

THROWING MUSES

Throwing Muses EP (Throwing Muses) 1984
Throwing Muses [tape] (Throwing Muses) 1985
Throwing Muses (UK 4AD) 1986
Chains Changed EP (UK 4AD) 1987
The Fat Skier (Sire) 1987
House Tornado (Sire) 1989
Hunkpapa (Sire) 1989
Dizzy EP (UK 4AD) 1989
The Real Ramona (Sire/Warner Bros.) 1991
Red Heaven (Sire/Warner Bros.) 1992
University (Sire/Reprise) 1995
Ruthie's Knocking EP (Rykodisc) 1996
Limbo (Rykodisc) 1996

KRISTEN HERSH

Hips and Makers (Sire/Reprise) 1994
Strings (Sire/Reprise) 1994

As the final Throwing Muses album before co-founder Tanya Donelly—having tested the world beyond her Rhode Island band home in the Breeders—moved out to form Belly, **The Real Ramona** betrays no special creative tension or gathering storm clouds, although the recording process was reportedly a high-wire balancing act. With Fred Abong replacing bassist Leslie Langston and producer Dennis Herring helping everyone play nice, singer/guitarist Kristin Hersh (Donelly's step-sister and the Muses' primary songwriter) sounds comfortably in charge on the group's fourth full-length album (not counting the seven-song **Fat Skier**). Engaged material ("Counting Backwards," the whooping drum-driven "Golden Thing," Donelly's peppy "Not Too Soon"), inventive arrangements and audible concentration in their delivery remedy the aloofness that made **Hunkpapa** a bland low point in the once-singular quartet's progress from intriguing artistry to alternapop ordinariness. With Hersh's folky voice as its main ingredient, the band's sonic personality is still anemic and dry, but **The Real Ramona** pumps in enough blood and guts for encouraging signs of life.

Donelly then left the group to Hersh and drummer David Narcizo; Langston plays lyrical bass on **Red Heaven** but isn't listed as an official member. (Abong also resigned, taking a short-term studio assignment from Donelly without actually joining Belly.) Sounding as if some enormous obstacle had been lifted out of Hersh's way, the self-produced album is a lively, passionate rockfest. Blowing away the Elizabethan wispiness of the previous two outings, Hersh sings out with throaty vibrato and surging confidence (reinforcing the Patti Smith aspect that has always lurked in her larynx), and slashes enthusiastically at her guitar as if she had just discovered the foot switch on her distortion pedal. Carried along on big, hearty melodies and the energized delivery, her bizarre thoughtdreams make an impression even when their purpose is far from clear: "I saw him first on Summer Street / He held my breath/A famous face and instant death." Although the middle of the quizzical "Pearl" surges with electric power, the resonant acoustic folk that begins and ends it ("Hot hands move things / I write on his wall / I have no mind at all") points the way to Hersh's solo career, which she began two years later.

If not for that preview, the revelation of **Hips and Makers** might have been even more dramatic. Hersh's stately debut is a beautiful album of family, madness and devotion sung with resounding emotional power over the scantiest allotments of acoustic guitar, piano and cello. Like a pre-Raphaelite painting, **Hips and Makers** is rendered in dusky browns, twilight yellows and muted reds, a deep dive into Hersh's mind that pulls out anxieties, uncertainties and dislocated bewilderment. "This hairdo's truly evil / I'm not sure it's mine," from "Teeth," seems whimsical enough, but the quiet ferocity of her determination, rushing ahead of the tempo in "Houdini Blues," is riveting: "Oh no, don't put me in that box / You know what you can do with those locks / Bet your life I'll come crawling out again / You'll have to deal with me then." The harrowing edge in her keen makes the first portion of the incalculable "A Loon" extra disturbing; her sudden mid-song switch to a girlish voice brings no relief from the feeling that something is seriously amiss. The diarist's reflections delivered in the form of "The Letter" send an unnerving current of surrealism flowing through a graceful melody: "Don't forget that I'm living inside the space where walls and floor meet / There's a box inside my chest / An animal stuffed with my frustration." Jane Scarpantoni is the album's cellist; Michael Stipe ups the ethereal quotient by singing on "Your Ghost"; Lenny Kaye did the exquisitely tasteful co-production.

Following **Hips and Makers** (and its sidecar, **Strings,** which contains two new originals, a bluesy Led Zeppelin cover, the album's "Beestung" and four other songs from it given appealing baroque makeovers with six British string players), Hersh did a solo tour and then returned to Throwing Muses, recording an album with Narcizo and new bassist

Bernard Georges the following year. Other than one related song ("Teller") and Scarpantoni's presence, **University** steers away from **Hips and Makers,** keeping the distinction between her group and solo work clear. That's ironic: the artistic triumph of Hersh's solo work now makes it hard to think of Throwing Muses as more than an equally weighted alter ego to her unaccompanied efforts. In fact, other than the surprising wah-wah workouts, **University** is of a piece with **Red Heaven.** Fragmentary lyrics about love, lust and family (while still alluding to troubled mental states: "I have nothing to offer but confusion/And the circus in my head") are less evocative in competition with full-bodied electric pop, but the active setting frees Hersh to write less ambitious songs that sometimes say as much. "No Way in Hell," a perplexing self-portrait ("I sleep with one hand on my clothes / I sleep with one hand on my heart / There's almost nothing left to guard"), evolves into a merry / angry round—something that would have been impossible in the unprotected starkness of her solo record. Having proven that she can keep two plates spinning at the same time, Hersh now has to decide whether she wants to integrate her musical selves or keep them apart. [i]

See also *Belly, Breeders; TPRG.*

THROWN-UPS

See *Mudhoney.*

THROW THAT BEAT IN THE GARBAGECAN!

Tweng! (Ger. September Gurls) 1988
Large Marge Sent Us! (Ger. September Gurls) 1989 (spinART) 1993
Not Particularly Silly (Ger. Electrola) 1991
Cool (Ger. Electrola) 1992
Cool EP (spinART) 1993
The Cool Album (spinART) 1993
Superstar (Ger. Electrola) 1994

KLAUS CORNFIELD & LOTSI LAPISLAZULI

Little Tigers (Ger. Musical Tragedies) 1991

Like Japan, another burgeoning post-war industrial giant looking for culture in all the wrong places, Germany has to do its global bit in the abject scavenging and silly recycling of American junk with merry abandon. A quick look at the early scrap operation mounted by this hyperactive Bremen sextet reveals a band name nicked from the B-52's, an album title skimmed off *Pee-wee's Big Adventure* and a record label named after a Big Star song. The group's colophon, however, is more locally relevant: the anti-fascist symbol of a swastika being dumpsterized.

And that's not even getting into the chipper and imaginatively loopy music contained on the **Large Marge Sent Us!** CD, which incorporates the crappy-sounding, rock'n'rolly seven-cut **Tweng!** mini-album and three single sides: a total of two dozen short blasts of derivative but original Anglo-American power-pop sung mainly in English by guitarist Klaus Cornfield. Introducing a liquid theme that evidently means a lot to him, Cornfield ventures "Under Water" amid splashy sound effects. Even when pining for transportation and affection ("I Wish I Had a Car"), Throw That Beat! keeps its smileyface spirit; a rudimentary resemblance to the Television Personalities stops at the point of the Germans' happy-go-lucky emotional outlook.

Strewing giddy ideas around like ticker tape ("A Chocolatbar for Breakfast," "You Only Think of Me, . . . When There's No Program on TV," "I Dedicate My Life to You," "Little Red Go-Cart," the comically self-aware "I'm Like a Baby" and the sci-fi miscegenation of "Some Alien . . . "), **Not Particularly Silly** refines the band's elements into pure pop joy, a danceable sugar rush of simple harmony singing, catchy tunes, hearty guitar elbow grease, organ accents (by the woman who calls herself Iwie Candy X07) and Alex Sticht's peppy drumming. Lotsi Lapislazuli steps up for more lead vocals, giving the band a two-headed sound and moving the seventeen-cut collection along without having to stop for breath. Don't pay any mind to the album title: they are and it is, and that's good for all concerned.

Released in the US (identical in contents save for the addition of an unlisted ode to a mouse, but minus the spectacular cartoon insert) as **The Cool Album** to differentiate it from the confusingly titled and half-overlapping four-song **Cool** EP, **Cool** takes a calmer, more considered musical approach (there's lots more Lotsi and a full dollop of ABBA in the blend) and allows adult uncertainty to infect the lyrics. With the piano bounce of "Je Pense Toujours à Toi" revealing another facet of the band's sound (and language skills), "It's Never Enough," "A Last Kiss," "Over & Over," "Angels Don't Cry" and "Too Blue" (heralded by trumpet blares) all rue love's losses in bittersweet pop confections.

With Lotsi gone, the quintet drafted guest vocalists Janas Hoyt (moonlighting from Indiana's Vulgar Boatmen) and Gina Vaporjieff D'orio to help on **Superstar.** Slickly produced to far more of a regular rock'n'roll sound than usual for Throw That Beat!, the record sacrifices a lot of the band's pop charm and most of its innocence; despite a few moments that are clearly intended as audio in-jokes (in the spirit of the Pooh Sticks), it's hard to tell how serious the squealing and roaring guitars, repetitive choruses, strings (on Iwie's "I'm Your Trip") and Cornfield's exaggerated singing are. Some of his songs aren't half bad ("I Won't Give Up," "Let Me Sit Next to Iwie," "Brand New Rock-'n'Roll Party"), but whimsy was never meant to sound this determined or muscular.

There's nothing remotely serious about **Little Tigers,** an absurd and amazing album recorded—literally—in Klaus' bathroom. (The veracious liner notes do acknowledge that one flute solo was actually committed to tape in his kitchen.) Sounding like they've been soaking in a bathtub full of gin, Klaus and Lotsi accompany their interwoven voices on a madcap mixture of acoustic guitar, toy piano, bells, harmonica, music box, bongos, kalimba and such handy percussion implements as "toilet-flush," "rhythmical root-brush" and "dry-shaver." More David Peel than Spike Jones, the pair's fanciful program of originals (plus a rendition of Queen's "You and I") about aliens ("Nanoo Nanoo," "Space Cadett"), animals ("I Buy Me a Dog") and amour ("I Love Your Smile in the Sun," "All that Love in My Heart," "Kissing Under the Tree") is unerringly adorable and, under the circumstances, more accomplished than it has any right to be. [i]

THUG LIFE

See *2Pac.*

JOHNNY THUNDERS & WAYNE KRAMER

See *Wayne Kramer.*

TIGER TRAP

Tiger Trap (K) 1993
Sour Grass EP (K) 1993

GO SAILOR

Fine Day for Sailing EP7 (Yo Yo) 1994
Long Distance EP7 (Slumberland) 1995
Don't Go EP7 (Lookout!) 1996
Go Sailor (Lookout!) 1996

SOFTIES

Loveseat EP7 (Slumberland) 1995
The Softies EP7 (K) 1995
It's Love (K) 1995
The Softies (Slumberland) 1996

Formed at a Flaming Lips show, named after a Beat Happening song and inspired by tweepop titans like Talulah Gosh, Sacramento's Tiger Trap exemplified the new generation of love-rockers in the early '90s. While the scene's starchier young women veered off to become riot grrrls, singer/guitarist Rose Melberg turned her quartet toward endearing, simple, sexually ambiguous post-adolescent odes to romance in all its heartrending joys and disappointments. Ebullient tunes like the Calvin Johnson–produced **Tiger Trap**'s "Super Crush," "For Sure" and "Words and Smiles" leave overt politics aside, making their points for dignity and individualism in subtler ways. Winsome but never wimpy, Melberg's sure, sweet voice and catchy melodies—energized by the band's upright and enterprising casual electric rock, firmly driven by drummer Heather Dunn (who later played with Lois and the reformed Raincoats)—make **Tiger Trap** a solid delight of potential appeal beyond the timorous realm of independent amateurism. As Colette did a century earlier in the first of her Claudine novels, Tiger Trap ennobles the obsessions of adolescent romance by not entirely succumbing to them.

The subsequent **Sour Grass** EP, a final salvo from the short-lived band, presents five fine (especially the title tune and "Don't Ask") new songs cut from the same cloth but produced a tad more ambitiously by Yo Yo Records magnate Pat Maley.

With that, Melberg bagged Tiger Trap, moved to Portland, Oregon, and continued on with a pair of new bands. Go Sailor, a trio with bassist Paul and drummer Amy, plays polite janglecharm—a sparser, toned-down (but no less peppy) version of Tiger Trap's punk-pop. Compiled along with a couple of compilation items on the nifty '96 album, Go Sailor's three four-song EPs benefit from Melberg's growing confidence, both as a writer and as a singer. (The sonic upgrade from 7-inch to CD is also advantageous.) There's nothing fancy here, but the songs are wonderful in their melodic and emotional purity.

Recycling the name of a minor '70s British new wave band, the Softies—Melberg's duo with fan-turned-partner vocalist Jen Sbragia—offers weightless guitar/harmony song sketches recalling the skeletal jazz-influenced pop that led Tracey Thorn of the Marine Girls to form Everything but the Girl. With no songs in common, the K 7-inch EP and **It's Love** (whose one non-original is a version of Talulah Gosh's "I Can't Get No Satisfaction, Thank God") are still awfully samey. While lovely in small doses, the unvarying translucence of the duo's quiet simplicity—which erases the differences between one lovely/cute love song and the next—is cloying in quantity.

Again, Melberg's abundant talent and increased self-assurance save the day. Stronger melodies and sweeter harmonies (both vocals and softly interwoven electric guitars), plus shifting rhythms and slightly more intricate chord structures, make the eight-song **The Softies** consistently engaging. The sheer fabric of the duo's romantic music is no more varied than on **It's Love,** but the patterns into which it is shaped here (the extra-dreamy "Half as Much," the peppy "Snow Like This," the breezy "All in Good Time") are easier to tell apart. [i]

See also *Lois, Raincoats.*

TIJUANA BIBLE

See *Mick Farren.*

TIMBUK 3

Greetings From Timbuk 3 (IRS) 1986
Eden Alley (IRS) 1988
Edge of Allegiance (IRS) 1989
Big Shot in the Dark (IRS) 1991
Field Guide: Some of the Best of Timbuk 3 (IRS) 1992
Espace Ornano (Watermelon) 1993
Looks Like Dark to Me EP (High Street) 1994
A Hundred Lovers (High Street) 1995

Pat and Barbara K. MacDonald are wryly rueful observers of society's ills; their dry, dusty voices have a down-home charm that makes up for occasional excesses in their lyrics. Using a rhythm box for backing, they burst out of the Austin, Texas, scene with the peppy, corrosively sarcastic hit "The Future's So Bright, I Gotta Wear Shades," only to see, like Randy Newman and Elvis Costello before them, how irony is typically ignored or misunderstood by mainstream audiences. Anyone digging into their excellent debut album, however, could hardly misconstrue the MacDonalds' intent. From the dour "Life Is Hard" to the fake cheer of "Hairstyles and Attitudes," the duo's contemporary vision is vivid and harrowing.

Eden Alley is more diverse (less countryfied), but the sense of dismay remains the same. Reflecting big trouble on both a personal and a global level, "Too Much Sex, Not Enough Affection," "Welcome to the Human Race," "Rev. Jack & His Roamin' Cadillac Church" and the rest of these smart, stinging songs are guaranteed to produce a case of the existential dreads.

Produced by the MacDonalds with drummer Denardo Coleman (Ornette's son), **Edge of Allegiance** oozes sardonic desperation, occasionally labored ("Standard White Jesus") but more often right on the money, whether it's a darkly humorous portrait of the lowest level of the underclass ("Dirty Dirty Rice") or a disdainful view of standard-issue patriotism ("National Holiday").

Big Shot in the Dark presents Timbuk 3 as a bona fide quartet (with drummer Wally Ingram and bassist/etc. Courtney Audain), offering looser, more soulful grooves in sharp contrast to the increasingly embittered content. Mocking power-seekers in the title track, social horror in "Dis***land (Was Made for You & Me)," aimless youth in "God Made an Angel" and other sources of stress, the MacDonalds almost seem overwhelmed by their moral outrage.

Field Guide: Some of the Best of Timbuk 3 is a straightforward thirteen-track compression of the first four albums, with a 1989 B-side ("Assholes on Parade") added for collectability. Recorded in 1991 in Paris, **Espace Ornano** (the name of the venue) is a nifty live set highlighted by snappy renditions of "Throw Down Gun" (a warning about police frame-ups), "Tarzan Was a Bluesman" and "Dirty Dirty Rice." "The Future's So Bright" is conspicuous by its absence.

The song *does* resurface in a newly deconstructed but still scathing version on the six-track **Looks Like Dark to Me.** In addition to an agreeably footloose reading of "Born to Be Wild," the EP provides a stunning companion piece to "The Future's So Bright" in the form of the brooding title track, wherein Pat MacDonald accurately describes himself as a "hopeful cynic."

A Hundred Lovers finds the MacDonalds in fine form, rockin' in a steadier fashion as they allow the superior rhythm section of Audain and Ingram more room to maneuver. Irritation at the state of the world remains the order of the day, but messages come wrapped in vibrant, funky sounds. Highlights include the driving "Not Yet Gone," with faux–ZZ Top guitar, "Legalize Our Love" (a rousing assault on homophobia) and the sly, sexy "Just Wanna Funk With Your Mind," featuring Barbara K's unsettling offer to "attempt a little amateur brain surgery." Yipes! [jy]

See also *TPRG*.

TIMCO

Friction Tape (Basura!/Priority) 1994
Gentleman Jim (Basura!/Priority) 1996

The unmistakable imprint of guitarist Kevin Thomson (ex–Nice Strong Arm) guides Timco through the eight songs of **Friction Tape.** Following Nice Strong Arm's dissolution, the Austin native relocated from New York to San Francisco and fell in with Red House Painters and American Music Club, whose Mark Eitzel assisted with production on the recorded-live-in-a-club debut LP. Combining the racket of Nice Strong Arm with the stark, measured reserve of his new pals, **Friction Tape** delivers lyrically introspective songs with melancholic melodies and instrumentation that lays in wait and then explodes in passionate fury. The forlorn "July" merges meditative, aching melodies with propulsive rhythms and Thomson's nimble, frenetic riffing. When "Bastard" or "Screw You" begin to fall into overwrought territory, Thomson saves the songs with energetic, emotional solos. Still, for all of the heart at its core, **Friction Tape** is hit and miss.

Gentleman Jim benefits enormously from clear studio sound; the record gets a powerful hit off Thomson's deep, resonant voice (especially on the dreamy "447") and draws a sharper, more exciting tension between the band's temperamental poles ("Louisiana" and "Marquis De Speed" are especially hair-raising examples of the yin yang). The growing cohesiveness between Thomson, drummer Ethel M.D. and bassist John Wischmann leads Timco to attempt more complex maneuvers (and some simpler ones, as well), most of which they pull off with casual aplomb. (Be sure not to miss the unlisted jazz noir/car instrumental that follows "Not for Me.") An intimate, seductive orchid that repeatedly snaps its piercing teeth shut on your finger, **Gentleman Jim** makes a most polite case for chaos. [mww/i]

TIMES

See *Ed Ball.*

SALLY TIMMS

See *Mekons.*

TINDERSTICKS

Marbles EP10 (UK Tippy Toe/Ché) 1993
Unwired EP7 (UK Domino) 1993
Tindersticks (UK This Way UP) 1993 (This Way Up/Bar/None) 1994
Kathleen EP (UK This Way Up) 1994
Amsterdam, 8th February 1994 (UK This Way Up) 1994
Tindersticks (This Way Up/London) 1995
The Bloomsbury Theatre 12th March 1995 (UK This Way Up) 1995

England's Tindersticks may not be the ideal band to invite to your next kegger, but it would be hard to imagine a finer convoy to guide you through those subdued moments of absinthe-accompanied repose. The Nottingham group makes a decidedly continental sound, polished chamber-pop settings punctuated by Gallic acoustic guitar flourishes and timeless port-city debauchery. That last element is particularly well typified by the beautiful-loser tales spun by frontman Stuart Staples, a sepulchral-voiced singer who makes Leonard Cohen sound like Smokey Robinson.

The fluid aggregation (generally a sextet, but often inflated to big-band proportions by full string and horn sections) began releasing limited-edition, intricately hand-packaged 7- and 10-inches in 1992. While portions of those earlier EPs would turn up on later releases, **Unwired** contains a pair of fascinating, otherwise unavailable songs that expose Staples' obsession with love's bleaker side ("Rottweilers and Mace") and his predilection for blacker-than-black humor ("Feeling Relatively Good").

Tindersticks (the first one) is nothing short of a revelation. Clocking in at nearly eighty minutes, it wends through the darkest recesses of Staples' psyche, revealing a fixation on bodily fluids—see "Blood," "Jism" and "Nectar"—as well as a windswept passion that brings to mind the seascapes of coastal England, postcards of gray cliffs and crashing whitecaps. Ancillary instruments like muted trumpet and violin lurk forebodingly in the background of songs like "Tyed," only to press to the fore on "Whiskey & Water" and the rapturously weary masterwork "City Sickness." The elegantly wasted atmosphere can grow a bit oppressive by the close of the album-ending "The Not Knowing" (a mournful sonnet spiced with the strains of bassoon and oboe), but the temptation to re-enter is still pretty powerful. The Amsterdam concert captured on the limited-edition live set is a good one, but adds little to the material—other than "For Those Not So Beautiful," drawn entirely from the studio album.

The 1995 **Tindersticks** (talk about letting the music speak for itself!) picks up where the debut left off—

with Staples muttering reticent epithets into the murky corners of "El Diablo en el Ojo." Every bit as diligent in its avoidance of standard rock shape-throwing, it's still a more sonically open set: "A Night In" evokes images of Scott Walker holding down a piano-bar stool in the wee hours of a French morning, while the flamboyant "Snowy in F# Minor" actually elicits images of the band sitting around passing a bottle of port as a celebration, rather than a prelude to a coma. Staples remains the focal point, although his duets with Carla Torgerson of the Walkabouts (on "Travelling Light") and Drugstore's Isobel Monteiro cast him as an agreeably heavy Lee Hazlewood analog—more such collaborations would indeed be welcome. The **Bloomsbury Theatre** concert is a rather remarkable undertaking, recorded with the support of a twenty-six-piece orchestra that's indispensable without being overwhelming. The arrangements of "El Diablo en el Ojo" (on which the classical musicians offer only subtle enhancements) and the first LP's "Drunk Tank" (utterly transformed by the stringed tempest) are enriched by the orchestral supplements, but they also retain their singularly intimate character, which is no mean feat. Maybe overkill isn't so bad after all. [dss]

See also *Walkabouts.*

TIN MACHINE

See *David Bowie.*

TINY LIGHTS

Prayer for the Halcyon Fear (Uriel/Temple) 1986
(Absolute A Go Go) 1990
Hazel's Wreath (Gaia) 1988
Know It You Love (unreleased) 1989
Hot Chocolate Massage (Absolute A Go Go) 1990
Stop the Sun, I Want to Go Home (Dr. Dream) 1992
Milky Juicy (Dr. Dream) 1994
The Young Person's Guide to Tiny Lights (Bar/None) 1995

Tiny Lights are a perfectly lovely jumble of plaintive pop, **Close to the Edge** epics, jazzy forays and neo-hippie lullabies that, if not for a procession of label failures, might have found an audience as broad as its tastes. Not as naïve as Donna Croughn's sweet, girlish vocals might indicate, these urban pastoralists from Hoboken, New Jersey, are pretty sophisticated, especially when arranging songs to fit Croughn's electric violin, cello (played by Jane Scarpantoni until the demand for her as a session player became too great and Stuart Hake replaced her in 1992), John Hamilton's surprisingly intricate guitar lines and a rhythm section that doubles on trumpet and saxophone.

Some hard touring in the early '90s added muscle and maturity to the band's enthusiasm and expansiveness, an effect first evident on the live-feeling, 8-track recording of **Hot Chocolate Massage.** The same process also weathered Croughn's voice into something not so cute, more earthy and evocative. The loose funk and backporch jazz of that record tempers the flights of fancy on the band's next album, **Stop the Sun, I Want to Go Home.** More adept at its acoustic numbers, better able to ground its joyous psychedelia within the rhythms of the increasingly impressive rhythm section (bassist Dave Dreiwitz and drummer Andy Damos), the band is at an accomplished peak. "Everybody's in the Park" is a song that bests 10,000 Maniacs—who at one time opened for Tiny Lights—at their own game, and "Better," sung by Hamilton, is the best pure rock song Tiny Lights has ever done.

Milky Juicy finds the band returning to a label for the first time (not counting a reissue and **Know It You Love,** which went unreleased after Gaia folded), but such continuity didn't encourage any careerist instincts: it's the band's most adventurous, eclectic record. Comfortable in what it can do but undaunted by what it can't, the band rifles through a sample-book's worth of styles, never sticking with one sound two songs in a row. The personality and family feel is never more evident (indeed, by this time Croughn and Hamilton had gotten married) or its sentiments and observations more accessible. **Milky Juicy** is the sound of a band following its heart.

Assembled as a tenth-anniversary present to its fans, **The Young Person's Guide to Tiny Lights** collects a handful of songs recorded for **Know It You Love** along with "hits" and favorites. Because Tiny Lights' records (and live shows, where the mix of sounds often make the most sense, and more important, inspires dancing) never stay in one groove for too long, the compilation's hodgepodge is about as formulaic as anything it's done. And that's a good thing. [sf]

See also *TPRG.*

TITANIC LOVE AFFAIR

Titanic Love Affair (Charisma) 1991
No Charisma EP (Crackpot) 1992
Their Titanic Majesties Request (No Alternative) 1996

If you don't want people to think your group sounds like a well-known band to which it bears an uncanny sonic resemblance, it may not be the wisest tactic to have that group's former drummer paint the back cover illustration for your debut album. Nonetheless, the caricature of the quartet from Urbana, Illinois, that brings up the rear on **Titanic Love Affair** bears the signature of one Chris Mars, late of the Replacements. Yeah, whatever.

Released not long after the Replacements ceased to exist (and before anyone much beyond Buffalo had heard of the Goo Goo Dolls, who made a similar gaffe by having Paul Westerberg write with them), **Titanic Love Affair** hovers between **Tim** and **Pleased to Meet Me** without ever breathing on the greatness of either. Ken Hartz (with backing vocals by the quartet's other guitarist, Jay Bennett) strains to evoke the sound of Westerberg's voice, only getting close enough to be obnoxious; the tame rock (capably produced by Albhy Galuten, a veteran whose studio résumé includes the Bee Gees) is too many notches below the Replacements' incendiary jizz to bolster the plainly derivative songwriting. In the album's weak defense, one good number ("Breakin' Down the Walls") is squandered in the effort.

After the short, disappointing corporate experience that attended **Titanic Love Affair,** the group issued the wryly titled five-song **No Charisma** on a St. Paul independent label. Co-produced to a healthier pop-rock tumult by Adam Schmitt, the surgingly melodic EP trades a borrowed personality for a sound that is less focused but much more exciting. The songs still bear Westerbergian traces, but the delivery of potent slacker rockers like "One Day" and the sardonic "Being Cool" is not aimed in any special direction.

Without leaving TLA (whose second full-length album appeared, after substantial delay, in 1996), Bennett began playing with Tommy Keene and joined Wilco. [i]

See also *Adam Schmitt, Uncle Tupelo.*

TOADIES

Velvet EP [tape] (no label) 1992
Pleather EP (Grass) 1993
Rubberneck (Interscope/Atlantic) 1994

Toadies' post-punk rock seemed a natural for radio, but the Dallas/Ft. Worth quartet had to tour for the better part of a year with Bush before **Rubberneck**'s virtues were exposed to such a broad audience. Certainly the songs—especially "Possum Kingdom"—are a bouncing good time, and guitarist Todd Lewis has the knack of singing forcefully without merely shouting. Better still, with co-writer/guitarist Darrel Herbert, Lewis has also solved the problem of how best to integrate guitar melodies back into loud music: solos are still too dated a gesture, but a catchy, tuneful scream fits the mood of the moment quite nicely.

Lewis and bassist Lisa Umbarger are all that remain of the original quartet that made the **Velvet** EP. By the time of **Pleather,** Herbert and drummer Mark Reznicek had been lifted from an inattentive Dallas band. [ga]

TOAD THE WET SPROCKET

Bread and Circus (Abe's/Columbia) 1989
Pale (Abe's/Columbia) 1990
Fear (Columbia) 1991
Dulcinea (Columbia) 1994
In Light Syrup (Columbia) 1995

Any band that finds its name in a Monty Python sketch deserves a point or two for taste—but that's about all Toad the Wet Sprocket had going for it early on. The Santa Barbara, California, quartet met in high school; singer/guitarist Glen Phillips, three years his bandmates' junior, took a proficiency exam to graduate along with them. The band was initially an R.E.M. clone: a little jangle in the guitars, some nice harmonies and not much else. Produced by Marvin Etzioni, **Pale** begins to refine their sound, exploring acoustic-electric dynamics, but seldom gets beyond pro forma folk-rock.

Fear is a significant step forward; without turning the band into overnight hard-rockers, the arrangements are gutsier within the framework of airy harmonies and shimmering guitars that defines the group's sound. The bracing anti-sexual-assault protest "Hold Her Down" snared the band some attention from those who misinterpreted it as glorifying rape, but the flowing, layered "Walk on the Ocean" and the smooth "All I Want" were fully embraced pop hits. Dean Dinning's propulsive bassline gives "Butterflies" some guts, while "Stories I Tell" builds hypnotically to guitarist Todd Nichols' edgy electric solo. Still, Toad's forte remains mostly lush, quieter fare, such as "Nightingale Song" and "I Will Not Take These Things for Granted."

The million-selling **Fear** kept Toad on the road for a while, and the live dates had an impact on the group's approach to **Dulcinea.** Slayer's safe, but Toad employs a far more electric edge on the dozen new songs; "Inside" is practically metallic when compared to the rest of Toad's canon. And the two singles, "Fall Down" and "Something's Always Wrong," are undeniably infectious. But the weaker material ("Reincarnation Song," "Windmills") is awfully ponderous, and the album's egghead quality ("You bend your words / Like Yuri Geller's spoons," from "Nanci") gets a little exasperating.

Conscious of its rep as a lightweight, Toad titled its odds'n'sods collection **In Light Syrup,** gathering up B-sides, soundtrack songs, fan club singles and a couple of previously unreleased numbers. Perhaps because the tracks weren't put together conceptually, it's actually a pretty entertaining album. "Good Intentions" is one of the better items on the *Friends* TV show LP, while "Hobbit on the Rocks" nods toward XTC. "Are We Afraid" and "All Right" kick up uncharacteristic heads of steam, while "Janitor" taps into a funk vein Toad has never really revealed on record. Seemingly filler on the surface, **In Light Syrup** actually provides surprising insights into some of Toad's veiled attributes. [gg]

See also *TPRG.*

TODAY IS THE DAY

Supernova (Amphetamine Reptile) 1994
Willpower (Amphetamine Reptile) 1995
Today Is the Day (Amphetamine Reptile) 1996

Nashville is called Music City USA, but that appellation doesn't seem to have made much impact on this trio, undoubtedly the most abrasive, amusical band to have ventured forth from that roots-conscious town. Today Is the Day is certainly not without precedent in terms of its basic tone. The group erects a Big Black–styled firewall in which all elements are given equal weight: jagged guitar corkscrews, sheets of cryptic, shimmering samples and heaving percussive effects. What sets the band apart is the vocals of Steve Austin, who screeches his way through life like he's on a one-man crusade to test the limits of otolaryngology. For long stretches of **Supernova,** Austin's otherworldly shriek will likely have you reflexively bringing your hand to your own throat. Songs like "6 Dementia Satyr" explode with cut-up tactics that don't always hold together, but the medium doesn't leave much doubt as to the message. When a breather is required, the band segues into ambient, forbidding instrumentals, like the viscous "Blind Man at Mystic Lake."

Willpower is slightly less claustrophobic in timbre, thanks in part to the atmospheric infiltration of White Room studio, the Detroit neo-psych mecca employed for the trio's second time around. Austin hasn't changed his delivery much—except to punctuate tracks like "Nothing to Lose" with the most hair-raising cackle this side of Robert Englund—but his subject matter has grown more concrete. Too bad, since his interests lie primarily in hackneyed domains like necrophilia ("Sidewinder") and suicide ("Golden Calf"). Extra points for subliminal use of motivational tapes—exactly what they're supposed to motivate is, of course, open to debate.

While the sound is a bit more focused, Austin's stream-of-subconsciousness ravings aren't any less intense on the self-titled third album. Not-so-vague threats like "Marked" and excruciating scab-picks like "Bugs" pack even more punch when they're leavened by such acoustic instrumental interludes as "A Man of Science." Pure hate for now people. [dss]

TOENUT

See *Drivin' n' Cryin'*.

TOILING MIDGETS

Sea of Unrest (Instant) 1982 (Fistpuppet) 1994
Four Track Mind [tape] (Mogul) 1984
Dead Beats (Thermidor) 1985
Son (Matador) 1992

SLEEPERS

Seventh World EP (Win) 1978
Painless Nights (Adolescent) 1981
The Less an Object (Tim/Kerr) 1996

The Toiling Midgets was spawned out of a congress between the Sleepers and Negative Trend, two of the Bay Area's most avowedly confrontational hardcore bands. Congruous to Flipper (two of whose founders played in Negative Trend), the new quintet boiled its songs down to their most primary elements, reassembling them if the mood struck but often allowing guitar solos to writhe somewhere in the middle distance as a disconnected rhythm cut in and out. For better or worse, however, the Midgets were distinguished almost entirely by singer Ricky Williams, a drug-addled, volatile-voiced figure of precarious mental balance. (Known as Ricky Tractor, he had previously drummed in Crime.)

Sea of Unrest, the only record released by the original lineup, shows Williams to be a truly "unique" talent. He uses an astoundingly powerful voice to invest songs like the disturbing "Trauma Girl" and the tortured "All the Girls Cry" (which obviously spent its share of time on Perry Farrell's turntable) with everything from operatic flourishes to *sotto voce* street-person babble. Beneath (and occasionally above) Williams' acrobatics, guitarists Craig Gray and Paul Hood unskein a particularly scraggy sheath of goth-inflected drone, characterized by haphazard circuits up and down the fretboard. The band parted ways with Williams (who died in 1992 after a long bout with respiratory illness), added guitarist Annie Unger and released **Dead Beats,** a portentous and quickly deleted all-instrumental album.

A decade later, original members Hood, Gray and Tim Mooney (a Sleepers veteran who went on to play drums in American Music Club) reunited to record **Son,** with AMC frontman Mark Eitzel as a suitably shirt-tearing stand-in for Williams. Harkening to the more excessive days of yore, Eitzel gnashes and wails through glacially paced, cavernous songs like "Faux Pony" and "Fabric," the moments of duress set off by a handful of stately, enigmatic instrumentals like "Slaughter on Sumner St." Bleak in the presence of beauty.

Williams' theatrical vocals and desperate lyrics were also the focal point of the Sleepers, a band whose harsh-but-crisp sound was reminiscent of early Joy Division (if that band had borrowed more from the Stooges and less from Sabbath). **The Less an Object** compiles most of the Sleepers' extant material (plus a pair of otherwise unreleased songs) into a harrowing profile in excess. [dss]

See also *American Music Club; TPRG.*

LYDIA TOMKIW

See *Algebra Suicide.*

TOM TOM CLUB

Tom Tom Club (Sire) 1980
Close to the Bone (Sire) 1983
Boom Boom Chi Boom Boom (UK Fontana) 1988
(Sire/Reprise) 1989
Dark Sneak Love Action (Sire/Reprise) 1992

Formed as a lighthearted family side project to Talking Heads by the band's rhythm section—bassist Tina Weymouth and her husband, drummer Chris Frantz—the beat-happening Tom Tom Club got off to a great start with the debut album, which contains two irresistibly infectious dance tracks, "Wordy Rappinghood" and "Genius of Love." Adrian Belew, Tyrone Downie and three Weymouth sisters contribute to the club grooves. Evidently delighted with the results, the same basic cast reconvened two years later and made the similar **Close to the Bone.**

Recorded by Weymouth and Frantz with a different gang of pals, **Boom Boom Chi Boom Boom** was issued first in the UK and then overhauled for its American release. The third chapter is a more ambitious and less focused record ("Challenge of the Love Warriors" is nothing more than percussion and heavy breathing; David Byrne and Jerry Harrison join their nominal bandmates for a cover of "Femme Fatale") that forces a reevaluation of the Tom Tom Club's goals and desires.

So did the end of the Heads' career at the close of the decade. No longer an alternate musical outlet for the couple, the Tom Tom Club—here configured as a quartet with guitarist Mark Roule and keyboardist Bruce Martin—became their primary creative endeavor on **Dark Sneak Love Action.** If there was any resulting tension about the undertaking, it's nowhere audible on this thoroughly delightful and diverse multi-cultural exposition on easygoing, sexy pop rhythmotics. Sung by Weymouth with assists from Kirsty MacColl and others, the new wave whispering of "Dark Sneak Love Action," the novelty pep of "As the Disco Ball Turns," the reggaefied "Who Wants an Ugly Girl?" and a gorgeous Bananarama-like cover of Hot Chocolate's "You Sexy Thing" are wonderful, sensual charmers. [i]

See also *TPRG.*

TONYALL

See *All.*

TOOL

Opiate EP (Zoo) 1992
Undertow (Zoo) 1993
Aenima (Zoo) 1996

"Seems like I've been here before / Seems so familiar," howls Tool singer Maynard James Keenan at the beginning of **Opiate,** and he's right. The Los Angeles quartet had to win its success by getting through a thicket of Metallica, Alice in Chains, Soundgarden and Rollins Band. While part of the pack, Tool's brand of moshable metal is not quite at its head. The rhythm section of bassist Paul D'Amour and drummer Danny Carey (whose credits also include Pygmy Love Circus and Green Jellÿ) is a synched, propulsive machine, and guitarist Adam Jones is as tasteful as metal players come, always looking for some sonic alternative to typical axe-hero wankerdom. Keenan isn't the most distinctive of singers, but he can growl with the best of 'em and deploys his voice as part of the overall package rather than as a force in its own right.

Opiate is the Tool appetizer, a six-song EP of studio and concert work. The slamfest never lets up, latching into some particularly powerful grooves on "Hush," "Sweat" and the live "Jerk-Off." The title track, a bit more layered and defined than the other five, introduces the religious fixation Keenan explores in greater depth on **Undertow.**

Tool's first full-length album is even more molten but not quite as consistent as the EP. While Keenan battles the church and inner demons ("In order to survive you/I must survive myself"), the musicians stretch out, taking most of the songs over the five-minute mark. **Undertow** misses **Opiate**'s brutal economy, though each track has at least a couple of slick tempo changes to help hold interest (sixteen minutes of "Disgustipated" is a hair too much, however). Henry Rollins co-wrote and guests on the roiling "Bottom," and "Prison Sex" wields a knife-edged guitar hook to excellent effect. (Those who leave the CD player running after the last songs on both **Opiate** and **Undertow** will find bizarre, unlisted tone poems at the end of each.)

While Tool worked on its unpleasantly titled next record (which very nearly topped the charts upon its 1996 release), D'Amour hooked up with some buddies—Ken Andrews and Greg Edwards from Failure and Chris Pitman from Zaum—and cut a covers LP as the Replicants. [gg]

See also *Failure.*

TOO MUCH JOY

Green Eggs and Crack (Stonegarden) 1987
Son of Sam I Am (Alias) 1988 (Alias/Giant/Warner Bros.) 1990
Cereal Killers (Alias/Giant/Warner Bros.) 1991
Nothing on My Mind EP (Giant/Warner Bros.) 1991
Mutiny (Giant) 1992
. . . finally (Discovery) 1996

The unreliability of humor as rock-it fuel (see?) usually dooms bands formed from *Mad*-magazine magma. Either not funny (Dead Milkmen), too clever by half (Half Man Half Biscuit) or overly abstruse (King Missile), few entrants in modern music's smileathon ever achieve anything near the sublime dada genius of the Bonzo Dog Band. Luckily for the genre's proponents, the audience receptors for sophomoric humor—college sophomores—are prone to giggle fits, and one cute idea can go a long way for bands that ultimately have nothing else to offer.

Prudently hedging middlebrow wit with credible electric pop songcraft rooted in the tuneful end of new wave energizers, Too Much Joy, four New York smart-alecks originally from suburban Scarsdale, refined their goofiness over the course of two indie albums in which they cracked jokes without becoming one. The unassuming **Green Eggs and Crack** (assembled from four years' worth of sessions) is a neat little record on which Tim Quirk sings wry odes like "James Dean's Jacket" in a personable boy-next-door voice. The more accomplished **Son of Sam I Am** mixes silly history lessons ("My Past Lives," "1964"), snotty social (un)consciousness ("Making Fun of Bums") and a poke at fallen rock idols ("Hugo!"). There's also an impressively melodic rewrite of LL Cool J's "That's a Lie." The reissue substitutes a remix of that track, removes the borrowed Bozo intro to "Clowns" and adds a cover of Terry Jacks' "Seasons in the Sun" and a tribute to the Mekons.

With the group moving to a major label, producer Paul Fox organizes TMJ's maturing humor and instrumental skills into presentable, catchy college rock on **Cereal Killers.** Whether griping good-naturedly about foreigners' unfair advantages ("Long Haired Guys From England"), recounting a sorry vacation story ("Thanksgiving in Reno") or revisiting a favorite topic ("King of Beers"), the band uses its puppy-dog personality to counteract the excess of foolishness, making **Cereal Killers** a lightweight pleasure. **Nothing on My Mind** builds an EP around the album's anthem to apathy.

Mutiny is marginally more serious, placing as much emphasis on straightforward melodicism and sly style-mongering as chucklehead topical indulgences. Even (or, more accurately, better off) ignoring the lyrics of numbers like the opening "Parachute" (ha), "Sort of Haunted House," "Unbeautiful" and the U2-quoting "Strong Thing," it's easy to enjoy the sound of a band that knows its giddy punk-era moves. Still, fandom doesn't excuse the band's new lyrics on the Records' classic "Starry Eyes."

Returning from a long absence with new bassist/album producer William Wittman replacing co-founder Sandy Smallens, Too Much Joy made the slightly grown-up **. . . finally.** Between them, guitarist Jay Blumenfield and drummer Tommy Vinton hammer together a loud go-cart of dense rock that challenges Quirk's ability to keep up; strain occasionally takes the charm out of his voice (see "Different Galaxies"). As if turning up the juice cancels out the humor—and perhaps it does—the lyrics don't press so hard and don't seem so stupid, even when they are. Proving the band's whimsy chops intact, though, "I'm Your Wallet" is a cute idea that works; most of the concepts aren't so ambitiously weird. The overpowering, sometimes nearly generic music obscures the progress, but **. . . finally** benefits from an organic focus not found on the others. Needless cover: Billy Bragg's "A New England." [i]

See also *TPRG.*

TOO $HORT

Born to Mack (Dangerous Music) 1987 (Dangerous Music/Jive/RCA) 1989
Life Is . . . Too $hort (Dangerous Music/RCA) 1988
Short Dog's in the House (Dangerous Music/Jive/RCA) 1990
Shorty the Pimp (Dangerous Music/Jive) 1992
Get in Where You Fit In (Dangerous Music/Jive) 1993
Greatest Hits Volume 1: The Player Years 1983–1988 (In-a-Minute) 1994
Cocktails (Dangerous Music/Jive) 1994
Gettin' It (Dangerous Music/Jive) 1996

Making up for his coast's late arrival in the game, Oakland rapper Too $hort (Todd Shaw) set about becoming the mackest daddy of them all, the big-money, fat-rope-wearing super-player who gets *all* the ho's. If record sales are the means by which such races are decided, the consistent platinum-winner is certainly up there in the same lewd, crude non-gangsta league as Sir Mix-a-Lot and the 2 Live Crew. It took Too $hort a few albums to wash the diffidence out of his mouth, but once he did, this larger-than-life character became an archetype for pottymouth banality. He's since become a major force in the free-fire-zone of rap's wild side, and his musical quality has been on the steady rise.

Busting rhymes of heartless sexin' with average skills in a nearly conversational style—that, ironically, owes a lot to the lighthearted old school, where his explicit verbiage would hardly have gone over—Too $hort has also demonstrated a surprisingly strong social conscience, although it's hard to imagine what good straight talk from the author of "Pimpology," "Blowjob Betty" and "Don't Fuck for Free" does anybody.

Following a trio of albums (compiled on **The Player Years**) for a California indie, he released **Born to Mack** on his own label, making weak work of simple beats and unconvincing boasts, big-booty fantasies ("Freaky Tales," "Partytime"), ugly put-downs ("Dope Fiend Beat") and jailbait concerns ("Little Girls"). With guest MCs, more diverse beats and ruder misogyny, **Life Is . . .** spins its wheels through the innocuous boasts and crack-criticism of "Nobody Does It Better" and "I Ain't Trippin'." On the vinyl's XXX side, however, T$ delivers mean-spirited tracks like "Cuss-Words" (in which he describes getting a blow job from Nancy Reagan), "Pimp the Ho" and "Don't Fight the Feelin'." **Short Dog's in the House** zips up his hot dog to concentrate on crack denunciations (see "The Ghetto") and a clever statement against censorship: "Ain't Nothin' but a Word to Me," a tag-team performance with Ice Cube in which the pair's stream of profanity is intentionally obliterated by maddening beeps.

After dicking around with better ideas, the entrepreneur seems to have settled for being a caricature with a small, crude vocabulary, a chip on his shoulder about his skills and a few simple desires in the world. **Get in Where You Fit In** doesn't bother to look up from a gutter-minded dedication to smoking dope and scoring with the ladies (if only T$ called them that: he throws around the word "bitch" like an interjection without regard to context or content, as in "We ain't leaving—*bitch!*") but benefits from a live combo augmenting the 808s and samplers. If Too $hort would shut up, the album would be entertainingly funky.

Like a fast-food restaurant, $hort Dog goes with what works on **Cocktails**—and hold everything else. A heap of producers delivers easygoing, nicely accented funk grooves that suit $horty to a T; he floats his slow flow like a promenading pimp inspecting his staff. With few interruptions, track after track—whether done solo or teamed up on the mic with 2Pac ("We Do This"), producer Ant Banks ("Can I Get a Bitch") or the Dangerous Crew ("Giving Up the Funk"), all of whom out-hustle the star hustler—spews out tedious sex talk with all the insipid imagination of a bathroom wall inscriber and the narrative content of a porno movie with all the extraneous scenes consigned to the editing room trash bin. The album's only ear-opener is "Thangs Change," in which T$ offers a moralistic complaint about women's loose behavior and trashy clothing. *Hunh?* What would have merely been absurdly arrogant hypocrisy turns out to be much weirder than that: "Rappers like me always disrespect ladies / Wonder why it's like that? / Well, so do I / But I just turn my back and then I go get high." For an illustration of the thinking that leads to countless social ills, $horty's shrugging lack of concern for his admitted irresponsibility is one trick of his that can't be beat. [i]

TORTOISE

Tortoise (Thrill Jockey) 1994
Rhythms, Resolutions & Clusters (Thrill Jockey) 1995
Millions Now Living Will Never Die (Thrill Jockey) 1996

Punk set its sights on killing a lot of things—disco, arena rock, singer/songwriter pabulum—but even the earliest anarcho-rumblers paid their respects to prog-rock icons as varied as Can (a fave rave of John Lydon) and the Red Crayola (a crucial influence on Pere Ubu, among others). In the '90s, a new generation of bands adheres more strictly to the tenet of pure sound as an end in itself. This all-instrumental Chicago-based aggregation is one of the most intriguing, given its willingness to cut across cultural lines to skim tricks from dub reggae and hip-hop—not to mention its virtually all-rhythm lineup.

On the quintet's debut, the beckoning warmth of the gently shifting rhythms (credit drummer John McEntire, also of Gastr del Sol, the Sea and Cake and Red Krayola, drummer/vibraphonist John Herndon, late of Poster Children and recently of 5Style, and percussionist Dan Bitney) makes it easy to forget that there's nary a whit of guitar and only the briefest whiff of standard-issue keyboards in play. The disc derives most of its melodicism from the interplay between bassists Douglas McCombs (of Eleventh Dream Day) and Bundy K. Brown (Gastr del Sol)—which reaches its apex on the (Jah) Wobbly "Spiderwebbed." Fragmentary blips of melodica (on the pastoral "Night Air") and prehistoric synthesizer break the surface now and again, but **Tortoise** is primarily a manifestation of the axiom that "it don't mean a thing if it ain't got that swing." Although the limited-edition **Rhythms, Resolutions & Clusters** is ostensibly a remixed version of the debut, such sonic architects as Steve Albini, Brad Wood and Jim O'Rourke treat each song as if it were a tabula rasa, rendering them virtually unrecognizable—but without perceptibly changing their spirits.

With Brown replaced by Dave Pajo (ex-Slint), **Millions Now Living Will Never Die** finds Tortoise messing with structure a bit more purposefully. McEntire, the foremost of three percussionists, steers clear of 4/4 beats, imbuing "The Taut and Tame" with a Canterbury school sense of jazzy playfulness. On the twenty-minute "Djed," which oscillates from dub reggae sensuality to TV-theme giddiness without a whole lot of square-peg/round-hole toil, he duels with fellow stickmen Herndon and Bitney on mallets, marimbas and more. [dss]

See also *Eleventh Dream Day, Gastr del Sol, Poster Children, Shrimp Boat, Slint.*

ALI FARKA TOURE

Ali Farka Toure (World Circuit/Mango) 1989
African Blues (Shanachie) 1990
The River (UK World Circuit) 1990
The Source (World Circuit/Hannibal) 1992
Radio Mali (UK World Circuit) 1996

ALI FARKA TOURE WITH RY COODER

Talking Timbuktu (World Circuit/Hannibal) 1994

It's a disservice to write off the Malian guitarist and singer Ali Farka Toure as simply a blues musician who happens to come from Africa. True, he understands the blues and has listened to John Lee Hooker and Muddy Waters and the whole canon; his guitar accompaniments borrow liberally from the folk-blues trickbag. But when he tackles even traditional twelve-bar, his serpentine voice and understated phrasing create a bridge between worlds—linking American blues conventions to their antecedents in African chant and ritual.

Born in 1939, Toure first gained international recognition on the European festival circuit in the late '80s but didn't attract US attention until the 1990 release of **African Blues**—like its eponymous predecessor, a solo acoustic recording. The blunt, lonesome vocals echo the plainspoken manner of Delta storytellers, but the forms are less familiar: many of the selections are built on droning single chords that become enchanting through repetition.

That same hypnotic quality opens Toure's more expansive 1990 album, **The River.** The first track, "Heygana," is a lilting, prayerful dirge that emulates the steady flow of a river. Still playing largely solo, Toure has help here from members of the Chieftains, whose contributions make "Kenouna" a multi-culti masterpiece.

The Source is the first recording to feature Toure's Groupe Asko, which includes hand drums, calabash and vocal chorus. The album also has guest stars—among them, Taj Mahal and tabla master Nitin Sawney. Though it continues Toure's unique conversational approach to the blues, **The Source** is most notable for the way it challenges the singer to move beyond blues ("Hawa Dolo") and to eschew simple guitar riffing for more intricate single-note lines ("Roucky").

If prior collaborations demonstrate a certain cautious openness, **Talking Timbuktu,** with Ry Cooder, shows that Toure can stretch with the best of 'em. Cooder pulls Toure in a more Eastern, raga-styled direction, turning his perpetually pained voice into a powerful melody instrument. The journey begins with Cooder's electric and slide guitars joining two-thirds of Groupe Asko (Hamma Sankare and Oumar Toure) but soon branches out: the heatedly rhythmic "Amandral" features drummer Jim Keltner and former Chick Corea bassist John Patitucci, while "Ai Du" finds Texas guitarist Clarence "Gatemouth" Brown adding (of all things) a searing viola solo. The result is absolutely transfixing music that defies glib categorization.

The music on the **Radio Mali** compilation dates from the 1970s. [tm]

TOWERING INFERNO

Kaddish (UK TI) 1994 (UK Island) 1995 (Island Independent) 1996

Englishmen Andy Saunders and Richard Wolfson—Towering Inferno—began performing *Kaddish,* a thematic multi-media piece about the Holocaust, in 1993. (The title is the Jewish prayer for the dead). Such a violently engaging work, so heavily dependent upon visuals and the visceral impact of live amplitude to make its impact felt, would seem doomed if abstracted into a single dimension, yet the transformation from performance piece to record album is thoroughly successful. Long, intricate and involving, **Kaddish** incorporates strange, dubby atmospherics, delicate piano melodicism and grinding metallic guitar passages with artistic ambience, dense, bellicose percussion, thudding electronica and newsreel-like voices—Foetus meets Philip Glass and Allen Ginsberg? Taken in toto, **Kaddish** is both remarkably horrifying (their point) and ultimately fascinating (their goal). One hopes that it represents the next logical step in that ever-morphing world of sound: a thoughtfully intense modern musical work that tests not only your ears but also your soul. [jf]

TRAGICALLY HIP

The Tragically Hip (MCA) 1987
Up to Here (MCA) 1989
Road Apples (MCA) 1991
Fully Completely (MCA) 1992
Day for Night (Atlantic) 1994
Trouble at the Henhouse (Atlantic) 1996

It's an article of faith for many Canadian rock fans that Kingston, Ontario's Tragically Hip is the best band north of the forty-ninth parallel—or at least the best band that people south of the border have yet to pay serious attention to. The quintet's chief allure is singer Gordon Downie, who brings an almost psychopathic intensity to his stream-of-consciousness lyrics. Yet he works very much in partnership with bandmates Bobby Baker (lead guitar), Paul Langlois (rhythm guitar), Gord Sinclair (bass) and Johnny Fay (drums). Together, they lay down a solid blues-rock foundation that never fails to support a mosh pit.

Few of the band's strengths are evident on the Hip's eponymous eight-song debut, an inauspicious start that only hints of the weight to come. Downie and Sinclair split the songwriting duties, a democracy not to be repeated on future albums, with Downie's "Killing Time" the strongest contribution and Sinclair's "Smalltown Bringdown" the most memorable in a concert setting.

Up to Here is a major improvement in all respects. Produced by journeyman rocker Don Smith, the album launched the band to Canadian stardom and introduced several songs that continue to be concert favorites: "Blow at High Dough" (with the incendiary hook, "Yeah, I can get behind anything"), "New Orleans Is Sinking" and "Boots or Hearts," an acoustic slide-guitar rouser that nails the emotion of a wounded lover ("But even babies raised by wolves / They know exactly when they've been used").

By the time of **Road Apples,** the Hip had reached do-no-wrong stature in their home country, and the disc—recorded in New Orleans—justifies the rep. Taking the classic approach of outsiders assessing the city, the Hip allow a southern rock influence to seep into songs like "Little Bones" and "On the Verge." But Downie's divining rod always leads his lyrics to warped images of Canadiana, so "Three Pistols" finds Canuck painter Tom Thompson paddling his canoe next to images of gunslingers and Shakespeare.

Comprehension of its ideas is evidently an open issue to the band: "It'd be better for us if you don't understand" is a memorable line from "Locked in the Trunk of a Car," the spooky serial killer meditation of **Fully Completely.** Recorded in London with producer Chris Tsangarides, the strong album places new emphasis on vocals, as Langlois and Sinclair step up for added harmonies to bring a sound more like R.E.M. than previously noted—a comparison the Hip strenuously turns back. Downie's lyrical flair again makes its mark, with even more examples of arcane Canadiana in such tracks as "Wheat Kings" (a song inspired by a wrongly imprisoned Canadian), "Fifty-Mission Cap" (the story of Bill Barilko, a champion Maple Leafs hockey player who disappeared on a fishing trip) and "At the Hundredth Meridian," a meditation on the vastness of America's great plains, and what a fine burial site they would make: "Get Ry Cooder to sing my eulogy."

Tragically Hip songs have often hinted at themes of death, but **Day for Night**—perhaps the band's finest work—is positively haunted by images of mortality. In its darkest hour, the band sets the imagination on a midnight ride: "Grace, Too," "Nautical Disaster" and "Inevitability of Death" all embrace the undertow of our worst fears. [ph]

TRANCE MISSION

Trance Mission (City of Tribes) 1993
Meanwhile . . . (City of Tribes) 1995
Head Light (City of Tribes) 1996

STEPHEN KENT

Landing (City of Tribes) 1994

Efforts to tag the many dimensions of San Francisco's Trance Mission have churned up amalgams of words like ethnic, ambient, techno, tribal, post-industrial and trance, but even tacking on the obvious "world music" designation wouldn't cover the half of it. At a time when the gaps between East and West, old world and new world, are closing in, Trance Mission stitches together instruments and atmospheres from the four corners of the earth to create a blanket of sounds that seems to exist beyond the stratosphere.

At the center of this mélange is the drone of Stephen Kent's didgeridoo. The Briton is credited with bringing the ancient Australian aboriginal horn—traditionally made from a termite-hollowed eucalyptus branch—to the fore in Western culture with Lights in a Fat City, a band that released two albums (**Somewhere,** since reissued by City of Tribes, and **Sound Column**) in the late '80s. In Trance Mission, Kent's sinuous rhythms are paired with the clarinets and trumpet of another virtuoso, Beth Custer, who also tours with Club Foot Orchestra, a band that primarily accompanies silent films in movie theaters. Percussionist John Loose and multi-instrumentalist Kenneth Newby—who plays everything from a *suling* (Indonesian bamboo flute) to electronic samples—add to the group's intricate mesh of sounds.

Trance Mission's debut strikes a perfect balance between grounded grooves and ethereal effects, rife as it is with explosive dance beats and moments of anarchy when, as with improvisational jazz, the players enter their own realms only to meet again later in each piece. The collage of sounds on tracks like "Bo Didgeley," "VeeDeeVu" and "Tjilpi II" exude a sense of immediacy. The didgeridoo and percussion set a tribal cadence behind primal barks, grunts and howls. Kent's playing is devoid of the constraints of time and space—especially on such tranquil pieces as "Tunnels" and the amorphous "Icaro." On "Folk Song" and the playful "Rig," the didg and percussion provide a backdrop to Custer's soulful clarinet.

Meanwhile . . . adds more layers of percussion and smooths out the compositions, pulling the band's hypnotic swirl further into Western territory. Producer Simon Tassano, co-founder of Lights in a Fat City, focuses a sleeker, more textured sound for the group. "Go Play Outside!" could pass for a nature program soundtrack—a constant stalking rhythm embellished with the spiritual wails of Kent's wife Eda Maxym and the oddly detached spoken word of Robert Anthony. The songs are subtle and haunting; on "Zozobra" and "Bindi," Custer's playing takes on a bluesy, lonesome feel. "No They There," with Custer switching to trumpet, is a tribute of sorts to Miles Davis. Though the album's tone is sweeping and consistent, it does lack the debut's funk and levity.

Between Trance Mission albums and stints with other local ensembles (Beasts of Paradise and Rocking Horse People), Kent released the solo **Landing,** a spotlight for his didgeridoo talents on which the power and intensity of this ancient ceremonial tool really penetrates. Again, the earthy drones contrast with Maxym's celestial cries; Loose and Newby join on a couple of tracks, but Kent handles most of the percussion, samples and drums himself. **Landing**'s importance lies not only in its presentation of the didgeridoo to Western ears, but also in its tribute to the aborigines. Didg solos like "Anthem for the People" and social statements like "Mabo," which celebrates a historic land-rights victory for the indigenous Australians, reflect Kent's respect for the instrument and culture he's helping popularize. [mg]

See also *Beasts of Paradise, Spacetime Continuum.*

TRANSGLOBAL UNDERGROUND

Dream of 100 Nations (UK Nation) 1993
International Times (UK Nation) 1994 (Epic) 1995

NATACHA ATLAS

Diaspora (UK Mantra/Beggars Banquet) 1995

The British music collective Transglobal Underground incorporates a variety of international sounds into its dancey, trancey electronica, focusing on the snaky melodies of traditional Arabic and Indian styles. At the group's core are Attiah Ahlan, Natacha Atlas (a former vocalist with Jah Wobble's Invaders of the Heart), Alex Kasiek (keyboards, guitar), Hamid Mantu (drums, programming) and Count Dubulah (bass/samples).

International Times, the group's first American release, brings together Atlas' Arabic-inspired vocals with bhangra rappers, hip-hop beats, violins, tablas and other disparate instrumentation. Though the album traverses the globe for inspiration, its songs blend seamlessly, both internally and collectively. The lead-off track, "Lookee Here," finds rapper Heitham Al-Sayed trading verses with Atlas, while behind them, tablas, congas and other percussion beat away gracefully. By way of a string section that marries the measured tones of Western classical music with the fluttery arrangements of traditional Eastern music, that track segues into "Taal Zaman," as Atlas' versatile voice snakes along with the strings through a warm bank of hypnotic percussion and relaxing electronics. Other tracks—including "Dustbowl" and the single "Temple Head"—incorporate such Western pop elements as deep, dubby bass, a funky keyboard, wailing guitar and spoken vocal samples into the ancient, timeless sound of chant. Rarely has a group so gracefully and respectfully blended traditional sounds with overt pop styles.

Although billed as an Atlas solo album, **Diaspora** was also made by the Transglobal central committee—Mantu, Dubulah and Kasiek co-wrote, produced and perform such strongly tradition-minded songs as the prayerful "Iskanderia" and "Leysh Nat'Arak" (a plea for peace between Arab and Jew) with her. [mrk]

See also *Love and Rockets, Jah Wobble's Invaders of the Heart.*

TRASH CAN SINATRAS

Cake (Go! Discs/London) 1990
I've Seen Everything (Go! Discs/London) 1993
A Happy Pocket (UK Go! Discs) 1996

This young coastal Scottish quintet from Irvine proudly reclaims the joyous pop sound of such early-'80s Postcard bands as Orange Juice and Aztec Camera; singer Frank Reader's voice bears an uncanny resemblance to Roddy Frame's. The pristine-sounding **Cake** is an exceptionally good debut, a refreshing mix of ringing guitars and rich broguish harmonies.

After such a promising start, **I've Seen Everything** blooms with even more depth and breadth. Deftly produced by Ray Shulman, the album boasts plenty of marvelous, grand-scale pop, especially the two splendid tracks that open it. Underneath Reader's resigned voice, "Easy Read" makes superb use of a dripping string section to wring every ounce of drama out of a wracking tune. But the Smiths-like "Hayfever" is the group's zenith; strings add warmth as this gorgeous, catchy track moves forcefully through dramatic verses and an arching chorus. While the LP takes a more somber, hushed turn thereafter, it never loses its thoughtful charm, and even returns to a more stomping dynamic level on the hypnotic neo-psychedelic "One at a Time."

The group subsequently self-produced a third album, released in mid-'96. [i/jr]

TREAT HER RIGHT

See *Morphine.*

TREEPEOPLE

Time Whore EP (Silence) 1990
Guilt Regret Embarrassment (Toxic Shock) 1991 + 1992
Something Vicious for Tomorrow (C/Z) 1992
Just Kidding (C/Z) 1993
Actual Re-enactment (C/Z) 1994

Three years before the great grunge rush of 1991, former members of a Boise, Idaho, punk band called State of Confusion moved to Seattle in search of an audience and a musical community. Their new band, Treepeople, lasted as long as the grunge hype did. Remarkably, the quartet's dense post-punk music (as well as its career) remained relatively unaffected by the Seattle scene of which it became a part.

Treepeople confidently established its sound with the **Time Whore** EP, blending aggressive punk, catchy pop and quirky art-rock. With both Doug Martsch and Scott Schmaljohn playing guitar and singing, the music is cluttered and busy. Screaming guitar solos lie buried beneath layers of fuzz; somewhere in the middle lies Martsch's strained, breaking voice, searching for a meaning to social relationships. "Party" and "Tongues on Thrones" both offer perfect balances of hooks and noise, though "Radio Man" shows the band in its most generic punk guise. On "Size of a Quarter," the band backs snippets of medical news banter from the radio and TV with some of the album's best guitar bedlam.

The twenty-one-track **Guilt Regret Embarrassment** CD is sprawling and less absorbing than **Time Whore.** The band adds David Bowie and Butthole Surfers covers to a mix of melody, guitar sonics, thoughtful angst and the occasional TV or radio sample.

The problem with much of the Treepeople's recorded music is that it constantly hints at originality and catharsis without actually ever offering them. On no album is this more clear than on **Something Vicious for Tomorrow** (which includes the **Time Whore** EP, resequenced and with one track substitution). On the title song and "It's Alright Now Ma," every interesting lyric, voice or guitar sound that emerges from the noisy swirl is pushed back under again. Schmaljohn adds more vocals to this album, and his regular-guy voice makes a good foil for Martsch's strangled cries. Together, the two turn the Smiths' "Bigmouth Strikes Again" from mannered to pissed-off.

Just Kidding is almost two albums in one: the first half is dominated by Schmaljohn (along with new drummer Eric Akre), the second by Martsch. The latter's "Anything's Impossible" is one of the album's strongest songs, full of the rapid tempo changes and twisted guitar lines that unhinged previous Treepeople songs; on "Neil's Down," he stops thinking and just screams "I hated you" between angsty explosions of guitar and drums. Despite its schism, **Just Kidding** is a more straightforward rock record than the Treepeople's previous albums, ending with what may be the closest thing to a ballad Treepeople has ever played, "Outside In."

Claiming that he was sick of Seattle and tired of touring, Martsch moved back to Boise to form Built to Spill. Schmaljohn, the only original member of the band remaining, recruited John Polle to fill in on guitar and vocals for Treepeople's final album, **Actual Re-enactment.** The result is more cohesive but less distinctive. Songs teeter between hard rock ("Wha'd I Mean to Think You Said") and indie-rock ("Bag of Wood"). As a last album, **Actual Re-enactment** sounds more like a first one, with the Treepeople no longer a band perfecting a dense post-punk fusion but one searching for an identity as a sensitive but aggressive alternative-rock group. [ns]

See also *Built to Spill, Halo Benders, Kill Sybil.*

TRENCHMOUTH

Construction of New Action (Skene!) 1991
Inside the Future (Skene!) 1993
Trenchmouth Vs. the Light of the Sun (Skene!/EastWest) 1994
Volumes, Amplifiers, Equalizers (It. Runt) 1995
The Broadcasting System (Skene!) 1996

Fueled by diverse influences and smart enough to experiment with them, the explicitly political Trenchmouth resembles the better-known Fugazi in several ways but is, perhaps bravely, more esoteric. The Chicago quartet fuses foxy rhythms (ska, Caribbean) with hardcore's energy, dub's mysterious intensity, funk's ass-grabbing power and jazzy variations of all of the above. The sonic results are ambitious, as if the band habitually issued itself challenges and succeeded, more or less, in rising to meet them.

Trenchmouth's calling card, **Construction of New Action,** establishes the group's genre-blending style. The ska-core/metal grooves of "Ultraman" give way to the more-frenzied "¡Friction!," in which Trenchmouth's radical program is most clearly articulated. Already developing his own vocal style—inspired (in part) by Fugazi's Ian MacKaye and Nation of Ulysses' Ian Svenonius—Damon Locks snaps, "I do solemnly swear that I will fuel reaction/I make noise in the night so I can shake hands with revolution." Latin rhythms (and vocals *en español*) fuel "Sordo Ciego"; guitarist Chris De Zutter suavely marries metallic chords with deft jazz riffs on "Bear in Mind." Locks' percussion (mostly congas) fuels drummer Fred Armisen and bassist Wayne Montana's fluid, soulful foundations.

Maybe they were already there, but **Inside the Future** seems more apocalyptic (or at least furturistic) in its lyrical themes, and is matched by more focused aggression and deeper instrumental stealth. Alienated (?) by daily life, Locks explores "The Dawning of a New Sound System," ponders "The future Vs. Centrifugal Force" and envisions totalitarianism in "Hit Men Will Suffocate the City," ironically deciding that "Mine's not to understand the intricacies of the modern world/ Just enjoy the luxury of the modern age where you can even eat the dishes." Caught in the post-modern moment of "In the Event of a Struggle," Locks declares, "it's always present tense, it's always now." The rhythm section is especially powerful; Montana's loping, taut bass riffs counter Armisen's dynamic support. **Inside the Future** percolates urgently, especially "Sea of Serenity (Swing Version)," but doesn't club the listener with dogma—Trenchmouth is like a good professor, making listeners work for their lessons. The closing instrumental, "Now I Have Tasted Life," is the band's first recorded foray into convincing dub.

Vs. the Light of the Sun steers Trenchmouth further toward infinity, with the frenzy of "Here Come the Automata," the jagged rhythms of "How I Became Invincible," the desperation of "The Effects of Radiation," the new Trench-dub "A Man Without Lungs" and the insistent tumult of "Doing the Flammability." De Zutter turns in his finest work here, from post-hardcore bombast to jazz-inspired inflection, and the band's earnest, precise approach is richer and more intriguing than before.

The Italian reissue **Volumes, Amplifiers, Equalizers** combines the first two LPs, along with a track from the band's second single and a cover of the Avengers' "I Believe in Me." [mww]

TRIBE 8

Pig Bitch EP7 (Harp) 1991
By the Time We Get to Colorado EP (Revolver) 1993
Fist City (Alternative Tentacles) 1995
Roadkill Cafe EP (Alternative Tentacles) 1995
Snarkism (Alternative Tentacles) 1996

The best thing about homocore is the unique context it provides for unfettered honesty: using punk's anything-goes forum and the up-front sexuality countenanced by gay activism, bands like San Francisco's Tribe 8 can trample over lyrical boundaries that would paint straight songwriters as pathetic sexual obsessives (what rocker short of Ted Nugent would have the gall to name a song "Barnyard Poontang"?) while simultaneously claiming the right to piss on the gay community's prevailing propriety. **Fist City,** the hard-rocking lesbian quintet's impressive first album, makes twin goals of singularity and hot sex and comes off as a blast of musical liberation. "Frat Pig" (date rape), "All I Can Do" (emotional scars), "Allen's Mom" (family collapse) and "Kick" (drugs) make serious work of serious issues, but Tribe 8 has its own heated agenda: "Neanderthal Dyke" rejects political correctness ("Feminist theory gets me uptight/Get in some heels and lipstick/And I'll spend the night"), "Manipulate" rejects human consideration ("I just want to objectify my girlfriend"), "Flippersnapper" rips apart fashion convention ("Let's all cut our hair like hers / We don't care about individuality / We want popularity and loads of promiscuity") and "Freedom" offers an offbeat equation ("I had my freedom when she was in my bed"). Behind growly singer Lynn Breedlove, the group's rock barrels along with as much intelligent raunch as the lyrics, a guitar-drenched punk charge that means business but stays well within safe musical boundaries.

The four-song **Roadkill Cafe** EP is a tour-snapshot goof: a lengthy funk joke about sexual misperceptions ("Wrong Bathroom"), a pointless cover of Golden Earring's "Radar Love," a live and sleazy "Ice Cream Man" and an exceedingly hoarse rendition of the debut album's "Manipulate," also recorded onstage. **Snarkism** gets the band back to full-scale operations with such bristly rock topicals as "Republican Lullaby," "Tranny Chaser," the rock-star legends of "Jim, Darby & Sid" and a reprise of "Wrong Bathroom." [i]

TRICK BABYS

See *Vacant Lot.*

TRICKY

Maxinquaye (UK Island) 1994 (Island) 1995
Tricky Presents Grassroots EP (Payday/ffrr) 1996
Pre-Millennium Tension (Island) 1996

NEARLY GOD

Heaven (Island Independent) 1996

The beat that initially gave birth to hip-hop was a subway train rumbling through the South Bronx: sturdy, inexorable and powerful enough to move loads of people with urgent efficiency. It took fifteen years for that beat to settle down enough to become an entirely different sort of conveyance. In the hands of artist/producer Tricky—the Bristol-born sound-system veteran of the legendary Wild Bunch and a contributor to Massive Attack—it becomes a pulsing heartbeat gently impelling a thick-pile carpet ride slowly through inner dreamscapes. Although rooted in some of the sounds and concepts of contemporary hip-hop, Tricky is an ingenious escape artist, and nothing about **Maxinquaye** is bound by convention. Generously sharing the mic with one Martine (as well as several other vocalists), he sets the controls for the heart of the mind, sublimating rhythms into the intricate atmospheric textures of such relaxed, trippy inventions as "Aftermath," "Strugglin'," "Hell Is Around the Corner," the hallucinatory "Feed Me" and the jazzy, Björk-like "Pumpkin." But lest he be mistaken for low-key groovers like P.M. Dawn or the rap pretensions of high-style acid jazzers, Tricky unloads a massive rock guitar attack in his drastic reconfiguration of Public Enemy's "Black Steel in the Hour of Chaos," makes like Marvin Gaye in the soulful dirt of "Abbaon Fat Track" and cranks up a bumping distorted club groove for "Brand New You're Retro." Fun facts: "Pumpkins" employs a Smashing Pumpkins drum sample, and the small list of session players includes guitarist James Stevenson (ex–Generation X) and bassist Pete Briquette (ex–Boomtown Rats).

Demonstrating a degree of activity to match his fervid stylistic imagination, Tricky greeted the summer of '96 with a pair of confusingly billed releases. **Tricky Presents Grassroots** is a collaborative EP on which he digs diverse, smoothly soulful grooves with singers Laveda Davis, Stephanie Cook and Roberto Malary Jr. and slides his own enervated version of hip-hop beats under a lame rap group called Hillfiguzes. The eclectic, meandering and deeply uneven **Nearly God,** billed to an entity of the same name, also involves plenty of outsiders (Björk, Alison Moyet, Terry Hall, Neneh Cherry and others), all of whom allow their individuality to become part of Tricky's increasingly Prince-like visions. [i]

See also *Massive Attack.*

TRIPL3FASTACTION

Broadcaster (Capitol) 1996

Tripl3fastaction formed from the remains of the late-'80s Chicago punk foursome Rights of the Accused. Matured a bit from ROTA's indelicate assault and solidly grounded in good old midwestern power-pop, singer/guitarist/songwriter Wes Kidd and drummer Brian St. Clair fashioned the aptly named Tripl3fastaction and—along with pals Loud Lucy and Veruca Salt—became a respected band-around-town after Smashing Pumpkins and Liz Phair put Chicago back on the rock'n'roll map in 1993.

The band's two early singles are quite good. "Aerosmith," in particular, is arresting: over a barely strummed guitar and some feedbacky guitar noise, Kidd plays the part of a canny but unsatisfied '90s Everykid baying at the moon ("I got my MTV/ My Q101/I got some DGC that I don't need"). The other single, "Revved Up," is just that. Although the band was snapped up in the great Chicago signing spree of 1994, **Broadcaster** didn't appear until the spring of 1996. TFA's sound is less unapologetically pop than Veruca's, and Kidd's musical vision is considerably less baroque than Billy Corgan's, but his punk beginnings emerge in the ferocity of the band's attack. New versions of "Aerosmith" and "Revved Up" hit harder than the originals; "Bird Again" is a fun slice of edgy, modernized Cheap Trick. On the dreamy "Don't Tell," the concussive "American City World" and the closing ten-minute "Superstar" (by turns wan and wild), Kidd shows that he can do propulsive, smartened-up modern rock as well as anyone else these days. [bw]

TRIPPING DAISY

Bill (Dragon Street) 1992 (Island Red) 1993
Get It On EP (Island Red) 1994
i am an ELASTIC FIRECRACKER (Island) 1995

Despite dissonant image-consciousness and a trace of Jane's Addiction in its sound, this Dallas pop-rock quartet is, at heart, as innocuous and virtuous as a troop of boy scouts. The late cover codger on the debut earns the band's dedication and the admonition to "Be Kind. Respect the elderly," while the unlisted hidden track—a surreal spoken fable—delivers a message about love overcoming racism. Cleanly co-produced by Texas scene veteran Patrick Keel (ex-Pool), the power-poppish **Bill** pairs the occasional quizzical lyric ("We are the brown-eyed pickle boy"???) with well-crafted melodies and sterling performances, aiming the group for mainstream accessibility while using Beatlesque psychedelia and other shreds of strangeness to lend offbeat credibility. Singer/lyricist Tim DeLaughter's acrobatic vocals and guitarist Wes Berggren's propulsive strumming lend **Bill** enough variety to keep it from sinking into blandlivion—but just barely.

The five tracks recorded live in Dallas for the harder-rocking **Get It On** include **Bill**'s "Blown Away" and "On the Ground," a cover of Bad Religion's "We're Only Gonna Die" and two new originals, including the bass-popping "Get It On," a maddening novelty number in which DeLaughter blurts the title over and over with barely a pause for breath.

Ted Nicely co-produced **i am an ELASTIC FIRECRACKER,** an uneven, unfocused followup that mounts a stronger rock attack and gives prominent play to the Perry Farrell aspect of DeLaughter's singing. But as the tortured "Prick" and other tracks head down Jane's road, Tripping Daisy can't muster the 'tude to match the sound, and the band's moral center remains unmoved by the keening melodies and blustery guitar. Thoughtful and colorfully expressed lyrical meditations on insecurity, motivation, love and addiction mark Tripping Daisy as smart, positive and socially aware. "Step Behind" and "I Got a Girl" revisit the poles of **Bill**'s pop (flowery psychedelia and surging power-pop); "Same Dress New Day" stitches in a doodly theremin for dinky charm. Throughout the album, Tripping Daisy comes off confused but intermittently entertaining. [vg/i]

TROLLIN WITHDRAWAL

See *Swirlies.*

TRUE BELIEVERS

See *Alejandro Escovedo.*

TRUE SOUNDS OF LIBERTY (TSOL)

T.S.O.L. EP (Posh Boy) 1981
Dance With Me (Frontier) 1981
Beneath the Shadows (Alternative Tentacles) 1982 (Restless) 1989
Change Today? (Enigma) 1984
Revenge (Enigma) 1986
Hit and Run (Enigma) 1987
Thoughts of Yesterday 1981–1982 (Posh Boy) 1988 + 1992
TSOL Live (Restless) 1988
Strange Love (Enigma) 1990
Hell and Back Together 1984–1990 (Restless) 1992

TSOL/SLAYER

Abolish Government EP7 (Sub Pop) 1996

TENDER FURY

Tender Fury (Posh Boy) 1988
Garden of Evil (Triple X) 1990
If Anger Were Soul, Id Be James Brown (Triple X) 1991

JACK GRISHAM/MIKE ROCHE/RON EMORY/TODD BARNES

Live 1991 (Triple X) 1991

JOYKILLER

The Joykiller (Epitaph) 1995
Static (Epitaph) 1996

Without California's True Sounds of Liberty (and Agent Orange, for that matter), it's safe to assume there would be no Offspring. One of the top five or so punk outfits this country has ever produced, the pioneering Long Beach group degenerated from a tight, rippling hardcore quartet to a lame hair-metal band with no original members by the end of its run, in 1990. In between, TSOL embraced new genres about as often as charismatic singer Jack Grisham switched surnames. **Dance With Me** wedded furious rhythms to goth imagery; the brilliant **Beneath the Shadows** saturated ambitious, slightly pretentious post-punk songs with a spooky organ; the hard-rock **Change Today?,** which lacked Grisham and drummer Todd Barnes, signaled the beginning of the end.

After leaving the group, Grisham formed Cathedral of Tears and then hooked up with Barnes for the metal-gilded Tender Fury, whose first album's punky promise was broken by a truly rotten followup. (The 1992 CD of TSOL's **Thoughts of Yesterday** includes **Tender Fury.**)

Legally prohibited from using the band's name, TSOL's charter members—Grisham, Barnes, guitarist Ron Emory and bassist Mike Roche—teamed up for a thrilling live reunion album in 1991. The reenergized crew blitzes through such early classics as "Superficial Love" and "Man and Machine" with a violent fury not heard since the days of the band's first EP. The most convincing equivalent to an aural moshpit you're likely to encounter.

The same year, Triple X released **If Anger Were Soul, Id Be James Brown,** the third and final Tender Fury album, a huge improvement over **Garden of Evil.** With ex-Adolescent Frank Agnew on guitar, the band rips through a batch of catchy melodic punk that admirably recaptures the classic SoCal sound. Also worth noting is the excellent cover of Neil Young's "Mr. Soul."

Perhaps hoping to ride the crest of the new punk wave, Grisham reteamed with Emory for the Joykiller, whose eponymous debut takes the band back to its hardcore roots. Unfortunately, this speedy collection of full-bore punkish rock wouldn't have much character were it not for Grisham's trademark melodramatic vocals. With the exception of the socially conscious "Show Me the System" and the salacious sing-along "Go Bang," the songs just don't stick. [db]

See also *Slayer; TPRG.*

TRULY

Heart and Lungs EP (Sub Pop) 1991
Leslie's Coughing Up Blood EP (Sub Pop) 1993
Blue Flame Ford EP10 (Revolution/Capitol) 1995
Fast Stories . . . From Kid Coma (Revolution/Capitol) 1995

From a marketing standpoint, Truly's claim to fame is that it features original Soundgarden bassist Hiro Yamamoto and ex–Screaming Trees drummer Mark Pickerel. While comparisons to both of those bands (and other Seattle peers) are inevitable, there's a lot more to Truly than its family tree. The band's focal point is Robert Roth, whose dark, semi-mumbled voice (not unlike a sleepy Mark Lanegan), oddly tuned guitar riffs and affection for wheezy vintage keyboards shape an unusual and varied sound. At different points, Truly sounds like it's from 1974, 1989 and 1999.

Actually formed in 1990, the band dribbled out a single and two EPs during the five years it took to record the sprawling and obscurely conceptual **Fast Stories . . . From Kid Coma.** The band's reference points are fairly obvious (Zeppelin, My Bloody Valentine and all things psychedelic) but never dominant—Truly exists pretty much in its own little world. The droning, low-end riffs contrast nicely with Roth's soft, multi-layered vocals, and although the elaborate instrumental work sometimes blurs the fine line between clever and stupid, Pickerel's strong, steady drumming holds it all together in places where a less tasteful player might have driven the band into complete overkill. (With thirteen songs splayed over seventy-two minutes, the album is excessive enough.) Oddest of all is the production: although Truly is essentially a driving, riff-heavy rock band, the sharp edges are subtly blunted by a miasmic, narco-haze mix. Heavy but never bludgeoning, melodic but never cheesy, excessive but never ridiculous, **Fast Stories** is an extended trip into several of rock's outer dimensions. [ja]

See also *Screaming Trees, Soundgarden.*

TRUMANS WATER

Of Thick Tum (Justice My Eye/Elevated Loin) 1992 (Homestead) 1993
Our Scars Like Badges EP7 (Homestead) 1992
Jubileeeee EP7 (Drunken Fish) 1993
Spasm Smash XXXOXOX Ox and Ass (Homestead) 1993
10X My Age EP (UK Elemental) 1993
Godspeed the Static (Drunken Fish) 1993
Godspeed the Hemorrhage (Homestead) 1993
Godspeed the Vortex (The Way Out Sound) 1993
Godspeed the Punchline (Homestead) 1994
Milktrain to Paydirt (Homestead) 1995

SOUL-JUNK

1950 (Holy Kiss) 1994
1951 (Shrimper) 1994
1952 (Homestead) 1995

There are plenty of reasons why rock has never been as fertile an improvisational canvas for musicians as jazz—chief among them, the hold of the 4/4 beat, the transience of attention spans (on the part of musicians and audience alike) and the fact that most aspiring bands would rather build a beer-can wall than a vertically soaring head. Despite a receding indie-rock orthodoxy, this San Diego quartet manages to successfully navigate the waters of improv with minimal listing toward the shores of pomp or shambling into silly lo-fi wankery.

The excitement of getting into a studio for the first time (or in front of a 4-track, to be more precise) to record **Of Thick Tum** proved to be such an overwhelming experience that no one in the band remembered to bring a tuner. It's clear someone had the Pavement songbook, though, since most of the album's songs follow the shuffle/spazz-out/shuffle map so closely it's a wonder Trumans Water didn't end up wandering the outskirts of Stockton, fuzzboxes in hand. The four-song **Our Scars Like Badges** EP tempers the Boswell-ism a tad, allowing for more visceral interplay between the three credited guitarists (Kirk Branstetter, the bass-doubling Kevin Branstetter and occasional singer Glen Galloway), particularly on the lengthy—for this band, that means over two minutes—"Sad Sailor Story."

Spasm Smash XXXOXOX Ox and Ass has some residual Malkmus-mania—most evident in the album's artwork and in blatant stylistic cops like "Mindstab Forklift" and "Athete Who Is Suck"—but aggression supplants irony for long patches of instrumental scree. Not to imply that the band doesn't have a formalized (and sometimes narrowcast) notion of what passes for cultural exchange in indie-land—just check out the opening "Aroma of Gina Arnold" for proof of that—but the Trumans aesthetic is obviously stretching.

Intended to be considered as a series—although not necessarily an identical litter of quadruplets—the improv-based (and mainly instrumental) **Godspeed** albums that tumbled out around the tail end of 1993 evince a dramatic advancement on the part of the Trumans as both musicians and theoreticians. The albums aren't "pure" improvisation on the order of Saccharine Trust's monumental **Worldbroken,** but at their best, they can approximate the feeling of finding yourself inserted under the glass of a pinball machine during a multi-ball bonus round. Once you get past the grating white noise of "Total X-Stasis" and the just-plain-silly "Soup of Volts," **Godspeed the Vortex** reveals itself as the best of the lot. Riddled with intriguingly abrasive guitar figures that apply Eastern modality ("Syrup Is Tangled") and post-Sharrock prolapse ("True-Star Down"), the album shifts from ambient to demanding with pinpoint precision: pop it into the cassette module of your clock radio and you'll never oversleep again. **Godspeed the Punchline** consists of eighteen short blasts of negasonic tumult, kicking off with the adrenalized "Destroy 1998" and winding through pieces both dreamily atmospheric ("Infinity Times Zero") and violently quaking ("Playboy Stabtone Bloodbath Go"). The unremittingly telescoped timeframes sometimes abort clever ideas just as they're kicking into gear, but as a sort of avant-skronk Whitman's sampler, it's a pretty nifty specimen.

Having reached a sort of Zen-like state with those releases, Trumans Water was able to stomach enough linear thought to allow record-store types to unapologetically file **Milktrain to Paydirt** under rock. The herky-jerky rhythms of "Unitraction Bath" and "Mnemonic Elf Lock" pack a particularly potent post-Fall punch, but that's not always enough to offset the self-congratulatory quirkiness that seems so ingrained in the band's approach.

Glen Galloway left the band midway through the **Godspeed** series in order to devote himself to performing Christian-themed material—but don't assume that constitutes a change in his musical ideology. Soul-Junk is just as mercurial, just as stimulating as Trumans Water at its best. The album **1950,** which takes most of its lyrics directly from Bible passages, isn't an ideal introduction, since the lopsided production situates Galloway's strangled vocals (reminiscent of Superchunk's Mac McCaughan) so far in front of the minimal guitar/drums backing (augmented by free-jazz sax honking on a few instrumental interludes) that you'd swear the instrumentalists were playing in a car parked outside the studio.

With slightly more structure and much better recording, **1951** leaves little doubt of Galloway's objective in songs like "Spirit of God Descend Upon Us" and "God Does Speak." His lyrical tone, however, has more in common with old-school gospel than Christian rock as such: there's plenty of joyful worship and virtually no brimstone. There's even plenty of sensory stimulation for heathens, as borne out by the squawking "Turn to Joy." Cohorts Ron Easterbrook and Brian Cantrell take more active roles on **1952,** which adds some much-needed conceptual tension. We're speaking strictly in terms of sound, of course—songs like "Spoiler!" and the instrumental "Pegasus on the Slow Tip" are dotted with blasts of Moog, trumpet and trombone. Thematically, Galloway sticks to songs of praise—getting in some especially effective licks on the funk-tinged "Sweet to My Soul" and "Cold-Coct the Coroner." Proof that positive thinking needn't rot your teeth. [dss]

JENNIFER TRYNIN

Cockamamie (Squint) 1995 (Squint/Warner Bros.) 1995

First issued independently on the Boston-based singer/songwriter's own label, Jennifer Trynin's **Cockamamie** was released nationally in June 1995, at precisely the same time as Alanis Morissette's **Jagged Little Pill.** This was initially a good thing: Trynin's smart, self-sufficient-woman rock songs were reviewed favorably next to Morissette's jilted-lover rants, and many critics wrote that Trynin was the one to watch. Then Morissette's single "You Oughta Know" clicked and pretty soon Trynin was invisible.

That's a shame, because **Cockamamie** (recorded as a trio with a rhythm section) is a vital, astonishingly mature debut, full of defiantly hooky power-pop kept in check by an endless supply of surly asides and Trynin's ear for bitter blues-soaked recrimination. The syrup-slow "Too Bad You're Such a Loser" finds Trynin enumerating all the ways a potential lover is inadequate; in "Happier," she asks "Aren't you the guy who robbed the Store 24?/Maybe the fuck who tried to jimmy my door?" Trynin may have a scrawny little voice, but like Matthew Sweet, she writes melodies that flatter her limited range and sings them with a blend of who-cares detachment and I-care conviction that transforms ordinary phrases into extraordinary events. [tm]

TSOL

See *True Sounds of Liberty.*

TSUNAMI

Cow Arcade [tape] (Simple Machines) 1991
Headringer EP7 (Simple Machines) 1991
Deep End (Simple Machines) 1993
The Heart's Tremolo (Simple Machines) 1994
World Tour and Other Destinations (Simple Machines) 1995

SLACK

Bates Stamper EP [tape] (Simple Machines) 1992

LIQUORICE

Listening Cap (4AD) 1995

That Jenny Toomey and Kristin Thomson have built a modest indie empire with their Simple Machines label is admirable enough; that a pair of young women could rise to the top of the straight-edge, terminally macho DC-area indie heap is nothing short of amazing. Amid the usual apprenticeships in assorted punk and folk bands (Toomey was in Geek), the roommates started the label and then formed Tsunami with bassist Andrew Webster and drummer John Palmer.

In 1991, Simple Machines released the cassette-demo **Cow Arcade** and the five-song **Headringer** 7-inch. The latter (reissued in '95 on the band's **World Tour** compilation) was quite a calling card, with its brash mixture of Pylonesque pop dissonance ("Flameproof Suit," "Candyman") and moody, pre–riot grrrl punk ("Kickball Babe"). The next two years kept Tsunami in a flurry of touring and recording, with four Simple Machines 45s (often in elaborate packaging) and assorted singles and compilation tracks for other labels.

Tsunami made its longplaying debut in mid-'93. **Deep End** not only reaffirms the band's indie-to-the-marrow ethics (assorted answering machine messages from scenesters appear), but also reveals a combo unwilling to fashion crude, scratchy documents merely for the sake of street cred. Toomey and Thomson's vocal harmonies approach choir-like complexity on "Lucky" and "Valentine"; furthermore, the group's thick, layered arrangements—an intoxicating blur of strummed/dirty guitars, sonorous basslines and catchy melodic hooks—mark Tsunami as pop experimentalists, not ossifying punk-rockers.

Preceded by another slew of singles and compilation appearances, Tsunami released **The Heart's Tremolo** in 1994. The harmonies and noisy guitars remain signatures, but Toomey's supple voice frequently takes center stage, a confident instrument skating over impressionistic lyrics designed to convey the vicissitudes of affection, devotion, disappointment and outright fury. The band explores artful pop terrain that is alternately lushly balladic and quirky in an almost avant-folk manner. "Quietnova" has a droning, mantra-like quality; "Fast Food Medicine" uses odd time signature shifts and unusual guitar effects.

The twenty-two-track **World Tour and Other Destinations** collects all of Tsunami's miscellaneous 7-inch cuts, non-album B-sides and compilation contributions to date. Highlights include the chiming, near-anthemic "Sometimes a Notion," a powerful version of the Minutemen's "Courage" (originally on the M-men tribute album **Our Band Could Be Your Life**) and the self-explanatory "Bossa Nova." By no means an anthology of afterthoughts, the CD also boasts fold-out artwork depicting a colorful US map with names of band pals at "rest areas" over the years.

Toomey has been compared to both Throwing Muses' Kristin Hersh and Belly's Tanya Donelly, but that does the workaholic a disservice. In addition to her Tsunami and Simple Machines duties, Toomey is one-third of loungecore combo Grenadine and co-collaborator with Nothing Painted Blue's Franklin Bruno on a political punk musical called *Indie Rock Summer Stock.* Around 1990, she got together with her pal Dan Littleton (late of Annapolis' Hated, later to form Brooklyn's Ida) as the offbeat folk duo Slack. A mail-order-only cassette, the five-song **Bates Stamper,** was issued in '92, but it wasn't until '94 that the pair would find times in their respective schedules for "serious" recording. With Slack rechristened Liquorice, Toomey and Littleton went into the Michigan studio of Warren Defever (His Name Is Alive) and, assisted by HNIA drummer Trey Many, recorded thirty songs in a week. While legend has it that producer Defever's remixing frenzy resulted in some seventy-seven "versions" of those thirty songs, **Listening Cap** consists of eight delightful, low-key originals plus covers of the Roches' "Jill of All Trades" (stately piano torch balladry at its most sentimental) and Bruno's "Keeping the Weekend Free," a sweet, affecting vocal duet between Toomey and Littleton. Throughout the record, Toomey is a reluctant star at the microphone. She slips from purr to trill, from muted frustration to smoky desire; when she dispassionately sings the lines "Honey, yeah, I got a trouble with you and it/Isn't what you are/It's what you do," it's easy to believe, as the singer is undoubtedly trying to convince herself, that the affair's breakup is someone else's fault. Accompanied by Littleton's warm, effects-free guitar tone and Many's sympathetic percussion murmurs (the snare is frequently brushed), Toomey is cast as a charismatic java hut chanteuse for lonely singles and troubled lovers alike. [fm]

See also *Grenadine, His Name Is Alive, Ida.*

TUBALCAIN

25 Assorted Needles (Verdugo) 1992
Left EP (Funky Mushroom) 1994

SPAHN RANCH

Collateral Damage (Cleopatra) 1993
Blackmail Starters Kit EP (Cleopatra) 1994
The Coiled One (Cleopatra) 1995
In Parts Assembled Solely (Cleopatra) 1996

EXECUTIVE SLACKS

Executive Slacks EP (Red) 1983
You Can't Hum When You're Dead (Fundamental) 1984
Nausea (Fundamental) 1985
Fire and Ice (Fundamental) 1986
Repressed (Cleopatra) 1994

Formed to supplant the final incarnation of harsh-edged Philadelphia techno-oriented dance-rockers Executive Slacks, Tubalcain brings back departed co-founder John Young (keyboards/programming) to join Slacks singer Athanasios Demetrios Maroulis (also the singer in the industrial electronics duo Spahn Ranch) and drummer Harry Lewis; guitarist Robb Jordan and bassist Stephen Lentz round out the new crew. Incorporating occasional thrashy rhythms rather than making a point of them, resigning electronics to an accent not a compelling force, Tubalcain takes a forthright rock course on **25 Assorted Needles**—Jordan's angry guitar energy slobbers all over the lumbering, goth-inflected songs—and sounds much less distinctive as a result. Athan was never the previous band's strongest feature; expecting his sturdy roar (and ludicrous cave-wall lyrics: "The painted eyes of snakes are born a serpents womb/And baring the swords of teeth see the flowers flame") to carry a plainer load just doesn't make sense. For all its exertions, Tubalcain's ominous temperament is scarcely unsettling; the chaotic heavy-gravity cover of the Rolling Stones' "2000 Light Years From Home" (or, as Athan sings it, "hoa-umm") is tragic. Also worth a complaint to the authorities: several tracks end in hasty fades that suggest sloppy mastering errors.

Repressed is a posthumous anthology of Executive Slacks, which ended its proto-industrial decade in 1991. Among the thirteen tracks making their way to CD for the first time are "Nausea" (a song used in an episode of *Miami Vice*), "The Bus" and the group's entertaining cover of Gary Glitter's "Rock and Roll." [i]

See also *TPRG*.

MAUREEN (MOE) TUCKER

Playin' Possum (Trash) 1981
MoeJadKateBarry EP (50 Skidillion Watts) 1987
Life in Exile After Abdication (50 Skidillion Watts) 1989
I Spent a Week There the Other Night (UK Rough Trade) 1991 (Sky) 1994
Dogs Under Stress (Sky) 1994

Unlike her more accomplished and ambitious fellow pioneers in the Velvet Underground, drummer Maureen (Moe) Tucker never became an international rock star or a distinguished new music composer. But neither did she go quietly into the history books. Instead, after a decade-long parenting hiatus, the New Jersey native launched a solo career founded on pretty much the same ideals of inspired amateurism and raw expression that originally motivated the Velvets. In Tucker's hands (and mouth), **Playin' Possum** came out sounding quite different from **White Light/White Heat:** the ramshackle home-made set of covers (Little Richard and Chuck Berry classics, a Dylan tune, a stunningly well-played Vivaldi concerto, "Heroin"), plus an original (well . . .) instrumental tribute to Bo Diddley is charming in its heartfelt solitary incompetence but plants its modest roots in an era the Velvets helped put in the past tense.

Discovering a kindred and supportive spirit in minimalist/naïve rock titan Jad Fair, Tucker returned to the studio (actually, a Florida garage) in 1986 to cut a similar batch of covers with his help. (Exactly why the red-vinyl 12-inch named for its four participants is attributed solely to her isn't clear, since she plays drums and sings only one of the five songs.) Motley as hell but reeking of credibility and unpolished spirit, the wonderful **MoeJadKateBarry** EP includes versions of VU obscurities ("Guess I'm Falling in Love," "Hey, Mr. Rain," "Why Don't You Smile Now"), a Jimmy Reed standard ("Baby What You Want Me to Do") and an impromptu instrumental, "Jad Is a Fink."

Lou Reed, Daniel Johnston and Sonic Youth joined Jad and Moe for the loose and unpredictable **Life in Exile After Abdication,** an historically significant intergenerational meeting of prophets and disciples. The eclectic disc contains wall-rattling noise, acoustic folk ("Goodnight Irene"), rock'n'roll (a return visit to "Bo Diddley" with Sonic Youth's rhythm section), even a whispery version of Reed's "Pale Blue Eyes." Tucker's six originals include "Andy," a droning guitar/piano tribute to an artist she once knew.

The thoroughly competent-sounding **I Spent a Week There the Other Night** brings Tucker into her own as a songwriter: other than a subdued version of "Waiting for the Man" and a rocking "Then He Kissed Me," the plain-spoken testimonials to normalcy (and Native Americans) are all hers. The classy musical cast includes enough VU alumni (Reed, John Cale, Sterling Morrison) to deem the effectively droney "I'm Not" a full-fledged reunion—if only Tucker had played drums. (She parks her sticks for the entire album, leaving Victor De Lorenzo of the Violent Femmes and John Sluggett of Half Japanese to the rhythmic task.) Rowdy and exciting, proletarian and pure in its true Tucker-ness, **I Spent a Week There the Other Night** shows the young'uns how it's done without preaching. "I hate to cook and I don't like to clean/And hangin' out the clothes just makes me mean/I don't wanna dust, don't wanna scrub/And why the hell would I clean the tub?" For a forty-six-year-old mother of five, "Lazy" is pure punk perfection.

Even with a less-legendary legion (Morrison, Don Fleming and Miriam Linna of the A-Bones are the marquee names here), Tucker improves on that feat with **Dogs Under Stress.** Giving an unpretentious, relatively consistent production charge to tuneful rock originals (plus a pumping Bo Diddley cover and an inexplicable, somber "Danny Boy"), Tucker comes into her own as a confident singer and firm bandleader. (Even her track's worth of alto sax work is credible.) In the most colorful tunes, she manages total parental (or spousal) indifference in "Me, Myself and I," describes a character called Crazy Hannah, enthuses about "Saturday Night" partydown and plans a trip to New York in "Train," which sounds like an R&B band imitating the Feelies. Moe power to her. [i]

See also *Half Japanese, Lou Reed, Sonic Youth, Velvet Underground, Violent Femmes; TPRG.*

TUMOR CIRCUS

See *Jello Biafra, Steel Pole Bath Tub.*

2PAC

2Pacalypse Now (TNT/Interscope/EastWest) 1991
Strictly 4 My N.I.G.G.A.Z. . . . (TNT/Interscope/Atlantic) 1993 (Restless) 1993
Me Against the World (Out da Gutta/Interscope/Atlantic) 1995
All Eyez on Me (Death Row/Interscope) 1996

THUG LIFE

Volume 1 (Out da Gutta/Interscope/Atlantic) 1994

Stepping out of a minor role in the whimsical Digital Underground, rapper 2Pac (Tupac Shakur), the native son of a Black Panther who carried him while incarcerated in a New York prison, went deadly serious on solo albums that made him a notorious and controversial bicoastal leader of the '90s gangsta school (and led him to a major second career as a compelling film actor). A hardass attitude, inflamed political anger, articulate intelligence, malignant charisma and calmly commanding vocals give 2Pac's records their undeniable power; contradictory pronouncements and numerous violent confrontations with legal (and otherwise) authorities turned him into an enigmatic lightning rod for the nation's anti-rap anxiety. Denying the need for a dividing line between life and art (or, for that matter, life and death), 2Pac's tumultuous existence and death-obsessed raps had a frightening synchronicity; it's impossible to hear his music without considering the crucible from which it spilled.

Produced and featuring appearances by the Digital Underground crew, **2Pacalypse Now** is a strong but scattered debut, an overzealous, musically unfocused first step by a young star who can't quite find his feet after leaving the nest. The Underground's greasyfinger grooves don't really suit 2Pac's lean delivery, and the songs are too derivative to stand completely on their own. Submerging political commentary ("Trapped," "Words of Wisdom," "Soulja's Story") and empathy for young mothers and their effect on the community ("Brenda's Got a Baby") in wanton gun-happy tales of violence, the album is cocky rather than confident—the least personal of 2Pac's missives.

Moving further outside the Underground's orbit (but not completely out of it), 2Pac hooked up with a variety of collaborators on **Strictly 4 My N.I.G.G.A.Z . . .**, assembling a riotous bustle of sound in which vocals and samples collide like fans at a Green Day show. The raps—many of them duets with peers like Ice Cube, Ice-T and Treach—don't so much flow as blurt, and few of the hasty, incoherent soundalikes leave a lasting impression, save for "Keep Ya Head Up," a distinctively low-key and uplifting track in which 2Pac preaches respect for black women and self-reliance over the Five Stairsteps' optimistic refrain, "Ooh child, things are gonna get easier." Otherwise, the threats, boasts, sexual bravado and despair set a malevolent mood only sporadically organized into clear communication. (The Restless edition is vinyl-only.)

Incarnating the code tattooed on his stomach, 2Pac then formed the free-floating (and short-lived) Thug Life, making **Volume 1** with his older brother Mopreme and three low-profile associates. In "Bury Me a G," the first of ten soul-grooving heartsinkers, 2Pac details his priorities: "I ain't got time for bitches / Gotta keep my mind on my muthafuckin riches." In "Stay True," he explains the program. "Thug life, y'all know the rules, gotta do what you gotta do: stay true." For 2Pac, staying true means loyalty to friends and the hard-nosed realness of being a gangsta, not weak ideals or emotions. "It's kinda hard to be optimistic when your homie's lying on the pavement, twisted . . . I'm trying hard to make amends but I'm losing all my muthafuckin friends." In the face of such grim fatalism (which triggers "How Long Will They Mourn Me?," a duet with Snoop pal Nate Dogg, as well as "Cradle to the Grave"), hopes and dreams are for suckers; thug life's fatalism rules out the possibility of failure by shooting straight for the abyss.

Volume 1 effectively sets off 2Pac's rhymes with spare, smooth, seductive jazz grooves swinging on '70s soul samples; the album is a sweet, summery ride through understated West Coast atmospheres in which the bass doesn't pump and the drums don't kick. The lyrics, in contrast, are violent, amoral and remorseless—a barrage of dismal and dispiriting images that never lets up. Sonically, **Volume 1** is a flat-out groove. Intellectually, it's like a subscription to the obituaries.

Back on his own, recovering from an ambush shooting and on his way to prison in connection with a sexual assault, 2Pac topped himself with the devastating **Me Against the World,** a solemn, doom-laden album that doesn't so much explain his tumultuous life as coolly observe it. Although it begins with news dispatches about his disastrous brushes with justice and violence, **Me Against the World** isn't actually about all that. "Temptations" is the only song to actually address the issues: speaking to someone he professes to really care about, 2Pac explains the context of his love life, sounding patient and beleaguered, careful not to impose himself the way a jury believed he did. "Ain't no time for commitment, I gotta go / Can't be wit' you, every minute's another show / And even though I'm known for my one-night stands / With you I wanna be an honest man."

In this grim dance, the future is ordained and the present scarcely matters. "If I Die 2Nite," "Death Around the Corner," "Me Against the World" and others ambivalently present mortality as everything from a fact of life to a desirable end. "I'm having visions of leaving in a hearse," 2Pac raps in "So Many Tears." But there's a surprisingly positive message amid the album's dense gloom. Picking up from a verse in the second album's "Keep Ya Head Up," "Dear Mama" is a tragic, tender expression of gratitude, regret and forgiveness to his mother, Afeni Shakur. "A poor single mother on welfare / Tell me how you did it / There's no way I can pay you back / But the plan is to show you that I understand." On this album, 2Pac is beginning to see the light, even if he expects it to be extinguished at any moment.

Spending most of a year in jail improved 2Pac's outlook, but not necessarily for the musical better. Upon emerging, he signed himself onto Death Row (Suge Knight's ultra-successful rap label, home to Snoop Doggy Dogg and, until '96, Dr. Dre) and made the excessive and uneven **All Eyez on Me,** which renounces cynicism in such tracks as "No More Pain," "Life Goes On" and "Only God Can Judge Me," concentrating instead on the things he's been missing: sex, freedom, friends and the good life. Filling two CDs with twenty-seven tracks (the better half of which would have been more than enough), it's an unpredictable and endless kitchen sink of overzealous producers and colliding styles: besides an R&B/hip-hop zone located between Montel Jordan and Warren G, the beats come in a variety of idioms, from electro-boogie to G-funk. Adding to the album's structural inconsistency, guests come and go: Snoop and 2Pac marvel at their mutual infamy in "2 of Amerikaz Most Wanted," Nate Dogg and Dru Down help 2Pac lodge a ludicrous complaint about women who appear in different artists' videos ("All Bout U") and George Clinton adds his voice to "Can't C Me." Not surprisingly, repetition is a problem—there are enough mentions of Alizé and Cristal cocktails to suggest the hand of a product placement consultant. The diminution of violence is encouraging on a personal and moral plane, but 2Pac the playboy is far less invigorating a figure than 2Pac the philosopher of death, which makes **All Eyez on Me** way too much of a not-altogether-good thing.

In early September 1996, Shakur was shot and killed in Las Vegas. [i]

See also *Digital Underground.*

TUSCADERO

The Pink Album (TeenBeat) 1994 + 1995 (TeenBeat/Elektra) 1996

Step Into My Wiggle Room (TeenBeat) 1995

"I dunno just what possessed you / If I were a cop, I'd arrest you / Mom, what's goin' on? / I know to you it seemed like trash / But did you have to do something quite so rash?" The misdemeanor being bemoaned by Tuscadero singer/guitarist Melissa Farris on the Washington, DC, punk-pop quartet's debut album is, of course, the parental disposal of childhood artifacts. But then you have to expect such topical issues from a group named for Suzi Quatro's *Happy Days* character. An unabashed member of the back-to-infancy junk-loving movement, Tuscadero does tuneful songs about board games, candy, crayolas, its namesake and monster crushes, counterbalancing the juvenilia with silly slices of adulthood ("Latex Dominatrix") and a serious bust-up put-down ("Dime a Dozen") on **The Pink Album.** Farris alternates mic duties with Margaret McCartney; neither of the two guitarists has a particularly strong or accurate voice, but that's in keeping with the band's amateurish and poorly recorded energetic rock hash. "Just My Size," "Game Song," "Crayola" and "Nancy Drew" are all sturdy constructions, but there isn't a song on this premature ejaculation that couldn't use a more accomplished, appealing performance. (After being signed by Elektra in '95, the group remixed and rerecorded some of **The Pink Album** for its substantially improved '96 reissue, actually the album's *third* version. Because of a producer's credit omitted from the booklet, the original CD ended with the band announcing the correct information. Subsequent copies amended the booklet and deleted the spoken bit from the disc, thereby shortening its length by a minute.)

Step Into My Wiggle Room resolves most of the band's sonic problems, arranging the two women's voices into stirring harmonies that recall the B-52's, clarifying and complicating their guitar tones and settling bassist Phil Satlof and drummer Jack Hornady into a supple, reliable rhythm team. Besides four group efforts—including the psychedelic "Poster Boy" and the wry character assassination of "Palmer: The All-Star Jam," which gets ten pals in to help move the swaying chantalong groove along—the arts-and-crafts assignment disc contains an individually created item from each member. Satlof's "Dreams of the Tanker" is a busy-bee blanket of guitar whooshing over a tinny electronic rhumba, while McCartney's "The Sways," Hornady's "Given Up" and Farris' "Sonic Yogurt" are catchy electric pop tunes of divergent stylistic impulses. Most annoying self-indulgence here: five minutes of ambient chatter that follow "Palmer." [i]

28TH DAY

See *Barbara Manning.*

24-7 SPYZ

Harder Than You (In-Effect) 1989
Gumbo Millennium (In-Effect) 1990
This Is . . . 24-7 Spyz! EP (EastWest) 1991
Strength in Numbers (EastWest) 1992
Temporarily Disconnected (Ger. Enemy) 1995
Heavy Metal Soul by the Pound (What Are Records?) 1996

A quartet hailing from the South Bronx and Manhattan, 24-7 Spyz come on like a leaner, meaner Living Colour on **Harder Than You,** mixing and matching hardcore punk and tough-minded funk to achieve a singularly potent "black rock" blend. Guitarist Jimi Hazel proves himself a better-than-average slice-and-dice man on tracks like "Pillage" and the instrumental "Jimi'z Jam," while singer/lyricist Peter Fluid keeps things politically wired on "Social Plague" (an anti-supremacist rant) and "Ballots Not Bullets," a reggae protest that journalistically details Haiti's bloody '87 election. But it's the band's freewheeling sense of fun that makes **Harder Than You** such a visceral joy: cock an ear to the giddily obscene "Spyz Dope," the bubblethrash goof "Tango Skin Polka" or the ode to a rock-savvy matriarch, "Grandma Dynamite," for a taste of the Spyz at their unfettered finest.

Gumbo Millennium finds the band stretching in new directions—and stretching for material. While bassist Rick Skatore's "Dude U Knew" is an appealing exercise in airy funk, throwaways like "Spyz on Piano" and drummer Anthony Johnson's unconvincing rap attempt "Don't Push Me" indicate a dearth of workable new ideas. Still, Hazel's shred-guitar work on "John Connelly's Theory" (a pointed reference to the Nuclear Assault guitarist) and "Heaven and Hell" show him blossoming into a bona fide axe hero.

The transitional **This Is . . . 24-7 Spyz!** EP introduces new members Jeff Broadnax and Joel Maitoza (replacing Fluid and Johnson, respectively) on five new songs for a different label. The lyrics of "Stuntman" provide some big clues to explain the band's acrimonious split with In-Effect: "Hardcore, grindcore, guitar pop/If you won't do metal, you'll get dropped." (Ironically, the quartet's subsequent work has been steeped in metallic production values.)

Co-produced by Terry Date and Jimi Hazel, the hard-hitting **Strength in Numbers** reprises "Stuntman" and "My Desire" from the EP, adding some worthy tunes, notably the Steely Dan–like ballad "Earth and Sky" and the soaring Hazel showcase "Sireality." Soon after the release of **Strength in Numbers,** Broadnax departed and Fluid returned to the fold. [ts]

27 VARIOUS

Hi. (Susstones) 1987
Yes, Indeed (Susstones) 1989
Approximately (Clean/Twin\Tone) 1990
Up (Clean/Twin\Tone) 1992
Fine (Clean/Twin\Tone) 1992

POLARA

Polara (Clean/Restless) 1995

Over the consistently improving course of five 27 Various albums, Minneapolis guitarist/singer Ed Ackerson grew from the ingenious retro-pop junior of **Hi.** and **Yes, Indeed** (a mild-mannered mix of garage psychedelia and offbeat Anglo-pop) to an assured and able multi-faceted rocker with a specialty in foot-pedal power. Still reveling in the past as a form of modern life, 27 Various came into its own on **Approximately,** respecting the derivative limitations of looking backward while acknowledging a few obvious touchstones: the Byrdsy connotation of twelve-street guitars, a nod to the lighter side of **Their Satanic Majesties Request** and a Rutlesque effort to adapt a couple of Beatles songs into "The Things I Wasn't Supposed to See."

Up is another excellent showcase for Ackerson's thoughtfully modulated guitar playing and genre-hopping songwriting. (In addition, he borrows a pair from Springfield-era Neil Young and Graham Day of England's Prisoners.) Whether kicking a nitrous two-car snarl in "Put Me Down," setting a sweet power-pop sound to sizzle-fry in "Happening/Sometime" (crossing the dB's with Let's Active in the process), doing bouncy country-rock in "Lay It On, Elaine," setting off a flower-carpet tremolo trip in "While You Can" or plastering fuzz all over the walls in "Doesn't Matter to You," 27 Various comes in as many flavors as Heinz but with far better jingles.

Although it was recorded with the same lineup as **Up** less than a year later, **Fine** has less to do with Ackerson's past than his future. Besides the introduction of Farfisa organ and Moog synthesizer to a mounting arsenal, he comes down hard on the distortion effects, erecting a monumental wall of roaring, pliable dream noise on which to paint his calm pop vocals. Occasionally sketching out the plan on acoustic guitar before opening the floodgates, the band sounds like My Bloody Valentine speeding on mood elevators. Carefully stretched across melodic frames, sterling songs like "You've Got It Bad" and "Out of Mohair" go over the top with marvelous, sensual results, holding their shape through the wobbly storms.

Ackerson then dissolved 27 Various, did road time playing loud guitar in Antenna and finally settled in to record a solo album under the name Polara. Using Matt Wilson (formerly a guitarist in Trip Shakespeare) on drums and Antenna/Velo-Deluxe leader John Strohm on guitar, with contributions from a female vocalist, an "electronics" player, a flautist and a few others, Ackerson lets keyboards, samplers, programming and "effect manipulation" spread the thick, disorienting jam without abandoning guitar or his commitment to the pop song. Basically, **Polara** uses the same elements as **Fine** to trigger soft explosions of a more convoluted and exploratory nature, and as a result is a more challenging, uneven and rewarding album. Without a standard formulation, the burbling additions, whirling thingamabobs and submarine descents come and go unpredictably, barely accenting some tracks and overloading others enough to sink them. At **Polara**'s most effective, strong songs are colored in with sparkly sounds from mystery galaxies; at the other end, adequate songs are drowned in random fingerpainting. The quiet noise washes lurking in "Taupe" put atmospheric pressure into a simple acoustic number; "Avenue E" weaves a pulsing sequencer figure through a song custom-designed for such embroidery. In this context, the throwback sound of "Source of Light" is a treat. Not so much a great leap forward as a door opening to many new possibilities, **Polara** delivers a talented pioneer to the world he was born to explore. [i]

See also *Antenna; TPRG.*

20/20

20/20 (Portrait) 1979
Look Out! (Portrait) 1981
Sex-Trap (Mainway) 1982
20/20/Look Out! (Oglio) 1995
4 Day Tornado (Oglio) 1995

20/20/Look Out! is a most welcome reissue of the first two releases by these Los Angeles (by way of Tulsa, Oklahoma) power-pop purveyors. The **20/20** LP stands proudly as one of the genre's best (and most unique-sounding, thanks to Earle Mankey's imaginative production trickery), with scads of tuneful songs from singer/guitarist Steve Allen and singer/bassist Ron Flynt. **Look Out!** doesn't quite reach the heights of the debut, but nevertheless has three or four songs (especially the big-beat "Nuclear Boy") that remain solid examples of decade-turning skinny-tie rock.

Shortly after the twofer reissue of those two albums, 20/20 released its first new music in over a decade. **4 Day Tornado** (named for its brief recording schedule) sounds completely different from the 20/20 of old. True to their pop roots but less British-sounding than on past efforts, Flynt and Allen (along with new drummer Bill Belknap) offer the mesmerizing, atmospheric "Watching the Headlights Burn" and the propulsive "Nothing at All." Whether or not 20/20 continues as a functioning unit beyond this point, **4 Day Tornado** proves there's life in these (not so) old boys yet. [jmb]

22 BRIDES

22 Brides (Zero Hour) 1994
Beaker (Zero Hour) 1995

Led by sisters Libby and Carrie Johnson (originally the entire band, subsequently expanded by an onboard rhythm section), New York's 22 Brides made encouraging progress from the electrified coffeehouse mundanity of the first album to the semi-stylish rock of **Beaker.** Joining their voices in close harmony to sing a lot of the lead parts in unison, the two singer/songwriters are nothing special on **22 Brides.** But set amid the swirling noise guitar that occasionally lights a fire under **Beaker,** the effect is a bit more distinctive. The graft of punky abandon to the trunk of folky preciousness doesn't mesh strongly enough to make the second album more than moderately intriguing ("Insomnia" and the stirring "Crash" are promising high points), but experimental hybrids do have a way of sprouting strange flowers. [i]

2 FOOT FLAME

See *Mecca Normal.*

TYPE O NEGATIVE

Slow, Deep and Hard (RoadRacer) 1991
The Origin of the Feces (RoadRacer) 1992
Bloody Kisses (Roadrunner) 1993
October Rust (Roadrunner) 1996

Bassist Peter Steele, frontman of this consummately nihilistic Brooklyn dirge-metal-cum-goth-rock quartet, lives by the rebel's credo so eloquently expressed by Marlon Brando in *The Wild One.* "Whaddaya got?" Steele's unilateral misanthropy has been mistaken for sexism, racism and simple-minded poppycock—but only the last interpretation holds any water at all.

Slow, Deep and Hard is one of the most extreme metal albums of the decade, rife as it is with such drawn-out death-knells as "Unsuccessfully Coping With the Natural Beauty of Infidelity," a funereal wail that finds Steele (who formerly fronted the thrash-metal outfit Carnivore) moaning in dismay about being spurned by the love of his life. His oft-repeated lament—"I know you're fuckin' someone else"—is matched by his bandmates' (who, not surprisingly, prefer to hide behind single initials here) interjections of "slut," "whore" and equivalent insults. Steele saves most of his venom for such self-immolation sessions as "Prelude to Agony." Steele's deep bass croon (he actually is a more-than-adequate singer), combined with the solemn, bass-heavy dirginess of the "melodies," often makes Type O Negative sound like an evil doppelgänger for fellow Sabbath-philes Joy Division. In what passes not for humor but for highbrow art here, "The Misinterpretation of Silence and Its Disastrous Consequences" is sixty-four seconds of nothing.

Type O Negative's "special" relationship with its audience manifests itself from the onset of the live **Origin of the Feces,** which fades in on a robust (and lengthy) crowd chant of "you suck," accompanied by the crashes of multiple breaking bottles. Clearly skilled at the ins and outs of taming the savage metal crowd, Steele offers up an a cappella verse of "I'm in the Mood for Love" (yes, *that* one) before leading the band into a painstakingly enunciated, keyboard-tinged version of "Unsuccessfully Coping." Unfortunately, he wastes a few minutes of space that could've been given over to post-Rickles banter on "Are You Afraid," a witless pro-suicide anthem that only serves to call to mind the adage about heeding one's own advice. Based on this, Brooklyn homeboy Andrew Dice Clay would likely enjoy the band's company. (Collector's note: the original sleeve, which featured an up-close and personal shot of Steele's anus, was later withdrawn and replaced with something less literally befitting the title.)

The quartet succumbs to its own worst inclinations on **Bloody Kisses,** an overblown, full-on goth record gravely (no pun intended) lacking in the band's past over-the-top attitude. Yes, "We Hate Everyone" jibes at the extreme left and far right, but the album is overrun with workaday sacrilege (like the three-part "Christian Woman") that could have been gleaned from a copy of *Crowley for Dummies.* Steele does, however, proffer just enough of his unique plasmaphilic sexual rumination—like the title track and "Blood & Fire"—to engender hope for a rosy (or is that gory?) future. [dss]

UB40

Signing Off (UK Graduate) 1980 (Virgin) 1994
Present Arms (UK DEP International) 1981 (DEP International/Virgin) 1992
Present Arms in Dub (UK DEP International) 1981 (DEP International/Virgin) 1992
The Singles Album (UK Graduate) 1982
UB44 (UK DEP International) 1982
Live (UK DEP International) 1983 (Virgin) 1994
1980–83 (A&M) 1983
Labour of Love (A&M) 1983
Geffery Morgan (A&M) 1984
The UB40 File (UK Graduate) 1985
Baggariddim (UK DEP International) 1985
Little Baggariddim EP (A&M) 1985
Rat in the Kitchen (DEP International/Virgin/A&M) 1986
UB40 CCCP—Live in Moscow (A&M) 1987
The Best of UB40 Volume One (UK DEP International) 1987 (Virgin) 1995
UB40 (DEP International/A&M) 1988
Labour of Love II (Virgin) 1989
Promises and Lies (DEP International/Virgin) 1993
Best of UB40 Volume Two (Virgin) 1995

ALI CAMPBELL

Big Love (Kuff/Virgin) 1995

It is a testament to either reggae's amazing elasticity, the sunny music's universal appeal or the efficacy of its modern pop co-option that UB40, a racially integrated octet from Birmingham, England, would, if not quite eclipse Bob Marley as the form's most commercially successful (we're talking multi-platinum here) practitioners, at least become reggae's longest-running hit machine. Not to put too fine a point on it, Marley lived only eight years after making the landmark **Catch a Fire** album; UB40 is already nine years past its first greatest-hits compilation.

Significantly, UB40 (the official name for a British unemployment form) has built its empire on laid-back covers of soul and pop classics and gentle love songs, not religion and revolution; there isn't a single item in the UB40 archive with the international social significance of "Redemption Song" or "Get Up Stand Up." Ultimately, UB40 is loyal not to a culture but to a beat. Unlike most pop behemoths who arrive through some exotic entrance way, UB40 has never rethought its basic approach of quietly percolating grooves garnished with sultry horn lines and centered on Ali Campbell's cool crooning (with harmonies from his guitar-playing brother Robin). Indicative of an abiding conservatism that has made no effort to follow the undertow of dancehall, the band's formula is mighty steady: recent albums sound enough like early ones that it would be impossible to guess their order of release.

At the outset, UB40's biggest problem was its weak songwriting, which seemed to rise to the occasion only for singles; as a result, **The Singles Album** is an especially fine LP (even though over half of it had already appeared on **Signing Off**). **Present Arms** is notable for more prominent use of toasting (continued on **UB44**) and little else, aside from two solid singles. **Present Arms in Dub,** though, attempts an alternative to the usual dub style, drastically changing the music to the point where some songs are hardly recognizable. (**The UB40 File** is a repackage of **Signing Off,** with a second disc compiling two 1980 singles.)

UB44, in addition to minor alterations (more Latin percussion, sparingly applied gurgling synth), displays wider lyrical range and increased verbal acuity, but the only truly striking tune is, naturally, a single ("So Here I Am"). The first live album (issued in America more than a decade later) was recorded on tour in Ireland in 1982 and features such tunes as "Food for Thought" and "One in Ten."

The **1980–83** compilation selects tracks from **UB44, Present Arms** and early singles—not bad, but not the introduction America wanted to hear. What finally did the trick was a novelty of sorts, one that sidestepped the band's material shortcomings. **Labour of Love** is an LP of cover versions, drawing on reggae (and previously reggaefied) hits from a number of diverse authors, including Neil Diamond ("Red Red Wine"), Jimmy Cliff ("Many Rivers to Cross") and Delroy Wilson ("Johnny Too Bad"). The resultant variety and melodic quality make the album easily and enduringly enjoyable, a rich mine of superbly played familiarity.

Geffery Morgan unveiled a vastly more creative UB40 at work. Inventive production, intriguing rock rhythms, powerful and memorable songwriting and a new outlook combine to make it a great record that remains rooted in reggae but is far more diverse—see the reggae/rock hybrids "Riddle Me" and "If It Happens Again" or "Nkomo a Go Go," a propulsive dance-rock beat with wailing saxophone.

Baggariddim consists of three new recordings (the catchy "Don't Break My Heart," "Mi Spliff" and a charmingly reggaefied "I Got You Babe" sung with Chrissie Hynde) on an EP plus a seven-song album of dub mixes from **Labour of Love** and **Geffery Morgan. Little Baggariddim** has the three new items, "One in Ten," "Hip Hop Lyrical Robot" and "I Got You Babe" in dub.

Rat in the Kitchen is another accomplished collection of originals that makes clear the maturity of UB40's songwriting. Bopping from start to finish with infectious warmth and top-notch musicianship, the album addresses employment and poverty; "Sing Our Own Song" vaguely discusses apartheid but it's clear

UB40 isn't deeply committed to commitment on its records.

Live in Moscow, a single disc recorded during a historic 1986 Russian tour, has lively performances but thin sound. In its original issue, **The Best of UB40 Volume One** compiles fourteen British hits (eighteen on CD); the belated American release is abridged.

In November 1987, UB40 bassist Earl Falconer drove his car into a Birmingham factory wall, killing his brother Ray ("Pablo"), the band's co-producer. Although he was eventually sentenced to prison for causing a death by reckless driving, Falconer was back in the group for the recording of **UB40,** a lightweight, restrained album with a return visit by Hynde, on "Breakfast in Bed."

Labour of Love II assembles another unassailable collection of reggae-ready songs that either came from or had previously found their way to Jamaica. Although **II** is less convincing than the first covers album, several tunes—Al Green's "Here I Am (Come and Take Me)" and Smokey Robinson's "The Way You Do the Things You Do" (originally a hit for the Temptations)—are able to locate that magical blend of song and style.

Following a lengthy studio layoff, UB40 made another album of originals, the lyrically downcast—but sounding none the worse for wear—**Promises and Lies.** For all the irresistible warm-bath appeal of the smooth grooves, no one should sing a line like "It's a long, black night, good people, descended on our land" with such glowing positive spirit. The unmovable Campbell delivers all of the lyrics—from the grim realities of "C'est la Vie" to the title track's deep disillusion ("All your promises were lies") to the racial oppression venom of "Sorry" ("You must prove it sign the cheque without delay / Most humbly yours, four hundred years back pay")—in exactly the same tone he's always used. The emotional soft-soap is disconcerting if not dishonest, leaving the album easy to hear but hard to take seriously. (Actually, the only number that receives a stirring reading is "Can't Help Falling in Love," the Elvis Presley oldie recorded for the soundtrack of *Sliver.*) UB40 breaks the mold here with samples (in "It's a Long Long Way") and Astro's occasional toasts: he waxes surprisingly sexy on "Bring Me Your Cup" and really wrecks shit in "Sorry." Furthermore, Falconer spells Campbell on the electronics-powered "Reggae Music," giving a warmhearted salute to the band in a husky voice.

In its American edition at least, the band's second greatest-hits compilation is nearly useless, drawing all but three of its tracks from **Labour of Love II** and **Promises and Lies.**

Campbell's solo album marks the first significant break in the group's close-knit insularity since Falconer's imprisonment; still, everyone in UB40 makes some contribution. Although the polished soul of **Big Love** doesn't break for any border, the album does give Campbell the freedom to work with some new people, slip out—just briefly—from reggae's rhythmic yoke, do without live drumming, promote hemp farming (I said, "promote hemp farming") and sing a broader range of material. He covers Syreeta Wright, Jimmy Cliff's "Let Your Yeah Be Yeah" and preserves the father/daughter tradition of Frank and Nancy Sinatra's "Somethin' Stupid" with his own progeny. For all that, Campbell doesn't maintain his usual air of sophisticated reserve. Left to explore his ambitions, he steps outside his strengths; the anti-racist fable "Talking Blackbird" and the tape collage PSA announcement "Stop the Guns" are witlessly obvious, and score no points beyond stating their messages. [jg/i]

See also *TPRG.*

UGLY KID JOE

As Ugly as They Wanna Be (Stardog) 1991
America's Least Wanted (Stardog/Mercury) 1992
Menace to Sobriety (Mercury) 1995
Motel California (Evilution) 1996

If one's only contact with this Santa Barbara quintet was the obnoxious image of its bird-flipping cartoon brat or the antagonistic lyrics of its 1992 hit single, "Everything About You," one might have felt a twinge of pity that Green Day came along and wrecked their party. In fact, Ugly Kid Joe (originally known as Suburban Alcoholic White Trash) is nothing more than a Mötley Halen wannabe, a bad-looking second-rate hair-metal band that prefers T-shirts and baggy shorts to frilly shirts and leather trousers. The six-track **As Ugly as They Wanna Be,** issued on a phony major-label street-cred imprint, has the hit and a bunch of other crud, the nadir being a pseudo-funky reprise of the single.

Their career momentum fizzling fast, the Joes released the increasingly aptly named **America's Least Wanted,** a formulaic rock/pop exercise that takes some cues from Guns n' Roses, repeats "Everything About You" and another EP track and fails to find wit or purpose in a cover of Harry Chapin's "Cat's in the Cradle." A one-joke joke that, like a comedian running short on material, keeps reusing the same punchline, Ugly Kid Joe doesn't have such a dark heart after all. The acoustic "Mr. Recordman" is, at worst, skeptical; the band gladly sides with downtrodden sorts like "Goddamn Devil" and "Panhandlin' Prince." Among the guests: Jane's Addiction's Stephen Perkins, Judas Priest's Rob Halford and actress Julia Sweeney.

It's frightening to think that grown men would take public pride in such abject stupidity, but the **Menace to Sobriety** booklet contains a real-looking hotel bill detailing $12,896.81 in damage caused in a "food fight." Skipping the hey-remember-us? angle after a lengthy absence (during which time drummer Mark Davis left and was replaced by Shannon Larkin), guitarists Klaus Eichstadt and Dave Fortman, bassist Cordell Crockett and singer Whitfield Crane (sporting a new and nasty W. Axl Rose vocal affliction on some songs) reintroduce themselves as a growly, serious rock lot attempting to fill the gap left by the Gunners' silence. The surprising reverence of "God" and "Jesus Rode a Harley" ("Noah used to rock the boat sometimes / Mary used to get undone / Yeah, and Jesus rode a Harley Davidson") is the real shocker here; a liner note thanking "positive, good-vibin', spiritually blessed" supporters adds to the suspicion that something in addition to alcohol is affecting the band's vision. Just when the memory of Stryper was fading out, isn't *that* special? [i]

UKRAINIANS

See *Wedding Present.*

JAMES BLOOD ULMER

Tales of Captain Black (Artists House) 1979 (Japan. DIW) 1996
Are You Glad to Be in America? (UK Rough Trade) 1980 (Artists House) 1981 (Japan. DIW) 1995
Free Lancing (Columbia) 1981
Black Rock (Columbia) 1982
Odyssey (Columbia) 1983 (Columbia/Legacy) 1996
Part Time (UK Rough Trade) 1984
Phalanx—Got Something Good for You (Ger. Moers Music) 1986
Live at the Caravan of Dreams (Caravan of Dreams) 1987
America—Do You Remember the Love? (Blue Note) 1987
In Touch (Japan. DIW) 1988
Original Phalanx (Japan. DIW) 1989
Blues Allnight (In + Out/Rounder) 1989
Revealing (Ger. In + Out) 1990 (In + Out/Rounder) 1996
Black and Blues (Japan. DIW) 1991
Harmolodic Guitar With Strings (Japan. DIW) 1993
Blues Preacher (DIW/Columbia) 1994
Live (In + Out/Rounder) 1994

MUSIC REVELATION ENSEMBLE

No Wave (Ger. Moers Music) 1980
Music Revelation Ensemble (Japan. DIW) 1988
Elec. Jazz (Japan. DIW) 1990
After Dark (Japan. DIW) 1992
In the Name of . . . (DIW/Columbia) 1994
Knights of Power (Japan. DIW) 1996

Although most of his early stints were with jazz organists like Hank Marr, Larry Young and Big John Patton, guitarist James Blood Ulmer is inextricably linked with pioneering saxophonist Ornette Coleman. Ostensibly the first electric guitarist to apply Coleman's harmolodics theory to his own music, Ulmer's debut finds him heavily indebted to the saxophonist. **Tales of Captain Black** offers Ulmer's trademark knotted, choked phrasing as a rough-hewn foil to Coleman's pure, free melodocism, but he hasn't fully discovered his own voice yet. **Revealing,** a 1977 session with the great tenor saxophonist George Adams and bassist Cecil McBee that went unreleased until 1990, offers a less cluttered, more effective example of early Ulmer.

After several fine albums flanked by ace avant-gardists like David Murray, Oliver Lake and Olu Dara, on which he began forging a more distinctive identity, Ulmer hit a high-water mark with the brilliant **Odyssey.** Along with drummer Warren Benbow and violinist Charles Burnham, the album combines Ulmer's innovative playing, a powerfully sweeping mix of cerebral probing and surging, bluesy expressiveness—a style that prompted many to call him the most important African-American guitarist since Jimi Hendrix—and his natural ease with, and interest in, post-country blues and soul fusions. The instrumentals pack plenty of free-jazz punch, imbuing his Coleman-derived concept with an invigorating accessibility; the vocal pieces gorgeously complement Ulmer's raggedly soulful singing with a lovely down-home feel. Burnham's warm electric violin, in particular, delivers a striking adaptation of the black string band tradition to a rich stew of blues, gospel, soul and jazz. In short, **Odyssey** is Ulmer's most complete record.

Ulmer always possessed a strong crossover potential, and **America—Do You Remember the Love?,** recorded with bassist Bill Laswell and Coleman alumnus Ronald Shannon Jackson on drums, attempted to blatantly cash in on it. It contains some of Ulmer's most measured, resonant singing, but the fiery urgency of his guitar playing is missing in action. Ulmer balanced his late-'80s search for commercial acceptance with several mostly instrumental collaborations—the Phalanx project with George Adams and the revived Music Revelation Ensemble with David Murray—but at best these records are only qualified successes.

In the '90s, Ulmer has mounted a two-pronged attack with uneven results. He has continued to veer closer to commercial rock territory and failed both financially and artistically. His more jazz-oriented outings, however, have redeemed many of his missteps. **Blues Allnight,** with second guitarist Ronnie Drayton, drummer Grant Calvin Weston and frequent Ulmer bassist Amin Ali, opts for straight-up rock production and employs cloying synth interjections, weak tunes and the occasional anthemic quality found in beer commercials. It's quite possibly Ulmer's worst album. But while **Black and Blues** was recorded with the same group a year later and goes for much the same over-the-top attack, the performances avoid the chintzy gloss of the previous effort. The effects-heavy guitar playing continues to flirt with mersh-metal sounds, but it's leavened with an unreconstructed hard funk wallop. Ulmer's singing exudes a renewed, raw vigor, and the propulsive support of Ali and Weston is impressive.

Blues Preacher, his first domestic major-label outing since the Blue Note record, is another misguided crossover attempt, transporting the old ideas into the '90s. While nothing matches the putrid excesses of the album's cringe-inducing closer "Angel"—a sad stab at slow-jam grooving—the record places the emphasis on Blood's vocals amid unwavering rock and funk rhythms and more faux-metal guitars (courtesy of Drayton). The flat production and dynamic-free performances do nothing to accentuate his rather bland, inexpressive vocalizing.

The title of **Harmolodic Guitar With Strings** sounds like a self-indulgent recipe for disaster, but the album is one of Ulmer's finest. Pairing his guitar with a somber string quartet led by violinist John Blake, the mostly instrumental record provides a highly effective framing device for the subtle intricacies of Ulmer's playing. In contrast to his forced efforts at playing upbeat rock and funk, this record embraces his strikingly dark impulses. Free of a heavy-handed rhythm section, Ulmer's sophisticated sense of rhythm gets highlighted almost matter-of-factly. Against the sorrowful strings, Ulmer's powerful playing exudes a frustrated expression; his guitar grapples with inchoate rage, sadness and joy.

Live is another terrific outing with Ali and drummer Aubrey Dayle. Free of studio trickery, this 1994 Munich club date focuses on Ulmer's still-present fire, an element all too often smothered on his '90s group albums. The record mixes old and new tunes; all of them drip with palpable electric urgency. Both Ulmer's singing and his guitar playing connect; although unlike **Odyssey,** it paints the same sort of full picture of Ulmer's abilities.

Elec. Jazz with Murray, Ali and drummer Cornell Rochester is a muscular set of fierce funk-based improvising. More linear and accessible than the Music Revelation Ensemble's 1980 debut and less indulgent than its eponymous 1988 followup, it's still largely uninspired. The same is true of the group's **After**

Dark. The title track, however, foreshadows **Harmolodic Guitar With Strings** by incorporating a string quartet, which sits rather uncomfortably with the full band.

Much as Ulmer's more recent solo work has delivered the goods, the MRE's **In the Name of . . .** proves its equal. Recorded with a revolving cast of saxophonists—Arthur Blythe (the alto player with whom Ulmer recorded in the early '80s), Sam Rivers and Hamiet Bluiett—the improvisations are explosive, and the hornmen, none of whom has played this sort of electric energy music much of late, inject the proceedings with palpable freshness. Many of the tunes situate loping, Ornette-like melodies over a furious rhythmic attack and Ulmer delivers some of his best straight-up guitar in years. [pm]

See also *TPRG.*

ULTRA BIDÉ

God Is God . . . Puke Is Puke (Alternative Tentacles) 1995

Formed in Kyoto by singer/bassist Hidé, Ultra Bidé released a pair of albums in Japan before he packed off to New York City and relaunched the group with two other expatriates, guitarist Satoru and drummer Tada, he found there. Playing intricate but engaging art-punk noise with domineering power *and* subtle control (but crudely profane and sketchy lyrics), the trio does a riveting high-wire act on **God Is God . . . Puke Is Puke,** dancing wildly over a pit of chaotic abandon and falling in only some of the time. At its best here ("Saigon Whore," "What the Hell," "Loop" and an Asian-shaped instrumental with an untranslated Japanese title), Ultra Bidé cracks its electric knuckles and plunges into fully formed songs, respecting the loud/soft dynamic spread while mustering the furious intensity of free-jazz nerds. Better skronk through responsibility. [i]

ULTRAMAGNETIC MC'S

Critical Beatdown (Next Plateau) 1988
Funk Your Head Up (Mercury) 1992
The Four Horsemen (Wild Pitch) 1993
The Basement Tapes 1984–1990 (Tuff City) 1994

The Ultramagnetic MC's was one of a flood of crews to emerge from the late-'80s New York–area scenes that included EPMD, Eric B. & Rakim and Public Enemy. The group made its early reputation on a number of classic 12-inch sides ("Ego Trippin'," "Mentally Mad," "Chorus Line") that blended unvarnished beats with offbeat lyrical deliveries. Like the more heralded Rakim, Kool Keith (Thornton)'s innovative flows and spacey, abstract lyrics became especially influential to the next generation of rhymers (maybe too influential: even before the Ultramagnetic MC's got to Wild Pitch, an unrelated duo called the UMC's released an album on the label).

The quartet's **Critical Beatdown** is an amazing debut. Producer Ced Gee (Cedric Miller) pushes sampling technology to its early limits, providing sonics that are less bassy and more breakbeat-heavy than most of their contemporaries. Kool Keith's shifty rhyme patterns (or "patterrins," as he calls them) drop in and around the third-line backbeats on "Ease Back" and "Give the Drummer Some." Complex polyrhythms fill "Kool Keith Housing Things" and "Ego Trippin'." Anyone listening too closely to "Feelin' It," in which Keith poetically turns his competitors into crawling roaches, shoeless ducks and exiled rabbits, is bound to get caught up in his whirlwind weirdness.

Funk Your Head Up sharpens (and recycles) the mid-tempo groove and rhyme attack. "Hahaha! MCs are funny to me/And on Easter they're like bunnies to me," laughs Keith on "Message From the Boss." Highlights include "MC Champion," "Bust the Facts," "Make It Happen" and "Poppa Large." The sex fetishes ("Porno Star") are less interesting. If hip-hop were only about clever lyrics and concrete breakbeats, the UMC's might have been on top of the world. But next to the street socio-politics of Ice Cube, the gangsta dramatics of Dr. Dre and the shock gimmickry of Geto Boys, Ultramagnetics were beginning to sound nostalgic.

The group's third album moves to a more studio-oriented sound and an ever-wider topical range. "We Are the Horsemen" finds Keith commanding his crew and followers to "Enter your spaceship!" While "One Two One Two" rocks a more traditional battle flow and "Raise It Up" and "Time to Catch a Body" are nods to the reality-rap school, "Saga of Dandy, the Devil and Day" pays tribute to baseball's Negro League.

The Basement Tapes is a compilation of the group's early sides, outtakes and demos; the uneven set of Ced Gee productions is badly packaged and mostly poorly recorded. [jzc]

UNCLE GREEN

Get It Together (New Vision) 1987
15 Dryden (New Vision/DB) 1988
You (DB) 1989
What an Experiment His Head Was (DB) 1991
Book of Bad Thoughts (Atlantic) 1992

3 LB. THRILL

Vulture (Fiftyseven/550 Music) 1995

Uncle Green was formed as a nondescript cover band by four New Jersey high-school freshmen; after graduation, the friends relocated to Atlanta and began spewing out equally nondescript pop originals. Using airy harmonies and acoustic strums to spiff up their mild-mannered mainstream creations, Uncle Green breezed through three blandly inoffensive albums produced in turn by John Keane and Brendan O'Brien, neither of whom was able to locate a strong personality among the group's assets.

O'Brien also oversaw **What an Experiment His Head Was,** focusing the maturing band's unexpectedly prickly, literate lyrics and energized musical attack into a sharp, hot beam. Using dense and diverse arrangements that owe equal debts to the Beatles and Elvis Costello, the band's two singer/songwriters—guitarists Matt Brown and Jeff Jensen—push the sturdily tuneful material toward accessible psychedelia and baroque folk-rock with enough emotional and musical bite to leave marks.

The band's move to a major label was accompanied by a deeper descent into romantic bitterness, distrust and disgust; **Book of Bad Thoughts,** complete with a needless remake of the previous album's catchy ode to willful relationship ignorance, "I Don't Wanna Know About It," continues the association with O'Brien (playing organ on enough tracks to count as a fifth member), who helps the group up its rock kick. At the album's most extreme point, Jensen's "In Good Time" roars with ferocious despair. Brown's "Bellingham" rests easily on a jaunty piano figure, but the band's dynamic range doesn't simply follow individual members' impulses: Brown punches out "He Woke Up Naked" with the chunky force of the Smithereens and slides into boogie mundanity on "A Good Man," while Jensen wraps his weedy voice around the temperate balladry of "The Blue Light." Although not a great album—too much of the writing is overweening, and there are times when it sounds like the work of two separate bands—**Book of Bad Thoughts** is a solid effort from a thoughtful and practical outfit.

Evidently convinced that Uncle Green had run its course (or perhaps feeling lonely in the record racks since the demise of the adjacent Uncle Tupelo), the four rechristened their group 3 lb. Thrill and, with O'Brien and co-producer Nick DiDia, made **Vulture,** a thick, powerful rock record that opens new lyrical vistas and sublimates pop into soaring electric onslaughts with stirring melodies. The opening "Born Again" heralds the new beginning more in the feedback and buzzing distortion than the religion-versus-evolution lyrics, but still makes it clear the group is on a new sonic mission and that Uncle Green's derivative digressions are a thing of the past. Big, modern guitars dominate the album, accompanied by forceful voicing of songs about suicidal depression ("Mary Tells Me"), incestuous child-abuse ("Diana"), nuclear testing ("Bikini Island"), abject alienation ("Coffin Nails") and societal imposition (the blustery bonus track that follows "Piñata"). What a difference putting on a couple of pounds can make. [ky/i]

See also *TPRG*.

UNCLE JOE'S BIG OL' DRIVER

Uncle Joe's Big Ol' Driver (Headhunter/Cargo) 1994
Chick Rock (Headhunter/Cargo) 1995

Reveling in the sort of post-punk disassembly of classic rock first effected in mid-'80s Minnesota, Uncle Joe's Big Ol' Driver digs into big'n'beefy sprawling riffwork with gusto and a knack for songs that stick on its all-fun first album. Nodding enthusiastically toward the full-frontal melodic rock of the Replacements and Soul Asylum (as well as the Lyres in "Divine"), the San Diego quartet makes fine use of crunching rhythm guitars and spirited frenzy in "Gone Sour," "Sweet Things Come in Small Packages" and the calamitous garage-powered "Jersey." (The band's stylistic inclination isn't too surprising, since Dave Jass, one of its two singer/guitarists, grew up in Minneapolis and did a stint with a nascent incarnation of Soul Asylum. Andrew McKeag is from Portland, but that doesn't make them sound like Poison Idea. So much for theories.)

Relocating to Seattle and landing another in a long series of drummers, UJBOD takes a more varied approach on **Chick Rock.** (**Dick Rock** if you like, girls.) Produced by the illustrious Kurt Bloch, UJBOD hits its stride with bar-fogged, meat'n'potatoes rock. "Head First," "Good Morning Headache" and "Thunderbolt Grease Slapper" all follow happily in the debut's footsteps, but "One Night Stand" makes a junior Dinosaur Jr bid and "Johnny the Man" hits a white-line-fever boogie groove, while the skeletal "AM" strikes a quiet, reflective tone that will sound familiar to fans of Paul Westerberg's maudlin side. [vg]

UNCLE TUPELO

No Depression (Rockville) 1990
Still Feel Gone (Rockville) 1991
March 16–20, 1992 (Rockville) 1992
Anodyne (Sire/Reprise) 1993

WILCO

A.M. (Sire/Reprise) 1995
Being There (Reprise) 1996

SON VOLT

Trace (Warner Bros.) 1995

How it was exactly that country became uncool is a subject for another time—suffice it to say that by the early 1990s, the utter banality of contemporary country music and the grunge era's distrust of nearly all things rootsy combined to marginalize just about any artist who possessed both a brain and a twang. Into this irony-laden juncture stepped a couple of kids country enough to love the music and punk enough to feel that so many people not liking it was a pretty good reason to play it.

The story of Uncle Tupelo is the story of these two principals, who grew up in Belleville, Illinois, a decaying working-class suburb just east of St. Louis. Jeff Tweedy and Jay Farrar roomed together for years in fraternal squalor. Their first group was a punk cover band called the Primitives; so doctrinaire were they that Tweedy admits he wouldn't even talk to anyone who didn't like Black Flag. The Primitives broke up when Farrar's brother went into the army. The pair opened their minds a bit and began crafting a fairly persuasive brand of country punk—not cowpunk, as too many novelty-tinged bands have envisioned it, but a slower and psychically intense style of punk-informed rural music.

Their first two albums are at once callow and weary, earnest and irresponsible, bashy workouts marked with a tired banjo or a distant mandolin. Each man brought a distinct sensibility to the band. Tweedy has the sweeter instincts, demonstrated in the shambling heck-yeah-we're-hicks charm of the debut's "Screen Door" and in the keening chorus of the winsome "Gun" and his scattery tribute song, "D. Boon," both on **Still Feel Gone.** But Farrar, with his big, indignant voice and pained tone, gives the early records their soul. His trademark move is a dead stop, a sharp intake of breath and a clenched-teeth bash at the nearest guitar; the move—part show, part genuine outrage—captures both his natural flair for drama and an implicit need for catharsis through rock. Tweedy, who wrote for a fanzine as a teen, has a critic's interest in music: his songs are dotted with musical references, both philosophical and specific. But Farrar is more fanatical; even when he's not actually singing about music, his delivery makes it clear that little else matters.

March 16–20, 1992, produced by Peter Buck, is a bit more subdued. It's almost entirely acoustic and marked by Farrar's ferocious readings of traditional folk tunes on such cheery subjects as moonshining, coal miners, nuclear power and Satan. In between, Tweedy essays his own brand of folk in a pair of gorgeously abstract ballads, "Wait Up" and "Black Eye," and tosses in a nice approximation of **Freewheelin'**-era Dylan in the cameo "I Wish My Baby Was Born." A moving, subtle, funny, sad and enormously enjoyable album. (That same year, Rockville issued a double-vinyl pairing of **Still Feel Gone** and **March 16–20, 1992** with new artwork specific to neither.)

Moving to a major label, Uncle Tupelo delivered **Anodyne.** The argument can be made that this well-produced and sparkling record finds the trio at a powerful and sure-footed peak. The punk is gone, and so is the country: what's left is something new, from the sweet, mournful violin that opens the record to the wan envoi, "Steal the Crumbs," that ends it. But Tweedy makes his allegiances plain with "Acuff-Rose," a tip-o'-the-hat to the venerable Nashville publishing house, and "We've Been Had," a cry of betrayal against big daddy rock'n'roll. Farrar duets with Doug Sahm on Sahm's classic "Give Back the Key to My Heart" and, on the title song, crafts Tupelo's finest moment: a floating, soaring melody that is somehow at once archaic and immediate. This was the band's legacy: the reworking of a branch of a historic music in a way that can fill our minds with meaning and resonance today.

Indeed, by this time the pair found themselves, somewhat discomfitingly, hailed as the catalyst of a potent new strain of serious alternative country, sometimes called Americana and sometimes called No Depression (after the Carter Family chestnut that gave Uncle Tupelo's first album its name). The music ranged from rock bands like the Bottle Rockets (led by former Tupelo guitar tech and guest instrumentalist Brian Henneman) and the Jayhawks (whose Gary Louris guested on **Still Feel Gone**) on the one side to neo-folk and -country singers like Iris DeMent and Jimmie Dale Gilmore on the other.

In mid-'94, the pair dissolved the band and went their separate ways, apparently at the abrupt demand of Farrar; both refuse to discuss the matter further. Tupelo heads liked Tweedy but considered Farrar the band's real talent; Wilco's **A.M.** is, in this context, a surprisingly substantive exposition of smart songcraft. Backed by the remnants of Tupelo (drummer Ken Coomer, bassist John Stirratt and multi-instrumentalist Max Johnson) and using Henneman well as lead guitarist, Tweedy offers at least a pair of tuneful wonders—the blithe "I Must Be High" and "Box Full of Letters," an oblique farewell to Farrar—that takes the Tupelo fusion further into the realm of pop.

What could the unrepentant Farrar do but delve deep into the past? The sound of **Trace,** unveiling his new quartet, Son Volt, displays an uncompromising devotion to the spirit of antediluvian American folk and country, conveyed most tellingly by his dark voice and a lonesome-sounding guitar or violin. Co-produced (as was **A.M.**) by Brian Paulson, the record doesn't refuse to rock: the trebly attack of songs like "Drown" and "Route" is reminiscent of the bashy splendor of Uncle Tupelo's earliest releases. But its overall feel is stark and regretful, letting sentimentality ("Live free or die") vie with mordancy ("Driving down sunny 44 highway/There's a beach there known for cancer") for dominance. The album's tone is set right away in the breathtaking "Windfall," a pretty yet seemingly casual genuflection to the sacred American trinity of a car, a road and a radio. But the song is less a hymn to the music than a blessing from it: "May the wind take your troubles away." Those who are not attuned to the sound Uncle Tupelo constructed may find this all contrarily non-modern, almost didactic in its intent; Farrar's guilty on both counts. But the greatest American music in general—and rock'n'roll in particular—is based on little else but people like him: fucked-up true believers who won't, or can't, do anything else. [bw]

See also *Golden Smog.*

UNCLE WIGGLY

He Went There So Why Don't We Go [tape] (Aut. Water Tapes/Nur Sch.) 1990
Across the Room and Into Your Lap (Shimmy-Disc) 1991
There Was an Elk (Shimmy-Disc) 1993
I Got Your Uncle Wiggly Right Here: Rare & Unreleased '88–'93 [tape] (D.U.) 1993
Non-Stuff (UK Hemiola) 1995
Jump Back, Baby (TeenBeat) 1996

New York's casual and eccentric Uncle Wiggly gets its strength from the full creative participation of all three members; each holds up his corner of the triangle. It's pretty easy to figure out who writes what. William Berger contributes krautish guitar-focused instrumentals and short pop songs. James Kavoussi creates fuzzy, crabbed meanderings in strange tunings. Mike Anzalone does the retro-pop sing-songs. (Kavoussi, who is the drummer of record in Uncle Wiggly, also works on his own as pHoaming Edison and is a singer/guitarist in Fly Ashtray, which originally included Anzalone as well. Berger was formerly in Smack Dab.)

He Went There So Why Don't We Go finds the stylistic troika firmly in place. While it initially sounds like an attempt to recreate **Magical Mystery Tour**–era Beatles ("Tongue and Teeth" includes a distant trumpet; most songs display an innocent surrealism), the sweet lilting and lurching melodies turn to earthier, more repetitive psychedelia. Besides a number of short, indistinct instrumentals, the album ranges from "The King's Loyal Moustache Clippings," a Kavoussi carbuncle of a song, to the stop-and-go prettiness of the unlisted "With My" and "Oatmeal Goddess," which works in both the guitar riff from "Help Me, Rhonda" and some wheezing harmonica.

Across the Room and Into Your Lap, Wiggly's cutest record, is largely characterized by Shimmy-lord Kramer's production, which pours on the reverb, especially on the vocals: "Ba Ba Ba" and "My, My, My, How Are You?" sound like Galaxie 500 outtakes. While dispensing with any nostalgic sounds, the album does include more than one song about ice cream. Again, the majority of the songs are catchy jam instrumentals with similar structures. Uncle Wiggly keeps working over basic patterns, coming up with different combinations, weaving a stiff, shiny and still-intricate chunky blanket.

The sprawling **There Was an Elk** turns more psychedelic in a rougher way. It's as if the trio wrote edgier songs and then took the edges off, leaving a flatter but still forceful sound. The vocals are nearly invisible, sketched in lightly, rather than articulated. There are golden moments in the constant matrix of Wiggly-ness—the gem "Small Factory" (sung by Sari from the Gamma Rays), the mechanics-repair-shop musique concrète of "Elephant Fly." There's also such untuned mush as "Peeking Over the Fence."

Consisting mainly of demos and live tracks, Wiggly's rarities cassette contains things that seem un-Wiggly but actually fit the group's idiosyncratic logic—a "country disco" melody, a Red Crayola cover. Somehow these end up sounding not out of the ordinary at all, and especially not out of the Uncle Wiggly aesthetic. In addition, the album includes several lovely songs not available anywhere else, and "Having a Swell Time" and "Greek Chorus II" are worth the price alone.

Joining the mass exodus from Shimmy-Disc, Uncle Wiggly made the very different **Non-Stuff** for a British label. The eight long songs are deeper (more tom-tom, less snare), sluggish and trippy. From the sounds of things, besides listening to more Amon Düül II, they've also been starting up a lot more lawnmowers and household appliances.

Jump Back, Baby has a bigger college-rock sound than anything else the band has done. The production is smoother and cleaner; there's less of the meandering and noodling found on other releases. The falsetto vocals kick in more often, and the vocals are more to the fore anyway, especially on "Yr Hed" and "Imbeciles." The usual assortment of quirks is still present: backward, smushing sounds, silly psychedelic lyrics and lots of little intricate noises behind the big pop themes. (Despite an art/info fuck-up, Kavoussi has *not* left the band.) [rxe]

See also *Fly Ashtray, Smack Dab.*

UNDERBELLY

See *Sidewinders.*

UNDERWORLD

Underneath the Radar (Sire) 1988
Change the Weather (Sire) 1989
dubnobasswithmyheadman (UK Junior Boy's Own) 1993 (Wax Trax!/TVT) 1994
Dirty Epic/Cowgirl EP (Wax Trax!/TVT) 1994
Second Toughest in the Infants (Wax Trax!/TVT) 1996

Underworld's roots are in the mid-'80s electro-pop new wave quintet Freur (which, in a prescient pre-Prince move, was initially identified only by an unpronounceable glyph), best known for the dreamy pop single "Doot Doot." The English band's 1983 album made less impact here than the song did, and a 1985 followup, **Get Us Out of Here,** was released only in Europe.

A few years later, four-fifths of Freur re-emerged with a dance beat as Underworld. **Underneath the Radar** is a by-the-numbers slice of polished late-'80s British dance-pop: unremarkable and inoffensive. **Change the Weather** boasts a little more enthusiasm but, at the end of the day, tracks like "Thrash" might as well be INXS on amphetamines. Given the relatively banal nature of the group's sound, Underworld met with some success, particularly in the US. During a 1990 tour with Eurythmics, singer/guitarist Karl Hyde and keyboard programmer Rick Smith simultaneously decided to call it a day, and Underworld dissolved.

Hyde kicked around the US as a session musician. While hanging out in Manhattan preparing for a Deborah Harry tour, he became enamored of the underground poetry scene thriving at clubs like Jackie 60. The mix of sex, verbal abuse and music inspired a new, more fragmented approach to lyricism. Back in England, he rejoined Smith and, augmented by DJ Darren Emerson, revived the Underworld name. Hyde and Smith developed a new artistic method, creating songs and handing them over to Emerson to deconstruct. They pressed and distributed five hundred copies of a single, "The Hump," themselves; the next, "Dirty," was released as Lemon Interrupt, with production credited to Underworld.

Following the release of "Mmm Skyscraper I Love You," the trio discovered that DJs were playing the version that favored Hyde's sketchy vocals and guitar as opposed to the beat-heavy club mixes. The band's full-length album, **dubnobasswithmyheadman,** makes it clear this realization had been taken into account. Tracks like "Dark & Long" and the agitated "Cowgirl" integrate Hyde's contributions alongside the beats and keyboards with dexterity and innovation ("Tongue" might even be mistaken for the Durutti Column at points), with subtle and sinister results. Fans of the album are encouraged to seek out the domestic CD single of "Dirty Epic"/"Cowgirl," which includes not only three mixes of each but also "Rez" (the stunning UK B-side of "Cowgirl") and the seductive "River of Bass."

Continuing in the direction suggested by a 1994 single ("Born Slippy"), **Second Toughest in the Infants** works within, but is not confined by, the palette of drum-and-bass/jungle sounds that had swelled in popularity. In line with such peers as Jonah Sharp (Spacetime Continuum) and Orbital, cuts like the spiraling "Juanita" use layers of skittish keyboard lines and breakneck rhythmic programming to disorienting effect. The album loses a degree of steam two-thirds of the way through, but ultimately stands as an important and entertaining chapter in the band's evolution. Hyde and Smith are also founding members of the Tomato design collective; in addition to producing Underworld videos and an art book, *Mmm Skyscraper I Love You,* the company has created everything from Nike TV spots to Rolling Stones album covers. [kbr]

See also *TPRG.*

UNITED FUTURE ORGANIZATION

United Future Organization (Brownswood/Talkin Loud/Verve Forecast) 1994
No Sound Is Too Taboo (Brownswood/Talkin Loud/Verve Forecast) 1995

Tokyo's United Future Organization produces and remixes artists, programs clubs and club nights, designs fashion and, as a sideline, has a hand in the future of international funk. Led by DJs Toshio Matsuura, Tadashi Yabe and Raphael Sebbag, UFO is a unique blend of hip-hop style, raw soul grooves and acid-jazz cool. While the elements are common enough, UFO's deployment of them is wildly creative. Much of acid-jazz is little more than homages to hard soul, bop and Roy Ayers paid via more recent influences; UFO strives to reattain the music's essential feel, recombining it with samplers, turntables, live musicians and whatever else is handy. **United Future Organization** samples Lenny Bruce on top of a Jack Kerouac beat monologue for "Poetry and All That Jazz" and still manages to outweigh the sum of the song's parts; Jon Hendricks steps in for a transcendent funk bop reprise of his "I'll Bet You Thought I'd Never Find You."

No Sound Is Too Taboo further entwines samples with live instrumentation, refining and expanding on the ideas central to the debut. Part of the fun is that the elements present are so varied and unlikely that the discs convey the excitement of a night out at a hip club. French, Portuguese, English and Japanese are sprinkled throughout, while samba, soul, hip-hop and jazz all bump into each other like acquaintances on line for the bathroom. This UFO is the musical equivalent of the party scene in *Breakfast at Tiffany's.* [sf]

UNREST

Unrest! [tape] (TeenBeat) 1985
Unrest EP7 (TeenBeat) 1985
Lisa Carol Freemont [tape] (TeenBeat) 1985
Tink of S.E. LP (TeenBeat) 1987
Malcolm X Park (Caroline) 1988
Catchpellet EP7 (TeenBeat) 1989
Twister [tape] (TeenBeat) 1989
Kustom Karnal Blackxploitation (Caroline) 1990
A Factory Record EP (Sub Pop) 1991
Imperial f.f.r.r. (TeenBeat/No. 6) 1992 (UK Guernica) 1992
Bavarian Mods EP (TeenBeat/Homestead) 1992
Isabel Bishop (TeenBeat/4AD) 1993
Cath Carroll EP (TeenBeat/4AD) 1993
Perfect Teeth (TeenBeat/4AD) 1993
Fuck Pussy Galore (& All Her Friends) (TeenBeat/Matador) 1993
B.P.M. {1991–1994} (TeenBeat) 1995

AIR MIAMI

Me. Me. Me. (TeenBeat/4AD) 1995
Fuck You, Tiger EP (TeenBeat/4AD) 1995
Niagara Falls Is Frozen EP (TeenBeat) 1996

MARK E

Sammy Supreme My Man EP7 (TeenBeat) 1990
Superstar [tape] (TeenBeat) 1991

PHIL KRAUTH

Cold Morning (TeenBeat) 1995
Silver Eyes (TeenBeat) 1996

OLYMPIC DEATH SQUAD

Blue (TeenBeat) 1996

At Unrest's inception, leader Mark Robinson was an Arlington teenager wedged between (punk) rock and an art place, struggling madly to satisfy his predilections for both the splenetic bashing of local harDCore and the vaporous waft of gray-overcoated Brit gloom-rock. Those elements would endure, in varying degrees, throughout the band's various lineups and moodswings, but what began as stylistic convolution gradually turned into intricacy, making Unrest—at its peak—one of the underground's most fruitfully unpredictable bands.

While **Tink of S.E.** is the commonly agreed-upon moniker bestowed upon the band's first widely available album, the diffuse art project was actually titled differently on each of the individually hand-drawn covers that swathed it upon release. The motley cluster of avant-rock tone bursts inside are reminiscent in theory of jazzbo prog-rockers Henry Cow (an album of whose gave Unrest its name), but in actuality, things like "Live on a Hot August Night" and "The Tundra" are little more than lazy clutter in dada drag. (The potent cover of King Crimson's "21st Century Schizoid Man" and a loopy dub incursion into "Wild Thing" are another matter, however.) Augmented by a handful of early singles (including an endearingly contorted version of "So You Want to Be a Rock'n'Roll Star" from the three-song **Unrest**) and tracks from cassettes (all on Robinson's TeenBeat label), the entire album—which is referred to in the liner notes as **State Champs**—is contained on **Fuck Pussy Galore (& All Her Friends).**

Malcolm X Park isn't much more focused, but the latent Anglophilia of the first outing is manifested in snappier fashion, from The Teardrop Explodes–styled space-pop of "Lucifer Rising" to the title track, which retools the Fall's astringent raving for the moshpit set. A cover of Kiss' "Strutter" denotes both an overly ironic worldview *and* a discouraging disposition to vapid muscle-flexing, but the rest of the album provides enough of a gray-matter workout to compensate. (**Twister** is a twenty-track collection of '80s outtakes.)

Robinson looked a bit closer to home when it came time to seek conceptual inspiration for **Kustom Karnal Blackxploitation,** an album mottled with ghetto-blasts of bizarro-world Afrocentric ranting (like "Kill Whitey" and "Black Power Dynamo") that border on minstrel-show caricature. The thing is, Robinson doesn't seem to carry a lot of malice—even when he's proclaiming himself omnipotent ruler of the universe. Drummer Phil Krauth and bassist David Park set up a fairly wide array of agreeably brittle rhythms for Robinson to splatter with guitar outbursts, ranging from purist hardcore like "Click Click (Fuck Like a Man)" to the fey bubble-pop of "She Makes Me Shake Like a Soul Machine." Talk about cognitive dissonance! **A Factory Record** allows Robinson to indulge his fetish for the Manchester label's seminal '70s work by covering songs by four of its artists: Crawling Chaos, Crispy Ambulance, ESG and Miaow, whose singer, Cath Carroll, would prove to be a lasting icon in the Unrest canon.

That EP pointed the way to the sea change that materialized on the wonderful **Imperial f.f.r.r. (An Imperial Full Frequency Range Recording),** a giddy blend of ethereal cotton-candy pop, go-go-influenced trance-grooves, new wavey white-funk and bracing guitar math; it's as if years of *New Musical Express* coverage had been boiled down and used to fertilize the band's rich creative loam. The album's crucial mechanism is Robinson's non-stop kinetic strumming, which provides the urgent underpinning for sexy tunes like "Cherry Cream On," a song that would appear, with slight variations, under several different titles on scattered singles. As Robinson plays the role of funk-driven shaman, new bassist Bridget Cross—fresh from a nascent version of Velocity Girl—judiciously peppers the mix with sweet bills and coos (as on the death-obsessed "June") that provide plenty of tension, given their disturbing subtext. The **Isabel Bishop** mini-album augments **Imperial**'s sweetly acoustic ode to the painter, whose granddaughter was Robinson's long-time girlfriend, with six archival tracks, including the carnal classic "Yes She Is My Skinhead Girl." (That song is one of the four added to **Imperial**'s expanded British edition, which has completely different artwork.)

The title track of **Bavarian Mods,** which ponders a world overrun by lederhosen-wearing rude boys, is one of the more bizarre entreaties to come down the pike in a Vespa's age; Robinson ups the ante by playing it off a cover of Argent's "God Gave Rock and Roll to You." On the heels of that, **Cath Carroll** seems positively normal (if slightly stalker-ish) in its lionizing of the singer/journalist, whom Robinson subsequently signed to record for TeenBeat. The commercial version of the EP contains but one song ("Where Are All Those Puerto Rican Boys?") that doesn't appear on **Perfect Teeth,** but a widely distributed promo edition adds a thirty-three-minute go-go/kraut-rock workout on "Hydro."

Beyond the sparkling pop perfection of "Cath Carroll" ("is going to take me for a ride!"), **Perfect Teeth** suffers from an energy shortage severe enough to make liquid No-Doz an ideal mouthwash. The album has its charming moments (like the gooey "Make Out Club"), but the pervasive sense of gentility keeps any of the songs from getting under the skin. Perfect for tea parties, but that's about it.

The trio then split, tying up some loose ends with **B.P.M.,** a compendium of remixes and previously unreleased cuts that reflects most of the band's many sides to good effect. Chugging through two versions of Family Fodder's giddy "Winona Ryder" and another version of "Hydrofoil," Unrest is at its most breezily unaffected. A nice way to bow out.

Robinson and Cross went on to form Air Miami with drummer Gabriel Stout; the new trio doesn't stray far from the path blazed by Unrest. The bubblegum aftertaste left by segments of **Me. Me. Me.** is a bit too strong when Robinson indulges his propensity for creating inconsequential chantalongs like "World Cup Fever," but he offsets that with reams of bracing, Fire Engines–styled guitar and a guileless new wave sensibility (see "Dolphin Expressway") that should sway all but the most diehard Anglophobe. Cross takes more vocal turns (most notably the creamy, Casio-flecked "Afternoon Train"), which is assuredly a good thing; the two also engage in some post-mod Sonny & Cher duets, which isn't. **Fuck You, Tiger** (which unfortunately has no title track) joins two fairly radical remixes of album tracks with a pair of lovely new songs, including the shimmering Jimmy Webb analogue "Warm Miami May." Robinson subsequently formed Olympic Death Squad, a one-man band he unveiled on 1996's **Blue** album.

As Mark E, Robinson channels the spirit of an airport lounge performer possessed with never-to-be-fulfilled Vegas ambitions. **Sammy Supreme My Man** is an oddly touching tribute to Sammy Davis, Jr., replete with Vegas-tinged raps and love-you-man banter that's strictly coolsville.

On his first solo album, Krauth also takes a shot at late '60s adult pop, betraying an unexpected affinity for the baroque stylings of AM confectioners like the Association and Fifth Dimension—either of whom would have had a ball swinging through something like the opening "Rainy Days." While Krauth's voice lacks range (to say the least), his enthusiasm is positively infectious, particularly on upbeat tracks like "You've Changed" and the mildly psychedelic "Taste of Beauty." [dss]

See also *Grenadine, Velocity Girl.*

UNSANE

Unsane (Matador) 1991
Singles 89–92 (Matador) 1992
Total Destruction (Matador/Atlantic) 1994
The Peel Sessions EP (Matador) 1994
Scattered, Smothered and Covered (Amphetamine Reptile) 1995

From the blood-soaked crime scene photos that adorn the sleeves of its releases to the unmitigated aggression of its sonic attack, New York's Unsane spends most of its time on the "wrong" side of the tracks separating mere catharsis from genuine menace. Metalheads and hardcore punks alike might find varying degrees of satisfaction in the grinding gears of the Unsane machine, but you'd be hard-pressed to fit the band—especially the early singles compiled on **89–92** (red-river bathtub)—into a genus with nearly as much socially redeeming value as either of those.

On its raw full-length debut (decapitated body on train tracks), the trio lurches through virtually structure-free material with a bipolar propensity for mixing precision and unbalance. Guitarist Chris Spencer's overly distorted vocals screech atop the graceful-yet-pugilistic rhythms anchored by drummer Charlie Ondras, who died of a heroin overdose shortly after the album's release. After an extended period of retrenchment, Spencer and bassist Pete Shore linked with ex-Swans drummer Vinny Signorelli for **Total Destruction** (gore-covered radiator grille), an even *more* abrasive collection of songs, a disconcerting number of which give off dumbed-down thrash-metal vibes. Still, feral tracks like "Body Bomb" run through the system with the speed (and side effects) of flesh-eating bacteria.

After parting ways with Matador, Unsane cast its lot with Amphetamine Reptile's hatecore HQ for **Scattered, Smothered and Covered.** The sonic tumult is still manifest, with the trio (including new bassist Dave Curran) lobbing contrapuntal grenades in what sounds like an aural game of *Rollerball.* The songs, however, lack some of their predecessors' inherent urgency. The **Peel Sessions** EP marries two of those BBC rituals—an incendiary eleven-minute, four-song medley recorded with Ondras in '91 and five slightly more measured tracks cut with Signorelli in '92. [dss]

See also *Action Swingers, Swans.*

UNWOUND

Fake Train (Kill Rock Stars) 1993
New Plastic Ideas (Kill Rock Stars) 1994
The Future of What (Kill Rock Stars) 1995
Unwound (Punk in My Vitamins) 1995
Repetition (Kill Rock Stars) 1996

The power trio of singer/guitarist Justin Trosper, bassist Vern Rumsey and drummer Sara Lund may not make memorable songs per se, but Unwound does make an indelible *sensation.* Flaunting serious noise science that recalls but rarely imitates Fugazi, Slint and Sonic Youth, this Tumwater, Washington (near Olympia), band exudes an almost palpable existential rage, largely dispensing with melody to rely on a tensely wrought wall of guitar clamor that overlaps like so many layers of steel fencing. Boldly experimental and yet emotionally vital, the band produces what the liner notes to its second album term "progressive Punk Rock."

The stark **Fake Train** boasts a formidable dynamic range, from the meditative instrumental "Were, Are and Was or Is," which pours sublimely chirping feedback over dappled guitar arpeggios, through the piledriving "Pure Pain Sugar" and up to the apoplectic heights of "Lucky Acid" and the schizo noise bursts of the aptly named "Nervous Energy." There are few hooks and Trosper's voice rarely veers from a generic indie-rock holler, but those deficiencies are more than compensated for by the band's inventive attack (especially by Lund) and the sheer number of cool sounds and textures that festoon every track.

New Plastic Ideas finds Unwound branching out

into propulsive, odd meters, a vastly bigger sound and even more traumatic contrasts between loud and soft, pulling the arty riffage into much tighter focus. There's even something resembling melody emerging on songs such as "Envelope," "Hexenzsene" and the downright Cure-ish instrumental "Abstraktions"—but the band's strength remains the art of noise, as in the staccato dissonance of "All Souls Day" and the way the roiling mass of distortion in "Usual Dosage" gives way to a lambent middle passage of tinkling, ringing tones.

Although **The Future of What** goes in for slightly more conventional song structures, the lung-shredding "New Energy" makes it clear straightaway that the band has only honed its edge. Trosper hits new heights with the cyclonic drone that closes "Natural Disasters," the prismatic harmonics of "Re-enact the Crime" and the masterful three-minute feedback aria that ends the record. And then there's the curious keyboard loop track, "Pardon My French"; the effect is of well-calculated disorientation—much like the rest of Unwound's music.

The band's 1995 self-titled album is actually its debut, recorded in 1992 with original drummer Brandt Sandeno but not released at the time because the group felt it was no longer representative of its sound after Sandeno left. Which is very true—**Unwound** is a manic, bilious spew, more straightforward and even catchy, with little of the tricky guitarchitecture and chiaroscuro dynamics the band would later make such a big part of its sound. Still, the relentless, intense anger makes it a revealing document of this band's stormy emotional roots. And truth be told, it's one of their best.

Continuing Unwound's onward-and-upward creative arc, **Repetition** raises the ante further from **The Future of What.** Clanging guitar noise is only one of the band's tools here; the album's taut structural designs are equally effective whether charged with carefully wielded aggression ("Fingernails on a Chalkboard," the febrile and funky "Message Received"), fed into comely barbed-wire pop songs ("Lowest Common Denominator," "Lady Elect"), translated into dubby instrumental grooves ("Sensible") or set free with saxophone in the jazz jam freakout "Go to Dallas and Take a Left." **Repetition** is a sharp kick in the head that clears out the cobwebs and stimulates the imagination. [ma/i]

UPPER CRUST

Let Them Eat Rock (Upstart) 1995

With their magisterial wigs, frilly shirts, made-up names and three-farthing British accents, Boston's Upper Crust evokes a long-gone era—namely, the '60s, when gimmick bands were as common as Sheep. Groups that dress up and write topical theme songs usually do so because they can't get anywhere on their music, and that would certainly seem to be the case with the five indolent artistocats of the Upper Crust, formerly a New England surf band called the Clamdiggers with roots in such credible combos as the Lyres, Bags and Titanics. The half-hour-long **Let Them Eat Rock** quotes liberally from AC/DC ("Let Them Eat Rock," "Little Lord Fauntleroy"), the Troggs ("RSVP," "Who's Who of Love"), Sex Pistols ("Minuet") and Vapors ("Little Rickshaw Boy"), adding nothing but *Mad*-level parody lyrics to the rote garage-rock. Off with their heads. [i]

URBAN DANCE SQUAD

Mental Floss for the Globe (Hol. Ariola) 1989 (Arista) 1990
Mental Relapse EP (Arista) 1991
Life 'n Perspectives of a Genuine Crossover (Arista) 1991
Persona Non Grata (Virgin) 1995

Cultural pluralists have been extolling the possibilities inherent in rap/metal fusion since the days of Run–DMC's "Rock Box," but few bands have come up with a hybrid as gleefully schizophrenic as that found on **Mental Floss for the Globe,** the first volley from this Holland-based five-piece. Noisy, funky and endlessly variegated, UDS's debut is possibly the quintessential hip-metal (heavy-hop?) album. On tracks like "Prayer for My Demo" (predating the Pooh Sticks song of the same name) and "No Kid," guitarist Tres Manos pulls everything from Hendrix to Ry Cooder out of his bag of tricks, while the fluid rhythm section keeps things percolating and rapper Rudeboy Remington rants atop the skronk-heavy effects assembled by DJ DNA. Country-western, raga rock, dub, free jazz—it all gets thrown into the multi-culti stew, making for a truly brain-blasting platter. **Mental Relapse** footnotes the LP with a pair of alternate versions and two live takes, plus the hip-hoppy slide-guitar blues tale entitled "Hitchhike H.D."

After headbangers and homeboys alike responded with a collective shrug to **Mental Floss**' everything-*and*-the-kitchen-sink approach, UDS came back with a more conventional-sounding funk-metal record that downplays DNA's wall-of-noise predilections. **Life 'n Perspectives of a Genuine Crossover** has some enjoyable tracks (notably the raging "Comeback" and the easy-grooving "Routine," a meditation on boredom that finds Rudeboy contemplating "taking a bath with my toaster"), but elsewhere the band sounds like a Red Hot Chili Peppers clone.

That trend continues on **Persona Non Grata,** which finds DJ DNA gone and Tres Manos making like a macho guitar hero at every turn. Produced by Phil Nicolo (Cypress Hill, Urge Overkill) and one, uh, Stiff Johnson, **Persona Non Grata** sounds like a shameless bid for acceptance by the metal market. The stripped-down approach yields some lowbrow kicks—the lumbering riffology of "No Honestly" and "Self-sufficient Snake" would do any band of Black Sabbath worshipers proud—but the embrace of such a one-dimensional strategy is disheartening. [ts]

URGE OVERKILL

Strange, I . . . EP (Ruthless) 1986
Jesus Urge Superstar (Touch and Go) 1989
Americruiser (Touch and Go) 1990
The SuperSonic Storybook (Touch and Go) 1991
The Urge Overkill Stull EP (Touch and Go) 1992
Saturation (Geffen) 1993
Exit the Dragon (Geffen) 1995

Of far more profound cultural relevance to semioticians and hometown pals than open-eared music fans outside Chicago, conceptual super-poseurs Urge Overkill have never let a serious or original musical thought get in the way of a flashy uniform, a swinging medallion, a styling hairstyle or other tropes of their camp-hip-cred '70s crud-rock pretensions. Though devoted to being one of the best-looking bands around, the trio has rarely shown more than passing concern for making records that sound like anything. Disinclined to do a lot more than occasionally simulate relevant archetypes, Urge is all fantasy and spin: a repeated promise that never delivers the goods. The band *has* gotten appreciably better at its studio game over the years—especially since the Geffen-coincident hookup with Philadelphia's no-nonsense Butcher Brothers (Joe and Phil Nicolo, better known as hip-hop producers)—but the records' paucity of content leaves even the band's most seemingly ambitious efforts sounding weak-willed and trivial.

Following a premature Steve-Albini-engineered-and-issued EP (he had a label called Ruthless before Eazy-E), National "Nash" Kato (vocals, guitar; real name Nathan Katruud), Eddie "King" Roeser (vocals, bass, later guitar) and drummer Jack Watt ("The Jaguar") cut the awful-sounding **Jesus Urge Superstar** with Albini; the murk of thick mid-tempo guitar rock does nothing to prove the existence of songs, much less any audible trace of junk-culture devotion. Lacking an audio personality, the band attaches promising titles ("Dump Dump Dump," "God Flintstone," "The Polaroid Doll") to shapeless, styleless tossoffs and leaves it at that.

Butch Vig's production of **Americruiser** (the CD of which includes the first LP and a cover of "Wichita Lineman" from a single) cleans the sound up enough to reveal the thin strings, clunky tempos and weak hooks holding the songs together. Sort of tuneful roots-punk (roughed-up Replacements minus the Stones impulse), the brief album sets out with the band's best idea yet ("Ticket to LA")—and then fails to catch the plane it's on. Clunky, unkempt and focused with all the accuracy of a drunk waving a shotgun, **Americruiser** would be nothing if not for its deluxe furnishings.

With drummer Blackie Onassis (Johnny Rowan) entering the picture, **The SuperSonic Storybook** throws even choppier rhythms into a poppier, more streamlined attack; for the first time, both the arrangements and the vocals seem premeditated. The self-production is competent if a bit wooly in spots; the song titles (including a straight-faced tribute to the new guy, "(Today Is) Blackie's Birthday") still read better than the tunes sound. "Henhough: The Greatest Story Ever Told" pushes the cooler-than-you envelope with a twangy but ponderous frontier-orphans ballad; a straight, melodramatic rendition of Hot Chocolate's "Emma" typifies the band's bone-dry sense of wit, which adds nothing to the original except the certainty that the parodic gesture is genius enough.

Following that same line of reasoning, the **Stull** EP begins with a shmeary, overbearing and irony-drenched rendition of Neil Diamond's "Girl, You'll Be a Woman Soon" that proved to be a charm for the group several years later when it fit in with the similarly smarmy obsessions of Quentin Tarantino, who folded it into *Pulp Fiction,* from where it become a breakout hit of sorts. Otherwise, the bright-sounding five-song batch (co-produced by Kramer) is most notable for the band's raging punk cover of the impossibly obscure "Stitches in My Head" (from a 1977 single by New York's Alan Milman Sect) and the rambling "Goodbye to Guyville," whose titular argot for the Chicago indie-rock scene was appropriated by Liz Phair for the name of her first album.

Successfully launched from **Stull**'s stabilizing orbit, **Saturation** leads Urge Overkill into the real world, with more credible songs than they've ever seen in one place and a distinctive mainstream rock sound that doesn't simply force its cool down your throat. With Kato's poised whiskey baritone—Gregg Allman meets Rob Tyner—leading the charge, "Sister Havana," "Positive Bleeding" and "Bottle of Fur" strap together memorable hard-rock melodies and self-conscious style footnotes to Kiss, T.Rex, the Cars and others. Even on the lesser songs, the Butcher Brothers hammer the riff-at-the-ready trio into concise, taut shapes, keeping numbers rolling along with solid centers and brassy surfaces. Still too arch and inconsistent for full-scale appreciation ("Erica Kane" is another great title wasted on a nothing song), **Saturation** is the first Urge album that isn't simply an embarrassment.

After that relative pinnacle, Urge took a calmer approach—more power-pop than flaming rock—on **Exit the Dragon,** letting the Butchers soften the edges and trim away the gloss for a warm'n'fuzzy tube distortion frig. Exchanging obvious highlights for a not-quite-adequate layer of songwriting stability, the trio gets by—barely—through the elevated skill of its diverse presentation. The Lemonheads-like custard is sprinkled with sonic references to the Cars, Sweet, Stones, Bowie and Replacements, which tart up commendable songs like "The Break," "Need Some Air," "Take Me," "And You'll Say" and the strenuously restrained "Somebody Else's Body." Otherwise, **Exit the Dragon**—ending ignominiously with the absurd and ineffectual nine-minute epic "Digital Black Epilogue"—drags along through various permutations of flat, tired, bland and weak. [i]

U.S. SAUCER

My Company Is Misery (Amarillo) 1992
Tender Places Come From Nothing (Amarillo) 1994
United States Saucer (Ger. Return to Sender/Normal) 1996

Taking drummerless inspiration from old-time country music and the freedom to make craggy noise from indie-rock, the Bay Area's U.S. Saucer—singer/bassist David Tholfsen, singer/guitarist Margaret Murray (also of SF Seals and the Zip Code Rapists spinoff, Three Doctors Band) and, moonlighting from Thinking Fellers Union Local 282, Brian Hageman on guitar and viola—drowsily explores diverse shades of soft and loud, firm and flexible, tight and loose on **My Company Is Misery.** Despite fascinating passages of cagey, distorted electricity, the album's predominant hue comes from skeins of nearly subliminal acoustic eloquence. If that suggests a ponderous artistry, Tholfsen's melodramatic voice, which smacks of condescending irony, pretentious wordplay ("Foregone Hormone," "Up Chuck," couplets like "Granger monger glides on a pool / Of effluent / Red Granger hordes fluids / To all corners") and the cow noises that gussy up a handsome, low-powered cover of Lowell George's "Willin'" all serve to undercut the implicit seriousness, making the ultimate dichotomy of **My Company Is Misery** its bewildering intent.

The second album takes fewer fliers and is thus a lot easier to live with. With Hageman resting his viola, Tholfsen partially tames his mannered vocals on **Tender Places Come From Nothing,** testing a delivery that doesn't scour the outback so hard; he occasionally organizes appealing harmonies with Murray. As she did the first time out, Murray offers a mournful lead vocal (on "His Room"); Hageman steps up to the mic as well, giving mostly spoken voice to his own atmospheric "Hell Rules." The gently propulsive electric arrangements of originals, traditionals (an egregiously off-key "Silent Night") and offbeat covers (the mock-Mexicana of Terry Gilkyson's "Ride Away Vaquero," "Hold on Dear Brother," written by Blondie Chaplin and Ricky Fataar, who once played together in the Beach Boys) maintain a reliably desirable consistency, leaving Tholfsen's two carefully noted solo turns—Tom T. Hall's "I Love . . ." and a bizarre string-bass-plus-baritone/falsetto deconstruction of Merle Haggard's "Today I Started Loving Her Again"—to carry the weirdness weight. File under unexplained phenomena. [i]

See also *Barbara Manning, Thinking Fellers Union Local 282, Zip Code Rapists.*

US3

Hand on the Torch (Blue Note) 1994

The so-called acid-jazz movement that peaked in the early '90s was a lot like the white blues revival of the late '60s: most of the prime movers, while respectful enough, were too young to really grasp the significance of their source material. Hence, it became as much a fashion statement as a bona fide musical (r)evolution. Working as US3, Londoners Geoff Wilkinson and Mel Simpson—thirtysomething jazzbos making their livelihoods in journalism and concert promotion (Wilkinson) and studio work (Simpson)—proved the exception to the rule. Commingling serious players, street-savvy rappers and cleverly deployed hard bop samples, they created a sound at once cerebrally and pelvically involving.

The fluid aggregation had its biggest hit with "Cantaloop (Flip Fantasia)," which spiraled an incredibly catchy—if somewhat fluffy—tune from a vintage Benny Green sample. For that song and the rest of **Hand on the Torch,** Simpson and Wilkinson dip deep into their record collections (contractually including the entire Blue Note archive) to bite from sides by Art Blakey and Thelonious Monk. Over the top of their tracks, the English and American rappers (Rahsaan, Tukka Yoot and Kobie Powell) spin tales that range from the intense (the penitentiary paean "Eleven Long Years") to the inane (the crotch-grabbing "I Got It Goin' On"). [dss]

UTAH SAINTS

Something Good EP (ffrr/London) 1992
Utah Saints (ffrr/London) 1992

Poised stylistically and chronologically between the cut-and-paste acid-house of Bomb the Bass and M/A/R/R/S and the towering trip-hop of the Chemical Brothers, Britain's Utah Saints—DJs/artists Jez Willis and Tim Garbutt—took samples of other people's records and fashioned them into great singles. The first, "What Can You Do for Me," incorporates sweet bits from Gwen Guthrie ("Ain't Nothin' Going on but the Rent") and Eurythmics ("There Must Be an Angel Playing With My Heart," a sample the boys would recycle again when they remixed Annie Lennox's "Little Bird" in 1994). The subsequent "Something Good" built its hook around a snippet of Kate Bush's "Cloudbusting," the first time Bush authorized any such appropriation of her work. Both those cuts, in multiple versions, appear on the **Something Good** EP and the eponymous album that followed it, alongside equally worthy tracks like "Trance Atlantic Glide" (meant to be played at either 45 or 33 rpm) and a surprisingly faithful cover of Simple Minds' "New Gold Dream (81–82–83–84)." Since that initial surge of activity, however, Willis and Garbutt have been relatively inactive as recording artists, devoting their energies to remixing (including a bizarre take on the Osmonds' "Crazy Horses"), although they did release a new single, "Ohio," in late 1995. [kbr]

U2

Boy (Island) 1980
October (Island) 1981
War (Island) 1983
Under a Blood Red Sky (Island) 1983
The Unforgettable Fire (Island) 1984
Wide Awake in America EP (Island) 1985
The Joshua Tree (Island) 1987
Rattle and Hum (Island) 1988
Achtung Baby (Island) 1991
One EP (Island) 1992
Zooropa (Island) 1993

PASSENGERS

Original Soundtracks 1 (Island) 1995

Empirical science recognizes two forms of testing, only one of which—weighing a pebble, say, or candling an egg—is considered non-destructive. It's the other investigative process that causes irreparable changes to the object being examined. In human terms, this can be characterized as the how-will-you-know-if-you-don't-try-it quandary. In the discipline of rock, the great what-if questions—like what happens to a fiery, idealistic young band that becomes unthinkably popular and still wants to respect itself in the morning—can only be answered by living through the experience and extracting whatever data and conclusions might emerge. If the career of U2 is seen as some sort of cosmic sociology project, the results are more confusing than illuminating, and the damage to the subjects is unmistakable. As pivotal collaborator Brian Eno might have observed in one of his oblique strategy sessions, the path from where you mean to go to where you ultimately wind up is rarely a straight line.

All the ironic prophecy anyone need hear regarding U2 is right there in "I Will Follow," the sweeping declaration that opens **Boy:** a tiny tape error and a nearly inaudible count-off signifying both the cavalier ignorance of buffed niceties and the commitment to live all-together-now music-making, the distant herald of the Edge's distinctive two-note riff drama, Larry Mullen Jr.'s firing drum reports, the weird-but-right glockenspiel tinkles, Bono's titular invocation and finally Adam Clayton's surprising bass propulsion. And then the lyrics, sung as a passionate teenager's soulful cry to unmarked heavens: "I was on the outside when you said, you said you needed me / I was looking at myself / I was blind I could not see / A boy tries hard to be a man."

Coming straight from the outside of rock convention, the unprecedented Dublin quartet followed nobody in its procession toward locating and satisfying a vast need among the world's three-chords-and-the-truth-seeking rock audience. The boys tried hard to be men, and within a few years had lost every bit of their childlike grace, with mounting self-obsession and the concomitant inability to see themselves develop into world-class prats. "If he stops to think he starts to cry."

A hasty reckoning of U2's past would note that the exploratory but uneven **Boy** mainly broke ground for the monumentally confident and focused **War** ("Sunday Bloody Sunday," "Two Hearts Beat as One," "New Year's Day"), one of the most original, exciting and emotional rock albums of the 1980s. Sandwiched between them, however, **October** served notice that the band's creative highs were going to exact a price; between the demonstrations of growing artistic power that begin and end the record ("Gloria," "I Fall Down," "I Threw a Brick Through a Window," "Is That All?"), the center is an effort to renounce rock's primacy in exaggerated indulgences that lead U2 nowhere. The Edge's emergence as a refined pianist and Bono's book-reading ("Stranger in a Strange Land") are especially bad omens.

U2 capped off this first era with a recapitulation and proof of their commanding live presence: **Under a Blood Red Sky,** eight dynamic numbers drawn from all three albums.

Abandoning the proven commercial intuition of producer Steve Lillywhite, U2 began a fascinating long-term studio alliance with Brian Eno and Daniel Lanois on **The Unforgettable Fire.** On this first collaboration, the band benefits immeasurably from its new friends' extravagant skill at subtle sound-shaping without being overwhelmed by it. The three-dimensional textures stay true to U2's origins for the most part but expand enthusiastically into new realms, and the album's smooth shifts—from the tricky shadings of "A Sort of Homecoming" to the direct rock power of "Pride (In the Name of Love)," the wally instrumental "4th of July" to the hypnotically gorgeous "Bad"—are accomplished with the aplomb of a well-tuned machine. The Edge, for one, takes to the richer canvases with abundant imagination, and his contributions to the album, both loudly extroverted and expressively fine, are stupendous. But then there's Bono. In addition to his overly studied singing—which is mostly fine but occasionally discloses too much obvious stage direction—his artistic pretensions (and a growing obsession with the US: "Pride" and "MLK" are both about Martin Luther King) head him the wrong way down such blinkered cul-de-sacs as "Elvis Presley and America" and "Indian Summer Sky."

For a budget-priced epiphany along similar lines, check out the mesmerizing eight-minute live version of "Bad" on **Wide Awake in America,** an odd release that also contains a concert version of "A Sort of Homecoming" and two worthwhile studio outtakes: "Three Sunrises" and "Love Comes Tumbling."

The Joshua Tree completes the second phase in U2's development, vaulting the group into the commercial stratosphere while delivering its final statement on the subject of basic guitar-bass-drums electric pop music. As Eno and Lanois keep a low stylistic profile, the album gets off to a magnificent start with "Where the Streets Have No Name," "I Still Haven't Found What I'm Looking For" and "With or Without You," tracks that crystallize U2's finest attributes into a triptych of absolutely perfect hit singles. But trouble lurks in the melodramatically recited "Bullet the Blue Sky," and the album alternates between preciousness and overstatement from there, with only a few balancing acts ("In God's Country," "Trip Through Your Wires") that don't teeter over. While **The Joshua Tree** brought U2 the success it always seemed to be preparing for, the album also raised the specter of dubious creative ambitions as yet unimagined.

You can watch U2's artistic equilibrium crumbling in **Rattle and Hum.** The dismaying documentary film (for which the half-live/half-studio album serves as soundtrack) reveals the messianic Bono to have become a superstar all too conscious of his position and power. Hinged by the unwarranted savior's introduction to "Helter Skelter" ("This is a song Charles Manson stole from the Beatles—we're stealing it back") and his disconcertingly authoritarian delivery of "Pride (In the Name of Love)," the album's concert tracks convey more of Bono's burgeoning demagoguery than the band's still-thrilling live presence. And beyond the bracingly direct "Desire," "When Love Comes to Town" (a bizarre collaboration with B. B. King) and a swinging horn-charged tribute to Billie Holiday ("Angel of Harlem"), the new songs produced by Jimmy Iovine aren't very good.

Achtung Baby inverts U2's usual album design: rather than tuck away its stylistic adventures and fingerpainting behind immediately recognizable pop offerings, the group announces its reinvention with the lead-off hitters: "Zoo Station" metal-plates an unfamiliar construction into a thick, disorienting tunnel of clattery drums and partially distorted vocals, while "Even Better Than the Real Thing" disguises a straightforward structure in skittering dance rhythms and slithery layered-soul vocals. Although there are more sonic shocks ("The Fly," the shamble-beat and clubbable funk elements of the pretty "Mysterious Ways"), a lot of what follows is more traditional than the arcane approaches of Eno/Lanois' production at first suggests. "One" is nothing new; the lovely "Who's Gonna Ride Your Wild Horses" rises and falls on the same elementary two-chord progression the Edge has been recycling productively for years; the reggae-informed "Tryin' to Throw Your Arms Around the World" is likewise uncomplicated, regardless of its surprising tonal balance.

More significant than the specific musical inventions inaugurated here, U2's great leap forward into the '90s is to free itself of the past, saving some treasured old bits but using them in a new context that should, by rights, not be considered the work of the same band. Taking inspiration from both Bowie's late-'70s Eno era (**Low, Heroes** and **Lodger**) and the recent sound of European techno, U2 funnels it into songs that are more consistently personal, intimate (most are unhappily addressed man-to-woman) and downhearted than those on any album in the band's prior catalogue. Stepping cleanly off the ledge with **Achtung Baby,** U2 finds itself able to fly into a new era rather than plummet to its destruction.

The **One** EP, with its royalties donated to AIDS research, contains the wacky/cool "Lady With the Spinning Head (UVI)," a cloying falsetto cover of Lou Reed's "Satellite of Love" and a seven-minute Youth remix of the already abstruse disco interpretation of "Night and Day," the Cole Porter song U2 recorded for the first **Red Hot + Blue** fund-raising album.

Having willed itself into a creative vacuum that could easily have turned into freefall (and very nearly did on the conceptually insane, musically weak Zoo TV tour), U2 made a strong landing on **Zooropa.** Three production hands—Eno, the Edge and Flood (Depeche Mode, Nine Inch Nails, Erasure)—guide the band out of rock's forest and into the uncertain world of rhythm-driven ambient soundscapes, challenging Bono to sing his way back to safety. It's as if the Edge were charging headlong into the future, shrugging off the stipulation of songs as U2's métier and daring his bandmates to keep up. And they do: Bono's lyrics and delivery come from an entirely new place. In "Lemon," he field-tests a hair-raising falsetto *and* a close simulation of David Bowie; evidently satisfied with the results, he adapts the same techniques elsewhere on the album. Borrowed back from the soundtrack to Wim Wenders' *Faraway, So Close,* the lazy "Stay (Faraway, So Close!)" encapsulates the small-scale cinematics that effectively replace the futile grand panoramas of yore: "Green light, 7-Eleven / You stop for a pack of cigarettes / You don't smoke, don't even want to / I see you check your change." The sense of ennui and global discomfort that infects much of the album—dedicated to Charles Bukowski, the nervous "Dirty Day" offers, "If you need somebody to blame / Throw a rock in the air / You're bound to hit someone guilty"—gives purpose and meaning to the music, an invigorating blend of samples, treatments, dance beats, alluring melodies, inside-out arrangements and an overall approach that disconnects rather than unifies the ten tracks.

Content-wise, the record is all over the place. Bono assesses the state of things in the believably genuine "Some Days Are Better Than Others" and declares his religious faith in "The First Time." Breaking custom in a big way, the Edge takes the mic to recite the completely unnatural-sounding and forbidding "Numb" in a grippingly sedated voice. Despite long odds, **Zooropa** makes most such why-not ideas pay off; still, it was a fool's bet for the band to have Johnny Cash sing "The Wanderer" to close the LP.

Although not commercially released, a CD of celebrity dance remixes (by Massive Attack, David Morales and others) was sent to members of U2's fan club in 1995. The hour-long **Melon: Remixes for Propaganda** contains alternate versions of **Zooropa**'s "Lemon" and "Numb," **Achtung Baby**'s "Mysterious Ways" and "Even Better Than the Real Thing" and two non-LP songs, eviscerating the band's careful creations for pointless club utility.

But even **Melon,** for those who heard it, was inadequate preparation for the eccentric orbit on which the group was about to embark. Treating the new world terra firma of **Zooropa** as if it were an especially springy trampoline, U2 and Eno used it to achieve escape velocity in the guise of Passengers on **Original Soundtracks 1.** Following the leader's well-documented expertise in creating music for nonexistent films (Eno's dryly detailed ersatz annotation underscores his role), the ad hoc quintet entertains itself mucking around in trendy ambient, techno and jungle grooves that are premixed to sound like the end results of a deconstruction process. That these rhythmic nothings have been whisked together by rock'n'roll superstars on a busman's holiday does nothing to elevate the tracks' listenability. Dilettantes should leave wordless dance music to more accomplished artisans. The album is, however, seeded with a handful of actual songs, which are flimsy **Zooropa** afterbirths ("Slug"), exotic adventures ("Ito Okashi," sung by Japan's Holi) or pure farce. "Miss Sarajevo" trundles Luciano Pavarotti into the bridge of a string-sodden ballad; "Elvis Ate America" isolates an ambivalent figure in Bono's semiotic sensibilities and, following the riff poetry prototype he unveiled in a 1994 speech inducting Bob Marley into the Rock and Roll Hall of Fame, sneers at him with condescending contempt. Last laughs can be mighty bitter, and Bono is hardly in a position to be pointing fingers at little rock gods who've lost their way. [i]

See also *Michael Brook, Brian Eno.*

UZI

See *Come.*

VACANT LOT

. . . Because They Can (Can. Shake/Cargo) 1992
Wrong (Can. Shake/Cargo) 1993
Shake Well (Can. Shake) 1995

TRICK BABYS

Player (Go-Kart) 1995

DA WILLYS

Satuhday Nite Palsy (Ger. Brake Out) 1990

Following in the great New York tradition of the Speedies (down to a common high school), the Vacant Lot purified the sound of pop-punk to its catchy essence, consigned the Ramones comic-book mentality to cartoon artwork and aspired to the panache of teen-dream stardom without ever truly outgrowing the city's clubs. Tight, energetic and bursting with cool tunes played fast enough to spin heads, the Vacant Lot—an outgrowth of the unrecorded Rat Bastards, which transmuted into the Devil Dogs when singer/guitarist Pete Ciccone left—is a phenomenal live band that very nearly managed to get the same charge going on the first of their three studio albums.

Recorded two years before its release, the twelve-song, twenty-seven-minute **. . . Because They Can** is an accurate taste of the quartet's rollicking exuberance. Singing calmly in an ordinary voice over Mitro's hot-wired guitar interjections, Ciccone gives originals like "Hard Hard Time," "I Won't Say I'm Sorry" and "Good as Gone" the same pep as superspeed covers of the We Five's "You Were on My Mind" and the Dictators' "Loyola." (That song's author, Andy Shernoff, is one of the album's producers.) A couple of obviously Ramones-styled numbers are distinctly sub-par, but the rest ring as true as '78 classics.

Recorded as the Lot was falling apart, the shabby-sounding **Wrong** lacks the earlier disc's sonic focus and drive. The album benefits from a growing '60s sensibility but overindulges the band's proto-Ramones fixation ("Dee Dee Said," the copycat "Do It Tomorrow") and buries the few worthwhile tracks ("Blue, My Mind," "Remember Me," "Believe In") in the harsh clatter of Nitebob's inept production.

The band's leaders split between the recording and release of **Wrong;** Mitro got custody of the original rhythm section (drummer Paul Corio and bassist Brett Wilder) and formed Trick Babys, leaving Ciccone to draft a new lineup under the Vacant Lot sign. To Ciccone's credit, the new quartet's **Shake Well** is very nearly as good as **. . . Because They Can**—solidly written, cleanly produced and spunkily performed. Highlights of an altogether swell collection of breathlessly revved-up romantic sparklers that take no chances and make no gaffes: "Anticipation," "Sweetest Sound" and "Feel Better."

Nitebob improves only marginally on his **Wrong** knob-twiddling as producer of the Trick Babys' debut, but the bluesy theatrics of big-voiced singer Lynne Von (Schlichting, formerly of Da Willys) are so domineering that it doesn't really matter how the band is recorded. Kitschy lyrical inventions ("Otto's Squid Pit," "Red Leather Couch"), a searing instrumental entitled "Camel Chips" and a neatly diverse trio of covers (the bubblegum chestnut "Quick Joey Small," Brenda Lee's "Sweet Nothin's" and the Isley Brothers' "Warpath") bathe the rough and randy **Player** in the pungent aroma of vintage rock'n'roll, and Mitro's guitar playing both outlines and fills in the songs. Ultimately, though, Von's throaty Shangri-La from hell growling is the deciding factor in the Trick Babys' lovability.

In her pre-Babys life, Lynne Von unleashed her gut-busting bellow in the company of a similarly configured quartet with a different orientation. Following a 7-inch EP, **A Case of Da Willys,** in the late '80s, the raucous scum-blues group made **Satuhday Nite Palsy** in the belated image of Big Brother and the Holding Company—if that group had grown up in Alphabet City and had copped different drugs on the way to the studio. While covering Captain Beefheart's "Frying Pan," Da Willys make up a '50s-informed blues-rockin' idiom all their own, giving the leather-lunged singer (who, it must be said, has excellent control) plenty of room to wail and roar on memorable originals like "Love Rollercoaster," "Cryin in the River" and "Finger Poppin." [i]

VANDALIAS

Mach V (Big Deal) 1995

The story that goes with the grand-mod-funk-squad cartoon characters portrayed on this Minneapolis band's first album is that JimJim (guitar/vocals), Bobby (bass) and Alan (guitar) Vandalia are brothers from rural Michigan—a fiction the concurrently published comic-book fable upholds. The liner notes of **Yellow Pills Vol. 1,** however, credits Dan Sarka (who wrote the story) and Peter Daniel, late of the Twin Cities' Raspberries-worshipping Sparrows, as the voices behind the Vandalias.

No matter. The brash but overpoweringly sincere power-pop of **Mach V** is played as if the Vandalias—whoever they are—had invented the form. Unlike most modern practitioners, the Vandalias harbor no brattiness or irony. Heartfelt sentiments like "Watch My Baby Cry," "Mighty Song of Joy" and "Build This House" are delivered straight, with no winking cynicism or spit-in-the-drink chaser. That may defeat the purpose of pop music that knows it will never be popular, but the Vandalias' midwestern forthrightness (a trait shared with the Smoking Popes) is refreshing. And the sweetly sung music—part Beatles-by-way-of-the-Raspberries, a bit Byrds-like and partly in the vein of Material Issue—is unfailingly swell. [i]

S. VAN GELDER

See *His Name Is Alive.*

VASELINES

See *Eugenius.*

BEN VAUGHN COMBO

The Many Moods of Ben Vaughn (Fever/Restless) 1986
Beautiful Thing (Restless) 1987

BEN VAUGHN

Ben Vaughn Blows Your Mind (Restless) 1988
Dressed in Black (Enigma) 1990
Mood Swings ('90–'85 & More) (Restless) 1992
Mono U-S-A (Bar/None) 1993
Instrumental Stylings (Bar/None) 1994
Rambler 65 (Sp. Munster) 1995

KIM FOWLEY AND BEN VAUGHN

Kings of Saturday Night (Sector 2) 1995

Ben Vaughn has been a journeyman singer, songwriter and all-around rock'n'roll classicist since 1978, when he issued his first record—an independent EP—as a member of a Brinsley Schwarz–ish New Jersey band called the Gertz Mountain Budguzzlers. Active as a player and producer in the Philadelphia area, Vaughn made a name for himself as a songwriter when the Morells covered "The Man Who Has Everything" on their classic 1982 album **Shake and Push** and Marshall Crenshaw recorded the witty "I'm Sorry (But So Is Brenda Lee)" on his '85 LP **Downtown.**

Vaughn's own sleepy acoustic/country rendition of "I'm Sorry" is a letdown and, contrary to its title, **The Many Moods** showcases only two main strengths: clever lyrics and catchy tunes, the latter usually grounded in vintage rockabilly and '60s pop-song strategies. Vaughn pokes fun at the tyranny of trendies ("Wrong Haircut," "I Dig Your Wig") and defines down-to-earth suburbanism ("Lookin' for a 7-11," "M-M-Motor Vehicle") with an implicit jab at Bruce Springsteen's poetic bombast. The Combo (Aldo Jones, later of Go to Blazes, on bass, Lonesome Bob on drums and Gus Cordovox on accordion) provides raucous support for Vaughn's unstylized singing and guitar.

Beautiful Thing has a fresh, easygoing feel, but too much restraint can be dangerous: halfway through the first side, this mild-sounding record threatens to slide right off the turntable. The LP has a shortage of sharp wordplay (two exceptions being "Shingaling With Me" and "Big House With a Yard") and too few raveups (a crazed polka called "Gimme, Gimme, Gimme" and the peppy guitar instrumental "Desert Boots" notwithstanding).

Actually recorded with help from his old Combo mates, Vaughn's first official solo album boasts more creative spine and studio energy than **Beautiful Thing,** earning a place in the pop pleasure dome somewhere between Jonathan Richman and Yo La Tengo. The relaxed love songs (like "She's Your Problem Now") on **Blows Your Mind** are delightful; the rootsy rockers ("Darlene," the gentle instrumental "El Rambler Dorado") are lively without getting out of hand.

Vaughn's ascendance into the high council of modern-pop auteurs was confirmed by the guest list on **Dressed in Black,** the cover of which inexplicably pictures him in blackface. Crenshaw, John Hiatt, Alex Chilton, Peter Holsapple, Foster and Lloyd and Gordon Gano of the Violent Femmes all make cameo appearances. Unfortunately, Vaughn's writing isn't up to snuff. Aside from the ripping title track and a great version of "The Man Who Has Everything," the best moments are the Velvet Underground quotation at the beginning of "Cashier Girl" (not exactly an original gimmick) and a fairly amusing ode to facial hair, "Growin' a Beard."

Given the inconsistency of his individual records, **Mood Swings** is the best sample of Vaughn's pithy, playful retro-vision. The twenty-one-track collection includes many of the aforementioned songs; the mix of Combo tracks, solo waxings and the 1984 single "My First Band" (literally recorded in Aldo Jones' parents' basement) captures Vaughn's genuine love of rock'n'roll history, the way he adroitly revitalizes the old ways with contemporary enthusiasm and the genial, anthemic quality of his finest writing. This best-of is truly Vaughn's best record.

Mono U-S-A is Vaughn's variation on the **Basement Tapes** idea crossed with David Bowie's **Pin-Ups:** homemade monaural tapes of obscure covers reflecting Vaughn's deep roots in country, blues and rockabilly. For added authenticity, he cut the album's eighteen songs in 7-track (an 8-track machine with one track on the fritz). The whole notion is entirely too precious, and the one-man-band act doesn't allow for dynamic instrumental interplay (the version of the Ventures' "Exploration in Fear" is soporific, not scary). But there is an intimate charm to these playful, unabashedly nostalgic performances ("Just a Little Bit of You" is Charlie Rich by way of the Sir Douglas Quintet) and admirable nerve in the way Vaughn tackles heavy complaints like Fred Neil's "Blues on the Ceiling" and Willie Nelson's "Suffer in Silence" all by his lonesome.

Rambler 65 is another production-concept project: Vaughn recorded the entire thing on 8-track in his car. With very audible nods to Nick Lowe, simple rock songs like "7 Days Without Love," "Perpetual Motion Machine" and "Heavy Machinery" prove that music can effectively be made, not just enjoyed, in the front seat of a jalopy, but the album isn't spectacular on its own merits. The use of a drum machine and cheap synthesizers in all their dinky splendor points the sound in some odd directions, and "Rock Is Dead" is a bit too corny for its own good, but **Rambler 65** does have its seconds of pleasure. The American model promised by Rhino for '97 is resequenced and remastered.

Even more minimalist in concept and tone, **Instrumental Stylings** does without words and—in many cases—arresting melodies. As a backing-track sketchbook covering everything from zydeco and spaghetti western twang to swinging-bachelor mush and Stax-cum-Creedence blues grooves, the album is okay aural wallpaper. But there is nothing here to make you whistle while you work—and that includes the bonus vocal track, a dull, heavy-rock pastiche called "Stretch Limo" featuring the robotic drone of Dean Ween.

The paucity of new original songs on recent Vaughn records may be due to his increased workload—and success—as a producer. In the early '90s, he worked on superb comeback records by rockabilly legend Charlie Feathers and the late R&B great Arthur Alexander, then Ween's Nashville LP. **Kings of Saturday Night,** a collaboration with LA gadfly Kim

Fowley, isn't in that league by a country mile. Recorded by long-distance, the album consists of instrumental tracks recorded by Vaughn and then overdubbed with Fowley's ghoulish vocals and superficial lyrics. The project must have looked like a fun idea on paper. That's where it should have stayed. [df/i]

SUZANNE VEGA

Suzanne Vega (A&M) 1985
Solitude Standing (A&M) 1987
Days of Open Hand (A&M) 1990
99.9F° (A&M) 1992
Nine Objects of Desire (A&M) 1996

VARIOUS ARTISTS

Tom's Album (A&M) 1991

With "Luka," the Top 5 hit from 1987's **Solitude Standing,** Suzanne Vega's star appeared to be ascendant. She had already outgrown an initial image and role as harbinger of a new folk-informed singer/songwriter era and wasn't about to be creatively seduced into stasis by chart success. While the New Yorker's voice has retained its warm tone and her songs their compassionate intelligence, her subsequent albums have shown her to be less interested in commercial achievement than in exploring increasingly idiosyncratic subjects and sounds.

Days of Open Hand, produced with keyboard player Anton Sanko, moves Vega from the subtle folk-rock of her first two albums to an artier, somewhat glacial sound owing more to Leonard Cohen records of the 1980s. Using an ambitious instrumental mix that includes bouzouki, accordion, strings, sequencers and Fairlights, the songs also venture further afield. "Institution Green" turns voting into a harsh, almost unnatural act; "Tired of Sleeping" evokes **Revolver**-era John Lennon and "Men in a War" is probably the jauntiest song ever written about amputation. About the only element that mars an otherwise fine album is a stiff, airless insularity that occasionally makes **Days of Open Hand** sound like a term paper written by an over-intellectual graduate student.

Moving forward from that flawed declaration of independence, **99.9F°** is a confident statement from a mature artist. Working with producer Mitchell Froom (now her husband), Vega sounds completely at ease in the studio. Many of the songs display a new interest in space and sound, using both in an almost sculptural fashion, creating a compelling amalgam that industrializes folk music. Clanging percussion, eerie effects and ghostly synthesizers jostle for position with more conventional guitars and drums. From the confrontational David and Goliath tale of "Rock in This Pocket" to the matter-of-fact "When Heroes Go Down," Vega explores the shifting dynamics of power, paying special attention to the roles played by doctors and patients. A frightened patient's skeptical response to questions in "Blood Makes Noise" (elsewhere, "Blood Sings") leads to the quiescence of a low-grade fever in "99.9F°" ("It could be normal / But it isn't quite"); the medical fantasy of "(If You Were) In My Movie" flips over into the terror of a girl being examined sexually in "Bad Wisdom." For all of the anxiety and intimations of mortality, though, Vega still shows a playful side in the surreal "Fat Man and Dancing Girl" and the gender-bending "As Girls Go."

In 1990, British dance-music collective DNA used Vega's vocal from "Tom's Diner" (an a cappella number from **Solitude Standing**) as the basis for an acid-jazz track that became a sizable UK hit. Despite her record's unathorized use, Vega proved to be a good sport and even wound up contributing to **Tom's Album,** a 1991 collection entirely composed of covers and mixes of the song. [sm]

See also *TPRG*.

VEGAS

See *Dave Stewart*.

VEGETARIAN MEAT

Let's Pet (No. 6) 1995

With far too many modern bands falling on the wrong side of Spinal Tap's "clever/stupid" demarcation, it's easy to mistake "uncategorizable" as a subgenre of the latter. Vegetarian Meat, the peripatetic basement-recording duo of Manish Kalvakota (guitar and drums) and Alex McAulay (everything else), doesn't help matters by hopping genre fences at random (not to mention an apparent aversion to playing live). But the quirky, slightly new wavey pop on the duo's lone long-player does display some admirable influences: Brian Wilson, Half Japanese and the whole New Zealand school of shambling popsters. Vegetarian Meat's off-beat tuneage charts the ups'n'downs of lurve, with the songs' protagonist frequently being on the receiving end of flagellation (sometimes self-inflicted). Loser or not, songwriter McAulay charms by matching the musical arrangements to the lyrical ambiance—a fuzzy wash of guitars to accompany a whiny mood in "Pet," metallic, punkish power chords for a nastier temperament in "Silver and Gold" and so forth. During an optimistic moment he soars with a rockist verve that recalls mid-period Who ("One Way Down"); feeling whimsical in "Trip," he channels vintage psychedelia and gives a passing nod to British folkies of the '60s. In a nutshell, no two songs on **Let's Pet** are alike, and the record would seem to signal the emergence of a talent worth citing in the same breath as Guided by Voices, the Grifters and Lou Barlow. [fm]

VEHICLE FLIPS

See *Wimp Factor 14*.

VELOCITY GIRL

Velocity Girl EP (Slumberland) 1993
Copacetic (Sub Pop) 1993
Sorry Again EP (Sub Pop) 1994
¡Simpatico! (Sub Pop) 1994
Gilded Stars and Zealous Hearts (Sub Pop) 1996

HEARTWORMS

Space Escapade (Darla) 1995

Just as devoted to swirling guitars as to writing great pop songs, Velocity Girl—formed at the University of Maryland in the late '80s (originally with future Unrest bassist Bridget Cross as its singer) and named after a Primal Scream song—effectively mixes melodies into churning noise. Though the band occasionally comes off as lightweight when delving into pop's sugary side, even its less interesting musical moments are catchy enough to be appealing.

Following the standard course for indie-label noise-poppers, Velocity Girl—singer Sarah Shannon, guitarist/bassist/singer Archie Moore, guitarist Brian Nelson, guitarist/bassist Kelly Riles and drummer Jim Spellman (ex–High Back Chairs)—released a slew of singles and compilation tracks before recording an album. Six of those early tunes are compiled on the **Velocity Girl** EP. "Always" and "I Don't Care If You Go" are great pop songs with intriguingly textured guitars; a jazzy acoustic version of the latter provides a nice change of pace. But the record's strongest song—and the most significant in terms of the band's first-album tenor—is "Forgotten Favorite," a pop gem enveloped in sheets of white noise.

Copacetic's cover photo is out of focus, and the album's music is equally abstract. On "Pretty Sister" and the title track, Shannon's voice has to fight to be heard over the sonic wash, yet there's no mistaking the material's catchiness. Despite being taken as shoegazers, Velocity Girl makes its songs here jump up and down rather than simply stare at the floor. "Pop Loser" is especially irresistible, thanks to its slightly sharper guitar sound and "la-la-la-la-la" ("I'll play my la-la shit for you any time") chorus.

Velocity Girl concentrated more on songwriting and less on pure sound for the uneven **¡Simpatico!**, which has some great tunes but less of the atmosphere that makes the first album so riveting. Shannon's increased vocal confidence (and deepening range) lets her rise above the guitars instead of getting caught among them, and the melodies—see "Sorry Again" and "Drug Girls"—jump right out instead of simply inviting listeners in. But that trend leaves a few songs (most notably "I Can't Stop Smiling") too sweet for their own good. The **Sorry Again** EP—the titular song plus three unimpressive non-album tracks—is recommended for completists only.

The band loses even more of its experimental edge on **Gilded Stars and Zealous Hearts,** an uninspired album of relatively straight-ahead mainstreamed pop. Though the album is perfectly presentable and has its catchy moments ("Nothing," "One Word"), Velocity Girl sounds far less distinctive without much noise in its noise-pop, and unbearably smooth production (by Clif Norrell) only worsens matters. The shift away from swirl would be far easier to accept if it were accompanied by stronger songwriting (as it was on the band's previous album), but **Gilded Stars** is big on endlessly repeated choruses and includes more filler than standouts.

In addition to Velocity Girl (which announced that it would disband in 1996), Moore plays in the Heartworms, a side project that also includes his younger brother Kevin, Trish Roy of Belmondo, Chip Porter of Sabine and Chris Norborg of Chisel. The band's aptly named debut album is spacier than anything Velocity Girl has ever recorded, but its mix of pop and noise is somewhat similar in thinking. Unfortunately, the material is weak, and only the trance-inducing title track really stands out here. Spellman also plays in a band called Piper Cub with Andrew Webster of Tsunami, John Dugan of Chisel and Steve Raskin of Edsel. The group has yet to record an album. [rl]

See also *High Back Chairs, Lilys, Unrest.*

VELO-DELUXE

See *Antenna.*

VELVET CRUSH

Ash and Earth EP7 (Bus Stop) 1991
The Soul Crusher e.p. EP7 (Aus. Summershine) 1991
In the Presence of Greatness (Ringers Lactate) 1991
The Post-Greatness e.p. EP (UK Creation) 1992
Teenage Symphonies to God (Creation/550 Music/Epic) 1994

REVERBS

The Happy Forest (Metro-America/Enigma) 1984

PAUL CHASTAIN

Halo EP (Pet Sounds) 1985

CHOO CHOO TRAIN

Briar Rose EP (UK Subway Organisation) 1988
High EP (UK Subway Organisation) 1988
Briar High (Singles 1988) (UK Subway Organisation) 1992

HONEYBUNCH

Time Trails (Summershine) 1996

Among power-pop's truest believers, Ric Menck is a visionary and a scholar, a brilliant pilgrim on a lifetime quest to understand and master that inscrutable fusion of allure, insight and energy that yields the most sublime melodic devotionals to the grand wizards of the two-minute single: Brian Wilson, Alex Chilton, Roger McGuinn, Ray Davies, Pete Townshend, Phil Spector, etc. That he has sought to do so from behind a small drum kit rather than with a guitar or piano only heightens the intensity of the Illinois native's efforts, sharpens the clarity of his perspective. Where other auteurs have found easy creative satisfaction in the imitation of some obvious aspect of their icons' formulae, Menck—who can both sing and play guitar but rarely does in public—demonstrates a keener, deeper obsession with the zen of pop.

Before joining forces, Menck and singer/bassist Paul Chastain pursued the pop muse separately in different parts of Illinois. Menck was half of the Reverbs; **The Happy Forest** (all seven tracks of it) is blandly produced and pedestrian mid-'80s power-pop dominated by John Brabeck's colorless vocals. Chastain reached 12-inch vinyl shortly thereafter, with a solo EP. Although teasingly brief, the six-song **Halo** is a real charmer, tender and skillfully realized originals that brush against R.E.M. pep, Beatlesque wistfulness and modest approximations of studio grandiloquence, all buoyed by Chastain's sweet voice and casual aplomb.

After working as Pop the Balloon with future solo artist Adam Schmitt for a time, Menck formed Choo Choo Train (and a couple of side groups, Bag O'Shells and the Springfields, for good measure) with Chastain in the late '80s and set out to conquer the world. Eleven simple tracks by the twinky trio (with guitarist Darren Cooper), including all of the **Briar Rose** and **High** EPs, were posthumously compiled as **Briar High** and issued over Menck's strenuous objections. Sanctioned or not, it documents the group's aerated Anglo-pop obsessions: light, well-formed tunes ("Flower Field," "When Sunday Comes (She Sighs)," "My Best Friend") given a sparkly dusting of jangly guitars and Chastain's wimpiest vocals. Jeff Murphy of kindred souls Shoes guests on "Every Little Knight"; Menck sings lead on "Big Blue Buzz" and "Wishing on a Star."

Concurrent with a move to Providence, Rhode Island, in 1990, Menck and Chastain retired Choo Choo Train and—with guitarist Jeffrey Borchardt, a Wisconsin native who had been in the White Sisters and was more recently leading the Honeybunch—inaugurated a new, more serious, group. As Velvet Crush, the trio embraces pop music as a living ideal, not a convenience or a nostalgic refuge. Awesomely catchy, genially level-headed and brashly electric, **In the Presence of Greatness**—produced with a minimum of muss and fuss by Matthew Sweet at home on his 8-track—suspends Chastain's rich, light vocals and Borchardt's slashing jangle chords over Menck's economical and musical beat-keeping. Entirely true to the form but distinctly original, the band's collaborative songwriting yields a steady stream of winners (the puerile lyrics of the acoustic "Asshole" do seem to have been imported from a discount broker, however): "Drive Me Down," "Window to the World," "Ash and Earth," "Blind Faith," "White Soul," "Superstar." Free of style-mongering, reference-dropping and retro-pandering, it's an exceptional album that ignores the '60s and the '90s as well, mapping out a pure electric pop sound of its own. As far as **Greatness** goes, this is the real thing, baby. The two prior 7-inches contain the same four songs from that November '90 Sweet session. Besides the first's title track, the EPs contain the non-LP "Circling the Sun" and equally rare covers of Teenage Fanclub's "Everything Flows" and Jonathan Richman's "She Cracked."

One of the three new songs wrapped around a remixed "Window to the World" on **The Post-Greatness e.p.** is "Atmosphere," a surging harmony workout that gets a stronger electric charge on the trio's second album. Co-produced by Mitch Easter (who also served as VC's second guitarist on the road, replacing Dave Gibbs of the Gigolo Aunts and preceding Tommy Keene and others in the slot), **Teenage Symphonies to God**—the title comes from something Brian Wilson once said—carries the group closer to Gram Parsons–influenced country-rock. Borrowing ex-Byrd Gene Clark's sad-eyed "Why Not Your Baby," co-writing a convincing country-soul charmer ("Faster Days") with Stephen Duffy of the Lilac Time and crafting its own pop and country-rock originals, Velvet Crush keeps one foot in its stylistic past while leaning in another direction entirely. Besides the idiom shift and noticeable improvement in technique, the second album's tone is warmer, more intimate. Songs face difficulties with equal parts compassion and confusion—and little emotional success. "My Blank Pages," a snarly poker of guitar pop, and "Keep on Lingerin'," a dusky pedal-steel bounce, face up to a universal sense of uncertainty ("Can't say just how I feel inside / I know there's something on my mind / But I can't put reason into rhyme," quips the former; "I'm not sure where I'm goin' / Bright neon lights / A lifetime passing me by," laments the latter)—and that's the buoyant side. While the gorgeous "Time Wraps Around You" announces "It's time to leave the past far behind," other numbers paint a lonely and bleak future: "This Life Is Killing Me," the bracing "Hold Me Up" ("One is too alone / Suffer as the days / Linger on and on"). In this context, the romantic folk-rock of "Weird Summer" and the Fanclubby self-deprecation of "Star Trip" pass for blinding bright spots. How this all adds up to an uplifting joy to hear is far from obvious; suffice it to say the soaring vocals, chiming guitars and snappy backbeat send a much happier message than the desolate lyrics. [i]

See also *Shoes, Matthew Sweet.*

VELVET UNDERGROUND

The Velvet Underground & Nico (Verve) 1967
White Light / White Heat (Verve) 1968
The Velvet Underground (MGM) 1969 (Verve) 1985
Loaded (Cotillion) 1970
The Velvet Underground Live at Max's Kansas City (Cotillion) 1972
Lou Reed and the Velvet Underground (Pride) 1973
Squeeze (UK Polydor) 1973
1969 Velvet Underground Live With Lou Reed (Mercury) 1974
VU (Verve) 1985
Another View (Verve) 1986
The Best of the Velvet Underground: Words and Music of Lou Reed (Verve) 1989
Live MCMXCIII (Sire/Warner Bros.) 1993
The Best Of (UK Global Television) 1995
Peel Slowly and See (Polydor) 1995

VARIOUS ARTISTS

A Tribute to the Velvet Underground: Heaven and Hell Volume One (Imaginary/Communion) 1990
Heaven and Hell Volume Two (UK Imaginary) 1991

Leaving well enough alone not being a dependable feature of human nature, it came to pass that one of rock's most sacred—and safely refrigerated—cows should defy all expectations and tamper with fate in 1993. As the sex-drugs-noise-literature-decadence-obsession template responsible for more offbeat groups than any institution other than art college, the Velvet Underground—which ended its five original years of seismic activity in 1970—remained frozen in history until the mid-'80s, when reissue producers in the process of putting three of the band's records on CD stumbled onto a bunch of "uncatalogued" tapes from a scrapped 1969 album and assembled two new albums of outtakes, the stupendous **VU** and **Another View.** After all those years in which its alumni had to grapple with the weight and onus of its legend, the band was suddenly in play again; the vivid memory of timeless records gained a modern aura as generations first jacking up the Velvets' dark, anarchic spume were greeted with present-tense releases providing stark contrast to the latest mature solo endeavors from primary architects Lou Reed and John Cale.

Those aftershocks seemed likely to be as far as the resurgence would go—after all, it's not as if Lou Reed, one of rock's most churlish and self-conscious enigmas, would ever deign to traffic in nostalgia or put the band's untarnished reputation at risk. But events conspired to push history down its inexorable path. Andy Warhol, a pivotal figure in the group's launch, died in 1987; Nico, the featured singer on its first album, died in 1988. Warhol's passing prompted Reed and Cale to join forces for the first time in years; they wrote and recorded a tribute album, 1990's **Songs for Drella.** That same year, safely out of view at a French Warhol event, Reed, Cale, drummer Maureen Tucker and original rhythm guitarist Sterling Morrison spent ten minutes doing "Heroin" together for old time's sake. The foursome subsequently recorded a track for Tucker's **I Spent a Week There One Night** (1991) and returned to their neutral corners. But momentum was gathering . . .

Then came the shocking announcement that the band would reunite for a short European tour in 1993. Despite the enormous odds against the quartet's ability to put the genie back in the bottle—or, more to the point, drop their adult defenses and whip themselves into the same massively fucked-up incompetent abandon engendered by decadent youthfulness in the psychotic environment of Warhol's '60s New York whirl—the live album extracted, without overdubs, from three Paris shows in June is fantastic. Released both as two discs and as a "hits"-oriented one-disc version, **Live MCMXCIII** completely upholds any illusions, no matter how outlandishly exaggerated by time and ignorance they may be, of how the Velvet Underground was supposed to sound.

Discarding the stiff-backed propriety that has come to characterize his solo projects, Cale throws himself into manic viola scraping (always the secret ingredient in the band's cacophony), driving the sonic asylum insurrection on "Heroin," "The Black Angel's Death Song" and "Hey Mr. Rain." He also makes able work of the vocals for such Nico-identified numbers as "All Tomorrow's Parties" and "Femme Fatale." (However, Reed's "I'm Waiting for the Man" has been sung far better by those who sound a shade less unlikely to have ever scored, or imagined scoring, smack in Harlem.) Cale even gives an enthusiastic recitation to his vicious shaggy-dog saga ("The Gift")—as if the O'Henry ending might still come as a surprise to listeners.

For his part, Reed tries *singing* again for a change. He makes a fine showing on "White Light/White Heat," "I'll Be Your Mirror," "Beginning to See the Light" and "Pale Blue Eyes," among others, but he trashes "The Black Angel's Death Song" and cruelly disrespects the folk-melody details of "Venus in Furs." He also plays guitar with the neck-wringing intensity and contemporary flair of any crazed young woollyburgher in a Velvets-cushioned noise band. (See "I Heard Her Call My Name" for a hair-raising example of feedback-riddled furiosity.) On rhythm guitar and bass, Morrison (who died of lymphoma in August '95) slashes away with the sturdy 4/4 downstroke that was one of the band's less noted but essential signatures. Meanwhile, Tucker maintains the economical tomtom backbeat for which she's always been treasured and sings "Afterhours" and, with Reed, an over-optimistic "I'm Sticking With You" set to tinkly Cale piano as light relief. Good for much more than a deep sigh of relief at a memory aired and unsullied, **Live MCMXCIII** (and don't stint by getting the half-pint issue—you'd miss Reed's shamelessly hysterical "Velvet Nursery Rhyme"—even in the plush plastic folder with peelable bananas) is an amazing triumph over nature.

The decade's other blast from the Velvets' past is **Peel Slowly and See,** a five-CD chronological retrospective that contains the band's four studio albums (**The Velvet Underground & Nico, White Light/White Heat, The Velvet Underground** and **Loaded,** rightly ignoring **Squeeze,** a sham involving no founding members) in their entirety, half of **VU,** previously unissued demos, six concert recordings (only one of them from the three official live albums), alternate versions and outtakes from **Loaded** plus a pair of Velvets-written-and-played tunes from Nico's first solo album.

The live artifacts are well-chosen and blindingly good, but—commendable though their excavation and exhibition may be—some of the archive discoveries are the wrong kind of revelatory. One entire disc is devoted to an excruciating six-song 1965 home demo session by Cale, Morrison and a short-tempered Reed. For eighty humiliating minutes, the three would-be folk-rockers repeatedly attempt to shape their new conception into something presentable; hearing it now sucks most of the mystery and some of the thrill out of what they finally came up with. The stirring campfire harmonies of "All Tomorrow's Parties" are amusing enough in light of the Teutonic sheen Nico later froze the song in, but when Cale sings "Venus in Furs" as a solemn Welsh ballad over acoustic guitar, what would become stylishly droning debauchery succumbs to laughably ponderous S&M coffeehouse chic. Reed's nasal delusions of channeling Jimmie Rodgers by way of a wizened Delta bluesman on a jugband arrangement of "Waiting for the Man" are equally off-the-mark ludicrous, embarrassing evidence that he was taking someone *else's* walk on the wild side—and being awfully condescending about it. "Heroin," though approached in much the same way, yields more credible results. But then there's "Wrap Your Troubles in Dreams," an egregious (and wisely discarded) Reed composition that forces Cale to sing such pseudo-poetic howlers as "Excrement filters through the brain / Hatred bends the spine / Filth covers the body pores / To be cleansed by dying time"—so *that's* where Trent Reznor learned to read.

No matter how good the songs or bizarre the performances ("Countess From Hong Kong"?), the later demos are easier to swallow in the sense that they come out of the group's aesthetic, not the other way around. Six hours of the Velvet Underground may be more than anyone need hear, but it's undeniable that decades of profound rock greatness and influence are inscribed in **Peel Slowly and See**'s grooves.

The two volumes of **Heaven and Hell,** both produced by England's Imaginary label, ignore all of the contemporary bands whose careers are essentially tributes to the Velvet Underground and instead assemble cover versions of a generally better cut than the usual let's-have-a-bash dross. The transoceanic **Volume One** includes Nirvana doing "Here She Comes Now," the Wedding Present, Ride, Screaming Trees, Telescopes and Buffalo Tom. The inferior all-British-Isles **Volume Two** features Echo and the Bunnymen doing the obscure "Foggy Notion," Fatima Mansions, Revenge, the Reegs and Bill Nelson. [i]

See also *John Cale, Lou Reed, Maureen Tucker; TPRG.*

TOM VERLAINE

See *Television.*

VERLAINES

Ten O'Clock in the Afternoon EP (NZ Flying Nun) 1984
Hallelujah All the Way Home (NZ Flying Nun) 1985 (Homestead) 1989
Juvenilia (Homestead) 1987 (NZ Flying Nun) 1993
Bird-Dog (NZ Flying Nun) 1987 (Homestead) 1988
Some Disenchanted Evening (Flying Nun/Homestead) 1990
Ready to Fly (Slash) 1991
Way Out Where (Slash) 1993

By the time some indie bands finally catch the attention of major labels, it's often too late—they've already used up their best material and shot their creative wad. Such, happily, has not been the case with New

Zealand's Verlaines. Following a series of promising but inconsistent import and indie albums (the best is 1987's **Juvenilia** compilation, expanded by five tracks for its NZ CD reissue), the group inked a deal with Warner Bros.–distributed Slash and proceeded to release the two finest albums of its career.

Ready to Fly kicks off with "Gloom Junky," a title that sets the mood for an album of glumly effective songs about lost love. While it's de rigueur to mention that singer/guitarist Graeme Downes has a doctorate in music, it's a point that bears repeating when discussing an album that pulls off so many potentially disastrous songwriting styles and production details so successfully: "Tremble" and "Moonlight on Snow" feature orchestration; "Such as I" is drawn purely from musical theater (one can almost see the chorus line dancing behind Downes); "See You Tomorrow" is a blues. Throw in Downes' strongest bunch of guitar-pop tunes and you've got the Verlaines' best LP.

Until **Way Out Where,** that is. After years of leading the Verlaines as a trio, Downes added a second guitarist to the group for this record, and the results are apparent from the very first moments of the album's bracing opener, "Mission of Love," by far the band's most electrified tune ever. With the strings, reeds and genre exercises largely shelved, this is a true rock'n'roll album (arguably the Verlaines' first), and Downes rises to the occasion with enough top-drawer material to mark him as one of the best singer/songwriters currently plying the trade. Choice cuts abound, including "This Valentine" (an exhortation for a romantic fool to get over it already), "Stay Gone" (a send-off to a departed lover) and the title track (one of rock's most effective odes to a raped environment). Highly recommended, and a good sign of more to come. [pl]

See also *Dead C; TPRG.*

VERMONSTER

See *Magic Hour.*

VERSUS

Let's Electrify! EP (Remora) 1993
The Stars Are Insane (TeenBeat) 1994
Dead Leaves (TeenBeat) 1995
Deep Red EP (TeenBeat) 1996
Secret Swingers (TeenBeat/Caroline) 1996

CONTAINE

I Want It All EP (Enchanté) 1994

FLOWER

Concrete (Bear) 1988
Hologram Sky (Ger. Semaphore) 1990
Concrete Sky (1987–1990) (Bear/Simple Machines) 1994

FRENCH

French EP (Bear) 1996

Although the New York trio's basic sound is close enough to textbook alternapop that you'd be none too surprised to see its photo illustrating the term in a twenty-first-century cultural encyclopedia, Versus usually does enough with those generic ingredients to merit a second listen. Using Mission of Burma's angular guitar attack as a blueprint, the band's debut EP works up ample tension—much of which comes from the skittering interplay between bassist Fontaine Toups and drummer Ed Baluyut—but the only real release comes during "That Girl Is Gone," where Toups' sugary vocals stretch across brother Richard Baluyut's jagged guitar lines like cotton candy skewered on a length of barbed wire.

On **The Stars Are Insane,** Versus takes fuller advantage of the trio format's biggest benefit—fewer notes to get in the way. Opening with "Thera," wherein the guitar enunciates with typical rigor over a Factory Records–like sheen, the album settles into a midtempo drift that's as seductively luxurious as a soak in a hot spring. Toups' vocal turns, like the sweet-and-sour "Circle," are still more involving than Richard Baluyut's sing-song recitations. He manages to summon up a modicum of emotion on the chiming "Deseret," but the guitarist usually sounds so uninvolved that he might as well be reading from a microbiology text. **Dead Leaves** collects some B-sides and outtakes from 1992 and 1993, including a handful from the band's experiments as a four-piece. While "Venus Victoria" and "Tin Foil Star" burble agreeably, most of this should have remained in the vaults.

Another Baluyut brother (littlest sibling James) joined the band on guitar in late '95, and his contributions to the five-song **Deep Red** (and the full-length **Secret Swingers**) make it clear that he wasn't just added to the lineup in order to maintain familial accord.The fuller sound works to the benefit of EP songs like the swooning "Shooting Star" and accentuates Toups' vocals exquisitely on the ballad "Lost Time." Maybe we've found the Osmonds of the '90s at last.

Containe is a Toups-led side project that makes the most of the concord between her poignant voice—particularly on the swoon-worthy "Tired Eyes"—and the sweeter tones of collaborator Connie Lovatt. While slightly too tranquil for its own good, **I Want It All** does have its share of restorative qualities.

Before forming Versus, both Richard and Ed Baluyut played guitar (Richard also sang) in the bracing, textured and not dissimilar-sounding Flower. Both of the quartet's albums are collected in full on **Concrete Sky,** with the non-LP compilation track "Concrete" added. Flower bassist Ian James went on to play guitar in Cell; after that group ended, he formed a loud pop trio, French, with Flower drummer Andrew Bordwin. [dss]

See also *Cell.*

VERTICAL SLIT

See *V-3.*

VERTIGO

Vertigo (Amphetamine Reptile) 1990
Rub EP (Amphetamine Reptile) 1991
Ventriloquist (Amphetamine Reptile) 1992
Nail Hole (Amphetamine Reptile) 1993

These unusually tightly wound proponents of the well-established AmRep mindset—laymen should imagine malicious smart guys who look like grad students but carry blackjacks to bludgeon unsuspecting bystanders—operate with the unconscious mindmeld of a free-jazz ensemble. Their "gimmick" (although they don't treat it as one) is the lack of a bass player: okay, guitarists Jared Aos and Gene Tangren occasionally resort to use of the four-stringed beast but, mostly, they lock horns and put the pedals to the treble. Let the eardrums beware.

The Minneapolis trio's self-titled debut (released hot on the heels of the improbably infectious "Bad Syd" single) charges the air with static electricity but fails to put that spark to much use, although a pair of garage-rock covers do muster a snotty snarl. **Rub** cuts back on the "rock" component of the band's sound, letting drummer Roy Llerandi lead a mostly fruitful sonic scavenger hunt along the banks of the River Skronk.

Although **Ventriloquist** begins with a head-turning change of pace—"Love Withdrawal," a fuzzed-out sliver of post-Mudhoney garage-punk—the album settles into a more familiar misanthropic rage by the middle of "Rocket V," a spoken (make that shouted) word diatribe about noisy neighbors (talk about the pot calling the kettle black!). Inspirational verse: "Open the door/Let me in/I swear I'll bash your brains out if I have to."

About halfway through the recording of **Ventriloquist,** Llerandi was replaced by Bill Beeman. Beeman's receptiveness to the simple 4/4—and the more widespread use of bass—makes **Nail Hole** more conventionally rhythmic than its predecessors, bounded by the midwestern punk swagger of "King of Terror" on one hand and the post-psychedelic spuzz of "Up the Road" on the other. [dss]

VERUCA SALT

American Thighs (Minty Fresh) 1994 (Minty Fresh/DGC) 1994
Blow It Out Your Ass It's Veruca Salt EP (Minty Fresh/DGC) 1996

The contrast of wispy pop vocals against sizzling pan-fried guitars gives Veruca Salt its immediate sensual appeal; catchy tunes that bend topics and themes into inscrutable shapes around a warped '70s rock-culture template add depth to the Chicago quartet's debut album. Accused of cloning the Breeders' genes and resented for the critical and A&R frenzy that brought the young band to a fat deal with a major label fifteen months after playing its first public show in a Chicago bar, Veruca Salt (named for a little girl character in Roald Dahl's *Charlie and the Chocolate Factory*) is neither the second coming nor devil spawn.

Talented and engaging, intelligent and educated, coy and painfully self-amused (witness the album's AC/DC lyric title and a music publishing company named Are You There God It's Me Music?), singer/guitarists Louise Post and Nina Gordon (joined by Steve Lack on bass and Gordon's brother, Jim Shapiro, on drums) come off like overachieving smarties forced to explain their weird behavior in front of the class without letting their true motives show. **American Thighs,** adroitly recorded by Brad Wood (of Liz Phair fame), showcases the pair's solo songwriting and sympathetically joined voices. The album drags its tail through some uninspired rockers at the start and finish, but the middle soars with pretty and powerful gems: "Seether," "Forsythia" (both by Gordon, who has a singular knack for offbeat melodies and sinister lyrics), the power-falsetto rock of "Victrola" and the simmering burn of "Spiderman '79," (typically tough and direct Post creations) and "Number One Blind" (a Gordon/Shapiro collaboration). A casually stylish link between insular underground sensibilities and MTV popularity, **American Thighs** is, as Gordon sings in "Seether," "neither loose nor tight . . . neither black nor white . . . neither big nor small . . . the center of it all."

The colorfully titled EP, a stopgap to keep the band in mind while awaiting the release of its second album in late '96, contains some nice pictures and four unspectacular new songs written two each by Post and Gordon and recorded with a loudly articulated rock edge by Steve Albini. [i]

VERVE

The Verve E.P. EP (Hut/Vernon Yard) 1992
Voyager 1 EP (Jolly Roger) 1993
A Storm in Heaven (Vernon Yard) 1993
No Come Down (B Sides & Outtakes) (Vernon Yard) 1994
A Northern Soul (Vernon Yard) 1995

This quartet from Wigan, England, was one of shoegazing's most dynamic proponents—even if that quality manifested itself in terms of soaring musical sweep rather than onstage theatrics. Amid the swirling, psychedelic music, solid songwriting and frontman Richard Ashcroft's hypnotic vocals helped the band's better soundscapes actually go someplace. The five-song '92 EP (compiling several British singles) does a great job of outlining the Verve's potential, even if the group doesn't quite live up to it. "Gravity Grave" and "She's a Superstar" are catchy enough to prove there's something behind the musical drift, and "Feel"—a slow, shifting ten-minute epic—never succumbs to self-indulgence.

The band—Ashcroft, guitarist Nick McCabe, bassist Simon Jones and drummer Peter Salisbury—really comes into its own on the wistful and organic-sounding **A Storm in Heaven.** The album doesn't provide aural wallpaper, it invites listeners to crawl inside its songs for a breather from reality. The engulfing "Slide Away" offers a chance to do just what its title suggests: it could be considered an anti-anthem of escapist music.

Few bands can put together a worthwhile compilation of mostly unreleased ephemera only one album into their careers, and the Verve proved to be no exception with **No Come Down (B Sides & Outtakes).** The appealing title track has an interesting Arabian flair, but little else on this nine-song anthology is as compelling as **A Storm in Heaven.** Also included are a live "Gravity Grave" and acoustic versions of the album's "Make It Till Monday" and "Butterfly," which make a good case for the Verve's versatility, if not for an entire "unplugged" album. The authorized bootleg **Voyager 1** (clear blue vinyl, no information other than song titles) contains live versions of six numbers recorded in New York and London.

The quartet meanders more on **A Northern Soul,** and the album suffers for it. As a whole, the record lacks the mystery and majesty of **A Storm in Heaven,** and it occasionally gets too grandiose for its own good. "On Your Own" and "No Knock on My Door" are catchy (especially for a band so addicted to sonic swirl), but they lack the atmospheric scope of the Verve's best work. In August 1995, shortly after **A Northern Soul**'s release, Ashcroft announced the band was breaking up. [rl]

VERVE PIPE

I've Suffered a Head Injury (LMNO Pop!) 1992
Pop Smear (LMNO Pop!) 1994
Villains (RCA) 1996

The Verve Pipe formed in East Lansing, Michigan, in 1992 when members of two popular area groups decided to work together. The sum was indeed greater than its parts, and the group quickly garnered a regional following for its textured rock sound, marked by inventive arrangements, frontman Brian Vander Ark's soul-searching lyrics and layered vocals. **I've Suffered a Head Injury** is clearly the work of a young band; the tempo shifts in "Martyr Material" get a bit too cute, and some of the album's new wave touches are out of date. But "Brian's Song" is driven by a solid, jangly rock groove and stirring guitar solos, while "The Freshmen" is an insightful treatise on accountability via the mistreatment of a woman by two young men.

Pop Smear is more fully realized and distinctive. The songs are sturdier and harder-hitting, the new muscle coming from plain old artistic growth plus the addition of guitarist A. J. Dunning. Vander Ark's vocals are more assured and commanding, and the sonic breadth—which seemed a bit willynilly on **Head Injury**—is more focused. The loud, murky rock of "Spoonful of Sugar," the Latin bop of "Honest" and the shimmering folk of "What You Wanted" all sound of a singular piece.

The Verve Pipe hit a timely peak as it was making its major-label debut. Produced by Jerry Harrison, **Villains** is a mature work marked by its substantial dynamic range—from the driving rock fury of "Barely (If at All)" and "Drive You Mild" to the layered ambience of "Veneer," the chiming balladry of "Penny Is Poison" and the tightly coiled build of the title track. "The Freshmen" shows up again, improved by a slower, more dramatic arrangement. **Villains** also marks the arrival of keyboardist / percussionist Doug Corella, which gives the Verve Pipe additional sonic textures to separate it from the standard two-guitar modern rock attack. Definitely one to watch. [gg]

VICTOR DIMISICH BAND

See *Terminals.*

VIDALIAS

(melodyland) (Upstart) 1995

There's a pungent point to the fact that this Atlanta quintet is named for a sweet southern genus of onion: hip western swing and country rock have rarely been played or sung with such tasty tear-inducing flavor. In a small-time variation on Lyle Lovett's wry charm, singer/guitarist Chuck Walston (in real life, a political reporter for an Atlanta newspaper) repeatedly takes it on the chin but still manages to hold his head high in modest, enormously appealing numbers like "Play Me for a Fool," "Loser Leave Town" and "Faking It." [i]

VIKINGS

See *Devil Dogs.*

HOLLY VINCENT

HOLLY AND THE ITALIANS

The Right to Be Italian (Virgin/Epic) 1981

HOLLY BETH VINCENT

Holly & the Italians (Virgin/Epic) 1982

OBLIVIOUS

America (Daemon) 1993

VOWEL MOVEMENT

Vowel Movement (Mammoth) 1995

Born in Chicago, peripatetic rocker Holly Vincent began her music career in the late-'70s punk scene, playing drums and guitar and singing in forgotten local bands like the Brothel Creepers and the all-female Backstage Pass. Along with drummer Steve Dalton (aka Steve Young), she first convened Holly and the Italians in California but was living in London when they recorded "Tell That Girl to Shut Up," the 1980 single for which Vincent is still best known.

The success of that belligerent charmer led to a deal and an album. Produced in roaring power-pop style by Richard Gottehrer, **The Right to Be Italian** is a new wave classic of romantic ups and downs, leather-jacket rebellion and kitsch culture, carried mightily on Vincent's tough-girl attitude, gale-force Brill Building melodies and chunky rhythm guitar presence. Her subsequent Mike Thorne–produced solo album (confusingly titled **Holly and the Italians,** although the band had dissolved) is light-years better, a mesmerizing and mature disc of baroque atmospheres, opaque introspection, sexual ambivalence and psychedelically distorted hallucinations. If Joni Mitchell and Ronnie Spector mated with Nick Cave and Leonard Cohen, the offspring of their offspring might have conceived something like this.

Vincent didn't release another album for more than a decade. In the meantime, she surfaced in New York, Los Angeles and elsewhere, duetting with Joey Ramone on a great 1982 single of "I Got You Babe," serving a brief, unrecorded stint in the Waitresses and forming a one-gig group called Bikey with her brother Nick, before his tenure as Frank Black's drummer. Through a number of undocumented bands, Vincent kept strings—mostly cello—as a distinctive counterpoint to her punky rock poise.

Vincent's return to the recording studio finally came, surprisingly enough, through the auspices of Indigo Girl Amy Ray. She encouraged (and funded) Vincent to form a band and record **America,** which was issued on Ray's label, Daemon. The Oblivious album is roughly produced with the vocals mixed low and the guitars loud and blurry, but it's hard-hitting, smartly played and marbled with some great songs. The reversion to primal rock directness is aerated by Vincent's self-harmonizing doubletracked singing and broken by the violinized delicacy of such numbers as "America (I'm Wasted)" and "Witness." In the obsessive desires of "Crush," "D.S.F." and "That Was," the wry disdain of "It's the Sound" ("This life is good for me / It said so on my record sleeve / It said so in my favorite books / And on the street when I get looks") and the taut violence of "Fired Away," Vincent displays the sinew, melodic acuity and raw nerve that make her music so compelling. A strong showing after such a long absence.

The strange (and unfortunately named) fruit of a brief alliance with Johnette Napolitano, then on her way out of Concrete Blonde, **Vowel Movement** is a minor album the pair improvised on bass (mostly played by Napolitano) and drums (mostly played by

Vincent). Both wrote lyrics and sang; Vincent overdubbed guitar. Sloppy and undeveloped, indulgent, haphazard and just flat-out noisy, the album occasionally happens onto terra firma ("Las Vegas," both versions of "Jackie Baby," "Jesus," "Death of a Surfer"), but too much of it flails along shapelessly, a doomed work in progress. [i]

See also *Concrete Blonde; TPRG.*

VIOLENT FEMMES

Violent Femmes (Slash) 1983
Hallowed Ground (Slash) 1984
The Blind Leading the Naked (Slash/Warner Bros.) 1986
3 (Slash/Warner Bros.) 1989
Why Do Birds Sing? (Slash/Reprise) 1991
Add It Up (1981–1993) (Slash/Reprise) 1993
New Times (Elektra) 1994

The Violent Femmes burst out of Milwaukee, Wisconsin, in the early '80s, a remarkably original folk-punk trio of buskers playing acoustic instruments and singing intense, personal songs with remarkable candor. Gordon Gano (vocals, guitar, songs), Brian Ritchie (bass) and Victor De Lorenzo (drums) started out stripped-down and sidewalk-simple, but grew more adventurous and uncommon over the years, fixing a flexible style that resembles no other band.

On the skeletal debut, Gano's articulate passion and lyrical maladjustment combine with the charged (but not very loud) playing to convey an incredible sense of desperation and rage. **Hallowed Ground** reveals his religious fervor, connecting it with traditional American folk music. **The Blind Leading the Naked** was produced by Talking Head Jerry Harrison with conscious mainstreaming intent. Of course, the Femmes at their most commercial are still pretty radical, although "I Held Her in My Arms" does sound unnervingly like Bruce Springsteen.

By this point, the group had slowed its collective productivity (three years elapsed before the next new album), addressing their efforts instead to solo projects. When the Femmes reconvened, the reversal of entropy brought only comfortable creative torpor. The trio revisits familiar terrain with easy confidence and very little evident artistic ambition or effort on **3.** Gano's songwriting and delivery have their usual odd character and some of the old passion, but the Femmes are hardly cooking with gas.

After another lengthy hiatus, the Femmes returned with **Why Do Birds Sing?,** a stripped-down effort that harks back to **Violent Femmes** and contains three tunes ("Girl Trouble," "Life Is a Scream" and "Flamingo Baby") Gano wrote during the creative frenzy that produced most of the tunes on the first two albums. Despite a decade in the biz, Gano still captures teen angst and frustration better, and more convincingly, than almost anybody. Standouts include "American Music," the Femme-ization of Culture Club's "Do You Really Want to Hurt Me" (with new lyrics by Gano), "Out the Window" (a cheery paean to suicide) and "I'm Free," a goofy, quasi-religious hymn that celebrates the power of love.

Add It Up is a generous and thoughtful twenty-three-track sampler of the band's career that includes the expected "hits" as well as gems like "Waiting for the Bus" (a 1981 demo that's been a staple of the band's live gigs for years), the leering "36-24-36," "America Is," a half-studio, half-live version of "Lies" with Ashwin Batish on sitar and the mysterious "Dance, Motherfucker, Dance!" featuring the Horns of Dilemma.

New Times introduces new drummer Guy Hoffman, formerly of BoDeans and the Oil Tasters, in place of De Lorenzo (who released his second solo album, **Pancake Day,** in 1996). With the exception of a compressed, pumped-up drum sound and a couple of keyboard accents, the trio's spartan style remains the same. Nihilism, wiseass bon mots and hopeless love affairs still churn through Gano's psyche to emerge as high art and low humor. "Don't Start Me on the Liquor" is typical folk-rock done Femmes style, "Mirror Mirror (I See a Damsel)" sounds like a Russian polka and "I'm Nothing" is as fine an expression of sputtering youthful rage as the band has ever done. The only anomaly is "Machine," a sophomoric electronic experiment that doesn't quite work. [i/jp]

See also *BoDeans, Maureen Tucker; TPRG.*

JOOST VISSER

See *Bettie Serveert.*

VIVA KNIEVAL

See *Bikini Kill.*

VIVA SATELLITE!

See *Eggs.*

VIVA SATURN

Viva Saturn EP (Heyday) 1988
Soundmind (Spirit/Heyday) 1992
Brightside (Restless) 1995

When California psyche-popsters Rain Parade came to an end, leader David Roback broke off to form Opal and then Mazzy Star; his bass-playing brother Steven (joined by bandmate John Thoman on guitar, future Continental Drifter drummer Carlo Nuccio and two others) reemerged as the guitar/keyboards-playing singer of Viva Saturn. The eponymous five-song 12-inch continues the former band's tastefully time-shifted folk-pop eloquence with cello shading, organ and backward tape manipulation casting a mild psychedelic swirl on quietly sung delicacies like "Brought It on Yourself" and the alluring "Remember I'm Dead."

Tightened up to a four-piece, the unprolific Viva Saturn finally released its debut album several years later, sounding like a slightly more energized West Coast version of Luna with mild shoegazer tendencies (and, in the memorably dispirited "Haven't Felt Like," a dusty '60s piano-pop affect). Firm songwriting and crisp drumming holds **Soundmind** together, as Roback's dreamy singing (supported by such guests as Barbara Manning, Chris Cacavas and Matt Piucci) and the layers of languid guitar could easily float apart into shapeless reveries. A remarkably calm and pretty record that masks its aggression in a delicate mix, the perplexing **Soundmind** soothes as it sears.

Contrary to its chipper title, the majority of songs on **Brightside** are mournful enough to send Morrissey into a funk. "Send a Message" and "Here Comes April" are sprightly and upbeat, but most of the material is bleak and lonely, with titles like "Black Cloud," "Mourn the Light," "Nothing Helps" and "Distracted."

The somber "String Me Out a Line" conveys aching loneliness with haunting clarity, its gentle acoustic instrumentation and quiet vocal harmonies making it **Brightside**'s most memorable track. [i/ky]

SUSAN VOELZ

13 Ribs (Fr. Voodoo) 1992 (Pravda) 1993
Summer Crashing (Pravda) 1995

Drummers may be the butt of endless musician jokes, but at least they're noticed enough to be teased. When was the last time anyone taunted the violin player? It's only in recent years that the DIY spirit began moving fiddlers to make vocal pop albums of their own, and to date the list of participants in the movement doesn't number much more than Lisa Germano, Alison Krauss, Tammy Rogers and Susan Voelz.

Reaching public attention as a member of Poi Dog Pondering (although, like Germano, she also played with John Mellencamp), the Wisconsin native made her solo debut with **13 Ribs,** a wonderful and eclectic record that showcases an appealing flyaway voice and intelligent, sensitive songwriting over her instrumental technique. Playing a little guitar and getting varied backing from Poi Dogs and other pals, Voelz sings about real things—a beloved pet, a river, a car crash, an old house—with articulate lyrics and exquisite musicianship. Sifting comfortably through mixes of folk and rock, a waltz, small-scale western swing, jugband eccentricity, elegiac grandeur and more, Voelz brings an intimacy and honesty to both sound and words that makes it all glisten like morning dew. "Good Day to Die" suggests where Natalie Merchant might aim if she drank more coffee; the swaying "Mr. Magoo" scrubs out the gooey stain of "Midnight at the Oasis" all by itself. "Let Me Be Your Bible," a breezy Brill Building harmony popper wryly constructed from Scripture, is amazing; the rest of the record is nearly as good.

Back in the studio after "a year of touring . . . that included a spectacular rollover and over car wreck" (the aftermath of which is pictured in the artwork), Voelz changed the timbre of her tune for **Summer Crashing.** This equally artful album has lots more electric guitar (by Jon Sanchez), drums, distortion—and a dampened spirit, expressed in abstractly emotional songs of affecting solemnity. "Happy" sets the brief attainment of joy as an uncertain goal ("I don't wanna feel bad/So I stop feelin' anything"), but acknowledges the danger of such desire; as if by way of explanation, "William" concerns a manic-depressive whose happiness gets him institutionalized. The low-key but powerfully atmospheric music orbits closely around a nucleus of Voelz's breezy voice and mournful violin, reflecting aspects of her personality with prismatic variety and occasional solar flares illuminating the twilight. Mighty fine. [i]

See also *Poi Dog Pondering.*

VOIVOD

War and Pain (Metal Blade) 1984
Rrröööaaarrr (Noise International/Combat) 1986
Thrashing Rage EP (Noise International/Combat) 1986
Killing Technology (Noise International/Combat) 1987
Dimension Hatröss (Noise International) 1988
Nothingface (Mechanic/MCA) 1989
Angel Rat (Mechanic) 1991
The Best of Voivod (Futurist/Mechanic) 1992
The Outer Limits (Mechanic/MCA) 1993
Negatron (Mausoleum/BMG) 1995

Evolutionary change has been a watchword with this band of French Canadian eccentrics since their crude mid-'80s beginnings in youthful Motörhead-meets-Mad-Max power thrash. By 1987's **Killing Technology,** the twin influences of progressive rock (Floyd/Crimson) and post-punk/industrial (Killing Joke/Foetus) had begun to mutate the metallic Montreal quartet, although they retained their quirky nicknames and drummer Michel "Away" Langevin's futuristic space-warrior lyrical concepts and artwork.

The exponential upward climb in imagination, complexity and experimentation continued on the '88 breakthrough, **Dimension Hatröss,** and the decade-closing career high point, **Nothingface.** The latter record cemented Voivod's status as a thrilling anomaly, staking out unique terrain on the post-modern frontier. Along with a stunning rendition of Syd Barrett's "Astronomy Domine," the album showcases a full-blown melodic sensibility, vibrant production, the integration of sampling technology and guitarist Denis "Piggy" D'Amour's status as the Robert Fripp of alternative metal.

Pruned down to a threesome (bassist Jean-Yves Theriault played on the disc, but departed before its release), Voivod entered the '90s with the brilliant **Angel Rat,** a dozen surprisingly evocative dream images ("Zoning in a hall of glass / Plasma flowing from a cask"), and a less dissonant, even more advanced and individualistic prog-alternative sound (like Faith No More without the funk leanings). The driving "Panorama," the robotic "Golem" and the jaunty mariner's reverie "The Prow" all signal a newfound commitment to melodic, atmospheric riff-rock, while upholding the band's essential science friction and spiraling chord changes. "Clouds in My House" and the title track hum with a keyboard-enhanced, semi-sweet drone, as Denis "Snake" Belanger's voice reaches a new level of linear melodicism. "Nuage Fractal" is threaded by D'Amour's delicate neo-gothicisms; he waxes Edge-like on the gentle "Freedom," using the pealing guitar motifs to accelerate the tune's dramatic **Dark Side of the Moon** mood.

Proceeding as a trio, Voivod pursued its playful, human side on **The Outer Limits.** The kitschy space-alien cover art and comic-book interior illustrations are printed in 3D (with appropriate viewing glasses included). Musically, the band continues the innovations of **Angel Rat**—albeit less homogeneously and welded to more basic rock power. The confident opener, "Fix My Heart," boasts a simple, effective metallic riff spiking introspective lyrical musings, which contrasts with "Moonbeam Rider," lushly energetic and rife with ethereal solos and staccato rhythms, and the Bauhausian "Le Pont Noir." For the second time in its career, Voivod dips into the Pink Floyd well, this time for a lucid version of **More**'s "The Nile Song." Meanwhile, at seventeen-plus minutes, "Jack Luminous" is the group's ultimate sci-fi opus—a **2112** for the '90s. Soon after the record's release, Belanger beamed off the Voivod ship for good.

Langevin and D'Amour are joined by new vocalist/bassist Eric Forrest for the disappointingly regressive **Negatron.** Songs like "Nanoman" and "Meteor" sound like outtakes from the **Dimension Hatröss** period, and the loss of Belanger's psychedelic melodicism is a systemic flaw the record never overcomes. Forrest's one-dimensional Pantera-style roaring adds little drama to the proceedings; there are a few decent industrial-metal riffs but little resonance. Jim Thirlwell co-wrote and performs on the dense closer "D.N.A.," not coincidentally the album's most engaging track. Although the disc boasts an extra multimedia track for CD-ROM users, Voivod—for the first time in its future-now existence—seems sonically remedial. (Foetus' involvement may have been a payback for Langevin's participation in his Steroid Maximus project. The Canadian added percussion and other bits to a couple of tracks each of **Quilombo** and **Gondwanaland.**)

The 1992 best-of, a solid overview up to that point, mainly sticks to a simple chronological format of two tracks per album (plus the menacing rarity "Cockroaches"), which clearly documents the band's stylistic growth. Be warned, though: newcomers may find it difficult to reconcile the sharp contrast between rough early noise-metal like "Ripping Headaches" and the more sophisticated later material. [gef]

See also *Foetus; TPRG.*

VOLUPTUOUS HORROR OF KAREN BLACK

A National Health Care (Beautiful) 1993 (Go-Kart) 1996
The Anti-Naturalists (Triple X) 1995

As New York's leading lurid theatrical club attraction since GG Allin flung his final feces, the Voluptuous Horror of Karen Black earned its reputation for the orificial paint egg-speriments performed on the blue-hued body of head-standing singer Kembra Pfahler. On record, however, the quartet sounds a lot like the Runaways auditioning an especially tuneless vocalist. While the musicians crank up an adequately anachronistic glop of chunky '70s punk sludge on **The Anti-Naturalists,** Pfahler concocts mildly amusing shock-buzzer lyrics like "Water Coffin," "Honky Tonk Biscuit Queen," "Gotta Get My Eyes Done" and "Sick Bed." Her clumsy, flat singing is the only real horror here. The debut contains such equally inspired inventions as "You Slay Me" and "One Man Lady." [i]

CHRIS VON SNEIDERN

Sight & Sound (Heyday) 1993
Big White Lies (Heyday) 1994

After serving (unrecorded) stints with such Bay Area pop stalwarts as Flying Color and the Sneetches, Syracuse, New York, native Chris Von Sneidern unleashed **Sight & Sound,** the first of two remarkably beautiful pop masterpieces, in 1993. Using his guitar and pen to fashion pretty, Badfinger-esque songs—the desperate "Bad Black Lonesome," the Merseybeat homage "Annalisa," the moving, lilting "Life Start Living" and the frightening, Big Star **3rd**-like "Never Again, My Love" to name just a few—Von Sneidern imbues the album with unparalleled pop vision and sheer melodic genius. A near-perfect beginning.

Big White Lies is every bit as strong as the debut; the dozen songs include a well-placed cover of Bread's "Everything I Own" alongside such lovely originals as the summery "Roll On," the dreamy (natch) "Dream Away" and the slightly more forceful "Hard Again." Von Sneidern has a definite gift for both songwriting and arranging; unobtrusive little touches include the exotic percussion on the catchy title track and Bryan Higgins' sweet french horn flourishes (à la the Beatles' "For No One") on "Here I Go." The whole package (purportedly the first to contain interactive CD-ROM liner notes) is an essential pop treasure from one of the most talented auteurs to come along in ages. [jmb]

VOWEL MOVEMENT

See *Holly Vincent.*

V-3

Unbroken Silence [tape] (Iron Press) 1989
Earth Muffin EP (Siltbreeze) 1991
Psychic Dancehall (Ropeburn) 1991
Negotiate Nothing (Ropeburn) 1992
Russian Roulette Chinese Style EP (Birdman) 1995
The Superhuman EP (Honeyman) 1995
Photograph Burns (Onion/American) 1996

VERTICAL SLIT

Slit and Pre-Slit (no label) 1977
The Live EP (Old Age) 1980
Under the Blood Red Lava Lamp [tape] (Iron Press) 1986
Basement 2215 [tape] (Iron Press) 1987
Vertical Slit and Beyond (Ropeburn) 1990
Your Wife Is Licking My Strobe Light and Grinning [tape] (Iron Press) 1991

JIM SHEPARD

Picking Through the Wreckage With a Stick (Siltbreeze) 1994
Evil Love Deeper (Thrill Jockey) 1995

Monomaniacal home-recordists-cum-outsider-musicians are getting to be a rather common breed, but Columbus, Ohio's Jim Shepard was hunkered down in his primordial lair back when most people thought "lo-fi" meant listening to music on a transistor radio. Far more devoted to noise than most one-man/4-track operations, Shepard has a flair for carving out blocks of blue-collar art-rock that rivals fellow rust-belt survivors like Destroy All Monsters and Pere Ubu (in its heyday). He also tempers the smart-guy sound-assemblage with a dark and smoky garage aesthetic born of toxin-laden practice spaces and beer-soaked lunch hours out behind the plant.

Shepard inaugurated his insular experimentation back in the late '70s with Vertical Slit, a free-ranging, amorphously constructed band that laid out its lattices of scree around the leader's extraordinary guitar constructions. You can hear bits of MC5er Fred "Sonic" Smith, Sonny Sharrock and Can's Michael Karoli in Shepard's alternately piercing and massaging use of feedback, while his lyrics coat everything in sight with overlapping bile and black humor. An array of cassette releases and micro-pressed records—in editions ranging from one hundred (**Slit and Pre-Slit**) to a whopping three hundred (**The Live EP**)—were excerpted for **Vertical Slit and Beyond,** a revelatory 1976–90 compendium of isolationist howl that would be impossible to replicate in an age of networking and back-slapping indie-rock support groups.

Not that the confronto-delic aesthetic that endures in V-3 (a combo Shepard put together) exactly conforms to that of the whippersnappers who have sprung up over the years. In fact, his last-sane-man-on-earth stance might be even more pronounced in this setting. The atypically clean-sounding **Psychic Dancehall** wastes no time in expounding Shepard's pronounced anti-social mindset: the weary opener, "Prime Minister Keyes" finds him continually muttering (to no one in particular) "I couldn't fit in if you gave me your name." His fellow travelers here seem to share those feelings: Bassist Nudge Squidfish (!) delivers a hollow-eyed plaint called "Dead Man," while singer/guitarist Roxanne Newman uses her tabula rasa voice to sap all emotion from defeatist anthems like "Tick Tock" and "Gotta Get Free." It's clearly Shepard's show, though, and he airs a stealthy virtuosity both as a guitarist, on the Ubu-esque "Another Exterminator (Eaten by Bugs)," and a scorched-earth prose writer (the glacial live version of "Photograph Burns").

Negotiate Nothing lowers the fi a notch or two, which actually enhances the hepatic tones that radiate from liquored-up portraits like "Girl in a Room" and "Harry" (both of which bear a trace of MX-80–style bluster). While it's easier to identify most of the album as punk-rock, Shepard and Squidfish throw a wrench (hell, a whole toolbox!) into the works on pieces like the tape-loop collage "Scrap Metal Radio" and the fuzzily suburbo-phobic "Your Uncle." Shepard's keen observations are more detailed than ever, as evidenced by the deceptively titled "Party at 15th and Summit," a real-time journey to rock bottom that introduces characters like Gene: "He plays in a local band / He's advanced to shooting heroin in the back of his hand."

After an enforced hiatus—the result of an industrial accident that nearly cost Shepard a hand at his day job—V-3 resurfaced on a major label. The cash influx didn't change the band's modus operandi, though—**Photograph Burns** was recorded for a hair under five hundred dollars, and it's got enough jaggedly dangling viscera (especially in a remake of "Superhuman") to prove it. Shepard's dark, mannered vocals add a detached menace to psychic jostles like "American Face" (a spiritual update of the MC5's bird-flipping "American Ruse") and a crescendo-upon-crescendo rendition of the title track. Interestingly, Shepard also allows a glimpse into his usually well-disguised introspective side on the foggy "Bristol Girl." He may not be on a first-name basis with the man downstairs, but you get the feeling Shepard knows a lot more about bad juju than labelmate Glenn Danzig ever will.

On his solo albums, both compiled from a battery of self-released cassettes, Shepard waxes more avant-garde, blending Chrome-plated tape gnash with perversely over-the-top fuzz guitar. Songs as such don't materialize very often on **Picking Through the Wreckage With a Stick,** but the sounds that do are pretty enthralling in their own right. Shepard works up some resonant Eastern modalities on "Exile on Brown Street" and leads a pickup group (including a couple of Strapping Fieldhands) through live versions of "U.F.O.logy" and "Dusted." The pulsing "Quotients & Numbers" (which exudes a fervor reminiscent of embryonic Modern Lovers) proves Shepard is better off with a melody. **Evil Love Deeper,** which compiles material recorded by a variety of Shepard's "lesser" groups (including Lacquer and Skullbank) meanders in a similar fashion, taking in post-Beat art pieces like "2001: A Long Island Oddysey" and spazzed-out noise ventures ("Panasonic"). As the songs get shorter—they range from four minutes down to fifty seconds—the attitude gets worse, and the results more rewarding. [dss]

VULGAR BOATMEN

You and Your Sister (Record Collect) 1989 (Safe House) 1989
Please Panic. (Safe House/Caroline) 1992
OppositeSex (UK Blanco y Negro/EastWest) 1995

If the band's songs weren't about such mundane things as the emotional maze of regular life, and if the writing and playing of them weren't accomplished with such exquisite subtlety and quietly obsessive focus, the bizarre story of the Vulgar Boatmen might seem simply odd, an attention-getting gimmick that would look intriguing on a record company bio. In fact, the saga of the group with a dual identity—a sporadic studio-centered entity convened by Florida college professor Robert Ray and a remarkable international touring outfit led by Indianapolis auteur Dale Lawrence—reads like a troubled family saga in which claims to a name weigh heavy, ties that bind overcome obstacles of time and distance, and a common vision proves to be the greatest power of all.

Formed and abandoned in Florida in the early '80s by future Silo Walter Salas-Humara, the Vulgar Boatmen eventually came to rest, in a most irregular remote collaboration, on the mutual shoulders of singer/guitarists Ray (at the time a graduate student in Indiana) and Lawrence (a veteran of Bloomington's goofy punk Gizmos who had taken a course taught by Ray). After Ray returned to Florida, the two exchanged tapes by mail, jointly crafting songs that took shape as a sublime semi-electric pop sound melding the patient intensity and precision of the Feelies, the driven certainty of quiet Velvet Underground and the shapely melodic force of classic pop artisans. While Ray maintained a Vulgar Boatmen in the Southeast, Lawrence formed a group called Right to Left (later renamed the Vulgar Boatmen) to play the material that would eventually appear on the band's first album. Over time, the Indiana contingent became an exceptional live act of diverse talents and unassuming intensity, augmenting its original creations with one of the most eclectic cover repertoires on the planet.

As heard on all three albums, the nebulous group's ability to grasp and shape simple elements into three-chord (often two-chord) songs of delicate grandeur is unmatched by any of the countless groups that have attempted the same feat. With Lawrence and Ray's high, clear voices singing intimately unrevealing lyrics about people and places, always raising more questions than they answer, the Vulgar Boatmen are as American as an Andrew Wyeth painting and as evocative as a Robert Frost poem.

The Florida quintet initially gained local notice through a pair of tiny-edition cassettes and contributed songs to **Lagartija,** the 1988 solo album by Salas-Humara, who had left the fold somewhere along the way but returned to co-produce and appear on **You and Your Sister.** If the results aren't fully refined, the Boatmen sound is essentially in place on gorgeous songs like the archetypal "Mary Jane," the alternately disquieting and explosive "Change the World All Around," the enigmatic "Decision by the Airport" and the mesmerizing ripple of "Drive Somewhere."

The debut's characteristic features—songs, named for women (including the trademark "Margaret Says" formation), that almost invariably involve cars, a firm backbeat ticking like a clock, handsome, transforming guitar fancies, translucently elusive lyrics, more than a hint of tension in the restrained demeanor—are all upheld on the perfectly pitched and absolutely superb **Please Panic.** Although three different memberships for the band are listed on the back cover (a total of fourteen musicians!), the album couldn't be more focused if it were the work of a solitary artist. The tonal equality of the singers' voices, the claustrophobic narrowness of the stylistic approach and the writers' consistent lyrical tenor all dispel any fear of organizational confusion. With viola adding a somber undercurrent to the airy guitars and vocals, the songs are masterpieces of carefully paced folk-pop economy, following clearly marked (if dimly lit) paths without faltering or allowing the slightest deviation from course. The better half of an unfailingly fine dozen—"You Don't Love Me Yet," "You're the One," "I'm Not Stuck on You" (all great mix-tape flirting songs), "Allison Says," "We Can Figure This Out" and "Stop Alternating"—circle around hard decisions and mixed understandings with maddening uncertainty, acknowledging flaws and desires without giving in to either. At their best, the Boatmen can make your breath catch with an unexpected pause or make your spirits leap with a single turn of phrase.

Except for the organ that alters the rhythmic texture of several songs, **OppositeSex** varies little, using many of the same musicians (sixteen in all) to maintain the Boatmen's singular course. The egregiously incongruous rock crunch and bluntly topical lyrics of the inexplicable title track (co-written and sung by first-album alumnus Carey Crane) stand out like a mastering error from someone else's tapes, and the explicit country accents of the dull "Call Back Instead" suggest the dangers of stretching the stylistic boundaries at all. That said, "When We Walk," "We Can Walk" (entirely different songs), "Wide Awake," an overhaul of the Gizmos' "Heartbeat" (a loving pop tune so instantly familiar that it must be a lost Buddy Holly or Jonathan Richman classic in some parallel world, and is an indication of how long Lawrence has been a brilliant songwriter), "Shake," the Dobro-and-harmonica-colored "In a Minute" and "Genie Says" (in a pre–"Free as a Bird" maneuver, the Salas-Humara vocal was reclaimed from one of the band's '80s cassettes) make it seem as if time had stood still after **Please Panic.** And maybe it had. More than a year after its UK release, the album still had not appeared in America. [i]

See also *Silos.*

WACO BROTHERS

. . . To the Last Dead Cowboy (Bloodshot) 1995

WRECK

Wreck EP (Play It Again Sam USA) 1989
Soul Train (Play It Again Sam USA) 1990
House of Boris (Wax Trax) 1991
El Mundo de los Niños (C/Z) 1994

Call 'em way-co or wack-o, it doesn't make much difference: this part-time Chicago-based ensemble funnels the diverse backgrounds of its membership—singer/guitarist Jon Langford and drummer Steve Goulding of the Mekons (the latter also lately in Poi Dog Pondering), bassist Tommy Ray of the Bottle Rockets (replaced on the road by Alan Doughty of Jesus Jones), singer/guitarist Dean Schlabowske of Wreck and British mandolinist Tracey Deare—into a frenzied wiseguy whack at sturdy country rock that proves equal to their wanton ministrations**. . . To the Last Dead Cowboy** loosens the band's wig to the point where it nearly blows off and then does a deft highwire jig on the edge of collapse. Settling down doesn't diminish the fun, however—the Elvis-oid "If You Don't Change Your Mind" is an easy highlight, while the breakup waltz of "K.T. Tennessee" and the sappy duet "Lake of Vinegar" twang all the right heartstrings with sardonic glee. Neither does the political slant (see "Harm's Way," "Plenty Tough Union Made," "$ Bill the Cowboy"). Ultimately, the Wacos' greatest strength is raving Poguesiness, sending tunes like "Too Sweet to Die" and "Bad Times (Are Comin' Round Again)" into turbocharger heaven.

Just before starting the Wacos, Langford co-produced Wreck's **El Mundo de los Niños,** doing nothing to dilute the Chicago group's jagged rock aggression. Although sporting a different lineup than on the Steve Albini–produced **Soul Train** (ex–Die Kreuzen bassist Keith Brammer went off to join Carnival Strippers, for one), the quartet remains an angular crab, intelligently scratching its way across a concrete track behind Schlabowske's tunelessly articulate shouts and trebly guitar noise. The funny Mekons-country chorus of "The Lonesome Death of Casey Kasem" and the dragass progress of "Brick" provide the only clues to his imminent Waco-dom; otherwise, this world of children is nothing like that one. [i]

See also *Carnival Strippers, Mekons; TPRG.*

TOM WAITS

Closing Time (Asylum) 1973 (Elektra) 1990
The Heart of Saturday Night (Asylum) 1974 (Elektra) 1989
Nighthawks at the Diner (Asylum) 1975 (Elektra) 1989
Small Change (Asylum) 1976 (Elektra) 1989
Foreign Affairs (Asylum) 1977 (Elektra) 1989
Blue Valentine (Asylum) 1978 (Elektra) 1990
Heartattack and Vine (Asylum) 1980 (Elektra) 1990
Bounced Checks (Ger. Asylum) 1981
Swordfishtrombones (Island) 1983
Rain Dogs (Island) 1985
Anthology of Tom Waits (Asylum/Elektra) 1985
Franks Wild Years (Island) 1987
Big Time (Island) 1988
The Early Years (Bizarre/Straight) 1991
Night on Earth (Island) 1992
Bone Machine (Island) 1992
The Early Years Vol. 2 (Bizarre/Straight) 1993
The Black Rider (Island) 1993

VARIOUS ARTISTS

Step Right Up: The Songs of Tom Waits (Manifesto) 1995

HOLLY COLE

Temptation (Metro Blue) 1995

Tom Waits is at once a throwback and a visionary. His gritty Everyman sing-song and tubercular jazzcat persona—fusing seedy imagery and a frankly boozy, druggy ambience in music that is somehow quite beautiful and often unfashionably sentimental—hail directly from both Kurt Weill and the Beat generation. On the other hand, Waits is a sterling songsmith who has downplayed his gift for melody to daringly explore a fashionably dark avantist compositional mode using wildly imaginative production techniques.

Like Captain Beefheart and Sonic Youth, Waits forges a new musicality out of the decay, clangor and chaos of the late twentieth century. Few musicians of his generation (he was born in 1949) have as much street cred—Waits is a crucial relay point between Beat writers, especially William S. Burroughs and Charles Bukowski, and today's young hipsters—and he gets props for occasionally proving that uncompromising art and successful commerce can coincide.

Both volumes of **The Early Years** hail from 1971, when Waits made some early (unreleased) recordings for Frank Zappa's Bizarre label before moving on to David Geffen's Asylum Records. The two belated collections find Waits singing in a higher, clearer voice with sparser, more conventional arrangements than he would later adopt, when dissonance and metallic percussion timbres became an intrinsic part of his compositions. The songs are early-'70s SoCal singer/songwriter pop in the Randy Newman vein, albeit overlaid with a fine layer of LA grit and distinguished by such characteristic titles as "I'm Your Late Night Evening Prostitute" and "Looks Like I'm Up Shit Creek Again." And even those sound like classics. (**Vol. 2** includes early versions of such well-known Waits numbers as "Ol' 55," "Grapefruit Moon" and "Old Shoes (& Picture Postcards)," all of which were rerecorded on **Closing Time.)**

Waits hit an artistic and commercial peak during

the watershed **Swordfishtrombones/Rain Dogs** period. On the latter, Waits' beatnik hobo poetry, Beefheart (by way of Satchmo) vocals and some just plain impeccable songwriting ("Downtown Train" has been covered many times) are bolstered by a phenomenal band—guitarist Marc Ribot and junkyard percussionist Michael Blair supply the album's most defining sounds, but the backing cast also includes Keith Richards, Chris Spedding, Robert Quine and chief Lounge Lizard John Lurie. **Franks Wild Years,** the music for a misconceived theater piece, is a decided step down. The soundtrack for the disappointing documentary film, **Big Time**—mostly composed of reworked (sometimes radically so) versions of songs from **Franks Wild Years** and **Rain Dogs**—continues the downward slide.

Especially in this context, the **Night on Earth** soundtrack sounds like a wise holding action. Three tracks for the Jim Jarmusch film have vocals; although two are different versions of the same song ("Good Old World," "Back in the Good Old World"), it's a damn good song. The crackerjack band, which features Bay Area notables Joe Gore on guitar and Ralph Carney on everything from trumpet to pan pipes, ably emits Waits' distinctive junkyard wino jazz. Of the instrumental pieces, only the perfectly noir "Los Angeles Theme (Another Private Dick)" and the darkly jaunty "Carnival (Brunello Del Montalcino)" stand out a bit, and although the album doesn't merit close scrutiny or even repeated listenings—it is, after all, a film score—**Night on Earth** can make you feel like you're a character in one of Waits' songs.

With guest appearances by Primus bassist Les Claypool, Los Lobos' David Hidalgo (on violin and accordion) and Keith Richards (who provides yowling alleycat harmonies on "That Feel") as well as Carney and Gore, **Bone Machine** is true to its title: skeletal but impeccably, artfully structured. The hellish, apocalyptic imagery of the opener, "Earth Died Screaming," pretty much sets the tone, although the gloom is somewhat relieved by at least one certifiable Waits classic: the delightful "I Don't Wanna Grow Up" (later covered by the Ramones). Waits' already fuzzy growl is often further distorted; combined with the percussion-heavy arrangements, the effect is very dark. Indeed, the album's claustrophobic, nightmarish feel may have been what put a damper on its initial reception, but in retrospect, **Bone Machine** ranks with Waits' finest work.

The Black Rider contains music written for a theater production by pioneering dramatist Robert Wilson and William S. Burroughs (who "sings" on the studiedly curious "'T'Ain't No Sin"). Perhaps the best track is the darkly hilarious opener, "Lucky Day (Overture)," a little carnival waltz with Waits as a freak-show barker. Wrought in Waits' now familiar Weill-on-the-Bowery style, some of the songs are quite moving, and the poetry is as good as ever. Elsewhere, though, Waits indulges some of his shmaltzier tendencies while Wilson's high-falutin' presence seems to have made the whole thing a bit more precious and pretentious than it need be. It ain't one of his best, but even mediocre Tom Waits merits fifty-five minutes and thirty-nine seconds of attention.

Waits' songs have proven amenable to some mainstream-minded pop singers, but the tribute-paying **Step Right Up** lays claim to his innovative eccentricity as an inspiration for undergrounders. Among those plundering the catalogue are Violent Femmes ("Step Right Up"), Archers of Loaf ("Big Joe and Phantom 309"), Pete Shelley ("Better off Without a Wife"), Alex Chilton ("Downtown"), Jeffrey Lee Pierce ("Pasties and a G-String") and Tindersticks ("Mockin' Bird"). In a twist, the Buckley recording tucked between Pale Saints and Frente! is not by young Jeff but by his old man, Tim: a 1973 album version of "Martha."

Taking a very different view of the same subject, cool Toronto song stylist Holly Cole explores Waits' compositional classicism and jazz orientation on **Temptation,** a languorous, spaciously rendered collection of his least pulpy numbers. Cole's smoky alto already paints the material in much different hues than Waits' froggy rasp, and the spare arrangements—as little as string bass and brushes for "Temptation" or piano for "Frank's Theme," as much as a rhythm section and horn trio for "Little Boy Blue"—push the bracing revisionism even further. [ma/i]

See also *TPRG*.

WAKE

Masked (Cleopatra) 1993
Christine EP (Cleopatra) 1995
Nine Ways (Cleopatra) 1996

The Wake does its best to modernize Bauhaus/Sisters of Mercy–style goth and, for the most part, succeeds. On **Masked,** the Columbus, Ohio, quintet's unique sound, simultaneously ambient and sinister, can mainly be attributed to guitarist Rich Witherspoon and keyboardist Robert Brothers. Carefully arranged and executed songs like "Sideshow," "Silent Siren" and "Masked" best display their densely layered, tightly intertwined melodies, which drape elegantly over the resounding, slightly tribal work of drummer Daniel C. and bassist James Tramel. Troy Payne's deep, detached vocals make him sound like a weary disciple of Sisters of Mercy singer Andrew Eldritch.

For **Christine,** the Wake got Rosetta Stone to remix songs from **Masked** (two versions each of "Watchtower" and "Masked," plus one instrumental reinterpretation of "Siren"); in addition, the EP contains two renditions of the new title track. The result is an uninspired, monotonous soft-industrial rendering of material best heard in its original form. "Christine (Remix 2.3 wHATEver)" is the only track here with any genuine vivacity or structure.

After that gaffe, the Wake reasserted control over its music and reverted to an all-gothic format for **Nine Ways.** Joining "Christine," bold, commanding offerings like "Curtain" and "Reverend Mother" are similarly shadowy. New bassist Steven Creighton adds a more forceful quality to the scheme, but the Wake otherwise sounds much as it did on the debut. There is, however, a subtle sense of self-confidence that hadn't been evident before—perhaps the **Christine** convulsion confirmed the band's original instincts that goth, although currently a much less accessible/acceptable genre than industrial, is its true way. [ky]

DAVE WAKELING

See *General Public.*

WAKE OOLOO

Hear No Evil (Pravda) 1994
What About It (Pravda) 1995
Stop the Ride (Pravda) 1996

After the Feelies' influential decade-plus of obsessively precise pop geometry, it's understandable that Wake Ooloo, the post-Feelies quartet formed by singer/guitarist Glenn Mercer and percussionist-turned-drummer/vocalist Dave Weckerman, should be a bit less anal in its exposition. Joined by barely audible keyboardist Russell Gambino and bassist Troy Meiss, the New Jersey pair adjusts the medication on **Hear No Evil,** following a tangent from the trajectory (Dylan plus textured rock) of end-time Feelies. The songs are familiar in melody and structure, but Wake Ooloo's dynamics and arrangements aren't so tightly controlled; feedback and distortion are more random commodities, and stray notes are allowed to stick wherever they land. **Hear No Evil** is sometimes unfocused and sloppy, a victim of Mercer's limitations as a rampant rocker. The ratio of songs that wander ("Time to Go," "Effigy" and "Rise," crudely built on the "You Really Got Me" chord riff) to songs that work ("Nobody Heard," "Forty Days," "Another Song") is about even.

Mercer severed the Feelies umbilical connection with **What About It,** but it took some radical surgery. Rather than sprinting down narrow melodic corridors, the quartet (with new bassist John Dean in the lineup) demonstrates its ability to lose control in an unrestrained MC5-ish rock frenzy ("Don't Look Now") *and* unwind to a pretty four-chord stroll ("Anything"). Overall, the pop is poppier and the rock is rockier: "Monday Morning," the finale, builds from an atmospheric nothing to a stunning crescendo. In a surprising show of democracy, the once-autocratic Mercer gives everyone a turn at the mic, stepping aside for four of the album's dozen numbers. The uneven songwriting and singing—Mercer is the only reasonably competent vocalist in the bunch, the others don't come close—precludes stylistic continuity, a situation Mercer exacerbates with "Down That Road," a deeply uncharacteristic acoustic blues. [i]

See also *Speed the Plough.*

WALKABOUTS

The Walkabouts EP [tape] (Necessity) 1984
22 Disasters EP (Necessity) 1985
See Beautiful Rattlesnake Gardens (PopLlama Products) 1988
Cataract (Sub Pop) 1989
Rag & Bone EP (Sub Pop) 1990
Where the Deep Water Goes EP (Sub Pop) 1991
Scavenger (Sub Pop) 1991
Dead Man Rise EP (Sub Pop) 1992
Jack Candy EP (Ger. Sub Pop) 1993
New West Motel (Ger. Sub Pop) 1993 (Creative Man/Cargo) 1996
Your Hope Shines EP (Ger. Sub Pop) 1993
Satisfied Mind (Ger. Sub Pop) 1993 (Creative Man/Cargo) 1996
Setting the Woods on Fire (Ger. Sub Pop) 1994 (Creative Man/Cargo) 1995
Good Luck Morning EP (Ger. Sub Pop) 1994
Devil's Road (Ger. Virgin) 1996

CHRIS AND CARLA

Shelter for an Evening (Ger. Sub Pop) 1993
Life Full of Holes (Ger. Glitterhouse) 1995

CHRIS & CARLA WITH THE MYLOS ALL-STARS

Nights Between Stations—Live in Thessaloniki (Gr. Hitch-Hyke/Ger. Glitterhouse) 1995

Seattle's Walkabouts play a quirkily personalized brand of updated folk-rock, distinguished by a darkly layered sound and the yin/yang vocals of founders Chris Eckman and Carla Torgerson. The early releases on Necessity and PopLlama find the band sounding a bit tentative and unformed, but contain enough flashes of inspiration to encourage further attention. **Cataract** and the six-song **Rag & Bone** (combined as **Rag & Bone Plus Cataract,** a single CD bearing the EP's original artwork) are more distinctive, mining a richly shadowy strain of Americana. The addition of keyboardist Glenn Slater is significant to the EP, helping to broaden the band's sound.

Scavenger (which adds a name producer, Gary Smith, and guest appearances by Brian Eno and Natalie Merchant) is impressive, even if the artificially speedy tempos of such numbers as "Dead Man Rise" and "Stir the Ashes" rob the songs of a certain amount of atmosphere. And even if Smith's bright, seamless production is unsuited to the subtle menace of tunes like "The Night Watch" and "Where the Deep Water Goes," the material is strong enough that the quintet's fundamental integrity still shines through, with Torgerson emerging as a particularly commanding presence. **Where the Deep Water Goes** combines two **Scavenger** tracks with non-album covers of Alex Chilton ("Big Black Car") and Neil Young ("On the Beach"), while **Dead Man Rise** contains the titular album track, a remix of another ("Train to Mercy") and three European radio-session recordings.

It's a shame that Sub Pop didn't see fit to release **New West Motel** domestically, since it's the album on which the Walkabouts truly come into their own. The more organic production approach showcases the band's instrumental strengths, giving songs like "Jack Candy," "Your Hope Shines" and "Break It Down Gently" new textures as well as a sense of aggression that's more conducive to the darker elements of the group's personality. The **Jack Candy** CD EP features Tom Waits and Neil Young tunes as well as an interesting reworking of a traditional gospel number.

The largely acoustic-flavored **Satisfied Mind** is an unsurprisingly eloquent collection of interpretations of songs from sources as diverse as the Carter Family, Charlie Rich, Patti Smith and Nick Cave. The Walkabouts' skillful renditions illuminate and extend the band's own vision; among the guests are R.E.M.'s Peter Buck and Screaming Trees singer Mark Lanegan.

Though its title quotes an old Hank Williams tune, the consistently ace **Setting the Woods on Fire** features all original material. It pretty much picks up where **New West Motel** leaves off, with strong tunes like "Firetrap," "Good Luck Morning" and the rousing, horn-driven "Hole in the Mountain" given a spiky, full-bodied grace. The **Good Luck Morning** EP includes two album tracks and two live numbers.

Devil's Road, the first Walkabouts disc on which the compositions are credited solely to Eckman, is its most ambitiously eclectic album and certainly one of its best. The band sounds stronger and more distinctive than ever, and the excellent use of strings on six tracks enhances the emotional potency of both restrained, aching Torgerson-sung songs ("The Light Will Stay On," "Christmas Valley") and more aggressive Eckman-led material like "Blue Head Flame."

The three Chris and Carla releases are worthy adjuncts to the Walkabouts' catalogue. **Shelter for an Evening** is an unadorned live recording from two acoustic duo shows in Germany, with an agreeable mix of Walkabouts material and songs by Dylan, Young, Jimmy Webb and Richard Thompson. **Life Full of Holes,** a full-blown studio effort, is not dissimilar to Walkabouts albums except for the more relaxed (though hardly complacent) sound. The pair is here joined by the rest of the Walkabouts, Tindersticks (who back up the duo on two tracks), Peter Buck and Scott McCaughey on a typically fine set of mostly original material. **Nights Between Stations** was recorded live in Greece with backing by local musicians. [ss]

See also *Tindersticks; TPRG.*

WALT MINK

Miss Happiness (Caroline) 1992
Bareback Ride (Caroline) 1993
El Producto (Atlantic) 1996

Marc Bolan understood the creative potential of setting wimpy vocals against decisive rock choogle, but the power-pop groups that followed the leader in the '70s (Milk 'n' Cookies, Shoes, 20/20 and so forth) and beyond reduced the electric offensive to tightly compressed guitar distortion that, in its gentle little-tiger roar, stayed as pretty as the singers' fey voices. Not Walt Mink. The trio—formed at Macalester College in St. Paul, Minnesota—pushes the walls of soft and strong so far apart that it's sometimes hard to believe the audible evidence of what's going on.

John Kimbrough (son of *Murphy Brown* actor Charles Kimbrough) manages the feat of singing like he's about to doze off after inhaling too much helium while playing guitar with a kinetic fervor that would make Jimi Hendrix kiss the sky. Armed with an equally explosive, turn-on-a-dime rhythm section—bassist Candice Belanoff and drummer Joey Waronker (whose sister leads that dog and whose father was president of Warner Bros. Records), Walt Mink debuted with **Miss Happiness.** The album is a marvel of winsome melodies set like precious jewels atop churning walls of intricate rock. In conception, the attack owes more to the fill-every-corner pressure of speed metal than the look-at-us-we're-cute world of pudding bowl haircuts. A couple of songs coagulate into thick puddles of shapeless gunk, but the best ones soak up several generations of rock style and carry it safely through Walt Mink's distinctive abyss. The funk-accented "Miss Happiness," the slabby "Love You Better," the nothing-of-the-sort "Quiet Time," the naggy "Smoothing the Ride," the railroading "Croton-Harmon (Local)" and "Showers Down" are all thrilling results of the band's original something-for-everyone formulation; a startling cover of Nick Drake's acoustic wisp "Pink Moon" collates divergent decades and sensibilities into a spectacular artifact.

Bareback Ride doesn't change anything substantial, but the songs aren't as strong or appealing and the playing is uninspired, making the album all but redundant. As if he had discharged too much of his initiative on **Miss Happiness** and not gotten enough back, Kimbrough weaves a simple, busy web of guitar, roaring just as loudly but concentrating his efforts into metallic vignettes rather than functionally stable textures. The radio-attacking "Disappear" is good enough, but the Indian music affectation of "Sunnymede" only adds novelty to a record that is in far greater need of substance. (The three female members of that dog guest on voices and strings.)

After **Bareback Ride,** Walt Mink signed to Columbia but left without releasing a record; the next stop was Atlantic, where the group—no longer including Waronker, off to play with Beck after guesting with 9-Iron—made **El Producto.** If not consistently engrossing, the third album is still easily Walt Mink's best. Stylistic variety is the key to the power trio's progress: while Kimbrough's hyperactive guitar swarms like a face full of angry electric bees in "Stood Up," "Betty" makes smart use of the loud/soft switch, "Me & My Dog" drops the curtain for a slithery raga-lead approach that works this time and "Love in the Dakota" (an inexplicable retelling of *Rosemary's Baby* made even more seductive by robust cello) is only one of several folky, or at least acoustic-based, arrangements. Still one of the most imaginative extreme-guitar activists in pop, Kimbrough has likewise expanded his vocal repertoire, adding Beatlesque stylings and a middle register to tether the higher reaches of his eccentric stop-start-hold-rush phrasing. Busy new drummer Orestes Morfín (ex–Bitch Magnet) fits in perfectly, and songwriting that isn't just a framework for instrumental exertions pushes the best tracks over the top. **El Producto** is close enough for that cigar. [i]

JUSTIN WARFIELD

My Field Trip to Planet 9 by Justin Warfield
(Qwest/Reprise) 1993

JUSTIN WARFIELD SUPERNAUT

The Justin Warfield Supernaut (Qwest/Reprise) 1995

Los Angeles native Justin Warfield was barely twenty when **My Field Trip to Planet 9** was released, and that record's promise, combined with his youth, led many to expect great things of the psychedelicized rapper. What *should* have been expected of his youth was some malleability and capriciousness; all his next record of **Sgt. Pepper**–influenced psychedelic rock shares with the debut is its reflexive title.

Produced by Prince Paul, **My Field Trip to Planet 9** is a joyously atypical hip-hop record: Warfield's trippy guitar loops take the place of shopworn soul/funk samples, he goes by his given name rather than a contrived street handle and his view of pop culture is as expanded as his mind—Ravi Shankar and *Joanie Loves Chachi* both get namechecked. Warfield's plain-spoken raps seek to lull rather than rouse, and his delivery sounds like a mid-afternoon stoner monologue that just happens to rhyme.

Dispensing with hip-hop, Warfield turned to rock with the four-piece Supernaut. Much of the material is as original as Lenny Kravitz—which is to say not very—and the lyrics are not much more intelligible. "Serpent's tongue just grazed the fire/Demon-shed tongue drip cornshoe dire" goes "Moontower." Warfield is a charmer, though, and both records' shortcomings can be written off as the miscalculations of an overenthusiastic rookie. [sf]

WATERBOYS

The Waterboys EP (Ensign/Island) 1983
The Waterboys (UK Ensign) 1983 (Ensign/Chrysalis) 1986
A Pagan Place (Ensign/Island) 1984 (Ensign/Chrysalis) 1987
This Is the Sea (Ensign/Island) 1985 (Ensign/Chrysalis) 1987
Fisherman's Blues (Ensign/Chrysalis) 1988
Room to Roam (Ensign/Chrysalis) 1990
The Best of the Waterboys '81–'90 (Ensign/Chrysalis) 1991
Dream Harder (Geffen) 1993
The Secret Lite of the Waterboys: 81–85 (Ensign/Chrysalis) 1994

MIKE SCOTT

Bring 'Em All In (Chrysalis/EMI) 1995

ANTHONY THISTLETHWAITE

Aesop Wrote a Fable (UK Rolling Acres) 1993

On its 1983 debut album, the Waterboys—a united kingdom of musicians from England, Scotland and Wales based in London—concocted a spirited combination of stirring rock and Celtic folk, a soaring, passionate blend that swelled dramatically under Mike Scott's unrestrained vocals and colorful guitar playing. The following year's equally electrifying **A Pagan Place** solidified the Waterboys' reputation for playing "The Big Music," as Scott aptly described it on the second album.

The Edinburgh native then introduced a bit of country and blues—and a barrow of Irish folk traditionalism—into the Waterboys, first as one of several approaches on the eclectic **This Is the Sea** and then full-blown on **Fisherman's Blues** and **Room to Roam.** Coincident with his relocation to County Galway in the mid-'80s, Scott moved to erase most traces of the former Waterboys formulation in favor of a wholesome acoustic folk sound, largely shaped by an important new arrival, Irish fiddler Steve Wickham. **Fisherman's Blues** features such rollicking songs as "And a Bang on the Ear," "Has Anybody Here Seen Hank?" and "When Will We Be Married?," which make the most of Scott's adopted heritage, while **Room to Roam** (notwithstanding two incongruous electric rockers) can claim a fine, unaffected rendition of the old "Raggle Taggle Gypsy," the bouncy romanticism of "A Man Is in Love" and the slow-moving epiphany "Bigger Picture."

In 1991, evidently having satisfied his unquenchable thirst for Gaelic culture, Scott packed himself off to New York and formed a completely new band to indulge his new passion: mainstream guitar rock. Beginning with an obligatory declaration of "The New Life," **Dream Harder** is a major drag, both musically and in its multiple flaky announcements of faith. Scott tries religion ("I just found God!," he shouts in "Glastonbury Song"); in "Corn Circles," a song whose exaggerated vintage theatricality *must* be an intentional pun, he prattles on about his belief in farm patterns made by aliens. "The Return of Jimi Hendrix," a nonsensical dream served up as a western clip-clop rocker, makes the late musician the object of Scott's desperate adoration; sitars and other flower-power implements join him for the simpleminded wordplay of "Spiritual City." With that, the Waterboys ceased to exist.

The two compilations cover, respectively, the obvious and the obscure. **The Best of the Waterboys '81–'90** evenly samples the first five albums, omitting some worthwhile tracks but basically following the winding progress of the band's first decade. For those already up to speed, **The Secret Life of the Waterboys 81–85** is an intriguing fifteen-song collection of outtakes, demos, radio sessions, concert takes and alternate mixes from the band's early years. (There's even a 1981 radio session item by Scott's pre-Waterboys band, Another Pretty Face.) Unfamiliar versions of "A Pagan Place" and "Don't Bang the Drum" provide an interesting look through the band's musical treasure chest, though nothing here is as powerful or convincing as the album versions.

After dissolving the band, Scott tried going it solo with **Bring 'Em All In.** The album's uncluttered, folk/acoustic style is much better suited to his increasingly mellow singing style, making it more enjoyable than anything he's done since **Fisherman's Blues.** Scott is still carried away with his new age idealism, though: the lyrics of "Long Way to the Light" and "Building the City of Light" are both so insufferably earnest and overpoweringly positive that they distract all attention away from any merits the music might have. Fortunately, the shimmery, evocative title track and the hushed, soothing "She Is So Beautiful" redeem the effort. The jaunty, exuberant "City Full of Ghosts (Dublin)" is another worthwhile track. The album's laid-back stance isn't as exciting as the Waterboys' salad days, and Scott's current infatuations aren't as inspiring as his Emerald Isle fixation, but this is a step back in the right direction.

When saxophonist/keyboardist/guitarist/etc. Anthony Thistlethwaite, a member of Scott's company from the outset through **Room to Roam** (and a busy session player with plenty of outside credits), put a song entitled "Muddy Waterboy" at the head of his 1993 solo album, it surely meant that he was ready to unload on his longtime employer's populist pretensions. No such luck: it turned out the Leicester native had been nursing an entirely different jones the whole time, one to do with McKinley Morganfield rather than Celtic traditionalism. **Aesop Wrote a Fable** is a straight-up Chicago blues album, mixing a few originals with classics of the canon from Willie Dixon and Sonny Boy Williamson as well as some from Peter Green and John Mayall. Thistlethwaite's a good enough singer, and the lively arrangements (three with horns) refresh the oldies enough to justify the effort. Former bandmate Karl Wallinger guests on piano. [ky/i]

See also *World Party; TPRG.*

WATERDOG

Waterdog (Atlantic) 1995

Of all the Green Day clones who streamed onto the major-label stage as **Dookie** kept on printing money—and, truth be told, there weren't that many, not like the swarm of grunge do-bees that sprang out of Pearl Jam's poo (I have absolutely no idea what that says about the two groups' relative merits)—Waterdog are . . . somewhere in the middle. The Providence, Rhode Island, quartet is both credible (meaning they didn't hear "Welcome to Paradise" on the clock radio and chuck away all those years of jam-funk practice to join the fun) and deft enough to ape the Clash, quote a Billy Bragg lyric, trot out a ska beat and lightfinger an East Bay melody or two without setting off burglar alarms. If that doesn't mean there are any major signs of originality or personality on Waterdog's fine-sounding debut, a few memorable tracks (most notably "Jessica" and the self-effacing, realistic "What's the Difference") and infectious enthusiasm give Waterdog the right to jump around the pop-punk playground with all the other kids. [i]

WATERLILLIES

Envoluptuousity (Kinetic/Sire/Reprise) 1992
Tempted (Kinetic/Sire/Reprise) 1994

On first listen, the music of New York City's Waterlillies—singer Sandra Jill Alikas-St. Thomas and instrumentalist Ray Carroll—could easily be shelved alongside Book of Love and A Flock of Seagulls: thin, catchy synthpop with a recently expired sell-by date. But **Envoluptuousity** is redeemed by several factors, including Alikas' flexible, disciplined soprano and Carroll's sterling production. Despite lyrics that tend toward the tone of diary entries (not always a bad thing), the stylistic range the two bring to their songwriting buoys the nine cuts, from the dreamy "Sunshine Like You" and "Hip to My Way" (Alikas' take on Carroll's life as a young urban homosexual) through the piano-based house of "Tired of You" and a couple of ballads, "The Only One (I Could Stand)" and "Mermaid Song."

Although the debut sank with barely a ripple, the two returned two years later with **Tempted.** The album kicks off with the title tune, a rousing dance track that garnered a fair share of radio and club play; released as the followup single, "Never Get Enough," fared even better thanks to a couple of minimal but muscular remixes by Junior Vasquez. Elsewhere, "Supersonic" incorporates elements of trance, "I Don't Want Your Love" uses a hip-hop beat, and Alikas flexes her developing diva chops on down-tempo numbers like "How Does It Feel?" and "Take My Breath Away" (not a Berlin cover). Except for a wholly unnecessary a cappella rendition of Bacharach/David's "Close to You," the Waterlillies' sophomore album stretches the boundaries of a limited aesthetic palette with greater returns than the debut. That wasn't enough to keep the duo together, however, and they parted ways in 1995. [kbr]

MIKE WATT

Ball-Hog or Tugboat? (Columbia) 1994

FIREHOSE

Ragin', Full-On (SST) 1986
if'n (SST) 1987
fROMOHIO (SST) 1989
Flyin' the Flannel (Columbia) 1991
Live Totem Pole (Columbia) 1992
Mr. Machinery Operator (Columbia) 1993

A blue-collar hero in an art-school world, bassist and working-joe conceptualist Mike Watt has been a titanic presence on the avant-rock scene since the dawn of the '80s—when he, guitarist D Boon and drummer George Hurley formed the Minutemen. That spectacularly prolific (a dozen records in just five years) band's heady mélange of skittery avant-garde rhythms, burly guitar assays and agit-prop sloganeering was as revelatory a development as any in punk rock's two-decade history. When Boon was killed in a van crash in December 1985, Watt considered abdicating his station, but he and Hurley were coaxed into perseverance by an Ohio-bred Minutemen fan, Ed Crawford, thus propagating fIREHOSE.

When that band wound down, the proud resident of San Pedro, California, reverted to his long-held position that the bassist—what he's often called "the lame guy's position"—was meant to be heard and not seen, which prompted the assembly of the promethean posse that appears on his solo debut, **Ball-Hog or Tugboat?** On the cast-of-dozens disc, Watt does his best to avoid the spotlight, ceding vocal chores to disciples as varied as Eddie Vedder (whose straight-faced reading of the anti-rockist "Against the 70's" vindicates him from Pearl Jam's excesses) and Evan Dando (an appropriate choice for the loopy-yet-loving "Piss-Bottle Man," which Watt wrote in tribute to his road-weary father). To Watt's credit, he never lets things degenerate into the sort of jam-session indolence so common to cronies-in-the-studio packages: even the faithful cover of Funkadelic's "Maggot Brain" (a chance for J Mascis to pump up the volume) maintains a clear sense of purpose. It's a dizzying compendium of hipster jive, balls-to-the-wall rock and asides like Bikini Kill leader Kathleen Hanna's impassioned spoken-word piece explaining why she *won't* appear on the album (a boys' club atmosphere and the presence of an alleged rapist). Still, the titular question posed by **Ball Hog or Tugboat?** makes it clear that Mike Watt will always be the latter—the kind of man-machine that rock needs to get it out of its axis-bending ruts.

The early fIREHOSE records are hampered by Crawford's chronic unwillingness to push his adolescent heroes. Thus, both **Ragin', Full-On** and **if'n** take flight only when Watt steps up to the mic (as on the disjointed "Me, You and Remembering") and exponentially increases both the energy and risk levels. Those moments also provide a breather from Crawford's sometimes charming, sometimes grating voice—an attribute that *does* allow him to successfully lampoon Michael Stipe on the latter disc's devastating "For the Singer of R.E.M."

For better and worse, **fROMOHIO** is a far more mature effort. Crawford has absorbed a bit of his bandmates' eccentricities, and his voice has lost some of its shriller edges (both thanks, no doubt, to the trio's constant touring). Watt and Hurley, however, seem to pull their punches a bit: "Understanding" and "Vastopol" reek of second-string '70s country-rock. **Flyin' the Flannel** reinstates some of the aggro in the form of Watt's hometown tribute "O'er the Town of Pedro" as well as fractious meanderings like "Tien an Man Dream Again." The trio even scored an unlikely hit of sorts with a subdued cover of Daniel Johnston's "Walking the Cow." The seven-song **Live Totem Pole** captures the band in a habitat much more natural than the studio (LA's Palomino, August '91), and fIREHOSE makes the most of the adrenaline rush, delivering solid versions of Public Enemy's "Sophisticated Bitch," Superchunk's "Slack Motherfucker" and Blue Öyster Cult's "The Red and the Black," a Minutemen perennial. Produced by J Mascis, the tired-sounding **Mr. Machinery Operator** is best forgotten. [dss]

See also *Sonic Youth; TPRG.*

WC AND THE MAAD CIRCLE

See *Coolio.*

WEB

See *Bill Laswell.*

WEDDING PRESENT

George Best (UK Reception) 1987
Tommy (UK Reception) 1988
Ukrainski Vistupi v Johna Peela (UK RCA) 1989
Janice Long Evening Show EP (UK Nighttracks/Strange Fruit) 1988
The BBC Sessions (Strange Fruit/Dutch East India Trading) 1988
Bizarro (UK RCA) 1989 (RCA) 1990 (Manifesto) 1996
Brassneck EP (UK RCA) 1990
Seamonsters (UK RCA) 1991 (First Warning) 1992 (Bizarre/Planet) 1994 (Manifesto) 1996
Hit Parade 1 (First Warning) 1992 (Bizarre/Planet) 1994 (Manifesto) 1996
Hit Parade 2 (UK BMG) 1993 (Bizarre/Planet) 1994 (Manifesto) 1996
Hit Parade 3 EP (UK BMG)
John Peel Sessions 1987–90 (Strange Fruit/Dutch East India Trading) 1993
Watusi (Island) 1994
Mini EP (UK Cooking Vinyl) 1996
Mini Plus (Cooking Vinyl) 1996
Saturnalia (Cooking Vinyl) 1996

UKRAINIANS

The Ukrainians (UK Cooking Vinyl) 1991
Pisni Iz the Smiths EP (Cooking Vinyl) 1992
Verony (UK Cooking Vinyl) 1993
Kultura (UK Cooking Vinyl) 1994 (Cooking Vinyl) 1995

When the Wedding Present chose iconoclastic soccer superstar George Best as the cover boy and namesake of its first album, the Leeds group wasn't just honoring a universal pop icon or a local childhood hero. (Singer Dave Gedge and guitarist Pete Solowka were raised near Manchester, for whose team Best played.) The British love their football in ways that go beyond fandom; only the most hopeless Red Sox or Cubs diehard could truly grasp the desperate post-conscious love/hate dedication detailed in Nick Hornby's *Fever Pitch* memoir. Whatever idealism has not yet been sucked dry from the youth of this fallen empire, its tattered and jaundiced remains have been invested heavily (if not equally) in pop and soccer. As a result, the campaigns that take place on their respective fields can become a lot more personal and close to home for adherents than an impartial observer might be able to gauge from the cheap seats.

Like the Smiths, the Jam, Slade and the Beatles before them, the Wedding Present came to have much greater resonance than a mere bunch of tunes with madly strummed guitars, some ordinary faces elevated by television, might suggest. With Mitty-esque aplomb, the quartet quickly became a part of England, musical evidence that dedication and imagination were still sewn into the nation's fiber, and that—like the possibility held out by the World Cup every four years—a brighter future just might lie one stealthy hit away.

When the Smiths stepped down from their perch in 1987, the Wedding Present—led by singer/songwriter/guitarist Gedge, now the foursome's only original member—was conveniently poised to fill the cultural void thus created. He came armed with a deft balance of arrogance and insouciance, archness and populism, art and artlessness. The band's catchy, rushed, offhand singles could not have been better suited to win the heart and minds of self-obsessed sensitivos. If the band's voluminous output hasn't been distinguished by memorable melodic exposition, the sameness of its work actually contributes to its no-frills familiarity, as does the group's avoidance of stardom's trappings in its generally anonymous and uninformative record packaging.

Solowka strums as if his hand were on fire throughout **George Best;** the unfussy rhythm section races to keep pace as Gedge delivers his offbeat flurries of small-scale perception ("Everyone Thinks He Looks Daft," "It's What You Want That Matters," "My Favourite Dress") in a gruff, semi-singing non-style that certainly owes a debt to some of Morrissey's idiosyncrasies. **Ukrainski Vistupi v Johna Peela,** a Solowka-led detour into traditional Ukrainian folk music, served early notice that the Weddoes were open to odd ideas, and unlikely to settle for a career of humdrum routine. (That particular ethnic impulse, however, was shunted off into the Ukrainians, a band formed by Solowka as a side project. After he left the Wedding Present at the turn of the decade, it became his main musical pursuit. The Ukrainians have since released three albums and a hysterical EP of translated Smiths covers.)

Tommy summarizes the prolific band's first two years in a collection of singles and radio sessions from '85 and '86. But the group's discography includes numerous other broadcast recordings and albums compiled from them. The eight-track **BBC Sessions** combines two prior British releases of 1986 sessions. The twelve-track 1993 album gathers together dates from '87, '88 and '90, and contains alternate versions of songs from **George Best** and **Seamonsters,** as well as such typically eclectic material choices as Altered Images' "Happy Birthday."

Just as it seemed the Wedding Present might succumb to an already tired stylistic formula in its primary work, American noise producer Steve Albini (whose four tracks, issued in the UK in 1990 as the **Brassneck** EP, were added to the American issue of the otherwise uneventful **Bizarro**) arrived to bring the Wedding Present in for a recharge. While Gedge's offhand ruminations are still delivered in something of an Ian-Curtis-fan-next-door voice, the sound of Solowka burning out amplifiers is far more distracting than his usual semi-cloying jangle.

Evidently satisfied with that test run, the Wedding Present engaged Albini for an entire album. A tangle of crossed relationship wires, **Seamonsters** is a stirring mixture that adds bruising instrumental aggression—seemingly at random—to the simple folk-rock and pop structures. Until the production idea turns into a gimmick halfway, uncertainty makes **Seamonsters** an exciting, multi-dimensional contradiction. When the faders suddenly burn out in the middle of "Dalliance," Gedge has to struggle to be heard in the exciting din; when all hell breaks loose in "Lovenest" and "Corduroy," he just stands aside and lets Solowka's replacement, Paul Dorrington, do his damage without further comment. Unlike most of the bands who choose to express themselves with paint-stripping intensity, the

Wedding Present is a pop group through and through; what's left when the fuzzboxes get switched off here is pretty, sweet even. The provocative song titles—"Dalliance," "Suck," "Octopussy"—suggest a stronger drive behind the congenial tone. The US edition of the ten-song album adds three British B-sides.

Instead of recording a new LP in 1992, the Wedding Present devoted the year to executing an ambitious project worthy of both Christo and Ed McMahon. On the first Monday of each month, from January to December, the group released a new 7-inch (the A-side an original, the B-side a cover) in the UK. The gimmick guaranteed the band extra-musical notoriety as well as unprecedented chart success: snowballing interest, coupled with the short shelf lives of these limited-edition issues, accelerated sales enough to vault the lot, if only for a week each, into the British Top 30 in turn, thereby earning the Wedding Present a Guinness Book citation for equalling Elvis Presley's feat of a dozen chart hits within a calendar year.

If only the records were as deliberate as the scheme. Enthusiasm for the concise, punchy 45 format does not equal a talent for it, and the Wedding Present's sketchy structures and casual indie sound do not make its pop craft timelessly memorable, even in pop's disposable aesthetic. Of the dozen A-sides produced in this effort, none are apotheoses of the art; some ("Blue Eyes," "California," "Boing!") would make good album filler. Given the opportunity, that's how some of them register. **Hit Parade 1** and **Hit Parade 2** compile, respectively, the first and second chronological halves of the campaign. Each disc presents six months' worth of originals, followed by their six flipsides—which at least have the benefit of songwriting variety and an imaginative selection process. Among the treats on **Hit Parade 1** are Neil Young's "Don't Cry No Tears," a revelatory rendition of Julee Cruise's "Falling" (the *Twin Peaks* theme) and an amusing swipe at the Monkees' "Pleasant Valley Sunday"; the catalogues of Altered Images, Close Lobsters and the Go-Betweens also cough up a tune each. Among **HP2**'s genre-spanning covers are the reverently wah-wahed "The Theme From Shaft," Bowie's "Chant of the Ever Circling Skeletal Family," Mud's "Rocket," Bow Wow Wow's "Go Wild in the Country" and Elton John's "Step Into Christmas." (As a byproduct of the band's standing invitation from the John Peel show, initial English copies of **Hit Parade 2** included a bonus disc of the series' songs remade for radio transmission.) Stretching the concept a tad, **Hit Parade 3** is a semi-related six-song collection of covers.

If Gedge can be observed to harbor some uncontrollable artistic urges, **Watusi** indulges two of the most evident—toward trendy Amerindie powerhouses and duplicitous romantic entanglements. Produced/organ-ized by Steve Fisk, with vocal assists on two tracks from Heather Lewis of Beat Happening, the Wedding Present downshifts into a winning compromise with the light, easygoing minimal pop known to emanate from Olympia, Washington. Frequently slow and spare, letting small-scale instrumental restraint release Gedge's most luminous melodies and performances, the album is a surprising charmer—except in the lyrics of songs that shrug off guilt while acknowledging its validity. "For a start I don't feel any remorse/But how can I resist/When she doesn't even know you exist," Gedge sings merrily in "Catwoman," which trots out the predictable feline sex metaphors. In "Big Rat," he tries to defuse a tearful row with the pathetic excuse that "she meant absolutely nothing to me . . . I'm not sure I even had any fun." In "Gazebo," he tells an ex "just how much you meant to me," offers the information that "I'm seeing someone here you don't know her" and then turns the tables: "She's one in a million, but she isn't you." Musically, **Watusi** has all the variety absent from prior Wedding Present albums, as if the group had suddenly discovered that an album could be more than one thing without breaking into little pieces. "Spangle," in which Gedge is the loser for a change, gets a crackling 78-rpm atmosphere that doesn't seem gimmicky; "So Long, Baby" gets away with a patchwork of a giddy power-pop refrain and a thick, tough Fall-like verse. This is the kind of excellent record the Wedding Present should have made years ago.

After another long break, the group picked up the other thread of its obsession, and did an EP of songs at least nominally about cars and driving. Released in the US with a Butterglory cover and two other added tracks (expanding the clever automotive joke of the title, **Mini**, to **Mini Plus** in the process), the record retains some of the open-toed architecture and delicate detailing of **Watusi,** but does it on cruise control, and fails—by a couple of microns—to spark the previous album's gratifying combustion. [i]

See also *TPRG.*

WEEN

God Ween Satan–The Oneness (Twin\Tone) 1990
The Pod (Shimmy-Disc) 1991 (Elektra) 1995
Pure Guava (Elektra) 1992
Chocolate and Cheese (Elektra) 1994
12 Golden Country Greats (Elektra) 1996

COGS

Absolute Ween: The Cogs Perform the Songs of Ween EP (Bear) 1994

After establishing that any monkeys with a Tascam 4-track and enough mind-expanding drugs *can* produce listenable sounds of arguable merit, Ween didn't stop there. Gene and Dean Ween (aka singer Mickey Melchiondo and guitarist Aaron Freeman)—the pride (er . . .) of New Hope, Pennsylvania—quickly progressed from extreme and outrageous self-indulgence to moderate and highly entertaining self-indulgence. All it took was a wicked, *Mad*-magazine-addled sense of what's amusing (just about everything) and what's too tasteless or crude (nothing), talented studio pals and their own skills. In the wig-tightening process, Ween stopped being a fringe-weird affront to all but the scruffiest indie-rock addicts and became a lovable college-radio fixture, inbred nephews of They Might Be Giants, raised in Juvenile Hall to create their own engaging fantasy world. Feckless ingenuity and a puerile sensibility make Dean and Gene unreliable musical friends—get too close and you might get retched on as they run off, cackling—but Ween has life-of-the-party stamped all over its low forehead.

God Ween Satan—The Oneness, a twenty-six-song debut produced by Andrew Weiss (better known for his bass role in Rollins Band), begins with the shrieked diatribe "You Fucked Up" and proceeds to thrash around in a dada sandbox, throwing out made-up voices and devolved musical idioms for more than an hour. The damage includes the munchkin dink-pop of "Don't Laugh (I Love You)," a funky cover of Prince's "Shockadelica," two lines of demento jazz-blues ("I Gots a Weasel"), more peeves ("Cold & Wet"), overweight metal ("Mushroom Festival in Hell"), breezy reggae ("Nicole") and fake flamenco ("El Camino"). There's even a Beastie Boys sendup ("Old Queen Cole") and an incisive nineteen-second Bruce Springsteen parody ("Old Man Thunder"). Like the true brats they are, Ween'll try anything and dare you to sit through it. Equally entertaining and infuriating, **The Oneness** is certainly unique.

The brats brewed up another batch of Weenness for **The Pod:** twenty-two new episodes of mindless drivel recorded at home on 4-track. Less inflamed and inspired than the first album (blame, perhaps, the five cans of Scotchgard the band claims to have inhaled), **The Pod** lurches, howls, fuzzes and strums through sloppy creations that are mostly one hit short of a high. When they're not roaring out of control, songs drift aimlessly. The Beatles parodies ("Right to the Ways and the Rules of the World" and "Pork Roll Egg and Cheese") are pretty funny, as is the straight-faced folk duet "Oh My Dear (Falling in Love)," but it says a lot about the album that "Pollo Asado," a Mexican restaurant menu order set to music, is one of its highlights. Many of the tracks are essentially tape manipulation experiments in sound (the pitch of "Demon Sweat" drifts unsettlingly downward throughout the track): since Ween can write actual songs, they're a waste.

Against all odds, major-label intervention didn't screw Ween up. **Pure Guava,** which is every bit as uninhibited, profane and absurd as its two predecessors—witness such delicacies as "Flies on My Dick," "Reggaejunkiejew" and "Hey Fat Boy (Asshole)"—is more judicious in its differentiation between keepers and the runts of the hellzapoppin' litter. Also, the audio quality of their self-contained home production is significantly improved. (Maybe they stopped having to record over old cassettes.) "Push th' Little Daisies," a peppy and irritating old-lady-voiced ode to flowers (or is it burial?), was presentable enough for radio play; "Don't Get 2 Close (2 My Fantasy)" continues the pair's affair with English-accented '60s pop; "I Saw Gener Cryin' in His Sleep" adds tenderness to the emotional palette; "Pumpin' 4 the Man" is a racing country dig at the local gas-jockey ("So get your fingers out your ass/And pump some faggot's gas/And think about how much New Hope sucks"). The sound effects (not what you think) of "Poop Ship Destroyer" are even more unforgivable. **Pure Guava**—obnoxiousness in excelsis.

Memorably dressed in a midriff-baring Ween wrestling belt, **Chocolate and Cheese** gets the band out of its claustrophobic solitude and into the real recording world, with assists from Andrew Weiss, drummer Claude Coleman (ex-Skunk) and others. Several tracks were cut in a real studio. Striking a sublime balance between sick invention and weirdly credible presentation, Ween unloads more cool and characteristic material here than on all three previous albums together. In fact, while there are certainly points contiguous to the earlier records, the duo sounds reborn, and this album is consistently brilliant. The super-creepy "Spinal Meningitis (Got Me Down)" and "Mister, Would You Please Help My Pony?" are as disturbing as anything in the Residents gallery; the creamy masterwork "Freedom of '76" could seriously pass for that era's Philly soul (in fact, the falsetto song is a literal tribute to the city). Elsewhere, "Baby Bitch" Weensterizes the folk-rock sound of Gordon Lightfoot or Crosby, Stills and Nash; "Drifter in the Dark" is a harmony cowboy classic; "Voodoo Lady" deconstructs disco; "I Can't Put My Finger on It," sung, like the tragic ballad "Buenas Tardes Amigo," in a Mexican accent, loads on the distortion and squiggly bits and contains what has come to be a Ween catchphrase: "Are you surprised when I touch the dwarf inside?" Never.

On the other hand, surprise is about all **12 Golden Country Greats** has going for it. Ween's Nashville album walks a disturbingly straight line between unadorned genre exercise and obnoxious put-on. Using top session pros to pave a smooth twang all the way down home, Ween allows a few moments of presentable dignity to intrude on the more familiar malice of such typical butt-busters as "Piss Up a Rope," "Fluffy" and "Help Me Scrape the Mucus off My Brain." Although funny enough on paper and of a creative piece with the Weensters' usual stupidity, the album is so beholden to the dissonance between sound and vision (shades of John Trubee's classic "A Blind Man's Penis") that it fails to register adequate irony or lack thereof.

Ween's brand of eccentricity so discourages imitation and defies parody that the idea of paying tribute to the group on record is too quixotic for words. (Although a dentist's office edition of **Pure Guava** would be worth hearing.) Yet that's what New York's Cogs took it upon themselves to do. **Absolute Ween** finds the duo stumbling aimlessly through the lo-fi haze, taking a properly dissolute (and thus fairly convincing) swipe at a career-spanning quintet of Ween tunes, including "Puffy Cloud," "Captain Fantasy" and "Pork Roll, Egg & Cheese." [i]

WEEZER

Weezer (DGC) 1994
Pinkerton (DGC) 1996

RENTALS

Return of the Rentals (Maverick/Reprise) 1995

It's the most obvious things that are the easiest to overlook. Like the early, underground days of the Ramones, when the bare-bones reduction of pop and punk seemed too simpleminded to matter but was quickly proven to be a brilliant, trailblazing invention, **Weezer** exists on two completely different levels of creative achievement. It's no coincidence that Ric Ocasek—whose Cars essentially took the same dryly ironic route by way of Roxy Music—produced the Los Angeles quartet's big-selling debut, which has a lot more going on than meets the ear.

Superficially, the by-the-numbers pop-punk record offers nothing beyond singer/guitarist Rivers Cuomo's crunchy up-and-down melodies and enigmatic teenish lyrics, thickly tendered mid-tempo rhythm guitar rock and the impression of a dweeby/bland offstage personality. (The album cover comes as close to generic as a blue-background band photo can be.) But twisted into the threadbare lucidity of seemingly pedestrian nonsense like the enervated frat-Val anxiety of "Undone—The Sweater Song," the incongruous hip-hop slang and giddy culture references of "Buddy Holly," the unconvincingly beach-crazed "Surf Wax America" and the Kiss-praising "In the Garage" (a '90s answer to Brian Wilson's "In My Room"), there's a sardonic disclaimer of responsibility. Weezer has perfected the art of pissing on itself, both embodying and renouncing the ethos of pop in one sly strum. **Weezer** is something of a '90s marker, a deliciously entertaining piece of crap that floats in the punchbowl like a rare jewel. "I got an electric guitar/I play my stupid songs/I write these stupid words and I love everyone waiting there for me." How post-modern can a band be?

Stepping over the irony-laden line—squaring the archness, as it were—with inadequate song ammo and no obvious stylistic purpose, Weezer bassist Matt Sharp and drummer Pat Wilson formed the Rentals, adding vintage Moog synthesizers, violin and female voices to their other band's thick guitar distortion and clocklike rhythms. **The Return of the Rentals** calls to mind such self-conscious nostalgists as the Pooh Sticks and Denim, letting the soft voices of Cherielynn Westrich and that dog's Petra Haden (as well as the latter's violin scrolling) add a nice counterpoint to the pedal-pushing. But rather than use the dated electronic keyboards to hammer home the Cars comparison, the Eno-esque squiggles do little more than accent the sizzling Weezerisms with pretentious '70s-goofing insincerity. On its basic merits, the album isn't significantly inferior to (or intrinsically different from) **Weezer,** but the gap between its ambition and its achievement makes it eminently resistible. [i]

See also *that dog.*

WE KNOW WHERE YOU LIVE

See *Wonder Stuff.*

PAUL WELLER

Paul Weller (Go! Discs/London) 1992
Wild Wood (UK Go! Discs) 1993 (Go! Discs/London) 1994
Live Wood (UK Go! Discs) 1994
Stanley Road (Go! Discs/London) 1995

JAM

Greatest Hits (Polydor) 1991
Extras (Polydor) 1992
Live Jam (Polydor) 1993

STYLE COUNCIL

The Singular Adventures of the Style Council (Greatest Hits Vol. 1) (Polydor) 1989
Here's Some That Got Away (Polydor) 1993

Ya couldn't say surprised. . . . Unlike other vital rock'n'roll veterans who habitually leap from style to guise as if turning the pages of a catalogue, Paul Weller has marked his progress with clearly linear—if unique—logic. As the angry young man grew to adulthood inside the modpunk cocoon of the Jam, his tastes ran (as the mods' had) toward American soul music, specifically the easy flowing melodic artistry of Curtis Mayfield and the preternatural cool of Marvin Gaye. By the time the Jam closed up shop—firmly ensconced as one of Britain's all-time hitmakers—at the end of '82, the singer/guitarist had turned down the heat enough to segue smoothly into the continental soul-pop pretensions of the suave Style Council.

Over the course of a handful of albums that got him to 1990, Weller (partnered with Mick Talbot) lost, in succession, his connection to rock, his creative judgment and his sense of humor. As of the Style Council's 1988 swan song, **Confessions of a Pop Group,** frustrated political activism and god knows what else (he *did* turn thirty that year) had left him cynical and disgusted, the leading contender to succeed Kingsley Amis as England's angriest curmudgeon. Weller was wise to back out of that dead end, but he left behind enough halfbaked odds and ends, many of them previously unreleased, to assemble **Here's Some That Got Away,** a sorry epilogue to the band. (The tracks didn't get away—they were hiding out, hoping no one would stumble on them.)

Weller took a couple of years to regain his composure (a stint leading the Paul Weller Movement produced only one 45; he also did some work with the Young Disciples) and then launched a solo career free of the Style Council's grand illusions and the negative ions he had built up. As he reports in "Uh Huh Oh Yeh," the song that begins **Paul Weller,** "I took a trip down boundary lane/Try an' find myself again/At least a part I left somewhere." Later on, he identifies the piece of himself that needed to be left behind: "Bitterness rising—you gotta shake those feelings off." That the album sounds a lot like the transitional point between Traffic and Steve Winwood's subsequent solo work is fair enough; the brightening of Weller's countenance needs the warm support of music this cozy. Shaping up as a sensitive pop romantic comfortably using old-school soul as his contemporary building blocks, Weller settles into the material like a calm patriarch in a favorite old chair. As Steve White (drums) and Jacko Peake (sax, flute) fetch his slippers and pipe, the kinder, gentler auteur reflects on his life and love with effortlessly engaging craft. (Incidentally, half of "Kosmos," the twelve-minute track that ends the album, is the maddening sound of a manual turntable popping on a record's end groove.)

Weller's upbeat mood didn't last long. The equivocal and indistinctly produced **Wild Wood** sucks him halfway back into doubt and discontent, and the music reflects that. While still rooted in elements of syncopation and organ-plus-horns instrumentation, the lonely "Sunflower" and "Can You Heal Us (Holy Man)" are tougher and less finespun than anything on **Paul Weller.** Elsewhere, the remote and unappealing album pulls clean away from soul. The title track, "Foot of the Mountain" and "Country" all allude to folky acoustic solitude; the anxious "Has My Fire Really Gone Out?" and the merely unsettled "5th Season" force out thick Bands of rustic rock. By the finish, when he fires off a scrabbly little guitar solo in "Hung Up," it's evident that Weller's balance mechanism needs another readjustment.

Most of the material on **Live Wood** does come from the preceding album, but the four shows recorded between December '93 and April '94 also yield songs from **Paul Weller** (including "Bull-Rush," here given a "Magic Bus" coda). Performing with a quartet, Weller does simple justice to his creations, putting himself into the mix with determined enthusiasm.

Back in a stock-taking mood, Weller opens the firmly focused **Stanley Road** with "The Changingman," a song that acknowledges his continuing instability ("I'm the changingman—built on shifting sands . . . What I can't be today—I can be tomorrow") amid a hail of caustic electric guitar, the most aggressive playing he's put on record since surrendering it a dozen years earlier. The self-appraisal gets more corrosive (in the next song, he's "a porcelain god that shatters when it falls"), but Weller wisely turns the spotlight away, covering the old voodoo-casting "I Walk on Gilded Splinters" and then letting memories sweep over him in the title track, "Time Passes . . ." and "Whirlpools' End." Following a fairly stable path of soulful rock (put it this way: Joe Cocker's voice could come roaring out of the speakers without incident here), the album skips wind instruments but employs a contingent of stars (Carleen Anderson, Steve Winwood, Oasis' Noel Gallagher, old partner Mick Talbot, ex–Blow Monkey Dr. Robert, Young Disciple Mark Nelson) to return Weller to a reassuringly solid middle ground. It's unnerving to think that Woking's most famous teenager is now a settled, mature family man able to look back with ponderous consideration, but Weller faces up to it manfully and makes music that befits his station.

The Jam's commercial stature in Great Britain explains why the flow of releases has continued, more than a decade after the band's demise. The ideal Jam album for neophytes and fans alike, **Greatest Hits** offers nineteen picture-perfect products (1977's "In the City" to 1982's "Beat Surrender") of a brash and brilliant band that was both of its time and quite contrary to it. **Extras** expands on the topic with good-to-great B-sides, demos, rarities and outtakes, including touchstone covers of songs by the Who, Small Faces, James Brown, Curtis Mayfield and the Chi-Lites. **Live Jam** consists of two dozen concert tracks, recorded at various shows between 1979 and 1982. [i]

See also *TPRG.*

PAUL WESTERBERG

14 Songs (Sire/Reprise) 1993
Eventually (Reprise) 1996

Had he not been the most important and compelling American punk-rock voice of the 1980s, a rebellious paradigm of trenchant, self-abusing irony, Paul Westerberg might be thoroughly admired (or at least forgiven) for his wistful, semi-acoustic pop solo career. Attempting to reconcile himself with such unforeseen personal developments as sobriety, independence and adulthood, the author of the Replacements' fiery gumption has turned into the James Taylor of post-punk, a sensitive, contemplative sweetheart who knows life can be hard but isn't unwilling to stop and smell its silver lining. As unfair as it is to judge an artist by standards he has since renounced, it's impossible to hear either of these albums without a major twinge of ain't-the-same resentment.

Writing **14 Songs** in the wake of the band's unceremonious collapse, Westerberg presumably had plenty on his mind. But what comes out here is stiff-upper-lip conviction, by-the-numbers music and glib lyrics that drift away toward remoteness and pretension. Having outgrown self-deprecation and self-destruction, Westerberg doesn't turn the guns around: his will to cause any serious damage to anyone is gone. "World Class Fad" and the Stonesy "Something Is Me" apply rock juice to anemic taunts, while "Mannequin Shop" takes easy aim into the bucket of cosmetic surgery and fires cotton balls. Turning the intensity knob down to a bland safety zone, Westerberg comes up with some nice melodies, but the transformation from brutal youth to restrained adult intimacy is hard to accept. To its credit, **14 Songs** has some gorgeous and affecting love songs ("First Glimmer," "Runaway Wind," the acoustic "Even Here We Are," the country-ish "Things") and one entertaining sub-punk raver ("Down Love," a protest against excess volume), but the surprising album neither illuminates nor ameliorates the Replacements' end.

Having quashed expectations once and for all, there's no way Westerberg could have disappointed (or, it seems, surprised) anyone on his next album. With heartfelt lines like "A good day is any day that you're alive," sung against a spare blend of piano, drums and strings, **Eventually** reduces the author of "Bastards of Young," "Unsatisfied" and "Hold My Life" (a song that gets a passing reference in "Good Day") to Hallmark sentimentality. Though the music floats along dreamily, the sardonic "MamaDaddyDid" ("decided not to raise any children—just like my-my-my Mom and Daddy did") hints at the broken bottle his songs used to wield, but there's no danger of bloodshed there, or in such equally tepid observations as "These Are the Days" and "Time Flies Tomorrow." The Minneapolitan's familiar skills as an affecting singer and catchy melodicist are intact—the album is very much of a piece with **14 Songs,** although it's more comfortable in the benign folk-rock center than escaping to louder climes—but the lyrics' resignation suits Westerberg to an entirely different audience than is likely to recognize his name (or, for that matter, the recycled tune of "Once Around the Weekend" or the guitar chords of "You've Had It With You"). [i]

See also *Goo Goo Dolls, Leatherwoods.*

WHALE

Pay for Me EP (Hut/Caroline) 1995
We Care (Virgin) 1995

Oh, those wacky Scandinavians. When they're not dominating the world's mush-pop charts with bands whose names begin with A, they're slyly undermining the reliability of genres (death metal, cocktail pop) in which their participation comes as something of a surprise. Whale's contribution to the region's cause is a playful crotch-first take on modern woman-sung rock. Meandering aimlessly between driven fuzz-guitar rock, stylish dance grooves and traces of imported hip-hop on **We Care**—imagine R. Kelly producing Alanis Morissette with backing by Portishead—the shameless Swedish trio levels such smarmy assaults on taste and intelligence as "I'll Do Ya," "Hobo Humpin' Slobo Babe" and "Young, Dumb & Full of Cum." In an accented, just-fucked voice, Cia Berg scatters topical references (Nine Inch Nails and Sarah Cracknell of Saint Etienne are both mentioned in "Eurodog"; MTV newsman Kurt Loder's name crops up in "That's Where It's At") and crude sexual euphemisms with a friendly wink that partly excuses the endeavor's essential obnoxiousness. What's harder to forgive is the trio's weakness for endless repetition of its simple choruses, but that's a whale of a different story. [i]

CARON WHEELER

See *Soul II Soul.*

WHEN PEOPLE WERE SHORTER AND LIVED NEAR THE WATER

When People Were Shorter and Lived Near the Water EP7 (Trace Elements) 1987
Uncle Ben EP7 (Shimmy-Disc) 1988
Bobby (Shimmy-Disc) 1989
Porgy (Shimmy-Disc) 1991
Bill Kennedy's Showtime (Shimmy-Disc) 1994

SHAPIR-O'RAMA

El Mundo de Vapor y Valentía (Old Vienna) (Mind of a Child) 1995

JAD FAIR AND THE SHAPIR-O'RAMA

We Are the Rage (Japan. Avant) 1996

When People Were Shorter and Lived Near the Water, the band of merry pranksters led by singer Kim M. Rancourt, is devoted to conceptual covers of material from outside sources. Depending on one's point of view, the New York group's work can be viewed as deconstructing the originals, partying with them or pummeling unsuspecting songs into submission. They sound like punch-drunk travelers who've taken a wrong turn and wandered into a quiet seacoast village, but, undaunted, come rolling out of their bus into the town square and begin singing songs of their homeland. But what seem, on first exposure, to be wildly exuberant first-take performances, are—when called for—actually smart arrangements. And dumb arrangements when they're called for. These workmen use the right tool for the job.

The first two releases are 7-inch EPs; **Uncle Ben** is included on the CD of **Bobby,** a full-length collection of Bobby Goldsboro numbers. Legal problems delayed the band's version of George Gershwin's *Porgy and Bess,* but **Porgy** finally emerged, a well-informed piece of work, not simply a cheap parody. Guitarist Dave Rick and keyboardist Chris Xefos (both also of King Missile) are clearly the invaluable musical heart of the proceedings.

Bill Kennedy's Showtime is a trip back to Rancourt's Detroit high-school days and displays the band at its strongest, covering songs by the Motor City bands that played the infamous Grande Ballroom. Passing over such obvious choices as the MC5 and Stooges, WPWSALNTW favors Mitch Ryder, Catfish, the Frost and SRC.

Rancourt's desire to work on original material with Dave Rick led to Shapir-O'Rama. Rick's quartet made a quick evolution from its previous incarnation as Wonderama when they booted out their lead singer and replaced him with Rancourt. In contrast to his other undertaking, Shapir-O'Rama allows Rancourt (responsible for all the lyrics) to be serious, and his writing on **El Mundo de Vapor y Valentía (Old Vienna)** is heartfelt. The album's sole cover is King Crimson's "I Talk to the Wind." [dbg]

See also *King Missile; TPRG.*

WHITE SHARK

See *Thinking Fellers Union Local 282.*

WHITE ZOMBIE

Psycho-Head Blowout (Silent Explosion) 1986
Soul-Crusher (Silent Explosion) 1987 (Caroline) 1988
Make Them Die Slowly (Caroline) 1989
"God of Thunder" (Caroline) 1989
La Sexorcisto: Devil Music Volume One (Geffen) 1992
Astro-Creep: 2000 (Geffen) 1995
Supersexy Swingin' Sounds (Geffen) 1996

When White Zombie crept into New York's then-vaunted scum-rock scene, the group was perceived as playing a kitsch in-joke on downtown types by enveloping a standard Birthday-Party-via-Blue-Cheer sludge onslaught in the gaudiest arena-rock trappings you could buy at the ninety-nine-cents store. But despite the art-school background shared by singer Rob Zombie (actually Rob Straker, aka Rob Dirt) and bassist Sean Yseult (Reynolds), it soon became evident that White Zombie viewed their capering with the ghost of metal past not as burlesque but as communion.

A pair of self-released singles put the Zombies on the Lower East Side map, situating them somewhere between, oh, Raging Slab and the Swans—with an uncommon flair for the visual manifested in the frontman's Big Daddy Roth–inspired cartooning and a bandwide affection for mangy threads that antedated "grunge" per se. When **Psycho-Head Blowout** was released, the foursome was just beginning to pay attention to its audio obligations: guitarist Tom Five started to pluck some sputtering MC5-esque leads from the unctuous sea of sonic muck, and drummer Ivan DePrume channeled some of his plentiful brute force into structured beats. By most standards, however, **Psycho-Head Blowout** is still a mess.

Soul Crusher brings the focus in tighter, splaying each instrument out side-by-side—roadkill-style, one might say—heightening the more unorthodox traits of each player. The muffled dance throb of Yseult's bass provides some of the album's most interesting pure sound, but it's Straker's guttural bellow that generates the most power. His magnetism—simultaneously forbidding and ludicrous—lends songs like "Scum-Kill" and "Ratmouth" an ambience not unlike a thrill-ride at an itinerant carnival where the operators look a little too jumpy for comfort.

Most of the avant peripherals fell by the wayside during the months leading up to **Make Them Die Slowly,** White Zombie's first unequivocal foray into metal. A guitarist swap brought in John Ricci (formerly with Chicago's Rights of the Accused), whose head-down riffing gave the band a rudder, facilitating full-speed-ahead (okay, *low*-speed, but you get the point). This newfound linearity enhances the brawn of anarcho-Steppenwolf swaggerfests like "Demonspeed" and "Murderworld" (on which Straker makes the barmy assertion "This is murderworld, buddy/Not just another traffic jam") and allows for a sudden burst of anthemic pugnacity on "Disaster Blaster." There are traces of the old art-damage—most perceptibly on the plodding "Godslayer," which is well-steeped in **Funhouse**-era Stoogery—but producer Bill Laswell keeps the band on track. The subsequent "God of Thunder" 12-inch single—withdrawn due to excessive plundering of the Kiss katalog—contains a cover of that band's rock-Valhalla hymn, as well as the new "Love Razor" and a Daniel Rey–produced remake of "Disaster Blaster."

All it took for the band to fully realize its splatter-comic *Mad Max* vision was an infusion of corporate cash, which rendered the White Zombie organism so garish and overblown that it fittingly struck the fancy of those kindred two-dimensional spirits Beavis and Butt-head. The influence of incessant reruns granted the cartoon duo's praise for the Zombies' "Thunder Kiss '65" video can't be overemphasized: more than a year after its release, **La Sexorcisto: Devil Music Volume One** took apocalypto-teen America by storm. It's not all that hard to understand the reasons: Rob Zombie's nihilistic caricatures are so broadly drawn—as on "Welcome to Planet Motherfucker"—that they inspire high-fives rather than high anxiety. Crucially, the band gloms on to enough synthetic sound—mostly sequenced percussion—to fit the future-shock wordplay of "Spiderbaby (Yeah-Yeah-Yeah)" and "Grindhouse (A Go-Go)" with plenty of sci-fi ammo. If Al Jourgensen's mind-alterer of choice were comic-book ink, he might be able to project a worldview this diverting.

The three years that led up to the release of **Astro-Creep: 2000** (*Songs of Love, Destruction and Other Synthetic Delusions of the Electric Head*) were filled with endless touring that not only revealed White Zombie as a welcome throwback to the days of the *rilly* big show (heavy on pyrotechnics and Vegas-worthy light displays) but intensified its desire to advance the more-is-more cause on all fronts. To that end, the album (which derives slightly more bottom from the production of Sasquatch-rock expert Terry Date) boasts more in the way of disorienting samples and far-out, Robert Williams–inspired lyric phantasmagoria. "Electric Head" (a suite divided into "The Agony" and "The Ecstasy") is straightforward enough in its assault, but when Yseult and the guitarist now referred to only as "J" precipitate the stun-gun onslaught of "Super-Charger Heaven" and "Grease Paint and Monkey Brains," the effect is galvanizing even for post-pubescents. A few of the songs ("Blood, Milk and Sky," "Blur the Technicolor") are shackled to the surfeit of technological gew-gaws, but that high-tech glow soon fades, leaving an image of White Zombie as unreconstructed show people who'll look just fine in Times Square when the next century kicks into high gear.

Supersexy Swingin' Sounds consists of **Astro-Creep: 2000** remixes by John Fryer, the Dust Brothers, P. M. Dawn and others. [dss]

BARRENCE WHITFIELD AND THE SAVAGES

Barrence Whitfield and the Savages (Mamou) 1984
Dig Yourself (Rounder) 1985
Call of the Wild EP (UK Demon/Rounder) 1987
Ow! Ow! Ow! (Rounder) 1987
Live Emulsified (Rounder) 1989
Let's Lose It (Fr. New Rose) 1990 (Stony Plain) 1991
Savage Tracks (Fr. New Rose) 1992
Ritual of the Savages (Ocean Music) 1995

BARRENCE WHITFIELD WITH TOM RUSSELL

Hillbilly Voodoo (East Side Digital) 1993
Cowboy Mambo (East Side Digital) 1993

Growing up in East Orange, New Jersey, Barry White spent his teen years fronting various funk and rock bands. When success eluded one outfit that had it almost within reach, he closed the door on the music business and headed for Boston to attend college. Studying to be a television news writer, he supported himself by working in a used record shop, where his inclination for singing along with records drew crowds. It also got the attention of then-Lyre Peter Greenberg, who encouraged his return to performing. Peter brought along the basis of the Savages in the form of disenfranchised Lyres, and Barry brought his record-collector's love of R&B. He also unveiled his new moniker, Barrence Whitfield, since the world just isn't big enough for two Barry Whites.

The band's furious debut threw down the gauntlet and rolled out the red carpet for the second coming of hopped-up, gut-bucket sweat-groovers; the loud-and-fast R&B drew from punk's adrenaline, not its anger. A new Savages lineup emerged on **Ow! Ow! Ow!** (actually the UK-only **Call of the Wild** EP plus five additional songs). The band broadened its palette with the addition of a keyboardist, making **Ow! Ow! Ow!** a strong and satisfying effort by a more versatile ensemble.

What should have followed was an album that built on **Ow! Ow! Ow!**'s strengths (Barrence Whitfield and the Savages) and learned from its weaknesses (dry production and some songs that simply didn't equal the invention of the performers). Instead, what appeared was **Live Emulsified,** a well-intentioned but unsuccessful attempt to capture the legendary proselytic qualities of the band's concerts.

A growing European following led the French New Rose label to underwrite **Let's Lose It,** a solid effort produced by Jim Dickinson, and **Savage Tracks,** a motley assortment of live and live-in-the-studio takes and demos. The latter has its moments, but is most decidedly not an album statement. New Rose also reissued Whitfield's debut on CD.

With the Savages more or less idle, Barrence began working in a number of other settings. He contributed tracks to Merle Haggard and Don Covay tributes and recorded two albums with singer/songwriter Tom Russell. This experience clearly afforded him an opportunity to work in genres (for example, country) that hadn't been part of the Savages repertoire. Not a songwriter himself, Whitfield displays his wide-ranging skills as a stylist on their two collaborative efforts. While some of the tracks don't prove more than great taste in material, it's great to hear him taking on the works of Jesse Winchester, Bob Dylan, Gram Parsons, Richard Thompson, Steve Earle and Pops Staples.

Returning with a revamped Savages, Whitfield rendered **Ritual of the Savages,** an album whose confidence and verve is helpfully coupled to sympathetic production. Ben Vaughn (one of the producers) contributed a number he co-wrote with Dave Alvin; there's also the usual mix of well-chosen covers, with the bulk of the originals by Whitfield's longtime guitarist, Milton Reder. [dbg]

See also *TPRG*.

CHRIS WHITLEY

Living With the Law (Columbia) 1991
Poison Girl EP (Columbia) 1992
Din of Ecstasy (Work) 1995

Chris Whitley learned to play guitar while living in a log cabin in Vermont; the first album he bought was the Jimi Hendrix Experience's **Smash Hits.** That disparity helps to make sense of the stunning sweep of musical extremes Whitley made during the first half of the '90s. The Houston native moved around a lot in his youth, including stays in Mexico and Belgium, where he was part of a techno-pop outfit. He returned to the US during the late '80s as something of a troubadour, reacting to his experiences overseas by concentrating on Dobro and acoustic guitar, developing his slide and finger-picking techniques.

Rootsy, dark and intense, **Living With the Law** is a magnificent debut. Whitley's fresh, dust-bowl balladry with modern grit gave a musical voice to angst a few months before Nirvana put the word in the collective teenage vocabulary. Whitley's spectral slide work is otherworldly, and his elastic vocals—gritty mumbles and falsetto yodels—can soothe or frighten, depending on a song's tone. For all the album's musical virtues, Whitley's songwriting is what really shines. Adopting an outlaw persona, he displays a knack for vivid, cinematic detail and chilling images ("Baby got a vision, child/Like a loaded gun/She use my body/Like carrion crow"). "Phone Call From Leavenworth" is a desolate one-character drama; "Big Sky Country" is a spiritual brimming with hope.

The **Poison Girl** EP shows what Whitley can do in a live setting. Half of the six songs were recorded solo in his living room, a perfect fit given the intimate nature of his material. The full-band tracks don't lose much of that feeling, either.

Whitley took a long break after **Living With the Law**—part of it spent in rehab—and emerged closer to the Hendrix side of his musical makeup on **Din of Ecstasy.** "Din" is the operative word: Whitley puts down the Dobro (most of the time), straps on a Stratocaster and lets wail with an electric rock fury steeped in classic rock influences and a variety of New York sounds from the Velvet Underground to Sonic Youth. (That Whitley covers the Jesus and Mary Chain's "Some Candy Talking" contributes to the album's Lou Reed aspect.) Dinosaur Jr is a touchstone for the song "Din," while "Know" and "Ultraglide" nod in the general direction of Seattle. **Din of Ecstasy** isn't entirely derivative: Whitley is a hot electric player, and the album retains his distinctive arranging touch in the fast funk groove of "O God My Heart Is Ready," the winding, hypnotic builds of "Guns & Dolls" and "WPL." "New Machine" shows he hasn't abandoned the first album's rootsiness, and his imagery is also intact, from the "red and yellow roses, nipple rings and tattoos" in "Narcotic Prayer" to the pagan sexual rites described in "WPL." With just two full-length albums, it's impossible to anticipate Whitley's next direction—or how long he'll take to get there—but he's hardly in danger of falling into a creative rut. [gg]

WIDESPREAD PANIC

Space Wrangler (Landslide) 1988 (Capricorn/Warner Bros.) 1992
Widespread Panic (Capricorn/Warner Bros.) 1991
Everyday (Capricorn/Warner Bros.) 1993
Ain't Life Grand (Capricorn) 1994

You can't blame these unpretentious rockers for coming from Athens, Georgia—R.E.M. doesn't hold the only license to export music from the college town it put on the rock'n'roll map. But it's hard to resist the irrational tug of resentment that Widespread Panic evinces no interest whatsoever in identifying with their superstar homies. Instead, the trio-turned-sextet tools along its own unchallenging rocky road, steering clear of moronic boogie *and* ironic pop (while rocking hard enough to at least imply the former) and upholding a modernized sense of the clarity and drive that made the Allman Brothers more than a simple jam band and Little Feat more than a groove party. If Widespread Panic's music is perfectly ordinary, at least the band seems proud of it.

Space Wrangler is a polite debut that takes few risks in showcasing the basic assets of a young but already confident combo: guitarist John Bell's easygoing vocals, the rhythm section's creative energy, keyboard accents and upbeat songwriting that doesn't neglect melody for instrumental precision. The reissue adds three subsequent studio cuts. **Widespread Panic** is better—bluesier, rockier, funkier, countrier. But diverse skill can't turn this uninspired blue-plate special into a pungent meal; bulky rather than satisfying, it hasn't got much flavor but probably travels well. (Cool scene footnote: a song named for Athens' Love Tractor.)

Everyday is the first Widespread Panic album that actually leaves a mark: Bell's voice, grown husky and expressive, lends the sturdy songs a measure of urgency they previously lacked. Having thus located a workable stylistic center, Widespread Panic spun itself in a number of different directions on **Ain't Life Grand,** produced, like the first album, by John Keane. "Little Kin" loads up a ZZ Top shotgun and fires off a bolt of buzzing rock, while "Airplane" is a gentle semi-acoustic harmony reverie. "Blackout Blues" recalls an old Allmans blues extravaganza; "Raise the Roof" finds a sultry hypnotic groove. And although the chorus comes straight from the Bon Jovi cliché book, "Heroes" musters a milder version of Pearl Jam's taut emotional ambience. Growing up in public is never a pretty sight, but Widespread Panic's fourth album almost makes the experience seem worthwhile. [i]

See also *Vic Chesnutt.*

JANE WIEDLIN

See *Go-Go's.*

WIG

Lying Next to You EP (Nocturnal) 1990
Deliverance (Island) 1994

There are two parts to the story of Wig, a band that's been around since 1989 but has only put out two records. The quartet formed in Ann Arbor, Michigan, blending genres (rock, punk and hip-hop) in the same manner as townmates Big Chief and coastal kindred spirits the Beastie Boys and Jane's Addiction. Wig's particular approach was an ensemble wall-of-sound—light on solos, heavy on dense sonic mass, with Preston Cleveland's guttural, angry and frequently distorted vocals fused into the mix rather than on top of it. **Lying Next to You** is filled with thick metallic funk ("John Shaft," "Sweet Francis" and "Bullet"); reasonably inventive stuff, even if the lumbering "Toy Boat" and "White Ring" are too self-consciously arty. Mixing feedback, effects and power chords, guitarist Rob Schurgin is notably inventive.

Cleveland left to form the group Mule, and Schurgin, bassist Fran Falls and drummer John Burke bided their time until they found the right singer. They met Clark S. Nova, a veteran of the Ann Arbor band Morsel, at a signing party for his self-published novel *Bone Cold* and began Wig's second phase. Nova is a more melodic singer than Cleveland, and **Deliverance** is bigger, louder, rockier and a little less subversive than its predecessor. This is textured, swirling music, ambient but aggressive. "Gun Groove" kicks things off with a fury, "10 Seconds" offers primal catharsis and "Tender Assassin" successfully treads the border of art rock and pop, a bit like U2 doing a Yes song. The remainder of **Deliverance** doesn't quite live up to those songs, but the album shows Wig is on to something. [gg]

See also *Mule.*

WILCO

See *Uncle Tupelo.*

WILD CARNATION

See *Speed the Plough.*

WEBB WILDER AND THE BEATNECKS

It Came From Nashville (Landslide) 1986 (Watermelon) 1993

WEBB WILDER

Hybrid Vigor (Island) 1989
Doo Dad (Praxis/Zoo) 1991
Acres of Suede (Watermelon) 1996

WEBB WILDER AND THE NASHVEGANS

Town & Country (Watermelon) 1995

Billing himself as "the last of the full-grown men," deep-voiced singer Webb Wilder—who could pass for Johnny Cash's cousin—specializes in jokey yet groove-solid country rock. If the concepts sometimes threaten to overshadow the content (he also makes long-form videos), Wilder's appealingly light touch and sense of fun invariably save the day. It's hard to resist someone whose credo is "Work Hard . . . Rock Hard . . . Eat Hard . . . Sleep Hard . . . Grow Big . . . Wear Glasses If You Need 'Em."

Ruled by a breezy, who-cares vibe, **It Came From Nashville** features incisive versions of Steve Earle's "The Devil's Right Hand" and the Jerry Lee Lewis classic "Move on Down the Line," along with such twangy new instrumentals as "Horror Hayride" and "Ruff Rider," dedicated to tough-guy Broderick Crawford. Guitarist Donny "The Twangler" Roberts struts his stuff with hot licks.

Wilder turns in some commanding vocals on **Hybrid Vigor,** but producer R. S. Field (who's worked on every Webb album to date, writes nearly all of the original material and guests on a variety of instruments, yet is never pictured—draw your own conclusions) goes for a heavier, arena-friendly sound that spoils the party. The drums are too loud and the Twangler's overheated guitars often suggest a hellish metal-country experiment. (Hence the album's title?)

Happily, all concerned got it right on the swell **Doo Dad.** Though the production remains emphatic for sure, a warmer vibe tempers any harshness, and Webb swaggers gloriously. The diverse menu includes the rousing boogie of "Tough It Out," a heart-rending plea for forgiveness in the form of "Everyday (I Kick Myself)," a spiffy display by the Twangler on the instrumental "Sputnik" and, against all odds, an exciting version of the warhorse "Baby Please Don't Go." The spirited yet pointless cover of the Electric Prunes "I Had Too Much to Dream (Last Night)" is probably a warmup for the next album.

Town & Country, a wide-ranging collection of covers, works beautifully. Wilder's at his authoritative best, doing expected stuff like Waylon Jennings' "Nashville Bum" and Ray Smith's rockabilly hit "Rockin' Little Angel," then sounding just as swell on the Flamin Groovies' chilling junkie ode, "Slow Death," the Small Faces' charming "My Mind's Eye" and Mott the Hoople's cornpone "The Original Mixed-Up Kid," which completes the circle from Nashville to London and back again. All in all, good fun, first note to last. [jy]

ROZZ WILLIAMS

See *Christian Death.*

VICTORIA WILLIAMS

Happy Come Home (Geffen) 1987
Swing the Statue! (Rough Trade) 1990 (Mammoth) 1994
Loose (Mammoth/Atlantic) 1994
This Moment in Toronto With Victoria Williams and the Loose Band (Mammoth/Atlantic) 1995

VARIOUS ARTISTS

Sweet Relief: A Benefit for Victoria Williams (Thirsty Ear/Chaos) 1993

Had it not been for the misfortune of illness (multiple sclerosis, diagnosed in 1992) and the generosity of friends, the uplifting magic of Victoria Williams' warbly jazz-country voice and unique musical observations might never have spread much beyond the tiny cult that had been attracted by her first two albums. A classic case of extravagant talent undersold by a humble personality, the two records are quietly remarkable and were commercially doomed on principle. Illogically overproduced with theatrical expansiveness—complete with Van Dyke Parks string arrangements—by Anton Fier and Steven Soles, **Happy Come Home** contains such delights as "Frying Pan," "Opelousas," "TC" (about a colorful oldtimer) and "Happy," about the confusion engendered by a neighborhood dog with that cheerful name. Produced by Williams and Michael Blair, **Swing the Statue!** gives songs like the enigmatic "Summer of Drugs" memoir, the narrative "Tarbelly and Featherfoot" and the reverent "Holy Spirit" all the room they need to breathe; if anything, the arrangements are almost too low-key.

Fortunately, among those whose hearts were captured by the exceptional charm and spiritual resonance of the Louisiana-born singer/songwriter's smalltown character studies were Lou Reed, Evan Dando and members of Soul Asylum, the Jayhawks, Giant Sand and Pearl Jam. With their participation, **Sweet Relief**—a touching album of Williams tunes (two of them not yet recorded by her) given heartfelt readings by those artists, as well as the Waterboys, Maria McKee, Michael Penn, Michelle Shocked, Shudder to Think and Matthew Sweet—helped defray the uninsured singer's medical expenses and provided the basis for an industry-wide organization, the Sweet Relief Musicians Trust Fund, which in '96 turned the spotlight on Vic Chesnutt, producing a fund-raising album of his music.

With her disease in remission, Williams made the absolutely wonderful **Loose,** a sublime masterpiece positively glowing with love and good feelings. Even when she's ruing the death of beloved friends (as in

"Happy to Have Known Pappy" and "Harry Went to Heaven"), Williams can only express her joy at the experience of knowing such fine folks. Navigating sentimentality with pure artistry, this gifted word painter gently breathes metaphysical life into the ordinary people on whom she sets her lyrical sights. Her songs amplify the emotional impact of letters from home with the spiritual intensity of a believer who has been delivered from her own crisis while weathering the pain of others. Working with a stellar company of musicians (including Dave Pirner, Andrew Williams, members of R.E.M. and the Jayhawks), producer Paul Fox demonstrates real ingenuity in helping to fashion diverse responses to Williams' inventions: "Crazy Mary" has pedal steel, loads of strings and a snarling Peter Buck electric guitar solo; "You R Loved" runs on Van Morrisonesque soul power with two organists, a horn section and a crisp backbeat; "What a Wonderful World" is given full standard honors with just piano and strings; "My Ally," a duet with Pirner, needs only the pair's acoustic guitars and an undercurrent of Wurlitzer organ. Throughout, Williams wields her idiosyncratic voice, with microtonal pitch control and time-out delayed phrasing, like a jazz instrument, begging comparison to Blossom Dearie, although *she*'s probably never sung Spirit's "Nature's Way," as Williams pointedly does here.

The '95 live album finds Williams holding cozy court with a sextet in an onstage living room with typical casual modesty: in the course of sixteen songs from her albums and elsewhere (including covers and two originals she has not previously recorded), Williams apologizes for an untuned guitar, denies (and then proves) her ability to play piano, improvises a song to her dog, worries about the Canadian comprehensibility of "Hitchhiker" and generally charms the pants off a rapturous Toronto audience. Encouraged by Williams' jazziest singing (check the graceful "Smoke Gets in Your Eyes"), however, the piano-based chamber-pop arrangements reach rarefied Joni Mitchell levels, and the album tilts dangerously toward the preciousness Williams' best studio work (and guitar-based concerts) so easily resists. [i]

See also *TPRG.*

CHRIS WILSON AND THE SNEETCHES

See *Sneetches.*

WIMP FACTOR 14

Ankle Deep (Harriet) 1993

VEHICLE FLIPS

In Action (Harriet) 1995

Pittsburgh's Wimp Factor 14 first made waves with a series of excellent early-'90s singles—the first of which, "Train Song" (each copy packaged with a genuine train-flattened penny), was among 1991's 7-inch best. On those records, the group mixes basic strum-pop with interesting instrumental touches (melodica, toy ukulele, zither, plastic bucket drums and so forth) to achieve an unusually inviting sound.

That sound, however, wouldn't have added up to much without the superior songcraft of singer Frank Boscoe. On the quintet's only CD, **Ankle Deep** (packaged in a six-by-nine-inch manila envelope, which probably didn't help its prospects any at retail), Boscoe displays a consistent knack for combining the introspective with the topical, resulting in a playfully conversational songwriting style. Many artists would be reduced to novelty when tackling such subjects as college term papers ("I Is for Incomplete"), day-job drudgery ("(It's Ok to Work for) Rockwell International") and how to avoid losing small objects ("How to Avoid Losing Small Objects"). But Boscoe, who had shown a knack for this sort of anecdotal approach on the group's 1992 "Botch" single (another day-job lament, about messing up a production run of chess pieces), is smart enough to make it work throughout the bulk of **Ankle Deep.**

The group disbanded shortly after the release of the album. Boscoe resurfaced in 1995 with the group Vehicle Flips, whose fine **In Action** sounds very much like WF14 without the oddball instruments. [pl]

WINDBREAKERS

Meet the Windbreakers EP (Big Monkey) 1982
Any Monkey With a Typewriter EP (Big Monkey) 1983
Terminal (Homestead) 1985
Disciples of Agriculture (Fr. Closer) 1985
Run (DB) 1986
A Different Sort . . . (DB) 1987
At Home With Bobby and Tim (DB) 1989
Electric Landlady (DB) 1991

BOBBY SUTLIFF

Another Jangly Mess EP (UK Tambourine) 1986
Only Ghosts Remain (PVC) 1987

TIM LEE

What Time Will Tell (Coyote/Twin\Tone) 1988
The New Thrill Parade (Fr. New Rose) 1992
Crawdad (DB) 1992

Balancing an accessible melodic sensibility with a more unhinged, unsettling edge, this Mississippi combo—centered on singer/writer/guitarists Tim Lee and Bobby Sutliff—was one of the most underappreciated gems of the '80s southern pop boom. After turning out a dandy series of rough gems with **Terminal, Run** and the early EPs—all produced by Mitch Easter—Lee and Sutliff split. Lee kept the Windbreakers name for the equally worthy **A Different Sort . . . ,** while Sutliff went solo with the five-song **Another Jangly Mess** in the UK and the full-length **Only Ghosts Remain** in the States. The latter disc incorporates the contents of the former; both are as good as power-pop gets. Lee dropped the band name (and much of its quirkiness) for the winsome and relatively straightforward **What Time Will Tell,** produced by ex-dB Gene Holder. Lee's second Holder-produced album, **The New Thrill Parade,** went unheard until New Rose issued it a few years later.

Lee and Sutliff were back together the following year for the confident-sounding, smoothly crafted **At Home With Bobby and Tim** (the CD of which adds all of **Terminal** as a bonus). The pair sounds as strong as ever on bittersweet originals like Lee's "Just Fine," Sutliff's "On the Wire" and a cover of Russ Tolman's "Portrait of Blue." Tolman returned the favor by producing **Electric Landlady**—equally strong material with a slightly harder-rocking edge. "Big Ideas" and "Colorblind" rank with the pair's strongest work, yet the album proved to be the Windbreakers' last gasp.

Lee made a strong return to solo action the following year with **Crawdad,** a rootsier, somewhat more acoustic record that highlights the confessional aspects of such numbers as "Friday Night" and "Like Sand." Also included are impassioned covers of Sutliff's "You Could've Told Me" and Mott the Hoople's "I Wish I Was Your Mother." [ss]

See also *TPRG*.

WIPERS

Is This Real? (Park Ave.) 1980 (Sub Pop) 1993
Alien Boy EP7 (Park Ave.) 1980
Youth of America EP (Park Avenue) 1981 (Restless) 1990
Over the Edge (Brain Eater) 1983 (Restless) 1987
Wipers (Enigma) 1985
Land of the Lost (Restless) 1986
Follow Blind (Restless) 1987
The Circle (Restless) 1988
The Best of Wipers and Greg Sage (Restless) 1990
Silver Sail (Tim/Kerr) 1993
The Herd (Tim/Kerr) 1996

GREG SAGE

Straight Ahead (Enigma) 1985
Sacrifice (For Love) (Restless) 1991

VARIOUS ARTISTS

Eight Songs for Greg Sage and the Wipers EP7 (Tim/Kerr) 1992
Fourteen Songs for Greg Sage and the Wipers (Tim/Kerr) 1993

Led by singer/guitarist Greg Sage, Portland, Oregon's Wipers began as a trio playing heavy rock that mixed high velocity and volume to obscure songs with introspective and intelligent lyrics. **Is This Real?** is a case in point. Raw, abrasive and hard-hitting, it's come to be considered such a touchstone in northwestern punk/grunge history that Sub Pop reissued it (adding the three non-LP B-sides from **Alien Boy**) fourteen years later, after Nirvana covered not one, but two, of its songs.

Youth of America shows much refinement, and is highlighted by Sage's weird guitar work on some long instrumental bridges. The title track is a simple, repetitive, colossal ten-minute monster, the Wipers' ultimate effort. **Over the Edge** is as appealing, with some of Sage's most memorable songs. The thick title track (later covered by Hole), plus the simmering "Doom Town" and the roaring "So Young" define the Wipers' dense, methodical, chunky aggression, with heavy, cloudy guitar.

Sage recorded the solo **Straight Ahead** while looking for a new label for the Wipers. Side One sounds like his band, which is fine, but Side Two is just the man and his guitar making hauntingly strange, consciousness-expanding, atmospheric space pieces such as "Astro Cloud." Intriguing. **Wipers** is a live album from a 1984 tour that includes three great songs never recorded in a studio.

Land of the Lost reveals no rust after a three-year layoff. "Way of Love" and "Nothing Left to Lose" are charging rockers fed by Sage's fire-breathing string work, while "Just Say" shows a prettier side of his playing. **Follow Blind** backsteps a bit, with more hypnotic guitar. On the first moody Wipers LP, Brad Davidson's prominent bass sets up subconscious undercurrents. The stunning title track and "Any Time You Find" mix Sage's solo atmospherics with his thicker, repetitive style and are highly affecting.

The Circle's scorching opener, "I Want a Way," and its tumultuous title track are red herrings for Wipers' business as usual. The album actually includes one of the band's rare, unabashed pop songs in "Time Marches On" and closes with the slow, somber shudder of three completely different-sounding songs: "Goodbye Again," "Be There" and "Blue & Red." Beautiful.

In compiling the 1990 retrospective, Sage favored his recent albums, but the collection includes such rarities as the band's blistering 1978 debut single "Better Off Dead," a long-forgotten compilation track and plenty of other goodies. A fine introduction.

After Sage relocated to Phoenix, Arizona, his second solo effort, **Sacrifice (For Love),** picks up where the last three tracks of **The Circle** left off, only with an unobtrusive drum machine this time. The LP delves further into more somber, reflective auras; even a cover of the Yardbirds' "For Your Love" comes off as desperate and scared, while only "This Planet Earth" mines the repressed anger of his long career. "Dreams" and "No Turning Back" typify the album's slow, barely restrained fits of alarmed passion and quiet frustration.

Come the Seattle explosion, the otherwise overlooked Sage (in America: in Europe he has always routinely sold out theaters) suddenly found himself considered a guru of sorts, despite his stylistic distance from the metallic and '70s-inspired hard-rock bands who held him in such esteem. Accordingly, Portland's Tim/Kerr label assembled the tribute CD (originally a four-single 7-inch box set) to pay homage. The obvious curiosities are Nirvana's "Return of the Rat" (the band's other **Is This Real?** cover, "D-7," came from a Peel session and was included on **Hormoaning**) and the aforementioned Hole cover, but the likes of Thurston Moore, Crackerbash, Poison Idea, Hazel and Nation of Ulysses keep the aggression coming. Perhaps the best and most ironic track is "Potential Suicide" by old Portland contemporaries Napalm Beach; that band's Sam Henry was the Wipers' first drummer and had played on the original a dozen years earlier.

Reclaiming the Wipers name (and getting back drummer Steve Plouf) didn't make **Silver Sail** Sage's attempt to capitalize on his newfound prestige. Rather, with characteristic independence, Sage went even prettier, spacier and moodier than his previous work in order to get away from the public desire for him to rock out with his new crop of admirers. A more deliberate pace allows Sage's virtuoso playing extra opportunity to bob and weave, float and tickle, tease and torment; he introduces hints of quiet surf music, spaghetti westerns and other lonely, timeless sounds. Likewise, his spooky voice sounds unusually beautiful, especially on the crescendos of "Prisoner." Finally, he lets loose with two vintage blasts, "Never Win" and "Silver Sail."

Again recorded as a duo with Plouf, Sage's tenth studio album, **The Herd,** swings his direction back around 180 degrees. He's bringing the fire this time, as evidenced by the clangorous roar of the angry, anthemic "Psychic Vampire" and "The Herd." The sterling pop melody of the bristlingly loud "Resist" conveys a strong anti-repression message; it's as if the MC5 had never gone away. For a guy/band approaching the twenty-year mark, these rocket-fueled smashers sound every bit as dynamic and pushy as his earliest choleric days, only using more intricate chord patterns and playing. One of America's greatest independent label talents just keeps getting better. [jr]

See also *TPRG*.

WIRE

Pink Flag (Harvest) 1977 (Restless Retro) 1989
Chairs Missing (UK Harvest) 1978 (Restless Retro) 1989
154 (Automatic/Warner Bros.) 1979 (Restless Retro) 1989
Document and Eyewitness (UK Rough Trade) 1981 (Mute) 1991
And Here It Is . . . Again . . . Wire (UK Sneaky Pete) 1984
Wire Play Pop (UK Pink) 1986
Snakedrill EP (UK Mute) 1986 (Mute/Enigma) 1987
The Ideal Copy (Mute/Enigma) 1987
The Peel Sessions EP (UK Strange Fruit) 1987
A Bell Is a Cup Until It Is Struck (Mute/Enigma) 1988
It's Beginning to and Back Again (Mute/Enigma) 1989
The Peel Sessions Album (UK Strange Fruit) 1989 (Strange Fruit/Dutch East India Trading) 1991
On Returning (1977–1979) (Restless Retro) 1989
Manscape (Mute/Enigma) 1990
Life in the Manscape EP (Mute/Enigma) 1990
The Drill (Mute) 1991
Wire 1985–1990: The A List (Mute/Elektra) 1993
Behind the Curtain: Early Versions 1977 & 78 (UK EMI) 1995
Turns and Strokes (WMO) 1996

WIR

The First Letter (Mute/Elektra) 1991

COLIN NEWMAN

A–Z (UK Beggars Banquet) 1980 (Restless) 1991
provisionally entitled the singing fish (UK 4AD) 1981
not to (UK 4AD) 1982
Commercial Suicide (Crammed Discs/Enigma) 1986
provisionally entitled the singing fish/not to (UK 4AD) 1988 (Restless) 1991
It Seems (Crammed Discs/Restless) 1988
Voice EP (UK Swim) 1995

DESMOND SIMMONS

Alone on Penguin Island (UK Dome) 1981 (WMO) 1995

MALKA SPIGEL

Rosh Ballata (UK Swim) 1993

ORACLE

Tree (UK Swim) 1994

IMMERSION

Oscillating (UK Swim) 1995
The Remixes Vol. 1 (UK Swim) 1995

DOME

Dome (UK Dome/Rough Trade) 1980
3R4 (UK 4AD) 1980
Dome 2 (UK Dome/Rough Trade) 1981
Dome 3 (UK Dome/Rough Trade) 1981
MZUI/Waterloo Gallery (UK Cherry Red) 1982 (UK These) 1995
Will You Speak This Word (Nor. Uniton) 1983
8 Time (UK 4AD) 1988
Dome 1.2 (UK Dome/Grey Area/Mute) 1992
Dome 3.4 (UK Dome/Grey Area/Mute) 1992

DUET EMMO

Or So It Seems (UK Mute) 1983 (UK Dome/Grey Area/Mute) 1992

P'O

Whilst Climbing Thieves Vie for Attention (UK Court) 1983 (UK These) 1995

LEWIS AND GILBERT

Pacific/Specific (in a different place) (WMO) 1995

BRUCE GILBERT

This Way (UK Mute) 1984
The Shivering Man (UK Mute) 1986
This Way to the Shivering Man (Mute/Restless) 1990
Insiding (Mute/Elektra) 1991
Music for Fruit EP (UK Mute) 1991
Ab Ovo (UK Mute) 1996

HE SAID

Hail (UK Mute) 1985 (Mute/Restless) 1989
Take Care (UK Mute) 1988 (Mute/Restless) 1990

H.A.L.O.

Immanent (Swed. MNW Zone) 1995

VARIOUS ARTISTS

Whore—Various Artists Play Wire (WMO) 1996

In the late '70s, Brian Eno said that although the Velvet Underground didn't sell a lot of records, it seemed as if everyone who bought one went out and started a band. In the '80s and '90s, it would not have been an exaggeration to say the same about London's Wire—or specifically, about the work that the group produced in its first and best incarnation. Formed in 1976 in the wake of the Sex Pistols, the quartet differed from many of its peers in England's initial punk uprising in that its members were older, smarter, more ambitious and more sophisticated. Singer/guitarist Colin Newman, bassist/lyricist Graham Lewis, guitarist Bruce Gilbert and drummer Robert Gotobed (yes, his real name) had no musical training, but like many of the psychedelic rockers of the '60s, they had all been to art school. A trippier vibe permeated some of their music, and that they were signed to Harvest by the same guy who had signed the Pink Floyd led some pundits to call them the Punk Floyd. In fact, their initial skeletal, brusque rock designs owed more to Eno, the Velvets, Roxy Music, Can and Captain Beefheart, although they'd be loath to admit any influences at all.

After paring down from a quintet (guitarist George Gill was given the boot) and making their recorded debut with two tracks on the live compilation **The Roxy, London WC2,** Wire set out to "cock a snoot at the history of rock'n'roll" on **Pink Flag,** a brilliant twenty-one-song suite crafted with the help of producer Mike Thorne, a virtual fifth member of the band through **154.** The group manipulates classic rock song structures by condensing them into brief, intense explosions of attitude and energy, coming up with a collection of unforgettable tunes ("12XU," "Lowdown," "Fragile," "Mannequin") that nevertheless function best as a whole. Having said what they wanted to say about punk, rock and punk-rock, the band got downright weird on **Chairs Missing**—this is where the psychedelic tag fits best—adding synthesizers, slowing things down and concentrating on textured vignettes such as "Sand in My Joints" and the near-hit, "Outdoor Miner" (an homage to a leaf-eating insect). Undercurrents of isolation and madness run through the album; the title is British slang for someone who's a bit disturbed, as in "that guy has a few chairs missing in his front room."

The soundscapes became lusher and grander ("Map Ref. 41°N 93°W"), the lyrics more impressionistic and Beat poetic ("On Returning") and the melodies even more memorable ("The 15th") on **154.** The final studio album by Wire's first incarnation was named for the number of gigs that the group had played to date. (The CD reissue includes an EP of experimental industrial drones originally released as a bonus with the vinyl LP.) Taken together, these first three albums are evidence of an amazing amount of growth in a span of less than three years. They account for Wire's vaunted reputation, and they have been cited as major influences by such diverse bands as R.E.M., Minor Threat, Mission of Burma, Sonic Youth, the Minutemen, Hüsker Dü and Big Black—'80s post-punk bands that were in turn substantial influences on '90s alternative rock.

Facing commercial indifference and growing tension between the "pop" camp (Newman and Gotobed) and the "noise" contingent (Gilbert and Lewis), Wire disbanded after a disjointed live release, **Document and Eyewitness.** This soundtrack to a mixed-media evening of "Dadaist cabaret" leaves you with the impression that you really had to be there to enjoy it. (The CD reissue notably includes the weird industrial dance single "Our Swimmer" b/w "Midnight Bahnhof Cafe," which predicts the direction the band would take when it reunited.) **And Here It Is . . . Again . . . Wire, Wire Play Pop** and **On Returning (1977–1979)** are all best-of collections drawing from the band's first period; the last is the most successful, though the songs on **Pink Flag** lose something when they're taken out of context. **The Peel Sessions Album** and **Behind the Curtain: Early Versions 1977 & 78** are both invaluable documents of Wire's rapid growth and fearless experimentation.

The story would have ended there had the group not reconvened after a six-year break. A three-day trial run yielded "Drill" and "Serious of Snakes," both of which appeared on the four-song **Snakedrill** EP, which featured a new, stripped-down sound based on rhythmic repetition and noise. **The Ideal Copy** expanded the sound with cold digital production that stresses the "dugga-dugga-dugga" dance rhythms. (The CD includes the four-song **Snakedrill.**) For the first time, Wire no longer sounded ahead of its time: New Order had already done this sort of thing better, and while the album has moments of tunefulness (including "Ahead" and "Ambitious"), a mechanical sameness replaces the old diversity. Cynics said Wire blew its status as cult heroes by coming back, but at least the band showed more courage and commitment than other reunited first-generation art-punks, steadfastly championing the old spirit of punk invention by moving forward and refusing to play any of its old material.

Wire continued along the dance-pop path with diminishing results on **A Bell Is a Cup** and **It's Beginning to and Back Again** (aka **IBTABA**). Their respective MTV-friendly singles, "Kidney Bingos" and "Eardrum Buzz," are among the few standout tracks. The band was starting to be more concerned with the artistic process than the finished results: **IBTABA** attempted to create "new" tracks by radically reworking digital live recordings from Chicago and Portugal. The studio trickery was more inspired than the music, and things soon got even worse. Convinced that the "beat combo" of two guitars, bass and drums had run its course, the band marginalized Gotobed, one of rock's great minimalist drummers, replacing him with a machine on the soulless **Manscape** (Wire's absolute nadir) and **The Drill,** an entire nine-track album of versions of "Drill," none of which better the original. Where Wire's music once abraded like sand in your joints, its electro-fizzle had the impact of slapping on some aftershave; lyrics that were once rewardingly abstract had grown simply incomprehensible. Evidently as fed up as many of the band's old fans, Gotobed quit, effectively ending Wire Mark II. The fan-selected and heavily annotated **Wire 1985–1990: The A List** compiles the best of Wire's second go-round; it's nowhere near as essential as the original three studio albums, but it's better than any of the proper second-generation albums. The era also produced numerous EPs featuring a song or two from each album along with live tracks or remixes; none are worth owning.

Newman, Gilbert and Lewis dropped the "e" from the band name and became Wir, a none-too-inspired gimmick used as a loophole to renege on an old promise to disband if the four original partners weren't involved. **The First Letter** is more spirited than anything since **A Bell Is a Cup,** but once again, the most interesting thing about the album is the way it was made: all three played MIDI guitars into a computer, creating digital loops that were later sliced up into songs. It must have dawned on each of them that they no longer needed the others to record this way; this realization and the time-honored creative and personal tensions put an end to Wir soon after the album's release. The official party line is that Wir is dead and buried, but it's said that Wire may rear its head again once everybody forgets why they got sick of each other. In the meantime, while the devoted WMO organization keeps fans fed with reissues and new solo and band releases (like the **Turns and Strokes** compendium of previously unissued live, studio and rehearsal efforts), a career can be made keeping track of Wire-related projects.

Everyone but Gotobed has been incredibly prolific (the drummer has taken up farming), but as a whole, Newman's output is the most rewarding. Several of the songs on the Thorne-produced **A–Z** and **not to** were performed during the first-generation Wire's final tours, and a few feature lyrics by Lewis. Both albums are inventive and full of hooks, and they continue the cinematic style of **Chairs Missing** and **154.** ("Alone" from **A–Z** was used to great effect by director Jonathan Demme in *The Silence of the Lambs*). The productions are clearly inspired by Eno, with layered vocals, treated guitars, percussion (including drums by Gotobed) and odd tape effects. Between the two albums, Newman paused to record an album of Eno-style ambient instrumentals called **provisionally entitled the singing fish;** 4AD reissued **fish** and **not to** on one CD in 1988. Desmond Simmons was a contributor to Newman's early solo projects; Simmons' Wiresque solo effort, **Alone on Penguin Island,** was originally issued on Lewis and Gilbert's Dome Records label. Just before Wire's reunion, Newman released **Commercial Suicide,** which combines his ambient and pop interests by bringing a more spacious, minimalist approach to vocal-driven tunes. **It Seems** refines this sound and features several songs ("Quite Unrehearsed," "Round & Round" and the title track) that are as striking as anything Wire recorded. These albums feature contributions from Newman's Israeli-born wife, Malka Spigel, and members of her dance-pop band Minimal Compact. Newman produced Spigel's debut solo album, **Rosh Ballata,** which the couple released on its own Swim label. Oracle was Newman, Spigel and

Samy Birnbach of Minimal Compact fooling around in a world-beat/techno vein, while Immersion is Newman and Spigel's ambient house alter ego. If their efforts fall short of such masters of the genre as the Orb and Aphex Twin, Newman and Spigel may just be warming up.

Gilbert and Lewis' activities are just as diverse and even harder to track. Working together in the early '80s as Dome, they released four albums of industrial experiments, noisy works-in-progress and occasional pop epiphanies ("Rolling Upon My Day"); **Dome, Dome 2, Dome 3** and **Will You Speak This Word** were reissued on CD in pairs by Mute in the UK in 1992. The **MZUI** record consists of "aural wallpaper" improvised in and for an art gallery show by Gilbert, Lewis and graphic artist Russell Mills (who illustrated Eno's book, *More Dark Than Shark*). **Pacific/Specific** contains tracks from the duo's 1980 Peel session and a 1982 Australian radio broadcast with Mills. The anagram-named Duet Emmo was an industrial dance collaboration with Daniel Miller, the founder of Mute Records. Gilbert and Lewis further confused things by releasing records under the names Cupol and 3R4 (compiled on **8 Time**) and P'O (a one-off band with drummer Peter Price, clarinetist David Tidball and vocalist A. C. Marias, aka video director Angela Conway, a guest vocalist on He Said's **Hail**) in addition to backing Marias on her 1989 album **One of Our Girls (Has Gone Missing).**

After the Dome albums, all of the Gibert/Lewis releases are for completists or insomniacs only. On his own, Lewis has released melodramatic, over-produced dance music as He Said and, after relocating to Sweden, H.A.L.O., essentially emphasizing the worst tendencies of Wire Mark II. In contrast, Gilbert's spartan, clangy soundscapes make the description "minimalist Muzak" sound like overstatement. He has also recorded gently throbbing backing tracks for dance productions, and these have been collected as **Music for Fruit, Insiding** and **Ab Ovo.** These albums are nearly devoid of guitar. The notion that Gilbert was Wire's guitar hero is a fallacy; he always played the role of the artistic wrench in the works, giving the project of the moment a perverse twist. Gilbert, who turned fifty in 1996, is currently making quite a name for himself as a DJ in techno clubs under the moniker the Beekeeper.

If there is a common thread in all of the Wire-related output after the first three albums, it's the notion that rock is dead and dance music is the future. Maybe that could be accepted if the stuff that followed **Pink Flag, Chairs Missing** and **154** had the same spark, but it doesn't. Certainly the rock bands that Wire influenced in the '80s didn't subscribe to that notion, and neither did the wave of Wire-influenced groups that emerged in the '90s, including Blur, Elastica and Menswe@r. Perhaps there's a generation of musicians yet to come who will be equally inspired by **The Ideal Copy** and **The First Letter.** Either way, the members of Wire maintain that it doesn't mean anything to them; they are true artists in the sense that they only make music to please themselves. [jdr]

See also *TPRG*.

WISEBLOOD

See *Foetus*.

BOB WISEMAN

Bob Wiseman Sings Wrench Tuttle: In Her Dream (Can. Risqué Disque) 1989 (Risqué Disque/Atlantic) 1990
Presented by Lake Michigan Soda (Can. Warner Music) 1991
Hits of the '60s and '70s [tape] (Can. Death of Vinyl Entertainment) 1992
City of Wood (Can. Warner Music) 1993
In By Of (Bar/None) 1994
Beware of Bob (Can. Warner Music) 1994
Accidentally Acquired Beliefs (Can. Warner Music) 1995

BRUCE MCCULLOCH

Shame-Based Man (Atlantic) 1995

It's lucky Bob Wiseman never got to be a contestant on *What's My Line.* When Arlene Dahl and Bennett Cerf pulled off their masks and looked eagerly for the correct answer to their futile supposings, the nondescript Canadian who stood before them might be hard-pressed to explain what exactly it is that he does, since it changes so radically depending on what he's doing. Until 1992's **Lost Together,** when the group's dedication to country-rock became definite and his outside interests grew too demanding, he contributed barrelhouse piano, florid organ and rustic accordion to Blue Rodeo. He's co-written, produced and played on records for a wide variety of artists, from Ron Sexsmith and Eugene Chadbourne to Barenaked Ladies, Jane Siberry and Edie Brickell; he's also created scores for Canadian television. According to record company bumpf, he's also a monologist, painter, photographer and jazz pianist. Far from seeming like a daunting over-achiever, this odd duck is a truly fascinating and unpredictable figure.

In 1989, Wiseman branched out of Blue Rodeo with **In Her Dream,** an album whose fictional conceit was that its lyrics came from letters written to Wiseman by "poet, traveller, activist and philosopher" Wrench Tuttle. ("Currently he lives in Atlanta where he studies movement classes.") **In Her Dream** is an offbeat mixture of heavy-duty political protest ("Just Tourists" and "No Commotion" both concern the fatal French bombing of a Greenpeace ship; "Bhopal (Driftnet Plan)" is an indictment of Union Carbide's greed as the cause of the disastrous poison leak in India) and rollicking, likable folk-to-rock, played mostly on acoustic guitar and piano, with phone messages, a news broadcast and other offbeat ingredients keeping the hops hopping. In a whimsical fantasy, Wiseman musters a dose of backward electric psychedelia for "Airplane on the Highway," which complains about the hassle of driving with wings: "They say there once were airplanes that in the sky flew." Wiseman sings in a casual but engaging voice that squawks a bit like Gordon Gano's but reeks of personality; among the guests are Mary Margaret O'Hara (vocals), Ben Mink (violin) and future Ani DiFranco drummer Andy Stochansky (voice).

Wiseman's next two solo albums, which find him turning down the giddiness in favor of devastating sardonicism and stand-your-ground current-events anger, weren't released in America, but all three are conveniently sampled on the cleverly titled and remarkably stirring **In By Of.** Although the topicals from **In Her Dream** were left behind, the six songs that represent it are good choices, and the nine selections from **Presented by Lake Michigan Soda** and **City of Wood** provide enough searing commentary to make up the difference. "How Round the Earth" uses the telling of an anti-Semitic beating Wiseman evidently suffered as a twelve-year-old as the context for a wry refutation of impersonal politics that remarks on a press conference at which Ice Cube "talked about . . . the Jewish conspiracy." Bob genially invites the rapper to tea so he can show him his bank account and his car: "And then maybe you'll decide/The earth isn't flat." Even more ardent about the carriage of injustice, "Have a Nice Day" is an intricate and detailed attack on an attorney who represents reality-denying reactionaries; the harshly worded "City of Wood" damns the blame-the-victim defense and the actual aggressor in a sex attack, using crudely thumped bass keys of a piano for creepy accompaniment. Able to make righteous rage and righteous rock go head to head as well as hand in hand, Wiseman sets up a compelling dichotomy that makes hard ideas very hard *not* to swallow.

Wiseman co-wrote, produced and plays on **Shame-Based Man,** the inexplicable, unclassifiable and barely defensible 1995 album by Bruce McCulloch (no, not him, the other one) from *Kids in the Hall.* Beyond an amusing vintage simulation of the Doors ("Doors"), Wiseman's part in abetting the dryly absurdist comic's nearly futile attempt to set his supposed-to-be-funny-and-touching nonsense to music—with all the bad words and rock references not found on the TV show—is well-crafted and inconspicuous, which is easily the best thing that can be said about the record. [i]

JAH WOBBLE'S INVADERS OF THE HEART

Without Judgement (Bel. KK) 1989 (Restless) 1994
Rising Above Bedlam (UK Oval/EastWest) 1991 (Oval/Atlantic) 1992
Take Me to God (Island) 1994
Heaven & Earth (UK Island) 1995 (Island Independent) 1996

ENO/WOBBLE

Spinner (All Saints/Gyroscope) 1995

The liner notes to **Rising Above Bedlam** make it clear that Jah Wobble underwent some kind of bizarre transformation around the end of the '80s, when he ended a period of supporting himself in such unglamorous jobs as driving a London taxi and sweeping a train station by founding his first full-time band, the Invaders of the Heart. First, some history. Jah Wobble (John Wardle) was a close friend and confidant of John Lydon when Lydon was still Johnny Rotten and the Sex Pistols were on the fast road to hell in a handbasket. When the singer left the Sex Pistols in 1978, he, Wobble and ex-Clash guitarist Keith Levene formed Public Image Limited, where the budding bassist first noodled with his trademark—a dub-influenced murky brand of languid low-end madness that he has perfected, but barely altered, in the two decades since.

Wobble stayed with PiL for nearly three years, departing after the band's tour in support of 1979's **Metal Box** (aka **Second Edition**). He then spent half a decade producing uneven solo records and collaborations with the likes of Can alumni Holger Czukay and Jaki Liebezeit, U2 guitarist the Edge, and Gary Clail and the stable of On-U Sound artists. He launched Invaders of the Heart with guitarist Justin Adams and recorded a debut album (using keyboard/percussionist David Harrow and Urban Dance Squad drummer Michael Schoots) in Holland. Originally released only in Belgium, **Without Judgment** is an accessible seventy-minute exercise in avant-garde experimentalism, sparse aural atmospheres informed by acid-house trance weirdness. Wobble's plodding bass and Adams' steady playing mingle with minimally deployed tape loops and synthesizers. Some pleasing pop sounds are to be found in this vast landscape ("So Many Years"), as are danceable numbers and tongue-in-cheek jabs at the English ("Burger Bar") and commercial culture. Keep an ear open for brief, uncredited appearances by a number of people, including someone who sounds remarkably like ex–Pop Group vocalist Mark Stewart on "Bungalow Park."

Consolidating the group as a trio with Adams and keyboardist Mark Ferda, Wobble made the ambitious **Rising Above Bedlam** a refreshing departure from some of the flat, occasionally tedious and self-conscious material he lobbed out in the '80s. The album is founded on North African rhythms, embellished with Latin, Middle Eastern and other stylistic elements. In the booklet, Wobble describes his self-appointed mission with spiritual fervor: "Music is a force in itself. My responsibility is to tune into this force, this power greater than myself, and by way of imagination help to make it of this time and place." That's a tall order, which the album unsurprisingly fails to fully meet. Still, what it lacks in imagination, it makes up for in charm.

Among the guests are Sinéad O'Connor. She's an asset on "Sweet Divinity," but in "Visions of You," she sounds like an irritable pond goose, while Wobble's clumsy lead vocals (he's more suited to musical speech than actual singing) could be Peter Lorre trying to make a desperate return to Rick's Cafe. The strongest tracks include the Iberian spice of "Relight the Flame," which is held up almost entirely by vocalist Natacha Atlas (later of Transglobal Underground), whose multilingual talents and unusually versatile range could have been used far more effectively. The Middle Eastern flavor and post-punk reproachfulness of "Everyman's an Island" also make for a terrific listen, as does the title track, which eschews international influence to momentarily resurrect the fractious sounds of **Metal Box.**

Take Me to God reconfigures the band as a floating collective with Wobble the only track-to-track stalwart; it broadens the first album's stylistic range while adding disjointed theological twists. God, who appears to have bolstered Wobble's resolve to be our conduit between the timeless power of music and the here and now, makes frequent lyrical appearances throughout the first portion of the lengthy disc. Wobble intones that he himself "is the music and the music is me" on "God in the Beginning," then announces "I've just remembered who I am," followed by a chorus of "Becoming more like God, becoming God" in "Becoming More Like God." Along with Atlas' return for "When the Storm Comes," the addition of singers Ximena Tascon and Anneli M. Drecker (among others) considerably tops **Rising**'s vocal variety. Gavin Friday also stops by for a couple of songs, as does Dolores O'Riordan of the Cranberries. The record takes on far too much to be thoroughly solid, but it is still recommended.

Produced in part by Bill Laswell, the eclectic and enervating **Heaven & Earth** contains only two vocals (by Atlas and Najma). The album is otherwise instrumental in structure and ambient in tone. While preserving the international breadth of the two previous records, Wobble and his cohorts delve into trancey soul-funk, turntable scratching, quiet storm elevator mush and other surprising realms, notably giving a spotlight to jazz saxophonist Pharoah Sanders in the somnolent fifteen-minute "Gone to Croatan." As Wobble grows increasingly sophisticated, his music gets less predictable—and, in this case, a lot less stimulating. [icm/i]

See also *Brian Eno, Transglobal Underground; TPRG.*

WOLFGANG PRESS

The Burden of Mules (UK 4AD) 1983
The Legendary Wolfgang Press & Other Tall Stories (UK 4AD) 1985
Standing Up Straight (UK 4AD) 1986
Bird Wood Cage (4AD/Rough Trade) 1988
Queer (4AD) 1991
Funky Little Demons (4AD/Warner Bros.) 1995

In the '80s, Britain's Wolfgang Press was one of the best dark funk bands around: the London-based trio of singer Michael Allen, guitarist/keyboardist Andrew Gray and keyboardist Mark Cox combined harsh electronics with even harsher live guitars and creepy, echoing vocals to create dance music that could inspire dancing if it didn't leave listeners too bummed out to move. At some point, the three decided to concentrate more on funk and rhythm than noise and nihilism, and now seem to have discarded the darkness they were carrying. As a cold British funk band without much underlying dissonance, the group's charm is considerably diminished.

Queer's cover of Randy Newman's "Mama Told Me (Not to Come)" upholds the band's penchant for remaking other people's songs in its own mold, while "Louis XIV" takes a remarkably arcane topic—in this case, France's famous Sun King—and works it into a sinuous rhythm track with a few sprightly samples underneath Allen's stream-of-consciousness lyrics. Bassist Leslie Langston (Throwing Muses) plays on nearly every track; as the three bandmembers perform several different instrumental tasks on each song, the sound is appreciably fuller than usual. Although the Wolfgang Press appears to be stretching its style, the scattered songs don't hang together as well as on previous releases. (Initial copies of the British vinyl issue, which contains a minorly different set of tracks than the US CD, came with a bonus 12-inch of remixes.)

On **Funky Little Demons,** the Wolfgang Press finally realized they had been trying to fit a square peg into a round hole and sought to make straight-ahead dance music with the correct materials. Unfortunately, songs that sound properly formed and constructed are much less interesting. No longer enigmatic risk-takers, the Wolfgang Press have become just another white post–new wave soul band. [mf]

See also *TPRG.*

WOLVERTON BROTHERS

The Wolverton Brothers (OKra) 1988
Sucking Hind Tit (OKra) 1990
Liarman (Atavistic) 1993
Glad EP (Atavistic) 1995

On their rickety and gutbuckety but nonetheless auspicious debut, this strange Cincinnati foursome (no Wolvertons and no brothers in the bunch, natch) set the general stage for the rest of their extant career. Blending hard-chooglin' boogie rock, country-fried riffage and feedback-soaked atmospherics, the Wolverton Brothers have shaped a distinct backwoods hoedown marked by a dissolute, unspecific sense of ennui. Covering Charlie Daniels' "Long Haired Country Boy" and singing about old-timey fishing excursions with girlfriends wearing "fancy earrings," the album suggests hickish small-town social decay without ever traipsing into clichéd celebrations of incest, buggery or moonshine.

The band sounds much tighter and more expansive on its terrific followup, **Sucking Hind Tit,** which includes an eighteen-minute cover of America's "A Horse With No Name." The compelling layers of twangy, contrapuntal riffing hit an apex on tunes like "Could've Had a Life" and "Peace March," while the eerie "Posse Comitatus" captures the chafing frustration of rural middle America that helped foment the militia movement.

Failing to suitably capture its thrilling live energy, the band eventually recorded a seven-song followup with producer Jon Langford of the Mekons. **Liarman** pares down the twang in favor of a decidedly punchier rhythmic attack, while placing greater emphasis on the textural, harmony-heavy lattice built from Bill Stuart and Tim Schwallie's guitar playing. Unfortunately lost in these thick, coloristic sounds is the nifty interplay between Stuart, Schwallie and bassist Jay McCubbin. On the other hand, a song like "Max Gomez Love" adds a novel, almost Spanish instrumental lyricism, and "Blackout" sports a nice gritty funk.

The five-song Glad EP continues the band's progression in much the same vein, calming some of the combo's manic attack while ripping some of its previously rigid structures wide open, particularly on "Cold Spring." The Wolverton Brothers have maintained the invigorating blueprint proposed on their debut while transforming themselves into something less obvious than the rootsy twang of the early days. [pm]

WONDERMINTS

Wondermints (Japan. Toy's Factory) 1995

Los Angeles is home to many pop-oriented artists, both old (the Plimsouls, 20/20) and new (Sugarplastic, the Negro Problem). The best of the current lot, however, may be the Wondermints. With a sound that's firmly rooted in mid- to late-'60s California pop (there's an endorsement from Brian Wilson in the CD booklet) with faint echoes of everything from Elvis Costello to bachelor pad music, Darian Sahanaja (vocals/keyboards) and Nick Walusko (vocals/guitar) manage to evoke summery good vibrations without ever sounding beholden to the '60s.

With rich, full sound that belies the fact that it was recorded on only four tracks, the twelve-song **Wondermints** was collected from various tapes the band had circulated; even though the LP is cobbled together, it still manages to flow nicely from beginning to end. Some of the treasures it contains are the dainty power-pop of "Proto-Pretty," Walusko's gently lilting ballad "She Opens Heaven's Door," the Middle Eastern-influenced "Shine" and the muscular, modern "Carnival of Souls." The album's crown jewel, though, is Sahanaja's stunningly beautiful "Tracy Hide," a tune that perfectly re-creates **Smile**-era Beach Boys, from the deliciously flowing melody to the yearning lead vocal. And following in the grand tradition of the Holy Modal Rounders' "Boobs a Lot" and Loudon Wainwright's "Rufus Is a Tit Man," Sahanaja also contributes the gentle, dreamy "Playtex Aviary." [jmb]

WONDER STUFF

The Eight Legged Groove Machine (Polydor) 1988
Hup (Polydor) 1989
Never Loved Elvis (Polydor) 1991
Construction for the Modern Idiot (Polydor) 1993
If the Beatles Had Read Hunter . . . The Singles (UK Polydor) 1994

WE KNOW WHERE YOU LIVE

Don't Be Too Honest EP (UK HMD) 1995

Led by sneering smartass and self-important singer/lyricist Miles Hunt, Birmingham's Wonder Stuff started out as a quartet playing speedy, hilariously mean punk-pop on **The Eight Legged Groove Machine.** The ambitious **Hup** added mild psychedelia and country-folk to the mix. But while the band may have continued to mature musically and expand its thematic repertoire, nothing the Wonder Stuff did later could match the biting humor and cleverness of that thrilling debut.

By the release of **Never Loved Elvis,** the Stuffies were stadium-filling UK superstars. They were also without the Bass Thing (aka Rob Jones, who moved to New York City, where he died of drug-related causes in 1993); the arrival of multi-instrumentalist Martin Bell and a new bassist transformed the band into a ten-legged groove machine. More than any other album, the Mick Glossop–produced **Never Loved Elvis** proves that this angry lot sure did have a sweet spot. There's the lovely, fiddle-filled "Mission Drive," the bouncy, accordion-powered "Welcome to the Cheap Seats" (with guest vocals by Kirsty MacColl) and the slavish Madness soundalike "The Size of a Cow," a hooky singalong tailor-made for adoring festival crowds.

Clearly enjoying its commercial success (though US fame always eluded them), the band took no artistic leaps on **Construction for the Modern Idiot,** a spotty collection whose chief flaw is its uninspired songwriting. In addition to an embarrassing rant against pedophiles ("I Wish Them All Dead"), the album offers a grotesque bit of Charles Bukowski idolatry ("A Great Drinker") that would likely have made the writer cringe. Providing a break in the filler, however, is "Full of Life (Happy Now)," a catchy complaint against drunken violence, and the gloriously anthemic "On the Ropes," the perfect swan song for a band that would soon throw in the towel.

Hunt became a host for MTV Europe and later started the aggressive hard-pop Vent with ex-Cult guitarist Billy Duffy and ex-Eat drummer Pete Howard. Three-fifths of the Stuffies resurfaced backing Eat singer Ange Dolittle in We Know Where You Live (the name sometimes appears all run together), whose debut EP, **Don't Be Too Honest,** sounds not much like the Wonder Stuff but an awful lot like Eat.

The worthwhile posthumous Wonder Stuff hits compilation offers eighteen tracks, some of them previously non-LP, including the band's playful remake of Tommy Roe's "Dizzy" with British TV comedian Vic Reeves. [db]

See also *Cult, Eat; TPRG.*

WOODEN LEG

See *Blood Oranges.*

WOOL

Budspawn EP (External/London) 1992
Box Set (London) 1994 (Bong Load) 1994

Punk cred was once good for a favorable writeup in *Flipside,* the adoration of scenesters—and just about nothing else. Come the '90s and a couple of breakthrough bands and, all of a sudden, a résumé with genuine indie-core experience is the major-label A&R equivalent of a Harvard MBA. Wool's pedigree comes from brothers Peter (vocals/guitar) and Franz (guitar/vocals) Stahl, who formerly led Scream, the Washington, DC, band that could claim the indulgence of Dischord Records and the end-time membership of future Nirvana/Foo Fighters star Dave Grohl.

The six-song **Budspawn** is a friendly little noise-monster, with lots of bellowing vocals, crashing guitar power and explosive rhythmic contortions—as well as a working knowledge of dynamics and a melodic underpinning that shapes and justifies the torrid aggression. If that still leaves the eight-minute sonic dare of "EFF" unwarranted, the hooky chorus of "Slightly Under" makes up for it.

The arrival of former Drive Like Jehu drummer Chris Bratton upped the quartet's cool factor one more notch, but weird production (the second Van Halen album would seem to be a significant model) and an ungainly stab at MTV presentability makes the de-punked **Box Set** a dreadfully uneven—and occasionally dreadful—album. For every tuneful pop incision like "B-350" or "Chances Are," there's a lump of numbskullery like "Superman Is Dead" ("Now that Superman is dead/Who will kick ass"—gee guys, I dunno, but if you're that worried . . .) or a dubious goof like covering "God Rest His Soul," Steve Alaimo's moldy tribute to Martin Luther King ("Memphis battleground was red/Blood came pouring from his head"). Likewise, a few impressive guitar exhibitions—Franz Stahl's snazzy solo in "Coalinga," the brothers' burnout noise fiesta in the twelve-minute "Take a Look"—are balanced by the obvious "Public Image" clip in "Blackeye" and the generic Big Rock sound elsewhere. Even the bright packaging concept—the mock-retrospective liner notes purport to detail the band's lengthy career—is a halfbaked idea that trips over itself. (The album's vinyl edition on Bong Load includes a three-song bonus single.) [i]

WORKDOGS

See *Gibson Bros.*

WORLD OF LEATHER

St. Mark's Place (UK Soundcakes) 1994

British power-pop auteur Tot Taylor is the man behind the throne in the World of Leather, a merry band floating around Liverpool singer/guitarist Mark Chase. The Tin Pan–loving Taylor co-wrote, plays keyboards on and produced **St. Mark's Place,** a bizarre glam-pop extravaganza that credits a couple of drummers and as many as eight (!) guitarists on a single track—not to mention a string quartet and horn trio—and still doesn't sound like anyone's Phil Spector fantasies got the better of them. Chase is more likely to ape early-'70s Bowie (which he does to cloying effect on "Baby Yamamoto") than Darlene Love, but that's just the beginning of this wild invention. Taylor wisely avoids burying the bright, amusing songs in overt style-mongering (which doesn't preclude witty asides, like the Raspberries/Wizzard seeds in the wry career projection of "Future Ex–Pop Star" or the Glitterized shoutalong stomp of "Boots in Space"), instead giving them room to stretch and breathe. The album occasionally drops the scrim of cleverness to reveal a pedestrian hack of no special sappy character (see "Paper Gun" or "When Saturday Comes"), but when the curtains go back up, **St. Mark's Place** is a colorful funhouse. [i]

WORLD OF POOH

See *Barbara Manning.*

WORLD OF SKIN

See *Swans.*

WORLD PARTY

Private Revolution (Ensign/Chrysalis) 1986
Goodbye Jumbo (Ensign/Chrysalis) 1990
Thank You World (Ensign/Chrysalis) 1991
Bang! (Ensign/Chrysalis) 1993

With **Private Revolution,** one-man-pop-orchestra Karl Wallinger proved that his post-Waterboys soirée was a place to be. **Goodbye Jumbo** upped the ante; the Welshman's three years in the studio were well-spent, yielding a pastiche of '60s influences—mostly the Beatles, the Beach Boys, the Rolling Stones and Bob Dylan—blended into a thoroughly contemporary mix that propels the lyrics of Wallinger's ripping and heartfelt journey from disillusion to hope. He protests any sort of hippie or retro tag, but there's no denying the paisley-tinged psychedelia—including pro-environment and peace-on-earth sloganeering—of "Put the Message in the Box," "Love Street" and "Thank You World," as well as the percolating "Sympathy for the Devil" shuffle groove of "Way Down Now." Sinéad O'Connor, Wire Train's Jeff Trott and Steve Wickham of the Waterboys are among the handful of guests that help flesh out Wallinger's mostly self-sufficient vision. (The **Thank You World** mini-album contains two mixes and a live version of the title track, a remix of the album's "Is It Too Late" and five other tracks, all originals save for a rendition of John Lennon's "Happiness Is a Warm Gun.")

Bang! is more of a group project, with tourmates Chris Sharrock (ex–Icicle Works) and Dave Catlin-Birch signing on as full-fledged Party members. Ironically, in light of Wallinger's newfound reliance on computer technology, the sound is a little softer, his worldview a tad darker ("Faith: you don't need to believe it/Faith: 'cos they're just going to deceive you"), but **Bang!** is still a work of estimable craft and infectious melodicism that draws less baldly from Wallinger's acknowledged influences. World Party's sonic stew now includes funk ("What Is Love All About," "Give It All Away," "Radio Days") and country ("Kingdom Come"). If **Bang!** isn't as consistently stirring as either **Private Revolution** or **Goodbye Jumbo,** it does redefine the band's expanding identity. [gg]

See also *Waterboys; TPRG.*

WRECK

See *Waco Brothers.*

WRECKLESS ERIC

Wreckless Eric (UK Stiff) 1978
The Wonderful World of Wreckless Eric (UK Stiff) 1978
The Whole Wide World (Stiff) 1979
Big Smash! (Stiff/Epic) 1980
The Peel Sessions EP (UK Strange Fruit) 1988
Le Beat Group Électrique (Fr. New Rose) 1989
At the Shop! (Fr. New Rose) 1990
The Donovan of Trash (Sympathy for the Record Industry) 1993

CAPTAINS OF INDUSTRY

A Roomful of Monkeys (UK Go! Discs) 1985

LEN BRIGHT COMBO

The Len Bright Combo Present the Len Bright Combo by the Len Bright Combo (UK Empire) 1986
Combo Time! (UK Ambassador) 1986

HITSVILLE HOUSE BAND

12 O'Clock Stereo (Casino) 1994

Eric Goulden has spent the past decade and a half taking his initial burst onto the music scene and treating it, well, recklessly. Emerging in England as part of the initial Stiff roster and with Nick Lowe on board as his producer, Wreckless Eric made his name in 1977 with the winsome and catchy "Whole Wide World." A series of producers was unable to help him equal that song's notoriety; after a layoff from recording, Goulden (minus the nickname) re-emerged fronting the short-lived Captains of Industry with former Ian Dury sidemen. Making no inroads on any front, the group threw in the towel after one album.

A move to France in the mid-'80s did little to dull Goulden's songcraft, or his imagination in billing his work with confusing invention. Two releases appeared from the Len Bright Combo, an enterprise that naturally involved no one named Len Bright. Their rough-and-tumble attitude and sonic values owed much to the confluence of Eric with the likeminded rhythm section of ex-Milkshakes. "You're Gonna Screw My Head Off" and "Someone Must Have Nailed Us Together" are two would-be classics, but the lo-fi production makes it sound as if the band was playing in the back of a station wagon while a car driving alongside recorded them through the window.

Reinstating the Wreckless appellation, Eric released two albums via France's New Rose label. **Le Beat Group Électrique** is comfortably spartan in the minimalist but professional studio setting that Len Bright avoided; the acoustic **At the Shop** was recorded live in New Rose's Paris record store. Backed by a bassist and Fabrice Bertran doubling on baritone sax and congas, Eric sings and strums his way through five originals, including "(Waiting for the Shit) (To Hit the Fan)" and "Big Old World." The record also contains solo renditions of the Stiff-vintage "Semaphore Signals," a French version of "Depression" and a cover of "Boney Maronie" that were "found in the warehouse."

Then, quietly, came **The Donovan of Trash,** Eric's first Stateside release in more than a decade. A natural-sounding ease imbues all aspects of the record, from material to arrangements and performance. This is as likably flip as Eric's ever been; likewise the excellent **12 O'Clock Stereo,** the first flowering of the unpretentious Hitsville House Band (Goulden, drummer Denis Baudrillart and bassist Fabrice Lombardo). [dbg]

See also *Ottoman Empire; TPRG.*

WRECK SMALL SPEAKERS ON EXPENSIVE STEREOS

See *Dead C.*

WRENS

The Low EP EP7 (Dow Boy) 1993
Silver (Grass) 1994
Secaucus (Grass) 1996

The Wrens are probably the only band to ask the musical question "Where's my fresh diner daisy?" The New Jersey foursome stacks up twenty-five songs on **Silver,** a most ambitious debut album. Frenetic guitar stylings in classic post-punk slapdash mode underpin most of the tracks; bassist Kevin Whelan, guitarists Greg Whelan and Charles Bissell and drummer Jerry MacDonnell take turns in the lead-singing slot; the predominantly strained, nasal vocals render a lot of the lyrics indiscernible but lend a heartfelt charm. At times loopy, the Wrens' breakneck approach here is most effective on "Adenoi." Who says Hebrew prayers can't rock?

Named for the quartet's home base, **Secaucus** is a streamlined progression from the first full-length. The album displays the Wrens' newly impressive range, from the racing shamble of the opening "Yellow Number Three" and the glammy, vamping "Built in Girls" to an ambient, spacey instrumental, "I'll Mind You." Vocal sheen of an almost Beach Boys proportion is achieved on the ballads "Won't Get Too Far" and "Jane Fakes a Hug," the spareness of which reveals what sounds like someone making cappucino noisily in the background. Unbridled pop fortitude is in full effect on "Surprise, Honeycomb" and the tick-tock pace of "Hats Off to Marriage, Baby." The musical-chairs vocals make the Wrens' output resemble the work of several different bands at once, but a group with this much quirky verve shouldn't limit itself. [re]

WU-TANG CLAN

Enter the Wu-Tang (36 Chambers) (Loud/RCA) 1993

METHOD MAN

Tical (Def Jam) 1994

OL' DIRTY BASTARD

Return to the 36 Chambers: The Dirty Version (Elektra) 1995

RAEKWON

Only Built 4 Cuban Linx . . . (Loud/RCA) 1995

GENIUS/GZA

Words From the Genius (Cold Chillin') 1991+1994
Liquid Swords (Geffen) 1995

GHOSTFACE KILLAH

Ironman (Razor Sharp/Epic) 1996

Historically, Staten Island hasn't contributed much except David Johansen to the music world, but after the prolific and massively successful Wu-Tang Clan, New York's forgotten borough doesn't really need to. As Buddy Holly did for Lubbock and Elvis for Tupelo, the rough-and-ready Wu-Tang Clan—named after a cinematic tribe of martial artists—has put Richmond County on the map with one group album and a steady stream of solo records, all of which typify '90s East Coast rap style: loping funk beats, a devotion to smoking pot ("tical") and gangsta boasting that doesn't trivialize sex or violence, dealing firmly with the big city's relentless intensity and leaving random explosions of lurid melodrama to the Californians.

Enter the Wu-Tang (36 Chambers) introduces the extended crew: Prince Rakeem (The RZA), Method Man, Ol' Dirty Bastard, Shallah Raekwon, U-God, Rebel INS, Ghost Face Killer and the Genius (GZA), only some of whom actually come from Staten Island. Surprisingly cohesive and organized given all the mic competition (credit producer Rakeem for cool beats and the take-a-number verbal discipline), the album uses film bites, TV references, team cheers and loosely arranged vocal weaves to shape inoffensive raps that flow loosely in carefully contained tracks. Maintaining a stylistic and literal connection to New York's old-school tradition, the crew pays tribute in the soulful "Can It Be All So Simple" (a song remade by Raekwon on his solo album) and follows through on the autobiographical "C.R.E.A.M." Otherwise, the band's head-swaying atmospheres are more effective than its rambling lyrics.

While watching the money pile up for that multi-platinum album, five Wu-Tang Clan members cut solo projects (and Rakeem was in the Gravediggaz and launched the Razor Sharp label). In light of their creative diversity, the unanimity of the group's album seems almost inconceivable in retrospect. With his husky voice, melodic flow and full-time sens-smoking hobby, Method Man is the most active and audible member on **Enter the Wu-Tang.** (His eponymous track begins with a comical series of memorably vulgar threats.) His solo record, produced in woozy, disorienting pass-it-over-here behind-a-wall-of-muslin style by Rakeem (Robert Diggs), is a slow simmer of odd sounds, muted beats and the rapper's cloudy delivery. Method Man spends a lot of the record smoking chronic and clearing his lyrical throat to no serious effect, but he occasionally coughs up a surprise: the heartfelt love jones of "All I Need," the "I Will Survive" melodies of "Release Yo' Delf," the falsetto crooning of the guest-heavy "Mr. Sandman." A convincing evocation of blunted oblivion, **Tical** makes the most of its blurry focus and casual progress.

Ol' Dirty Bastard (Russell Jones) has it hectic in real life (he was shot by robbers in Brooklyn in late '94 and later arrested for breaking into a Queens house). He keeps it reckless on his riotous solo album, the cover of which pictures him on a welfare ID card. A bizarre outrage joke of rowdy vulgarity and raw self-indulgence that uses some of the scratchiest old records for its tracks, **Return to the 36 Chambers:**

The Dirty Version, produced with feverish invention by the RZA and others, includes a rude Blowfly song, nostalgic romantic crooning, kids' voices, girlfriends discussing his merits, gunfire, chronic, silly noises, theatrically rendered boasts and this financial statement: "Who the fuck wanna be an MC if you can't get paid to be a fuckin' MC? . . . 26 years old, *still* on welfare/So I gotta get paid fully."

Raekwon's **Only Built 4 Cuban Linx . . .** begins with a dramatic prayer and then launches into "Knuckleheadz," a gangsta spiel performed over curtly simple drums, string bass and a bit of piano. Although produced by the RZA and featuring verbal contributions from Tony Starks (Ghost Face Killer), Method Man and other bandmates (not to mention Blue Raspberry, the lame female group that has sung on various Wu-Tang joints, and the usual cinematic samples), Raekwon's album is way different from his cohorts' (something he makes a point of in a studio conversation entitled "Shark Niggas [Biters]"); the lyrics—which casually incorporate the argot of the 5% Nation Muslim sect—are harsher and more frightful than other Clan members, the beats firmer. Without the personality of Ol' Dirty Bastard or the distinctive flow of Method Man, Raekwon plays it gangsta straight, bringing nothing more than energy, conviction and smart studio support to his project.

The Genius/GZA (Gary Grice) also brings drug-dealer action, gunplay and fervent religious philosophy to his tough, provocative and deceptively low-key album, **Liquid Swords,** setting it all up as cinematic narratives. "You witness the saga/Casualties and drama/Life is a script/I'm not an actor but the author of a modern day opera/With a main character/It's presidents and papers the dominant factor," he explains in "Cold World." Far more compelling than the likeminded Raekwon, GZA tumbles out his words like a Martin Scorsese/Abel Ferrara student armed with a rhyming dictionary. Over spare, inventive, subtly atmospheric tracks (produced, in further proof of his incredible diversity, by RZA, who should get his own record together asap) and numerous snatches of ninja film dialogue and TV news reports, GZA—deploying a low, conversational voice ominous with taut intensity—reveals an intriguing sense of what constitutes fair rap game: the bizarre "Labels" merely strings together several dozen record-company names: "from EastWest to Atco, I bring it to the Next Plateau."

The tracks on **Words From the Genius** predate the Wu-Tang album, although its release didn't. Produced mainly by Easy Mo Bee (but with Prince Rakeem doing the honors with the rapper on the blunt-puffing "Pass the Bone," billed on the front cover as a "smash hit"), it's an unstylish, all-over-the-place collection with little of **Liquid Swords'** slashing damage. The Genius tells how he came to be an MC ("Those Were the Days"), paints women as gold-diggers ("What Are Silly Girls Made Of?," using female spoken-word inserts to confirm his faith), paints himself as a hood ("Life of a Drug Dealer"), picks up a drunk nymphomaniac on the subway ("Superfreak") and details the ups and downs of tavern life ("Stay Out of Bars"). The rhymes are rude but involving (especially when he's recounting stories), the beats blandly adequate: not prime, but not simply a cash-in. [i]

See also *Gravediggaz.*

STEVE WYNN

Kerosene Man (Rhino) 1990
Kerosene Man EP (Rhino) 1991
Dazzling Display (RNA) 1992
Fluorescent (Mute) 1994
Take Your Flunky and Dangle (Ger. Return to Sender/Normal) 1995
Melting in the Dark (Zero Hour/Universal) 1996

"Post-punk" has always been more of a chronological term than an aesthetic one—when it comes to the actual music, "pre-punk" might be a better tag for the way many Reagan-era bands chose to cast new light and darkness on the classic rock and seminal obscurities of the '60s and early '70s. Case in point: Steve Wynn. As the leader of Los Angeles psychedelic-cum-feedback blues combo Dream Syndicate, the singer/guitarist looked primarily to influences like Bob Dylan, Neil Young and (definitively) the Velvet Underground. What he took from punk had more to do with attitude, noisy energy, abyss-skirting emotions and musical riskiness—qualities, of course, present in the best rock'n'roll of any scene, era or sub-genre.

Since Dream Syndicate dissolved in '89, Wynn has traced the same kind of edges, his continuing spirit of mutable classicism propped up by a further emphasis on crafty songwriting and stout production contexts. **Kerosene Man** rounds up a passel of guest contributors (to name, believe it or not, just a handful: bassist Fernando Saunders, sax player Steve Berlin of Los Lobos, former Divine Horsemen vocalist Julie Christensen, Concrete Blonde's Johnette Napolitano, Giant Sand's Howe Gelb and drummers D. J. Bonebrake and Denny Fongheiser) for a varied, song-strong exercise in snappy guitar pop ("Carolyn," "Killing Time"), narrative mood pieces ("The Blue Drifter," "Anthem") and unsettling ballads (the vengeful "Something to Remember Me By" and the lovely "Conspiracy of the Heart"). It's a darn good record of multiple resonances—some listeners might come away remembering the hummable hooks, others the insinuating shards of guitar, still others the doleful lyricism. The adjacent EP packages the wordplay-driven bar-room rock of the title cut with four tracks from various radio sessions, including covers of Sonic Youth's "Kool Thing" and Paul Simon's "The Boy in the Bubble."

Dazzling Display is exactly that, though not always in a good way. Sometimes the ambitious arrangements—horns and strings and layered harmonies and track-upon-track of guitar ornamentation—achieve a bright, swollen grandiosity. Elsewhere, returning producer Joe Chiccarelli's work is merely slick, which hardly seems appropriate for a record of pulpy character sketches (separate songs are devoted to Hubert Selby Jr. and James Ellroy). The material is equally inconsistent—many songs just don't get where they're supposed to go, or never leave the starting blocks. They are, however, balanced by high points like the infectious, Beatlesque "Tuesday," the rolling carnival of "Dandy in Disguise" and a suitably bizarre duet with Napolitano on Serge Gainsbourg's "Bonnie and Clyde" (putting Wynn a few years ahead of the hipness curve—plus he did the English translation himself!).

Wynn pared things back considerably after that, turning his attention to the all-star garage band Gutterball while also co-producing **Fluorescent,** a spare, solid exercise in songwriting (especially lyrics) that doesn't quite take off. It's an objectively good record of terse, rootsy guitar rock, lacking in either flash or roughness—"tasteful" would be the appropriate word for the perky, finely wrought road story "Collision Course" and the sweetly restrained "Wedding Bells." Other tracks (the appropriately foreboding "That's Why I Wear Black," the country-inflected "The Sun Rises in the West") walk a fine line between subtle and prosaic. The fine supporting cast this time out includes Gelb, John Wesley Harding, Victoria Williams and several Continental Drifters. Check out Wynn's singing on "Look Both Ways" for one of the most entertainingly blatant Dylan imitations ever. The Return to Sender disc, mostly outtakes from **Fluorescent** and **Kerosene Man,** is a better record, with a bunch of loose, rollicking songs, a real campfire-band feel to the music and some of Wynn's warmest, most liquid vocals. Despite its rarity, **Take Your Flunky and Dangle** is solid enough to be of interest to even casual fans.

Wynn finally realized long-standing plans to use the band Come—guitarists Thalia Zedek and Chris Brokaw, bassist Sean O'Brien and drummer Arthur Johnson—as his backing group on **Melting in the Dark.** Although something of a return to the Dream Syndicate's savage guitar-frenzy, the album is flightier, with dry, laconic vocals, jauntily aggressive tempos and a joyous garage-crud vibe that suggests it was a lot of fun to make. The vocal pairing of Wynn and Zedek is spookily effective; with his dramatic songs anchoring the three-guitar sparks, you'd never know the music was being made by a band that can be so brooding and gothic on its own. Come subsequently lost O'Brien and Johnson (which makes **Melting in the Dark** that lineup's final work together), and Wynn put together a short-lived touring band with Zedek, Brokaw, Gutterball's Armistead Welliford and erstwhile Dream Syndicate drummer Dennis Duck. [jc]

See also *Come, Gutterball; TPRG.*

X

Los Angeles (Slash) 1980
Wild Gift (Slash) 1981
Under the Big Black Sun (Elektra) 1982
More Fun in the New World (Elektra) 1983
Ain't Love Grand (Elektra) 1985
See How We Are (Elektra) 1987
Live at the Whisky A Go-Go on the Fabulous Sunset Strip (Elektra) 1988
Los Angeles/Wild Gift (Slash) 1988
Hey Zeus! (Big Life/Mercury) 1993
Unclogged (Infidelity/Sunset Blvd.) 1995

EXENE CERVENKA + WANDA COLEMAN

Twin Sisters (Freeway) 1985

EXENE CERVENKA

Old Wives' Tales (Rhino) 1989
Running Sacred (RNA) 1990
Rage EP7 (Kill Rock Stars) 1994
Surface to Air Serpents (213CD) 1996

EXENE CERVENKOVA

Excerpts From the Unabomber Manifesto (Year One) 1995

LYDIA LUNCH/EXENE CERVENKA

Rude Hieroglyphics (Rykodisc) 1995

JOHN DOE

Meet John Doe (DGC) 1990

JOHN DOE THING

Kissingsohard (Forward) 1995

KNITTERS

Poor Little Critter on the Road (Slash) 1985

VARIOUS ARTISTS

Live From the Masque Volume 2: WeWeCanCan-DoDoWhatWhat WeWe Wanna Do (Year One) 1996

Though X was perhaps the most important band to emerge from the Los Angeles punk scene, its members were never genuine punks per se. Too self-conscious and artsy to simply spew, leaders John Doe (bass/vocals) and Exene Cervenka (vocals) repackaged their bohemian tendencies in new wave guise, delivering desperate meditations on sex and society at high velocity, happy to ride the coattails of more instinctual performers. Since withdrawing from the scene after their '88 live album (regrouping to make **Hey Zeus!** in '93), X no longer prowls the cutting edge of anything, but Doe and Cervenka's tart tandem vocals—suggesting either psychotic bluegrass music or a less accomplished variant of the Jefferson Airplane—retain their signature sting.

Produced by Doors organist Ray Manzarek, who would do the same honors on the subsequent three albums, **Los Angeles** finds the gang rushing to dispatch their tunes as if eager to catch the next train out of town. Featuring such ambitious yet messy originals as "Sex and Dying in High Society" and "Johny Hit and Run Paulene," plus a high-octane demolition of the Doors' "Soul Kitchen," this overheated debut also establishes big-beat drummer D. J. Bonebrake and guitarist Billy Zoom, a slick rockabilly/Chuck Berry disciple, as important elements in the mix. **Wild Gift** brings X's vision into sharper focus, with "We're Desperate" and the atypically understated "White Girl" capturing the grit'n'grime of ordinary stressed-out lives. (The two albums were subsequently paired on a single CD.)

While **Under the Big Black Sun** displays more polish, it's hardly bland. Doe and Cervenka's best material achieves an arresting cinematic vividness—see the cheesy "Motel Room in My Bed" and "The Have Nots," a poignant lament for the common man highlighted by a surprisingly swingin' groove. And Exene's touching performance of the heartbroken pre-rock chestnut "Dancing With Tears in My Eyes" is sentimental in the best possible way. X finally stumbled: **More Fun in the New World** has erratic material and less sparkle in both singing and playing. "I Must Not Think Bad Thoughts" is a sardonic exception, though it suggests they must have been thinking a few of them about their music and its place in the cultural big picture.

Reflecting a growing uncertainty about how to proceed, the band got metalmeister Michael Wagener, who doesn't show much of an affinity for X's style, to produce **Ain't Love Grand.** (Maybe that's why they chose him.) **See How We Are** constitutes an enormous improvement. With Zoom gone, ex-Blasters leader Dave Alvin stands in (although Tony Gilkyson is credited on the cover as the fourth X-er). Alvin contributes two of his most heart-rending compositions (the title track and "4th of July") and generally brings the band down to earth, restoring its confidence. Too bad he'd split by the time X recorded their fine 1988 live album, which features Gilkyson's less distinctive but suitably driving axework. (The **Masque** compilation, recorded live in '78 and released on a label in which Cervenka has an interest, has seven X songs amid tracks by F-Word, the Alleycats and Zeroes.)

Released during X's extended leave, Cervenka's first two solo albums filled the void for fans without resorting to outright mimicry. Both produced by Tony Gilkyson, **Old Wives' Tales** and **Running Sacred** range from country and blues roots to more modern sounds; her vocals, once characterized by a charmingly unsteady sense of pitch, display greater technical prowess while retaining their warmth.

In her other life as a published poet, Cervenka has made spoken-word albums in tandem with Wanda Coleman and Lydia Lunch. **Rage** is a solo wordcore single; the twenty-two-track **Surface to Air Serpents** essays audio collage by combining poetry, sound manipulation, actualities and music into a woozy portfolio of creative observations. Using her new (?) name, Exene entered the current events realm with a limited edition recording of her reading **Excerpts From the Unabomber Manifesto.**

Doe, who's built himself a solid little acting career in a number of cool films, doesn't fare as well as Cervenka on his first solo album. Produced by Davitt Sigerson and featuring a high-powered support crew that includes guitarist Richard Lloyd, **Meet John Doe** is a misguided attempt to sell him as a slick album-rock star. Despite passionate singing, originals like "Let's Be Mad" and "A Matter of Degrees" would've sounded much better on an X album than in these over-produced versions. Credited to the John Doe Thing, the crackling **Kissingsohard** makes a far stronger case for his solo career. Avoiding the kind of sweeping statements that tend to bring such proceedings to a screeching halt, Doe zeroes in on the details of lives under extreme stress. "Fallen Tears" strikes a twangy country groove, while the punky "Love Knows" and the don't-give-a-damn chaos of "Beer, Gas, Ride Forever" show he hasn't forgotten the thrilling uproar of the old days. The standout track, however, is "Willamette," a heart-rending anthem that peaks with the refrain "Will work for food." It'll leave a tear in your beer.

Not surprisingly, X (with Gilkyson returning) seems a bit creaky on **Hey Zeus!,** its first album in five years. Sluggish tempos indicate the result of both passing years and, perhaps, a desire to reel in new, less adventurous listeners. Still, Doe and Cervenka mesh well, just like the good old days, making at least "Country at War," "Lettuce and Vodka" and "Baby You Lied" worthy additions to the canon.

Despite the now-tiresome (but apparently endless) "unplugged" gambit, **Unclogged** constitutes a triumphant about-face from the lackluster **Hey Zeus!** These shaggy, stripped-down renditions of such classics as "White Girl," "I Must Not Think Bad Thoughts" and "Burning House of Love" are infused with a liberating playfulness never found in the band's more ambitious work. Fifteen years after their debut, it looks as if X has finally learned to enjoy music for its own sake.

The Knitters' **Poor Little Critter on the Road,** by an ad hoc group that is essentially the Zoom-era X plus Dave Alvin, mixes acoustic originals and roots tunes, but is surprisingly forgettable. [jy]

See also *Dave Alvin, Lydia Lunch; TPRG.*

XANAX 25

Denial Fest (Futurist) 1995

The '90s affectation for naming bands after drugs (Codeine, Morphine, Halcion and so on) found its most self-conscious proponent in this New York quartet, whose only audibly distinctive feature is singer Jaik Miller, the second coming of Aqualung (or is that Live's Ed Kowalczyk?). A lumbering rhythm section, Matt Stein's chunky guitar routines and revealingly self-abusive songs about night sweats and suicidal tendencies actually add up to a dull but commercial "alternative" sound, rooted in the purity of passion. The nine-song **Denial Fest** (an appealing title that gives further indication of X25's Live-ly tendencies) includes a cover of Madder Rose's "Swim" and a brief, meaningless guest vocal by Cher son Elijah Blue Allman. On sound alone, Xanax 25 is the kind of band that's easy to dismiss until it suddenly sells a million records; it's safe to assume, however, that the name precludes any such mainstream acceptance. [i]

XC-NN

XC-NN (550 Music/Epic) 1994
Lifted (550 Music/Epic) 1996

Formed in 1992 by former Sisters of Mercy guitarist Tim Bricheno and Glasgow-born singer David Tomlinson (ex–Jellyfish Kiss), the trio (completed by drummer Neill Lambert—a bassist joined later) named CNN popped out two UK singles before being forced to change its name by Ted Turner. Regardless of the nomenclature, **XC-NN** is no great shakes, another cynical but lame runner in the we-can-outsmart-the-market steeplechase. Slapping dramatic, reality-invoking spoken samples into burly British hard rock distinguished mainly by its conceptual surliness and attempts at sensationalism ("Logic Bomb," "Unnatural Passions"), **XC-NN** is less convincing than Sigue Sigue Sputnik and twice as tuneless. Even Billy Idol couldn't make a record this tiresomely unpersuasive. As Tomlinson sings—with a sneering attempt at irony—in "Young, Stupid & White," "This ain't rock'n'roll / This is stupid." Sho 'nuff.

Produced by Guns n' Roses intimate Mike Clink, **Lifted** eliminates the first album's color commentary for faceless American dumb-rock, an uninspired scrapheap assembled from various Generation Pearl Jam influences. "All Over the Place" slaps a catchy chorus tune onto a ticking sequencer chug, and the Creedence-styling "Love Sick" cranks up a stunning storm of chaotic noise guitar over twanging synthesizers, but otherwise the excursions into dance beats, acoustic pop and suchlike are hapless and futile. [i]

XORCIST

Damned Souls (21st Circuitry) 1991
Bitches EP (21st Circuitry) 1993
Phantoms (21st Circuitry) 1994

San Francisco's Xorcist (actually just Peter Stone, who sometimes goes by the name "Bat") specializes in "torture tech," the most brutal, unrelenting form of industrial music. **Damned Souls** would make a fine soundtrack to any Clive Barker film: death and destruction imagery pops up all over the place, wanting nothing more than to scare the water out of hapless listeners. Between the bludgeoning beats, creepy synth melodies snake around distorted, caustic vocals. Samples lifted from films like *The Dead Zone, Death Wish, Blade Runner,* several porn flicks and, naturally, *The Exorcist* series further add to the unsettling mayhem.

On the **Bitches** EP, Xorcist briefly takes a break from all the pain and chaos long enough to do a whimsical industrial version of Nirvana's "Smells Like Teen Spirit" that must be heard to be believed. But the rest of the album—the title track, another new song titled "U R the 1 (Fux Version)," along with remixes of "Xorcist" and "UNGDSOB" from **Damned Souls**—reverts to style, wallowing in danceable ditties saturated with violence, perversion and despair.

As with other Xorcist releases, **Phantoms** unleashes nightmare-inducing chaos in powerful portions. It's violent, it's disturbing, it stops at nothing to terrify—and it works, especially on the edgy opener,

"Bitchend." Scary as this material sounds, though, the truly frightening thing about it is its ability to make such awful visions so compelling. [ky]

XTC

3D EP (UK Virgin) 1977
White Music (Virgin International) 1978 (Virgin/Geffen) 1984
Go 2 (Virgin International) 1978 (Virgin/Geffen) 1984
Drums and Wires (Virgin) 1979 (Virgin/Geffen) 1984
Black Sea (Virgin/RSO) 1980 (Virgin/Geffen) 1984
English Settlement (Virgin/Epic) 1982 (Virgin/Geffen) 1984
Waxworks/Beeswax (UK Virgin) 1982 (Virgin/Geffen) 1984
Mummer (UK Virgin) 1983 (Virgin/Geffen) 1984
The Big Express (Virgin/Geffen) 1984
The Compact XTC—The Singles 1978–85 (UK Virgin) 1985
Skylarking (Virgin/Geffen) 1986
Oranges & Lemons (Virgin/Geffen) 1989
Explode Together: The Dub Experiments 78–80 (UK Virgin) 1990
Rag & Bone Buffet (UK Virgin) 1990 (Virgin/Geffen) 1991
Nonsuch (Geffen) 1992
XTC: Live in Concert (Windsong) 1992

DUKES OF STRATOSPHEAR

Psonic Psunspot (Virgin/Geffen) 1987
Chips from the Chocolate Fireball (UK Virgin) 1987 (Geffen) 1988

MR. PARTRIDGE

'Take Away'/'The Lure of Salvage' (UK Virgin) 1980

ANDY PARTRIDGE/HAROLD BUDD

Through the Hill (All Saints/Gyroscope) 1994

ANDY PARTRIDGE

EP (Hello Recording Club) 1994

VARIOUS ARTISTS

A Testimonial Dinner (Thirsty Ear) 1995

Hailing from the bland English exurb of Swindon, XTC emerged from an early manic post-punk phase to produce several classics: the spiky art-pop gems **Drums and Wires** and **Black Sea,** the flawed epic **English Settlement** and the exquisite pop pastorale **Skylarking,** an album that—despite its detractors—may stand as the band's greatest triumph. For many years now a trio of Andy Partridge (guitar/vocals), Colin Moulding (bass/vocals) and Dave Gregory (keyboards/guitar), XTC—one band that made the description "clever" a criticism—is one of the last of England's original class of '77 still in active and unbroken existence. By this point, though, the group's increasingly safe, mellow music is a candidate for the Adult Alternative chart; as time goes on, XTC's studio-bound perfectionism flirts more and more heavily with soullessness—imagine Steely Dan playing the Beatles songbook.

Compiling two dozen rarities from throughout the band's career, **Rag & Bone Buffet** (*Rare Cuts & Leftovers*) is an XTC freak's dream—but probably no one else's. There's a wealth of disposable material here, with some exceptions: the mad ska workout "Too Many Cooks in the Kitchen," the fine **English Settlement** outtakes "Tissue Tigers (The Arguers)" and "Blame the Weather," the creepy "Pulsing Pulsing," and the wonderfully jolly "Take This Town" from the **Times Square** soundtrack. Rare versions of album cuts like "Ten Feet Tall," "Scissor Man" and "Respectable Street" provide even more bait for hardcore gourmands.

Nonsuch, the sole XTC studio album of the '90s so far, was released during the commercial explosion of American underground rock; produced by Elton John veteran Gus Dudgeon, the album's mannered, polished Angloisms stood in direct opposition—emotionally, musically and sonically—to the prevailing raw edge. The often oversweet group had long since begun to overplay the McCartney side of its Beatlesque musical psyche. "The Ballad of Peter Pumpkinhead" rocks out in that amiably nerdish way that only XTC can manage, the eloquent anti-censorship anthem "Books Are Burning" attains a certain majesty and "Wrapped in Grey" wears its Beach Boys influences well. But the preachy, wordy "The Smartest Monkeys" (sung by Moulding) and precious, overwrought pop IQ tests like "Rook" and "Crocodile" are more the rule.

XTC: Live in Concert, documenting a fierce 1980 show, stands in stark contrast. Goaded by Terry Chambers' workmanlike yet brutally crafty drum work, the band sprints with tight, adrenalized velocity through a tuneful set of post-punk classics including "Life Begins at the Hop," "Burning With Optimism's Flame" and "Making Plans for Nigel." Partridge's droll blow-by-blow liner notes clinch this nifty release. Oh, for the good old days.

Meanwhile, back to the future. Unexpected and unprecedented, **Through the Hill,** a joint album by Partridge and California-born avant-garde composer Budd (known in rock circles for his 1986 collaboration with the Cocteau Twins and work with Brian Eno), is a generally placid but occasionally pepped-up set of ambient instrumentals performed mostly on guitar and keyboards. Budd's reading of two poems by Partridge and the merest wisps of "aaahing" vocals offer the only discernible evidence of the latter's presence. Partridge's recent solo EP, released by John Flansburgh's subscription-only CD club, contains four otherwise unavailable tracks, including two from the rumored but unreleased **Bubble Gum Album.**

The brief 1995 tribute album offers an impressive array of sophisticated commercial heavyweights and critical favorites doing a bizarre assortment of XTC oldies. Freedy Johnston countryfies "Earn Enough for Us," Sarah McLachlan embraces "Dear God" as if it were one of her own and the Rembrandts take the nervous edge off "Making Plans for Nigel" in a cloyingly sweet treatment. The Crash Test Dummies make handsome work of "All You Pretty Girls," They Might Be Giants throw a vintage kitchen sink at "25 O'Clock" (by XTC's alter ego, the psychedelic Dukes of Stratosphear), Ruben Blades puts Latin rhythm and energy into "The Man Who Sailed Around His Soul" and Joe Jackson, who was actually on the English new wave scene when XTC released the original on its debut album, treats "Statue of Liberty" with utmost respect. But if there's something awfully familiar about the sound of "The Good Things," recorded by the previously unknown Terry & the Lovemen in—of all places—Swindon, that's just as it should be. [ma/i]

See also *Martin Newell; TPRG.*

Y'ALL

An Evening of Stories & Songs [tape] (no label) 1993
The Next Big Thing (no label) 1994
Big Apple Pie (no label) 1995

The importance of family values in country music has not been lost on Y'all, a couple of small-town emigrés from Indiana and Texas facing life together in New York. Harmony-singing gentle, mildly funny folk songs of life, love and the "white trash country gospel" over simple acoustic instruments on self-released records, they're not They Might Be Giants, but they're not the Proclaimers, either. (Actually, their sound *is* close to the Kingston Trio, only there's two of 'em and John Stewart never sang about being "Queen of the Rodeo.") Exactly what they are is hard to settle on, but James Dean Jay Byrd and Steven Cheslik-DeMeyer have angelic voices, the temperament of concerned candy stripers and some of the ugliest dresses to be found in the Aunt Bee rack of America's Salvation Armies. Campy in principle not execution, Y'all is winningly weird in the nicest possible way.

The bare-bones '93 cassette, a studio version of the duo's live act, is unassumingly pretty, but the songs (except for "My Family Tree" and "Eduardo") are too quiet and nondescript. **The Next Big Thing** offers a second version of the debut's "My Man, Our Horses, And Me" (this time backed by the eight-strong Cow-Girl Chorus) and such friskier compositions as "The Egg Man (for Edith Massey)," the poverty-stricken "Food Stamp Blues," the twangy "Are You on the Top 40 of Your Lord?" and the coyly sexual "Do It." Much more engaging than the debut.

Big Apple Pie, all seven slices of it, brings Y'all into the modern world with excellent results. Sounding like an old-timey band with such useful implements as fiddle, banjo, mandolin and washboard, the good-singing duo and their friends wax homesick in "The Map of the U.S. of A." and "Gotta Be a Big Man," flipping the sexual script with Loretta Lynn's "You Ain't Woman Enough to Take My Man." Supported more simply, Byrd and Cheslik-DeMeyer also poke genial fun at their adopted city in "God Bless New York City (My Big Apple Pie)," sing a folk ballad about a southeastern town called "Graham" and take a third crack at "My Man, Our Horses, And Me." Once was enough, guys. [i]

YELLO

Solid Pleasure (Ralph) 1980 (Mercury) 1988
Claro Que Si (Ralph) 1981 (Mercury) 1988
Bostich EP (Stiff) 1982
You Gotta Say Yes to Another Excess (Elektra) 1983 (Mercury) 1988
Yello EP (Elektra) 1983 (UK Mercury) 1983
Stella (Elektra) 1985 (Mercury) 1988
Yello 1980–1985: The New Mix in One Go (UK Mercury) 1986
One Second (Mercury) 1987
Flag (Mercury) 1988
Baby (UK Mercury) 1991
Essential (Smash) 1992
Zebra (4th & B'way) 1994
Hands on Yello (UK Mercury) 1995

Hailing originally from the worlds of performance and fine art, the Swiss trio Yello (Boris Blank on electronics, Dieter Meier on vocals and Carlos Peron on effects and tapes) is second only to Kraftwerk in the annals of primary European synthpop. Their initial releases, **Solid Pleasure** and the more discofied **Claro Que Si,** blend a pop sensibility with electronic innovation, distinguished by an apparent disregard for musical convention. Sometimes dark in tone, at other times just plain silly ("Pinball Cha Cha," "Bananas to the Beat"), those early Yello records—issued domestically on the Residents' label—never fail to amuse and entertain. The **Bostich** EP offers new versions of four songs from those two LPs.

Yello's international profile began to rise with a label change and **You Gotta Say Yes to Another Excess.** Leading off with the dance hit "I Love You"—a bizarre concoction of whispered vocals, pulsing electronic beats and squealing tires—the album is exceptional, blending the light and dark in Yello's sound without sacrificing humor or atmosphere (particularly on the swirling "Lost Again"). The record's second half (side), featuring "Swing," the minimal "Heavy Whispers" and the neo-funk of "Pumping Velvet," is especially strong. There are two different **Yello** EPs: both contain longer versions of three **Excess** songs; the import adds the non-LP "Base for Alec," the domestic replaces it with "Bostich" (again).

With the departure of Peron, the band lost its more eccentric sonic impulses, replaced by guest musicians and increasing continental polish. The stylized Europop of **Stella** is respectable (the urgent "Vicious Games" and "Angel No"), theatrical ("Domingo") and evocative ("Desert Inn"), but only the moderately irritating "Koladi-Ola (Low Blow)" smacks of the old Yello. **Stella** also includes "Oh Yeah," a catchy tune that resurfaced with aggravating frequency in films and TV commercials for several years. **The New Mix in One Go** is a diplomatic assortment of tracks from the first four albums, some in remixed or rerecorded form, plus a few fresh cuts, including "Live at the Roxy."

One Second finds the duo mining an increasingly conservative stylistic vein, serving up sophisticated adult pop with occasional Latin accents that do little to distinguish the material. Billy Mackenzie of the Associates contributes lyrics and histrionic vocals to the romantic ballad "Moon on Ice," while Shirley Bassey outdoes him with an even bigger diva turn on "The

Rhythm Divine," the album's grandiose high point. (Mackenzie subsequently recorded that tune, for which he also wrote lyrics, with the exact same arrangement).

The segued tracks of **Flag** are meant to be listened to as a whole; as such, the album makes for compelling background music and nothing more. Even the best cut, "The Race," is merely a composite of elements Yello has used time and again: Latin rhythms, whispered vocals, horn accents.

Baby didn't even receive an American release, but the three tracks—"Drive/Driven," "Rubberbandman" and "Jungle Bill"—from it on the incorrectly titled **Essential** compilation show little evolution in Yello's increasingly homogeneous sound. The anthology's sixteen tracks draw far too heavily from the mediocre later albums, with only one cut each from **Claro Que Si** and **Solid Pleasure** and two from **Excess.**

Zebra doesn't stray too far, but a couple of factors elevate it slightly. Playful cuts like "How How" border on self-parody, but Meier's audible smile redeems them; more important, Blank seems to have been listening to the sorts of European trance and techno artists Yello's earlier efforts influenced, introducing contemporary dancefloor timbres and rhythms into tracks like "Suite 909" and "Do It." Not surprisingly, the techno nation eventually paid homage to Yello with a remix album. **Hands on Yello** includes new incarnations of assorted tracks, created by Cosmic Baby, Jam & Spoon, the Grid, Carl Cox and the Orb; Moby's jazzy reinterpretation of "Lost Again" is especially entertaining. [kbr]

See also *TPRG*.

Y KANT TORI READ

See *Tori Amos.*

YO LA TENGO

Ride the Tiger (Coyote/Twin\Tone) 1986 (Matador) 1996
New Wave Hot Dogs (Coyote/Twin\Tone) 1987 (Matador) 1996
President Yo La Tengo (Coyote) 1989 (Matador) 1996
Fakebook (Bar/None/Restless) 1990
That Is Yo La Tengo (Ger. City Slang) 1991
May I Sing With Me (Alias) 1992
Upside-Down EP (Alias) 1992
Painful (Matador/Atlantic) 1993
Electr-o-Pura (Matador) 1995
Tom Courtenay EP (Matador) 1995
Camp Yo La Tengo EP (Matador) 1995
Genius + Love = Yo La Tengo (Matador) 1996

DUMP

Superpowerless (Hol. Brinkman) 1993
Dump EP7 (18 Wheeler) 1995
International Airport EP10 (Smells Like) 1995
I Can Hear Music (Hol. Brinkman) 1995

The dialectic progress of Hoboken's Yo La Tengo from one end of the Velvet Underground (preternaturally calm pop) to the other (guitar-noise world domination) has described a curvy creative arc that goes off in various digressive directions and defies connect-the-dots simplicity. Beginning in earnest with the group's third album, ex–rock critic Ira Kaplan's introverted singing and demonstrative guitar work, held in gravitational orbit by Georgia Hubley's straightforward drumming and the married couple's fannish enthusiasms, have led Yo La Tengo to nose around many fascinating corners of the noise-pop universe. Keeping cool heads even when rising distortion levels threaten the established order of things, Kaplan and Hubley (joined, over the years, by a small circle of friends) make increasingly ambitious records that invariably deliver textural thrills, entertaining reference points and occasional blasts of wholly original invention.

Ride the Tiger, produced as modest dinkypop by ex–Mission of Burma bassist Clint Conley, benefits from Dave Schramm's sterling guitarings and contains an obscure Kinks cover ("Big Sky"). His absence costs the self-produced **New Wave Hot Dogs** some of its instrumental flair, but smart, effective songwriting makes up the difference. Kaplan plugs tentatively into roiling vats of skronk chaos for "Let's Compromise" (with help from then-Bongwater guitarist Dave Rick), "House Fall Down" and "The Story of Jazz," but the album mostly relaxes around the Feelies' neighborhood, acting shy and fidgety but finding a seductive melodic groove. Typical of the band's real-life sensibilities, "Lewis" ends by listing oldies titles in the hopes of someday forgetting "every hit song America ever had."

Gene Holder produced and plays bass on **President Yo La Tengo** (later repackaged on one CD with **New Wave Hot Dogs** and "The Asparagus Song" from a 1987 single). The seven-song mixture of studio efforts and two concert items ranges far and wide, starting with the droney tug of "Barnaby, Hardly Working" and ending with a serious, spare rendition (with accordion by John Baumgartner of Speed the Plough) of Bob Dylan's "I Threw It All Away." As if to underscore Yo La's multi-faceted personality, Kaplan's "The Evil That Men Do" appears twice: as a concise '60s guitar and organ instrumental and as ten mind-bending minutes of onstage feedback fury.

Schramm returned to join Hubley and Kaplan (bringing along standup bassist Al Greller from his own group, the Schramms) for **Fakebook,** a delightful, low-key covers collection. Besides an eclectic stack of tuneful arcanities from the Kinks, Flying Burrito Brothers, John Cale, NRBQ, Cat Stevens and the Flamin Groovies, the group also lends an interpretive ear to The Scene Is Now and (were they the first?) Daniel Johnston. In a conceptual coup, Yo La even covers itself, rerecording a song each from the prior two albums. The simple arrangements are ideal for Kaplan's genial singing; Hubley's harmonies contribute to the friendly folks-at-home ambience.

Coincident with the arrival of permanent bassist James McNew (ex-Christmas) and Hubley's emergence as a lead vocalist, **May I Sing With Me** finds the trio splashing around the noisy end of rock's pool. On the album's pièce de resistance, "Mushroom Cloud of Hiss," Kaplan spews feedback and guitar noise like he's losing his grip on a steaming runaway firehose; powered along by Hubley's newly insistent drumming, he affects an aggressive singing style that undercuts the song's shock wave frenzy by failing to contrast with it. That lack of dynamic variation is the album's problem—several songs in need of gentle succoring are rattled off the tracks by clamorous arrangements, while others designed to withstand heat treatment (like "Out the Window") don't have much else to recommend them. Segments of the record balance the band's divergent impulses to good effect (the feedback-laced instrumental "Sleeping Pill" and the Hubley-sung

"Satellite," for instance). But Kaplan's inability to keep his hands off his instrument cocks up the mild-mannered appeal of "Five-Cornered Drone (Crispy Duck)," needlessly threatens the tranquility of "Always Something" and disperses the airy cloud of Hubley's vocals on "Detouring America With Horns."

Upside-Down footnotes **May I Sing With Me** with a substantial remix and a complete rerecording of its comely lead-off track—thereby making "Upside-Down" available in distinct loud and soft variations rather than any blend of the two. The EP's three other tracks are covers (wan pop and fierce punk) and "Sun-squashed," twenty-four minutes of dark, stormy, string-bending improvisation that introduces organ into the band's regular bag o' tricks. **That Is Yo La Tengo,** released overseas before the album, previews three songs from it and adds two outtakes from the same January 1991 sessions for which producer Gene Holder served as the band's pre-McNew bassist.

Having been left to its own idiosyncratic creative devices for so long, Yo La Tengo suddenly sounds supremely confident, stylistically settled and—dare it be said?—*trendy* on **Painful,** a serenely atmospheric album most British shoegazer stars would kill to have in their catalogue. Using simply held organ chords as a basic structural element, keeping vocals right in the breezeway and filtering dramatic, moany waves of barbed guitar extrusion over placid songs in no hurry to reveal themselves, the trio invents an exquisite world of decorum and revelation, a cool sonic oasis that occasionally catches fire. Hardly a collection of singalongs, **Painful** does drift somewhat more than it probably ought to, but it does contain such sturdy compositions as "From a Motel 6" (cute Dylan road pun, that), Hubley's "Nowhere Near" and the shapely instrumental "I Heard You Looking." Finessing harmonic layers of melodic noise that put Sonic Youth's strenuous exertions to shame, Kaplan ambles right into the advanced-placement pantheon of guitar mistreaters and is the main reason **Painful** is such a joy.

With some exceptions, **Electr-o-Pura** undoes that progress, redividing the band into loud/soft alternation with a looser, edgier feel in tracks that aren't nearly as worked over or carefully thought out. Hubley sings more than usual, holding down the folky fort in songs like "Pablo and Andrea" (a lovely breeze carried on Kaplan's most graceful guitar picking) and the fuzzier "(Straight Down to the) Bitter End." Kaplan does a great job singing "Tom Courtenay," a euphoric harmony-pop tribute to '60s Britville that is by far the band's catchiest-ever composition, and brings Tom Verlaine-y aplomb to "Flying Lesson (Hot Chicken #1)," "Paul Is Dead," "The Ballad of Red Buckets" and the tenderly romantic "My Heart's Reflection." But he devotes greater creative energy to shaping songs like "Decora" and "Blue Line Swinger" with tremolo, feedback and experimental forays into "patterns of sound." **Tom Courtenay** the EP adds two non-LP originals and a Dead C cover; **Camp Yo La Tengo** presents a remix of "Blue Line Swinger," a Hubley-sung acoustic remake of "Tom Courtenay," a tremolo-timed garage cover of the Seeds' "Can't Seem to Make You Mine" and a long, somber jam (with found-sound samples) entitled "Mr. Ameche Plays the Stranger."

Genius + Love = Yo La Tengo is a thoroughly fine two-CD (one vocal, one instrumental) compendium of rare and unreleased tracks.

Dump is bassist James McNew's sweet-as-kittens solo side project. Working at home on what he pointedly refers to as a "weary" 4-track cassette machine, he displays proficiency on a multitude of instruments (mainly guitar, bass, drums and Acetone organ) and a wavery tenor voice that wouldn't hurt a fly, assembling pop tunes (original and covers) and sound collages to a please-yourself-first aesthetic. **Superpowerless** is simply wonderful, a soothing and minimally produced nineteen-track collection of delightfully forlorn originals (the brisk "Secret Blood," "Good Medicine" and the escalating title track are easy highlights) and covers as far-reaching as the Shaggs, Sun Ra, Wreckless Eric, NRBQ and Henry Mancini. McNew gets a bit of assistance from his Yo La bandmates and Dave Ramirez of Hypnolovewheel, but Dump's charm is all his fault.

Following a 7-inch quartet of covers (songs by Silver Apples, Barbara Manning, Jandek and Hypnolovewheel), the **International Airport** 10-inch eschews even the modest ambitions of **Superpowerless,** using bits of droney organ and noise guitar, plus occasional drums and vocals, to bring rudimentary life to four originals, a Versus number and the Kinks' obscure "The Way Love Used to Be." The title track, a twelve-and-a-half-minute extravaganza, builds handsomely to an invigorating weave of instrumental layers and begins to wind down before McNew begins singing, turning what could have been a minor outing into a compelling epic.

While fleshier arrangements return the gentle-cycle **I Can Hear Music** album (initially fortified with a second CD of bonus tunes) to the easy access of **Superpowerless,** McNew's wan singing isn't quite as assured or engaging as before. Still, his private world here is riddled with impressive powderpuff songwriting ("Don't Let On," "Slow Down," "Curl") and fine ideas: a gorgeous Fugs cover ("Morning Morning"), the Moody Blues citation of "Hope, Joe," the grubby synth pulse of "It's Not Alright" and the country bounce given Bob Dylan's "Wanted Man." And don't miss the unlisted version of Ultravox's "Vienna." [i]

See also *Combustible Edison, Schramms; TPRG.*

YONA-KIT

See *Jim O'Rourke.*

YOU AND WHAT ARMY

Kinda Wanna (Big Deal) 1996

New York City's versatile You and What Army plays mild-mannered indie-pop with a smart center. Gentle without getting too cuddly about it, the skilled band proffers enticing casual harmony vocals by guitarist Gary Meister and bassist Ken Weinstein, a mocking lyrical sensibility ("American Car Crash Little Girl," "Love and Anarchy," "Turning Blue") and diverting accents: things like country and classical violin, continental accordion and punk fuzz guitar crop up often enough to keep stylistic things in motion. **Kinda Wanna** is a bit less equivocal than its title, but the quartet aims to beguile, not demand, and modesty becomes them. Best cultural couplet, from the bewildering finale "Swingset": "Be like clean, not unclear/Be like Schnabel, not Vermeer." [tr]

GARY YOUNG

See *Pavement.*

NEIL YOUNG (AND CRAZY HORSE)

Neil Young (Reprise) 1968
Everybody Knows This Is Nowhere (Reprise) 1969
After the Gold Rush (Reprise) 1970
Harvest (Reprise) 1972
Journey Through the Past (Reprise) 1972
Time Fades Away (Reprise) 1973
On the Beach (Reprise) 1974
Tonight's the Night (Reprise) 1975
Zuma (Reprise) 1975
American Stars 'n Bars (Reprise) 1977
Decade (Reprise) 1977
Comes a Time (Reprise) 1978
Rust Never Sleeps (Reprise) 1979
Live Rust (Reprise) 1979
Hawks & Doves (Reprise) 1980
Re•ac•tor (Reprise) 1981
Trans (Geffen) 1982
Neil and the Shocking Pinks: Everybody's Rockin' (Geffen) 1983
Old Ways (Geffen) 1985
Landing on Water (Geffen) 1986
Life (Geffen) 1987
This Note's for You (Reprise) 1988
Eldorado EP (Japan. Reprise) 1989
Freedom (Reprise) 1989
Ragged Glory (Reprise) 1990
Weld (Reprise) 1991
Arc (Reprise) 1991
Harvest Moon (Reprise) 1992
Lucky Thirteen (Geffen) 1993
Unplugged (Reprise) 1993
Sleeps With Angels (Reprise) 1994
Mirror Ball (Reprise) 1995
Dead Man (Vapor) 1996
Broken Arrow (Reprise) 1996

VARIOUS ARTISTS

The Bridge: A Tribute to Neil Young (No. 6/Caroline) 1989

Dirty rock 'n' roller—hippie narcissist. Rockabilly hepcat—techno troubadour. Folkie romantic—bluesy bad boy. Harmony supergroup sore thumb—beloved bandleader. Cultural analyst—grandfather of grunge.

Neil Young has been all of these things and more in the course of an insanely prolific solo career that's approaching the three-decade mark with more than two dozen studio albums under his belt. Though his output during the '80s was particularly erratic, he has never stopped placing personal expression before commercial success or the need to accommodate expectations. As a result, through all his unpredictability, Young is never (well, hardly ever) boring, and that's a state of grace few veteran musicians can claim. Holding to his lyrical axiom that it's better to burn out than fade away, Young is one of the few oldtimers to make real peace with punk-rockers half his age, finding rejuvenation and comradeship in their fountain of wild youth. Virtually alone among his generation, Young has never given up an iota of his intensity or faltered in the ability and inclination to pulverize eardrums with furious energy. (If anything, he's turned up.) Young's reckless path demonstrates far less self-conscious orthodoxy than many underground bands. It's almost miraculous that after several lifetimes of iconography for drippy love children and hardened country rockers, Neil Young became a hero to an alternative nation that hadn't been born when he was first balladeering about rivers and roads.

Beginning in the late '60s, Young made an initial series of alternately tender, idealistic, haunted and howling albums (compiled on the sprawling, arcana-laden and indispensable **Decade**), culminating in 1979's **Rust Never Sleeps.** Forged in the reflected glow of punk's waning embers, the record contains some unusually strong ballads ("Thrasher," "Powderfinger") and devilish rockers like "Hey Hey, My My (Into the Black)." With the unflappable Crazy Horse—guitarist Frank Sampedro, drummer Ralph Molina and bassist Billy Talbot—joining him to unleash whirlwinds of thrilling noise, Young used the song to announce that he had some ideas of his own about '70s rebellion. If the old guy was a bit awkward in his approach, unfettered passion and intensity got the message across, regardless of details. **Live Rust** is a career-spanning double live set that includes lethal versions of "Cortez the Killer," "Like a Hurricane" and "Tonight's the Night."

Young spent the 1980s ricocheting around his art like a pinball, trying on a sample sale of musical styles that didn't always fit him. The folk and country turf of **Hawks & Doves** and the big, nasty electric noise of **Re•ac•tor** roll on familiar turf but are hindered by inconsistent material. Coincident with a tradition-breaking change of labels, **Trans** presents Neil as electro-man, complete with synths, vocoder and songs about computers and future shock; the easily likable **Everybody's Rockin'** salutes rockabilly with a lightweight, good-natured set of originals and oldies. **Old Ways** takes him back up the country for some down-home silliness and guest shots by Waylon Jennings and Willie Nelson; **Landing on Water** suggests he'd been listening to the Cars.

Just when it seemed he'd completely lost his marbles, Young reunited with Crazy Horse for **Life,** a tough-edged album compromised by overblown production, and began his re-entry approach. Young later recapitulated his Geffen era with **Lucky Thirteen,** an adroit and effective selection wryly subtitled *Excursions Into Alien Territory.* Boiling down five years of experimentation (replacing several chapters with otherwise unissued or rare—like from a videodisc—live recordings and one unheard studio track, "Depression Blues") makes for a brazenly eclectic compilation in which good ideas and bad ideas are clearly distinguished but treated with equal respect. If the electronic age still doesn't suit Mr. Soul, this is at least a serious and largely successful attempt to extract the credible essence from Young's sabbatical in space.

After circling around back for one more stylistic detour—the pointless set of big-band blues (co-billed with the Bluenotes) on **This Note's for You**—Young was ready to strip down, plant his feet on terra firma and stop horsing around. Which immediately made the world a better place. He wanged out **Eldorado,** five live-in-the-studio numbers recorded in New York with a rhythm section dubbed the Restless and released only in Japan, as a waters-tester. That, and the carefully considered and deftly sequenced **Freedom**—the desire for it, not an expression of it—put an end to his era of itinerant exploration by reclaiming old domains, setting the stage for his astonishing rebirth. While not heavy with enduring Young standards, the hearty album (performed with a non–Crazy Horse rhythm section and such guests as Linda Ronstadt and Ben Keith) is bookended by two versions—short/acoustic and long/paint-peeling—of "Rockin' in the Free World," an anguished observation of homelessness, and contains strung-out balladry ("Too Far Gone"), a gentle invitation to the "Wrecking Ball," a spooky acoustic saga of social strife ("Crime in the City") and a harsh guitar-bass-drums reinterpretation of the Drifters' "On Broadway."

Leaving behind the topical concerns of **Freedom** and reuniting with Crazy Horse, Young offered additional encouragement on the more consistently personal and joyously simple **Ragged Glory.** The band thrashes away like there's no tomorrow as Young yanks all sorts of exciting noises from his guitar on "Country Home," "Love to Burn," "Mansion on the Hill," "Over and Over" and other strong songs, some capably stretched to seven or ten minutes by the organic quartet's instrumental enthusiasms. Although widely regarded as his best in a blue moon, the album isn't perfect. A few tracks don't work; the quartet's offhand sloppiness occasionally seems forced. (Singing about "F*!#in' Up" is a lot easier than doing it.) Still, **Ragged Glory** serves as a bracing reminder that Neil Young can shake the rafters with more heart than anybody.

Which is exactly what he did in the early '91 tour (utterly upstaged opening act: Sonic Youth) documented on the two CDs of **Weld.** Moving on up from the intensity of **Live Rust,** Young and Crazy Horse planted a flag in previously uncharted worlds of ear-cleaning guitar distortion and stomping rock furiosity. The set list draws solidly (and productively) from **Ragged Glory** but repeats numbers from the previous concert record ("Cinnamon Girl," "Like a Hurricane," "Cortez the Killer," "Powderfinger" and "Tonight's the Night") and borrows Bob Dylan's "Blowin' in the Wind" for a haunting answer to Hendrix's Woodstock address. Stunning in its sheer sensual energy and gripping in its improvised facility, **Weld** is a high-water mark of live albums, a purgatory colonic that somehow captures everything unique and magical in Young's artistry. The same recording project produced **Arc,** an amazing piece of audio detritus fully deserving of a place next to Lou Reed's classic patience-tester, **Metal Machine Music.** Editing together thirty-five seamless minutes of introductions, guitar crashes, vocal fragments, feedback, drum windups, crescendos and climaxes, the aging veteran demonstrates *his* sonic youth by creating a sustained abstract buildup from the concerts' release; nothing much happens, but the atmospheric tension of this adventure is awesome.

With all that excitement out of his system, Young settled down to make **Harvest Moon,** a sublimely gentle and romantic country sequel to his 1972 chart-topper, **Harvest.** He rounded up alumni of that album (James Taylor and Linda Ronstadt, the rhythm section of Kenny Buttrey and Tim Drummond, steel guitarist/vocalist Ben Keith); there's even an orchestral number ("Such a Woman") to recall the London Symphony's role on "A Man Needs a Maid." Lovely, affecting and as warm as a family reunion, **Harvest Moon**—which, it must be said, drags at times—puts some of Young's finest melodies to typically remarkable lyrics. In "Unknown Legend," he makes note of "The chrome and steel she rides/Collidin' with the very air she breathes." "Dreamin' Man" contains the acute observation that "I can't tell when I'm not being real." Whether ruing the death of a dog ("Old King") in a hick voice or describing himself in the third person ("You and Me") in a wavery falsetto, Young succumbs fully to his transcendent artistry: whether he rocks the house or whispers to the walls, he never lacks the necessary tools to convey what's in his heart. Using the long-gone archetype of the late-'60s singer/songwriter, Young manages to both update and honor his—and others'—past.

The irony of getting "unplugged" was evidently not lost on Young when he sat down to tape a formal acoustic program for MTV. Proffering simple ground-zero rearrangements that make it sound as if he whipped up the fourteen songs that afternoon, Young uses the opportunity to register an alternate career sampler, dredging up obscurities like "Transformer Man" (from **Trans**), "Pocahontas" (from **Rust Never Sleeps**) and his first album's "Old Laughing Lady." Amid such poignant standards as "Helpless," "Like a Hurricane," "The Needle and the Damage Done" and Buffalo Springfield's "Mr. Soul," Young charts a course that is neither easy, obvious nor arbitrary. If **Unplugged** is too close to his stylistic base to be an eye-opener, it is nonetheless a substantial original effort that isn't just for insatiable fans.

As mercurial as Young's muse is, Crazy Horse has always proven equal to every twist in his road; on the enigmatic and strange-sounding **Sleeps With Angels,** the foursome modulate comfortably from wispy plaints ("My Heart," "Driveby" and "Western Hero") to the ominously noisy title track and the snorting consumer outrage of "Piece of Crap." The dynamic key is the album's softly firm center: "Prime of Life" and "Change Your Mind," an emotional fifteen-minute opus in which Young pleads the case for love as crucial life support. Under the album's mournful shroud of death, the song can be taken as part of a vague and oblique commentary (guilt?) on the death of Kurt Cobain (who quoted Young's burn out/fade away advice in his suicide note). Though uninviting at first, **Sleeps With Angels** rewards patience and attention. More than any album in Young's recent history, this one has to be taken whole; the unevenness of individual songs fades to its pervasive pall, an acid that slowly strips away layers of significance to reveal crucial elements of seemingly offhand but subtle invention. (**The Complex Sessions,** a promo-only EP recorded live while shooting videos for the record, offers a different perspective on four songs from the album.)

Mirror Ball cements Young's union with the new generation, borrowing Pearl Jam to serve as a second-rate stand-in for Crazy Horse on a thick, tough rock record whose appeal is more obvious than its qualities. Producer Brendan O'Brien locates a steady dynamic plateau, and the musicians ride around it, clutching a stack of songs whose melodies are largely wasted on trivial lyrics. Ultimately, Young's material is stimulating more than satisfying, and the album suffers from a hastiness at the wrong point in the process. Instead of just being recorded in a hurry (usually a good thing for Young, and an apt approach here), the *songs* sound hasty and ill-considered, expressing simple ideas far too simply. Among the album's frustrations are "Big Green Country" ("Sometimes I feel like a piece of paper/Sometimes I feel like my own name"), "Downtown" ("where the hippies all go") and "Peace and Love" ("flying so high/too young to die"), into which

Eddie Vedder's clenched-teeth clumsiness ("Broke walls of pain to walk") is utterly out of keeping with Young's own ungainly musings. "Act of Love" is a masterful piece of music and "Throw Your Hatred Down" is commendable in its sincerity, but you have to wish Neil had brought a better stash to the studio.

It makes sense that a powerful iconoclast should have an unfettered conduit for expression, and in early '96, Young unveiled Vapor Records, his own independent label. Unfortunately, there's a thin line between freedom and indulgence, and **Dead Man**—music from, and inspired by, the Jim Jarmusch film of the same name—flounces over the median strip like a rotting fish in its death throes. As Johnny Depp and unidentified actors recite poetry and do scenes from the film, Young fools around aimlessly on echoed electric guitar (plus pump organ and "detuned piano") for an hour of shapeless, seemingly unskilled and nearly random sound that is far more discouraging than **Arc.**

Whatever *that* was about, a restorative bout with Crazy Horse produced the pliably rough **Broken Arrow** soon after, and washed away the bad taste of **Dead Man**'s aimless noodling with some forthright electric jamming. (Yes, there's a difference.) An exceedingly loose ambience that draws seven new songs, plus an unexpected live cover of Jimmy Reed's "Baby What You Want Me to Do," out to nearly fifty minutes tests the unexceptional (save for the gorgeous "Slip Away") material's mettle, but these old pals have no trouble tuning in on each other's hallucinations and keeping it all moving together in raw and sloppy eddies of melodic invention. (The vinyl edition boasts a bonus track, "Interstate.")

The bands chosen to honor Young's songs on **The Bridge,** a fundraiser for a California school for physically challenged children, paint an offbeat picture of his influence. Soul Asylum makes a solid country-roots connection with "Barstool Blues," Victoria Williams and the Williams Brothers make a beautiful issue of "Don't Let It Bring You Down" and Nick Cave sucks "Helpless" into a grim torpor. But Sonic Youth's rendition of "Computer Age" is a failed stab at irony, Flaming Lips trivializes "After the Gold rush" and Psychic TV so lacks the ability to feign sincerity that "Only Love Can Break Your Heart" feels like a parody, not a tribute. [jy/i]

See also *Pearl Jam; TPRG.*

YOUNG DISCIPLES

Road to Freedom (UK Talkin Loud) 1992 (Talkin Loud/ Mercury) 1993

CARLEEN ANDERSON

True Spirit (Circa/Virgin) 1994

A band only in the loosest sense of the term, the Young Disciples consisted at its core of club DJs Femi Williams, bassist Marc O. Nelson and singer Carleen Anderson, the deep-voiced young daughter of James Brown funk diva Vicki Anderson. If Soul II Soul found its niche in the sound system mix of early '80s Island singles that merged street reggae and elegant disco, the Young Disciples seemed the logical extension of the British rare groove movement that mined southern American funk and jazz. Recorded in 1991, **Road to Freedom** is a masterpiece of understated soul, a seamless blend of samplers and studio musicians and a blueprint for the nascent acid-jazz and trip-hop movements. (Around the same time, the group also helped Des'ree on her first album.)

Although the US edition contains mixes with Anderson's vocals, "All I Have" and "Step Right On" appear on the original British issue only as instrumental dubs; oddly enough, these mixes demonstrate Williams and Nelson's clever deployment of sampled and live sounds, presaging Britain's turn toward abstract hip-hop-influenced instrumentals. Elsewhere, they make good use of a stellar supporting cast, including New York rapper Masta Ace, Paul Weller, Fred Wesley, Pee Wee Ellis and Maceo Parker. By the time **Road to Freedom** appeared in America, Anderson (a prominent guest on two Bryan Ferry albums) had herself hit the road, and, working with full-service producer Ian Green, released a dull, mainstream solo dance-pop album the following year. [jzc]

See also *Bryan Ferry.*

YOUNG FRESH FELLOWS

The Fabulous Sounds of the Pacific Northwest (PopLlama Products) 1984 (East Side Digital) 1988
Topsy Turvy (PopLlama Products) 1985 (East Side Digital) 1988
The Men Who Loved Music (PopLlama Products/Frontier) 1987
Refreshments (PopLlama Products/Frontier) 1987
Totally Lost (Frontier) 1988
Beans and Tolerance (PopLlama Products/Frontier) 1989
This One's for the Ladies (Frontier) 1989
Includes a Helmet (UK Utility) 1990
Electric Bird Digest (Frontier) 1991
Somos los Mejores! (Sp. Munster) 1991
It's Low Beat Time (Frontier) 1992
Gleich Jetzt (Japan. 1+2) 1992
Take It Like a Matador (Sp. Impossible) 1993
Pop (PopLlama Products) 1993

SCOTT MCCAUGHEY

My Chartreuse Opinion (PopLlama Products) 1989 (East Side Digital) 1989

MINUS 5

The Minus Five EP (Hello Recording Club) 1993
Old Liquidator (East Side Digital) 1995
Emperor of the Bathroom EP (East Side Digital) 1995

SQUIRRELS

Ernest Anyway and the Mighty Squirrels Sing the Hits of Johnny Kidd and the Pirates/Five Virgins (PopLlama Products) 1986
What Gives? (PopLlama Products) 1990
Harsh Toke of Reality (PopLlama Products) 1993
Scrapin' for Hits (Poplust Audio) 1996

Seattle's Young Fresh Fellows combine punk-derived recklessness and a bubbly garage-pop sensibility with an absurdist lyrical wit and a bittersweet vulnerable streak that has grown increasingly resonant as the band confronts the inconvenient realities of adult life. **The Fabulous Sounds of the Pacific Northwest** and **Topsy Turvy** (subsequently paired on an ESD CD) abound with short, memorable ditties whose gentle humor doesn't completely camouflage their underlying angst; the latter record features slightly more ambitious compositions (several even exceed the three-minute mark) and sees the band expanding from a trio to a quartet.

The Men Who Loved Music, which remains the

Fellows' strongest album to date, is more ambitious. Singer/guitarist Scott McCaughey provides cheerfully self-deprecating lyrics for his combo's tongue-in-cheek stabs at ska ("TV Dream"), funk ("Amy Grant"), country ("Hank, Karen and Elvis") and frat rock, "I Got My Mojo Working (And I Thought You'd Like to Know)." The CD version appends six of the seven outtakes and rarities that make up the **Refreshments** EP, plus the previously unreleased "Happy Death Theme."

Totally Lost is less overtly wacky and more outfront in its darker lyrical underpinnings; though lacking much of its predecessors' garagey rush, the album is not without its moments, "Take My Brain Away" and "No Help at All" among them. The blank-sleeved, white-label limited-edition authorized vinyl bootleg generally known as **Beans and Tolerance** (recorded after guitarist Chuck Carroll's departure temporarily left the Fellows a threesome) is a therapeutically sloppy session that recaptures the band's original nutty fervor. **This One's for the Ladies**—with long-serving Fastbacks great Kurt Bloch replacing Carroll—is a heartening return to form, cheerfully balancing hooks, humor and self-doubt on tunes like "Middle Man of Time," "The Family Gun" and a fab cover of the Kinks' "Picture Book."

The Butch Vig–produced **Electric Bird Digest** rocks solidly throughout but sounds more workmanlike than inspired, and it's hard to ignore the sense of ennui that suffuses the album. The melancholy in McCaughey compositions like "Whirlpool" and "Thirsty" seems genuine, but that doesn't make the songs compelling. Seattle scene pal Jimmy Silva contributed one of the album's best songs ("The Telephone Tree") and co-wrote another ("Fear, Bitterness and Hatred") with drummer Tad Hutchinson. Bloch's three compositions don't stand out.

It's Low Beat Time—apparently the Fellows' studio swan song—is an odd farewell, teaming the Fellows with five different producers, including Vig and, strangely enough, Memphis R&B veteran Willie Mitchell. Despite the patchwork approach, the album does restore some of the energy missing from **Electric Bird Digest.** Things get engagingly weird about halfway through, with a spacey cocktail-jazz instrumental ("The Crafty Clerk"), a straightforwardly groovy Mitchell-produced cover of the Young Rascals' "Love Is a Beautiful Thing," a collaboration with New York's A-Bones on "Monkey Say," and a pair recorded live to lo-fi two-track with Kearney Barton, who engineered the Sonics' classic '60s garage-punk sides. Flamboyant septuagenarian soul legend Rufus Thomas pops up to sing lead on the bizarre finale, which starts out as a rendition of the trad-folk "Green Green" but eventually devolves into . . . well, whatever.

The Fellows' discography also includes a number of one-off albums and singles for a variety of domestic and overseas labels. The Spanish sixteen-track **Somos los Mejores!** best-of includes a handful of non-album gems, while the British eight-song **Includes a Helmet** sampler (including one previously unreleased tune) is a bit too skimpy to function as a useful introduction. **Gleich Jetzt** is a Japanese release consisting of motley but spirited live-in-the-studio covers and rerecordings of some old Fellows numbers. **Take It Like a Matador** is a slapdash but fun live set recorded in Spain. The seven-song **Pop** (actually, the front cover and spine are filled with other words, but you have to read Japanese; the word "pop" is prominently printed on the disc) was produced as an export item to coincide with the band's December 1993 dates in Osaka and Tokyo; the nifty grab-bag of odds and ends includes the invigorating studio pop of "Dear Red" and "Everybody Said Was Wrong," a sharp dose of beat-group nostalgia ("Rabbit Run") and spot-on live covers of Jonathan Richman's "Roller Coaster by the Sea" and the Dictators' "Teengenerate."

McCaughey made his solo debut in 1989 with **My Chartreuse Opinion,** on which he plays various instruments and Dennis Diken (Smithereens) mans the drum kit. It doesn't sound all that different from the Fellows, and displays some of the gleeful unpredictability of the band's early days. The ESD reissue adds six tracks, two on which McCaughey is backed by the Ben Vaughn Combo and four from records by Seattle legend and Fellows pal Jimmy Silva, with McCaughey on guitar and vocals.

With the Fellows either defunct or on hold, McCaughey resurfaced at the helm of the Minus 5, a free-floating aggregation that at various times has involved such pals as Peter Buck of R.E.M. (on whose 1995 world tour McCaughey served as sideman) and members of NRBQ, Posies and Walkabouts (not to mention Fellows bassist Jim Sangster and, on the John Lennon tribute album, Mary Lou Lord, Lee Ranaldo and Dennis Diken). Despite the all-star personnel, though, the Minus 5's work largely favors sober introspection over super-session tomfoolery. On the four-song subscription-only Hello Recording Club CD, McCaughey's past lyrical irony blossoms into full-blown adult disillusionment, without the Fellows' buoyant garage-pop sensibility to cushion the impact. The full-length **Old Liquidator,** which formalizes the 5 as a quartet with Buck and the Posies (Ken Stringfellow and Jon Auer), continues McCaughey's slump into self-flagellation. But this time he allows somewhat more whimsical music to help emotionally naked tunes like "Vulture," "Worse" (co-written by Silva) and "No More Glory" go down painlessly; in this context, an elegantly disheartened cover of Nick Lowe's "Basing Street" is entirely appropriate. **Emperor of the Bathroom** follows the title track—**Old Liquidator**'s only real pop-rocker—with another album cut ("Story"), a spare remake of "Vulture," a jokey country weeper ("Heartache for Sale") and McCaughey's solo acoustic cover of the Fantastic Baggys' "This Little Woody."

Using the Fellows, Posies, Roy Loney and others for studio support, Seattle singer Rob Morgan (aka Ernest Anyway) occasionally chucks up a high-concept/ low-rent Squirrels album of loopy covers. If the staff of *Mad* magazine—back when it was good—set out to make furshlugginer indie-rock records, these'd be them. The brilliant 1986 outing presents one vinyl side of pre-Beatles classics borrowed from Johnny Kidd and the Pirates and a prescient dose of such later-in-the-'60s tunes as "Hair" and "Spirit in the Sky" done as cocktail lounge laxative sleaze.

The second Squirrels LP is even better. For such an irreverent assault on pop music, **What Gives?** has great playing and production, excellent vocals by Morgan and enough revisionist imagination to fuel a dozen such undertakings. There's a rollicking rendition of a gospel standard, a spunky revamp of Gilbert O'Sullivan's "Get Down," a chaotic monster-heavy assault on Bill Withers' "Lean on Me" (dissolving into Alice Cooper's "Eighteen"), a relatively straight version of

Paul Revere and the Raiders' pushy "Let Me!" and the positively inspired (Wizard of) "Oz '90" medley.

Moving out of the Fellows' orbit (although McCaughey does contribute a tad), **Harsh Toke of Reality** varies the Squirrels' recipe with a greater proportion of eclectically styled originals and a new cast of cohorts, including Loney and singer Re Styles of the Tubes. The small and seemingly random selection of oldies includes an all-out Bee Gees disco version of Paul McCartney's "Coming Up," a speeding cornpone rendition of "Let It Be," an extravagant reconsideration of Tommy James' "Draggin' the Line" and a relatively mild take on the Vogues' "Five O'Clock World." Witty rock'n'roll citations and funny bits abound as Morgan and his pals keep the joint jumping from jokey metal ("Bone of Contention") to jokey boogie ("Bobo") to jokey godknowswhat ("Swallowing Tadpoles, Poopin' Out Frogs"), but **Harsh Toke of Reality** isn't quite as effortless a blast as its predecessors. [ss/i]

See also *Fastbacks, Roy Loney and the Phantom Movers, Posies, R.E.M., Jimmy Silva, Smithereens; TPRG.*

YOUNG GODS

The Young Gods (UK Product Inc.) 1987 (Play It Again Sam/Wax Trax!) 1989 (Play It Again Sam/Interscope) 1995
L'Eau Rouge (Play It Again Sam) 1989 (Play It Again Sam/Interscope) 1995
Longue Route EP (Play It Again Sam) 1990
The Young Gods Play Kurt Weill (Play It Again Sam/Caroline) 1991 (Play It Again Sam/Interscope) 1995
T.V. Sky (Play It Again Sam/Caroline) 1992 (Play It Again Sam/Interscope) 1995
Live Sky Tour (UK Play It Again Sam) 1993 (Play It Again Sam/Interscope) 1995
Only Heaven (Play It Again Sam/Interscope) 1995

Switzerland's Young Gods are nothing if not ambitious. Grafting rock, classical and electronic influences, the group's unusual vocals/sampler/drums configuration reconstructs rock from the ground up, producing a fiery collage of roaring guitars, blistering rhythms and Wagnerian orchestras, all presided over by Franz Treichler's leering, guttural voice. Irreverent, abrasive and years ahead of its time, the group's music has sometimes worked better in theory than practice. From the very beginning, however, the Young Gods have rocked their technology every bit as hard as Public Enemy did theirs. Although the Young Gods owe more than just their name to Swans, the trio has used the influence to its own ends, sharing only some *sturm und drang* samples and a flair for the melodramatic.

The group debuted in 1985 with the awesome "Envoyé!" single (imaginatively translated as "Go for it and fuck off" in the first album's lyrics), which in many ways remains its ultimate statement. Clocking in at less than two minutes, the song's snarling guitars, shotgun samples and jackhammer beat is like techno played by a speedmetal band. The album is less immediate, taking the *götterdämmerung* vibe to almost ludicrous extremes through blaring classical samples and beats that sting like an interrogator's slaps. After seven overwhelmingly mean-spirited songs, a bizarre cover of Gary Glitter's "Did You Miss Me" prances surreally onto the set, evoking a vision of Quasimodo reeling drunkenly across a regal ballroom. "Bombastic" would be a gross understatement, but when ability matches ambition, **The Young Gods** has a uniquely menacing majesty.

It all snaps into focus on **L'Eau Rouge** ("Red Water," a charming reference to menstruation), which is far more assured and coherent but just as shocking as the debut. Thundering guitars dominate many tracks—Treichler has not inaccurately referred to the album as "metal cabaret"—but the group also brings in crazed Shostakovich samples, the whipcrack grind of "L'Amourir" and some quaintly sinister Kurt Weill–isms. The CDs of **L'Eau Rouge** and **The Young Gods** include concurrent single tracks not available on the vinyl versions; **Longue Route** includes an ass-kicking remix, two raunchy live tracks and, by way of transition, a cover of Weill's "September Song."

The Young Gods Play Kurt Weill, part of a tribute organized by Switzerland's Festival du Bois de la Bàtie, features studio versions of the Gods' live set at the festival. Far from a one-off indulgence, the inventive interpretations veer from comparatively straightforward to neo-metal ("Mackie Messer," aka "Mack the Knife") to a gorgeous sitar collage ("Ouverture"); the opening "Prologue" features an eerie juxtaposition of a neo-Nazi rally overlaid with Guns n' Roses riffs.

T.V. Sky, the first Young Gods album to be sung entirely in English, dispenses with the orchestras, showing a tasteful dance influx (the grinding "Skinflowers") and even further refined riff technology. The album closes with the sprawling "Summer Eyes," a generally engaging twenty-minute song cycle. Three multi-remix singles were released from the album; **Live Sky Tour** is a decent if unnecessary live LP.

Apart from a perfunctory flirtation with ambient, the disappointing **Only Heaven** generally rehashes previously mastered styles, the only strong track being the pulsing "Donnez les Esprits." Initial copies did come in a very cool white plastic case, however.

A tongue-in-cheek anonymity has always distinguished the band's public profile; since late '89 the lineup has been Treichler, drummer Üse Hiestand and samplerist Alain Monod. Although the band is nominally a trio, Roli Mosimann—the former Swans drummer who has long been a reigning industrial-era producer—is unquestionably the fourth God, having produced the band's entire output and co-written most of it. [ja]

See also *TPRG.*

YOU'VE GOT FOETUS ON YOUR BREATH

See *Foetus.*

YO YO

Make Way for the Motherlode (EastWest) 1991
Black Pearl (EastWest) 1992
You Better Ask Somebody (EastWest) 1993
Total Control (EastWest) 1996

With her golden braids, hazel eyes, singsong delivery and complicated feminist consciousness, Yo Yo (Yolanda Whitaker) cuts an unusual figure in roughneck rap. After making her star-is-born cameo on Ice Cube's "It's a Man's World" in 1990, the Los Angeles MC declared herself the leader of a sisters-are-doing-it-for-themselves movement of Intelligent Black

Women and set about leveling hip-hop's sexual playground on **Make Way for the Motherlode,** a strong debut enthusiastically produced by Cube, Sir Jinx and Del tha Funkee Homosapien. Something of a West Coast analogue to Queen Latifah, Yo works out the details of her position on the fly, offering advice ("Girl, Don't Be No Fool"), romantic negotiations ("Tonight's the Night," "I Got Played") and declarations of independence ("Sisterland," "You Can't Play With My Yo-Yo") that flow too easily into generic boasting ("Make Way for the Motherlode," "Ain't Nobody Better"). Repeatedly announcing one's intelligence isn't the same as consistently demonstrating it.

Recorded with Cube, Jinx and DJ Pooh, **Black Pearl** serves Yo Yo up on a more ambitious plate of fashions and funk, setting her cautionary romantic insights to verse in "You Should Have Listened," scanning the decimation of her environment in "A Few Good Men," bristling with step-off toughness on tracks like "Cleopatra" and "Black Pearl" and humorously debating the issues with an unnamed male foil in "Hoes." But "Woman to Woman" forgets all that high-minded stuff about intelligent black womanhood and descends to tart-tongued wrassling over an unfaithful man; "Will You Be Mine" gets all mushy (and oily) without any intent beyond the obvious. Yo Yo is a sharp, energetic rhymer with lots of ideas, but she's a commercial artist first and a reliable commentator second; there are limits to taking her seriously.

The disappointing **You Better Ask Somebody** picks up the remaining slack in a concerted attempt to join the profitable gangsta world of strapped insensibility. Converting the IBW acronym to a meaningless verb ("IBWin' wit My Crewin'"), Yo Yo grabs her Uzi and chronic, jumps in her ride and starts threatening people. There are gunplay sounds on "Can You Handle It?"; "Girls Got a Gun" tries a Sister Souljah–like racial rationale for learning how to shoot. As a procession of producers keeps her moving to varied beats from scratchy old-school to slinky G-funk, the self-declared "Mackstress" sells herself out with dismaying speed and obviousness for someone who once claimed a principled mission. Comedian Martin Lawrence provides crude running commentary in "Letter to the Pen," Yo's solidarity missive to someone behind bars; Ice Cube plays Barrow to Yo Yo's Parker in "The Bonnie and Clyde Theme," which paints violence as romantic devotion.

Total Control brings Cube back for a second chapter of "Bonnie and Clyde," and otherwise continues Yo Yo's progress into an all-purpose sampler of current cushy R&B grooves, making for Long Beach with guest Breed on "Tre Ride" and going the related Montel Jordan route on "One for the Cuties." Yo's rap skills are intact (see "Da Risin'" and the sexy "Body Work"), but she relegates them to a subordinate role, undercutting her once-distinctive approach with too many generic moves. [i]

See also *Ice Cube.*

Z

Shampoohorn (Barking Pumpkin) 1993
Music for Pets (Zappa) 1996

DWEEZIL ZAPPA

Havin' a Bad Day (Chrysalis) 1986 (Rykodisc) 1987
My Guitar Wants to Kill Your Mama (Chrysalis) 1988
Confessions . . . (Barking Pumpkin) 1991

Following three solo albums, shred guitarist and MTV star Dweezil Zappa teamed up with his brother Ahmet Zappa (jovial vocals) to lead this zany band of manic-excessive rockers. When they're not trying to mimic the droll mock-stupidity of their late father's early work ("Singer in the Woods," "Kidz Cereal") or playing it straight (the pop-lite of "Doomed to Be Together"), the junior Zappas sound like hair-metal parodists making a hash of their borrowed in-joke on **Shampoohorn.**

Music for Pets tones down the brothers' hyperactive outer child and gets on to music-making with more applied intelligence and, dare it be said, restraint. While glibly eclectic to a fault, the album is at least tolerable and, in "Father Time"—a touching and angry song about death—poignantly sincere. [i]

ZAHAR

Zahar (Knitting Factory Works) 1992

HASSAN HAKMOUN AND ZAHAR

Trance (Real World) 1993

HASSAN HAKMOUN

The Fire Within: Gnawa Music of Morocco (Music of the World) 1995

Hassan Hakmoun is a Gnawa, a descendant of the African slaves Arabs carried north into Morocco. Like the Santerías in Cuba, the Africans converted to the dominant religion, in this case Islam, but infused the music of the masters with the remembered rhythms of their own rituals. This new culture spread over much of North Africa in various forms. Hakmoun grew up in Marrakech, surrounded by the trance-inducing music of his people, which draws on sounds from their original homelands, including Mali, Sudan, Niger, Senegal and Guinea. As a boy, he learned the *sintir* (a three-stringed cross between bass guitar and lute with a body hollowed out of a single piece of wood and covered with camel skin), various hand drums and Gnawa chants and religious ceremonies. In the '60s, British and American music flooded Morocco, and youthful groups that mixed Gnawa, Arabic, Berber and rock became the rage. Before leaving for America, Hakmoun played in several such fusion bands.

Hakmoun came to New York in 1987 and set to work creating an international hybrid of Gnawa, hip-hop, dancehall reggae and other dance rhythms. His domestic debut, **Zahar,** was recorded live at the Knitting Factory with drummer Bill McClellan and guitarist Anthony Michael Peterson, joined on several tracks by three guest players. The well-recorded music is oriented as much toward rock and jazz-rock fusion as droney ethnic traditionalism, but it's clear Hakmoun has an original voice and an eclectic sensibility.

Trance augments McClellan and Peterson with percussionists Kweyao Agyapon and Hossam Ramzy. On "Soudan Minitara" and "Alal Wahya Alal," funky tracks that incorporate Arabic rap, Hakmoun's experiment works remarkably well. **The Fire Within** is traditional acoustic Gnawa music, programmed to give the impression of a *derdeba,* a ceremony to dedicate ceremonial robes. Thanks to multi-tracking, Hakmoun plays *sintir, qaraqeb* (metal castanets) and a drum that sounds like a bass *dumbek.* The tunes are soothing, mid-tempo excursions accented by impassioned vocals that combine Arabic ululations with chants that likely owe their origins to West African call-and-response singing. [jp]

ZAMBONIS

See *Philistines Jr.*

DAN ZANES

Cool Down Time (Private Music) 1995

In what is becoming an altogether too predictable creative course, the former frontman of Boston's rock'n'rolling Del Fuegos was reborn as a rootsy singer/songwriter on his first solo album. The band's 1989 swan song dipped a toe in such waters; to his credit, Zanes has the sincerity and the sensitivity to make something more than an adult refuge of the idiom. The quietly downcast **Cool Down Time** has its problems, most notably Mitchell Froom's clichéd production sound (his signature here—familiar from records by Los Lobos and Elvis Costello—is more immediately recognizable than Zanes') and keyboard work, which draws too much attention away from the low-key singer/guitarist. Though the tasteful Louisiana swampfunk arrangements gently overwhelm many of the modest songs, Zanes ably holds the spotlight on "Darkness Before Dawn," "Carelessly," "No Sense of Time" and "Treasures of Love," tenderly painting their spare country soul in gorgeous romanticism. [i]

ZAP MAMA

Zap Mama (Bel. Crammed Discs) 1991
Adventures in Afropea 1 (Crammed/Luaka Bop/Warner Bros.) 1993
Sabsylma (Crammed/Luaka Bop/Warner Bros.) 1994

Zap Mama is an intercultural five-woman a cappella ensemble that sings songs from all over Africa, Europe and North America. Group founder and leader Marie Daulne is of mixed African and European heritage. During the civil war in Zaire, her Belgian father was killed; her mother sought refuge with the Pygmies in the rain forest and eventually brought her daughter to Belgium where Daulne grew up singing African folk songs, jazz standards and Catholic hymns. Before starting Zap Mama, she studied polyphony in Arabic, Asian and African music, took formal jazz training at the Antwerp School of Jazz and learned about ethnomusicology. After a return visit to Zaire to meet the Pygmies who saved her family and learn their songs—only to find the tribe had vanished along with the rain forest—Daulne began teaching singing at a private school in Antwerp and put the group together for a one-off gig at a local coffeehouse. They created a sensation and have been touring and recording ever since. Like Daulne, other members of the quintet come from multi-ethnic families; genuine multiculturalism allows them to sound authentic in a variety of languages and contexts, including Syrian folk music, Zairean Pygmy chants, vocalese, Arabic pop tunes and Afro-Cuban mouth music.

Adventures in Afropea 1 is a vocal tour de force. The group's smooth harmonies and the pops, clicks, chirps, tweets and other onomatopoetic sounds they use to accent their harmonies make the disc a unique listening experience. Polyphonic Pygmy chants like "Babanzélé" brush up against Syrian and Zulu folk tunes, jazzy African-American spirituals like "Bottom," a sixteenth-century Spanish song that sounds like a Gregorian chant and free-form improvisations like "Brrrlak!," "I Ne Suhe" and "Plekete."

Two replacement members, from Cameroon and Portugal, joined for **Sabsylma.** The group's increased (although still quite understated) use of percussion adds extra bottom, and a few sound effects are tossed in to add the odd aural surprise, but the vocals remain the main attraction. "India" mixes Indian drum-scat interludes, sweet harmonies and subtle tablas to the mix; the vocalese "De la Vie à la Mort" displays incredible rhythmic technique; "Mr. Brown" is a softly thumpin' bit of acid-jazz with South African and Pygmy flava. Everything Zap Mama touches—whether it be hip-hop, swing, reggae, African, Indian, Pygmy polyphony, aboriginal chants or smooth jazz harmonizing—is delivered with easy grace and soulful fire. [jp]

DWEEZIL ZAPPA

See *Z.*

FRANK ZAPPA (AND THE MOTHERS OF INVENTION)

Freak Out! (Verve) 1966 (Rykodisc) 1988 + 1995
Absolutely Free (Verve) 1967 (Rykodisc) 1989 + 1995
Lumpy Gravy (Verve) 1967 (Rykodisc) 1995
We're Only in It for the Money (Verve) 1968 (Rykodisc) 1995
Cruising With Ruben & the Jets (Verve) 1968 (Rykodisc) 1988 + 1995
Uncle Meat (Bizarre) 1969 (Rykodisc) 1988 + 1995
The **** of the Mothers (Verve) 1969
Hot Rats (Bizarre) 1969 (Rykodisc) 1987 + 1995
Burnt Weeny Sandwich (Bizarre) 1970 (Rykodisc) 1995
Weasels Ripped My Flesh (Bizarre) 1970 (Rykodisc) 1990 + 1995
Chunga's Revenge (Bizarre/Reprise) 1970 (Rykodisc) 1990 + 1995
Fillmore East–June 1971 (Bizarre) 1971 (Rykodisc) 1990 + 1995
200 Motels (Bizarre/United Artists) 1971
Just Another Band From LA (Bizarre) 1972 (Rykodisc) 1990 + 1995
Waka/Jawaka (Bizarre) 1972 (Rykodisc) 1989 + 1995
The Grand Wazoo (Bizarre) 1972 (Rykodisc) 1986 + 1995
Over-nite Sensation (DiscReet) 1973 (Rykodisc) 1995
Apostrophe (') (DiscReet) 1974 (Rykodisc) 1995
Roxy & Elsewhere (DiscReet) 1974 (Rykodisc) 1995
One Size Fits All (DiscReet) 1975 (Rykodisc) 1989 + 1995
Zoot Allures (Warner Bros.) 1976 (Rykodisc) 1990 + 1995
Zappa in New York (DiscReet) 1978 (Rykodisc) 1995
Studio Tan (DiscReet) 1978 (Rykodisc) 1995
Sleep Dirt (DiscReet) 1979 (Rykodisc) 1995
Sheik Yerbouti (Zappa) 1979 (Rykodisc) 1990 + 1995
Orchestral Favorites (DiscReet) 1979 (Rykodisc) 1995
Joe's Garage Act I (Zappa) 1979 (Rykodisc) 1995
Joe's Garage Acts II & III (Zappa) 1979 (Rykodisc) 1995
Tinseltown Rebellion (Barking Pumpkin) 1981 (Rykodisc) 1990 + 1995
Shut Up 'N Play Yer Guitar (Barking Pumpkin) 1981 (Rykodisc) 1986 + 1995
You Are What You Is (Barking Pumpkin) 1981 (Rykodisc) 1990 + 1995
Ship Arriving Too Late to Save a Drowning Witch (Barking Pumpkin) 1982 (Rykodisc) 1995
The Man From Utopia (Barking Pumpkin) 1983 (Rykodisc) 1995
Baby Snakes (Barking Pumpkin) 1983 (Rykodisc) 1995
London Symphony Orchestra (Barking Pumpkin) 1983 (Rykodisc) 1986 + 1995
Boulez Conducts Zappa: The Perfect Stranger (Angel) 1984 (Rykodisc) 1995
Them or Us (Barking Pumpkin) 1984 (Rykodisc) 1986 + 1995
Thing-Fish (Barking Pumpkin) 1984 (Rykodisc) 1986 + 1995
Francesco Zappa (Barking Pumpkin) 1984 (Rykodisc) 1995
Frank Zappa Meets the Mothers of Prevention (Barking Pumpkin) 1985 (Rykodisc) 1986 + 1995
Does Humor Belong in Music? (UK EMI) 1986 (Rykodisc) 1995
Jazz From Hell (Barking Pumpkin) 1986 (Rykodisc) 1987 + 1995
We're Only in It for the Money/Lumpy Gravy (Rykodisc) 1986
Over-nite Sensation/Apostrophe (') (Rykodisc) 1986
Joe's Garage Acts I, II & III (Barking Pumpkin) 1987 (Rykodisc) 1988
London Symphony Orchestra Vol. II (Barking Pumpkin) 1987 (Rykodisc) 1995
Guitar (Barking Pumpkin) 1988 (Rykodisc) 1988 + 1995
You Can't Do That on Stage Anymore Vol. 1 (Barking Pumpkin) 1988 (Rykodisc) 1991 + 1995
You Can't Do That on Stage Anymore Vol. 2 (Barking Pumpkin) 1988 (Rykodisc) 1991 + 1995
Broadway the Hard Way (Barking Pumpkin) 1988 (Rykodisc) 1989 + 1995
You Can't Do That on Stage Anymore Vol. 3 (Barking Pumpkin) 1989 (Rykodisc) 1991 + 1995
The Best Band You Never Heard in Your Life (Barking Pumpkin) 1991 (Rykodisc) 1995

You Can't Do That on Stage Anymore Vol. 4 (Barking Pumpkin) 1991 (Rykodisc) 1991 + 1995
Make a Jazz Noise Here (Barking Pumpkin) 1991 (Rykodisc) 1995
As An Am (31 October 1981) (Foo-eee/Rhino) 1991
The Ark—Boston 1968 (July 1968) (Foo-eee/Rhino) 1991
Freaks & Mother f*#@%! (5 November 1970) (Foo-eee/Rhino) 1991
Unmitigated Audacity (12 May 1974) (Foo-eee/Rhino) 1991
Anyway the Wind Blows–Frank in Paris (24 February 1979) (Foo-eee/Rhino) 1991
'Tis the Season to Be Jelly (30 September 1967) (Foo-eee/Rhino) 1991
Saarbrücken 1978 (3 September 1978) (Foo-eee/Rhino) 1991
Piquantique (21 August 1973) (Foo-eee/Rhino) 1991
Disconnected Synapses (1970) (Foo-eee/Rhino) 1992
Tengo No Minchia Tanta (June 1971) (Foo-eee/Rhino) 1992
Electric Aunt Jemima (1968) (Foo-eee/Rhino) 1992
At the Circus (1978/1970) (Foo-eee/Rhino) 1992
Swiss Cheese/Fire! (12 April 1971) (Foo-eee/Rhino) 1992
Our Man in Nirvana (8 November 1968) (Foo-eee/Rhino) 1992
Conceptual Continuity (19 November 1977) (Foo-eee/Rhino) 1992
You Can't Do That on Stage Anymore Vol. 5 (Barking Pumpkin) 1992 (Rykodisc) 1995
You Can't Do That on Stage Anymore Vol. 6 (Barking Pumpkin) 1992 (Rykodisc) 1995
Playground Psychotics (Barking Pumpkin) 1992 (Rykodisc) 1995
Ahead of Their Time (Rykodisc) 1993 + 1995
Civilization Phase III (Rykodisc) 1994 + 1995
London Symphony Orchestra Vol. I & II (Rykodisc) 1995
Strictly Commercial: The Best of Frank Zappa (Rykodisc) 1995
The Lost Episodes (Rykodisc) 1996
Läther (Rykodisc) 1996

ZAPPA/BEEFHEART/MOTHERS

Bongo Fury (DiscReet) 1975 (Rykodisc) 1989 + 1995

ZAPPA/ENSEMBLE MODERN

The Yellow Shark (Barking Pumpkin) 1993 (Rykodisc) 1995

ZAPPA'S UNIVERSE

Zappa's Universe (Verve) 1993

The late composer/guitarist Frank Zappa's role as a spiritual godfather of punk has been largely obscured by the genre-vaulting scope of his voluminous output. His predilection for uber-fusion, avant-garde classicism, pornographic fandangos and what he called "jazz from hell" helped make the very mention of Zappa's name anathema to large segments of the rock audience. Nonetheless, Zappa, who died of cancer in 1993, was a punk of the first order, and a singularly nasty one at that. Dragging highbrow musical concepts through the gutter (and vice versa), Zappa filled his oeuvre with scathing satire, puerile scatology, annoying noise and enough general misanthropy to make John Lydon seem like a choir boy.

The Baltimore-born, California-bred autocrat's entire catalogue of officially released albums (except for the currently unavailable **200 Motels** movie soundtrack) was reissued in a massive 1995 undertaking after years of sporadic availability. With many albums baited with bonus tracks and other goodies, they constitute an impressive argument for the man's generally acknowledged (though rarely investigated) reputation as the quintessential musical maverick/genius of his era. Parsing Zappa's vaunted "conceptual continuity" (the arcane system of cross-references that links his albums) is daunting even for adepts, but diving into his catalogue is invariably a true listening adventure. His subversive influence can still be felt throughout the underground music scene; everything from the Butthole Surfers' jeering burlesques to Steve Albini's uncompromising iconoclasm is to some extent in debt to Zappa's original aesthetic. He also presaged the indie-label boom, forming his own record companies years before the DIY aesthetic came into vogue.

The early Mothers of Invention albums—**Freak Out!, Absolutely Free** and **We're Only in It for the Money**—form the triad that cemented Zappa's reputation as the ultimate freak, an outsider repulsed by both the straight world and the burgeoning hippie movement. Mixing '50/'60s R&B sendups with crude attempts at jazz-rock fusion and elaborate (for the time) rock operettas (for example, **Absolutely Free**'s "Brown Shoes Don't Make It"), the Mothers—signed to a jazz label—posited themselves as a highly individual alternative at a time when such rebellion earned no credit in the straight world. Looking back, it's impossible to overestimate just how devastating the anti-hippie jabs ("Flower Punk," "Who Needs the Peace Corps?") of **We're Only in It for the Money** must have been to nouveau longhairs.

Zappa's first "solo" effort, **Lumpy Gravy** (originally conceived as a second disc to be paired with **We're Only in It for the Money** and ultimately issued on a single CD with it), is a spotty combination of nonsensical dialogue and ambitious orchestral maneuvers in the vein of classical experimentalist (and Zappa icon) Edgard Varèse. **Cruising With Ruben & the Jets,** a collection of doo-wop/R&B pastiches, comes off as both sincere and sardonic, a snotty homage to the music of Zappa's youth.

The double-LP **Uncle Meat,** identified as "most of the music from the Mothers' movie of the same name which we haven't got enough money to finish yet" (the film was completed years later and released on video), finds Zappa coming into his own as a composer and the Mothers maturing as improvisers, particularly on the free-form workouts of the six-part "King Kong" suite that fills most of the second disc. The mostly instrumental **Burnt Weeny Sandwich** is even better, and includes the panoramic, nineteen-minute "Little House I Used to Live In," complete with a high-flying violin solo by Don "Sugar Cane" Harris.

By almost any yardstick, **Hot Rats,** Zappa's second solo album, is a masterpiece. With sparkling melodies and stellar musicianship, it's every bit the "movie for your ears" that Zappa envisioned. Opening with the lush "Peaches en Regalia," a staple of Zappa's live set, **Hot Rats** also includes "Willie the Pimp," notable for both its inclusion of an ace Captain Beefheart vocal and Zappa's first extended guitar solo. The smokin' sax and violin workouts on "The Gumbo Variations" still sound up-to-the-minute.

Weasels Ripped My Flesh, a fascinating hodgepodge of live and studio recordings, represents the last gasp of the Mothers' '60s lineup; faux free-jazz numbers such as "The Eric Dolphy Memorial Barbecue" indicate just how far outside the mainstream the band was operating. With a rocking electric violin-drenched version of Little Richard's "Directly From My Heart to You" sitting alongside such ineffable weirdness as "Prelude to the Afternoon of a Sexually Aroused Gas Mask" and "My Guitar Wants to Kill Your Mama," **Weasels Ripped My Flesh** is a truly distinctive last will and testament for the group. (Historical footnote: Mothers Lowell George and Roy Estrada went on to form Little Feat, while other members of the group later became the ill-fated Grandmothers.)

Along with the rest of a mostly new batch of Mothers-to-be, ex-Turtles Mark Volman and Howard Kaylan (the vocalists dubbed themselves the Phlorescent Leech & Eddie) made their debut on Zappa's solo **Chunga's Revenge.** Concurrent with their arrival came a nose-dive into the crass sexual humor of **200 Motels, Fillmore East—June 1971** and **Just Another Band From LA.**

Following the demise of the Flo and Eddie–period Mothers, Zappa began a tradition of hiring top-shelf musicians—sometimes identified as Mothers, sometimes not—to play his increasingly complex music. (He retired the Mothers' name for good in 1976.) **Waka/Jawaka,** conceived as a sequel to **Hot Rats,** features trumpeter Sal Marquez on "Big Swifty," an impressive Miles Davis parody/homage. **The Grand Wazoo,** however, ranks as the superior **Hot Rats'** followup, with a battery of more than twenty musicians and vocalists contributing to this oft-overlooked fusion masterpiece.

Though heavy on mean-spirited sex songs, **Overnite Sensation** includes the memorable "Montana," a silly-but-enjoyable ditty about a "dental floss tycoon" (with uncredited backing vocals by Tina Turner and the Ikettes!). **Apostrophe (')**, the title track of which features Jack Bruce on bass, yielded Zappa's first "hit" single, "Don't Eat the Yellow Snow." The live two-disc **Roxy & Elsewhere** finds Zappa in top form as both ringleader and conductor, shepherding the Mothers though mind-spinningly complex number like "Be-Bop Tango (of the Old Jazzmen's Church)."

One Size Fits All continues in the vein of **Overnite Sensation,** albeit with less vulgarity. The mostly live-in-Austin **Bongo Fury** reunites Zappa with his old crony Captain Beefheart (whose **Trout Mask Replica** Zappa produced); Beefheart's psycho-blues vocalizing and dada poesy—and the inclusion of the catchy "Muffin Man"—help make it one of Zappa's most enjoyable efforts.

Zoot Allures is a fairly straightforward (for Zappa) rock jam album, with Beefheart adding harmonica to "Find Her Finer." Zappa then ran into a conflict with his record label; withdrawing four new albums he had created—**Zappa in New York, Studio Tan, Orchestral Favorites** and another sequel to **Hot Rats**—Zappa designed an ambitious multi-disc set from them and deemed it **Läther.** That didn't come out either (until 1996), but the individual albums did. **Zappa in New York** is live from '76, **Studio Tan** is something of a grab-bag and **Sleep Dirt** consists of instrumentals subsequently augmented with vocals. **Sheik Yerbouti** contains both the disco parody "Dancin' Fool" (a turntable hit) and the notorious "Jewish Princess," which drew the wrath of the Anti-Defamation League.

Orchestral Favorites is a mostly instrumental effort that pairs a thirty-seven-piece orchestra with a rock combo, offering a taste of the full-fledged classical recordings Zappa would essay in the '80s. **Joe's Garage Act I,** a concept album about a hapless rock band, features the likable title track and the hilarious "Why Does It Hurt When I Pee?" (a tragically ironic title for a man who would ultimately die of prostate cancer). The sprawling **Joe's Garage Acts II & III** offers "Catholic Girls" as a sort of followup to "Jewish Princess." (All three albums were later consolidated into a double CD.)

The '80s saw Zappa's workaholism in full bloom; some years he spewed forth as many as four new albums. With the formation of the Barking Pumpkin label, he was able to operate entirely outside the realm of the majors, and he reveled in the total artistic freedom he had always sought. **Tinseltown Rebellion** is a live album (with the exception of the studio single "Fine Girl") that features a young Steve Vai on rhythm guitar. The title track finds Zappa weighing in (with predictable disdain) on the subject of punk.

Offering blessed relief from the dense verbal overload of prior albums, the three-disc **Shut Up 'N Play Yer Guitar** (and its 1988 sequel, **Guitar**) showcases Zappa's snaky six-string solos, often grafted onto totally unrelated rhythm tracks. A wanker's delight.

The short, snappy songs that make up **You Are What You Is** operate much like a long suite; there are several gems here, notably the country-western parody "Harder Than Your Husband" and the merciless poseur denunciation of "Mudd Club."

While **Ship Arriving Too Late to Save a Drowning Witch** is one of Zappa's lesser albums, it contains his biggest hit, "Valley Girl," in which his then-fourteen-year-old daughter Moon Unit does a delicious—and mass culture–influencing—demonstration of spoiled-brat Southern California speech pathology. **The Man From Utopia** (which credits Steve Vai with "impossible guitar parts") offers a glib sampling of Zappa's perennial obsessions, containing more porno pap ("The Jazz Discharge Party Hats"), doo-wop parodies ("Luigi & the Wise Guys") and tinker-toy instrumentals ("Moggio"), every song clocking in at under five minutes.

There is little to recommend **Baby Snakes,** a movie soundtrack consisting primarily of rehashed versions of old songs ("Disco Boy," "Dinah-Moe Humm"). The next two albums put Zappa back on classical terrain: **London Symphony Orchestra** (and its 1987 sequel, both now available in a two-disc package) turns the 102-piece LSO, conducted by Kent Nagano, loose on Zappa's slippery compositions, while **The Perfect Stranger** puts Pierre Boulez in the conductor's seat with similar results. Those who truly can't hack modern classical music are advised to avoid these albums, as well as the later **Francesco Zappa.**

Them or Us begins with a straightforward cover of the Channels' 1956 single "The Closer You Are" and ends with a walloping rendition of the Allman Brothers Band's "Whipping Post," sandwiching a hefty helping of the usual mischief between those two poles. One of Zappa's sons, Dweezil, contributes guitar to several tracks, including the Steve Vai showcase, "Stevie's Spanking."

The obnoxious **Thing-Fish** (originally a three-record set, now on two CDs) may well be brilliant, but the album's insufferable mixture of *Amos & Andy*–inspired double-talk (courtesy of vocalist Ike Willis) and sexual fetishism renders it nearly impenetrable to all but hardcore Zappaphiles. For masochists only.

Snippets of Zappa's testimony before the PMRC-inspired 1985 Senate hearings on record-rating can be heard on "Porn Wars," a twelve-minute musical collage from the otherwise unremarkable **Frank Zappa Meets the Mothers of Prevention. Does Humor Belong in Music?,** yet another live album (from 1984), was originally released only in the United Kingdom.

The claustrophobic-sounding, all-instrumental **Jazz From Hell** was composed and played entirely on Synclavier sampling synthesizer and holds the distinction of being Zappa's only Grammy-winning album.

Documenting the abortive 1988 tour of Zappa's horn-enhanced big band, the next three albums—**Broadway the Hard Way, The Best Band You Never Heard in Your Life** and **Make a Jazz Noise Here**—are brashly inventive affairs brimming with humor, political satire and amazing chops. The first features almost all-new material, including brutal excoriations of Elvis Presley ("Elvis Has Just Left the Building"), Jesse Jackson ("Rhymin' Man") and Michael Jackson ("Why Don't You Like Me?"). **Best Band** reprises old favorites ("Cosmik Debris," "Zomby Woof") and includes goofy covers of "Purple Haze" and "Sunshine of Your Love," culminating with an infamous nine-minute version of "Stairway to Heaven" that serves notice Zappa's sense of humor remains as perverse as ever. **Make a Jazz Noise Here** highlights the band's tightly controlled approach to improvisation on tracks like the sprawling "When Yuppies Go to Hell" and a retooled "King Kong."

Both **Playground Psychotics** and **Ahead of Their Time** are, if not essential, of definite archival interest. The two-CD former collects live music and backstage banter from the comedic Flo and Eddie–period Mothers and includes several tracks recorded in 1971 with John Lennon and Yoko Ono at the Fillmore East. **Ahead of Their Time** is a 1968 recording of the Mothers live at London's Royal Festival Hall, on which the group is heard working out material that would later appear on **Uncle Meat, Burnt Weeny Sandwich** and **Weasels Ripped My Flesh.**

The challenging **Civilization Phase III** is a sprawling mess that mixes smut and Synclavier sounds in equal measure.

The six double-CDs that constitute the all-live **You Can't Do That on Stage Anymore** series draw material in chronological order from all stages of Zappa's career, offering a kaleidoscopic view of the great man's many musical incarnations. True diehards may want to also investigate the **Beat the Boots** series (the only releases on the Foo-eee/Rhino consortium), fifteen unauthorized concert albums that Zappa came across and co-opted with his own authorized releases in 1991 and 1992. As might be expected, the albums—also packaged as two vinyl and cassette boxes—boast bootleg-quality sound, tape hiss and all.

The Yellow Shark, another classical effort, was recorded live by Frankfurt's Ensemble Modern under Zappa's direction and production and released posthumously. Made without the composer's participation, **Zappa's Universe** is a live recording of his music performed in late 1991 as a tribute by various associates, relatives and fans.

Strictly Commercial, a choice nineteen-song selection of Zappa's most accessible material, makes a dandy primer for the uninitiated, covering as it does a gamut of eras, from **Hot Rats'** "Peaches en Regalia" and **Apostrophe**'s "Don't Eat the Yellow Snow" through "Dancin' Fool," "Valley Girl" and **Them or Us**' "Be in My Video."

Personally compiled by Zappa near the end of his life, **The Lost Episodes** is a richly annotated collection of thirty rare studio recordings, outtakes and other curiosities from the great man's long and windy career. A treasure trove for devoted fans, it includes several Zappa/Beefheart collaborations ("Lost in a Whirlpool" dates from the late '50s). Among the other goodies: "Lil' Clanton Shuffle," a swell jam originally intended for inclusion on **Hot Rats,** a twelve-minute "Sharleena" sung by Sugar Cane Harris and the original mix of the controversial 1980 single "I Don't Wanna Get Drafted." With scads of unheard recordings presumably gathering dust in the vaults, it's a safe bet **The Lost Episodes** is only the beginning of an onslaught of esoterica. In the words of Edgard Varèse, the present-day composer refuses to die. [ts]

MARTIN ZELLAR

Born Under (Rykodisc) 1994

MARTIN ZELLAR AND THE HARDWAYS

Martin Zellar and the Hardways (Rykodisc) 1996

Shifting out of the Gear Daddies (but hanging on to the quartet's bassist), Minnesota singer/guitarist Martin Zellar went solo on **Born Under,** heading further down the simple backroad paths of rustic country and heartland rock, sometimes mixing styles in a single song. A sensitive, observant songwriter devoted to personal issues no greater than "East Side Boys," Zellar has a grit-strewn voice with a mannered catch better suited to the harsh honesty of his lyrics than the placid curves of his melodies. Guitarist Dan Murphy of Soul Asylum guests on "Lie to Me"; Adam and Noah Levy of the Honeydogs are all over the record. [i]

See also *Honeydogs.*

ZENI GEVA

Maximum Money Monster (Pathological/Revolver) 1990
Total Castration (Public Bath) 1991
Live in Amerika (Nux Organization/Charnel Music) 1993
Desire for Agony (Alternative Tentacles) 1994
Trance Europe Experience (Nux Organization/Charnel Music) 1995
Freedom Bondage (Alternative Tentacles) 1995

The IBAS—the International Brotherhood of Aggressive Skronk—helps explain why several albums by this dark-hearted Tokyo noise trio would wind up being produced to an indistinct roar by Steve Albini in his Chicago basement. Led by singer/guitarist Kazuyuki (KK) Null with guitarist Tabata and drummer Eito (which doesn't explain the sometimes audible bass throbs), Zeni Geva extrudes venomous thrash with a death-metal sensibility and the kick-pedal frequency of hardcore industrialism. Exaggerated beyond the point of horribility, Zeni Geva is pure radioactive sonic grub, a malevolent sonic horror show as pointlessly unpleasant as any band going.

Tucked behind a stunningly crude cover, **Total Castration** is a groaning mass of gory riff decimation over which Null bellows his harsh, elemental lyrics: "I

Want You," "I Hate You," the labored and relatively intricate "Shoot Me With Your Blood," "Godflesh" (which might be a tribute, but it's hard to tell). **Desire for Agony** commits similar crimes: "Autopsy Love," "Heathen Blood," "The Body." The six tracks recorded in a Dutch studio by Ronal Trijber for **Trance Europe Experience** are appealingly toned-down versions of old faves, mostly from **Desire for Agony;** the disc also includes three rough'n'raw live tracks.

Null has also released albums solo, in collaboration with other musicians and with his former trio, ANP (Absolut Null Punkt). [i]

See also *Jim O'Rourke.*

ZIP CODE RAPISTS

Sing and Play the Three Doctors and Other Sounds of Today (Amarillo) 1992
The Man Can't Bust Our Music! EP7 (Ectoplasm) 1993
Sing and Play the Matador Records Catalog EP7 (Hol. Ecstatic Piss) 1994
94124 EP (Amarillo) 1995

THERAPIST JOHN'S ZIP CODE REVUE

Abundance (Amarillo) 1994

THREE DOCTOR'S BAND

Back to Basics "Live" (Amarillo) 1994
Archaeology of the Infinite (Amarillo) 1995

The reasons why people feel compelled to play rock music are many and varied, but the desire for public humiliation has rarely been indulged with quite as much enthusiasm as it has by the Zip Code Rapists, the entertaining San Francisco duo of Gregg Turkington (mainly vocals) and John Harris Singer (mainly music—pretty ironic given his name, hunh?). To call the Rapists a Ween tribute band is actually unfair—the lo-fi wailing of their first phase is hardly as skilled or ambitious as Dean and Gene's. Since music sure ain't it, the pair's main talent seems to be for pathological put-ons, atrocious cover songs and carefree self-abasement. You want high-concept absurdity? After thumbing their noses at the kings of corporate cool by knocking off an ingeniously awful 7-inch covering four songs originally released by Pavement, Liz Phair, Bettie Serveert and Thinking Fellers Union Local 282 on Matador Records, the hoaxers orchestrated their own fraudulent breakup, a feud between two competing spin-off bands and the long-rumored reunion—all in the space of a year.

When not rubbishing songs by Chris Isaak, Dawn, Circle Jerks and Gordon Lightfoot, the duo spends the live side of **Sing and Play the Three Doctors** apologizing for their name, performance and existence. Lest anyone take them seriously, however, they also claim to have driven twelve hundred miles (the gig's in San Francisco) and signed a contract with Columbia Records. The studio side affords them a chance to overdub a drum machine, lay on the noise guitar and improve the vocals, producing a minimal mess with such amusing items as the revisionist history of "President's Song," the swingin' anti-egg-salad diatribe "Office Party", and the noise-guitar desperation of "Wired," in which someone repeatedly interjects "I can't breathe" with convincing constriction between coughs.

Although it crams ten short studio songs onto a 7-inch, **The Man Can't Bust Our Music!** is the best of the band's litter, a far more accomplished effort than the 12-inch debut. The duo manages to make surprisingly varied and inventive music from originals—the punkin' "Kick in the Heads," Turkington's botched piano piece "Tuesday Street" and the profane Anglofried cartoon theme "Darn It Duck," the bluegrass blipvert "Hotel One"—and a raucous freakout decimation of Mike Nesmith's "Listen to the Band." Anyway, no track lasts long enough to become a nuisance.

The Zip Code Rapists then pretended to tear apart in an acrimonious split. Singer formed the shockingly professional Zip Code Revue, a seductively sweet-sounding country-roots-acoustic ensemble that conscientiously spoils that illusion on **Abundance** by covering the parent group's "Wired" and adding such hair-raising noise fiascoes as "Adams II" and "Tea in Djibouti." (The CD also wrecks shit further with a skronky version of Led Zeppelin's "When the Levee Breaks" and an obsequious lounge lunge at the Doors' "Touch Me.") Otherwise, the album is presentably sung and handsomely played by a bunch of sympathetic pals (including David Tholfsen of U.S. Saucer, whose "Begging Song" is on the program here, plus guests from Counting Crows and American Music Club). If not for the destructive digressions and occasionally bizarre lyrics (most conspicuously "Doctors Are Spreading Disease"), **Abundance** could generally pass in contemporary twang-pop circles—an amazing case of urban renewal.

Although Turkington's contribution to the feud—the Three Doctor's Band—has an intermittent country accent as well, he stays a lot closer to the Rapists' minimalist crud in hashing away noisily at songs by Madonna, the Bee Gees, the Monkees and others on the supposed quartet's (mostly studio) **Back to Basics "Live."** (Typical ZCR humor: "All songs written by the Three Doctors Band . . . except . . ." [followed by a credit list for all but one of the record's selections].) Other than a dicey two-song concert singalong that features the band's three other guitarists (moonlighters from Faith No More and Caroliner as well as a different member of U.S. Saucer), the album is an elementary effort that sounds like one talentless teenager's bedroom-mirror rehearsal session, and is about that much fun to endure.

With their "differences" settled, the two Zip Code Rapists made a back-together-again-for-the-first-time comeback with the disarmingly competent **94124** EP, taking the opportunity to announce a new morality in the bozo-funky "Zip Code Gentlemen." Of course, it's a joke, and the skimpy record (six songs, a one-minute live fragment plus a self-described "filler" remix) soon finds the two up to their old tricks, faking their way through a dubious Nashville two-step ("I Need Him"), a muck-slinging product endorsement ("Ranch Style Beans"), sick-puppy pop ("Happy Like Larry") and fucked-up live covers ("The Look of Love," the Doors' "Riders on the Storm"). With that, plus the significant inclusion of a perverted southwestern ballad ("Henderson"), the Zip Code Rapists finally reach their ultimate destination—they're a Ween tribute band, after all. [i]

See also *Caroliner, Faith No More, Thinking Fellers Union Local 282, U.S. Saucer.*

ZIPGUN

8 Track Player (eMpTy) 1992
Baltimore (eMpTy) 1993

Kicking a solid smear of vintage Stooges/MC5/Heartbreakers into a potent fast roar of Jack-Endino-co-produced grunge, this Seattle quartet (containing ex-Derelicts guitarist Neil Rogers and ex–Final Warning drummer Dan Cunnen) comes out, naturally enough, sounding a bit like Mudhoney, but with a tighter, more focused and less ambitious assault that gets the job done just as well. Robbe Clarke has a rough, deep Iggy Pop voice, and Rogers gets a good hit off Mark Wooten's powerful bassisms; only the traps' overly gated click has the wrong kind of shit sound. The quartet's sturdy songwriting on **8 Track Player** (the cover design of which was recycled by Nyack a few years later and has been adapted by others as well) never loses its grasp on engaging structures or workable melodies—check "The End," "Put Me Away" and the thrashy "Ego a Go Go." The spoken-word bit beginning "Cool in the Cell" is a cute idea; "Backwards" (three guesses) isn't.

Other than a gruesomely throttled saxophone (on a painful jam reasonably entitled "Hades") and two guest blasts from Tom Price's organ, **Baltimore** keeps up the good work without frills. Zipgun fries up a trebly side of relentless razorstun guitar aggro in short, fast, semi-tuneful originals that push Clarke to punkier (occasionally Thundering) Popisms than on **8 Track Player.** The material's slapped-together quality works to the band's advantage on "Long Hot Kiss," "Highball," "Through the Roof," "Shadey" and "I Can't Wait," but pushing **Baltimore** too hard in Mudhoney's direction cuts down on what made the band so cool the first time out. [i]

JOHN ZORN

Pool/Hockey (Parachute) 1980
Archery (Parachute) 1982
Locus Solus (Rift) 1983 (Tzadik) 1995
The Classic Guide to Strategy, Vol. 1 (Lumina) 1983
The Classic Guide to Strategy, Vol. 2 (Lumina) 1985
The Big Gundown (Icon/Nonesuch) 1986
Spillane (Nonesuch/Elektra) 1987
Spy Vs. Spy (Musician/Elektra) 1989
Cynical Hysterie Hour (Japan. Sony/CBS) 1989
Film Works 1986–1990 (Japan. Wave) 1991 (Elektra) 1992
Elegy EP (Japan. Eva) 1992 (Tzadik) 1995
Kristallnacht (Japan. Eva) 1993 (Tzadik) 1995
Masada Alef (Japan. DIW) 1994
Masada Beit (Japan. DIW) 1995
Masada Gimel (Japan. DIW) 1995
Masada Daled EP (Japan. DIW) 1995
The Book of Heads (Tzadik) 1995
First Recordings 1973 (Tzadik) 1995
Redbird (Tzadik) 1995
Masada Hei (Japan. DIW) 1995
Masada Vav (Japan. DIW) 1996
Filmworks 2 (Tzadik) 1996

EUGENE CHADBOURNE AND JOHN ZORN

School (Parachute) 1978

DEREK BAILEY/GEORGE LEWIS/JOHN ZORN

Yankees (Celluloid) 1983

DEREK BAILEY/JOHN ZORN/WILLIAM PARKER

Harras (Japan. Avant) 1996

MICHIHIRO SATO AND JOHN ZORN

Ganryu Island (Yukon) 1985

SONNY CLARK MEMORIAL QUARTET

Voodoo (Black Saint) 1986

STEVE BERESFORD/DAVID TOOP/JOHN ZORN/TONIE MARSHALL

Deadly Weapons (Fr. Nato) 1986 + 1991

VARIOUS ARTISTS (COBRA)

Cobra (Sw. Hat Hut) 1987 + 1991
John Zorn's Cobra Live at the Knitting Factory (Knitting Factory Works) 1995
John Zorn's Cobra Tokyo Operations '94 (Japan. Avant) 1996

JOHN ZORN/GEORGE LEWIS/BILL FRISELL

News for Lulu (Sw. Hat Hut) 1988 + 1993
More News for Lulu (Sw. Hat Hut) 1992

JOHN ZORN/FRED FRITH

Art of Memory (UK Incus) 1995

DEKOBOKO HAJIME/YAMANTAKA EYE

Nani Nani (Tzadik) 1995

MYSTIC FUGU ORCHESTRA

Zohar (Tzadik) 1995

The mindbogglingly prolific John Zorn is the undisputed king of the downtown New York art-music scene, a sonic omnivore who's absorbed all of the extremes of twentieth-century music and processed it into "blocks of sound." Zorn has worked with and influenced uncountable numbers of musicians. As a composer, he's written pieces for everyone from Albert Collins to Guy Klucevsek; as a saxophonist, he's played everything from free improvisation to thrash-metal to traditional jazz to licks on Joe Piscopo's "Honeymooners Rap." He's also become something of a cottage industry, masterminding two labels: Avant (in Japan) and Tzadik (in the US). Though his way-too-self-conscious eclecticism is sometimes hard to take, he's always battering against the walls of music's capabilities and is capable of both random bullshit and work of surpassing brilliance and even beauty.

The **Pool/Hockey** record is, like so many of Zorn's lesser albums, a document rather than a listenable record. In this case, it captures two of his early "game pieces," which are played the way one plays a game rather than the way one plays a composition, often with a prompter helping to direct the action. There are fragments of notation, but it's mostly a set of rules for improvisation. Squeak, blat, pop, thud, honk. It also captures a scene: the 2000 Statues experimental music collective, for which many of Zorn's early compositions were written. "Pool" is played by Zorn with violinist Polly Bradfield, percussionists Mark E. Miller and Charles K. Noyes and Bob Ostertag on electronics. The trio piece "Hockey" appears in two versions: one with Zorn, Miller and Bradfield, and one with Ostertag, guitar-improv headcase Eugene Chadbourne (who'd played with Zorn on his earliest release, 1978's **School,** which includes three takes on another game piece, "Lacrosse") and keyboardist Wayne Horvitz. Zorn notes in his liners that "Hockey" has had "over 11 performances." That's one way of putting it. **Archery,** dating from around the same time, has a dozen players, including bassist Bill Laswell and cellist Tom Cora; its rules are very different, but it sounds about the same.

Locus Solus is Zorn's first major leap forward, and his first stab at something like rock (though it's not really recognizable as such). A series of trios play improvised "songs," often with vocals, all of which clock in under three minutes (many under two). The results are often hard to take—especially the eight tracks by the first trio, which pits Peter Blegvad's intonations and Zorn's sax, clarinet and game calls against warped turntable manipulations by Christian Marclay. Still, these infinitesimal-attention-span pieces don't just bear up under careful examination, they *demand* it. It's easy to hear how some of the thirty-eight pieces, like "The Violent Death of Dutch Schultz" and a set of James Bond–influenced tracks, led toward Naked City, but others represent equally fascinating paths not taken. Also noteworthy: the presence of "singer"/"guitarist" Arto Lindsay, formerly of DNA, and drummer Anton Fier, on their way to the Golden Palominos (on whose first record Zorn also played).

Zorn was still keeping his hand in more traditional free improv, though. The two **Classic Guide to Strategy** records (scheduled to be reissued on a single Tzadik CD in 1996) are strangely calm solo meditations for saxophone, clarinet and his ever-present game calls; **Yankees** teams him with two improv legends from earlier schools, British guitarist Derek Bailey and trombonist George Lewis, for a playful, rule-free workout.

Ganryu Island is Zorn's first major bow toward the East (Japanese music, film and record labels would later have a tremendous impact on his work). The album's seven duets between Zorn (on various reeds) and Michihiro Sato (on the three-stringed *shamisen*) probably seemed like a fascinating idea, and they are—for about the first five minutes. Beyond that, the record is just more documentation.

Credited to the Sonny Clark Memorial Quartet, **Voodoo** is something new for Zorn: jazz. Clark was a fairly obscure pianist of the '50s and '60s; here, a quartet led by pianist Horvitz (also including bassist Ray Drummond and drummer Bobby Previte) plays perfectly straightforward versions of seven of his pieces. Zorn, on alto, plays it straight too, almost entirely avoiding his signature squawks, and proves himself capable of some very nice, if un-life-changing, traditional improvisation and a sharp, distinctive tone.

As with **Voodoo,** Zorn is essentially a sideman on **Deadly Weapons,** recorded with a quartet including Francophone vocalist Tonie Marshall and multi-instrumentalists Steve Beresford and David Toop; Zorn co-wrote only three of its eleven tracks and doesn't appear at all on four of them. It's a beautiful, unique record, and, despite its title, mostly very quiet—built on sinuous keyboard and drum machine parts. Oddity: Zorn playing keyboards on "Chen Pe'i Pe'i." High point: the sensuous, creepy keyboard riff that glides "Jayne Mansfield" along.

Zorn's next big compositional breakthrough was the arrangement of "Der kleine Leutnant des lieben Gottes" that he came up with for the 1985 Kurt Weill tribute album **Lost in the Stars**—tossing the original into a blender, pulling out the little squirmy bits and alchemizing them into something recognizable only to those intimately familiar with the pre-mangled piece. Like Weill, Zorn is perpetually dragging "high" forms of composition into "low" forms, and vice versa; the next person he pulled that arranging strategy on was Ennio Morricone, whose spaghetti-western film music he tackles on **The Big Gundown.** The cast of a few billion musicians includes old pals (Horvitz, Bradfield, Sato, Lindsay), emerging downtown types (trombonist Jim Staley, keyboardist Anthony Coleman) and a whole bunch of ringers (a Latin American percussion section, Toots Thielemans whistling and playing harmonica, several members of Living Colour).

Zorn's best-known game piece is undoubtedly "Cobra," whose rules (involving a complicated set of hand signals that players can use to indicate who should play what when) have been incorporated into many improvisers' vocabularies for the sake of convenience. Written for (roughly) twelve players and a prompter, it's a hell of a lot of fun to play and to watch (headbands! gesticulations! dirty looks!); without the visual side and an easy indication of who's playing what when, it can be dry and confusing to hear. Despite delightful and ornate packaging, the 1987 **Cobra** pretty much falls into the latter camp. It's got two recordings, one studio (with a lineup of Staley, Marclay, guitarists Bill Frisell, Elliott Sharp and Arto Lindsay, Coleman, Horvitz and David Weinstein all playing keyboards of various types, harpists Carol Emanuel and Zeena Parkins, Bob James manipulating tapes, percussionist Bobby Previte and accordionist Guy Klucevsek) and one live (with Frisell, Sharp, Coleman, Horvitz, Weinstein, Klucevsek, James, Marclay and Previte, plus J. A. Deane playing trombone synthesizer). The CD edition adds six tracks.

Much more enjoyable is the later **John Zorn's Cobra Live at the Knitting Factory.** "Cobra" was played at the New York club at least once a month for several years, each time by a different lineup; the 1995 disc collects short movements from '92 performances. The sound is sometimes dodgy but the tremendous variation in lineups and the "greatest-hits" nature of the selection process gives a good sense of what the game's dynamics are like, even for those who've never seen it played. For a treat, check out "Taipan" and "D. Popylepis," by an all-vocal Cobra lineup including Jeff Buckley, Brutal Truth's Kevin Sharp and a pre–Soul Coughing M. Doughty (back in the days when he was the Knitting Factory's ticket clerk).

Tokyo Operations '94 is a full-length live Cobra performance recorded at Tokyo's Shibuya La Mama with a dozen Japanese musicians, mostly playing traditional instruments and often improvising in a pre-twentieth-century style. After they get the everybody-make-a-lot of-noise-*now!* thing out of their systems, some worthwhile, unusual music gets made, though fifty minutes of a single Cobra lineup is still a bit much to take if you can't watch the musicians' visual interactions.

Spillane is one of Zorn's most show-offish albums and not one of his best. Zorn gets across the fact that he's capable of a very broad range of styles, but seems over-anxious: look how many things I can do and how quickly! The side-long title piece is a somewhat more together take on **The Big Gundown**'s everything-and-the-kitchen-sink film-music-isms with another very large cast; the other two tracks are a shifting series of settings for blues guitarist Albert Collins and "Forbidden Fruit," played by the Kronos Quartet with additional vocals and turntables.

The News for Lulu trio formed around this time; though it has played only rarely, the group is one of Zorn's most interesting projects. The eponymous first album finds Zorn (alto sax), George Lewis (trombone) and Bill Frisell (guitar) playing improvisations on seventeen pieces by Sonny Clark and his fellow '60s Blue Note not-quite-household-names Kenny Dorham, Hank Mobley and Freddie Redd; three are reprised in live versions recorded two days later. Similar to the kind of deconstruction Zorn worked on Weill and Morricone, this time it's constantly pretty and coherent. Without a rhythm section, all three musicians have to lean on each other to support the songs' structure, but nobody ever quite solos in a standard way: they're just all *on,* all the time, finding fresh moments of startling loveliness within every song. And Zorn, it turns out, can *really* play.

More News for Lulu, recorded in 1989 but not issued until three years later, includes two live performances. It adds Misha Mengelberg's "Gare Guillemins" and Big John Patton's "Minor Swing" to the group's repertoire and takes a few tunes further out; otherwise, it's more of the glorious same.

Spy Vs. Spy seems at first like a better idea for a single track than for an album: take a bunch of Ornette Coleman's wild, tricky jazz compositions, throw them to a double-alto-sax/bass/double-drum lineup (in order: Zorn, Tim Berne, Mark Dresser, Joey Baron and Michael Vatcher), speed them up to hardcore punk velocity, tell everyone to play as loud as they possibly can and see what happens. What happens is a wonderful, invigorating record. It steamrollers over the subtleties of Coleman's writing (though Zorn and Berne are amazingly deft at these high speeds) and doesn't exactly shed any new light on the tunes, but the energy of the recording is beyond belief. "Fucking hardcore *rules,*" Zorn declares on the back cover, and who would doubt him?

The Japanese **Cynical Hysterie Hour** contains a few dozen very short pieces Zorn wrote for animated cartoon shows—an excuse for him to take after his idol Carl Stalling, who scored Warner Bros.' greatest cartoons. The lineup is pretty much the usual suspects (Frisell, Horvitz, Lindsay and a host of others); the eight pieces making up the "Trip Coaster" sequence were also issued as a separate 3-inch CD.

Recorded over a five-year span with more or less the same crew (though guitarist Robert Quine appears on most of it), **Film Works** collects Zorn's scores to the movies *White and Lazy, The Golden Boat* and *She Must Be Seeing Things,* plus a version of Morricone's theme song for *The Good, the Bad and the Ugly* recorded for a Southeast Asian ad for Camel cigarettes! Unfortunately, Zorn's love for film music gets the better of him: there's too much of his favorite composers here, and not enough of him. The *White and Lazy* score is interesting as another pointer toward Naked City, though.

Elegy, Zorn's first non–Naked City recording in several years, is a half-hour piece recorded with several members of Faith No More and Mr. Bungle (Mike Patton and Trey Spruance), as well as turntable manipulator David Shea and a few others. Inspired by the beauty-in-torture imagery of Jean Genet's *Thief's Journal,* it's a slow, quiet, menacing composition that ends up being boring as hell, meandering all over the place and not ending up anywhere in particular.

Kristallnacht is another single long piece, this time about the Holocaust and the formation of the Jewish state. It is a very, very literal-minded piece of program music—the Jewish ghettos are represented by a mournful melody from klezmer musicians David Krakauer and Frank London with tapes of Hitler's speeches played over the top, and the "Night of Broken Windows" of the title is represented by keyboardist Anthony Coleman (in a heartstopping passage) repeatedly playing a sample of glass being smashed. There are certain topics suited to literalism, and this is one of them—it's a tremendously powerful work. The other musicians here include percussionist William Winant (also on **Elegy**), bassist Mark Dresser (of the **Spy Vs. Spy** band), guitarist Mark Ribot and violinist Mark Feldman.

Zorn's fascination with Jewish history extended to the name and the content of his next major group of works, **Masada,** named after the site where Jews committed mass suicide rather than submit to Roman rule. **Alef, Beit, Gimel** and **Daled** (the first four letters of the Hebrew alphabet) were all released in Japan within a single year with matching graphics; the eighteen-minute EP **Daled** was only available by mail with proofs of purchase of the first three. That they're all pretty interchangeable may have something to do with the fact that they were all recorded on the same day, with the core lineup of Zorn (alto sax), Dave Douglas (trumpet), Greg Cohen (bass) and Joey Baron (drums). As for the music? In short and in long, harmolodic klezmer: Jewish-sounding minor-key themes, developed in ways that usually could have come straight off Ornette Coleman records. All four are terrific musicians (though Baron deserves special commendation), and they played together in public for a long time before they ever recorded, so the records are totally solid. You may not need to hear all of them, that's all.

The **Masada** record to start with is probably **Hei.** Though its packaging is uniform with the first four and has the same lineup, the album was recorded more than a year later. The band is both looser and tighter, even more confident and daring than before, and they've toned down the Ornette-worship a *little* bit. The record's centerpiece is "Hobah," an eleven-minute almost-free workout in which Zorn's wall-leveling squawking keeps resolving itself into a vague but present tonal structure.

Vav (what will Zorn do when he runs out of letters?), recorded at the **Hei** session, is more of the same, only slightly less so. Again, nothing here doesn't deserve to be released or to be heard; it's all beautifully played, and it all rewards careful listening. It's just that there's a hell of a lot of **Masada,** and it's all very similar. If you love it, great—there's that much more of it to love. If you don't, you're not missing anything if you've only heard one of the records.

The Zorn/Fred Frith alto/guitar improv album **The Art of Memory** is dedicated to "Derek and Evan"—that would be English free-improv masters Derek Bailey (the guitarist whose Incus label released the album) and Evan Parker (the saxophonist whose style Zorn tries very hard to cop, especially on "The Chain," though he doesn't quite have Parker's circular-breathing technique). Lots of interesting noises get made; not much of lasting consequence happens.

Harras, improvised live at the Knitting Factory, is proof that even if you put together Bailey, a saxophonist and a guy named Parker, you don't quite get a Derek Bailey/Evan Parker record. The saxophonist is Zorn and the Parker is bassist William Parker, probably best known for his work with David S. Ware's quartet. It's a curious combination: Bailey and Parker's playing is pretty much totally free, but Zorn, for all his noise-making proclivities, is at heart a melodicist. At times, he almost seems to be improvising on some kind of melodic theme, while Parker and Bailey play off Zorn's and each other's textures. There's some terrific chemistry going on, though, particularly on the thirty-six-minute "Evening Harras."

On a similar tip, Zorn wrote the thirty-five solo guitar études of **The Book of Heads** for Eugene Chadbourne in 1978, but they weren't recorded until 1995—by Marc Ribot, rather than Chadbourne. The pieces are an attempt to notate the language of guitar free-improv (and its attendant props: balloons, rice, pencils, that kind of thing); while it's good to know that it's possible to do and that somebody did it, no one actually has to hear it.

Released at the same time, **First Recordings 1973** is even more time-delayed, although two of its five pieces actually date from 1974: the long collage "Mikhail Zoetrope" and the very short genre-hop "Automata of Al-Jazari." Though they're certainly juvenilia (Zorn was about twenty at the time he recorded them, all by himself) and occasionally embarrassing, these pieces hold up awfully well, and they anticipate his later work with nearly disturbing clarity.

That same year (1995) also saw two albums on which Zorn collaborated with the Boredoms' (and Naked City's) mic-swallowing vocal-sound-maker Eye, who had by this point changed his first name to Yamantaka. **Nani Nani,** on which Zorn appears as Dekoboko Hajime, was recorded in two days and is pretty much what you'd expect: screech, rattle, gulp, blurt, squawk. It lets Eye do his thing all over a dozen different settings of varying levels of interest (the best is the video-game-gone-berserk "Propolution"). Almost half the record is taken up by a single-note drone (with a little Eye hollering) imaginatively titled "Bad Hawkwind."

The twenty-four-minute **Zohar** is much stranger and more interesting. It's credited to Mystic Fugu Orchestra; Zorn and Eye are respectively billed as Rav Tzizit and Rav Yechida. The idea is to approximate very early Jewish liturgical recordings; this means that every track consists of very faint Eye wailing, Zorn quietly playing harmonium lines loosely based on traditional Jewish modalities and incredibly loud surface-noise effects (they all but obliterate "Ayin"). There are a few surprises—a drum machine seems to be buried somewhere in "Frog Doina," for instance—but it mostly sticks to the program. There's no other record anything like it.

The most recent major Zorn composition to be recorded is 1995's "Redbird," which appears on the CD of the same name, introduced by a nearly silent eight-minute percussion piece (played to zen perfection by James Pugliese). This time, Zorn's inspiration is painter Agnes Martin, whose work's merciless calm is shared by the music. A chamber ensemble plays a single note or chord every few seconds, then lets it gradually decay; this process goes on for forty minutes. Depending on the amount of attention you pay to it, "Redbird" can be either soothing or maddening. In any case, when a composer who made his name with his short attention span pulls off something sustained this long and this well, it's a real achievement. [ddw]

See also *Boredoms, God Is My Co-Pilot, Golden Palominos, Naked City, Painkiller, Marc Ribot.*

ZUMPANO

Look What the Rookie Did (Scratch/Sub Pop) 1995
Goin' Through Changes (Sub Pop) 1996

More important than its simply effective re-creation of breezy '60s guitar-pop harmony atmospheres, this young Vancouver quartet (named after ex-Glee drummer Jason Zumpano; singer Carl Newman is also in Superconductor) subtly taps into the imaginary frivolity of that bygone era on its debut with such songs of incidental teen angst as "Oh That Atkinson Girl," "The Party Rages On" and "Wraparound Shades." With production by Kevin Kane of Grapes of Wrath on **Look What the Rookie Did,** Zumpano is able to fight off the potential for coyness in its polka dot endeavors and ambitious enough to raise the ante with dramatic horns and pedal steel, treating period evocation as an intermediate goal rather than the stylistic finish line. Between the non-linear lyrics, blasts of freak-out rock excitement (especially the two minutes of bonus feedback and meltdown noise that follows the last listed track) and a sense that more is going on here than meets the ears, it's clear that Zumpano are not mere stylistic burrowers. An apt Jimmy Webb cover ("Rosecrans Boulevard" fits in here like an original) and the loaded-gun ethnicity of "(She's a) Full-blooded Sicilian" (complete with strummed banjo) defines an intriguing band with more on its mind than "Snowflakes & Heartaches."

Goin' Through Changes goes further down the same time tunnel, but with more ambition, confidence and intuitive skill. Another absolute delight. [i]

See also *Superconductor.*

ZUZU'S PETALS

When No One's Looking (Twin\Tone) 1992
The Music of Your Life (Twin\Tone) 1994

It's easy to see where ZuZu's Petals stand on the whole femininity-versus-feminism debate. They're carefully styled and attended by unabashedly girly accouterments (in the CD booklet of one record, they're sitting around sipping tea; the sleeve of another gathers three pocketbooks around an old tube radio). But the Minneapolis trio never slips into cutesy character when its time to get down to business. Sure, they're a little poppier than most of their Twin Cities counterparts, but that's more a function of nurture (they've clearly spent a fair share of time in the coffeehouse) than nature.

On the trio's full-length debut (produced by Lou Giordano), guitarist Laurie Lindeen's songwriting contributions tend to be quite a bit lighter than bassist Coleen Elwood's; emphasizing the folky trills inherent in her sing-song delivery fits Lindeen's diary-like musings nicely. While there's not much in songs like "Cinderella's Daydream" and the woe-is-the-world "God Cries" that you haven't heard before, Lindeen's ardor is difficult to resist. Elwood has more of a rocker's bias—albeit not as overwrought as that of homegirls Babes in Toyland—which manifests itself on the blunt eccentric's rallying cry "Psycho Tavern."

Both women loosen up significantly on **The Music of Your Life,** a less-polished recording (by Albhy Galuten) that consequently shows a lot more life: the tremolo-infused "Chatty Cathy" (written by the entire trio) tears into its trashy title target with merciless glee, while Lindeen's "Do Not" musters a mysterioso pulse that tickles the pleasure center in a manner that probably would not get the Jimmy Stewart seal of approval. [dss]